MW01618442

CLINICAL MANUAL OF ORIENTAL MEDICINE

AN INTEGRATIVE APPROACH

THIRD EDITION

中西醫結合臨床手冊

Lotus Institute Of Integrative Medicine

PO Box 92493
City of Industry, CA 91715, USA
Tel: (626) 780-7182
Fax: (626) 363-9751
Web: www.eLotus.org
Email: info@eLotus.org

中西醫結合臨床手冊

Copyright: Copyright © 1998, 2002, 2006, 2016 by the Lotus Institute of Integrative Medicine. Third Edition. All rights reserved. No part of this publication may be reproduced, stored in a retrieval system, or transmitted, in any form or by any means, electronic, mechanical, photocopying, recording, or otherwise, except for brief review, without the prior written permission of the Lotus Institute of Integrative Medicine.

Professional Use Only: This Clinical Manual of Oriental Medicine is intended as an educational guide for licensed healthcare practitioners only, as professional training and expertise are essential to the safe recommendation of and effective guidance for use of herbs. All herbal products discussed within this Clinical Manual must be used only through licensed healthcare practitioners.

The information in this Clinical Manual is presented in an accurate, truthful and non-misleading manner. The information is supported by modern research whenever possible and referenced accordingly throughout the entire Clinical Manual. Nonetheless, the FDA requires the following statements:

These statements have not been evaluated by the Food and Drug Administration.
These products are not intended to diagnose, treat, cure or prevent any disease.

General Disclaimer: Great care has been taken to maintain the accuracy of the information contained in this Clinical Manual. The information as presented in this Clinical Manual is for educational purposes only. We cannot anticipate all conditions under which this may be used. In view of ongoing research, changes in governmental regulation, and the constant flow of information relating to Chinese and Western medicine, the reader is urged to check with other sources for all up-to-date information. The staff and authors of Lotus Institute of Integrative Medicine recognize that practitioners accessing this information will have varying levels of training and expertise; therefore, we accept no responsibility for the results obtained by the application of the information within this Clinical Manual. Nor are we liable for the safety and suitability of the products, either alone or in combination with others, with single herbs or with the products of other manufacturers. Neither the Lotus Institute of Integrative Medicine nor the authors of this Clinical Manual can be held responsible for errors of fact or omission, nor for any consequences arising from the use or misuse of the information herein.

Caution: Use of herbs during pregnancy or while nursing is not recommended.

Special Thanks: We would like to offer our appreciation to the following practitioners: Alex Yuan-Da Chen, Cathy McNease, Ching-Chang Tung, Hua-Long Zhang, Jimmy Wei-Yen Chang, John K. Chen, Jun-Qing Luo, Laraine Crampton, Li-Chun Huang, Maoshing Ni, Matt Van Benschoten, Richard Tan, Victor Meng-Chau Jang, and Xiao-Ping Zhang. We would also like to thank all the practitioners for submitting their case studies.

ISBN-10: 0-9772270-6-5
ISBN-13: 978-0-9772270-6-8
Illustrator: Charles O. Funk
Design: Chien-Hui Liao, Rick Friesen
Publisher: Lotus Institute of Integrative Medicine
PO Box 92493, City of Industry, CA, USA 91715
Tel: (626) 780-7182
Order: (866) 905-6887
Fax: (626) 363-9751
Web: www.eLotus.org
Email: info@eLotus.org

Formula Name Changes

To provide more clarity and consistency, several formula names have been changed, as summarized in the following table:

Old Names	New Names
Adrenoplex	*Adrenal +*
Back Support (Acute)	*Back Support (AC)*
Back Support (Chronic)	*Back Support (CR)*
Corydalin	*Corydalin (AC)*
Flex (Spur)	*Flex (SPR)*
Herbal Analgesic	*Herbal ANG*
Knee & Ankle (Acute)	*Knee & Ankle (AC)*
Knee & Ankle (Chronic)	*Knee & Ankle (CR)*
Menotrol	*Menatrol*
Migratrol	*Corydalin (CR)*
Neck & Shoulder (Acute)	*Neck & Shoulder (AC)*
Neck & Shoulder (Chronic)	*Neck & Shoulder (CR)*
P-Statin	*P-Support*
Traumanex	*Flex (TMX)*
V-Statin	*V-Support*

Preface

The cultural climate of contemporary healthcare is changing rapidly. As the North American public increasingly discovers the validity and efficacy of traditional Chinese medicine (TCM), both patients and practitioners here are catching glimpses of the potential for a comprehensive cooperation between the previously separate worlds of allopathic (that is, 'Western' or 'modern') medicine and traditional Chinese medicine. This partnership has begun not only here but is also in progress in many of the nations in which modern and ancient medicines co-exist. There are notable examples of forward-looking hospitals and medical centers that are welcoming the assistance of TCM practitioners, and of TCM medical schools placing additional emphasis on the importance of training graduates who possess a broad understanding of both medical worlds, and being able to welcome and effectively communicate with partners within the allopathic model.

There are layers of action and potential throughout both worlds, but some are less 'integrated' than others. An acupuncturist need not know surgical techniques in order to appropriately address the presenting problems of a patient who desires assistance in recovering from surgery. A surgeon need not know how to do acupuncture in order to recommend that the surgical patient pursue a course of acupuncture to assist in resolving post-surgical pain and swelling. The partnership across this line is assisted by, but not ultimately completely dependent upon, communication between the two professionals.

However, when the TCM practitioner specializing in internal medicine, endocrinology, or gynecology turns to prescribing herbal medicines while the internist, endocrinologist, or gynecologist turns to prescribing pharmaceuticals, the potential for enhancing, exaggerating, undermining, or complicating the other's efforts becomes much more apparent and potentially serious. When it comes to co-treating with medicines meant to be ingested, the need for communication becomes much clearer, and more urgent. The reasonable nexus of these two very different worlds would seem to be at the point of diagnosis, but even here it seems there could be a confounding welter of confusing terminology and approaches for both parties, creating a gulf between sincere professionals on either side.

While a neurologist would view and treat a headache patient from one angle, a TCM doctor would consider the same patient in light of a whole series of both similar and very different criteria. Neither is 'right' or 'wrong' for having a different approach than the other, and both have valuable healing services to offer. Although it is prohibitively expensive in terms of both time and life energy for all M.D.s to learn TCM and all practitioners of Chinese medicine to earn medical degrees, there can and must increasingly be a shared vocabulary of understanding accessible to both medical traditions. This common ground can enhance the ability of both TCM and allopathic doctors to cooperate in providing the highest quality care to their patients while observing the utmost care to safeguard all patients from untoward reactions, interactions or complications resulting from co-treatment.

The following pages are certainly aimed primarily at TCM practitioners who are functioning either in independent or group practices, in complimentary care group practices or centers, or in hospitals incorporating both medical traditions. However, those nurses, M.D.s, chiropractors, naturopaths, nutritionists and others who find themselves practicing alongside or in cooperation with TCM professionals will find the material in this text to be of help as they consider the purposes and actions of herbal medicines previously veiled by the mysteries of unfamiliarity, unique terminology and distinctive diagnostic strategies.

There is no disputing the superiority of combining individual skill, excellent training, and extensive experience in selecting precisely the right combination of herbs for the particular patient and precise condition, tailoring treatments to fit the surrounding climate, circumstances, unique patient constitution, and previous patient responses to individual herbs or combinations.

Preface

However, there is also a long-respected broader territory of reliable treatment using pre-processed combinations of herbs for very effective application to a specific range of action and symptomology. This middle ground, appropriately catalogued, documented and explained, can be very useful to the practitioner.

An M.D. debating whether a particular pharmaceutical product is appropriate for a patient who is already taking an herbal formula need not return to TCM school to learn the individual characteristics of 5,000 herbal substances and the myriad applications of each substance and of combinations thereof if appropriate information is available to her or him regarding the constituents and pharmaceutical actions of the herbal formula that the patient is taking.

Similarly, a doctor of TCM need not obtain a degree in pharmacology in an allopathic medical school in order to gain precise and adequate information as to the potential for enhanced or conflicting actions of the herbal medicines under consideration for a patient who has already begun taking pharmaceutical products to address symptoms. Having a clear and extensive resource for understanding the nature and TCM-context actions of commonly used pharmaceuticals is a key asset for this practitioner.

We have selected the Evergreen herbal formulas as the exemplars in this Clinical Manual because these formulas represent the most recent and innovative approach of TCM to address modern illnesses. For these new formulas, though their effectiveness has been documented by much clinical and laboratory research, there is not currently sufficient English-language explanation to ensure understanding and proper usage among practitioners. In other words, it is necessary to make sure contemporary practitioners understand how these newest formulas work so they can make correct diagnoses and treat accordingly.

We choose to keep a simple focus in this volume. Thus, neither classical formulas, nor formulas from multiple sources are covered in order to avoid repetition or unnecessary complication of the discussion. There is abundant documentation that exists for classical formulas from centuries of clinical application. There is no need to revisit those classics here, as we already know what they do and how they work. Naturally, a practitioner taking careful note of the details of this volume will find that he or she can take general principles or specific information for use in considering other formulas, which is a positive by-product, though not the central focus of this text.

The Lotus Institute of Integrative Medicine intends for this Clinical Manual to provide not only a helpful resource for TCM practitioners and others, but also to form a bridge of communication precisely at the point of convergence of traditional Chinese medicine and other medical traditions. The thorough documentation and extensive discussion available for the products from Evergreen Herbs offer a broad and useful base from which to begin. It is our hope that the indexes, guidelines, and supplementary material will make this volume even more accessible and helpful; we welcome your feedback and suggestions for future editions.

Sincere regards and best wishes for your endeavors in providing superlative healthcare,

Lotus Institute of Integrative Medicine
PO Box 92493, City of Industry, CA USA 91715
Tel: (626) 780-7182
Order: (866) 905-6887
Fax: (626) 363-9751
Web: www.eLotus.org
Email: info@eLotus.org

Contributors

JIMMY WEI-YEN CHANG, M.P.H., PH.D., O.M.D., L.AC. [張蔚炎]

Dr. Jimmy Wei-Yen Chang, a renowned pulse diagnostician and herbalist with over 30 years of innovative clinical experience, is one of the very few licensed practitioners who is able to integrate TCM pulse diagnosis with Western biomedical conditions and also correlate definitive pulses with herbal prescriptions. He has made pulse diagnosis, Chinese medicine's cardinal diagnostic technique, into a reliable diagnostic tool in itself. For additional information, please attend his online courses and read his book:

- **Online courses:** www.elotus.org/speaker-bio
  - Allergy, Stress, and Depression: Pulse Dx & Herbal Tx
  - Cardiovascular & Respiratory Disorders: Pulse Dx & Herbal Tx
  - Dermatological, Endocrine, and Genito-Urinary Disorders: Pulse Dx & Herbal Tx
  - *Fang Jia Fang*: The Art and Science of Herbal Combinations, Part I-II
  - Gastrointestinal & Hepatic Disorders: Pulse Dx & Herbal Tx
  - Pain, Endocrinology, Dermatology: Pulse Dx & Herbal Tx
  - Pulsynergy Made Easy Part I-IV
  - The Successful Practice Pharmacy: Jimmy Chang's Latest Herbal Discoveries, Part I-IV
  - Women's Health & Infertility: Pulse Dx & Herbal Tx
- **Website:** www.pulsynergy.com
- **Book:** *Pulsynergy* by Dr. Jimmy Wei-Yen Chang and Marcus Brinkman

JOHN CHEN, PHARM.D., PH.D., O.M.D., L.AC. [陳冠生]

Dr. John Chen is a recognized authority in both Western pharmacology and Chinese herbal medicine, having combined formal training in both fields with extensive research in China. He teaches at the USC School of Pharmacy, Emperor's College, Yo San University of TCM, OCOM, Five Branches, AOMA and ACTCM, and has taught numerous professional seminars across the U.S. and abroad. Integrating medicines of the East and the West, Dr. Chen shares his invaluable knowledge of drug-herb interactions and herbal alternatives to drugs. Presently, Dr. Chen maintains his consulting practice in Southern California. For additional information, please attend his online courses and read his books:

- **Online courses:** www.elotus.org/speaker-bio
  - Recognition and Prevention of Herb-Drug Interactions
  - Herb-Drug Interactions: An Advanced Class
  - Herb-Drug Interactions for the Collection Formulas, Part I-II
  - Internal Medicine: Herbal Alternatives to Drugs, Part I-II
  - Meet the Masters: Classic Formulas and Their Contemporary Applications
  - Evolution of Chinese Herbs in Treating Modern Diseases
- **Books:** www.aompress.com
  - *Chinese Medical Herbology and Pharmacology* by John Chen and Tina Chen
  - *Chinese Herbal Formulas and Applications* by John Chen and Tina Chen
  - *Chinese Herbal Formulas for Veterinarians* by Signe Beebe, Michael Salewski, John Chen, and Tina Chen

Contributors

LI-CHUN HUANG, M.D. (CHINA), L.AC. [黄麗春]

Auricular medicine is a scientific medical system which can diagnose and treat many different diseases of the body and the mind solely through the ears. After more than 40 years of research and practice, Dr. Li-Chun Huang, an internationally renowned physician, founded this unique art of healing. Dr. Huang developed this complete system of auricular diagnosis with visual examination, palpation, and electrical probe diagnosis. Auricular medicine can precisely diagnosis and treat over 400 symptoms and over 200 diseases. The ears are one of the few areas where a practitioner can conduct diagnosis and treatment at the same time. It is very fast, effective, and safe. With vaccaria seed application, in which Dr. Huang uses two seeds per point, the therapy is minimally invasive while providing long-lasting stimulation to promote healing. Dr. Huang is very generous in sharing her knowledge and has recommended point prescriptions associated with formulas and conditions mentioned in this Clinical Manual. For in-depth study of auricular medicine, please refer to her books and online courses:

- **Online courses:** www.elotus.org/speaker-bio
  - Auricular Medicine Class I: Introduction to Auricular Medicine
  - Auricular Medicine Class II: Auricular Points
  - Auricular Medicine Class III: Functions of Auricular Points, Part I
  - Auricular Medicine Class IV: Functions of Auricular Points, Part II
  - Auricular Medicine Class V: Auricular Diagnosis
  - Auricular Medicine Class VI: Auricular Diagnosis and Techniques
  - Auricular Medicine Class VII: Auricular Treatment
  - Auricular Medicine Class VIII: Auricular Treatment and Manipulations
- **Website:** www.earmedicine.us/
- **Books:**
  - *Auricular Medicine (second edition)* by Li-Chun Huang
  - *Handbook of Auricular Treatment, Prescriptions & Formulae* by Li-Chun Huang
  - *Auricular Diagnosis with Color Photos* by Li-Chun Huang
  - *Color Ear Chart (Left Ear)* by Li-Chun Huang
  - *Color Ear Chart (Right Ear)* by Li-Chun Huang

CATHY MCNEASE

Cathy McNease is a nationally certified herbalist and the co-author of books: *The Tao of Nutrition* and *101 Vegetarian Delights*. She is currently on the faculty of Yo San University and a professional member of the American Herbalists Guild. In addition to her teaching profession, she also runs a private practice focusing on nutrition and dietary modifications. For additional information, please attend her online courses and read her book:

- **Online courses:** www.elotus.org/speaker-bio
  - The Tao of Nutrition: Harmonizing the Seasons
  - The Tao of Nutrition: Healing with Food Energy
- **Book:** *The Tao of Nutrition* by Dr. Maoshing Ni and Cathy McNease

Contributors

MAOSHING NI, L.AC., D.O.M., PH.D., DIPL. C.H., DIPL. ABAAP

Dr. Maoshing Ni, known as Dr. Mao, is a 38th-generation doctor of Chinese medicine, an authority on Taoist anti-aging medicine, a Diplomat of Chinese Herbology and a Diplomat in Anti-Aging. He was awarded the Outstanding Acupuncturist of the Year Award in 1987. Dr. Mao is a co-founder of Yo San University and the Tao of Wellness, the acclaimed center for nutrition, Chinese medicine, and acupuncture, located in Santa Monica, CA. He is currently director and professor of Chinese medicine at Yo San University and runs a general practice with a special interest in immune, hormonal and aging related conditions. For additional information, please visit his website or read his book:

- **Website:** www.taoofwellness.com/
- **Book:** *The Tao of Nutrition* by Dr. Maoshing Ni and Cathy McNease

RICHARD TEH-FU TAN, O.M.D., L.AC. [譚特夫]

The late Dr. Richard Tan was a leading acupuncture authority in our profession. His skills represented the culmination of years of study. At age seven, he began his studies in Chinese Medicine with his family in Taiwan, and apprenticed with numerous masters in herbal medicine, five element theory, acupuncture channel theory, *zang fu* energetics, *feng shui*, and qi cultivation. Early in his career, he treated hundreds of patients who were also receiving Western medical care in an army hospital. Upon coming to the U.S., Dr. Tan revolutionized the acupuncture community with Balance Method Acupuncture. This school of acupuncture was derived from the *I Ching*, which consisted of six logical systems based on TCM Channel relationships and the Chinese Clock. He practiced in San Diego for over 25 years while leading many interns to become successful practitioners. Dr. Tan also lectured extensively throughout the U.S. and the world. For additional information, please attend his online courses, and read his books:

- **Online courses:** www.elotus.org/speaker-bio
  - Dr. Tan's Balance Method: As Simple As 1-2-3! [Introduction]
  - Intro to Master Tung's Acupuncture: Richard Tan's Applications [Introduction]
  - Master Tung's Acupuncture - Dr. Tan Style [Introduction]
- **Books:**
  - *Twelve and Twelve in Acupuncture* by Richard Teh-Fu Tan and Stephen Rush
  - *Twenty-Four More in Acupuncture* by Richard Teh-Fu Tan and Stephen Rush
  - *Dr. Tan's Strategy of Twelve Magical Points* by Richard Teh-Fu Tan
  - *Acupuncture 1, 2, 3* by Richard Teh-Fu Tan

Contributors

MATT VAN BENSCHOTEN, O.M.D., L.AC.

The late Dr. Matt Van Benschoten was a graduate of the California Acupuncture College of Los Angeles, with over 30 years of clinical, research, and teaching experience in acupuncture, Chinese herbal medicine, and medical *qi gong*. He was the author of more than fifty papers on acupoint diagnostic methods, chronic fatigue syndrome, AIDS, autoimmune disease, breast cancer, mercury toxicity, and indoor mold exposure. His clinical practice focused on multidrug resistance infections, immune dysfunction, and environmental illness. For additional information, please attend his online courses, or visit his website:

- **Online courses:** www.elotus.org/speaker-bio
  - Autoimmune Disorders, Multiple Chemical Sensitivities & Chinese Medicine
  - Chronic Fatigue and Chinese Herbal Medicine
  - Immunology and Chinese Herbal Medicine
  - Laboratory Test Results and Chinese Herbal Medicine
  - Multiple Drug Resistance and Chinese Herbal Medicine
- **Website:** www.mmvbs.com/

CHUAN-MIN WANG, D.C., L.AC. [王全民]

Born in Taiwan, Dr. Chuan-Min Wang received a Philosophy B.S. degree from Fu-Jen Catholic University in 1974 and an Education Master degree from National Taiwan Normal University in 1977. During his college years, Dr. Wang studied Chinese Philosophy and *I-Ching* from Master Hwai-Jin Nan. During 1972-1974, **Dr. Wang learned Tung's acupuncture directly with Master Ching-Chang Tung**. After his studies, Dr. Wang taught philosophy at a local college and practice acupuncture at home in Taiwan. After immigrating to the US, Dr. Wang studied chiropractic techniques and received a Doctor of Chiropractic degree in 1999. Soon after, Dr. Wang received his chiropractic physician and acupuncture licenses and began a practice in Illinois. Dr. Wang has also visited Peru, El Salvador, the Dominican Republic, and Bolivia as a volunteer physician 7 times and received the Humanitarian Physician Award from the Buddhist Compassion Relief *Tzu Chi* Foundation Taiwan in 2004 for his volunteer works. In addition, Dr. Wang was invited to promote Tung's Acupuncture three days in He'nan Traditional Chinese Medicine by The World Federation of Acupuncture-Moxibustion Society (WFAS). For additional information, please attend his online courses and read his book:

- **Online courses:** www.elotus.org/speaker-bio
  - Master Tung's Acupuncture: Five *Zang* System
  - Master Tung's Unique Points for Female Conditions
  - Top 30 Master Tung Points & Their Clinical Indications
- **Website:** www.acup-chiro.com/
- **Book:** *Introduction to Tung's Acupuncture* by Chuan-Min Wang

Table of Contents

Table of Contents

Section 1

INTRODUCTION

Introduction

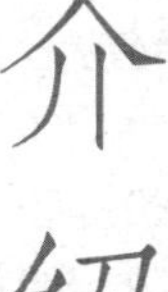

Strategic Dosing Guidelines

The standard dose of herbal extracts for an average adult is 6 to 10 grams per day. In treating acute or severe cases, the dosage may be increased up to 20 grams per day. Since not everybody is an "average adult," the fundamental concept in dosing is to realize that one size does not fit all. Every person is unique and must be treated individually.

The principle behind the Age-To-Dose Dosing Guideline is assessment of the maturity of the organs' ability to metabolize, utilize and eliminate herbs. This detailed chart is especially useful for adjusting dosages for infants and younger children. The recommendations are taken from *Zhong Yao Xue* [Chinese Herbology], published by Nanjing College of Traditional Chinese Medicine.

The principle underlying the Weight-To-Dose Dosing Guideline is based on gauging the effective concentration of the herb after it is distributed throughout the body. This dosing strategy is especially useful for patients whose body weight falls outside of the normal range. All calculations are based on Clark's Rule in *Pharmaceutical Calculations*, by Mitchell Stoklosa and Howard Ansel.

These two charts provide the herbal practitioner with a handy reference for calculating dosages for those patients who fall outside the definition of an "average adult." It is still important to keep in mind, however, that these charts serve only as a guideline - not an absolute rule. Every person is unique and must be treated as such. One must always remember to treat each patient as an individual, not as a chart!

*Suggestion for pediatric patients to improve compliance: Mix some honey into the herbal tea and have them drink it with a straw.

Table I. Age-to-Dose Dosing Guideline

Age	Recommended Daily Dosage	Fine Granules	Capsules
0 - 1 month	1/18 - 1/14 of adult dose	0.3 - 0.4 grams	N/R*
1 - 6 months	1/14 - 1/7 of adult dose	0.4 - 0.9 grams	N/R*
6 - 12 months	1/7 - 1/5 of adult dose	0.9 - 1.2 grams	N/R*
1 - 2 years	1/5 - 1/4 of adult dose	1.2 - 1.5 grams	N/R*
2 - 4 years	1/4 - 1/3 of adult dose	1.5 - 2.0 grams	N/R*
4 - 6 years	1/3 - 2/5 of adult dose	2.0 - 2.4 grams	N/R*
6 - 9 years	2/5 - 1/2 of adult dose	2.4 - 3.0 grams	5 - 6 capsules**
9 - 14 years	1/2 - 2/3 of adult dose	3.0 - 4.0 grams	6 - 8 capsules**
14 - 18 years	2/3 - full adult dose	4.0 - 6.0 grams	8 - 12 capsules**
18 - 60 years	***adult dose***	***6.0 grams***	***12 capsules****
60 years and over	3/4 or less of adult dose	4.5 - 6.0 grams	9 - 12 capsules**

Table II. Weight-to-Dose Dosing Guideline

Weight	Recommended Daily Dosage	Fine Granules	Capsules
30 - 40 lbs	20% - 27% of adult dose	1.2 - 1.6 grams	N/R*
40 - 50 lbs	27% - 33% of adult dose	1.6 - 1.9 grams	N/R*
50 - 60 lbs	33% - 40% of adult dose	1.9 - 2.4 grams	N/R*
60 - 70 lbs	40% - 47% of adult dose	2.4 - 2.8 grams	N/R*
70 - 80 lbs	47% - 53% of adult dose	2.8 - 3.2 grams	5 - 6 capsules**
80 - 100 lbs	53% - 67% of adult dose	3.2 - 4.0 grams	6 - 8 capsules**
100 - 120 lbs	67% - 80% of adult dose	4.0 - 4.8 grams	8 - 10 capsules**
120 - 150 lbs	80% - 100% of adult dose	4.8 - 6.0 grams	10 - 12 capsules**
150 lbs	***adult dose***	***6.0 grams***	***12 capsules****
150 - 200 lbs	100% - 133% of adult dose	6.0 - 7.9 grams	12 - 16 capsules**
200 - 250 lbs	133% - 167% of adult dose	7.9 - 10.0 grams	16 - 20 capsules**
250 - 300 lbs	167% - 200% of adult dose	10.0 - 12.0 grams	20 - 24 capsules**

* N/R: Not Recommended for infants and young children since they may have difficulty swallowing.
** Each capsule weighs 500 mg or 0.5 gram.

List of Formulas (Alphabetical Order)

Names	Clinical Applications	Therapeutic Functions
Adrenal +	An adrenal support formula for individuals who are "burned out," with fatigue, no energy, and lack of interest, drive and satisfaction	Tonifies Kidney qi
Arm Support	General musculoskeletal disorders of the arm (shoulders, elbows, and wrists)	Dispels cold and damp, activates qi and blood circulation, relieves pain
Astringent Complex	Used as an adjunct formula to treat acute and chronic inflammation with swelling	Clears fire, damp-heat, toxic heat, and deficiency heat
Back Support (AC)	Acute pain and inflammation of the lower back; or chronic pain with acute flare-up	Activates blood circulation, disperses painful obstruction in the lower back
Back Support (CR)	Chronic pain and inflammation of the lower back with weakness, degeneration, and decreased mobility and range of motion	Invigorates channel circulation, tonifies Kidney and Liver yin
Back Support (HD)	Herniated disk, lumbar radiculopathy, prolapsed or bulging disk, or slipped disk; localized or radiating pain from the spine	Activates blood circulation, eliminates blood stasis, reduces inflammation, relieves pain, strengthens the soft tissues
Balance (Heat)	Menopause with manifestations of heat (hot flashes, irritability, insomnia, and mood swings)	Clears deficiency heat
Balance Spring	Atrophic vaginitis or vulvovaginitis with vaginal dryness, itching, and burning sensations	Nourishes blood, softens the Liver, tonifies Kidney yin and *jing* (essence)
Blossom (Phase 1)	Female infertility: regulates menstruation and promotes fertility during the menstrual phase	Regulates menstruation, relieves pain
Blossom (Phase 2)	Female infertility: regulates menstruation and promotes fertility during the follicular phase	Tonifies qi and blood, nourishes Kidney *jing* (essence)
Blossom (Phase 3)	Female infertility: regulates menstruation and promotes fertility during the ovulatory phase	Tonifies *ming men* (life gate) fire and Kidney yang
Blossom (Phase 4)	Female infertility: regulates menstruation and promotes fertility during the luteal phase	Moves qi and blood
CA Support	Cancer support formula for individuals who suffer extreme weakness and deficiency and cannot receive chemotherapy, radiation treatments, or surgery	Clears heat, eliminates toxins, tonifies the underlying deficiencies (qi, blood, yin, and yang)
C/R Support	Chemotherapy/radiation support formula	Tonifies qi and yin, harmonizes the Stomach
Calm	Stress, frustration, restlessness, anxiety, and emotional disturbance; also a support formula for PMS (breast distension, irritability and/or mood swings)	Spreads Liver qi, relieves stagnation
Calm (ES)	Extra-strength formula for severe restlessness, stress, and anxiety; also a support formula for craving and withdrawal associated with addiction	Purges Liver fire, calms the *shen* (spirit)
Calm (Jr)	ADD (attention deficit disorder) and ADHD (attention deficit hyperactivity disorder) with difficulty focusing and concentrating	Extinguishes Liver wind, nourishes the *shen* (spirit)
Calm ZZZ	Stress, insomnia, and an overactive mind in individuals with underlying weakness and deficiencies	Calms the *shen* (spirit), regulates Liver qi, sedates Liver fire, tonifies deficiencies
Cholisma	High cholesterol and triglycerides levels	Dispels dampness, invigorates blood circulation

List of Formulas (Alphabetical Order)

Names	Clinical Applications	Therapeutic Functions
Cholisma (ES)	High cholesterol and triglycerides levels in individuals with fatty liver and obesity	Dissolves damp, eliminates phlegm, invigorates blood circulation
Circulation	Cardiovascular and circulatory disorders with decreased blood flow to the heart	Invigorates blood circulation in the upper *jiao*
Circulation (SJ)	Cardiovascular and circulatory disorders with severe blood stasis and impaired blood circulation throughout the entire body	Invigorates blood and qi circulation and eliminates blood and qi stagnation in the upper, middle and lower *jiaos*
Cordyceps 3	General support to improve respiratory, immune and reproductive functions	Tonifies Lung and Kidney qi
Corydalin (AC)	Acute headaches: vertex, occipital, frontal, and temporal	Invigorates qi and blood circulation in the head
Corydalin (CR)	Chronic or deficient headaches: migraine, tension, and cluster	Invigorates qi and blood circulation in the head, tonifies blood
Dermatrol (Clear)	Clears the skin, treats acne	Clears Lung heat and detoxifies the skin
Dermatrol (Damp)	Relieves skin conditions that appear to be visibly wet and purulent, or contain pus, abscesses or fluid	Clears heat, eliminates toxins, dries dampness, dispels wind, relieves itching
Dermatrol (Dry)	Relieves skin conditions that appear red and dry, and may be flaky or scaly with underlying damage to and atrophy of the skin	Clears heat, moistens dryness, eliminates toxins, dispels wind, relieves itching
Dermatrol (HZ)	Shingles (herpes zoster) with skin lesions and nerve pain	Drains damp-heat, purges fire, eliminates toxins, tonifies the underlying deficiencies
Dermatrol (PS)	Psoriasis and skin disorders with sores, abscesses, lesions, blisters, and severe itching	Clears heat and detoxifies, nourishes blood
Dissolve (GS)	Gallstones (cholelithiasis) and inflammation of the gallbladder and bile duct (cholecystitis)	Spreads Liver qi, clears damp-heat in the Gallbladder
Dissolve (KS)	Kidney and urinary stones (nephrolithiasis and urolithiasis)	Dissolves stones and promotes urination
Enhance Memory	Forgetfulness and poor memory	Tonifies Heart and Kidney *jing* (essence)
Equilibrium	Diabetes mellitus	Nourishes yin, dispels dampness
Flex (CD)	Arthritis and joint pain that worsens with exposure to cold and dampness	Warms the channels and relieves *bi zheng* (painful obstruction syndrome) with cold and dampness
Flex (GT)	Gout, gouty arthritis	Drains damp-heat, opens the channels and collaterals, relieves pain
Flex (Heat)	Arthritis and joint pain with redness, swelling, and inflammation	Clears heat and relieves *bi zheng* (painful obstruction syndrome) with heat
Flex (MLT)	Weakness, atrophy and degeneration of the muscles, tendons and ligaments	Tonifies qi and blood, activates qi and blood circulation, nourishes yin, strengthens muscles, ligaments, and tendons
Flex (NP)	Neuropathy and nerve-related pain and numbness	Invigorates blood circulation in the extremities, relieves pain

List of Formulas (Alphabetical Order)

Names	Clinical Applications	Therapeutic Functions
Flex (SC)	Muscle spasms and cramps	Nourishes Liver yin and blood, unblocks stagnation
Flex (SPR)	Bone spurs with swelling, inflammation and pain	Invigorates blood in the channels, disperses stagnation and relieves pain
Flex (TMX)	Trauma and injuries with bruises, swelling, inflammation; damages to soft tissues and bones	Invigorates qi and blood circulation, relieves pain
Gardenia Complex	Any excess conditions characterized by heat, fire and toxins, such as infection, inflammation, metabolic disorders and autoimmune diseases	Purges fire in all three *jiaos*
Gastrodia Complex	Hypertension in individuals with deficient conditions	Reduces Liver yang rising, tonifies Liver and Kidney yin
Gentiana Complex	Hypertension in individuals with excess conditions. Also effective for genito-urinary infection and inflammation with pain and dysuria	Dispels Liver channel damp-heat
Gentle Lax (Deficient)	Chronic or habitual constipation with mild to moderate severity	Moistens the Intestines by nourishing yin and blood
Gentle Lax (Excess)	Acute and severe constipation	Purges the Intestines and unblocks stagnation
GI Care	Acid reflux, stomach ulcer and duodenal ulcer due to excessive amount of gastric acid	Clears Stomach fire and relieves pain
GI Care II	Gastrointestinal disorders with infection and inflammation	Clears damp-heat, relieves diarrhea
GI Care (HMR)	Hemorrhoids, including internal or external hemorrhoids, with or without swelling, inflammation or bleeding	Clears damp-heat, eliminates toxic heat from the Intestines, regulates bowel movements
GI Care (UC)	Ulcerative colitis with diarrhea, mucus, blood, and abdominal cramps	Clears damp-heat, binds the Intestines, stops bleeding
GI DTX	Cleanses the bowel and promotes gastrointestinal health	Clears toxic heat in the Intestines
GI Harmony	Irritable bowel syndrome (IBS) with gas, pain, and alternating diarrhea and constipation	Spreads Liver qi, regulates the bowels
GI Tonic	General weakness of the gastrointestinal system with poor appetite, indigestion, loose stools and diarrhea	Tonifies Spleen qi, binds the Intestines
Herbal ABX	An herbal antibiotic [mainly antibacterial] formula for bacterial and viral infection; may be used by itself or with another formula	Clears fire, damp-heat and toxic heat, reduces swelling and redness
Herbal ANG	An herbal analgesic formula that relieves pain and reduces inflammation; may be used by itself or as an adjunct to another formula	Strongly unblocks stagnation and relieves pain
Herbal AVR	An herbal antibiotic [mainly antiviral] formula that treats various types of infections; may be used by itself or with another formula	Releases wind-heat, clears deficiency heat, eliminates toxic heat
Herbal DRX	An herbal diuretic formula for edema, swelling, and water accumulation	Drains dampness, eliminates water accumulation
Herbal DTX	Herbal detox to relieve adverse reactions caused by exposure to drugs, chemicals, heavy metals, environmental or airborne toxins	Clears heat, detoxifies, and nourishes yin

List of Formulas (Alphabetical Order)

Names	Clinical Applications	Therapeutic Functions
Herbal ENT	Herbal antibiotic formula [antibacterial and antiviral] for ear, nose, throat, and lung infections and inflammations	Clears heat in the head and the upper *jiao*, eliminates toxins
Herbalite	Promotes weight loss and treats obesity by suppressing appetite and increasing metabolic and energy levels	Clears heat in the Stomach, dispels dampness
Immune +	Promotes and strengthens immune function	Tonifies *wei* (defensive) *qi*
Imperial Tonic	A comprehensive and balanced tonic to promote optimal health and wellness	Tonifies qi, blood, yin, and yang
Kidney DTX	Herbal detox to treat chronic kidney diseases with elevated creatinine and blood urea nitrogen	Clears heat, detoxifies the Kidney, dispels dampness
Kidney Tonic (Yang)	Kidney yang deficiency with coldness, low libido, premature ejaculation, weakness and soreness of the back and knees, pale complexion, and polyuria	Tonifies Kidney yang
Kidney Tonic (Yin)	Kidney yin deficiency with blurry vision, weakness of the back and knees, tinnitus, dryness, flushed cheeks, possible low-grade fever	Tonifies Kidney yin
Knee & Ankle (AC)	Acute knee and ankle injuries with swelling, inflammation and pain; or chronic pain with acute flare-up	Clears heat, activates blood circulation, eliminates blood stasis, drains fluids
Knee & Ankle (CR)	Chronic knee and ankle disorders with weakness, degeneration, and decreased mobility and range of motion	Tonifies qi, blood and yin; activates qi and blood circulation, opens channels and collaterals to relieve pain
Liver DTX	Liver detox to treat hepatic diseases with elevated liver enzymes and compromised liver functions	Clears heat, detoxifies the Liver
Lonicera Complex	Common cold, influenza, oral herpes, sore throat and infection in the early stages	Dispels wind-heat
LPS Support	Systemic lupus erythematosus (SLE) with inflammation affecting various tissues and organs in the body	Clears heat, eliminates toxins, nourishes yin, tonifies blood, promotes generation of body fluids
Lycium Support	Atrophic and degenerative eye disorders with impaired or blurred vision, excessive tearing, dry eyes	Tonifies Liver and Kidney yin to brighten the eyes
Magnolia Clear Sinus	Allergic sinusitis or rhinitis with nasal congestion and clear nasal discharge	Disperses wind-cold, opens nasal orifices
Menatrol	Amenorrhea, polycystic ovarian disease, and infertility with cold and blood stasis	Tonifies Kidney yang, invigorates blood
Mense-Ease	Dysmenorrhea with pain and discomfort	Invigorates blood circulation and removes stasis, relieves pain
Neck & Shoulder (AC)	Acute neck and shoulder pain; or chronic pain with acute flare-up	Activates blood circulation, disperses painful obstruction in the neck and shoulders
Neck & Shoulder (CR)	Chronic neck and shoulder pain with weakness, degeneration, and decreased mobility and range of motion	Invigorates channel circulation, tonifies Kidney and Liver yin

List of Formulas (Alphabetical Order)

Names	Clinical Applications	Therapeutic Functions
Neuro Plus	Neuro-degenerative disorders with impaired mental and/or physical functions, such as Alzheimer's disease, Parkinson's disease, and sequelae of stroke	Tonifies Kidney yang, opens channels and collaterals
Notoginseng 9	Bleeding disorders, including internal and external bleeding	Cools the blood, disperses blood stasis, stops bleeding
Nourish	General endocrine and hormonal imbalances (i.e., menopause) and atrophy of the organs (i.e., eyes, ears, kidneys, pancreas, and others)	Nourishes Liver and Kidney yin
Nourish (Fluids)	Chronic consumptive disorders characterized by dryness, such as thirst, dry mouth, post-infective cough, and non-productive cough	Nourishes Lung and Stomach yin, replenishes body fluids, harmonizes the middle *jiao*
Osteo 8	Osteoporosis, bone fractures, and broken bones	Replenishes Kidney *jing* (essence)
Pinellia Complex	Disorders characterized by accumulation of fluids, exudation and effusion [damp and phlegm]	Dries dampness and dissolves phlegm
Pinellia XPT	Lung infection and inflammation with profuse, thick, yellow phlegm, post-nasal drip, chest fullness, and breathing difficulties	Clears Lung heat and phlegm
Polygonum 14	A general hair tonic to treat hair loss, premature grey hair, and unhealthy hair with split ends	Tonifies Liver blood and Kidney yin
P-Support	Enlarged prostate with urinary difficulties	Disperses stagnation and relieves *lin zheng* (dysuria syndrome)
Pueraria Clear Sinus	Sinus infection with yellow, purulent nasal discharge and nasal congestion	Disperses wind and heat, opens nasal orifices
Resolve (AI)	Hardness and nodules caused by general infectious or inflammatory disorders; lymph edema and swelling	Disperses phlegm stagnation, clears heat, and detoxifies
Resolve (Lower)	Ovarian and uterine cysts, fibroids and mass	Disperses blood stasis and phlegm accumulation in the lower *jiao*
Resolve (Upper)	Breast lumps and cysts	Spreads Liver qi, disperses phlegm accumulation in the upper *jiao*
Respitrol (CF)	Cough due to various causes; it may be used by itself or with another formula	Releases exterior wind, eliminates phlegm, nourishes yin
Respitrol (Cold)	Acute respiratory conditions with dyspnea, chills, nasal congestion, and clear or white nasal discharge	Warms the Lung, dispels wind and cold
Respitrol (Deficient)	Chronic and deficient-type respiratory conditions with dyspnea, wheezing, shallow inhalation, and general weakness	Tonifies and descends Lung qi
Respitrol (Heat)	Acute respiratory conditions with dyspnea, wheezing, fever, dry mouth, and thirst	Clears Lung heat, descends Lung qi
Schisandra ZZZ	Insomnia with excessive worries, fear and pensiveness	Tonifies Spleen and Heart blood, tranquilizes the *shen* (spirit)
Shine	Depression	Disperses phlegm and stagnation of qi, blood, food and damp

List of Formulas (Alphabetical Order)

Names	Clinical Applications	Therapeutic Functions
Shine (DS)	Depression and stress	Spreads Liver qi, clears Heart fire
Silerex	Itching from rashes, eczema, urticaria, dermatitis, allergies	Clears heat and disperses wind, stops itching
Symmetry	Bell's palsy, facial paralysis, TMJ (temporomandibular joint) pain, and trigeminal neuralgia	Dispels wind attack, relieves pain
Thyrodex	Hyperthyroidism	Drains Liver fire, softens hardness
Thyro-forte	Hypothyroidism	Tonifies Kidney and Spleen yang
Venus	Small and underdeveloped breasts, lactation difficulties	Tonifies Kidney yang, invigorates blood circulation
Vibrant	A quick and immediate tonic to boost energy and vitality	Tonifies qi
Vital Essence	Reproductive disorders (infertility, low sperm count, poor sperm motility, mobility, and morphology)	Tonifies Kidney yin, yang, and *jing* (essence)
Vitality	Sexual disorders (impotence, decreased libido, spermatorrhea, and premature ejaculation)	Tonifies Kidney yang and *jing* (essence)
V-Support	Genito-urinary infection and inflammation with itching and pain	Dispels damp-heat in the lower *jiao*

List of Formulas (Diseases/Disorders)

MUSCULOSKELETAL DISORDERS		
Names	**Clinical Applications**	**Therapeutic Functions**
Arm Support	General musculoskeletal disorders of the arm (shoulders, elbows, and wrists)	Dispels cold and damp, activates qi and blood circulation, relieves pain
Back Support (AC)	Acute pain and inflammation of the lower back; or chronic pain with acute flare up	Activates blood circulation, disperses painful obstruction in the lower back
Back Support (CR)	Chronic pain and inflammation of the lower back	Invigorates channel circulation, tonifies Kidney and Liver yin
Back Support (HD)	Herniated disk, lumbar radiculopathy, prolapsed or bulging disk, or slipped disk; localized or radiating pain from the spine	Activates blood circulation, eliminates blood stasis, reduces inflammation, relieves pain, strengthens the soft tissues
Corydalin (AC)	Acute headaches: vertex, occipital, frontal, and temporal	Invigorates qi and blood circulation in the head
Corydalin (CR)	Chronic or deficient headaches: migraine, tension, and cluster	Invigorates qi and blood circulation in the head, tonifies blood
Flex (CD)	Arthritis and joint pain that worsens with exposure to cold and dampness	Warms the channels and relieves *bi zheng* (painful obstruction syndrome) with cold and dampness
Flex (GT)	Gout, gouty arthritis	Drains damp-heat, opens the channels and collaterals, relieves pain
Flex (Heat)	Arthritis and joint pain with redness, swelling, and inflammation	Clears heat and relieves *bi zheng* (painful obstruction syndrome) with heat
Flex (MLT)	Musculoskeletal disorders affecting the muscles, tendons and ligaments, including atrophy and wasting, chronic wear and tear, and decreased range of motion and mobility	Tonifies qi and blood, activates qi and blood circulation, nourishes yin, strengthens muscles, ligaments, and tendons
Flex (NP)	Neuropathy and nerve-related pain and numbness	Invigorates blood circulation in the extremities, relieves pain
Flex (SC)	Muscle spasms and cramps	Nourishes Liver yin and blood, unblocks stagnation
Flex (SPR)	Bone spurs with swelling, inflammation and pain	Invigorates blood in the channels, disperses stagnation and relieves pain
Flex (TMX)	Trauma and sports injuries with bruises, swelling, inflammation; damages to soft tissues and bones	Invigorates qi and blood circulation, relieves pain
Herbal ANG	An herbal analgesic formula that relieves pain and reduces inflammation; may be used individually or as an adjunct to another formula	Strongly unblocks stagnation and relieves pain
Knee & Ankle (AC)	Acute knee and ankle injuries with swelling, inflammation and pain; or chronic pain with acute flare up	Clears heat, activates blood circulation, eliminates blood stasis, drains fluids
Knee & Ankle (CR)	Chronic knee and ankle disorders, including atrophy and degeneration of the soft tissues, decreased range of motion and mobility, and generalized weakness and pain	Tonifies qi, blood and yin; activates qi and blood circulation, opens channels and collaterals to relieve pain
Neck & Shoulder (AC)	Acute neck and shoulder pain; or chronic pain with acute flare up	Activates blood circulation, disperses painful obstruction in the neck and shoulders
Neck & Shoulder (CR)	Chronic neck and shoulder pain	Invigorates channel circulation, tonifies Kidney and Liver yin
Notoginseng 9	Bleeding disorders, including internal and external bleeding	Cools the blood, disperses blood stasis, stops bleeding
Osteo 8	Osteoporosis, bone fractures, and broken bones	Replenishes Kidney *jing* (essence)

List of Formulas (Diseases/Disorders)

CARDIOVASCULAR / CIRCULATORY DISORDERS		
Names	**Clinical Applications**	**Therapeutic Functions**
Cholisma	Elevated cholesterol and triglycerides levels	Dispels dampness, invigorates blood circulation
Cholisma (ES)	High cholesterol and triglycerides levels in individuals with fatty liver and obesity	Dissolves damp, eliminates phlegm, invigorates blood circulation
Circulation	Cardiovascular and circulatory disorders with decreased blood flow to the heart	Invigorates blood circulation in the upper *jiao*
Circulation (SJ)	Cardiovascular and circulatory disorders with blood stasis and impaired blood circulation in upper, middle and lower *jiaos*	Invigorates blood and qi circulation and eliminates blood and qi stagnation in the upper, middle and lower *jiaos*
Gastrodia Complex	Hypertension in individuals with deficient conditions	Reduces Liver yang rising, tonifies Liver and Kidney yin
Gentiana Complex	Hypertension in individuals with excess conditions	Dispels Liver channel damp-heat
Notoginseng 9	Bleeding disorders, including internal and external bleeding	Cools the blood, disperses blood stasis, stops bleeding

RESPIRATORY DISORDERS		
Names	**Clinical Applications**	**Therapeutic Functions**
Cordyceps 3	General support to improve respiratory and immune functions	Tonifies Lung and Kidney qi
Herbal ABX	An herbal antibiotic [mainly antibacterial] formula for bacterial and viral infection; may be used by itself or with another formula	Clears fire, damp-heat and toxic heat, reduces swelling and redness
Herbal AVR	An herbal antibiotic [mainly antiviral] formula that treats various types of infections; may be used by itself or with another formula	Releases wind-heat, clears deficiency heat, eliminates toxic heat
Herbal ENT	Herbal antibiotic formula [antibacterial and antiviral] for ear, nose, throat, and lung infections and inflammations	Clears heat in the head and the upper *jiao*, eliminates toxins
Lonicera Complex	Initial stage of respiratory infection with fever and sore throat	Disperses wind-heat
Magnolia Clear Sinus	Allergic sinusitis or rhinitis with nasal congestion and clear nasal discharge	Disperses wind-cold, opens nasal orifices
Notoginseng 9	Bleeding disorders, including internal and external bleeding	Cools the blood, disperses blood stasis, stops bleeding
Nourish (Fluids)	Chronic consumptive disorders characterized by dryness, such as thirst, dry mouth, post-infective cough, and non-productive cough	Nourishes Lung and Stomach yin, replenishes body fluids, harmonizes the middle *jiao*
Pinellia Complex	Disorders characterized by accumulation of fluids, exudation and effusion [damp and phlegm]	Dries dampness and dissolves phlegm
Pinellia XPT	Lung infection with profuse, thick, yellow phlegm, post-nasal drip, chest fullness, and breathing difficulties	Clears Lung heat and phlegm
Pueraria Clear Sinus	Sinus infection with yellow, purulent nasal discharge and nasal congestion	Disperses wind and heat, opens nasal orifices
Respitrol (CF)	Cough due to various causes with different complications; may be used by itself or with another formula	Releases exterior wind, eliminates phlegm, nourishes yin
Respitrol (Cold)	Acute respiratory conditions with dyspnea, chills, nasal congestion, and clear or white nasal discharge	Warms the Lungs, dispels wind and cold
Respitrol (Deficient)	Chronic and deficient-type respiratory conditions with dyspnea, wheezing, shallow inhalation, and general weakness	Tonifies and descends Lung qi
Respitrol (Heat)	Acute respiratory conditions with dyspnea, wheezing, fever, dry mouth, and thirst	Clears Lung heat, descends Lung qi

List of Formulas (Diseases/Disorders)

LIVER / GALLBLADDER DISORDERS		
Names	**Clinical Applications**	**Therapeutic Functions**
Dissolve (GS)	Gallstones and inflammation of the gallbladder and bile duct	Spreads Liver qi, clears damp-heat in the Gallbladder
Liver DTX	Liver detox for hepatic diseases with elevated liver enzymes and compromised liver functions	Clears heat, detoxifies the Liver
GASTROINTESTINAL DISORDERS		
Names	**Clinical Applications**	**Therapeutic Functions**
Gentle Lax (Deficient)	Chronic or habitual constipation with mild to moderate severity	Moistens the Intestines by nourishing yin and blood
Gentle Lax (Excess)	Acute and severe constipation	Purges the Intestines and unblocks stagnation
GI Care	Acid reflux, stomach ulcer, duodenal ulcer, stomach pain	Clears Stomach fire and relieves pain
GI Care II	Burning diarrhea due to infection or improper food intake, inflammatory bowel conditions	Clears damp-heat, relieves diarrhea
GI Care (HMR)	Hemorrhoids, including internal or external hemorrhoids, with or without swelling, inflammation or bleeding	Clears damp-heat, eliminates toxic heat from the Intestines, regulates bowel movements
GI Care (UC)	Ulcerative colitis with diarrhea, mucus, blood, and abdominal cramps	Clears damp-heat, binds the Intestines, stops bleeding
GI DTX	Cleanses the bowel and promotes gastrointestinal health	Clears toxic heat in the Intestines
GI Harmony	Irritable bowel syndrome with gas, pain, and alternating loose stools and constipation	Spreads Liver qi, regulates the bowels
GI Tonic	General weakness of the gastrointestinal system with poor appetite, indigestion, loose stools and diarrhea	Tonifies Spleen qi, binds the Intestines
Herbal ABX	An herbal antibiotic [mainly antibacterial] formula for bacterial and viral infection; may be used by itself or with another formula	Clears fire, damp-heat and toxic heat, reduces swelling and redness
Herbal AVR	An herbal antibiotic [mainly antiviral] formula that treats various types of infections; may be used by itself or with another formula	Releases wind-heat, clears deficiency heat, eliminates toxic heat
Herbal ANG	An herbal analgesic formula that relieves pain and reduces inflammation; may be used individually or as an adjunct to another formula	Strongly unblocks stagnation and relieves pain
Notoginseng 9	Bleeding disorders, including internal and external bleeding	Cools the blood, disperses blood stasis, stops bleeding
GENITO-URINARY DISORDERS		
Names	**Clinical Applications**	**Therapeutic Functions**
Balance Spring	Atrophic vaginitis or vulvovaginitis with vaginal dryness, itching, and burning sensations	Nourishes blood, softens the Liver, tonifies Kidney yin and *jing* (essence)
Dissolve (KS)	Kidney and urinary stones	Dissolves stones, promotes urination, relieves pain
Gentiana Complex	Urinary tract infection, inflammation and infection of the genito-urinary tract	Clears damp-heat in lower *jiao*
P-Support	Enlarged prostate with urinary discomfort	Disperses stagnation and relieves *lin zheng* (dysuria syndrome)
V-Support	Genito-urinary infection and inflammation with itching and pain	Dispels damp-heat in the lower *jiao*

List of Formulas (Diseases/Disorders)

DERMATOLOGICAL DISORDERS		
Names	**Clinical Applications**	**Therapeutic Functions**
Dermatrol (Clear)	Clears the skin, treats acne	Clears Lung heat and detoxifies the skin
Dermatrol (Damp)	Relieves skin conditions that appear to be visibly wet and purulent, or contain pus, abscesses or fluid	Clears heat, eliminates toxins, dries dampness, dispels wind, relieves itching
Dermatrol (Dry)	Relieves skin conditions that appear red and dry, and may be flaky or scaly with underlying damage to and atrophy of the skin	Clears heat, moistens dryness, eliminates toxins, dispels wind, relieves itching
Dermatrol (HZ)	Shingles (herpes zoster) with skin lesions and nerve pain	Drains damp-heat, purges fire, eliminates toxins, tonifies the underlying deficiencies
Dermatrol (PS)	Psoriasis and skin disorders with sores, abscesses, lesions, blisters, and severe itching	Clears heat and detoxifies, nourishes blood
Herbal ABX	An herbal antibiotic [mainly antibacterial] formula for bacterial and viral infection; may be used by itself or with another formula	Clears fire, damp-heat and toxic heat, reduces swelling and redness
Herbal AVR	An herbal antibiotic [mainly antiviral] formula that treats various types of infections; may be used by itself or with another formula	Releases wind-heat, clears deficiency heat, eliminates toxic heat
Silerex	Itching from rashes, eczema, urticaria	Clears heat and disperses wind, stops itching

ENDOCRINE DISORDERS		
Names	**Clinical Applications**	**Therapeutic Functions**
Adrenal +	An adrenal support formula for individuals who are "burned out," with fatigue, no energy, lack of interest, lack of drive and satisfaction	Tonifies Kidney qi
Equilibrium	Diabetes mellitus	Nourishes yin, dispels dampness
Kidney Tonic (Yang)	Kidney yang deficiency with coldness, low libido, premature ejaculation, weakness and soreness of the back and knees, pale complexion, and polyuria	Tonifies Kidney yang
Kidney Tonic (Yin)	Kidney yin deficiency with blurry vision, weakness of the back and knees, tinnitus, dryness, flushed cheeks, possible low-grade fever	Tonifies Kidney yin
Nourish	General endocrine and hormonal imbalances (i.e., menopause) and atrophy of the organs (i.e., eyes, ears, kidneys, pancreas, and others)	Nourishes Liver and Kidney yin
Thyrodex	Hyperthyroidism	Drains Liver fire, softens hardness
Thyro-forte	Hypothyroidism	Tonifies Kidney and Spleen yang
Please refer to "Formulas for Women" and "Formulas for Men" for other hormone-balancing formulas		

STRESS / PSYCHOLOGICAL / SLEEP DISORDERS		
Names	**Clinical Applications**	**Therapeutic Functions**
Calm	Stress, frustration, irritability, anxiety, and emotional disturbance	Spreads Liver qi, relieves stagnation
Calm (ES)	Extra-strength formula for severe restlessness, stress, and anxiety	Purges Liver fire, calms the *shen* (spirit)
Calm (Jr)	ADD and ADHD, restlessness with difficulty focusing and concentrating	Extinguishes Liver wind, nourishes the *shen* (spirit)
Calm ZZZ	Stress, insomnia, and an overactive mind in individuals with underlying weakness and deficiencies	Calms the *shen* (spirit), regulates Liver qi, sedates Liver fire, tonifies deficiencies

List of Formulas (Diseases/Disorders)

Names	Clinical Applications	Therapeutic Functions
Schisandra ZZZ	Insomnia with excessive worries, pensiveness	Tonifies Spleen and Heart blood, tranquilizes the *shen* (spirit)
Shine	Depression	Disperses phlegm and stagnation of qi, blood, food and damp
Shine (DS)	Depression and stress	Spreads Liver qi, clears Heart fire
INFECTIOUS DISEASES		
Names	**Clinical Applications**	**Therapeutic Functions**
Gardenia Complex	Any excess conditions characterized by heat, fire and toxins, including infectious diseases and inflammatory conditions	Purges fire in all three *jiaos*
Gentiana Complex	Genito-urinary infection and inflammation with pain and dysuria	Clears damp-heat and Liver fire
GI Care II	General intestinal disorders such as burning diarrhea due to infection, food poisoning, or food sensitivities	Clears damp-heat in the Intestines
Herbal ABX	An herbal antibiotic [mainly antibacterial] formula for bacterial and viral infection; may be used by itself or with another formula	Clears fire, damp-heat and toxic heat, reduces swelling and redness
Herbal AVR	An herbal antibiotic [mainly antiviral] formula that treats various types of infections; may be used by itself or with another formula	Releases wind-heat, clears deficiency heat, eliminates toxic heat
Herbal ENT	Herbal antibiotic formula [antibacterial and antiviral] for ear, nose, throat, and lung infections and inflammations	Clears toxic-heat in the upper *jiao*
Lonicera Complex	Common cold, influenza, oral herpes, cold sores, and fever blisters in the early stages	Dispels wind-heat
Respitrol (Heat)	Acute respiratory conditions with dyspnea, wheezing, fever, dry mouth, and thirst	Clears Lung heat
V-Support	Genito-urinary infection and inflammation with itching and pain	Dispels damp-heat in the lower *jiao*
IMMUNE / ENERGY DISORDERS		
Names	**Clinical Applications**	**Therapeutic Functions**
CA Support	Cancer support formula for individuals who suffer extreme weakness and deficiency and cannot receive chemotherapy, radiation treatments, or surgery	Clears heat, eliminates toxins, tonifies the underlying deficiencies (qi, blood, yin, and yang)
C/R Support	Chemotherapy and radiation support formula	Tonifies qi and yin, harmonizes the Stomach
Cordyceps 3	General support to improve respiratory, immune and reproductive functions	Tonifies Lung and Kidney qi
GI Tonic	Gastrointestinal tonic formula to improve digestion of foods and absorption of nutrients	Tonifies Spleen qi, binds the Intestines
Immune +	Promotes and strengthens immune function	Tonifies *wei* (defensive) *qi*
Imperial Tonic	A comprehensive and balanced tonic to improve mental and physical performances	Tonifies qi, blood, yin, and yang
Vibrant	A quick and immediate tonic to boost energy and vitality	Tonifies qi

List of Formulas (Diseases/Disorders)

FORMULAS FOR WOMEN		
Names	**Clinical Applications**	**Therapeutic Functions**
Balance (Heat)	Menopause with manifestations of heat (hot flashes, irritability, insomnia, and mood swings)	Clears deficiency heat
Balance Spring	Atrophic vaginitis or vulvovaginitis with vaginal dryness, itching, and burning sensations	Nourishes blood, softens the Liver, tonifies Kidney yin and *jing* (essence)
Blossom (Phase 1)	Female infertility: regulates menstruation and promotes fertility during the menstrual phase	Regulates menstruation, relieves pain
Blossom (Phase 2)	Female infertility: regulates menstruation and promotes fertility during the follicular phase	Tonifies qi and blood, nourishes Kidney *jing* (essence)
Blossom (Phase 3)	Female infertility: regulates menstruation and promotes fertility during the ovulatory phase	Tonifies *ming men* (life gate) fire and Kidney yang
Blossom (Phase 4)	Female infertility: regulates menstruation and promotes fertility during the luteal phase	Moves qi and blood, relieves PMS
Calm	Premenstrual syndrome (PMS)	Spreads Liver qi, relieves stagnation
Menatrol	Amenorrhea, polycystic ovarian disease, and infertility with cold and blood stasis	Tonifies Kidney yang, invigorates blood
Mense-Ease	Dysmenorrhea with pain and discomfort	Invigorates blood circulation and removes stasis, relieves pain
Nourish	General endocrine and hormonal imbalances (i.e., menopause) and atrophy of the organs (i.e., eyes, ears, kidneys, pancreas, and others)	Nourishes Liver and Kidney yin
Polygonum 14	A general hair tonic to treat hair loss, premature grey hair, and unhealthy hair with split ends	Tonifies Liver blood and Kidney yin
Resolve (Lower)	Ovarian and uterine cysts and fibroids	Disperses blood stasis and phlegm accumulation
Resolve (Upper)	Breast lumps and cysts	Spreads Liver qi, disperses phlegm accumulation
Schisandra ZZZ	Pale complexion, anemia, insomnia, post-menstrual deficiencies	Tonifies Spleen and Heart blood, tranquilizes the *shen* (spirit)
Venus	Small and underdeveloped breasts, lactation difficulties	Tonifies Kidney yang, invigorates blood circulation
Vitality	Female sexual disorders, such as decreased libido, lack of interest and vitality	Tonifies Kidney yang and *jing* (essence)
FORMULAS FOR MEN		
Names	**Clinical Applications**	**Therapeutic Functions**
Kidney Tonic (Yang)	Kidney yang deficiency with coldness, low libido, premature ejaculation, weakness and soreness of the back and knees, pale complexion, and polyuria	Warms and tonifies Kidney yang, replenishes *jing* (essence) and tonifies blood
Kidney Tonic (Yin)	Kidney yin deficiency with blurry vision, weakness of the back and knees, tinnitus, dryness, flushed cheeks, possible low-grade fever	Tonifies the Kidney yin
Polygonum 14	A general hair tonic to treat hair loss, premature grey hair, and unhealthy hair with split ends	Tonifies Liver blood and Kidney yin
P-Support	Enlarged prostate with urinary discomfort	Disperses stagnation and relieves *lin zheng* (dysuria syndrome)
Vital Essence	Male reproductive disorders (infertility, low sperm count, poor sperm motility, mobility, and morphology)	Tonifies Kidney yin, yang, and *jing* (essence)
Vitality	Male sexual disorders (impotence, decreased libido, spermatorrhea, and premature ejaculation)	Tonifies Kidney yang and *jing* (essence)

List of Formulas (Diseases/Disorders)

HEALTH / BEAUTY / ANTI-AGING FORMULAS		
Names	**Clinical Applications**	**Therapeutic Functions**
Adrenal +	An adrenal support formula for individuals who are "burned out," with fatigue, no energy, lack of interest, lack of drive and satisfaction	Tonifies Kidney qi
Balance Spring	Atrophic vaginitis or vulvovaginitis with vaginal dryness, itching, and burning sensations	Nourishes blood, softens the Liver, tonifies Kidney yin and *jing* (essence)
Cordyceps 3	General support to improve respiratory, immune and reproductive functions	Tonifies Lung and Kidney qi
Dermatrol (Clear)	Clears the skin, treats acne	Clears Lung heat and detoxifies the skin
Enhance Memory	Forgetfulness and poor memory	Tonifies Heart and Kidney *jing* (essence)
Herbalite	Obesity, promotes weight loss by suppressing appetite and increasing metabolic and energy levels	Clears heat in the Stomach, dispels dampness
Imperial Tonic	A comprehensive and balanced tonic to improve mental and physical performances	Tonifies qi, blood, yin, and yang
Kidney Tonic (Yang)	Kidney yang deficiency with coldness, low libido, premature ejaculation, weakness and soreness of the back and knees, pale complexion, and polyuria	Warms and tonifies Kidney yang, replenishes *jing* (essence) and tonifies blood
Kidney Tonic (Yin)	Kidney yin deficiency with blurry vision, weakness of the back and knees, tinnitus, dryness, flushed cheeks, possible low-grade fever	Tonifies the Kidney yin
Lycium Support	Atrophic and degenerative eye disorders, such as glaucoma and cataract, with impaired or blurred vision, excessive tearing, and dry eyes	Tonifies Liver and Kidney yin to brighten the eyes
Polygonum 14	A general hair tonic to treat hair loss, premature grey hair, and unhealthy hair with split ends	Tonifies Liver blood and Kidney yin
Venus	Small and underdeveloped breasts, lactation difficulties	Tonifies Kidney yang, invigorates blood circulation

DETOX / CLEANSING DISORDERS		
Names	**Clinical Applications**	**Therapeutic Functions**
Circulation (SJ)	Chronic blood stagnation with multiple and complex symptoms	Invigorates blood and qi circulation, and eliminates blood and qi stagnation in the upper, middle and lower *jiaos*
Gardenia Complex	Any excess conditions characterized by heat, fire and toxins, including infectious diseases and inflammatory conditions	Clears heat, purges fire, eliminates toxins
GI DTX	Herbal detox to cleanse the bowel and promote gastrointestinal health	Clears toxic heat in the Intestines
Herbal DTX	Herbal detox to relieve adverse reactions to exposure to drugs, chemicals, heavy metals, environmental or airborne toxins	Clears heat, detoxifies, and nourishes yin
Kidney DTX	Herbal detox for chronic kidney diseases with elevated creatinine and blood urea nitrogen	Clears heat, detoxifies the Kidney, dispels dampness
Liver DTX	Herbal detox for liver diseases with elevated liver enzymes and compromised liver functions	Clears heat, detoxifies the Liver
Resolve (AI)	Herbal detox to cleanse the lymphatic system and resolve hardness and nodules	Disperses phlegm stagnation, clears heat, and detoxifies

List of Formulas (Diseases/Disorders)

SPECIALTY FORMULAS		
Names	**Clinical Applications**	**Therapeutic Functions**
Astringent Complex	Acute and chronic inflammation with swelling	Clears fire, damp-heat, toxic heat, and deficiency heat
Circulation (SJ)	Cardiovascular and circulatory disorders with blood stasis and impaired blood circulation in upper, middle and lower *jiaos*	Invigorates blood and qi circulation, and eliminates blood and qi stagnation in the upper, middle, and lower *jiaos*
Gardenia Complex	Any excess conditions characterized by heat, fire and toxins, including infectious diseases and inflammatory conditions	Clears heat, purges fire, eliminates toxins
Herbal DRX	An herbal diuretic formula for edema, swelling, and water accumulation	Drains dampness, eliminates water accumulation
Kidney Tonic (Yang)	Kidney yang deficiency with coldness, low libido, premature ejaculation, weakness and soreness of the back and knees, pale complexion, and polyuria	Tonifies Kidney yang
Kidney Tonic (Yin)	Kidney yin deficiency with blurry vision, weakness of the back and knees, tinnitus, dryness, flushed cheeks, possible low-grade fever	Tonifies Kidney yin
LPS Support	Systemic lupus erythematosus (SLE), autoimmune disorders	Clears heat, eliminates toxins, nourishes yin, tonifies blood, promotes generation of body fluids
Lycium Support	Atrophic and degenerative eye disorders, such as glaucoma and cataract, with impaired or blurred vision, excessive tearing, and dry eyes	Tonifies Liver and Kidney yin to brighten the eyes
Neuro Plus	Neuro-degenerative disorders with impaired mental and/or physical functions, such as Alzheimer's disease, Parkinson's disease, and sequelae of stroke	Tonifies Kidney yang, opens channels and collaterals
Notoginseng 9	Bleeding disorders, including internal and external bleeding	Cools the blood, disperses blood stasis, stops bleeding
Nourish (Fluids)	Chronic consumptive disorders characterized by dryness, such as thirst, dry mouth, post-infective cough, and non-productive cough	Nourishes Lung and Stomach yin, replenishes body fluids, harmonizes the middle *jiao*
Pinellia Complex	Disorders characterized by accumulation of fluids, exudation and effusion [damp and phlegm]	Dries dampness and dissolves phlegm
Resolve (AI)	Formation of hardness and nodules from general infectious or inflammatory disorders	Disperse phlegm stagnation, clears heat, and detoxifies
Symmetry	Bell's palsy, facial paralysis, TMJ (temporomandibular joint) pain, and trigeminal neuralgia	Dispels wind attack, relieves pain

Section 2

Symptom / Disease Index

病症索引

Symptom / Disease Index

Conditions	Symptoms/Disease Description	TCM Diagnosis	Herbal Formulas
Abdominal Pain	Lower abdominal pain due to menstrual cramps	Blood stagnation in the uterus or lower *jiao*	***Mense-Ease***
	Lower abdominal pain due to endometriosis, fibroids, or cysts	Qi and blood stagnation in the lower *jiao*	***Resolve (Lower)***
	Lower abdominal pain due to pelvic inflammatory disease	Damp-heat in the lower *jiao*	***V-Support***
	Intestinal spasms and cramps	Intestinal qi stagnation	***Flex (SC)***
	Due to gallstones	Damp-heat in the Liver and Gallbladder	***Dissolve (GS)***
	Due to food poisoning, traveler's diarrhea, or infection	Damp-heat in the Intestines	***GI Care II***
	Due to constipation	Heat in the Large Intestine	***Gentle Lax (Excess)***
	Due to constipation and fecal compaction	Heat in the Large Intestine	***GI DTX***
	Due to irritable bowel syndrome (IBS)	Liver qi stagnation	***GI Harmony***
	Due to ulcerative colitis (UC), Crohn's disease	Damp-heat in the Large Intestine	***GI Care (UC)***
	With hypochondriac pain, fidgeting, restlessness, and irritability	Liver qi stagnation	***Calm***
	With acid regurgitation, belching	Stomach heat	***GI Care***
	Dull pain with fatigue and diarrhea	Spleen qi deficiency	***GI Tonic***
	Due to Kidney stone	Qi stagnation with dampness accumulation	***Dissolve (KS)***
	Severe abdominal pain	Severe qi and blood stagnation	*add* **Herbal ANG**
	With severe blood stagnation	Blood stasis	*add* **Circulation (SJ)**
Abscess	General abscess	Phlegm accumulation	***Resolve (AI)***
	Lung abscess, profuse yellow phlegm	Phlegm and heat in the Lung	***Pinellia XPT***
	Breast abscess	Phlegm stagnation in the upper *jiao*	***Resolve (Upper)***
	Ulcerative colitis with mucus and blood in the stools	Damp-heat in the Large Intestine	***GI Care (UC)***
	All swelling and inflammation of the lymph nodes and glands	Phlegm accumulation	***Resolve (AI)***
	Irritable bowel syndrome with mucus and pus in the stools	Damp-heat in the Small and Large Intestine	***GI Harmony***
	Anorectal abscess	Toxic heat with damp accumulation	***Resolve (AI)*** with ***Astringent Complex***
	Skin abscess	Toxic heat with phlegm	***Dermatrol (Damp)***
	With infection	Accumulation of toxic heat	*add* **Herbal ABX** or **Herbal AVR**
Abuse (Substance)	*See* Addiction		
AC Separation	Shoulder pain from injury	Qi and blood stagnation	***Arm Support*** and ***Flex (TMX)***
	With severe pain	Severe qi and blood stagnation	*add* **Herbal ANG**
Acid Reflux	Heartburn, belching, indigestion, gastritis, ulcers, foul breath	Stomach heat	***GI Care***
	Caused by stress	Liver qi stagnation	*add* **Calm**

Symptom / Disease Index

Conditions	Symptoms/Disease Description	TCM Diagnosis	Herbal Formulas
Acid Reflux *(cont'd)*	With excess heat, constipation, sweating, thirst, possible fever	Excess fire	*add* ***Gardenia Complex***
	With bleeding	Excess heat	*add* ***Notoginseng 9***
Acne	General acne	Toxic and damp-heat accumulation (mild)	***Dermatrol (Clear)***
	With pus and redness	Toxic and damp-heat accumulation (severe)	*add* ***Dermatrol (PS)***
	With infection and abscess	Toxic heat	*add* ***Herbal ABX***
	Due to stress	Liver qi stagnation	*add* ***Calm*** or ***Calm (ES)***
	Due to hormone imbalance	Liver qi stagnation	*add* ***Calm*** *or* ***Gardenia Complex***
ADD/ADHD (Children/Adults)	Inability to focus and concentrate	Liver qi stagnation	***Calm (Jr)***
	With hyperactivity	Liver wind with *shen* (spirit) disturbance	*add* ***Calm (ES)***
	With poor memory	Liver qi stagnation with Heart deficiency	*add* ***Enhance Memory***
	With insomnia	Liver wind with *shen* (spirit) disturbance	*add* ***Calm ZZZ***
	With excess heat in all three *jiaos* manifesting in red face, constipation, hyperactivity, and short temper	Excess heat	*add* ***Gardenia Complex***
	With blood stagnation manifesting in signs of purplish tongue, possible distended sublingual veins	Blood stagnation	*add* ***Circulation (SJ)***
Addiction	Withdrawal symptoms associated with smoking, drug or alcohol addiction	Toxic heat in the Liver and *shen* (spirit) disturbance	***Liver DTX*** *and* ***Calm (ES)***
	Liver damage with elevated liver enzymes	Toxic heat in the Liver	***Liver DTX***
	Kidney damage with proteinuria	Toxic heat in the Kidney	***Kidney DTX***
	See also specific addiction		
Addison's Disease	Symptoms of adrenal insufficiency	Kidney yang deficiency	***Adrenal +***
Adrenal Insufficiency	Diminished function of the adrenal glands and endocrine system	Deficiencies of Kidney yin, yang and *jing* (essence)	***Adrenal +***
Aging	Early signs of aging with weakness, fatigue, forgetfulness, dizziness, etc.	Deficiencies of qi, blood, yin and yang	***Imperial Tonic***
	Neurodegeneration with early signs of dementia and Alzheimer's disease	Deficiencies of Kidney yin, yang and *jing* (essence)	***Neuro Plus***
	Poor memory and forgetfulness	Heart and Kidney deficiencies	***Enhance Memory***
	Premature aging with chronic fatigue	Kidney and Lung deficiencies	***Cordyceps 3***
	Premature aging with decreased mental and physical performances	Deficiencies of Kidney yin, yang and *jing* (essence)	***Adrenal +***
	Degeneration of soft tissue (muscles, ligaments, tendons, cartilage)	Kidney and Liver yin deficiencies	***Flex (MLT)***
	Decrease in bone density	Kidney *jing* (essence) deficiency	***Osteo 8***
	Premature gray or white hair	Kidney *jing* (essence) and Liver blood deficiencies	***Polygonum 14***
	Thirst with dry skin	Stomach and Lung yin deficiencies	***Nourish (Fluids)***
	Diminished vision, dry eyes, visual problems	Liver and Kidney yin deficiencies	***Lycium Support***

Symptom / Disease Index

Conditions	Symptoms/Disease Description	TCM Diagnosis	Herbal Formulas
Aging *(cont'd)*	Diminished hearing, auditory problems	Liver and Kidney yin deficiencies	***Nourish***
	Vaginal dryness, lack of lubrication leading to painful intercourse	Kidney yin deficiency	***Balance Spring***
	Kidney yin deficiency with blurry vision, weakness of the back and knees, tinnitus, dryness, flushed cheeks, possible low-grade fever	Kidney yin deficiency	***Kidney Tonic (Yin)***
	Kidney yang deficiency with coldness, low libido, premature ejaculation, weakness and soreness of the back and knees, pale complexion, and polyuria	Kidney yang deficiency	***Kidney Tonic (Yang)***
Agitation	Short temper, flushed face, possible constipation	Liver qi stagnation or Liver yang rising	***Calm*** or ***Calm (ES)***
AIDS	Compromised immune system; frequent viral and bacterial infections	*Wei* (defensive) *qi* deficiency	***Immune +***
	With viral infection	Heat	*add* ***Herbal AVR***
	With bacterial infection	Heat	*add* ***Herbal ABX***
	See specific diseases and symptoms for complications		
Alcohol Abuse	*See* Addiction		
Allergy	Allergic rhinitis or sinusitis, clear or white watery nasal discharge, stuffy nose, sneezing	Wind-cold with fluid congestion	***Magnolia Clear Sinus***
	Allergic rhinitis or sinus infection, yellow nasal discharge, stuffy nose	Damp-heat with fluid congestion	***Pueraria Clear Sinus***
	Skin allergy, rash, itching, eczema, and other dermatological disorders	Wind-heat at the skin level, heat in the blood	***Silerex*** or ***Dermatrol (PS)***
	Dry lesions on the skin	Wind toxin	***Dermatrol (Dry)***
	Wet lesions on the skin	Damp-heat toxin	***Dermatrol (Damp)***
	Allergic reactions from exposure to drugs, chemicals, heavy metals, environmental and airborne toxins	Toxic heat	***Herbal DTX***
	Asthma due to allergy with heat symptoms such as redness of the face, yellow phlegm, and red tongue	Lung heat	***Respitrol (Heat)***
	Asthma due to allergy with cold symptoms such as clear or white sputum	Cold in the Lung	***Respitrol (Cold)***
	Profuse post-nasal drip and sputum in the throat	Phlegm accumulation	***Pinellia XPT***
	Ears plugged, nose and throat with yellow nasal discharge, and ticklish sore throat	Toxic heat accumulation in the upper *jiao*	***Herbal ENT***
	Allergy with cough	Lung qi reversal	***Respitrol (CF)***
	Food allergy with underlying digestive weakness and loose stools	Spleen qi deficiency	***GI Tonic***
Alopecia	Hair loss, premature gray hair, split ends, dry and dull hair	Blood deficiency with dryness	***Polygonum 14***
	Due to stress	Blood deficiency with Liver qi stagnation	*add* ***Calm***
Alzheimer's Disease	Forgetfulness, poor concentration, compromised mental and physical functions	Deficiencies of Kidney yin, yang and *jing* (essence) with phlegm obstruction	***Neuro Plus***

Symptom / Disease Index

Conditions	Symptoms/Disease Description	TCM Diagnosis	Herbal Formulas
Amenorrhea	Amenorrhea with a history of irregular or delayed menstruation with scanty discharge, cold extremities	Kidney yang deficiency and blood stagnation	***Menatrol***
	Caused by stress or change of environment	Liver qi stagnation	*add **Calm***
	With severe blood stagnation, purplish tongue, dark complexion, or past history of surgery	Severe blood stasis	*add **Circulation (SJ)***
	With yang deficient signs	Kidney yang deficiency	*add **Kidney Tonic (Yang)***
	With yin deficient signs	Kidney yin deficiency	*add **Kidney Tonic (Yin)***
Anemia	With fatigue, lack of energy, poor appetite	Blood and qi deficiencies	***Imperial Tonic***
	With insomnia, excessive worries, disturbed sleep	Spleen and Heart blood deficiencies	***Schisandra ZZZ***
	With chronic headache	Blood deficiency	*add **Corydalin (CR)***
	With excessive stress, anxiety, and insomnia	Liver qi stagnation with underlying deficiency	*add **Calm ZZZ***
Ankle	Acute ankle pain	Qi and blood stagnation	***Knee & Ankle (AC)***
	Chronic ankle pain	Qi and blood stagnation	***Knee & Ankle (CR)***
	Acute sprain and strain with bruises and swelling	Qi and blood stagnation	***Knee & Ankle (AC)*** and ***Flex (TMX)***
	Recovery from ligament or connective tissue injury	Qi and blood stagnation	***Knee & Ankle (CR)*** and ***Flex (MLT)***
Anorexia	Poor to no appetite, weight loss, sallow complexion	Spleen deficiency	***GI Tonic***
	With fatigue, thirst, dryness, dizziness, and general deficiencies	Qi, yin, yang and blood deficiencies	***GI Tonic*** and ***Imperial Tonic***
	Due to constipation, abdominal fullness and distension, and intestinal toxin build-up	Spleen deficiency with toxic-heat in the Intestines	***GI DTX***
	Due to depression	Accumulation of damp and phlegm	***Shine*** or ***Shine (DS)***
	Due to stress and anxiety	Liver qi stagnation	***Calm*** or ***Calm (ES)***
Anxiety	Stress, irritability, restlessness, nervousness	Liver qi stagnation	***Calm***
	With pronounced anger, neurosis or insomnia	Liver fire with *shen* (spirit) disturbance	***Calm (ES)***
	Anxiety and stress with inability to calm down, "overactive mind" in patients with deficiency	Liver qi stagnation with qi deficiency	***Calm ZZZ***
	With insomnia, excessive worrying, pensiveness, and indecisiveness	Liver qi stagnation with Spleen and Heart deficiencies	*add **Schisandra ZZZ***
	With forgetfulness	Heart and Kidney deficiencies	*add **Enhance Memory***
	With depression	Qi, blood, phlegm stagnation	*add **Shine** or **Shine (DS)***
Appendicitis (Chronic)	Chronic, dull pain in the lower right quadrant of the abdomen	Damp-heat	***Resolve (AI)***
	With moderate to severe infection	Toxic heat	*add **Herbal ABX***
	With severe pain	Severe qi and blood stagnation	*add **Herbal ANG***
	With fever	Toxic heat accumulation	*add **Gardenia Complex***

SYMPTOM / DISEASE

Symptom / Disease Index

Conditions	Symptoms/Disease Description	TCM Diagnosis	Herbal Formulas
Appetite	Loss of appetite with generalized weakness and loose stools in chronic illness or in children	Spleen qi deficiency	***GI Tonic***
	Loss of appetite from stress and nervousness	Liver overacting on the Spleen	***Calm***
	Loss of appetite from depression	Accumulation of damp and phlegm	***Shine*** or ***Shine (DS)***
	Loss of appetite due to excessive worrying	Spleen and Heart deficiencies	***Schisandra ZZZ***
	Excessive appetite with weight gain	Stomach heat	***Herbalite***
Apprehension	*See* Anxiety		
Arm	Arm pain	Qi and blood stagnation	***Arm Support***
	With severe pain	Qi and blood stagnation	*add* ***Herbal ANG***
	Due to injury	Qi and blood stagnation	*add* ***Flex (TMX)***
	Recovery from broken bone	Qi and blood stagnation with Kidney *jing* (essence) deficiency	*add* ***Osteo 8***
	Recovery from weakness or atrophy of muscles, tendons and ligaments	Qi and blood stagnation with Liver and Kidney yin and deficiencies	*add* ***Flex (MLT)***
Arteries (Blockage)	In angina pectoris	*Xiong bi* (painful obstruction of the chest)	***Circulation***
	With excessive blood stagnation manifesting in purplish tongue, dark complexion	Blood stasis	***Circulation (SJ)***
	With high cholesterol/triglycerides	Damp accumulation	***Cholisma***
	With high cholesterol, fatty liver, and obesity	Excessive damp accumulation	***Cholisma (ES)***
	In peripheral vascular disease	Qi and blood stagnation	***Flex (NP)***
	With deficient-type hypertension	Liver yang rising with Liver and Kidney yin deficiencies	***Gastrodia Complex***
	With excess-type hypertension	Liver heat and fire rising	***Gentiana Complex***
Arteriosclerosis	*See* Cholesterol		
Arthralgia	*See* Arthritis		
Arthritis	Arthritis with pain, swelling, inflammation, redness with heat sensations	*Bi zheng* (painful obstruction syndrome) due to heat	***Flex (Heat)***
	Arthritis with weakness, soreness, pain; worsens during cold and rainy seasons	*Bi zheng* (painful obstruction syndrome) due to cold and damp	***Flex (CD)***
	Of the neck and shoulder	*Bi zheng* (painful obstruction syndrome) with qi and blood stagnation	***Neck & Shoulder (CR)*** with a ***Flex*** formula
	Of the arm	*Bi zheng* (painful obstruction syndrome) with qi and blood stagnation	***Arm Support*** with a ***Flex*** formula
	Of the back	*Bi zheng* (painful obstruction syndrome) with qi and blood stagnation	***Back Support (CR)*** with a ***Flex*** formula
	Of the knee and ankle	*Bi zheng* (painful obstruction syndrome) with qi and blood stagnation	***Knee & Ankle (CR)*** with a ***Flex*** formula
	Osteoarthritis	Qi and blood stagnation with Kidney *jing* (essence) deficiency	***Osteo 8*** with a ***Flex*** formula
	Gouty arthritis	*Re bi* (heat painful obstruction)	***Flex (GT)***

Symptom / Disease Index

Conditions	Symptoms/Disease Description	TCM Diagnosis	Herbal Formulas
Arthritis (*cont'd*)	With degeneration of soft tissue (muscles, ligaments, tendon, cartilage)	Liver and Kidney yin deficiencies	***Flex (MLT)*** with a ***Flex*** formula
	With blood stagnation manifesting in purplish tongue, previous trauma or history of surgery, and dark complexion.	Blood stasis	***Circulation (SJ)*** with a ***Flex*** formula
	With severe pain	*Bi zheng* (painful obstruction syndrome) with severe qi and blood stagnation	*add* ***Herbal ANG***
	To reduce inflammation	Heat accumulation	*add* ***Astringent Complex***
	With hyperactive immunity in an autoimmune condition	Toxic heat	*add* ***Gardenia Complex***
AST, ALT	Elevated levels of liver enzymes, AST and ALT (SGPT and SGOT)	Toxic heat in the Liver	***Liver DTX***
	Elevated liver enzymes due to exposure to drugs, chemicals, heavy metals, environmental and airborne toxins	Toxic heat	***Liver DTX*** and ***Herbal DTX***
Asthma	Wheezing, dyspnea, yellow sputum, heat sensations	Lung heat	***Respitrol (Heat)***
	Wheezing, dyspnea, white sputum, chills	Lung cold	***Respitrol (Cold)***
	Chronic asthma with wheezing, shortness of breath, shallow inhalation	Deficiencies of the Lung and the Kidney	***Respitrol (Deficient)***
	Maintenance formula for asthma triggered by over-exertion	Lung and Kidney deficiencies	***Cordyceps 3***
	Maintenance formula for asthma triggered by allergies	Lung qi deficiency	***Immune +***
	Maintenance formula for asthma triggered by exposure to chemicals, heavy metals, environmental and airborne toxins	Toxic heat	***Herbal DTX***
	With cough	Lung qi reversal	***Respitrol (CF)*** with a ***Respitrol*** formula
	With excessive phlegm or sputum that may or may not be easy to cough out	Excessive phlegm accumulation	***Pinellia XPT*** with a ***Respitrol*** formula
	With allergy, sinusitis or rhinitis manifesting in yellow nasal discharge	Lung heat	***Pueraria Clear Sinus*** with a ***Respitrol*** formula
	With allergy, sinusitis or rhinitis manifesting in clear or white nasal discharge	Lung cold	***Magnolia Clear Sinus*** with a ***Respitrol*** formula
	With severe dry throat, mouth and skin	Stomach and Lung yin deficiencies	***Nourish (Fluids)*** with a ***Respitrol*** formula
Atherosclerosis	*See* Cholesterol		
Attention Deficit	*See* ADD		
Atrophy	Degeneration and atrophy of soft tissue (muscles, ligaments, tendons, cartilage)	Kidney *jing* (essence) deficiency and Liver yin deficiencies	***Flex (MLT)***
	Muscle atrophy due to stroke	*Wei* (atrophy) syndrome	*add* ***Neuro Plus***
	Muscle atrophy with weakness, poor appetite	Spleen qi deficiency	*add* ***GI Tonic***
	Congenital deficiency with weakness of the bones	Kidney *jing* (essence) deficiency	*add* ***Osteo 8***

Symptom / Disease Index

Conditions	Symptoms/Disease Description	TCM Diagnosis	Herbal Formulas
Atrophy (*cont'd*)	Muscle atrophy with weakness, dizziness, blurry vision, listlessness, palpitation, shortness of breath, spontaneous sweating	Qi, blood, yin and yang deficiencies	*add* ***Imperial Tonic***
	Of the arm	*Wei* (atrophy) syndrome	*add* ***Arm Support***
	Of the neck and shoulder area	*Wei* (atrophy) syndrome	*add* ***Neck & Shoulder (CR)***
	Of the back area	*Wei* (atrophy) syndrome	*add* ***Back Support (CR)***
	Of the knee and ankle area	*Wei* (atrophy) syndrome	*add* ***Knee & Ankle (CR)***
	With numbness	Blood stagnation	*add* ***Flex (NP)***
	Vaginal dryness or atrophy	Kidney yin deficiency	***Balance Spring***
	Optic atrophy: dry eyes, floaters, visual disturbance	Kidney and Liver yin deficiencies	***Lycium Support***
Atrophic Vaginitis	Vaginal dryness or atrophy	Kidney yin deficiency	***Balance Spring***
	During menopause	Kidney yin deficiency with heat	*add* ***Nourish*** *or* ***Balance (Heat)***
Autism	Developmental delays and learning disabilities	*Shen* (spirit) disturbance	***Calm (Jr)***
Autoimmune Diseases	Hyperactive immune system	Excess heat in all three *jiaos*	***Gardenia Complex***
	Systemic lupus erythematosus	Heat and toxins	***LPS Support***
	Rheumatoid arthritis	*Bi zheng* (painful obstruction syndrome) due to heat	***Flex (Heat)***
	Myasthenia gravis	*Zhong* (central) *qi* deficiency	***C/R Support***
	Sjögren's syndrome	Lung yin deficiency with heat	***Nourish (Fluids)*** and ***Herbal ENT***
	Type I diabetes mellitus	Stomach, Lung, and Kidney yin deficiencies	***Equilibrium***
	Multiple sclerosis	Qi and blood stagnation	***Neuro Plus***
	Grave's disease	Excess Liver yang	***Thyrodex***
	Hashimoto's thyroiditis, chronic thyroiditis	Kidney yang deficiency	***Thyro-forte***
	General low-grade fever, fatigue, malaise	Yin deficiency with heat	***Nourish*** and ***Balance (Heat)***
	Psoriasis	Toxic heat	***Dermatrol (PS)***
	Ulcerative colitis and Crohn's disease	Damp-heat in the Intestines	***GI Care (UC)***
	See also specific disease		
Aversion to Cold/Wind	Weak immune system with increased susceptibility to catching colds	*Wei* (defensive) *qi* deficiency	***Immune +***
	With fever and chills from bacterial infection	Wind-heat	***Herbal ABX***
	With fever and chills from viral infection	Wind-heat	***Herbal AVR***
Back Pain	Acute low back pain	Qi and blood stagnation	***Back Support (AC)***
	Due to recent traumatic injury	Qi and blood stagnation	*add* ***Flex (TMX)***

Symptom / Disease Index

Conditions	Symptoms/Disease Description	TCM Diagnosis	Herbal Formulas
Back Pain (*cont'd*)	With spasms and cramps	Qi and blood stagnation with Liver yin and body fluid deficiencies	add ***Flex (SC)***
	Chronic aches, weakness, and soreness of the lower back	Qi and blood stagnation with Liver and Kidney deficiencies	***Back Support (CR)***
	Due to osteoporosis	Kidney yin, yang and *jing* (essence) deficiencies	add ***Osteo 8***
	Due to slipped disk	Qi and blood stagnation	***Back Support (HD)***
	Due to bone spurs	Qi and blood stagnation	***Flex (SPR)***
	Due to kidney stones	Qi and blood stagnation	***Dissolve (KS)***
	Due to kidney infection	Heat in the lower *jiao*	***V-Support***
	Due to chronic nephritis or nephritic syndrome	Toxic heat in the Kidney	***Kidney DTX***
	Due to dysmenorrhea	Qi and blood stagnation	***Mense-Ease***
	Due to fibroids, cysts and endometriosis	Blood and phlegm stagnation	***Resolve (Lower)***
	With symptoms such as blurry vision, flushed cheeks, soreness and weakness of the back and knees, low-grade fever, and night sweats	Kidney yin deficiency	***Kidney Tonic (Yin)***
	With symptoms such as coldness, low libido, polyuria, and weakness of the back and knees	Kidney yang deficiency	***Kidney Tonic (Yang)***
	With severe blood stagnation from previous injury	Qi and blood stagnation	add ***Circulation (SJ)***
	Severe back pain	Severe qi and blood stagnation	add ***Herbal ANG***
Balance	Poor balance with dizziness and vertigo	Liver wind rising	***Gastrodia Complex***
Baldness	*See* Hair		
Bed-wetting	Bed-wetting, frequent urination, terminal dripping of urine	Kidney yang deficiency	***Kidney Tonic (Yang)***
Behavior	Disruptive, rude or aggressive behavior	Liver yang rising with *shen* (spirit) disturbance	***Calm (ES)***
	ADD or ADHD	Liver wind with *shen* (spirit) disturbance	***Calm (Jr)***
Belching	With acid reflux, heartburn, foul breath, indigestion	Stomach heat	***GI Care***
	With poor appetite, loose stools, fatigue	Spleen qi deficiency	***GI Tonic***
	With dry throat, thirst	Stomach yin deficiency	***Nourish (Fluids)***
	With hypochondriac distension, irritability, stress, anxiety	Liver qi stagnation	***Calm***
	With gas, indigestion, irritable bowel syndrome	Food stagnation	***GI Harmony***
	With constipation	Heat in the Intestines	***Gentle Lax (Excess)*** or ***Gentle Lax (Deficient)***
	With constipation and fecal compaction	Heat in the Intestines	***GI DTX***
	Chronic, stubborn belching with blood stagnation (purplish tongue) or for unknown reasons	Blood stasis	***Circulation (SJ)***
Bell's Palsy	Facial paralysis	Wind attack with qi and blood stagnation	***Symmetry***

Symptom / Disease Index

Conditions	Symptoms/Disease Description	TCM Diagnosis	Herbal Formulas
Benign Prostatic Hyperplasia (BPH)	With difficult, painful, and burning urination	Damp-heat in the lower *jiao*	***P-Support***
	With back soreness, terminal dripping of urine, coldness	Kidney yang deficiency	add ***Kidney Tonic (Yang)***
	Moderate to severe cases of infection and inflammation	Accumulation of toxic heat	add ***Resolve (AI)***
	With more swelling and inflammation	Excess stagnation	add ***Astringent Complex*** and ***Resolve (Lower)***
Bile Duct	Inflammation or obstruction of the bile duct	Damp-heat in the Liver and Gallbladder	***Dissolve (GS)***
	With severe pain due to bile duct obstruction	Severe qi and blood stagnation	***Dissolve (GS)*** and ***Herbal ANG***
Binge Eating	Excessive appetite	Stomach heat	***Herbalite***
Bipolar Disorder	Manic behavior	Liver yang rising with *shen* (spirit) disturbance	***Calm (ES)***
	Depression	Stagnation of phlegm, qi, blood, and food with deficiencies of the Spleen and the Heart	***Shine*** or ***Shine (DS)***
Bladder	*See* Urinary stone, Urinary tract infection (UTI), and Urination (frequent)		
Bladder Stone	Kidney or urinary stones	*Shi lin* (stone dysuria)	***Dissolve (KS)***
	With severe pain due to kidney stone	Severe qi and blood stagnation	add ***Herbal ANG***
	With bleeding	Qi and blood stagnation with heat pushing blood out of the vessels	add ***Notoginseng 9***
	With fever or heat sensation	Qi and blood stagnation with heat or fire accumulation	add ***Herbal ABX***
Bleeding	General bleeding	All causes	***Notoginseng 9***
	Abnormal uterine bleeding due to heat	Heat in the lower *jiao*	add ***V-Support***
	Bleeding from peptic and duodenal ulcers	Stomach heat	add ***GI Care***
	Intestinal bleeding with diarrhea due to food poisoning	Toxic heat in the Large Intestine	add ***GI Care II***
	Rectal bleeding due to hemorrhoids	Heat in the Large Intestine	add ***GI Care (HMR)***
	Lower gastrointestinal bleeding due to ulcerative colitis	Damp-heat in the Large Intestine	add ***GI Care (UC)***
	Subcutaneous bleeding, purpura	Spleen qi deficiency with inability to keep blood in the vessels	add ***Schisandra ZZZ***
	Bleeding and bruises from traumas	Qi and blood stagnation	add ***Flex (TMX)***
	Excessive bleeding leading to anemia or fatigue and weakness	Qi and blood deficiency	add ***Imperial Tonic***
Blister(s)	Oral herpes	Toxic heat	***Lonicera Complex***
	Genital herpes	Damp-heat in the lower *jiao* and Liver channel	***Gentiana Complex***
	Herpes zoster	Toxic heat	***Dermatrol (HZ)***

Symptom / Disease Index

Conditions	Symptoms/Disease Description	TCM Diagnosis	Herbal Formulas
Blister(s) *(cont'd)*	Nerve pain from herpes infection	Qi and blood stagnation	***Flex (NP)***
	Dermatitis	Toxic and damp-heat accumulation	***Dermatrol (Damp)*** or ***Dermatrol (Dry)***
Bloating	With epigastric fullness, heartburn	Stomach heat with qi stagnation	***GI Care***
	With PMS, mood swings, breast distension, stress	Liver qi stagnation	***Calm***
	With dysmenorrhea	Liver qi stagnation with blood stasis	***Mense-Ease***
	Due to endometriosis	Qi and blood stagnation in the lower *jiao*	***Resolve (Lower)***
	Due to irritable bowel syndrome (IBS)	Liver qi stagnation	***GI Harmony***
	Due to ulcerative colitis	Damp-heat in the Large Intestine	***GI Care (UC)***
	Due to weakness of the digestive system	Spleen qi deficiency	***GI Tonic***
	With constipation	Food stagnation	***Gentle Lax (Excess), Gentle Lax (Deficient)***
	With constipation and fecal compaction	Food stagnation	***GI DTX***
	Severe bloating and pain	Qi stagnation	*add* ***Herbal ANG***
Blood Clot	In the extremities	Blood stagnation	***Flex (NP)***
	In the heart	Blood stagnation	***Circulation***
	Throughout the body	Blood stagnation	***Circulation (SJ)***
Blood Pressure	*See* Hypertension		
Blood Sugar Level	*See* Diabetes mellitus		
Bone Disorder	Osteoporosis	Kidney yin and *jing* (essence) deficiencies	***Osteo 8***
	Delayed healing of bone fracture	Deficiency of Kidney *jing* (essence)	***Osteo 8***
	Recovery phase of external injuries in all parts of the body; strengthens the bones, tendons and ligaments	Liver and Kidney deficiencies	***Osteo 8*** plus ***Flex (MLT)***
	Acute phase of traumatic injuries with severe pain, inflammation and bruises	Qi and blood stagnation	***Flex (TMX)***
	Herniated disk of the spine	Qi and blood stagnation	***Back Support (HD)***
	Bone spur	Qi and blood stagnation	***Flex (SPR)***
	Bone spur with severe pain	Severe qi and blood stagnation	***Flex (SPR)*** plus ***Herbal ANG***
Bone Spur	Bone spur anywhere in the body	Qi and blood stagnation	***Flex (SPR)***
	Accompanied by severe pain	Severe qi and blood stagnation	*add* ***Herbal ANG***
	Neck and shoulder pain	Qi and blood stagnation in the upper *jiao*	*add* ***Neck & Shoulder (AC)***
	Low back pain	Qi and blood stagnation in the lower *jiao*	*add* ***Back Support (AC)***
	Arm (shoulder, elbow, wrist) pain	Qi and blood stagnation in the upper *jiao*	*add* ***Arm Support***
	Knee and ankle pain	Qi and blood stagnation in the lower *jiao*	*add* ***Knee & Ankle (AC)***

Symptom / Disease Index

Conditions	Symptoms/Disease Description	TCM Diagnosis	Herbal Formulas
Borborygmi	Due to food poisoning or gastrointestinal infection	Damp-heat in the Intestines	***GI Care II***
	Due to stress and anxiety	Liver overacting on Spleen	***Calm***
	Due to irritable bowel syndrome (IBS)	Liver overacting on Spleen	***GI Harmony***
	Due to weakness of the digestive system	Spleen qi deficiency	***GI Tonic***
	Due to constipation	Food stagnation	***Gentle Lax (Excess)***, ***Gentle Lax (Deficient)*** or ***GI DTX***
Bowel Cleansing	Intestinal/colon detox	Toxic heat in the Intestines	***GI DTX***
Bowel Movement	*See* Constipation, Diarrhea, Ulcerative colitis (UC), Irritable bowel syndrome (IBS), Hemorrhoids, Crohn's disease		
BPH	*See* Benign prostatic hyperplasia (BPH)		
Brain	Alzheimer's, dementia, Parkinson's, post-stroke complications and other neurodegenerative disorders with compromised mental and physical functions	Kidney yin, yang and *jing* (essence) deficiencies	***Neuro Plus***
	Poor memory, forgetfulness	Heart and Kidney deficiencies	***Enhance Memory***
Breast	Under-developed breasts	Kidney yang and *jing* (essence) deficiencies	***Venus***
	Breast distension, PMS, irritability	Liver qi stagnation	***Calm***
	Breast lumps, benign breast disorder, fibrocystic disorders	Liver qi stagnation with phlegm and heat	***Resolve (Upper)***
	Breast cancer patients receiving chemotherapy or radiation	*Wei* (defensive) *qi* and *zhong* (central) *qi* deficiencies	***C/R Support***
	End stage breast cancer	*Yuan* (source) *qi* deficiency	***CA Support***
Breath, Bad	Foul breath with excessive hunger	Stomach heat	***Herbalite***
	Excess heat in the body	Heat in all three *jiaos*	***Gardenia Complex***
	With bitter taste in the mouth, short temper	Liver fire	***Gentiana Complex***
	With dry mouth	Lung and Stomach yin deficiencies	***Nourish (Fluids)***
	With throat infection	Toxic heat accumulation	***Herbal ENT***
Breathing	*See* Asthma, Dyspnea, Cough		
Bronchitis / Bronchiectasis	Cough	Lung qi reversal	***Respitrol (CF)***
	Cough, dyspnea, fever, yellow sputum	Lung heat	***Respitrol (Heat)***
	Cough, dyspnea, clear white sputum, intolerance to cold, chills	Lung cold	***Respitrol (Cold)***
	Cough, profuse yellow sputum, chest congestion	Lung heat with phlegm	***Pinellia XPT***
	Chronic bronchitis with dryness and scanty sputum	Lung qi and yin deficiency	***Respitrol (Deficient)*** and ***Nourish (Fluids)***
	Moderate to severe cases of chronic bronchitis with infection and inflammation	Accumulation of toxic heat	***Respitrol (Deficient)*** and ***Herbal ABX***
	Coughing of blood	Lung heat	***Notoginseng 9*** with a ***Respitrol*** formula

Symptom / Disease Index

Conditions	Symptoms/Disease Description	TCM Diagnosis	Herbal Formulas
Bronchitis / Bronchiectasis (*cont'd*)	To enhance the antibiotic effect	Toxic heat in the Lung	*add* ***Herbal ABX***
	To enhance the antiviral effect	Toxic heat in the Lung	*add* ***Herbal AVR***
	To enhance the anti-inflammatory effect	Heat in the Lung	*add* ***Astringent Complex***
Bruises	Due to blood stasis	Blood stasis	***Flex (TMX)***
	Due to blood deficiency	Spleen qi deficiency	***Schisandra ZZZ***
Bruxism (Teeth Grinding)	With stress	Liver qi stagnation	***Calm***
	With severe stress and insomnia	Liver qi stagnation with *shen* (spirit) disturbance	***Calm (ES)***
Bulimia	Binge eating followed by abdominal pain or self-induced vomiting	*Shen* (spirit) disturbance	***Calm (ES)***
	Obesity, excess appetite with mental disorder	*Shen* (spirit) disturbance with Stomach heat	***Calm (ES)*** with ***Herbalite***
"Burned Out"	Fatigue, over-exhaustion, lack of interest, and decreased vitality	Kidney yang deficiency	***Adrenal +***
	Chronic fatigue	Lung and Kidney deficiencies	***Cordyceps 3***
	Overall weakness and deficiency	Qi, blood, yin and yang deficiencies	***Imperial Tonic***
	Short term fatigue and tiredness	Qi deficiency	***Vibrant***
Bursitis	Inflammation and redness of the joints	*Bi zheng* (painful obstruction syndrome) due to heat	***Flex (Heat)***
	Of the shoulder	Qi and blood stagnation	***Neck & Shoulder (AC)***
	Of the arm	Qi and blood stagnation	***Arm Support***
	Of the hip	Qi and blood stagnation	***Back Support (AC)***
	Of the knee	Qi and blood stagnation	***Knee & Ankle (AC)***
	With degeneration of the soft tissue (muscle, ligaments, tendons, cartilage)	Liver and Kidney yin deficiencies	***Flex (MLT)***
	With severe pain	Severe qi and blood stagnation	*add* ***Herbal ANG***
	With severe inflammation	Heat accumulation	*add* ***Astringent Complex***
Calcification	Calcification of joints	Phlegm accumulation	***Flex (SPR)***
Calcium	Calcium deficiency seen in osteoporosis or decreased bone density	Deficiency of Kidney yin and *jing* (essence)	***Osteo 8***
Calculi	*See* Stones		
Calf	Spasms and cramps	Qi and blood stagnation	***Flex (SC)***
	With severe pain	Severe qi and blood stagnation	*add* ***Herbal ANG***
	Chronic stiffness from old injuries with blood stagnation	Blood stasis	*add* ***Circulation (SJ)***
	With knee or ankle pain	Qi and blood stagnation	*add* ***Knee & Ankle (AC)***

Symptom / Disease Index

Conditions	Symptoms/Disease Description	TCM Diagnosis	Herbal Formulas
Cancer / Carcinoma	Side effects of chemotherapy and radiation: nausea, vomiting, compromised immune system, generalized weakness, and others	Deficiencies of yin, *yuan* (source) *qi*, and *wei* (defensive) *qi*	***C/R Support***
	Weakened or compromised immune system	*Wei* (defensive) *qi* deficiency	***Immune +***
	Compromised respiratory and reproductive systems	Lung and Kidney deficiencies	***Cordyceps 3***
	Dry mouth and thirst	Stomach yin deficiency	***Nourish (Fluids)***
	End stage cancer in patients who are too weak to receive chemotherapy or radiation	*Yuan* (source) *qi* deficiency	***CA Support***
Candidiasis	Genital itching and yellow discharge	Damp-heat in the lower *jiao* and Liver channel	***V-Support***
Canker Sore	Ulcers in the mouth	Stomach heat	***Lonicera Complex***
Capsulitis	Frozen shoulder with pain	Qi and blood stagnation	***Arm Support*** and ***Neck & Shoulder (AC)***
	With severe pain	Qi and blood stagnation	*add* ***Herbal ANG***
Carbuncles	Carbuncles with painful inflammation	Toxic heat with phlegm accumulation	***Resolve (AI)*** and ***Dermatrol (Damp)***
	Non-healing carbuncles after rupturing	Spleen qi deficiency	*add* ***Immune +***
Carpal Tunnel Syndrome	Wrist pain	Qi and blood stagnation	***Arm Support***
	With severe pain	Severe qi and blood stagnation	***Arm Support*** and ***Herbal ANG***
Cartilage	Enhancing the growth of muscles, tendons, ligaments, and cartilages	Liver blood and Kidney yin deficiencies	***Flex (MLT)***
Cataract	With blurry vision, dry eyes, weakness of the lower back and knees, tinnitus	Liver and Kidney yin deficiencies	***Lycium Support***
	With hypertension, flushed face, possible constipation	Liver yang rising	***Gentiana Complex***
Cellulite	Accumulation of cellulite with excessive hunger	Stomach heat	***Herbalite***
Cellulitis	Swelling, inflammation, and enlarged glands	Phlegm fire stagnation	***Herbal ABX*** and ***Resolve (AI)***
	With wet or oozing appearance	Damp-heat toxin	***Herbal ABX*** and ***Dermatrol (Damp)***
	With severe inflammation	Toxic heat accumulation	*add* ***Astringent Complex***
	With fever	Excess heat accumulation	*add* ***Gardenia Complex***
Cerebral Circulation Insufficiency	Forgetfulness, poor concentration associated with dementia or Alzheimer's disease	Poor circulation with deficiencies of Kidney yin, yang and *jing* (essence)	***Neuro Plus***
	Poor memory and forgetfulness	Heart and Kidney deficiencies	***Enhance Memory***
	Severe blood stagnation	Blood stagnation	***Circulation (SJ)***
Chancre	Chancre of mouth	Toxic heat accumulation	***Herbal ABX*** and ***Lonicera Complex***
	Chancre in the genital region	Damp-heat in the lower *jiao* and Liver channel	***Herbal ABX*** with ***Gentiana Complex***

Symptom / Disease Index

Conditions	Symptoms/Disease Description	TCM Diagnosis	Herbal Formulas
Chemical	*See* Poisoning		
Chemotherapy	To alleviate side effects associated with chemotherapy and radiation	Deficiencies of yin, *yuan* (source) *qi* and *wei* (defensive) *qi*	***C/R Support***
	End stage cancer in patients who are too weak to receive chemotherapy or radiation	*Yuan* (source) *qi* deficiency	***CA Support***
	See also Cancer / Carcinoma		
Chest Pain	Coronary heart disorders	Blood stagnation in the chest	***Circulation***
	Cardiovascular/coronary heart disorders with severe pain	Qi and blood stagnation	***Circulation*** with ***Herbal ANG***
	Asthma with fever, yellow phlegm	Heat in the Lung	***Respitrol (Heat)***
	Asthma with chills, white or clear phlegm	Cold in the Lung	***Respitrol (Cold)***
	Chest pain due to cough	Lung qi reversal	***Respitrol (CF)***
	Chronic respiratory condition	Lung qi deficiency	***Respitrol (Deficient)***
	Chest congestion, pain with coughing, yellow sputum	Heat and phlegm in the Lung	***Pinellia XPT***
	Severe blood stagnation or past history of injury or surgery in the chest area	Blood stagnation	***Circulation (SJ)***
	Due to acid reflux and erosive esophagitis	Stomach fire	***GI Care***
	After eating greasy or fatty food; due to gallstones	Damp-heat in the Gallbladder	***Dissolve (GS)***
Chickenpox	Blisters with itching	Toxic heat invading the Lung	***Lonicera Complex***
	With severe itching	Wind-heat invasion	*add* ***Silerex***
	To enhance the antiviral effect	Toxic deficiency heat	*add* ***Herbal AVR***
	See also Shingles		
Chills	Common cold/flu with ticklish throat, fever, chills	Wind-heat invasion	***Lonicera Complex***
	Common cold/flu with clear or white nasal discharge, sneezing	Wind-cold invasion	***Respitrol (Cold)***
	Fever and chills from stomach flu or food poisoning with diarrhea	Damp-heat in the Intestine	***GI Care II***
	With fever, sore throat, ear pain	Toxic heat accumulation	***Herbal ENT***
	Infectious mononucleosis	Phlegm heat accumulation	***Resolve (AI)***
Chinese Restaurant Syndrome	Hypersensitivity to MSG with headache, thirst and abdominal discomfort	Toxic, damp-heat	***GI Care II*** with ***Liver DTX***
Chlamydia	Burning sensation with urination, discharge, and pain	Damp-heat in the lower *jiao* and Liver channel	***V-Support***
Cholecystitis	Inflammation of the gallbladder with or without gallstones	Damp-heat in the Gallbladder	***Dissolve (GS)***
	With elevated liver enzymes, possibly with liver impairment	Damp-heat in the Liver and the Gallbladder	*add* ***Liver DTX***
	With fatty liver and high cholesterol	Damp-heat in the Liver and the Gallbladder	*add* ***Cholisma (ES)***

Symptom / Disease Index

Conditions	Symptoms/Disease Description	TCM Diagnosis	Herbal Formulas
Cholelithiasis	Gallstones with or without cholecystitis	Damp-heat in the Gallbladder drying up the fluid	***Dissolve (GS)***
	Gallstones with elevated liver enzymes, possibly with liver impairment	Damp-heat in the Liver and the Gallbladder	*add **Liver DTX***
	With severe pain due to gallstones	With qi and blood stagnation	*add **Herbal ANG***
	With fatty liver and high cholesterol	Damp-heat in the Liver and the Gallbladder	*add **Cholisma (ES)***
	With fever	Liver fire	*add **Gardenia Complex***
Cholestasis	*See* Cholecystitis, Cholelithiasis		
Cholesterol / Triglycerides	Elevated levels	Accumulation of damp and phlegm	***Cholisma***
	With excess-type hypertension	Damp and phlegm with Liver fire	*add **Gentiana Complex***
	With deficient-type hypertension	Damp and phlegm with Liver yang rising	*add **Gastrodia Complex***
	With coronary heart disease	Damp and phlegm with blood stagnation	*add **Circulation***
	With obesity and excessive appetite	Damp and phlegm with Stomach heat	*add **Herbalite***
	With fatigue	Damp and phlegm with Lung and Kidney deficiencies	*add **Cordyceps 3***
	With fatty liver and obesity	Damp and phlegm in the Liver	***Cholisma (ES)***
Chronic Fatigue Syndrome	Short-term tiredness and lack of energy	Qi deficiency	***Vibrant***
	Chronic fatigue with generalized weakness	Qi, blood, yin and yang deficiencies	***Imperial Tonic***
	Chronic fatigue with reproductive and respiratory deficiencies	Lung and Kidney qi deficiencies	***Imperial Tonic*** with ***Cordyceps 3***
	Adrenal insufficiency	Kidney qi deficiency	***Adrenal +***
	Forgetfulness and inability to concentrate	Heart and Kidney deficiencies	***Enhance Memory***
	Chronic fatigue with low-grade fever due to viral infection	Toxic deficiency heat	***Herbal AVR***
	Sluggishness, poor blood circulation, purplish tongue	Blood stasis	***Circulation (SJ)***
	Stress-related	Liver qi stagnation	***Calm*** or ***Calm (ES)***
	Due to weakness of the digestive tract	Spleen qi deficiency	***GI Tonic***
	Due to accumulation of toxins and allergens	Toxic heat accumulation	***Herbal DTX***
Cigarette Smoking	With wheezing, dyspnea, shortness of breath, phlegm	Lung heat with damp and phlegm	***Respitrol (Heat)*** or ***Respitrol (Cold)***
	To eliminate storage of phlegm and sputum in the Lung	Accumulation of damp and phlegm	***Pinellia XPT***
	To stop production of phlegm and sputum in the Spleen	Accumulation of damp and phlegm	***Pinellia Complex***
	Withdrawal symptoms associated with smoking, drug, or alcohol addiction	Toxic heat in the Liver and *shen* (spirit) disturbance	***Calm (ES)*** and ***Liver DTX***
	To restore lung health and respiratory functions	Lung deficiency	***Cordyceps 3*** or ***Respitrol (Deficient)***

Symptom / Disease Index

Conditions	Symptoms/Disease Description	TCM Diagnosis	Herbal Formulas
Circulation, Poor	Poor blood circulation to the heart	Qi and blood stagnation in the upper *jiao*	***Circulation***
	Poor blood circulation throughout the body	Qi and blood stagnation in the upper, middle and lower *jiao*	***Circulation (SJ)***
	Poor blood circulation to the limbs	Qi and blood stagnation	***Flex (NP)***
Cleansing	Intestinal/colon detox	Toxic heat in the Intestines	***GI DTX***
	Liver detox	Toxic heat in the liver	***Liver DTX***
	Kidney detox	Toxic heat in the kidney	***Kidney DTX***
	Accumulation of allergens, chemicals and toxins in the body	Toxic heat in the body	***Herbal DTX***
Clot, Blood	Coronary heart condition	Blood stagnation	***Circulation***
	Severe blood stagnation in the body	Blood stagnation	***Circulation (SJ)***
	Severe blood stagnation in the extremities	Blood stagnation	***Flex (NP)***
Cluster Headache	Acute cluster headache	Qi and blood stagnation	***Corydalin (AC)***
	Chronic cluster headache with blood deficiency	Qi and blood stagnation with blood deficiency	***Corydalin (CR)***
	Severe cluster headache	Severe qi and blood stagnation	*add* ***Herbal ANG***
	Caused by stress	Liver qi stagnation or Liver yang rising	*add* ***Calm*** or ***Calm (ES)***
	With extreme stress, heat, short temper, irritability, red face, red eyes, and possible constipation	Liver fire	*add* ***Gentiana Complex***
Cognitive Impairment	Memory impairment due to neurodegenerative disorders	Deficiencies of Kidney yin, yang and *jing* (essence) with phlegm	***Neuro Plus***
	Poor memory and forgetfulness	Heart and Kidney deficiencies	***Enhance Memory***
Cold	*See* Common cold or specific diseases		
Cold Sores	Fever blisters with pain and inflammation	Wind-heat	***Lonicera Complex***
	Moderate to severe cases of infection and inflammation	Accumulation of toxic heat	***Lonicera Complex*** and ***Herbal AVR***
Colic Pain	*See* Stones		
Colitis	Ulcerative colitis or Crohn's disease	Damp-heat in the Large Intestine	***GI Care (UC)***
	With diarrhea due to infection	Damp-heat in the Large Intestine	*add* ***GI Care II***
	With moderate to severe cases of infection and inflammation	Accumulation of toxic heat	*add* ***Herbal ABX***
	With bleeding	Heat accumulation pushing blood out of the vessels	*add* ***Notoginseng 9***
	To enhance anti-inflammatory effect	Excess heat accumulation	*add* ***Astringent Complex***
Colon	Cleansing	Toxic heat accumulation in the colon	***GI DTX***
	See also Constipation, Diarrhea, Colitis, Diverticulitis, Irritable bowel syndrome (IBS), Crohn's disease, Ulcerative colitis (UC), etc.		

Symptom / Disease Index

Conditions	Symptoms/Disease Description	TCM Diagnosis	Herbal Formulas
Common Cold	Sore throat, headache	Wind-heat	***Lonicera Complex***
	Dyspnea, chest congestion, fever	Lung heat	***Respitrol (Heat)***
	Runny nose with clear watery discharge, sneezing, nasal congestion	Lung cold	***Respitrol (Cold)***
	Chest congestion, profuse yellow sputum, cough	Lung heat with phlegm	***Pinellia XPT***
	With cough	Reversed flow of Lung qi	*add* ***Respitrol (CF)***
	With severe sore throat and possible ear ache	Toxic heat in the Lung	*add* ***Herbal ENT***
	Due to viral infection	Toxic deficiency heat	*add* ***Herbal AVR***
	With severe inflammation	Excess heat accumulation	*add* ***Astringent Complex***
	Prevention of common cold and flu	*Wei* (defensive) *qi* deficiency	***Immune +***
Complexion	Pale with fatigue and weakness	Qi deficiency	***Imperial Tonic***
	Pale with dizziness and anemia	Blood deficiency	***Schisandra ZZZ***
	Dark circles under the eyes, soreness and weakness of the lower back and knees, dizziness, tinnitus, possible spermatorrhea, hair loss and dryness	Kidney yin deficiency	***Nourish*** or ***Kidney Tonic (Yin)***
	Dark complexion with purplish tongue, dry hair, coldness; menstrual cramps and blood clots in women	Blood stagnation	***Menatrol***
	Dark complexion from chronic blood stagnation resulting from surgery or old injuries	Blood stasis	***Circulation (SJ)***
	Red complexion with high blood pressure and fast heart rate	Heat in all three *jiaos*	***Gardenia Complex***
Conception	*See* Infertility		
Conjunctivitis	Redness and swelling of the eyes, "red eyes"	Liver fire rising	***Gentiana Complex***
	Inflammation and swelling of the eyes	Heat in all three *jiaos*	***Gardenia Complex***
	Moderate to severe cases of infection and inflammation	Accumulation of toxic heat	***Gardenia Complex*** and ***Herbal ABX***
Constipation	Excess-type constipation with yellow tongue coat and red face	Excess heat in the Large Intestine	***Gentle Lax (Excess)***
	Deficient-type constipation with dryness	Heat in the Large Intestine with yin deficiency	***Gentle Lax (Deficient)***
	Irritable bowel syndrome (IBS)	Liver qi stagnation	*add* ***GI Harmony***
	With cold extremities, pale complexion, preference for warmth, polyuria and excessive urinary urges at night	Kidney yang deficiency	*add* ***Kidney Tonic (Yang)***
	With thirst, dryness, dizziness; in postpartum or convalescing patients	Blood deficiency	*add* ***Schisandra ZZZ***
	Post-surgical constipation	Qi and blood stagnation	*add* ***Flex (TMX)***
	With hemorrhoids	Blood stagnation	*add* ***GI Care (HMR)***
	With dryness and thirst	Stomach yin deficiency	*add* ***Nourish (Fluids)***
	With bleeding	Heat in the Intestines	*add* ***Notoginseng 9***
	Intestinal/colon detox	Toxic heat in the Intestines	***GI DTX***

Symptom / Disease Index

Conditions	Symptoms/Disease Description	TCM Diagnosis	Herbal Formulas
Contact Dermatitis	Wet lesions	Damp-heat toxin	***Dermatrol (Damp)***
	Dry lesions	Wind-toxin	***Dermatrol (Dry)***
	With itching	Wind-heat	*add **Silerex***
Contagious Disease	*See* Infection		
Convulsion	Childhood convulsion	Liver wind	***Calm (Jr)***
	High blood pressure, redness of the face and eyes, tremors	Liver wind with Liver yang rising	***Symmetry*** with ***Gastrodia Complex***
	Dryness of the eyes, soreness of the back and knees, tinnitus	Liver and Kidney yin deficiency	***Symmetry*** with ***Nourish***
Coronary Heart Disease	Chest pain with numbness due to poor blood circulation	Blood stagnation	***Circulation***
	Chest pain with high cholesterol/triglycerides	Blood stagnation with damp and phlegm	*add **Cholisma***
	Chest pain with high cholesterol/triglycerides, fatty liver and obesity	Blood stagnation with damp and phlegm	*add **Cholisma (ES)***
	Chest pain with deficient-type hypertension, dizziness, tinnitus	Blood stagnation with Liver yang rising	*add **Gastrodia Complex***
	Chest pain with excess-type hypertension, headache, flushed face, red eyes, anger	Blood stagnation with Liver fire	*add **Gentiana Complex***
	Chest pain with generalized weakness	Blood stagnation with qi deficiency	*add **Imperial Tonic***
	Severe blood stasis manifesting in dark, purplish complexion, purplish tongue, possible distended sublingual veins	Blood stasis	***Circulation (SJ)***
Cough	General cough	Reversed flow of Lung qi	***Respitrol (CF)***
	Dyspnea, yellow nasal discharge or sputum, fever	Lung heat	*add **Respitrol (Heat)***
	Dyspnea, white nasal discharge or sputum, chills	Lung cold	*add **Respitrol (Cold)***
	Early stage of infection, cough with pronounced sore throat	Wind-heat	*add **Herbal ENT***
	Mid-to-late stage of infection, cough with chest congestion and yellow sputum	Lung heat with phlegm	*add **Pinellia XPT***
	Chronic dry and non-productive cough, chest pain	Lung yin deficiency	*add **Nourish (Fluids)***
	Moderate to severe cases of infection and inflammation	Accumulation of toxic heat	*add **Herbal ABX***
	Cough due to exposure to drugs, chemicals, heavy metals, environmental and airborne toxins	Toxic heat	*add **Herbal DTX***
	Chronic respiratory disease with weakness	Lung and Kidney deficiencies	*add **Respitrol (Deficient)***
	With phlegm or feeling of plum-pit syndrome, hypochondriac distension, short temper	Liver qi stagnation or Liver fire	*add **Calm (ES)***
	Dry cough, thirst, dryness	Lung and Stomach yin deficiencies	*add **Nourish (Fluids)***
	With severe inflammation	Excess heat	*add **Astringent Complex***
	With post-nasal drip	Damp and phlegm	*add **Pinellia Complex***

Symptom / Disease Index

Conditions	Symptoms/Disease Description	TCM Diagnosis	Herbal Formulas
Cramps	Muscle spasms and cramps	Liver yin and body fluid deficiencies	***Flex (SC)***
	Menstrual cramps	Blood stagnation	*add* ***Mense-Ease***
	Stomach cramp with acid reflux or ulcer	Stomach heat	*add* ***GI Care***
	Intestinal cramps from irritable bowel syndrome (IBS)	Liver qi stagnation	*add* ***GI Harmony***
	Intestinal cramps from ulcerative colitis	Damp-heat in the intestine	*add* ***GI Care (UC)***
	With severe pain	Severe qi and blood stagnation	*add* ***Herbal ANG***
	From yin/fluid deficiency	Yin and fluid deficiencies	*add* ***Nourish (Fluids)***
Crohn's Disease	Diarrhea, rectal bleeding, poor appetite, fever, night sweats, weight loss	Toxic heat accumulation in the Intestines with yin-deficient heat	***GI Care (UC)***
	With pronounced poor appetite and weakness	Spleen qi deficiency	*add* ***GI Tonic***
	With severe bleeding	Heat pushing blood out of the vessels	*add* ***Notoginseng 9***
	With stress	Liver qi stagnation	*add* ***Calm***
	With more fever	Heat accumulation	*add* ***Gardenia Complex***
	With more inflammation	Heat accumulation	*add* ***Astringent Complex***
	With damp and phlegm accumulation	Spleen qi deficiency with dampness	*add* ***Pinellia Complex***
Crying	Emotional disturbance during menopause	Kidney yin deficiency with *shen* (spirit) disturbance	***Balance (Heat)***
	From stress	Liver qi stagnation	***Calm*** or ***Calm (ES)***
	With stress, fatigue, insomnia	Liver qi stagnation with qi deficiency	***Calm ZZZ***
	Depression	Qi, blood, food, phlegm stagnation	***Shine*** or ***Shine (DS)***
Cyst	Cysts in the breast	Liver qi stagnation with phlegm accumulation	***Resolve (Upper)***
	Ovarian or uterine cysts	Qi and blood stagnation in the lower *jiao*	***Resolve (Lower)***
	Cysts elsewhere in the body	Qi and phlegm stagnation	***Resolve (AI)***
	With damp and phlegm accumulation	Spleen qi deficiency with dampness	*add* ***Pinellia Complex***
Cystic Acne	General acne	Toxic and damp-heat accumulation (mild)	***Dermatrol (Clear)***
	With pus and redness	Toxic and damp-heat accumulation (severe)	*add* ***Dermatrol (PS)***
	With lesions that are wet	Damp-heat	*add* ***Dermatrol (Damp)***
	Due to stress	Liver qi stagnation	*add* ***Calm*** or ***Calm (ES)***
	Due to hormone imbalance	Liver qi stagnation	*add* ***Calm***
	With damp and phlegm accumulation	Spleen qi deficiency with dampness	*add* ***Pinellia Complex***
Cystitis	Acute stage with urinary urgency, burning and painful urination	Damp-heat in the Urinary Bladder	***V-Support***
	Interstitial cystitis	Damp-heat accumulation and blood stagnation in the lower *jiao*	*add* ***Circulation (SJ)***

Symptom / Disease Index

Conditions	Symptoms/Disease Description	TCM Diagnosis	Herbal Formulas
Cystitis (*cont'd*)	With bleeding	Heat pushing blood out of the vessels	add ***Notoginseng 9***
	With fever	Fire accumulation in the lower *jiao*	add ***Gardenia Complex***
	Chronic stage with urinary urgency, frequent re-infection	Damp-heat in the Urinary Bladder with yin deficiency	***Gentiana Complex*** with ***Nourish***
	Moderate to severe cases of infection and inflammation	Accumulation of toxic heat	***Gentiana Complex*** and ***Herbal ABX***
Degeneration	Of the nervous system	Kidney yin, yang and *jing* (essence) deficiencies	***Neuro Plus***
	Poor memory and forgetfulness	Heart and Kidney deficiencies	***Enhance Memory***
	Decrease in function of adrenal glands and the endocrine system	Kidney qi deficiency	***Adrenal +***
	Hypothyroidism	Kidney yang deficiency	***Thyro-forte***
	Pre-mature aging with gray hair and hair loss	Liver blood deficiency with Kidney yin deficiency	***Polygonum 14***
	Degenerative arthritis of the upper body	Liver yin and Kidney yin deficiencies	***Neck & Shoulder (CR)*** with a ***Flex*** formula
	Degenerative arthritis of the lower body	Liver yin and Kidney yin deficiencies	***Back Support (CR)*** with a ***Flex*** formula
	Degenerative arthritis of the legs	Liver yin and Kidney yin deficiencies	***Knee & Ankle (CR)*** with a ***Flex*** formula
	Of soft tissue (muscle, tendon, ligament, cartilage)	Liver and Kidney yin deficiencies	***Flex (MLT)***
	Of the bones	Kidney yin and *jing* (essence) deficiencies	***Osteo 8***
	Decreased or absence of libido	Kidney yang deficiency	***Vitality***
	Vaginal atrophy and dryness	Kidney yin and *jing* (essence) deficiencies	***Balance Spring***
	Blurred vision and deteriorated eye functions	Liver and Kidney yin deficiencies	***Lycium Support***
Dehydration	Resulting in excessive thirst and dryness	Yin and fluid deficiencies	***Nourish (Fluids)***
	Causing cramps	Blood deficiency with qi and blood stagnation	add ***Flex (SC)***
	From diarrhea due to food poisoning	Damp-heat in the Intestines	add ***GI Care II***
	Due to chronic diarrhea with weak digestion and poor appetite	Spleen qi deficiency	add ***GI Tonic***
	Due to excess fire, fever, inflammation or infection	Fire in the *qi* (energy) level	add ***Gardenia Complex***
Delirium	With anxiety, irritability, restlessness and insomnia	Liver fire	***Calm (ES)***
	With constipation	Qi stagnation and excess fire	add ***Gentle Lax (Excess)***
	With heat sensation	Excess fire	add ***Gardenia Complex***
	With severe blood stagnation manifesting in purplish tongue, dark complexion or in cases where other herbs don't seem to work	Severe blood stasis	add ***Circulation (SJ)***

Symptom / Disease Index

Conditions	Symptoms/Disease Description	TCM Diagnosis	Herbal Formulas
Dementia	Memory impairment due to neurodegenerative disorders	Deficiencies of Kidney yin, yang and *jing* (essence) with phlegm	***Neuro Plus***
	Poor memory and forgetfulness	Heart and Kidney deficiencies	***Enhance Memory***
Dependence	*See* Addiction		
Depression	Depression	Stagnation of phlegm, qi, blood and food	***Shine***
	Depression and stress	Liver qi stagnation with Heart fire	***Shine (DS)***
	Severe depression	Stagnation of phlegm, qi, blood and food	*add* ***Circulation (SJ)***
	With alcohol or drug abuse	Stagnation of phlegm, qi, blood and food with toxic heat	*add* ***Liver DTX***
Dermatitis	Mild to moderate rash, itching, redness	Wind-heat or damp-heat at the skin level	***Silerex***
	With moderate to severe cases of infection and inflammation	Accumulation of toxic heat	*add* ***Herbal ABX***
	With lesions that are wet	Damp-heat	*add* ***Dermatrol (Damp)***
	With lesions that are dry	Dry-heat accumulation	*add* ***Dermatrol (Dry)***
	With abscesses, sores and pus	Toxic heat	*add* ***Dermatrol (PS)***
	With redness and heat sensation	Excess heat accumulation	*add* ***Gardenia Complex***
	With more inflammation and swelling	Excess heat accumulation	*add* ***Astringent Complex***
Detox	Accumulation of toxic substances in the body leading to compromised liver function (from alcohol, drugs, medication, and smoking.)	Toxic heat in the Liver	***Liver DTX***
	Accumulation of toxic substances in the body leading to compromised kidney function	Toxic heat in the Kidney	***Kidney DTX***
	Adverse reactions from exposure to drugs, chemicals, heavy metals, hormones in meat, environmental and airborne toxins	Toxic heat in the Intestines	***Herbal DTX***
	Accumulation of toxic substances in the gastrointestinal tract; colon detox	Toxic heat accumulation	***GI DTX***
	To invigorate blood circulation and promote self healing	Blood stagnation	***Circulation (SJ)***
	To cleanse the lymphatic system	Damp and phlegm accumulation	***Resolve (AI)***
	For weight loss	Stomach fire	***Herbalite***
	For bacterial detox	Excessive heat	***Herbal ABX***
	For viral detox	Toxic heat	***Herbal AVR***
Diabetes Mellitus	High blood glucose	Lung, Stomach, and Kidney yin deficiencies	***Equilibrium***
	With impotence	With Kidney yang deficiency	*add* ***Vitality***
	With urinary tract infection	With damp-heat in the Urinary Bladder	*add* ***V-Support***
	With high cholesterol	With damp and phlegm accumulation	*add* ***Cholisma***
	With excessive thirst	With yin and fluid deficiencies	*add* ***Nourish (Fluids)***
	With retinopathy	With Liver and Kidney yin deficiencies	*add* ***Lycium Support***

Symptom / Disease Index

Conditions	Symptoms/Disease Description	TCM Diagnosis	Herbal Formulas
Diabetes Mellitus (*cont'd*)	With neuropathy	With qi and blood stagnation	*add* ***Flex (NP)***
	With nephropathy	With toxic heat in the blood	*add* ***Kidney DTX***
	With obesity	With damp and phlegm accumulation	*add* ***Herbalite***
	With coronary artery disease	With blood stasis	*add* ***Circulation***
	With infection	With toxic heat	*add* ***Herbal ABX***
Diarrhea	Loose stools or diarrhea with poor appetite and weakness	Spleen qi deficiency	***GI Tonic***
	With foul-smelling stools, burning sensation of anus, abdominal discomfort and pain, nausea and vomiting, traveler's diarrhea, food poisoning, stomach flu	Damp-heat in the Intestines	***GI Care II***
	Due to ulcerative colitis, Crohn's disease, diarrhea with pus and blood	Toxic heat in the Intestines	***GI Care (UC)***
	Due to irritable bowel syndrome (IBS)	Liver qi stagnation	***GI Harmony***
	Due to side effect of chemotherapy and radiation	Yin deficiency heat	***C/R Support***
	Moderate to severe cases of infection and inflammation	Accumulation of toxic heat	*add* ***Herbal ABX***
	With bleeding	Heat pushing blood out of the vessels	*add* ***Notoginseng 9***
	Extreme thirst and dryness from diarrhea	Yin and fluid deficiency	*add* ***Nourish (Fluids)***
Diet	Excessive appetite, overweight	Damp accumulation with Stomach heat	***Herbalite***
	Excessive appetite with high cholesterol	Damp accumulation	*add* ***Cholisma***
	Excessive appetite with high cholesterol, fatty liver and obesity	Damp phlegm accumulation	*add* ***Cholisma (ES)***
	Excessive appetite with gallstones	Damp-heat in the Gallbladder	*add* ***Dissolve (GS)***
	Excessive appetite with hepatitis	Toxic heat in the Liver	*add* ***Liver DTX***
	Poor appetite due to food poisoning or traveler's diarrhea	Damp-heat in the Intestines	***GI Care II***
	Poor dietary choices resulting in fecal impaction	Toxic heat in the Large Intestine	***GI DTX***
	Poor appetite, fatigue, loose stools	Spleen qi deficiency	***GI Tonic***
Discharge	Clear and watery nasal discharge	Wind-cold at the exterior	***Magnolia Clear Sinus***
	Thick and yellow nasal discharge	Damp-heat at the nose	***Pueraria Clear Sinus***
	Ear discharge from infection	Toxic heat invasion	***Herbal ENT***
	Yellow or yellow/greenish vaginal discharge	Damp-heat in the lower *jiao*	***V-Support***
	Nipple discharge from fibrocystic disorder	Phlegm accumulation and Liver qi stagnation	***Resolve (Upper)***
Distension	Head: distension and pain	Qi and blood stagnation	***Corydalin (AC)***
	Head: due to deficient type of hypertension	Liver yang rising with yin deficiency	***Gastrodia Complex***
	Head: due to excess type of hypertension	Liver fire	***Gentiana Complex***
	Chest: coronary heart disease	*Xiong bi* (painful obstruction of the chest)	***Circulation***
	Chest: wheezing or dyspnea with fever, yellow sputum	Lung heat	***Respitrol (Heat)*** with ***Pinellia XPT***

Symptom / Disease Index

Conditions	Symptoms/Disease Description	TCM Diagnosis	Herbal Formulas
Distension *(cont'd)*	Chest: wheezing or dyspnea with white sputum	Lung cold	***Respitrol (Cold)*** with ***Pinellia XPT***
	Chest: chronic respiratory disorder with dyspnea	Lung qi deficiency	***Respitrol (Deficient)***
	Hypochondriac area	Liver qi stagnation	***Calm***
	Abdomen: due to irritable bowel syndrome (IBS)	Liver qi stagnation	***GI Harmony***
	Abdomen: due to ulcerative colitis (UC) or Crohn's disease	Damp-heat in the intestine	***GI Care (UC)***
	Abdomen: with weakness of digestion	Spleen qi deficiency	***GI Tonic***
	Abdomen: with constipation	Heat in the intestine	***Gentle Lax (Excess)***, ***Gentle Lax (Deficient)***
	Lower abdomen: due to fibroids, cysts or endometriosis	Qi and blood stagnation	***Resolve (Lower)***
	Breast distension	Liver qi stagnation	***Calm***
	Severe breast distension	Liver qi stagnation	***Calm*** and ***Resolve (Upper)***
	Swelling and edema	Fluid and damp accumulation	***Herbal DRX***
Diverticulitis	Diverticulitis with inflammation	Damp-heat in the intestine	***Resolve (AI)***
	With acute constipation	Qi stagnation with heat	*add* ***Gentle Lax (Excess)***
	With chronic constipation or dry stools	Yin deficiency with stagnation	*add* ***Gentle Lax (Deficient)***
	With severe pain	Severe qi and blood stagnation	*add* ***Herbal ANG***
	With severe inflammation	Damp-heat in the intestine	*add* ***Astringent Complex***
Dizziness	Due to anemia	Spleen and Heart deficiencies	***Schisandra ZZZ***
	Due to hypertension or Meniere's syndrome	Liver yang rising or Liver fire	***Gastrodia Complex*** or ***Gentiana Complex***
	From exposure to drugs, chemicals, heavy metals, environmental and airborne toxins	Toxic heat	***Herbal DTX***
	With migraine or headache from blood deficiency	Blood deficiency	***Corydalin (CR)***
	With ear, nose or throat infection	Wind-heat and toxic heat invasion	***Herbal ENT***
	With blurry vision, tinnitus, hot flashes, low-grade fever or night sweats	Kidney yin-deficient heat	***Balance (Heat)*** or ***Nourish***
	With flu or common cold	Wind-heat or wind-cold invasion	***Lonicera Complex*** or ***Respitrol (Cold)***
	From anxiety, stress	Liver qi stagnation	***Calm (ES)***
Dreams	Increased dreams, difficulty falling and staying asleep, poor appetite, epigastric fullness and distension, fatigue	Spleen and Heart deficiencies	***Schisandra ZZZ***
	Nervousness, forgetfulness, restlessness, weakness	Heart and Kidney deficiencies	***Enhance Memory***
	Anger, short temper, hypochondriac discomfort	Liver fire	***Calm (ES)***

Symptom / Disease Index

Conditions	Symptoms/Disease Description	TCM Diagnosis	Herbal Formulas
Dreams (*cont'd*)	Difficulty falling or staying asleep, stress, anxiety, restlessness with deficiency	Liver qi stagnation with qi deficiency	***Calm ZZZ***
Drooling of Saliva	With paralysis, Bell's palsy	Liver wind	***Symmetry***
	With profuse saliva, poor appetite, pale complexion, loose stools	Spleen qi deficiency	***GI Tonic*** and ***Pinellia Complex***
	With ulceration in the tongue, bitter taste, constipation, irritability	Stomach heat	***Herbal ENT*** and ***Gentle Lax (Excess)***
Dryness	Dry eyes	Liver and Kidney yin deficiencies	***Lycium Support***
	Dry skin, hair, nails	Liver blood and Kidney yin deficiencies	***Polygonum 14***
	Vaginal dryness	Liver blood and Kidney *jing* (essence) deficiencies	***Balance Spring***
	General dryness with thirst	Lung and Stomach yin deficiency	***Nourish (Fluids)***
	Severe dryness with tinnitus, hair loss, blurry vision, weakness and soreness of back and knees, hot flashes, low-grade fever, malar flush, and night sweats	Kidney yin deficiency	***Kidney Tonic (Yin)*** and ***Balance (Heat)***
Duodenum	Ulcer with abdominal pain	Stomach heat	***GI Care***
	See also specific diseases and conditions		
Dysentery	Diarrhea with foul-smelling stools, burning sensation of anus, abdominal discomfort and pain, nausea and vomiting	Damp-heat in the Intestines	***GI Care II***
	Moderate to severe cases of infection and inflammation	Accumulation of toxic heat	*add* ***Herbal ABX***
	With bleeding	Heat pushing blood out of the vessels	*add* ***Notoginseng 9***
	With fever	Excess heat accumulation	*add* ***Gardenia Complex***
Dysmenorrhea	With bloating and blood clots	Qi and blood stagnation	***Mense-Ease***
	Due to cysts, fibroids, or endometriosis	Qi and blood stagnation	*add* ***Resolve (Lower)***
	With pelvic infection or inflammation	Toxic heat accumulation and blood stagnation	*add* ***V-Support***
	With severe pain	Severe qi and blood stagnation	*add* ***Herbal ANG***
	With back pain	Kidney deficiency	*add* ***Back Support (CR)***
Dyspnea	With cough, chest congestion, yellow sputum, with or without fever	Lung heat	***Respitrol (Heat)***
	With cough, white sputum or nasal discharge, chills	Lung cold	***Respitrol (Cold)***
	With cough and no other significant signs	Lung qi reversal	***Respitrol (CF)***
	With profuse amount of phlegm and sputum	Damp and phlegm accumulation	***Pinellia XPT***
	Chronic respiratory disorder; dyspnea with light physical exertion	Deficiencies of the Lung and the Kidney	***Respitrol (Deficient)***
	Chronic respiratory disorder with underlying Lung and Kidney deficiency	Lung and Kidney qi deficiency	***Cordyceps 3***

Symptom / Disease Index

Conditions	Symptoms/Disease Description	TCM Diagnosis	Herbal Formulas
Dysuria	Painful urination due to infection	Damp-heat in the Urinary Bladder	***V-Support***
	Due to kidney or urinary stones	*Shi lin* (stone dysuria)	***Dissolve (KS)***
	Chronic nephritis	Toxic heat with dampness and Kidney deficiency	***Kidney DTX***
	Due to prostate enlargement	Damp accumulation and qi stagnation	***P-Support***
	Post menopausal	Yin-deficient heat	***Balance (Heat)*** with ***Nourish***
	Due to post-surgical adhesion	Blood stagnation	***Flex (TMX)***
	Due to yeast infection	Damp-heat or damp in the lower *jiao*	***V-Support***
	With infection and inflammation	Accumulation of toxic heat	*add* ***Herbal ABX***
	With bleeding	Heat pushing blood out of the vessels	*add* ***Notoginseng 9***
	With fever	Excess heat accumulation	*add* ***Gardenia Complex***
	With severe pain	Severe qi and blood stagnation	*add* ***Herbal ANG***
Ear Infection	Ear infection with fever, pain	Damp-heat in the Liver and Gallbladder channels	***Herbal ENT***
	Moderate to severe cases of infection and inflammation	Accumulation of toxic heat	*add* ***Gentiana Complex***
	With swelling	Damp-heat accumulation	*add* ***Resolve (AI)***
	With fever	Excess heat accumulation	*add* ***Gardenia Complex***
Eating Disorder	*See* Anorexia, Bulimia, Obesity		
Eczema	Mild to moderate general itching and skin conditions	Wind-heat at the skin level, heat in the blood	***Silerex***
	Moderate to severe skin condition with wet or oozing appearance	Damp-heat toxin	***Dermatrol (Damp)***
	Moderate to severe skin condition with dry or flaky appearance	Wind toxin with dryness	***Dermatrol (Dry)***
	Of the genital area	Damp-heat in the lower *jiao*	***V-Support***
	Skin reaction due to exposure to drugs, chemicals, heavy metals, environmental and airborne toxins	Toxic heat accumulation	*add* ***Herbal DTX***
	Chronic eczema with underlying blood deficiency or anemia	Toxic heat accumulation with blood deficiency	*add* ***Schisandra ZZZ***
	With redness, burning or fever	Excess heat accumulation	*add* ***Gardenia Complex***
	Stubborn eczema due to blood stagnation with dark appearance and purplish tongue	Blood stagnation	*add* ***Circulation (SJ)***
	Stress related	Liver qi stagnation	*add* ***Calm*** or ***Calm (ES)***
Edema	General edema with swelling	Water accumulation	***Herbal DRX***
	Edema in hypothyroid patients	Kidney yang deficiency with damp accumulation	*add* ***Thyro-forte***

Symptom / Disease Index

Conditions	Symptoms/Disease Description	TCM Diagnosis	Herbal Formulas
Edema (*cont'd*)	Due to hypertension	Liver yin deficiency with Liver yang rising	*add* ***Gastrodia Complex***
	Due to obesity and excess appetite	Stomach heat with damp	*add* ***Herbalite***
	With coldness and weakness	Kidney yang deficiency	*add* ***Kidney Tonic (Yang)***
	Due to chronic kidney disease	Kidney deficiency	*add* ***Kidney DTX***
	With weak digestive system and diarrhea	Spleen deficiency	*add* ***GI Tonic***
	With lymphedema	Damp and phlegm accumulation	*add* ***Resolve (AI)***
	Due to diabetes mellitus	Yin deficiency with damp	*add* ***Equilibrium***
	With poor blood flow	Blood stagnation	*add* ***Circulation(SJ)***
Elbow	Tennis elbow, golfer's elbow, pain	Qi and blood stagnation	***Arm Support***
	With severe pain	Severe qi and blood stagnation	*add* ***Herbal ANG***
	Soft tissue degeneration (muscles, tendons, ligaments and cartilage)	Liver and Kidney yin deficiencies	*add* ***Flex (MLT)***
Emaciation	Weight loss, fatigue, overall deficiency	Qi, blood, yin and yang deficiencies	***Imperial Tonic***
	Weight loss, loose stools, poor appetite, fatigue, anorexia, anemia, weak digestive system	Spleen deficiency	***GI Tonic***
	Chronic fatigue with compromised lung and kidney functions	Lung and Kidney deficiencies	***Cordyceps 3***
	Kidney yin deficiency with blurry vision, weakness of the back and knees, tinnitus, dryness, flushed cheeks, possible low-grade fever	Kidney yin deficiency	***Kidney Tonic (Yin)***
	Kidney yang deficiency with coldness, low libido, premature ejaculation, weakness and soreness of the back and knees, pale complexion, and polyuria	Kidney yang deficiency	***Kidney Tonic (Yang)***
Emotion	Instability with stress, PMS, nervousness	Liver qi stagnation	***Calm***
	Instability with restlessness, insomnia, and anger	Liver and Heart fire	***Calm (ES)***
	Instability with mood swings in menopause patients	Kidney and Liver yin deficiencies	***Balance (Heat)***
	Instability, over-active mind, stress and insomnia in patients with deficiency	Liver qi stagnation with qi deficiency	***Calm ZZZ***
	Excessive worrying, pensiveness, anemia	Spleen and Heart blood deficiencies	***Schisandra ZZZ***
	Depression	Qi, blood, phlegm, food, fire and damp accumulation	***Shine***
	Depression and stress	Liver qi stagnation and Heart fire	***Shine (DS)***
	Pent-up emotion with red face, constipation, excess anger	Excess accumulation of fire	*add* ***Gardenia Complex***
	Chronic, stubborn emotional imbalance that doesn't seem to respond to any treatment	Blood stagnation	*add* ***Circulation (SJ)***
Emphysema	Dyspnea, wheezing, scanty or no sputum, weakness	Deficiencies of the Lung and the Kidney	***Respitrol (Deficient)***
	Dyspnea, wheezing, white sputum	Lung cold	***Respitrol (Cold)***
	Dyspnea, wheezing, fever, yellow sputum	Lung heat	***Respitrol (Heat)***

Symptom / Disease Index

Conditions	Symptoms/Disease Description	TCM Diagnosis	Herbal Formulas
Emphysema (*cont'd*)	Maintenance formula to improve breathing	Lung and Kidney deficiencies	***Cordyceps 3***
	Cough with no other pronounced symptoms	Lung qi reversal	***Respitrol (CF)***
	To eliminate storage of sputum and phlegm in the Lung	Accumulation of damp and phlegm	***Pinellia XPT***
	To stop production of sputum and phlegm by the Spleen	Accumulation of damp and phlegm	***Pinellia Complex***
Endocrine Disorders	Diminished function of the adrenal glands and endocrine system	Deficiencies of Kidney yin, yang and *jing* (essence)	***Adrenal +***
	Diabetes mellitus	Yin deficiency with dampness and heat	***Equilibrium***
	Hyperthyroidism, Graves disease	Excess heat	***Thyrodex***
	Hypothyroidism, Hashimoto's disease	Kidney yang deficiency	***Thyro-forte***
	Addison's disease	Kidney deficiency	***Adrenal +***
	Menopause	Kidney deficiency	***Nourish*** or ***Balance (Heat)***
Endometriosis	Cramps and pain with or without menstruation	Blood stagnation in the lower *jiao*	***Resolve (Lower)***
	Severe menstrual cramps	Blood stagnation in the lower *jiao*	*add* ***Mense-Ease*** during the period
	With back pain	Blood stagnation in the lower *jiao*	*add* ***Back Support (AC)***
	Causing infertility	Blood stagnation in the lower *jiao*	*add* ***Blossom (Phase 1-4)***
Energy	Short-term tiredness and lack of energy	Qi deficiency	***Vibrant***
	Chronic fatigue with generalized weakness and deficiency in qi, blood, yin and yang	Qi, blood, yin and yang deficiencies	***Imperial Tonic***
	Patients who are burned out with fatigue, lack of energy and drive	Deficiencies of Kidney yin, yang and *jing* (essence)	***Adrenal +***
	Chronic fatigue with Lung and Kidney weakness	Lung and Kidney deficiencies	***Cordyceps 3***
	Low energy and weak immune system	*Wei* (defensive) *qi* deficiency	***Immune +***
	Low energy and weak digestive function	Spleen qi deficiency	***GI Tonic***
	Chronic sluggishness with blood stagnation signs of purplish tongue, dark complexion, past history of trauma or surgery	Blood stagnation	***Circulation (SJ)***
	Too much energy, hyperactivity, overexcitement	Liver and Heart fire	***Gardenia Complex***
Enhancement (Breast)	To enhance the size and the shape of the breasts	Kidney yang and *jing* (essence) deficiencies	***Venus***
Enteritis	Diarrhea with foul-smelling stools, burning sensation of anus, abdominal discomfort and pain, nausea and vomiting	Damp-heat in the Intestines	***GI Care II***
	Chronic enteritis with weakness, poor appetite, and diarrhea	Spleen qi deficiency	*add* ***GI Tonic***
	With fever, excess heat and inflammation	Excess heat	*add* ***Herbal ABX***

Symptom / Disease Index

Conditions	Symptoms/Disease Description	TCM Diagnosis	Herbal Formulas
Enteritis (*cont'd*)	With pain	Qi and blood stagnation	add ***Herbal ANG***
	With bleeding	Heat pushing blood out of the vessels	add ***Notoginseng 9***
	Ulcerative colitis, Crohn's disease	Damp-heat in the Large Intestine	***GI Care (UC)***
	Moderate to severe cases of ulcerative colitis and Crohn's disease	Accumulation of toxic heat	***GI Care (UC)*** and ***Herbal ABX***
	Due to chemotherapy	Qi deficiency and heat accumulation	***C/R Support***
Epicondylitis (Lateral or Medial)	Tennis elbow, golfer's elbow	Qi and blood stagnation	***Arm Support***
	For degeneration of the joint and related soft tissue (muscle, ligaments, tendons, cartilages)	*Wei* (atrophy) syndrome	***Flex (MLT)***
	From trauma or recent sports injury	Qi and blood stagnation	add ***Flex (TMX)***
	For severe pain	Qi and blood stagnation	add ***Herbal ANG***
	For severe inflammation	Heat accumulation in the body	add ***Astringent Complex***
Epididymitis	Inflammation and swelling of the epididymis	Heat in the lower *jiao*	***V-Support*** and ***Herbal ABX*** or ***Astringent Complex***
Epigastric Pain	Epigastric fullness and pain, stomach ulcer, gastritis, acid reflux	Stomach heat	***GI Care***
	Irritable bowel syndrome (IBS)	Liver qi stagnation	***GI Harmony***
	Pain due to gallstones	Damp-heat in the Liver and Gallbladder	***Dissolve (GS)***
	With severe pain	Severe qi and blood stagnation	add ***Herbal ANG***
	Due to stress	Liver qi stagnation	add ***Calm***
Epilepsy	Prevention of epilepsy and seizures	Liver wind	***Gastrodia Complex***
	Treatment of epilepsy and seizures	Liver wind	***Symmetry***
Erectile Dysfunction	*See* Impotence		
Erysipelas	Skin and lymph infection	Toxic heat accumulation with phlegm	***Resolve (AI)*** and ***Herbal ABX***
	With dry lesions on the skin	Wind toxin	***Dermatrol (Dry)***
	With wet lesions on the skin	Damp-heat toxin	***Dermatrol (Damp)***
Esophageal Reflux	*See* Acid reflux		
Estrogen	Breast discomfort with PMS	Liver qi stagnation	***Calm***
	Breast discomfort with lumps, possible fibroids	Liver qi stagnation with phlegm stagnation	***Resolve (Upper)***
	Infertility	Depends on each phase	***Blossom (Phase 1-4)***
	Menopause	Kidney yin deficiency	***Nourish***
	Menopause with hot flashes and mood swings	Kidney yin deficiency with heat	***Balance (Heat)***
	Osteoporosis	Kidney *jing* (essence) deficiency	***Osteo 8***
	Dryness of the eyes with blurred vision	Liver and Kidney yin deficiencies	***Lycium Support***
	Deficiency manifesting in vaginal dryness or atrophy	Kidney yin deficiency	***Balance Spring***

Symptom / Disease Index

Conditions	Symptoms/Disease Description	TCM Diagnosis	Herbal Formulas
Eyes	Dry eyes, blurred vision, floaters, spots in front of the eyes, lasik recovery, photophobia, cataracts, and night blindness	Liver and Kidney yin deficiencies	***Lycium Support***
	Hypertensive patients with red eyes, blurred vision, dizziness or vertigo	Liver yang rising	***Gastrodia Complex***
	Hypertensive patients with red eyes, flushed face, short temper	Liver fire rising	***Gentiana Complex***
	Red eyes due to infection	Accumulation of toxic heat	***Herbal ABX***
Eyes, with Dark Circles	With generalized weakness, possible tinnitus, blurry vision, night sweating, low-grade fever	Kidney yin deficiency	***Kidney Tonic (Yin)***
	With coldness, soreness and weakness of the low back and knees, spermatorrhea, low libido, polyuria, hair loss	Kidney yang deficiency	***Kidney Tonic (Yang)***
Facial Paralysis	Bell's palsy	External wind attack with qi and blood stagnation	***Symmetry***
	Post stroke sequelae	Internal wind attack with qi and blood stagnation	***Neuro Plus***
Fainting	*See* Hypoglycemia, Hypotension		
Fallopian Tubes	Obstruction of the fallopian tubes	Qi and blood stagnation of the lower *jiao*	***Resolve (Lower)***
	Inflammation of the fallopian tubes	Damp-heat in the lower *jiao*	***V-Support***
	Abscess and inflammation	Phlegm obstruction	***Resolve (AI)*** and ***V-Support***
	Infertility due to scarring, coldness and weakness	Blood stagnation with Kidney yang deficiency	***Menatrol***
Fat	Obesity with excessive appetite	Damp-heat accumulation with heat	***Herbalite***
	High cholesterol and triglycerides levels	Damp-heat accumulation	***Cholisma***
	High cholesterol and triglycerides levels with obesity and fatty liver	Damp-heat accumulation	***Cholisma (ES)***
	Fatty tissue deposit, such as lipomas	Phlegm stagnation	***Resolve (AI)***
	Excessive damp and phlegm in the body	Accumulation of damp and phlegm	***Pinellia Complex***
Fatigue	Short-term tiredness and lack of energy	Qi deficiency	***Vibrant***
	Chronic fatigue with generalized weakness	Qi, blood, yin and yang deficiencies	***Imperial Tonic***
	Anemia, weakness, insomnia, excess worries	Spleen and Heart qi deficiencies	***Schisandra ZZZ***
	Burned out with fatigue, lack of energy and drive	Deficiencies of Kidney yin, yang and *jing* (essence)	***Adrenal +***
	Chronic fatigue with Lung and Kidney weakness	Lung and Kidney deficiencies	***Cordyceps 3***
	Low energy and weak immune system	*Wei* (defensive) *qi* deficiency	***Immune +***
	Low energy and weak digestive function, poor appetite, loose stools, anorexia	Spleen qi deficiency	***GI Tonic***
	With chest pain due to coronary artery disease	*Xiong bi* (painful obstruction of the chest)	***Circulation***
	Due to chronic nephritis	Toxic heat in the Kidney	***Kidney DTX***

Symptom / Disease Index

Conditions	Symptoms/Disease Description	TCM Diagnosis	Herbal Formulas
Fatigue (*cont'd*)	In cancer patients	*Yuan* (source) *qi* and *wei* (defensive) *qi* deficiencies	***C/R Support*** or ***CA Support***
	With severe blood stagnation manifesting in purplish tongue	Blood stasis	***Circulation (SJ)***
	General feeling of heaviness, lassitude and weakness	Damp accumulation with Spleen qi deficiency	***Pinellia Complex***
	In hypothyroidism	Kidney yang deficiency	***Thyro-forte***
	From depression	Qi, blood, food, phlegm stagnation	***Shine*** or ***Shine (DS)***
	Chronic fatigue due to viral infection	Qi, blood, yin and yang deficiencies	***Herbal AVR***
Fatty Liver	Fatty liver with high cholesterol and obesity	Damp and phlegm accumulation	***Cholisma (ES)***
	With hepatitis	Toxic heat in the Liver	*add* ***Liver DTX***
Fear	Fear, restlessness, anxiety	*Shen* (spirit) disturbance with fire	***Calm (ES)***
	Easily frightened, poor sleep, excessive dreams	Spleen and Heart blood deficiency with *shen* (spirit) disturbance	***Schisandra ZZZ***
Fecal Compaction	Intestinal/colon detox	Toxic heat in the Intestines	***GI DTX***
Fertility	*See* Infertility		
Fever	General fever	Heat in all three *jiaos*	***Gardenia Complex***
	Viral infections, common cold and influenza	Wind-heat	***Lonicera Complex***
	Ear infection	Toxic heat accumulation	***Herbal ENT***
	Infectious mononucleosis	Toxic damp-heat invasion	***Resolve (AI)*** with ***Herbal ENT***
	Skin infections	Toxic heat accumulation	***Dermatrol (Dry)*** or ***Dermatrol (Damp)***
	Urinary tract infection	Damp-heat in the lower *jiao*	***V-Support***
	Gastrointestinal infection	Damp-heat and toxic heat invasion	***GI Care II***
	Fever in bacterial infections, pneumonia, or bronchitis, cough, dyspnea	Lung heat	***Respitrol (Heat)***
	Fever, chest congestion, yellow sputum	Damp-heat in the Lung	***Pinellia XPT***
	Low-grade fever in the evening with perspiration	Yin-deficient heat	***Nourish***
	Low-grade fever in the evening or with hot flashes in menopause	Yin-deficient heat	***Balance (Heat)***
	Due to hyperthyroidism	Liver fire excess	***Thyrodex***
	Due to exposure to drugs, chemicals, heavy metals, environmental and airborne toxins	Toxic heat	***Herbal DTX***
	With swelling and inflammation	Heat with phlegm stagnation	***Gardenia Complex*** with ***Resolve (AI)***
	Unremitting fever due to blood stagnation manifesting in purplish tongue	Blood stasis	***Circulation (SJ)*** with ***Gardenia Complex***
	Ulcerative colitis	Damp-heat in the Intestines	***GI Care (UC)***

Symptom / Disease Index

Conditions	Symptoms / Disease Description	TCM Diagnosis	Herbal Formulas
Fever (*cont'd*)	Crohn's disease	Damp-heat in the Intestines	***GI Harmony***
	Due to various types of bacterial infection	Heat at various parts of body	*add* ***Herbal ABX***
	Due to various types of viral infection	Toxic heat at various parts of body	*add* ***Herbal AVR***
	With inflammation	Heat accumulation in the body	*add* ***Astringent Complex***
Fever Blister	Cold sores with pain and inflammation	Wind-heat	***Lonicera Complex***
	Moderate to severe cases of infection and inflammation	Accumulation of toxic heat	*add* ***Herbal AVR***
	With severe pain	Qi and blood stagnation	*add* ***Herbal ANG***
Fibrocystic Disease	Fibrocystic breast masses	Liver qi stagnation with phlegm	***Resolve (Upper)***
	Fibroids in the uterus and ovaries	Blood stagnation in the lower *jiao*	***Resolve (Lower)***
Fibromyalgia	With coldness and/or numbness	*Bi zheng* (painful obstruction syndrome) with cold and deficiency	***Flex (CD)***
	With heat sensations	*Bi zheng* (painful obstruction syndrome) with heat	***Flex (Heat)***
	With spasms and cramps	*Bi zheng* (painful obstruction syndrome) with Liver yin and body fluid deficiencies	***Flex (SC)***
	Due to bone spurs	Qi and blood stagnation	***Flex (SPR)***
	Due to stress	*Bi zheng* (painful obstruction syndrome) with Liver qi stagnation	*add* ***Calm*** *or* ***Calm (ES)***
	Due to heat	Heat and fire	*add* ***Gardenia Complex***
	With severe pain	Severe qi and blood stagnation	*add* ***Herbal ANG***
	Due to blood stagnation manifesting in purplish tongue	Blood stasis	*add* ***Circulation (SJ)***
Fidgeting	*See* Irritability, Stress, Anxiety		
Filatov's Disease	Fever, pharyngitis, enlarged lymph	Toxic heat accumulation with dampness	***Resolve (AI)*** and ***Herbal ENT***
Fissures (Anal)	With dryness	Yin deficiency	***Nourish*** or ***Nourish (Fluids)***
	With ulceration or from hemorrhoids	Damp-heat in the lower *jiao*	***GI Care (HMR)*** and ***V-Support***
	With acute constipation	Qi and blood stagnation	***Gentle Lax (Excess)***
	With chronic constipation or dry stools	Yin deficiency	***Gentle Lax (Deficient)***
	With infection	Toxic heat	*add* ***Herbal ABX***
Five-Center Heat	With sweating, irritability	Yin deficiency with heat	***Balance (Heat)***
	With thirst, dryness	Yin deficiency	*add* ***Nourish (Fluids)***
	With extreme Kidney yin deficiency	Kidney yin deficiency	*add* ***Kidney Tonic (Yin)***

Symptom / Disease Index

Conditions	Symptoms/Disease Description	TCM Diagnosis	Herbal Formulas
Flatulence	Due to irritable bowel syndrome	Liver qi stagnation	***GI Harmony***
	With burning diarrhea or infection	Damp-heat in the Intestine	***GI Care II***
	With weakness, poor appetite with diarrhea	Spleen qi deficiency	***GI Tonic***
	With ulcerative colitis, Crohn's disease	Damp-heat accumulation	***GI Care (UC)***
	With stress-related bloating and distension	Liver qi stagnation	***Calm***
	With gallstones	Damp-heat in the Liver	***Dissolve (GS)***
Floaters	With dry eyes and visual disturbance	Kidney and Liver yin deficiency	***Lycium Support***
	With red eyes	Liver yang rising	***Gentiana Complex***
Flu	*See* Common Cold, Infection		
Focus	ADD, ADHD	Liver wind with *shen* (spirit) disturbance	***Calm (Jr)***
	Inability to focus, poor memory, forgetfulness	Heart and Kidney deficiencies	***Enhance Memory***
	Alzheimer's disease, dementia	Kidney yang deficiency	***Neuro Plus***
Food Poisoning	Diarrhea, abdominal pain, nausea, vomiting	Damp-heat in the Intestines	***GI Care II***
	Moderate to severe cases of infection and inflammation	Accumulation of toxic heat	*add* ***Herbal ABX***
	With fever	Accumulation of toxic heat	*add* ***Gardenia Complex***
Forgetfulness	Poor memory	Heart and Kidney deficiencies	***Enhance Memory***
	Poor memory, poor concentration associated with Alzheimer's disease, dementia	Deficiencies of Kidney yin, yang and *jing* (essence)	***Neuro Plus***
	With dizziness, weakness, difficulty sleeping, anemia, excessive thinking and worrying	Spleen and Heart deficiency	***Schisandra ZZZ***
	ADD or ADHD in children	Liver wind with *shen* (spirit) disturbance	***Calm (Jr)***
	Diminished mental and physical functions	Deficiencies of Kidney yin, yang and *jing* (essence)	***Adrenal +***
	With Kidney yin deficient signs of blurry vision, weakness of the back and knees, tinnitus, dryness, flushed cheeks, and possible low-grade fever	Kidney yin deficiency	***Kidney Tonic (Yin)***
	With Kidney yang deficient signs of coldness, low libido, premature ejaculation, weakness and soreness of the back and knees, pale complexion, and polyuria	Kidney yang deficiency	***Kidney Tonic (Yang)***
Fracture	*See* Bone disorder		
Frozen Shoulders	Acute pain and immobility	Qi and blood stagnation	***Neck & Shoulder (AC)***
	Chronic, dull pain, immobility, numbness	Qi and blood stagnation with Liver yin deficiency	***Neck & Shoulder (CR)***
	Pain due to bone spur	Qi and blood stagnation	*add* ***Flex (SPR)***
	With severe pain	Severe qi and blood stagnation	*add* ***Herbal ANG***

Symptom / Disease Index

Conditions	Symptoms/Disease Description	TCM Diagnosis	Herbal Formulas
Fullness	Due to peptic ulcers	Stomach heat	***GI Care***
	With irritability and stress	Liver overacting on the Spleen and Stomach	***Calm***
	With constipation	Qi stagnation of the Large Intestine	***Gentle Lax (Excess), Gentle Lax (Deficient)***
	Before or during menstruation	Liver qi stagnation	***Calm***
	Due to endometriosis, uterine or ovarian fibroids	Blood stagnation in the lower *jiao*	***Resolve (Lower)***
	Due to gallstone	Damp-heat in the Gallbladder	***Dissolve (GS)***
	Due to irritable bowel syndrome (IBS), Crohn's disease	Liver qi stagnation	***GI Harmony***
	Due to ulcerative colitis	Damp-heat accumulation	***GI Care (UC)***
	With weakness, poor appetite and loose stools	Spleen qi deficiency	***GI Tonic***
	From chemotherapy/radiotherapy	Stomach yin and qi deficiencies	***C/R Support***
Fungal Infection	*See* Infection		
Furuncles	Swelling with redness and pain	Damp-heat	***Resolve (AI)*** and ***Dermatrol (Damp)***
	Moderate to severe infection	Toxic heat	***Resolve (AI)*** and ***Herbal ABX***
	With severe pain	Severe qi and blood stagnation	***Resolve (AI)*** and ***Herbal ANG***
	Chronic, non-healing cases with blood stagnation manifesting in purplish tongue	Blood stasis	***Resolve (AI)*** and ***Circulation (SJ)***
	Chronic, non-healing, furuncles in deficient patients	Spleen and Lung qi deficiencies	***Resolve (AI)*** and ***Cordyceps 3***
Gallbladder	*See* Cholecystitis, Cholelithiasis		
Gallstones	*See* Stones		
Gas	*See* Flatulence		
Gastritis	Heartburn, acid reflux, stomach pain	Stomach fire	***GI Care***
	Due to stress	Stomach fire with Liver qi stagnation	add ***Calm***
	With weakness, poor appetite and loose stools	Spleen qi deficiency	add ***GI Tonic***
	With dryness and thirst	Stomach yin deficiency	add ***Nourish (Fluids)***
	With severe pain	Qi and blood stasis	add ***Herbal ANG***
	With bleeding	Heat pushing blood out of the vessels	add ***Notoginseng 9***
Gastroenteritis	Diarrhea with foul-smelling stools, burning sensation of anus, abdominal discomfort and pain, nausea and vomiting	Damp-heat in the Intestines	***GI Care II***
	Ulcerative colitis, Crohn's disease or similar symptoms	Damp-heat accumulation	***GI Care (UC)***
	Gastrointestinal symptoms associated with exposure to drugs, chemicals, heavy metals, environmental and airborne toxins	Toxic heat	***Herbal DTX***

Symptom / Disease Index

Conditions	Symptoms/Disease Description	TCM Diagnosis	Herbal Formulas
Gastroenteritis *(cont'd)*	With bleeding	Heat in the blood	*add* ***Notoginseng 9***
	With fever or excess heat	Excess accumulation of heat	*add* ***Gardenia Complex***
	To enhance the antibacterial effect	Accumulation of toxic heat	*add* ***Herbal ABX***
	To enhance the antiviral effect	Accumulation of toxic heat	*add* ***Herbal AVR***
Gastroesophageal Reflux Disease (GERD)	Acid reflux, heartburn, stomach pain and discomfort	Stomach fire with rising Stomach qi	***GI Care***
	Due to stress	Liver qi stagnation	*add* ***Calm***
Gastroptosis	Downward displacement of the stomach	Qi and yang deficiency	***C/R Support*** and ***GI Tonic***
Genital Herpes	*See* Herpes (Genital)		
Genital Itching	Itching and discomfort in the genital area	Damp-heat in the lower *jiao*	***V-Support*** or ***Gentiana Complex***
Germs	*See* Infection		
Glandular Fever	Fever, pharyngitis, enlarged lymph nodes	Toxic heat accumulation with dampness	***Resolve (AI)*** and ***Herbal ABX***
Glomerulo-nephritis	Compromised kidney function with proteinuria and edema	Toxic heat accumulation	***Kidney DTX***
	Drug-related	Toxic heat accumulation	*add* ***Herbal DTX***
Glucose	*See* Diabetes mellitus, Hypoglycemia		
Goiter	Due to hyperthyroidism	Liver qi and phlegm stagnation	***Thyrodex***
	Due to hypothyroidism	Spleen and Kidney yang deficiencies	***Thyro-forte***
Gonorrhea	Discharge, dysuria with burning sensation and pain	Damp-heat in the lower *jiao*	***Gentiana Complex*** or ***V-Support***
Gout	Pain and redness	*Re bi* (heat painful obstruction)	***Flex (GT)***
	With more swelling and inflammation	Heat	*add* ***Astringent Complex***
	With severe pain	Severe qi and blood stagnation	*add* ***Herbal ANG***
Grave's Disease	*See* Hyperthyroidism		
Growth (Delayed)	Delayed growth compared to the peers	Kidney yin, yang and *jing* (essence) deficiencies	***Osteo 8***
Gums	Bleeding or swollen gums	Stomach heat	***Gardenia Complex***
Hair	Premature gray hair, dry scalp, hair loss	Liver yin and blood deficiencies	***Polygonum 14***
	Stress-related hair disorders	Liver qi stagnation with yin and blood deficiencies	*add* ***Calm***
Halitosis	Foul breath with excessive hunger	Stomach heat	***Herbalite***
	Excess heat in the body	Heat in all three *jiaos*	***Gardenia Complex***
	With bitter taste in the mouth, short temper	Liver fire	***Gentiana Complex***
	With dry mouth	Lung and Stomach yin deficiencies	***Nourish (Fluids)***
	With throat infection	Toxic heat accumulation	***Herbal ENT***

Symptom / Disease Index

Conditions	Symptoms/Disease Description	TCM Diagnosis	Herbal Formulas
Hands	Cold hands due to poor circulation	Qi and blood stagnation	***Flex (NP)***
	Feeling of heat in the palms and feet	Yin deficiency with heat	***Balance (Heat)*** or ***Nourish***
	Pain or numbness of the arm	Qi and blood stagnation	***Arm Support***
	Tingling, pain, or numbness of the hands originating from cervical disorder	Qi and blood stagnation	***Neck & Shoulder (AC)***
	Stiffness of hand and fingers from arthritis	*Bi zheng* (painful obstruction syndrome)	***Flex*** formulas
Hangover	Excessive consumption of alcohol	Toxic heat in the Liver	***Liver DTX***
	With headache	Toxic heat in the Liver with qi and blood stagnation	*add* ***Corydalin (AC)***
	With stomach pain, nausea and vomiting	Heat in the Liver and the Stomach	*add* ***GI Care***
	With excess heat and fire signs	Excess fire accumulation	*add* ***Gardenia Complex***
	With excessive thirst	Yin and fluid deficiencies	*add* ***Nourish (Fluids)***
Hardness	*See* Nodules		
Hashimoto's Thyroiditis	*See* Hypothyroidism		
Hay Fever	*See* Allergy		
Headache	Acute headache	Qi and blood stagnation	***Corydalin (AC)***
	Due to hypertension with dizziness	Liver yin deficiency with Liver yang rising	*add* ***Gastrodia Complex***
	Due to stress	Liver qi stagnation	*add* ***Calm***
	Temporal or vertex headache with flushed face, anger	Damp-heat in the Liver channel	*add* ***Gentiana Complex***
	Due to common cold, fever, sore throat	Wind-heat	*add* ***Lonicera Complex***
	Sinus headache with white watery nasal discharge	Wind-cold with fluid congestion	*add* ***Magnolia Clear Sinus***
	Sinus headache with yellow thick nasal discharge	Damp-heat with fluid congestion	*add* ***Pueraria Clear Sinus***
	With ear, nose, or throat infection	Toxic heat invasion	*add* ***Herbal ENT***
	Stubborn, stabbing headache due to previous trauma to the head or blood stagnation	Blood stasis	*add* ***Circulation (SJ)***
	With excess heat signs manifesting in red face, fast heartbeat, and possible constipation	Excess heat	*add* ***Gardenia Complex***
	With facial paralysis, Bell's palsy, TMJ or trigeminal neuralgia	Qi and blood stagnation	*add* ***Symmetry***
	Due to neck stiffness or pain	Qi and blood stagnation	*add* ***Neck & Shoulder (AC)***
	Chronic headache	Blood deficiency with qi and blood stagnation	***Corydalin (CR)***

Symptom / Disease Index

Conditions	Symptoms/Disease Description	TCM Diagnosis	Herbal Formulas
Hearing Loss	Diminished hearing or ringing of the ear	Kidney yin deficiency	***Nourish***
	Tinnitus, mostly low pitched	Lung and Kidney qi deficiencies	*add* ***Cordyceps 3***
	Tinnitus, mostly high pitched	Liver yang rising	*add* ***Gentiana Complex***
Heart	*See* Coronary heart disease, Cholesterol, Hypertension, Hypotension		
Heart Attack (Prevention)	Coronary heart disease	Blood stagnation in the upper *jiao*	***Circulation***
Heartbeat	Fast with high blood pressure	Excess fire	***Gardenia Complex***
	Fast with low blood pressure	Yin deficiency	***Nourish***
	Slow with low blood pressure	Qi and blood deficiencies	***Imperial Tonic***
	Slow with high blood pressure	Blood stagnation	***Circulation (SJ)***
Heartburn	Acid reflux with stomach pain and discomfort	Stomach fire	***GI Care***
	Due to stress	Liver overacting on Spleen and Stomach	*add* ***Calm***
Heaviness	Heaviness and/or sluggish feeling	Damp accumulation	***Herbal DRX***
	Obesity with excessive appetite	Stomach heat	***Herbalite***
	General feeling of heaviness, lassitude and weakness	Damp accumulation with Spleen qi deficiency	***Pinellia Complex***
Heavy Metal	*See* Poisoning, Detox		
Hematemesis	Vomiting of blood	Stomach heat	***Notoginseng 9***
	Due to peptic ulcer	Stomach heat	*add* ***GI Care***
	Due to trauma	Qi and blood stasis	*add* ***Flex (TMX)***
Hematochezia	Blood in the stools	Heat in the Intestines	***Notoginseng 9***
	In ulcerative colitis, Crohn's disease	Damp-heat and toxic heat in the Intestines	*add* ***GI Care (UC)***
	Due to peptic ulcer	Stomach heat	*add* ***GI Care***
	With hemorrhoids	Heat and blood stagnation in the lower *jiao*	*add* ***GI Care (HMR)***
Hematuria	Blood in the urine with infection	Heat in the bladder or lower *jiao*	***Notoginseng 9*** with ***V-Support***
	Blood in the urine due to kidney or bladder stones	*Shi lin* (stone dysuria)	*add* ***Dissolve (KS)***
Hemiplegia	Muscle stiffness, paralysis, difficult movement	Qi and blood stagnation	***Neuro Plus***
	Facial paralysis, Bell's palsy	Qi and blood stagnation	***Symmetry***
Hemoptysis	Coughing of blood	Heat in the Lung or deficiency	***Notoginseng 9*** and ***Respitrol (CF)***
Hemorrhage	*See* Bleeding		
Hemorrhoids	Hemorrhoids	Heat in the Large Intestine	***GI Care (HMR)***
	With excess type of constipation	Heat in the Large Intestine	*add* ***Gentle Lax (Excess)***
	With deficient type of constipation	Heat in the Large Intestine with yin deficiency	*add* ***Gentle Lax (Deficient)***

Symptom / Disease Index

Conditions	Symptoms/Disease Description	TCM Diagnosis	Herbal Formulas
Hemorrhoids *(cont'd)*	With severe pain	Severe qi and blood stagnation	*add **Herbal ANG***
	With bleeding	Heat pushing blood out of the vessels	*add **Notoginseng 9***
	Severe hemorrhoids	Damp-heat accumulation	*add **Resolve (AI)*** and ***Astringent Complex***
Hepatitis	With elevated liver enzymes	Toxic heat in the Liver	***Liver DTX***
	With gallstones or cholecystitis	Toxic heat in the Liver, damp-heat in the Gallbladder	*add **Dissolve (GS)***
	Due to exposure to drugs, chemicals, heavy metals, environmental and airborne toxins	Toxic heat	*add **Herbal DTX***
	With fatigue and weakness	Qi, yin, yang and blood deficiency	*add **Imperial Tonic***
	Moderate to severe cases of infection and inflammation	Accumulation of toxic heat	*add **Herbal AVR***
Herbicide Poisoning	Adverse reactions from exposure to insecticide, pesticide, herbicide and other toxins	Toxic heat in the Liver	***Herbal DTX***
	Compromised liver function due to exposure to toxins	Toxic heat in the Liver	***Liver DTX***
	Compromised kidney function due to exposure to toxins	Toxic heat in the Kidney	***Kidney DTX***
Herniated Disk	Slipped disk with pain	Qi and blood stagnation	***Back Support (HD)***
	Due to bone spurs	Qi and blood stagnation	*add **Flex (SPR)***
	With back sprain and strain	Qi and blood stagnation	*add **Back Support (AC)***
	With shooting pain	Qi and blood stagnation	*add **Flex (NP)***
	With severe pain	Severe qi and blood stagnation	*add **Herbal ANG***
Herpes (Genital)	Genital herpes outbreak with lesions and pain	Damp-heat in the Liver and Gallbladder channels	***Gentiana Complex***
	Frequent genital herpes outbreaks	Damp-heat in the Liver and Gallbladder channels with underlying yin deficiency	*add **Nourish***
	Moderate to severe cases of infection and inflammation	Accumulation of toxic heat	*add **Herbal AVR***
	With severe pain	Severe qi and blood stagnation with heat	*add **Herbal ANG***
Herpes (Oral)	Fever blisters with pain and inflammation	Wind-heat	***Lonicera Complex***
	Frequent oral herpes outbreaks	Wind-heat with *wei* (defensive) *qi* deficiency	*add **Immune +***
	Moderate to severe cases of infection and inflammation	Accumulation of toxic heat	*add **Herbal AVR***
	With severe pain	Severe qi and blood stagnation with heat	*add **Herbal ANG***
Herpes Zoster	Acute pain and inflammation of herpes zoster	Damp-heat	***Dermatrol (HZ)***
	With wet lesions	Damp-heat	*add **Dermatrol (Damp)***
	Moderate to severe cases of infection and inflammation	Accumulation of toxic heat	*add **Herbal AVR***
	With severe pain	Severe qi and blood stagnation with heat	*add **Herbal ANG***

Symptom / Disease Index

Conditions	Symptoms/Disease Description	TCM Diagnosis	Herbal Formulas
Hiccup	With foul breath, hunger, redness of the face	Stomach heat	***Herbalite*** or ***GI Care***
	With poor appetite, loose stool or diarrhea, generalized weakness	Spleen qi deficiency	***GI Tonic***
	Chronic and unknown in cause	Blood stagnation	***Circulation (SJ)***
	With fullness and distension	Damp and phlegm accumulation	***Pinellia Complex***
High Blood Pressure	*See* Hypertension		
Hip Fracture	Post-traumatic care	Qi and blood stagnation	***Flex (TMX)***
	With bleeding	Qi and blood stagnation	*add* ***Notoginseng 9***
	With severe pain	Severe qi and blood stagnation with heat	*add* ***Herbal ANG***
	To strengthen and rebuild the bones and connective tissues (muscles, ligaments, tendons, cartilage) during recovery	Kidney *jing* (essence) deficiency	***Osteo 8*** and ***Flex (MLT)***
HIV	Viral infection	Toxic heat	***Herbal AVR***
	Immune deficiency with frequent infections	*Wei* (defensive) *qi* deficiency	*add* ***Immune +***
	Chronic fatigue with immune deficiency	Lung and Kidney deficiencies	*add* ***Cordyceps 3***
Hives	*See* Itching		
Hordeolum (Sty)	Localized infection of one or more sebaceous glands	Toxic heat accumulation	***Herbal ABX*** and ***Resolve (AI)***
Hormones	Estrogen deficiency in menopause	Kidney yin deficiency	***Kidney Tonic (Yin)*** or ***Nourish***
	Estrogen deficiency in atrophic vaginitis	Kidney yin deficiency	***Balance Spring***
	Testosterone deficiency	Kidney yang deficiency	***Vitality*** or ***Kidney Tonic (Yang)***
	Low libido in men or women	Kidney yang deficiency	***Vitality***
	Hypothyroidism with decreased thyroid hormone	Kidney yang deficiency	***Thyro-forte***
	Hyperthyroidism with increased thyroid hormone	Liver fire	***Thyrodex***
	Diabetes mellitus with decreased insulin	Yin deficiency	***Equilibrium***
	Adrenal insufficiency	Kidney yin, yang, and *jing* (essence) deficiencies	***Adrenal +***
	Hormone irregularity	Liver qi stagnation	***Calm***
Hospital-acquired Infection	*See* Infection and specific types of diseases and conditions		
Hot Flashes	With menopause signs	Yin deficiency with deficiency heat	***Balance (Heat)***
	With thirst, dryness, and sweating	Yin deficiency with deficiency heat and dryness	*add* ***Nourish***
	With irritability and restlessness	Yin deficiency with Liver qi stagnation	*add* ***Calm (ES)***
	With insomnia due to deficiency	Yin deficiency with Spleen and Heart deficiencies	*add* ***Schisandra ZZZ***
	With insomnia due to excess	Yin deficiency with *shen* (spirit) disturbances	*add* ***Calm ZZZ***
	See also Menopausal syndrome		

SYMPTOM / DISEASE

Symptom / Disease Index

Conditions	Symptoms/Disease Description	TCM Diagnosis	Herbal Formulas
Hyperactivity	Restlessness with inability to concentrate	Liver wind with *shen* (spirit) disturbance	***Calm (Jr)***
	See also ADD/ADHD		
Hyperglycemia	*See* Diabetes mellitus		
Hyperhydrosis	Excessive sweating with a weak immune system	Lung qi deficiency and *wei* (defensive) *qi* deficiency	***Immune +***
	Excessive sweating during menopause	Yin-deficient heat	***Nourish*** and ***Balance (Heat)***
	Due to excess heat manifesting in red face, fast heartbeat, possible high blood pressure and constipation	Excess heat accumulation	***Gardenia Complex***
Hyperlipidemia	*See* Cholesterol		
Hypertension	Excess type with flushed face, anger, redness of eyes	Damp-heat in the Liver	***Gentiana Complex***
	Deficient type with dizziness, vertigo, tinnitus, and blurry vision	Liver yang rising with Liver and Kidney yin deficiencies	***Gastrodia Complex***
	With chronic kidney disorder	Toxic heat in the Kidney	add ***Kidney DTX***
	With excess fire manifesting in red face, red eyes, heat sensation, fast heart rate, high blood pressure and possible constipation	Excess fire in all three *jiaos*	add ***Gardenia Complex***
	With high cholesterol	Damp and phlegm accumulation	add ***Cholisma*** or ***Cholisma (ES)***
	With coronary heart disease	Blood stagnation	add ***Circulation***
	With headache	Qi and blood stagnation	add ***Corydalin (AC)***
	With blood stagnation manifesting in purplish tongue	Blood stasis	add ***Circulation (SJ)***
Hyperthermia	*See* Fever		
Hyperthyroidism	With elevated T3 and T4 levels and enlarged thyroid gland	Qi and phlegm stagnation	***Thyrodex***
	With irritability	Qi and phlegm stagnation with *shen* (spirit) disturbance and Liver qi stagnation	add ***Calm***
	With hypertension	Qi and phlegm stagnation with rising Liver yang	add ***Gastrodia Complex***
	With excess heat or fever	Excess fire	add ***Gardenia Complex***
Hyper-triglyceridemia	*See* Cholesterol		
Hypochondriac Pain	With fidgeting, restlessness, irritability	Liver qi stagnation	***Calm***
	With anger, neurosis	Liver fire	***Calm (ES)***
	Due to hepatitis	Toxic heat in the Liver	***Liver DTX***
	With cholecystitis or gallstones	Damp-heat in the gallbladder	***Dissolve (GS)***
	Due to irritable bowel syndrome (IBS)	Liver qi stagnation	***GI Harmony***
	Due to mass accumulation	Damp and phlegm accumulation	***Resolve (AI)***

Symptom / Disease Index

Conditions	Symptoms/Disease Description	TCM Diagnosis	Herbal Formulas
Hypochondriac Pain *(cont'd)*	Chronic pain with blood stagnation	Blood stagnation	***Circulation (SJ)*** and ***Calm***
	With severe pain	Severe qi and blood stagnation	*add* ***Herbal ANG***
Hypoglycemia	Low blood sugar level, dizziness	Spleen and Heart blood deficiencies	***Schisandra ZZZ***
	With overall weakness and deficiencies of yin, yang, qi and blood	Qi, blood, yin and yang deficiencies	***Imperial Tonic***
Hypotension	Low blood pressure with dizziness, fatigue	Deficiencies of qi and yang	***Imperial Tonic***
Hypothermia	Coldness of the body and extremities	Cold accumulation with Kidney yang deficiency	***Kidney Tonic (Yang)*** or ***Adrenal +***
Hypothyroidism	With fatigue, aversion to cold, decreased heart rate and blood pressure, muscle weakness or sluggishness, and other related symptoms	Yang deficiency of Heart, Spleen, and Kidney	***Thyro-forte***
	With low energy	Qi deficiency	*add* ***Imperial Tonic***
	With depression	Qi, blood, food, and phlegm stagnation	*add* ***Shine*** or ***Shine (DS)***
	With coldness or slow metabolism	Yang deficiency	*add* ***Adrenal +***
Hysterectomy	Post-operative healing	Blood stagnation	***Flex (TMX)***
	Decrease in bone density following the operation	Kidney yin and *jing* (essence) deficiencies	***Osteo 8***
	Hot flashes, irritabilities, mood swings, night sweating	Kidney yin deficiency with deficient fire	***Balance (Heat)*** with ***Nourish***
	With dryness and thirst	Yin and body fluids deficiencies	***Nourish (Fluids)***
	With dry hair or graying of hair	Kidney *jing* (essence) and Liver blood deficiencies	***Polygonum 14***
	Vaginal dryness	Kidney yin deficiency	***Balance Spring***
	Depression	*Shen* (spirit) disturbance	***Shine*** or ***Shine (DS)***
	Emotional instability with stress, anxiety and anger	Liver qi stagnation	***Calm*** or ***Calm (ES)***
	Low or no libido	Kidney yang deficiency	***Vitality***
Hysteria	Mild to moderate cases of irritability and stress	Liver qi stagnation	***Calm***
	Moderate to severe cases of mood swings, anger, restlessness, irritability	Liver fire with *shen* (spirit) disturbance	***Calm (ES)***
	Disorientation, crying spells, inability to control oneself, and restless sleep in menopause	Yin deficiency with false heat	***Calm (ES)*** with ***Balance (Heat)***
	Stress, anxiety, restlessness, insomnia due to deficiency	Liver qi stagnation with qi deficiency	***Calm ZZZ***
	Excessive worrying, pensiveness, dreams, anemia, mostly in women	Spleen and Heart blood deficiencies with *shen* (spirit) disturbance	***Schisandra ZZZ***
	With heat symptoms of flushed face, red tongue, heat sensations	Excessive heat accumulation	*add* ***Gardenia Complex***
IBS (Irritable Bowel Syndrome)	*See* Irritable bowel syndrome		

Symptom / Disease Index

Conditions	Symptoms/Disease Description	TCM Diagnosis	Herbal Formulas
Immune System (Deficiency)	With frequent viral or bacterial infections	*Wei* (defensive) *qi* deficiency	***Immune +***
	With weak constitution	Qi, blood, yin and yang deficiencies	*add* ***Imperial Tonic***
	Due to chemotherapy and radiation	Qi and yin deficiencies	*add* ***C/R Support***
	With respiratory and reproductive weakness	Lung and Kidney deficiencies	*add* ***Cordyceps 3***
	End-stage cancer patients who cannot receive chemotherapy or radiation	*Yuan* (source) *qi* deficiency	*add* ***CA Support***
	With an active bacterial infection	Heat invasion	***Herbal ABX***
	With an active viral infection	Heat invasion	***Herbal AVR***
Immune System (Excess)	*See* Autoimmune and specific diseases		
Impotence	Generalized male sexual dysfunction	Kidney yang deficiency	***Vitality***
	Due to complications of diabetes mellitus	Kidney yin and yang deficiencies	*add* ***Equilibrium***
	With decreased sexual desire and stamina due to adrenal depletion	Kidney yang deficiency	*add* ***Adrenal +***
	Due to nervousness and anxiety	Liver fire with *shen* (spirit) disturbance	*add* ***Calm*** or ***Calm (ES)***
	With poor appetite, weakness, loose stools or diarrhea	Spleen qi deficiency with Kidney yang deficiency	*add* ***GI Tonic***
	With palpitation, shortness of breath, spontaneous sweating, sallow complexion, emaciation, listlessness, poor appetite, loose stools	Spleen and Heart deficiencies	*add* ***Schisandra ZZZ***
	Concurrent sexual dysfunction and reproductive disorder	Kidney yin, yang and *jing* (essence) deficiencies	*add* ***Vital Essence***
Incomplete Emptying (Urine)	Urinary symptoms due to benign prostatic hypertrophy	Stagnation or damp-heat in the lower *jiao*	***P-Support***
	Burning sensations and pain during urination	Damp-heat in the lower *jiao*	***V-Support***
Incomplete Evacuation (Stools)	With acute, severe constipation	Excess heat in the Intestines	***Gentle Lax (Excess)***
	With chronic, habitual constipation	Deficiency heat in the Intestines	***Gentle Lax (Deficient)***
	With fecal compaction	Toxic heat in the Intestines	***GI DTX***
	Due to irritable bowel syndrome (IBS) or stress	Liver qi stagnation	*add* ***GI Harmony***
	Due to ulcerative colitis, Crohn's disease	Toxic heat in the Intestines	*add* ***GI Care (UC)***
	Due to food poisoning, improper food intake, traveler's diarrhea or colitis	Damp-heat in the Intestines	*add* ***GI Care II***
	Due to weakness, poor appetite	Spleen qi deficiency	*add* ***GI Tonic***
Incontinence	With coldness symptoms such as cold extremities, weakness and coldness of the lower back and knees, light-colored urine	Kidney yang deficiency	***Kidney Tonic (Yang)***
Indigestion	Loose stools, poor appetite, weak digestion, and generalized weakness	Spleen qi deficiency	***GI Tonic***
	Indigestion and burning diarrhea with stomach pain, fullness and discomfort due to improper food intake	Damp-heat in the Intestines	***GI Care II***
	Food stagnation	Food stagnation	***Shine***

Symptom / Disease Index

Conditions	Symptoms/Disease Description	TCM Diagnosis	Herbal Formulas
Indigestion (*cont'd*)	Slow digestion, or due to irritable bowel syndrome (IBS)	Liver qi stagnation	***GI Harmony***
	Due to stomach and duodenal ulcer	Stomach heat	***GI Care***
	Due to stress	Liver qi stagnation	***Calm***
Infection	Sinus infection with clear and watery discharge	Wind-cold at exterior	***Magnolia Clear Sinus***
	Sinus infection with sticky and yellowish discharge	Damp-heat in the interior	***Pueraria Clear Sinus***
	Ear, nose and throat infection	Toxic heat invasion	***Herbal ENT***
	Lung infection with fever, dyspnea, chest congestion	Lung heat	***Respitrol (Heat)***
	Lung infection with runny nose with clear watery discharge, sneezing, nasal congestion	Lung cold	***Respitrol (Cold)***
	Lung infection with chest congestion, profuse yellow sputum, cough	Lung heat with phlegm	***Pinellia XPT***
	Common cold and influenza	Wind-heat or wind-cold at the exterior	***Lonicera Complex***
	Gastrointestinal infection with abdominal pain and diarrhea	Damp-heat in the Intestines	***GI Care II***
	Viral hepatitis	Toxic heat in the Liver	***Liver DTX***
	Oral herpes with blisters	Wind-heat or Stomach heat	***Lonicera Complex***
	Genital herpes with lesions	Damp-heat in lower *jiao*	***Gentiana Complex***
	Herpes zoster (shingles)	Toxic heat invasion	***Dermatrol (HZ)***
	Genitourinary infection	Damp-heat in the lower *jiao*	***Gentiana Complex*** or ***V-Support***
	Skin infections	Toxic heat invasion	***Dermatrol (Dry)*** or ***Dermatrol (Damp)***
	Acne from infection	Heat and toxins	***Dermatrol (Clear)***
	Yeast infection	Damp or damp-heat in the lower *jiao*	***V-Support*** and ***Pinellia Complex***
	Bacterial infection	Heat at various parts of body	***Herbal ABX***
	Viral infection	Heat at various parts of body	***Herbal AVR***
	With fever	Excess heat accumulation	*add* ***Gardenia Complex***
	With inflammation	Heat	*add* ***Astringent Complex***
	With inflammation and swelling	Damp-heat	*add* ***Resolve (AI)***
	Frequent or recurrent infection due to weakened immunity	*Wei* (defensive) *qi* deficiency	***Immune +***
Infertility (Female)	Irregular menstrual cycle (Menstrual Phase)	Qi and blood stagnation	***Blossom (Phase 1)***
	Irregular menstrual cycle (Follicular Phase)	Qi and blood deficiency, Kidney *jing* (essence) deficiencies	***Blossom (Phase 2)***
	Irregular menstrual cycle (Ovulatory Phase)	Kidney yang deficiency	***Blossom (Phase 3)***

Symptom / Disease Index

Conditions	Symptoms/Disease Description	TCM Diagnosis	Herbal Formulas
Infertility (Female) *(cont'd)*	Irregular menstrual cycle (Luteal Phase)	Liver qi stagnation	***Blossom (Phase 4)***
	Due to obstruction (including cysts, endometriosis, tubal obstruction, and fibroids)	Blood stagnation in the lower *jiao*	***Resolve (Lower)*** followed by ***Blossom (Phase 1-4)***
	With coldness; irregular or absence of menstruation with scanty discharge	Kidney yang deficiency and blood stagnation	***Menatrol*** followed by ***Blossom (Phase 1-4)***
	With extreme stress	Liver qi stagnation	***Blossom (Phase 1-4)*** with **Calm**
	With inflammation or infection of the pelvis (ovaries, uterus, fallopian tubes)	Heat accumulation in the lower *jiao*	***Blossom (Phase 1-4)*** with ***V-Support***
	Women past 35 years of age with more prominent signs of yin deficiency and heat signs	Kidney yin deficiency	***Blossom (Phase 1-4)*** with ***Kidney Tonic (Yin)***
	Women past 35 years of age with more prominent signs of yang deficiency and cold signs	Kidney yang deficiency	***Blossom (Phase 1-4)*** with ***Kidney Tonic (Yang)***
Infertility (Male)	Generalized male sexual dysfunction with low libido, erectile dysfunction, and others	Kidney yang deficiency	***Vitality***
	Generalized male reproductive dysfunction with low sperm count, and poor sperm motility, morphology	Kidney yin and *jing* (essence) deficiencies	***Vital Essence***
Inflammation	Soft tissue or joint inflammation with pain and redness	*Bi zheng* (painful obstruction syndrome) due to heat	***Flex (Heat)***
	Joint pain that worsens with cold and dampness	*Bi zheng* (painful obstruction syndrome) due to cold and dampness	***Flex (CD)***
	Muscle spasm and cramps	Liver yin and body fluid deficiencies	***Flex (SC)***
	Inflammation and pain due to external injuries	Qi and blood stagnation	***Flex (TMX)***
	Inflammation of soft tissue (muscle, ligaments, tendon, cartilage)	Qi and blood stagnation	***Flex (MLT)***
	Herniated disk	Qi and blood stagnation	***Back Support (HD)***
	Gout	*Re bi* (heat painful obstruction)	***Flex (GT)***
	Pelvic inflammatory disease	Damp-heat in the lower *jiao*	***V-Support***
	With swelling and redness	Damp-heat	***Resolve (AI)***
	Inflammation in ulcerative colitis	Damp-heat in the Intestines	***GI Care (UC)***
	Inflammation due to gastroenteritis or traveler's diarrhea	Damp-heat in the Intestines	***GI Care II***
	Chronic nephritis or nephrotic syndrome	Toxic heat in the Kidney	***Kidney DTX***
	Hepatitis	Toxic heat in the Liver	***Liver DTX***
	Inflammation with severe pain	Qi and blood stagnation	*add* **Herbal ANG**
	Moderate to severe cases of infection and inflammation	Accumulation of toxic heat	*add* **Herbal ABX**
	With fever and other heat signs of red face, fast heartbeat, high blood pressure or constipation	Excess heat	*add* **Gardenia Complex**

Symptom / Disease Index

Conditions	Symptoms/Disease Description	TCM Diagnosis	Herbal Formulas
Inflammation (*cont'd*)	General inflammation with a thick and forceful pulse	Heat	add ***Astringent Complex***
	See also specific diseases		
Influenza	*See* Common cold, Infection		
Injury	Bone fracture, severe pain, bruises	Blood stagnation	***Flex (TMX)***
	Of the neck and shoulder area	Qi and blood stagnation	add ***Neck & Shoulder (AC)***
	Of the low back	Qi and blood stagnation	add ***Back Support (AC)***
	Of the arm	Qi and blood stagnation	add ***Arm Support***
	Of the leg, knee or ankle	Qi and blood stagnation	add ***Knee & Ankle (AC)***
	With severe pain	Severe qi and blood stagnation	add ***Herbal ANG***
	Chronic history of injury/trauma with residual pain	Qi and blood stagnation	add ***Circulation (SJ)***
	Sprain and strain of muscles	Qi and blood stagnation	add ***Flex (SC)***
	Recovery from bone fracture	Kidney *jing* (essence) deficiency	***Osteo 8***
	Recovery from soft tissue injuries, such as muscles, ligaments, and tendons	Liver and Kidney yin deficiencies	***Flex (MLT)***
Inner Ear Disorder	Inner ear infection and pain	Toxic fire accumulation	***Herbal ENT***
	Dizziness, vertigo, and poor balance	Liver wind rising	***Gastrodia Complex***
	With severe pain	Severe qi and blood stagnation	add ***Herbal ANG***
	Swelling and feeling of pressure	Dampness accumulation	add ***Resolve (AI)***
	High-pitched tinnitus	Liver yang rising	***Gentiana Complex***
	Low-pitched tinnitus	Kidney yin deficiency	***Nourish*** or ***Kidney Tonic (Yin)***
Insecticide Poisoning	Adverse reactions from exposure to insecticide, pesticide, herbicide and other toxins	Toxic heat	***Herbal DTX***
	Compromised liver function due to exposure to toxins	Toxic heat in the Liver	***Liver DTX***
	Compromised kidney function due to exposure to toxins	Toxic heat in the Kidney	***Kidney DTX***
Insomnia	Due to excessive worries and dreams, fatigue, pensiveness, poor appetite	*Shen* (spirit) disturbance due to Spleen and Heart deficiencies	***Schisandra ZZZ***
	Due to fatigue with stress and an overactive mind with difficulty falling or staying asleep	Liver qi stagnation and qi deficiency	***Calm ZZZ***
	Due to restlessness, stress, anxiety	*Shen* (spirit) disturbance with Liver fire	add ***Calm*** or ***Calm (ES)***
	Due to depression	Stagnation of phlegm, qi, blood, and food	add ***Shine*** or ***Shine (DS)***
	Due to hyperthyroidism	*Shen* (spirit) disturbance with qi and phlegm stagnation	add ***Thyrodex***
	Chronic insomnia with blood stagnation manifesting in dark complexion, purplish tongue	Blood stagnation	add ***Circulation (SJ)***

SYMPTOM / DISEASE

Symptom / Disease Index

Conditions	Symptoms/Disease Description	TCM Diagnosis	Herbal Formulas
Insulin	*See* Diabetes mellitus		
Intercourse	Painful intercourse due to vaginal dryness	Kidney yin deficiency	***Balance Spring***
	Causing bladder infection	Damp-heat in the lower *jiao*	***V-Support***
	Painful intercourse due to endometriosis	Qi and blood stagnation	***Resolve (Lower)***
	See also Infertility, Impotence, Libido, Sexual dysfunction		
Intermittent Claudication	With pain due to blood clot	Qi and blood stagnation	***Circulation (SJ)***
	With severe pain	Severe qi and blood stagnation	*add* ***Herbal ANG***
	See also Blood clot		
Intestinal Cleanse	Intestinal/colon detox	Toxic heat in the Intestines	***GI DTX***
Intestinal Flu	Nausea, vomiting, diarrhea and abdominal discomfort	Damp-heat in the Intestines	***GI Care II***
	Moderate to severe cases of infection and inflammation	Accumulation of toxic heat	*add* ***Herbal ABX***
Intestines	*See* Constipation, Diarrhea, or specific disorders		
Irritability	With stress, anxiety, restlessness, insomnia, nervousness, poor appetite	Liver qi stagnation	***Calm***
	With the above symptoms, but more severe, with or without neurosis	Liver fire and *shen* (spirit) disturbance	***Calm (ES)***
	ADD, ADHD	Liver wind and *shen* (spirit) disturbance	***Calm (Jr)***
	With anxiety, stress, insomnia and an over-active mind in patients with deficiency	Liver qi stagnation with qi deficiency	***Calm ZZZ***
	With crying spells and melancholy attacks during menopause	Liver yin deficiency with false heat	***Balance (Heat)***
	With fidgeting, restlessness, short temper, high blood pressure	Liver fire	***Gentiana Complex***
	With high blood pressure, excess heat, red face, fast heartbeat and possible constipation	Excess heat accumulation	*add* ***Gardenia Complex***
	With depression	Qi, blood, phlegm stagnation	*add* ***Shine*** or ***Shine (DS)***
Irritable Bowel Syndrome (IBS)	Alternating diarrhea and constipation with abdominal bloating, pain, and flatulence	Damp-heat in the Intestines	***GI Harmony***
	Due to stress	Damp-heat in the Intestines with Liver qi stagnation	*add* ***Calm***
Itching	General skin itching	Wind-heat at the skin level, heat in the blood	***Silerex***
	Genital itching	Damp-heat in the lower *jiao*	***V-Support***
	Wet skin lesions	Damp-heat toxin	***Dermatrol (Damp)***
	Dry skin lesions	Wind-heat toxin	***Dermatrol (Dry)***
	Psoriasis	Toxic heat	***Dermatrol (PS)***
	Moderate to severe cases of viral infection and inflammation	Accumulation of toxic heat	*add* ***Herbal AVR*** and ***Astringent Complex***

Symptom / Disease Index

Conditions	Symptoms/Disease Description	TCM Diagnosis	Herbal Formulas
Itching (*cont'd*)	Moderate to severe cases of infection and inflammation	Accumulation of toxic heat	*add* ***Herbal ABX*** and ***Astringent Complex***
	With fever	Toxic heat	*add* ***Gardenia Complex***
	With oozing fluids	Damp accumulation	*add* ***Pinellia Complex***
IVF	To increase the success of *in vitro* fertilization	Kidney *jing* (essence) deficiency	***Blossom (Phase 1-4)***
	See also Infertility		
Jaundice	Yellow skin and sclera with hepatitis	Damp-heat in the Liver	***Liver DTX***
	Yellow skin and sclera with cholecystitis or gallstones	Damp-heat in the Gallbladder	***Dissolve (GS)***
	Infectious jaundice	Toxic heat	***Liver DTX*** and ***Herbal ABX***
Jock Itch	Genital itching	Damp-heat in the lower *jiao* and Liver channel	***V-Support***
Joint	*See* specific disease and location of the disorder		
Kidney	Chronic nephritis or nephritic syndrome	Toxic heat	***Kidney DTX***
	Compromised kidney function	Kidney deficiency	***Cordyceps 3***
	Kidney or urinary stones	*Shi lin* (stone dysuria)	***Dissolve (KS)***
	Moderate to severe cases of infection and inflammation	Accumulation of toxic heat	***Kidney DTX*** and ***Herbal ABX***
Kissing Disease	Fever, pharyngitis, enlarged lymph glands	Toxic heat accumulation with dampness	***Herbal ENT***
Knee	Acute knee pain	Qi and blood stagnation	***Knee & Ankle (AC)***
	Acute sprain and strain or other traumas to the knee	Qi and blood stagnation	*add* ***Flex (TMX)***
	With severe pain	Severe qi and blood stagnation	*add* ***Herbal ANG***
	Chronic knee pain	Qi and blood stagnation	***Knee & Ankle (CR)***
	Recovery from soft tissue injuries, such as muscles, ligaments, and tendons	Liver and Kidney yin deficiencies	*add* ***Flex (MLT)***
	Recovery from bone fracture	Kidney *jing* (essence) deficiency	*add* ***Osteo 8***
	Due to gout	*Re bi* (heat painful obstruction)	***Flex (GT)***
Lactation	Swelling and pain during nursing period	Blockage	***Venus***
	Insufficient lactation due to deficiency	Qi, blood, yin and yang deficiency	*add* ***Imperial Tonic***
Large Intestine	*See* Diarrhea, Constipation, Ulcerative colitis, Colitis, Crohn's disease, Enteritis, or the specific disorder		
Lasik Recovery	Dry eyes, floaters, visual disturbance	Kidney and Liver yin deficiency	***Lycium Support***
Lassitude	Due to weak digestive system	Spleen deficiency	***GI Tonic***
	Due to qi and blood deficiency	Qi and blood deficiency	***Imperial Tonic***
	Due to Kidney deficiency	Kidney yin or yang deficiency	***Kidney Tonic (Yang)*** or ***Kidney Tonic (Yin)***
	Due to dampness accumulation with Spleen qi deficiency	Dampness with Spleen qi deficiency	***Pinellia Complex***
	See also Fatigue		

Symptom / Disease Index

Conditions	Symptoms/Disease Description	TCM Diagnosis	Herbal Formulas
Lateral Epicondylitis	Tennis elbow	Qi and blood stagnation	***Arm Support***
	With severe pain	Qi and blood stagnation	*add* ***Herbal ANG***
	For degeneration of the joint and related soft tissue (muscle, ligaments, tendons, cartilage)	*Wei* (atrophy) syndrome	***Flex (MLT)*** *and* ***Osteo 8***
LDL Cholesterol	Elevated levels	Damp accumulation	***Cholisma***
	With hypertension due to deficiency	Liver yang rising with yin deficiency	*add* ***Gastrodia Complex***
	With hypertension due to excess	Liver fire with dampness	*add* ***Gentiana Complex***
	With hepatitis	Toxic heat in the Liver	*add* ***Liver DTX***
	With fatty liver and obesity	Damp-heat accumulation	***Cholisma (ES)***
Leg	*See* Restless leg, Cramps, Knee, Ankle, Pain, Osteoporosis, Circulation (poor), and specific conditions		
Lesions	Dry lesions on the skin	Wind-toxin	***Dermatrol (Dry)***
	Wet lesions on the skin	Damp-heat toxin	***Dermatrol (Damp)***
	Lesions from oral herpes	Stomach fire flaring upward	***Lonicera Complex***
	Lesions from genital herpes	Damp-heat in the lower *jiao* and Liver channel	***Gentiana Complex***
	Lesions from herpes zoster	Toxic heat	***Dermatrol (HZ)***
Libido	Decreased libido	Kidney yang deficiency	***Vitality***
	Excess libido	Kidney yin deficiency with rising fire	***Gardenia Complex***
Ligament	Acute injuries to muscles, tendons, ligaments, and cartilages	Qi and blood stagnation	***Flex (TMX)***
	Recovery from injuries to muscles, tendons, ligaments, and cartilages	Liver blood and Kidney yin deficiencies	***Flex (MLT)***
	See also specific parts of the body		
Lipid	*See* Cholesterol		
Lipoprotein	*See* Cholesterol		
Lithiasis	*See* Stones		
Liver	*See* Hepatitis, Fatty liver, Cancer, Detox, and specific diseases		
Low Back Pain	*See* Back pain		
Low-Grade Fever	*See* Fever		
Lubrication	Vaginal dryness, painful intercourse due to hormonal irregularity, estrogen deficiency or menopause	Kidney yin deficiency	***Balance Spring***
Lumbago	*See* Back pain		
Lumbar Radiculopathy	Herniated disk with pain	Qi and blood stagnation	***Back Support (HD)***
	With acute back pain	Qi and blood stagnation	*add* ***Back Support (AC)***

Symptom / Disease Index

Conditions	Symptoms/Disease Description	TCM Diagnosis	Herbal Formulas
Lumbar Radiculopathy *(cont'd)*	With chronic back pain	Qi and blood stagnation	*add* ***Back Support (CR)***
	With recent trauma	Qi and blood stagnation	*add* ***Flex (TMX)***
	With severe back pain	Qi and blood stagnation	*add* ***Herbal ANG***
	Due to bone spurs	Qi and blood stagnation	*add* ***Flex (SPR)***
Lump	Hard swelling with redness and pain	Dampness accumulation	***Resolve (AI)***
	In the breast	Damp and phlegm accumulation	***Resolve (Upper)***
Lung	*See* Asthma, Cough, Dyspnea, Bronchitis, Pneumonia, and specific diseases		
Lupus	Systemic lupus erythematosus	Toxic heat accumulation with yin deficiency	***LPS Support***
	With hyperactive immunity in an autoimmune condition	Heat	***Gardenia Complex***
Lyme Disease	Early symptoms of rash, fever, malaise, body ache	Toxic heat invasion	***Herbal ABX***
Lymph Nodes	Swelling	Damp accumulation	***Resolve (AI)***
Lymphadenitis	Swelling and pain	Dampness with toxic heat	***Resolve (AI)*** with ***Herbal ABX***
Lymph-adenopathy	All types of inflammation and swelling with heat sensation	Damp accumulation	***Resolve (AI)***
	Moderate to severe cases of infection and inflammation	Accumulation of toxic heat	*add* ***Herbal ABX***
	Swelling and enlarged lymph nodes with possible nodules or fibroids in the breasts	Liver qi and phlegm stagnation	*add* ***Resolve (Upper)***
	Swelling and enlarged lymph nodes with possible nodules or fibroids in the reproductive organs	Blood and phlegm stagnation in the lower *jiao*	*add* ***Resolve (Lower)***
	With immune deficiency	*Wei* (defensive) *qi* deficiency	*add* ***Immune +***
	With edema	Damp and water accumulation	*add* ***Herbal DRX***
Lymphedema	Accumulation of lymphatic fluids causing swelling	Dampness and phlegm accumulation	***Resolve (AI)***
Macular Degeneration	Degeneration of macula and diminished vision	Liver and Kidney yin deficiencies with heat	***Nourish***
	Degeneration of macula and diminished vision	Liver and Kidney yin deficiencies without heat	***Lycium Support***
Malabsorption Syndrome	Malabsorption, diarrhea, fatigue, poor appetite	Spleen qi deficiency	***GI Tonic***
Malignancy	*See* Cancer / Carcinoma		
Malnutrition	With fatigue, poor energy, lack of appetite	Spleen qi deficiency	***GI Tonic***
	With generalized deficiency and overall constitutional weakness	Qi, blood, yin and yang deficiencies	***Imperial Tonic***
Mammary Gland	*See* Breast		
Mania	Mild cases of hyperactivity with anger and irritability	Liver heat with *shen* (spirit) disturbance	***Calm (ES)***
	In severe cases with blood stagnation, signs of dark complexion, purplish tongue	Blood stagnation	*add* ***Circulation (SJ)***

Symptom / Disease Index

Conditions	Symptoms/Disease Description	TCM Diagnosis	Herbal Formulas
Manic Depressive Illness	*See* Bipolar disorder		
Mastitis	*See* Breast		
Mass	Mass, swelling, or nodules	Phlegm and damp accumulation	***Resolve (AI)***
	In the breast	Liver qi stagnation with phlegm accumulation	***Resolve (Upper)***
	In the female reproductive organs (ovarian cysts, uterine fibroids, myomas, etc)	Qi and blood stagnation with phlegm accumulation	***Resolve (Lower)***
Medial Epicondylitis	Golfer's elbow	Qi and blood stagnation	***Arm Support***
	With severe pain	Qi and blood stagnation	*add* ***Herbal ANG***
	Recent injury	Qi and blood stagnation	*add* ***Flex (TMX)***
Memory	Forgetfulness, poor memory	Heart and Kidney deficiencies	***Enhance Memory***
	Decreased mental function due to injury and/or degeneration	Deficiency of Kidney yin and *jing* (essence)	***Neuro Plus***
	See also Forgetfulness		
Meniere's Disease	Dizziness, vertigo, and loss of balance	Liver wind rising	***Gastrodia Complex***
	With dampness in the body	Damp accumulation	*add* ***Pinellia Complex***
Menopausal Syndrome	Mood swings, emotional instability, hot flashes, night sweating	Yin deficiency with deficiency heat	***Balance (Heat)***
	With thirst and dryness with yin deficient signs listed above	Yin deficiency with deficiency heat and dryness	*add* ***Nourish***
	With pronounced irritability and mood swings	Yin deficiency with Liver qi stagnation	*add* ***Calm***
	With pronounced anger, restlessness	Yin deficiency with *shen* (spirit) disturbance	*add* ***Calm (ES)***
	With tiredness, insomnia, and excessive worrying	Yin deficiency with Spleen and Heart blood deficiencies	*add* ***Schisandra ZZZ***
	With qi deficiency, insomnia, irritability, restlessness, stress, restless mind	Liver qi stagnation with qi deficiency	*add* ***Calm ZZZ***
	Vaginal dryness or atrophy	Kidney yin deficiency	***Balance Spring***
	Osteoporosis	Kidney *jing* (essence) deficiency	***Osteo 8***
Menstrual Disorders	**Diarrhea**: Loose stools or diarrhea with lower abdominal fullness, profuse menstrual amount, sallow complexion, edema, bland taste in the mouth, poor appetite	Spleen qi deficiency	***GI Tonic***
	Diarrhea: Watery stools, lower abdominal coldness and feeling of prolapse, coldness of limbs, delayed menstruation	Spleen and Kidney yang deficiencies	*add* ***Kidney Tonic (Yang)***
	Diarrhea: Abdominal pain followed by loose stools, abdominal pain lessens with defecation, hypochondriac distension and pain, nausea, breast tenderness	Liver qi stagnation	*add* ***Calm***

Symptom / Disease Index

Conditions	Symptoms/Disease Description	TCM Diagnosis	Herbal Formulas
Menstrual Disorders (*cont'd*)	**Edema**: Edema of the face and limbs, loose stools, scanty urine, light in color	Spleen qi deficiency with deficiency cold	*add* ***Herbal DRX***
	Fever: Low-grade fever during the period and subsides after each cycle, period usually comes early, profuse in amount, purplish in color and thick in texture, chest and hypochondriac distension, irritability, dizziness, redness of the face and eyes, bitter taste in the mouth, dry throat	Liver fire	***Gentiana Complex***
	Fever: Low-grade fever or heat sensation which is exacerbated before each cycle, early periods, dark in color and scanty in amount, irritability, dry mouth, throat, emaciation	Kidney yin deficiency with deficiency heat	***Balance (Heat)*** and ***Nourish***
	Headache: Usually occurs before or during each cycle, fixed in location and stabbing in nature, blood clots with lower abdominal pain	Blood stagnation	***Resolve (Lower)*** or ***Mense-Ease***
	Headache: Dizziness, distension and pain before the period, irritability, short temper, restless sleep, tinnitus, hypochondriac pain, bitter taste in the mouth, bright red menstrual color, yellow vaginal discharge	Liver yang rising	***Calm***
	Headache: Feeling of emptiness and pain after cycles, dizziness, fear of light and prefers quiet environments, palpitation, insomnia, dry mouth, poor appetite, sallow complexion, light menstrual amount	Blood deficiency	***Schisandra ZZZ*** with ***Corydalin (CR)***
	Low back pain: Acute pain, lower abdominal bloating, possible blood clots	Qi and blood stagnation	***Back Support (AC)***
	Low back pain: Soreness and weakness sensation with fatigue	Kidney deficiency	***Back Support (CR)***
	Nose bleeding: Bleeding occurs usually during or before periods, bitter taste in the mouth, dry throat, redness of the face, eyes, dizziness, irritability, short temper, insomnia, breast tenderness or hypochondriac pain	Liver fire	***Gentiana Complex***
	Nose bleeding: Bleeding occurs usually during or after periods, dizziness, tinnitus, dry mouth, throat, afternoon fever	Yin deficiency	***Nourish***
	Nose bleeding: Bleeding usually occurs during or after periods, light colored menstrual blood, fatigue, loose stools, poor appetite	Spleen qi deficiency with inability to keep blood within the vessels	***Schisandra ZZZ***
Menstrual Disorders (Amount)	**Profuse**: Early and profuse in amount or incessant bleeding, bright red in color, emaciation, flushed cheeks, *wu xin re* (five-center heat), dizziness, tinnitus, tidal fever, night sweating, insomnia, soreness of the lower back and knees, dry eyes, dry stools	Kidney and Liver yin deficiency	***Balance (Heat)*** and ***Notoginseng 9***

Symptom / Disease Index

Conditions	Symptoms/Disease Description	TCM Diagnosis	Herbal Formulas
Menstrual Disorders (Amount) *(cont'd)*	**Profuse**: Early, profuse in amount or prolonged in length, bright red or dark and black in color, thick in texture with clots, redness of the face, irritability, short temper, stifling sensation in the chest, breast tenderness, dizziness, headache, bitter taste in the mouth	Liver fire	***Gardenia Complex*** and ***Notoginseng 9***
	Profuse: Prolonged duration, light in color, sensations of emptiness in the lower abdomen, preference for pressure, pale complexion, listlessness, shortness of breath, spontaneous sweating, poor appetite, loose stools, edema	Spleen qi deficiency	***GI Tonic*** and ***Notoginseng 9***
	Profuse: Profuse yellow vaginal discharge before and after cycles, fetid in smell and thick in texture, genital itching, epigastric fullness, heaviness sensation	Damp-heat in the lower *jiao*	***V-Support*** and ***Notoginseng 9***
	Scanty: As little as a few drops, light in color, delayed onset, dull abdominal pain, preference for pressure, pale complexion, dizziness, blurry vision, palpitation, forgetfulness, insomnia, dry skin and hair	Blood deficiency	***Schisandra ZZZ***
	Scanty: Dark purple with clots, delayed onset, thick in texture, stabbing or needling pain in the lower abdomen, dark complexion, breast distension	Blood stagnation	***Resolve (Lower)*** or ***Mense-Ease***
	Scanty: Light red or dark red in color, scanty in amount, lower abdominal pain after each cycle, irregular menstruation, dizziness, tinnitus, weakness of the back and extremities	Kidney yin deficiency	***Kidney Tonic (Yin)***
	Scanty: Thick yellow in texture, turbid vaginal discharge, overweight, epigastric fullness, nausea, heaviness sensation	Damp-heat in the lower *jiao*	***V-Support***
Menstrual Disorders (Color)	**Light red**: Scanty in amount, delayed, lower abdominal dull pain, lusterless complexion, dizziness, palpitation, insomnia, dry skin, hair, and nails	Blood deficiency	***Schisandra ZZZ***
	Light red: Scanty, early and profuse in amount, pale complexion, fatigue, spontaneous sweating, aversion to wind, feeling of emptiness in the lower abdomen	Qi deficiency	***Imperial Tonic***
	Light red: Clots, coldness of the limbs, lower abdominal pain that is alleviated by warmth, soreness and weakness of the lower back, clear leukorrhea, loose stools	Kidney and Spleen yang deficiency	***GI Tonic*** and ***Kidney Tonic (Yang)***
	Dark purple: Thick with clots, lower abdominal pain, irritability, thirst, low grade fever before menstrual cycles, thick yellow vaginal discharge	Damp-heat accumulation	***V-Support***
	Dark purple: Clots, lower abdominal fullness, distension and pain that worsens with pressure, emotional instability, breast distension and tenderness	Liver qi stagnation	***Calm***

Symptom / Disease Index

Conditions	Symptoms/Disease Description	TCM Diagnosis	Herbal Formulas
Menstrual Disorders (Color) (*cont'd*)	**Dark purple:** Blood clots with coldness in the lower abdomen, purplish tongue, symptoms alleviated with warmth	Cold accumulation with blood stasis	***Menatrol***
Menstrual Disorders (Cramps)	Menstrual pain with bloating and blood clots	Blood and qi stagnation in the lower *jiao*	***Mense-Ease***
	With severe pain and cramps due to endometriosis	Severe qi and blood stagnation	*add* ***Resolve (Lower)***
	Pain with water retention	Qi and blood stagnation with damp accumulation	*add* ***Herbal DRX***
Menstrual Disorders (Duration)	**Prolonged**: Bright red or purplish red in color, thick in texture with blood clots, soreness and weakness of low back and extremities, dizziness, five-center heat, thirst	Kidney yin deficiency with heat	***Nourish***
	Prolonged: Light in color, coldness of extremities, low back pain, slightly overweight	Kidney yang deficiency	***Kidney Tonic (Yang)***
	Prolonged: Dark purple with clots, lower abdominal pain which worsens with pressure, pain lessens with passage of clots	Blood stagnation	***Resolve (Lower)***
	Shortened: Light in color, low-grade fever, night sweats, flushed cheeks, tinnitus	Kidney yin deficiency	***Kidney Tonic (Yin)***
Menstrual Disorders (Irregularity)	**Early**: Profuse in amount, dark red or purplish in color, thick with fetid odor, irritability, dry mouth, preference for coldness, constipation, yellow urine	Damp-heat in the lower *jiao*	***V-Support***
	Early: Scanty in amount, red in color with no clots, dizziness, palpitation, insomnia, soreness of the lower back, *wu xin re* (five-center heat), flushed cheeks	Yin deficiency	***Balance (Heat)*** and ***Nourish***
	Early: Amount may be profuse or scanty, color may be red or purplish with clots, breast distension and tenderness, chest, hypochondriac and lower abdominal fullness and pain, emotional instability with possible short temper, bitter taste in the mouth or dryness	Liver qi stagnation	***Calm***
	Early: Light in color, scanty in amount, feeling of emptiness in the lower abdomen, listlessness, palpitation, shortness of breath, poor appetite, loose stools	Qi deficiency	***Imperial Tonic***
	Early: Profuse during the first day and dramatically decreases later or incessant bleeding that is purple with clots, lower abdominal fullness, distension and pain	Blood stagnation	***Resolve (Lower)***
	Delayed: Scanty in amount, light in color, absence of abdominal pain, dizziness, palpitation	Blood deficiency	***Schisandra ZZZ***
	Delayed: Scanty in amount, purplish in color, lower abdominal pain which worsens with pressure and lessens with warmth, purplish complexion	Excess cold	***Menatrol***
	Delayed: Purplish red blood with lower abdominal distension and pain, chest and hypochondriac pain, breast tenderness	Liver qi stagnation	***Calm***

Symptom / Disease Index

Conditions	Symptoms/Disease Description	TCM Diagnosis	Herbal Formulas
Menstrual Disorders (Irregularity) *(cont'd)*	**Irregular**: May be twice a month or once in two months, may be profuse or scanty in amount with breast tenderness, lower abdominal distension and pain, hypochondriac distension, or lower back soreness	Liver qi stagnation with Kidney yin deficiency	***Calm*** and ***Kidney Tonic (Yin)***
	Irregular: Pale in color and scanty in amount, dizziness, palpitation, fatigue, listlessness, loose stools	Heart and Spleen deficiency	***Schisandra ZZZ***
	Absence of menstruation during menopause	Yin deficiency with false heat	***Balance (Heat)*** or ***Nourish***
Mental Health Disorders	Anxiety	Liver qi stagnation	***Calm***
	Delusion	*Shen* (spirit) disturbance	***Calm (ES)***
	Depression	Qi, blood, phlegm, and food stagnation	***Shine*** or ***Shine (DS)***
	With high blood pressure, fast heart rate, high temperature	Excess heat accumulation	*add* ***Gardenia Complex***
	Chronic case with blood stasis signs of dark complexion, purplish tongue with distended sublingual veins	Blood stagnation	*add* ***Circulation (SJ)***
	See also specific diseases		
Metabolic Disorder	Diabetes with elevated blood glucose	Dampness accumulation	***Equilibrium***
	Obesity with excessive appetite	Dampness accumulation	***Herbalite***
	Hyperlipidemia	Dampness and phlegm accumulation	***Cholisma***
	Hyperlipidemia with obesity and fatty liver	Dampness and phlegm accumulation	***Cholisma (ES)***
	Slow metabolism with low energy	Qi deficiency	***Vibrant***
	Slow metabolism in chronic fatigue syndrome	Severe qi deficiency	***Cordyceps 3***
	Slow metabolism with overall weakness and deficiency	Qi and blood deficiencies	***Imperial Tonic***
	Slow metabolism with adrenal insufficiency	Kidney qi deficiency	***Adrenal +***
	Slow metabolism due to hypothyroidism	Kidney yang deficiency	***Thyro-forte***
	Rapid metabolism due to hyperthyroidism	Excess heat	***Thyrodex***
Metastasis	*See* Cancer		
Migraine	*See* Headache		
Miscarriage	Habitual miscarriage with yin deficient signs of low-grade fever, night sweats, flushed cheeks, dizziness, and tinnitus	Kidney yin deficiency	***Kidney Tonic (Yin)***
	Habitual miscarriage with yang deficient signs of coldness, low libido, soreness and weakness of the back and knees, and polyuria	Kidney yang deficiency	***Kidney Tonic (Yang)***
Molds	*See* Allergy		
Mononucleosis	Infection causing swelling of lymph glands with fatigue	Toxic heat with dampness	***Herbal ENT*** with ***Resolve (AI)***
Mood Swing	Mood swings, irritability	Liver qi stagnation	***Calm***
	Insomnia, restlessness and anger in excess conditions	Liver fire	***Calm (ES)***

Symptom / Disease Index

Conditions	Symptoms/Disease Description	TCM Diagnosis	Herbal Formulas
Mood Swing (*cont'd*)	Insomnia, stress, overactive mind, anxiety with weakness in patients with deficiency	Liver qi stagnation with qi deficiency	***Calm ZZZ***
	Excessive worrying, pensiveness, dream-disturbed sleep	Spleen and Heart blood deficiencies	***Schisandra ZZZ***
	During menopause	Kidney yin deficiency with Liver qi stagnation	***Balance (Heat)***
	In depression	Food, phlegm, qi and blood stagnation	***Shine*** or ***Shine (DS)***
	In chronic cases with blood stagnation signs of dark complexion, purplish tongue, distended sublingual veins	Blood stagnation	*add* ***Circulation (SJ)***
Mouth	Dry mouth	Stomach yin deficiency	***Nourish (Fluids)***
	Ulcers or gum disease	Stomach fire	***Gardenia Complex***
	Fever blisters	Lung heat	***Lonicera Complex***
	Oral thrush	Damp and phlegm	***Pinellia Complex***
Mucus	Profuse yellow phlegm, chest congestion, cough and possible fever	Phlegm and heat in the Lung	***Pinellia XPT***
	Cough, dyspnea, chest congestion, yellow sputum	Lung heat	***Respitrol (Heat)***
	Clear or white phlegm, nasal congestion, sneezing	Lung cold	***Respitrol (Cold)***
	Irritable bowel syndrome with mucus in stools	Liver qi stagnation	***GI Harmony***
	Ulcerative colitis or Crohn's disease with mucus in stools	Damp-heat in the intestine	***GI Care (UC)***
	Mucus in stools due to food poisoning or traveler's diarrhea	Damp-heat in the intestine	***GI Care II***
	Moderate to severe cases of infection and inflammation	Accumulation of toxic heat	*add* ***Herbal ABX*** or ***Herbal AVR***
	With bleeding	Heat forcing blood out of the vessels	*add* ***Notoginseng 9***
	Dampness in the body	Damp accumulation	*add* ***Pinellia Complex***
Mumps	Swollen, painful glands with infection and inflammation	Toxic heat with phlegm accumulation	***Herbal ENT*** with ***Resolve (AI)***
Muscle, Tense	Muscle tightness and tension	Liver yin and body fluid deficiencies	***Flex (SC)***
	Due to stress	Liver qi stagnation	*add* ***Calm***
	Tightness or degeneration of soft tissues: muscles, tendons, ligaments and cartilages	Liver blood and Kidney yin deficiencies	*add* ***Flex (MLT)***
Muscle, Weak	Low energy and fatigue, weakness and soreness	Qi, blood, yin and yang deficiencies	***Imperial Tonic***
	Weakness of muscle due to adrenal gland under-activity	Kidney yang deficiency	***Adrenal +***
	Lack of muscle tone, digestive weakness, loose stools, fatigue	Spleen qi deficiency	***GI Tonic***
	Post-stroke complications	Qi and blood stagnation	***Neuro Plus***
	Degeneration of soft tissue (muscles, ligaments, tendons, cartilage)	Liver blood and Kidney *jing* (essence) deficiencies	***Flex (MLT)***
Myasthenia Gravis	General weakness and fatigability after exercise	*Yuan* (source) *qi* deficiency	***C/R Support*** or ***Imperial Tonic***

SYMPTOM / DISEASE

Symptom / Disease Index

Conditions	Symptoms/Disease Description	TCM Diagnosis	Herbal Formulas
Nasal Congestion	Thick yellow nasal discharge, nasal obstruction, sinus infection	Damp-heat with fluid congestion	***Pueraria Clear Sinus***
	Clear watery nasal discharge, nasal obstruction, allergy	Wind-cold with fluid congestion	***Magnolia Clear Sinus***
	Infection of the ear, nose and throat	Toxic heat	*add* ***Herbal ENT***
	Moderate to severe cases of infection and inflammation	Toxic heat	*add* ***Herbal ABX*** or ***Herbal AVR***
Nausea	With stomach pain, acid regurgitation	Stomach heat	***GI Care***
	With vomiting due to chemotherapy	Stomach yin deficiency	***C/R Support***
	With vomiting, abdominal pain and diarrhea due to food poisoning	Damp-heat in the lower *jiao*	***GI Care II***
	With vomiting and abdominal pain due to gallstones	Damp-heat in the Liver and Gallbladder	***Dissolve (GS)***
	With poor appetite and weakness	Spleen qi deficiency	***GI Tonic***
	With dryness and thirst	Stomach yin deficiency	***Nourish (Fluids)***
	With excessive dampness, thick tongue coating, possible excessive drooling of saliva	Damp accumulation	***Pinellia Complex***
	Unexplained cause, exhibiting dark complexion, purplish tongue	Blood stagnation	***Circulation (SJ)***
Neck Pain	Acute neck and shoulder pain	Qi and blood stagnation	***Neck & Shoulder (AC)***
	From external injuries	Qi and blood stagnation	*add* ***Flex (TMX)***
	With severe pain	Severe qi and blood stagnation	*add* ***Herbal ANG***
	Due to bone spurs	Qi and blood stagnation	*add* ***Flex (SPR)***
	Chronic neck and shoulder pain	Qi and blood stagnation with Liver yin deficiency	***Neck & Shoulder (CR)***
	Due to osteoporosis	Kidney yin and *jing* (essence) deficiencies	*add* ***Osteo 8***
Nephritis	Compromised kidney function with edema and proteinuria	Kidney deficiency with dampness	***Kidney DTX***
	With compromised liver function	Kidney deficiency with damp-heat in the Liver	*add* ***Liver DTX***
	Due to exposure to drugs, chemicals and other toxins	Kidney deficiency with toxic heat	*add* ***Herbal DTX***
	To improve kidney function for recovery	Kidney deficiency	*add* ***Cordyceps 3***
	With edema	Water accumulation	*add* ***Herbal DRX***
	With high blood pressure	Kidney and Liver yin deficiency with Liver yang rising	*add* ***Gastrodia Complex***
	With lupus	Toxic heat accumulation	*add* ***LPS Support***
Nephrotic Syndrome	*See* Nephritis		
Nerves	Oral herpes	Stomach fire flaring upward	***Lonicera Complex***
	Genital herpes	Damp-heat in the lower *jiao* and Liver channel	***Gentiana Complex***
	Herpes zoster (shingles)	Toxic and damp heat accumulation	***Dermatrol (HZ)***

Symptom / Disease Index

Conditions	Symptoms/Disease Description	TCM Diagnosis	Herbal Formulas
Nerves (*cont'd*)	Neuropathy with numbness and pain of extremities; post-herpetic neuralgia	Qi and blood stagnation	***Flex (NP)***
	Pain due to multiple sclerosis with generalized weakness and deficiency	Qi and blood stagnation with Kidney deficiency	***Neuro Plus***
Nervousness	*See* Stress, Anxiety		
Neuralgia	Peripheral neuralgia with pain, numbness, tingling and swelling	Qi and blood stagnation	***Flex (NP)***
	Due to bone spurs	Qi and blood stagnation	***Flex (SPR)***
	Due to herniated disks	Qi and blood stagnation	***Back Support (HD)***
	With severe pain	Severe qi and blood stagnation	*add* ***Herbal ANG***
	From diabetes mellitus	Qi and blood stagnation	*add* ***Equilibrium***
	From genital herpes	Qi and blood stagnation	*add* ***Gentiana Complex***
	From herpes zoster	Qi and blood stagnation	*add* ***Dermatrol (HZ)***
Neuropathy	*See* Neuralgia		
Neurosis	Stress, irritability, restlessness, insomnia, nervousness	Liver qi stagnation	***Calm***
	Above symptoms, but more severe	Liver fire	***Calm (ES)***
	Excessive worrying, pensiveness, over thinking, poor appetite	Spleen and Heart deficiencies	***Schisandra ZZZ***
	Insomnia, nervousness, anxiety, overactive mind, stress, and weakness	Liver qi stagnation with qi deficiency	***Calm ZZZ***
	Severe or chronic condition with blood stagnation signs of dark complexion, purplish tongue, distended sublingual veins	Blood stagnation	***Circulation (SJ)***
Night Sweat	Perspiration at night	Yin deficiency with false heat	***Nourish*** and ***Balance (Heat)***
Nocturnal Emission	Nocturnal emission	Kidney yin deficiency	***Nourish*** or ***Kidney Tonic (Yin)***
Nodules	Anywhere in the body due to infection and inflammation	Phlegm stagnation	***Resolve (AI)***
	In the breast	Phlegm stagnation	***Resolve (Upper)***
	In the lower abdominal area	Phlegm and blood stagnation	***Resolve (Lower)***
	In the neck due to hyperthyroidism	Liver fire with phlegm stagnation	***Thyrodex***
	In the neck due to hypothyroidism	Yang deficiency with phlegm stagnation	***Thyro-forte***
	In the lymphatic system	Phlegm stagnation	***Resolve (AI)***
Nose	Profuse white or clear nasal discharge, sneezing	Lung cold	***Respitrol (Cold)***
	Allergy with clear or white nasal discharge	Wind-cold attacking the Lung	***Magnolia Clear Sinus***
	Allergy with yellow nasal discharge	Wind-heat attacking the Lung	***Pueraria Clear Sinus***
	Sinus infection	Toxic heat	***Herbal ENT***
	Nose bleeding	Heat pushing blood out of the vessels	***Notoginseng 9***
	Dry nose, throat, thirst	Lung and Stomach yin deficiencies	***Nourish (Fluids)***

Symptom / Disease Index

Conditions	Symptoms/Disease Description	TCM Diagnosis	Herbal Formulas
Nutrition	*See* Malnutrition		
Obesity	With excessive hunger	Stomach fire	***Herbalite***
	With high cholesterol	Stomach fire with phlegm and damp	*add* ***Cholisma***
	With fatty liver and high cholesterol	Damp-phlegm accumulation	*add* ***Cholisma (ES)***
	With diabetes mellitus	Stomach fire with yin deficiency	*add* ***Equilibrium***
	With excess type hypertension	Stomach fire with damp-heat	*add* ***Gentiana Complex***
	With deficient type hypertension	Stomach fire with Liver yin deficiency	*add* ***Gastrodia Complex***
	With coronary artery disease	Stomach fire with phlegm stagnation	*add* ***Circulation***
Obsessive-Compulsive Disorder (OCD)	Presence of recurrent, unwanted and intrusive physical and mental activities	*Shen* (spirit) disturbance	***Calm (ES)***
Ocular Disturbance	Dry eyes, floaters, visual disturbance	Kidney and Liver yin deficiency	***Lycium Support***
Olecranon Bursitis	Painful elbow	Qi and blood stagnation	***Arm Support***
	With severe pain	Severe qi and blood stagnation	*add* ***Herbal ANG***
	Due to trauma	Qi and blood stagnation	*add* ***Flex (TMX)***
Operation (Post-Op Care)	Enhances recovery and prevents adhesions and complications	Qi and blood stagnation	***Flex (TMX)***
	To treat or reduce the risk of infection in post-operative patients	Toxic heat	***Herbal ABX***
	To enhance growth of bones	Kidney *jing* (essence) deficiency	***Osteo 8***
	To enhance the recovery and growth of soft tissue (muscles, tendons, ligaments and cartilage)	Kidney yin and Liver blood deficiencies	***Flex (MLT)***
	Post-operative recovery in deficient and weak patients	Qi and blood deficiency	***Imperial Tonic***
	With constipation	Heat and dryness in the Intestines	***Gentle Lax (Excess), Gentle Lax (Deficient)***
	Post-operative pain: *See* Pain or the affected parts of the body		
Optic Atrophy	Dry eyes, floaters, visual disturbance	Kidney and Liver yin deficiency	***Lycium Support***
Orchitis	Inflammation and swelling of the testicles	Heat in the lower *jiao*	***V-Support*** and ***Astringent Complex***
Osteoarthritis	Joint pain	Qi and blood stagnation with Kidney *jing* (essence) deficiency	***Osteo 8*** and a ***Flex*** formula
Osteoporosis	Decreased density of bones	Deficiency of Kidney *jing* (essence)	***Osteo 8***
	With bone fracture or broken bone	Deficiency of Kidney *jing* (essence) with blood stagnation	*add* ***Flex (TMX)***
	With low libido	Kidney *jing* (essence) deficiency	*add* ***Vitality***

Symptom / Disease Index

Conditions	Symptoms/Disease Description	TCM Diagnosis	Herbal Formulas
Osteoporosis (*cont'd*)	With menopause symptoms such as hot flashes, irritability, and night sweating	Kidney *jing* (essence) deficiency and deficiency heat flaring	add ***Balance (Heat)***
	With vaginal dryness	Kidney yin deficiency	add ***Balance Spring***
Otitis Media	Inflammation of the ear with pain, fever or hearing impairment	Toxic heat accumulation	***Herbal ENT***
	With bacterial infection	Toxic heat accumulation	add ***Herbal ABX***
	With viral infection	Toxic heat accumulation	add ***Herbal AVR***
Otolaryngological Disorders	Disorders of the ear, nose, and throat	Toxic heat accumulation	***Herbal ENT***
Ovaries	*See* Fibrocystic disease, Endometriosis, Infertility, Menstrual irregularity, Menopausal syndrome		
Overdose	Overdose of drugs or other toxic materials	Toxic heat	***Herbal DTX*** or ***Liver DTX***
Overeating	Excessive appetite	Stomach heat	***Herbalite***
Overweight	*See* Obesity		
Ovulation Disorders	Due to coldness, weakness and blood clots during menstruation	Blood stagnation with Kidney yang deficiency	***Menatrol***
	Due to stress	Liver qi stagnation	***Calm***
	Due to endometriosis or fibroids	Qi and blood stagnation	***Resolve (Lower)***
	Infertility	Varies	***Blossom (Phase 1-4)***
Pain	A general formula to relieve pain	Qi and blood stagnation	***Herbal ANG***
	See Specific conditions, diseases, or body parts		
Palpitation	With insomnia, fatigue, and overthinking	Heart and Spleen blood deficiencies	***Schisandra ZZZ***
	With chest pain, coronary heart disorder	Blood stagnation	***Circulation***
	With increased blood pressure due to hyperthyroidism	Qi and phlegm stagnation	***Thyrodex***
	In menopausal women	Deficiency heat	***Balance (Heat)***
Pancreas	*See* Diabetes mellitus		
Papules	Acne	Wind–heat with damp	***Dermatrol (Clear)***
Paralysis	Impaired function of the extremities or the face in post-stroke	Qi and blood stagnation	***Neuro Plus***
	Facial paralysis	Qi and blood stagnation	***Symmetry***
Paranoia	Personality disorder	*Shen* (spirit) disturbance with heat	***Calm (ES)***
Parkinson's Disease	Tremor, muscle rigidity, poor balance, impaired mental and physical functions	Deficiencies of Kidney yin, yang and *jing* (essence) with Liver yang rising	***Neuro Plus***
Parotitis	Inflammation or infection of the parotid salivary gland	Toxic heat with phlegm accumulation	***Herbal ENT*** with ***Resolve (AI)***
Patella	Acute knee pain	Qi and blood stagnation	***Knee & Ankle (AC)***
	Chronic knee pain	Qi and blood stagnation	***Knee & Ankle (CR)***
	With severe pain	Severe qi and blood stagnation	add ***Herbal ANG***

Symptom / Disease Index

Conditions	Symptoms/Disease Description	TCM Diagnosis	Herbal Formulas
Pelvic Inflammatory Disease (PID)	Yellow discharge with foul odor	Damp-heat in the lower *jiao*	***V-Support***
	Foul smelling yellow discharge, pelvic pain in patients with excess conditions	Damp-heat in the lower *jiao*	***Gentiana Complex***
	With endometriosis	Qi and blood stagnation	*add* ***Resolve (Lower)***
	With weakness and thirst	Damp-heat accumulation in the lower *jiao* with Kidney yin deficiency	*add* ***Nourish***
	With moderate to severe cases of infection and inflammation	Accumulation of toxic heat	*add* ***Herbal ABX***
	With severe pain	Severe qi and blood stagnation	*add* ***Herbal ANG***
Pelvic Pain	Due to pelvic inflammatory disease	Damp-heat in the lower *jiao*	***V-Support***
	Due to dysmenorrhea	Blood stagnation in the lower *jiao*	***Mense-Ease***
	Due to fibroids or endometriosis	Blood and phlegm stagnation in the lower *jiao*	***Resolve (Lower)***
	Due to genitourinary infection	Damp-heat in the lower *jiao*	***V-Support*** or ***Gentiana Complex***
	Due to irritable bowel syndrome	Spleen qi deficiency	***GI Harmony***
	Due to prostate issues	Qi and blood stagnation	***P-Support***
	Post-surgical pelvic pain or scar tissues	Qi and blood stagnation	***Flex (TMX)***
	With severe pain	Severe qi and blood stagnation	*add* ***Herbal ANG***
	Moderate to severe cases of infection and inflammation	Accumulation of toxic heat	*add* ***Herbal ABX***
	With high fever	Excess heat accumulation	*add* ***Gardenia Complex***
Penis	*See* Impotence, Premature ejaculation, Sexual dysfunction, Sexually transmitted disease		
Peptic Ulcer	Gastric and duodenal ulcer	Stomach heat	***GI Care***
	Due to stress	Stomach heat with Liver qi stagnation	*add* ***Calm***
	With poor appetite, fatigue, loose stools	Stomach heat with Spleen qi deficiency	*add* ***GI Tonic***
	With severe pain	Severe qi and blood stagnation	*add* ***Herbal ANG***
	With bleeding	Heat forcing blood out of the vessels	*add* ***Notoginseng 9***
Period	*See* Menstrual irregularity, Menstrual cramps/pain, Amenorrhea, Menopausal syndrome		
Peripheral Neuropathy	Neuropathy with pain, numbness, tingling and swelling	Qi and blood stagnation	***Flex (NP)***
	With severe pain	Severe qi and blood stagnation	*add* ***Herbal ANG***
	From diabetes mellitus	Qi and blood stagnation	*add* ***Equilibrium***
	From genital herpes	Qi and blood stagnation	*add* ***Gentiana Complex***
	From herpes zoster	Qi and blood stagnation	*add* ***Dermatrol (HZ)***
Personality Disorder	*See* Mental health disorders		

Symptom / Disease Index

Conditions	Symptoms/Disease Description	TCM Diagnosis	Herbal Formulas
Pesticide Poisoning	Adverse reactions from exposure to insecticide, pesticide, herbicide and other toxins	Toxic heat	***Herbal DTX***
	Compromised liver function due to exposure to toxins	Toxic heat in the Liver	***Liver DTX***
	Compromised kidney function due to exposure to toxins	Toxic heat in the Kidney	***Kidney DTX***
	Intestinal detox	Toxic heat in the Intestines	***GI DTX***
Pfeiffer's Disease	Fever, pharyngitis, enlarged lymph	Toxic heat accumulation with dampness	***Resolve (AI)*** and ***Herbal ENT***
Pharyngitis	With sore throat	Wind-heat invasion	***Lonicera Complex*** or ***Herbal ENT***
	With fever, cough, dyspnea	Lung heat	*add* ***Respitrol (Heat)***
	Moderate to severe cases of infection and inflammation	Accumulation of toxic heat	*add* ***Herbal ABX***
	With severe pain	Toxic heat with severe qi and blood stagnation	*add* ***Herbal ANG***
Phlegm	Profuse yellow phlegm, chest congestion, cough, and possible fever	Phlegm and heat in the Lung	***Pinellia XPT***
	Yellow phlegm, cough, dyspnea, chest congestion	Lung heat	***Respitrol (Heat)***
	Clear or white phlegm, nasal congestion, sneezing	Lung cold	***Respitrol (Cold)***
	Chronic cases of dyspnea with phlegm	Lung and Kidney deficiencies	***Respitrol (Deficient)***
	Moderate to severe cases of infection and inflammation	Accumulation of toxic heat	*add* ***Herbal ABX***
	With cough	Lung qi reversal	*add* ***Respitrol (CF)***
	Nodules or swellings	Phlegm accumulation	***Resolve (AI)***
	Damp phlegm in the body in general	Damp/phlegm accumulation	***Pinellia Complex***
Photophobia	With dry eyes, floaters, visual disturbance	Kidney and Liver yin deficiency	***Lycium Support***
Pituitary Gland	Diminished function of the adrenal glands and endocrine system	Deficiencies of Kidney yin, yang and *jing* (essence)	***Adrenal +***
	Diabetes mellitus	Yin deficiency with dampness and heat	***Equilibrium***
	Hyperthyroidism	Excess heat	***Thyrodex***
	Hypothyroidism	Kidney yang deficiency	***Thyro-forte***
	Sexual and reproductive disorders	Kidney yin and yang deficiencies	***Vitality*** and ***Vital Essence***
	Menstrual disorders	Various	***Blossom Phase 1-4***
Plaque	*See* Cholesterol		
Plasma	*See* Blood clots, bleeding, and specific conditions		

Symptom / Disease Index

Conditions	Symptoms/Disease Description	TCM Diagnosis	Herbal Formulas
PMS (Premenstrual Syndrome)	Breast distension, bloating, mood swings	Liver qi stagnation	***Calm***
	Insomnia, restlessness, and anger	Liver fire	***Calm (ES)***
	With insomnia, anxiety, stress, irritability, overactive mind, and weakness with underlying deficiency	Liver qi stagnation with qi deficiency	*add* ***Calm ZZZ***
	With lower abdominal pain and dysmenorrhea	Liver qi stagnation with blood stagnation	*add* ***Mense-Ease***
	With edema	Liver qi stagnation with water accumulation	*add* ***Herbal DRX***
Pneumonia	Cough, dyspnea, fever	Lung heat	***Respitrol (Heat)***
	Chest congestion, fever, cough with yellow sputum	Phlegm and heat in the Lung	***Pinellia XPT***
	With high fever	Excess heat accumulation	*add* ***Gardenia Complex***
	With severe cough	Lung heat with reversed flow of qi	*add* ***Respitrol (CF)***
	Due to bacterial infection	Heat	*add* ***Herbal ABX***
	Due to viral infection	Heat	*add* ***Herbal AVR***
Poison Oak/Ivy	Skin itching	Wind-heat	***Silerex***
	Severe skin itching	Toxic heat	***Dermatrol (PS)***
Poisoning	Food poisoning with abdominal pain and diarrhea	Damp-heat in the Intestines	***GI Care II***
	Adverse reactions from exposure to insecticide, pesticide, herbicide, heavy metal, and other toxins	Toxic heat	***Herbal DTX***
	Compromised liver function due to exposure to toxins	Toxic heat in the Liver	***Liver DTX***
	Compromised kidney function due to exposure to toxins	Toxic heat in the Kidney	***Kidney DTX***
	Toxicity in the intestines, colon	Toxic heat in the Intestines	***GI DTX***
	Itching of the skin	Wind-heat attacking the exterior	***Silerex***
	Moderate to severe cases of infection and inflammation of the skin	Accumulation of toxic heat	*add* ***Herbal ABX***
	With fever	Excess heat accumulation	*add* ***Gardenia Complex***
	Chronic cases with blood stagnation signs of dark complexion, purplish tongue with distended sublingual veins	Blood stagnation	*add* ***Circulation (SJ)***
Pollution	*See* Detox, Poisoning		
Polycystic Ovary Syndrome	Absence of menstruation with severe pain and coldness	Blood stagnation with cold accumulation	***Menatrol***
	Irregular menstruation with pain but no coldness	Qi, blood and phlegm stagnation	***Resolve (Lower)***
	Infertility	Varies	*add* ***Blossom (Phase 1-4)***
	See also Fibrocystic disease, Endometriosis, Infertility, Menstrual irregularity		
Polydipsia	Increased intake of fluid and thirst	Lung yin deficiency with heat	***Nourish (Fluids)***
	Increased intake of fluid and thirst in diabetes mellitus	Lung yin deficiency with heat	*add* ***Equilibrium***

Symptom / Disease Index

Conditions	Symptoms/Disease Description	TCM Diagnosis	Herbal Formulas
Polyneuropathy	Neuropathy with pain, numbness, tingling and swelling	Qi and blood stagnation	***Flex (NP)***
	With severe pain	Severe qi and blood stagnation	*add* ***Herbal ANG***
	From diabetes mellitus	Qi and blood stagnation	*add* ***Equilibrium***
	From genital herpes	Qi and blood stagnation	*add* ***Gentiana Complex***
	From herpes zoster	Qi and blood stagnation	*add* ***Dermatrol (HZ)***
Polyphagia	Increased intake of food in diabetes mellitus	Stomach yin deficiency with heat	***Equilibrium***
	Increased hunger in obesity	Stomach heat	***Herbalite***
Polyps	Intestinal polyps	Damp accumulation	***Resolve (AI)*** and ***GI DTX***
	Nasal polyps	Damp accumulation	***Resolve (AI)*** and ***Pueraria Clear Sinus***
Polyuria	In diabetes mellitus	Kidney yin deficiency	***Equilibrium***
	With coldness and weakness	Kidney yang deficiency	***Kidney Tonic (Yang)***
	Due to enlarged prostate	Damp-heat in the lower *jiao*	***P-Support*** and ***Astringent Complex***
	Due to chronic nephritis or nephritic syndrome	Toxic heat in the Kidney	***Kidney DTX***
	Due to infection with dark urine and pain	Damp-heat in the lower *jiao*	***V-Support***
	Moderate to severe cases of infection and inflammation	Accumulation of toxic heat	*add* ***Herbal ABX***
Poor Memory	*See* Forgetfulness, Memory		
Post-Menstrual Care	Dizziness with signs of anemia, poor sleep, excessive dreams, and worrying	Blood deficiency	***Schisandra ZZZ***
	Fatigue and generalized weakness	Qi and blood deficiencies	***Imperial Tonic***
	Soreness and weakness of the back and knees, feeling of emptiness in the lower abdomen	Kidney yin deficiency	***Kidney Tonic (Yin)***
Post-Nasal Drip	Yellow in color due to sinus infection	Damp-heat with fluid congestion	***Pueraria Clear Sinus***
	White in color with nasal obstruction	Wind-cold with fluid congestion	***Magnolia Clear Sinus***
	Moderate to severe cases of infection and inflammation	Accumulation of toxic heat	*add* ***Herbal ENT***
	To enhance the phlegm/damp eliminating effect	Damp phlegm accumulation	*add* ***Pinellia Complex***
Postpartum Care	Residual blood stagnation with pain	Blood stagnation	***Flex (TMX)***
	To treat or reduce the risk of infection	Toxic heat	***Herbal ABX***
	Generalized weakness, dizziness, post-partum tonic	Blood, qi, yin and yang deficiencies	***Imperial Tonic***
	Pale face, insomnia with anemia	Blood deficiency	***Schisandra ZZZ***
	Post-partum depression	Qi, blood, phlegm and food stagnation	***Schisandra ZZZ*** and ***Shine***
	Insufficient lactation due to blockage or deficiency	Qi and blood deficiencies with qi stagnation	***Venus*** and ***Imperial Tonic***

Symptom / Disease Index

Conditions	Symptoms/Disease Description	TCM Diagnosis	Herbal Formulas
Postpartum Care (*cont'd*)	Constipation	Qi and blood stagnation and deficiencies	***Imperial Tonic, Gentle Lax (Deficient)***
	With severe pain	Severe qi and blood stagnation	*add* ***Herbal ANG***
	With bleeding	Qi deficiency	*add* ***Notoginseng 9***
Premature Aging	Premature gray hair, hair loss, brittle hair with split ends	Liver blood deficiency	***Polygonum 14***
	Premature gray hair, hair loss due to stress	Liver blood deficiency with Liver qi stagnation	***Polygonum 14*** and ***Calm***
	With decreased mental and physical functions	Qi, blood, yin and yang deficiencies	***Imperial Tonic***
	With poor memory and forgetfulness	Kidney yin and *jing* (essence) deficiencies	***Enhance Memory***
	With decreased libido in men and women	Kidney yang deficiency	***Vitality***
	To prevent osteoporosis	Kidney *jing* (essence) deficiency	***Osteo 8***
	General Kidney yin deficiency signs such as blurry vision, weakness of the back and knees, tinnitus, dryness, flushed cheeks, possible low-grade fever	Kidney yin deficiency	***Kidney Tonic (Yin)***
	General Kidney yang deficiency signs such as coldness, low libido, premature ejaculation, weakness and soreness of the back and knees, pale complexion, and polyuria	Kidney yang deficiency	***Kidney Tonic (Yang)***
Premature Ejaculation	Generalized male sexual dysfunction with low libido	Kidney yang deficiency	***Vitality***
	With soreness and weakness of the low back and knees, hair loss, coldness, polyuria, or loose stools	Kidney yang deficiency	***Kidney Tonic (Yang)***
	With *wu xin re* (five-center heat), night sweating, dry mouth, dizziness, tinnitus, dry stools	Kidney yin deficiency	***Kidney Tonic (Yin)***
	With irritability, bitter taste in the mouth, yellow urine, possible genital itching	Damp-heat in the lower *jiao*	***V-Support***
	With emaciation, fatigue, weakness of limbs, poor appetite, loose stools	Spleen qi deficiency	***GI Tonic***
Premenstrual Syndrome (PMS)	Breast distension, bloating, mood swings	Liver qi stagnation	***Calm***
	Insomnia, restlessness and anger	Liver fire	***Calm (ES)***
	With lower abdominal pain and dysmenorrhea	Liver qi stagnation with blood stagnation	*add* ***Mense-Ease***
	With edema	Liver qi stagnation with water accumulation	*add* ***Herbal DRX***
	With insomnia, anxiety, stress, irritability, overactive mind and weakness in patients with deficiency	Liver qi stagnation with qi deficiency	*add* ***Calm ZZZ***
Prolapse	Organ prolapse, such as stomach, uterus, or anus	Spleen qi deficiency with inability to hold the organs in place	***C/R Support***
Prostate	Enlarged prostate with difficult, painful urination	Damp-heat in the lower *jiao*	***P-Support***
	Enlarged prostate with back soreness, terminal dripping of urine, overall coldness	Kidney yang deficiency	*add* ***Kidney Tonic (Yang)***

Symptom / Disease Index

Conditions	Symptoms/Disease Description	TCM Diagnosis	Herbal Formulas
Prostate *(cont'd)*	Moderate to severe cases of infection and inflammation or burning urination	Accumulation of toxic heat	*add **V-Support***
	Excessive swelling with thick tongue coating	Phlegm accumulation	*add **Resolve (AI)***
Proteinuria	Due to nephritis	Kidney deficiency with dampness	***Kidney DTX***
	With edema	Damp accumulation	***Kidney DTX*** and ***Herbal DRX***
Psoriasis	Itching, silvery, scaling papules and plaques on the skin	Toxic heat	***Dermatrol (PS)***
	With heat sensation, red discoloration of the skin, possible burning sensation	Excess heat accumulation	*add **Gardenia Complex***
	Severe flaking and dryness of the skin	Dryness and toxic heat accumulation	*add **Dermatrol (Dry)***
Psychological Disorder	*See* Mental health disorders		
Psychosis	Mental impairment and confusion	*Shen* (spirit) disturbance with Liver fire	***Calm (ES)***
Pulmonary Disorders	*See* Asthma, Cough, Dyspnea, Pneumonia, Bronchitis, Common cold, Influenza or other specific disorders		
Purple Tongue	Severe blood stagnation manifesting in chronic symptoms	Severe blood stagnation	***Circulation (SJ)***
Purpura	With fatigue and weakness	Spleen qi deficiency	***Schisandra ZZZ***
	Subcutaneous bleeding	Heat pushing blood out of the vessels	***Schisandra ZZZ*** and ***Notoginseng 9***
	Excess heat with feverish sensation, red face, red tongue, rapid pulse	Excess heat accumulation	***Gardenia Complex*** and ***Notoginseng 9***
Pus	Lung abscesses, profuse yellow phlegm	Phlegm and heat in the Lung	***Pinellia XPT***
	Breast abscesses	Phlegm stagnation in the upper *jiao*	***Resolve (Upper)***
	With hard mass	Phlegm and damp accumulation	***Resolve (AI)***
	Weepy skin lesions	Damp-heat toxin	***Dermatrol (Damp)***
	General formation of abscess due to infection and inflammation	Accumulation of toxic heat	*add **Herbal ABX***
	Generalized dampness in the body	Damp/phlegm accumulation	*add **Pinellia Complex***
Pustules	Acne	Wind-heat with damp	***Dermatrol (Clear)***
Pyelonephritis	Chronic nephritis or nephritic syndrome	Toxic heat in the Kidney	***Kidney DTX***
	Moderate to severe cases of infection and inflammation	Accumulation of toxic heat	***Kidney DTX*** and ***Herbal ABX***
Radiation Therapy	To alleviate side effects associated with chemotherapy and radiation	Deficiencies of yin, *yuan* (source) *qi* and *wei* (defensive) *qi*	***C/R Support***
	End stage cancer in patients who are too weak to receive chemotherapy or radiation	*Yuan* (source) *qi* deficiency	***CA Support***
	See also Cancer / Carcinoma		
Rash	Itching, redness, and swelling of skin	Wind-heat at the skin level, heat in the blood	***Silerex***
	Any wet lesions	Damp-heat	***Dermatrol (Damp)***

Symptom / Disease Index

Conditions	Symptoms/Disease Description	TCM Diagnosis	Herbal Formulas
Rash (*cont'd*)	Any dry lesions	Dryness with heat	***Dermatrol (Dry)***
	Psoriasis	Toxic heat	***Dermatrol (PS)***
	Genital rash and itching	Damp-heat in the lower *jiao*	***V-Support***
	For rash due to exposure to or accumulation of drugs, chemicals, heavy metals, environmental and airborne toxins in the blood	Toxic heat	*add* ***Herbal DTX***
	To facilitate metabolism and break down of drugs, chemicals, heavy metals, environmental and airborne toxins in the body	Toxic heat	*add* ***Liver DTX***
	To facilitate elimination of drugs, chemicals, heavy metals, environmental and airborne toxins from the kidneys	Toxic heat	*add* ***Kidney DTX***
Raynaud's Syndrome	Coldness of the extremities	Yang deficiency	***Kidney Tonic (Yang)***
	To increase peripheral blood circulation	Qi and blood stagnation	*add* ***Flex (NP)***
Red Blood Cells	Deficiency of red blood cells in anemia	Blood deficiency	***Schisandra ZZZ***
Regurgitation	*See* Nausea, Vomiting, Acid reflux		
Rehabilitation	*See* Detox, Addiction and specific conditions		
Reiter's Syndrome	Urinary urgency, burning urination, redness and painful eyes, ulcers, and pain	Toxic heat accumulation	***Gardenia Complex, Gentiana Complex***
Renal Colic	With severe pain in the flank due to kidney stones	*Shi lin* (stone dysuria)	***Dissolve (KS)***
	With severe pain	Severe qi and blood stagnation	*add* ***Herbal ANG***
	With edema	Damp accumulation	*add* ***Herbal DRX***
Reproductive System	*See* Sexual dysfunction, Infertility, Infection, and other related organs		
Respiratory Disorders	*See* Asthma, Cough, Dyspnea, Pneumonia, Bronchitis, Common cold, Infection		
Restless Leg Syndrome	Constant movement of the legs	Liver wind rising with lack of nourishment to the tendons and muscles	***Flex (SC)*** and ***Gastrodia Complex***
Restlessness	*See* Stress, ADD/ADHD		
Retinopathy, Diabetic	Reduced visual acuity, diminished or impaired vision, blurred vision, excessive tearing, optic atrophy	Liver and Kidney yin deficiencies	***Lycium Support*** and ***Equilibrium***
Rheumatism	*See* Arthritis		
Rheumatoid Arthritis	*See* Arthritis		
Rhinitis	*See* Sinusitis		
Rib Pain	From external injuries	Qi and blood stagnation	***Flex (TMX)***
	With severe pain	Severe qi and blood stagnation	*add* ***Herbal ANG***
	With spasms	Liver blood deficiency	*add* ***Flex (SC)***
Ringing of Ears	*See* Tinnitus		

Symptom / Disease Index

Conditions	Symptoms/Disease Description	TCM Diagnosis	Herbal Formulas
Rosacea	Redness on the central face with domed papules and pustules	Wind-heat with damp	***Dermatrol (Clear)***
Rotator Cuff Tear / Tendonitis	Acute pain and immobility	Qi and blood stagnation	***Arm Support*** and ***Neck & Shoulder (AC)***
	Chronic, dull pain, immobility, numbness	Qi and blood stagnation with Liver yin deficiency	***Arm Support*** and ***Neck & Shoulder (CR)***
	With shooting pain	Qi and blood stagnation	*add* ***Flex (NP)***
	With severe pain	Severe qi and blood stagnation	*add* ***Herbal ANG***
	With degeneration of soft tissue (muscle, ligaments, tendons, cartilage)	Liver blood deficiency and Kidney yin deficiency	***Flex (MLT)***
Runny Nose	*See* Common cold		
Sadness	*See* Depression		
Salpingitis	Inflammation of the fallopian tube	Damp-heat in the lower *jiao*	***V-Support***
	To reduce adhesions and scar tissue	Blood stagnation	*add* ***Resolve (Lower)***
	With fever	Excess heat accumulation	*add* ***Gardenia Complex***
Scapular Pain	Pain in the scapula or in between the scapulas	Qi and blood stagnation	***Neck & Shoulder (AC)***
	Due to external injuries	Qi and blood stagnation	*add* ***Flex (TMX)***
	With severe pain	Severe qi and blood stagnation	*add* ***Herbal ANG***
Schizophrenia	Disturbed thoughts, delusion, hallucination, bizarre behavior	*Shen* (spirit) disturbance with Liver fire	***Calm (ES)***
Sciatica	With back pain	Qi and blood stagnation	***Back Support (HD)***
	With arthritis that worsens during cold and rainy seasons	Coldness and deficiency of the lower back	*add* ***Flex (CD)***
	Due to bone spurs	Qi and blood stagnation with phlegm formation	*add* ***Flex (SPR)***
	With severe pain	Severe qi and blood stagnation	*add* ***Herbal ANG***
	With shooting pain	Qi and blood stagnation	*add* ***Flex (NP)***
Scrofula	Scrofula	Dampness accumulation	***Resolve (AI)***
	With redness and heat sensation	Heat accumulation	*add* ***Herbal ABX***
Scrotum	Itching of the scrotum	Damp-heat in the lower *jiao*	***V-Support***
	Infection of the scrotum, swelling with pain with possible eczema or oozing of fluids, yellow urine, constipation	Damp-heat in the lower *jiao* and Liver channel	*add* ***Herbal ABX***
Seborrheic Dermatitis	With lesions that are wet	Damp-heat	***Dermatrol (Damp)***
Seizures	For prevention and treatment of seizure	Liver wind rising	***Gastrodia Complex*** or ***Symmetry***
Semen	*See* Sexual dysfunction, Infertility		

Symptom / Disease Index

Conditions	Symptoms/Disease Description	TCM Diagnosis	Herbal Formulas
Sexual Dysfunction	Impotence, premature ejaculation, inability to sustain erection, decreased libido	Kidney yin, yang and *jing* (essence) deficiencies	***Vitality***
	Due to stress	Liver qi stagnation	*add* ***Calm*** or ***Calm (ES)***
	Due to complications of diabetes mellitus	Kidney yin and yang deficiencies	*add* ***Equilibrium***
	With chronic fatigue	Kidney and Lung deficiencies	*add* ***Cordyceps 3***
	Male infertility due to sperm disorder (morphology, motility and mobility)	Kidney *jing* (essence) deficiency	***Vital Essence***
	Excess libido in men and women with emaciation, dry stools or constipation, dry mouth, yellow urine	Kidney yin deficiency with deficiency fire	***Balance (Heat)*** and ***Nourish***
	Excess libido in men and women with dysuria, thirst, decreased appetite	Damp-heat in the lower *jiao*	***Gentiana Complex, Gardenia Complex***
	Female infertility	Varies	***Blossom (Phase 1-4)***
	Vaginal dryness	Kidney yin deficiency	***Balance Spring***
Sexually Transmitted Disease (STD)	Infection in the genital area with itching, pus, discharge, and pain	Damp-heat in the lower *jiao*	***V-Support*** or ***Gentiana Complex***
	From bacterial infection	Toxic heat	*add* ***Herbal ABX***
	From viral infection	Toxic heat	*add* ***Herbal AVR***
SGPT, SGOT	Elevated levels of liver enzymes SGPT and SGOT (AST and ALT)	Toxic heat in the Liver	***Liver DTX***
	Moderate to severe cases of infection and inflammation	Accumulation of toxic heat	*add* ***Herbal ABX***
	Elevated liver enzymes due to exposure to drugs, chemicals and other toxins	Toxic heat	*add* ***Herbal DTX***
Shingles	Pain of the affected area with or without lesions	Damp-heat in the Liver channel	***Dermatrol (HZ)***
	With wet lesions	Damp-heat	*add* ***Dermatrol (Damp)***
	With severe pain	Severe qi and blood stagnation	*add* ***Herbal ANG***
	To enhance the antiviral effect	Toxic deficiency heat	*add* ***Herbal AVR***
Shortness of Breath	*See* Asthma, Cough, Dyspnea		
Shoulder Pain	With acute pain and immobility	Qi and blood stagnation	***Neck & Shoulder (AC)***
	With chronic dull pain	Qi and blood stagnation with Liver yin deficiency	***Neck & Shoulder (CR)***
	Caused by external injuries	Qi and blood stagnation	*add* ***Flex (TMX)***
	Bone spurs	Qi and blood stagnation	*add* ***Flex (SPR)***
	With severe pain	Severe qi and blood stagnation	*add* ***Herbal ANG***
	Shoulder pain radiating down the arm	Qi and blood stagnation	*add* ***Arm Support***
	With degeneration or for maintenance of soft tissue (muscle, tendons, cartilage, ligaments)	Liver blood deficiency and Kidney yin deficiency	*add* ***Flex (MLT)***

Symptom / Disease Index

Conditions	Symptoms/Disease Description	TCM Diagnosis	Herbal Formulas
Sigh	Frequent sighing with chest or hypochondriac distension, poor appetite	Liver qi stagnation	***Calm***
	With anxiety, stress, restlessness, overactive mind, insomnia and weakness	Liver qi stagnation with qi deficiency	***Calm ZZZ***
	Due to depression	Qi, blood, food, phlegm stagnation	***Shine*** or ***Shine (DS)***
	With shortness of breath, spontaneous sweating, fatigue	Lung qi deficiency	***Immune +***
Sinusitis	Thick yellow nasal discharge, nasal obstruction, sinus infection	Damp-heat with fluid congestion	***Pueraria Clear Sinus***
	Clear watery nasal discharge, nasal obstruction, allergy	Wind-cold with fluid congestion	***Magnolia Clear Sinus***
	Moderate to severe cases of infection and inflammation	Accumulation of toxic heat	*add* ***Herbal ENT***
	With headache	Qi and blood stagnation	*add* ***Corydalin (AC)***
Sjögren's Syndrome	Dry mouth, itchy eyes, swollen glands, dental cavity, fatigue	Lung and Stomach yin deficiency	***Nourish (Fluids)*** and ***Herbal ENT***
	With hyperactive immunity in an autoimmune condition	Heat	***Gardenia Complex***
Skin	Itching, redness and swelling of skin, dermatitis	Wind-heat at the skin level, heat in the blood	***Silerex***
	Psoriasis	Toxic heat	***Dermatrol (PS)***
	Rash in the lower body and genital region	Damp-heat in the lower *jiao*	***Gentiana Complex***
	Skin lesions from shingles	Toxic heat	***Dermatrol (HZ)***
	Any skin condition that is wet or oozing	Toxic and damp-heat accumulation	***Dermatrol (Damp)***
	Any skin condition that is dry	Dry heat invasion	***Dermatrol (Dry)***
	Yellow discoloration of the skin in jaundice patients	Damp-heat in the Liver and Gallbladder	***Liver DTX***
	Dry skin	Blood deficiency	***Nourish (Fluids)***
	Nodules, swellings and redness	Phlegm heat accumulation	***Resolve (AI)***
	Acne	Wind-heat	***Dermatrol (Clear)***
	Skin conditions with moderate to severe cases of infection and inflammation	Accumulation of toxic heat	*add* ***Herbal ABX***
	Adverse reactions on the skin from exposure to drugs, chemicals, heavy metals, environmental and airborne toxins	Toxic heat	*add* ***Herbal DTX***
	With fever, redness and burning sensation all over the body	Excess heat accumulation	*add* ***Gardenia Complex***
Sleep	Insomnia in weak or deficient patients with excessive worrying, pensiveness and poor or dream-disturbed sleep	Heart and Spleen blood deficiency	***Schisandra ZZZ***
	Insomnia with stress, anxiety, irritability, overactive mind and restlessness in patients with overall weakness and deficiency	Liver qi stagnation with deficiency	***Calm ZZZ***

Symptom / Disease Index

Conditions	Symptoms/Disease Description	TCM Diagnosis	Herbal Formulas
Sleep (*cont'd*)	Insomnia due to stress and anxiety in excess conditions	*Shen* (spirit) disturbance	***Calm (ES)***
	Hypersomnia, constant sleepiness, poor appetite, loose stools, weakness	Spleen qi deficiency	***GI Tonic***
	Generalized coldness, tinnitus, polyuria, edema	Kidney yang deficiency	***Kidney Tonic (Yang)***
Slipped Disk	Herniated disk with pain	Qi and blood stagnation	***Back Support (HD)***
	With severe pain	Severe qi and blood stagnation	*add* ***Herbal ANG***
	With shooting pain	Qi and blood stagnation	*add* ***Flex (NP)***
Sluggishness	With edema and heavy sensation in the body	Damp accumulation	***Herbal DRX***
	With poor appetite, loose stools, and edema	Spleen qi deficiency with water accumulation	***GI Tonic***
	With fatigue	Qi deficiency	***Vibrant*** or ***Imperial Tonic***
	Due to damp and phlegm accumulation	Damp and phlegm accumulation	*add* ***Pinellia Complex***
Small Intestine	*See* Diarrhea, Constipation, Enteritis, Crohn's disease		
Smoking	With wheezing, dyspnea, shortness of breath, phlegm	Lung heat with damp and phlegm	***Respitrol (Heat)*** or ***Respitrol (Deficient)***
	To eliminate storage of phlegm and sputum	Accumulation of damp and phlegm in the Lung	***Pinellia XPT***
	To stop production of phlegm and sputum	Production of damp and phlegm by the Spleen	***Pinellia Complex***
	Withdrawal symptoms associated with smoking, drugs or alcohol cessation	Toxic heat in the Liver and *shen* (spirit) disturbance	***Calm (ES)*** and ***Liver DTX***
	To restore lung health and respiratory functions	Lung deficiency	***Cordyceps 3***
Soft Tissues	Enhancing the growth of muscles, tendons, ligaments, and cartilages	Liver blood and Kidney yin deficiencies	***Flex (MLT)***
	See also specific diseases and locations		
Sore Throat	*See* Throat		
Spasm	Spasms and cramps of the skeletal or intestinal muscles	Liver yin and body fluid deficiencies	***Flex (SC)***
	Spastic colon or irritable bowel syndrome (IBS)	Liver qi stagnation	***GI Harmony***
	Menstrual spasms and cramps	Liver qi stagnation	***Mense-Ease***
Sperm Count (Low)	Infertility, generalized male sexual dysfunction	Kidney yang deficiency	***Vital Essence***
	Infertility, generalized male sexual dysfunction with chronic fatigue	Lung and Kidney deficiencies	*add* ***Cordyceps 3***
	Infertility with impotence	Kidney yang deficiency	*add* ***Vitality***
Spermatorrhea	With emaciation, fatigue, listlessness, pale complexion, shortness of breath, spontaneous sweating, poor appetite, forgetfulness	Qi, blood, yin and yang deficiencies	***Vitality*** with ***Imperial Tonic***
	Easily aroused, bitter taste in the mouth, yellow urine, low grade fever	Kidney yin deficiency	***Nourish*** with ***Balance (Heat)***
	Irritability, genital itching or feeling of dampness	Damp-heat in the lower *jiao*	***V-Support***

Symptom / Disease Index

Conditions	Symptoms/Disease Description	TCM Diagnosis	Herbal Formulas
Spider bite	Toxic reactions locally	Toxic heat	***Herbal ABX*** and ***Dermatrol (PS)***
	Toxic reactions systemically	Toxic heat	***Herbal ABX*** and ***Gardenia Complex***
Spleen	*See* Anemia, Immune system (deficiency)		
Sports Formulas	Short-term boost for energy and athletic performance	Qi deficiency	***Vibrant***
	Long-term enhancement of energy and durability	Qi, blood, yin and yang deficiencies	***Imperial Tonic***
	Sports injuries, trauma	Blood stagnation	***Flex (TMX)***
	Spasms, muscle cramps, sprains and strains	Liver yin and body fluid deficiencies	***Flex (SC)***
	Severe muscle pain	Qi and blood stagnation	***Flex (SC)*** and ***Herbal ANG***
	To strengthen the soft tissue (muscles, tendons, ligaments and cartilages)	Liver blood deficiency and Kidney *jing* (essence) deficiency	***Flex (MLT)***
	To strengthen the bones	Kidney *jing* (essence) deficiency	***Osteo 8***
Sprain and Strain	Acute muscle, tendon or ligaments sprain and strain	Qi and blood stagnation	***Flex (TMX)***
	For maintenance of healthy soft tissue (muscles, tendons, ligaments and cartilage)	Liver blood deficiency and Kidney *jing* (essence) deficiency	***Flex (MLT)***
	See also specific conditions and body parts		
Spur (Bone)	Bone spurs	Qi and blood stagnation	***Flex (SPR)***
	With severe pain	Severe qi and blood stagnation	*add* ***Herbal ANG***
	Neck and shoulder	Qi and blood stagnation in the upper *jiao*	*add* ***Neck & Shoulder (AC)***
	Low back pain	Qi and blood stagnation in the lower *jiao*	*add* ***Back Support (AC)***
	Arm pain	Qi and blood stagnation in the upper *jiao*	*add* ***Arm Support***
	Knee or ankle pain	Qi and blood stagnation in the lower *jiao*	*add* ***Knee & Ankle (AC)***
Sputum	Yellow, profuse, purulent sputum, chest congestion	Phlegm and heat in the Lung	***Pinellia XPT***
	Yellow sputum in cases of wheezing, dyspnea, cough, and fever	Lung heat	*add* ***Respitrol (Heat)***
	White sputum in cases of nasal obstruction or discharge, sneezing	Lung cold	*add* ***Respitrol (Cold)***
	Moderate to severe cases of infection and inflammation	Accumulation of toxic heat	*add* ***Herbal ABX***
	Profuse white or clear sputum with poor appetite, fatigue, loose stools	Spleen qi deficiency	***Pinellia Complex*** with ***GI Tonic***
Stiffness	*See* Neck, Shoulder, Back, Arthritis, Bone spur, Spasms		
Stomach	Heartburn, acid reflux, stomach pain, ulcers, gastritis	Stomach fire	***GI Care***
	Stomach pain due to stress	Stomach fire with Liver qi stagnation	***GI Care*** and ***Calm***

SYMPTOM / DISEASE

Symptom / Disease Index

Conditions	Symptoms/Disease Description	TCM Diagnosis	Herbal Formulas
Stomach (*cont'd*)	Stomach pain due to gallstones	Damp-heat in the Liver and Gallbladder	***Dissolve (GS)***
	Dull stomach pain with poor appetite, fatigue, and loose stools	Spleen qi deficiency	***GI Tonic***
	General stomach problem with thirst and dryness	Stomach yin deficiency	***Nourish (Fluids)***
	Severe stomach pain	Qi and blood stagnation	*add* ***Herbal ANG***
	With dark, tarry stool due to bleeding	Stomach heat	*add* ***Notoginseng 9***
	Chronic, stubborn stomach pain with manifestations of blood stagnation such as dark complexion, purplish tongue with distended sublingual veins	Blood stagnation	*add* ***Circulation (SJ)***
Stones	Kidney or urinary stones	*Shi lin* (stone dysuria)	***Dissolve (KS)***
	Gallstones	Damp-heat in the Liver and Gallbladder	***Dissolve (GS)***
	Moderate to severe cases of infection and inflammation	Accumulation of toxic heat	*add* ***Herbal ABX***
	With severe pain	Severe qi and blood stagnation	*add* ***Herbal ANG***
	With bleeding	Heat in the blood	*add* ***Notoginseng 9***
Stools	*See* Diarrhea, Constipation		
Strep Throat	*See* Throat (sore), Infection		
Stress	Moderate cases of stress, anxiety, irritability, restlessness, nervousness	Liver qi stagnation	***Calm***
	Severe cases of stress, anxiety, irritability, restlessness, nervousness	Liver fire with *shen* (spirit) disturbance	***Calm (ES)***
	Stress, anxiety, restlessness, insomnia in patients with deficiency	Liver qi stagnation with qi deficiency	***Calm ZZZ***
	With acute headache	Liver qi stagnation with qi and blood stagnation	*add* ***Corydalin (AC)***
	With chronic headache	Liver qi stagnation with qi and blood stagnation	*add* ***Corydalin (CR)***
	With stomach or duodenal ulcer	Liver overacting on the Stomach	*add* ***GI Care***
	With deficient-type hypertension	Liver qi stagnation with damp-heat	*add* ***Gastrodia Complex***
	With excess-type hypertension	Liver fire with damp-heat	*add* ***Gentiana Complex***
	With weakness of the digestive system due to stress	Spleen qi deficiency with Liver qi stagnation	*add* ***GI Tonic***
	Irritable bowel syndrome (IBS) due to stress	Liver qi stagnation	*add* ***GI Harmony***
	Ulcerative colitis (UC) or Crohn's disease due to stress	Liver qi stagnation with damp-heat accumulation	*add* ***GI Care (UC)***
	With depression	Qi, blood, phlegm stagnation	*add* ***Shine*** or ***Shine (DS)***
Stroke	Prevention of stroke in patients with increased risk due to excess-type hypertension	Liver fire rising	***Gentiana Complex***
	Prevention of stroke in patients with increased risk due to deficient-type hypertension	Liver yang rising with Liver and Kidney yin deficiencies	***Gastrodia Complex***
	Prevention of stroke in patients with increased risk due to high cholesterol levels	Phlegm and damp	***Cholisma*** or ***Cholisma (ES)***

Symptom / Disease Index

Conditions	Symptoms/Disease Description	TCM Diagnosis	Herbal Formulas
Stroke (*cont'd*)	Prevention of stroke in patients with increased risk due to coronary heart disease	Blood stagnation	***Circulation***
	Treatment of stroke complications; to be used only after hemorrhage stops	Deficiencies of Kidney yin, yang and *jing* (essence) with qi and blood stagnation	***Neuro Plus***
	Treatment of stroke complications; facial paralysis	Qi and blood stagnation	***Symmetry***
Subluxation	Neck, cervical vertebrae	Qi and blood stagnation	***Neck & Shoulder (AC)***
	Low back, lumbar vertebrae	Qi and blood stagnation	***Back Support (AC)***
	Herniated disk	Qi and blood stagnation	***Back Support (HD)***
	With severe pain	Severe qi and blood stagnation	*add* ***Herbal ANG***
	With shooting pain	Severe qi and blood stagnation	*add* ***Flex (NP)***
Sugar	*See* Diabetes mellitus, Hypoglycemia		
Surgery, recovery from	Enhances post-surgical recovery, reduces adhesions	Qi and blood stagnation	***Flex (TMX)***
	With severe pain during post-surgical recovery	Severe qi and blood stagnation	*add* ***Herbal ANG***
	With post-surgical weakness	Qi, blood, yin and yang deficiencies	*add* ***Imperial Tonic***
	Enhances bone growth	Kidney *jing* (essence) deficiencies	*add* ***Osteo 8***
	Enhances soft tissue growth (muscles, tendons, ligaments, cartilage)	Liver blood and Kidney *jing* (essence) deficiencies	*add* ***Flex (MLT)***
	Post-surgical constipation	Qi and blood stagnation	*add* ***Gentle Lax (Deficient)***
Sweating	Night sweating, irritability, hot flashes	Yin deficiency with deficiency heat	***Balance (Heat)***
	Spontaneous sweating with impaired immune system	*Wei* (defensive) *qi* deficiency	***Immune +***
	Sweating due to hyperthyroidism	Qi and phlegm stagnation	***Thyrodex***
	Profuse sweating due to excess heat, red face, possible constipation, rapid heart rate, high blood pressure	Excess heat	***Gardenia Complex***
	With thirst, dryness	Stomach and Lung yin deficiencies	***Nourish (Fluids)***
Swelling	Swelling with pain and inflammation	Damp-heat accumulation	***Resolve (AI)***
	Moderate to severe infection	Toxic heat accumulation	*add* ***Herbal ABX***
	With severe pain	Severe qi and blood stagnation	*add* ***Herbal ANG***
	With severe inflammation	Heat accumulation	*add* ***Astringent Complex***
	Swelling with edema	Water accumulation	***Herbal DRX***
	Edema of the lower body with coldness	Kidney yang deficiency	***Kidney Tonic (Yang)***
	Swelling and inflammation of the upper body with heat sensation and redness	Toxic heat invasion	***Herbal ENT***
Swimmer's Ear	Infection with pain	Toxic heat invasion	***Herbal ENT***
	With severe pain	Severe qi and blood stagnation with toxic heat	*add* ***Herbal ANG***

Symptom / Disease Index

Conditions	Symptoms/Disease Description	TCM Diagnosis	Herbal Formulas
Systemic Lupus Erythematosus (SLE)	Lupus with inflammation in joints, tendons, and other connective tissues and organs	Toxic heat accumulation with yin deficiency	***LPS Support***
	With hyperactive immunity in an autoimmune condition	Heat	***Gardenia Complex***
Tachycardia	*See* Palpitation		
***Tan Yin* (Phlegm Retention)**	Generalized damp/phlegm in the body	Damp/phlegm accumulation with Spleen qi deficiency	***Pinellia Complex***
	Yellow phlegm and sputum in the chest	Phlegm and damp retention in the chest	***Pinellia XPT***
	Swelling with edema	Phlegm, damp and water retention	***Herbal DRX***
Taste	Bitter taste, short temper, headache, hypochondriac pain, possible sticky sensation in the mouth	Liver fire	***Gentiana Complex*** or ***Liver DTX***
	Above symptoms with constipation	Excess heat with stagnation	add ***Gentle Lax (Excess)***
	Sweet taste, fatigue, poor appetite, epigastric distension, irregular bowel movements, possible stickiness sensation in the mouth	Spleen qi deficiency	***GI Tonic***
	Sour taste	Qi, blood, phlegm and food stagnation	***Shine*** or ***Shine (DS)***
Tearing	Excessive tearing in the eyes	Liver fire with Kidney yin deficiency	***Lycium Support***
Teeth Grinding	See Bruxism		
Tendon	Enhancing the growth of muscles, tendons, ligaments, and cartilages	Liver blood and Kidney yin deficiencies	***Flex (MLT)***
Tendonitis	*See* Neck, Shoulder, Arm, Wrist, Elbow, Ankle, Knee, Back		
Tenesmus	Due to food poisoning or traveler's diarrhea	Damp-heat in the Intestines	***GI Care II***
	With feeling of incomplete evacuation, hypochondriac pain, bloating, pain which lessens with defecation	Liver qi stagnation	***Calm*** and ***GI Harmony***
	With pain, feeling of rectal prolapse, fatigue	Spleen qi deficiency	***GI Tonic***
Tension	Stress, irritability, anxiety	Liver qi stagnation	***Calm***
	Severe restlessness with insomnia, redness of the face, anger	Liver fire	***Calm (ES)***
	See also Stress, Anxiety, Insomnia		
Tension Headache	Acute headache	Qi and blood stagnation	***Corydalin (AC)***
	Headache with stress and anxiety	Liver qi stagnation	add ***Calm***
	Headache with excessive emotional distress, insomnia	Liver qi stagnation with *shen* (spirit) disturbance	add ***Calm (ES)***
	With severe pain	Severe qi and blood stagnation	add ***Herbal ANG***
	Chronic headache with possible previous head injuries manifesting in dark complexion, purplish tongue, and distended sublingual veins	Blood stagnation	add ***Circulation (SJ)***
	Maintenance formula for chronic pain or in cases of deficient-type headaches with dull and hollow pain	Blood deficiency	***Corydalin (CR)***
	See also Headache		

Symptom / Disease Index

Conditions	Symptoms/Disease Description	TCM Diagnosis	Herbal Formulas
Terminal Cancer	Terminal, end-stage cancer patients with extreme weakness	*Yuan* (source) *qi* deficiency	***CA Support***
	See also Cancer / Carcinoma		
Terminal Dribbling	Urinary symptoms, painful urination that is dark in color due to benign prostatic hypertrophy and heat	Damp-heat in the lower *jiao*	***P-Support***
	With polyuria, coldness and frequent urinary urges at night and coldness	Kidney yang deficiency	***Kidney Tonic (Yang)***
Testicles	*See* Impotence, Premature Ejaculation, Infection		
Testosterone	Impotence due to lack of testosterone	Kidney yang deficiency	***Vitality***
Thirst	General thirst and dryness	Lung and Stomach yin deficiency	***Nourish (Fluids)***
	Increased desire and intake of water in diabetic mellitus	Lung yin deficiency with heat	***Equilibrium***
Thoracic Pain	Pain in the chest, ribs, thoracic area	Qi and blood stagnation	***Neck & Shoulder (AC)***
	For severe pain	Severe qi and blood stagnation	*add* ***Herbal ANG***
	For stabbing pain with previous trauma history, purplish tongue, dark distended sublingual vein, dark complexion	Blood stagnation	*add* ***Circulation (SJ)***
Throat (Sore)	Redness and swelling of the throat from common cold or influenza	Wind-heat invasion	***Lonicera Complex***
	Moderate to severe cases of infection and inflammation	Accumulation of toxic heat	***Herbal ENT***
	With swollen tonsils	Toxic heat accumulation	*add* ***Resolve (AI)***
	With fever	Excess heat accumulation	*add* ***Gardenia Complex***
	With yellow or greenish phlegm	Toxic heat with phlegm accumulation	*add* ***Pinellia XPT***
	From bacterial infection	Toxic heat	*add* ***Herbal ABX***
	From viral infection	Toxic heat	*add* ***Herbal AVR***
Thrombo-cytopenia	Decrease in number of blood platelets	Blood deficiency	***Schisandra ZZZ*** or ***Imperial Tonic***
Thrombosis	Obstruction in the vessels	Blood stagnation	***Circulation*** or ***Flex (TMX)***
Throwing Up	*See* Vomiting, Nausea		
Thyroid Gland	Hyperthyroidism	Liver fire rising	***Thyrodex***
	Hypothyroidism	Kidney, Heart, and Spleen yang deficiencies	***Thyro-forte***
	Thyroid nodules	Phlegm accumulation	***Resolve (AI)***
Tidal Fever	Afternoon fever with sweating, irritability	Yin deficiency with heat	***Balance (Heat)***
	With thirst, dryness	Yin deficiency	*add* ***Nourish (Fluids)***
	See also Fever		

Symptom / Disease Index

Conditions	Symptoms/Disease Description	TCM Diagnosis	Herbal Formulas
Tinnitus	Dizziness and vertigo in hypertensive patients	Liver yin deficiency with Liver yang rising	***Gastrodia Complex***
	Dizziness, night sweats, and generalized weakness	Liver and Kidney yin deficiencies	***Nourish***
	Due to compromised kidney and ear functions	Kidney deficiency	***Cordyceps 3***
	Due to exposure to drugs, chemical, and other toxins	Toxic heat	***Kidney DTX***
	General Kidney yin deficiency signs such as blurry vision, weakness of the back and knees, tinnitus, dryness, flushed cheeks, possible low-grade fever	Kidney yin deficiency	***Kidney Tonic (Yin)***
TMJ	Temporomandibular joint pain	Wind attack with qi and blood stagnation	***Symmetry***
Tonsillitis	Sore throat with redness and swelling	Wind-heat invasion	***Lonicera Complex*** or ***Herbal ENT***
	Moderate to severe cases of infection and inflammation	Accumulation of toxic heat	*add* ***Herbal ABX***
	With severe pain and swelling	Toxic heat with phlegm stagnation	*add* ***Astringent Complex***
Toothache	With swelling and pain, worsens with intake of spicy food and lessens with coldness	Wind-heat invasion	***Gardenia Complex***
	Pain with stomach ulcer	Stomach heat	***GI Care***
	Toothache especially at the root, dry throat, palpitation, dizziness, irritability, insomnia	Kidney yin deficiency	***Nourish*** or ***Balance (Heat)***
	With bleeding	Heat forcing blood out of the vessels	*add* ***Notoginseng 9***
Toxins	Adverse reactions from exposure to drugs, chemicals, heavy metals, environmental and airborne toxins	Toxic heat	***Herbal DTX***
	Compromised liver function due to exposure to toxins	Toxic heat in the Liver	*add* ***Liver DTX***
	Compromised kidney function due to exposure to toxins	Toxic heat in the Kidney	*add* ***Kidney DTX***
	Toxins in the intestines/colon	Toxic heat	*add* ***GI DTX***
	Headache from exposure to toxic substances	Toxic heat with qi and blood stagnation	*add* ***Corydalin (AC)***
	Respiratory symptoms from exposure to toxic substances	Toxic heat in the Lung	*add* ***Respitrol (Heat)***
	Dermatological reactions from exposure to toxic substances	Toxic heat in the exterior	*add* ***Silerex***
	For chronic exposure to toxins with blood stagnation signs of dark complexion, purplish tongue and distended sublingual veins	Blood stagnation	*add* ***Circulation (SJ)***
	Toxins manifesting on the skin as dry lesions	Dry/toxic heat accumulation	*add* ***Dermatrol (Dry)***
	Toxins manifesting on the skin as wet lesions	Damp and toxic heat accumulation	*add* ***Dermatrol (Damp)***
	To strengthen the immune system to guard against toxic invasion	*Wei* (defensive) *qi* deficiency	***Immune +***
Traumatic Injuries	With severe pain, inflammation, bruises, broken bones	Blood stagnation	***Flex (TMX)***
	Moderate to severe cases of infection and inflammation	Accumulation of toxic heat	*add* ***Herbal ABX***

Symptom / Disease Index

Conditions	Symptoms/Disease Description	TCM Diagnosis	Herbal Formulas
Traumatic Injuries *(cont'd)*	With severe pain	Severe qi and blood stagnation	*add* ***Herbal ANG***
	Chronic, old injury with recurrent pain	Chronic blood stagnation	*add* ***Circulation (SJ)***
	Injury to the head	Qi and blood stagnation	*add* ***Corydalin (AC)***
	Injury to the neck and shoulder area	Qi and blood stagnation	*add* ***Neck & Shoulder (AC)***
	Injury to the arm	Qi and blood stagnation	*add* ***Arm Support***
	Injury to the back	Qi and blood stagnation	*add* ***Back Support (AC)***
	Herniated disk	Qi and blood stagnation	*add* ***Back Support (HD)***
	Injury to the knees or ankles	Qi and blood stagnation	*add* ***Knee & Ankle (AC)***
	To facilitate recovery following traumatic injuries to the bones	Kidney yin and *jing* (essence) deficiencies	***Osteo 8***
	To enhance recovery of connective tissue (muscles, tendons, ligaments, cartilage)	Liver blood and Kidney yin deficiencies	***Flex (MLT)***
Traveler's Diarrhea	Diarrhea with foul-smelling stools, burning sensation of anus, abdominal discomfort and pain, nausea and vomiting	Damp-heat in the Intestines	***GI Care II***
	Moderate to severe cases of infection and inflammation	Accumulation of toxic heat	*add* ***Herbal ABX***
	For severe pain	Qi and blood stagnation and toxic heat	*add* ***Herbal ANG***
	With bleeding	Toxic heat	*add* ***Notoginseng 9***
	See also Diarrhea		
Trichomoniasis	Infection in the genital region	Damp-heat in the lower *jiao* and Liver channel	***V-Support***
	Moderate to severe cases of infection and inflammation	Accumulation of toxic heat	*add* ***Herbal ABX***
Trigeminal Neuralgia	Facial nerve pain	Wind attack with qi and blood stagnation	***Symmetry***
	Severe pain	Severe qi and blood stagnation	*add* ***Flex (NP)*** or ***Herbal ANG***
Triglycerides	*See* Cholesterol/triglycerides		
Tuberculosis	Dry cough with scanty sputum, dyspnea	Yin and qi deficiencies of the Lung	***Respitrol (Deficient)***
	Cough, yellow-greenish sputum, dyspnea	Phlegm and heat in the Lung	*add* ***Pinellia XPT***
	Moderate to severe cases of infection and inflammation	Accumulation of toxic heat	*add* ***Herbal ABX***
Tumor	*See* Cancer / Carcinoma		
Twitching	Of the face, dizziness, tinnitus, short temper	Liver yang rising	***Gastrodia Complex*** and ***Flex (SC)***
	Of the face, intermittent in nature, dizziness, wiry, possible stiffness and cramping of other parts of the body	Liver blood deficiency	***Symmetry***

Symptom / Disease Index

Conditions	Symptoms/Disease Description	TCM Diagnosis	Herbal Formulas
Twitching (*cont'd*)	With underlying damp/phlegm accumulation	Damp accumulation with Spleen qi deficiency	***Pinellia Complex***
Type "A" Personality	Excessive competitive drive, impatience, overactive mind, stressed but with deficient constitution	Liver qi stagnation with qi deficiency	***Calm ZZZ***
	All the above symptoms but excess in body constitution also manifesting in possible red face, eyes, constipation, high blood pressure, fast heart rate	Liver and Heart fire	***Calm (ES)***
Ulcerative Colitis (UC)	With mucus, pus and blood in the stools with feeling of incomplete evacuation and abdominal cramps	Damp-heat in the Intestines	***GI Care (UC)***
	Due to stress	Stomach heat with Liver qi stagnation	*add **Calm***
	With bleeding	Stomach heat	*add **Notoginseng 9***
Ulcers, Gastric and Duodenal	Gastric and duodenal ulcers	Stomach heat with yin deficiency	***GI Care***
	Due to stress	Stomach heat with Liver qi stagnation	*add **Calm***
	With bleeding	Stomach heat	*add **Notoginseng 9***
	With severe pain	Severe qi and blood stagnation	*add **Herbal ANG***
	Moderate to severe cases of infection and inflammation	Accumulation of toxic heat	*add **Herbal ABX***
	With dry mouth and thirst	Stomach yin deficiency	*add **Nourish (Fluids)***
	See also Skin for ulcers and lesions on the skin		
Upper Respiratory Infection	Initial stage of infection with slight sore throat, feverish sensation, cough, yellow phlegm	Wind-heat invasion	***Lonicera Complex***
	Severe sore throat, ear infection and yellow nasal discharge	Toxic heat	***Herbal ENT***
	Fever, cough, dyspnea	Lung heat	***Respitrol (Heat)***
	Sneezing, white or clear nasal discharge	Wind-cold invasion	***Respitrol (Cold)***
	Cough	Lung qi reversal	***Respitrol (CF)***
	For bacterial infection	Toxic heat	*add **Herbal ABX***
	For viral infection	Toxic heat	*add **Herbal AVR***
	With severe inflammation	Excess heat	*add **Astringent Complex***
Urinary Stone	Kidney or urinary stones	*Shi lin* (stone dysuria)	***Dissolve (KS)***
	Moderate to severe cases of infection and inflammation	Accumulation of toxic heat	*add **V-Support***
	With severe pain	Severe qi and blood stagnation	*add **Herbal ANG***
	With bleeding	Heat pushing blood out of the vessels	*add **Notoginseng 9***
Urinary Tract Infection (UTI)	Painful and difficult urination with itching and discharge	Damp-heat in the lower *jiao*	***Gentiana Complex*** or ***V-Support***
	With severe pain	Severe qi and blood stagnation	*add **Herbal ANG***
	With bleeding	Heat pushing blood out of the vessels	*add **Notoginseng 9***
	With fever	Excess heat accumulation	*add **Gardenia Complex***

Symptom / Disease Index

Conditions	Symptoms/Disease Description	TCM Diagnosis	Herbal Formulas
Urinary Tract Infection (UTI) (*cont'd*)	Frequent recurrences of urinary tract infection due to diabetes mellitus	Damp-heat in the lower *jiao* with yin deficiency	*add* ***Equilibrium***
	For bacterial infection	Toxic heat	*add* ***Herbal ABX***
	For viral infection	Toxic heat	*add* ***Herbal AVR***
	Recurrent infection with yin-deficient heat signs of thirst, dryness, flushed cheeks, low-grade fever	Yin-deficient heat	***Nourish***
Urination (Frequent)	Frequent urinary urges, especially at night, coldness, clear urination	Kidney yang deficiency	***Kidney Tonic (Yang)***
	Due to prostate enlargement	Damp-heat in the lower *jiao*	***P-Support***
	In diabetic patients	Kidney yang deficiency	***Equilibrium***
	Chronic nephritis or nephritic syndrome	Toxic heat in the Kidney	***Kidney DTX***
	Frequent urination with burning sensations, cystitis, urinary tract infection (UTI)	Damp-heat in the lower *jiao*	***V-Support***
	Moderate to severe cases of infection and inflammation	Accumulation of toxic heat	*add* ***Herbal ABX***
	Interstitial cystitis	Blood stagnation	*add* ***Resolve (Lower)***
Urination (Incontinent)	With coldness, weakness and soreness of the lower back and knees, clear urination	Kidney yang deficiency	***Kidney Tonic (Yang)***
Urine	Clear, profuse, frequent urges especially at night, coldness	Kidney yang deficiency	***Kidney Tonic (Yang)***
	Dark, yellow, painful urination	Damp-heat in the lower *jiao*	***V-Support***
	High urine ketone level or high blood glucose level	Deficient fire with damp accumulation	***Equilibrium***
Urolithiasis	Kidney or urinary stones	*Shi lin* (stone dysuria)	***Dissolve (KS)***
	Moderate to severe cases of infection and inflammation	Accumulation of toxic heat	*add* ***V-Support***
	With severe pain	Severe qi and blood stagnation	*add* ***Herbal ANG***
	With bleeding	Heat pushing blood out of the vessels	*add* ***Notoginseng 9***
Urticaria	Rash, itching of the body	Wind-heat at the skin level, heat in the blood	***Silerex***
	Rash of the lower body and genital region	Damp-heat in the lower *jiao*	***Gentiana Complex***
	Dry lesions	Wind toxin	***Dermatrol (Dry)***
	Wet lesions	Damp-heat toxin	***Dermatrol (Damp)***
	Severe heat with red tongue, fever	Excess heat	*add* ***Gardenia Complex***
	Due to accumulation of toxins and allergens	Toxic heat	*add* ***Herbal DTX, Liver DTX*** and/or ***Kidney DTX***
Uterus	*See* Fibrocystic disease, Infertility, Menopausal syndrome, Dysmenorrhea, Endometriosis, Pelvic inflammatory disease, Menstruation		

Symptom / Disease Index

Conditions	Symptoms/Disease Description	TCM Diagnosis	Herbal Formulas
Vaginitis	Foul smelling, yellow discharge, pelvic pain, itching due to infection	Damp-heat in the lower *jiao*	***V-Support***
	Due to complications of diabetes mellitus	Damp-heat in the lower *jiao* with yin deficiency	*add* ***Equilibrium***
	Moderate to severe cases of infection and inflammation	Accumulation of toxic heat	*add* ***Herbal ABX***
	With lower abdominal pain	Qi and blood stagnation	*add* ***Herbal ANG***
	For bacterial infection	Toxic heat	*add* ***Herbal ABX***
	For viral infection	Toxic heat	*add* ***Herbal AVR***
Vaginitis, Atrophic	Vaginal dryness or atrophy with painful intercourse due to hormonal irregularity, estrogen deficiency or menopause	Kidney yin deficiency	***Balance Spring***
Varicocele	Causing male infertility	Blood stagnation	***Resolve (Lower)***
Varicose Veins	Distended purplish black veins mostly on the legs	Blood stagnation	***Circulation (SJ)***
	With water retention	Blood stagnation with water accumulation	*add* ***Herbal DRX***
Vein	Distended sublingual vein	Blood stagnation	***Circulation (SJ)***
Venereal Diseases	*See* Sexually transmitted disease (STD)		
Vertigo	With headache, flushed face, and anger	Liver fire rising	***Gentiana Complex***
	With or without nausea and vomiting and yin deficiency	Liver yin deficiency with Liver wind rising	***Gastrodia Complex***
	With underlying dampness/phlegm and Spleen qi deficiency	Damp/phlegm accumulation with Spleen qi deficiency	*add* ***Pinellia Complex***
Vision	Dry, blurry vision, reduced acuity	Kidney deficiency with false heat	***Lycium Support***
	Vision impairment due to diabetes mellitus	Yin deficiency	*add* ***Equilibrium***
	Blurry vision due to deficient-type hypertension	Liver yin deficiency with Liver yang rising	*add* ***Gastrodia Complex***
	Blurry vision due to excess-type hypertension	Liver fire	*add* ***Gentiana Complex***
Voice	Hoarseness due to a common cold/flu with itching, painful throat	Wind-heat invasion	***Lonicera Complex***
	Hoarseness due to overuse, dry throat, scanty sputum	Yin deficiency	***Nourish (Fluids)***
Vomiting	Nausea and vomiting due to chemotherapy	Stomach yin deficiency	***C/R Support***
	Nausea, vomiting, abdominal pain and diarrhea due to food poisoning	Damp-heat in the Intestines	***GI Care II***
	Nausea, vomiting, epigastric, chest and hypochondriac distension and pain, due to stress	Liver qi stagnation	***Calm***
	With dryness and thirst	Stomach yin deficiency	***Nourish (Fluids)***
	From exposure to toxic materials	Toxic heat invasion	***Liver DTX*** with ***Herbal DTX***
	Caused by gallstones	Damp-heat in the Liver and Gallbladder	***Dissolve (GS)***
Vulvitis	Inflammation of the vulva	Damp-heat in the lower *jiao*	***V-Support***
	Moderate to severe cases of infection and inflammation	Accumulation of toxic heat	*add* ***Herbal ABX***
	Severe itching	Toxic heat	*add* ***Silerex***

Symptom / Disease Index

Conditions	Symptoms/Disease Description	TCM Diagnosis	Herbal Formulas
Vulvovaginitis	Vaginal dryness or atrophy	Kidney yin deficiency	***Balance Spring***
Wasting Syndrome	Due to cancer with chemotherapy and radiation treatments	*Yuan* (source) *qi* and yin deficiencies	***C/R Support***
	End-stage cancer	*Yuan* (source) *qi* deficiency	***CA Support***
	Weight loss, decreased energy, overall weakness	Qi, blood, yin and yang deficiencies	***Imperial Tonic***
	Digestive weakness, loose stools, fatigue	Spleen qi deficiency	***GI Tonic***
	Degeneration of soft tissue (muscles, ligaments, tendons, cartilage)	Liver blood and Kidney *jing* (essence) deficiencies	***Flex (MLT)***
	Degeneration of bones	Kidney *jing* (essence) deficiency	***Osteo 8***
	Due to immune deficiency	*Wei* (defensive) *qi* deficiency	***Immune +***
Water Retention	*See* Edema		
Weak Muscle	*See* Muscle		
Weakness	For immediate boost of energy	Qi deficiency	***Vibrant***
	Decreased energy, overall weakness of constitution	Qi, yin, yang and blood deficiencies	***Imperial Tonic***
	Poor appetite, loose stools	Spleen qi deficiency	***GI Tonic***
	Respiratory and reproductive weakness	Lung and Kidney deficiencies	***Cordyceps 3***
	Anemia, restless sleep, pale complexion	Blood deficiency	***Schisandra ZZZ***
	Adrenal insufficiency in patients who are "burned-out" with decreased mental and physical functions	Kidney deficiency	***Adrenal +***
	Weakness of the immune system	*Wei* (defensive) *qi* deficiency	***Immune +***
	End stage cancer patients who cannot receive chemotherapy or radiation	*Yuan* (source) *qi* deficiency	***CA Support***
	Weakness in cancer patients receiving chemotherapy or radiation	*Yuan* (source) *qi* deficiency	***C/R Support***
	Weakness of the bones	Kidney *jing* (essence) deficiency	***Osteo 8***
	Degeneration of soft tissue (muscles, ligaments, tendons, cartilage)	Liver blood and Kidney *jing* (essence) deficiencies	***Flex (MLT)***
	Weakness of the back and knees	Kidney deficiency	***Back Support (CR)***
	Weakness of the legs, knees, and ankles	Kidney deficiency	***Knee & Ankle (CR)***
	Weakness of the neck and shoulders	Liver blood deficiency	***Neck & Shoulder (CR)***
	General Kidney yin deficiency signs such as blurry vision, weakness of the back and knees, tinnitus, dryness, flushed cheeks, and low-grade fever	Kidney yin deficiency	***Kidney Tonic (Yin)***
	General Kidney yang deficiency signs such as coldness, low libido, premature ejaculation, weakness and soreness of the back and knees, pale complexion, and polyuria	Kidney yang deficiency	***Kidney Tonic (Yang)***
Weight Control	*See* Obesity		
Wheezing	*See* Asthma		
Whiplash	*See* Neck pain		

Symptom / Disease Index

Conditions	Symptoms/Disease Description	TCM Diagnosis	Herbal Formulas
White Blood Cells	Low white blood cells count in immunocompromised patients	Qi deficiency	***Immune +***
	Low white blood cells count in patients with compromised respiratory and reproductive functions	Lung and Kidney qi deficiencies	***Cordyceps 3***
Withdrawal	*See* Addiction		
Wrist	Wrist pain	Qi and blood stagnation	***Arm Support***
	Degeneration of soft tissue (muscles, ligaments, tendons, cartilage)	Liver blood & Kidney *jing* (essence) deficiencies	*add* **Flex (MLT)**
	With severe pain	Severe qi and blood stagnation	*add* **Herbal ANG**
	Acute trauma/injury	Qi and blood stagnation	*add* **Flex (TMX)**
Worrying	With insomnia, weakness, poor appetite	Spleen and Heart deficiency	***Schisandra ZZZ***
Yawning	Short-term fatigue and lack of energy	Qi deficiency	***Vibrant***
	Overall weakness of the constitution	Qi, blood, yin and yang deficiencies	***Imperial Tonic***
	Fatigue, coldness, decreased dietary intake, loose stools, frequent urinary urges especially at night, decreased libido	Kidney yang deficiency	***Vitality***
	With listlessness, stifling sensation in the chest, sighing, abdominal distension, plum-pit sensation, emotional instability	Liver qi stagnation	***Calm***
	With chest congestion and stabbing pain in a fixed location, palpitation, shortness of breath, dizziness, intermittent pulse	Chest *bi zheng* (painful obstruction syndrome)	***Circulation***
	Lack of exercise, sedentary lifestyle, poor blood flow and metabolism	Blood stasis	***Circulation (SJ)***
Yeast Infection (Vaginal)	Itching and pain in the genital region	Damp-heat in the lower *jiao*	***Gentiana Complex*** or ***V-Support***
	Frequent yeast infection due to complications of diabetes mellitus	Damp-heat in the lower *jiao* with yin deficiency	*add* **Equilibrium**
	Moderate to severe cases of infection and inflammation	Accumulation of toxic heat	*add* **Herbal ABX**
	With damp and phlegm accumulation	Spleen qi deficiency with dampness	*add* **Pinellia Complex**

Section 3

Laboratory Tests Index

檢驗報告索引

Introduction

Medical laboratory testing is an important part of medicine today. It plays a crucial role in the detection, diagnosis, and treatment of disease in patients. It is estimated that 60 to 70% of all decisions regarding a patient's diagnosis and treatment, hospital admission, and discharge are based on laboratory test results.

There are two common categories of medical tests. Screening tests are used to detect disease when there are little or no signs and symptoms of the disease present. Diagnostic tests are used when a disease is suspected, to confirm or rule out the diagnosis. **In this index, these tests are organized into three tables: Blood Tests, Urine Tests, and Stool Tests.**

Despite advancements in technology, it is extremely important to remember that no test is completely accurate. It is not uncommon to have results that are either false-positives or false-negatives. A false-positive result is one that is incorrectly abnormal in a person who does not have the disease. A false-negative result is one that is incorrectly normal in a person who has the disease. Therefore, it is extremely important to remember that we are treating a "person" and not a "lab value," and that decisions should always be made based on the totality of all data (i.e., symptoms, signs, tongue, pulse, and all others), and never just on lab test alone, especially in light of false-positive or false-negative results.

The reference range refers to a range of numbers that encompass 95% of healthy people in the population. Reference values should be used as guidelines only, as they vary due to many factors, such as demographics of the healthy population, specific methods and/or instruments used to measure the specimens, and variations among the laboratories. Therefore, the test results should be interpreted based on the reference range of the laboratory that actually performed the tests.

This index is written by Dr. Matt Van Benschoten. Additional information on Laboratory Test Results and Chinese Herbal Medicine is available as an online course by Dr. Van Benschoten at www.elotus.org.

This section provides valuable information for practitioners who use laboratory tests to assist in diagnosis and treatment. The index offers a guideline on lab tests, reference range, possible diagnosis, and suggested herbal formulas. However, it is important to note that laboratory results do not equate to diagnosis, as one result may indicate multiple possible diagnoses. Furthermore, one diagnosis does not equate to one herbal formula, as any one disease may have significantly different clinical manifestations and may need to be treated differently. Informed professional judgment and careful evaluation must be exercised prior to recommending any herbal formulas to patients.

Blood Tests

Tests	Reference Range	Result	Possible Diagnosis	Herbal Formulas
Albumin	3.5–5.5 g/dL	Low	due to liver disorders	***Liver DTX***
			due to kidney disorders	***Kidney DTX***
			due to inflammation	***Gardenia Complex*** or ***Astringent Complex***
			due to acute, severe diarrhea	***GI Care II***
			due to chronic, mild diarrhea	***GI Tonic***
Alkaline phosphatase (ALP)	36–92 U/L	Elevated	due to liver disorders, if GGTP is also elevated	***Liver DTX***
			due to gallstones	***Dissolve (GS)***
			Bone disorders with increased frequency of fractures, if GGTP is normal or low	***Osteo 8***
Aminotransferase, alanine (ALT) [formerly SGOT]	0–35 U/L	Elevated	due to liver disorders	***Liver DTX***
			due to liver disorders such as fatty liver	*add* ***Cholisma (ES)***
			due to liver disorders with cholecystitis or cholelithiasis	*add* ***Dissolve (KS)***
Aminotransferase, aspartate (AST) [formerly SGPT]	0–35 U/L	Elevated	due to liver disorders	***Liver DTX***
			due to liver disorders such as fatty liver	*add* ***Cholisma (ES)***
			due to liver disorders with cholecystitis or cholelithiasis	*add* ***Dissolve (KS)***
Antinuclear antibodies (ANA)	≤ 1.0 units	Positive	due to autoimmune disease	***Gardenia Complex***
			due to Lupus	***LPS Support***
			with atrophy and damage of tissues and organs	***Nourish*** or ***Nourish (Fluids)***
			with blood stasis	***Circulation (SJ)*** or ***Flex (NP)***
Basophils	0-2%	High	due to allergy of the nose	***Magnolia Clear Sinus*** or ***Pueraria Clear Sinus***
			due to allergy of the skin	***Silerex***
Bicarbonate (carbon dioxide)	23–28 mEq/L	Elevated	due to lung disorders	***Respitrol (Heat)***, ***(Cold)*** or ***(Deficient)***
			due to adrenal insufficiency	***Adrenal +***
			due to acute, severe diarrhea	***GI Care II***
			due to chronic, mild diarrhea	***GI Tonic***
			due to kidney disorders	***Kidney DTX***
Bilirubin	0–0.3 mg/dL (direct) 0.3–1.2 mg/dL (total)	Elevated	due to liver disorders (cirrhosis, viral hepatitis)	***Liver DTX***
			due to liver disorders (gallstones)	***Liver DTX*** and ***Dissolve (GS)***
BUN			*see* Urea nitrogen	
Calcium	9–10.5 mg/dL	High	due to hyperparathyroidism from tumor or low vitamin D levels	***Corydalin (AC)***
			due to kidney disorders	***Kidney DTX***
			due to cancer	***CA Support***
		Low	due to low blood protein levels	***Imperial Tonic***
			with increased risk of osteoporosis	***Osteo 8***

Blood Tests

Tests	Reference Range	Result	Possible Diagnosis	Herbal Formulas
CD4+ T-cell count	640–1175/μL	Low	low T-cell count	***Immune +***
CD8+ T-cell count	335–875/μL	Low	low T-cell count	***Immune +***
Chloride	98–106 mEq/L	High	due to anemia	***Imperial Tonic***
			due to dehydration from diarrhea	***GI Tonic*** or ***GI Care II***
			due to kidney disorders	***Kidney DTX***
		Low	Occurs with any disorder that causes low blood sodium	*see* Sodium
			due to adrenal insufficiency	***Adrenal +***
			due to chronic lung disorders (i.e., emphysema)	***Respitrol (Deficient)*** or ***Cordyceps 3***
			due to acute, severe diarrhea	***GI Care II***
			due to chronic, mild diarrhea	***GI Tonic***
			due to ulcerative colitis	***GI Care (UC)***
			due to fever	***Gardenia Complex***
Cholesterol	Total: 150–199 mg/dL	>200 mg/dL	Hyperlipidemia	***Cholisma*** or ***Cholisma (ES)***
			Hyperlipidemia with increased risk of heart disease	*add* ***Circulation***
			Hyperlipidemia with kidney disorders	*add* ***Kidney DTX***
			Hyperlipidemia with diabetes	*add* ***Equilibrium***
			Hyperlipidemia with obesity	*add* ***Herbalite***
			Hyperlipidemia with hypertension	*add* ***Gastrodia Complex*** or ***Gentiana Complex***
		Low	due to liver disorders	***Liver DTX***
			due to hyperthyroidism	***Thyrodex***
			due to anemia	***Imperial Tonic***
			due to stress	***Calm*** or ***Calm (ES)***
	HDL: ≥ 40 mg/dL	<40 mg/dL	Dyslipidemia	***Cholisma*** or ***Cholisma (ES)***
			Dyslipidemia with increased risk of heart disease	*add* ***Circulation***
	LDL: ≤ 130 mg/dL	>130 mg/dL	Hyperlipidemia	***Cholisma*** or ***Cholisma (ES)***
			Hyperlipidemia with increased risk of heart disease	*add* ***Circulation***
Complete blood cell count (CBC)			*see* individual tests	
C-reactive protein (CRP)	< 0.5 mg/dL	>2.4 mg/dL	significantly higher risk of coronary event	***Circulation***
Creatine kinase (CK or CPK)	30–170 U/L	High	due to acute heart attack	n/a
			due to muscular dystrophy	***Flex (MLT)***
			due to trauma	***Flex (TMX)***
			due to chronic alcoholism	***Liver DTX***

Blood Tests

Tests	Reference Range	Result	Possible Diagnosis	Herbal Formulas
Creatinine	0.7–1.3 mg/dL	Elevated	due to kidney damage	***Kidney DTX***
			due to kidney damage from kidney stones	*add* ***Dissolve (KS)***
Electrolytes			*see* individual tests	
Eosinophils	0-7%	Low	due to bacterial infection	***Herbal ABX***
		High	due to allergy of the nose	***Magnolia Clear Sinus*** or ***Pueraria Clear Sinus***
			due to allergy of the skin	***Silerex***
Erythrocyte sedimentation rate (ESR)	0–20 mm/h (female) 0–15 mm/h (male)	High	Red blood cell (RBC) aggregation [blood stasis]	***Circulation (SJ)***
			RBC aggregation due to infection	*add* ***Herbal ABX*** or ***Herbal AVR***
			RBC aggregation due to inflammation	*add* ***Gardenia Complex*** or ***Astringent Complex***
			RBC aggregation due to arthritis	*add* a ***Flex*** formula
			RBC aggregation due to nephritis	*add* ***Kidney DTX***
			RBC aggregation due to autoimmune disease	*add* ***Gardenia Complex*** or ***LPS Support***
			RBC aggregation due to inflammatory bowel disease	*add* ***GI Harmony*** or ***GI Care (UC)***
			RBC aggregation due to anemia	*add* ***Imperial Tonic***
			RBC aggregation due to heavy metal poisoning	*add* ***Herbal DTX***
		Low	Inhibited RBC sedimentation due to polycythemia, leukocytosis, sickle cell anemia	Formula varies depending on TCM diagnosis
Ferritin	15–200 µg/L	High	High ferritin due to infection	***Herbal ABX*** or ***Herbal AVR***
			High ferritin due to inflammation	***Gardenia Complex*** or ***Astringent Complex***
			High ferritin due to arthritis	***Flex (Heat)***, ***Flex (CD)*** and other formulas
			High ferritin due to liver disorders	***Liver DTX***
		Low	Low ferritin due to anemia	***Imperial Tonic***
			Low ferritin due to bleeding	***Notoginseng 9***
Gamma-glutamyl transpeptidase (GGT or GGTP)	8–78 U/L	High	Liver disorders, especially due to alcohol consumption	***Liver DTX***
Glucose	70–105 mg/dL (fasting) < 140 mg/dL (2 hour postprandial)	High	Pre-diabetes (>105) or diabetes (>125)	***Equilibrium***
			due to acute stress	***Calm*** or ***Calm (ES)***
			due to hyperthyroidism	***Thyrodex***
			due to chronic liver disorders	***Liver DTX***
		Low	due to Addison's disease	***Adrenal +***
			due to hypothyroidism	***Thyro-forte***

Blood Tests

Tests	Reference Range	Result	Possible Diagnosis	Herbal Formulas
Hematocrit	36–47% (female) 41–51% (male)	Low	Anemia	***Imperial Tonic***
			Anemia due to bone marrow damage during chemotherapy or radiation	*add* ***C/R Support***
			Anemia due to hyperthyroidism	*add* ***Thyrodex***
			Anemia due to liver disorders	*add* ***Liver DTX***
			Anemia due to bleeding	***Notoginseng 9*** followed by ***Imperial Tonic***
		High	Dehydration (#1 cause of high hematocrit)	***Imperial Tonic*** with increased fluid intake
Hemoglobin	12–16 g/dL (female) 14–17 g/dL (male)	Low	Anemia	***Imperial Tonic***
			Anemia due to bone marrow damage during chemotherapy or radiation	*add* ***C/R Support***
			Anemia due to kidney disorders	*add* ***Kidney DTX***
			Anemia due to liver disorders	*add* ***Liver DTX***
			Anemia due to hyperthyroidism	*add* ***Thyrodex***
			Anemia due to bleeding	***Notoginseng 9*** followed by ***Imperial Tonic***
Lipids			*see* Cholesterol, Triglycerides	
Liver function tests			*see* individual tests	
Lymphocytes	21-49%	Low	due to diseases that affect the immune system	***Immune +***
			due to autoimmune disorders	***LPS Support***
		High	due to viral infection	***Herbal AVR***
Magnesium	1.5–2.4 mg/dL	High	due to hypothyroidism	***Thyro-forte***
			due to Addison's disease	***Adrenal +***
			due to kidney disorders	***Kidney DTX***
		Low	due to kidney disorders	***Kidney DTX***
			due to thyroid disorders	***Thyrodex*** or ***Thyro-forte***
			due to acute, severe diarrhea	***GI Care II***
			due to chronic, mild diarrhea	***GI Tonic***
			due to excessive urination in diabetes	***Equilibrium***
			due to ulcerative colitis	***GI Care (UC)***
Mean corpuscular volume (MCV)	80–100 fL	High	Macrocytic RBC due to liver disorders	***Imperial Tonic*** with ***Liver DTX***
		Low	Microcytic RBC due to blood loss	***Imperial Tonic*** with ***Notoginseng 9***
Monocyte	0-14%	High	due to inflammatory conditions	***Gardenia Complex*** or ***Astringent Complex***

Blood Tests

Tests	Reference Range	Result	Possible Diagnosis	Herbal Formulas
Neutrophils	38-70%	High	due to bacterial infection	***Herbal ABX***
			due to inflammatory conditions	***Gardenia Complex*** or ***Astringent Complex***
		Low	due to chemotherapy or radiation therapy	***C/R Support***
Platelet count	150–350 x 10^3 /µL	High	due to cardiovascular and circulatory diseases	***Circulation***, ***Circulation (SJ)*** or ***Flex (NP)***
			due to cancer	***CA Support*** or ***C/R Support***
			due to trauma	***Flex (TMX)***
			due to arthritis	***Flex (Heat)***, ***Flex (CD)*** or others
			due to infection	***Herbal ABX*** or ***Herbal AVR***
		Low	low platelet count	***Imperial Tonic***
			with risks of bleeding and bruising	*add* ***Notoginseng 9***
			due to autoimmune disorders	*add* ***LPS Support***
			due to chemotherapy or radiation therapy	*add* ***C/R Support***
			due to kidney disorders	*add* ***Kidney DTX***
			due to allergy of the nose	*add* ***Magnolia Clear Sinus*** or ***Pueraria Clear Sinus***
			due to allergy of the skin	*add* ***Silerex***
			due to exposure to chemicals, toxins, or drugs	*add* ***Herbal DTX***
			due to infection	*add* ***Herbal ABX*** or ***Herbal AVR***
			due to bone marrow damage	*add* ***Osteo 8***
Potassium	3.5–5 mEq/L	High	due to kidney disorders	***Kidney DTX***
			due to adrenal insufficiency	***Adrenal +***
			due to infection	***Herbal ABX*** or ***Herbal AVR***
			due to diabetes	***Equilibrium***
			due to chemotherapy	***C/R Support***
		Low	due to acute, severe diarrhea	***GI Care II***
			due to chronic, mild diarrhea	***GI Tonic***
			due to liver disorders	***Liver DTX***
			due to chronic stress	***Calm***, ***Calm (ES)***, or ***Calm ZZZ***
			due to fever	***Gardenia Complex***
Prostate-specific antigen, total (PSA-T)	0–4 ng/mL	High	due to enlarged prostate	***P-Support***

Blood Tests

Tests	Reference Range	Result	Possible Diagnosis	Herbal Formulas
Protein, total	6–7.8 g/dL	High	due to chronic inflammation	***Gardenia Complex*** or ***Astringent Complex***
			due to autoimmune disease	***LPS Support***
			due to rheumatoid arthritis	***Flex (Heat)***, ***Flex (CD)***, or ***Flex (NP)***
			due to chronic infection	***Herbal ABX*** or ***Herbal AVR***
			due to hepatitis or acute liver disorders	***Liver DTX***
		Low	due to liver disorders	***Liver DTX***
			due to kidney disorders	***Kidney DTX***
			Malabsorption due to irritable bowel syndrome (IBS)	***GI Harmony***
			Malabsorption due to weakened digestive system	***GI Tonic***
			due to hemorrhage	***Notoginseng 9***
			due to acute, severe diarrhea	***GI Care II***
			due to chronic, mild diarrhea	***GI Tonic***
Red blood cell (RBC) count	4.2–5.9 x 10^6 cells/μL	Low	Anemia	***Imperial Tonic***
			Anemia due to chemotherapy or radiation	*add* ***C/R Support***
			Anemia due to bone marrow damage	*add* ***Osteo 8***
			Anemia due to chronic inflammatory conditions	*add* ***Astringent Complex***
			Anemia due to kidney disorders	*add* ***Kidney DTX***
			Anemia due to trauma	*add* ***Flex (TMX)***
			Anemia due to bleeding	***Notoginseng 9*** followed by ***Imperial Tonic***
		High	Lung disorders	***Respitrol (Heat)***, ***(Cold)*** or ***(Deficient)***
			Coronary artery conditions	***Circulation*** or ***Circulation (SJ)***
			Poisoning	***Herbal DTX***
SGOT			*see* Aminotransferase, alanine (ALT)	
SGPT			*see* Aminotransferase, aspartate (AST)	
Sequential multiple analyzer (SMA-6, 12, 20)			*see* individual tests	
Sodium	136–145 mEq/L	High	due to frequent urination in diabetes	***Equilibrium***
		Low	due to adrenal insufficiency	***Adrenal +***
			due to acute, severe diarrhea	***GI Care II***
			due to chronic, mild diarrhea	***GI Tonic***
			excessive fluid accumulation due to liver disorders (cirrhosis)	***Herbal DRX*** and ***Liver DTX***
			excessive fluid accumulation due to kidney disorders	***Herbal DRX*** and ***Kidney DTX***

Blood Tests

Tests	Reference Range	Result	Possible Diagnosis	Herbal Formulas
Thyroid-stimulating hormone (TSH)	0.5–5.0 μIU/mL	High	Hypothyroidism with high TSH and low T_3 and T_4	***Thyro-forte***
		Low	Hyperthyroidism with low TSH and high T_3 and T_4	***Thyrodex***
Thyroxine (T_4)	0.9–2.4 ng/dL (free) 4–11 μg/dL (free index) 5–12 μg/dL (total)	High	Hyperthyroidism with low TSH and high T_3 and T_4	***Thyrodex***
		Low	Hypothyroidism with high TSH and low T_3 and T_4	***Thyro-forte***
Triiodothyronine (T_3)	25–35% (uptake) 70–195 ng/dL (total)	High	Hyperthyroidism with low TSH and high T_3 and T_4	***Thyrodex***
		Low	Hypothyroidism with high TSH and low T_3 and T_4	***Thyro-forte***
Triglycerides	< 250 mg/dL	Elevated	Hypertriglyceridemia	***Cholisma*** or ***Cholisma (ES)***
			due to obesity	*add* ***Herbalite***
			with diabetes	*add* ***Equilibrium***
			due to hypothyroidism	*add* ***Thyro-forte***
			with increased risk of heart disease	*add* ***Circulation***
Urea nitrogen (BUN)	8–20 mg/dL	Elevated	due to acute or chronic kidney disease, damage, failure	***Kidney DTX***
			due to kidney damage from kidney stones	*add* ***Dissolve (KS)***
			due to kidney damages from diabetes	*add* ***Equilibrium***
			due to kidney damages from chronic gout	*add* ***Flex (GT)***
			due to gastrointestinal bleeding	***GI Care*** and ***Notoginseng 9***
			due to infection	***Herbal ABX*** or ***Herbal AVR***
			decreased blood flow to kidneys due to cardiovascular conditions	***Kidney DTX*** and ***Circulation (SJ)***
		Low	due to liver failure	***Liver DTX***
Uric acid	2.5–8 mg/dL	Elevated	due to gout	***Flex (GT)***
			due to recurring kidney stones	*add* ***Dissolve (KS)***
			due to kidney disorders	*add* ***Kidney DTX***
			due to chemotherapy	*add* ***C/R Support***
			due to lead poisoning	*add* ***Herbal DTX***

Blood Tests

Tests	Reference Range	Result	Possible Diagnosis	Herbal Formulas
White blood cell (WBC) count	3.9–10.7 x 10^3 cells/μL	High	due to bacterial infection	*Herbal ABX*
			due to inflammation	*Gardenia Complex* or *Astringent Complex*
			due to stress	*Calm* or *Calm (ES)*
			due to hemorrhage	*Notoginseng 9*
			due to trauma	*Flex (TMX)*
			due to cancer	*CA Support* or *C/R Support*
			due to accumulation of toxins, chemicals, or drugs	*Herbal DTX*
			due to allergy of the nose	*Magnolia Clear Sinus* or *Pueraria Clear Sinus*
			due to allergy of the skin	*Silerex*
			due to hepatitis	*Liver DTX*
			due to heavy metal toxicities	*Herbal DTX*
		Low	due to viral infection	*Herbal AVR*
			with weaken immune system	*Immune +*
			due to chemotherapy or radiation therapy	*CA Support* or *C/R Support*
			due to bone marrow damage	*Osteo 8*
			due to heavy metal toxicities	*Herbal DTX*
			due to alcoholism	*Liver DTX*
			due to diabetes	*Equilibrium*
			due to autoimmune disorders	*LPS Support*

Urine Tests

Tests	Reference Range	Result	Possible Diagnosis	Herbal Formulas
Acetone	Negative	Positive	due to diabetes	***Equilibrium***
Bacteria	Negative	Positive	due to urinary tract infection	***Gentiana Complex*** or ***V-Support***
Bilirubin (total)	0.3-1.2 mg/dL	Elevated	due to liver disorders	***Liver DTX***
Blood (occult)	Negative	Positive	due to urinary tract disorders	***Gentiana Complex*** or ***V-Support***
			due to kidney disorders	***Kidney DTX***
			due to kidney stones	***Dissolve (KS)***
Epithelial cells	0-6 /HPF	High	due to urinary tract disorders	***Gentiana Complex*** or ***V-Support***
Glucose	Negative	Positive	due to diabetes	***Equilibrium***
			due to kidney disorders	***Kidney DTX***
Nitrite	Negative	Positive	due to urinary tract infection	***Gentiana Complex*** or ***V-Support***
Protein	Negative	Positive	due to kidney disorders	***Kidney DTX***
Red blood cells (RBC)	0-3 /HPF	High	due to urinary tract disorders	***Gentiana Complex*** or ***V-Support***
			due to kidney disorders	***Kidney DTX***
			due to kidney stones	***Dissolve (KS)***
			due to benign prostatic hyperplasia	***P-Support***
Urobilinogen	0.05-2.5 mg/24 h	High	due to liver disorders	***Liver DTX***
White blood cells (WBC)	0-3 /HPF	Many	due to urinary tract infection	***Gentiana Complex*** or ***V-Support***

Stool Tests

Tests	Reference Range	Result	Possible Diagnosis	Herbal Formulas
Bacteria	Negative	Positive	Peptic ulcer due to *H. pylori* infection	***GI Care***
			due to bacterial infection in the gastrointestinal tract	***GI Care II*** with ***Herbal ABX***
Blood (occult)	Negative	Positive	due to gastric or duodenal bleeding	***Notoginseng 9*** and ***GI Care***
			due to irritable bowel syndrome (IBS)	***Notoginseng 9*** and ***GI Harmony***
			due to inflammatory bowel disease (i.e., Crohn's disease, ulcerative colitis)	***Notoginseng 9*** and ***GI Care (UC)***
			due to hemorrhoids	***Notoginseng 9*** and ***GI Care (HMR)***
Fat	< 5 g/day for 100g fat diet	High	due to malabsorption syndrome	***GI Tonic***
Parasite	Negative	Positive	due to parasitic infestation in the gastrointestinal tract	*Wu Mei Wan* (Mume Pill)
Virus	Negative	Positive	due to viral infection in the gastrointestinal tract	***GI Care II*** with ***Herbal AVR***

Section 4

Drug – Herb Index

中西藥索引

Introduction

It is estimated that 25% of all drugs originate from natural sources. From this information, we can draw two conclusions. One, herbal medicine possesses tremendous healing powers. Two, the use of herbal medicine should never be taken lightly. Even though herbs are classified by the U.S. Food and Drug Administration as "dietary supplements," they do possess strong medicinal properties. When used correctly, they can treat a wide variety of diseases and ailments; but if used incorrectly, they may contribute to unwanted side effects and adverse reactions.

The ultimate responsibility of a healthcare practitioner is to prevent illness and heal individuals who have become ill or injured. We are blessed today with a wide selection of treatment modalities, including herbs and drugs. It is our duty as healthcare practitioners to inform the patients of the treatment options available, as well as the advantages and disadvantages of each course of action.

In recent years the use of Chinese herbs has become a more and more popular option. To facilitate professional understanding of the choices between drugs and herbs, we have created this section entitled the *Drug-Herb Index.* Our goal in creating this section is to point out the similarities between drug and herbal treatments, so if a patient wishes to discontinue drug treatment, the practitioner has alternative treatment options available. ***Knowing herbal alternatives to drugs gives the practitioner treatment options so they can decide with their patients on the best therapy possible.***

There are two sections in the Drug-Herb Index:

1. **Drug-Herb Interactions:**
   This section includes an excerpt on the fundamental concepts of drug-herb from *Chinese Medical Herbology and Pharmacology* published by Art of Medicine Press, Inc. It also includes a Drug-Herb Interaction Chart that lists drugs that have higher risks of interactions with herbs. It is important to note that the study of drug-herb interaction is still in its infancy, and the absence of information does not imply lack of interactions. Rather, the practitioners are strongly urged to check other sources for more detailed and updated information.

2. **Drug-Herb Index:**
   Drugs are listed alphabetically according to **Brand Names** or *Generic Names*. The "*Clinical Application*" column describes common uses of each drug. The "*Herb Alternative*" column lists the herbal formula having functions similar to the drug. Detailed information on the herbal formula(s) can be found in Section 5 Exemplar Formulas.

This section provides valuable information for doctors and patients who prefer to use herbs rather than drugs, or to use herbs as supplements to the regular prescription medication. The indexes compare the similarities between drugs and herbs. However, it is important to note that the indexes do not imply therapeutic equivalence, and the herbal alternatives as listed are not substitutes for their corresponding drugs. Informed professional judgment and careful evaluation must be exercised prior to recommending any herbal formulas to patients.

Drug – Herb Interactions

The practice of medicine is now at a crossroads: countless patients are being treated simultaneously with both Western and Oriental medicine. It is quite common for a patient to seek herbal treatment while taking several prescription medications. According to Journal of American Medical Association (JAMA), an estimated 15 million adults in the United States (representing 18.4% of all prescription pharmaceutical users) took prescription drugs concurrently with herbal remedies and/or vitamins in 1997.[1]

As the general public grows increasingly open to the use of herbs and supplements, both patients and the health professionals who care for them are becoming more alert to the potential for occasional adverse herb-drug interactions. Safety has become a major topic of discussion. Even though herbal remedies are classified as dietary supplements, it must be noted that if used incorrectly, herbs, like any substance, may affect patients adversely. The safest route of access to herbal therapy is through a well-qualified herbalist.

Although Chinese herbal medicine has been prescribed safely by professionals in the West for many years now and a great deal of research has been amassed in China, there are still few formal studies published in English to document the safety and efficacy of combining herbs with prescription drugs. Some questions posed by Western healthcare professionals or patients are difficult to answer quickly with documented specifics. However, with some general insights into pharmacology, one can foresee possible interactions and take appropriate precautions to prevent incompatible combinations.

The concept of 'interaction' refers to the possibility that, when two (or more) substances are given concurrently, one substance may interact with another, or alter its bioavailability or clinical action. The net result may be an increase or a decrease in the effectiveness of one or both substances. It is important to note that interactions may yield positive effects (achieving better therapeutic effects at lower dosage) or negative results (creating unwanted side effects or adverse reactions). Most of the possible interactions may be classified in two major categories: pharmacokinetic and pharmacodynamic.[2, 3]

PHARMACOKINETIC INTERACTIONS

'Pharmacokinetic interaction' refers to the fluctuation in bioavailability of herb/drug molecules in the body as a result of changes in absorption, distribution, metabolism and elimination.[4,5]

Absorption

Absorption is the term that describes the process of the physical passage of herbs or drugs from the outside to the inside of the body. The majority of all absorption occurs in the intestines, where herbs or drugs must pass through the intestinal wall to enter the bloodstream. Several mechanisms may interfere with the absorption of drugs or herbs through the intestines.[6,7]

The absorption of herbs may be adversely affected if herbs are administered with drugs that may promote binding in the gastrointestinal (GI) tract. Drugs such as ezetimibe (Zetia), ezetimibe/simvastatin (Vytorin), cholestyramine (Questran), colestipol (Colestid) and sucralfate (Carafate) may bind to certain herbs, forming an insoluble complex that decreases absorption of both substances. Because of the large size of the insoluble complex, few or no molecules of either substance pass through the intestinal wall.[8,9,10]

Herb absorption may be adversely affected in the presence of drugs that change the pH of the stomach. Antacids, cimetidine (Tagamet), famotidine (Pepcid), nizatidine (Axid), ranitidine (Zantac), omeprazole (Prilosec), esomeprazole (Nexium), pantoprazole (Protonix), and lansoprazole (Prevacid), may neutralize, decrease or inhibit the secretion of stomach acids.[11,12] With this subsequent decrease in stomach acidity, herbs may not be broken down properly in the stomach, leading to poor absorption in the intestines. To minimize this interaction, herbs are best taken separately from these drugs by approximately two hours.

Drugs that affect gastrointestinal motility may also affect the absorption of herbs. GI motility is the rate at which the intestines contract to push food products from the stomach to the rectum. Slower GI motility means that the herbs stay in the intestines for a longer period of time, thereby increasing the potential absorption. Conversely, more rapid GI motility means that the herbs stay in the intestines for a shorter time, which may decrease absorption. Drugs such as haloperidol (Haldol) decrease GI motility and may increase herb absorption; while drugs such as metoclopramide (Reglan) increase GI motility and possibly decrease herb absorption.

Therefore, it may be necessary to decrease the dosage of herbs when the patient is taking a drug that decreases GI motility and increases overall absorption. Likewise, it is probably helpful to increase the dosage of herbs when the patient is taking a drug that increases GI motility and thus decreases overall absorption.

Distribution

After absorption, herbs or drugs must be delivered to the targeted area in order to exert their influence. 'Distribution' refers to the processes by which herbs or drugs (once absorbed) are carried and released to different parts of the body. Currently, it appears that the majority of herbs and drugs do not have any clinically-significant interactions affecting distribution and thus can safely be taken together. The exception seems to be if a drug has a narrow range-of-safety index, and is highly protein-bound, in which case interaction with other substances might occur during the distribution phase. Examples of drugs that have both a narrow range-of-safety index and a high protein-bound ratio include warfarin (Coumadin) and phenytoin (Dilantin). Unfortunately, it is very difficult to predict whether an individual herb will interact

Drug – Herb Interactions

with either one of these drugs because there are no known tests or experiments documenting such interactions.[13,14]

Metabolism

Once metabolized by the liver, most herbs and drugs become inactive derivatives. The rate at which the liver metabolizes a substance determines the length of time it stays active in the body. If the liver was induced to speed up its metabolic rate, herbs and drugs would be deactivated at a more rapid pace, and the overall effectiveness of ingested substances would be lower. On the other hand, if the liver was made to slow its metabolism, herbs and drugs would be deactivated at a slower pace and the overall impact of the substances would be greater.

In general, drugs that induce greater liver metabolism do not exert an immediate effect. The metabolism rate of the liver changes slowly, over several weeks. Therefore, the effect of accelerated liver metabolism is not seen until weeks after the initiation of drug therapy. Some examples of pharmaceuticals that speed hepatic metabolism are: phenytoin (Dilantin), carbamazepine (Tegretol), phenobarbitals and rifampin (Rifadin).[15,16] Therefore, herbs given in the presence of one of these products may be deactivated more rapidly, and their overall effectiveness lowered. Under these circumstances, a higher dose of herbs may be required to achieve the desired effect.

In great contrast, drugs that inhibit liver metabolism have an immediate onset of action. The rate of liver metabolism may be greatly impaired within a few days. Pharmaceuticals that slow or inhibit liver metabolism include: cimetidine (Tagamet), erythromycin, ethanol, fluconazole (Diflucan), itraconazole (Sporanox) and ketoconazole (Nizoral), among others.[17,18] When a patient takes these drugs concurrently with herbs, there is a higher risk of herbal components accumulating in the body, as the ability of the liver to neutralize them is compromised. If the herbs are metabolized more slowly, their overall effectiveness may be prolonged. In this case, one may need to lower the dosage of herbs to avoid unwanted side effects.

Depending on the half-life in the body of drugs that influence liver metabolism, it may be necessary to increase or decrease the dosages of herbs for weeks or even months after discontinuation of the pharmaceutical substance, along with consistent monitoring.

Elimination

While the liver neutralizes incoming drugs and herbs, the kidneys are responsible for eliminating the substances and their metabolites from the body. If the kidneys are damaged, then the rate of elimination is slowed, leading to an accumulation of active substances in the body. Important examples of drugs that damage the kidneys include amphotericin B, methotrexate, tobramycin and gentamicin.[19,20] As a safety precaution, when prescribing herbs for a patient who is currently taking or has recently taken one of these drugs, it may be wise to lower the dose of herbs to avoid unnecessary and unwanted side effects.

SUMMARY OF PHARMACOKINETIC INTERACTIONS

The pharmacokinetic interactions listed above include both theoretical and actual interactions. Though such interactions are possible, the extent and severity of each interaction will vary depending on the specific circumstances, such as the dosages of all substances, the inherent sensitivity of each patient, individual body weight, and metabolic rate.

PHARMACODYNAMIC INTERACTIONS

The study of pharmacodynamics gives us insight into the dynamic behavior of drugs inside the human body. The phrase 'pharmacodynamic interactions' refers in our context to fluctuations in the bioavailability of ingested substances as a result of synergistic or antagonistic interactions between herb and drug molecules. Pharmacodynamic interactions are generally more difficult to predict and prevent than pharmacokinetic interactions. Most of the currently-known pharmacodynamic interactions have been documented through actual cases, not by laboratory experiments. The best way to prevent pharmacodynamic interactions is to follow the patient closely and monitor all clinical signs and symptoms, and particularly any abnormal reactions.

A ***synergistic*** interaction occurs when two drugs with similar properties show an additive or even exponential increase in clinical impact when given together. An ***antagonistic*** interaction occurs when two drugs with similar properties are administered simultaneously and show lessened or no clinical effectiveness.[21]

Synergistic or antagonistic interactions may occur with any concurrent use of medicinal substances, regardless of whether they are herbs, drugs, or both.

Herb-to-Herb Interactions

Oriental medicine has tracked cases of herb-to-herb pharmacodynamic interactions for centuries. The additive effect is generally referred to as *xiang xu* (mutual accentuation) or *xiang shi* (mutual enhancement), such as in the combination of *Shi Gao* (Gypsum Fibrosum) and *Zhi Mu* (Radix Anemarrhenae) to clear heat and purge fire. The antagonistic effect is generally referred to as *xiang wei* (mutual counteraction), *xiang sha* (mutual suppression) or *xiang wu* (mutual antagonism), such as in the combination of *Lai Fu Zi* (Semen Raphani) and *Ren Shen* (Radix Ginseng), in which the therapeutic action of the latter herb is decreased by the addition of *Lai Fu Zi* (Semen Raphani).

Classic Chinese texts describe numerous other herb-to-herb interactions, such as the *Shi Ba Fan* (Eighteen Incompatibles) and *Shi Jiu Wei* (Nineteen Counteractions), discussed in greater detail in most textbooks of Chinese herbology. Ill-advised combinations of these herbs will likely lead to adverse side effects and/or toxic reactions.

Drug – Herb Interactions

Herb-to-Drug Interactions

Pharmacodynamic herb-to-drug interactions are best identified by analyzing the therapeutic profile of the herbs as well as that of the drugs. Concurrent use of herbs and drugs with similar therapeutic actions poses potential for herb-drug interactions. In these cases, the increased potency of treatment may interfere with optimal outcome, as the desired effect becomes less predictable and harder to obtain with precision. The highest risk of clinically-significant interactions occurs between herbs and drugs that have **sympathomimetic, anticoagulant, antiplatelet, diuretic** and **antidiabetic** effects.[22]

Herbs that exert **sympathomimetic** effects may interfere with antihypertensive and antiseizure drugs. The classic example of this type of herb is *Ma Huang* (Herba Ephedrae), containing ephedrine, pseudoephedrine, norephedrine and other ephedrine alkaloids. *Ma Huang* (Herba Ephedrae) may interact with other drugs and disease conditions and should always be used with caution in patients vulnerable to hypertension, seizures, diabetes, thyroid conditions, and similar regulatory imbalances.[23]

Herbs with **anticoagulant** and **antiplatelet** effects include herbs that have blood-activating and blood-stasis-removing functions, such as *Dan Shen* (Radix Salviae Miltiorrhizae), *Dang Gui* (Radix Angelicae Sinensis), *Chuan Xiong* (Rhizoma Ligustici Chuanxiong), *Tao Ren* (Semen Persicae), *Hong Hua* (Flos Carthami) and *Shui Zhi* (Hirudo). These herbs may interfere with anticoagulant and antiplatelet drugs, including warfarin (Coumadin), enoxaparin (Lovenox), aspirin, dipyridamole (Persantine), clopidogrel (Plavix) and lepirudin (Refludan). Without proper supervision, concurrent use of these herbs and drugs may lead to prolonged and excessive bleeding. Thus, individuals taking anticoagulant or antiplatelet drugs must be very cautious about concurrently using herbs, and would be wise to do so only under the supervision of well-trained healthcare professionals.[24]

Concomitant use of **diuretic** herbs and diuretic drugs may create additive or synergistic effects, making hypertension more difficult to control, or hypotensive episodes more likely.[25] The dosage of herbs and/or drugs must be adjusted to achieve optimal treatment outcome. Commonly-used diuretic herbs include *Fu Ling* (Poria), *Zhu Ling* (Polyporus), *Che Qian Zi* (Semen Plantaginis), and *Ze Xie* (Rhizoma Alismatis).

Antidiabetic herbs may interfere with antidiabetic drugs by accentuating the decrease of plasma glucose levels. The dosage of these herbs and drugs must be balanced carefully to effectively control blood glucose levels without causing hyper- or hypoglycemia.[26] Herbs with definite antidiabetic effects include the following pairs of herbs: *Zhi Mu* (Radix Anemarrhenae) and *Shi Gao* (Gypsum Fibrosum); *Xuan Shen* (Radix Scrophulariae) and *Cang Zhu* (Rhizoma Atractylodis); and *Shan Yao* (Rhizoma Dioscoreae) and *Huang Qi* (Radix Astragali).

SUMMARY OF PHARMACODYNAMIC INTERACTIONS

Understanding synergistic and antagonistic interactions from both an Oriental medicine perspective and the realm of pharmaceutical medicines helps practitioners to anticipate, prevent, and/or monitor for unwanted interactions in patients who need or elect to rely on multiple therapeutic substances.

SUMMARY: CONCURRENT USE OF HERBAL MEDICINES AND PHARMACEUTICALS

Historically, herbs and drugs have been presumed to be very different treatment modalities that have rarely, if ever, been used together. The line that separates use of herbs and drugs, however, has blurred in recent decades as the lay public gains increased accessibility to multiple treatment modalities. It is not uncommon for one patient to seek care from several health professionals for an ailment. As a result, a patient may easily be taking multiple drugs, herbs, supplements, and vitamins concurrently. It becomes difficult to predict whether the combination of all these substances will lead to unwanted side effects and/or interactions. It is imprudent to assume that there will be no interactions. On the other hand, it is just as unwise to abandon treatment simply for fear of possible interactions. The solution to this situation is in the understanding of pharmacokinetic and pharmacodynamic herb-drug interactions. By understanding these mechanisms, one can recognize potential interactions and take proper actions to prevent their occurrence.

References

1. David M. Eisenberg, et al. *Trends in Alternative Medicine Use in the United States,* 1990-1997. JAMA. November 11, 1998.
2. Robert Berkow and Andrew J. Fletcher: *The Merck Manual of Diagnosis and Therapy 16th Edition.* Merck Research Laboratories, 1992.
3. Anthony S. Fauci, et al: *Harrison's Principles of Internal Medicine 14th Edition.* McGraw-Hill Health Professions Division, 1998.
4. Robert Berkow and Andrew J. Fletcher: *The Merck Manual of Diagnosis and Therapy 16th Edition.* Merck Research Laboratories, 1992.
5. Anthony S. Fauci, et al: *Harrison's Principles of Internal Medicine 14th Edition.* McGraw-Hill Health Professions Division, 1998.
6. Philip D. Hansten: *Understanding Drug-Drug Interactions. Science and Medicine* 16-25. January-February 1998.
7. Philip D. Hansten: *Chapter Three Drug Interactions. Applied Therapeutics.* Applied Therapeutics, Inc. 1993.
8. Philip D. Hansten: *Understanding Drug-Drug Interactions. Science and Medicine* 16-25. January-February 1998.
9. Philip D. Hansten: *Chapter Three Drug Interactions. Applied Therapeutics.* Applied Therapeutics, Inc. 1993.
10. Sophia Segal and Susan Kaminski: *Drug-Nutrient Interactions.* American Druggist 42-49. July 1996.
11. Philip D. Hansten: *Understanding Drug-Drug Interactions. Science and Medicine* 16-25. January-February 1998.
12. Philip D. Hansten: *Chapter Three Drug Interactions. Applied Therapeutics.* Applied Therapeutics, Inc. 1993.
13. Philip D. Hansten: *Understanding Drug-Drug Interactions. Science and Medicine* 16-25. January-February 1998.

Drug – Herb Interactions

14. Philip D. Hansten: *Chapter Three Drug Interactions. Applied Therapeutics.* Applied Therapeutics, Inc. 1993.
15. Philip D. Hansten: *Understanding Drug-Drug Interactions. Science and Medicine* 16-25. January-February 1998.
16. Philip D. Hansten: *Chapter Three Drug Interactions. Applied Therapeutics.* Applied Therapeutics, Inc. 1993.
17. Philip D. Hansten: *Understanding Drug-Drug Interactions. Science and Medicine* 16-25. January-February 1998.
18. Philip D. Hansten: *Chapter Three Drug Interactions. Applied Therapeutics.* Applied Therapeutics, Inc. 1993.
19. Philip D. Hansten: *Understanding Drug-Drug Interactions. Science and Medicine* 16-25. January-February 1998.
20. Philip D. Hansten: *Chapter Three Drug Interactions. Applied Therapeutics.* Applied Therapeutics, Inc. 1993.
21. Harold Kalant and Walter H.E. Roschlau: *Principles of Medical Pharmacology Sixth Edition.* Oxford University Press, 1998.
22. P.F.D'Arcy: Adverse Reactions and Interactions With Herbal Medicine. Part 2 – Drug Interactions. *Adverse Drug React. Toxicol.* Rev. 1993, 12(3) 147-162 Oxford University Press.
23. P.F.D'Arcy: Adverse Reactions and Interactions With Herbal Medicine. Part 2 – Drug Interactions. *Adverse Drug React. Toxicol.* Rev. 1993, 12(3) 147-162 Oxford University Press.
24. P.F.D'Arcy: Adverse Reactions and Interactions With Herbal Medicine. Part 2 – Drug Interactions. *Adverse Drug React. Toxicol.* Rev. 1993, 12(3) 147-162 Oxford University Press.
25. P.F.D'Arcy: Adverse Reactions and Interactions With Herbal Medicine. Part 2 – Drug Interactions. *Adverse Drug React. Toxicol.* Rev. 1993, 12(3) 147-162 Oxford University Press.
26. P.F.D'Arcy: Adverse Reactions and Interactions With Herbal Medicine. Part 2 – Drug Interactions. *Adverse Drug React. Toxicol.* Rev. 1993, 12(3) 147-162 Oxford University Press.

Drug – Herb Interaction Chart

Brand Name	Generic Name	Type Of Drugs	Effect of Interaction	Comment
Aciphex	*Rabeprazole*	acid-reducer	may interfere with absorption of herbs	adjust herb doses accordingly
Amphotericin	*Amphotericin*	antifungal	may reduce elimination of herbs	decrease dose of herbs if necessary
Aspirin	*Aspirin*	antiplatelet	this effect may change with herbs	monitor aspirin effectiveness closely
Axid	*Nizatidine*	acid-reducer	may interfere with absorption of herbs	adjust herb doses accordingly
Carafate	*Sucralfate*	anti-ulcer	may interfere with absorption of herbs	separate taking herbs and drugs by two hours
Cholestid	*Colestipol*	antihyperlipidemic	may interfere with absorption of herbs	separate taking herbs and drugs by two hours
Coumadin	*Warfarin*	anticoagulant	this effect may change with herbs	monitor Coumadin effectiveness closely
Dexilant	*Dexlansoprazole*	acid-reducer	may interfere with absorption of herbs	adjust herb doses accordingly
Diflucan	*Fluconazole*	antifungal	may slow the metabolism of herbs	decrease dose of herbs if necessary
Dilantin	*Phenytoin*	anticonvulsant	may increase the metabolism of herbs	increase dose of herbs if necessary
EES	*Erythromycin*	antibiotic	may slow the metabolism of herbs	decrease dose of herbs if necessary
E-Mycin	*Erythromycin*	antibiotic	may slow the metabolism of herbs	decrease dose of herbs if necessary
Eryc	*Erythromycin*	antibiotic	may slow the metabolism of herbs	decrease dose of herbs if necessary
Ethanol	*Alcohol*	alcohol	may slow the metabolism of herbs	decrease dose of herbs if necessary
Haldol	*Haloperidol*	antipsychotic	may interfere with absorption of herbs	decrease dose of herbs if necessary
Lovenox	*Enoxaparin*	anticoagulant	this effect may change with herbs	monitor Lovenox effectiveness closely
Maalox	*Antacid*	antacid	may interfere with absorption of herbs	separate taking herbs and drugs by two hours
Methotrexate	*Methotrexate*	antineoplastic	may reduce elimination of herbs	decrease dose of herbs if necessary
Mylanta	*Antacid*	antacid	may interfere with absorption of herbs	separate taking herbs and drugs by two hours
Nexium	*Esomeprazole*	acid-reducer	may interfere with absorption of herbs	adjust herb doses accordingly
Nizoral	*Ketoconazole*	antifungal	may slow the metabolism of herbs	decrease dose of herbs if necessary
Pepcid	*Famotidine*	acid-reducer	may interfere with absorption of herbs	adjust herb doses accordingly
Persantine	*Dipyridamole*	antiplatelet	this effect may change with herbs	monitor Persantine effectiveness closely
Phenobarbital	*Phenobarbital*	anticonvulsant	may increase the metabolism of herbs	increase dose of herbs if necessary
Plavix	*Clopidogrel*	antiplatelet	this effect may change with herbs	monitor Plavix effectiveness closely
Prevacid	*Lansoprazole*	acid-reducer	may interfere with absorption of herbs	adjust herb doses accordingly
Prilosec	*Omeprazole*	acid-reducer	may interfere with absorption of herbs	adjust herb doses accordingly
Protonix	*Pantoprazole*	GI stimulant	may interfere with absorption of herbs	increase dose of herbs if necessary
Questran	*Cholestyramine*	antihyperlipidemic	may decrease absorption of herbs	separate taking herbs and drugs by two hours
Reglan	*Metoclopramide*	GI stimulant	may interfere with absorption of herbs	increase dose of herbs if necessary
Rifadin	*Rifampin*	antibiotic	may increase the metabolism of herbs	increase dose of herbs if necessary
Sporanox	*Itraconazole*	antifungal	may slow the metabolism of herbs	decrease dose of herbs if necessary
Tagamet	*Cimetidine*	acid-reducer	may interfere with absorption of herbs	adjust herb doses accordingly
Tagamet	*Cimetidine*	acid-reducer	may slow the metabolism of herbs	decrease dose of herbs if necessary
Tegretol	*Carbamazepine*	anticonvulsant	may increase the metabolism of herbs	increase dose of herbs if necessary
Tums	*Antacid*	antacid	may interfere with absorption of herbs	separate taking herbs and drugs by two hours
Vytorin	*Ezetimibe/ Simvastatin*	antihyperlipidemic	may decrease absorption of herbs	separate taking herbs and drugs by two hours
Zantac	*Ranitidine*	acid-reducer	may interfere with absorption of herbs	adjust herb doses accordingly
Zetia	*Ezetimibe*	antihyperlipidemic	may decrease absorption of herbs	separate taking herbs and drugs by two hours

Drug – Herb Index

Brand Names / *Generic Names*		**Clinical Applications**	**Herb Alternatives**
Abatacept	**Orencia**	*See* **Orencia**	
Abilify	*Aripiprazole*	Moderate levels of stress, anxiety, nervousness, tension	***Calm***
		Moderate to severe emotional and psychological disorders	***Calm (ES)***
Abreva	*Docosanol*	Cold sores	***Lonicera Complex***
Acamprosate	**Campral**	*See* **Campral**	
Accolate	*Zafirlukast*	Dyspnea and shortness of breath in cases of chronic asthma	***Respitrol (Deficient)***
		Management and prevention of chronic asthma	***Cordyceps 3***
Accupril	*Quinapril*	Cardiovascular disorders, such as hypertension	***Gastrodia Complex***
Acetaminophen + Codeine	**Tylenol + Codeine**	*See* **Tylenol + Codeine**	
Aciphex	*Rabeprazole*	Various gastrointestinal disorders, such as heartburn, acid reflux and peptic ulcer	***GI Care***
Actigall	*Ursodiol*	To dissolve and expel gallstones; cholecystitis	***Dissolve (GS)***
Actonel	*Risedronate*	Osteoporosis	***Osteo 8***
Actos	*Pioglitazone*	Elevated blood glucose levels in non-insulin dependent diabetes mellitus	***Equilibrium***
Acutrim	*Phenylpropanolamine*	Obesity; elevated body weight; slow basal metabolism; lack of energy	***Herbalite***
Acyclovir	**Zovirax**	*See* **Zovirax**	
Adalimumab	**Humira**	*See* **Humira**	
Adapalene	**Differin**	*See* **Differin**	
Adderall	*Amphetamine + Dextroamphetamine*	To promote concentration and focus in ADD (attention deficit disorder) and ADHD (attention deficit-hyperactivity disorder)	***Calm (Jr)***
Adefovir	**Hepsera**	*See* **Hepsera**	
Adipex	*Phentermine*	Obesity; elevated body weight; slow basal metabolism; lack of energy	***Herbalite***
Advair	*Fluticasone + Salmeterol*	Dyspnea and shortness of breath in cases of chronic asthma	***Respitrol (Deficient)***
		Management and prevention of chronic asthma	***Cordyceps 3***
		For astringent and non-steroidal anti-inflammatory effect	***Astringent Complex***
Advil	*Ibuprofen*	Various types of headaches: migraine, tension, stress, vertex, occipital	***Corydalin (AC)*** or ***(CR)***
		Musculoskeletal pain with redness, swelling and inflammation	***Flex (Heat)***
		Musculoskeletal pain that worsens during cold and rainy days	***Flex (CD)***
		Neuropathy	***Flex (NP)***
		Chronic injuries of soft tissues (muscles, ligaments, and tendons)	***Flex (MLT)***
		Arm pain (shoulder, elbow, and wrist)	***Arm Support***
		Acute or chronic pain of the leg (knee and ankle)	***Knee & Ankle (AC)*** or ***(CR)***
		Acute or chronic upper and lower back pain	***Back Support (AC)*** or ***(CR)***
		Acute or chronic neck and shoulder pain	***Neck & Shoulder (AC)*** or ***(CR)***
		Menstrual pain and cramps in dysmenorrhea	***Mense-Ease***
		Pain associated with amenorrhea	***Menatrol***
		Pain associated with endometriosis	***Resolve (Lower)***
		Severe pain	*add* ***Herbal ANG***
		Pain due to trauma	*add* ***Flex (TMX)***

Drug – Herb Index

Brand Names / *Generic Names*		**Clinical Applications**	**Herb Alternatives**
Albuterol	**Proventil, Ventolin, ProAir**	*See* **Proventil, Ventolin, ProAir**	
Aldactone	*Spironolactone*	Edema and fluid retention	***Herbal DRX***
Alefacept	**Amevive**	*See* **Amevive**	
Alendronate	**Fosamax**	*See* **Fosamax**	
Aleve	*Naproxen*	Various headaches: migraine, tension, stress, vertex, occipital	***Corydalin (AC) or (CR)***
		Musculoskeletal pain with redness, swelling and inflammation	***Flex (Heat)***
		Musculoskeletal pain that worsens during cold and rainy days	***Flex (CD)***
		Neuropathy	***Flex (NP)***
		Chronic injuries of soft tissues (muscles, ligaments, and tendons)	***Flex (MLT)***
		Arm pain (shoulder, elbow, and wrist)	***Arm Support***
		Acute or chronic pain of the leg (knee and ankle)	***Knee & Ankle (AC)*** or ***(CR)***
		Acute or chronic upper and lower back pain	***Back Support (AC)*** or ***(CR)***
		Acute or chronic neck and shoulder pain	***Neck & Shoulder (AC)*** or ***(CR)***
		Menstrual pain and cramps in dysmenorrhea	***Mense-Ease***
		Pain associated with amenorrhea	***Menatrol***
		Pain associated with endometriosis	***Resolve (Lower)***
		Severe pain	*add* ***Herbal ANG***
		Pain due to trauma	*add* ***Flex (TMX)***
Alfuzosin	**Uroxatral**	*See* **Uroxatral**	
Allegra	*Fexofenadine*	Nasal congestion with yellow, sticky discharge	***Pueraria Clear Sinus***
		Nasal congestion with white, watery discharge	***Magnolia Clear Sinus***
		Allergic or hypersensitive skin problems such as rash, itching, eczema, etc.	***Silerex***
Allopurinol	**Zyloprim**	*See* **Zyloprim**	
Almotriptan	**Axert**	*See* **Axert**	
Alprazolam	**Xanax**	*See* **Xanax**	
Altace	*Ramipril*	Cardiovascular disorders, such as hypertension	***Gastrodia Complex***
Aluminum + Magnesium	**Maalox, Mylanta**	*See* **Maalox, Mylanta**	
Alupent	*Metaproterenol*	Heat-type asthma with fever, dry mouth, thirst, red face and red tongue	***Respitrol (Heat)***
		Cold-type asthma with chills, intolerance to cold, cyanotic complexion of the face and body	***Respitrol (Cold)***
		Chronic asthma with frequent attacks of wheezing and dyspnea	***Respitrol (Deficient)*** or ***Cordyceps 3***
Amantadine	**Symmetrel**	*See* **Symmetrel**	
Amaryl	*Glimepiride*	Elevated blood glucose levels in non-insulin dependent diabetes mellitus	***Equilibrium***

DRUG-HERB

Drug – Herb Index

Brand Names / *Generic Names*		**Clinical Applications**	**Herb Alternatives**
Ambien	*Zolpidem*	Insomnia due to Liver qi stagnation (stress, anxiety, nervousness, restlessness)	***Calm ZZZ***
		Insomnia due to *shen* (spirit) disturbance with qi and blood deficiencies	***Schisandra ZZZ***
Amevive	*Alefacept*	Psoriasis	***Dermatrol (PS)***
Amitiza	*Lubiprostone*	Moderate to severe constipation	***Gentle Lax (Excess)*** or ***(Deficient)***
Amitriptyline	**Elavil**	*See* **Elavil**	
Amlodipine	**Norvasc**	*See* **Norvasc**	
Amlodipine + Olmesartan	**Azor**	*See* **Azor**	
Amlodipine + Valsartan	**Exforge**	*See* **Exforge**	
Amoxicillin	**Amoxil**	*See* **Amoxil**	
Amoxicillin + Clavulanic Acid	**Augmentin**	*See* **Augmentin**	
Amoxil	*Amoxicillin*	Generalized bacterial infection	***Herbal ABX***
		Upper respiratory tract infection with fever, headache, sore throat	***Lonicera Complex***
		Respiratory tract infection with sinus congestion, watery nasal discharge, sneezing and chills	***Respitrol (Cold)***
		Lower respiratory tract infection with high fever, copious yellow sputum, cough and perspiration	***Respitrol (Heat)***
		Lower respiratory tract infection with chest congestion, cough, yellow phlegm and fever	***Pinellia XPT***
		Infection in the gastrointestinal tract	***GI Care II***
		Genito-urinary infections, such as urinary tract infection or sexually-transmitted diseases	***Gentiana Complex*** or ***V-Support***
		Ear, nose and throat infections	***Herbal ENT***
		General skin conditions associated with infection and inflammation	***Dermatrol (Damp)*** or ***Dermatrol (Dry)***
		With more swelling and inflammation	*add* ***Astringent Complex***
Amphetamine + Dextroamphetamine	**Adderall**	*See* **Adderall**	
Ampicillin	**Principen**	*See* **Principen**	
Anafranil	*Clomipramine*	Depression with low energy, prolonged sadness and lack of interest	***Shine***
		Depression with stress and anxiety	***Shine (DS)***
		Nerve related pain, such as neuralgia and neuropathy	***Flex (NP)***
Anaprox	*Naproxen*	Various headaches: migraine, tension, stress, vertex, occipital	***Corydalin (AC)*** or ***(CR)***
		Musculoskeletal pain with redness, swelling and inflammation	***Flex (Heat)***
		Musculoskeletal pain that worsens during cold and rainy days	***Flex (CD)***

Drug – Herb Index

Brand Names / *Generic Names*		**Clinical Applications**	**Herb Alternatives**
Anaprox *(cont'd)*	*Naproxen*	Neuropathy	***Flex (NP)***
		Chronic injuries of soft tissues (muscles, ligaments, and tendons)	***Flex (MLT)***
		Arm pain (shoulder, elbow, and wrist)	***Arm Support***
		Acute or chronic pain of the leg (knee and ankle)	***Knee & Ankle (AC)*** or ***(CR)***
		Acute or chronic upper and lower back pain	***Back Support (AC)*** or ***(CR)***
		Acute or chronic neck and shoulder pain	***Neck & Shoulder (AC)*** or ***(CR)***
		Menstrual pain and cramps in dysmenorrhea	***Mense-Ease***
		Pain associated with amenorrhea	***Menatrol***
		Pain associated with endometriosis	***Resolve (Lower)***
		Severe pain	*add* ***Herbal ANG***
		Pain due to trauma	*add* ***Flex (TMX)***
Anastrozole	**Arimidex**	*See* **Arimidex**	
Ansaid	*Flurbiprofen*	Various headaches: migraine, tension, stress, vertex, occipital	***Corydalin (AC) or (CR)***
		Musculoskeletal pain with redness, swelling and inflammation	***Flex (Heat)***
		Musculoskeletal pain that worsens during cold and rainy days	***Flex (CD)***
		Neuropathy	***Flex (NP)***
		Chronic injuries of soft tissues (muscles, ligaments, and tendons)	***Flex (MLT)***
		Arm pain (shoulder, elbow, and wrist)	***Arm Support***
		Acute or chronic pain of the leg (knee and ankle)	***Knee & Ankle (AC)*** or ***(CR)***
		Acute or chronic upper and lower back pain	***Back Support (AC)*** or ***(CR)***
		Acute or chronic neck and shoulder pain	***Neck & Shoulder (AC)*** or ***(CR)***
		Menstrual pain and cramps in dysmenorrhea	***Mense-Ease***
		Pain associated with amenorrhea	***Menatrol***
		Pain associated with endometriosis	***Resolve (Lower)***
		Severe pain	*add* ***Herbal ANG***
		Pain due to trauma	*add* ***Flex (TMX)***
Antitussive Combination	**Phenergan, Poly-Histine, Robitussin**	*See* **Phenergan, Poly-Histine, Robitussin**	
Anusol-HC	*Hydrocortisone*	Hemorrhoids	***GI Care (HMR)***
		For astringent and non-steroidal anti-inflammatory effect	***Astringent Complex***
Apidra	*Insulin Glulisine*	Diabetes	***Equilibrium***
Aprepitant	**Emend**	*See* **Emend**	
Aredia	*Pamidronate*	Osteoporosis	***Osteo 8***
Aricept	*Donepezil*	Mental and physical deteriorations in Alzheimer's disease and dementia	***Neuro Plus***
		Mental deteriorations with aging	***Enhance Memory***
Arimidex	*Anastrozole*	To resolve fibrocystic benign breast disorder	***Resolve (Upper)***

Drug – Herb Index

Brand Names / *Generic Names*		**Clinical Applications**	**Herb Alternatives**
Aripiprazole	**Abilify**	*See* **Abilify**	
Armour Thyroid	*Thyroid Desiccated*	Hypothyroidism	***Thyro-forte***
Asacol	*Mesalamine*	Inflammatory bowel disease with diarrhea	***GI Care II*** or ***GI Harmony***
Aspirin	*Aspirin*	Various headaches: migraine, tension, stress, vertex, occipital	***Corydalin (AC)*** or ***(CR)***
		Musculoskeletal pain with redness, swelling and inflammation	***Flex (Heat)***
		Musculoskeletal pain that worsens during cold and rainy days	***Flex (CD)***
		Neuropathy	***Flex (NP)***
		Chronic injuries of soft tissues (muscles, ligaments, and tendons)	***Flex (MLT)***
		Arm pain (shoulder, elbow, and wrist)	***Arm Support***
		Acute or chronic pain of the leg (knee and ankle)	***Knee & Ankle (AC)*** or ***(CR)***
		Acute or chronic upper and lower back pain	***Back Support (AC)*** or ***(CR)***
		Acute or chronic neck and shoulder pain	***Neck & Shoulder (AC)*** or ***(CR)***
		Menstrual pain and cramps in dysmenorrhea	***Mense-Ease***
		Pain associated with amenorrhea	***Menatrol***
		Pain associated with endometriosis	***Resolve (Lower)***
		Severe pain	*add* ***Herbal ANG***
		Pain due to trauma	*add* ***Flex (TMX)***
Atarax	*Hydroxyzine*	Allergic or hypersensitive skin problems such as rash, itching, and eczema	***Silerex***
Atenolol	**Tenormin**	*See* **Tenormin**	
Ativan	*Lorazepam*	Moderate levels of stress, anxiety, nervousness, and tension	***Calm***
		Moderate to severe emotional and psychological disorders	***Calm (ES)***
		Moderate levels of stress, anxiety, and insomnia	***Calm ZZZ***
Atomoxetine	**Strattera**	*See* **Strattera**	
Augmentin	*Amoxicillin + Clavulanic Acid*	Generalized bacterial infection	***Herbal ABX***
		Upper respiratory tract infection with fever, headache, sore throat	***Lonicera Complex***
		Respiratory tract infection with sinus congestion, watery nasal discharge, sneezing and chills	***Respitrol (Cold)***
		Lower respiratory tract infection with high fever, copious yellow sputum, cough and perspiration	***Respitrol (Heat)***
		Lower respiratory tract infection with chest congestion, cough, yellow phlegm and fever	***Pinellia XPT***
		Infection in the gastrointestinal tract	***GI Care II***
		Genitourinary infections, such as urinary tract infection or sexually-transmitted diseases	***Gentiana Complex*** or ***V-Support***
		Ear, nose and throat infections	***Herbal ENT***
		General skin conditions associated with infection and inflammation	***Dermatrol (Damp)*** or ***Dermatrol (Dry)***
		With more swelling and inflammation	*add* ***Astringent Complex***
Avalide	*Hydrochlorothiazide + Irbesartan*	Cardiovascular disorders with water accumulation	***Gastrodia Complex*** and ***Herbal DRX***

Drug – Herb Index

Brand Names / *Generic Names*		**Clinical Applications**	**Herb Alternatives**
Avandia	*Rosiglitazone*	Elevated blood glucose levels in non-insulin dependent diabetes mellitus	***Equilibrium***
Avapro	*Irbesartan*	Cardiovascular disorders, such as hypertension	***Gastrodia Complex***
Avelox	*Moxifloxacin*	Generalized bacterial infection	***Herbal ABX***
		Upper respiratory tract infection with fever, headache, sore throat	***Lonicera Complex***
		Respiratory tract infection with sinus congestion, watery nasal discharge, sneezing and chills	***Respitrol (Cold)***
		Lower respiratory tract infection with high fever, copious yellow sputum, cough and perspiration	***Respitrol (Heat)***
		Lower respiratory tract infection with chest congestion, cough, yellow phlegm and fever	***Pinellia XPT***
		Infection in the gastrointestinal tract	***GI Care II***
		Genitourinary infections, such as urinary tract infection or sexually-transmitted diseases	***Gentiana Complex*** or ***V-Support***
		Ear, nose and throat infections	***Herbal ENT***
		General skin conditions associated with infection and inflammation	***Dermatrol (Damp)*** or ***Dermatrol (Dry)***
Avita	*Retinoid*	Acne	***Dermatrol (Clear)***
Avodart	*Dutasteride*	Benign prostatic hypertrophy (BPH)	***P-Support***
Axert	*Almotriptan*	Treatment of acute migraine attack	***Corydalin (AC)***
		Prevention of chronic migraine recurrence	***Corydalin (CR)***
Azithromycin	**Zithromax**	*See* **Zithromax**	
Azor	*Amlodipine + Olmesartan*	Cardiovascular disorders, such as hypertension	***Gastrodia Complex***
Baclofen	**Lioresal**	*See* **Lioresal**	
Bactrim, Bactrim DS	*Sulfamethoxazole + Trimethoprim*	Generalized bacterial infection	***Herbal ABX***
		Upper respiratory tract infection with fever, headache, sore throat	***Lonicera Complex***
		Respiratory tract infection with sinus congestion, watery nasal discharge, sneezing and chills	***Respitrol (Cold)***
		Lower respiratory tract infection with high fever, copious yellow sputum, cough and perspiration	***Respitrol (Heat)***
		Lower respiratory tract infection with chest congestion, cough, yellow phlegm and fever	***Pinellia XPT***
		Infection in the gastrointestinal tract	***GI Care II***
		Genitourinary infections, such as urinary tract infection or sexually-transmitted diseases	***Gentiana Complex*** or ***V-Support***
		Ear, nose, and throat infections	***Herbal ENT***
		General skin conditions associated with infection and inflammation	***Dermatrol (Damp)*** or ***Dermatrol (Dry)***
		With more swelling and inflammation	*add* ***Astringent Complex***
Benadryl	*Diphenhydramine*	Allergic or hypersensitive skin problems such as rash, itching, and eczema	***Silerex***
		Nasal congestion with yellow, sticky discharge	***Pueraria Clear Sinus***
		Nasal congestion with white, watery discharge	***Magnolia Clear Sinus***

Drug – Herb Index

Brand Names / *Generic Names*		**Clinical Applications**	**Herb Alternatives**
Benazepril	**Lotensin**	*See* **Lotensin**	
Benicar	*Olmesartan*	Cardiovascular disorders, such as hypertension	***Gastrodia Complex***
Bentyl	*Dicyclomine*	General relief of muscle spasm and cramps	***Flex (SC)***
Benzonatate	**Tessalon Perles**	*See* **Tessalon Perles**	
Benzoyl Peroxide	**Brevoxyl, Triaz**	*See* **Brevoxyl, Triaz**	
Benzatropine	**Cogentin**	*See* **Cogentin**	
Biaxin	*Clarithromycin*	Generalized bacterial infection	***Herbal ABX***
		Upper respiratory tract infection with fever, headache, sore throat	***Lonicera Complex***
		Respiratory tract infection with sinus congestion, watery nasal discharge, sneezing and chills	***Respitrol (Cold)***
		Lower respiratory tract infection with high fever, copious yellow sputum, cough and perspiration	***Respitrol (Heat)***
		Lower respiratory tract infection with chest congestion, cough, yellow phlegm and fever	***Pinellia XPT***
		Infection in the gastrointestinal tract	***GI Care II***
		Genitourinary infections, such as urinary tract infection or sexually-transmitted diseases	***Gentiana Complex*** or ***V-Support***
		Ear, nose, and throat infections	***Herbal ENT***
		General skin conditions associated with infection and inflammation	***Dermatrol (Damp)*** or ***Dermatrol (Dry)***
		With more swelling and inflammation	*add **Astringent Complex***
Bisacodyl	**Dulcolax**	*See* **Dulcolax**	
Bisoprolol	**Zebeta**	*See* **Zebeta**	
Boniva	*Ibandronate*	Osteoporosis	***Osteo 8***
Brethine	*Terbutaline*	Heat-type asthma with fever, dry mouth, thirst, red face and red tongue	***Respitrol (Heat)***
		Cold-type asthma with chills, intolerance to cold, cyanotic complexion of the face and body	***Respitrol (Cold)***
		Chronic asthma with frequent attacks of wheezing and dyspnea	***Respitrol (Deficient)*** or ***Cordyceps 3***
Brevoxyl	*Benzoyl Peroxide*	Acne	***Dermatrol (Clear)***
Bromfed	*Pseudoephedrine + Brompheniramine*	Lower respiratory tract infection with chest congestion, cough, yellow phlegm and fever	***Pinellia XPT***
		To stop the production of phlegm	***Pinellia Complex***
		Nasal congestion with yellow, sticky discharge	***Pueraria Clear Sinus***
		Nasal congestion with white, watery discharge	***Magnolia Clear Sinus***
		Cough and dyspnea	***Respitrol (CF)***
Budeprion	*Bupropion*	Depression with low energy, prolonged sadness and lack of interest	***Shine***
		Depression with stress and anxiety	***Shine (DS)***
Budesonide + Formoterol	**Symbicort**	*See* **Symbicort**	
Bumex	*Bumetanide*	Edema and fluid retention	***Herbal DRX***

Drug – Herb Index

Brand Names / *Generic Names*		**Clinical Applications**	**Herb Alternatives**
Buprenorphine + Naloxone	**Suboxone**	*See* **Suboxone**	
Bupropion	**Budeprion, Wellbutrin**	*See* **Budeprion, Wellbutrin**	
BuSpar	*Buspirone*	Moderate levels of stress, anxiety, nervousness, and tension	***Calm***
		Moderate to severe emotional and psychological disorders	***Calm (ES)***
		Moderate levels of stress, anxiety, and insomnia	***Calm ZZZ***
Buspirone	**BuSpar**	*See* **BuSpar**	
Butalbital + APAP + Caffeine	**Fioricet**	*See* **Fioricet**	
Butalbital + Aspirin + Caffeine	**Fiorinal**	*See* **Fiorinal**	
Bystolic	*Nebivolol*	Elevated blood pressure in patients with hyperactive adrenergic system	***Gentiana Complex***
Caffeine	**NoDoz, Vivarin**	*See* **NoDoz, Vivarin**	
Calan	*Verapamil*	Cardiovascular disorders, such as hypertension	***Gastrodia Complex***
Calcium Carbonate	**Tums**	*See* **Tums**	
Calcium Sennosides	**Ex-Lax**	*See* **Ex-Lax**	
Campral	*Acamprosate*	Craving and withdrawal symptoms associated with alcohol addiction	***Calm (ES)***
Capoten	*Captopril*	Cardiovascular disorders, such as hypertension	***Gastrodia Complex***
Captopril	**Capoten**	*See* **Capoten**	
Carbamazepine	**Tegretol**	*See* **Tegretol**	
Carbidopa + Levodopa	**Sinemet**	*See* **Sinemet**	
Cardizem	*Diltiazem*	Cardiovascular disorders, such as hypertension	***Gastrodia Complex***
Cardura	*Doxazosin*	Elevated blood pressure in patients with hyperactive adrenergic system	***Gentiana Complex***
Carisoprodol	**Soma**	*See* **Soma**	
Cartia XT	*Diltiazem*	Cardiovascular disorders, such as hypertension	***Gastrodia Complex***
Carvedilol	**Coreg**	*See* **Coreg**	
Cataflam	*Diclofenac*	Various headaches: migraine, tension, stress, vertex, occipital	***Corydalin (AC)*** or ***(CR)***
		Musculoskeletal pain with redness, swelling and inflammation	***Flex (Heat)***
		Musculoskeletal pain that worsens during cold and rainy days	***Flex (CD)***
		Neuropathy	***Flex (NP)***
		Chronic injuries of soft tissues (muscles, ligaments, and tendons)	***Flex (MLT)***
		Arm pain (shoulder, elbow, and wrist)	***Arm Support***
		Acute or chronic pain of the leg (knee and ankle)	***Knee & Ankle (AC)*** or ***(CR)***
		Acute or chronic upper and lower back pain	***Back Support (AC)*** or ***(CR)***
		Acute or chronic neck and shoulder pain	***Neck & Shoulder (AC)*** or ***(CR)***
		Menstrual pain and cramps in dysmenorrhea	***Mense-Ease***
		Pain associated with amenorrhea	***Menatrol***

Drug – Herb Index

Brand Names / *Generic Names*		**Clinical Applications**	**Herb Alternatives**
Cataflam *(cont'd)*	*Diclofenac*	Pain associated with endometriosis	***Resolve (Lower)***
		Severe pain	*add* ***Herbal ANG***
		Pain due to trauma	*add* ***Flex (TMX)***
Catapres	*Clonidine*	Elevated blood pressure in patients with hyperactive adrenergic system	***Gentiana Complex***
Ceclor	*Cefaclor*	Generalized bacterial infection	***Herbal ABX***
		Upper respiratory tract infection with fever, headache, sore throat	***Lonicera Complex***
		Respiratory tract infection with sinus congestion, watery nasal discharge, sneezing and chills	***Respitrol (Cold)***
		Lower respiratory tract infection with high fever, copious yellow sputum, cough and perspiration	***Respitrol (Heat)***
		Lower respiratory tract infection with chest congestion, cough, yellow phlegm and fever	***Pinellia XPT***
		Infection in the gastrointestinal tract	***GI Care II***
		Genitourinary infections, such as urinary tract infection or sexually-transmitted diseases	***Gentiana Complex*** or ***V-Support***
		Ear, nose and throat infections	***Herbal ENT***
		General skin conditions associated with infection and inflammation	***Dermatrol (Damp)*** or ***Dermatrol (Dry)***
		With more swelling and inflammation	*add* ***Astringent Complex***
Cefaclor	**Ceclor**	*See* **Ceclor**	
Cefadroxil	**Duricef**	*See* **Duricef**	
Cefdinir	**Omnicef**	*See* **Omnicef**	
Cefixime	**Suprax**	*See* **Suprax**	
Cefprozil	**Cefzil**	*See* **Cefzil**	
Ceftin	*Cefuroxime*	Generalized bacterial infection	***Herbal ABX***
		Upper respiratory tract infection with fever, headache, sore throat	***Lonicera Complex***
		Respiratory tract infection with sinus congestion, watery nasal discharge, sneezing and chills	***Respitrol (Cold)***
		Lower respiratory tract infection with high fever, copious yellow sputum, cough and perspiration	***Respitrol (Heat)***
		Lower respiratory tract infection with chest congestion, cough, yellow phlegm and fever	***Pinellia XPT***
		Infection in the gastrointestinal tract	***GI Care II***
		Genitourinary infections, such as urinary tract infection or sexually-transmitted diseases	***Gentiana Complex*** or ***V-Support***
		Ear, nose, and throat infections	***Herbal ENT***
		General skin conditions associated with infection and inflammation	***Dermatrol (Damp)*** or ***Dermatrol (Dry)***
		With more swelling and inflammation	*add* ***Astringent Complex***
Cefuroxime	**Ceftin**	*See* **Ceftin**	

Drug – Herb Index

Brand Names / *Generic Names*		**Clinical Applications**	**Herb Alternatives**
Cefzil	*Cefprozil*	Generalized bacterial infection	***Herbal ABX***
		Upper respiratory tract infection with fever, headache, sore throat	***Lonicera Complex***
		Respiratory tract infection with sinus congestion, watery nasal discharge, sneezing and chills	***Respitrol (Cold)***
		Lower respiratory tract infection with high fever, copious yellow sputum, cough and perspiration	***Respitrol (Heat)***
		Lower respiratory tract infection with chest congestion, cough, yellow phlegm and fever	***Pinellia XPT***
		Infection in the gastrointestinal tract	***GI Care II***
		Genitourinary infections, such as urinary tract infection or sexually-transmitted diseases	***Gentiana Complex*** or ***V-Support***
		Ear, nose, and throat infections	***Herbal ENT***
		General skin conditions associated with infection and inflammation	***Dermatrol (Damp)*** or ***Dermatrol (Dry)***
		With more swelling and inflammation	*add* ***Astringent Complex***
Celebrex	*Celecoxib*	Various headaches: migraine, tension, stress, vertex, occipital	***Corydalin (AC)*** or ***(CR)***
		Musculoskeletal pain with redness, swelling and inflammation	***Flex (Heat)***
		Musculoskeletal pain that worsens during cold and rainy days	***Flex (CD)***
		Neuropathy	***Flex (NP)***
		Chronic injuries of soft tissues (muscles, ligaments, and tendons)	***Flex (MLT)***
		Arm pain (shoulder, elbow, and wrist)	***Arm Support***
		Acute or chronic pain of the leg (knee and ankle)	***Knee & Ankle (AC)*** or ***(CR)***
		Acute or chronic upper and lower back pain	***Back Support (AC)*** or ***(CR)***
		Acute or chronic neck and shoulder pain	***Neck & Shoulder (AC)*** or ***(CR)***
		Menstrual pain and cramps in dysmenorrhea	***Mense-Ease***
		Pain associated with amenorrhea	***Menatrol***
		Pain associated with endometriosis	***Resolve (Lower)***
		Severe pain	*add* ***Herbal ANG***
		Pain due to trauma	*add* ***Flex (TMX)***
Celecoxib	**Celebrex**	*See* **Celebrex**	
Celexa	*Citalopram*	Depression with low energy, prolonged sadness and lack of interest	***Shine***
		Depression with stress and anxiety	***Shine (DS)***
Cephalexin	**Keflex**	*See* **Keflex**	
Cetirizine	**Zyrtec**	*See* **Zyrtec**	
Chantix	*Varenicline*	Craving and withdrawal symptoms associated with cigarette smoking addiction	***Calm (ES)***
Chlorpheniramine + Hydrocodone	**Tussionex**	*See* **Tussionex**	
Chlorpromazine	**Thorazine**	*See* **Thorazine**	
Chlorzoxazone	**Parafon Forte DSC**	*See* **Parafon Forte DSC**	

Drug – Herb Index

Brand Names / *Generic Names*		**Clinical Applications**	**Herb Alternatives**
Cialis	*Tadalafil*	Male sexual disorder (i.e., erectile dysfunction, impotence)	***Vitality***
		Male reproductive disorder (i.e., infertility)	***Vital Essence***
		Male sexual and reproductive dysfunctions with cold signs and symptoms	***Kidney Tonic (Yang)***
Cimetidine	**Tagamet**	*See* **Tagamet**	
Cipro	*Ciprofloxacin*	Generalized bacterial infection	***Herbal ABX***
		Upper respiratory tract infection with fever, headache, sore throat	***Lonicera Complex***
		Respiratory tract infection with sinus congestion, watery nasal discharge, sneezing and chills	***Respitrol (Cold)***
		Lower respiratory tract infection with high fever, copious yellow sputum, cough and perspiration	***Respitrol (Heat)***
		Lower respiratory tract infection with chest congestion, cough, yellow phlegm and fever	***Pinellia XPT***
		Infection in the gastrointestinal tract	***GI Care II***
		Genitourinary infections, such as urinary tract infection or sexually-transmitted diseases	***Gentiana Complex*** or ***V-Support***
		Ear, nose, and throat infections	***Herbal ENT***
		General skin conditions associated with infection and inflammation	***Dermatrol (Damp)*** or ***Dermatrol (Dry)***
Ciprofloxacin	**Cipro**	*See* **Cipro**	
Citalopram	**Celexa**	*See* **Celexa**	
Clarinex	*Desloratadine*	Nasal congestion with yellow, sticky discharge	***Pueraria Clear Sinus***
		Nasal congestion with white, watery discharge	***Magnolia Clear Sinus***
		Allergic or hypersensitive skin problems such as rash, itching, and eczema	***Silerex***
Clarithromycin	**Biaxin**	*See* **Biaxin**	
Claritin	*Loratadine*	Nasal congestion with yellow, sticky discharge	***Pueraria Clear Sinus***
		Nasal congestion with white, watery discharge	***Magnolia Clear Sinus***
		Allergic or hypersensitive skin problems such as rash, itching, and eczema	***Silerex***
Cleocin	*Clindamycin*	Generalized bacterial infection	***Herbal ABX***
		Upper respiratory tract infection with fever, headache, sore throat	***Lonicera Complex***
		Respiratory tract infection with sinus congestion, watery nasal discharge, sneezing and chills	***Respitrol (Cold)***
		Lower respiratory tract infection with high fever, copious yellow sputum, cough and perspiration	***Respitrol (Heat)***
		Lower respiratory tract infection with chest congestion, cough, yellow phlegm and fever	***Pinellia XPT***
		Infection in the gastrointestinal tract	***GI Care II***
		Genitourinary infections, such as urinary tract infection or sexually-transmitted diseases	***Gentiana Complex*** or ***V-Support***
		Ear, nose, and throat infections	***Herbal ENT***

Drug – Herb Index

Brand Names / *Generic Names*		**Clinical Applications**	**Herb Alternatives**
Cleocin (*cont'd*)	*Clindamycin*	General skin conditions associated with infection and inflammation	***Dermatrol (Damp)*** or ***Dermatrol (Dry)***
		With more swelling and inflammation	*add* ***Astringent Complex***
Clindamycin	**Cleocin**	*See* **Cleocin**	
Clinoril	*Sulindac*	Various headaches: migraine, tension, stress, vertex, occipital	***Corydalin (AC)*** or ***(CR)***
		Musculoskeletal pain with redness, swelling and inflammation	***Flex (Heat)***
		Musculoskeletal pain that worsens during cold and rainy days	***Flex (CD)***
		Neuropathy	***Flex (NP)***
		Chronic injuries of soft tissues (muscles, ligaments, and tendons)	***Flex (MLT)***
		Arm pain (shoulder, elbow, and wrist)	***Arm Support***
		Acute or chronic pain of the leg (knee and ankle)	***Knee & Ankle (AC)*** or ***(CR)***
		Acute or chronic upper and lower back pain	***Back Support (AC)*** or ***(CR)***
		Acute or chronic neck and shoulder pain	***Neck & Shoulder (AC)*** or ***(CR)***
		Menstrual pain and cramps in dysmenorrhea	***Mense-Ease***
		Pain associated with amenorrhea	***Menatrol***
		Pain associated with endometriosis	***Resolve (Lower)***
		Severe pain	*add* ***Herbal ANG***
		Pain due to trauma	*add* ***Flex (TMX)***
Clobetasol	**Temovate**	*See* **Temovate**	
Clomid	*Clomiphene*	Amenorrhea or ovulatory failure	***Menatrol***
		Female infertility due cysts, fibroids or blocked fallopian tube	***Resolve (Lower)***
		Female infertility due to ovulatory failure	***Blossom (Phase 1-4)***
Clomiphene	**Clomid**	*See* **Clomid**	
Clomipramine	**Anafranil**	*See* **Anafranil**	
Clonazepam	**Klonopin**	*See* **Klonopin**	
Clonidine	**Catapres**	*See* **Catapres**	
Clotrimazole	**Gyne-Lotrimin, Mycelex**	*See* **Gyne-Lotrimin, Mycelex**	
Clotrimazole + Betamethasone	**Lotrisone**	*See* **Lotrisone**	
Cogentin	*Benzatropine*	To improve mental and physical functions in Parkinson's disease	***Neuro Plus***
Cognex	*Tacrine*	Mental and physical deteriorations in Alzheimer's disease and dementia	***Neuro Plus***
		Mental deteriorations with aging	***Enhance Memory***
Colace	*Docusate*	Excess-type constipation with yellow tongue coat and red face	***Gentle Lax (Excess)***
		Deficient-type constipation with dryness	***Gentle Lax (Deficient)***
		Fecal compaction	***GI DTX***
Colchicine	*Colchicine*	Gout	***Flex (GT)***
Colesevelam	**Welchol**	*See* **Welchol**	

DRUG-HERB

Drug – Herb Index

Brand Names / *Generic Names*		**Clinical Applications**	**Herb Alternatives**
Combivent	*Ipratropium + Salbutamol*	Heat-type asthma with fever, dry mouth, thirst, red face and red tongue	***Respitrol (Heat)***
		Cold-type asthma with chills, intolerance to cold, cyanotic complexion of the face and body	***Respitrol (Cold)***
		Chronic asthma with frequent attacks of wheezing and dyspnea	***Respitrol (Deficient)*** or ***Cordyceps 3***
Concerta	*Methylphenidate*	To promote concentration and focus in ADD (attention deficit disorder) and ADHD (attention deficit-hyperactivity disorder)	***Calm (Jr)***
Coreg	*Carvedilol*	Elevated blood pressure in patients with hyperactive adrenergic system	***Gentiana Complex***
Corticosteroid	*Corticosteroid*	For astringent and non-steroidal anti-inflammatory effect	***Astringent Complex***
		Arthritis	***Flex (Heat), Flex (CD)*** or ***Flex (NP)***
		Management of acute asthma	***Respitrol (Heat)*** or ***(Cold)***
		Management and prevention of chronic asthma	***Respitrol (Deficient)*** or ***Cordyceps 3***
		Sinusitis or rhinitis	***Magnolia Clear Sinus*** or ***Pueraria Clear Sinus***
		Inflammatory bowel disorders in general	***GI Care II***
		Irritable bowel syndrome	***GI Harmony***
		Ulcerative colitis	***GI Care (UC)***
		Hemorrhoids	***GI Care (HMR)***
		Skin rash and eczema	***Silerex***
		Skin conditions with lesions, infections, and inflammations	***Dermatrol (Damp)*** or ***Dermatrol (Dry)***
		Psoriasis	***Dermatrol (PS)***
Cozaar	*Losartan*	Cardiovascular disorders, such as hypertension	***Gastrodia Complex***
Crestor	*Rosuvastatin*	Elevated serum cholesterol and triglycerides levels	***Cholisma***
		Elevated serum cholesterol and triglycerides levels with fatty liver and obesity	***Cholisma (ES)***
Cyclobenzaprine	**Flexeril**	*See* **Flexeril**	
Cymbalta	*Duloxetine*	Depression with low energy, prolonged sadness and lack of interest	***Shine***
		Depression with stress and anxiety	***Shine (DS)***
Dalmane	*Flurazepam*	Insomnia due to Liver qi stagnation (stress, anxiety, nervousness, restlessness)	***Calm ZZZ***
		Insomnia due to *shen* (spirit) disturbance with qi and blood deficiencies	***Schisandra ZZZ***
Danazol	**Danocrine**	*See* **Danocrine**	
Danocrine	*Danazol*	Fibrocystic benign breast disorder	***Resolve (Upper)***
		Endometriosis or cysts in the uterus and ovaries	***Resolve (Lower)***
Darvocet	*Propoxyphene + Acetaminophen*	Various headaches: migraine, tension, stress, vertex, occipital	***Corydalin (AC)***
		Musculoskeletal pain due to sports or traumatic injuries	***Flex (TMX)***
		Arthritis, especially if condition worsens with cold and dampness	***Flex (CD)***

Drug – Herb Index

Brand Names / *Generic Names*		**Clinical Applications**	**Herb Alternatives**
Darvocet (*cont'd*)	*Propoxyphene + Acetaminophen*	Acute or chronic upper and lower back pain	***Back Support (AC)***
		Acute or chronic neck and shoulder pain	***Neck & Shoulder (AC)***
		Arm pain (shoulder, elbow, and wrist)	***Arm Support***
		Acute pain from herniated disk in the back	***Back Support (HD)***
		Acute pain of the leg (knee and ankle)	***Knee & Ankle (AC)***
		Severe pain	*add* ***Herbal ANG***
Darvon	*Propoxyphene*	Various headaches: migraine, tension, stress, vertex, occipital	***Corydalin (AC)***
		Musculoskeletal pain due to sports or traumatic injuries	***Flex (TMX)***
		Arthritis, especially if condition worsens with cold and dampness	***Flex (CD)***
		Acute or chronic upper and lower back pain	***Back Support (AC)***
		Acute or chronic neck and shoulder pain	***Neck & Shoulder (AC)***
		Arm pain (shoulder, elbow, and wrist)	***Arm Support***
		Acute pain from herniated disk in the back	***Back Support (HD)***
		Acute pain of the leg (knee and ankle)	***Knee & Ankle (AC)***
		Severe pain	*add* ***Herbal ANG***
Daypro	*Oxaprozin*	Various headaches: migraine, tension, stress, vertex, occipital	***Corydalin (AC)*** or ***(CR)***
		Musculoskeletal pain with redness, swelling and inflammation	***Flex (Heat)***
		Musculoskeletal pain that worsens during cold and rainy days	***Flex (CD)***
		Neuropathy	***Flex (NP)***
		Chronic injuries of soft tissues (muscles, ligaments, and tendons)	***Flex (MLT)***
		Arm pain (shoulder, elbow, and wrist)	***Arm Support***
		Acute or chronic pain of the leg (knee and ankle)	***Knee & Ankle (AC)*** or ***(CR)***
		Acute or chronic upper and lower back pain	***Back Support (AC)*** or ***(CR)***
		Acute or chronic neck and shoulder pain	***Neck & Shoulder (AC)*** or ***(CR)***
		Menstrual pain and cramps in dysmenorrhea	***Mense-Ease***
		Pain associated with endometriosis	***Resolve (Lower)***
		Severe pain	*add* ***Herbal ANG***
		Pain due to trauma	*add* ***Flex (TMX)***
Demadex	*Torsemide*	Edema and fluid retention	***Herbal DRX***
Denavir	*Penciclovir*	Treatment of oral herpes	***Lonicera Complex***
		Treatment of genital herpes	***Gentiana Complex***
		Prevention of recurrent genital herpes	***Nourish***
		Treatment of herpes zoster (shingles)	***Dermatrol (HZ)***
		For post-herpetic neuralgia	*add* ***Flex (NP)***
		Generalized viral infection	*add* ***Herbal AVR***
		To enhance immunity during remission	***Immune +***
Desipramine	**Norpramin**	*See* **Norpramin**	
Desloratadine	**Clarinex**	*See* **Clarinex**	

DRUG–HERB

Drug – Herb Index

Brand Names / *Generic Names*		**Clinical Applications**	**Herb Alternatives**
Desvenlafaxine	**Pristiq**	*See* **Pristiq**	
Desyrel	*Trazodone*	Depression with low energy, prolonged sadness and lack of interest	***Shine***
		Depression with stress and anxiety	***Shine (DS)***
		Nerve-related pain, such as neuralgia and neuropathy	***Flex (NP)***
Detrol	*Tolterodine*	Frequent urination and inability to control urination	***Kidney Tonic (Yang)***
Dexedrine	*Dextroamphetamine*	To promote concentration and focus in ADD (attention deficit disorder) and ADHD (attention deficit-hyperactivity disorder)	***Calm (Jr)***
Dexilant	*Dexlansoprazole*	Various gastrointestinal disorders, such as heartburn, acid reflux and peptic ulcer	***GI Care***
Dexlansoprazole	**Dexilant**	*See* **Dexilant**	
Dexmethylphenidate	**Focalin**	*See* **Focalin**	
Dextroamphetamine	**Dexedrine**	*See* **Dexedrine**	
DiaBeta	*Glyburide*	Elevated blood glucose levels in non-insulin dependent diabetes mellitus	***Equilibrium***
Diazepam	**Valium**	*See* **Valium**	
Diclofenac	**Cataflam, Voltaren**	*See* **Cataflam, Voltaren**	
Dicyclomine	**Bentyl**	*See* **Bentyl**	
Didronel	*Etidronate*	Osteoporosis	***Osteo 8***
Diethylpropion	**Tenuate**	*See* **Tenuate**	
Differin	*Adapalene*	Acne	***Dermatrol (Clear)***
Diflunisal	**Dolobid**	*See* **Dolobid**	
Dilantin	*Phenytoin*	Nerve-related pain, such as neuralgia and neuropathy	***Flex (NP)***
Diltiazem	**Cardizem**	*See* **Cardizem**	
Dimetapp	*Phenylpropanolamine + Brompheniramine*	Lower respiratory tract infection with chest congestion, cough, yellow phlegm and fever	***Pinellia XPT***
		To stop the production of phlegm	***Pinellia Complex***
		Nasal congestion with yellow, sticky discharge	***Pueraria Clear Sinus***
		Nasal congestion with white, watery discharge	***Magnolia Clear Sinus***
		Cough and dyspnea	***Respitrol (CF)***
Diovan	*Valsartan*	Cardiovascular disorders, such as hypertension	***Gastrodia Complex***
Diphenhydramine	**Benadryl, Sominex**	*See* **Benadryl, Sominex**	
Docosanol	**Abreva**	*See* **Abreva**	
Docusate	**Colace**	*See* **Colace**	
Dolobid	*Diflunisal*	Various headaches: migraine, tension, stress, vertex, occipital	***Corydalin (AC)*** or ***(CR)***
		Musculoskeletal pain with redness, swelling and inflammation	***Flex (Heat)***
		Musculoskeletal pain that worsens during cold and rainy days	***Flex (CD)***
		Neuropathy	***Flex (NP)***
		Chronic injuries of soft tissues (muscles, ligaments, and tendons)	***Flex (MLT)***
		Arm pain (shoulder, elbow, and wrist)	***Arm Support***
		Acute or chronic pain of the leg (knee and ankle)	***Knee & Ankle (AC)*** or ***(CR)***

Drug – Herb Index

Brand Names / *Generic Names*		**Clinical Applications**	**Herb Alternatives**
Dolobid (*cont'd*)	*Diflunisal*	Acute or chronic upper and lower back pain	***Back Support (AC)*** or ***(CR)***
		Acute or chronic neck and shoulder pain	***Neck & Shoulder (AC)*** or ***(CR)***
		Menstrual pain and cramps in dysmenorrhea	***Mense-Ease***
		Pain associated with amenorrhea	***Menatrol***
		Pain associated with endometriosis	***Resolve (Lower)***
		Severe pain	*add* ***Herbal ANG***
		Pain due to trauma	*add* ***Flex (TMX)***
Donepezil	**Aricept**	*See* **Aricept**	
Doxazosin	**Cardura**	*See* **Cardura**	
Doxepin	**Sinequan**	*See* **Sinequan**	
Doxycycline	**Vibramycin**	*See* **Vibramycin**	
Doxylamine	**Unisom**	*See* **Unisom**	
Dulcolax	*Bisacodyl*	Moderate to severe constipation	***Gentle Lax (Excess)*** or ***(Deficient)***
Dulera	*Formoterol + Mometasone*	Heat-type asthma with fever, dry mouth, thirst, red face and red tongue	***Respitrol (Heat)***
		Cold-type asthma with chills, intolerance to cold, cyanotic complexion of the face and body	***Respitrol (Cold)***
		Chronic asthma with frequent attacks of wheezing and dyspnea	***Respitrol (Deficient)***
Duloxetine	**Cymbalta**	*See* **Cymbalta**	
Duphalac	*Lactulose*	Moderate to severe constipation	***Gentle Lax (Excess)*** or ***(Deficient)***
Duragesic	*Fentanyl (Transdermal)*	Various headaches: migraine, tension, stress, vertex, occipital	***Corydalin (AC)***
		Musculoskeletal pain due to sports or traumatic injuries	***Flex (TMX)***
		Arthritis, especially if condition worsens with cold and dampness	***Flex (CD)***
		Acute or chronic upper and lower back pain	***Back Support (AC)***
		Acute or chronic neck and shoulder pain	***Neck & Shoulder (AC)***
		Arm pain (shoulder, elbow, and wrist)	***Arm Support***
		Acute pain from herniated disk in the back	***Back Support (HD)***
		Acute pain of the leg (knee and ankle)	***Knee & Ankle (AC)***
		Severe pain	*add* ***Herbal ANG***
Duratuss	*Expectorant Combination*	Lower respiratory tract infection with chest congestion, cough, yellow phlegm and fever	***Pinellia XPT***
		To stop the production of phlegm	***Pinellia Complex***
		Cough and dyspnea	***Respitrol (CF)***
Duricef	*Cefadroxil*	Generalized bacterial infection	***Herbal ABX***
		Upper respiratory tract infection with fever, headache, sore throat	***Lonicera Complex***
		Respiratory tract infection with sinus congestion, watery nasal discharge, sneezing and chills	***Respitrol (Cold)***
		Lower respiratory tract infection with high fever, copious yellow sputum, cough and perspiration	***Respitrol (Heat)***

DRUG–HERB

Drug – Herb Index

Brand Names / *Generic Names*		**Clinical Applications**	**Herb Alternatives**
Duricef *(cont'd)*	*Cefadroxil*	Lower respiratory tract infection with chest congestion, cough, yellow phlegm and fever	***Pinellia XPT***
		Infection in the gastrointestinal tract	***GI Care II***
		Genitourinary infections, such as urinary tract infection or sexually-transmitted diseases	***Gentiana Complex*** or ***V-Support***
		Ear, nose, and throat infections	***Herbal ENT***
		General skin conditions associated with infection and inflammation	***Dermatrol (Damp)*** or ***Dermatrol (Dry)***
		With more swelling and inflammation	*add* ***Astringent Complex***
Dutasteride	**Avodart**	*See* **Avodart**	
Dyazide	*Triamterene + Hydrochlorothiazide*	Edema and fluid retention	***Herbal DRX***
Dyrenium	*Triamterene*	Edema and fluid retention	***Herbal DRX***
EES	*Erythromycin*	*See* **E-Mycin**	
Efalizumab	**Raptiva**	*See* **Raptiva**	
Effexor	*Venlafaxine*	Depression with low energy, prolonged sadness and lack of interest	***Shine***
		Depression with stress and anxiety	***Shine (DS)***
Elavil	*Amitriptyline*	Depression with low energy, prolonged sadness and lack of interest	***Shine***
		Depression with stress and anxiety	***Shine (DS)***
		Nerve-related pain, such as neuralgia and neuropathy	***Flex (NP)***
Eldepryl	*Selegiline*	To improve mental and physical functions in Parkinson's disease	***Neuro Plus***
Eletriptan	**Relpax**	*See* **Relpax**	
Elidel	*Pimecrolimus*	Allergic or hypersensitive skin problems such as rash, itching, and eczema	***Silerex***
Emend	*Aprepitant*	Chemotherapy-induced emesis	***C/R Support***
E-Mycin	*Erythromycin*	Generalized bacterial infection	***Herbal ABX***
		Upper respiratory tract infection with fever, headache, sore throat	***Lonicera Complex***
		Respiratory tract infection with sinus congestion, watery nasal discharge, sneezing and chills	***Respitrol (Cold)***
		Lower respiratory tract infection with high fever, copious yellow sputum, cough and perspiration	***Respitrol (Heat)***
		Lower respiratory tract infection with chest congestion, cough, yellow phlegm and fever	***Pinellia XPT***
		Infection in the gastrointestinal tract	***GI Care II***
		Genito-urinary infections, such as urinary tract infection or sexually-transmitted diseases	***Gentiana Complex*** or ***V-Support***
		Ear, nose, and throat infections	***Herbal ENT***
		General skin conditions associated with infection and inflammation	***Dermatrol (Damp)*** or ***Dermatrol (Dry)***
		With more swelling and inflammation	*add* ***Astringent Complex***
Enalapril	**Vasotec**	*See* **Vasotec**	

Drug – Herb Index

Brand Names / *Generic Names*		**Clinical Applications**	**Herb Alternatives**
Enbrel	*Etanercept*	Treatment of autoimmune diseases, such as rheumatoid arthritis	***Flex (Heat)*** or ***Flex (CD)***
		Treatment of autoimmune diseases, such as psoriasis	***Dermatrol (PS)***
		Treatment of autoimmune diseases, such as ulcerative colitis and Crohn's disease	***GI Care (UC)***
		Treatment of autoimmune diseases, such as Sjögren's syndrome	***Nourish (Fluids)***
		Treatment of autoimmune diseases, such as scleroderma and Raynaud's syndrome	***Circulation (SJ)***
		Treatment of autoimmune diseases, such as systemic lupus erythematosus	***LPS Support***
		Treatment of autoimmune diseases, such as multiple sclerosis	***Neuro Plus***
		To suppress acute inflammation in autoimmune diseases	*add* ***Gardenia Complex***
		To manage chronic inflammation in autoimmune diseases	*add* ***Nourish***
		To promote generation of new cells, tissues, and organs	*add* ***Kidney Tonic (Yin)*** or ***Nourish***
		To promote blood circulation and facilitate repair and regeneration	*add* ***Circulation (SJ)***
Entex	*Guaifenesin + Phenylephrine + Phenylpropanolamine*	Lower respiratory tract infection with chest congestion, cough, yellow phlegm and fever	***Pinellia XPT***
		To stop the production of phlegm	***Pinellia Complex***
		Nasal congestion with yellow, sticky discharge	***Pueraria Clear Sinus***
		Nasal congestion with white, watery discharge	***Magnolia Clear Sinus***
		Cough and dyspnea	***Respitrol (CF)***
Epoetin alfa	**Epogen**	*See* **Epogen**	
Epogen	*Epoetin alfa*	To strengthen the overall constitution of the person	***Schisandra ZZZ*** or ***Imperial Tonic***
		To enhance the immune system during chemotherapy and radiation treatment	***C/R Support***
		To tonify the body for individuals who are too weak to receive chemotherapy and radiation treatment	***CA Support***
Erythromycin	**E-Mycin, EES, PCE**	*See* **E-Mycin**	
Escitalopram	**Lexapro**	*See* **Lexapro**	
Esomeprazole	**Nexium**	*See* **Nexium**	
Estrace	*Estradiol*	Menopausal symptoms such as hot flashes, irritability and mood swings	***Balance (Heat)*** or ***Nourish***
		Osteoporosis	***Osteo 8***
		Vaginal dryness and atrophy	***Balance Spring***
Estradiol	**Estrace, Estring, Vivelle, Vagifem**	*See* **Estrace** (Oral), **Estring** (Vaginal Ring), **Vivelle** (Transdermal), **Vagifem** (Vaginal Tablets)	
Estratab	*Estrogens, Esterified*	Menopausal symptoms such as hot flashes, irritability and mood swings	***Balance (Heat)*** or ***Nourish***
		Osteoporosis	***Osteo 8***
		Vaginal dryness and atrophy	***Balance Spring***
Estring	*Estradiol Vaginal Ring*	Vaginal dryness and atrophy	***Balance Spring***

Drug – Herb Index

Brand Names / *Generic Names*		**Clinical Applications**	**Herb Alternatives**
Estrogens + Progestins	**Prempro**	*See* **Prempro**	
Estrogens, Conjugated	**Premarin**	*See* **Premarin**	
Estrogens, Esterified	**Estratab**	*See* **Estratab**	
Estropipate	**Ogen**	*See* **Ogen**	
Eszopiclone	**Lunesta**	*See* **Lunesta**	
Etanercept	**Enbrel**	*See* **Enbrel**	
Etidronate	**Didronel**	*See* **Didronel**	
Etodolac	**Lodine**	*See* **Lodine**	
Evista	*Raloxifene*	Osteoporosis	***Osteo 8***
Exelon	*Rivastigmine*	Mental and physical deteriorations in Alzheimer's disease and dementia	***Neuro Plus***
		Mental deteriorations due to aging	***Enhance Memory***
Exforge	*Amlodipine + Valsartan*	Cardiovascular disorders, such as hypertension	***Gastrodia Complex***
Ex-Lax	*Calcium Sennosides*	Moderate to severe constipation	***Gentle Lax (Excess)*** or ***(Deficient)***
Expectorant Combination	**Duratuss, Zephrex**	*See* **Duratuss, Zephrex**	
Ezetimibe	**Zetia**	*See* **Zetia**	
Ezetimibe + Simvastatin	**Vytorin**	*See* **Vytorin**	
Famciclovir	**Famvir**	*See* **Famvir**	
Famotidine	**Pepcid**	*See* **Pepcid**	
Famvir	*Famciclovir*	Treatment of oral herpes	***Lonicera Complex***
		Treatment of genital herpes	***Gentiana Complex***
		Prevention of recurrent genital herpes	***Nourish***
		Treatment of herpes zoster (shingles)	***Dermatrol (HZ)***
		For post-herpetic neuralgia	*add* ***Flex (NP)***
		Generalized viral infection	*add* ***Herbal AVR***
		To enhance immunity during remission	***Immune +***
Fastin	*Phentermine*	Obesity, elevated body weight, slow basal metabolism, lack of energy	***Herbalite***
Febuxostat	**Uloric**	*See* **Uloric**	
Feldene	*Piroxicam*	Various headaches: migraine, tension, stress, vertex, occipital	***Corydalin (AC)*** or ***(CR)***
		Musculoskeletal pain with redness, swelling and inflammation	***Flex (Heat)***
		Musculoskeletal pain that worsens during cold and rainy days	***Flex (CD)***
		Neuropathy	***Flex (NP)***
		Chronic injuries of soft tissues (muscles, ligaments, and tendons)	***Flex (MLT)***
		Arm pain (shoulder, elbow, and wrist)	***Arm Support***

Drug – Herb Index

Brand Names / *Generic Names*		**Clinical Applications**	**Herb Alternatives**
Feldene (*cont'd*)	*Piroxicam*	Acute or chronic pain of the leg (knee and ankle)	***Knee & Ankle (AC)*** or ***(CR)***
		Acute or chronic upper and lower back pain	***Back Support (AC)*** or ***(CR)***
		Acute or chronic neck and shoulder pain	***Neck & Shoulder (AC)*** or ***(CR)***
		Menstrual pain and cramps in dysmenorrhea	***Mense-Ease***
		Pain associated with amenorrhea	***Menatrol***
		Pain associated with endometriosis	***Resolve (Lower)***
		Severe pain	*add* ***Herbal ANG***
		Pain due to trauma	*add* ***Flex (TMX)***
Felodipine	**Plendil**	*See* **Plendil**	
Fenofibrate	**Tricor**	*See* **Tricor**	
Fenofibric Acid	**Trilipix**	*See* **Trilipix**	
Fentanyl (Transdermal)	**Duragesic**	*See* **Duragesic**	
Fexofenadine	**Allegra**	*See* **Allegra**	
Filgrastim	**Neupogen**	*See* **Neupogen**	
Finasteride	**Proscar**	*See* **Proscar**	
Fioricet	*Butalbital + APAP + Caffeine*	Acute headaches	***Corydalin (AC)***
		Chronic headaches	***Corydalin (CR)***
Fiorinal	*Butalbital + Aspirin + Caffeine*	Acute headaches	***Corydalin (AC)***
		Chronic headaches	***Corydalin (CR)***
Flagyl	*Metronidazole*	Infection in the gastrointestinal tract	***GI Care II***
Flexeril	*Cyclobenzaprine*	General relief of muscle spasm and cramps	***Flex (SC)***
Flomax	*Tamsulosin*	Benign prostatic hypertrophy (BPH)	***P-Support***
Flonase	*Fluticasone*	Nasal congestion with yellow, sticky discharge	***Pueraria Clear Sinus***
		Nasal congestion with white, watery discharge	***Magnolia Clear Sinus***
Flovent	*Fluticasone*	Dyspnea and shortness of breath in cases of chronic asthma	***Respitrol (Deficient)***
		Management and prevention of chronic asthma	***Cordyceps 3***
		For astringent and non-steroidal anti-inflammatory effect	***Astringent Complex***
Floxin	*Ofloxacin*	Generalized bacterial infection	***Herbal ABX***
		Upper respiratory tract infection with fever, headache, sore throat	***Lonicera Complex***
		Respiratory tract infection with sinus congestion, watery nasal discharge, sneezing and chills	***Respitrol (Cold)***
		Lower respiratory tract infection with high fever, copious yellow sputum, cough and perspiration	***Respitrol (Heat)***
		Lower respiratory tract infection with chest congestion, cough, yellow phlegm and fever	***Pinellia XPT***
		Infection in the gastrointestinal tract	***GI Care II***
		Genitourinary infections, such as urinary tract infection or sexually-transmitted diseases	***Gentiana Complex*** or ***V-Support***

Drug – Herb Index

Brand Names / *Generic Names*		**Clinical Applications**	**Herb Alternatives**
Floxin (*cont'd*)	*Ofloxacin*	Ear, nose, and throat infections	***Herbal ENT***
		General skin conditions associated with infection and inflammation	***Dermatrol (Damp)*** or ***Dermatrol (Dry)***
		With more swelling and inflammation	*add* ***Astringent Complex***
Fluoxetine	**Prozac**	*See* **Prozac**	
Flurazepam	**Dalmane**	*See* **Dalmane**	
Flurbiprofen	**Ansaid**	*See* **Ansaid**	
Fluticasone	**Flonase, Flovent**	*See* **Flonase, Flovent**	
Fluticasone + Salmeterol	**Advair**	*See* **Advair**	
Fluvastatin	**Lescol**	*See* **Lescol**	
Focalin	*Dexmethylphenidate*	To promote concentration and focus in ADD (attention deficit disorder) and ADHD (attention deficit-hyperactivity disorder)	***Calm (Jr)***
Formoterol + Mometasone	**Dulera**	*See* **Dulera**	
Fosamax	*Alendronate*	Osteoporosis	***Osteo 8***
Fosinopril	**Monopril**	*See* **Monopril**	
Frova	*Frovatriptan*	Treatment of acute migraine attack	***Corydalin (AC)***
		Prevention of chronic migraine recurrence	***Corydalin (CR)***
Frovatriptan	**Frova**	*See* **Frova**	
Furadantin	*Nitrofurantoin*	Genitourinary infections, such as urinary tract infection	***Gentiana Complex*** or ***V-Support***
Gabapentin	**Neurontin**	*See* **Neurontin**	
Galantamine	**Reminyl**	*See* **Reminyl**	
Gemfibrozil	**Lopid**	*See* **Lopid**	
Geodon	*Ziprasidone*	Moderate levels of stress, anxiety, nervousness, tension, etc.	***Calm***
		Moderate to severe emotional and psychological disorders	***Calm (ES)***
Glimepiride	**Amaryl**	*See* **Amaryl**	
Glipizide	**Glucotrol**	*See* **Glucotrol**	
Glucophage	*Metformin*	Elevated blood glucose levels in non-insulin dependent diabetes mellitus	***Equilibrium***
Glucotrol	*Glipizide*	Elevated blood glucose levels in non-insulin dependent diabetes mellitus	***Equilibrium***
Glyburide	**DiaBeta, Micronase**	*See* **DiaBeta, Micronase**	
Glycolax	*Polyethylene Glycol*	Moderate to severe constipation	***Gentle Lax (Excess)*** or ***(Deficient)***
Guaifenesin + Phenylephrine + Phenylpropanolamine	**Entex**	*See* **Entex**	
Guanfacine	**Tenex**	*See* **Tenex**	
Gyne-Lotrimin	*Clotrimazole*	Vaginitis	***V-Support***

Drug – Herb Index

Brand Names / *Generic Names*		**Clinical Applications**	**Herb Alternatives**
Haldol	*Haloperidol*	Moderate to severe emotional and psychological disorders	***Calm (ES)***
Haloperidol	**Haldol**	*See* **Haldol**	
Hamamelis	**Tucks**	*See* **Tucks**	
Hepsera	*Adefovir*	Hepatitis B	***Liver DTX***
Humira	*Adalimumab*	Treatment of autoimmune diseases, such as rheumatoid arthritis	***Flex (Heat)*** or ***Flex (CD)***
		Treatment of autoimmune diseases, such as psoriasis	***Dermatrol (PS)***
		Treatment of autoimmune diseases, such as ulcerative colitis and Crohn's disease	***GI Care (UC)***
		Treatment of autoimmune diseases, such as Sjögren's syndrome	***Nourish (Fluids)***
		Treatment of autoimmune diseases, such as scleroderma and Raynaud's syndrome	***Circulation (SJ)***
		Treatment of autoimmune diseases, such as systemic lupus erythematosus	***LPS Support***
		Treatment of autoimmune diseases, such as multiple sclerosis	***Neuro Plus***
		To suppress acute inflammation in autoimmune diseases	*add* ***Gardenia Complex***
		To manage chronic inflammation in autoimmune diseases	*add* ***Nourish***
		To promote generation of new cells, tissues, and organs	*add* ***Kidney Tonic (Yin)*** or ***Nourish***
		To promote blood circulation and facilitate repair and regeneration	*add* ***Circulation (SJ)***
Hydrochlorothiazide	**Microzide**	*See* **Microzide**	
Hydrochlorothiazide + Irbesartan	**Avalide**	*See* **Avalide**	
Hydrochlorothiazide + Triamterene	**Maxzide, Dyazide**	*See* **Maxzide, Dyazide**	
Hydrocodone + Acetaminophen	**Lorcet, Lortab, Vicodin**	*See* **Lorcet, Lortab, Vicodin**	
Hydrocortisone	*Hydrocortisone*	For astringent and non-steroidal anti-inflammatory effect	***Astringent Complex***
		Skin conditions with allergy, rash, itching, eczema, dermatitis	***Silerex***
		Skin conditions with lesions, infections and inflammations	***Dermatrol (Damp)*** or ***Dermatrol (Dry)***
		Psoriasis	***Dermatrol (PS)***
		Hemorrhoids	***GI Care (HMR)***
Hydroxychloroquine	**Plaquenil**	*See* **Plaquenil**	
Hydroxyzine	**Atarax**	*See* **Atarax**	
Hytrin	*Terazosin*	Benign prostatic hypertrophy (BPH)	***P-Support***
		Elevated blood pressure in patients with hyperactive adrenergic system	***Gentiana Complex***
Hyzaar	*Losartan + Hydrochlorothiazide*	Cardiovascular disorders with water accumulation	***Gastrodia Complex*** and ***Herbal DRX***
Ibandronate	**Boniva**	*See* **Boniva**	
Ibuprofen	**Advil, Motrin**	*See* **Advil, Motrin**	

Drug – Herb Index

Brand Names / *Generic Names*		**Clinical Applications**	**Herb Alternatives**
Imipramine	**Tofranil**	*See* **Tofranil**	
Imitrex	*Sumatriptan*	Treatment of acute migraine attack	***Corydalin (AC)***
		Prevention of chronic migraine recurrence	***Corydalin (CR)***
Imodium	*Loperamide*	Acute diarrhea from gastrointestinal infection	***GI Care II***
		Chronic diarrhea from general weakness and deficiency	***GI Tonic***
Inderal	*Propranolol*	Elevated blood pressure in patients with hyperactive adrenergic system	***Gentiana Complex***
Indocin	*Indomethacin*	Various headaches: migraine, tension, stress, vertex, occipital	***Corydalin (AC)*** or ***(CR)***
		Musculoskeletal pain with redness, swelling and inflammation	***Flex (Heat)***
		Musculoskeletal pain that worsens during cold and rainy days	***Flex (CD)***
		Neuropathy	***Flex (NP)***
		Chronic injuries of soft tissues (muscles, ligaments, and tendons)	***Flex (MLT)***
		Arm pain (shoulder, elbow, and wrist)	***Arm Support***
		Acute or chronic pain of the leg (knee and ankle)	***Knee & Ankle (AC)*** or ***(CR)***
		Acute or chronic upper and lower back pain	***Back Support (AC)*** or ***(CR)***
		Acute or chronic neck and shoulder pain	***Neck & Shoulder (AC)*** or ***(CR)***
		Menstrual pain and cramps in dysmenorrhea	***Mense-Ease***
		Pain associated with amenorrhea	***Menatrol***
		Pain associated with endometriosis	***Resolve (Lower)***
		Gout	***Flex (GT)***
		Severe pain	*add* ***Herbal ANG***
		Pain due to trauma	*add* ***Flex (TMX)***
Indomethacin	**Indocin**	*See* **Indocin**	
Infliximab	**Remicade**	*See* **Remicade**	
Insulin Glulisine	**Apidra**	*See* **Apidra**	
Ionamin	*Phentermine*	Obesity, elevated body weight, slow basal metabolism, lack of energy	***Herbalite***
Ipratropium + Salbutamol	**Combivent**	*See* **Combivent**	
Irbesartan	**Avapro**	*See* **Avapro**	
Isometheptene + Apap + Dichloraphenazone	**Midrin**	*See* **Midrin**	
Isoptin	*Verapamil*	Cardiovascular disorders, such as hypertension	***Gastrodia Complex***
Janumet	*Metformin + Sitagliptin*	Elevated blood glucose levels in non-insulin dependent diabetes mellitus	***Equilibrium***
Januvia	*Sitagliptin*	Elevated blood glucose levels in non-insulin dependent diabetes mellitus	***Equilibrium***

Drug – Herb Index

Brand Names / *Generic Names*		**Clinical Applications**	**Herb Alternatives**
Keflex	*Cephalexin*	Generalized bacterial infection	***Herbal ABX***
		Upper respiratory tract infection with fever, headache, sore throat	***Lonicera Complex***
		Respiratory tract infection with sinus congestion, watery nasal discharge, sneezing and chills	***Respitrol (Cold)***
		Lower respiratory tract infection with high fever, copious yellow sputum, cough and perspiration	***Respitrol (Heat)***
		Lower respiratory tract infection with chest congestion, cough, yellow phlegm and fever	***Pinellia XPT***
		Infection in the gastrointestinal tract	***GI Care II***
		Genitourinary infections, such as urinary tract infection or sexually-transmitted diseases	***Gentiana Complex*** or ***V-Support***
		Ear, nose, and throat infections	***Herbal ENT***
		General skin conditions associated with infection and inflammation	***Dermatrol (Damp)*** or ***Dermatrol (Dry)***
		With more swelling and inflammation	add ***Astringent Complex***
Kenalog	*Triamcinolone*	For astringent and non-steroidal anti-inflammatory effect	***Astringent Complex***
		Skin conditions with allergy, rash, itching, eczema, dermatitis	***Silerex***
		Skin conditions with lesions, infections, and inflammations	***Dermatrol (Damp)*** or ***Dermatrol (Dry)***
		Psoriasis	***Dermatrol (PS)***
		Hemorrhoids	***GI Care (HMR)***
Ketek	*Telithromycin*	Generalized bacterial infection	***Herbal ABX***
		Upper respiratory tract infection with fever, headache, sore throat	***Lonicera Complex***
		Respiratory tract infection with sinus congestion, watery nasal discharge, sneezing and chills	***Respitrol (Cold)***
		Lower respiratory tract infection with high fever, copious yellow sputum, cough and perspiration	***Respitrol (Heat)***
		Lower respiratory tract infection with chest congestion, cough, yellow phlegm and fever	***Pinellia XPT***
		Infection in the gastrointestinal tract	***GI Care II***
		Genitourinary infections, such as urinary tract infection or sexually-transmitted diseases	***Gentiana Complex*** or ***V-Support***
		Ear, nose, and throat infections	***Herbal ENT***
		General skin conditions associated with infection and inflammation	***Dermatrol (Damp)*** or ***Dermatrol (Dry)***
		With more swelling and inflammation	add ***Astringent Complex***
Ketoprofen	**Orudis**	*See* **Orudis**	
Klonopin	*Clonazepam*	Moderate levels of stress, anxiety, nervousness, and tension	***Calm***
		Moderate to severe emotional and psychological disorders	***Calm (ES)***
		Moderate levels of stress, anxiety, and insomnia	***Calm ZZZ***
Lactulose	**Duphalac**	*See* **Duphalac**	

DRUG–HERB

Drug – Herb Index

Brand Names / *Generic Names*		**Clinical Applications**	**Herb Alternatives**
Lansoprazole	**Prevacid**	*See* **Prevacid**	
Lasix	*Furosemide*	Edema and fluid retention	***Herbal DRX***
Lescol	*Fluvastatin*	Elevated serum cholesterol and triglycerides levels	***Cholisma***
		Elevated serum cholesterol and triglycerides levels with fatty liver and obesity	***Cholisma (ES)***
Leuprolide	**Lupron**	*See* **Lupron**	
Levalbuterol	**Xopenex**	*See* **Xopenex**	
Levaquin	*Levofloxacin*	Generalized bacterial infection	***Herbal ABX***
		Upper respiratory tract infection with fever, headache, sore throat	***Lonicera Complex***
		Respiratory tract infection with sinus congestion, watery nasal discharge, sneezing and chills	***Respitrol (Cold)***
		Lower respiratory tract infection with high fever, copious yellow sputum, cough and perspiration	***Respitrol (Heat)***
		Lower respiratory tract infection with chest congestion, cough, yellow phlegm and fever	***Pinellia XPT***
		Infection in the gastrointestinal tract	***GI Care II***
		Genitourinary infections, such as urinary tract infection or sexually-transmitted diseases	***Gentiana Complex*** or ***V-Support***
		Ear, nose, and throat infections	***Herbal ENT***
		General skin conditions associated with infection and inflammation	***Dermatrol (Damp)*** or ***Dermatrol (Dry)***
		With more swelling and inflammation	*add* ***Astringent Complex***
Levitra	*Vardenafil*	Male sexual disorder (i.e., erectile dysfunction, impotence)	***Vitality***
		Male reproductive disorder (i.e., infertility)	***Vital Essence***
		Male sexual and reproductive dysfunctions with cold signs and symptoms	***Kidney Tonic (Yang)***
Levofloxacin	**Levaquin**	*See* **Levaquin**	
Levothyroxine	**Synthroid**, **Levoxyl**	*See* **Synthroid**, **Levoxyl**	
Levoxyl	*Levothyroxine*	Hypothyroidism	***Thyro-forte***
Lexapro	*Escitalopram*	Depression with low energy, prolonged sadness and lack of interest	***Shine***
		Depression with stress and anxiety	***Shine (DS)***
Linagliptin	**Tradjenta**	*See* **Tradjenta**	
Lioresal	*Baclofen*	General relief of muscle spasm and cramps	***Flex (SC)***
Liotrix	**Thyrolar**	*See* **Thyrolar**	
Lipitor	*Atorvastatin*	Elevated serum cholesterol and triglycerides levels	***Cholisma***
		Elevated serum cholesterol and triglycerides levels with fatty liver and obesity	***Cholisma (ES)***
Liraglutide	**Victoza**	*See* **Victoza**	
Lisdexamfetamine	**Vyvanse**	*See* **Vyvanse**	
Lisinopril	**Prinivil**, **Zestril**	*See* **Prinivil**, **Zestril**	
Lodine	*Etodolac*	Various headaches: migraine, tension, stress, vertex, occipital	***Corydalin (AC)*** or ***(CR)***
		Musculoskeletal pain with redness, swelling and inflammation	***Flex (Heat)***

Drug – Herb Index

Brand Names / *Generic Names*		**Clinical Applications**	**Herb Alternatives**
Lodine (*cont'd*)	*Etodolac*	Musculoskeletal pain that worsens during cold and rainy days	***Flex (CD)***
		Neuropathy	***Flex (NP)***
		Chronic injuries of soft tissues (muscles, ligaments, and tendons)	***Flex (MLT)***
		Arm pain (shoulder, elbow, and wrist)	***Arm Support***
		Acute or chronic pain of the leg (knee and ankle)	***Knee & Ankle (AC)*** or ***(CR)***
		Acute or chronic upper and lower back pain	***Back Support (AC)*** or ***(CR)***
		Acute or chronic neck and shoulder pain	***Neck & Shoulder (AC)*** or ***(CR)***
		Menstrual pain and cramps in dysmenorrhea	***Mense-Ease***
		Pain associated with amenorrhea	***Menatrol***
		Pain associated with endometriosis	***Resolve (Lower)***
		Severe pain	*add* ***Herbal ANG***
		Pain due to trauma	*add* ***Flex (TMX)***
Loperamide	**Imodium**	*See* **Imodium**	
Lopid	*Gemfibrozil*	Elevated serum cholesterol and triglycerides levels	***Cholisma***
		Elevated serum cholesterol and triglycerides levels with fatty liver and obesity	***Cholisma (ES)***
Lopressor	*Metoprolol*	Elevated blood pressure in patients with hyperactive adrenergic system	***Gentiana Complex***
Lorabid	*Loracarbef*	Generalized bacterial infection	***Herbal ABX***
		Upper respiratory tract infection with fever, headache, sore throat	***Lonicera Complex***
		Respiratory tract infection with sinus congestion, watery nasal discharge, sneezing and chills	***Respitrol (Cold)***
		Lower respiratory tract infection with high fever, copious yellow sputum, cough and perspiration	***Respitrol (Heat)***
		Lower respiratory tract infection with chest congestion, cough, yellow phlegm and fever	***Pinellia XPT***
		Infection in the gastrointestinal tract	***GI Care II***
		Genitourinary infections, such as urinary tract infection or sexually-transmitted diseases	***Gentiana Complex*** or ***V-Support***
		Ear, nose, and throat infections	***Herbal ENT***
		General skin conditions associated with infection and inflammation	***Dermatrol (Damp)*** or ***Dermatrol (Dry)***
		With more swelling and inflammation	*add* ***Astringent Complex***
Loracarbef	**Lorabid**	*See* **Lorabid**	
Loratadine	**Claritin**	*See* **Claritin**	
Lorazepam	**Ativan**	*See* **Ativan**	
Lorcet	*Hydrocodone + Acetaminophen*	Various headaches: migraine, tension, stress, vertex, occipital	***Corydalin (AC)***
		Musculoskeletal pain due to sports or traumatic injuries	***Flex (TMX)***
		Arthritis, especially if condition worsens with cold and dampness	***Flex (CD)***
		Acute or chronic upper and lower back pain	***Back Support (AC)***
		Acute or chronic neck and shoulder pain	***Neck & Shoulder (AC)***

Drug – Herb Index

Brand Names / *Generic Names*		**Clinical Applications**	**Herb Alternatives**
Lorcet (*cont'd*)	*Hydrocodone + Acetaminophen*	Arm pain (shoulder, elbow, and wrist)	***Arm Support***
		Acute pain from herniated disk in the back	***Back Support (HD)***
		Acute pain of the leg (knee and ankle)	***Knee & Ankle (AC)***
		Severe pain	*add **Herbal ANG***
Lortab	*Hydrocodone + Acetaminophen*	Various headaches: migraine, tension, stress, vertex, occipital	***Corydalin (AC)***
		Musculoskeletal pain due to sports or traumatic injuries	***Flex (TMX)***
		Arthritis, especially if condition worsens with cold and dampness	***Flex (CD)***
		Acute or chronic upper and lower back pain	***Back Support (AC)***
		Acute or chronic neck and shoulder pain	***Neck & Shoulder (AC)***
		Arm pain (shoulder, elbow, and wrist)	***Arm Support***
		Acute pain from herniated disk in the back	***Back Support (HD)***
		Acute pain of the leg (knee and ankle)	***Knee & Ankle (AC)***
		Severe pain	*add **Herbal ANG***
Losartan	**Cozaar**	*See* **Cozaar**	
Losartan + Hydrochlorothiazide	**Hyzaar**	*See* **Hyzaar**	
Lotensin	*Benazepril*	Cardiovascular disorders, such as hypertension	***Gastrodia Complex***
Lotrisone	*Clotrimazole + Betamethasone*	For astringent and non-steroidal anti-inflammatory effect	***Astringent Complex***
		Skin conditions with allergy, rash, itching, eczema, dermatitis	***Silerex***
		Skin conditions with lesions, infections and inflammations	***Dermatrol (Damp)*** or ***Dermatrol (Dry)***
		Psoriasis	***Dermatrol (PS)***
		Hemorrhoids	***GI Care (HMR)***
Lovastatin	**Mevacor**	*See* **Mevacor**	
Lovaza	*Omega-3-Acid Ethyl Esters*	Elevated serum cholesterol and triglycerides levels	***Cholisma***
		Elevated serum cholesterol and triglycerides levels with fatty liver and obesity	***Cholisma (ES)***
Lozol	*Indapamide*	Edema and fluid retention	***Herbal DRX***
Lubiprostone	**Amitiza**	*See* **Amitiza**	
Lunesta	*Eszopiclone*	Insomnia due to Liver qi stagnation (stress, anxiety, nervousness, restlessness)	***Calm ZZZ***
		Insomnia due to *shen* (spirit) disturbance with qi and blood deficiencies	***Schisandra ZZZ***
Lupron	*Leuprolide*	To resolve cysts in the uterus and ovaries	***Resolve (Lower)***
Lyrica	*Pregabalin*	Nerve related pain, such as neuralgia and neuropathy	***Flex (NP)***
Maalox	*Aluminum + Magnesium*	Various gastrointestinal disorders, such as heartburn and acid reflux	***GI Care***
Magnesia	**Milk of Magnesia**	*See* **Milk of Magnesia**	
Maxzide	*Triamterene + Hydrochlorothiazide*	Edema and fluid retention	***Herbal DRX***

Drug – Herb Index

Brand Names / *Generic Names*		**Clinical Applications**	**Herb Alternatives**
Medrol	*Methylprednisolone*	For astringent and non-steroidal anti-inflammatory effect	***Astringent Complex***
		Arthritis	***Flex (Heat), Flex (CD)*** or ***Flex (NP)***
		Management of acute asthma	***Respitrol (Heat)*** or ***(Cold)***
		Management and prevention of chronic asthma	***Respitrol (Deficient)*** or ***Cordyceps 3***
		Sinusitis or rhinitis	***Magnolia Clear Sinus*** or ***Pueraria Clear Sinus***
		Inflammatory bowel disorders in general	***GI Care II***
		Irritable bowel syndrome	***GI Harmony***
		Ulcerative colitis	***GI Care (UC)***
		Hemorrhoids	***GI Care (HMR)***
		Skin rash and eczema	***Silerex***
		Skin conditions with lesions, infections, and inflammations	***Dermatrol (Damp)*** or ***Dermatrol (Dry)***
		Psoriasis	***Dermatrol (PS)***
Meloxicam	**Mobic**	*See* **Mobic**	
Memantine	**Namenda**	*See* **Namenda**	
Mephyton	*Vitamin K*	Bleeding disorders	***Notoginseng 9***
Mesalamine	**Asacol**	*See* **Asacol**	
Metaproterenol	**Alupent**	*See* **Alupent**	
Metaxalone	**Skelaxin**	*See* **Skelaxin**	
Metformin	**Glucophage**	*See* **Glucophage**	
Metformin + Sitagliptin	**Janumet**	*See* **Janumet**	
Methimazole	**Tapazole**	*See* **Tapazole**	
Methocarbamol	**Robaxin**	*See* **Robaxin**	
Methotrexate	**Rheumatrex**	*See* **Rheumatrex**	
Methylphenidate	**Concerta**	*See* **Concerta**	
Methylprednisolone	**Medrol**	*See* **Medrol**	
Metoprolol	**Lopressor**, **Toprol**	*See* **Lopressor**, **Toprol**	
Metronidazole	**Flagyl**	*See* **Flagyl**	
Mevacor	*Lovastatin*	Elevated serum cholesterol and triglycerides levels	***Cholisma***
		Elevated serum cholesterol and triglycerides levels with fatty liver and obesity	***Cholisma (ES)***
Micardis	*Telmisartan*	Cardiovascular disorders, such as hypertension	***Gastrodia Complex***
Miconazole	**Monistat**	*See* **Monistat**	
Micronase	*Glyburide*	Elevated blood glucose levels in non-insulin dependent diabetes mellitus	***Equilibrium***
Microzide	*Hydrochlorothiazide*	Edema and fluid retention	***Herbal DRX***

Drug – Herb Index

Brand Names / *Generic Names*		**Clinical Applications**	**Herb Alternatives**
Midrin	*Isometheptene + Apap + Dichloraphenazone*	Various headaches: migraine, tension, stress, vertex, occipital	***Corydalin (AC)***
		Migraine headache	***Corydalin (CR)***
Milk of Magnesia	*Magnesia*	Moderate to severe constipation	***Gentle Lax (Excess)*** or ***(Deficient)***
Minipress	*Prazosin*	Benign prostatic hypertrophy (BPH)	***P-Support***
		Elevated blood pressure in patients with hyperactive adrenergic system	***Gentiana Complex***
Minocin	*Minocycline*	Antibiotic to treat acne	***Dermatrol (Clear)***
Minocycline	**Minocin**	*See* **Minocin**	
Minoxidil	**Rogaine**	*See* **Rogaine**	
Mirtazapine	**Remeron**	*See* **Remeron**	
Mobic	*Meloxicam*	Various headaches: migraine, tension, stress, vertex, occipital	***Corydalin (AC)*** or ***(CR)***
		Musculoskeletal pain with redness, swelling and inflammation	***Flex (Heat)***
		Musculoskeletal pain that worsens during cold and rainy days	***Flex (CD)***
		Neuropathy	***Flex (NP)***
		Chronic injuries of soft tissues (muscles, ligaments, and tendons)	***Flex (MLT)***
		Arm pain (shoulder, elbow, and wrist)	***Arm Support***
		Acute or chronic pain of the leg (knee and ankle)	***Knee & Ankle (AC)*** or ***(CR)***
		Acute or chronic upper and lower back pain	***Back Support (AC)*** or ***(CR)***
		Acute or chronic neck and shoulder pain	***Neck & Shoulder (AC)*** or ***(CR)***
		Menstrual pain and cramps in dysmenorrhea	***Mense-Ease***
		Pain associated with amenorrhea	***Menatrol***
		Pain associated with endometriosis	***Resolve (Lower)***
		Severe pain	*add* ***Herbal ANG***
		Pain due to trauma	*add* ***Flex (TMX)***
Mometasone	**Nasonex**	*See* **Nasonex**	
Mometasone + Formoterol	**Dulera**	*See* **Dulera**	
Monistat	*Miconazole*	Vaginitis	***V-Support***
Monopril	*Fosinopril*	Cardiovascular disorders, such as hypertension	***Gastrodia Complex***
Montelukast	**Singulair**	*See* **Singulair**	
Motrin	*Ibuprofen*	Various headaches: migraine, tension, stress, vertex, occipital	***Corydalin (AC)*** or ***(CR)***
		Musculoskeletal pain with redness, swelling and inflammation	***Flex (Heat)***
		Musculoskeletal pain that worsens during cold and rainy days	***Flex (CD)***
		Neuropathy	***Flex (NP)***
		Chronic injuries of soft tissues (muscles, ligaments, and tendons)	***Flex (MLT)***
		Arm pain (shoulder, elbow, and wrist)	***Arm Support***
		Acute or chronic pain of the leg (knee and ankle)	***Knee & Ankle (AC)*** or ***(CR)***

Drug – Herb Index

Brand Names / *Generic Names*		**Clinical Applications**	**Herb Alternatives**
Motrin *(cont'd)*	*Ibuprofen*	Acute or chronic upper and lower back pain	***Back Support (AC)*** or ***(CR)***
		Acute or chronic neck and shoulder pain	***Neck & Shoulder (AC)*** or ***(CR)***
		Menstrual pain and cramps in dysmenorrhea	***Mense-Ease***
		Pain associated with amenorrhea	***Menatrol***
		Pain associated with endometriosis	***Resolve (Lower)***
		Severe pain	*add* ***Herbal ANG***
		Pain due to trauma	*add* ***Flex (TMX)***
Moxifloxacin	**Avelox**, **Vigamox**	*See* **Avelox**, **Vigamox**	
Mycelex	*Clotrimazole*	Vaginitis	***V-Support***
Mylanta	*Aluminum + Magnesium*	Various gastrointestinal disorders, such as heartburn and acid reflux	***GI Care***
Nabumetone	**Relafen**	*See* **Relafen**	
Nafarelin	**Synarel**	*See* **Synarel**	
Namenda	*Memantine*	Mental and physical deteriorations in Alzheimer's disease and dementia	***Neuro Plus***
		Mental deteriorations due to aging	***Enhance Memory***
Naprosyn	*Naproxen*	Various headaches: migraine, tension, stress, vertex, occipital	***Corydalin (AC)*** or ***(CR)***
		Musculoskeletal pain with redness, swelling and inflammation	***Flex (Heat)***
		Musculoskeletal pain that worsens during cold and rainy days	***Flex (CD)***
		Neuropathy	***Flex (NP)***
		Chronic injuries of soft tissues (muscles, ligaments, and tendons)	***Flex (MLT)***
		Arm pain (shoulder, elbow, and wrist)	***Arm Support***
		Acute or chronic pain of the leg (knee and ankle)	***Knee & Ankle (AC)*** or ***(CR)***
		Acute or chronic upper and lower back pain	***Back Support (AC)*** or ***(CR)***
		Acute or chronic neck and shoulder pain	***Neck & Shoulder (AC)*** or ***(CR)***
		Menstrual pain and cramps in dysmenorrhea	***Mense-Ease***
		Pain associated with amenorrhea	***Menatrol***
		Pain associated with endometriosis	***Resolve (Lower)***
		Severe pain	*add* ***Herbal ANG***
		Pain due to trauma	*add* ***Flex (TMX)***
Naproxen	**Naprosyn**, **Anaprox**	*See* **Naprosyn**, **Anaprox**	
Nasacort	*Triamcinolone*	Nasal congestion with yellow, sticky discharge	***Pueraria Clear Sinus***
		Nasal congestion with white, watery discharge	***Magnolia Clear Sinus***
		For astringent and non-steroidal anti-inflammatory effect	*add* ***Astringent Complex***
Nasonex	*Mometasone*	Nasal congestion with yellow, sticky discharge	***Pueraria Clear Sinus***
		Nasal congestion with white, watery discharge	***Magnolia Clear Sinus***
		For astringent and non-steroidal anti-inflammatory effect	*add* ***Astringent Complex***
Nateglinide	**Starlix**	*See* **Starlix**	
Nebivolol	**Bystolic**	*See* **Bystolic**	

Drug – Herb Index

Brand Names / *Generic Names*		**Clinical Applications**	**Herb Alternatives**
Neupogen	*Filgrastim*	To strengthen the overall constitution of the person	***Imperial Tonic*** or ***Cordyceps 3***
		To boost the immune system to prevent bacterial and viral infections	***Cordyceps 3*** or ***Immune +***
		To enhance the immune system during chemotherapy and radiation treatment	***C/R Support***
		To tonify the individuals who are too weak to receive chemotherapy and radiation treatment	***CA Support***
Neurontin	*Gabapentin*	Nerve-related pain, such as neuralgia and neuropathy	***Flex (NP)***
Nexium	*Esomeprazole*	Various gastrointestinal disorders, such as heartburn, acid reflux and peptic ulcer	***GI Care***
Niacin	*Niacin*	Elevated serum cholesterol and triglycerides levels	***Cholisma***
		Elevated serum cholesterol and triglycerides levels with fatty liver and obesity	***Cholisma (ES)***
Niaspan	*Niacin*	Elevated serum cholesterol and triglycerides levels	***Cholisma***
		Elevated serum cholesterol and triglycerides levels with fatty liver and obesity	***Cholisma (ES)***
Nifedipine	**Procardia**	*See* **Procardia**	
Nitrofurantoin	**Furadantin**	*See* **Furadantin**	
NoDoz	*Caffeine*	Lack of energy levels, decreased mental and physical performance	***Vibrant***
		Chronic fatigue and weakness	***Imperial Tonic***
Nolvadex	*Tamoxifen*	To resolve fibrocystic benign breast disorder	***Resolve (Upper)***
Norflex	*Orphenadrine*	General relief of muscle spasm and cramps	***Flex (SC)***
Norpramin	*Desipramine*	Depression with low energy, prolonged sadness and lack of interest	***Shine***
		Depression with stress and anxiety	***Shine (DS)***
		Nerve-related pain, such as neuralgia and neuropathy	***Flex (NP)***
Nortriptyline	**Pamelor**	*See* **Pamelor**	
Norvasc	*Amlodipine*	Cardiovascular disorders, such as hypertension	***Gastrodia Complex***
Ofloxacin	**Floxin**	*See* **Floxin**	
Ogen	*Estropipate*	Menopausal symptoms such as hot flashes, irritability and mood swings	***Balance (Heat)*** or ***Nourish***
		Osteoporosis	***Osteo 8***
		Vaginal dryness and atrophy	***Balance Spring***
Olanzapine	**Zyprexa**	*See* **Zyprexa**	
Olmesartan	**Benicar**	*See* **Benicar**	
Olmesartan + Amlodipine	**Azor**	*See* **Azor**	
Omega-3-Acid Ethyl Esters	**Lovaza**	*See* **Lovaza**	
Omeprazole	**Prilosec**	*See* **Prilosec**	
Omnicef	*Cefdinir*	Generalized bacterial infection	***Herbal ABX***
		Upper respiratory tract infection with fever, headache, sore throat	***Lonicera Complex***

Drug – Herb Index

Brand Names / *Generic Names*		**Clinical Applications**	**Herb Alternatives**
Omnicef (*cont'd*)	*Cefdinir*	Respiratory tract infection with sinus congestion, watery nasal discharge, sneezing and chills	***Respitrol (Cold)***
		Lower respiratory tract infection with high fever, copious yellow sputum, cough and perspiration	***Respitrol (Heat)***
		Lower respiratory tract infection with chest congestion, cough, yellow phlegm and fever	***Pinellia XPT***
		Infection in the gastrointestinal tract	***GI Care II***
		Genitourinary infections, such as urinary tract infection or sexually-transmitted diseases	***Gentiana Complex*** or ***V-Support***
		Ear, nose, and throat infections	***Herbal ENT***
		General skin conditions associated with infection and inflammation	***Dermatrol (Damp)*** or ***Dermatrol (Dry)***
		With more swelling and inflammation	*add* ***Astringent Complex***
Ondansetron	**Zofran**	*See* **Zofran**	
Onglyza	*Saxagliptin*	Elevated blood glucose levels in non-insulin dependent diabetes mellitus	***Equilibrium***
Orencia	*Abatacept*	Treatment of autoimmune diseases, such as rheumatoid arthritis	***Flex (Heat)*** or ***Flex (CD)***
		Treatment of autoimmune diseases, such as psoriasis	***Dermatrol (PS)***
		Treatment of autoimmune diseases, such as ulcerative colitis and Crohn's disease	***GI Care (UC)***
		Treatment of autoimmune diseases, such as Sjögren's syndrome	***Nourish (Fluids)***
		Treatment of autoimmune diseases, such as scleroderma and Raynaud's syndrome	***Circulation (SJ)***
		Treatment of autoimmune diseases, such as systemic lupus erythematosus	***LPS Support***
		Treatment of autoimmune diseases, such as multiple sclerosis	***Neuro Plus***
		To suppress acute inflammation in autoimmune diseases	*add* ***Gardenia Complex***
		To manage chronic inflammation in autoimmune diseases	*add* ***Nourish***
		To promote generation of new cells, tissues, and organs	*add* ***Kidney Tonic (Yin)*** or ***Nourish***
		To promote blood circulation and facilitate repair and regeneration	*add* ***Circulation (SJ)***
Orinase	*Tolbutamide*	Elevated blood glucose levels in non-insulin dependent diabetes mellitus	***Equilibrium***
Orlistat	**Xenical**	*See* **Xenical**	
Orphenadrine	**Norflex**	*See* **Norflex**	
Orudis	*Ketoprofen*	Various headaches: migraine, tension, stress, vertex, occipital	***Corydalin (AC)*** or ***(CR)***
		Musculoskeletal pain with redness, swelling and inflammation	***Flex (Heat)***
		Musculoskeletal pain that worsens during cold and rainy days	***Flex (CD)***
		Neuropathy	***Flex (NP)***
		Chronic injuries of soft tissues (muscles, ligaments, and tendons)	***Flex (MLT)***
		Arm pain (shoulder, elbow, and wrist)	***Arm Support***

Drug – Herb Index

Brand Names / *Generic Names*		**Clinical Applications**	**Herb Alternatives**
Orudis (*cont'd*)	*Ketoprofen*	Acute or chronic pain of the leg (knee and ankle)	***Knee & Ankle (AC)*** or ***(CR)***
		Acute or chronic upper and lower back pain	***Back Support (AC)*** or ***(CR)***
		Acute or chronic neck and shoulder pain	***Neck & Shoulder (AC)*** or ***(CR)***
		Menstrual pain and cramps in dysmenorrhea	***Mense-Ease***
		Pain associated with amenorrhea	***Menatrol***
		Pain associated with endometriosis	***Resolve (Lower)***
		Severe pain	*add* ***Herbal ANG***
		Pain due to trauma	*add* ***Flex (TMX)***
Oseltamivir	**Tamiflu**	*See* **Tamiflu**	
Oxaprozin	**Daypro**	*See* **Daypro**	
Oxycodone	**OxyContin**	*See* **OxyContin**	
Oxycodone+ APAP	**Percocet**	*See* **Percocet**	
OxyContin	*Oxycodone*	Various headaches: migraine, tension, stress, vertex, occipital	***Corydalin (AC)***
		Musculoskeletal pain due to sports or traumatic injuries	***Flex (TMX)***
		Arthritis, especially if condition worsens with cold and dampness	***Flex (CD)***
		Acute or chronic upper and lower back pain	***Back Support (AC)***
		Acute or chronic neck and shoulder pain	***Neck & Shoulder (AC)***
		Arm pain (shoulder, elbow, and wrist)	***Arm Support***
		Acute pain from herniated disk in the back	***Back Support (HD)***
		Acute pain of the leg (knee and ankle)	***Knee & Ankle (AC)***
		Severe pain	*add* ***Herbal ANG***
Pamelor	*Nortriptyline*	Depression with low energy, prolonged sadness and lack of interest	***Shine***
		Depression with stress and anxiety	***Shine (DS)***
		Nerve-related pain, such as neuralgia and neuropathy	***Flex (NP)***
Pamidronate	**Aredia**	*See* **Aredia**	
Pantoprazole	**Protonix**	*See* **Protonix**	
Parafon Forte DSC	*Chlorzoxazone*	General relief of muscle spasm and cramps	***Flex (SC)***
Paroxetine	**Paxil**	*See* **Paxil**	
Paxil	*Paroxetine*	Depression with low energy, prolonged sadness and lack of interest	***Shine***
		Depression with stress and anxiety	***Shine (DS)***
PCE	*Erythromycin*	*See* **E-Mycin**	
Pen VK	*Penicillin*	Generalized bacterial infection	***Herbal ABX***
		Upper respiratory tract infection with fever, headache, sore throat	***Lonicera Complex***
		Respiratory tract infection with sinus congestion, watery nasal discharge, sneezing and chills	***Respitrol (Cold)***
		Lower respiratory tract infection with high fever, copious yellow sputum, cough and perspiration	***Respitrol (Heat)***
		Lower respiratory tract infection with chest congestion, cough, yellow phlegm and fever	***Pinellia XPT***

Drug – Herb Index

Brand Names / *Generic Names*		**Clinical Applications**	**Herb Alternatives**
Pen VK (*cont'd*)	*Penicillin*	Infection in the gastrointestinal tract	***GI Care II***
		Genitourinary infections, such as urinary tract infection or sexually-transmitted diseases	***Gentiana Complex*** or ***V-Support***
		Ear, nose, and throat infections	***Herbal ENT***
		General skin conditions associated with infection and inflammation	***Dermatrol (Damp)*** or ***Dermatrol (Dry)***
		With more swelling and inflammation	*add **Astringent Complex***
Penciclovir	**Denavir**	*See* **Denavir**	
Penicillin	**Pen VK**	*See* **Pen VK**	
Pepcid	*Famotidine*	Various gastrointestinal disorders, such as heartburn, acid reflux and peptic ulcer	***GI Care***
Percocet	*Oxycodone + APAP*	Various headaches: migraine, tension, stress, vertex, occipital	***Corydalin (AC)***
		Musculoskeletal pain due to sports or traumatic injuries	***Flex (TMX)***
		Arthritis, especially if condition worsens with cold and dampness	***Flex (CD)***
		Acute or chronic upper and lower back pain	***Back Support (AC)***
		Acute or chronic neck and shoulder pain	***Neck & Shoulder (AC)***
		Arm pain (shoulder, elbow, and wrist)	***Arm Support***
		Acute pain from herniated disk in the back	***Back Support (HD)***
		Acute pain of the leg (knee and ankle)	***Knee & Ankle (AC)***
		Severe pain	*add **Herbal ANG***
Phenergan	*Antitussive Combination*	Lower respiratory tract infection with chest congestion, cough, yellow phlegm and fever	***Pinellia XPT***
		To stop the production of phlegm	***Pinellia Complex***
		Cough and dyspnea	***Respitrol (CF)***
Phentermine	**Fastin, Ionamin, Adipex**	*See* **Fastin, Ionamin, Adipex**	
Phenyl-propanolamine	**Acutrim**	*See* **Acutrim**	
Phenyl-propanolamine + Brompheniramine	**Dimetapp**	*See* **Dimetapp**	
Phenytoin	**Dilantin**	*See* **Dilantin**	
Pimecrolimus	**Elidel**	*See* **Elidel**	
Pioglitazone	**Actos**	*See* **Actos**	
Piroxicam	**Feldene**	*See* **Feldene**	
Plaquenil	*Hydroxychloroquine*	Rheumatoid arthritis or lupus due to autoimmune disorder	***LPS Support***
		Rheumatoid arthritis with redness, swelling and inflammation	***Flex (Heat)***
		Rheumatoid arthritis that worsens during cold and rainy days	***Flex (CD)***
Plendil	*Felodipine*	Cardiovascular disorders, such as hypertension	***Gastrodia Complex***
Polyethylene Glycol	**Glycolax**	*See* **Glycolax**	

DRUG-HERB

Drug – Herb Index

Brand Names / *Generic Names*		**Clinical Applications**	**Herb Alternatives**
Poly-Histine	*Antitussive Combination*	Lower respiratory tract infection with chest congestion, cough, yellow phlegm and fever	***Pinellia XPT***
		To stop the production of phlegm	***Pinellia Complex***
		Cough and dyspnea	***Respitrol (CF)***
Pravachol	*Pravastatin*	Elevated serum cholesterol and triglycerides levels	***Cholisma***
		Elevated serum cholesterol and triglycerides levels with fatty liver and obesity	***Cholisma (ES)***
Pravastatin	**Pravachol**	*See* **Pravachol**	
Prazosin	**Minipress**	*See* **Minipress**	
Prednisone, Prednisolone	*Prednisone, Prednisolone*	For astringent and non-steroidal anti-inflammatory effect	***Astringent Complex***
		Arthritis	***Flex (Heat), Flex (CD)*** or ***Flex (NP)***
		Management of acute asthma	***Respitrol (Heat)*** or ***Respitrol (Cold)***
		Management and prevention of chronic asthma	***Respitrol (Deficient)*** or ***Cordyceps 3***
		Sinusitis or rhinitis	***Magnolia Clear Sinus*** or ***Pueraria Clear Sinus***
		Inflammatory bowel disorders in general	***GI Care II***
		Irritable bowel syndrome	***GI Harmony***
		Ulcerative colitis	***GI Care (UC)***
		Hemorrhoids	***GI Care (HMR)***
		Skin rash and eczema	***Silerex***
		Skin conditions with lesions, infections, and inflammations	***Dermatrol (Damp)*** or ***Dermatrol (Dry)***
		Psoriasis	***Dermatrol (PS)***
Pregabalin	**Lyrica**	*See* **Lyrica**	
Premarin	*Estrogens, Conjugated*	Menopausal symptoms such as hot flashes, irritability and mood swings	***Balance (Heat)*** or ***Nourish***
		Osteoporosis	***Osteo 8***
		Vaginal dryness and atrophy	***Balance Spring***
Prempro	*Estrogens + Progestins*	Menopausal symptoms such as hot flashes, irritability and mood swings	***Balance (Heat)*** or ***Nourish***
		Osteoporosis	***Osteo 8***
		Vaginal dryness and atrophy	***Balance Spring***
Prevacid	*Lansoprazole*	Various gastrointestinal disorders, such as heartburn, acid reflux and peptic ulcer	***GI Care***
Prilosec	*Omeprazole*	Various gastrointestinal disorders, such as heartburn, acid reflux and peptic ulcer	***GI Care***
Principen	*Ampicillin*	Generalized bacterial infection	***Herbal ABX***
		Upper respiratory tract infection with fever, headache, sore throat	***Lonicera Complex***

Drug – Herb Index

Brand Names / *Generic Names*		**Clinical Applications**	**Herb Alternatives**
Principen *(cont'd)*	*Ampicillin*	Respiratory tract infection with sinus congestion, watery nasal discharge, sneezing and chills	***Respitrol (Cold)***
		Lower respiratory tract infection with high fever, copious yellow sputum, cough and perspiration	***Respitrol (Heat)***
		Lower respiratory tract infection with chest congestion, cough, yellow phlegm and fever	***Pinellia XPT***
		Infection in the gastrointestinal tract	***GI Care II***
		Genitourinary infections, such as urinary tract infection or sexually-transmitted diseases	***Gentiana Complex*** or ***V-Support***
		Ear, nose, and throat infections	***Herbal ENT***
		General skin conditions associated with infection and inflammation	***Dermatrol (Damp)*** or ***Dermatrol (Dry)***
		With more swelling and inflammation	*add* ***Astringent Complex***
Prinivil	*Lisinopril*	Cardiovascular disorders, such as hypertension	***Gastrodia Complex***
Pristiq	*Desvenlafaxine*	Depression with low energy, prolonged sadness and lack of interest	***Shine***
		Depression with stress and anxiety	***Shine (DS)***
ProAir	*Albuterol*	Heat-type asthma with fever, dry mouth, thirst, red face and red tongue	***Respitrol (Heat)***
		Cold-type asthma with chills, intolerance to cold, cyanotic complexion of the face and body	***Respitrol (Cold)***
		Chronic asthma with frequent attacks of wheezing and dyspnea	***Respitrol (Deficient)***
Procardia	*Nifedipine*	Cardiovascular disorders, such as hypertension	***Gastrodia Complex***
Propa pH	*Salicylic Acid*	Acne	***Dermatrol (Clear)***
Propoxyphene	**Darvon**	*See* **Darvon**	
Propoxyphene + Acetaminophen	**Darvocet**	*See* **Darvocet**	
Propranolol	**Inderal**	*See* **Inderal**	
Propylthiouracil	**PTU**	*See* **PTU**	
Proscar	*Finasteride*	Benign prostatic hypertrophy (BPH)	***P-Support***
Protonix	*Pantoprazole*	Various gastrointestinal disorders, such as heartburn, acid reflux and peptic ulcer	***GI Care***
Proventil	*Albuterol*	Heat-type asthma with fever, dry mouth, thirst, red face and red tongue	***Respitrol (Heat)***
		Cold-type asthma with chills, intolerance to cold, cyanotic complexion of the face and body	***Respitrol (Cold)***
		Chronic asthma with frequent attacks of wheezing and dyspnea	***Respitrol (Deficient)***
Prozac	*Fluoxetine*	Depression with low energy, prolonged sadness and lack of interest	***Shine***
		Depression with stress and anxiety	***Shine (DS)***
Pseudoephedrine	**Sudafed**	*See* **Sudafed**	
Pseudoephedrine + Brompheniramine	**Bromfed**	*See* **Bromfed**	
PTU	*Propylthiouracil*	Mild-to-moderate cases of hyperthyroidism	***Thyrodex***

Drug – Herb Index

Brand Names / *Generic Names*		**Clinical Applications**	**Herb Alternatives**
Quetiapine	**Seroquel**	*See* **Seroquel**	
Quinapril	**Accupril**	*See* **Accupril**	
Rabeprazole	**Aciphex**	*See* **Aciphex**	
Raloxifene	**Evista**	*See* **Evista**	
Ramipril	**Altace**	*See* **Altace**	
Ranexa	*Ranolazine*	Treatment of chronic angina	***Circulation***
Ranitidine	**Zantac**	*See* **Zantac**	
Ranolazine	**Ranexa**	*See* **Ranexa**	
Raptiva	*Efalizumab*	Psoriasis	***Dermatrol (PS)***
Rebetol	*Ribavirin*	Treatment of chronic hepatitis C	***Liver DTX***
Relafen	*Nabumetone*	Various headaches: migraine, tension, stress, vertex, occipital	***Corydalin (AC)*** or ***(CR)***
		Musculoskeletal pain with redness, swelling and inflammation	***Flex (Heat)***
		Musculoskeletal pain that worsens during cold and rainy days	***Flex (CD)***
		Neuropathy	***Flex (NP)***
		Chronic injuries of soft tissues (muscles, ligaments, and tendons)	***Flex (MLT)***
		Arm pain (shoulder, elbow, and wrist)	***Arm Support***
		Acute or chronic pain of the leg (knee and ankle)	***Knee & Ankle (AC)*** or ***(CR)***
		Acute or chronic upper and lower back pain	***Back Support (AC)*** or ***(CR)***
		Acute or chronic neck and shoulder pain	***Neck & Shoulder (AC)*** or ***(CR)***
		Menstrual pain and cramps in dysmenorrhea	***Mense-Ease***
		Pain associated with amenorrhea	***Menatrol***
		Pain associated with endometriosis	***Resolve (Lower)***
		Severe pain	*add* ***Herbal ANG***
		Pain due to trauma	*add* ***Flex (TMX)***
Relenza	*Zanamivir*	Common cold or influenza with fever, headache, sore throat	***Lonicera Complex***
		Generalized viral infection	***Herbal AVR***
Relpax	*Eletriptan*	Treatment of acute migraine attack	***Corydalin (AC)***
		Prevention of chronic migraine recurrence	***Corydalin (CR)***
Remeron	*Mirtazapine*	Depression with low energy, prolonged sadness and lack of interest	***Shine***
		Depression with stress and anxiety	***Shine (DS)***
Remicade	*Infliximab*	Treatment of autoimmune diseases, such as rheumatoid arthritis	***Flex (Heat)*** or ***Flex (CD)***
		Treatment of autoimmune diseases, such as psoriasis	***Dermatrol (PS)***
		Treatment of autoimmune diseases, such as ulcerative colitis and Crohn's disease	***GI Care (UC)***
		Treatment of autoimmune diseases, such as Sjögren's syndrome	***Nourish (Fluids)***
		Treatment of autoimmune diseases, such as scleroderma and Raynaud's syndrome	***Circulation (SJ)***

Drug – Herb Index

Brand Names / *Generic Names*		**Clinical Applications**	**Herb Alternatives**
Remicade (*cont'd*)	*Infliximab*	Treatment of autoimmune diseases, such as systemic lupus erythematosus	***LPS Support***
		Treatment of autoimmune diseases, such as multiple sclerosis	***Neuro Plus***
		To suppress acute inflammation in autoimmune diseases	*add* ***Gardenia Complex***
		To manage chronic inflammation in autoimmune diseases	*add* ***Nourish***
		To promote generation of new cells, tissues, and organs	*add* ***Kidney Tonic (Yin)*** or ***Nourish***
		To promote blood circulation and facilitate repair and regeneration	*add* ***Circulation (SJ)***
Reminyl	*Galantamine*	Mental and physical deteriorations in Alzheimer's disease and dementia	***Neuro Plus***
		Mental deterioration due to aging	***Enhance Memory***
Renova	*Retinoid*	Acne	***Dermatrol (Clear)***
Requip	*Ropinirole*	To improve mental and physical functions in Parkinson's disease	***Neuro Plus***
Restoril	*Temazepam*	Insomnia due to Liver qi stagnation (stress, anxiety, nervousness, restlessness)	***Calm ZZZ***
		Insomnia due to *shen* (spirit) disturbance with qi and blood deficiencies	***Schisandra ZZZ***
Retin-A	*Retinoid*	Acne	***Dermatrol (Clear)***
Retinoid	**Retin-A, Avita, Renova**	*See* **Retin-A, Avita, Renova**	
Rheumatrex	*Methotrexate*	Rheumatoid arthritis with redness, swelling, and inflammation	***Flex (Heat)***
		Rheumatoid arthritis that worsens during cold and rainy days	***Flex (CD)***
		Rheumatoid arthritis or lupus due to autoimmune disorder	***LPS Support***
Ribavirin	**Rebetol**	*See* **Rebetol**	
Rifaximin	**Xifaxan**	*See* **Xifaxan**	
Risedronate	**Actonel**	*See* **Actonel**	
Risperdal	*Risperidone*	Moderate levels of stress, anxiety, nervousness, and tension	***Calm***
		Moderate to severe emotional and psychological disorders	***Calm (ES)***
Risperidone	**Risperdal**	*See* **Risperdal**	
Ritalin	*Methylphenidate*	To promote concentration and focus in ADD (attention deficit disorder) and ADHD (attention deficit-hyperactivity disorder)	***Calm (Jr)***
Rituxan	*Rituximab*	Treatment of autoimmune diseases, such as rheumatoid arthritis	***Flex (Heat)*** or ***Flex (CD)***
		Treatment of autoimmune diseases, such as psoriasis	***Dermatrol (PS)***
		Treatment of autoimmune diseases, such as ulcerative colitis and Crohn's disease	***GI Care (UC)***
		Treatment of autoimmune diseases, such as Sjögren's syndrome	***Nourish (Fluids)***
		Treatment of autoimmune diseases, such as scleroderma and Raynaud's syndrome	***Circulation (SJ)***
		Treatment of autoimmune diseases, such as systemic lupus erythematosus	***LPS Support***
		Treatment of autoimmune diseases, such as multiple sclerosis	***Neuro Plus***
		To suppress acute inflammation in autoimmune diseases	*add* ***Gardenia Complex***

DRUG–HERB

Drug – Herb Index

Brand Names / *Generic Names*		**Clinical Applications**	**Herb Alternatives**
Rituxan (*cont'd*)	*Rituximab*	To manage chronic inflammation in autoimmune diseases	*add* ***Nourish***
		To promote generation of new cells, tissues, and organs	*add* ***Kidney Tonic (Yin)*** or ***Nourish***
		To promote blood circulation and facilitate repair and regeneration	*add* ***Circulation (SJ)***
Rituximab	**Rituxan**	*See* **Rituxan**	
Rivastigmine	**Exelon**	*See* **Exelon**	
Robaxin	*Methocarbamol*	General relief of muscle spasm and cramps	***Flex (SC)***
Robitussin	*Antitussive Combination*	Lower respiratory tract infection with chest congestion, cough, yellow phlegm and fever	***Pinellia XPT***
		To stop the production of phlegm	***Pinellia Complex***
		Cough and dyspnea	***Respitrol (CF)***
Rogaine	*Minoxidil*	To promote growth of healthy and shiny new hair	***Polygonum 14***
Ropinirole	**Requip**	*See* **Requip**	
Rosiglitazone	**Avandia**	*See* **Avandia**	
Rosuvastatin	**Crestor**	*See* **Crestor**	
Salicylic Acid	**Propa pH, Stridex**	*See* **Propa pH, Stridex**	
Saxagliptin	**Onglyza**	*See* **Onglyza**	
Selegiline	**Eldepryl**	*See* **Eldepryl**	
Senna	**Senokot**	*See* **Senokot**	
Senokot	*Senna*	Excess-type constipation with yellow tongue coat and red face	***Gentle Lax (Excess)***
		Deficient-type constipation with dryness	***Gentle Lax (Deficient)***
		Fecal compaction	***GI DTX***
Septra, Septra DS	*Sulfamethoxazole + Trimethoprim*	Generalized bacterial infection	***Herbal ABX***
		Upper respiratory tract infection with fever, headache, sore throat	***Lonicera Complex***
		Respiratory tract infection with sinus congestion, watery nasal discharge, sneezing and chills	***Respitrol (Cold)***
		Lower respiratory tract infection with high fever, copious yellow sputum, cough and perspiration	***Respitrol (Heat)***
		Lower respiratory tract infection with chest congestion, cough, yellow phlegm and fever	***Pinellia XPT***
		Infection in the gastrointestinal tract	***GI Care II***
		Genitourinary infections, such as urinary tract infection or sexually-transmitted diseases	***Gentiana Complex*** or ***V-Support***
		Ear, nose, and throat infections	***Herbal ENT***
		General skin conditions associated with infection and inflammation	***Dermatrol (Damp)*** or ***Dermatrol (Dry)***
		With more swelling and inflammation	*add* ***Astringent Complex***
Seroquel	*Quetiapine*	Moderate levels of stress, anxiety, nervousness, and tension	***Calm***
		Moderate to severe emotional and psychological disorders	***Calm (ES)***
Sertraline	**Zoloft**	*See* **Zoloft**	
Sildenafil	**Viagra**	*See* **Viagra**	

Drug – Herb Index

Brand Names / *Generic Names*		**Clinical Applications**	**Herb Alternatives**
Simvastatin	**Zocor**	*See* **Zocor**	
Sinemet	*Carbidopa + Levodopa*	To improve mental and physical functions in Parkinson's disease	***Neuro Plus***
Sinequan	*Doxepin*	Depression with low energy, prolonged sadness and lack of interest	***Shine***
		Depression with stress and anxiety	***Shine (DS)***
		Nerve-related pain, such as neuralgia and neuropathy	***Flex (NP)***
Singulair	*Montelukast*	Dyspnea and shortness of breath in cases of chronic asthma	***Respitrol (Deficient)***
		Management and prevention of chronic asthma	***Cordyceps 3***
Sitagliptin	**Januvia**	*See* **Januvia**	
Skelaxin	*Metaxalone*	General relief of muscle spasm and cramps	***Flex (SC)***
Slo-Phylline	*Theophylline*	Heat-type asthma with fever, dry mouth, thirst, red face and red tongue	***Respitrol (Heat)***
		Cold-type asthma with chills, intolerance to cold, cyanotic complexion of the face and body	***Respitrol (Cold)***
		Chronic asthma with frequent attacks of wheezing and dyspnea	***Respitrol (Deficient)*** or ***Cordyceps 3***
Soma	*Carisoprodol*	General relief of muscle spasm and cramps	***Flex (SC)***
Sominex	*Diphenhydramine*	Insomnia due to Liver qi stagnation (stress, anxiety, nervousness, restlessness)	***Calm ZZZ***
		Insomnia due to *shen* (spirit) disturbance with qi and blood deficiencies	***Schisandra ZZZ***
Spiriva	*Tiotropium*	Heat-type asthma with fever, dry mouth, thirst, red face and red tongue	***Respitrol (Heat)***
		Cold-type asthma with chills, intolerance to cold, cyanotic complexion of the face and body	***Respitrol (Cold)***
		Chronic asthma with frequent attacks of wheezing and dyspnea	***Respitrol (Deficient)*** or ***Cordyceps 3***
Spironolactone	**Aldactone**	*See* **Aldactone**	
Starlix	*Nateglinide*	Elevated blood glucose levels in non-insulin dependent diabetes mellitus	***Equilibrium***
Sterapred	*Prednisone*	For astringent and non-steroidal anti-inflammatory effect	***Astringent Complex***
		Arthritis	***Flex (Heat), Flex (CD)*** or ***Flex (NP)***
		Management of acute asthma	***Respitrol (Heat)*** or ***Respitrol (Cold)***
		Management and prevention of chronic asthma	***Respitrol (Deficient)*** or ***Cordyceps 3***
		Sinusitis or rhinitis	***Magnolia Clear Sinus*** or ***Pueraria Clear Sinus***
		Inflammatory bowel disorders in general	***GI Care II***
		Irritable bowel syndrome	***GI Harmony***
		Ulcerative colitis	***GI Care (UC)***
		Hemorrhoids	***GI Care (HMR)***
		Skin rash and eczema	***Silerex***
		Skin conditions with lesions, infections, and inflammations	***Dermatrol (Damp)*** or ***Dermatrol (Dry)***
		Psoriasis	***Dermatrol (PS)***

Drug – Herb Index

Brand Names / *Generic Names*		**Clinical Applications**	**Herb Alternatives**
Strattera	*Atomoxetine*	To promote concentration and focus in ADD (attention deficit disorder) and ADHD (attention deficit-hyperactivity disorder)	***Calm (Jr)***
Stridex	*Salicylic Acid*	Acne	***Dermatrol (Clear)***
Suboxone	*Buprenorphine + Naloxone*	Craving and withdrawal symptoms associated with opioid dependence	***Calm (ES)***
Sudafed	*Pseudoephedrine*	Nasal congestion with yellow, sticky discharge	***Pueraria Clear Sinus***
		Nasal congestion with white, watery discharge	***Magnolia Clear Sinus***
Sulfamethoxazole + Trimethoprim	**Bactrim, Septra**	*See* **Bactrim, Septra**	
Sulindac	**Clinoril**	*See* **Clinoril**	
Sumatriptan	**Imitrex**	*See* **Imitrex**	
Suprax	*Cefixime*	Generalized bacterial infection	***Herbal ABX***
		Upper respiratory tract infection with fever, headache, sore throat	***Lonicera Complex***
		Respiratory tract infection with sinus congestion, watery nasal discharge, sneezing and chills	***Respitrol (Cold)***
		Lower respiratory tract infection with high fever, copious yellow sputum, cough and perspiration	***Respitrol (Heat)***
		Lower respiratory tract infection with chest congestion, cough, yellow phlegm and fever	***Pinellia XPT***
		Infection in the gastrointestinal tract	***GI Care II***
		Genitourinary infections, such as urinary tract infection or sexually-transmitted diseases	***Gentiana Complex*** or ***V-Support***
		Ear, nose, and throat infections	***Herbal ENT***
		General skin conditions associated with infection and inflammation	***Dermatrol (Damp)*** or ***Dermatrol (Dry)***
		With more swelling and inflammation	*add* ***Astringent Complex***
Symbicort	*Budesonide + Formoterol*	Heat-type asthma with fever, dry mouth, thirst, red face and red tongue	***Respitrol (Heat)***
		Cold-type asthma with chills, intolerance to cold, cyanotic complexion of the face and body	***Respitrol (Cold)***
		Chronic asthma with frequent attacks of wheezing and dyspnea	***Respitrol (Deficient)*** or ***Cordyceps 3***
Symmetrel	*Amantadine*	Common cold or influenza with fever, headache, sore throat	***Lonicera Complex***
		Generalized viral infection	***Herbal AVR***
Synarel	*Nafarelin*	Endometriosis	***Resolve (Lower)***
		Amenorrhea	***Menatrol***
Synthroid	*Levothyroxine*	Hypothyroidism	***Thyro-forte***
Tacrine	**Cognex**	*See* **Cognex**	
Tadalafil	**Cialis**	*See* **Cialis**	
Tagamet	*Cimetidine*	Various gastrointestinal disorders, such as heartburn, acid reflux, and peptic ulcer	***GI Care***

Drug – Herb Index

Brand Names / *Generic Names*		**Clinical Applications**	**Herb Alternatives**
Tamiflu	*Oseltamivir*	Common cold or influenza with fever, headache, sore throat	***Lonicera Complex***
		Generalized viral infection	***Herbal AVR***
Tamoxifen	**Nolvadex**	*See* **Nolvadex**	
Tamsulosin	**Flomax**	*See* **Flomax**	
Tapazole	*Methimazole*	Mild-to-moderate cases of hyperthyroidism	***Thyrodex***
Tazarotene	**Tazorac**	*See* **Tazorac**	
Tazorac	*Tazarotene*	Acne	***Dermatrol (Clear)***
Tegaserod	**Zelnorm**	*See* **Zelnorm**	
Tegretol	*Carbamazepine*	Nerve-related pain, such as neuralgia and neuropathy	***Flex (NP)***
Telithromycin	**Ketek**	*See* **Ketek**	
Telmisartan	**Micardis**	*See* **Micardis**	
Temazepam	**Restoril**	*See* **Restoril**	
Temovate	*Clobetasol*	Skin conditions with lesions, infections, and inflammations	***Dermatrol (Damp)*** or ***Dermatrol (Dry)***
		Psoriasis	***Dermatrol (PS)***
		Skin rash and eczema	***Silerex***
		For astringent and non-steroidal anti-inflammatory effect	*add* ***Astringent Complex***
Tenex	*Guanfacine*	Elevated blood pressure in patients with hyperactive adrenergic system	***Gentiana Complex***
Tenormin	*Atenolol*	Elevated blood pressure in patients with hyperactive adrenergic system	***Gentiana Complex***
Tenuate	*Diethylpropion*	Obesity, elevated body weight, slow basal metabolism, lack of energy	***Herbalite***
Terazosin	**Hytrin**	*See* **Hytrin**	
Terbutaline	**Brethine**	*See* **Brethine**	
Tessalon Perles	*Benzonatate*	Cough	***Respitrol (CF)***
Theo-Dur	*Theophylline*	Heat-type asthma with fever, dry mouth, thirst, red face and red tongue	***Respitrol (Heat)***
		Cold-type asthma with chills, intolerance to cold, cyanotic complexion of the face and body	***Respitrol (Cold)***
		Chronic asthma with frequent attacks of wheezing and dyspnea	***Respitrol (Deficient)*** or ***Cordyceps 3***
Theophylline	**Slo-Phylline, Theo-Dur**	*See* **Slo-Phylline, Theo-Dur**	
Thorazine	*Chlorpromazine*	Moderate to severe emotional and psychological disorders	***Calm (ES)***
Thyroid Desiccated	**Armour Thyroid**	*See* **Armour Thyroid**	
Thyrolar	*Liotrix*	Hypothyroidism	***Thyro-forte***
Tiotropium	**Spiriva**	*See* **Spiriva**	
Tofranil	*Imipramine*	Depression with low energy, prolonged sadness and lack of interest	***Shine***
		Depression with stress and anxiety	***Shine (DS)***
		Nerve-related pain, such as neuralgia and neuropathy	***Flex (NP)***
Tolbutamide	**Orinase**	*See* **Orinase**	

DRUG–HERB

Drug – Herb Index

Brand Names / *Generic Names*		**Clinical Applications**	**Herb Alternatives**
Tolectin	*Tolmetin*	Various headaches: migraine, tension, stress, vertex, occipital	***Corydalin (AC)*** or ***(CR)***
		Musculoskeletal pain with redness, swelling and inflammation	***Flex (Heat)***
		Musculoskeletal pain that worsens during cold and rainy days	***Flex (CD)***
		Neuropathy	***Flex (NP)***
		Chronic injuries of soft tissues (muscles, ligaments, and tendons)	***Flex (MLT)***
		Arm pain (shoulder, elbow, and wrist)	***Arm Support***
		Acute or chronic pain of the leg (knee and ankle)	***Knee & Ankle (AC)*** or ***(CR)***
		Acute or chronic upper and lower back pain	***Back Support (AC)*** or ***(CR)***
		Acute or chronic neck and shoulder pain	***Neck & Shoulder (AC)*** or ***(CR)***
		Menstrual pain and cramps in dysmenorrhea	***Mense-Ease***
		Pain associated with amenorrhea	***Menatrol***
		Pain associated with endometriosis	***Resolve (Lower)***
		Severe pain	*add* ***Herbal ANG***
		Pain due to trauma	*add* ***Flex (TMX)***
Tolmetin	**Tolectin**	*See* **Tolectin**	
Tolterodine	**Detrol**	*See* **Detrol**	
Toprol	*Metoprolol*	Elevated blood pressure in patients with hyperactive adrenergic system	***Gentiana Complex***
Tradjenta	*Linagliptin*	Elevated blood glucose levels in non-insulin dependent diabetes mellitus	***Equilibrium***
Tramadol	**Ultram**	*See* **Ultram**	
Trazodone	**Desyrel**	*See* **Desyrel**	
Triamcinolone	**Kenalog, Nasacort**	*See* **Kenalog, Nasacort**	
Triamterene	**Dyrenium**	*See* **Dyrenium**	
Triamterene + Hydrochlorothiazide	**Dyazide, Maxzide**	*See* **Dyazide, Maxzide**	
Triaz	*Benzoyl Peroxide*	Acne	***Dermatrol (Clear)***
Tricor	*Fenofibrate*	Elevated serum cholesterol and triglycerides levels	***Cholisma***
		Elevated serum cholesterol and triglycerides levels with fatty liver and obesity	***Cholisma (ES)***
Trilipix	*Fenofibric Acid*	Elevated serum cholesterol and triglycerides levels	***Cholisma***
		Elevated serum cholesterol and triglycerides levels with fatty liver and obesity	***Cholisma (ES)***
Trimox	*Amoxicillin*	*See* **Amoxil**	
Tucks	*Hamamelis*	Hemorrhoids	***GI Care (HMR)***
Tums	*Calcium Carbonate*	Various gastrointestinal disorders, such as heartburn and acid reflux	***GI Care***
Tussionex	*Chlorpheniramine + Hydrocodone*	Lower respiratory tract infection with chest congestion, cough, yellow phlegm and fever	***Pinellia XPT***
		To stop the production of phlegm	***Pinellia Complex***
		Cough and dyspnea	***Respitrol (CF)***

Drug – Herb Index

Brand Names / *Generic Names*		**Clinical Applications**	**Herb Alternatives**
Tylenol + Codeine	*Acetaminophen + Codeine*	Various headaches: migraine, tension, stress, vertex, occipital	***Corydalin (AC)***
		Musculoskeletal pain due to sports or traumatic injuries	***Flex (TMX)***
		Arthritis, especially if condition worsens with cold and dampness	***Flex (CD)***
		Acute or chronic upper and lower back pain	***Back Support (AC)***
		Acute or chronic neck and shoulder pain	***Neck & Shoulder (AC)***
		Arm pain (shoulder, elbow, and wrist)	***Arm Support***
		Acute pain from herniated disk in the back	***Back Support (HD)***
		Acute pain of the leg (knee and ankle)	***Knee & Ankle (AC)***
		Severe pain	*add* ***Herbal ANG***
Uloric	*Febuxostat*	Gout	***Flex (GT)***
Ultram	*Tramadol*	Various headaches: migraine, tension, stress, vertex, occipital	***Corydalin (AC)*** or ***(CR)***
		Musculoskeletal pain with redness, swelling and inflammation	***Flex (Heat)***
		Musculoskeletal pain that worsens during cold and rainy days	***Flex (CD)***
		Chronic injuries of soft tissues (muscles, ligaments, and tendons)	***Flex (MLT)***
		Arm pain (shoulder, elbow, and wrist)	***Arm Support***
		Acute or chronic pain of the leg (knee and ankle)	***Knee & Ankle (AC)*** or ***(CR)***
		Acute or chronic upper and lower back pain	***Back Support (AC)*** or ***(CR)***
		Acute or chronic neck and shoulder pain	***Neck & Shoulder (AC)*** or ***(CR)***
		Acute pain from herniated disk in the back	***Back Support (HD)***
		Severe pain	*add* ***Herbal ANG***
		Pain due to trauma	*add* ***Flex (TMX)***
Unisom	*Doxylamine*	Insomnia due to Liver qi stagnation (stress, anxiety, nervousness, restlessness)	***Calm ZZZ***
		Insomnia due to *shen* (spirit) disturbance with qi and blood deficiencies	***Schisandra ZZZ***
Uroxatral	*Alfuzosin*	Benign prostatic hypertrophy (BPH)	***P-Support***
Ursodiol	**Actigall**	*See* **Actigall**	
Vagifem	*Estradiol Vaginal Tablets*	Vaginal dryness and atrophy	***Balance Spring***
Valacyclovir	**Valtrex**	*See* **Valtrex**	
Valium	*Diazepam*	Moderate to severe emotional and psychological disorders	***Calm (ES)***
		Moderate levels of stress, anxiety, nervousness, and tension	***Calm***
		Moderate levels of stress, anxiety, and insomnia	***Calm ZZZ***
Valsartan	**Diovan**	*See* **Diovan**	
Valtrex	*Valacyclovir*	Treatment of oral herpes	***Lonicera Complex***
		Treatment of genital herpes	***Gentiana Complex***
		Prevention of recurrent genital herpes	***Nourish***
		Treatment of herpes zoster (shingles)	***Dermatrol (HZ)***
		For post-herpetic neuralgia	*add* ***Flex (NP)***

Drug – Herb Index

Brand Names / *Generic Names*		**Clinical Applications**	**Herb Alternatives**
Valtrex (*cont'd*)	*Valacyclovir*	Generalized viral infection	*add* ***Herbal AVR***
		To enhance immunity during remission	***Immune +***
Vardenafil	**Levitra**	*See* **Levitra**	
Varenicline	**Chantix**	*See* **Chantix**	
Varicella Zoster Immune Globulin	**Varizig**	*See* **Varizig**	
Varizig	*Varicella Zoster Immune Globulin*	To reduce severity of chickenpox infections	***Dermatrol (HZ)***
		Generalized viral infection	*add* ***Herbal AVR***
		For post-herpetic neuralgia	*add* ***Flex (NP)***
Vasotec	*Enalapril*	Cardiovascular disorders, such as hypertension	***Gastrodia Complex***
Venlafaxine	**Effexor**	*See* **Effexor**	
Ventolin	*Albuterol*	Heat-type asthma with fever, dry mouth, thirst, red face and red tongue	***Respitrol (Heat)***
		Cold-type asthma with chills, intolerance to cold, cyanotic complexion of the face and body	***Respitrol (Cold)***
		Chronic asthma with frequent attacks of wheezing and dyspnea	***Respitrol (Deficient)***
Verapamil	**Calan, Isoptin, Verelan**	*See* **Calan, Isoptin, Verelan**	
Verelan	*Verapamil*	Cardiovascular disorders, such as hypertension	***Gastrodia Complex***
Viagra	*Sildenafil*	Male sexual disorder (i.e., erectile dysfunction, impotence)	***Vitality***
		Male reproductive disorder (i.e., infertility)	***Vital Essence***
		Male sexual and reproductive dysfunctions with cold signs and symptoms	***Kidney Tonic (Yang)***
Vibramycin	*Doxycycline*	Antibiotic used to treat acne	***Dermatrol (Clear)***
Vicodin	*Hydrocodone + Acetaminophen*	Various headaches: migraine, tension, stress, vertex, occipital	***Corydalin (AC)***
		Musculoskeletal pain due to sports or traumatic injuries	***Flex (TMX)***
		Arthritis, especially if condition worsens with cold and dampness	***Flex (CD)***
		Acute or chronic upper and lower back pain	***Back Support (AC)***
		Acute or chronic neck and shoulder pain	***Neck & Shoulder (AC)***
		Arm pain (shoulder, elbow, and wrist)	***Arm Support***
		Acute pain from herniated disk in the back	***Back Support (HD)***
		Acute pain of the leg (knee and ankle)	***Knee & Ankle (AC)***
		Severe pain	*add* ***Herbal ANG***
Victoza	*Liraglutide*	Elevated blood glucose levels in non-insulin dependent diabetes mellitus	***Equilibrium***
Vigamox	*Moxifloxacin*	Generalized bacterial infection	***Herbal ABX***
		Upper respiratory tract infection with fever, headache, sore throat	***Lonicera Complex***
		Respiratory tract infection with sinus congestion, watery nasal discharge, sneezing and chills	***Respitrol (Cold)***
		Lower respiratory tract infection with high fever, copious yellow sputum, cough and perspiration	***Respitrol (Heat)***

Drug – Herb Index

Brand Names / *Generic Names*		**Clinical Applications**	**Herb Alternatives**
Vigamox (*cont'd*)	*Moxifloxacin*	Lower respiratory tract infection with chest congestion, cough, yellow phlegm and fever	***Pinellia XPT***
		Infection in the gastrointestinal tract	***GI Care II***
		Genitourinary infections, such as urinary tract infection or sexually-transmitted diseases	***Gentiana Complex*** or ***V-Support***
		Ear, nose, and throat infections	***Herbal ENT***
		General skin conditions associated with infection and inflammation	***Dermatrol (Damp)*** or ***Dermatrol (Dry)***
Viibryd	*Vilazodone*	Depression with low energy, prolonged sadness and lack of interest	***Shine***
		Depression with stress and anxiety	***Shine (DS)***
Vilazodone	**Viibryd**	*See* **Viibryd**	
Vistaril	*Hydroxyzine*	Allergic or hypersensitive skin problems such as rash, itching, and eczema	***Silerex***
Vitamin K	**Mephyton**	*See* **Mephyton**	
Vivarin	*Caffeine*	Lack of energy levels, decreased mental and physical performance	***Vibrant***
		Chronic fatigue and weakness	***Imperial Tonic***
Vivelle	*Estradiol Transdermal*	Menopausal symptoms such as hot flashes, irritability and mood swings	***Balance (Heat)*** or ***Nourish***
		Vaginal dryness and atrophy	***Balance Spring***
		Osteoporosis	***Osteo 8***
Voltaren	*Diclofenac*	Various headaches: migraine, tension, stress, vertex, occipital	***Corydalin (AC)*** or ***(CR)***
		Musculoskeletal pain with redness, swelling and inflammation	***Flex (Heat)***
		Musculoskeletal pain that worsens during cold and rainy days	***Flex (CD)***
		Neuropathy	***Flex (NP)***
		Chronic injuries of soft tissues (muscles, ligaments, and tendons)	***Flex (MLT)***
		Arm pain (shoulder, elbow, and wrist)	***Arm Support***
		Acute or chronic pain of the leg (knee and ankle)	***Knee & Ankle (AC)*** or ***(CR)***
		Acute or chronic upper and lower back pain	***Back Support (AC)*** or ***(CR)***
		Acute or chronic neck and shoulder pain	***Neck & Shoulder (AC)*** or ***(CR)***
		Menstrual pain and cramps in dysmenorrhea	***Mense-Ease***
		Pain associated with amenorrhea	***Menatrol***
		Pain associated with endometriosis	***Resolve (Lower)***
		Severe pain	*add* ***Herbal ANG***
		Pain due to trauma	*add* ***Flex (TMX)***
Vytorin	*Ezetimibe + Simvastatin*	Elevated serum cholesterol and triglycerides levels	***Cholisma***
		Elevated serum cholesterol and triglycerides levels with fatty liver and obesity	***Cholisma (ES)***
Vyvanse	*Lisdexamfetamine*	To promote concentration and focus in ADD (attention deficit disorder) and ADHD (attention deficit-hyperactivity disorder)	***Calm (Jr)***

Drug – Herb Index

Brand Names / *Generic Names*		**Clinical Applications**	**Herb Alternatives**
Welchol	*Colesevelam*	Elevated serum cholesterol and triglycerides levels	***Cholisma***
		Elevated serum cholesterol and triglycerides levels with fatty liver and obesity	***Cholisma (ES)***
Wellbutrin	*Bupropion*	Depression with low energy, prolonged sadness and lack of interest	***Shine***
		Depression with stress and anxiety	***Shine (DS)***
		Craving and withdrawal symptoms associated with cigarette smoking addiction	***Calm (ES)***
Xanax	*Alprazolam*	Moderate to severe emotional and psychological disorders	***Calm (ES)***
		Moderate levels of stress, anxiety, nervousness, and tension	***Calm***
		Moderate levels of stress, anxiety, and insomnia	***Calm ZZZ***
Xenical	*Orlistat*	Obesity	***Herbalite***
Xifaxan	*Rifaximin*	Traveler's diarrhea	***GI Care II***
Xopenex	*Levalbuterol*	Heat-type asthma with fever, dry mouth, thirst, red face and red tongue	***Respitrol (Heat)***
		Cold-type asthma with chills, intolerance to cold, cyanotic complexion of the face and body	***Respitrol (Cold)***
		Chronic asthma with frequent attacks of wheezing and dyspnea	***Respitrol (Deficient)***
Yocon	*Yohimbine*	Male sexual disorder (i.e., erectile dysfunction, impotence)	***Vitality***
		Male reproductive disorder (i.e., infertility)	***Vital Essence***
		Male sexual and reproductive dysfunctions with cold signs and symptoms	***Kidney Tonic (Yang)***
Yohimbine	**Yocon**	*See* **Yocon**	
Zafirlukast	**Accolate**	*See* **Accolate**	
Zanamivir	**Relenza**	*See* **Relenza**	
Zantac	*Ranitidine*	Various gastrointestinal disorders, such as heartburn, acid reflux and peptic ulcer	***GI Care***
Zebeta	*Bisoprolol*	Elevated blood pressure in patients with hyperactive adrenergic system	***Gentiana Complex***
Zelnorm	*Tegaserod*	Irritable bowel syndrome	***GI Harmony***
Zephrex	*Expectorant Combination*	Lower respiratory tract infection with chest congestion, cough, yellow phlegm and fever	***Pinellia XPT***
		To stop the production of phlegm	***Pinellia Complex***
		Cough and dyspnea	***Respitrol (CF)***
Zestril	*Lisinopril*	Cardiovascular disorders, such as hypertension	***Gastrodia Complex***
Zetia	*Ezetimibe*	Elevated serum cholesterol and triglycerides levels	***Cholisma***
		Elevated serum cholesterol and triglycerides levels with fatty liver and obesity	***Cholisma (ES)***
Zileuton	**Zyflo**	*See* **Zyflo**	
Ziprasidone	**Geodon**	*See* **Geodon**	
Zithromax	*Azithromycin*	Generalized bacterial infection	***Herbal ABX***
		Upper respiratory tract infection with fever, headache, sore throat	***Lonicera Complex***

Drug – Herb Index

Brand Names / *Generic Names*		**Clinical Applications**	**Herb Alternatives**
Zithromax (*cont'd*)	*Azithromycin*	Respiratory tract infection with sinus congestion, watery nasal discharge, sneezing and chills	***Respitrol (Cold)***
		Lower respiratory tract infection with high fever, copious yellow sputum, cough and perspiration	***Respitrol (Heat)***
		Lower respiratory tract infection with chest congestion, cough, yellow phlegm and fever	***Pinellia XPT***
		Infection in the gastrointestinal tract	***GI Care II***
		Genitourinary infections, such as urinary tract infection or sexually-transmitted diseases	***Gentiana Complex*** or ***V-Support***
		Ear, nose, and throat infections	***Herbal ENT***
		General skin conditions associated with infection and inflammation	***Dermatrol (Damp)*** or ***Dermatrol (Dry)***
		With more swelling and inflammation	*add* ***Astringent Complex***
Zocor	*Simvastatin*	Elevated serum cholesterol and triglycerides levels	***Cholisma***
		Elevated serum cholesterol and triglycerides levels with fatty liver and obesity	***Cholisma (ES)***
Zofran	*Ondansetron*	Nausea due to chemotherapy	***C/R Support***
Zoloft	*Sertraline*	Depression with low energy, prolonged sadness and lack of interest	***Shine***
		Depression with stress and anxiety	***Shine (DS)***
Zolpidem	**Ambien**	*See* **Ambien**	
Zostavax	*Zoster Vaccine Live*	Treatment of herpes zoster (shingles)	***Dermatrol (HZ)***
Zovirax	*Acyclovir*	Treatment of oral herpes	***Lonicera Complex***
		Treatment of genital herpes	***Gentiana Complex***
		Prevention of recurrent genital herpes	***Nourish***
		Treatment of herpes zoster (shingles)	***Dermatrol (HZ)***
		Generalized viral infection	*add* ***Herbal AVR***
		To enhance immunity during remission	***Immune +***
Zyflo	*Zileuton*	Dyspnea and shortness of breath in cases of chronic asthma	***Respitrol (Deficient)***
		Management and prevention of chronic asthma	***Cordyceps 3***
Zyloprim	*Allopurinol*	Gout	***Flex (GT)***
Zyprexa	*Olanzapine*	Moderate levels of stress, anxiety, nervousness, tension, etc.	***Calm***
		Moderate to severe emotional and psychological disorders	***Calm (ES)***
Zyrtec	*Cetirizine*	Nasal congestion with yellow, sticky discharge	***Pueraria Clear Sinus***
		Nasal congestion with white, watery discharge	***Magnolia Clear Sinus***
		Allergic or hypersensitive skin problems such as rash, itching, and eczema	***Silerex***

Section 5

Exemplar Formulas

標
準
方
劑

Guide To Formula Monographs

The information regarding herbal formulas on the following pages is intended for use by licensed healthcare practitioners only, as professional training and expertise are essential for correct interpretation of the material and optimal use of the herbs. All information is presented in an accurate and truthful manner. Therapeutic claims are supported by modern research and referenced accordingly throughout the entire text. The advantages and disadvantages of each herbal formula are disclosed in full so that practitioners and their patients can make informed decisions.

Traditional Chinese Medicine (TCM) Terminology

Because traditional Chinese medicine and Western medicine have distinct cultural and philosophical influences, it is challenging to accurately convey some TCM terms and concepts by using English or allopathic clinical language. We have made sincere efforts to provide consistent standards for terms and concepts to bridge the gap, as follows:

- Terms that have become an accepted part of English language discourse and are well understood by the general public, such as qi, yin and yang, are neither italicized nor capitalized.
- Terms unique to the profession, understood primarily by TCM practitioners, are given in pinyin, italicized and translated, but not capitalized; for example, *bi zheng* (painful obstruction syndrome), *xiao ke* (wasting and thirsting) syndrome, and *lin zheng* (dysuria syndrome).
- Nouns distinct to herbal medicine are italicized, capitalized and translated, such as *Ren Shen* (Radix et Rhizoma Ginseng) and *Bu Zhong Yi Qi Tang* (Tonify the Middle and Augment the Qi Decoction).
- It is important to note that anatomical organ names in TCM imply functions distinct from their common understanding in Western medicine. Therefore, organ names are capitalized when discussed within the context of traditional Chinese medicine but not when referring exclusively to anatomical function. For example, *Huang Qin* (Radix Scutellariae) is commonly used to clear **Lung** heat because the herb has shown antibiotic effect to treat infection of the **lungs**.

CLINICAL APPLICATIONS

This section outlines the indications for use of the herbal formulas, including symptoms, diseases, and diagnoses according to Western and traditional Chinese medicine.

WESTERN THERAPEUTIC ACTIONS

The functions of the herbal formulas are summarized according to allopathic criteria. Therapeutic functions and clinical effects stated are supported by modern research and clinical studies. Additional information and a detailed explanation are provided in the Modern Research section.

CHINESE THERAPEUTIC ACTIONS

This section summarizes the functions of the herbal formulas according to traditional Chinese medicine. Diagnoses, therapeutic functions, and clinical effects are stated in Chinese medical terminology and are supported by historical references and modern textbooks.

DOSAGE

The dosage of herbal extract for an average adult ranges from 4 to 8 capsules [2 to 4 grams] three to four times daily, taken with warm water on an empty stomach, one hour before or two hours after meals. However, it is important to keep in mind that the dosage must be adjusted to reflect the age and body weight of the patient, and the severity and nature of the illness.

The average adult is roughly defined as an individual between 18 and 60 years of age, with a body weight of 120 to 180 pounds. However, since not everybody is an "average adult," dosing of herbs must be individualized based on age and body weight. Generally speaking, the dosage should be reduced if the patient is younger than 18 years of age or weighs less than 120 pounds. Conversely, the dosage should be increased if the patient weighs more than 180 pounds. For more information on dosing, please refer to *Strategic Dosing Guidelines* on page 14.

The dosage should be adjusted according to the type and severity of the illness. For treating acute or severe illnesses, such as severe low back pain, the dosage may be doubled to enhance the therapeutic effect. Depending on the patient and the disease, some herbal formulas may be taken in dosages of up to 40 capsules [20 grams] per day. Similarly, the dosage frequency may be adjusted to reflect the nature of the illness. For example, a person with insomnia should take more herbs before bedtime and less during the day. Finally, for patients who have allergies or food sensitivities, or for someone who has never taken herbs before, it is prudent to start with a lower dosage of herbs.

INGREDIENTS

The ingredients of the formulas are listed in alphabetical order by their *pinyin* and pharmaceutical names. The nomenclature of herbs and formulas are taken from the following primary sources:

- *Zhong Hua Ren Min Gong He Guo Yao Dian* (Chinese Herbal Pharmacopoeia by People's Republic of China), People's Republic of China, 2010. Our standard reference for nomenclature of *pinyin* and pharmaceutical names, this text offers the most precise, accurate, and current information on the identification of Chinese herbs and other medicinal substances.
- *Xian Dai Zhong Yao Yao Li Xue* (Contemporary Pharmacology of Chinese Herbs) by Wang Ben-Yang, Tianjing Science and Technology Press, 1999.
- *Chinese Medical Herbology and Pharmacology*, by John Chen and Tina Chen, Art of Medicine Press, 2004.
- *Chinese Herbal Formulas and Applications*, by John Chen and Tina Chen, Art of Medicine Press, 2009.

Guide To Formula Monographs

- *Chinese Herbal Medicine Materia Medica*, by Dan Bensky and Andrew Gamble, Eastland Press, 2004.
- *Chinese Herbal Medicine Formulas & Strategies*, by Dan Bensky and Randall Barolet, Eastland Press, 2009.
- *A Practical Dictionary of Chinese Medicine* 2nd Edition, by Nigel Wiseman and Feng Ye, Paradigm Publications, 1998.

BACKGROUND

This section provides introductory and background information on the disease.

FORMULA EXPLANATION

This section explains the rationale for and the treatment strategy of the herbal formula. The therapeutic function of each ingredient is discussed in detail to provide a comprehensive understanding of each herbal formula. The explanations include both Chinese and Western medical terminology and are intended for readers with medical training.

CAUTIONS & CONTRAINDICATIONS

This section discusses relevant cautions for use of the herbal formula, including (but not limited to) side effects, adverse reactions, contraindications and herb-drug interactions. In addition, this section addresses how to discern circumstances in which to treat or ***not*** to treat with a particular formula. It provides valuable information for prevention of wrong diagnosis and malpractice. Information is presented in an accurate and truthful manner so that healthcare practitioners can evaluate risks versus benefits, and so that their patients can make informed decisions. Lastly, the use of herbs during pregnancy or while nursing is ***not*** recommended.

CLINICAL NOTES

This section includes quick and easy tips for practitioners to boost the effectiveness and overall success of the treatment. This section also provides valuable information on differential diagnosis, treatment, and prognosis, based on the clinical experience of masters of traditional Chinese medicine.

Pulse Diagnosis by Dr. Jimmy Wei-Yen Chang:

This section provides the pulses associated with the disease. Dr. Jimmy Wei-Yen Chang, a renowned pulse diagnostician and herbalist with over 30 years of innovative, clinical, and practical experience, is one of the very few licensed practitioners who is able to integrate TCM pulse diagnosis with Western biomedical conditions and correlate definitive pulses with herbal prescriptions. He has made pulse diagnosis, Chinese medicine's cardinal diagnostic technique, into a reliable diagnostic tool in itself.

Dr. Chang's unique pulse diagnostic method has some differences from the pulse diagnosis that is traditionally taught in TCM schools. The biggest and probably the most crucial difference is the location of the *cun*, *guan*, and *chi* positions of the pulse. For Dr. Chang's pulse diagnosis, the pulse positions are found by first locating the styloid process. The index finger is then placed distal to the styloid process, which corresponds to the *cun* position and relates to the Lungs on the right hand and to the Heart on the left hand; the middle finger is placed proximal to the styloid process, which corresponds to the *guan* position and relates to the Stomach on the right hand and to the Liver on the left hand; lastly, the ring finger is then placed proximal to the middle finger and corresponds to the *chi* position, which relates to the Kidney's urinary function and upper body on the right hand, and to the Kidney's reproductive function and lower body on the left hand. With this slight difference between Dr. Chang's pulse positions and the traditional pulse positions, it can make the difference between reaching the correct or incorrect diagnosis.

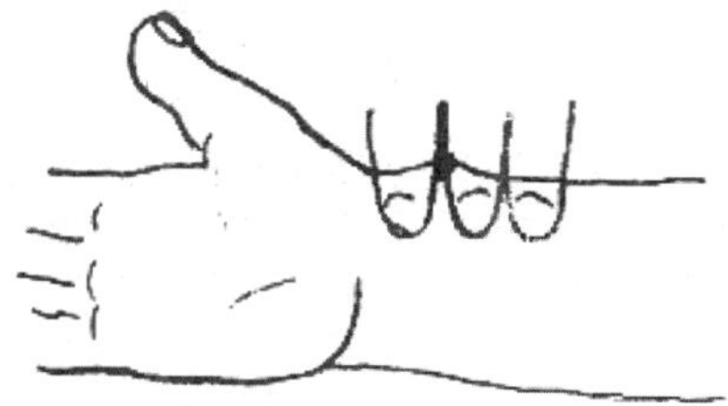

Dr. Chang's Pulse Positions

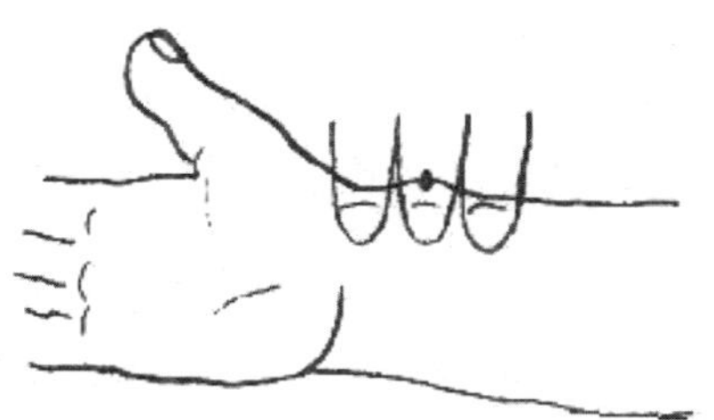

Traditional Pulse Positions

According to Dr. Chang, a complete pulse is made up of three basic components: 1) the shape of the pulse, 2) the jump of the pulse, and 3) the level of the pulse. The shape of the pulse includes convex-shaped pulses (i.e., turtle pulse, bird's beak pulse), concave-shaped pulses, straight wiry pulses (i.e., pulse within a pulse, *taiyang* pulse, big pulse), and shapeless pulses (i.e., dispersing pulse, greasy pulse). The jump of the pulse includes its velocity (fast or slow), strength (i.e., forceful, weak, impetuous), resistance (i.e., tight, flowing), and amplitude (high or low). The level of the pulse describes the depth at which the pulse can be felt – superficial (floating) or deep (sunken). Based on these three components and the position in which the pulse is felt, Dr. Chang is able to arrive at a definitive pulse and its diagnosis. For additional information, please attend his online courses or read his book:

- Online courses: http://www.elotus.org/speaker-bio
- Book: *Pulsynergy* by Dr. Jimmy Wei-Yen Chang and Marcus Brinkman.

Guide To Formula Monographs

SUPPLEMENTARY FORMULAS

This section emphasizes the modification of herbal treatment. As two or more patients having the same disease may have different clinical manifestations, it is often necessary to choose an alternate formula, combine two formulas for synergistic effects, or add another formula to treat complications or progression of the disease.

ACUPUNCTURE TREATMENT

Traditional Points:

These are textbook recommendations for body and ear points. This section lists and explains the suggested acupuncture treatments to be used with herbal therapy. The translation and abbreviations of the vessels follow the system established by the World Health Organization (WHO):

Lung (LU)	Pericardium (PC)
Large Intestine (LI)	Triple Heater [*San Jiao*] (TH)
Stomach (ST)	Gallbladder (GB)
Spleen (SP)	Liver (LR)
Heart (HT)	Governor Vessel (GV) [a.k.a. *Du* Channel]
Small Intestine (SI)	
Bladder (BL)	Conception Vessel (CV) [a.k.a. *Ren* Channel]
Kidney (KI)	

Classic Master Tung's Points:

This section highlights Master Tung's main treatment strategy and acupuncture points. Master Tung Ching-Chang (1916–1975) was born and raised in Shandong, China. He inherited generations of family-style acupuncture and continued the legacy after he moved to Taiwan in 1949. With his relocation to Taiwan, Master Tung was able to avoid the Cultural Revolution and preserved the clinical pearls of traditional healing. Tung Style Acupuncture is known for its outstanding therapeutic effects using very few refined acupuncture points. It is often grouped with the distal acupuncture style for its stress on points on the hands and feet. Even though many of Tung Style Acupuncture points still follow the 14 channel relationships, the locations and applications are very different from the unified TCM school tradition. Master Tung is best known for his "*Dao Ma*" technique, which utilizes three needles in adjacent areas on the channel to enhance the treatment effect. He treated over 400,000 patients during his lifetime and trained many practitioners along the way. Master Tung is famous for the miraculous and spontaneous results he would obtain by using few needles. The acupuncture points and techniques he used are unique while remaining in accord with orthodox acupuncture. In most cases, the patient notices instant relief upon insertion of the needle. Even though Master Tung passed away in 1975, his students and disciples continue to practice his style of acupuncture around the world. Master Tung's life-long research and clinical experiences were complied into many books and other works. Tung Style Acupuncture has also been recognized by the NCCAOM and was added to the continuing education list in 2003. For those who are interested in further study of Tung Style Acupuncture, the following books are available:

- *Advanced Tung Style Acupuncture: The Dao Ma Needling Technique of Master Tung Ching Chang* by James H Maher
- *Advanced Tung Style Acupuncture Vol. 2: Obstetrics & Gynecology* by James H Maher
- *Advanced Tung Style Acupuncture Vol. 3: Nephrology Urology & Andrology* by James H Maher
- *Advanced Tung Style Acupuncture Vol. 4: Neurology* by James H Maher
- *Advanced Tung Style Acupuncture Vol. 5: Anesthesiology/Pain Management* by James H Maher
- *Advanced Tung Style Acupuncture Vol. 6A: Internal Medicine* by James H Maher
- *Advanced Tung Style Acupuncture Vol. 6B: Internal Medicine* by James H Maher
- *Introduction to Tung's Acupuncture* by Dr. Chuan-Min Wang
- *Illustrated Tung's Acupuncture Points* by Wei-Chieh Young
- *Lectures On Tung's Acupuncture: Points Study* by Wei-Chieh Young
- *Lectures On Tung's Acupuncture: Therapeutic System* by Wei-Chieh Young
- *Practical Atlas of Tung's Acupuncture* by Henry McCann & Hans-Georg Ross
- *Pricking the Vessels: Bloodletting Therapy in Chinese Medicine* by Henry McCann
- *Mastering Tung Acupuncture – Distal Imaging for Fast Pain Relief* by Brad Whisnant

* Note: Though there are many books on Master Tung's style of acupuncture and Master Tung's points, there are still some points that have not been translated in English. These points are marked with (*) and additional information is available at the Lotus Institute website: www.elotus.org.

Master Tung's Numbering System

Throughout the manual, the letter "T" will appear in front of the numbers indicating it's a Master Tung point. The numbers below give a general idea where the points are located on the body.

T 11.00	Fingers	T 77.00	Lower leg
T 22.00	Hand	T 88.00	Thigh
T 33.00	Forearm	T 99.00	Ear
T 44.00	Upper arm	T 1010.00	Head/Face
T 55.00	Plantar of the foot	T DT.00	Back
T 66.00	Dorsum of the foot	T VT.00	Chest

Guide To Formula Monographs

Master Tung's Bloodletting Therapy

While the use of special points and synergistic needling (*dao ma)* are hallmarks of Master Tung's acupuncture style, any discussion of his approach is incomplete without mention of his bloodletting techniques. Especially in chronic, severe, or difficult cases that do not respond well to acupuncture and herbs, bloodletting is indispensible.

Points for bloodletting are found in two main areas. First, individual points, usually found on the trunk of the body, can be used for bloodletting based on specific indications. Second, various zones of the limbs have corresponding effects on the *zang* and *fu* organs, allowing the practitioner to treat according to organ patterns. The best areas for bloodletting will show local signs of blood stasis, such as visible spider nevi or small dark purple veins. Veins that are thick, distended, and may be green in color should not be bled. Upon palpation, the skin in these areas may feel rough, indicating blood stasis, or hot, indicating heat. It is important that bloodletting is done on the veins, not the arteries. Unlike Tung's needling technique, bloodletting is applied ipsilaterally to the site of disease.

Master Tung used three-edged needles exclusively for bloodletting. However, lancet needles are safer for beginners because the depth can be controlled. Advanced practitioners may choose to use three-edged needles, body piercing or syringe needles.

Bloodletting is contraindicated in patients with bleeding disorders (i.e., hemophilia), and patients who are on anticoagulant or antiplatelet therapies, such as Coumadin (warfarin), or on any medications that may cause excessive bleeding. Caution should be taken in deficient patients, patients who are hungry, anemic, and pregnant, and also elderly patients. Bloodletting should be stopped when the following signs are presented: pale face, fainting pulse, cold limbs, sweating, lowering blood pressure, or unconsciousness.

Note: State regulatory boards and agencies have differing perspectives on whether bloodletting is part of your acupuncture scope of practice. Understanding this skill and its therapeutic value does not guarantee that it is legal for you to practice it in your state. Please check with your licensing board.
In addition, adhere to clean needle technique protocols, including but not limited to wearing disposable gloves, using disposable needles, and using one needle per point, when bloodletting. Please review your clean needle technique for bloodletting.

For more information on bloodletting, please visit www.elotus.org

Zones of the Trunk

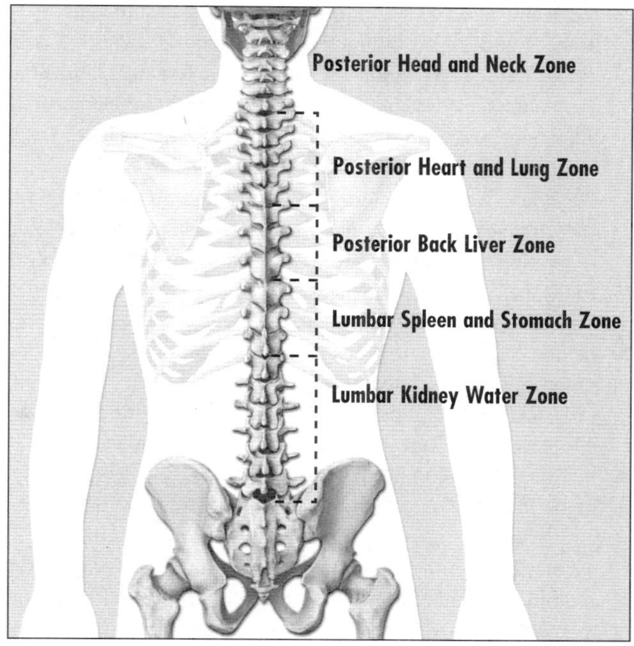

Zones of the Lower Limbs

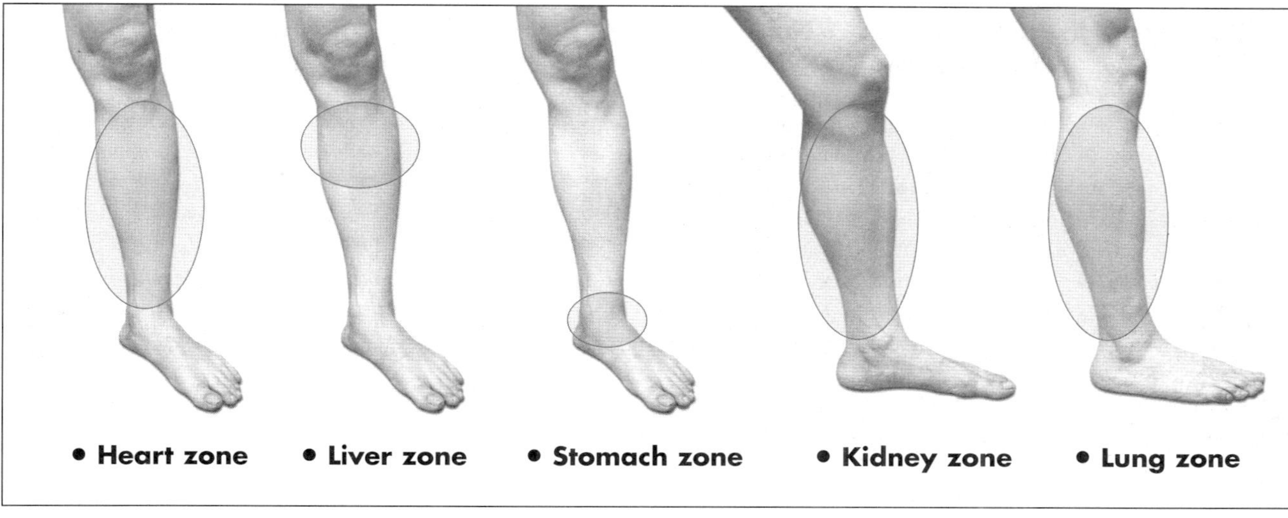

FORMULAS

Guide To Formula Monographs

Master Tung's Points by Dr. Chuan-Min Wang:

This section illustrates clinical application of Master Tung's points by Dr. Chuan-Min Wang, **an official apprentice who learned Tung's acupuncture directly with Master Ching-Chang Tung from 1972-1974**. Born in Taiwan, Dr. Chuan-Min Wang received a Philosophy B.S. degree from Fu-Jen Catholic University in 1974 and an Education Master degree from National Taiwan Normal University in 1977. During his college years, Dr. Wang studied Chinese Philosophy and *I-Ching* from Master Hwai-Jin Nan. After his studies, Dr. Wang taught philosophy at a local college and practice acupuncture at home in Taiwan. After immigrating to the U.S., Dr. Wang studied chiropractic techniques and received a Doctor of Chiropractic degree in 1999. Soon after, Dr. Wang received his chiropractic physician and acupuncture licenses and began a practice in Illinois. Dr. Wang has also visited Peru, El Salvador, the Dominican Republic, and Bolivia as a volunteer physician 7 times and received the Humanitarian Physician Award from the Buddhist Compassion Relief *Tzu Chi* Foundation Taiwan in 2004 for his volunteer works. In addition, Dr. Wang was invited to promote Tung's Acupuncture three days in He'nan Traditional Chinese Medicine by The World Federation of Acupuncture-Moxibustion Society (WFAS). For additional information, please attend his online courses and read his book:

- Online courses: www.elotus.org/speaker-bio
  - Master Tung's Acupuncture: Five *Zang* System
  - Master Tung's Unique Points for Female Conditions
  - Top 30 Master Tung Points & Their Clinical Indications
- Website: www.acup-chiro.com/
- Book: *Introduction to Tung's Acupuncture* by Chuan-Min Wang

* Note: Though there are many books on Master Tung's style of acupuncture and Master Tung's points, there are still some points that have not been translated in English. These points are marked with (*) and additional information is available at the Lotus Institute website: www.elotus.org.

Balance Method by Dr. Richard Teh-Fu Tan:

The late Dr. Richard Tan was a leading acupuncture authority in our profession. His skills represented the culmination of years of study. At age seven, he began his studies in Chinese Medicine with his family in Taiwan, and apprenticed with numerous masters in herbal medicine, five element theory, acupuncture channel theory, *zang fu* energetics, *feng shui*, and qi cultivation. Early in his career, he treated hundreds of patients who were also receiving Western medical care in an army hospital. Upon coming to the U.S., Dr. Tan revolutionized the acupuncture community with Balance Method Acupuncture. This school of acupuncture was derived from the *I Ching*, which consisted of six logical systems based on TCM Channel relationships and the Chinese Clock. He practiced in San Diego for over 25 years while leading many interns to become successful practitioners. Dr. Tan also lectured extensively throughout the U.S. and the world. For additional information, please attend his online courses, and read his books:

- **Online courses:** www.elotus.org/speaker-bio
  - Dr. Tan's Balance Method: As Simple As 1-2-3! [Introduction]
  - Intro to Master Tung's Acupuncture: Richard Tan's Applications [Introduction]
  - Master Tung's Acupuncture - Dr. Tan Style [Introduction]
- **Books:**
  - *Twelve and Twelve in Acupuncture* by Richard Teh-Fu Tan and Stephen Rush
  - *Twenty-Four More in Acupuncture* by Richard Teh-Fu Tan and Stephen Rush
  - *Dr. Tan's Strategy of Twelve Magical Points* by Richard Teh-Fu Tan
  - *Acupuncture 1, 2, 3* by Richard Teh-Fu Tan

Ear Acupuncture:

These are the textbook recommendations for ear points.

Auricular Medicine by Dr. Li-Chun Huang:

This section highlights clinical applications of Auricular Medicine, a scientific medical system which can diagnose and treat many different diseases of the body and the mind solely through the ears. After more than 40 years of research and practice, Dr. Li-Chun Huang, an internationally renowned physician, founded this unique art of healing. Dr. Huang developed this complete system of auricular diagnosis with visual examination, palpation, and electrical probe diagnosis. Auricular medicine can precisely diagnosis and treat over 400 symptoms and over 200 diseases. The ears are one of the few areas where a practitioner can conduct diagnosis and treatment at the same time. It is very fast, effective, and safe. Dr. Huang is very generous in sharing her knowledge and has recommended point prescriptions associated with formulas and conditions mentioned in this Clinical Manual. For additional information, please attend her online courses and read her books:

- Online courses: http://www.elotus.org/speaker-bio
- Website: http://www.earmedicine.us/
- Books:
  - *Auricular Medicine (second edition)* by Li-Chun Huang
  - *Handbook of Auricular Prescriptions and Formulae* by Li-Chun Huang
  - *Auricular Diagnosis with Color Photos* by Li-Chun Huang
  - *Color Ear Chart (Left Ear)* by Li-Chun Huang
  - *Color Ear Chart (Right Ear)* by Li-Chun Huang

> Note: Unlike traditional protocol, Dr. Huang uses two vaccaria seeds per ear point to provide stronger stimulation and faster healing.

Guide To Formula Monographs

NUTRITION

This section describes the dietary changes recommended to facilitate short-term and long-term recovery. Detailed information is available on what foods to consume and what foods to avoid.

The Tao of Nutrition by Dr. Maoshing Ni and Cathy McNease:

This section highlights foods and nutrients that should be consumed and avoided. Recommendations include common foods, as well as those that are unique to Chinese culture and traditional Chinese medicine. For additional information, please attend her online courses or read their publication:

- Online courses: http://www.elotus.org/speaker-bio
- Book: *The Tao of Nutrition* by Dr. Maoshing Ni and Cathy McNease

LIFESTYLE INSTRUCTIONS

This section highlights lifestyle changes recommended to enhance herbal treatment. Lifestyle instructions are recommended to enhance the effectiveness of herbal treatment and to prevent recurrence of illnesses.

CASE STUDIES

- This section includes actual case reports submitted by healthcare practitioners. It enables the readers to understand the response to, and efficacy of, the herbal formulas in clinical settings, rather than in research studies alone. Note: As these are original reports submitted by practitioners, the formality of the presentation varies from one case study to another.

ADDITIONAL INFORMATION

This section provides any other additional and helpful information regarding the formula and the treatment.

PHARMACOLOGICAL AND CLINICAL RESEARCH

This section summarizes clinical and laboratory studies on the effectiveness of the herbs. Therapeutic claims are explained in detail and referenced accordingly in this section.

References: The references cited include human clinical trials that are randomized, double-blind, and placebo-controlled, with a large number of subjects and sound statistical design. Such studies provide meaningful results with conclusions that can be extrapolated to patients with similar conditions. In addition to human clinical trials, references cited include clinical observations, case studies, credible textbooks, *in-vivo* and *in-vitro* studies, and clinical and laboratory studies.

Scientific and Medical Terminology: For the occasional allopathic term that readers might find puzzling, we recommend accessing any standard allopathic medical dictionary (*see* next entry for example). Since there is no need for translation or interpretation of these terms, we concluded that it was unnecessary to explain such terms in this text. Medical Abbreviations and Symbols are used in accordance with *Dorland's Illustrated Medical Dictionary*, by Saunders.

Drug Names are designated in this text by generic names only, or the combination of Proprietary (Generic) names. The Proprietary (Generic) names are referenced according to *Drug Facts and Comparisons*, updated monthly by Facts and Comparisons, a Wolters Kluwer Company.

Pharmacological Effects: Most pharmacological studies focus on the anatomical and physiological influences of the herbs 1) on the body, or 2) against pathogens. For example, many herbs are described as having antihypertensive effects, as the administration of the herbs leads directly to a decrease in blood pressure. Others are said to have antibacterial effects, as the introduction of the herb leads to the inhibition or death of bacteria. However, the exact mechanisms of action for many herbs are still not well understood at this time.

COMPARATIVE ANALYSIS

Written by Dr. John Chen, who holds doctorate degrees in both Western pharmacology and traditional Chinese medicine, this section compares and contrasts the advantages and disadvantages of drug and herbal medicines. Dr. Chen strongly believes in "medicine without borders," and concludes without bias the "bottom line" on the treatment options for any given condition, whether it is drugs, herbs, or both. Learning the benefits and risks of both medicines empowers practitioners and patients to make more educated and informed decisions for optimal treatment results.

Dr. Chen is the author of three important textbooks: *Chinese Medical Herbology and Pharmacology*, *Chinese Herbal Formulas and Applications*, and *Chinese Herbal Formulas for Veterinarians*. He is also the founder and president of Art of Medicine Press. For more information, please visit his website at www.aompress.com. He is also a regular speaker of the Lotus Institute, as well as many colleges and professional associations.

GENERAL DISCLAIMER

Great care has been taken to maintain the accuracy of the information contained in this *Clinical Manual*. The information as presented in this *Clinical Manual* is for educational purposes only. We cannot anticipate all conditions under which it may be used. In view of ongoing research, changes in governmental regulation, and the constant flow of information related to Chinese and Western medicine, the reader is urged to check with other sources for all up-to-date information. The staff and authors of the Lotus Institute of Integrative Medicine recognize that practitioners accessing this information will have varying levels of training and expertise; therefore, we accept no responsibility for the results obtained by the application of the information within this *Clinical Manual*. Nor are we liable for the safety and suitability of the products, either alone or in combination with others, with single herbs or with the

Guide To Formula Monographs

products of other manufacturers. Neither the Lotus Institute of Integrative Medicine nor the authors of this *Clinical Manual* can be held responsible for errors of fact or omission, nor for any consequences arising from the use or misuse of the information herein.

PROFESSIONAL USE ONLY

This *Clinical Manual of Oriental Medicine* is intended as an educational guide for licensed healthcare practitioners only, as professional training and expertise are essential to the safe recommendation and effective guidance for use of herbs. All herbal products discussed within this *Clinical Manual* must be used only through licensed healthcare practitioners.

The information in this *Clinical Manual* is presented in an accurate, truthful and non-misleading manner. The information is supported by modern research whenever possible and referenced accordingly throughout the entire *Clinical Manual*. Nonetheless, the FDA requires the following statements:

> *These statements have not been evaluated by the Food and Drug Administration. These products are not intended to diagnose, treat, cure or prevent any disease.*

Adrenal +™

CLINICAL APPLICATIONS

- **Adrenal insufficiency or low adrenal functions**
- **Premature aging**
- **Diminished sexual and reproductive functions**
- Patients who are "burned out," with fatigue, no energy, lack of interest, lack of drive and satisfaction

WESTERN THERAPEUTIC ACTIONS

- Regulates and improves the function of the adrenal glands and the endocrine system
- Improves mental acuity and physical performance
- Restores normal sexual and reproductive functions
- Enhances the immune system

CHINESE THERAPEUTIC ACTIONS

- Tonifies Kidney yin, yang, and *jing* (essence)
- Tonifies the qi and blood
- Strengthens the Spleen and Stomach

DOSAGE

Take 3 to 4 capsules three times daily on an empty stomach with warm water. The dosage may be increased to 6 to 8 capsules three times daily, if necessary. For maintenance, take 1 to 2 capsules daily.

INGREDIENTS

Ba Ji Tian (Radix Morindae Officinalis)
Da Zao (Fructus Jujubae)
Du Zhong (Cortex Eucommiae)
Fu Ling (Poria)
Fu Zi (Radix Aconiti Lateralis Praeparata)
Gou Qi Zi (Fructus Lycii)
Mu Dan Pi (Cortex Moutan)
Niu Xi (Radix Achyranthis Bidentatae)
Ren Shen (Radix et Rhizoma Ginseng)
Rou Gui (Cortex Cinnamomi)
Shan Yao (Rhizoma Dioscoreae)
Shan Zhu Yu (Fructus Corni)
Shi Chang Pu (Rhizoma Acori Tatarinowii)
Shu Di Huang (Radix Rehmanniae Praeparata)
Suo Yang (Herba Cynomorii)
Wu Wei Zi (Fructus Schisandrae Chinensis)
Xiao Hui Xiang (Fructus Foeniculi)
Yuan Zhi (Radix Polygalae)
Ze Xie (Rhizoma Alismatis)
Zhi Gan Cao (Radix et Rhizoma Glycyrrhizae Praeparata cum Melle)

BACKGROUND

The adrenal glands, two triangular glands on top of the kidneys, are responsible for the production and release of cortisol in response to stress. If an individual suffers from chronic stress or manages stress poorly, the function of the adrenal glands will be affected, resulting in adrenal insufficiency or adrenal fatigue. Clinical manifestations including anxiety, depression, fatigue, intolerance for stress, increased allergy and sensitivity to foods and chemicals, and a tendency to feel cold.

FORMULA EXPLANATION

Adrenal + is designed to treat patients who are "burned out," with symptoms of premature aging, fatigue, no energy, lack of interest, drive, and satisfaction. Such conditions may be caused by excessive stress, anxiety, tension, overwork, and lack of rest. From the traditional Chinese medicine perspective, there is an excessive consumption of qi, blood, yin, yang, and Kidney *jing* (essence), accompanied by deficiency of Spleen, Stomach, Heart and Kidney. Deficiency of the Spleen and Stomach leads to an inadequate supply of qi, shown by symptoms of generalized weakness, fatigue, and anorexia. Deficiency of Heart qi and blood may contribute to forgetfulness, being easily frightened, low-grade fever, and night sweats. Deficiency of yin and yang leads to premature aging. Lastly, the lack of *jing* (essence) contributes further to Kidney deficiency, leading to decreased libido, spermatorrhea, and other sexual disorders.

In this formula, a large portion of *Ren Shen* (Radix et Rhizoma Ginseng) is used because it is the most effective and potent herb to tonify qi, strengthen the Lung and the Spleen, and improve mental functioning. It has excellent adaptogenic functions to help the body adjust to various stressful situations. Studies have shown that *Ren Shen* (Radix et Rhizoma Ginseng) improves both mental and physical functions.

In addition, *Suo Yang* (Herba Cynomorii), *Ba Ji Tian* (Radix Morindae Officinalis), and *Xiao Hui Xiang* (Fructus Foeniculi) strengthen the Spleen and the Kidney. *Shu Di Huang* (Radix Rehmanniae Praeparata) and *Gou Qi Zi* (Fructus Lycii) nourish the Kidney and benefit qi. *Du Zhong* (Cortex Eucommiae) and *Niu Xi* (Radix Achyranthis Bidentatae) tonify the Kidney and strengthen the knees and the lower back. *Fu Ling* (Poria) and *Shan Yao* (Rhizoma Dioscoreae) strengthen the Spleen and dissolve dampness. *Shan Yao* (Rhizoma Dioscoreae) and *Wu Wei Zi* (Fructus Schisandrae Chinensis) tonify the Lung and prevent leakage of Lung qi. Furthermore, they reduce the loss of fluids from the Kidney, particularly via spermatorrhea. *Yuan Zhi* (Radix Polygalae) tonifies the Heart and calms the *shen* (spirit). *Shi Chang Pu* (Rhizoma Acori Tatarinowii) opens the sensory orifices, improves mental functioning, and increases alertness. *Da Zao* (Fructus Jujubae) tonifies both qi and blood, and strengthens the Lung and Spleen functions.

Furthermore, *Ze Xie* (Rhizoma Alismatis) settles turbidity in the Kidney and controls the potential stagnation that may be associated with the use of *Shu Di Huang* (Radix Rehmanniae Praeparata). *Mu Dan Pi* (Cortex Moutan) sedates deficiency fire of the Liver; it also balances the astringent property of *Shan Zhu*

Adrenal +™

Yu (Fructus Corni). *Fu Ling* (Poria), as a sedating herb used with *Shan Yao* (Rhizoma Dioscoreae), dispels damp through urination and tonifies the middle *jiao*.

Hot in nature, *Fu Zi* (Radix Aconiti Lateralis Praeparata) and *Rou Gui* (Cortex Cinnamomi) revitalize Kidney yang and warm the lower body. *Fu Zi* (Radix Aconiti Lateralis Praeparata) is excellent for treatment of various chronic cold-type disorders associated with the endocrine, cardiovascular and musculoskeletal systems. *Rou Gui* (Cortex Cinnamomi) strengthens the Spleen and tonifies Kidney yang.

Lastly, *Zhi Gan Cao* (Radix et Rhizoma Glycyrrhizae Praeparata cum Melle) tonifies qi and harmonizes the actions of the other herbs.

CAUTIONS & CONTRAINDICATIONS

- This formula is contraindicated during pregnancy and nursing.
- This formula is not recommended in cases with exterior or excess conditions. It should not be used in cases of infections and inflammations.
- This formula should be used with caution in patients with yin deficiency, since this formula is warm in nature.
- This formula may be taken with a small amount of salt as a channel-guiding substance to enhance the Kidney-tonic properties.
- Patients who wear a pacemaker, or individuals who take antiarrhythmic drugs or cardiac glycosides such as Lanoxin (digoxin), should not take this formula. *Fu Zi* (Radix Aconiti Lateralis Praeparata) may interact with these drugs by affecting the rhythm and potentiating the contractile strength of the heart.[1]

CLINICAL NOTES

Pulse Diagnosis by Dr. Jimmy Wei-Yen Chang:

- Overall thin and weak pulse

SUPPLEMENTARY FORMULAS

- For an immediate boost of energy, use with ***Vibrant***.
- For long-term restoration of vitality, use with ***Imperial Tonic***.
- For patients with hypothyroidism, use with ***Thyro-forte***.
- For sexual and reproductive disorders, use with ***Vitality***.
- For compromised immune system, use with ***Immune +***.
- For stomach and duodenal ulcers, use with ***GI Care***.
- For stress and anxiety, use with ***Calm***.
- For severe stress and anxiety, use with ***Calm (ES)***.
- For stress, anxiety, and insomnia, use with ***Calm ZZZ***.
- For insomnia, use with ***Schisandra ZZZ***.
- For obesity, use with ***Herbalite***.
- For weakness and deficiency of the Lung, use with ***Cordyceps 3***.
- For poor memory, use with ***Enhance Memory***.
- For general Kidney yang deficiency, add ***Kidney Tonic (Yang)***.
- For general Kidney yin deficiency, add ***Kidney Tonic (Yin)***.
- For male infertility, add ***Vital Essence***.

ACUPUNCTURE TREATMENT

Traditional Points:

- Apply moxa to *Mingmen* (GV 4), *Shenshu* (BL 23), *Guanyuan* (CV 4)
- Needle *Shenshu* (BL 23), *Sanyinjiao* (SP 6), *Zusanli* (ST 36), *Qihai* (CV 6), *Mingmen* (GV 4), *Shenque* (CV 8)

Classic Master Tung's Points:

- **Fatigue:** *Tianhuang* (T 77.17), *Dihuang* (T 77.19), *Renhuang* (T 77.21), *Minghuang* (T 88.12), *Tianhuang* (T 88.13), *Qihuang* (T 88.14), *Beimian* (T 44.07), *Sanyan* (T 11.21), *Zhitong* (T 44.13)
- **Diminished sexual function:**
  - Female: *Fuke* (T 11.24), *Qimen* (T 33.01), *Qijiao* (T 33.02), *Qizheng* (T 33.03), *Tianhuang* (T 77.17), *Dihuang* (T 77.19), *Renhuang* (T 77.21)
  - Male: *Tianhuang* (T 77.17), *Dihuang* (T 77.19), *Renhuang* (T 77.21), *Tianhuang* (T 88.13), *Minghuang* (T 88.12), *Qihuang* (T 88.14), *Tongshen* (T 88.09), *Tongwei* (T 88.10), *Sanshen* (T 44.27)*
  - Bleed tender points on the Kidney area of the back from L1-L5 with cupping.
  - Long-term treatment with moxa to the Kidney area on the back from L1-L5, *Guanyuan* (CV 4), *Zhongji* (CV 3)

Master Tung's Points by Dr. Chuan-Min Wang:

- **Mild to moderate adrenal insufficiency:** *Tianhuangfu [shenguan]* (T 77.18)
- **Moderate to severe adrenal insufficiency:** *Tianhuang* (T 77.17), *Dihuang* (T 77.19), *Renhuang* (T 77.21)

Balance Method by Dr. Richard Tan:

- Left side: *Hegu* (LI 4), *Fuliu* (KI 7), *Ligou* (LR 5), and Kidney point on the ear
- Right side: *Zusanli* (ST 36), *Yanglingquan* (GB 34), *Tongli* (HT 5)
- Left and right sides can be alternated from treatment to treatment.

Auricular Medicine by Dr. Li-Chun Huang:

- **Addison's disease:** Adrenal Gland, Endocrine, Pituitary, Exciting Point, Thalamus, *San Jiao*, Kidney, Liver
- **Regulating the function of endocrine glands:** Endocrine, Pituitary, Thalamus, Kidney, Gonadotropin, Liver, Corresponding points selected based on the focus.
- **Improving fatigue:** Sympathetic, Kidney, Liver, Spleen, *San Jiao*, Anxious, Nervous Subcortex, Speed Recovered Fatigue. Bleed Ear Apex.

NUTRITION

- Increase the consumption of fresh fruits, vegetables, grains, seeds, and nuts.
- Eat more fish and fish oils, onions, garlic, olives, olive oil, herbs, spices, yogurt, fiber, and tofu or other soy products.

Adrenal +™

- Sea vegetables, such as kelp and dulse, replenish the body with minerals like magnesium, potassium, calcium, iodine, and iron.
- Ensure adequate intake of vitamin B complex to process and utilize energy.
- Decrease intake of alcohol, fats, and highly processed foods.
- Avoid the use of stimulants, such as coffee, caffeine, and high-sugar products.
- Food allergies or chemical hypersensitivity can drain energy and cause fatigue. Additional tests are necessary to rule out allergy and/or hypersensitivity.

The Tao of Nutrition by Dr. Maoshing Ni and Cathy McNease:

- **Kidney yang deficiency:** Consume warming foods such as chicken, lamb, scallions, sesame seeds, fish, baked tofu, soybeans, walnuts, eggs, lentils, black beans, lotus seeds, a little wine, ginger, cinnamon bark tea.
- **Kidney yin deficiency:** Consume cooling foods such as mulberries, apples, peaches, pears, fresh vegetables, mung beans, soybeans, tofu, soy sprouts, chrysanthemum flowers.

LIFESTYLE INSTRUCTIONS

- Get regular exercise and adequate rest.
- For relaxation and better sleep, take a warm bath for about 20 minutes before bedtime. Sea salt or Epsom salt can also be added.
- Engage in activities such as *tai chi chuan* [*tai ji chuan*], walking, or meditation that allow calming of the mind without creating stagnation or excessive fatigue.
- Avoid exposure to heavy metals such as lead, cadmium, aluminum, copper, and arsenic, all of which can suppress the immune system and cause fatigue. Those who have already been exposed should take ***Herbal DTX*** to eliminate these toxins.

CASE STUDIES

- M.H., a 66-year-old female patient, presented with tiredness, weakness, inability to exercise with desire to rest frequently, and some anxiety. Her blood pressure was 145/70 mmHg and her heart rate was 88 beats per minute. Laboratory results showed K 5 mmol/L, Na 140 mmol/L, Cl 103 mmol/L, CO_2 26 mmol/L, and Anion gap 15.8 mmol/L. According to the results, high potassium signified adrenal stress, and high anion gap showed dysglycemia. The practitioner diagnosed this condition as Kidney qi deficiency with yin and yang deficiencies. Other objective findings were cold hands and feet. ***Adrenal +*** was prescribed at three capsules three times daily and as needed after exercising. The results were good. The patient reported that she was satisfied with the herbs and noticed the difference in energy it had given her. Submitted by N.H., Chatsworth, California.
- L.D., a 31-year-old female, presented with fatigue, dizziness, low body temperature, coldness, and muscle weakness. Her blood pressure was 100/60 mmHg and her heart rate was 65 beats per minute. Her Western diagnosis was hypotension and hypoglycemia. Laboratory result showed she had decreased thyroid activity and adrenal medullary insufficiency. The diagnosis was yang deficiency. She was prescribed ***Thyro-forte*** and ***Adrenal +*** at 2.5 and 1.5 grams per day, respectively. She did not receive any acupuncture. After two months, she felt much more energized and the dizziness was gone. She no longer felt cold. Submitted by W.F., Bloomfield, New Jersey.

PHARMACOLOGICAL AND CLINICAL RESEARCH

Adrenal + is designed to treat patients who are "burned out," with fatigue and lethargy accompanied by premature aging and a decline in mental acuity and physical performance. It contains herbs that stimulate the mind, improve physical strength, restore sexual prowess, and enhance the immune system.

The endocrine system has a significant impact on the regulation of various glands in the body, including, but not limited to, the hypothalamus, pituitary, thyroid, parathyroid, the adrenal glands, gonads, pancreas, and paraganglia.[2] The imbalance of the endocrine system will affect the glands, and disorder of the glands will also affect the endocrine system. To properly address such conditions, this formula uses many herbs to regulate and restore the endocrine system and the glands. For example, *Shu Di Huang* (Radix Rehmanniae Praeparata) has been shown to increase plasma levels of adrenal cortical hormone.[3] *Ba Ji Tian* (Radix Morindae Officinalis) has a stimulating effect on the pituitary gland and the adrenal cortex, and its administration has been associated with an increase in plasma levels of corticosteroids.[4] Administration of glycyrrhizin and glycyrrhetinic, two active ingredients in *Zhi Gan Cao* (Radix et Rhizoma Glycyrrhizae Praeparata cum Melle), clearly enhances the overall duration and influence of cortisone as demonstrated by various laboratory studies.[5] One clinical trial showed that patients with declining pituitary gland function were successfully treated by continuous use of *Ren Shen* (Radix et Rhizoma Ginseng) and *Zhi Gan Cao* (Radix et Rhizoma Glycyrrhizae Praeparata cum Melle) for two to three months.[6] Since the long-term use of *Zhi Gan Cao* (Radix et Rhizoma Glycyrrhizae Praeparata cum Melle) is sometimes associated with cellular accumulation of water, *Ze Xie* (Rhizoma Alismatis) is added for its diuretic action to alleviate this potential side effect.[7] Other herbs that affect and improve the endocrine system include *Shan Zhu Yu* (Fructus Corni), *Du Zhong* (Cortex Eucommiae), and *Ba Ji Tian* (Radix Morindae Officinalis).[8,9]

In addition to regulating the endocrine system, it is also important to restore optimal mental and physical functioning. *Shi Chang Pu* (Rhizoma Acori Tatarinowii) and *Ren Shen* (Radix et Rhizoma Ginseng) improve mental acuity. In laboratory studies, administration of *Shi Chang Pu* (Rhizoma Acori Tatarinowii) is associated with improvement of memory.[10] In clinical studies, use of *Ren Shen* (Radix et Rhizoma Ginseng) is associated with marked effectiveness in improving memory and learning ability.[11] In one study on mental retardation, 30 children with low IQ took a formula comprised of *Ren Shen* (Radix et Rhizoma Ginseng)

Adrenal +™

and three other herbs and showed mild to moderate improvement in classroom performance.[12] Furthermore, *Da Zao* (Fructus Jujubae) and *Ba Ji Tian* (Radix Morindae Officinalis) improve physical performance. In comparison with placebo substances, both of these herbs showed significant capacity to increase body weight, muscle strength, and physical endurance.[13,14]

Furthermore, many herbs in this formula function to improve sexual and reproductive functions. Use of *Gou Qi Zi* (Fructus Lycii) is highly effective to improve low sperm count and poor motility.[15] *Wu Wei Zi* (Fructus Schisandrae Chinensis) has a stimulating effect on reproductive organs, increasing the weight of the testicles in males and inducing ovulation in females.[16] In another study, patients with impotence were treated with *Ren Shen* (Radix et Rhizoma Ginseng) with marked success. Out of 27 patients, 15 regained normal function, 9 had moderate improvement, and 3 showed no effect. Lastly, in one clinical study, 24 patients with low sperm count, treated with a preparation of *Ren Shen* (Radix et Rhizoma Ginseng), demonstrated an increase in sperm count in 70% of the patients, and an increase in sperm motility in 67% of the patients.[17]

Since patients who are weak and deficient often have a suppressed immune system, herbs are included in this formula to strengthen the body and enhance the immune system. According to studies, use of a *Rou Gui* (Cortex Cinnamomi) preparation for five days increased white blood cell count by 150 to 200%, and use of *Ren Shen* (Radix et Rhizoma Ginseng) increased the total count of IgM.[18,19] Additionally, *Gou Qi Zi* (Fructus Lycii) and *Du Zhong* (Cortex Eucommiae) increase non-specific immunity, as they promote phagocytic activity by the macrophages, and increase the total number of T cells.[20,21,22]

In summary, ***Adrenal*** + contains herbs that have excellent effects of regulating the adrenal glands and balancing the endocrine system. It is a key formula to treat patients experiencing premature aging, declining mental and physical functioning, or who are simply "burned out" with fatigue, no energy, lack of interest, lack of drive and satisfaction.

COMPARATIVE ANALYSIS

Adrenal insufficiency or low adrenal functions are general terms used to describe individuals who have premature aging or are "burned out," with fatigue, no energy, lack of interest, lack of drive and satisfaction. These conditions affect overall health, and often lead to diminished mental and physical functions.

Adrenal insufficiency technically and specifically refers to conditions such as Addison's disease. Such serious conditions are often treated with various types of intravenous or oral adrenocortical hormones. Though effective, they often have a great number of side effects, including immune suppression, increased frequency of and decreased resistance to infections, decreased or blurred vision, filling or rounding out of the face, frequent urination, increased thirst, abdominal or stomach pain, acne, bloody or black (tarry) stools, headache, irregular heartbeat, menstrual problems, muscle cramps or pain, muscle weakness, nausea, pain throughout the body, sensitivity of eyes to light, stunting of growth (in children), swelling of feet or lower legs, tearing of eyes, thin and shiny skin, difficulty sleeping, unusual bruising, unusual increase in hair growth, unusual tiredness or weakness, rapid weight gain, and non-healing wounds. Therefore, unless the patients are diagnosed with the biomedical condition of adrenal cortical hypofunction, potent drugs such as adrenocortical hormones are not used.

Adrenal insufficiency is used here to describe the general signs and symptoms of qi, blood, yin, yang, and Kidney *jing* (essence) depletion accompanied by Spleen, Stomach, Heart and Kidney deficiencies. As described above, ***Adrenal*** + has excellent functions to regulate the endocrine system, stimulate the adrenal glands, and improve mental and physical functions. Though herbs do not treat specific and serious conditions such as Addison's disease, they do offer excellent preventative and treatment effects for individuals who are "burned out," with fatigue, no energy, lack of interest, lack of drive and satisfaction. Most importantly, herbal therapy has a significantly better safety profile in comparison with drug treatments.

References

1. *Forensic Science International*, 1994 June 28; 55-8.
2. *Dorland's Illustrated Medical Dictionary, 28th Edition*. W.B.Saunders Company, 1994.
3. *Zhong Yao Xue* (Chinese Herbology), 1998; 156:158.
4. *Guo Wai Yi Xue Zhong Yi Zhong Yao Fen Ce* (Monograph of Chinese Herbology from Foreign Medicine), 1990; 12(6):48.
5. *Zhong Yao Zhi* (Chinese Herbology Journal), 1993; 358.
6. *Zhong Hua Yi Xue Za Zhi* (Chinese Journal of Medicine), 1975; 10:718.
7. *Sheng Yao Xue Za Zhi* (Journal of Raw Herbology), 1982; 36(2):150.
8. *Zhong Yao Yao Li Yu Lin Chuang* (Pharmacology and Clinical Applications of Chinese Herbs), 1989; 5(1):36.
9. *Zhong Yi Xue* (Chinese Herbal Medicine), 1982; 13(6):24.
10. *Zhong Yi Xue* (Chinese Herbal Medicine), 1992; 23(8):417.
11. *Zhong Yao Ci Hai* (Encyclopedia of Chinese Herbs), 1994.
12. *Zhong Cheng Yao Yan Jiu* (Research of Chinese Patent Medicine), 1982; 6:22.
13. *Guo Wai Yi Xue Zhong Yi Zhong Yao Fen Ce* (Monograph of Chinese Herbology from Foreign Medicine), 1985; 7(4):48.
14. *Zhong Xi Yi Jie He Za Zhi* (Journal of Integrated Chinese and Western Medicine), 1991; 11(7):415.
15. *Xin Zhong Yi* (New Chinese Medicine), 1988; 2:20.
16. *Shang Hai Zhong Yi Yao Za Zhi* (Shanghai Journal of Chinese Medicine and Herbology), 1989; 2:43.
17. *Ji Lin Yi Xue* (Jilin Medicine), 1983; 5:54.
18. *Zhong Yao Yao Li Yu Ying Yong* (Pharmacology and Applications of Chinese Herbs), 1983;443.
19. *Zhong Yao Xue* (Chinese Herbology), 1998; 729:736.
20. *Zhong Yi Xue* (Chinese Herbal Medicine), 1983;19(7):25.
21. *Zhong Yi Xue* (Chinese Herbal Medicine), 1983;14(8):27.
22. *Zhong Xi Yi Jie He Za Zhi* (Journal of Integrated Chinese and Western Medicine), 1988; 8(12):736.

Arm Support™

CLINICAL APPLICATIONS

- **Shoulder**: periarthritis of the shoulder, frozen shoulder, capsulitis, rotator cuff tear, rotator cuff tendonitis, bursitis, inflammation and pain of the shoulder, subluxation or dislocation, AC (acromioclavicular) separation
- **Elbow**: lateral epicondylitis (tennis elbow), medial epicondylitis (golfer's elbow), olecranon bursitis, tendonitis
- **Wrist**: carpal tunnel syndrome, tendonitis, sprain and strain
- **General pain and discomfort of the arm:** tendonitis, bursitis, arthritis, numbness, decreased range of motion, and atrophy

WESTERN THERAPEUTIC ACTIONS

- Analgesic effect to alleviate pain
- Anti-inflammatory function to reduce swelling and inflammation
- Muscle-relaxant property to relieve spasms and cramps
- Protects and facilitates the recovery of cartilages from repetitive damages

CHINESE THERAPEUTIC ACTIONS

- Dispels cold and damp
- Activates qi and blood circulation
- Opens peripheral channels and collaterals
- Relieves pain

DOSAGE

Take 3 to 4 capsules, three times daily as needed to relieve pain. The dosage may be increased up to 6 to 8 capsules every four to six hours if necessary, especially in the early stages of injury when there is severe and excruciating pain. When the pain subsides, the dosage should be reduced to 3 or 4 capsules, three times daily. For maximum effectiveness, take the herbs on an empty stomach with two tall glasses of warm water. In chronic cases or for consolidation of treatment efficacy, the dosage can be reduced to 2 capsules twice daily on an empty stomach.

INGREDIENTS

Bai Shao (Radix Paeoniae Alba)
Dan Shen (Radix et Rhizoma Salviae Miltiorrhizae)
E Zhu (Rhizoma Curcumae)
Ge Gen (Radix Puerariae Lobatae)
Gui Zhi (Ramulus Cinnamomi)
Ji Xue Teng (Caulis Spatholobi)
Jiang Huang (Rhizoma Curcumae Longae)
Luo Shi Teng (Caulis Trachelospermi)
Sang Shen (Fructus Mori)
Sang Zhi (Ramulus Mori)
Shan Zha (Fructus Crataegi)
Wu Jia Pi (Cortex Acanthopanacis)
Xi Xian Cao (Herba Siegesbeckiae)
Yan Hu Suo (Rhizoma Corydalis)

BACKGROUND

Musculoskeletal and connective tissue disorders are major causes of pain and physical disability. Causes of these bone, muscle, and joint disorders vary greatly, depending on the exact disease. Simple causes include trauma and external injuries, such as pulled muscles, strained ligaments, dislocated joints, and bone fractures. Complicated causes include infection, autoimmune disorders, crystal-induced inflammation, and non-inflammatory tissue degeneration. Optimal treatment must address the symptoms (pain and inflammation) and the underlying causes. After the disorder is stabilized, physical therapy and exercise are important to maintain flexibility and strengthen surrounding muscles.

FORMULA EXPLANATION

Arm Support is designed specifically to treat disorders of the arms, including shoulders, elbows, and wrists. Disorders of the arms are usually characterized by swelling, inflammation, pain, decreased range of motion with movement difficulty, and in severe cases, atrophy of the muscles and soft tissues. To successfully treat this condition, herbs are used to activate qi and blood circulation, dispel qi and blood stagnation, open channels and collaterals, and relieve pain.

In this formula, *Dan Shen* (Radix et Rhizoma Salviae Miltiorrhizae), *E Zhu* (Rhizoma Curcumae), and *Yan Hu Suo* (Rhizoma Corydalis) activate qi and blood circulation, dispel qi and blood stagnation, and relieve pain. *Shan Zha* (Fructus Crataegi) enters the *xue* (blood) level, moves blood, and reduces inflammation and swelling. *Sang Shen* (Fructus Mori), *Ji Xue Teng* (Caulis Spatholobi) and *Wu Jia Pi* (Cortex Acanthopanacis) tonify yin and blood, and strengthen soft tissues (muscles, tendons, and ligaments). *Gui Zhi* (Ramulus Cinnamomi), *Sang Zhi* (Ramulus Mori), *Xi Xian Cao* (Herba Siegesbeckiae), *Jiang Huang* (Rhizoma Curcumae Longae) and *Luo Shi Teng* (Caulis Trachelospermi) open the channels and collaterals and relieve pain. *Bai Shao* (Radix Paeoniae Alba) relaxes muscles and *Ge Gen* (Radix Puerariae Lobatae) relieves pain in the upper *jiao*. Lastly, *Gui Zhi* (Ramulus Cinnamomi) and *Sang Zhi* (Ramulus Mori) act as channel-guiding herbs, leading the effect of the formula to the upper body and the extremities to directly treat the affected area.

In summary, ***Arm Support*** is an excellent formula to treat all types of musculoskeletal disorders affecting the arms, including shoulders, elbows, and wrists.

CAUTIONS & CONTRAINDICATIONS

- This formula has strong qi and blood activating herbs and is contraindicated during pregnancy and nursing.
- *Dan Shen* (Radix et Rhizoma Salviae Miltiorrhizae) may enhance the overall effectiveness of Coumadin (warfarin), an anticoagulant drug. Patients who take anticoagulant or antiplatelet medications should ***not*** take this herbal formula without supervision by a licensed healthcare practitioner.[1]

Arm Support™

- Shoulder pain that originates from a heart condition is known as referred pain. The left shoulder is mostly affected and there will be other accompanying symptoms of chest pain, palpitation, or shortness of breath. Referred pain due to liver or gallbladder problems may also reflect in the shoulder, but especially the right shoulder. These potential differential diagnoses should be investigated and ruled out during initial evaluations. This formula is ***not*** designed for referred pain caused by acute internal organ problems.

CLINICAL NOTES

- This formula is most effective when used as an adjunct formula to acupuncture treatment. Optimal results will show when acupuncture, electro-stimulation, and herbs are included in the treatment regimen.
- Avoid repetitive movements that may contribute to further injuries, such as in cases of inflammation of the joint, tennis elbow, or carpal tunnel syndrome.
- Cold packs may be used for acute injuries to reduce swelling and inflammation. In general, only during the first 24 to 48 hours of the injury where there is prominent inflammation should ice be used. On the other hand, hot packs should be used for chronic injuries to promote blood circulation and enhance healing in the affected area.
- *Tui-na* and acupuncture can add tremendous relief for the patient immediately. Herbs can then be administered to consolidate the effect.
- This formula is designed for pain in the arm starting from the shoulder down to the wrist. ***Neck & Shoulder (AC)*** and ***Neck & Shoulder (CR)*** are formulated for pain in the cervical and shoulder area.

Pulse Diagnosis by Dr. Jimmy Wei-Yen Chang:

- **Frozen shoulder:** scattered pulse, a pulse with no border, soft and weak, on the right *chi* position
- **Soft tissue damage of the shoulder:** turtle pulse, a convex-shaped pulse, on the right *chi* position
- **Cervical disk problem or spur with radiating pain down the arm:** thin, straight, tight pulse extending proximally to the right *chi* position

SUPPLEMENTARY FORMULAS

- For headache, combine with ***Corydalin (AC)***.
- With acute pain or numbness of neck and shoulders, combine with ***Neck & Shoulder (AC)***.
- With radiating or tingling pain of the arm caused by cervical spondylosis, combine with ***Neck & Shoulder (AC)***.
- With chronic pain of neck and shoulders, combine with ***Neck & Shoulder (CR)***.
- For acute disorders of the arm with severe pain, combine with ***Herbal ANG***.
- For chronic disorders of the arm with atrophy and tearing of soft tissues (muscles, ligaments, tendons), combine with ***Flex (MLT)***.
- For arthritis or *bi zheng* (painful obstruction syndrome) due to heat, add ***Flex (Heat)***.
- For arthritis or *bi zheng* (painful obstruction syndrome) due to cold, add ***Flex (CD)***.
- For tightness and spasms of the muscles, tendons and ligaments, add ***Flex (SC)***.
- For bone spurs and calcific tendonitis, add ***Flex (SPR)***.
- For nerve pain, add ***Flex (NP)***.
- For bone fractures or bruises, add ***Flex (TMX)***.
- For osteoarthritis, add ***Osteo 8***.
- With severe inflammation, add ***Astringent Complex***.

ACUPUNCTURE TREATMENT

Traditional Points:

- **Shoulder pain:** *Jianyu* (LI 15), *Jianliao* (TH 14), *Jianzhen* (SI 9) and any other *ah shi* points
- **Elbow pain:** *Quchi* (LI 11), *Xiaohai* (SI 8), *Tianjing* (TH 10), *Shousanli* (LI 10), *Hegu* (LI 4) and any other *ah shi* points
- **Wrist pain:** *Yangchi* (TH 4), *Yangxi* (LI 5), *Yanggu* (SI 5) and any other *ah shi* points

Classic Master Tung's Points:

- Needle contralateral to the pain. If the pain is present on both sides, needle bilaterally or the side with the more *ah shi* points.
- **General arm pain:** *Zuwujin* (T 77.25), *Shangjiuli* (T 88.26), *Zhongjiuli* (T 88.25), *Xiajiuli* (T 88.27), *Shangqu* (T 44.16)
- **Lateral upper arm pain:** *Tongtian* (T 88.03), *Tongshan* (T 88.02), *Tongguan* (T 88.01), *Simashang* (T 88.18), *Simazhong* (T 88.17), *Simaxia* (T 88.19), *Sihuashang* (T 77.08), *Sihuaxia* (T 77.11), *Sihuazhong* (T 77.09)
- **Medial upper arm pain:** *Shangquan* (T 88.22), *Zhongquan* (T 88.21), *Xiaquan* (T 88.20), *Simashang* (T 88.18), *Simazhong* (T 88.17), *Simaxia* (T 88.19), *Yizhong* (T 77.05), *Erzhong* (T 77.06), *Sanzhong* (T 77.07)
- **Lateral forearm pain:** *Waisanguan* (T 77.27), *Zuqianjin* (T 77.24), *Zuwujin* (T 77.25), *Sihuazhong* (T 77.09)
- **Medial forearm pain:** *Huoshan* (T 33.06), *Tianhuang* (T 77.17), *Dihuang* (T 77.19), *Renhuang* (T 77.21), *Waisanguan* (T 77.27)
- **Frozen shoulder:** *Linggu* (T 22.05), *Dabai* (T 22.04), *Fanhoujue* (T 22.12)*, *Tianhuangfu [Shenguan]* (T 77.18), *Minghuang* (T 88.12), *Tianhuang* (T 88.13), *Qihuang* (T 88.14), *Quchi* (LI 11), *Xiyan*, *Huantiao* (GB 30), *Renhuang* (T 77.21), *Sihuashang* (T 77.08), *Waisanguan* (T 77.27), *Sizhi* (T 77.20), *ah shi* points around the second metacarpal phalangeal joint, *Baguansan* (T 11.30)*, *Baguansi* (T 11.31)*. Bleed the affected area with cupping. Bleed before needling for best result.
- **Tennis elbow:** *Shuanglongyi* (T 77.29)*, *Shuanglonger* (T 77.30)*, *Shangchun* (T 77.15), *Xiachun* (T 77.16), *Sizhi* (T 77.20), *Waisanguan* (T 77.27)
- **Golfer's elbow:** *Shuanglongyi* (T 77.29)*, *Shuanglonger* (T 77.30)*, *Waisanguan* (T 77.27), *Tianhuang* (T 88.13), *Shangchun* (T 77.15), *Xiachun* (T 77.16), *Yinlingquan* (SP 9), *Quling* (T 33.16)

Arm Support™

- **Wrist pain:** *Sizhi* (T 77.20), *Waisanguan* (T 77.27), three points around the *ah shi* points on the front of the ankle
- **Finger numbness:** *Minghuang* (T 88.12), *Tianhuang* (T 88.13), *Qihuang* (T 88.14), *Sifeng, Xinling* (T 33.17)*, *Zhongjiuli* (T 88.25)
- **Index finger pain:** *Sihuazhong* (T 77.09)
- **Middle finger pain:** *Dan* (T 11.13), *Tongguan* (T 88.01), *Tongshan* (T 88.02)

Master Tung's Points by Dr. Chuan-Min Wang:

- **Shoulder pain:** Needle contralaterally *Jianzhong* (T 44.06), *Zhongjiuli* (T 88.25), *Qili* (T 88.51)*, *Tianhuangfu [shenguan]* (T 77.18), *Sizhi* (T 77.20).
- **Elbow pain:** Needle contralaterally *Quling* (T 33.16), *Cesanli* (T 77.22), *Cexiasanli* (T 77.23).
- **Wrist pain:** Needle contralaterally *Cesanli* (T 77.22), *Cexiasanli* (T 77.23), *Tung's Wantong* (T 66.16)*.

Balance Method by Dr. Richard Tan:

- **Shoulder pain:**
  - Needle *ah shi* points on the opposite wrist: *Yangxi* (LI 5), *Yangchi* (TH 4), *Wangu* (SI 4) to *Yanggu* (SI 5), *Jingqu* (LU 8) to *Taiyuan* (LU 9), *Shenmen* (HT 7), *Daling* (PC 7)
  - Needle all *ah shi* points on the opposite ankle: *Zhongfeng* (LR 4), *Shangqiu* (SP 5), *Taixi* (KI 3), *Kunlun* (BL 60), *Qiuxu* (GB 40), *Jiexi* (ST 41)
- **Elbow pain:**
  - Needle *ah shi* points on the opposite knee: *Yinlingquan* (SP 9) to *Xuehai* (SP 10), *Ququan* (LR 8), *Yingu* (KI 10), *Weiyang* (BL 39) to *Weizhong* (BL 40), *Xiyangguan* (GB 33) to *Yanglingquan* (GB 34), *Dubi* (ST 35) to *Zusanli* (ST 36)
- **Wrist pain:**
  - Needle on the opposite side of the pain: *Shangqiu* (SP 5), *Zhongfeng* (LR 4), *Rangu* (KI 2), *Taixi* (KI 3), *Yangxi* (LI 5), *Yanggu* (SI 5), *Yangchi* (TH 4)
  - Needle on the same side of the pain: *Kunlun* (BL 60), *Qiuxu* (GB 40), *Jiexi* (ST 41)

Auricular Medicine by Dr. Li-Chun Huang:

- **Tennis elbow (external humeral epicondylitis):** Tennis Elbow Point, Elbow. Bleed Helix 2.
- **Carpal tunnel syndrome:** Wrist (front and back of ear). Bleed Helix 1.
- **Trigger finger:** Wrist (front and back), Finger (front & back). Bleed Ear Apex.

NUTRITION

- Eat plenty of whole grains, seafood, dark green vegetables, and nuts. These foods are rich in vitamin B complex and magnesium, which are essential for nerve health and relaxation of tense muscles, respectively.
- Adequate intake of minerals, such as calcium and potassium, are essential for pain management. Deficiency of these minerals will lead to spasms, cramps, and tense muscles.

LIFESTYLE INSTRUCTIONS

- Patients should avoid exposing affected areas to cold or drafts. Wear adequate clothing to cover the arms, shoulders, and neck to avoid exposure to cold.
- Patients with disorders of the elbows or wrists should be encouraged to gently exercise the affected area as much as possible.
- Frozen shoulder is one condition in which the patient should be advised to exercise the joint frequently. Because the shoulder has the greatest range of motion of any joint in the body, stretching and strengthening exercises are essential in keeping the shoulders healthy. Prolonged immobilization causes adhesions, which makes treatment very difficult and painful. Patients should be advised to move their shoulder(s) in all directions (external and internal rotation, abduction and extension) to improve pain free range of motion. Heat packs are often helpful in this condition.
- Hot baths with *Ai Ye* (Folium Artemisiae Argyi) or Epsom salt help to relax tense muscles, invigorate blood flow, and draw toxins from tissues. Rest and relax in the bath for about 30 minutes. About 2 to 3 tablespoons of *Ai Ye* (Folium Artemisiae Argyi) powdered extract can be mixed in the hot water each time.
- Patients should note their sleeping position, as poor sleeping position may lead to shoulder and neck pain in the morning.

CASE STUDIES

- R.T., a 48-year-old male patient, presented with pain in his right elbow, which began four months prior. Over a short period of time it got progressively worse to the point where he couldn't use his hand and arm at all. Objective findings were tenderness to the touch around the lateral epicondyle and *Chize* (LU 5) area, and weakness of the hand. The Western diagnosis was lateral epicondylitis; the TCM diagnosis was qi and blood stagnation. The patient was prescribed ***Arm Support***. After two bottles, the patient reported that almost all of the arm function had returned and only felt minor pain when working out. Consideration was then made to switch to ***Flex (MLT)*** for future maintenance. Submitted by E.C., Lake Forest, California.
- B.L., a 25-year-old male patient, presented with pain in the left shoulder which had begun one month prior. On a scale from 1 to 10 (with 10 being the most painful), the patient rated his pain as a 7. He was involved in boxing and packaging activity and noted that he was unable to perform with his left arm at work. Objective findings were limited range of motion reduced to about 30% mobility, and positive signs for supraspinatus injury. The Western diagnosis was rotator cuff injury; the TCM diagnosis was local qi and blood stagnation. ***Arm Support*** was prescribed at three capsules three times daily. After nine days of taking the herbs, the patient reported he was experiencing no pain in his left shoulder and his range of motion had increased to 100% mobility. Submitted by E.C., Lake Forest, California.
- D.S., a 65-year-old female, presented with discomfort fluctuating between the areas of the neck, shoulder, and lower back. It was

Arm Support™

noted that this condition had been affected by sitting at her desk job throughout the day. Objective findings included limited range of motion, and a positive reaction when palpating her rotator muscles. The practitioner diagnosed this condition as damp-cold *bi zheng* (painful obstruction syndrome); her Western diagnosis was fibromyalgia. For treatment, ***Herbal ANG*** and ***Arm Support*** were prescribed. After taking the herbs, the patient has reduced the amount of her anti-inflammatory drugs and other prescription drugs by 70%. When lower back pain was also present, the patient was given ***Back Support (CR)***. Overall the patient reported her pain has decreased by 50% and continues taking the herbs for more relief. Submitted by J.L., San Diego, California.

- ☯ S.C., a 62-year-old female, presented with pain in the right wrist due to practicing yoga, along with high stress and insomnia. The patient had not yet seen a Western doctor for this condition, but her TCM diagnosis was qi and blood stagnation in the Lung, Pericardium, and Heart channels. For treatment, ***Arm Support*** and ***Calm ZZZ*** were prescribed at 3 to 4 capsules three times a day for each formula. After taking the herbs for one week, the wrist pain had completely resolved and did not return. The additional symptoms of stress and sleep had improved during the course of the following two weeks. The patient has stopped taking the ***Arm Support*** and continues taking only the ***Calm ZZZ***. Submitted by B.S., Niceville, Florida.
- ☯ A.M., a 40-year-old female, presented with pain in the wrist due to giving massages, in which any rest was helpful in pain relief. The TCM diagnosis was qi and blood stagnation in the Lung, Pericardium, and Heart channels along the wrist. For treatment, ***Arm Support*** was prescribed at 3 to 4 capsules three times per day. Pain had decreased with taking the herbs; however, the pain returned when she resumed massaging and discontinued taking the herbs. In response, the patient continued to take the herbs for pain management while massaging due to not being able to refrain from massaging. Submitted by B.S., Niceville, Florida.
- ☯ C.C., a 47-year-old female, who is overweight, presented with arthritis pain in her thumb. The practitioner diagnosed this condition as qi stagnation along the wrist and along the Lung, Pericardium, and Small Intestine channels, and also phlegm fluid retention. For treatment, ***Herbalite*** and ***Arm Support*** were prescribed. After taking the ***Arm Support***, the pain in her wrist had stopped and her thumb's range of motion had increased when combined with acupuncture treatment. Submitted by B.S., Niceville, Florida.

PHARMACOLOGICAL AND CLINICAL RESEARCH

Arm Support is designed specifically to treat disorders of the arms, including shoulders, elbows, and wrists. Clinical manifestations of such disorders include swelling, inflammation, and pain; decreased range of motion with movement difficulties, and in severe cases, atrophy of the muscles and soft tissues. Clinical applications of this formula include periarthritis of the shoulders, frozen shoulder, tennis elbow, carpal tunnel syndrome, and general conditions such as tendonitis, bursitis, and arthritis.

Yan Hu Suo (Rhizoma Corydalis) is one of the strongest and most potent herbs for treatment of pain. Its effects are well documented in both historical references and modern research studies. According to classical texts, *Yan Hu Suo* (Rhizoma Corydalis) has been used to treat chest and hypochondriac pain, epigastric and abdominal pain, hernial pain, menstrual pain, amenorrhea and pain of the extremities. According to laboratory studies, the extract of *Yan Hu Suo* (Rhizoma Corydalis) has been found to effectively treat both acute and chronic phases of inflammation. The mechanism of its anti-inflammatory effect is attributed to its inhibitory action on the release of histamine and pro-inflammatory mediators.[2,3] Furthermore, it has a strong analgesic effect. With adjustment in dosage, the potency of *Yan Hu Suo* (Rhizoma Corydalis) has been compared to that of morphine. In fact, the analgesic effect of *Yan Hu Suo* (Rhizoma Corydalis) is so strong and reliable that it has been used with satisfactory anesthetic effect in 98 out of 105 patients (93.4%) who underwent surgery.[4] The analgesic effect can be potentiated further with concurrent acupuncture therapy. In one research study, it is demonstrated that the analgesic effect is increased significantly with concurrent treatments using *Yan Hu Suo* (Rhizoma Corydalis) and electro-acupuncture, when compared to a control group, which received electro-acupuncture only.[5] Overall, it is well understood that *Yan Hu Suo* (Rhizoma Corydalis) has a marked effect to treat pain. Though the maximum analgesic effect of *Yan Hu Suo* (Rhizoma Corydalis) is not as strong as morphine, it has been determined that the herb is much safer, with significantly less side effects, less risk of tolerance, and no evidence of physical dependence even with long-term use.[6]

In addition to *Yan Hu Suo* (Rhizoma Corydalis), ***Arm Support*** contains many other herbs with analgesic and anti-inflammatory effects. *Bai Shao* (Radix Paeoniae Alba) has excellent anti-inflammatory effect to treat arthritis by modulating the production of pro-inflammatory mediators from macrophage-like synoviocytes.[7] *Ge Gen* (Radix Puerariae Lobatae) contains many isoflavonoid compounds which have significant analgesic and muscle relaxant activities.[8] *Xi Xian Cao* (Herba Siegesbeckiae) has both analgesic and anti-inflammatory effects. It reduces swelling and inflammation through significant inhibition of the productions of nitric oxide, prostaglandin E(2), tumor necrosis factor-alpha (TNF-α), inducible nitric oxide synthase and cyclo-oxygenase-2 proteins.[9,10] In comparison with drugs, the topical application of *Xi Xian Cao* (Herba Siegesbeckiae) shows comparable analgesic effect to piroxicam gel and methyl salicylate ointment.[11]

Beyond alleviating the pain and reducing inflammation, ***Arm Support*** utilizes herbs to facilitate the recovery from repetitive damages to the cartilages. *Xi Xian Cao* (Herba Siegesbeckiae) has

Arm Support™

a marked effect to protect the cartilages in collagenase-induced osteoarthritis. This herb contributes to a significant increase in proteoglycan, aggrecan, and type II collagen expression. In comparison with Celebrex (celecoxib), the drug showed anti-inflammatory effect but had no effect on cartilage protection.[12]

In terms of clinical applications, the herbs in ***Arm Support*** have shown marked effects to treat a wide variety of disorders. According to one clinical study, herbs such as *Sang Zhi* (Ramulus Mori), *Ji Xue Teng* (Caulis Spatholobi), *Gui Zhi* (Ramulus Cinnamomi) and others demonstrate marked success to treat 15 patients with tendonitis of the elbow.[13] According to another study, herbs such as *Gui Zhi* (Ramulus Cinnamomi) have been used with good success in a study of 30 patients with arthritis.[14] Lastly, one study reported that use of *Xi Xian Cao* (Herba Siegesbeckiae) and others resulted in a positive effect to treat generalized *bi zheng* (painful obstruction syndrome) characterized by wind-damp.[15]

Overall, ***Arm Support*** is considered as one of the best formulas to treat various musculoskeletal disorders of the arms. Clinical applications of this formula include, but are not limited to, periarthritis of the shoulder, frozen shoulder, tennis elbow, carpal tunnel syndrome, and general conditions such as tendonitis, bursitis, and arthritis.

COMPARATIVE ANALYSIS

Pain is a basic bodily sensation induced by a noxious stimulus that causes physical discomfort (as pricking, throbbing, or aching). Pain may be of acute or chronic state, and may be of nociceptive, neuropathic, or psychogenic origin. NSAIDs are generally prescribed for musculoskeletal disorders of the arm, including shoulders, elbows, and wrists. NSAIDs [such as Motrin (ibuprofen) and Voltaren (diclofenac)] treat pain of mild to moderate intensity, and are most effective to reduce inflammation and swelling. Though effective, these drugs cause serious side effects such as gastric ulcer, duodenal ulcer, gastrointestinal bleeding, tinnitus, blurred vision, dizziness, and headache. Furthermore, the newer NSAIDs, also known as COX-2 inhibitors [such as Celebrex (celecoxib)], are associated with significantly higher risk of cardiovascular events, including heart attack and stroke. Therefore, practitioners and patients must evaluate the potential benefit versus risk before prescribing and taking these drugs. In short, it is important to remember that while drugs offer reliable and potent symptomatic pain relief, they should only be used if and when needed. Frequent use and abuse leads to unnecessary side effects and complications.

Treatment of pain is a sophisticated balance of art and science. Proper treatment of pain requires a careful evaluation of the type of disharmony (excess or deficiency, cold or heat, exterior or interior), characteristics (qi and/or blood stagnations), and location (upper body, lower body, extremities, or internal organs). Furthermore, optimal treatment requires integrative use of herbs, acupuncture, and *tui-na* therapies. All these therapies work together to tonify underlying deficiencies, strengthen the body, and facilitate recovery from chronic pain. TCM pain management targets both the symptom and the cause of pain, and as such, often achieves immediate and long-term success. Furthermore, TCM pain management is often associated with few or no side effects.

In conclusion, for treatment of mild to severe pain due to various causes, TCM pain management offers similar treatment effects as Western medicine with significantly fewer side effects.

References

1. Chan K, Lo AC, Yeung JH, Woo KS. Journal of Pharmacy and Pharmacology 1995 May;47(5):402-406.
2. *Biol Pharm Bull*, Feb 1994; 17(2):262-5.
3. Oh YC, Choi JG, Lee YS, Brice OO, Lee SC, Kwak HS, Byun YH, Kang OH, Rho JR, Shin DW, Kwon DY. Tetrahydropalmatine inhibits pro-inflammatory mediators in lipopolysaccharide-stimulated THP-1 cells. Department of Oriental Pharmacy, College of Pharmacy, Wonkwang University Wonkwang Oriental Medicines Research Institute, Iksan, Republic of Korea. J Med Food. 2010 Oct;13(5):1125-32.
4. *He Bei Xin Yi Yao* (Hebei New Medicine and Herbology), 1973; 4:34.
5. *Chen Tzu Yen Chiu* (Acupuncture Research), 1994;19(1):55-8.
6. *Zhong Yao Yao Li Yu Ying Yong* (Pharmacology and Applications of Chinese Herbs), 1983; 447.
7. Zheng YQ, Wei W. Total glucosides of paeony suppresses adjuvant arthritis in rats and intervenes cytokine-signaling between different types of synoviocytes. Int Immunopharmacol. 2005 Sep;5(10):1560-73.
8. Yasuda T, Endo M, Kon-no T, Kato T, Mitsuzuka M, Ohsawa K. Antipyretic, analgesic and muscle relaxant activities of pueraria isoflavonoids and their metabolites from Pueraria lobata Ohwi-a traditional Chinese drug. Biol Pharm Bull. 2005 Jul;28(7):1224-8.
9. Li H, Kim JY, Hyeon J, Lee HJ, Ryu JH. In Vitro Antiinflammatory Activity of a New Sesquiterpene Lactone Isolated from Siegesbeckia glabrescens. College of Pharmacy, Sookmyung Women's University, 52 Hyochangwon-Gil, Yongsan-Gu, Seoul, 140-742, Korea. Phytother Res. 2011 Feb 10. doi: 10.1002/ptr.3420.
10. Park HJ, Kim IT, Won JH, Jeong SH, Park EY, Nam JH, Choi J, Lee KT. Anti-inflammatory activities of ent-16alphaH,17-hydroxy-kauran-19-oic acid isolated from the roots of Siegesbeckia pubescens are due to the inhibition of iNOS and COX-2 expression in RAW 264.7 macrophages via NF-kappaB inactivation. Division of Applied Plant Sciences, Sang-Ji University, Wonju, Republic of Korea. Eur J Pharmacol. 2007 Mar 8;558(1-3):185-93.
11. Wang J, Cai Y, Wu Y. Antiinflammatory and analgesic activity of topical administration of Siegesbeckia pubescens. Department of Pharmacognosy, School of Pharmacy, Huazhong University of Science and Technology, Wuhan-430030, People's Republic of China. Pak J Pharm Sci. 2008 Apr;21(2):89-91.
12. Huh JE, Baek YH, Lee JD, Choi DY, Park DS. Therapeutic effect of Siegesbeckia pubescens on cartilage protection in a rabbit collagenase-induced model of osteoarthritis. Oriental Medicine Research Center for Bone and Joint Disease, KyungHee University, Seoul, Korea. J Pharmacol Sci. 2008 Jul;107(3):317-28.
13. *Hei Long Jiang Zhong Yi Yao* (Heilongjiang Chinese Medicine and Herbology), 1991; (1):27.
14. *Shi Zhen Guo Yao Yan Jiu* (Research of Shizhen Herbs), 1991; 5(4):36.
15. *Shang Hai Zhong Yi Yao Za Zhi* (Shanghai Journal of Chinese Medicine and Herbology), 1982; 9:33.

Astringent Complex™

CLINICAL APPLICATIONS

- **Swelling and inflammation:** acute or chronic, may present with or without redness, heat sensation, and/or pain
- All excess heat (acute) and deficiency heat (chronic) conditions presenting with fire, heat, damp-heat, or toxic heat
- Any swelling, exudate, fluids, pus, abscess from water or damp accumulation as a result of inflammation

WESTERN THERAPEUTIC ACTIONS

- Anti-inflammatory effect to reduce swelling and inflammation
- Suppressant effect on the pro-inflammatory cytokines, such as tumor necrosis factor-α (TNF-α) and interleukin-1 beta (IL-1β)
- Antioxidant effect to fix free-radical-mediated peroxidation of membrane lipids and oxidative damage of DNA and proteins

CHINESE THERAPEUTIC ACTIONS

- Clears fire, damp-heat, toxic heat, and deficiency heat
- Reduces swelling and redness
- Cools the blood

DOSAGE

Take 2 to 4 capsules three times daily on an empty stomach with warm water. Dosage may be increased to 6 to 8 capsules three times daily, if necessary. The herbs should be taken with meals for those with sensitive digestive system.

INGREDIENTS

Bai Wei (Radix et Rhizoma Cynanchi Atrati)
Ce Bai Ye (Cacumen Platycladi)
He Zi (Fructus Chebulae)
Ma Chi Xian (Herba Portulacae)
Tian Hua Fen (Radix Trichosanthis)
Wu Bei Zi (Galla Chinensis)

BACKGROUND

Inflammation is a complex biological response that protects the host organism from harmful stimuli, such as infections or irritations. Inflammation may be classified as either acute or chronic. Acute inflammation is the initial response of the body to harmful stimuli. Chronic inflammation, on the other hand, is a disease.

Acute inflammation begins with increased blood perfusion to the affected areas, leading to localized redness and heat. In cases of infection, the blood vessels become more permeable and allow various immune cells to leave the blood vessels and enter the affected areas. Some cells, such as macrophages and neutrophils, engulf and digest micro-organisms. Other cells release hydrogen peroxide (and other oxidative chemicals) to kill micro-organisms so they can be consumed and cleaned up by phagocytes. In cases of irritation, such as an allergy, there is an inappropriate immune response that triggers inflammation. When exposed to an allergen (an irritation factor), pre-sensitized mast cells respond by degranulating and releasing histamines, which in turn propagate an excessive inflammatory response. This is characterized by blood vessel dilation, production of pro-inflammatory molecules, and recruitment of leukocytes.[1] In both cases, the initial inflammatory response is a healthy and natural response against infections and irritants, and without it, the body would not be able to properly defend and heal itself.

Once the threat of infection has passed or the presence of the irritant has been removed, the body returns to its normal condition. In cases of chronic inflammatory disease, the immune system develops an inappropriate response to something it has been exposed to in the past, and becomes confused. Instead of protecting the body, the immune system begins to attack the healthy cells. The immune system can attack various tissues and organs, and cause a wide range of problems to the external and internal parts of the body. Examples of chronic inflammatory diseases include arthritis, rheumatoid arthritis, tendonitis, bursitis, gouty arthritis, polymyalgia rheumatica, systemic lupus erythematosus, osteoarthritis, celiac disease, vasculitis, bronchiolitis, irritable bowel disease, atherosclerosis, psoriasis, myocarditis, nephritis, colitis, iritis, hay fever, and many more. In fact, Dr. Andrew Weil has stated that chronic inflammation may be "the root of all degenerative disease," and the "cause of the two greatest killers in America: cancer and heart disease."[2]

FORMULA EXPLANATION

Inflammation is a part of the body's natural defense system against injury and disease. It is mostly recognized with symptoms of pain, redness, and swelling that is the result of injury or infection. However, inflammation can also be chronic, present throughout the body, and contribute to various diseases. ***Astringent Complex*** is an herbal formula designed specifically with anti-inflammatory effects to address both acute and chronic inflammation, targeting the chief signs and symptoms of swelling, redness, heat, and pain.

Acute inflammation is characterized by marked changes in the vascular system, noticeably increased blood flow, increased heat, and increased exudation of plasma proteins and fluids into tissues, causing swelling. In traditional Chinese medicine (TCM), acute inflammation from trauma is diagnosed as qi and blood stagnation with heat and dampness. Qi and blood stagnation results in the pain associated with trauma or poor blood flow. Heat is the redness and/or hot sensation while dampness is the edema or excess accumulation of fluid. Dampness may also be the acute inflammatory exudates causing swelling, which can also manifest as pus, sores, abscesses, and boils.

Infection and inflammation have two different pathologies. While infections and inflammations are both treated with heat-clearing herbs in Chinese medicine, the biggest difference is that heat-clearing, detoxifying herbs are mostly used for their antibiotic or antiviral effects against infections, while heat-clearing herbs with sour taste and astringent/binding property are

Astringent Complex™

employed to address inflammation, as the symptoms involve heat sensation, redness, and swelling.

Tian Hua Fen (Radix Trichosanthis) reduces acute inflammation by clearing heat and purging fire. *Ce Bai Ye* (Cacumen Platycladi) cools blood and stops bleeding that may be associated with acute inflammation. *Wu Bei Zi* (Galla Chinensis) and *He Zi* (Fructus Chebulae) are two key herbs that address swelling, as they have sour taste and astringent/binding property which function to shrink the inflamed and expanded tissue. *Ma Chi Xian* (Herba Portulacae) and *Tian Hua Fen* (Radix Trichosanthis) treat acute inflammatory exudates by clearing heat, draining pus, and dispelling abscesses and sores through urination. Acute inflammation coupled with infection is diagnosed as toxic heat accumulation with damp accumulation. Two herbs in this formula have heat-clearing and detoxifying effects, namely *Ma Chi Xian* (Herba Portulacae) and *Bai Wei* (Radix et Rhizoma Cynanchi Atrati). For noticeably clear signs of bacterial or viral infection, ***Herbal ABX*** or ***Herbal AVR*** should be used concurrently.

Chronic systemic inflammation represents yin-deficient heat or heat in the blood. As the body's resources are taxed from chronic inflammation, yin becomes deficient, and deficiency heat or heat in the blood can manifest. *Bai Wei* (Radix et Rhizoma Cynanchi Atrati) and *Ma Chi Xian* (Herba Portulacae) cool blood and clear deficiency heat in the *ying* (nutritive) level; they are two key herbs to address chronic inflammation. *Tian Hua Fen* (Radix Trichosanthis) helps to generate body fluids, which is a yin substance that is essential for tissue growth. *Wu Bei Zi* (Galla Chinensis) and *He Zi* (Fructus Chebulae) are two important herbs that address swelling as both herbs have sour taste and astringent/binding property to prevent the drying of yin from heat in cases of chronic inflammation.

Together, these six herbs clear excess heat, deficiency heat, damp-heat, and toxic heat; they also cool the blood, and drain and reduce swelling.

CAUTIONS & CONTRAINDICATIONS

- This formula should be used with caution if infection is involved. Due to the sour and binding properties of the herbs in this formula, it may cause retention of pathogenic factors if used alone. Other formulas to address the cause of the infection should be added, such as ***Herbal ABX*** or ***Herbal AVR***.
- This formula is contraindicated during pregnancy and nursing.

CLINICAL NOTES

- ***Astringent Complex*** is designed by Dr. Jimmy Wei-Yen Chang to reduce signs and symptoms of acute and chronic inflammation.
- ***Astringent Complex*** is a formula that treats the symptoms of inflammation, and is most effective if taken with another formula to treat the cause of inflammation. If ***Astringent Complex*** is taken with another formula, keep the dosage ratio at 1:2 or 1:1, respectively.
- This herbal formula is rarely used alone. It is designed to be used as a supplementary formula for treatment of various inflammatory condition. In TCM, inflammation can be characterized by excess heat in the qi level, toxic heat, heat in the blood, deficiency heat, qi and blood stagnation, and/or damp accumulation. The cause of inflammation should be determined and a primary formula used to address the condition. Causes of inflammation range widely, including inflammation/infection of various organs, arthritis, rheumatoid arthritis, gout, bursitis, tendonitis, trauma, chronic inflammation, cough, Crohn's disease, inflammatory bowel diseases, hemorrhoids, pelvic inflammatory disease, hypertension, prostatitis, asthma, autoimmune diseases, sinus conditions, and vasculitis.

Pulse Diagnosis by Dr. Jimmy Wei-Yen Chang:

- **Acute inflammation:** big pulse, a thick, straight pulse that is expanding and forceful on all levels. The thicker and more forceful the pulse, the more acute or severe the inflammation in the body.
- **Chronic inflammation:** dispersing pulse, a soft, borderless pulse

SUPPLEMENTARY FORMULAS

- With bacterial infection, add ***Herbal ABX***.
- With viral infection, add ***Herbal AVR***.
- With severe heat conditions, add ***Gardenia Complex***.
- With dampness, add ***Pinellia Complex***.
- With severe pain, add ***Herbal ANG***.
- For inflammation due to trauma, add ***Flex (TMX)***.
- For fibrous tissue, add ***Circulation (SJ)***.
- For edema, add ***Herbal DRX***.
- With abscess, nodule, or hard swelling, add ***Resolve (AI)***.
- With acute arthritis, add ***Flex (Heat)***, ***Flex (CD)***, or ***Flex (GT)***.
- With pain in the arms, add ***Arm Support***.
- With acute neck and/or shoulder pain, add ***Neck & Shoulder (AC)***.
- With acute back pain, add ***Back Support (AC)***.
- With knee and/or ankle pain, add ***Knee & Ankle (AC)***.
- With asthma or respiratory conditions, add ***Respitrol (Heat)***, ***Respitrol (Deficient)***, or ***Respitrol (Cold)***.
- With sinusitis or rhinitis, add ***Magnolia Clear Sinus*** or ***Pueraria Clear Sinus***.
- For inflammatory condition of the gums or gastrointestinal track, add ***GI Care***.
- With inflammatory bowel disease, such as irritable bowel syndrome or Crohn's disease, add ***GI Harmony*** or ***GI Care (UC)***.
- For inflammatory conditions of the heart, add ***Circulation***.
- With lupus, add ***LPS Support***.
- With liver disease, add ***Liver DTX***.
- With kidney disease, add ***Kidney DTX***.
- With chemical poisoning or hypersensitivity, add ***Herbal DTX***.
- With genito-urinary inflammation or pelvic inflammatory diseases, add ***V-Support***.

Astringent Complex™

ACUPUNCTURE TREATMENT

Traditional Points:

- Please refer to other formulas for acupuncture points depending on each specific condition.

Master Tung's Points by Dr. Chuan-Min Wang:

- **Inflammation:** Bleed Ear Apex or *Wuling* (T DT.04) area. Needle *Muliu* (T 66.06), *Mudou* (T 66.07).

Balance Method by Dr. Richard Tan:

- Left side: *Houxi* (SI 3), *Xiaohai* (SI 8), *Taichong* (LR 3), *Ququan* (LR 8)
- Right side: *Shaohai* (HT 3), *Shenmen* (HT 7), *Yanglingquan* (GB 34), *Zulinqi* (GB 41)
- Left and right sides can be alternated from treatment to treatment.
- The above acupuncture prescription is for general inflammation. Please refer to other formulas for acupuncture points depending on each specific condition.

Ear Acupuncture:

- Please refer to other formulas for acupuncture points depending on each specific condition.

Auricular Medicine by Dr. Li-Chun Huang:

- **General anti-inflammatory points:** Allergic Area, Endocrine, Adrenal Gland, Spleen, corresponding points (to the area affected). Bleed Ear Apex.
- Please refer to other formulas for acupuncture points depending on each specific condition.

NUTRITION

- Increase the consumption of the following foods: fresh fruits and vegetables, mushrooms, whole grains such as brown rice and bulgur wheat. Choose organic produce if possible.
- Eat whole foods, and minimize the consumption of processed foods and fast foods. Avoid processed meats, such as lunch meats, hot dogs and sausages, as they contain nitrites, which are associated with inflammation and chronic diseases.
- Drink green or oolong tea, and avoid coffee whenever possible.
- Increase intake of berries, especially blueberries and strawberries. They are an excellent source for anti-inflammatory phytochemicals and antioxidants.
- Increase intake of nourishing, cooling foods/roots such as Mexican yams, yams, radishes, potatoes, carrots, melons, cucumbers, beets, turnips, malanga, celeriac, taro, and rutabaga.
- Avoid spicy, deep-fried, or greasy foods. Avoid sugar as it contributes to production of damp and phlegm. Also avoid cold or raw foods that may compromise the Spleen and as a result produce more dampness.
- Avoid alcohol, coffee, energy drinks or other stimulants.
- Avoid spicy, pungent, aromatic vegetables such as pepper, garlic, onions, basil, rosemary, cumin, fennel, anise, leeks, chives, scallions, thyme, saffron, wormwood, mustard, chili pepper, and wasabi.

LIFESTYLE INSTRUCTIONS

- Avoid drinking, smoking, staying up late, and stress, which all contribute to heat.

CASE STUDIES

- A 59-year-old male was stung by a sea urchin while diving in Hawaii four months prior to coming in for treatment. The spines of the sea urchin went into his hand. The black markings of the sting are all gone, but he has difficulty moving his fingers with limited movement of his fingers and hand. His tongue is dusky and swollen with a sticky coat. His pulses are wiry and slippery. After taking ***Flex (NP)*** and ***Astringent Complex*** for 15 days, in conjunction with acupuncture, the patient is completely healed. Submitted by K.M., Albany, California.
- A 50-year-old female presented with persistent proctitis, which she had suffered from for two years. Her right and left pulse were superficial and wiry, and her left *cun* position was convex and forceful at both the middle and superficial positions. She was prescribed ***GI Care*** and ***Astringent Complex***, 50:50. After three 100 gram bottles of the mixed formula, her symptoms disappeared. It has been four months since she finished the herbs and her symptoms never returned, and her medical tests came back negative as well. Submitted by S.B., Berkeley, California.

PHARMACOLOGICAL AND CLINICAL RESEARCH

To effectively and properly treat chronic inflammatory disease, ***Astringent Complex*** uses many anti-inflammatory herbs to control unnecessary and unchecked inflammatory reactions. Traditionally, these anti-inflammatory herbs are described as "heat-clearing" or "astringent" herbs. Today, their pharmacological effects have been discovered through laboratory reports and their indications are validated through clinical studies.

Ce Bai Ye (Cacumen Platycladi) exerts a potent anti-inflammatory effect by suppressing the expressions of tumor necrosis factor (TNF)-α, interleukin (IL)-6, and cyclo-oxygenase (COX)-2.[3] *Ma Chi Xian* (Herba Portulacae) has comparable analgesic and anti-inflammatory effects to diclofenac sodium (Voltaren), one of the most frequently used non-steroidal-anti-inflammatory drugs in the world.[4] According to one study, topical application of an herbal paste made from equal portions of *Ma Chi Xian* (Herba Portulacae) and *Mang Xiao* (Natrii Sulfas) showed 93% rate of effectiveness among 128 patients to reduce swelling and inflammation from external or trauma injuries within 3 to 7 days.[5] Lastly, many herbs in this formula play significant roles in treatment of chronic inflammatory diseases. *Ce Bai Ye* (Cacumen Platycladi) and *Ma Chi Xian* (Herba Portulacae) have been used to treat various inflammatory conditions associated with infection.[6]

He Zi (Fructus Chebulae) has both antihistamine and anti-anaphylactic effects. In a dose-dependent manner, administration

Astringent Complex ™

of water extract of *He Zi* (Fructus Chebulae) significantly inhibited histamine release from mast cells, and effectively prevented and/or treated systemic and local anaphylaxis.[7] *He Zi* (Fructus Chebulae) also has anti-inflammatory effects and disease-modifying activity for the treatment of rheumatoid arthritis. According to one study in subjects with artificiallyinduced arthritis, it significantly inhibited joint swelling by modulating the pro-inflammatory cytokine expression in the synovium, reducing serum levels of TNF-α, TNF-R1, IL-6 and IL-1β.[8] According to another study, chebulagic acid isolated from the immature seeds of *He Zi* (Fructus Chebulae) significantly suppressed the onset and progression of collagen-induced arthritis.[9] Chebulagic acid also showed potent activity to inhibit both cyclo-oxygenase and 5-lipoxygenase, the key enzymes involved in inflammation and carcinogenesis.[10]

Finally, *Tian Hua Fen* (Radix Trichosanthis) has a marked anti-inflammatory effect and has been used to treat various chronic inflammatory conditions.[11,12] *Tian Hua Fen* (Radix Trichosanthis) also has immunoregulatory functions. Trichosanthin, an active component extracted from this herb, has illustrated a beneficial immunoregulatory effect in subjects who received skin transplantation by significantly delaying allograft rejection and minimizing other inflammatory conditions. The mechanism of this action is attributed to the reduced levels of interleukin (IL)-2 and interferon-gamma, and increased levels of IL-4 and IL-10 in splenic T cells.[13]

In summary, ***Astringent Complex*** contains many herbs with excellent binding and retaining effects to reduce swelling and inflammation and treat various types of inflammatory disorders.

COMPARATIVE ANALYSIS

Western medicine is very effective in treating acute inflammatory conditions. Non-steroidal anti-inflammatory drugs (NSAIDs) effectively relieve pain and reduce swelling to treat various joint diseases. These drugs, however, are not safe or effective for treating chronic inflammatory disease. NSAIDs, such as Motrin (ibuprofen), Naprosyn (naproxen) and Voltaren (diclofenac), cause serious side effects such as gastric ulcer, duodenal ulcer, gastrointestinal bleeding, tinnitus, blurred vision, dizziness, and headache. Furthermore, the newer NSAIDs, also known as Cox-2 inhibitors [such as Celebrex (celecoxib)], are associated with significantly higher risk of cardiovascular events, including heart attack and stroke. In fact, these side effects are so serious that two Cox-2 inhibitors have already been withdrawn from the market [Vioxx (rofecoxib) and Bextra (valdecoxib)].

Severe or systemic inflammation is often treated with corticosteroids, such as prednisone, to quickly and effectively suppress inflammation. Though effective for short-term use, long-term use of corticosteroids causes numerous side effects: increased appetite and weight gain, deposits of fatty tissues, water and salt retention leading to swelling and edema, high blood pressure, diabetes, black and blue marks, slow healing of wounds, osteoporosis, cataracts, acne, muscle weakness, thinning of the skin, increased susceptibility to infection, stomach ulcers, increased sweating, mood swings, psychological problems such as depression, and adrenal suppression and crisis. Therefore, corticosteroids should be used cautiously and only for acute and severe inflammatory disorders.

Chinese herbs work well to treat both acute and chronic inflammatory conditions. In cases of acute inflammation, it is important to identify the cause and characteristics of the inflammation. For example, treatment for acute infection and inflammation of the lungs is very different from the treatment for acute injury and inflammation of the knees. When the acute inflammation subsides, and is transformed into a chronic inflammatory disease, careful observation must be made to differentiate constitutional imbalance. By using herbs that correct the underlying imbalance, the deterioration of chronic inflammatory disease will be reversed and healing can finally begin.

Drugs are more powerful and should be used in cases of serious and acute inflammatory disease. However, they should only be used when absolutely necessary as they cause significant side effects. On the other hand, herbs are more effective to gradually alter the underlying constitution of the body to positively affect the long-term course of chronic inflammatory disease. Herbs are also much gentler, and will not cause significant side effects even with long-term use.

References

1. Cotran; Kumar, Collins (1998). *Robbins Pathologic Basis of Disease.* Philadelphia: W.B Saunders Company.
2. Andrew Weil — www.drweil.com.
3. Choi Y, Moon A, Kim YC. A pinusolide derivative, 15-methoxypinusolidic acid from Biota orientalis inhibits inducible nitric oxide synthase in microglial cells: implication for a potential anti-inflammatory effect. College of Pharmacy, Seoul National University, 599 Gwanangno, Gwanak-gu, Seoul 151-742, Republic of Korea. Int Immunopharmacol. 2008 Apr;8(4):548-55.
4. Chan K, Islam MW, Kamil M, Radhakrishnan R, Zakaria MN, Habibullah M, Attas A. The analgesic and anti-inflammatory effects of Portulaca oleracea L. subsp. Sativa (Haw.) Celak. Department of Biomedical Sciences, Zayed Complex for Herbal Research and Traditional Medicine, Ministry of Health, PO Box 29300, Abu Dhabi, United Arab Emirates. J Ethnopharmacol. 2000 Dec;73(3):445-51.
5. *Shan Dong Zhong Yi Za Zhi* (Shandong Journal of Chinese Medicine), 1996; 15(6):282.
6. Chen J, Chen T. *Chinese Medical Herbology and Pharmacology.* City of Industry, CA: Art of Medicine Press, 2004.
7. Shin TY, Jeong HJ, Kim DK, Kim SH, Lee JK, Kim DK, Chae BS, Kim JH, Kang HW, Lee CM, Lee KC, Park ST, Lee EJ, Lim JP, Kim HM, Lee YM. Inhibitory action of water soluble fraction of Terminalia chebula on systemic and local anaphylaxis. College of Pharmacy, Woosuk University, Chonju, 565-701, Chonbuk, South Korea. J Ethnopharmacol. 2001 Feb;74(2):133-40.
8. Nair V, Singh S, Gupta YK. Antiarthritic and disease modifying activity of Terminalia chebula Retz. in experimental models. Department of Pharmacology, All India Institute of Medical Sciences, New Delhi, India. J Pharm Pharmacol. 2010 Dec;62(12):1801-6. doi: 10.1111/j.2042-7158.2010.01193.x.
9. Lee S.I., Hyun P.M., Kim S.H., Kim K.S., Lee S.K., Kim B.S., Maeng P.J. & Lim J.S. Suppression of the onset and progression of collagen-induced arthritis by

FORMULAS

Astringent Complex™

chebulagic acid screened from a natural product library. *Arthritis Rheum.* 2005, 52(1): 345-353.

10. Reddy DB, Reddy TC, Jyotsna G, Sharan S, Priya N, Lakshmipathi V, Reddanna P. Chebulagic acid, a COX-LOX dual inhibitor isolated from the fruits of Terminalia chebula Retz., induces apoptosis in COLO-205 cell line. Department of Animal Sciences, School of Life Sciences, University of Hyderabad, Hyderabad 500046, India. J Ethnopharmacol. 2009 Jul 30;124(3):506-12.
11. Akihisa T, Yasukawa K, Kimura Y, Takido M, Kokke WC, Tamura T. Five D:C-friedo-oleanane triterpenes from the seeds of Trichosanthes kirilowii Maxim. and their anti-inflammatory effects. College of Science and Technology, Nihon University, Tokyo, Japan. Chem Pharm Bull (Tokyo). 1994 May;42(5):1101-5.
12. Chen J, Chen T. *Chinese Medical Herbology and Pharmacology.* City of Industry, CA: Art of Medicine Press, 2004.
13. Gong Q, Deng D, Ding J, Wang C, Bian Z, Ye Z, Xu J. Trichosanthin, an extract of Trichosanthes kirilowii, effectively prevents acute rejection of major histocompatibility complex-mismatched mouse skin allograft. Transplant Proc. 2008 Dec;40(10):3714-8.

Back Support (AC)™

CLINICAL APPLICATIONS

- **Acute low back pain (lumbago)**
- **Back pain** from sports or traumatic injuries, sprains and strains, subluxation
- **Back pain** due to strenuous exercise or repetitive movements (e.g., grocery checkers/packers, warehouse and assembly line workers, and others in similarly demanding occupations)
- **Back pain** with inflammation, swelling, or redness
- **Chronic back pain with acute exacerbation or re-injury**

WESTERN THERAPEUTIC ACTIONS

- Analgesic influence to relieve pain
- Anti-inflammatory action to reduce pain and inflammation
- Muscle-relaxant effect to alleviate muscle spasms and cramps

CHINESE THERAPEUTIC ACTIONS

- Relieves pain
- Opens channels
- Disperses qi and blood stagnation

DOSAGE

Take 3 to 4 capsules, three times daily as needed to relieve pain. The dosage may be increased up to 6 to 8 capsules every four to six hours if necessary, especially in the early stages of injury when there is severe and excruciating pain. When the pain subsides, the dosage can then be decreased to 3 or 4 capsules three times daily. For maximum effectiveness, take the herbs on an empty stomach with two tall glasses of warm water.

INGREDIENTS

Bai Shao (Radix Paeoniae Alba)
Chuan Niu Xi (Radix Cyathulae)
Du Zhong (Cortex Eucommiae)
Ge Gen (Radix Puerariae Lobatae)
Gui Zhi (Ramulus Cinnamomi)
Huang Jin Gui (Caulis Vanieriae)
Ji Xue Teng (Caulis Spatholobi)
Liu Zhi Huang (Herba Solidaginis)
Mo Gu Xiao (Caulis Hyptis Capitatae)
Mu Gua (Fructus Chaenomelis)
Wei Ling Xian (Radix et Rhizoma Clematidis)
Yan Hu Suo (Rhizoma Corydalis)
Zhi Gan Cao (Radix et Rhizoma Glycyrrhizae Praeparata cum Melle)

BACKGROUND

Musculoskeletal and connective tissue injuries lead to over 10 million clinic visits per year in the United States.[1] Causes of these injuries may be external (sports injuries, car accidents, trauma), internal (chronic wear and tear of muscles, ligaments and tendons; bones weakened by osteoporosis), or both. Acute injuries are characterized by severe pain, swelling and inflammation, and in some cases, internal bleeding. Treatment of acute injuries should focus on relieving pain, reducing swelling and inflammation, and stopping bleeding. Chronic injuries are characterized by dull pain, stiffness and numbness, and decreased muscle mass and strength. Treatment of chronic injuries includes relief of pain, and restoration of physical and physiological functions.

FORMULA EXPLANATION

Back Support (AC) is formulated specifically to relieve acute low back pain caused by sports or traumatic injuries, strenuous exercise, repetitive movements, or accidents. ***Back Support (AC)*** contains herbs that regulate qi and blood circulation, remove qi and blood stagnation, and relieve pain.

Yan Hu Suo (Rhizoma Corydalis) activates qi and blood circulation, and is one of the strongest analgesic herbs to relieve pain. *Mo Gu Xiao* (Caulis Hyptis Capitatae), *Liu Zhi Huang* (Herba Solidaginis) and *Huang Jin Gui* (Caulis Vanieriae) are indigenous Taiwanese herbs that have anti-inflammatory and analgesic properties and are often used to treat the acute pain associated with traumatic injuries or sprains and strains. *Gui Zhi* (Ramulus Cinnamomi) warms the channels, facilitates the flow of qi, and relieves painful obstruction. *Ge Gen* (Radix Puerariae Lobatae) alleviates muscle tightness. *Bai Shao* (Radix Paeoniae Alba) and *Zhi Gan Cao* (Radix et Rhizoma Glycyrrhizae Praeparata cum Melle) nourish the muscles and relieve stiffness and pain of the back. *Mu Gua* (Fructus Chaenomelis), *Wei Ling Xian* (Radix et Rhizoma Clematidis) and *Ji Xue Teng* (Caulis Spatholobi) increase qi and blood circulation to relax the muscles and the tendons. *Chuan Niu Xi* (Radix Cyathulae) invigorates the blood. *Du Zhong* (Cortex Eucommiae) is not only a channel-guiding herb to direct the actions of the formula to the lumbar region, it also has the effect of tonifying and strengthening the back.

Together, these herbs effectively treat acute pain and inflammation affecting the lower back.

CAUTIONS & CONTRAINDICATIONS

- Because of the blood-invigorating nature of this formula, ***Back Support (AC)*** is not recommended during pregnancy and nursing.
- ***Back Support (AC)*** is not designed for long-term use. If the pain lasts for a long period of time and becomes chronic in nature, ***Back Support (CR)*** should be used.
- If the patient presents with fever and a one-sided back pain, consider a possible kidney infection and do not use this herbal formula. Patients with acute nephritis should be referred to their medical doctor immediately.
- Patients who have pain radiating to the extremities accompanied by a sudden loss of bladder or bowel control may have a pinched nerve or spinal injury, and must be referred out to emergency care. This condition, known as cauda equina syndrome, can lead to permanent disability and must be evaluated and treated immediately.

Back Support (AC)™

CLINICAL NOTES

- Take ***Back Support (AC)*** with 2 tall glasses of warm water, as back pain can be related to dehydration.
- Many patients may seek treatment for a chronic back condition that has recently been exacerbated. In such cases, ***Back Support (AC)*** should be prescribed for one or two weeks to relieve the acute pain. After the pain subsides, switch to ***Back Support (CR)*** to consolidate the effect.
- For musculoskeletal injuries to the back, ***Back Support (AC)*** can be given to the patient prior to each acupuncture treatment. The muscle-relaxant influence from the herbs will take effect within about 30 minutes. By relaxing the muscles and invigorating qi and blood circulation with the herbs, there will be less stagnation in the channels, and the acupuncture and *tui-na* treatments will be more effective.
- There are several causes for back pain. This formula is designed to treat back pain due to musculoskeletal injuries. For back pain resulting from other causes, please refer to the Supplementary Formula section for appropriate formulas.

Pulse Diagnosis by Dr. Jimmy Wei-Yen Chang:

- **Soft tissue damage:** turtle pulse, a convex-shaped pulse on the left *chi*; the more forceful the pulse, the more recent the injury, with more inflammation and pain
- **Bone spurs or disk problems:** guitar string / steel wire pulse on the left *chi*
- **Low back pain due to blood stasis from old injuries:** dispersing pulse, a pulse in which its border is difficult to perceive, soft, weak, and deep, on the left *chi*

SUPPLEMENTARY FORMULAS

- For acute back pain due to herniated disk, combine with ***Back Support (HD)***.
- To enhance the analgesic action, use with ***Herbal ANG***.
- For acute back pain due to traumatic injuries, sprain and strain with or without bruises and bone fractures, use with ***Flex (TMX)***.
- For pain due to bone spurs, add ***Flex (SPR)***.
- For back pain associated with osteoporosis, use with ***Osteo 8***.
- For back pain with severe cramps, take with ***Flex (SC)***.
- For arthritic pain that worsens during cold and rainy weather, use with ***Flex (CD)***.
- For arthritis with redness, swelling and inflammation, use with ***Flex (Heat)***.
- For back pain due to menstrual discomfort, use ***Mense-Ease***.
- For back pain aggravated by obesity, use ***Herbalite*** for weight loss.
- For back pain caused by kidney stones, use ***Dissolve (KS)*** instead.
- For back pain or soreness resulting from chronic nephritis, use ***Kidney DTX***.
- For chronic, stubborn back pain with blood stagnation, add ***Circulation (SJ)***.
- With severe inflammation, combine with ***Astringent Complex***.

ACUPUNCTURE TREATMENT

Traditional Points:

- *Yaotongxue*, *Huantiao* (GB 30), *Yaoyan* (Extra 9), *Shenshu* (BL 23), *Weizhong* (BL 40)

Classic Mater Tung's Points:

- Needle contralateral to the pain. If the pain is in the center, needle bilaterally or the side with the more *ah shi* points. If the pain is bilateral, needle bilaterally.
- *Linggu* (T 22.05), *Zhongbai* (T 22.06), *Xiabai* (T 22.07), *Wanshunyi* (T 22.08), *Wanshuner* (T 22.09), *Chongzi* (T 22.01), *Chongxian* (T 22.02), *Erjiaoming* (T 11.12), *Tianhuangfu [Shenguan]* (T 77.18), *Zhongjiuli* (T 88.25), *Zhengjin* (T 77.01), *Zhengzong* (T 77.02), *Weizhong* (BL 40), *Majinshui* (T 1010.13), *Makuaishui* (T 1010.14), *Shuiqu* (T 66.09)
- Bleed *Weizhong* (BL 40) or dark veins nearby. Bleed painful area on the back with cupping. Bleed before needling for best result.

Master Tung's Points by Dr. Chuan-Min Wang:

- For acute pain, bleed first then needle.
- For chronic pain, needle first then bleed.
- **Mid back pain:** Needle contralaterally *Chongzi* (T 22.01), *Chongxian* (T 22.02), *Zhengjin* (T 77.01), *Zhengzong* (T 77.02). Bleed ipsilaterally popliteal fossa or local tender spot.
- **Low back pain:** Bleed ipsilaterally popliteal fossa or local tender spot.
  - L1-L3 pain: Needle contralaterally *Zhongbai* (T 22.06), *Xiabai* (T 22.07).
  - L4-L5 pain: Needle contralaterally *Dabai* (T 22.04), *Linggu* (T 22.05).
  - S1-S2 pain: Needle contralaterally *Wanshunyi* (T 22.08), *Wanshuner* (T 22.09).
- **Hip pain:** Needle contralaterally *Jianzhong* (T 44.06), *Xiaqu* (T 44.15), *Shangqu* (T 44.16), *Yunbai* (T 44.11), *Libai* (T 44.12). Bleed ipsilaterally popliteal fossa or local tender spot.
- **Sciatic pain:** Needle contralaterally *Dabai* (T 22.04), *Linggu* (T 22.05), *Wanshunyi* (T 22.08). Needle ipsilaterally *Weizhong* (BL 40), *Kunlun* (BL 60), *Zuqianjin* (T 77.24), *Zuwujin* (T 77.25).

Balance Method by Dr. Richard Tan:

- Needle the following points on the side opposite the pain: *Hegu* (LI 4), *Houxi* (SI 3), *Wangu* (SI 4), *Linggu* (T 22.05), *Dabai* (T 22.04), *Zhongbai* (T 22.06), *Dazhong* (KI 4) or *ah shi* points nearby, *Fuliu* (KI 7), *Ququan* (LR 8) or *ah shi* points nearby
- Needle the following points on the same side as the pain: All *ah shi* points nearby *Chize* (LU 5), *Kongzui* (LU 6), *Shaohai* (HT 3) to *Lingdao* (HT 4), *Shugu* (BL 65)
- Needle *ah shi* points around *Fengfu* (GV 16) to *Houding* (GV 19).

Ear Acupuncture:

- **Sciatic pain:** Lower Back, Hip, Sciatic, and Pituitary Gland. Embed needles or use ear seeds in both ears, and instruct the

Back Support (AC)™

patient to massage the points three to four times daily for two to three minutes each time.

- **Tailbone injury:** Coccyx, Adrenal Gland, Pituitary Gland

Auricular Medicine by Dr. Li-Chun Huang:

- Occiput, Lesser Occiput Nerve, Large Auricular Nerve, *Shenmen*. Corresponding area of pain in the lumbar, sacral, sciatic area in the front and back of the ear. Bleed Ear Apex.

NUTRITION

- Eat a diet with a wide variety of raw vegetables and fruits, and whole grain cereals to ensure a complete supply of nutrients for the bones, nerves, and muscles.
- Adequate intake of calcium is essential for the repair and rebuilding of bones, tendons, cartilage, and connective tissues.
- Fresh pineapples are recommended as they contain bromelain, an enzyme that is excellent in reducing inflammation. If the consumption of fresh pineapples causes stomach upset, eat it after meals.
- To relieve cramps and spasms, eat plenty of fruits and vegetables, especially those high in potassium, such as bananas and oranges. Also drink an adequate amount of warm water.
- Adequate intake of minerals, such as calcium and potassium, is essential for pain management. Deficiency of these minerals will lead to spasms, cramps, and tense muscles.
- Avoid red meat and seafood in the diet as they contain high levels of uric acid, which puts added strain on the kidneys.
- Avoid cold beverages, ice cream, caffeine, sugar, tomatoes, milk, and dairy products.
- The following is a folk remedy to treat acute back pain from sprain and strain. Crack open 2 crabs (ocean) with a wooden stick (do not use a knife or any metal instruments) and put them into a clay pot with enough vodka or whiskey to cover both crabs. Place the clay pot into another larger pot with water, and steam it for one hour. Serve the crab meat along with the liquor soup.

LIFESTYLE INSTRUCTIONS

- Patients are advised to use their legs (instead of bending from the waist or back) when lifting heavy objects.
- Patients are encouraged to wear clothing that covers their backs completely and to tuck their shirts into their pants or skirts to avoid *any* wind exposure to their backs, which will further aggravate the condition.
- Stretching and strengthening exercises for the back muscles are essential for long-term recovery. Strengthening the abdominal muscles is also beneficial to reduce strain on the lower back.
- Mild exercise such as swimming, yoga, or *tai chi chuan* [*tai ji quan*] on a regular basis is recommended.
- For those who are overweight, weight loss is strongly recommended to decrease pressure on the joints and relieve pain.
- Proper balance of work and rest is very important. While sitting, make sure the back is straight and the elbows and knees are bent at a 90° angle. Take a break at least once every hour to alleviate pressure on the vertebrae and disks.
- Finally, adequate rest is essential to recovery. It is wise to review the sleeping postures to ensure that the back is being appropriately supported and relaxed.
- Hot baths with *Ai Ye* (Folium Artemisiae Argyi) or Epsom salts help to relax tense muscles, invigorate blood flow and draw toxins from tissues. Rest and relax in the bath for about 15 to 30 minutes, but avoid becoming over-tired from the heat and soaking. Mix about 2 to 3 tablespoons of *Ai Ye* (Folium Artemisiae Argyi) extract powder in the hot water each time.
- Firm beds are recommended over soft ones for patients with back pain.

CASE STUDIES

- N.I., a 34-year-old patient, presented with muscle spasms and tightness in the lower back, creating difficulty to move or bend over on a daily basis. Upon assessment, there was limited range of motion while bending forward as well as pain upon palpation of erector spinalis and quadratus lumborum muscles. The TCM diagnosis was Kidney yin deficiency and the patient was prescribed ***Back Support (AC)***. Within one day the pain had lessened and the range of motion had increased rapidly. After three days of taking the herbal formula the patient was back to normal. Submitted by A.I., Hilo, Hawaii.
- L.S., a 27-year-old male electrician, complained of bad back spasms, which then lead to being unable to stand up straight for two days. This occurred after a recent job he had been bending over for while working and was in extreme pain. This condition was diagnosed as Liver yin deficiency. The patient was treated with ***Back Support (AC)*** and ***Herbal ANG***, four capsules three times a day. It took one week for complete recovery, with the pain decreasing in intensity until alleviated during the one week of treatment. Submitted by A.I., Hilo, Hawaii.
- B.B., a 54-year-old female, presented with chronic back spasms, occurring since a discectomy between L2-L3 ten years prior. Complete disabling pain four to five times a day was also present. Objective findings were pain on the right side of the lower back at the inner BL channel, and tension from *Xinshu* (BL 15) to *Dachangshu* (BL 25) on the right side. The practitioner diagnosed the condition as qi and blood stagnation in the BL channel of the lower back. The patient was given ***Back Support (AC)***, 3 to 4 capsules, four times a day. She took the herbs for four weeks consistently. The patient had a 90% reduction in spasms with occasional flare-ups only if she did activities that she knew would cause it. The patient was able to stand in her kitchen and bake for five hours, which she was unable to do previously. Submitted by L.M., Lafayette, Colorado.
- R.K., 55-year-old female, presented with insomnia due to low back pain and stress. The practitioner diagnosed this condition as qi and blood stagnation in the Urinary Bladder channel and Liver qi stagnation. ***Calm ZZZ*** and ***Back Support (AC)*** were

FORMULAS

Back Support (AC)™

prescribed. After taking the herbs for two weeks, the back pain resolved temporarily; however, occasional flare-ups of pain will occur due to overuse. Over time, as her back pain decreased, her sleep improved as well. Submitted by B.S., Niceville, Florida.

- A 50-year-old female acupuncturist sustained an injury to her sacrum and coccyx. She fell from a chair hammock 3 to 4 feet above ground onto cement. A sensation similar to a lightening bolt was felt in the sacral area as well as a feeling of electricity from her sacrum to her knees. She was in acute pain and thought she was paralyzed. As an acupuncturist, she diagnosed herself as qi and blood stagnation resulting from trauma. She was immediately treated by a chiropractor. She also took 6 capsules of ***Back Support (AC)*** three times a day. After just two doses, the patient experienced tremendous relief. Although the patient still complained of slight lingering pain that persisted for a while, she stated that ***Back Support (AC)*** made a remarkable difference in her recovery process. Within one month, the patient improved almost 95%. Submitted by M.T.B., Alpine, California.
- An injury caused by a fall resulted in acute low back pain to a 29-year-old male blackjack dealer. Sequelae included local swelling, redness, and limited lumbar range of motion. Skin and muscle bruising was quite noticeable. The TCM diagnosis of qi and blood stagnation was confirmed through tongue analysis that showed a pale, purple tongue body, a wiry pulse, as well as pain upon palpation. Administration of ***Back Support (AC)*** reduced the pain immediately the same day. Low back pain was completely resolved within a week, with full lumbar range of motion recovery within only four days. Submitted by T.G., Albuquerque, NM.
- D.D., a 41-year-old nurse, presented with a work-related injury. She had severe back pain that was the result of a fall from lifting a patient. She said she heard a popping sound in her back when she fell. MRI confirmed her diagnosis of lumbar herniated disc. By the time she came for treatment, she was nine weeks post-injury and had scheduled for steroid epidurals. She refused injections and came to our clinic for 'safe and non-invasive care.' Her blood pressure was 140/80 mmHg and her heart rate was 80 beats per minute. The TCM diagnoses include qi and blood stagnation and soft tissue damage. ***Back Support (AC)***, ***Flex (SC)***, and ***Flex (TMX)*** were prescribed at 3 capsules each three times a day. After the herbs, the patient was able to reduce Vicodin (APAP/Hydrocodone) use from 2 to 0.5 tablets per day, and none at all on some days. She had increased blood pressure from stress over the injury, which was up to 170/110 mmHg. After the herbs and massage, the blood pressure came down to normal and is staying down. She had received no additional physical therapy. She did remarkably well in a short period of time. Submitted by M.H., West Palm Beach, Florida.
- J.M., a 36-year-old female massage therapist, presented with pain from a recent automobile accident (second accident in six months). She exhibited neck, back, arm, and leg pain. Airbags bent her right thumb. Her blood pressure was 120/70 mmHg and her heart rate was 72 beats per minute. X-rays showed herniation and soft tissue damage. She also complained of muscle spasms, hot sensation on trigger points, inability to move the right thumb and decreased range of motion of the neck and trunk. ***Flex (TMX)***, ***Neck & Shoulder (AC)***, and ***Back Support (AC)*** were all prescribed at 2 capsules each three times daily. J.M. responded quickly to these formulas and acupuncture treatments. Pain levels were reduced by half in a short period of time. Submitted by M.H., West Palm Beach, Florida.
- A 36-year-old female college professor reported back pain for a period of one week. The cause of injury involved her reaching for an item and a sudden severe back pain followed. Tenderness upon palpation was noted at T12 to L2 region along with paraspinal hypertonicity. Although no X-rays were taken, she initially got chiropractic treatment for a slipped disc, which included ultrasound and chiropractic manipulative adjustments. Though her back pain was still present, it was not as severe. Her pulse was wiry, slippery, and slightly weak. The TCM diagnoses for her condition include Liver qi stagnation, local qi and blood stagnation, and qi deficiency. After taking a prescription of ***Back Support (AC)*** for a couple of days, the patient noticed slight improvement. By the fourth and fifth day on the formula, her mobility had markedly improved along with a decrease in pain. Submitted by N.M., Torrance, California.
- A 47-year-old female office manager complained of neck pain and low back pain that were aggravated by prolonged sitting. She has a past history of two whiplash injuries that could also have attributed to causing her neck pain. Upon examination, the practitioner found extreme spasms of the erector muscles, bilateral weakness of her sternocleidomastoid muscles and a lack of muscle tone in her lower back. With these symptoms, the patient was diagnosed with right-sided sciatica, arthralgia of the spine and stress-induced muscle spasms. The TCM diagnosis was concluded to be Liver qi stagnation. The treatment included acupuncture, moxa, and infrared heat. ***Back Support (AC)*** and ***Neck & Shoulder (AC)*** were prescribed for this patient. The results were as follows:

  3/29/01: stress: 8; pain: 9-10 (on a scale of 1 to 10; 10 rating = worse condition)
  5/05/01: 50% improvement
  5/19/01: 70% improvement
  8/16/01: No more pain. However, slight intermittent flaring of her condition was noted.

  The practitioner and the patient both concluded that the ***Back Support (AC)*** and ***Neck & Shoulder (AC)*** have really helped. Submitted by T.W., Santa Monica, California.
- G.A., a 51-year-old female patient, presented with bilateral lower back pain ranging from 7 to 9 out of 10 on a pain scale. She described the pain as stabbing and spasmodic. She could barely walk or sit, and even lying down was uncomfortable. In fact, the patient stated she couldn't find relief in any position. She'd had intermittent back pain and spasms for much of her adult life, with the first serious episode occurring in her late twenties.

Back Support (AC)™

The patient had recently missed several days of work and could concentrate on nothing but the pain. Objective findings included X-rays that revealed arthritis at L4 possibly as the result of trauma. The patient reported that she had injured her back when she was in first grade – a classmate had pulled a chair out from under her as she prepared to sit down. Tongue body color was unremarkable with scalloped edges. The tongue coating was thick and white with hairline cracks. Pulse was deep and small on both sides. Her lower back pain was too painful to palpate. The TCM diagnosis was severe qi and blood stagnation in the lower back with mild Kidney qi and yang deficiencies. ***Back Support (CR)*** was prescribed at 4 capsules three to four times a day. The practitioner wanted to prescribe ***Back Support (AC)***, but had only ***Back Support (CR)*** in the pharmacy. Rather than wait a few days for the herbs to arrive, ***Back Support (CR)*** was given first to begin the herbal therapy. ***Back Support (CR)*** reduced the patient's pain level dramatically within 24 hours. This case exemplifies the principle of therapeutic diagnosis – the patient's excellent response to this formula demonstrated the degree to which underlying Kidney deficiency played a role in the pathology. However, she wasn't conscientious about taking the herbs and when the pain was gone and the bottle was empty, she didn't resume taking the herbs and the deficiency persisted.

The same patient returned some months later with another flare-up of stabbing and spasmodic bilateral lower back pain. Again, she could hardly walk nor could she find a position that relieved her pain at all. This time she reported that the pain was probably the result of her new job as an esthetician – she was now spending her workdays sitting on a stool bending to give facials to customers. Her tongue appeared pale and scalloped, and peeled on the edges with thin white coating and hairline cracks. Her pulses were still deep on both sides. The blood pressure was 118/72 mmHg and the heart rate was 62 beats per minute. The TCM diagnosis was severe qi and blood stagnation of the lumbar region, which probably resulted from working under ergonomically unsound conditions. She also suffered from mild Kidney qi and yang deficiencies. This time, ***Back Support (AC)*** was prescribed at 4 capsules three to four times a day. Though the patient responded well to ***Back Support (CR)*** during her previous lumbar pain flare-up, the practitioner chose to give the patient ***Back Support (AC)*** instead this time. Though the formula reduced her pain, it took longer to do so and the pain, though milder, lingered. This case was submitted by the practitioner as an example of the importance of treating the underlying deficiency in chronic cases. Submitted by H.H., San Francisco, California.

PHARMACOLOGICAL AND CLINICAL RESEARCH

Back Support (AC) is formulated to treat low back pain caused by trauma, sports injuries, sprains and strains, or subluxation. The herbs in ***Back Support (AC)*** have analgesic influence to relieve pain, anti-inflammatory action to reduce pain and inflammation, and antispasmodic effect to relax muscles and tendons.

Yan Hu Suo (Rhizoma Corydalis) is one of the most potent herbs for treatment of pain. Its effects are well documented in both historical references and modern research studies. According to classical texts, *Yan Hu Suo* (Rhizoma Corydalis) has been used to treat chest and hypochondriac pain, epigastric and abdominal pain, hernial pain, dysmenorrhea or menstrual pain, and pain of the extremities. According to laboratory studies, the extract of *Yan Hu Suo* (Rhizoma Corydalis) has been found to be effective in both acute and chronic phases of inflammation. The mechanism of its anti-inflammatory effect is attributed to its inhibitory activities on the release of histamine and pro-inflammatory mediators.[2,3] Furthermore, it has a strong analgesic effect. With adjustment in dosage, the potency of *Yan Hu Suo* (Rhizoma Corydalis) has been compared to that of morphine. In fact, the analgesic effect of *Yan Hu Suo* (Rhizoma Corydalis) is so strong and reliable that it has been used with satisfactory anesthetic effect in 98 out of 105 patients (93.4%) who underwent surgery.[4] The analgesic effect can be potentiated further with concurrent acupuncture therapy. In one research study, it is demonstrated that the analgesic effect is increased significantly with concurrent treatments using *Yan Hu Suo* (Rhizoma Corydalis) and electro-acupuncture, when compared to a control group, which received electro-acupuncture only.[5] Overall, it is well understood that *Yan Hu Suo* (Rhizoma Corydalis) has a marked effect to treat pain. Though the maximum analgesic effect of *Yan Hu Suo* (Rhizoma Corydalis) is not as strong as morphine, it has been determined that the herb is much safer, with significantly less side effects, less risk of tolerance, and no evidence of physical dependence even with long-term use.[6]

Bai Shao (Radix Paeoniae Alba) and *Zhi Gan Cao* (Radix et Rhizoma Glycyrrhizae Praeparata cum Melle) are two of the most effective herbs to relieve pain, reduce inflammation, and alleviate spasms and cramps. Pharmacologically, these two herbs have shown marked analgesic effect, anti-inflammatory effect, and muscle-relaxant effect.[7,8] *Bai Shao* (Radix Paeoniae Alba) exhibits excellent anti-inflammatory effect to treat arthritis by modulating the pro-inflammatory mediators production from macrophage-like synoviocytes.[9] *Zhi Gan Cao* (Radix et Rhizoma Glycyrrhizae Praeparata cum Melle) illustrates marked anti-inflammatory effects by enhancing the effect of glucocorticoids through increased production and secretion as well as decreased metabolism by the liver, along with increased plasma concentration caused by decreased protein binding.[10] Clinically, these two herbs have been used to treat a wide variety of musculoskeletal disorders. According to one study, use of these herbs via intramuscular injection was associated with 84.67% rate of effectiveness (105 out of 124 subjects) to treat the general complaint of pain.[11] More specifically, these two herbs have also been found to effectively treat pain in the lower back and legs among 33 elderly patients,[12] as well as severe pain of the back and legs in 27 patients.[13] Furthermore, the combination of these two herbs was effective in relieving nerve pain (neuralgia) in 30 out of 42 patients.[14] According to

Back Support (AC)™

another study, the use of these two herbs was also effective for muscle spasms and cramps in various areas of the body, including muscle spasms and twitching in the facial region in 11 patients,[15] intestinal spasms in 254 patients,[16] and intestinal cramps and spasms in 85 patients.[17]

Lastly, ***Back Support (AC)*** contains several herbs for their adjunct effect to alleviate pain, reduce inflammation, and relieve spasms and cramps. *Gui Zhi* (Ramulus Cinnamomi) has an analgesic effect to relieve pain. According to one study, it has been used successfully to treat arthritis among 30 patients.[18] According to another study, use of this herb is effective to treat numbness among 30 patients.[19] *Ji Xue Teng* (Caulis Spatholobi) exhibits an anti-inflammatory effect through its inhibitory activities against a panel of key enzymes relating to inflammation, including cyclo-oxygenase, phospholipase, and lipoxygenase.[20] *Mu Gua* (Fructus Chaenomelis) reduces inflammation and relieves arthritis via prevention of ultrastructural changes of synoviocytes and inhibition of secretion of pro-inflammatory cytokines, such as interleukin-1, tumor necrosis factor-alpha (TNF-α), and prostaglandin E2.[21] Furthermore, *Mu Gua* (Fructus Chaenomelis) has been shown to effectively treat rheumatic and rheumatoid arthritis by reducing inflammation in subjects with collagen-induced arthritis.[22] *Wei Ling Xian* (Radix et Rhizoma Clematidis) exerts its significant anti-inflammatory effect by blocking the production of the pro-inflammatory mediators, nitric oxide, and prostaglandin.[23] Lastly, *Ge Gen* (Radix Puerariae Lobatae) has also been shown to have a muscle-relaxant effect to relieve muscle spasms and cramps.[24]

In summary, ***Back Support (AC)*** is an excellent formula for acute and severe pain in the lower back region, as it contains herbs with excellent analgesic effect to relieve pain, anti-inflammatory effect to reduce swelling and inflammation, and muscle-relaxant effect to alleviate spasms and cramps.

COMPARATIVE ANALYSIS

Pain is a basic bodily sensation induced by a noxious stimulus that causes physical discomfort (such as pricking, throbbing, or aching). Pain may be of acute or chronic state. For acute back pain, two classes of drugs commonly used for treatment include non-steroidal anti-inflammatory agents (NSAID) and opioid analgesics. NSAIDs [such as Motrin (ibuprofen) and Voltaren (diclofenac)] are generally used for mild to moderate pain, and are most effective to reduce inflammation and swelling. Though effective, they may cause such serious side effects as gastric ulcer, duodenal ulcer, gastrointestinal bleeding, tinnitus, blurred vision, dizziness, and headache. Furthermore, the newer NSAIDs, also known as COX-2 inhibitors [such as Celebrex (celecoxib)], are associated with significantly higher risk of cardiovascular events, including heart attack and stroke. Opioid analgesics [such as Vicodin (APAP/hydrocodone) and morphine] are usually used for severe to excruciating pain. While they may be the most potent agents for pain, they also have the most serious risks and side effects, including but not limited to dizziness, lightheadedness, drowsiness, upset stomach, vomiting, constipation, stomach pain, rash, difficult urination, and respiratory depression resulting in difficult breathing. Furthermore, long-term use of these drugs leads to tolerance and addiction. In brief, it is important to remember that while drugs offer reliable and potent symptomatic pain relief, they should only be used if and when needed. Frequent use and abuse leads to unnecessary side effects and complications.

Treatment of pain is a sophisticated balance of art and science. Proper treatment of pain requires a careful evaluation of the type of disharmony (excess or deficiency, cold or heat, exterior or interior), characteristics (qi and/or blood stagnation), and locations (upper body, lower body, extremities, or internal organs). Furthermore, optimal treatment requires integrative use of herbs, acupuncture, and *tui-na* therapies. All these therapies work together to tonify the underlying deficiencies, strengthen the body, and facilitate recovery from chronic pain. TCM pain management targets both the symptom and the cause of pain, and as such, often achieves immediate and long-term success. Furthermore, TCM pain management is often associated with few or no side effects.

In conclusion, for treatment of mild to severe pain due to various causes, TCM pain management offers similar treatment effects as Western medicine with significantly fewer side effects.

References

1. Berkow R. et al. The Merck Manual of Medical Information. Merck Research Laboratories. 1999 February.
2. *Biol Pharm Bull*, Feb 1994; 17(2):262-5.
3. Oh YC, Choi JG, Lee YS, Brice OO, Lee SC, Kwak HS, Byun YH, Kang OH, Rho JR, Shin DW, Kwon DY. Tetrahydropalmatine inhibits pro-inflammatory mediators in lipopolysaccharide-stimulated THP-1 cells. Department of Oriental Pharmacy, College of Pharmacy, Wonkwang University Wonkwang Oriental Medicines Research Institute, Iksan, Republic of Korea. J Med Food. 2010 Oct;13(5):1125-32.
4. *He Bei Xin Yi Yao* (Hebei New Medicine and Herbology), 1973; 4:34.
5. *Chen Tzu Yen Chiu* (Acupuncture Research), 1994;19(1):55-8.
6. *Zhong Yao Yao Li Yu Ying Yong* (Pharmacology and Applications of Chinese Herbs), 1983; 447.
7. *Zhong Yao Xue* (Chinese Herbology), 1998; 759:765.
8. *Zhong Cao Yao* (Chinese Herbal Medicine), 1991; 22(10):452.
9. Zheng YQ, Wei W. Total glucosides of paeony suppresses adjuvant arthritis in rats and intervenes cytokine-signaling between different types of synoviocytes. Int Immunopharmacol. 2005 Sep;5(10):1560-73.
10. *Zhong Yao Zhi* (Chinese Herbology Journal), 1993; 358.
11. *Shang Hai Zhong Yi Yao Za Zhi* (Shanghai Journal of Chinese Medicine and Herbology), 1983; 4:14.
12. *Yun Nan Zhong Yi* (Yunnan Journal of Traditional Chinese Medicine), 1990; 4:15.
13. *Zhe Jiang Zhong Yi Za Zhi* (Zhejiang Journal of Chinese Medicine), 1980; 2:60.
14. *Zhong Yi Za Zhi* (Journal of Chinese Medicine), 1983; 11:9.
15. *Hu Nan Zhong Yi* (Hunan Journal of Traditional Chinese Medicine), 1989; 2:7.
16. *Zhong Hua Nei Ke Za Zhi* (Chinese Journal of Internal Medicine), 1960; 4:354.
17. *Zhong Yi Za Zhi* (Journal of Chinese Medicine), 1985; 6:50.
18. *Zhong Yao Xue* (Chinese Herbology), 1998; 65:67.
19. *Hu Nan Zhong Yi Za Zhi* (Hunan Journal of Chinese Medicine), 1987; 8(2):4.
20. Li RW, David Lin G, Myers SP, Leach DN. Anti-inflammatory activity of Chinese medicinal vine plants. Australian Centre for Complementary Medicine

Back Support (AC)™

Education and Research, A Joint Venture of the University of Queensland and Southern Cross University. J Ethnopharmacol. 2003 Mar;85(1):61-7.

21. Dai M, Wei W, Shen YX, Zheng YQ. Glucosides of Chaenomeles speciosa remit rat adjuvant arthritis by inhibiting synoviocyte activities. Institute of Clinical Pharmacology, Anhui Medical University, Hefei 230032, China. Acta Pharmacol Sin. 2003 Nov;24(11):1161-6.
22. Chen Q. & Wei W. Effects and mechanisms of glucosides of *Chaenomeles speciosa* on collagen- induced arthritis in rats. *Int Immunopharmacol.* 2003, 3(4): 593-608.
23. Park EK, Ryu MH, Kim YH, Lee YA, Lee SH, Woo DH, Hong SJ, Han JS, Yoo MC, Yang HI, Kim KS. Anti-inflammatory effects of an ethanolic extract from Clematis mandshurica Rupr. East-West Bone and Joint Research Center, College of Medicine, Kyung Hee University, Hoegi-1 dong, Dongdaemun-gu, Seoul 130-701, South Korea. J Ethnopharmacol. 2006 Nov 3;108(1):142-7.
24. *Zhong Yao Xue* (Chinese Herbology), 1998; 101:103.

FORMULAS

Back Support (CR)™

CLINICAL APPLICATIONS

- **Chronic low back pain (lumbago)**
- Weakness and soreness of the lower back and knees
- Dull achy back pain, stiffness, and limited range of motion
- Slow and incomplete recovery from back injuries
- Sciatica, osteoarthritis, lumbago, lower back pain resulting from osteoporosis

WESTERN THERAPEUTIC ACTIONS

- Chondroprotective function to prevent joint destruction and cartilage erosion
- Osteogenic function to promote generation of new bones
- Anti-inflammatory effect to reduce pain, swelling, and redness
- Analgesic influence to relieve pain
- Antispasmodic effect to stop muscle spasm and cramping

CHINESE THERAPEUTIC ACTIONS

- Disperses painful obstruction
- Relieves pain
- Invigorates qi and blood circulation
- Tonifies Liver and Kidney deficiencies

DOSAGE

Take 3 to 4 capsules three times daily. Patients who have chronic back pain from repetitive movement from their job should take this formula at a maintenance dose of two capsules a day to strengthen the muscles and tendons in the back to prevent injury. For maximum effectiveness, take the herbs on an empty stomach with warm water. This formula should not be taken during the acute phase of injury, where there is still bleeding, inflammation, and bruising.

INGREDIENTS

Bai Shao (Radix Paeoniae Alba)
Chuan Niu Xi (Radix Cyathulae)
Di Huang (Radix Rehmanniae)
Du Huo (Radix Angelicae Pubescentis)
Du Zhong (Cortex Eucommiae)
Ji Xue Teng (Caulis Spatholobi)
Mu Gua (Fructus Chaenomelis)
Qian Nian Jian (Rhizoma Homalomenae)
Sang Ji Sheng (Herba Taxilli)
Wei Ling Xian (Radix et Rhizoma Clematidis)
Zhi Gan Cao (Radix et Rhizoma Glycyrrhizae Praeparata cum Melle)

BACKGROUND

Musculoskeletal and connective tissue injuries lead to over 10 million clinic visits per year in the United States.[1] Causes of these injuries may be external (sports injuries, car accidents, trauma), internal (chronic wear and tear of muscles, ligaments and tendons; bones weakened by osteoporosis), or both. Acute injuries are characterized by severe pain, swelling and inflammation, and in some cases, internal bleeding. Treatment of acute injuries should focus on relieving pain, reducing swelling and inflammation, and stopping bleeding. Chronic injuries are characterized by dull pain, stiffness and numbness, and decreased muscle mass and strength. Treatment of chronic injuries includes relief of pain and restoration of physical and physiological functions.

FORMULA EXPLANATION

Back Support (CR) is formulated based on *Du Huo Ji Sheng Tang* (Angelica Pubescens and Taxillus Decoction), the historical herbal formula used to treat chronic low back pain, sciatica, rheumatoid arthritis, and osteoarthritis.[2] ***Back Support (CR)*** contains herbs that activate qi and blood circulation, remove qi and blood stagnation, relieve pain, and nourish the muscles and tendons.

In this formula, a large dose of *Du Huo* (Radix Angelicae Pubescentis) is used to dispel wind, cold, and dampness in the back and lower parts of the body. *Du Zhong* (Cortex Eucommiae), *Sang Ji Sheng* (Herba Taxilli), *Qian Nian Jian* (Rhizoma Homalomenae), and *Di Huang* (Radix Rehmanniae) replenish the vital functions of the Liver and the Kidney, which are responsible for strengthening the bones, sinews, and muscles of the lower back and knees. *Bai Shao* (Radix Paeoniae Alba) has analgesic, antispasmodic and anti-inflammatory effects. Together with the harmonizing effect of *Zhi Gan Cao* (Radix et Rhizoma Glycyrrhizae Praeparata cum Melle), they nourish and relax the tendons and muscles in the back. *Mu Gua* (Fructus Chaenomelis), *Wei Ling Xian* (Radix et Rhizoma Clematidis), and *Ji Xue Teng* (Caulis Spatholobi) increase qi and blood circulation in order to relax the muscles and tendons in the back. *Chuan Niu Xi* (Radix Cyathulae) invigorates the blood and acts as a channel-guiding herb to direct the effects of the formula to the lumbar region. Together, these herbs treat chronic pain affecting the lower back.

CAUTIONS & CONTRAINDICATIONS

- Because of the blood-invigorating nature of this formula, ***Back Support (CR)*** is not recommended during pregnancy and nursing.
- ***Back Support (CR)*** is a warm formula, and use of this warm formula may be associated with a slight increase in blood pressure. Therefore, blood pressure should be monitored while taking this formula.
- Patients who have pain radiating to the extremities accompanied by a sudden loss of bladder or bowel control may have a pinched nerve or spinal injury, and must be referred out to emergency care if they have not already been evaluated by a specialist. This condition, known as cauda equina syndrome, can lead to permanent disability and must be evaluated and treated immediately.
- If the patient presents with fever and one-sided back pain, consider a possible kidney infection and do not use this herbal formula. Patients with acute nephritis should be referred to their medical doctor immediately.

Back Support (CR)™

CLINICAL NOTES

- ***Back Support (AC)*** is for acute cases with inflammation and pain. It is the best formula for recent injury or acute exacerbation with excruciating pain.
- ***Back Support (CR)*** is usually used for chronic pain or dull pain. In addition to having herbs that relieve pain, this formula also has herbs to nourish and strengthen the underlying structures and tissues so the back becomes less fragile.

Pulse Diagnosis by Dr. Jimmy Wei-Yen Chang:

- **Soft tissue damage:** turtle pulse, a convex-shaped pulse on the left *chi*; the more forceful the pulse, the more recent the injury, with more inflammation and pain
- **Bone spurs or disk problems:** guitar string / steel wire pulse on the left *chi*
- **Low back pain due to blood stasis from old injuries:** dispersing pulse, a pulse in which its border is difficult to perceive, soft, weak, and deep, on the left *chi*

SUPPLEMENTARY FORMULAS

- For chronic low back pain with weakness and soreness of the knees, add ***Knee & Ankle (CR)***.
- For chronic low back pain with weakened soft tissues (muscles, tendons, and ligaments), add ***Flex (MLT)***.
- To enhance the analgesic effect, add ***Herbal ANG***.
- For osteoporosis or weakness of the bones, add ***Osteo 8***.
- For chronic low back pain due to herniated disk, combine with ***Back Support (HD)***.
- For soreness and weakness of the lower back and knees and/or low sex drive because of Kidney yang deficiency, combine with ***Kidney Tonic (Yang)***.
- For soreness and weakness of the lower back and knees due to yin deficiency, add ***Kidney Tonic (Yin)***.
- For bone fractures and internal bruises, add ***Flex (TMX)***.
- For arthritis that worsens during cold or rainy seasons, add ***Flex (CD)***.
- For arthritis with redness, inflammation, swelling, and burning pain, add ***Flex (Heat)***.
- For muscle spasms and cramps, add ***Flex (SC)***.
- For pain related to bone spurs, add ***Flex (SPR)***.
- For back pain due to kidney stones, use ***Dissolve (KS)***.
- For back pain or soreness because of nephritis, use ***Kidney DTX***.
- For dull back pain during menstruation, add ***Mense-Ease***.
- For back pain resulting from obesity, use ***Herbalite*** to help with weight loss.
- For chronic, stubborn back pain with blood stagnation, add ***Circulation (SJ)***.
- With inflammation, add ***Astringent Complex***.

ACUPUNCTURE TREATMENT

Traditional Points:

- *Huatuojiaji* points (Extra 15) in the back from L3 to L5 for lower back pain. *Huatuojiaji* points (Extra 15) from T1 to T12 for upper back pain.
- *Hegu* (LI 4), *Yaotongxue* (Extra 29), *Huantiao* (GB 30), *Yaoyen* (Extra 21), *Shenshu* (BL 23), *Weizhong* (BL 40)

Classic Master Tung's Points:

- Needle contralateral to the pain. If the pain is in the center, needle bilaterally or the side with the more *ah shi* points. If the pain is bilateral, needle bilaterally.
- *Linggu* (T 22.05), *Chongzi* (T 22.01), *Chongxian* (T 22.02), *Wanshunyi* (T 22.08), *Wanshuner* (T 22.09), *Zhongbai* (T 22.06), *Zhengjin* (T 77.01), *Zhengzong* (T 77.02), *Zhongjiuli* (T 88.25), *Tongshen* (T 88.09), *Tongwei* (T 88.10), *Simashang* (T 88.18), *Simazhong* (T 88.17), *Simaxia* (T 88.19), *Shuijin* (T 1010.20), *Shuitong* (T 1010.19), *Chengshan* (BL 57), *Biyi* (T 1010.22), *Zhitong* (T 44.13)

Master Tung's Points by Dr. Chuan-Min Wang:

- For acute pain, bleed first then needle.
- For chronic pain, needle first then bleed.
- **Mid back pain:** Needle contralaterally *Chongzi* (T 22.01), *Chongxian* (T 22.02), *Zhengjin* (T 77.01), *Zhengzong* (T 77.02). Bleed ipsilaterally popliteal fossa or local tender spot.
- **Low back pain:** Bleed ipsilaterally popliteal fossa or local tender spot.
  - L1-L3 pain: Needle contralaterally *Zhongbai* (T 22.06), *Xiabai* (T 22.07).
  - L4-L5 pain: Needle contralaterally *Dabai* (T 22.04), *Linggu* (T 22.05).
  - S1-S2 pain: Needle contralaterally *Wanshunyi* (T 22.08), *Wanshuner* (T 22.09).
- **Hip pain:** Needle contralaterally *Jianzhong* (T 44.06), *Xiaqu* (T 44.15), *Shangqu* (T 44.16), *Yunbai* (T 44.11), *Libai* (T 44.12). Bleed ipsilaterally popliteal fossa or local tender spot.
- **Sciatic pain:** Needle contralaterally *Dabai* (T 22.04), *Linggu* (T 22.05), *Wanshunyi* (T 22.08). Needle ipsilaterally *Weizhong* (BL 40), *Kunlun* (BL 60), *Zuqianjin* (T 77.24), *Zuwujin* (T 77.25).

Balance Method by Dr. Richard Tan:

- Needle the following points on the side opposite the pain: *Hegu* (LI 4), *Houxi* (SI 3), *Wangu* (SI 4), *Linggu* (T 22.05), *Dabai* (T 22.04), *Zhongbai* (T 22.06), *Dazhong* (KI 4) or *ah shi* points nearby, and *Fuliu* (KI 7), *Ququan* (LR 8) or *ah shi* points nearby.
- Needle the following points on the same side as the pain: All *ah shi* points nearby *Chize* (LU 5), *Kongzui* (LU 6), *Shaohai* (HT 3) to *Lingdao* (HT 4), *Shugu* (BL 65).
- Needle *ah shi* points around *Fengfu* (GV 16) to *Houding* (GV 19).

Ear Acupuncture:

- Back, Lumbago, Small Intestine, Adrenal Gland, Pituitary Gland
- Embed ear needles or use ear seeds.
- Ten treatments equal one course.

FORMULAS

Back Support (CR)™

Auricular Medicine by Dr. Li-Chun Huang:

- **Low back pain due to Kidney qi deficiency:** Corresponding points (to the area of pain in the Lumbar and Lumbar Muscle Area), Kidney, Liver, Spleen, Endocrine, Coronary Vascular Subcortex, Large Auricular Nerve, Lumbar Area

NUTRITION

- Eat a diet with a wide variety of raw vegetables and fruits, and whole grain cereals to ensure a complete supply of nutrients for the bones, nerves, and muscles.
- Adequate intake of calcium is essential for the repair and rebuilding of bones, tendons, cartilage, and connective tissues.
- Fresh pineapples are recommended as they contain bromelain, an enzyme that is excellent in reducing inflammation.
- To relieve cramps and spasms, eat plenty of fruits and vegetables, especially those high in potassium such as bananas and oranges. Also drink an adequate amount of water, as back pain may be due in part to dehydration.
- Adequate intake of minerals, such as calcium and potassium, are essential for pain management. Deficiency of these minerals will lead to spasms, cramps, and tense muscles.
- Avoid red meat and seafood in the diet as they contain high levels of uric acid, which adds strain on the kidneys.
- Avoid cold beverages, ice cream, caffeine, sugar, tomatoes, milk, and dairy products.

The Tao of Nutrition by Dr. Maoshing Ni and Cathy McNease:

- To help tonify the Kidney
  - Make soup with green beans, black beans, azuki beans, and a pinch of cinnamon.
  - Slowly cook (2 to 3 hours) ½ cup black beans, ½ cup water, and ¾ cup rice wine.
  - Eat a handful of curry cashews daily. Make curry cashews by dry roasting cashews in a pan and sprinkle with curry powder for a couple of minutes on high flame. Remove promptly and avoid burning the cashews.
  - Eat a small handful daily of pecans that have been soaked in sherry or port for one week or more.

LIFESTYLE INSTRUCTIONS

- Patients are advised to use their legs (instead of bending their back) when lifting heavy objects.
- Exercises for stretching and strengthening the back muscles are essential for long-term recovery. Strengthening the stomach muscles is also beneficial as it reduces the strain on the lower back.
- Mild exercise such as swimming, yoga, or *tai chi chuan* [*tai ji quan*] is recommended.
- Weight loss is suggested to decrease the pressure on the joints and relieve pain.
- Proper balance of work and rest is very important. While sitting, make sure the back is straight and the elbows and knees are bent at a 90° angle. Take a break at least once every hour to alleviate the pressure on the vertebrae and disks.
- Mild back pain can be relieved with application of heat to stimulate the blood circulation. Massage, hot packs, saunas and whirlpools are recommended.
- Hot baths with *Ai Ye* (Folium Artemisiae Argyi) or Epsom salts help to relax tense muscles, invigorate blood flow and draw toxins from tissues. Rest and relax in the bath for about 15 to 30 minutes, but avoid becoming over-tired from the heat and soaking. Mix about 2 to 3 tablespoons of *Ai Ye* (Folium Artemisiae Argyi) extract powder in the hot water each time.
- Patients are encouraged to wear clothing that cover their back completely, and tuck their shirts into their pants or skirts to avoid any wind exposure to their back, which can further aggravate the condition.
- Firm beds are recommended over soft ones for patients with back pain.
- Finally, adequate rest is essential to recovery.

CASE STUDIES

- G.P., a 57-year-old female patient, presented with low back pain she had been experiencing for ten years. Her blood pressure was 116/62 mmHg. Objective findings included tenderness upon palpation of L4/L5 area, as well as limited range of motion while performing lateral flexion on both the left and right side. The practitioner diagnosed this condition as Kidney deficiency. After taking ***Back Support (CR)***, the patient felt improvement in her mobility and was able to move around in confidence. She also reported that she was able to walk and stand for longer periods of time. The patient stopped taking Vicodin (hydrocodone/acetaminophen) she was prescribed by her medical doctor and continued to take two more bottles of ***Back Support (CR)***. Submitted by G.S., Pasadena, California.
- B.F., a 35-year-old male, presented with mid-back pain, especially during exhaustion and stress. Patient has no desire to take pain killer and was looking for alternative medicine to help. No recent injuries were mentioned; however, he had a history of a sports injury 15 years ago. The practitioner diagnosed his condition as Kidney yang deficiency, blocked channels, and Spleen qi deficiency. After taking ***Back Support (CR)*** for six weeks, the patient reported his pain decreasing from 6 to 0, based on a scale from 0 to 10 (with 10 being the most painful). He now only takes the herbs and receives acupuncture as needed. Additional lifestyle changes recommended were applying heat, and core strengthening exercises. Submitted by L.M., Las Vegas, Nevada.
- J.J., a 55-year-old female, presented with pain in the back, neck and shoulder areas. The practitioner diagnosed this condition as qi and blood stagnation located in the Urinary Bladder and Small Intestine channels. Upon diagnosis, ***Back Support (CR)*** was prescribed for treatment. As a result of taking ***Back Support (CR)*** and also receiving acupuncture, cupping, and electrical stimulation, the patient's posture improved and was able to stand up straighter,

Back Support (CR)™

and experienced an overall decrease in pain. Submitted by B.S., Niceville, Florida.

- A 58-year-old female presented with back pain she'd had for 15 years, that was worse upon waking and better with activity. Most recently, she had hip pain for five months that felt deep in the acetabulum region. Tendon pain located antero-medially near the groin was also noted. No structural abnormalities were found upon further investigation. The practitioner diagnosed the condition as qi and blood stagnation in the Urinary Bladder and Gallbladder channels. After taking ***Back Support (CR)***, her back pain decreased and since then, she experienced less muscle stiffness, especially in the morning. Her previous radiating hip pain is now less severe and infrequent. She has also noticed that walking, which was painful for her in the past, has become almost pain-free. In addition to ***Back Support (CR)***, she also took Wobenzyme and has improved her diet. Submitted by J.M., Baltimore, Maryland.
- A 56-year-old female presented with severe back pain, joint pain, morning stiffness, and difficulty walking, which were all attributed to degenerative joint disease. Standing and bending aggravated her pain. She found relief with rest. Severe irritation and discomfort were evoked during lumbar range of motion. The practitioner diagnosed the condition as cold-damp stagnation in the Urinary Bladder channel with underlying Kidney deficiency. The patient was treated with ***Back Support (CR)*** along with acupuncture. Soon after, the patient reported that she was able to walk without difficulty and stand without pain for longer periods of time (30 to 60 minutes). Eventually she was able to return to a painless level of activity and function. Submitted by M.I., San Pedro, California.
- A 45-year-old male presented with pain in the low back and buttocks. On a pain scale from 0-10 (with 10 being the most painful), the patient rated his pain as a 7. There were decreased range of motion in the lumbar spine, and radicular pain on the right side. He was diagnosed with a herniated disc in the lumbar spine. After taking ***Back Support (CR)***, the patient stated that the severity of the pain decreased on a daily basis from 7 to 4. Submitted by G.P., Lawndale, California.
- A female patient suffering from lower back (L4 area) pain radiating down the left hip was unable to lie on her back. On examination, her left leg was shorter than the right. The patient reported that the pain was caused by a twisted pelvis from a tailbone injury years before: her tailbone projected outwards, and her knees were swollen and painful. She also suffered from gout. X-ray showed bone spurs in the lower spine. After taking ***Back Support (CR)***, she was able to lie on her back for almost an hour without pain, sit for a longer period of time with less pain, and sleep restfully. She also experienced more flexibility in the lower spine while doing yoga. Submitted by S.M., Midline, Michigan.

PHARMACOLOGICAL AND CLINICAL RESEARCH

Back Support (CR) is an excellent formula for rehabilitation from chronic back injuries, such as repetitive injuries or long-term wear and tear of the muscles and joints. As a result, the chronic nature of this condition may eventually contribute to atrophy and degeneration, accompanied by decreased mobility of the joints, and generalized weakness and pain of the muscles. ***Back Support (CR)*** contains herbs with chondroprotective, osteogenic, anti-inflammatory, analgesic, and muscle-relaxant functions.

Back Support (CR) contains many herbs to strengthen and rebuild soft tissues, including muscles, tendons, and ligaments. *Chuan Niu Xi* (Radix Cyathulae) shows a great chondroprotective effect against cartilage-degrading disorders, and is an excellent herb to protect the cartilage from repetitive and stress-induced injuries. According to one study, the extract of this herb has a potent effect to inhibit the induction of MMP-13, an important enzyme for the degradation of the cartilage collagen matrix, especially under arthritic conditions by down-regulating the MMP-13 activity.[3] *Wei Ling Xian* (Radix et Rhizoma Clematidis) also has an excellent chondroprotective effect. According to one study, the saponin fraction from *Wei Ling Xian* (Radix et Rhizoma Clematidis) is effective in ameliorating joint destruction and cartilage erosion in subjects with osteoarthritis. The mechanisms of action for protecting articular cartilage are through preventing extracellular matrix degradation and chondrocyte injury.[4] Another study demonstrates that the acetone extract of *Wei Ling Xian* (Radix et Rhizoma Clematidis) has significant and dose-dependent inhibitory effects on the pro-inflammatory and degradative mediators associated with inflammatory arthritis. *Wei Ling Xian* (Radix et Rhizoma Clematidis) inhibits prostaglandin E(2), metalloproteinase (MMP-3 and -13), and cyclo-oxygenase-2 production by primary human chondrocytes stimulated by lipopolysaccharide.[5] Lastly, *Wei Ling Xian* (Radix et Rhizoma Clematidis) also shows a beneficial effect for the treatment of osteoarthritis by preventing apoptosis in primary cultured articular chondrocytes induced by adenoviral TNF-related apoptosis-inducing ligand.[6]

Back Support (CR) also has many herbs to strengthen and rebuild bones. *Du Zhong* (Cortex Eucommiae) has significant osteogenic and antiosteoporotic effects to promote generation of new bones and prevent osteoporosis. According to a bone cells culture experiment, administration of *Du Zhong* (Cortex Eucommiae) shows a potential effect to increase the proliferation and differentiation of the osteoblasts without affecting osteoclast activity. The researchers conclude that these herbs can effectively increase the rate of tissue regeneration of damaged bones.[7] According to another study, use of *Du Zhong* (Cortex Eucommiae) for 16 weeks shows a marked effect to protect subjects from estrogen deficiency-induced osteoporosis. In a dose-dependent manner, the herb improves bone biomechanical quality through modifications of bone mineral density and trabecular microarchitecture

Back Support (CR)™

without hyperplastic effects on the uterus. The researchers suggest that *Du Zhong* (Cortex Eucommiae) might be a potential alternative medicine for treatment of postmenopausal osteoporosis.[8] *Sang Ji Sheng* (Herba Taxilli) has significant osteogenic and antiosteoporotic actions to promote generation of new bones and prevent osteoporosis. According to a bone cells culture experiment, administration of *Sang Ji Sheng* (Herba Taxilli) shows a potential effect to increase the proliferation and differentiation of the osteoblasts without affecting osteoclast activity. The researchers conclude that these herbs can effectively increase the rate of tissue regeneration of damaged bones.[9]

Back Support (CR) utilizes many herbs with anti-inflammatory effects to treat pain and inflammation in the lower back. *Ji Xue Teng* (Caulis Spatholobi) exhibits an anti-inflammatory effect through its inhibitory activities against a panel of key enzymes relating to inflammation, including cyclo-oxygenase, phospholipase A(2), and lipoxygenase (5-LO).[10] *Mu Gua* (Fructus Chaenomelis) reduces inflammation and relieves arthritis via prevention of ultrastructural changes of synoviocytes and inhibition of secretion of pro-inflammatory cytokines, such as interleukin-1 (IL-1), tumor necrosis factor-alpha (TNF-α), and prostaglandin E2.[11] *Wei Ling Xian* (Radix et Rhizoma Clematidis) exerts its significant anti-inflammatory effect by blocking the production of the pro-inflammatory mediators, nitric oxide and prostaglandin E(2).[12] Furthermore, *Du Zhong* (Cortex Eucommiae) demonstrates marked anti-inflammatory effects through its stimulating effect on the endocrine system and consequent secretion of steroids from the adrenal cortex.[13] *Di Huang* (Radix Rehmanniae) exerts an anti-inflammatory effect to reduce swelling and inflammation via its influence on the endocrine system.[14] Lastly, *Du Huo* (Radix Angelicae Pubescentis) has a mild sedative effect and marked analgesic and anti-inflammatory effects.[15] Clinically, *Du Zhong* (Cortex Eucommiae) has been used successfully in an herbal formula to treat six patients with sciatica,[16] *Di Huang* (Radix Rehmanniae) has been used in an herbal formula to successfully treat 12 patients with rheumatoid arthritis,[17] and *Wei Ling Xian* (Radix et Rhizoma Clematidis) has significant effect to inhibit pro-inflammatory compounds and prevent rheumatoid arthritis.[18]

Bai Shao (Radix Paeoniae Alba) and *Zhi Gan Cao* (Radix et Rhizoma Glycyrrhizae Praeparata cum Melle) are two of the most effective herbs to relieve pain, reduce inflammation, and alleviate spasms and cramps. Pharmacologically, these two herbs have shown marked analgesic, anti-inflammatory, and muscle-relaxant effects.[19,20] *Bai Shao* (Radix Paeoniae Alba) exhibits an excellent anti-inflammatory effect to treat arthritis by modulating the pro-inflammatory mediators production from macrophage-like synoviocytes.[21] *Zhi Gan Cao* (Radix et Rhizoma Glycyrrhizae Praeparata cum Melle) illustrates marked anti-inflammatory effects by enhancing the effect of glucocorticoids through increased production and secretion as well as decreased metabolism by the liver, along with increased plasma concentration caused by decreased protein binding.[22] Clinically, these two herbs have been used to treat a wide variety of musculoskeletal disorders. According to one study, use of these herbs via intramuscular injection was associated with an 84.67% rate of effectiveness (105 out of 124 subjects) to treat general complaints of pain.[23] More specifically, these two herbs have also been found to effectively treat pain in the lower back and legs among 33 elderly patients,[24] as well as severe pain of the back and legs in 27 patients.[25] Furthermore, the combination of these two herbs was effective in relieving nerve pain (neuralgia) in 30 out of 42 patients.[26] According to another study, the use of these two herbs was also effective for muscle spasms and cramps in various areas of the body, including muscle spasms and twitching in the facial region in 11 patients,[27] intestinal spasms in 254 patients,[28] and intestinal cramps and spasms in 85 patients.[29]

In summary, ***Back Support (CR)*** is an excellent formula that contains herbs with analgesic and anti-inflammatory effects to relieve pain and inflammation associated with back pain. Furthermore, it also utilizes herbs with chondroprotective and osteogenic functions to repair cartilage erosion, protect joint destruction, and promote generation of new bones.

COMPARATIVE ANALYSIS

Pain is a basic bodily sensation induced by a noxious stimulus that causes physical discomfort (such as pricking, throbbing, or aching). Pain may be of acute or chronic state, and may be of nociceptive, neuropathic, or psychogenic origin. For acute pain, use of non-steroidal anti-inflammatory agents (NSAID), and opioid analgesics offer immediate and reliable effects to relieve pain. Though these drugs have serious side effects, short-term use can be justified because the benefits often outweigh the risks. For chronic pain, on the other hand, use of NSAIDs and opioid analgesics are usually not the desired treatment options, as they symptomatically relieve pain, but do not change the underlying course of illness. Unfortunately, the convenience of these drugs contributes to the vicious cycle of pain, followed by continuous and repetitive use of drugs to symptomatically relieve pain. When the effect of the drugs dissipates, patients are often left with nothing but more pain and more complications from side effects. Therefore, it is important to understand that while these drugs may be beneficial for acute pain, they do not adequately address most cases of chronic pain. Additional treatment modalities must be incorporated to ensure effective and complete recovery from chronic pain conditions. [Note: Common side effects of NSAIDs include gastric ulcer, duodenal ulcer, gastrointestinal bleeding, tinnitus, blurred vision, dizziness, and headache. Serious side effects of newer NSAIDs, also known as COX-2 inhibitors [such as Celebrex (celecoxib)], include significantly higher risk of cardiovascular events, including heart attack and stroke. Side effects of opioid analgesics [such as Vicodin (APAP/Hydrocodone) and morphine] include dizziness, lightheadedness, drowsiness, upset stomach, vomiting, constipation, stomach pain, rash, difficult urination, and respiratory depression resulting in difficult breathing. Furthermore, long-term use of these drugs leads to tolerance and addiction.]

Treatment of chronic pain is a sophisticated balance of art and science. Proper treatment of pain requires a careful evaluation of the type of disharmony (excess or deficiency, cold or heat, exterior or interior), characteristics (qi and/or blood stagnation), and locations (upper body, lower body, extremities, or internal organs). Furthermore, optimal treatment requires integrative use of herbs, acupuncture, and *tui-na* therapies. All these therapies work together to tonify the underlying deficiencies, strengthen the body, and facilitate recovery from chronic pain. TCM pain management targets both the symptom and the cause of pain, and as such, often achieves immediate and long-term success. Furthermore, TCM pain management is often associated with few or no side effects.

In conclusion, for treatment of mild to severe pain due to various causes, TCM pain management offers similar treatment effects as Western medicine with significantly fewer side effects. Though TCM therapies may not be as potent as the drugs for acute pain management, they are often superior [better effects with fewer side effects] for chronic pain management.

References

1. Berkow R. et al. The Merck Manual of Medical Information. Merck Research Laboratories. 1999 February.
2. Bensky, D. et al. *Chinese Herbal Medicine Formulas & Strategies*. Eastland Press. 1990.
3. Park HY, Lim H, Kim HP, Kwon YS. Downregulation of Matrix Metalloproteinase-13 by the Root Extract of Cyathula officinalis Kuan and its Constituents in IL-1β-treated Chondrocytes. College of Pharmacy, Kangwon National University, Chunchon, Korea. Planta Med. 2011 Feb 23.
4. Wu W, Xu X, Dai Y, Xia L. Therapeutic effect of the saponin fraction from Clematis chinensis Osbeck roots on osteoarthritis induced by monosodium iodoacetate through protecting articular cartilage. Department of Pharmacology of Chinese Materia Medica, College of Traditional Chinese Medicine, China Pharmaceutical University, Nanjing. Phytother Res. 2010 Apr;24(4):538-46.
5. Hsieh MS, et al. Using (18)F-FDG microPET imaging to measure the inhibitory effects of Clematis chinensis Osbeck on the pro-inflammatory and degradative mediators associated with inflammatory arthritis. School of Medicine, Taipei Medical University, Taipei, Taiwan; Orthopedics Research Center, Taipei Medical University Hospital, Taipei, Taiwan. J Ethnopharmacol. 2010 Jul 3.
6. Lee SW, et al. Purified extract from Clematis mandshurica prevents adenoviral-TRAIL induced apoptosis on rat articular chondrocytes. Department of Rheumatology, Dong-A University College of Medicine and Institute of Medical Science, Busan, South Korea. Am J Chin Med. 2008;36(2):399-410.
7. Yao CH, Tsai HM, Chen YS, Liu BS. Fabrication and evaluation of a new composite composed of tricalcium phosphate, gelatin, and Chinese medicine as a bone substitute. Institute of Biomedical Engineering and Material Science, Chungtai Institute of Health Science and Technology, Taichung, Taiwan, Republic of China. J Biomed Mater Res B Appl Biomater. 2005 Nov;75(2):277-88.
8. Zhang R, Liu ZG, Li C, Hu SJ, Liu L, Wang JP, Mei QB. Du-Zhong (Eucommia ulmoides Oliv.) cortex extract prevent OVX-induced osteoporosis in rats. Bone. 2009 Sep;45(3):553-9.
9. Yao CH, Tsai HM, Chen YS, Liu BS. Fabrication and evaluation of a new composite composed of tricalcium phosphate, gelatin, and Chinese medicine as a bone substitute. Institute of Biomedical Engineering and Material Science, Chungtai Institute of Health Science and Technology, Taichung, Taiwan, Republic of China. J Biomed Mater Res B Appl Biomater. 2005 Nov;75(2):277-88.
10. Li RW, David Lin G, Myers SP, Leach DN. Anti-inflammatory activity of Chinese medicinal vine plants. Australian Centre for Complementary Medicine Education and Research, A Joint Venture of the University of Queensland and Southern Cross University, P.O. Box 157, Lismore, NSW 2480, Australia. J Ethnopharmacol. 2003 Mar;85(1):61-7.
11. Dai M, Wei W, Shen YX, Zheng YQ. Glucosides of Chaenomeles speciosa remit rat adjuvant arthritis by inhibiting synoviocyte activities. Institute of Clinical Pharmacology, Anhui Medical University, Hefei 230032, China. Acta Pharmacol Sin. 2003 Nov;24(11):1161-6.
12. Park EK, Ryu MH, Kim YH, Lee YA, Lee SH, Woo DH, Hong SJ, Han JS, Yoo MC, Yang HI, Kim KS. Anti-inflammatory effects of an ethanolic extract from Clematis mandshurica Rupr. East-West Bone and Joint Research Center, College of Medicine, Kyung Hee University, Hoegi-1 dong, Dongdaemun-gu, Seoul 130-701, South Korea. J Ethnopharmacol. 2006 Nov 3;108(1):142-7.
13. *Zhong Cao Yao* (Chinese Herbal Medicine), 1982; 13(6):24.
14. *Zhong Yao Yao Li Yu Ying Yong* (Pharmacology and Applications of Chinese Herbs), 1983: 400.
15. *Zhong Yao Yao Li Yu Ying Yong* (Pharmacology and Applications of Chinese Herbs), 1983; 796.
16. *Zhong Yao Xue* (Chinese Herbology), 1998; 797:799.
17. *Zhong Yao Lin Chuan Xin Yong* (New Clinical Applications of Chinese Medicine), 2001; 242-243.
18. Sun SX, Li YM, Fang WR, Cheng P, Liu L, Li F. Effect and mechanism of AR-6 in experimental rheumatoid arthritis. Department of Physiology, China Pharmaceutical University, 210009 Nanjing, China. Clin Exp Med. 2010 Jun;10(2):113-21.
19. *Zhong Yao Xue* (Chinese Herbology), 1998; 759:765.
20. *Zhong Cao Yao* (Chinese Herbal Medicine), 1991; 22(10):452.
21. Zheng YQ, Wei W. Total glucosides of paeony suppresses adjuvant arthritis in rats and intervenes cytokine-signaling between different types of synoviocytes. Int Immunopharmacol. 2005 Sep;5(10):1560-73.
22. *Zhong Yao Zhi* (Chinese Herbology Journal), 1993; 358.
23. *Shang Hai Zhong Yi Yao Za Zhi* (Shanghai Journal of Chinese Medicine and Herbology), 1983; 4:14.
24. *Yun Nan Zhong Yi* (Yunnan Journal of Traditional Chinese Medicine), 1990; 4:15.
25. *Zhe Jiang Zhong Yi Za Zhi* (Zhejiang Journal of Chinese Medicine), 1980; 2:60.
26. *Zhong Yi Za Zhi* (Journal of Chinese Medicine), 1983; 11:9.
27. *Hu Nan Zhong Yi* (Hunan Journal of Traditional Chinese Medicine), 1989; 2:7.
28. *Zhong Hua Nei Ke Za Zhi* (Chinese Journal of Internal Medicine), 1960; 4:354.
29. *Zhong Yi Za Zhi* (Journal of Chinese Medicine), 1985; 6:50.

Back Support (HD)™

CLINICAL APPLICATIONS

- **Back pain due to herniated disk**
- **Herniated disk, lumbar radiculopathy, prolapsed or bulging disk, or slipped disk** with possible severe back pain which may worsen with coughing, straining or laughing, tingling or numbness in the legs or feet, muscle spasm or weakness
- **Pain originating from the spinal cord and radiating down the legs**

WESTERN THERAPEUTIC ACTIONS

- Analgesic effect to relieve pain
- Anti-inflammatory effect to reduce swelling and inflammation
- Spasmolytic effect to relax muscles
- Chondroprotective effect to protect the cartilages
- Osteogenic effect to promote generation of bones

CHINESE THERAPEUTIC ACTIONS

- Activates blood circulation and eliminates blood stasis
- Reduces swelling and inflammation
- Strengthens soft tissues and relieves pain

DOSAGE

Take 3 to 4 capsules, three times daily, as needed to relieve pain. The dosage may be increased up to 6 to 8 capsules every four to six hours if necessary, especially in the early stages of injury when there is severe and excruciating pain. When the pain subsides, reduce the dosage to 3 or 4 capsules, three times daily. For maximum effectiveness, take the herbs on an empty stomach, with two tall glasses of warm water.

INGREDIENTS

Bai Shao (Radix Paeoniae Alba)
Che Qian Zi (Semen Plantaginis)
Chuan Niu Xi (Radix Cyathulae)
Chuan Xiong (Rhizoma Chuanxiong)
Dan Shen (Radix et Rhizoma Salviae Miltiorrhizae)
Dang Gui (Radix Angelicae Sinensis)
Du Zhong (Cortex Eucommiae)
E Zhu (Rhizoma Curcumae)
Gan Cao (Radix et Rhizoma Glycyrrhizae)
Gui Zhi (Ramulus Cinnamomi)
San Leng (Rhizoma Sparganii)
Shen Jin Cao (Herba Lycopodii)
Yan Hu Suo (Rhizoma Corydalis)
Yi Yi Ren (Semen Coicis)
Ze Xie (Rhizoma Alismatis)

BACKGROUND

Herniated disk, also known as slipped, prolapsed or ruptured disk, refers to the damaged disks that cushion the spine. A herniated disk may be caused by acute injuries to, or chronic wear and tear of, the spine. When the disk becomes herniated and presses on a nerve, it can cause pain, swelling, numbness, weakness, and loss of physical functions served by the nerve. Optimal treatment should include use of herbs and acupuncture to relieve pain and swelling, and utilization of physical medicine (*tui-na*, adjustment, surgery) to correct the underlying problem.

FORMULA EXPLANATION

Back Support (HD) is designed to treat herniated disk. It contains herbs to activate blood circulation and eliminate blood stasis, reduce swelling and inflammation, strengthen soft tissue and relieve pain. It is most effective for acute injuries that are mild to moderate in severity.

Dang Gui (Radix Angelicae Sinensis), *Chuan Xiong* (Rhizoma Chuanxiong) and *Dan Shen* (Radix et Rhizoma Salviae Miltiorrhizae) tonify blood and activate blood circulation. *Yan Hu Suo* (Rhizoma Corydalis), *San Leng* (Rhizoma Sparganii) and *E Zhu* (Rhizoma Curcumae) are among the strongest pain-relieving herbs that also eliminate blood stasis. *Bai Shao* (Radix Paeoniae Alba) and *Gan Cao* (Radix et Rhizoma Glycyrrhizae) nourish yin to relieve muscle spasms and cramps. They also nourish Liver yin and benefit soft tissues. *Ze Xie* (Rhizoma Alismatis), *Che Qian Zi* (Semen Plantaginis), and *Yi Yi Ren* (Semen Coicis) drain water accumulation to reduce swelling and inflammation associated with herniated disk. *Shen Jin Cao* (Herba Lycopodii) and *Gui Zhi* (Ramulus Cinnamomi) open the channels and collaterals to unblock obstructions, especially of the extremities to treat radiating pain and/or numbness. *Du Zhong* (Cortex Eucommiae) and *Chuan Niu Xi* (Radix Cyathulae) are channel-guiding herbs that direct to the back and strengthen soft tissues, such as muscles, tendons, and ligaments. They also tonify the Kidney, dominate the marrow and directly benefit the bones and disks.

Back Support (HD) is an excellent formula to treat herniated disk, prolapsed disk, or slipped disk. It is most effective for acute injuries that are mild to moderate in severity.

CAUTIONS & CONTRAINDICATIONS

- Because of the blood-invigorating nature of this formula, it is contraindicated during pregnancy and nursing.
- Patients who have pain radiating to the extremities accompanied by a sudden loss of bladder or bowel control may have a pinched nerve or spinal injury and must be referred out to emergency care if they have not already been evaluated by a specialist. This condition, known as cauda equina syndrome, can lead to permanent disability and must be evaluated and treated immediately.
- This herbal formula contains herbs that invigorate blood circulation, such as *Dan Shen* (Radix et Rhizoma Salviae Miltiorrhizae) and *Dang Gui* (Radix Angelicae Sinensis). Therefore, patients who are on anticoagulant or antiplatelet therapies, such as Coumadin (warfarin), should use this formula with caution, or not at all, as there may be a higher risk of bleeding and bruising.[1,2,3]

Back Support (HD)™

CLINICAL NOTES

- Herniated disk can be caused by a prolapsed or slipped disk pressing on the nerves. As a result, there may be shooting pain that starts from the vertebrae and travels outwards to the extremities. While the use of herbs and acupuncture are helpful to relieve pain and reduce inflammation, physical treatment (such as *tui-na* or chiropractic adjustments) may be necessary to correct the underlying problem. In overt cases of radiculopathy, manipulation to the spinal area is contraindicated.
- To maximize the therapeutic effect, this formula can be given to patients before acupuncture treatments. The muscle-relaxant influence from the herbs takes effect within about 30 minutes. By relaxing the muscles and invigorating qi and blood circulation, there is less stagnation in the channels, and the acupuncture and *tui-na* treatments will be more effective.
- Cold packs may be used for acute injuries during the first 24 to 48 hours to reduce swelling and inflammation. Afterwards, hot packs should be used to promote blood circulation and enhance healing in the affected area.
- The most common areas of injury for herniated disk are L4-L5 and L5-S1.
- This formula is an adjunct to acupuncture treatment. Optimal results are obtained when acupuncture, electro-stimulation and herbs are included in the treatment regimen.

Pulse Diagnosis by Dr. Jimmy Wei-Yen Chang:

- **In the neck:** guitar string / steel wire tight pulse on, or extending proximal to, the right *chi*
- **In the low back:** guitar string / steel wire tight pulse, on extending proximal to, the left *chi*

SUPPLEMENTARY FORMULAS

- For severe back pain, add ***Back Support (AC)*** and ***Herbal ANG***.
- For external or traumatic injuries, use with ***Flex (TMX)***.
- For acute neck, shoulder and upper back pain, combine with ***Neck & Shoulder (AC)***.
- For neuropathy, add ***Flex (NP)***.
- For bone spurs, add ***Flex (SPR)***.
- For degeneration of disks, add ***Osteo 8***.
- To enhance and support soft tissues and cartilages, combine with ***Flex (MLT)***.
- With severe inflammation, combine with ***Astringent Complex***.
- With severe blood stagnation, add ***Circulation (SJ)***.

ACUPUNCTURE TREATMENT

Traditional Points:

- *Ah shi* points on the back, *Yinmen* (BL 37), *Chengshan* (BL 57). Strongly stimulate and remove the needles.
- *Shenshu* (BL 23), *Yaoyangguan* (GV 3), *Weizhong* (BL 40), *Huantiao* (GB 30), *Chengfu* (BL 36)

Classic Master Tung's Points:

- Needle contralateral to the pain. If the pain is in the center, needle bilaterally or the side with the more *ah shi* points. If the pain is bilateral, needle bilaterally.
- *Linggu* (T 22.05), *Chongzi* (T 22.01), *Chongxian* (T 22.02), *Xiabai* (T 22.07), *Chengshan* (BL 57), *Zhengjin* (T 77.01), *Zhengzong* (T 77.02), *Zhengshi* (T 77.03), *Zhongjiuli* (T 88.25), *Minghuang* (T 88.12), *Tianhuang* (T 88.13), *Qihuang* (T 88.14), *Tianhuang* (T 77.17), *Dihuang* (T 77.19), *Renhuang* (T 77.21), *Zhoushui* (T 1010.25)

Master Tung's Points by Dr. Chuan-Min Wang:

- **Herniated disk:** Needle *Minghuang* (T 88.12), *Tianhuang* (T 88.13), *Qihuang* (T 88.14). Bleed popliteal fossa or around fibula head area.

Balance Method by Dr. Richard Tan:

- Needle the following points on the side opposite the pain: *Hegu* (LI 4), *Houxi* (SI 3), *Wangu* (SI 4), *Linggu* (T 22.05), *Dabai* (T 22.04), *Zhongbai* (T 22.06), *Dazhong* (KI 4) or *ah shi* points nearby, *Fuliu* (KI 7), *Ququan* (LR 8) or *ah shi* points nearby
- Needle the following points on the same side as the pain: All *ah shi* points nearby *Chize* (LU 5), *Kongzui* (LU 6), *Shaohai* (HT 3) to *Lingdao* (HT 4), *Shugu* (BL 65)
- Needle *ah shi* points around *Fengfu* (GV 16) to *Houding* (GV 19).

Ear Acupuncture:

- Lower back (search for the most sensitive and painful point), *Shenmen*, Adrenals

Auricular Medicine by Dr. Li-Chun Huang:

- Occiput, Lesser Occiput Nerve, Large Auricular Nerve, *Shenmen*, Golden, Silver and Bronze triangles, corresponding point of pain. Bleed Ear Apex.
- **Sciatic nerve pain:** Triangle Area Sciatic Nerve of the Posterior. Bleed Ear Apex.

NUTRITION

- Eat whole grain cereals and a wide variety of raw vegetables and fruits to ensure a complete supply of nutrients for the bones, nerves, and muscles.
- Fresh pineapples are recommended as they contain bromelain, an enzyme that is excellent in reducing inflammation. If the consumption of fresh pineapples causes stomach upset, eat it after meals.
- To relieve cramps and spasms, eat plenty of fruits and vegetables, especially those high in potassium, such as bananas and oranges. Also, drink an adequate amount of warm water.
- The following is a folk remedy to treat acute back pain from sprain and strain: Crack open 2 ocean crabs with a wooden stick (do not use a knife or any metal instruments) and put them into

FORMULAS

Back Support (HD)™

a clay pot with enough vodka or whiskey to cover both crabs. Place the clay pot into another bigger pot with water and steam for one hour. Serve the crab meat along with the liquor soup.

- Adequate intake of minerals, such as calcium and potassium, is essential for pain management. Deficiency of these minerals leads to spasms, cramps, and tense muscles.
- Avoid cold beverages, ice cream, caffeine, sugar, tomatoes, milk, and dairy products.

LIFESTYLE INSTRUCTIONS

- Stretching and strengthening exercises for the back muscles are essential for long-term recovery.
- Mild exercise such as swimming, yoga, or *tai chi chuan* [*tai ji chuan*] on a regular basis is recommended.
- Avoid engaging in activities that may lead to re-injury, such as improper lifting with turning or twisting, or excessive strain on the back. Advise the patient that lifting should involve the use of the knees, not the back. Avoid all strenuous physical activity.
- For those who are overweight, weight loss is strongly recommended to decrease pressure on the joints and relieve pain.
- Finally, adequate rest is essential to recovery. It is wise to review sleeping postures to ensure that the back is appropriately supported and relaxed in sleep. Firm beds are recommended over soft ones.
- Heat pad use is recommended to warm the affected area and provide better blood circulation for pain relief.

CASE STUDIES

- R.B., a 70-year-old male, presented with sciatica, causing him to have right leg and hip pain, along with spasms of the lower back. It was noted that it was worse with exercise and better with heat application. Objective findings included pain upon palpation of the piriformis muscle, as well as during extension and flexion of the muscles. The TCM diagnosis was Liver and Kidney yin deficiencies, in addition to qi and blood stagnation. ***Back Support (HD)*** was prescribed at 4 capsules two times per day. The patient experienced improvement of his pain after two weeks of taking the herbs. Submitted by M.P., Muskego, Wisconsin.
- K.T., a 52-year-old female, presented with severe low back pain due to traumatic injury along the spine. The practitioner diagnosed this condition as qi and blood stagnation along the Urinary Bladder and Small Intestine channels. ***Back Support (CR)***, ***Back Support (HD)***, and ***Herbal ANG*** were prescribed for treatment. As a result, the patient had reported most relief coming from taking the ***Back Support (HD)***. The pain continued to swap between improving and worsening. The patient discontinued taking the herbs before even considering taking only the ***Back Support (HD)*** long term. Submitted by B.S., Niceville, Florida.

PHARMACOLOGICAL AND CLINICAL RESEARCH

Back Support (HD) is developed specifically to treat herniated, prolapsed, or slipped disk. It contains herbs with marked analgesic effects to relieve pain, and anti-inflammatory effects to reduce swelling and inflammation. Furthermore, many of these herbs have the effect to treat other related conditions, such as sciatica, arthritis, and neuralgia.

Yan Hu Suo (Rhizoma Corydalis) is one of the strongest and most potent herbs for treatment of pain. Its effects are well documented in both historical references and modern research studies. According to classical texts, *Yan Hu Suo* (Rhizoma Corydalis) can be used to treat chest and hypochondriac pain, epigastric and abdominal pain, hernial pain, amenorrhea or menstrual pain, and pain of the extremities. According to laboratory studies, the extract of *Yan Hu Suo* (Rhizoma Corydalis) has been found to be effective in both acute and chronic phases of inflammation. The mechanism of its anti-inflammatory effect is attributed to its effect to inhibit the release of histamine and pro-inflammatory mediators.[4,5] Furthermore, it has a strong analgesic effect. With adjustment in dosage, the potency of *Yan Hu Suo* (Rhizoma Corydalis) has been compared to that of morphine. In fact, the analgesic effect of *Yan Hu Suo* (Rhizoma Corydalis) is so strong and reliable that it has been used with satisfactory anesthetic effect in 98 out of 105 patients (93.4%) who underwent surgery.[6] The analgesic effect can be potentiated further with concurrent acupuncture therapy. In one research study, it is demonstrated that the analgesic effect is increased significantly with concurrent treatments using *Yan Hu Suo* (Rhizoma Corydalis) and electro-acupuncture, when compared to a control group, which received electro-acupuncture only.[7] Overall, it is well understood that *Yan Hu Suo* (Rhizoma Corydalis) has a marked effect to treat pain. Though the maximum analgesic effect of *Yan Hu Suo* (Rhizoma Corydalis) is not as strong as morphine, it has been determined that the herb is much safer, with significantly less side effects, less risk of tolerance, and no evidence of physical dependence even with long-term use.[8]

In addition to *Yan Hu Suo* (Rhizoma Corydalis), ***Back Support (HD)*** uses other herbs with analgesic effects to relieve pain. *Du Huo* (Radix Angelicae Pubescentis) has a mild sedative effect and moderate analgesic activity.[9] *San Leng* (Rhizoma Sparganii) has a marked analgesic effect to inhibit pain.[10] The combination of *Bai Shao* (Radix Paeoniae Alba) and *Gan Cao* (Radix et Rhizoma Glycyrrhizae) has a marked analgesic effect to relieve pain. The effectiveness is increased significantly when combined with acupuncture.[11] Clinically, these two herbs have been used successfully to treat conditions such as pain,[12] neuralgia,[13] trigeminal neuralgia,[14,15] neck pain,[16] acute back pain,[17] heel pain,[18] pain in the lower back and legs,[19] sciatica,[20] gastric and abdominal pain,[21] and dysmenorrhea.[22]

Since herniated disk is often complicated with local swelling and inflammation, ***Back Support (HD)*** uses many herbs with

Back Support (HD)™

anti-inflammatory effects. *Dang Gui* (Radix Angelicae Sinensis) exerts both analgesic and anti-inflammatory effects through the inhibition of pro-inflammatory mediators, including nitric oxide and prostaglandin E2 in peritoneal macrophages.[23,24] In comparison with acetylsalicylic acid, the anti-inflammatory effect of *Dang Gui* (Radix Angelicae Sinensis) is approximately 1.1 times stronger, and its analgesic effect is approximately 1.7 times stronger.[25] According to clinical studies, *Dang Gui* (Radix Angelicae Sinensis) has been used successfully to treat menstrual pain in 112 patients,[26] migraine headache in 35 patients,[27] different types of headache in 36 patients,[28] and general complaint of pain in 105 patients.[29] In addition, *Chuan Xiong* (Rhizoma Chuanxiong) exerts an anti-inflammatory effect via inhibitory activity on TNF-α production and TNF-α bioactivity, and shows a promising effect to treat inflammation and related diseases.[30] Clinically, it has been used in various formulas to effectively treat various types and causes of headache,[31,32] trigeminal nerve pain,[33] trigeminal neuralgia,[34] and angina.[35]

To treat local spasms and cramps, *Bai Shao* (Radix Paeoniae Alba) and *Gan Cao* (Radix et Rhizoma Glycyrrhizae) are used as they have an excellent muscle-relaxant effect to relax both smooth and skeletal muscles.[36,37] Clinically, these two herbs have been used successfully to treat conditions such as leg cramps in the calf,[38] muscle cramps in hemodialysis,[39] restless leg syndrome,[40] intestinal spasm,[41] facial spasms and twitching,[42] and menstrual cramps and pain.[43]

Lastly, individuals with herniated disks may also have damages to their cartilage and bones. *Chuan Niu Xi* (Radix Cyathulae) is an excellent herb to protect the cartilage from repetitive and stress-induced injuries. According to one study, the extract of *Chuan Niu Xi* (Radix Cyathulae) has a potent effect to inhibit the induction of MMP-13, an important enzyme for the degradation of the cartilage collagen matrix, especially under arthritic conditions. By down-regulating the MMP-13 activity, *Chuan Niu Xi* (Radix Cyathulae) showed great chondroprotection against cartilage degrading disorders.[44] *Dang Gui* (Radix Angelicae Sinensis) is an effective herb to promote the generation of bones. According to one study, the water extract of *Dang Gui* (Radix Angelicae Sinensis) has been found to contribute to the formation of bones and treatment of bone injuries. It directly stimulates the proliferation, alkaline phosphatase activity, protein secretion, and particularly type I collagen synthesis of human osteoprecursor cells in a dose-dependent manner.[45] According to another study, *Dang Gui* (Radix Angelicae Sinensis) shows a marked stimulatory effect in osteoblast proliferation and differentiation systems, as well as in a fibroblast-secreted hyaluronic acid assay. This herb enhances the deposition of hyaluronic acid and proliferation of osteoblasts *in vitro*, as well as bone regeneration.[46]

In summary, ***Back Support (HD)*** is developed specifically to treat herniated disk, prolapsed disk, or slipped disk. It contains herbs with marked analgesic effects to relieve pain, anti-inflammatory effects to reduce swelling and inflammation, spasmolytic effects to relax muscles, chondroprotective effect to protect the cartilages and osteogenic promote the generation of bones.

COMPARATIVE ANALYSIS

Pain is a basic bodily sensation induced by a noxious stimulus that causes physical discomfort (such as pricking, throbbing, or aching). Pain may be of nociceptive, neuropathic, or psychogenic origin. For neuropathic pain due to herniated disks, drugs [aspirin, non-steroidal anti-inflammatory agents (NSAID) and opioid analgesics] offer few benefits. Use of drugs do not change the underlying condition [herniated disk], they only mask the symptom [pain]. Most patients are simply told to relax at home, stay confined to bed, and take drugs as needed for pain. If the pain persists, more and more drugs are needed, thereby creating more side effects and complications. If the pain becomes worse, invasive treatment such as surgery is often suggested. In other words, Western medicine offers few or no options. [Note: Common side effects of aspirin and NSAIDs include gastric ulcer, duodenal ulcer, gastrointestinal bleeding, tinnitus, blurred vision, dizziness, and headache. Serious side effects of newer NSAIDs, also known as COX-2 inhibitors [such as Celebrex (celecoxib)], include significantly higher risk of cardiovascular events, including heart attack and stroke. Side effects of opioid analgesics [such as Vicodin (APAP/hydrocodone) and morphine] include dizziness, lightheadedness, drowsiness, upset stomach, vomiting, constipation, stomach pain, rash, difficult urination, and respiratory depression resulting in difficult breathing. Furthermore, long-term use of these drugs leads to tolerance and addiction.]

Treatment of pain is a sophisticated balance of art and science. Proper treatment of pain requires a careful evaluation of the type of disharmony (excess or deficiency, cold or heat, exterior or interior), characteristics (qi and/or blood stagnations), and locations (upper body, lower body, extremities, or internal organs). Furthermore, optimal treatment requires integrative use of herbs, acupuncture and *tui-na* therapies. All these treatments work together to tonify the underlying deficiencies, strengthen the body, and facilitate recovery from chronic pain. Herbs and acupuncture are effective to treat the symptom (pain), and *tui-na* is effective to correct the underlying cause (herniation). By addressing both symptom and cause, TCM therapies achieve immediate and long-term success. Furthermore, TCM therapies are often associated with few or no side effects. However, it is important to also recognize the limitation of TCM therapies. Integrative use of herbs, acupuncture, and *tui-na* are excellent for initial stages of herniated disks of mild to moderate severity. When applied properly, they are often very successful to treat pain, correct the underlying problem, and restore normal physical functions. However, certain conditions may still require surgical treatment, such as in severe cases of herniated disks (such as ruptured disk) or chronic conditions where all other options have failed.

Back Support (HD)™

Optimal treatment of herniated disks is to understand all available options (from Western and traditional Chinese medicine), and utilize the most effective modality for each specific condition.

References

1. Chan K, Lo AC, Yeung JH, Woo KS. Journal of Pharmacy and Pharmacology 1995 May;47(5):402-6.
2. Pharmacotherapy 1999 July;19(7):870-876.
3. European Journal of Drug Metabolism and Pharmacokinetics 1995; 20(1):55-60.
4. *Biol Pharm Bull*, Feb 1994; 17(2):262-5.
5. Oh YC, Choi JG, Lee YS, Brice OO, Lee SC, Kwak HS, Byun YH, Kang OH, Rho JR, Shin DW, Kwon DY. Tetrahydropalmatine inhibits pro-inflammatory mediators in lipopolysaccharide-stimulated THP-1 cells. Department of Oriental Pharmacy, College of Pharmacy, Wonkwang University Wonkwang Oriental Medicines Research Institute, Iksan, Republic of Korea. J Med Food. 2010 Oct;13(5):1125-32.
6. *He Bei Xin Yi Yao* (Hebei New Medicine and Herbology), 1973; 4:34.
7. *Chen Tzu Yen Chiu* (Acupuncture Research), 1994;19(1):55-8.
8. *Zhong Yao Yao Li Yu Ying Yong* (Pharmacology and Applications of Chinese Herbs), 1983; 447.
9. *Zhong Yao Yao Li Yu Ying Yong* (Pharmacology and Applications of Chinese Herbs), 1983; 796.
10. Lu T, Mao C, Qiu L. The research of analgestic action of different processed products of Sparganium stoloniferum. Nanjing Univesity of Traditional Chinese Medicine, Nanjing 210029. Zhong Yao Cai. 1997 Mar;20(3):135-7.
11. *Guo Wai Yi Xue* (Foreign Medicine) 1984;6(1):58.
12. *Shang Hai Zhong Yi Yao Za Zhi* (Shanghai Journal of Chinese Medicine and Herbology), 1983; 4:14.
13. *Zhong Yi Ming Fang Lin Chuang Xin Yong* (Contemporary Clinical Applications of Classic Chinese Formulas) 2001;313.
14. *Jiang Xi Yi Yao* (Jiangxi Medicine and Herbology) 1965;5(7):909.
15. *Zhong Yi Za Zhi* (Journal of Chinese Medicine), 1983; 11:9.
16. *Jiang Su Zhong Yi* (Jiangsu Chinese Medicine), 1990; (10):29.
17. *Zhe Jiang Zhong Yi Za Zhi* (Zhejiang Journal of Chinese Medicine) 1995;(11):524.
18. *Si Chuan Zhong Yi* (Sichuan Chinese Medicine) 1996;11:38.
19. *Yun Nan Zhong Yi* (Yunnan Journal of Traditional Chinese Medicine), 1990; 4:15.
20. *Fu Jian Zhong Yi Yao* (Fujian Chinese Medicine and Herbology), 1994; (1):7.
21. *Fu Jian Zhong Yi Yao* (Fujian Chinese Medicine and Herbology) 1961;9(4):44.
22. Tanaka T. A novel anti-dysmenorrhea therapy with cyclic administration of two Japanese herbal medicines. Clinical & Experimental Obstetrics & Gynecology 2003;30(2-3):95-8.
23. *Xin Yi Yao Xue Za Zhi* (New Journal of Medicine and Herbology), 1975; (6):34.
24. Chao WW, Kuo YH, Li WC, Lin BF. The production of nitric oxide and prostaglandin E2 in peritoneal macrophages is inhibited by Andrographis paniculata, Angelica sinensis and Morus alba ethyl acetate fractions. Department of Biochemical Science and Technology, Institute of Microbiology and Biochemistry, National Taiwan University, Taipei 106, Taiwan, ROC. J Ethnopharmacol. 2009 Feb 25;122(1):68-75.
25. *Yao Xue Za Zhi* (Journal of Medicinals), 1971; (91):1098.
26. *Lan Zhou Yi Xue Yuan Xue Bao* (Journal of Lanzhou University of Medicine), 1988; 1:36.
27. *Bei Jing Yi Xue* (Beijing Medicine), 1988; 2:95.
28. *Hu Bei Zhong Yi Za Zhi* (Hubei Journal of Chinese Medicine), 1993; (2):9.
29. *Xin Yi Yao Xue Za Zhi* (New Journal of Medicine and Herbology), 1976; 12:26.
30. Liu L, Ning ZQ, Shan S, Zhang K, Deng T, Lu XP, Cheng YY. Phthalide Lactones from Ligusticum chuanxiong inhibit lipopolysaccharide-induced TNF-alpha production and TNF-alpha-mediated NF-kappaB Activation. Planta Med. 2005 Sep;71(9):808-13.
31. *Si Chuan Zhong Yi* (Sichuan Chinese Medicine), 1996; (11):27.
32. *Zhong Xi Yi Jie He Za Zhi* (Journal of Integrated Chinese and Western Medicine), 1991; (1):52.
33. *He Bei Zhong Yi Za Zhi* (Hebei Journal of Chinese Medicine), 1982; 4:34.
34. *Zhong Yao Lin Chuan Xin Yong* (New Clinical Applications of Chinese Medicine), 2001; 65.
35. *Xin Yi Yao Xue Za Zhi* (New Journal of Medicine and Herbology), 1977; 1:15.
36. *Guo Wai Yi Xue* (Foreign Medicine) 1984;6(1):58.
37. *He Nan Zhong Yi* (Henan Chinese Medicine) 1986;(6):15.
38. *Zhong Yi Za Zhi* (Journal of Chinese Medicine) 1985;6:450.
39. Inoshita F, et al. Effect of orally administered shao-yao-gan-cao-tang (Shakuyaku-kanzo-to) on muscle cramps in maintenance hemodialysis patients: a preliminary study. American Journal of Chinese Medicine 2003;31(3):445-53.
40. *He Bei Zhong Yi* (Hebei Chinese Medicine) 1984;3:29.
41. *Zhong Yi Za Zhi* (Journal of Chinese Medicine), 1985; 6:50.
42. *Zhong Xi Yi Jie He Za Zhi* (Journal of Integrated Chinese and Western Medicine), 1991; (1):43.
43. *Bei Jing Zhong Yi* (Beijing Chinese Medicine) 1983;(1):33.
44. Park HY, Lim H, Kim HP, Kwon YS. Downregulation of Matrix Metalloproteinase-13 by the Root Extract of Cyathula officinalis Kuan and its Constituents in IL-1β-treated Chondrocytes. College of Pharmacy, Kangwon National University, Chunchon, Korea. Planta Med. 2011 Feb 23.
45. Yang Q, Populo SM, Zhang J, Yang G, Kodama H. Effect of Angelica sinensis on the proliferation of human bone cells. Clin Chim Acta. 2002 Oct;324(1-2):89-97.
46. Zhao H, Alexeev A, Sharma V, Guzman LD, Bojanowski K. Effect of SBD.4A--a defined multicomponent preparation of Angelica sinensis--in periodontal regeneration models. Phytother Res. 2008 Jul;22(7):923-8.

Balance (Heat)™

CLINICAL APPLICATIONS

- **Menopause and its associated conditions:**
  - **Hot flashes**
  - **Night sweats**
  - **Insomnia**
  - **Mood swings, emotional instability and irritability**
- Related symptoms such as restless sleep, crying spells, and disorientation

WESTERN THERAPEUTIC ACTIONS

- Endocrine activities to balance female hormones and ease common symptoms associated with menopause
- Antidepressant action to settle the emotions and stabilize moods
- Sedative function to treat insomnia and restless sleep
- Osteoprotective function to promote bone formation and antiosteoporotic effect to treat osteoporosis

CHINESE THERAPEUTIC ACTIONS

- Nourishes yin
- Clears deficiency heat
- Calms the *shen* (spirit)
- Stops perspiration

DOSAGE

Take 3 to 4 capsules three times daily on an empty stomach with warm water. Take the last dose half an hour before bedtime if hot flashes, insomnia, restless sleep or night sweating are especially worse at night. For severe conditions, gradually increase the dosage to 8 to 10 capsules three times daily until symptoms are controlled. After relief of symptoms, dosage can then be reduced to 3 to 4 capsules daily.

INGREDIENTS

Bai Shao (Radix Paeoniae Alba)
Bie Jia (Carapax Trionycis)
Chai Hu (Radix Bupleuri)
Da Zao (Fructus Jujubae)
Di Gu Pi (Cortex Lycii)
Di Huang (Radix Rehmanniae)
Fu Xiao Mai (Fructus Tritici Levis)
Gan Cao (Radix et Rhizoma Glycyrrhizae)
Huang Bo (Cortex Phellodendri Chinensis)
Mu Dan Pi (Cortex Moutan)
Qing Hao (Herba Artemisiae Annuae)
Shou Wu Teng (Caulis Polygoni Multiflori)
Xiao Mai (Fructus Tritici)
Zhi Mu (Rhizoma Anemarrhenae)

BACKGROUND

Menopause is the cessation of menses (amenorrhea) for at least one year due to decreasing ovarian function. Clinical symptoms include hot flashes, night sweats, mood swings, emotional instability, irritability, and osteoporosis. Menopause generally begins at approximately 49 to 50 years of age, and the transition may last between three to five years.

FORMULA EXPLANATION

The chief cause of imbalance in women during menopause is Kidney yin deficiency with deficiency heat. The treatment protocol to address the hot flashes, mood swings and night sweats is to clear the deficiency heat and nourish the yin. The patient may also have irritability and emotional instability because of Liver qi stagnation.

Xiao Mai (Fructus Tritici) nourishes the *shen* (spirit) of the Heart and treats excessive worrying or anxiety. *Chai Hu* (Radix Bupleuri) works with *Xiao Mai* (Fructus Tritici) to regulate nervousness, irritability, and mood swings by spreading the stagnant Liver qi. *Qing Hao* (Herba Artemisiae Annuae), *Zhi Mu* (Rhizoma Anemarrhenae) and *Mu Dan Pi* (Cortex Moutan) reduce hot flashes and heat sensations by clearing deficiency heat. *Bie Jia* (Carapax Trionycis) and *Di Huang* (Radix Rehmanniae) nourish the Kidney *jing* (essence) and replenish vitality that is lost through normal aging. *Fu Xiao Mai* (Fructus Tritici Levis) stops abnormal perspiration. *Shou Wu Teng* (Caulis Polygoni Multiflori) nourishes the Heart blood, pacifies nerves, and treats insomnia and nervousness. *Gan Cao* (Radix et Rhizoma Glycyrrhizae), *Xiao Mai* (Fructus Tritici) and *Da Zao* (Fructus Jujubae), the three herbs that make up the formula *Gan Mai Da Zao Tang* (Licorice, Wheat, and Jujube Decoction), nourish the blood of the Heart and moisten internal organ dryness. Finally, *Di Gu Pi* (Cortex Lycii) and *Huang Bo* (Cortex Phellodendri Chinensis) drain yin-deficient fire to control flare-ups of hot flashes.

In summary, ***Balance (Heat)*** is an excellent formula to address all imbalances associated with menopause.

CAUTIONS & CONTRAINDICATIONS

- This formula is contraindicated in cases of cold and deficiency.
- Allergy warning: *Xiao Mai* (Fructus Tritici) used in this product contains wheat. Persons with allergy to wheat should not take this product.

CLINICAL NOTES

- ***Balance (Heat)*** and ***Nourish*** are two of the most commonly used formulas for menopause.
  - ***Balance (Heat)*** is stronger to clear deficiency heat, and relieve symptoms such as hot flashes and emotional disturbance.
  - ***Nourish*** is more effective to tonify the underlying Kidney yin deficiency, and alleviate conditions such as thirst, dryness, and atrophy of genitourinary tissues.
- ***Balance (Heat)*** and ***Nourish*** are both safe formulas that can be used throughout the entire menopause period. Generally, ***Balance (Heat)*** is given first to alleviate the menopause symptoms. When the condition is under control, then switch over to ***Nourish*** to tonify yin and consolidate the effect.

Balance (Heat)™

Pulse Diagnosis by Dr. Jimmy Wei-Yen Chang:

- **Kidney yang deficiency:** small pulse on the left *chi*
- **Kidney yin deficiency:** *Taiyang* pulse, a thick, long, wiry, forceful pulse on the left *chi* is often associated with hormone imbalance. If the *Taiyang* pulse is found on both *chi* positions and the palms are hot, advice the patient to avoid estrogen drugs as they significantly increase the risk of breast cancer.

SUPPLEMENTARY FORMULAS

- To address the cause of menopause by tonifying the Kidney yin and reduce deficiency heat, add ***Nourish***.
- To only tonify Kidney yin and *jing* (essence), combine with ***Kidney Tonic (Yin)***.
- For emotional instability, irritability, and mood swings, combine with ***Calm***.
- For severe *shen* (spirit) disturbance with insomnia, combine with ***Calm (ES)***.
- For menopause with stress, insomnia and fatigue, add ***Calm ZZZ***.
- For depression or crying spells, add ***Shine.***
- For vaginal dryness, add ***Balance Spring***.
- For vaginitis, add ***V-Support***.
- For prevention and treatment of osteoporosis, add ***Osteo 8***.
- For fibrocystic disorders of the female reproductive organs, use ***Resolve (Lower)***.
- For benign breast tumors, mastitis, and nodules, use ***Resolve (Upper)***.
- For hair loss, combine with ***Polygonum 14***.
- For constipation, use ***Gentle Lax (Deficient)***.
- For lack of libido, or Kidney yang deficiency, add ***Vitality***.
- For poor memory and forgetfulness, use with ***Enhance Memory***.
- For hypertension, add ***Gastrodia Complex***.
- For thirst and dryness due to Lung and Stomach yin deficiencies, add ***Nourish (Fluids)***.

ACUPUNCTURE TREATMENT

Traditional Points:

- *Taixi* (KI 3), *Taichong* (LR 3)
- *Shenmen* (HT 7), *Sanyinjiao* (SP 6), *Xinshu* (BL 15), *Ganshu* (BL 18), *Pishu* (BL 20), *Feishu* (BL 13), *Shenshu* (BL 23), *Taixi* (KI 3), *Yinlingquan* (SP 9)

Classic Master Tung's Points:

- **Menopause (general):** *Tianhuang* (T 77.17), *Dihuang* (T 77.19), *Renhuang* (T 77.21), *Tianhuang* (T 88.13), *Minghuang* (T 88.12), *Qihuang* (T 88.14), *Shuijin* (T 1010.20), *Zhenjing* (T 1010.08), *Xinling* (T 33.17)*, *Simashang* (T 88.18), *Simazhong* (T 88.17), *Simaxia* (T 88.19)
- **Hot flashes:** *Tianhuang* (T 77.17), *Dihuang* (T 77.19), *Renhuang* (T 77.21), *Tianhuang* (T 88.13), *Minghuang* (T 88.12), *Qihuang* (T 88.14), *Shuijin* (T 1010.20), *Zhenjing* (T 1010.08), *Xinling* (T 33.17)*, *Simashang* (T 88.18), *Simazhong* (T 88.17), *Simaxia* (T 88.19)
- **Mood swings:** *Tianhuang* (T 77.17), *Dihuang* (T 77.19), *Renhuang* (T 77.21), *Tianhuang* (T 88.13), *Minghuang* (T 88.12), *Qihuang* (T 88.14), *Shuijin* (T 1010.20), *Zhenjing* (T 1010.08), *Xinling* (T 33.17)*, *Simashang* (T 88.18), *Simazhong* (T 88.17), *Simaxia* (T 88.19), *Fuke* (T 11.24), *Wanshunyi* (T 22.08), *Wanshuner* (T 22.09), *Shuixiang* (T 66.14)
- **Irregular menstruation:** *Fuke* (T 11.24), *Tianhuang* (T 77.17), *Dihuang* (T 77.19), *Renhuang* (T 77.21), *Tianhuang* (T 88.13), *Minghuang* (T 88.12), *Qihuang* (T 88.14), *Shuijin* (T 1010.20), *Zhenjing* (T 1010.08), *Xinling* (T 33.17)*, *Simashang* (T 88.18), *Simazhong* (T 88.17), *Simaxia* (T 88.19), *Wanshunyi* (T 22.08), *Wanshuner* (T 22.09)
- **Osteoporosis:** *Tianhuang* (T 77.17), *Dihuang* (T 77.19), *Renhuang* (T 77.21), *Tianhuang* (T 88.13), *Minghuang* (T 88.12), *Qihuang* (T 88.14), *Fuke* (T 11.24), *Zhengji* (T 44.24)*

Master Tung's Points by Dr. Chuan-Min Wang:

- **Menopause:** *Tianhuang* (T 77.17), *Dihuang* (T 77.19), *Renhuang* (T 77.21), *Minghuang* (T 88.12)

Balance Method by Dr. Richard Tan:

- Left side: *Waiguan* (TH 5), *Hegu* (LI 4), *Yangxi* (LI 5), *Linggu* (T 22.05), *Sanyinjiao* (SP 6), *Yinlingquan* (SP 9), *Fuliu* (KI 7), *Rangu* (KI 2), *Dazhong* (KI 4), *Fuliu* (KI 7)
- Right side: *Tongli* (HT 5), *Daling* (PC 7), *Tianquan* (PC 2), *Zulinqi* (GB 41), *ah shi* points from *Zusanli* (ST 36) to *Fenglong* (ST 40)
- **Hot flashes**
  - Left side: *Houxi* (SI 3), *Xiaohai* (SI 8), *Taichong* (LR 3), *Ququan* (LR 8)
  - Right side: *Shaohai* (HT 3), *Shenmen* (HT 7), *Yanglingquan* (GB 34), *Zulinqi* (GB 41)
- Left and right sides can be alternated from treatment to treatment.

Ear Acupuncture:

- Uterus, Ovary, Endocrine, Sympathetic, Subcortex
  - For emotional disorders, add *Shenmen* and Heart.
  - For palpitations and irregular heartbeat, add Heart and Small Intestine.
  - For flushed cheeks, excess perspiration, add Cheeks and Lung.

Auricular Medicine by Dr. Li-Chun Huang:

- **Menopause:** Uterus, Endocrine, Ovary, Gonadotropin, Pituitary, Sympathetic, Anxious, Kidney, Liver, Heart
- **Relieving excessive sweating:** Sympathetic, Thalamus, Heart, Lung, Spleen, Nervous Subcortex, corresponding sweating areas

NUTRITION

- Encourage a diet with a high content of raw foods, fruits and vegetables to stabilize blood sugar. Wild yam is very helpful to nourish yin and reduce menopause symptoms. Increase intake

Balance (Heat)™

of nourishing roots such as radishes, potatoes, carrots, melons, cucumbers, beets, turnips, malanga, celeriac, taro, and rutabaga.

- Increase the intake of soy products such as tofu, soymilk and soy nuts. Soy products regulate the estrogen levels and are beneficial for menopause.
- Increase intake of cooling foods: tofu, tomato, celery, asparagus, bamboo, seaweed, kelp, bitter melon, cucumber, gourd, luffa, winter melon, oranges, grapefruit, pear, banana, papaya, watermelon, white radish, mustard leaf, potherb mustard, Chinese kale, napa cabbage, and bamboo sprout.
- Take *Gou Qi Zi* (Fructus Lycii) on a daily basis (mix with cereal or trail mix) to nourish Kidney yin.
- *Gan Mai Da Zao Tang* (Licorice, Wheat, and Jujube Decoction) can be used as tea on a daily basis.
- Avoid spicy/pungent/aromatic fruits and vegetables that are warm and may aggravate the condition, such as mango, durian, lychee, longan fruit, pepper, garlic, onions, basil, rosemary, cumin, fennel, anise, leeks, chives, scallions, thyme, saffron, wormwood, mustard, chili pepper, and wasabi.
- Avoid food/drinks with artificial coloring.
- Discourage dairy products and red meats, as they promote hot flashes.

The Tao of Nutrition by Dr. Maoshing Ni and Cathy McNease:

- **Menopause**
  - Eat black beans, sesame seeds, soybeans, walnuts, goji berries, mulberries, yams, licorice, lotus seeds, and chrysanthemum flowers.

LIFESTYLE INSTRUCTIONS

- Avoid stress, tension, and anxiety as much as possible.
- Avoid cigarette smoking or exposure to second-hand smoke, as they may dry yin and body fluids.
- Natural progesterone cream can be applied every 15 minutes to help relieve hot flashes.
- Eliminate things that are potentially toxic (e.g., alcohol, coffee, cigarettes, refined sugars, saturated fats, and chemical-based household cleaners and personal hygiene products).

CASE STUDIES

- J.J., a 49-year-old female, presented with constipation and abdominal bloating. The patient had a history of having a bowel movement every other day to every three days since childhood. She was experiencing cold sensation and had been taking birth control pills for heavy bleeding. As a result of taking birth control pills, she would experience night sweats when she was taking the sugar pills or during her menses. Her blood pressure was 118/72 mmHg and her heart rate was 75 beats per minute. The practitioner diagnosed this condition as yin deficiency and stagnation; the western diagnosis was chronic constipation. ***Gentle Lax (Deficient)*** was prescribed at three capsules three times daily with warm water in combination with ***Balance (Heat)*** three to five capsules at night when she is not taking birth control pills. The patient was amazed with the results; she reported having regular daily bowl movements and relief of her bloating. In addition, she was no longer experiencing night sweats when she was on the sugar pill days of her birth control pills. Along with taking herbs the patient also received acupuncture twice weekly. Submitted by L.W., Arroyo Grande, California.
- J.M., a 54-year-old female, presented with hot flashes, which were especially bad at night, causing her to wake up constantly throughout the night. Pulse was deep and thin, and her tongue was dusky pink with a center crack. The practitioner diagnosed this condition as Kidney yin deficiency; her western diagnosis was menopause. Upon diagnosis, the patient was prescribed ***Nourish*** and ***Balance (Heat)*** up to five capsules three times a day. After taking the herbs for four weeks, the duration of the hot flashes was shorter and she was sleeping through the night. Submitted by T.W., Perrysburg, Ohio.
- S.S., a 55-year-old female, presented with menopause symptoms and experiencing hot flashes ten times a day. Additional symptoms included irritability and difficulty staying asleep. The patient also relied heavily on sleeping aids which resulted in grogginess. Furthermore, there was arthritis in her thumbs, a constant need to clear her throat, and some acid reflux. Her blood pressure was 120/80 mmHg and her heart rate was 78 beats per minute. The practitioner diagnosed the condition as yin deficiency and Liver qi stagnation. ***Balance (Heat)*** was prescribed at three capsules three times daily, combined with ***Calm***, three capsules three times daily. The patient had very positive results. She reported feeling less irritable and was no longer experiencing hot flashes. Her sleep had also improved where she only needed to take sleeping aids occasionally. Lastly, her acid reflux had improved; however, it was still present when taking certain foods and wine. Submitted by L.W., Arroyo Grande, California.
- J.N., a 56-year-old female, presented with menopause symptoms, including hot flashes, night sweats, inability to stay asleep, and moodiness. The practitioner diagnosed this condition as Kidney yin deficiency. For treatment, the patient was prescribed ***Balance (Heat)***. As a result, her hot flashes and night sweats were reduced. Her sleep had improved slowly as well as her moodiness. Patient felt she had to continue taking the herbs since the symptoms returned once she stopped taking them. Submitted by S.L., Yuma, Arizona.
- F.R., a 56-year-old female, presented with multiple symptoms consisting of night sweats, irritability, and difficulty staying asleep. The practitioner diagnosed this condition as Liver yin deficiency. Upon diagnosis the patient was directed to take ***Balance (Heat)*** four capsules three times a day. As a result of taking the herbs for three months, she reported not having any more night sweats and only occasional sleeplessness and irritability. Submitted by S.L., Yuma, Arizona.

Balance (Heat)™

- C.R., a 56-year-old female, presented with hot flashes. Additional symptoms included difficulty sleeping, dry mouth, anxiety, and depression. It was noted that her palpitations and sweating were constant. The practitioner diagnosed this condition as Kidney yin-deficient heat. ***Nourish (Fluids)***, ***Kidney Tonic (Yin)***, and ***Balance (Heat)*** were prescribed. As a result of taking the ***Kidney Tonic (Yin)*** with ***Balance (Heat)***, she noticed less heat sensation, decrease in both anxiety and sleep difficulty, but she was still sweating slightly. Afterwards, taking ***Kidney Tonic (Yin)*** with ***Nourish (Fluids)***, the patient was no longer experiencing dry mouth and thirst. Submitted by J.C., Rosemead, California.
- M.K., a 50-year-old female, presented with a hot and flushed face, and very mild sweat one week before her menstrual cycle. Due to the sweating, she was unable to wear nylon or silk clothes. Blood pressure was 120/80 mmHg and her heart rate was 82 beats per minute. The pulse was thready and weak in the Kidney yin positions. The TCM diagnosis was Kidney yin deficiency with deficiency heat. ***Balance (Heat)*** was prescribed at 8 capsules twice daily. Symptoms resolved quickly after taking the herbs. She was then instructed to reduce the dosage to 4 capsules twice daily. Dietary changes were also made. Patient felt extremely grateful to the practitioner for prescribing the formula. Submitted by M.H., West Palm Beach, Florida.
- A 62-year-old saleslady initially presented with neck pain resulting from a car accident. She also had symptoms of night sweats and dry skin. The patient complained of feeling frustrated and had been gaining weight. Besides having smoked 1½ packs of cigarettes a day her whole life, the patient had been diagnosed with hypothyroid and was on 100 mcg of levothyroxine (Synthroid) per day. Her tongue was dusky red with a thick coat. Her pulse was choppy and rapid. The TCM diagnosis included Liver qi stagnation, Kidney yin and yang deficiency, and qi and blood stagnation. After 2 weeks of taking ***Balance (Heat)***, the patient commented, "I feel much better overall and I definitely sleep better and am less irritable." Submitted by F.A., Calabasas, California.
- A 44-year-old female nurse presented with irritability and approximately 60 hot flashes per day. Her tongue body was red with no coating and the pulse was slippery and rapid. The practitioner diagnosed this as Kidney and Liver yin deficiency. Because of the severity of her condition, she was given a higher dose of a modified ***Balance (Heat)*** formula. The formula contained ***Balance (Heat)*** along with 15 grams of *Gui Ban* (Plastrum Testudinis) and 9 grams of *Qing Hao* (Herba Artemisiae Annuae). The prescribed dosage was 6 capsules at three times a day. After taking ***Balance (Heat)***, the frequency of hot flashes reduced dramatically, from 60 per day to two to three per week! Submitted by K.S., Encinitas, California.
- A 49-year-old female social worker presented with stress, anxiety, dizziness, and irregular menses. The patient reported occasional irritability, hot flashes, night sweats, and painful menses. Dry eyes and muscle cramps were also present. The patient was diagnosed with Kidney and Liver yin deficiency with Liver qi stagnation. With ***Balance (Heat)*** and ***Calm (ES)***, the patient experienced a reduction of hot flashes and had less irritability, stress, anxiety, and dizziness. She also stated that she slept much better and that her menses were not as painful. The practitioner concluded that the combination of ***Balance (Heat)*** and ***Calm (ES)*** was quite effective in treating the patient's condition. Submitted by D.W., Raton, New Mexico.
- M.M., a 41-year-old female, presented with "adrenaline-rush" sensations, characterized by heat flushes to her face, associated with mood swings and anxiety. Her tongue was red and purple, and her face was red. The Western diagnosis was stress-related anxiety attack; the TCM diagnosis was Liver stagnation and yin deficiency. After beginning herbal therapy with ***Calm***, two capsules three times daily, and ***Balance (Heat)***, two capsules three times daily, the patient stated that her affect and personality became calmer. Furthermore, she reported "feeling good," with increased energy levels and sound sleep. Submitted by C.L., Chino Hills, California.
- J.D., a 48-year-old post-menopausal female, complained of severe hot flashes. She stated that even during cooler temperatures at night, she needed to cool down by constantly using a hand-held battery-operated fan directed at her face. However, she did not complain of insomnia, mood swings, or palpitations. She confessed that, as a nurse, she was leery of trying herbal treatment. However, she had already tried hormone replacement therapy and OTC supplements with no success, and finally decided to try herbs. ***Balance (Heat)*** was prescribed, at three capsules three times daily. During a follow-up visit two weeks later, the patient stated that the hot flashes were completely resolved. Submitted by C.L., Chino Hills, California.
- A 51-year-old female nuclear medicine technician presented with hot flashes, night sweats, and insomnia. The practitioner diagnosed her with Kidney yin and Heart yin deficiency with deficiency heat signs. Before the patient's treatment, she had irregular periods for 1½ years. During treatment, no periods occurred for 6 months. The patient had tried *Liu Wei Di Huang Wan* (Rehmannia Six Formula) with minimal results. Next, she tried *Zhi Bai Di Huang Wan* (Anemarrhena Phellodendron and Rehmannia Formula) and the hot flashes were reduced from 10-12 episodes to 4 episodes per day. The practitioner then switched the patient to ***Balance (Heat)*** at 6 capsules twice a day. Within 1 week the hot flashes and night sweats were gone. *Tian Wang Bu Xin Dan* (Emperor of Heaven's Special Pill to Tonify the Heart) was also supplemented, which in turn helped her sleep better. ***Balance (Heat)*** proved to be very effective for clearing heat. Submitted by R.M., San Rafael, California.
- A 50-year-old female interior designer presented with peri-menopausal symptoms of hot flashes, night sweats, insomnia, and emotional fragility. The patient still had residual hot flashes despite correct dosing with hormone replacement therapy. With this clinical picture, the practitioner diagnosed this case as yin

Balance (Heat)™

deficiency with deficiency heat. ***Balance (Heat)*** was prescribed at 3 capsules in the afternoon and 3 capsules before bedtime. Abatement of all residual heat symptoms occurred within one day. The practitioner found that ***Balance (Heat)*** was an excellent addition to the hormone replacement therapy. Submitted by C.W., San Diego, California.

PHARMACOLOGICAL AND CLINICAL RESEARCH

Balance (Heat) is formulated specifically for female imbalances and disorders such as menopausal syndrome with hot flashes, insomnia, irritability, emotional disturbances, and osteoporosis.

Balance (Heat) contains *Gan Cao* (Radix et Rhizoma Glycyrrhizae), *Xiao Mai* (Fructus Tritici) and *Da Zao* (Fructus Jujubae) as three main ingredients in this formula. These three herbs have been used with excellent results to treat a wide variety of conditions, including but not limited to menopause, insomnia, emotional instability, and psychological disorders. According to a clinical study, 133 patients in menopause were treated with these three herbs with good success. The effectiveness rate was 92.7% for insomnia, 84.1% for perspiration, 94.4% for tidal fever, 86.85% for headache, 67.8% for irritability and restlessness, and 70.2% for abdominal fullness.[1] According to another clinical study, use of these herbs in 54 menopause patients was associated with complete relief in 35 cases, improvement in 14 cases, and no effect in 5 cases.[2] Furthermore, 22 of 30 women (73.3%) with menopause experienced significant relief when treated with a formula that contains these three herbs.[3] Other conditions effectively treated by these three herbs include insomnia (74.2% rate of effectiveness),[4] neurasthenia (92% rate of effectiveness,[5] hysteria (88.8% rate of effectiveness),[6] and *zang zao* (restless organ syndrome) (92.1% rate of effectiveness).[7]

Balance (Heat) incorporates other herbs to alleviate other conditions associated with menopause. *Da Zao* (Fructus Jujubae) and *Chai Hu* (Radix Bupleuri) both have sedative effects, and are helpful to reduce spontaneous motor activities,[8] prolong sleeping time and relieve insomnia.[9] *Qing Hao* (Herba Artemisiae Annuae) and *Di Gu Pi* (Cortex Lycii) help to regulate body temperature and relieve warm body sensations and fever.[10,11] Lastly, *Zhi Mu* (Rhizoma Anemarrhenae) has showed significant antidepressant activity.[12] The proposed mechanism of the antidepressant activity involves a marked increase of noradrenaline and serotonin levels in both the hypothalamus and the hippocampus.[13]

Finally, since the hormonal changes during menopause increases risks of osteoporosis, herbs are used in ***Balance (Heat)*** to counter those risks. *Di Huang* (Radix Rehmanniae), *Zhi Mu* (Rhizoma Anemarrhenae) and *Gan Cao* (Radix et Rhizoma Glycyrrhizae) are three herbs that have beneficial effects to regulate the endocrine system to balance the hormones during the menopause transition.[14,15] Furthermore, *Di Huang* (Radix Rehmanniae) has an antiosteoporotic effect, as it potently stimulates osteoblast proliferation to increase bone mass density.[16] *Zhi Mu* (Rhizoma Anemarrhenae) has an osteoprotective effect, as the herb suppresses the descent of bone mineral density, and corrects the decreased concentration of calcium and E(2) in serum without altering the number of osteoclasts. The researchers concluded that *Zhi Mu* (Rhizoma Anemarrhenae) is effective to prevent bone loss through the promotion of bone formation without the inhibition of bone resorption.[17]

In summary, ***Balance (Heat)*** is an excellent formula to soothe the transition of menopause and associated conditions, such as hot flashes, irritability, insomnia, emotional disturbances, and osteoporosis.

COMPARATIVE ANALYSIS

As life expectancy continues to increase, women are expected to spend more and more of their life in post-menopausal years. Therefore, it is becoming increasingly important to ensure a smooth transition during the menopausal years.

Hormone replacement therapy (HRT) was long considered the standard treatment for menopause and its related conditions. However, there is no longer a consensus as to when and how to use these drugs. While these drugs may alleviate hot flashes, they significantly increase the risk of breast cancer, ovarian cancer, uterine cancer, and have a number of significant side effects. For most physicians and patients, the risks are simply far greater than the potential benefits. The bottom line is – synthetic hormones can never replace endogenous hormones. Therefore, no matter how or when they are prescribed, the potential for adverse reactions is always present.

TCM offers a gentle yet effective way to address menopause and its related conditions. Chinese herbs have demonstrated, via numerous *in vivo* and *in vitro* studies, marked effects to alleviate hot flashes, vasomotor instability, loss of bone mass, and other conditions associated with menopause. Most importantly, they are much gentler and safer on the body.

Menopause is simply a transition in the journey of life. It is a not a disease, and therefore, should not be treated with synthetic drugs that pose significantly higher risks of cancer and other side effects. Herbs should be considered the primary option, and not the secondary alternative, as they are safe and natural, and more than sufficient to address almost all cases of menopause.

References

1. *Fu Jian Zhong Yi Yao* (Fujian Chinese Medicine and Herbology) 1985;4:34.
2. *Xin Zhong Yi* (New Chinese Medicine) 1988;9:51.
3. *Fu Jian Zhong Yi Yao* (Fujian Chinese Medicine and Herbology) 1960;10:17.
4. *Zhe Jiang Zhong Yi Za Zhi* (Zhejiang Journal of Chinese Medicine) 1982;9:412.
5. *Jiang Su Yi Yao* (Jiangsu Journal of Medicine and Herbology) 1976;1:47.
6. *Jiang Su Yi Yao* (Jiangsu Journal of Medicine and Herbology) 1978;1:3.
7. *Nan Jing Zhong Yi Yao Da Xue Xue Bao* (Journal of Nanjing University of Traditional Chinese Medicine and Medicinals) 1996;6:22.
8. *Guo Wai Yi Xue Zhong Yi Zhong Yao Fen Ce* (Monograph of Chinese Herbology from Foreign Medicine), 1985; 7(4):48.
9. *Zhong Yao Yao Li Yu Ying Yong* (Pharmacology and Applications of Chinese Herbs), 1983; 888.

FORMULAS

Balance (Heat)™

10. *Zhong Yao Yao Li Yu Ying Yong* (Pharmacology and Applications of Chinese Herbs), 1983:59.
11. *Yi Xue Zhong Yang Za Zhi* (Central Journal of Medicine), 1967; 223:664.
12. Ren LX, Luo YF, Li X, Wu YL. Antidepressant activity of sarsasapogenin from Anemarrhena asphodeloides Bunge (Liliaceae). School of Pharmacy, Shenyang Pharmaceutical University, Shenyang, China. Pharmazie. 2007 Jan;62(1):78-9.
13. Ren LX, Luo YF, Li X, Zuo DY, Wu YL. Antidepressant-like effects of sarsasapogenin from Anemarrhena asphodeloides BUNGE (Liliaceae). School of Pharmacy, Shenyang Pharmaceutical University, China. Biol Pharm Bull. 2006 Nov;29(11):2304-6.
14. *Zhong Yao Xue* (Chinese Herbology), 1998; 156:158.
15. *Zhong Hua Yi Xue Za Zhi* (Chinese Journal of Medicine), 1975; 10:718.
16. Yin J, Tezuka Y, Kouda K, Tran QL, Miyahara T, Chen Y, Kadota S. Antiosteoporotic activity of the water extract of Dioscorea spongiosa. Biol Pharm Bull. 2004 Apr;27(4):583-6.
17. Nian H, et al. Protective effect of steroidal saponins from rhizome of Anemarrhena asphodeloides on ovariectomy-induced bone loss in rats. Department of Pharmacognosy, School of Pharmacy, Second Military Medical University, Shanghai 200433, China. Acta Pharmacol Sin. 2006 Jun;27(6):728-34.

Balance Spring™

CLINICAL APPLICATIONS

- **Atrophic vaginitis or vulvovaginitis** with vaginal dryness, itching, and burning sensations
- **Vaginal dryness and atrophy** due to hormonal irregularity, estrogen deficiency, or menopause
- Painful intercourse due to vaginal dryness and atrophy, or insufficient vaginal lubrication

WESTERN THERAPEUTIC ACTIONS

- Regulates and restores hormone balance
- Promotes health of soft tissues
- Phytoestrogen activity to treat vaginal dryness
- Phytoestrogen activity to treat irregular menstruation, menstrual pain, amenorrhea, and osteoporosis

CHINESE THERAPEUTIC ACTIONS

- Nourishes the blood to soften the Liver
- Strengthens the Spleen
- Tonifies Kidney yin and *jing* (essence)
- Moves blood to the lower *jiao*

DOSAGE

Take 3 to 4 capsules three times daily. Dosage can be increased up to 6 to 8 capsules three times daily. Most women see improvement within one to two months. Dosage then can be reduced to 1 to 2 capsules once or twice a day for maintenance.

INGREDIENTS

Bai Shao (Radix Paeoniae Alba)
Bai Zhu (Rhizoma Atractylodis Macrocephalae)
Chuan Xiong (Rhizoma Chuanxiong)
Dang Gui (Radix Angelicae Sinensis)
Fu Ling (Poria)
Shan Yao (Rhizoma Dioscoreae)
Wang Bu Liu Xing (Semen Vaccariae)
Ze Xie (Rhizoma Alismatis)

BACKGROUND

Vaginal dryness and atrophy is a common condition that affects approximately 40% of perimenopausal women and 55% of postmenopausal women. While most menopause symptoms such as hot flashes and night sweats last only for a few years, symptoms of vaginal dryness and atrophy often persist for decades after menopause. As the production of estrogen decreases with menopause, local genital tissues become dry and thin, which in turn leads to vaginal atrophy or atrophic vaginitis (inflammation of the mucosa). Vaginal dryness and atrophy is usually associated with symptoms of itching, discomfort, decreased elasticity of local tissues, painful intercourse, and increased risk of injury and infection with intercourse. In addition, vaginal dryness and atrophy will also affect urinary functions, causing symptoms such as irritation, dyspareunia, and dysuria. Lastly, vaginal dryness and atrophy presents physical as well as emotional challenges, as pain, injuries, and infections associated with intercourse discourage sexual activities and may cause a strain on personal relationships. In summary, this condition greatly affects the quality of life for women, and is a medical condition that requires effective treatment.

FORMULA EXPLANATION

In traditional Chinese medicine (TCM), menstruation begins after the 2nd cycle of a woman's life (14 years of age) and ends after the 7th cycle (49 years of age), as each cycle is seven years. This occurs as *Tian Kui* (天癸), the substance that governs growth, maturation, and reproduction, gradually becomes depleted until menstruation stops and the uterus is no longer nourished by the blood. Other substances in the body also decline during this time, particularly the Kidney yin, yang, and *jing* (essence). Related symptoms may include hot flashes, irritability, night sweats, insomnia, vaginal thinning, and dryness.

Balance Spring is an anti-aging formula designed to increase vaginal fluids by tonifying Kidney yin and *jing* (essence). By restoring the body's own ability to provide lubrication naturally, ***Balance Spring*** offers a safe and effective solution to treat vaginal dryness and atrophy on a long-term basis.

Dang Gui (Radix Angelicae Sinensis) tonifies the blood and activates blood circulation to the reproductive organs. This is the chief herb for any gynecological disorder and one of the best herbs to balance women's hormones. *Bai Shao* (Radix Paeoniae Alba) nourishes the blood and consolidates yin. *Shan Yao* (Rhizoma Dioscoreae) tonifies Kidney yin. *Bai Zhu* (Rhizoma Atractylodis Macrocephalae) and *Fu Ling* (Poria) strengthen the Spleen so the body can extract, absorb, and utilize nutrients from the foods. *Fu Ling* (Poria) and *Ze Xie* (Rhizoma Alismatis) strengthen the Spleen and dispel water retention. Also, by tonifying the Spleen, it can in turn help produce more blood. *Chuan Xiong* (Rhizoma Chuanxiong) activates and regulates blood circulation. It also helps *Dang Gui* (Radix Angelicae Sinensis) regulate hormones. *Wang Bu Liu Xing* (Semen Vaccariae) activates blood circulation, opens channels, and has a uterine stimulant effect. Both of these herbs also serve as channel-guiding herbs to the Liver and the lower abdomen where more blood flow means better delivery of nutrients and tonics to the affected area.

In summary, ***Balance Spring*** effectively treats vaginal dryness, atrophy, and many other menopausal symptoms by tonifying Kidney yin, yang, and *jing* (essence), nourishing blood, and improving blood circulation.

CAUTIONS & CONTRAINDICATIONS

- Because this formula aims to regulate women's own ability to produce estrogen, menstruation may briefly return for some individuals in premenopausal or perimenopausal states. They

Balance Spring™

should not be alarmed as this is part of the antiaging effect of this formula. However, if the patient notices abnormal or irregular bleeding, discontinue use and refer to a medical doctor for further testing.

- This formula is not recommended for lack of vaginal secretion due to radiation therapy, chemotherapy, and immunologic disorders.
- This herbal formula contains herbs that invigorate blood circulation, such as *Dang Gui* (Radix Angelicae Sinensis). Therefore, patients who are on anticoagulant or antiplatelet therapies, such as Coumadin (warfarin), should use this formula with caution, or not at all, as there may be a higher risk of bleeding and bruising.[1,2,3]
- The safety status of using *Dang Gui* (Radix Angelicae Sinensis) in individuals with hormone-dependent cancer is unclear.[4,5,6] According to one reference, use of *Dang Gui* (Radix Angelicae Sinensis) is not associated with thickening of the endometrium or vaginal cell maturation, both of which would indicate an estrogenic effect. Furthermore, there is no confirmation of the presence of a phytoestrogen component or effect on hormone-dependent cancer when ferulic acid is evaluated as the main component of *Dang Gui* (Radix Angelicae Sinensis).[7] According to another reference, the water extract of *Dang Gui* (Radix Angelicae Sinensis) has a weak estrogen-agonistic activity to stimulate the growth of breast cancer cells (MCF-7).[8] In summary, due to conflicting and insufficient data, use of *Dang Gui* (Radix Angelicae Sinensis) in patients with hormone-dependent cancer warrants caution pending further study.

CLINICAL NOTES

- In contrast with hormone replacement therapy, use of yam, such as *Shan Yao* (Rhizoma Dioscoreae) in this formula, is not only effective to treat menopause symptoms, but also safe in regards to risks of cancer and cardiovascular diseases. In one study, the extract of yam has been shown to act as a weak phytoestrogen and to protect against proliferation in human breast cancer (MCF-7) cells.[9] In another study, use of yam was found to reduce the risk of breast cancer and cardiovascular diseases in postmenopausal women.[10]
- Women with infection or inflammation of the urogenital regions should be properly treated first, prior to taking this formula.
- Normal vaginal secretion may briefly return after taking the herbs, and if so, patients are encouraged to participate in normal sexual activity as it invigorates and stimulates the Kidney *jing* (essence), which in turn has a positive effect on all the systems in the body.

Pulse Diagnosis by Dr. Jimmy Wei-Yen Chang:

- Small pulse, a thin and weak pulse, on the left *chi*

SUPPLEMENTARY FORMULAS

- With hot flashes and night sweats, add ***Balance (Heat)*** and/or ***Nourish***.
- With vaginal or urinary tract infection and inflammation, add ***V-Support***.
- With Kidney yin deficiency, add ***Nourish*** or ***Kidney Tonic (Yin)***.
- With Kidney yang deficiency or low libido, add ***Vitality*** or ***Kidney Tonic (Yang)***.
- With irritability and emotional swings, add **Calm**.
- With osteoporosis, add ***Osteo 8***.
- With dry, brittle hair, add ***Polygonum 14***.
- With insomnia, add ***Schisandra ZZZ***.
- With forgetfulness, add ***Enhance Memory***.

ACUPUNCTURE TREATMENT

Traditional Points:

- *Ququan* (LR 8), *Taixi* (KI 3), *Sanyinjiao* (SP 6)
- *Xingjian* (LR 2), *Fuliu* (KI 7), *Chize* (LU 5), *Lianquan* (CV 23), *Shenshu* (BL 23)

Classic Master Tung's Points:

- **General:** *Tianhuang* (T 77.17), *Dihuang* (T 77.19), *Renhuang* (T 77.21), *Tianhuang* (T 88.13), *Minghuang* (T 88.12), *Qihuang* (T 88.14), *Shuijin* (T 1010.20), *Zhenjing* (T 1010.08), *Xinling* (T 33.17)*, *Simashang* (T 88.18), *Simazhong* (T 88.17), *Simaxia* (T 88.19)
- **Vaginitis:** *Fuke* (T 11.24), *Huanchao* (T 11.06), *Jiemeiyi* (T 88.04), *Jiemeier* (T 88.05), *Jiemeisan* (T 88.06), *Libai* (T 44.12), *Yunbai* (T 44.11), *Jianzhong* (T 44.06), *Haibao* (T 66.01), *Renzong* (T 44.08), *Dizong* (T 44.09), *Tianzong* (T 44.10). Bleed tender points on the sacral region with cupping. Bleed before needling for best result.
- **Painful intercourse:** *Fuke* (T 11.24), *Tianhuang* (T 77.17), *Dihuang* (T 77.19), *Renhuang* (T 77.21), *Tianhuang* (T 88.13), *Minghuang* (T 88.12), *Qihuang* (T 88.14)

Master Tung's Points by Dr. Chuan-Min Wang:

- **Vaginal dryness:** *Tianzong* (T 44.10), *Yunbai* (T 44.11)

Balance Method by Dr. Richard Tan:

- Left side: *Zusanli* (ST 36), *Lieque* (LU 7)
- Right side: *Hegu* (LI 4), *Yinlingquan* (SP 9), *Lougu* (SP 7) or *ah shi* points nearby, *Sanyinjiao* (SP 6)
- Left and right sides can be alternated from treatment to treatment.

Ear Acupuncture:

- Uterus, Ovary, Endocrine, *Shenmen*, Subcortex, Sympathetic

Auricular Medicine by Dr. Li-Chun Huang:

- Uterus, Endocrine, Ovary, Pituitary, Sympathetic, Anxious, Gonadotropin
- Supplementary points: Kidney, Liver, Heart

Balance Spring™

NUTRITION

- Increase the intake of soy and red clover, which have estrogen-like properties (phytoestrogens). They are helpful for certain menopausal symptoms, including vaginal atrophy.
- Vitamin D helps with many conditions associated with menopause, including vaginal dryness and osteoporosis. Foods rich in vitamin D include fortified milk, breakfast cereals, and other fortified foods and supplements.
- Increase intake of nourishing, cooling foods, such as Mexican yams, wild yams, radishes, potatoes, carrots, melons, cucumbers, beets, turnips, malanga, celeriac, taro, and rutabaga.
- Avoid spicy foods, alcohol, and processed and deep-fried foods.
- Avoid spicy, pungent, and aromatic vegetables, such as pepper, garlic, onions, basil, rosemary, cumin, fennel, anise, leeks, chives, scallions, thyme, saffron, wormwood, mustard, chili pepper, and wasabi.
- Avoid alcohol, coffee, and any drinks that have a stimulant effect.

The Tao of Nutrition by Dr. Maoshing Ni and Cathy McNease:

- Increase the intake of black beans, sesame seeds, soybeans, walnuts, goji berries, mulberries, yams, licorice, Chinese black dates, lotus seeds, chrysanthemum flowers.
- Cook black beans with rice into porridge. Eat twice daily.
- Roast sesame seeds and add to rice porridge for breakfast.
- Steam chicken with goji berries and yam.
- Take walnuts, lotus seeds, and sunflower seeds and make porridge with rice.
- Stew millet, mulberries, lamb, and goji berries.
- Make tea from chrysanthemum and cassia seeds and drink three times daily.
- Make tea from licorice, Chinese black dates, and wheat. This will help to alleviate extreme mood swings and depression.

LIFESTYLE INSTRUCTIONS

- Avoid stress or tension if possible.
- Avoid scented soaps, lotions, perfumes or douches in the genital area to prevent irritation or possible infection.
- Adequate sleep of seven to eight hours daily starting before 10:00 p.m. is recommended.
- Engage in at least 30 minutes of daily mild exercises like *tai chi chuan* [*tai ji quan*], yoga, walking, or stretching.
- Regular sexual activity enhances blood flow to the vagina, which helps keep vaginal tissues healthy and decrease problems with vaginal atrophy.

PHARMACOLOGICAL AND CLINICAL RESEARCH

Vaginal dryness and atrophy is a common condition that affects perimenopausal women and postmenopausal women. With decreased production of estrogen, vaginal and vulvar tissues become thin and dry, leading to vaginal atrophy or atrophic vaginitis (inflammation of the mucosa). Clinical manifestations include itching, discomfort, decreased elasticity of local tissues, painful intercourse, and increased risks of injury and infection with intercourse. As these symptoms can persist for decades after menopause, treatment is absolutely essential to maintain and improve quality of life. To effectively treat vaginal dryness and atrophy, ***Balance Spring*** uses herbs with marked effects to regulate and restore hormone balance and promote health of the soft tissues.

Wild yam (*Dioscorea* spp., including *Dioscorea alata, Dioscorea japonica, Dioscorea villosa and Dioscorea opposita*) has been used as a "natural alternative" to estrogen therapy throughout the world. Diosgenin, the main active compound in wild yam, has been shown to have estrogen-like activity, and can be used to treat vaginal dryness, night sweats, hot flashes, and other symptoms associated with menopause.[11] In one study, the ethyl acetate extracts of various types of yam were found to activate estrogen receptors alpha and beta to various extents, thus providing basic evidence for the beneficial effect of yam for menopausal women.[12] According to another study in 24 postmenopausal women, daily ingestion of yam as food for 30 days was associated with an estrogenic effect. There were significant increases in serum concentrations of estrone (26%), sex hormone binding globulin (SHBG) (9.5%), and near significant increase in estradiol (27%). However, no significant changes were observed in serum concentrations of dehydroepiandrosterone sulfate, androstenedione, testosterone, follicular stimulating hormone, and luteinizing hormone.[13]

In addition to yam, ***Balance Spring*** contains other herbs to regulate and restore hormone balance. The extracts of *Wang Bu Liu Xing* (Semen Vaccariae) have an estrogen-like activity,[14] and can be used to treat conditions such as irregular menstruation, menstrual pain, amenorrhea, and osteoporosis. In fact, the therapeutic benefits of *Wang Bu Liu Xing* (Semen Vaccariae) are comparable to 17beta-estradiol.[15] Specifically, segetalins G and H, cyclic peptides from *Wang Bu Liu Xing* (Semen Vaccariae), are compounds with estrogen-like activity.[15] In addition, administration of *Chuan Xiong* (Rhizoma Chuanxiong) is associated with progestogenic activity *in vivo*, and may have utility for progesterone-replacement therapy.[17] Lastly, according to a placebo-controlled experiment on 55 postmenopausal women who complained of hot flashes and refused hormonal therapy, use of a preparation with *Dang Gui* (Radix Angelicae Sinensis) showed decrease in number and intensity of hot flashes from baseline to completion of treatment (90-96% vs 15-25%, $p < 0.001$), when compared to placebo. In addition, there was also a marked alleviation of sleep disturbances and fatigue, and no apparent major adverse effects were noted. The researchers concluded that the herb treatment may be used as an important modality for menopausal women with contraindications for hormone replacement therapy.[18]

Balance Spring utilizes many herbs with marked influences over soft tissues. *Chuan Xiong* (Rhizoma Chuanxiong) has a

FORMULAS

significant effect to promote blood circulation throughout the body to facilitate general healing.[19,20] *Chuan Xiong* (Rhizoma Chuanxiong) also has marked influences to relax the smooth muscles.[21] In addition, *Dang Gui* (Radix Angelicae Sinensis) is an excellent herb to promote wound healing.[22] It has been shown to facilitate skin repair and regeneration by increasing type I collagen production in human dermal fibroblasts.[23] Lastly, in cases of injuries, use of *Chuan Xiong* (Rhizoma Chuanxiong) has been shown to suppress hypertrophic scarring.[24] Overall, these herbs all contribute to the health and healing of tissues throughout the body.

In summary, ***Balance Spring*** is a great formula to treat vaginal dryness and atrophy associated with perimenopausal and postmenopausal women. It contains herbs with marked effects to regulate and restore hormone balance and promote health of the soft tissues.

COMPARATIVE ANALYSIS

Vaginal dryness and atrophy is a painful condition that affects the physical and emotional health of women during perimenopausal and postmenopausal time periods. Unlike most other menopause symptoms, such as hot flashes and night sweats, which last only for a few months to years, vaginal dryness and atrophy generally persists for decades after menopause. Therefore, treatment is essential to improve quality of life.

In Western medicine, hormone replacement therapy (HRT) is long considered the standard treatment for menopause and its related conditions. However, there is no longer a consensus as to when and how to use these drugs. While these drugs may alleviate hot flashes and vaginal dryness, they significantly increase the risk of breast cancer, ovarian cancer, uterine cancer, stroke, heart attack, and have a number of significant side effects. For most physicians and patients, the risks are simply far greater than the potential benefits. The bottom line: synthetic hormones can never replace endogenous hormones. Therefore, no matter how or when they are prescribed, the potential for adverse reactions is always present.

Traditional Chinese medicine offers a gentle yet effective way to address menopause and its related conditions. Chinese herbs have demonstrated via numerous *in vivo* and *in vitro* studies to have marked effects to alleviate vaginal dryness and atrophy, hot flashes, vasomotor instability, loss of bone mass, and other conditions associated with menopause. Most importantly, they are much gentler and safer on the body.

Menopause is simply a transition in the journey of life. It is not a disease, and therefore, should not be treated with synthetic drugs that pose significant risks of cancer and other side effects. Herbs should be considered the primary option, and not the secondary alternative, as they are safe and natural, and more than sufficient to address almost all cases of menopause.

References

1. Chan K, Lo AC, Yeung JH, Woo KS. Journal of Pharmacy and Pharmacology 1995 May;47(5):402-6.
2. Pharmacotherapy 1999 July;19(7):870-876.
3. European Journal of Drug Metabolism and Pharmacokinetics 1995; 20(1):55-60.
4. Natural Standard (www.naturalstandard.com).
5. National Institutes of Health.
6. U.S National Library of Medicine.
7. American Herbal Pharmacopoeia. *Dang Gui* (Radix Angelicae Sinensis) monograph.
8. Lau CB, Ho TC, Chan TW, Kim SC. Use of dong quai (Angelica sinensis) to treat peri- or postmenopausal symptoms in women with breast cancer: is it appropriate? Menopause 2005 Nov-Dec;12(6):734-40.
9. Park MK, Kwon HY, Ahn WS, Bae S, Rhyu MR, Lee Y. Estrogen activities and the cellular effects of natural progesterone from wild yam extract in mcf-7 human breast cancer cells. Am J Chin Med. 2009;37(1):159-67.
10. Wu WH, Liu LY, Chung CJ, Jou HJ, Wang TA. Estrogenic effect of yam ingestion in healthy postmenopausal women. J Am Coll Nutr. 2005 Aug;24(4):235-43.
11. MedlinePlus. A service of the U.S. National Library of Medicine and National Institute of Health.
12. Cheng WY, Kuo YH, Huang CJ. Isolation and identification of novel estrogenic compounds in yam tuber (Dioscorea alata Cv. Tainung No. 2). J Agric Food Chem. 2007 Sep 5;55(18):7350-8.
13. Wu WH, Liu LY, Chung CJ, Jou HJ, Wang TA. Estrogenic effect of yam ingestion in healthy postmenopausal women. J Am Coll Nutr. 2005 Aug;24(4):235-43.
14. Itokawa H, Yun Y, Morita H, Takeya K, Yamada K. Estrogen-like activity of cyclic peptides from Vaccaria segetalis extracts. Department of Pharmacognosy, Tokyo University of Pharmacy and Life Science, Japan. Planta Med. 1995 Dec;61(6):561-2.
15. Shih CC, Lin CH, Lin WL. Ameliorative effects of Vaccaria segetalis extract on osteopenia in ovariectomized rats. Institute of Pharmaceutical Science and Technology, College of Health Science, Central Taiwan University of Science and Technology, 11, Po-Tze Lane, Takun, Taichung, Taiwan, ROC. J Nat Med. 2009 Oct;63(4):386-92.
16. Morita H, Yun YS, Takeya K, Itokawa H. Conformational preference for segetalins G and H, cyclic peptides with estrogen-like activity from seeds of Vaccaria segetalis. Department of Pharmacognosy, School of Pharmacy, Tokyo University of Pharmacy and Life Science, Japan. Bioorg Med Chem. 1997 Nov;5(11):2063-7.
17. Lim LS, Shen P, Gong YH, Lee LS, Yong EL. Dynamics of progestogenic activity in serum following administration of Ligusticum chuanxiong. Life Sci. 2006 Aug 22;79(13):1274-80.
18. Kupfersztain C, Rotem C, Fagot R, Kaplan B. The immediate effect of natural plant extract, Angelica sinensis and Matricaria chamomilla (Climex) for the treatment of hot flushes during menopause. A preliminary report. Clin Exp Obstet Gynecol. 2003;30(4):203-6.
19. *Zhong Yao Xue* (Chinese Herbology), 1989; 535:539.
20. Tian JW, Fu FH, Jiang WL, Wang CY, Sun F, Zhang TP. Protective effect of ligusticum chuanxiong phthalides on focai cerebral ischemia in rats and its related mechanism of action. Zhongguo Zhong Yao Za Zhi. 2005 Mar;30(6):466-8.
21. *Hua Xue Xue Bao* (Journal of Chemistry), 1957; 23:246.
22. Hsiao CY, Hung CY, Tsai TH, Chak KF. A Study of the Wound Healing Mechanism of a Traditional Chinese Medicine, Angelica sinensis, Using a Proteomic Approach. Evid Based Complement Alternat Med. 2012;2012:467531.
23. Zhao H, et al. Angelica sinensis isolate SBD.4: composition, gene expression profiling, mechanism of action and effect on wounds, in rats and humans. Eur J Dermatol. 2012 Jan-Feb;22(1):58-67.
24. Wu JG, Wei YJ, Ran X, Zhang H, Nian H, Qin LP. Inhibitory effects of essential oil from rhizomes of Ligusticum chuanxiong on hypertrophic scarring in the rabbit ear model. Pharm Biol. 2011 Jul;49(7):764-9.

Blossom ™ Introduction

INTRODUCTION

Infertility is defined as failure to become pregnant after one or more years of regular sexual activity conducted during the time of ovulation. Infertility afflicts over 6 million American couples, of which approximately 40% is attributed to male and 60% to female partners.

Many reasons contribute to female infertility, including but not limited to ovulatory failure, faulty or blocked fallopian tubes, endometriosis, uterine fibroids, polyps, pelvic adhesions, pelvic inflammatory diseases, chlamydia, hormonal imbalance, age, and psychological issues. Sometimes infertility is simply unexplained. There is often more than one cause that contributes to female infertility.

According to traditional Chinese medicine, treatment of female infertility must focus on regulation of the menses. Essential keys in becoming pregnant include a healthy menstrual cycle along with strong Kidney qi, an abundance of blood in the *chong* (thoroughfare) channel, and an unblocked *ren* (conception) channel.

The four principles of treatment for infertility are:

- **Phase 1 - Menstrual Phase** (the week of menstruation): In this phase, it is important to ensure proper shedding of the uterine lining to prepare an optimal surrounding for implantation. Qi and blood moving herbs are utilized to achieve this effect to clear and prevent any stagnation in the lower *jiao*.
- **Phase 2 - Follicular Phase** (the week following the last day of menstruation): During this phase, the key strategy is to tonify the Kidney yin, *jing* (essence), and blood, which are lost during the period. This stage is essential in fortifying the body to ensure healthy conception.
- **Phase 3 - Ovulatory Phase** (week of ovulation): The primary treatment plan during the ovulatory phase is to help the eggs mature and to promote ovulation. Kidney yang tonic herbs have the effect to enhance the surge of luteinizing hormone (LH), which then stimulates ovulation. Herbs should be taken during the week of ovulation.
- **Phase 4 - Luteal Phase** (the week before the onset of the menstruation): The focus during this phase is to regulate Liver qi and treat any possible premenstrual syndrome (PMS) and ensure proper flow of qi and blood in the Liver, *chong* (thoroughfare) and *ren* (conception) channels. When patients are more relaxed and at ease throughout the month, conception will more likely happen.

Blossom Phases 1-4 are designed to match the four phases of the average 28-day menstrual cycle. The goal of ***Phase 1*** is to clear up any blood stagnation in the uterus during menstruation and prepare an optimal environment for implantation to occur later. After menstruation, the uterine lining must rebuild itself to prepare for implantation. During this time it is important to tonify the Kidney yin and yang with ***Blossom Phases 2*** and ***3*** respectively. Then ***Blossom Phase 4*** may be used to regulate the smooth flow of qi and blood and prepare the uterus for the next cycle. However, not every woman's cycle is exactly 28 days, and therefore the ***Blossom*** series should be utilized according to the relative phases of the patient.

Scenario 1: Regular menstrual cycles (28 days)

Broken into four phases of seven days each, patients should take ***Blossom Phases 1-4*** accordingly if the menstrual cycle follows the 28-day cycle and ovulation is predictable.

- Day 1 to 7: ***Blossom (Phase 1)***
- Day 8 to 14: ***Blossom (Phase 2)***
- Day 15 to 21: ***Blossom (Phase 3)***
- Day 22 to 28: ***Blossom (Phase 4)***

Scenario 2: Regular menstrual cycles of variable length (25 to 35 days)

Some patients have cycles that come on a regular basis but do not follow the 28-day pattern. This type of patient should take the ***Blossom*** series as follows:

HOW TO USE THE BLOSSOM SERIES

Menstrual Cycle Patterns	Phase 1 – Menstrual Phase	Phase 2 – Follicular Phase	Phase 3 – Ovulatory Phase	Phase 4 – Luteal Phase
Scenario 1: Regular menstrual cycles (28 days)	Take ***Blossom (Phase 1)*** from day 1-7 of menstrual cycle.	Take ***Blossom (Phase 2)*** from day 8-14 of menstrual cycle.	Take ***Blossom (Phase 3)*** from day 15-21 of menstrual cycle.	Take ***Blossom (Phase 4)*** from day 22-28 of menstrual cycle.
Scenario 2: Regular menstrual cycles of variable length (25-35 days)	Take ***Blossom (Phase 1)*** from first to last day of the period.	Divide the number of days from the last day of the menstrual period to the first day of the next menstrual period into three equal parts, and take ***Blossom Phases 2, 3,*** and ***4*** successively during those three phases.		
Scenario 3: Irregular, unpredictable cycles	Treat the underlying cause of irregular cycles first before using the ***Blossom*** series for infertility.			

Note: Specific information regarding each of the four ***Blossom*** formulas is listed in the following sections.

Blossom™ Introduction

- Begin taking ***Blossom (Phase 1)*** on the first day of menstrual bleeding and stop when the period ends.
- Since the exact number of days of each phase is difficult to predict, simply divide the number of days from the last day of the menstrual period to the first day of the next menstrual period into three equal parts, and take ***Blossom Phases 2***, ***3***, and ***4*** successively during those three phases. If the calculation of the next menstrual cycle is off by a few days, it is fine to continue onto the next cycle and begin taking ***Blossom (Phase 1)*** again. Since Chinese herbs are all natural and cause few to no side effects, it is not necessary to take the dosages of herbs as rigidly as artificial hormone pills, where timing is much more important.

Scenario 3: Irregular and unpredictable cycles

If the patient's cycles are completely irregular and unpredictable, the underlying cause should be treated first before starting the ***Blossom*** series.

SUMMARY

When ***Blossom*** formulas are used to promote fertility, one course of treatment is three months. Efficacy can be seen ranging from one to three courses (three to nine months) of treatment. The couple should not try to conceive in the first three months of herbal treatment. Since there is only one brief window of opportunity to conceive each month, patients are advised to wait and give the herbs enough time to regulate the hormones, nourish the *jing* (essence), and bring the body into balance. Patients should be advised to not feel anxious, nervous, depressed, or worried as these are contributors to qi stagnation and may lessen the chances of becoming pregnant. Advise patients that proper pre-conception care by taking herbs will enable the body to be at optimal health, and is extremely important to ensure a healthy conception and course of pregnancy. Usually when the body is ready, a vacation should be suggested so that the patient is not in her normal environment and can relax and be more likely to become pregnant. When the time is right and the couple is trying to conceive, advise the patient to continue taking ***Blossom (Phase 1)***, and also to spread out the days of ***Blossom (Phase 2)*** and ***Blossom (Phase 3)*** until she finds out if she is pregnant or has her next period. Do not take ***Blossom (Phase 4)*** when the woman is trying to conceive.

Use of these four fertility formulas will strengthen the underlying condition, regulate menstruation, balance hormones, and significantly improve the probability of a successful pregnancy. These four formulas can be used for patients who suffer from habitual miscarriage, patients who simply experience infertility for unknown reasons, or support patients who opt for IVF treatment.

Note: Additional information, such as Supplementary Formulas, Nutrition, Lifestyle Instructions, and Clinical Notes, are listed after the text of ***Blossom (Phase 1-4)*** provided in the Blossom Summary section.

Blossom (Phase 1)™

CLINICAL APPLICATIONS

- **Female infertility - menstrual phase formula**

WESTERN THERAPEUTIC ACTIONS

- Regulates menstruation and treats related complications
- Relieves pain, reduces inflammation, and eliminates water accumulation

CHINESE THERAPEUTIC ACTIONS

- Invigorates blood circulation and relieves pain
- Regulates the *chong* (thoroughfare) and *ren* (conception) channels
- Regulates menstruation

DOSAGE

Take 4 to 6 capsules three times daily on an empty stomach. Discontinue use when the patient becomes pregnant.

INGREDIENTS

Bai Shao (Radix Paeoniae Alba)
Chi Shao (Radix Paeoniae Rubra)
Chong Wei Zi (Fructus Leonuri)
Chuan Xiong (Rhizoma Chuanxiong)
Dang Gui (Radix Angelicae Sinensis)
Fu Ling (Poria)
Xiang Fu (Rhizoma Cyperi)
Ze Lan (Herba Lycopi)

FORMULA EXPLANATION

Blossom (Phase 1) is to be used during phase 1 - menstrual phase, the week of menstruation. This formula contains herbs that are mild yet effective to regulate the menstrual flow and promote healthy shedding of endometrial tissue. *Dang Gui* (Radix Angelicae Sinensis) tonifies and moves blood. *Chong Wei Zi* (Fructus Leonuri) promotes blood circulation, and regulates menstruation. When combined with *Dang Gui* (Radix Angelicae Sinensis), they treat various types of gynecological disorders ranging from irregular menstruation, dysmenorrhea, and amenorrhea to postpartum abdominal pain. *Ze Lan* (Herba Lycopi) moves blood to dispel clots. It also works with *Fu Ling* (Poria) to reduce water retention and edema associated with menstruation. *Chi Shao* (Radix Paeoniae Rubra) and *Chuan Xiong* (Rhizoma Chuanxiong) also treat a wide variety of gynecological disorders by relieving pain. *Xiang Fu* (Rhizoma Cyperi) enters the Liver and regulates qi to relieve bloating and emotional imbalances during the menstrual period. *Bai Shao* (Radix Paeoniae Alba) nourishes blood, softens the Liver and has an antispasmodic effect to relax the uterus and relieve pain.

In short, ***Blossom (Phase 1)*** moves qi and blood to regulate the menses and ensure proper shedding of the uterine lining during the menstrual phase.

CAUTIONS & CONTRAINDICATIONS

- This formula should be discontinued when the patient becomes pregnant.
- This formula may cause more bleeding in some patients. In cases where there is excessive bleeding, reduce the dosage to half or discontinue its use temporarily.
- This herbal formula contains herbs that invigorate blood circulation, such as *Dang Gui* (Radix Angelicae Sinensis). Therefore, patients who are on anticoagulant or antiplatelet therapies, such as Coumadin (warfarin), should use this formula with caution, or not at all, as there may be a higher risk of bleeding and bruising.[1,2,3]

ACUPUNCTURE TREATMENT

Traditional Points:

- *Guanyuan* (CV 4), *Qihai* (CV 6), *Sanyinjiao* (SP 6), *Zusanli* (ST 36), *Shenshu* (BL 23), *Taixi* (KI 3), *Taichong* (LR 3), *Neiguan* (PC 6)

Classic Master Tung's Points:

- **Infertility:** *Fuke* (T 11.24), *Huanchao* (T 11.06), *Tongshen* (T 88.09), *Tongbei* (T 88.11), *Tianhuang* (T 77.17), *Dihuang* (T 77.19), *Renhuang* (T 77.21), *Jiemeiyi* (T 88.04), *Jiemeier* (T 88.05), *Jiemeisan* (T 88.06), *Mufu* (T 88.38)*, *Tianhuang* (T 88.13), *Minghuang* (T 88.12), *Qihuang* (T 88.14). Moxa the lower abdomen for at least 30 minutes each day.
- **Menstruation (excess amount):** *Fuke* (T 11.24), *Xinling* (T 33.17)*, *Tianhuang* (T 77.17), *Dihuang* (T 77.19), *Renhuang* (T 77.21)
- **Menstruation (scanty amount):** *Fuke* (T 11.24), *Wanshunyi* (T 22.08), *Wanshuner* (T 22.09), *Jiemeiyi* (T 88.04), *Jiemeier* (T 88.05), *Jiemeisan* (T 88.06), *Tianhuang* (T 77.17), *Dihuang* (T 77.19), *Renhuang* (T 77.21), *Tianhuang* (T 88.13), *Minghuang* (T 88.12), *Qihuang* (T 88.14)
- **Menstruation (delayed):** *Linggu* (T 22.05), *Renhuang* (T 77.21), *Sihuashang* (T 77.08), *Menjin* (T 66.05). Moxa the sacral area.
- **Menstruation (absence):** *Fuke* (T 11.24), *Jiemeiyi* (T 88.04), *Jiemeier* (T 88.05), *Jiemeisan* (T 88.06), *Tianhuang* (T 77.17), *Dihuang* (T 77.19), *Renhuang* (T 77.21), *Tianhuang* (T 88.13), *Minghuang* (T 88.12), *Qihuang* (T 88.14)
- **Menstruation (flooding and spotting):** *Jiemeiyi* (T 88.04), *Jiemeier* (T 88.05), *Jiemeisan* (T 88.06), *Liuwan* (T 66.08), *Yinbai* (SP 1), *Renhuang* (T 77.21), *Dihuang* (T 77.19)

Master Tung's Points by Dr. Chuan-Min Wang:

- **Infertility:** *Huanchao* (T 11.06), *Fuke* (T 11.24), *Tongshen* (T 88.09)

Balance Method by Dr. Richard Tan:

- Left side: *Hegu* (LI 4), *Linggu* (T 22.05), *Yinlingquan* (SP 9), *Lougu* (SP 7), *Sanyinjiao* (SP 6)

Blossom (Phase 1)™

- Right side: *Neiguan* (PC 6), *Lieque* (LU 7), *Tongli* (HT 5), *Zusanli* (ST 36), *Fenglong* (ST 40)
- Alternate sides from treatment to treatment.

Auricular Medicine by Dr. Li-Chun Huang:

- **Infertility:** Uterus, Kidney, Liver, Endocrine, Lower *Jiao*, Ovary, Gonadotropin, Thalamus, Pituitary
- **Irregular menstruation:** Pituitary, Endocrine, Ovary, Uterus, Kidney, Liver, Lower *Jiao*, Gonadotropin
- **Hypomenorrhea and amenorrhea:** Uterus, Ovary, Exciting, Pituitary, Endocrine, Kidney, Liver, Sympathetic, Gonadotropin, Coronary Vascular Subcortex, Nervous Subcortex
- **Excessive menstruation or bleeding in between periods:** Uterus, Spleen, Diaphragm, Endocrine, Pituitary, Liver, Kidney, Ovary, Adrenal Gland

NUTRITION

- During this stage, it is especially important to not eat foods that are cold (sushi, uncooked vegetables, salad, tomatoes, watermelon, cucumbers, winter melon, strawberries, tofu, crabs, bananas, pear, soy milk, kiwi, ice cream, cold beverages) or sour (all citrus) in nature. They create stagnation and cause pain.

The Tao of Nutrition by Dr. Maoshing Ni and Cathy McNease:

- Make a fertility-enhancing trail mix consisting of equal parts of dried cranberries, walnuts, sesame seeds, longan fruits, and cashews.

LIFESTYLE INSTRUCTION

- During menstruation, avoid sports that may expose the body to the cold environment, such as skiing or cold-water sports.
- Wear clothing that promotes warmth in cold weather, and covers the abdomen and low back.

PHARMACOLOGICAL AND CLINICAL RESEARCH

Blossom (Phase 1) is the first of four formulas to treat infertility. It is formulated with herbs that have a marked influence to regulate the menstruation. According to several studies, administration of *Dang Gui* (Radix Angelicae Sinensis) is associated with both stimulating and inhibiting effects on the uterus, thereby exhibiting an overall regulatory effect on menstruation.[4] Furthermore, use of *Dang Gui* (Radix Angelicae Sinensis) in essential oil form was effective in relieving menstrual pain with a 76.79% rate of effectiveness among 112 patients.[5] The mechanism of this action is attributed in part to the analgesic and anti-inflammatory effects of the herb, which has been cited to be similar or stronger than acetylsalicylic acid.[6]

In addition to *Dang Gui* (Radix Angelicae Sinensis), many other herbs are used in this formula to treat menstruation-related symptoms. For example, *Xiang Fu* (Rhizoma Cyperi) has an inhibitory effect on the uterus to relax the muscles and relieve pain.[7] *Bai Shao* (Radix Paeoniae Alba) and *Chi Shao* (Radix Paeoniae Rubra) have an antispasmodic effect to alleviate spasms and cramps.[8,9] *Xiang Fu* (Rhizoma Cyperi) and *Bai Shao* (Radix Paeoniae Alba) have analgesic effects to effectively relieve pain.[10,11] *Chi Shao* (Radix Paeoniae Rubra) and *Chuan Xiong* (Rhizoma Chuanxiong) have antiplatelet effects to reduce clotting and pain.[12,13] *Chuan Xiong* (Rhizoma Chuanxiong) and *Xiang Fu* (Rhizoma Cyperi) have sedative effects to relieve stress, anxiety and general discomfort.[14,15] Lastly, *Fu Ling* (Poria) has a diuretic effect, and is helpful to reduce water accumulation and treat edema.[16,17]

In short, ***Blossom (Phase 1)*** is an excellent formula for phase 1 - menstrual phase. It contains herbs to regulate menstruation and treat related complications.

References

1. Chan K, Lo AC, Yeung JH, Woo KS. Journal of Pharmacy and Pharmacology 1995 May;47(5):402-6.
2. Pharmacotherapy 1999 July;19(7):870-876.
3. European Journal of Drug Metabolism and Pharmacokinetics 1995; 20(1):55-60.
4. *Zhong Yao Xue* (Chinese Herbology), 1998; 815:823.
5. *Lan Zhou Yi Xue Yuan Xue Bao* (Journal of Lanzhou University of Medicine), 1988; 1:36.
6. *Yao Xue Za Zhi* (Journal of Medicinals), 1971; (91):1098.
7. *Zhong Hua Yi Xue Za Zhi* (Chinese Journal of Medicine), 1935; 12:1351.
8. *Zhong Cheng Yao Yan Jiu* (Research of Chinese Patent Medicine), 1980; 1:32.
9. *Zhong Yi Za Zhi* (Journal of Chinese Medicine), 1985; 6:50.
10. *Gui Yang Yi Xue Yuan Xue Bao* (Journal of Guiyang Medical University), 1959;113.
11. *Shang Hai Zhong Yi Yao Za Zhi* (Shanghai Journal of Chinese Medicine and Herbology), 1983; 4:14.
12. *Zhong Xi Yi Jie He Za Zhi* (Journal of Integrated Chinese and Western Medicine), 1984; 4(12):745.
13. *Hua Xi Yi Xue Za Zhi* (Huaxi Medical Journal), 1993; 8(3):170.
14. *Zhong Yao Yao Li Yu Ying Yong* (Pharmacology and Applications of Chinese Herbs), 1983;123.
15. *Zhong Guo Yao Ke Da Xue Xue Bao* (Journal of University of Chinese Herbology), 1989; 20(1):48.
16. *Chang Yong Zhong Yao Cheng Fen Yu Yao Li Shou Ce* (A Handbook of the Composition and Pharmacology of Common Chinese Drugs), 1994; 1383:1391.
17. *Shang Hai Zhong Yi Yao Za Zhi* (Shanghai Journal of Chinese Medicine and Herbology), 1986; 8:25.

Blossom (Phase 2)™

CLINICAL APPLICATIONS

- **Female infertility - follicular phase formula**

WESTERN THERAPEUTIC ACTIONS

- Regulatory effect to promote normal menstruation
- Hematopoietic effect to promote the production of white and red blood cells
- Adaptogenic effect to address emotional and physical stress associated with menstruation

CHINESE THERAPEUTIC ACTIONS

- Nourishes blood
- Tonifies Kidney yin
- Replenishes Kidney *jing* (essence)

DOSAGE

Take 4 to 6 capsules three times daily on an empty stomach. Discontinue use when the patient becomes pregnant.

INGREDIENTS

Bai Zhu (Rhizoma Atractylodis Macrocephalae)
Chong Wei Zi (Fructus Leonuri)
Chuan Xiong (Rhizoma Chuanxiong)
Dang Gui (Radix Angelicae Sinensis)
E Jiao (Colla Corii Asini)
Fu Ling (Poria)
Gou Qi Zi (Fructus Lycii)
Lu Jiao Shuang (Cornu Cervi Degelatinatum)
Mu Dan Pi (Cortex Moutan)
Niu Xi (Radix Achyranthis Bidentatae)
Nu Zhen Zi (Fructus Ligustri Lucidi)
Shan Yao (Rhizoma Dioscoreae)
Shan Zhu Yu (Fructus Corni)
Shu Di Huang (Radix Rehmanniae Praeparata)
Tu Si Zi (Semen Cuscutae)
Wu Wei Zi (Fructus Schisandrae Chinensis)
Ze Xie (Rhizoma Alismatis)

FORMULA EXPLANATION

Blossom (Phase 2) is designed to be used during phase 2 - follicular phase, the week after finishing menstruation. This formula contains herbs that tonify blood, nourish yin, and replenish *jing* (essence). Mild qi and blood-moving herbs are also used to prevent stagnation as a result of the rich tonics.

In this formula, *Dang Gui* (Radix Angelicae Sinensis), *Shu Di Huang* (Radix Rehmanniae Praeparata) and *E Jiao* (Colla Corii Asini) are among the most effective blood-tonifying herbs to replenish what was lost through menstruation. *Bai Zhu* (Rhizoma Atractylodis Macrocephalae), *Fu Ling* (Poria) and *Shan Yao* (Rhizoma Dioscoreae) are used to strengthen the Spleen. A healthy Spleen is essential in the production of blood and extraction of post-natal qi from food. *Shan Zhu Yu* (Fructus Corni), *Nu Zhen Zi* (Fructus Ligustri Lucidi) and *Gou Qi Zi* (Fructus Lycii) nourish the Kidney yin and *jing* (essence). *Tu Si Zi* (Semen Cuscutae) and *Lu Jiao Shuang* (Cornu Cervi Degelatinatum) are two mild yang-tonic herbs to support the Kidney yang. Without yang tonics, yin tonics cannot achieve their maximum effect. *Wu Wei Zi* (Fructus Schisandrae Chinensis) is an astringent herb added to consolidate, bind and prevent the leakage of *jing* (essence). *Ze Xie* (Rhizoma Alismatis) is used to offset the stagnating nature of *Shu Di Huang* (Radix Rehmanniae Praeparata). *Chuan Xiong* (Rhizoma Chuanxiong), *Mu Dan Pi* (Cortex Moutan) and *Chong Wei Zi* (Fructus Leonuri) are mild blood-moving herbs used to ensure that the tonics do not become stagnant. Finally, *Niu Xi* (Radix Achyranthis Bidentatae) guides the effect of the herbs to the lower *jiao*, namely the Kidney.

In short, this formula successfully tonifies the body to ensure healthy conception by using herbs that supplement the Kidney yin, *jing* (essence), and blood.

CAUTIONS & CONTRAINDICATIONS

- This formula should be discontinued when the patient becomes pregnant.
- This herbal formula contains herbs that invigorate blood circulation, such as *Dang Gui* (Radix Angelicae Sinensis). Therefore, patients who are on anticoagulant or antiplatelet therapies, such as Coumadin (warfarin), should use this formula with caution, or not at all, as there may be a higher risk of bleeding and bruising.[1,2,3]

ACUPUNCTURE TREATMENT

Traditional Points:

- *Guanyuan* (CV 4), *Qihai* (CV 6), *Sanyinjiao* (SP 6), *Zusanli* (ST 36), *Shenshu* (BL 23), *Taixi* (KI 3), *Taichong* (LR 3), *Neiguan* (PC 6)

Classic Master Tung's Points:

- **Infertility:** *Fuke* (T 11.24), *Huanchao* (T 11.06), *Tongshen* (T 88.09), *Tongbei* (T 88.11), *Tianhuang* (T 77.17), *Dihuang* (T 77.19), *Renhuang* (T 77.21), *Jiemeiyi* (T 88.04), *Jiemeier* (T 88.05), *Jiemeisan* (T 88.06), *Mufu* (T 88.38)*, *Tianhuang* (T 88.13), *Minghuang* (T 88.12), *Qihuang* (T 88.14). Moxa the lower abdomen for at least 30 minutes each day.
- **Menstruation (excess amount):** *Fuke* (T 11.24), *Xinling* (T 33.17)*, *Tianhuang* (T 77.17), *Dihuang* (T 77.19), *Renhuang* (T 77.21)
- **Menstruation (scanty amount):** *Fuke* (T 11.24), *Wanshunyi* (T 22.08), *Wanshuner* (T 22.09), *Jiemeiyi* (T 88.04), *Jiemeier* (T 88.05), *Jiemeisan* (T 88.06), *Tianhuang* (T 77.17), *Dihuang* (T 77.19), *Renhuang* (T 77.21), *Tianhuang* (T 88.13), *Minghuang* (T 88.12), *Qihuang* (T 88.14)
- **Menstruation (delayed):** *Linggu* (T 22.05), *Renhuang* (T 77.21), *Sihuashang* (T 77.08), *Menjin* (T 66.05). Moxa the sacral area.
- **Menstruation (absence):** *Fuke* (T 11.24), *Jiemeiyi* (T 88.04), *Jiemeier* (T 88.05), *Jiemeisan* (T 88.06), *Tianhuang* (T 77.17),

Blossom (Phase 2)™

Dihuang (T 77.19), *Renhuang* (T 77.21), *Tianhuang* (T 88.13), *Minghuang* (T 88.12), *Qihuang* (T 88.14)

- **Menstruation (flooding and spotting):** *Jiemeiyi* (T 88.04), *Jiemeier* (T 88.05), *Jiemeisan* (T 88.06), *Liuwan* (T 66.08), *Yinbai* (SP 1), *Renhuang* (T 77.21), *Dihuang* (T 77.19)

Master Tung's Points by Dr. Chuan-Min Wang:

- **Infertility:** *Huanchao* (T 11.06), *Fuke* (T 11.24), *Tongshen* (T 88.09)

Balance Method by Dr. Richard Tan:

- Left side: *Hegu* (LI 4), *Linggu* (T 22.05), *Yinlingquan* (SP 9), *Lougu* (SP 7), *Sanyinjiao* (SP 6)
- Right side: *Neiguan* (PC 6), *Lieque* (LU 7), *Tongli* (HT 5), *Zusanli* (ST 36), *Fenglong* (ST 40)
- Alternate sides from treatment to treatment.

Auricular Medicine by Dr. Li-Chun Huang:

- **Infertility:** Uterus, Kidney, Liver, Endocrine, Lower *Jiao*, Ovary, Gonadotropin, Thalamus, Pituitary
- **Irregular menstruation:** Pituitary, Endocrine, Ovary, Uterus, Kidney, Liver, Lower *Jiao*, Gonadotropin
- **Hypomenorrhea and amenorrhea:** Uterus, Ovary, Exciting, Pituitary, Endocrine, Kidney, Liver, Sympathetic, Gonadotropin, Coronary Vascular Subcortex, Nervous Subcortex
- **Excessive menstruation or bleeding in between periods:** Uterus, Spleen, Diaphragm, Endocrine, Pituitary, Liver, Kidney, Ovary, Adrenal Gland

NUTRITION

The Tao of Nutrition by Dr. Maoshing Ni and Cathy McNease:

- Make a fertility-enhancing trail mix consisting of equal parts of dried cranberries, walnuts, sesame seeds, longan fruits, and cashews.

PHARMACOLOGICAL AND CLINICAL RESEARCH

Blossom (Phase 2) is formulated with herbs that have marked influence to facilitate and restore normal health and well-being after menstruation. This formula contains herbs with regulatory effects to promote normal menstruation, hematological effects to promote the production of white and red blood cells, and adaptogenic effects to address mental and physical stresses associated with menstruation.

According to several studies, administration of *Dang Gui* (Radix Angelicae Sinensis) is associated with both stimulating and inhibiting effects on the uterus, thereby exhibiting an overall regulatory effect on menstruation.[4] Because of this regulatory effect, *Dang Gui* (Radix Angelicae Sinensis) is beneficial and can be used before, during, and after menstruation.

Since most women have pronounced weakness and deficiencies after their menstruation during the follicular phase, many herbs in this formula promote the production of the various types of blood cells. According to one study, *Gou Qi Zi* (Fructus Lycii) has a marked hematopoietic effect to increase the production of red blood cells and white blood cells.[5] According to another study, administration of *E Jiao* (Colla Corii Asini) is associated with a marked hematopoietic effect to increase the production of red blood cells and white blood cells,[6] and its use has been shown to effectively treat leukopenia and anemia.[7] Furthermore, *Bai Zhu* (Rhizoma Atractylodis Macrocephalae) has an immunostimulant effect by increasing the activity of macrophages and the reticulo-endothelial system, and it also increases the number of white blood cells, lymphocytes, and IgG.[8,9] *Wu Wei Zi* (Fructus Schisandrae Chinensis) has an immunostimulant effect to heighten non-specific immunity.[10] Lastly, *Gou Qi Zi* (Fructus Lycii) has an immuno-stimulant effect to increase non-specific immunity, the phagocytic activity of macrophages, and the total number of T cells.[11]

As stated above, ***Blossom (Phase 2)*** contains herbs with an adaptogenic effect to help the body cope with mental and physical stress during and after menstruation. Examples of herbs with such effect include *Bai Zhu* (Rhizoma Atractylodis Macrocephalae) and *Tu Si Zi* (Semen Cuscutae).[12,13] In addition, *Shan Yao* (Rhizoma Dioscoreae) has a stimulating effect on the gastrointestinal tract to promote normal digestion and absorption of nutrients.[14] *Chuan Xiong* (Rhizoma Chuanxiong) and *Mu Dan Pi* (Cortex Moutan) stimulate blood circulation and promote delivery of oxygen and essential nutrients to various parts of the body.[15,16] *Wu Wei Zi* (Fructus Schisandrae Chinensis) stimulates the central nervous system and increases mental alertness, improves work efficiency, and quickens reflexes.[17] *Fu Ling* (Poria) and *Ze Xie* (Rhizoma Alismatis) have diuretic effects, and treat edema frequently associated with menstruation.[18,19]

In short, ***Blossom (Phase 2)*** is an excellent formula to facilitate and restore normal health and well-being after menstruation. This formula contains herbs with regulatory effects to promote normal menstruation, hematopoietic effects to promote the production of white and red blood cells, and adaptogenic effects to address mental and physical stresses associated with menstruation.

References

1. Chan K, Lo AC, Yeung JH, Woo KS. Journal of Pharmacy and Pharmacology 1995 May;47(5):402-6.
2. Pharmacotherapy 1999 July;19(7):870-876.
3. European Journal of Drug Metabolism and Pharmacokinetics 1995; 20(1):55-60.
4. *Zhong Yao Xue* (Chinese Herbology), 1998; 815:823.
5. *Zhong Yao Xue* (Chinese Herbology), 1998; 860:862.
6. *Zhong Cheng Yao Yan Jiu* (Research of Chinese Patent Medicine), 1981; (5):31.
7. *Shan Dong Yi Yao Gong Ye* (Shandong Pharmaceutical Industry), 1986; 3:21.
8. *Jun Shi Yi Xue Jian Xun* (Military Medicine Notes), 1977; 2:5.
9. *Xin Yi Yao Xue Za Zhi* (New Journal of Medicine and Herbology), 1979; 6:60.
10. *Zhong Yao Xue* (Chinese Herbology), 1998; 878:881.
11. *Zhong Cao Yao* (Chinese Herbal Medicine), 19(7):25.
12. *Xin Yi Yao Xue Za Zhi* (New Journal of Medicine and Herbology), 1974; 8:13.
13. *Chang Yong Zhong Yao Cheng Fen Yu Yao Li Shou Ce* (A Handbook of the Composition and Pharmacology of Common Chinese Drugs), 1994; 1563:1564.

Blossom (Phase 2)™

14. *Zhi Wu Zi Yuan Yu Huan Jing* (Source and Environment of Plants), 1992; 1(2):10.
15. *Zhong Yao Xue* (Chinese Herbology), 1989; 535:539.
16. *Guo Wai Yi Xue Zhong Yi Zhong Yao Fen Ce* (Monograph of Chinese Herbology from Foreign Medicine), 1983; (3):5,1984;(5):54.
17. *Zhong Yao Xue* (Chinese Herbology), 1998; 878:881.
18. *Sheng Yao Xue Za Zhi* (Journal of Raw Herbology), 1982; 36(2):150.
19. *Chang Yong Zhong Yao Cheng Fen Yu Yao Li Shou Ce* (A Handbook of the Composition and Pharmacology of Common Chinese Drugs), 1994; 1383:1391.

Blossom (Phase 3)™

CLINICAL APPLICATIONS

- **Female infertility - ovulatory phase formula**

WESTERN THERAPEUTIC ACTIONS

- Regulatory effect to promote normal menstruation
- Regulatory effect on the endocrine system to promote production and secretion of hormones

CHINESE THERAPEUTIC ACTIONS

- Tonifies Kidney yang
- Replenishes Kidney *jing* (essence)
- Mildly moves blood in the lower *jiao*

DOSAGE

Take 4 to 6 capsules three times daily on an empty stomach. Discontinue use when the patient becomes pregnant.

INGREDIENTS

Ba Ji Tian (Radix Morindae Officinalis)
Bai Shao (Radix Paeoniae Alba)
Dang Gui (Radix Angelicae Sinensis)
Gou Qi Zi (Fructus Lycii)
Lu Jiao Shuang (Cornu Cervi Degelatinatum)
Shan Zhu Yu (Fructus Corni)
Shu Di Huang (Radix Rehmanniae Praeparata)
Suo Yang (Herba Cynomorii)
Tu Si Zi (Semen Cuscutae)
Xiao Hui Xiang (Fructus Foeniculi)
Xu Duan (Radix Dipsaci)
Yi Mu Cao (Herba Leonuri)
Yin Yang Huo (Herba Epimedii)

FORMULA EXPLANATION

Blossom (Phase 3) is developed specifically for phase 3 – the ovulatory phase, during the week of ovulation. The ovulatory stage is when Kidney yin is turning into yang and ovulation occurs with a peak in temperature. The primary treatment strategy is to help the eggs mature and promote ovulation. Kidney yang tonic herbs have the effect to enhance the surge of luteinizing hormone (LH), which then stimulates ovulation. To facilitate ovulation, mild blood-moving herbs are also added.

Suo Yang (Herba Cynomorii) is traditionally used for infertility, low libido, lack of Kidney *jing* (essence) and other Kidney yang deficiency conditions. It is used here with *Yin Yang Huo* (Herba Epimedii), *Lu Jiao Shuang* (Cornu Cervi Degelatinatum), *Xu Duan* (Radix Dipsaci) and *Ba Ji Tian* (Radix Morindae Officinalis) to boost the yang and promote ovulation. *Tu Si Zi* (Semen Cuscutae) tonifies both Kidney yin and yang and is an essential herb for treating infertility. *Xiao Hui Xiang* (Fructus Foeniculi) warms the Kidney and the womb in preparation for pregnancy. *Shu Di Huang* (Radix Rehmanniae Praeparata), *Gou Qi Zi* (Fructus Lycii), *Bai Shao* (Radix Paeoniae Alba) and *Shan Zhu Yu* (Fructus Corni) support Kidney yin for two purposes: first, to enhance the effects of the yang tonics, as both Kidney yin and yang should always be tonified together for maximum effect; second, to prevent the yang tonics from creating deficiency fire. Yang tonics as described above promote the release of the egg. *Dang Gui* (Radix Angelicae Sinensis) tonifies blood and *Yi Mu Cao* (Herba Leonuri) moves the blood, which increases blood supply to the ovaries to induce the contraction of the muscles pulling the ovaries closer to the fallopian tubes, thus facilitating the movement of the egg into the fallopian tube.

CAUTIONS & CONTRAINDICATIONS

- This formula should be discontinued when the patient becomes pregnant.
- This herbal formula contains herbs that invigorate blood circulation, such as *Dang Gui* (Radix Angelicae Sinensis). Therefore, patients who are on anticoagulant or antiplatelet therapies, such as Coumadin (warfarin), should use this formula with caution, or not at all, as there may be a higher risk of bleeding and bruising.[1,2,3]

ACUPUNCTURE TREATMENT

Traditional Points:

- *Guanyuan* (CV 4), *Qihai* (CV 6), *Sanyinjiao* (SP 6), *Zusanli* (ST 36), *Shenshu* (BL 23), *Taixi* (KI 3), *Taichong* (LR 3), *Neiguan* (PC 6)

Classic Master Tung's Points:

- **Infertility:** *Fuke* (T 11.24), *Huanchao* (T 11.06), *Tongshen* (T 88.09), *Tongbei* (T 88.11), *Tianhuang* (T 77.17), *Dihuang* (T 77.19), *Renhuang* (T 77.21), *Jiemeiyi* (T 88.04), *Jiemeier* (T 88.05), *Jiemeisan* (T 88.06), *Mufu* (T 88.38)*, *Tianhuang* (T 88.13), *Minghuang* (T 88.12), *Qihuang* (T 88.14). Moxa the lower abdomen for at least 30 minutes each day.
- **Menstruation (excess amount):** *Fuke* (T 11.24), *Xinling* (T 33.17)*, *Tianhuang* (T 77.17), *Dihuang* (T 77.19), *Renhuang* (T 77.21)
- **Menstruation (scanty amount):** *Fuke* (T 11.24), *Wanshunyi* (T 22.08), *Wanshuner* (T 22.09), *Jiemeiyi* (T 88.04), *Jiemeier* (T 88.05), *Jiemeisan* (T 88.06), *Tianhuang* (T 77.17), *Dihuang* (T 77.19), *Renhuang* (T 77.21), *Tianhuang* (T 88.13), *Minghuang* (T 88.12), *Qihuang* (T 88.14)
- **Menstruation (delayed):** *Linggu* (T 22.05), *Renhuang* (T 77.21), *Sihuashang* (T 77.08), *Menjin* (T 66.05). Moxa the sacral area.
- **Menstruation (absence):** *Fuke* (T 11.24), *Jiemeiyi* (T 88.04), *Jiemeier* (T 88.05), *Jiemeisan* (T 88.06), *Tianhuang* (T 77.17), *Dihuang* (T 77.19), *Renhuang* (T 77.21), *Tianhuang* (T 88.13), *Minghuang* (T 88.12), *Qihuang* (T 88.14)
- **Menstruation (flooding and spotting):** *Jiemeiyi* (T 88.04), *Jiemeier* (T 88.05), *Jiemeisan* (T 88.06), *Liuwan* (T 66.08), *Yinbai* (SP 1), *Renhuang* (T 77.21), *Dihuang* (T 77.19)

Master Tung's Points by Dr. Chuan-Min Wang:

- **Infertility:** *Huanchao* (T 11.06), *Fuke* (T 11.24), *Tongshen* (T 88.09)

Blossom (Phase 3)™

Balance Method by Dr. Richard Tan:

- Left side: *Hegu* (LI 4), *Linggu* (T 22.05), *Yinlingquan* (SP 9), *Lougu* (SP 7), *Sanyinjiao* (SP 6)
- Right side: *Neiguan* (PC 6), *Lieque* (LU 7), *Tongli* (HT 5), *Zusanli* (ST 36), *Fenglong* (ST 40)
- Alternate sides from treatment to treatment.

Auricular Medicine by Dr. Li-Chun Huang:

- **Infertility:** Uterus, Kidney, Liver, Endocrine, Lower *Jiao*, Ovary, Gonadotropin, Thalamus, Pituitary
- **Irregular menstruation:** Pituitary, Endocrine, Ovary, Uterus, Kidney, Liver, Lower *Jiao*, Gonadotropin
- **Hypomenorrhea and amenorrhea:** Uterus, Ovary, Exciting, Pituitary, Endocrine, Kidney, Liver, Sympathetic, Gonadotropin, Coronary Vascular Subcortex, Nervous Subcortex
- **Excessive menstruation or bleeding in between periods:** Uterus, Spleen, Diaphragm, Endocrine, Pituitary, Liver, Kidney, Ovary, Adrenal Gland

NUTRITION

- During the ovulatory phase, patients are advised to eat more lamb, which increases warmth of the body.

The Tao of Nutrition by Dr. Maoshing Ni and Cathy McNease:

- Make a fertility-enhancing trail mix consisting of equal parts of dried cranberries, walnuts, sesame seeds, longan fruits, and cashews.

PHARMACOLOGICAL AND CLINICAL RESEARCH

Blossom (Phase 3) is developed for phase 3 - the ovulatory phase, during the week of ovulation. To ensure proper maturation of eggs and subsequent ovulation, this formula uses herbs with a regulatory effect on the endocrine system to promote normal menstruation along with the production and secretion of hormones.

According to several studies, administration of *Dang Gui* (Radix Angelicae Sinensis) is associated with both stimulating and inhibiting effects on the uterus, thereby exhibiting an overall regulatory effect on menstruation.[4] Because of this regulatory effect, *Dang Gui* (Radix Angelicae Sinensis) is beneficial and can be used before, during and after menstruation.

To regulate ovulation, ***Blossom (Phase 3)*** uses many herbs with marked endocrinological effects to promote the production and secretion of various hormones. For example, use of *Shu Di Huang* (Radix Rehmanniae Praeparata) is associated with a marked stimulating effect on the endocrine system, with the mechanism of action attributed to inhibiting negative feedback signals to the pituitary gland.[5] According to another study, administration of *Ba Ji Tian* (Radix Morindae Officinalis) also has a stimulant effect on the endocrine system and increases the production and release of hormones.[6] Most importantly, use of *Yin Yang Huo* (Herba Epimedii) has a stimulant effect on the endocrine system by increasing the production and secretion of endogenous hormones such as corticosterone, cortisol, and testosterone.[7] Lastly, this formula uses many herbs to facilitate and enhance the overall effect of therapy. *Gou Qi Zi* (Fructus Lycii) and *Yi Mu Cao* (Herba Leonuri) both have stimulating effects on the reproductive organs, namely the uterus, to prepare for conception.[8,9]

In short, this is an excellent formula specifically designed for women in phase 3 – the ovulatory phase of the menstrual cycle. It contains herbs that regulate menstruation, promote the production and secretion of hormones, and prepare the uterus for conception.

References

1. Chan K, Lo AC, Yeung JH, Woo KS. Journal of Pharmacy and Pharmacology 1995 May;47(5):402-6.
2. Pharmacotherapy 1999 July;19(7):870-876.
3. European Journal of Drug Metabolism and Pharmacokinetics 1995; 20(1):55-60.
4. *Zhong Yao Xue* (Chinese Herbology), 1998; 815:823.
5. *Zhong Yao Xue* (Chinese Herbology), 1998; 156:158.
6. *Guo Wai Yi Xue Zhong Yi Zhong Yao Fen Ce* (Monograph of Chinese Herbology from Foreign Medicine), 1990; 12(6):48.
7. *Zhong Xi Yi Jie He Za Zhi* (Journal of Integrated Chinese and Western Medicine), 1989; 9(12):737-8,710.
8. *Zhong Yao Xue* (Chinese Herbology), 1998; 860:862.
9. *Zhong Yao Yan Jiu* (*Research of Chinese Herbology*), 1979; 581.

Blossom (Phase 4)™

CLINICAL APPLICATIONS

- **Female infertility - luteal phase formula**

WESTERN THERAPEUTIC ACTIONS

- Regulates menstruation to relieve premenstrual syndrome (PMS)
- Regulates menstruation to prepare for proper shedding of the uterine lining
- Analgesic effect to relieve pain
- Anti-inflammatory effect to relieve inflammation
- Muscle-relaxant effect to relieve spasms and cramps

CHINESE THERAPEUTIC ACTIONS

- Regulates Liver qi
- Invigorates blood

DOSAGE

Take 4 to 6 capsules three times daily on an empty stomach. Discontinue use when the patient becomes pregnant.

INGREDIENTS

Bai Shao (Radix Paeoniae Alba)
Bai Zhu (Rhizoma Atractylodis Macrocephalae)
Chai Hu (Radix Bupleuri)
Chuan Niu Xi (Radix Cyathulae)
Chuan Xiong (Rhizoma Chuanxiong)
Dang Gui (Radix Angelicae Sinensis)
Fu Ling (Poria)
Gan Cao (Radix et Rhizoma Glycyrrhizae)
He Huan Pi (Cortex Albiziae)
Ju He (Semen Citri Reticulatae)
Lu Lu Tong (Fructus Liquidambaris)
Xiang Fu (Rhizoma Cyperi)
Yi Mu Cao (Herba Leonuri)
Yu Jin (Radix Curcumae)

FORMULA EXPLANATION

Blossom (Phase 4) is formulated specifically for phase 4 – the luteal phase, the week before the period. Regulating Liver qi is the most important treatment strategy during this stage. Liver qi stagnation is characterized by irregular menstruation, abdominal bloating, irritability, emotional instability, short temper, and breast distension. This formula is designed to relieve premenstrual syndrome (PMS), release tension and stagnation, and prepare the uterus for proper shedding the following week.

In this formula, *Chai Hu* (Radix Bupleuri) and *Xiang Fu* (Rhizoma Cyperi) smooth the Liver qi and disperse qi stagnation. *He Huan Pi* (Cortex Albiziae) relieves Liver qi stagnation and reduces anxiety and irritability associated with PMS. *Dang Gui* (Radix Angelicae Sinensis) tonifies blood and relieves pain. *Bai Shao* (Radix Paeoniae Alba) nourishes the blood to soften the Liver to relieve distension and pain. *Bai Zhu* (Rhizoma Atractylodis Macrocephalae) and *Fu Ling* (Poria) tonify the Spleen and dispel dampness to facilitate the transportation and transformation of nutrients. *Gan Cao* (Radix et Rhizoma Glycyrrhizae) supplements qi and helps *Bai Shao* (Radix Paeoniae Alba) soften the Liver to relieve pain.

Yu Jin (Radix Curcumae), *Chuan Xiong* (Rhizoma Chuanxiong), *Lu Lu Tong* (Fructus Liquidambaris) and *Yi Mu Cao* (Herba Leonuri) move blood and break blood stasis in the lower *jiao* to ensure proper shedding of the endometrial lining during the period. *Chuan Niu Xi* (Radix Cyathulae) and *Ju He* (Semen Citri Reticulatae) are channel-guiding herbs that help direct the effect of the herbs to the lower *jiao*.

CAUTIONS & CONTRAINDICATIONS

- Do not take this formula while trying to conceive. Also, it should be discontinued when the patient finds out she is pregnant.
- This herbal formula contains herbs that invigorate blood circulation, such as *Dang Gui* (Radix Angelicae Sinensis). Therefore, patients who are on anticoagulant or antiplatelet therapies, such as Coumadin (warfarin), should use this formula with caution, or not at all, as there may be a higher risk of bleeding and bruising.[1,2,3]

CLINICAL NOTES

- If the patient does not have Liver qi stagnation, she does not need to take ***Blossom (Phase 4)*** and can take ***Blossom (Phase 2)*** and ***Blossom (Phase 3)*** for more days instead.

ACUPUNCTURE TREATMENT

Traditional Points:

- *Guanyuan* (CV 4), *Qihai* (CV 6), *Sanyinjiao* (SP 6), *Zusanli* (ST 36), *Shenshu* (BL 23), *Taixi* (KI 3), *Taichong* (LR 3), *Neiguan* (PC 6)

Classic Master Tung's Points:

- **Infertility:** *Fuke* (T 11.24), *Huanchao* (T 11.06), *Tongshen* (T 88.09), *Tongbei* (T 88.11), *Tianhuang* (T 77.17), *Dihuang* (T 77.19), *Renhuang* (T 77.21), *Jiemeiyi* (T 88.04), *Jiemeier* (T 88.05), *Jiemeisan* (T 88.06), *Mufu* (T 88.38)*, *Tianhuang* (T 88.13), *Minghuang* (T 88.12), *Qihuang* (T 88.14). Moxa the lower abdomen for at least 30 minutes each day.
- **Menstruation (excess amount):** *Fuke* (T 11.24), *Xinling* (T 33.17)*, *Tianhuang* (T 77.17), *Dihuang* (T 77.19), *Renhuang* (T 77.21)
- **Menstruation (scanty amount):** *Fuke* (T 11.24), *Wanshunyi* (T 22.08), *Wanshuner* (T 22.09), *Jiemeiyi* (T 88.04), *Jiemeier* (T 88.05), *Jiemeisan* (T 88.06), *Tianhuang* (T 77.17), *Dihuang* (T 77.19), *Renhuang* (T 77.21), *Tianhuang* (T 88.13), *Minghuang* (T 88.12), *Qihuang* (T 88.14)
- **Menstruation (delayed):** *Linggu* (T 22.05), *Renhuang* (T 77.21), *Sihuashang* (T 77.08), *Menjin* (T 66.05). Moxa the sacral area.
- **Menstruation (absent):** *Fuke* (T 11.24), *Jiemeiyi* (T 88.04), *Jiemeier* (T 88.05), *Jiemeisan* (T 88.06), *Tianhuang* (T 77.17), *Dihuang* (T 77.19), *Renhuang* (T 77.21), *Tianhuang* (T 88.13), *Minghuang* (T 88.12), *Qihuang* (T 88.14)

Blossom (Phase 4)™

- **Menstruation (flooding and spotting):** *Jiemeiyi* (T 88.04), *Jiemeier* (T 88.05), *Jiemeisan* (T 88.06), *Liuwan* (T 66.08), *Yinbai* (SP 1), *Renhuang* (T 77.21), *Dihuang* (T 77.19)

Master Tung's Points by Dr. Chuan-Min Wang:

- **Infertility:** *Huanchao* (T 11.06), *Fuke* (T 11.24), *Tongshen* (T 88.09)

Balance Method by Dr. Richard Tan:

- Left side: *Hegu* (LI 4), *Linggu* (T 22.05), *Yinlingquan* (SP 9), *Lougu* (SP 7), *Sanyinjiao* (SP 6)
- Right side: *Neiguan* (PC 6), *Lieque* (LU 7), *Tongli* (HT 5), *Zusanli* (ST 36), *Fenglong* (ST 40)
- Alternate sides from treatment to treatment.

Auricular Medicine by Dr. Li-Chun Huang:

- **Infertility:** Uterus, Kidney, Liver, Endocrine, Lower *Jiao*, Ovary, Gonadotropin, Thalamus, Pituitary
- **Irregular menstruation:** Pituitary, Endocrine, Ovary, Uterus, Kidney, Liver, Lower *Jiao*, Gonadotropin
- **Hypomenorrhea and amenorrhea:** Uterus, Ovary, Exciting, Pituitary, Endocrine, Kidney, Liver, Sympathetic, Gonadotropin, Coronary Vascular Subcortex, Nervous Subcortex
- **Excessive menstruation or bleeding in between periods:** Uterus, Spleen, Diaphragm, Endocrine, Pituitary, Liver, Kidney, Ovary, Adrenal Gland

NUTRITION

The Tao of Nutrition by Dr. Maoshing Ni and Cathy McNease:

- Make a fertility-enhancing trail mix consisting of equal parts of dried cranberries, walnuts, sesame seeds, longan fruits, and cashews.

PHARMACOLOGICAL AND CLINICAL RESEARCH

Blossom (Phase 4) is formulated specifically for phase 4 – luteal phase, the week before the period. This formula uses herbs to regulate menstruation to relieve premenstrual syndrome (PMS) and prepare for proper shedding. Furthermore, it incorporates additional herbs with analgesic effects to relieve pain, anti-inflammatory effects to relieve inflammation, and spasmolytic effects to relieve spasms and cramps.

According to several studies, administration of *Dang Gui* (Radix Angelicae Sinensis) is associated with both stimulating and inhibiting effects on the uterus, thereby exhibiting an overall regulatory effect on menstruation.[4] Furthermore, use of *Dang Gui* (Radix Angelicae Sinensis) in essential oil form was effective in relieving menstrual pain with a 76.79% rate of effectiveness among 112 patients.[5] The mechanism of this action is attributed in part to the analgesic and anti-inflammatory effects of the herb, which has been cited to be similar to or stronger than acetylsalicylic acid.[6]

Blossom (Phase 4) contains many herbs to address premenstrual syndrome (PMS) with analgesic effects to relieve pain, anti-inflammatory effects to relieve inflammation, and muscle-relaxant effects to relieve spasms and cramps. Herbs with an analgesic effect to relieve pain include *Xiang Fu* (Rhizoma Cyperi),[7] *Gan Cao* (Radix et Rhizoma Glycyrrhizae),[8] *Chai Hu* (Radix Bupleuri),[9] and *Bai Shao* (Radix Paeoniae Alba).[10] Herbs with an anti-inflammatory effect to reduce swelling and inflammation include *Gan Cao* (Radix et Rhizoma Glycyrrhizae),[11] *Chai Hu* (Radix Bupleuri),[12] and *Bai Shao* (Radix Paeoniae Alba).[13] Lastly, herbs with a muscle-relaxant effect to relieve spasms and cramps include *Bai Shao* (Radix Paeoniae Alba) and *Gan Cao* (Radix et Rhizoma Glycyrrhizae).[14,15] In addition, *Fu Ling* (Poria) is added for its mild sedative effect to relieve the general pain and discomfort associated with PMS.[16] Lastly, *Yi Mu Cao* (Herba Leonuri) has been used specifically to treat irregular menstruation and hypermenorrhea.[17]

Furthermore, this formula uses many herbs to treat menstruation-related complications. For example, *Fu Ling* (Poria) and *Bai Zhu* (Rhizoma Atractylodis Macrocephalae) have diuretic effects, and are used to drain water accumulation and treat edema.[18,19,20] *Chuan Xiong* (Rhizoma Chuanxiong), *Yi Mu Cao* (Herba Leonuri) and *Bai Zhu* (Rhizoma Atractylodis Macrocephalae) have antiplatelet effects, and are used to prevent clotting and pain before and during menstruation.[21,22]

Lastly, *Yi Mu Cao* (Herba Leonuri) has a stimulating effect, while *Xiang Fu* (Rhizoma Cyperi) has an inhibiting effect, on the uterus. The regulatory effects of these two herbs ensure proper and smooth transition throughout changes in the menstrual cycle.[23,24]

In short, this is a great formula to conclude the four phases of menstruation and promote fertility. It regulates menstruation to relieve premenstrual syndrome and prepare for proper shedding. Furthermore, it incorporates additional herbs with analgesic effects to relieve pain, anti-inflammatory effects to relieve inflammation, and muscle-relaxant effects to relieve spasms and cramps.

References

1. Chan K, Lo AC, Yeung JH, Woo KS. Journal of Pharmacy and Pharmacology 1995 May;47(5):402-6.
2. Pharmacotherapy 1999 July;19(7):870-876.
3. European Journal of Drug Metabolism and Pharmacokinetics 1995; 20(1):55-60.
4. *Zhong Yao Xue* (Chinese Herbology), 1998; 815:823.
5. *Lan Zhou Yi Xue Yuan Xue Bao* (Journal of Lanzhou University of Medicine), 1988; 1:36.
6. *Yao Xue Za Zhi* (Journal of Medicinals), 1971; (91):1098.
7. *Gui Yang Yi Xue Yuan Xue Bao* (Journal of Guiyang Medical University), 1959; 113.
8. *Zhong Yao Xue* (Chinese Herbology), 1998; 759:765.
9. *Shen Yang Yi Xue Yuan Xue Bao* (Journal of Shenyang University of Medicine), 1984; 1(3):214.
10. *Shang Hai Zhong Yi Yao Za Zhi* (Shanghai Journal of Chinese Medicine and Herbology), 1983; 4:14.
11. *Zhong Cao Yao* (Chinese Herbal Medicine), 1991; 22(10):452.

FORMULAS

Blossom (Phase 4)™

12. *Zhong Yao Yao Li Yu Ying Yong* (Pharmacology and Applications of Chinese Herbs), 1983; 888.
13. *Zhong Yao Zhi* (Chinese Herbology Journal), 1993; 183.
14. *Zhong Yi Za Zhi* (Journal of Chinese Medicine), 1985; 6:50.
15. *Hu Nan Zhong Yi* (Hunan Journal of Traditional Chinese Medicine), 1989; 2:7.
16. *Zhong Yao Da Ci Dian* (Dictionary of Chinese Herbs), 1977; 1596.
17. *Zhong Hua Fu Chan Ke Za Zhi* (*Chinese Journal of OB/GYN*), 1958; 1:1.
18. *Chang Yong Zhong Yao Cheng Fen Yu Yao Li Shou Ce* (A Handbook of the Composition and Pharmacology of Common Chinese Drugs), 1994; 1383:1391.
19. *Shang Hai Zhong Yi Yao Za Zhi* (Shanghai Journal of Chinese Medicine and Herbology), 1986; 8:25.
20. *Zhong Hua Yi Xue Za Zhi* (Chinese Journal of Medicine), 1961; 47(1):7.
21. *Hua Xi Yi Xue Za Zhi* (Huaxi Medical Journal), 1993; 8(3):170.
22. *Zhong Xi Yi Jie He Za Zhi* (Journal of Integrated Chinese and Western Medicine), 1986; 6(1):39.
23. *Zhong Yao Yan Jiu* (*Research of Chinese Herbology*), 1979; 581.
24. *Zhong Hua Yi Xue Za Zhi* (Chinese Journal of Medicine), 1935; 12:1351.

Blossom ™ Summary

CLINICAL NOTES

- There are many causes of infertility according to Western medicine, all with different corresponding diagnosis in traditional Chinese medicine (TCM). For example, an inability to ovulate often indicates Kidney yang deficiency, while tubal obstruction means qi and blood or phlegm stagnation. A specific diagnosis is necessary in selecting the right herbal formula for the patient.
- One course of treatment is three months. Efficacy ranges from one to three courses. The couple should not try excessively to become pregnant during the first three months of herbal treatment. They should be psychologically prepared to not expect results too soon, and therefore help relax the Liver qi. In such cases, the chances of becoming pregnant would be greater. Advise patients that proper pre-conception care enables the body to be at its optimal health and is extremely important to ensure healthy conception and course of pregnancy.
- In cases where the period is irregular and there is no clear distinction of the phases, treat the underlying cause first by using a supplementary formula. When a menstrual pattern is established, use ***Blossom (Phases 1-4)*** accordingly.
- Women who were on oral contraceptives previously may not become pregnant as quickly as those who did not take any because the body needs a period of time to re-adjust and begin to secrete hormones regularly without the interference of contraceptives. Herbs will help speed up this process.
- Pelvic inflammatory disease (PID), usage of intrauterine devices (IUDs), ruptured appendix, lower abdominal surgery, and ectopic pregnancy can all be causative factors to tubal dysfunction. A hysterosalpingogram is taken as a definitive test for tubal dysfunction. *See* Supplementary Formulas section for the most appropriate formula to use.
    1. PID includes endometritis, salpingitis, mucopurulent cervicitis, oophoritis, and upper female genital tract infection. Transmitted sexually through gonococcal, chlamydial, or bacterial infection, acute PID may present with no symptoms and in many instances be barely discernible. Consequently, pathogenic factors infiltrate and cause damage within the endocervix, and also weaken tubal integrity.
    2. IUD complications include bleeding and pain as well as potential for a perforated uterus. The most common side effects of IUDs include cramping and irregular vaginal bleeding. Complications ensue if other extenuating pathogens are introduced into the endometrial cavity. The possibility of rupturing a tubo-ovarian abscess may also occur during insertion.
    3. Pre- and post-surgical impediments also impair tubal patency. A thorough medical history should be taken, including past surgical procedures, especially of the lower abdominal region, for complete diagnostic assessment.
- Taking the formulas throughout the four phases also enhances the success rate of *in vitro* fertilization (IVF). ***Blossom (Phases 1-4)*** formulas have the following effects:
    1. Tonify the Kidney to help the ovaries produce better-quality eggs.
    2. Increase blood flow to the lower *jiao*/uterus and prepare the uterine lining for implantation.
    3. Regulate Liver qi for relaxation.
    4. Help consolidate the pregnancy, to decrease the chances of miscarriage.
- If it is unexplained infertility or there is no other significant underlying cause to the infertility, simply following the four formulas for each phase will be sufficient.
- Note: For sexual and reproductive disorders of the male partner, please refer to ***Vitality*** and ***Vital Essence***.

CAUTIONS & CONTRAINDICATIONS

- ***Blossom (Phases 1-4)*** should be discontinued when the patient becomes pregnant.
- Women who take these fertility formulas may experience more bleeding during their period, which is a normal response of the herbs.
- It is important to remember that these formulas are designed to treat infertility. They do not offer any protection against sexually transmitted diseases.
- These formulas are ineffective for infertility caused by immune dysfunction.

SUPPLEMENTARY FORMULAS

Supplementary formulas are crucial to successful treatment of infertility. In addition to taking the primary formulas, ***Blossom (Phases 1-4)*** for the four corresponding phases, one or two [maximum] supplementary formula(s) should be added for optimal effect. The following are some recommendations. The patient should take 4 to 6 capsules of the primary formula and 2 to 4 capsules of the supplementary formula three times daily throughout the month.

- With Kidney yang deficiency manifesting as cold body and extremities, low libido, polyuria, hair loss, pale and cold appearance, and other cold symptoms, add ***Kidney Tonic (Yang)***.
- With Kidney yin deficiency or women over 40 years of age manifesting heat sensations, dryness, scanty menstruation, flushed cheeks, thin appearance, night sweats or dry mouth, add ***Kidney Tonic (Yin)***.
- With dampness accumulation where the patient shows overweight tendency or phlegm accumulation with thick tongue coating, heaviness sensation, add ***Herbal DRX***.
- With uterine fibroids, polycystic ovaries, endometriosis, fallopian tube blockage, tuberculosis of the fallopian tube, post-surgical adhesions or other stagnations, add ***Resolve (Lower)***.
- With generalized tiredness and fatigue due to qi and blood deficiencies, add ***Imperial Tonic***.
- With high levels of stress and Liver qi stagnation, add ***Calm***.
- With chronic pelvic inflammatory disease, add ***Herbal ABX*** and ***Resolve (Lower)***.

Blossom™ Summary

- For Liver qi stagnation causing infertility in patients who have had abortions or miscarriages, add ***Calm***.
- For infertility with coldness and blood stagnation, add ***Menatrol***.
- With anemia or blood deficiency, add ***Schisandra ZZZ***.
- For painful menstruation, add ***Mense-Ease***.
- With post-abortion, post-surgical, or chronic infection/inflammation causing infertility, add ***Herbal ABX***.
- For women with past history of miscarriage, herbal formulas may be used to stabilize pregnancy, such as with *Bao Chan Wu You Fang* (Preserve Pregnancy and Care-Free Decoction).

NUTRITION

- Foods that are cold (sushi, uncooked vegetables, salad, tomatoes, watermelon, cucumbers, winter melon, strawberries, tofu, crabs, bananas, pear, soybean milk, kiwi, ice cream, cold beverages) or sour (all citrus) in nature should be avoided one week before and during menstruation. Cold and sour foods create stagnation and cause pain.
- Eat more nuts, seeds, lamb, and seafood, especially clams.
- Avoid overly spicy and pungent food as they may cause excessive bleeding.
- Decrease the intake of processed food and increase the consumption of organic food.
- Avoid alcohol, coffee, and cigarette smoking.
- Always eat breakfast! According to the TCM clock, the most optimal time for the digestive system is in the morning from 8:00 to 10:00 a.m.
- According to Dr. Richard Tan's mirror concept, a diet high in small eggs such as fish eggs may be beneficial to women who suffer from infertility due to ovulatory or ovarian dysfunctions.

LIFESTYLE INSTRUCTIONS

- Eliminate things that are potentially toxic or unhealthy (e.g., alcohol, coffee, cigarettes, refined sugars, saturated fats, and chemical-based household cleaners and personal hygiene products).
- Sleep by 10:00 p.m. In TCM, 11:00 p.m. to 1:00 a.m. is when the yin shifts to yang. It is crucial for the body to be at rest during this time for optimal health.
- Avoid sports that may expose the body to cold environments, such as skiing and all water sports.
- It is important to understand that the body is like a garden. No seed can properly sprout and grow without fertilized soil, water and sunshine. Taking these herbs to regulate the menses and fortify the body with these nutrients and *jing* (essence) are steps one must take to ensure a healthy pregnancy. Because there is only one window of opportunity to become pregnant each month, it is important to be patient and to give herbs enough time to regulate and bring the body back to balance. Advise the patient to not feel so anxious, nervous, depressed, or worried. Encourage her to engage in yoga, meditation, *tai chi chuan* [*tai ji chuan*] or other activities that help her relax and focus on something else other than constantly thinking about trying to become pregnant.
- A positive attitude and low stress level can contribute greatly to a successful pregnancy. If taking a vacation will help, they should be advised to do so.

CASE STUDIES

- L.D., 27-year-old female, presented with a difficulty in conceiving for three years. The patient had a history of kidney stones and a high fasting blood sugar, which resulted in her taking Glucophage (metformin), a Western drug. Objective findings were warm body temperature and RLQ pain that would come and go, with a desire for heat and pressure. Urgent stools with watery consistency were also present. Blood pressure was 108/66 mmHg and her heart rate was 84 beats per minute. Lab testing showed blood sugar levels of 108 without the Glucophage (metformin), and her basal body temperature showed luteal phase on day ten with ovulation on days 13-15. The practitioner diagnosed the condition as Kidney yin and yang deficiencies with blood stagnation and Spleen qi deficiency with dampness. Her Western diagnosis was infertility due to luteal phase defect. The patient was given ***Blossom (Phases 1-4)*** corresponding with the four phases of the cycle. With the ***Blossom (Phases 1-4)*** the patient conceived a baby within five months of initiating the herbal intake. She had a healthy pregnancy free of complications compared to her first pregnancy where she experienced pre-eclampsia and a low birth weight baby. The patient did not take any herbs during pregnancy but continued with acupuncture treatment. Submitted by L.M., Lafayette, Colorado.
- J.P., a 43-year-old female, presented with a past history of three miscarriages within the past year. Her records showed that her FSH was high and she hadn't had a menstrual period in three months. Since her last miscarriage she has had hot flashes, insomnia, and night sweats. The patient was looking for a way to get pregnant. The practitioner diagnosed this condition as Liver qi stagnation, Liver and Kidney deficiencies. ***Blossom (Phases 1-4)*** were prescribed at 4 capsules three times a day. Her period returned within two months of taking the herbs. After acupuncture treatments and dietary changes, the patient was now six months pregnant. Her HCG was increasing and heart beat was present on the ultrasounds. None of her past pregnancies lasted longer than six weeks before ending in miscarriages. Submitted by M.R., Santa Cruz, California.
- S.M., a 43-year-old female, presented with infertility. It was noted that the patient had other health concerns of weight gain, irritability due to high stress, and undergoing IVF cycles. She had been experiencing high risk pregnancy, consisting of nine failed IUIs, and was currently taking DHEA hormonal drugs. The TCM diagnosis was Heart qi and blood deficiencies, blood stagnation, Liver and Kidney yin deficiencies, and Spleen deficiency. Her Western diagnosis was undefined infertility, possibly due to old age. For treatment, ***Blossom (Phases 1-4)*** was prescribed with the

Blossom ™ Summary

addition of ***Schisandra ZZZ***. After six weeks of taking the herbs, she had successful conception implantation. The patient reported she was able to sleep more, moods were more stabilized, she was less fatigued, and her weight became more stable. As a result, she gave birth to a healthy baby girl. Submitted by N.T., Bethesda, Maryland.

- A.S., a 29-year-old female, presented with PCOS, consisting of multiple sacs, no ripening of the eggs, irregular cycles, and fatigue. It was also mentioned that she had two unsuccessful IUIs due to two chemical pregnancies. Additional symptoms included cystic ovaries, acne, increase facial and body hair, deficiencies of both vitamin D and DHEA, and short temperatured luteal phase. The TCM diagnosis was blood deficiency, phlegm and damp accumulation, Spleen and Kidney deficiencies, and *ren* (conception) and *chong* (thoroughfare) channels dysregulation. Her Western diagnosis was cystic ovaries infertility, low follicular and luteal temperatured irregular menstruation, and elevated prolactin. ***Blossom (Phases 1-4)*** was prescribed to her for the entire month, with ***Imperial Tonic*** to replenish the *jing* (essence), and ***Nourish*** to tonify the blood and Kidney yin. The six-month protocol was used to clear heat, tonify the qi/blood/*jing* (essence), and regulate the cycle. As a result, her temperatures had re-established to create normal cycles again. Secondly, after three months of balanced cycles, her cystic ovaries had reduced; she also had nourished her qi/blood/*jing* (essence), and her other deficiencies, which were also restored. As a result, she had a successful IUI and was now two months pregnant. The ***Blossom (Phases 1-4)*** and ***Nourish*** were very helpful. Submitted by N.T., Bethesda, Maryland.
- D.C., a 36-year-old female, presented with infertility which had been occurring for five years. It was also noted that she had an unstable luteal phase in addition to a slightly high TSH level of 2.81. Tongue was puffy with red tip; pulse was wiry. The practitioner diagnosed this condition as Liver and Heart qi stagnation along with Kidney yang deficiency. ***Blossom (Phases 1-4)*** were prescribed at three capsules three times per day. After taking the herbs for one month, her premenstrual symptoms had dissipated, followed by an increase of her progesterone level after two months. She had continued to take the herbs to achieve a pregnancy with a full term birth. The herbs were very helpful. Submitted by M.R., Santa Cruz, California.
- L.K., a 35-year-old female, presented with symptoms including unstable hormones, PMS with mood swings, swelling and sharp cramping. Her blood pressure was 106/68 mmHg and her heart rate was 62 beats per minute. Her menstruation consisted of dark blood, clots and was considered an irregular cycle varying between 26 to 36 days. Occasional breakthrough bleeding and spotting also occurred. In addition, she had a desire to become pregnant within one year. The TCM diagnosis was Liver qi and blood stasis. ***Blossom (Phase 1)*** was prescribed, starting with her menstruation at 4 capsules three times daily taken until the bleeding had ceased. The remaining ***Blossom (Phases 2-4)*** were taken to continue the treatment. After two months of taking the ***Blossom*** formulas, the patient's cycle returned to 28 days with minimal mood swings and pre-menstrual cramps. Three months after taking the herbs, she noticed the color of her blood became bright red and no clots were present. She is now starting to attempt getting pregnant after five months into the treatment. Submitted by A.G., Solana Beach, California.

COMPARATIVE ANALYSIS

Infertility is a common disorder that may be due to a wide variety of causes. Before treatment, both partners should be examined, evaluated, and treated if necessary. Each course of treatment is three months, and efficacy can usually be seen within one to three courses. Continuous and persistent use of these four fertility formulas will regulate menstruation, balance hormones, and strengthen the underlying condition. Not only will they significantly improve the possibility of successful fertilization, they will also increase the probability of a smooth pregnancy with minimal complications.

Female infertility is a complicated disorder that has numerous causes. In Western medicine, those with physiological disorders, such as irregular or absence of ovulation, are usually treated with Clomid (clomiphene). Though it induces ovulation, it causes side effects such as hot flashes, abdominal swelling, breast tenderness, nausea, vision disturbance, and headaches. Furthermore, those with physical disorders, such as problems with the fallopian tubes or cervix, are treated with physical intervention, such as surgery, intrauterine insemination, and *in vitro* fertilization. Though these methods are effective, they are more invasive, more expensive, and have more risks.

In TCM, female infertility is very complicated, and requires multiple treatment plans to ensure optimal success. Therefore, four formulas are used to address all possible causes of infertility. Together, they regulate menstruation, promote ovulation, nourish the body, and ensure optimal conditions for fertilization. This comprehensive method has been used with tremendous success throughout the history of traditional Chinese medicine.

Western and traditional Chinese medicine are both effective for female infertility. In general, herbal therapy is an excellent option for mild to severe cases of infertility, as it is very effective and has few or no side effects. However, if the women do not respond to herbal therapy, physical intervention may be considered as the last alternative.

CA Support™

CLINICAL APPLICATIONS

- **Cancer support formula:** patients with cancer who suffer extreme weakness and deficiency and cannot withstand surgery or chemotherapy and radiation treatments
- **Late stage, terminally-ill cancer patients with pain and suffering**
- **Maintainance and preventative formula** to be used at the conclusion of chemotherapy and radiation treatments

WESTERN THERAPEUTIC ACTIONS

- Immunostimulant effect to boost white blood cells
- Hematopoietic function to increase red blood cells
- Antineoplastic activity to suppress cancer cells
- Antiangiogenic property to inhibit tumor growth, invasion, and metastasis

CHINESE THERAPEUTIC ACTIONS

- Clears heat
- Eliminates toxins
- Tonifies the underlying deficiencies (qi, blood, yin and yang)

DOSAGE

Take 3 to 4 capsules three times daily. It should be taken on an empty stomach with warm water for maximum effectiveness.

INGREDIENTS

Bai Hua She She Cao (Herba Hedyotis)
Bai Zhu (Rhizoma Atractylodis Macrocephalae)
Ban Zhi Lian (Herba Scutellariae Barbatae)
Chong Lou (Rhizoma Paridis)
Dong Chong Xia Cao (Cordyceps)
E Zhu (Rhizoma Curcumae)
Fu Ling (Poria)
Huang Jing (Rhizoma Polygonati)
Huang Qi (Radix Astragali)
Ji Xue Teng (Caulis Spatholobi)
Xi Yang Shen (Radix Panacis Quinquefolii)
Yi Yi Ren (Semen Coicis)

BACKGROUND

Cancer is the second leading cause of death, according to a report by CDC published in January 11, 2012.[1] In Western medicine, treatment options for cancer include surgery, chemotherapy and radiation. Though these treatments may be effective, they are invasive to the body and often cause severe and serious damage to many organs and cells. Therefore, additional interventions are extremely important to alleviate the side effects of these invasive treatments, support the body and its health, and improve the overall quality of life.

FORMULA EXPLANATION

CA Support is developed specifically for individuals who have extreme weakness and deficiency after prolonged battles with cancer and its treatments (chemotherapy and radiation). This condition is characterized by both extreme excess (cancer is often considered as accumulation of phlegm, heat, and toxins) and extreme deficiency (qi, blood, yin and yang deficiencies caused by chemotherapy and radiation). Therefore, optimal treatment requires use of herbs to gently clear heat and eliminate toxins, and greatly tonify the underlying deficiencies.

In this formula, *Huang Qi* (Radix Astragali) and *Xi Yang Shen* (Radix Panacis Quinquefolii) are both used to greatly tonify qi. Both tonics are light, and have very strong immune-enhancing effects. Though potent, they do not create the general stagnating side-effects associated with tonics. *Bai Zhu* (Rhizoma Atractylodis Macrocephalae), *Fu Ling* (Poria), and *Yi Yi Ren* (Semen Coicis) strengthen the middle *jiao*, and further enhance the qi-tonifying effect of *Huang Qi* (Radix Astragali) and *Xi Yang Shen* (Radix Panacis Quinquefolii). By strengthening the middle *jiao*, the digestive system can function properly and appetite will increase. *Ji Xue Teng* (Caulis Spatholobi) tonifies blood, *Huang Jing* (Rhizoma Polygonati) nourishes yin, and *Dong Chong Xia Cao* (Cordyceps) strengthens yang. Together, these herbs tonify and treat the underlying qi, blood, yin and yang deficiencies. Small amounts of *E Zhu* (Rhizoma Curcumae), *Chong Lou* (Rhizoma Paridis), *Ban Zhi Lian* (Herba Scutellariae Barbatae) and *Bai Hua She She Cao* (Herba Hedyotis) are added to clear heat, relieve pain, and eliminate toxins. These three herbs also have shown promising anticancer effects according to various *in vitro* and *in vivo* studies.[2,3]

In summary, ***CA Support*** is developed specifically to address the difficult and challenging cases of cancer in which the patients are too weak to continue with chemotherapy and/or radiation treatments. Use of this formula will strengthen the underlying constitution, improve quality of life, and decrease pain and suffering.

CAUTIONS & CONTRAINDICATIONS

- This formula is ***not*** designed to treat cancer, nor is it designed to replace chemotherapy and/or radiation. The focus of this formula is to support patients with cancer who are too weak to continue with chemotherapy and radiation treatments. This formula contains herbs that tonify the underlying deficiencies to improve quality of life and reduce pain and suffering.
- This formula is contraindicated in patients with severe infection or inflammation with excess heat.

CLINICAL NOTE

- Chinese or Korean *Ren Shen* (Radix et Rhizoma Ginseng) should not be used in individuals who suffer from extreme weakness and deficiency from chemotherapy and radiation treatments. These individuals often have severe yin deficiency, and use of a warm herb [such as *Ren Shen* (Radix et Rhizoma Ginseng)] may create more side effects such as dry nose and mouth, nosebleeds and ulcerations in the mouth. Therefore, American *Xi Yang Shen*

CA Support™

(Radix Panacis Quinquefolii) will be much more beneficial and is the herb used in this formula instead of *Ren Shen* (Radix et Rhizoma Ginseng).

Pulse Diagnosis by Dr. Jimmy Wei-Yen Chang:

- Tent pulse, a convex-shaped pulse that collapses under pressure

SUPPLEMENTARY FORMULAS

- To enhance the immune system and increase white blood cell count, take with ***Cordyceps 3*** or ***Immune +***.
- To increase red blood cell count, add *Dang Gui Bu Xue Tang* (Tangkuei Decoction to Tonify the Blood) or ***Schisandra ZZZ***.
- For hair loss from chemotherapy or radiation, take with ***Polygonum 14***.
- For loose stools because of Spleen deficiency, add ***GI Tonic***.
- For pain due to cancer, add ***Herbal ANG***.
- With acute headache, add ***Corydalin (AC)***.
- With chronic headache, add ***Corydalin (CR)***.
- For dry skin, add ***Nourish (Fluids)***.

ACUPUNCTURE TREATMENT

Traditional Points:

- *Zusanli* (ST 36)
- Patients in many cases are too weak to receive acupuncture. It is recommended to just perform gentle massage or acupressure.

Classic Master Tung's Points:

- **Bladder cancer/tumor:** *Simazhong* (T 88.17), *Tongshen* (T 88.09), *Wanshunyi* (T 22.08), *Tianhuangfu [Shenguan]* (T 77.18), *Shuangling* (T 11.28)*, *Waisanguan* (T 77.27), *Zhiwu* (T 11.26)
- **Bone cancer/tumor:** Bilateral *Simashang* (T 88.18), *Simazhong* (T 88.17), *Simaxia* (T 88.19), *Minghuang* (T 88.12), *Tianhuang* (T 88.13), *Qihuang* (T 88.14), *Shuangling* (T 11.28)*, *Tianhuangfu [Shenguan]* (T 77.18), *Zhiwu* (T 11.26). Needle everyday. Bleed HT and LU area below the knee. The more the blood is let out, the better the result.
- **Brain cancer/tumor:** *Shangliu* (T 55.06), *Zhengjin* (T 77.01), *Zhengzong* (T 77.02) with strong stimulation, *Yizhong* (T 77.05), *Erzhong* (T 77.06), *Sanzhong* (T 77.07), *Shuangling* (T 11.28)*, *Zhiwu* (T 11.26). Bleed dark veins nearby the medial malleolus or *Shuijing* (T 66.13). Bleed before needling for best result.
- **Breast cancer/tumor:** *Simashang* (T 88.18), *Simazhong* (T 88.17), *Simaxia* (T 88.19), *Yizhong* (T 77.05), *Erzhong* (T 77.06), *Sanzhong* (T 77.07), *Shuanglongyi* (T 77.29)*, *Shuanglonger* (T 77.30)*, *Zhiwu* (T 11.26). Bleed all dark veins nearby the HT, LU area on the legs [maximum of 150 mL for each time of bleeding]. Bleed before needling for best result.
- **Chondroma:** *Simashang* (T 88.18), *Simazhong* (T 88.17), *Dihuang* (T 77.19), *Renhuang* (T 77.21), *Tianhuangfu [Shenguan]* (T 77.18), *Fuyuan* (T 11.22), *Shuangling* (T 11.28), *Zhiwu* (T 11.26). Bleed the affected area. Bleed before needling for best result.
- **Colon cancer/tumor:** *Sanzhong* (T 77.07), *Zuwujin* (T 77.25), *Zuqianjin* (T 77.24), *Tianhuang* (T 88.13), *Minghuang* (T 88.12), *Cesanli* (T 77.22), *Simazhong* (T 88.17), *Shuangling* (T 11.28)*, *Zhiwu* (T 11.26). Bleed *Sihuashang* (T 77.08), *Sihuazhong* (T 77.09), *Sihuaxia* (T 77.11), *Fuchang* (T 77.12), or dark veins nearby. Bleed the LU area below the knee. Bleed before needling for best result. The more the blood is let out, the better the effect.
- **Fallopian tube cancer/tumor:** *Fuke* (T 11.24), *Huanchao* (T 11.06), *Sanzhong* (T 77.07), *Jiemeiyi* (T 88.04), *Jiemeier* (T 88.05), *Jiemeisan* (T 88.06), *Shuangling* (T 11.28)*, *Zhiwu* (T 11.26). Bleed dark veins nearby *Daling* (PC 7), *Yinxi* (HT 6). Bleed before needling for best result. The more the blood is let out, the better the effect.
- **Gallbladder cancer/tumor:** *Minghuang* (T 88.12), *Qihuang* (T 88.14), *Huozhi* (T 88.15), *Shuangling* (T 11.28)*, *Zhiwu* (T 11.26)
- **Kidney cancer/tumor:** *Tianhuang* (T 77.17), *Dihuang* (T 77.19), *Renhuang* (T 77.21), *Tongshen* (T 88.09), *Wanshunyi* (T 22.08), *Shuangling* (T 11.28)*, *Zhiwu* (T 11.26)
- **Liver cancer/tumor:** *Minghuang* (T 88.12), *Tianhuang* (T 88.13), *Qihuang* (T 88.14), *Huoying* (T 66.03), *Tianhuangfu [Shenguan]* (T 77.18), *Shuangling* (T 11.28)*, *Zhiwu* (T 11.26). Needle everyday.
- **Lung cancer/tumor:** *Simashang* (T 88.18), *Simazhong* (T 88.17), *Simaxia* (T 88.19), *Linggu* (T 22.05), *Dabai* (T 22.04), *Shuangling* (T 11.28)*, *Waisanguan* (T 77.27), *Xinchang* (T 11.19), *Zhiwu* (T 11.26). Bleed the LU area below the knee. Bleed before needling for best result. The more the blood is let out, the better the effect.
- **Lymphatic cancer/tumor:** *Wanshunyi* (T 22.08), *Yizhong* (T 77.05), *Erzhong* (T 77.06), *Sanzhong* (T 77.07), *Cesanli* (T 77.22), *Tianhuangfu [Shenguan]* (T 77.18), *Huoying* (T 66.03), *Shuangling* (T 11.28)*, *Zhiwu* (T 11.26). Bleed the LU area below the knee. The more the blood is let out, the better the effect.
- **Nasal cancer/tumor:** *Linggu* (T 22.05), *Dabai* (T 22.04), *Simashang* (T 88.18), *Simazhong* (T 88.17), *Simaxia* (T 88.19), *Fugesan* (T 44.30)*, *Shuangling* (T 11.28)*, *Zhiwu* (T 11.26). Bleed the LU area below the knee. Bleed before needling for best result. The more the blood is let out, the better the effect.
- **Oral cancer/tumor:** Bleed *Shaoshang* (LU 11), *Sihuazhong* (T 77.09), mouth area, *Zhiwu* (T 11.26). Bleed before needling for best result. The more the blood is let out, the better the effect.
- **Osteosarcoma:** *Piyi* (T 88.35)*, *Pier* (T 88.36)*, *Simazhong* (T 88.17), *Tianhuangfu [Shenguan]* (T 77.18), *Huoying* (T 66.03), *Fuyuan* (T 11.22), *Shuangling* (T 11.28)*, *Zhiwu* (T 11.26). Bleed around affected area. The more blood that is let out, the better the result.
- **Ovarian, uterus, cervix cancer/tumor:** *Fuke* (T 11.24), *Huanchao* (T 11.06), *Zhiwu* (T 11.26), *Shuangling* (T 11.28)*, *Qimen* (T 33.01), *Qijiao* (T 33.02), *Qizheng* (T 33.03), *Yunbai* (T 44.11), *Menjin* (T 66.05), *Waisanguan* (T 77.27), *Tianhuang* (T 77.17), *Dihuang* (T 77.19), *Renhuang* (T 77.21), *Jiemeiyi* (T 88.04), *Jiemeier* (T 88.05), *Jiemeisan* (T 88.06), *Mufu* (T 88.38)*, *Tongshen* (T 88.09), *Tongbei* (T 88.11). Bleed the dark veins nearby the web between the first and second toes; and the second and third toes. Bleed

FORMULAS

CA Support™

sacral area with cupping. Bleed before needling for best result. The more the blood is let out, the better the effect.

- **Pancreatic cancer/tumor:** *Piyi* (T 88.35)*, *Pier* (T 88.36)*, *Pisan* (T 88.37)*, *Yizhong* (T 77.05), *Erzhong* (T 77.06), *Sanzhong* (T 77.07), *Minghuang* (T 88.12), *Qihuang* (T 88.14), *Shuangling* (T 11.28)*, *Zhiwu* (T 11.26)
- **Stomach cancer/tumor:** *Cesanli* (T 77.22), *Waisanguan* (T 77.27), *Shuangling* (T 11.28)*, *Zhiwu* (T 11.26). Bleed dark veins nearby the ST area in the lower limb. Bleed before needling for best result. The more the blood is let out, the better the effect.
- **Testicular cancer/tumor:** *Dajian* (T 11.01), *Xiaojian* (T 11.02), *Waijian* (T 11.04), *Fujian* (T 11.03), *Shuangling* (T 11.28)*, *Zhiwu* (T 11.26)
- **Throat cancer/tumor:** *Tongguan* (T 88.01), *Cesanli* (T 77.22), *Yizhong* (T 77.05), *Erzhong* (T 77.06), *Sanzhong* (T 77.07), *Linggu* (T 22.05), *Dabai* (T 22.04), *Sihuashang* (T 77.08), *Zuqianjin* (T 77.24), *Zuwujin* (T 77.25), *Waisanguan* (T 77.27), *Shuangling* (T 11.28)*, *Zhiwu* (T 11.26). Bleed dark veins nearby *Shaoshang* (LU 11), nine points evenly on the neck, or the back of the neck or the ST channel on the lower limb. Bleed before needling for best result. The more the blood is let out, the better the effect.
- **Thyroid cancer/tumor:** *Xinling* (T 33.17)*, *Simashang* (T 88.18), *Simazhong* (T 88.17), *Simaxia* (T 88.19), *Waisanguan* (T 77.27), *Shuangling* (T 11.28)*, *Zhiwu* (T 11.26). Bleed *Sihuazhong* (T 77.09) and back of the neck. Bleed before needling for best result. The more the blood is let out, the better the effect.
- **Tongue cancer/tumor:** *Cesanli* (T 77.22), *Houjian* (T 44.29)*, *Minghuang* (T 88.12), *Qihuang* (T 88.14), *Shuangling* (T 11.28)*, *Zhiwu* (T 11.26). Bleed the LU area below the knee. Bleed before needling for best result. The more the blood is let out, the better the effect.
- **Vaginal cancer/tumor:** *Fuke* (T 11.24), *Huanchao* (T 11.06), *Libai* (T 44.12), *Yunbai* (T 44.11), *Sanzhong* (T 77.07), *Shuangling* (T 11.28)*, *Zhiwu* (T 11.26). Bleed dark veins nearby *Daling* (PC 7), *Yinxi* (HT 6). Bleed before needling for best result. The more the blood is let out, the better the effect.

Master Tung's Points by Dr. Chuan-Min Wang:

- **Terminal cancer:** *Yizhong* (T 77.05), *Erzhong* (T 77.06), *Sanzhong* (T 77.07), *Waisanguan* (T 77.27).

Balance Method by Dr. Richard Tan:

- Left side: *Hegu* (LI 4), *Zusanli* (ST 36), *Taixi* (KI 3), *Yinlingquan* (SP 9)
- Right side: *Lieque* (LU 7), *Tongli* (HT 5), *Zusanli* (ST 36)
- Left and right side can be alternated from treatment to treatment.

Auricular Medicine by Dr. Li-Chun Huang:

- **Fatigue:** Sympathetic, Kidney, Liver, Spleen, *San Jiao*, Anxious, Nervous Subcortex, Speed Recovered Fatigue. Bleed Ear Apex.
- **Promoting immunity:** Allergic Area, Endocrine, Adrenal Gland, Spleen, Liver. Bleed Ear Apex and Helix 1-6.

NUTRITION

- Eat a variety of fresh, organic fruits and vegetables of all colors.
- Incorporate more high fiber whole grains and nuts into the diet.
- Drink warm or hot liquids with meals. Putting cold and ice on any part of the body will immediately constrict the flow of blood to that region. Similarly, drinking cold or iced drinks with meals will hinder the natural peristaltic movements of the digestive system.
- Foods with antioxidant effects, such as vitamin A, C and E are beneficial as they neutralize the free radicals and minimize damage to cells. Beneficial foods include citrus fruits, carrots, green leafy vegetables, and green tea.
- Chew food completely and thoroughly. The digestive tract can process and absorb smaller pieces of food much better than food that is incompletely chewed. Larger pieces of food can lead to incomplete digestion and digestive discomfort.
- Always eat breakfast. According to the TCM clock, the most optimal time for the digestive system is in the morning from 8 to 10 a.m.
- Give the body two to three hours between the last meal of the day and bedtime. During sleep, the digestive system slows down as well. Make sure the body has adequate time to digest the food before going into sleep mode.
- If the patient is allergic to any food or feels uncomfortable after eating certain foods, avoid eating them.
- Avoid fast food, processed foods, junk food, artificial sugars, and carbonated drinks. Stay away from meat, greasy food, alcohol, caffeine, dairy products (except for unsweetened low-fat yogurt), tap water, iron supplements and vegetables and fruits with pesticides.
- For patients who have breast cancer, the following foods are especially beneficial: all mushrooms, whole grains, broccoli, brussel sprouts, cabbage, cauliflower, yellow/orange vegetables (carrots, pumpkins, squash, sweet potatoes), fresh garlic, onions, fresh berries, apples, cherries, grapes, and plums.
- Ginger can always be used to relieve nausea. Boil ten slices of ginger for five minutes and mix with brown sugar. Slices of fresh ginger can also be chewed or sucked on for a stronger and immediate effect.
- The Spleen is responsible for generating post-natal qi and good Spleen function also contributes to a healthy immune system. Foods that damage the Spleen should be avoided:
  - Avoid any and all foods that contain sugar, such as cake, dessert, candy, chocolate, canned juice, soft drinks, caffeinated drinks, stevia, sugar substitutes, agave, xylitol, and corn syrup.
  - Avoid raw or uncooked meats, such as sashimi, sushi, steak tartar, and seared meat. Minimize consumption of foods that are cooling in nature, including tofu, tomato, celery, asparagus, bamboo, seaweed, kelp, bitter melon, cucumber, gourd, luffa, eggplant, winter melon, honeydew, citrus, oranges, guava, grapefruit, pineapple, plums, pear, banana, papaya, watermelon, white radish, mustard leaf, potherb mustard, Chinese kale, napa,

CA Support™

bamboo sprout. Do not eat foods straight from the refrigerator. Long-term intake of cold fruits and vegetables like the ones listed above may be damaging to the Spleen. The cooling property of foods can be neutralized by cooking or adding 20 pieces of *Gou Qi Zi* (Fructus Lycii).
  - Avoid carbohydrates like white rice or bread as they may produce dampness.
  - No seafood especially shellfish, like crabs, oyster, scallops, clams, lobster and shrimp (they enter the *yangming* Stomach channel).
  - Avoid fermented foods like cheese or fermented tofu.
  - Do not eat dairy products, such as milk, cream, yogurt, cheese, and ice cream.
  - No lamb, beef, goose or duck.
  - Avoid fried or greasy foods.
- Warm and hot natured foods that damage qi and yin should be avoided, such as:
  - Avoid certain fruits like mango and durian that produce heat.
  - Avoid spicy foods and stimulants like coffee, alcohol, and energy drinks.
  - Avoid spicy/pungent/aromatic vegetables such as pepper, garlic, onions, basil, rosemary, cumin, funnel, anise, leeks, chives, scallions, thyme, saffron, wormwood, mustard, chili pepper, and wasabi.
- Avoid food and drinks with artificial coloring.
- Consume as few meat products as possible. Do not eat processed meats, such as lunch meats, hot dogs and sausages, as they contain nitrites that are associated with inflammation and chronic disease.
- Patients are encourages to eat millet porridge with dioscorea and poria daily for breakfast. Millet has been used for the military traditionally in the past and the present. It has high nutritional value, is easy to digest, and extremely beneficial to the Spleen. The millet porridge contains the following ingredients: millet 100 grams, *Shan Yao* (Rhizoma Dioscoreae) 50 grams for fresh root or 25 grams for dried root, and *Fu Ling* (Poria) 25 grams. Cook all ingredients in 4 cups of water. Bring it to a boil for 5 minutes, and simmer on medium fire for 20 minutes.

The Tao of Nutrition by Dr. Maoshing Ni and Cathy McNease:

- Consume foods that help strengthen the body so that it is able to fight against the cancer cells. A detoxifying diet is also recommended to rid the body of the toxin (cancer cells).
- Blend shiitake or ganoderma mushrooms and white fungus, boil and drink the soup three times daily.
- Boil together mung beans, pearl barley, azuki beans, and figs. This makes a delicious dessert that will aid appetite and sustain energy level.
- Make tea from dandelion, burdock, and chrysanthemum flowers; also can add beet tops or carrot tops. Drink this as the regular beverage every day.
- Always wash commercially grown fruits and vegetables in salt water to neutralize chemicals.
- Eat garlic and seaweed, slightly stir-fried in water.
- Drink carrot and celery juice.
- Make blender juice from a mixture of fresh vegetables and drink warm.
- For breast cancer, make tea from asparagus and dandelion and apply poultice to breast.
- For breast tumor, charcoal the pumpkin cap into powder, take one teaspoon of powder in one small glass of rice wine twice daily.
- Make tea from seaweed, peach kernel, and green orange peels.
- For externally visible tumors, make a poultice from seaweed, ginger and dandelion, and apply locally.
- Avoid the following foods: meat (a little fish can be eaten), coffee, cinnamon, anise, pepper, dairy products, spicy foods (except garlic), high fat foods, cooked oils, chemical additives and moldy foods.
- Avoid smoking, stress, and all irritants.

LIFESTYLE INSTRUCTIONS

- Avoid radiation from microwaves and limit prolonged exposure to appliances with high electromagnetic output, such as television, computer monitors, electric stoves, cellular phones, and other popular electronic devices.
- Relax, exercise regularly (*tai chi chuan* [*tai ji quan*], *qi gong* or yoga). Maintain a positive outlook on life.
- Avoid consumption of alcohol and exposure to tobacco in any form.
- Avoid stress and anxiety whenever possible. They suppress the immune system, slow down the metabolic process, and foster the development of cancer.
- Avoid wearing tight bras that can cut off lymphatic flow, obstruct elimination of toxins and increase risk of tumor growth.
- Sleep by 10:00 p.m. In TCM, 11:00 p.m. to 1:00 a.m. is when the yin shifts to yang. It is crucial for the body to be at rest during this time for optimal health.

PHARMACOLOGICAL AND CLINICAL RESEARCH

CA Support is developed specifically for individuals who have extreme weakness and deficiency after prolonged battles with cancer and its treatments (chemotherapy and radiation). At this moment, though the patient still has cancer, their constitution is too fragile to continue with chemotherapy and radiation. Optimal treatment requires use of herbs to suppress the growth of cancer cells while stimulating the production of healthy cells. To achieve this goal, ***CA Support*** uses herbs with immunostimulant effects to increase white blood cells, hematopoietic effects to increase red blood cells, and antineoplastic effects to suppress cancer cells.

Huang Qi (Radix Astragali), one of the most commonly used herbs, has been shown in many clinical studies to effectively increase white blood cells, multinuclear leukocytes, and IgM.[4,5] Use of *Huang Qi* (Radix Astragali) has been shown to restore normal immune system function in 115 patients with leukopenia.[6] Furthermore, use of *Huang Qi* (Radix Astragali) is also associated with a marked hematopoietic effect, as it stimulates the bone marrow and increases the production and maturity of blood cells.[7] In addition to *Huang Qi* (Radix Astragali), ***CA Support*** contains many other herbs with immunostimulant effects. *Ji Xue Teng* (Caulis Spatholobi) has been shown to increase both neutrophils and eosinophils after three days of the herbal therapy.[8] *Ji Xue Teng* (Caulis Spatholobi) also has a hematopoietic effect to distinctly stimulate the proliferation of hematopoietic progenitor cells in subjects with bone marrow depression.[9] *Dong Chong Xia Cao* (Cordyceps) is another herb that has demonstrated immunomodulatory functions. It enhances the overall immunity by increasing the number of lymphocytes and natural killer cells, and the production of interleukin, interferon and tumor-necrosis-factor.[10,11,12,13,14] Cordysinocan, a polysaccharide isolated from cultured *Dong Chong Xia Cao* (Cordyceps), activates immune responses in cultured T-lymphocytes and macrophages to signal the cascade and induction of cytokines.[15] *Bai Zhu* (Rhizoma Atractylodis Macrocephalae) increases the number of white blood cells, lymphocytes, and IgG, as well as enhancing the activity of macrophages and the reticuloendothelial system.[16,17] *Chong Lou* (Rhizoma Paridis) exerts a stimulating effect on the immune system in relation to phagocytosis, respiratory burst, and nitric oxide production.[18] Finally, *Bai Hua She She Cao* (Herba Hedyotis) has both immunomodulatory and antitumor effects by stimulating the immune system to kill or engulf tumor cells.[19]

In addition to strengthening the body, ***CA Support*** also incorporates many herbs with antineoplastic effects to fight cancer. *Ban Zhi Lian* (Herba Scutellariae Barbatae) and *Bai Hua She She Cao* (Herba Hedyotis) have potent antineoplastic effects, and have shown a promising effect to treat various types of cancer according to both *in vitro* and *in vivo* studies.[20,21] Clinical applications of *Ban Zhi Lian* (Herba Scutellariae Barbatae) and *Bai Hua She She Cao* (Herba Hedyotis) include: breast cancer,[22,23] liver cancer,[24,25] nasopharyngeal cancer,[26] colorectal cancer,[27] leukemia,[28] prostate cancer,[29] lung cancer,[30] uterine leiomyoma,[31] skin cancer,[32] and many others. *E Zhu* (Rhizoma Curcumae) has a marked antineoplastic effect to induce apoptosis and inhibits proliferation of human cancer cells.[33,34] It has been used with satisfactory results for treatment of stomach, lung, liver, and esophageal cancers.[35] *Dong Chong Xia Cao* (Cordyceps) has a cytotoxic effect, and shows a significant and dose-dependent inhibitory effect on the proliferation of four cancer cell lines: breast cancer, mouse melanoma, human premyelocytic leukemia, and human hepatocellular carcinoma.[36] *Chong Lou* (Rhizoma Paridis) has a dose-dependent anticancer activity against lung adenocarcinoma cells,[37] human promyelocytic leukemia cells,[38] and breast cancer cells.[39] *Bai Zhu* (Rhizoma Atractylodis Macrocephalae) has marked inhibitory action against esophageal cancer according to several *in vitro* studies.[40] *Yi Yi Ren* (Semen Coicis) and *Fu Ling* (Poria) have antineoplastic activity, and are generally more effective when combined with other therapies.[41,42] Lastly, *E Zhu* (Rhizoma Curcumae) and *Fu Ling* (Poria) have antiangiogenic activity, which inhibit the formation of new blood vessels from a pre-existing vascular network to suppress tumor growth, invasion, and metastasis.[43,44]

Overall, ***CA Support*** is developed specifically to address the difficult and challenging cases of cancer in which the patient is too weak to continue with chemotherapy and radiation treatments. Use of ***CA Support*** will strengthen the underlying constitution and suppress the growth of cancer cells. In conclusion, ***CA Support*** is an excellent formula to decrease pain and suffering, and improve quality of life for patients with cancer.

COMPARATIVE ANALYSIS

Despite all the advances in medicine, treatment of cancer is still in its infancy in both Western and traditional Chinese medicine.

Optimal treatment methods may include chemotherapy, radiation, and/or surgery. Though they may be effective, they are extremely harsh and create a tremendous number of side effects, including severe nausea, vomiting, hair loss, and most importantly, bone marrow suppression with decreased count of red and white blood cells. Serious cases of bone marrow suppression often necessitate the termination of chemotherapy and radiation treatments, a scenario where the patient now suffers from both cancer and the side effects of its treatments at the same time.

For patients with cancer who are too weak to receive chemotherapy, radiation, and/or surgery, use of herbal therapies is extremely beneficial to alleviate the side effects of drugs, strengthen the body, and improve overall quality of life.

Optimal therapy in cases of cancer is not to choose between Western ***or*** traditional Chinese medicine, but to use Western ***and*** traditional Chinese medicines together. These two modalities of medicine complement each others, and provide the brightest outlook and prognosis for successful treatment of cancer.

References

1. Center of Disease Control and Prevention (CDC). National Vital Statistics Report. Volume 60, Number 4. January 11, 2012.
2. Wong BY, Lau BH, Jia TY, Wan CP. Oldenlandia diffusa and Scutellaria barbata augment macrophage oxidative burst and inhibit tumor growth. *Cancer Biother Radiopharm* 1996 Feb; 11(1):51-6.
3. Wong BY, Lau BH, Jia TY, Wan CP. Oldenlandia diffusa and Scutellaria barbata augment macrophage oxidative burst and inhibit tumor growth. *Cancer Biother Radiopharm* 1996 Feb; 11(1):51-6.
4. *Shan Xi Yi Yao Za Zhi* (Shanxi Journal of Medicine and Herbology), 1974; 5-6:57.
5. *Biol Pharm Bull*, 1977; 20(11)-1178-82.
6. *Zhong Guo Zhong Xi Yi Jie He Za Zhi* (Chinese Journal of Integrative Chinese and Western Medicine), 1995 Aug.; 15(8):462-4.
7. *Nan Jing Zhong Yi Xue Yuan Xue Bao* (Journal of Nanjing University of Traditional Chinese Medicine), 1989; 1:43.
8. *Shang Hai Zhong Yi Yao Za Zhi* (Shanghai Journal of Chinese Medicine and Herbology), 1965; 9:16.

CA Support™

9. Wang DX, Chen ML, Yin JF, Liu P. Effect of SS8, the active part of Spatholobus suberectus Dunn, on proliferation of hematopoietic progenitor cells in mice with bone marrow depression. Zhongguo Zhong Yao Za Zhi. 2003 Feb;28(2): 152-5.
10. Kuo,YC. et al. Cordyceps sinensis as an immuno-modulatory agent. *American Journal Of Chinese Medicine*. 24(2):111-25, 1996.
11. Guan, YJ. et al. Effect of cordyceps sinensis on T-lymphocyte subsets in chronic renal failure. *Chung-Kuo Chung His I Chieh Ho Tsa Chih*. Jun. 1992; 12(6):338-9,323.
12. Liu, C. et al. Effects of cordyceps sinensis (CS) on in vitro natural killer cells. *Chung-Kuo Chung His I Chieh Ho Tsa Chih*. May. 1992; 12(5):267-9,259.
13. Xu, RH. et al. Effects of cordyceps sinensis on natural killer activity and colony formation of B16 melanoma. *Chinese Medical Journal*. Feb. 1992; 105(2):97-101.
14. Liu, P. et al. Influence of cordyceps sinensis (berk.) sacc. and rat serum containing same medicine on IL-1, IFN and TNF produced by rat Kupffer's cells. *Chung Kuo Chung Yao Tsa Chih*, June 1996; 21(6):367-9, 384.
15. Cheung JK, Li J, Cheung AW, Zhu Y, Zheng KY, Bi CW, Duan R, Choi RC, Lau DT, Dong TT, Lau BW, Tsim KW. Cordysinocan, a polysaccharide isolated from cultured Cordyceps, activates immune responses in cultured T-lymphocytes and macrophages: signaling cascade and induction of cytokines. J Ethnopharmacol. 2009 Jul 6;124(1):61-8.
16. *Xin Yi Yao Xue Za Zhi* (New Journal of Medicine and Herbology), 1979; 6:60.
17. *Jun Shi Yi Xue Jian Xun* (Military Medicine Notes), 1977; 2:5.
18. Zhang XF, Cui Y, Huang JJ, Zhang YZ, Nie Z, Wang LF, Yan BZ, Tang YL, Liu Y. Immuno-stimulating properties of diosgenyl saponins isolated from Paris polyphylla. State Key laboratory for SCUSS, Institute of Chemistry, The Chinese Academy of Sciences, Beijing 100080, China. Bioorg Med Chem Lett. 2007 May 1;17(9):2408-13.
19. Shan BE, Zhang JY, Du XN. Immunomodulatory activity and anti-tumor activity of Oldenlandia diffusa in vitro. Zhongguo Zhong Xi Yi Jie He Za Zhi. 2001 May;21(5):370-4.
20. Wong BY, Lau BH, Jia TY, Wan CP. Oldenlandia diffusa and Scutellaria barbata augment macrophage oxidative burst and inhibit tumor growth. *Cancer Biother Radiopharm* 1996 Feb; 11(1):51-6.
21. Wong BY, Lau BH, Jia TY, Wan CP. Oldenlandia diffusa and Scutellaria barbata augment macrophage oxidative burst and inhibit tumor growth. *Cancer Biother Radiopharm* 1996 Feb; 11(1):51-6.
22. Liu Z, Liu M, Liu M, Li J. Methylanthraquinone from Hedyotis diffusa WILLD induces Ca(2+)-mediated apoptosis in human breast cancer cells. Toxicol In Vitro. 2010 Feb;24(1):142-7.
23. Fong S, Shoemaker M, Cadaoas J, Lo A, Liao W, Tagliaferri M, Cohen I, Shtivelman E. Molecular mechanisms underlying selective cytotoxic activity of BZL101, an extract of Scutellaria barbata, towards breast cancer cells. Cancer Biol Ther. 2008 Apr;7(4):577-86.
24. Yu Hsueh-Chiu, Suzuki S., Okubo T., Kawashima I., Tsuda M., Borai N.E., Yamamura M. & Yu H.C. Anti-tumor effect of Chinese herbal medicines " *Scutellaria barbata* and *Oldenlandia diffusa* " on cancer cell lines and C3H-AVy mouse with spontaneous hepatocellular carcinoma. *J of Traditional Medicines*. 2000, 17: 165-169.
25. Tang PM, Chan JY, Au SW, Kong SK, Tsui SK, Waye MM, Mak TC, Fong WP, Fung KP. Pheophorbide a, an active compound isolated from Scutellaria barbata, possesses photodynamic activities by inducing apoptosis in human hepatocellular carcinoma. Cancer Biol Ther. 2006 Sep;5(9):1111-6.
26. Dai SJ, Peng WB, Zhang DW, Shen L, Wang WY, Ren Y. Cytotoxic neo-clerodane diterpenoid alkaloids from Scutellaria barbata. J Nat Prod. 2009 Oct;72(10):1793-7.
27. Dai SJ, Liang DD, Ren Y, Liu K, Shen L. New neo-clerodane diterpenoid alkaloids from Scutellaria barbata with cytotoxic activities. Chem Pharm Bull (Tokyo). 2008 Feb;56(2):207-9.
28. *Ren Min Wei Sheng Chu Ban She* (Journal of People's Public Health), 1988:302.
29. Wong BY, Nguyen DL, Lin T, Wong HH, Cavalcante A, Greenberg NM, Hausted RP, Zheng J. Chinese medicinal herb Scutellaria barbata modulates apoptosis and cell survival in murine and human prostate cancer cells and tumor development in TRAMP mice. Eur J Cancer Prev. 2009 Aug;18(4):331-41.
30. Chen LG, Hung LY, Tsai KW, Pan YS, Tsai YD, Li YZ, Liu YW. Wogonin, a bioactive flavonoid in herbal tea, inhibits inflammatory cyclooxygenase-2 gene expression in human lung epithelial cancer cells. Mol Nutr Food Res. 2008 Nov;52(11):1349-57.
31. Kim KW, Jin UH, Kim DI, Lee TK, Kim MS, Oh MJ, Kim MS, Kwon DY, Lee YC, Kim CH. Antiproliferative effect of Scutellaria barbata D. Don. on cultured human uterine leiomyoma cells by down-regulation of the expression of Bcl-2 protein. Phytother Res. 2008 May;22(5):583-90.
32. Suh SJ, Yoon JW, Lee TK, Jin UH, Kim SL, Kim MS, Kwon DY, Lee YC, Kim CH. Chemoprevention of Scutellaria bardata on human cancer cells and tumorigenesis in skin cancer. Phytother Res. 2007 Feb;21(2):135-41.
33. *Xin Yi Yao Xue Za Zhi* (New Journal of Medicine and Herbology), 1976; 12:28.
34. Lim CB, Ky N, Ng HM, Hamza MS, Zhao Y. Curcuma wenyujin extract induces apoptosis and inhibits proliferation of human cervical cancer cells in vitro and in vivo. Integr Cancer Ther. 2010 Mar;9(1):36-49.
35. *Shan Dong Zhong Yi Xue Yuan Xue Bao* (Journal of Shandong University School of Chinese Medicine), 1980; 1:30.
36. Wu JY, Zhang QX, Leung PH. Inhibitory effects of ethyl acetate extract of Cordyceps sinensis mycelium on various cancer cells in culture and B16 melanoma in C57BL/6 mice. Phytomedicine. 2007 Jan;14(1):43-9.
37. Yan LL, Zhang YJ, Gao WY, Man SL, Wang Y. In vitro and in vivo anticancer activity of steroid saponins of Paris polyphylla var. yunnanensis. School of Pharmaceutical Science and Technology, Tianjin University, Tianjin 300072, China. Exp Oncol. 2009 Mar;31(1):27-32.
38. Zhao Y, Kang LP, Liu YX, Liang YG, Tan DW, Yu ZY, Cong YW, Ma BP. Steroidal saponins from the rhizome of Paris polyphylla and their cytotoxic activities. Department of Biotechnology, Beijing Institute of Radiation Medicine, Beijing, PR China. Planta Med. 2009 Mar;75(4):356-63.
39. Lee MS, Yuet-Wa JC, Kong SK, Yu B, Eng-Choon VO, Nai-Ching HW, Chung-Wai TM, Fung KP. Effects of polyphyllin D, a steroidal saponin in Paris polyphylla, in growth inhibition of human breast cancer cells and in xenograft. Department of Biochemistry, The Chinese University of Hong Kong, Shatin, NT, Hong Kong SAR, China. Cancer Biol Ther. 2005 Nov;4(11):1248-54.
40. *Zhong Liu Yu Zhi Tong Xun* (Journal of Prevention and Treatment of Cancer), 1976; 2:40.
41. *Zhong Cao Yao Xue* (Study of Chinese Herbal Medicine), 1976; 15.
42. *Zhong Xi Yi Jie He Za Zhi* (Journal of Integrated Chinese and Western Medicine), 1985; 2:115.
43. Varinska L, Mirossay L, Mojzisova G, Mojzis J. Antiangogenic effect of selected phytochemicals. Pharmazie. 2010 Jan;65(1):57-63.
44. Yance D.R., Sagar S.M. Targeting angiogenesis with integrative cancer therapies. *Integr Cancer Ther.* 2006, 5(1):9-29.

C/R Support™

CLINICAL APPLICATIONS

- **Chemotherapy/radiation support:** side effects and adverse reactions associated with these treatments
- **Myasthenia gravis**
- **Chronic fatigue syndrome**
- **Prolapse of organs** such as the stomach, rectum, uterus and bladder
- **Anorexia and wasting syndrome**

WESTERN THERAPEUTIC ACTIONS

- Chemoprotective and radioprotective benefits to prevent, minimize, or reverse adverse reactions associated with chemotherapy or radiation
- Immunostimulant effect to increase both specific and non-specific immunity
- Hematopoietic function to increase the production of red blood cells

CHINESE THERAPEUTIC ACTIONS

- Tonifies the Spleen and the Stomach
- Tonifies yin and moistens dryness
- Tonifies the *wei* (defensive) *qi*
- Harmonizes the middle *jiao*

DOSAGE

Take 3 to 4 capsules three times daily as a maintenance dose. Dosage may be increased to 5 to 6 capsules three times daily for cancer patients receiving chemotherapy, or radiation treatments. ***C/R Support*** should be taken on an empty stomach with warm water for maximum effectiveness. Honey can also be added to enhance the taste of the herbs, tonify qi and harmonize the middle *jiao*.

INGREDIENTS

Bai Zhu (Rhizoma Atractylodis Macrocephalae)
Chen Pi (Pericarpium Citri Reticulatae)
Dang Gui (Radix Angelicae Sinensis)
Di Huang (Radix Rehmanniae)
Dong Chong Xia Cao (Cordyceps)
Gou Qi Zi (Fructus Lycii)
Huang Qi (Radix Astragali)
Ling Zhi (Ganoderma)
Mai Dong (Radix Ophiopogonis)
Ren Shen (Radix et Rhizoma Ginseng)
Shi Di (Calyx Kaki)
Zhi Gan Cao (Radix et Rhizoma Glycyrrhizae Praeparata cum Melle)
Zhu Ru (Caulis Bambusae in Taenia)

BACKGROUND

Cancer is the second leading cause of death, according to a report by the CDC published in January 11, 2012.[1] In Western medicine, treatment options for cancer include surgery, chemotherapy, and radiation. Though these treatments may be effective, they are invasive to the body and often cause severe and serious damages to many organs and cells. Therefore, additional interventions are extremely important to alleviate the side effects of these invasive treatments, support the body and its health, and improve the overall quality of life.

FORMULA EXPLANATION

C/R Support is an herbal formula specifically designed to support patients with cancer as they undergo chemotherapy and radiation treatments. Though effective against cancer cells, chemotherapy and radiation destroy normal tissue and healthy cells and cause a wide array of side effects and adverse reactions, including but not limited to nausea, vomiting, hair loss, weakness and fatigue. For cancer patients receiving chemotherapy and radiation, ***C/R Support*** complements the overall treatment by enhancing the immune system, reducing the side effects of the drug treatment, inhibiting the growth of cancer cells, and boosting the energy and vitality of the patient.

Huang Qi (Radix Astragali) is the chief herb in this formula. It replenishes the vital qi, consolidates the *wei* (defensive) *qi*, and protects against external pathogenic factors. It has anticancer effects to increase the content of cAMP and inhibit the growth of tumor cells. *Ling Zhi* (Ganoderma) tonifies blood and vital energy, increases the white blood cell count, and inhibits the growth of various viruses and bacteria. *Dong Chong Xia Cao* (Cordyceps) is essential in rebuilding the patient's constitution and is used for chronically debilitated patients. *Shi Di* (Calyx Kaki), *Zhi Gan Cao* (Radix et Rhizoma Glycyrrhizae Praeparata cum Melle) and *Zhu Ru* (Caulis Bambusae in Taenia) tonify the Spleen and Stomach of the middle *jiao* to prevent nausea, vomiting and stomach discomfort. *Chen Pi* (Pericarpium Citri Reticulatae) strengthens the Spleen and dispels phlegm. *Di Huang* (Radix Rehmanniae), *Gou Qi Zi* (Fructus Lycii), and *Mai Dong* (Radix Ophiopogonis) treat thirst and dryness by replenishing body fluids. *Dang Gui* (Radix Angelicae Sinensis) augments the yin and blood and relieves thirst and dryness. *Ren Shen* (Radix et Rhizoma Ginseng) and *Bai Zhu* (Rhizoma Atractylodis Macrocephalae) tonify the Spleen qi to increase both energy and appetite during radiation treatments.

C/R Support can also be used to treat prolapse of internal organs, such as the stomach, rectum, bladder, or uterus. *Huang Qi* (Radix Astragali), *Ling Zhi* (Ganoderma), *Ren Shen* (Radix et Rhizoma Ginseng), and *Bai Zhu* (Rhizoma Atractylodis Macrocephalae) tonify qi, ascend yang, and raise the prolapse of internal organs. Similarly, qi and yang tonic herbs in this formula help to relieve chronic fatigue syndrome, anorexia, wasting syndrome, and myasthenia gravis.

CAUTIONS & CONTRAINDICATIONS

- ***C/R Support*** is ***not*** designed to treat cancer or replace chemotherapy and radiation. Its main focus is to complement

C/R Support™

chemotherapy and radiation treatments by strengthening the overall constitution of the patient and minimize the side effects.

- This formula is contraindicated in cases of excessive heat, damp heat, infection or inflammation.
- This herbal formula contains herbs that invigorate blood circulation, such as *Dang Gui* (Radix Angelicae Sinensis). Therefore, patients who are on anticoagulant or antiplatelet therapies, such as Coumadin (warfarin), should use this formula with caution, or not at all, as there may be a higher risk of bleeding and bruising.[2,3,4]
- The safety status of using *Dang Gui* (Radix Angelicae Sinensis) in individuals with hormone-dependent cancer is unclear.[5,6,7] According to one reference, use of *Dang Gui* (Radix Angelicae Sinensis) is not associated with thickening of the endometrium or vaginal cell maturation, both of which would indicate an estrogenic effect. Furthermore, there is no confirmation of the presence of a phytoestrogen component or effect on hormone-dependent cancer when ferulic acid is evaluated as the main component of *Dang Gui* (Radix Angelicae Sinensis).[8] According to another reference, the water extract of *Dang Gui* (Radix Angelicae Sinensis) has a weak estrogen-agonistic activity to stimulate the growth of breast cancer cells (MCF-7).[9] In summary, due to conflicting and insufficient data, use of *Dang Gui* (Radix Angelicae Sinensis) in patients with hormone-dependent cancer warrants caution pending further study.

CLINICAL NOTES

- ***C/R Support*** has a wide range of clinical applications. Its use is not limited to cancer patients receiving chemotherapy and radiation.
- ***C/R Support*** contains herbs with immune-enhancing, anticancer activities, and energy-boosting properties. It will benefit cancer patients, whether or not they are receiving chemotherapy and radiation treatments.

Pulse Diagnosis by Dr. Jimmy Wei-Yen Chang:

- **Overall weakness, including weak immune system:** tent pulse, a convex-shaped pulse that collapses upon pressure
- **Weak digestion:** small pulse, a weak and thin pulse that disappears upon pressure, on the right *guan*

SUPPLEMENTARY FORMULAS

- For patients with cancer who have extreme weakness and deficiency and cannot tolerate chemotherapy or radiation treatment, use ***CA Support***.
- To enhance the immune system during or after chemotherapy or radiation treatment, add ***Immune +***.
- For cancer of the lung and reproductive systems, add ***Cordyceps 3*** to strengthen the constitution of these two organs.
- For hair loss during chemotherapy or radiation treatment, combine with ***Polygonum 14*** to nourish qi and blood and prevent hair damage.
- For maintenance at the conclusion of chemotherapy or radiation treatment, take ***Cordyceps 3***, ***Imperial Tonic*** and ***Immune +*** on a long-term basis.
- For poor appetite and loose stools from Spleen deficiency caused by chemotherapy or radiation, add ***GI Tonic***.
- For Kidney yin deficiency, add ***Kidney Tonic (Yin)***.
- For Kidney yang deficiency, add ***Kidney Tonic (Yang)***.
- For constipation, add ***Gentle Lax (Deficient)***.
- For pain due to cancer, add ***Herbal ANG***.
- For stress and anxiety, use ***Calm***.
- For stress, anxiety, and insomnia, use ***Calm ZZZ***.
- For a quick boost of energy and vitality, use ***Vibrant***.

ACUPUNCTURE TREATMENT

Traditional Points:

- *Zusanli* (ST 36), *Fuliu* (KI 7), *Neiguan* (PC 6), *Pishu* (BL 20), *Weishu* (BL 21), *Hegu* (LI 4), *Shanzhong* (CV 17)

Classic Master Tung's Points:

- **Bladder cancer/tumor:** *Simazhong* (T 88.17), *Tongshen* (T 88.09), *Wanshunyi* (T 22.08), *Tianhuangfu [Shenguan]* (T 77.18), *Shuangling* (T 11.28)*, *Waisanguan* (T 77.27), *Zhiwu* (T 11.26)
- **Bone cancer/tumor:** Bilateral *Simashang* (T 88.18), *Simazhong* (T 88.17), *Simaxia* (T 88.19), *Minghuang* (T 88.12), *Tianhuang* (T 88.13), *Qihuang* (T 88.14), *Shuangling* (T 11.28)*, *Tianhuangfu [Shenguan]* (T 77.18), *Zhiwu* (T 11.26). Needle everyday. Bleed HT and LU area below the knee. The more the blood is let out, the better the result.
- **Brain cancer/tumor:** *Shangliu* (T 55.06), *Zhengjin* (T 77.01), *Zhengzong* (T 77.02) with strong stimulation, *Yizhong* (T 77.05), *Erzhong* (T 77.06), *Sanzhong* (T 77.07), *Shuangling* (T 11.28)*, *Zhiwu* (T 11.26). Bleed dark veins nearby the medial malleolus or *Shuijing* (T 66.13). Bleed before needling for best result.
- **Breast cancer/tumor:** *Simashang* (T 88.18) *Simazhong* (T 88.17), *Simaxia* (T 88.19), *Yizhong* (T 77.05), *Erzhong* (T 77.06), *Sanzhong* (T 77.07), *Shuanglongyi* (T 77.29)*, *Shuanglonger* (T 77.30)*, *Zhiwu* (T 11.26). Bleed all dark veins nearby the HT, LU area on the legs [maximum of 150 mL for each time of bleeding]. Bleed before needling for best result.
- **Chondroma:** *Simashang* (T 88.18), *Simazhong* (T 88.17), *Dihuang* (T 77.19), *Renhuang* (T 77.21, *Tianhuangfu [Shenguan]* (T 77.18), *Fuyuan* (T 11.22), *Shuangling* (T 11.28), *Zhiwu* (T 11.26). Bleed the affected area. Bleed before needling for best result.
- **Colon cancer/tumor:** *Sanzhong* (T 77.07), *Zuwujin* (T 77.25), *Zuqianjin* (T 77.24), *Tianhuang* (T 88.13), *Minghuang* (T 88.12), *Cesanli* (T 77.22), *Simazhong* (T 88.17), *Shuangling* (T 11.28)*, *Zhiwu* (T 11.26). Bleed *Sihuashang* (T 77.08), *Sihuazhong* (T 77.09), *Sihuaxia* (T 77.11), *Fuchang* (T 77.12), or dark veins nearby. Bleed the LU area below the knee. Bleed before needling for best result. The more the blood is let out, the better the effect.
- **Fallopian tube cancer/tumor:** *Fuke* (T 11.24), *Huanchao* (T 11.06), *Sanzhong* (T 77.07), *Jiemeiyi* (T 88.04), *Jiemeier* (T 88.05),

FORMULAS

C/R Support™

Jiemeisan (T 88.06), *Shuangling* (T 11.28)*, *Zhiwu* (T 11.26). Bleed dark veins nearby *Daling* (PC 7), *Yinxi* (HT 6). Bleed before needling for best result. The more the blood is let out, the better the effect.

- **Gallbladder cancer/tumor:** *Minghuang* (T 88.12), *Qihuang* (T 88.14), *Huozhi* (T 88.15), *Shuangling* (T 11.28)*, *Zhiwu* (T 11.26)
- **Kidney cancer/tumor:** *Tianhuang* (T 77.17), *Dihuang* (T 77.19), *Renhuang* (T 77.21), *Tongshen* (T 88.09), *Wanshunyi* (T 22.08), *Shuangling* (T 11.28)*, *Zhiwu* (T 11.26)
- **Liver cancer/tumor:** *Minghuang* (T 88.12), *Tianhuang* (T 88.13), *Qihuang* (T 88.14), *Huoying* (T 66.03), *Tianhuangfu [Shenguan]* (T 77.18), *Shuangling* (T 11.28)*, *Zhiwu* (T 11.26). Needle everyday.
- **Lung cancer/tumor:** *Simashang* (T 88.18), *Simazhong* (T 88.17), *Simaxia* (T 88.19), *Linggu* (T 22.05), *Dabai* (T 22.04), *Shuangling* (T 11.28)*, *Waisanguan* (T 77.27), *Xinchang* (T 11.19), *Zhiwu* (T 11.26). Bleed the LU area below the knee. Bleed before needling for best result. The more the blood is let out, the better the effect.
- **Lymphatic cancer/tumor:** *Wanshunyi* (T 22.08), *Yizhong* (T 77.05), *Erzhong* (T 77.06), *Sanzhong* (T 77.07), *Cesanli* (T 77.22), *Tianhuangfu [Shenguan]* (T 77.18), *Huoying* (T 66.03), *Shuangling* (T 11.28)*, *Zhiwu* (T 11.26). Bleed the LU area below the knee. The more the blood is let out, the better the effect.
- **Nasal cancer/tumor:** *Linggu* (T 22.05), *Dabai* (T 22.04), *Simashang* (T 88.18), *Simazhong* (T 88.17), *Simaxia* (T 88.19), *Fugesan* (T 44.30)*, *Shuangling* (T 11.28)*, *Zhiwu* (T 11.26). Bleed the LU area below the knee. Bleed before needling for best result. The more the blood is let out, the better the effect.
- **Oral cancer/tumor:** Bleed *Shaoshang* (LU 11), *Sihuazhong* (T 77.09), mouth area, *Zhiwu* (T 11.26). Bleed before needling for best result. The more the blood is let out, the better the effect.
- **Osteosarcoma:** *Piyi* (T 88.35)*, *Pier* (T 88.36)*, *Simazhong* (T 88.17), *Tianhuangfu [Shenguan]* (T 77.18), *Huoying* (T 66.03), *Fuyuan* (T 11.22), *Shuangling* (T 11.28)*, *Zhiwu* (T 11.26). Bleed around affected area. The more the blood is let out, the better the result.
- **Ovarian, uterus, cervix cancer/tumor:** *Fuke* (T 11.24), *Huanchao* (T 11.06), *Zhiwu* (T 11.26), *Shuangling* (T 11.28)*, *Qimen* (T 33.01), *Qijiao* (T 33.02), *Qizheng* (T 33.03), *Yunbai* (T 44.11), *Menjin* (T 66.05), *Waisanguan* (T 77.27), *Tianhuang* (T 77.17), *Dihuang* (T 77.19), *Renhuang* (T 77.21), *Jiemeiyi* (T 88.04), *Jiemeier* (T 88.05), *Jiemeisan* (T 88.06), *Mufu* (T 88.38)*, *Tongshen* (T 88.09), *Tongbei* (T 88.11). Bleed the dark veins nearby the web between the first and second toes; and second and third toes. Bleed sacral area with cupping. Bleed before needling for best result. The more the blood is let out, the better the effect.
- **Pancreatic cancer/tumor:** *Piyi* (T 88.35)*, *Pier* (T 88.36)*, *Pisan* (T 88.37)*, *Yizhong* (T 77.05), *Erzhong* (T 77.06), *Sanzhong* (T 77.07), *Minghuang* (T 88.12), *Qihuang* (T 88.14), *Shuangling* (T 11.28)*, *Zhiwu* (T 11.26)
- **Stomach cancer/tumor:** *Cesanli* (T 77.22), *Waisanguan* (T 77.27), *Shuangling* (T 11.28)*, *Zhiwu* (T 11.26). Bleed dark veins nearby the ST area in the lower limb. Bleed before needling for best result. The more the blood is let out, the better the effect.
- **Testicular cancer/tumor:** *Dajian* (T 11.01), *Xiaojian* (T 11.02), *Waijian* (T 11.04), *Fujian* (T 11.03), *Shuangling* (T 11.28)*, *Zhiwu* (T 11.26)
- **Throat cancer/tumor:** *Tongguan* (T 88.01), *Cesanli* (T 77.22), *Yizhong* (T 77.05), *Erzhong* (T 77.06), *Sanzhong* (T 77.07), *Linggu* (T 22.05), *Dabai* (T 22.04), *Sihuashang* (T 77.08), *Zuqianjin* (T 77.24), *Zuwujin* (T 77.25), *Waisanguan* (T 77.27), *Shuangling* (T 11.28)*, *Zhiwu* (T 11.26). Bleed dark veins nearby *Shaoshang* (LU 11), nine points evenly on the neck, or the back of the neck or the ST channel on the lower limb. Bleed before needling for best result. The more the blood is let out, the better the effect.
- **Thyroid cancer/tumor:** *Xinling* (T 33.17)*, *Simashang* (T 88.18), *Simazhong* (T 88.17), *Simaxia* (T 88.19), *Waisanguan* (T 77.27), *Shuangling* (T 11.28)*, *Zhiwu* (T 11.26). Bleed *Sihuazhong* (T 77.09) and back of the neck. Bleed before needling for best result. The more the blood is let out, the better the effect.
- **Tongue cancer/tumor:** *Cesanli* (T 77.22), *Houjian* (T 44.29)*, *Minghuang* (T 88.12), *Qihuang* (T 88.14), *Shuangling* (T 11.28)*, *Zhiwu* (T 11.26). Bleed the LU area below the knee. Bleed before needling for best result. The more the blood is let out, the better the effect.
- **Vaginal cancer/tumor:** *Fuke* (T 11.24), *Huanchao* (T 11.06), *Libai* (T 44.12), *Yunbai* (T 44.11), *Sanzhong* (T 77.07), *Shuangling* (T 11.28)*, *Zhiwu* (T 11.26). Bleed dark veins nearby *Daling* (PC 7), *Yinxi* (HT 6). Bleed before needling for best result. The more the blood is let out, the better the effect.

Master Tung's Points by Dr. Chuan-Min Wang:

- **Chemotherapy, radiation, myasthenia gravis, organ prolapse, anorexia, wasting:** *Zhenghui* (T 1010.01), *Zhengben* (T 1010.12), *Zhongbai* (T 22.06)

Balance Method by Dr. Richard Tan:

- **Digestive symptoms due to chemotherapy or radiation**
  - Left side: *Neiguan* (PC 6), *Lieque* (LU 7), *Zusanli* (ST 36), *Yanglingquan* (GB 34)
  - Right side: *Zhigou* (TH 6), *Hegu* (LI 4), *Yinlingquan* (SP 9), *Ququan* (LR 8)
  - Left and right sides can be alternated from treatment to treatment.

Ear Acupuncture:

- **Pain due to cancer**
  - Main points: Subcortex, Heart, correlating diseased organ
  - Adjunct points: Sympathetic, Liver, *Shenmen*
- Select four to six points each time. Alternate the ear treatments every two days.

Auricular Medicine by Dr. Li-Chun Huang:

- **Nausea:** Cardia, Stomach, Liver, *Shenmen*, Occiput, Digestive Subcortex

C/R Support™

- **Fatigue:** Sympathetic, Kidney, Liver, Spleen, *San Jiao*, Anxious, Nervous Subcortex, Speed Recovered Fatigue. Bleed Ear Apex.
- **Edema at arm pit after breast cancer surgery:** *San Jiao*, Arm Pit, Spleen, Endocrine, Large Auricular Nerve. Bleed Helix 4.
- **Promoting immunity:** Allergic Area, Endocrine, Adrenal Gland, Spleen, Liver. Bleed Ear Apex and Helix 1-6.

NUTRITION

- Eat a variety of fresh, organic fruits and vegetables of all colors.
- Incorporate more high fiber whole grains and nuts into the diet.
- Drink warm or hot liquids with meals. Putting cold and ice on any part of the body will immediately constrict the flow of blood to that region. Similarly, drinking cold or iced drinks with meals will hinder the natural peristaltic movements of the digestive system.
- Foods with antioxidant effects, such as vitamin A, C and E are beneficial as they neutralize the free radicals and minimize damage to cells. Beneficial foods include citrus fruits, carrots, green leafy vegetables, and green tea.
- Chew food completely and thoroughly. The digestive tract can process and absorb smaller pieces of food much better than food that is incompletely chewed. Larger pieces of food can lead to incomplete digestion and digestive discomfort.
- Always eat breakfast. According to the TCM clock, the most optimal time for the digestive system is in the morning from 8 to 10 a.m.
- Give the body two to three hours between the last meal of the day and bedtime. During sleep, the digestive system slows down as well. Make sure the body has adequate time to digest the food before going into sleep mode.
- If the patient is allergic to any food or feels uncomfortable after eating certain foods, avoid eating them.
- Avoid fast food, processed foods, junk food, artificial sugars, and carbonated drinks. Stay away from meat, greasy food, alcohol, caffeine, dairy products (except for unsweetened low-fat yogurt), tap water, iron supplements and vegetables and fruits with pesticides.
- For patients who have breast cancer, the following foods are especially beneficial: all mushrooms, whole grains, broccoli, brussel sprouts, cabbage, cauliflower, yellow/orange vegetables (carrots, pumpkins, squash, sweet potatoes), fresh garlic, onions, fresh berries, apples, cherries, grapes, and plums.
- Ginger can always be used to relieve nausea. Boil ten slices of ginger for five minutes and mix with brown sugar. Slices of fresh ginger can also be chewed or sucked on for a stronger and immediate effect.
- The Spleen is responsible for generating post-natal qi and good Spleen function also contributes to a healthy immune system. Foods that damage the Spleen should be avoided:
  - Avoid any and all foods that contain sugar, such as cake, dessert, candy, chocolate, canned juice, soft drinks, caffeinated drinks, stevia, sugar substitutes, agave, xylitol, and corn syrup.
  - Avoid raw or uncooked meats, such as sashimi, sushi, steak tartar, and seared meat. Minimize consumption of foods that are cooling in nature, including tofu, tomato, celery, asparagus, bamboo, seaweed, kelp, bitter melon, cucumber, gourd, luffa, eggplant, winter melon, watermelon, honeydew, citrus, oranges, guava, grapefruit, pineapple, plums, pear, banana, papaya, white radish, mustard leaf, potherb mustard, Chinese kale, napa, bamboo sprout. Do not eat foods straight from the refrigerator. Long-term intake of cold fruits and vegetables like the ones listed above may be damaging to the Spleen. The cooling property of foods can be neutralized by cooking or adding 20 pieces of *Gou Qi Zi* (Fructus Lycii).
  - Avoid carbohydrates like white rice or bread as they may produce dampness.
  - No seafood especially shellfish, like crabs, oyster, scallops, clams, lobster and shrimp (they enter the *yangming* Stomach channel).
  - Avoid fermented foods like cheese or fermented tofu.
  - Do not eat dairy products, such as milk, cream, yogurt, cheese, and ice cream.
  - No lamb, beef, goose or duck.
  - Avoid fried or greasy foods.
- Warm and hot natured foods that damage qi and yin hould be avoided, such as:
  - Avoid certain fruits like mango and durian that produce heat.
  - Avoid spicy foods and stimulants like coffee, alcohol, and energy drinks.
  - Avoid spicy/pungent/aromatic vegetables such as pepper, garlic, onions, basil, rosemary, cumin, funnel, anise, leeks, chives, scallions, thyme, saffron, wormwood, mustard, chili pepper, and wasabi.
- Avoid food and drinks with artificial coloring.
- Consume as few meat products as possible. Do not eat processed meats, such as lunch meats, hot dogs and sausages, as they contain nitrites that are associated with inflammation and chronic disease.

The Tao of Nutrition by Dr. Maoshing Ni and Cathy McNease:

- Blend shitake or ganoderma mushrooms and white fungus, boil and drink the soup three times a day.
- Boil together mung beans, pearl barley, azuki beans, and figs. This makes a delicious dessert that will aid appetite and sustain energy levels.
- Avoid meat, chicken, coffee, cinnamon, anise, pepper, dairy products, spicy foods (except garlic), high fat foods, cooked oils, chemical additives, moldy foods, smoking, constipation, stress, and all irritations.

LIFESTYLE INSTRUCTIONS

- Avoid radiation from microwaves and limit prolonged exposure to appliances with high electromagnetic output, such as television,

C/R Support™

computer monitors, electric stoves, cellular phones, and other popular electronic devices.

- Relax, exercise regularly (*tai chi chuan* [*tai ji quan*], *qi gong* or yoga). Maintain a positive outlook on life.
- Avoid the consumption of alcohol and exposure to tobacco or nicotine in any form.
- Avoid stress and anxiety whenever possible. They suppress the immune system, slow down the metabolic process, and foster the development of cancer.
- Avoid wearing tight bras, which can cut off lymphatic flow, obstruct elimination of toxins and increase risk of tumor growth.
- Sleep by 10:00 p.m. In TCM, 11:00 p.m. to 1:00 a.m. is when the yin shifts to yang. It is crucial for the body to be at rest during this time for optimal health.

CASE STUDIES

- E.F., a 47-year-old female with uterine cancer, had been receiving chemotherapy for the previous ten months. She was experiencing numbness of her mouth and jaw, and losing her sense of taste and smell as a result of the chemotherapy. The practitioner diagnosed the condition as Kidney and Spleen qi deficiencies. She was instructed to take ***C/R Support***. At first, she was only taking the herbs sporadically, but once she noticed the pain went away when taking them, she took them regularly. Her Western doctor commented that the patient's appetite had increased, compliments to the herbs, which was very important when undergoing her chemotherapy. Submitted by C.W., Santa Barbara, California.
- In July 1999, a 66-year-old retired business woman was brought in for acupuncture and herbal treatments. She was seriously ill from severe chronic anorexia triggered by intolerance to chemotherapeutic treatment following radiation and surgery for cancer of the vocal cords. Approximately 5'4" tall, the woman was curled up in the fetal position, weighing 85 lbs., cold, lethargic, nauseous and exceedingly anxious. She had had one previous occurrence of the cancer two years before, and felt she was in danger of dying, if not from the cancer, then from the treatment. She began taking small doses of ***C/R Support*** granules stirred into warm water, as she could not swallow anything but liquids. She continued with ***C/R Support*** for several weeks, later augmented with *Bu Zhong Yi Qi Tang* (Tonify the Middle and Augment the Qi Decoction), but found it difficult to incorporate a second herbal formula, so she relied on ***C/R Support*** for approximately eight months. No further chemotherapeutic or radiation treatment was attempted, at the direction of her M.D. oncologist and at the patient's wishes. Within three weeks of beginning treatment, the woman was able to resume eating small meals of well-cooked foods, and within two months, she was gaining weight noticeably and regaining color in her face. Her voice was a strained whisper initially, gradually regaining some volume and tone. Because the underlying pathogens in her case were Lung heat, Heart fire, and dryness with persistent phlegm, her herbal formula was gradually changed to half ***C/R Support***, and half additional ingredients to address the heat, dryness and phlegm. At approximately 24 months into treatment, ***C/R Support*** was discontinued, although the patient continues to take herbs specific to her imbalance and seek acupuncture weekly. Because of emotional issues related to her throat, compliance with her herbal regime is difficult for the patient: she seldom takes the full dosage or recommended frequency; however, she states she tries to become more and more consistent. She has regained normal weight and vitality, returning to an active 'retired' home and social life. As of January 2002, she continues to receive 'cancer free' reports from her oncologist and surgeon, and is seeing gradual improvement in her voice, thirst levels and phlegm. Submitted by L.C., Santa Monica, California.
- A 69-year-old male presented in July 1999 with advanced multiple myeloma, brittle bones, chronic intense pain in his back and hips, digestive difficulties, deficient constipation and hair loss. He is an entertainment professional and concerned about being able to preserve his career in the face of medical expenses and the emotional satisfaction of continuing to work. His blood cancer count was high and remained somewhat high through February 2001, when it was 2,100. He began taking ***C/R Support*** at the normal dosage in July 1999, combined over time with a normal dosage of either ***Nourish***, *Shou Wu Pian* (Polygonum Pills), or *You Gui Wan* (Restore the Right [Kidney] Pill), depending on the symptoms presented at his weekly visits for acupuncture and herbal consultation. He continued on ***C/R Support*** through the middle of 2001, transitioning at that point to individualized formulas specific to his underlying digestive weakness, osteoporosis and pain. Although the osteoporotic aspects of his illness continue to make him vulnerable to skeletal injury and pain, he has maintained 80% of the hairline he had upon presenting for treatment, and has been able to continue working in his profession. His blood cancer counts in December 2001 were below 300. He states he continues to feel he is improving. Submitted by L.C., Santa Monica, California.
- K.E., a 45-year-old female, presented with ovarian cancer and ***C/R Support*** was prescribed at 2 grams three times a day. She was instructed to take 4 grams three times daily if her white blood cell count was low. She also received acupuncture treatment in addition to the herbs. Patient reported that she felt okay during the chemotherapy and stayed relatively healthy and kept the white blood cell count healthy. Submitted by W.F., Bloomfield, New Jersey.

PHARMACOLOGICAL AND CLINICAL RESEARCH

C/R Support is formulated specifically to offer chemotherapy or radiation support for patients with cancer. Chemotherapy or radiation work by killing cancer cells that multiply rapidly. Unfortunately, as these treatments destroy fast-growing cancer cells, they can also cause serious damages to fast-growing healthy cells, such as red blood cells, white blood cells, bone marrow

C/R Support™

cells, hair follicles and cells in the digestive tract (mouth, throat, stomach and intestines). So while it may be important to use chemotherapy or radiation to treat cancer, it is equally important to use herbs to alleviate the side effects of these harsh treatments and improve the quality of life.

C/R Support is formulated with many herbs specifically to alleviate the side effects of many chemotherapy drugs and radiation treatments. *Dong Chong Xia Cao* (Cordyceps) is effective to alleviate leukopenia caused by Taxol (paclitaxel) by protecting both hematopoietic progenitor cells directly and the bone marrow stem cell niche through its effects on osteoblast differentiation.[10] *Gou Qi Zi* (Fructus Lycii) shows a protective effect against Adriamycin (doxorubicin)-induced cardiotoxicity through antioxidant-mediated mechanisms.[11] *Gou Qi Zi* (Fructus Lycii) is also an excellent option to treat myelosuppression induced by chemotherapy or radiation.[12] *Ling Zhi* (Ganoderma) has shown many benefits to support patients treated with chemotherapy or radiation. It prevents nephrotoxicity caused by Platinol (cisplatin) by reversing the increase in urea, creatinine levels and ALP activity and also maintaining the renal antioxidant defense.[13] *Ling Zhi* (Ganoderma) also alleviates many Cytoxan (cyclophosphamide)-induced toxicities, such as decrease in body weight, natural killer activity, interferon-gamma production, and cytotoxic T lymphocyte activity.[14] *Ren Shen* (Radix et Rhizoma Ginseng) has a significant effect to protect the gastrointestinal tract of cancer patients who receive radiation treatment. It also protects the hematopoietic system and increases the number of bone marrow cells and spleen cells.[15] Lastly, *Huang Qi* (Radix Astragali) has been shown in multiple studies to alleviate side effects associated with chemotherapy. *Huang Qi* (Radix Astragali) significantly attenuated cardiotoxicity induced by Cerubidine (daunorubicin) by decreasing free radical release and apoptosis in cultured neonatal cardiomyocytes.[16] It is also effective to restore the depressed immune functions in subjects with tumor treated with Cytoxan (cyclophosphamide).[17] Finally, *Huang Qi* (Radix Astragali) promotes myelopoiesis and enhances hematopoiesis in subjects with myelosuppression caused by Cytoxan (cyclophosphamide).[18]

C/R Support contains many herbs with general immunostimulant and immunomodulatory effects. *Huang Qi* (Radix Astragali) has been shown repeatedly through modern research to increase both specific and non-specific immunity.[19,20,21] *Bai Zhu* (Rhizoma Atractylodis Macrocephalae) has been shown to increase the activity of the macrophages and reticuloendothelial system, and elevate the number of white blood cells, lymphocytes, and IgG.[22,23] *Gou Qi Zi* (Fructus Lycii) has an effect to increase non-specific immunity and boost phagocytic activity of the macrophages and the total number of T cells.[24] *Ren Shen* (Radix et Rhizoma Ginseng) has immune-enhancing effects to increase the function of the reticuloendothelial system and increases the total count of IgM.[25] *Dong Chong Xia Cao* (Cordyceps) is another herb that has demonstrated immunomodulatory functions. It enhances the overall immunity by increasing the number of lymphocytes and natural killer cells, and the production of interleukin, interferon and tumor-necrosis-factor.[26,27,28,29,30] Cordysinocan, a polysaccharide isolated from cultured *Dong Chong Xia Cao* (Cordyceps), activates immune responses in cultured T-lymphocytes and macrophages to signal the cascade and induction of cytokines.[31] Lastly, *Ling Zhi* (Ganoderma) has a wide range of therapeutic effects in the treatment of cancer. Various clinical studies have demonstrated the effects of *Ling Zhi* (Ganoderma) to enhance the immune system.[32,33,34,35] The specific effects of *Ling Zhi* (Ganoderma) include an increase in monocytes, macrophages, and T lymphocytes as well as an increased production of cytokine, interleukin, tumor-necrosis-factor, and interferon. *Ling Zhi* (Ganoderma) has also been used to successfully treat leukopenia.[36]

In addition, ***C/R Support*** also contains many herbs with hematopoietic effects to increase the production of red blood cells. Specifically, administration of *Gou Qi Zi* (Fructus Lycii) in decoction has been shown to increase the production of red blood cells and white blood cells.[37] *Huang Qi* (Radix Astragali) has been shown to increase the production and maturity of blood cells from the bone marrow.[38] Furthermore, use of *Dang Gui* (Radix Angelicae Sinensis) in *Si Wu Tang* (Four-Substance Decoction) showed a marked hematopoietic effect to increase red blood cells for the treatment of anemia.[39] The mechanism of action is attributed to increased activity of colony-stimulating factors (CSF).[40]

In summary, ***C/R Support*** is an important formula for chemotherapy or radiation support. It contains herbs that alleviate the side effects of chemotherapy and radiation, and improves the quality of life for the patient.

COMPARATIVE ANALYSIS

Despite all the advances in medicine, treatment of cancer is still in its relative infancy in both Western and traditional Chinese medicine.

Optimal treatment methods may include chemotherapy, radiation and/or surgery. Though they may be effective, they are extremely harsh and create a huge number of side effects, including severe nausea, vomiting, hair loss, and most importantly, bone marrow suppression with decreased counts of red and white blood cells. Serious cases of bone marrow suppression often necessitate the termination of chemotherapy and radiation treatments, a scenario where the patient suffers from both cancer and its treatments at the same time.

Use of herbs is extremely effective to complement chemotherapy and radiation. Not only do they alleviate many side effects of chemotherapy and radiation, they strengthen the overall constitution of the body so they can tolerate and finish the entire course of therapies.

Optimal therapy in cases of cancer is not to choose between Western ***or*** traditional Chinese medicine, but to integrate Western ***and*** traditional Chinese medicines together. These two modalities

C/R Support™

of medicine complement each others, and provide the brightest outlook and prognosis for successful treatment of cancer.

References

1. Center of Disease Control and Prevention (CDC). National Vital Statistics Report. Volume 60, Number 4. January 11, 2012.
2. Chan K, Lo AC, Yeung JH, Woo KS. Journal of Pharmacy and Pharmacology 1995 May;47(5):402-6.
3. Pharmacotherapy 1999 July;19(7):870-876.
4. European Journal of Drug Metabolism and Pharmacokinetics 1995; 20(1):55-60.
5. Natural Standard (www.naturalstandard.com).
6. National Institutes of Health.
7. U.S National Library of Medicine.
8. American Herbal Pharmacopoeia. *Dang Gui* (Radix Angelicae Sinensis) monograph.
9. Lau CB, Ho TC, Chan TW, Kim SC. Use of dong quai (Angelica sinensis) to treat peri- or postmenopausal symptoms in women with breast cancer: is it appropriate? Menopause 2005 Nov-Dec;12(6):734-40.
10. Liu WC, Chuang WL, Tsai ML, Hong JH, McBride WH, Chiang CS. Cordyceps sinensis health supplement enhances recovery from taxol-induced leukopenia. Exp Biol Med (Maywood). 2008 Apr;233(4):447-55.
11. Xin YF, Zhou GL, Deng ZY, Chen YX, Wu YG, Xu PS, Xuan YX. Protective effect of Lycium barbarum on doxorubicin-induced cardiotoxicity. Phytother Res. 2007 Nov;21(11):1020-4.
12. Gong H, Shen P, Jin L, Xing C, Tang F. Therapeutic effects of Lycium barbarum polysaccharide (LBP) on irradiation or chemotherapy-induced myelosuppressive mice. Cancer Biother Radiopharm. 2005 Apr;20(2):155-62.
13. Pillai TG, John M, Sara Thomas G. Prevention of cisplatin induced nephrotoxicity by terpenes isolated from Ganoderma lucidum occurring in Southern Parts of India. College of Veterinary and Animal Sciences, Mannuthy, Thrissur, Kerala, India. Exp Toxicol Pathol. 2011 Jan;63(1-2):157-60.
14. Nonaka Y, Ishibashi H, Nakai M, Shibata H, Kiso Y, Abe S. Effects of the antlered form of Ganoderma lucidum on tumor growth and metastasis in cyclophosphamide-treated mice. Institute for Health Care Science, Suntory Ltd., Mishima-gun, Osaka 618-8503, Japan. Biosci Biotechnol Biochem. 2008 Jun;72(6):1399-408.
15. Park E, Hwang I, Song JY, Jee Y. Acidic polysaccharide of Panax ginseng as a defense against small intestinal damage by whole-body gamma irradiation of mice. Applied Radiological Science Research Institute, Cheju National University, Jeju, South Korea. Acta Histochem. 2011 Jan;113(1):19-23.
16. Luo Z, Zhong L, Han X, Wang H, Zhong J, Xuan Z. Astragalus membranaceus prevents daunorubicin-induced apoptosis of cultured neonatal cardiomyocytes: role of free radical effect of Astragalus membranaceus on daunorubicin cardiotoxicity. Shanghai Institute of Hematology, School of Medicine, Shanghai Jiao Tong University, Shanghai 20001, China. Phytother Res. 2009 Jun;23(6):761-7.
17. Cho WC, Leung KN. In vitro and in vivo immunomodulating and immunorestorative effects of Astragalus membranaceus. Department of Clinical Oncology, Queen Elizabeth Hospital, Hong Kong, SAR, China. J Ethnopharmacol. 2007 Aug 15;113(1):132-41.
18. Zhu XL, Zhu BD. Mechanisms by which Astragalus membranaceus injection regulates hematopoiesis in myelosuppressed mice. Department of Pharmacology, School of Basic Medical Science, Peking University Health Science Center, 38 Xueyuan Road, Haidian Qu, Beijing 100083, China. Phytother Res. 2007 Jul;21(7):663-7.
19. Chu, DT. et al. Immunotherapy with Chinese medicinal herbs. I. immune restoration of local xenogenetic graft-versus-host reaction in cancer patients by fractionated astragalus membranaceus in vitro. *Journal of Clinical & Laboratory Immunology*. Mar. 1988; 25(3):119-23.
20. Sun, Y. et al. Immune restoration and/or augmentation of local graft versus host reaction by traditional Chinese medicinal herbs. *Cancer*. July 1983; 52(1): 70-3.
21. Sun, Y. et al. Preliminary observations on the effects of the Chinese medicinal herbs astragalus membranaceus and ganoderma lucidum on lymphocyte blastogenic responses. *Journal of Biological Response Modifiers*. 1983; 2(3):227-37.
22. *Jun Shi Yi Xue Jian Xun* (Military Medicine Notes), 1977; 2:5.
23. *Xin Yi Yao Xue Za Zhi* (New Journal of Medicine and Herbology), 1979; 6:60.
24. *Zhong Cao Yao* (Chinese Herbal Medicine), 19(7):25.
25. *Zhong Yao Xue* (Chinese Herbology), 1998; 729:736.
26. Kuo,YC. et al. Cordyceps sinensis as an immuno-modulatory agent. *American Journal Of Chinese Medicine*. 24(2):111-25, 1996
27. Guan, YJ. et al. Effect of cordyceps sinensis on T-lymphocyte subsets in chronic renal failure. *Chung-Kuo Chung His I Chieh Ho Tsa Chih*. Jun. 1992; 12(6):338-9,323.
28. Liu, C. et al. Effects of cordyceps sinensis (CS) on in vitro natural killer cells. *Chung-Kuo Chung His I Chieh Ho Tsa Chih*. May. 1992; 12(5):267-9,259.
29. Xu, RH. et al. Effects of cordyceps sinensis on natural killer activity and colony formation of B16 melanoma. *Chinese Medical Journal*. Feb. 1992; 105(2):97-101.
30. Liu, P. et al. Influence of cordyceps sinensis (berk.) sacc. and rat serum containing same medicine on IL-1, IFN and TNF produced by rat Kupffer's cells. *Chung Kuo Chung Yao Tsa Chih*, June 1996; 21(6):367-9, 384.
31. Cheung JK, Li J, Cheung AW, Zhu Y, Zheng KY, Bi CW, Duan R, Choi RC, Lau DT, Dong TT, Lau BW, Tsim KW. Cordysinocan, a polysaccharide isolated from cultured Cordyceps, activates immune responses in cultured T-lymphocytes and macrophages: signaling cascade and induction of cytokines. J Ethnopharmacol. 2009 Jul 6;124(1):61-8.
32. Wang, SY. et al. The anti-tumor effect of ganoderma lucidum is mediated by cytokines released from activated macrophages and t-lymphocytes. *International Journal Of Cancer*. Mar 17. 1997; 70(6):699-705.
33. Van Der Hem, LG. et al. Ling Zhi-8: Studies of a new immunomodulating agent. *Transplantation*. Sep 15. 1995; 60(5):438-43.
34. Haak-Frendscho, M. et al. Ling Zhi-8: A novel t-cell mitogen induces cytokine production and up-regulation of ICAM-1 expression. *Cellular Immunology*. Aug. 1993; 150(1):101-13.
35. Tanaka, S. et al. Complete amino acid sequence of a novel immuno-modulatory protein, ling zhi-9. an immuno-modulator from a fungus, ganoderma lucidum, having similar effect to immunoglobulin variable regions.
36. *Zhong Hua Xue Yi Za Zhi* (Chinese Journal of Hematology), 1985; 7:428.
37. *Zhong Yao Xue* (Chinese Herbology), 1998; 860:862.
38. *Nan Jing Zhong Yi Xue Yuan Xue Bao* (Journal of Nanjing University of Traditional Chinese Medicine), 1989; 1:43.
39. *Shan Xi Zhong Yi Xue Yuan Xue Bao* (Journal of Shanxi University School of Chinese Medicine) 1986;2:40.
40. *Zhong Yao Yao Li Yu Lin Chuang* (Pharmacology and Clinical Applications of Chinese Herbs) 1992;152.

Calm™

CLINICAL APPLICATIONS

- **Stress, anxiety, nervousness, restlessness**
- **General symptoms associated with stress,** such as poor appetite, headache, tension, and insomnia
- **Premenstrual syndrome (PMS)** with breast distension, irritability and/or mood swings

WESTERN THERAPEUTIC ACTIONS

- Calming effect to relieve restlessness and irritability
- Anxiolytic function to relieve stress, nervousness and anxiety
- Analgesic action to relieve pain, headache and muscle tension associated with stress

CHINESE THERAPEUTIC ACTIONS

- Spreads Liver qi
- Nourishes Liver blood
- Clears heat
- Harmonizes middle *jiao*

DOSAGE

Take 3 to 4 capsules three times daily on an empty stomach with warm water. Dosage may be increased to 6 to 8 capsules three times daily if necessary to alleviate symptoms for a few days. Once stabilized, reduce dosage back down to 3 to 4 capsules three times daily.

INGREDIENTS

Bai Shao (Radix Paeoniae Alba)
Bai Zhu (Rhizoma Atractylodis Macrocephalae)
Bo He (Herba Menthae)
Chai Hu (Radix Bupleuri)
Dang Gui (Radix Angelicae Sinensis)
Fu Ling (Poria)
Mu Dan Pi (Cortex Moutan)
Sheng Jiang (Rhizoma Zingiberis Recens)
Zhi Gan Cao (Radix et Rhizoma Glycyrrhizae Praeparata cum Melle)
Zhi Zi (Fructus Gardeniae)

BACKGROUND

Stress is a normal physical and psychological reaction to demands of life. Most people experience challenges with mental or physical stress on a regular basis. When confronted with stress, the body responds with a burst of hormones to empower the organism to cope and survive – a reaction that is labeled as the "fight-or-flight" response. Once the stress is gone, however, the body is supposed to return to a normal relaxed state. Unfortunately, the nonstop stress of modern life often keeps the body in a constant stressed state. Over time, constantly living in a stressed state coupled with an absence of relaxed states leads to serious health problems. Acute and chronic stress can affect the brain (feelings and emotions), heart (hypertension, arrhythmia, atherosclerosis, coronary artery disease), muscles (stiffness and pain), stomach (acid reflux, peptic ulcer disease, irritable bowel syndrome), and immune system (weakened immune system, frequent infection).

FORMULA EXPLANATION

According to the Five-Elements Theory, the Liver is the most sensitive of all organs to emotional distress. Stress and pressure can easily lead to Liver qi stagnation, which can overact on the Spleen and the Stomach. The treatment protocol is to spread the Liver qi, harmonize the middle *jiao*, and nourish the blood.

Calm is formulated based on *Xiao Yao San* (Rambling Powder), a classic Chinese formula for Liver qi stagnation. In this formula, *Chai Hu* (Radix Bupleuri) enters the Liver and disperses stagnant qi. *Bai Shao* (Radix Paeoniae Alba) and *Dang Gui* (Radix Angelicae Sinensis) nourish the blood and soften the Liver. *Bai Zhu* (Rhizoma Atractylodis Macrocephalae) and *Fu Ling* (Poria) strengthen the Spleen and the Stomach to prevent the overacting of the Liver (Wood element) on the Spleen and the Stomach (Earth element). The fragrant and acrid properties of *Bo He* (Herba Menthae) and *Sheng Jiang* (Rhizoma Zingiberis Recens) help disperse Liver qi stagnation. The combination of *Zhi Gan Cao* (Radix et Rhizoma Glycyrrhizae Praeparata cum Melle) and *Bai Shao* (Radix Paeoniae Alba) produces an analgesic effect to treat hypochondriac distension. *Zhi Zi* (Fructus Gardeniae) and *Mu Dan Pi* (Cortex Moutan) clear heat and reduce irritability, anger and other heat signs.

Overall, ***Calm*** is an excellent formula to concurrently treat the excess (Liver qi stagnation) and the deficiency (blood deficiency).

CAUTIONS & CONTRAINDICATIONS

- ***Calm*** is a qi-regulating formula, and prolonged use (4 to 6 months) may cause qi deficiency in some patients. Such patients with stressful lifestyles or jobs who cannot be without ***Calm*** should be advised to take a qi tonic formula, such as ***GI Tonic*** or ***Cordyceps 3*** at 1 to 2 capsules daily, to help maintain optimal qi levels in the body.
- This herbal formula contains herbs that invigorate blood circulation, such as *Dang Gui* (Radix Angelicae Sinensis). Therefore, patients who are on anticoagulant or antiplatelet therapies, such as Coumadin (warfarin), should use this formula with caution, or not at all, as there may be a higher risk of bleeding and bruising.[1,2,3]

CLINICAL NOTES

- ***Calm*** is one of the most effective and popular herbal formulas for stress. It relieves Liver qi stagnation, which manifests in a wide range of clinical signs and symptoms, including but not limited to stress, anxiety, nervousness, restlessness, PMS, insomnia, fidgeting, and irritability.

Calm ™

Pulse Diagnosis by Dr. Jimmy Wei-Yen Chang:

- **Outward display of emotional conditions** (i.e., patients who express how they feel and do not hold their feelings inside): convex and forceful pulse on the left *guan*
- **Internalized emotional conditions** (i.e., patients who hold their feelings inside): concave and deep pulse on the left *guan*

SUPPLEMENTARY FORMULAS

- For stomach pain, heartburn, gastric and duodenal ulcers, add ***GI Care***.
- For severe emotional disturbance with anger and neurosis or insomnia, use ***Calm (ES)***.
- For stress, anxiety and insomnia in patients with deficiency, use ***Calm ZZZ***.
- For constant worrying with excessive dreams, combine with ***Schisandra ZZZ***.
- For hypertension, add ***Gastrodia Complex*** or ***Gentiana Complex***.
- With depression, add ***Shine*** or ***Shine (DS)***.
- For women experiencing hot flashes and night sweating during menopause, add ***Balance (Heat)***.
- For lack of vaginal lubrication during menopause, combine with ***Balance Spring***.
- For infertility due to stress, use ***Blossom (Phase 1-4)***.
- In cases of prolonged Liver qi stagnation causing benign breast lumps, breast tumor and/or mastitis, use ***Resolve (Upper)***.
- For dysmenorrhea, add ***Mense-Ease***.
- If the patient has hyperthyroidism, add ***Thyrodex***.
- With acute headache, add ***Corydalin (AC)***.
- With chronic headache, add ***Corydalin (CR)***.
- For ADD/ADHD, add ***Calm (Jr)***.
- For irritable bowel syndrome (IBS) due to stress, add ***GI Harmony***.
- For ulcerative colitis due to stress, add ***GI Care (UC)***.
- For excess heat, add ***Gardenia Complex***.
- With blood stagnation, add ***Circulation (SJ)***.
- For stress- or hormonal-related acne, combine with ***Dermatrol (Clear)***.

ACUPUNCTURE TREATMENT

Traditional Points:

- *Hegu* (LI 4), *Taichong* (LR 3), *Yintang*
- *Taichong* (LR 3), *Xingjian* (LR 2), *Qimen* (LR 14), *Zhangmen* (LR 13), *Feishu* (BL 13), *Shangwan* (CV 13), *Shanzhong* (CV 17)

Classic Master Tung's Points:

- **Insomnia:** *Linggu* (T 22.05), *Xinling* (T 33.17)*, *Shenjian* (T 44.19), *Zhenjing* (T 1010.08), *Zhenghui* (T 1010.01), *Tianhuang* (T 77.17), *Dihuang* (T 77.19), *Renhuang* (T 77.21), *Huoying* (T 66.03), *Tianhuangfu [Shenguan]* (T 77.18), *Shenmen* on the ear. Bleed *du* (governing) channel and back of the knee area. Bleed before needling for best result.
- **PMS:** *Fuke* (T 11.24), *Xinling* (T 33.17)*, *Zhenjing* (T 1010.08), *Tianhuang* (T 77.17), *Dihuang* (T 77.19), *Renhuang* (T 77.21), *Linggu* (T 22.05), *Sihuashang* (T 77.08), *Jiemeiyi* (T 88.04), *Jiemeier* (T 88.05), *Jiemeisan* (T 88.06). Bleed *Huobao* (T 55.01) or dark veins nearby. Bleed before needling for best result.
- **Stress:** *Zhenjing* (T 1010.08), *Tianhuangfu [Shenguan]* (T 77.18), *Huoying* (T 66.03), *Dizong* (T 44.09), *Dan* (T 11.13)

Master Tung's Points by Dr. Chuan-Min Wang:

- **Anxiety, stress, irritability, insomnia:** *Zhenjing* (T 1010.08), *Tianhuangfu [shenguan]* (T 77.18), *Zhongjiuli* (T 88.25)
- **PMS:** *Zhenghui* (T 1010.01), *Zhenjing* (T 1010.08), *Huanchao* (T 11.06), *Fuke* (T 11.24)

Balance Method by Dr. Richard Tan:

- Left side: *Zhongzhu* (TH 3), *Tianjing* (TH 10), *Hegu* (LI 4), *Taichong* (LR 3), *Ququan* (LR 8), *Sanyinjiao* (SP 6)
- Right side: *Quze* (PC 3), *Daling* (PC 7), *Neiguan* (PC 6), *Shenmen* (HT 7), *Yanglingquan* (GB 34), *Zulinqi* (GB 41), *Xiangu* (ST 43)
- Left and right sides can be alternated from treatment to treatment.

Ear Acupuncture:

- *Shenmen*

Auricular Medicine by Dr. Li-Chun Huang:

- **Liver qi stagnation, stress, anxiety, restlessness:** *Shenmen*, Heart, Nervous Subcortex, Anxious, Be Happy, Liver, Occiput. Bleed Ear Apex.
- **Menopause:** Uterus, Endocrine, Ovary, Gonadotropin, Pituitary, Sympathetic, Anxious, Kidney, Liver, Heart.

NUTRITION

- A diet high in calcium, magnesium, phosphorus, potassium, and vitamins B and E is recommended. These nutrients are easily depleted by stress.
- Encourage the consumption of fruits and vegetables such as apricots, winter melon, asparagus, avocados, bananas and broccoli in addition to brown rice, dried fruit, figs, salmon, garlic, green leafy vegetables, and soy products.
- Avoid any and all foods that contain sugar, such as cake, desserts, candy, chocolate, canned juice, soft drinks, caffeinated drinks, stevia, sugar substitutes, agave, xylitol, and corn syrup.
- Avoid fermented foods like cheese or fermented tofu.
- Do not eat dairy products, such as milk, cream, yogurt, cheese, and ice cream.
- Warm and hot natured foods that damage qi and yin should be avoided, such as:
  - certain fruits like mango and durian that produce heat.
  - stimulants like coffee, alcohol, and energy drinks.
  - spicy/pungent/aromatic vegetables such as pepper, garlic, onions, basil, rosemary, cumin, funnel, anise, leeks, chives, scallions, thyme, saffron, wormwood, mustard, chili pepper, and wasabi.
- Avoid food and drinks with artificial coloring.

Calm ™

- Consume as few meat products as possible. Do not eat processed meats, such as lunch meats, hot dogs and sausages, as they contain nitrites that are associated with inflammation and chronic disease.

The Tao of Nutrition by Dr. Maoshing Ni and Cathy McNease:

- **Premenstrual syndrome (PMS)**
  - At least one week prior to the usual onset of PMS symptoms, consume foods such as ginger, green onions, fennel, orange peel, spinach, walnuts, hawthorn berries, cinnamon, black pepper, and Chinese date.
  - Avoid cold foods, raw foods, excessive consumption of fruits, vinegar, all shellfish, coffee, stimulants, sugar, dairy products, and smoking.
- **Restlessness and emotional instability:** Make a tea of wheat bran, licorice root, and dates. Drink three times daily until symptoms are relieved.

LIFESTYLE INSTRUCTIONS

- Regular exercise, adequate rest, and normal sleep patterns are beneficial for stress reduction.
- Relax the mind and the body through meditation, yoga, breathing exercises, imagery exercises, and other activities such as *tai chi chuan [tai ji chuan]* and *qi gong*.
- Get away from the daily routine to do something different and enjoyable to relieve stress whenever possible. Laughter really is the best medicine.
- Noise can be disturbing to mental health and cause stress. Noise greater than 65-decibels can cause psychological disturbance, greater than 90-decibels can cause emotional damages, and greater than 120-decibels can cause nervous system and hearing damages.
- Shift outlook on life and look at changes in a positive way and as challenges rather than threats.

CASE STUDIES

- B.C., a 74-year-old female, presented with insomnia, irritability, and neck and shoulder tension. Neck and shoulders were tender and tight upon palpation. The patient was overweight and drank vodka every night which increased the intensity of her condition. This condition was diagnosed as Liver qi stagnation. After taking ***Calm,*** four capsules three times daily, she was able to relax and went to sleep easier. Her neck and shoulders felt a lot looser as well. Submitted by A.I., Hilo, Hawaii.
- S.P., a 42-year-old female, presented with insomnia and restlessness. This person had a Type A personality which needed to be calmed down. The TCM diagnosis was Liver depression affecting the Heart. After taking ***Calm***, the restlessness and emotions decreased in intensity. The patient felt more balanced through the day and slept better at night. She was not up at night as often, and had less desire to want to clean the house at night. She has continued to take the herbs as needed. Submitted by L.M., Portland, Oregon.
- S.S., a 55-year-old female, presented with menopause symptoms and experienced hot flashes ten times a day. Additional symptoms included irritability and difficulty staying asleep. The patient also relied heavily on sleeping aids which resulted in grogginess. Furthermore, she had arthritis in her thumbs, a constant need to clear her throat, and acid reflux. Her blood pressure was 120/80 mmHg and her heart rate was 78 beats per minute. The practitioner diagnosed the condition as yin deficiency and Liver qi stagnation. ***Balance (Heat)*** was prescribed at three capsules three times daily, along with ***Calm,*** three capsules three times daily with warm water. The patient had very positive results. She reported feeling less irritable and was no longer experiencing hot flashes. Her sleep had also improved where she only needed to take sleeping aids occasionally. Lastly, her acid reflux had improved; however, it was still present when taking certain foods and wine. Submitted by L.W., Arroyo Grande, California.
- S.F., a 32-year-old male, presented with stress, anger and irritability. The patient was prescribed ***Calm***, up to eight capsules as needed. After taking two bottles of the herbs, the patient reported being less stressed and a decreased anger. He would forget to take the herbs at times but admitted to being calmer when he took them. The patient was very pleased with the results. Submitted by S.L., Yuma, Arizona.
- J.C., a 57-year-old female, presented with nervousness, insomnia, and anxiety with a desire to stop smoking. Night sweats were also present. Her tongue was red with no coating present. The practitioner diagnosed the condition as Kidney yin deficiency with heat and Liver qi stagnation. Her Western diagnosis was menopause and hypothyroidism. The patient was given a combination of ***Calm***, ***Shine***, and ***Nourish***. ***Nourish*** was taken daily while ***Shine*** and ***Calm*** were taken as needed. After taking the herbs for six months, the patient reported improvement in sleep; she was calmer and more balanced overall with a positive attitude. Submitted by K.F., Honolulu, Hawaii.
- S.T., a 27-year-old female, presented with PMS symptoms consisting of severe cramping and moodiness. Pulse was choppy and the tongue was purple. The practitioner diagnosed this condition as Liver qi and blood stagnation. ***Mense-Ease*** was prescribed at 4 to 6 capsules three times a day, along with ***Calm*** to take as needed. After taking ***Mense-Ease*** for one cycle, the patient reported less menstrual pain and less cramping and moodiness. In addition, she reported that ***Calm*** had immediate effectiveness. Submitted by S.L., Yuma, Arizona.
- L.S., a 36-year-old female, presented with tight upper back muscles, tension in the neck, and fatigue. It was also noted that she has a very stressful job, was easily irritated and had no patience at all. Objective findings included knots in the upper back muscles and stiff neck with limited range of motion. The practitioner diagnosed it as Liver qi stagnation. After taking

Calm™

Calm, three capsules a day for a week, the patient reported feeling much more at ease, being able to handle the stress both at home and at work. The overall tension was lifted and her muscles felt more relaxed. She asked for a second bottle of the herbs to continue taking it as needed. Submitted by L.M., Gresham, Oregon.

- S.M., a 52-year-old female, presented with irritability and had a tendency to be easily stressed. Tongue was red with a peeled coating. The practitioner diagnosed this condition as Liver qi stagnation and prescribed the patient to take ***Calm***, three capsules three times a day. After taking the herbs for two days the patient reported being much calmer and not as angry. The patient had also received acupuncture 2 to 3 times a week. Submitted by S.L., Yuma, Arizona.
- S.F., a 42-year-old female, presented with a gastrointestinal disorder with symptoms consisting of diarrhea with extreme urgency, especially worse with stress. Pulse was wiry and thready and her tongue was red with a long center crack. An additional objective finding was dark circles under her eyes. The practitioner diagnosed this condition as Liver overacting on Spleen. Upon diagnosis the patient was given ***GI Harmony*** and ***Calm***. Taking the herbs, the patient is doing well, having a bowel movement which is well formed. Additional lifestyle changes she had made were avoiding caffeine and going to bed before 11:00 p.m. Submitted by T.W., Perrysburg, Ohio.
- D.H., an 18-year-old male, presented with stress and anxiety due to feeling overwhelmed by life. Pulse was wiry and his tongue was reddish purple. The practitioner diagnosed this condition as Liver blood and qi stagnation and prescribed the patient ***Calm*** at three to eight capsules, three times a day. After one week of taking the herb, the patient reported being less stressed and having less anxiety. The patient had also started counseling at the beginning of treatment as well. Submitted by S.L., Yuma, Arizona.
- A 35-year-old male manager presented with stress, anxiety and anger. His pulse was rapid and face was red. The practitioner diagnosed the condition as Liver qi stagnation and Liver yang rising. When the patient began the initial treatment one year ago, he and his wife noticed a significant improvement. Through the course of the one-year treatment, the patient noticed a regression of his improvement when not taking his dose of ***Calm*** and felt as though he had "less control of his life." The patient was recommended to continue taking ***Calm*** at 4 capsules two times a day. Consequently, his condition showed signs of improvement. Submitted by K.S., San Diego, California.
- A new job and concurrent relationship problems had created quite a stressful situation for a 27-year-old female restaurant cook, who was diagnosed with Liver qi stagnation. Her tongue was purple and her pulse was wiry. Constantly thinking about her problems made her unable to relax. Placed on a two week regimen of ***Calm*** has improved her condition tremendously. Although the patient reported that her stress has not changed, she felt more relaxed after taking ***Calm***. Submitted by T.G., Albuquerque, New Mexico.
- A 40-year-old housewife presented with migraines, stress, and a lack of sleep. She woke up frequently and had many stress-related headaches for years. The practitioner diagnosed the condition as Liver qi stagnation with heat rising. The practitioner felt the treatment should revolve around calming the *shen* (spirit). After two weeks of taking ***Calm***, the headaches were less severe and less frequent. However, sleep was still poor. At four weeks, her headaches were very mild and under control. She no longer needed to take any Western medications. The patient appeared more calm and reported sleeping better and feeling less stressful. She was recommended to continue taking ***Calm*** for two to three more months. As an adjunct to the treatment, the practitioner also suggested taking ***Corydalin (AC)*** for her headaches, as well as reducing her caffeine intake. Submitted by D.S., Flagstaff, Arizona.
- A 38-year-old female administrator presented with insomnia and TMJ. The practitioner diagnosed her as having Liver fire rising, Kidney and Heart not communicating, and depression. When the patient initially came to the office, she had not slept that same night. She was nervous and had jawbone pain, which was caused by sleeping with a clenched jaw. The acupuncture treatment calmed the patient. To reinforce her acupuncture treatment, ***Calm*** was also given at a dose of 3 capsules, three times a day. On the second treatment, the patient was much calmer and more relaxed. The same acupuncture treatment was given, with the advice to continue taking ***Calm***. As a result, the practitioner concluded that ***Calm*** was effective for her depression, anxiety, and other symptoms of Liver fire. Submitted by A.D., La Crescenta, California.
- S.C., a 42-year-old female, presented with stress due to domestic situations. Clinical manifestations included constipation, bloating, neck tension, insomnia, anorexia, fatigue, tearfulness and sadness. Her tongue was pale and scalloped, with a mid-line crack; her pulse was soft and soggy. The Western diagnosis was depressive disorder; the TCM diagnosis was Liver qi stagnation. After taking ***Calm*** at three capsules, three times daily, the patient reported feeling much better. Her voice became more animated, there was more character in her face, and more shine to her eyes. Furthermore, the patient stated that her neck tension, insomnia, constipation, and sadness were gone. Submitted by C.L., Chino Hills, California.
- M.M., a 41-year-old female, presented with "adrenaline-rush" sensations, characterized by heat flushes to her face, associated with mood swings and anxiety. Her tongue was red and purple, and her face was red. The Western diagnosis was stress-related anxiety attack; the TCM diagnosis was Liver stagnation and yin deficiency. After beginning herbal therapy with ***Calm***, two capsules three times daily, and ***Balance (Heat)***, two capsules, three times daily, the patient stated that her affect and personality became calmer. Furthermore, she reported "feeling good," with increased energy levels and sound sleep. Submitted by C.L., Chino Hills, California.

Calm™

- L.A., a 37-year-old female patient, presented with insomnia, with difficulty falling and staying asleep. Other symptoms included neck and shoulder stiffness, TMJ pain, heavy menstrual flow, and cramping with blood clots. She complained of marital problems and held the stress and sadness inside. She was also seeing a psychotherapist. The blood pressure was 123/86 mmHg and her heart rate was 88 beats per minute. The tongue appeared to be salmon pink in color, moist with numerous fissures from the center to the tip. The tongue was swollen and the tip was red. The pulse was slippery and thin. The TCM diagnosis was Spleen qi and Heart blood deficiencies with Liver qi stagnation. ***Calm*** was prescribed. ***Calm*** alone eased her tension, but did not help much with her energy. Her sleep improved slightly. The TMJ resolved after eight acupuncture treatments. After two months, ***Schisandra ZZZ*** was added. The patient then slept through the night much more soundly. Submitted by J.C.O., Whittier, California.
- A female presented with stress, irritability, premenstrual syndrome (PMS), loose stool, crying for no reason, muscle tension, and nervous trembling in the hands. She stated that she felt overwhelmed in life and worried incessantly. Her blood pressure was 115/75 mmHg and her heart rate was 87 beats per minute. Her tongue was pink with a red tip and a thin white coating. Pulse was wiry on the left side and slippery on the right side. The TCM diagnosis was Spleen qi deficiency with Liver qi stagnation. ***Calm*** was prescribed. The patient responded immediately, stating her "nerves" calmed down, stomach settled, and began to feel more "emotionally stable." She took only 3 capsules three times a day the week before her period. Submitted by J.C., Whittier, California.
- D.S., a 45-year-old female, presented with insomnia, mood swings, cramps and fatigue. The tongue was slightly purplish and pale with teeth marks. The coating was thin and white. The pulse was deep and wiry. She was diagnosed with Spleen qi deficiency and blood deficiency. ***Nourish***, ***Calm***, and ***Schisandra ZZZ*** were prescribed. The patient reported her sleep pattern improved, her moods balanced, and her energy level increased. She was very happy with the herbs. Submitted by B.F., Newport Beach, California.
- A 36-year-old female patient presented with a long history of anxiety, irritability, insomnia, mood swings, and dream-disturbed sleep. Her pulse was slow, full and wiry; tongue was red on the tip and sides. The TCM diagnosis was Liver qi stagnation. After taking three capsules of ***Calm*** three times daily, the patient reported subtle changes in moods, including that she was not as irritable, and was able to focus on work and maintain higher productivity. She was also able to sleep better, without disturbing dreams. Submitted by C.L., Chino Hills, California.
- J.W., a 44-year-old patient, presented with infertility and a history of miscarriage. She experienced high stress which she "bottled up" inside. Her hands and feet were cold. She also had back pain, low energy, severe menstrual cramps and premenstrual syndrome (PMS). Her tongue was pale and purplish, swollen with teeth marks. The tip was red. Pulse was wiry on both sides and slippery on the right. Her blood pressure was 125/86 mmHg and heart rate was 83 beats per minute. Lab report showed she had low FSH levels. The diagnosis was Spleen and Kidney yang deficiencies with Liver qi and blood stagnation. ***Menatrol*** was prescribed. After one month on ***Menatrol***, the patient reported her menstrual cramping "miraculously disappeared" and her estrogen levels increased dramatically. She was afraid the herbs would interfere with her *in vitro* fertilization (IVF) procedure so she stopped taking them for six weeks. After the IVF was not successful and her tongue color became very purple in the center, the practitioner suggested she take the formula ***Calm***. She was open to it. Within a week, her stress level decreased and her energy level increased. Her tongue color changed from purple to pink and slightly dusky. She is presently continuing to take ***Calm*** and is actively trying to conceive naturally. Submitted by J.C.O., Whittier, California.
- E.P., a 32-year-old female, presented with a 2½-year history of vertigo, associated with insomnia, palpitations, anxiety, and nausea. She also suffered from irritable bowel syndrome with alternating diarrhea and constipation. She had an unsteady gait and was unable to drive. For the Western diagnosis of anxiety disorder, the TCM diagnosis was Liver fire Initially, ***Calm*** and ***Gentiana Complex*** were prescribed at two capsules each, three times daily, but then the dosage was increased to three capsules of each, three times daily. After three weeks, the signs and symptoms of irritable bowel syndrome were resolved, and ***Gentiana Complex*** was discontinued. On the sixth treatment, the patient reported all symptoms improved. However, work-related stress and anxiety remained. On the 15th visit, ***Calm*** was changed to ***Schisandra ZZZ*** to help with her insomnia. After taking this formula for nine days, the patient reported much improvement in her sleeping patterns, from five to six hours of interrupted sleep to six to seven hours of uninterrupted sleep. The patient was treated with acupuncture five times throughout the course of herbal treatment. Submitted by C.L., Chino Hills, California.

PHARMACOLOGICAL AND CLINICAL RESEARCH

Nonstop stress in the modern world places a tremendous burden on the mind and the body to always function in a heightened and alarmed state. Over time, the mind and the body are unable to relax, leading to a wide variety of dysfunction throughout the body, including brain (feelings and emotions), heart (hypertension, arrhythmia, atherosclerosis, coronary artery disease), stomach (acid reflux, peptic ulcer disease, irritable bowel syndrome), muscles (stiffness and pain), and immune system (weakened immune system, frequent infection). Therefore, optimal treatment requires use of herbs to rescue the mind from stress and restore the body to its optimal health.

Calm has herbs with adaptogenic effects to help the patients cope with nonstop stress. *Chai Hu* (Radix Bupleuri) and *Zhi Zi* (Fructus Gardeniae) have a calming effect on the brain to help the patients manage mental stress by promoting relaxation and improving sleeping.[4,5] *Gan Cao* (Radix et Rhizoma Glycyrrhizae)

FORMULAS

has a positive cognitive effect to improve mental functions and ameliorate memory impairment.[6] Furthermore, *Bai Zhu* (Rhizoma Atractylodis Macrocephalae) and *Fu Shen* (Poria Paradicis) have adaptogenic effects to help the patients deal with physical stress by enhancing duration and relieving restlessness.[7,8]

In addition, ***Calm*** contains herbs with various cardiovascular and circulatory functions to decrease the adverse effect of stress on the heart. In one laboratory study, intravenous injection of *Dang Gui* (Radix Angelicae Sinensis) is associated initially with an inhibitory influence on the heart, followed by a negative chronotropic effect and a positive inotropic effect. It improves overall blood circulation by decreasing the whole blood specific viscosity, or improving the hemorrheological changes associated with blood stagnation. It also has an antiarrhythmic effect, especially against arrhythmia induced by epinephrine, cardiac glycosides, aconitine, and barium chloride. Administration of *Dang Gui* (Radix Angelicae Sinensis) is associated with reduction of plasma cholesterol and triglyceride levels, and a decreased risk of atherosclerosis, as demonstrated in laboratory studies.[9,10,11,12] Furthermore, *Zhi Zi* (Fructus Gardeniae) has demonstrated marked antihypertensive action in numerous studies. One proposed mechanism of this hypotensive effect is its stimulation of the parasympathetic nervous system.[13] In addition, *Zhi Gan Cao* (Radix et Rhizoma Glycyrrhizae Praeparata cum Melle) has shown marked effectiveness in treating subjects with palpitations and artificially-induced arrhythmia.[14,15] Finally, *Bai Shao* (Radix Paeoniae Alba) and *Chai Hu* (Radix Bupleuri) have antihyperlipidemic activities, and have been shown to lower total cholesterol, low-density lipoprotein, and triglyceride levels.[16,17]

To alleviate adverse effect of stress on the digestive system, ***Calm*** contains many herbs with gastroprotective effects. *Gan Cao* (Radix et Rhizoma Glycyrrhizae) has a proven effect to prevent and treat gastric and duodenal ulcers. The mechanisms of this action include inhibition of gastric acid secretion, binding and deactivation of gastric acid, and promotion of recovery from ulceration.[18] According to one study, 100 patients with gastric or duodenal ulcers were treated with *Gan Cao* (Radix et Rhizoma Glycyrrhizae) extract with 90% rate of effectiveness.[19] Another study also reported good results using *Gan Cao* (Radix et Rhizoma Glycyrrhizae) to treat patients with peptic ulcers. The treatment protocol was to administer 2.5 to 5 grams of powdered *Gan Cao* (Radix et Rhizoma Glycyrrhizae) three times daily for 3 to 4 weeks.[20] In addition, *Zhi Zi* (Fructus Gardeniae) has a gastroprotective effect to protect the stomach from gastritis and gastric lesions. *Zhi Zi* (Fructus Gardeniae) has acid-neutralizing capacities, antioxidant activities, inhibitory effects on the growth of *Helicobacter pylori*, and reversal of ethanol-induced gastric lesions.[21] Furthermore, *Bai Zhu* (Rhizoma Atractylodis Macrocephalae) has a dual effect to regulate the digestive tract,[22] and is effective to treat either constipation or diarrhea.[23,24]

Lastly, ***Calm*** contains many herbs with analgesic and anti-inflammatory effects to relieve various aches and pain caused by stress. *Dang Gui* (Radix Angelicae Sinensis) has both analgesic and anti-inflammatory effects with potency comparable to or greater than acetylsalicylic acid.[25,26] It has been used successfully to treat low back and leg pain,[27] vascular headache,[28] migraine headache,[29] and the general complaint of pain.[30] *Bai Shao* (Radix Paeoniae Alba) and *Gan Cao* (Radix et Rhizoma Glycyrrhizae) have anti-inflammatory and spasmolytic functions.[31,32] Clinically, these two herbs have a marked effect to treat neck pain,[33] acute back pain,[34] sciatica,[35] pain in the lower back and legs,[36] leg cramps in the calf,[37] restless leg syndrome,[38] heel pain,[39] gastric and abdominal pain,[40] intestinal spasm,[41] menstrual cramps and pain,[42] neuralgia,[43] facial spasms and twitching,[44] trigeminal neuralgia,[45,46] and dysmenorrhea.[47] *Bai Zhu* (Rhizoma Atractylodis Macrocephalae) also has anti-inflammatory activity and its mechanism of action is attributed to the inhibition of tumor necrosis factor-alpha (TNF-α) and nitric oxide production.[48] *Zhi Zi* (Fructus Gardeniae) also has anti-inflammatory activity, as this herb suppresses vascular inflammation via inhibition of TNF-α.[49] Lastly, *Chai Hu* (Radix Bupleuri) demonstrates both analgesic and anti-inflammatory functions,[50,51] and the saikosaponins appear to be the main compounds for these actions.[52]

To enhance the immune system and maintain optimal health, many herbs with immunostimulant effects are used in this formula. *Chai Hu* (Radix Bupleuri) stimulates both humoral and cellular immunity.[53] *Dang Gui* (Radix Angelicae Sinensis) increases the phagocytic activity of the macrophages.[54] Lastly, *Bai Zhu* (Rhizoma Atractylodis Macrocephalae) increases the activity of the macrophages and reticuloendothelial system, and elevates the number of white blood cells, lymphocytes, and IgG.[55,56]

In summary, ***Calm*** is an excellent formula to treat stress and manage its related conditions and complications. ***Calm*** relaxes the mind and restores the body to its optimal health.

COMPARATIVE ANALYSIS

Stress and anxiety are two of the most common emotional disorders. Clinical signs and symptoms include recurrent and intrusive thoughts, insomnia, disturbed sleep, illusions, hallucinations, difficulty concentrating, hypervigilance, restlessness, anger, and irritability.

Pharmaceutical drug treatments for stress and anxiety focus primarily on use of sedative and hypnotic drugs, such as Valium (diazepam) and Ativan (lorazepam). Though these drugs are very potent and have an immediate effect to sedate patients, they do not address the underlying conditions. Furthermore, long-term use of these medications are associated with many side effects, including drowsiness, dizziness, tiredness, blurred vision, changes in sex drive or ability, shuffling walk, persistent, fine tremor or inability to sit still, difficulty breathing or swallowing, severe skin rash, yellowing of the skin or eyes, irregular heartbeat, and addiction. Therefore, these drugs should only be used when necessary, and only for a short period of time.

Calm ™

Use of herbs is extremely effective to treat stress and anxiety. Herbs regulate mood and emotions, and alleviate stress and anxiety by enhancing the body's own ability to deal with these external factors. Unlike drugs that have an immediate effect to treat stress and anxiety by sedating the mind and decreasing its responsiveness, herbs do not have an immediate effect, and require two or more weeks of continuous use to gradually treat these conditions. In contrast, one of the main advantages of herbs is they are safe and natural, and do not have negative side effects like drugs.

Stress and anxiety are two very common disorders. While drugs and herbs are both effective, they have contrasting differences of benefits and risks. While drugs are more effective for short-term treatment, herbs are more successful for long-term management. Furthermore, counseling (behavioral and psychotherapy) is extremely important toward the understanding of, and complete recovery from, these conditions.

References

1. Chan K, Lo AC, Yeung JH, Woo KS. Journal of Pharmacy and Pharmacology 1995 May;47(5):402-6.
2. Pharmacotherapy 1999 July;19(7):870-876.
3. European Journal of Drug Metabolism and Pharmacokinetics 1995; 20(1):55-60.
4. *Zhong Yao Yao Li Yu Ying Yong* (Pharmacology and Applications of Chinese Herbs), 1983; 888.
5. *Jiang Su Yi Yao* (Jiangsu Journal of Medicine and Herbology), 1976; (1):28.
6. Zhu Z, Li C, Wang X, Yang Z, Chen J, Hu L, Jiang H, Shen X. 2,2',4'-trihydroxychalcone from Glycyrrhiza glabra as a new specific BACE1 inhibitor efficiently ameliorates memory impairment in mice. J Neurochem. 2010 Jul;114(2):374-85.
7. *Xin Yi Yao Xue Za Zhi* (New Journal of Medicine and Herbology), 1974; 8:13.
8. *Zhong Yao Da Ci Dian* (Dictionary of Chinese Herbs), 1977:1596.
9. *Jiang Su Zhong Yi* (Jiangsu Chinese Medicine), 1965; (3):22.
10. Xue, JX. et al. Effects of the combination of astragalus membranaceus (Fisch.) Bge. (AM), angelica sinensis (Oliv.) Diels (TAS), cyperus rotundus L. (CR), ligusticum chuanxiong Hort (LC) and paeonia veitchii lynch (PV) on the hemorrheological changes in "blood stagnating" rats. *Chung Kuo Chung Yao Tsa Chih*; 19(2):108-10, 128. Feb 1994.
11. *Lan Zhou Yi Xue Yuan Xue Bao* (Journal of Lanzhou University of Medicine), 1989; 15(3):125.
12. *Zhong Cao Yao Tong Xun* (Journal of Chinese Herbal Medicine), 1976; (3):30.
13. *Zhong Yao Yao Li Yu Ying Yong* (Pharmacology and Applications of Chinese Herbs), 1983; 934.
14. *Shang Hai Yi Yao Za Zhi* (Shanghai Journal of Medicine and Herbology), 1988; (2):12.
15. *Jiang Su Zhong Yi Za Zhi* (Jiangsu Journal of Chinese Medicine), 1987; 8(10):688.
16. Yang HO, Ko WK, Kim JY, Ro HS. Paeoniflorin: an antihyperlipidemic agent from Paeonia lactiflora. Fitoterapia. 2004 Jan;75(1):45-9.
17. *Zhong Yao Xue* (Chinese Herbology), 1998; 103:106.
18. *Zhong Yao Zhi* (Chinese Herbology Journal), 1993; 358.
19. *Zhong Hua Nei Ke Xue Za Zhi* (Journal of Chinese Internal Medicine), 1960; 3:226.
20. *Zhong Yao Lin Chuan Xin Yong* (New Clinical Applications of Chinese Medicine), 2001; 163.
21. Lee JH, Lee DU, Jeong CS. Gardenia jasminoides Ellis ethanol extract and its constituents reduce the risks of gastritis and reverse gastric lesions in rats. Plant Resources Research Institute, Duksung Women's University, Seoul, 132-714, Korea. Food Chem Toxicol. 2009 Feb 4.
22. *Chang Yong Zhong Yao Cheng Fen Yu Yao Li Shou Ce* (A Handbook of the Composition and Pharmacology of Common Chinese Drugs), 1994; 739:742.
23. *Xin Yi Yao Xue Za Zhi* (New Journal of Medicine and Herbology), 1978; 4:9.
24. *Shan Dong Zhong Yi Za Zhi* (Shandong Journal of Chinese Medicine), 1982; 2:107.
25. *Xin Yi Yao Xue Za Zhi* (New Journal of Medicine and Herbology), 1975; (6):34.
26. *Yao Xue Za Zhi* (Journal of Medicinals), 1971; (91):1098.
27. *Xin Zhong Yi* (New Chinese Medicine), 1980; 2:34.
28. *Hu Bei Zhong Yi Za Zhi* (Hubei Journal of Chinese Medicine), 1993; (2):9.
29. *Bei Jing Yi Xue* (Beijing Medicine), 1988; 2:95.
30. *Xin Yi Yao Xue Za Zhi* (New Journal of Medicine and Herbology), 1976; 12:26.
31. Zheng YQ, Wei W. Total glucosides of paeony suppresses adjuvant arthritis in rats and intervenes cytokine-signaling between different types of synoviocytes. Int Immunopharmacol. 2005 Sep;5(10):1560-73.
32. Leem K, Kim H, Boo Y, Lee HS, Kim JS, Yoo YC, Ahn HJ, Park HJ, Seo JC, Kim HK, Jin SY, Park HK, Chung JH, Cho JJ. Effects of Paeonia lactiflora root extracts on the secretions of monocyte chemotactic protein-1 and -3 in human nasal fibroblasts. Phytother Res. 2004 Mar;18(3):241-3.
33. *Jiang Su Zhong Yi* (Jiangsu Chinese Medicine), 1990; (10):29.
34. *Zhe Jiang Zhong Yi Za Zhi* (Zhejiang Journal of Chinese Medicine) 1995;(11):524.
35. *Fu Jian Zhong Yi Yao* (Fujian Chinese Medicine and Herbology), 1994; (1):7.
36. *Yun Nan Zhong Yi* (Yunnan Journal of Traditional Chinese Medicine), 1990; 4:15.
37. *Zhong Yi Za Zhi* (Journal of Chinese Medicine) 1985;6:450.
38. *He Bei Zhong Yi* (Hebei Chinese Medicine) 1984;3:29.
39. *Si Chuan Zhong Yi* (Sichuan Chinese Medicine) 1996;11:38.
40. *Fu Jian Zhong Yi Yao* (Fujian Chinese Medicine and Herbology) 1961;9(4):44.
41. *Zhong Yi Za Zhi* (Journal of Chinese Medicine), 1985; 6:50.
42. *Bei Jing Zhong Yi* (Beijing Chinese Medicine) 1983;(1) 33.
43. *Zhong Yi Ming Fang Lin Chuang Xin Yong* (Contemporary Clinical Applications of Classic Chinese Formulas) 2001;313.
44. *Zhong Xi Yi Jie He Za Zhi* (Journal of Integrated Chinese and Western Medicine), 1991; (1):43.
45. *Jiang Xi Yi Yao* (Jiangxi Medicine and Herbology) 1965;5(7):909.
46. *Zhong Yi Za Zhi* (Journal of Chinese Medicine), 1983; 11:9.
47. Tanaka T. A novel anti-dysmenorrhea therapy with cyclic administration of two Japanese herbal medicines. Clinical & Experimental Obstetrics & Gynecology 2003;30(2-3):95-8.
48. Li CQ, He LC, Jin JQ. Atractylenolide I and atractylenolide III inhibit Lipopolysaccharide-induced TNF-alpha and NO production in macrophages. Phytother Res. 2007 Apr;21(4):347-53.
49. Hwang SM, Lee YJ, Yoon JJ, Lee SM, Kang DG, Lee HS. Gardenia jasminoides inhibits tumor necrosis factor-alpha-induced vascular inflammation in endothelial cells. Professional Graduate School of Oriental Medicine, Wonkwang University, Chonbuk, Republic of Korea. Phytother Res. 2010 Jun;24 Suppl 2:S214-9.
50. *Shen Yang Yi Xue Yuan Xue Bao* (Journal of Shenyang University of Medicine), 1984; 1(3):214.
51. *Zhong Yao Yao Li Yu Ying Yong* (Pharmacology and Applications of Chinese Herbs), 1983; 888.
52. Yamamoto M., Kumagai A. & Yamamura Y. () Structure and actions of saikosaponins isolated from *Bupleurum falcatum* L. I. Anti-inflammatory action of saikosaponins. *Arzneim Forsch.* 1975, 25: 1021-1023.
53. *Shang Hai Yi Ke Da Xue Xue Bao* (Journal of Shanghai University of Medicine), 1986; 13(1):20.
54. *Zhong Hua Yi Xue Za Zhi* (Chinese Journal of Medicine), 1978; 17(8):87.
55. *Jun Shi Yi Xue Jian Xun* (Military Medicine Notes), 1977; 2:5.
56. *Xin Yi Yao Xue Za Zhi* (New Journal of Medicine and Herbology), 1979; 6:60.

Calm (ES)™

CLINICAL APPLICATIONS

- **Stress** with poor appetite, headache, tension, insomnia, and similar stress responses
- **Extreme or severe emotional and psychological disorders,** such as hysteria, neurosis, and schizophrenia
- **Insomnia** with disturbed sleep and night awakenings
- **Withdrawal signs and symptoms** associated with alcohol, drug, and smoking addiction

WESTERN THERAPEUTIC ACTIONS

- Sedative effect to relieve nervousness and irritability
- Anxiolytic function to relieve stress and anxiety
- Tranquilizing effect to alleviate severe emotional and psychological disorders
- Antispasmodic effect to relieve muscle tension and cramping
- Calming effect to ease withdrawal signs and symptoms associated with alcohol, drug, and smoking addiction

CHINESE THERAPEUTIC ACTIONS

- Spreads Liver qi, purges excess Liver fire
- Calms the *shen* (spirit) and tranquilizes the Heart

DOSAGE

For stress- and anxiety-related disorders, take 3 to 4 capsules three times daily. For severe emotional and psychological disorders, or patients with withdrawal signs and symptoms because of drug or alcohol addiction, the dosage may be increased to 6 to 8 capsules every four to six hours or as needed. Dosage can then be dropped down to 3 to 4 capsules three times daily when symptoms are stabilized.

INGREDIENTS

Bai Zhu (Rhizoma Atractylodis Macrocephalae)
Chai Hu (Radix Bupleuri)
Chuan Xiong (Rhizoma Chuanxiong)
Da Huang (Radix et Rhizoma Rhei)
Da Zao (Fructus Jujubae)
Dang Gui (Radix Angelicae Sinensis)
Fu Ling (Poria)
Gan Cao (Radix et Rhizoma Glycyrrhizae)
Gou Teng (Ramulus Uncariae cum Uncis)
Gui Zhi (Ramulus Cinnamomi)
Huang Qin (Radix Scutellariae)
Long Gu (Os Draconis)
Mu Li (Concha Ostreae)
Sheng Jiang (Rhizoma Zingiberis Recens)
Suan Zao Ren (Semen Ziziphi Spinosae)
Xi Yang Shen (Radix Panacis Quinquefolii)
Xie Cao (Radix et Rhizoma Valerianae)
Zhu Ru (Caulis Bambusae in Taenia)

BACKGROUND

Stress is a normal physical and psychological reaction to demands of life. Most people experience challenges with mental or physical stress on a regular basis. When confronted with stress, the body responds with a burst of hormones to empower the organism to cope and survive – a reaction that is labeled as the "fight-or-flight" response. Once the stress is gone, however, the body is supposed to return to a normal relaxed state. Unfortunately, the nonstop stress of modern life often keeps the body in a constantly stressed state. Over time, constantly living in a stressed state coupled with an absence of relaxed states leads to serious health problems.

FORMULA EXPLANATION

Calm (ES) is one of the strongest herbal formulas to treat emotional and psychological disorders. In addition to regulating Liver qi and purging Liver fire, it also calms the *shen* (spirit) and tranquilizes the Heart. Clinically, it is commonly used for patients with severe emotional distress or mild psychological disorders. Furthermore, it can also be used to treat withdrawal signs and symptoms commonly associated with substance addiction.

Long Gu (Os Draconis) and *Mu Li* (Concha Ostreae) are mineral medicinal substances commonly used to anchor the floating *shen* (spirit). They have tranquilizing and sedative effects, which can subdue the hyperactivity of Liver fire. *Gou Teng* (Ramulus Uncariae cum Uncis) treats headache associated with a sudden rise of blood pressure. *Huang Qin* (Radix Scutellariae) and *Da Huang* (Radix et Rhizoma Rhei) clear heat and relieve irritability. *Chai Hu* (Radix Bupleuri) disperses stagnant Liver qi and *Dang Gui* (Radix Angelicae Sinensis) nourishes Liver blood. *Xi Yang Shen* (Radix Panacis Quinquefolii), *Bai Zhu* (Rhizoma Atractylodis Macrocephalae), *Fu Ling* (Poria), *Sheng Jiang* (Rhizoma Zingiberis Recens), and *Da Zao* (Fructus Jujubae) strengthen and harmonize the middle *jiao* and prevent the Liver from overacting on the Spleen. *Gui Zhi* (Ramulus Cinnamomi) and *Chuan Xiong* (Rhizoma Chuanxiong) promote qi and blood circulation. *Suan Zao Ren* (Semen Ziziphi Spinosae) and *Xie Cao* (Radix et Rhizoma Valerianae) calm the Heart and nourish the *shen* (spirit). *Gan Cao* (Radix et Rhizoma Glycyrrhizae) harmonizes all the herbs in the formula and protects the stomach against the harshness of the mineral medicinal substances in this formula.

CAUTIONS & CONTRAINDICATIONS

- This formula is contraindicated during pregnancy and nursing.
- Patients with a weak digestive system may experience mild gastrointestinal disturbances. In such cases, reduce the dosage or take this formula with ***GI Care*** for nausea, and ***Gentle Lax (Deficient)*** for constipation.
- This herbal formula contains herbs that invigorate blood circulation, such as *Dang Gui* (Radix Angelicae Sinensis). Therefore, patients who are on anticoagulant or antiplatelet therapies, such as Coumadin (warfarin), should use this formula

Calm (ES)™

with caution, or not at all, as there may be a higher risk of bleeding and bruising.[1,2,3]

- The following warning statement is required by the State of California: "This product contains *Da Huang* (Radix et Rhizoma Rhei). Read and follow directions carefully. Do not use if you have or develop diarrhea, loose stools, or abdominal pain because *Da Huang* (Radix et Rhizoma Rhei) may worsen these conditions and be harmful to your health. Consult your physician if you have frequent diarrhea or if you are pregnant, nursing, taking medication, or have a medical condition."

CLINICAL NOTES

- In addition to using ***Calm (ES)***, efforts should be made to identify the underlying cause of illness. Both the symptoms and the cause should be treated concurrently to ensure optimal results.

Pulse Diagnosis by Dr. Jimmy Wei-Yen Chang:

- **Outward display of emotional conditions** (i.e., patients who express how they feel and do not hold their feelings inside): convex and forceful pulse on the left *guan*
- **Internalized emotional conditions** (i.e., patients who hold their feelings inside): concave and deep pulse on the left *guan*

SUPPLEMENTARY FORMULAS

- For moderate amounts of stress and anxiety or PMS, use ***Calm***.
- For stress and anxiety with insomnia in deficiency patients, use ***Calm ZZZ***.
- For insomnia arising from blood deficiency, add ***Schisandra ZZZ***.
- For crying spells or depression, add ***Shine*** or ***Shine (DS)***.
- For ADD/ADHD, add ***Calm (Jr)***.
- For stress-related irritable bowel syndrome (IBS), add ***GI Harmony***.
- For stress-related ulcerative colitis, add ***GI Care (UC)***.
- For chronic, stubborn insomnia with blood stagnation, add ***Circulation (SJ)***.
- For menopausal signs, add ***Balance (Heat)***.
- For hypertension, add ***Gentiana Complex*** or ***Gastrodia Complex***.
- For headache, add ***Corydalin (AC)*** or ***Corydalin (CR)***.
- For constipation, combine with ***Gentle Lax (Excess)*** or ***Gentle Lax (Deficient)***.
- If the patient has hyperthyroidism, add ***Thyrodex***.
- For heartburn or gastric ulcers, add ***GI Care***.
- For excess fire in the body, add ***Gardenia Complex***.
- For thirst and dryness, add ***Nourish (Fluids)***.

ACUPUNCTURE TREATMENT

Traditional Points:

- *Yintang* (Extra 1), *Xingjian* (LR 2)
- *Shenmen* (HT 7), *Taichong* (LR 3), *Ganshu* (BL 18), *Baihui* (GV 20), *Xinshu* (BL 15), *Pishu* (BL 20)

Classic Master Tung's Points:

- **Stress:** *Dizong* (T 44.09), *Neiguan* (PC 6), *Huoying* (T 66.03), *Tongshan* (T 88.02), *Tongtian* (T 88.03), *Tianhuangfu [Shenguan]* (T 77.18), *Huoxi* (T 11.16)
- **Insomnia:** *Linggu* (T 22.05), *Xinling* (T 33.17)*, *Shenjian* (T 44.19), *Zhenjing* (T 1010.08), *Zhenghui* (T 1010.01), *Tianhuang* (T 77.17), *Dihuang* (T 77.19), *Renhuang* (T 77.21), *Huoying* (T 66.03), *Tianhuangfu [Shenguan]* (T 77.18), *Shenmen* on the ear. Bleed *du* (governing) channel and back of the knee area. Bleed before needling for best result.
- **Alcohol, drug, and smoking addiction:** *Simashang* (T 88.18), *Simaxia* (T 88.19), *Simazhong* (T 88.17), *Tongshan* (T 88.02), *Tongguan* (T 88.01), *Tongtian* (T 88.03), *Tianhuang* (T 88.13), *Minghuang* (T 88.12), *Qihuang* (T 88.14)

Master Tung's Points by Dr. Chuan-Min Wang:

- **Anxiety, stress, irritability, insomnia:** *Zhenjing* (T 1010.08), *Tianhuangfu [shenguan]* (T 77.18), *Zhongjiuli* (T 88.25)

Balance Method by Dr. Richard Tan:

- Left side: *Zulinqi* (GB 41), *Yanglingquan* (GB 34), *Shenmen* (HT 7), *Tongli* (HT 5), *Shaohai* (HT 3), *Quze* (PC 3), *Daling* (PC 7)
- Right side: *Taichong* (LR 3), *Ligou* (LR 5), *Ququan* (LR 8), *Zhongzhu* (TH 3), *Waiguan* (TH 5), *Tianjing* (TH 10)
- *Yintang* (Extra 1), bilateral ear *Shenmen, Anmian*
- Left and right sides can be alternated from treatment to treatment.

Ear Acupuncture:

- **Insomnia:** Heart, Kidney, Parietal Lobe. Place magnetic ear balls or embedded ear needles on one or both sides of the ear every evening and remove in the morning. Five days of consecutive therapy equals one treatment course.
- **Psychiatric disorders:** *Shenmen*, Heart, Subcortex, Brain Stem. Strongly stimulate the points every other day. Fifteen treatments equal one course. Ear seeds can also be used. Alternate ears every week.
- **To quit cigarette smoking:** Mouth, Bronchi, Lung, Pituitary Gland, *Shenmen*, Subcortex. Switch ear every five days. Instruct the patient to massage the points for one to two minutes when smoking urges occur.
- **Select six points from the following and needle both ears:** Stomach, Adrenal Gland, *Shenmen*, Kidney, Subcortex to Endocrine, Brain Stem, Heart.

Auricular Medicine by Dr. Li-Chun Huang:

- **Improving depression, anxiety, stress, nervousness:** *Shenmen*, Heart, Nervous Subcortex, Anxious, Be Happy, Liver, Occiput. Bleed Ear Apex.
- **Improving sleep:** *Shenmen*, Heart, Kidney, Occiput, Neurasthenia Area, Neurasthenia Point, Nervous Subcortex. Bleed Ear Apex.

Calm (ES)™

- **Hysteria:** Heart, Liver, *Shenmen*, Brain Stem, Anxious Point, Forehead, Nervous Subcortex. Bleed Ear Apex.
  - For hysterical paralysis, add Knee Joint, Hip Joint, Lumbosacral
  - For hysterical aphasia, add Mouth, Glottis, *San Jiao*
  - For hysterical blindness, add Vision 2, Eyes, Occiput
- **Psychosis:** Forehead, Nervous Subcortex, Heart, Liver, *Shenmen*, Occiput, Anxious. Bleed Ear Apex.
  - For manic type, add Brain Stem
  - For depressive type, add Be Happy
- **Addiction**
  - **Smoking addiction (smoking withdrawal):** Sympathetic, *Shenmen*, Mouth, Lower Lung, Nervous Subcortex, Anxious
  - **Alcohol addiction:** Sympathetic, *Shenmen*, Drunk Point, Liver, Nervous Subcortex, Anxious Point
  - **Drug addiction:** Sympathetic, *Shenmen*, Kidney, Liver, Lower Lung, Anxious Point, Nervous Subcortex. Bleed Ear Apex.

NUTRITION

- A diet high in calcium, magnesium, phosphorus, potassium, and vitamins B and E is recommended. These vitamins and minerals are easily depleted by stress.
- Encourage the consumption of fruits and vegetables such as apricots, asparagus, avocados, bananas and broccoli. Brown rice, dried fruit, figs, salmon, garlic, green leafy vegetables, soy products, and yogurt are also recommended.
- Avoid caffeine (coffee, tea, cola, chocolate), tobacco, alcohol and sugar whenever possible.[4]
- Warm and hot natured foods that damage qi and yin should be avoided, such as:
  - certain fruits like mango and durian that produce heat.
  - stimulants like coffee, alcohol, and energy drinks.
  - spicy/pungent/aromatic vegetables such as pepper, garlic, onions, basil, rosemary, cumin, funnel, anise, leeks, chives, scallions, thyme, saffron, wormwood, mustard, chili pepper, and wasabi.
- Avoid food and drinks with artificial coloring.
- Consume as few meat products as possible. Do not eat processed meats, such as lunch meats, hot dogs and sausages, as they contain nitrites that are associated with inflammation and chronic disease.

The Tao of Nutrition by Dr. Maoshing Ni and Cathy McNease:

- **Restlessness and emotional instability:** Make a tea of wheat bran, licorice root, and dates. Drink three times daily until symptoms are relieved.

LIFESTYLE INSTRUCTIONS

- If insomnia is related to work or stress, advise the patient not to work in the bedroom and remove anything that may be a reminder of the office or work. A warm bath or light snack before bedtime may also be helpful.
- Regular exercise, adequate rest, and normal sleep patterns are beneficial for stress reduction.
- Relax the mind and the body through meditation, yoga, breathing exercises, imagery exercises, and other activities such as *tai chi chuan [tai ji chuan]* and *qi gong*.
- Get away from daily routines to do something enjoyable to relieve stress whenever possible. Laughter really is the best medicine.
- Noise can be disturbing to mental health and cause stress. Noise greater than 65-decibels can cause psychological disturbance, greater than 90-decibels can cause emotional damages, and greater than 120-decibels can cause nervous system and hearing damages.
- Sleep by 10 p.m. In TCM, 11 p.m. to 1 a.m. is when the yin shifts to yang. It is crucial for the body to be at rest during this time for optimal health.

CASE STUDIES

- C.K., a 54-year-old female, presented with obsessive compulsive disorder, anxiety and over thinking. Patient had been taking Celexa (citalopram) and Effexor (venlafaxine) for many years for anxiety and depression. The practitioner diagnosed the condition as disturbance of the *shen* (spirit). She was treated with ***Calm (ES)***, four capsules three times daily based upon her small frame and weight of 120 pounds. She was also recommended to take vitamin B_{12}. After one year of taking the herbs and returning to the Western drugs occasionally, the patient began to handle and recognize her emotions and no longer uses the drugs. In her five-year follow-up treatment, she was only taking two capsules two times daily, doing her spiritual work, breathing properly, and was much happier. Submitted by N.H., Chatsworth, California.
- A 65-year-old female patient, whose husband had recently died and was left to run their business, presented with high blood pressure and was not interested in Western medicine for treatment. Her blood pressure was 160/92 mmHg and her heart rate was 78 beats per minute. She frequently experienced stress at work, sleeping difficulties, and would wake up feeling very anxious during the night. The practitioner diagnosed the condition as Liver qi stagnation and phlegm fire. The patient was treated with ***Calm (ES)*** four capsules three times daily. After seeing results from the herbs, her Western doctor stopped pushing her to take the Western drugs. Occasionally the patient experienced an increase in her blood pressure due to stress, and would come in to receive acupuncture treatment. The patient was also encouraged to exercise and lose weight to help with her overall health. Submitted by L.W., Arroyo Grande, California.
- P.I., a 46-year-old female, presented with spotting and uterine bleeding between menstrual cycles, which were irregular short cycles ranging from 15 to 27 days long. She had been experiencing heavy bleeding, no clots during her cycles, night sweats, and chronic anxiety, which was worse before her menses. Her Western diagnosis was perimenopausal syndrome with

Calm (ES)™

chronic anxiety; the TCM diagnosis was Liver and Kidney yin deficiencies with deficiency heat, blood stagnation, Liver qi stagnation, and *shen* (spirit) disturbance. The practitioner prescribed ***Calm (ES)***, two grams three times a day and has been taking this formula for anxiety the past two years. In addition, she was also prescribed ***Nourish*** and ***Notoginseng 9***, same dosage as the other formula, for six months to stop the uterine bleeding. ***Notoginseng 9*** successfully stopped the irregular bleeding and night sweats, which had been gradually reduced over the six month period. Her periods have returned to normal with light flow and her anxiety is also much better ever since adding ***Nourish***. The patient had excellent wellness and lifestyle habits, including her diet and exercise, and she was very compliant with taking her herbs. Submitted by E.Z., Portland, Oregon.

- J.K., a 35-year-old male, presented with alcoholism, with a constant urge to drink. However, he did not want to attend AA meetings. Other than this, the patient was considered to be healthy. The patient had also just previously quit smoking cold turkey. For treatment the patient was given ***Calm (ES)*** and ***Liver DTX*** in conjunction with receiving acupuncture. As a result, the patient reported that he no longer had the urge to drink. The practitioner had also counseled the patient that this was not a stand alone treatment for alcoholism and advised the patient to go seek more help. Submitted by B.L., Fort Myers, Florida.
- J.H., a 37-year-old female, presented with anxiety, depression and addiction symptoms. There was also a history of ulcerative colitis. Pulse was weak and wiry, and her tongue had a red tip with a center crack and white coat. The practitioner diagnosed this condition as qi and blood stagnation, Liver qi stagnation, and *shen* (spirit) disturbance. For treatment the patient was prescribed a combination of ***Astringent Complex***, ***Calm (ES)***, and *Gui Pi Tang* (Restore the Spleen Decoction). The patient had completely changed for the better as she had stopped taking Western medication, quit smoking, and felt stable and happy after two months of treatment. Submitted by T.W., Perrysburg, Ohio.
- M.D., a 41-year-old female, presented with manic depressive disorder. PMS symptoms, constipation and a history of depression and addiction were also noted. Pulse was wiry and her tongue had a red tip. The practitioner diagnosed this condition as Liver qi stagnation with heat disturbing the *shen* (spirit) and consuming fluids. Upon diagnosis, the patient was given ***Calm (ES)*** along with *Zhi Zi* (Fructus Gardeniae) and *Da Huang* (Radix et Rhizoma Rhei). With taking the herbs the patient had stated she had never felt this good naturally before. She was very thankful. Submitted by T.W., Perrysburg, Ohio.
- A.D., a 58-year-old female, presented with nervousness, along with worrisome scattered thoughts throughout the day. It was noted that the patient was anorexic as well. Blood pressure was 112/74 mmHg and heart rate was 60 beats per minute. The practitioner diagnosed this condition as Spleen and Heart qi deficiencies with Liver qi stagnation agitating the *shen* (spirit). The patient was prescribed ***Calm (ES)*** to take as she was dealing with her mother's health condition and their strained relationship as well. During the times she took the ***Calm (ES)***, the patient responded very well and continues to use them during times of stress. Submitted by L.H., Chicago, Illinois.
- L.H., a 43-year-old female, presented with anxiety symptoms consisting of restless thoughts, insomnia and waking up at 3 a.m. almost every night. It was noted that the patient's anxiety was related to a business situation involving traveling and that she felt very overwhelmed at work. Blood pressure was 110/72 mmHg and heart rate was 62 beats per minute. The practitioner diagnosed the condition as Liver qi stagnation with fire harassing the *shen* (spirit). Upon diagnosis, ***Calm (ES)*** was prescribed and she was directed to take it before and during the business trip. After taking the herbs, the patient experienced immediate effect of relief from stress and insomnia. The herbs also gave her a peaceful feeling with her work situation. Submitted by L.H., Chicago, Illinois.
- S.L., a 42-year-old female, presented with a sensation of insanity, grief and sadness. Objective findings were wide-opened eyes and shaking hands. The practitioner diagnosed this condition as disturbance of the *shen* (spirit). Upon diagnosis the patient was directed to take ***Calm (ES)*** as needed. As a result of taking the herbs for four days, the patient noticed herself feeling calmer and less hysterical. However, the patient had noted that in order for ***Calm (ES)*** to be effective, she needed to take it several times a day. Submitted by S.L., Yuma, Arizona.
- A.L., a 36-year-old female, presented with PMS symptoms including stomach cramping, moodiness and breast tenderness. Pulse was wiry and the tip and sides of her tongue were both slightly red. The TCM diagnosis was Liver qi stagnation. For treatment, ***Calm (ES)*** was prescribed at two capsules two times a day. As a result of taking the herbs, it was noticed one week before her next menstrual cycle that the patient felt more relaxed, with no breast tenderness or cramping. Submitted by M.P., Muskego, Wisconsin.
- W.Y., a 62-year-old male, presented with insomnia due to stress and anxiety, which caused him to wake two to three times per night. Objective findings included red cheeks and purple lips. The TCM diagnosis was blood stagnation with Liver fire. For treatment ***Circulation*** was prescribed to treat the blood stagnation as well as ***Calm (ES)*** to treat the anxiety. Both were prescribed at a dosage of 2 capsules two times a day. Within the first week of taking the herbs the patient's sleep had improved to waking up only once during the night. His legs were still blue so the dosage of ***Circulation*** was increased. Submitted by M.P., Muskego, Wisconsin.
- A.B., a 22-year-old female, presented with anxiety and fear of failure. Additional symptoms she had been experiencing were depression, insomnia, and poor eating habits. It was noted that her *shen* (spirit) was not settled and she had dysglycemia. The practitioner diagnosed this condition as Liver qi stagnation and Spleen qi deficiency; Western diagnosis was low self-esteem

Calm (ES)™

along with low caloric diet. ***Calm (ES)*** was prescribed to take during the day and then ***Calm ZZZ*** to take at night. After two weeks she was then instructed to take ***Schisandra ZZZ*** at night and ***Shine*** during the day. *Bu Zhong Yi Qi Tang* (Tonify the Middle and Augment the Qi Decoction) was taken as well until she began eating at regular intervals. After one month of taking the herbs, the insomnia had resolved and regular sleeping habits were occurring. In addition, her depression was lifted. She started experiencing major changes in attitude, life purpose and direction. Six weeks later she maintained her results by taking ***Calm***. The anxiety had also reduced, only being anxious during stressful situations, which she had been resolving. She had also established regular eating habits, her energy had improved and her menses became regular without pain. Overall, the patient was very pleased with the outcome of taking the herbs. Submitted by N.T., Bethesda, Maryland.

- S.B., a 49-year-old female, presented with mood swings. It was also noted that she had night sweats and ringing in the ears. She was borderline diabetic, which she managed well through her diet. The practitioner diagnosed this condition as Kidney and Liver yin deficiencies with Liver qi stagnation. ***Calm (ES)*** was prescribed in combination with *Zhi Bai Di Huang Wan* (Anemarrhena, Phellodendron, and Rehmannia Pill). By the end of the first week taking the herbs, she had reported feeling less volatile, a decrease in night sweating, and was sleeping more deeply. Submitted by N.V., Muir Beach, California.
- L.L., a 56-year-old female, presented with frustration, anger and sadness over losing her home in the hurricanes. She was unable to move through these emotions. She was also diagnosed with hypertension, high cholesterol, and post-traumatic stress syndrome recently, and refused to take medications. Her blood pressure was 138/78 mmHg and her heart rate was 82 beats per minute. She also suffered from headaches in the temporal region and the vertex. Other symptoms included twitching of the eyes, agitation, red eyes, and a scalloped tongue with thick yellow tongue coating. The TCM diagnoses were damp-heat in the Liver and Gallbladder, Kidney yin deficiency, and excess fire and wind rising. She was prescribed the following formulas: ***Calm (ES)*** at 1 to 3 capsules, as needed, ***Cholisma*** at 4 capsules twice daily, and ***Gentiana Complex*** at 5 capsules twice daily. The patient gained control of her emotions immediately after taking ***Calm (ES)***. Blood pressure gradually reduced over time to 120/72 mmHg. The practitioner commented that the combination of these formulas is phenomenal. Submitted by M.H., West Palm Beach, Florida.
- A 49-year-old female social worker presented with stress, anxiety, dizziness and irregular menses. The patient reported occasional irritability, hot flashes, night sweats and dysmenorrhea. Dry eyes and muscle cramps were also present. The patient was diagnosed with Kidney and Liver yin deficiencies with Liver qi stagnation. With ***Balance (Heat)*** and ***Calm (ES)***, the patient experienced a reduction of hot flashes and had less irritability, stress, anxiety and dizziness. She also stated that she slept better and her menses were not as painful. The practitioner concluded that ***Balance (Heat)*** and ***Calm (ES)*** were an excellent combination for the condition. Submitted by D.M., Raton, New Mexico.
- A 44-year-old female police officer presented with chronic headaches located in the occipital/temporal regions. She stated that stress aggravated the problem. There was acute tenderness at the *Fengchi* (GB 20) area as well as in the cervical spine. She also experienced pain on her zygoma. The practitioner diagnosed the condition as qi and blood stagnation in Gallbladder, Urinary Bladder, and Small Intestine channels in addition to myofascial syndrome, which was stress-induced because of the nature of her job. She was treated with ***Corydalin (AC), Neck & Shoulder (AC)*** and ***Calm (ES)***, which were all so effective that they subsequently replaced her medication, Imitrex (sumatriptan). The practitioner concluded that a critical aspect in the treatment was to assist the patient in coping with stress, which in turn made the herbal treatment more effective. Submitted by S.C., La Crescenta., California.
- An 18-year-old female presented with vivid visual hallucinations at night, mainly when going alone from her car to the house. The Western diagnosis was paranoia with visual hallucination; the TCM diagnosis was Liver qi stagnation with *shen* (spirit) disturbance. The practitioner prescribed three capsules of ***Calm (ES)***, three times daily for two weeks, and taught the patient to engage in positive visual imagery and mental clarification. After the integrative therapies, the patient reported that her hallucinations and fears had resolved. Submitted by C.L., Chino Hills, California.
- A 40-year-old male presented with severe insomnia, restlessness, and hyperactivity. Tongue body appeared red while his pulse felt rapid and wiry. Western assessment of his condition was schizophrenia. The TCM diagnosis was Heart fire and Liver fire. Within a week of taking ***Calm (ES)***, his sleep time increased from 2 to 3 hours a night to 7 to 8 hours a night. His restlessness and hyperactivity also subsided. Submitted by T.G., Albuquerque, New Mexico.
- M.C., a 53-year-old female, presented with anxiety. She was very anxious and fearful of flying. Otherwise healthy, she had to take her son up north to begin college and had to fly, and came to my office for treatment. Her blood pressure was 120/78 mmHg and her heart rate was 76 beats per minute. The TCM diagnosis was Liver fire. ***Calm (ES)*** was prescribed at 4 to 6 capsules before the flight. She reported later that she took 4 capsules one hour before her flight, and that her anxiety was under control. She was able to fly out more often to see her son as she felt she could handle the flights when she takes ***Calm (ES)***. Submitted by M.H., West Palm Beach, Florida.
- A 53-year-old male miner presented with insomnia, depression, stress, anxiety and fatigue. He had difficulty falling asleep, which was aggravated by relentless worrying. Other symptoms included

Calm (ES)™

palpitations and occasional dizziness. A choppy pulse and a pale tongue were present, along with a pale complexion. The practitioner diagnosed the condition as Heart and Spleen blood deficiency. After the initial treatment, his sleep improved from two to three hours per night to five to six hours per night. The patient was no longer fatigued and felt much calmer. Because of his occupation and the nature of his condition, he was unable to take the Western medication since drowsiness was one side effect. The combination of ***Schisandra ZZZ*** and ***Calm (ES)*** made it possible to manage his condition with no known side effects. The practitioner recommended continuous application of the herbal combination of ***Schisandra ZZZ*** and ***Calm (ES)*** for his medical condition. Submitted by D.M., Raton, New Mexico.

- A 78-year-old female with a past history of stroke presented with memory loss, insomnia, and nightmares. She was easily frightened and frequently woke up in the middle of the night because of her dreams. Her Western medical diagnosis was dementia. The TCM diagnosis included qi and blood stagnation, Liver and Kidney yin deficiency, and Heart fire. She was given ***Calm (ES)*** and ***Neuro Plus***. After taking the herbs for approximately one month, the patient was able to recall the practitioner's name for the very first time! In addition, her sleep, mood, complexion, and energy level improved greatly. The patient was much calmer and less irritable. Despite the fact that she still did not know the name of her town or the correct month, there were many improvements in all other areas. The practitioner concluded that the combination of ***Calm (ES)*** and ***Neuro Plus*** has enhanced the patient's quality of life. Submitted by P.R., Encinitas, California.
- B.B., a 51-year-old female, presented with daily, moderate headaches. She suffered from breast tenderness and a headache that worsened before each period. She also had insomnia and would waken and stay awake for an hour, several times a night. She suffered from irritability that may have arisen from her recent quitting of tobacco smoking. Her tongue was purplish red; her pulse was rapid and wiry. The TCM diagnosis was Liver fire and Liver qi stagnation. *Jia Wei Xiao Yao San* (Augmented Rambling Powder) and ***Calm (ES)*** were prescribed at 2 grams each, daily. After taking the herbs, the patient reported the breast soreness was gone. Her headache began to diminish, especially after she was past nicotine detox. Irritability was also greatly reduced. The patient continued taking the herbs for a year, and noticed that if she stopped taking the herbs, the irritability would return but not the headache or sore breasts. She continues with the formulas at 1 gram per day each, and is very impressed with the results. Submitted by C.D., Phoenix, Oregon.

PHARMACOLOGICAL AND CLINICAL RESEARCH

Nonstop stress in the modern world places a tremendous burden on the mind and the body to always function in a heightened and alarmed state. Over time, the mind and the body are unable to relax, leading to a wide variety of dysfunction throughout the body, including brain (feelings and emotions), heart (hypertension, arrhythmia, atherosclerosis, coronary artery disease), muscles (stiffness and pain), stomach (acid reflux, peptic ulcer disease, irritable bowel syndrome), and immune system (weakened immune system, frequent infection). Therefore, optimal treatment requires use of herbs to rescue the mind from stress and restore the body to its optimal health.

Calm (ES) contains herbs with adaptogenic effects to help the patients cope with nonstop stress. *Bai Zhu* (Rhizoma Atractylodis Macrocephalae) and *Fu Shen* (Poria Paradicis) have an adaptogenic effect to help the patients deal with physical stress by enhancing duration and relieving restlessness.[5,6] *Chai Hu* (Radix Bupleuri), *Gou Teng* (Ramulus Uncariae cum Uncis), *Suan Zao Ren* (Semen Ziziphi Spinosae), *Da Zao* (Fructus Jujubae), *Xie Cao* (Radix et Rhizoma Valerianae) and *Zhi Zi* (Fructus Gardeniae) have calming effects on the brain to help the patients manage mental stress by promoting relaxation and improving sleeping.[7,8,9,10,11,12] To improve mental functions and ameliorate memory impairment, herbs are used in this formula for their positive cognitive effect, such as *Da Zao* (Fructus Jujubae) and *Gan Cao* (Radix et Rhizoma Glycyrrhizae).[13,14]

In addition, herbs with anxiolytic and antidepressant effects are used in this formula to combat stress, anxiety and depression. *Suan Zao Ren* (Semen Ziziphi Spinosae) and *Xi Yang Shen* (Radix Panacis Quinquefolii) both have an anxiolytic effect to relieve stress and anxiety.[15,16] *Huang Qin* (Radix Scutellariae) exerts its anxiolytic effect through positive allosteric modulation of the GABA(A) receptor complex.[17] *Xie Cao* (Radix et Rhizoma Valerianae) has both anxiolytic and antidepressant activities.[18] According to neurobiological research, administration of *Xie Cao* (Radix et Rhizoma Valerianae) and its active valerenic acid is associated with a significant reduction in anxious behavior. The herb and its active compounds exert their anxiolytic effects by interacting with the GABA(A)-ergic system, a mechanism of action similar to the benzodiazepine drugs.[19]

To restore normal functions of the heart, ***Calm (ES)*** has herbs with various cardiovascular and circulatory functions. In one laboratory study, intravenous injection of *Dang Gui* (Radix Angelicae Sinensis) was associated initially with an inhibitory influence on the heart, followed by a negative chronotropic effect and a positive inotropic effect. It improves overall blood circulation by decreasing the whole blood specific viscosity, or improving the hemorrheological changes in "blood stagnation." It also has an antiarrhythmic effect, especially against arrhythmia induced by epinephrine, cardiac glycosides, aconitine, and barium chloride. Administration of *Dang Gui* (Radix Angelicae Sinensis) is associated with reduction of plasma cholesterol and triglyceride levels, and a decreased risk of atherosclerosis, as demonstrated in laboratory studies.[20,21,22,23] *Zhi Zi* (Fructus Gardeniae) has demonstrated marked antihypertensive action in numerous studies. One proposed mechanism of this hypotensive effect is its stimulation of the parasympathetic nervous system.[24]

Calm (ES)™

Zhi Gan Cao (Radix et Rhizoma Glycyrrhizae Praeparata cum Melle) has shown marked effectiveness in treating subjects with palpitations and artificially-induced arrhythmia.[25,26] *Chai Hu* (Radix Bupleuri) has an antihyperlipidemic effect, and has been shown to lower total cholesterol, low-density lipoprotein (LDL) and triglyceride levels.[27] Lastly, *Gou Teng* (Ramulus Uncariae cum Uncis) has a moderate and prolonged antihypertensive effect to treat hypertension by decreasing heart rate and reducing peripheral vascular resistance.[28,29] *Gou Teng* (Ramulus Uncariae cum Uncis) also has a cardioprotective effect for prevention and treatment of vascular proliferative disorders, such as atherosclerosis and restenosis after angioplasty.[30]

Calm (ES) contains many herbs with analgesic and anti-inflammatory effects to help the body cope with muscle aches and pain due to stress. *Dang Gui* (Radix Angelicae Sinensis) has both analgesic and anti-inflammatory effects with potency comparable to or greater than acetylsalicylic acid.[31,32] It has been used successfully to treat low back and leg pain,[33] vascular headache,[34] migraine headache,[35] and the general complaint of pain.[36] *Bai Zhu* (Rhizoma Atractylodis Macrocephalae) also has anti-inflammatory activity and its mechanism of action is attributed to the inhibition of tumor necrosis factor-alpha (TNF-α) and nitric oxide production.[37] Lastly, *Chai Hu* (Radix Bupleuri) demonstrates both analgesic and anti-inflammatory functions,[38,39] and the saikosaponins appear to be the main compounds for these actions.[40] *Huang Qin* (Radix Scutellariae) exhibits significant and potent anti-inflammatory activity via inhibition of nitric oxide, cyclo-oxygenase-2, prostaglandin E2, and proinflammatory cytokines.[41] Finally, *Chuan Xiong* (Rhizoma Chuanxiong) illustrates an anti-inflammatory effect through its inhibitory activity on TNF-α production and bioactivity.[42] *Chuan Xiong* (Rhizoma Chuanxiong) has been used successfully to treat many different types of headaches.[43,44,45]

To alleviate adverse effect of stress on the digestive system, ***Calm (ES)*** contains many herbs with gastroprotective effects. *Bai Zhu* (Rhizoma Atractylodis Macrocephalae) has a dual effect to regulate the digestive tract,[46] and is effective to treat either constipation or diarrhea.[47,48] *Mu Li* (Concha Ostreae) has a significant effect to neutralize gastric acid, and is commonly used to treat gastric and duodenal ulcers.[49,50] *Da Huang* (Radix et Rhizoma Rhei) has a remarkable laxative and purgative effect, as it works directly on the large intestine to increase peristalsis and induce bowel movements.[51] *Gan Cao* (Radix et Rhizoma Glycyrrhizae) has a proven effect to prevent and treat peptic ulcers. The mechanisms of this action include inhibition of gastric acid secretion, binding and deactivation of gastric acid, and promotion of recovery from ulceration.[52] According to one study, 100 patients with gastric or duodenal ulcers were treated with *Gan Cao* (Radix et Rhizoma Glycyrrhizae) extract with 90% rate of effectiveness.[53] Another study also reported good results using *Gan Cao* (Radix et Rhizoma Glycyrrhizae) to treat patients with peptic ulcers. The treatment protocol was to administer 2.5 to 5 grams of powdered *Gan Cao* (Radix et Rhizoma Glycyrrhizae) three times daily for 3 to 4 weeks.[54]

To enhance the immune system and maintain optimal health, many herbs with immunostimulant effects are used in this formula. *Chai Hu* (Radix Bupleuri) stimulates both humoral and cellular immunity.[55] *Dang Gui* (Radix Angelicae Sinensis) increases the phagocytic activity of the macrophages.[56] Lastly, *Bai Zhu* (Rhizoma Atractylodis Macrocephalae) increases the activity of the macrophages and reticuloendothelial system, and elevates the number of white blood cells, lymphocytes, and IgG.[57,58]

In summary, ***Calm (ES)*** is an excellent formula to relax the mind and restore the body to its optimal health.

COMPARATIVE ANALYSIS

Stress and anxiety are two of the most common emotional disorders. Clinical signs and symptoms include recurrent and intrusive thoughts, insomnia, disturbed sleep, illusions, hallucinations, difficulty concentrating, hypervigilance, restlessness, anger, and irritability.

Pharmaceutical drug treatment for stress and anxiety focuses primarily on the use of sedative and hypnotic drugs, such as Valium (diazepam) and Ativan (lorazepam). Though these drugs are very potent and have an immediate effect to sedate patients, they do not address the underlying conditions. Furthermore, long-term use of these medications are associated with many side effects, including drowsiness, dizziness, tiredness, blurred vision, changes in sex drive or ability, shuffling walk, persistent, fine tremor or inability to sit still, difficulty breathing or swallowing, severe skin rash, yellowing of the skin or eyes, irregular heartbeat, and addiction. Therefore, these drugs should only be used when necessary, and only for a short period of time.

Use of herbs is extremely effective to treat stress and anxiety. Herbs regulate mood and emotions, and alleviate stress and anxiety by enhancing the body's own ability to deal with these external factors. Unlike drugs that have an immediate effect to treat stress and anxiety by sedating the mind and decreasing its responsiveness, herbs do not have an immediate effect, and require two or more weeks of continuous use to gradually treat these conditions. In contrast, one of the main advantages of herbs is they are safe and natural, and do not have negative side effects like drugs.

Stress and anxiety are two very common disorders. While drugs and herbs are both effective, they have contrasting differences of benefits and risks. While drugs are more effective for short-term treatment, herbs are more successful for long-term management. Furthermore, counseling (behavioral and psychotherapy) is extremely important toward the understanding of, and complete recovery from, these conditions.

References

1. Chan K, Lo AC, Yeung JH, Woo KS. Journal of Pharmacy and Pharmacology 1995 May;47(5):402-6.
2. Pharmacotherapy 1999 July;19(7):870-876.

Calm (ES)™

3. European Journal of Drug Metabolism and Pharmacokinetics 1995; 20(1):55-60.
4. Balch, JF. et al. *Prescription for Nutritional Healing*. Avery Publishing Group. 1997.
5. *Xin Yi Yao Xue Za Zhi* (New Journal of Medicine and Herbology), 1974; 8:13.
6. *Zhong Yao Da Ci Dian* (Dictionary of Chinese Herbs), 1977:1596.
7. *Zhong Yao Yao Li Yu Ying Yong* (Pharmacology and Applications of Chinese Herbs), 1983; 888.
8. *Zhong Yao Yao Li Yu Ying Yong* (Pharmacology and Applications of Chinese Herbs), 1983; 786.
9. *Chang Yong Zhong Yao Xian Dai Yan Jiu Yu Lin Chuan* (Recent Study & Clinical Application of Common Traditional Chinese Medicine), 1995; 489:491.
10. Cao JX, Zhang QY, Cui SY, Cui XY, Zhang J, Zhang YH, Bai YJ, Zhao YY. Hypnotic effect of jujubosides from Semen Ziziphi Spinosae. Department of Pharmacology, Peking University, School of Basic Medical Science, 38 Xueyuan Lu, Beijing 100191, China. J Ethnopharmacol. 2010 Jul 6;130(1):163-6.
11. *Xian Dai Zhong Yao Yao Li Xue* (Contemporary Pharmacology of Chinese Herbs), 1997; 1092.
12. *Jiang Su Yi Yao* (Jiangsu Journal of Medicine and Herbology), 1976; (1):28.
13. Heo HJ, Park YJ, Suh YM, Choi SJ, Kim MJ, Cho HY, Chang YJ, Hong B, Kim HK, Kim E, Kim CJ, Kim BG, Shin DH. Effects of oleamide on choline acetyltransferase and cognitive activities. Biosci Biotechnol Biochem. 2003 Jun;67(6):1284-91.
14. Zhu Z, Li C, Wang X, Yang Z, Chen J, Hu L, Jiang H, Shen X. 2,2',4'-trihydroxychalcone from Glycyrrhiza glabra as a new specific BACE1 inhibitor efficiently ameliorates memory impairment in mice. J Neurochem. 2010 Jul;114(2):374-85.
15. Peng WH, Hsieh MT, Lee YS, Lin YC, Liao J. Anxiolytic effect of seed of Ziziphus jujuba in mouse models of anxiety. Institute of Chinese Pharmaceutical Sciences, China Medical College, Taichung, Taiwan, PR China. J Ethnopharmacol. 2000 Oct;72(3):435-41.
16. Wei XY, et al. Anxiolytic effect of saponins from Panax quinquefolium in mice. Department of Pharmacology, Shenyang Pharmaceutical University, Shenyang 110016, PR China. J Ethnopharmacol. 2007 May 22;111(3):613-8.
17. Hui KM, Huen MS, Wang HY, Zheng H, Sigel E, Baur R, Ren H, Li ZW, Wong JT, Xue H. Anxiolytic effect of wogonin, a benzodiazepine receptor ligand isolated from Scutellaria baicalensis Georgi. Department of Biochemistry, Hong Kong University of Science and Technology, Clear Water Bay, Kowloon, Hong Kong, China. Biochem Pharmacol. 2002 Nov 1;64(9):1415-24.
18. Hattesohl M, Feistel B, Sievers H, Lehnfeld R, Hegger M, Winterhoff H. Extracts of Valeriana officinalis L. s.l. show anxiolytic and antidepressant effects but neither sedative nor myorelaxant properties. Department of Pharmacology and Toxicology, Universitätsklinikum Münster, Westfälische Wilhelms-Universität Münster, Domagkstr. 12, 48149 Münster, Germany. Phytomedicine. 2008 Jan;15(1-2):2-15.
19. Murphy K, Kubin ZJ, Shepherd JN, Ettinger RH. Valeriana officinalis root extracts have potent anxiolytic effects in laboratory rats. Department of Psychology, Eastern Oregon University, LaGrande, OR 97850, USA. Phytomedicine. 2010 Jul;17(8-9):674-8.
20. *Jiang Su Zhong Yi* (Jiangsu Chinese Medicine), 1965; (3):22.
21. Xue, JX. et al. Effects of the combination of astragalus membranaceus (Fisch.) Bge. (AM), angelica sinensis (Oliv.) Diels (TAS), cyperus rotundus L. (CR), ligusticum chuanxiong Hort (LC) and paeonia veitchii lynch (PV) on the hemorrheological changes in "blood stagnating" rats. *Chung Kuo Chung Yao Tsa Chih*; 19(2):108-10, 128. Feb 1994.
22. *Lan Zhou Yi Xue Yuan Xue Bao* (Journal of Lanzhou University of Medicine), 1989; 15(3):125.
23. *Zhong Cao Yao Tong Xun* (Journal of Chinese Herbal Medicine), 1976; (3):30.
24. *Zhong Yao Yao Li Yu Ying Yong* (Pharmacology and Applications of Chinese Herbs), 1983; 934.
25. *Shang Hai Yi Yao Za Zhi* (Shanghai Journal of Medicine and Herbology), 1988; (2):12.
26. *Jiang Su Zhong Yi Za Zhi* (Jiangsu Journal of Chinese Medicine), 1987; 8(10):688.
27. *Zhong Yao Xue* (Chinese Herbology), 1998; 103:106.
28. *Chang Yong Zhong Yao Cheng Fen Yu Yao Li Shou Ce* (A Handbook of the Composition and Pharmacology of Common Chinese Drugs), 1994; 1419:1423.
29. *Zhong Cao Yao Tong Xun* (Journal of Chinese Herbal Medicine), 1976; 7:45.
30. Kim TJ, Lee JH, Lee JJ, Yu JY, Hwang BY, Ye SK, Shujuan L, Gao L, Pyo MY, Yun YP. Corynoxeine isolated from the hook of Uncaria rhynchophylla inhibits rat aortic vascular smooth muscle cell proliferation through the blocking of extracellular signal regulated kinase 1/2 phosphorylation. Biol Pharm Bull. 2008 Nov;31(11):2073-8.
31. *Xin Yi Yao Xue Za Zhi* (New Journal of Medicine and Herbology), 1975; (6):34.
32. *Yao Xue Za Zhi* (Journal of Medicinals), 1971; (91):1098.
33. *Xin Zhong Yi* (New Chinese Medicine), 1980; 2:34.
34. *Hu Bei Zhong Yi Za Zhi* (Hubei Journal of Chinese Medicine), 1993; (2):9.
35. *Bei Jing Yi Xue* (Beijing Medicine), 1988; 2:95.
36. *Xin Yi Yao Xue Za Zhi* (New Journal of Medicine and Herbology), 1976; 12:26.
37. Li CQ, He LC, Jin JQ. Atractylenolide I and atractylenolide III inhibit Lipopolysaccharide-induced TNF-alpha and NO production in macrophages. Phytother Res. 2007 Apr;21(4):347-53.
38. *Shen Yang Yi Xue Yuan Xue Bao* (Journal of Shenyang University of Medicine), 1984; 1(3):214.
39. *Zhong Yao Yao Li Yu Ying Yong* (Pharmacology and Applications of Chinese Herbs), 1983; 888.
40. Yamamoto M., Kumagai A. & Yamamura Y. () Structure and actions of saikosaponins isolated from *Bupleurum falcatum* L. I. Anti-inflammatory action of saikosaponins. *Arzneim Forsch.* 1975, 25: 1021-1023
41. Kim EH, Shim B, Kang S, Jeong G, Lee JS, Yu YB, Chun M. Anti-inflammatory effects of Scutellaria baicalensis extract via suppression of immune modulators and MAP kinase signaling molecules. Department of Biological Sciences, Seoul National University, Seoul 151-742, Republic of Korea. J Ethnopharmacol. 2009 Nov 12;126(2):320-31.
42. Liu L, Ning ZQ, Shan S, Zhang K, Deng T, Lu XP, Cheng YY. Phthalide Lactones from Ligusticum chuanxiong inhibit lipopolysaccharide-induced TNF-alpha production and TNF-alpha-mediated NF-kappaB Activation. Planta Med. 2005 Sep;71(9):808-13.
43. *Zhong Xi Yi Jie He Za Zhi* (Journal of Integrated Chinese and Western Medicine), 1991; (1):52.
44. *Shan Xi Zhong Yi Za Zhi* (Shanxi Journal Chinese Medicine), 1985; 10:447.
45. *Si Chuan Zhong Yi* (Sichuan Chinese Medicine), 1986; (11):27.
46. *Chang Yong Zhong Yao Cheng Fen Yu Yao Li Shou Ce* (A Handbook of the Composition and Pharmacology of Common Chinese Drugs), 1994; 739:742.
47. *Xin Yi Yao Xue Za Zhi* (New Journal of Medicine and Herbology), 1978; 4:9.
48. *Shan Dong Zhong Yi Za Zhi* (Shandong Journal of Chinese Medicine), 1982; 2:107.
49. *Zhong Yao Xue* (Chinese Herbology), 1998; 686:688.
50. *Zhong Yi Za Zhi* (Journal of Chinese Medicine), 1983; 3:36.
51. *Zhong Yao Xue* (Chinese Herbology), 1998; 251:256.
52. *Zhong Yao Zhi* (Chinese Herbology Journal), 1993; 358.
53. *Zhong Hua Nei Ke Xue Za Zhi* (Journal of Chinese Internal Medicine), 1960; 3:226.
54. *Zhong Yao Lin Chuan Xin Yong* (New Clinical Applications of Chinese Medicine), 2001; 163.
55. *Shang Hai Yi Ke Da Xue Xue Bao* (Journal of Shanghai University of Medicine), 1986; 13(1):20.
56. *Zhong Hua Yi Xue Za Zhi* (Chinese Journal of Medicine), 1978; 17(8):87.
57. *Jun Shi Yi Xue Jian Xun* (Military Medicine Notes), 1977; 2:5.
58. *Xin Yi Yao Xue Za Zhi* (New Journal of Medicine and Herbology), 1979; 6:60.

Calm (Jr)™

CLINICAL APPLICATIONS

- **ADD** (attention deficit disorder)
- **ADHD** (attention deficit hyperactivity disorder)
- **Hyperactivity, anxiety, impulsiveness, difficulty in focusing, inattentiveness, restlessness**

WESTERN THERAPEUTIC ACTIONS

- Cognitive effect to improve memory and treat learning impairment
- Neuroprotective effect to protect and prevent damages to the nerves and the brain
- Anxiolytic activity to relieve anxiety and hyperactivity
- Detoxifying effect to eliminate unwanted toxic compounds, chemical substances, and artificial food additives

CHINESE THERAPEUTIC ACTIONS

- Extinguishes Liver wind
- Nourishes Liver yin
- Tranquilizes the *shen* (spirit)

DOSAGE

For adults, take 3 to 4 capsules three times daily. For children, please refer to the Strategic Dosing Guidelines section to determine the proper dose based on age or body weight. For maximum effect, take the herbs on an empty stomach. The herbs should be taken for three months continuously prior to an evaluation on the progress of the individual.

INGREDIENTS

Bai Shao (Radix Paeoniae Alba)
Bie Jia (Carapax Trionycis)
Chuan Xiong (Rhizoma Chuanxiong)
Di Huang (Radix Rehmanniae)
Gou Teng (Ramulus Uncariae cum Uncis)
Gui Ban (Plastrum Testudinis)
Jue Ming Zi (Semen Cassiae)
Mai Dong (Radix Ophiopogonis)
Mu Li (Concha Ostreae)
Shi Chang Pu (Rhizoma Acori Tatarinowii)
Tai Zi Shen (Radix Pseudostellariae)
Yu Jin (Radix Curcumae)
Yuan Zhi (Radix Polygalae)
Zhi Gan Cao (Radix et Rhizoma Glycyrrhizae Praeparata cum Melle)

BACKGROUND

Introduction: ADD/ADHD is a developmental condition in which the affected person is unable to concentrate and is easily distracted, with or without accompanying hyperactivity. Adults or children must have had an onset of symptoms before the age of seven that caused significant social or academic impairment. More recently, increasing attention has been focused on adult forms of ADHD, which have probably been under-diagnosed. The incidence is 3 to 7% in school-age children, and 2 to 7% in adults.

Pathophysiology: The pathology of ADHD is not clear. Findings indicating that psychostimulants (which facilitate dopamine release) and noradrenergic tricyclics treat this condition have led to speculation that certain areas of the brain related to attention are deficient in neural transmission. The neurotransmitters dopamine and norepinephrine have been associated with ADD/ADHD.

Mortality/Morbidity: There is no clear correlation with mortality in ADD/ADHD. However, studies suggest that childhood ADD/ADHD is a risk factor for subsequent conduct and substance abuse problems, which can carry significant mortality and morbidity. ADD/ADHD may lead to difficulties with academic or employment performance and social difficulties that can profoundly affect normal development. However, exact morbidity has not been established.

Age and Gender Distribution: ADD/ADHD is a developmental disorder diagnosis that requires an onset of symptoms before age seven. After childhood, symptoms may persist into adolescence and adulthood, or they may ameliorate or disappear. The percentages in each group are not well established, but at least an estimated 15-20% of children with ADD/ADHD will maintain the full diagnosis in adulthood. Up to 65% of these children will have ADD/ADHD or some residual symptoms of ADD/ADHD as adults. In children, ADD/ADHD is three to five times more common in boys than girls. Some studies report incidences as high as 5:1. In adults, the gender ratio is closer to even.

Treatment: Stimulants such as Ritalin (methylphenidate) and Dexedrine (dextroamphetamine), are generally prescribed for treatment of ADD/ADHD. Though they may be effective, there are certain risks involved. Common short-term side effects include significant insomnia, appetite suppression and weight loss, headaches, mood fluctuations (depression, irritability), and these substances can exacerbate tics in children. Long-term risks include possible growth retardation, especially with prolonged use. Furthermore, stimulants such as Ritalin (methylphenidate) and Dexedrine (dextroamphetamine) have significant abuse potential and must be used and regulated carefully.

FORMULA EXPLANATION

According to traditional Chinese medicine, ADD/ADHD is diagnosed as Liver wind rising with *shen* (spirit) disturbance arising from Liver yin deficiency. To treat these disorders, both calming and nourishing herbs must be used together to restore normal balance in the body.

To extinguish Liver wind and calm down Liver yang rising (manifesting in muscle twitching or restlessness), *Mu Li* (Concha Ostreae), *Jue Ming Zi* (Semen Cassiae) and *Gou Teng* (Ramulus Uncariae cum Uncis) are used. These three herbs neutralize the mood, addressing the emotional aspects of ADD/ADHD such

Calm (Jr)™

as irritability, hyperactivity and short temper. *Bie Jia* (Carapax Trionycis) and *Gui Ban* (Plastrum Testudinis) are used to tonify Liver yin and further assist the first three herbs in extinguishing Liver wind. To address yin deficiency, *Bai Shao* (Radix Paeoniae Alba), *Di Huang* (Radix Rehmanniae) and *Mai Dong* (Radix Ophiopogonis) are used. *Bai Shao* (Radix Paeoniae Alba) also softens the Liver to relieve spasms, cramps and stiffness that may be associated with anxiety or hyperactivity. *Mai Dong* (Radix Ophiopogonis) also sedates Heart fire to relieve *shen* (spirit) disturbance. *Shi Chang Pu* (Rhizoma Acori Tatarinowii) and *Yuan Zhi* (Radix Polygalae) are two aromatic herbs used to disperse phlegm obstructing the orifices and help restore cognitive and sensory functions. They are often used for forgetfulness and inability to concentrate. *Yu Jin* (Radix Curcumae) clears Heart heat, opens orifices and promotes consciousness. *Tai Zi Shen* (Radix Pseudostellariae) is neutral and tonifies both qi and yin. *Chuan Xiong* (Rhizoma Chuanxiong) promotes blood circulation and relieves stagnation and pain in the channels that may be caused by the long-term stiffening or twitching of the muscles. *Zhi Gan Cao* (Radix et Rhizoma Glycyrrhizae Praeparata cum Melle) nourishes the Heart and harmonizes the entire formula.

In summary, ***Calm (Jr)*** is an effective and sophisticated formula with many herbs that address different aspects of ADD/ADHD. Herbs are used to tonify qi to treat the underlying deficiency, calm the *shen* (spirit) to improve focus and concentration, and sedate Liver wind and fire to reduce hyperactivity.

CAUTIONS & CONTRAINDICATIONS

- This formula should be discontinued once the condition is stabilized, or when the desired effects are achieved.
- This formula is contraindicated during pregnancy and nursing.
- This formula is contraindicated in individuals with yang deficiency or coldness.

CLINICAL NOTES

- It has been proposed that the environment is one of the major factors contributing to the cause of ADD/ADHD. In utero exposures to chemical and/or toxic substances, food additives or colorings, or allergens may increase the risk of the disorder. Environmental factors, such as diet, education and media influences (such as television), may also influence behavior in children.
- Proper treatment of ADD/ADHD is important to ensure proper academic performance, vocational success, and social-emotional development. Lack of or delayed treatment may contribute to incomplete development of such skills.
- There is great controversy on whether children with ADD/ADHD should receive drug treatment because of the possible risks and side effects. Herbs are a safe alternative as they restore the natural balance in the body without being addictive.
- It is important to educate and/or treat the parents who are over-anxious about the academic achievements of their children. If necessary, ***Calm*** or ***Calm (ES)*** can be used to calm the *shen* (spirit) of the parents.
- This formula should be used only as needed during school. However, use of this formula is not necessary during vacations, such as summer and winter vacations.
- ***Calm (Jr)*** is an herbal formula developed by Dr. Feng Bu-Zhen, a master of traditional Chinese medicine in Shanxi, China. It is commonly used to reduce hyperactivity, improve memory and increase attention span. According to one clinical trial published in *Shanxi Medicine and Herbology* in 1990, children with ADD/ADHD were treated daily for one month with herbs in ***Calm (Jr)***. At the end of the clinical trial, it was reported that out of 68 children, 61 showed no presentation of ADD/ADHD, three showed some improvement, and four had no response. No significant side effects were reported. Submitted by B.F., Shanxi, China.

SUPPLEMENTARY FORMULAS

- For poor memory or forgetfulness, use ***Enhance Memory***.
- With anger and/or insomnia, add ***Calm (ES)***.
- For stress, add ***Calm***.
- For stress and insomnia with underlying deficiency and weakness, add ***Calm ZZZ***.
- For depression, add ***Shine*** or ***Shine (DS)***.
- With muscle stiffness, cramps and spasms, add ***Flex (SC)***.
- With acute headache, add ***Corydalin (AC)***.
- With chronic headache, add ***Corydalin (CR)***.
- With constipation, add ***Gentle Lax (Excess)*** or ***Gentle Lax (Deficient)***.
- With fatigue, excessive worrying and/or restless sleep due to blood deficiency, add ***Schisandra ZZZ***.
- For Liver and Kidney yin deficiencies, add ***Nourish***.
- For individuals with chronic exposure to chemical and/or toxic substances, add ***Herbal DTX***.
- With blood stagnation, add ***Circulation (SJ)***.
- With hyperactivity and impulsivity due to excess heat in the body, add ***Gardenia Complex***.

ACUPUNCTURE TREATMENT

Traditional Points:

- *Baihui* (GV 20), *Si Shen Cong*
- *Neiguan* (PC 6), *Taichong* (LR 3), *Dazhui* (GV 14), *Quchi* (LI 11), *Baihui* (GV 20), *Mingmen* (GV 4), *Daling* (PC 7)

Classic Master Tung's Points:

- *Zhenjing* (T 1010.08), *Tianhuangfu [Shenguan]* (T 77.18), *Huoying* (T 66.03), *Dizong* (T 44.09), *Dan* (T 11.13), *Yintang*

Master Tung's Points by Dr. Chuan-Min Wang:

- **ADD, ADHD:** *Zhenghui* (T 1010.01), *Zhengben* (T 1010.12), *Zhongbai* (T 22.06)

Calm (Jr)™

Balance Method by Dr. Richard Tan:

- Left side: *Taichong* (LR 3), *Ligou* (LR 5), *Ququan* (LR 8), *Houxi* (SI 3), ear *Shenmen*
- Right side: *Qiuxu* (GB 40), *Yanglingquan* (GB 34), *Shenmen* (HT 7)
- Left and right sides can be alternated from treatment to treatment.

Auricular Medicine by Dr. Li-Chun Huang:

- **Attention deficit disorder:** *Shenmen*, Occiput, Brain Stem, Brain, Nervous Subcortex, Neurasthenia Point. Bleed Ear Apex.
- **Asperger syndrome:** Brain, Forehead, Occiput, *Shenmen*, Nervous Subcortex, Neurasthenia Point, Anxious, Be Happy Point, Groove of Brain Posterior. Bleed Ear Apex.
- **Epilepsy:** Epilepsy Point, Brain, Brain Stem, Nervous Subcortex, Occiput, *Shenmen*, Kidney, Liver. Bleed Ear Apex.
- **Autism in infants:** Thalamus, Brain, Forehead, Exciting, Anxious, Be Happy, Endocrine.
- **Convulsion and hyperactivity:** *Shenmen*, Occiput, Nervous Subcortex, Lesser Occipital Nerve, Liver, Brain Stem, Brain. Bleed Ear Apex.

NUTRITION

- Make sure the diet has an adequate amount of calcium and magnesium, which have a calming effect.
- Cold-water fish, such as tuna, salmon, and herring, are great sources of docosahexaenenoic acid (DHA). This essential fatty acid is vital for proper development of the brain.
- Increase consumption of complex carbohydrates, such as fresh vegetables, fresh fruits, beans, and whole grains. Decrease consumption of simple carbohydrates, such as glucose, fructose, sugars, and processed grains.
- Avoid exposure to chemical and/or toxic substances, food additives or coloring, or allergens, which increase the risk of developing ADD/ADHD.
- Eliminate from the diet: sugar, candy, junk food, foods with artificial color and flavor, and fried foods. Also avoid antacids, cough drops, throat lozenges, and carbonated beverages.
- Warm and hot natured foods that damage qi and yin should be avoided, such as:
  - certain fruits like mango and durian that produce heat.
  - stimulants like coffee, alcohol, and energy drinks.
  - spicy/pungent/aromatic vegetables such as pepper, garlic, onions, basil, rosemary, cumin, funnel, anise, leeks, chives, scallions, thyme, saffron, wormwood, mustard, chili pepper, and wasabi.
- Avoid food and drinks with artificial coloring.
- Consume as few meat products as possible. Do not eat processed meats, such as lunch meats, hot dogs and sausages, as they contain nitrites that are associated with inflammation and chronic disease.

The Tao of Nutrition by Dr. Maoshing Ni and Cathy McNease:

- Incorporate ¼ cup of either fresh or frozen blueberries into breakfast daily for two to four weeks.

LIFESTYLE INSTRUCTIONS

- Psychosocial support is extremely important for complete and long-term treatment of ADD/ADHD. Such approaches include contingency management (e.g., reward and timeout systems), parent training (educating the parent on child management skills), clinical behavior therapy (coordinated contingency management by both parents and teachers), and cognitive-behavioral treatment (e.g., self-monitoring, verbal self-instruction, problem-solving strategies, self-reinforcement).
- Encourage activities that foster calm and concentration, such as reading, meditation, *qi gong* and *tai chi chuan [tai ji chuan]*.
- Discourage activities that impose disruption and short attention span, such as playing video games and watching television.

CASE STUDIES

- B.K., a 36-year-old male, presented with ADD along with poor memory. Pulse was rapid and wiry. The practitioner diagnosed this condition as Liver yin deficiency. ***Calm (Jr)*** was prescribed at 3 to 4 capsules three times per day. After taking the herbs for three months, the patient reported a calmer, more focused personality. His memory had also improved. Submitted by S.L., Yuma, Arizona.
- J.S., a 9-year-old male, presented with inability to complete tasks, inability to focus on school work, irritability and restlessness. He was easily angered and also had insomnia. He was skinny and had a pale complexion and dark circles under his eyes. Western diagnosis was ADHD. The TCM diagnosis was Liver wind rising, Liver yin deficiency, and *shen* (spirit) disturbance. ***Calm (Jr)*** was prescribed, and he showed great improvement in his ability to stay on tasks, with less irritability and fewer outbursts of anger. Sleep also improved. This patient continued to eat a diet high in simple carbohydrates and fats. His parents have not reached a point where they are willing to consider dietary changes. However, with ***Calm (Jr)*** and acupuncture, the child is improving. Submitted by J.S., Milwaukee, Oregon.
- S.A., a 5-year-old female, was diagnosed with her first seizure attack on May 2, 2002 and spent two days in the hospital. She was put on Tegretol (carbamazepine). Shortly after beginning the medication, the child started to have stomachaches and was not her usual self. The mother thought the seizure might have been caused by immunization shots the child had received earlier. The TCM diagnosis was Liver wind. While taking ***Calm (Jr)***, the child was able to decrease the dosage of Tegretol (carbamazepine). The mother noticed the seizures diminishing in frequency and intensity. The child was able to endure the seizures in a more relaxed manner. The patient also received cranio-sacral therapy. Submitted by M.C., Sarasota, Florida.

Calm (Jr)™

PHARMACOLOGICAL AND CLINICAL RESEARCH

Calm (Jr) is formulated to treat and prevent ADD/ADHD. It contains herbs with cognitive effects to improve memory and treat learning impairment, neuroprotective effect to protect and prevent damages to the nerves and the brain, and anxiolytic activity to relieve anxiety and hyperactivity. Furthermore, ***Calm (Jr)*** also contains herbs with detoxifying effects to eliminate unwanted toxic compounds, chemical substances, and artificial food additives.

Calm (Jr) contains many herbs that directly improve cognitive functions. Pharmacologically, utilization of the herbs has shown to improve cognition, treat aging-induced learning deficit, and ameliorate drug-induced memory impairment. In one laboratory study, administration of *Shi Chang Pu* (Rhizoma Acori Tatarinowii) is associated with a dose-dependent effect in improving memory.[1] Paeoniflorin, a compound from *Bai Shao* (Radix Paeoniae Alba), has been shown to enhance aging-induced learning deficit.[2] *Jue Ming Zi* (Semen Cassiae) contains numerous compounds, such as obtusifolin, that showed a marked effect to improve learning and attenuate scopolamine-induced memory impairment.[3] *Gan Cao* (Radix et Rhizoma Glycyrrhizae) also has a marked cognitive effect to efficiently ameliorate memory impairment.[4] *Yuan Zhi* (Radix Polygalae) is another herb with excellent neuroprotective and cognitive effects. It has a dose-dependent effect to protect the neurons from Abeta-induced neuronal damages.[5] It also inhibited acetylcholinesterase (AChE) activity in a dose-dependent and non-competitive manner.[6] Lastly, *Yuan Zhi* (Radix Polygalae) shows a beneficial cognitive effect on memory impairment induced by scopolamine or dysfunction of the cholinergic system in the brain.[7] Clinically, according to one study, 30 children with low IQ were treated, resulting in mild to moderate improvement in classroom performance using an herbal formula containing herbs such as *Shi Chang Pu* (Rhizoma Acori Tatarinowii) and *Yuan Zhi* (Radix Polygalae). The treatment protocol was to administer the formula twice daily for two weeks per course of treatment, for a total of three months of treatment.[8] According to another clinical trial, administration of 10 to 15 mL of a syrup made from *Yuan Zhi* (Radix Polygalae) and *Shi Chang Pu* (Rhizoma Acori Tatarinowii) three times daily was effective in managing 90 of 100 children with hyperactivity disorders.[9]

In addition, ***Calm (Jr)*** has many herbs that indirectly improve cognitive functions by protecting the nerves and the brain. *Shi Chang Pu* (Rhizoma Acori Tatarinowii) contains beta-asarone, which has shown to have a neuroprotective effect by attenuating neuronal apoptosis in the hippocampus induced by beta-amyloid (Abeta).[10] Ferulic acid, a component present in both *Dang Gui* (Radix Angelicae Sinensis) and *Chuan Xiong* (Rhizoma Chuanxiong), exerts a marked effect to reduce the cerebral infarct area and minimize neurological deficit following transient focal cerebral ischemia.[11] According to one study, administration of *Gou Teng* (Ramulus Uncariae cum Uncis) demonstrates a neuroprotective effect against chemical-induced neuronal damages.[12] *Gou Teng* (Ramulus Uncariae cum Uncis) is also effective to protect and alleviate damage to hippocampal neurons induced by acute hypoxia.[13] *Gou Teng* (Ramulus Uncariae cum Uncis) also has a marked anxiolytic effect, and may be helpful to calm those who have anxiety or hyperactivity.[14] Clinically, *Jue Ming Zi* (Semen Cassiae) demonstrates a marked protective effect to prevent dopaminergic neurons against the toxicities involved in Parkinson's disease.[15] *Di Huang* (Radix Rehmanniae) shows a neuroprotective effect to ameliorate cognition deficits and attenuate oxidative damages in brain to treat senescence or neurodegenerative diseases, such as Alzheimer's and Parkinson's diseases.[16]

According to the Merck Manual, the exposure to toxic substances and food additives or colorings is one of the main causes of ADD/ADHD. Therefore, the importance of eliminating environmental toxins cannot be over-emphasized. In ***Calm (Jr)***, herbs are added to specifically protect the liver and improve the detoxification of environmental toxins. *Zhi Gan Cao* (Radix et Rhizoma Glycyrrhizae Praeparata cum Melle) has been used successfully for thousands of years for detoxification. More recently, it has been documented that *Zhi Gan Cao* (Radix et Rhizoma Glycyrrhizae Praeparata cum Melle) has a marked detoxifying effect to treat a variety of poisonings, including but not limited to drug poisoning (chloral hydrate, urethane, cocaine, picrotoxin, caffeine, pilocarpine, nicotine, barbiturates, mercury and lead), food poisoning (tetrodotoxin, snake, and mushrooms), and others (enterotoxin, herbicides, pesticides).[17] Furthermore, *Zhi Gan Cao* (Radix et Rhizoma Glycyrrhizae Praeparata cum Melle) and *Yu Jin* (Radix Curcumae) have also been shown to have hepatoprotective effects against chemical- or tetrachloride-induced liver damage and liver cancer.[18]

Since ADD/ADHD is characterized by an imbalance of neurotransmitters leading to a disharmony of the entire body, herbs that harmonize and balance the entire body have been used for treatment with good success. *Mai Dong* (Radix Ophiopogonis), *Bai Shao* (Radix Paeoniae Alba), *Shi Chang Pu* (Rhizoma Acori Tatarinowii) and *Chuan Xiong* (Rhizoma Chuanxiong) balance the central nervous system and calm hyperactivity. They have been used to effectively reverse drug-induced excitation.[19,20,21,22] *Mai Dong* (Radix Ophiopogonis), *Bai Shao* (Radix Paeoniae Alba) and *Chuan Xiong* (Rhizoma Chuanxiong) harmonize the cardiovascular system and minimize the fluctuation of heart rate and blood pressure.[23,24,25,26] *Di Huang* (Radix Rehmanniae) regulates the endocrine system to ensure normal production and release of endogenous hormones.[27]

In summary, ***Calm (Jr)*** treats and prevents ADD/ADHD by improving memory and learning ability, relieving hyperactivity, and balancing the entire body. The effects of the formula have been documented with clinical trials, and the functions of the individual herbs have been shown by numerous clinical studies.

Calm (Jr) ™

COMPARATIVE ANALYSIS

ADD/ADHD is a developmental condition in which the affected person is unable to concentrate and is easily distracted, with or without accompanying hyperactivity.

Stimulants such as Ritalin (methylphenidate) and Dexedrine (dextroamphetamine) are generally prescribed for treatment of ADD/ADHD. Though they may be effective, there are certain risks involved. Common short-term side effects include significant insomnia, appetite suppression and weight loss, headaches, mood fluctuations (depression, irritability), and exacerbation of tics in children. Long-term risks include possible growth retardation, especially with prolonged use. Furthermore, stimulants such as Adderall (dextroamphetamine), Focalin (dexmethylphenidate), Concerta (methylphenidate), have significant abuse potentials and must be used and regulated carefully.

From traditional Chinese medicine perspectives, ADD and ADHD are characterized by Liver wind rising with *shen* (spirit) disturbance arising from Liver yin deficiency. Therefore, herbs that calm the mind and nourish the underlying deficiencies are used. Many herbs in this formula have been shown via *in vitro* and *in vivo* studies to be effective in enhancing concentration and memory. Furthermore, these herbs are safe and natural, and do not have the harsh side effects of drugs.

It is important to realize that though drugs may be effective, they have serious short- and long-term side effects. Furthermore, these drugs have significant abuse potentials, and their use must be monitored carefully. On the other hand, use of herbs is not only effective to improve focus and attention, they also improve memory and learning ability. Furthermore, herbs are much safer than drugs, both for short- and long-term uses. Lastly, practitioners and parents must both recognize that optimal treatment of ADD and ADHD requires more than just taking drugs or herbs, it also requires dietary, environmental and behavior changes. Combination of all these modalities ensures long-term success.

References

1. *Zhong Cao Yao* (Chinese Herbal Medicine), 1992; 23(8):417.
2. Ohta H., Matsumoto K., Shimizu M. & Watanabe H.Paeoniflorin attenuates learning impairment of aged rats in operant brightness discrimination task. *Pharmacol Biochem Behav.* 1994, 49(1): 213-217.
3. Kim DH, Hyun SK, Yoon BH, Seo JH, Lee KT, Cheong JH, Jung SY, Jin C, Choi JS, Ryu JH. Gluco-obtusifolin and its aglycon, obtusifolin, attenuate scopolamine-induced memory impairment. Department of Life and Nanopharmaceutical Sciences, College of Pharmacy, Kyung Hee University, Seoul, Korea. J Pharmacol Sci. 2009 Oct;111(2):110-6.
4. Zhu Z, Li C, Wang X, Yang Z, Chen J, Hu L, Jiang H, Shen X. 2,2',4'-trihydroxychalcone from Glycyrrhiza glabra as a new specific BACE1 inhibitor efficiently ameliorates memory impairment in mice. J Neurochem. 2010 Jul;114(2):374-85.
5. Naito R, Tohda C. Characterization of anti-neurodegenerative effects of Polygala tenuifolia in Abeta(25-35)-treated cortical neurons. Division of Biofunctional Evaluation, Research Center for Ethnomedicine, Institute of Natural Medicine, University of Toyama, Toyoma, Japan. Biol Pharm Bull. 2006 Sep;29(9):1892-6.
6. Park CH, Choi SH, Koo JW, Seo JH, Kim HS, Jeong SJ, Suh YH. Novel cognitive improving and neuroprotective activities of Polygala tenuifolia Willdenow extract, BT-11. Department of Pharmacology, College of Medicine, National Creative Research Initiative Center for Alzheimer's Dementia and Neuroscience Research Institute, MRC, Seoul National University, Seoul, South Korea. J Neurosci Res. 2002 Nov 1;70(3):484-92.
7. Sun XL, Ito H, Masuoka T, Kamei C, Hatano T. Effect of Polygala tenuifolia root extract on scopolamine-induced impairment of rat spatial cognition in an eight-arm radial maze task. Department of Pharmacognosy, Okayama University Graduate School of Medicine, Dentistry and Pharmaceutical Sciences, Tsushima, Okayama 700-8530, Japan. Biol Pharm Bull. 2007 Sep;30(9):1727-31.
8. *Zhong Cheng Yao Yan Jiu* (Research of Chinese Patent Medicine), 1982; 6:22.
9. *Jiang Su Zhong Yi* (Jiangsu Chinese Medicine), 1989, (1):29.
10. Geng Y, Li C, Liu J, Xing G, Zhou L, Dong M, Li X, Niu Y. Beta-asarone improves cognitive function by suppressing neuronal apoptosis in the beta-amyloid hippocampus injection rats. The Institute of Medicine, Qiqihar Medical University, Qiqihar 161006, China. Biol Pharm Bull. 2010;33(5):836-43.
11. Cheng CY, Ho TY, Lee EJ, Su SY, Tang NY, Hsieh CL. Ferulic acid reduces cerebral infarct through its antioxidative and anti-inflammatory effects following transient focal cerebral ischemia in rats. Am J Chin Med. 2008;36(6):1105-19.
12. Tang NY, Liu CH, Su SY, Jan YM, Hsieh CT, Cheng CY, Shyu WC, Hsieh CL. Uncaria rhynchophylla (miq) Jack plays a role in neuronal protection in kainic acid-treated rats. Am J Chin Med. 2010;38(2):251-63.
13. Liu W, Zhang ZQ, Zhao XM, Gao YS. Protective effect of Uncaria rhynchophylla total alkaloids pretreatment on hippocampal neurons after acute hypoxia. Zhongguo Zhong Yao Za Zhi. 2006 May;31(9):763-5.
14. Jung JW, Ahn NY, Oh HR, Lee BK, Lee KJ, Kim SY, Cheong JH, Ryu JH. Anxiolytic effects of the aqueous extract of Uncaria rhynchophylla. J Ethnopharmacol. 2006 Nov 24;108(2):193-7.
15. Ju MS, Kim HG, Choi JG, Ryu JH, Hur J, Kim YJ, Oh MS. Cassiae semen, a seed of Cassia obtusifolia, has neuroprotective effects in Parkinson's disease models. Department of Oriental Pharmaceutical Science, College of Pharmacy, Kyung Hee University, #1 Hoegi-dong, Dongdaemun-gu, Seoul 130-701, Republic of Korea. Food Chem Toxicol. 2010 Aug-Sep;48(8-9):2037-44.
16. Zhang X, Zhang A, Jiang B, Bao Y, Wang J, An L. Further pharmacological evidence of the neuroprotective effect of catalpol from Rehmannia glutinosa. School of Environmental and Biological Science & Technology, Dalian University of Technology, Dalian 116024, China. Phytomedicine. 2008 Jun;15(6-7):484-90.
17. *Zhong Yao Tong Bao* (Journal of Chinese Herbology), 1986; 11(10):55.
18. *Zhong Guo Mian Yi Xue Za Zhi* (Chinese Journal of Immunology), 1989; 5(2):121.
19. *Guang Zhou Zhong Yi Xue Yuan Xue Bao* (Journal of Guangzhou University of Chinese Medicine), 1986; (23):29.
20. *Zhong Yao Tong Bao* (Journal of Chinese Herbology), 1985; 10(6):43.
21. *Zhong Yao Yao Li Yu Ying Yong* (Pharmacology and Applications of Chinese Herbs), 1983; 477.
22. *Zhong Yao Yao Li Yu Ying Yong* (Pharmacology and Applications of Chinese Herbs), 1983; 123.
23. *Zhong Yao Yao Li Yu Ying Yong* (Pharmacology and Applications of Chinese Herbs); 1983; 35.
24. *Hua Xi Yao Xue Za Zhi* (Huaxi Herbal Journal), 1991; 6(1):13.
25. *Zhong Guo Yao Li Xue Tong Bao* (Journal of Chinese Herbal Pharmacology), 1986; 2(5):26.
26. *Zhong Yao Yao Li Yu Ying Yong* (Pharmacology and Applications of Chinese Herbs), 1989; (2):40.
27. *Zhong Yao Xue* (Chinese Herbology), 1998; 156:158.

Calm ZZZ™

CLINICAL APPLICATIONS

- **Chronic and constant stress, anxiety and depression with underlying deficiency**
- **Insomnia with difficulty falling or staying asleep** in patients who are stressed or have things on their minds
- **Type A personality** with excessive competitive drive, impatience, sense of urgency without the body strength and constitution to cope with their stress

WESTERN THERAPEUTIC ACTIONS

- Anxiolytic effect to relieve stress and anxiety
- Antidepressant function to lift emotions
- Sedative and hypnotic benefits to treat insomnia
- Muscle-relaxant action to alleviate tension and stiffness

CHINESE THERAPEUTIC ACTIONS

- Calms the *shen* (spirit)
- Regulates Liver qi
- Sedates Liver fire
- Tonifies the deficiencies

DOSAGE

Take 3 to 4 capsules three times daily for stress, anxiety, emotional instability and similar mental disorders. For insomnia, another dose may be taken 30 minutes before bedtime. This formula is safe for long-term use.

INGREDIENTS

Bai Shao (Radix Paeoniae Alba)
Chai Hu (Radix Bupleuri)
Da Zao (Fructus Jujubae)
Deng Xin Cao (Medulla Junci)
Fu Shen (Poria Paradicis)
Gan Cao (Radix et Rhizoma Glycyrrhizae)
Gou Teng (Ramulus Uncariae cum Uncis)
He Huan Hua (Flos Albiziae)
Shou Wu Teng (Caulis Polygoni Multiflori)
Suan Zao Ren (Semen Ziziphi Spinosae)
Xiang Fu (Rhizoma Cyperi)
Xiao Mai (Fructus Tritici)
Zhi Mu (Rhizoma Anemarrhenae)

BACKGROUND

Nonstop stress in the modern world places a tremendous burden on the mind and the body to always function in a heightened and alarmed state. Overtime, the mind and the body are unable to relax, leading to a wide variety of dysfunctions throughout the body, including brain (feelings and emotions), heart (hypertension, arrhythmia, atherosclerosis, coronary artery disease), muscles (stiffness and pain), stomach (acid reflux, peptic ulcer disease, irritable bowel syndrome), and immune system (weakened immune system, frequent infection). Therefore, optimal treatment requires use of herbs to rescue the mind from stress and restore the body to its optimal health.

FORMULA EXPLANATION

Calm ZZZ is designed to treat individuals who are under constant stress but also have a deficient constitution. This is one of the best formulas to treat *shen* (spirit) disturbance both during the day and at night. *Shen* (spirit) disturbance during the day can manifest as stress, anxiety and emotional instability. *Shen* (spirit) disturbance at night manifests as insomnia with difficulty falling asleep and/or staying asleep. Many of these patients will also have underlying deficiencies as a result of Liver excess consuming yin and body fluids on a long-term basis. Therefore, optimal treatment requires use of herbs to calm the *shen* (spirit), regulate Liver qi, sedate Liver fire, and tonify the deficiencies.

In this formula, *Chai Hu* (Radix Bupleuri) and *Xiang Fu* (Rhizoma Cyperi) are used to regulate qi circulation and relieve Liver qi stagnation. *Gou Teng* (Ramulus Uncariae cum Uncis) calms Liver yang, *Deng Xin Cao* (Medulla Junci) sedates Heart fire, and *Zhi Mu* (Rhizoma Anemarrhenae) clears deficiency fire. These three herbs treat the excess aspects of *shen* (spirit) disturbance and relieve irritability.

In addition, *Bai Shao* (Radix Paeoniae Alba), *Fu Shen* (Poria Paradicis), *Suan Zao Ren* (Semen Ziziphi Spinosae), *He Huan Hua* (Flos Albiziae), and *Shou Wu Teng* (Caulis Polygoni Multiflori) calm the *shen* (spirit) and relieve stress and anxiety by nourishing the Heart. *Xiao Mai* (Fructus Tritici), *Gan Cao* (Radix et Rhizoma Glycyrrhizae) and *Da Zao* (Fructus Jujubae) calm the *shen* (spirit) and control emotional instability and prevent the drastic shifting of moods. Together, these eight herbs address the deficiency aspects of *shen* (spirit) disturbance.

In short, ***Calm ZZZ*** uses an integrative approach to treat both the excess and deficient aspects of *shen* (spirit) disturbance. Clinical applications include stress, anxiety, emotional disturbance, mental disorders, and insomnia.

CAUTIONS & CONTRAINDICATIONS

- This herbal formula may cause drowsiness in individuals who are sensitive to herbs. Patients are advised not to drive or operate heavy machinery while taking this herbal formula. Similarly, alcohol is not recommended as it may intensify the effect.
- ***Calm ZZZ*** is ***not*** to be used as "sleeping pills." Do ***not*** ingest a large amount of this formula, as this will only increase the risk of potential side effects, such as drowsiness.
- Allergy warning: *Xiao Mai* (Fructus Tritici) used in this product contains wheat. Persons with allergy to wheat should not take this product.

Calm ZZZ™

CLINICAL NOTES

- *Calm ZZZ* is an excellent formula to treat insomnia associated with stress and anxiety. However, it will generally take a few days before this formula nourishes the underlying deficiency and restores the normal sleeping patterns accordingly.

Pulse Diagnosis by Dr. Jimmy Wei-Yen Chang:

- **Internalized emotional conditions** (i.e., patients who hold their feelings inside): concave and deep pulse on the left *guan*

SUPPLEMENTARY FORMULAS

- For mild to moderate cases of stress and anxiety, combine with ***Calm***.
- For moderate to severe cases of stress and anxiety, combine with ***Calm (ES)***.
- For severe cases of insomnia, combine with ***Schisandra ZZZ***.
- For headache, add ***Corydalin (AC)*** or ***Corydalin (CR)***.
- For heartburn or gastric ulcers, add ***GI Care***.
- For depression, add ***Shine*** or ***Shine (DS)***.
- For constipation, combine with ***Gentle Lax (Deficient)*** or ***Gentle Lax (Excess)***.
- For irritable bowel syndrome (IBS) due to stress, combine with ***GI Harmony***.
- For ulcerative colitis due to stress, add ***GI Care (UC)***.
- For menopausal symptoms, combine with ***Balance (Heat)***.
- For forgetfulness, add ***Enhance Memory***.
- For hypertension, add ***Gastrodia Complex*** or ***Gentiana Complex***.
- To tonify the overall body constitution, add ***Imperial Tonic***.

ACUPUNCTURE TREATMENT

Traditional Points:

- *Shenmen* (HT 7), *Sanyinjiao* (SP 6), *Ganshu* (BL 18), *Danshu* (BL 19), *Wangu* (GB 12), *Anmian*, *Yintang*, ear *Shenmen*

Classic Master Tung's Points:

- **Stress, anxiety, irritability, depression and emotional instability:** *Dizong* (T 44.09), *Neiguan* (PC 6), *Huoying* (T 66.03), *Tongshan* (T 88.02), *Tongtian* (T 88.03), *Tianhuangfu [Shenguan]* (T 77.18), *Huoxi* (T 11.16)
- **Insomnia:** *Linggu* (T 22.05), *Xinling* (T 33.17)*, *Shenjian* (T 44.19), *Zhenjing* (T 1010.08), *Zhenghui* (T 1010.01), *Tianhuang* (T 77.17), *Dihuang* (T 77.19), *Renhuang* (T 77.21), *Huoying* (T 66.03), *Tianhuangfu [Shenguan]* (T 77.18), *Shenmen* on the ear. Bleed *du* (governing) channel and back of the knee area.

Master Tung's Points by Dr. Chuan-Min Wang:

- **Anxiety, stress, irritability, insomnia:** *Zhenjing* (T 1010.08), *Tianhuangfu [shenguan]* (T 77.18), *Zhongjiuli* (T 88.25)

Balance Method by Dr. Richard Tan:

- Left side: *Shenmen* (HT 7), *Shaohai* (HT 3), *Zulinqi* (GB 41), *Yanglingquan* (GB 34), *Weizhong* (BL 40), *Shugu* (BL 65).
- Right side: *Zhongzhu* (TH 3), *Tianjing* (TH 10), *Houxi* (SI 3), *Xiaohai* (SI 8), *Taixi* (KI 3), *Yingu* (KI 10)
- Left and right sides can be alternated from treatment to treatment.

Ear Acupuncture:

- *Shenmen*

Auricular Medicine by Dr. Li-Chun Huang:

- **Tranquilizing the mind:** Nervous Subcortex, *Shenmen*, Brain Stem, Occiput, Anxious. Bleed Ear Apex.
- **Improving sleep:** *Shenmen*, Heart, Kidney, Occiput, Neurasthenia Area, Neurasthenia Point, Nervous Subcortex. Bleed Ear Apex.
- **Neurasthenia:** *Shenmen*, Heart, Occiput, Nervous Subcortex, Neurasthenia Area (Front & Back), Neurasthenia Point (Front & Back). Bleed Ear Apex.
- **Improving depression, anxiety, stress, nervousness:** *Shenmen*, Heart, Nervous Subcortex, Anxious, Be Happy, Liver, Occiput. Bleed Ear Apex.

NUTRITION

- A diet high in calcium, magnesium, phosphorus, potassium, and vitamins B and E is recommended. These vitamins and minerals are easily depleted by stress.
- Encourage the consumption of fruits and vegetables such as apricots, winter melon, asparagus, avocados, bananas and broccoli in addition to brown rice, dried fruit, figs, salmon, garlic, green leafy vegetables, soy products, and yogurt.
- A glass of warm milk with honey before bedtime is helpful for mild insomnia.
- Advise the patient to avoid foods that contain tyramine near bedtime. Tyramine increases the release of the brain stimulant norepinephrine. Food with high tyramine content include: bacon, cheese, chocolate, eggplant, ham, potatoes, sugar, sausage, spinach, and tomatoes.
- Avoid caffeine (coffee, tea, cola, chocolate), tobacco, alcohol and sugar whenever possible.
- Warm and hot natured foods that damage qi and yin should be avoided, such as:
  - certain fruits like mango and durian that produce heat.
  - stimulants like coffee, alcohol, and energy drinks.
  - spicy/pungent/aromatic vegetables such as pepper, garlic, onions, basil, rosemary, cumin, funnel, anise, leeks, chives, scallions, thyme, saffron, wormwood, mustard, chili pepper, and wasabi.
- Avoid food and drinks with artificial coloring.
- Consume as few meat products as possible. Do not eat processed meats, such as lunch meats, hot dogs and sausages, as they contain nitrites that are associated with inflammation and chronic disease.

Calm ZZZ™

The Tao of Nutrition by Dr. Maoshing Ni and Cathy McNease:

- **Restlessness and emotional instability:** Make a tea of wheat bran, licorice root, and dates. Drink three times daily until symptoms are relieved.
- **Insomnia:** Boil mulberry tea and drink 1/2 cup.
- **Anxiety and/or insomnia:** Toast 1/4 cup amaranth in the oven until slightly brown, remove and steep in a cup of hot water for five minutes and sip for immediate relief of anxiety or before bedtime for insomnia.

LIFESTYLE INSTRUCTIONS

- Regular exercise, adequate rest, and normal sleep patterns are beneficial for stress reduction.
- Relax the mind and the body through meditation, yoga, breathing exercises, imagery exercises, and other activities such as *tai chi chuan [tai ji chuan]* and *qi gong.*
- Get away from the daily routine to do something different and enjoyable to relieve stress whenever possible. Laughter really is the best medicine!
- Noise can be disturbing to mental health and cause stress.
- If insomnia is due to overwork, do not work in the bedroom, and remove anything that may be a reminder of the office or work. A warm bath or light snack before bedtime may also be helpful.
- Advise the patients to not worry and to do their best to prepare for upcoming events they know may be stressful. Try to ask for help from friends, family and colleagues when stress in life becomes intolerable.
- Shift outlook on life and look at changes in a positive way and as challenges rather than threats.
- Sleep by 10 p.m. In TCM, 11 p.m. to 1 a.m. is when the yin shifts to yang. It is crucial for the body to be at rest during this time for optimal health.

CASE STUDIES

- C.W., a 39-year-old female, presented with difficulty in both falling and staying asleep, which she believed was due to stress. The practitioner diagnosed this condition as Liver qi stagnation and *shen* (spirit) disturbance; the Western diagnosis was insomnia. ***Calm ZZZ*** was prescribed at three capsules three times a day. After taking the herbs for two weeks, the patient reported being able to sleep for four to six hours undisturbed. She had also mentioned having better personal relationships. Submitted by S.L., Yuma, Arizona.
- M.S., a 49-year-old female, presented with severe muscle spasms on the side of her neck and shoulder area. Objective findings included limited range of motion (ROM). It was mentioned that she had been under a lot of stress and was experiencing difficulty sleeping. Other findings included pale face, low voice, and tension on the trapezius muscle. The practitioner diagnosed this condition as qi and blood deficiencies, along with qi and blood stagnation. ***Calm ZZZ*** was prescribed, in which after one week of taking it, the patient had reported a dramatic improvement. Her ROM became 90% normal, and the other symptoms almost diminished. Submitted by N.V., Muir Beach, California.
- A.B., a 22-year-old female, presented with anxiety and fear of failure. Additional symptoms she had been experiencing were depression, insomnia, and poor eating habits. It was noted that her *shen* (spirit) was not settled and she had dysglycemia. The practitioner diagnosed this condition as Liver qi stagnation and Spleen qi deficiency; Western diagnosis was low self-esteem along with low caloric diet. ***Calm (ES)*** was prescribed to take during the day and then ***Calm ZZZ*** to take at night. After two weeks she was then instructed to take ***Schisandra ZZZ*** at night and ***Shine*** during the day. *Bu Zhong Yi Qi Tang* (Tonify the Middle and Augment the Qi Decoction) was taken as well until she began eating at regular intervals. After one month of taking the herbs, the insomnia had resolved and regular sleeping habits were occurring. In addition, her depression was lifted. She started experiencing major changes in attitude, life purpose and direction. Six weeks later she maintained her results by taking ***Calm.*** The anxiety had also reduced, only being anxious during stressful situations, which she had been resolving. She had also established regular eating habits, her energy had improved and her menses became regular without pain. Overall, the patient was very pleased with the outcome of taking the herbs. Submitted by N.T., Bethesda, Maryland.
- S.C., a 62-year-old female, presented with pain in the right wrist due to practicing yoga, along with high stress and insomnia. The patient had not yet seen a Western doctor for this condition, but her TCM diagnosis was qi and blood stagnation in the Lung, Pericardium, and Heart channels. For treatment, ***Arm Support*** and ***Calm ZZZ*** were prescribed at 3 to 4 capsules three times a day each. After taking the herbs for one week, the wrist pain had completely resolved and did not return. The additional symptoms of stress and sleep had improved during the course of the following two weeks. Afterwards, the patient no longer needed to take the ***Arm Support*** and only continued taking the ***Calm ZZZ.*** Submitted by B.S., Niceville, Florida.
- R.K., a 55-year-old female, presented with insomnia due to low back pain and stress. The practitioner diagnosed this condition as qi and blood stagnation in the Urinary Bladder channel and Liver qi stagnation. ***Calm ZZZ*** and ***Back Support (AC)*** were prescribed. After taking the herbs for two weeks, the back pain resolved temporarily. However, it still would come and go due to overuse. Over time, her sleep had improved as her back pain had gotten better. Submitted by B.S., Niceville, Florida.
- J.F., a 38-year-old female, presented with sleep issues, difficulty falling asleep and staying asleep. Premenstrual irritability, mood swings, and anxiety during the day were also present. Other symptoms included palpitations and racing heart beat at night when working at 3:30 a.m. and 5:00 a.m. Blood pressure was 100/62 mmHg and heart rate was 70 beats per minute. Objective

FORMULAS

Calm ZZZ™

findings were pale face, jitteriness and difficulty sitting still. The practitioner diagnosed this condition as Liver blood and yin deficiencies as well as Heart blood and yin deficiencies. The patient was given **Calm ZZZ** three capsules three times a day. *Jia Wei Xiao Yao San* (Augmented Rambling Powder) was given at the onset of her PMS symptoms until day three of her period. With **Calm ZZZ** she was sleeping seven hours in a row consistently with some nights eight to ten hours as well as falling asleep after just 20 minutes vs. one to two hours before she took the herbs. The PMS symptoms also improved dramatically with much more even emotions. Submitted by L.M., Lafayette, Colorado.

PHARMACOLOGICAL AND CLINICAL RESEARCH

Calm ZZZ is an excellent formula to treat both the emotional and physical aspects of mental and psychological disorders. Pharmacological effects of this formula include anxiolytic effect to relieve stress and anxiety, antidepressant function to lift emotions, sedative and hypnotic benefits to treat insomnia, and muscle-relaxant action to relieve tension and stiffness. Clinical applications include stress, anxiety, depression and insomnia.

Calm ZZZ has herbs with anxiolytic, antidepressant, and sedative effects to combat stress, anxiety, depression and insomnia. *Suan Zao Ren* (Semen Ziziphi Spinosae) has an anxiolytic effect to relieve stress and anxiety.[1] *Zhi Mu* (Rhizoma Anemarrhenae) has demonstrated significant antidepressant activity on two experimental models of depression.[2] The proposed mechanism of the antidepressant activity of *Zhi Mu* (Rhizoma Anemarrhenae) involves marked increase of noradrenaline and serotonin levels in both the hypothalamus and the hippocampus.[3] *Chai Hu* (Radix Bupleuri), *Gou Teng* (Ramulus Uncariae cum Uncis), *Suan Zao Ren* (Semen Ziziphi Spinosae) and *Da Zao* (Fructus Jujubae) have a calming effect on the brain to help the patients manage mental stress by promoting relaxation and improving sleeping.[4,5,6,7,8] Clinically, *Suan Zao Ren* (Semen Ziziphi Spinosae) has been used in many studies to successfully treat insomnia.[9,10]

Gan Cao (Radix et Rhizoma Glycyrrhizae), *Xiao Mai* (Fructus Tritici) and *Da Zao* (Fructus Jujubae) are the three principle herbs in this formula. Together, these three herbs have been shown to have an excellent anxiolytic effect to treat disorders such as neurasthenia, hysteria, and insomnia. For neurasthenia, use of *Gan Cao* (Radix et Rhizoma Glycyrrhizae), *Xiao Mai* (Fructus Tritici), *Da Zao* (Fructus Jujubae) and others was shown to effectively treat 92 out of 100 patients.[11] For hysteria, concurrent use of acupuncture and these herbs effectively stabilized the condition and resolved the clinical signs and symptoms in all 60 patients, with no recurrence in follow-up visits 6 months after the conclusion of treatments.[12] For insomnia, use of *Gan Cao* (Radix et Rhizoma Glycyrrhizae), *Xiao Mai* (Fructus Tritici), *Da Zao* (Fructus Jujubae) and others was associated with a 74.2% overall rate of effectiveness in 110 patients.[13] Furthermore, concurrent use of *Da Zao* (Fructus Jujubae) and *Gan Cao* (Radix et Rhizoma Glycyrrhizae) also has a positive cognitive effect to improve mental functions and ameliorate memory impairment.[14,15]

In addition, **Calm ZZZ** contains many herbs with analgesic, anti-inflammatory, and muscle-relaxant effects to help the body cope with muscle aches and pain due to stress. *Bai Shao* (Radix Paeoniae Alba) and *Gan Cao* (Radix et Rhizoma Glycyrrhizae) have anti-inflammatory and muscle-relaxant functions.[16,17] Clinically, these two herbs have marked effect to treat neck pain,[18] acute back pain,[19] sciatica,[20] pain in the lower back and legs,[21] leg cramps in the calf,[22] restless leg syndrome,[23] heel pain,[24] gastric and abdominal pain,[25] intestinal spasm,[26] menstrual cramps and pain,[27] neuralgia,[28] facial spasms and twitching,[29] trigeminal neuralgia,[30,31] and dysmenorrhea.[32] *Xiang Fu* (Rhizoma Cyperi) illustrates its anti-inflammatory effect in dose- and time-dependent manners by inhibiting the production of nitric oxide and superoxide (O2-), two important mediators in the pathogenesis of inflammatory diseases.[33] *Zhi Mu* (Rhizoma Anemarrhenae) exerts significant anti-inflammatory action by inhibiting cyclo-oxygenase-2, inducible nitric oxide synthase, and 5-lipoxygenase.[34] Lastly, *Chai Hu* (Radix Bupleuri) demonstrates both analgesic and anti-inflammatory functions,[35,36] and the saikosaponins appear to be the main compounds for these actions.[37]

Lastly, to alleviate the adverse effects of stress on the digestive system, **Calm ZZZ** contains many herbs with gastroprotective effects. *Gan Cao* (Radix et Rhizoma Glycyrrhizae) has a proven effect to prevent and treat peptic ulcers. The mechanisms of this action include inhibition of gastric acid secretion, binding and deactivation of gastric acid, and promotion of recovery from ulceration.[38] According to one study, 100 patients with gastric or duodenal ulcers were treated with *Gan Cao* (Radix et Rhizoma Glycyrrhizae) with a 90% rate of effectiveness.[39] Another study also reported good results using *Gan Cao* (Radix et Rhizoma Glycyrrhizae) to treat patients with peptic ulcers. The treatment protocol was to administer 2.5 to 5 grams of powdered *Gan Cao* (Radix et Rhizoma Glycyrrhizae) three times daily for three to four weeks.[40]

In summary, **Calm ZZZ** is an excellent formula that treats both the emotional and physical aspects of mental and psychological disorders. Treatment of the emotional aspects of mental disorder includes use of herbs with anxiolytic effects to relieve stress and anxiety, and sedative and hypnotic effects to treat insomnia. Furthermore, treatment of the physical aspects of mental disorder includes use of herbs with muscle-relaxant effects to relieve tension and stiffness.

COMPARATIVE ANALYSIS

Stress, anxiety, and insomnia are three conditions that often contribute to and aggravate each other. Clinical signs and symptoms include intrusive thoughts, illusions, hallucinations, difficulty concentrating, hypervigilance, restlessness, anger, irritability, and inability to fall and/or stay asleep.

Calm ZZZ ™

Pharmaceutical drug treatments for stress, anxiety, and insomnia focus primarily on use of benzodiazepines such as Valium (diazepam), Ativan (lorazepam), Halcion (triazolam), Restoril (temazepam), and Dalmane (flurazepam). Though these drugs are very potent and have an immediate effect to sedate patients, they do not address the underlying conditions. Furthermore, long-term use of these medications are associated with many side effects, including drowsiness, dizziness, tiredness, blurred vision, changes in sex drive or ability, shuffling walk, persistent, fine tremor or inability to sit still, difficulty breathing or swallowing, severe skin rash, yellowing of the skin or eyes, irregular heartbeat, and addiction. Therefore, these drugs should only be used when necessary, and only for a short period of time.

Use of herbs is extremely effective to treat stress, anxiety, and insomnia. Herbs regulate mood and emotions, and alleviate stress and anxiety by enhancing the body's own ability to deal with these external factors. Furthermore, many herbs calm the *shen* (spirit) and help to restore normal sleeping patterns. Unlike benzodiazepine drugs that have immediate and potent sedative effects, herbs are moderate in potency, and may require one to two weeks to relieve stress, anxiety, and insomnia. In contrast, one of the main advantages of herbs is they are safe and natural, and do not have negative side effects like drugs.

Stress, anxiety, and insomnia are very common disorders. While drugs and herbs are both effective, they have contrasting differences of benefits and risks. While drugs are more effective for short-term treatment, herbs are more successful for long-term management. Furthermore, counseling (behavioral and psychotherapy) is extremely important toward the understanding of, and complete recovery from, these conditions.

References

1. Peng WH, Hsieh MT, Lee YS, Lin YC, Liao J. Anxiolytic effect of seed of Ziziphus jujuba in mouse models of anxiety. Institute of Chinese Pharmaceutical Sciences, China Medical College, Taichung, Taiwan, PR China. J Ethnopharmacol. 2000 Oct;72(3):435-41.
2. Ren LX, Luo YF, Li X, Wu YL. Antidepressant activity of sarsasapogenin from Anemarrhena asphodeloides Bunge (Liliaceae). School of Pharmacy, Shenyang Pharmaceutical University, Shenyang, China. Pharmazie. 2007 Jan;62(1):78-9.
3. Ren LX, Luo YF, Li X, Zuo DY, Wu YL. Antidepressant-like effects of sarsasapogenin from Anemarrhena asphodeloides BUNGE (Liliaceae). School of Pharmacy, Shenyang Pharmaceutical University, China. Biol Pharm Bull. 2006 Nov;29(11):2304-6.
4. *Zhong Yao Yao Li Yu Ying Yong* (Pharmacology and Applications of Chinese Herbs), 1983; 888.
5. *Zhong Yao Yao Li Yu Ying Yong* (Pharmacology and Applications of Chinese Herbs), 1983; 786.
6. *Chang Yong Zhong Yao Xian Dai Yan Jiu Yu Lin Chuan* (Recent Study & Clinical Application of Common Traditional Chinese Medicine), 1995; 489:491.
7. Cao JX, Zhang QY, Cui SY, Cui XY, Zhang J, Zhang YH, Bai YJ, Zhao YY. Hypnotic effect of jujubosides from Semen Ziziphi Spinosae. Department of Pharmacology, Peking University, School of Basic Medical Science, 38 Xueyuan Lu, Beijing 100191, China. J Ethnopharmacol. 2010 Jul 6;130(1):163-6.
8. *Xian Dai Zhong Yao Yao Li Xue* (Contemporary Pharmacology of Chinese Herbs), 1997; 1092.
9. *Xin Zhong Yi* (New Chinese Medicine), 1982; (11):35.
10. *Shang Hai Zhong Yi Yao Za Zhi* (Shanghai Journal of Chinese Medicine and Herbology), 1984; (10):30.
11. *Jiang Su Yi Yao* (Jiangsu Journal of Medicine and Herbology), 1976; 1:47.
12. *Shan Dong Zhong Yi Za Zhi* (Shandong Journal of Chinese Medicine), 1994; 5:237.
13. *Zhe Jiang Zhong Yi Za Zhi* (Zhejiang Journal of Chinese Medicine), 1982; 9:412.
14. Heo HJ, Park YJ, Suh YM, Choi SJ, Kim MJ, Cho HY, Chang YJ, Hong B, Kim HK, Kim E, Kim CJ, Kim BG, Shin DH. Effects of oleamide on choline acetyltransferase and cognitive activities. Biosci Biotechnol Biochem. 2003 Jun;67(6):1284-91.
15. Zhu Z, Li C, Wang X, Yang Z, Chen J, Hu L, Jiang H, Shen X. 2,2',4'-trihydroxychalcone from Glycyrrhiza glabra as a new specific BACE1 inhibitor efficiently ameliorates memory impairment in mice. J Neurochem. 2010 Jul;114(2):374-85.
16. Zheng YQ, Wei W. Total glucosides of paeony suppresses adjuvant arthritis in rats and intervenes cytokine-signaling between different types of synoviocytes. Int Immunopharmacol. 2005 Sep;5(10):1560-73.
17. Leem K, Kim H, Boo Y, Lee HS, Kim JS, Yoo YC, Ahn HJ, Park HJ, Seo JC, Kim HK, Jin SY, Park HK, Chung JH, Cho JJ. Effects of Paeonia lactiflora root extracts on the secretions of monocyte chemotactic protein-1 and -3 in human nasal fibroblasts. Phytother Res. 2004 Mar;18(3):241-3.
18. *Jiang Su Zhong Yi* (Jiangsu Chinese Medicine), 1990; (10):29.
19. *Zhe Jiang Zhong Yi Za Zhi* (Zhejiang Journal of Chinese Medicine) 1995;(11):524.
20. *Fu Jian Zhong Yi Yao* (Fujian Chinese Medicine and Herbology), 1994; (1):7.
21. *Yun Nan Zhong Yi* (Yunnan Journal of Traditional Chinese Medicine), 1990; 4:15.
22. *Zhong Yi Za Zhi* (Journal of Chinese Medicine) 1985;6:450.
23. *He Bei Zhong Yi* (Hebei Chinese Medicine) 1984;3:29.
24. *Si Chuan Zhong Yi* (Sichuan Chinese Medicine) 1996;11:38.
25. *Fu Jian Zhong Yi Yao* (Fujian Chinese Medicine and Herbology) 1961;9(4):44.
26. *Zhong Yi Za Zhi* (Journal of Chinese Medicine), 1985; 6:50.
27. *Bei Jing Zhong Yi* (Beijing Chinese Medicine) 1983;(1):33.
28. *Zhong Yi Ming Fang Lin Chuang Xin Yong* (Contemporary Clinical Applications of Classic Chinese Formulas) 2001;313.
29. *Zhong Xi Yi Jie He Za Zhi* (Journal of Integrated Chinese and Western Medicine), 1991; (1):43.
30. *Jiang Xi Yi Yao* (Jiangxi Medicine and Herbology) 1965;5(7):909.
31. *Zhong Yi Za Zhi* (Journal of Chinese Medicine), 1983; 11:9.
32. Tanaka T. A novel anti-dysmenorrhea therapy with cyclic administration of two Japanese herbal medicines. Clinical & Experimental Obstetrics & Gynecology 2003;30(2-3):95-8.
33. Seo WG, et al. Inhibitory effects of methanol extract of Cyperus rotundus rhizomes on nitric oxide and superoxide productions by murine macrophage cell line, RAW 264.7 cells. Department of Microbiology, Wonkwang University School of Medicine, Iksan, 570-749, Chonbuk, South Korea. J Ethnopharmacol. 2001 Jun;76(1):59-64.
34. Lim H, Nam JW, Seo EK, Kim YS, Kim HP. (-)-Nyasol (cis-hinokiresinol), a norneolignan from the rhizomes of Anemarrhena asphodeloides, is a broad spectrum inhibitor of eicosanoid and nitric oxide production. College of Pharmacy, Kangwon National University, Chunchon 200-701, Korea. Arch Pharm Res. 2009 Nov;32(11):1509-14.
35. *Shen Yang Yi Xue Yuan Xue Bao* (Journal of Shenyang University of Medicine), 1984; 1(3):214.
36. *Zhong Yao Yao Li Yu Ying Yong* (Pharmacology and Applications of Chinese Herbs), 1983; 888.
37. Yamamoto M., Kumagai A. & Yamamura Y. () Structure and actions of saikosaponins isolated from *Bupleurum falcatum* L. I. Anti-inflammatory action of saikosaponins. *Arzneim Forsch.* 1975, 25: 1021-1023.
38. *Zhong Yao Zhi* (Chinese Herbology Journal), 1993; 358.

FORMULAS

39. *Zhong Hua Nei Ke Xue Za Zhi* (Journal of Chinese Internal Medicine), 1960; 3:226.

40. *Zhong Yao Lin Chuan Xin Yong* (New Clinical Applications of Chinese Medicine), 2001; 163.

Cholisma ™

CLINICAL APPLICATIONS

- **Dyslipidemia**
  - **Hyperlipidemia** (high cholesterol and triglycerides levels)
  - **Hypercholesterolemia** (high cholesterol levels)
  - **Hypertriglyceridemia** (high triglycerides levels)
- **Arteriosclerosis and atherosclerosis**

WESTERN THERAPEUTIC ACTIONS

- Antihyperlipidemic effect to reduce plasma levels of cholesterol and triglycerides
- Reduces absorption of fatty foods and enhances breakdown of fatty tissues
- Antiatherosclerotic effect to prevent arteriosclerosis and atherosclerosis
- Vasodilating, antiplatelet, and anticoagulant effects to prevent angina

CHINESE THERAPEUTIC ACTIONS

- Dissolves dampness and eliminates phlegm
- Invigorates blood circulation

DOSAGE

Take 3 to 4 capsules three times daily on an empty stomach. For maximum effectiveness, take the last dose one hour prior to bedtime, as synthesis of cholesterol is most active at night. Maintenance dose is 2 capsules two times a day.

INGREDIENTS

Cang Zhu (Rhizoma Atractylodis)
Dan Shen (Radix et Rhizoma Salviae Miltiorrhizae)
Ge Gen (Radix Puerariae Lobatae)
He Ye (Folium Nelumbinis)
Hu Zhang (Rhizoma et Radix Polygoni Cuspidati)
Jiao Gu Lan (Rhizoma seu Herba Gynostemmatis)
Ju Hua (Flos Chrysanthemi)
Jue Ming Zi (Semen Cassiae)
Shan Zha (Fructus Crataegi)
Yi Yi Ren (Semen Coicis)
Ze Xie (Rhizoma Alismatis)
Zhi He Shou Wu (Radix Polygoni Multiflori Praeparata)
Zi Mu Xu (Herba Medicaginis)

BACKGROUND

Dyslipidemia is the elevation of cholesterol and/or triglycerides levels that contributes to the development of arteriosclerosis and atherosclerosis and increases the risks of coronary artery disorder. Causes of dyslipidemia may be primary (genetic) or secondary (including diet, obesity, diabetes). Optimal treatment requires dietary changes, exercise, and if necessary, use of herbs or drugs to lower lipids.

FORMULA EXPLANATION

According to traditional Chinese medicine, cholesterol is considered as an excess deposit of dampness and phlegm in the blood vessels. To effectively reduce plasma levels of cholesterol and triglycerides, treatment must focus on dissolving dampness, eliminating phlegm, and invigorating blood circulation.

To dissolve dampness, diuretic and digestive herbs are used in ***Cholisma***. *Shan Zha* (Fructus Crataegi) is the primary digestive herb used to break down animal fat. It has been found to be effective in lowering serum cholesterol and blood pressure. *Ze Xie* (Rhizoma Alismatis) and *Yi Yi Ren* (Semen Coicis) are two diuretic herbs that have actions similar to choline and lecithin to lower blood sugar and cholesterol. *Jue Ming Zi* (Semen Cassiae), *He Ye* (Folium Nelumbinis), *Ju Hua* (Flos Chrysanthemi) and *Jiao Gu Lan* (Rhizoma seu Herba Gynostemmatis) clear damp-heat, lower serum cholesterol and blood pressure. *Zhi He Shou Wu* (Radix Polygoni Multiflori Praeparata) is a unique herb that tonifies Kidney *jing* (essence) and reduces cholesterol and triglycerides at the same time. With its aromatic property, *Cang Zhu* (Rhizoma Atractylodis) dries up dampness and eliminates phlegm. *Dan Shen* (Radix et Rhizoma Salviae Miltiorrhizae) invigorates blood circulation, improves microcirculation, inhibits coagulation of blood, and lowers blood cholesterol. *Hu Zhang* (Rhizoma et Radix Polygoni Cuspidati) detoxifies the Liver and lowers the cholesterol. *Ge Gen* (Radix Puerariae Lobatae) dilates blood vessels to lower blood pressure. *Zi Mu Xu* (Herba Medicaginis) may reduce cholesterol absorption from food and atherosclerotic formation.

Overall, ***Cholisma*** effectively lowers cholesterol and triglyceride levels by dissolving dampness, eliminating phlegm, and invigorating blood circulation.

CAUTIONS & CONTRAINDICATIONS

- *Jue Ming Zi* (Semen Cassiae), *Zhi He Shou Wu* (Radix Polygoni Multiflori Praeparata) and *Ju Hua* (Flos Chrysanthemi) may cause loose stools or diarrhea for those with sensitive gastrointestinal tracts. Should this occur, reduce the dosage to 2 capsules three times daily.
- Hypertension should also be suspected if the patient has high cholesterol. Treat both hypertension and dyslipidemia simultaneously for maximum results.
- This herbal formula contains herbs that invigorate blood circulation, such as *Dan Shen* (Radix et Rhizoma Salviae Miltiorrhizae). Therefore, patients who are on anticoagulant or antiplatelet therapies, such as Coumadin (warfarin), should use this formula with caution, or not at all, as there may be a higher risk of bleeding and bruising.[1]
- According to most textbooks and contemporary references, the classic entry of "*He Shou Wu*" is now separated into two entries: the unprepared *Sheng Shou Wu* (Radix Polygoni Multiflori) and the prepared *Zhi He Shou Wu* (Radix Polygoni Multiflori

FORMULAS

Cholisma™

Praeparata), as they have significantly different therapeutic effects and side effects. *Sheng Shou Wu* (Radix Polygoni Multiflori) is a stimulant laxative that treats constipation, but may cause nausea, vomiting, abdominal pain, diarrhea, and in rare cases, liver disorder (dose- and time-dependent, and reversible upon discontinuation).[2] On the other hand, *Zhi He Shou Wu* (Radix Polygoni Multiflori Praeparata) is a tonic herb that is safe and well-tolerated. The dramatic changes in the therapeutic effect and safety profile are attributed to the long and complicated processing of the root with *Hei Dou* (Semen Sojae) through repeated blending, cooking, and drying procedures. When properly processed, the chemical composition of the root changes significantly. Many new compounds are generated from the Maillard reaction (four furanones, two furans, two nitrogen compounds, one pyran, one alcohol and one sulfur compound). Furthermore, the preparation process causes changes in the composition of sugars and 16 kinds of amino acids; it also reduces the pH of the herb from 6.28 to 5.61.[3,4] In summary, these changes give rise to the tonic effects of the prepared roots, and eliminate the adverse reactions associated with the unprepared roots. **Note:** Due to medical risks and legal liabilities, it is prudent to exercise caution and ***not*** use this herb in either prepared or unprepared forms in patients with pre-existing or risk factors of liver diseases.

CLINICAL NOTES

- The baseline cholesterol level should be established prior to the initiation of herbal therapy; and the first follow-up test should be done one month after the initiation of herbal therapy. Subsequent follow-ups can be done every two to three months to determine overall effectiveness. Cholesterol testing kits are available over-the-counter in most pharmacies. Results may vary from patient to patient. Lifestyle and dietary changes are also crucial for satisfactory results.
- ***Cholisma*** is specifically formulated to reduce blood cholesterol and triglyceride levels. Patients must take this herbal formula on a long-term basis for maximum results.
- Dyslipidemia has many secondary causes (obesity, diabetes, hypothyroidism, and use of drugs such as thiazides, beta-blockers, estrogen and progestins, and glucocorticoids) and multiple complications (atherosclerosis, arteriosclerosis, coronary artery disease, angina pectoris and hypertension). Therefore, optimal treatment must address both the causes and the complications. *See* Supplementary Formulas for more details.

Pulse Diagnosis by Dr. Jimmy Wei-Yen Chang:

- The overall general feel of the pulse is greasy. A greasy pulse is a pulse in which its border is not clear due to plaque built-up on the arterial wall. The more forceful and harder the pulse is, the worse the plaque built-up. The amplitude of the pulse is also limited.

SUPPLEMENTARY FORMULAS

- For obese patients with an excess appetite, add ***Herbalite***.
- For fatty liver and obesity, use ***Cholisma (ES)***.
- For diabetes mellitus and high blood glucose, add ***Equilibrium***.
- For hypothyroidism, add ***Thyro-forte***.
- For hypertension with dizziness or vertigo, combine with ***Gastrodia Complex***.
- For hypertension with anger or flushed face, combine with ***Gentiana Complex***.
- For edema, add ***Herbal DRX***.
- For excess heat in the body, add ***Gardenia Complex***.
- For excessive blood stagnation in the body, add ***Circulation (SJ)***.
- For coronary heart disorders, add ***Circulation***.

ACUPUNCTURE TREATMENT

Traditional Points:

- Bleed *Weizhong* (BL 40) or wherever there is a visible, dilated vein in the area of the transverse crease of the popliteal fossa.
- *Taichong* (LR 3), *Xingjian* (LR 2), *Zusanli* (ST 36), *Quchi* (LI 11), *Fenglong* (ST 40)
- *Gongsun* (SP 4), *Sanyinjiao* (SP 6), *Zhongwan* (CV 12), *Ququan* (LR 8)

Classic Master Tung's Points:

- *Fuding* (T 44.04), *Houzhi* (T 44.05), *Luotong* (T 44.14), *Zhitong* (T 44.13), *Xinling* (T 33.17)*, *Linggu* (T 22.05), *Jianzhong* (T 44.06), *Dizong* (T 44.09)

Master Tung's Points by Dr. Chuan-Min Wang:

- **Elevated cholesterol or triglyceride:** Bleed *Sihuashang* (T 77.08), *Sihuazhong* (T 77.09), *Sihuafu* (T 77.10), *Sihuaxia* (T 77.11). Needle *Qimen* (T 33.01), *Qijiao* (T 33.02), *Qizheng* (T 33.03), *Muliu* (T 66.06), *Mudou* (T 66.07).

Balance Method by Dr. Richard Tan:

- Left side: *Yinlingquan* (SP 9), *Xuehai* (SP 10), *Waiguan* (TH 5)
- Right side: *Zusanli* (ST 36), *Fenglong* (ST 40), *Daling* (PC 7), *Laogong* (PC 8)
- Alternate sides from treatment to treatment.

Auricular Medicine by Dr. Li-Chun Huang:

- **Coronary heart disease:** Heart, Liver, Chest, Small Intestine, Sympathetic, Coronary Vascular Subcortex

NUTRITION

- Increase the daily intake of cholesterol-lowering foods such as apples, bananas, carrots, cold-water fish, dried beans, garlic, grapefruit, olive oil, and fibers such as bran and oats.
- Increase the intake of niacin, which can lower total cholesterol levels by up to 18%, increase HDL cholesterol by up to 32%, and lower triglycerides by up to 26%. Slow release form of niacin is

Cholisma™

preferred to minimize side effects such as flushing and stomach pain.

- Other supplements that are beneficial are vitamin B5, vitamin C, vitamin E, chromium picolinate, lecithin, and coenzyme Q10.
- Increase the intake of vinegar, as it will help to soften the blood vessels and prevent atherosclerosis.
- Decrease the intake of food that will raise cholesterol levels, including but not limited to: beer, wine, cheese, tobacco products, meat, aged and cured meats, sugar, and greasy or fried foods.
- Avoid greasy, fatty, fried and oily foods. Seafood should also be reduced.

The Tao of Nutrition by Dr. Maoshing Ni and Cathy McNease:

- Make soup with diced artichoke hearts, sliced ginger, and 1/2 head of cabbage. Eat a bowl daily.
- Drink one glass daily of pureed asparagus juice, including the pulp; add one teaspoon of honey.
- Use white mushrooms and corn silk to make soup or tea regularly.
- Add rice bran to a grain dish every day for at least two months.
- Incorporate pinto beans and other beans that are high in fiber and rich in folate that lowers cholesterol into the diet regularly.

LIFESTYLE INSTRUCTIONS

- Exercise is the best way to decrease the buildup of cholesterol in the arteries. It also helps to reduce weight.
- Drink tea on a daily basis, especially after meals, to facilitate the elimination of fatty foods from the diet. Beneficial teas include *pu-er*, black, *oolong* or green tea.
- Avoid the use of alcohol and exposure to tobacco. They increase cholesterol buildup and hardening of the arteries.

CASE STUDIES

- A 39-year-old male patient presented with a history of loose stools, allergies, and poor circulation with high cholesterol. His reports showed 263 mg/dL for total cholesterol levels. The practitioner diagnosed this condition as Spleen qi deficiency with damp and phlegm accumulation. ***Cholisma*** was prescribed at 6 grams a day for about five months. After taking the herbs for five months, the patient retested his cholesterol levels and it had dropped to 228 mg/dL. He was very happy with the results, which he attributed mostly to ***Cholisma***. He had also increased his exercise and was eating healthier as well. Submitted by A.Z., Los Angeles, California.
- P.Z., a 61-year-old male, presented with high triglycerides. His tongue was red with yellow tongue coating. His pulse was wiry and slippery. The patient was overweight. ***Cholisma*** was prescribed at 4 capsules three times daily. His triglycerides dropped from 250 to 136 mg/dL after herbal and acupuncture treatments. Submitted by W.F., Bloomfield, New Jersey.
- A 31-year-old female who went to her medical doctor for a postpartum check-up had a blood cholesterol level of 375 mg/dL. Since she was nursing, her doctor refused to prescribe any drugs. She decided to begin herbal treatment with marked changes to the diet and lifestyle. She was instructed to take ***Cholisma***, 2 grams three times daily. In addition, she exercised for 30 minutes three times per week. Furthermore, she avoided red meat and carbohydrate as much as possible, and increased the intake of fresh fruits and vegetables. Two months after the initial check-up, her cholesterol was reduced from 375 to 266 mg/dL. The patient continued to take ***Cholisma***. Submitted by J.C., Diamond Bar, California.
- K.N., a 69-year-old female, presented with left hand trigger finger and low back pain. It was also noted that she had high cholesterol shown by lab results and borderline high blood pressure. The TCM diagnosis was Liver and Kidney yin deficiencies with Lung heat; her Western diagnosis was hypertension and arthritis. ***Cholisma*** was prescribed, in which a reduction of her cholesterol levels were experienced as well as normal blood pressure again. In addition to taking the herbs, the patient was swimming for exercise. Submitted by M.P., Muskego, Wisconsin.
- R.L., a 79-year-old female, presented with post-stroke symptoms of paralysis on the right side (leg, arm, and face). Her blood pressure was 140/80 mmHg and the heart rate was 90 beats per minute. She also had high cholesterol. She was diagnosed with wind-stroke with blood stagnation. ***Neuro Plus*** and ***Cholisma*** were prescribed at 4.5 grams and 1.5 grams each day, respectively. This patient also received acupuncture. After ten weeks of treatment, the patient regained movement of her leg and partial movement of her arm and almost full movement of her face and mouth. ***Neuro Plus*** also helped the patient regain strength. These were very quick results. In addition, the cholesterol level dropped from 250 to 180 mg/dL. Submitted by W.F., Bloomfield, New Jersey.
- A 46-year-old female speech therapist presented with weight gain, pain in the left arm and a slow metabolism. Her cholesterol reading was noted at 280 mg/dL. The TCM diagnosis included damp and phlegm stagnation as well as blood stagnation as indicated by a red tongue body with a thick tongue coating and a "rolling" pulse. Within three months of taking ***Cholisma***, her cholesterol reading decreased to 220 mg/dL. Within six months of exclusively taking ***Cholisma***, her cholesterol reading fell to 198 mg/dL. Submitted by T.G., Albuquerque, New Mexico.
- A 22-year-old female presented with high triglycerides and high ALT. The patient appeared thin and pale. Her limbs were always cold and she was easily agitated. Her blood pressure was 115/70 mmHg and the heart rate was 72 beats per minute. The TCM diagnosis was yang deficiency with heat in the Liver. She was prescribed ***Liver DTX*** at 3 capsules three times a day with ***Cholisma*** at 2 capsules twice a day. She also received acupuncture. After six weeks, her liver enzymes and triglycerides levels returned to normal. Submitted by W.F., Bloomfield, New Jersey.

Cholisma™

Lab Tests for E.S.	10-21-2004	11-04-2004	01-13-2005
Cholesterol	221 mg/dL	Herbal Treatment	206 mg/dL
HDL	66 mg/dL		69 mg/dL
LDL	141 mg/dL		123 mg/dL
Triglycerides	73 mg/dL		68 mg/dL
Blood Pressure	140/100 mm Hg		118/80 mm Hg

- E.S., a 48-year-old male, presented with hypercholesterolemia and hypertension. His pulse was deep and slippery; his tongue was normal. The patient refused acupuncture treatment, requesting only herbal treatment. ***Cholisma*** was prescribed at two grams, three times daily on November 4, 2004, along with recommendations for improved diet and exercise habits. After two months of herbal therapy, lab reports [table above] showed significant reduction of total cholesterol, LDL and triglyceride levels, and an increase of healthy HDL. There was also a reduction of blood pressure. The patient continues to take the herbs. Lab reports before and after commencement of herbal treatments show significant improvements. Submitted by C.L., Chino Hills, California.
- A 50-year-old unemployed male presented with a family history of heart disease and diabetes. He was also described as overweight and extremely irritated. With increased levels of triglycerides, cholesterol and VLDL, the practitioner diagnosed the patient with dyslipidemia. The TCM diagnosis was Liver and Kidney yin deficiency. The patient took ***Cholisma*** continuously for one year, but refused to do another laboratory test in order to note any significant changes. Without any changes to his diet and physical activities, he was still able to lose weight. The practitioner recommended ***Cholisma*** to his other patients with similar conditions. He also noted that ***Cholisma*** worked slower in comparison with drugs such as Lipitor (atorvastatin) and Zocor (simvastatin). Submitted by F.A., Calabasas, California.
- J.L., an 86-year-old male, presented with hypertension, insomnia, anxiety and high cholesterol. His blood pressure was 180/90 mmHg and the heart rate was 60 beats per minute. The blood pressure was higher in the morning (180-190/90-95 mmHg) than in the evening (170-180/85-90 mmHg). The TCM diagnosis was damp-heat accumulation. ***Gastrodia Complex*** at 4.5 grams a day and ***Cholisma*** at 1.5 grams a day were prescribed. This patient also received acupuncture. After six weeks of treatment, both morning and evening blood pressure were down to an average of 147/80 mmHg. Submitted by W.F., Bloomfield, New Jersey.
- L.L., a 56-year-old female, presented with frustration, anger and sadness over losing her home in the hurricanes. She was unable to move through these emotions. She was also diagnosed with hypertension, high cholesterol, and post-traumatic stress syndrome recently, and refused to take medications. Her blood pressure was 138/78 mmHg and her heart rate was 82 beats per minute. She also suffered from headaches in the temporal region and the vertex. Other symptoms included twitching of the eyes, agitation, red eyes, and a scalloped tongue with thick yellow tongue coating. The TCM diagnoses were damp-heat in the Liver and Gallbladder, Kidney yin deficiency, and excess fire and wind rising. She was prescribed the following formulas: ***Calm (ES)*** at 1 to 3 capsules, as needed, ***Cholisma*** at 4 capsules twice daily, and ***Gentiana Complex*** at 5 capsules twice daily. The patient gained control of her emotions immediately after taking ***Calm (ES)***. Blood pressure gradually reduced over time to 120/72 mmHg. The practitioner commented that the combination of these formulas is phenomenal. Submitted by M.H., West Palm Beach, Florida.
- M.C., a 49-year-old highly-stressed executive, presented with elevated SGPT, LDL and cholesterol levels. He stated he frequently checked his blood pressure and it ranged from 135-148/85-91 mmHg. He was never diagnosed with hypertension but had an upcoming insurance physical and wanted to lower his blood pressure naturally [without using drugs]. He also complained of low-grade temporal headaches, a pressured feeling in the head, and neck and shoulder tension. His blood pressure at the time of examination was 148/94 mmHg and his heart rate was 72 beats per minute. He worried excessively, in part because his son was diagnosed with a brain tumor ten years ago. He also suffered from insomnia, and fist clenching that lasted throughout the day. He said that his stress caused numbness and tension of his left shoulder and rhomboid area. The TCM diagnoses include Liver qi stagnation and Spleen qi deficiency. ***Cholisma*** at 4 capsules three times daily and ***Liver DTX*** at 5 capsules at night were prescribed. He reported after taking the herbs that he passed his insurance exam. Blood pressure has stayed down at 120/72 mmHg. His stress was manageable and there were no more headaches. His energy level was also excellent. His cholesterol levels also dropped from 216 to 186 mg/dL. The practitioner reported that the patient is now a believer of herbs. Submitted by M.H., West Palm Beach, Florida.

PHARMACOLOGICAL AND CLINICAL RESEARCH

Cholisma is formulated with both Chinese and Western herbs that have been proven to reduce blood cholesterol and triglyceride levels. All the herbs work in synergy to reduce blood cholesterol and triglycerides levels by reducing the absorption of fatty foods,

Cholisma ™

enhancing the breakdown of fatty tissues and decreasing the synthesis of cholesterol.

Cholisma contains many herbs with multiple mechanisms of actions to lower plasma cholesterol and triglycerides. *Zi Mu Xu* (Herba Medicaginis) has been shown to reduce cholesterol absorption and decrease atherosclerotic formation.[5,6,7] It significantly reduces cholesterol absorption through direct binding in the gastrointestinal tract.[8] *Zi Mu Xu* (Herba Medicaginis) also reduces the cholesterol level by decreasing the accumulation and synthesis of cholesterol in the liver.[9] *Zhi He Shou Wu* (Radix Polygoni Multiflori Praeparata) reduces intestinal absorption of dietary cholesterol, and has been shown to decrease triglycerides and low-density lipoproteins but increase high-density lipoproteins.[10,11,12] *He Ye* (Folium Nelumbinis) has an antihyperlipidemic effect and effectively ameliorates lipid metabolic disorders (dyslipidemia, hypercholesterolemia, and fatty liver) caused by high fat diet, with efficacy similar to that of silymarin and Zocor (simvastatin).[13] *Hu Zhang* (Rhizoma et Radix Polygoni Cuspidati) and *Jiao Gu Lan* (Rhizoma seu Herba Gynostemmatis) have similar effects, as they both lower triglyceride, total cholesterol, and low-density lipoprotein levels.[14,15,16] *Jue Ming Zi* (Semen Cassiae) has multiple therapeutic benefits: it decreases low-density lipoproteins, increases high-density lipoproteins, and lowers blood pressure without any serious adverse effects.[17,18,19] *Shan Zha* (Fructus Crataegi) also has marked effectiveness for reduction of plasma cholesterol levels. It enhances LDL-receptor activity, increases hepatic breakdown, and decreases synthesis of cholesterol.[20,21]

Clinically, many studies have been conducted to demonstrate the therapeutic benefits of these herbs. According to one study, administration of *Zhi He Shou Wu* (Radix Polygoni Multiflori Praeparata) showed a 90.93% rate of effectiveness to treat 32 patients with elevated cholesterol levels.[22] According to another study, 48 patients treated with *Jue Ming Zi* (Semen Cassiae) in syrup for two months reported reduction in blood cholesterol in 95.8% of the patients, reduction in triglycerides in 86.7%, and reduction of beta-lipoprotein in 89.5%.[23] Lastly, 30 patients with elevated cholesterol levels were treated with 90% rate of effectiveness using an herbal formula that contained *Shan Zha* (Fructus Crataegi), *Dan Shen* (Radix et Rhizoma Salviae Miltiorrhizae), and *Ge Gen* (Radix Puerariae Lobatae).[24]

In addition to lowering plasma cholesterol and triglycerides, ***Cholisma*** contains herbs to treat arteriosclerosis and atherosclerosis and reduce risks of heart attacks. *Zhi He Shou Wu* (Radix Polygoni Multiflori Praeparata) has antiatherosclerotic benefits and has been shown to prevent development of atherosclerotic lesions.[25] The mechanism of action is the inhibition of the expression of intercellular adhesion molecule (ICAM)-1 and vascular endothelial growth factor (VEGF) in foam cells.[26] Furthermore, several herbs in this formula, such as *Dan Shen* (Radix et Rhizoma Salviae Miltiorrhizae), have antiplatelet and anticoagulant activities to prevent formation of blood clots.[27,28] In addition, *Ge Gen* (Radix Puerariae Lobatae) and *Shan Zha* (Fructus Crataegi) have a vasodilating effect to dilate coronary artery and prevent heart attack.[29,30,31] Clinically, these herbs have been used successfully to treat many cardiovascular disorders, such as angina,[32] thrombosis,[33] coronary artery disorder,[34] and transient ischemic attack.[35]

In summary, ***Cholisma*** is an excellent formula to treat dyslipidemia, arteriosclerosis and atherosclerosis, and prevent heart attack.

COMPARATIVE ANALYSIS

Dyslipidemia is the accumulation of abnormally high levels of fats (cholesterols, triglycerides, or both) in the blood. If untreated, dyslipidemia can lead to the development of arteriosclerosis and atherosclerosis and significantly increase the risk of coronary artery disease (CAD). One of the most common misconceptions about dyslipidemia is that this condition is "genetically predetermined," and therefore, can only be treated with pharmaceutical drugs. This is incorrect because diet and lifestyle changes are the most effective prevention and treatment modalities. However, most practitioners and patients are "commercially preconditioned" into believing drugs are the best and only treatment. As such, drugs for dyslipidemia are now among the most commonly prescribed drugs in the United States.

There are several categories of drugs that may be used to treat dyslipidemia. The most commonly used category is HMG-CoA reductase inhibitors, with examples such as Lipitor (atorvastatin), Zocor (simvastatin), and Pravachol (pravastatin). Also known as "statin" drugs, these drugs reduce plasma cholesterol and triglyceride levels by reducing their synthesis in the liver. In most cases, these drugs are effective and are well tolerated. However, these drugs have been shown to cause serious and potentially life-threatening side effects in a small number of patients, such as rhabdomyolysis with kidney failure (0.5%), liver impairment (2.3%), and increased risk of liver cancer.[36] Furthermore, discontinuation of these drugs is frequently associated with a rebound increase of cholesterol and triglyceride levels. Given the potential risks versus benefits, it is important to take drugs only when necessary, and once on drug therapy, be monitored closely by a medical doctor so the drug can be discontinued immediately if these serious side effects begin to develop.

According to TCM, dyslipidemia is diagnosed as the accumulation of damp and phlegm in the blood vessels. This condition may be treated effectively with herbs, with gradual and consistent reduction of plasma cholesterol levels by an average of 10 to 15 mg/dL per month. However, the therapeutic effects of herbs may require two to three months before they become more noticeable. The herbs in ***Cholisma*** are very well tolerated by patients, and are associated with few or no known side effects.

Dyslipidemia is a serious condition that requires treatment. The best and most effective treatment is diet and lifestyle changes, as outlined earlier in this monograph. Herbal therapy

Cholisma™

may be added to facilitate and enhance the overall results. Lastly, and only if necessary, drug therapy may be used but only with careful screening and supervision.

References

1. Chan K, Lo AC, Yeung JH, Woo KS. Journal of Pharmacy and Pharmacology 1995 May;47(5)::402-406.
2. Lei X, et al. Liver Damage Associated with Polygonum multiflorum Thunb.: A Systematic Review of Case Reports and Case Series. Evid Based Complement Alternat Med. 2015;2015:459749. doi: 10.1155/2015/459749.
3. Liu Z, Chao Z, Liu Y, Song Z, Lu A. Maillard reaction involved in the steaming process of the root of Polygonum multiflorum. Institution of Basic Theory, China Academy of Chinese Medical Sciences, Beijing, PR China. Planta Med. 2009 Jan;75(1):84-8. Epub 2008 Nov 25.
4. Liu Z, et al. In vitro antioxidant activities of maillard reaction products produced in the steaming process of Polygonum multiflorum root. Nat Prod Commun. 2011 Jan;6(1):55-8.
5. Malinow, MR. et al. Effect of alfalfa saponins on intestinal cholesterol absorption in rats. *Am J Clin Nutr.* 1977; 30::2061.
6. Malinow, MR. et al. Cholesterol and bile acid balance in macaca fascicularis; effects of alfalfa saponins. *J Clin Invest.* 1981; 67::156.
7. Wilcox, MR. et al. Serum and liver cholesterol, total lipids and lipid phosphorus levels of rats under various dietary regimes. *Am J Clin Nutr.* 1961; 9::236.
8. Story, JA. et al. Adsorption of bile acids by components of alfalfa and wheat bran in vitro. *J Food Sci.* 1982; 47::1276.
9. Story, JA. et al. Interactions of alfalfa plant and sprout saponins with cholesterol in vitro and in cholesterol-fed rats. *Am J Clin Nutr.* 1984; 39::917.
10. Kee Chang Huang. The pharmacology of Chinese herbs. CRC publishers. 1992, 388 pp.
11. *Zhong Cao Yao* (Chinese Herbal Medicine), 1991; 22(3)::117.
12. Yin J.H., Zhou X.Y. & Zhu X.Q. Pharmacological and clinical studies on the processed products of radix Polygoni multiflori. *Zhongguo Zhong Yao Za Zhi.* 1992, 17(12):: 722-4, 762-3.
13. Lin MC, Kao SH, Chung PJ, Chan KC, Yang MY, Wang CJ. Improvement for high fat diet-induced hepatic injuries and oxidative stress by flavonoid-enriched extract from Nelumbo nucifera leaf. Department of Internal Medicine, Chung-Shan Medical University Hospital, Taichung, Taiwan. J Agric Food Chem. 2009 Jul 8;57(13)::5925-32.
14. Xing WW, Wu JZ, Jia M, Du J, Zhang H, Qin LP. Effects of polydatin from Polygonum cuspidatum on lipid profile in hyperlipidemic rabbits. Department of Pharmacognosy, School of Pharmacy, Second Military Medical University, Shanghai 200433, PR China. Biomed Pharmacother. 2009 Aug;63(7)::457-62.
15. Du J, Sun LN, Xing WW, Huang BK, Jia M, Wu JZ, Zhang H, Qin LP. Lipid-lowering effects of polydatin from Polygonum cuspidatum in hyperlipidemic hamsters. Department of Pharmacognosy, School of Pharmacy, Second Military Medical University, No. 325 Guohe Road, Shanghai 200433, PR China. Phytomedicine. 2009 Jun;16(6-7)::652-8.
16. Megalli S, Davies NM, Roufogalis BD. Anti-hyperlipidemic and hypoglycemic effects of Gynostemma pentaphyllum in the Zucker fatty rat. Faculty of Pharmacy and Herbal Medicines Research and Education Centre University of Sydney, Building Al5, Sydney NSW 2006. J Pharm Pharm Sci. 2006;9(3):281-91.
17. *Zhong Yao Zhi* (Chinese Herbology Journal), 1984::352.
18. *Zhong Cao Yao* (Chinese Herbal Medicine), 1991; 22(2)::72.
19. Cho S.H., Kim T.H., Lee N.H., Son H.S., Cho I.J. & Ha T.Y. Effects of *Cassia tora* fiber supplement on serum lipids in Korean diabetic patients. *J Med Food.* 2005, 8(3):: 311-318.
20. *Zhong Yi Yao Xue Bao* (Report of Chinese Medicine and Herbology), 1989; 2::45.
21. Rajendran, S. et al. Effect of tincture of crataegus on the LDL-receptor activity of the hepatic plasma membrane of rats fed on atherogenic diet. *Atherosclerosis.* 123(1-2)::235-41, June 1997.
22. *Zhe Jiang Zhong Yi Za Zhi* (Zhejiang Journal of Chinese Medicine), 1991; (6)::245.
23. *Zhong Guo Yi Yuan Yao Xue Za Zhi* (Chinese Hospital Journal of Herbology), 1987, 9::395.
24. *Hei Long Jiang Zhong Yi Yao* (Heilongjiang Chinese Medicine and Herbology), 1997; (2)::49.
25. Yang P.Y., Almofti M.R., Lu L., Kang H., Zhang J., Li T.J., Rui Y.C., Sun L.N. & Chen W.S. Reduction of atherosclerosis in cholesterol-fed rabbits and decrease of expressions of intracellular adhesion molecule-1 and vascular endothelial growth factor in foam cells by a water-soluble fraction of *Polygonum multiflorum. J Pharmacol Sci.* 2005, 99(3):: 294-300.
26. Yang PY, Almofti MR, Lu L, Kang H, Zhang J, Li TJ, Rui YC, Sun LN, Chen WS. Reduction of atherosclerosis in cholesterol-fed rabbits and decrease of expressions of intracellular adhesion molecule-1 and vascular endothelial growth factor in foam cells by a water-soluble fraction of Polygonum multiflorum. School of Pharmacy, Second Military Medical University, Shanghai, China. J Pharmacol Sci. 2005 Nov;99(3)::294-300.
27. *Shang Hai Di Yi Xue Yuan Xue Bao* (Journal of First Shanghai Medical College), 1979; 6(3)::144.
28. *Shang Hai Di Yi Xue Yuan Xue Bao* (Journal of First Shanghai Medical College), 1982; 9(1)::14.
29. *Yi Xue Yan Jiu Tong Xun* (Report of Medical Studies), 1972; (2)::14.
30. *Zhong Hua Yi Xue Za Zhi* (Chinese Journal of Medicine), 1979; 59(8)::479.
31. *Guang Xi Zhong Yi Yao* (Guangxi Chinese Medicine and Herbology), 1990; 13(3)::45.
32. *Zhong Yao Lin Chuan Xin Yong* (New Clinical Applications of Chinese Medicine), 2001; 51-52.
33. *An Hui Zhong Yi Xue Yuan Xue Bao* (Journal of Anhui University School of Medicine), 1986; 5(4)::45.
34. *Zhong Hua Xin Xue Guan Bing Za Zhi* (Chinese Journal of Cardiology), 1985; 3::175.
35. Xu G, Zhao W, Zhou Z, Zhang R, Zhu W, Liu X. Danshen extracts decrease blood C reactive protein and prevent ischemic stroke recurrence:: a controlled pilot study. Phytother Res. 2009 Dec;23(12)::1721-5.
36. Drug Facts and Comparisons, Updated Monthly. A Wolters Kluwer Company. Page 538. June 2001.

Cholisma (ES)™

CLINICAL APPLICATIONS

- **Dyslipidemia**
  - **Hyperlipidemia** (high cholesterol and triglycerides levels)
  - **Hypercholesterolemia** (high cholesterol levels)
  - **Hypertriglyceridemia** (high triglyceride levels)
- **Dyslipidemia with obesity, diabetes mellitus, or fatty liver**

WESTERN THERAPEUTIC ACTIONS

- Antihyperlipidemic effect to reduce plasma levels of cholesterol and triglycerides
- Antiobesity effect to reduce body weight and inhibit lipid accumulation
- Hypoglycemic effect to lower blood glucose levels to manage diabetes mellitus
- Prevents and treats fatty liver

CHINESE THERAPEUTIC ACTIONS

- Dissolves dampness
- Eliminates phlegm
- Invigorates blood circulation
- Clears heat

DOSAGE

Take 3 to 4 capsules three times daily on an empty stomach. For maximum effectiveness, take the last dose one hour before bedtime, as synthesis of cholesterol is most active at night. As a preventative formula, take 2 capsules twice daily on an empty stomach.

INGREDIENTS

Da Huang (Radix et Rhizoma Rhei)
Dan Shen (Radix et Rhizoma Salviae Miltiorrhizae)
Ge Gen (Radix Puerariae Lobatae)
Hai Zao (Sargassum)
Huang Qin (Radix Scutellariae)
Jue Ming Zi (Semen Cassiae)
Shan Zha (Fructus Crataegi)
Yin Chen (Herba Artemisiae Scopariae)
Yu Jin (Radix Curcumae)
Ze Xie (Rhizoma Alismatis)

BACKGROUND

Dyslipidemia is the elevation of cholesterol and/or triglycerides levels that contributes to the development of arteriosclerosis and atherosclerosis and increases the risks of coronary artery disorder. Causes of dyslipidemia may be primary (genetic) or secondary (including diet, obesity, and diabetes). Complications of dyslipidemia include atherosclerosis, arteriosclerosis, coronary artery disease, angina pectoris, hypertension and fatty liver. Optimal treatment requires dietary changes, exercise, and if necessary, use of herbs or drugs to lower lipids.

FORMULA EXPLANATION

According to traditional Chinese medicine, cholesterol and triglycerides are considered as excess accumulations of dampness (hyperglycemia) and phlegm in the blood vessels (dyslipidemia), liver (fatty liver), and body (obesity). To effectively reduce plasma levels of cholesterol and triglycerides, treat fatty liver, and reduce body weight, treatment must focus on dissolving dampness, eliminating phlegm, invigorating blood circulation, and clearing heat.

In ***Cholisma (ES)***, *Ze Xie* (Rhizoma Alismatis) resolves dampness and *Hai Zao* (Sargassum) eliminates phlegm. *Dan Shen* (Radix et Rhizoma Salviae Miltiorrhizae), *Yu Jin* (Radix Curcumae), and *Shan Zha* (Fructus Crataegi) activate blood circulation and eliminate blood stasis; keeping the flow of blood smooth will prevent plaque buildup on the vessel walls and ensure a healthy cardiovascular system. In addition, the liver has a remarkable power to regenerate itself, and it does so even faster when blood movers are used to ensure the proper supply of nutrients and elimination of waste. Long-term stagnation of damp, phlegm, and blood will create heat. Therefore, several herbs are used to clear heat, such as *Jue Ming Zi* (Semen Cassiae), *Da Huang* (Radix et Rhizoma Rhei), *Yin Chen* (Herba Artemisiae Scopariae), *Ge Gen* (Radix Puerariae Lobatae) and *Huang Qin* (Radix Scutellariae). *Yin Chen* (Herba Artemisiae Scopariae) and *Da Huang* (Radix et Rhizoma Rhei) ensure the healthy function of the liver and gallbladder by promoting the secretion of bile, digestion of fat, and the dispelling of damp-heat accumulation in the Liver and Gallbladder.

In summary, ***Cholisma (ES)*** is an excellent formula to treat individuals with an overall condition characterized by elevated cholesterol and triglyceride levels, accompanied by a fatty liver and obesity.

CAUTIONS & CONTRAINDICATIONS

- ***Cholisma (ES)*** is contraindicated during pregnancy.
- *Jue Ming Zi* (Semen Cassiae) and *Da Huang* (Radix et Rhizoma Rhei) may cause loose stool or diarrhea for those with sensitive gastrointestinal tracts. Should this occur, reduce the dosage to 2 to 3 capsules three times daily.
- The following warning statement is required by the State of California: "This product contains *Da Huang* (Radix et Rhizoma Rhei). Read and follow directions carefully. Do not use if you have or develop diarrhea, loose stools, or abdominal pain because *Da Huang* (Radix et Rhizoma Rhei) may worsen these conditions and be harmful to your health. Consult your physician if you have frequent diarrhea or if you are pregnant, nursing, taking medication, or have a medical condition."
- This herbal formula contains herbs that invigorate blood circulation, such as *Dan Shen* (Radix et Rhizoma Salviae Miltiorrhizae). Therefore, patients who are on anticoagulant or antiplatelet therapies, such as Coumadin (warfarin), should use this formula with caution, or not at all, as there may be a higher risk of bleeding and bruising.[1]

Cholisma (ES)™

CLINICAL NOTES

- ***Cholisma (ES)*** is specifically formulated to reduce blood cholesterol and triglyceride levels in individuals with fatty liver and/or obesity. Patients must take this herbal formula on a long-term basis for maximum results.
- The baseline cholesterol levels should be established before the initiation of herbal therapy; the first follow-up test should be done one month after the initiation of herbal therapy. Subsequent follow-ups can be done every two to three months to determine overall effectiveness. Cholesterol testing kits are available over-the-counter in most pharmacies. Results may vary from patient to patient. Lifestyle and dietary changes are also crucial for satisfactory result.
- Dyslipidemia has many secondary causes (obesity, diabetes, hypothyroidism, and use of drugs such as thiazides, beta-blockers, estrogen and progestins, and glucocorticoids) and multiple complications (atherosclerosis, arteriosclerosis, coronary artery disease, angina pectoris, hypertension and fatty liver). Therefore, optimal treatment must address both the causes and the complications. *See* Supplementary Formulas for more details.

Pulse Diagnosis by Dr. Jimmy Wei-Yen Chang:

- The overall general feel of the pulse is greasy. A greasy pulse is a pulse in which its border is not clear due to plaque built-up on the arterial wall. The more forceful and harder the pulse is, the worse the plaque built-up.
- **Fatty liver:** deep and forceful pulse on the left *guan*

SUPPLEMENTARY FORMULAS

- For high cholesterol and triglyceride levels without fatty liver or obesity, use ***Cholisma*** instead.
- For obese patients with an excess appetite, add ***Herbalite***.
- For patients with diabetes mellitus, add ***Equilibrium***.
- For deficient-type hypertension with dizziness or vertigo, combine with ***Gastrodia Complex***.
- For excess-type hypertension with anger or flushed face, combine with ***Gentiana Complex***.
- For coronary heart disorders, add ***Circulation***.
- For excess heat everywhere in the body, add ***Gardenia Complex***.
- For hepatitis or other liver dysfunction, add ***Liver DTX***.

ACUPUNCTURE TREATMENT

Traditional Points:

- **Hyperlipidemia:**
  - Bleed *Weizhong* (BL 40) or wherever there is visible, dilated vein in the transverse crease of the popliteal fossa.
  - *Taichong* (LR 3), *Xingjian* (LR 2), *Zusanli* (ST 36), *Quchi* (LI 11), *Fenglong* (ST 40)
  - Alternate the following two sets of points:
    1) *Sanyinjiao* (SP 6), *Zusanli* (ST 36), and *Neiguan* (PC 6)
    2) *Taibai* (SP 3), *Yanglingquan* (GB 34), and *Fenglong* (ST 40)
- **Obesity:** *Shenmen* (HT 7), *Liangqiu* (ST 34), *Gongsun* (SP 4), *Tianshu* (ST 25), *Daling* (PC 7), *Qihai* (CV 6), *Guanyuan* (CV 4)

Classic Master Tung's Points:

- **Hyperlipidemia:** *Fuding* (T 44.04), *Houzhi* (T 44.05), *Luotong* (T 44.14), *Zhitong* (T 44.13), *Xinling* (T 33.17)*, *Linggu* (T 22.05), *Jianzhong* (T 44.06), *Dizong* (T 44.09)
- **Obesity (general):** *Linggu* (T 22.05), *Huaguyi* (T 55.02), *Huagusi* (T 55.05), *Yizhong* (T 77.05), *Erzhong* (T 77.06), *Sanzhong* (T 77.07), *Zusanli* (ST 36), *Menjin* (T 66.05), *Liangqiu* (ST 34), *Renhuang* (T 77.21), *Tongguan* (T 88.01), *Tianhuangfu [Shenguan]* (T 77.18), *Mufu* (T 88.38)*, *Minghuang* (T 88.12). Bleed SP and ST areas on the back and dark veins nearby *Weizhong* (BL 40), *Sihuashang* (T 77.08), *Sihuazhong* (T 77.09), *Sihuaxia* (T 77.11), *Yizhong* (T 77.05), *Erzhong* (T 77.06) and *Sanzhong* (T 77.07). Bleed before needling for best result.
- **Fatty liver:** *Ganmen* (T 33.11), *Minghuang* (T 88.12), *Huoquan* (T 88.16). Bleed the LR area in the back wtih cupping. Bleed before needling for best result.

Master Tung's Points by Dr. Chuan-Min Wang:

- **Elevated cholesterol or triglyceride:** Bleed *Sihuashang* (T 77.08), *Sihuazhong* (T 77.09), *Sihuafu* (T 77.10), *Sihuaxia* (T 77.11). Needle *Qimen* (T 33.01), *Qijiao* (T 33.02), *Qizheng* (T 33.03), *Muliu* (T 66.06), *Mudou* (T 66.07).

Balance Method by Dr. Richard Tan:

- **Hyperlipidemia**
  - Left side: *Yinlingquan* (SP 9), *Xuehai* (SP 10), *Waiguan* (TH 5)
  - Right side: *Zusanli* (ST 36), *Fenglong* (ST 40), *Daling* (PC 7), *Laogong* (PC 8)
  - Alternate sides from treatment to treatment.
- **Obesity**
  - Left side: *Waiguan* (TH 5), *Hegu* (LI 4), *Yinlingquan* (SP 9)
  - Right side: *Zusanli* (ST 36), *Neiguan* (PC 6)
  - Alternate sides from treatment to treatment.
- **Fatty liver**
  - Right side: *ah shi* points around *Quze* (PC 3) to *Ximen* (PC 4), *Yanglingquan* (GB 34)
  - Left side: *Tianjing* (TH 10), *Shanglian* (LI 9), *Shousanli* (LI 10), *Xiguan* (LR 7), *Yinlingquan* (SP 9)
  - Alternate sides from treatment to treatment.

Auricular Medicine by Dr. Li-Chun Huang:

- **Obesity:** Pituitary, Endocrine, Forehead, Exciting Point, Hunger Point, Thalamus, *Sanjiao*, Kidney, Large Intestine, Lung, areas that have fat deposit such as the Abdomen or Buttock

NUTRITION

- Increase the daily intake of cholesterol-lowering foods such as apples, bananas, carrots, cold-water fish, dried beans, garlic, grapefruit, olive oil, and fibers such as bran and oat.

Cholisma (ES)™

- Advise the patients to consume large quantities of fresh fruits and vegetables.
- Decrease the intake of food that will raise cholesterol levels, including but not limited to: beer, wine, cheese, aged and cured meats, sugar, and greasy or fried foods. Avoid eating red meat, fatty foods, processed or fried foods, soda, pastries, pies, doughnuts, candy, and other sweets.
- Eat small, frequent meals throughout the day instead of a few large ones. Eat slowly and chew thoroughly.
- Increase the intake of niacin, which can lower total cholesterol levels by up to 18%, increase HDL cholesterol by up to 32%, and lower triglycerides by up to 26%. Slow release form of niacin is preferred to minimize side effects such as flushing and stomach pain.
- Other supplements that are beneficial are vitamin B5, vitamin C, vitamin E, chromium picolinate, lecithin, and coenzyme Q10.
- Avoid greasy, fatty, fried and oily foods. Seafood should also be reduced.

The Tao of Nutrition by Dr. Maoshing Ni and Cathy McNease:

- Make soup with diced artichoke hearts, sliced ginger, and 1/2 head of cabbage. Eat a bowl daily.
- Drink one glass daily of pureed asparagus juice, including the pulp; add one teaspoon of honey.
- Use white mushrooms and corn silk to make soup or tea regularly.
- Add rice bran to a grain dish everyday for at least two months.
- Incorporate pinto beans and other beans that are high in fiber and contain rich folate that lowers cholesterol into the diet regularly.

LIFESTYLE INSTRUCTIONS

- Drink tea on a daily basis, especially after meals, to decrease the absorption of fatty foods from the diet. Beneficial teas include *pu-er*, black, *oolong* or green tea.
- Avoid the consumption of alcohol and exposure to tobacco. They increase cholesterol buildup and hardening of arteries.
- The importance of a regular exercise routine cannot be over-emphasized. Exercise will improve energy levels, normalize metabolic functions, reduce fat, and burn calories.
- Change dietary and exercise habits to avoid rebound weight gain.
- Do not lose weight drastically. Rapid weight loss may be hazardous and is more likely to lead to rebound weight gain.

CASE STUDY

- A 57-year-old female presented with an enlarged liver. She has a history of hepatitis and a cholecystectomy previously. Symptoms included shortness of breath, edema in the upper body and liver enzyme elevation. The TCM diagnosis was Spleen qi deficiency with phlegm. ***Liver DTX*** and ***Cholisma (ES)*** were both prescribed for five months. Her liver was normal in size without any discrete mass. As a result of taking the herbs, the patient's overall condition had improved. It was confirmed through another testing that her liver enzyme levels were back to normal. She hasn't had any issues since. Submitted by H.C., Sydney, New York.

PHARMACOLOGICAL AND CLINICAL RESEARCH

Cholisma (ES) is formulated to treat dyslipidemia (hyperlipidemia, hypercholesterolemia and hypertriglyceridemia). This formula incorporates many herbs with excellent antihyperlipidemic effects to reduce plasma levels of cholesterol and triglycerides. Furthermore, ***Cholisma (ES)*** is also beneficial to treat related conditions and compilations, such as obesity, diabetes mellitus, and fatty liver.

Cholisma (ES) contains many herbs with multiple mechanisms of actions to lower plasma cholesterols and triglycerides. *Ze Xie* (Rhizoma Alismatis) has a remarkable antihyperlipidemic effect, and has been shown in various clinical studies to effectively treat dyslipidemia, hypercholesterolemia, arteriosclerosis and fatty liver.[2,3] *Jue Ming Zi* (Semen Cassiae) has multiple therapeutic benefits: it lowers low-density lipoproteins, increases high-density lipoproteins, and lowers blood pressure without any serious adverse effects.[4,5,6] *Ge Gen* (Radix Puerariae Lobatae) and *Shan Zha* (Fructus Crataegi) have both shown marked effectiveness for reduction of plasma cholesterol levels, with mechanisms of action attributed to enhancement of LDL-receptor activity, increased hepatic breakdown and decreased synthesis of cholesterol.[7,8] *Yu Jin* (Radix Curcumae) has potent antioxidant and antihyperlipidemic functions, and demonstrates a comparable effect to that of Mevacor (lovastatin) to decrease plasma levels of cholesterol, triacylglycerol, and low-density lipoprotein cholesterol.[9] Lastly, *Yu Jin* (Radix Curcumae), *Da Huang* (Radix et Rhizoma Rhei) and *Yin Chen* (Herba Artemisiae Scopariae) are all effective in lowering plasma and liver content of cholesterols and triglycerides.[10,11,12] Clinical applications of these herbs include dyslipidemia, hypercholesterolemia, and coronary artery disease.[13,14,15]

Clinically, many studies have been conducted to demonstrate the therapeutic benefits of these herbs to treat dyslipidemia. According to one clinical study, use of *Jue Ming Zi* (Semen Cassiae) effectively reduces cholesterol levels to normal within 6 weeks in 98 of 100 patients.[16] According to another clinical study, use of *Jue Ming Zi* (Semen Cassiae) in 48 patients is associated with reduction in blood cholesterol in 95.8% of the patients, reduction in triglycerides in 86.7%, and reduction of beta-lipoprotein in 89.5%.[17] Lastly, 30 patients with elevated cholesterol levels were treated with a 90% rate of effectiveness using an herbal formula that contained *Shan Zha* (Fructus Crataegi), *Dan Shen* (Radix et Rhizoma Salviae Miltiorrhizae) and *Ge Gen* (Radix Puerariae Lobatae).[18]

Cholisma (ES) also has herbs to lower blood glucose to treat diabetes mellitus and reduce body weight to treat obesity, conditions commonly associated with dyslipidemia. Oral administration

Cholisma (ES)™

of *Ge Gen* (Radix Puerariae Lobatae) in herbal decoction has been shown to lower blood glucose levels.[19] In addition, administration of puerariafuran from *Ge Gen* (Radix Puerariae Lobatae) is associated with a preventative effect against diabetic complications, such as cataracts.[20] *Yin Chen* (Herba Artemisiae Scopariae) has an antiobesity effect, and has been shown to effectively reduce body weight and inhibit lipid accumulation, according to one study in subjects fed a high fat diet.[21] According to one clinical study, successful reduction of body weight was reported in 79 of 96 patients using a combination of herbal therapy, diet changes, and exercise regimens. The herbal formula contained *Jue Ming Zi* (Semen Cassiae), *Ze Xie* (Rhizoma Alismatis), *Shan Zha* (Fructus Crataegi) and others.[22]

In summary, ***Cholisma (ES)*** is one of the best formulas to treat elevated cholesterol and triglyceride levels with complications such as fatty liver, obesity, and diabetes. The formula is most effective if combined with lifestyle and dietary changes as described above.

COMPARATIVE ANALYSIS

Dyslipidemia, obesity, and fatty liver are three conditions that are often closely linked to each others. Dyslipidemia is the accumulation of abnormally high levels of fats (cholesterols, triglycerides, or both) in the blood, fatty liver is the excess accumulation of fat in the liver cells, and obesity is the abnormal increase in body weight. If untreated, these conditions increase risk of diabetes, coronary artery disease, and cardiovascular and cerebrovascular disorders.

In Western medicine, dyslipidemia is usually treated with HMG-CoA reductase inhibitors, a category of drugs that includes Lipitor (atorvastatin), Zocor (simvastatin), and Pravachol (pravastatin). Also known as "statin" drugs, these drugs reduce plasma cholesterol and triglyceride levels by reducing their synthesis in the liver. In most cases, these drugs are effective and are well tolerated. However, these drugs have been shown to cause serious and potentially life-threatening side effects in a small number of patients, such as rhabdomyolysis with kidney failure (0.5%), liver impairment (2.3%), and increased risk of liver cancer.[23] Furthermore, discontinuation of these drugs is frequently associated with a rebound increase of cholesterol and triglyceride levels. Given the potential risks versus benefits, it is important to take drugs only when necessary, and once on drug therapy, be monitored closely by the medical doctor so the drug can be discontinued immediately if these serious side effects begin to develop.

Obesity, a common health problem that is quickly becoming an epidemic, has few treatment options available. There are only a few drugs approved by the Food and Drug Administration for long-term weight loss, and they have serious side effects. Xenical (orlistat) reduces body weight by blocking absorption of fat in the digestive tract. Because it interferes with the normal absorption process, this drug is known to cause many gastrointestinal side effects, such as fecal incontinence, fecal urgency, flatulence with discharge, increased defecation, oily evacuation, oily rectal leakage, steatorrhea, and projectile diarrhea. Meridia (sibutramine) is a stimulant agent that causes weight loss by increasing metabolism and suppressing appetite. Similar to many other stimulant weight-loss drugs, use of Meridia (sibutramine) may cause anorexia, anxiety, constipation, dizziness, headache, insomnia, irritability, nervousness, rhinitis, xerostomia, hypertension, congestive heart failure, arrhythmias, seizure and stroke.

Fatty liver is a potentially serious condition that, if untreated, may lead to liver cirrhosis. Unfortunately, there is no drug treatment for fatty liver in Western medicine.

Dyslipidemia, obesity, and fatty liver are all characterized by the presence of damp and phlegm affecting various parts of the body. Use of herbs has been shown to be extremely effective to slowly and steadily improve all three of these conditions.

For treatment of dyslipidemia and obesity, drugs are more potent but have significantly more side effects, in comparison with herbs. However, the higher potency of the drugs is not necessary an advantage because these conditions are chronic in nature and require persistent and long-term treatment, not aggressive and short-term treatment. Therefore, long-term evaluation will often show comparable efficacy of both treatments. For fatty liver, herbal treatment is superior, especially since there are no treatment options available in Western medicine. Lastly, it is extremely important to remember there is no magic bullet. Without commitment to changing diet and lifestyles, use of either drugs or herbs will have limited effectiveness. The practitioners and patients must work together to achieve significant and sustainable clinical results.

References

1. Chan K, Lo AC, Yeung JH, Woo KS. Journal of Pharmacy and Pharmacology 1995 May;47(5):402-406.
2. He, XY. Effects of alisma plantago l. on hyperlipidemia, arteriosclerosis and fatty liver. *Chinese Journal of Modern Developments in Traditional Medicine.* 1(2):114-7, Oct. 1981.
3. *Zhong Hua Yi Xue Za Zhi* (Chinese Journal of Medicine), 1976; 11:693.
4. *Zhong Yao Zhi* (Chinese Herbology Journal), 1984:352.
5. *Zhong Cao Yao* (Chinese Herbal Medicine), 1991; 22(2):72.
6. Cho S.H., Kim T.H., Lee N.H., Son H.S., Cho I.J. & Ha T.Y. Effects of *Cassia tora* fiber supplement on serum lipids in Korean diabetic patients. *J Med Food.* 2005, 8(3): 311-318.
7. *Zhong Yi Yao Xue Bao* (Report of Chinese Medicine and Herbology), 1989; 2:45.
8. Rajendran, S. et al. Effect of tincture of crataegus on the LDL-receptor activity of the hepatic plasma membrane of rats fed on atherogenic diet. *Atherosclerosis.* June 1997; 123(1-2):235-41.
9. Xu C, Haiyan Z, Hua Z, Jianhong Z, Pin D. Effect of Curcuma kwangsiensis polysaccharides on blood lipid profiles and oxidative stress in high-fat rats. Int J Biol Macromol. 2009 Mar 1;44(2):138-42.
10. *Xin Yi Yao Xue Za Zhi* (New Journal of Medicine and Herbology), 1978; (9):540.
11. *Shang Hai Zhong Yi Yao Za Zhi* (Shanghai Journal of Chinese Medicine and Herbology), 1986; 12:40.
12. *Zhong Yao Yao Li Yu Ying Yong* (Pharmacology and Applications of Chinese Herbs), 1990; 15(6):52.

Cholisma (ES)™

13. *Shang Hai Zhong Yi Yao Za Zhi* (Shanghai Journal of Chinese Medicine and Herbology), 1988; 8:2.
14. *Zhong Yi Za Zhi* (Journal of Chinese Medicine), 1980; 1:39.
15. *Shang Hai Zhong Yi Yao Za Zhi* (Shanghai Journal of Chinese Medicine and Herbology), 1986; 12:40.
16. *Xin Yi Yao Xue Za Zhi* (New Journal of Medicine and Herbology), 1974; 3:30.
17. *Zhong Guo Yi Yuan Yao Xue Za Zhi* (Chinese Hospital Journal of Herbology), 1987; 9:395.
18. *Hei Long Jiang Zhong Yi Yao* (Heilongjiang Chinese Medicine and Herbology), 1997; (2):49.
19. *Zhong Yao Xue* (Chinese Herbology), 1998; 101:103.
20. Kim NH, Kim YS, Lee YM, Jang DS, Kim JS. Inhibition of aldose reductase and xylose-induced lens opacity by puerariafuran from the roots of Pueraria lobata. Biol Pharm Bull. 2010;33(9):1605-9.
21. Hong JH, Hwang EY, Kim HJ, Jeong YJ, Lee IS. Artemisia capillaris inhibits lipid accumulation in 3T3-L1 adipocytes and obesity in C57BL/6J mice fed a high fat diet. The Center for Traditional Microorganism Resources Center, Keimyung University, Daegu, Republic of Korea. J Med Food. 2009 Aug;12(4):736-45.
22. *Zhong Yao Lin Chuan Xin Yong* (New Clinical Applications of Chinese Medicine), 2001; 284-285.
23. Drug Facts and Comparisons, Updated Monthly. A Wolters Kluwer Company. Page 538. June 2001.

Circulation™

CLINICAL APPLICATIONS

- **Cardiovascular disorders:** coronary heart disease, angina pectoris, ischemia, and atherosclerosis
- **Circulatory disorders:** poor cerebral and body circulation, numbness of the limbs, peripheral neuropathy and similar problems

WESTERN THERAPEUTIC ACTIONS

- Vasodilating action to increase blood perfusion and decrease peripheral resistance
- Positive cardiotonic property to strengthen cardiac contraction and improve blood circulation
- Antiplatelet and anticoagulant effects to reduce the risk of blood clots
- Antihyperlipidemic function to lower plasma cholesterols and triglycerides

CHINESE THERAPEUTIC ACTIONS

- Invigorates blood circulation in the upper *jiao* and eliminates blood stasis
- Unblocks meridians and relieves pain
- Warms Heart yang and dispels damp and phlegm

DOSAGE

Take 2 to 4 capsules three times daily on an empty stomach with warm water. This formula is to be taken on a daily basis for maintenance of cardiovascular and circulatory health. Do ***not*** use this formula to treat acute myocardial infarction.

INGREDIENTS

Bai Shao (Radix Paeoniae Alba)
Chuan Xiong (Rhizoma Chuanxiong)
Dan Shen (Radix et Rhizoma Salviae Miltiorrhizae)
Dang Gui (Radix Angelicae Sinensis)
Ge Gen (Radix Puerariae Lobatae)
Gui Zhi (Ramulus Cinnamomi)
Hong Hua (Flos Carthami)
Hou Po (Cortex Magnoliae Officinalis)
Jiang Xiang (Lignum Dalbergiae Odoriferae)
Mao Dong Qing (Radix Ilicis Pubescentis)
Ren Shen (Radix et Rhizoma Ginseng)
Sha Ren (Fructus Amomi)
Xie Bai (Bulbus Allii Macrostemonis)
Zhi Shi (Fructus Aurantii Immaturus)

BACKGROUND

Heart disease is the number one cause of death in the United States, according to a report by CDC published in January 11, 2012.[1] Heart disease refers to a class of diseases that involves the heart and/or blood vessels, such as coronary heart disease and atherosclerosis. Risk factors that contribute to coronary heart disease include hypercholesterolemia, hypertension, obesity, smoking, and physical inactivity. As a result, blood flow to the heart is impaired, leading to ischemia, angina, and in severe cases, myocardial infarction and sudden death. Therefore, proper management of heart disease requires integration of preventative and treatment measures, such as lifestyle changes, diet modifications, and medical intervention.

FORMULA EXPLANATION

Cardiovascular and circulatory disorders, such as coronary heart disease, angina pectoris, ischemia, and atherosclerosis, are characterized by Heart yang deficiency with blood stagnation and damp and phlegm accumulation. To effectively treat these disorders, treatment must focus on warming Heart yang, dissolving damp, eliminating phlegm, and invigorating blood circulation.

Ren Shen (Radix et Rhizoma Ginseng) replenishes the vital qi and mimics the effect of cardiac glycosides, making the heart beat stronger and more rhythmically. *Xie Bai* (Bulbus Allii Macrostemonis) disperses painful obstructions due to turbid-phlegm congealing in the chest. *Xie Bai* (Bulbus Allii Macrostemonis) and *Gui Zhi* (Ramulus Cinnamomi) warm and facilitate the flow of yang qi in the chest to improve the function of the heart. *Dan Shen* (Radix et Rhizoma Salviae Miltiorrhizae) improves microcirculation, strengthens myocardial contraction, and adjusts the heart rate. *Mao Dong Qing* (Radix Ilicis Pubescentis) dilates the blood vessels, lowers blood pressure and reduces the oxygen consumption of cardiac muscles. *Ge Gen* (Radix Puerariae Lobatae) dilates blood vessels to lower blood pressure. *Hong Hua* (Flos Carthami), *Dang Gui* (Radix Angelicae Sinensis), *Jiang Xiang* (Lignum Dalbergiae Odoriferae) and *Chuan Xiong* (Rhizoma Chuanxiong) invigorate general blood circulation and dispel blood stasis. *Bai Shao* (Radix Paeoniae Alba) nourishes the blood and relieves pain. *Gui Zhi* (Ramulus Cinnamomi) promotes the peripheral blood circulation and unblocks stagnation in the channels and collaterals. *Sha Ren* (Fructus Amomi) regulates qi and dissolves dampness. *Zhi Shi* (Fructus Aurantii Immaturus) and *Hou Po* (Cortex Magnoliae Officinalis) regulate qi, expand the chest, and relieve congestion.

Together, these herbs effectively treat cardiovascular and circulatory disorders that affect the heart.

CAUTIONS & CONTRAINDICATIONS

- Acute myocardial infarction is a medical emergency. Call 911 to send patients to emergency room as soon as possible. Monitor their condition until emergency medical personnel arrive.
- Do ***not*** use this formula to treat acute myocardial infarction. ***Circulation*** is to be used to promote cardiovascular and circulatory health, ***not*** to treat acute heart attacks.
- This herbal formula contains herbs that invigorate blood circulation, such as *Dang Gui* (Radix Angelicae Sinensis) and *Dan Shen* (Radix et Rhizoma Salviae Miltiorrhizae). Therefore, patients who are on anticoagulant or antiplatelet therapies, such as Coumadin (warfarin), should use this formula with caution,

Circulation ™

or not at all, as there may be a higher risk of bleeding and bruising.[2,3,4]
- ***Circulation*** is contraindicated during pregnancy and nursing.

CLINICAL NOTES
- Maintenance of the herbal treatment is necessary for approximately six months in order to stabilize the condition. One should always address the secondary causes and/or complications of coronary artery disease.
- Patients with high risk of cardiovascular disorders may benefit from preventative treatments by taking low doses of ***Circulation***. Risk factors of cardiovascular disorders include family history, obesity, sedentary lifestyle, and cigarette smoking.

Pulse Diagnosis by Dr. Jimmy Wei-Yen Chang:
- Pulse within a pulse on the left *cun*. A pulse within a pulse feels like there is a bundle of electric wires, which are thin, straight, and tight, within the artery.

SUPPLEMENTARY FORMULAS
- For cardiovascular or circulatory disorders affecting the entire body, add ***Circulation (SJ)***.
- For hypertension with dizziness or vertigo, combine with ***Gastrodia Complex***.
- For hypertension with anger or flushed face, combine with ***Gentiana Complex***.
- For edema and water accumulation, add ***Herbal DRX***.
- For high cholesterol and triglycerides, add ***Cholisma***.
- For high cholesterol and triglycerides with fatty liver and obesity, add ***Cholisma (ES)***.
- For diabetes mellitus, add ***Equilibrium***.
- For obesity, ***Herbalite*** may be used to suppress appetite and facilitate weight loss.
- For excess heat accumulation, add ***Gardenia Complex***.
- For excess damp/phlegm in the body, add ***Pinellia Complex***.

ACUPUNCTURE TREATMENT
Traditional Points:
- *Liangqiu* (ST 34), *Renzhong* (GV 26), *Xinshu* (BL 15), *Tongli* (HT 5), *Qihai* (CV 6), *Fenglong* (ST 40)
  - Acute: Needle *Ximen* (PC 4). Bleed *Quze* (PC 3) or the vein nearby.
  - Chronic: *Shanzhong* (CV 17), *Neiguan* (PC 6)

Classic Master Tung's Points:
- **Arteriosclerosis:** *Fuding* (T 44.04), *Houzhi* (T 44.05), *Luotong* (T 44.14), *Zhitong* (T 44.13), *Xinling* (T 33.17)*, *Linggu* (T 22.05), *Jianzhong* (T 44.06), *Dizong* (T 44.09)
- **Coronary heart disease:** *Huofu* (T 88.41)*, *Huoliang* (T 88.42)*, *Huochang* (T 88.43)*, *Mufu* (T 88.38)*, *Muliang* (T 88.39)*, *Muchang* (T 88.40)*, *Tongshan* (T 88.02), *Tongtian* (T 88.03), *Tongguan* (T 88.01)
- **Angina pectoris:** *Xinmen* (T 33.12), *Xinling* (T 33.17)*, *Sihuashang* (T 77.08), *Sihuawai* (T 77.14), *Sihuazhong* (T 77.09), *Sihuali* (T 77.13), *Sihuafu* (T 77.10), *Sihuaxia* (T 77.11), *Huobao* (T 55.01), *Xinchang* (T 11.19), *Dizong* (T 44.09), *Shangqi* (T 88.44)*, *Xiaqi* (T 88.45)*, *Tongtian* (T 88.03), *Neiguan* (PC 6) towards the heart or penetrate through to *Waiguan* (TH 5), *Sanling* (T 44.18)*. Bleed the HT and LU area in the upper back T3 – T6 with cupping. Bleed visible dark veins in the elbow and back of the knee. Do not use cupping methods here. Bleed before needling for best result.
- **Peripheral neuropathy:** *Erjiaoming* (T 11.12), *Wanshunyi* (T 22.08), *Wanshuner* (T 22.09), *Tianhuang* (T 77.17), *Dihuang* (T 77.19), *Renhuang* (T 77.21), *Zhengshi* (T 77.03), *Zhengjin* (T 77.01), *Zhengzong* (T 77.02). Bleed *Weizhong* (BL 40), *Sihuashang* (T 77.08), *Sihuawai* (T 77.14), *Sihuazhong* (T 77.09), *Sihuali* (T 77.13), *Sihuafu* (T 77.10), *Sihuaxia* (T 77.11) or dark veins nearby. Bleed before needling for best result.
- **Palpitation:** *Dizong* (T 44.09), *Xinling* (T 33.17)*, *Tongtian* (T 88.03), *Tongguan* (T 88.01), *Sihuashang* (T 77.08), *Sihuawai* (T 77.14), *Sihuazhong* (T 77.09), *Sihuali* (T 77.13), *Sihuafu* (T 77.10), *Sihuaxia* (T 77.11), *Huochuan* (T 33.04), *Tianshi* (T 33.15), *Dishi* (T 33.14), *Renshi* (T 33.13), *Xinchang* (T 11.19)
- **Arrhythmia:** *Xinling* (T 33.17)*, *Tongguan* (T 88.01), *Dizong* (T 44.09), *Xinmen* (T 33.12), *Neiguan* (PC 6), *Tongtian* (T 88.03), *Tianshi* (T 33.15), *Dishi* (T 33.14), *Renshi* (T 33.13), *Tongshan* (T 88.02). Bleed dark veins visible on ST channel on the lower limb. Bleed before needling for best result.

Master Tung's Points by Dr. Chuan-Min Wang:
- **Coronary artery disease**
  - Acute: Bleed *Houxin* (T DT.11) on the left. Needle bilaterally *Shuixiang* (T 66.14), *Huoying* (T 66.03), *Huosan* (T 66.12), *Shangbai* (T 22.03).
  - Chronic or prevention: *Tongguan* (T 88.01), *Tongshan* (T 88.02), *Tongtian* (T 88.03)

Balance Method by Dr. Richard Tan:
- Left side: *Neiguan* (PC 6), *Tongli* (HT 5), *Zusanli* (ST 36), *Yanglingquan* (GB 34), *Weizhong* (BL 40) or *ah shi* points nearby
- Right side: *Sanjian* (LI 3), *Hegu* (LI 4), *Houxi* (SI 3), *Sanyinjiao* (SP 6), and *Ligou* (LR 5), *Fuliu* (KI 7) or *ah shi* points nearby
- Needle Heart point on the ear.
- Alternate sides between treatments.

Ear Acupuncture:
- **Main points:** Heart, Small Intestine, Sympathetic, Carotid Artery, Anterior Pituitary, Subcortex
- **Adjunct points:** Brain Stem, Lung, Liver, Chest, Occipital
- Needle every other day three to five points for an hour. Twelve treatments equal one course.

Circulation™

Auricular Medicine by Dr. Li-Chun Huang:

- **Coronary heart disease:** Heart, Liver, Chest, Small Intestine, Sympathetic, Coronary Vascular Subcortex
- **Reducing heart rate:** Occiput, Heart, Chest, Small Intestine, *Shenmen*, Coronary Vascular Subcortex, Reduce Heart Rate Point. Bleed Ear Apex.
- **Arrhythmia:** Heart, Chest, Small Intestine, Sympathetic, Coronary Vascular Subcortex
- **Tachycardia, fibrillation:** *Shenmen*, Small Intestine, Heart, Chest, Occiput, Reduce Heart Rate, Coronary Vascular Subcortex. Bleed Ear Apex.
- **Bradycardia:** Sympathetic, Heart, Chest, Adrenal Gland, Coronary Vascular Subcortex

NUTRITION

- Individuals with arteriosclerosis should eat foods high in fiber (fruits and vegetables) and low in fat and cholesterol. Avoid sweets, chips, fried and greasy foods, junk foods, ice cream, and alcohol. Stay away from smoking and exposure to second-hand smoke. Regular exercise with close monitoring of weight is recommended.
- Increase intake of garlic and onions, as they can reduce serum cholesterol levels. Raw nuts (except peanuts), olive oil, pink salmon, trout, tuna, Atlantic herring, and mackerel are also rich in essential fatty acids that are good for patients with cardiovascular disorders.
- Eliminate sodium, MSG, baking soda, canned vegetables, diet soft drinks, preservatives, meat tenderizers, saccharin, and softened water from the diet.
- Patients on anticoagulants drugs, such as Coumadin (warfarin), should not fluctuate their daily consumption of vitamin K, which is found in alfalfa, cauliflower, liver, and in all dark green vegetables including broccoli and spinach.
- Increase the intake of niacin, which can lower total cholesterol levels by up to 18%, increase HDL cholesterol by up to 32%, and lower triglycerides by up to 26%. Slow release form of niacin is preferred to minimize side effects such as flushing and stomach pain.
- Other supplements that are beneficial include vitamin B5, vitamin C, vitamin E, chromium picolinate, lecithin, and coenzyme Q10.
- Give the body two to three hours between the last meal of the day and bedtime. During sleep, the digestive system slows down. Make sure the body has adequate time to digest the food before going into sleep mode.

The Tao of Nutrition by Dr. Maoshing Ni and Cathy McNease:

- **Coronary heart disease**
  - Increase the intake of American ginseng, brown rice, black fungus, sea cucumber, vinegar, shiitake mushrooms, celery, seaweed, lotus root, cassia seeds, jelly fish, chrysanthemums, hawthorn berries, water chestnuts, mung beans, pearl barley, peach kernels, ginger, soy sprouts, mung sprouts, other sprouts, wheat bran, persimmons, bananas, watermelon, sunflower seeds, and lotus seeds.
  - Avoid fatty foods, stimulating foods, spicy foods, coffee, smoking, alcohol, simple carbohydrates (sugar and white flour), salt, stress, tension, worrying, emotional stimulation, and lack of sleep.

LIFESTYLE INSTRUCTIONS

- Exercise helps blood circulation and is the key to keeping the blood vessels elastic, flexible, and unclogged.
- Avoid the use of alcohol and exposure to tobacco. They increase cholesterol buildup and hardening of arteries.
- Healthy diet and lifestyle changes can reverse arteriosclerosis and its complications. However, they must be applied daily and continuously for a long time, without interruptions.

CASE STUDIES

- W.Y., a 62-year-old male, presented with insomnia due to stress and anxiety, which caused him to wake 2 to 3 times per night. Objective findings included red cheeks and purple lips. The TCM diagnosis was blood stagnation with Liver fire. For treatment, ***Circulation*** was prescribed to treat blood stagnation and ***Calm (ES)*** was prescribed to treat anxiety. Both were prescribed at a dosage of 2 capsules two times a day. Within the first week of taking the herbs, the patient's sleep had improved to waking up only once during the night. His legs were still blue so the dosage of ***Circulation*** was increased. Submitted by M.P., Muskego, Wisconsin.
- F.L., a 53-year-old female patient, presented with recent history of TIA (transient ischemic attack). Objective findings included right-sided pulling and numbness of the face with difficulty smiling and closing the right eye, as well as drooping of facial muscles on the right side when smiling, and partial facial flaccidity. Treatment using three capsules of ***Circulation***, three times daily, was successful: no recurring episodes were noted during subsequent follow-up visits. This patient also had constipation with hard, difficult to move stools, abdominal pain, and cramps with bloating. All these gastrointestinal symptoms were resolved with ***Gentle Lax (Deficient)*** taken at four capsules, three times daily. Submitted by C.L., Chino Hills, California.

PHARMACOLOGICAL AND CLINICAL RESEARCH

Circulation is formulated to treat cardiovascular and circulatory disorders. It contains herbs with vasodilating effects to increase blood perfusion and improve blood circulation, cardiotonic effects to strengthen cardiac contraction, antiplatelet and anticoagulant effects to reduce the risk of blood clots, and antihyperlipidemic effects to lower plasma cholesterols and triglycerides.

One of the fastest and most effective ways to increase and improve blood circulation is to dilate the blood vessels and strengthen the heart contraction. Dilated blood vessels allow the blood to flow smoothly with decreased resistance, and strong heart contraction enables the blood to reach peripheral parts of the body. In this formula, many herbs have a strong vasodilating effect, such as *Bai Shao* (Radix Paeoniae Alba), *Chuan Xiong* (Rhizoma Chuanxiong) and *Mao Dong Qing* (Radix Ilicis Pubescentis). *Bai Shao* (Radix Paeoniae Alba) has demonstrated a marked action to dilate aorta and peripheral blood vessels, and cause a slight decrease in blood pressure.[5,6] *Chuan Xiong* (Rhizoma Chuanxiong) dilates blood vessels to lower blood pressure, increases blood perfusion to coronary arteries, and decreases oxygen consumption by the cardiac muscle.[7] *Mao Dong Qing* (Radix Ilicis Pubescentis) has shown marked effectiveness to dilate blood vessels and increase blood perfusion to the coronary arteries.[8] Lastly, *Dang Gui* (Radix Angelicae Sinensis) has a positive inotropic effect to strengthen cardiac contraction and improve overall blood circulation.[9,10]

Blood clot formation is a significant risk of coronary heart disease. Blood clots may be prevented and treated with herbs that have antiplatelet and anticoagulant effects. *Dan Shen* (Radix et Rhizoma Salviae Miltiorrhizae) has antiplatelet, anticoagulant, and thrombolytic effects, and is also one of the most effective herbs to improve blood circulation.[11,12] *Dang Gui* (Radix Angelicae Sinensis) also has a significant antiplatelet effect, similar to that of aspirin.[13] *Chuan Xiong* (Rhizoma Chuanxiong) has a marked effect to inhibit thrombus formation and platelet aggregation in a dose-dependent manner.[14] Lastly, *Xie Bai* (Bulbus Allii Macrostemonis) has been shown to markedly inhibit platelet aggregation and prevent clotting.[15]

Atherosclerosis is also another cause of coronary heart disease. Therefore, proper precaution must be taken to ensure normal levels of plasma cholesterols and triglycerides. In this formula, *Bai Shao* (Radix Paeoniae Alba) exerts a significant effect to lower total cholesterol, low-density lipoprotein and triglyceride levels, compared with a control group.[16] *Hou Po* (Cortex Magnoliae Officinalis) has demonstrated marked effect to prevent and treat atherosclerosis by lowering the plasma lipids, decreasing arterial lesions, and suppressing aortic oxidative stress (measured by free radical, malondialdehyde, and oxidative DNA damage).[17] Administration of *Ren Shen* (Radix et Rhizoma Ginseng) in humans at 6 grams per day for 8 weeks is associated with increased high-density lipoprotein (HDL) and decreased serum total cholesterol, triglyceride, low-density lipoprotein (LDL) and plasma malondialdehyde (MDA) levels.[18] Lastly, *Xie Bai* (Bulbus Allii Macrostemonis) has demonstrated marked effectiveness to lower plasma cholesterol and triglyceride levels.[19]

Clinically, use of herbs in ***Circulation*** has been shown to effectively treat various types of coronary heart disease. According to one study, use of *Dan Shen* (Radix et Rhizoma Salviae Miltiorrhizae) was effective to treat 323 patients with coronary artery disease,[20] and use of *Dan Shen* (Radix et Rhizoma Salviae Miltiorrhizae) and *Ge Gen* (Radix Puerariae Lobatae) effectively treated 100 consecutive coronary patients (mean age 58 +/- 8 years).[21] According to another study, 106 patients with ischemic heart disease were treated with 99.06% rate of effectiveness using an herbal formula that contained *Dang Gui* (Radix Angelicae Sinensis), *Chuan Xiong* (Rhizoma Chuanxiong), *Xie Bai* (Bulbus Allii Macrostemonis), *Dan Shen* (Radix et Rhizoma Salviae Miltiorrhizae) and others.[22] Furthermore, *Mao Dong Qing* (Radix Ilicis Pubescentis) has been shown to effectively treat cardiovascular diseases, such as coronary artery disease and ischemic stroke.[23,24] Lastly, *Chuan Xiong* (Rhizoma Chuanxiong) has been used in various formulas to effectively treat angina,[25] coronary artery disease,[26] cerebral embolism,[27] and ischemic stroke.[28]

In summary, ***Circulation*** is an excellent formula that helps to prevent and treat cardiovascular and circulatory diseases.

COMPARATIVE ANALYSIS

Cardiovascular and circulatory disorders are complex illnesses that affect various parts of the body. In Western medicine, these disorders are treated with medications such as antiplatelets [aspirin and Ticlid (ticlopidine)] and anticoagulants [heparin and Coumadin (warfarin)]. In emergencies, nitroglycerin and thrombolytic drugs may be used to dilate blood vessels and dissolve blood clots, respectively. Though these drugs have serious side effects, their use can be justified because they offer major benefits, especially in urgent situations.

Use of herbs is also beneficial to treat cardiovascular and circulatory disorders. In fact, many drugs used for treatment of cardiovascular and circulatory disorders are originally derived from natural sources. Similarly, these herbs have similar pharmacological effects to those of the drugs, such as antiplatelet, anticoagulant, thrombolytic, and vasodilating effects. Furthermore, herbs are much safer than drugs, as they have a regulatory effect on blood hemodynamics, thereby achieving desired effects with minimal side effects.

Both drugs and herbs are effective for prevention and treatment of mild to moderate cases of cardiovascular and circulatory disorders. Drug therapies are more potent and precise, but do have more side effects. However, drugs are simply the most effective and most reliable therapy in emergency cases such as in acute heart attack. On the other hand, herbs are effective for both prevention and treatment of cardiovascular and circulatory disorders. However, they should not be used in emergencies, as Western medicine is more suitable for crisis management.

References

1. Center of Disease Control and Prevention (CDC). National Vital Statistics Report. Volume 60, Number 4. January 11, 2012.
2. Chan K, Lo AC, Yeung JH, Woo KS. Journal of Pharmacy and Pharmacology 1995 May;47(5):402-6.
3. Pharmacotherapy 1999 July;19(7):870-876.
4. European Journal of Drug Metabolism and Pharmacokinetics 1995; 20(1):55-60.

5. Goto H., Shimada Y., Akechi Y., Kohta K., Hattori M. & Terasawa K. Endothelium-dependent vasodilator effect of extract prepared from the roots of *Paeonia lactiflora* on isolated rat aorta. *Planta Med.* 1996, 62(5): 436-439.
6. *Zhong Guo Yao Li Xue Tong Bao* (Journal of Chinese Herbal Pharmacology), 1986; 2(5):26.
7. *Zhong Yao Yao Li Yu Ying Yong* (Pharmacology and Applications of Chinese Herbs), 1989;(2):40.
8. *Zhong Yao Xue* (Chinese Herbology), 1998; 588:589.
9. *Jiang Su Zhong Yi* (Jiangsu Chinese Medicine), 1965; (3):22.
10. Xue, JX. et al. Effects of the combination of astragalus membranaceus (Fisch.) Bge. (AM), angelica sinensis (Oliv.) Diels (TAS), cyperus rotundus L. (CR), ligusticum chuanxiong Hort (LC) and paeonia veitchii lynch (PV) on the hemorrheological changes in "blood stagnating" rats. *Chung Kuo Chung Yao Tsa Chih*; 19(2):108-10, 128. Feb 1994.
11. *Shang Hai Di Yi Xue Yuan Xue Bao* (Journal of First Shanghai Medical College), 1979; 6(3):144.
12. *Shang Hai Di Yi Xue Yuan Xue Bao* (Journal of First Shanghai Medical College), 1982; 9(1):14.
13. *Yao Xue Xue Bao* (Journal of Herbology), 1980; 15(6):321.
14. Tian JW, Fu FH, Jiang WL, Wang CY, Sun F, Zhang TP. Protective effect of ligusticum chuanxiong phthalides on focai cerebral ischemia in rats and its related mechanism of action. Zhongguo Zhong Yao Za Zhi. 2005 Mar;30(6):466-8.
15. *Bai Qiu En Yi Ke Da Xue Xue Bao* (Journal of Baiqiuen University of Medicine), 1984; 10(16):609.
16. Yang HO, Ko WK, Kim JY, Ro HS. Paeoniflorin: an antihyperlipidemic agent from Paeonia lactiflora. Fitoterapia. 2004 Jan;75(1):45-9.
17. Chang WC, Yu YM, Hsu YM, Wu CH, Yin PL, Chiang SY, Hung JS. Inhibitory effect of Magnolia officinalis and lovastatin on aortic oxidative stress and apoptosis in hyperlipidemic rabbits. Department of Biological Science and Technology, China Medical University and Hospital, Taichung, Taiwan. J Cardiovasc Pharmacol. 2006 Mar;47(3):463-8.
18. Kim SH, Park KS. Effects of Panax ginseng extract on lipid metabolism in humans. Department of Health & Kinesiology, Purdue University, 1362 Lambert, West Lafayette, IN, 47907-1362,USA. Pharmacol Res. 2003 Nov;48(5):511-3.
19. *Prostaglandins*, 1976; 12:685.
20. *Xin Zhang Xue Guan Ji Bing* (Cardiovascular Diseases), 1974; 2(1):5.
21. Tam WY, Chook P, Qiao M, Chan LT, Chan TY, Poon YK, Fung KP, Leung PC, Woo KS. The efficacy and tolerability of adjunctive alternative herbal medicine (Salvia miltiorrhiza and Pueraria lobata) on vascular function and structure in coronary patients. J Altern Complement Med. 2009 Apr;15(4):415-21.
22. *Zhong Guo Zhong Xi Yi Jie He Za Zhi* (Chinese Journal of Integrative Chinese and Western Medicine), 1994; (12):742.
23. *Xin Yi Yao Xue Za Zhi* (New Journal of Medicine and Herbology), 1979; 11:48.
24. *Guang Dong Yi Xue* (Guangdong Medicine), 1983; 4(8):28.
25. *Chong Qing Yi Yao* (Chongching Medicine and Herbology), 1978; 1:23.
26. *Zhong Yao Lin Chuan Xin Yong* (New Clinical Applications of Chinese Medicine), 2001; 65.
27. *Zhong Xi Yi Jie He Za Zhi* (Journal of Integrated Chinese and Western Medicine), 1986; 6(4):234.
28. Chen KJ, Chen K. Ischemic stroke treated with Ligusticum chuanxiong. Chin Med J (Engl). 1992 Oct;105(10):870-3.

Circulation (SJ) ™

CLINICAL APPLICATIONS

- **Severe blood stasis and stagnant blood circulation in upper, middle and lower *jiaos* (*San Jiao*):**
  - Severe blood stasis in the upper *jiao*: headache, angina pectoris, rheumatic heart disease, thrombosis, embolism, cardiac ischemia, bradyarrhythmia, stroke, concussion, post-concussion syndrome, cerebral atherosclerosis, hyperlipidemia, and physical injury to the chest
  - Severe blood stasis in the middle *jiao*: pleural adhesion, acute and chronic hepatitis, liver cirrhosis, hepatic hemangioma, cholecystitis, jaundice, and splenomegalia
  - Severe blood stasis in the lower *jiao*: female infertility, male infertility, amenorrhea, dysmenorrhea, irregular menstruation, uterine bleeding, ectopic pregnancy, hysteromyoma, endometriosis, oophoritic cyst, ovarian cyst, pelvic inflammatory disease, hyperplastic tuberculosis of intestine, ulcerative colitis, and urinary stones
- **Chronic traumatic injury** that was not treated properly back in the acute phase and now re-exacerbates off and on
- **Cardiovascular, circulatory or clotting disorders**
- **Chronic musculoskeletal injuries, joint injuries** (such as knee, ankle, wrist, elbow, shoulder, and back)
- **Post-surgical pain and adhesions**
- **Severe, chronic or unusual conditions that do not respond to standard herbal treatment** [use ***Circulation (SJ)*** as an adjunct formula to boost the overall therapeutic effect]

WESTERN THERAPEUTIC ACTIONS

- Treats cardiovascular and circulatory disorders throughout the entire body
- Antiplatelet and anticoagulant effects to reduce the risk of blood clots and decrease blood viscosity
- Vasodilating action to lower blood pressure and increase blood perfusion
- Positive cardiotonic function to strengthen cardiac contraction and improve blood circulation

CHINESE THERAPEUTIC ACTIONS

- Invigorates blood and qi circulation in the upper, middle, and lower *jiaos*
- Dispels blood stasis and qi stagnation
- Unblocks meridians and relieves pain

DOSAGE

Take 3 to 4 capsules three times daily. For severe cases, dosage may be increased to 7 to 8 capsules three times daily to relieve pain. This formula should be taken for no more than one month continuously. As an adjunct to another formula to invigorate blood, the recommended dose is 1 to 2 capsules in addition to the regular dose of the base formula.

INGREDIENTS

Bai Shao (Radix Paeoniae Alba)
Chai Hu (Radix Bupleuri)
Chi Shao (Radix Paeoniae Rubra)
Chuan Niu Xi (Radix Cyathulae)
Chuan Xiong (Rhizoma Chuanxiong)
Dang Gui (Radix Angelicae Sinensis)
Di Huang (Radix Rehmanniae)
Gan Cao (Radix et Rhizoma Glycyrrhizae)
Hong Hua (Flos Carthami)
Jie Geng (Radix Platycodonis)
Mo Yao (Myrrha)
Mu Dan Pi (Cortex Moutan)
Pu Huang (Pollen Typhae)
Rou Gui (Cortex Cinnamomi)
Shui Zhi (Hirudo)
Tao Ren (Semen Persicae)
Wu Yao (Radix Linderae)
Xiang Fu (Rhizoma Cyperi)
Yan Hu Suo (Rhizoma Corydalis)
Zhi Qiao (Fructus Aurantii)

BACKGROUND

Cardiovascular and circulatory disorders are common and complex illnesses that affect various parts of the body. Cardiovascular and circulatory disorders include hypertension, arteriosclerosis, coronary artery disease, embolism and many others. Furthermore, cardiovascular and circulatory disorders are often complicated with other conditions, such as diabetes mellitus, obesity, dyslipidemia, etc. As the number one cause of death in the United States, prevention and treatment of cardiovascular disease simply cannot be underestimated.[1]

FORMULA EXPLANATION

Circulation (SJ) is an herbal formula specifically formulated with herbs that invigorate blood circulation, dispel blood stasis, unblock meridians, and relieve pain. It promotes normal blood circulation in the upper, middle, and lower *jiaos*. Its formulation follows the principles of three classic formulas: *Xue Fu Zhu Yu Tang* (Drive Out Stasis in the Mansion of Blood Decoction) to treat blood stasis in the upper *jiao*, *Ge Xia Zhu Yu Tang* (Drive Out Blood Stasis Below the Diaphragm Decoction) to treat blood stasis in the middle *jiao*, and *Shao Fu Zhu Yu Tang* (Drive Out Blood Stasis in the Lower Abdomen Decoction) to treat blood stasis in the lower *jiao*.

Tao Ren (Semen Persicae) and *Hong Hua* (Flos Carthami) are used to activate the blood circulation. These two herbs have excellent synergistic effect and are often used together. *Shui Zhi* (Hirudo) is one of the strongest blood stasis removing herbs, and is added to enhance the overall effect to break down blood stasis. *Dang Gui* (Radix Angelicae Sinensis), *Chuan Xiong* (Rhizoma

Circulation (SJ)™

Chuanxiong) and *Di Huang* (Radix Rehmanniae) nourish blood, activate blood circulation and eliminate blood stasis. *Mu Dan Pi* (Cortex Moutan) and *Chi Shao* (Radix Paeoniae Rubra) clear heat, cool blood, and dispel blood stasis. Since blood stasis and qi stagnation often occur simultaneously, *Zhi Qiao* (Fructus Aurantii), *Wu Yao* (Radix Linderae) and *Xiang Fu* (Rhizoma Cyperi) are used to activate and regulate qi circulation. To effectively treat qi and blood stasis in all three *jiaos*, *Jie Geng* (Radix Platycodonis), *Chai Hu* (Radix Bupleuri), and *Chuan Niu Xi* (Radix Cyathulae) are used to guide the formula to the upper, middle and lower *jiaos*, respectively. In addition, because pain is often associated with qi and blood stasis, *Yan Hu Suo* (Rhizoma Corydalis), *Mo Yao* (Myrrha), *Pu Huang* (Pollen Typhae) and *Rou Gui* (Cortex Cinnamomi) are used to unblock the channels and collaterals to relieve pain. Furthermore, the combination of *Bai Shao* (Radix Paeoniae Alba) and *Gan Cao* (Radix et Rhizoma Glycyrrhizae) also has great effect to relieve spasms and cramps. Lastly, *Gan Cao* (Radix et Rhizoma Glycyrrhizae) tonifies qi and harmonizes all the herbs in this formula.

In summary, ***Circulation (SJ)*** is an excellent formula to treat various types of disorders characterized by blood stasis anywhere in the upper, middle, and lower *jiaos* of the body.

CAUTIONS & CONTRAINDICATIONS

- This herbal formula contains herbs that invigorate blood circulation, such as *Dang Gui* (Radix Angelicae Sinensis). Therefore, patients who are on anticoagulant or antiplatelet therapies, such as Coumadin (warfarin), should use this formula with caution, or not at all, as there may be a higher risk of bleeding and bruising.[2,3,4]
- Patients on anticoagulant drugs, such as Coumadin (warfarin), should not fluctuate their daily consumption of vitamin K, which is found in alfalfa, cauliflower, liver, and in all dark green vegetables including broccoli and spinach.
- This formula is contraindicated during pregnancy and nursing. It should be used with caution during menstruation as it may cause excessive bleeding. In such cases, discontinue use immediately and resume after menstruation is over.
- This formula is contraindicated in patients with bleeding disorders, such as hypermenorrhea, uterine bleeding, hemophilia, and others.
- This formula should be discontinued one to two weeks before surgery.
- Use with caution or add ***GI Tonic*** if the patient has a weak digestive system or Spleen qi deficiency with diarrhea.
- During the course of treatment with this formula, some patients with chronic "dead blood" might notice pain in places of past injuries. Advise the patient of this possible experience before giving the formula that it is a positive sign as it is clearing away the residual stagnation and bringing in fresh blood supply to the chronically injured place. In some cases where patients cannot tolerate the pain, reduce the dosage of the formula by 20%. After experiencing the initial pain, the patient will later experience a total clearing sensation. This is especially prevalent in those suffering from chronic headaches due to previous head injuries. Failure to advise the patient on the potential experience of pain may result in misunderstanding by the patient, who may think the herbal treatment is causing them more pain in an adverse way.
- This formula should be taken for no more than one month continuously, since the use of strong blood moving herbs may sometimes cause blood deficiency.
- Due to its potent effect, this formula is contraindicated in weak and elderly patients.

CLINICAL NOTES

- The sedentary lifestyle of modern society is characterized by sitting for long hours and lack of exercise. Most people spend many hours of the day sitting in their cars, office, and home. With lack of movement, blood circulation is impaired and gradually leads to a large number of illnesses. Therefore, this formula is not only an excellent formula to improve blood circulation and treat clot related disorders, it is also a wonderful formula for prevention of chronic illness. In addition, this formula can be combined with many other formulas to improve blood circulation and deliver the herbs to the affected areas that may be hard to reach.
- ***Circulation (SJ)*** has a wide range of therapeutic actions and may be used to treat many different diseases. One common presentation among all these diseases is blood stasis characterized by either a light or dark purplish tongue. There are also cases where the tongue may appear normal but the sublingual veins are distended and dark in appearance. The patient's face may appear dark and lusterless. Lips may be dark or purplish. Axillae, transverse cubital crease and the popliteal fossa may all appear slightly darker than the rest of the skin.
- Patients with intermittent claudication, chronic pain in the calf when walking, should be checked for cardiovascular disorders.
- ***Circulation (SJ)*** works similarly like the "restart" function on the computer. When too many programs are open and running, the computer may freeze. The body works the same way in that it breaks down when there are too many aggravating factors or symptoms. This formula works like the "restart" function on the computer to clear away stagnation so the body has a chance to start new again. In breaking down the blood clot, it then should become clear what condition needs to be addressed instead of being confused with multiple symptoms that may not point to any clear diagnosis.

Pulse Diagnosis by Dr. Jimmy Wei-Yen Chang:

- Dispersing or scattered pulse found in the pulse position corresponding to the location of the blood stasis. Dispersing and scattered pulses are shapeless pulses in which their borders are hard to perceive and are thick, weak, and deep. A scattered pulse is weaker than a dispersing pulse, indicating a more chronic injury with blood stasis.

Circulation (SJ) ™

SUPPLEMENTARY FORMULAS

Circulation (SJ) can be used individually, or in combination with any other formulas that treat disorders of the *zang fu* organs or diseases of the body.

- Cardiovascular disorders:
  - Angina, atherosclerosis: add ***Circulation***.
  - High cholesterol: add ***Cholisma*** or ***Cholisma (ES)***.
  - Hypertension with dizziness or vertigo: add ***Gastrodia Complex***.
  - Hypertension with anger or flushed face: add ***Gentiana Complex***.
- Gynecological disorders:
  - Dysmenorrhea: add ***Mense-Ease***.
  - Fibrocystic disorder in the breast: add ***Resolve (Upper)***.
  - Endometriosis, fibroids or cysts in the uterus or other mass: add ***Resolve (Lower)***.
- Musculoskeletal disorders:
  - Pain of arm, elbow, wrist or hand: add ***Arm Support***.
  - Neck, shoulder and upper back pain: add ***Neck & Shoulder (AC)*** or ***Neck & Shoulder (CR)***.
  - Back pain: add ***Back Support (AC)*** or ***Back Support (CR)***.
  - Headache: add ***Corydalin (AC)*** or ***Corydalin (CR)***.
  - Neuropathy: add ***Flex (NP)***.
  - *Bi zheng* (painful obstruction syndrome) due to cold: combine with ***Flex (CD)***.
  - *Bi zheng* (painful obstruction syndrome) due to heat: combine with ***Flex (Heat)***.
  - Muscle stiffness, cramps and spasms: add ***Flex (SC)***.
  - For excruciating pain: add ***Herbal ANG***.
  - Bone spurs: add ***Flex (SPR)***.
  - Knee pain: add ***Knee & Ankle (AC)*** or ***Knee & Ankle (CR)***.
  - Gout: add ***Flex (GT)***.
  - Trauma, post-surgical recovery: add ***Flex (TMX)***.
- Others:
  - For extreme anxiety, stress, emotional or psychological issues: add ***Calm*** or ***Calm (ES)***. If heat is evident from the tongue, use ***Circulation (SJ)*** with ***Gardenia Complex*** first until heat is purged. Then follow up with ***Calm*** or ***Calm (ES)***.
  - Insomnia: add ***Calm (ES)***, ***Calm ZZZ***, or ***Schisandra ZZZ***.
  - Depression: add ***Shine*** or ***Shine (DS)***.
  - Post-stroke care: add ***Neuro +***.
  - For nodules or swelling: add ***Resolve (AI)***.
  - With excess heat or fever: add ***Gardenia Complex***.
  - Psoriasis or chronic skin condition: add ***Dermatrol (PS)***.
  - For weepy skin conditions: add ***Dermatrol (Damp)***.
  - For dry skin conditions: add ***Dermatrol (Dry)***.
  - For edema or swelling: add ***Herbal DRX***.
  - Varicose veins: add *Shan Zha* (Fructus Crataegi).
  - For forgetfulness: add ***Enhance Memory***.
  - With cold extremities: add ***Kidney Tonic (Yang)***.
  - Hair loss: add ***Polygonum 14***.

ACUPUNCTURE TREATMENT

Traditional Points:

- For varicose veins, bleeding technique should be performed once a week on the small, distended vein while taking ***Circulation (SJ)*** and *Shan Zha* (Fructus Crataegi).

Master Tung's Points by Dr. Chuan-Min Wang:

- **Blood stasis:** Needle and moxa *Huofuhai* (T 33.07).

Balance Method by Dr. Richard Tan:

- Left side: *Shaoshang* (LU 11), *Zhongchong* (PC 9), *Shaochong* (HT 9), *Zusanli* (ST 36), *Yanglingquan* (GB 34), *Weizhong* (BL 40)
- Right side: *Hegu* (LI 4), *Houxi* (SI 3), *Zhongzhu* (TH 3), *Sanyinjiao* (SP 6), *Zhongfeng* (LR 4), *Taixi* (KI 3)
- Alternate sides from treatment to treatment.

Auricular Medicine by Dr. Li-Chun Huang:

- **Invigorating blood circulation:** Heart, Liver, Hot Point, Lung, Coronary Vascular Subcortex, Sympathetic, Large Auricular Nerve, Lesser Occipital Nerve, corresponding points (to the area affected)
- **Thromboangiitis obliterans:** corresponding point (to the area affected), Sympathetic, Coronary Vascular Subcortex, Lesser Occipital Nerve, Large Auricular Nerve, Hot Point, Heart
  - Supplementary points: Lung, Liver, Spleen, Endocrine
- **Thrombophlebitis:** corresponding point (to the area affected), Sympathetic, Endocrine, *San Jiao*, Heart, Lung, Liver, Kidney, Spleen, Hot Point, Coronary Vascular Subcortex. Bleed Ear Apex.
- **Phantom limb pain:** Sympathetic, *Shenmen*, Occiput, Lesser Occipital Nerve, Large Auricular Nerve, Nervous Subcortex. Bleed Ear Apex.

NUTRITION

- L-carnitine is helpful to strengthen the heart muscle and to promote circulation.
- Coenzyme Q10 improves tissue oxygenation.
- A multienzyme complex supplement helps enhance use of oxygen in body tissue.
- Multivitamins are very beneficial for various aspects of proper circulation, such as formation of red blood cells, restoration of normal blood viscosity, and prevention of blood clots.
- Minerals, such as calcium, magnesium, and potassium, are essential for normal heartbeat.
- Drink warm or hot liquids with meals. Putting cold and ice on any part of the body will immediately constrict the flow of blood to that region. Similarly, drinking cold or iced drinks with meals will hinder the natural peristaltic movements of the digestive system.
- Avoid any and all foods that contain sugar, such as cake, dessert, candy, chocolate, canned juice, soft drinks, caffeinated drinks, stevia, sugar substitutes, agave, xylitol, and corn syrup.

Circulation (SJ)™

- Avoid raw or uncooked meats, such as sashimi, sushi, steak tartar, and seared meat. Minimize consumption of foods that are cooling in nature, including tofu, tomato, celery, asparagus, bamboo, seaweed, kelp, bitter melon, cucumber, gourd, luffa, eggplant, winter melon, watermelon, honeydew, citrus, oranges, guava, grapefruit, pineapple, plums, pear, banana, papaya, white radish, mustard leaf, potherb mustard, Chinese kale, napa, and bamboo sprout. Do not eat foods straight from the refrigerator.
- Avoid fried or greasy foods.
- Warm and hot natured foods that damage qi and yin should be avoided, such as:
  - certain fruits like mango and durian that produce heat.
  - stimulants like coffee, alcohol, and energy drinks.
  - spicy/pungent/aromatic vegetables such as pepper, garlic, onions, basil, rosemary, cumin, funnel, anise, leeks, chives, scallions, thyme, saffron, wormwood, mustard, chili pepper, and wasabi.
- Avoid food and drinks with artificial coloring.
- Consume as few meat products as possible. Do not eat processed meats, such as lunch meats, hot dogs and sausages, as they contain nitrites that are associated with inflammation and chronic disease.

LIFESTYLE INSTRUCTIONS

- Exercise helps blood circulation and is the key to keeping the blood vessels elastic, flexible and unclogged.
- Avoid the consumption of alcohol and exposure to tobacco. They increase cholesterol buildup and hardening of arteries.
- Healthy diet and lifestyle changes can reverse arteriosclerosis and its complications. However, they must be practiced daily and continuously for a long time without interruptions.

CASE STUDIES

- L.P., a 28-year-old female, presented with severe sharp and stabbing headaches. After a few years, they have become more frequent and intense, described as her whole head getting sore and unable to function. Upon palpation, pain and tenderness was found on the trapezius, occipital, and temporal areas. Her Western diagnosis was migraines, and the TCM diagnosis was Liver yang rising with blood stasis. ***Circulation (SJ)*** was prescribed at four capsules three times a day. The headaches immediately decreased, the frequency of the pain was a major difference in tolerance, and she was able to function more. ***Circulation (SJ)*** was used to address the symptoms initially before addressing the root of the condition and it made a great difference. Submitted by A.I., Hilo, Hawaii.
- An 81-year-old female patient presented with pain and numbness in her feet. The condition is affected by the patient's blood sugar level, for which the patient was taking medication. The symptoms were reported as chronic; however, it still only comes and goes. Her Western diagnosis was peripheral neuropathy and the TCM diagnosis was blood stasis and Kidney deficiency. The patient was treated with ***Circulation (SJ)***, which reduced the pain and numbness until her blood sugar remained under control. Submitted by A.I., Hilo, Hawaii.
- D.A., a 55-year-old female, presented with extreme pain in both heels, radiating up the calf area. Symptoms of night sweats, problems with staying asleep, low energy, and depression were also present. Her pulse was weak and thin and her tongue was red with thin white coating. The practitioner diagnosed this condition as Liver qi stagnation and Kidney yin deficiency. Upon diagnosis, the patient was prescribed ***Flex (NP)*** and ***Circulation (SJ)***. The patient reported less pain; however, it was still present especially in the morning and late in the day after standing a lot. Her sleep improved as well, waking up only once during the night. The patient continued to improve; however, effort on her part was necessary to improve more. Submitted by B.L., Fort Myers, Florida.
- D.D., a 72-year-old male, presented with shortness of breath and cough with frothy, clear white sputum. It was noted that this patient was diabetic, post-stroke, with a heart function of 77%, and creatinine level of 1.8 mg/dL. Objective findings included left leg hot to the touch, right leg cold to the touch, and difficulty with inhaling. He had recently taken two rounds of antibiotics. The practitioner diagnosed this condition as Kidney not grasping the qi, Lung and Spleen qi deficiencies with phlegm accumulation; his Western diagnosis was COPD. For treatment he was given a combination of ***Cordyceps 3***, ***Respitrol (Deficient)***, ***Circulation (SJ)*** and ***Neuro Plus***, just one bottle at a time. The patient gradually improved, getting stronger each week and continued taking the herbs for about three months. Submitted by T.W., Perrysburg, Ohio.
- After recently attending Dr. Jimmy Chang's seminar in Austin, Texas, I decided to try ***Circulation (SJ)*** with a client I had been working with since March. He was a 25-year-old who had been diagnosed with Reflex Sympathetic Dystrophy (RSD) of the right ankle. This was the result of a fall from a cliff five years ago in which he sustained extensive crushing injury to the bones of the ankle and fibula. He had three surgeries to attempt to repair the damage that were unsuccessful to the extent that amputation just below the knee was strongly encouraged by his physicians. Most of the time he could not stand anything touching his right leg so he was in shorts and barefoot, and in a wheelchair. I started working with him with acupuncture only using Dr. Tan's 12 Magic Points since he was reluctant to try herbs since he was using painkillers, even though they were not very effective. We had made some progress: he had been able to reduce his medications and sometimes he could put on a sock and loose shoe. Then two weeks ago I put him on ***Circulation (SJ)***. The first week some diminishment of pain occurred, but the second week was the miracle! He came to his appointment with shoes and socks on, and was walking with a slight limp. His face and eyes were clearer then I had ever seen, he was laughing and calm. Later that day the massage therapist who had originally referred him to me called

Circulation (SJ) ™

to tell me for the first time in the two years she had been working with him she was able to touch his leg without him screaming in pain. She said his entire body was different - the tension and rigidity that was always there in the past was gone. Her statement to me was "it was like massaging a normal person." She stated that she had been contemplating discontinuing working with him because she "felt like all she was doing was grinding bone on bone and causing him pain." My client and I thank you and Dr. Chang for your continuing efforts in the field of Asian medicine. Please do not let Dr. Chang stop teaching. Thanks again!

As an update, this week when I saw this young man, he had continued improvement. While we were talking before his treatment he was sitting there with his legs crossed as only men can do, stroking and playing with his damaged ankle and toes. When I commented on this, he said that it was just so amazing to him to be able to be touched without it causing pain for the first time in years. Submitted by A.G., Austin, Texas.

ADDITIONAL INFORMATION

- ***Circulation (SJ)*** is designed by Dr. Jimmy Wei-Yen Chang to treat a wide variety of disorders characterized by severe or chronic blood and qi stagnation. He calls this condition "dead blood syndrome" where there is chronic blood stasis in the body with no outlet. With this stagnation, the homeostasis of the body is disturbed and multiple symptoms may appear.
- ***Circulation (SJ)*** has three main functions:
  1. It treats chronic persistent pain that is the result of previous traumatic injuries, which were not treated properly. Chronic qi and blood stagnation lead to pain which worsens with exacerbation or when the body is not in optimal health. This formula contains strong blood-moving herbs, which effectively drive away chronic blood stasis.
  2. It treats multiple chronic disorders or complex patterns with no clear diagnosis. These cases have multiple symptoms and each is very severe. However, there may be conflicting signs and symptoms, which prevent clear diagnosis of the exact cause. Such cases are best treated with blood-moving herbs. By clearing away chronic "dead blood" that may be complicating the condition, the true illness will surface, which then makes it possible to diagnose and prescribe an appropriate formula.
  3. It treats complex conditions where the diagnosis is clear but after using the correct herbs following differentiation principles, the condition still does not improve. For example, a patient may suffer from insomnia and appropriate *shen* (spirit) calming herbs are given but the patient shows no result after several treatments. Alternatively, a patient suffers from high fever and *Bai Hu Tang* (White Tiger Decoction) is given but the high fever persists. In such cases where the diagnostic signs clearly match the herbal prescription but the patient shows no result, then one might consider that there is underlying "dead blood" disrupting the balance of the body. "Dead blood" might be blocking the blood flow and preventing it from nourishing the Heart *shen* (spirit) in the first case. It might also be the "dead blood" that is creating so much stagnation that the fever persists because there is a lack of proper circulation. In any case, removing the root cause is the only long-term solution to the problem.

PHARMACOLOGICAL AND CLINICAL RESEARCH

Circulation (SJ) is designed to treat various types of illnesses characterized by cardiovascular and circulatory disorders. Pharmacologically, many herbs in this formula have marked antiplatelet, anticoagulant and thrombolytic effects, and are excellent for treating clotting disorders. Furthermore, these herbs also have vasodilating effects to lower blood pressure and increase blood perfusion, and cardiotonic action to strengthen cardiac contraction and improve blood circulation. Clinically, the herbs in the formula have been shown to treat cardiovascular, circulatory, clotting disorders, and many other illnesses.

Circulation (SJ) incorporates many herbs with antiplatelet and anticoagulant effects to inhibit thrombus formation and treat clotting disorders. Herbs with antiplatelet effects include *Dang Gui* (Radix Angelicae Sinensis),[5] *Hong Hua* (Flos Carthami),[6] and *Chi Shao* (Radix Paeoniae Rubra).[7] Herbs with anticoagulant effects include *Shui Zhi* (Hirudo) and *Tao Ren* (Semen Persicae).[8,9] There are many herbs in this formula that also have a marked influence on the cardiovascular system. For example, *Dang Gui* (Radix Angelicae Sinensis) has a positive inotropic and a negative chronotropic effect.[10] Furthermore, it has been shown to improve overall blood circulation by decreasing the whole blood specific viscosity, or improving the hemorrheological changes in "blood stasis."[11] Use of *Zhi Qiao* (Fructus Aurantii) showed a marked ability to lower the oxygen requirement of cardiac muscle.[12] *Jie Geng* (Radix Platycodonis) has been shown to dilate blood vessels and increase blood perfusion to peripheral parts of the body.[13] Lastly, *Chuan Xiong* (Rhizoma Chuanxiong) dilates blood vessels to lower blood pressure, increases blood perfusion to coronary arteries, and decreases oxygen consumption by the cardiac muscle.[14]

Clinically, ***Circulation (SJ)*** may be used individually, or as an adjunct to other formulas to treat a wide variety of cardiovascular, circulatory, clotting, and related disorders. *Dang Gui* (Radix Angelicae Sinensis) has been used in formulas with good success to treat 40 patients with cerebral vascular accident.[15] *Hong Hua* (Flos Carthami) has been used in formulas with a 94.7% rate of effectiveness to treat 137 patients with cerebral thrombosis,[16] and an 80.8% rate of effectiveness in relieving chest pain in 100 patients with coronary artery disease.[17] *Chi Shao* (Radix Paeoniae Rubra) has been used with a 92.01% rate of effectiveness for prevention of thrombus formation in 263 patients.[18] *Chuan Xiong* (Rhizoma Chuanxiong), when given via injection, was associated with relief of pain in 92.5% of patients with angina,[19] a 94.5% rate of effectiveness among 400 patients with cerebral thrombosis,[20]

Circulation (SJ)™

and a 90% rate of effectiveness for 50 patients with acute cerebral embolisms.[21] Lastly, coronary artery disorder may be effectively treated with formulas that contain *Yan Hu Suo* (Rhizoma Corydalis) or *Pu Huang* (Pollen Typhae).[22,23]

Circulation (SJ) is formulated following the principles of three classic formulas: *Xue Fu Zhu Yu Tang* (Drive Out Stasis in the Mansion of Blood Decoction), *Ge Xia Zhu Yu Tang* (Drive Out Blood Stasis Below the Diaphragm Decoction), and *Shao Fu Zhu Yu Tang* (Drive Out Blood Stasis in the Lower Abdomen Decoction). Because of this formulation strategy, ***Circulation (SJ)*** can also be explained from the perspective of how it is used to treat disorders of the upper, middle, and lower *jiaos*.

Circulation (SJ) uses *Xue Fu Zhu Yu Tang* (Drive Out Stasis in the Mansion of Blood Decoction) to treat blood stasis in the upper *jiao*, a condition characterized by circulatory disorders in the upper parts of the body. Clinically, *Xue Fu Zhu Yu Tang* (Drive Out Stasis in the Mansion of Blood Decoction) has been shown to have a 89.3% rate of effectiveness to treat cardiac ischemia in 84 patients,[24] a 92.8% rate of effectiveness to treat bradyarrhythmia in 28 patients,[25] a 90% rate of effectiveness to treat vascular headache in 50 patients,[26] a 93.33% rate of effectiveness to treat headache in 15 patients,[27] a 92.3% rate of effectiveness to treat concussion in 12 patients,[28] an 87% rate of effectiveness to treat cerebral atherosclerosis in 63 patients,[29] and a 95% rate of effectiveness to treat hyperlipidemia with elevated cholesterol and triglyceride levels in 20 patients.[30]

Circulation (SJ) uses *Ge Xia Zhu Yu Tang* (Drive Out Blood Stasis Below the Diaphragm Decoction) to treat blood stasis in the middle *jiao*. Clinical researches have been shown that *Ge Xia Zhu Yu Tang* (Drive Out Blood Stasis Below the Diaphragm Decoction) has an 86% rate of effectiveness to treat hepatic hemangioma in 32 patients,[31] a marked effect to treat chronic active hepatitis in 25 patients,[32] good success to treat pleural adhesion in 60 patients,[33] a 90.6% rate of effectiveness to treat chronic pelvic inflammatory disease in 64 patients,[34] a 90% rate of effectiveness to treat prostatic hypertrophy in 22 patients,[35] a 96% rate of effectiveness to treat chronic colitis in 75 patients,[36] and a 90% rate of effectiveness to treat gastric or duodenal ulcer in 30 patients.[37]

Circulation (SJ) uses *Shao Fu Zhu Yu Tang* (Drive Out Blood Stasis in the Lower Abdomen Decoction) to treat blood stasis in the lower *jiao*, a condition characterized by circulatory disorders in the lower parts of the body. According to numerous clinical research studies, *Shao Fu Zhu Yu Tang* (Drive Out Blood Stasis in the Lower Abdomen Decoction) has a marked effect to treat both male and female infertility.[38,39,40] Furthermore, it may also be used to treat various other disorders with great success, such as a 97.5% rate of effectiveness in 40 women with endometriosis,[41] a 92% rate of effectiveness in 50 women with oophoritic cyst,[42] a 97% rate of effectiveness in 100 patients with dysmenorrhea,[43] a 94% rate of effectiveness in 14 patients with hysteromyoma,[44] a 92% rate of effectiveness in 42 women with pelvic inflammatory disease,[45] and a marked effect in 32 women with uterine bleeding associated with functional disorder.

In summary, ***Circulation (SJ)*** is an herbal formula with a wide range of therapeutic applications to address numerous disorders characterized by qi stagnation and blood stasis. Pharmacologically, many herbs in this formula have marked antiplatelet, anticoagulant, thrombolytic and vasodilating effects. Clinically, the herbs in ***Circulation (SJ)*** have been shown to treat cardiovascular, circulatory, clotting, and many other disorders.

COMPARATIVE ANALYSIS

Cardiovascular and circulatory disorders are complex illnesses that affect various parts of the body. In Western medicine, these disorders are treated with medications such as antiplatelets [aspirin and Ticlid (ticlopidine)] and anticoagulants [heparin and Coumadin (warfarin)]. In emergencies, nitroglycerin and thrombolytic drugs may be used to dilate blood vessels and dissolve blood clots, respectively. Though these drugs have serious side effects, their use can be justified because they offer tremendous benefits, especially in urgent situations.

Use of herbs is also beneficial to treat cardiovascular and circulatory disorders. In fact, many drugs used for treatment of cardiovascular and circulatory disorders are originally derived from natural sources. Similarly, these herbs have similar pharmacological effects to those of the drugs, such as antiplatelet, anticoagulant, thrombolytic, and vasodilating effects. Furthermore, herbs are much safer than drugs, as they have a regulatory effect on blood hemodynamics, thereby achieving desired effects with minimal side effects.

Both drugs and herbs are effective for prevention and treatment of mild to moderate cases of cardiovascular and circulatory disorders. Drug therapies are more potent and precise, but do have more side effects. However, drugs are simply the most effective and most reliable therapy in emergency cases such as in acute heart attack. On the other hand, herbs are effective for both prevention and treatment of cardiovascular and circulatory disorders. However, they should not be used in emergencies, as Western medicine is more suitable for crisis management.

References

1. Center of Disease Control and Prevention (CDC). National Vital Statistics Report. Volume 60, Number 4. January 11, 2012.
2. Chan K, Lo AC, Yeung JH, Woo KS. Journal of Pharmacy and Pharmacology 1995 May;47(5):402-6.
3. Pharmacotherapy 1999 July;19(7):870-876.
4. European Journal of Drug Metabolism and Pharmacokinetics 1995; 20(1):55-60.
5. *Zhong Guo Yao Li Xue Tong Bao* (Journal of Chinese Herbal Pharmacology), 1981; 2(1):35.
6. *Zhong Cheng Yao Yan Jiu* (Research of Chinese Patent Medicine), 1983; 12:31.
7. *Zhong Yao Xue* (Chinese Herbology), 1998; 831:836.
8. *Pharmazie*, 1988; 43:737.
9. *Shang Hai Zhong Yi Yao Za Zhi* (Shanghai Journal of Chinese Medicine and Herbology), 1985; 7:45.

Circulation (SJ)™

10. *Jiang Su Zhong Yi* (Jiangsu Chinese Medicine), 1965; (3):22.
11. Xue, JX. et al. Effects of the combination of astragalus membranaceus (Fisch.) Bge. (AM), angelica sinensis (Oliv.) Diels (TAS), cyperus rotundus L. (CR), ligusticum chuanxiong Hort (LC) and paeonia veitchii lynch (PV) on the hemorrheological changes in "blood stagnating" rats. *Chung Kuo Chung Yao Tsa Chih*; Feb 1994; 19(2):108-10, 128.
12. *Zhi Wu Yao You Xiao Cheng Fen Shou Ce* (Manual of Plant Medicinals and Their Active Constituents), 1986; 725.
13. *Zhong Yao Yao Li Yu Ying Yong* (Pharmacology and Applications of Chinese Herbs), 1983; 866.
14. *Zhong Yao Xue* (Chinese Herbology), 1989; 535:539.
15. *Shen Jing Jing Shen Ji Bing Za Zhi* (Journal of Psychiatric Disorders), 1981; 4:222.
16. *Shan Xi Yi Yao Za Zhi* (Shanxi Journal of Medicine and Herbology), 1983; 5:297.
17. *Xin Zhang Xue Guan Ji Bing* (Cardiovascular Diseases), 1976; 4(4):265.
18. *Zhong Xi Yi Jie He Za Zhi* (Journal of Integrated Chinese and Western Medicine), 1986; 9:561.
19. *Xin Yi Yao Xue Za Zhi* (New Journal of Medicine and Herbology), 1977; 1:15.
20. *Zhong Xi Yi Jie He Za Zhi* (Journal of Integrated Chinese and Western Medicine), 1986; 6(4):234.
21. *Zhong Yi Yan Jiu Yuan* (Research Hospital of Chinese Medicine), 1976; 4(4):261.
22. *Zhong Yao Tong Bao* (Journal of Chinese Herbology), 1980; 4:192.
23. *Hu Nan Yi Yao Za Zhi* (Hunan Journal of Medicine and Herbology), 1982; 9:(3):6.
24. *Zhe Jiang Zhong Yi Za Zhi* (Zhejiang Journal of Chinese Medicine), 1997; 10:445.
25. *Zhe Jiang Zhong Yi Xue Yuan Xue Bao* (Journal of Zhejiang University of Chinese Medicine), 1992; 16(3):19.
26. *Zhong Guo Zhong Xi Yi Jie He Za Zhi* (Chinese Journal of Integrative Chinese and Western Medicine), 1995; 15(7):438.
27. *Guang Xi Zhong Yi Yao* (Guangxi Chinese Medicine and Herbology), 1996; 5:22.
28. *Shan Xi Zhong Yi* (Shanxi Chinese Medicine), 1993; 14(5):222.
29. *Hu Nan Zhong Yi Za Zhi* (Hunan Journal of Chinese Medicine), 1993; 9(1):41.
30. *Zhong Xi Yi Jie He Za Zhi* (Journal of Integrated Chinese and Western Medicine), 1988; 8(10):601.
31. *Jiang Su Zhong Yi* (Jiangsu Chinese Medicine), 1997; 8:21.
32. *Xin Yi Yao Xue Za Zhi* (New Journal of Medicine and Herbology), 1978; 9:44.
33. *Bei Jing Zhong Yi* (Beijing Chinese Medicine), 1987; 4:24
34. *Jiang Xi Zhong Yi Yao* (Jiangxi Chinese Medicine and Herbology), 1988; 2:28
35. *Si Chuan Zhong Yi* (Sichuan Chinese Medicine), 1998; 1:36.
36. *Shan Xi Zhong Yi* (Shanxi Chinese Medicine), 1991; 7(5):16.
37. *Xin Zhong Yi* (New Chinese Medicine), 1976; 4:35.
38. *Hu Nan Yi Yao Za Zhi* (Hunan Journal of Medicine and Herbology), 1983; 3:52.
39. *He Nan Zhong Yi* (Henan Chinese Medicine), 1985; 3:29.
40. Yang CC. Chen JC. Chen GW. Chen YS. Chung JG. Effects of Shao-Fu-Zhu-Yu-Tang on motility of human sperm. American Journal of Chinese Medicine. 2003; 31(4):573-9.
41. *Zhong Xi Yi Jie He Za Zhi* (Journal of Integrated Chinese and Western Medicine), 1988; 10:639.
42. *Xin Zhong Yi* (New Chinese Medicine), 1995; 8:40.
43. *Zhe Jiang Zhong Yi Za Zhi* (Zhejiang Journal of Chinese Medicine), 1964; 11:17.
44. *Bei Jing Zhong Yi* (Beijing Chinese Medicine), 1987; 5:34.
45. *Hu Bei Zhong Yi Za Zhi* (Hubei Journal of Chinese Medicine), 1993; 15(3):23.

Cordyceps 3™

CLINICAL APPLICATIONS

- **Kidney disorders:** nephritis, glomerulonephritis, nephropathy, diabetic nephropathy, diabetic microalbuminuria, proteinuria, and compromised kidney functions
- **Sexual and reproductive disorders:** low sperm count, poor sperm motility, insufficient sex hormones
- **Metabolic disorders:** fatigue, dyslipidemia and hyperglycemia
- **Respiratory disorders:** asthma, tracheitis, prevention of infection
- **Immune disorders:** chronic, compromised and/or low immunity

WESTERN THERAPEUTIC ACTIONS

- Improves kidney and ear functions
- Increases sperm count and sperm motility
- Enhances energy and increases the basal metabolism
- Prevents and treats elevated cholesterol levels
- Prevents and treats respiratory disorders
- Stimulates the immune system

CHINESE THERAPEUTIC ACTIONS

- Tonifies Kidney yang and augments Kidney *jing* (essence)
- Tonifies Lung, stops bleeding and dissolves phlegm
- Tonifies qi

DOSAGE

Take 3 to 4 capsules three times daily on an empty stomach with warm water. ***Cordyceps 3*** is safe for long-term use.

INGREDIENTS

Dong Chong Xia Cao (Cordyceps)
Huang Qi (Radix Astragali)
Ren Shen (Radix et Rhizoma Ginseng)

BACKGROUND

Cordyceps 3 is an herbal formula that tonifies the Lung, the Spleen, and the Kidney. In traditional Chinese medicine, Lung imbalance corresponds to respiratory and immune disorders in Western medicine; Spleen imbalance refers to metabolic disorders; and Kidney imbalance is often related to renal disorders as well as sexual and reproductive disorders.

FORMULA EXPLANATION

Dong Chong Xia Cao (Cordyceps), *Huang Qi* (Radix Astragali) and *Ren Shen* (Radix et Rhizoma Ginseng) are three of the most precious herbs in Chinese herbal medicine. The combination of these three herbs has a wide spectrum of beneficial effects, including but not limited to increasing energy, strengthening the overall constitution of the body, and improving overall well-being. Clinically, these herbs are commonly used to treat deficiencies of the Lung, Spleen and/or Kidney.

Dong Chong Xia Cao (Cordyceps) has a remarkable effect to tonify both the Lung and the Kidney, and to treat chronic deficiency of both organs. *Dong Chong Xia Cao* (Cordyceps) tonifies the Kidney to treat impotence, spermatorrhea, frequent urination, nocturnal emission, premature ejaculation, tinnitus, forgetfulness, and early signs of aging. Furthermore, it tonifies the Lung to treat chronic respiratory disorders, such as chronic cough and frequent respiratory infections. *Huang Qi* (Radix Astragali) tonifies the qi to improve energy levels, strengthens the Lung to prevent and treat infections, and enhances the immune system to fight against cancer. It is one of the most potent and effective herbs for patients with generalized weakness and deficiencies. *Ren Shen* (Radix et Rhizoma Ginseng) is one of the oldest and most recognized herbs in Chinese herbal medicine. It has a tremendous ability to tonify qi to improve energy, strengthen the Spleen to improve digestion, tonify the Lung to prevent infection, and calm the *shen* (spirit) to improve mental function.

In short, ***Cordyceps 3*** is formulated with three of the best tonic herbs in the Chinese herbal pharmacopoeia. The tonic effect is gentle and potent, allowing the herbs to be taken safely for a long period of time. ***Cordyceps 3*** has a wide range of therapeutic effects and can be used on a long-term basis. Lastly, it is also an antiaging tonic to ensure optimal health.

CAUTIONS & CONTRAINDICATIONS

- This formula should be used with caution with the following conditions: in the presence of an exterior pathogen, excess internal heat or dampness, and with infectious or inflammatory diseases.
- Some patients may notice headache and irritability after taking ***Cordyceps 3*** because of its warm and tonic properties. If that is the case, reduce the dosage to 1 to 2 capsules three times daily.

CLINICAL NOTES

- ***Cordyceps 3*** is most effective when used on a long-term basis for prevention of various cardiovascular, reproductive, and respiratory disorders. Furthermore, it is one of the best herbal formulas to stimulate the immune system to fight against cancer. It should be taken continuously for at least 4 to 6 months for maximum effectiveness.
- ***Cordyceps 3*** is excellent for treating many disorders, such as cardiovascular, reproductive, and respiratory diseases. However, though it is useful if taken individually, results can be enhanced by combining it with other appropriate formulas as listed in Supplementary Formulas.

Pulse Diagnosis by Dr. Jimmy Wei-Yen Chang:

- Tent pulse, a convex-shaped pulse that collapses under pressure on the right *cun*.

SUPPLEMENTARY FORMULAS

- To tonify the yin, yang, qi and blood of the body, combine with ***Imperial Tonic***.
- For patients with cancer undergoing chemotherapy or radiation, add ***C/R Support***.

Cordyceps 3™

- For patients with cancer who are unable to receive chemotherapy or radiation due to generalized weakness or deficiency, combine with ***CA Support***.
- Kidney disorders (proteinuria, nephritis, glomerulonephritis, nephropathy, diabetic nephropathy, diabetic microalbuminuria, and compromised kidney functions), add ***Kidney DTX***.
- For Kidney yin deficiency, add ***Kidney Tonic (Yin)***.
- For Kidney yang deficiency, add ***Kidney Tonic (Yang)***.
- For dry, brittle, or gray hair, add ***Polygonum 14***.
- To enhance the immune system, add ***Immune +***.
- For chronic cough or asthma arising from Kidney and Lung yin deficiencies, add ***Respitrol (Deficient)***.
- For cough with unknown etiology, add ***Respitrol (CF)***.
- For tinnitus, add ***Nourish***.
- For patients who are "burned out" with adrenal insufficiency, add ***Adrenal +***.
- For impotence and reproductive disorders in men, add ***Vitality***.
- For lack of libido in women, add ***Vitality***.
- For male infertility, low sperm count, poor sperm quality, add ***Vital Essence***.
- For female infertility, add ***Blossom (Phases 1-4)***.
- For thirst or dryness, add ***Nourish (Fluids)***.
- For anemia, add ***Schisandra ZZZ***.

ACUPUNCTURE TREATMENT

Traditional Points:

- *Shenshu* (BL 23), *Feishu* (BL 13)

Classic Master Tung's Points:

- **Nephritis (chronic):** *Tianhuangfu [Shenguan]* (T 77.18), *Dihuang* (T 77.19), *Renhuang* (T 77.21), *Huoying* (T 66.03), *Tongshen* (T 88.09), *Houzhui* (T 44.02), *Shouying* (T 44.03), *Shuixiang* (T 66.14), *Shuixian* (T 66.15), *Tongwei* (T 88.10), *Tongbei* (T 88.11)
- **Pyelonephritis:** *Shuijin* (T 1010.20), *Shuitong* (T 1010.19), *Wanshunyi* (T 22.08), *Wanshuner* (T 22.09), *Tongshen* (T 88.09), *Tongguan* (T 88.01), *Houzhui* (T 44.02), *Shouying* (T 44.03)
- **Proteinuria:** *Tongshen* (T 88.09), *Tongwei* (T 88.10), *Tianhuang* (T 77.17), *Dihuang* (T 77.19), *Renhuang* (T 77.21), *Shuijin* (T 1010.20), *Shuitong* (T 1010.19), *Shuixiang* (T 66.14), *Shuixian* (T 66.15), *Tongbei* (T 88.11)
- **Spermatorrhea:** *Tianhuang* (T 77.17), *Dihuang* (T 77.19), *Renhuang* (T 77.21), *Tongshen* (T 88.09), *Tongwei* (T 88.10), *Shuijin* (T 1010.20), *Shuitong* (T 1010.19), *Tianhuangfu [Shenguan]* (T 77.18). Moxa *Guanyuan* (CV 4), *Zhongji* (CV 3), *Zhongshu* (GV 7)
- **Impotence:** *Tianhuang* (T 77.17), *Dihuang* (T 77.19), *Renhuang* (T 77.21), *Tianhuang* (T 88.13), *Minghuang* (T 88.12), *Qihuang* (T 88.14), *Tongshen* (T 88.09), *Tongwei* (T 88.10), *Sanshen* (T 44.27)*. Bleed tender points on the Kidney area of the back from L1-L5 with cupping. Bleed before needling for best result. Moxa the Kidney area on the back from L1-L5, *Guanyuan* (CV 4), *Zhongji* (CV 3)
- **Fatigue:** *Tianhuang* (T 77.17), *Dihuang* (T 77.19), *Renhuang* (T 77.21), *Minghuang* (T 88.12), *Tianhuang* (T 88.13), *Qihuang* (T 88.14), *Beimian* (T 44.07), *Sanyan* (T 11.21), *Zhitong* (T 44.13)

Ear Acupuncture:

- Nose, Spleen, Bone Marrow

Auricular Medicine by Dr. Li-Chun Huang:

- **Asthma:** Bronchus, Stop Asthma, Sympathetic, Adrenal Gland, Allergic Area, Chest, Endocrine, Coronary Vascular Subcortex. Bleed Ear Apex.
- **Improving fatigue:** Sympathetic, Kidney, Liver, Spleen, *San Jiao*, Anxious, Nervous Subcortex, Speed Recovered
- **Promoting immunity:** Allergic Area, Endocrine, Adrenal Gland, Spleen, Liver. Bleed Ear Apex and Helix 1-6.
- **Preventing common cold:** Spleen, Lung, Endocrine, Allergic Area, Adrenal Gland. Bleed Ear Apex.
- **Impaired hearing:** Internal Ear, External Ear, *San Jiao*, Vision I, Kidney, Gallbladder, Sympathetic, External Sympathetic, Cardiovascular Subcortex, Temple (Auditory Center), Speed Hearing (Elbow)
- **Tinnitus:** Internal Ear, Temple (Auditory Center), *San Jiao*

NUTRITION

- Include more nuts and seeds like walnuts and pine nuts in the diet.

LIFESTYLE INSTRUCTIONS

- Sleep by 10:00 p.m. In TCM, 11:00 p.m. to 1:00 a.m. is when the yin shifts to yang. It is crucial for the body to be at rest during this time for optimal health.
- Since there is such a wide range of therapeutic benefits associated with this formula, please refer to other related formulas for detailed descriptions of nutrition and lifestyle instructions pertinent to the specific imbalance being addressed.

CASE STUDIES

- J.L., a 36-year-old male, presented with fatigue due to working long hours at work. Additional symptoms included cold sensation and low sperm mobility. This condition was diagnosed as Lung and Kidney yin deficiencies and was treated with ***Cordyceps 3***. The patient has been taking the herbs for six months and has noticed improved energy and less fatigue. He is continuing to take them to improve his sperm mobility. Submitted by L.M., Portland, Oregon.
- S.W, a 61-year-old female, presented with fatigue, weak sensation of the lungs, sighing, and sweating easily at times. In addition, she was also experiencing some low back pain and frequent colds with immune system disorders. The Western diagnosis was chronic fatigue syndrome; the TCM diagnosis was Lung and Kidney qi deficiencies. This condition was treated with

Cordyceps 3™

Cordyceps 3 and *Ba Wei Di Huang Wan* (Eight-Ingredient Pill with Rehmannia). After taking the herbs she noticed the duration of the fatigue was shorter each day, her sleep had improved, lungs felt great with breathing and she felt stronger emotionally. The patient continued taking the herbs for three months. Submitted by L.M., Portland, Oregon.

☯ D.D., a 72-year-old male, presented with shortness of breath and cough with frothy, clear white sputum. It was noted that this patient was diabetic, post-stroke, with a heart function of 77%, and creatinine level of 1.8 mg/dL. Objective findings included left leg hot to the touch, right leg cold to the touch, and difficulty with inhaling. He had recently taken two rounds of antibiotics. The practitioner diagnosed this condition as Kidney not grasping the qi, Lung and Spleen qi deficiencies with phlegm accumulation; his Western diagnosis was COPD. For treatment he was given a combination of ***Cordyceps 3***, ***Respitrol (Deficient)***, ***Circulation (SJ)*** and ***Neuro Plus***, just one bottle at a time. The patient gradually improved, getting stronger each week and continued taking the herbs for about three months. Submitted by T.W., Perrysburg, Ohio.

PHARMACOLOGICAL AND CLINICAL RESEARCH

Cordyceps 3 has a wide spectrum of therapeutic effects and clinical applications. Historically, the herbs in this formula have been used to treat disorders of the Kidney (renal, sexual and reproductive disorders), Spleen (metabolic disorders) and Lung (respiratory and immune disorders). More recently, it has been used to support cancer patients with great results.

Cordyceps 3 contains herbs to tonify the Kidney and restore renal functions. In one study, daily ingestion of *Dong Chong Xia Cao* (Cordyceps) for 30 days effectively reduced protein in the urine from 4.3g to 1.32g in 18 patients with nephritis and proteinuria.[1] In another study, 117 patients with compromised kidney function were treated with *Dong Chong Xia Cao* (Cordyceps) three times daily with good results.[2] Furthermore, 23 patients with tinnitus were treated with *Dong Chong Xia Cao* (Cordyceps) three times daily for four weeks with significant improvement.[3] Besides *Dong Chong Xia Cao* (Cordyceps), *Huang Qi* (Radix Astragali) is also regarded as one of the most effective herbs for the treatment of kidney-related disorders, such as proteinuria, nephritis, and glomerulonephritis. The clinical benefits of *Huang Qi* (Radix Astragali) in treating kidney disorders include decreased amount of protein in the urine, increased volume of urine, and decreased excretion of chloride and ammonia.[4] According to clinical studies, use of *Huang Qi* (Radix Astragali) is associated with beneficial actions against nephropathy and glomerulonephritis.[5] In one clinical trial, 20 patients with nephritis were treated with *Huang Qi* (Radix Astragali) decoction for 15 to 90 days with improvements noted in 16 patients.[6] In another study, 56 patients with chronic glomerulonephritis were treated with intramuscular injections of *Huang Qi* (Radix Astragali) for one month with marked reduction of protein in the urine (effective rate of 61.7%) and an improvement of kidney functions.[7] *Huang Qi* (Radix Astragali) also shows a marked effect to ameliorate the pathological changes of early diabetic nephropathy by reducing fasting blood glucose and albuminuria levels, and reversing the glomerular hyperfiltration state.[8] Diabetic microalbuminuria in type II diabetes can also be effectively treated with *Huang Qi* (Radix Astragali) and *Chuan Xiong* (Rhizoma Chuanxiong). The mechanism of action may relate with the therapeutic effects of herbs on anti-inflammation, antioxidation and alleviation of the hypo-fibrinolytic/pro-thrombotic state.[9]

Cordyceps 3 also tonifies the Kidney to treat sexual and reproductive disorders. Pharmacologically, it has been shown that the use of *Dong Chong Xia Cao* (Cordyceps) is associated with an increase in sperm count and sperm motility.[10] In one clinical study, 197 patients with sexual disorders were treated with *Dong Chong Xia Cao* (Cordyceps) three times daily for 40 days, with an effective rate of 64.15%.[11] In addition, the use of *Ren Shen* (Radix et Rhizoma Ginseng) is associated with stimulation of the pituitary gland to increase the secretion of gonadotropin. According to laboratory studies, it increases the production of sperm in males, and it lengthens the estrus period in females.[12] Furthermore, *Ren Shen* (Radix et Rhizoma Ginseng) is also effective in the treatment of sexual dysfunction. According to one clinical study, 24 patients with low sperm count were treated with a preparation of *Ren Shen* (Radix et Rhizoma Ginseng). An increase in sperm count was noted in 70% of patients, and an increase in sperm motility in 67% of the patients.[13]

Cordyceps 3 has a strong tonic effect on the Spleen to treat metabolic disorders. Increased energy, elevated metabolism, and improved general well-being are three of the most immediate and recognizable benefits of this formula. *Huang Qi* (Radix Astragali) and *Ren Shen* (Radix et Rhizoma Ginseng) have direct effects to increase energy and elevate metabolism. *Huang Qi* (Radix Astragali) is an excellent tonic that raises the energy level by increasing the basal metabolic rate and cAMP.[14] *Ren Shen* (Radix et Rhizoma Ginseng) awakens the central nervous system which improves both mental and physical performances.[15,16] It has been demonstrated in one laboratory study that the administration of *Ren Shen* (Radix et Rhizoma Ginseng) is associated with a marked effect in improving memory and learning abilities.[17] Furthermore, *Ren Shen* (Radix et Rhizoma Ginseng) has a marked influence on the endocrine system to balance many hormones in the body. It stimulates the pituitary gland to increase the secretion of adrenocorticotropic hormone (ACTH), which in turn stimulates the adrenal glands and their activities.[18] In another study, use of *Ren Shen* (Radix et Rhizoma Ginseng) has been associated with an increase in adrenal cortical hormone (ACH) and ACTH, and subsequently better physical performance.[19] Lastly, *Dong Chong Xia Cao* (Cordyceps) has been shown to stimulate the secretion of adrenal gland hormones.[20] Together, these herbs help the body to achieve a healthy balance of its endocrine system.

Cordyceps 3™

Cordyceps 3 contains herbs to treat metabolic disorders, such as dyslipidemia and hyperglycemia. *Dong Chong Xia Cao* (Cordyceps) is effective in the treatment of hyperlipidemia.[21] In one clinical study, 273 patients with hyperlipidemia were treated with 1 gram of *Dong Chong Xia Cao* (Cordyceps) three times daily, and showed a marked decrease of LDL and triglycerides and increase of HDL.[22] Another study of 204 patients reported that *Dong Chong Xia Cao* (Cordyceps) is effective in lowering LDL.[23] Similarly, *Ren Shen* (Radix et Rhizoma Ginseng) is effective in treating atherosclerosis and hypercholesterolemia. In one study, use of a *Ren Shen* (Radix et Rhizoma Ginseng) preparation twice daily was beneficial in patients with hypertension, atherosclerosis, and chest pain. Furthermore, *Ren Shen* (Radix et Rhizoma Ginseng) has also been found to have a moderate effect in lowering blood cholesterol levels, with a significant influence to lower triglycerides.[24] *Huang Qi* (Radix Astragali) has been shown to effectively lower blood glucose levels and increase blood insulin levels in subjects with streptozotocin-induced diabetes. The antihyperglycemic action appeared to be due to increased release of insulin.[25] *Ren Shen* (Radix et Rhizoma Ginseng) is also effective in lowering blood glucose in subjects with hyperglycemia.[26] Ginsenoside Rc, an active component of *Ren Shen* (Radix et Rhizoma Ginseng), significantly enhances glucose uptake by inducing ROS generation, which leads to AMPK and p38 MAPK activation.[27]

Finally, ***Cordyceps 3*** contains herbs to tonify the Lung and treat various respiratory disorders. Pharmacologically, *Dong Chong Xia Cao* (Cordyceps) has demonstrated bronchodilating and antibiotic effects.[28,29] *Dong Chong Xia Cao* (Cordyceps) is beneficial for the treatment of asthma. The mechanism of action is attributed to the regulation of bronchoalveolar lavage fluids cell function by the immunomodulatory agents from the herb.[30] In one clinical trial, 656 patients with chronic respiratory tract disorders were treated with *Dong Chong Xia Cao* (Cordyceps) three times daily for 40 days with good success.[31] In another study, 43 patients with allergic rhinitis were treated with 6 grams of *Dong Chong Xia Cao* (Cordyceps) three times daily for four weeks with 93% effective rate.[32] In addition, one study reported an 84.4% rate of effectiveness using *Dong Chong Xia Cao* to treat 109 patients with chronic tracheitis.[33] Furthermore, the use of *Huang Qi* (Radix Astragali) was found through numerous clinical trials to be effective in prevention of respiratory tract disorders. In one study, the use of *Huang Qi* (Radix Astragali) was associated with a decreased risk of infection as well as shortened duration of infection.[34] In another study, daily use of *Huang Qi* (Radix Astragali) showed a 94% effectiveness in prevention of respiratory tract infections in 100 children.[35] Lastly, in a clinical trial of 41 patients with asthma, injection of *Huang Qi* (Radix Astragali) daily for three months showed significant improvement in 85.4% of patients.[36]

Most importantly, *Dong Chong Xia Cao* (Cordyceps) is one of the few herbs that have demonstrated an exceptional stimulant effect on the immune system to fight cancer. *Dong Chong Xia Cao* (Cordyceps) has a direct cytotoxic effect. It has a significant and dose-dependent inhibitory effect on the proliferation of many cancer cell lines: breast cancer, melanoma, human premyelocytic leukemia, human hepatocellular carcinoma, leukemia, and human oral squamous cancer cells.[37,38,39] *Dong Chong Xia Cao* (Cordyceps) also enhances the immune system by stimulating and increasing the phagocytic activities of macrophages against foreign substances.[40] This effect is further potentiated with the addition of *Huang Qi* (Radix Astragali) and *Ren Shen* (Radix et Rhizoma Ginseng). *Huang Qi* (Radix Astragali) is extremely effective in enhancing the immune system and reversing immune deficiency.[41,42,43] In patients with leukopenia, administration of *Huang Qi* (Radix Astragali) was associated with an obvious rise of white blood cell count in 115 patients.[44] *Ren Shen* (Radix et Rhizoma Ginseng) also has an immune-enhancing effect for increasing the function of the reticuloendothelial system and the total IgM count.[45] In one clinical study, 52 cancer patients who have leukopenia caused by chemotherapy were able to continue and complete the entire course of chemotherapy treatment with the intake of *Ren Shen* (Radix et Rhizoma Ginseng) to prevent bone marrow suppression.[46]

In summary, ***Cordyceps 3*** is a diversified formula that can be used for treatment and prevention of numerous conditions. It is also one of the best general tonic formulas to take on a long-term basis to ensure health and well-being.

COMPARATIVE ANALYSIS

One striking difference between Western and traditional Chinese medicine is that Western medicine focuses and excels in crisis management, while traditional Chinese medicine emphasizes and shines in holistic and preventative treatments. Therefore, in emergencies, such as gunshot wounds or surgery, Western medicine is generally the treatment of choice. However, for treatment of chronic idiopathic illness of unknown origins, where all lab tests are normal and a clear diagnosis cannot be made, traditional Chinese medicine is distinctly superior.

Cordyceps 3 is an herbal tonic that has a broad spectrum of therapeutic effects. It may be used as maintenance and preventive treatment for various conditions, including but not limited to chronic immune deficiency, chronic fatigue syndrome, and sexual and/or reproductive dysfunctions. For many of these conditions, traditional Chinese medicine is superior to Western medicine, as there are limited drug options available.

References

1. *Zhong Yao Lin Chuan Xin Yong* (New Clinical Applications of Chinese Medicine), 2001; 196-197.
2. *Shang Hai Zhong Yi Yao Za Zhi* (Shanghai Journal of Chinese Medicine and Herbology), 1986; 8:29.
3. *Fu Jian Yi Yao Za Zhi* (Fujian Journal of Medicine and Herbology), 1985; 6:42.
4. *Jiang Su Yi Xue* (Jiangsu Medical Journal), 1989; 15(1):12.
5. *Jiang Su Yi Xue* (Jiangsu Medical Journal), 1989; 15(1):12.

Cordyceps 3™

6. *Hei Long Jiang Zhong Yi Yao* (Heilongjiang Chinese Medicine and Herbology), 1982; 1:39.
7. *Zhong Xi Yi Jie He Za Zhi* (Journal of Integrated Chinese and Western Medicine), 1987; 7:403.
8. Zhang J, Xie X, Li C, Fu P. Systematic review of the renal protective effect of Astragalus membranaceus (root) on diabetic nephropathy in animal models. Department of Nephrology, West China Hospital of Sichuan University, Chengdu 610041, China. J Ethnopharmacol. 2009 Nov 12;126(2):189-96.
9. Lu ZM, Yu YR, Tang H, Zhang XX. The protective effects of Radix Astragali and Rhizoma Ligustici chuanxiong on endothelial dysfunction in type 2 diabetic patients with microalbuminuria. Sichuan Da Xue Xue Bao Yi Xue Ban. 2005 Jul;36(4):529-32.
10. *Zhong Yao Xue* (Chinese Herbology), 1998; 785:788.
11. *Jiang Su Zhong Yi Yao* (Jiangsu Medicine and Herbology), 1985; 5:46.
12. *Zhong Cheng Yao* (Study of Chinese Patent Medicine), 1989; 11(9):30.
13. *Ji Lin Yi Xue* (Jilin Medicine), 1983; 5:54.
14. *Zhong Yao Yao Li Yu Lin Chuang* (Pharmacology and Clinical Applications of Chinese Herbs), 1985:193.
15. *Zhong Yao Yao Li Yu Ying Yong* (Pharmacology and Applications of Chinese Herbs), 1983; 16.
16. *Zhong Hua Yi Xue Za Zhi* (Chinese Journal of Medicine), 1985; 42(12):13.
17. *Zhong Yao Ci Hai* (Encyclopedia of Chinese Herbs), 1994.
18. *Bai Qiu En Yi Ke Da Xue Xue Bao* (Journal of Baiqiuen University of Medicine), 1980; 6(2):32.
19. *Planta Med*, 1979; 30:43.
20. *Zhong Xi Yi Jie He Za Zhi* (Journal of Integrated Chinese and Western Medicine), 1990; 10(9):570.
21. *Zhong Yao Xue* (Chinese Herbology), 1998; 785:788.
22. *Zhong Xi Yi Jie He Za Zhi* (Journal of Integrated Chinese and Western Medicine), 1985; 11:652.
23. *Qing Hai Yi Yao Za Zhi* (Qinghai Journal of Medicine and Herbology), 1986; 3:22.
24. *Ji Lin Yi Xue* (Jilin Medicine), 1983; 5:54.
25. Ma W, Nomura M, Takahashi-Nishioka T, Kobayashi S. Combined effects of fangchinoline from Stephania tetrandra Radix and formononetin and calycosin from Astragalus membranaceus Radix on hyperglycemia and hypoinsulinemia in streptozotocin-diabetic mice. Biol Pharm Bull. 2007 Nov;30(11):2079-83.
26. *Zhong Yao Xue* (Chinese Herbology), 1998; 729:736.
27. Lee MS, Hwang JT, Kim SH, Yoon S, Kim MS, Yang HJ, Kwon DY. Ginsenoside Rc, an active component of Panax ginseng, stimulates glucose uptake in C2C12 myotubes through an AMPK-dependent mechanism. Biogeron Research Center, Korea Food Research Institute, Bundang-ku, Songnam, Republic of Korea. J Ethnopharmacol. 2010 Feb 17;127(3):771-6.
28. *Fu Jian Yi Yao Za Zhi* (Fujian Journal of Medicine and Herbology), 1983; 5:311.
29. *Ren Min Wei Sheng Chu Ban She* (Journal of People's Public Health), 1983; 358.
30. Kuo YC, Tsai WJ, Wang JY, Chang SC, Lin CY, Shiao MS. Regulation of bronchoalveolar lavage fluids cell function by the immunomodulatory agents from Cordyceps sinensis. Life Sci. 2001 Jan 19;68(9):1067-82.
31. *Zhong Cao Yao* (Chinese Herbal Medicine), 1987; 10:8.
32. *Zhong Xi Yi Jie He Za Zhi* (Journal of Integrated Chinese and Western Medicine), 1987; 1:43.
33. *Zhong Yao Lin Chuan Xin Yong* (New Clinical Applications of Chinese Medicine), 2001; 197.
34. *Zhong Yi Za Zhi* (Journal of Chinese Medicine), 1980; 1:71.
35. *Jiang Su Zhong Yi* (Jiangsu Chinese Medicine), 1988; 9:32.
36. *Zhong Hua Er Ke Za Zhi* (Chinese Journal of Pediatrics), 1978; 2:87.
37. Wu JY, Zhang QX, Leung PH. Inhibitory effects of ethyl acetate extract of Cordyceps sinensis mycelium on various cancer cells in culture and B16 melanoma in C57BL/6 mice. Phytomedicine. 2007 Jan;14(1):43-9.
38. Lui JC, Wong JW, Suen YK, Kwok TT, Fung KP, Kong SK. Cordycepin induced eryptosis in mouse erythrocytes through a Ca2+-dependent pathway without caspase-3 activation. Arch Toxicol. 2007 Dec;81(12):859-65.
39. Wu WC, Hsiao JR, Lian YY, Lin CY, Huang BM. The apoptotic effect of cordycepin on human OEC-M1 oral cancer cell line. Cancer Chemother Pharmacol. 2007 Jun;60(1):103-11.
40. *Shang Hai Zhong Yi Za Zhi* (Shanghai Journal of Chinese Medicine), 1988; 1:48.
41. *Biol Pharm Bull*, 1977; 20(11)-1178-82.
42. *Yun Nan Zhong Yi Za Zhi* (Yunan Journal of Chinese Medicine), 1980; 2:28.
43. *Journal of Clinical and Laboratory Immunology*, 1988 Mar.; 25(3):125-9.
44. *Zhong Guo Zhong Xi Yi Jie He Za Zhi* (Chinese Journal of Integrative Chinese and Western Medicine), 1995 Aug.; 15(8):462-4.
45. *Zhong Yao Xue* (Chinese Herbology), 1998; 729:736.
46. *Te Chan Ke Xue Shi Yan* (Research of Special Scientific Projects), 1984; 4:24.

Corydalin (AC)™

CLINICAL APPLICATIONS

- **Acute headache:**
  - Various kinds of acute headaches (according to Western medicine): sinus, vascular, stress, supraorbital, orbital, tension, menstrual-related or migraine headaches
  - Various types of acute headaches (according to traditional Chinese medicine): vertex, occipital, frontal, wind-cold, wind-heat, damp-phlegm, *jueyin*, Liver yang rising and blood stagnation headaches

WESTERN THERAPEUTIC ACTIONS

- Analgesic effect to relieve pain
- Anti-inflammatory effect to reduce swelling and pain
- Muscle-relaxant effect to relieve stiffness, spasms and cramps
- Improves peripheral and micro-circulation to relieve headache and prevent cerebral ischemia

CHINESE THERAPEUTIC ACTIONS

- Relieves pain
- Invigorates qi and blood circulation
- Removes qi and blood stagnation

DOSAGE

Take 3 to 4 capsules three times daily on an empty stomach. The dosage may be increased up to 6 to 8 capsules every four to six hours as needed for severe pain.

INGREDIENTS

Bai Zhi (Radix Angelicae Dahuricae)
Chuan Xiong (Rhizoma Chuanxiong)
Dan Shen (Radix et Rhizoma Salviae Miltiorrhizae)
Ge Gen (Radix Puerariae Lobatae)
Yan Hu Suo (Rhizoma Corydalis)

BACKGROUND

Headache is pain in any part of the head, including the scalp, face, and interior of the head. Causes of headache vary, including hypertension, stress, anxiety, injuries, infection, glaucoma, hematoma, tumor, and others. Proper diagnosis requires careful review of medical history and physical exam. Optimal treatment combines elimination of cause and relief of pain.

FORMULA EXPLANATION

Corydalin (AC) is an empirical formula designed to relieve a variety of headaches. ***Corydalin (AC)*** contains herbs which activate qi and blood circulation, remove qi and blood stagnation, and relieve pain.

Yan Hu Suo (Rhizoma Corydalis) is the principle herb in this formula and is used to activate qi and blood circulation, remove blood stasis, and relieve pain. *Bai Zhi* (Radix Angelicae Dahuricae) is used as a channel-guiding herb, which leads the effectiveness of the formula to the head. In addition, *Bai Zhi* (Radix Angelicae Dahuricae) has a strong effect to dispel wind and other exterior pathogenic factors. *Chuan Xiong* (Rhizoma Chuanxiong) and *Dan Shen* (Radix et Rhizoma Salviae Miltiorrhizae) activate blood circulation in the peripheral parts of the body and remove stasis. *Ge Gen* (Radix Puerariae Lobatae) relieves pain in the upper body and dispels wind-cold or wind-heat from the exterior parts of the body.

CAUTIONS & CONTRAINDICATIONS

- This formula is contraindicated during pregnancy and nursing.
- Patients with persistent pain not relieved by ***Corydalin (AC)*** should seek further examination to rule out structural or functional abnormalities.
- Should other prominent signs of diminishing eyesight and vomiting occur in addition to the headache, refer the patient to a medical doctor immediately for a CT scan or MRI to rule out intra-cranial pressure due to tumor, aneurysms, or cerebral stenosis.
- ***Corydalin (AC)*** is designed for short-term management of acute pain, not for long-term treatment of chronic pain. Therefore, once the acute pain has subsided, ***Corydalin (AC)*** should be discontinued and another maintenance formula should be initiated.
- This herbal formula contains herbs that invigorate blood circulation, such as *Dan Shen* (Radix et Rhizoma Salviae Miltiorrhizae). Therefore, patients who are on anticoagulant or antiplatelet therapies, such as Coumadin (warfarin), should use this formula with caution, or not at all, as there may be a higher risk of bleeding and bruising.[1]

CLINICAL NOTES

- ***Corydalin (AC)*** contains herbs that exert analgesic function directly on the central nervous system. ***Corydalin (AC)*** works synergistically with acupuncture to provide pain relief for various aches and pain.
- ***Corydalin (AC)*** is best for acute headaches with severe pain, and is most effective for symptomatic relief. ***Corydalin (CR)*** is most effective when taken on a long-term basis to control and prevent the recurrence of headaches.
- In addition to treating the acute symptom of pain, efforts should be made to identify the underlying cause of pain. For optimal results, another formula should be prescribed to target the cause while using ***Corydalin (AC)*** to address the symptoms.

Pulse Diagnosis by Dr. Jimmy Wei-Yen Chang:

- **Headache due to wind-heat:** floating and forceful pulse on the right *cun*, and long and forceful pulse on the right *chi*. Temperature above the elbows and the back of the neck will feel hot.
- **Headache due to wind-cold:** floating and tight pulse on the right *cun*, and thready and long pulse on the right *chi*. Temperature above the elbows and the back of the neck will feel cold.
- **Headache due to Liver fire:** forceful and floating pulse on the left *guan*. Temperature of the entire arm will feel hot.

Corydalin (AC)™

- **Headache due to poisoning:** forceful pulse on both *chi* and left *guan* positions.

SUPPLEMENTARY FORMULAS

- For migraine headaches, add ***Corydalin (CR)***.
- For headache caused by recent traumatic or musculoskeletal injury, add ***Flex (TMX)***.
- For severe, long-term headache from previous traumatic injury or blood stagnation, add ***Circulation (SJ)***.
- For headache with excess heat, add ***Gardenia Complex***.
- For headache due to stress and tension, add ***Calm***, ***Calm (ES)***, or ***Calm ZZZ***.
- For headache due to Liver fire, add ***Gentiana Complex***.
- For migraine headache with Liver wind rising, combine with ***Gastrodia Complex***.
- For headache due to wind-heat, add ***Lonicera Complex***.
- For headache due to sinus congestion, add ***Pueraria Clear Sinus*** or ***Magnolia Clear Sinus***.
- For headache with neck and shoulder stiffness, combine with ***Neck & Shoulder (AC)***.
- For headache due to environmental or toxic poisoning, add ***Herbal DTX***.
- For headache due to underlying damp and phlegm with Spleen qi deficiency, add ***Pinellia Complex***.

ACUPUNCTURE TREATMENT

Traditional Points:

- *Hegu* (LI 4). Needle 1 to 1.5 *cun* deep. Massage the affected area on the head.
- *Renzhong* (GV 26), *Lieque* (LU 7), *Taichong* (LR 3), *Xingjian* (LR 2), *Geshu* (BL 17), *Baihui* (GV 20), *Taiyang* (Extra 2), *Yintang* (Extra 1)

Classic Master Tung's Points:

- Needle contralateral to the pain. If the pain is in the center, needle bilaterally or the side with the more *ah shi* points. If the pain is bilateral, needle bilaterally.
- **Headache (general):** *Linggu* (T 22.05), *Dabai* (T 22.04), *Huolian* (T 66.10), *Huoju* (T 66.11), *Huosan* (T 66.12). Bleed dark veins on the dorsal aspect of the feet. Bleed before needling for best result.
- **Headache (occipital):** *Linggu* (T 22.05), *Dabai* (T 22.04), *Fanhoujue* (T 22.12)*, *Zhengjin* (T 77.01), *Zhengzong* (T 77.02), *Wanshunyi* (T 22.08), *Wanshuner* (T 22.09), *Tongbei* (T 88.11), *Huofu* (T 88.41)*, *Huochang* (T 88.43)*, *Huoliang* (T 88.42)*, *Dihuang* (T 77.19), *Boqiu* (T 77.04), *Zhengshi* (T 77.03). Bleed the sacral region or *Weizhong* (BL 40) or dark veins nearby. Bleed before needling for best result.
- **Headache (frontal):** *Linggu* (T 22.05), *Dabai* (T 22.04), *Biyi* (T 1010.22), *Xinling* (T 33.17)*, *Zhongbai* (T 22.06), *Taiyang*, *Huoju* (T 66.11), *Wuhu* (T 11.27), *Zhenjing* (T 1010.08), *Sifuyi* (T 1010.11), *Sifuer* (T 1010.10), *Tongtian* (T 88.03). Bleed *Sihuashang* (T 77.08), *Sihuaxia* (T 77.11), *Sihuazhong* (T 77.09), *Fuchang* (T 77.12), ST channel on the lower limb and dark veins nearby. Bleed before needling for best result.
- **Headache (temporal):** *Linggu* (T 22.05), *Shangbai* (T 22.03), *Zhongbai* (T 22.06), *Xinling* (T 33.17)*, *Cesanli* (T 77.22), *Cexiasanli* (T 77.23), *Shangjiuli* (T 88.26), *Zhongjiuli* (T 88.25), *Xiajiuli* (T 88.27), *Jianzhong* (T 44.06), *Sihuawai* (T 77.14), *Liuwan* (T 66.08), *Menjin* (T 66.05), *Huoying* (T 66.03), *Qihu* (T 77.26), *Waisanguan* (T 77.27), *Yizhong* (T 77.05), *Erzhong* (T 77.06), *Sanzhong* (T 77.07), *Taiyang*, *Waiguan* (TH 5) penetrating through *Neiguan* (PC 6). Bleed any dark veins or tender points nearby the lateral malleolus. Bleed at a 45 degree angle the dark veins nearby the other temporal area. Patient needs to lean downwards, hold his/her breath and exhale to help push blood out. Bleed before needling for best result.
- **Headache (vertex):** *Linggu* (T 22.05), *Dabai* (T 22.04), *Xinling* (T 33.17)*, *Zhenghui* (T 1010.01), *Qianhui* (T 1010.05), *Shuitong* (T 1010.19), *Shuijin* (T 1010.20), *Zhengjin* (T 77.01), *Shenting* (GV 24), *Shangxing* (GV 23), *Huozhu* (T 66.04), *Huolian* (T 66.10), *Huoju* (T 66.11), *Huosan* (T 66.12), *Zhengzong* (T 77.02)
- **Headache (migraine):** *Linggu* (T 22.05), *Dabai* (T 22.04), *Cesanli* (T 77.22), *Yizhong* (T 77.05), *Erzhong* (T 77.06), *Sanzhong* (T 77.07), *Liuwan* (T 66.08), *Zhongjiuli* (T 88.25)
- **Headache (supraorbital):** *Erjiaoming* (T 11.12), *Shangbai* (T 22.03), *Sanchayi* (T 22.15)*, *Huaguyi* (T 55.02), *Shangli* (T 1010.09), *Tianhuangfu [Shenguan]* (T 77.18)
- **Headache (hypertension):** *Linggu* (T 22.05), *Dabai* (T 22.04), *Xinling* (T 33.17)*, *Zhenghui* (T 1010.01), *Qianhui* (T 1010.05), *Shuitong* (T 1010.19), *Shuijin* (T 1010.20), *Sansheng* (T 55.07)*, *Weizhong* (BL 40), *Shenting* (GV 24), *Shangxing* (GV 23), *Huozhu* (T 66.04), *Tongtian* (T 88.03), *Fuding* (T 44.04), *Houzhi* (T 44.05), *Jianfeng* (T 44.31)*, *Tongshan* (T 88.02), *Tongguan* (T 88.01), *Zhitong* (T 44.13). Bleed *Huoshan* (T 33.06), *Huoling* (T 33.05) or dark veins nearby. Bleed before needling for best result.
- **Headache (common cold):** *Linggu* (T 22.05), *Dabai* (T 22.04), *Xinling* (T 33.17)*, *Zhenghui* (T 1010.01), *Qianhui* (T 1010.05), *Shuitong* (T 1010.19), *Shuijin* (T 1010.20), *Sanzhong* (T 77.07), *Sihuashang* (T 77.08), *Sihuazhong* (T 77.09), *Sihuawai* (T 77.14), *Sihuaxia* (T 77.11), *Shenting* (GV 24), *Shangxing* (GV 23), *Huozhu* (T 66.04), *Dizong* (T 44.09)
- **Headache (menstruation):** *Linggu* (T 22.05), *Dabai* (T 22.04), *Xinling* (T 33.17)*, *Zhenghui* (T 1010.01), *Qianhui* (T 1010.05), *Shuitong* (T 1010.19), *Shuijin* (T 1010.20), *Sanzhong* (T 77.07), *Sihuashang* (T 77.08), *Sihuazhong* (T 77.09), *Sihuawai* (T 77.14), *Sihuaxia* (T 77.11), *Shenting* (GV 24), *Shangxing* (GV 23), *Huozhu* (T 66.04), *Dizong* (T 44.09)
- **Headache (injury):** *Zhengjin* (T 77.01), *Zhengzong* (T 77.02) with strong stimulation, *Yizhong* (T 77.05), *Erzhong* (T 77.06), *Sanzhong* (T 77.07), *Zhengshi* (T 77.03). Bleed dark veins nearby the medial malleolus or *Shuijing* (T 66.13). Bleed before needling for best result.

Corydalin (AC)™

Master Tung's Points by Dr. Chuan-Min Wang:

- **Headache**
  - Frontal: *Cesanli* (T 77.22), *Tianhuangfu [shenguan]* (T 77.18)
  - Temporal: *Cesanli* (T 77.22), *Zhongjiuli* (T 88.25)
  - Occipital: *Cesanli* (T 77.22), *Zhengjin* (T 77.01), *Zhengzong* (T 77.02)
  - Vertex: Needle bilaterally *Cesanli* (T 77.22), *Huozhu* (T 66.04).
  - Migraine: *Cesanli* (T 77.22), *Menjin* (T 66.05)
  - Behind the eyes: *Cesanli* (T 77.22), *Tianhuangfu [shenguan]* (T 77.18)

Balance Method by Dr. Richard Tan:

- Left side: *Zhongchong* (PC 9), *Shaochong* (HT 9), *Shaoshang* (LU 11), *Zusanli* (ST 36), *Weizhong* (BL 40), *Yanglingquan* (GB 34)
- Right side: *Hegu* (LI 4), *Houxi* (SI 3), *Zhongzhu* (TH 3), *Fuliu* (KI 7), *Zhongfeng* (LR 4), *Sanyinjiao* (SP 6)
- Left and right sides can be alternated from treatment to treatment.

Ear Acupuncture:

- *Taiyang*, Adrenal Gland, Hypothalamus, Temporal Lobe
- Use metal ear balls. Switch ears every three days. Five sessions equals one treatment course.

Auricular Medicine by Dr. Li-Chun Huang:

- **Frontal headache:** Sympathetic, Forehead, Nervous Subcortex. Bleed Ear Apex.
  - For sinus headaches, add Internal Nose.
- **Temporal headache:** Temple, Sympathetic, External Sympathetic, Nervous Subcortex, Coronary Vascular Subcortex. Bleed Ear Apex.
- **Occipital headache:** Occiput, Lesser Occipital Nerve, Nervous Subcortex. Bleed Ear Apex.
- **Vertex headache:** Vertex, External Sympathetic, Nervous Subcortex. Bleed Ear Apex.

NUTRITION

- Avoid intake of ice drinks or cold food, as they constrict vessels, channels and collaterals.
- Drink plenty of water throughout the day to avoid dehydration.
- Diet is important to control and prevent headaches that are food related.
- Encourage the patient to consume an adequate amount of fruits, vegetables, grains, and raw nuts and seeds.
- Caffeine withdrawal is one of the most common causes of headache. In such cases, gradually decrease and stop the consumption of caffeine-containing foods, such as coffee, tea, soda and energy drinks.
- Avoid foods containing tyramine, which can cause headaches, such as alcohol, chocolate, banana, citrus fruits, avocado, cabbage, and potato. Also, avoid the consumption of cakes, coffee, dairy products (except yogurt), processed or packaged foods, tobacco, or any junk foods.
- Monosodium glutamate (MSG) should be avoided in individuals who are sensitive to it. MSG is generally found in canned soups, TV dinners, some meats, and restaurant foods.

The Tao of Nutrition by Dr. Maoshing Ni and Cathy McNease:

- Make tea from ginger and green onions, boiling for five minutes; drink and try to sweat.
- Steam aching portion of head over mint and cinnamon tea that is cooking, then dry head afterwards, avoiding drafts.
- Drink tea made from chrysanthemum flowers and cassia seeds.
- Make buckwheat meal into a paste and apply to painful area until it sweats.
- Drink green tea.
- Make rice porridge and add garlic and green onions. Eat while hot then get under covers and sweat.
- Avoid spicy food, lack of sleep, alcohol, smoking, excessive stimulation, eye strain, and stress.

LIFESTYLE INSTRUCTIONS

- Avoid allergens as much as possible if the headache is triggered by allergy. Installation of an air purifier will minimize the presence of allergens in the air and reduce the risk of allergy and headache.
- Avoid direct exposure to air conditioning, fans, or wind to the head or neck region.
- Avoid stressful situations and environments whenever possible. Ease the tension with massage, warm baths, and an exercise program.
- Tension headaches can be relieved by gentle massage of the neck and shoulders to relax the muscles. A hot Epsom salts bath is also helpful.
- Headache due to poor circulation will respond to vigorous scalp massage.
- Regular exercise, adequate rest, and normal sleeping habits are essential for optimal health.

CASE STUDIES

- M.M., a 42-year-old female, presented with chronic jaw pain located on the left side of her face. The patient had been experiencing it for ten years and was grinding her teeth at night. Upon palpation, nodules were found around *Jiache* (ST 6), the jaw was visibly misaligned, and it was difficult for the patient to open her mouth. The practitioner diagnosed this condition as Liver qi stagnation, blood stasis, and Liver and Kidney yin deficiencies. Her Western diagnosis was temporomandibular joint disorder (TMJ). ***Corydalin (AC)*** was given at a dosage of two spoonfuls, as needed, for her tension and pain. Administration of the recommended doses produced excellent results. The patient reported a decrease in tension, circulation to the area returned,

FORMULAS

Corydalin (AC)™

and being able to open her mouth easier immediately after drinking the herbs. The combination of doing acupuncture and self-massage also helped the jaw's alignment and caused many of the nodules to disappear. Submitted by M.M., Alameda, California.

- F.R., a 48-year-old female, presented with tension cluster headaches, about five to seven headaches per week. The practitioner diagnosed this condition as qi and blood stagnation, along with Liver blood and yin deficiencies. For treatment, ***Corydalin (CR)*** was prescribed at three capsules three times per day, as well as taking ***Corydalin (AC)***, as needed. Acupuncture treatment was received as well. During the first two weeks of taking the herbs, the patient reported four to six headaches per week. By the 5th week of taking the herbs, the headaches reduced to only one per week. After eight weeks of taking the herbs, she seldom experienced headaches. Submitted by S.L., Yuma, Arizona.
- A 55-year-old female, M.V., presented with acute pounding headaches with no known cause. The practitioner diagnosed this condition as Liver overacting on Spleen. Upon diagnosis, ***Corydalin (AC)*** was prescribed. Within 24 hours of taking the herbs, the onset of the headaches were either delayed or not present. The results were very quick and effective. Later, it was discovered that the headaches were triggered by lack of sleep and by increased consumption of processed food. Submitted by V.G., Virginia Beach, Virginia.
- N.P., a 51-year-old perimenopausal female, presented with hot flashes, joint pain, difficulty sleeping, and headaches that would last 2 to 3 days. Her cycle was currently every 28 days, with heavy bleeding and clots. The patient was also overweight. The TCM diagnosis was qi, blood and yin deficiencies; the Western diagnosis was perimenopausal hormonal headaches. ***Corydalin (AC)*** was prescribed, and she was directed to take it at the first sign of a headache and continue taking it for a few days following. By taking the ***Corydalin (AC)*** as instructed, it prevented her headaches from occurring. Due to its effectiveness, she continues taking the ***Corydalin (AC)*** four days before her menstruation. Submitted by N.V., Muir Beach, California.
- A 43-year-old female nurse presented with severe menstrual cramping and pain, along with nausea and vomiting. She was unable to work because of her illness. Tenderness and pain were felt in the abdominal region with *Zhongfeng* (LR 4) and *Ligou* (LR 5) being the most tender distal points upon palpation. The practitioner diagnosed the condition as qi and blood stagnation in the abdomen and Liver qi stagnation. In addition to the stagnation were damp accumulation with multiple uterine fibroids (7.3 cm in size) and an ovarian cyst. She was instructed to take ***Corydalin (AC)***, 6 to 8 capsules, two to four times a day, which helped to control the pain and, in turn, reduced the need for her missing more work. With the help of the herbs, not only did the severity and intensity of her menstrual cramping subsided, but the occurrence lasted only for a few hours instead of one to two days. Eventually the patient did not experience any more vomiting associated with pain. The practitioner concluded that ***Corydalin (AC)*** worked as a superb analgesic herbal formula during the treatment. Submitted by T.W., Santa Monica, California.
- A 31-year-old male administrative assistant with migraines since the age of six had been treated with Imitrex (sumatriptan) with limited success. The migraines were diagnosed as qi and blood stagnation with Liver qi stagnation stirring up wind. The doctor prescribed ***Corydalin (AC)***, upon which the patient experienced almost immediate and positive results! The patient subsequently stopped using Imitrex (sumatriptan) completely which, in turn, reduced occurrences of rebound headaches. Submitted by J.K., Woodland Hills, California.
- A 47-year-old female acupuncturist presented with one-sided severely debilitating migraines, which occurred particularly during the weekends. The TCM diagnosis was Kidney yin deficiency leading to Liver yang rising. A dose of ***Corydalin (AC)*** relieved the pain especially when the drug Imitrex (sumatriptan) was unsuccessful. Within two weeks of taking ***Corydalin (AC)***, she was free from headaches. She supplemented her treatment with ***Gastrodia Complex*** in addition to acupuncture treatments. She has experienced no migraine episodes for more than six months, and continues using the herbal combination of ***Corydalin (AC)*** and ***Gastrodia Complex***. Submitted by D.W., Hashbrouck Heights, New Jersey.
- A 44-year-old female police officer presented with chronic headaches located in the occipital and temporal regions. She stated that stress aggravated the problem. There was acute tenderness at the *Fengchi* (GB 20) area as well as in the cervical spine. She also experienced pain on her zygoma. The practitioner diagnosed the condition as qi and blood stagnation in Gallbladder, Urinary Bladder, and Small Intestine channels in addition to myofascial syndrome, which was stress-induced because of the nature of her job. She was treated with ***Corydalin (AC)***, ***Neck & Shoulder (AC)***, and ***Calm (ES)***, which were all so effective that they subsequently replaced her medication, Imitrex (sumatriptan). The practitioner concluded that a critical aspect in the treatment was to assist the patient in coping with her stress, which in turn made the herbal treatment more effective. Submitted by S.C., La Crescenta, California.
- A 64-year-old female retired editor presented with severe sinus headaches and acute/chronic sinusitis. There was severe sinus pain on palpation above and below her eyebrows. Her tongue had a reddish tip, and the coat was thin with a whitish yellow color. Pulse diagnosis was slightly elevated at the Lung position. The practitioner diagnosed the condition as damp-heat in the upper *jiao*. Administration of the recommended doses of ***Corydalin (AC)*** produced excellent results. The patient also reported that the most immediate relief from her sinus headaches occurred upon taking the ***Corydalin (AC)*** formula exclusively. The practitioner also noted similar positive outcomes from other patients. Submitted by R.K., San Diego, California.

Corydalin (AC)™

- A 50-year-old female public information specialist who was emotionally labile presented with pain in the shoulder, neck, thoracic area, lumbar area, and foot. Her lumbar discs at L4 and L5 were herniated. In addition to migraines and bouts of constipation, she also complained of anxiety, depression and insomnia, all of which may be attributed to some side effects of taking multiple pharmaceuticals. The practitioner diagnosed her condition as qi and blood stagnation as well as Liver depression. ***Corydalin (AC)*** and ***Schisandra ZZZ*** were given. ***Corydalin (AC)*** significantly reduced her pain. She was able to lessen the use of oxycontin and Duragesic (fentanyl) patches significantly. In fact, the dosages of oxycontin and Duragesic (fentanyl) patches were reduced by as much as 75%. Furthermore, the practitioner observed that ***Corydalin (AC)*** was also effective to maintain other patients who suffered from occasional pain. The majority of patients (about 90%) who took ***Corydalin (AC)*** responded favorably, especially since most were experiencing digestive side effects with ibuprofen. Submitted by F.G., Sykesville, Maryland.
- An 85-year-old retired female presented with excruciating pain in the neck and shoulder that causes difficulty sleeping. Objective findings included limited range of motion of the neck. The tongue had a dirty yellow coat and a red tip. The Western diagnosis included psoriatic arthritis, arthritis, fibromyalgia, hiatal hernia, hypertension, depression, chronic constipation, leaky gut syndrome, sciatica, and insomnia. The patient was instructed to take ***Neck & Shoulder (AC)*** and ***Corydalin (AC)***, 3 capsules of each three times daily in between meals. ***Calm (ES)*** was given at night to help sleep. The patient responded that the formulas were effective in reducing the acute pain in the neck and shoulder region. After the acute phase two weeks later, the patient was switched to *Gan Mai Da Zao Tang* (Licorice, Wheat, and Jujube Decoction) and *Shao Yao Gan Cao Tang* (Peony and Licorice Decoction), a combination recommended by Dr. Richard Tan that consistently helped patients with fibromyalgia. Submitted by J.B., Camarillo, California.
- L.N., a 42-year-old female, had a history of headaches and migraines triggered by stress and/or environmental factors. She presented with sinus headache for two days following a migraine headache. Clinical manifestations included orbital pain with photophobia, and neck and shoulder pain. The TCM diagnosis was qi and blood stagnation. Acupuncture treatment was combined with ***Corydalin (AC)*** at three capsules, three times daily, or as needed for headache. The practitioner commented that all symptoms were resolved after treatments. Submitted by C.L., Chino Hills, California.
- At a seminar in Providence, Rhode Island, a question was raised as whether *Yan Hu Suo* (Rhizoma Corydalis) would cause a person treated with this herb to test positive in a drug screen (as do a number of analgesic substances). A very small study was conducted in a laboratory at the Rhode Island Clinical Research Center: two people taking 6 capsules of ***Corydalin (AC)*** were screened for drugs three hours later. Both were completely negative in the seven drug panels. A solution of 5% *Yan Hu Suo* (Rhizoma Corydalis) powdered extract (freed from excessive carbohydrate) was also tested in the drug-screening test, again with negative results. It was concluded by the researchers that a person being treated for pain with the usual dosage of ***Corydalin (AC)*** would not risk testing positive for substances such as opiates, benzodiazepines, and barbiturates. [Note: *Yan Hu Suo* (Rhizoma Corydalis) is the main ingredient that is present in both ***Corydalin (AC)*** and ***Herbal ANG***.] Submitted by D.W., Hadley, Massachusetts.

PHARMACOLOGICAL AND CLINICAL RESEARCH

Corydalin (AC) is an empirical formula designed to relieve various kinds of headaches. ***Corydalin (AC)*** contains herbs with strong effects to relieve pain, reduce inflammation, and improve blood circulation.

Yan Hu Suo (Rhizoma Corydalis) is one of the strongest and most potent herbs for treatment of pain. Its effects are well documented in both historical references and modern research studies. According to classical texts, *Yan Hu Suo* (Rhizoma Corydalis) has been shown to treat chest and hypochondriac pain, epigastric and abdominal pain, hernial pain, amenorrhea or menstrual pain, and pain of the extremities. According to laboratory studies, the extract of *Yan Hu Suo* (Rhizoma Corydalis) has been found to be effective in both acute and chronic phases of inflammation. The mechanism of its anti-inflammatory effect is attributed to its effect to inhibit the release of histamine and pro-inflammatory mediators.[2,3] Furthermore, it has a strong analgesic effect. With adjustment in dosage, the potency of *Yan Hu Suo* (Rhizoma Corydalis) has been compared to that of morphine. In fact, the analgesic effect of *Yan Hu Suo* (Rhizoma Corydalis) is so strong and reliable that it has been used with satisfactory anesthetic effect in 98 out of 105 patients (93.4%) who underwent surgery.[4] The analgesic effect can be potentiated further with concurrent acupuncture therapy. In one research study, it is demonstrated that the analgesic effect is increased significantly with concurrent treatments using *Yan Hu Suo* (Rhizoma Corydalis) and electro-acupuncture, when compared to a control group, which received electro-acupuncture only.[5] Overall, it is well understood that *Yan Hu Suo* (Rhizoma Corydalis) has a marked effect to treat pain. Though the maximum analgesic effect of *Yan Hu Suo* (Rhizoma Corydalis) is not as strong as morphine, it has been determined that the herb is much safer, with significantly less side effects, less risk of tolerance, and no evidence of physical dependence even with long-term use.[6] Clinically, 47 patients with angioneurotic headache were treated successfully (24 had complete relief of pain, 22 had partial relief, and 1 had no effect) using an herbal formula with *Yan Hu Suo* (Rhizoma Corydalis) as the chief ingredient.[7]

Bai Zhi (Radix Angelicae Dahuricae), an important herb in ***Corydalin (AC)***, has both analgesic and anti-inflammatory

Corydalin (AC)™

properties.[8] The mechanism of action is attributed in part to the inhibition of lipopolysaccharide-induced production of nitric oxide, prostaglandin E2 and tumor necrosis factor-alpha (TNF-α) via mitogen-activated protein kinases and nuclear factor-kappaB in macrophages.[9] Clinically, *Bai Zhi* (Radix Angelicae Dahuricae) is used to treat vertex headache, sinus headache, orbital headache, and headache due to wind-heat or wind-cold.[10] In one study of 73 patients with occipital headache, after receiving two doses of *Bai Zhi* (Radix Angelicae Dahuricae), 69 patients experienced complete relief, 3 patients experienced partial relief, and 1 patient noted no relief.[11] In another study involving 62 patients with chronic headache, 54 patients reported satisfactory results after approximately two weeks of herbal treatment.[12] Furthermore, 130 patients with vascular headache were treated with complete recovery in 84 cases, significant improvement in 25 cases, and moderate improvement in 21 cases. The herbal formula contained *Bai Zhi* (Radix Angelicae Dahuricae), *Chuan Xiong* (Rhizoma Chuanxiong) and others as needed. The treatment protocol was to administer one dose (approximately 6.9 grams of the powdered herbs) two times daily with warm water.[13] Lastly, a 5% solution of *Bai Zhi* (Radix Angelicae Dahuricae) was given to 62 patients with headaches. One course of treatment ranged from 10 to 15 days, and patients received one to two courses of treatment. Of 62 patients, 54 showed significant improvement.[14]

Chuan Xiong (Rhizoma Chuanxiong) is a potent herb to relieve pain and reduce inflammation. It exerts an anti-inflammatory effect via an inhibitory activity on TNF-α production and bioactivity, and shows a promising effect to treat inflammation and related diseases.[15] Clinically, it has been used in various formulas to effectively treat various types and causes of headaches. One study reports 95.1% success rate to treat various types and causes of headache using *Chuan Xiong* (Rhizoma Chuanxiong) and *Dang Gui* (Radix Angelicae Sinensis) as the chief herbs.[16] In another study, 50 patients with headaches were treated with great success using herbal formulas with *Chuan Xiong* (Rhizoma Chuanxiong) as the main ingredient.[17] Lastly, one herbal formula with *Chuan Xiong* (Rhizoma Chuanxiong) demonstrated a 96.3% rate of effectiveness for treatment of vascular headache among 54 patients (40 showed complete recovery, 12 showed improvement, and 2 had no effect).[18]

Ge Gen (Radix Puerariae Lobatae) is an excellent herb to relax the muscle and reduce stiffness. It contains many isoflavonoid compounds which have significant analgesic and muscle-relaxant activities.[19] Traditionally, it has been commonly used to treat stiffness and pain in the neck and shoulder regions. Today, by relaxing the neck and shoulder muscles, it has also been shown to treat migraine headache with an 83% rate of effectiveness.[20] According to one study, 44 patients (83%) reported significant reduction in pain after taking *Ge Gen* (Radix Puerariae Lobatae) three times daily for 2 to 22 days.[21]

Dan Shen (Radix et Rhizoma Salviae Miltiorrhizae) is used primarily to improve peripheral blood circulation.[22] *Dan Shen* (Radix et Rhizoma Salviae Miltiorrhizae) improves microcirculation and is commonly used to increase blood perfusion to the brain.[23] Two studies showed *Dan Shen* (Radix et Rhizoma Salviae Miltiorrhizae) to offer protection against cerebral ischemia by increasing cerebral perfusion and reducing ultra-structural abnormalities.[24,25] Other studies demonstrated that by increasing cerebral perfusion, *Dan Shen* (Radix et Rhizoma Salviae Miltiorrhizae) reduces neurological deficits and repairs cellular damage.[26,27]

In summary, ***Corydalin (AC)*** is an excellent formula to treat pain in patients suffering from headaches. It contains herbs with analgesic effects to alleviate pain, anti-inflammatory effects to reduce swelling and inflammation, and muscle-relaxant effects to relieve stiffness, spasms and cramps.

COMPARATIVE ANALYSIS

Pain is a basic bodily sensation induced by a noxious stimulus that causes physical discomfort (such as pricking, throbbing, or aching). Pain may be of acute or chronic state, and may be of nociceptive, neuropathic, or psychogenic origin. Two classes of drugs commonly used to treat pain include non-steroidal anti-inflammatory drugs (NSAID) and opioid analgesics. NSAIDs [such as Motrin (ibuprofen) and Voltaren (diclofenac)] are generally used for mild to moderate pain, and are most effective to reduce inflammation and swelling. Though effective, they may cause such serious side effects as gastric ulcer, duodenal ulcer, gastrointestinal bleeding, tinnitus, blurred vision, dizziness and headache. Furthermore, the newer NSAIDs, also known as COX-2 inhibitors [such as Celebrex (celecoxib)], are associated with significantly higher risk of cardiovascular events, including heart attack and stroke. Opioid analgesics [such as Vicodin (APAP/hydrocodone) and morphine] are usually used for severe to excruciating pain. While they may be the most potent agents for pain, they also have the most serious risks and side effects, including but not limited to dizziness, lightheadedness, drowsiness, upset stomach, vomiting, constipation, stomach pain, rash, difficult urination, and respiratory depression resulting in difficult breathing. Furthermore, long-term use of these drugs leads to tolerance and addiction. In brief, it is important to remember that while drugs offer reliable and potent symptomatic pain relief, they should only be used if and when needed. Frequent use and abuse leads to unnecessary side effects and complications.

Treatment of pain is a sophisticated balance of art and science. Proper treatment of pain requires a careful evaluation of the type of disharmony (excess or deficiency, cold or heat, exterior or interior), characteristics (qi and/or blood stagnations), and location (upper body, lower body, extremities, or internal organs). Furthermore, optimal treatment requires integrative use of herbs, acupuncture and *tui-na* therapies. All these therapies work together to tonify the underlying deficiencies, strengthen the body, and facilitate recovery from chronic pain. TCM pain management targets both the symptom and the cause of pain,

Corydalin (AC)™

and as such, often achieves immediate and long-term success. Furthermore, TCM pain management is often associated with few or no side effects.

For treatment of mild to severe pain due to various causes, TCM pain management offers similar treatment effects with significantly fewer side effects than Western medicine. However, as in any therapeutic approach, it is important to recognize the limitations of TCM pain management. In some cases, such as excruciating cancer pain in terminally ill patients, drugs are simply superior to herbs. Under these circumstances, potent and consistently reliable pain relief is the main objective, and this can be accomplished more effectively by use of drugs such as intravenous injection of morphine. Herbs should be used to support the underlying constitution of the body, and to alleviate the side effects of the drugs.

References

1. Chan K, Lo AC, Yeung JH, Woo KS. Journal of Pharmacy and Pharmacology 1995 May;47(5):402-406.
2. *Biol Pharm Bull*, Feb 1994; 17(2):262-5.
3. Oh YC, Choi JG, Lee YS, Brice OO, Lee SC, Kwak HS, Byun YH, Kang OH, Rho JR, Shin DW, Kwon DY. Tetrahydropalmatine inhibits pro-inflammatory mediators in lipopolysaccharide-stimulated THP-1 cells. Department of Oriental Pharmacy, College of Pharmacy, Wonkwang University Wonkwang Oriental Medicines Research Institute, Iksan, Republic of Korea. J Med Food. 2010 Oct;13(5):1125-32.
4. *He Bei Xin Yi Yao* (Hebei New Medicine and Herbology), 1973; 4:34.
5. *Chen Tzu Yen Chiu* (Acupuncture Research), 1994;19(1):55-8.
6. *Zhong Yao Yao Li Yu Ying Yong* (Pharmacology and Applications of Chinese Herbs), 1983; 447.
7. *Zhe Jiang Zhong Yi Za Zhi* (Zhejiang Journal of Chinese Medicine), 1986; (4):158.
8. *Zhong Guo Zhong Yao Za Zhi* (People's Republic of China Journal of Chinese Herbology), 1991; 16(9):560.
9. Kang OH, Lee GH, Choi HJ, Park PS, Chae HS, Jeong SI, Kim YC, Sohn DH, Park H, Lee JH, Kwon DY. Ethyl acetate extract from Angelica Dahuricae Radix inhibits lipopolysaccharide-induced production of nitric oxide, prostaglandin E2 and tumor necrosis factor-alphavia mitogen-activated protein kinases and nuclear factor-kappaB in macrophages. Pharmacol Res. 2007 Apr;55(4):263-70.
10. Bensky, D. et al. *Chinese Herbal Medicine Materia Medica*. Eastland Press 1993.
11. Effectiveness of angelica (bai zhi) in treating occipital headache: a report of 73 cases. Airforce Hospital in Hengyang, China. (Xin Zhong Yi) *Modern Medical Journal*; 1976; 3:128.
12. Effectiveness of angelica (bai zhi) in treating chronic headache: a report of 62 cases. National Defense Hospital. (Xin Yi Xue Yao Za Zi) *Journal of Modern* Medicine, 1976;8:35.
13. *Hu Bei Zhong Yi Za Zhi* (Hubei Journal of Chinese Medicine), 1989; (1):8.
14. *Xin Yi Yao Xue Za Zhi* (New Journal of Medicine and Herbology), 1976; 8:35.
15. Liu L, Ning ZQ, Shan S, Zhang K, Deng T, Lu XP, Cheng YY. Phthalide Lactones from Ligusticum chuanxiong inhibit lipopolysaccharide-induced TNF-alpha production and TNF-alpha-mediated NF-kappaB Activation. Planta Med. 2005 Sep;71(9):808-13.
16. *Zhong Xi Yi Jie He Za Zhi* (Journal of Integrated Chinese and Western Medicine), 1991; (1):52.
17. *Shan Xi Zhong Yi Za Zhi* (Shanxi Journal Chinese Medicine), 1985; 10:447.
18. *Si Chuan Zhong Yi* (Sichuan Chinese Medicine), 1996; (11):27.
19. Yasuda T, Endo M, Kon-no T, Kato T, Mitsuzuka M, Ohsawa K. Antipyretic, analgesic and muscle relaxant activities of pueraria isoflavonoids and their metabolites from Pueraria lobata Ohwi-a traditional Chinese drug. Biol Pharm Bull. 2005 Jul;28(7):1224-8.
20. *Zhong Hua Nei Ke Za Zhi* (Chinese Journal of Internal Medicine), 1977; 6:326.
21. Gao, XX. et al. Effectiveness of pueraria root (ge gen) in treating migraine headache: a case report of 53 patients. (Zhong Hua Nei Ke Za Zi) *Journal of TCM Internal Medicine*. 1977; 6:326.
22. Yeung, HC. *Handbook of Chinese Herbs*. Institute of Chinese Medicine. 1983.
23. Nagai, M. et al. Vasodilator effects of des(alpha-carboxy-3'4-dihydroxyphenethyl) lithospermic acid (8-epiblechnic acid)' a derivative of lithospermic acids in Salviae miltiorrhizae radix. *Biol Pharm Bull*, Feb. 1996; 19(2):228-32.
24. Wu, W. et al. the effect of radix salviae miltiorrhizae on the changes of ultra-structure in rat brain after cerebral ischemia. *J. Tradit Chin Med*, Sept. 1992; 12(3):183-6.
25. Kuang, PG. et al. The effect of radix salviae miltiorrhizae on vasoactive intestinal peptide in cerebral ischemia: an animal experiment. *J Tradit Chin Med*, Sept. 1989; 9(3):203-6.
26. Kuang, P. et al. Effect of radix salviae miltiorrhizae on nitric oxide in cerebral ischemia-reperfusion injury. *J Tradit Chin Med*, Sept. 1996; 16(3):224-7.
27. Protective effect of radix saliva miltiorrhizae on nitric oxide in cerebral ischemia-reperfusion injury. *J Tradit Chin Med*, Jun. 1995; 15(2):135-40.

Corydalin (CR)™

CLINICAL APPLICATIONS

- **Chronic headache with underlying deficiency**
  - Migraine headache
  - Tension headache
  - Cluster headache

WESTERN THERAPEUTIC ACTIONS

- Analgesic action to relieve pain
- Anti-inflammatory influence to reduce inflammation

CHINESE THERAPEUTIC ACTIONS

- Relieves pain
- Subdues hyperactive yang qi
- Tonifies blood and yin
- Extinguishes Liver wind
- Relieves qi and blood stagnation

DOSAGE

Take 3 to 4 capsules three times daily. For severe pain, the dosage may be increased to 6 to 8 capsules every four to six hours as necessary. For maximum effectiveness, take the herbs on an empty stomach with warm water.

INGREDIENTS

Bai Shao (Radix Paeoniae Alba)
Bai Zhi (Radix Angelicae Dahuricae)
Chuan Xiong (Rhizoma Chuanxiong)
Dang Gui (Radix Angelicae Sinensis)
Ge Gen (Radix Puerariae Lobatae)
Ju Hua (Flos Chrysanthemi)
Long Gu (Os Draconis)
Man Jing Zi (Fructus Viticis)
Sang Ji Sheng (Herba Taxilli)
Shu Di Huang (Radix Rehmanniae Praeparata)
Tian Ma (Rhizoma Gastrodiae)
Yan Hu Suo (Rhizoma Corydalis)
Yu Jin (Radix Curcumae)

BACKGROUND

Headache is pain in any part of the head, including the scalp, face and interior of the head. Causes of headache vary, including hypertension, stress, anxiety, injuries, infection, glaucoma, hematoma, and tumor. Proper diagnosis requires careful review of medical history and physical exam. Optimal treatment combines elimination of cause and relief of pain.

FORMULA EXPLANATION

Corydalin (CR) is designed specifically to relieve the most common forms of migraine and tension headaches. The focus of this formula is directed at the *jueyin* and *shaoyang* meridians, the ones most commonly affected in migraine and tension headache syndromes. ***Corydalin (CR)*** contains herbs that tonify Liver blood and yin, subdue hyperactive yang qi, extinguish Liver wind, regulate Liver qi and blood, and relieve pain.

Corydalin (CR) is an empirical formula based on the classic Chinese herbal formula *Si Wu Tang* (Tangkuei Four Combination). The four main herbs in this formula, *Shu Di Huang* (Radix Rehmanniae Praeparata), *Dang Gui* (Radix Angelicae Sinensis), *Bai Shao* (Radix Paeoniae Alba) and *Chuan Xiong* (Rhizoma Chuanxiong), tonify Liver blood and yin. In addition, *Chuan Xiong* (Rhizoma Chuanxiong) and *Yan Hu Suo* (Rhizoma Corydalis) regulate and invigorate the blood, and are two of the primary herbs in the Chinese pharmacopoeia to treat headache. *Yu Jin* (Radix Curcumae) regulates wood element qi (Gallbladder/*shaoyang*), and relieves blood stasis. In combination with *Chuan Xiong* (Rhizoma Chuanxiong), *Yu Jin* (Radix Curcumae) serves to invigorate and harmonize yin and yang, and Liver blood and qi. *Ju Hua* (Flos Chrysanthemi) tonifies Liver yin, clears Liver heat, and subdues hyperactive Liver yang. *Man Jing Zi* (Fructus Viticis), *Bai Zhi* (Radix Angelicae Dahuricae) and *Ge Gen* (Radix Puerariae Lobatae) are combined for their benefits in relieving pain, relaxing muscle tension and relieving spasms by increasing peripheral blood circulation. *Tian Ma* (Rhizoma Gastrodiae) and *Long Gu* (Os Draconis) are added to extinguish Liver wind and subdue and anchor hyperactive Liver yang. *Sang Ji Sheng* (Herba Taxilli) is added to tonify Liver yin.

In summary, ***Corydalin (CR)*** contains herbs that address both acute and chronic aspects of headaches by treating excess and deficiency. It contains herbs to relieve pain by activating qi and blood circulation, calming hyperactive yang qi, and extinguishing Liver wind. Furthermore, it treats the underlying cause of headache by tonifying the blood and yin to remedy deficiencies in those areas.

CAUTIONS & CONTRAINDICATIONS

- Patients with persistent pain not relieved by ***Corydalin (AC)*** or ***Corydalin (CR)*** should seek further examination to rule out structural or functional abnormalities.
- Should prominent signs of diminishing vision and vomiting occur in addition to the headache, refer the patient to a medical doctor immediately for a CT scan or MRI to rule out intracranial pressure due to a tumor, aneurysm, or cerebral stenosis.
- This herbal formula contains herbs that invigorate blood circulation, such as *Dang Gui* (Radix Angelicae Sinensis). Therefore, patients who are on anticoagulant or antiplatelet therapies, such as Coumadin (warfarin), should use this formula with caution, or not at all, as there may be a higher risk of bleeding and bruising.[1,2,3]

CLINICAL NOTES

- ***Corydalin (CR)*** is a great formula for chronic headache, especially if the headache is due in part to blood deficiency. It can be taken on a long-term basis to minimize recurrences and the severity of pain. The maintenance dose is 2 capsules twice daily.

Corydalin (CR)™

- *Corydalin (AC)* is best for acute headaches with severe pain, and is most effective for symptomatic relief. ***Corydalin (CR)*** is most effective when taken on a long-term basis to control and prevent the recurrence of headaches.
- For headache in which herbs cannot achieve maximum relief, the cervical vertebrae (C1 to C3) should be checked for any abnormality. Check for specific trigger points in the neck or any uneven tension of cervical muscles bilaterally. If one side is stiffer than the other, this may be an indication of a cervical disorder. In cases where the neck and shoulder are also stiff due to misalignment resulting in headaches, ***Neck & Shoulder (AC)*** can be added.
- For women who suffer from periodic headaches, especially preceding menstrual cycles, it is important to treat blood stagnation. The headaches usually subside with the passage of blood clots. The recommended formulas include ***Mense-Ease*** and ***Resolve (Lower)***.
- The late Dr. John H.F. Shen created this formula. The formula explanation was provided by Dr. Ray Rubio. This is an effective formula to treat migraine, tension, and cluster headaches.

Pulse Diagnosis by Dr. Jimmy Wei-Yen Chang:

- **Migraine headache:** a pulse next to a pulse on the right *chi*. A pulse next to a pulse is when a thin pulse can be felt next to a thick pulse.
- **Headache due to Liver fire:** forceful and floating pulse on the left *guan*. Temperature of the entire arm will feel hot.
- **Headache due to wind-heat:** floating and forceful pulse on the right *cun*, and long and forceful pulse on the right *chi*. Temperature above the elbows and the back of the neck will feel hot.
- **Headache due to wind-cold:** floating and thready pulse on the right *cun*, and thready and long pulse on the right *chi*. Temperature above the elbows and the back of the neck will feel cold.
- **Headache due to poisoning:** forceful pulse on both *chi* and left *guan* positions.

SUPPLEMENTARY FORMULAS

- For acute headache with severe pain, add ***Corydalin (AC)***.
- For headache from wind-heat, add ***Lonicera Complex***.
- For headache from excess and heat conditions, combine with ***Gardenia Complex***.
- For headache associated with infection, add ***Herbal ABX*** or ***Herbal AVR***.
- For headache associated with infection of ear, nose and throat, add ***Herbal ENT***.
- For headache caused by stress and tension, add ***Calm***, ***Calm (ES)***, or ***Calm ZZZ***.
- For headache related to sinus congestion, add ***Pueraria Clear Sinus*** or ***Magnolia Clear Sinus***.
- For headache with neck and shoulder stiffness, combine with ***Neck & Shoulder (AC)***.
- For migraine headache with Liver wind rising, combine with ***Gastrodia Complex*** or ***Gentiana Complex***.
- If headache is caused by recent traumatic or musculoskeletal injury, add ***Flex (TMX)***.
- For headache due to old trauma or injury or blood stagnation, add ***Circulation (SJ)***.
- For Kidney yin deficiency, add ***Nourish*** or ***Kidney Tonic (Yin)***.
- With headache due to underlying damp and phlegm with Spleen qi deficiency, add ***Pinellia Complex***.

ACUPUNCTURE TREATMENT

Traditional Points:

- *Renzhong* (GV 26), *Lieque* (LU 7), *Zusanli* (ST 36), *Xingjian* (LR 2), *Taichong* (LR 3), *Geshu* (BL 17), *Baihui* (GV 20), *Xuehai* (SP 10)

Classic Master Tung's Points:

- Needle contralateral to the pain. If the pain is in the center, needle bilaterally or the side with the more *ah shi* points. If the pain is bilateral, needle bilaterally.
- **Headache (general):** *Linggu* (T 22.05), *Dabai* (T 22.04), *Huolian* (T 66.10), *Huoju* (T 66.11), *Huosan* (T 66.12). Bleed dark veins on the dorsal aspect of the feet. Bleed before needling for best result.
- **Headache (occipital):** *Linggu* (T 22.05), *Dabai* (T 22.04), *Fanhoujue* (T 22.12)*, *Zhengjin* (T 77.01), *Zhengzong* (T 77.02), *Wanshunyi* (T 22.08), *Wanshuner* (T 22.09), *Tongbei* (T 88.11), *Huofu* (T 88.41)*, *Huochang* (T 88.43)*, *Huoliang* (T 88.42)*, *Dihuang* (T 77.19), *Boqiu* (T 77.04), *Zhengshi* (T 77.03). Bleed the sacral region or *Weizhong* (BL 40) or dark veins nearby. Bleed before needling for best result.
- **Headache (frontal):** *Linggu* (T 22.05), *Dabai* (T 22.04), *Biyi* (T 1010.22), *Xinling* (T 33.17)*, *Zhongbai* (T 22.06), *Taiyang*, *Huoju* (T 66.11), *Wuhu* (T 11.27), *Zhenjing* (T 1010.08), *Sifuyi* (T 1010.11), *Sifuer* (T 1010.10), *Tongtian* (T 88.03). Bleed *Sihuashang* (T 77.08), *Sihuaxia* (T 77.11), *Sihuazhong* (T 77.09), *Fuchang* (T 77.12), ST channel on the lower limb and dark veins nearby. Bleed before needling for best result.
- **Headache (temporal):** *Linggu* (T 22.05), *Shangbai* (T 22.03), *Zhongbai* (T 22.06), *Xinling* (T 33.17)*, *Cesanli* (T 77.22), *Cexiasanli* (T 77.23), *Shangjiuli* (T 88.26), *Zhongjiuli* (T 88.25), *Xiajiuli* (T 88.27), *Jianzhong* (T 44.06), *Sihuawai* (T 77.14), *Liuwan* (T 66.08), *Menjin* (T 66.05), *Huoying* (T 66.03), *Qihu* (T 77.26), *Waisanguan* (T 77.27), *Yizhong* (T 77.05) *Erzhong* (T 77.06), *Sanzhong* (T 77.07), *Taiyang*, *Waiguan* (TH 5) penetrating through *Neiguan* (PC 6). Bleed any dark veins or tender points nearby the lateral malleolus. Bleed at a 45 degree angle the dark veins nearby the other temporal area. Patient needs to lean downwards, hold his/her breath and exhale to help push blood out. Bleed before needling for best result.
- **Headache (vertex):** *Linggu* (T 22.05), *Dabai* (T 22.04), *Xinling* (T 33.17)*, *Zhenghui* (T 1010.01), *Qianhui* (T 1010.05), *Shuitong*

FORMULAS

Corydalin (CR)™

(T 1010.19), *Shuijin* (T 1010.20), *Zhengjin* (T 77.01), *Shenting* (GV 24), *Shangxing* (GV 23), *Huozhu* (T 66.04), *Huolian* (T 66.10), *Huoju* (T 66.11), *Huosan* (T 66.12), *Zhengzong* (T 77.02)

- **Headache (migraine):** *Linggu* (T 22.05), *Dabai* (T 22.04), *Cesanli* (T 77.22), *Yizhong* (T 77.05), *Erzhong* (T 77.06), *Sanzhong* (T 77.07), *Liuwan* (T 66.08), *Zhongjiuli* (T 88.25)
- **Headache (supraorbital):** *Erjiaoming* (T 11.12), *Shangbai* (T 22.03), *Sanchayi* (T 22.15)*, *Huaguyi* (T 55.02), *Shangli* (T 1010.09), *Tianhuangfu [Shenguan]* (T 77.18)
- **Headache (hypertension):** *Linggu* (T 22.05), *Dabai* (T 22.04), *Xinling* (T 33.17)*, *Zhenghui* (T 1010.01), *Qianhui* (T 1010.05), *Shuitong* (T 1010.19), *Shuijin* (T 1010.20), *Sansheng* (T 55.07)*, *Weizhong* (BL 40), *Shenting* (GV 24), *Shangxing* (GV 23), *Huozhu* (T 66.04), *Tongtian* (T 88.03), *Fuding* (T 44.04), *Houzhi* (T 44.05), *Jianfeng* (T 44.31)*, *Tongshan* (T 88.02), *Tongguan* (T 88.01), *Zhitong* (T 44.13). Bleed *Huoshan* (T 33.06), *Huoling* (T 33.05) or dark veins nearby. Bleed before needling for best result.
- **Headache (common cold):** *Linggu* (T 22.05), *Dabai* (T 22.04), *Xinling* (T 33.17)*, *Zhenghui* (T 1010.01), *Qianhui* (T 1010.05), *Shuitong* (T 1010.19), *Shuijin* (T 1010.20), *Sanzhong* (T 77.07), *Sihuashang* (T 77.08), *Sihuazhong* (T 77.09), *Sihuawai* (T 77.14), *Sihuaxia* (T 77.11), *Shenting* (GV 24), *Shangxing* (GV 23), *Huozhu* (T 66.04), *Dizong* (T 44.09)
- **Headache (menstruation):** *Linggu* (T 22.05), *Dabai* (T 22.04), *Xinling* (T 33.17)*, *Zhenghui* (T 1010.01), *Qianhui* (T 1010.05), *Shuitong* (T 1010.19), *Shuijin* (T 1010.20), *Sanzhong* (T 77.07), *Sihuashang* (T 77.08), *Sihuazhong* (T 77.09), *Sihuawai* (T 77.14), *Sihuaxia* (T 77.11), *Shenting* (GV 24), *Shangxing* (GV 23), *Huozhu* (T 66.04), *Dizong* (T 44.09)
- **Headache (injury):** *Zhengjin* (T 77.01), *Zhengzong* (T 77.02) with strong stimulation, *Yizhong* (T 77.05), *Erzhong* (T 77.06), *Sanzhong* (T 77.07), *Zhengshi* (T 77.03). Bleed dark veins nearby the medial malleolus or *Shuijing* (T 66.13). Bleed before needling for best result.

Master Tung's Points by Dr. Chuan-Min Wang:

- **Headache**
  - Frontal: *Cesanli* (T 77.22), *Tianhuangfu [shenguan]* (T 77.18)
  - Temporal: *Cesanli* (T 77.22), *Zhongjiuli* (T 88.25)
  - Occipital: *Cesanli* (T 77.22), *Zhengjin* (T 77.01), *Zhengzong* (T 77.02)
  - Vertex: Needle bilaterally *Cesanli* (T 77.22), *Huozhu* (T 66.04).
  - Migraine: *Cesanli* (T 77.22), *Menjin* (T 66.05)
  - Behind the eyes: *Cesanli* (T 77.22), *Tianhuangfu [shenguan]* (T 77.18)

Balance Method by Dr. Richard Tan:

- On the same side of the migraine, needle *Fengshi* (GB 31), *Diwuhui* (GB 42), and *Shaofu* (HT 8).
- On the opposite side, needle *Taichong* (LR 3), *Xiguan* (LR 7), *Waiguan* (TH 5), and *Tianjing* (TH 10).

Ear Acupuncture:

- Adrenal Gland, Hypothalamus, Temporal Lobe
- Use metal ear pellets. Alternate ears every three days. Five sessions equals one treatment course.

Auricular Medicine by Dr. Li-Chun Huang:

- **Migraine:** Temple, Sympathetic, External Sympathetic, Nervous Subcortex, Coronary Vascular Subcortex. Bleed Ear Apex.
- **Frontal headache:** External Sympathetic, Forehead, Nervous Subcortex. Bleed Ear Apex.
  - For headache due to sinus or rhinitis, add Internal Nose.
  - For headache due to ametropia, add Vision II.
- **Occipital headache:** Occiput, Lesser Occipital Nerve, Nervous Subcortex. Bleed Ear Apex.
  - For occiput headache due to cervical vertebral C3 to C4 degeneration, add Cervical Vertebral C3 and C4 (frontal and back of ear).
- **Temporal headache:** Temple, Sympathetic, External Sympathetic, Nervous Subcortex, Coronary Vascular Subcortex. Bleed Ear Apex.
- **Vertex headache:** Vertex, External Sympathetic, Nervous Subcortex. Bleed Ear Apex.

NUTRITION

- Avoid intake of cold drinks, cold foods, and sour fruits. Cold and sour substances constrict vessels, channels and collaterals.
- If headaches are food related, the diet must be regulated and controlled to reduce or eliminate triggers.
- Consume adequate amounts of fruits, vegetables, grains, and raw nuts and seeds.
- One of the most common causes of headache is caffeine. Gradually decrease and stop consumption of caffeine-containing drinks, such as coffee, tea, cola, energy drinks, and specialty beverages with caffeine.
- Avoid foods containing tyramine, which can trigger headaches, such as alcohol, chocolate, bananas, citrus, avocado, cabbage, and potatoes. Also avoid cakes, dairy products (except yogurt), processed or packaged foods (because of colorants, preservatives and other additives), tobacco and junk food.
- Monosodium glutamate (MSG) should be avoided by individuals sensitive to it. MSG is generally found in canned soups, TV dinners, some meats, many pre-prepared frozen dishes and restaurant foods.

The Tao of Nutrition by Dr. Maoshing Ni and Cathy McNease:

- Migraines or headaches due to high blood pressure, menstrual cycles, emotional stress or tension
  - Recommendations: chrysanthemum flowers, mint, green onions, oyster shells, pearl barley, carrots, prunes, buckwheat, peach kernels.
  - Take lemon juice and 1/2 tablespoon baking soda mixed in a glass of water and drink.
  - Make tea of Chinese prunes, mint, and green tea.

Corydalin (CR)™

- Mash peach kernels and walnuts, mix with rice wine and lightly roast; take two tablespoons three times daily.
- Avoid spicy food, lack of sleep, alcohol, smoking, excess stimulation, eye strain, and stress.

LIFESTYLE INSTRUCTIONS

- Avoid allergens as much as possible, as allergens may trigger headache.
- Installation of an air purifier will minimize the presence of allergens in the air and reduce the risk of allergy and headache.
- Avoid stressful situations and environments whenever possible. Ease tension with massage, warm baths, and an exercise program.
- Avoid direct exposure to air conditioning, fans, drafts or wind blowing on the head and neck region.
- Tension headaches can be relieved by gentle massage of the neck and shoulders to relax the muscles. A hot Epsom salts bath or soaking the feet is also helpful.
- Headache due to poor circulation will respond to a vigorous scalp massage.
- Regular exercise, adequate rest, and normal sleeping habits are essential for optimal health.

CASE STUDIES

- M.M., a 42-year-old female, presented with recurring tension headaches, which worsened with lack of sleep and overwork. Daily activities such as using her computer and iPad were straining her neck which then aggravated the headaches more. Yoga and breathing techniques were used temporarily to help improve the headaches. Additional symptoms included malaise and a desire to lie down. The location started in the occipital area, throbbing pain around the vertex, forehead and behind the eyes. The TCM diagnosis was Kidney and Liver yin deficiencies with Liver yang rising. This condition was treated with ***Corydalin (CR)*** four spoons once daily. The patient reported immediate relief and improved sensation of well being. Overall the frequency of headaches was less and the patient felt more balanced. Submitted by M.M., Alameda, California.
- S.G., a 29-year-old female, presented with headaches, which she had been experiencing three to four times per week and 50% of them were migraines. It was also noted that she had low back and neck pain, as well as insomnia with sleep duration of only four hours each night. Her pulse was thin and wiry and her tongue was pale with thick white coat. The practitioner diagnosed the condition as Liver overacting on the Spleen, Spleen qi and Liver blood deficiency with dampness. ***Corydalin (CR)*** was prescribed at four capsules three times per day. She received acupuncture treatment as well. With taking the herbs the patient had only one episode of a headache and one episode of a migraine in the following month. She has not needed to return for any additional treatment since. Submitted by C.C., San Diego, California.
- F.R., a 48-year-old female, presented with tension and cluster headaches, about five to seven days per week. The practitioner diagnosed this condition as qi and blood stagnation, along with Liver blood and yin deficiencies. For treatment, ***Corydalin (CR)*** was prescribed at three capsules three times per day, as well as taking ***Corydalin (AC)*** as needed. Acupuncture treatment was received as well. During the first two weeks of taking the herbs, the patient reported four to six headaches. By the fifth week of taking the herbs, the headaches reduced to only one per week. After eight weeks she seldom experienced any headaches. Submitted by S.L., Yuma, Arizona.
- A 44-year-old female presented with chronic migraines, described as a tight sharp pain. It was mentioned that she had been having headaches for the past 30 years and she was also experiencing neck and arm pain. Objective findings included tight muscles upon palpation of the sternocleidomastoid, trapezius, biceps and deltoid muscles. The TCM diagnosis was Liver qi stagnation along with qi and blood stagnation; Western diagnosis was repetitive muscle syndrome. ***Corydalin (CR)*** for headaches and ***Herbal ANG*** for muscle discomfort were prescribed and directed to take as needed. The patient had been treated on and off by these herbs for the past six months and had finally gotten off all her medications. She had sworn by them, mentioning they gave better results than her anti-inflammatories. Submitted by J.L., San Diego, California.
- J.A., a 52-year-old female, presented with having migraines with a pain level of 10 out of 10. They were described as throbbing, beginning at the occipital region, travelling down the Urinary Bladder and Gallbladder channels. The practitioner diagnosed this condition as Liver yin deficiency and Liver yang rising. Liver overacting on Spleen and Gallbladder damp-heat were also present. For treatment, ***Corydalin (CR)*** was prescribed. In response to receiving acupuncture and taking the herbs, the patient's migraines were well controlled. After an analysis of her diet, it was discovered that she had food allergies to certain foods which had increased onset of her migraines. Since then she has been limiting these foods from her diet. Submitted by V.G., Virginia Beach, Virginia.
- M.L., a 13-year-old female, presented with migraine headache with no other significant complaints. She was diagnosed with qi and blood stagnation. ***Corydalin (CR)*** was prescribed at 6 grams daily. In the first two weeks, the patient reported the headache occurred approximately four times a week. During the third and fourth week of herbal treatment, the headache reduced to twice a week. During the fifth week, the headache was completely gone and the patient felt she had more energy. She also received acupuncture throughout the five weeks. Submitted by W.F., Bloomfield, New Jersey.
- V.B., a 49-year-old female, presented with migraines she had been experiencing for the previous five years, lasting every month for four to six days and usually occurring prior to the onset of her period. She worked as an on-site manager in a large complex and stated the migraines were aggravated by the stress of her job. She also suffered from uterine prolapse and

Corydalin (CR)™

was experiencing significant tension in her neck and shoulders as well. In addition, she had difficulty falling and staying asleep so she was taking Ambien (zolpidem) on a regular basis. The TCM diagnosis was primarily Spleen qi deficiency with blood deficiency, accumulation of dampness, and central qi sinking; Liver blood deficiency generating wind, and Liver qi stagnation were also present. An additional assessment from the practitioner was that the migraines had been due to a histamine response. She was prescribed both ***Corydalin (CR)*** and *Bu Zhong Yi Qi Tang* (Tonify the Middle and Augment the Qi Decoction). She was also taking Ferro Food, a product for anemia recommended by her alternative medicine practitioner. While taking ***Corydalin (CR)*** along with receiving three or four acupuncture treatments, cupping, and body therapy for her upper body tension over a four month period, the patient reported she did not have any migraines. During one of the last treatments she had just contracted a headache prior to the visit, and it had completely resolved afterwards within one day. She said she was able to stop taking the prescribed medication Topamax (topiramate). It was advised by the practitioner that the patient increase her intake of foods containing magnesium, and reduce any foods containing tyramine. Submitted by M.M., Burlington, Wisconsin.

PHARMACOLOGICAL AND CLINICAL RESEARCH

Corydalin (CR) is formulated to treat a variety of headaches, including but not limited to migraine, tension and cluster headaches. The mechanism of action of the herbs includes an analgesic effect to relieve pain, anti-inflammatory action to reduce inflammation, and specific constituents to target and treat headache.

Yan Hu Suo (Rhizoma Corydalis) is one of the strongest and most potent herbs for treatment of pain. It has a strong analgesic effect that is comparable to morphine. In fact, the analgesic effect of *Yan Hu Suo* (Rhizoma Corydalis) is so strong and reliable that it has been used with satisfactory anesthetic effect in 98 out of 105 patients (93.4%) who underwent surgery.[4] The analgesic effect can be potentiated further with concurrent acupuncture therapy. Overall, it is well understood that *Yan Hu Suo* (Rhizoma Corydalis) has a marked effect to treat pain.

Dang Gui (Radix Angelicae Sinensis) is a commonly used herb in Chinese medicine and has notable strength to relieve various types of pain, including but not limited to migraine, pain of the low back and legs, and menstrual cramps.[5,6] Pharmacologically, it has shown analgesic and anti-inflammatory actions.[7] The anti-inflammatory property of *Dang Gui* (Radix Angelicae Sinensis) is attributed to the inhibition of pro-inflammatory mediators, including nitric oxide and prostaglandin E2 in peritoneal macrophages.[8] In comparison to aspirin, the anti-inflammatory action of *Dang Gui* (Radix Angelicae Sinensis) is approximately 1.1 times stronger and its analgesic effect is approximately 1.7 times stronger.[9] Clinically, a preparation of *Dang Gui* (Radix Angelicae Sinensis) was found to have an 82.9% effective rate in treating 35 patients with migraine headache.[10]

Dang Gui (Radix Angelicae Sinensis) and *Chuan Xiong* (Rhizoma Chuanxiong) are two herbs frequently used together to treat headaches. Pharmacologically, *Chuan Xiong* (Rhizoma Chuanxiong) has a marked effect to suppress inflammation via its inhibitory activity on tumor necrosis factor-alpha (TNF-α) production and bioactivity.[11] Clinically, one study reported 95.1% success rate to treat various types and causes of headache using an herbal formula that contained *Dang Gui* (Radix Angelicae Sinensis) and *Chuan Xiong* (Rhizoma Chuanxiong).[12] In another clinical study, 50 patients with headache were treated with herbal formulas with great success using such ingredients as *Dang Gui* (Radix Angelicae Sinensis), *Chuan Xiong* (Rhizoma Chuanxiong), *Bai Zhi* (Radix Angelicae Dahuricae), and *Ju Hua* (Flos Chrysanthemi).[13]

Bai Shao (Radix Paeoniae Alba) is commonly used for its analgesic and antispasmodic effects.[14] Common applications include pain, spasms and cramps, and trigeminal pain.[15] Paeonol, one of the main active compounds of *Bai Shao* (Radix Paeoniae Alba), has anti-inflammatory and antioxidant activities.[16] In addition, the total glucosides of *Bai Shao* (Radix Paeoniae Alba) exert anti-inflammatory effects by modulating the production of pro-inflammatory mediators.[17] Clinically, *Bai Shao* (Radix Paeoniae Alba) helps relieve pain and stiffness of neck and shoulder muscles associated with headache.

Bai Zhi (Radix Angelicae Dahuricae) has definite analgesic and anti-inflammatory activities, and is frequently used for a variety of headaches.[18] Pharmacologically, *Bai Zhi* (Radix Angelicae Dahuricae) reduce inflammation by inhibiting lipopolysaccharide-induced production of nitric oxide, prostaglandin E2 and TNF-α via mitogen-activated protein kinases and nuclear factor-kappaB in macrophages.[19] Clinically, there have been various clinical studies proving *Bai Zhi* (Radix Angelicae Dahuricae) effectively treats headache. In one clinical study, patients with occipital headache were treated twice daily with *Bai Zhi* (Radix Angelicae Dahuricae). Out of 73 patients, 69 showed significant improvements, 3 showed slight improvement, and 1 showed no effect.[20] In another study, 54 out of 62 patients with chronic headache showed significant improvement using a 5% solution of *Bai Zhi* (Radix Angelicae Dahuricae) for 10 to 15 days per course of treatment, for one to two courses total.[21] In short, *Bai Zhi* (Radix Angelicae Dahuricae) is an extremely useful and effective herb for headache treatment.

In addition to the herbs listed above, ***Corydalin (CR)*** utilizes many other herbs with marked analgesic and anti-inflammatory activities. *Ge Gen* (Radix Puerariae Lobatae) has a strong analgesic effect and is effective to treat migraine headache. Many isoflavonoid compounds from *Ge Gen* (Radix Puerariae Lobatae), including daidzin, daidzein, dihydrodaidzein, and p-ethylphenol, demonstrated significant analgesic and muscle-relaxant activities.[22]

Corydalin (CR)™

In a clinical study of migraine headache, a *Ge Gen* (Radix Puerariae Lobatae) preparation containing 100 mg of puerarin was reported 83% effective when used three times daily for 2 to 22 days.[23] Furthermore, *Tian Ma* (Rhizoma Gastrodiae) has analgesic and anti-inflammatory activities. The mechanism of action is attributed to the inhibition of cyclo-oxygenase (COX) I and II activities.[24] Gastrodin, one compound from *Tian Ma* (Rhizoma Gastrodiae), shows good results in treating 156 patients with neurasthenic headache and 72 patients with vascular headache.[25] Lastly, the methanol extract of *Yu Jin* (Radix Curcumae) showed a significant effect to inhibit cyclo-oxygenase-2 activity and reduce inflammation and relieve pain.[26]

In summary, ***Corydalin (CR)*** contains herbs that have shown through historical applications and clinical trials to be effective in treating a variety of headaches, including but not limited to migraine, tension, and cluster headaches.

COMPARATIVE ANALYSIS

Pain is a basic bodily sensation induced by a noxious stimulus that causes physical discomfort (such as pricking, throbbing, or aching). Pain may be of acute or chronic state, and may be of nociceptive, neuropathic, or psychogenic origin. For migraine, three classes of drugs commonly used to treat pain include non-steroidal anti-inflammatory agents (NSAID), opioid analgesics, and serotonin agonists. NSAIDs [such as Motrin (ibuprofen) and Voltaren (diclofenac)] are generally used for mild to moderate pain, and are most effective to reduce inflammation and swelling. Though effective, they may cause such serious side effects as gastric ulcer, duodenal ulcer, gastrointestinal bleeding, tinnitus, blurred vision, dizziness and headache. Opioid analgesics [such as Vicodin (APAP/hydrocodone) and morphine] are usually used for severe to excruciating pain. While they may be the most potent agents for pain, they also have the most serious risks and side effects, including but not limited to dizziness, lightheadedness, drowsiness, upset stomach, vomiting, constipation, stomach pain, rash, difficult urination, and respiratory depression resulting in difficult breathing. Furthermore, long-term use of these drugs leads to tolerance and addiction. Lastly, serotonin agonists, such as Imitrex (sumatriptan), are specifically used for migraine. Common side effects of this drug include flushing, tingling feeling, feeling of warmth or heaviness, drowsiness, dizziness, upset stomach, diarrhea, vomiting, irritation of the nose, and muscle cramps. Though effective, these drugs do not change the course of illness, and do not reduce the frequency or severity of recurrent migraine attacks. In brief, it is important to remember that while drugs offer reliable and potent pain relief, they only treat symptoms and not the cause. They should only be used if and when needed. Frequent use and abuse leads to unnecessary side effects and complications.

Treatment of migraine is a sophisticated balance of art and science. Proper treatment of pain requires a careful evaluation of the type of disharmony (excess or deficiency, cold or heat, exterior or interior), characteristics (qi and/or blood stagnations), and location (upper body, lower body, extremities, or internal organs). Furthermore, optimal treatment requires integrative use of herbs, acupuncture and *tui-na* therapies. All these therapies work together to tonify underlying deficiencies, strengthen the body, and facilitate recovery from chronic pain. TCM pain management targets both symptoms and the causes of pain, and as such, often achieves immediate and long-term success. Furthermore, TCM pain management is often associated with few or no side effects.

For treatment of mild to severe pain due to various causes, TCM pain management offers similar treatment effects with significantly fewer side effects. However, as is true of any therapeutic modality, it is important to recognize the limitations of TCM pain management. In some cases, such as acute, excruciating migraine, drugs are superior to herbs, as they are more immediately potent and have a more rapid onset of action (especially if given via injection). Therefore, optimal treatment may require the integration of Western medicine to treat acute pain, and herbal medicine to provide long-term healing of underlying causes and prevent recurrence of migraines.

References

1. Chan K, Lo AC, Yeung JH, Woo KS. Journal of Pharmacy and Pharmacology 1995 May;47(5):402-6.
2. Pharmacotherapy 1999 July;19(7):870-876.
3. European Journal of Drug Metabolism and Pharmacokinetics 1995; 20(1):55-60.
4. *He Bei Xin Yi Yao* (Hebei New Medicine and Herbology), 1973; 4:34.
5. *Xin Zhong Yi* (New Chinese Medicine), 1980; 2:34.
6. *Lan Zhou Yi Xue Yuan Xue Bao* (Journal of Lanzhou University of Medicine), 1988; 1:36.
7. *Xin Yi Yao Xue Za Zhi* (New Journal of Medicine and Herbology), 1975; (6):34.
8. Chao WW, Kuo YH, Li WC, Lin BF. The production of nitric oxide and prostaglandin E2 in peritoneal macrophages is inhibited by Andrographis paniculata, Angelica sinensis and Morus alba ethyl acetate fractions. Department of Biochemical Science and Technology, Institute of Microbiology and Biochemistry, National Taiwan University, Taipei 106, Taiwan, ROC. J Ethnopharmacol. 2009 Feb 25;122(1):68-75.
9. *Yao Xue Za Zhi* (Journal of Medicinals), 1971; (91):1098.
10. *Bei Jing Yi Xue* (Beijing Medicine), 1988; 2:95.
11. Liu L, Ning ZQ, Shan S, Zhang K, Deng T, Lu XP, Cheng YY. Phthalide Lactones from Ligusticum chuanxiong inhibit lipopolysaccharide-induced TNF-alpha production and TNF-alpha-mediated NF-kappaB Activation. Planta Med. 2005 Sep;71(9):808-13.
12. *Zhong Xi Yi Jie He Za Zhi* (Journal of Integrated Chinese and Western Medicine), 1991; (1):52.
13. *Shan Xi Zhong Yi Za Zhi* (Shanxi Journal Chinese Medicine), 1985; 10:447.
14. *Shang Hai Zhong Yi Yao Za Zhi* (Shanghai Journal of Chinese Medicine and Herbology), 1983; 4:14.
15. *Zhong Yi Za Zhi* (Journal of Chinese Medicine), 1983; 11:9.
16. Nizamutdinova IT, Oh HM, Min YN, Park SH, Lee MJ, Kim JS, Yean MH, Kang SS, Kim YS, Chang KC, Kim HJ. Paeonol suppresses intercellular adhesion molecule-1 expression in tumor necrosis factor-alpha-stimulated human umbilical vein endothelial cells by blocking p38, ERK and nuclear factor-kappaB signaling pathways. Int Immunopharmacol. 2007 Mar;7(3):343-50.
17. Zheng YQ, Wei W. Total glucosides of paeony suppresses adjuvant arthritis in rats and intervenes cytokine-signaling between different types of synoviocytes. Int Immunopharmacol. 2005 Sep;5(10):1560-73.

Corydalin (CR)™

18. *Zhong Guo Zhong Yao Za Zhi* (People's Republic of China Journal of Chinese Herbology), 1991; 16(9):560.
19. Kang OH, Lee GH, Choi HJ, Park PS, Chae HS, Jeong SI, Kim YC, Sohn DH, Park H, Lee JH, Kwon DY. Ethyl acetate extract from Angelica Dahuricae Radix inhibits lipopolysaccharide-induced production of nitric oxide, prostaglandin E2 and tumor necrosis factor-alphavia mitogen-activated protein kinases and nuclear factor-kappaB in macrophages. Pharmacol Res. 2007 Apr;55(4):263-70.
20. *Xin Yi Xue* (New Medicine), 1976; 1:8.
21. *Xin Yi Yao Xue Za Zhi* (New Journal of Medicine and Herbology), 1976; 8:35.
22. Yasuda T, Endo M, Kon-no T, Kato T, Mitsuzuka M, Ohsawa K. Antipyretic, analgesic and muscle relaxant activities of pueraria isoflavonoids and their metabolites from Pueraria lobata Ohwi-a traditional Chinese drug. Biol Pharm Bull. 2005 Jul;28(7):1224-8.
23. *Zhong Hua Nei Ke Za Zhi* (Chinese Journal of Internal Medicine), 1977; 6:326.
24. Lee JY, Jang YW, Kang HS, Moon H, Sim SS, Kim CJ. Anti-inflammatory action of phenolic compounds from Gastrodia elata root. Division of Pathophysiology and Pharmacology, College of Pharmacy, Chung-Ang University, Seoul 156-756, Korea. Arch Pharm Res. 2006 Oct;29(10):849-58.
25. *Zhong Guo Shen Jing Jing Shen Ke Za Zhi* (Chinese Journal of Psychiatric Disorders), 1986; 5:265.
26. Lou Y, Zhao F, He H, Peng KF, Zhou XH, Chen LX, Qiu F. Guaiane-type sesquiterpenes from Curcuma wenyujin and their inhibitory effects on nitric oxide production. J Asian Nat Prod Res. 2009 Aug;11(8):737-47.

Dermatrol (Clear)™

CLINICAL APPLICATIONS

- **Acne vulgaris (acne or pimples)** in youth and adults
  - Inflammatory types (papules, pustules, cysts)
  - Non-inflammatory types (black heads, white heads)
- **Rosacea**

WESTERN THERAPEUTIC ACTIONS

- Regulates and balances the hormones
- Antibiotic effect to treat infection
- Anti-inflammatory effect to reduce swelling and inflammation

CHINESE THERAPEUTIC ACTIONS

- Clears Lung heat and detoxifies the skin
- Clears Liver and Kidney fire
- Drains pus
- Purges heat

DOSAGE

Take 3 to 4 capsules three times daily. Dosage can be increased up to 6 to 8 capsules three times daily in acute cases. This formula should not be taken for more than two months continuously.

INGREDIENTS

Bai Zhi (Radix Angelicae Dahuricae)
Bo He (Herba Menthae)
Chuan Xiong (Rhizoma Chuanxiong)
Da Huang (Radix et Rhizoma Rhei)
Hu Zhang (Rhizoma et Radix Polygoni Cuspidati)
Huang Bo (Cortex Phellodendri Chinensis)
Huang Lian (Rhizoma Coptidis)
Huang Qin (Radix Scutellariae)
Jie Geng (Radix Platycodonis)
Lian Qiao (Fructus Forsythiae)
Yi Yi Ren (Semen Coicis)
Yin Yang Huo (Herba Epimedii)
Zao Jiao (Fructus Gleditsiae)
Zhi Zi (Fructus Gardeniae)

BACKGROUND

Acne vulgaris (acne) is the formation of comedones, papules, pustules, nodules, and/or cysts as a result of obstruction and inflammation of hair follicles and the sebaceous gland. Acne is a common disorder in youths, and is becoming more common in older individuals (up to age 40), due to modern dietary and lifestyle habits that consist of rich foods, and dietary and environmental toxins. Individuals who are more prone to be affected include youths who are experiencing hormonal fluctuations, women who have irregular menstruation, and people who suffer from excessive stress due to work, family, or other emotional factors.

Commonly seen types of acne in the clinic include inflammatory types (papules, pustules, cysts) and non-inflammatory types (black heads, white heads). Modern research has found that acne is closely tied to hormonal imbalances – acne in young women is most often related to menstrual cycles, and overproduction of testosterone can cause pore enlargement and overproduction of sebaceous glands, leading to acne all over the body. Acne can also be caused by improper hygiene, leading to the excessive growth of acne-causing bacteria. Regrettably, acne is not viewed as a serious disorder, with most people carrying the viewpoint that it will naturally dissipate after age 25. However, if not treated properly, acne may leave behind scarring [physically and emotionally], leading to a lifetime of self-esteem issues.

FORMULA EXPLANATION

Dermatrol (Clear) is an herbal formula that treats acne by releasing wind-heat from the exterior and clearing heat and fire from the interior.

Bo He (Herba Menthae) and *Lian Qiao* (Fructus Forsythiae) are two herbs that effectively clear wind-heat from the exterior. As the skin and the Lung are closely related, *Huang Qin* (Radix Scutellariae) clears heat and eliminates toxins from the Lung, and *Jie Geng* (Radix Platycodonis) guides these herbs to the Lung. By clearing heat from the Lung and the skin, these herbs help to directly treat acne.

Huang Qin (Radix Scutellariae), *Huang Lian* (Rhizoma Coptidis), and *Huang Bo* (Cortex Phellodendri Chinensis) are all bitter and cold herbs that clear heat and fire from upper, middle, and lower *jiaos*, respectively. Furthermore, *Zhi Zi* (Fructus Gardeniae) clears excess heat and fire throughout the body, and *Da Huang* (Radix et Rhizoma Rhei) drains all the heat out of the body through its laxative and purgative functions. Overall, these herbs clear and drain heat and fire from the interior aspects of the entire body.

Beyond clearing heat from the exterior and the interior, additional herbs are utilized to clear heat from specific areas of the body. The location of acne may indicate pathology relating to the organ systems of that particular region. Acne on the forehead indicates a problem in the Heart. The Heart dominates the *shen* (spirit), and people who have acne in this area tend to think and worry excessively, such as students who are under a lot of academic and social stress. This condition can be treated with *Zhi Zi* (Fructus Gardeniae), which sedates fire in all three *jiaos*, especially the Heart. Acne around the nose indicates heat in the Stomach and Spleen, or the digestive system. Individuals with acne in this region tend to stay up late, and have inflammatory bowels after ingesting foods that are pungent and spicy. This condition is best treated with *Huang Lian* (Rhizoma Coptidis), an herb that clears fire from the middle *jiao*. Acne on the chin indicates Kidney imbalance, or hormonal dysfunction. This type of acne tends to happen in females around their menstrual cycles when hormone levels fluctuate. *Huang Bo* (Cortex Phellodendri Chinensis) is the best herb to treat this condition, since it clears heat in the lower *jiao*. Liver is the organ that is responsible

Dermatrol (Clear)™

for feelings and emotions. Therefore, acne on the cheeks or acne outbreak associated with stress and anxiety tends to be characterized by Liver qi stagnation or Liver fire. *Hu Zhang* (Rhizoma et Radix Polygoni Cuspidati) is included to clear Liver heat and Liver fire.

In addition to clearing heat and fire, this formula uses *Bai Zhi* (Radix Angelicae Dahuricae), *Yi Yi Ren* (Semen Coicis), *Yin Yang Huo* (Herba Epimedii) and *Zao Jiao* (Fructus Gleditsiae) to clear dampness and drain pus. *Chuan Xiong* (Rhizoma Chuanxiong) is added to invigorate blood circulation, remove blood stasis, and relieve pain. Finally, *Da Huang* (Radix et Rhizoma Rhei) clears fire and drains toxic heat downward through defecation.

Overall, ***Dermatrol (Clear)*** is an excellent formula to treat acne by releasing wind-heat from the exterior, clearing heat and fire from the interior, and draining heat downward.

CAUTIONS & CONTRAINDICATIONS

- This formula is contraindicated in cases of cold or deficiency.
- Do not use this formula during pregnancy and nursing.
- The following warning statement is required by the State of California: "This product contains *Da Huang* (Radix et Rhizoma Rhei). Read and follow directions carefully. Do not use if you have or develop diarrhea, loose stools, or abdominal pain because *Da Huang* (Radix et Rhizoma Rhei) may worsen these conditions and be harmful to your health. Consult your physician if you have frequent diarrhea or if you are pregnant, nursing, taking medication, or have a medical condition."

CLINICAL NOTES

- One very effective folk remedy for acne is to use high quality, wild honey with extra virgin olive oil. Mix two drops of honey and olive oil in a clean bowl thoroughly. Apply to the acne before bedtime and leave it on overnight. This is very effective for acne that has just started to develop and is painful but has not yet manifested in redness or swelling on the face. During the day time, apply a thinner amount on the local area to prevent the acne from breaking out. This method is only useful when the honey and the olive oil are mixed and used right away. Using the same mixture the day after, or applying honey on the face first, and then olive oil next are all ineffective and may contribute to more breakouts. Note: Be sure to pick high quality honey and extra virgin olive oil to see results.

Pulse Diagnosis by Dr. Jimmy Wei-Yen Chang:

- Deep, short and convex pulse on the right *cun*
- **Acne due to poor diet (Stomach fire):** convex, forceful, and superficial pulse on the right *guan*
- **Acne due to hormones (Kidney fire):** *Taiyang* pulse, a thick, long wiry, and forceful pulse, on both *chi* positions
- **Acne due to stress (Liver qi stagnation):** convex and forceful in the left *guan*

SUPPLEMENTARY FORMULAS

- For pimples that are hard and painful, add ***Resolve (AI)***.
- For pimples that are infected with pus and abscesses, combine with ***Herbal ABX***.
- For excessive heat manifesting in red face, red tongue and/or heat sensation and irritability, add ***Gardenia Complex***.
- For excess heat in the Liver, add ***Liver DTX***.
- For deficiency heat in the Kidney, add ***Balance (Heat)***.
- With constipation, add ***Gentle Lax (Excess)***.
- With stress, add ***Calm (ES)***.
- For hormone-related acne where breakouts occur during or before menstruation, add ***Calm***.

ACUPUNCTURE TREATMENT

Traditional Points:

- **Main points:** *Baihui* (GV 20), *Chize* (LU 5), *Quchi* (LI 11), *Dazhui* (GV 14), *Hegu* (LI 4), *Feishu* (BL 13), *Weizhong* (BL 40)
- **Supplementary points:** *Sibai* (ST 2), *Xiaguan* (ST 7), *Jiache* (ST 6)
- Use the sedation method, retain needles for 30 minutes, one time daily for ten days, or until symptoms decrease, then switch to one time every other day.

Classic Master Tung's Points:

- *Yizhong* (T 77.05), *Erzhong* (T 77.06), *Sanzhong* (T 77.07), *Simashang* (T 88.18), *Simazhong* (T 88.17), *Simaxia* (T 88.19), *Waisanguan* (T 77.27), *Linggu* (T 22.05), *Dabai* (T 22.04), *Huoying* (T 66.03), *Tianhuangfu [Shenguan]* (T 77.18)

Balance Method by Dr. Richard Tan:

- Right side: *Sanjian* (LI 3), *Quchi* (LI 11), *Taibai* (SP 3), *Yinlingquan* (SP 9), *Dadun* (LR 1), *Zhongfeng* (LR 4)
- Left side: *Chize* (LU 5), *Taiyuan* (LU 9), *Zusanli* (ST 36), *Xiangu* (ST 43)
- Alternate sides from treatment to treatment.

Ear Acupuncture:

- Lung, *Shenmen*, Adrenal, Endocrine

Auricular Medicine by Dr. Li-Chun Huang:

- Endocrine, Cheek Area, Liver, Spleen, Lung, Large Intestine, Adrenal Gland. Bleed Ear Apex, Helix 4, or Cheek Area.
  - For acne that worsen during the menstrual cycle, add Uterus, Ovary, Pituitary

NUTRITION

- Besides establishing a normal pattern of work and rest, individuals should incorporate more fresh fruits and vegetables into their diets. Cook and eat fresh foods by steaming, boiling, and light dry-frying.
- Drink more water to maintain normal bowel movements.

Dermatrol (Clear)™

- Consume foods that are low calorie, low fat, and low carbohydrate.
- Incorporate more of the following cooling foods in the diet: tofu, tomato, celery, asparagus, bamboo, seaweed, kelp, bitter melon, cucumber, gourd, luffa, winter melon, orange, grapefruit, pear, banana, papaya, watermelon, white radish, mustard leaf, potherb mustard, cactus, Chinese kale, napa, and bamboo sprout. However, long-term consumption of cold fruits and vegetables like the ones listed above may be damaging to the Spleen. To make the property more neutral, add about 20 pieces of *Gou Qi Zi* (Fructus Lycii) when cooking.
- Avoid certain fruits that produce heat and aggravate acne, such as mango, lychee, and durian.
- Avoid spicy foods, deep-fried foods, and canned foods.
- Avoid spicy, pungent, aromatic vegetables such as pepper, garlic, onions, ginger, basil, rosemary, cumin, fennel, anise, leeks, chives, scallions, thyme, saffron, wormwood, mustard, chili pepper, wasabi, and cardamon.
- Avoid drinks such as coffee, alcohol, sodas, and energy drinks.
- Avoid foods that may trigger a skin response, such as chocolate, sweets, and peanuts.
- Avoid foods and drinks with artificial coloring. Limit the intake of foods high in sugar and carbohydrates.
- Consume as few meat products as possible, especially meats high in fat. Do not eat processed meats, such as lunch meats, hot dogs and sausages, as they contain nitrites that are associated with inflammation and chronic disease.

The Tao of Nutrition by Dr. Maoshing Ni and Cathy McNease:

- Eat more squash, cucumbers, watermelon, winter melon, celery, carrots, cabbage, beet tops, dandelions, aloe vera, mulberry leaf, carrot tops, lettuce, potato, cherries, papaya, pear, persimmon, raspberries, buckwheat, alfalfa sprouts, millet, brown rice, and mung beans.
- Drink plenty of water.
- Blend a cucumber, apply externally; leave on for 20 minutes then wash off.
- Apply plain, low fat organic yogurt; leave on for 20 minutes then wash off.
- Rub watermelon rind on the acne.
- Apply aloe vera to the affected area.
- Eat watermelon or drink watermelon juice.
- Drink dandelion and beet top tea.
- Boil raspberries to a concentrate and wash area with it.
- For oozing acne conditions, cover area with pearl barley powder overnight, wash off with water; or mix pearl barley powder with aloe vera gel into a paste and leave on area overnight, then wash off with water.

LIFESTYLE INSTRUCTIONS

- Wash the face often, but not excessively. Excessive washing may lead to more oil production.
- After perspiring or washing the face, make sure to dry the face with a clean towel or cloth.
- Use natural skin care products instead of products that contain chemicals and artificial ingredients.
- Use proper moisturizers, e.g., moisturizers that are suitable for the skin type.
- Be sure to rinse off excess facial cleanser, soap, and lotion from the face as the chemical or the oil may contribute to more breakouts.
- Always remove cosmetic products from the face before bedtime.
- Go to bed before 10:00 p.m. and make sure to have adequate amount of sleep.
- Drink more water throughout the day.
- Avoid humidity and sweating, which may trigger acne.

PHARMACOLOGICAL AND CLINICAL RESEARCH

Acne vulgaris (acne) is the formation of comedones, papules, pustules, nodules, and/or cysts as a result of obstruction and inflammation of hair follicles and the sebaceous glands. Optimal treatment requires use of herbs to target various aspects of acne, including herbs with regulatory effects on the hormones, herbs with antibiotic effects to treat the infection, herbs with anti-inflammatory effects to reduce swelling and inflammation.

The most common cause of acne in puberty is the overproduction of sebum due to the stimulation of androgen. Therefore, use of herbs to regulate and balance the hormones will greatly reduce the number and severity of acne outbreaks. *Yin Yang Huo* (Herba Epimedii) is one of the most effective herbs to influence the production and release of sex hormones, including corticosterone, cortisol, testosterone, and estrogen.[1,2,3] Another herb of great importance is *Huang Qin* (Radix Scutellariae), which has an antiandrogenic effect through inhibition of the androgen receptor signaling pathway.[4] Together, these two herbs regulate and balance the endogenous hormones, which in turn control sebaceous gland function and excessive production of sebum.[5]

Infection is an important cause and complication of acne. As a cause, proliferation of *Propionibacterium acnes* in the keratinocytes directly contributes to infection and inflammation of the follicles. As a complication, cases of acne with open comedones are prone to contact infection from skin bacteria, which in turn form abscesses and increase the risks of scarring. Therefore, the use of herbs with antibiotic effects is very important for optimal treatment of acne. According to a study that evaluated 119 plants, *Yin Yang Huo* (Herba Epimedii) and *Hu Zhang* (Rhizoma et Radix Polygoni Cuspidati) have been identified as two herbs with potent antibiofilm activity against *Propionibacterium acnes*. In fact, these two herbs showed marked antibiofilm activity when used in subinhibitory concentrations, indicating that killing of microbial cells is not their only mode of action.[6] Furthermore, this formula contains many other herbs with antibiotic effects, including but not limited to *Huang*

FORMULAS

Dermatrol (Clear)™

Bo (Cortex Phellodendri Chinensis),[7,8] *Huang Lian* (Rhizoma Coptidis),[9] *Huang Qin* (Radix Scutellariae),[10,11] and *Lian Qiao* (Fructus Forsythiae).[12]

Obstruction of pilosebaceous duct is also an important aspect of acne. Therefore, use of herbs with anti-inflammatory effects is important to reduce swelling and inflammation, and eliminate the obstruction. In this formula, *Bo He* (Herba Menthae) and *Zao Jiao* (Fructus Gleditsiae) have antiallergic and anti-inflammatory effects to suppress histamine release and prostaglandin D(2) synthesis from mast cells.[13,14,15] *Da Huang* (Radix et Rhizoma Rhei), *Huang Lian* (Rhizoma Coptidis), and *Huang Qin* (Radix Scutellariae) all have anti-inflammatory activity to reduce swelling and inflammation and treat skin disorders.[16] Finally, other herbs with anti-inflammatory effects include *Bai Zhi* (Radix Angelicae Dahuricae),[17] *Chuan Xiong* (Rhizoma Chuanxiong),[18] *Hu Zhang* (Rhizoma et Radix Polygoni Cuspidati),[19] *Yi Yi Ren* (Semen Coicis),[20] *Zhi Zi* (Fructus Gardeniae),[21] and *Yin Yang Huo* (Herba Epimedii).[22] Together, these herbs reduce swelling and inflammation to eliminate obstruction of the pilosebaceous duct in acne.

In summary, ***Dermatrol (Clear)*** has an excellent effect to treat acne through its pharmacological effect to regulate the hormones, control and suppress infection, and reduce swelling and inflammation.

COMPARATIVE ANALYSIS

Acne vulgaris (acne) is the formation of comedones, papules, pustules, nodules, and/or cysts characterized as inflammatory (papules, pustules, cysts) and non-inflammatory types (black heads, white heads). Common causes of acne include hormonal imbalance, use of occlusive cosmetics, cleansing agents, clothing, and environment (humidity). Proper treatment of acne is important for many reasons: to avoid infection, to prevent scarring, and possible short- and long-term self-esteem issues.

In Western medicine, acne is treated with four main types of drugs. First are topical antibacterial drugs, such as benzoyl peroxide, clindamycin, and erythromycin. Though the use of these drugs topically is generally well tolerated, they may still cause adverse reactions such as dry skin and allergic responses. Second is the use of topical exfoliants to remove the old and dead skin cells, such as Retin A (tretinoin) or Tazorac (tazarotene). The main adverse reactions of these types of drugs are skin irritation, increased sun sensitivity, and stinging sensations. Third is the use of oral antibiotics, such as tetracycline, doxycycline, or erythromycin. Though these drugs are effective and inexpensive, use of them will likely cause increased sun sensitivity and upset stomach. Finally, when all else fails, oral retinoid such as Accutane (isotretinoin) may be prescribed. However, this should be avoided if at all possible because this drug causes many short- and long-term side effects, such as damages to the blood cells, the liver, arthralgias, depression, and risks of birth defects.

In Chinese herbal medicine, acne is generally diagnosed as a heat condition. As such, herbs that dispel wind-heat from the exterior and clear damp-heat from the interior are generally prescribed with great success. From pharmacological perspectives, these heat-clearing herbs are ones with antibiotic and anti-inflammatory effects. Furthermore, since hormonal imbalance is also a common cause of acne, an effective, but often under-utilized approach, is the use of herbs to regulate and balance the hormones. In this formula, herbs are used to clear heat from the exterior and balance the hormones from the interior to achieve a synergistic and optimal result for acne treatment.

Overall, both herbs and drugs treat acne safely and effectively. In most cases, herbs can be used to treat mild to moderate cases of acne with good effect and little or no side effects. Short-term use of antibiotic drugs or topical exfoliants is also well-tolerated in most cases. However, oral retinoid such as Accutane (isotretinoin) or oral corticosteroids such as prednisone should not be used unless the acne condition is very severe, and all other options have been proven ineffective, as these drugs often carry more long-term risks than short-term benefits.

References

1. *Zhong Yao Da Ci Dian* (Dictionary of Chinese Herbs), 1977:2251.
2. *Zhong Xi Yi Jie He Za Zhi* (Journal of Integrated Chinese and Western Medicine), 1989; 9(12):737-8,710.
3. De Naeyer A, Pocock V, Milligan S, De Keukeleire D. Estrogenic activity of a polyphenolic extract of the leaves of Epimedium brevicornum. Fitoterapia. 2005 Jan;76(1):35-40.
4. Bonham M, Posakony J, Coleman I, Montgomery B, Simon J, Nelson PS. Characterization of chemical constituents in Scutellaria baicalensis with antiandrogenic and growth-inhibitory activities toward prostate carcinoma. Clin Cancer Res. 2005 May 15;11(10):3905-14.
5. Porter, R. et al. The Merck Manual of Diagnosis and Therapy 19th Edition. Merck Sharp & Dohme Corp. 2011.
6. Coenye T, Brackman G, Rigole P, De Witte E, Honraet K, Rossel B, Nelis HJ. Eradication of Propionibacterium acnes biofilms by plant extracts and putative identification of icariin, resveratrol and salidroside as active compounds. Phytomedicine. 2012 Mar 15;19(5):409-12.
7. *Zhong Yao Da Ci Dian* (Dictionary of Chinese Herbs), 1977: 2032.
8. *Zhong Cao Yao* (Chinese Herbal Medicine), 1985; 16(1):34.
9. Zhang S, Zhang B, Xing K, Zhang X, Tian X, Dai W. Inhibitory effects of golden thread (Coptis chinensis) and berberine on Microcystis aeruginosa. Fisheries College, Ocean University of China, Qingdao 266003, P. R. China. Water Sci Technol. 2010;61(3):763-9.
10. *Zhong Yao Xue* (Chinese Herbology), 1988; 137:140.
11. *J Pharm Pharmacol* 2000 Mar;52(3):361-6.
12. *Shan Xi Xin Yi Yao* (New Medicine and Herbology of Shanxi), 1980; 9(11):51.
13. Chan BC, Hon KL, Leung PC, Sam SW, Fung KP, Lee MY, Lau HY. Traditional Chinese medicine for atopic eczema: PentaHerbs formula suppresses inflammatory mediators release from mast cells. J Ethnopharmacol. 2008 Oct 30;120(1):85-91.
14. Lee MY, Lee JA, Seo CS, Ha H, Lee NH, Shin HK. Protective effects of Mentha haplocalyx ethanol extract (MH) in a mouse model of allergic asthma. Phytother Res. 2011 Jun;25(6):863-9. doi: 10.1002/ptr.3341.
15. Dai Y., Chan Y.P., Chu L.M. & Bu P.P. Antiallergic and anti-inflammatory properties of the ethanolic extract from *Gleditsia sinensis. Biol Pharm Bull.* 2002, 25(9): 1179-1182.

Dermatrol (Clear) ™

16. Cuéllar MJ, Giner RM, Recio MC, Máñez S, Ríos JL. Topical anti-inflammatory activity of some Asian medicinal plants used in dermatological disorders. Departament de Farmacologia, Facultat de Farmàcia, Universitat de València, Avda. Vicent Andrés Estellés, s/n. 46100 Burjassot, Valencia, Spain. Fitoterapia. 2001 Mar;72(3):221-9.

17. Kang OH, Lee GH, Choi HJ, Park PS, Chae HS, Jeong SI, Kim YC, Sohn DH, Park H, Lee JH, Kwon DY. Ethyl acetate extract from Angelica Dahuricae Radix inhibits lipopolysaccharide-induced production of nitric oxide, prostaglandin E2 and tumor necrosis factor-alphavia mitogen-activated protein kinases and nuclear factor-kappaB in macrophages. Pharmacol Res. 2007 Apr;55(4):263-70.

18. Liu L, Ning ZQ, Shan S, Zhang K, Deng T, Lu XP, Cheng YY. Phthalide Lactones from Ligusticum chuanxiong inhibit lipopolysaccharide-induced TNF-alpha production and TNF-alpha-mediated NF-kappaB Activation. Planta Med. 2005 Sep;71(9):808-13.

19. Kim KW, Ha KT, Park CS, Jin UH, Chang HW, Lee IS, Kim CH. Polygonum cuspidatum, compared with baicalin and berberine, inhibits inducible nitric oxide synthase and cyclooxygenase-2 gene expressions in RAW 264.7 macrophages. Molecular and Cellular Glycobiology Unit, Department of Biological Science, Sungkyunkwan University, Chunchun-Dong 300, Suwon City, Kyunggi-Do 440-746, South Korea. Vascul Pharmacol. 2007 Aug-Sep;47(2-3):99-107.

20. Seo W.G., Pae H.O., Chai K.Y., Yun Y.G., Kwon T.H. & Chung H.T. Inhibitory effects of methanol extract of seeds of Job's Tears (*Coix lachryma-jobi* L. var. *ma-yuen*) on nitric oxide and superoxide production in RAW 264.7 macrophages. *Immunopharmacol Immunotoxicol.* 2000, 22(3): 545-554.

21. Hwang SM, Lee YJ, Yoon JJ, Lee SM, Kang DG, Lee HS. Gardenia jasminoides inhibits tumor necrosis factor-alpha-induced vascular inflammation in endothelial cells. Professional Graduate School of Oriental Medicine, Wonkwang University, Chonbuk, Republic of Korea. Phytother Res. 2010 Jun;24 Suppl 2:S214-9.

22. Yuk SS, Lim EM, Lee JY, Lee YJ, Kim YS, Lee TH, Park SK, Bae H, Kim HM, Ko SG, Oh MS, Park W. Antiinflammatory effects of Epimedium brevicornum water extract on lipopolysaccharide-activated RAW264.7 macrophages. College of Oriental Medicine, Kyungwon University, Seongnam, Republic of Korea. Phytother Res. 2010 Dec;24(12):1781-7. doi: 10.1002/ptr.3161.

FORMULAS

Dermatrol (Damp)™

CLINICAL APPLICATIONS

- **Any skin conditions that appear to be visibly wet and purulent, or contain pus, abscesses or oozing fluids.**
- **Skin conditions considered as wet**, such as infectious eczema, lesions, ulcers, carbuncles, furuncles, cellulitis, rash, candidal infections, contact and stasis dermatitis, seborrheic dermatitis, herpes zoster, and acne vulgaris.

WESTERN THERAPEUTIC ACTIONS

- Antiallergic effect to relieve allergy
- Antipruritic function to relieve itching
- Anti-inflammatory activity to reduce skin swelling and inflammation
- Antibiotic effect to treat skin infection
- Antitoxin and antidote benefits to neutralize and antagonize chemicals, allergens and toxins

CHINESE THERAPEUTIC ACTIONS

- Clears heat, eliminates toxins
- Dispels wind, relieves itching
- Strengthens the Spleen, dispels dampness

DOSAGE

Take 3 to 4 capsules three times daily. Dosage can be increased up to 6 to 8 capsules three times daily in acute cases. This formula should not be taken for more than two months continuously.

INGREDIENTS

Bai Shao (Radix Paeoniae Alba)
Bo He (Herba Menthae)
Chai Hu (Radix Bupleuri)
Che Qian Zi (Semen Plantaginis)
Chi Shao (Radix Paeoniae Rubra)
Chuan Mu Tong (Caulis Clematidis Armandii)
Chuan Xiong (Rhizoma Chuanxiong)
Dang Gui (Radix Angelicae Sinensis)
Di Huang (Radix Rehmanniae)
Du Huo (Radix Angelicae Pubescentis)
Fang Feng (Radix Saposhnikoviae)
Fu Ling (Poria)
Gan Cao (Radix et Rhizoma Glycyrrhizae)
Geng Mi (Semen Oryzae)
Huang Bo (Cortex Phellodendri Chinensis)
Huang Lian (Rhizoma Coptidis)
Huang Qin (Radix Scutellariae)
Jie Geng (Radix Platycodonis)
Jing Jie (Herba Schizonepetae)
Lian Qiao (Fructus Forsythiae)
Long Dan (Radix et Rhizoma Gentianae)
Mu Dan Pi (Cortex Moutan)
Niu Bang Zi (Fructus Arctii)
Qian Hu (Radix Peucedani)
Qiang Huo (Rhizoma et Radix Notopterygii)
Shan Yao (Rhizoma Dioscoreae)
Shan Zhu Yu (Fructus Corni)
Sheng Jiang (Rhizoma Zingiberis Recens)
Shi Gao (Gypsum Fibrosum)
Shu Di Huang (Radix Rehmanniae Praeparata)
Tian Hua Fen (Radix Trichosanthis)
Yi Yi Ren (Semen Coicis)
Ze Xie (Rhizoma Alismatis)
Zhi Gan Cao (Radix et Rhizoma Glycyrrhizae Praeparata cum Melle)
Zhi Mu (Rhizoma Anemarrhenae)
Zhi Qiao (Fructus Aurantii)
Zhi Zi (Fructus Gardeniae)

BACKGROUND

The skin is the largest organ in the body, and it functions as a protective barrier that keeps undesirable substances from entering. Because the skin is the physical barrier that separates the exterior from the interior, skin health can be affected by factors from both the outside and the inside. External factors that affect the skin include infection (bacteria, virus, and parasites), external exposure to allergens (poison ivy, poison oak, chemicals used in cosmetics or cleaning agents, and drugs used in skin creams), insect bites (spiders and ticks), or trauma. Internal factors that affect the skin include inhalation of allergens (dust, pollen, and dander), ingestion of allergens (peanuts, nuts, fish, wheat, eggs, and milk), intake of certain drugs (penicillin, sulfa drugs, aspirin, and opioids), autoimmune diseases (systemic lupus erythematosus, Sjögren's syndrome, and psoriasis), and emotional or physical imbalance (stress and anxiety).

Although there are multiple and complicated causes of skin disorders, the clinical manifestations are usually simple and straight-forward: most skin disorders have either wet or dry characteristics. Optimal treatment requires the use of medicinal substances to treat both the cause and the symptoms.

Skin disorders with damp/wet characteristics may have open lesions with infection, inflammation, ulceration, pus, and abscesses; and they often affect areas with excessive moisture, such as toes, buttocks, armpits, groin, and under the breast. Examples of skin disorders with damp/wet characteristics include skin infection, skin ulcers, exudative skin lesions, sores, abscesses, carbuncles, furuncles, cellulitis, seborrheic dermatitis, and acne vulgaris.

Skin disorders with dry characteristics often appear to be dry, red, flaky, and scaly with underlying damages to and atrophy of the skin. Examples of skin disorders with dry characteristics include psoriasis, atopic dermatitis, urticaria, rosacea, warts, tinea versicolor, erysipelas, and eczema.

FORMULA EXPLANATION

Acute dermatological disorders are generally due to wind-heat and toxic heat invasion, which is usually associated with

Dermatrol (Damp)™

physical contact or oral ingestion of allergen(s). On the other hand, chronic dermatological conditions involve more with the accumulation of dampness in the body, which is the result of improper diet or Spleen's weakness in metabolism and transporting water. ***Dermatrol (Damp)*** has four groups of herbs to address both acute and chronic skin conditions with wet lesions.

The first group of herbs drains dampness, strengthens the Spleen, and helps the body metabolize water. They include *Che Qian Zi* (Semen Plantaginis), *Chuan Mu Tong* (Caulis Clematidis Armandii), *Fu Ling* (Poria), *Yi Yi Ren* (Semen Coicis), *Ze Xie* (Rhizoma Alismatis) and *Sheng Jiang* (Rhizoma Zingiberis Recens). These herbs have diuretic and anti-inflammatory activities to reduce skin swelling and water retention.

The second group of herbs expels wind and relieves itching: *Bo He* (Herba Menthae), *Chai Hu* (Radix Bupleuri), *Qian Hu* (Radix Peucedani), *Chuan Xiong* (Rhizoma Chuanxiong), *Jie Geng* (Radix Platycodonis), *Du Huo* (Radix Angelicae Pubescentis), *Qiang Huo* (Rhizoma et Radix Notopterygii), *Fang Feng* (Radix Saposhnikoviae), and *Jing Jie* (Herba Schizonepetae). These herbs have an antihistamine effect to treat allergy, and an antipruritic effect to relieve itching.

The third group clears heat and eliminates toxins. Herbs in this group include *Chi Shao* (Radix Paeoniae Rubra), *Huang Bo* (Cortex Phellodendri Chinensis), *Huang Lian* (Rhizoma Coptidis), *Huang Qin* (Radix Scutellariae), *Lian Qiao* (Fructus Forsythiae), *Long Dan* (Radix et Rhizoma Gentianae), *Mu Dan Pi* (Cortex Moutan), *Niu Bang Zi* (Fructus Arctii), *Shi Gao* (Gypsum Fibrosum), *Tian Hua Fen* (Radix Trichosanthis), *Zhi Mu* (Rhizoma Anemarrhenae), and *Zhi Zi* (Fructus Gardeniae). These herbs have an antibiotic function to treat skin infection, and anti-inflammatory function to reduce skin swelling and inflammation.

The fourth group of herbs aims to tonify blood and nourish yin, which is the underlying cause for chronic, non-healing rashes, sores, and dermatological problems. With abundant blood, wind cannot rise to cause further itching. This group of herbs tonifies yin and nourishes blood to prevent heat from flaring up and aggravating the symptoms. Herbs in this group include *Bai Shao* (Radix Paeoniae Alba), *Dang Gui* (Radix Angelicae Sinensis), *Di Huang* (Radix Rehmanniae), *Geng Mi* (Semen Oryzae), *Shan Yao* (Rhizoma Dioscoreae), *Shan Zhu Yu* (Fructus Corni), and *Shu Di Huang* (Radix Rehmanniae Praeparata). *Chuan Xiong* (Rhizoma Chuanxiong) and *Zhi Qiao* (Fructus Aurantii) promote qi and blood circulation and remove stagnation. Finally, *Gan Cao* (Radix et Rhizoma Glycyrrhizae) and *Zhi Gan Cao* (Radix et Rhizoma Glycyrrhizae Praeparata cum Melle) are used to harmonize the formula. As these herbs strengthen the underlying body constitution, they also regulate and balance the endocrine system, and in turn facilitate the release of endogenous corticosteroids as necessary to reduce swelling and inflammation.

In summary, ***Dermatrol (Damp)*** effectively treats damp/wet skin disorders by using herbs to strengthen the Spleen and dry dampness, clear heat and eliminate toxins, and dispel wind and relieve itching.

CAUTIONS & CONTRAINDICATIONS

- This formula is contraindicated in patients with cold or deficiency cold signs.
- This formula is contraindicated during pregnancy and nursing.
- In addition to external factors (dry skin, atopic dermatitis, contact dermatitis, infections) and internal factors (allergic reactions through ingestion or inhalation), skin disorders may be caused by conditions such as cholestasis, chronic renal failure, hyper- or hypothyroidism, diabetes, iron deficiency, and polycythemia vera. Optimal treatment requires these conditions to be ruled out, or confirmed and treated.
- This formula is contraindicated for long-term use. Identification and elimination of the cause is the best long-term solution. When symptoms clear up, re-evaluate the condition and prescribe some other formulas to address the underlying cause of the skin condition. Many times the patient may have another attack and it is usually due to poor dietary habit, so it is essential to ask the patient to be extremely careful with what they eat in order to prevent future break outs.
- This herbal formula contains herbs that invigorate blood circulation, such as *Dang Gui* (Radix Angelicae Sinensis). Therefore, patients who are on anticoagulant or antiplatelet therapies, such as Coumadin (warfarin), should use this formula with caution, or not at all, as there may be a higher risk of bleeding and bruising.[1,2,3]

CLINICAL NOTES

- *Yin Care*, a topical herbal solution, may be applied topically to help relieve itching.
- This formula is designed by Dr. Jimmy Wei-Yen Chang and has worked effectively for over 90% of his patients who suffer from various dermatological conditions with damp/wet lesions. However, it is not to be used long term as the heat-clearing herbs may weaken the Spleen and Stomach. After the symptoms and signs improve or are alleviated, one must find the underlying cause and treat it so the lesions do not return. Taking the herbs at a large dosage or for a prolonged period of time may not be necessary as the triggering factors are either due to exposure to allergen or improper diet and lifestyle. Please refer to Nutrition and Lifestyle Instructions sections to help maintain a healthy constitution and clear skin.

Pulse Diagnosis by Dr. Jimmy Wei-Yen Chang:

- **Wet skin lesions** due to damp-heat accumulation: deep and forceful pulse on all three pulse positions (*cun, guan, chi*)

FORMULAS

Dermatrol (Damp)™

SUPPLEMENTARY FORMULAS

- For severe itching, add ***Silerex***.
- For acne, add ***Dermatrol (Clear)***.
- To enhance the overall antibacterial function, add ***Herbal ABX***.
- To enhance the overall antiviral function, add ***Herbal AVR***.
- For severe inflammation, add ***Astringent Complex***.
- With additional signs of fire manifesting in red eyes, red tongue, anger and/or constipation, combine with ***Gardenia Complex*** and ***Gentle Lax (Excess)***.
- With additional signs of damp accumulation due to Spleen and Stomach qi deficiencies, add ***Pinellia Complex***.
- In chronic dermatological conditions where the surrounding skin of the lesion appears purple and the tongue is purple, add ***Circulation (SJ)***.
- For weakened immune system, *wei* (defensive) *qi* deficiency, or chronic overall deficient patients with inability to heal lesions and wounds, add a high dose of ***Immune +***.
- For skin conditions due to exposure to chemicals, such as paint, nail polish, glue, drugs, pain killers, bleach, or aerosol, combine with ***Herbal DTX***.
- For skin condition associated with stress, add ***Calm***.

ACUPUNCTURE TREATMENT

Traditional Points:

- *Quchi* (LI 11), *Xuehai* (SP 10), *Hegu* (LI 4), *Sanyinjiao* (SP 6), *Fengchi* (GB 20), *Dazhui* (GV 14), *Fengmen* (BL 12), *Fengshi* (GB 31), *Jianyu* (LI 15), *Zusanli* (ST 36)

Classic Master Tung's Points:

- **Eczema:** *Simashang* (T 88.18), *Simazhong* (T 88.17), *Simaxia* (T 88.19), *Linggu* (T 22.05), *Minghuang* (T 88.12), *Tianhuang* (T 88.13), *Qihuang* (T 88.14), *Tianhuang* (T 77.17), *Dihuang* (T 77.19), *Renhuang* (T 77.21), *Jinqianshang* (T 88.24), *Jinqianxia* (T 88.23)
- **Atopic dermatitis:** *Simashang* (T 88.18), *Simazhong* (T 88.17), *Simaxia* (T 88.19), *Linggu* (T 22.05), *Zhisima* (T 11.07)
- **Herpes zoster:** *Linggu* (T 22.05), *Tianhuang* (T 88.13), *Minghuang* (T 88.12), *Qihuang* (T 88.14), *Simashang* (T 88.18), *Simazhong* (T 88.17), *Simaxia* (T 88.19), *Shuitong* (T 1010.19), *Shuijin* (T 1010.20)
- **Tinea versicolor:** *Tianhuang* (T 88.13), *Minghuang* (T 88.12), *Qihuang* (T 88.14), *Simashang* (T 88.18), *Simaxia* (T 88.19), *Simazhong* (T 88.17), *Shuijin* (T 1010.20), *Shuitong* (T 1010.19). Bleed the LR area T5 – T9 and KI area T9 – T12 on the back with cupping. Bleed before needling for best result.
- **Hives:** *Simashang* (T 88.18), *Simaxia* (T 88.19), *Simazhong* (T 88.17), *Tianhuang* (T 77.17), *Dihuang* (T 77.19), *Renhuang* (T 77.21), *Tianhuang* (T 88.13), *Minghuang* (T 88.12), *Qihuang* (T 88.14), *Zhisima* (T 11.07)
- **Dry, cracking hands/fingers:** *Mu* (T 11.17), *Zhisima* (T 11.07)

Master Tung's Points by Dr. Chuan-Min Wang:

- **Wet, oozing lesions:** Bleed *Zhiwu* (T 11.26). Needle *Waisanguan* (T 77.27).

Balance Method by Dr. Richard Tan:

- Right side: *Sanjian* (LI 3), *Quchi* (LI 11), *Zhongzhu* (TH 3), *Tianjing* (TH 10), *Taibai* (SP 3), *Yinlingquan* (SP 9)
- Left side: *Chize* (LU 5), *Taiyuan* (LU 9), *Shaoshang* (LU 11), *Jingqu* (LU 8), *Zusanli* (ST 36), *Xiangu* (ST 43), *Jinggu* (BL 64), *Zhiyin* (BL 67)
- Alternate sides from treatment to treatment.

Ear Acupuncture:

- *Ah shi* points, Endocrine, Subcortex, Lung, *Shenmen*, Sympathetic

Auricular Medicine by Dr. Li-Chun Huang:

- **Rash and itching:** Allergy Area, *Shenmen*, Sympathetic, Occiput, Nervous Subcortex, Lung, Diaphragm, Spleen, Liver. Bleed Ear Apex.
- **Contact dermatitis:** Allergic Area, Sympathetic, Adrenal Gland, Liver, Spleen, Lung, Endocrine, corresponding points (to the area affected). Bleed Ear Apex.
  - For dermatitis with severe pain, add *Shenmen* and Occiput.
- **Eczema:** Allergic Area, Lung, Sympathetic, Spleen, *Shenmen*, Endocrine, Occiput, Diaphragm, corresponding points (to the area affected). Bleed Ear Apex.
- **Cutaneous pruritis:** *Shenmen*, Occiput, Liver, Spleen, Lung, Endocrine, Diaphragm, Allergic Area. Bleed Ear Apex.
- **Urticaria:** Liver, Lung, Spleen, Diaphragm, *Shenmen*, Occiput, Allergic Area, Sympathetic, Endocrine, Adrenal Gland. Bleed Ear Apex.
- **Severe itching:** Prick five times on the ear apex, five times each on the helix near the Great Auricular Nerve and Lesser Occipital Nerve.

Taoist Ear Points by Jun-Qing Luo:

- Bleed the back of the ear for any visible veins. This is very effective for relieving itching and treatment of any dermatological disorders.

NUTRITION

- According to the five elements theory, the Spleen (earth element) generates the Lung (metal element). In order to be free of any skin condition, which is governed by the Lung (metal element), the Spleen (earth element) must be free from damaging foods. Consumption of these damaging foods, such as ones listed below, will worsen the patient's condition and possibly make herbal treatment less effective or ineffective.
  - Seafood: especially shellfish, like crabs, oyster, scallops, clams, lobster, and shrimp (they enter the *yangming* Stomach channel).
  - Fermented foods: cheese or fermented tofu.

Dermatrol (Damp)™

- Dairy: milk, cream, yogurt, cheese, and ice cream.
- Sugar: any and all foods containing sugar, such as cake and dessert.
- Meat: lamb, beef, goose, and duck.
- Deep-fried or greasy food.
- Certain fruits: mango and durian.
- Stimulants: coffee, alcohol, and energy drinks.
- Carbohydrates: white rice or bread as they may damage the Spleen and in turn produce more dampness.
- Spicy, pungent, aromatic vegetables: pepper, garlic, onions, basil, rosemary, cumin, fennel, anise, leeks, chives, scallions, thyme, saffron, wormwood, mustard, chili pepper, and wasabi.

- If the patient is allergic to any food or feels uncomfortable after eating certain foods, then it is best to avoid eating them.

The Tao of Nutrition by Dr. Maoshing Ni and Cathy McNease:

- Increase consumption of potatoes, broccoli, dandelion, mung beans, seaweed, pearl barley, azuki beans, corn silk, water chestnuts, winter melon, and watermelon.
- Mash fresh potato and apply locally, changing every four hours, for three days.
- Apply honey to affected area.
- Apply mashed daikon radish to affected area.
- Make tea from dandelion and corn silk.
- Boil soup from seaweed and winter melon, drinking at least one time per day for ten days.
- Externally, wash with equal portions of salt and borax, dissolved in warm water; wash area two to three times daily. Do not use internally.

LIFESTYLE INSTRUCTIONS

- To properly restore the immune function, the patient is advised to sleep by 10:00 p.m. so they may enter deep sleep by 1:00 a.m. (Liver time according to the Chinese Anatomical Clock) to fully rest the Liver to restore its detoxification functions.
- Avoid being overly tired from working or stress whenever possible.
- Do not scratch or irritate lesions as it might lead to scar formation and further infection.
- Proper skin care is important for treatment of skin conditions. Use cool or lukewarm water when bathing, mild or moisturizing soap, limited bathing duration and frequency, and avoid tight or irritating clothing.

PHARMACOLOGICAL AND CLINICAL RESEARCH

Skin disorders with damp/wet characteristics, such as skin infection, skin ulcers and exudative skin lesions, have open lesions with infection, inflammation, ulceration, pus, and abscesses. Causes of skin disorders with damp/wet characteristics may be external (infection, direct contact, trauma) or internal (ingestion or inhalation of allergens, autoimmune diseases, emotional or physical imbalance). Optimal treatment requires the use of medicinal substances to treat both the cause and the symptoms. ***Dermatrol (Damp)*** contains herbs with multiple pharmacological effects, including but not limited to antiallergic, antipruritic, anti-inflammatory, antibiotic, antitoxin, and antidotal.

Dermatrol (Damp) contains many herbs with direct and general effects to treat skin disorders. *Sheng Jiang* (Rhizoma Zingiberis Recens) has a stimulant effect to promote and facilitate human normal epidermal keratinocytes and dermal fibroblasts cell growths.[4] *Bo He* (Herba Menthae) has been shown to increase local blood circulation to the skin to relieve itching and pain.[5] *Jing Jie* (Herba Schizonepetae) has a general effect on the skin, and has been used successfully to treat dermatological disorders, such as measles, pruritic rash, and itching.[6] *Dang Gui* (Radix Angelicae Sinensis) has an antipimple and an antieczema effect exerted through the regulation of nuclear factor kappa B, maleic dialdehyde (MDA), polymorphonuclear cells, interleukin-1β, inducible nitric oxide synthase, and tumor necrosis factor-α.[7] Lastly, *Di Huang* (Radix Rehmanniae) has been used with good success to treat rashes, urticaria, and contact dermatitis.[8]

Dermatrol (Damp) utilizes many herbs with antiallergic and antipruritic effects to treat various skin disorders. *Huang Qin* (Radix Scutellariae) has a remarkable effect as an antiallergic agent. It inhibits histamine and leukotriene release from mast cells, with greater potency than Intal (cromolyn), a drug that prevents the release of inflammatory chemicals such as histamine from mast cells.[9] Furthermore, *Huang Qin* (Radix Scutellariae) also inhibits the passive cutaneous anaphylaxis reaction through its downregulation of the expression of various inflammatory mediators.[10] *Jie Geng* (Radix Platycodonis) also has a significant effect – it treats allergies by inhibiting the inflammatory cytokines and the Syk-dependent signaling cascades, according to *in vivo* and *in vitro* studies.[11] *Shu Di Huang* (Radix Rehmanniae Praeparata) has been shown to inhibit systemic allergic reactions in a dose-dependent manner through the inhibition of histamine release from the peritoneal mast cells and significant suppression of tumor necrosis factor-alpha (TNF-α) production.[12] Topical application of extract from *Di Huang* (Radix Rehmanniae) and *Shu Di Huang* (Radix Rehmanniae Praeparata) shows marked anti-inflammatory and antiallergic activities to treat atopic dermatitis by suppressing the expression of cytokines, chemokines, and adhesion molecules.[13] *Niu Bang Zi* (Fructus Arctii) has a significant antiallergic effect to reduce the release of inflammatory mediators through inhibition of degranulation and cys-leukotriene release.[14] It effectively treats allergic diseases, including atopic dermatitis, by inhibiting the expression of IL-4 and IL-5.[15] Furthermore, *Zhi Mu* (Rhizoma Anemarrhenae) has a strong antiallergic effect, and can be used to inhibit the passive cutaneous anaphylaxis reaction induced by the antigen-immunoglobulin E (IgE) complex.[16] Lastly, *Jing Jie* (Herba Schizonepetae) and *Lian Qiao* (Fructus Forsythiae) have an antipruritic effect to inhibit itch-scratch response induced by substance P.[17]

Dermatrol (Damp)™

Dermatrol (Damp) incorporates many herbs with anti-inflammatory effects to treat inflammatory skin disorders. *Huang Qin* (Radix Scutellariae), *Huang Lian* (Rhizoma Coptidis) and *Huang Bo* (Cortex Phellodendri Chinensis) all have anti-inflammatory activities, and may be used to treat different skin disorders.[18] *Fu Ling* (Poria) and *Lian Qiao* (Fructus Forsythiae) are two herbs with beneficial effects to treat skin diseases involving chronic inflammation. These two herbs have inhibitory effects on lipoxygenase, cyclo-oxygenase, and elastase activities, which are therapeutic targets in dermatological disorders.[19] *Chai Hu* (Radix Bupleuri) reduces inflammation by decreasing capillary permeability caused by histamine and 5-hydroxy-tryptamine.[20] Glycyrrhizin and glycyrrhetinic acid, two compounds from *Gan Cao* (Radix et Rhizoma Glycyrrhizae), have demonstrated marked anti-inflammatory effects by enhancing the overall duration of effect of cortisone. There are two proposed mechanisms of actions: they may enhance cortisone's effect by decreasing liver metabolism, or they may increase plasma concentration by affecting protein binding.[21] The anti-inflammatory influence of glycyrrhizin and glycyrrhetinic acid is approximately 1/10th that of cortisone.[22] Lastly, other herbs with anti-inflammatory effects include *Dang Gui* (Radix Angelicae Sinensis),[23] *Di Huang* (Radix Rehmanniae),[24] *Jing Jie* (Herba Schizonepetae),[25] *Fang Feng* (Radix Saposhnikoviae),[26] *Mu Dan Pi* (Cortex Moutan),[27] *Niu Bang Zi* (Fructus Arctii),[28] *Shan Yao* (Rhizoma Dioscoreae),[29] *Shan Zhu Yu* (Fructus Corni),[30] *Zhi Mu* (Rhizoma Anemarrhenae),[31] and *Zhi Zi* (Fructus Gardeniae).[32]

Dermatrol (Damp) utilizes many herbs with antibiotic effects to treat skin infections. Herbs with antibacterial effect include *Huang Bo* (Cortex Phellodendri Chinensis),[33,34] *Huang Lian* (Rhizoma Coptidis),[35] *Huang Qin* (Radix Scutellariae),[36,37] *Tian Hua Fen* (Radix Trichosanthis),[38,39] *Jing Jie* (Herba Schizonepetae),[40] *Lian Qiao* (Fructus Forsythiae),[41] *Long Dan* (Radix et Rhizoma Gentianae),[42] *Mu Dan Pi* (Cortex Moutan),[43] *Zhi Zi* (Fructus Gardeniae),[44] and *Zhi Mu* (Rhizoma Anemarrhenae).[45,46] Herbs with antiviral effect include *Huang Lian* (Rhizoma Coptidis),[47,48,49] *Chai Hu* (Radix Bupleuri),[50] *Che Qian Zi* (Semen Plantaginis),[51] *Fang Feng* (Radix Saposhnikoviae),[52] *Huang Bo* (Cortex Phellodendri Chinensis),[53] *Huang Qin* (Radix Scutellariae),[54] *Lian Qiao* (Fructus Forsythiae),[55] *Long Dan* (Radix et Rhizoma Gentianae),[56] *Tian Hua Fen* (Radix Trichosanthis),[57,58] and *Zhi Mu* (Rhizoma Anemarrhenae).[59] Herbs with antifungal effect include *Huang Lian* (Rhizoma Coptidis),[60] *Huang Qin* (Radix Scutellariae),[61] *Niu Bang Zi* (Fructus Arctii),[62] *Zhi Zi* (Fructus Gardeniae),[63] and *Zhi Mu* (Rhizoma Anemarrhenae).[64]

Lastly, in today's industrialized world, many cases of skin disorders are directly associated with exposure to certain allergens, chemicals, and toxins. Therefore, *Gan Cao* (Radix et Rhizoma Glycyrrhizae) and *Fang Feng* (Radix Saposhnikoviae) are used as they have antitoxin and antidotal effects to treat skin disorders caused by exposure to certain toxins and chemicals. Glycyrrhizin, generally considered to be one of the main constituents of *Gan Cao* (Radix et Rhizoma Glycyrrhizae), has a marked detoxifying effect to treat poisoning, including but not limited to drug poisoning (chloral hydrate, urethane, cocaine, picrotoxin, caffeine, pilocarpine, nicotine, barbiturates, mercury, and lead), food poisoning (tetrodotoxin, snake, and mushrooms), and others (enterotoxin, herbicides, and pesticides).[65] Furthermore, the use of *Gan Cao* (Radix et Rhizoma Glycyrrhizae), *Fang Feng* (Radix Saposhnikoviae), and *Lu Dou* (Semen Phaseoli Radiati) has been shown to be an effective antidote for arsenic poisoning.[66]

In summary, ***Dermatrol (Damp)*** is a great formula to treat various skin disorders with damp/wet appearance. It has many herbs with a general dermatological effect to promote the growth and healing of human normal epidermal keratinocytes and dermal fibroblasts cell growths. It contains herbs with antiallergic and antipruritic effects to treat symptoms of itching and irritation. It utilizes herbs with anti-inflammatory effects to reduce swelling and inflammation. It incorporates herbs with antibiotic effects to treat skin infections. Finally, it incorporates herbs with antitoxin and antidote activities to treat skin disorders caused by exposure to certain toxins and chemicals.

COMPARATIVE ANALYSIS

Though there are many skin disorders with different causes and clinical manifestations, most skin disorders are treated with antibiotics, antihistamines, and anti-inflammatory drugs. Antibiotic substances (antibacterial, antiviral, and antifungal) are effective treatment options for skin infection caused by bacteria, virus and/or fungus. Antibiotics can be ingested orally or applied topically. Since skin disorders are often accompanied by itching, antihistamines are often used to block allergic reactions and to relieve itching through their sedative effects. For more severe cases of skin inflammatory disorders, topical or oral corticosteroids are used to reduce swelling and inflammation. In addition to these three main categories of drugs, moisturizing agents or drying agents are prescribed to treat dry and wet skin conditions, respectively. Moisturizing agents, such as creams or lotions with oil, put a thin film of oil on the skin and help the skin hold on to its natural moisture. Drying agents, such as talcum powder or aluminum salts, help to dry up excessive moisture and minimize infections in areas such as toes, buttocks, armpits and/or groins.

In TCM, successful treatment of skin disorders requires the use of herbs to treat wind-heat at the exterior and toxic heat in the interior. Herbs that dispel wind-heat from the exterior generally have antihistamine and antipruritic effects, and are great to treat symptoms of itching and irritation. Herbs that clear toxic heat from the interior generally have an antibiotic effect to treat the infection and an anti-inflammatory function to reduce swelling and inflammation. Overall, herbs are a safe and effective option to treat skin disorders without the harsh side effects and adverse reactions of drugs.

Dermatrol (Damp)™

Drugs and herbs are both effective to treat skin disorders, and each has its inherent advantages and disadvantages. For skin disorders characterized by acute, severe or isolated incidence, such as exposure to poison oak, insect bite, and severe allergic or anaphylactic reactions, drugs are more effective as they are more potent and have a faster onset of action. Furthermore, such conditions are often treated aggressively but only for a short period of time, and therefore, side effects and adverse reactions of drugs can be managed and are not likely to create long-term problems. In contrast, skin disorders characterized by chronic and persistent nature, such as chronic idiopathic dermatitis or urticaria, will respond favorably to herbs. Finally, though drugs and herbs are both effective to symptomatically treat skin disorders characterized by allergic reactions, the only cure is to identify the allergen(s) and avoid any exposure to it if at all possible.

References

1. Chan K, Lo AC, Yeung JH, Woo KS. Journal of Pharmacy and Pharmacology 1995 May;47(5):402-6.
2. Pharmacotherapy 1999 July;19(7):870-876.
3. European Journal of Drug Metabolism and Pharmacokinetics 1995; 20(1):55-60.
4. Chen CY, Cheng KC, Chang AY, Lin YT, Hseu YC, Wang HM. 10-Shogaol, an Antioxidant from Zingiber officinale for Skin Cell Proliferation and Migration Enhancer. Int J Mol Sci. 2012;13(2):1762-77.
5. *Zhong Cao Yao Xue* (Study of Chinese Herbal Medicine), 1980; 932.
6. *Zhong Yi Za Zhi* (Journal of Chinese Medicine), 12:18.
7. Han C, Guo J. Antibacterial and Anti-inflammatory Activity of Traditional Chinese Herb Pairs, Angelica sinensis and Sophora flavescens. Inflammation. 2011 Oct 6.
8. *Tian Jing Yi Xue Za Zhi* (Journal of Tianjing Medicine and Herbology), 1966; 3:209.
9. Kim DS, Son EJ, Kim M, Heo YM, Nam JB, Ro JY, Woo SS. Antiallergic herbal composition from Scutellaria baicalensis and Phyllostachys edulis. Unigen Inc., Cheonan, 330-863 Chungnam, Korea. Planta Med. 2010 May;76(7):678-82.
10. Jung HS, Kim MH, Gwak NG, Im YS, Lee KY, Sohn Y, Choi H, Yang WM. Antiallergic effects of Scutellaria baicalensis on inflammation in vivo and in vitro. J Ethnopharmacol. 2012 May 7;141(1):345-9.
11. Han EH, Park JH, Kim JY, Chung YC, Jeong HG. Inhibitory mechanism of saponins derived from roots of Platycodon grandiflorum on anaphylactic reaction and IgE-mediated allergic response in mast cells. BK21 Project Team, Department of Pharmacy, College of Pharmacy, Chosun University, Gwangju, South Korea. Food Chem Toxicol. 2009 Feb 4.
12. Kim H, Lee E, Lee S, Shin T, Kim Y, Kim J. Effect of Rehmannia glutinosa on immediate type allergic reaction. Department of Oriental Pharmacy, College of Pharmacy, Wonkwang University, Iksan, Chonbuk, South Korea. Int J Immunopharmacol. 1998 Apr-May;20(4-5):231-40.
13. Sung YY, Yoon T, Jang JY, Park SJ, Kim HK. Topical application of Rehmannia glutinosa extract inhibits mite allergen-induced atopic dermatitis in NC/Nga mice. Center of Herbal Resources Research, Korea Institute of Oriental Medicine, Daejeon 305-811, Republic of Korea. J Ethnopharmacol. 2011 Mar 8;134(1):37-44.
14. Knipping K, van Esch EC, Wijering SC, van der Heide S, Dubois AE, Garssen J. In vitro and in vivo antiallergic effects of Arctium lappa L. University of Utrecht, Department of Pharmaceutical Sciences, Sorbonnelaan 16, 3508 TC Utrecht, The Netherlands. Exp Biol Med (Maywood). 2008 Nov;233(11):1469-77.
15. Sohn EH, Jang SA, Joo H, Park S, Kang SC, Lee CH, Kim SY. Antiallergic and anti-inflammatory effects of butanol extract from Arctium Lappa L. Department of Pediatrics, College of Medicine, Hanyang University, Seoul, 133-792, Korea. Clin Mol Allergy. 2011 Feb 8;9(1):4.
16. Lee B, Trinh HT, Jung K, Han SJ, Kim DH. Inhibitory effects of steroidal timosaponins isolated from the rhizomes of Anemarrhena asphodeloides against passive cutaneous anaphylaxis reaction and pruritus. Department of Life and Nanopharmaceutical Sciences, Kyung Hee University, Seoul, South Korea. Immunopharmacol Immunotoxicol. 2010 Sep;32(3):357-63.
17. Tohda C, Kakihara Y, Komatsu K, Kuraishi Y. Inhibitory effects of methanol extracts of herbal medicines on substance P-induced itch-scratch response. Research Center for Ethnomedicines, Institute of Natural Medicine, Toyama Medical and Pharmaceutical University, Sugitani, Japan. Biol Pharm Bull. 2000 May;23(5):599-601.
18. Cuéllar MJ, Giner RM, Recio MC, Máñez S, Ríos JL. Topical anti-inflammatory activity of some Asian medicinal plants used in dermatological disorders. Departament de Farmacologia, Facultat de Farmàcia, Universitat de València, Avda. Vicent Andrés Estellés, s/n. 46100 Burjassot, Valencia, Spain. Fitoterapia. 2001 Mar;72(3):221-9.
19. Prieto JM, Recio MC, Giner RM, Máñez S, Giner-Larza EM, Ríos JL. Influence of traditional Chinese anti-inflammatory medicinal plants on leukocyte and platelet functions. J Pharm Pharmacol. 2003 Sep;55(9):1275-82.
20. *Zhong Yao Yao Li Yu Ying Yong* (Pharmacology and Applications of Chinese Herbs), 1983; 888.
21. *Zhong Yao Zhi* (Chinese Herbology Journal), 1993; 358.
22. *Zhong Cao Yao* (Chinese Herbal Medicine), 1991; 22(10):452.
23. Chao WW, Kuo YH, Li WC, Lin BF. The production of nitric oxide and prostaglandin E2 in peritoneal macrophages is inhibited by Andrographis paniculata, Angelica sinensis and Morus alba ethyl acetate fractions. Department of Biochemical Science and Technology, Institute of Microbiology and Biochemistry, National Taiwan University, Taipei 106, Taiwan, ROC. J Ethnopharmacol. 2009 Feb 25;122(1):68-75.
24. Baek GH, et al. Rehmannia glutinosa Suppresses Inflammatory Responses Elicited by Advanced Glycation End Products. Inflammation. 2012 Feb 14.
25. Ge WH, Guo JY, Shen YJ, Chen ML, Shi SL, Han YH, Lin J. Effects of volatie oil of Schizonepeta tenuifolia Briq herb and Saposhnikovia divaricata Schischke root on proinflammatory cytokine expression and regulation. Zhongguo Zhong Yao Za Zhi. 2007 Sep;32(17):1777-9.
26. Wang CC, Chen LG, Yang LL. Inducible nitric oxide synthase inhibitor of the Chinese herb I. Saposhnikovia divaricata (Turcz.) Schischk. Cancer Lett. 1999 Oct 18;145(1-2):151-7.
27. Chan BC, Hon KL, Leung PC, Sam SW, Fung KP, Lee MY, Lau HY. Traditional Chinese medicine for atopic eczema: PentaHerbs formula suppresses inflammatory mediators release from mast cells. J Ethnopharmacol. 2008 Oct 30;120(1):85-91.
28. Zhao F, Wang L, Liu K. In vitro anti-inflammatory effects of arctigenin, a lignan from Arctium lappa L., through inhibition on iNOS pathway. School of Pharmacy, Yantai University, Yantai, Shandong, China. J Ethnopharmacol. 2009 Apr 21;122(3):457-62.
29. Yang MH, Yoon KD, Chin YW, Park JH, Kim J. Phenolic compounds with radical scavenging and cyclooxygenase-2 (COX-2) inhibitory activities from Dioscorea opposita. College of Pharmacy and Research Institute of Pharmaceutical Science, Seoul National University, Seoul 151-742, South Korea. Bioorg Med Chem. 2009 Apr 1;17(7):2689-94.
30. *Chang Yong Zhong Yao Cheng Fen Yu Yao Li Shou Ce* (A Handbook of the Composition and Pharmacology of Common Chinese Drugs), 1994, 368:376.
31. Kim JY, Shin JS, Ryu JH, Kim SY, Cho YW, Choi JH, Lee KT. Anti-inflammatory effect of anemarsaponin B isolated from the rhizomes of Anemarrhena asphodeloides in LPS-induced RAW 264.7 macrophages is mediated by negative regulation of the nuclear factor-kappaB and p38 pathways. Department of Pharmaceutical Biochemistry, College of Pharmacy, Kyung-Hee University, Dongdaemun-Ku, Hoegi-Dong, Seoul 130-701, South Korea. Food Chem Toxicol. 2009 Jul;47(7):1610-7.

Dermatrol (Damp)™

32. Hwang SM, Lee YJ, Yoon JJ, Lee SM, Kang DG, Lee HS. Gardenia jasminoides inhibits tumor necrosis factor-alpha-induced vascular inflammation in endothelial cells. Professional Graduate School of Oriental Medicine, Wonkwang University, Chonbuk, Republic of Korea. Phytother Res. 2010 Jun;24 Suppl 2:S214-9.
33. Chen ML, Xian YF, Ip SP, Tsai SH, Yang JY, Che CT. Chemical and biological differentiation of Cortex Phellodendri Chinensis and Cortex Phellodendri Amurensis. School of Chinese Medicine, The Chinese University of Hong Kong, Shatin, N.T., Hong Kong. Planta Med. 2010 Oct;76(14):1530-5.
34. Yu HH, Kim KJ, Cha JD, Kim HK, Lee YE, Choi NY, You YO. Antimicrobial activity of berberine alone and in combination with ampicillin or oxacillin against methicillin-resistant Staphylococcus aureus. Department of Food and Nutrition, Kunsan National University, Kunsan. J Med Food. 2005 Winter; 8(4):454-61.
35. Zhang S, Zhang B, Xing K, Zhang X, Tian X, Dai W. Inhibitory effects of golden thread (Coptis chinensis) and berberine on Microcystis aeruginosa. Fisheries College, Ocean University of China, Qingdao 266003, P. R. China. Water Sci Technol. 2010;61(3):763-9.
36. *Zhong Yao Xue* (Chinese Herbology), 1988; 137:140.
37. *J Pharm Pharmacol* 2000 Mar;52(3):361-6.
38. *Zhong Yao Yao Li Yu Ying Yong* (Pharmacology and Applications of Chinese Herbs), 1983:149.
39. *Proc Natl Acad Sci*, 1991; 88(15):6570.
40. *Zhong Yao Yao Li Yu Ying Yong* (Pharmacology and Applications of Chinese Herbs), 1983; 744.
41. *Shan Xi Xin Yi Yao* (New Medicine and Herbology of Shanxi), 1980; 9(11):51.
42. *Zhong Yao Yao Li Yu Ying Yong* (Pharmacology and Applications of Chinese Herbs), 1983; 295.
43. *Zhong Yao Cai* (Study of Chinese Herbal Material), 1991; 14(2):41.
44. *Zhong Yao Zhi* (Chinese Herbology Journal), 1984; 578.
45. *Yao Xue Qing Bao Tong Xun* (Journal of Herbal Information), 1987; 5(4):62.
46. *Zhong Hua Xin Yi Xue Bao* (Chinese Journal of New Medicine), 1950; 1(5):95.
47. *Zhong Yao Xue* (Chinese Herbology), 1988, 140:144.
48. *Zhong Hua Yi Xue Za Zhi* (Chinese Journal of Medicine), 1958; 44(9):888.
49. *Zhong Xi Yi Jie He Za Zhi* (Journal of Integrated Chinese and Western Medicine), 1989; 9(8):494.
50. *Zhong Yao Xue* (Chinese Herbology), 1998; 103:106.
51. Chiang LC, Chiang W, Chang MY, Lin CC. In vitro cytotoxic, antiviral and immunomodulatory effects of Plantago major and Plantago asiatica. Am J Chin Med. 2003;31(2):225-34.
52. *Zhong Yao Tong Bao* (Journal of Chinese Herbology), 1988; 13(6):364.
53. *Zhong Yao Xue* (Chinese Herbology), 1998; 144:146.
54. Błach-Olszewska Z, Jatczak B, Rak A, Lorenc M, Gulanowski B, Drobna A, Lamer-Zarawska E. Production of cytokines and stimulation of resistance to viral infection in human leukocytes by Scutellaria baicalensis flavones. Ludwik Hirszfeld Institute of Immunology and Experimental Therapy, Polish Academy of Sciences, Wrocław, Poland. J Interferon Cytokine Res. 2008 Sep;28(9):571-81.
55. *Shan Xi Xin Yi Yao* (New Medicine and Herbology of Shanxi), 1980; 9(11):51.
56. Li X, Zhou JY, Yang QW, Chen Y, Piao YA, Li HY. Inhibition activities of polysaccharide (RG4-1) from Gentiana rigescens against RSV. J Asian Nat Prod Res. 2011 Jun;13(6):512-22.
57. Zheng YT, Ben KL, Jin SW. Anti-HIV-1 activity of trichobitacin, a novel ribosome-inactivating protein. Acta Pharmacol Sin. 2000 Feb;21(2):179-82.
58. Li ZH, Nie BM, Chen H, Chen SY, He P, Lu Y, Guo XK, Liu JX. In vitro anti-coxsackievirus B(3) effect of ethyl acetate extract of Tian-hua-fen. Department of Microbiology and Parasitology, Shanghai Second Medical University, Shanghai 200025, China. World J Gastroenterol. 2004 Aug 1;10(15):2263-6.
59. Bae G, Yu JR, Lee J, Chang J, Seo EK. Identification of nyasol and structurally related compounds as the active principles from Anemarrhena asphodeloides against respiratory syncytial virus (RSV). The Center for Cell Signaling & Drug Discovery Research, College of Pharmacy, Ewha Womans University, Seoul 120-750, Korea. Chem Biodivers. 2007 Sep;4(9):2231-5.
60. Yu H.H., Kim K.J., Cha J.D., Kim H.K., Lee Y.E., Choi N.Y. & You Y.O. Antimicrobial Activity of Berberine Alone and in Combination with Ampicillin or Oxacillin Against Methicillin-Resistant *Staphylococcus aureus* . *J Med Food.* 2005, 8(4): 454-461.
61. Wong KS, Tsang WK. In vitro antifungal activity of the aqueous extract of Scutellaria baicalensis Georgi root against Candida albicans. Int J Antimicrob Agents. 2009 Sep;34(3):284-5.
62. *Zhong Yao Zhi* (Chinese Herbology Journal), 1984; 250.
63. Lelono RA, Tachibana S, Itoh K. Isolation of antifungal compounds from Gardenia jasminoides. United Graduate School of Agricultural Sciences, Ehime University, 3-5-7 Tarumi, Matsuyama, Ehime 790-8566, Japan. Pak J Biol Sci. 2009 Jul 1;12(13):949-56.
64. Iida Y, Oh KB, Saito M, Matsuoka H, Kurata H, Natsume M, Abe H. Detection of antifungal activity in Anemarrhena asphodeloides by sensitive BCT method and isolation of its active compound. Department of Biotechnology, Faculty of Technology, Tokyo University of Agriculture and Technology, Japan. J Agric Food Chem. 1999 Feb;47(2):584-7.
65. *Zhong Yao Tong Bao* (Journal of Chinese Herbology), 1986; 11(10):55.
66. *Xin Yi Xue* (New Medicine), 1973; 7:6.

Dermatrol (Dry)™

CLINICAL APPLICATIONS

- **Any skin conditions that appear red and dry, and may be flaky or scaly with underlying damage and atrophy of the skin**
- **Skin conditions considered as dry**, such as dermatitis, eczema, urticaria, hives, rash, and allergic rash caused by skin irritants such as detergents or other chemicals

WESTERN THERAPEUTIC ACTIONS

- Antiallergic effect to relieve allergy
- Antipruritic function to relieve itching
- Anti-inflammatory activities to reduce skin swelling and inflammation
- Antibiotic effect to treat skin infection
- Antitoxin and antidote effects to neutralize and antagonize chemicals, allergens, and toxins

CHINESE THERAPEUTIC ACTIONS

- Clears heat, moistens dryness, eliminates toxins
- Dispels wind, relieves itching
- Strengthens the Spleen, dispels dampness

DOSAGE

Take 3 to 4 capsules three times daily. Dosage can be increased up to 6 to 8 capsules three times daily in acute cases. This formula should not be taken for more than two months continuously.

INGREDIENTS

Bai Shao (Radix Paeoniae Alba)
Cang Zhu (Rhizoma Atractylodis)
Chai Hu (Radix Bupleuri)
Chan Tui (Periostracum Cicadae)
Che Qian Zi (Semen Plantaginis)
Chi Shao (Radix Paeoniae Rubra)
Chuan Mu Tong (Caulis Clematidis Armandii)
Chuan Xiong (Rhizoma Chuanxiong)
Dang Gui (Radix Angelicae Sinensis)
Di Huang (Radix Rehmanniae)
Fang Feng (Radix Saposhnikoviae)
Fu Ling (Poria)
Gan Cao (Radix et Rhizoma Glycyrrhizae)
Geng Mi (Semen Oryzae)
Hei Zhi Ma (Semen Sesami Nigrum)
Huang Bo (Cortex Phellodendri Chinensis)
Huang Lian (Rhizoma Coptidis)
Huang Qin (Radix Scutellariae)
Jing Jie (Herba Schizonepetae)
Ku Shen (Radix Sophorae Flavescentis)
Lian Qiao (Fructus Forsythiae)
Long Dan (Radix et Rhizoma Gentianae)
Mu Dan Pi (Cortex Moutan)
Niu Bang Zi (Fructus Arctii)
Shan Yao (Rhizoma Dioscoreae)
Shan Zhu Yu (Fructus Corni)
Shi Gao (Gypsum Fibrosum)
Shu Di Huang (Radix Rehmanniae Praeparata)
Tian Hua Fen (Radix Trichosanthis)
Yi Yi Ren (Semen Coicis)
Ze Xie (Rhizoma Alismatis)
Zhi Gan Cao (Radix et Rhizoma Glycyrrhizae Praeparata cum Melle)
Zhi Mu (Rhizoma Anemarrhenae)
Zhi Zi (Fructus Gardeniae)

BACKGROUND

The skin is the largest organ in the body, and it functions as a protective barrier that keeps undesirable substances from entering. Because the skin is the physical barrier that separates the exterior from the interior, skin health can be affected by factors from both the outside and the inside. External factors that affect the skin include infection (bacteria, virus, and parasites), external exposure to allergens (poison ivy, poison oak, chemicals used in cosmetics or cleaning agents, and drugs used in skin creams), insect bites (spiders and ticks), or trauma. Internal factors that affect the skin include inhalation of allergens (dust, pollen, and dander), ingestion of allergens (peanuts, nuts, fish, wheat, eggs, and milk), intake of certain drugs (penicillin, sulfa drugs, aspirin, and opioids), autoimmune diseases (systemic lupus erythematosus, Sjögren's syndrome, and psoriasis), and emotional or physical imbalance (stress and anxiety).

Although there are multiple and complicated causes of skin disorders, the clinical manifestations are relatively simple and straight forward: most skin disorders have either wet or dry characteristics. Optimal treatment requires the use of medicinal substances to treat both the cause and the symptoms.

Skin disorders with damp/wet characteristics may have open lesions with infection, inflammation, ulceration, pus and abscesses; and they often affect areas with excessive moisture, such as toes, buttocks, armpits, groin, and under the breast. Examples of skin disorders with damp/wet characteristics include skin infection, skin ulcers, exudative skin lesions, sores, abscesses, carbuncles, furuncles, cellulitis, seborrheic dermatitis, and acne vulgaris.

Skin disorders with dry characteristics often appear to be dry, red, flaky, and scaly with underlying damages to and atrophy of the skin. Examples of skin disorders with dry characteristics include psoriasis, atopic dermatitis, urticaria, rosacea, warts, tinea versicolor, erysipelas, and eczema.

FORMULA EXPLANATION

In most cases, acute dermatological disorders are generally due to wind and/or heat invasion, which is generally associated with physical contact or oral ingestion of allergen(s). On the other hand, chronic dermatological conditions involve the accumulation of dampness in the body as well as dryness resulting from fire

Dermatrol (Dry)™

and toxin drying out the yin in the body for a prolonged period of time. ***Dermatrol (Dry)*** is formulated with four groups of herbs to address both acute and chronic cases of skin disorders with dry lesions.

The first group of herbs aims to relieve itching by releasing exterior wind: *Chai Hu* (Radix Bupleuri), *Chan Tui* (Periostracum Cicadae), *Fang Feng* (Radix Saposhnikoviae), *Jing Jie* (Herba Schizonepetae) and *Chuan Xiong* (Rhizoma Chuanxiong). These herbs have antihistamine effect to treat allergy, and antipruritic effect to relieve itching.

The second group of herbs clears heat and eliminates toxins to address localized inflammation and infection: *Chi Shao* (Radix Paeoniae Rubra), *Chuan Mu Tong* (Caulis Clematidis Armandii), *Huang Bo* (Cortex Phellodendri Chinensis), *Huang Lian* (Rhizoma Coptidis), *Huang Qin* (Radix Scutellariae), *Ku Shen* (Radix Sophorae Flavescentis), *Lian Qiao* (Fructus Forsythiae), *Long Dan* (Radix et Rhizoma Gentianae), *Mu Dan Pi* (Cortex Moutan), *Niu Bang Zi* (Fructus Arctii), *Shi Gao* (Gypsum Fibrosum), *Tian Hua Fen* (Radix Trichosanthis), *Zhi Mu* (Rhizoma Anemarrhenae), and *Zhi Zi* (Fructus Gardeniae). These herbs clear heat and eliminate toxins throughout the entire body, including upper, middle, and lower *jiaos*. Furthermore, *Zhi Mu* (Rhizoma Anemarrhenae) and *Tian Hua Fen* (Radix Trichosanthis) both effectively moisten and purge fire to address the dry nature of the lesions. These herbs have antibiotic function to treat skin infection, and an anti-inflammatory function to reduce skin swelling and inflammation.

Furthermore, despite the dry appearance of the rash, almost all patients suffering from dermatological disorders have some form of dampness inside. Therefore, the third group of herbs is used to strengthen the Spleen and drain dampness: *Cang Zhu* (Rhizoma Atractylodis), *Fu Ling* (Poria), *Yi Yi Ren* (Semen Coicis), *Che Qian Zi* (Semen Plantaginis), and *Ze Xie* (Rhizoma Alismatis). These herbs have diuretic and anti-inflammatory activities to reduce skin swelling and water retention.

Finally, the fourth group of herbs aims to tonify blood and nourish yin, which addresses the underlying causes of chronic, non-healing rashes, sores, and dermatological problems. Blood deficiency leads to malnourishment of the skin, characterized by dryness, coarseness, lack of moisture, and lack of skin tone. With the dry nature of the skin condition, blood must be tonified. Also with abundant blood, wind cannot rise to cause further itching. This group of herbs tonifies yin and nourishes blood to prevent heat from flaring up causing the symptoms to become worse. Herbs in this group include *Bai Shao* (Radix Paeoniae Alba), *Dang Gui* (Radix Angelicae Sinensis), *Di Huang* (Radix Rehmanniae), *Geng Mi* (Semen Oryzae), *Hei Zhi Ma* (Semen Sesami Nigrum), *Shan Yao* (Rhizoma Dioscoreae), *Shan Zhu Yu* (Fructus Corni) and *Shu Di Huang* (Radix Rehmanniae Praeparata). *Gan Cao* (Radix et Rhizoma Glycyrrhizae) and *Zhi Gan Cao* (Radix et Rhizoma Glycyrrhizae Praeparata cum Melle) harmonize the formula. As these herbs strengthen the underlying body constitution, they also regulate and balance the endocrine system, and in turn, facilitate the release of endogenous corticosteroids to reduce swelling and inflammation.

In summary, ***Dermatrol (Dry)*** is an excellent formula to treat dry skin disorders by using herbs that moisten dryness, clear heat and eliminate toxins, and dispel wind and relieve itching.

CAUTIONS & CONTRAINDICATIONS

- This formula is contraindicated in patients with cold or deficiency cold signs.
- This formula is contraindicated during pregnancy and nursing.
- In addition to external factors (dry skin, atopic dermatitis, contact dermatitis, infections) or internal factors (allergic reactions through ingestion or inhalation), skin disorders may be caused by conditions such as cholestasis, chronic renal failure, hyper- or hypothyroidism, diabetes, iron deficiency, and polycythemia vera. Optimal treatment requires these conditions to be ruled out, or confirmed and treated.
- This formula is contraindicated for long-term use. Identification and elimination of the cause is the best long-term solution. When symptoms clear up, re-evaluate the condition and prescribe some other formulas to address the underlying cause of the skin condition. Many times the patient may have another attack and it is usually due to poor dietary habit, so it is essential to ask the patient to be extremely careful with what they eat in order to prevent future break outs.
- This herbal formula contains herbs that invigorate blood circulation, such as *Dang Gui* (Radix Angelicae Sinensis). Therefore, patients who are on anticoagulant or antiplatelet therapies, such as Coumadin (warfarin), should use this formula with caution, or not at all, as there may be a higher risk of bleeding and bruising.

CLINICAL NOTES

- *Yin Care*, a topical herbal solution, may be applied topically to help relieve itching. Also, toothpaste may also be applied topically to relieve temporary itching.
- This formula is designed by Dr. Jimmy Wei-Yen Chang and has worked effectively for over 90% of his patients who suffer from various dermatological conditions with dry, red lesions. However, it is not to be used for long term as the heat clearing effect may damage the Spleen and Stomach. After the symptoms/signs improve or are alleviated, one must find the underlying cause and treat it so the lesions do not return. Taking the herbs at a large dosage or for a prolonged period of time may not be necessary as the triggering factors are either due to exposure to allergen or improper diet and lifestyle. Please refer to Nutrition and Lifestyle Instructions sections to help maintain a healthy constitution and clear skin.

Pulse Diagnosis by Dr. Jimmy Wei-Yen Chang:

- **Dry skin lesions** due to dryness and heat in the Lung and Large Intestine: floating and forceful pulse on the right *cun*.

Dermatrol (Dry)™

SUPPLEMENTARY FORMULAS

- For severe itching, add ***Silerex***.
- With additional signs of fire manifesting in red eyes, red tongue, anger and/or constipation, combine with ***Gardenia Complex*** and ***Gentle Lax (Excess)***.
- In chronic dermatological conditions where the surrounding skin of the lesions appears purple and the tongue is purple, add ***Circulation (SJ)***.
- To enhance the overall antibacterial function, add ***Herbal ABX***.
- To enhance the overall antiviral function, add ***Herbal AVR***.
- For severe inflammation, add ***Astringent Complex***.
- With more yin and fluid deficiencies, combine with ***Nourish*** or ***Nourish (Fluids)***.
- Due to exposure to chemicals such as paint, nail polish, glue, drugs, pain killers, bleach, aerosol, new house syndrome, etc., add ***Herbal DTX***.
- For low immune system, *wei* (defensive) *qi* deficiency, or chronic overall deficient patients with inability to heal lesions/wounds, add a high dose of ***Immune +***.
- For skin condition associated with stress, add ***Calm***.

ACUPUNCTURE TREATMENT

Traditional Points:

- *Quchi* (LI 11), *Xuehai* (SP 10), *Hegu* (LI 4), *Sanyinjiao* (SP 6), *Fengchi* (GB 20), *Dazhui* (GV 14), *Fengmen* (BL 12), *Fengshi* (GB 31), *Jianyu* (LI 15), *Zusanli* (ST 36)

Classic Master Tung's Points:

- **Eczema:** *Simashang* (T 88.18), *Simazhong* (T 88.17), *Simaxia* (T 88.19), *Linggu* (T 22.05), *Minghuang* (T 88.12), *Tianhuang* (T 88.13), *Qihuang* (T 88.14), *Tianhuang* (T 77.17), *Dihuang* (T 77.19), *Renhuang* (T 77.21), *Jinqianshang* (T 88.24), *Jinqianxia* (T 88.23)
- **Atopic dermatitis:** *Simashang* (T 88.18), *Simazhong* (T 88.17), *Simaxia* (T 88.19), *Linggu* (T 22.05), *Zhisima* (T 11.07)
- **Herpes zoster:** *Linggu* (T 22.05), *Tianhuang* (T 88.13), *Minghuang* (T 88.12), *Qihuang* (T 88.14), *Simashang* (T 88.18), *Simazhong* (T 88.17), *Simaxia* (T 88.19), *Shuitong* (T 1010.19), *Shuijin* (T 1010.20)
- **Tinea versicolor:** *Tianhuang* (T 88.13), *Minghuang* (T 88.12), *Qihuang* (T 88.14), *Simashang* (T 88.18), *Simaxia* (T 88.19), *Simazhong* (T 88.17), *Shuijin* (T 1010.20), *Shuitong* (T 1010.19). Bleed the LR area T5 – T9 and KI area T9 – T12 on the back with cupping. Bleed before needling for best result.
- **Hives:** *Simashang* (T 88.18), *Simaxia* (T 88.19), *Simazhong* (T 88.17), *Tianhuang* (T 77.17), *Dihuang* (T 77.19), *Renhuang* (T 77.21), *Tianhuang* (T 88.13), *Minghuang* (T 88.12), *Qihuang* (T 88.14), *Zhisima* (T 11.07)

Master Tung's Points by Dr. Chuan-Min Wang:

- **Dry, flaky lesions:** *Simazhong* (T 88.17), *Simashang* (T 88.18), *Simaxia* (T 88.19)

Balance Method by Dr. Richard Tan:

- Right side: *Sanjian* (LI 3), *Quchi* (LI 11), *Houxi* (SI 3), *Xiaohai* (SI 8), *Taibai* (SP 3), *Yinlingquan* (SP 9), *Taichong* (LR 3), *Ququan* (LR 8)
- Left side: *Chize* (LU 5), *Taiyuan* (LU 9), *Zusanli* (ST 36), *Xiangu* (ST 43)
- Alternate sides from treatment to treatment.

Ear Acupuncture:

- *Ah shi* points, Endocrine, Subcortex, Lung, *Shenmen*, Sympathetic

Auricular Medicine by Dr. Li-Chun Huang:

- **Rash and itching:** Allergy Area, *Shenmen*, Sympathetic, Occiput, Nervous Subcortex, Lung, Diaphragm, Spleen, Liver. Bleed Ear Apex.
- **Contact dermatitis:** Allergic Area, Sympathetic, Adrenal Gland, Liver, Spleen, Lung, Endocrine, corresponding points (to the area affected). Bleed Ear Apex.
  - For dermatitis with severe pain, add *Shenmen* and Occiput.
- **Eczema:** Allergic Area, Lung, Sympathetic, Spleen, *Shenmen*, Endocrine, Occiput, Diaphragm, corresponding points (to the area affected). Bleed Ear Apex.
- **Cutaneous pruritis:** *Shenmen*, Occiput, Liver, Spleen, Lung, Endocrine, Diaphragm, Allergic Area. Bleed Ear Apex.
- **Urticaria:** Liver, Lung, Spleen, Diaphragm, *Shenmen*, Occiput, Allergic Area, Sympathetic, Endocrine, Adrenal Gland. Bleed Ear Apex.
- **Severe itching:** Prick five times on the ear apex, five times each on the helix near the Great Auricular Nerve and Lesser Occipital Nerve.

Taoist Ear Points by Jun-Qing Luo:

- Bleed the back of the ear for any visible veins. This is very effective for relieving itching and treatment of any dermatological disorders.

NUTRITION

- According to the five elements theory, the Spleen (earth element) is what generates the Lung (metal element). In order to be free of any skin condition, which is governed by the Lung (metal element), the Spleen (earth element) must be free from damaging foods. Consumption of damaging foods, such as ones listed below, will worsen the patient's condition and possibly make herbal treatment less or ineffective.
  - Seafood: especially shellfish, like crabs, oyster, scallops, clams, lobster, and shrimp (they enter the *yangming* Stomach channel).
  - Fermented foods: cheese or fermented tofu.
  - Dairy: milk, cream, yogurt, cheese, and ice cream.
  - Sugar: any and all foods containing sugar, such as cake and dessert.
  - Meat: lamb, beef, goose, and duck.
  - Deep-fried or greasy food.

FORMULAS

Dermatrol (Dry)™

- Certain fruits: mango and durian.
- Stimulants: coffee, alcohol, and energy drinks.
- Carbohydrates: white rice or bread as they may damage the Spleen and in turn produce more dampness.
- Spicy, pungent, aromatic vegetables: pepper, garlic, onions, basil, rosemary, cumin, fennel, anise, leeks, chives, scallions, thyme, saffron, wormwood, mustard, chili pepper, and wasabi.

- If the patient is allergic to any food or feels uncomfortable after eating certain foods, then it is best to avoid eating it.

The Tao of Nutrition by Dr. Maoshing Ni and Cathy McNease:

- Increase consumption of Chinese prunes, guava skins, pearl barley, vinegar, garlic, walnuts, cucumber, beet tops, dandelion greens, squash, and mung beans.
- Take fifteen peeled and sliced water chestnuts and one cup of vinegar, slowly simmer in a non-metal pot for 20 minutes until the water chestnuts absorb most of the vinegar. Then mash into a paste and seal in a jar. Spread evenly on a gauze pad and apply to affected area, changing daily if not too serious, three times daily if serious. Mild cases should show improvement within five days.
- Apply mashed garlic to affected area, changing twice daily for one week.

LIFESTYLE INSTRUCTIONS

- To properly restore the immune function, the patient is advised to sleep by 10:00 p.m. so they may enter deep sleep by 1:00 a.m. (Liver time according to the Chinese Anatomical Clock) to fully rest the Liver to restore its detoxification functions.
- Avoid being overly tired from working or stress whenever possible.
- Do not scratch or irritate lesions as it might lead to scar formation and further infection.
- Proper skin care is important for treatment of skin conditions. Use cool or lukewarm water when bathing, mild or moisturizing soap, limited bathing duration and frequency, and avoid tight or irritating clothing.

PHARMACOLOGICAL AND CLINICAL RESEARCH

Skin disorders with dry characteristics, such as psoriasis, atopic dermatitis and urticaria, often appear to be dry, red, flaky, and scaly. Skin disorders with dry characteristics are usually characterized by underlying damages to and atrophy of the skin, caused by external (infection, direct contact, trauma) or internal (ingestion or inhalation of allergens, autoimmune diseases, emotional or physical imbalance) factors. Optimal treatment requires the use of medicinal substances to treat both the cause and the symptoms. ***Dermatrol (Dry)*** contains herbs with multiple pharmacological effects, including but not limited to antiallergic, antipruritic, anti-inflammatory, antibiotic, antitoxin and antidotal.

Dermatrol (Dry) contains many herbs with direct and general effects to treat skin disorders. *Jing Jie* (Herba Schizonepetae) has a general effect on the skin, and has been used successfully to treat dermatological disorders, such as measles, pruritic rash and itching.[1] *Chan Tui* (Periostracum Cicadae) has been used effectively to treat chronic urticaria.[2] *Dang Gui* (Radix Angelicae Sinensis) has an antipimple and an antieczema effect exerted through the regulation of nuclear factor kappa B, maleic dialdehyde (MDA), polymorphonuclear cells, interleukin-1β, inducible nitric oxide synthase, and tumor necrosis factor-α.[3] *Di Huang* (Radix Rehmanniae) has been used with good success to treat rashes, urticaria and contact dermatitis.[4] Lastly, *Ku Shen* (Radix Sophorae Flavescentis) has been used with a 79% effective rate in 148 patients to treat dermatological disorders, such as rashes, itching, and eczema.[5]

Dermatrol (Dry) utilizes many herbs with antiallergic and antipruritic effects to treat various skin disorders. *Ku Shen* (Radix Sophorae Flavescentis) has both antipruritic and antiallergic effects, and is one of the best herbs to treat skin disorders. According to a study in subjects with artificially-induced dermatitis, the extract from *Ku Shen* (Radix Sophorae Flavescentis) shows an antipruritic effect to inhibit scratching in a dose-dependent manner.[6] The antipruritic effect is attributed in part to its effect to reduce several eicosanoid-related skin inflammation, such as atopic dermatitis.[7] Furthermore, topical application of *Ku Shen* (Radix Sophorae Flavescentis) has been shown to treat artificially-induced contact dermatitis through inhibition against recruitment and degranulation of mast cells.[8] *Huang Qin* (Radix Scutellariae) has a remarkable effect as an antiallergic agent. It inhibits histamine and leukotriene release from mast cells with greater potency than Intal (cromolyn), a drug that prevents the release of inflammatory chemicals such as histamine from mast cells.[9] Furthermore, *Huang Qin* (Radix Scutellariae) also inhibits the passive cutaneous anaphylaxis reaction through its downregulation of the expression of various inflammatory mediators.[10] *Shu Di Huang* (Radix Rehmanniae Praeparata) has been shown to inhibit systemic allergic reactions in a dose-dependent manner through the inhibition of histamine release from the peritoneal mast cells and significant suppression of tumor necrosis factor-alpha (TNF-α) production.[11] Topical application of an extract from *Di Huang* (Radix Rehmanniae) and *Shu Di Huang* (Radix Rehmanniae Praeparata) shows marked anti-inflammatory and antiallergic activities to treat atopic dermatitis by suppressing the expression of cytokines, chemokines, and adhesion molecules.[12] *Niu Bang Zi* (Fructus Arctii) has a significant antiallergic effect to reduce the release of inflammatory mediators through inhibition of degranulation and cys-leukotriene release.[13] It effectively treats allergic diseases, including atopic dermatitis, by inhibiting the expression of IL-4 and IL-5.[14] Furthermore, *Zhi Mu* (Rhizoma Anemarrhenae) has a strong antiallergic effect, and can be used to inhibit the

Dermatrol (Dry)™

passive cutaneous anaphylaxis reaction induced by the antigen-immunoglobulin E (IgE) complex.[15] Lastly, *Jing Jie* (Herba Schizonepetae) and *Lian Qiao* (Fructus Forsythiae) have an antipruritic effect to inhibit itch-scratch response induced by substance P.[16]

Dermatrol (Dry) incorporates many herbs with anti-inflammatory effects to treat inflammatory skin disorders. *Huang Qin* (Radix Scutellariae), *Huang Lian* (Rhizoma Coptidis), and *Huang Bo* (Cortex Phellodendri Chinensis) all have anti-inflammatory activities, and may be used to treat different skin disorders.[17] *Fu Ling* (Poria) and *Lian Qiao* (Fructus Forsythiae) are two herbs with beneficial effects to treat skin diseases involving chronic inflammation. These two herbs have inhibitory effects on lipoxygenase, cyclo-oxygenase, and elastase activities, which are therapeutic targets in dermatological disorders.[18] *Chai Hu* (Radix Bupleuri) reduces inflammation by decreasing capillary permeability caused by histamine and 5-hydroxy-tryptamine.[19] Glycyrrhizin and glycyrrhetinic acid, two compounds from *Gan Cao* (Radix et Rhizoma Glycyrrhizae), have demonstrated marked anti-inflammatory effects by enhancing the overall duration of effect of cortisone. There are two proposed mechanisms of actions: they may enhance cortisone's effect by decreasing liver metabolism, or they may increase plasma concentration by affecting protein binding.[20] The anti-inflammatory influence of glycyrrhizin and glycyrrhetinic acid is approximately 1/10th that of cortisone.[21] Lastly, other herbs with anti-inflammatory effects include *Dang Gui* (Radix Angelicae Sinensis),[22] *Di Huang* (Radix Rehmanniae),[23] *Jing Jie* (Herba Schizonepetae),[24] *Fang Feng* (Radix Saposhnikoviae),[25] *Mu Dan Pi* (Cortex Moutan),[26] *Niu Bang Zi* (Fructus Arctii),[27] *Shan Yao* (Rhizoma Dioscoreae),[28] *Shan Zhu Yu* (Fructus Corni),[29] *Zhi Mu* (Rhizoma Anemarrhenae),[30] and *Zhi Zi* (Fructus Gardeniae).[31]

Dermatrol (Dry) utilizes many herbs with antibiotic effects to treat skin infections. Herbs with antibacterial effect include *Huang Bo* (Cortex Phellodendri Chinensis),[32,33] *Huang Lian* (Rhizoma Coptidis),[34] *Huang Qin* (Radix Scutellariae),[35,36] *Ku Shen* (Radix Sophorae Flavescentis),[37,38] *Tian Hua Fen* (Radix Trichosanthis),[39,40] *Jing Jie* (Herba Schizonepetae),[41] *Lian Qiao* (Fructus Forsythiae),[42] *Long Dan* (Radix et Rhizoma Gentianae),[43] *Mu Dan Pi* (Cortex Moutan),[44] *Zhi Zi* (Fructus Gardeniae),[45] and *Zhi Mu* (Rhizoma Anemarrhenae).[46,47] Herbs with antiviral effect include *Huang Lian* (Rhizoma Coptidis),[48,49,50] *Huang Bo* (Cortex Phellodendri Chinensis),[51] *Huang Qin* (Radix Scutellariae),[52] *Ku Shen* (Radix Sophorae Flavescentis),[53,54] *Chai Hu* (Radix Bupleuri),[55] *Che Qian Zi* (Semen Plantaginis),[56] *Fang Feng* (Radix Saposhnikoviae),[57] *Lian Qiao* (Fructus Forsythiae),[58] *Long Dan* (Radix et Rhizoma Gentianae),[59] *Tian Hua Fen* (Radix Trichosanthis),[60,61] and *Zhi Mu* (Rhizoma Anemarrhenae).[62] Herbs with antifungal effect include *Huang Lian* (Rhizoma Coptidis),[63] *Huang Qin* (Radix Scutellariae),[64] *Niu Bang Zi* (Fructus Arctii),[65] *Zhi Zi* (Fructus Gardeniae),[66] and *Zhi Mu* (Rhizoma Anemarrhenae).[67] Lastly, *Ku Shen* (Radix Sophorae Flavescentis) also has antiparasitic,[68] antiprotozoal,[69] and antimalarial effects.[70]

Lastly, in today's industrialized world, many cases of skin disorders are directly associated with exposure to certain allergens, chemicals, and toxins. Therefore, *Gan Cao* (Radix et Rhizoma Glycyrrhizae) and *Fang Feng* (Radix Saposhnikoviae) are used as they have antitoxin and antidotal effects to treat skin disorders caused by exposure to certain toxins and chemicals. Glycyrrhizin, generally considered to be one of the main constituents of *Gan Cao* (Radix et Rhizoma Glycyrrhizae), has a marked detoxifying effect to treat poisoning, including but not limited to drug poisoning (chloral hydrate, urethane, cocaine, picrotoxin, caffeine, pilocarpine, nicotine, barbiturates, mercury, and lead), food poisoning (tetrodotoxin, snake and mushrooms), and others (enterotoxin, herbicides and pesticides).[71] Furthermore, the use of *Gan Cao* (Radix et Rhizoma Glycyrrhizae), *Fang Feng* (Radix Saposhnikoviae), and *Lu Dou* (Semen Phaseoli Radiati) has been shown to be an effective antidote for arsenic poisoning.[72]

In summary, ***Dermatrol (Dry)*** is a great formula to treat various skin disorders with dry appearance. It contains herbs with antiallergic and antipruritic effects to treat symptoms of itching and irritation. It utilizes herbs with anti-inflammatory effects to reduce swelling and inflammation. It incorporates herbs with antibiotic effects to treat skin infections. Finally, it incorporates herbs with antitoxin and antidotal activities to treat skin disorders caused by exposure to certain toxins and chemicals.

COMPARATIVE ANALYSIS

Though there are many skin disorders with different causes and clinical manifestations, most skin disorders are treated with antibiotics, antihistamines, and anti-inflammatory drugs. Antibiotic substances (antibacterial, antiviral, and antifungal) are effective treatment options for skin infection caused by bacteria, virus, and/or fungus. Antibiotics can be ingested orally or applied topically. Since skin disorders are often accompanied by itching, antihistamines are often used to block allergic reactions and to relieve itching through their sedative effects. For more severe cases of skin inflammatory disorders, topical or oral corticosteroids are used to reduce swelling and inflammation. In addition to these three main categories of drugs, moisturizing agents or drying agents are prescribed to treat dry and wet skin conditions, respectively. Moisturizing agents, such as creams or lotions with oil, put a thin film of oil on the skin and help the skin hold on to its natural moisture. Drying agents, such as talcum powder or aluminum salts, help to dry up excessive moisture and minimize infections in areas such as toes, buttocks, armpits and/or groins.

In TCM, successful treatment of skin disorders requires the use of herbs to treat wind-heat at the exterior and toxic heat in the interior. Herbs that dispel wind-heat from the exterior

Dermatrol (Dry)™

generally have antihistamine and antipruritic effects, and are great to treat symptoms of itching and irritation. Herbs that clear toxic heat from the interior generally have an antibiotic effect to treat the infection and an anti-inflammatory function to reduce swelling and inflammation. Overall, herbs are a safe and effective option to treat skin disorders, without the harsh side effects and adverse reactions of drugs.

Drugs and herbs are both effective to treat skin disorders, and each has its inherent advantages and disadvantages. For skin disorders characterized by acute, severe or isolated incidence, such as exposure to poison oak, insect bite, and severe allergic or anaphylactic reactions, drugs are more effective as they are more potent and have a faster onset of action. Furthermore, such conditions are often treated aggressively but only for a short period of time, and therefore, side effects and adverse reactions of drugs can be managed and are not likely to create long-term problems. In contrast, skin disorders characterized by chronic and persistent nature, such as chronic idiopathic dermatitis or urticaria, will respond favorably to herbs. Finally, though drugs and herbs are both effective to symptomatically treat skin disorders characterized by allergic reactions, the only cure is to identify the allergen(s) and avoid any exposure to it if at all possible.

References

1. *Zhong Yi Za Zhi* (Journal of Chinese Medicine), 12:18.
2. *Pi Fu Bing Fang Zhi Yan Jiu Tong Xun* (Research Journal on Prevention and Treatment of Dermatological Disorders), 1972; 3:215.
3. Han C, Guo J. Antibacterial and Anti-inflammatory Activity of Traditional Chinese Herb Pairs, Angelica sinensis and Sophora flavescens. Inflammation. 2011 Oct 6.
4. *Tian Jing Yi Xue Za Zhi* (Journal of Tianjing Medicine and Herbology), 1966; 3:209.
5. *Zhong Cao Yao Tong Xun* (Journal of Chinese Herbal Medicine), 1976; 1:35.
6. Yamaguchi-Miyamoto T, Kawasuji T, Kuraishi Y, Suzuki H. Antipruritic effects of Sophora flavescens on acute and chronic itch-related responses in mice. Japan Society for the Promotion of Science, Domestic Research Fellow, Honmachi, Kawaguchi, Saitama, Japan. Biol Pharm Bull. 2003 May;26(5):722-4.
7. Kim DW, Chi YS, Son KH, Chang HW, Kim JS, Kang SS, Kim HP. Effects of sophoraflavanone G, a prenylated flavonoid from Sophora flavescens, on cyclooxygenase-2 and in vivo inflammatory response. College of Pharmacy, Kangwon National University, Chunchon, Korea. Arch Pharm Res. 2002 Jun;25(3):329-35.
8. Kim H, Lee MR, Lee GS, An WG, Cho SI. Effect of Sophora flavescens Aiton extract on degranulation of mast cells and contact dermatitis induced by dinitrofluorobenzene in mice. J Ethnopharmacol. 2012 May 9.
9. Kim DS, Son EJ, Kim M, Heo YM, Nam JB, Ro JY, Woo SS. Antiallergic herbal composition from Scutellaria baicalensis and Phyllostachys edulis. Unigen Inc., Cheonan, 330-863 Chungnam, Korea. Planta Med. 2010 May;76(7):678-82.
10. Jung HS, Kim MH, Gwak NG, Im YS, Lee KY, Sohn Y, Choi H, Yang WM. Antiallergic effects of Scutellaria baicalensis on inflammation in vivo and in vitro. J Ethnopharmacol. 2012 May 7;141(1):345-9.
11. Kim H, Lee E, Lee S, Shin T, Kim Y, Kim J. Effect of Rehmannia glutinosa on immediate type allergic reaction. Department of Oriental Pharmacy, College of Pharmacy, Wonkwang University, Iksan, Chonbuk, South Korea. Int J Immunopharmacol. 1998 Apr-May;20(4-5):231-40.
12. Sung YY, Yoon T, Jang JY, Park SJ, Kim HK. Topical application of Rehmannia glutinosa extract inhibits mite allergen-induced atopic dermatitis in NC/Nga mice. Center of Herbal Resources Research, Korea Institute of Oriental Medicine, Daejeon 305-811, Republic of Korea. J Ethnopharmacol. 2011 Mar 8;134(1):37-44.
13. Knipping K, van Esch EC, Wijering SC, van der Heide S, Dubois AE, Garssen J. In vitro and in vivo antiallergic effects of Arctium lappa L. University of Utrecht, Department of Pharmaceutical Sciences, Sorbonnelaan 16, 3508 TC Utrecht, The Netherlands. Exp Biol Med (Maywood). 2008 Nov;233(11):1469-77.
14. Sohn EH, Jang SA, Joo H, Park S, Kang SC, Lee CH, Kim SY. Antiallergic and anti-inflammatory effects of butanol extract from Arctium Lappa L. Department of Pediatrics, College of Medicine, Hanyang University, Seoul, 133-792, Korea. Clin Mol Allergy. 2011 Feb 8;9(1):4.
15. Lee B, Trinh HT, Jung K, Han SJ, Kim DH. Inhibitory effects of steroidal timosaponins isolated from the rhizomes of Anemarrhena asphodeloides against passive cutaneous anaphylaxis reaction and pruritus. Department of Life and Nanopharmaceutical Sciences, Kyung Hee University, Seoul, South Korea. Immunopharmacol Immunotoxicol. 2010 Sep;32(3):357-63.
16. Tohda C, Kakihara Y, Komatsu K, Kuraishi Y. Inhibitory effects of methanol extracts of herbal medicines on substance P-induced itch-scratch response. Research Center for Ethnomedicines, Institute of Natural Medicine, Toyama Medical and Pharmaceutical University, Sugitani, Japan. Biol Pharm Bull. 2000 May;23(5):599-601.
17. Cuéllar MJ, Giner RM, Recio MC, Máñez S, Ríos JL. Topical anti-inflammatory activity of some Asian medicinal plants used in dermatological disorders. Departament de Farmacologia, Facultat de Farmàcia, Universitat de València, Avda. Vicent Andrés Estellés, s/n. 46100 Burjassot, Valencia, Spain. Fitoterapia. 2001 Mar;72(3):221-9.
18. Prieto JM, Recio MC, Giner RM, Máñez S, Giner-Larza EM, Ríos JL. Influence of traditional Chinese anti-inflammatory medicinal plants on leukocyte and platelet functions. J Pharm Pharmacol. 2003 Sep;55(9):1275-82.
19. *Zhong Yao Yao Li Yu Ying Yong* (Pharmacology and Applications of Chinese Herbs), 1983; 888.
20. *Zhong Yao Zhi* (Chinese Herbology Journal), 1993; 358.
21. *Zhong Cao Yao* (Chinese Herbal Medicine), 1991; 22(10):452.
22. Chao WW, Kuo YH, Li WC, Lin BF. The production of nitric oxide and prostaglandin E2 in peritoneal macrophages is inhibited by Andrographis paniculata, Angelica sinensis and Morus alba ethyl acetate fractions. Department of Biochemical Science and Technology, Institute of Microbiology and Biochemistry, National Taiwan University, Taipei 106, Taiwan, ROC. J Ethnopharmacol. 2009 Feb 25;122(1):68-75.
23. Baek GH, et al. Rehmannia glutinosa Suppresses Inflammatory Responses Elicited by Advanced Glycation End Products. Inflammation. 2012 Feb 14.
24. Ge WH, Guo JY, Shen YJ, Chen ML, Shi SL, Han YH, Lin J. Effects of volatie oil of Schizonepeta tenuifolia Briq herb and Saposhnikovia divaricata Schischke root on proinflammatory cytokine expression and regulation. Zhongguo Zhong Yao Za Zhi. 2007 Sep;32(17):1777-9.
25. Wang CC, Chen LG, Yang LL. Inducible nitric oxide synthase inhibitor of the Chinese herb I. Saposhnikovia divaricata (Turcz.) Schischk. Cancer Lett. 1999 Oct 18;145(1-2):151-7.
26. Chan BC, Hon KL, Leung PC, Sam SW, Fung KP, Lee MY, Lau HY. Traditional Chinese medicine for atopic eczema: PentaHerbs formula suppresses inflammatory mediators release from mast cells. J Ethnopharmacol. 2008 Oct 30;120(1):85-91.
27. Zhao F, Wang L, Liu K. In vitro anti-inflammatory effects of arctigenin, a lignan from Arctium lappa L., through inhibition on iNOS pathway. School of Pharmacy, Yantai University, Yantai, Shandong, China. J Ethnopharmacol. 2009 Apr 21;122(3):457-62.
28. Yang MH, Yoon KD, Chin YW, Park JH, Kim J. Phenolic compounds with radical scavenging and cyclooxygenase-2 (COX-2) inhibitory activities from Dioscorea opposita. College of Pharmacy and Research Institute of Pharmaceutical Science, Seoul National University, Seoul 151-742, South Korea. Bioorg Med Chem. 2009 Apr 1;17(7):2689-94.
29. *Chang Yong Zhong Yao Cheng Fen Yu Yao Li Shou Ce* (A Handbook of the Composition and Pharmacology of Common Chinese Drugs), 1994, 368:376.

Dermatrol (Dry)™

30. Kim JY, Shin JS, Ryu JH, Kim SY, Cho YW, Choi JH, Lee KT. Anti-inflammatory effect of anemarsaponin B isolated from the rhizomes of Anemarrhena asphodeloides in LPS-induced RAW 264.7 macrophages is mediated by negative regulation of the nuclear factor-kappaB and p38 pathways. Department of Pharmaceutical Biochemistry, College of Pharmacy, Kyung-Hee University, Dongdaemun-Ku, Hoegi-Dong, Seoul 130-701, South Korea. Food Chem Toxicol. 2009 Jul;47(7):1610-7.
31. Hwang SM, Lee YJ, Yoon JJ, Lee SM, Kang DG, Lee HS. Gardenia jasminoides inhibits tumor necrosis factor-alpha-induced vascular inflammation in endothelial cells. Professional Graduate School of Oriental Medicine, Wonkwang University, Chonbuk, Republic of Korea. Phytother Res. 2010 Jun;24 Suppl 2:S214-9.
32. Chen ML, Xian YF, Ip SP, Tsai SH, Yang JY, Che CT. Chemical and biological differentiation of Cortex Phellodendri Chinensis and Cortex Phellodendri Amurensis. School of Chinese Medicine, The Chinese University of Hong Kong, Shatin, N.T., Hong Kong. Planta Med. 2010 Oct;76(14):1530-5.
33. Yu HH, Kim KJ, Cha JD, Kim HK, Lee YE, Choi NY, You YO. Antimicrobial activity of berberine alone and in combination with ampicillin or oxacillin against methicillin-resistant Staphylococcus aureus. Department of Food and Nutrition, Kunsan National University, Kunsan. J Med Food. 2005 Winter; 8(4):454-61.
34. Zhang S, Zhang B, Xing K, Zhang X, Tian X, Dai W. Inhibitory effects of golden thread (Coptis chinensis) and berberine on Microcystis aeruginosa. Fisheries College, Ocean University of China, Qingdao 266003, P. R. China. Water Sci Technol. 2010;61(3):763-9.
35. *Zhong Yao Xue* (Chinese Herbology), 1988; 137:140.
36. *J Pharm Pharmacol* 2000 Mar;52(3):361-6.
37. Oh I, Yang WY, Chung SC, Kim TY, Oh KB, Shin J. In vitro sortase a inhibitory and antimicrobial activity of flavonoids isolated from the roots of Sophora flavescens. Arch Pharm Res. 2011 Feb;34(2):217-22.
38. *Zhong Yao Xue* (Chinese Herbology), 1998; 148:151.
39. *Zhong Yao Yao Li Yu Ying Yong* (Pharmacology and Applications of Chinese Herbs), 1983:149.
40. *Proc Natl Acad Sci*, 1991; 88(15):6570.
41. *Zhong Yao Yao Li Yu Ying Yong* (Pharmacology and Applications of Chinese Herbs), 1983; 744.
42. *Shan Xi Xin Yi Yao* (New Medicine and Herbology of Shanxi), 1980; 9(11):51.
43. *Zhong Yao Yao Li Yu Ying Yong* (Pharmacology and Applications of Chinese Herbs), 1983; 295.
44. *Zhong Yao Cai* (Study of Chinese Herbal Material), 1991; 14(2):41.
45. *Zhong Yao Zhi* (Chinese Herbology Journal), 1984; 578.
46. *Yao Xue Qing Bao Tong Xun* (Journal of Herbal Information), 1987; 5(4):62.
47. *Zhong Hua Xin Yi Xue Bao* (Chinese Journal of New Medicine), 1950; 1(5):95.
48. *Zhong Yao Xue* (Chinese Herbology), 1988, 140:144.
49. *Zhong Hua Yi Xue Za Zhi* (Chinese Journal of Medicine), 1958; 44(9):888.
50. *Zhong Xi Yi Jie He Za Zhi* (Journal of Integrated Chinese and Western Medicine), 1989; 9(8):494.
51. *Zhong Yao Xue* (Chinese Herbology), 1998; 144:146.
52. Błach-Olszewska Z, Jatczak B, Rak A, Lorenc M, Gulanowski B, Drobna A, Lamer-Zarawska E. Production of cytokines and stimulation of resistance to viral infection in human leukocytes by Scutellaria baicalensis flavones. Ludwik Hirszfeld Institute of Immunology and Experimental Therapy, Polish Academy of Sciences, Wrocław, Poland. J Interferon Cytokine Res. 2008 Sep;28(9): 571-81.
53. Chen C., Guo S.M. & Liu B. A randomized controlled trial of kurorinone versus interferon-alpha2a treatment in patients with chronic hepatitis B. *J Viral Hepat.* 2000, 7(3): 225-229.
54. Liu J., Zhu M., Shi R. & Yang M. Radix Sophorae flavescentis for chronic hepatitis B: a systematic review of randomized trials. *Am J Chin Med.* 2003, 31(3): 337-354.
55. *Zhong Yao Xue* (Chinese Herbology), 1998; 103:106.
56. Chiang LC, Chiang W, Chang MY, Lin CC. In vitro cytotoxic, antiviral and immunomodulatory effects of Plantago major and Plantago asiatica. Am J Chin Med. 2003;31(2):225-34.
57. *Zhong Yao Tong Bao* (Journal of Chinese Herbology), 1988; 13(6):364.
58. *Shan Xi Xin Yi Yao* (New Medicine and Herbology of Shanxi), 1980; 9(11):51.
59. Li X, Zhou JY, Yang QW, Chen Y, Piao YA, Li HY. Inhibition activities of polysaccharide (RG4-1) from Gentiana rigescens against RSV. J Asian Nat Prod Res. 2011 Jun;13(6):512-22.
60. Zheng YT, Ben KL, Jin SW. Anti-HIV-1 activity of trichobitacin, a novel ribosome-inactivating protein. Acta Pharmacol Sin. 2000 Feb;21(2):179-82.
61. Li ZH, Nie BM, Chen H, Chen SY, He P, Lu Y, Guo XK, Liu JX. In vitro anti-coxsackievirus B(3) effect of ethyl acetate extract of Tian-hua-fen. Department of Microbiology and Parasitology, Shanghai Second Medical University, Shanghai 200025, China. World J Gastroenterol. 2004 Aug 1;10(15):2263-6.
62. Bae G, Yu JR, Lee J, Chang J, Seo EK. Identification of nyasol and structurally related compounds as the active principles from Anemarrhena asphodeloides against respiratory syncytial virus (RSV). The Center for Cell Signaling & Drug Discovery Research, College of Pharmacy, Ewha Womans University, Seoul 120-750, Korea. Chem Biodivers. 2007 Sep;4(9):2231-5.
63. Yu H.H., Kim K.J., Cha J.D., Kim H.K., Lee Y.E., Choi N.Y. & You Y.O. Antimicrobial Activity of Berberine Alone and in Combination with Ampicillin or Oxacillin Against Methicillin-Resistant *Staphylococcus aureus* . *J Med Food.* 2005, 8(4): 454-461.
64. Wong KS, Tsang WK. In vitro antifungal activity of the aqueous extract of Scutellaria baicalensis Georgi root against Candida albicans. Int J Antimicrob Agents. 2009 Sep;34(3):284-5.
65. *Zhong Yao Zhi* (Chinese Herbology Journal), 1984; 250.
66. Lelono RA, Tachibana S, Itoh K. Isolation of antifungal compounds from Gardenia jasminoides. United Graduate School of Agricultural Sciences, Ehime University, 3-5-7 Tarumi, Matsuyama, Ehime 790-8566, Japan. Pak J Biol Sci. 2009 Jul 1;12(13):949-56.
67. Iida Y, Oh KB, Saito M, Matsuoka H, Kurata H, Natsume M, Abe H. Detection of antifungal activity in Anemarrhena asphodeloides by sensitive BCT method and isolation of its active compound. Department of Biotechnology, Faculty of Technology, Tokyo University of Agriculture and Technology, Japan. J Agric Food Chem. 1999 Feb;47(2):584-7.
68. *Zhong Yao Xue* (Chinese Herbology), 1998; 148:151.
69. Youn HJ, Lakritz J, Rottinghaus GE, Seo HS, Kim DY, Cho MH, Marsh AE. Anti-protozoal efficacy of high performance liquid chromatography fractions of Torilis japonica and Sophora flavescens extracts on Neospora caninum and Toxoplasma gondii. College of Veterinary Medicine, Seoul National University, Seoul 151-742, Republic of Korea. Vet Parasitol. 2004 Nov 10;125(3-4):409-14.
70. Kim YC, Kim HS, Wataya Y, Sohn DH, Kang TH, Kim MS, Kim YM, Lee GM, Chang JD, Park H. Antimalarial activity of lavandulyl flavanones isolated from the roots of Sophora flavescens. College of Pharmacy, Wonkwang University, Iksan, Korea. Biol Pharm Bull. 2004 May;27(5):748-50.
71. *Zhong Yao Tong Bao* (Journal of Chinese Herbology), 1986; 11(10):55.
72. *Xin Yi Xue* (New Medicine), 1973; 7:6.

FORMULAS

Dermatrol (HZ)™

CLINICAL APPLICATIONS

- **Shingles (herpes zoster)**
- Shingles with skin lesions and nerve pain

WESTERN THERAPEUTIC ACTIONS

- Antiviral effect to shorten the duration and suppress the severity of shingles
- Anti-inflammatory effect to reduce inflammation
- Analgesic effect to relieve pain

CHINESE THERAPEUTIC ACTIONS

- Drains damp-heat
- Purges fire
- Eliminates toxins
- Tonifies the underlying deficiencies

DOSAGE

Take 4 capsules three times daily during the entire course of infection. The herbal therapy should begin immediately upon the notice of the first warning signs. If necessary, the dosage may be doubled on the first two days of herbal therapy to achieve a faster onset of action. However, this formula should be discontinued when the course of infection is terminated.

INGREDIENTS

Chi Shao (Radix Paeoniae Rubra)
Chong Lou (Rhizoma Paridis)
Dao Di Wu Gong (Rhizoma Heliminthostachytis)
Di Huang (Radix Rehmanniae)
Gan Cao (Radix et Rhizoma Glycyrrhizae)
Huang Bo (Cortex Phellodendri Chinensis)
Huang Lian (Rhizoma Coptidis)
Huang Qin (Radix Scutellariae)
Jin Qian Cao (Herba Lysimachiae)
Jin Yin Hua (Flos Lonicerae Japonicae)
Jing Jie (Herba Schizonepetae)
Lian Qiao (Fructus Forsythiae)
Long Dan (Radix et Rhizoma Gentianae)
Mu Dan Pi (Cortex Moutan)
Niu Bang Zi (Fructus Arctii)
Pu Gong Ying (Herba Taraxaci)
Zhi Zi (Fructus Gardeniae)
Zi Hua Di Ding (Herba Violae)

BACKGROUND

Shingles, also known as chickenpox, herpes zoster, zona zoster, is caused by re-activation of the varicella-zoster virus (human herpes virus type 3). Shingles is an acute viral inflammation of the sensory ganglia of spinal and cranial nerves associated with a vesicular eruption and neuralgic pain. Optimal treatment requires use of medicinal substances to treat both the cause and the symptoms. Treating the cause requires use of antiviral agents to suppress the virus and shorten the duration of infection. Treating the symptoms requires use of medicines to reduce inflammation and pain.

FORMULA EXPLANATION

Dermatrol (HZ) is an herbal formula specifically formulated to treat shingles (herpes zoster). In traditional Chinese medicine, the history of treating shingles is well-documented, with the first recorded treatment in *Huang Di Nei Jing* (Yellow Emperor's Inner Classic) from the second century A.D. Shingles is generally diagnosed as the presence of damp-heat, fire and toxins, accompanied by underlying deficiencies. Therefore, ***Dermatrol (HZ)*** incorporates herbs specifically to drain damp-heat, purge fire, eliminate toxins, and tonify the underlying deficiencies.

In this formula, *Dao Di Wu Gong* (Rhizoma Heliminthostachytis) is used as the principle herb as it has a unique effect to clear heat and eliminate toxins. The use of this herb has been documented to effectively treat shingles, both in internal and topical formulations. *Long Dan* (Radix et Rhizoma Gentianae) and *Jin Qian Cao* (Herba Lysimachiae) clear damp-heat from the Liver and Gallbladder channels. Together, they drain damp-heat through urination. *Huang Lian* (Rhizoma Coptidis), *Huang Qin* (Radix Scutellariae), *Huang Bo* (Cortex Phellodendri Chinensis) and *Zhi Zi* (Fructus Gardeniae) clear damp-heat from upper, middle and lower *jiaos*, and enable this formula to treat shingles affecting different parts of the body. *Jin Yin Hua* (Flos Lonicerae Japonicae), *Lian Qiao* (Fructus Forsythiae) and *Jing Jie* (Herba Schizonepetae) clear heat and toxins from the exterior to treat lesions and sores. *Niu Bang Zi* (Fructus Arctii), *Pu Gong Ying* (Herba Taraxaci), *Zi Hua Di Ding* (Herba Violae) and *Chong Lou* (Rhizoma Paridis) clear heat and eliminate toxins from the interior to treat lesions and sores. *Chi Shao* (Radix Paeoniae Rubra) activates blood circulation and relieves pain. Adequate blood circulation will ensure proper healing of the lesions. *Di Huang* (Radix Rehmanniae) and *Mu Dan Pi* (Cortex Moutan) nourish yin and clear deficiency heat. They also prevent all the bitter and cold herbs from consuming the yin and fluids of the body. Lastly, *Gan Cao* (Radix et Rhizoma Glycyrrhizae) harmonizes all the herbs in this formula.

In short, ***Dermatrol (HZ)*** is an herbal formula that utilizes thousands of years of clinical experiences to treat shingles. It shortens the duration and reduces the severity of illness by using herbs to drain damp-heat, purge fire, eliminate toxins and tonify the underlying deficiencies.

CAUTIONS & CONTRAINDICATIONS

- This formula is bitter and cold, and may cause nausea and vomiting in individuals who have a sensitive stomach. Therefore, it may be taken with food to minimize such adverse reactions.
- This formula should be stopped once symptoms are cleared. It is not recommended for long-term use.

Dermatrol (HZ)™

CLINICAL NOTES

- *Dermatrol (HZ)* is a potent herbal formula that treats shingles. It should be used immediately with the first warning signs of herpes outbreak, and continued until the remission. However, it should not be taken indefinitely as this formula is relatively strong, and may weaken the overall constitution if taken for a long period of time. Discontinue use after symptoms have cleared. However, if there is still pain, herbs can be continued for a few more days. Acupuncture is a more effective method for treating the pain after herpetic lesions have cleared.
- Herbal therapy is most effective if it is started immediately, upon experiencing the first warning signs. The dosage may be doubled on the first two days to speed up the initial onset of action. The herbal therapy should be continued until the course of infection is terminated. Possible warning signs and symptoms may include: headache, flu-like symptoms (usually without a fever), and sensitivity to light, followed by itching, tingling, or even severe pain in the area of the rash.
- Herpetic lesions can also be treated topically, in conjunction with taking herbs orally. There are two topical treatments that are quite effective:
  - The first topical treatment uses an herbal paste made from mixing the extract granules of 2 parts *Da Huang* (Radix et Rhizoma Rhei), 2 parts *Huang Bo* (Cortex Phellodendri Chinensis), 1 part *Wu Bei Zi* (Galla Chinensis), and 1 part *Mang Xiao* (Natrii Sulfas) with petroleum jelly. The herbal paste is to be applied topically and covered with gauze. The herbal paste should be changed on a daily basis.
  - The second topical treatment uses *Hai Jin Sha* (Spora Lygodii) as an herbal wash. Mix 1 tablespoon of the extract granule of *Hai Jin Sha* (Spora Lygodii) with 1 cup of water and apply topically as a wash after shower.
- It is important to see an ophthalmologist if the shingles lesions appear near the eyes. If untreated, herpes zoster infection of the eye may lead to blindness.

SUPPLEMENTARY FORMULAS

- To enhance the overall effect to treat genital herpes, combine with ***Gentiana Complex***.
- To enhance the overall effect to treat oral herpes, combine with ***Lonicera Complex***.
- To enhance the antiviral effect, add ***Herbal AVR***.
- For post-herpetic nerve pain, combine with ***Flex (NP)***.
- To strengthen the immune system and minimize the recurrences of shingles, use ***Immune +*** and ***Nourish*** on a regular basis at low doses.
- For chronic pain without blisters but dark appearance at the place of the lesions, add ***Circulation (SJ)***.
- For fever, add ***Gardenia Complex***.

ACUPUNCTURE TREATMENT

Bleeding technique is very effective in the treatment of shingles. Wear gloves and bleed the local area with a lancet needle. Finish by applying *Zi Yun Gao* (Purple Cloud Ointment).

Traditional Points:

- *Hegu* (LI 4), *Zhigou* (TH 6), *Yanglingquan* (GB 34). Insert needles 0.5 *cun* deep all along the sides of the shingles (use between 4 and 16 needles).
- Tap plum-blossom needles all along the sides of the shingles. Be careful ***not*** to tap directly on the lesions. Tap until there is slight bleeding from the skin.
  - Shingles with more itching (wind): *Quchi* (LI 11), *Fengchi* (GB 20), *Hegu* (LI 4), *Waiguan* (TH 5), *Yanglingquan* (GB 34), *Xuehai* (SP 10)
  - Shingles with more burning sensations (toxic heat): *ah shi* points, *Huatuojiaji*, *Quchi* (LI 11), *Waiguan* (TH 5), *Yanglingquan* (GB 34)
  - Shingles with more pain (qi and blood stagnation): *Zhangmen* (LR 13), *Yifeng* (TH 17), *Zhigou* (TH 6), *Yanglingquan* (GB 34)
  - Shingles with wet lesions (dampness and Spleen deficiency): *Zusanli* (ST 36), *Qimen* (LR 14), *Yuanye* (GB 22), *Fenglong* (ST 40), *Zhigou* (TH 6), *ah shi* points

Classic Master Tung's Points:

- **Herpes zoster:** *Linggu* (T 22.05), *Tianhuang* (T 88.13), *Minghuang* (T 88.12), *Qihuang* (T 88.14), *Simashang* (T 88.18), *Simazhong* (T 88.17), *Simaxia* (T 88.19), *Shuitong* (T 1010.19), *Shuijin* (T 1010.20)
- **Herpes of the eyes:** *Shangbai* (T 22.03), *Tianhuangfu [Shenguan]* (T 77.18), *Huoying* (T 66.03), *Simazhong* (T 88.17)
- Bleed the LU area below the knees. Bleed before needling for best result.

Master Tung's Points by Dr. Chuan-Min Wang:

- **Shingles:** Bleed *Zhiwu* (T 11.26) or around shingles area, 1 *cun* away from the border of the shingles rash. Needle around shingles area, 0.5 *cun* away from the border of the shingles rash.

Balance Method by Dr. Richard Tan:

- **Shingles on the rib cage:** Needle bilaterally *ah shi* points from *Chize* (LU 5) to *Kongzui* (LU 6), *Tongli* (HT 5) to *Shaohai* (HT 3), and from *Waiguan* (TH 5) to *Sidu* (TH 9), and *Yanggu* (SI 5) to *Xiaohai* (SI 8)

Ear Acupuncture:

- **Herpes zoster:** Lung (three needles), Subcortex, Endocrine, affected area. Strong stimulation should be applied for two hours every other day. Ten to fifteen treatments equal one course of treatment.

Dermatrol (HZ)™

Auricular Medicine by Dr. Li-Chun Huang:

- **Herpes zoster:** Allergic Area, Endocrine, Adrenal Gland, *Shenmen*, Occiput, Liver, Gallbladder, Spleen, Lung, corresponding point (to the area affected). Bleed Ear Apex.
  - For herpes zoster with insomnia, add Neurasthenia Area, Neurasthenia Point, and Nervous Subcortex.

NUTRITION

- There are many nutrients that are essential for preventing, fighting, and healing of shingles. Some examples include garlic, L-lysine, calcium, magnesium, and vitamins A, B, C, and E.
- The following foods are also beneficial: brewer's yeast, brown rice, garlic, raw fruits and vegetables, whole grains, and foods rich in vitamins.
- Avoid foods that are spicy, fried or greasy. Refrain from foods that are high in L-carnitine, such as peanuts, chocolate, and corn. Shellfish and seafood are also contraindicated. Foods high in L-arginine should also be avoided, as there is a correlation between L-arginine consumption and herpetic viral activity.
- Avoid spicy/pungent/aromatic vegetables such as pepper, garlic, onions, basil, rosemary, cumin, funnel, anise, leeks, chives, scallions, thyme, saffron, wormwood, mustard, chili pepper, and wasabi.

The Tao of Nutrition by Dr. Maoshing Ni and Cathy McNease:

- Apply grated, raw yam locally or mix with a pinch of borax.

LIFESTYLE INSTRUCTIONS

- Shingles attack may be triggered by many factors, including but not limited to emotional or physical stress, spinal cord injuries, and conditions that cause immunodeficiency. All these conditions and situations should be avoided, if at all possible.
- Individuals with shingles should avoid direct skin contact with others, as the fluid from shingles blisters is contagious, and exposure to it can cause chickenpox (but not shingles).
- It is important to take good general care of skin sores, such as not scratching blisters and keeping the skin clean and dry.
- Be careful at the gym, as the virus may be transmitted through physical contact, such as via exercise mats.
- Wet and cold compresses are helpful and soothing.
- Avoid alcohol and tobacco products.

CASE STUDIES

- A 65-year-old male farmer complained of shingles lesions that started one week ago at the left chest area, which then spread throughout the ribs and the back. The pain was described as burning, stabbing, and extremely painful. The patient had yellow urine, normal bowel movement, and a wiry-forceful pulse. This condition was diagnosed as damp-heat and Liver fire. The patient was treated with ***Dermatrol (HZ)*** orally. The patient was also instructed to use *Hai Jin Sha* (Spora Lygodii) as an herbal wash topically to the affected area once daily. After four days of internal and external treatments, the shingles lesions decreased in size, and the pain was reduced significantly. After seven days, the patient reported complete recovery. Anonymous.
- E.S., a 58-year-old female, presented with itching and severe burning on the right side of her face as well as other parts of her scalp. Objective findings included red discoloration at the sites of pain. Allopathic antiviral and analgesic medicines had been taken, yet unsatisfactory results were obtained. The practitioner diagnosed this condition as deficiency of yin and blood with rising damp/heat/fire/toxins. For treatment, ***Dermatrol (HZ)*** was prescribed. After the second acupuncture treatment, pain was reduced by 50%. Her pain was nearly eliminated after one month of treatment, with the addition of ***Dermatrol (HZ)*** having a synergistic effect as well. Submitted by J.B., Camarillo, California.

PHARMACOLOGICAL AND CLINICAL RESEARCH

Dermatrol (HZ) is formulated with many herbs that address the overall condition of herpes infection, including use of herbs to treat the virus, reduce the inflammation, relieve pain, and facilitate the healing of lesions and sores. Proper use of herbs has been shown to decrease the severity of symptoms, shorten the duration of infection, and reduce the frequency of recurrences.

Since herpes is a viral infection, ***Dermatrol (HZ)*** is formulated with many herbs that have marked antiviral effects. Pharmacologically, both the ethanol and water extract of *Huang Bo* (Cortex Phellodendri Chinensis) has been shown to have specific antiviral activity against the herpes virus.[1] Extracts of *Huang Qin* (Radix Scutellariae) have displayed a wide spectrum of antiviral activity. Specifically, baicalein and wogonin, two compounds from the herb, boost innate antiviral immunity by stimulating the production of cytokines and increasing the resistance to viral infection in human leukocytes.[2] *Pu Gong Ying* (Herba Taraxaci) has been described as "highly effective" against the herpes virus, according to a study that evaluate 472 traditional medicinal herbs for their antiviral effect.[3] Clinically, topical application of herbs is also effective for treatment of herpes zoster, such as with topical application of *Dao Di Wu Gong* (Rhizoma Heliminthostachytis) and *Long Dan* (Radix et Rhizoma Gentianae).[4] Other herbs with antiviral effects include *Huang Lian* (Rhizoma Coptidis), *Chi Shao* (Radix Paeoniae Rubra), *Gan Cao* (Radix et Rhizoma Glycyrrhizae), and *Zi Hua Di Ding* (Herba Violae). These herbs have been shown to effectively suppress the replication of the virus and reduce the duration of viral infections.[5,6,7,8]

To reduce inflammation and relieve pain, ***Dermatrol (HZ)*** incorporates many herbs with excellent anti-inflammatory and analgesic effects. *Huang Qin* (Radix Scutellariae), *Huang Lian* (Rhizoma Coptidis) and *Huang Bo* (Cortex Phellodendri Chinensis) all have significant anti-inflammatory effects, and have been used to treat different skin disorders.[9] *Huang Qin* (Radix

Dermatrol (HZ)™

Scutellariae) exerts its anti-inflammatory effect via inhibition of nitric oxide, cyclo-oxygenase-2, prostaglandin E2, and proinflammatory cytokines.[10] *Huang Lian* (Rhizoma Coptidis) illustrates its anti-inflammatory effect through suppression of tumor necrosis factor-α, interleukin-1β and nitrite oxide.[11] *Huang Bo* (Cortex Phellodendri Chinensis) reduces inflammation by inhibiting the production of proinflammatory cytokines in a dose-dependent manner.[12] Together, these three herbs have an excellent synergistic effect to treat many inflammatory disorders. In addition to these three herbs, *Gan Cao* (Radix et Rhizoma Glycyrrhizae) is also used to reduce inflammation, though its mechanism of action is completely different. *Gan Cao* (Radix et Rhizoma Glycyrrhizae) enhances the overall duration of effect of cortisone and decreases sensitivity to stimuli. The anti-inflammatory influence of glycyrrhizin and glycyrrhetinic acid, two compounds in this herb, is approximately 1/10th that of cortisone.[13,14] Furthermore, ***Dermatrol (HZ)*** uses herbs with analgesic effects to relieve pain. *Jing Jie* (Herba Schizonepetae) has been shown to reduce inflammation and relieve pain by decreasing levels of cyclo-oxygenase and nitric oxide synthase.[15] *Lian Qiao* (Fructus Forsythiae) has both anti-inflammatory and analgesic effects.[16] *Zhi Zi* (Fructus Gardeniae) has a marked analgesic effect to relieve pain, and may be used either internally or externally.[17,18] Clinically, one study reported a marked effect to treat neuralgia affecting various parts of the body by using an herbal formula that contains *Chi Shao* (Radix Paeoniae Rubra), *Huang Qin* (Radix Scutellariae) and others.[19]

Lastly, ***Dermatrol (HZ)*** uses many herbs to facilitate the healing of herpetic lesions and sores and to shorten the duration of illness, such as *Dao Di Wu Gong* (Rhizoma Heliminthostachytis), *Zi Hua Di Ding* (Herba Violae), and *Chong Lou* (Rhizoma Paridis). *Jing Jie* (Herba Schizonepetae) is also added for its function to relieve itching and general skin discomfort.[20]

In summary, ***Dermatrol (HZ)*** is an herbal formula that treats both the cause and the symptoms of shingles. It contains herbs with antiviral effects to treat the herpes infection. Furthermore, it contains herbs with anti-inflammatory and analgesic effects to treat the symptoms of shingles.

COMPARATIVE ANALYSIS

Shingles, also known as chickenpox or herpes zoster, is a viral infection with an acute inflammation of the sensory ganglia of spinal and cranial nerves associated with a vesicular eruption and neuralgic pain. There is no specific treatment in Western medicine. However, certain drugs may be used to treat the symptoms. Wet compresses are soothing when applied topically. Aspirin and Elavil (amitriptyline) are sometimes used to relieve pain. Antiviral drugs, such as Zovirax (acyclovir) and Valtrex (valacyclovir), are recommended only in individuals with weakened immune systems, such as geriatric and pediatric patients. In short, most of these drugs relieve symptoms, but do not change the course of infection or reduce its severity.

Herbs are very effective to treat the cause and the symptoms of shingles. As described above, many herbs have been shown via *in vitro* and *in vivo* studies to effectively treat viral infections by reducing its severity and duration. Furthermore, many herbs have excellent analgesic effects to relieve pain and anti-inflammatory effects to reduce inflammation. Though there is no cure, herbs do offer excellent short- and long-term relief. Finally, after the shingles are resolved, patients should follow the guidelines established in Nutrition and Lifestyles Instructions sections to strengthen the body and reduce recurrences.

References

1. Wang W, Zu Y, Fu Y, Reichling J, Suschke U, Nokemper S, Zhang Y. In vitro antioxidant, antimicrobial and anti-herpes simplex virus type 1 activity of Phellodendron amurense Rupr. from China. Key Laboratory of Forest Plant Ecology, Northeast Forestry University, Hexing Road 26, 150040 Harbin, China. Am J Chin Med. 2009;37(1):195-203.
2. Błach-Olszewska Z, Jatczak B, Rak A, Lorenc M, Gulanowski B, Drobna A, Lamer-Zarawska E. Production of cytokines and stimulation of resistance to viral infection in human leukocytes by Scutellaria baicalensis flavones. Ludwik Hirszfeld Institute of Immunology and Experimental Therapy, Polish Academy of Sciences, Wrocław, Poland. J Interferon Cytokine Res. 2008 Sep;28(9):571-81.
3. Zheng M. Experimental study of 472 herbs with antiviral action against the herpes simplex virus. Dept. of Microbiology, Jiangxi Medical College, Nanchang. Zhong Xi Yi Jie He Za Zhi. 1990 Jan;10(1):39-41, 6.
4. *Zhong Yao Lin Chuan Xin Yong* (New Clinical Applications of Chinese Medicine), 2001; 183.
5. *Zhong Xi Yi Jie He Za Zhi* (Journal of Integrated Chinese and Western Medicine), 1989; 9(8):494.
6. *Zhong Yao Xue* (Chinese Herbology), 1998; 162:164.
7. Kuo KK, Chang JS, Wang KC, Chiang LC. Water extract of Glycyrrhiza uralensis inhibited enterovirus 71 in a human foreskin fibroblast cell line. Am J Chin Med. 2009;37(2):383-94.
8. Wang CK, Colgrave ML, Gustafson KR, Ireland DC, Goransson U, Craik DJ. Anti-HIV cyclotides from the Chinese medicinal herb Viola yedoensis. Institute for Molecular Bioscience, Australian Research Council Special Research Centre for Functional and Applied Genomics, University of Queensland, Brisbane, Australia. J Nat Prod. 2008 Jan;71(1):47-52.
9. Cuéllar MJ, Giner RM, Recio MC, Máñez S, Ríos JL. Topical anti-inflammatory activity of some Asian medicinal plants used in dermatological disorders. Departament de Farmacologia, Facultat de Farmàcia, Universitat de València, Avda. Vicent Andrés Estellés, s/n. 46100 Burjassot, Valencia, Spain. Fitoterapia. 2001 Mar;72(3):221-9.
10. Kim EH, Shim B, Kang S, Jeong G, Lee JS, Yu YB, Chun M. Anti-inflammatory effects of Scutellaria baicalensis extract via suppression of immune modulators and MAP kinase signaling molecules. Department of Biological Sciences, Seoul National University, Seoul 151-742, Republic of Korea. J Ethnopharmacol. 2009 Nov 12;126(2):320-31.
11. Zhang Q, Piao XL, Piao XS, Lu T, Wang D, Kim SW. Preventive effect of Coptis chinensis and berberine on intestinal injury in rats challenged with lipopolysaccharides. State Key Laboratory of Animal Nutrition, China Agricultural University, No. 2, West Road Yuanmingyuan, Beijing 100193, China. Food Chem Toxicol. 2010 Oct 25.
12. Hsiang CY, Wu SL, Cheng SE, Ho TY. Acetaldehyde-induced interleukin-1beta and tumor necrosis factor-alpha production is inhibited by berberine through nuclear factor-kappaB signaling pathway in HepG2 cells. Graduate Institute of Medical Science, China Medical University, Taichung 404, Taiwan. J Biomed Sci. 2005 Oct;12(5):791-801.
13. *Zhong Yao Zhi* (Chinese Herbology Journal), 1993; 358.
14. *Zhong Cao Yao* (Chinese Herbal Medicine), 1991; 22(10):452.

FORMULAS

Dermatrol (HZ) ™

15. Ge WH, Guo JY, Shen YJ, Chen ML, Shi SL, Han YH, Lin J. Effects of volatie oil of Schizonepeta tenuifolia Briq herb and Saposhnikovia divaricata Schischke root on proinflammatory cytokine expression and regulation. Zhongguo Zhong Yao Za Zhi. 2007 Sep;32(17):1777-9.
16. Ozaki Y, Rui J, Tang Y, Satake M. Antiinflammatory effect of Forsythia suspensa Vahl and its active fraction. Biol Pharm Bull. 1997 Aug;20(8):861-4.
17. *Zhong Yao Zhi* (Chinese Herbology Journal), 1984; 578.
18. *Zhong Yi Za Zhi* (Journal of Chinese Medicine), 1964; 12:450.
19. *Zhong Yao Lin Chuan Xin Yong* (New Clinical Applications of Chinese Medicine), 2001; 318.
20. *Zhong Yi Za Zhi* (Journal of Chinese Medicine), 1964; 12:18.

Dermatrol (PS)™

CLINICAL APPLICATIONS

- **Psoriasis, parapsoriasis and other scaling diseases**
- **Severe acne with pus, abscesses and redness**
- **Dermatological disorders** with sores, abscesses, lesions, blisters, and severe itching

WESTERN THERAPEUTIC ACTIONS

- Antiproliferative action to suppress proliferation of the psoriatic cells
- Immunosuppressive and immunomodulatory activities to control hyperactive immune system
- Antipruritic effect to inhibit scratching
- Antiallergic effect to alleviate allergies
- Antihistamine effect to relieve itching
- Anti-inflammatory effect to reduce tissue inflammation

CHINESE THERAPEUTIC ACTIONS

- Clears heat and detoxifies
- Invigorates blood circulation and nourishes blood

DOSAGE

Take 3 to 4 capsules three times daily on an empty stomach with warm water. In acute conditions, dosage may be increased to 8 to 10 capsules three times daily for one week, or until symptoms subside. After relief of symptoms, dosage then can be reduced to 3 or 4 capsules daily.

INGREDIENTS

Bai Hua She She Cao (Herba Hedyotis)
Bai Xian Pi (Cortex Dictamni)
Ban Lan Gen (Radix Isatidis)
Chan Tui (Periostracum Cicadae)
Chi Shao (Radix Paeoniae Rubra)
Da Qing Ye (Folium Isatidis)
Feng Fang (Nidus Vespae)
Gan Cao (Radix et Rhizoma Glycyrrhizae)
Jin Yin Hua (Flos Lonicerae Japonicae)
Ku Shen (Radix Sophorae Flavescentis)
Mu Dan Pi (Cortex Moutan)
Quan Xie (Scorpio)
Wu Shao She (Zaocys)
Zhi He Shou Wu (Radix Polygoni Multiflori Praeparata)

BACKGROUND

Psoriasis, parapsoriasis and other scaling diseases are skin disorders with well-circumscribed, scaling papules or plaques without wetness, crusts, and fissures. The cause is unclear but involves immune stimulation of epidermal keratinocytes. Common triggers include emotional stress, sunburn, infection and use of certain drugs (alcohol, beta-blockers, lithium, ACE inhibitors, indomethacin, and interferon α).

FORMULA EXPLANATION

Psoriasis and scaling diseases with severe itching in traditional Chinese medicine are amongst the most difficult disorders to treat since there may be various pathogenic factors involved. In addition, most conditions are chronic and may be complicated by the presence of both excess and deficient factors simultaneously, such as wind, toxic heat, dampness, and blood deficiency. To successfully treat such stubborn and complicated conditions, ***Dermatrol (PS)*** contains many strong and potent herbs to treat both the cause and the symptoms concurrently.

Dermatrol (PS) contains many medicinal substances that have potent actions to eliminate the heat and toxins that contribute directly to psoriasis or other dermatological conditions. *Wu Shao She* (Zaocys) has excellent dispersing functions that enter the internal organs and travel to the skin to relieve itching. It disperses wind, which is the predominant cause for itching. To further relieve itching and disperse wind, *Ku Shen* (Radix Sophorae Flavescentis), *Bai Xian Pi* (Cortex Dictamni) and *Chan Tui* (Periostracum Cicadae) are used. *Da Qing Ye* (Folium Isatidis), *Ban Lan Gen* (Radix Isatidis) and *Bai Hua She She Cao* (Herba Hedyotis) are used to clear heat and detoxify. *Jin Yin Hua* (Flos Lonicerae Japonicae) is commonly used to treat toxic heat in the exterior characterized by all dermatological sores, lesions, ulcerations, warts, and furuncles. To cool the blood and prevent further spreading of lesions, *Mu Dan Pi* (Cortex Moutan) and *Chi Shao* (Radix Paeoniae Rubra) are used. *Quan Xie* (Scorpio) and *Feng Fang* (Nidus Vespae) are used together to relieve toxicity, dispel wind and relieve pain. The use of these two substances is effective because in traditional Chinese medicine, it is sometimes necessary to "use toxin to attack toxin." These two herbs are used to treat a wide range of dermatological disorders ranging from toxic sores, mastitis, mumps, swellings and scrofula. *Zhi He Shou Wu* (Radix Polygoni Multiflori Praeparata) tonifies blood and prevents flaring of wind associated with blood deficiency. Finally, *Gan Cao* (Radix et Rhizoma Glycyrrhizae) is used to harmonize the formula, reduce the toxicity of *Quan Xie* (Scorpio) and protect the stomach from the cold properties of the heat-clearing herbs.

CAUTIONS & CONTRAINDICATIONS

- This formula is contraindicated during pregnancy and nursing.
- Patients with weak Spleen and Stomach should take this formula with food to avoid stomach upset.
- Patients with yang deficiency or coldness should use this formula with caution. A yang tonic formula such as ***Kidney Tonic (Yang)*** is recommended to be taken with ***Dermatrol (PS)*** for maximum effect.
- According to most textbooks and contemporary references, the classic entry of "*He Shou Wu*" is now separated into two entries: the unprepared *Sheng Shou Wu* (Radix Polygoni Multiflori) and the prepared *Zhi He Shou Wu* (Radix Polygoni Multiflori

Dermatrol (PS)™

Praeparata), as they have significantly different therapeutic effects and side effects. *Sheng Shou Wu* (Radix Polygoni Multiflori) is a stimulant laxative that treats constipation, but may cause nausea, vomiting, abdominal pain, diarrhea, and in rare cases, liver disorder (dose- and time-dependent, and reversible upon discontinuation).[1] On the other hand, *Zhi He Shou Wu* (Radix Polygoni Multiflori Praeparata) is a tonic herb that is safe and well-tolerated. The dramatic changes in the therapeutic effect and safety profile are attributed to the long and complicated processing of the root with *Hei Dou* (Semen Sojae) through repeated blending, cooking, and drying procedures. When properly processed, the chemical composition of the root changes significantly. Many new compounds are generated from the Maillard reaction (four furanones, two furans, two nitrogen compounds, one pyran, one alcohol and one sulfur compound). Furthermore, the preparation process causes changes in the composition of sugars and 16 kinds of amino acids; it also reduces the pH of the herb from 6.28 to 5.61.[2,3,4] In summary, these changes give rise to the tonic effects of the prepared roots, and eliminate the adverse reactions associated with the unprepared roots. **Note:** Due to medical risks and legal liabilities, it is prudent to exercise caution and ***not*** use this herb in either prepared or unprepared forms in patients with pre-existing or risk factors of liver diseases.

CLINICAL NOTES

- Because psoriasis is a difficult and stubborn disease, the treatment period is set at three months at a time, between intervals for evaluation and modification of the herbal formula(s).
- After the condition has stabilized, it is recommended that the patient take 2 capsules per day of ***Dermatrol (PS)***. Furthermore, those with qi deficiency or blood deficiency should take ***Immune +*** or ***Schisandra ZZZ***, respectively.

Pulse Diagnosis by Dr. Jimmy Wei-Yen Chang:

- **Wet skin lesions due to damp-heat accumulation:** deep and forceful pulse on all three pulse positions (*cun, guan, chi*)
- **Dry skin lesions due to dryness and heat accumulation in the Lung and Large Intestine:** floating and forceful pulse on the right *cun*
- **Allergy lesions due to fire and dryness in the Lung, Large Intestine and Liver:** floating, forceful, and jumpy on the right *cun* and left *guan*
- **Toxic lesions due to Liver fire:** thick, long, wiry, forceful, and jumpy on both *chi*; and floating, forceful, and jumpy on the left *guan*
- **Skin problems due to stress:** forceful on the left *guan*

SUPPLEMENTARY FORMULAS

- For itching due to wind-heat, add ***Silerex***.
- For acne with redness, pain and pus, add ***Dermatrol (Clear)***.
- For toxic heat with redness and pain, or skin infection, add ***Herbal ABX*** and ***Gardenia Complex***.
- For excess heat manifesting in redness, add ***Gardenia Complex***.
- For chronic skin condition with blood stagnation, combine with ***Circulation (SJ)***.
- For blood or yin deficiency with dry skin, flaking, and dry throat, add ***Schisandra ZZZ*** and/or ***Nourish (Fluids)***.
- For yin deficiency with heat and dryness, add ***Nourish***.
- For ulcerations and wet lesions on the skin due to damp-heat, add ***Gentiana Complex***.
- For dry stools or constipation, add ***Gentle Lax (Excess)*** or ***Gentle Lax (Deficient)***.
- For shingles, use ***Dermatrol (HZ)*** instead.
- For lupus, use ***LPS Support*** instead.
- Use ***Dermatrol (Dry)*** instead if desired effect is not obvious with ***Dermatrol (PS)***.

ACUPUNCTURE TREATMENT

Traditional Points:

- *Quchi* (LI 11), *Xuehai* (SP 10), *Zusanli* (ST 36), *Neiguan* (PC 6), *Shenmen* (HT 7), *Sanyinjiao* (SP 6), *Feiyang* (BL 58)

Classic Master Tung's Points:

- **Eczema:** *Simashang* (T 88.18), *Simazhong* (T 88.17), *Simaxia* (T 88.19), *Linggu* (T 22.05), *Minghuang* (T 88.12), *Tianhuang* (T 88.13), *Qihuang* (T 88.14), *Tianhuang* (T 77.17), *Dihuang* (T 77.19), *Renhuang* (T 77.21), *Jinqianshang* (T 88.24), *Jinqianxia* (T 88.23)
- **Atopic dermatitis:** *Simashang* (T 88.18), *Simazhong* (T 88.17), *Simaxia* (T 88.19), *Linggu* (T 22.05), *Zhisima* (T 11.07)
- **Herpes zoster:** *Linggu* (T 22.05), *Tianhuang* (T 88.13), *Minghuang* (T 88.12), *Qihuang* (T 88.14), *Simashang* (T 88.18), *Simazhong* (T 88.17), *Simaxia* (T 88.19), *Shuitong* (T 1010.19), *Shuijin* (T 1010.20)
- **Tinea versicolor:** *Tianhuang* (T 88.13), *Minghuang* (T 88.12), *Qihuang* (T 88.14), *Simashang* (T 88.18), *Simaxia* (T 88.19), *Simazhong* (T 88.17), *Shuijin* (T 1010.20), *Shuitong* (T 1010.19). Bleed the LR area T5 – T9 and KI area T9 – T12 on the back with cupping. Bleed before needling for best result.
- **Hives:** *Simashang* (T 88.18), *Simaxia* (T 88.19), *Simazhong* (T 88.17), *Tianhuang* (T 77.17), *Dihuang* (T 77.19), *Renhuang* (T 77.21), *Tianhuang* (T 88.13), *Minghuang* (T 88.12), *Qihuang* (T 88.14), *Zhisima* (T 11.07)

Master Tung's Points by Dr. Chuan-Min Wang:

- **Psoriasis:** *Simazhong* (T 88.17), *Simashang* (T 88.18), *Simaxia* (T 88.19)

Balance Method by Dr. Richard Tan:

- Left side: *Dadun* (LR 1), *Zhongfeng* (LR 4), *Shangyang* (LI 1), *Hegu* (LI 4)

Dermatrol (PS)™

- Right side: *Zuqiaoyin* (GB 44), *Qiuxu* (GB 40), *Shaoshang* (LU 11), *Jingqu* (LU 8)
- Left and right sides can be alternated from treatment to treatment.

Ear Acupuncture:

- Main points: Lung, Endocrine, *Shenmen*, Occipital
- Adjunct points: Adrenal Gland, Liver, Spleen, Brain Stem, Heart
- Select four to five points each time, and needle for 30 to 60 minutes every other day. Ear seeds can also be used. Alternate ears every three to seven days.

Auricular Medicine by Dr. Li-Chun Huang:

- **Psoriasis:** corresponding points (to the areas affected), Gallbladder, Liver, Spleen, Lung, Large Intestine, Endocrine. Bleed Ear Apex and Helix 4.
- **Cutaneous pruritis:** *Shenmen*, Occiput, Liver, Spleen, Lung, Endocrine, Diaphragm, Allergic Area. Bleed Ear Apex.
- **Urticaria:** Liver, Lung, Spleen, Diaphragm, *Shenmen*, Occiput, Allergic Area, Sympathetic, Endocrine, Adrenal Gland. Bleed Ear Apex.
- **Contact dermatitis:** Liver, Spleen, Lung, Endocrine, Sympathetic, Adrenal Gland, Allergic Area, corresponding points (to the area affected). Bleed Ear Apex.
- **Eczema:** Allergic Area, Lung, Sympathetic, Spleen, *Shenmen*, Endocrine, Occiput, Diaphragm, corresponding points (to the area affected). Bleed Ear Apex.

NUTRITION

- Successful treatment of psoriasis or any dermatological disorders with herbs is highly dependent on the patient's cooperation in maintaining a proper diet. During the treatment period, alcohol, spicy food, seafood and anything that may be stimulating, or that may cause allergies should be avoided completely.
- Fish oil, flax seed oil, and primrose oil help to reduce inflammation, and are beneficial for the treatment of psoriasis.
- Make sure the diet contains adequate amount of fruits, vegetables, whole grains, and dietary fiber.
- Avoid citrus fruits, fried foods, processed foods, and saturated fats.

The Tao of Nutrition by Dr. Maoshing Ni and Cathy McNease:

- **Psoriasis**
  - Recommendations: Chinese prunes, guava skin, pearl barley, vinegar, garlic, walnuts, cucumber, beet tops, dandelions, squash, and mung beans.
  - Take 15 peeled and sliced water chestnuts and 1 cup of vinegar (preferably aged rice vinegar), slowly simmer in a non-metal pot for 20 minutes until water chestnuts absorb most of the vinegar. Then mash into a paste and seal in a jar. Spread evenly on a gauze pad and apply to affected area, changing daily for mild to moderate condition, and three times daily for serious condition. Mild cases should show improvement within five days, but serious conditions may take up to two weeks.
  - Take peels from guava, char and powder it, mix with sesame oil into a paste and apply twice daily for one week.
  - Apply mashed garlic to the affected area, changing twice daily for one week.
  - Avoid spicy food, stimulating food, alcohol, caffeine, smoking, and excessive sun exposure.
- **Acne**
  - Recommendations: squash, cucumbers, watermelon, winter melon, celery, carrots, cabbage, beet tops, dandelions, aloe vera, mulberry leaf, carrot tops, lettuce, potato, cherries, papaya, pear, persimmon, raspberries, buckwheat, alfalfa sprouts, millet, brown rice, mung beans, and plenty of water.
  - Apply plain, low-fat, no chemical yogurt to the affected area. Leave on for 20 minutes then wash off.
  - Rub watermelon rind on the acne.
  - Apply aloe vera.
  - Eat watermelon or drink watermelon juice.
  - Roast buckwheat, grind to powder and mix with rice vinegar into a paste, then apply to area.
  - For oozing acne condition, cover area with pearl barley powder over night, wash off with water.
  - For infected acne, apply a dandelion poultice to the area.
  - Avoid fried foods, fatty or oily foods, spicy foods, coffee, alcohol, sugar, smoking, stress, constipation, make-up, washing with chemicals, chocolate, ice cream, soft drinks, and emotional stress.

LIFESTYLE INSTRUCTIONS

- Do not scratch the affected area, which increase risk of infection and scarring.
- Avoid factors that trigger psoriasis outbreak whenever possible: alcohol consumption, emotional stress, sunburn, infection and drugs (beta-blockers, lithium, ACE inhibitors, indomethacin, and interferon α).
- Prevention of respiratory infections is also important. Adequate rest is essential.

CASE STUDIES

- D.D., a 45-year-old business owner, who is a single mom and received less than four hours of sleep for herself each night, presented with chronic eczema and itchy skin. Objective findings were red and heavy eyes and the location of her rash was mainly on her hands and feet. She had recently lost over 50 pounds and was still trying to lose more weight. The practitioner diagnosed this condition as damp-heat and Liver disharmony. ***Dermatrol (PS)*** was prescribed at three capsules three times daily along with ***Liver DTX*** at the same dosage. The results were positive; she experienced less itching and her rashes were less. However, during times of stress and lack of sleep the rash and itching

Dermatrol (PS)™

symptoms would return. The patient's compliance with her lifestyle was needed for prolonged results. Submitted by L.W., Arroyo Grande, California.

- A.K., a 13-year-old male, presented with acne, consisting of red and purulent appearance along with irritable sensation. The practitioner diagnosed this condition as Liver qi stagnation. Liver yang rising and dampness were also present. ***Dermatrol (PS)*** was prescribed for treatment. After taking the herbs, the acne had cleared more than 50% with minimal pus and redness; itching was no longer present. He was also receiving acupuncture twice a week. Submitted by A.D., Phoenix, Arizona.
- M.Z., a 15-year-old male, presented with a large amount of pimples over his face. Objective findings included blemishes and dark discoloration on the cheeks, forehead, and chin. It was mentioned that he had already tried Western topical creams and antibiotics. The practitioner diagnosed this condition as damp-heat. For treatment, ***Lonicera Complex*** and ***Dermatrol (PS)*** were both prescribed. It was reported after three weeks that his condition had improved; the blemishes and purple patches had vanished. He continued taking the ***Dermatrol (PS)*** at two capsules daily for maintenance. Submitted by G.G., East Lansing, Michigan.
- S.W., a 54-year-old female, presented with psoriasis in which she had been experiencing since she was a child. It consisted of patches that were scaly, dry, red, and itchy on different parts of her body. It was noted that gluten would aggravate her condition. The patient had restricted her diet by avoiding excess sugar, spicy food, and alcohol. Objective findings included pale face and agitated demeanor. The practitioner diagnosed this condition as blood heat, blood deficiency, and Liver qi stagnation. ***Dermatrol (PS)*** was prescribed at 6 capsules two times per day. Within two weeks of taking the herbs and receiving acupuncture, her skin had cleared. After four months of continuing, it was free of all signs of psoriasis. Submitted by N.V., Muir Beach, California.
- A 33-year-old female presented with eczema on localized areas of the hands, wrists and face. The affected skin was itchy and dry, and appeared thicker and paler than surrounding areas. The woman had tried steroid creams and prescription drugs for four years without satisfactory results. The Western diagnosis was eczema and atopic dermatitis; the TCM diagnosis was blood deficiency leading to blood dryness and wind. After taking ***Dermatrol (PS)***, the patient reported complete resolution of eczema on the face and arms. The skin on the wrists and hands may remain discolored. Overall, ***Dermatrol (PS)*** helped tremendously. [Note: This formula should be used with caution in patients with yin deficiency as it may cause hot flashes.] Submitted by M.M., Randolph, New Jersey.
- L.W., a 22-year-old male, presented with septic facial acne. Very depressed, he did not want to be seen in public. The TCM diagnosis was damp-heat with Liver qi stagnation. After one week of taking ***Dermatrol (PS)*** and ***Shine***, the acne was 80% resolved and the depression was improving. After washing his face with a mild soap, the patient applied a topical skin wash [*Yin Care*] diluted with tea tree oil. The acne was gone in 28 days. The patient now socializes happily with family and friends. Submitted by H.C., Stephens City, Virginia.
- A 26-year-old farmer with a history of alcohol consumption reported a rash and itchiness of the body without any obvious cause. He was initially diagnosed with a skin rash, and treated with topical steroids without success. As the condition continued to deteriorate, with formation of white skin flakes, the diagnosis was changed to psoriasis. After three months of unsuccessful treatment with drugs, the patient then sought herbal treatment. The patient subsequently presented with severe itching, thirst, irritability, constipation, dysuria, and the presence of psoriatic flakes throughout his head and body. Open lesions resulted as a consequence of constant scratching. The tongue was red with a yellow, greasy coat, while the pulse was thready and rapid. The TCM diagnosis was accumulation of heat and toxins. After two weeks of herbal treatment with ***Dermatrol (PS)***, the patient reported marked improvement with reduction of itching and skin irritation, healing of skin lesions, and less psoriatic flakes. The patient was advised to continue with the herbs for another week until the psoriasis resolved completely. Submitted by C.S., Jilin, China.
- A 31-year-old female presented with a family history of chronic psoriasis, and outbreaks mainly on her elbows, knees and sacrum. She also suffered from vaginal itching and burning sensations. The TCM diagnosis was toxic damp-heat in the Liver. ***V-Support*** and ***Dermatrol (PS)*** were prescribed. A topical wash, *Yin Care*, was prescribed for external application for the psoriasis and vaginally for local itching. The patient had acupuncture treatments and was on the herbal formulas for two years. The patient was advised to stop smoking, eat less spicy food, and refrain from alcohol intake, but was unable to change her lifestyle. Nonetheless, her condition continued to improve, and she noticed that if she did not take the herbs, the symptoms would return. Submitted by M.C., Sarasota, Florida.

PHARMACOLOGICAL AND CLINICAL RESEARCH

Psoriasis is defined as a chronic and recurrent disease characterized by dry, well-circumscribed, silvery, scaling papules and plaques of varying sizes.[5] Areas commonly affected by psoriasis include the scalp, sacral area, extensor surface of the extremities, buttocks, and penis. The exact cause of psoriasis is unknown, but the lesions are characterized by increased epidermal cell proliferation and inflammation involving immune stimulation. Therefore, optimal treatment must focus on controlling the immune system, suppressing cell proliferation and reducing tissue inflammation.

Psoriasis is directly associated with hyperactivity of the immune system. Therefore, successful treatment of psoriasis must include use of herbs to control and regulate the immune system. *Bai Xian Pi* (Cortex Dictamni) is an excellent herb with remark-

Dermatrol (PS)™

able immunosuppressive activity to inhibit the proliferation of T-cells.[6] In addition, *Bai Hua She She Cao* (Herba Hedyotis) is also used in this formula for its immunomodulatory effect.[7]

Dermatrol (PS) contains many herbs with marked characteristics to treat psoriasis by suppressing the proliferation of cells. The inhibitory effect of these herbs slows or stops the abnormally high rate cell proliferation, as in cases of psoriasis. Herbs with this inhibitory effect include *Ku Shen* (Radix Sophorae Flavescentis),[8,9,10,11] *Da Qing Ye* (Folium Isatidis),[12] *Bai Hua She She Cao* (Herba Hedyotis),[13,14] and *Fang Feng* (Radix Saposhnikoviae).[15]

Dermatrol (PS) also employs many herbs with marked traits for treatment of psoriasis by suppressing the inflammation of tissue. The anti-inflammatory effect of the herbs helps to reduce swelling and facilitate recovery. Herbs with this anti-inflammatory activity include *Bai Xian Pi* (Cortex Dictamni),[16] *Da Qing Ye* (Folium Isatidis),[17] *Jin Yin Hua* (Flos Lonicerae Japonicae),[18] *Ku Shen* (Radix Sophorae Flavescentis),[19] *Mu Dan Pi* (Cortex Moutan),[20] and *Gan Cao* (Radix et Rhizoma Glycyrrhizae).[21] These herbs have excellent anti-inflammatory influences with differing mechanisms of action. Some reduce inflammation by inhibiting prostaglandin synthesis and decreasing the permeability of the blood vessels.[22] Others reduce swelling by stimulating the release of glucocorticoids and delaying their breakdown. [17]

In addition to herbs that suppress cell proliferation and tissue inflammation, ***Dermatrol (PS)*** contains many herbs that have excellent effects to treat general dermatological disorders. Pharmacologically, *Ku Shen* (Radix Sophorae Flavescentis) has an antipruritic effect to inhibit scratching in a dose-dependent manner.[23] The antipruritic effect is attributed in part to its effect to reduce several eicosanoid-related skin inflammation, such as atopic dermatitis.[24] *Bai Xian Pi* (Cortex Dictamni) has an antiallergic effect. It inhibits the scratching behavior in subjects with artificially-induced allergic atopic dermatitis and other allergy-related diseases in a dose-dependent manner.[25] *Mu Dan Pi* (Cortex Moutan) has an antihistamine effect to significantly suppress histamine release and prostaglandin D(2) synthesis from mast cells.[26] Indolinone, an alkaloid isolated from *Da Qing Ye* (Folium Isatidis), has been shown to block mast cell degranulation *in vitro*.[27] Clinically, according to one study, the use of *Chan Tui* (Periostracum Cicadae) was successful in treating 27 out of 30 patients with chronic urticaria.[28] In another study, use of *Ku Shen* (Radix Sophorae Flavescentis) was found to have a 79% effective rate in treating 148 patients with dermatological disorders, such as rash, itching and eczema.[29] Furthermore, topical application of *Bai Xian Pi* (Cortex Dictamni) was found to be 100% effective in treating 33 cases of suppurative dermatological disorders.[30] Lastly, 56 patients with pustular psoriasis of the palms were treated with great success (10 had complete recovery, 24 had significant improvement, 13 had moderate improvement, and 9 had no effect) using an herbal formula with *Da Qing Ye* (Folium Isatidis), *Ban Lan Gen* (Radix Isatidis), *Bai Hua She She Cao* (Herba Hedyotis), *Bai Xian Pi* (Cortex Dictamni), *Chi Shao* (Radix Paeoniae Rubra), and others.[31]

In summary, ***Dermatrol (PS)*** is a well-balanced formula that addresses multiple aspects of psoriasis and other scaling diseases or dermatological disorders with severe itching. ***Dermatrol (PS)*** contains herbs that suppress the proliferation of cells, reduce the inflammation of tissue, and relieve itching and discomfort. It is one of the most effective formulas for the treatment of the challenging and stubborn disorder of psoriasis.

COMPARATIVE ANALYSIS

Successful treatment of psoriasis is one of the most challenging conditions for both Western and traditional Chinese medicine. There is no cure in Western medicine, and only a few effective treatments to control symptoms. Drug options include lubricants, keratolytics and corticosteroids. Lubricating cream is usually combined with coal tar, followed by exposure to ultraviolet (UV) light. Though this method may be effective, excessive exposure to UV light may cause sunburn and induce exacerbations. Keratolytics such as anthralin may be beneficial, but it is irritating and should not be used in intertriginous areas. Lastly, topical corticosteroids help to reduce itching and inflammation. However, they cause local side effects such as atrophy and telangiectases. Furthermore, continuous use of topical corticosteroids for just one to two weeks results in loss of steroid effectiveness.

Herbs are effective to treat both the causes and the symptoms of psoriasis. However, despite both short- and long-term improvements, herbs do not cure psoriasis. Therefore, it is necessary to periodically re-initiate herbal therapy to control psoriasis and prevent flare-ups. With persistent prevention and aggressive treatments, it will be possible to control psoriasis by reducing the frequency and severity of recurrences.

References

1. Lei X, et al. Liver Damage Associated with Polygonum multiflorum Thunb.: A Systematic Review of Case Reports and Case Series. Evid Based Complement Alternat Med. 2015;2015:459749. doi: 10.1155/2015/459749.
2. Liu Z, et al. Maillard reaction involved in the steaming process of the root of Polygonum multiflorum. Institution of Basic Theory, China Academy of Chinese Medical Sciences, Beijing, PR China. Planta Med. 2009 Jan;75(1):84-8. Epub 2008 Nov 25.
3. Liu Z, et al. In vitro antioxidant activities of maillard reaction products produced in the steaming process of Polygonum multiflorum root. Nat Prod Commun. 2011 Jan;6(1):55-8.
4. Liu Z, et al. Comparative analyses of chromatographic fingerprints of the roots of Polygonum multiflorum Thunb. and their processed products using RRLC/DAD/ESI-MS(n). Planta Med. 2011 Nov;77(16):1855-60. doi: 10.1055/s-0030-1271200.
5. Beers, M. and Berkow, R. *The Merck Manual of Diagnosis and Therapy 17th Edition*. 1999.
6. Chang J, Xuan LJ, Xu YM, Zhang JS. Cytotoxic terpenoid and immunosuppressive phenolic glycosides from the root bark of Dictamnus dasycarpus. Planta Med. 2002 May;68(5):425-9.
7. Shi Y, Wang CH, Gong XG. Apoptosis-inducing effects of two anthraquinones from Hedyotis diffusa WILLD. Biol Pharm Bull. 2008 Jun;31(6):1075-8.

FORMULAS

Dermatrol (PS)™

8. *Yao Xue Za Zhi* (Journal of Medicinals), 1961; 81:1635.
9. *Bei Jing Yi Ke Da Xue Xue Bao* (Journal of Beijing University of Medicine), 1986; 18(2):127.
10. *Zhong Hua Xue Yi Xue Za Zhi* (Chinese Journal on Study of Hematology), 1991; 12(2):89.
11. *Zhong Guo Zhong Yao Za Zhi* (People's Republic of China Journal of Chinese Herbology), 1990; 15(10):49.
12. *Zhi Wu Yao You Xiao Cheng Fen Shou Ce* (Manual of Plant Medicinals and Their Active Constituents), 1986: 608,1084.
13. *Zhong Yao Xue* (Chinese Herbology), 1998; 204:205.
14. Liu Z, Liu M, Liu M, Li J. Methylanthraquinone from Hedyotis diffusa WILLD induces Ca(2+)-mediated apoptosis in human breast cancer cells. Toxicol In Vitro. 2010 Feb;24(1):142-7.
15. Tai J, Cheung S. Anti-proliferative and antioxidant activities of Saposhnikovia divaricata. Oncol Rep. 2007 Jul;18(1):227-34.
16. Kim JH, Park YM, Shin JS, Park SJ, Choi JH, Jung HJ, Park HJ, Lee KT. Fraxinellone inhibits lipopolysaccharide-induced inducible nitric oxide synthase and cyclooxygenase-2 expression by negatively regulating nuclear factor-kappa B in RAW 264.7 macrophages cells. Biol Pharm Bull. 2009 Jun;32(6): 1062-8.
17. Recio MC, Cerdá-Nicolás M, Potterat O, Hamburger M, Ríos JL. Anti-inflammatory and antiallergic activity in vivo of lipophilic Isatis tinctoria extracts and tryptanthrin. Planta Med. 2006 May;72(6):539-46.
18. *Shan Xi Yi Kan* (Shanxi Journal of Medicine), 1960; (10):22.
19. Jiang H, Meng F, Li J, Sun X. Anti-apoptosis effects of oxymatrine protect the liver from warm ischemia reperfusion injury in rats. World J Surg. 2005 Nov;29(11):1397-401.
20. *Sheng Yao Xue Za Zhi* (Journal of Raw Herbology), 1979; 33(3):178.
21. *Zhong Yao Zhi* (Chinese Herbology Journal), 1993; 358.
22. *Zhong Guo Yao Ke Da Xue Xue Bao* (Journal of University of Chinese Herbology), 1990; 21(4):222.
23. Yamaguchi-Miyamoto T, Kawasuji T, Kuraishi Y, Suzuki H. Antipruritic effects of Sophora flavescens on acute and chronic itch-related responses in mice. Japan Society for the Promotion of Science, Domestic Research Fellow, Hon-machi, Kawaguchi, Saitama, Japan. Biol Pharm Bull. 2003 May;26(5):722-4.
24. Kim DW, Chi YS, Son KH, Chang HW, Kim JS, Kang SS, Kim HP. Effects of sophoraflavanone G, a prenylated flavonoid from Sophora flavescens, on cyclooxygenase-2 and in vivo inflammatory response. College of Pharmacy, Kangwon National University, Chunchon, Korea. Arch Pharm Res. 2002 Jun;25(3):329-35.
25. Jiang S, Nakano Y, Rahman MA, Yatsuzuka R, Kamei C. Effects of a Dictamnus dasycarpus T. extract on allergic models in mice. Biosci Biotechnol Biochem. 2008 Mar;72(3):660-5.
26. Chan BC, Hon KL, Leung PC, Sam SW, Fung KP, Lee MY, Lau HY. Traditional Chinese medicine for atopic eczema: PentaHerbs formula suppresses inflammatory mediators release from mast cells. J Ethnopharmacol. 2008 Oct 30;120(1):85-91.
27. Kiefer S, Mertz AC, Koryakina A, Hamburger M, Küenzi P. (E,Z)-3-(3',5'-Dimethoxy-4'-hydroxy-benzylidene)-2-indolinone blocks mast cell degranulation. Eur J Pharm Sci. 2010 May 12;40(2):143-7.
28. *Pi Fu Bing Fang Zhi Yan Jiu Tong Xun* (Research Journal on Prevention and Treatment of Dermatological Disorders), 1972; 3:215.
29. *Zhong Cao Yao Tong Xun* (Journal of Chinese Herbal Medicine), 1976; 1:35.
30. *Chi Jiao Yi Sheng Za Zhi* (Journal of Barefoot Doctors), 1975; 6:21.
31. *Zhong Yi Za Zhi* (Journal of Chinese Medicine), 1995; (6):338.

Dissolve (GS)™

CLINICAL APPLICATIONS

- **Cholelithiasis** – gallstones
- **Cholecystitis** – inflammation of the gallbladder and bile duct
- Other liver and gallbladder conditions: cholestasis, bile stasis, biliary sludge

WESTERN THERAPEUTIC ACTIONS

- Dissolves and drains stones
- Cholagogic effect to promote bile flow and prevent biliary stasis and sludge
- Antihyperlipidemic function to treat and prevent cholesterol-type gallstones
- Reduces inflammation of the gallbladder and bile duct

CHINESE THERAPEUTIC ACTIONS

- Dissolves gallstones
- Facilitates the passage of gallstones
- Spreads Liver qi
- Clears damp-heat

DOSAGE

Take 4 capsules three times daily on an empty stomach with warm water. ***Dissolve (GS)*** must be taken continuously for at least three months. In cases of multiple or large stones, the treatment should be continued until the stones are dissolved or passed out. In cases where the patient feels severe discomfort, pain or sensation of obstruction after taking the herbs, reduce the dosage as they may be signs that the big stones are becoming obstructed. In such cases, reduce the dosage to a level comfortable to the patient and stretch the treatment period so the stones can be dissolved and flushed slowly. ***Dissolve (GS)*** can also be taken after surgery to prevent formation of new stones. In such cases, take 2 capsules a day for three months and 1 capsule per day for another six months.

INGREDIENTS

Da Huang (Radix et Rhizoma Rhei)
Hai Jin Sha (Spora Lygodii)
Jin Qian Cao (Herba Lysimachiae)
Li Zhi He (Semen Litchi)
Long Dan (Radix et Rhizoma Gentianae)
Wei Ling Xian (Radix et Rhizoma Clematidis)
Yin Chen (Herba Artemisiae Scopariae)
Zhi Qiao (Fructus Aurantii)

BACKGROUND

Cholelithiasis and cholecystitis are two of the most common disorders affecting the gallbladder and the bile duct. Signs and symptoms of cholelithiasis and cholecystitis include fullness and pain in the right hypochondriac region, low-grade fever, constipation and leukorrhea. Acute onset is characterized by jaundice, severe colicky pain in the upper right quadrant that may radiate to the right shoulder and back, nausea, vomiting, aversion to oily and greasy foods, lack of appetite, anxiety and related symptoms. Diagnostic signs and symptoms include a positive response to Murphy's sign and tenderness at the inferior right scapula.

FORMULA EXPLANATION

The fundamental etiology of cholecystitis and cholelithiasis is damp-heat. Cholecystitis is characterized by damp-heat in the Gallbladder and cholelithiasis is characterized by damp-heat drying up fluids in the Gallbladder.

Long Dan (Radix et Rhizoma Gentianae) enters the Liver and the Gallbladder to clear damp-heat. *Yin Chen* (Herba Artemisiae Scopariae), an empirical herb for treating hepatic and gallbladder disorders, has a cholagogic function that increases the secretion of bile and the excretion of bile salt and bilirubin. It also lowers serum cholesterol and beta-lipoprotein. *Jin Qian Cao* (Herba Lysimachiae) dissolves gallstones and increases the secretion of bile by the liver cells. *Wei Ling Xian* (Radix et Rhizoma Clematidis) unblocks the channels and helps to dissolve stones. *Li Zhi He* (Semen Litchi) relieves abdominal and epigastric pain due to Liver qi constraint. *Zhi Qiao* (Fructus Aurantii) unblocks qi obstruction and facilitates the passage of gallstones. *Hai Jin Sha* (Spora Lygodii) transforms hardness and dissolves stones. *Da Huang* (Radix et Rhizoma Rhei) lowers cholesterol and eliminates damp-heat accumulation by its purgative action.

CAUTIONS & CONTRAINDICATIONS

- This formula is contraindicated during pregnancy and nursing.
- Regardless of size and number of stones, surgery may be the treatment of choice for the following conditions:
  - acute onset with severe colic
  - sudden deterioration in the overall health of the patient
  - sudden deterioration in cholecystitis or cholelithiasis
  - poor results from previous treatments and initial signs of liver damage
- The following warning statement is required by the State of California: "This product contains *Da Huang* (Radix et Rhizoma Rhei). Read and follow directions carefully. Do not use if you have or develop diarrhea, loose stools, or abdominal pain because *Da Huang* (Radix et Rhizoma Rhei) may worsen these conditions and be harmful to your health. Consult your physician if you have frequent diarrhea or if you are pregnant, nursing, taking medication, or have a medical condition."

CLINICAL NOTES

- Cholelithiasis is the presence of gallstones, which are formed as a result of cholesterol and pigments in bile bind to each others. While most gallstones are asymptomatic, some may cause symptoms such as biliary colic, and complications such as cholecystitis, biliary tract obstruction, cholangitis, and gallstone pancreatitis. Successful treatment of cholelithiasis requires

FORMULAS

Dissolve (GS)™

dissolution and draining of gallstones, alleviation of the symptoms and complications, and prevention of future gallstones.

- Cholecystitis and cholelithiasis commonly occur simultaneously. They are most commonly seen in women over 30 to 40 years of age, and in individuals who are obese. Often times they are un-diagnosed or mis-diagnosed as gastritis, peptic ulcers, viral hepatitis, angina or acute pancreatitis. X-ray results are not always accurate. Ultrasound of the gallbladder is more reliable and has approximately 90 to 95% accuracy. Conditions most suitable for Chinese herbal treatment include chronic cholecystitis, the presence of gallstones in the liver, gallstones composed primarily of calcium, small gallstones, and the presence of gallstones after removal of the gallbladder. Ideal candidates for herbal treatment are individuals who are asymptomatic with stone(s) less than 30 mm in diameter. Elderly or weak patients not suitable for surgical treatment can also benefit from Chinese herbal treatment.
- Individuals with high risk of developing cholecystitis or gallstones will benefit from prophylactic treatment by taking ***Dissolve (GS)*** on a preventative basis. Risk factors of cholecystitis or gallstones include the four F's: female, fair, fertile, and fat.
- Ultrasound should be performed prior to using herbs so the size of the stones can be determined. Non-aggressive dosing of herbs is optimal in cases of large stones. Never prescribe a high dose of herbs to flush large stones as it may result in obstruction, which may then require immediate surgical intervention.
- ***Dissolve (GS)*** is an herbal formula developed by Professor Xiao-Ping Zhang of Anhui Hospital of Traditional Chinese Medicine. ***Dissolve (GS)*** is an empirical formula designed to treat cholecystitis and cholelithiasis. It has been used for over 30 years in China and has helped several thousand patients with cholecystitis and cholelithiasis. It is imperative, however, that patients comply with instructions and continue to take the herbal formula for at least three months for optimal results.

Pulse Diagnosis by Dr. Jimmy Wei-Yen Chang:

- Bird's beak / pen tip pulse, a convex-shaped pulse that is approximately 0.1 cm in length that feels like a pen's tip, on the deep level of the left *guan*.

SUPPLEMENTARY FORMULAS

- For hepatitis, jaundice, or high liver enzyme levels, combine with ***Liver DTX***.
- For constipation, combine with ***Gentle Lax (Excess)***.
- With blood stagnation, add ***Circulation (SJ)***.
- With excess heat, add ***Gardenia Complex***.
- With prominent signs and symptoms of Liver fire or damp-heat in the Liver and Gallbladder, combine with ***Gentiana Complex***.
- To reduce blood cholesterol and triglyceride levels, use ***Cholisma***.
- To reduce cholesterol and triglyceride levels in individuals with fatty liver and obesity, use ***Cholisma (ES)***.
- For peptic ulcers or gastritis, combine with ***GI Care***.
- For severe pain, use with ***Herbal ANG***.
- For bloating and distension, add ***GI Harmony***.
- For angina or chest pain, combine with ***Circulation***.
- For excess damp and phlegm in the body, add ***Pinellia Complex***.
- For obese patients with an excess appetite, add ***Herbalite***.
- For diabetes mellitus and high blood glucose, add ***Equilibrium***.

ACUPUNCTURE TREATMENT

Traditional Points:

- *Zulinqi* (GB 41), *Zhigou* (TH 6), *Dannangxue*, *Zusanli* (ST 36), *Zhangmen* (LR 13), *Qimen* (LR 14), *Ganshu* (BL 18), *Danshu* (BL 19), *Zhongwan* (CV 12)

Classic Master Tung's Points:

- **Gallstones:** *Huozhi* (T 88.15), *Tianhuang* (T 88.13), *Minghuang* (T 88.12), *Qihuang* (T 88.14), *Muzhi* (T 1010.18), *Makuaishui* (T 1010.14), *Yizhong* (T 77.05), *Erzhong* (T 77.06), *Sanzhong* (T 77.07), *Tianhuang* (T 77.17), *Dihuang* (T 77.19), *Renhuang* (T 77.21), *Ganmen* (T 33.11). Bleed *Majinshui* (T 1010.13), *Makuaishui* (T 1010.14) or dark veins nearby. Bleed before needling for best result.
- **Cholecystitis:** *Huozhi* (T 88.15), *Tianhuang* (T 88.13), *Minghuang* (T 88.12), *Qihuang* (T 88.14), *Muhuang* (T 88.47)*, *Ganmen* (T 33.11), *Changmen* (T 33.10), *Waisanguan* (T 77.27), *Muzhi* (T 1010.18), *Huoying* (T 66.03), *Huozhu* (T 66.04), *Sansheng* (T 55.07)*, *Huoquan* (T 88.16). Bleed tender points on the LR area in the back with cupping. Bleed before needling for best result.

Master Tung's Points by Dr. Chuan-Min Wang:

- **Gallstones:** *Qihuang* (T 88.14), *Huozhi* (T 88.15), *Huoquan* (T 88.16)

Balance Method by Dr. Richard Tan:

- Left side: *Hegu* (LI 4) or *ah shi* points nearby, *Sanyangluo* (TH 8) or *ah shi* points nearby, *Zhongdu* (LR 6) or *ah shi* points nearby
- Right side: *Yanglingquan* (GB 34) or *ah shi* points nearby, *Yangjiao* (GB 35) or *ah shi* points nearby, *Quze* (PC 3) or *ah shi* points nearby

Ear Acupuncture:

- Pancreas, Gallbladder, Duodenum, Liver. Use ear seeds.
- Alternate sets between ears every seven days and instruct the patient to massage the points several times a day. Strongly stimulate the points or use electric stimulation.
  - Set 1: *Shenmen*, Abdomen, Endocrine, Gallbladder
  - Set 2: Liver, Adrenal Gland, Upper Abdomen, Shoulder
- On the right ear, needle *Shenmen* towards the Abdomen, Sympathetic, Gallbladder. Needle 0.2 mm below the Gallbladder towards the Duodenum.
- On the left ear, needle Gallbladder towards the Duodenum.

Dissolve (GS)™

Auricular Medicine by Dr. Li-Chun Huang:

- **Gallstones:** Sympathetic, *San Jiao*, Digestive Subcortex, Gallbladder, Gallbladder Node of the Posterior, Bile Duct, Duodenum
- **Cholecystitis, cholangitis:** Bile Duct, Liver, Duodenum, Stomach, Spleen, *San Jiao*, Endocrine, Gallbladder (Front and Back), Digestive Subcortex
- **Improving the function of gallbladder:** Gallbladder, Duodenum, *San Jiao*, Spleen, Digestive Subcortex, Upper Back and Shoulder, Gallbladder Area of Posterior, Bile Duct, Stomach, Liver, Endocrine

NUTRITION

- For patients with cholecystitis, advise against eating solid foods for a few days. They should drink distilled water and fresh juices. Liquid foods can be introduced slowly after three or four days.
- For patients with gallstones, advise taking three tablespoons of olive oil with lemon juice before going to bed and upon awakening. Small gallstones can sometimes be passed and eliminated with this method. Ultrasound should be performed prior to using this method to prevent large stones from obstructing the bile duct which may then require immediate surgery.
- Increase the consumption of applesauce, yogurt, fresh apples, and beets.
- Avoid eating red meat, shrimp, lobsters, oysters, fatty or greasy foods, fried foods, spicy foods, margarine, soft drinks, commercial oils and processed foods.
- Food allergies can cause inflammation and obstruction of the bile duct. Avoid foods that commonly cause gallbladder disorders, such as eggs, pork, onion, fowl, milk, coffee, and citrus fruits.

The Tao of Nutrition by Dr. Maoshing Ni and Cathy McNease:

- Recommendations: corn silk, water chestnuts, seaweed, beet tops, watermelon, celery, watercress, winter melon, pearl barley, walnuts, watermelon rind, winter melon rind, green tea powder, and distilled water.
- Drink watermelon juice.
- Drink celery, carrot, and water chestnut juice.
- Drink corn silk tea for water; three to five glasses daily.
- Drink tea from beet tops, winter melon rind, and watermelon rind.
- Take two teaspoons ground walnuts in corn silk tea.
- Take one teaspoon green tea powder in warm water three times daily.
- After consuming any of the above diuretics remedies, do some mild jumping exercise to help loosen up the stones.
- Avoid spicy foods, fried foods, oily foods, coffee, hard water, spinach, citrus, tomatoes, spinach combined with tofu or dairy products.

LIFESTYLE INSTRUCTIONS

- Individuals with gallbladder colic should fast, keep warm, and rest in bed.
- Detoxification of liver and colon are helpful for long-term management.
- Sitz bath is helpful to decongest and detoxify the intestines.

CASE STUDIES

- S.T., a 54-year-old female, presented with complaints of waking at 3:00 a.m., feeling cold easily, craving sweets, overweight, and hot flashes in the morning. Her blood pressure was 125/80 mmHg and her heart rate was 75 beats per minute. Her lab report revealed gallstones and elevated liver enzymes. The TCM diagnosis was cold and damp in the Spleen with Spleen deficiency, and damp-heat in the Liver. ***Dissolve (GS)*** was prescribed at 12 grams a day for a week. The patient reported she passed two gallstones, which were recovered, through the stool. The practitioner concluded that patients with gallstones should take ***Dissolve (GS)*** prior to considering surgery because it is less invasive and less expensive. Submitted by S.C., Colonie, New York.
- J.J., a 55-year-old female patient, presented with right upper quadrant stomach pain. After visiting the Urgent Care it was confirmed that she had three gallstones present, 2 to 4 cm each. It was suggested by the Western doctor that she remove them with surgery. After discussing with the patient about trying an herbal formula before two weeks prior to receiving surgery, she was prescribed ***Dissolve (GS)***. The patient was directed to take 5 capsules three times daily until her pain was gone. Once the pain subsided, she was told to continue for two more weeks at 5 capsules two times daily. Following three days of taking the herbs, the patient's symptoms of nausea, acid feeling in the throat, and right upper quadrant pain were resolved. Ten days after taking the formula she felt 100% better, followed by her visit to her primary care physician confirming that there were no gallstones anywhere via ultrasound. The patient has not had a recurrence since. Submitted by B.W., St. Helens, Oregon.
- A 51-year-old female housekeeper presented with pain in the upper right quadrant of the abdomen within the gallbladder region. The practitioner diagnosed the condition as damp-heat in the Gallbladder. After taking ***Dissolve (GS)*** for a period of nine months, there was a complete cessation of upper right quadrant pain. Submitted by D.K., Forestville, California.
- C.B., a 72-year-old female, presented with gallstones, pain under the right ribcage, poor digestion, and pain in the right shoulder. Her blood pressure was 180/95 mmHg and the heart rate was 85 beats per minute. Ultrasound was performed to confirm the stones. The Western diagnosis was gallstones and high cholesterol. The TCM diagnosis was damp-heat accumulation with Liver qi stagnation. She was prescribed ***Dissolve (GS)*** at 4.5 grams daily and ***Cholisma*** at 1.5 grams daily. The patient also

Dissolve (GS)™

received acupuncture. After eight weeks, the patient reported the pain in the right shoulder had improved fully. Digestion was much better with no more bloating or constipation. Submitted by W.F., Bloomfield, New Jersey.

PHARMACOLOGICAL AND CLINICAL RESEARCH

Dissolve (GS) is formulated to treat cholelithiasis (gallstones) and cholecystitis (inflammation of the gallbladder and bile duct). It contains many herbs with significant effects to dissolve and drain the gallstones, reduce inflammation of the gallbladder and bile duct, and relieve pain.

Pharmacologically, *Jin Qian Cao* (Herba Lysimachiae) has a cholagogic effect that increases the production and excretion of bile acid, which in turn help to resolve the current gallstones and prevent the formation of new ones.[1] *Long Dan* (Radix et Rhizoma Gentianae) and *Da Huang* (Radix et Rhizoma Rhei) also have marked cholagogic activities when administered via oral ingestion or intravenous injection.[2,3] *Yin Chen* (Herba Artemisiae Scopariae) has a stimulating effect on gallbladder function, as the use of this herb is associated in the flow of bile to prevent biliary stasis and sludge.[4] Clinically, oral administration of *Wei Ling Xian* (Radix et Rhizoma Clematidis) in decoction showed 87% effective in treating 120 patients with cholelithiasis.[5]

Dissolve (GS) also contains many herbs to treat the symptoms and complications of gallstones. *Da Huang* (Radix et Rhizoma Rhei), *Wei Ling Xian* (Radix et Rhizoma Clematidis) and *Yin Chen* (Herba Artemisiae Scopariae) all have significant anti-inflammatory effects to reduce inflammation and relieve pain. *Da Huang* (Radix et Rhizoma Rhei) shows a significant anti-inflammatory effect via inhibition of inducible nitric oxide synthase.[6] *Wei Ling Xian* (Radix et Rhizoma Clematidis) exhibits its anti-inflammatory effect by blocking the production of the pro-inflammatory mediators, nitric oxide and prostaglandin E(2).[7] The essential oils of *Yin Chen* (Herba Artemisiae Scopariae) show significant anti-inflammatory effect by blocking the expression of cyclo-oxygenase-2 and inhibiting the production of inflammatory mediators, such as nitric oxide and prostaglandin E(2).[8] Clinically, one study showed that ten patients with acute cholecystitis were treated with marked success using *Da Huang* (Radix et Rhizoma Rhei). The clinical signs and symptoms were resolved after an average of 2.3 days, the patients' temperature returned to normal after 2 days, and the WBC count returned to normal after 3.4 days. The treatment protocol was to administer 30 to 60 grams of *Da Huang* (Radix et Rhizoma Rhei) decoction every 1 to 2 hours until the abdominal pain was resolved. Another clinical study reported complete recovery in all 41 cases of acute cholecystitis using the following formula in decoction three times daily: *Da Huang* (Radix et Rhizoma Rhei) 20-50g, *Yin Chen* (Herba Artemisiae Scopariae) 25g, *Jin Qian Cao* (Herba Lysimachiae) 25g, and others.[9]

Finally, as over 85% of gallstones are cholesterol stones in the Western world, proper management of cholesterol levels is important for treatment and prevention.[10] Pharmacologically, *Yin Chen* (Herba Artemisiae Scopariae) has an antihyperlipidemic effect to lower both plasma cholesterols and beta-lipoproteins.[11] It also has an antiobesity function to effectively reduce body weight and inhibit lipid accumulation.[12] Clinically, a preparation of *Da Huang* (Radix et Rhizoma Rhei) given three times daily for three weeks was 76% effective in reducing plasma triglycerides and beta-lipoprotein levels in 47 patients.[13] According to another study, daily consumption of *Yin Chen* (Herba Artemisiae Scopariae) as a tea for one month per course of treatment was effective in reducing serum cholesterol levels. Of 82 patients, the study reported an average reduction of 42.4 mg/dL, or a 14.3% decrease, per person.[14]

In summary, ***Dissolve (GS)*** is an herbal formula with many herbs that dissolve gallstones, manage the symptoms, and treat the complications. ***Dissolve (GS)*** may be taken in regular doses for treatment of gallstones, or lower doses for their prevention.

COMPARATIVE ANALYSIS

Cholelithiasis and cholecystitis are two conditions that often occur together. In Western medicine, if these two conditions are asymptomatic, treatment may not be necessary, as risks often outweigh the benefits. If symptomatic, bile acids [such as Ursodiol (ursodeoxycholic acid)] are usually given to dissolve stones. However, these drugs must be given for a long period of time, and have only limited success rate of about 30%. Furthermore, these drugs may cause side effects such as bladder pain, bloody or cloudy urine, burning or painful urination, dizziness, fast heartbeat, indigestion, lower back or side pain, severe nausea, shortness of breath, skin rash, stomach pain, vomiting, weakness, wheezing, and others. Lastly, if drugs fail, invasive treatments, such as surgery and sonic shock wave, are the last alternatives.

Cholelithiasis and cholecystitis are two conditions that are successfully treated with herbs. The mechanisms of action of herbs are to dissolve and expel stones from the gallbladder and bile duct. Herbal therapies are effective to treat and to prevent stones. Depending on the number and size of the stones, the duration of treatment ranges from days to months. Nonetheless, use of herbs should be limited to individuals with mild to moderate cases of cholelithiasis and cholecystitis. If there are acute manifestations, or if herbal therapy is ineffective after three months, then patients should be referred to Western medicine for surgery and sonic shock wave treatments.

References

1. *Zhong Yao Yao Li Yu Ying Yong* (Pharmacology and Applications of Chinese Herbs), 1983:: 696.
2. *Xin Yi Yao Xue Za Zhi* (New Journal of Medicine and Herbology), 1974; (5)::34.
3. *Yun Nan Yi Yao* (Yunan Medicine and Herbology), 1991; 12(5)::304.
4. *Sheng Yao Xue Za Zhi* (Journal of Raw Herbology), 1978; 32(2)::177.
5. *He Nan Zhong Yi* (Henan Chinese Medicine), 1987; 6::22.

Dissolve (GS)™

6. Wang CC, Huang YJ, Chen LG, Lee LT, Yang LL. Inducible nitric oxide synthase inhibitors of Chinese herbs III. Rheum palmatum. Planta Med. 2002 Oct;68(10)::869-74.
7. Park EK, Ryu MH, Kim YH, Lee YA, Lee SH, Woo DH, Hong SJ, Han JS, Yoo MC, Yang HI, Kim KS. Anti-inflammatory effects of an ethanolic extract from Clematis mandshurica Rupr. East-West Bone and Joint Research Center, College of Medicine, Kyung Hee University, Hoegi-1 dong, Dongdaemun-gu, Seoul 130-701, South Korea. J Ethnopharmacol. 2006 Nov 3;108(1)::142-7.
8. Cha JD, Moon SE, Kim HY, Lee JC, Lee KY. The essential oil isolated from Artemisia capillaris prevents LPS-induced production of NO and PGE(2) by inhibiting MAPK-mediated pathways in RAW 264.7 macrophages. Oral Cancer Research Institute, College of Dentistry, Yonsei University, Seoul, Korea. Immunol Invest. 2009;38(6)::483-97.
9. *Zhong Yao Lin Chuan Xin Yong* (New Clinical Applications of Chinese Medicine), 2001; 29.
10. Porter R, Kaplan J. The Merck Manual of Diagnosis and Therapy, Nineteenth Edition. Merck Sharp & Dohme Corp.
11. *Zhong Yao Yao Li Yu Ying Yong* (Pharmacology and Applications of Chinese Herbs), 1990; 15(6)::52.
12. Hong JH, Hwang EY, Kim HJ, Jeong YJ, Lee IS. Artemisia capillaris inhibits lipid accumulation in 3T3-L1 adipocytes and obesity in C57BL/6J mice fed a high fat diet. The Center for Traditional Microorganism Resources Center, Keimyung University, Daegu, Republic of Korea. J Med Food. 2009 Aug;12(4)::736-45.
13. *Shang Hai Zhong Yi Yao Za Zhi* (Shanghai Journal of Chinese Medicine and Herbology), 1988; 8::2.
14. *Zhong Yi Za Zhi* (Journal of Chinese Medicine), 1980; 1::39.

FORMULAS

Dissolve (KS)™

CLINICAL APPLICATIONS

- **Nephrolithiasis (kidney stones)**
- **Urolithiasis (bladder stones)**
- **Painful urination** with difficulty initiating or maintaining a good urinary stream; sudden stopping or blockage of urination with passage of a stone(s); lower abdominal pain
- **Renal colic** characterized by excruciating, one-sided, intermittent pain in the flank area that spreads across the abdomen and to the genital area and inner thigh

WESTERN THERAPEUTIC ACTIONS

- Dissolves and drains stones
- Diuretic effect to promote urination and passage of stones
- Analgesic and anti-inflammatory effects to relieve pain from blockage of tubes and ducts

CHINESE THERAPEUTIC ACTIONS

- Dissolves stones
- Treats dysuria due to *shi lin* (stone dysuria)
- Promotes normal urination
- Relieves spasms and pain

DOSAGE

Take 3 to 4 capsules three times daily on an empty stomach, with two glasses of warm water. Dosage may be increased up to 6 to 8 capsules three times daily, when necessary. Patients should continue to take these herbs until the stones are dissolved or passed out in the urine. For maintenance purposes, herbs can be taken at 1 to 2 capsules a day for six months to prevent the formation of new stones.

INGREDIENTS

Chuan Lian Zi (Fructus Toosendan)
Fu Ling (Poria)
Hai Jin Sha (Spora Lygodii)
Jin Qian Cao (Herba Lysimachiae)
Shi Wei (Folium Pyrrosiae)
Wei Ling Xian (Radix et Rhizoma Clematidis)
Yan Hu Suo (Rhizoma Corydalis)
Ze Xie (Rhizoma Alismatis)
Zhi Qiao (Fructus Aurantii)
Zhu Ling (Polyporus)

BACKGROUND

Nephrolithiasis (kidney stones) and/or urolithiasis (bladder stones) are formed when there is an increased accumulation or decreased elimination of calcium oxalate, calcium phosphate, cystine, magnesium ammonium phosphate and uric acid. As these substances harden to form stones, they cause pain, nausea, vomiting, hematuria and infection. Optimal treatment requires dissolution and draining of stones, alleviation of the symptoms and complications, and prevention of future kidney stones.

FORMULA EXPLANATION

Dissolve (KS) is an effective formula to dissolve and facilitate the passage of kidney and bladder stones, relieve pain and promote normal urination.

According to traditional Chinese medicine, kidney and urinary stones are known as "*shi lin*," which literally means dysuria due to stones. *Jin Qian Cao* (Herba Lysimachiae), *Hai Jin Sha* (Spora Lygodii), and *Shi Wei* (Folium Pyrrosiae), are three principle herbs used in this formula to dissolve and pass the stones. *Jin Qian Cao* (Herba Lysimachiae) dissolves stones and helps to clear damp-heat in the lower *jiao* to relieve burning dysuria. *Hai Jin Sha* (Spora Lygodii) dissolves and dispels stones. *Hai Jin Sha* (Spora Lygodii) also reduces swelling caused by obstruction. *Shi Wei* (Folium Pyrrosiae) softens and dissolves stones.

Ze Xie (Rhizoma Alismatis), *Zhu Ling* (Polyporus) and *Fu Ling* (Poria) are diuretic herbs used here to facilitate the passage and elimination of stones. Together, they promote urination, flush out the stones, and reduce edema and/or water retention in the body caused by kidney stone obstruction.

Zhi Qiao (Fructus Aurantii) relieves the distension and pressure caused by kidney stones by activating qi circulation. It also breaks up stagnant qi to resolve accumulations in the abdomen. *Wei Ling Xian* (Radix et Rhizoma Clematidis) is one of the strongest herbs to enter and open all the channels and collaterals in the body. With its penetrating characteristics, it breaks up stagnation to relieve pain caused by obstruction.

To relieve pain, *Yan Hu Suo* (Rhizoma Corydalis) and *Chuan Lian Zi* (Fructus Toosendan) are added to the formula. *Yan Hu Suo* (Rhizoma Corydalis) is one of the strongest analgesic herbs for pain relief, while *Chuan Lian Zi* (Fructus Toosendan) has an antispasmodic effect to relieve spasms of the smooth muscle of the ureter.

Together, the herbs in ***Dissolve (KS)*** effectively treat the cause and the symptoms of kidney and bladder stones.

CAUTIONS & CONTRAINDICATIONS

- This formula is not suitable for stones that are too big to be passed. Surgical intervention may be the treatment of choice for acute pain associated with stones greater than 2.5 cm in diameter.
- Patients with kidney infection or acute pain from the kidney stone should seek medical help immediately.
- This formula is contraindicated during pregnancy and nursing.

CLINICAL NOTES

- Patients with kidney stones may be asymptomatic. They may or may not experience pain, bleeding, obstruction of urine flow or any sign of infection. Patients who are asymptomatic but have stones may take this formula to dissolve kidney stones.
- Kidney stones without pain usually indicate that the stone is still in the kidney. When pain is experienced in the flank area, radiating across the abdomen down to the genitals, it is an

Dissolve (KS)™

indication that the stone is passing or is obstructed in its passage from the kidney to the ureter.

- If the stones are too big to pass through the ureter and urethra, sonic wave therapy (lithotripsy) is one treatment option to break the stones into smaller fragments, in combination with taking the herbal formula to facilitate elimination. The patient should drink plenty of fluids regularly to help flush stone fragments out of the kidney and urinary tract.
- If the stones are too big to pass through the ureter and urethra, and are causing severe pain, surgery may be the best treatment option, as herbal treatment may require a prolonged period of time to show effectiveness.
- If the stones are small enough to pass through the urinary ducts, the patient may begin taking this formula. Some patients may feel slight pain or discomfort during this process, as the herbs work to dispel the stones. Continue taking the herbs until the stones pass out of the body.
- Pain associated with kidney stones may occur after rigorous exercise that promotes movement of the stone.
- Back pain due to kidney stones should be differentiated from sprain, strain or trauma. Colicky pain due to kidney stones is usually one-sided, and radiates across the abdomen down to the genitals. Patients with sprain and strain will report that the pain is due to trauma or over-exertion. Reports from current X-rays or other imaging can also provide a clue to the cause of the pain.
- Recurrence of kidney stones may be prevented by taking ***Dissolve (KS)*** 2 to 3 capsules, once a day.

Pulse Diagnosis by Dr. Jimmy Wei-Yen Chang:

- Bird's beak / pen tip pulse, a convex-shaped pulse that is approximately 0.1 cm in length that feels like a pen's tip, on the deep level of either left or right *chi*. Detection of this pulse on the left *chi* indicates kidney stones in the left ureter; on the right *chi* indicates stones in the right ureter.
- If there is also inflammation, the pulse will be forceful.

SUPPLEMENTARY FORMULAS

- For kidney or bladder stones with infection and inflammation, use with ***Herbal ABX***.
- For burning dysuria, dark yellow urine, urinary tract infection, use with ***V-Support***.
- For kidney or bladder stones with edema, use with ***Herbal DRX***.
- For excess heat or fever, add ***Gardenia Complex***.
- For hypertension, use ***Gastrodia Complex*** or ***Gentiana Complex***
- For flank or back pain and spasms, use with ***Flex (SC)***.
- To relieve pain, use with ***Herbal ANG***.
- For bleeding, add ***Notoginseng 9***.
- For chronic nephritis, chronic nephrotic syndrome or proteinuria, use ***Kidney DTX*** instead.

ACUPUNCTURE TREATMENT

Traditional Points:

- Needle and strongly stimulate *Quanliao* (SI 18) and *Yangchi* (TH 4)
- *Shenshu* (BL 23), *Yaoyan* (Extra 9), *Renzhong* (GV 26), *Guanyuan* (CV 4), *Zusanli* (ST 36), *Zhongji* (CV 3), *Sanyinjiao* (SP 6)

Classic Master Tung's Points:

- *Liukuai* (T 1010.16), *Qikuai* (T 1010.17), *Shuiyu* (T 44.17), *Sanshen* (T 44.27)*, *Majinshui* (T 1010.13), *Makuaishui* (T 1010.14), *Tianhuang* (T 77.17), *Dihuang* (T 77.19), *Renhuang* (T 77.21). Bleed dark veins on or nearby *Liukuai* (T 1010.16), *Qikuai* (T 1010.17), *Shuiyu* (T 44.17). Bleed before needling for best result.

Master Tung's Points by Dr. Chuan-Min Wang:

- **Kidney stones:** Bleed *Xiaquan* (T 88.20), *Zhongquan* (T 88.21), *Shangquan* (T 88.22) or *Shuizhong* (T DT.13), *Shuifu* (T DT.14). Needle *Majinshui* (T 1010.13), *Makuaishui* (T 1010.14).

Balance Method by Dr. Richard Tan:

- Left side: *Chengshan* (BL 57), *Jinggu* (BL 64), *Chize* (LU 5) or *ah shi* points nearby, *Kongzui* (LU 6) or *ah shi* points nearby
- Right side: *Sanyinjiao* (SP 6), *Rangu* (KI 2), *Dazhong* (KI 4), *Fuliu* (KI 7), *Zhubin* (KI 9), *Hegu* (LI 4), Kidney point on the ear
- Sides can be alternated between treatments.

Ear Acupuncture:

- Kidney, Abdomen, Sympathetic, Subcortex. Stimulate these points strongly for 20 to 40 minutes.
- Kidney, Ureter, Urethra. Needle bilaterally

Auricular Medicine by Dr. Li-Chun Huang:

- Ureter, Kidney, Bladder, Sympathetic, Nervous Subcortex, External Abdomen, *Shenmen*, Lower *Jiao*, *San Jiao*. Bleed Ear Apex.

NUTRITION

- Patients with calcium stones should refrain from eating foods containing high amounts of oxalates, such as rhubarb, spinach (especially in combination with calcium-rich foods), nuts, cocoa, tea, and pepper. These foods contribute to calcium stone formation in the body.
- Patients with uric acid stones should refrain from foods that increase the level of uric acid in the urine, such as meat, poultry, pork, liver, beef, sardines, meat broth, clams, crabs, peas, various beans, cauliflower, coffee and tea.
- Patients who are prone to forming kidney stones should drink eight to ten glasses of water a day. Chronic dehydration increases the risk of stone formation.
- Potassium citrate makes the urine more alkaline, and helps to flush out uric acid. Fruits and vegetables should be increased, while protein, eggs, and milk should be reduced in the diet.

Dissolve (KS)™

- Vitamin A is essential to prevent formation and deposit of stones in the kidneys. Increase the consumption of foods high in vitamin A, such as carrots, yams, apricots, peaches, and mango.

The Tao of Nutrition by Dr. Maoshing Ni and Cathy McNease:

- Recommendations: corn-silk, water chestnuts, seaweed, beet tops, watermelon, celery, watercress, winter melon, pearl barley, walnuts, watermelon rind, winter melon rind, green tea powder, and distilled water.
- Drink celery, carrot, watermelon, and water chestnut juice.
- Drink cornsilk tea for water; three to five glasses daily.
- Drink tea from beet tops, winter melon rind, and watermelon rind.
- Take two teaspoons ground walnuts in cornsilk tea.
- Take one teaspoon green tea powder in warm water three times daily.
- After consuming any of the above diuretics remedies, do some mild jumping exercise to help loosen up the stones.
- Avoid spicy foods, fried foods, oily foods, coffee, hard water, spinach, citrus, tomatoes, spinach combined with tofu or dairy products.

LIFESTYLE INSTRUCTIONS

- Patients should drink plenty of water throughout the day to help flush out the stones.
- Patients should urinate whenever necessary (or more frequently than usual, if they do not feel strong urges to urinate), and not hold their urine.
- Sitz-baths may be helpful if there is shooting pain in the kidney and bladder areas with fever and chills. However, if the condition is not alleviated, the patient should seek medical help immediately to rule out kidney infection.

CASE STUDIES

- A 42-year-old male computer specialist presented with pain indicative of kidney stones. The patient's medical doctor suggested immediate surgery. The patient was placed on a treatment plan with ***Dissolve (KS)*** for ten days. He was checked by his medical doctor two weeks later and discovered that the stones were completely gone. The practitioner also commented that many of her colleagues have used ***Dissolve (KS)*** on their patients with similar results. Submitted by C.B., Santa Barbara, California.
- A 38-year-old female had a 20-year history of kidney stones. Her kidney stone condition had a familiar cycle that started with low back pain, retention of urine, and ended with passing of a stone five to six months later. She was in her first two weeks of the cycle when she came for treatment. Her condition included low back pain, edema in her lower legs, swollen eyes, retention of urine, and night sweats. Her Western medical diagnosis was kidney stones with pyelonephritis. Her TCM diagnosis was Kidney yang deficiency. After taking ***Dissolve (KS)*** for three days, her condition began to improve. Edema in the lower legs disappeared with only slight swelling in the eyes. Night sweats and tearing in the eyes resolved. Her low back pain diminished. Furthermore, her lab analysis tested negative for any presence of kidney stones. Submitted by M.J., Brooklyn, New York.
- D.B., a 43-year-old male, presented with kidney stones which he had been diagnosed with five years prior. Pain was described as severe and gripping in the abdomen area. His blood pressure was 125/85 mmHg and the heart rate was 84 beats per minute. The practitioner diagnosed his condition as *shi lin* (stone dysuria) with damp-heat. After taking ***Dissolve (KS)*** at 3 grams twice daily, the patient's pain diminished within a few hours of starting the formula. Dietary and lifestyle recommendations were also given. The patient had experienced passing of several stones over the first 24 hours without extreme pain but mild discomfort. He has needed to use ***Dissolve (KS)*** occasionally; however, there was a significant difference in pain reduction and recurrence. Submitted by B.E., Reno, Nevada.
- M.E., a 58-year-old male, presented with lower back pain of severity leading to impaired mobility. Recent diagnostic imaging had revealed the patient had kidney stones. The practitioner diagnosed this condition as Urinary Bladder damp-heat and prescribed ***Dissolve (KS)***. After taking the herbs, the patient reported a significant reduction in symptoms; however, he has not had any further diagnostic testing to determine whether they are completely gone. He has had a history of tumors in his lungs, so he is constantly being evaluated for his ongoing medical condition. The patient had refused acupuncture treatment and he didn't think he believed in Chinese Medicine. However, after taking ***Dissolve (KS)***, he has become a convert to Chinese Medicine. He works as an engineer and is no longer immobilized by pain. Submitted by M.M., Burlington, Wisconsin.
- A 72-yr-old patient (a former nurse) had a long history of kidney stones and kidney infections. In 1979, she had surgery to remove a kidney stone "the size of a small gumball." This was before laproscopic or arthroscopic surgery, so it was quite an ordeal for her, and appeared to have caused significant trauma to her kidneys. She described the surgery as "slitting open her entire left side and cutting open the kidney." She was hospitalized for a long time and also developed a staph infection. In recent years, she continued to have recurrent stones in both kidneys (a combination of calcium phosphate and oxalate stones) despite lithotripsy treatment. In the last five months, she was treated with ***Dissolve (KS), Herbal ABX*** and ***Kidney DTX***. These formulas completely dissolved her latest kidney stones and significantly reduced the frequency of kidney infections. Submitted by S.B., Palmer, Alaska.
- A 21-year-old female art gallery manager complained of kidney pain, which was severe at times. Other symptoms included lumbar pain and heat. The diagnosis for her case was renal lithiasis. After taking ***Dissolve (KS)*** for six months, there was a complete cessation of the heat sensation and pain. Submitted by D.K., Forestville, California.

Dissolve (KS)™

- A female came to the practitioner's office for treatment of kidney stones. A chronic low back pain condition had plagued the patient for five years, shuffling in and out of the emergency room and being treated with painkillers. The practitioner prescribed ***Dissolve (KS)*** formula along with two homeopathic compositions. Within 36 hours, she was able to pass a kidney stone. Another patient with the same condition was given the same treatment protocol. Again, a kidney stone was passed within the same time frame. Submitted by I.B., Miami, Florida.
- A 73-year-old female veterinarian presented with severe low back and abdominal pain due to renal calculi [kidney stone]. There was redness and swelling over the right kidney on her back. Tenderness over the right kidney region was also noted upon palpation. The pain referred along the belt channel, which traveled around the lower abdomen. The patient's pulse was wiry, particularly on the right side with the kidney pulse weak but tight. The practitioner diagnosed the condition as Kidney deficiency resulting in damp-heat in the lower *jiao* along with qi obstruction. After the patient took ***Dissolve (KS)*** for 4 weeks, she began experiencing a cessation of pain and an increased urine flow. Subsequent X-ray findings showed a decrease in size of stones in her right kidney, the site that originally contained much larger and a higher number of renal calculi. There was no apparent change in the stones in her left kidney. Upon discontinuing treatment of ***Dissolve (KS)***, the severe pain returned and urination again became scanty. The patient re-started her treatment with ***Dissolve (KS)***, which immediately stopped the pain and an easy urine flow resumed. The patient's condition continued to fluctuate before it finally returned to some form of normalcy three months later. Submitted by V.W., Princeville, Hawaii.
- A 25-year-old male computer technician presented with left-sided low back pain radiating to the left testicle. There was also frequent painful urination with dribbling. The symptoms had been present for six days. Kidney stones tested positive by way of Computerized Electrodermal Screening (EAV). The practitioner diagnosed the condition as damp-heat in the lower *jiao*. After three days of taking ***Dissolve (KS)*** at 3 capsules three times daily with meals, the low back pain and dysuria were completely relieved. Frequency of urination and dribbling were also resolved. Application of ***Dissolve (KS)*** appeared to have accelerated the patient's recovery. Submitted by D.H., Fort Myers, Florida.
- A female patient presented with severe right-sided lumbar pain that she described as 'cutting' in nature. She also had frequent, painful and yellow urination. The western diagnosis was kidney stones; the TCM diagnosis was *lin zheng* (dysuria syndrome), with damp-heat in the Urinary Bladder. After two bottles of ***Dissolve (KS)*** and *Ba Zheng San* (Eight-Herb Powder for Rectification), the pain subsided and urine was clear. The patient felt some stones may have passed in her urine. Submitted by M.C., Sarasota, Florida.

PHARMACOLOGICAL AND CLINICAL RESEARCH

Dissolve (KS) is formulated specifically to treat nephrolithiasis (kidney stones) and/or urolithiasis (bladder stones). It contains herbs that have shown great effectiveness for dissolving stones and promoting urination to flush out stones.

Ze Xie (Rhizoma Alismatis) is a diuretic herb with great effect to dissolve and flush out stones. According to one study, one preparation of *Ze Xie* (Rhizoma Alismatis) extract significantly inhibits urinary calcium oxalate stone formation induced by ethylene glycol and ammonium chloride.[1] According to another study, *Ze Xie* (Rhizoma Alismatis) inhibits the renal stone formation by down-regulating the bikunin mRNA expression and decreasing the calcium oxalate formation in the kidney.[2] To further promote normal urination and facilitate drainage of stones, many herbs with diuretic benefits are used. *Fu Ling* (Poria) and *Zhu Ling* (Polyporus) have diuretic effects, causing significant increases in urine output.[3,4] In addition, the use of *Zhu Ling* (Polyporus) is also associated with increased excretion of sodium, chloride, potassium and calcium.[5,6] *Jin Qian Cao* (Herba Lysimachiae) is another excellent herb to prevent and treat kidney and bladder stones. Pharmacologically, the aqueous extract of *Jin Qian Cao* (Herba Lysimachiae) has a potent effect to reduce plasma levels of uric acid in hyperuricemia in subjects pretreated with oxonate.[7] Clinically, the decoction of *Jin Qian Cao* (Herba Lysimachiae) is effective in preventing and treating urinary stones, with better action against kidney stones than bladder stones.[8] Furthermore, according to a clinical study, seven patients with stones in the urinary tract were treated with an herbal formula containing *Jin Qian Cao* (Herba Lysimachiae), *Hai Jin Sha* (Spora Lygodii), and others. After ten days of herbal treatment, stones were eliminated in all patients.[9]

Dissolve (KS) contains herbs that reduce inflammation and relieve pain. *Chuan Lian Zi* (Fructus Toosendan) has obvious anti-inflammatory and analgesic activities,[10] and has been used successfully to treat pain associated with blockage of tubes and ducts, such as pain in the testicles,[11] hydrocele testis,[12] blocked fallopian tubes,[13] and acute and chronic cholecystitis.[14] *Wei Ling Xian* (Radix et Rhizoma Clematidis) exhibits its anti-inflammatory effect by blocking the production of the pro-inflammatory mediators.[15] *Yan Hu Suo* (Rhizoma Corydalis) demonstrates a strong analgesic effect to relieve pain and a marked anti-inflammatory effect to reduce swelling and inflammation.[16,17]

Dissolve (KS) also has herbs to treat infection. *Jin Qian Cao* (Herba Lysimachiae) has an antibiotic effect as it inhibits the growth of numerous bacteria.[18] *Fu Ling* (Poria) has a bacteriostatic effect.[19] *Chuan Lian Zi* (Fructus Toosendan) also has significant antibacterial activity.[20] Lastly, 50 patients with urinary tract infection (40 with acute and 10 with chronic infection) were treated with an herbal formula with complete recovery in 48 cases. The herbal formula contained *Shi Wei* (Folium Pyrrosiae)

Dissolve (KS)™

and others, and was administered in decoction daily for a range of 3 to 15 packs.[21]

In summary, ***Dissolve (KS)*** is an herbal formula with many herbs that treat the cause of kidney and bladder stones, manage the symptoms and the complications. ***Dissolve (KS)*** may be taken in larger doses for treatment of stones, or lower doses for prevention.

COMPARATIVE ANALYSIS

Urinary stones (kidney and bladder stones) are two conditions that often occur together. In Western medicine, if these two conditions are asymptomatic, treatment may not be necessary, as risks often outweigh the benefits. If symptomatic, alkalinization of the urine may be effective for uric acid stones, but not for other types of stones. In most cases, urinary stones (kidney and bladder stones) can only be treated with invasive treatments such as surgery or ultrasound disruption therapy.

Kidney and bladder stones are two conditions that are successfully treated with herbs. The mechanisms of action of herbs are to dissolve and expel stones from the kidney and urinary bladder. Herbal therapies are effective to treat and to prevent stones. Depending on the number and size of the stones, the duration of treatment ranges from days to months. Nonetheless, use of herbs should be limited to individuals with mild to moderate cases of kidney and bladder stones. If there is acute manifestations, or if herbal therapy is ineffective after three months, then patients should be referred to Western medicine for surgery or ultrasound disruption therapy.

References

1. Cao ZG, Liu JH, Radman AM, Wu JZ, Ying CP, Zhou SW. An experimental study of effect of different extracts of Alisma orientalis on urinary calcium oxalate stones formation in rats. Department of Urology, Tongji Hospital, Tongji Medical College, Huazhong University of Science and Technology, Wuhan 430030, Hubei, China. Zhongguo Zhong Yao Za Zhi. 2003 Nov;28(11):1072-5.
2. Cao ZG, Liu JH, Zhou SW, Wu W, Yin CP, Wu JZ. The effects of the active constituents of Alisma orientalis on renal stone formation and bikunin expression in rat urolithiasis model. Department of Urology, Tongji Hospital, Tongji Medical College, Huazhong University of Science and Technology, Wuhan 430030, China. Zhonghua Yi Xue Za Zhi. 2004 Aug 2;84(15):1276-9.
3. *Chang Yong Zhong Yao Cheng Fen Yu Yao Li Shou Ce* (A Handbook of the Composition and Pharmacology of Common Chinese Drugs), 1994; 1383:1391.
4. *Sheng Yao Xue Za Zhi* (Journal of Raw Herbology), 1982; 36(2):150.
5. *Yao Xue Xue Bao* (Journal of Herbology), 1964; 11(12):815.
6. Zhang G, Zeng X, Han L, Wei JA, Huang H. Diuretic activity and kidney medulla AQP1, AQP2, AQP3, V2R expression of the aqueous extract of sclerotia of Polyporus umbellatus FRIES in normal rats. J Ethnopharmacol. 2010 Mar 24;128(2):433-7.
7. Wang HD, Ge F, Guo YS, Kong LD. Effects of aqueous extract in herba of Lysimachia christinae on hyperuricemia in mice. State Key Laboratory of Pharmaceutical Biotechnology, School of Life Sciences, Nanjing University, Nanjing 210093, Jiangsu, China. Zhongguo Zhong Yao Za Zhi. 2002 Dec;27(12):939-41, 944.
8. *Guang Xi Zhong Yi Yao* (Guangxi Chinese Medicine and Herbology), 1990; 13(6):40.
9. *Zhe Jiang Zhong Yi Za Zhi* (Zhejiang Journal of Chinese Medicine), 1983; (11):493.
10. Xie F, Zhang M, Zhang CF, Wang ZT, Yu BY, Kou JP. Anti-inflammatory and analgesic activities of ethanolic extract and two limonoids from Melia toosendan fruit. J Ethnopharmacol. 2008 May 22;117(3):463-6.
11. *Zhong Yao Lin Chuan Xin Yong* (New Clinical Applications of Chinese Medicine), 2001; 69.
12. *Zhong Yao Lin Chuan Xin Yong* (New Clinical Applications of Chinese Medicine), 2001; 70.
13. *Shang Hai Zhong Yi Yao Za Zhi* (Shanghai Journal of Chinese Medicine and Herbology), 1992; (3):19.
14. *Zhong Yao Lin Chuan Xin Yong* (New Clinical Applications of Chinese Medicine), 2001; 68.
15. Park EK, Ryu MH, Kim YH, Lee YA, Lee SH, Woo DH, Hong SJ, Han JS, Yoo MC, Yang HI, Kim KS. Anti-inflammatory effects of an ethanolic extract from Clematis mandshurica Rupr. East-West Bone and Joint Research Center, College of Medicine, Kyung Hee University, Hoegi-1 dong, Dongdaemun-gu, Seoul 130-701, South Korea. J Ethnopharmacol. 2006 Nov 3;108(1):142-7.
16. Huang JY, Fang M, Li YJ, Ma YQ, Cai XH. Analgesic effect of Corydalis yanhusuo in a rat model of trigeminal neuropathic pain. Department of Stomatology, Zhujiang Hospital, Southern Medical University, Guangzhou 510282, China. Nan Fang Yi Ke Da Xue Xue Bao. 2010 Sep;30(9):2161-4.
17. Kubo M, Matsuda H, Tokuoka K, Ma S, Shiomoto H. Anti-inflammatory activities of methanolic extract and alkaloidal components from Corydalis tuber. Faculty of Pharmaceutical Sciences, Kinki University, Osaka, Japan. Biol Pharm Bull. 1994 Feb;17(2):262-5.
18. *Zhong Yao Xue* (Chinese Herbology), 1998, 334:336.
19. *Zhong Yao Da Ci Dian* (Dictionary of Chinese Herbs), 1977:1596.
20. Zhang Q, Shi Y, Liu XT, Liang JY, Ip NY, Min ZD. Minor limonoids from Melia toosendan and their antibacterial activity. Planta Med. 2007 Oct;73(12): 1298-303.
21. *Shan Dong Zhong Yi Za Zhi* (Shandong Journal of Chinese Medicine), 1986; (5):12.

Enhance Memory™

CLINICAL APPLICATIONS

- **Cognitive impairment** with forgetfulness, poor memory and difficulty concentrating or focusing
- **Delayed mental development in children**
- **Deteriorating cognition in elderly patients**
- Adjunct formula for individuals who wish to improve their memory, cognitive function, and mental alertness
- Support formula for periods of mental stress, such as long work hours, impending deadlines, and exams

WESTERN THERAPEUTIC ACTIONS

- Cognitive effect to improve memory and learning ability
- Circulatory effect to improve blood perfusion and deliver oxygen and essential nutrients to the brain
- Neuroprotective effect to prevent and treat neurodegenerative disorders and drug-induced memory impairments

CHINESE THERAPEUTIC ACTIONS

- Nourishes the Heart
- Tonifies the Kidney *jing* (essence)
- Invigorates blood circulation to the head

DOSAGE

For adults, take 3 to 4 capsules three times daily with warm water for treatment. For maintenance, take 2 capsules twice daily. For children, take 2 capsules twice daily. This formula is most effective when taken on a continuous basis for three to six months.

INGREDIENTS

Bai Zi Ren (Semen Platycladi)
Dan Shen (Radix et Rhizoma Salviae Miltiorrhizae)
Dang Gui (Radix Angelicae Sinensis)
Di Huang (Radix Rehmanniae)
Fu Ling (Poria)
Jie Geng (Radix Platycodonis)
Mai Dong (Radix Ophiopogonis)
Ren Shen (Radix et Rhizoma Ginseng)
Shi Chang Pu (Rhizoma Acori Tatarinowii)
Suan Zao Ren (Semen Ziziphi Spinosae)
Tian Dong (Radix Asparagi)
Wu Wei Zi (Fructus Schisandrae Chinensis)
Xuan Shen (Radix Scrophulariae)
Yin Xing Ye (Folium Ginkgo)
Yuan Zhi (Radix Polygalae)

BACKGROUND

Mild cognitive impairment is a condition characterized by poor memory, mild memory loss, forgetfulness, and difficulty concentrating or focusing. Mild cognitive impairment may be caused by many factors, including stress, lack of sleep, lack of exercise, overeating, insufficient intake of vitamin B_{12}, headache, head injury, stroke, and seizures. Mild cases of cognitive impairment can be reversed with lifestyle changes or diet modifications. However, moderate cases of cognitive impairment will require herbal treatment.

FORMULA EXPLANATION

According to traditional Chinese medicine, the Kidney produces marrow and the brain is the sea of marrow. Strong Kidney *jing* (essence) is vital to the nourishment of the brain, memory, concentration and alertness. The Kidney is also essential in helping the Heart house the *shen* (spirit) and maintain clear mental activity, consciousness, memory and thinking.

Forgetfulness and inability to concentrate or focus are usually the result of deficiency and lack of nourishment due to overwork, lack of rest, or aging. ***Enhance Memory*** contains herbs that tonify the Kidney and Heart, invigorate blood circulation to the head, and open orifices to improve alertness. *Di Huang* (Radix Rehmanniae), *Xuan Shen* (Radix Scrophulariae), *Mai Dong* (Radix Ophiopogonis) and *Tian Dong* (Radix Asparagi) nourish Kidney yin and *jing* (essence). *Ren Shen* (Radix et Rhizoma Ginseng) and *Fu Ling* (Poria) tonify Heart qi. *Dan Shen* (Radix et Rhizoma Salviae Miltiorrhizae) and *Dang Gui* (Radix Angelicae Sinensis) invigorate the blood, and *Yin Xing Ye* (Folium Ginkgo) acts as a channel-guiding herb to the brain. Furthermore, the flavonoids in *Yin Xing Ye* (Folium Ginkgo) provide antioxidant protection to the brain and its related vascular structure. These blood-moving herbs keep adequate amounts of oxygenated blood to the brain cells to ensure healthy brain functions. *Yuan Zhi* (Radix Polygalae) and *Shi Chang Pu* (Rhizoma Acori Tatarinowii) improve mental alertness because they have aromatic dispelling functions to clear phlegm obstructing the orifices. *Bai Zi Ren* (Semen Platycladi), *Suan Zao Ren* (Semen Ziziphi Spinosae) and *Wu Wei Zi* (Fructus Schisandrae Chinensis) tranquilize the *shen* (spirit) and prevent the leakage of Heart qi. *Jie Geng* (Radix Platycodonis) acts as a channel-guiding herb to bring other herbs to the Heart.

In conclusion, ***Enhance Memory*** is a well-balanced formula to improve memory and increase cognition. ***Enhance Memory*** contains herbs that nourish the Heart, tonify the Kidney *jing* (essence), and invigorate blood circulation to the head.

CAUTIONS & CONTRAINDICATIONS

- This formula is contraindicated in cases of excess heat or existing exterior pathogenic conditions.
- This formula is contraindicated during pregnancy and nursing.
- This herbal formula contains herbs that invigorate blood circulation, such as *Dan Shen* (Radix et Rhizoma Salviae Miltiorrhizae) and *Dang Gui* (Radix Angelicae Sinensis). Therefore, patients who are on anticoagulant or antiplatelet therapies, such as Coumadin (warfarin), should use this formula with caution, or not at all, as there may be a higher risk of bleeding and bruising.[1,2,3]

Enhance Memory™

CLINICAL NOTES

- It is important to note that the maximum benefit of ***Enhance Memory*** is derived from continuous use, not from one excessive dose. In other words, use the normal dose continuously for three to six months for optimal effect. Increasing the dose exponentially will not necessarily accelerate the desired effect.
- This formula is safe for long-term use.

Pulse Diagnosis by Dr. Jimmy Wei-Yen Chang:

- **Poor memory and concentration** due to Heart blood deficiency: small pulse, a thin and weak pulse on the left *cun*

SUPPLEMENTARY FORMULAS

- With Alzheimer's disease, add ***Neuro Plus***.
- With Kidney yang deficiency, add ***Kidney Tonic (Yang)***.
- With Kidney yin deficiency, add ***Kidney Tonic (Yin)***.
- With patients who are "burned out," add ***Adrenal +***.
- With stress or Liver qi stagnation, add ***Calm***.
- With stress and anxiety in patients with excess heat, fire and *shen* (spirit) disturbance, add ***Calm (ES)***.
- With stress and insomnia in patients with deficiency, add ***Calm ZZZ***.
- With ADD/ADHD and poor memory, add ***Calm (Jr)***.
- With blood stagnation, add ***Circulation (SJ)***.
- For visual disturbances, blurriness, redness or pain, combine with ***Lycium Support***.

ACUPUNCTURE TREATMENT

Traditional Points:

- *Si Shen Cong*, scalp points
- *Taichong* (LR 3), *Xingjian* (LR 2), *Yinlingquan* (SP 9), *Yanglingquan* (GB 34), *Renzhong* (GV 26), *Baihui* (GV 20)

Classic Master Tung's Points:

- *Dizong* (T 44.09), *Tianhuangfu [Shenguan]* (T 77.18), *Zhenghui* (T 1010.01), *Piyi* (T 88.35)*, *Pier* (T 88.36)*

Master Tung's Points by Dr. Chuan-Min Wang:

- **Forgetfulness, poor memory:** Bleed *Huosan* (T 66.12), *Chongxiao* (T DT.17). Needle *Shuixiang* (T 66.14), *Shuixian* (T 66.15).

Balance Method by Dr. Richard Tan:

- Left side: *Shenmen* (HT 7), *Shaohai* (HT 3), *Zulinqi* (GB 41), *Yanglingquan* (GB 34), *Weizhong* (BL 40), *Shugu* (BL 65)
- Right side: *Zhongzhu* (TH 3), Tianjing (TH 10), *Houxi* (SI 3), *Xiaohai* (SI 8), *Taixi* (KI 3), *Yingu* (KI 10), ear *Shenmen*
- Alternate sides from treatment to treatment.

Auricular Medicine by Dr. Li-Chun Huang:

- **Invigorating the brain function:** Brain, Thalamus, Pituitary, Forehead, Heart, Kidney, Smart, Nervous Subcortex, Groove of Brain Posterior

NUTRITION

- Make sure the diet contains an adequate amount of lecithin, which is essential for transmission of nerve impulses that control memory. Good sources of lecithin include flax seed oil, walnut oil, sesame oil, egg yolk, soybean, and raw wheat germ.
- Do not overeat. Adults who consume between 2,100 and 6,000 calories each day are twice as likely to develop memory problems, according to American Academy of Neurology.[4]
- The B vitamins are also important for energy and proper brain function.
- Ensure adequate intake of vitamin B_{12}. Brain shrinkage and age-related memory declines have been linked with vitamin B_{12} deficiency, according to a report done by researchers at Chicago's Rush University Medical Center and published in *Neurology*. Foods rich in vitamin B_{12} include meat, fish, poultry, milk, eggs, and fortified breakfast cereals.

The Tao of Nutrition by Dr. Maoshing Ni and Cathy McNease:

- **Poor concentration:** Incorporate 1/4 cup of either fresh or frozen blueberries into breakfast daily for two to four weeks.
- **Memory decline:** Make trail mix of equal portions of dried blueberries, walnuts, pine nuts, goji berries, and pumpkin seeds.
- **Memory decline:** Make a brain tonic bean soup by cooking equal portions of navy beans, black beans, and kidney beans seasoned with rosemary, thyme, and turmeric. Eat a bowl daily.
- **Memory and focus issues:** Eat hardboiled quail eggs regularly.

LIFESTYLE INSTRUCTIONS

- Patients are recommended to have a good balance between exercise, rest, and relaxation.
- Encourage patients to continuously stay mentally active. Go back to school, get a part time job, solve crossword puzzles, play chess, and engage in other mentally-fulfilling activities.
- Encourage patients to stay physically active. Exercises that are good for the heart are also good for the brain.
- Avoid a stressful and hectic lifestyle. A poor memory is often related to an excessive amount of stress on a daily basis.
- Avoid physical activities or contact sports that cause direct injuries to the brain, such as boxing.
- Stay away from environments with dramatic and sudden change of temperature, from hot to cold and vice versa.
- Develop healthy sleeping habit. Sleep is necessary to consolidate memories so that they can be recalled in the future. Lack of sleep impairs a person's ability to focus and learn.
- Smoking and alcoholic beverages are not recommended.

CASE STUDIES

- J.H., a 35-year-old female, presented with memory loss due to trauma from a car accident. Her blood pressure was 120/70 mmHg and the heart rate was 72 beats per minute. Additional symptoms included heart flutters and night sweats. The patient

Enhance Memory™

was diagnosed with Kidney yin deficiency and Heart qi and *jing* (essence) deficiencies. ***Enhance Memory*** was prescribed for eight weeks, at 3 capsules three times daily for the first four weeks followed by a reduction to 2 capsules three times daily the next four weeks. After nine days her heart flutters and night sweats resolved. In conjunction with acupuncture treatments the patient's healing process was positive on many levels. Submitted by B.S., Albuquerque, New Mexico.

☯ A professional singer in her early 70's years of age had been complaining of memory loss. She was prescribed ***Enhance Memory***. After taking this formula for two weeks, she exclaimed that "she was able to recall lyrics and felt mentally confident again." Submitted by K.F., Honolulu, Hawaii.

PHARMACOLOGICAL AND CLINICAL RESEARCH

Enhance Memory is carefully crafted with herbs that have shown marked ability to enhance cognitive functions. Herbs in ***Enhance Memory*** have been shown to improve blood circulation to deliver oxygen and essential nutrients to the brain. Furthermore, herbs in ***Enhance Memory*** have a positive cognitive effect to improve mental functions and a neuroprotective effect to prevent damages to the neurons. Lastly, many herbs in ***Enhance Memory*** have been found to be effective in treating neurodegenerative disorders and drug-induced memory impairments.

Dang Gui (Radix Angelicae Sinensis) and *Dan Shen* (Radix et Rhizoma Salviae Miltiorrhizae) are two herbs in ***Enhance Memory*** that have shown pronounced ability to improve blood circulation. *Dang Gui* (Radix Angelicae Sinensis) improves overall blood circulation by decreasing blood viscosity, or improving the hemorrheological changes in "blood stagnation."[5] Administration of *Dan Shen* (Radix et Rhizoma Salviae Miltiorrhizae) is associated with marked vasodilation of the coronary arteries, a negative chronotropic and an inotropic effect, and a reduction of blood pressure.[6] In addition to improving blood circulation to the brain, ***Enhance Memory*** contains *Shi Chang Pu* (Rhizoma Acori Tatarinowii) to help guide the herbs into the brain. Administration of *Shi Chang Pu* (Rhizoma Acori Tatarinowii) is associated with an increased permeability of the blood-brain barrier by opening the tight junctions of the endothelial cells.[7] This action helps to enhance the overall effect of the formula. Overall, these three herbs act to improve microcirculation, thus delivering oxygen and essential nutrients to the brain to ensure the health and optimal performance of brain cells.

Enhance Memory contains many herbs with positive cognitive effects to improve memory. Administration of *Ren Shen* (Radix et Rhizoma Ginseng) for three days has demonstrated marked impact in improving memory and learning ability.[8] Another study shows that administration of *Ren Shen* (Radix et Rhizoma Ginseng) enhances cognitive performance and ameliorates the increase in subjective feelings of mental fatigue experienced by participants during the later stages of sustained, cognitively demanding task performance.[9] *Ren Shen* (Radix et Rhizoma Ginseng) has also been used successfully to improve classroom performance in a clinical trial of 30 children with low IQ and mental retardation.[10] In addition, *Shi Chang Pu* (Rhizoma Acori Tatarinowii) has a dose-dependent effect on improving cognition and memory.[11] Furthermore, a preparation of *Wu Wei Zi* (Fructus Schisandrae Chinensis) has a stimulating effect on the central nervous system to increase mental alertness, improve work efficiency, and quicken reflexes.[12] *Wu Wei Zi* (Fructus Schisandrae Chinensis) has also been shown to significantly reduce memory impairment in laboratory studies.[13] Lastly, *Yin Xing Ye* (Folium Ginkgo) has shown a positive cognitive effect to improve attention and memory in 52 young, healthy volunteers.[14]

Enhance Memory also contains many herbs with neuroprotective effects to prevent damages to the neurons. *Yuan Zhi* (Radix Polygalae) has potential as a drug to treat dementia and Alzheimer's disease via several mechanisms of actions. It has a dose-dependent effect to protect the neurons from Abeta-induced neuronal damage.[15] It also inhibits acetylcholinesterase (AChE) activity in a dose-dependent and non-competitive manner.[16] *Shi Chang Pu* (Rhizoma Acori Tatarinowii) shows a neuroprotective effect by attenuating neuronal apoptosis in hippocampus induced by beta-amyloid (Abeta), and helps to manage cognitive impairment associated with conditions such as Alzheimer's disease.[17] *Dang Gui* (Radix Angelicae Sinensis) reduces the neurotoxicity induced by amyloid beta-peptide in a dose-dependent manner and has potential to prevent Alzheimer's disease. *Di Huang* (Radix Rehmanniae) contains catapol, a compound with potential to treat senescence or neurodegenerative diseases, such as Alzheimer's and Parkinson's diseases, by ameliorating cognitive deficits and attenuating oxidative damage in the brain.[18] Finally, *Jie Geng* (Radix Platycodonis) demonstrates a marked neuroprotective effect by rescuing the neurons in the hippocampal region from ischemic damage.[19]

In addition to having a direct cognitive effect to improve brain functions and an indirect neuroprotective effect to prevent damage, ***Enhance Memory*** has many herbs to treat various neurodegenerative disorders. *Yin Xing Ye* (Folium Ginkgo) has been used in China and Europe for treatment of dementia. Pharmacologically, it has an antiplatelet effect to reduce blood viscosity and a vasodilative effect to increase perfusion to peripheral parts of the body, including the brain.[20,21] Clinically, numerous studies have shown *Yin Xing Ye* (Folium Ginkgo) to be safe and effective in treating various types of neurodegenerative disorders. According to a placebo-controlled, double-blind, randomized clinical trial with 309 patients over 52 weeks, *Yin Xing Ye* (Folium Ginkgo) was concluded to be "safe" and capable of "improving the cognitive performance and the social functioning of demented patients for six months to one year." The study was published by JAMA in October 1997.[22] According to another randomized, placebo-controlled, double-blind clinical trial, 400 patients aged 50 years or older with dementia with neuropsychiatric features were treated with *Yin Xing Ye* (Folium

Ginkgo) extract or placebo for 22 weeks. The results showed that *Yin Xing Ye* (Folium Ginkgo) extract was significantly superior to placebo on all secondary outcome measures, including the Neuropsychiatric Inventory and an activities-of-daily-living scale. Furthermore, *Yin Xing Ye* (Folium Ginkgo) extract was well tolerated. Incidence of adverse effects was comparable to placebo.[23] Another study conducted at the University of Southern California Keck School of Medicine also showed that use of *Yin Xing Ye* (Folium Ginkgo) was significantly better than placebo to improve cognitive performance and global assessment scores in patients with dementia accompanied by neuropsychiatric symptoms.[24]

Lastly, the use of herbs in ***Enhance Memory*** has also been found to be effective in preventing and treating drug-induced memory impairment. *Jie Geng* (Radix Platycodonis) ameliorates scopolamine-induced amnesia via inhibition of acetylcholinesterase (AChE) activity and inhibition of thiobarbituric acid-reactive substance in the serum and brain.[25] *Dang Gui* (Radix Angelicae Sinensis) is effective in treating scopolamine- and cycloheximide-induced amnesia in laboratory subjects.[26] *Yuan Zhi* (Radix Polygalae) is beneficial in treating memory impairment caused by scopolamine or dysfunction of the cholinergic system in the brain.[27] Finally, in an *in vitro* study, a traditional Chinese medicinal preparation [composed of *Ren Shen* (Radix et Rhizoma Ginseng), *Yuan Zhi* (Radix Polygalae), *Shi Chang Pu* (Rhizoma Acori Tatarinowii), and *Fu Ling* (Poria)] reduced the ethanol-induced impairment of memory registration. It also ameliorated the scopolamine-induced memory registration deficit. These results suggest that the herbal preparation ameliorates the impairing effect of ethanol on learning and memory processes.[28]

In summary, ***Enhance Memory*** is an excellent formula to improve cognition and treat memory-related disorders such as memory impairment, dementia, and Alzheimer's disease.

COMPARATIVE ANALYSIS

One striking difference between Western and traditional Chinese medicine is that Western medicine focuses and excels in crisis management, while traditional Chinese medicine emphasizes and shines in holistic and preventative treatments. Therefore, in emergencies, such as gunshot wounds or surgery, Western medicine is generally the treatment of choice. However, for treatment of chronic idiopathic illness of unknown origins, where all lab tests are normal and a clear diagnosis cannot be made, traditional Chinese medicine is distinctly superior.

In cases of gradual deterioration of mental acuity (with forgetfulness and poor memory), there are no diagnostic signs or symptoms, no laboratory abnormalities, and no functional or anatomical disorders. Under these circumstances, Western medicine struggles to identify a specific diagnosis and offers no drug treatments. On the other hand, traditional Chinese medicine is beneficial as it excels in maintenance and preventative therapies. Herbs can be used to improve blood circulation to the brain, nourish underlying deficiencies, and improve cognitive functions. In comparison with Western medicine, traditional Chinese medicine offers safe and effective treatment options. Therefore, herbal therapy should definitely be employed to prevent deterioration of this condition, and to restore optimal health.

References

1. Chan K, Lo AC, Yeung JH, Woo KS. Journal of Pharmacy and Pharmacology 1995 May;47(5)::402-6.
2. Pharmacotherapy 1999 July;19(7)::870-876.
3. European Journal of Drug Metabolism and Pharmacokinetics 1995; 20(1)::55-60.
4. American Academy of Neurology. Annual meeting report in February, 2012.
5. Xue, JX. et al. Effects of the combination of astragalus membranaceus (Fisch.) Bge. (AM), angelica sinensis (Oliv.) Diels (TAS), cyperus rotundus L. (CR), ligusticum chuanxiong Hort (LC) and paeonia veitchii lynch (PV) on the hemorrheological changes in "blood stagnating" rats. *Chung Kuo Chung Yao Tsa Chih*; 19(2):: Feb 1994; 108-10, 128.
6. *Shang Hai Di Yi Xue Yuan Xue Bao (Journal of First Shanghai Medical College)*, 1980; 7(5)::347.
7. Hu Y, Yuan M, Liu P, Mu L, Wang H. Effect of Acorus tatarinowii schott on ultrastructure and permeability of blood-brain barrier. Department of Clinical Pharmacology and Pharmacy, Chinese PLA General Hospital, Beijing 100853, China. Zhongguo Zhong Yao Za Zhi. 2009 Feb;34(3)::349-51.
8. *Zhong Yao Ci Hai (Encyclopedia of Chinese Herbs)*, 1994.
9. Reay JL, Kennedy DO, Scholey AB. Effects of Panax ginseng, consumed with and without glucose, on blood glucose levels and cognitive performance during sustained 'mentally demanding' tasks. Human Cognitive Neuroscience Unit, Northumbria University, Newcastle upon Tyne, NE1 8ST, UK. J Psychopharmacol. 2006 Nov;20(6)::771-81.
10. *Zhong Cheng Yao Yan Jiu (Research of Chinese Patent Medicine)*, 1982; 6::22.
11. *Zhong Yi Xue (Chinese Herbal Medicine)*, 1992; 23(8)::417.
12. *Zhong Yao Xue (Chinese Herbology)*, 1998; 878::881.
13. Kang S.Y., Lee K.Y., Koo K.A., Yoon J.S., Lim S.W., Kim Y.C. & Sung S.H. ESP-102, a standardized combined extract of *Angelica gigas*, *Saururus chinensis* and *Schizandra chinensis*, significantly improved scopolamine-induced memory impairment in mice. *Life Sci.* 2005, 76(15):: 1691-1705.
14. Elsabagh S, Hartley DE, Ali O, Williamson EM, File SE. Differential cognitive effects of Ginkgo biloba after acute and chronic treatment in healthy young volunteers. Psychopharmacology Research Unit, Centre for Neuroscience, Hodgkin Building, King's College London, Guy's Campus, London, SE1 1UL, UK. Psychopharmacology (Berl). 2005 May;179(2)::437-46.
15. Naito R, Tohda C. Characterization of anti-neurodegenerative effects of Polygala tenuifolia in Abeta(25-35)-treated cortical neurons. Division of Biofunctional Evaluation, Research Center for Ethnomedicine, Institute of Natural Medicine, University of Toyama, Toyoma, Japan. Biol Pharm Bull. 2006 Sep;29(9)::1892-6.
16. Park CH, Choi SH, Koo JW, Seo JH, Kim HS, Jeong SJ, Suh YH. Novel cognitive improving and neuroprotective activities of Polygala tenuifolia Willdenow extract, BT-11. Department of Pharmacology, College of Medicine, National Creative Research Initiative Center for Alzheimer's Dementia and Neuroscience Research Institute, MRC, Seoul National University, Seoul, South Korea. J Neurosci Res. 2002 Nov 1;70(3)::484-92.
17. Geng Y, Li C, Liu J, Xing G, Zhou L, Dong M, Li X, Niu Y. Beta-asarone improves cognitive function by suppressing neuronal apoptosis in the beta-amyloid hippocampus injection rats. The Institute of Medicine, Qiqihar Medical University, Qiqihar 161006, China. Biol Pharm Bull. 2010;33(5)::836-43.
18. Zhang X, Zhang A, Jiang B, Bao Y, Wang J, An L. Further pharmacological evidence of the neuroprotective effect of catalpol from Rehmannia glutinosa. School of Environmental and Biological Science & Technology, Dalian University of Technology, Dalian 116024, China. Phytomedicine. 2008 Jun;15(6-7)::484-90.

Enhance Memory™

19. Choi JH, Yoo KY, Park OK, Lee CH, Won MH, Hwang IK, Ryu SY, Kim YS, Yi JS, Bae YS, Kang IJ. Platycodin D and 2"-O-acetyl-polygalacin D2 isolated from Platycodon grandiflorum protect ischemia/reperfusion injury in the gerbil hippocampus. Department of Anatomy and Neurobiology, Institute of Neurodegeneration and Neuroregeneration, College of Medicine, Hallym University, Chuncheon, South Korea. Brain Res. 2009 Jul 7;1279:: 197-208.
20. Kudolo GB, Wang W, Barrientos J, Elrod R, Blodgett J. The ingestion of Ginkgo biloba extract (EGb 761) inhibits arachidonic acid-mediated platelet aggregation and thromboxane B2 production in healthy volunteers. Department of Clinical Laboratory Sciences, MSC 6246, University of Texas HSC at San Antonio, 7703 Floyd Curl Drive, San Antonio, TX 78229-3900, USA. J Herb Pharmacother. 2004;4(4)::13-26.
21. *Guo Wai Yi Xue Zhong Yi Zhong Yao Fen Ce* (Monograph of Chinese Herbology from Foreign Medicine), 1979; 4::200.
22. Le Bars, P. et al. A placebo-controlled, double-blind, randomized trial of an extract of ginkgo biloba for dementia. *JAMA* (Journal of American Medical Association);278::1327-1332. October 22, 1997.
23. Napryeyenko O, Borzenko I; GINDEM-NP Study Group. Ginkgo biloba special extract in dementia with neuropsychiatric features. A randomised, placebo-controlled, double-blind clinical trial. Psychiatry Department, National Medical University, Kyiv, Ukraine. Arzneimittelforschung. 2007;57(1)::4-11.
24. Schneider LS, DeKosky ST, Farlow MR, Tariot PN, Hoerr R, Kieser M. A randomized, double-blind, placebo-controlled trial of two doses of Ginkgo biloba extract in dementia of the Alzheimer's type. Curr Alzheimer Res. 2005 Dec;2(5)::541-51.
25. Moon MK, Ahn JY, Kim S, Ryu SY, Kim YS, Ha TY. Ethanol extract and saponin of Platycodon grandiflorum ameliorate scopolamine-induced amnesia in mice. Functional Food Technology Research Group, Korea Food Research Institute, Sungnam-Si, Republic of Korea. J Med Food. 2010 Jun;13(3)::584-8.
26. Hsieh MT, et al. Radix Angelica Sinensis extracts ameliorate scopolamine- and cycloheximide-induced amnesia, but not p-chloroamphetamine-induced amnesia in rats. American Journal of Chinese Medicine 2000;28(2)::263-72.
27. Sun XL, Ito H, Masuoka T, Kamei C, Hatano T. Effect of Polygala tenuifolia root extract on scopolamine-induced impairment of rat spatial cognition in an eight-arm radial maze task. Department of Pharmacognosy, Okayama University Graduate School of Medicine, Dentistry and Pharmaceutical Sciences, Tsushima, Okayama 700-8530, Japan. Biol Pharm Bull. 2007 Sep;30(9)::1727-31.
28. *Biological and Pharmaceutical Bulletin.* 1994 Nov.; 17(11)::1472-6,

FORMULAS

Equilibrium™

CLINICAL APPLICATIONS

- **Diabetes mellitus**
- **High blood glucose levels** and/or **high urine ketone levels**
- **Polyuria, polydipsia** and/or **polyphagia**

WESTERN THERAPEUTIC ACTIONS

- Antihyperglycemic effect to lower plasma glucose levels by increasing the production and the release of insulin
- Antidiabetic function to alleviate insulin resistance
- Neuroprotective benefit to protect the nerves
- Nephroprotective activity to protect the kidneys
- Circulatory effect to improve blood circulation to peripheral parts of the body
- Treats the cause and the complications of diabetes mellitus, such as neurological, renal, and microvascular disorders

CHINESE THERAPEUTIC ACTIONS

- Nourishes Lung, Stomach, and Kidney yin
- Clears deficiency fire
- Dries damp

DOSAGE

Take 3 to 4 capsules three times daily on an empty stomach [one hour before or two hours after meals]. To effectively control blood glucose level, it is important to keep in mind that dosing must be adjusted to reflect the condition of the patient and the response to the treatment, as the severity of diabetes is different in every case.

INGREDIENTS

Bai Zhu (Rhizoma Atractylodis Macrocephalae)
Cang Zhu (Rhizoma Atractylodis)
Dan Shen (Radix et Rhizoma Salviae Miltiorrhizae)
Hong Hua (Flos Carthami)
Huang Qi (Radix Astragali)
Lian Xu (Stamen Nelumbinis)
Lian Zi Xin (Plumula Nelumbinis)
Shan Yao (Rhizoma Dioscoreae)
Shi Gao (Gypsum Fibrosum)
Xi Yang Shen (Radix Panacis Quinquefolii)
Xuan Shen (Radix Scrophulariae)
Zhi Mu (Rhizoma Anemarrhenae)

BACKGROUND

Diabetes mellitus is defined as a rise in blood glucose levels due to impaired insulin secretion and peripheral insulin resistance. The clinical manifestation, however, is much more complicated than its definition. Patients with chronic diabetes mellitus are frequently plagued by various complications, such as visual disturbances, prolonged delay in healing of wounds, frequent recurrence of infections, and impotence. Treatment of diabetes mellitus, therefore, must focus on treating both the cause and the complications simultaneously.

FORMULA EXPLANATION

According to traditional Chinese medicine, diabetes mellitus is classified as upper, middle or lower *xiao ke* (wasting and thirsting) syndromes. Upper *xiao ke* (wasting and thirsting) syndrome is characterized by Lung heat drying up the moisture, leading to polydipsia; middle *xiao ke* (wasting and thirsting) syndrome is characterized by Stomach heat damaging fluid, leading to polyphagia; and lower *xiao ke* (wasting and thirsting) syndrome is characterized by Kidney deficiency, leading to polyuria. Furthermore, patients with high blood glucose commonly show signs of damp accumulation and Spleen deficiency. Overall, the clinical presentation of patients with diabetes can be summarized as yin deficiency with damp and heat.

Xi Yang Shen (Radix Panacis Quinquefolii) greatly replenishes the vital essence of the body and promotes the secretion of body fluids to treat polydipsia. *Shi Gao* (Gypsum Fibrosum) and *Zhi Mu* (Rhizoma Anemarrhenae) are a pair commonly used to clear heat in the middle *jiao*. They sedate Stomach fire and suppress appetite to relieve polyphagia. *Xuan Shen* (Radix Scrophulariae) enters the Lung, the Stomach, and the Kidney to replenish the vital essence and clear heat simultaneously. *Huang Qi* (Radix Astragali) and *Shan Yao* (Rhizoma Dioscoreae) strengthen the Spleen and enhance its function of transportation and transformation. *Bai Zhu* (Rhizoma Atractylodis Macrocephalae) and *Cang Zhu* (Rhizoma Atractylodis) strengthen the Spleen and dry up dampness. *Dan Shen* (Radix et Rhizoma Salviae Miltiorrhizae) and *Hong Hua* (Flos Carthami) activate blood circulation and enhance the overall effectiveness of the herbs. Activation of blood circulation also reduces the risk of atherosclerosis by preventing buildup of cholesterol on the inner walls of blood vessels. Proper blood circulation also helps to prevent diabetic neuropathy. Lastly, *Lian Zi Xin* (Plumula Nelumbinis) and *Lian Xu* (Stamen Nelumbinis) tonify the Kidney and control frequent urination.

Together, the herbs in ***Equilibrium*** effectively treat the cause and the complications of diabetes mellitus.

CAUTIONS & CONTRAINDICATIONS

- This formula is contraindicated during pregnancy and nursing.
- Patients should not stop using their drug treatment abruptly as there is a risk of hyperglycemia or diabetic ketoacidosis. Herbal and drug treatments should overlap for one to two weeks before patients begin tapering off their drug treatment, in order to ensure adequate control of blood glucose levels.
- ***Equilibrium*** may reduce the dosage and frequency of insulin injection needed; however, ***Equilibrium*** can never replace insulin, especially in type I diabetes mellitus patients. Patients with type I diabetes mellitus should always be treated with

Equilibrium ™

insulin, or the combination of insulin and herbs, and should continue to test their blood glucose regularly.

- This herbal formula contains herbs that invigorate blood circulation, such as *Dan Shen* (Radix et Rhizoma Salviae Miltiorrhizae). Therefore, patients who are on anticoagulant or antiplatelet therapies, such as Coumadin (warfarin), should use this formula with caution, or not at all, as there may be a higher risk of bleeding and bruising.[1]

CLINICAL NOTES

- For patients with type II diabetes, ***Equilibrium*** in combination with diet and exercise provide excellent clinical results. Most patients will experience satisfactory clinical results within three to four weeks of herbal treatment. Clinical effects include a significant reduction in blood glucose levels and less fluctuations throughout the day.
- In Western medicine, diabetes is defined simply as an increase in blood glucose levels. Diagnosis, however, can be difficult because diabetes has many complications, including impairment of vision, impotence, chronic infections, neuropathy, poor healing of wounds, and risk of coma.
- In traditional Chinese medicine, diabetes is commonly referred as *xiao ke* (wasting and thirsting) syndrome. However, it is important to keep in mind that even though these two conditions share many similarities, they are not equivalent. Both diabetes and *xiao ke* (wasting and thirsting) syndrome are characterized by the presence of three P's: polyuria, polydipsia and polyphagia. Diabetes is defined as an increase in blood glucose level, with or without the presence of the three P's. In addition, diabetes may have many complications that are not present in *xiao ke* (wasting and thirsting) syndrome, such as visual disturbance, impotence, amenorrhea, and frequent or chronic infections. Conversely, *xiao ke* (wasting and thirsting) syndrome is diagnosed based on the presence of three P's. Polyuria, polydipsia and polyphagia may be caused by factors other than diabetes, such as fever, dehydration, or kidney diseases. Understanding the similarities and differences between the two is essential to achieving optimal treatment of the patient.
- Patients with diabetes mellitus can be treated with drugs, herbs, or both. However, if both drugs and herbs are used, it is important to monitor the patient's condition frequently to ensure proper control of the signs and symptoms. Over-dosage with drugs and/or herbs may cause "hypoglycemic" signs and symptoms, and under-dosage may contribute to "hyperglycemic" signs and symptoms.
- ***Equilibrium*** is an herbal formula developed by Professor Xiao-Ping Zhang of Anhui Hospital of Traditional Chinese Medicine. It is an empirical formula designed to treat patients with diabetes mellitus. It has been used for over 30 years in China and has helped several thousand patients with diabetes by lowering their blood glucose level and reducing the long-term risks and complications associated with diabetes.

Pulse Diagnosis by Dr. Jimmy Wei-Yen Chang:

- **Type II diabetes:** wiry, forceful, and deep pulse on the right *guan*

SUPPLEMENTARY FORMULAS

- For high cholesterol and triglycerides, add ***Cholisma***.
- For high cholesterol and triglycerides with fatty liver and obesity, add ***Cholisma (ES)***.
- For hypertension, add ***Gastrodia Complex***.
- For chronic buildup of cholesterol leading to coronary artery disease, add ***Circulation***.
- With thirst and dry mouth, add ***Nourish (Fluids)***.
- For blurred vision or visual impairment, add ***Lycium Support***.
- For impotence due to impaired blood circulation, combine with ***Circulation (SJ)***.
- For neuropathy, add ***Flex (NP)***.
- For infection, add ***Herbal ABX***.
- For recurrent yeast infections, add ***V-Support***.
- For urinary tract infection, add ***Gentiana Complex***.
- For infection of ear, nose and throat, add ***Herbal ENT***.
- With compromised kidney functions, add ***Kidney DTX***.

ACUPUNCTURE TREATMENT

Traditional Points:

- *Quchi* (LI 11), *Sanyinjiao* (SP 6), *Yanglingquan* (GB 34)
- *Shenshu* (BL 23), *Taixi* (KI 3)
- *Pishu* (BL 20), *Shenshu* (BL 23), *Qihai* (CV 6), *Sanyinjiao* (SP 6), *Yanglingquan* (GB 34), *Shenque* (CV 8)
  - For excessive thirst, add *Feishu* (BL 13), *Yishe* (BL 49), *Chengjiang* (CV 24).
  - For hunger, add *Weishu* (BL 21), *Fenglong* (ST 40).
  - For polyuria, add *Guanyuan* (CV 4), *Fuliu* (KI 7).

Classic Master Tung's Points:

- **Diabetes (general):** *Tianhuang* (T 77.17), *Dihuang* (T 77.19), *Renhuang* (T 77.21), *Tianhuang* (T 88.13), *Minghuang* (T 88.12), *Qihuang* (T 88.14), *Tongshen* (T 88.09), *Tongwei* (T 88.10), *Shuijin* (T 1010.20), *Shuitong* (T 1010.19), *Piyi* (T 88.35)*, *Pier* (T 88.36)*, *Pisan* (T 88.37)*, *Tianhuangfu [Shenguan]* (T 77.18). Moxa *Tianhuangfu [Shenguan]* (T 77.18), *Zhongwan* (CV 12), *Guanyuan* (CV 4), *Zusanli* (ST 36)
- **Diabetes (vision problem):** *Linggu* (T 22.05), *Dabai* (T 22.04), *Shuitong* (T 1010.19), *Shuijin* (T 1010.20), *Minghuang* (T 88.12), *Tianhuang* (T 88.13), *Qihuang* (T 88.14), *Tianhuang* (T 77.17), *Dihuang* (T 77.19), *Renhuang* (T 77.21)
- **Diabetes insipidus:** *Simazhong* (T 88.17), *Simaxia* (T 88.19), *Tianhuangfu [Shenguan]* (T 77.18), *Renhuang* (T 77.21), *Zusanli* (ST 36)

Master Tung's Points by Dr. Chuan-Min Wang:

- **Diabetes:** *Tianhuangfu [shenguan]* (T 77.18), *Dihuang* (T 77.19), *Renhuang* (T 77.21)

Equilibrium™

Balance Method by Dr. Richard Tan:

- Left side: *Sanyinjiao* (SP 6), *Yinlingquan* (SP 9) or *ah shi* points nearby, *Fuliu* (KI 7), *Hegu* (LI 4), *Waiguan* (TH 5)
- Right side: *Zusanli* (ST 36), *Weizhong* (BL 40), *Zulinqi* (GB 41)
- Left and right sides can be alternated from treatment to treatment.

Ear Acupuncture:

- Main points: Pancreas, Endocrine
- Adjunct points: Kidney, *Sanjiao*, *Shenmen*, Heart, Liver
- Select three to four points for three to seven days.

Auricular Medicine by Dr. Li-Chun Huang:

- **Reducing blood sugar:** Pancreas, Diabetes, Ear Center (Vagus), *San Jiao*, Pituitary, Endocrine, Thalamus
- **Diabetes insipidus:** Pituitary, Thalamus, Endocrine, Thirst, Mouth, Bladder, Urethra, *San Jiao*
- **Diabetes mellitus:** Diabetes, Pancreas, Ear Center, Pituitary, Thalamus, *San Jiao*, Endocrine

NUTRITION

- Avoid the consumption of simple sugars, which have an adverse effect on glucose tolerance.
- Eat a low-fat, high-fiber diet including plenty of raw fruits and vegetables.
- Avoid supplements containing the amino acid cysteine, which interferes with absorption of insulin by the cells.
- Avoid excessive amounts of vitamin B_1 (thiamine) and C, which may inactivate insulin.
- Avoid the consumption of alcohol and use of tobacco in any form as they increase nerve damage.
- Increase intake of nourishing, cooling foods/roots such as Mexican yam, yam, radishes, potatoes, carrots, melons, cucumbers, beets, turnips, malanga, celeriac, taro, and rutabaga.
- Avoid spicy/pungent/aromatic vegetables such as pepper, garlic, onions, basil, rosemary, cumin, funnel, anise, leeks, chives, scallions, thyme, saffron, wormwood, mustard, chili pepper, and wasabi.

The Tao of Nutrition by Dr. Maoshing Ni and Cathy McNease:

- Recommendations: pumpkin, wheat, mung beans, winter melon, celery, pears, spinach, yams, peas, sweet rice, soybeans, tofu, mulberries, squash, daikon radish, cabbage, peach, and organic pig or chicken pancreas.
- Eat a slice of pumpkin with each meal.
- Make pumpkin and yam pie with no sweeteners.
- Prepare soup with cabbage, yam, winter melon, and lentils.
- Drink daikon, celery, carrot, and spinach juice.
- Make soup from mung beans, peas, and barley.
- Drink chrysanthemum tea.
- Steam millet with yam and a few dates.
- Avoid sweets, sugar, honey, molasses, caffeine, and spicy foods.

LIFESTYLE INSTRUCTIONS

- Regular exercise, a sensible, healthy diet, and weight control are essential for long-term management of diabetes.
- Hot baths may be beneficial to regulate pancreatic functions.
- Avoid smoking and drinking.

CASE STUDIES

- R.C., a 55-year-old male, presented with high blood sugar. Objective findings included being overweight as well as pain in the right heel, which was the reason he couldn't work out. Pulse was soft and his tongue was red with a center crack. The practitioner diagnosed this condition as Spleen qi deficiency with damp accumulation; his Western diagnosis was pre-diabetes. Upon diagnosis the patient was given ***Equilibrium*** for treatment. With taking the herbs and receiving acupuncture for two weeks, the patient saw improvement overall, which lead to increase in energy and being able to run again. Two weeks after, the patient had received blood work confirming everything was normal and he didn't have to return until another year. The patient was very pleased. Submitted by T.W., Perrysburg, Ohio.
- L.M., a 72-year-old female, presented with high blood pressure, being stressed and overwhelmed. She had also mentioned having an intense sugar craving. The TCM diagnosis was Kidney yin deficiency with Liver yin deficiency. Gallbladder damp-heat and Liver yang rising was also present. ***Equilibrium*** was prescribed for treatment. In response to taking the herbs for two months, her cravings were controlled and her blood sugar level started to maintain from 250 to 140 mg/dL. Submitted by V.G., Virginia Beach, Virginia.
- A 45-year-old female with type I diabetes mellitus presented with night sweats and aching feet with a blood sugar level of 200 to 300 mg/dL. The practitioner diagnosed her condition as Kidney yin deficiency. Within one week of taking ***Equilibrium***, the patient's blood sugar level dropped so drastically that she needed to ingest some sugar in order to elevate her blood sugar level. Her condition stabilized during the second week of treatment at which point her blood sugar level reading was around 160 mg/dL. Surprisingly, her night sweats also subsided. Submitted by S.T., Morgan Hill, California.
- J.K., a 45-year-old female, was 5' 3" and weighed 160 pounds. She had urinary tract infections once or twice each month within the last 12 months. Her other symptoms and signs included constant thirst, increased fluid intake, and increased frequency and volume of urination. She was diagnosed with diabetes mellitus after testing positive for high levels of blood glucose. She was prescribed ***Equilibrium***, 4 capsules three times daily before meals. Two weeks after the initial treatment, she reported significant improvement of her signs and symptoms. Two months after the initial treatment, her blood glucose levels were within the ideal range. She did not have any urinary tract infections during these two months. She continues to take ***Equilibrium***,

Equilibrium ™

4 capsules three times daily before meals. Submitted by J.C., Diamond Bar, California.

- A 45-year-old female with type I diabetes mellitus presented with malaise, fatigue, night sweats, hot flashes and low back pain. Other signs and symptoms included abdominal bloating, red eyes, weak nails and a pale complexion. She was diagnosed with hepatitis C. The practitioner prescribed ***Liver DTX*** (3 capsules three times daily) and ***Equilibrium*** (3 capsules three times daily). The treatment regimen also integrated a pancreatic homeopathic prescription (10 drops six times a day) as well as another homeopathic prescription, Hepan Comp (1 drop three times daily). Two and a half months later, the patient was able to cease her insulin intake. Once her viral load reached a normal range, she discontinued taking all her prescribed pharmaceuticals. There was a total reversal of her clinical picture. Submitted by I.B., Miami, Florida.
- A 49-year-old male computer analyst presented with chronic skin lesions over his entire body. Visual inspection of his body exposed scars from past lesions as well as fresh, red, edematous sores especially on the lower extremities. The severity of his lesions appeared to fluctuate. He also complained of pain in both legs and right arm, which were all indicative of peripheral neuropathy. He was diagnosed with type I diabetes mellitus and had a history of kidney problems. The patient was also reported to be overweight. His tongue was dusky with purple veins on the underside. His tongue coating was scanty and his pulse was deep, weak, thready, and slippery. The practitioner diagnosed the patient's condition as Liver and Kidney yin deficiencies, qi deficiency, damp-heat in the skin, and qi and blood stagnation. Along with acupuncture, the patient started a combination of ***Equilibrium*** and ***Silerex*** at one-third the dose since he was on a large variety of other herbal treatments. After one week, no improvement of his lesions was noted and fluctuations of his blood sugar levels were minimal. After the second week, the herbal dose was increased to two-thirds the recommended dose. The patient's lesions slightly improved along with the blood sugar levels. The severity of the arm and leg pain also decreased. His pulse was also noticeably stronger. The practitioner concluded that some of the symptoms might have been due to other medications, which were taken concurrently by the patient. Nevertheless, the practitioner hypothesized that by clearing the skin condition, the patient would eventually decrease use of other skin medications. Submitted by N.M., Torrance, CA.
- A.G., a 60-year-old male, was 6' 1" and weighed 280 pounds. He was always hungry and ate two or three bowls of rice with every meal. He noticed that his cuts or scratches required a longer period of time to heal, sometimes up to one month. His diagnoses were diabetes mellitus and high cholesterol. He was given ***Equilibrium***, 4 capsules three times daily for his diabetes; and ***Cholisma***, 4 capsules three times daily for his cholesterol. After taking the herbs for three months, his blood glucose levels were within the ideal range and his cholesterol level dropped from 260 to 220 mg/dL. His weight also dropped from 280 to 255 pounds. He ate less and did not feel constantly hungry. He continues to take both ***Equilibrium*** and ***Cholisma***. Submitted by J.C., Diamond Bar, California.

PHARMACOLOGICAL AND CLINICAL RESEARCH

Equilibrium is formulated to treat diabetes mellitus by helping the body to regulate blood glucose levels and manage symptoms such as polyuria, polydipsia and polyphagia. It contains many herbs with marked effects to stimulate production and release of insulin, reduce blood glucose levels, and decrease insulin resistance. Furthermore, it also utilizes many herbs to treat common complications of diabetes mellitus, such as diabetic nephropathy, diabetic microalbuminuria, chronic glomerulonephritis, and neurotoxicity.

Huang Qi (Radix Astragali) has multiple benefits to manage plasma glucose and diabetes mellitus. Use of *Huang Qi* (Radix Astragali) is associated with a marked effect to lower plasma glucose levels and alleviate insulin resistance. The antihyperglycemic action appears to be due to increased production and release of insulin.[2] Other benefits of *Huang Qi* (Radix Astragali) include antiobesity and hypolipidemia activities.[3] *Zhi Mu* (Rhizoma Anemarrhenae) also has a significant antidiabetic effect. Therapeutic benefits include increased insulin secretion,[4] decreased insulin resistance,[5] and prevention of pancreatic atrophy.[6,7] *Shan Yao* (Rhizoma Dioscoreae) has an antidiabetic effect, and is effective in controlling the normally sharp increase of blood glucose following intraperitoneal injection of glucose.[8] *Xi Yang Shen* (Radix Panacis Quinquefolii) has exhibited significant hypoglycemic activity in normal and hyperglycemic subjects.[9] Finally, *Bai Zhu* (Rhizoma Atractylodis Macrocephalae) and *Cang Zhu* (Rhizoma Atractylodis) have antidiabetic effects and have been shown to decrease blood glucose levels.[10,11]

Clinically, these herbs have been used in many studies to treat diabetes mellitus. According to one study, one formula with *Xi Yang Shen* (Radix Panacis Quinquefolii) showed a 77% rate of effectiveness to lower plasma glucose levels in 105 patients.[12] According to another study, adult onset diabetes mellitus was treated with a 92% rate of effectiveness using an herbal formula that contained *Cang Zhu* (Rhizoma Atractylodis), *Huang Qi* (Radix Astragali), *Shan Yao* (Rhizoma Dioscoreae), *Xuan Shen* (Radix Scrophulariae) and others. Of 52 patients, 25 had complete recovery, 23 had improvement, and 4 had no effect.[13]

Equilibrium uses many herbs to treat several common complications of diabetes mellitus, such as microvascular, neurological, and renal complications. *Dan Shen* (Radix et Rhizoma Salviae Miltiorrhizae) and *Hong Hua* (Flos Carthami) have powerful effects to promote blood circulation and inhibit the aggregation of platelets and formation of thrombi.[14] Together, they effectively manage microvascular complications of diabetes. *Shan Yao* (Rhizoma Dioscoreae) and *Huang Qi* (Radix Astragali) have neuroprotective and neurological effects. Administration of *Shan Yao* (Rhizoma Dioscoreae) shows significant protection against drug-induced neurotoxicity, according to *in vivo* and *in vitro* studies.[15] Use of *Huang Qi* (Radix Astragali) is associated with a marked enhancement of the growth of axons in the peripheral nerve, according to *in vitro* and *in vivo* studies in subjects with nerve defects.[16] *Huang Qi* (Radix Astragali) is one of the most effective nephroprotective herbs.[17] *Huang Qi* exerts its nephroprotective effect by reducing fasting blood glucose and albuminuria levels, reversing the glomerular hyperfiltration state, and ameliorating the pathological changes of early diabetic nephropathy.[18] Clinically, *Huang Qi* (Radix Astragali) has been shown in clinical studies to successfully treat diabetic nephropathy,[19] diabetic microalbuminuria,[20] chronic glomerulonephritis,[21] and drug-induced nephrotoxicity.[22]

In summary, ***Equilibrium*** is an effective formula for treating diabetes mellitus and many of its complications.

COMPARATIVE ANALYSIS

Diabetes mellitus is one of the most common disorders in developed countries. The disease is well understood, and there are numerous treatment options. For type I diabetes (juvenile onset), insulin is the drug of choice. For type II (adult onset), drug treatment usually begins with oral medications, followed by insulin if necessary. Oral medications, such as Glucotrol (glipizide) and Diabeta (glyburide), are beneficial to control blood glucose levels, but may cause side effects such as seizures, loss of consciousness, skin rash, itching or redness, exaggerated sunburn, yellowing of the skin or eyes, light-colored stools, dark urine, unusual bleeding or bruising, fever, and sore throat. Furthermore, long-term use of these medications may lead to weight gain and insulin resistance, thereby decreasing overall effectiveness. Insulin is an effective and reliable drug to control blood glucose. However, once insulin injection therapy begins, endogenous production of insulin slowly decreases and the body becomes more and more dependent on exogenous sources. Eventually, the patient will become dependent on insulin for life. Lastly, there are many complications of diabetes mellitus. Some are well controlled by drugs, others are not.

Many herbs effectively treat both diabetes and its complications. For diabetes, herbs have shown marked effects to stimulate the endocrine system, increase production of insulin from the pancreas, and control blood glucose. Furthermore, many herbs are effective to alleviate symptoms of diabetes, such as thirst, hunger, frequent urination, and other manifestations of *xiao ke* (wasting and thirsting) syndrome. Lastly, as described in this monograph, many other formulas may be used as adjuncts to successfully treat complications of diabetes. However, herbal therapy has its limitations. Because herbs work primarily by stimulating the pancreas to produce insulin, it is only effective for type II diabetes. Therefore, for type I diabetic patients, herbs should be used to manage complications, but herbs cannot cure diabetes itself.

For type I diabetic patients, insulin must be used for diabetes, and both drugs and herbs may be used to treat complications. For type II diabetes patients, both drugs and herbs may be used to treat both the disease and complications. Optimal treatment requires integration of both medicines and selection of the most effective agents with the least number of side effects.

References

1. Chan K, Lo AC, Yeung JH, Woo KS. Journal of Pharmacy and Pharmacology 1995 May;47(5):402-406.
2. Ma W, Nomura M, Takahashi-Nishioka T, Kobayashi S. Combined effects of fangchinoline from Stephania tetrandra Radix and formononetin and calycosin from Astragalus membranaceus Radix on hyperglycemia and hypoinsulinemia in streptozotocin-diabetic mice. Biol Pharm Bull. 2007 Nov;30(11):2079-83.
3. Mao XQ, Yu F, Wang N, Wu Y, Zou F, Wu K, Liu M, Ouyang JP. Hypoglycemic effect of polysaccharide enriched extract of Astragalus membranaceus in diet induced insulin resistant C57BL/6J mice and its potential mechanism. Department of Pathophysiology, Medical College of Wuhan University, Hubei Provincial Key Laboratory of Allergy and Immune-Related Diseases, Wuhan, China. Phytomedicine. 2009 May;16(5):416-25.
4. Hoa NK, Phan DV, Thuan ND, Ostenson CG. Insulin secretion is stimulated by ethanol extract of Anemarrhena asphodeloides in isolated islet of healthy Wistar and diabetic Goto-Kakizaki Rats. Department of Pharmacology, Hanoi Medical University, Hanoi, Vietnam. Exp Clin Endocrinol Diabetes. 2004 Oct;112(9):520-5.
5. Miura T, Ichiki H, Iwamoto N, Kato M, Kubo M, Sasaki H, Okada M, Ishida T, Seino Y, Tanigawa K. Antidiabetic activity of the rhizoma of Anemarrhena asphodeloides and active components, mangiferin and its glucoside. Department of Clinical Nutrition, Suzuka University of Medical Science, Mie, Japan. Biol Pharm Bull. 2001 Sep;24(9):1009-11.
6. *Ri Ben Yao Wu Xue Za Zhi* (Japan Journal of Pharmacology), 1971; 67(6):223p.
7. *Planta med*, 1985; 51(2):100.
8. *Zhong Guo Yao Ke Da Xue Xue Bao* (Journal of University of Chinese Herbology), 1991; 22(3):158.
9. Oshima Y, Sato K, Hikino H. Isolation and hypoglycemic activity of quinquefolans A, B, and C, glycans of Panax quinquefolium roots. Pharmaceutical Institute, Tohoku University, Sendai, Japan. J Nat Prod. 1987 Mar-Apr;50(2):188-90.
10. Shan J.J. & Tian G.Y. Studies on physico-chemical properties and hypoglycemic activity of complex polysaccharide AMP-B from *Atractylodes macrocephala* Koidz. *Yao Xue Xue Bao.* 2003, 38(6): 438-441.
11. *Zhong Hua Yi Xue Za Zhi* (Chinese Journal of Medicine), 19858; 44(2):150.
12. *Zhong Yao Lin Chuan Xin Yong* (New Clinical Applications of Chinese Medicine), 2001; 257.
13. *Zhong Yao Lin Chuan Xin Yong* (New Clinical Applications of Chinese Medicine), 2001; 309.
14. Zhang RJ, You C, Cai BW, Wan Y, He M, Li H. Effect of compound Salvia injection on blood coagulation in patients with traumatic cerebral infarction. Zhongguo Zhong Xi Yi Jie He Za Zhi. 2004 Oct;24(10):882-4.
15. Yang MH, Yoon KD, Chin YW, Park JH, Kim SH, Kim YC, Kim J. Neuroprotective effects of Dioscorea opposita on scopolamine-induced memory impairment in in vivo behavioral tests and in vitro assays. College of Pharmacy and Research Institute of Pharmaceutical Science, Seoul National University, Seoul, Republic of Korea. J Ethnopharmacol. 2009 Jan 12;121(1):130-4.
16. Lu MC, Yao CH, Wang SH, Lai YL, Tsai CC, Chen YS. Effect of Astragalus membranaceus in rats on peripheral nerve regeneration: in vitro and in vivo studies. School of Post Baccalaureate Chinese Medicine, Changhua Christian Hospital, Changhua. J Trauma. 2010 Feb;68(2):434-40.

17. *Zhong Guo Sheng Li Ke Xue Hui, Di Er Ci Hui* (Chinese Convention on Biophysiology, 2nd Annual Convention), 1963:63.
18. Zhang J, Xie X, Li C, Fu P. Systematic review of the renal protective effect of Astragalus membranaceus (root) on diabetic nephropathy in animal models. Department of Nephrology, West China Hospital of Sichuan University, Chengdu 610041, China. J Ethnopharmacol. 2009 Nov 12;126(2):189-96.
19. Li M, Wang W, Xue J, Gu Y, Lin S. Meta-analysis of the clinical value of Astragalus membranaceus in diabetic nephropathy. Division of Nephrology, Huashan Hospital, Fudan University, Shanghai, China. J Ethnopharmacol. 2010 Oct 13.
20. Lu ZM, Yu YR, Tang H, Zhang XX. The protective effects of Radix Astragali and Rhizoma Ligustici chuanxiong on endothelial dysfunction in type 2 diabetic patients with microalbuminuria. Sichuan Da Xue Xue Bao Yi Xue Ban. 2005 Jul;36(4):529-32.
21. *Zhong Xi Yi Jie He Za Zhi* (Journal of Integrated Chinese and Western Medicine), 1987; 7:403.
22. Xuan W, Dong M, Dong M. Annals of Otology, Rhinology and Laryngology 1995 May;104(5):374-80.

Flex (CD)™

CLINICAL APPLICATIONS

- **Chronic cold-type of arthritis or arthralgia that worsens with cold and damp weather**
- **Chronic low back pain and sciatica with underlying deficiencies**
- **Degenerative disorders** with weakness of the lower back and knees with reduced mobility
- **General aches and pains** characterized by cold manifestations
- **Fibromyalgia** characterized by cold or numbness

WESTERN THERAPEUTIC ACTIONS

- Analgesic function to relieve pain
- Anti-inflammatory function to reduce swelling and inflammation
- Antirheumatic and antiarthritic effects to treat connective tissue disorders
- Chondroprotective and osteogenic functions to strengthen soft connective tissues and repair joints

CHINESE THERAPEUTIC ACTIONS

- Expels wind, cold and damp
- Warms channels and collaterals, disperses painful obstruction
- Tonifies Kidney yin and yang
- Invigorates the blood circulation and relieves pain

DOSAGE

Take 3 to 4 capsules three times daily with a glass of warm water. The dosage may be increased up to 6 capsules every six hours as needed for pain.

INGREDIENTS

Bai Shao (Radix Paeoniae Alba)
Chuan Niu Xi (Radix Cyathulae)
Chuan Xiong (Rhizoma Chuanxiong)
Dang Gui Wei (Extremitas Radix Angelicae Sinensis)
Di Huang (Radix Rehmanniae)
Du Huo (Radix Angelicae Pubescentis)
Du Zhong (Cortex Eucommiae)
Fang Feng (Radix Saposhnikoviae)
Ji Xue Teng (Caulis Spatholobi)
Qian Nian Jian (Rhizoma Homalomenae)
Qin Jiao (Radix Gentianae Macrophyllae)
Ren Shen (Radix et Rhizoma Ginseng)
Sang Ji Sheng (Herba Taxilli)
Wei Ling Xian (Radix et Rhizoma Clematidis)
Wu Jia Pi (Cortex Acanthopanacis)
Yan Hu Suo (Rhizoma Corydalis)
Zhi Cao Wu (Radix Aconiti Kusnezoffii Praeparata)
Zhi Chuan Wu (Radix Aconiti Praeparata)

BACKGROUND

Musculoskeletal and connective tissue disorders are major causes of pain and physical disability. Causes of these bone, muscle, and joint disorders vary greatly, depending on the exact disease. Simple causes include trauma and external injuries, such as pulled muscles, strained ligaments, dislocated joints, and bone fractures. Complicated causes include infection, autoimmune disorders, crystal-induced inflammation, and non-inflammatory tissue degeneration. Optimal treatment must address the symptom (pain and inflammation) and the underlying causes. After the disorder is stabilized, physical therapy and exercise are important to maintain flexibility and strengthen surrounding muscles.

FORMULA EXPLANATION

Flex (CD) is formulated specifically to treat musculoskeletal disorders characterized by cold and dampness. It contains herbs with functions to eliminate cold and dampness, tonify Kidney yin and yang, warm up channels and collaterals, activate qi and blood circulation, and relieve pain.

Du Huo (Radix Angelicae Pubescentis), *Qin Jiao* (Radix Gentianae Macrophyllae), and *Fang Feng* (Radix Saposhnikoviae) have antirheumatic, anti-inflammatory, and analgesic functions. They expel wind, dampness, and cold from the lower back, and remove painful obstruction. *Du Zhong* (Cortex Eucommiae), *Di Huang* (Radix Rehmanniae), *Chuan Niu Xi* (Radix Cyathulae), and *Sang Ji Sheng* (Herba Taxilli) replenish the vital essence of the Liver and the Kidney, which are responsible for strengthening the bones, sinews, and the muscles of the lower back and knees. *Bai Shao* (Radix Paeoniae Alba) has analgesic, antispasmodic, and anti-inflammatory effects. *Wei Ling Xian* (Radix et Rhizoma Clematidis), *Yan Hu Suo* (Rhizoma Corydalis), *Dang Gui Wei* (Extremitas Radix Angelicae Sinensis), *Chuan Xiong* (Rhizoma Chuanxiong), *Qian Nian Jian* (Rhizoma Homalomenae), *Wu Jia Pi* (Cortex Acanthopanacis), and *Ji Xue Teng* (Caulis Spatholobi) increase qi and blood circulation to the extremities to relax the muscles and the tendons. *Ren Shen* (Radix et Rhizoma Ginseng) and *Wu Jia Pi* (Cortex Acanthopanacis) tonify qi and address the underlying deficiencies. *Zhi Cao Wu* (Radix Aconiti Kusnezoffii Praeparata) and *Zhi Chuan Wu* (Radix Aconiti Praeparata) restore Kidney yang, dispel cold, and warm up the channels and collaterals to relieve pain.

In summary, the herbs in ***Flex (CD)*** dispel cold and dampness to treat various types of musculoskeletal and connective tissue disorders.

CAUTIONS & CONTRAINDICATIONS

- Side effects of this herbal formula may include nausea, vomiting, stomach discomfort and irritability. Discontinue using this formula if these adverse reactions occur.
- Do not use this formula if the patient presents with heat signs such as redness, burning or inflammation of the joints that worsens with heat.
- This formula is contraindicated during pregnancy and nursing.
- This herbal formula contains herbs that invigorate blood circulation, such as *Dang Gui Wei* (Extremitas Radix Angelicae Sinensis). Therefore, patients who are on anticoagulant or

Flex (CD)™

antiplatelet therapies, such as Coumadin (warfarin), should use this formula with caution, or not at all, as there may be a higher risk of bleeding and bruising.[1,2,3]

- Patients who wear a pacemaker, take antiarrhythmic drugs or cardiac glycosides, such as Lanoxin (digoxin), and have pre-existing cardiovascular problems should not take this formula. *Zhi Cao Wu* (Radix Aconiti Kusnezoffii Praeparata) and *Zhi Chuan Wu* (Radix Aconiti Praeparata) may interact with these drugs by affecting the rhythm and potentiating the contractile strength of the heart.[4]

CLINICAL NOTES

- Avoid exposure to rain, wind, and cold weather whenever possible.
- Always wear warm clothes and cover up the body and joints.
- Ice packs should never be used in patients with joint pain due to coldness and pain. Use heat pads instead.

Pulse Diagnosis by Dr. Jimmy Wei-Yen Chang:

- **Knee and ankle joint arthritis:** left *yangwei* pulse, which is an extra meridian pulse found distal to the *cun* position towards the thumb

SUPPLEMENTARY FORMULAS

- For neck and shoulder pain, add ***Neck & Shoulder (AC)*** or ***Neck & Shoulder (CR)***.
- For lower back pain, combine with ***Back Support (AC)*** or ***Back Support (CR)***.
- For herniated disk in the back with swelling and inflammation, add ***Back Support (HD)***.
- For arm pain, add ***Arm Support***.
- For knee pain, add ***Knee & Ankle (AC)*** or ***Knee & Ankle (CR)***.
- For spasms and cramps, combine with ***Flex (SC)***.
- For bone fractures, injuries, and bruises, combine with ***Flex (TMX)***.
- For post-stroke numbness and atrophy, use ***Neuro Plus***.
- For bone spurs, add ***Flex (SPR)***.
- For prevention and treatment of osteoporosis, add ***Osteo 8***.
- For degeneration of muscles, ligaments and tendons, combine with ***Flex (MLT)***.
- To potentiate the effect to relieve pain, add ***Herbal ANG***.
- For arthritic pain with inflammation, swelling, redness and pain, use ***Flex (Heat)*** instead.
- With severe Kidney yin or yang deficiency, combine with ***Kidney Tonic (Yin)*** or ***Kidney Tonic (Yang)***, respectively.

ACUPUNCTURE TREATMENT

Traditional Points:

- Moxa and needle *ah shi* points.

Classic Master Tung's Points:

- Needle contralateral to the pain. If the pain is in the center, needle bilaterally or the side with the more *ah shi* points. If the pain is bilateral, needle bilaterally.
- **General arthritis:** *Tianhuang* (T 88.13), *Minghuang* (T 88.12), *Fugesan* (T 44.30)*, *Simazhong* (T 88.17), *Dihuang* (T 77.19), *Jianzhong* (T 44.06), *Wuhu* (T 11.27). Bleed the affected area.
- **Arthritis (legs):** *Minghuang* (T 88.12), *Tianhuang* (T 88.13), *Qihuang* (T 88.14), *Zhongjiuli* (T 88.25), *Jianzhong* (T 44.06), *Wuhu* (T 11.27). Bleed dark veins on the legs. Bleed before needling for best result.
- **Arthritis (degenerative):** *Wanshunyi* (T 22.08), *Wanshuner* (T 22.09), *Simashang* (T 88.18), *Minghuang* (T 88.12), *Tianhuangfu [Shenguan]* (T 77.18), *Wuhu* (T 11.27). Bleed the affected area.

Master Tung's Points by Dr. Chuan-Min Wang:

- **Cold, damp *bi zheng* (painful obstruction syndrome), arthritis, fibromyalgia**
  - Shoulder: Needle contralaterally *Jianzhong* (T 44.06), *Shangjiuli* (T 88.26).
  - Elbow: Needle contralaterally *Cesanli* (T 77.22), *Cexiasanli* (T 77.23). Needle ipsilaterally *Huofuhai* (T 33.07), *Xinmen* (T 33.12).
  - Wrist: Needle contralaterally *Tung's Wantong* (T 66.16)*. Needle ipsilaterally *Huochuan* (T 33.04).
  - Knee: Needle contralaterally *Jianzhong* (T 44.06), *Tongguan* (T 88.01), *Tongshan* (T 88.02).
  - Ankle: Needle contralaterally *Zhongbai* (T 22.06), *Xiabai* (T 22.07). Needle ipsilaterally *Xuanzhong* (GB 39) for lateral ankle, *Sizhi* (T 77.20) for medial ankle.
  - Ankle not able to flex or extend: Needle contralaterally *Xiaqu* (T 44.15), *Shangqu* (T 44.16), *Zhongbai* (T 22.06), *Xiabai* (T 22.07), *Wuhu* 5 (T 11.27). Needle ipsilaterally *Zuwujin* (T 77.25).
  - Finger: Needle contralaterally *Tongshan* (T 88.02), *Tongtian* (T 88.03). Needle ipsilaterally *Huochuan* (T 33.04).

Balance Method by Dr. Richard Tan:

- Use Dr. Tan's Balance Method accordingly as determined by where the pain is (use mirror or image system).

Ear Acupuncture:

- Related joints, Adrenal Glands.
- Embed magnetic ear balls and switch ear every three days.

Auricular Medicine by Dr. Li-Chun Huang:

- Spleen, Liver, Kidney, *San Jiao*, Allergic Area, Endocrine, Adrenal Gland, and corresponding points to the affected area. Bleed Ear Apex.

NUTRITION

- Sulfur helps the absorption of calcium, and adequate intake and absorption of calcium is essential for the repair and the rebuilding of bones, tendons, cartilage, and connective tissues. Patients are encouraged to consume foods high in sulfur such as asparagus, eggs, fresh garlic, and onions.

Flex (CD)™

- Histidine, an amino acid, is responsible for removing the high levels of copper and iron found in arthritic patients. Patients are encouraged to consume foods high in histidine such as rice, wheat, and rye.
- Fresh pineapples are recommended as they contain bromelain, an enzyme that is excellent in reducing inflammation.
- Patients with gout should increase their intake of cherries and strawberries. Both of them are excellent in neutralizing uric acid. Increase the intake of water, as it helps to flush out uric acid.
- Foods that contain purines or uric acid, such as meat, anchovies, herring, meat gravies and broths, mushrooms, mussels, sardines, sweetbreads, and fried foods, should be avoided. Alcohol also increases the production of uric acid and should also be avoided.
- Avoid cold beverages, uncooked foods, ice cream, caffeine, sugar, tomatoes, milk, dairy products, and red meat.
- Intake of sour food, drinks or fruits (citrus) should be decreased as its nature constricts and may contribute to further stagnation in the channels and collaterals.
- Fish oil may help to alleviate pain associated with rheumatoid arthritis. It can be taken in conjunction with the herbs.

The Tao of Nutrition by Dr. Maoshing Ni and Cathy McNease:

- Recommendations: garlic, green onions, pepper, black beans, sesame seeds, chicken, lamb, mustard greens, ginger, and a small amount of rice wine (if individual does not have hypertension).
- Rub garlic or ginger on the painful areas. Or moxa could be burned on a slice of ginger over the painful areas.
- Drink scallion tea and rub it on the painful areas.
- Rub rice wine on the painful areas and drink one small glassful in the evening.
- Drink grape vine tea added to red wine.
- Make tea from parsnip, cinnamon, black pepper, and dried ginger.
- Avoid cold foods, raw foods, and cold weather elements.

LIFESTYLE INSTRUCTIONS

- Weight loss is strongly recommended in individuals who are overweight. This lessens the pressure on the joints, which can then help in relieving pain.
- Exercise is recommended. However, sports such as swimming or skiing that expose affected joints to cold and dampness should be avoided.

CASE STUDIES

- F.L., a 57-year-old female, presented with fibromyalgia. It was also noted that she had a tendency to feel cold all the time. Her TCM diagnosis was Spleen qi deficiency with damp, in addition to Kidney yin and yang deficiencies. For treatment, ***Flex (CD)*** was prescribed. The patient took the herbs with good results and continued to take the formula for two years to maintain the results. She no longer felt cold and, overall, had less pain as long as she followed the nutritional guidance as well. The patient was very pleased with the results. Submitted by V.G., Virginia Beach, Virginia.
- P.M., an 89-year-old male, presented with chronic back pain and sciatica for the past four months. He also experienced two other episodes of the same type of pain, once after sitting outside in cold weather for a football game and the other at the funeral for his wife. The pain was in both legs and knees, down the sides of the legs and into the buttocks. Right leg pain was worse than the left. Knee pain was bilateral. Pitting edema on both ankles was noticed. His blood pressure was 130/80 mmHg and the heart rate was 80 beats per minute. Trigger points were felt at the left quadratus lumborum and glute, L3, and L4 areas. In general, he was a very healthy and active 89-year old. The diagnoses were *bi zheng* (painful obstruction syndrome) due to cold, Kidney qi deficiency, and qi and blood stagnation on the Gallbladder channel. ***Flex (CD)*** was prescribed at 4 capsules twice a day. He had a total of three acupuncture visits and felt 90% better. He then planned a European walking vacation so he can get better even faster to avoid seeing a physical therapist. Submitted by M.H., West Palm Beach, Florida.
- C.M., a 48-year-old female, presented with joint pain (hands, feet, knees) that worsened in cold and rainy weather. She also had a family history of arthritis and osteoporosis. She also suffered from tendonitis of both forearms. She had decreased range of motion, with calcification of joints in her fingers. Her Western diagnosis was rheumatoid arthritis; the TCM diagnosis was cold and damp obstruction. ***Osteo 8*** and ***Flex (CD)*** were prescribed at four capsules each, twice daily. Within one day, the symptoms began improving. After one week, joints and tendons were not stiff, and almost pain free. During the winter (the season in which her condition usually deteriorated), the symptoms even improved. The patient reported later that if she stopped taking the herbs, the symptoms returned. Submitted by C.D., Phoenix, Oregon
- A 73-year-old female daycare worker presented with constant pain in the low back, right hip, and right knee due to osteoarthritis. Her pain was aggravated especially after any type of activity or prolonged sitting. Sharp pain was also elicited upon walking. Other signs and symptoms included fatigue, dizziness, and an intermittent high blood pressure. Her tongue body appeared red with a scanty tongue coating. Her left pulse was irregular, hesitant and thready at the Liver and Kidney positions. The right pulse was choppy, irregular, and weak at the Spleen position. The practitioner diagnosed her condition as Kidney and Liver yin deficiencies, qi and blood stagnation, and damp-cold *bi zheng* (painful obstruction syndrome) in the joints. Along with acupuncture treatment, the patient was instructed to take ***Flex (CD)*** at 3 spoonfuls, two times a day. The patient experienced a reduction in joint pain by almost 30%. Submitted by N.M., Torrance, California.
- A 63-year-old female homemaker presented with sciatica-like pain in the lumbar and left sacral region, which was worse in

Flex (CD)™

the evening and cold to the touch. The patient also reported swelling in her left ankle, which was also cold upon palpation and had been the source of her chronic pain for almost a year. She mentioned that her cold symptoms were relieved by warmth. A disc herniation was also diagnosed at her L3 to L4 lumbar level. Her tongue was thin, red with a thick tongue coat especially at the base. The pulse was tight and deep. The practitioner diagnosed this case as Liver and Kidney yin deficiencies, Kidney yang deficiency, and wind-damp *bi zheng* (painful obstruction syndrome). The patient was given ***Flex (CD)*** at 3 capsules three times daily. A significant decrease in pain level was quite evident during the initial treatment. Although the patient did experience minor indigestion in the beginning, the side effect resolved after only a short while. After taking three bottles of ***Flex (CD)***, the patient felt her pain was manageable enough that she was able to return to exercising in order to prevent further relapse. Submitted by J.T., Kingsport, Tennessee.

PHARMACOLOGICAL AND CLINICAL RESEARCH

Flex (CD) treats musculoskeletal and connective tissue disorders with cold and damp manifestations. ***Flex (CD)*** contains herbs with strong analgesic, anti-inflammatory, antirheumatic, chondroprotective, and osteogenic functions.

Yan Hu Suo (Rhizoma Corydalis) is one of the strongest and most potent herbs for treatment of pain. Its effects are well documented in both historical references and modern research studies. According to classical texts, *Yan Hu Suo* (Rhizoma Corydalis) has been shown to treat chest and hypochondriac pain, epigastric and abdominal pain, hernial pain, amenorrhea or menstrual pain, and pain of the extremities. According to laboratory studies, the extract of *Yan Hu Suo* (Rhizoma Corydalis) has been found to be effective in both acute and chronic phases of inflammation. The mechanism of its anti-inflammatory effect is attributed to its effect to inhibit the release of histamine and pro-inflammatory mediators.[5,6] Furthermore, it has a strong analgesic effect. With adjustment in dosage, the potency of *Yan Hu Suo* (Rhizoma Corydalis) has been compared to that of morphine. In fact, the analgesic effect of *Yan Hu Suo* (Rhizoma Corydalis) is so strong and reliable that it has been used with satisfactory anesthetic effect in 98 out of 105 patients (93.4%) who underwent surgery.[7] The analgesic effect can be potentiated further with concurrent acupuncture therapy. In one research study, it is demonstrated that the analgesic effect is increased significantly with concurrent treatments using *Yan Hu Suo* (Rhizoma Corydalis) and electro-acupuncture, when compared to a control group, which received electro-acupuncture only.[8] Overall, it is well understood that *Yan Hu Suo* (Rhizoma Corydalis) has a marked effect to treat pain. Though the maximum analgesic effect of *Yan Hu Suo* (Rhizoma Corydalis) is not as strong as morphine, it has been determined that the herb is much safer, with significantly fewer side effects, less risk of tolerance, and no evidence of physical dependence even with long-term use.[9]

Flex (CD) also contains many herbs with excellent antirheumatic and anti-inflammatory effects to treat arthritic and inflammatory disorders. *Du Huo* (Radix Angelicae Pubescentis) and *Sang Ji Sheng* (Herba Taxilli), two herbs commonly used together, have antirheumatic and anti-inflammatory functions and are especially effective in treating general body aches and pains.[10,11] *Wei Ling Xian* (Radix et Rhizoma Clematidis) has marked antiarthritic and antirheumatic activities, as the herbs have been shown to significantly inhibit proinflammatory compounds and prevent rheumatoid arthritis.[12] *Dang Gui* (Radix Angelicae Sinensis) exerts both analgesic and anti-inflammatory effects through the inhibition of pro-inflammatory mediators, including nitric oxide and prostaglandin E2 in peritoneal macrophages.[13,14] In comparison with acetylsalicylic acid, the anti-inflammatory effect of *Dang Gui* (Radix Angelicae Sinensis) is approximately 1.1 times stronger, and its analgesic effect is approximately 1.7 times stronger.[15] *Chuan Xiong* (Rhizoma Chuanxiong) illustrates an anti-inflammatory effect via an inhibitory activity on TNF-α production and TNF-α bioactivity, and shows a promising effect to treat inflammation and related diseases.[16] *Du Zhong* (Cortex Eucommiae) demonstrates marked anti-inflammatory effects through its stimulating effect on the endocrine system and consequent secretion of steroids from the adrenal cortex.[17] *Fang Feng* (Radix Saposhnikoviae) shows a marked effect to suppress inflammation via the inhibition of nitrite production by inducible nitric oxide synthase.[18] *Ji Xue Teng* (Caulis Spatholobi) exhibits an anti-inflammatory effect through its inhibitory activities against a panel of key enzymes relating to inflammation, including cyclo-oxygenase, phospholipase, and lipoxygenase.[19] Lastly, *Di Huang* (Radix Rehmanniae) has an anti-inflammatory effect to reduce swelling and inflammation.[20] The mechanism of action is attributed to its influence on the endocrine system. It has been shown that the use of *Di Huang* (Radix Rehmanniae) increases the plasma levels of adrenocortical hormone, even in the presence of dexamethasone.[21] Clinically, *Di Huang* (Radix Rehmanniae) was used in an herbal formula to successfully treat 12 patients with rheumatoid arthritis.[22]

Zhi Cao Wu (Radix Aconiti Kusnezoffii Praeparata) and *Zhi Chuan Wu* (Radix Aconiti Praeparata) have excellent analgesic and anti-inflammatory properties and are commonly used to treat a wide variety of aches and pains. The analgesic effect of aconitine, a compound present in both herbs, is related to its effect on the central nervous system. The anti-inflammatory effect of aconitine is stronger than aspirin, and its mechanism of action is unrelated to the production of steroids from the adrenal glands.[23,24] Clinically, *Zhi Chuan Wu* (Radix Aconiti Praeparata) has been used successfully to treat arthritis, inflammation of the shoulder, and heel spurs.[25,26] *Zhi Cao Wu* (Radix Aconiti

Flex (CD)™

Kusnezoffii Praeparata) has been used in topical applications to effectively treat periarthritis of the shoulders and sciatica.[27,28] Furthermore, it was demonstrated in one study of 225 patients with low back pain that the use of *Zhi Chuan Wu* (Radix Aconiti Praeparata) or *Zhi Cao Wu* (Radix Aconiti Kusnezoffii Praeparata) is up to 87.4% effective in relieving pain when used on a daily basis for 10 to 15 days.[29] Lastly, *Zhi Chuan Wu* (Radix Aconiti Praeparata) and *Zhi Cao Wu* (Radix Aconiti Kusnezoffii Praeparata) have been used topically to treat frozen shoulder. Out of 35 patients, 22 reported significant improvement, 8 reported moderate improvement, 4 reported slight improvement, and 1 reported no effect.[30]

Finally, ***Flex (CD)*** incorporates herbs to repair cartilages and rebuild bones, since chronic musculoskeletal and connective tissue disorders are often associated with wear and tear of the joints. *Chuan Niu Xi* (Radix Cyathulae) shows great chondroprotection against cartilage-degrading disorders. It is an excellent herb to protect the cartilage from repetitive and stress-induced injuries.[31] *Wei Ling Xian* (Radix et Rhizoma Clematidis) has an excellent chondroprotective effect. One study showed that the saponin fraction from *Wei Ling Xian* (Radix et Rhizoma Clematidis) is effective in ameliorating joint destruction and cartilage erosion in subjects with osteoarthritis, protecting articular cartilage by preventing extracellular matrix degradation and chondrocyte injury.[32] *Dang Gui* (Radix Angelicae Sinensis) is an effective herb to promote the generation of bones. According to one study, the water extract of *Dang Gui* (Radix Angelicae Sinensis) was found to contribute to the formation of bones and treatment of bone injuries. It directly stimulates the proliferation, alkaline phosphatase activity, protein secretion, and particularly type I collagen synthesis of human osteoprecursor cells in a dose-dependent manner.[33] *Du Zhong* (Cortex Eucommiae) has significant osteogenic and antiosteoporotic effects that promote generation of new bones and prevent osteoporosis. According to a bone cell culture experiment, administration of *Du Zhong* (Cortex Eucommiae) shows a potential effect to increase the proliferation and differentiation of osteoblasts without affecting osteoclast activity. The researchers conclude that these herbs can effectively increase the rate of tissue regeneration of damaged bones.[34]

In summary, ***Flex (CD)*** is an empirical herbal formula with excellent function to treat musculoskeletal and joint disorders characterized by cold and damp.

COMPARATIVE ANALYSIS

Pain is a basic bodily sensation induced by a noxious stimulus that causes physical discomfort (such as pricking, throbbing, or aching). Pain may be of acute or chronic state, and may be of nociceptive, neuropathic, or psychogenic origin.

Non-steroidal anti-inflammatory agents (NSAID), such as Motrin (ibuprofen), Naprosyn (naproxen), and Voltaren (diclofenac) are very frequently used to treat mild to moderate pain characterized by inflammation and swelling. Clinical applications include headache, arthritis, dysmenorrhea, and general aches and pain. Though effective, they may cause such serious side effects as gastric ulcer, duodenal ulcer, gastrointestinal bleeding, tinnitus, blurred vision, dizziness, and headache. Furthermore, the newer NSAIDs, also known as COX-2 inhibitors [such as Celebrex (celecoxib)], are associated with significantly higher risk of cardiovascular events, including heart attack and stroke. In fact, these side effects are so serious that two COX-2 inhibitors have already been withdrawn from the market [Vioxx (rofecoxib) and Bextra (valdecoxib)]. In brief, it is important to remember that while drugs offer reliable and potent symptomatic pain relief, they should only be used if and when needed. Frequent use and abuse leads to unnecessary side effects and complications.

Treatment of pain is a sophisticated balance of art and science. Proper treatment of pain requires a careful evaluation of the type of disharmony (excess or deficiency, cold or heat, exterior or interior), characteristics (qi and/or blood stagnations), and location (upper body, lower body, extremities, or internal organs). Furthermore, optimal treatment requires integrative use of herbs, acupuncture, and *tui-na* therapies. All these therapies work together to tonify the underlying deficiencies, strengthen the body, and facilitate recovery from chronic pain. TCM pain management targets both the symptom and the cause of pain, and as such, often achieves immediate and long-term success. Furthermore, TCM pain management is often associated with few or no side effects.

For treatment of mild to severe pain due to various causes, TCM pain management offers similar treatment effects with significantly fewer side effects.

References

1. Chan K, Lo AC, Yeung JH, Woo KS. Journal of Pharmacy and Pharmacology 1995 May;47(5):402-6.
2. Pharmacotherapy 1999 July;19(7):870-876.
3. European Journal of Drug Metabolism and Pharmacokinetics 1995; 20(1):55-60.
4. *Forensic Science International*, 1994 June 28; 55-8.
5. *Biol Pharm Bull*, Feb 1994; 17(2):262-5.
6. Oh YC, Choi JG, Lee YS, Brice OO, Lee SC, Kwak HS, Byun YH, Kang OH, Rho JR, Shin DW, Kwon DY. Tetrahydropalmatine inhibits pro-inflammatory mediators in lipopolysaccharide-stimulated THP-1 cells. Department of Oriental Pharmacy, College of Pharmacy, Wonkwang University Wonkwang Oriental Medicines Research Institute, Iksan, Republic of Korea. J Med Food. 2010 Oct;13(5):1125-32.
7. *He Bei Xin Yi Yao* (Hebei New Medicine and Herbology), 1973; 4:34.
8. *Chen Tzu Yen Chiu* (Acupuncture Research), 1994;19(1):55-8.
9. *Zhong Yao Yao Li Yu Ying Yong* (Pharmacology and Applications of Chinese Herbs), 1983; 447.
10. Bensky, D. et al. *Chinese Herbal Medicine Formulas & Strategies*. Eastland Press. 1990.
11. Yeung, HC. *Handbook of Chinese Herbs*. Institute of Chinese Medicine. 1996.
12. Sun SX, Li YM, Fang WR, Cheng P, Liu L, Li F. Effect and mechanism of AR-6 in experimental rheumatoid arthritis. Department of Physiology, China Pharmaceutical University, 210009 Nanjing, China. Clin Exp Med. 2010 Jun;10(2):113-21.
13. *Xin Yi Yao Xue Za Zhi* (New Journal of Medicine and Herbology), 1975; (6):34.

14. Chao WW, Kuo YH, Li WC, Lin BF. The production of nitric oxide and prostaglandin E2 in peritoneal macrophages is inhibited by Andrographis paniculata, Angelica sinensis and Morus alba ethyl acetate fractions. Department of Biochemical Science and Technology, Institute of Microbiology and Biochemistry, National Taiwan University, Taipei 106, Taiwan, ROC. J Ethnopharmacol. 2009 Feb 25;122(1):68-75.
15. *Yao Xue Za Zhi* (Journal of Medicinals), 1971; (91):1098.
16. Liu L, Ning ZQ, Shan S, Zhang K, Deng T, Lu XP, Cheng YY. Phthalide Lactones from Ligusticum chuanxiong inhibit lipopolysaccharide-induced TNF-alpha production and TNF-alpha-mediated NF-kappaB Activation. Planta Med. 2005 Sep;71(9):808-13.
17. *Zhong Cao Yao* (Chinese Herbal Medicine), 1982; 13(6):24.
18. Wang CN, Shiao YJ, Kuo YH, Chen CC, Lin YL. Inducible nitric oxide synthase inhibitors from Saposhnikovia divaricata and Panax quinquefolium. Planta Med. 2000 Oct;66(7):644-7.
19. Li RW, David Lin G, Myers SP, Leach DN. Anti-inflammatory activity of Chinese medicinal vine plants. Australian Centre for Complementary Medicine Education and Research, A Joint Venture of the University of Queensland and Southern Cross University, P.O. Box 157, Lismore, NSW 2480, Australia. J Ethnopharmacol. 2003 Mar;85(1):61-7.
20. *Zhong Yao Yao Li Yu Ying Yong* (Pharmacology and Applications of Chinese Herbs), 1983: 400.
21. *Zhong Yao Xue* (Chinese Herbology), 1998; 156:158.
22. *Zhong Yao Lin Chuan Xin Yong* (New Clinical Applications of Chinese Medicine), 2001; 242-243.
23. *Xian Dai Zhong Yao Yao Li Xue* (Contemporary Pharmacology of Chinese Herbs), 1997; 425.
24. Shi H, Zhou C, Li Y, Wang G, Sun Y. Anti-inflammatory effect of aconitines. Zhongguo Zhong Yao Za Zhi. 1990 Mar;15(3):174-7, 192.
25. *Nei Meng Gu Zhong Yi Yao* (Traditional Chinese Medicine and Medicinals of Inner Mongolia), 1986; (3):7.
26. *Nei Meng Gu Zhong Yi Yao* (Traditional Chinese Medicine and Medicinals of Inner Mongolia), 1986; (3):7.
27. *Bei Jing Zhong Yi* (Beijing Chinese Medicine), 1986; (5):31.
28. *Hei Long Jiang Zhong Yi Yao* (Heilongjiang Chinese Medicine and Herbology), 1995; (5):45.
29. Military Hospital Unit #64. Effectiveness of aconite wu tou (chuan wu) in treating low back pain, a report with 225 patients. *New Journal of Medicine and Pharmacology*. 1975; 4:45.
30. Zhang, HT. et al. Treatment of frozen shoulders with aconite wu tou (chuan wu) and camphor (zhang nao). *Shanghai Journal of Medicine and Pharmacolog.* 1987; 1:29.
31. Park HY, Lim H, Kim HP, Kwon YS. Downregulation of Matrix Metalloproteinase-13 by the Root Extract of Cyathula officinalis Kuan and its Constituents in IL-1β-treated Chondrocytes. College of Pharmacy, Kangwon National University, Chunchon, Korea. Planta Med. 2011 Feb 23.
32. Wu W, Xu X, Dai Y, Xia L. Therapeutic effect of the saponin fraction from Clematis chinensis Osbeck roots on osteoarthritis induced by monosodium iodoacetate through protecting articular cartilage. Department of Pharmacology of Chinese Materia Medica, College of Traditional Chinese Medicine, China Pharmaceutical University, Nanjing. Phytother Res. 2010 Apr;24(4):538-46.
33. Yang Q, Populo SM, Zhang J, Yang G, Kodama H. Effect of Angelica sinensis on the proliferation of human bone cells. Clin Chim Acta. 2002 Oct;324(1-2): 89-97.
34. Yao CH, Tsai HM, Chen YS, Liu BS. Fabrication and evaluation of a new composite composed of tricalcium phosphate, gelatin, and Chinese medicine as a bone substitute. Institute of Biomedical Engineering and Material Science, Chungtai Institute of Health Science and Technology, Taichung, Taiwan, Republic of China. J Biomed Mater Res B Appl Biomater. 2005 Nov;75(2):277-88.

Flex (GT)™

CLINICAL APPLICATIONS

- **Gout**
- **Gouty arthritis**

WESTERN THERAPEUTIC ACTIONS

- Decreases the absorption and increases the elimination of uric acid and other unwanted substances
- Analgesic effect to relieve pain
- Anti-inflammatory effect to reduce swelling and inflammation
- Antipyretic effect to relieve burning sensations and reduce inflammation

CHINESE THERAPEUTIC ACTIONS

- Strengthens the Spleen and Stomach
- Drains damp-heat
- Opens the channels and collaterals
- Relieves pain

DOSAGE

Take 4 capsules three times daily. The herbal therapy should begin immediately upon noticing the first warning signs of gout. The dosage may be doubled on days one and two of herbal therapy to achieve faster onset of action. If necessary, this formula may be taken at reduced dosages for maintainance and prevention.

INGREDIENTS

Cang Zhu (Rhizoma Atractylodis)
Che Qian Zi (Semen Plantaginis)
Chi Shao (Radix Paeoniae Rubra)
Di Huang (Radix Rehmanniae)
He Zi (Fructus Chebulae)
Huang Bo (Cortex Phellodendri Chinensis)
Ji Xue Teng (Caulis Spatholobi)
Jin Qian Cao (Herba Lysimachiae)
Shi Gao (Gypsum Fibrosum)
Wu Bei Zi (Galla Chinensis)
Yi Yi Ren (Semen Coicis)
Ze Xie (Rhizoma Alismatis)
Zhi Mu (Rhizoma Anemarrhenae)

BACKGROUND

Gout is a form of arthritis that is characterized by sudden, severe attacks of pain, tenderness, redness, warmth and swelling (inflammation) in certain joints. Gout usually affects the large toe, but it can affect other joints in the leg (knee, ankle, and foot) and sometimes also joints in the arm (hand, wrist, and elbow). Gout is caused in part by excessive intake of food rich in uric acid, or decreased excretion of uric acid through the kidneys. As uric acid deposits in the joints, it causes severe pain known as gout.

FORMULA EXPLANATION

According to traditional Chinese medicine, gout is generally considered as *bi zheng* (painful obstruction syndrome) with damp-heat. The presence of damp-heat begins with the inability of the Spleen and Stomach to adequately transform and transport food, followed by accumulation of damp-heat blocking the channels and collaterals leading to severe pain. This correlates with the Western medicine concept of gout, which starts with improper diet followed by excessive accumulation of uric acid. Therefore, optimal treatment requires use of herbs to strengthen the Spleen and Stomach, drain damp-heat, open the channels and collaterals, and relieve pain.

In this formula, *Cang Zhu* (Rhizoma Atractylodis) and *Yi Yi Ren* (Semen Coicis) strengthen the Spleen and Stomach to resolve dampness and swelling. *Jin Qian Cao* (Herba Lysimachiae), *Ze Xie* (Rhizoma Alismatis) and *Che Qian Zi* (Semen Plantaginis) drain damp-heat and help expel uric acid from the body through urination. *Shi Gao* (Gypsum Fibrosum), *Zhi Mu* (Rhizoma Anemarrhenae), *Huang Bo* (Cortex Phellodendri Chinensis) and *Di Huang* (Radix Rehmanniae) clear heat and sedate fire. Together they reduce the inflammation and burning sensation. *Ji Xue Teng* (Caulis Spatholobi) opens the channels and collaterals. *Chi Shao* (Radix Paeoniae Rubra) activates blood circulation and relieves pain. Lastly, *He Zi* (Fructus Chebulae) and *Wu Bei Zi* (Galla Chinensis) are two astringent herbs that reduce swelling and inflammation.

In summary, ***Flex (GT)*** is a comprehensive formula that targets both the cause and the symptoms of gout. It incorporates herbs to strengthen the Spleen and Stomach, drain damp-heat, open the channels and collaterals, and relieve pain.

CAUTIONS & CONTRAINDICATIONS

- This formula should not be used in cases of deficiency and cold.
- This formula is not designed to treat acute gout attacks. It is formulated to prevent gout.
- Heat packs should not be used in patients with gout, as it is a condition characterized by heat.

CLINICAL NOTES

Pulse Diagnosis by Dr. Jimmy Wei-Yen Chang:

- Turtle pulse, a convex-shaped pulse that has a "tail" (a thin, forceful, pulse proximal to the *chi* position), is 3-D, but flat on the bottom, on the left *chi*.
- If the pulse is forceful, the condition is acute with more inflammation and greater pain.
- If the pulse is weak, the condition is chronic with less inflammation and pain.

SUPPLEMENTARY FORMULAS

- For severe pain, combine with ***Herbal ANG***.
- With severe swelling and inflammation, add ***Astringent Complex***.

Flex (GT)™

- For gout in individuals with obesity, use with ***Herbalite*** to reduce body weight.
- For gout in individuals with diabetes, use with ***Equilibrium*** to control blood glucose levels.
- For gout in individuals with hyperlipidemia, use with ***Cholisma*** to reduce cholesterol and triglyceride levels.
- For gout in individuals with obesity and high cholesterol, add ***Cholisma (ES)***.
- For gout with kidney stones, add ***Dissolve (KS)***.
- With hypertension, add ***Gastrodia Complex*** or ***Gentiana Complex***.

ACUPUNCTURE TREATMENT

Traditional Points:

- Needle *ah shi* points using the sedating technique counter-clockwise.

Classic Master Tung's Points:

- Needle contralateral to the pain. If the pain is in the center, needle bilaterally or the side with the more *ah shi* points. If the pain is bilateral, needle bilaterally.
- *Tianhuang* (T 77.17), *Dihuang* (T 77.19), *Renhuang* (T 77.21), *Tianhuang* (T 88.13), *Minghuang* (T 88.12), *Qihuang* (T 88.14), *Simashang* (T 88.18), *Simazhong* (T 88.17), *Simaxia* (T 88.19), *Sizhi* (T 77.20). Bleed the affected area. The more the bleeding, the better the result.

Master Tung's Points by Dr. Chuan-Min Wang:

- **Gout**
  - **Big toe:** Bleed *Taichong* (LR 3) area. Needle contralaterally *Linggu* (T 22.05), *Sanchasan* (T 22.17)*.
  - **Knee:** Bleed popliteal fossa. Needle *Quchi* (LI 11), *Sanchasan* (T 22.17)*.

Balance Method by Dr. Richard Tan:

- Use Dr. Tan's Balance Method accordingly as determined by where the pain is (use mirror or image system). If the pain is in the big toes, needle around the thumb. If the pain is in the knees, needle the elbow. Needle the *ah shi* points.

Auricular Medicine by Dr. Li-Chun Huang:

- *San Jiao*, Endocrine, Kidney, Liver, Spleen, Coronary Vascular Subcortex, and corresponding points to the area of pain. Bleed Ear Apex.

NUTRITION

- *Hai Zao* (Sargassum) and *Kun Bu* (Thallus Eckloniae) are helpful, as they contain protein and vital minerals to reduce uric acid levels in the blood.
- Adequate amounts of vitamin C and bioflavonoids (3,000 to 5,000 mg daily) should be taken, as they help to reduce uric acid levels in the blood.
- Essential fatty acids are beneficial for gout, as they are needed to repair tissues and heal joint disorders.
- Since gout attack is caused by excessive deposit of uric acid in the joints, increased intake of food rich in uric acid will increase the risk of gout attacks. Purine-rich food should be avoided, including meat, soup (bone broth), gravies, meat extracts, seafood (anchovies, fish roes, herring, sardine, mussels), shellfish, internal organ meats (liver and kidneys), beer and other alcoholic beverages, spinach, asparagus, mushrooms, and cauliflower.
- Patients with gout should increase their intake of cherries, blueberries and strawberries, all of which are excellent in neutralizing uric acid.
- It is important to always consume an adequate amount of distilled water, and avoid tap water whenever possible. This will help flush out the uric acid crystals.
- After an attack of gout, it is recommended to eat only raw fruits and vegetables for about one to two weeks.

CASE STUDY

- Y.J., 63-year-old female, presented with arthritis and gout pain located throughout her feet, fingers, wrists, and arms. Objective findings included inflammation on the joints, redness and an inability to extend the joints. The pain was described as a sharp burning sensation. Blood pressure was 132/61 mmHg with heart rate of 73 beats per minute. The practitioner diagnosed this condition as qi and blood stagnation. ***Flex (GT)*** and ***Herbal ANG*** were prescribed. After taking the herbs and receiving acupuncture just a few times, the patient reported that her pain alleviated from a 9 to a 5 level. It was also noted that her range of motion had improved and was not as stiff as she was during the initial treatment. Submitted by J.C., Rosemead, California.

PHARMACOLOGICAL AND CLINICAL RESEARCH

Flex (GT) is a comprehensive formula that treats various aspects of gout. It incorporates herbs that decrease the absorption and increase the elimination of uric acid. Furthermore, it contains herbs with analgesic effects to relieve pain, anti-inflammatory effects to reduce swelling and inflammation, and antipyretic effects to relieve burning sensations and reduce inflammation.

Huang Bo (Cortex Phellodendri Chinensis), *Jin Qian Cao* (Herba Lysimachiae) and *Ze Xie* (Rhizoma Alismatis) are the key herbs in ***Flex (GT)*** for treating gout. *Huang Bo* (Cortex Phellodendri Chinensis) has a marked effect to treat gout. According to a study in subjects with artificially-induced gout, administration of *Huang Bo* (Cortex Phellodendri Chinensis) reduces serum uric acid levels and inhibits activities of liver xanthine oxidase for the treatment of gout.[1] The water extract of *Jin Qian Cao* (Herba Lysimachiae) has a potent hypouricemic effect to reduce plasma levels of uric acid in subjects with hyperuricemia.[2] *Jin Qian Cao* (Herba Lysimachiae) is also one of the most effective herbs to treat accumulation of uric acid crystals and stones in the body, such as gallstones, urinary stones,

Flex (GT)™

and bladder stones.[3,4,5] In addition, *Ze Xie* (Rhizoma Alismatis) has a marked effect to inhibit the formation of crystal and stones by downregulating the bikunin mRNA expression and decreasing the calcium oxalate formation in the kidney.[6] Furthermore, *Che Qian Zi* (Semen Plantaginis) and *Ze Xie* (Rhizoma Alismatis) have significant diuretic effects to flush out all these substances, including but not limited to sodium, potassium and calcium oxalate.[7,8,9,10] Together, these herbs work to prevent and treat gout.

Gout often occurs with pain, swelling and inflammation. Therefore, ***Flex (GT)*** uses many herbs with analgesic and anti-inflammatory effects. *Zhi Mu* (Rhizoma Anemarrhenae) shows significant anti-inflammatory action by inhibiting cyclo-oxygenase-2, inducible nitric oxide synthase and 5-lipoxygenase.[11] *Huang Bo* (Cortex Phellodendri Chinensis) has a marked effect to reduce inflammation by inhibiting the production of proinflammatory cytokines, including interleukin-1beta and tumor necrosis factor-alpha (TNF-α), in a dose-dependent manner.[12] *Ji Xue Teng* (Caulis Spatholobi) exhibits an anti-inflammatory effect through its inhibitory activities against a panel of key enzymes relating to inflammation, including cyclo-oxygenase, phospholipase, and lipoxygenase.[13] *Che Qian Zi* (Semen Plantaginis) shows a significant anti-inflammatory effect via its inhibitory effects on nitric oxide production *in vitro*.[14] Lastly, *Di Huang* (Radix Rehmanniae) has an anti-inflammatory effect to reduce swelling and inflammation.[15] The mechanism of action is attributed to its influence on the endocrine system. It has been shown that the use of *Di Huang* (Radix Rehmanniae) increases the plasma levels of adrenocortical hormones, even in the presence of dexamethasone.[16]

In summary, ***Flex (GT)*** prevents and treats gout by decreasing plasma levels of uric acid via reduced absorption and increased elimination of uric acid.

COMPARATIVE ANALYSIS

Gout is a form of arthritis that is characterized by sudden, severe attacks of pain, tenderness, redness, warmth and swelling (inflammation) in some joints. Gout is caused in part by excessive intake of food rich in uric acid, or decreased excretion of uric acid through the kidneys. As uric acid deposits accumulate in the joints, they cause severe pain known as gout.

Acute gout may be treated with colchicine, but use of this drug is not recommended as it may cause severe bone marrow suppression and possibly death. Non-steroidal anti-inflammatory agents (NSAID), such as Indocin (indomethacin), Motrin (ibuprofen), and Naprosyn (naproxen), are very frequently used to treat mild to moderate pain characterized by inflammation and swelling. However, they may cause such serious side effects as gastric ulcer, duodenal ulcer, gastrointestinal bleeding, tinnitus, blurred vision, dizziness, and headache. In short, drug treatment of gout is limited and less than satisfactory.

Treatment of gout must focus on treating the symptom and the cause. In this formula, many herbs with strong analgesic effects treat pain. Furthermore, many herbs with draining effects flush out excess uric acid. Though herbs are not as potent as the drugs, they offer both short- and long-term improvement for treatment of gout.

It is important to remember that optimal treatment lies not in use of drugs or herbs, but in commitment to make diet and lifestyle changes. Long-term success can be accomplished only if changes are made to decrease intake and increase elimination of uric acid.

References

1. Yang C, Zhu JX, Wang Y, Wen YL, Kong LD. Effects of processing Phellodendron amurense with salt on anti-gout. State Key Laboratory of Pharmaceutical Biotechnology, School of Life Sciences, Nanjing University, Nanjing 210093, China. Zhongguo Zhong Yao Za Zhi. 2005 Jan;30(2):145-8.
2. Wang HD, Ge F, Guo YS, Kong LD. Effects of aqueous extract in herba of Lysimachia christinae on hyperuricemia in mice. State Key Laboratory of Pharmaceutical Biotechnology, School of Life Sciences, Nanjing University, Nanjing 210093, Jiangsu, China. Zhongguo Zhong Yao Za Zhi. 2002 Dec;27(12):939-41, 944.
3. *Zhong Yao Yao Li Yu Ying Yong* (Pharmacology and Applications of Chinese Herbs), 1983: 696.
4. *Zhong Yi Za Zhi* (Journal of Chinese Medicine), 1958; 11:749.
5. *Guang Xi Zhong Yi Yao* (Guangxi Chinese Medicine and Herbology), 1990; 13(6):40.
6. Cao ZG, Liu JH, Zhou SW, Wu W, Yin CP, Wu JZ. The effects of the active constituents of Alisma orientalis on renal stone formation and bikunin expression in rat urolithiasis model. Department of Urology, Tongji Hospital, Tongji Medical College, Huazhong University of Science and Technology, Wuhan 430030, China. Zhonghua Yi Xue Za Zhi. 2004 Aug 2;84(15):1276-9.
7. *Zhong Yao Da Ci Dian* (Dictionary of Chinese Herbs), 1975: 403.
8. *Zhong Yao Xue* (Chinese Herbology), 1998; 340:341.
9. *Sheng Yao Xue Za Zhi* (Journal of Raw Herbology), 1982; 36(2):150.
10. Cao ZG, Liu JH, Radman AM, Wu JZ, Ying CP, Zhou SW. An experimental study of effect of different extracts of Alisma orientalis on urinary calcium oxalate stones formation in rats. Department of Urology, Tongji Hospital, Tongji Medical College, Huazhong University of Science and Technology, Wuhan 430030, Hubei, China. Zhongguo Zhong Yao Za Zhi. 2003 Nov;28(11):1072-5.
11. Lim H, Nam JW, Seo EK, Kim YS, Kim HP. (-)-Nyasol (cis-hinokiresinol), a norneolignan from the rhizomes of Anemarrhena asphodeloides, is a broad spectrum inhibitor of eicosanoid and nitric oxide production. College of Pharmacy, Kangwon National University, Chunchon 200-701, Korea. Arch Pharm Res. 2009 Nov;32(11):1509-14.
12. Hsiang CY, Wu SL, Cheng SE, Ho TY. Acetaldehyde-induced interleukin-1beta and tumor necrosis factor-alpha production is inhibited by berberine through nuclear factor-kappaB signaling pathway in HepG2 cells. Graduate Institute of Medical Science, China Medical University, Taichung 404, Taiwan. J Biomed Sci. 2005 Oct;12(5):791-801.
13. Li RW, David Lin G, Myers SP, Leach DN. Anti-inflammatory activity of Chinese medicinal vine plants. Australian Centre for Complementary Medicine Education and Research, A Joint Venture of the University of Queensland and Southern Cross University, P.O. Box 157, Lismore, NSW 2480, Australia. J Ethnopharmacol. 2003 Mar;85(1):61-7.
14. Tezuka Y., Irikawa S., Kaneko T., Banskota A.H., Nagaoka T., Xiong Q., Hase K., Kadota S. Screening of Chinese herbal drug extracts for inhibitory activity on nitric oxide production and identification of an active compound of *Zanthoxylum bungeanum*. *J Ethnopharmacol*. 2001, 77(2-3): 209-217.
15. *Zhong Yao Yao Li Yu Ying Yong* (Pharmacology and Applications of Chinese Herbs), 1983: 400.
16. *Zhong Yao Xue* (Chinese Herbology), 1998; 156:158.

Flex (Heat)™

CLINICAL APPLICATIONS

- **Acute muscle aches and pain with heat manifestations,** such as swelling, burning sensation, and inflammation
- **Acute *re bi* (heat painful obstruction), arthritis, arthralgia or gout** with redness and swelling
- **Fibromyalgia** with heat manifestations
- **Rheumatic heat disorders**

WESTERN THERAPEUTIC ACTIONS

- Analgesic function to relieve pain
- Anti-inflammatory effect to reduce inflammation and swelling
- Antirheumatic and antiarthritic functions to treat disorders of the connective tissue such as joints, muscles, bursae, tendons and fibrous tissues
- Immunomodulatory and immunosuppressive properties to treat joint disorders due to autoimmune disease
- Chondroprotective and osteoprotective benefits to strengthen connective tissues and repair joints

CHINESE THERAPEUTIC ACTIONS

- Expels wind and heat
- Disperses *bi zheng* (painful obstruction syndrome)
- Clears damp-heat and reduces swelling
- Alleviates pain

DOSAGE

Take 3 to 4 capsules three times daily. Dosage may be increased up to 5 to 6 capsules every four to six hours as needed. For quick and maximum effectiveness, take the herbs on an empty stomach with warm water.

INGREDIENTS

Cang Zhu (Rhizoma Atractylodis)
Dang Gui Wei (Extremitas Radix Angelicae Sinensis)
Du Huo (Radix Angelicae Pubescentis)
Fang Ji (Radix Stephaniae Tetrandrae)
Huang Bo (Cortex Phellodendri Chinensis)
Lu Lu Tong (Fructus Liquidambaris)
Luo Shi Teng (Caulis Trachelospermi)
Qiang Huo (Rhizoma et Radix Notopterygii)
Qin Jiao (Radix Gentianae Macrophyllae)
Sang Zhi (Ramulus Mori)
Shi Gao (Gypsum Fibrosum)
Wei Ling Xian (Radix et Rhizoma Clematidis)
Wu Jia Pi (Cortex Acanthopanacis)
Xi Xian Cao (Herba Siegesbeckiae)
Yi Yi Ren (Semen Coicis)
Zhi Mu (Rhizoma Anemarrhenae)

BACKGROUND

Musculoskeletal and connective tissue disorders are major causes of pain and physical disability. Causes of these bone, muscle and joint disorders vary greatly, depending on the exact disease. Simple causes include trauma and external injuries, such as pulled muscles, strained ligaments, dislocated joints and bone fractures. Complicated causes include infection, autoimmune disorders, crystal-induced inflammation, and non-inflammatory tissue degeneration. Optimal treatment must address the symptoms (pain and inflammation) and the underlying causes. After the disorder is stabilized, physical therapy and exercise are important to maintain flexibility and strengthen surrounding muscles.

FORMULA EXPLANATION

Flex (Heat) is formulated specifically to treat musculoskeletal disorders characterized by heat. It contains herbs with functions to eliminate wind, heat and dampness, remove painful obstructions, and relieve pain.

Cang Zhu (Rhizoma Atractylodis) dries dampness and *Huang Bo* (Cortex Phellodendri Chinensis) clears damp-heat in the lower parts of the body. These two herbs have an excellent effect to treat pain in the lower half of the body, as in the classic formula *Er Miao San* (Two-Marvel Powder). *Qiang Huo* (Rhizoma et Radix Notopterygii), *Du Huo* (Radix Angelicae Pubescentis), and *Sang Zhi* (Ramulus Mori) have antirheumatic, anti-inflammatory, and analgesic functions. They remove painful obstruction by expelling wind, damp, and heat in the upper and lower body. *Shi Gao* (Gypsum Fibrosum) and *Zhi Mu* (Rhizoma Anemarrhenae) have anti-inflammatory functions to clear heat and reduce painful swelling sensation of the joints. *Yi Yi Ren* (Semen Coicis) and *Fang Ji* (Radix Stephaniae Tetrandrae) are diuretics that reduce swelling of the joints. *Wei Ling Xian* (Radix et Rhizoma Clematidis), *Luo Shi Teng* (Caulis Trachelospermi) and *Dang Gui Wei* (Extremitas Radix Angelicae Sinensis) have antirheumatic and blood-invigorating effects to clear the channels and collaterals and enhance the flexibility and integrity of the joints. *Xi Xian Cao* (Herba Siegesbeckiae), *Lu Lu Tong* (Fructus Liquidambaris), and *Qin Jiao* (Radix Gentianae Macrophyllae) dredge the channels and scour residual blood stagnation. They are often used in wind disorders including paralysis or hemiplegia. *Wu Jia Pi* (Cortex Acanthopanacis) strengthens sinews and bones and helps relieve chronic pain.

In summary, the herbs in ***Flex (Heat)*** eliminate wind, heat and dampness to treat various types of musculoskeletal and connective tissue disorders.

CAUTIONS & CONTRAINDICATIONS

- This formula is contraindicated during pregnancy and nursing.
- This herbal formula contains herbs that invigorate blood circulation, such as *Dang Gui Wei* (Extremitas Radix Angelicae Sinensis). Therefore, patients who are on anticoagulant or antiplatelet therapies, such as Coumadin (warfarin), should use this formula with caution, or not at all, as there may be a higher risk of bleeding and bruising.[1,2,3]

Flex (Heat)™

CLINICAL NOTES

- *Flex (Heat)* can be combined with ***Flex (TMX)*** in the early stages of sports injuries when there is severe pain with inflammation, swelling, and redness. Begin treating the patient immediately for maximum effectiveness.
- Internal hemorrhage must be ruled out first prior to treating patients with head injuries.
- The use of ice packs is recommended to reduce redness, swelling, and inflammation.
- Heat packs should not be used in patients with joint pain due to heat.

Pulse Diagnosis by Dr. Jimmy Wei-Yen Chang:

- **Knee and ankle joint arthritis:** left *yangwei* pulse, which is an extra meridian pulse found distal to the *cun* position towards the thumb
- **Damp-heat accumulation:** deep and forceful pulse
- **Rheumatoid arthritis with excess heat:** deep and forceful pulse on both *chi*. Left *yangwei* pulse is fast and forceful.

SUPPLEMENTARY FORMULAS

- To potentiate the effect to relieve pain, add ***Herbal ANG***.
- With severe inflammation, combine with ***Astringent Complex***.
- With excess heat, add ***Gardenia Complex***.
- For severe pain with blood stagnation, add ***Circulation (SJ)***.
- For gout, use ***Flex (GT)*** instead.
- For neck and shoulder pain, combine with ***Neck & Shoulder (AC)*** or ***Neck & Shoulder (CR)***.
- For lower back pain, add ***Back Support (AC)*** or ***Back Support (CR)***.
- For herniated disk in the back with swelling and inflammation, add ***Back Support (HD)***.
- For knee pain, add ***Knee & Ankle (AC)*** or ***Knee & Ankle (CR)***.
- For spasms and cramps, combine with ***Flex (SC)***.
- For bone fractures, injuries, and bruises, add ***Flex (TMX)***.
- For bone spurs, add ***Flex (SPR)***.
- For post-stroke numbness and atrophy, use ***Neuro Plus***.
- For osteoporosis, add ***Osteo 8***.
- For degeneration of muscles, ligaments and tendons, combine with ***Flex (MLT)***.
- For arthritic pain that worsens during cold and rainy weather, use ***Flex (CD)*** instead of ***Flex (Heat)***.

ACUPUNCTURE TREATMENT

Traditional Points:

- Needle *ah shi* points.
- *Taichong* (LR 3), *Xingjian* (LR 2), *Zusanli* (ST 36), *Geshu* (BL 17)

Classic Master Tung's Points:

- Needle contralateral to the pain. If the pain is in the center, needle bilaterally or the side with the more *ah shi* points. If the pain is bilateral, needle bilaterally.
- **General arthritis:** *Tianhuang* (T 88.13), *Minghuang* (T 88.12), *Fugesan* (T 44.30)*, *Simazhong* (T 88.17), *Dihuang* (T 77.19), *Jianzhong* (T 44.06), *Wuhu* (T 11.27). Bleed the affected area.
- **Arthritis (legs):** *Minghuang* (T 88.12), *Tianhuang* (T 88.13), *Qihuang* (T 88.14), *Zhongjiuli* (T 88.25), *Jianzhong* (T 44.06), *Wuhu* (T 11.27). Bleed dark veins on the legs. Bleed before needling for best result.
- **Arthritis (degenerative):** *Wanshunyi* (T 22.08), *Wanshuner* (T 22.09), *Simashang* (T 88.18), *Minghuang* (T 88.12), *Tianhuangfu [Shenguan]* (T 77.18), *Wuhu* (T 11.27). Bleed the affected area.

Master Tung's Points by Dr. Chuan-Min Wang:

- **Hot *bi zheng* (painful obstruction syndrome), arthritis, fibromyalgia, rheumatic heat disorders**
  - Shoulder: Bleed *Chize* (LU 5) or *Quchi* (LI 11) area. Needle contralaterally *Tianhuangfu [shenguan]* (T 77.18), *Sizhi* (T 77.20).
  - Elbow: Bleed *Quchi* (LI 11) area. Needle contralaterally *Renzong* (T 44.08).
  - Wrist: Bleed *Shuiyu* (T 44.17) area. Needle contralaterally *Tung's Wantong* (T 66.16)*.
  - Knee: Bleed popliteal fossa or fibula head area. Needle contralaterally *Chongzi* (T 22.01), *Chongxian* (T 22.02).
  - Ankle: Bleed *Xuanzhong* (GB 39) area. Needle contralaterally *Zhongbai* (T 22.06), *Xiabai* (T 22.07), *Wuhu* 4, 5 (T 11.27).
  - Finger: Bleed tips of the fingers. Needle contralaterally *Wuhu* 1, 2 (T 11.27).

Balance Method by Dr. Richard Tan:

- Use Dr. Tan's Balance Method accordingly as determined by where the pain is (use mirror or image system).

Ear Acupuncture:

- Related joints, Adrenal Glands
- Embed magnetic ear balls and switch ears every three days.

Auricular Medicine by Dr. Li-Chun Huang:

- **Rheumatic arthritis:** Spleen, Liver, Kidney, *San Jiao*, Allergic Area, Endocrine, Adrenal Gland, and corresponding points to the affected area. Bleed Ear Apex.

NUTRITION

- Sulfur helps the absorption of calcium, and adequate intake and absorption of calcium is essential for the repair and the rebuilding of bones, tendons, cartilage, and connective tissues. Patients are encouraged to consume foods high in sulfur such as asparagus, eggs, fresh garlic, and onions.
- Histidine, an amino acid, is responsible for removing the high levels of copper and iron found in arthritic patients. Patients are encouraged to consume foods high in histidine such as rice, wheat and rye.
- Fresh pineapples are recommended as they contain bromelain, an enzyme that is excellent in reducing inflammation.

Flex (Heat) ™

- Increase intake of nourishing, cooling foods/roots such as Mexican yam, yam, radishes, potatoes, carrots, melons, cucumbers, beets, turnips, malanga, celeriac, taro, and rutabaga.
- Avoid spicy food, caffeine, citrus fruits, sugar, milk, dairy products, and red meat.
- Fish oil may help to alleviate pain associated with rheumatoid arthritis. It can be taken in conjunction with the herbs.
- Decrease the intake of sour foods, drinks or fruits (citrus) as their nature constricts and may contribute to further stagnation in the channels and collaterals.
- Avoid spicy/pungent/aromatic vegetables such as pepper, garlic, onions, basil, rosemary, cumin, funnel, anise, leeks, chives, scallions, thyme, saffron, wormwood, mustard, chili pepper, and wasabi.

The Tao of Nutrition by Dr. Maoshing Ni and Cathy McNease:

- Recommendations: plenty of fresh fruits and vegetables, dandelion, cabbage, mung beans, winter melon, and soybean sprouts.
- Apply poultices of crushed dandelion greens, changing every two hours.
- Avoid spicy foods, green onions, alcohol, smoking and all types of stress.

LIFESTYLE INSTRUCTIONS

- For obese patients, weight loss is suggested as it lessens the pressure on the joints, which can then help in relieving pain.

CASE STUDIES

- E.K., a 54-year-old female, presented with severe, burning, sacral pain. MRI evaluation revealed a bulging lumbar disk. The patient stated she had previously been managing her chronic low back pain but that this was the first time she had had the burning sensation. The TCM diagnosis was heat in the lower *jiao*. The patient reported that taking ***Flex (Heat)*** at four capsules, four times daily, took away the burning sensation but did not completely resolve the pain. She then used this formula from time to time, when the burning sensation came back. Submitted by M.C., Sarasota, Florida.
- A female broker presented with pain, heat and swelling in her joints that would flare-up and subside intermittently. Limited range of motion were also present along with joint rigidity. The pain and swelling was felt especially in the fourth finger bilaterally and occasionally on either ankles. There was a butterfly rash (yin deficiency) on her face. Other symptoms included hot flashes and night sweats. The practitioner diagnosed the condition as *bi zheng* (painful obstruction syndrome) due to wind-damp-heat with underlying Kidney yin deficiency. The patient was given ***Flex (Heat)*** to treat the pain, and *Zhi Bai Di Huang Wan* (Anemarrhena Phellodendron and Rehmannia Formula) to nourish yin. The patient had been treated with various medications previously and found that ***Flex (Heat)*** produced the best results. Past treatments for her condition also showed diminished efficacy after a period of four to six months. With ***Flex (Heat)*** she was able to continue treatment for almost a year while still maintaining its therapeutic value. The practitioners noted that ***Flex (Heat)*** was a very effective formula for inflammatory joint conditions. Submitted by T.W., Santa Monica, California.
- An 85-year-old female patient presented with severe pain in her right toe, with difficulty walking. Blood pressure was 140/90 mmHg with heart rate of 76 beats per minute. The TCM diagnosis was damp-heat arthritis; Western diagnosis was uric acid build up. ***Flex (Heat)*** was prescribed at 4 capsules three times a day for two weeks. The patient reported improvement after a few days and continued taking the remainder of the herbs. Additional treatment included applying *Zheng Gu Shui* (literally, rectify bones liquid) to the big toe area, drinking distilled water and pure cherry juice, and refraining from drinking alcoholic beverages. Submitted by L.W., Arroyo Grande, California.

PHARMACOLOGICAL AND CLINICAL RESEARCH

Flex (Heat) treats musculoskeletal and connective tissue disorders with heat manifestations. ***Flex (Heat)*** contains herbs with multiple therapeutic functions: analgesic, anti-inflammatory, antirheumatic, immunomodulatory, chondroprotective and osteogenic functions.

Flex (Heat) contains many herbs with analgesic effects to relieve pain and anti-inflammatory effects to reduce swelling and inflammation. Pharmacologically, *Zhi Mu* (Rhizoma Anemarrhenae) shows significant anti-inflammatory action by inhibiting cyclo-oxygenase-2, inducible nitric oxide synthase and 5-lipoxygenase.[4] *Huang Bo* (Cortex Phellodendri Chinensis) has a marked effect to reduce inflammation by inhibiting the production of proinflammatory cytokines, including interleukin-1beta and tumor necrosis factor-alpha (TNF-α), in a dose-dependent manner.[5] *Qiang Huo* (Rhizoma et Radix Notopterygii) has an analgesic effect to relieve muscle aches and pain.[6] It also has an anti-inflammatory effect to reduce swelling and inflammation. The mechanism is attributed to the inhibition of 5-lipoxygenase and cyclo-oxygenase.[7] *Dang Gui* (Radix Angelicae Sinensis) exerts both analgesic and anti-inflammatory effects through the inhibition of pro-inflammatory mediators, including nitric oxide and prostaglandin E2 in peritoneal macrophages.[8,9] In comparison with acetylsalicylic acid, the anti-inflammatory effect of *Dang Gui* (Radix Angelicae Sinensis) is approximately 1.1 times stronger, and its analgesic effect is approximately 1.7 times stronger.[10] *Xi Xian Cao* (Herba Siegesbeckiae) has both analgesic and anti-inflammatory effects. It reduces swelling and inflammation through significant inhibition of the productions of nitric oxide, prostaglandin E(2), TNF-α and cyclo-oxygenase-2.[11,12] Clinically, *Zhi Mu* (Rhizoma Anemarrhenae) exhibits significant analgesic and anti-inflammatory effects for the treatment of osteoarthritis. According to one clinical study, *Zhi Mu* (Rhizoma Anemarrhenae) is used in one formula to successfully

Flex (Heat)™

treat 56 patients with acute onset of rheumatism with 71.4% effectiveness.[13]

In addition to relieving pain and reducing inflammation, ***Flex (Heat)*** utilizes many herbs with antirheumatic, antiarthritic, immunosuppressive and immunomodulatory effects to treat more complicated inflammatory disorders. *Fang Ji* (Radix Stephaniae Tetrandrae) has antirheumatic and immunomodulatory effects to reduce and treat collagen-induced arthritis *in vivo*.[14] According to a recent human study, administration of *Fang Ji* (Radix Stephaniae Tetrandrae) for 12 weeks is beneficial for treatment of rheumatoid arthritis through its suppressive effect on excessive granulocyte activation and subsequent reduction of inflammation.[15] *Wei Ling Xian* (Radix et Rhizoma Clematidis) has marked antiarthritic activity, as the herb significantly inhibited proinflammatory compounds and prevented rheumatoid arthritis.[16] Lastly, *Xi Xian Cao* (Herba Siegesbeckiae) has an immunosuppressive effect to inhibit both cellular and humoral immunities and may help to treat joint disorder due to autoimmune disease.[17]

In addition to using herbs with analgesic and anti-inflammatory effects, ***Flex (Heat)*** contains herbs to treat gout. According to a study in subjects with artificially-induced gout, administration of *Huang Bo* (Cortex Phellodendri Chinensis) reduced serum uric acid levels and inhibited activities of liver xanthine oxidase for the treatment of gout.[18]

Lastly, chronic musculoskeletal and connective tissue disorders are often associated with wear and tear of the joints; therefore, ***Flex (Heat)*** incorporates herbs to repair cartilages and rebuild bones. *Wei Ling Xian* (Radix et Rhizoma Clematidis) has an excellent chondroprotective effect. One study showed that the saponin fraction from *Wei Ling Xian* (Radix et Rhizoma Clematidis) is effective in ameliorating joint destruction and cartilage erosion in subjects with osteoarthritis, protecting articular cartilage by preventing extracellular matrix degradation and chondrocyte injury.[19] *Xi Xian Cao* (Herba Siegesbeckiae) has a marked effect to protect the cartilages in collagenase-induced osteoarthritis. This herb contributes to a significant increase in proteoglycan, aggrecan, and type II collagen expression.[20] *Dang Gui* (Radix Angelicae Sinensis) is an effective herb to promote the generation of bones. According to one study, the water extract of *Dang Gui* (Radix Angelicae Sinensis) has been found to contribute to the formation of bones and treatment of bone injuries. It directly stimulates the proliferation, alkaline phosphatase activity, protein secretion and particularly type I collagen synthesis of human osteoprecursor cells in a dose-dependent manner.[21] *Zhi Mu* (Rhizoma Anemarrhenae) has an osteoprotective effect. According to a study in subjects with ovariectomy-induced bone loss, administration of steroidal saponins from *Zhi Mu* (Rhizoma Anemarrhenae) suppresses the atrophy of the uterus and descent of bone mineral density, corrects the decreased concentration of calcium and E(2) in serum, without altering the number of osteoclasts. The researchers conclude that *Zhi Mu* (Rhizoma Anemarrhenae) is effective to prevent bone loss through the promotion of bone formation but not the inhibition of bone resorption.[22]

In summary, ***Flex (Heat)*** is an empirical herbal formula with excellent function to treat musculoskeletal and joint disorders characterized by heat.

COMPARATIVE ANALYSIS

Pain is a basic bodily sensation induced by a noxious stimulus that causes physical discomfort (such as pricking, throbbing, or aching). Pain may be of acute or chronic state, and may be of nociceptive, neuropathic, or psychogenic origin.

Non-steroidal anti-inflammatory agents (NSAID), such as Motrin (ibuprofen), Naprosyn (naproxen) and Voltaren (diclofenac) are very frequently used to treat mild to moderate pain characterized by inflammation and swelling. Clinical applications include headache, arthritis, dysmenorrhea, and general aches and pain. Though effective, they may cause such serious side effects as gastric ulcer, duodenal ulcer, gastrointestinal bleeding, tinnitus, blurred vision, dizziness and headache. Furthermore, the newer NSAIDs, also known as COX-2 inhibitors [such as Celebrex (celecoxib)], are associated with significantly higher risk of cardiovascular events, including heart attack and stroke. In fact, these side effects are so serious that two COX-2 inhibitors have already been withdrawn from the market [Vioxx (rofecoxib) and Bextra (valdecoxib)]. In brief, it is important to remember that while drugs offer reliable and potent symptomatic pain relief, they should only be used if and when needed. Frequent use and abuse leads to unnecessary side effects and complications.

Treatment of pain is a sophisticated balance of art and science. Proper treatment of pain requires a careful evaluation of the type of disharmony (excess or deficiency, cold or heat, exterior or interior), characteristics (qi and/or blood stagnations), and location (upper body, lower body, extremities, or internal organs). Furthermore, optimal treatment requires integrative use of herbs, acupuncture and *tui-na* therapies. All these therapies work together to tonify the underlying deficiencies, strengthen the body, and facilitate recovery from chronic pain. TCM pain management targets both the symptoms and the causes of pain, and as such, often achieves immediate and long-term success. Furthermore, TCM pain management is often associated with few or no side effects.

For treatment of mild to severe pain due to various causes, TCM pain management offers similar treatment effects with significantly fewer side effects.

References

1. Chan K, Lo AC, Yeung JH, Woo KS. Journal of Pharmacy and Pharmacology 1995 May;47(5):402-6.
2. Pharmacotherapy 1999 July;19(7):870-876.
3. European Journal of Drug Metabolism and Pharmacokinetics 1995; 20(1): 55-60.

Flex (Heat) ™

4. Lim H, Nam JW, Seo EK, Kim YS, Kim HP. (-)-Nyasol (cis-hinokiresinol), a norneolignan from the rhizomes of Anemarrhena asphodeloides, is a broad spectrum inhibitor of eicosanoid and nitric oxide production. College of Pharmacy, Kangwon National University, Chunchon 200-701, Korea. Arch Pharm Res. 2009 Nov;32(11):1509-14.
5. Hsiang CY, Wu SL, Cheng SE, Ho TY. Acetaldehyde-induced interleukin-1beta and tumor necrosis factor-alpha production is inhibited by berberine through nuclear factor-kappaB signaling pathway in HepG2 cells. Graduate Institute of Medical Science, China Medical University, Taichung 404, Taiwan. J Biomed Sci. 2005 Oct;12(5):791-801.
6. *Zhong Cao Yao* (Chinese Herbal Medicine), 1991; 22(1):28.
7. Zschocke S, Lehner M, Bauer R. 5-Lipoxygenase and cyclooxygenase inhibitory active constituents from Qianghuo (Notopterygium incisum). Planta Med. 1997 Jun;63(3):203-6.
8. *Xin Yi Yao Xue Za Zhi* (New Journal of Medicine and Herbology), 1975; (6):34.
9. Chao WW, Kuo YH, Li WC, Lin BF. The production of nitric oxide and prostaglandin E2 in peritoneal macrophages is inhibited by Andrographis paniculata, Angelica sinensis and Morus alba ethyl acetate fractions. Department of Biochemical Science and Technology, Institute of Microbiology and Biochemistry, National Taiwan University, Taipei 106, Taiwan, ROC. J Ethnopharmacol. 2009 Feb 25;122(1):68-75.
10. *Yao Xue Za Zhi* (Journal of Medicinals), 1971; (91):1098.
11. Li H, Kim JY, Hyeon J, Lee HJ, Ryu JH. In Vitro Antiinflammatory Activity of a New Sesquiterpene Lactone Isolated from Siegesbeckia glabrescens. College of Pharmacy, Sookmyung Women's University, 52 Hyochangwon-Gil, Yongsan-Gu, Seoul, 140-742, Korea. Phytother Res. 2011 Feb 10. doi: 10.1002/ptr.3420.
12. Park HJ, Kim IT, Won JH, Jeong SH, Park EY, Nam JH, Choi J, Lee KT. Anti-inflammatory activities of ent-16alphaH,17-hydroxy-kauran-19-oic acid isolated from the roots of Siegesbeckia pubescens are due to the inhibition of iNOS and COX-2 expression in RAW 264.7 macrophages via NF-kappaB inactivation. Division of Applied Plant Sciences, Sang-Ji University, Wonju, Republic of Korea. Eur J Pharmacol. 2007 Mar 8;558(1-3):185-93.
13. *Ji Lin Zhong Yi Yao* (Jilin Chinese Medicine and Herbology), 1992; (1):16.
14. Niizawa A, Kogure T, Hai LX, Fujinaga H, Takahashi K, Shimada Y, Terasawa K. Clinical and immunomodulatory effects of fun-boi, an herbal medicine, on collagen-induced arthritis in vivo. Clin Exp Rheumatol. 2003 Jan-Feb;21(1):57-62.
15. Sekiya N, Shimada Y, Niizawa A, Kogure T, Mantani N, Sakai S, Hikiami H, Terasawa K. Suppressive effects of Stephania tetrandra on the neutrophil function in patients with rheumatoid arthritis. Phytother Res. 2004 Mar;18(3):247-9.
16. Sun SX, Li YM, Fang WR, Cheng P, Liu L, Li F. Effect and mechanism of AR-6 in experimental rheumatoid arthritis. Department of Physiology, China Pharmaceutical University, 210009 Nanjing, China. Clin Exp Med. 2010 Jun;10(2):113-21.
17. *Zhong Guo Zhong Yao Za Zhi* (People's Republic of China Journal of Chinese Herbology), 1989; 14(3):44.
18. Yang C, Zhu JX, Wang Y, Wen YL, Kong LD. Effects of processing Phellodendron amurense with salt on anti-gout. State Key Laboratory of Pharmaceutical Biotechnology, School of Life Sciences, Nanjing University, Nanjing 210093, China. Zhongguo Zhong Yao Za Zhi. 2005 Jan;30(2):145-8.
19. Wu W, Xu X, Dai Y, Xia L. Therapeutic effect of the saponin fraction from Clematis chinensis Osbeck roots on osteoarthritis induced by monosodium iodoacetate through protecting articular cartilage. Department of Pharmacology of Chinese Materia Medica, College of Traditional Chinese Medicine, China Pharmaceutical University, Nanjing. Phytother Res. 2010 Apr;24(4):538-46.
20. Huh JE, Baek YH, Lee JD, Choi DY, Park DS. Therapeutic effect of Siegesbeckia pubescens on cartilage protection in a rabbit collagenase-induced model of osteoarthritis. Oriental Medicine Research Center for Bone and Joint Disease, KyungHee University, Seoul, Korea. J Pharmacol Sci. 2008 Jul;107(3):317-28.
21. Yang Q, Populo SM, Zhang J, Yang G, Kodama H. Effect of Angelica sinensis on the proliferation of human bone cells. Clin Chim Acta. 2002 Oct;324(1-2):89-97.
22. Nian H, Qin LP, Chen WS, Zhang QY, Zheng HC, Wang Y. Protective effect of steroidal saponins from rhizome of Anemarrhena asphodeloides on ovariectomy-induced bone loss in rats. Department of Pharmacognosy, School of Pharmacy, Second Military Medical University, Shanghai 200433, China. Acta Pharmacol Sin. 2006 Jun;27(6):728-34.

Flex (MLT)™

CLINICAL APPLICATIONS

- **Atrophy and wasting of muscles, ligaments, and tendons**
- **Cartilage damage** from chronic wear and tear
- **Decreased range of motion and mobility** of the joints
- **Rehabilitation** from chronic or late-stages of musculoskeletal injuries
- Prevention against wear and tear or breakdown of cartilage and soft tissue surrounding joints
- Individuals engaging in repetitive motions who wish to maintain healthy joints and connective tissue

WESTERN THERAPEUTIC ACTIONS

- Chondroprotective effect to protect cartilages
- Osteogenic and antiosteoporotic functions to promote generation of bones
- Neuroregenerative effect to facilitate healing of nerves and neurons
- Adaptogenic effect to facilitate rehabilitation
- Analgesic, anti-inflammatory, and muscle-relaxant effects

CHINESE THERAPEUTIC ACTIONS

- Tonifies qi and blood
- Activates qi and blood circulation
- Nourishes yin
- Dispels wind-damp
- Strengthens muscles, tendons, ligaments, and bones

DOSAGE

Take 4 to 6 capsules three times daily. This formula should be taken during the mid-to-late stages of recovery and rehabilitation. It should not be taken during the acute phases of injuries, where there may be bleeding and bruises.

INGREDIENTS

Bai Shao (Radix Paeoniae Alba)
Chu Shi Zi (Fructus Broussonetiae)
Chuan Niu Xi (Radix Cyathulae)
Dang Gui (Radix Angelicae Sinensis)
Dang Shen (Radix Codonopsis)
Di Huang (Radix Rehmanniae)
Qian Nian Jian (Rhizoma Homalomenae)
Wu Jia Pi (Cortex Acanthopanacis)
Xu Duan (Radix Dipsaci)
Zhi He Shou Wu (Radix Polygoni Multiflori Praeparata)

BACKGROUND

Musculoskeletal and connective tissue injuries lead to over 10 million clinic visits per year in the United States.[1] Causes of these injuries may be external (sports injuries, car accidents, trauma), internal (chronic wear and tear of muscles, ligaments and tendons; bones weakened by osteoporosis), or both. Acute injuries are characterized by severe pain, swelling and inflammation, and in some cases, internal bleeding. Treatment of acute injuries should focus on relieving pain, reducing swelling and inflammation, and stopping bleeding. Chronic injuries are characterized by dull pain, stiffness and numbness, and decreased muscle mass and strength. Treatments of chronic injuries include relief of pain and restoration of physical and physiological functions.

FORMULA EXPLANATION

Flex (MLT) is designed specifically to treat chronic or mid-to-late stages of musculoskeletal injuries, with atrophy of the soft tissues (muscles, tendons, ligaments, and cartilage), decreased mobility of the joints, cartilage degeneration, and generalized weakness and pain. This formula contains herbs to tonify blood, activate blood circulation, nourish yin, and dispel wind-damp.

In this formula, many herbs are used to tonify the underlying deficiencies. *Dang Shen* (Radix Codonopsis) tonifies qi. *Dang Gui* (Radix Angelicae Sinensis), *Di Huang* (Radix Rehmanniae), and *Bai Shao* (Radix Paeoniae Alba) nourish blood and yin. Healthy joints depend on healthy surrounding cartilage and soft tissue. Because there is no blood supply to the cartilage, it gets nutrition and oxygen from the surrounding joint fluids. Therefore, adequate blood supply to the surrounding areas of the cartilage will ensure a healthy joint. *Dang Gui* (Radix Angelicae Sinensis) tonifies blood and promotes blood circulation to generate new tissues. *Chuan Niu Xi* (Radix Cyathulae) tonifies the Liver and Kidney, strengthens tendons and bones, and helps *Dang Gui* (Radix Angelicae Sinensis) move blood. Together, they stimulate soft tissue (tendons, ligaments and cartilage) growth and restoration. Furthermore, *Wu Jia Pi* (Cortex Acanthopanacis), *Qian Nian Jian* (Rhizoma Homalomenae), and *Xu Duan* (Radix Dipsaci) dispel wind-damp, strengthen bones and tendons, and relieve pain. *Chu Shi Zi* (Fructus Broussonetiae) and *Zhi He Shou Wu* (Radix Polygoni Multiflori Praeparata) tonify Liver and Kidney to strengthen muscles, tendons, cartilage, and ligaments. The yin tonics of this formula, *Bai Shao* (Radix Paeoniae Alba), *Zhi He Shou Wu* (Radix Polygoni Multiflori Praeparata), and *Chuan Niu Xi* (Radix Cyathulae), prevent the narrowing of the space between joints, especially in the vertebrae or the knee joint due to degeneration.

In summary, ***Flex (MLT)*** works to support connective tissues around the joints. It contains herbs that tonify the underlying deficiencies and facilitate healing and recovery. It treats chronic or mid-to-late stages of musculoskeletal injuries with soft tissue degeneration as it encourages repair and restoration.

CAUTIONS & CONTRAINDICATIONS

- This formula should ***not*** be taken during the acute phases of injuries with bleeding and bruises, as there are many tonic or warm herbs that may worsen the condition.
- This herbal formula contains herbs that invigorate blood circulation, such as *Dang Gui* (Radix Angelicae Sinensis). Therefore, patients who are on anticoagulant or antiplatelet therapies, such

Flex (MLT)™

as Coumadin (warfarin), should use this formula with caution, or not at all, as there may be a higher risk of bleeding and bruising.[2,3,4]

CLINICAL NOTES

- Cold packs should be used during the first 24 to 48 hours of acute injuries to reduce swelling and inflammation. On the other hand, hot packs should be used for chronic injuries to promote blood circulation and enhance healing in the affected area.
- This formula should be taken during the recovery and rehabilitation phases after an injury, but not during the acute phases with acute pain and severe inflammation.
- There are three excellent formulas for post-surgical recovery. ***Flex (TMX)*** should be taken after the surgery for 5 to 10 days to facilitate the immediate healing of wounds. Continue herbal treatment with ***Flex (MLT)*** and ***Osteo 8*** for one to three month to facilitate healing and recovery of soft tissues and bones, respectively.
- According to most textbooks and contemporary references, the classic entry of "*He Shou Wu*" is now separated into two entries: the unprepared *Sheng Shou Wu* (Radix Polygoni Multiflori) and the prepared *Zhi He Shou Wu* (Radix Polygoni Multiflori Praeparata), as they have significantly different therapeutic effects and side effects. *Sheng Shou Wu* (Radix Polygoni Multiflori) is a stimulant laxative that treats constipation, but may cause nausea, vomiting, abdominal pain, diarrhea, and in rare cases, liver disorder (dose- and time-dependent, and reversible upon discontinuation).[5] On the other hand, *Zhi He Shou Wu* (Radix Polygoni Multiflori Praeparata) is a tonic herb that is safe and well-tolerated. The dramatic changes in the therapeutic effect and safety profile are attributed to the long and complicated processing of the root with *Hei Dou* (Semen Sojae) through repeated blending, cooking, and drying procedures. When properly processed, the chemical composition of the root changes significantly. Many new compounds are generated from the Maillard reaction (four furanones, two furans, two nitrogen compounds, one pyran, one alcohol and one sulfur compound). Furthermore, the preparation process causes changes in the composition of sugars and 16 kinds of amino acids; it also reduces the pH of the herb from 6.28 to 5.61.[6,7] In summary, these changes give rise to the tonic effects of the prepared roots, and eliminate the adverse reactions associated with the unprepared roots. **Note:** Due to medical risks and legal liabilities, it is prudent to exercise caution and ***not*** use this herb in either prepared or unprepared forms in patients with pre-existing or risk factors of liver diseases.

SUPPLEMENTARY FORMULAS

- For recovery from chronic neck and shoulder injuries, combine with ***Neck & Shoulder (CR)***.
- For recovery from chronic low back pain, combine with ***Back Support (CR)***.
- For recovery from chronic arm (shoulder, elbow, and wrist) injuries, combine with ***Arm Support***.
- For recovery from chronic knee and ankle injuries, combine with ***Knee & Ankle (CR)***.
- With osteoarthritis, add ***Osteo 8***.
- With bone spur, add ***Flex (SPR)***.
- For individuals with severe weakness and deficiencies, combine with ***Imperial Tonic***.

ACUPUNCTURE TREATMENT

Master Tung's Points by Dr. Chuan-Min Wang:

- **Tendon, ligament disorders:** *Cesanli* (T 77.22), *Cexiasanli* (T 77.23), *Zhengjin* (T 77.01), *Zhengzong* (T 77.02)

Balance Method by Dr. Richard Tan:

- Left side: *Ququan* (LR 8), *Rangu* (KI 2), *Dazhong* (KI 4), *Fuliu* (KI 7), *Neiguan* (PC 6), *Tongli* (HT 5)
- Right side: *Waiguan* (TH 5), *Yangxi* (LI 5), *Zusanli* (ST 36), *Yanglingquan* (GB 34)

Auricular Medicine by Dr. Li-Chun Huang:

- **Low back pain, lumbar ligaments disease:** Lumbar Vertebral Area near the antihelix middle line positive point, Lumbar Vertebral Area of the Groove of Spinal Posterior (select the positive point).

NUTRITION

- Sea cucumber is very beneficial because it has a rich amount of lubricating compounds that are needed in all connective tissues, especially joints and joint fluids. Gelatin is also recommended.
- It is important to consume an adequate amount of multiple vitamins and minerals, as they are essential to prevent bone loss and promote bone growth.
- Glucosamine sulfate and chondroitin sulfate are great nutritional supports. They are important for the formation of bones, tendons, ligaments, and cartilages.

LIFESTYLE INSTRUCTION

- While it is important to relax and rest during the recovery process of injuries, it is also important not to stay completely bedridden. Gentle exercises will not only facilitate recovery, but will also prevent muscle atrophy and muscle wasting.

CASE STUDIES

- K.L., a 42-year-old male, presented with right hip and leg pain and numbness. He was using crutches with decreased impaired mobility for the previous three months. Symptoms of stiff neck, frozen ankle, and pain affecting his sleep were present. The patient had a tendency to get injuries due to his poor balance. The practitioner diagnosed the condition as *bi zheng* (painful obstruction syndrome) with blood deficiency and blood stasis with qi constraint. His Western diagnosis was muscle atrophy. The patient was given ***Flex (MLT)*** and directed to take it for eight weeks with the addition of ***Knee Ankle (CR)*** for four weeks. With both formulas and receiving acupuncture treatment for the eight weeks, the patient regained 100% use of his leg, moving from crutches to a cane. The patient resumed sleeping flat after three weeks and riding a bicycle after eight weeks. Pain reduced from 10 to 0 on a 1-10 scale. The patient was very pleased with the herbs, started practicing yoga, and has become more enthusiastic towards life. Submitted by K.F., Honolulu, Hawaii.

- M.K., a 39-year-old female, presented with a previously treated ankle sprain; however, the pain was still present due to increase of pressure and activity. Objective findings include swelling and pain upon palpation on the lateral side of the right ankle. The practitioner diagnosed this condition as qi and damp *bi zheng* (painful obstruction syndrome). Upon diagnosis the practitioner prescribed ***Flex (MLT)*** for the recovery stage of the patient's ankle sprain. With the addition of ***Flex (MLT)***, the swelling and pain reduced and the patient was able to tolerate standing for long periods of time without pain or fatigue. Submitted by L.H., Chicago, Illinois.
- B.B., 62-year-old female, presented with multiple symptoms including a stiff lower back, low grade pain bilaterally on both legs, as well as pain on the heel of the left foot. The patient had been previously diagnosed with plantar fasciitis. Objective findings included areas of the legs having knots within the muscles. The practitioner diagnosed this condition as qi and blood stasis, with underlying Liver and Kidney yin deficiencies. For treatment, the patient had received acupuncture, which had relieved the pain for only a few days. With the addition of ***Flex (MLT)***, it had accelerated the progress and reduction of the pain. The patient had commented that her legs had never felt as loose before. Submitted by L.H., Chicago, Illinois.
- M.W., a 58-year-old male, presented with pain located on the right knee. He had mentioned that he had had ten previous operations on it, one being a knee replacement in 2009. The TCM diagnosis was qi and blood stagnation; Western diagnosis was arthritis of the knee. ***Flex (MLT)*** was prescribed, followed with taking ***Knee & Ankle (CR)***. Overall the herbs reduced the pain, especially when walking, and it continued to improve. Submitted by M.P., Muskego, Wisconsin.
- K.W., a 50-year-old female, presented with a swollen right ankle. She mentioned she had broken it about a month ago and it had become stiff as well, making it hard to drive and run. Objective findings were swelling and pain upon palpation. The practitioner diagnosed the condition as qi and blood stagnation, as well as Liver and Kidney yin deficiencies. ***Flex (MLT)*** was prescribed at 3 capsules twice daily. After one week of taking the herbs as directed, the pain had resolved and the swelling had improved. The patient stopped taking the herbs after two weeks. Submitted by M.P., Muskego, Wisconsin.

PHARMACOLOGICAL AND CLINICAL RESEARCH

Flex (MLT) is an excellent formula for rehabilitation of patients who suffer from chronic musculoskeletal injuries. After acute injuries (such as broken bones, bone fracture, and tear of muscles, tendons or ligaments), patients are often asked to rest for an extended amount of time. As a result, lack of movement on a long-term basis often contributes to atrophy of the soft tissues (muscles, tendons, ligaments, and cartilage), decreased mobility of the joints, and generalized weakness and pain. ***Flex (MLT)*** is designed specifically to treat this condition, and it contains herbs with chondroprotective effects to benefit cartilages, osteogenic activity to promote generation of bones, neuroregenerative benefit for healing of nerves, and adaptogenic functions to facilitate rehabilitation.

Flex (MLT) incorporates many herbs to facilitate the healing and recovery from chronic musculoskeletal injuries. *Chu Shi Zi* (Fructus Broussonetiae) and *Qian Nian Jian* (Rhizoma Homalomenae) have been used traditionally to strengthen the soft tissues, such as muscles, ligaments and tendons.[8] *Chuan Niu Xi* (Radix Cyathulae) is an excellent herb to protect the cartilage from repetitive and stress-induced injuries. According to one study, the extract of *Chuan Niu Xi* (Radix Cyathulae) has a potent effect to inhibit the induction of MMP-13, an important enzyme for the degradation of the cartilage collagen matrix, especially under arthritic conditions. By down-regulating the MMP-13 activity, *Chuan Niu Xi* (Radix Cyathulae) shows great chondroprotection against cartilage degrading disorders.[9] *Dang Gui* (Radix Angelicae Sinensis) is an effective herb to promote the generation of bones. According to one study, the water extract of *Dang Gui* (Radix Angelicae Sinensis) has been found to contribute to the formation of bones and treatment of bone injuries. It directly stimulates the proliferation, alkaline phosphatase activity, protein secretion and particularly type I collagen synthesis of human osteoprecursor cells in a dose-dependent manner.[10] According to another study, *Dang Gui* (Radix Angelicae Sinensis) shows a marked stimulatory effect in osteoblast proliferation and differentiation systems, as well as in a fibroblast-secreted hyaluronic acid assay. This herb enhanced the deposition of hyaluronic acid and proliferation of osteoblasts *in vitro*, as well as bone regeneration.[11] *Xu Duan* (Radix Dipsaci) has significant osteogenic and antiosteoporotic properties to promote generation of new bones and prevent osteoporosis. According to a bone cells culture experiment, administration of *Xu Duan* (Radix Dipsaci) shows a potential effect to increase the proliferation and differentiation of osteoblasts without affecting osteoclast activity. The researchers conclude that these herbs can effectively increase the rate of tissue regeneration of damaged bones.[12] Lastly, *Dang Shen* (Radix Codonopsis) has been shown in one study to promote neuron regeneration in a dose-dependent manner.[13]

The rehabilitation of chronic musculoskeletal and connective tissue disorders is often accompanied by mental and physical

Flex (MLT) ™

stress. *Dang Shen* (Radix Codonopsis) has a regulatory effect on the central nervous system to help with adaptation to various stressful environments.[14] *Wu Jia Pi* (Cortex Acanthopanacis) enhances physical adaptation by increasing endurance and performance.[15] Together, these two herbs exert adaptogenic effects to help patients cope with mental and physical stress during the transition of rehabilitation.

In addition, many herbs in this formula have marked analgesic effects to relieve pain, and anti-inflammatory effects to reduce swelling and inflammation. *Dang Gui* (Radix Angelicae Sinensis) has marked analgesic and anti-inflammatory effects, with potency similar to or stronger than that of acetylsalicylic acid.[16,17] *Wu Jia Pi* (Cortex Acanthopanacis) also has excellent analgesic and anti-inflammatory effects, with duration of action lasting up to five hours.[18,19] *Bai Shao* (Radix Paeoniae Alba) and *Di Huang* (Radix Rehmanniae) have anti-inflammatory and antipyretic effects to reduce inflammation and swelling and relieve burning sensations in the affected areas.[20,21] Clinically, these herbs have been used with great success to treat a wide variety of musculoskeletal conditions, including but not limited to muscle wasting, muscle atrophy, chronic soft tissue injuries, and various types of pain.[22,23] Lastly, *Bai Shao* (Radix Paeoniae Alba) has an excellent muscle-relaxant effect to relieve spasms, cramps, and muscle stiffness.[24] This efficacy has been demonstrated in both smooth and skeletal muscles.

In summary, ***Flex (MLT)*** is an excellent formula for chronic or mid-to-late stages of musculoskeletal injuries. With chronic injuries, degeneration of the soft tissues (muscles, tendons, ligaments, and cartilage) leads to decreased range of motion and mobility of the joints. With mid-to-late stages of musculoskeletal injuries, muscle wasting and muscle atrophy due to lack of exercise and physical movement are the main concern. ***Flex (MLT)*** is developed specifically to address all of these conditions by using herbs that compliment the rehabilitation process and complete the recovery from these illnesses.

COMPARATIVE ANALYSIS

Pain is a basic bodily sensation induced by a noxious stimulus that causes physical discomfort (such as pricking, throbbing or aching). Pain may be of acute or chronic state, and may be of nociceptive, neuropathic, or psychogenic origin.

Western medicine excels in treatment of acute pain. There are many drugs with potent and reliable analgesic effects. Furthermore, many drugs are available as injection for immediate pain relief. However, these drugs treat the symptom of pain but do not alter the underlying disease. Furthermore, long-term use of these drugs for chronic pain are likely to cause more side effects, and complicate the condition further. In short, while drugs are effective for treating acute pain, they should be used sparingly to manage chronic pain.

Treatment of pain is a sophisticated balance of art and science. Proper treatment of pain requires a careful evaluation of the type of disharmony (excess or deficiency, cold or heat, exterior or interior), characteristics (qi and/or blood stagnations), and location (upper body, lower body, extremities, or internal organs). Furthermore, optimal treatment requires integrative use of herbs, acupuncture, and *tui-na* therapies. All these therapies work together to tonify the underlying deficiencies, strengthen the body, and facilitate recovery from chronic pain. TCM pain management targets both the symptom and the cause of pain, and as such, often achieves immediate and long-term success. Furthermore, TCM pain management is often associated with few or no side effects.

For treatment of mild to severe pain due to various causes, TCM pain management offers similar treatment effects with significantly fewer side effects.

References

1. Berkow R. et al. The Merck Manual of Medical Information. Merck Research Laboratories. 1999 February.
2. Chan K, Lo AC, Yeung JH, Woo KS. Journal of Pharmacy and Pharmacology 1995 May;47(5):402-6.
3. Pharmacotherapy 1999 July;19(7):870-876.
4. European Journal of Drug Metabolism and Pharmacokinetics 1995; 20(1): 55-60.
5. Lei X, et al. Liver Damage Associated with Polygonum multiflorum Thunb.: A Systematic Review of Case Reports and Case Series. Evid Based Complement Alternat Med. 2015;2015:459749. doi: 10.1155/2015/459749.
6. Liu Z, Chao Z, Liu Y, Song Z, Lu A. Maillard reaction involved in the steaming process of the root of Polygonum multiflorum. Institution of Basic Theory, China Academy of Chinese Medical Sciences, Beijing, PR China. Planta Med. 2009 Jan;75(1):84-8. Epub 2008 Nov 25.
7. Liu Z, et al. In vitro antioxidant activities of maillard reaction products produced in the steaming process of Polygonum multiflorum root. Nat Prod Commun. 2011 Jan;6(1):55-8.
8. Chen J, Chen T. Chinese Medical Herbology and Pharmacology. Art of Medicine Press. 2004.
9. Park HY, Lim H, Kim HP, Kwon YS. Downregulation of Matrix Metalloproteinase-13 by the Root Extract of Cyathula officinalis Kuan and its Constituents in IL-1β-treated Chondrocytes. College of Pharmacy, Kangwon National University, Chunchon, Korea. Planta Med. 2011 Feb 23.
10. Yang Q, Populo SM, Zhang J, Yang G, Kodama H. Effect of Angelica sinensis on the proliferation of human bone cells. Clin Chim Acta. 2002 Oct;324(1-2): 89-97.
11. Zhao H, Alexeev A, Sharma V, Guzman LD, Bojanowski K. Effect of SBD.4A--a defined multicomponent preparation of Angelica sinensis--in periodontal regeneration models. Phytother Res. 2008 Jul;22(7):923-8.
12. Yao CH, Tsai HM, Chen YS, Liu BS. Fabrication and evaluation of a new composite composed of tricalcium phosphate, gelatin, and Chinese medicine as a bone substitute. Institute of Biomedical Engineering and Material Science, Chungtai Institute of Health Science and Technology, Taichung, Taiwan, Republic of China. J Biomed Mater Res B Appl Biomater. 2005 Nov;75(2): 277-88.
13. Chen HT, Tsai YL, Chen YS, Jong GP, Chen WK, Wang HL, Tsai FJ, Tsai CH, Lai TY, Tzang BS, Huang CY, Lu CY. Dangshen (Codonopsis pilosula) activates IGF-I and FGF-2 pathways to induce proliferation and migration effects in RSC96 Schwann cells. Am J Chin Med. 2010;38(2):359-72.
14. *Zhong Yao Tong Bao* (Journal of Chinese Herbology), 1986; 11(8):53.
15. *Zhong Cao Yao* (Chinese Herbal Medicine), 1987; 18(3):28.
16. *Xin Yi Yao Xue Za Zhi* (New Journal of Medicine and Herbology), 1975; (6):34.
17. *Yao Xue Za Zhi* (Journal of Medicinals), 1971; (91):1098.

FORMULAS

Flex (MLT)™

18. *Zhong Guo Yao Li Xue Tong Bao* (Journal of Chinese Herbal Pharmacology), 1986; 2(2):21.
19. *Zhong Cheng Yao Yan Jiu* (Research of Chinese Patent Medicine), 1984; 10:22.
20. *Zhong Yao Yao Li Yu Ying Yong* (Pharmacology and Applications of Chinese Herbs), 1983; 400.
21. *Zhong Yao Zhi* (Chinese Herbology Journal), 1993; 183.
22. *Xin Yi Yao Xue Za Zhi* (New Journal of Medicine and Herbology), 1976; 12:26.
23. *Shang Hai Zhong Yi Yao Za Zhi* (Shanghai Journal of Chinese Medicine and Herbology), 1983; 4:14.
24. *Zhong Yi Za Zhi* (Journal of Chinese Medicine), 1983; 11:9.

Flex (NP)™

CLINICAL APPLICATIONS

- **Neuropathy:** peripheral neuropathy, polyneuropathy, diabetic neuropathy, drug-induced neuropathy
- **Neuralgia:** trigeminal neuralgia, postherpetic neuralgia
- **Peripheral vascular disease**
- General pain, numbness, tingling, swelling, and muscle wasting, especially in the extremities

WESTERN THERAPEUTIC ACTIONS

- Analgesic function to relieve pain
- Anti-inflammatory function to reduce swelling and inflammation
- Circulatory effect to improve peripheral blood circulation to facilitate healing and recovery
- Treats causes of peripheral neuropathy, such as trauma, infection, and accumulation of drugs and toxic chemicals

CHINESE THERAPEUTIC ACTIONS

- Invigorates blood circulation
- Relieves pain
- Opens channels and collaterals

DOSAGE

Take 3 to 4 capsules three times daily on an empty stomach, with warm water. Dosage may be increased to 6 to 8 capsules three times daily, if necessary.

INGREDIENTS

Bai Shao (Radix Paeoniae Alba)
Chuan Mu Xiang (Radix Vladimiriae)
Chuan Niu Xi (Radix Cyathulae)
Chuan Xiong (Rhizoma Chuanxiong)
Da Huang (Radix et Rhizoma Rhei)
Da Zao (Fructus Jujubae)
Dang Gui (Radix Angelicae Sinensis)
Dang Gui Wei (Extremitas Radix Angelicae Sinensis)
Er Cha (Catechu)
Fu Ling (Poria)
Gan Cao (Radix et Rhizoma Glycyrrhizae)
Hong Hua (Flos Carthami)
Huang Jin Gui (Caulis Vanieriae)
Liu Zhi Huang (Herba Solidaginis)
Lu Lu Tong (Fructus Liquidambaris)
Mo Gu Xiao (Caulis Hyptis Capitatae)
Mo Yao (Myrrha)
Mu Dan Pi (Cortex Moutan)
Qiang Huo (Rhizoma et Radix Notopterygii)
Qin Jiao (Radix Gentianae Macrophyllae)
Ru Xiang (Gummi Olibanum)
Sheng Ma (Rhizoma Cimicifugae)
Tao Ren (Semen Persicae)
Xue Jie (Sanguis Draconis)
Yan Hu Suo (Rhizoma Corydalis)

BACKGROUND

Neuropathy is defined as a functional disturbance or pathological change in the peripheral nervous system.[1] Symptoms of neuropathy include sensory loss, muscle weakness and atrophy, and pain. Etiologies of neuropathy include trauma, infection by micro-organisms, drugs, nutritional deficiency, metabolic disorders, malignancy, and unknown causes.[2] Due to the wide range of causes, treatment varies. Herbal treatment of neuropathy focuses on relieving symptoms (pain) and the cause (such as poor circulation, increased cellular pressure, trauma, and infection).

FORMULA EXPLANATION

According to traditional Chinese medicine, peripheral neuropathy, polyneuropathy, diabetic neuropathy, distal polyneuropathy, neuralgia, and fibromyalgia have various etiologies. However, they all share one common factor – pain due to blood stagnation. Therefore, ***Flex (NP)*** is formulated to treat nerve pain by activating blood circulation and eliminating blood stagnation.

Tao Ren (Semen Persicae) and *Hong Hua* (Flos Carthami) are often paired together to synergistically invigorate blood circulation and remove blood stagnation. *Ru Xiang* (Gummi Olibanum), *Mo Yao* (Myrrha), *Chuan Niu Xi* (Radix Cyathulae), and *Yan Hu Suo* (Rhizoma Corydalis) together invigorate blood circulation and relieve pain. *Er Cha* (Catechu) and *Xue Jie* (Sanguis Draconis) promote the generation of new tissues. *Mu Dan Pi* (Cortex Moutan) moves blood and clears heat associated with local inflammation due to blood stagnation. *Dang Gui* (Radix Angelicae Sinensis), *Dang Gui Wei* (Extremitas Radix Angelicae Sinensis), *Chuan Xiong* (Rhizoma Chuanxiong), and *Lu Lu Tong* (Fructus Liquidambaris) open the channels and collaterals to relieve pain by invigorating blood circulation to the extremities. *Fu Ling* (Poria) is used to strengthen the middle *jiao* to promote absorption of the herbs.

Da Huang (Radix et Rhizoma Rhei) clears heat, removes blood stasis and helps with blood circulation. *Bai Shao* (Radix Paeoniae Alba) softens the Liver and benefits the tendons and sinews to relieve tightness, numbness, tingling, and pain. *Chuan Mu Xiang* (Radix Vladimiriae) invigorates qi circulation in the channels to assist the overall pain-relieving effects of this formula.

Qin Jiao (Radix Gentianae Macrophyllae), *Qiang Huo* (Rhizoma et Radix Notopterygii), *Huang Jin Gui* (Caulis Vanieriae), *Mo Gu Xiao* (Caulis Hyptis Capitatae), and *Liu Zhi Huang* (Herba Solidaginis) are used to relieve pain in the joints and extremities. *Da Zao* (Fructus Jujubae) and *Gan Cao* (Radix et Rhizoma Glycyrrhizae) are used to harmonize the formula and the middle *jiao*.

In summary, ***Flex (NP)*** contains herbs that invigorate blood circulation and eliminate blood stasis to treat various presentations of nerve pain.

Flex (NP)™

CAUTIONS & CONTRAINDICATIONS

- This formula is contraindicated during pregnancy and nursing.
- This herbal formula contains herbs that invigorate blood circulation, such as *Dang Gui* (Radix Angelicae Sinensis) and *Dang Gui Wei* (Extremitas Radix Angelicae Sinensis). Therefore, patients who are on anticoagulant or antiplatelet therapies, such as Coumadin (warfarin), should use this formula with caution, or not at all, as there may be a higher risk of bleeding and bruising.[3,4,5]
- The following warning statement is required by the State of California: "This product contains *Da Huang* (Radix et Rhizoma Rhei). Read and follow directions carefully. Do not use if you have or develop diarrhea, loose stools, or abdominal pain because *Da Huang* (Radix et Rhizoma Rhei) may worsen these conditions and be harmful to your health. Consult your physician if you have frequent diarrhea or if you are pregnant, nursing, taking medication, or have a medical condition."

CLINICAL NOTES

- It is essential to identify and eliminate the cause(s) of neuropathy, especially if it is induced by drugs or toxic agents. Without elimination of the offending agent, treatment will offer only symptomatic relief.
- Neuropathy due to nutritional deficiency must be identified and treated accordingly. Adequate intake of vitamin B complex is beneficial. Though it is uncommon in developed countries, patients with polyneuropathy due to nutritional deficiency should be put on vitamin B supplementation.
- Neuropathy due to metabolic disorders, such as diabetic neuropathy, must be identified, and the root cause treated accordingly. Blood glucose levels must be monitored to ensure that the patient's levels stay within an acceptable range.
- Acupuncture is sometimes more effective than herbs in cases of neuropathy. *See* Acupuncture Treatment for treatment protocols.

Pulse Diagnosis by Dr. Jimmy Wei-Yen Chang:

- *Yinqiao* pulse, a thin, straight, wiry pulse found on or extends proximally to the *chi* position. *Yinqiao* pulse is one of the eight extra meridian pulses.

SUPPLEMENTARY FORMULAS

- For neuropathy due to chronic exposure to harmful toxins and chemicals, add ***Herbal DTX***.
- For diabetic neuropathy, use with ***Equilibrium***.
- To potentiate the effect to relieve pain, add ***Herbal ANG***.
- For nerve pain in the neck and shoulder area, combine with ***Neck & Shoulder (AC)*** or ***Neck & Shoulder (CR)***.
- For nerve pain in the arm (shoulder, elbow, and wrist), combine with ***Arm Support***.
- For nerve pain in the lower back, add ***Back Support (AC)*** or ***Back Support (CR)***.
- For nerve pain in the back from herniated disk, combine with ***Back Support (HD)***.
- For nerve pain in the knees, combine with ***Knee & Ankle (AC)*** or ***Knee & Ankle (CR)***.
- For nerve pain with chronic musculoskeletal disorder with damaged soft tissues (muscles, tendons, ligaments), add ***Flex (MLT)***.
- With excess heat, add ***Gardenia Complex***.
- With severe blood stagnation, add ***Circulation (SJ)***.
- For lymphedema, add ***Resolve (AI)***.

ACUPUNCTURE TREATMENT

Traditional Points:

- *Hua Tou Jia Ji*, local *ah shi* points
- *Hegu* (LI 4), *Shenshu* (BL 23), *Pishu* (BL 20), *Sanyinjiao* (SP 6), *Taichong* (LR 3)

Classic Master Tung's Points:

- Needle contralateral to the pain. If the pain is in the center, needle bilaterally or the side with the more *ah shi* points. If the pain is bilateral, needle bilaterally.
- **Peripheral neuropathy:** *Erjiaoming* (T 11.12), *Wanshunyi* (T 22.08), *Wanshuner* (T 22.09), *Tianhuang* (T 77.17), *Dihuang* (T 77.19), *Renhuang* (T 77.21), *Zhengshi* (T 77.03), *Zhengjin* (T 77.01), *Zhengzong* (T 77.02). Bleed *Weizhong* (BL 40), *Sihuashang* (T 77.08), *Sihuawai* (T 77.14), *Sihuazhong* (T 77.09), *Sihuali* (T 77.13), *Sihuafu* (T 77.10), *Sihuaxia* (T 77.11) or dark veins nearby. Bleed before needling for best result.

Master Tung's Points by Dr. Chuan-Min Wang:

- **Neuropathy:** *Zhongjiuli* (T 88.25), *Qili* (T 88.51)*, *Sizhi* (T 77.20), *Renhuang* (T 77.21)

Balance Method by Dr. Richard Tan:

- Use Dr. Tan's Balance Method accordingly as determined by where the pain is (use mirror or image system).

Ear Acupuncture:

- Affected area, Adrenal Gland, Lung
- Embed magnetic balls and switch ears every five days.

Auricular Medicine by Dr. Li-Chun Huang:

- **Peripheral neuropathy:** Large Auricular Nerve, Lesser Occipital Nerve, and corresponding points (fingers, toes). Bleed Ear Apex.
- **Intercostal neuralgia:** Intercostal Area, Large Auricular Nerve, corresponding points (to the area affected)
  - Supplementary points: Liver, Gallbladder, Chest, Occiput
- **Diabetes mellitus:** Diabetes Point, Pancreas, Ear Center, Pituitary, Thalamus, *San Jiao*, Endocrine
  - For numbness in the extremities, add Lesser Occipital Nerve, Large Auricular Nerve

Flex (NP)™

NUTRITION

- Nutritional balance is essential in the treatment and prevention of neuropathy. It is important to make sure that there is adequate intake of various nutrients in a well-balanced diet. If necessary, supplement the diet with vitamins and minerals.
- Increase the intake of foods that contain thiamine (vitamin B_1), such as whole grains and green vegetables, to maintain nerve health. Do not consume white sugar and white flour products, as they deplete the body of B vitamins.

LIFESTYLE INSTRUCTIONS

- Tight control over blood glucose levels is essential in patients with diabetic neuropathy. Diet, exercise, and herbal treatment will be extremely beneficial in maintaining normal blood glucose levels.
- Nerve pain can be relieved with light massage using a solution of apple cider vinegar water, which is made by mixing ½ cup apple cider vinegar with 2 cups of warm water.
- Application of hot wraps for half an hour is also effective to relieve pain.
- Avoid exposure to toxic agents or industrial poisons that cause nerve damage, such as carbon monoxide, heavy metals (especially lead or mercury), and many chemical solvents.
- Do not take harmful drugs that cause nerve damage, such as antibiotics (sulfonamides, nitrofurantoin, chlorobutanol), anti-seizure drugs (phenytoin), sedatives (barbital, hexobarbital) and anticancer drugs (vinca alkaloids).

CASE STUDIES

- F.T., a 44-year-old female marathon runner, presented with a Baker's cyst on her left knee, previously diagnosed by an MRI, measuring out to be 4 cm in diameter. Objective findings were pain and swelling that were limiting her ability to walk and run. The practitioner diagnosed this condition as stagnation of qi and blood within the channels, as well as heat toxin and accumulation of phlegm. ***Resolve (AI)*** and ***Flex (NP)*** were prescribed at 3 grams three times a day at a 2:1 ratio. After one month of taking the herbs, the cyst was almost completely resolved. The formula was then modified to address the residual inflammation and stagnation in the channels. Thereafter, the client was able to begin long distance running again without further problems. Other than that condition, the patient was in excellent health. She had eliminated coffee from her diet and started eating anti-inflammatory foods while being treated for the cyst. Submitted by E.Z., Portland, Oregon.
- D.A., a 55-year-old female, presented with extreme pain in both heels, radiating up the calf area. Symptoms of night sweats, problems with staying asleep, low energy, and depression were also present. Her pulse was weak and thin, and her tongue was red with thin white coating. The practitioner diagnosed this condition as Liver qi stagnation and Kidney yin deficiency. Upon diagnosis, the patient was prescribed ***Flex (NP)*** and ***Circulation (SJ)***. The patient reported less pain; however, it was still present especially in the morning and late in the day after standing a lot. Her sleep improved as well to waking up only once during the night. The patient continued to improve; however, effort on her part was necessary to improve more. Submitted by B.L., Fort Myers, Florida.
- J.B., a 55-year-old female, presented with pain located on the right foot, numbness and tingling along the neck, and pain shooting down the back legs. The patient was also complaining about hot flashes and night sweating. Objective findings included pain upon palpation of the joints and red cheeks. The TCM diagnosis was qi and blood stagnation with yin deficiency; her Western diagnosis was RSD (reflex sympathetic dystrophy). ***Flex (NP)*** was prescribed at 2 to 3 capsules twice a day. After taking the herbs, the patient experienced less pain in the arm and neck, but pain in the right foot was still present, and she was experiencing slight stomach discomfort. The patient was directed to take a higher dosage if tolerable. Submitted by M.P., Muskego, Wisconsin.
- L.L., a 52-year-old female, presented with body aches over the entire body along with swelling of the legs. Additional symptoms included low grade fever, sore throat, and low energy. The patient had been previously diagnosed with Lyme disease. Her pulse was thin and weak and her tongue was pale and dull with thin white coating. The practitioner diagnosed this condition as general qi and blood stagnation with Spleen qi deficiency. For treatment, patient was instructed to take ***Resolve (AI)*** and ***Flex (NP)*** in conjunction with acupuncture treatment. As a result, the patient's energy increased, the pain lessened, and the sore throat was no longer present. Additional treatment the patient had received was lymphatic massage which also had helped her improve. Submitted by B.L., Fort Myers, Florida.
- J.R., a male patient, suffered from intolerable neuropathy after receiving chemotherapy and radiation for throat cancer. He conducted an empirical test on himself in which he took ***Flex (NP)*** for one week and did not take it for another. He reported that the week without the ***Flex (NP)*** was nearly intolerable. But with it, he is "in the zone" and is able to sleep. ***Flex (NP)*** has reduced his neuropathic symptoms by a good 50%. Submitted by C.W., Carpinteria, California.
- A 59-year-old male was stung by a sea urchin while diving in Hawaii four months prior to coming in for treatment. The spines of the sea urchin went into his hand. The black marking of the sting are all gone, but he had difficulty moving his fingers with limited movement of his fingers and hand. His tongue was dusky and swollen with a sticky coat. His pulses were wiry and slippery. After taking ***Flex (NP)*** and ***Astringent Complex*** for 15 days, in conjunction with acupuncture, the patient was completely healed. Submitted by K.M., Albany, California.
- A 36-year-old diabetic (Type 1) female presented with severe neuropathy of her hands along with chronic fungal and bacterial infections, sores all over her lower limbs, feet numbness, severe fatigue, malaise and weakness. Besides her diabetes, she also

Flex (NP)™

was diagnosed with kidney failure as well as immune deficiency due to immuno-suppressants. She had a kidney transplant as a result of her kidney failure. The TCM practitioner diagnosed her condition as severe Kidney *jing* (essence) deficiency with underlying Spleen qi deficiency, damp-heat, and qi and blood stagnation. Her circulation was severely impaired along with noticeable signs of wasting and thirsting. The patient prescribed an herbal combination of ***Flex (NP)*** (3 to 4 capsules three times daily) and a customized special formula to tonify her Spleen qi, move the blood, and circulate the qi. The patient experienced relief from her hand pain within two to three days. Although stinging sensations still persisted, the pain was less in occurrence and intensity. Her sores and warts displayed signs of improvement as well as becoming less visible. Submitted by A.R., Encinitas, California.

- M.F., a 57-year-old female, presented with pain in the leg and big toe with pressure, metallic taste, absence of thirst, heat sensations except in the hands and feet, and upper body sweating. She had been exposed to toxic chemicals and pesticides for six months. The TCM diagnosis was yin deficiency with heat, damp-heat and toxic heat accumulation, and *bi zheng* (painful obstruction syndrome) of the legs. After six weeks of taking ***Liver DTX***, ***Balance (Heat)*** and ***Flex (NP)***, she experienced less leg pain, decreased sweating, subsiding heat sensations, and warmer hands. The patient still had a metallic taste in the mouth. The patient was also advised to increase her intake of carrot juice and cucumbers. Submitted by M.C., Sarasota, Florida.

PHARMACOLOGICAL AND CLINICAL RESEARCH

Flex (NP) is formulated specifically to treat nerve pain, such as in various presentations of neuropathy and neuralgia. The main signs and symptoms include pain, numbness, sensory loss, and muscle weakness and atrophy. Optimal treatment of neuropathy and neuralgia requires use of herbs to alleviate the symptom (pain) and the cause (poor circulation, increased cellular pressure, trauma, infection, and others).

Pharmacologically, ***Flex (NP)*** utilizes many herbs with excellent analgesic effects to alleviate pain and anti-inflammatory activity to reduce inflammation. *Dang Gui* (Radix Angelicae Sinensis), *Bai Shao* (Radix Paeoniae Alba), *Gan Cao* (Radix et Rhizoma Glycyrrhizae) and *Qiang Huo* (Rhizoma et Radix Notopterygii) all have an analgesic effect to alleviate pain.[6,7,8,9,10,11] *Mu Dan Pi* (Cortex Moutan) and *Qin Jiao* (Radix Gentianae Macrophyllae) have an anti-inflammatory effect to reduce swelling and inflammation.[12,13,14] More specifically, nerve-related pain, such as trigeminal pain, responds remarkably to such herbs as *Chuan Xiong* (Rhizoma Chuanxiong), *Bai Shao* (Radix Paeoniae Alba), and *Gan Cao* (Radix et Rhizoma Glycyrrhizae).[15,16] Injury-related pain, such as pain of the extremities, responds equally well to herbs such as *Ru Xiang* (Gummi Olibanum), *Mo Yao* (Myrrha), *Yan Hu Suo* (Rhizoma Corydalis), *Bai Shao* (Radix Paeoniae Alba), and *Gan Cao* (Radix et Rhizoma Glycyrrhizae).[17,18]

Clinically, many herbs in ***Flex (NP)*** have been used successfully to treat various types of nerve pain. The combination of *Bai Shao* (Radix Paeoniae Alba) and *Gan Cao* (Radix et Rhizoma Glycyrrhizae) has a marked analgesic effect, and has been used successfully to treat neuralgia,[19] trigeminal neuralgia,[20,21] and sciatica.[22] *Chuan Xiong* (Rhizoma Chuanxiong) exerts an anti-inflammatory effect via an inhibitory activity on TNF-α production and TNF-α bioactivity,[23] and is used clinically to treat trigeminal nerve pain and trigeminal neuralgia.[24,25] *Dang Gui* (Radix Angelicae Sinensis) exerts both analgesic and anti-inflammatory effects through the inhibition of pro-inflammatory mediators, including nitric oxide and prostaglandin E2 in peritoneal macrophages.[26,27] In comparison with acetylsalicylic acid, the anti-inflammatory effect of *Dang Gui* (Radix Angelicae Sinensis) is approximately 1.1 times stronger, and its analgesic effect is approximately 1.7 times stronger.[28] Lastly, *Yan Hu Suo* (Rhizoma Corydalis) is one of the strongest and most potent herbs for treatment of pain. According to laboratory studies, the extract of *Yan Hu Suo* (Rhizoma Corydalis) has been found to be effective in both acute and chronic phases of pain and inflammation. Furthermore, with appropriate adjustment of dosage, its analgesic effect is comparable to that of morphine.[29] Lastly, it has been demonstrated that the analgesic effect of *Yan Hu Suo* (Rhizoma Corydalis) is increased significantly with concurrent treatments with electro-acupuncture.[30]

In addition to relieving the symptoms (pain), ***Flex (NP)*** contains many herbs to treat the causes of neuropathy and neuralgia (poor circulation, increased cellular pressure, trauma, infection, and others). Poor circulation is a significant factor contributing to neuropathy and hindering its recovery. *Tao Ren* (Semen Persicae), *Hong Hua* (Flos Carthami), *Chuan Xiong* (Rhizoma Chuanxiong) and *Mu Dan Pi* (Cortex Moutan) have pronounced influence on improving blood circulation, increasing microcirculation to peripheral parts of the body, eliminating blood stasis, and facilitating recovery.[31,32,33,34] Increased cellular pressure is another contributor to neuropathy. *Mu Dan Pi* (Cortex Moutan) is used to reduce swelling and pressure in the periphery of the body by inhibiting prostaglandin synthesis and decreasing permeability of the blood vessels.[35,36] Trauma is another common cause of neuropathy. *Ru Xiang* (Gummi Olibanum), *Mo Yao* (Myrrha) and *Yan Hu Suo* (Rhizoma Corydalis) are commonly used in treatment of trauma and sports injuries.[37] *Tao Ren* (Semen Persicae) is also effective to facilitate recovery from injuries.[38] Certain injuries that damage both nerves and soft tissue, such as frostbite, can be treated with *Dang Gui* (Radix Angelicae Sinensis), *Gan Cao* (Radix et Rhizoma Glycyrrhizae), and other herbs.[39,40] Furthermore, infection and its complications also contribute to neuropathy. There are many herbs with remarkable antibiotic properties, such as *Er Cha* (Catechu),[41] *Xue Jie* (Sanguis Draconis),[42] and *Mu Dan Pi* (Cortex Moutan).[43] Lastly, exposure to drugs and toxic agents are two of the main causes of neuropathy. While elimination of these

Flex (NP)™

offending agents is the best solution, it is not always possible to discontinue the drugs or completely eliminate exposure to toxic chemicals. Under these circumstances, the drugs and the toxic chemicals accumulate in the body and adversely affect the nerves. *Gan Cao* (Radix et Rhizoma Glycyrrhizae) is prescribed to remedy these kinds of poisoning. It is one of the most effective detoxifying herbs for treatment of physiological insults, including drug poisoning (chloral hydrate, urethane, cocaine, picrotoxin, caffeine, pilocarpine, nicotine, barbiturates, mercury and lead), food poisoning (tetrodotoxin, snake, and mushrooms), and others (enterotoxin, herbicides, pesticides). The exact mechanism of this action is unclear, but it is thought that it is related to the regulatory effect of *Gan Cao* (Radix et Rhizoma Glycyrrhizae) on the endocrine or hepatic systems.[44]

In summary, ***Flex (NP)*** is an effective formula for treatment of neuropathy and neuralgia. It contains herbs that relieve the symptoms and the cause, and achieves both short- and long-term improvements.

COMPARATIVE ANALYSIS

Pain is a basic bodily sensation induced by a noxious stimulus that causes physical discomfort (such as pricking, throbbing, or aching). Pain may be of acute or chronic state, and may be of nociceptive, neuropathic, or psychogenic origin. For neuropathic pain of acute or chronic origins, the drugs of choice include antiseizure [Dilantin (phenytoin) and Neurontin (gabapentin)] and antidepressant drugs [Elavil (amitriptyline)]. Though effective, these drugs are associated with numerous and significant side effects. Antiseizure drugs cause side effects such as bleeding, burning sensations, clumsiness or unsteadiness, confusion, irregular eye movements, blurred or double vision, swollen glands in neck or underarms, slurred speech, delusions, dementia, bone malformations, and many others. Antidepressant drugs cause blurred vision, confusion or delirium, hallucinations, constipation (especially in the elderly), problems in urinating, decreased sexual ability, difficulty in speaking or swallowing, eye pain, fainting, fast or irregular heartbeat, loss of balance control, mask-like face, nervousness or restlessness, slowed movements, stiffness of arms and legs, and shortness of breath or troubled breathing. In short, these drugs should be prescribed only when benefits significantly outweigh the risks. Furthermore, use of these drugs must be monitored carefully to avoid developing serious side effects and complications.

Treatment of pain is a sophisticated balance of art and science. Proper treatment of pain requires a careful evaluation of the type of disharmony (excess or deficiency, cold or heat, exterior or interior), characteristics (qi and/or blood stagnations), and location (upper body, lower body, extremities, or internal organs). Furthermore, optimal treatment requires integrative use of herbs, acupuncture and *tui-na* therapies. All these therapies work together to tonify the underlying deficiencies, strengthen the body, and facilitate recovery from chronic pain. TCM pain management targets both the symptom and the cause of pain, and as such, often achieves immediate and long-term success. Furthermore, TCM pain management is often associated with few or no side effects.

For treatment of mild to severe pain due to neuropathic causes, TCM pain management offers similar treatment effects to those of pharmaceuticals, with significantly fewer side effects.

References

1. *Dorland's Illustrated Medical Dictionary 28th Edition*. W.B. Saunders Company, 1994.
2. Berkow, R. *The Merck Manual of Diagnosis and Therapy 16th Edition*. 1992.
3. Chan K, Lo AC, Yeung JH, Woo KS. Journal of Pharmacy and Pharmacology 1995 May;47(5):402-6.
4. Pharmacotherapy 1999 July;19(7):870-876.
5. European Journal of Drug Metabolism and Pharmacokinetics 1995; 20(1): 55-60.
6. *Xin Yi Yao Xue Za Zhi (New Journal of Medicine and Herbology)*, 1975; (6):34.
7. *Gui Yang Yi Xue Yuan Xue Bao (Journal of Guiyang Medical University)*, 1959; 113.
8. *Zhong Yao Xue (Chinese Herbology)*, 1998; 380:382.
9. *Zhong Yao Xue (Chinese Herbology)*, 1998; 386:387.
10. *Shang Hai Zhong Yi Yao Za Zhi (Shanghai Journal of Chinese Medicine and Herbology)* 1983; 4:14.
11. *Zhong Cao Yao (Chinese Herbal Medicine)*, 1991; 22( ):28.
12. *Sheng Yao Xue Za Zhi (Journal of Raw Herbology)*, 1979; 33(3):178.
13. *Chang Yong Zhong Yao Cheng Fen Yu Yao Li Shou Ce (A Handbook of the Composition and Pharmacology of Common Chinese Drugs)*, 1994; 1479:1482.
14. *Yao Xue Xue Bao* (Journal of Herbology), 1982; 17(1):12.
15. *He Bei Zhong Yi Za Zhi (Hebei Journal of Chinese Medicine)*, 1982; 4:34.
16. *Zhong Yi Za Zhi (Journal of Chinese Medicine)*, 1983;11:9.
17. *He Nan Zhong Yi Xue Yuan Xue Bao (Journal of University of Henan School of Medicine)*, 1980; 3:38.
18. *Yun Nan Zhong Yi (Yunnan Journal of Traditional Chinese Medicine)*, 1990; 4:15.
19. *Zhong Yi Ming Fang Lin Chuang Xin Yong* (Contemporary Clinical Applications of Classic Chinese Formulas) 2001;313.
20. *Jiang Xi Yi Yao* (Jiangxi Medicine and Herbology) 1965;5(7):909.
21. *Zhong Yi Za Zhi* (Journal of Chinese Medicine), 1983; 11:9.
22. *Fu Jian Zhong Yi Yao* (Fujian Chinese Medicine and Herbology), 1994; (1):7.
23. Liu L, Ning ZQ, Shan S, Zhang K, Deng T, Lu XP, Cheng YY. Phthalide Lactones from Ligusticum chuanxiong inhibit lipopolysaccharide-induced TNF-alpha production and TNF-alpha-mediated NF-kappaB Activation. Planta Med. 2005 Sep;71(9):808-13.
24. *He Bei Zhong Yi Za Zhi* (Hebei Journal of Chinese Medicine), 1982; 4:34.
25. *Zhong Yao Lin Chuan Xin Yong* (New Clinical Applications of Chinese Medicine), 2001; 65.
26. *Xin Yi Yao Xue Za Zhi* (New Journal of Medicine and Herbology), 1975; (6):34.
27. Chao WW, Kuo YH, Li WC, Lin BF. The production of nitric oxide and prostaglandin E2 in peritoneal macrophages is inhibited by Andrographis paniculata, Angelica sinensis and Morus alba ethyl acetate fractions. Department of Biochemical Science and Technology, Institute of Microbiology and Biochemistry, National Taiwan University, Taipei 106, Taiwan, ROC. J Ethnopharmacol. 2009 Feb 25;122(1):68-75.
28. *Yao Xue Za Zhi* (Journal of Medicinals), 1971; (91):1098.
29. *He Bei Xin Yi Yao* (Hebei New Medicine and Herbology), 1973; 4:34.
30. *Chen Tzu Yen Chiu* (Acupuncture Research), 1994;19(1):55-8.
31. *Zhong Guo Zhong Yi Yao Xue Bao (Chinese Journal of Chinese Medicine and Herbology)*, 1985; 7:45.
32. *Zhong Yao Yao Li Yu Ying Yong (Pharmacology and Applications of Chinese Herbs)*, 1989; (2):40.

Flex (NP)™

33. *Zhong Yao Xue (Chinese Herbology)*, 1989; 535:539.
34. *Guo Wai Yi Xue Zhong Yi Zhong Yao Fen Ce (Monograph of Chinese Herbology from Foreign Medicine)*, 1983; (3):5,1984;(5):54.
35. *Sheng Yao Xue Za Zhi (Journal of Raw Herbology)*, 1979; 33(3):178.
36. *Zhong Guo Yao Ke Da Xue Xue Bao (Journal of University of Chinese Herbology)*, 1990; 21(4):222.
37. *He Nan Zhong Yi Xue Yuan Xue Bao (Journal of University of Henan School of Medicine)*, 1980; 3:38.
38. *Shang Hai Zhong Yi Yao Za Zhi (Shanghai Journal of Chinese Medicine and Herbology)*, 1985; 7:45.
39. *Zhong Hua Yi Xue Za Zhi (Chinese Journal of Medicine)*, 1956; 10:978.
40. *Xin Zhong Yi (New Chinese Medicine)*, 1980.
41. *Zhong Cao Yao Xue (Study of Chinese Herbal Medicine)*, 1976; 431.
42. *Zhong Yao Xue (Chinese Herbology)*, 1998; 987:988.
43. *Zhong Yao Cai (Study of Chinese Herbal Material)*, 1991; 14(2):41.
44. *Zhong Yao Tong Bao (Journal of Chinese Herbology)*, 1986; 11(10):55.

Flex (SC)™

CLINICAL APPLICATIONS

- **Spasms and cramps:**
  - Skeletal muscles in the extremities
  - Smooth muscles in the internal organs
- **Muscle tightness and stiffness** due to repetitive movements
- External injuries with muscle sprain and strain

WESTERN THERAPEUTIC ACTIONS

- Muscle-relaxant effect to treat muscle spasms and cramps
- Anti-inflammatory function to reduce inflammation and swelling
- Analgesic effect to relieve pain

CHINESE THERAPEUTIC ACTIONS

- Tonifies Liver yin and Liver blood
- Relieves spasms and cramps
- Tonifies the blood
- Warms the meridians and unblocks stagnation
- Invigorates blood circulation

DOSAGE

Take 3 to 4 capsules every four to six hours as needed for muscle spasms and cramps. The dosage may be increased up to 5 to 6 capsules every two to four hours if necessary. For maximum effectiveness, take ***Flex (SC)*** on an empty stomach with a tall glass of warm water.

INGREDIENTS

Bai Shao (Radix Paeoniae Alba)
Dang Gui Wei (Extremitas Radix Angelicae Sinensis)
Hua Jiao (Pericarpium Zanthoxyli)
Zhi Gan Cao (Radix et Rhizoma Glycyrrhizae Praeparata cum Melle)

BACKGROUND

Muscle spasms and cramps are involuntary and sometimes painful contractions of the muscles. Spasms and cramps affect many muscle groups, including but not limited to leg, calf, thigh, hands, arms, abdomen, and intestines. Common causes of muscle spasms and cramps include overuse or injury of a muscle, dehydration, electrolyte imbalance, excessive consumption of alcohol, certain disease state (hypothyroidism, kidney failure), and use of drugs (diuretics). Stretching and adequate intake of fluids with sufficient amount of potassium are the best preventative measures for spasms and cramps. If necessary, herbs that relax the muscles can also be used.

FORMULA EXPLANATION

Flex (SC) is formulated to relieve muscle spasms and cramps. According to traditional Chinese medicine, the etiology of muscle spasms and cramps is Liver yin and Liver blood deficiencies. Effective treatment, therefore, must focus on nourishing Liver yin and Liver blood deficiencies, activating qi and blood circulation, and removing stagnation.

Bai Shao (Radix Paeoniae Alba) tonifies Liver yin and Liver blood to relieve spasms and cramps. Paeoniflorin, the active constituent in *Bai Shao* (Radix Paeoniae Alba), has strong analgesic, antispasmodic and anti-inflammatory effects. Together with the harmonizing function of *Zhi Gan Cao* (Radix et Rhizoma Glycyrrhizae Praeparata cum Melle), they nourish and relax the tendons and smooth muscles. *Hua Jiao* (Pericarpium Zanthoxyli) and *Dang Gui Wei* (Extremitas Radix Angelicae Sinensis) are used to warm peripheral channels and collaterals and invigorate qi and blood circulation.

CAUTIONS & CONTRAINDICATIONS

- This formula should not be taken long-term in patients who have hypertension, as prolonged use of *Zhi Gan Cao* (Radix et Rhizoma Glycyrrhizae Praeparata cum Melle) may be associated with water retention.
- This herbal formula contains herbs that invigorate blood circulation, such as *Dang Gui Wei* (Extremitas Radix Angelicae Sinensis). Therefore, patients who are on anticoagulant or antiplatelet therapies, such as Coumadin (warfarin), should use this formula with caution, or not at all, as there may be a higher risk of bleeding and bruising.[1,2,3]

SUPPLEMENTARY FORMULAS

- To enhance the analgesic effect, add ***Herbal ANG***.
- For neck and shoulder pain, add ***Neck & Shoulder (AC)*** or ***Neck & Shoulder (CR)***.
- For lower back pain, combine with ***Back Support (AC)*** or ***Back Support (CR)***.
- For pain in the arm (shoulder, elbow and wrist), add ***Arm Support***.
- For knee pain, combine with ***Knee & Ankle (AC)*** or ***Knee & Ankle (CR)***.
- For chronic musculoskeletal disorder with damaged soft tissues (muscles, tendons, ligaments, and cartilage), add ***Flex (MLT)***.
- For arthritis with inflammation, swelling, redness and pain, combine with ***Flex (Heat)***.
- For arthritic pain that worsens during cold and rainy weather, combine with ***Flex (CD)***.
- For bone fractures, injuries, and bruises, add ***Flex (TMX)***.
- To improve blood circulation to the extremities, combine with ***Flex (NP)***.
- For bone spurs, add ***Flex (SPR)***.
- For osteoporosis, add ***Osteo 8***.
- For severe blood stagnation, add ***Circulation (SJ)***.
- For dryness and thirst, add ***Nourish (Fluids)***.

ACUPUNCTURE TREATMENT

Traditional Points:

- *Shousanli* (LI 10), *Waiguan* (TH 5), *Zusanli* (ST 36)
- *Zhigou* (TH 6), *Zusanli* (ST 36), *Zhongwan* (CV 12), *Neiguan* (PC 6), *Guanyuan* (CV 4), *Taichong* (LR 3), *Shenque* (CV 8)

Flex (SC)™

Classic Master Tung's Points:

- Needle contralateral to the pain. If the pain is in the center, needle bilaterally or the side with the more *ah shi* points. If the pain is bilateral, needle bilaterally.
- *Linggu* (T 22.05), *Wanshunyi* (T 22.08), *Wanshuner* (T 22.09), *Zhongguan* (T 22.25)*, *Zhengjin* (T 77.01), *Zhengzong* (T 77.02), *Zhengshi* (T 77.03), *Tianhuang* (T 77.17), *Dihuang* (T 77.19), *Renhuang* (T 77.21)
- **Medial calf pain:** *Ganlingsan* (T 33.18)*, *Xinmen* (T 33.12), *Changmen* (T 33.10), *Ganmen* (T 33.11)

Master Tung's Points by Dr. Chuan-Min Wang:

- **Spasms, cramps:** *Zhongjiuli* (T 88.25), *Qili* (T 88.51)*, *Sanchasan* (T 22.17)*

Balance Method by Dr. Richard Tan:

- Use Dr. Tan's Balance Method accordingly as determined by where the pain is (use mirror or image system).

Auricular Medicine by Dr. Li-Chun Huang:

- **Spasm:** Sympathetic, Nervous Subcortex, *Shenmen*, corresponding points (to the area affected). Bleed Ear Apex.
- **Calf cramps:** Calf, Popliteal Fossa, Lesser Occipital Nerve, Liver, Spleen, Coronary Vascular Subcortex

NUTRITION

- Drink large amounts of water throughout the day (steam-distilled) to hydrate the muscles and flush out toxins residing in the muscles.
- To prevent muscle cramps and spasms, eat plenty of fruits and vegetables, especially those high in potassium, such as bananas and oranges.
- Avoid foods that increase the acidity of the body, such as red meat, baked goods, sweet foods, and processed foods.
- Increase the intake of foods rich in alkaline minerals, such as fresh raw vegetables, alfalfa sprouts, and seaweed.

LIFESTYLE INSTRUCTIONS

- Cigarette smoking and alcohol intake should be avoided as they dry out yin and may cause more cramping.
- Warm baths relax the tense muscles and relieve spasms and cramps.
- Avoid tight shoes and clothing, which impair normal circulation of blood to peripheral parts of the body.
- Stretch for at least 30 minutes daily, especially before exercising.

CASE STUDIES

- E.B., a 79-year-old female, presented with stiffness of the middle and ring fingers on the right hand. She was neither able to close her hand and make a fist, nor was she also able to extend her fingers. The range of motion was greatly reduced, and she was unable to sculpt. The patient refused to see a medical doctor. The previous carpal tunnel syndrome (CTS) surgery in 1983 left a small scar in the palm of her hand. The tendons of the palm were very tight, ropy in quality, enlarged and swollen. The palms were red, the skin was dry and the nails were brittle. She also complained of dry mouth and throat at night. The Western diagnoses were contraction of the palmar fascia and Dupuytren's Contracture. The TCM diagnoses were *bi zheng* (painful obstruction syndrome), Liver and Kidney yin deficiencies, and blood stagnation. Acupuncture, micro-current, massage, and ***Flex (SC)*** were all part of the treatment regime that helped her gain 90% range of motion within one week. She was almost able to close her hands and make a fist. The palm was less red and the swelling decreased. The patient was thrilled. Submitted by M.H., West Palm Beach, Florida.
- A 44-year-old female presented with upper back spasm. The patient stated: "It feels like creepy crawlers." In addition to her upper back dysfunction, floaters were also present with bright lights disturbing her eyes. The practitioner diagnosed her condition as Liver qi stagnation with Liver yin deficiency. After taking ***Flex (SC)***, the patient was calmer, more relaxed, and had fewer moods swings. Consequently, she was not as irritable and had less muscle spasms in her mid back. She also slept much better. Submitted by D.M., Raton, New Mexico.
- L.P., a 77-year-old female, presented with severe pain in the left wrist and right rib cage after a fall. She had numbness of the wrist and palm where she landed on the cement. The patient showed bruises on the right eye. The right wrist was painful to light movement and palpation. There were tender points on the right subclavicular area. There were no visible contusions on the right rib cage. The diagnoses were qi and blood stagnation with soft tissue damage. ***Flex (TMX)***, ***Neck & Shoulder (AC)*** and ***Flex (SC)*** were prescribed at 2 capsules of each formula three times daily. The patient reported daily lowering of pain levels. Numbness was reduced to a light tingling after two days. She reported continuous and steady improvement each day. She was instructed to reduce the dosage to 2 capsules of each formula twice a day when the pain subsided. After the swelling was reduced, the patient was referred to a chiropractor for cervical and occipital adjustments. Submitted by M.H., West Palm Beach, Florida.
- D.D., a 41-year-old nurse, presented with a work-related injury. She had severe back pain that was the result of a fall from lifting a patient. She said she heard a popping sound in her back when she fell. MRI confirmed her diagnosis of lumbar herniated disc. She was nine weeks post-injury and had scheduled for steroid epidurals. She refused injections and came to our clinic for 'safe and non-invasive care.' Her blood pressure was 140/80 mmHg and the heart rate was 80 beats per minute. The TCM diagnoses include qi and blood stagnation and soft tissue damage. ***Back Support (AC)***, ***Flex (SC)*** and ***Flex (TMX)*** were prescribed at 3 capsules each three times a day. After the herbs, the patient was able to reduce Vicodin (APAP/hydrocodone) use from 2 to 0.5 tablets per day, and none at all on some days. She had increased blood pressure from stress over the injury, which was up to

Flex (SC)™

170/110 mmHg. After the herbs and massage, the blood pressure came down to normal and is staying down. She had received no additional physical therapy. She did remarkably well in a short period of time. Submitted by M.H., West Palm Beach, Florida.

PHARMACOLOGICAL AND CLINICAL RESEARCH

Flex (SC) is formulated based on a classic Chinese herbal formula, *Shao Yao Gan Cao Tang* (Peony and Licorice Decoction), which has been used for approximately two thousands years to treat spasms and cramps of skeletal and intestinal muscles. Modern research has confirmed the ingredients of ***Flex (SC)*** to have excellent muscle-relaxant, analgesic and anti-inflammatory effects.

The combination of *Bai Shao* (Radix Paeoniae Alba) and *Gan Cao* (Radix et Rhizoma Glycyrrhizae) has an excellent muscle-relaxant effect to relax both smooth and skeletal muscles.[4,5] Clinically, these two herbs have been used successfully to treat conditions such as leg cramps in the calf,[6] muscle cramps in hemodialysis,[7] restless leg syndrome,[8] intestinal spasms,[9] facial spasms and twitching,[10] and menstrual cramps and pain.[11]

Bai Shao (Radix Paeoniae Alba) and *Gan Cao* (Radix et Rhizoma Glycyrrhizae) also have a marked analgesic effect to relieve pain. The effectiveness is increased significantly when combined with acupuncture.[12] Clinically, these two herbs have been used successfully to treat conditions such as pain,[13] neuralgia,[14] trigeminal neuralgia,[15,16] neck pain, [17] acute back pain,[18] heel pain,[19] pain in the lower back and legs,[20] sciatica,[21] gastric and abdominal pain,[22] and dysmenorrhea.[23]

Lastly, *Bai Shao* (Radix Paeoniae Alba) and *Gan Cao* (Radix et Rhizoma Glycyrrhizae) are commonly used to treat inflammatory disorders, as they have a synergistic effect when used together. *Bai Shao* (Radix Paeoniae Alba) has an excellent anti-inflammatory effect to reduce swelling and inflammation by modulating the pro-inflammatory mediators production from macrophage-like synoviocytes.[24] *Gan Cao* (Radix et Rhizoma Glycyrrhizae) has marked anti-inflammatory function by enhancing the effect of glucocorticoid through increased production and secretion, as well as decreased metabolism by the liver, or increased plasma concentration caused by decreased protein binding.[25] Clinical applications include pain, inflammation, edema, arthritis, spasms, cramps and others.[26,27]

Flex (SC) incorporates *Dang Gui* (Radix Angelicae Sinensis) and *Hua Jiao* (Pericarpium Zanthoxyli) to enhance the analgesic and anti-inflammatory effects. *Hua Jiao* (Pericarpium Zanthoxyli) exerts its anti-inflammatory effect by inhibiting the pro-inflammatory cytokines and suppressing the vascular inflammatory process.[28] *Dang Gui* (Radix Angelicae Sinensis) reduces inflammation through the inhibition of pro-inflammatory mediators, including nitric oxide and prostaglandin E2 in peritoneal macrophages.[29,30] In comparison with acetylsalicylic acid, the anti-inflammatory effect of *Dang Gui* (Radix Angelicae Sinensis) is approximately 1.1 times stronger, and its analgesic effect is approximately 1.7 times stronger.[31] According to clinical studies, *Dang Gui* (Radix Angelicae Sinensis) has been used successfully to treat menstrual pain in 112 patients,[32] migraine headache in 35 patients,[33] different types of headache in 36 patients,[34] and general complaint of pain in 105 patients.[35]

In summary, ***Flex (SC)*** is an excellent formula to treat spasms and cramps affecting both skeletal and smooth muscles.

COMPARATIVE ANALYSIS

Spasms and cramps are common musculoskeletal complaints that can be treated effectively with both drug and herbal therapies. In Western medicine, muscle relaxants such as Soma (carisoprodol) and Flexeril (cyclobenzaprine) are generally prescribed for spasms and cramps. These drugs are only mild to moderate in potency. However, they are also relatively safe, with relatively mild side effects such as blurred or double vision, dizziness, lightheadedness, and drowsiness.

Herbs that nourish yin and replenish fluids are most effective to relax the muscles. These herbs are also of mild to moderate potency, and are associated with few or no side effects.

Drugs and herbs have a comparable effect to treat spasms and cramps, and both are associated with few side effects. In addition to drug or herbal therapies, one can incorporate non-medicine modalities to enhance overall effectiveness, such as drinking water, stretching affected muscles, and taking potassium, magnesium and calcium supplements.

References

1. Chan K, Lo AC, Yeung JH, Woo KS. Journal of Pharmacy and Pharmacology 1995 May;47(5):402-6.
2. Pharmacotherapy 1999 July;19(7):870-876.
3. European Journal of Drug Metabolism and Pharmacokinetics 1995; 20(1): 55-60.
4. *Guo Wai Yi Xue* (Foreign Medicine) 1984;6(1):58.
5. *He Nan Zhong Yi* (Henan Chinese Medicine) 1986;(6) 15.
6. *Zhong Yi Za Zhi* (Journal of Chinese Medicine) 1985;6:450.
7. Inoshita F, Ogura Y, Suzuki Y, Hara S, Yamada A, Tanaka N, Yamashita A, Marumo F. Effect of orally administered shao-yao-gan-cao-tang (Shakuyaku-kanzo-to) on muscle cramps in maintenance hemodialysis patients: a preliminary study. American Journal of Chinese Medicine 2003;31(3):445-53.
8. *He Bei Zhong Yi* (Hebei Chinese Medicine) 1984;3:29.
9. *Zhong Yi Za Zhi* (Journal of Chinese Medicine), 1985; 6:50.
10. *Zhong Xi Yi Jie He Za Zhi* (Journal of Integrated Chinese and Western Medicine), 1991; (1):43.
11. *Bei Jing Zhong Yi* (Beijing Chinese Medicine) 1983;(1):33.
12. *Guo Wai Yi Xue* (Foreign Medicine) 1984;6(1):58.
13. *Shang Hai Zhong Yi Yao Za Zhi* (Shanghai Journal of Chinese Medicine and Herbology), 1983; 4:14.
14. *Zhong Yi Ming Fang Lin Chuang Xin Yong* (Contemporary Clinical Applications of Classic Chinese Formulas) 2001;313.
15. *Jiang Xi Yi Yao* (Jiangxi Medicine and Herbology) 1965;5(7):909.
16. *Zhong Yi Za Zhi* (Journal of Chinese Medicine), 1983; 11:9.
17. *Jiang Su Zhong Yi* (Jiangsu Chinese Medicine), 1990; (10):29.
18. *Zhe Jiang Zhong Yi Za Zhi* (Zhejiang Journal of Chinese Medicine) 1995;(11):524.
19. *Si Chuan Zhong Yi* (Sichuan Chinese Medicine) 1996;11:38.

FORMULAS

Flex (SC)™

20. *Yun Nan Zhong Yi* (Yunnan Journal of Traditional Chinese Medicine), 1990; 4:15.
21. *Fu Jian Zhong Yi Yao* (Fujian Chinese Medicine and Herbology), 1994; (1):7.
22. *Fu Jian Zhong Yi Yao* (Fujian Chinese Medicine and Herbology) 1961;9(4):44.
23. Tanaka T. A novel anti-dysmenorrhea therapy with cyclic administration of two Japanese herbal medicines. Clinical & Experimental Obstetrics & Gynecology 2003;30(2-3):95-8.
24. Zheng YQ, Wei W. Total glucosides of paeony suppresses adjuvant arthritis in rats and intervenes cytokine-signaling between different types of synoviocytes. Int Immunopharmacol. 2005 Sep;5(10):1560-73.
25. *Zhong Yao Zhi* (Chinese Herbology Journal), 1993; 358.
26. *Zhe Jiang Zhong Yi Za Zhi* (Zhejiang Journal of Chinese Medicine), 1980; 2:60.
27. *Zhong Hua Nei Ke Za Zhi* (Chinese Journal of Internal Medicine), 1960; 4:354.
28. Cao LH, Lee YJ, Kang DG, Kim JS, Lee HS. Effect of Zanthoxylum schinifolium on TNF-alpha-induced vascular inflammation in human umbilical vein endothelial cells. Professional Graduate School of Oriental Medicine, Wonkwang University, Iksan, Jeonbuk, 570-749, Republic of Korea. Vascul Pharmacol. 2009 May-Jun;50(5-6):200-7.
29. *Xin Yi Yao Xue Za Zhi* (New Journal of Medicine and Herbology), 1975; (6):34.
30. Chao WW, Kuo YH, Li WC, Lin BF. The production of nitric oxide and prostaglandin E2 in peritoneal macrophages is inhibited by Andrographis paniculata, Angelica sinensis and Morus alba ethyl acetate fractions. Department of Biochemical Science and Technology, Institute of Microbiology and Biochemistry, National Taiwan University, Taipei 106, Taiwan, ROC. J Ethnopharmacol. 2009 Feb 25;122(1):68-75.
31. *Yao Xue Za Zhi* (Journal of Medicinals), 1971; (91):1098.
32. *Lan Zhou Yi Xue Yuan Xue Bao* (Journal of Lanzhou University of Medicine), 1988; 1:36.
33. *Bei Jing Yi Xue* (Beijing Medicine), 1988; 2:95.
34. *Hu Bei Zhong Yi Za Zhi* (Hubei Journal of Chinese Medicine), 1993; (2):9.
35. *Xin Yi Yao Xue Za Zhi* (New Journal of Medicine and Herbology), 1976; 12:26.

Flex (SPR) ™

CLINICAL APPLICATIONS

- **Bone spurs** with pain and inflammation
- **Joint stiffness**
- **Calcification of joints**
- **Plantar fasciitis**
- **Spine pain**

WESTERN THERAPEUTIC ACTIONS

- Analgesic action to relieve pain associated with bone spurs
- Anti-inflammatory influence to reduce inflammation

CHINESE THERAPEUTIC ACTIONS

- Invigorates blood circulation and breaks up blood stagnation
- Relieves pain
- Dispels phlegm

DOSAGE

Take 3 to 4 capsules three times daily as needed to relieve pain. For maximum effectiveness, take the herbs on an empty stomach with two tall glasses of warm water.

INGREDIENTS

Bai Zhi (Radix Angelicae Dahuricae)
Chen Pi (Pericarpium Citri Reticulatae)
Da Ding Huang (Caulis Euonymi)
Dang Gui (Radix Angelicae Sinensis)
Fang Feng (Radix Saposhnikoviae)
Gan Cao (Radix et Rhizoma Glycyrrhizae)
Huang Jin Gui (Caulis Vanieriae)
Jin Yin Hua (Flos Lonicerae Japonicae)
Liu Zhi Huang (Herba Solidaginis)
Mo Gu Xiao (Caulis Hyptis Capitatae)
Mo Yao (Myrrha)
Po Bu Zi Ye (Folium Cordia Dichotoma)
Ru Xiang (Gummi Olibanum)
Tong Cao (Medulla Tetrapanacis)
Zao Jiao (Fructus Gleditsiae)
Zao Jiao Ci (Spina Gleditsiae)
Zhe Bei Mu (Bulbus Fritillariae Thunbergii)

BACKGROUND

Bone spurs form in response to pressure, rubbing, or stress on the same joint over a long period of time. As the body tries to protect and repair itself, it builds extra bone on top of normal bone. Most bone spurs are smooth and do not cause pain. However, some bone spurs may press or rub on other bones or soft tissues, causing pain, inflammation and burning sensations.

FORMULA EXPLANATION

Flex (SPR) is formulated to relieve pain due to bone spurs and joint stiffness arising from overuse. According to theories in traditional Chinese medicine, bone spurs form as the result of repetitive use and are diagnosed as stagnation of blood and phlegm.

Po Bu Zi Ye (Folium Cordia Dichotoma) regulates qi circulation and relieves pain. Unbeknownst to most practitioners, it is one of the most effective herbs in the Chinese *Materia Medica* to treat bone spurs. *Mo Gu Xiao* (Caulis Hyptis Capitatae), *Liu Zhi Huang* (Herba Solidaginis), and *Huang Jin Gui* (Caulis Vanieriae) have anti-inflammatory and analgesic effects and are often used to treat acute pain associated with traumatic injuries or sprains and strains. *Da Ding Huang* (Caulis Euonymi) further reduces inflammation and relieves pain. *Ru Xiang* (Gummi Olibanum), *Mo Yao* (Myrrha), and *Dang Gui* (Radix Angelicae Sinensis) have potent effects to move blood, disperse blood stagnation, and relieve pain. *Jin Yin Hua* (Flos Lonicerae Japonicae), *Bai Zhi* (Radix Angelicae Dahuricae), *Zhe Bei Mu* (Bulbus Fritillariae Thunbergii), *Zao Jiao* (Fructus Gleditsiae), and *Zao Jiao Ci* (Spina Gleditsiae) break up phlegm that is obstructing the channels and joints to restore proper qi and blood circulation. *Chen Pi* (Pericarpium Citri Reticulatae) regulates qi, while *Fang Feng* (Radix Saposhnikoviae) disperses wind and releases pain lodged in peripheral levels of the body. *Tong Cao* (Medulla Tetrapanacis) drains accumulation of damp and phlegm out of the body via urination. Lastly, *Gan Cao* (Radix et Rhizoma Glycyrrhizae) relieves pain and harmonizes the entire formula.

In summary, ***Flex (SPR)*** is an effective formula with both immediate and long-term therapeutic benefits.

CAUTIONS & CONTRAINDICATIONS

- This formula is contraindicated during pregnancy and nursing.
- Though there are no known side effects or adverse reactions, it is prudent to not recommend this formula for infants or young children, as the long-term impact on the growth of teeth and the skeleton is unclear.
- This herbal formula contains herbs that invigorate blood circulation, such as *Dang Gui* (Radix Angelicae Sinensis). Therefore, patients who are on anticoagulant or antiplatelet therapies, such as Coumadin (warfarin), should use this formula with caution, or not at all, as there may be a higher risk of bleeding and bruising.[1,2,3]

CLINICAL NOTES

- ***Flex (SPR)*** is formulated by Dr. Jimmy Wei-Yen Chang with herbs that treat bone spurs, relieve pain, and reduce swelling. ***Flex (SPR)*** has helped many patients with bone spurs to relieve pain and improve their range of movement.
- The primary purpose of ***Flex (SPR)*** is to relieve pain related to bone spurs. However, it can be taken as a supplemental formula to relieve pain. Some patients may experience immediate relief, while others may require as much as half a year for relief of the pain. Adequate rest of affected joints is essential to a complete recovery.

Flex (SPR)™

- According to clinical experience, patients taking ***Flex (SPR)*** generally have an all-or-none response for treating bone spurs. Most patients will experience varying degrees of relief from pain and inflammation. Up to 20 to 30% will experience long-term resolution of pain. However, it is possible that some patients will not notice any change. Evaluation of patients' condition should be done every one to two months to determine the progress of the patient and the efficacy of the formula.
- ***Flex (SPR)*** has been used with good success to treat animals with joint pain.
- According to Dr. Luo Jun-Qing, a *tui-na* master from China, patients who suffer from bone spur of the knee should not over-exercise their knee. Mild to moderate movements such as those in *tai chi chuan [tai ji chuan]* and walking should suffice.
- In addition to taking ***Flex (SPR)*** orally, herbs should also be applied topically to enhance the overall treatment. The topical preparation is made by cooking herbs in water and filtering out the herb residue. Use the herbal decoction topically by soaking a towel in the decoction while hot, and apply the decoction-soaked towel to the affected area while warm. The towel should be re-soaked in the decoction as needed to keep warm, for a total duration of 30 minutes. Perform this procedure twice per day. One herbal formula that has been used with good results contains the following herbs: *Dang Gui* (Radix Angelicae Sinensis) 15g, *Chi Shao* (Radix Paeoniae Rubra) 15g, *Chuan Xiong* (Rhizoma Chuanxiong) 12g, *Hong Hua* (Flos Carthami) 12g, *Dan Nan Xing* (Arisaema cum Bile) 12g, *Bai Jie Zi* (Semen Sinapis) 15g, *Ji Xue Teng* (Caulis Spatholobi) 20g, *Wei Ling Xian* (Radix et Rhizoma Clematidis) 15g, *Ru Xiang* (Gummi Olibanum) 15g, *Mo Yao* (Myrrha) 15g, *Gui Zhi* (Ramulus Cinnamomi) 15g and *Du Huo* (Radix Angelicae Pubescentis) 15g.

Pulse Diagnosis by Dr. Jimmy Wei-Yen Chang:

- **Upper body bone spur:** *Ren* pulse, a thin, straight, long, wiry pulse that extends proximally to the right *chi*.
- **Lower body bone spur:** *Ren* pulse, a thin, straight, long, wiry pulse that extends proximally to the left *chi*.
- Note: *Ren* pulse is one of the eight extra meridian pulses.

SUPPLEMENTARY FORMULAS

- For bone spurs in the neck and shoulder, add ***Neck & Shoulder (AC)***.
- For bone spurs in the lower back, add ***Back Support (AC)***.
- For bone spurs in the back with herniated disks, combine with ***Back Support (HD)***.
- For bone spurs in the arm (shoulder, elbow or wrist), combine with ***Arm Support***.
- For bone spurs in the knees, add ***Knee & Ankle (AC)***.
- For arthritis, add ***Flex (Heat)*** or ***Flex (CD)***.
- For bone spurs with nerve pain, combine with ***Flex (NP)***.
- For severe pain, add ***Herbal ANG***.
- For degeneration of muscles, tendons, ligaments, and cartilage, add ***Flex (MLT)***.
- For severe blood stagnation, add ***Circulation (SJ)***.
- With excess heat, add ***Gardenia Complex***.
- With severe inflammation, combine with ***Astringent Complex***.

ACUPUNCTURE TREATMENT

Traditional Points:

- **Bone spurs in the neck:** *Dazhui* (GV 14), *Fengchi* (GB 20), *Jianjing* (GB 21)
  - With numbness and pain in the arms, add *Jianyu* (LI 15), *Quchi* (LI 11), and *Hegu* (LI 4).
- **Bone spurs in the back:** *Yaoyangguan* (GV 3), *shu* (transport) points on the back; *ah shi* points on the affected areas
- **Sciatica with bone spurs:** *Huantiao* (GB 30), *Yanglingquan* (GB 34), *Quchi* (LI 11)
- **Bone spurs of the knees:** *Xiyan, Heding, Zusanli* (ST 36)
- Technique: use even method. Leave the needle in place for 30 minutes. Perform one acupuncture treatment daily or every other day, for 12 treatments per course of treatment prior to evaluation.

Classic Master Tung's Points:

- Needle contralateral to the pain. If the pain is in the center, needle bilaterally or the side with the more *ah shi* points. If the pain is bilateral, needle bilaterally.
- **General spur:** *Minghuang* (T 88.12) and two points 5 *cun* above and below it; *Linggu* (T 22.05), *Dabai* (T 22.04), *Zhongbai* (T 22.06), *Xiabai* (T 22.07), *Wanshunyi* (T 22.08), *Wanshuner* (T 22.09), *Zhengjin* (T 77.01), *Zhengzong* (T 77.02), *Houhui* (T 1010.06), *Simashang* (T 88.18), *Simazhong* (T 88.17), *Simaxia* (T 88.19), *Guciyi* (T 44.21)*, *Gucier* (T 44.22)*, *Gucisan* (T 44.23)*
- **Back spur:** *Linggu* (T 22.05), *Chongzi* (T 22.01), *Chongxian* (T 22.02), *Chengshan* (BL 57), *Zhengjin* (T 77.01), *Zhengzong* (T 77.02), *Zhongjiuli* (T 88.25), *Dan* (T 11.13), *Minghuang* (T 88.12), *Tianhuang* (T 88.13), *Qihuang* (T 88.14), *Guciyi* (T 44.21)*, *Gucier* (T 44.22)*, *Gucisan* (T 44.23)*, *Zhengji* (T 44.24)*
- **Neck spur:** *Wanshunyi* (T 22.08), *Wanshuner* (T 22.09), *Huochuan* (T 33.04), *Tianhuang* (T 88.13), *Sizhi* (T 77.20), *Minghuang* (T 88.12), *Qihuang* (T 88.14), *Guciyi* (T 44.21)*, *Gucier* (T 44.22)*, *Gucisan* (T 44.23)*, *Huofu* (T 88.41)*, *Huoliang* (T 88.42)*, *Huochang* (T 88.43)*, *Sojingdian* (T 22.19)*
- **Heel spur:** *Muguan* (T 22.26)*, *Guguan* (T 22.24)*, *Zhongguan* (T 22.25)*, *nuxi* point (where the red and white skin meet at the bottom of the Achilles tendon on the foot), *Guciyi* (T 44.21)*, *Gucier* (T 44.22)*, *Gucisan* (T 44.23)*
- **Plantar fasciitis:** *Muguan* (T 22.26)*, *Guguan* (T 22.24)*, *Zhongguan* (T 22.25)*, *nuxi* point (where the red and white skin meet at the bottom of the achilles tendon on the foot)

Master Tung's Points by Dr. Chuan-Min Wang:

- **Neck spur:** *Minghuang* (T 88.12), *Tianhuang* (T 88.13), *Qihuang* (T 88.14), *Houzhi* (T 44.05), *Jianzhong* (T 44.06)

Flex (SPR)™

- **Back spur:** *Minghuang* (T 88.12), *Tianhuang* (T 88.13), *Qihuang* (T 88.14), *Houzhui* (T 44.02), *Shouying* (T 44.03)
- **Heel spur:** *Minghuang* (T 88.12), *Tianhuang* (T 88.13), *Qihuang* (T 88.14), *Wuhu* 5 (T 11.27)
- **Plantar fasciitis:** Bleed local tender area. Needle ipsilaterally *Huoquan* (T 88.16), *Tianhuangfu [shenguan]* (T 77.18), *Sizhi* (T 77.20), *Taixi* (KI 3).

Balance Method by Dr. Richard Tan:

- Treatment depends on the individual presentation and the location of the spur.

Auricular Medicine by Dr. Li-Chun Huang:

- **Spurs:** Large Auricular Nerve, Lesser Occipital Nerve, Sympathetic, Nervous Subcortex, *Shenmen*, and corresponding point (seed the front and the back). Bleed Ear Apex.

NUTRITION

- Patients are encouraged to increase their intake of vinegar.
- Discourage the intake of bamboo and acidic fruits, such as orange or grapefruit.
- Minimize the consumption of seafood and red meat to avoid creating additional deposits of uric acid.

LIFESTYLE INSTRUCTIONS

- Rest is essential to the recovery of bone spurs. If possible, discontinue repetitive movement and overuse of the joint where the bone spur is located.
- Slow stretching exercises of the affected area are effective to reduce or diminish pain.
- Initially in the first 24 hours, use ice packs to reduce swelling and inflammation. However, long-term use of ice packs is not recommended, as it may cause more stagnation.

CASE STUDIES

- E.L., a 40-year-old female patient, presented with pain at the bottom of her heel due to a bone spur along with right hip flexor pain. It was reported that her pain level was a seven out of ten. She was formerly diagnosed with calcaneum calcium deposit. The TCM diagnosis was qi and blood stasis as well as Kidney yin deficiency. For treatment, ***Flex (SPR)*** was given at 4 capsules three times daily for two weeks. It was noted that the patient had almost immediate cessation of her pain, the swelling decreased, and she was able to return to her regular activity of running after five days. Submitted by J.W., San Francisco, California.
- M.A., a 60-year-old female, presented with pain located on her left foot due to a heel spur. X-rays had confirmed the presence of a calcaneal spur. The practitioner diagnosed this condition as phlegm and qi and blood stagnation. ***Flex (SPR)*** was prescribed at 4 capsules three times per day. Over the course of two months, the patient had noticed a decrease in her foot pain and after three months noticed that the pain had resolved. She was very pleased with the herbs and how they helped her. Submitted by M.P., Muskego, Wisconsin.
- E.F., a 60-year-old male, presented with knee pain located above the right patella beginning two days prior. X-rays had confirmed there was a bone spur present. It was noted that it became aggravated by any weight bearing or change of position. Objective findings included slight swelling and warm temperature. There was no trauma preceding the condition. The practitioner diagnosed this condition as qi and blood stagnation. ***Knee & Ankle (AC)*** and ***Flex (SPR)*** were prescribed at 2 capsules each three times per day. After taking the herbs for six weeks the condition had resolved. Submitted by L.L., Greenwich, Connecticut.
- A 53-year-old female presented with neck and shoulder pain which had been occurring for the previous 12 years. Current X-rays had shown a bone spur located in the C6-7 area. No curvature of the spine was seen. The practitioner had diagnosed the condition as yin and qi deficiencies with local qi and blood stagnation. ***Neck & Shoulder (CR)*** and ***Flex (SPR)*** were both prescribed. After taking the herbs, the patient had reported that her pain had decreased from a 7-8/10 to a 3-4/10 pain level. Submitted by H.C., Sydney, New York.

PHARMACOLOGICAL AND CLINICAL RESEARCH

Flex (SPR) is specifically designed to treat bone spurs. Pharmacologically, this formula contains herbs with analgesic effects to relieve pain and anti-inflammatory effects to reduce swelling and inflammation. Clinically, it resolves bone spurs characterized by "hardness and nodules," as described in traditional Chinese medicine.

Po Bu Zi Ye (Folium Cordia Dichotoma) is an indigenous herb in Taiwan. It has been used historically for treatment of "sharp pain of the heel." This traditional use has been expanded as *Po Bu Zi Ye* (Folium Cordia Dichotoma) is now recognized by many experts as the chief and most effective herb for treating bone spurs affecting various parts of the body. *Mo Gu Xiao* (Caulis Hyptis Capitatae), *Liu Zhi Huang* (Herba Solidaginis), *Huang Jin Gui* (Caulis Vanieriae), and *Da Ding Huang* (Caulis Euonymi) are four other indigenous herbs from Taiwan. These four herbs are commonly used to treat various types of musculoskeletal conditions with pain and inflammation.[4]

Zao Jiao Ci (Spina Gleditsiae), *Zao Jiao* (Fructus Gleditsiae) and *Po Bu Zi Ye* (Folium Cordia Dichotoma) are three important herbs for treating bone spurs. Historically, these herbs have been used to treat various types of "hardness and nodules." Today, they have been used successfully to treat various conditions characterized by pain and inflammation. Pharmacologically, *Zao Jiao Ci* (Spina Gleditsiae) and *Zao Jiao* (Fructus Gleditsiae) both exert marked anti-inflammatory effects.[5] Clinically, *Zao Jiao Ci* (Spina Gleditsiae) has been used successfully to treat sciatica in 117 patients (73 had complete recovery, 20 had significant improvement, 18 had moderate improvement, and 6

FORMULAS

Flex (SPR)™

had no improvement).[6,7] Furthermore, it has also been used with good success to treat hyperosteogeny. According to one study, 41 patients with hyperosteogeny were treated with significant improvement in 26 cases, improvement in 12 cases, and no effect in 3 cases. The herbal formula was administered as a decoction daily, and contained the following ingredients: *Zao Jiao Ci* (Spina Gleditsiae), *Dang Gui* (Radix Angelicae Sinensis), *Hong Hua* (Flos Carthami), *Shan Zhu Yu* (Fructus Corni), *Chuan Xiong* (Rhizoma Chuanxiong), *Ji Xue Teng* (Caulis Spatholobi), and others as needed.[8]

Flex (SPR) contains many herbs with analgesic effects to relieve pain and anti-inflammatory effects to reduce swelling. *Fang Feng* (Radix Saposhnikoviae) shows a marked effect to suppress inflammation via the inhibition of nitrite production by inducible nitric oxide synthase.[9] *Jin Yin Hua* (Flos Lonicerae Japonicae) demonstrates significant analgesic and anti-inflammatory effects via the inhibition of cylcooxygenase-2, inducible nitric oxide synthase, and 5-lipoxyfenase activities.[10] *Gan Cao* (Radix et Rhizoma Glycyrrhizae) has demonstrated a marked anti-inflammatory effect by enhancing the effect of glucocorticoid through increased production and secretion as well as decreased metabolism by the liver.[11] In terms of anti-inflammatory actions, the comparison of cortisone to glycyrrhizin and glycyrrhetinic acid, two compounds from *Gan Cao* (Radix et Rhizoma Glycyrrhizae), is approximately 10:1.[12] Clinical applications of *Gan Cao* (Radix et Rhizoma Glycyrrhizae) include pain, inflammation, edema, arthritis, spasms, and cramps.[13,14] Lastly, *Ru Xiang* (Gummi Olibanum) and *Mo Yao* (Myrrha) have an analgesic effect to relieve pain and an anti-inflammatory effect to reduce swelling and inflammation.[15,16] These two herbs also show an antiarthritic effect by reducing edema and decreasing arthritic scores in subjects with adjuvant-induced arthritis. The mechanism of action is attributed to the suppression of pro-inflammatory cytokines, such as tumor necrosis factor-alpha (TNF-α) and interleukin-1beta (IL-1β).[17] Furthermore, use of *Ru Xiang* (Gummi Olibanum) and *Mo Yao* (Myrrha) is also beneficial to facilitate wound healing by stimulating maturation and differentiation of white blood cells.[18] Clinically, they have been used effectively to treat pain associated with various types of trauma and external injuries.[19]

In summary, there are very few treatments available for bone spurs. ***Flex (SPR)*** offers a much-needed treatment option for those who suffer from this disorder.

COMPARATIVE ANALYSIS

Pain is a basic bodily sensation induced by a noxious stimulus that causes physical discomfort (such as pricking, throbbing, or aching). Pain may be of acute or chronic state, and may be of nociceptive, neuropathic, or psychogenic origin. For neuropathic pain due to bone spurs, drugs such as antiseizure [Dilantin (phenytoin) and Neurontin (gabapentin)] and antidepressant medications [Elavil (amitriptyline)] are prescribed. Though effective, these drugs are associated with numerous and significant side effects. Antiseizure drugs cause side effects such as bleeding, burning sensations, clumsiness or unsteadiness, confusion, irregular eye movements, blurred or double vision, swollen glands in neck or underarms, slurred speech, delusions, dementia, bone malformations, and many others. Antidepressant drugs cause blurred vision, confusion or delirium, hallucinations, constipation (especially in the elderly), problems in urinating, decreased sexual ability, difficulty in speaking or swallowing, eye pain, fainting, fast or irregular heartbeat, loss of balance control, mask-like face, nervousness or restlessness, slowed movements, stiffness of arms and legs, and shortness of breath or troubled breathing. In short, these drugs should be prescribed only when benefits significantly outweigh the risks. Furthermore, use of these drugs must be monitored carefully to avoid developing serious side effects and complications. Lastly, these drugs treat the symptom (pain) and not the cause (bone spurs). When the pain becomes intolerable, or if drugs cause too many side effects, the last option is surgery.

Bone spurs are caused by repetitive use of, or recurrent injuries to, the affected joint(s). Bone spurs are diagnosed as blood and phlegm stagnation, and are treated with herbs that activate blood circulation, resolve phlegm, and relieve pain. Clinically, herbal treatment of bone spurs has been shown to be relatively effective, though the required duration of treatment must be longer than one to two months.

Treatment of bone spurs is a challenge to both drug and herbal medicine. While drugs do not treat bone spurs, they do offer potent and effective means to control pain. On the other hand, herbs are relatively effective to treat pain and resolve spurs, but may require a prolonged period of treatment. In light of limited options, herbs should definitely be tried before considering surgery.

References

1. Chan K, Lo AC, Yeung JH, Woo KS. Journal of Pharmacy and Pharmacology 1995 May;47(5):402-6.
2. Pharmacotherapy 1999 July;19(7):870-876.
3. European Journal of Drug Metabolism and Pharmacokinetics 1995; 20(1): 55-60.
4. Chen, J. and Chen, T. Chinese Medical Herbology and Pharmacology, Art of Medicine Press, 2004.
5. Ha HH, Park SY, Ko WS, Kim Y. Gleditsia sinensis thorns inhibit the production of NO through NF-kappaB suppression in LPS-stimulated macrophages. Department of Molecular Biology, College of Natural Sciences, Pusan National University, Jangjeon-dong, Keumjeong-gu, Pusan, Republic of Korea. J Ethnopharmacol. 2008 Aug 13;118(3):429-34.
6. *Bei Jing Zhong Yi Yao Da Xue Xue Bao* (Journal of Beijing University of Medicine and Medicinals), 1994; 17(4):21.
7. *Si Chuan Zhong Yi* (Sichuan Chinese Medicine), 1994; (1):45.
8. *Si Chuan Zhong Yi* (Sichuan Chinese Medicine), 1994; (1):45.
9. Wang CN, Shiao YJ, Kuo YH, Chen CC, Lin YL. Inducible nitric oxide synthase inhibitors from Saposhnikovia divaricata and Panax quinquefolium. Planta Med. 2000 Oct;66(7):644-7.
10. Ryu KH, Rhee HI, Kim JH, Yoo H, Lee BY, Um KA, Kim K, Noh JY, Lim KM, Chung JH. Anti-inflammatory and analgesic activities of SKLJI, a highly

purified and injectable herbal extract of Lonicera japonica. Pharmacology Team, Life Science R&D Center, SK Chemical Suwon, Korea. Biosci Biotechnol Biochem. 2010 Oct 23;74(10):2022-8.

11. *Zhong Yao Zhi* (Chinese Herbology Journal), 1993; 358.
12. *Zhong Cao Yao* (Chinese Herbal Medicine), 1991; 22(10):452.
13. *Zhe Jiang Zhong Yi Za Zhi* (Zhejiang Journal of Chinese Medicine), 1980; 2:60.
14. *Zhong Hua Nei Ke Za Zhi* (Chinese Journal of Internal Medicine), 1960; 4:354.
15. *Zhong Yao Xue* (Chinese Herbology), 1998; 539:540.
16. Yoshikawa M, Morikawa T, Oominami H, Matsuda H. Absolute stereostructures of olibanumols A, B, C, H, I, and J from olibanum, gum-resin of Boswellia carterii, and inhibitors of nitric oxide production in lipopolysaccharide-activated mouse peritoneal macrophages. Kyoto Pharmaceutical University, Japan. Chem Pharm Bull (Tokyo). 2009 Sep;57(9):957-64.
17. Fan AY, Lao L, Zhang RX, Zhou AN, Wang LB, Moudgil KD, Lee DY, Ma ZZ, Zhang WY, Berman BM. Effects of an acetone extract of Boswellia carterii Birdw. (Burseraceae) gum resin on adjuvant-induced arthritis in lewis rats. Center for Integrative Medicine, School of Medicine, University of Maryland, 3rd Floor, James Kernan Hospital Man, 2200 Kernan Drive, Baltimore, MD 21201, USA. J Ethnopharmacol. 2005 Oct 3;101(1-3):104-9.
18. Haffor A-S. 2010. Effect of myrrh (Commiphora molmol) on leukocyte levels before and during healing from gastric ulcer skin injury. J Immunotoxicol 7: 68-75.
19. *He Nan Zhong Yi Xue Yuan Xue Bao* (Journal of University of Henan School of Medicine), 1980; 3:38.

Flex (TMX)™

CLINICAL APPLICATIONS

- **Traumatic injuries** including external and physical injuries with bruises, contusions, and sprains
- **Broken bones or fractures** with severe pain, inflammation and swelling
- **Post-surgical recovery:** prevents adhesion and scar tissue formations

WESTERN THERAPEUTIC ACTIONS

- Analgesic effect to alleviate pain
- Anti-inflammatory action to reduce inflammation and swelling
- Antispasmodic function to relieve muscle spasms and cramps
- Hemostatic effect to stop bleeding from trauma and injuries
- Circulatory effect to invigorates blood circulation to facilitate healing

CHINESE THERAPEUTIC ACTIONS

- Invigorates the blood circulation
- Removes blood stagnation
- Relieves pain
- Helps regenerate bones and soft tissues

DOSAGE

Take 5 to 6 capsules every six hours at the initial stage of injury. After the condition stabilizes, reduce the dosage to 3 to 4 capsules three times daily. For maximum effectiveness, take the herbs on an empty stomach with warm water. The herbs can be taken after meals if stomach discomfort should occur.

INGREDIENTS

Bai Shao (Radix Paeoniae Alba)
Chuan Mu Xiang (Radix Vladimiriae)
Da Huang (Radix et Rhizoma Rhei)
Dang Gui Wei (Extremitas Radix Angelicae Sinensis)
Er Cha (Catechu)
Fu Ling (Poria)
Gan Cao (Radix et Rhizoma Glycyrrhizae)
Hong Hua (Flos Carthami)
Mo Yao (Myrrha)
Mu Dan Pi (Cortex Moutan)
Ru Xiang (Gummi Olibanum)
Su Mu (Lignum Sappan)
Tao Ren (Semen Persicae)
Yan Hu Suo (Rhizoma Corydalis)

BACKGROUND

Musculoskeletal and connective tissue injuries lead to over 10 million clinic visits per year in the United States.[1] Causes of these injuries may be external (sports injuries, car accidents, trauma), internal (chronic wear and tear of muscles, ligaments and tendons; bones weakened by osteoporosis), or both. Acute injuries are characterized by severe pain, swelling and inflammation, and in some cases, internal bleeding. Treatment of acute injuries should focus on relieving pain, reducing swelling and inflammation, and stopping bleeding. Chronic injuries are characterized by dull pain, stiffness and numbness, and decreased muscle mass and strength. Treatment of chronic injuries includes relief of pain and restoration of physical and physiological functions.

FORMULA EXPLANATION

Flex (TMX) is formulated to treat both internal and external injuries, such as broken bones, bone fractures, sports injuries, bruises, contusions, and sprains. It can be used to enhance recovery and prevent scarring. This is an excellent formula to activate qi and blood circulation, remove qi and blood stagnation, relieve pain, and facilitate healing by regenerating bone and soft tissues.

Yan Hu Suo (Rhizoma Corydalis) and *Su Mu* (Lignum Sappan) dispel blood stasis and alleviate pain. *Er Cha* (Catechu) reduces swelling, drains dampness and absorbs seepage from sores or wounds. *Ru Xiang* (Gummi Olibanum), *Mo Yao* (Myrrha), *Chuan Mu Xiang* (Radix Vladimiriae), *Dang Gui Wei* (Extremitas Radix Angelicae Sinensis), *Hong Hua* (Flos Carthami) and *Tao Ren* (Semen Persicae) promote the healing of wounds and relieve pain by invigorating blood circulation. *Da Huang* (Radix et Rhizoma Rhei) and *Mu Dan Pi* (Cortex Moutan) reduce inflammation by clearing heat. *Bai Shao* (Radix Paeoniae Alba) has strong analgesic, antispasmodic and anti-inflammatory effects. *Fu Ling* (Poria) tonifies the Spleen and indirectly promotes the regeneration of muscles. *Gan Cao* (Radix et Rhizoma Glycyrrhizae) relaxes the tendons and muscles and harmonizes the formula.

Together, ***Flex (TMX)*** effectively treats trauma injuries by using herbs that relieve pain, reduce inflammation, alleviate spasms and cramps, and speed up recovery.

CAUTIONS & CONTRAINDICATIONS

- This formula is contraindicated during pregnancy and nursing.
- In cases of concussions, send the patient to the hospital immediately. Do not use ***Flex (TMX)*** until the condition is stabilized (usually 7-10 days later).
- Do not use this formula if the patient has serious internal hemorrhage. ***Flex (TMX)*** has many herbs that activate blood circulation and may delay coagulation.
- This formula is not designed for long-term use. It should be used only during the acute phases of injuries, and discontinued when the desired effects are achieved.
- This herbal formula contains herbs that invigorate blood circulation, such as *Dang Gui Wei* (Extremitas Radix Angelicae Sinensis). Therefore, patients who are on anticoagulant or antiplatelet therapies, such as Coumadin (warfarin), should use this formula with caution, or not at all, as there may be a higher risk of bleeding and bruising.[2,3,4]

Flex (TMX)™

- This formula may cause mild gastrointestinal discomfort, which can be minimized by taking the herbs with food or decreasing the dosage.
- The following warning statement is required by the State of California: "This product contains *Da Huang* (Radix et Rhizoma Rhei). Read and follow directions carefully. Do not use if you have or develop diarrhea, loose stools, or abdominal pain because *Da Huang* (Radix et Rhizoma Rhei) may worsen these conditions and be harmful to your health. Consult your physician if you have frequent diarrhea or if you are pregnant, nursing, taking medication, or have a medical condition."

CLINICAL NOTES

- ***Flex (TMX)*** is an herbal formula originally used by *kung fu [gong fu]* masters and monks in the *Shaolin* temple to treat various internal and external injuries. It has excellent functions to relieve pain, treat soft tissue injuries, and facilitate the healing of broken bones or bone fractures.
- There are three excellent formulas for post-surgical recovery. ***Flex (TMX)*** should be taken after the surgery for 5 to 10 days to facilitate the immediate healing of wounds. Continue herbal treatment with ***Flex (MLT)*** and ***Osteo 8*** for one month to facilitate healing and recovery of soft tissues and bones, respectively.
- In cases of concussions, use a lancet needle and bleed the area that was injured and squeeze out some blood. Send the patient to the hospital and advise the patient not to eat anything greasy for at least 1 month. It is best if their diet only includes porridge and completely cooked and soft vegetables. Do not use this formula until the condition has stabilized in 7 to 10 days to avoid bleeding.
- The following is a folk remedy to treat acute back pain from sprain and strain. Crack open 2 crabs (ocean) with a wooden stick (do not use a knife or any metal instruments) and put then into a clay pot with enough vodka or whiskey to cover both crabs. Place the clay pot into another bigger pot with water and steam it for one hour. Serve the crab meat along with the soup.

SUPPLEMENTARY FORMULAS

- To stop bleeding, add ***Notoginseng 9***.
- For severe pain, use with ***Herbal ANG***.
- With severe inflammation, combine with ***Astringent Complex***.
- For headache, use with ***Corydalin (AC)*** or ***Corydalin (CR)***.
- For neck and shoulder pain, add ***Neck & Shoulder (AC)*** or ***Neck & Shoulder (CR)***.
- For lower back pain, combine with ***Back Support (AC)*** or ***Back Support (CR)***.
- For pain in the arm (shoulder, elbow, wrist, and hand), combine with ***Arm Support***.
- For severe pain due to herniated disk, add ***Back Support (HD)***.
- For pain due to knee injuries, add ***Knee & Ankle (AC)*** or ***Knee & Ankle (CR)***.
- For chronic pain due to damaged soft tissues (muscles, ligaments, tendons, and cartilages), add ***Flex (MLT)***.
- For muscle spasms and cramps, combine with ***Flex (SC)***.
- For chronic arthritic pain that worsens during cold and rainy weather, combine with ***Flex (CD)***.
- For inflammation of joints with redness and swelling, consider using ***Flex (Heat)*** instead.
- For bone spurs, use with ***Flex (SPR)***.
- For external injury with open wound and/or infection, use with ***Herbal ABX***.
- During the recovery phase of bone fractures or broken bones, use with ***Osteo 8***.
- For post-surgical constipation, add ***Gentle Lax (Deficient)***.
- For severe blood stagnation and bruising, add ***Circulation (SJ)***.
- For signs and symptoms of excess fire, add ***Gardenia Complex***.

ACUPUNCTURE TREATMENT

Traditional Points:

- *Ah shi* points

Classic Master Tung's Points:

- **Head:** *Zhengjin* (T 77.01), *Zhengzong* (T 77.02) with strong stimulation, *Yizhong* (T 77.05), *Erzhong* (T 77.06), *Sanzhong* (T 77.07), *Zhengshi* (T 77.03). Bleed dark veins nearby the medial malleolus or *Shuijing* (T 66.13). Bleed before needling for best result.

Master Tung's Points by Dr. Chuan-Min Wang:

- **Trauma, broken bones, post-surgical rehab:** Needle bilaterally *Tianhuangfu [shenguan]* (T 77.18), *Minghuang* (T 88.12), *Tianhuang* (T 88.13), *Qihuang* (T 88.14).

Balance Method by Dr. Richard Tan:

- The treatment protocol is different for each case, depending on the location and severity of injuries.

Ear Acupuncture:

- **Knee injuries:** Knees, Adrenal Gland, Pituitary Gland
- **Post-operative pain:** Needle the reflective location of the surgery, Subcortex, *Shenmen*, and Lung. Needle twice a day with strong stimulation and leave the needles in for one to two hours. These points are more effective to relieve sharp pain associated with surgery and not as well for distension and pain as the result of abdominal surgery.
- **Post-operative flatulence:** Select and needle the sensitive points along the Large Intestine and Small Intestine, Stomach, Sympathetic, and Spleen. Strongly stimulate for one to two hours to help alleviate distension and promote passage of gas.

Auricular Medicine by Dr. Li-Chun Huang:

- **Acute sprain and contusion:** corresponding points (to the area of injury)

Flex (TMX)™

- For pain, add Large Auricular Nerve, Lesser Occipital Nerve. Bleed Ear Apex.
- For tranquilizing the mind, add *Shenmen.*

NUTRITION

- Advise the patients to eat half of a fresh pineapple on an empty stomach daily. Pineapple is rich in bromelain and will reduce swelling and inflammation.
- Patients with broken bones or fractures should consume an adequate amount of calcium during recovery.
- Patients with broken bones or fractures should avoid foods with preservatives because phosphorus in preservatives can lead to bone loss.
- Patients are advised to avoid cold food and drinks, as cold will cause more stagnation. They should also avoid spicy food to prevent aggravating the inflammatory condition.

LIFESTYLE INSTRUCTIONS

- Avoid exercise with a high risk of injury, especially during the recovery phase.
- For external injury with open wounds, be sure to clean the affected area thoroughly to prevent infection.
- Vitamin E oil can be applied to the wounds to minimize scarring. However, vitamin E oil should be applied only after the open wounds have closed or healed.

CASE STUDIES

- A.S., a 45-year-old female, presented with a right lateral ankle sprain that had occurred three days prior. Objective findings included purplish color and swelling around the ankle. The practitioner diagnosed this condition as local blood stagnation. For treatment, ***Flex (TMX)*** and ***Knee & Ankle (AC)*** were prescribed. After taking the herbs for three days, the patient reported her ankle was feeling 50% better. She discontinued taking the ***Flex (TMX)*** after eight days since her ankle was then 90% better. For an additional week she continued to take the ***Knee & Ankle (CR)*** and her ankle was 100% better. Submitted by S.L., Yuma, Arizona.
- D.G., a 59-year-old male, presented with an acute ankle sprain on the left ankle due to a recent fall. Objective findings included swelling, black and blue coloring, and abrasions around the left ankle. The TCM diagnosis was qi and blood stagnation. For treatment, ***Flex (TMX)*** was prescribed at 3 capsules three times per day. As a result of taking the herbs, the patient reported that the swelling had resolved in four days and the bruising resolved in one week. Overall, the herbs helped his pain decrease within two days of taking the herbs. Submitted by M.P., Muskego, Wisconsin.
- S.P., a 32-year-old male, presented with pain located on his neck and back due to an injury while working out. The practitioner diagnosed this condition as qi and blood stagnation. ***Flex (TMX)*** was prescribed at 4 capsules three times a day, while also taking ***Neck Shoulder (AC)*** at 6 capsules three times a day. After taking the herbs, there was an immediate decrease in pain. The patient discontinued taking ***Flex (TMX)*** after two weeks and continued taking ***Neck Shoulder (AC)*** for an additional four weeks until the pain was gone. Submitted by S.L., Yuma, Arizona.
- C.K., a 12-year-old boy, presented with a painful and swollen elbow, with bruises due to a go-cart accident in which he was pinned under the roll bar. The patient was asked to take three capsules of ***Flex (TMX)***, four times a day, with food to avoid stomach upset. The accident happened on Thursday. The boy was able to return to school on Monday with 100% recovery, and experienced no stomach upset. A topical herbal tincture *Po Sum On*, along with acupuncture, massage and homeopathic remedies, were all part of the treatment regimen. Submitted by M.C., Sarasota, Florida.
- D.D., a 41-year-old nurse, presented with a work-related injury. She had severe back pain that was the result of a fall from lifting a patient. She said she heard a popping sound in her back when she fell. MRI confirmed her diagnosis of a herniated lumbar disc. She was nine weeks post-injury and had scheduled for steroid epidurals. She refused injections and came to our clinic for 'safe and non-invasive care.' Her blood pressure was 140/80 mmHg and the heart rate was 80 beats per minute. The TCM diagnoses included qi and blood stagnation and soft tissue damage. ***Back Support (AC)***, ***Flex (SC)*** and ***Flex (TMX)*** were prescribed at 3 capsules each three times a day. After the herbs, the patient was able to reduce Vicodin (APAP/hydrocodone) use from 2 to 0.5 tablets per day, and none at all on some days. She had increased blood pressure from stress over the injury, which was up to 170/110 mmHg. After the herbs and massage, the blood pressure came down to normal and is staying down. She had received no additional physical therapy. She did remarkably well in a short period of time. Submitted by M.H., West Palm Beach, Florida.
- An 18-year-old male chef presented with neck and shoulder pain from a skateboard fall. X-rays revealed a diminished cervical curvature as well as a hypokyphotic curve at T2 to T3. The practitioner diagnosed the condition as a cervical sprain/strain. The patient was treated with ***Neck & Shoulder (AC)*** and ***Flex (TMX)***, which produced a reduction in pain. The patient found it necessary to take the herbs with food to avoid stomach discomfort. Submitted by M.H., Jupiter, Florida.
- J.M., a 36-year-old female massage therapist, presented with pain from a recent automobile accident (second accident in 6 months). She exhibited neck, back, arm and leg pain. Airbags bent her right thumb. Her blood pressure was 120/70 mmHg and her heart rate was 72 beats per minute. X-rays showed herniation and soft tissue damage. She also complained of muscle spasms, hot sensation on trigger points, inability to move the right thumb and the range of motion for the neck and trunk were both decreased. ***Flex (TMX)***, ***Neck & Shoulder (AC)*** and ***Back Support (AC)*** were all prescribed at 2 capsules each three times daily. She responded quickly to these formulas and acupuncture

Flex (TMX)™

treatments. Pain levels were reduced by half in a short period of time. Submitted by M.H., West Palm Beach, Florida.

- L.P., a 77-year-old female, presented with severe pain in the left wrist and right rib cage after a fall. She had numbness of the wrist and palm where she landed on the cement. The patient showed bruises on the right eye. The right wrist was painful to light movement and palpation. There were tender points on the right subclavicular area. There were no visible contusions on the right rib cage. The diagnoses were qi and blood stagnation with soft tissue damage. ***Flex (TMX)***, ***Neck & Shoulder (AC)*** and ***Flex (SC)*** were prescribed at 2 capsules of each formula three times daily. The patient reported daily lowering of pain levels. Numbness was reduced to a light tingling after two days. She reported continuous and steady improvement each day. She was instructed to reduce the dosage to 2 capsules of each formula twice a day when the pain subsided. After the swelling was reduced, the patient was referred to a chiropractor for cervical and occipital adjustments. Submitted by M. H., West Palm Beach, Florida.

PHARMACOLOGICAL AND CLINICAL RESEARCH

Flex (TMX) is formulated specifically to treat both internal and external injuries, such as muscle aches and pain, bruises, sprains, contusions, and in severe cases, bone fractures or broken bones. Pharmacologically, herbs in this formula have an analgesic effect to relieve pain, anti-inflammatory action to reduce inflammation and swelling, and antispasmodic function to relieve muscle spasms and cramps.

Yan Hu Suo (Rhizoma Corydalis) is one of the strongest and most potent herbs for treatment of pain. Its effects are well documented in both historical references and modern research studies. According to classical texts, *Yan Hu Suo* (Rhizoma Corydalis) has been shown to treat chest and hypochondriac pain, epigastric and abdominal pain, hernial pain, amenorrhea or menstrual pain, and pain of the extremities. According to laboratory studies, the extract of *Yan Hu Suo* (Rhizoma Corydalis) has been found to be effective in both acute and chronic phases of inflammation. The mechanism of its anti-inflammatory effect is attributed to its effect to inhibit the release of histamine and pro-inflammatory mediators.[5,6] Furthermore, it has a strong analgesic effect. With adjustment in dosage, the potency of *Yan Hu Suo* (Rhizoma Corydalis) has been compared to that of morphine. In fact, the analgesic effect of *Yan Hu Suo* (Rhizoma Corydalis) is so strong and reliable that it has been used with a satisfactory anesthetic effect in 98 out of 105 patients (93.4%) who underwent surgery.[7] The analgesic effect can be potentiated further with concurrent acupuncture therapy. In one research study, it is demonstrated that the analgesic effect is increased significantly with concurrent treatments using *Yan Hu Suo* (Rhizoma Corydalis) and electro-acupuncture, when compared to a control group, which received electro-acupuncture only.[8] Overall, it is well understood that *Yan Hu Suo* (Rhizoma Corydalis) has a marked effect to treat pain. Though the maximum analgesic effect of *Yan Hu Suo* (Rhizoma Corydalis) is not as strong as morphine, it has been determined that the herb is much safer, with significantly less side effects, less risk of tolerance, and no evidence of physical dependence even with long-term use.[9]

In addition to *Yan Hu Suo* (Rhizoma Corydalis), there are many herbs with analgesic effect to alleviate pain. *Ru Xiang* (Gummi Olibanum) and *Mo Yao* (Myrrha) have an analgesic effect to relieve pain and an anti-inflammatory effect to reduce swelling and inflammation.[10,11] Clinically, they have been used effectively to treat pain associated with various types of trauma and external injuries.[12] Furthermore, use of *Ru Xiang* (Gummi Olibanum) and *Mo Yao* (Myrrha) is also beneficial to facilitate wound healing by stimulating maturation and differentiation of white blood cells.[13] The combination of *Bai Shao* (Radix Paeoniae Alba) and *Gan Cao* (Radix et Rhizoma Glycyrrhizae) also has a marked analgesic effect to relieve pain. The effectiveness is increased significantly when combined with acupuncture.[14] Clinically, these two herbs have been used successfully to treat conditions such as pain,[15] neuralgia,[16] trigeminal neuralgia,[17,18] neck pain, [19] acute back pain,[20] heel pain,[21] pain in the lower back and legs,[22] sciatica,[23] gastric and abdominal pain,[24] and dysmenorrhea.[25]

Flex (TMX) contains many herbs with excellent anti-inflammatory effects to reduce swelling and inflammation. *Dang Gui* (Radix Angelicae Sinensis) exerts both analgesic and anti-inflammatory effects through the inhibition of pro-inflammatory mediators, including nitric oxide and prostaglandin E2 in peritoneal macrophages.[26,27] In comparison with acetylsalicylic acid, the anti-inflammatory effect of *Dang Gui* (Radix Angelicae Sinensis) is approximately 1.1 times stronger, and its analgesic effect is approximately 1.7 times stronger.[28] *Er Cha* (Catechu) exerts a remarkable anti-inflammatory effect via dual inhibition of cyclo-oxygenase and 5-lipoxygenase enzymes to reduce production of pro-inflammatory eicosanoids and attenuate edema.[29] *Mu Dan Pi* (Cortex Moutan) has demonstrated strong anti-inflammatory actions through inhibition of prostaglandin synthesis and decreased permeability of the blood vessels.[30,31] *Chuan Mu Xiang* (Radix Vladimiriae) exhibited an anti-inflammatory effect through significant inhibitory effects on INF-γ-induced nitric oxide production.[32] *Su Mu* (Lignum Sappan) has both anti-inflammatory and antiarthritic effects. It suppresses inflammation through the inhibition of nitric oxide activity,[33] and attenuates collagen-induced arthritis by decreasing the levels of IL-1β, IL-6, TNF-α and PGE2 in serum and the expression of cyclo-oxygenase-2 and transcription factor NF-κB.[34] Finally, *Gan Cao* (Radix et Rhizoma Glycyrrhizae) has demonstrated marked anti-inflammatory effects by enhancing the effect of glucocorticoid through increased production and secretion as well as decreased metabolism by the liver.[35] In terms of anti-inflammatory actions, the comparison of cortisone to glycyrrhizin and glycyrrhetinic acid, two compounds from

FORMULAS

Flex (TMX)™

Gan Cao (Radix et Rhizoma Glycyrrhizae), is approximately 10:1.[36] Clinical applications of *Gan Cao* (Radix et Rhizoma Glycyrrhizae) include pain, inflammation, edema, arthritis, spasms, cramps and others.[37,38]

To relieve spasms and cramps, ***Flex (TMX)*** utilizes the muscle-relaxant effect of *Bai Shao* (Radix Paeoniae Alba) and *Gan Cao* (Radix et Rhizoma Glycyrrhizae) to relax both smooth and skeletal muscles.[39,40] Clinically, these two herbs have been used successfully to treat conditions such as leg cramps in the calf,[41] muscle cramps in hemodialysis,[42] restless leg syndrome,[43] intestinal spasm,[44] facial spasms and twitching,[45] and menstrual cramps and pain.[46]

In addition to all the functions listed above, ***Flex (TMX)*** contains other herbs with supportive functions. *Tao Ren* (Semen Persicae) and *Hong Hua* (Flos Carthami) have excellent functions to invigorate blood circulation and facilitate healing. It was demonstrated in a clinical study with 775 cases of swelling and subcutaneous hemorrhage due to acute sprains that *Hong Hua* (Flos Carthami) can effectively improve and/or cure the condition within three to five days. *Da Huang* (Radix et Rhizoma Rhei) has a wide range of effects on the treatment of sports or traumatic injuries. Taken internally, it shortens coagulation time or stops bleeding. Used externally (as powder or paste), it treats traumatic hemorrhage with no adverse reactions or side effects. Lastly, *Dang Gui* (Radix Angelicae Sinensis) is an effective herb to promote the generation of bones. According to one study, the water extract of *Dang Gui* (Radix Angelicae Sinensis) is found to contribute to the formation of bones and treatment of bone injuries. It directly stimulates the proliferation, alkaline phosphatase activity, protein secretion and particularly type I collagen synthesis of human osteoprecursor cells in a dose-dependent manner.[47]

In summary, ***Flex (TMX)*** is not only effective for treating acute pain and inflammation associated with trauma and external injuries, it also contains herbs to facilitate healing and recovery.

COMPARATIVE ANALYSIS

Trauma injuries are generally treated with drugs that reduce inflammation and relieve pain. Two classes of drugs commonly used for treatment include non-steroidal anti-inflammatory agents (NSAID) and opioid analgesics. NSAIDs [such as Motrin (ibuprofen) and Voltaren (diclofenac)] are generally used for mild to moderate pain, and are most effective to reduce inflammation and swelling. Though effective, they may cause such serious side effects as gastric ulcer, duodenal ulcer, gastrointestinal bleeding, tinnitus, blurred vision, dizziness and headache. Furthermore, newer NSAIDs, also known as COX-2 inhibitors [such as Celebrex (celecoxib)], are associated with significantly higher risk of cardiovascular events, including heart attack and stroke. Opioid analgesics [such as Vicodin (APAP/hydrocodone) and morphine] are usually used for severe to excruciating pain. While they may be the most potent agents for pain, they also have the most serious risks and side effects, including but not limited to dizziness, lightheadedness, drowsiness, upset stomach, vomiting, constipation, stomach pain, rash, difficult urination, and respiratory depression resulting in difficult breathing. Furthermore, long-term use of these drugs leads to tolerance and addiction. In brief, it is important to remember that while drugs offer reliable and potent symptomatic pain relief, they should be used only if and when needed. Frequent use and abuse leads to unnecessary side effects and complications.

In TCM, treatment of trauma injuries is focused on relieving acute symptoms and promoting long-term recovery. Symptoms of pain, inflammation and swelling are usually treated with herbs that activate qi and blood circulation, as these herbs have excellent analgesic and anti-inflammatory effects. Furthermore, herbs that activate qi and blood also promote blood circulation to the affected area to facilitate and speed up the recovery process. In other words, by relieving symptoms and promoting recovery, use of herbs achieves both immediate and prolonged benefits.

Both drugs and herbs are effective and play slightly different roles in trauma management. In mild to moderate cases, drugs and herbs are approximately equally effective. In severe cases, such as bone fractures or severe physical injuries, drugs have a stronger analgesic effect. After the acute condition stabilizes, herbs should definitely be used as they facilitate and shorten the recovery process. In short, drugs and herbs have contrasting benefits, and may be utilize in different stages of trauma recovery for optimal care.

References

1. Berkow R. et al. The Merck Manual of Medical Information. Merck Research Laboratories. 1999 February.
2. Chan K, Lo AC, Yeung JH, Woo KS. Journal of Pharmacy and Pharmacology 1995 May;47(5):402-6.
3. Pharmacotherapy 1999 July;19(7):870-876.
4. European Journal of Drug Metabolism and Pharmacokinetics 1995; 20(1): 55-60.
5. *Biol Pharm Bull*, Feb 1994; 17(2):262-5.
6. Oh YC, Choi JG, Lee YS, Brice OO, Lee SC, Kwak HS, Byun YH, Kang OH, Rho JR, Shin DW, Kwon DY. Tetrahydropalmatine inhibits pro-inflammatory mediators in lipopolysaccharide-stimulated THP-1 cells. Department of Oriental Pharmacy, College of Pharmacy, Wonkwang University Wonkwang Oriental Medicines Research Institute, Iksan, Republic of Korea. J Med Food. 2010 Oct;13(5):1125-32.
7. *He Bei Xin Yi Yao* (Hebei New Medicine and Herbology), 1973; 4:34.
8. *Chen Tzu Yen Chiu* (Acupuncture Research), 1994;19(1):55-8.
9. *Zhong Yao Yao Li Yu Ying Yong* (Pharmacology and Applications of Chinese Herbs), 1983; 447.
10. *Zhong Yao Xue* (Chinese Herbology), 1998; 539:540.
11. Yoshikawa M, Morikawa T, Oominami H, Matsuda H. Absolute stereostructures of olibanumols A, B, C, H, I, and J from olibanum, gum-resin of Boswellia carterii, and inhibitors of nitric oxide production in lipopolysaccharide-activated mouse peritoneal macrophages. Kyoto Pharmaceutical University, Japan. Chem Pharm Bull (Tokyo). 2009 Sep;57(9):957-64.
12. *He Nan Zhong Yi Xue Yuan Xue Bao* (Journal of University of Henan School of Medicine), 1980; 3:38.

Flex (TMX)™

13. Haffor A-S. 2010. Effect of myrrh (Commiphora molmol) on leukocyte levels before and during healing from gastric ulcer skin injury. J Immunotoxicol 7: 68-75.
14. *Guo Wai Yi Xue* (Foreign Medicine) 1984;6(1):58.
15. *Shang Hai Zhong Yi Yao Za Zhi* (Shanghai Journal of Chinese Medicine and Herbology), 1983; 4:14.
16. *Zhong Yi Ming Fang Lin Chuang Xin Yong* (Contemporary Clinical Applications of Classic Chinese Formulas) 2001;313.
17. *Jiang Xi Yi Yao* (Jiangxi Medicine and Herbology) 1965;5(7):909.
18. *Zhong Yi Za Zhi* (Journal of Chinese Medicine), 1983; 11:9.
19. *Jiang Su Zhong Yi* (Jiangsu Chinese Medicine), 1990; (10):29.
20. *Zhe Jiang Zhong Yi Za Zhi* (Zhejiang Journal of Chinese Medicine) 1995; (11):524.
21. *Si Chuan Zhong Yi* (Sichuan Chinese Medicine) 1996;11:38.
22. *Yun Nan Zhong Yi* (Yunnan Journal of Traditional Chinese Medicine), 1990; 4:15.
23. *Fu Jian Zhong Yi Yao* (Fujian Chinese Medicine and Herbology), 1994; (1):7.
24. *Fu Jian Zhong Yi Yao* (Fujian Chinese Medicine and Herbology) 1961;9(4):44.
25. Tanaka T. A novel anti-dysmenorrhea therapy with cyclic administration of two Japanese herbal medicines. Clinical & Experimental Obstetrics & Gynecology 2003;30(2-3):95-8.
26. *Xin Yi Yao Xue Za Zhi* (New Journal of Medicine and Herbology), 1975; (6):34.
27. Chao WW, Kuo YH, Li WC, Lin BF. The production of nitric oxide and prostaglandin E2 in peritoneal macrophages is inhibited by Andrographis paniculata, Angelica sinensis and Morus alba ethyl acetate fractions. Department of Biochemical Science and Technology, Institute of Microbiology and Biochemistry, National Taiwan University, Taipei 106, Taiwan, ROC. J Ethnopharmacol. 2009 Feb 25;122(1):68-75.
28. *Yao Xue Za Zhi* (Journal of Medicinals), 1971; (91):1098.
29. Burnett BP, Jia Q, Zhao Y, Levy RM. A medicinal extract of Scutellaria baicalensis and Acacia catechu acts as a dual inhibitor of cyclooxygenase and 5-lipoxygenase to reduce inflammation. J Med Food. 2007 Sep;10(3):442-51.
30. *Sheng Yao Xue Za Zhi* (Journal of Raw Herbology), 1979; 33(3):178.
31. *Zhong Guo Yao Ke Da Xue Xue Bao* (Journal of University of Chinese Herbology), 1990; 21(4):222.
32. Xu J, Jin D, Shi D, Ma Y, Yang B, Zhao P, Guo Y. Sesquiterpenes from Vladimiria souliei and their inhibitory effects on NO production. Fitoterapia. 2011 Apr;82(3):508-11.
33. Hong C.H., Hur S.K., Oh O.J., Kim S.S., Nam K.A & Lee S.K. Evaluation of natural products on inhibition of inducible cyclooxygenase (COX-2) and nitric oxide synthase (iNOS) in cultured mouse macrophage cells. *J Ethnopharmacol.* 2002, 83(1-2): 153-159.
34. Wang YZ, Sun SQ, Zhou YB. Extract of the dried heartwood of Caesalpinia sappan L. attenuates collagen-induced arthritis. Department of Pharmacy, Daqing Campus of Harbin Medical University, Daqing 163319, China. J Ethnopharmacol. 2011 Jun 14;136(1):271-8.
35. *Zhong Yao Zhi* (Chinese Herbology Journal), 1993; 3:58.
36. *Zhong Cao Yao* (Chinese Herbal Medicine), 1991; 22(10):452.
37. *Zhe Jiang Zhong Yi Za Zhi* (Zhejiang Journal of Chinese Medicine), 1980; 2:60.
38. *Zhong Hua Nei Ke Za Zhi* (Chinese Journal of Internal Medicine), 1960; 4:354.
39. *Guo Wai Yi Xue* (Foreign Medicine) 1984;6(1):58.
40. *He Nan Zhong Yi* (Henan Chinese Medicine) 1986;(6):15.
41. *Zhong Yi Za Zhi* (Journal of Chinese Medicine) 1985;6:450.
42. Inoshita F, Ogura Y, Suzuki Y, Hara S, Yamada A, Tanaka N, Yamashita A, Marumo F. Effect of orally administered shao-yao-gan-cao-tang (Shakuyaku-kanzo-to) on muscle cramps in maintenance hemodialysis patients: a preliminary study. American Journal of Chinese Medicine 2003;31(3):445-53.
43. *He Bei Zhong Yi* (Hebei Chinese Medicine) 1984;3:29.
44. *Zhong Yi Za Zhi* (Journal of Chinese Medicine), 1985; 6:50.
45. *Zhong Xi Yi Jie He Za Zhi* (Journal of Integrated Chinese and Western Medicine), 1991; (1):43.
46. *Bei Jing Zhong Yi* (Beijing Chinese Medicine) 1983;(1):33.
47. Yang Q, Populo SM, Zhang J, Yang G, Kodama H. Effect of Angelica sinensis on the proliferation of human bone cells. Clin Chim Acta. 2002 Oct;324(1-2): 89-97.

FORMULAS

Gardenia Complex™

CLINICAL APPLICATIONS

- **Excess conditions with heat and fire in all three *jiaos***
- **Infectious diseases** with fever
- **Inflammatory conditions** with swelling, inflammation, burning sensations and pain
- **Disorders with high blood pressure and fast heart rate**

WESTERN THERAPEUTIC ACTIONS

- Antibiotic effect to treat infection
- Anti-inflammatory and analgesic effects to reduce swelling and relieve pain
- Antihypertensive effect to reduce blood pressure
- Hepatoprotective effect to treat hepatitis and liver cirrhosis
- Cholagogic effect to treat jaundice
- Gastrointestinal effect to decrease production and secretion of stomach acid
- Antipyretic effect to reduce body temperature

CHINESE THERAPEUTIC ACTIONS

- Clears heat
- Purges fire
- Eliminates toxins
- Nourishes yin and tonifies blood

DOSAGE

Take 3 to 4 capsules three times daily. Dosage may be increased up to 6 to 8 capsules three times daily in acute cases. This formula should not be taken for more than two months continuously.

INGREDIENTS

Bian Xu (Herba Polygoni Avicularis)
Chai Hu (Radix Bupleuri)
Che Qian Zi (Semen Plantaginis)
Dang Gui (Radix Angelicae Sinensis)
Di Huang (Radix Rehmanniae)
Fu Ling (Poria)
Gan Cao (Radix et Rhizoma Glycyrrhizae)
Geng Mi (Semen Oryzae)
Huang Bo (Cortex Phellodendri Chinensis)
Huang Qin (Radix Scutellariae)
Long Dan (Radix et Rhizoma Gentianae)
Mu Dan Pi (Cortex Moutan)
Shan Yao (Rhizoma Dioscoreae)
Shan Zhu Yu (Fructus Corni)
Shi Gao (Gypsum Fibrosum)
Shu Di Huang (Radix Rehmanniae Praeparata)
Ze Xie (Rhizoma Alismatis)
Zhi Mu (Rhizoma Anemarrhenae)
Zhi Zi (Fructus Gardeniae)

BACKGROUND

From traditional Chinese medicine perspectives, "excess" represents conditions with presentations of heat, fire, and toxins in various *zang fu* organs. From Western medical perspectives, these "excess" conditions are often characterized by infection, inflammation, increased metabolic rate, and hyperactivity of various organ systems, such as respiratory, gastrointestinal, hepatic, and others. Though the terminologies are different, these concepts can be integrated together. For example, "Lung heat" generally indicates infection and inflammation of the upper respiratory tract; "Stomach heat" often refers to gastric ulcer, duodenal ulcer or acid reflux; "damp-heat in the intestines" corresponds to various types of inflammatory bowel disorders; "damp-heat in the Liver and Gallbladder" suggests hepatitis or jaundice types of disorders; and "heat in the channels and collaterals" implies inflammatory and arthritic conditions affecting the joints. Similarly, herbs that clear heat, purge fire, and eliminate toxins often have antibacterial, antiviral, antipyretic, and anti-inflammatory effects.

FORMULA EXPLANATION

Gardenia Complex is designed for conditions manifesting in excess heat and fire in the body. This formula clears heat, purges fire, drains damp-heat, and eliminates toxins from the *zang fu* organs that are most susceptible to heat invasion, namely the Heart, Liver and Stomach.

Zhi Zi (Fructus Gardeniae) clears heat in all three *jiaos*. *Shi Gao* (Gypsum Fibrosum), *Zhi Mu* (Rhizoma Anemarrhenae), and *Geng Mi* (Semen Oryzae) represent the effect of the classic formula *Bai Hu Tang* (White Tiger Decoction) to drain *yangming* Stomach fire. *Chai Hu* (Radix Bupleuri) is a channel-guiding herb to the Liver to enhance *Long Dan* (Radix et Rhizoma Gentianae) and *Huang Qin* (Radix Scutellariae) in sedating Liver fire. *Mu Dan Pi* (Cortex Moutan) and *Huang Bo* (Cortex Phellodendri Chinensis) are added to clear deficiency heat from the Kidney. *Di Huang* (Radix Rehmanniae), *Shu Di Huang* (Radix Rehmanniae Praeparata), and *Dang Gui* (Radix Angelicae Sinensis) are added to tonify the blood and prevent the harsh herbs from damaging Liver blood. *Che Qian Zi* (Semen Plantaginis), *Ze Xie* (Rhizoma Alismatis), *Bian Xu* (Herba Polygoni Avicularis), and *Fu Ling* (Poria) drain dampness and eliminate heat through urination. *Shan Zhu Yu* (Fructus Corni) nourishes Kidney yin to prevent the herbs that drain dampness from damaging the yin. *Shan Yao* (Rhizoma Dioscoreae) with *Gan Cao* (Radix et Rhizoma Glycyrrhizae) protect the middle *jiao* from the harsh heat-clearing herbs and harmonize the formula.

In summary, ***Gardenia Complex*** is an excellent formula to clear excess fire and heat in the body affecting various *zang fu* organs such as the Heart, Liver and Stomach. ***Gardenia Complex*** can also be used with another formula to enhance the overall effect to clear excess fire and heat.

Gardenia Complex™

CAUTIONS & CONTRAINDICATIONS

- This formula is contraindicated in patients who have generalized weakness and deficiency. It is also contraindicated during pregnancy and nursing.
- This herbal formula contains herbs that invigorate blood circulation, such as *Dang Gui* (Radix Angelicae Sinensis). Therefore, patients who are on anticoagulant or antiplatelet therapies, such as Coumadin (warfarin), should use this formula with caution, or not at all, as there may be a higher risk of bleeding and bruising.[1,2,3]

CLINICAL NOTES

- ***Gardenia Complex*** and ***Herbal ABX*** are two formulas with strong and broad-spectrum heat-clearing effects.
  - ***Gardenia Complex*** is designed to purge heat in the organs due to internal imbalances or improper dietary intake such as excessive spicy or greasy food or lifestyle (including lack of sleep, and excessive smoking).
  - ***Herbal ABX*** clears heat and detoxifies, and is best for infection that is contracted from outside sources, such as influenza or urinary tract infection.
  - Therefore, although both formulas clear heat, their use should still be distinguished.
- ***Gardenia Complex*** incorporates numerous antibiotic herbs for two important reasons. First, the use of multiple herbs within an herbal formula has been shown to increase the antibiotic effect more than tenfold. Second, isolated use of single ingredients is often ineffective and increases the risk of development of bacterial and viral resistance.[4] Given these two reasons, it is necessary to combine herbs with appropriate properties to ensure effectiveness in treating the infection and minimizing the potential risk of the micro-organisms developing resistance.

Pulse diagnosis by Dr. Jimmy Wei-Yen Chang:

- Big pulse, a thick, expanding, forceful, and fast pulse on all three pulse positions, *cun*, *guan*, and *chi*.

SUPPLEMENTARY FORMULAS

- With lung infection, add ***Respitrol (Heat)*** or ***Pinellia XPT***.
- With infection of the ear, nose, and throat, add ***Herbal ENT***.
- With acid reflux, stomach ulcer, or duodenal ulcer, combine with ***GI Care***.
- With stomach or intestinal infection, combine with ***GI Care II***.
- With urinary tract infection or damp-heat in the lower *jiao*, combine with ***V-Support***.
- With hypertension, combine with ***Gastrodia Complex*** or ***Gentiana Complex***.
- With psychological disorder or emotional instability with excess nature, combine with ***Calm*** or ***Calm (ES)***.
- With depression, add ***Shine*** or ***Shine (DS)***.
- With liver and gallbladder disorders such as hepatitis, liver cirrhosis, and jaundice, add ***Liver DTX***.
- With coronary artery disease, add ***Circulation***.
- With *re bi* (heat painful obstruction), add ***Flex (Heat)***.
- With constipation, add ***Gentle Lax (Excess)***.
- With kidney stone, add ***Dissolve (KS)***.
- With acne, add ***Dermatrol (Clear)***.
- To address any dermatological disorders that are wet in appearance, add ***Dermatrol (Damp)***.
- To address any dermatological disorders that are dry in appearance, add ***Dermatrol (Dry)***.
- With unknown swelling or hard lesions, add ***Resolve (AI)***.
- With inflammation, add ***Astringent Complex***.
- With excessive damp and phlegm, add ***Pinellia Complex***.
- With bacterial infections, add ***Herbal ABX***.
- With viral infections, add ***Herbal AVR***.

ACUPUNCTURE TREATMENT

Traditional Points:

- *Quchi* (LI 11), *Hegu* (LI 4), *Neiguan* (PC 6), *Shousanli* (LI 10), *Zusanli* (ST 36), *Yanglingquan* (GB 34), *Sanyinjiao* (SP 6)
- *Dazhui* (GV 14), *Quchi* (LI 11), *Hegu* (LI 4), *Yuji* (LU 10), *Waiguan* (TH 5), *Zhongchong* (PC 9), *Xiangu* (ST 43)
- Bleed *Shaoshang* (LU 11), *Quchi* (LI 11), *Weizhong* (BL 40), and *Shixuan*.
- *Gua-sha* can be performed all along the Urinary Bladder channel and medial sides of *Weizhong* (BL 40) until bruises are apparent. (Note: *Gua-sha* is the act of scraping the skin with a small board or with a coin after applying oil on the skin).

Classic Master Tung's Points:

- **Fever:** *Dabai* (T 22.04). Bleed T1 area with cupping. Bleed before needling for best result.

Master Tung's Points by Dr. Chuan-Min Wang:

- **Excess heat:** *Huosan* (T 66.12)

Balance Method by Dr. Richard Tan:

- Left side: *Houxi* (SI 3), *Xiaohai* (SI 8), *Taichong* (LR 3), *Ququan* (LR 8)
- Right side: *Shaohai* (HT 3), *Shenmen* (HT 7), *Yanglingquan* (GB 34), *Zulinqi* (GB 41)
- Left and right sides can be alternated from treatment to treatment.
- The above acupuncture prescription is for general inflammation. Please refer to other formulas for acupuncture points depending on each specific condition.

Ear Acupuncture:

- *Shenmen*, Adrenals, Ear Apex. Use strong stimulation and remove the needles after 15 minutes.

Gardenia Complex™

Auricular Medicine by Dr. Li-Chun Huang:

- **Elevated body temperature:** Thalamus, Brain Stem, Lung, Sympathetic, Endocrine, corresponding points (to the area affected), Tragic Apex and Adrenal Gland. Bleed Ear Apex.
- **Excessive sweating:** Sympathetic, Thalamus, Heart, Lung, Spleen, Nervous Subcortex
- **Hyperhidrosis:** Sympathetic, Kidney, Heart, Spleen, Lung, Nervous Subcortex, corresponding points (to the area that is sweating)

NUTRITION

- Avoid hot, spicy, and fried foods, which aggravate excess conditions of heat and fire. Foods that are hot in nature such as pepper and lamb should be avoided.
- Foods that are cold in nature may be helpful in expelling fire in the body. These include cucumber, tomato, cactus, celery, and tofu.
- Increase intake of nourishing, cooling foods/roots such as Mexican yam, yam, radishes, potatoes, carrots, melons, cucumbers, beets, turnips, malanga, celeriac, taro, and rutabaga.
- Avoid spicy/pungent/aromatic vegetables such as pepper, garlic, onions, basil, rosemary, cumin, funnel, anise, leeks, chives, scallions, thyme, saffron, wormwood, mustard, chili pepper, and wasabi.

LIFESTYLE INSTRUCTIONS

- Avoid stress and stressful situations whenever possible.
- Refrain from alcoholic beverages and cigarette smoking.

CASE STUDIES

- K.B., a 62-year-old patient, presented with a chronic bilateral rash located on her arms. The rash occurred daily with a description of purple and dark in color. Daily lifestyle habits consisted of light alcohol drinking, cigarette smoking, and eating spicy foods. Other symptoms included pain with itching and peeling of the skin towards the end of the day. The TCM diagnosis was Lung and Liver fire. The practitioner administered ***Gardenia Complex*** and ***Silerex***, both at four capsules three times a day. Within two weeks, the patient reported that her skin had completely cleared up. The patient continued with the same herbal combination for an additional two months. Submitted by A.I., Hilo, Hawaii.
- K.B., a 62-year-old female, presented with constant daily fever for two weeks. There were no signs of infection; however, additional symptoms of slight anger, irritability, thirst, and slight red eyes were present. Her blood pressure was 132/72 mmHg. Though the fever was of unknown origin, the TCM diagnosis was Liver fire. ***Gardenia Complex*** was administered at four capsules three times daily. The fever cleared in two days and did not return. Her anger and irritability had also lessened. Submitted by A.I., Hilo, Hawaii.
- J.P., a 59-year-old male, presented with tooth pain located within the right molar. It was also noted that the patient had an infected gum in the same area. Objective finding was a red swollen jaw. The TCM diagnosis was Stomach heat; Western diagnosis was gum infection as well as gingivitis. Upon diagnosis the patient was prescribed ***Gardenia Complex***. After one week of taking the herbs, the infection had resolved. Submitted by M.P., Muskego, Wisconsin.

ADDITIONAL INFORMATION

Interpreting Blood Pressure and Heart Rate Readings:

Dr. Jimmy Wei-Yen Chang, author of *Pulsynergy* and creator of this formula, explains that excess heat can be defined by the objective findings of fast heart rate and high blood pressure. This formula is designed for any condition with the finding of high blood pressure and fast heart rate. The following is an article written by Dr. Chang entitled: "Interpreting Blood Pressure and Heart Rate Readings by Eight Principle Diagnostic Standards."

Whether approached by a seasoned practitioner or a novice, there are always cases that are difficult to differentiate and diagnose based on the classic *Ba Gang Bian Zheng* (Eight Principle Differentiation). When a patient presents complex symptoms, it is not always easy to sort out the tangle to come up with a confident, simple diagnosis and herbal prescription. Maybe the patient is taking one or more pharmaceuticals that complicate the clinical presentation, so that it is difficult to know which symptoms are true and which ones are side effects of the drug(s). Alternatively, maybe the patient is just not telling their entire history or complaints for one reason or another.

Conversely, maybe the difficulty in reaching a diagnosis is because the patient is describing too many symptoms, whether related to the chief complaint or not. In other cases, contradictory elements are in play, such as when a patient exhibits all excess signs but states that he or she suffers from chronic fatigue syndrome. On the other hand, maybe they feel cold, but their pulse is forceful and rapid, and their tongue is extremely red, with a definite yellow coating. One way or another, subjective complaints from patients may not always point to an immediate correct diagnosis.

One objective way to find out exactly whether the patient is truly suffering from deficiency, excess, heat or cold is to measure the blood pressure and the heart rate. Dr. Jimmy Wei-Yen Chang uses this method daily on all of his patients and has confirmed its practical usefulness through thousands of cases in his 30+ years of practice. Below is a brief summary of the patterns representing the most commonly seen complex types in the clinic.

Four Types of Blood Pressure + Heart Rate:

- **Type 1: Systolic (High) + Diastolic (High) + Heart Rate (Fast) = Excess Heat.** Patients with both high blood pressure and a fast heart rate are, without exception, suffering from an excess heat condition. Please note that these patients may complain that they are tired and depressed. However, if they have high blood pressure and a fast heart rate, tonic herbs should *never*

Gardenia Complex™

Blood Pressure and Heart Rate Chart for *Ba Gang Bian Zheng* (Eight Principle Differentiation)

	Systolic Pressure	Diastolic Pressure	Heart Rate	Diagnosis	Herbs
Type 1	High	High	Fast	Excess Heat	Heat-Clearing Herbs
Type 2	Low	Low	Slow	Yang Deficiency	Tonic Herbs
Type 3	High	Normal	Slow	Deficient heat + Blood stasis	Blood moving herbs + Deficiency heat-clearing herbs
Type 4	Low	Low	Fast	Yin deficiency heat	Tonify yin and sedate deficiency heat

be used, despite the fact that the patient complains of tiredness. The diagnosis is excess fire, which should be addressed with heat-clearing herbs.

- **Type 2: Systolic (Low) + Diastolic (Low) + Heart Rate (Slow) = Yang Deficiency.** Patients who have low blood pressure and a slow heart rate are experiencing deficiency, mostly qi or yang deficiency. These deficiencies are best helped by tonic herbs; never give these patients purging and sedating herbs.
- **Type 3: Systolic (High) + Diastolic (Normal) + Heart Rate (Slow) = Deficiency Heat + Blood Stasis.** Patients who belong to this category usually suffer from blood stasis, which may be the result of an old injury or surgery. The heart rate is slow because of blood stasis and obstruction of the flow. In turn, systolic pressure is increased, as the body attempts to maintain balance. The increased pressure and lack of flow result in heat from deficiency. Carefully selecting appropriate blood-moving and stasis-resolving herbs with herbs to clear deficiency heat will be the most helpful strategy for treating these patients.
- **Type 4: Systolic (Low) + Diastolic (Low) + Heart Rate (Fast) = Yin Deficiency Heat.** The last group might appear to reflect heat because of the rapid heart rate, but the low blood pressure tells a different story: the insufficient quantities of blood and yin in circulation require a rapid heart rate to maintain positive circulation. This is similar to a car engine running with insufficient oil: eventually, heat begins to build up from the deficiency of lubricating yin. These patients are suffering from yin deficiency heat, and must be treated with herbs that tonify yin and sedate the deficiency heat.

Summary:

This approach provides a guideline to follow when confronted with a confusing presentation in the patient. Tongue and pulse diagnoses should be combined with this approach to reach an accurate diagnostic conclusion. Here is an example of a recent case that was addressed using this method:

A 45-year-old female states that she suffers from chronic fatigue syndrome, is extremely tired, and has no energy even for driving or simple activities. She complains of how stressful life is, how depressed she feels, and states that everything in life is "just not right." Tonic herbs might be the first approach that comes to mind. However, the objective findings of her blood pressure (170/120 mmHg) and heart rate (110 beats per minute) suggest otherwise. It is important to look at the tongue and take the pulse to arrive at an accurate diagnosis. If the tongue is red and the pulse rapid, then the patient's complaint of tiredness and fatigue can be ruled out. In this particular case, it would be important to avoid using a warming, drying tonic formula like ***Vitality*** or ***Venus***. Heat-clearing formulas like ***Gardenia Complex*** and ***Herbal ABX*** would appropriately provide sedation for this patient. Although it seems wrong on the surface of things to use a sedating formula for someone identifying herself as having chronic fatigue syndrome, this would be the correct and effective approach.

Please remember that this is a guideline to follow when the presentation of the illness is complicated and confusing. It is important to gather all the details (signs, symptoms, tongue diagnosis, pulse diagnosis, and objective readings of blood pressure and heart rate) so the diagnosis will be accurate.

PHARMACOLOGICAL AND CLINICAL RESEARCH

Gardenia Complex is designed to treat all excess conditions, including presentations of heat, fire, and toxins in various *zang fu* organs. From Western medical perspectives, these disorders are often characterized by infection, inflammation, and hyperactivity of various organ systems. As such, ***Gardenia Complex*** has an extremely broad range of action, and may be used to treat many disorders.

Infection is a common presentation of heat, fire and toxins. ***Gardenia Complex*** contains many herbs with marked antibiotic effects to treat many types of infections, such as bacterial, viral, and fungal infections. Among herbs with marked antibiotic effects are *Zhi Zi* (Fructus Gardeniae),[5] *Zhi Mu* (Rhizoma Anemarrhenae),[6,7] *Chai Hu* (Radix Bupleuri),[8] *Mu Dan Pi* (Cortex Moutan),[9] *Huang Qin* (Radix Scutellariae),[10] *Long Dan* (Radix et Rhizoma Gentianae),[11] and *Shan Zhu Yu* (Fructus Corni).[12] In terms of clinical applications, these herbs have been used to treat various types of infections throughout the body, including, but not limited to, diseases such as common cold and influenza,[13] infectious hepatitis,[14] pneumonia,[15] bronchitis,[16] and encephalitis.[17]

Inflammatory conditions with swelling, inflammation, burning sensations and pain are also presentations of heat

FORMULAS

Gardenia Complex™

and fire. Many herbs in ***Gardenia Complex*** have a marked anti-inflammatory effect to treat such conditions, such as *Chai Hu* (Radix Bupleuri),[18] *Di Huang* (Radix Rehmanniae),[19] *Shan Zhu Yu* (Fructus Corni),[20] *Huang Qin* (Radix Scutellariae),[21] and *Mu Dan Pi* (Cortex Moutan).[22] Clinically, these herbs have been used with great success to treat various inflammatory conditions, including but not limited to, lymphadenitis, cellulitis, and erysipelas.[23] Furthermore, many of these herbs also have an analgesic effect to relieve pain, such as *Chai Hu* (Radix Bupleuri) and *Zhi Zi* (Fructus Gardeniae), which are beneficial for treatment of arthritis and rheumatism.[24,25,26]

Cardiovascular diseases are also considered excess in nature, such as hypertension and coronary artery disease. ***Gardenia Complex*** contains many herbs with a marked antihypertensive effect, such as *Huang Qin* (Radix Scutellariae),[27] *Huang Bo* (Cortex Phellodendri Chinensis),[28] *Mu Dan Pi* (Cortex Moutan),[29] and *Zhi Zi* (Fructus Gardeniae).[30] Though their mechanisms of action differ, they have all been shown to reduce blood pressure. According to one study, use of *Huang Qin* (Radix Scutellariae) three times daily was effective in treating 51 patients with hypertension.[31] According to another study, administration of *Mu Dan Pi* (Cortex Moutan) effectively lowered blood pressure within five days among 20 patients with hypertension.[32] Furthermore, *Mu Dan Pi* (Cortex Moutan) and *Zhi Zi* (Fructus Gardeniae) have cardiovascular effects to increase blood perfusion to the coronary arteries, decrease cardiac output and decrease load on the left ventricle.[33,34] These actions offer a protective effect against ischemia of the heart and coronary artery disorders.[35]

Liver and **gallbladder disorders**, such as hepatitis, liver cirrhosis, and jaundice, are often diagnosed as damp-heat in traditional Chinese medicine. ***Gardenia Complex*** incorporates many herbs with marked effects to treat these types of disorders. Pharmacologically, *Zhi Zi* (Fructus Gardeniae) and *Huang Qin* (Radix Scutellariae) are two herbs with excellent hepatoprotective effects.[36,37] Clinically, *Zhi Zi* (Fructus Gardeniae), *Huang Qin* (Radix Scutellariae), *Chai Hu* (Radix Bupleuri), and *Long Dan* (Radix et Rhizoma Gentianae) have all been used with great success to treat hepatitis and liver cirrhosis.[38,39,40,41] Furthermore, *Zhi Zi* (Fructus Gardeniae), *Chai Hu* (Radix Bupleuri), *Long Dan* (Radix et Rhizoma Gentianae), and *Huang Qin* (Radix Scutellariae) all have a cholagogic effect to stimulate the production of bile, enhance contraction of the gallbladder, increase excretion of bile into the intestines, and may be used to treat jaundice.[42,43,44]

Hyperacidity of the stomach is also a presentation of heat and fire rising upwards and damaging the surrounding area. Hyperacidity of the stomach may present in such diseases as acid reflux, belching, stomach ulcer, duodenal ulcer, and gastrointestinal bleeding. Lastly, *Zhi Zi* (Fructus Gardeniae) decreases the secretion of gastric acid and increases pH in the stomach.[45]

Hyperactivity of the central nervous system is another presentation of excess, and may be treated with herbs in ***Gardenia Complex***. *Zhi Zi* (Fructus Gardeniae) has an inhibitory effect on the central nervous system to decrease spontaneous activity, increase sleeping time, and decrease body temperature.[46] *Chai Hu* (Radix Bupleuri) has a sedative effect and prolongs sleeping time induced by barbiturates.[47]

Fever is one of the most typical symptoms of heat, and may be treated effectively with heat-clearing herbs in this formula. Many herbs in this formula have an excellent antipyretic effect to reduce fever and lower body temperature, such as *Shi Gao* (Gypsum Fibrosum),[48] *Zhi Mu* (Rhizoma Anemarrhenae),[49] and *Huang Qin* (Radix Scutellariae).[50]

In summary, ***Gardenia Complex*** has an extremely broad range of action, and may be used to treat many disorders characterized by fever, infection, inflammation, pain, and hyperactivity of various organ systems, such as the respiratory, cardiovascular, hepatic, and gastrointestinal systems.

COMPARATIVE ANALYSIS

One striking difference between Western and traditional Chinese medicine is that Western medicine focuses and excels in crisis management, while traditional Chinese medicine emphasizes and shines in holistic and preventative treatments. Therefore, in emergencies, such as gunshot wounds or surgery, Western medicine is generally the treatment of choice. However, for treatment of chronic idiopathic illness of unknown origins, where all lab tests are normal and a clear diagnosis cannot be made, traditional Chinese medicine is distinctly superior.

In cases of general presentations of inflammation, increased metabolism and elevated body temperature, where there are definite signs and symptoms of illness but not a clear diagnosis, Western medicine offers few treatment options. Under these circumstances, traditional Chinese medicine is beneficial as it excels in regulating imbalances and alleviating associated signs and symptoms. Therefore, herbal therapy should definitely be employed to prevent deterioration of this condition, and to restore optimal health. Because this formula has a broad spectrum of therapeutic effect (including antipyretic, antibiotic, and anti-inflammatory effects), it treats a wide variety of disorders. If a specific imbalance can be identified, treatment is most effective if this formula is combined with another formula that targets the identified imbalance.

References

1. Chan K, Lo AC, Yeung JH, Woo KS. Journal of Pharmacy and Pharmacology 1995 May;47(5):402-6.
2. Pharmacotherapy 1999 July;19(7):870-876.
3. European Journal of Drug Metabolism and Pharmacokinetics 1995; 20(1):55-60.
4. *Zhong Yao Xue* (Chinese Herbology), 1988; 140:144.
5. *Zhong Yao Zhi* (Chinese Herbology Journal), 1984; 578.
6. *Zhong Yao Xue* (Chinese Herbology), 1998; 115:119.

Gardenia Complex™

7. *Yao Xue Qing Bao Tong Xun* (Journal of Herbal Information), 1987; 5(4):62.
8. *Zhong Yao Xue* (Chinese Herbology), 1998; 103:106.
9. *Zhong Yao Cai* (Study of Chinese Herbal Material), 1991; 14(2):41.
10. *Zhong Yao Xue* (Chinese Herbology), 1988; 137:140.
11. *Zhong Yao Da Ci Dian* (Dictionary of Chinese Herbs), 1977; 2032.
12. *CA*, 1953; 47:12652g.
13. *Zhong Yi Za Zhi* (Journal of Chinese Medicine), 1985; 12:13.
14. *Xin Yi Yao Xue Za Zhi* (New Journal of Medicine and Herbology), 1974; 2:18.
15. *Zhong Yao Xue* (Chinese Herbology), 1998; 105.
16. *Zhong Guo Zhong Xi Yi Jie He Za Zhi* (Chinese Journal of Integrative Chinese and Western Medicine), 1984; 4:222.
17. *Xin Yi Xue* (New Medicine), 1972; 8:11.
18. *Zhong Yao Yao Li Yu Ying Yong* (Pharmacology and Applications of Chinese Herbs), 1983; 888.
19. *Zhong Yao Yao Li Yu Ying Yong* (Pharmacology and Applications of Chinese Herbs), 1983; 400.
20. *Chang Yong Zhong Yao Cheng Fen Yu Yao Li Shou Ce* (A Handbook of the Composition and Pharmacology of Common Chinese Drugs), 1994; 368:376.
21. *Chem Pharm Bull*, 1984; 32(7):2724.
22. *Sheng Yao Xue Za Zhi* (Journal of Raw Herbology), 1979; 33(3):178.
23. *Zhong Hua Wai Ke Za Zhi* (Chinese Journal of External Medicine), 1960; 4:366.
24. *Si Chuan Zhong Yi* (Sichuan Chinese Medicine), 1988; 9:11.
25. *Shen Yang Yi Xue Yuan Xue Bao* (Journal of Shenyang University of Medicine), 1984; 1(3):214.
26. *Ji Lin Zhong Yi Yao* (Jilin Chinese Medicine and Herbology), 1992; (1):16.
27. *Zhong Yao Xue* (Chinese Herbology), 1988; 137:140.
28. *Zhong Guo Yao Li Xue Tong Bao* (Journal of Chinese Herbal Pharmacology), 1989; 10(5):385.
29. *Guo Wai Yi Xue Zhong Yi Zhong Yao Fen Ce* (Monograph of Chinese Herbology from Foreign Medicine), 1983; (3):5,1984;(5):54.
30. *Zhong Yao Yao Li Yu Ying Yong* (Pharmacology and Applications of Chinese Herbs), 1983; 934.
31. *Shang Hai Zhong Yi Yao Za Zhi* (Shanghai Journal of Chinese Medicine and Herbology), 1956; 1:24.
32. *Liao Ning Yi Xue Za Zhi* (Liaoning Journal of Medicine), 1960; (7):48.
33. *Guo Wai Yi Xue Zhong Yi Zhong Yao Fen Ce* (Monograph of Chinese Herbology from Foreign Medicine), 1983; (3):5,1984;(5):54.
34. *Shan Xi Yi Yao Za Zhi* (Shanxi Journal of Medicine and Herbology), 1984; 13(4):359.
35. *Zhong Ji Yi Kan* (Medium Medical Journal); 4:19.
36. *Yun Nan Yi Yao* (Yunan Medicine and Herbology), 1991; 12(5):304.
37. *Ri Ben Yao Wu Xue Za Zhi* (Japan Journal of Pharmacology), 1957; 53(6):215.
38. *Xin Yi Yao Xue Za Zhi* (New Journal of Medicine and Herbology), 1974; 2:18.
39. *Xin Yi Yao Xue Za Zhi* (New Journal of Medicine and Herbology), 1974; 2:18.
40. *Shang Hai Zhong Yi Yao Za Zhi* (Shanghai Journal of Chinese Medicine and Herbology), 1965; 4:4.
41. *Zhong Hua Nei Ke Za Zhi* (Chinese Journal of Internal Medicine), 1978; 2:127.
42. *Zhong Yao Yao Li Yu Ying Yong* (Pharmacology and Applications of Chinese Herbs), 1983; 934.
43. *Zhong Yi Yao Xue Bao* (Report of Chinese Medicine and Herbology), 1988; (1):45.
44. *Ri Ben Yao Wu Xue Za Zhi* (Japan Journal of Pharmacology), 1957; 53(6):215.
45. *Zhong Yao Yao Li Yu Ying Yong* (Pharmacology and Applications of Chinese Herbs), 1983; 934.
46. *Jiang Su Yi Yao* (Jiangsu Journal of Medicine and Herbology), 1976; (1):28.
47. *Zhong Yao Yao Li Yu Ying Yong* (Pharmacology and Applications of Chinese Herbs), 1983; 888.
48. *Zhong Yao Xue* (Chinese Herbology), 1998; 115:119.
49. *Zhong Yao Xue* (Chinese Herbology), 1998; 115:119.
50. *Zhong Hua Yi Xue Za Zhi* (Chinese Journal of Medicine), 1956; 42(10):964.

Gastrodia Complex™

CLINICAL APPLICATIONS

- **Hypertension (deficient-type)** with dizziness, vertigo, blurred vision, headache, and/or generalized weakness
- Prevention of seizures, epilepsies and convulsions in hypertensive patients

WESTERN THERAPEUTIC ACTIONS

- Antihypertensive effect to lower blood pressure
- Vasodilating effect to increase blood perfusion and lower blood pressure
- Diuretic effect to increase water elimination and lower blood pressure
- Antiseizure, antiepileptic, and anticonvulsant effects to prevent seizures, epilepsies and convulsions

CHINESE THERAPEUTIC ACTIONS

- Extinguishes Liver wind
- Calms Liver yang
- Clears heat
- Nourishes Liver and Kidney yin

DOSAGE

Take 3 to 4 capsules three times daily with warm water on an empty stomach.

INGREDIENTS

Cha Chi Huang (Herba Stellariae Aquaticae)
Chuan Niu Xi (Radix Cyathulae)
Dan Shen (Radix et Rhizoma Salviae Miltiorrhizae)
Di Huang (Radix Rehmanniae)
Ge Gen (Radix Puerariae Lobatae)
Gou Qi Zi (Fructus Lycii)
Gou Teng (Ramulus Uncariae cum Uncis)
Jue Ming Zi (Semen Cassiae)
Sha Yuan Zi (Semen Astragali Complanati)
Shan Zhu Yu (Fructus Corni)
Shi Jue Ming (Concha Haliotidis)
Tian Ma (Rhizoma Gastrodiae)
Xia Ku Cao (Spica Prunellae)
Zhen Zhu Mu (Concha Margaritiferae)

BACKGROUND

Hypertension is the sustained elevation of resting blood pressure (systolic BP>140 mmHg and/or diastolic BP>90 mmHg). According to CDC, there are approximately 70 million people (29%) with hypertension in the United States. There are many factors that contribute to hypertension, including heredity, diet, obesity, stress, lack of exercise and pre-existing diseases. Hypertension is usually asymptomatic, but some may experience symptoms such as dizziness, flushed face, headache, fatigue, epistaxis, and nervousness.

FORMULA EXPLANATION

Gastrodia Complex is designed to extinguish Liver wind, calm Liver yang, and nourish Liver and Kidney yin. The main clinical applications of ***Gastrodia Complex*** are hypertension and headache. It can also be used in hypertensive patients to reduce the risks of seizure, convulsion, stroke, angina, and myocardial infarction.

Tian Ma (Rhizoma Gastrodiae), *Gou Teng* (Ramulus Uncariae cum Uncis), *Zhen Zhu Mu* (Concha Margaritiferae), and *Shi Jue Ming* (Concha Haliotidis) are the chief herbs used to calm or anchor Liver yang and extinguish the wind. Together they function to lower the blood pressure and relieve headache and dizziness caused by hypertension. *Cha Chi Huang* (Herba Stellariae Aquaticae), *Xia Ku Cao* (Spica Prunellae), and *Jue Ming Zi* (Semen Cassiae) have antihypertensive effects, which can clear red, painful, or swollen eyes associated with hypertension. *Sha Yuan Zi* (Semen Astragali Complanati) and *Gou Qi Zi* (Fructus Lycii) are used to alleviate visual problems associated with hypertension. *Di Huang* (Radix Rehmanniae) and *Shan Zhu Yu* (Fructus Corni) tonify the Liver and Kidney yin to prevent Liver yang rising. *Dan Shen* (Radix et Rhizoma Salviae Miltiorrhizae) improves microcirculation, myocardial contraction, and heart rate. *Ge Gen* (Radix Puerariae Lobatae) dilates blood vessels to lower blood pressure. It also relieves neck and occipital stiffness and tension commonly associated with hypertension. *Chuan Niu Xi* (Radix Cyathulae) directs the blood downward and gives this formula a descending property.

In short, ***Gastrodia Complex*** is a great formula that treats many diseases characterized by Liver wind and Liver yang excess with Liver and Kidney yin deficiency.

CAUTIONS & CONTRAINDICATIONS

- Some patients may experience mild stomach discomfort, which may be alleviated by reducing the dosage of herbs or taking the herbs with food.
- Herbal treatment is ineffective for malignant hypertension and certain cases of secondary hypertension, such as renal stenosis or pheochromocytoma. Refer the patients to a medical doctor as surgical intervention may be necessary.
- If untreated, hypertension can lead to various complications such as myocardial infarction, cerebral hemorrhage, renal failure, and premature death from these or other developments. Effective treatment must include both lifestyle changes and herbal therapy.
- This formula may be used as an adjunct for prevention of seizure, epilepsy, and convulsion; however, it is ***not*** suitable to treat acute onset of these conditions.
- This herbal formula contains herbs that invigorate blood circulation, such as *Dan Shen* (Radix et Rhizoma Salviae Miltiorrhizae). Therefore, patients who are on anticoagulant or antiplatelet therapies, such as Coumadin (warfarin), should use this formula with caution, or not at all, as there may be a higher risk of bleeding and bruising.[1]

Gastrodia Complex™

CLINICAL NOTES

- Western medicine classifies hypertension into two types: "red" and "pale" high blood pressure. "Red" high blood pressure corresponds with the TCM diagnosis of excess, and generally occurs in energetic and stressed individuals with marked redness and vascularized skin. "Pale" high blood pressure corresponds with the TCM diagnosis of deficiency, and generally occurs in individuals with compromised kidneys, glands, or metabolism.
- For treatment of hypertension, it is important to monitor the blood pressure and adjust the dosage based on age, body weight, severity of condition, and response to treatment.

Pulse Diagnosis by Dr. Jimmy Wei-Yen Chang:

- Big pulse, a thick, expanding, forceful, and fast pulse on all three pulse positions, *cun*, *guan*, and *chi*. The harder the pulse, the higher the blood pressure and the more severe the condition. In renal hypertension, *shaoyin* brachial pulse at the elbow may also be thick, forceful and expanding.

SUPPLEMENTARY FORMULAS

- For high cholesterol and triglycerides, add ***Cholisma***.
- For high cholesterol and triglycerides in individuals with fatty liver and obesity, add ***Cholisma (ES)***.
- For acute headache, add ***Corydalin (AC)***.
- For chronic headache, add ***Corydalin (CR)***.
- For hypertension with edema and water accumulation, combine with ***Herbal DRX***.
- For high blood pressure and fast heart rate due to excess heat, add ***Gardenia Complex***.
- For deviation of the eyes and mouth in post-stroke or Bell's palsy patients, add ***Symmetry***.
- For coronary heart disorders, combine with ***Circulation***.
- For cardiovascular and circulatory disorders throughout the entire body, or for stubborn hypertension with blood stagnation, combine with ***Circulation (SJ)***.
- For qi and blood deficiencies, combine with a small amount of ***Imperial Tonic***.
- For constipation, combine with ***Gentle Lax (Excess)*** or ***Gentle Lax (Deficient)***.
- For stress and anxiety, combine with ***Calm (ES)***.
- For insomnia due to stress and anxiety in individuals with underlying deficiencies, combine with ***Calm ZZZ***.
- For insomnia due to anemia, generalized weakness or excessive worrying, combine with ***Schisandra ZZZ***.
- To treat stroke complications, use ***Neuro Plus***.
- For trigeminal neuralgia or hemiplegia in hypertensive patients, combine with ***Flex (NP)***.
- With Kidney yin deficiency, add ***Kidney Tonic (Yin)*** or ***Nourish***.
- For visual disturbances such as redness, pain or blurriness, add ***Lycium Support***.

ACUPUNCTURE TREATMENT

Traditional Points:

- *Baihui* (GV 20), *Zusanli* (ST 36), *Renying* (ST 9), *Taichong* (LR 3).
- *Taichong* (LR 3), *Xingjian* (LR 2), *Fenglong* (ST 40), *Ganshu* (BL 18), *Yongquan* (KI 1), *Zusanli* (ST 36)

Classic Master Tung's Points:

- **Hypertension:** *Linggu* (T 22.05), *Dabai* (T 22.04), *Xinling* (T 33.17)*, *Quchi* (LI 11), *Tianhuang* (T 88.13), *Minghuang* (T 88.12), *Qihuang* (T 88.14), *Sanzhong* (T 77.07), *Yizhong* (T 77.05), *Erzhong* (T 77.06), *Sihuashang* (T 77.08), *Sihuazhong* (T 77.09), *Sihuaxia* (T 77.11), *Zhengjin* (T 77.01), *Zhengzong* (T 77.02), *Sansheng* (T 55.07)*, *Weizhong* (BL 40), *Huoying* (T 66.03), *Tianhuang* (T 77.17), *Dihuang* (T 77.19), *Renhuang* (T 77.21), *Tongtian* (T 88.03). Bleed the back of the neck, LU and HT, LR and SP, ST areas with cupping. Bleed dark veins nearby the ST, BL channels on the lower limbs. Bleed before needling for best result.
- **Headache:** *Linggu* (T 22.05), *Dabai* (T 22.04), *Xinling* (T 33.17)*, *Zhenghui* (T 1010.01), *Qianhui* (T 1010.05), *Shuitong* (T 1010.19), *Shuijin* (T 1010.20), *Sansheng* (T 55.07)*, *Weizhong* (BL 40), *Shenting* (GV 24), *Shangxing* (GV 23), *Huozhu* (T 66.04), *Tongtian* (T 88.03), *Fuding* (T 44.04), *Houzhi* (T 44.05), *Jianfeng* (T 44.31)*, *Tongshan* (T 88.02), *Tongguan* (T 88.01), *Zhitong* (T 44.13). Bleed *Huoshan* (T 33.06), *Huoling* (T 33.05) or dark veins nearby. Bleed before needling for best result.
- **Vertigo:** *Linggu* (T 22.05), *Dabai* (T 22.04), *Zhenghui* (T 1010.01), *Shuitong* (T 1010.19), *Shuijin* (T 1010.20), *Tongshan* (T 88.02), *Tongtian* (T 88.03), *Lieque* (LU 7), *Taiyuan* (LU 9), *Yongquan* (KI 1), *Quchi* (LI 11)
- **Epilepsy:** *Linggu* (T 22.05), *Zhengjin* (T 77.01), *Zhengzong* (T 77.02), *Zhenghui* (T 1010.01), *Qianhui* (T 1010.05), *Houhui* (T 1010.06), *Tianhuang* (T 77.17), *Dihuang* (T 77.19), *Renhuang* (T 77.21), *Yizhong* (T 77.05), *Erzhong* (T 77.06), *Sanzhong* (T 77.07), *Tianhuang* (T 88.13), *Minghuang* (T 88.12), *Qihuang* (T 88.14), *Tongshan* (T 88.02), *Tongguan* (T 88.01), *Sifuyi* (T 1010.11), *Sifuer* (T 1010.10), *Tianhuangfu [Shenguan]* (T 77.18). Bleed *du* (governing) channel, temporal region and back of the knee for dark veins. Bleed before needling for best result.

Master Tung's Points by Dr. Chuan-Min Wang:

- **High systolic pressure, hypertension due to Liver deficiency, dizziness:** *Fuding* (T 44.04), *Houzhi* (T 44.05)
- **High diastolic pressure, hypertension due to Kidney deficiency:** *Tianhuang* (T 77.17), *Tianhuangfu [shenguan]* (T 77.18)
- **High systolic and diastolic pressure:** Bleed *Wuling* (T DT.04) first. Then needle *Quchi* (LI 11), *Huoying* (T 66.03).

Balance Method by Dr. Richard Tan:

- Left side: *Xuanzhong* (GB 39), *Fenglong* (ST 40), *Chengshan* (BL 57), *Lieque* (LU 7), *Tongli* (HT 5)

Gastrodia Complex™

- Right side: *Taichong* (LR 3), *Rangu* (KI 2), *Gongsun* (SP 4), *Waiguan* (TH 5), *Binao* (LI 14)
- Left and right sides can be alternated from treatment to treatment.

Ear Acupuncture:

- Bleed the depression groove in the back of the ear to lower blood pressure.
- Use magnetic ear seeds. Switch ear every five days. Advise patient to massage the points until he/she feels a hot or distended sensation.
- Adrenal Gland, Heart, *Shenmen*, Endocrine, *Taiyang*, Liver, Kidney. Bleed the depression groove in the back of the ear to lower blood pressure. Select four or five points for each treatment, which lasts three days. Ten treatments equal one treatment course. Rest for one week in between treatment courses.

Auricular Medicine by Dr. Li-Chun Huang:

- **Reducing blood pressure:** Heart, *Shenmen*, Kidney, Liver, Occiput, Forehead, Decrease BP Point, Sympathetic, Coronary Vascular Subcortex. Bleed Ear Apex.
- **Auditory vertigo:** Internal Ear, Dizziness Area, Occiput, *San Jiao*, Liver, Kidney, Gallbladder. Bleed Ear Apex.
- **Dizziness and vertigo from cerebral arteriosclerosis:** Brain, Dizziness Area, Coronary Vascular Subcortex, Neck Triangle, External Sympathetic, Liver, Occiput. Bleed Ear Apex.

NUTRITION

- Eliminate salt from the diet in cases of hypertension. Avoid MSG, baking soda, meat, fat, aged foods, alcohol, diet soft drinks, preservatives, sugar substitutes, meat tenderizers, and soy sauce.
- Over-the-counter medications that contain ibuprofen, such as Advil or Motrin, should not be used.
- Aspartame should also be avoided, since a high level may increase blood pressure.
- Increase the intake of fresh, raw vegetables and fruits to control blood pressure. Nuts and seeds should be consumed daily as a source of protein.
- Vitamin C and bioflavonoids help to reduce blood pressure by stabilizing the blood vessel walls.
- Garlic is effective to lower blood pressure and thin the blood.

The Tao of Nutrition by Dr. Maoshing Ni and Cathy McNease:

- **Hypertension**
  - Recommendations: celery, spinach, garlic, bananas, sunflower seeds, honey, tofu, mung beans, bamboo shoots, seaweed, vinegar, tomatoes, water chestnuts, corn, apples, persimmons, peas, buckwheat, jellyfish, watermelon, hawthorn berries, eggplant, plums, mushrooms, lemons, lotus root, chrysanthemums, and cassia seeds.
  - Take black or white mushrooms and cook soup daily.
  - Steam or bake jellyfish about 12 minutes, add vinegar, soy sauce, and sesame oil; take daily for about two months.
  - Make tea from chrysanthemum flowers and cassia seeds and drink daily.
  - Avoid smoking, alcohol, spicy foods, coffee, caffeine, all stimulants, fatty or fried foods, salty foods, potatoes, pork, and over-eating.
- **Headache**
  - Recommendations: chrysanthemum flowers, mint, green onions, oyster shells, pearl barley, carrots, prunes, buckwheat, peach kernels, and green tea.
  - Avoid spicy food, alcohol, and smoking.

LIFESTYLE INSTRUCTIONS

- Normal bowel and urinary functions help to reduce blood pressure. Diuretics and stool softeners should be taken as needed.
- Maintain a positive attitude and outlook. Control emotions and reduce stress. Emotional fluctuations should be reduced whenever possible.
- Individuals who are aware of circumstances or activities that trigger tension and hypertensive responses need to initiate patterns in their lives that help them avoid or reduce the impact of those triggers.
- Stop alcohol consumption and cigarette smoking.
- Weight loss is highly recommended to help lower blood pressure.
- Exercises such as swimming and brisk walking are excellent for hypertension.
- Practices such as meditation, *tai chi chuan [tai ji chuan]*, and yoga are beneficial to relax, reduce stress, and lower blood pressure.

CASE STUDIES

- M.M., a 53-year-old female patient, presented with high blood pressure. Her blood pressure was 150/80 mmHg. The patient works in a high stress environment and lives a fast-paced lifestyle. Her energy is high but her sleep is sometimes restless. Other findings included elevated yet still favorable HDL and LDL levels. The diagnosis according to traditional Chinese medicine was Liver and Kidney yin deficiencies with Liver yang rising. ***Gastrodia Complex*** was prescribed at 4 spoonfuls twice daily for two months' duration. After two months, the patient's blood pressure was measured at 125/82 mmHg, she was sleeping better and her energy level increased. Submitted by M.M., Alameda, California.
- A 29-year-old male patient presented with chronic headaches, which he had been experiencing lifelong. Additional symptoms included lower back ache, dry eyes, neck tension, and slight dizziness. The practitioner diagnosed this condition as Liver and Kidney yin deficiencies with Liver yang rising. ***Gastrodia Complex*** was prescribed at 4 capsules three times per day. As a result of taking the herbs, the patient had reported relief of his headaches within four days. After taking only one bottle of the

Gastrodia Complex™

herbs, the patient had noted his relief lasted for about a month. Submitted by C.V., Concord, North Carolina.

- A 45-year-old male presented with headache, high blood pressure, and high cholesterol. The patient was diagnosed with Liver yang rising with stagnation of qi and blood. ***Cholisma*** and ***Gastrodia Complex*** were prescribed for the patient with positive results reported by the physician. Submitted by R.C., MD, Ph.D., New York, New York.
- J.L., an 86-year-old male, presented with hypertension, insomnia, anxiety, and high cholesterol. His blood pressure was 180/90 mmHg and the heart rate was 60 beats per minute. The blood pressure was higher in the morning (180-190/90-95 mmHg) than in the evening (170-180/85-90 mmHg). The TCM diagnosis was damp-heat accumulation. ***Gastrodia Complex*** at 4.5 grams a day and ***Cholisma*** at 1.5 grams a day were prescribed. This patient also received acupuncture. After six weeks of treatment, both morning and evening blood pressure were down to an average of 147/80 mmHg. Submitted by W.F., Bloomfield, New Jersey.
- S.O., a 51-year-old female patient, presented with extremely painful migraine headaches four to six times a month for three years. The pain developed during a time of intense involvement with a job that required serious focus and long hours. The pain was pounding and throbbing at her temples and behind her eyes. Her head itself felt "big" and each headache was accompanied by photosensitivity and occasionally nosebleeds and nausea. The patient didn't want to take any pharmaceutical drugs so she "rode out" the headaches by sleeping all day. Objective findings included sogginess and softness with palpation at the vertex where one would expect to feel only bone hardness of the skull. Blood pressure was 128/78 mmHg with a heart rate of 76 to 80 beats per minute. Tongue was red and peeled, especially at the sides. Pulse was wiry/floating and the left side was very thin. The patient appeared debilitated. Her diagnosis according to traditional Chinese medicine was Liver yang rising with Liver and Kidney yin deficiencies. The practitioner felt her episodic stress-related migraine headaches probably were due to poor regulation of blood vessel dilation/constriction in the head. ***Gastrodia Complex*** was prescribed at 4 capsules three times a day. After six weeks of herbal treatment, the patient reported that her headaches diminished in ferocity. During the next four weeks, the patient reported only one headache and it lasted only a few hours instead of putting her to bed for the entire day. Over the months that the patient continued the treatment, headaches became a rare event and she felt stronger overall. Submitted by H.H., San Francisco, California.
- A 39-year-old female presented with elevated blood pressure, palpitations, hot flashes, anxiety, and swelling in her neck, with a heart rate of 92 beats per minute. The Western diagnosis was hyperthyroidism; the TCM diagnosis was Liver and Kidney yin deficiencies. After she began taking ***Thyrodex***, the patient experienced diminished hot flashes and anxiety. Her blood pressure remained unchanged but the goiter diminished in size. After ***Gastrodia Complex*** was added to the herbal treatment, the patient noticed improvement after just one bottle. Submitted by P.W., Paulet, Vermont.
- A 47-year-old female acupuncturist presented with one-sided severely debilitating migraines, which occurred particularly during the weekends. The TCM diagnosis was Kidney yin deficiency leading to Liver yang rising. A dose of ***Corydalin (AC)*** relieved the pain especially when the drug Imitrex (sumatriptan) was unsuccessful. Within two weeks of taking ***Corydalin (AC)***, she was free from headaches. She supplemented her treatment with ***Gastrodia Complex*** in addition to acupuncture treatments. She has experienced no migraine episodes for more than six months, and continues using the herbal combination of ***Corydalin (AC)*** and ***Gastrodia Complex***. Submitted by D.W., Hashbrouck Heights, New Jersey.

PHARMACOLOGICAL AND CLINICAL RESEARCH

Gastrodia Complex is an herbal formula that has significant influence on the cardiovascular system to treat hypertension. It contains herbs with marked effects to decrease heart rate, reduce peripheral vascular resistance, dilate blood vessels, and promote diuresis.

Tian Ma (Rhizoma Gastrodiae) and *Gou Teng* (Ramulus Uncariae cum Uncis) are the two primary ingredients in this formula. *Tian Ma* (Rhizoma Gastrodiae) has many positive cardiovascular effects.[2] It increases the volume of blood flow to the cardiac muscle, increases resistance to hypoxia, and therefore reduces the risks of myocardial ischemia and myocardial infarction.[3] *Gou Teng* (Ramulus Uncariae cum Uncis) has a potent and prolonged antihypertensive effect. The decrease in blood pressure is attributed to decreased heart rate and a reduced peripheral vascular resistance.[4] Specifically, the vasodilative effect of *Gou Teng* (Ramulus Uncariae cum Uncis) can be attributed to its α-adrenoceptor blocking and calcium channel blocking activities.[5,6] Rhynchophylline and isorhynchophylline, two indole alkaloids from the hook of *Gou Teng* (Ramulus Uncariae cum Uncis), exert hypotensive and vasodilatory effects.[7] Administration of *Gou Teng* (Ramulus Uncariae cum Uncis) has been shown to reduce both systolic and diastolic blood pressure as well as slowing the heart rate.[8,9] Clinically, the use of these two herbs has been shown to effectively treat hypertension. One study reported marked effect using an herbal formula for 30 days to treat hypertension characterized by yin deficiency and yang excess. The herbal formula contained *Tian Ma* (Rhizoma Gastrodiae), *Gou Teng* (Ramulus Uncariae cum Uncis), and others. Of 60 patients, the blood pressure was reduced in 76.67% of patients. The average reduction was 20.87 mmHg for diastolic, and 10.21 mmHg for systolic blood pressure.[10] According to another study, 245 patients with hypertension were treated with a preparation of *Gou Teng* (Ramulus Uncariae cum Uncis), with

Gastrodia Complex ™

marked effectiveness in 38.2%, and an overall rate of effectiveness of 77.2%. Effectiveness was defined as significant and prolonged reduction of blood pressure.[11]

Gastrodia Complex contains many other herbs with significant influences over the cardiovascular system. *Ge Gen* (Radix Puerariae Lobatae) has shown marked effectiveness in lowering blood pressure by dilating coronary artery and relieving spasms of blood vessels.[12,13,14] In one study, 222 patients with hypertension accompanied by neck stiffness and pain were treated with *Ge Gen* (Radix Puerariae Lobatae) with a rate of effectiveness between 78 and 90%.[15] *Gou Qi Zi* (Fructus Lycii) has a significant effect to prevent the increase of blood pressure by decreasing vascular contraction and tension.[16,17] *Xia Ku Cao* (Spica Prunellae) illustrates the rapid onset of an antihypertensive effect through vasodilation.[18,19] It has been used as a single herb to treat hypertension in 42 patients with good results.[20] *Jue Ming Zi* (Semen Cassiae) and *Shan Zhu Yu* (Fructus Corni) lower blood pressure through their diuretic effect.[21,22] *Sha Yuan Zi* (Semen Astragali Complanati) exerts its antihypertensive action through a decrease in total peripheral resistance.[23,24] *Dan Shen* (Radix et Rhizoma Salviae Miltiorrhizae) dilates blood vessels and increases blood perfusion to peripheral blood vessels.[25] It has a significant protective effect on conditions such as cerebral infarct,[26] coronary artery disease,[27] angina,[28] and many others. Lastly, *Gou Teng* (Ramulus Uncariae cum Uncis) has a significant cardioprotective effect for the prevention and treatment of vascular proliferative disorders.[29] *Gou Teng* (Ramulus Uncariae cum Uncis) is also an effective herb for inducing angiogenesis, accelerating vascular wound healing, and promoting the growth of collateral blood vessel in ischemic tissues.[30]

Primary hypertension does not have a singular cause but many contributing factors, such as obesity, stress, anxiety, and dyslipidemia. Therefore, ***Gastrodia Complex*** contains many herbs to manage these contributing factors. *Jue Ming Zi* (Semen Cassiae) has been used in an herbal formula to successfully reduce body weight in 79 of 96 patients.[31] *Gou Teng* (Ramulus Uncariae cum Uncis) has a marked anxiolytic effect to treat stress and anxiety. According to one study, it has a therapeutic effect comparable to Buspar (buspirone).[32] *Jue Ming Zi* (Semen Cassiae) has been shown to lower blood cholesterol levels in both animal and human studies.[33,34] According to one study, 48 patients were treated with 20 mL of *Jue Ming Zi* (Semen Cassiae) preparation three times daily for two months. The study reported reduction in blood cholesterol in 95.8% of the patients, reduction in triglycerides in 86.7%, and reduction of beta-lipoprotein in 89.5%.[35] According to another study, daily administration of *Jue Ming Zi* (Semen Cassiae) helped to lower serum lipid status in type II diabetic subjects without serious adverse effects.[36]

In addition to treating hypertension and related conditions, ***Gastrodia Complex*** also contains herbs with excellent effects for prevention and/or treatment of seizures, epilepsy, and convulsions. *Tian Ma* (Rhizoma Gastrodiae), given via intraperitoneal or intravenous injection, has a marked effectiveness in treating seizures and convulsions.[37] *Tian Ma* (Rhizoma Gastrodiae) has also demonstrated an antiepileptic effect to prevent post-traumatic epilepsy.[38] Studies have shown *Tian Ma* (Rhizoma Gastrodiae) to have a positive effect in the treatment of seizures, cranial-cerebral injury, cervical spondylosis and cerebrovascular diseases.[39,40] *Gou Teng* (Ramulus Uncariae cum Uncis) has a preventative effect in the management of seizures. The duration of action was approximately three days following subcutaneous injection.[41] *Gou Teng* (Ramulus Uncariae cum Uncis) also has an anticonvulsant effect by suppressing the lipid peroxidation in the brain.[42] Rhynchophylline, a major component of *Gou Teng* (Ramulus Uncariae cum Uncis), is believed to be the main anticonvulsive compound.[43,44] Lastly, it has been shown that the combination of *Tian Ma* (Rhizoma Gastrodiae) and *Gou Teng* (Ramulus Uncariae cum Uncis) has a synergistic anticonvulsive and free-radical scavenging action, as demonstrated in laboratory studies.[45] Clinically, the use of *Tian Ma* (Rhizoma Gastrodiae) and *Gou Teng* (Ramulus Uncariae cum Uncis) in formulas has shown a marked effectiveness to treat seizures.[46,47]

In summary, ***Gastrodia Complex*** is an excellent formula to treat hypertension and related conditions and complications.

COMPARATIVE ANALYSIS

Hypertension is one of the most common disorders in developed countries. In Western medicine, many different categories of drugs may be used to treat hypertension, including but not limited to diuretics [Lasix (furosemide) and hydrochlorothiazide], beta-blockers [Tenormin (atenolol) and Inderal (propranolol)], calcium channel blockers [Procardia (nifedipine) and Calan (verapamil)], ACE inhibitors [Vasotec (enalapril)] and Capoten (captopril)], and vasodilators [hydralazine and minoxidil]. All these drugs have benefits and risks, and may be given individually or in combinations to control blood pressure. The main advantage of drug therapy is its potency to suppress blood pressure. The main disadvantages, however, are that the drugs cause a great number of side effects, and they do not change the underlying constitution of the patient. Therefore, while they are effective to suppress blood pressure, they must be used continuously and cannot be stopped. Discontinuing use of these drugs often leads to rebound hypertension.

In TCM, hypertension may be characterized by both excess and deficiency. Excess refers to Liver yang rising, and deficiency refers to Liver and Kidney yin deficiencies. Both conditions may be treated effectively with herbal medicine. The main advantage of using herbs is the effective ability to change the fundamental constitution of the body, thereby achieving long-term efficacy to reduce blood pressure, even after the herbs are discontinued. The main disadvantage, however, is that herbs are less immediately potent than drugs for the treatment of hypertensive crisis, or secondary hypertension, thus they should not be used in lieu of drugs in these cases.

Gastrodia Complex™

Both drugs and herbs are effective for treating hypertension, and they have their distinct advantages and disadvantages. In addition to choosing either drugs or herbal therapy, it is also important to make diet and lifestyle changes to ensure successful long-term management of hypertension.

References

1. Chan K, Lo AC, Yeung JH, Woo KS. Journal of Pharmacy and Pharmacology 1995 May;47(5):402-406.
2. Huang, JH. Comparison studies on the pharmacological properties of injected gastrodia elata, gastrodin-free fraction and gastrodin. *Acta Academiae Medicinae Sinicae*. 11(2):147-50, Apr. 1989.
3. Luo, H. et al. Effects of tian-ma injection on myocardial ischemia and lipid peroxidation in rabbits. *Journal of West China University of Medical Sciences*. 23(1):53-6, Mar. 1992.
4. *Chang Yong Zhong Yao Cheng Fen Yu Yao Li Shou Ce* (A Handbook of the Composition and Pharmacology of Common Chinese Drugs), 1994; 1419:1423.
5. Ozaki, Y. Vasodilative effects of indole alkaloids obtained from domestic plants uncaria rhynchophylla miq. and amsonia elliptica roem. et schult. *Nippon Yakurigaku Zasshi*, 95(2):47-54 Feb. 1990.
6. Horie, S. et al. Effects of hirsutine and antihypertensive indol alkaloid from uncaria rhynchophylla on intracellular calcium in rat thoracic aorta. *Life Science*, 50(7):491-8 1992.
7. Zhang WB, Chen CX, Sim SM, Kwan CY. In vitro vasodilator mechanisms of the indole alkaloids rhynchophylline and isorhynchophylline, isolated from the hook of Uncaria rhynchophylla (Miquel). Naunyn Schmiedebergs Arch Pharmacol. 2004 Feb;369(2):232-8.
8. Yano, S. et al. Calcium channel blocking effects of hirsutine and indol alkaloid from uncaria genus in the isolated rat aorta. *Planta Med*, 57(5):403-5 Oct. 1991.
9. Mok, SJ. et al. Cardiovascular responses in the normotensive rat produced by intravenous injection of gambirine isolated from uncariae bl. ex korth.
10. *Zhong Guo Zhong Xi Yi Jie He Za Zhi* (Chinese Journal of Integrative Chinese and Western Medicine), 1992; (6):409.
11. *Zhong Cao Yao Tong Xun* (Journal of Chinese Herbal Medicine), 1976; 7:45.
12. *Zhong Yao Xue* (Chinese Herbology), 1998; 101:103.
13. *Yi Xue Yan Jiu Tong Xun* (Report of Medical Studies), 1972; (2):14.
14. *Zhong Hua Yi Xue Za Zhi* (Chinese Journal of Medicine), 1979; 59(8):479.
15. *Zhong Cao Yao Tong Xun* (Journal of Chinese Herbal Medicine), 1975; 2:34.
16. Jia YX, Dong JW, Wu XX, Ma TM, Shi AY. The effect of lycium barbarum polysaccharide on vascular tension in two-kidney, one clip model of hypertension. Sheng Li Xue Bao. 1998 Jun;50(3):309-14.
17. *Zhong Yao Zhi* (Chinese Herbology Journal), 1984:484.
18. *Zhong Yao Yao Li Yu Ying Yong* (Pharmacology and Applications of Chinese Herbs), 1983:883.
19. *Zhong Yao Xue* (Chinese Herbology), 1998; 128:130.
20. *Fu Jian Zhong Yi Yao* (Fujian Chinese Medicine and Herbology), 1959; 4:41.
21. *Zhong Yao Zhi* (Chinese Herbology Journal), 1984:352.
22. Li C.P. Chinese herbal medicine. A publication of the John E. Fogarty International Center for Advanced Study in the Health Sciences (US Depart of Health, Education & Welfare). 1974, 120 pp.
23. Xue B., Li J.X. & Chen L.B. Depressive effect of total flavonoid fraction of *Astragalus complanatus* R. Br and its influence upon hemodynamics in SHR. *Zhongguo Zhong Yao Za Zhi*. 2002, 27(11): 855-858.
24. Li JX, Xue B, Chai Q, Liu ZX, Zhao AP, Chen LB. Antihypertensive effect of total flavonoid fraction of Astragalus complanatus in hypertensive rats. Institute of Physiology, School of Medicine, Shandong University, Shandong 250012, P.R. China. Chin J Physiol. 2005 Jun 30;48(2):101-6.
25. *Guo Wai Yi Xue Zhong Yi Zhong Yao Fen Ce* (Monograph of Chinese Herbology from Foreign Medicine), 1991; 13(3):41.
26. Lo CJ, Lin JG, Kuo JS, Chiang SY, Chen SC, Liao ET, Hsieh CL. Effect of salvia miltiorrhiza bunge on cerebral infarct in ischemia-reperfusion injured rats. Am J Chin Med. 2003;31(2):191-200.
27. *Xin Zhang Xue Guan Ji Bing* (Cardiovascular Diseases), 1974; 2(1):5.
28. *Zhong Cao Yao Tong Xun* (Journal of Chinese Herbal Medicine), 1978; 1:37.
29. Kim TJ, Lee JH, Lee JJ, Yu JY, Hwang BY, Ye SK, Shujuan L, Gao L, Pyo MY, Yun YP. Corynoxeine isolated from the hook of Uncaria rhynchophylla inhibits rat aortic vascular smooth muscle cell proliferation through the blocking of extracellular signal regulated kinase 1/2 phosphorylation. Biol Pharm Bull. 2008 Nov;31(11):2073-8.
30. Choi DY, Huh JE, Lee JD, Cho EM, Baek YH, Yang HR, Cho YJ, Kim KI, Kim DY, Park DS. Uncaria rhynchophylla induces angiogenesis in vitro and in vivo. Biol Pharm Bull. 2005 Dec;28(12):2248-52.
31. *Zhong Yao Lin Chuan Xin Yong* (New Clinical Applications of Chinese Medicine), 2001; 284-285.
32. Jung JW, Ahn NY, Oh HR, Lee BK, Lee KJ, Kim SY, Cheong JH, Ryu JH. Anxiolytic effects of the aqueous extract of Uncaria rhynchophylla. J Ethnopharmacol. 2006 Nov 24;108(2):193-7.
33. *Zhong Yao Zhi* (Chinese Herbology Journal), 1984:352.
34. *Zhong Cao Yao* (Chinese Herbal Medicine), 1991; 22(2):72.
35. *Zhong Guo Yi Yuan Yao Xue Za Zhi* (Chinese Hospital Journal of Herbology), 1987, 9:395.
36. Cho S.H., Kim T.H., Lee N.H., Son H.S., Cho I.J. & Ha T.Y. Effects of *Cassia tora* fiber supplement on serum lipids in Korean diabetic patients. *J Med Food*. 2005, 8(3): 311-318.
37. *Zhong Yao Yao Li Yu Ying Yong* (Pharmacology and Applications of Chinese Herbs), 1983:164.
38. Mori A, Yokoi I, Noda Y, Willmore LJ. Natural antioxidants may prevent posttraumatic epilepsy: a proposal based on experimental animal studies. Acta Med Okayama. 2004 Jun;58(3):111-8.
39. Wu, HQ. et al. The effect of vanillin on the fully amygdala-kindled seizures in the rat. *Acta Pharmaceutica Sinica*. 24(7):482-6, 1989.
40. Lu, SL. et al. The development of *nao li shen* and its clinical application. *J Pharm Pharmacol* 1997 Nov; 49(11):1162-4.
41. *Pharm Pharmacol*, 1985; 37; 401.
42. Hsieh C.L., Chen M.F., Li T.C., Li S.C., Tang N.Y., Hsieh C.T., Pon C.Z. & Lin J.G. Anticonvulsant effect of *Uncaria rhynchophylla* (Miq) Jack. in rats with kainic acid-induced epileptic seizure. *Am J Chin Med*. 1999, 27(2): 257-264.
43. Lo WY, Tsai FJ, Liu CH, Tang NY, Su SY, Lin SZ, Chen CC, Shyu WC, Hsieh CL. Uncaria rhynchophylla upregulates the expression of MIF and cyclophilin A in kainic acid-induced epilepsy rats: A proteomic analysis. Am J Chin Med. 2010;38(4):745-59.
44. Hsieh CL, Ho TY, Su SY, Lo WY, Liu CH, Tang NY. Uncaria rhynchophylla and Rhynchophylline inhibit c-Jun N-terminal kinase phosphorylation and nuclear factor-kappaB activity in kainic acid-treated rats. Am J Chin Med. 2009;37(2):351-60.
45. *Life Sci* 1999; 65(20):2071-82.
46. *Hei Long Jiang Zhong Yi Yao* (Heilongjiang Chinese Medicine and Herbology), 1995; (1):35.
47. *Zhong Guo Shen Jing Jing Shen Ke Za Zhi* (Chinese Journal of Psychiatric Disorders), 1985; 3:139.

Gentiana Complex™

CLINICAL APPLICATIONS

- **Hypertension (excess-type)** with anger, flushed face, dizziness, and throbbing headache
- **Viral infection,** such as genital herpes and herpes zoster
- **Bacterial or fungal infections,** such as urinary tract infection, vaginal infection, yeast infection, herpes infection, boils, carbuncles, acute cystitis, urethritis, and related discomforts or dysfunctions
- **Liver and gallbladder disorders,** such as acute icteric hepatitis, and acute cholecystitis

WESTERN THERAPEUTIC ACTIONS

- Antihypertensive effect to lower blood pressure
- Antibiotic, antibacterial, antiviral, and antifungal effects for a variety of infections
- Hepatoprotective and cholagogic functions to treat liver and gallbladder disorders
- Anti-inflammatory properties to treat inflammation of the internal organs and soft tissue

CHINESE THERAPEUTIC ACTIONS

- Drains fire from the Liver and the Gallbladder channels
- Clears damp-heat from the lower *jiao*
- Nourishes yin

DOSAGE

Take 4 capsules three times daily. For treatment of infections and inflammation of internal organs, the dosage may be increased to 6 to 8 capsules three to four times daily. Treatment is most effective if herbal therapy begins immediately with the first sign of outbreak and continues throughout the entire course of infection. Advise the patients to take the herbs with meals if they experience stomach discomfort.

INGREDIENTS

Che Qian Zi (Semen Plantaginis)
Da Huang (Radix et Rhizoma Rhei)
Dan Shen (Radix et Rhizoma Salviae Miltiorrhizae)
Di Huang (Radix Rehmanniae)
Ge Gen (Radix Puerariae Lobatae)
Hua Shi (Talcum)
Huang Bo (Cortex Phellodendri Chinensis)
Huang Qin (Radix Scutellariae)
Long Dan (Radix et Rhizoma Gentianae)
Niu Xi (Radix Achyranthis Bidentatae)
Shi Jue Ming (Concha Haliotidis)
Ze Xie (Rhizoma Alismatis)
Zhen Zhu Mu (Concha Margaritiferae)
Zhi Zi (Fructus Gardeniae)

BACKGROUND

Gentiana Complex contains herbs with multiple therapeutic functions. Primary clinical applications include cardiovascular disorders, infectious diseases, inflammatory disorders, and disorders affecting the liver, gallbladder and pancreas. From traditional Chinese medicine perspectives, heart, liver, gallbladder and pancreas disorders are considered as fire in the Liver and the Gallbladder channels, while infection and inflammation are diagnosed as damp-heat of the affected area(s) or organ(s).

FORMULA EXPLANATION

Gentiana Complex is formulated to treat fire in the Liver and the Gallbladder channels and damp-heat in the lower *jiao*. Fire in the Liver and Gallbladder is characterized by headache, red eyes, hypochondriac pain, a bitter taste in the mouth, deafness, and swollen or painful inner ears. Damp-heat in the lower *jiao* manifest with swelling and itching of the external genitalia, sweating in the groin, dysuria, turbid urine, and yellow, foul-smelling leukorrhea in women.

Shi Jue Ming (Concha Haliotidis) and *Zhen Zhu Mu* (Concha Margaritiferae) descend and anchor the rising Liver yang to treat dizziness and headache. *Da Huang* (Radix et Rhizoma Rhei) eliminates damp-heat and purges toxic fire. The active ingredient puerarin in *Ge Gen* (Radix Puerariae Lobatae) has been found to effectively relieve neck stiffness, pain, headache, and dizziness associated with hypertension. *Dan Shen* (Radix et Rhizoma Salviae Miltiorrhizae) adjusts the heart rate and improves microcirculation and myocardial contraction.

Damp-heat is considered to be the cause of various bacterial, viral, and fungal infections in traditional Chinese medicine. A large quantity of *Long Dan* (Radix et Rhizoma Gentianae) is used in this formula to drain damp-heat in the Liver channel and the lower *jiao*, to treat herpes, urinary tract infection, cystitis, and other infections. *Huang Qin* (Radix Scutellariae), *Huang Bo* (Cortex Phellodendri Chinensis) and *Zhi Zi* (Fructus Gardeniae) clear heat and drain dampness. *Ze Xie* (Rhizoma Alismatis), *Che Qian Zi* (Semen Plantaginis), *Hua Shi* (Talcum) and *Niu Xi* (Radix Achyranthis Bidentatae) eliminate damp-heat in the lower *jiao* and drain the damp-heat out of the body through urination. *Di Huang* (Radix Rehmanniae) protects the Liver from the strong sedative nature of the rest of the herbs in this formula.

In summary, ***Gentiana Complex*** is a great formula that clears fire in the Liver and the Gallbladder channels and damp-heat in the lower *jiao* to treat numerous Western biomedical disease such as hypertension, infection, and liver and gallbladder disorders.

CAUTIONS & CONTRAINDICATIONS

- Herbal treatment is ineffective for malignant hypertension and some secondary hypertension, such as renal stenosis or pheochromocytoma. Refer the patient to a medical doctor, as surgical intervention may be necessary.

Gentiana Complex™

- *Gentiana Complex* should be taken for approximately one to two weeks when treating viral, bacterial or fungal infection. Once the infection subsides, the patient should be placed on a maintenance regimen using *Nourish* to prevent future attacks.
- *Gentiana Complex* is contraindicated for long-term use when treating viral, bacterial or fungal infection. This formula is designed to treat only the acute conditions, and should not be used for long-term or prophylactic treatments.
- Some patients may experience mild stomach discomfort or loose stools, which may be alleviated by reducing the dosage of herbs or taking the herbs with food.
- This formula is contraindicated during pregnancy and nursing.
- This herbal formula contains herbs that invigorate blood circulation, such as *Dan Shen* (Radix et Rhizoma Salviae Miltiorrhizae). Therefore, patients who are on anticoagulant or antiplatelet therapies, such as Coumadin (warfarin), should use this formula with caution, or not at all, as there may be a higher risk of bleeding and bruising.[1]
- The following warning statement is required by the State of California: "This product contains *Da Huang* (Radix et Rhizoma Rhei). Read and follow directions carefully. Do not use if you have or develop diarrhea, loose stools, or abdominal pain because *Da Huang* (Radix et Rhizoma Rhei) may worsen these conditions and be harmful to your health. Consult your physician if you have frequent diarrhea or if you are pregnant, nursing, taking medication, or have a medical condition."

CLINICAL NOTES

- Western medicine classifies hypertension into two types: "red" and "pale" high blood pressure. "Red" high blood pressure corresponds with the TCM diagnosis of excess, and generally occurs in energetic and stressed individuals with marked redness and vascularized skin. "Pale" high blood pressure corresponds with the TCM diagnosis of deficiency, and generally occurs in individuals with compromised kidneys, glands, or metabolism.
- For treatment of hypertension, it is important to monitor the blood pressure and adjust the dosage based on age, body weight, severity of condition, and response of treatment.
- *Gentiana Complex* may be applied topically for treatment of genital herpes. Break open the capsules and apply the powder directly onto the lesion. Or, mix the powder with water to make a paste and apply to the lesions.
- *Gentiana Complex* and *V-Support* are very similar in treating damp-heat of the lower *jiao*. *Gentiana Complex* has an additional function to treat hypertension. Therefore, in patients who have normal blood pressure or low blood pressure suffering from damp-heat of the lower *jiao*, *V-Support* would be a more appropriate formula to use. In patients who have both hypertension (Liver yang rising) and also damp-heat in the lower *jiao*, *Gentiana Complex* should be used.
- *Gentiana Complex* and *V-Support* both have strong effect to treat damp-heat affecting the lower *jiao*:
  - *Gentiana Complex* has a broader effect to treat damp-heat along the Liver and Gallbladder channels from the head to the genital area.
  - *V-Support* has a localized effect to treat damp-heat in the genital area.
- Vaginitis may be caused by different micro-organisms:
  - Viral vaginitis is best treated with *Gentiana Complex*.
  - Bacterial vaginitis is more effectively treated with *V-Support*.
- *Gentiana Complex* incorporates numerous antibiotic herbs for two important reasons. First, the use of multiple herbs within an herbal formula has been shown to increase the antibiotic effect more than tenfold. Second, isolated use of single ingredients is often ineffective and increases the risk of development of bacterial and viral resistance.[2] Given these two reasons, it is necessary to combine herbs with appropriate properties to ensure effectiveness in treating the infection and minimizing the potential risk of the micro-organisms developing resistance and/or mutation.

Pulse Diagnosis by Dr. Jimmy Wei-Yen Chang:

- Big pulse, a thick, expanding, forceful, and fast pulse on all three pulse positions, *cun*, *guan*, and *chi*. The harder the pulse, the higher the blood pressure and the more severe the condition.

SUPPLEMENTARY FORMULAS

- For long-term treatment of hypertension, use *Gastrodia Complex*.
- For coronary heart disorders, combine with *Circulation*.
- For cardiovascular and circulatory disorders throughout the entire body, combine with *Circulation (SJ)*.
- For high blood pressure and fast heart rate due to excess fire, add *Gardenia Complex*.
- For severe blood stagnation, add *Circulation (SJ)*.
- For hypertension with edema and water accumulation, combine with *Herbal DRX*.
- For hypertension with high cholesterol and triglycerides, add *Cholisma*.
- For hypertension with high cholesterol and triglycerides in individuals with fatty liver and obesity, add *Cholisma (ES)*.
- For acute headache, add *Corydalin (AC)*.
- For chronic headache, add *Corydalin (CR)*.
- To treat shingles and herpetic lesions, add *Dermatrol (HZ)*.
- To relieve post-herpetic pain, add *Flex (NP)*.
- To prevent herpes attacks, use *Nourish* and *Immune +* when the patient is asymptomatic.
- To treat ear infection, combine with *Herbal ENT*.
- To enhance the antibacterial effect, combine with *Herbal ABX*.
- To enhance the antiviral effect, add *Herbal AVR*.
- For icteric hepatitis, acute cholecystitis or liver cirrhosis, combine with *Liver DTX*.
- For cholecystitis or gallstones, combine with *Dissolve (GS)*.
- For visual disturbances, add *Lycium Support*.

Gentiana Complex™

- For increased thirst and constipation, add ***Gentle Lax (Excess)***.
- To address any dermatological disorders that are wet in appearance, add ***Dermatrol (Damp)***.
- To address any dermatological disorders that are dry in appearance, add ***Dermatrol (Dry)***.
- For more dampness/phlegm in the body, add ***Pinellia Complex***.

ACUPUNCTURE TREATMENT

Traditional Points:

- *Quchi* (LI 11), *Hegu* (LI 4), *Taichong* (LR 3), *Renying* (ST 9)
- *Taichong* (LR 3), *Qihai* (CV 6), *Zhongwan* (CV 12), *Fenglong* (ST 40), *Geshu* (BL 17), *Renzhong* (GV 26), *Ganshu* (BL 18), *Pishu* (BL 20), *Danshu* (BL 19)

Classic Master Tung's Points:

- **Hypertension:** *Linggu* (T 22.05), *Dabai* (T 22.04), *Xinling* (T 33.17)*, *Quchi* (LI 11), *Tianhuang* (T 88.13), *Minghuang* (T 88.12), *Qihuang* (T 88.14), *Sanzhong* (T 77.07), *Yizhong* (T 77.05), *Erzhong* (T 77.06), *Sihuashang* (T 77.08), *Sihuazhong* (T 77.09), *Sihuaxia* (T 77.11), *Zhengjin* (T 77.01), *Zhengzong* (T 77.02), *Sansheng* (T 55.07)*, *Weizhong* (BL 40), *Huoying* (T 66.03), *Tianhuang* (T 77.17), *Dihuang* (T 77.19), *Renhuang* (T 77.21), *Tongtian* (T 88.03). Bleed the back of the neck, LU and HT, LR and SP, ST areas with cupping. Bleed dark veins nearby the ST, BL channels on the lower limbs. Bleed before needling for best result.
- **Viral infection (genital herpes and herpes zoster):** *Linggu* (T 22.05), *Tianhuang* (T 88.13), *Minghuang* (T 88.12), *Qihuang* (T 88.14), *Simashang* (T 88.18), *Simazhong* (T 88.17), *Simaxia* (T 88.19), *Shuitong* (T 1010.19), *Shuijin* (T 1010.20)
- **Herpes of the eyes:** *Shangbai* (T 22.03), *Tianhuangfu [Shenguan]* (T 77.18), *Huoying* (T 66.03), *Simazhong* (T 88.17). Bleed the LU area below the knees. Bleed before needling for best result.
- **UTI:** *Libai* (T 44.12), *Yunbai* (T 44.11), *Tianhuang* (T 77.17), *Dihuang* (T 77.19), *Renhuang* (T 77.21), *Simashang* (T 88.18), *Simazhong* (T 88.17), *Simaxia* (T 88.19), *Tongbei* (T 88.11), *Tongwei* (T 88.10), *Tongshen* (T 88.09), *Liukuai* (T 1010.16), *Qikuai* (T 1010.17), *Tianhuangfu [Shenguan]* (T 77.18). Bleed dark veins nearby the KI channel on the lower limb. Bleed before needling for best result.
- **Yeast infection:** *Fuke* (T 11.24), *Linggu* (T 22.05), *Yunbai* (T 44.11), *Libai* (T 44.12), *Simashang* (T 88.18), *Simazhong* (T 88.17), *Simaxia* (T 88.19), *Minghuang* (T 88.12), *Tianhuang* (T 88.13), *Qihuang* (T 88.14)
- **Cystitis:** *Tianhuang* (T 77.17), *Dihuang* (T 77.19), *Renhuang* (T 77.21), *Simashang* (T 88.18), *Simazhong* (T 88.17), *Simaxia* (T 88.19), *Tongbei* (T 88.11), *Tongwei* (T 88.10), *Tongshen* (T 88.09), *Liukuai* (T 1010.16), *Qikuai* (T 1010.17), *Liuwan* (T 66.08), *Fenzhishang* (T DT.01), *Yunbai* (T 44.11), *Libai* (T 44.12), *Tianhuangfu [Shenguan]* (T 77.18). Bleed tender points on the KI area of the back between L1-L5 with cupping. Bleed before needling for best result.
- **Genital swelling and infection:** *Huanchao* (T 11.06), *Fuke* (T 11.24), *Yunbai* (T 44.11), *Jiemeiyi* (T 88.04), *Jiemeier* (T 88.05), *Jiemeisan* (T 88.06), *Haibao* (T 66.01). Bleed sacral area with cupping. Bleed before needling for best result.
- **Boil and carbuncle:** *Jianzhong* (T 44.06), *Waisanguan* (T 77.27), *Zhiwu* (T 11.26)

Master Tung's Points by Dr. Chuan-Min Wang:

- **High systolic pressure, hypertension due to Liver deficiency, dizziness:** *Fuding* (T 44.04), *Houzhi* (T 44.05)
- **High diastolic pressure, hypertension due to Kidney deficiency:** *Tianhuang* (T 77.17), *Tianhuangfu [shenguan]* (T 77.18)
- **High systolic and diastolic pressure:** Bleed *Wuling* (T DT.04) first. Then needle *Quchi* (LI 11), *Huoying* (T 66.03).

Balance Method by Dr. Richard Tan:

- Left side: Bleed *Dadun* (LR 1). Needle *Taichong* (LR 3) and *Hegu* (LI 4).
- Right side: Bleed *Zhongchong* (PC 9). Needle *Neiguan* (PC 6) and *Zulinqi* (GB 41).
- Left and right sides can be alternated from treatment to treatment.

Ear Acupuncture:

- **Hypertension:** Adrenal gland, bleed the depression groove in the back of the ear to lower blood pressure, Heart, *Shenmen*, Endocrine, *Taiyang*, Liver, Kidney. Select four or five points for each treatment, which lasts three days. Ten treatments equal one treatment course. Rest for one week in between treatment courses.
- **Eczema of the rectum:** Rectum, Anus, Spleen, Lung, and Adrenal Gland. Embed steel balls or ear needle and switch ears every three to five days. Instruct the patient to massage the points three to four times daily for two minutes each time.

Auricular Medicine by Dr. Li-Chun Huang:

- **Reducing blood pressure:** Heart, *Shenmen*, Occiput, Kidney, Liver, Coronary Vascular Subcortex, Decrease BP. Bleed Ear Apex.
- **Hypertension:** *Shenmen*, Kidney, Liver, Heart, Occiput, Forehead, Decrease BP, Sympathetic, Coronary Vascular Subcortex. Bleed Ear Apex.
- **Cystitis:** Bladder, Urethra, Lower *Jiao*, Endocrine. Bleed Ear Apex.
- **Auditory vertigo:** Internal Ear, Dizziness Area, Occiput, *San Jiao*, Liver, Kidney, Gallbladder. Bleed Ear Apex.
- **Conjunctivitis:** Eye, Vision 2, Lower Lung. Bleed Ear Apex.
- **Cataract:** Kidney, Liver, Eye, Vision 2, Endocrine, Sympathetic. Bleed Ear Apex.
- **Glaucoma:** Eye, Decrease BP, Kidney, Liver, Occiput, Vision 1, Coronary Vascular Subcortex. Bleed Ear Apex.

NUTRITION

- Increase the intake of fresh, raw vegetables and fruits to control

Gentiana Complex ™

blood pressure. Nuts and seeds should be consumed daily as a source of protein. Vitamin C and bioflavonoids help to reduce blood pressure by stabilizing the blood vessel walls. Garlic is also effective to lower blood pressure and thin the blood.

- Patients with hypertension should minimize intake of salt from the diet. Avoid MSG, baking soda, meat, fat, aged foods, alcohol, diet soft drinks, preservatives, sugar substitutes, meat tenderizers, and soy sauce. Aspartame should also be avoided, since a high level may increase blood pressure. Over-the-counter medications, such as Advil or Motrin (ibuprofen), should not be used because they may increase the blood pressure.
- Individuals with cystitis should increase the intake of cranberries or cranberry juice. Cranberry produces hippuric acid in the urine that prohibits the growth of bacteria, thus preventing bacteria from adhering to the lining of the bladder. Juices that contain a large percentage of high-fructose syrup, sugar or sweeteners, on the other hand, should be avoided as they provide nutrients for bacterial growth.
- Patients should drink plenty of fluids, as it helps to flush out the bacteria in the bladder. Women are encouraged to empty the bladder before and after intercourse, and wash the genitalia thoroughly.
- For patients with herpes infection, avoid citrus fruits and juices while the virus is active.

The Tao of Nutrition by Dr. Maoshing Ni and Cathy McNease:

- **Hypertension**
  - Recommendations: celery, spinach, garlic, bananas, sunflower seeds, honey, tofu, mung beans, bamboo shoots, seaweed, vinegar, tomatoes, water chestnuts, corn, apples, persimmons, peas, buckwheat, jellyfish, watermelon, hawthorn berries, eggplant, plums, mushrooms, lemons, lotus root, chrysanthemums, and cassia seeds.
  - Steam or bake jellyfish about 12 minutes, add vinegar, soy sauce, and sesame oil; take daily for about two months.
  - Make tea from chrysanthemum flowers and cassia seeds and drink daily.
  - Take black or white mushrooms and cook soup daily.
  - Avoid smoking, alcohol, spicy foods, coffee, caffeine, all stimulants, fatty or fried foods, salty foods, stress, constipation, potatoes, strong emotions, pork, and overeating.
- **Candida yeast infection**
  - Recommendations: dandelions, beet tops, carrot tops, barley, garlic, rice vinegar, mung beans, citrus fruits.
  - Avoid sugar, excessive fruits, yeast-containing foods, processed foods, cheese, fermented foods, soy sauce, smoking, alcohol, caffeine, and constipation.
- **Chronic bladder infections**
  - Recommendations: watermelon, pears, carrots, celery, corn, mung beans, corn silk, squash, wheat, water chestnuts, barley, red beans, millet, oranges, cantaloupe, grapes, strawberries, lotus roots, loquats, and plenty of water.
  - Avoid heavy proteins, meat, dairy products, onions, scallions, ginger, black pepper, and alcohol.

LIFESTYLE INSTRUCTIONS

- Weight loss is highly recommended to help lower blood pressure.
- Normal bowel and urinary functions help to reduce blood pressure. Diuretics and stool softeners should be taken as needed.
- Maintain a positive attitude and outlook. Control emotions and reduce stress. Emotional fluctuations should be reduced whenever possible.
- Stop alcohol consumption and cigarette smoking.
- Exercise such as swimming and brisk walking are excellent exercises for hypertension.
- Practices such as meditation, *tai chi chuan [tai ji chuan]*, and yoga are also beneficial to relax, reduce stress, and lower blood pressure.
- Individuals with herpes should stay away from heat, over-exertion, stress, spicy and greasy foods, alcohol, coffee, or anything else that may trigger an attack. Patients should keep the infected area clean and dry in order to promote healing and avoid secondary infections. It is also recommended that patients abstain from sex during the outbreak period.
- For leukorrhea, yogurt and sour products should be included in the diet.
- Cotton underwear, instead of nylon, is recommended to promote air circulation in the genital region.
- Ointments containing cortisone or petroleum jelly should not be used on genital sores as oil-based products reduce air flow and slows healing. Cortisone inhibits the immune system and can encourage the virus to grow.
- Advise the patient to wipe from front to back after a bowel movement to avoid infection.
- Strengthening the immune system is the key to preventing another herpes attack. *See* Supplementary Formulas for an appropriate formula.

CASE STUDIES

- S.S., a 38-year-old female, presented with recurring genital herpes breakouts. Symptoms included painful burning sores along the inner surface of the thigh and buttocks which flare-up during menses and cause pain along the nerve radiating down the leg. The patient also experienced constipation and hemorrhoids during the event of a breakout. Her menses were heavy with bright red blood and bad cramps. She had also been trying to get pregnant and had not succeeded, leading to more stress. The TCM diagnosis was damp-heat in the Liver channel. This condition was treated with ***Gentiana Complex***, four spoons twice daily when the symptoms occur. After taking the herbs the patient reported that the sores and nerve pain were subsiding

FORMULAS

Gentiana Complex™

within a few days of starting them. She continued to keep the formula available throughout the year as it continued to help with the outbreaks. Submitted by M.M., Alameda, California.

- J.B., a 68-year-old female, presented with post-herpetic neuralgia. The pain was felt especially along the Gallbladder channel on the head, above the ear. There was sharp pain following the shingles outbreak. Other objective findings were small red spots along the Gallbladder channel around *Wangu* (GB 12) area. The practitioner diagnosed the condition as damp-heat in the Gallbladder and Liver. The patient was given ***Gentiana Complex*** at three capsules three times a day and took the herbs for three months. With ***Gentiana Complex***, the post-herpetic neuralgia went away, although the change was gradual. Submitted by L.M., Lafayette, Colorado.
- M.G., a 30-year-old female, presented with chronic sinus infection and sore throat. It was noted that she was not well rested and was experiencing digestive disorders as well, including belching, burping, and acid reflux. Objective findings were wiry pulse and mild acne on the face. The practitioner diagnosed this condition as damp-heat in the Liver. For treatment, the patient was first prescribed ***Magnolia Clear Sinus***, followed by a bottle of ***Gentiana Complex*** and ***Calm*** combined. She was directed to take three capsules at three times per day. With taking the herbs, the patient reported not having felt this good in years. Her sleep has improved and she no longer experienced digestive or sinus issues. Submitted by T.W., Perrysburg, Ohio.
- C.K., a 61-year-old female, presented with pelvic pain during intercourse at a level of 8 out of 10. Additional symptoms were digestive symptoms such as gas and bloating, nail fungus, and bad breath. She had a history of candida, low libido and fatigue. The practitioner diagnosed this condition as Liver and Gallbladder heat, damp-heat in the lower *jiao*, and Spleen qi deficiency. For treatment the patient was given a combination of ***Gentiana Complex***, ***Herbal ABX***, and *Yin Care* for one week; secondly, ***V-Support*** and ***Herbal ABX*** for the week after. Within 20 days the patient reported no more pain with intercourse or digestive issues. The patient continues to use the *Yin Care* for her nails as they are still healing. Submitted by T.W., Perrysburg, Ohio.
- A 27-year-old female with a history of genital warts due to HPV (human papilloma virus) presented with small growths around the perineum. The patient reported this as the third or fourth outbreak. After six rounds of ***Gentiana Complex***, three capsules, three times daily, the patient reported that the genital warts were completely resolved. Furthermore, the patient did not suffer from another outbreak for nine years following this treatment. Submitted by C.L., Chino Hills, California.
- L.L., a 56-year-old female, presented with frustration, anger and sadness over losing her home in the hurricanes. She was unable to move through these emotions. She was also diagnosed with hypertension, high cholesterol, and post-traumatic stress syndrome recently, and refused to take medications. Her blood pressure was 138/78 mmHg and her heart rate was 82 beats per minute. She also suffered from headaches in the temporal region and the vertex. Other symptoms included twitching of the eyes, agitation, red eyes, and a scalloped tongue with thick yellow tongue coating. TCM diagnoses were damp-heat in the Liver and Gallbladder, Kidney yin deficiency, and excess fire and wind rising. She was prescribed the following formulas: ***Calm (ES)*** at 1 to 3 capsules, as needed, ***Cholisma*** at 4 capsules twice daily, and ***Gentiana Complex*** at 5 capsules twice daily. The patient gained control of her emotions immediately after taking ***Calm (ES)***. Blood pressure gradually reduced over time to 120/72 mmHg. The practitioner commented that the combination of these formulas is phenomenal. Submitted by M.H., West Palm Beach, Florida.
- A 27-year-old female healthcare provider presented with genital herpes. The affected area in the genital region was itchy, red and swollen with thick white discharge. She was also having menstrual pain. Her pulse was slippery, deep and strong. Her tongue was pale purple with a red tip, and the sides were swollen with scalloped edges. The practitioner diagnosed the condition as damp-heat in the Liver and Liver qi stagnation. After taking ***Nourish*** and ***Gentiana Complex***, there was a decrease in symptoms. Symptoms flared up when the patient stopped using the formulas. Submitted by B.H., Pearl City, Hawaii.
- A 36-year-old female patient presented with a yeast infection characterized by vaginal itching for two days. The TCM diagnosis was damp-heat in the lower *jiao*. ***Gentiana Complex*** was prescribed at three capsules, three times daily. Within a couple of doses, the patient reported that both the vaginal discharge and itching were resolved. Submitted by C.L., Chino Hills, California.
- A.T., a 34-year-old female, had a history of oral herpes outbreaks that usually lasted two to three weeks. She presented with tingling sensations of the lips, progressing to burning sensation, with eruption of fever blisters. The TCM diagnosis was damp-heat in the middle *jiao* with Stomach fire. ***Gentiana Complex*** was prescribed at three capsules, three times daily. After one or two doses, the patient reported the symptoms were relieved without further exacerbation of fever blisters. Furthermore, there was no return or spread of lesions to other areas of the lips. ***Gentiana Complex*** was discontinued after only three days. Submitted by C.L., Chino Hills, California.
- A 41-year-old female presented with headaches that had been persistent for almost two weeks. She noted that her headache was more localized to the top of her head. Aside from the headaches, she also reported having large amounts of yellowish, foul-smelling, vaginal discharge. The practitioner diagnosed her condition as damp-heat in the lower *jiao* with underlying excess Liver fire. Within two weeks of taking ***Gentiana Complex***, the fetid discharge had stopped along with the headaches. Although the patient experienced some diarrhea during the first three days of treatment, her condition improved overall. Submitted by T.G., Albuquerque, New Mexico.

Gentiana Complex ™

☯ E.P., a 32-year-old female, presented with a 2½-year history of vertigo, associated with insomnia, palpitations, anxiety and nausea. She also suffered from irritable bowel syndrome with alternating diarrhea and constipation. She had an unsteady gait and was unable to drive. For the Western diagnosis of anxiety disorder, the TCM diagnosis was Liver fire. Initially, ***Calm*** and ***Gentiana Complex*** were prescribed at two capsules each, three times daily, but then the dosage was increased to three capsules of each, three times daily. After three weeks, the signs and symptoms of irritable bowel syndrome were resolved, and ***Gentiana Complex*** was discontinued. On the sixth treatment, the patient reported all symptoms improved. However, work-related stress anxiety remained. On the 15th visit, ***Calm*** was changed to ***Schisandra ZZZ*** to help with her insomnia. After taking this formula for nine days, the patient reported much improvement in her sleeping patterns, from five to six hours of interrupted sleep to six to seven hours of uninterrupted sleep. The patient was treated with acupuncture five times throughout the course of herbal treatment. Submitted by C.L., Chino Hills, California.

PHARMACOLOGICAL AND CLINICAL RESEARCH

Gentiana Complex has multiple therapeutic functions and clinical indications. It treats hypertension by using herbs with antihypertensive effect to lower blood pressure. It treats various types of infections by using herbs with antibacterial, antiviral, and antifungal effects. It also treats liver and gallbladder disorders with herbs that have hepatoprotective and cholagogic functions.

Hypertension: *Long Dan* (Radix et Rhizoma Gentianae) and *Ze Xie* (Rhizoma Alismatis) both have a diuretic effect to eliminate water and lower blood pressure.[3,4] *Long Dan* (Radix et Rhizoma Gentianae) has been used in an herbal formula with an 80.4% rate of effectiveness to treat 56 patients with hypertension (24 with significant improvement, 21 with moderate improvement, and 11 with no effect).[5] *Ge Gen* (Radix Puerariae Lobatae) has shown a marked effectiveness in lowering blood pressure by dilating coronary artery and relieving spasms of blood vessels.[6,7,8] In one study, 222 patients with hypertension accompanied by neck stiffness and pain were treated with *Ge Gen* (Radix Puerariae Lobatae) with a rate of effectiveness between 78 and 90%.[9] *Dan Shen* (Radix et Rhizoma Salviae Miltiorrhizae) dilates blood vessels and increases blood perfusion to peripheral blood vessels.[10] It has a significant protective effect on conditions such as cerebral infarct,[11] coronary artery disease,[12] angina,[13] and many others. *Huang Qin* (Radix Scutellariae) lowers blood pressure through dilation of blood vessels and inhibition of the sympathetic nervous system.[14] It has been used to treat 51 patients with hypertension with good results.[15] *Huang Bo* (Cortex Phellodendri Chinensis) demonstrates marked effectiveness to lower blood pressure via its effect on the central nervous system.[16] *Zhi Zi* (Fructus Gardeniae) exerts its antihypertensive action through the stimulation of the parasympathetic nervous system.[17] *Che Qian Zi* (Semen Plantaginis) also has significant angiotensin-converting enzyme inhibitory activity to lower blood pressure.[18] Clinically, administration of *Che Qian Zi* (Semen Plantaginis) as tea showed a marked effect to treat 50 patients with elevated blood pressure.[19] Lastly, *Da Huang* (Radix et Rhizoma Rhei) has various impacts on the cardiovascular system. It has been shown to lower blood pressure, reduce heart rate, and decrease peripheral vascular resistance.[20,21]

Bacterial infection: *Huang Qin* (Radix Scutellariae) has a wide-spectrum inhibitory effect against many bacteria, but is most effective against *Staphylococcus aureus* and *Pseudomonas aeruginosa*. Furthermore, it has been discovered that the effectiveness of standard antibiotics such as ampicillin, amoxicillin, methicillin and cefotaxime can be potentiated with the addition of baicalin, a flavone isolated from this herb. With the addition of baicalin, the effectiveness of these beta-lactam antibiotics was restored against beta-lactam-resistant *Staphylococcus aureus* and methicillin-resistant *Staphylococcus aureus* (MRSA).[22,23] *Huang Bo* (Cortex Phellodendri Chinensis) has antibacterial action against *Staphylococcus aureus, Diplococcus pneumoniae, Corynebacterium diphtheriae, Bacillus dysenteriae*, beta-hemolytic streptococcus, *Diplococcus meningitidis, Vibrio cholerae, Bacillus anthracis*, and others.[24,25] Berberine, a compound present in *Huang Bo* (Cortex Phellodendri Chinensis), has antimicrobial activity against numerous strains of MRSA. Furthermore, berberine markedly lowered the minimum inhibition concentrations of ampicillin and oxacillin against MRSA. Berberine and ampicillin exhibited an additive effect, and berberine and oxacillin showed a synergistic effect against MRSA. These results suggest that berberine may have antimicrobial activity and the potential to restore the effectiveness of beta-lactam antibiotics against MRSA.[26,27] Other herbs with antibacterial effects include *Da Huang* (Radix et Rhizoma Rhei),[28] *Long Dan* (Radix et Rhizoma Gentianae),[29] and *Zhi Zi* (Fructus Gardeniae).[30]

Viral infection: *Huang Qin* (Radix Scutellariae) has a wide spectrum of antiviral activity. Specifically, baicalein and wogonin, two compounds from the herb, boost innate antiviral immunity by stimulating the production of cytokines and increasing the resistance to viral infection in human leukocytes.[31] *Huang Bo* (Cortex Phellodendri Chinensis) has antiviral activity against herpes simplex virus type 1 (HSV-1).[32] The polysaccharide sulfate derived from *Niu Xi* (Radix Achyranthis Bidentatae) has an antiviral effect against many viruses, including simple herpes virus type-I and human immunodeficiency virus type 1 (HIV-1).[33,34] *Che Qian Zi* (Semen Plantaginis) has a strong antiviral effect against a series of viruses, namely herpesviruses (HSV-1 and HSV-2) and adenoviruses (ADV-3, ADV-8 and ADV-11).[35] Lastly, *Ge Gen* (Radix Puerariae Lobatae) has antiviral and cytotoxic effects, and can inhibit enterovirus 71 (EV71) when given before, simultaneously with, or after viral infection.[36]

Fungal infection: The aqueous extract of *Huang Qin* (Radix Scutellariae) has an *in vivo* antifungal effect against *Candida*

Gentiana Complex™

albicans.[37] Genipin and geniposide, two compounds from *Zhi Zi* (Fructus Gardeniae), have a potent inhibitory effect on pathogenic fungi, such as *Pleurotus ostreatus*, *Fusarium oxysporum* and *Corynespora cassiicola*.[38]

Liver and gallbladder disorders: *Long Dan* (Radix et Rhizoma Gentianae) has a hepatoprotective effect to protect the liver in acute liver injury and against carbon tetrachloride-induced liver damage.[39,40] *Long Dan* (Radix et Rhizoma Gentianae) also has cholagogic effects to increase the production and excretion of bile.[41] According to one report, 26 patients with chronic infectious hepatitis and persistent high liver enzymes levels were treated with an herbal formula with *Long Dan* (Radix et Rhizoma Gentianae) as the main herb, with good results.[42] *Da Huang* (Radix et Rhizoma Rhei) has a hepatoprotective effect to treat chemical-induced liver damage.[43] It also has cholagogic effect to increase the flow and excretion of bile.[44] Clinically, *Da Huang* (Radix et Rhizoma Rhei) has been used in formulas to effectively treat acute icteric hepatitis in 80 patients,[45] acute hepatitis A in 67 patients,[46] and acute cholecystitis in 10 patients.[47] *Dan Shen* (Radix et Rhizoma Salviae Miltiorrhizae) has a marked hepatoprotective effect to lower liver enzyme and to treat liver cirrhosis. The hepatoprotective function of *Dan Shen* (Radix et Rhizoma Salviae Miltiorrhizae) is attributed in part to its effect at improving blood circulation and promoting regeneration of liver cells.[48,49,50] Clinically, *Dan Shen* (Radix et Rhizoma Salviae Miltiorrhizae) has been used effectively to treat 104 patients with acute viral hepatitis and 22 patients with chronic active hepatitis.[51,52] *Huang Qin* (Radix Scutellariae) has a remarkable effect to protect and prevent various types of liver injuries. It protects against mutagenesis of liver cells induced by the mycotoxin aflatoxin-B_1,[53] it protects against fibrosis and lipid peroxidation in liver induced by bile duct ligation and scission or carbon tetrachloride,[54] and it inhibits hemin-nitrite-H_2O_2 induced liver injury in dose-dependent manners.[55] Use of *Huang Qin* (Radix Scutellariae) was associated with a 63.6% and a 73.3% rate of effectiveness to treat infectious hepatitis and chronic hepatitis among 268 patients, respectively.[56] Lastly, administration of *Zhi Zi* (Fructus Gardeniae) is associated with a marked hepatoprotective function as it lowers serum bilirubin, liver enzymes, and prevents the death of hepatocytes.[57,58] *Zhi Zi* (Fructus Gardeniae) also has a marked cholagogic effect to stimulate the production of bile, enhance contraction of the gallbladder, and increase excretion of bile into the intestines.[59]

Pancreatic disorders: *Zhi Zi* (Fructus Gardeniae) has a marked effect to protect the pancreas. Therapeutic benefits included reduction in pancreatic edema, neutrophil infiltration, serum amylase and lipase levels, serum cytokine levels, and mRNA expression of multiple inflammatory mediators.[60] Clinically, *Da Huang* (Radix et Rhizoma Rhei) is effective to treat acute pancreatitis in 100 patients. Initial treatment included decoction of 30 to 60 grams of *Da Huang* (Radix et Rhizoma Rhei) every one to two hours until symptoms returned to normal. After the condition stabilized, they were switched to tablets of *Da Huang* (Radix et Rhizoma Rhei), 3 grams twice daily. The total dosage of *Da Huang* (Radix et Rhizoma Rhei) per patient was 450 grams. The study reported close to 100% effectiveness. The time required was two days for normalization of amylase in urine and three days for pain relief.[61]

In summary, ***Gentiana Complex*** is an herbal formula with a wide range of clinical applications, including but not limited to cardiovascular disorders, infectious diseases, inflammatory disorders, and disorders affecting the liver, gallbladder, and pancreas.

COMPARATIVE ANALYSIS

Hypertension: Hypertension is one of the most common disorders in developed countries. In Western medicine, many different categories of drugs may be used to treat hypertension, including but not limited to diuretics [Lasix (furosemide) and hydrochlorothiazide], beta-blockers [Tenormin (atenolol) and Inderal (propranolol)], calcium channel blockers [Procardia (nifedipine) and Calan (verapamil)], ACE inhibitors [Vasotec (enalapril)] and Capoten (captopril)], and vasodilators [hydralazine and minoxidil]. All these drugs have benefits and risks, and may be given individually or in combinations to control blood pressure. The main advantage of drug therapy is its potency to suppress blood pressure. The main disadvantages, however, are that the drugs cause a great number of side effects, and they do not change the underlying constitution of the patient. Therefore, while they are effective to suppress blood pressure, they must be used continuously and cannot be stopped. Discontinuing use of these drugs often leads to rebound hypertension.

In TCM, hypertension may be characterized by both excess and deficiency. Excess refers to Liver yang rising, and deficiency refers to Liver and Kidney yin deficiencies. Both conditions may be treated effectively with herbal medicine. The main advantage of using herbs is the effective ability to change the fundamental constitution of the body, thereby achieving long-term efficacy to reduce blood pressure, even after the herbs are discontinued. The main disadvantage, however, is that herbs are less immediately potent than drugs for the treatment of hypertensive crisis, and should not be used in lieu of drugs for these cases or for individuals with secondary hypertension.

Both drugs and herbs are effective to treat hypertension, and they have their distinct advantages and disadvantages. In addition to choosing either drugs or herbal therapy, it is also important to make diet and lifestyle changes to ensure successful long-term management of hypertension.

Infection and inflammation: There are many disorders characterized by infection and inflammation of genital regions, including vaginitis, cystitis, pelvic inflammatory disease, and urinary tract infection. In Western medicine, these conditions are

Gentiana Complex ™

generally treated with antibiotic drugs, including antibacterial, antiviral, and antifungal agents. As a category, these drugs are effective to treat such infections and inflammations. However, these drugs are very potent, and may cause many side effects, such as secondary infection.

Herbal therapy is also very effective for treating these infections and inflammations. Many herbs have been shown to have marked antibacterial, antiviral, and antifungal properties. Furthermore, some have an analgesic effect to relieve pain, and others have a diuretic effect to relieve dysuria. Lastly, though these herbs are generally safe, they should be discontinued once the desired effects are achieved, as extended use may consume and weaken the body.

Drugs and herbs are both effective for treating infections and inflammations of the genitourinary system. In general, drugs are more effective for bacterial and fungal infections, but their safety profiles vary depending on the exact antibiotic prescribed. Herbs are equally effective for bacterial, viral, and fungal infections. For severe infections and inflammations, they are slightly less immediately potent than drugs, but are much safer and have significantly fewer side effects. Lastly, in both therapies, the chosen substance(s) should always be taken until the course of therapy is completed. Those who have weakness and deficiency from the infection and/or its treatment should take herbs to strengthen the body and facilitate recovery.

Liver and gallbladder disorders: Liver diseases, such as hepatitis, are serious and very complicated diseases. In Western medicine, these conditions are usually treated with interferon therapy. These drugs, however, have limited success, but are extremely expensive and create significant number of serious side effects, including dizziness, confusion, coma, arrhythmia, heart failure, leukopenia, thrombocytopenia, and many others. In severe and life threatening cases, such as liver cirrhosis and liver cancer, surgery may be performed.

In traditional Chinese medicine, treatment of liver disorders is also a very challenging and complicated matter. These conditions are usually treated with herbs that drain damp-heat from the Liver. Pharmacologically, these herbs have hepatoprotective effects that remove toxins from the liver, prevent the entrance of toxins into liver cells, and increase blood circulation to the liver to facilitate recovery. In most cases, herbs are most effective in the early stage of liver disorders characterized by increased liver enzymes. Immediate and aggressive treatment with herbs generally lowers liver enzyme levels and reverses the illness. Once the disease progresses into various stages of hepatitis and/or liver cirrhosis, individualized treatments specific to the clinical manifestations of the patient should be considered for maximum effectiveness.

Liver diseases, such as hepatitis, are serious and very complicated diseases that are challenging to both Western and traditional Chinese medicines. Herbal treatment is generally more effective for early stages of liver diseases, and ones with mild to moderate severity. Drug treatments, such as interferon therapy, are generally not utilized unless there is moderate to severe liver disease, because the risks of side effects are generally greater than the potential benefits. Unfortunately, severe cases of liver diseases are extremely difficult to manage for both Western medicine and traditional Chinese medicine. Under these circumstances, customized treatment with careful supervision is most effective.

References

1. Chan K, Lo AC, Yeung JH, Woo KS. Journal of Pharmacy and Pharmacology 1995 May;47(5):402-406.
2. *Zhong Yao Xue* (Chinese Herbology), 1988; 140:144.
3. *Sheng Yao Xue Za Zhi* (Journal of Raw Herbology), 1982; 36(2):150.
4. *Zhong Yao Yao Li Yu Ying Yong* (Pharmacology and Applications of Chinese Herbs), 1983: 718.
5. *Zhong Yao Lin Chuan Xin Yong* (New Clinical Applications of Chinese Medicine), 2001; 242.
6. *Zhong Yao Xue* (Chinese Herbology), 1998; 101:103.
7. *Yi Xue Yan Jiu Tong Xun* (Report of Medical Studies), 1972; (2):14.
8. *Zhong Hua Yi Xue Za Zhi* (Chinese Journal of Medicine), 1979; 59(8):479.
9. *Zhong Cao Yao Tong Xun* (Journal of Chinese Herbal Medicine), 1975; 2:34.
10. *Guo Wai Yi Xue Zhong Yi Zhong Yao Fen Ce* (Monograph of Chinese Herbology from Foreign Medicine), 1991; 13(3):41.
11. Lo CJ, Lin JG, Kuo JS, Chiang SY, Chen SC, Liao ET, Hsieh CL. Effect of salvia miltiorrhiza bunge on cerebral infarct in ischemia-reperfusion injured rats. Am J Chin Med. 2003;31(2):191-200.
12. *Xin Zhang Xue Guan Ji Bing* (Cardiovascular Diseases), 1974; 2(1):5.
13. *Zhong Cao Yao Tong Xun* (Journal of Chinese Herbal Medicine), 1978; 1:37.
14. *Zhong Yao Xue* (Chinese Herbology), 1988; 137:140.
15. *Shang Hai Zhong Yi Yao Za Zhi* (Shanghai Journal of Chinese Medicine and Herbology), 1956; 1:24.
16. *Zhong Guo Yao Li Xue Tong Bao* (Journal of Chinese Herbal Pharmacology), 1989; 10(5):385.
17. *Zhong Yao Yao Li Yu Ying Yong* (Pharmacology and Applications of Chinese Herbs), 1983; 934.
18. Geng F, Yang L, Chou G, Wang Z. Bioguided isolation of angiotensin-converting enzyme inhibitors from the seeds of Plantago asiatica L. Phytother Res. 2010 Jul;24(7):1088-94.
19. *Zhong Yao Lin Chuan Xin Yong* (New Clinical Applications of Chinese Medicine), 2001; 110.
20. *Chang Yong Zhong Yao Cheng Fen Yu Yao Li Shou Ce* (A Handbook of the Composition and Pharmacology of Common Chinese Drugs), 1994; 226:323.
21. *Zhong Guo Zhong Yao Za Zhi* (People's Republic of China Journal of Chinese Herbology), 1989; 14(10):46.
22. *Zhong Yao Xue* (Chinese Herbology), 1988; 137:140.
23. *J Pharm Pharmacol* 2000 Mar;52(3):361-6.
24. *Zhong Yao Da Ci Dian* (Dictionary of Chinese Herbs), 1977: 2032.
25. *Zhong Cao Yao* (Chinese Herbal Medicine), 1985; 16(1):34.
26. Chen ML, Xian YF, Ip SP, Tsai SH, Yang JY, Che CT. Chemical and biological differentiation of Cortex Phellodendri Chinensis and Cortex Phellodendri Amurensis. School of Chinese Medicine, The Chinese University of Hong Kong, Shatin, N.T., Hong Kong. Planta Med. 2010 Oct;76(14):1530-5.
27. Yu HH, Kim KJ, Cha JD, Kim HK, Lee YE, Choi NY, You YO. Antimicrobial activity of berberine alone and in combination with ampicillin or oxacillin against methicillin-resistant Staphylococcus aureus. Department of Food and Nutrition, Kunsan National University, Kunsan. J Med Food. 2005 Winter;8(4):454-61.
28. *Zhong Yao Xue* (Chinese Herbology), 1998; 251:256.

Gentiana Complex™

29. *Zhong Yao Yao Li Yu Ying Yong* (Pharmacology and Applications of Chinese Herbs), 1983; 295.
30. *Zhong Yao Zhi* (Chinese Herbology Journal), 1984; 578.
31. Błach-Olszewska Z, Jatczak B, Rak A, Lorenc M, Gulanowski B, Drobna A, Lamer-Zarawska E. Production of cytokines and stimulation of resistance to viral infection in human leukocytes by Scutellaria baicalensis flavones. Ludwik Hirszfeld Institute of Immunology and Experimental Therapy, Polish Academy of Sciences, Wrocław, Poland. J Interferon Cytokine Res. 2008 Sep;28(9):571-81.
32. Wang W, Zu Y, Fu Y, Reichling J, Suschke U, Nokemper S, Zhang Y. In vitro antioxidant, antimicrobial and anti-herpes simplex virus type 1 activity of Phellodendron amurense Rupr. from China. Key Laboratory of Forest Plant Ecology, Northeast Forestry University, Hexing Road 26, 150040 Harbin, China. Am J Chin Med. 2009;37(1):195-203.
33. Tian GY, Li ST, Song ML, Zheng MS, Li W. Synthesis of Achyranthes bidentata polysaccharide sulfate and its antivirus activity. Shanghai Institute of Oganic Chemistry, Chinese Academy of Sciences. Yao Xue Xue Bao. 1995;30(2):107-11.
34. Peng ZG, Chen HS, Guo ZM, Dong B, Tian GY, Wang GQ. Anti-HIV activities of Achyranthes bidentata polysaccharide sulfate in vitro and in vivo. Institute of Medicinal Biotechnology, Chinese Academy of Medical Sciences and Peking Union Medical College, Beijing 100050, China. Yao Xue Xue Bao. 2008 Jul;43(7):702-6.
35. Chiang LC, Chiang W, Chang MY, Lin CC. In vitro cytotoxic, antiviral and immunomodulatory effects of Plantago major and Plantago asiatica. Am J Chin Med. 2003;31(2):225-34.
36. Su FM, Chang JS, Wang KC, Tsai JJ, Chiang LC. A water extract of Pueraria lobata inhibited cytotoxicity of enterovirus 71 in a human foreskin fibroblast cell line. Kaohsiung J Med Sci. 2008 Oct;24(10):523-30.
37. Wong KS, Tsang WK. In vitro antifungal activity of the aqueous extract of Scutellaria baicalensis Georgi root against Candida albicans. Int J Antimicrob Agents. 2009 Sep;34(3):284-5.
38. Lelono RA, Tachibana S, Itoh K. Isolation of antifungal compounds from Gardenia jasminoides. United Graduate School of Agricultural Sciences, Ehime University, 3-5-7 Tarumi, Matsuyama, Ehime 790-8566, Japan. Pak J Biol Sci. 2009 Jul 1;12(13):949-56.
39. Jiang WX, Xue BY. Hepatoprotective effects of Gentiana scabra on the acute liver injuries in mice. Zhongguo Zhong Yao Za Zhi. 2005 Jul;30(14): 1105-7.
40. *Yun Nan Yi Yao* (Yunan Medicine and Herbology), 1991; 12(5):304.
41. *Yun Nan Yi Yao* (Yunan Medicine and Herbology), 1991; 12(5):304.
42. *Shang Hai Zhong Yi Yao Za Zhi* (Shanghai Journal of Chinese Medicine and Herbology), 1965; 4:4.
43. *Zhong Guo Zhong Yao Za Zhi* (People's Republic of China Journal of Chinese Herbology), 1989; 14(10):46.
44. *Xin Yi Yao Xue Za Zhi* (New Journal of Medicine and Herbology), 1974; (5):34.
45. *Zhong Xi Yi Jie He Za Zhi* (Journal of Integrated Chinese and Western Medicine), 1983; 1:19.
46. *Si Chuan Zhong Yi* (Sichuan Chinese Medicine), 1994; (3):21.
47. *Zhong Yao Lin Chuan Xin Yong* (New Clinical Applications of Chinese Medicine), 2001; 29.
48. *Zhong Yi Za Zhi* (Journal of Chinese Medicine), 1982; (1):67.
49. *Zhong Xi Yi Jie He Za Zhi* (Journal of Integrated Chinese and Western Medicine), 1988; 8(3):161.
50. *Zhong Xi Yi Jie He Za Zhi* (Journal of Integrated Chinese and Western Medicine), 1983; 3(3):180.
51. *Shan Xi Zhong Yi* (Shanxi Chinese Medicine), 1980; 6:15.
52. *Zhong Xi Yi Jie He Za Zhi* (Journal of Integrated Chinese and Western Medicine), 1984; 2:86.
53. de Boer JG, Quiney B, Walter PB, Thomas C, Hodgson K, Murch SJ, Saxena PK. Protection against aflatoxin-B1-induced liver mutagenesis by Scutellaria baicalensis. Centre for Biomedical Research, University of Victoria, P.O. Box 3020 STN CSC, Victoria, BC, Canada. Mutat Res. 2005 Oct 15;578(1-2):15-22.
54. Nan JX, Park EJ, Kim YC, Ko G, Sohn DH. Scutellaria baicalensis inhibits liver fibrosis induced by bile duct ligation or carbon tetrachloride in rats. Department of Pharmacy, Wonkwang University, Iksan, Cheonbuk, South Korea. J Pharm Pharmacol. 2002 Apr;54(4):555-63.
55. Zhao Y, Li H, Gao Z, Gong Y, Xu H. Effects of flavonoids extracted from Scutellaria baicalensis Georgi on hemin-nitrite-H2O2 induced liver injury. Department of Chemistry, Huazhong University of Science and Technology, Wuhan, 430074, PR China. Eur J Pharmacol. 2006 Apr 24;536(1-2):192-9.
56. *Zhong Hua Nei Ke Za Zhi* (Chinese Journal of Internal Medicine), 1978; 2:127.
57. *Zhong Yao Xue* (Chinese Herbology), 1998; 126:128.
58. *CA*, 1982; 97:16912n.
59. *Zhong Yao Yao Li Yu Ying Yong* (Pharmacology and Applications of Chinese Herbs), 1983; 934.
60. Jung WS, Chae YS, Kim DY, Seo SW, Park HJ, Bae GS, Kim TH, Oh HJ, Yun KJ, Park RK, Kim JS, Kim EC, Hwang SY, Park SJ, Song HJ. Gardenia jasminoides protects against cerulein-induced acute pancreatitis. Department of Biochemistry, Institute of Medical Science, Chonbuk National University Medical School, Jeonju, 570-749 Jeonbuk, South Korea. World J Gastroenterol. 2008 Oct 28;14(40):6188-94.
61. *Zhong Xi Yi Jie He Za Zhi* (Journal of Integrated Chinese and Western Medicine), 1982; 2:85.

Gentle Lax (Deficient)™

CLINICAL APPLICATIONS

- **Constipation**
- **Chronic, habitual constipation** with dry, hard stool
- **Deficient-type constipation** in postpartum, postsurgical, or convalescing individuals
- **Mild colon cleanser**

WESTERN THERAPEUTIC ACTIONS

- Emollient effect to lubricate the bowel and moisten the Intestines
- Laxative effect to relieve mild to moderate constipation
- Treats chronic constipation associated with hemorrhoids by reducing inflammation

CHINESE THERAPEUTIC ACTIONS

- Moistens the Intestines
- Unblocks the bowels
- Drains heat
- Nourishes yin and blood

DOSAGE

Take 4 capsules three times daily on an empty stomach with warm water. Individuals with sensitive gastrointestinal tracts should decrease the dosage and increase the dosing frequency to avoid stomach discomfort. For example, take 2 capsules four or five times daily, instead of taking 4 capsules three times daily.

INGREDIENTS

Bai Shao (Radix Paeoniae Alba)
Bai Zi Ren (Semen Platycladi)
Da Huang (Radix et Rhizoma Rhei)
Dang Gui Wei (Extremitas Radix Angelicae Sinensis)
Hou Po (Cortex Magnoliae Officinalis)
Jue Ming Zi (Semen Cassiae)
Ku Xing Ren (Semen Armeniacae Amarum)
Mai Dong (Radix Ophiopogonis)
Tao Ren (Semen Persicae)
Xuan Shen (Radix Scrophulariae)
Yu Li Ren (Semen Pruni)
Zhi He Shou Wu (Radix Polygoni Multiflori Praeparata)
Zhi Shi (Fructus Aurantii Immaturus)

BACKGROUND

Constipation is the infrequent or incomplete passage of stools. The stools are usually dry and hard, and are difficult to pass even with straining. Individuals with constipation often have two or fewer bowel movements per week, and will usually have feelings of incomplete evacuation after bowel movement. Common causes of constipation include lack of exercise, insufficient intake of water and fiber, stress, overuse of laxatives, and use of certain drugs (including opioids, antipsychotics, antidepressants, and anticholinergics).

FORMULA EXPLANATION

Gentle Lax (Deficient) is a mild formula suitable for deficient-type constipation. Deficient-type constipation is defined as chronic or habitual constipation, constipation in geriatric patients, or constipation in patients with red tongue, pale or sallow face, and general signs and symptoms of weakness.

Yu Li Ren (Semen Pruni) and *Bai Zi Ren* (Semen Platycladi) moisten the Intestines and unblock the bowels. *Ku Xing Ren* (Semen Armeniacae Amarum) and *Tao Ren* (Semen Persicae) lubricate the Large Intestine and direct qi downward. *Zhi Shi* (Fructus Aurantii Immaturus) and *Hou Po* (Cortex Magnoliae Officinalis) dissipate stagnation and reduce distension and bloating. *Xuan Shen* (Radix Scrophulariae) and *Mai Dong* (Radix Ophiopogonis) clear heat, cool the blood and nourish the yin. *Bai Shao* (Radix Paeoniae Alba) nourishes blood and relieves pain, which may be associated with constipation. *Da Huang* (Radix et Rhizoma Rhei) is a purgative that clears toxic heat lodged in the Intestines. *Jue Ming Zi* (Semen Cassiae) moistens the Intestines and facilitates the passage of stools. *Dang Gui Wei* (Extremitas Radix Angelicae Sinensis) and *Zhi He Shou Wu* (Radix Polygoni Multiflori Praeparata) enrich blood and act as gentle laxatives by moistening the desiccated intestines.

CAUTIONS & CONTRAINDICATIONS

- Individuals with a sensitive gastrointestinal tract should take this formula with caution, as it may be irritating to the stomach and intestinal mucosa. Those who experience stomach discomfort should reduce the dosage and take the herbs with food.
- A more serious etiology should be suspected if the constipation is accompanied by vomiting, blood in the stools, weight loss, or a distended, tympanitic abdomen.
- This formula is contraindicated during pregnancy and nursing.
- This herbal formula contains herbs that invigorate blood circulation, such as *Dang Gui Wei* (Extremitas Radix Angelicae Sinensis). Therefore, patients who are on anticoagulant or antiplatelet therapies, such as Coumadin (warfarin), should use this formula with caution, or not at all, as there may be a higher risk of bleeding and bruising.[1,2,3]
- The following warning statement is required by the State of California: "This product contains *Da Huang* (Radix et Rhizoma Rhei). Read and follow directions carefully. Do not use if you have or develop diarrhea, loose stools, or abdominal pain because *Da Huang* (Radix et Rhizoma Rhei) may worsen these conditions and be harmful to your health. Consult your physician if you have frequent diarrhea or if you are pregnant, nursing, taking medication, or have a medical condition."
- According to most textbooks and contemporary references, the classic entry of "*He Shou Wu*" is now separated into two entries: the <u>unprepared</u> *Sheng Shou Wu* (Radix Polygoni Multiflori) and the <u>prepared</u> *Zhi He Shou Wu* (Radix Polygoni Multiflori Praeparata), as they have significantly different therapeutic effects and side effects. *Sheng Shou Wu* (Radix Polygoni

Gentle Lax (Deficient)™

Multiflori) is a stimulant laxative that treats constipation, but may cause nausea, vomiting, abdominal pain, diarrhea, and in rare cases, liver disorder (dose- and time-dependent, and reversible upon discontinuation).[4] On the other hand, *Zhi He Shou Wu* (Radix Polygoni Multiflori Praeparata) is a tonic herb that is safe and well-tolerated. The dramatic changes in the therapeutic effect and safety profile are attributed to the long and complicated processing of the root with *Hei Dou* (Semen Sojae) through repeated blending, cooking, and drying procedures. When properly processed, the chemical composition of the root changes significantly. Many new compounds are generated from the Maillard reaction (four furanones, two furans, two nitrogen compounds, one pyran, one alcohol and one sulfur compound). Furthermore, the preparation process causes changes in the composition of sugars and 16 kinds of amino acids; it also reduces the pH of the herb from 6.28 to 5.61.[5,6,7] In summary, these changes give rise to the tonic effects of the prepared roots, and eliminate the adverse reactions associated with the unprepared roots. **Note:** Due to medical risks and legal liabilities, it is prudent to exercise caution and ***not*** use this herb in either prepared or unprepared forms in patients with pre-existing or risk factors of liver diseases.

CLINICAL NOTES

- Use of herbs is very effective to prevent drug-induced constipation. There are two types of drugs that are most likely to cause constipation: opioids [i.e., Vicodin (hydrocodone/acetaminophen), Darvocet (propoxyphene/acetaminophen), Tylenol/Codeine (acetaminophen/codeine)] and antipsychotic drugs [i.e., Haldol (haloperidol), Thorazine (chlorpromazine)].

Pulse Diagnosis by Dr. Jimmy Wei-Yen Chang:

- **Constipation due to constriction:** *Yinqiao* pulse, a thin, straight, wiry pulse on or extends proximal to the left *chi*
- **Constipation due to dryness in the Stomach and Large Intestine:** floating and forceful on the right *cun* and *guan*

SUPPLEMENTARY FORMULAS

- For excess types of constipation, use ***Gentle Lax (Excess)***.
- To detox the colon, use ***GI DTX*** instead.
- For constipation due to stress, add ***Calm***.
- For gastrointestinal disorders such as acid reflux or ulcers, use ***GI Care*** instead.
- For irritable bowel syndrome (IBS), use ***GI Harmony*** instead.
- For ulcerative colitis, use ***GI Care (UC)*** instead.
- For hemorrhoids and pain, use ***GI Care (HMR)*** and ***Herbal ANG*** instead.
- To tonify blood, combine with ***Schisandra ZZZ***.
- For constipation due to neurodegenerative disorders, Alzheimer's, Parkinson's and stroke, use ***Neuro Plus***.
- With excess fire, add ***Gardenia Complex***.
- For rectal bleeding, add ***Notoginseng 9***.
- For severe blood stagnation, add ***Circulation (SJ)***.
- For constipation in postpartum women with deficiency, add ***Imperial Tonic***.
- For constipation and postpartum depression, add ***Shine***.

ACUPUNCTURE TREATMENT

Traditional Points:

- *Zhigou* (TH 6), *Zhaohai* (KI 6)
- *Qihai* (CV 6), *Zhongwan* (CV 12), *Geshu* (BL 17), *Renzhong* (GV 26), *Zhigou* (TH 6), *Tianshu* (ST 25), *Taichong* (LR 3), *Zusanli* (ST 36), *Dachangshu* (BL 25)

Classic Master Tung's Points:

- **Constipation (general):** *Tushui* (T 22.11), *Qimen* (T 33.01), *Qijiao* (T 33.02), *Qizheng* (T 33.03), *Simashang* (T 88.18), *Simazhong* (T 88.17), *Simaxia* (T 88.19), *Tongtian* (T 88.03), *Fuchang* (T 77.12), *Huochuan* (T 33.04)
- **Constipation (post-partum):** *Simashang* (T 88.18), *Simazhong* (T 88.17), *Simaxia* (T 88.19)

Master Tung's Points by Dr. Chuan-Min Wang:

- **Constipation:** *Shuitong* (T 1010.19), *Shuijin* (T 1010.20), *Shuizhong* (T DT.13), *Shuifu* (T DT.14)

Balance Method by Dr. Richard Tan:

- Left side: *Waiguan* (TH 5), *Zhigou* (TH 6), *Zhaohai* (KI 6), *Hegu* (LI 4)
- Right side: *Zusanli* (ST 36), *Shangjuxu* (ST 37), *Kongzui* (LU 6) or *ah shi* points nearby
- Left and right sides can be alternated from treatment to treatment.

Ear Acupuncture:

- Large Intestine, Colon, Rectum, Sympathetic. Tape magnetic balls onto the points and switch ears every three days. If both ears are taped at the same time, rest one day in between the three-day treatments.
- Large Intestine, Rectum. Strong stimulation is necessary two or three times daily. Leave the needles in for one hour. Embed ear seeds in Spleen, Large Intestine and Rectum. Switch ear every week.

Auricular Medicine by Dr. Li-Chun Huang:

- Abdomen, Spleen, Lung, Liver, *San Jiao*, Large Intestine, Sigmoid, Digestive Subcortex

NUTRITION

- Eat plenty of foods with high fiber, such as fresh fruits, green leafy vegetables, cabbage, peas, sweet potatoes, and whole grains.
- Drink plenty of water, at least eight glasses per day.
- Prunes or prune juice are very effective to regulate bowels and relieve mild cases of constipation.
- A combination of wild or raw honey with fresh grapefruit will also relieve dry stool or constipation.

Gentle Lax (Deficient)™

- Black sesame with wild honey is a helpful combination to soften stool and facilitate bowel movement.
- Increase intake of nourishing, cooling foods/roots such as Mexican yam, yam, radishes, potatoes, carrots, melons, cucumbers, beets, turnips, malanga, celeriac, taro, and rutabaga.
- Avoid deep-fried foods. Follow a low-fat diet.
- Avoid fatty and spicy foods that may irritate the mucous membranes of the intestines.
- Avoid spicy/pungent/aromatic vegetables such as pepper, garlic, onions, basil, rosemary, cumin, funnel, anise, leeks, chives, scallions, thyme, saffron, wormwood, mustard, chili pepper, and wasabi.

The Tao of Nutrition by Dr. Maoshing Ni and Cathy McNease:

- Recommendations: bananas, apples, walnuts, figs, spinach, peaches, pears, pine nuts, sesame seeds, mulberries, grapefruit, yams, honey, apricot kernel, milk, yogurt, alfalfa sprouts, beets, cabbage, bok-choy, cauliflower, and potato.
- Eat two bananas on an empty stomach, followed by a glass of water.
- Drink a glass of lukewarm water with two teaspoons of honey on an empty stomach.
- Drink blended beets and cabbage on an empty stomach.
- Eat 5 to 10 figs on an empty stomach, followed by a glass of water.
- Eat a fresh apple on an empty stomach daily.
- Drink mulberry juice.
- Eat lightly steamed asparagus and cabbage at night before retiring.
- Avoid spicy foods, fried foods, and meat.

LIFESTYLE INSTRUCTIONS

- Avoid stress, anxiety and tension whenever possible.
- Exercise regularly to increase peristalsis of the intestines. Walking is one of the best exercises as it massages the intestines to regulate the bowels.
- Do not suppress the urge to relieve the bowels. Suppressing the urge is one of the main causes of chronic constipation. Empty the bowels whenever there is a desire, especially in the morning when the digestive system is most active.
- Massaging the abdomen along the directional flow of the large intestine (clock-wise) will also help.
- Patients with hemorrhoids should not lift anything heavy.

CASE STUDIES

- J.J., a 49-year-old female, presented with constipation and abdominal bloating. The patient had a history of having a bowel movement every other day to every three days since childhood. She was experiencing cold sensation and had been taking birth control pills for heavy bleeding. As a result of taking birth control pills, she would experience night sweats when she was taking the sugar pills or during her menses. Her blood pressure was 118/72 mmHg and her heart rate was 75 beats per minute. The practitioner diagnosed this condition as yin deficiency and stagnation; the Western diagnosis was chronic constipation. ***Gentle Lax (Deficient)*** was prescribed at three pills three times daily with warm water in combination with ***Balance (Heat)*** three to five capsules at night when she is not taking birth control pills. The patient was amazed with the results; she reported having regular daily bowel movements and relief of her bloating. In addition, she was no longer experiencing night sweats when she was on the sugar pill days of her birth control pills pills. Along with taking herbs the patient also received acupuncture twice weekly. Submitted by L.W., Arroyo Grande, California.
- A 32-year-old female presented with chronic constipation, which started since her early teens. Her bowel movements had occurred every three to four days. The practitioner diagnosed her condition as Spleen qi deficiency. After taking ***Gentle Lax (Deficient)***, her bowel movements became daily and regular. She noted that using ***Gentle Lax (Deficient)*** did not cause a feeling of fullness. After two months, her bowel movements have maintained a regular and daily schedule. Submitted by S.T., San Jose, California.
- A 49-year-old female teacher presented with constipation and gas as her chief complaints. Other signs and symptoms included bloating, low back pain, stress, anger, irritability, and fatigue. Her overall condition was indicative of irritable bowel syndrome. The practitioner attributed the patient's constipation and gas to Liver qi stagnation. The patient was previously treated with a combination of *Xiao Yao San* (Rambling Powder) and *Ma Zi Ren Wan* (Hemp Seed Pill) with little success. Once the practitioner substituted ***Gentle Lax (Deficient)*** and ***GI Care***, the patient's chief complaints abated. Her stress level lessened as well. Submitted by D.M., Raton, New Mexico.
- F.L., a 53-year-old female patient, presented with recent history of TIA (transient ischemic attack). Objective findings included right-sided pulling and numbness of the face with difficulty smiling and closing the right eye, as well as drooping of facial muscles on the right side when smiling, and partial facial flaccidity. Treatment using three capsules of ***Circulation***, three times daily, was successful: no recurring episodes were noted during subsequent follow-up visits. This patient also had constipation with hard, difficult to move stools, abdominal pain, and cramps with bloating. All these gastrointestinal symptoms were resolved with ***Gentle Lax (Deficient)*** taken at four capsules, three times daily. Submitted by C.L., Chino Hills, California.
- J.N., a 68-year-old male patient, presented with constipation and bloating. His blood pressure was 176/86 mmHg and the heart rate was 54 beats per minute. The practitioner diagnosed him with constipation and bloating due to blood deficiency, dryness, and from side effects of the high blood pressure medications. ***Gentle Lax (Deficient)*** was prescribed at 2 grams three times daily. Acupuncture was also given to balance the system. Patient reported that the formula helped him go to the bathroom daily and that it took less effort to pass stools. Submitted by W.F., Bloomfield, New Jersey.

Gentle Lax (Deficient) ™

PHARMACOLOGICAL AND CLINICAL RESEARCH

Gentle Lax (Deficient) is composed of herbs with mild laxative functions to promote regular bowel movements in individuals who have chronic or habitual constipation.

Pharmacologically, many of these herbs have excellent laxative, purgative, and lubricant effects. *Da Huang* (Radix et Rhizoma Rhei) has direct laxative and purgative effects to quickly and powerfully treat constipation.[8] *Da Huang* (Radix et Rhizoma Rhei) works mainly on the transverse and descending colon as it inhibits the re-absorption of water and causes evacuation of the stool.[9,10] In addition, *Da Huang* (Radix et Rhizoma Rhei) increases peristalsis of the large intestine without interfering with absorption of nutrients in the small intestine.[11] Furthermore, *Yu Li Ren* (Semen Pruni) increases peristalsis and promotes bowel movement.[12] *Bai Zi Ren* (Semen Platycladi) has a mild effect to lubricate the bowel and relieve constipation.[13] *Zhi Shi* (Fructus Aurantii Immaturus) stimulates smooth muscle and increases intestinal peristalsis.[14]

Clinically, herbs in this formula have been used successfully to treat chronic constipation, habitual constipation, and constipation with bloating. According to one study, 50 elderly patients with chronic constipation were treated with a 94% rate of effectiveness. [15] According to another study, 60 patients with chronic habitual constipation were treated with great success using herbs such as *Bai Shao* (Radix Paeoniae Alba), *Gan Cao* (Radix et Rhizoma Glycyrrhizae), and others as needed. [16] Furthermore, use of *Jue Ming Zi* (Semen Cassiae) as tea throughout the day also showed a marked effect to relieve chronic constipation.[17] Lastly, administration of *Hou Po* (Cortex Magnoliae Officinalis) in 36 women greatly reduced incidence of constipation and abdominal bloating following surgery.[18]

In summary, ***Gentle Lax (Deficient)*** is excellent for chronic or habitual constipation of mild to moderate severity.

COMPARATIVE ANALYSIS

Constipation is a very common problem that may be treated effectively using Western and traditional Chinese medicines. In Western medicine, bulking agents (bran, psyllium, and methylcellulose) are the gentlest and safest. These drugs are not habit forming, and may be used safely on a long-term basis. However, they act slowly and are not very strong. Laxatives (docusate and mineral oil) soften the stool by increasing the implementation of intestinal water. However, these drugs must be used carefully, as they interfere with the absorption of nutrients and other drugs. Lastly, cathartics (senna, cascara, and bisacodyl) are used for severe cases of constipation by increasing intestinal peristalsis and intraluminal fluids. However, these drugs should only be used on a short-term basis, as prolonged use will cause "lazy bowel" syndrome and serious fluid and electrolyte imbalance.

Constipation is treated with great success in TCM. Those with mild to moderate constipation are usually treated with herbs that moisten the Intestines and regulate bowel movement. Those with moderate to severe constipation are generally treated with herbs that purge the Intestines and induce bowel movement. These formulas should be used as needed, and discontinued when desired effects are achieved. Herbal formulas that contain *Da Huang* (Radix et Rhizoma Rhei) should be taken with meals, as it may irritate the stomach if taken on an empty stomach. Prolonged use of formula with *Da Huang* (Radix et Rhizoma Rhei) is not recommended, as it may increase the risk of habitual constipation and fluid and electrolyte imbalance.

Both drugs and herbs are equally effective in treating constipation. Both modalities of medicines should be used sparingly, and when needed, as prolonged use may cause side effects. Once a bowel movement is induced, herbal therapy may be initiated to change the fundamental constitution of the body in those with habitual constipation. Lastly, diet and lifestyle adjustments are also needed to ensure regular bowel movement.

References

1. Chan K, Lo AC, Yeung JH, Woo KS. Journal of Pharmacy and Pharmacology 1995 May;47(5):402-6.
2. Pharmacotherapy 1999 July;19(7):870-876.
3. European Journal of Drug Metabolism and Pharmacokinetics 1995; 20(1):55-60.
4. Lei X, et al. Liver Damage Associated with Polygonum multiflorum Thunb.: A Systematic Review of Case Reports and Case Series. Evid Based Complement Alternat Med. 2015;2015:459749. doi: 10.1155/2015/459749.
5. Liu Z, et al. Maillard reaction involved in the steaming process of the root of Polygonum multiflorum. Institution of Basic Theory, China Academy of Chinese Medical Sciences, Beijing, PR China. Planta Med. 2009 Jan;75(1):84-8. Epub 2008 Nov 25.
6. Liu Z, et al. In vitro antioxidant activities of maillard reaction products produced in the steaming process of Polygonum multiflorum root. Nat Prod Commun. 2011 Jan;6(1):55-8.
7. Liu Z, et al. Comparative analyses of chromatographic fingerprints of the roots of Polygonum multiflorum Thunb. and their processed products using RRLC/DAD/ESI-MS(n). Planta Med. 2011 Nov;77(16):1855-60. doi: 10.1055/s-0030-1271200.
8. *Zhong Xi Yi Jie He Za Zhi* (Journal of Integrated Chinese and Western Medicine), 1983; 1:19.
9. Yeung, HC. *Handbook of Chinese Herbs*. Institute of Chinese Medicine. 1996.
10. Bensky, D. et al. *Chinese Herbal Medicine Materia Medica*. Eastland Press. 1993.
11. Yang, ZH. et al. *Chinese Herbology*. Zhi Yin Publishing Company. 1990.
12. *Zhong Yao Tong Bao* (Journal of Chinese Herbology), 1988; 13(8):43.
13. *Zhong Yao Xue* (Chinese Herbology), 1998; 673:674.
14. *Zhong Guo Yi Yao Xue Bao* (Chinese Journal of Medicine and Herbology), 1991; 6(1):39.
15. *Tian Jin Zhong Yi* (Tianjin Chinese Medicine), 1996; (2):33.
16. *Zhong Yi Za Zhi* (Journal of Chinese Medicine), 1983; 8:79.
17. *Zhong Yao Lin Chuan Xin Yong* (New Clinical Applications of Chinese Medicine), 2001; 284.
18. *Xin Yi Yao Xue Za Zhi* (New Journal of Medicine and Herbology), 1973; 4:25.

Gentle Lax (Excess)™

CLINICAL APPLICATIONS

- **Constipation**
- **Excess-type constipation** with red tongue, yellow tongue coat, and red face
- **Food stagnation or indigestion** with abdominal distension and pain

WESTERN THERAPEUTIC ACTIONS

- Strong laxative effect which treats moderate to severe constipation
- Emollient effect which lubricates the bowels and promotes normal peristalsis of intestines
- Increases intestinal peristalsis and removes food stagnation

CHINESE THERAPEUTIC ACTIONS

- Relieves constipation
- Disperses lower abdominal distension and pain
- Purges accumulation of stagnant heat

DOSAGE

Take 3 to 4 capsules three times daily with warm water. To avoid stomach discomfort for individuals with sensitive gastrointestinal tract, take the herbs with meals, or decrease dosage and increase frequency of intake. The recommended starting dosage is 2 capsules four times daily.

INGREDIENTS

Bai Shao (Radix Paeoniae Alba)
Da Huang (Radix et Rhizoma Rhei)
Fan Xie Ye (Folium Sennae)
Hou Po (Cortex Magnoliae Officinalis)
Mang Xiao (Natrii Sulfas)
Tao Ren (Semen Persicae)
Zhi Shi (Fructus Aurantii Immaturus)

BACKGROUND

Constipation is the infrequent or incomplete passage of stools. The stools are usually dry and hard, and are difficult to pass even with straining. Individuals with constipation often have two or fewer bowel movements per week, and will usually have feelings of incomplete evacuation after bowel movement. Common causes of constipation include lack of exercise, insufficient intake of water and fiber, stress, overuse of laxatives, and use of certain drugs (opioids, antipsychotics, antidepressants, and anticholinergics).

FORMULA EXPLANATION

Gentle Lax (Excess) is an herbal formula designed to treat patients with excess-type constipation. Excess-type constipation is defined as acute and severe constipation, constipation in young adults, constipation with abdominal distension or pain, or constipation in patients with a red tongue, red face, and yellow tongue coat.

Da Huang (Radix et Rhizoma Rhei) is a strong purgative that clears heat and detoxifies. *Mang Xiao* (Natrii Sulfas) softens and facilitates the passage of stool. *Zhi Shi* (Fructus Aurantii Immaturus) and *Hou Po* (Cortex Magnoliae Officinalis) dissipate stagnation and reduce distension. *Bai Shao* (Radix Paeoniae Alba) nourishes blood and relieves abdominal or intestinal pain, which may be associated with constipation. *Fan Xie Ye* (Folium Sennae) and *Tao Ren* (Semen Persicae) are emollients used to lubricate the Large Intestine to facilitate the passage of stool.

CAUTIONS & CONTRAINDICATIONS

- This is a strong herbal formula that should be reserved for those with severe constipation. Stop taking the herbs when the desired effect is achieved. Use of ***Gentle Lax (Excess)*** at a large dosage or for a prolonged period of time is not recommended as it may cause diarrhea and dehydration.
- Patients with intestinal obstruction should be referred to a medical doctor for immediate help. Surgical intervention may be necessary in some cases.
- Patients with hemorrhoids should only take ***Gentle Lax (Excess)*** to relieve constipation. Should more bleeding occur, stop taking the formula immediately and switch to ***Notoginseng 9*** instead.
- A more serious etiology should be suspected if the constipation is accompanied by vomiting, blood in the stools, weight loss, or a distended, tympanitic abdomen.
- This formula is contraindicated during pregnancy and nursing.
- ***Gentle Lax (Excess)*** may be irritating to the intestinal mucosa. Patients should take this formula with caution by starting with a lower dosage or taking it with food.
- The following warning statement is required by the State of California: "This product contains *Da Huang* (Radix et Rhizoma Rhei) and *Fan Xie Ye* (Folium Sennae). Read and follow directions carefully. Do not use if you have or develop diarrhea, loose stools, or abdominal pain because *Da Huang* (Radix et Rhizoma Rhei) and *Fan Xie Ye* (Folium Sennae) may worsen these conditions and be harmful to your health. Consult your physician if you have frequent diarrhea or if you are pregnant, nursing, taking medication, or have a medical condition."

CLINICAL NOTES

- Use of herbs is very effective to prevent drug-induced constipation. There are two types of drugs that are most likely to cause constipation: opioids [i.e., Vicodin (hydrocodone/acetaminophen), Darvocet (propoxyphene/acetaminophen), Tylenol/Codeine (acetaminophen/codeine)] and antipsychotic drugs [i.e., Haldol (haloperidol), Thorazine (chlorpromazine)].

Pulse Diagnosis by Dr. Jimmy Wei-Yen Chang:

- Constipation due to constriction: *Yinqiao* pulse, a thin, straight, wiry pulse on or extends proximal to the left *chi*
- Constipation due to dryness in the Large Intestine and Stomach: floating and forceful on the right *cun* and *guan*

Gentle Lax (Excess)™

SUPPLEMENTARY FORMULAS

- For deficient types of constipation, use ***Gentle Lax (Deficient)***.
- To detox the colon, use ***GI DTX*** instead.
- For constipation due to stress, add ***Calm***.
- For gastrointestinal disorders such as acid reflux or ulcers, use ***GI Care*** instead.
- For irritable bowel syndrome (IBS), use ***GI Harmony*** instead.
- For ulcerative colitis, use ***GI Care (UC)*** instead.
- For hemorrhoids and pain, use ***GI Care (HMR)*** and ***Herbal ANG*** instead.
- For hemorrhoid bleeding, use ***GI Care (HMR)*** and ***Notoginseng 9*** instead.
- For hypertension, add ***Gastrodia Complex***.
- To help with detoxification, add ***Liver DTX***.
- For constipation due to neuro-degenerative disorders such as Alzheimer's disease, Parkinson's disease or stroke, use with ***Neuro Plus***.
- With excess fire, add ***Gardenia Complex***.
- For severe blood stagnation, add ***Circulation (SJ)***.
- For acne, add ***Dermatrol (Clear)***.

ACUPUNCTURE TREATMENT

Traditional Points:

- *Tianshu* (ST 25), *Shangjuxu* (ST 37)
- *Tianshu* (ST 25), *Dachangshu* (BL 25), *Zusanli* (ST 36), *Hegu* (LI 4), *Zhigou* (TH 6), *Taichong* (LR 3), *Xingjian* (LR 2)

Classic Master Tung's Points:

- **Constipation (general):** *Tushui* (T 22.11), *Qimen* (T 33.01), *Qijiao* (T 33.02), *Qizheng* (T 33.03), *Simashang* (T 88.18), *Simazhong* (T 88.17), *Simaxia* (T 88.19), *Tongtian* (T 88.03), *Fuchang* (T 77.12), *Huochuan* (T 33.04)

Master Tung's Points by Dr. Chuan-Min Wang:

- **Constipation:** *Qimen* (T 33.01), *Qijiao* (T 33.02), *Qizheng* (T 33.03), *Huochuan* (T 33.04) , *Dabai* (T 22.04)

Balance Method by Dr. Richard Tan:

- Left side: *Waiguan* (TH 5), *Zhigou* (TH 6), *Zhaohai* (KI 6), *Quchi* (LI 11)
- Right side: *Shangjuxu* (ST 37), *Tiaokou* (ST 38), *Kongzui* (LU 6) or *ah shi* points nearby, *Quze* (PC 3)
- Left and right sides can be alternated from treatment to treatment.

Ear Acupuncture:

- Large Intestine, Colon, Rectum, Sympathetic. Tape magnetic balls onto the points and switch ears every three days. If both ears are taped at the same time, rest one day in between the three-day treatments.
- Large Intestine, Rectum. Strong stimulation is necessary two or three times daily. Leave the needles in for one hour. Embed ear seeds in Spleen, Large Intestine and Rectum. Switch ear every week.

Auricular Medicine by Dr. Li-Chun Huang:

- Abdomen, Spleen, Lung, Liver, *San Jiao*, Large Intestine, Sigmoid, Digestive Subcortex

NUTRITION

- Eat plenty of foods with high fiber, such as fresh fruits, green leafy vegetables, cabbage, peas, sweet potatoes, and whole grains.
- Drink plenty of water, at least 8 glasses per day.
- A combination of honey with grapefruit will also relieve dry stool or constipation.
- Prunes or prune juice are very effective to regulate bowels and relieve mild cases of constipation.
- Long-term use of laxatives wipes out the normal flora of the intestines and leads to frequent constipation and/or secondary infections. Therefore, if purgatives are to be used for a prolonged period of time, acidophilus should also be used to replenish the "good" intestinal flora.
- Increase intake of nourishing, cooling foods/roots such as Mexican yam, yam, radishes, potatoes, carrots, melons, cucumbers, beets, turnips, malanga, celeriac, taro, and rutabaga.
- Avoid deep-fried foods. Follow a low-fat diet.
- Avoid fatty and spicy foods, which may irritate the mucous membranes of the intestines.
- Avoid spicy/pungent/aromatic vegetables such as pepper, garlic, onions, basil, rosemary, cumin, funnel, anise, leeks, chives, scallions, thyme, saffron, wormwood, mustard, chili pepper, and wasabi.

The Tao of Nutrition by Dr. Maoshing Ni and Cathy McNease:

- Recommendations: bananas, apples, walnuts, figs, spinach, peaches, pears, pine nuts, sesame seeds, mulberries, grapefruit, yams, honey, apricot kernel, milk, yogurt, alfalfa sprouts, beets, cabbage, bok-choy, cauliflower, and potato.
- Eat two bananas on an empty stomach, followed by a glass of water.
- Drink a glass of lukewarm water with 2 teaspoons of honey on an empty stomach.
- Drink blended beets and cabbage on an empty stomach.
- Eat 5 to 10 figs on an empty stomach, followed by a glass of water.
- Eat a fresh apple on an empty stomach daily.
- Drink mulberry juice.
- Eat lightly steamed asparagus and cabbage at night before retiring.
- Avoid spicy foods, fried foods, and meat.

LIFESTYLE INSTRUCTIONS

- Avoid stress, anxiety and tension whenever possible.
- Exercise regularly to increase peristalsis of the intestines. Walking is one of the best exercises as it massages the intestines to regulate the bowels.
- Do not suppress the urge to relieve the bowels. Suppressing the urge is one of the main causes of chronic constipation. Empty

Gentle Lax (Excess)™

the bowels whenever there is a desire, especially in the morning when the digestive system is most active.

- Massaging the abdomen along the directional flow of the large intestine (clock-wise) will also help.
- Patients with hemorrhoids should not lift anything heavy.

CASE STUDIES

- A 63-year-old retired male presented with lower abdominal pain, abdominal swelling, foul-smelling flatulence and constipation persistent for almost three days. His diet consisted of large amounts of chili. His tongue body appeared red with a thick, white, dry, tongue coating. His pulse was noted to be deep, "rolling," and wiry. Pain was elicited upon abdominal palpation. The practitioner diagnosed his condition as excess heat in the Large Intestine. Bowel movement was induced after three doses of ***Gentle Lax (Excess)***. The herbal treatment was continued for another week with smaller doses. The patient soon experienced a daily bowel movement activity. Submitted by T.G., Albuquerque, New Mexico.
- A 50-year-old female patient presented with bowel obstruction and constipation that had persisted for five or six days. On a scale of severity of 1 to 10, with one being minimal or no severity, the patient described her condition as 10+. The TCM diagnosis was qi deficiency with internal heat. In the beginning, she took four capsules of ***Gentle Lax (Excess)*** four times daily, and she had a bowel movement the next day. Dosage was then reduced to three capsules, three times daily until bowel functioning normalized. Submitted by M.C., Sarasota, Florida.

PHARMACOLOGICAL AND CLINICAL RESEARCH

Gentle Lax (Excess) is a potent formula that has laxative, purgative, and osmotic effects to treat constipation and intestinal obstruction.

Pharmacologically, many of these herbs have excellent laxative, purgative, and osmotic effects. *Da Huang* (Radix et Rhizoma Rhei) has direct laxative and purgative effects to quickly and powerfully treat constipation.[1] *Da Huang* (Radix et Rhizoma Rhei) works mainly on the transverse and descending colon as it inhibits the re-absorption of water and causes evacuation of the stools.[2,3] In addition, it increases peristalsis of the large intestine without interfering with absorption of nutrients in the small intestine.[4] *Mang Xiao* (Natrii Sulfas) is an osmotic agent and has a marked purgative effect. As an osmotic agent, it increases water content and pressure in the intestines, thus inducing peristalsis and bowel movement.[5] *Mang Xiao* (Natrii Sulfas) works best when it is taken with plenty of extra fluids. Together, *Da Huang* (Radix et Rhizoma Rhei) and *Mang Xiao* (Natrii Sulfas) have a synergistic effect to "push" and "pull," and have a powerful and reliable effect to treat all types of acute and/or severe constipation. In addition, *Fan Xie Ye* (Folium Sennae) and *Zhi Shi* (Fructus Aurantii Immaturus) are used in this formula as they have a stimulant effect on the large intestine to increase contraction and peristalsis.[6,7] Lastly, *Hou Po* (Cortex Magnoliae Officinalis) has an excitatory effect on the smooth muscles of the gastrointestinal tract. It promotes strong, forceful, and rhythmic peristalsis.

Clinically, the herbs in ***Gentle Lax (Excess)*** have been used successfully to treat constipation and intestinal obstruction. One study reported great success using *Da Huang* (Radix et Rhizoma Rhei) and *Mang Xiao* (Natrii Sulfas) to treat 72 patients with constipation from hospitalization.[8] Another study reported 95.6% rate of effectiveness using *Fan Xie Ye* (Folium Sennae) to treat 276 patients with post-surgical patients.[9] Furthermore, 60 patients with chronic habitual constipation were treated with great success using herbs such as *Bai Shao* (Radix Paeoniae Alba), *Gan Cao* (Radix et Rhizoma Glycyrrhizae), and others as needed.[10] Lastly, 44 patients with intestinal obstruction were treated with 97.7% rate of effectiveness using *Da Huang* (Radix et Rhizoma Rhei) and *Feng Mi* (Mel).[11]

In summary, ***Gentle Lax (Excess)*** is an excellent formula to treat acute and/or severe constipation in patients who are otherwise healthy.

COMPARATIVE ANALYSIS

Constipation is a very common problem that may be treated effectively using Western and traditional Chinese medicines. In Western medicine, bulking agents (bran, psyllium, and methylcellulose) are the gentlest and safest. These drugs are not habit forming, and may be used safely on a long-term basis. However, they act slowly and are not very strong. Laxatives (docusate and mineral oil) soften stool by increasing the implementation of intestinal water. However, these drugs must be used carefully, as they interfere with the absorption of nutrients and other drugs. Lastly, cathartics (senna, cascara, and bisacodyl) are used for severe cases of constipation by increasing intestinal peristalsis and intraluminal fluids. However, these drugs should only be used on a short-term basis, as prolonged use will cause "lazy bowel" syndrome and serious fluid and electrolyte imbalance.

Constipation is treated with great success in TCM. Those with mild to moderate constipation are usually treated with herbs that moisten the Intestines and regulate bowel movement. Those with moderate to severe constipation are generally treated with herbs that purge the intestines and induce bowel movement. These formulas should be used as needed, and discontinued when the desired effects have been achieved. Herbal formulas that contain *Da Huang* (Radix et Rhizoma Rhei) should be taken with meals, as it may irritate the stomach if taken on an empty stomach. Prolonged use of formulas with *Da Huang* (Radix et Rhizoma Rhei) are not recommended, as this may increase the risk of habitual constipation and fluid and electrolyte imbalance.

Both drugs and herbs are equally effective in treating constipation. Both modalities of medicines should be used sparingly, and when needed, as prolonged use may cause side

Gentle Lax (Excess)™

effects. Once a bowel movement is induced, herbal therapy may be initiated to change the fundamental constitution of the body in those with habitual constipation. Lastly, diet and lifestyle adjustments are also needed to ensure regular bowel movement.

References

1. *Zhong Xi Yi Jie He Za Zhi* (Journal of Integrated Chinese and Western Medicine), 1983; 1:19.
2. Yeung, HC. *Handbook of Chinese Herbs*. Institute of Chinese Medicine. 1996.
3. Bensky, D. et al. *Chinese Herbal Medicine Materia Medica*. Eastland Press. 1993.
4. Yang, ZH. et al. *Chinese Herbology*. Zhi Yin Publishing Company. 1990.
5. *Chang Yong Zhong Yao Xian Dai Yan Jiu Yu Lin Chuang* (Recent Study & Clinical Application of Common Traditional Chinese Medicine), 1995; 190:192.
6. *Ri Ben Yao Wu Xue Za Zhi* (Japan Journal of Pharmacology), 1963; (4):91.
7. *Zhong Guo Yi Yao Xue Bao* (Chinese Journal of Medicine and Herbology), 1991; 6(1):39.
8. *Zhong Xi Yi Jie He Za Zhi* (Journal of Integrated Chinese and Western Medicine), 1983; 1:19.
9. *Zhong Guo Xiang Cun Xin Xi* (Suburb Doctors of China), 1988; 1:35.
10. *Zhong Yi Za Zhi* (Journal of Chinese Medicine), 1983; 8:79.
11. *Zhong Yao Lin Chuan Xin Yong* (New Clinical Applications of Chinese Medicine), 2001; 30.

GI Care™

CLINICAL APPLICATIONS

- **Peptic ulcer disease (gastric ulcer and duodenal ulcer)**
- **Gastritis**
- **Acid reflux** with heartburn, foul breath, bitter taste in the mouth, indigestion
- **Generalized gastrointestinal (GI) disorders,** such as nausea, vomiting, indigestion, belching, bloating, epigastric fullness, and food sensitivities.

WESTERN THERAPEUTIC ACTIONS

- Antiulcer effect to decrease production and release of gastric acid
- Antacid effect to neutralize gastric acid
- Antibiotic effect against *Helicobacter pylori* (*H. pylori*)
- Analgesic effect to relieve pain
- Gastroprotective effect to restore normal digestion and gastrointestinal functions

CHINESE THERAPEUTIC ACTIONS

- Quells Stomach fire
- Spreads Liver qi stagnation and relieves pain
- Strengthens middle *jiao* to promote digestion

DOSAGE

Take 4 capsules three times daily on an empty stomach one to two hours before meals. For maximum effect, advise the patient to lie down for 10 minutes following ingestion of ***GI Care***.

INGREDIENTS

Bai Hua She She Cao (Herba Hedyotis)
Bai Shao (Radix Paeoniae Alba)
Chai Hu (Radix Bupleuri)
Di Yu (Radix Sanguisorbae)
Hai Piao Xiao (Endoconcha Sepiae)
Huang Lian (Rhizoma Coptidis)
Huang Qi (Radix Astragali)
Huang Qin (Radix Scutellariae)
Pu Gong Ying (Herba Taraxaci)
Sha Ren (Fructus Amomi)
Shen Qu (Massa Fermentata)
Wu Bei Zi (Galla Chinensis)
Wu Zhu Yu (Fructus Evodiae)
Xiang Fu (Rhizoma Cyperi)
Yan Hu Suo (Rhizoma Corydalis)
Zhe Bei Mu (Bulbus Fritillariae Thunbergii)

BACKGROUND

Gastrointestinal disorders, such as gastritis, gastric reflux, gastric ulcer and duodenal ulcer, are common disorders caused by many factors, such as infection (*H. pylori*), lifestyle (stress, cigarette smoking, alcohol), diet (spicy and pungent food), and drugs (NSAIDs). These factors damage mucosa and disrupt its defense and repair functions. As a result, various parts of the gastrointestinal tract may be affected, such as the esophagus (gastroesophageal reflux disease), stomach (gastritis, gastric ulcer) and duodenum (duodenal ulcer). Optimal treatment requires lifestyle changes, diet modifications, and medical intervention to treat the infection and repair mucosal damage.

FORMULA EXPLANATION

Gastrointestinal disorders are complex patterns of imbalance characterized by both excess and deficiency: excess refers to the Stomach heat (hyperacidity), and yin deficiency refers to the damaged mucosa of the digestive tract. This condition may be caused by external factors (infection, alcohol, smoking, drugs) or internal conditions (stress). Therefore, herbs are used in this formula to clear heat, regulate Liver qi circulation, strengthen the Stomach, and restore normal digestive functions.

Huang Lian (Rhizoma Coptidis) drains fire from the Stomach and the Liver. *Wu Zhu Yu* (Fructus Evodiae) directs the Stomach qi downward to treat vomiting, nausea and acid regurgitation. *Hai Piao Xiao* (Endoconcha Sepiae), *Bai Shao* (Radix Paeoniae Alba), and *Zhe Bei Mu* (Bulbus Fritillariae Thunbergii) are used to neutralize excessive stomach acid and ease heartburn. *Yan Hu Suo* (Rhizoma Corydalis) has antiulcer as well as strong analgesic effects similar to those of morphine and codeine. *Huang Qin* (Radix Scutellariae), *Bai Hua She She Cao* (Herba Hedyotis), and *Pu Gong Ying* (Herba Taraxaci) have an antibacterial effect that clears heat and eliminates toxins. *Huang Qin* (Radix Scutellariae) has also been shown through research to be effective against *H. pylori*, a bacteria known to cause gastritis, gastric ulcer, and duodenal ulcer. *Huang Qi* (Radix Astragali) tonifies the Spleen, augments the qi, and is essential in rebuilding the gastrointestinal system. *Sha Ren* (Fructus Amomi) promotes the movement of qi, strengthens the Stomach and helps with gastrointestinal symptoms such as abdominal distension, pain, nausea, and diarrhea. *Di Yu* (Radix Sanguisorbae) and *Wu Bei Zi* (Galla Chinensis) provide a coating for the stomach and are used to stop bleeding, generate flesh and expedite the recovery of peptic and duodenal ulcers. *Shen Qu* (Massa Fermentata) aids digestion and protects the stomach lining. *Chai Hu* (Radix Bupleuri) and *Xiang Fu* (Rhizoma Cyperi) spread the constrained Liver qi and relieve abdominal pain and distension.

CAUTIONS & CONTRAINDICATIONS

- ***GI Care*** should not be used to treat patients with atrophic gastritis with decreased or lack of secretion of stomach acid. ***GI Care*** contains herbs that neutralize and stop the secretion of stomach acid and may worsen the condition.
- Patients with cholecystitis and cholelithiasis are often misdiagnosed as having gastrointestinal problems. Correct diagnosis is critical in the overall success of the treatment.
- Allergy warning: *Shen Qu* (Massa Fermentata) used in this product contains wheat. Persons with allergy to wheat should not take this product.

GI Care™

CLINICAL NOTES

- When treating gastric or duodenal ulcers, it is imperative to rule out atrophic gastritis. Ulcers and atrophic gastritis share many similar signs and symptoms. The underlying etiologies, however, are completely different. Ulcers are caused by an excessive secretion of gastric acid and must be treated by neutralizing or reducing the acid secretion. Conversely, atrophic gastritis is caused by decreased (or lack of secretion) of gastric acid and must be treated by increasing the production of gastric acid. If untreated, atrophic gastric may lead to gastric carcinoma.
- Patients with ulcers induced by the use of non-steroidal anti-inflammatory drugs (NSAIDs) are often asymptomatic. These drugs cause peptic ulcers and gastrointestinal bleeding, but they mask these symptoms because they also have pain-relieving effects. Therefore, those who use these drugs on regular basis should be checked to rule out gastric or duodenal ulcers.

Pulse Diagnosis by Dr. Jimmy Wei-Yen Chang:

- **Acid reflux or heartburn:** half bump between the left *cun* and *guan* positions.
- **Gastroesophageal reflux disease (GERD)** due to damp-heat in the Stomach: deep, concave, and forceful pulse on the right *guan*.
- **Peptic ulcer** due to damp-heat in the Stomach with wood element overacting on earth element: deep, wiry, and forceful pulse on the right *guan*.

SUPPLEMENTARY FORMULAS

- For stress related Stomach problems, irritability, nervousness, and/or anxiety, add ***Calm*** or ***Calm (ES)***.
- With restlessness, stress, and insomnia with underlying deficiency, add ***Calm ZZZ***.
- For bleeding, add ***Notoginseng 9***.
- With severe pain, add ***Herbal ANG***.
- For gallbladder disorders such as cholecystitis or gallstones, combine with ***Dissolve (GS)***.
- For hepatic disorders such as hepatitis or liver cirrhosis, combine with ***Liver DTX***.
- For irritable bowel syndrome (IBS), use ***GI Harmony*** instead.
- For ulcerative colitis, use ***GI Care (UC)*** instead.
- To tonify the constitution of the body and nourish blood, combine with ***Schisandra ZZZ*** or ***Imperial Tonic***.
- For constipation, combine with ***Gentle Lax (Excess)*** or ***Gentle Lax (Deficient)***.
- For hemorrhoids, add ***GI Care (HMR)***.
- For nausea, vomiting and poor appetite due to chemotherapy, use ***C/R Support*** instead.
- For excess appetite, obesity, combine with ***Herbalite***.
- For excess fire, add ***Gardenia Complex***.
- With excessive damp/phlegm, add ***Pinellia Complex***.
- With bacterial infection in the digestive tract, add ***Herbal ABX***.
- With viral infection in the digestive tract, add ***Herbal AVR***.

ACUPUNCTURE TREATMENT

Traditional Points:

- *Xiangu* (ST 43), *Liangqiu* (ST 34), *Zhongwan* (CV 12), *Weishu* (BL 21), *Pishu* (BL 20), *Hegu* (LI 4), *Zusanli* (ST 36), *Shenque* (CV 8), *Neiguan* (PC 6), *Gongsun* (SP 4), *Qihai* (CV 6), *Quze* (PC 3), *Yanglingquan* (GB 34), *Zhaohai* (KI 6), *Dadu* (SP 2), *Shangwan* (CV 13), *Youmen* (KI 21), *Neiting* (ST 44), *Geshu* (BL 17), *Liangmen* (ST 21), *Sanyinjiao* (SP 6)

Classic Master Tung's Points:

- **Acid reflux:** *Tushui* (T 22.11), *Tianhuang* (T 88.13), *Tongguan* (T 88.01), *Tianhuangfu [Shenguan]* (T 77.18)
- **Duodenal ulcer:** *Linggu* (T 22.05), *Dabai* (T 22.04), *Tushui* (T 22.11), *Tongwei* (T 88.10), *Tongshen* (T 88.09), *Sihuashang* (T 77.08), *Shuitong* (T 1010.19), *Shuijin* (T 1010.20), *Xinmen* (T 33.12), *Changmen* (T 33.10), *Ganmen* (T 33.11). Bleed dark veins nearby the ST channel on the lower limb. Bleed before needling for best result.
- **Gastritis:** *Linggu* (T 22.05), *Tushui* (T 22.11), *Changmen* (T 33.10), *Menjin* (T 66.05), *Sihuashang* (T 77.08), *Sihuazhong* (T 77.09), *Sihuaxia* (T 77.11). Bleed *Sihuashang* (T 77.08) or nearby dark veins. Bleed before needling for best result.
- **Nausea:** *Tushui* (T 22.11), *Xinling* (T 33.17)*, *Sihuashang* (T 77.08), *Menjin* (T 66.05), *Linggu* (T 22.05), *Xinmen* (T 33.12), *Tianhuangfu [Shenguan]* (T 77.18)
- **Vomiting:** *Tushui* (T 22.11), *Xinling* (T 33.17)*, *Sihuashang* (T 77.08), *Menjin* (T 66.05), *Linggu* (T 22.05), *Xinmen* (T 33.12). Bleed near *Yamen* (GV 15). Bleed before needling for best result.
- **Bloating:** *Pizhong* (T 11.18), *Sihuashang* (T 77.08), *Sihuazhong* (T 77.09), *Sihuaxia* (T 77.11), *Fuchang* (T 77.12), *Menjin* (T 66.05), *Huoju* (T 66.11), *Changmen* (T 33.10), *Minghuang* (T 88.12), *Tianhuang* (T 88.13), *Qihuang* (T 88.14), *Beimian* (T 44.07), *Fukuai* (T 1010.15), *Shangjiuli* (T 88.26), *Zhongjiuli* (T 88.25), *Xiajiuli* (T 88.27), *Sifuyi* (T 1010.11), *Sifuer* (T 1010.10)

Master Tung's Points by Dr. Chuan-Min Wang:

- **Gastritis:** Bleed *Sihuashang* (T 77.08), *Sihuazhong* (T 77.09), *Sihuafu* (T 77.10), *Sihuaxia* (T 77.11), *Sihuali* (T 77.13), *Sihuawai* (T 77.14). Needle *Tushui* (T 22.11) or *Cesanli* (T 77.22) towards the ST channel.
- **Acid reflux:** *Tianhuang* (T 77.17), *Tianhuangfu [shenguan]* (T 77.18), *Tongshan* (T 88.02), *Tongtian* (T 88.03)
- **Duodenal ulcer:** *Menjin* (T 66.05), *Fuchang* (T 77.12)

Balance Method by Dr. Richard Tan:

- Left side: *Neiguan* (PC 6), *Lieque* (LU 7), *Zusanli* (ST 36), *Yanglingquan* (GB 34)
- Right side: *Zhigou* (TH 6), *Hegu* (LI 4), *Yinlingquan* (SP 9), *Ququan* (LR 8)
- Left and right sides can be alternated from treatment to treatment.

GI Care™

Ear Acupuncture:

- Stomach, Adrenal Gland, Prostate Gland, Duodenum. Use ear seeds.
- Nausea, vomiting: Stomach, Liver, Spleen, *Shenmen*. Needle once a day for three to five days. For severe cases, needle two or three times daily. These points can also be used for morning sickness during pregnancy. However, ear seeds with mild massage are recommended.

Auricular Medicine by Dr. Li-Chun Huang:

- **Gastritis:** Stomach, Spleen, Digestive Subcortex
  - For acute gastritis, add Sympathetic and bleed Ear Apex.
  - For superficial gastritis, add Sympathetic.
  - For atrophic gastritis, add Pancreas, Endocrine, Mouth (Sympathetic point is contraindicated).
  - For disharmony between the Liver and Stomach, add Stomach, Abdominal Distension Area, and *San Jiao*.
- **Gastric and duodenal ulcers:** Stomach, Spleen, Duodenum, Sympathetic, Digestive Subcortex
  - For disharmony between the Liver and Stomach, add Liver and *San Jiao*.
  - For Stomach yin deficiency, add Pancreas and Endocrine.
  - For gastric ulcer and duodenal ulcer due to abdominal pain, add Groove of Stomach and Intestine, and Duodenum Ball of Posterior. Bleed Ear Apex.
- **Reducing excessive gastric acid secretion:** Cardia, Sympathetic, Stomach, Duodenum, Gallbladder, Digestive Subcortex.
- **Invigorating the Spleen and promoting digestion:** Spleen, Stomach, Mouth, Pancreas, Endocrine, Digestive Subcortex, Small Intestine

NUTRITION

- Drinking a large amount of water often helps when the first sign of heartburn appears.
- Avoid fried, spicy or greasy foods, refined sugar, tea, coffee, caffeine, salt, chocolate, strong spices, and carbonated drinks. Stay away from sour and acidic food and fruits.
- Plan regular meals and chew slowly and thoroughly.
- Increase intake of nourishing, cooling foods/roots such as Mexican yam, yam, radishes, potatoes, carrots, melons, cucumbers, beets, turnips, malanga, celeriac, taro, and rutabaga.
- Increase the intake of papayas and pineapples as they contain bromelain, a digestive enzyme that helps with indigestion. Acidophilus is also helpful for digestion. Avoid lentils, peanuts and soybeans because they contain enzyme inhibitors.
- Avoid spicy/pungent/aromatic vegetables such as pepper, garlic, onions, basil, rosemary, cumin, funnel, anise, leeks, chives, scallions, thyme, saffron, wormwood, mustard, chili pepper, and wasabi.
- Avoid drinking alcohol and caffeine-containing beverages whenever possible. Alcohol and caffeine increase stomach acid and interfere with ulcer treatment.

The Tao of Nutrition by Dr. Maoshing Ni and Cathy McNease:

- **Peptic ulcers**
  - Recommendations: potatoes, honey, cabbage, ginger, figs, papayas, squid bone, peanut oil, kale, and persimmons. Drink fig juice.
  - Drink potato juice daily on an empty stomach for at least two weeks.
  - Drink warm kale juice or cabbage juice on an empty stomach to help heal the ulcer.
  - Take two teaspoons of peanut oil every morning on an empty stomach to help close the wound.
  - Take two tablespoons of steamed honey on an empty stomach in the mornings.
  - Cook ginger (an amount the size of the thumb) with rice and have for breakfast every morning on an empty stomach.
  - Dry and charcoal persimmon and grind into powder; take one tablespoon in a glass of warm water.
  - Avoid spicy foods, hot foods, stimulants, shellfish, coffee, smoking, alcohol, fried foods, and stress.

LIFESTYLE INSTRUCTIONS

- Avoid consumption of alcohol completely. Stop smoking cigarettes and avoid exposure to second-hand smoke whenever possible.
- Avoid stress as it may trigger stomach discomfort. Do not eat when angry, overly tired or stressed, and always chew food thoroughly.
- Non-steroidal anti-inflammatory drugs, such as aspirin, Motrin (ibuprofen) or Naprosyn (naproxen), should not be ingested as they are very damaging to the stomach.
- Use of antacids may suppress the symptoms of ulcer, but do not treat the cause. Do not rely on or use antacids excessively.
- Infection in the oral region, emotional disturbance, and diet may trigger gastritis and should be controlled.
- Keep the digestive tract warm at all times. Whenever possible, place a hot compress or a hot water bottle on the stomach.

CASE STUDIES

- A 50-year-old female presented with persistent proctitis, which she had had for two years. Her right and left pulse were superficial and wiry, and her left *cun* position was convex and forceful at both the middle and superficial positions. She was prescribed ***GI Care*** and ***Astringent Complex***, 50:50. After three 100 gram bottles of the mixed formula, her symptoms disappeared. It has been four months since she finished the herbs and her symptoms never returned, and her medical tests came back negative as well. Submitted by S.B., Berkeley, California.
- W.M, a 54-year-old female, presented with stomach aches and pains along with some IBS-type symptoms. The pain usually occurred shortly after eating, as either a dull or sharp sensation, more often with cold, sweet type foods. The patient's blood pressure was within normal range and heart beat was at 60

GI Care™

beats per minute. Patient had high stress and was given a TCM diagnosis of Stomach qi deficiency and cold, as well as Kidney yang deficiency, possibly leading to a developing ulcer. She was treated with ***GI Care*** at 4 capsules three times daily along with other dietary recommendations. After about a month, the patient only experienced occasional discomfort, usually from over-indulging. The patient continued on a smaller dose for another month. Submitted by M.E., Little Rock, Arizona.

- A 54-year-old female clerk presented with belching, esophageal reflux and acid regurgitation. Sleep was disturbed due to relentless nighttime cough with thick and sticky phlegm. At times, the patient would also experience vomiting. Her medical doctor prescribed Prilosec (omeprazole), but the patient preferred not to take pharmaceuticals if possible. The patient was given ***GI Care***, 4 capsules daily. Within two weeks, the patient was able to refrain from Prilosec (omeprazole) and continued with just ***GI Care***. Subsequently, the patient experienced no discomfort, slept well and has had no acid reflux. She was no longer expelling phlegm or mucus. Four months later, she was still taking ***GI Care*** and doing fine. The practitioner's intention was to slowly reduce her dosage and monitor her symptoms. Submitted by J.Y., Vancouver, Washington.
- T.T., a 48-year-old female, presented with symptoms consisting of bloating, burping, and other discomfort in the upper and lower quadrant area. Pulse was wiry and tongue was swollen with a dusky look. The practitioner diagnosed this condition as Liver qi stagnation with underlying Spleen and Kidney yang deficiencies; her Western diagnosis was GERD. For treatment, ***GI Care*** was prescribed. Being opposed to Western prescription drugs, the patient had been trying different remedies, but was interested in finding a natural remedy. She had tried OTC antacid, which had only helped a little bit. After taking ***GI Care***, the patient had noticed that it was more effective than the other medication she had been taking. Submitted by L.H., Chicago, Illinois.
- A.F., a 35-year-old female, presented with multiple symptoms consisting of poor appetite, fatigue, and weight loss. It was also noted that she had been experiencing diarrhea and rectal bleeding. Blood pressure was 108/59 mmHg and heart rate 60 beats per minute. Pulse was thin and thready; tongue had a geographic look, red color and no coating. The practitioner diagnosed this condition as Liver and Kidney yin deficiencies along with damp-heat in the lower *jiao*. Her Western diagnosis was Crohn's disease. For treatment, ***GI Care*** was prescribed. After one week of taking the herbs the diarrhea had improved; it became normal after five weeks. The patient also mentioned her fatigue had improved but she still got tired when stressed. Submitted by M.P., Muskego, Wisconsin.
- R.S., a 62-year-old female, presented with chronic heartburn, which had been occurring most of her adult life since she had been diagnosed with hepatitis C years ago. The TCM diagnosis was Liver qi stagnation with Stomach fire; Western diagnosis was acid reflux. ***GI Care*** was prescribed at three capsules three times per day. With a change of her diet and taking this formula, the patient noticed her heartburn was kept away 80% of the time. Submitted by J.L., San Diego, California.
- J.R., a 17-year-old female, presents with various gastrointestinal complaints including nausea, epigastric fullness with sensations of "pulling or tightness," abdominal pain that is "annoying and dull," intermittent abdominal pain, and alternating diarrhea and constipation. The TCM diagnosis was Liver qi stagnation with Stomach fire rising. The practitioner prescribed ***GI Care***. After one month of care, including three acupuncture treatments and steady herbal therapy, the patient reported improvement in the abdominal pain, to the point that it is now minimal, with increased periods of relief between exacerbations. Furthermore, the nausea resolved and bowel movements became normal. [Note: The practitioner commented that the patient improved although she was not totally compliant, and forgot to take the herbs once in a while.] Submitted by C.L., Chino Hills, California.
- A 45-year-old female presented with stomach sensitivity that worsened with stress. The Western diagnosis was acid reflux; the TCM diagnosis was Liver qi stagnation with heat. After beginning to take ***GI Care***, the patient reported it to be a gentle formula that helped her be free of stomach pain for two years. Due to financial reasons, the patient stopped coming in for acupuncture but remained on ***GI Care*** consistently. Submitted by M.C., Sarasota, Florida.

PHARMACOLOGICAL AND CLINICAL RESEARCH

GI Care is designed to treat gastrointestinal disorders, such as gastric ulcer, duodenal ulcer, gastritis, acid reflux, heartburn, nausea, vomiting, indigestion, belching, bloating, epigastric fullness, and food sensitivities. To address various causes and complications of these gastrointestinal disorders, ***GI Care*** incorporates herbs with multiple functions, including antiulcer, antacid, antibiotic, and gastroprotective activities.

While gastric acid is essential for digestion, an excessive amount will cause damages to various parts of the digestive tract, including the esophagus, stomach, and duodenum. Therefore, it is essential to use herbs to manage the production and release of gastric acid. *Huang Lian* (Rhizoma Coptidis) inhibits the secretion of gastric acid and is commonly used to treat peptic ulcers.[1] The mechanisms of actions include inhibiting the secretion of gastric acid, blunting the increase of malonyldialdehyde (MDA) and hydroxyl ion (OH), and decreasing nitric oxide level and superoxide dismutase activity from gastric mucus.[2] Clinically, *Huang Lian* (Rhizoma Coptidis) has a marked protective effect against gastric lesions and ulcerative formation induced by stress and alcohol consumption.[3] *Wu Zhu Yu* (Fructus Evodiae) and *Hai Piao Xiao* (Endoconcha Sepiae) also have significant antiulcer effects. Administration of *Wu Zhu Yu* (Fructus Evodiae) is associated with marked effectiveness in preventing and treating stomach ulcers by reducing gastric acid secretion.[4] *Hai Piao Xiao*

GI Care ™

(Endoconcha Sepiae) has a high content of calcium carbonate, and is an effective antacid to neutralize gastric acid.[5] Lastly, because an excessive amount of gastric acid will often damage the mucosa and cause pain, *Yan Hu Suo* (Rhizoma Corydalis) is added for its strong analgesic effect to relieve pain.[6]

Since *H. pylori* infection is a common cause of many gastrointestinal disorders, ***GI Care*** is formulated with many herbs with antibiotic effects, such as *Huang Lian* (Rhizoma Coptidis), *Huang Qin* (Radix Scutellariae) and *Bai Hua She She Cao* (Herba Hedyotis).[7,8,9] Pharmacologically, *Huang Lian* (Rhizoma Coptidis) has a marked effect to protect and treat gastric lesion induced by *H. pylori* lipopolysaccharide. *Huang Lian* (Rhizoma Coptidis) has been shown to inhibit epithelial cell apoptosis and suppress gastric mucosal inflammation.[10] Clinically, *H. pylori* infection was treated with a 75.9% rate of effectiveness using an herbal formula that contained *Huang Qin* (Radix Scutellariae), *Bai Hua She She Cao* (Herba Hedyotis), and others.[11]

To strengthen the digestive tract and restore its functions, *Shen Qu* (Massa Fermentata) and *Wu Zhu Yu* (Fructus Evodiae) are used in this formula. *Shen Qu* (Massa Fermentata) contains many different enzymes to facilitate digestion of starches and carbohydrates.[12] *Wu Zhu Yu* (Fructus Evodiae) has a significant gastroprotective effect. It protects the stomach against gastric lesions by strengthening the gastric mucosal lining and promoting the nitric oxide synthesis in local gastric mucosa.[13] In addition, use of *Wu Zhu Yu* (Fructus Evodiae) and *Huang Lian* (Rhizoma Coptidis) has been shown to have marked protective effect against aspirin-induced damages to the stomach mucus membrane.[14]

Lastly, severe cases of gastric or duodenal ulcers are sometimes complicated with hemorrhage. Therefore, a small amount of *Di Yu* (Radix Sanguisorbae) and *Wu Bei Zi* (Galla Chinensis) are added to this formula for their hemostatic effect to stop bleeding.[15] According to one study, *Di Yu* (Radix Sanguisorbae) and *Huang Lian* (Rhizoma Coptidis) have been used in one herbal formula to effectively treat 117 patients with acute bleeding from the gastrointestinal tract.[16] According to another study, use of *Wu Bei Zi* (Galla Chinensis) for one week successfully stopped bleeding in 29 out of 33 (91%) patients.[17]

In summary, herbs in ***GI Care*** have demonstrated significant pharmacological effects to treat various gastrointestinal disorders, including but not limited to peptic ulcer disease,[18,19] gastritis,[20,21] *H. pylori* infection,[22] gastrointestinal bleeding,[23] and others.[24]

COMPARATIVE ANALYSIS

Gastrointestinal conditions, such as gastric or duodenal ulcers, stress ulcers, gastritis and heartburn, are extremely common complaints in developed countries. As a result, many new drugs have been developed in recent years to treat these conditions. Antacids (such as Maalox and Mylanta) neutralize stomach acid and have a quick onset of action but only a short duration. Histamine-2 antagonists [such as Zantac (ranitidine) and Tagamet (cimetidine)] have a potent effect and medium duration of action and are well tolerated in most cases. However, they inhibit liver metabolism, and may cause drug-drug and drug-herb interactions and must be monitored carefully. Proton-pump inhibitors [such as Prilosec (omeprazole) and Protonix (pantoprazole)] have potent and irreversible effects to inhibit production of stomach acid. Unfortunately, prolonged use may cause atrophic gastritis, and in laboratory studies, stomach cancer in animal subjects. In brief, though these drugs are effective to reduce stomach acid and treat several gastrointestinal conditions, they must be prescribed and monitored carefully.

These gastrointestinal disorders may be treated effectively with herbs. According to numerous clinical studies, herbs neutralize stomach acid, decrease production and secretion of stomach acid, relieve pain, kill *H. pylori*, and in severe cases of bleeding ulcers, stop bleeding. Furthermore, herbs are also effective to treat drug- and stress-induced gastrointestinal disorders, two of the main causes. In short, by targeting both symptoms and causes, herbs achieve short- and long-term success to treat many gastrointestinal disorders. However, herbs do have their limitations. In cases of severe peptic ulcers, herbs are not as potent as, and do not last as long as, proton-pump inhibitors. Furthermore, acute cases of profuse gastrointestinal bleeding are medical emergencies, and require immediate medical intervention. Use of herbs is not recommended in these two scenarios.

References

1. *Zhong Yao Xue* (Chinese Herbology), 1988, 140:144.
2. Li B, Liu HR, Pan YQ, Jiang QS, Shang JC, Wan XH, He BC, Yang JQ, Zhou QX. Protective effects of total alkaloids from rhizoma Coptis chinensis on alcohol-induced gastric lesion in rats. Chongqing University of Medical Sciences, China. Zhongguo Zhong Yao Za Zhi. 2006 Jan;31(1):51-4.
3. Li B, Shang JC, Zhou QX. Study of total alkaloids from Rhizoma Coptis Chinensis on experimental gastric ulcers. Department of Pharmacology, Chongqing University of Medical Sciences, Chongqing 400016, China. Chin J Integr Med. 2005 Sep;11(3):217-21.
4. *Zhong Yao Yao Li Du Li Yu Lin Chuang* (Pharmacology, Toxicology and Clinical Applications of Chinese Herbs), 1988; 4(3):9.
5. *Zhong Yao Xue* (Chinese Herbology), 1998; 903:904.
6. Huang JY, Fang M, Li YJ, Ma YQ, Cai XH. Analgesic effect of Corydalis yanhusuo in a rat model of trigeminal neuropathic pain. Department of Stomatology, Zhujiang Hospital, Southern Medical University, Guangzhou 510282, China. Nan Fang Yi Ke Da Xue Xue Bao. 2010 Sep;30(9):2161-4.
7. *Zhong Yao Xue* (Chinese Herbology), 1998; 204:205.
8. Zhang S, Zhang B, Xing K, Zhang X, Tian X, Dai W. Inhibitory effects of golden thread (Coptis chinensis) and berberine on Microcystis aeruginosa. Fisheries College, Ocean University of China, Qingdao 266003, P. R. China. Water Sci Technol. 2010;61(3):763-9.
9. *Zhong Yao Xue* (Chinese Herbology), 1988; 137:140.
10. Lu JS, Liu YQ, Li M, Li BS, Xu Y. Protective effects and its mechanisms of total alkaloids from rhizoma Coptis chinensis on Helicobacter pylori LPS induced gastric lesion in rats. Dongzhimen Hospital Affiliated to Beijing University of Chinese Medicine, Beijing 100700, China. Zhongguo Zhong Yao Za Zhi. 2007 Jul;32(13):1333-6.

FORMULAS

GI Care ™

11. *Jiang Su Zhong Yi Za Zhi* (Jiangsu Journal of Chinese Medicine), 1997; 18(4):14.
12. *Zhong Yao Xue* (Chinese Herbology), 1998; 436:437.
13. Yu X, Wu DZ. Protective effects of Evodia rutaecarpa water extract on ethanol-induced rat gastric lesions. Institute of Chinese Materia Medica, Shanghai University of Traditional Chinese Medicine, Shanghai 201203, China. Zhongguo Zhong Yao Za Zhi. 2006 Nov;31(21):1801-3.
14. *Zhong Yao Yao Li Yu Lin Chuang* (Pharmacology and Clinical Applications of Chinese Herbs) 1993;9(4):9.
15. *Zhong Yao Yao Li Yu Ying Yong* (Pharmacology and Applications of Chinese Herbs), 1983; 406.
16. *Zhong Yao Lin Chuan Xin Yong* (New Clinical Applications of Chinese Medicine), 2001; 246.
17. *Zhe Jiang Zhong Yi Xue Yuan Xue Bao* (Journal of Zhejiang University of Chinese Medicine), 1987; 6:20.
18. *Si Chuan Zhong Yi* (Sichuan Chinese Medicine), 1987; (1):29.
19. *Hu Nan Yi Yao Za Zhi* (Hunan Journal of Medicine and Herbology), 1977; 2:35.
20. *Shan Xi Zhong Yi* (Shanxi Chinese Medicine) 1997;4:14.
21. *Hu Nan Zhong Yi Za Zhi* (Hunan Journal of Chinese Medicine), 1992; (2):33.
22. *Jiang Su Zhong Yi Za Zhi* (Jiangsu Journal of Chinese Medicine), 1997; 18(4):14.
23. *Hei Long Jiang Zhong Yi Yao* (Heilongjiang Chinese Medicine and Herbology), 1993; (1):34.
24. *Zhong Cao Yao Fang Ji De Ying Yong* (Applications of Chinese Herbal Formulas), 1976; 101.

GI Care II™

CLINICAL APPLICATIONS

- **GI infection and inflammation:** traveler's diarrhea, gastroenteritis, enteritis, dysentery, food poisoning and other gastrointestinal disorders with diarrhea, foul-smelling stools with burning sensations of the anus, abdominal discomfort, pain, borborygmus, possibly nausea, vomiting and a feeling of incomplete defecation
- **GI disorders with damp-heat**
- **All excess types of diarrhea characterized by heat and dampness**
- **Monosodium glutamate (MSG) poisoning**

WESTERN THERAPEUTIC ACTIONS

- Treats diarrhea, dysentery, enteritis, stomach flu, and other gastrointestinal disorders
- Antibiotic effect to treat acute diarrhea due to bacterial or viral infection
- Antitoxic effect to treat acute diarrhea due to drug or food poisoning
- Gastroprotective benefit to treat acute diarrhea with mucus or blood present in the stools
- Alleviates the signs and symptoms of acute diarrhea, such as nausea, vomiting, abdominal pain, intestinal cramps and spasms, and fever

CHINESE THERAPEUTIC ACTIONS

- Dispels damp-heat in the Intestines
- Binds the Intestines and stops diarrhea
- Promotes digestion and relieves pain

DOSAGE

Take 3 to 4 capsules three times daily on an empty stomach, with warm water. Dosage may be increased to 6 to 8 capsules three times daily, if necessary. Herbs should be taken for at least seven days in cases of acute infection to completely expel the pathogens.

INGREDIENTS

Bai Shao (Radix Paeoniae Alba)
Bai Zhi (Radix Angelicae Dahuricae)
Bai Zhu (Rhizoma Atractylodis Macrocephalae)
Chen Pi (Pericarpium Citri Reticulatae)
Chuan Mu Xiang (Radix Vladimiriae)
Chun Pi (Cortex Ailanthi)
Da Huang (Radix et Rhizoma Rhei)
Da Zao (Fructus Jujubae)
Dang Gui (Radix Angelicae Sinensis)
Fu Ling (Poria)
Gan Cao (Radix et Rhizoma Glycyrrhizae)
Ge Gen (Radix Puerariae Lobatae)
Guang Huo Xiang (Herba Pogostemonis)
Hou Po (Cortex Magnoliae Officinalis)
Huang Lian (Rhizoma Coptidis)
Huang Qin (Radix Scutellariae)
Jie Geng (Radix Platycodonis)
Qing Pi (Pericarpium Citri Reticulatae Viride)
Rou Gui (Cortex Cinnamomi)
Shen Qu (Massa Fermentata)
Sheng Jiang (Rhizoma Zingiberis Recens)
Wu Bei Zi (Galla Chinensis)
Zhi Qiao (Fructus Aurantii)
Zi Su Ye (Folium Perillae)

BACKGROUND

Gastrointestinal disorders, such as traveler's diarrhea, dysentery, gastroenteritis, and enteritis, are generally caused by invasion of foreign substances or micro-organisms that cause inflammation of the lining of the stomach, small intestine and large intestine. Common causes of these gastrointestinal disorders include infection (bacteria, virus, or parasites), plant toxins (mushrooms), chemical toxins (heavy metals, MSG), and drugs (antibiotics, antihelminthics, cytotoxic agents, colchicine, digoxin, NSAIDs). Clinical manifestations include nausea, vomiting, abdominal pain and discomfort, diarrhea with foul-smelling stools with burning sensations of the anus, and in some cases, presence of blood, mucus, WBC or RBC in the stools. Depending on the cause, proper treatment may include fluid replacement, antidiarrheals and antibiotics.

FORMULA EXPLANATION

GI Care II is formulated specifically to treat diarrhea, dysentery, enteritis, and other intestinal disorders. According to traditional Chinese medicine, such conditions are often characterized by damp-heat in the Intestines, leading to such symptoms as pain, nausea, vomiting, abdominal pain, fever, urgency, tenesmus, burning sensation of the anus after defecation, and diarrhea with or without the presence of mucus or blood. Therefore, this formula uses herbs to dispel damp-heat in the Intestines, promote digestion, relieve pain, and bind the Intestines to stop diarrhea.

Ge Gen (Radix Puerariae Lobatae) raises the yang qi of the Spleen to stop diarrhea. It generates fluids to replenish the loss of water due to diarrhea. With its ability to relieve the exterior, it also works for patients with intestinal flu or traveler's diarrhea. *Ge Gen* (Radix Puerariae Lobatae) works synergistically with *Bai Shao* (Radix Paeoniae Alba) and *Gan Cao* (Radix et Rhizoma Glycyrrhizae) to relieve abdominal and intestinal pain, spasms and tenesmus associated with diarrhea or dysentery.

Huang Qin (Radix Scutellariae) and *Huang Lian* (Rhizoma Coptidis) clear damp-heat in the Intestines to relieve burning sensations, feelings of incomplete defecation and frequent urges to defecate. This pair of herbs also relieves pain by reducing inflammation and infection. *Rou Gui* (Cortex Cinnamomi) and *Dang Gui* (Radix Angelicae Sinensis) are used to moderate the heat-clearing effect to prevent damages to the Spleen and Stomach.

GI Care II™

Chun Pi (Cortex Ailanthi) and *Wu Bei Zi* (Galla Chinensis) are astringents used symptomatically to bind the Intestines for relief of diarrhea. *Chun Pi* (Cortex Ailanthi) and *Wu Bei Zi* (Galla Chinensis), sticky by nature, patches ulcerations to repair the intestinal walls.

Chuan Mu Xiang (Radix Vladimiriae), *Hou Po* (Cortex Magnoliae Officinalis), *Chen Pi* (Pericarpium Citri Reticulatae), *Qing Pi* (Pericarpium Citri Reticulatae Viride), and *Zhi Qiao* (Fructus Aurantii) promote the movement of qi and help eliminate stagnation, turbidity, bloating and gas in the Intestines. *Da Huang* (Radix et Rhizoma Rhei), *Chuan Mu Xiang* (Radix Vladimiriae) and *Hou Po* (Cortex Magnoliae Officinalis) dispel turbidity and remove the bacteria causing the infection or inflammation. With their descending and purgative functions, they prevent the retention of pathogenic factors in the Intestines. A small amount of *Da Huang* (Radix et Rhizoma Rhei) is used in this formula to completely purge damp-heat.

Jie Geng (Radix Platycodonis) raises the qi of both the Lung and Large Intestine, two organs connected by their *zang fu* relationship. It is commonly used to treat diarrhea and tenesmus, due to its function of lifting the sunken qi. *Bai Zhi* (Radix Angelicae Dahuricae) dispels pus and has an ascending effect to help *Jie Geng* (Radix Platycodonis) lift the sunken qi to treat diarrhea and tenesmus.

Chen Pi (Pericarpium Citri Reticulatae), *Sheng Jiang* (Rhizoma Zingiberis Recens), *Da Zao* (Fructus Jujubae), and *Shen Qu* (Massa Fermentata) harmonize the middle *jiao* to relieve nausea and vomiting. *Guang Huo Xiang* (Herba Pogostemonis) and *Zi Su Ye* (Folium Perillae) are both fragrant and wake the Spleen. They are used to harmonize the middle *jiao*, dispel dampness, and relieve vomiting and nausea. Finally, *Fu Ling* (Poria) and *Bai Zhu* (Rhizoma Atractylodis Macrocephalae) strengthen the Spleen to relieve diarrhea.

In conclusion, ***GI Care II*** is a great formula to treat damp-heat affecting the gastrointestinal tract with infection and inflammation.

CAUTIONS & CONTRAINDICATIONS

- This formula is contraindicated for patients who have diarrhea caused by deficiency and cold, Spleen qi deficiency, or Spleen and Kidney yang deficiencies.
- This formula is contraindicated for patients who are pregnant or nursing.
- Allergy warning: *Shen Qu* (Massa Fermentata) used in this product contains wheat. Persons with allergy to wheat should not take this product.
- This herbal formula contains herbs that invigorate blood circulation, such as *Dang Gui* (Radix Angelicae Sinensis). Therefore, patients who are on anticoagulant or antiplatelet therapies, such as Coumadin (warfarin), should use this formula with caution, or not at all, as there may be a higher risk of bleeding and bruising.[1,2,3]
- The following warning statement is required by the State of California: "This product contains *Da Huang* (Radix et Rhizoma Rhei). Read and follow directions carefully. Do not use if you have or develop diarrhea, loose stools, or abdominal pain because *Da Huang* (Radix et Rhizoma Rhei) may worsen these conditions and be harmful to your health. Consult your physician if you have frequent diarrhea or if you are pregnant, nursing, taking medication, or have a medical condition."

CLINICAL NOTES

- Diarrhea is a symptom, not a disease. Therefore, if it persists after taking this formula for one to two weeks, have a stool sample examined microscopically for cells, mucus, fat, blood, infectious organisms and other substances to determine the exact cause.
- Patients taking ***GI Care II*** for colitis or traveler's diarrhea should continue taking the formula for an additional two to three days after all the symptoms have subsided. This is to ensure that all the pathogenic factors are cleared out from the Intestines in order to prevent development of chronic colitis in the future. To strengthen the Spleen afterwards, ***GI Tonic*** should be administered for three to five days.
- ***GI Care II*** is a great formula to have while traveling to prevent or treat traveler's diarrhea and other gastrointestinal infections.
- ***GI Care II*** incorporates numerous antibiotic herbs for two important reasons. First, the use of multiple herbs within an herbal formula has been shown to increase the antibiotic effect more than tenfold. Second, isolated use of single ingredients is often ineffective and increases the risk of development of bacterial and viral resistance.[4] Given these two reasons, it is necessary to combine herbs with appropriate properties to ensure effectiveness in treating the infection and minimizing the potential risk of the micro-organisms developing resistance and/or mutation.
- There are two formulas that can be used to treat inflammation of the bowel.
  - ***GI Care II*** is designed more for an active infection and inflammation of the intestines due to improper food intake. Because bacteria lodged in the intestines need to be purged out, purgative herbs such as *Da Huang* (Radix et Rhizoma Rhei) are used.
  - ***GI Care (UC)*** is designed more for patients suffering from chronic ulcerative colitis and Crohn's disease without the active infection. Therefore, it contains many herbs that would generate new tissue and repair the normal flora of the intestines.

Pulse Diagnosis by Dr. Jimmy Wei-Yen Chang:

- **Traveler's diarrhea, enteritis, colitis, or gas:** rainbow pulse, a convex-shaped pulse that is thick, forceful, and expanding on and extends distally to the left *cun*
- **Inflammation of the digestive system:** floating and forceful pulse on the right and left *guan*

GI Care II™

SUPPLEMENTARY FORMULAS

- For bacterial infection of the gastrointestinal tract, combine with ***Herbal ABX***.
- For viral infections of the gastrointestinal tract, add ***Herbal AVR***.
- With more inflammation, add ***Astringent Complex***.
- Fistula or diverticulitis, or pain with pus-filled pockets of infection or abscess, fever or inflammation, use with ***Resolve (AI)*** and ***Astringent Complex***.
- For irritable bowel syndrome (IBS) with bloating and gas, use with ***GI Harmony***.
- With stress, add ***Calm*** or ***Calm (ES)***.
- For irritable bowel syndrome with constipation, use ***GI Harmony*** and ***Gentle Lax (Deficient)*** instead.
- For intestinal and abdominal cramping and pain, use with ***Flex (SC)***.
- In monosodium glutamate (MSG) poisoning, combine with ***Herbal DTX***.
- For ulcerative colitis, add ***GI Care (UC)***.
- For hemorrhoids, add ***GI Care (HMR)***.
- For excess heat, add ***Gardenia Complex***.
- For dryness and thirst, add ***Nourish (Fluids)***.
- For bleeding, add ***Notoginseng 9***.

ACUPUNCTURE TREATMENT

Traditional Points:

- *Shangjuxu* (ST 37), *Tianshu* (ST 25), *Zusanli* (ST 36), *Shangwan* (CV 13), *Guanyuan* (CV 4)
- Needle *Tianshu* (ST 25), *Shangjuxu* (ST 37), and *Xiajuxu* (ST 39). Bleed veins next to *Zusanli* (ST 36)

Classic Master Tung's Points:

- **Gastroenteritis (acute):** *Huozhi* (T 88.15), *Qihuang* (T 88.14), *Zusanli* (ST 36), *Ganmen* (T 33.11), *Changmen* (T 33.10), *Fuchang* (T 77.12) , *Zhiwujin* (T 11.08), *Zuqianjin* (T 77.24), *Zuwujin* (T 77.25), *Sihuashang* (T 77.08), *Sihuazhong* (T 77.09), *Jinyingshang* (T 88.33)* and *Jinyingxia* (T 88.34)*. Bleed the LU area on the lower limb.
- **Gastroenteritis (chronic):** *Piyi* (T 88.35)*, *Pier* (T 88.36)*, *Pisan* (T 88.37)*, *Cesanli* (T 77.22), *Menjin* (T 66.05), *Linggu* (T 22.05), *Changmen* (T 33.10), *Zhiwujin* (T 11.08). Bleed the dark veins nearby the ST channel on the lower limb.
- **Bloating:** *Pizhong* (T 11.18), *Sihuashang* (T 77.08), *Sihuazhong* (T 77.09), *Sihuaxia* (T 77.11), *Fuchang* (T 77.12), *Menjin* (T 66.05), *Huoju* (T 66.11), *Changmen* (T 33.10), *Minghuang* (T 88.12), *Tianhuang* (T 88.13), *Qihuang* (T 88.14), *Beimian* (T 44.07), *Fukuai* (T 1010.15), *Shangjiuli* (T 88.26), *Zhongjiuli* (T 88.25), *Xiajiuli* (T 88.27), *Sifuyi* (T 1010.11), *Sifuer* (T 1010.10)

Master Tung's Points by Dr. Chuan-Min Wang:

- **Traveler's diarrhea:** *Changmen* (T 33.10), *Menjin* (T 66.05)

Balance Method by Dr. Richard Tan:

- Left side: *Liangqiu* (ST 34), *Zusanli* (ST 36), *Shangjuxu* (ST 37), *Tiaokou* (ST 38), *Ximen* (PC 4), *Neiguan* (PC 6) or *ah shi* points nearby, and Large Intestine on the left ear.
- Right side: *Taibai* (SP 3), *Gongsun* (SP 4), *Xuehai* (SP 10), *Hegu* (LI 4), *Quchi* (LI 11), *Shousanli* (LI 10) or *ah shi* points nearby, and Small Intestine on the right ear.
- Left and right sides can be alternated from treatment to treatment.

Ear Acupuncture:

- Stomach, Small Intestine, Large Intestine, Spleen. Use ear seeds.
- Stomach, Large Intestine, lower part of the Rectum, Spleen. Use three needles on different parts of the Large Intestine. Large Intestine and Stomach are the main points. Strength of stimulation should be determined by the patient's constitution and tolerance. Both needles and seeds can be used. Strong stimulation is necessary if ear seeds are selected. If diarrhea is severe, points should be massaged every two to four hours. After symptoms subside, needle every other day or twice a week. Ten days equals one treatment course.

Auricular Medicine by Dr. Li-Chun Huang:

- **Acute gastroenteritis:** Spleen, Stomach, Sympathetic, Rectum, Large Intestine, Small Intestine, Sigmoid, Digestive Subcortex. Bleed Ear Aplex.
  - Abdominal spasm: add *Shenmen*, Occiput
  - Bearing down sensation in the abdomen: add Abdominal Distension and Lower *Jiao*

NUTRITION

- Patients with diarrhea should keep taking in plenty of pure water and appropriate foods to prevent dehydration and malnutrition.
- During the recovery phase of diarrhea, eat foods that are easy to digest early in the meal, such as soup, porridge, and cooked fruits and vegetables.
- Avoid foods that may trigger diarrhea or are hard to digest, such as sorbitol, dairy products, spicy food, alcohol, and caffeine.
- Avoid eating raw, cold or unsanitary food and beverages.
- Use a separate chopping board to prepare raw foods and fruits to prevent contamination with other foods.
- Do not eat foods with refined sugar during the recovery phase, especially if the diarrhea is caused by bacterial infection.
- Incorporate probiotics into the diet. Different strands of probiotics should be taken while on herbs. At least double or triple the normal recommended dosage.

The Tao of Nutrition by Dr. Maoshing Ni and Cathy McNease:

- **Diarrhea**
  - Recommendations: garlic, black pepper, blueberries, cinnamon, raspberry leaves, lotus seeds, burned rice, yams, sweet potatoes,

GI Care II™

fresh fig leaves, peas, buckwheat, litchi, guava peel, apple, charcoaled bread, ginger, pearl barley, basil, and unripe prunes.

- Cook rice porridge with lotus seed and yam or with barley.
- Cook rice porridge with ginger and black pepper.
- Eat burnt rice or bread.
- Take two tablespoons dried apples, three times daily on an empty stomach with warm water.
- Drink black tea.
- Take two bulbs of garlic, bake until black. Then boil in water and drink the tea.
- Make tea from dried litchi and Chinese black dates.
- Make tea from guava peel.
- Make tea from ginger, fennel, basil, and Chinese black dates.
- Make tea from unripe prunes.
- Eat sweet rice porridge.
- Avoid cold, raw foods, most fruits, juices, and overeating.

LIFESTYLE INSTRUCTIONS

- Remind patients of the importance of washing their hands prior to eating.
- Patients with intestinal disturbance due to stress should engage in regular exercise, adequate rest, and normal sleep patterns. Practicing meditation exercises at least twice daily will also be beneficial. Get away from the daily routine to do something enjoyable to relieve stress whenever possible.
- Relax, rest and drink plenty of water until the condition clears up.

CASE STUDIES

- M.K., a 52-year-old female, presented with traveler's diarrhea as well as hyperactive bowel sounds. Blood work results were monocytes at level 18, whereas normal would be less than 7; neutrophils 66 (40-60%), lymphocytes 18 (25-40%). This concluded that with the imbalance ratio of neutrophils high and lymphocytes low she was experiencing a bacterial infection. Monocytes at high levels usually signify a parasitic problem. The TCM diagnosis was damp-heat in the Intestines. The patient was prescribed ***GI Care II*** at four capsules three times daily on an empty stomach with a glass of water. After taking the herbs for five days the dosage was modified to three capsules three times daily to finish the bottle. The patient has no longer been experiencing intestinal problems. Submitted by N.H., Chatsworth, California.
- T.P., a 6-year-old female, presented with profuse diarrhea, cramping, and fever for four days. She had been on a trip to Mexico and was recommended to bring a bottle of ***GI Care II*** with her just in case. The practitioner diagnosed this condition as damp-heat in the Intestines. For treatment of the infection, she took 2 capsules three times per day. After the second day of taking the herbs, the fever had subsided and her stools and cramping improved. She continued taking it for the remainder of the trip. Submitted by N.V., Muir Beach, California.
- A 35-year-old male with a history of digestive problems presented with severe abdominal pain, nausea, and vomiting after eating sushi during dinner. This condition was immediately diagnosed as food poisoning due to damp-heat in the Intestines. ***GI Care II*** was prescribed at 4 grams three times daily until the symptoms resolve. One hour after taking the first dose, the patient felt much better with decreased abdominal pain. After the second dose, all symptoms were completely resolved. Submitted by J.C., Diamond Bar, California.

PHARMACOLOGICAL AND CLINICAL RESEARCH

GI Care II treats gastrointestinal disorders, such as traveler's diarrhea, dysentery, gastroenteritis and enteritis with clinical manifestations of nausea, vomiting, abdominal pain, fever, and diarrhea with or without mucus or blood. According to Western medicine, the most common causes of these acute gastrointestinal disorders are infection (bacteria, virus, or parasites), chemical toxins (heavy metals, MSG), and drugs (antibiotics, antihelminthics, cytotoxic agents, colchicine, digoxin, NSAIDs).[5] The purpose of this formula is to simultaneously address both the causes and symptoms of diarrhea, for immediate relief and recovery.

GI Care II contains herbs with excellent effects to treat the causes and the symptoms of various gastrointestinal disorders. *Huang Lian* (Rhizoma Coptidis), individually or in an herbal formula, exhibits excellent clinical results in treating over 1,000 patients with bacterial dysentery. The treatments are associated with marked effectiveness with low incidence of side effects.[6,7] Diarrhea can be addressed with many herbs, such as *Fu Ling* (Poria) and *Bai Zhu* (Rhizoma Atractylodis Macrocephalae). In a clinical study, 93 infants with diarrhea were treated with *Fu Ling* (Poria) three times daily. Complete recovery was documented in 79 cases, improvement in 8 cases, and no effect in 6 cases.[8] In another study, 320 infants with diarrhea responded well to treatment with 3 to 4 grams of an herbal powder that contained *Bai Zhu* (Rhizoma Atractylodis Macrocephalae) and other herbs.[9]

Infection is one of the most common causes of gastrointestinal disorders. Therefore, ***GI Care II*** uses many herbs with marked antibiotic properties to eradicate the offending micro-organisms. Herbs with antibiotic effects include *Bai Shao* (Radix Paeoniae Alba), *Huang Qin* (Radix Scutellariae), *Huang Lian* (Rhizoma Coptidis), *Hou Po* (Cortex Magnoliae Officinalis), and *Fu Ling* (Poria).[10,11,12,13,14,15,16] Of these herbs, *Huang Qin* (Radix Scutellariae) and *Huang Lian* (Rhizoma Coptidis) are the most potent and have the widest spectrum of antibiotic properties. In fact, their effectiveness is comparable to antibiotics such as ampicillin, amoxicillin, methicillin and cefotaxime.[17]

Another common reason for gastrointestinal disorders is drug or food poisoning. Ideally, the offending agent should be eliminated to remove the cause of the diarrhea. However,

GI Care II ™

if discontinuation of the implicated drug is not possible, or if the poisonous food has already been absorbed, herbs should be used to remove the buildup of drugs and/or minimize toxicity. *Gan Cao* (Radix et Rhizoma Glycyrrhizae) is one of the best herbs to treat poisoning from toxic agents, including, but not limited to, drug poisoning (chloral hydrate, urethane, cocaine, picrotoxin, caffeine, pilocarpine, nicotine, barbiturates, mercury and lead), food poisoning (tetrodotoxin, snake, and mushrooms), and others (enterotoxin, herbicides, pesticides). The exact mechanism of this action is unclear, but it is thought to be related to the regulatory effect of *Gan Cao* (Radix et Rhizoma Glycyrrhizae) on the endocrine and/or hepatic systems.[18,19,20]

In addition to eliminating the causes of gastrointestinal disorders, it is also necessary to prescribe herbs to alleviate the symptoms. Use of *Sheng Jiang* (Rhizoma Zingiberis Recens) has been demonstrated by many studies to be one of the safest and most effective ways to relieve nausea and vomiting.[21] Abdominal pain may be relieved with herbs that have analgesic and antispasmodic effects. *Gan Cao* (Radix et Rhizoma Glycyrrhizae) relieves pain; additional herbs that relieve spasms and cramps of the intestines include *Ge Gen* (Radix Puerariae Lobatae), *Bai Shao* (Radix Paeoniae Alba), and *Bai Zhi* (Radix Angelicae Dahuricae).[22,23,24,25] According to one clinical trial, these herbs are so effective that 241 out of 254 patients (94.8%) with intestinal spasms showed significant improvement within 3 to 6 days of beginning herbal treatment.[26] To reduce fever and inflammation associated with acute diarrhea, *Ge Gen* (Radix Puerariae Lobatae), *Bai Shao* (Radix Paeoniae Alba), *Huang Qin* (Radix Scutellariae), and *Zi Su Ye* (Folium Perillae) are added for their antipyretic and anti-inflammatory effects.[27,28,29,30]

Diarrhea is sometimes accompanied by mucus or blood in the stool, which can be treated with *Da Huang* (Radix et Rhizoma Rhei) and *Wu Bei Zi* (Galla Chinensis). *Da Huang* (Radix et Rhizoma Rhei), if processed appropriately, has strong properties for treatment of hemorrhagic necrotic enteritis. In this disease syndrome, most patients who take *Da Huang* (Radix et Rhizoma Rhei) report lessened pain and diminished levels of blood in the stool within two to six doses.[31] Similarly, according to one clinical study on gastrointestinal bleeding, the use of *Wu Bei Zi* (Galla Chinensis) was over 90% effective in stopping bleeding in 33 patients within nine days.[32]

In conclusion, ***GI Care II*** is a great formula to treat the cause and relieve the symptoms of gastrointestinal disorders such as traveler's diarrhea, dysentery, gastroenteritis, and enteritis.

COMPARATIVE ANALYSIS

Gastrointestinal disorders, such as food poisoning, traveler's diarrhea, dysentery, gastroenteritis, and enteritis, are generally caused by ingestion of a foreign substance that causes symptoms such as nausea, vomiting, diarrhea with foul-smelling stools with burning sensations of the anus, and abdominal pain and discomfort. In Western medicine, these conditions are often treated symptomatically. For example, diarrhea is usually treated with antidiarrheal drugs, such as Lomotil (diphenoxylate) and Imodium (loperamide). Nausea and vomiting are treated with injection of antiemetics, such as Thorazine (chlorpromazine). Lastly, for gastrointestinal infections, antibiotics are used to kill the microorganism. Overall, these gastrointestinal disorders are acute problems that require immediate and aggressive treatments. While drugs are effective to treat the symptoms and the cause, they are likely to consume and weaken the body, therefore requiring a prolonged period of time for complete recovery.

From traditional Chinese medicine perspectives, these gastrointestinal disorders are considered to be damp-heat in the Intestines. The herbs that treat damp-heat are effective to address both the symptoms and the cause. As described above, these herbs have been shown to have an antiemetic effect to treat nausea and vomiting, an antidiarrheal effect to stop diarrhea, an analgesic effect to relieve pain, a muscle-relaxant effect to alleviate spasms and cramps, and an antibiotic effect to kill the pathogens. In addition to having marked therapeutic effects, these herbs are gentle and are well tolerated by those individuals who are already under a tremendous amount of stress. In short, herbal treatment offer immediate relieve, and facilitate long-term recovery from these gastrointestinal disorders.

Drugs and herbs are both effective to treat gastrointestinal disorders by addressing both symptoms and cause. In addition to these treatments, it is extremely important to make sure patients receive plenty of rest and fluids, as excessive vomiting and diarrhea may lead to dehydration. Fluids can be replenished orally in most cases, or intravenously in severe cases. Furthermore, because these gastrointestinal disorders are consuming and depleting in nature, it is important to use herbs to strengthen the body and supplement deficiencies once the patients begin the recovery process.

References

1. Chan K, Lo AC, Yeung JH, Woo KS. Journal of Pharmacy and Pharmacology 1995 May;47(5):402-6.
2. Pharmacotherapy 1999 July;19(7):870-876.
3. European Journal of Drug Metabolism and Pharmacokinetics 1995; 20(1): 55-60.
4. *Zhong Yao Xue* (Chinese Herbology), 1988; 140:144.
5. Fauci, A. et al. *Harrison's Principles of Internal Medicine, 14th Edition*. McGraw-Hill Health Professions Division. 1998.
6. *Zhong Hua Nei Ke Za Zhi* (Chinese Journal of Internal Medicine), 1976; 4: 219.
7. *Si Chuan Yi Xue Yuan Xue Bao* (Journal of Sichuan School of Medicine), 1959; 1: 102.
8. *Bei Jing Zhong Yi* (Beijing Chinese Medicine), 1985; 3:31.
9. *Shan Dong Zhong Yi Za Zhi* (Shandong Journal of Chinese Medicine), 1982; 2:107.
10. *Xin Zhong Yi* (New Chinese Medicine), 1989; 21(3):51.
11. *Zhong Yao Xue* (Chinese Herbology), 1988; 137:140.
12. *Zhong Yao Xue* (Chinese Herbology), 1988, 140:144.
13. *Planta med*, 1982; 44(2):100.
14. *Yao Jian Gong Zuo Tong Xun* (Journal of Herbal Preparations), 1980; 10(4):209.

GI Care II™

15. *Xin Hua Ben Cao Gang Mu* (New Chinese Materia Medica), 1988; 58.
16. *Zhong Yao Da Ci Dian* (Dictionary of Chinese Herbs), 1977; 1596.
17. *J Pharm Pharmacol* 2000 Mar; 52(3):361-6.
18. *Zhong Yao Tong Bao* (Journal of Chinese Herbology), 1986; 11(10):55.
19. *Xin Zhong Yi* (New Chinese Medicine), 1985; 2:34.
20. *Xin Zhong Yi* (New Chinese Medicine), 1978; 1:36.
21. *Xin Zhong Yi* (New Chinese Medicine), 1986; 12:24.
22. *Zhong Yao Xue* (Chinese Herbology), 1998; 101:103.
23. *Zhong Yao Zhi* (Chinese Herbology Journal), 1993; 358.
24. *Zhong Yao Yao Li Yu Ying Yong* (Pharmacology and Applications of Chinese Herbs), 1983; 796.
25. *Zhi Wu Yao You Xiao Cheng Fen Shou Ce* (Manual of Plant Medicinals and Their Active Constituents), 1986; 624,603,197.
26. *Zhong Hua Wai Ke Za Zhi* (Chinese Journal of External Medicine), 1960; 4:354.
27. *Zhong Yao Xue* (Chinese Herbology), 1998; 101:103.
28. *Zhong Yao Zhi* (Chinese Herbology Journal), 1993:183.
29. *Zhong Hua Yi Xue Za Zhi* (Chinese Journal of Medicine), 1956; 42(10):964.
30. *Planta Med*, 1985; (6):4.
31. *Fu Jian Zhong Yi Yao* (Fujian Chinese Medicine and Herbology), 1985; 1:36.
32. *Zhe Jiang Zhong Yi Xue Yuan Xue Bao* (Journal of Zhejiang University of Chinese Medicine), 1987; 6:20.

GI Care (HMR)™

CLINICAL APPLICATIONS

- **Hemorrhoids:** internal or external, with or without swelling, inflammation or bleeding

WESTERN THERAPEUTIC ACTIONS

- Anti-inflammatory effect to reduce the swelling and inflammation of hemorrhoid tissues
- Hemostatic effect to stop rectal bleeding
- Mild laxative effect to relieve constipation

CHINESE THERAPEUTIC ACTIONS

- Clears damp-heat and eliminates toxic-heat from the Intestines
- Stops bleeding
- Regulates bowel movements

DOSAGE

Take 4 capsules three times daily on an empty stomach with warm water.

INGREDIENTS

Chun Pi (Cortex Ailanthi)
Dang Gui (Radix Angelicae Sinensis)
Di Yu Tan (Radix Sanguisorbae Carbonisatum)
He Zi (Fructus Chebulae)
Huai Hua Tan (Flos Sophorae Carbonisatum)
Huang Qin (Radix Scutellariae)
Jin Yin Hua (Flos Lonicerae Japonicae)
Lian Qiao (Fructus Forsythiae)
Pu Gong Ying (Herba Taraxaci)
Wu Bei Zi (Galla Chinensis)
Xian He Cao (Herba Agrimoniae)
Yu Li Ren (Semen Pruni)

BACKGROUND

Hemorrhoids are painful, swollen veins in the lower portion of the rectum or anus. Hemorrhoids are usually asymptomatic, but may also cause pain while sitting, itching, and bleeding. Hemorrhoids can be caused by straining during bowel movements, constipation, sitting for long periods of time, and certain diseases, such as liver cirrhosis.

FORMULA EXPLANATION

GI Care (HMR) is designed as a first-line therapy to treat various presentations of hemorrhoids, including internal and external hemorrhoids, and with or without swelling, inflammation and bleeding. In traditional Chinese medicine, hemorrhoids are generally considered as a condition characterized by damp-heat and toxic-heat attacking the Intestines, leading to signs and symptoms such as enlarged and protruding tissues in the rectum, constipation, and rectal bleeding.

In this formula, *Jin Yin Hua* (Flos Lonicerae Japonicae), *Lian Qiao* (Fructus Forsythiae), *Pu Gong Ying* (Herba Taraxaci), and *Huang Qin* (Radix Scutellariae) clear damp-heat and eliminate toxic-heat from the Intestines. *Huai Hua Tan* (Flos Sophorae Carbonisatum), *Di Yu Tan* (Radix Sanguisorbae Carbonisatum), *Chun Pi* (Cortex Ailanthi) and *Xian He Cao* (Herba Agrimoniae) clear heat, cool the blood, and stop rectal bleeding. *Dang Gui* (Radix Angelicae Sinensis) tonifies blood and replenishes blood lost through rectal bleeding. It also moves blood to treat the blood clots around the anus that are associated with the hemorrhoidal condition. *Yu Li Ren* (Semen Pruni) moistens the Intestines and relieves constipation. *He Zi* (Fructus Chebulae) and *Wu Bei Zi* (Galla Chinensis) have an astringent effect to reduce inflammation of swollen hemorrhoid tissues.

Overall, ***GI Care (HMR)*** is an excellent formula that treats various presentations of hemorrhoids, including internal or external hemorrhoids, with or without swelling, inflammation or bleeding.

CAUTIONS & CONTRAINDICATIONS

- This formula is contraindicated during pregnancy.
- Individuals with bleeding hemorrhoids should ***not*** take drugs with anticoagulant or antiplatelet effects, such as aspirin, Motrin/Advil (ibuprofen) and Aleve (naproxen). These drugs may cause more bleeding.
- This herbal formula contains herbs that invigorate blood circulation, such as *Dang Gui* (Radix Angelicae Sinensis). Therefore, patients who are on anticoagulant or antiplatelet therapies, such as Coumadin (warfarin), should use this formula with caution, or not at all, as there may be a higher risk of bleeding and bruising.[1,2,3]

CLINICAL NOTES

Pulse Diagnosis by Dr. Jimmy Wei-Yen Chang:

- *Yinqiao* pulse is a thin, straight, wiry pulse that extends proximally to the *chi* positions. It is one of the eight extra meridian pulses.

SUPPLEMENTARY FORMULAS

- With mild to moderate constipation, add ***Gentle Lax (Deficient)***.
- With moderate to severe constipation, add ***Gentle Lax (Excess)***.
- With severe and profuse bleeding, combine with ***Notoginseng 9***.
- For hemorrhoids in individuals with extreme weakness and deficiency, use with ***Imperial Tonic***.
- With blood deficiency, add ***Schisandra ZZZ***.
- With ulcerative colitis, add ***GI Care (UC)***.
- With irritable bowel syndrome, add ***GI Harmony***.
- With severe inflammation, combine with ***Astringent Complex***.

ACUPUNCTURE TREATMENT

Traditional Points:

- *Changqiang* (GV 1), *Chengshan* (BL 57), *Sanyinjiao* (SP 6), *Kunlun* (BL 60), *Huiyang* (BL 35), *Erbai*, *Taichong* (LR 3), *Ciliao* (BL 32), *Fuliu* (KI 7), *Yaoyangguan* (GV 3), *Weizhong* (BL 40), *Qihai* (CV 6), *Dachangshu* (BL 25), *Shangqiu* (SP 5)

FORMULAS

GI Care (HMR)™

Classic Master Tung's Points:

- *Qimen* (T 33.01), *Qijiao* (T 33.02), *Qizheng* (T 33.03), *Waisanguan* (T 77.27), *Yizhong* (T 77.05), *Erzhong* (T 77.06), *Sanzhong* (T 77.07), *Kongzui* (LU 6), *Huofu* (T 88.41)*, *Huoliang* (T 88.42)*, and *Huochang* (T 88.43)*. Bleed dark veins on the back of the knees. Bleed dark veins on the KI channel of the lower limb. Bleed before needling for best result.

Master Tung's Points by Dr. Chuan-Min Wang:

- **Hemorrhoids:** Bleed the popliteal fossa. Needle *Qimen* (T 33.01), *Qijiao* (T 33.02), *Qizheng* (T 33.03) toward the TH channel.

Balance Method by Dr. Richard Tan:

- Left side: *Houxi* (SI 3), *Xiaohai* (SI 8), *Taichong* (LR 3), *Ququan* (LR 8)
- Right side: *Shaohai* (HT 3), *Shenmen* (HT 7), *Yanglingquan* (GB 34), *Zulinqi* (GB 41)
- Place 12 needles around the umbilicus at 0.5 to 1 *cun* deep.
- Left and right sides can be alternated from treatment to treatment.

Ear Acupuncture:

- Large Intestine, Rectum, Spleen, Adrenals, Subcortex

Auricular Medicine by Dr. Li-Chun Huang:

- Anus, Rectum, Spleen, Large Intestine, Diaphragm, Pituitary, Adrenal Gland. Bleed Ear Apex and Anus area.

NUTRITION

- It is very beneficial to eat foods that are high in fiber to ensure regular bowel movements, such as wheat bran, fresh fruits, and nearly all vegetables. A diet high in fiber is one of the most important factors for the prevention and treatment of hemorrhoids.
- It is important to make sure the diet contains an adequate amount of vitamins and minerals, as many of them are essential for blood clotting and coagulation. Vitamins and minerals that are especially important are vitamin B complex, vitamin C, vitamin K, and calcium.
- Advise the patient to increase water intake.
- A folk remedy that may be helpful in treating hemorrhoids involves eating one fresh cucumber (not peeled with ends removed) each morning and evening.
- Another folk remedy states to eat two to three pieces of banana (the riper the better) with wild honey daily. Treatment course is 30 to 50 days.
- Foods that should be avoided include fats, animal products, coffee, alcohol, pepper, mustard, and things that are spicy or pungent. These foods are generally harder to digest, and are more likely to irritate the digestive system. Alcohol consumption may worsen the pain and cause further bleeding.
- Warm and hot natured foods that damage qi and yin should be avoided, such as:
  - certain fruits like mango and durian that produce heat.
  - stimulants like coffee, alcohol, and energy drinks.
  - spicy/pungent/aromatic vegetables such as pepper, garlic, onions, basil, rosemary, cumin, funnel, anise, leeks, chives, scallions, thyme, saffron, wormwood, mustard, chili pepper, and wasabi.
- Avoid food and drinks with artificial coloring.
- Consume as few meat products as possible. Do not eat processed meats, such as lunch meats, hot dogs and sausages, as they contain nitrites that are associated with inflammation and chronic disease.

The Tao of Nutrition by Dr. Maoshing Ni and Cathy McNease:

- **Hemorrhoids**
  - Recommendations: sea cucumber, black fungus, water chestnut, buckwheat, tangerines, figs, plums, fish, prunes, guavas, bamboo shoots, mung beans, winter melon, black sesame seeds, persimmons, bananas, squash, cucumbers, taro, tofu, and cooling foods.
  - Avoid stimulating foods, spicy foods, alcohol, smoking, constipation, stress, lack of exercise, and standing or sitting too long.

LIFESTYLE INSTRUCTIONS

- It is important to maintain normal and soft bowel movements on a regular basis, as straining during bowel movement will often worsen hemorrhoids. Empty the bowels as soon as the urge to defecate occurs to avoid unnecessary straining. Bowel movements should take no more than three to five minutes. Refrain from reading on the toilet.
- Avoid excessive wiping after a bowel movement. Avoid using rough toilet paper, since it may cause more irritation and bleeding. Use soft and moist toilet paper or baby wipes.
- Regular walking helps to stimulate peristalsis and promote normal bowel movements.
- Soak in a sitz bath with hot water for 20 minutes each night to focus blood circulation in the area of the anus. This helps clear the blue, ballooned veins. It also helps disperse the blood clots that cause the firm, tender mass in the anal area.
- Prolonged sitting or standing is not recommended as it may aggravate the condition. Rest face down on a bed whenever possible in times of flare-ups.
- Sit on soft cushions or surfaces whenever possible. Avoid sitting on hard surfaces, which increases pressure upon the hemorrhoidal blood vessels and tissues. Also, when it is necessary to sit for a long period of time, always try to leave the seat for five minutes each hour or shift the buttocks often from side to side to help relieve the constant rectal pressure.
- Patients should learn to exhale and not hold their breath when straining or lifting heavy objects.

GI Care (HMR)™

CASE STUDIES

- B.R., a 38-year-old female, complained of an acute hemorrhoid after a short bout of constipation. Blood pressure was 116/78 mmHg with a heart rate of 62 beats per minute. Even when her normal bowel movements were present, the hemorrhoid remained along with itching and constant discomfort. Her first hemorrhoid occurred after giving birth to her baby two years prior to this treatment. The TCM diagnosis was damp-heat. Patient was given ***GI Care (HMR)*** at 3 grams twice a day. After one dose the hemorrhoid receded completely and all discomfort, itching, and swelling was resolved. Patient took one more dose twelve hours later to solidify the effect. Her hemorrhoid did not return. Submitted by E.R., Kula, Hawaii.
- A.R., a 53-year-old male, presented with constipation and hemorrhoids. His pulse was slippery and wiry and his tongue was scalloped with a dry center. The patient had recently had surgery for his shoulder and as a result he had spent a considerable amount of time sitting. Excess sitting coupled with his long term Spleen qi deficiency lead to hemorrhoids. The practitioner diagnosed this condition as Spleen qi deficiency with dampness and slight heat. After taking ***GI Care (HMR)*** for one week, the patient resumed normal bowel movement and no longer suffered from hemorrhoids. Submitted by L.H., Chicago, Illinois.
- A 65-year-old woman has a seven to eight year history of constipation and occasional rectal bleeding. In the last 10 days, the passing of stools has become increasingly more difficult, with severe pain and straining, and accompanied by rectal bleeding of bright red blood. The tongue coat was yellow and greasy, and the pulse was wiry and fine. The patient was diagnosed with damp-heat and toxic-heat in the Intestines, with stagnation of qi and blood. After taking ***GI Care (HMR)*** for seven days, the patient reported complete recovery with normal bowel movement, absence of bleeding, and resolution of hemorrhoids. Submitted Anonymously.
- A.R., a 50-year-male, presented with hemorrhoids due to a lifestyle consisting of sitting constantly and rarely taking part in any exercise. He has had long term Spleen qi deficiency with poor dietary habits and bowel movements only two to three times per week. Pulse was thin and wiry and his tongue showed a thick sticky yellow coating. The practitioner diagnosed this condition as Spleen qi deficiency with damp-heat obstruction in the lower *jiao*. After two weeks of taking ***GI Care (HMR)***, the hemorrhoid had greatly reduced in size, discomfort, and itching; however, very little effect on his bowel movements was noted. Submitted by L.H., Chicago, Illinois.
- B.K., an 85-year-old female, presented with hemorrhoids including the symptoms of itching and distending pain. Pulse was irregular and her tongue had a thick, turbid coating. The practitioner diagnosed this condition as Kidney qi deficiency with damp-heat accumulation in the lower *jiao*. For treatment, the patient was prescribed ***GI Care (HMR)***, and received acupuncture and dietary recommendations as well. After taking the herbs for two days, the patient reported relief of distending pain, and itching was reduced but not eliminated. Submitted by L.H., Chicago, Illinois.

PHARMACOLOGICAL AND CLINICAL RESEARCH

GI Care (HMR) is a formula developed specifically to treat hemorrhoids. It contains many herbs with a marked anti-inflammatory effect to reduce the swelling and inflammation of hemorrhoidal tissues, a hemostatic effect to stop rectal bleeding, and a mild laxative effect to relieve constipation.

Di Yu (Radix Sanguisorbae), *Huang Qin* (Radix Scutellariae), *Jin Yin Hua* (Flos Lonicerae Japonicae) and *Lian Qiao* (Fructus Forsythiae) are four herbs in this formula that have an anti-inflammatory effect to reduce the swelling and inflammation of hemorrhoidal tissues.[4,5,6] The mechanism of this action has been attributed in part to the decreased permeability of the blood vessels and subsequent reduction of swelling and inflammation.[7] Specifically, the extract of *Di Yu* (Radix Sanguisorbae) has a significant effect to suppress the production of nitric oxide and prostaglandin from lipopolysaccharide-activated cells and peritoneal macrophages in a dose-dependent manner.[8] *Huang Qin* (Radix Scutellariae) exerts significant and potent anti-inflammatory properties via inhibition of nitric oxide, cyclo-oxygenase-2, prostaglandin E2, and proinflammatory cytokines.[9] *He Zi* (Fructus Chebulae) has potent activity to inhibit both cyclo-oxygenase and 5-lipoxygenase, the key enzymes involved in inflammation and carcinogenesis.[10] Clinically, use of herbs has shown excellent success to treat hemorrhoids. In one study, 400 patients with hemorrhoids were treated with an herbal decoction once daily with good success. The study reported that 61% showed significant improvement, 31% showed moderate improvement and 8% experienced no improvement. The formula contained *Huai Hua* (Flos Sophorae), *Dang Gui* (Radix Angelicae Sinensis), *Huang Qin* (Radix Scutellariae), and others.[11] In another study, hemorrhoids were treated with an 84.3% rate of effectiveness using a formula that contained *Wu Bei Zi* (Galla Chinensis), *Di Yu* (Radix Sanguisorbae), and others.[12]

In addition to reducing inflammation, ***GI Care (HMR)*** uses herbs to relieve pain associated with hemorrhoids. *Lian Qiao* (Fructus Forsythiae) and *Dang Gui* (Radix Angelicae Sinensis) both have analgesic and anti-inflammatory effects. In fact, the anti-inflammatory effect of *Dang Gui* (Radix Angelicae Sinensis) is approximately 1.1 times stronger than acetylsalicylic acid, and its analgesic effect is approximately 1.7 times stronger than acetylsalicylic acid.[13,14]

Bleeding is a typical symptom that occurs after a bowel movement, producing blood-streaked stools or blood on the toilet paper. Therefore, ***GI Care (HMR)*** contains several herbs with marked hemostatic function to stop bleeding, such as *Huai Hua* (Flos Sophorae), *Di Yu* (Radix Sanguisorbae), *Chun Pi* (Cortex Ailanthi), and *Xian He Cao* (Herba Agrimoniae). Specifically, *Huai Hua* (Flos Sophorae) and *Di Yu* (Radix Sanguisorbae)

FORMULAS

GI Care (HMR)™

have a marked hemostatic effect to stop bleeding, and have been shown to reduce time of bleeding by as much as 31.9 to 45.5% when ingested orally.[15,16] For clinical applications, use of *Di Yu* (Radix Sanguisorbae) and *Xian He Cao* (Herba Agrimoniae) has been shown to effectively treat gastrointestinal bleeding.[17,18] *Chun Pi* (Cortex Ailanthi), *Di Yu* (Radix Sanguisorbae), *Huai Hua* (Flos Sophorae) and *Xian He Cao* (Herba Agrimoniae) have an excellent effect to stop bleeding among patients with hematochezia due to various causes.[19,20,21,22,23]

Furthermore, individuals with hemorrhoids often have constipation, and straining during a bowel movement will often make hemorrhoids worse. Therefore, ***GI Care (HMR)*** includes two herbs to lubricate the intestines and restore normal bowel movement. *Dang Gui* (Radix Angelicae Sinensis) and *Yu Li Ren* (Semen Pruni) both have mild to moderate laxative effects to increase intestinal peristalsis and promote bowel movement.[24] Lastly, *Lian Qiao* (Fructus Forsythiae) has antipruritic activity and is helpful to relieve itching associated with hemorrhoids.[25]

In summary, ***GI Care (HMR)*** is an excellent formula to treat hemorrhoids as it contains herbs that address both the causes and the complications of hemorrhoids.

COMPARATIVE ANALYSIS

In Western medicine, hemorrhoids are generally not treated except with use of over-the-counter (OTC) stool softeners and soothing agents. These methods offer only temporary and symptomatic relief. In more severe cases, invasive treatments may be performed, such as injection sclerotherapy, rubber-band ligation, laser destruction, infrared photocoagulation, and surgical hemorrhoidectomy. In other words, there are few options between mild OTC drugs that offer only temporary and symptomatic relief, and serious invasive treatments that completely eradicate body tissues.

Herbs offer effective treatment options for various presentations of hemorrhoids, including internal and/or external hemorrhoids, with or without swelling, inflammation or bleeding, and in both acute and chronic conditions. As described above, herbs have been shown to have a mild laxative effect to relieve constipation, an anti-inflammatory effect to reduce the swelling and inflammation of hemorrhoid tissues, and a hemostatic effect to stop rectal bleeding. Therefore, not only are the herbs beneficial, they provide additional treatment options not available in Western medicine.

The therapeutic benefits of herbs should be explored for the treatment of hemorrhoids, as they offer great relief with few or no side effects. When necessary, and only in the most severe cases of hemorrhoids that do not respond to any other therapies, should the patient consider invasive treatment options.

References

1. Chan K, Lo AC, Yeung JH, Woo KS. Journal of Pharmacy and Pharmacology 1995 May;47(5):402-6.
2. Pharmacotherapy 1999 July;19(7):870-876.
3. European Journal of Drug Metabolism and Pharmacokinetics 1995; 20(1): 55-60.
4. *Shan Xi Yi Kan* (Shanxi Journal of Medicine), 1960; (10):22.
5. *Ke Yan Tong Xun* (Journal of Science and Research), 1982; (3):35.
6. *Chem Pharm Bull*, 1984; 32(7):2724.
7. *Ke Yan Tong Xun* (Journal of Science and Research), 1982; (3):35.
8. Yu T, Lee YJ, Yang HM, Han S, Kim JH, Lee Y, Kim C, Han MH, Kim MY, Lee J, Cho JY. Inhibitory effect of Sanguisorba officinalis ethanol extract on NO and PGE(2) production is mediated by suppression of NF-κB and AP-1 activation signaling cascade. J Ethnopharmacol. 2010 Sep 9.
9. Kim EH, Shim B, Kang S, Jeong G, Lee JS, Yu YB, Chun M. Anti-inflammatory effects of Scutellaria baicalensis extract via suppression of immune modulators and MAP kinase signaling molecules. Department of Biological Sciences, Seoul National University, Seoul 151-742, Republic of Korea. J Ethnopharmacol. 2009 Nov 12;126(2):320-31.
10. Reddy DB, Reddy TC, Jyotsna G, Sharan S, Priya N, Lakshmipathi V, Reddanna P. Chebulagic acid, a COX-LOX dual inhibitor isolated from the fruits of Terminalia chebula Retz., induces apoptosis in COLO-205 cell line. Department of Animal Sciences, School of Life Sciences, University of Hyderabad, Hyderabad 500046, India. J Ethnopharmacol. 2009 Jul 30;124(3):506-12.
11. *Si Chuan Zhong Yi* (Sichuan Chinese Medicine), 1985; 3(5):49.
12. *Zhe Jiang Zhong Yi Za Zhi* (Zhejiang Journal of Chinese Medicine), 1985; (1):22.
13. *Yao Xue Za Zhi* (Journal of Medicinals), 1971; (91):1098.
14. Ozaki Y, Rui J, Tang YT. Antiinflammatory effect of Forsythia suspensa V(AHL) and its active principle. Biol Pharm Bull. 2000 Mar;23(3):365-7.
15. *Guang Xi Zhong Yi Yao* (Guangxi Chinese Medicine and Herbology), 1990; 13(1):44.
16. *Zhong Yao Yao Li Yu Ying Yong* (Pharmacology and Applications of Chinese Herbs), 1983; 406.
17. *Zhe Jiang Zhong Yi Xue Yuan Xue Bao* (Journal of Zhejiang University of Chinese Medicine), 1985; 9(4):26.
18. *Shang Hai Zhong Yi Yao Za Zhi* (Shanghai Journal of Chinese Medicine and Herbology), 1979; 4:28.
19. *An Hui Zhong Yi Xue Yuan Xue Bao* (Journal of Anhui University School of Medicine); 1985; 2:62.
20. *Zhong Yao Xue* (Chinese Herbology), 1988; 469-473.
21. *Zhong Yao Lin Chuan Xin Yong* (New Clinical Applications of Chinese Medicine), 2001; 246.
22. *Zhong Yao Lin Chuan Xin Yong* (New Clinical Applications of Chinese Medicine), 2001; 247.
23. *Shang Hai Zhong Yi Yao Za Zhi* (Shanghai Journal of Chinese Medicine and Herbology), 1979; 4:28.
24. *Zhong Yao Tong Bao* (Journal of Chinese Herbology), 1988; 13(8):43.
25. Tohda C, Kakihara Y, Komatsu K, Kuraishi Y. Inhibitory effects of methanol extracts of herbal medicines on substance P-induced itch-scratch response. Research Center for Ethnomedicines, Institute of Natural Medicine, Toyama Medical and Pharmaceutical University, Sugitani, Japan. Biol Pharm Bull. 2000 May;23(5):599-601.

GI Care (UC)™

CLINICAL APPLICATIONS

- **Ulcerative colitis**
- **Crohn's disease**
- **Other inflammatory bowel disease,** such as diverticulitis, fistula, colitis
- Chronic diarrhea with mucus, pus and blood, feeling of incomplete evacuation and abdominal cramps

WESTERN THERAPEUTIC ACTIONS

- Anti-inflammatory effect to reduce swelling and inflammation
- Antispasmodic action to alleviate abdominal spasms and cramps
- Antibiotic effect to treat infection
- Gastroprotective benefit to promote normal digestion and absorption of nutrients
- Antidiarrheal function to relieve diarrhea
- Antidotal function to eliminate toxins

CHINESE THERAPEUTIC ACTIONS

- Dispels damp-heat in the Intestines
- Relieves diarrhea
- Disperses stagnation and detoxifies
- Tonifies yin

DOSAGE

Take 3 to 4 capsules three times daily on an empty stomach with warm water. Dosage may be increased up to 8 to 10 capsules three times daily in acute conditions for no more than four days or until symptoms subside. After relief of symptoms the dosage then can be reduced to 3 to 4 capsules daily. For prevention or maintenance, take 2 capsules daily.

INGREDIENTS

Bai Shao (Radix Paeoniae Alba)
Chun Pi (Cortex Ailanthi)
Di Yu Tan (Radix Sanguisorbae Carbonisatum)
Dong Gua Zi (Semen Benincasae)
Fang Feng (Radix Saposhnikoviae)
Hou Po (Cortex Magnoliae Officinalis)
Huang Lian (Rhizoma Coptidis)
Ma Chi Xian (Herba Portulacae)
Mai Ya (Fructus Hordei Germinatus)
Nan Sha Shen (Radix Adenophorae)
Shan Yao (Rhizoma Dioscoreae)
Shan Zha Tan (Fructus Crataegi Carbonisatum)
Shi Liu Pi (Pericarpium Granati)
Wu Bei Zi (Galla Chinensis)
Yi Yi Ren (Semen Coicis)

BACKGROUND

Inflammatory bowel disease, which includes ulcerative colitis and Crohn's disease, is a condition characterized by chronic inflammation affecting various parts of the gastrointestinal tract. Ulcerative colitis and Crohn's disease are chronic, non-specific, inflammatory, ulcerative diseases that have no known etiology. Possible risk factors include immunological factors, infectious agents (such as bacteria, virus or amoeba), dietary factors (including chemicals and drugs), and psychosomatic factors. Ulcerative colitis and Crohn's disease usually occur between ages 14 to 24, or between 50 to 70. Clinical presentations of ulcerative colitis and Crohn's disease vary greatly depending on the extent and severity of the illness. The initial presentation begins with gradual onset of diarrhea with mucus and blood. There are symptomatic and asymptomatic intervals of diarrhea. Patients may also experience tenesmus and left lower quadrant pain and cramps.[1] Optimal treatment requires use of herbs to address the cause, the symptoms, and the complications.

FORMULA EXPLANATION

According to traditional Chinese medicine, ulcerative colitis and Crohn's disease are diagnosed as disorders characterized by the disharmony between the Spleen/Stomach and the Liver. Liver qi stagnation overacts on the Spleen and Stomach to impair the normal transformation and transportation of food. Over a long period of time, this dampness combines with heat to lodge in the Large Intestine to cause diarrhea with inflammation. Because of prolonged diarrhea and loss of fluids, yin also becomes deficient.

Nan Sha Shen (Radix Adenophorae) nourishes yin and dries up dampness. *Shan Yao* (Rhizoma Dioscoreae) nourishes the Spleen yin and relieves diarrhea. *Mai Ya* (Fructus Hordei Germinatus) and *Shan Zha Tan* (Fructus Crataegi Carbonisatum) promote digestion and stop bleeding. *Ma Chi Xian* (Herba Portulacae) and *Huang Lian* (Rhizoma Coptidis) dispel damp-heat in the Intestines to relieve intestinal irritations. *Di Yu Tan* (Radix Sanguisorbae Carbonisatum), *Chun Pi* (Cortex Ailanthi), *Shi Liu Pi* (Pericarpium Granati) and *Wu Bei Zi* (Galla Chinensis) are used to bind the Intestines to stop diarrhea, dispel pus, stop bleeding and generate new tissue. *Yi Yi Ren* (Semen Coicis) and *Dong Gua Zi* (Semen Benincasae) are traditionally used to treat intestinal abscess and are used here to dispel pus and mucus present in the stool. They both enter the Lung, which is connected to the Large Intestine via the *zang fu* relationship. These two herbs help to dry up dampness and enhance the ability of the Lung to metabolize water and prevent further accumulation of dampness, especially in the Large Intestine. *Fang Feng* (Radix Saposhnikoviae) is used to stop diarrhea and relieve pain. Together with *Bai Shao* (Radix Paeoniae Alba), these two herbs relieve abdominal and intestinal spasms, cramps, and pain. *Hou Po* (Cortex Magnoliae Officinalis) regulates qi in the abdomen to relieve bloating, distension, and pain.

GI Care (UC) effectively treats ulcerative colitis and Crohn's disease by targeting both the cause and the symptoms. Herbs are used to treat the underlying cause of disharmony between the Spleen/Stomach and the Liver, and accumulation of damp-heat in the Intestines. In addition, herbs are used to symptomatically

GI Care (UC)™

relieve diarrhea, treat intestinal abscess, dispel pus, and alleviate pain and distension.

CAUTIONS & CONTRAINDICATIONS

- This formula is contraindicated during pregnancy and nursing.
- This formula is contraindicated in cases of diarrhea due to Spleen qi deficiency or Kidney yang deficiency.
- While the use of herbs is effective in treating mild to moderate ulcerative colitis and Crohn's disease, it may not be appropriate for treating certain complications, such as toxic colitis, toxic megacolon, massive hemorrhage, free perforation, or fulminating toxic colitis. Surgical intervention may be necessary for such complications, but will require permanent ileostomy in addition to physical and emotional burden.

CLINICAL NOTES

- There are two formulas that can be used to treat inflammation of the bowel.
  - ***GI Care (UC)*** is designed more for patients suffering from chronic ulcerative colitis and Crohn's disease without the active infection. Therefore, it contains many herbs that would generate new tissue and repair the normal flora of the intestines.
  - ***GI Care II*** is designed more for an active infection and inflammation of the intestines due to improper food intake. Because bacteria lodged in the intestines need to be purged out, purgative herbs such as *Da Huang* (Radix et Rhizoma Rhei) are used.

Pulse Diagnosis by Dr. Jimmy Wei-Yen Chang:

- Rainbow pulse, a convex-shaped pulse that is thick, forceful, and expanding on and extends distally to the left *cun*.
- Floating and forceful pulse on the right *cun* and *guan*.

SUPPLEMENTARY FORMULAS

- With bleeding, add ***Notoginseng 9***.
- For diverticulitis and fistula, combine with ***Resolve (AI)*** and ***Astringent Complex***.
- For burning diarrhea with tenesmus, add ***GI Care II***.
- For hemorrhoids, add ***GI Care (HMR)***.
- For stress related ulcerative colitis and Crohn's disease, combine with ***Calm*** or ***Calm (ES)***.
- For bloating, add ***GI Harmony***.
- For constipation, add ***Gentle Lax (Deficient)***.
- For low-grade fever or night fever, add ***Balance (Heat)***.
- For excess heat or fever, add ***Gardenia Complex***.
- For perirectal abscesses, fever, add ***Resolve (AI)*** and ***Herbal ABX***.
- For chronic diarrhea with overall weakness and deficiency, add ***Imperial Tonic***.
- For chronic diarrhea with qi deficiency manifesting in weight loss, malaise, fatigue and poor appetite, add ***GI Tonic***. This formula should be taken to tonify the Spleen qi when the symptoms are in remission or under control.
- For intestinal spasms or abdominal cramping, add ***Flex (SC)***.
- With anemia, add ***Schisandra ZZZ***.
- With excessive damp/phlegm, add ***Pinellia Complex***.
- With severe inflammation, combine with ***Astringent Complex***.

ACUPUNCTURE TREATMENT

Traditional Points:

- *Zusanli* (ST 36), *Dadun* (LR 1), *Daimai* (GB 26), *Weizhong* (BL 40), *Huangshu* (KI 16), *Guilai* (ST 29), *Fushe* (SP 13), *Tianshu* (ST 25), *Sanyinjiao* (SP 6), *Yinlingquan* (SP 9)
- *Tianshu* (ST 25), *Zusanli* (ST 36), *Yinlingquan* (SP 9), *Zhongwan* (CV 12), *Neiguan* (PC 6), *Hegu* (LI 4)

Classic Master Tung's Points:

- **Ulcerative colitis:** *Qimen* (T 33.01), *Qijiao* (T 33.02), *Qizheng* (T 33.03), *Sihuashang* (T 77.08), *Sihuazhong* (T 77.09), *Sihuaxia* (T 77.11), *Menjin* (T 66.05), *Changmen* (T 33.10)
- **Gastroenteritis (acute):** *Huozhi* (T 88.15), *Qihuang* (T 88.14), *Zusanli* (ST 36), *Ganmen* (T 33.11), *Changmen* (T 33.10), *Fuchang* (T 77.12), *Zhiwujin* (T 11.08), *Zuqianjin* (T 77.24), *Zuwujin* (T 77.25)
- **Gastroenteritis (chronic):** *Piyi* (T 88.35)*, *Pier* (T 88.36)*, *Pisan* (T 88.37)*, *Cesanli* (T 77.22), *Menjin* (T 66.05), *Linggu* (T 22.05), *Changmen* (T 33.10), *Zhiwujin* (T 11.08). Bleed the dark veins nearby the ST channel on the lower limb.
- **Bloating:** *Pizhong* (T 11.18), *Sihuashang* (T 77.08), *Sihuazhong* (T 77.09), *Sihuaxia* (T 77.11), *Fuchang* (T 77.12), *Menjin* (T 66.05), *Huoju* (T 66.11), *Changmen* (T 33.10), *Minghuang* (T 88.12), *Tianhuang* (T 88.13), *Qihuang* (T 88.14), *Beimian* (T 44.07), *Fukuai* (T 1010.15), *Shangjiuli* (T 88.26), *Zhongjiuli* (T 88.25), *Xiajiuli* (T 88.27), *Sifuyi* (T 1010.11), *Sifuer* (T 1010.10)
- **Enteritis (acute):** *Changmen* (T 33.10), *Sihuashang* (T 77.08), *Sihuazhong* (T 77.09), *Zusanli* (ST 36), *Ganmen* (T 33.11), *Fuchang* (T 77.12), *Jinyingshang* (T 88.33)* and *Jinyingxia* (T 88.34)*. Bleed the LU area on the lower limb.

Master Tung's Points by Dr. Chuan-Min Wang:

- **Crohn's disease, ulcerative colitis:** *Menjin* (T 66.05), *Zuqianjin* (T 77.24)

Balance Method by Dr. Richard Tan:

- Left side: *Zhongfeng* (LR 4), *Gongsun* (SP 4), *Yinlingquan* (SP 9), *Hegu* (LI 4), *Linggu* (T 22.05)
- Right side: *Lieque* (LU 7), *Kongzui* (LU 6), *Neiguan* (PC 6), *Zusanli* (ST 36), *Tiaokou* (ST 38) or *ah shi* points nearby.
- Left and right sides can be alternated from treatment to treatment.
- Ear points: *Shenmen*, Intestine

Ear Acupuncture:

- Main points: Large Intestine, Small Intestine, Sympathetic
- Adjunct points: Spleen, Rectum, *San Jiao*, Endocrine

GI Care (UC)™

Auricular Medicine by Dr. Li-Chun Huang:

- **Ulcerative colitis:** Large Intestine, Sigmoid, Lower *Jiao*, Sympathetic, Spleen, Rectum, Endocrine, Digestive Subcortex. Bleed Ear Apex.
- **Crohn's disease:** Large Intestine, Lower *Jiao*, Small Intestine, Spleen, Sympathetic, Endocrine, Ileum, Digestive Subcortex. Bleed Ear Apex.
- **Relieving diarrhea:** Spleen, Occiput, Large Intestine, Sympathetic, Rectum, *Shenmen*, Digestive Subcortex. Bleed Ear Apex.
- **Invigorating the Spleen and promoting the digestion:** Spleen, Stomach, Mouth, Pancreas, Endocrine, Digestive Subcortex, Small Intestine
- **Stop bleeding:** Pituitary, Diaphragm, Adrenal Gland, Spleen, Large Intestine, Rectum

NUTRITION

- Encourage the consumption of fruits and vegetables such as apricots, winter melon, asparagus, avocados, bananas and broccoli in addition to brown rice, dried fruit, figs, salmon, garlic, green leafy vegetables, soy products, and yogurt.
- Avoid any and all foods that contain sugar, such as cake, dessert, candy, chocolate, canned juice, soft drinks, caffeinated drinks, stevia, sugar substitutes, agave, xylitol, and corn syrup.
- Avoid fermented foods like cheese or fermented tofu.
- Do not eat dairy products, such as milk, cream, yogurt, cheese, and ice cream.
- Warm and hot natured foods that damage qi and yin should be avoided, such as:
  - certain fruits like mango and durian that produce heat.
  - stimulants like coffee, alcohol, and energy drinks.
  - spicy/pungent/aromatic vegetables such as pepper, garlic, onions, basil, rosemary, cumin, funnel, anise, leeks, chives, scallions, thyme, saffron, wormwood, mustard, chili pepper, and wasabi.
- Avoid food and drinks with artificial coloring.
- Consume as few meat products as possible. Do not eat processed meats, such as lunch meats, hot dogs and sausages, as they contain nitrites that are associated with inflammation and chronic disease.

The Tao of Nutrition by Dr. Maoshing Ni and Cathy McNease:

- **Diarrhea**
  - Recommendations: garlic, black pepper, blueberries, cinnamon, raspberry leaves, lotus seeds, burned rice, yams, sweet potatoes, fresh fig leaves, peas, buckwheat, litchi, guava peel, apple, charcoaled bread, ginger, pearl barley, basil, and unripe prunes.
  - Cook rice porridge with lotus seed and yam or with barley.
  - Cook rice porridge with ginger and black pepper.
  - Eat sweet rice porridge.
  - Eat burnt rice or bread.
  - Take two tablespoons of dried apples, three times daily on an empty stomach with warm water.
  - Drink black tea.
  - Take two bulbs of garlic, bake until black. Then boil in water and drink the tea.
  - Make tea from guava peel.
  - Make tea from ginger, fennel, basil, and Chinese black dates.
  - Make tea from unripe prunes.
  - Make tea from dried litchi and Chinese black dates.
  - Avoid cold, raw foods, most fruits, juices, and overeating.
- **Gastritis and colitis:** drink diluted lotus root juice.

LIFESTYLE INSTRUCTIONS

- Avoid the use of certain drugs and chemicals that cause and/or aggravate ulcerative colitis and Crohn's disease. The list of offending drugs and/or chemicals may be different for every patient.
- Certain over-the-counter or prescription antidiarrheal drugs may worsen the condition and create a toxic megacolon. These drugs should not be taken unless supervised by a qualified health care provider.
- Bed rest and relaxation are helpful for short- and long-term recovery.

CASE STUDIES

- S.C., a 62-year-old female, presented with chronic intestinal pain, including blood in the stool and rectal bleeding. The patient had been hospitalized back in March due to a blood clot in her leg. Additional notations while at the hospital include decrease of hemoglobin, infusion of two pints of blood, and weight decrease from 90 to 79 pounds. The doctors had noted she was at increased risk for stroke. Peripheral neuropathy, edema on the dorsal foot, hair loss, and insomnia symptoms were also present. The practitioner diagnosed this condition as damp-heat in the Intestines, Kidney deficiency, and blood stasis in the lower *jiao*; her Western diagnosis was ulcerative colitis. For treatment, ***GI Care (UC)*** was prescribed at 4 capsules three times a day. Patient continued to take Remicade (infliximab) 10-15 mg, iron, and Pepcid (famotidine). After taking the herbs for one month the patient's colon was saved and no longer needed a colostomy. The frequency of her bowel movement decreased from twelve to two per day. Bleeding had stopped within two weeks of taking the herbs and the stools went from being very watery to full formed and soft. The patient was very pleased with the outcome. Submitted by D.K., Lincroft, New Jersey.
- A 49-year-old female has chronic ulcerative colitis as well as epigastric and abdominal pain and bloody stool. In the past 12 months, the patient has been treated with various herbs and drugs. The patient stated that while the treatments were effective, bloody stools returned as soon as the treatment was discontinued. The patient had two to three bowel movements per day and was constantly tired. The tongue was dark purple with thick greasy yellow coat. The pulse was deep and slippery. The diagnosis was accumulation of damp-heat and toxins in the Large Intestine. After taking ***GI Care (UC)*** for 30 days,

GI Care (UC)™

the patient reported significant improvement of all symptoms. Furthermore, her bowel movement returned to normal without blood. In the follow-up session one year later, the patient noted that she has remained healthy and without a relapse of her original chief complaint. Submitted by Y.L., Hebei, China.

PHARMACOLOGICAL AND CLINICAL RESEARCH

GI Care (UC) is designed to treat inflammatory bowel disease (including ulcerative colitis and Crohn's disease), a condition characterized by chronic, non-specific, and idiopathic inflammation affecting the gastrointestinal tract. Because there are no known causes in Western medicine, drugs are used mainly to treat only the symptoms and complications.

In treating ulcerative colitis and Crohn's disease, ***GI Care (UC)*** incorporates many herbs with marked effect to treat inflammation of the gastrointestinal tract. *Huang Lian* (Rhizoma Coptidis) and *Huang Bo* (Cortex Phellodendri Chinensis) both have marked anti-inflammatory effects,[2] with potency comparable to dexamethasone for treatment of both acute and chronic inflammation-related diseases.[3] According to one clinical study, 100 patients with inflammation of the gastrointestinal tract were treated with *Huang Lian* (Rhizoma Coptidis) and *Dou Kou* (Fructus Amomi Rotundus), 2 to 3 grams per dose for four to six doses per day, with all patients reporting improvement.[4] According to another study, 276 patients with chronic colitis were treated with 90% rate of effectiveness using an herbal formula with *Huang Bo* (Cortex Phellodendri Chinensis), *Di Yu* (Radix Sanguisorbae) and others.[5] *Bai Shao* (Radix Paeoniae Alba) and *Hou Po* (Cortex Magnoliae Officinalis) are two other herbs that are very helpful for treatment of inflammatory bowel disease. Both herbs have anti-inflammatory effects to suppress inflammation,[6,7] and antispasmodic effect to relieve spasms and cramps of the intestines.[8,9]

Since infection is one of the common causes of ulcerative colitis and Crohn's disease, ***GI Care (UC)*** uses many herbs with marked antibiotic effects. Herbs in this formula have shown marked antibacterial, antiviral, and antifungal effects. Examples of such herbs include *Bai Shao* (Radix Paeoniae Alba),[10] *Hou Po* (Cortex Magnoliae Officinalis),[11] *Ma Chi Xian* (Herba Portulacae),[12] *Huang Lian* (Rhizoma Coptidis),[13,14] and *Shi Liu Pi* (Pericarpium Granati).[15] In fact, many herbs have been used successfully for treatment of infection and inflammation of the gastrointestinal tract. In one study, *Shan Zha* (Fructus Crataegi) was used to treat 100 patients with acute bacterial enteritis with satisfactory results. [16] In another study, use of *Ma Chi Xian* (Herba Portulacae) was 83.62% effective in treating 403 patients with chronic bacterial dysentery, and 89.12% effective in treating 331 patients with acute bacterial dysentery. [17] Lastly, use of *Huang Lian* (Rhizoma Coptidis), individually or in an herbal formula, is associated with excellent clinical results in treating over 1,000 patients with bacterial dysentery. The treatments are characterized by marked effectiveness, short duration of treatment, and low incidence of side effects. [18]

GI Care (UC) also employs herbs to promote normal digestion and absorption, and reduce the stress of the intestines. *Shan Yao* (Rhizoma Dioscoreae) is used to treat indigestion and reduce the stress of the intestines. In one study, it has been found that use of *Shan Yao* (Rhizoma Dioscoreae) and other herbs were effective in treating 101 infants with indigestion and related complications.[19] *Mai Ya* (Fructus Hordei Germinatus) improves digestion by increasing gastric emptying time and intestinal peristalsis. *Shan Zha* (Fructus Crataegi) facilitates digestion and absorption by inducing the production of gastric acid.[20] Lastly, *Shi Liu Pi* (Pericarpium Granati) has a gastroprotective effect, and use of this herb protects the stomach from alcohol-, indomethacin-, and aspirin-induced ulcers by increasing the pH and mucus secretion.[21]

In addition to treating the cause, ***GI Care (UC)*** incorporates herbs that address the symptoms of ulcerative colitis and Crohn's disease. *Shan Yao* (Rhizoma Dioscoreae) and *Shan Zha* (Fructus Crataegi) consolidate the stool and treat diarrhea.[22,23] *Wu Bei Zi* (Galla Chinensis) has a marked effect to suppress diarrhea due to enterotoxigenic *Escherichia coli*, the most frequently isolated enteropathogen that accounts for approximately 210 million diarrhea episodes annually.[24] Lastly, *Fang Feng* (Radix Saposhnikoviae) is added to facilitate the elimination of heavy metals,[25] which may irritate the bowel and cause inflammation of the intestines.

In summary, ***GI Care (UC)*** is a carefully crafted formula with many herbs that treat the cause and the symptoms of ulcerative colitis and Crohn's disease. ***GI Care (UC)*** contains herbs that reduce the inflammation of the gastrointestinal tract, treat the infection, promote normal digestion and absorption, relieve diarrhea, alleviate abdominal spasms and cramps, and eliminate irritating toxins.

COMPARATIVE ANALYSIS

Ulcerative colitis and Crohn's disease are chronic, non-specific, idiopathic, inflammatory and ulcerative diseases of the gastro-intestinal tract.[26] Because Western medicine recognizes no known etiology, drug treatments are focused primarily to treat symptoms. Three classes of drugs used to treat ulcerative colitis and Crohn's disease include antidiarrheals, 5-Aminosalicylates, and corticosteroids. Antidiarrheal agents [such as Lomotil (diphenoxylate) and Imodium (loperamide)] stop diarrhea, but may cause dizziness, drowsiness, sedation, and in some cases, dependence with long-term use. 5-Aminosalicylates [such as Azulfidine (sulfasalazine), Dipentum (olsalazine) and Pentasa (mesalamine)] suppress low-grade inflammation, but are not used often because of side effects such as anorexia, dyspepsia, nausea and vomiting. Lastly, oral or intravenous corticosteroids are used to suppress moderate to severe cases of ulcerative colitis

GI Care (UC)™

and Crohn's disease. However, long-term use of corticosteroids has numerous side effects, including but not limited to osteoporosis, glucose intolerance, cataract formation, fluid retention, dependence and muscle wasting. Finally, surgical colectomy is performed in severe and emergency cases of massive hemorrhage, free perforation, or fulminating toxic colitis. The disadvantages of surgery include permanent ileostomy, possible sexual dysfunction in males, and physical and emotional burden.

Use of acupuncture and herbs is effective to treat inflammatory conditions of the gastrointestinal tract, including ulcerative colitis, Crohn's disease, and other inflammatory bowel diseases. While acupuncture and herbal treatments are effective for both prevention and treatment, they do have limitations. Certain complications of ulcerative colitis and Crohn's disease are considered medical emergencies, and should not be treated with acupuncture and herbs. Complications such as toxic colitis or toxic megacolon require immediate hospitalization. Furthermore, serious complications such as massive hemorrhage, free perforation, or fulminating toxic colitis require immediate surgical intervention.

References

1. Beers, M. and Berkow, R. *The Merck Manual of Diagnosis and Therapy 19th Edition*. 2011.
2. *Yao Xue Za Zhi* (Journal of Medicinals), 1981, 101(10):883.
3. Park EK, Rhee HI, Jung HS, Ju SM, Lee YA, Lee SH, Hong SJ, Yang HI, Yoo MC, Kim KS. Antiinflammatory effects of a combined herbal preparation (RAH13) of Phellodendron amurense and Coptis chinensis in animal models of inflammation. East-West Bone and Joint Research Center, East-West Neo Medical Center, Kyung Hee University, 149 Sangil-dong, Gangdong-gu, Seoul 134-727, Korea. Phytother Res. 2007 Aug;21(8):746-50.
4. *Si Chuan Yi Xue Yuan Xue Bao* (Journal of Sichuan School of Medicine), 1959; 1:102.
5. *Zhe Jiang Zhong Yi Za Zhi* (Zhejiang Journal of Chinese Medicine), 1996; (10):438.
6. Zheng YQ, Wei W. Total glucosides of paeony suppresses adjuvant arthritis in rats and intervenes cytokine-signaling between different types of synoviocytes. Int Immunopharmacol. 2005 Sep;5(10):1560-73.
7. Oh JH, Kang LL, Ban JO, Kim YH, Kim KH, Han SB, Hong JT. Anti-inflammatory effect of 4-O-methylhonokiol, compound isolated from Magnolia officinalis through inhibition of NF-kappaB. College of Pharmacy, CBITRC, Chungbuk National University, 12, Gaesin-dong, Heungduk-gu, Cheongju, Chungbuk 361-763, Republic of Korea. Chem Biol Interact. 2010 Dec 5;188(3):677.
8. *Zhong Yi Za Zhi* (Journal of Chinese Medicine), 1985; 6:50.
9. Chan SS, Zhao M, Lao L, Fong HH, Che CT. Magnolol and honokiol account for the anti-spasmodic effect of Magnolia officinalis in isolated guinea pig ileum. School of Chinese Medicine, The Chinese University of Hong Kong, Hong Kong, P.R. China. Planta Med. 2008 Mar;74(4):381-4.
10. *Xin Zhong Yi* (New Chinese Medicine), 1989; 21(3):51.
11. *Yao Jian Gong Zuo Tong Xun* (Journal of Herbal Preparations), 1980; 10(4):209.
12. *Ji Lin Zhong Yi Yao* (Jilin Chinese Medicine and Herbology), 1985; 3:28.
13. *Zhong Guo Yi Yao Bao* (Chinese Journal of Medicine and Medicinals), 1958; 44(9):888.
14. *Zhong Xi Yi Jie He Za Zhi* (Journal of Integrated Chinese and Western Medicine), 1989; 9(8):494).
15. *Zhong Cao Yao Xue* (Study of Chinese Herbal Medicine), 1976; 694.
16. *Xin Yi Xue* (New Medicine), 1975; 2:111.
17. *Fu Jian Zhong Yi Yao* (Fujian Chinese Medicine and Herbology), 1959; 6:1.
18. *Zhong Hua Nei Ke Za Zhi* (Chinese Journal of Internal Medicine), 1976; 4:219.
19. *Zhong Yi Za Zhi* (Journal of Chinese Medicine), 1984 5:9.
20. *Ying Yang Xue Bao* (Report of Nutrition), 1984; 6(2):109.
21. Alam MS, Alam MA, Ahmad S, Najmi AK, Asif M, Jahangir T. Protective effects of Punica granatum in experimentally-induced gastric ulcers. Department of Ilmul Advia, Faculty of Medicine, Jamia Hamdard, New Delhi - 110062, India. Toxicol Mech Methods. 2010 Nov;20(9):572-8.
22. *Hu Nan Yi Yao Za Zhi* (Hunan Journal of Medicine and Herbology), 1982; 4:17.
23. *Yun Nan Zhong Yao Zhi* (Yunan Journal of Chinese Herbal Medicine), 1973; 3:31.
24. Chen JC, Ho TY, Chang YS, Wu SL, Hsiang CY. Anti-diarrheal effect of Galla Chinensis on the Escherichia coli heat-labile enterotoxin and ganglioside interaction. Graduate Institute of Chinese Pharmaceutical Sciences, China Medical University, Taichung, Taiwan. J Ethnopharmacol. 2006 Feb 20;103(3): 385-91.
25. *Xin Yi Yao Tong Xun* (Journal of New Medicine and Herbology), 1973; 7:6.
26. Beers, M. and Berkow, R. *The Merck Manual of Diagnosis and Therapy 19th Edition*. 2011.

GI DTX ™

CLINICAL APPLICATIONS

- **Bowel cleansing formula** to promote intestinal health (especially those with poor dietary habits resulting in an accumulation of toxins in the colon)
- **Abdominal distension and rigidity** due to fecal compaction and constipation
- **Polyps or inflammation in the colon** due to toxic build-up
- **Short-term intestinal detoxification**

WESTERN THERAPEUTIC ACTIONS

- Promotes healthy elimination of intestinal toxins
- Cleanses the intestines and promotes healthy bowel function
- Provides temporary relief of occasional, mild constipation
- Promotes regular intestinal motility and elimination
- Prevents and treats intestinal polyps

CHINESE THERAPEUTIC ACTIONS

- Clears toxic heat in the Intestines
- Strengthens and tonifies the Spleen and Stomach

DOSAGE

Take 3 to 4 capsules three times daily. Dosage can be increased up to 6 to 8 capsules three times daily. One round of cleansing is for one week. The treatment may be repeated every six months if necessary.

INGREDIENTS

Bai Hua She She Cao (Herba Hedyotis)
Bai Jiang Cao (Herba cum Radice Patriniae)
Da Huang (Radix et Rhizoma Rhei)
Feng Wei Cao (Herba Pteris)
Fu Ling (Poria)
Shan Yao (Rhizoma Dioscoreae)
Wu Wei Zi (Fructus Schisandrae Chinensis)
Zhi He Shou Wu (Radix Polygoni Multiflori Praeparata)

BACKGROUND

Constipation and fecal compaction are two of the most common intestinal problems in developed countries. Although constipation may be caused by a variety of factors, the most common and preventable factor is diet. Refined sugar, white flour, chemical food additives, and preservatives are all ingredients found in many modern foods. Overindulgence in these types of foods may often lead to intestinal upset and constipation. When waste materials stay within the colon for an extended period of time, they become toxic material through putrefaction and fermentation, and the toxic materials are absorbed into the blood and the body.

When intestinal peristalsis becomes slow and the bowel movements become stagnant, it is possible for the large intestine to retain 15 pounds or more of waste. Constipation may lead to a host of health issues, including indigestion, skin problems, unexplained fatigue, and aches and pains. Today, with the increase of environmental and food toxins, it is very important for individuals who already experience stagnant bowel movements to detoxify and regulate their digestive tract.

A healthy colon is vital for the general health and well-being of an individual. A healthy colon detoxifies the body by extracting excess water and salt from solid wastes, and effectively expelling these waste materials and toxins from the body. Good bowel movements are an indicator of great health, and a healthy individual should experience one to two bowel movements per day. With the incidence of colon cancer on the rise, it is becoming more and more evident that maintaining colon health is an important preventative health measure.

FORMULA EXPLANATION

The first and foremost important strategy to cleanse the colon is to purge out the toxic accumulation in the colon. ***GI DTX*** contains unprocessed *Da Huang* (Radix et Rhizoma Rhei) to achieve the maximum effect to purge downward and eliminate toxins. It also has qi invigorating effects to increase peristalsis and enhance the overall detoxifying effect. Additionally, it can also drain damp and help eliminate toxins through urination. To prevent the purging effect of *Da Huang* (Radix et Rhizoma Rhei) from injuring the yin, *Wu Wei Zi* (Fructus Schisandrae Chinensis) is added. Additionally, with its sour taste, it provides a check and balance to prevent the overly bitter and purging *Da Huang* (Radix et Rhizoma Rhei) from injuring the qi. *Wu Wei Zi* (Fructus Schisandrae Chinensis) also has an excellent effect to protect the liver and help in the detox process. Lastly, *Zhi He Shou Wu* (Radix Polygoni Multiflori Praeparata) nourishes yin and tonifies the blood.

Bai Jiang Cao (Herba cum Radice Patriniae), *Feng Wei Cao* (Herba Pteris) and *Bai Hua She She Cao* (Herba Hedyotis) all enter the Large Intestine channel to enhance the detoxifying effect of *Da Huang* (Radix et Rhizoma Rhei). *Bai Jiang Cao* (Herba cum Radice Patriniae) and *Bai Hua She She Cao* (Herba Hedyotis) drain pus and abscesses to treat intestinal polyps. *Feng Wei Cao* (Herba Pteris) effectively reduces inflammation in the colon.

Shan Yao (Rhizoma Dioscoreae) and *Fu Ling* (Poria) function to tonify the Spleen and Stomach to restore balance after toxins are purged from the colon. Both of these herbs also prevent the harsh effects of the heat-clearing and detoxifying herbs from injuring the digestive system.

Overall, ***GI DTX*** achieves the delicate balance to simultaneously cleanse the intestines and protect the digestive tract.

CAUTIONS & CONTRAINDICATIONS

- *GI DTX* is recommended to be used for seven days per course of treatment within a six-month period. Though it may be used more frequently in severe cases, it should not be used more than one course every other month.

GI DTX ™

- Use of this formula at a large dosage or for a prolonged period of time is contraindicated.
- This formula is contraindicated during pregnancy, nursing, and menstruation. It is also contraindicated in individuals who have weak body constitutions, such as children or geriatric individuals.
- The following warning statement is required by the State of California: "This product contains *Da Huang* (Radix et Rhizoma Rhei). Read and follow directions carefully. Do not use if you have or develop diarrhea, loose stools, or abdominal pain because *Da Huang* (Radix et Rhizoma Rhei) may worsen these conditions and be harmful to your health. Consult your physician if you have frequent diarrhea or if you are pregnant, nursing, taking medication, or have a medical condition."
- According to most textbooks and contemporary references, the classic entry of "*He Shou Wu*" is now separated into two entries: the unprepared *Sheng Shou Wu* (Radix Polygoni Multiflori) and the prepared *Zhi He Shou Wu* (Radix Polygoni Multiflori Praeparata), as they have significantly different therapeutic effects and side effects. *Sheng Shou Wu* (Radix Polygoni Multiflori) is a stimulant laxative that treats constipation, but may cause nausea, vomiting, abdominal pain, diarrhea, and in rare cases, liver disorder (dose- and time-dependent, and reversible upon discontinuation).[1] On the other hand, *Zhi He Shou Wu* (Radix Polygoni Multiflori Praeparata) is a tonic herb that is safe and well-tolerated. The dramatic changes in the therapeutic effect and safety profile are attributed to the long and complicated processing of the root with *Hei Dou* (Semen Sojae) through repeated blending, cooking, and drying procedures. When properly processed, the chemical composition of the root changes significantly. Many new compounds are generated from the Maillard reaction (four furanones, two furans, two nitrogen compounds, one pyran, one alcohol and one sulfur compound). Furthermore, the preparation process causes changes in the composition of sugars and 16 kinds of amino acids; it also reduces the pH of the herb from 6.28 to 5.61.[2,3] In summary, these changes give rise to the tonic effects of the prepared roots, and eliminate the adverse reactions associated with the unprepared roots. **Note:** Due to medical risks and legal liabilities, it is prudent to exercise caution and ***not*** use this herb in either prepared or unprepared forms in patients with pre-existing or risk factors of liver diseases.

CLINICAL NOTES

- After using ***GI DTX*** for one week, incorporate probiotics in the diet to replenish the intestinal flora.
- In the first three days of intestinal cleansing, patients may notice passage of more than normal amount of stool that may be foul smelling. After the third day, there should be passage of normal amount of stool with little smell.
- ***GI DTX*** is designed as a short-term intestinal detoxification for patients who suffer from long-term constipation and fecal compaction. As a short-term treatment, this formula has a strong and powerful effect to drain downwards to eliminate accumulation of stools, fecal compaction, and other toxins in the intestines. For long-term benefit, patients are strongly advised to engage in dietary and lifestyles changes so the same conditions do not recur.

Pulse Diagnosis by Dr. Jimmy Wei-Yen Chang:

- **Dryness in the Large Intestine and Stomach:** superficial and forceful on the right *cun* and *guan* positions
- **Constipation due to constriction:** *yinqiao* pulse, a thin, straight and wiry pulse, on or proximal to the *chi* positions

SUPPLEMENTARY FORMULAS

- To detox the Liver and support liver functions, add ***Liver DTX***.
- To detox the Kidney and improve kidney functions, combine with ***Kidney DTX***.
- To facilitate elimination of heavy metals, chemical, and other toxins, add ***Herbal DTX***.
- For individuals with underlying qi deficiency, add ***GI Tonic***.
- For individuals with underlying qi, blood, yin and yang deficiencies, add ***Imperial Tonic***.

ACUPUNCTURE TREATMENT

Traditional Points:

- *Dachangshu* (BL 25), *Tianshu* (ST 25), *Zhigou* (TH 6), *Zhaohai* (KI 6), *Shangjuxu* (ST 37), *Zusanli* (ST 36), *Hegu* (LI 4)

Classic Master Tung's Points:

- **Colon detox:** *Tushui* (T 22.11), *Qimen* (T 33.01), *Qijiao* (T 33.02), *Qizheng* (T 33.03), *Simashang* (T 88.18), *Simazhong* (T 88.17), *Simaxia* (T 88.19), *Tongtian* (T 88.03), *Fuchang* (T 77.12), *Huochuan* (T 33.04)
- **Bloating:** *Pizhong* (T 11.18), *Sihuashang* (T 77.08), *Sihuazhong* (T 77.09), *Sihuaxia* (T 77.11), *Fuchang* (T 77.12), *Menjin* (T 66.05), *Huoju* (T 66.11), *Changmen* (T 33.10), *Minghuang* (T 88.12), *Tianhuang* (T 88.13), *Qihuang* (T 88.14), *Beimian* (T 44.07), *Fukuai* (T 1010.15), *Shangjiuli* (T 88.26), *Zhongjiuli* (T 88.25), *Xiajiuli* (T 88.27), *Sifuyi* (T 1010.11), *Sifuer* (T 1010.10)

Master Tung's Points by Dr. Chuan-Min Wang:

- **Colon cleanse:** *Menjin* (T 66.05), *Changmen* (T 33.10)

Balance Method by Dr. Richard Tan:

- Left side: *Waiguan* (TH 5), *Zhigou* (TH 6), *Zhaohai* (KI 6), *Quchi* (LI 11)
- Right side: *Shangjuxu* (ST 37), *Tiaokou* (ST 38), *Kongzui* (LU 6) or *ah shi* points nearby, *Quze* (PC 3)
- Left and right sides can be alternated from treatment to treatment.

Ear Acupuncture:

- Sympathetic, *Shenmen*, Large Intestine, Small Intestine, Endocrine

GI DTX ™

Auricular Medicine by Dr. Li-Chun Huang:

- **Increase bowel movement:** Large Intestine, Sigmoid, Liver, Spleen, Lung, *San Jiao*, Digestive Subcortex

NUTRITION

- Increase fiber intake, and avoid fast foods, processed foods, artificial sugars, and carbonated drinks.
- Give the body two to three hours between the last meal of the day and bedtime. When a person sleeps, the digestive system slows down as well. Make sure to give the body adequate time to digest the food before going into sleep mode.
- Always eat breakfast! According to the TCM clock, the most optimal time for the digestive system is in the morning from 8:00 to 10:00 a.m.
- Drink warm or hot liquids with meals. Putting cold and ice on any part of the body will immediately constrict the flow of blood to that region. Similarly, drinking cold or iced drinks with meals will hinder the natural peristaltic movements of the digestive system.
- Chew food completely. The digestive system can process and absorb smaller pieces of food much better than food that is incompletely chewed. Larger pieces of food can lead to incomplete digestion and digestive discomfort.
- Incorporate fresh organic fruits and vegetables as well as high-fiber whole grains into diet.
- Drink at least two quarts of water daily.
- Do not eat processed meats, such as lunch meats, hot dogs and sausages, as they contain nitrites that are associated with inflammation and chronic disease.
- Avoid deep-fried or greasy foods whenever possible.

The Tao of Nutrition by Dr. Maoshing Ni and Cathy McNease:

- Recommendations: bananas, apples, walnuts, figs, spinach, peaches, pears, pine nuts, sesame seeds, mulberries, grapefruit, yams, honey, azuki beans, apricot kernel, milk, yogurt, alfalfa sprouts, beets, cabbage, bok choy, cauliflower, potato, Chinese cabbage, and salt water.
- Eat two bananas on an empty stomach, followed by a glass of water.
- Drink a glass of lukewarm water with two teaspoonfuls of honey on an empty stomach.
- Drink blended beets and cabbage on an empty stomach daily.
- Make beet soup.
- Eat 5 to 10 figs on an empty stomach, followed by a glass of water.
- Eat a fresh apple on an empty stomach.
- Drink mulberry juice.
- Eat lightly steamed asparagus and cabbage at night before retiring.
- Drink a glass of lukewarm water with 2 teaspoons of salt, on an empty stomach. This remedy should be used as a last resort when nothing else has worked and should not be used by those with edema or hypertension.
- Avoid spicy foods, fried foods and meat.

LIFESTYLE INSTRUCTIONS

- Eliminate things that are unhealthy (e.g., alcohol, coffee, cigarettes, refined sugars, and saturated fats) or potentially toxic (e.g., chemical-based household cleaners and personal hygiene products).
- Regular use of steam rooms or saunas can help to eliminate toxins through sweating.
- Take a 30-minute walk after meals to help stimulate the circulatory and digestive systems.
- Incorporate some form of cardiovascular exercise.
- Do not postpone bowel movements, respond to the urge immediately.

PHARMACOLOGICAL AND CLINICAL RESEARCH

GI DTX is an herbal formula designed to cleanse the bowel and promote gastrointestinal health for someone with chronic constipation, fecal impaction, intestinal polyps, and/or inflammatory bowel.

To successfully remove the chronic buildup of dry and hard stools, ***GI DTX*** uses herbs to moisten the bowel, stimulate intestinal peristalsis, and purge downwards. *Shan Yao* (Rhizoma Dioscoreae) and *Zhi He Shou Wu* (Radix Polygoni Multiflori Praeparata) are two tonic herbs with marked gastrointestinal effects. They moisten the bowels to soften the dry stools, and they stimulate the intestinal peristalsis to facilitate the passage of stools.[4,5] To ensure success to cleanse the bowel, *Da Huang* (Radix et Rhizoma Rhei) is used for its strong purgative and laxative activities. *Da Huang* (Radix et Rhizoma Rhei) contains sennoside A, aloe-emodin, and rhein, compounds with a potent effect to directly stimulate the large intestine to increase contraction and peristalsis.[6] Together, these herbs achieve the effect of gently moistening and softening the dry stools, and strongly and potently purging them out of the body.

Chronic constipation and fecal impaction are often accompanied by complications, such as inflammation, as long-term buildup of stools is toxic to the intestines. To reduce inflammation and swelling, several herbs with anti-inflammatory effects are used. *Bai Jiang Cao* (Herba cum Radice Patriniae) has remarkable anti-inflammatory activity, especially at colorectal sites, and has been shown to have therapeutic value for treatment of ulcerative colitis and other types of inflammatory bowel disease (IBD).[7] *Da Huang* (Radix et Rhizoma Rhei), in addition to having a potent purgative effect, also has significant anti-inflammatory effects via inhibition of inducible nitric oxide synthase.[8] *Shan Yao* (Rhizoma Dioscoreae) exerts anti-inflammatory effects through its antioxidant activities.[9] Lastly, *Wu Wei Zi* (Fructus Schisandrae Chinensis) demonstrates anti-inflammatory effects

GI DTX ™

through inhibition of nitric oxide production, prostaglandin E(2) release, cyclo-oxygenase-2 and inducible nitric oxide synthase expression.[10]

Formation of intestinal polyps is another complication of long-term constipation and fecal impaction. To stop the formation and growth of intestinal polyps, ***GI DTX*** utilizes herbs with antiproliferative effects. *Wu Wei Zi* (Fructus Schisandrae Chinensis) contains benzocyclooctadiene lignans, which have been shown to exert antiproliferative activity against human colorectal cancer cells.[11] *Bai Hua She She Cao* (Herba Hedyotis) also has a strong antiproliferative effect to inhibit the growth and induce the apoptosis of abnormal cells in the body.[12] Lastly, *Da Huang* (Radix et Rhizoma Rhei) is an herb with a broad spectrum of antiproliferative, cytotoxicity, and anticancer effects.[13,14,15,16]

Finally, after cleansing the bowel and removal of toxic substances in the intestines, it is necessary to rebuild the intestines and restore its normal health. Interestingly, in addition to having purgative, laxative, anti-inflammatory and antiproliferative functions, *Da Huang* (Radix et Rhizoma Rhei) also has cytoprotective activity to protect human intestinal epithelial cells from damage. The cytoprotective effect of *Da Huang* (Radix et Rhizoma Rhei) is attributed to the inhibition of cell apoptosis and necrosis.[17] *Da Huang* (Radix et Rhizoma Rhei) has also illustrated a significant protective effect in subjects with artificially-induced ulcerative colitis.[18]

In summary, ***GI DTX*** cleanses the bowel and promotes intestinal health to treat chronic constipation, fecal impaction, intestinal polyps, and/or inflammatory bowel conditions.

COMPARATIVE ANALYSIS

Constipation and fecal compaction are very common problems affecting many people in developed countries. Common causes include lack of exercise, insufficient intake of water and fiber, stress, overuse of laxatives, and use of certain drugs (such as opioids, antipsychotics, antidepressants, and anticholinergics). As constipation becomes a long-term problem, complications will begin to rise, including but not limited to slowed or irregular intestinal peristalsis, fecal impaction, re-absorption of toxins, and formation of intestinal polyps. Therefore, optimal treatment requires treatment of constipation and its complications.

In Western medicine, there are many options for treatment of constipation. Bulking agents (bran, psyllium and methylcellulose) are the gentlest and safest. These drugs are non-habit forming, and may be used safely on a long-term basis. However, they act slowly and are not very strong. Laxatives (docusate and mineral oil) soften stools by increasing the implementation of intestinal water. However, these drugs must be used carefully, as they interfere with absorption of nutrients and other drugs. Lastly, cathartics (senna, cascara, and bisacodyl) are used for severe cases of constipation by increasing intestinal peristalsis and intraluminal fluids. However, these drugs should only be used on a short-term basis, as prolonged use will cause "lazy bowel" syndrome and serious fluid and electrolyte imbalance. Unfortunately, while these drugs are effective for treating constipation, they do not regulate the peristalsis or restore the intestines to its normal health. As a result, long-term use or abuse of cathartics will often cause dependence on these drugs.

In traditional Chinese medicine, constipation can be treated with great success. Those with mild to moderate constipation are usually treated with herbs that moisten the Intestines and regulate bowel movement. Those with moderate to severe constipation are generally treated with herbs that purge the Intestines and induce bowel movement. These formulas should be used as needed, and discontinued when the desired effects have been achieved. In addition to treating constipation, many herbs are beneficial for regulating the peristalsis and restoring the normal health of the intestines. These preventative and maintenance measures are what ensure long-term success of the treatment and recovery of the health conditions.

Both drugs and herbs are equally effective in treating constipation. Both modalities of medicines should be used sparingly, and only when needed, as prolonged use may cause side effects. However, Chinese herbs are generally more effective to correct the underlying problems associated with chronic and habitual constipation, fecal impaction and other complications of constipation. Lastly, diet and lifestyle adjustments are also needed to ensure regular bowel movement.

References

1. Lei X, et al. Liver Damage Associated with Polygonum multiflorum Thunb.: A Systematic Review of Case Reports and Case Series. Evid Based Complement Alternat Med. 2015;2015:459749. doi: 10.1155/2015/459749.
2. Liu Z, Chao Z, Liu Y, Song Z, Lu A. Maillard reaction involved in the steaming process of the root of Polygonum multiflorum. Institution of Basic Theory, China Academy of Chinese Medical Sciences, Beijing, PR China. Planta Med. 2009 Jan;75(1):84-8. Epub 2008 Nov 25.
3. Liu Z, et al. In vitro antioxidant activities of maillard reaction products produced in the steaming process of Polygonum multiflorum root. Nat Prod Commun. 2011 Jan;6(1):55-8.
4. *Zhi Wu Zi Yuan Yu Huan Jing* (Source and Environment of Plants), 1992; 1(2):10.
5. *Chang Yong Zhong Yao De Ying Yong* (Application of Commonly-Used Chinese Herbs), 1983:117-118.
6. *Zhong Yao Xue* (Chinese Herbology), 1998; 251:256.
7. Cho EJ, Shin JS, Noh YS, Cho YW, Hong SJ, Park JH, Lee JY, Lee JY, Lee KT. Anti-inflammatory effects of methanol extract of Patrinia scabiosaefolia in mice with ulcerative colitis. J Ethnopharmacol. 2011 Jul 14;136(3):428-35.
8. Wang CC, Huang YJ, Chen LG, Lee LT, Yang LL. Inducible nitric oxide synthase inhibitors of Chinese herbs III. Rheum palmatum. Planta Med. 2002 Oct;68(10):869-74.
9. Yang MH, Yoon KD, Chin YW, Park JH, Kim J. Phenolic compounds with radical scavenging and cyclooxygenase-2 (COX-2) inhibitory activities from Dioscorea opposita. College of Pharmacy and Research Institute of Pharmaceutical Science, Seoul National University, Seoul 151-742, South Korea. Bioorg Med Chem. 2009 Apr 1;17(7):2689-94.
10. Guo LY, Hung TM, Bae KH, Shin EM, Zhou HY, Hong YN, Kang SS, Kim HP, Kim YS. Anti-inflammatory effects of schisandrin isolated from the fruit of Schisandra chinensis Baill. Natural Products Research Institute, College

FORMULAS

GI DTX ™

of Pharmacy, Seoul National University, Seoul 151-747, South Korea. Eur J Pharmacol. 2008 Sep 4;591(1-3):293-9.

11. Gnabre J, Unlu I, Chang TC, Lisseck P, Bourne B, Scolnik R, Jacobsen NE, Bates R, Huang RC. Isolation of lignans from Schisandra chinensis with anti-proliferative activity in human colorectal carcinoma: Structure-activity relationships. Department of Biology, Johns Hopkins University, Mudd Hall, 3400 N. Charles Street, Baltimore, MD 21218, USA. J Chromatogr B Analyt Technol Biomed Life Sci. 2010 Oct 15;878(28):2693-700.
12. Gupta S, Zhang D, Yi J, Shao J. Anticancer activities of Oldenlandia diffusa. J Herb Pharmacother. 2004;4(1):21-33.
13. Lin ML, Lu YC, Chung JG, Wang SG, Lin HT, Kang SE, Tang CH, Ko JL, Chen SS. Down-regulation of MMP-2 through the p38 MAPK-NF-kappaB-dependent pathway by aloe-emodin leads to inhibition of nasopharyngeal carcinoma cell invasion. Mol Carcinog. 2010 Sep;49(9):783-97.
14. Lu GD, Shen HM, Chung MC, Ong CN. Critical role of oxidative stress and sustained JNK activation in aloe-emodin-mediated apoptotic cell death in human hepatoma cells. Carcinogenesis. 2007 Sep;28(9):1937-45.
15. Guo J, Xiao B, Zhang S, Liu D, Liao Y, Sun Q. Growth inhibitory effects of gastric cancer cells with an increase in S phase and alkaline phosphatase activity repression by aloe-emodin. Cancer Biol Ther. 2007 Jan;6(1):85-8.
16. Hsu CM, Hsu YA, Tsai Y, Shieh FK, Huang SH, Wan L, Tsai FJ. Emodin inhibits the growth of hepatoma cells: finding the common anti-cancer pathway using Huh7, Hep3B, and HepG2 cells. Biochem Biophys Res Commun. 2010 Feb 19;392(4):473-8.
17. Liu LN, Mei QB, Liu L, Zhang F, Liu ZG, Wang ZP, Wang RT. Protective effects of Rheum tanguticum polysaccharide against hydrogen peroxide-induced intestinal epithelial cell injury. World J Gastroenterol. 2005 Mar 14;11(10):1503-7.
18. Liu L, Wang ZP, Xu CT, Pan BR, Mei QB, Long Y, Liu JY, Zhou SY. Effects of Rheum tanguticum polysaccharide on TNBS -induced colitis and CD4+T cells in rats. World J Gastroenterol. 2003 Oct;9(10):2284-8.

GI Harmony™

CLINICAL APPLICATIONS

- **Irritable bowel syndrome (IBS)**
- **Disharmony of the GI tract:** alternating diarrhea and constipation with abdominal bloating, pain, flatulence and a feeling of incomplete evacuation, and straining and urgency of bowel movements
- Various bowel disorders, such as diverticulitis, mucous colitis, nervous bowel, irritable colon, and spastic colon

WESTERN THERAPEUTIC ACTIONS

- Soothes the irritation of the gastrointestinal tract caused by drugs, chemicals, and certain foods
- Regulates and restores gastrointestinal functions
- Relieves diarrhea and constipation
- Alleviates pain, inflammation, spasms and cramps
- Relieves bloating, flatulence, and inflammation

CHINESE THERAPEUTIC ACTIONS

- Tonifies the Spleen
- Regulates Liver qi
- Stops diarrhea
- Clears damp-heat

DOSAGE

Take 3 to 4 capsules three times daily with warm water. Dosage can be increased up to 8 to 10 capsules three times daily in acute cases until symptoms subside. For maximum effectiveness, take the herbs on an empty stomach.

INGREDIENTS

Bai Shao (Radix Paeoniae Alba)
Bai Zhi (Radix Angelicae Dahuricae)
Bai Zhu (Rhizoma Atractylodis Macrocephalae)
Bo He (Herba Menthae)
Chai Hu (Radix Bupleuri)
Che Qian Zi (Semen Plantaginis)
Chen Pi (Pericarpium Citri Reticulatae)
Chuan Mu Xiang (Radix Vladimiriae)
Dang Gui (Radix Angelicae Sinensis)
Dang Shen (Radix Codonopsis)
Fang Feng (Radix Saposhnikoviae)
Fu Ling (Poria)
Hou Po (Cortex Magnoliae Officinalis)
Huang Bo (Cortex Phellodendri Chinensis)
Huang Lian (Rhizoma Coptidis)
Huo Xiang (Herba Agastaches)
Pao Jiang (Rhizoma Zingiberis Praeparatum)
Qin Pi (Cortex Fraxini)
Wu Wei Zi (Fructus Schisandrae Chinensis)
Yi Yi Ren (Semen Coicis)
Yin Chen (Herba Artemisiae Scopariae)
Zhi Gan Cao (Radix et Rhizoma Glycyrrhizae Praeparata cum Melle)

BACKGROUND

Irritable bowel syndrome (IBS) is a motility disorder involving the entire gastrointestinal tract causing varying degrees of abdominal discomfort and pain, constipation and/or diarrhea and abdominal bloating. In addition, patients often notice a change in the pattern of bowel movement, mucus in the stool, and sensation of incomplete evacuation after defecation. Though the exact cause is unknown and the pathophysiology is not completely understood, it has been found that emotional factors, diet, drugs, chemicals or toxic substances often precipitate or aggravate the condition. Optimal treatment, therefore, must focus on alleviating the gastrointestinal symptoms and eliminating the factors that trigger the bowel irritation.

FORMULA EXPLANATION

According to traditional Chinese medicine, irritable bowel syndrome (IBS) is a condition caused by Spleen qi deficiency and Liver qi stagnation. Gastrointestinal symptoms such as loose stools, mucus in the stool, pain, incomplete evacuation and bloating are all results of Liver overacting on the Spleen and Stomach. In addition to IBS, many other bowel disorders exhibit similar signs and symptoms described above. ***GI Harmony*** focuses on tonifying the Spleen, harmonizing the Stomach, spreading the Liver qi to relieve bloating and pain, and draining damp-heat in the Intestines to reduce inflammation.

Dang Shen (Radix Codonopsis), *Bai Zhu* (Rhizoma Atractylodis Macrocephalae), *Fu Ling* (Poria), and *Yi Yi Ren* (Semen Coicis) tonify the Spleen and dispel dampness. Dampness in the body is manifested by the presence of mucus in the stool. Dampness in the Intestines also causes feelings of incomplete evacuation. The above herbs strengthen Spleen qi and avoid the conditions characterized by Wood overacting on the Earth element. *Huo Xiang* (Herba Agastaches) , *Fang Feng* (Radix Saposhnikoviae), and *Wu Wei Zi* (Fructus Schisandrae Chinensis) stop diarrhea. *Chai Hu* (Radix Bupleuri), *Hou Po* (Cortex Magnoliae Officinalis), *Chen Pi* (Pericarpium Citri Reticulatae), *Bo He* (Herba Menthae), and *Chuan Mu Xiang* (Radix Vladimiriae) are qi-regulating herbs used to relieve bloating, pain, gas and stress. *Bai Shao* (Radix Paeoniae Alba) and *Dang Gui* (Radix Angelicae Sinensis) nourish blood to soften the Liver and relieve cramps. To reduce the inflammation in the intestines, heat-clearing herbs, such as *Huang Bo* (Cortex Phellodendri Chinensis), *Huang Lian* (Rhizoma Coptidis), *Yin Chen* (Herba Artemisiae Scopariae), *Che Qian Zi* (Semen Plantaginis), and *Qin Pi* (Cortex Fraxini), are used. *Yin Chen* (Herba Artemisiae Scopariae) also increases the production of bile to help digestion. *Che Qian Zi* (Semen Plantaginis) also dispels water through urination to consolidate stool. *Pao Jiang* (Rhizoma Zingiberis Praeparatum) and *Zhi Gan Cao* (Radix et Rhizoma Glycyrrhizae Praeparata cum Melle) harmonize the middle *jiao*. Finally, *Bai Zhi* (Radix Angelicae Dahuricae) enters the Stomach and the Spleen channels to stop diarrhea, eliminate pus, and relieve pain.

GI Harmony™

GI Harmony is a comprehensive formula that addresses irritable bowel syndrome and many other bowel disorders. This formula treats the cause of the disorder by tonifying the Spleen and spreading Liver qi stagnation. Furthermore, this formula treats the symptoms by relieving bloating and flatulence, regulating bowel movement, and alleviating abdominal pain.

CAUTIONS & CONTRAINDICATIONS

- This formula is contraindicated during pregnancy and nursing.
- This herbal formula contains herbs that invigorate blood circulation, such as *Dang Gui* (Radix Angelicae Sinensis). Therefore, patients who are on anticoagulant or antiplatelet therapies, such as Coumadin (warfarin), should use this formula with caution, or not at all, as there may be a higher risk of bleeding and bruising.[1,2,3]

CLINICAL NOTES

- ***GI Harmony*** is an herbal formula derived from the standard treatment of IBS used in a clinical trial conducted by University of Western Sydney MacArthur in Australia. In this randomized, double-blind, placebo-controlled study, 116 patients who fulfilled the Rome criteria were allocated to one of three groups: individualized treatment, standard treatment, or placebo. After 16 weeks of treatment, the gastroenterologists evaluated the patients and concluded that both the individualized treatment and the standard treatment, in comparison with placebo, showed significant improvement in bowel symptom score, global improvement, and reduced degree of interference with life. This study is published on November 11, 1998 by Journal of American Medical Association (JAMA).[4]
- Patients should take ***Calm*** to continually relieve Liver qi stagnation, especially if they have a stressful lifestyle or career. ***GI Harmony*** and ***Calm*** can be taken at equal portions for patients who have IBS and are constantly stressed.
- Female patients suffering from IBS are likely to note aggravation of symptoms before each menstrual cycle. ***Calm*** is recommended with ***GI Harmony*** for maximum effect.

Pulse Diagnosis by Dr. Jimmy Wei-Yen Chang:

- Rainbow pulse, a convex-shaped pulse that is thick, forceful, and expanding on and extends distally to the left *cun*.
- Floating and forceful pulse on the right *cun* and *guan*.

SUPPLEMENTARY FORMULAS

- For irritable bowel due to stress, add ***Calm***.
- For irritable bowel with insomnia due to *shen* (spirit) disturbance in patients with excess, add ***Calm (ES)***.
- For irritable bowel with insomnia due to stress in patients with deficiency, add ***Calm ZZZ***.
- For constipation, add ***Gentle Lax (Deficient)***.
- For hemorrhoids, add ***GI Care (HMR)***.
- For fistula and diverticulitis, combine with ***Resolve (AI)*** and ***Astringent Complex***.
- For peptic ulcer, add ***GI Care***.
- For burning diarrhea or dysentery, add ***GI Care II***.
- For fatigue or weakness, add ***Imperial Tonic***.
- For excess fire, add ***Gardenia Complex***.
- For bleeding, add ***Notoginseng 9***.
- For excessive damp and phlegm, add ***Pinellia Complex***.

ACUPUNCTURE TREATMENT

Traditional Points:

- *Dachangshu* (BL 25), *Tianshu* (ST 25), *Zhongji* (CV 3), *Shenque* (CV 8)
  - For diarrhea, add *Zusanli* (ST 36) and *Sanyinjiao* (SP 6).
  - For Spleen and Stomach deficiencies, add *Pishu* (BL 20) and *Zhangmen* (LR 13).
  - For Spleen and Kidney yang deficiencies, add *Shenshu* (BL 23), *Mingmen* (GV 4) and *Guanyuan* (CV 4).
  - For epigastric distension and discomfort, add *Gongsun* (SP 4).
  - For stress and emotional disturbances, add *Ganshu* (BL 18) and *Xingjian* (LR 2).

Classic Master Tung's Points:

- **Irritable bowel syndrome (with diarrhea):** *Qimen* (T 33.01), *Qijiao* (T 33.02), *Qizheng* (T 33.03), *Sihuashang* (T 77.08), *Sihuazhong* (T 77.09), *Sihuaxia* (T 77.11), *Menjin* (T 66.05), *Simazhong* (T 88.17), *Minghuang* (T 88.12), *Ganmen* (T 33.11), *Changmen* (T 33.10)
- **Irritable bowel syndrome (with constipation):** *Tushui* (T 22.11), *Qimen* (T 33.01), *Qijiao* (T 33.02), *Qizheng* (T 33.03), *Simashang* (T 88.18), *Simazhong* (T 88.17), *Simaxia* (T 88.19), *Tongtian* (T 88.03), *Fuchang* (T 77.12), *Huochuan* (T 33.04)
- **Bloating:** *Pizhong* (T 11.18), *Sihuashang* (T 77.08), *Sihuazhong* (T 77.09), *Sihuaxia* (T 77.11), *Fuchang* (T 77.12), *Menjin* (T 66.05), *Huoju* (T 66.11), *Changmen* (T 33.10), *Minghuang* (T 88.12), *Tianhuang* (T 88.13), *Qihuang* (T 88.14), *Beimian* (T 44.07), *Fukuai* (T 1010.15), *Shangjiuli* (T 88.26), *Zhongjiuli* (T 88.25), *Xiajiuli* (T 88.27), *Sifuyi* (T 1010.11), *Sifuer* (T 1010.10)

Master Tung's Points by Dr. Chuan-Min Wang:

- **Irritable bowel syndrome, diverticulitis:** *Changmen* (T 33.10), *Ganmen* (T 33.11), *Sihuazhong* (T 77.09)

Balance Method by Dr. Richard Tan:

- Left side: *Dadun* (LR 1), *Zhongfeng* (LR 4), *Gongsun* (SP 4), *Sanyinjiao* (SP 6), *Yinlingquan* (SP 9), *Hegu* (LI 4), *Shangyang* (LI 1)
- Right side: *Lieque* (LU 7), *Kongzui* (LU 6), *Neiguan* (PC 6), *Zhongchong* (PC 9), *Liangqiu* (ST 34), *Zusanli* (ST 36), *Tiaokou* (ST 38), *Chongyang* (ST 42), *Lidui* (ST 45)
- Left and right sides can be alternated from treatment to treatment.
- Ear points: *Shenmen* and Intestine.

GI Harmony™

The selection of points may be alternated with the points below from treatment to treatment.

- Left side: *Neiguan* (PC 6), *Zhongchong* (PC 9), *Chongyang* (ST 42), *Lidui* (ST 45)
- Right side: *Shangyang* (LI 1), *Hegu* (LI 4), *Dadun* (LR 1), *Zhongfeng* (LR 4)

Ear Acupuncture:

- Sympathetic, *Shenmen*, Endocrine, Small Intestine, Large Intestine
- Select two to three points per treatment. Leave in the needles for 20 minutes. Treat daily or every other day.

Auricular Medicine by Dr. Li-Chun Huang:

- **Relaxing the bowels:** Abdomen, Spleen, Lung, Liver, *San Jiao*, Large Intestine, Sigmoid, Digestive Subcortex
- **Relieving diarrhea:** Spleen, Occiput, Large Intestine, Sympathetic, Rectum, *Shenmen*, Digestive Subcortex. Bleed Ear Apex.
- **Invigorating the Spleen and promoting the digestion:** Spleen, Stomach, Mouth, Pancreas, Endocrine, Digestive Subcortex, Small Intestine
- **Bloating and distension:** Liver, Stomach, Spleen, Lung, Gallbladder, *San Jiao*, Large Intestine, Abdominal Distension Area, Digestive Subcortex
- **Intestine dysfunction:** Large Intestine, Small Intestine, Sigmoid, Liver, Spleen, *San Jiao*, Digestive Subcortex, Sympathetic
- **Constipation:** Large Intestine, Sigmoid, Liver, Spleen, Lung, *San Jiao*, Digestive Subcortex
- **Stop bleeding:** Pituitary, Diaphragm, Adrenal Gland, Spleen, corresponding point where there is bleeding

NUTRITION

- Diet is essential to complete recovery. Foods that are associated with gas production should not be consumed, such as onions, soda, beans, cabbage, brussel sprouts, cauliflower and broccoli. Use of probiotics helps to relieve bloating and other symptoms of IBS.
- Eat a variety of fresh, organic fruits and vegetables of all colors.
- Incorporate more high-fiber whole grains and nuts into diet.
- Drink warm or hot liquids with meals. Putting cold and ice on any part of the body will immediately constrict the flow of blood to that region. Similarly, drinking cold or iced drinks with meals will hinder the natural peristaltic movements of the digestive system.
- Foods with antioxidant effects, such as vitamin A, C and E are beneficial as they neutralize the free radicals and minimize damage to cells. Beneficial foods include citrus fruits, carrots, green leafy vegetables, and green tea.
- Chew food completely and thoroughly. The digestive tract can process and absorb smaller pieces of food much better than food that is incompletely chewed. Larger pieces of food can lead to incomplete digestion and digestive discomfort.
- Always eat breakfast. According to the TCM clock, the most optimal time for the digestive system is in the morning from 8 to 10 a.m.
- Give the body two to three hours between the last meal of the day and bedtime. During sleep, the digestive system slows down as well. Make sure the body has adequate time to digest the food before going into sleep mode.
- If the patient is allergic to any food or feel uncomfortable after eating certain foods, avoid eating them.
- Avoid fast food, processed foods, junk food, artificial sugars, and carbonated drinks. Stay away from meat, greasy food, alcohol, caffeine, dairy products (except for unsweetened low-fat yogurt), tap water, iron supplements, and vegetables and fruits with pesticides.
- The Spleen is responsible for generating post-natal qi and good Spleen function also contributes to a healthy immune system. Foods that damage the Spleen should be avoided:
  - Avoid any and all foods that contain sugar, such as cake, dessert, candy, chocolate, canned juice, soft drinks, caffeinated drinks, stevia, sugar substitutes, agave, xylitol, and corn syrup.
  - Avoid raw or uncooked meats, such as sashimi, sushi, steak tartar, and seared meat.
  - Minimize consumption of foods that are cooling in nature, including tofu, tomato, celery, asparagus, bamboo, seaweed, kelp, bitter melon, cucumber, gourd, luffa, eggplant, winter melon, watermelon, honeydew, citrus, oranges, guava, grapefruit, pineapple, plums, pear, banana, papaya, white radish, mustard leaf, potherb mustard, Chinese kale, napa, and bamboo sprout. Do not eat foods straight from the refrigerator. Long-term intake of cold fruits and vegetables like the ones listed above may be damaging to the Spleen. The cooling property of foods can be neutralized by cooking or adding 20 pieces of *Gou Qi Zi* (Fructus Lycii).
  - Avoid carbohydrates like white rice or bread as they may produce dampness.
  - No seafood especially shellfish, like crabs, oyster, scallops, clams, lobster and shrimp (they enter the *yangming* Stomach channel).
  - Avoid fermented foods like cheese or fermented tofu.
  - Do not eat dairy products, such as milk, cream, cheese, and ice cream.
  - No lamb, beef, goose or duck.
  - Avoid deep-fried or greasy foods.
- Warm and hot natured foods that damage qi and yin should be avoided, such as:
  - certain fruits like mango and durian that produce heat.
  - stimulants like coffee, alcohol, and energy drinks.
  - spicy/pungent/aromatic vegetables such as pepper, garlic, onions, basil, rosemary, cumin, funnel, anise, leeks, chives, scallions, thyme, saffron, wormwood, mustard, chili pepper, and wasabi.
- Avoid food and drinks with artificial coloring.

GI Harmony™

- Consume as few meat products as possible. Do not eat processed meats, such as lunch meats, hot dogs and sausages, as they contain nitrites that are associated with inflammation and chronic disease.

The Tao of Nutrition by Dr. Maoshing Ni and Cathy McNease:

- **Diarrhea**
  - Recommendations: garlic, black pepper, blueberries, cinnamon, raspberry leaves, lotus seeds, burned rice, yams, sweet potatoes, fresh fig leaves, peas, buckwheat, litchi, guava peel, apple, charcoaled bread, ginger, pearl barley, basil, unripe prunes.
  - Cook rice porridge with lotus seed and yam or with barley.
  - Eat burnt rice or bread.
  - Make tea from dried litchi and Chinese black dates.
  - Take two tablespoons of dried apples, three times daily on an empty stomach with warm water.
  - Cook rice porridge with ginger and black pepper.
  - Drink black tea.
  - Take two bulbs of garlic, bake until black. Then boil in water and drink the tea.
  - Make tea from guava peel.
  - Make tea from ginger, fennel, basil, and Chinese black dates.
  - Make tea from unripe prunes.
  - Eat sweet rice porridge.
  - Avoid cold, raw foods, most fruits, juices, and overeating.
- **Constipation**
  - Recommendations: bananas, apples, walnuts, figs, spinach, peaches, pears, pine nuts, sesame seeds, mulberries, grapefruit, yams, honey, apricot kernel, milk, yogurt, alfalfa sprouts, beets, cabbage, bok choy, cauliflower, and potato.
  - Eat two bananas on an empty stomach, followed by a glass of water.
  - Drink a glass of lukewarm water with 2 teaspoons of honey on an empty stomach.
  - Drink blended beets and cabbage on an empty stomach.
  - Make beet soup.
  - Eat 5 to 10 figs on an empty stomach, followed by a glass of water.
  - Eat a fresh apple on an empty stomach daily.
  - Drink mulberry juice.
  - Eat lightly steamed asparagus and cabbage at night before retiring.
  - Avoid spicy foods, fried foods, and meat.

LIFESTYLE INSTRUCTIONS

- Stress is a major factor in patients suffering from IBS. A relaxed or positive outlook on life is very important to recovery. Patients should be advised to learn to become more relaxed.
- Application of a heat pad to the abdomen may help with relieving pain associated with bloating and distension. Light abdominal massage in circular motions clockwise and then counterclockwise starting from small circles gradually becoming bigger may also help relieve distension, discomfort and pain. A five-minute abdominal massage is recommended daily. Patients should be advised to pass gas whenever needed to relieve qi stagnation.
- Chronic diarrhea may be alleviated with topical application of herbs. Grind *She Chuang Zi* (Fructus Cnidii) or *Wu Zhu Yu* (Fructus Evodiae) into a fine powder, dry fry the powder until it is warm, and place the powder on the umbilicus covered by gauze or tape. Change the powder every 24 hours. If the herbs are unavailable, 60g of sea salt may be used as a substitute.

CASE STUDIES

- A female patient complained of irritable bowel syndrome (IBS) for the past 20 years. Symptoms included diarrhea 10 to 15 times per day immediately after meals. This condition was diagnosed as Liver overacting on Spleen and Stomach. The patient was treated with ***GI Harmony***, four capsules three times a day. Within one month of acupuncture and ***GI Harmony*** the patient noticed more time elapsed before the diarrhea occurred after meals. By the end of two months, only two or three episodes had occurred during a two week period, followed by only one or two episodes each month after three months of treatment. Today the patient only keeps ***GI Harmony*** available if needed, but she has not had any flare-ups in two months. Submitted by C.C., Cromwell, Connecticut.
- S.F., a 42-year-old female, presented with a gastrointestinal disorder with symptoms consisting of diarrhea with extreme urgency, especially worse with stress. Pulse was wiry and thready and her tongue was red with a long center crack. An additional objective finding was dark circles under her eyes. The practitioner diagnosed this condition as Liver overacting on Spleen. Upon diagnosis the patient was given ***GI Harmony*** and ***Calm***. With taking the herbs, the patient is doing well, having a bowel movement which is well formed. Additional lifestyle changes she had made were avoiding caffeine and going to bed before 11:00 p.m. Submitted by T.W., Perrysburg, Ohio.
- D.S., a 65-year old female, presented with chronic irritable bowel syndrome consisting of mostly loose stools and constipation occasionally. It was also noted she had her gallbladder removed. Objective findings included minimal discomfort in all quadrants. The practitioner diagnosed this condition as Spleen qi deficiency and damp-cold. ***GI Harmony*** was prescribed, in which the patient needed to take at higher amounts and for a longer period of time in order to experience quiet digestions. She was very pleased with the results of the formula. Submitted by J.L., San Diego, California.
- P.Q., a 42-year-old female, presented with acid reflux and a 20-year history of irritable bowel syndrome. She had been on Xanax (alprazolam), Nexium (esomeprazole) and other Western medications. After only four days of taking ***GI Harmony*** at four capsules, three times daily, the patient saw improvement.

GI Harmony™

She is now successfully off all Western medications. The doctor commented that this formula is a "miracle in a bottle." Submitted by H.C., Stephens City, Virginia.

- G.M., a 42-year-old female, presented with pain in the lower *jiao*, extreme fatigue, constipation, depression, poor concentration, pain with diarrhea, palpitations and night sweats. The Western diagnosis was chronic fatigue syndrome [as the doctors couldn't find anything specifically wrong]; the TCM diagnosis was yin deficiency with deficiency heat. After taking ***Balance (Heat)***, ***GI Harmony*** and ***Gentle Lax (Deficient)***, the patient reported little to no night sweats within three weeks. Her bowels normalized, and the GI tract pain was much better. She stated that she felt she could now smile and face the day. Submitted by M.C., Sarasota, Florida.
- X.L., a 7.5-year-old dog, presented with irritable bowel syndrome consisting of both loose sticky stools and constipation. The practitioner diagnosed this condition as Liver qi stagnation with Spleen qi deficiency. Upon diagnosis, ***GI Harmony*** was prescribed. The pet was given half a capsule whenever an event of IBS symptoms came about. With taking the herbs the stools would usually clear up right away and would have perfect stools for many days. Submitted by J.L., San Diego, California.

PHARMACOLOGICAL AND CLINICAL RESEARCH

GI Harmony is formulated to treat irritable bowel syndrome (IBS) and other bowel disorders, such as diverticulitis, mucous colitis, nervous bowel, irritable colon, and spastic colon. It contains herbs that neutralize factors that trigger and aggravate these bowel disorders, such as emotional disturbances, diet imbalance, and exposure to drugs, chemicals or toxic substances.

Irritable bowel syndrome is a disorder characterized by irritable and irregular bowel movement with alternating diarrhea and constipation. Therefore, the primary treatment emphasis must be to regulate and restore normal gastrointestinal functions. *Bai Zhu* (Rhizoma Atractylodis Macrocephalae) is one of the most important herbs to balance gastrointestinal dysfunction. This herb is well known for its dual effect on the digestive tract: it treats diarrhea at low doses and constipation at high doses. With this dual effect to balance the intestines, *Bai Zhu* (Rhizoma Atractylodis Macrocephalae) is the ideal herb for cases where there is alternation of diarrhea and constipation.[5] In addition to *Bai Zhu* (Rhizoma Atractylodis Macrocephalae), ***GI Harmony*** uses many other herbs to influence and support the gastrointestinal tract. Diarrhea can be prevented and treated with herbs such as *Bai Zhu* (Rhizoma Atractylodis Macrocephalae), *Wu Wei Zi* (Fructus Schisandrae Chinensis), *Che Qian Zi* (Semen Plantaginis), and *Fu Ling* (Poria). In one study, 320 infants with diarrhea were treated with an herbal powder containing *Bai Zhu* (Rhizoma Atractylodis Macrocephalae) three times daily before meals with good results.[6] In another study, 63 out of 69 infants with diarrhea showed complete recovery within one to two days following treatment using an herbal decoction containing 30 grams of *Che Qian Zi* (Semen Plantaginis) and a small amount of sugar.[7] Furthermore, in a clinical study, 93 infants with diarrhea were treated with *Fu Ling* (Poria) with good symptomatic relief and a shortened duration of diarrhea.[8] On the other hand, constipation can be alleviated and treated with herbs such as *Bai Shao* (Radix Paeoniae Alba), *Gan Cao* (Radix et Rhizoma Glycyrrhizae), *Dang Gui* (Radix Angelicae Sinensis) and *Pao Jiang* (Rhizoma Zingiberis Praeparatum). According to one report, over 60 patients with chronic habitual constipation were treated with great success using an herbal formula with 24 to 40 grams of fresh *Bai Shao* (Radix Paeoniae Alba) and 10 to 15 grams of fresh *Gan Cao* (Radix et Rhizoma Glycyrrhizae) in decoction.[9] Use of *Dang Gui* (Radix Angelicae Sinensis), *Gan Cao* (Radix et Rhizoma Glycyrrhizae) and others in an herbal formula showed 94% rate of effectiveness for treatment of chronic constipation in 50 elderly patients.[10]

Beyond constipation and diarrhea, ***GI Harmony*** contains other herbs that regulate and restore normal gastrointestinal functions. *Dang Shen* (Radix Codonopsis) has marked preventative and treatment effects on peptic ulcers. It increases gastric emptying time, decreases severity of ulceration, and increases the amount of prostaglandin in the stomach.[11] Deoxyschizandrin, one ingredient of *Wu Wei Zi* (Fructus Schisandrae Chinensis), inhibits the secretion of gastric acid, and has shown beneficial effects in treatment of gastric ulcer.[12] *Hou Po* (Cortex Magnoliae Officinalis) has an inhibitory effect on the gastrointestinal system, leading to decreased secretion of gastric acid.[13] Many components of *Gan Cao* (Radix et Rhizoma Glycyrrhizae) have shown protective and treatment effects for peptic ulcers. The mechanisms of action include inhibition of gastric acid secretion, binding and deactivation of gastric acid, and promotion of recovery from ulceration [14] *Hou Po* (Cortex Magnoliae Officinalis) decreases incidence of intestinal bloating.[15] Administration of *Chuan Mu Xiang* (Radix Vladimiriae) shows 100% effectiveness in 29 patients to reduce flatulence due to indigestion, acute gastroenteritis, gastric nervosa, and post-surgical complications.[16] Lastly, an herbal formula composed of 80% *Huang Lian* (Rhizoma Coptidis) demonstrates effective in treating 100 patients with inflammatory bowel condition, such as acute gastroenteritis or enteritis.[17] Lastly, *Pao Jiang* (Rhizoma Zingiberis Praeparatum) has been shown to enhance intestinal peristalsis, increase production of gastric mucous membranes, and restore normal intestinal activity.[18,19]

From Western medicine perspectives, though the cause and pathophysiology of irritable bowel syndrome are not completely known and understood, the severity of the disease and frequency of attacks are clearly associated with factors such as emotion, diet, drugs, chemicals or toxic substances. Therefore, ***GI Harmony*** contains many herbs to specifically address these factors. *Chai Hu* (Radix Bupleuri) is one of the most effective and most frequently used herbs to regulate the emotion and treat psychological disorders, including but not limited to depression,[20] neurosis,[21]

GI Harmony™

schizophrenia,[22] and psychosis.[23] Since the bowel irritation may be associated with intake of certain foods, drugs, chemicals or other toxic substances, ***GI Harmony*** contains herbs to detoxify these offending substances. Administration of *Dan Shen* (Radix et Rhizoma Salviae Miltiorrhizae) shows a marked protective effect against irritation of the gastrointestinal tract caused by aspirin and non-steroidal-anti-inflammatory drugs (NSAIDs).[24] In addition, glycyrrhizin, one of the main constituents of *Gan Cao* (Radix et Rhizoma Glycyrrhizae), has a remarkable detoxifying effect to treat various kinds of poisonings, including but not limited to drug poisoning (chloral hydrate, urethane, cocaine, picrotoxin, caffeine, pilocarpine, nicotine, barbiturates, mercury and lead), food poisoning (tetrodotoxin, snake, and mushrooms), and others (enterotoxin, herbicides, pesticides).[25]

Lastly, to treat pain and inflammation, ***GI Harmony*** uses many herbs with analgesic, anti-inflammatory and antispasmodic effects. *Dang Gui* (Radix Angelicae Sinensis) has a strong analgesic and anti-inflammatory effect, with potency and efficacy similar or greater than aspirin.[26,27] *Bai Zhi* (Radix Angelicae Dahuricae) has potent analgesic, anti-inflammatory and antispasmodic effects.[28,29,30,31] Use of *Bai Zhi* (Radix Angelicae Dahuricae) in an herbal formula has been shown to effectively treat 40 patients with gastric pain due to gastric ulcer, duodenal ulcer, and chronic gastritis.[32] *Bai Shao* (Radix Paeoniae Alba) and *Gan Cao* (Radix et Rhizoma Glycyrrhizae) are two herbs with strong and synergistic, analgesic, and antispasmodic activities.[33,34] In fact, the use of these two herbs show great success in treating 85 patients with intestinal cramps and spasms in one clinical study.[35] To harmonize the gastrointestinal tract and normalize its functions, ***GI Harmony*** uses many herbs with different mechanisms of action to reduce inflammation and relieve irritation. *Fang Feng* (Radix Saposhnikoviae) and *Che Qian Zi* (Semen Plantaginis) show a marked effect to suppress inflammation via the inhibition of nitrite production.[36,37] *Hou Po* (Cortex Magnoliae Officinalis) illustrates its anti-inflammatory properties through the inactivation of NF-kappaB, which is an important factor in the regulation of inflammatory reaction.[38] *Huang Lian* (Rhizoma Coptidis) and *Huang Bo* (Cortex Phellodendri) both have a great effect to reduce inflammation by inhibiting the production of proinflammatory cytokines, such as interleukin-1beta and tumor necrosis factor-alpha (TNF-α).[39] In fact, the combination of *Huang Lian* (Rhizoma Coptidis) and *Huang Bo* (Cortex Phellodendri) exert anti-inflammatory activity as potent as the effects associated with dexamethasone (Decadron) or celecoxib (Celebrex) for treating both acute and chronic inflammatory diseases.[40] Lastly, *Gan Cao* (Radix et Rhizoma Glycyrrhizae) demonstrates marked anti-inflammatory effects. The exact mechanisms of action vary among experts. Some believe that the enhanced cortisone effect is due to decreased metabolism by the liver, or increased plasma concentration caused by decreased protein binding.[41] Nonetheless, *Gan Cao* (Radix et Rhizoma Glycyrrhizae) has potent steroid-like effect, with potency of glycyrrhizin and glycyrrhetinic acid comparable to 1/10th that of cortisone.[42]

In summary, ***GI Harmony*** contains herbs with marked effectiveness to treat irritable bowel syndrome. ***GI Harmony*** regulates the bowel movement, and relieves abdominal discomfort and pain, and neutralizes the irritation caused by toxic and other offending substances (such as drugs and chemicals).

COMPARATIVE ANALYSIS

Irritable bowel syndrome (IBS) is a motility disorder that affects the entire gastrointestinal tract. This disorder has no known anatomic cause. Therefore, most drug treatments focus on relieving symptoms. Anticholinergic drugs [such as Pro-Banthine (propantheline)], tranquilizers [such as Librium (chlordiazepoxide)], and sedatives [such as phenobarbital] are frequently given to relieve gastrointestinal symptoms and to calm patients. Those with depression are treated with antidepressants, and ones with diarrhea are treated with antidiarrheals. While this discussion of drug treatment is an oversimplification, it nonetheless illustrates that these drugs only treat symptoms, and not the cause, of irritable bowel syndrome. Therefore, though they offer short-term effectiveness, symptoms often flare-up again once the drugs are discontinued.

Use of acupuncture and herbs is effective to treat various gastrointestinal disorders, including but not limited to irritable bowel syndrome, diverticulitis, mucous colitis, nervous bowel, irritable colon, and spastic colon. Not only do they control the symptoms, they often change the underlying constitution of the body to achieve long-term results. In fact, most patients remain symptom free for at least several months after the herbs are discontinued.

It is important to remember that stress and diet are two main factors that trigger irritable bowel syndrome. In addition to considering drugs or herbal treatment, it is important to follow the guidelines described in this monograph, and make diet and lifestyle changes. Only then will treatment successfully ensure short- and long-term effectiveness, and minimize the frequency and severity of irritable bowel syndrome.

References

1. Chan K, Lo AC, Yeung JH, Woo KS. Journal of Pharmacy and Pharmacology 1995 May;47(5):402-6.
2. Pharmacotherapy 1999 July;19(7):870-876.
3. European Journal of Drug Metabolism and Pharmacokinetics 1995; 20(1): 55-60.
4. Bensoussan, A. Talley, N. et al. Treatment of Irritable Bowel Syndrome with Chinese Herbal Medicine. JAMA, November 11, 1998. Vol 280, No 18.
5. *Chang Yong Zhong Yao Cheng Fen Yu Yao Li Shou Ce* (A Handbook of the Composition and Pharmacology of Common Chinese Drugs), 1994; 739:742.
6. *Shan Dong Zhong Yi Za Zhi* (Shandong Journal of Chinese Medicine), 1982; 2:107.
7. *Zhong Xi Yi Jie He Za Zhi* (Journal of Integrated Chinese and Western Medicine), 1987; 11:697.
8. *Bei Jing Zhong Yi* (Beijing Chinese Medicine), 1985; 5:31.

GI Harmony ™

9. *Zhong Yi Za Zhi* (Journal of Chinese Medicine), 1983; 8:79.
10. *Tian Jin Zhong Yi* (Tianjin Chinese Medicine), 1996; (2):33.
11. *Zhong Yao Yao Li Yu Lin Chuang* (Pharmacology and Clinical Applications of Chinese Herbs), 1990; 6(6):9.
12. *Ri Ben Yao Li Xue Za Zhi* (Japanese Journal of Herbology), 1986; 87(3):209.
13. *Guo Wai Yi Yao Zhi Wu Yao Fen Ce* (Monograph of Foreign Botanical Medicine), 1988; 10(1):43.
14. *Zhong Yao Zhi* (Chinese Herbology Journal), 1993; 358.
15. *Xin Yi Yao Xue Za Zhi* (New Journal of Medicine and Herbology), 1973; 4:25.
16. *Yun Nan Zhong Yao Zhi* (Yunan Journal of Chinese Herbal Medicine), 1979; 3:37.
17. *Si Chuan Yi Xue Yuan Xue Bao* (Journal of Sichuan School of Medicine), 1959; 1:102.
18. *Zhong Yao Xue* (Chinese Herbology), 1998; 376:378.
19. *Zhong Cao Yao* (Chinese Herbal Medicine), 1988; 13(11):17.
20. *Bei Jing Zhong Yi* (Beijing Chinese Medicine) 1996;2:22.
21. *Fu Jian Zhong Yi Yao* (Fujian Chinese Medicine and Herbology) 1999;5:26.
22. *Zhong Xi Yi Jie He Za Zhi* (Journal of Integrated Chinese and Western Medicine) 1982;(3):170.
23. *Xin Zhong Yi* (New Chinese Medicine) 1983;(1):37.
24. *Zhong Yao Yao Li Yu Lin Chuang* (Pharmacology and Clinical Applications of Chinese Herbs), 1991; 14(5):47.
25. *Zhong Yao Tong Bao* (Journal of Chinese Herbology), 1986; 11(10):55.
26. *Xin Yi Yao Xue Za Zhi* (New Journal of Medicine and Herbology), 1975; (6):34.
27. *Yao Xue Za Zhi* (Journal of Medicinals), 1971; (91):1098.
28. *Zhong Guo Zhong Yao Za Zhi* (People's Republic of China Journal of Chinese Herbology), 1991; 16(9):560.
29. *Zhong Guo Zhong Yao Za Zhi* (People's Republic of China Journal of Chinese Herbology), 1991; 16(9):560.
30. *Zhong Yao Yao Li Yu Ying Yong* (Pharmacology and Applications of Chinese Herbs), 1983:796.
31. *Zhi Wu Yao You Xiao Cheng Fen Shou Ce* (Manual of Plant Medicinals and Their Active Constituents), 1986: 624,603,197.
32. *Zhong Yao Lin Chuan Xin Yong* (New Clinical Applications of Chinese Medicine), 2001; 207.
33. *Shang Hai Zhong Yi Yao Za Zhi* (Shanghai Journal of Chinese Medicine and Herbology), 1983; 4:14.
34. *Zhong Yao Xue* (Chinese Herbology), 1998, 759:765.
35. *Zhong Yi Za Zhi* (Journal of Chinese Medicine), 1985; 6:50.
36. Tezuka Y., Irikawa S., Kaneko T., Banskota A.H., Nagaoka T., Xiong Q., Hase K., Kadota S. Screening of Chinese herbal drug extracts for inhibitory activity on nitric oxide production and identification of an active compound of *Zanthoxylum bungeanum. J Ethnopharmacol.* 2001, 77(2-3): 209-217.
37. Wang CC, Chen LG, Yang LL. Inducible nitric oxide synthase inhibitor of the Chinese herb I. Saposhnikovia divaricata (Turcz.) Schischk. Cancer Lett. 1999 Oct 18;145(1-2):151-7.
38. Oh JH, Kang LL, Ban JO, Kim YH, Kim KH, Han SB, Hong JT. Anti-inflammatory effect of 4-O-methylhonokiol, compound isolated from Magnolia officinalis through inhibition of NF-kappaB. College of Pharmacy, CBITRC, Chungbuk National University, 12, Gaesin-dong, Heungduk-gu, Cheongju, Chungbuk 361-763, Republic of Korea. Chem Biol Interact. 2010 Dec 5;188(3):677.
39. Hsiang CY, Wu SL, Cheng SE, Ho TY. Acetaldehyde-induced interleukin-1beta and tumor necrosis factor-alpha production is inhibited by berberine through nuclear factor-kappaB signaling pathway in HepG2 cells. Graduate Institute of Medical Science, China Medical University, Taichung 404, Taiwan. J Biomed Sci. 2005 Oct;12(5):791-801.
40. Park EK, Rhee HI, Jung HS, Ju SM, Lee YA, Lee SH, Hong SJ, Yang HI, Yoo MC, Kim KS. Antiinflammatory effects of a combined herbal preparation (RAH13) of Phellodendron amurense and Coptis chinensis in animal models of inflammation. East-West Bone and Joint Research Center, East-West Neo Medical Center, Kyung Hee University, 149 Sangil-dong, Gangdong-gu, Seoul 134-727, Korea. Phytother Res. 2007 Aug;21(8):746-50.
41. *Zhong Yao Zhi* (Chinese Herbology Journal), 1993; 358.
42. *Zhong Cao Yao* (Chinese Herbal Medicine), 1991; 22(10):452.

FORMULAS

GI Tonic™

CLINICAL APPLICATIONS

- **General gastrointestinal deficiency and weakness:** fatigue, poor appetite, loose stools or diarrhea, anorexia, borborygmus, bloating, weight loss, sallow complexion, weak pulse, and scalloped tongue
- **Spleen qi deficiency** causing various gastrointestinal disorders: diarrhea, superficial gastritis, and chronic colitis
- **Malnutrition** in children or those with poor appetite and loose stools

WESTERN THERAPEUTIC ACTIONS

- Balancing effect to regulate and restore gastrointestinal functions
- General supportive effect to treat gastrointestinal disorders
- Strengthens the gastrointestinal tract to improve appetite, digestion, and absorption

CHINESE THERAPEUTIC ACTIONS

- Tonifies Spleen qi
- Stops diarrhea
- Promotes digestion
- Dispels dampness and stagnation

DOSAGE

Take 2 to 4 capsules three times daily on an empty stomach, one hour before or two hours after meals. The formula can be used to treat diarrhea symptomatically. However, to achieve long-term and lasting effect, ***GI Tonic*** should be taken continuously for three to six months to change the constitution of the Spleen and the Stomach.

INGREDIENTS

Bai Zhu (Rhizoma Atractylodis Macrocephalae)
Bian Dou (Semen Lablab Album)
Fu Ling (Poria)
Gan Cao (Radix et Rhizoma Glycyrrhizae)
Jie Geng (Radix Platycodonis)
Lian Zi (Semen Nelumbinis)
Ren Shen (Radix et Rhizoma Ginseng)
Sha Ren (Fructus Amomi)
Shan Yao (Rhizoma Dioscoreae)
Yi Yi Ren (Semen Coicis)
Zhi Huang Qi (Radix Astragali Praeparata cum Melle)

BACKGROUND

Fatigue is a general symptom that may be caused by many underlying disorders, including but not limited to anemia, fibromyalgia, depression, stress and anxiety, chronic infection, and gastrointestinal and endocrine disorders. Though the causes vary widely, they share one thing in common – compromised digestion of food and absorption of nutrients. As a result, the body becomes increasingly weaker and the patient feels chronically fatigued. Therefore, the first step toward recovery is to restore gastrointestinal health so the patient can absorb nutrients from foods and begin the healing process.

FORMULA EXPLANATION

GI Tonic is designed to treat Spleen deficiency leading to symptoms of fatigue, poor appetite, diarrhea, loose stools, borborygmus, bloating and other gastrointestinal disorders. In traditional Chinese medicine, the main function of the Spleen is to extract qi from the food and turn it into energy. When the Spleen and the Stomach are deficient, they will not be able to carry out the normal gastrointestinal functions. As a result, food may travel quickly out of the body without being digested or absorbed. A weak digestive system would directly result in low appetite. Lack of nutrients would lead to weak extremities, weight loss and sallow facial appearance. Deficiency of the Spleen may cause accumulation of dampness, which may obstruct the qi flow and cause fullness in the chest.

GI Tonic contains many herbs to strengthen the Spleen and dispel dampness to restore normal gastrointestinal functions. *Ren Shen* (Radix et Rhizoma Ginseng) and *Zhi Huang Qi* (Radix Astragali Praeparata cum Melle) tonify the *yuan* (source) *qi* and Spleen qi to relieve weakness and fatigue. They also have a strong effect to increase energy and vitality. *Bai Zhu* (Rhizoma Atractylodis Macrocephalae) and *Fu Ling* (Poria) strengthen the Spleen, dispel dampness and relieve diarrhea. As they strengthen the Spleen, they also help increase appetite as well. *Shan Yao* (Rhizoma Dioscoreae), *Bian Dou* (Semen Lablab Album) and *Lian Zi* (Semen Nelumbinis) tonify both qi and Spleen yin. They are also slightly astringent in taste, and therefore have stabilizing and binding effect to relieve diarrhea or loose stools. *Yi Yi Ren* (Semen Coicis) dispels dampness, promotes urination and expels excess fluid retention in the body. *Sha Ren* (Fructus Amomi) is aromatic as it dries up dampness and stops diarrhea. It also regulates qi to relieve bloating and borborygmus. *Jie Geng* (Radix Platycodonis) raises qi and prevents prolapse that may be caused by diarrhea. *Gan Cao* (Radix et Rhizoma Glycyrrhizae) is used to harmonize the middle *jiao* and also the entire formula.

In short, ***GI Tonic*** contains herbs with great effect to tonify Spleen qi, stop diarrhea, promote digestion, and dispel dampness and stagnation. It is an excellent formula to treat gastrointestinal disorder characterized by generalized weakness and deficiency.

CAUTIONS & CONTRAINDICATIONS

- This formula is contraindicated in cases of interior heat accumulation, exterior wind-cold, or exterior wind-heat.
- This formula should not be used by itself in cases of diarrhea due to damp-heat in the Intestines, with such symptoms as burning sensations in the anus, tenesmus and foul-smelling stool. This condition is an indication of infection, and must be treated first with herbs that clear damp-heat from the Intestines.

GI Tonic ™

CLINICAL NOTES

- *GI Tonic* may be used on a short-term basis (one to two weeks) to treat diarrhea symptomatically, or on a long-term basis (three to six months) to restore gastrointestinal health.
- *GI Tonic* is beneficial for patients suffering from all kinds of gastrointestinal disorders involving Spleen qi deficiency. By strengthening the Spleen, it increases the production of post-natal qi and improves the wellness of the patient.

Pulse Diagnosis by Dr. Jimmy Wei-Yen Chang:

- Small pulse, a thin and weak pulse that disappears upon pressure on the right *guan*.

SUPPLEMENTARY FORMULAS

- For early morning diarrhea with coldness, combine with ***Kidney Tonic (Yang)***.
- For constipation with irritable bowel syndrome, combine with ***Gentle Lax (Deficient)*** and ***GI Harmony***.
- For hemorrhoids, add ***GI Care (HMR)***.
- For irritable bowel syndrome with irritability and stress, combine with ***GI Harmony*** and ***Calm***.
- Diarrhea or dysentery due to infection of the gastrointestinal tract, use ***GI Care II*** instead.
- For inflammatory bowel syndrome or ulcerative colitis caused by damp-heat in the Intestines, use ***GI Care (UC)*** instead.
- For extreme fatigue and deficiency in qi, blood, yin and yang, add ***Imperial Tonic***.
- For an immediate boost of energy, add ***Vibrant***.
- For depression, add ***Shine*** or ***Shine (DS)***.
- For hepatitis, add ***Liver DTX***.
- For bleeding, add ***Notoginseng 9***.
- For excess damp and phlegm, add ***Pinellia Complex***.

ACUPUNCTURE TREATMENT

Traditional Points:

- *Pishu* (BL 20), *Shenshu* (BL 23), *Zhongwan* (CV 12), *Tianshu* (ST 25), *Shangjuxu* (ST 37), *Yinlingquan* (SP 9), *Guanyuan* (CV 4), *Mingmen* (GV 4)

Classic Master Tung's Points:

- **Diarrhea:** *Qimen* (T 33.01), *Qijiao* (T 33.02), *Qizheng* (T 33.03), *Sihuashang* (T 77.08), *Sihuazhong* (T 77.09), *Sihuaxia* (T 77.11), *Menjin* (T 66.05), *Tianhuang* (T 77.17), *Dihuang* (T 77.19), *Renhuang* (T 77.21)
- **Poor appetite:** *Sihuashang* (T 77.08), *Sihuazhong* (T 77.09), *Sihuaxia* (T 77.11)

Master Tung's Points by Dr. Chuan-Min Wang:

- **Poor digestion:** *Tongwei* (T 88.10)
- **Poor appetite:** *Pizhong* (T 11.18), *Linggu* (T 22.05)
- **Loose stool:** *Changmen* (T 33.10)

Balance Method by Dr. Richard Tan:

- Left side: *Neiguan* (PC 6), *Lieque* (LU 7), *Zusanli* (ST 36), *Yanglingquan* (GB 34),
- Right side: *Hegu* (LI 4), *Waiguan* (TH 5), *Yinlingquan* (SP 9), *Ququan* (LR 8)
- Left and right sides can be alternated from treatment to treatment.

Ear Acupuncture:

- Large Intestine, Small Intestine, Lung, Spleen

Auricular Medicine by Dr. Li-Chun Huang:

- **Relieving diarrhea:** Spleen, Occiput, Large Intestine, Sympathetic, Rectum, *Shenmen*, Digestive Subcortex. Bleed Ear Apex.
- **Strengthen the Spleen and promoting digestion:** Spleen, Stomach, Mouth, Pancreas, Endocrine, Digestive Subcortex, Small Intestine

NUTRITION

- Eat a variety of fresh, organic fruits and vegetables of all colors.
- Incorporate more high-fiber whole grains and nuts into diet.
- Drink warm or hot liquids with meals. Putting cold and ice on any part of the body will immediately constrict the flow of blood to that region. Similarly, drinking cold or iced drinks with meals will hinder the natural peristaltic movements of the digestive system.
- Foods with antioxidant effects, such as vitamin A, C and E are beneficial as they neutralize the free radicals and minimize damage to cells. Beneficial foods include citrus fruits, carrots, green leaf vegetables, and green tea.
- Chew food completely and thoroughly. The digestive tract can process and absorb smaller pieces of food much better than food that is incompletely chewed. Larger pieces of food can lead to incomplete digestion and digestive discomfort.
- Always eat breakfast. According to the TCM clock, the most optimal time for the digestive system is in the morning from 8 to 10 a.m.
- Give the body two to three hours between the last meal of the day and bedtime. During sleep, the digestive system slows down as well. Make sure the body has adequate time to digest the food before going into sleep mode.
- If the patient is allergic to any food or feel uncomfortable after eating certain foods, then avoid eating it.
- Avoid fast food, processed foods, junk food, artificial sugars, and carbonated drinks. Stay away from meat, greasy food, alcohol, caffeine, dairy products (except for unsweetened low-fat yogurt), tap water, iron supplements, and vegetables and fruits with pesticides.
- The Spleen is responsible for generating post-natal qi, and good Spleen function also contributes to a healthy immune system. Foods that damage the Spleen should be avoided:

GI Tonic™

- Avoid any and all foods that contain sugar, such as cake, dessert, candy, chocolate, canned juice, soft drinks, caffeinated drinks, stevia, sugar substitutes, agave, xylitol, and corn syrup.
- Avoid raw or uncooked meats, such as sashimi, sushi, steak tartar, and seared meat.
- Minimize consumption of foods that are cooling in nature, including tofu, tomato, celery, asparagus, bamboo, seaweed, kelp, bitter melon, cucumber, gourd, luffa, eggplant, winter melon, watermelon, honeydew, citrus, oranges, guava, grapefruit, pineapple, plums, pear, banana, papaya, white radish, mustard leaf, potherb mustard, Chinese kale, napa, and bamboo sprout. Do not eat foods straight from the refrigerator. Long-term intake of cold fruits and vegetables like the ones listed above may be damaging to the Spleen. The cooling property of foods can be neutralized by cooking or adding 20 pieces of *Gou Qi Zi* (Fructus Lycii).
- Avoid carbohydrates like white rice or bread as they may produce dampness.
- No seafood especially shellfish, like crabs, oyster, scallops, clams, lobster and shrimp (they enter the *yangming* Stomach channel).
- Avoid fermented foods like cheese or fermented tofu.
- Do not eat dairy products, such as milk, cream, cheese, and ice cream.
- No lamb, beef, goose or duck.
- Avoid deep-fried or greasy foods.

☯ Warm and hot natured foods that damage qi and yin should be avoided, such as:

- certain fruits like mango and durian that produce heat.
- stimulants like coffee, alcohol, and energy drinks.
- spicy/pungent/aromatic vegetables such as pepper, garlic, onions, basil, rosemary, cumin, funnel, anise, leeks, chives, scallions, thyme, saffron, wormwood, mustard, chili pepper, and wasabi.

☯ Avoid food and drinks with artificial coloring.

☯ Consume as few meat products as possible. Do not eat processed meats, such as lunch meats, hot dogs and sausages, as they contain nitrites that are associated with inflammation and chronic disease.

The Tao of Nutrition by Dr. Maoshing Ni and Cathy McNease:

☯ **Weak digestion:** make a soupy porridge with cornmeal. Especially good for recovery from flu or cold.

☯ **Weak digestion and diarrhea:** toast 2 tablespoonfuls of quinoa until slightly brown, steep in hot water with 3 slices of ginger and a pinch of cardamom.

LIFESTYLE INSTRUCTIONS

☯ Sanitation of food is important to prevent further damage to the digestive system.

☯ Do not sit directly on wet cement or marble floors to prevent invasion of damp-cold.

☯ A positive outlook on life is important. Worrying and thinking too much consume Spleen qi.

☯ Individuals suffering from irritable bowel syndrome with alternating spells of constipation and diarrhea should stay away from stress as it may aggravate the symptoms.

CASE STUDIES

☯ J.S., a 67-year-old female, presented with gas, bloating, and diarrhea. She had already been to a Western doctor to rule out any internal abnormalities. The practitioner diagnosed this condition as Spleen qi deficiency; the Western diagnosis was irritable bowel syndrome. ***GI Tonic*** was prescribed to treat the condition symptomatically and it produced excellent results. The patient was also aware of her trigger foods and attempted to avoid them. The patient continues to keep the ***GI Tonic*** available, especially when traveling, in case of traveler's diarrhea. Submitted by S.R., Waterbury, Connecticut.

☯ A 25-years-old female with a long-term history of digestive problems presented with indigestion and diarrhea. She stated that she experienced abdominal pain and diarrhea whenever she eats food that is slightly unclean or spoiled. In addition, she has poor appetite and indigestion. She has a skinny appearance and an aversion to cold. The diagnosis was diarrhea due to Spleen and Stomach deficiencies. She started taking ***GI Tonic***, and began to improve within one week. She continued to take the herbs for one month to strengthen the underlining deficiencies. Submitted by J.C., Diamond Bar, California.

PHARMACOLOGICAL AND CLINICAL RESEARCH

GI Tonic is an herbal formula designed to improve the overall health of the body by supporting the gastrointestinal tract. It contains herbs with a balancing effect to regulate and restore gastrointestinal functions. Clinically, ***GI Tonic*** addresses both the causes and the symptoms of gastrointestinal problems, such as diarrhea, gastritis and colitis characterized by weakness and deficiency. Lastly, ***GI Tonic*** is also effective in relieving anorexia and malnutrition secondary to gastrointestinal disorders.

Optimal health cannot be restored unless the underlying gastrointestinal disorders are first corrected. Without proper absorption of food and nutrients, the body simply cannot heal and recover. Thus, ***GI Tonic*** uses many herbs to restore physical and physiological functions of the gastrointestinal tract. *Bai Zhu* (Rhizoma Atractylodis Macrocephalae) and *Sha Ren* (Fructus Amomi) have dual effects to regulate the gastrointestinal tract. At low doses, they have a stimulating effect on the stomach and the intestines, and at high doses, they have an inhibiting effect. Because of this balancing effect, these two herbs can be used for various gastrointestinal disorders, including both diarrhea and constipation.[1,2]

GI Tonic contains many herbs that have been shown in clinical studies to treat various gastrointestinal disorders. In one clinical

GI Tonic ™

study, 95 patients with chronic diarrhea were treated using this formula with an overall effective rate of 71.6%.[3] In another study, 42 children with diarrhea due to deficiency of the Spleen were treated, resulting in improvement in all cases.[4] The individual herbs in ***GI Tonic*** have also shown great promise for treatment of gastrointestinal conditions. For example, 93 infants with diarrhea were treated with *Fu Ling* (Poria) with complete recovery in 79 cases, improvement in 8 cases, and no effect in 6 cases (93.4% effective rate).[5] In another study, 320 infants with diarrhea were treated three times daily with *Bai Zhu* (Rhizoma Atractylodis Macrocephalae) and *Shan Yao* (Rhizoma Dioscoreae) with good results.[6] Furthermore, 10 children diagnosed with Spleen deficiency according to traditional Chinese medicine were treated with a decoction of *Ren Shen* (Radix et Rhizoma Ginseng) twice daily for 7 to 14 days. At the end of the study, it was reported that all had an increase in appetite, cessation of spontaneous perspiration, increase in body weight, and improvement of facial complexion.[7]

Herbs in ***GI Tonic*** have also shown a marked effect for treatment of gastrointestinal disorders, such as superficial gastritis and peptic ulcer disease. In one study, 32 patients were treated with complete recovery in 15 cases (46.8%), a marked effect in 9 cases (28.1%), a moderate effect in 7 cases (21.8%), and no effect in 1 case. The overall effective rate was 96.7%.[8] In another study, 43 patients with gastric or duodenal ulcer were treated successfully using *Sha Ren* (Fructus Amomi) in powder form. The study reported significant improvement in such symptoms as epigastric pain, abdominal distension, and acid reflux.[9] Furthermore, *Gan Cao* (Radix et Rhizoma Glycyrrhizae) and *Jie Geng* (Radix Platycodonis) have gastroprotective effects. Many components of *Gan Cao* (Radix et Rhizoma Glycyrrhizae) prevent and treat peptic ulcers. The mechanisms of this action include inhibition of gastric acid secretion, binding and deactivation of gastric acid, and promotion of recovery from ulceration.[10] Administration of *Jie Geng* (Radix Platycodonis) is beneficial in the treatment of stomach and duodenal ulcers via inhibition of gastric acid secretion.[11] Lastly, administration of *Huang Qi* (Radix Astragali) for one month is also associated with a marked effect for the treatment of peptic ulcer disease.

Ren Shen (Radix et Rhizoma Ginseng) is one of the most effective herbs to improve the overall health of the body. Traditionally, it used to tonify *yuan* (source) *qi* to strengthen the body and restore vitality. Today, this effect is often described as "adaptogenic effect," implying that it helps the body to adapt and cope with mental and physical stress.[12,13] In Germany, *Ren Shen* (Radix et Rhizoma Ginseng) is approved by the Commission E to treat lack of stamina in individuals with declining performance, capacity for work, and concentration; and during convalescence.[14] Furthermore, to manage mental stress, *Ren Shen* (Radix et Rhizoma Ginseng) has been shown a positive cognitive effect to improve memory and learning ability.[15] This herb also alleviates feelings of mental fatigue experienced by participants during the later stages of the sustained, cognitively demanding task performance.[16] To manage physical stress, *Ren Shen* (Radix et Rhizoma Ginseng) has demonstrated a marked influence on the endocrine system. It stimulates the pituitary gland to increase the secretion of ACTH, which in turn stimulates the adrenal glands to produce cortisol.[17] According to studies, subjects that are given *Ren Shen* (Radix et Rhizoma Ginseng) show 132 to 179% better physical performance in swimming than ones that are not.[18] Lastly, *Ren Shen* (Radix et Rhizoma Ginseng) is frequently coupled with *Bai Zhu* (Rhizoma Atractylodis Macrocephalae), as both herbs have an adaptogenic effect and synergistically enhance each other.[19]

In summary, ***GI Tonic*** is an essential formula for the treatment of various gastrointestinal disorders, including but not limited to diarrhea, colitis, superficial gastritis, and inflammatory condition of the intestines. ***GI Tonic*** contains herbs that will address both the cause and the symptoms of such gastrointestinal problems, thereby providing both immediate and long-term relief.

COMPARATIVE ANALYSIS

One striking difference between Western and traditional Chinese medicine is that Western medicine focuses and excels in crisis management, while traditional Chinese medicine emphasizes and shines in holistic and preventative treatments. Therefore, in emergencies, such as gunshot wounds or surgery, Western medicine is generally the treatment of choice. However, for treatment of chronic idiopathic illness of unknown origins, where all lab tests are normal and a clear diagnosis cannot be made, traditional Chinese medicine is distinctly superior.

In cases of chronic energetic and gastrointestinal disorders, where all tests are normal but there are still general and non-diagnostic signs and symptoms, Western medicine offers few treatment options since there is not a clear diagnosis. On the other hand, traditional Chinese medicine is beneficial as it excels in maintainance and preventative therapies. Herbs can be used to regulate imbalances and alleviate associated signs and symptoms. Therefore, herbal therapy should definitely be employed to prevent deterioration of this condition, and to restore optimal health.

References

1. *Chang Yong Zhong Yao Cheng Fen Yu Yao Li Shou Ce* (A Handbook of the Composition and Pharmacology of Common Chinese Drugs), 1994; 739:742.
2. *Zhong Yao Xue* (Chinese Herbology), 1998; 326:327.
3. *Xin Yi Yao Xue Za Zhi* (New Journal of Medicine and Herbology), 1979; 3:129.
4. *Jiang Xi Zhong Yi Yao* (Jiangxi Chinese Medicine and Herbology), 1959; 4:36.
5. *Bei Jing Zhong Yi* (Beijing Chinese Medicine), 1985; 5:31.
6. *Shan Dong Zhong Yi Za Zhi* (Shandong Journal of Chinese Medicine), 1982; 2:107.
7. *Chong Qing Yi Yao* (Chongching Medicine and Herbology), 1984; 6:41.
8. *Zhong Yi Fang Ji Xian Dai Yan Jiu* (Modern Study of Medical Formulae in Traditional Chinese Medicine), 1997; 507.
9. *Fu Jian Zhong Yi Yao* (Fujian Chinese Medicine and Herbology), 1983; (6):36.

FORMULAS

GI Tonic™

10. *Zhong Yao Zhi* (Chinese Herbology Journal), 1993; 358.
11. *Zhong Yao Yao Li Yu Ying Yong* (Pharmacology and Applications of Chinese Herbs), 1983; 866.
12. *Zhong Yao Yao Li Yu Ying Yong* (Pharmacology and Applications of Chinese Herbs), 1983; 16.
13. *Zhong Hua Yi Xue Za Zhi* (Chinese Journal of Medicine), 1985; 42(12):13.
14. Blumenthal M. The Complete German Commission E Monographs. Therapeutic Guide to Herbal Medicines. The American Botanical Council. 1998.
15. *Zhong Yao Ci Hai* (Encyclopedia of Chinese Herbs), 1994.
16. Reay JL, Kennedy DO, Scholey AB. Effects of Panax ginseng, consumed with and without glucose, on blood glucose levels and cognitive performance during sustained 'mentally demanding' tasks. Human Cognitive Neuroscience Unit, Northumbria University, Newcastle upon Tyne, NE1 8ST, UK. J Psychopharmacol. 2006 Nov;20(6):771-81.
17. *Bai Qiu En Yi Ke Da Xue Xue Bao* (Journal of Baiqiuen University of Medicine), 1980; 6(2):32.
18. *Planta Med*, 1979; 30:43.
19. *Xin Yi Yao Xue Za Zhi* (New Journal of Medicine and Herbology), 1974; 8:13.

Herbal ABX™

CLINICAL APPLICATIONS

- **All types of infection,** with or without fever, inflammation, redness and swelling
- **All excess conditions,** with fire, heat, damp-heat, or toxic heat
- Conditions with red tongue, yellow or greasy yellow tongue coating or forceful, rapid pulse
- This combination is used as an adjunct formula to clear heat

WESTERN THERAPEUTIC ACTIONS

- Broad spectrum antibiotic functions
- Antibacterial effects
- Antiviral effects
- Antifungal effects

CHINESE THERAPEUTIC ACTIONS

- Clears fire, damp-heat and toxic heat
- Reduces swelling and redness

DOSAGE

Take 3 to 4 capsules three times daily on an empty stomach, with warm water. Dosage may be increased to 6 to 8 capsules three times daily, if necessary. The herbs should be taken with meals for those with a sensitive stomach.

INGREDIENTS

Cha Chi Huang (Herba Stellariae Aquaticae)
Da Qing Ye (Folium Isatidis)
Feng Wei Cao (Herba Pteris)
Hu Yao Huang (Herba Leucas Mollissimae)
Huang Lian (Rhizoma Coptidis)
Liu Zhi Huang (Herba Solidaginis)
Pao Zai Cao (Herba Physalis Angulatae)
Pu Gong Ying (Herba Taraxaci)
Shu Wei Huang (Herba Rostellulariae)
Xian Feng Cao (Herba Bidentis)
Ya She Huang (Herba Lippiae)

BACKGROUND

A healthy person has numerous defense mechanisms that protect against the invasion of micro-organisms. These host defense mechanisms include natural barriers (i.e., skin), non-specific immunity (i.e., phagocytic cells) and specific immunity (i.e., antibodies). However, if the host defenses are defective or becomes disrupted, the micro-organisms may enter and affect various parts of the body. Therefore, optimal treatment of infective disorders requires use of treatment agents to kill the micro-organisms and preventative agents that restore the host defense mechanisms.

FORMULA EXPLANATION

Herbal ABX is designed specifically as an antibiotic formula for the treatment of infections. According to traditional Chinese medicine, infection is characterized by the presentation of fire, damp-heat and/or toxic heat attacking various parts of the body. Therefore, treatment requires use of herbs that eliminate the offending pathogens. Furthermore, it is important to also treat the complications of infection, such as swelling, inflammation, and fever.

Many herbs in this formula focus on eliminating the fire, damp-heat or toxic heat causes of infection. *Huang Lian* (Rhizoma Coptidis) clears heat, sedates fire, and eliminates toxic heat. *Da Qing Ye* (Folium Isatidis) clears heat, eliminates toxins and cools the blood. *Pu Gong Ying* (Herba Taraxaci) enters the Liver, detoxifies and helps promote the Liver's function to clear toxins. *Xian Feng Cao* (Herba Bidentis) reduces inflammation, clears heat, reduces swelling, drains pus, and promotes urination. *Feng Wei Cao* (Herba Pteris) clears heat, drains dampness, reduces inflammation, cools the blood, and detoxifies. *Shu Wei Huang* (Herba Rostellulariae) invigorates the blood and reduces inflammation. *Ya She Huang* (Herba Lippiae) reduces inflammation. *Liu Zhi Huang* (Herba Solidaginis) relieves pain, reduces inflammation and swelling, and eliminates toxins. *Hu Yao Huang* (Herba Leucas Mollissimae) clears heat, eliminates toxins, and invigorates blood circulation. *Cha Chi Huang* (Herba Stellariae Aquaticae) clears heat, detoxifies invigorates blood, and reduces swelling. *Pao Zai Cao* (Herba Physalis Angulatae) reduces inflammation and eliminates toxins.

SPECIFIC INDICATIONS

Herbal ABX has a broad spectrum of antibiotic effect, and is used to treat respiratory tract infections, gastrointestinal infections, hepatic disorders, reproductive system infections, sexually-transmitted diseases, urinary tract infections, and other infectious disease.

Respiratory tract infections: *Da Qing Ye* (Folium Isatidis), *Feng Wei Cao* (Herba Pteris), *Ya She Huang* (Herba Lippiae), *Pao Zai Cao* (Herba Physalis Angulatae) and *Shu Wei Huang* (Herba Rostellulariae) treat respiratory infections. Clinical presentations include common cold, influenza, bacterial or viral infections, bronchitis, pneumonia, encephalitis, upper respiratory tract infection, fever, sore and swollen throat, laryngitis, middle-ear infections, oral sores, parotitis, rhinitis, sinusitis, pharyngitis, and cough with yellow sputum.

Gastrointestinal infections: *Huang Lian* (Rhizoma Coptidis), *Hu Yao Huang* (Herba Leucas Mollissimae), *Pao Zai Cao* (Herba Physalis Angulatae), *Cha Chi Huang* (Herba Stellariae Aquaticae), *Feng Wei Cao* (Herba Pteris), and *Pu Gong Ying* (Herba Taraxaci) clear fire and damp-heat in the digestive tract. These toxins cause gastritis, peptic ulcers, duodenal ulcers, esophagitis, gastroenteritis, pancreatitis, enteritis, dysentery, colitis, diarrhea, ulcerative colitis, Crohn's disease, irritable bowel syndrome, acute and chronic appendicitis, hemorrhoids, vomiting, foul breath, swollen or bleeding gums, and abdominal pain.

Herbal ABX™

Hepatic disorders: *Huang Lian* (Rhizoma Coptidis), *Da Qing Ye* (Folium Isatidis), *Pu Gong Ying* (Herba Taraxaci), *Hu Yao Huang* (Herba Leucas Mollissimae), *Cha Chi Huang* (Herba Stellariae Aquaticae), *Xian Feng Cao* (Herba Bidentis), and *Liu Zhi Huang* (Herba Solidaginis) enter the Liver channel to treat Liver fire. Manifestations of Liver fire include hepatitis, cholecystitis, jaundice, erysipelas, herpes zoster, fibrocystic breast disorder, migraine, acid reflux, conjunctivitis, bitter taste in the mouth, tinnitus, irritability, and hypochondriac pain.

Reproductive system infections: *Pao Zai Cao* (Herba Physalis Angulatae), *Ya She Huang* (Herba Lippiae), *Cha Chi Huang* (Herba Stellariae Aquaticae), *Hu Yao Huang* (Herba Leucas Mollissimae), and *Feng Wei Cao* (Herba Pteris) treat inflammation or infections of the reproductive organs. In women, symptoms include vaginitis, foul-smelling yellow or white leukorrhea, inflammation of the pelvis, ovaries, uterus, fallopian tubes, inflammation or infection following abortion or delivery, lower abdominal pain, genital itching, cervicitis, hypermenorrhea, yeast infections, prolapse of the uterus with inflammation and infection. In men, disorders include prostatitis, genital itching, and orchitis.

Sexually-transmitted diseases (STDs): This formula is a useful adjunct formula to clear toxic or damp-heat associated with STDs such as gonorrhea, genital herpes, trichomoniasis, candidiasis, and chancroid lesions.

Urinary tract infections (UTI): *Huang Lian* (Rhizoma Coptidis), *Ya She Huang* (Herba Lippiae), *Shu Wei Huang* (Herba Rostellulariae), *Pao Zai Cao* (Herba Physalis Angulatae), *Hu Yao Huang* (Herba Leucas Mollissimae), *Xian Feng Cao* (Herba Bidentis), and *Cha Chi Huang* (Herba Stellariae Aquaticae) treat infection of the urinary system manifesting in dysuria and frequent urges to urinate. In such cases, the urine is mostly yellow and turbid. Disorders include nephritis, cystitis, UTI and kidney stones.

Other: This formula is effective for treatment of Lyme disease, cellulitis, sores, carbuncles, hypertension, environmental poisoning, pericarditis, arteritis, gout, paronychia, phlebitis, toxic insect bites, hordeolum, keratitis, trachomata, ear infection, perichondritis, aural eczematoid dermatitis, conjunctivitis and external otitis.

In summary, ***Herbal ABX*** consists of a wide array of herbs with marked antibiotic properties, beneficial for the treatment of various infections.

CAUTIONS & CONTRAINDICATIONS

- This formula is contraindicated in cases of deficiency and coldness. It should be used with caution for those who have weak digestive systems.
- This formula is contraindicated during pregnancy and nursing.
- Because antibiotic therapy may decrease the absorption of birth control pills by interfering with the normal flora in the intestines, women should use additional prophylactics if they are on antibiotic therapy and birth control pills concurrently.

CLINICAL NOTES

- In individuals with constipation, purgative herbs such as ***Gentle Lax (Excess)*** should be used first before selecting an appropriate formula.
- ***Herbal ABX*** should be taken for at least seven to ten days to ensure complete eradication of micro-organisms. Early discontinuation may increase the risk of mutation and subsequent resistance by the micro-organisms.
- Many herbs in ***Herbal ABX*** are indigenous herbs from the island of Taiwan. Because of their geographic isolation, they maintain potent antibiotic effect without any tolerance or resistance of micro-organisms. Therefore, for infections that do not respond to antibiotic drugs or classic herbal formulas, ***Herbal ABX*** will often provide excellent clinical results.
- If the condition does not improve after seven to ten days, re-evaluate the condition and modify the formula or select another formula as needed.
- This herbal combination is designed as a supplementary formula for treatment of various infections. In traditional Chinese medicine, such infectious diseases are characterized by heat, fire, damp-heat or toxic heat with elevated temperatures and/or inflammation.
- In gynecological disorders, this formula should be continued for two or three days more, after the symptoms subside.
- There is no evidence thus far that use of heat-clearing herbs may permit secondary infections to arise (as is the case with antibiotics). However, those who have recurrent infections should take acidophilus prophylactically, especially if they have a history of repeated antibiotic usage.
- When boils or cysts break and are draining, keep the local area clean to prevent the spread of infection to other parts of the body. After handling a boil, hands should be washed thoroughly, as staph bacteria may infect other areas or cause food poisoning.
- Use of a yin tonic formula, such as ***Nourish***, is recommended after the use of antibiotics to restore the normal balance of yin and yang in the body.
- ***Herbal ABX*** incorporates numerous antibiotic herbs for two important reasons. First, the use of multiple herbs within an herbal formula has been shown to increase the antibiotic effect more than ten-fold. Second, isolated use of single ingredients is often ineffective and increases the risk of development of bacterial and viral resistance.[1] Given these two reasons, it is necessary to combine herbs with appropriate properties to ensure effectiveness in treating the infection and minimizing the potential risk of the micro-organisms developing resistance and/or mutation.
- Patients with encephalitis or meningitis should be sent to the emergency room for immediate medical treatment. Warning signs and symptoms of encephalitis or meningitis include fever,

Herbal ABX™

headache, stiff neck, sore throat, vomiting, and mental confusion. In addition to soreness, the stiffness is also characterized by severe pain with gentle taps to the neck, and extreme stiffness and immobility when the patient tries to lower the chin to the chest.

Pulse Diagnosis by Dr. Jimmy Wei-Yen Chang:

- Superficial, thick, and forceful pulse on any of the pulse position depending on the location of the inflammation and infection.

SUPPLEMENTARY FORMULAS

- For viral infections, add ***Herbal AVR***.
- For infection of the ear, nose, and throat, add ***Herbal ENT***.
- For common cold or influenza with sore throat, combine with ***Lonicera Complex***.
- For sinus infections, combine with ***Magnolia Clear Sinus*** or ***Pueraria Clear Sinus***.
- For respiratory tract infections, combine with ***Respitrol (Heat)*** or ***Respitrol (Cold)***.
- For cough, add ***Respitrol (CF)***.
- For inflammation and swelling, combine with ***Resolve (AI)*** or ***Astringent Complex***.
- For yellow phlegm due to respiratory tract infections, use with ***Pinellia XPT***.
- For damp and phlegm accumulation, add ***Pinellia Complex***.
- For genital infections, use with ***Gentiana Complex*** or ***V-Support***.
- For gastric or duodenal ulcers with *H. pylori* infection, use with ***GI Care***.
- For hepatitis, add ***Liver DTX***.
- For chronic nephritis or nephritic syndrome, add ***Kidney DTX***.
- For kidney or bladder stones, use with ***Dissolve (KS)***.
- For shingles, use with ***Dermatrol (HZ)***.
- For dermatological disorders that appear wet, combine with ***Dermatrol (Damp)***.
- For dermatological disorders that appear dry, combine with ***Dermatrol (Dry)***.
- For chemical or heavy metal poisoning, add ***Herbal DTX***.
- For gallstones, combine with ***Dissolve (GS)***.
- For infection from external injuries or surgeries, combine with ***Flex (TMX)***.
- For unknown condition with blood stagnation, combine with ***Circulation (SJ)***.
- For bleeding, use ***Notoginseng 9***.
- For high blood pressure and fast heart rate due to excess fire, add ***Gardenia Complex***.
- This formula can be combined with other herbal formulas to enhance its heat clearing, fire purging and detoxifying actions.

ACUPUNCTURE TREATMENT

Traditional Points:

- *Hegu* (LI 4), *Zusanli* (ST 36), *Quchi* (LI 11), *Neiguan* (PC 6), *Shousanli* (LI 10), *Yanglingquan* (GB 34), *Sanyinjiao* (SP 6)

Balance Method by Dr. Richard Tan:

- Left side: *Houxi* (SI 3), *Xiaohai* (SI 8), *Taichong* (LR 3), *Ququan* (LR 8)
- Right side: *Shaohai* (HT 3), *Shenmen* (HT 7), *Yanglingquan* (GB 34), *Zulinqi* (GB 41)
- Left and right sides can be alternated from treatment to treatment.
- The above acupuncture prescription is for general inflammation. Please refer to other formulas for acupuncture points depending on each specific condition.

Ear Acupuncture:

- **Chronic middle ear infection:** Eustachian Tube, Middle Ear, Mastoid Process, Kidney
- **Acute conjunctivitis:** Bleed protruding vein in the back of the ear once a day. Needle for 30 minutes the following points: Eyes, *Shenmen*, and apex of tragus.
- **Acute tonsillitis:** Bleed the protruding vein in the back of the ear, and apex of the tragus once a day. Needle and strongly stimulate the Throat, Pharynx and Tonsil.

Auricular Medicine by Dr. Li-Chun Huang:

- **Reduce fever:** Thalamus, Brain Stem, Lung, Sympathetic, Endocrine, corresponding points to infection. Bleed Ear Apex, Tragic Apex and Adrenal Gland.
- **Erysipelas:** Lung, Allergic Area, Liver, Spleen, Adrenal Gland, Endocrine. Bleed Ear Apex.

NUTRITION

- Avoid spicy, fried or greasy foods.
- Be sure to include foods and beverages that are cool or cold in nature. Among these are watermelon, lotus nodes, melon, seaweed, cranberries, celery, cucumber, cactus and winter melon.
- Drink plenty of water and urinate often.
- Increase supplementation with Vitamin C and B complex.
- Increase intake of nourishing, cooling foods/roots such as Mexican yam, yam, radishes, potatoes, carrots, melons, cucumbers, beets, turnips, malanga, celeriac, taro, and rutabaga.
- Avoid spicy/pungent/aromatic vegetables such as pepper, garlic, onions, basil, rosemary, cumin, funnel, anise, leeks, chives, scallions, thyme, saffron, wormwood, mustard, chili pepper, and wasabi.

The Tao of Nutrition by Dr. Maoshing Ni and Cathy McNease:

- **Yeast infection/candidiasis:** eat a steamed artichoke daily for two weeks.
- **Vaginal infection:** boil a bulb of garlic, cool to lukewarm, then douche with the liquid.
- **Bladder infection:** drink one cup cranberry juice, unsweetened and diluted, along with 1,000 mg vitamin C every three to four hours a day. Drink an additional 5 to 6 cups of water daily.
- **Chronic bladder infection:**
  - Drink watermelon and pear juice three times daily.

Herbal ABX™

- Drink carrot and celery juice three times daily.
- Eat squash soup for at least seven days.
- Eat steamed lotus root and water chestnuts twice daily.
- Drink blended mung bean juice.
- Drink tea made from wheat and pearl barley.

☯ **Chronic sinus infection:**
- Make tea from magnolia flower, basil, ginger, and green onion. Drink three times daily for at least one week.
- Combine magnolia flowers and eggs, cook and eat.
- Make tea from mulberry leaves and chrysanthemums, then cook rice porridge in the tea, adding apricot kernels.
- Boil tea of mint, basil, and ginger. While boiling the tea, inhale the steam through the nose, three times daily for at least two months.

LIFESTYLE INSTRUCTIONS

☯ Sleep by 10:00 p.m. In TCM, 11:00 p.m. to 1:00 a.m. is when the yin shifts to yang. It is crucial for the body to be at rest during this time for optimal health. There is no better way to restore or enhance the immune system other than resting and sleeping before 10:00 p.m.

☯ Afternoon naps for about 30 minutes are also recommended.

CASE STUDIES

☯ S.O., a 3-year-old female, presented with constant coughing for two weeks. After being taken to the emergency room, she was diagnosed with whooping cough; however, no medication was prescribed. Other assessments included veins seen on her chest. The TCM diagnosis was Lung heat and the parents were instructed to give her ***Respitrol (Heat)*** and ***Herbal ABX*** mixed with juice. Initially there was no change noted. However, after two days the symptoms began to lessen and she was back to normal within a week. Submitted by A.I., Hilo, Hawaii.

☯ N.T., a 36-year old female patient, presented with a painful rash located on the center of her abdomen. She had been experiencing emotional stress as well. Her Western doctor had already diagnosed her with shingles and prescribed her an antiviral, which didn't seem to help and created lung pain. The TCM diagnosis was damp-heat, which the practitioner treated with ***Herbal ABX***. After taking the herbs daily and receiving acupuncture twice a week, the patient's rash and pain disappeared in seven days. To maintain these results, the patient took ***Immune +*** to boost her immune system. Submitted by S.R., Waterbury, Connecticut.

☯ L.R., a 53-year-old female patient, who was a smoker and a fast-paced business woman, presented with frequent urinary tract infections (UTI) and herpes breakouts. Her eating habits consisted of spicy food, coffee, and wine. The patient had been experiencing burning and pressure, and had been taking antibiotics. The practitioner diagnosed the condition as damp-heat in the lower *jiao*. She was treated with ***Herbal ABX*** three pills four times daily along with ***V-Support*** at the same dosage. For topical treatment to the affected area, Yin Care was applied three times daily at 50% the recommended amount. After the infection had cleared, the patient was then directed to take ***Nourish*** three pills three times daily. The patient healed quickly, complete relief of pain was present, and she had committed to eliminate smoking, coffee, and spicy food from her lifestyle. Submitted by L.W., Arroyo Grande, California.

☯ M.I., a 29-year-old female, presented with pus-filled sores located on her scalp. It had been occurring for a week along with symptoms of pain, slight itching, and fever. The cause was unknown. The sores were described as filled with white pus and 3 to 4 mm width. Her Western diagnosis was seborrheic dermatitis (capiti) and the TCM diagnosis was blood heat with wind dryness. The patient was prescribed the combination of ***Resolve (AI)*** and ***Herbal ABX*** both at three pills three times a day. After three days the inflammation and sores had gone down and within one week the sores had completely resolved. Submitted by A.I., Hilo, Hawaii.

☯ D.D., a 37-year-old male, presented with severe ongoing autoimmune reactions from a spider bite which had occurred six months prior to his first treatment. He had been suffering from psoriasis the past years and episodes occurred where his entire body swelled up which made it hard for him to breathe. The patient also reported that he had just recently recovered from pink eye as well. He was desperate for relief as he had been on prednisone for three months, 20 mg a day. Additional medication he had been recently placed on was methotrexate at 2.5 mg to stop the symptoms. Objective findings included fang marks present near the olecranon, although the spider had not been identified as the patient was sleeping in bed. The area was red and inflamed still after six months of the incident. The TCM diagnosis was toxic heat and the practitioner prescribed ***Herbal ABX*** initially to rid the toxin. After only two weeks of taking ***Herbal ABX*** and receiving acupuncture, the patient reported he was no longer experiencing any episodes of autoimmune response. After a month he was no longer taking Western drugs and there has been no re-occurrence of the symptoms. Submitted by M.M., Burlington, Wisconsin.

☯ J.O., a 34-year-old male, presented with sinus drainage with thin watery consistency. Ear clogging and pressure were also present. Blood pressure was 122/72 mmHg and heart rate was 84 beats per minute. The practitioner diagnosed the condition as wind-cold invasion, phlegm damp in the *San Jiao* and Stomach channels, and Spleen qi and Kidney yin deficiencies with damp constitution. The patient was given ***Herbal ABX*** and *Xiao Chai Hu Tang* (Minor Bupleurum Decoction) at three capsules four times a day for seven days. With ***Herbal ABX*** the sinus drainage resolved and the ears cleared within four days. The patient continued taking the herbs for an additional seven days. Submitted by L.M., Lafayette, Colorado.

Herbal ABX™

- M.B., a 37-year-old male, had presented with pain located on the forehead that had been occurring for three days. Additional symptoms included thick yellow mucus and a fever of 102°F. Pain was also found upon palpation of his sinus cavities. His Western diagnosis was sinusitis and the TCM diagnosis was wind-heat. Upon the diagnosis, the patient was administered ***Pueraria Clear Sinus*** and ***Herbal ABX*** both at four pills three times a day. In one day the fever had cleared followed by decreased in pain in two days. The sinuses finally resolved within a week. Submitted by A.I., Hilo, Hawaii.
- M.C., a 60-year-old male, presented with cough and nasal congestion with yellow discharge. He had been previously diagnosed with sinusitis and bronchitis and was currently taking antibiotics. There had been a chronic case of allergies triggering repeated episodes of his sinus infections and bronchitis. The patient would get an episode every two to three months and had been on a lot of antihistamine and cortisone medications. The practitioner diagnosed this condition as exterior wind-heat with phlegm heat. Upon diagnosis, the patient was prescribed ***Pueraria Clear Sinus*** and ***Herbal ABX***. With taking the herbs, the patient reported his sinusitis and bronchitis had cleared, the discharge lessened in the amount and the color became clear. Submitted by B.L., Fort Myers, Florida.
- J.V., a 56-year-old female patient with diabetes and obesity, presented with sores located in the genital region. The sores were affected by her blood sugar levels. The TCM diagnoses included wind and damp-heat. ***Resolve (AI)*** and ***Herbal ABX*** at four pills three times a day were prescribed. This condition is ongoing and occurs each time the patient doesn't control her diet or blood sugar level. The ***Resolve (AI)*** and ***Herbal ABX*** greatly reduced the sores and alleviated the discomfort when needed. She kept this combination on hand and they always work for her. Submitted by A.I., Hilo, Hawaii.
- C.K., a 61-year-old female, presented with pelvic pain during intercourse at a level of 8 out of 10. Additional symptoms were digestive symptoms such as gas and bloating, nail fungus, and bad breath. She had a history of candida, low libido, and fatigue. The practitioner diagnosed this condition as Liver and Gallbladder heat, damp-heat in the lower *jiao*, and Spleen qi deficiency. For treatment the patient was given a combination of ***Gentiana Complex***, ***Herbal ABX***, and Yin Care for one week; secondly, ***V-Support*** and ***Herbal ABX*** for the week after. Within 20 days the patient reported no more pain with intercourse or digestive issues. The patient continues to use the Yin Care for her nails as they are still healing. Submitted by T.W., Perrysburg, Ohio.
- M.H., a 34-year-old female, presented with a rash located on the inner thigh that had been in existence for three days. Additional symptoms included pustules, redness, and itchiness. Objective findings were raised, oozing patches beginning to spread upward towards the trunk. The practitioner diagnosed this condition as wind-heat with dampness; her Western diagnosis was a staph infection. ***Herbal ABX*** was prescribed at 5 grams four times a day. The patient was also directed to apply a mix of ***Herbal ABX*** with water on gauze to the effected area. After one day of taking the herbs, less oozing and redness was present. After three days, the ulcer had healed and there was no longer oozing. Following 21 days the rash had resolved. He was very thankful for the effects of the ***Herbal ABX***. Submitted by M.R., Santa Cruz, California.
- M.C., a 60-year-old male, presented with chronic sinusitis, consisting of yellow green discharge. Additional symptoms included sensation of heat in the upper neck area, some tightness in the chest, and a tickling of the throat but no cough. The practitioner diagnosed this condition as Lung qi deficiency and Kidney yin deficiency. Patient was given ***Herbal ABX*** when the discharge was present and ***Immune +*** when the discharge wasn't present. After taking the herbs, the patient stopped having sinus infections and bronchitis. The patient still came in for follow ups occasionally. Submitted by B.L., Fort Myers, Florida.
- A.G., a 36-year-old male, presented with a combination of symptoms, including fever, chills, sore throat, and malaise. He was also experiencing ear pain and sinus congestion. It was also noted that the patient was allergic to sulfur drugs and was weary of taking Western medication. Pulse was superficial and rapid; tongue was swollen with a red tip. The practitioner diagnosed this condition as toxic heat. His Western diagnosis was laryngitis. After taking two bottles ***Herbal ABX*** and ***Herbal ENT***, the patient's symptoms had resolved. He still continued to use ***Herbal ABX*** periodically as it had worked well for him. Submitted by V.G., Virginia Beach, Virginia.
- M.V., a 48-year-old female, presented with a cut on her foot which had occurred while showering. The following day she had noticed redness, swelling, and soreness to the touch. It was clear that she had an infection. ***Herbal ABX*** was prescribed at 6 capsules three times per day. As a result, the redness and inflammation had begun to recede. She continued taking the herbs for the full ten days. The TCM diagnosis was heat in the blood. ***Herbal ABX*** successfully reversed the course of the infection, while clearing the toxic heat in the blood completely. Submitted by N.V., Muir Beach, California.
- A 35-year-old female presented with an ear infection with pain. The patient was given ten days of antibiotics with no relief. After antibiotic therapy, she continued to have a slight fever and body aches. Her medical doctor diagnosed her with an ear infection, but upon examination, not much fluid was observed. The practitioner diagnosed the patient's condition as phlegm heat in the Lung and *San Jiao*. After taking ***Herbal ABX***, her ear pain, congestion and infection all cleared up. The practitioner has found ***Herbal ABX*** quite effective in treating other patients for ear infections. Submitted by M.K., Sherman Oaks, California.
- A 42-year-old midwife presented with sinus infection (for ten days) with yellow green discharge, increased pressure and pain in the sinus cavity and the ears, and severe pain. Upon examination,

it was found that there was also lymph node swelling and pain. The TCM diagnosis was phlegm heat in the Lung and toxic heat in the throat. The patient was instructed to take ***Pueraria Clear Sinus*** (4 capsules three times daily) and ***Herbal ABX*** (4 capsules three times daily). Within one day, the patient responded that there was a lot less pain and marked decrease in swelling. She continued to improve with each dose and stated that she felt "all better" by the third day. The practitioner commented the formulas were "very amazing and powerful." Submitted by M.N., Knoxville, Tennessee.

- B.F., a 55-year-old male, presented with cough, thick nasal discharge, headache and fatigue. The tongue was pale, flabby and slightly purple. The pulse was slow. He was diagnosed with common cold and wind-cold invasion. ***Magnolia Clear Sinus***, ***Respitrol (Cold)*** and ***Herbal ABX*** were prescribed. The patient reported that the sinus cleared in three days. Submitted by B.F., Newport Beach, California.
- H.M., a 59-year-old female, presented with seasonal nasal allergies, rhinitis, stuffy sinuses, and profuse, clear, nasal mucus. She was allergic to mold and mildew. ***Herbal ABX*** and ***Magnolia Clear Sinus*** were prescribed. They brought about relief after ten days, when the patient would usually be battling the symptoms for months and would have to take antibiotics. Submitted by H.C., Stephens City, Virginia.
- The owner brought in a male cat that had oozing sores and ulcers filled with yellow pus that started after a fight with another cat. The TCM diagnosis was toxic damp-heat at the skin level. ***Herbal ABX*** was prescribed topically. The cat licked it off, so it worked internally as well. After one day, the condition became much better as the sores began drying up. After three days, the cat was 90% better. After five days, all sores healed completely. Submitted by M.C., Sarasota, Florida.

PHARMACOLOGICAL AND CLINICAL RESEARCH

Herbal ABX is an herbal antibiotic formula to treat infections. Pharmacological effects of this formula include antibacterial, antiviral and antifungal effects.

Huang Lian (Rhizoma Coptidis) is one of the most commonly used and effective herbs for many infections. Pharmacologically, it has potent, broad-spectrum antibacterial action against *Bacillus dysenteriae, Mycobacterium tuberculosis, Salmonella typhi, E. coli, Vibrio cholerae, Bacillus proteus, Pseudomonas aeruginosa, Diplococcus meningitidis, Staphylococcus aureus, beta-hemolytic streptococcus, Diplococcus pneumoniae, Corynebacterium diphtheriae, Bordetella pertussis, Bacillus anthracis,* and *Leptospira.* The aqueous extracts of *Huang Lian* (Rhizoma Coptidis) also exhibited strong inhibition on cariogenic bacteria.[2] Furthermore, berberine, a compound from *Huang Lian* (Rhizoma Coptidis), shows antimicrobial activity against numerous strains of methicillin-resistant *Staphylococcus aureus* (MRSA). Berberine markedly lowers the minimum inhibition concentrations of ampicillin and oxacillin against MRSA. Berberine and ampicillin exhibit additive effect, and berberine and oxacillin show a synergistic effect against MRSA. These results suggest that berberine may have antimicrobial activity and the potential to restore the effectiveness of beta-lactam antibiotics against MRSA.[3] In addition to its antibacterial properties, *Huang Lian* (Rhizoma Coptidis) has antifungal and antiviral actions.[4] It is effective against numerous pathogenic fungi and dermatophytes.[5] According to another reference, the extracts and decoctions of *Huang Lian* have demonstrated significant antimicrobial activity against a variety of organisms including bacteria, influenza viruses, hepatitis viruses, fungi, protozoans, helminths, and chlamydia.[6,7]

Clinically, *Huang Lian* (Rhizoma Coptidis) has been used to treat a wide variety of infections. It showed excellent results in treating bacterial dysentery in over 1,000 patients, with short course of treatment and low incidence of side effects.[8] It was shown to be effective in treating acute gastroenteritis or enteritis in over 100 patients.[9] Good results were reported when a constituent of *Huang Lian* (Rhizoma Coptidis) was used to treat over 100 patients suffering from pulmonary tuberculosis.[10] *Huang Lian* (Rhizoma Coptidis) is also effective when used topically in treating suppurative otitis media.[11]

Da Qing Ye (Folium Isatidis) has broad-spectrum antibacterial, antiviral and antifungal applications. It is effective against *Staphylococcus aureus, α-hemolytic streptococcus, Diplococcus meningitidis, Salmonella typhi, E. coli, Corynebacterium diphtheriae, Bacillus dysenteriae,* and *leptospirosis.*[12] *Da Qing Ye* (Folium Isatidis) also has a significant activity in a concentration-dependent manner against *Trichophyton schoen leinii, Aspergillus niger, Candida albicans, Trichophyton simii,* and *Macrophomina phaseolina.*[13] The effectiveness of *Da Qing Ye* (Folium Isatidis) is reflected in numerous clinical research reports. In one study, 168 children with upper respiratory infections were treated, with great results.[14] In another study, 51 children between the ages of one and thirteen were treated for encephalitis B, with marked effectiveness.[15]

Pu Gong Ying (Herba Taraxaci) has a bactericidal effect *in vitro* against *Staphylococcus aureus, beta-hemolytic streptococcus, Diplococcus pneumoniae, Diplococcus meningitidis, Corynebacterium diphtheriae, Pseudomonas aeruginosa, Bacillus dysenteriae* and *Salmonella typhi.*[16] *Pu Gong Ying* (Herba Taraxaci) also has a highly effective antiviral effect, especially against herpes simplex virus.[17] Clinical research has shown this herb to be 83% effective against acute tonsillitis,[18] and 98% effective for sore throat.[19] Similar successes were reported using *Pu Gong Ying* (Herba Taraxaci) for topical treatment of parotitis or of burn patients with concurrent infection.[20,21]

In summary, ***Herbal ABX*** is an excellent formula with marked antibiotic properties, including antibacterial, antiviral, and antifungal effects. It can be used individually, or in combination with another formula to treat the infection and the related complications.

Herbal ABX™

COMPARATIVE ANALYSIS

Discovery of antibiotic drugs is one of the major breakthroughs in modern medicine. It enables doctors to effectively treat many different types of infections. Unfortunately, decades of misuse and abuse have led to growing problems of bacterial mutation and resistance. At this moment, many of these "super bugs" can only be treated with the newest and most potent antibiotic drugs, and unfortunately, many of them have potent side effects as well. Due to the number of antibiotic drugs, and the various species of micro-organisms, it is beyond the scope of this monograph to discuss the benefits and risks of each individual drug. As a category, antibiotic drugs are extremely effective against most types of bacterial infections. The key points are to select the correct antibiotic drug with least potential side effects, and make sure that the patient finishes the entire course of therapy.

Herbs are also extremely effective for treatment of various infections. In fact, many modern pharmaceutical drugs were originally derived from natural sources, including penicillin [the oldest antibiotic] and gentamicin [one of the most potent]. One of the main benefits of using herbs is their wide spectrum of antibiotic effect, with indications for bacterial, viral and fungal infections. Furthermore, most of these herbs are extremely safe, and do not have the same harsh side effects as drugs.

Both drugs and herbs are effective to treat mild to moderate cases of bacterial infections. However, drugs are more appropriate for life-threatening infections, such as meningitis or encephalitis, because drugs are more immediately potent and can be prescribed with more laboratory precision (via cultures and sensitivity tests). On the other hand, use of herbs is far more effective than drugs for treating certain viral infections, such as the common cold and influenza, as drugs are essentially ineffective for these conditions. Most importantly, herbs are much gentler to the body and safer than drugs. In other words, herbs treat infection without damaging the patient's underlying constitution. This allows the patient to recover faster, and become more resistant to re-current or secondary infections.

References

1. *Zhong Yao Xue* (Chinese Herbology), 1988; 140:144.
2. Wang S., Fan M. & Bian Z. Experimental study of bacteriostatic activity of Chinese herbal medicines on primary cariogenic bacteria *in vitro* . *Zhonghua Kou Qiang Yi Xue Za Zhi.* 2001, 36(5): 385-387.
3. Yu HH, Kim KJ, Cha JD, Kim HK, Lee YE, Choi NY, You YO. Antimicrobial activity of berberine alone and in combination with ampicillin or oxacillin against methicillin-resistant Staphylococcus aureus. Department of Food and Nutrition, Kunsan National University, Kunsan. J Med Food. 2005 Winter;8(4):454-61.
4. *Zhong Yao Xue* (Chinese Herbology), 1988, 140:144.
5. *Zhong Hua Yi Xue Za Zhi* (Chinese Journal of Medicine), 1958; 44(9):888.
6. *Zhong Xi Yi Jie He Za Zhi* (Journal of Integrated Chinese and Western Medicine), 1989; 9(8):494.
7. Yu H.H., Kim K.J., Cha J.D., Kim H.K., Lee Y.E., Choi N.Y. & You Y.O. Antimicrobial Activity of Berberine Alone and in Combination with Ampicillin or Oxacillin Against Methicillin-Resistant *Staphylococcus aureus* . *J Med Food.* 2005, 8(4): 454-461.
8. *Zhong Hua Nei Ke Za Zhi* (Chinese Journal of Internal Medicine), 1976; 4:219.
9. *Si Chuan Yi Xue Yuan Xue Bao* (Journal of Sichuan School of Medicine), 1959; 1:102.
10. *Zhe Jiang Zhong Yi Za Zhi* (Zhejiang Journal of Chinese Medicine), 1964; 10:51.
11. *Zhong Hua Er Bi Hou Ke Za Zhi* (Chinese Journal of ENT), 1954; 4:272.
12. *Zhong Yao Xue* (Chinese Herbology), 1998; 174:175.
13. Ahmad I, Fatima I. Butyrylcholinesterase, lipoxygenase inhibiting and antifungal alkaloids from Isatis tinctoria. J Enzyme Inhib Med Chem. 2008 Jun;23(3): 313-6.
14. *Fu Jian Zhong Yi Yao* (Fujian Chinese Medicine and Herbology), 1965; 4:14.
15. *Fu Jian Zhong Yi Yao* (Fujian Chinese Medicine and Herbology), 1965; 4:11.
16. *Zhong Yi Yao Xue Bao* (Report of Chinese Medicine and Herbology), 1991; (1):41.
17. Zheng M. Experimental study of 472 herbs with antiviral action against the herpes simplex virus. Dept. of Microbiology, Jiangxi Medical College, Nanchang. Zhong Xi Yi Jie He Za Zhi. 1990 Jan;10(1):39-41, 6.
18. *Xin Yi Yao Xue Za Zhi* (New Journal of Medicine and Herbology), 1977; 8:8.
19. *Liao Ning Zhong Yi Za Zhi* (Liaoning Journal of Chinese Medicine), 1988; 9:27.
20. *Xin Yi Xue* (New Medicine), 1972; 10:49.
21. *Zhong Xi Yi Jie He Za Zhi* (Journal of Integrated Chinese and Western Medicine), 1987; 5:301.

Herbal ANG™

CLINICAL APPLICATIONS

- **Pain:** acute or chronic
- **Pain:** dull, sharp, stabbing, numbing, burning, and fixed, moving or radiating
- **Pain** of skeletal and smooth muscles

WESTERN THERAPEUTIC ACTIONS

- Potent analgesic effect to relieve pain
- Strong anti-inflammatory effect to reduce swelling and inflammation

CHINESE THERAPEUTIC ACTIONS

- Invigorates blood circulation
- Relieves pain

DOSAGE

When taken alone, the recommended dosage is 3 to 4 capsules three times daily as needed to relieve pain. For severe pain, dosage can be increased to 7 to 8 capsules every four to six hours as needed to relieve pain. As an adjunct with other formulas to relieve pain, the recommended dose is 2 to 3 capsules in addition to the regular dose of the base formula. Take the herbs on an empty stomach with two tall glasses of warm water. This formula should be discontinued when the desired effects are achieved.

INGREDIENTS

Dang Gui (Radix Angelicae Sinensis)
Mo Yao (Myrrha)
Ru Xiang (Gummi Olibanum)
Sheng Ma (Rhizoma Cimicifugae)
Yan Hu Suo (Rhizoma Corydalis)

BACKGROUND

Pain is the most common reason for physician consultation in the United States.[1] Pain is the unpleasant feeling often caused by intense or damaging stimuli, such as burning a finger or stepping on a sharp object. Acute pain is a beneficial and necessary warning signal for survival – it alerts the individual to withdraw from harmful situations, to protect a damaged body part while it heals, and to avoid similar experiences in the future. Chronic pain, however, may persist after the stimulus has been removed or after the body has been healed. In these cases, chronic pain can significantly interfere with a person's quality of life and general functioning, causing complications such as anxiety, stress, depression, anger, fatigue, sleep disturbance, immune suppression, and many others. Because chronic pain affects the body and the mind, effective treatment requires treatment of psychological and physical aspects of the condition.

FORMULA EXPLANATION

"Where there is pain, there is stagnation. When stagnation is cleared, so will the pain." For practitioners of traditional Chinese medicine, this is one of the most important fundamental principles for treatment of pain. ***Herbal ANG*** is designed as an adjunct formula to relieve severe pain. It can be used alone, or with other formulas for pain in the body.

Yan Hu Suo (Rhizoma Corydalis) is the strongest and the most effective herb in the entire Chinese herbal pharmacopoeia to relieve pain. It enters both *xue* (blood) and *qi* (energy) levels to effectively invigorate blood circulation, regulate qi and relieve pain in the chest, abdomen, and limbs. It is effective to relieve pain of the visceral organs and the musculoskeletal system. To enhance the analgesic effect of *Yan Hu Suo* (Rhizoma Corydalis), *Ru Xiang* (Gummi Olibanum) and *Mo Yao* (Myrrha) are added to ***Herbal ANG***. This pair of herbs is often used together synergistically to relieve a wide range of pain that may be caused by qi or blood stagnation, trauma or arthritic syndrome. *Dang Gui* (Radix Angelicae Sinensis) tonifies and moves blood. Finally, *Sheng Ma* (Rhizoma Cimicifugae) is used as a channel-guiding herb. It moves upwards and outwards and has a dispersing nature, which helps break up stagnation and relieve pain.

In short, ***Herbal ANG*** is an extremely effective formula to relieve pain. It can be used individually, or in combination with another formula for pain at a specific location.

CAUTIONS & CONTRAINDICATIONS

- This formula should be discontinued one week prior to surgery.
- This formula is contraindicated during pregnancy and nursing.
- This formula is designed for short-term symptomatic treatment of pain. It is not recommended for long-term use.
- For patients with chronic pain, it is essential to identify the cause of pain and treat it accordingly.
- This herbal formula contains herbs that invigorate blood circulation, such as *Dang Gui* (Radix Angelicae Sinensis). Therefore, patients who are on anticoagulant or antiplatelet therapies, such as Coumadin (warfarin), should use this formula with caution, or not at all, as there may be a higher risk of bleeding and bruising.[2,3,4]

CLINICAL NOTES

- ***Herbal ANG*** is an excellent formula to treat both internal and external injuries leading to pain of the body and the extremities. The diagnosis for such conditions is often qi and blood stagnation. Therefore, ***Herbal ANG*** can be used safely and effectively to relieve pain.
- If the pain is located in the trunk of the body, such as in the chest or abdominal regions, additional examination is necessary to diagnose the underlying cause of the pain. While ***Herbal ANG*** is still effective to relieve pain, it will not address the underlying illness and may delay the treatment. For example, patients with kidney stones may have tremendous pain in the lower back. Though it is important to relieve pain, it is even more important to address kidney stones. In other words, while it is important to treat pain in acute cases, it is equally important to identify the underlying cause so the overall treatment will not be delayed.

Herbal ANG™

- *Herbal ANG* is an extra-strength formula to be used in with other formulas to relieve severe pain. It will begin to show effectiveness within 30 minutes. It can be used in conjunction with acupuncture treatment for a synergistic analgesic effect.
- Pain from cancer is often severe and excruciating, which may not be relieved effectively by herbs. Under these circumstances, opioid drugs should be used for pain management if necessary. ***CA Support*** and ***C/R Support*** may be used as adjunct treatments.

SUPPLEMENTARY FORMULAS

- For headache, add ***Corydalin (AC)*** or ***Corydalin (CR)***.
- For pain in the neck and shoulder area, add ***Neck & Shoulder (AC)*** or ***Neck & Shoulder (CR)***.
- For pain in the arm (shoulder, elbow and wrist), combine with ***Arm Support***.
- For pain in the lower back, add ***Back Support (AC)*** or ***Back Support (CR)***.
- For pain in the back from herniated disk, combine with ***Back Support (HD)***.
- For pain in the knees, combine with ***Knee & Ankle (AC)*** or ***Knee & Ankle (CR)***.
- For gout, add ***Flex (GT)***.
- For pain with chronic musculoskeletal disorder with damaged soft tissues (muscles, tendons, ligaments and cartilage), combine with ***Flex (MLT)***.
- For arthritic syndrome or fibromyalgia due to coldness, combine with ***Flex (CD)***.
- For arthritic syndrome or fibromyalgia due to heat, combine with ***Flex (Heat)***.
- For spasms and cramps, add ***Flex (SC)***.
- For neuropathy, add ***Flex (NP)***.
- For bone spurs, add ***Flex (SPR)***.
- For dysmenorrhea, add ***Mense-Ease***.
- For pain due to gallstones, use with ***Dissolve (GS)***.
- For pain due to kidney stones, use with ***Dissolve (KS)***.
- For external or trauma injuries, use with ***Flex (TMX)***.
- For post-surgical care, ***Flex (TMX)*** can be added to invigorate blood circulation or relieve pain, and ***Herbal ABX*** can be added to prevent infection.
- For pain in the gastric region, add ***GI Care***.
- For pain or bloating due to irritable bowel syndrome, combine with ***GI Harmony***.
- For abdominal pain due to food poisoning or traveler's diarrhea, add ***GI Care II***.
- For pain due to ulcerative colitis, add ***GI Care (UC)***.
- For hemorrhoids, add ***GI Care (HMR)***.
- For pain due to endometriosis, uterine fibroids, ovarian cysts or mass, add ***Resolve (Lower)***.
- For fibrocystic breast disorder, add ***Resolve (Upper)***.
- For unknown pain with blood stagnation, add ***Circulation (SJ)***.
- For pain due to Bell's Palsy or TMJ (temporo-mandibular joint) pain, add ***Symmetry***.

ACUPUNCTURE TREATMENT

Traditional Points:

- *Ah shi* points; *Taibai* (SP 3), *Neiguan* (PC 6), *Waiguan* (TH 5), *Hegu* (LI 4)
- *Hegu* (LI 4), *Neiguan* (PC 6), *Ximen* (PC 4), *Sanyangluo* (TH 8), *Guangming* (GB 37) and local points:
  - Head: add *Quanliao* (SI 18), *Yifeng* (TH 17), *Guangming* (GB 37), *Hegu* (LI 4), *Lieque* (LU 7), *Jinmen* (BL 63)
  - Neck: add *Hegu* (LI 4), *Neiguan* (PC 6), *Futu* (ST 32)
  - Chest and thoracic: add *Hegu* (LI 4), *Neiguan* (PC 6), *Ximen* (PC 4)
  - Abdomen: add *Zusanli* (ST 36), *Shangjuxu* (ST 37), *Hegu* (LI 4), *Neiguan* (PC 6), *Taichong* (LR 3), *Yinlingquan* (SP 9)
  - Lower limbs: add *Huantiao* (GB 30), *Chengshan* (BL 57), *Sanyinjiao* (SP 6)

Master Tung's Points by Dr. Chuan-Min Wang:

- **Generalized pain**
  - Wind: *Shouwujin* (T 33.08), *Shouqianjin* (T 33.09)
  - Damp: *Shuiqu* (T 66.09), *Minghuang* (T 88.12), *Tianhuang* (T 88.13), *Qihuang* (T 88.14)
  - Cold: *Huofuhai* (T 33.07), *Jianzhong* (T 44.06)

Balance Method by Dr. Richard Tan:

- Left side: *Fengchi* (GB 20), *Zhongchong* (PC 9), *Shaochong* (HT 9), *Shaoshang* (LU 11), *Zusanli* (ST 36), *Weizhong* (BL 40), *Yanglingquan* (GB 34), ear *Shenmen*
- Right side: *Fengchi* (GB 20), *Hegu* (LI 4), *Houxi* (SI 3), *Zhongzhu* (TH 3), *Taixi* (KI 3), *Zhongfeng* (LR 4), *Sanyinjiao* (SP 6), *Yintang* (Extra 1), ear *Shenmen*

Auricular Medicine by Dr. Li-Chun Huang:

- Corresponding point of the pain, Sympathetic, *Shenmen*, Occiput. Bleed Ear Apex.
- Phantom limb pain: Sympathetic, *Shenmen*, Occiput, Lesser Occipital Nerve, Large Auricular Nerve, Nervous Subcortex. Bleed Ear Apex.

NUTRITION

- If pain is characterized by cold, avoid cold or raw foods (vegetables and salads), fruits (watermelon and pear), drinks and exposure to cold weather or surface. Avoid taking cold showers or swimming in cold water. Foods that are warm or hot in nature such as lamb, pepper, onions and scallions are recommended.
- If pain is characterized by heat, avoid eating spicy food. Increase the intake of vegetables or fruits that are cold in nature such as watermelon and cucumber.
- If pain is due to dampness, avoid eating greasy fatty or fried food. Dairy products are not recommended.
- Increase the intake of minerals such as calcium and magnesium, which calm the nerves and reduce sensitivity to pain.

Herbal ANG™

LIFESTYLE INSTRUCTIONS

- Proper diet and exercise are extremely important in preventing recurrent pain syndrome. Chronic pain is often the result of occupations that require repetitive use of the same joints or repeated injuries to the same area. Strong efforts should be made to eliminate or improve such working conditions.
- Exercise is always helpful in keeping qi and blood circulating properly in the body.
- Other therapies that are effective for pain management include massage, relaxation techniques, deep breathing, and heat/cold therapy.

CASE STUDIES

- R.B., a 25-year-old female, presented with severe head and neck pain. The patient had also been experiencing tension headaches in the frontal and occipital area. Objective findings included a pain level of 7/10, decreased mobility, and increased heart rate. Diagnostic tests had been received, which ruled out infection and meningitis. She had also joined a yoga group and was receiving psychotherapy and massage. The practitioner diagnosed the condition as chronic neck and back pain; her Western diagnosis was occipital neuralgia. For treatment, the patient was instructed to make certain dietary changes, received acupuncture twice a week and was prescribed ***Herbal ANG*** and ***Neck Shoulder (AC)***. The patient reported that with taking the herbs she experienced a slow, steady improvement to a healthier lifestyle. She felt her tendons and ligaments were getting stronger due to enhanced blood flow. She was very happy with the results of taking the herbs. Submitted by E.S., Castro Valley, California.
- Y.J., a 63-year-old female, presented with arthritis and gout pain located throughout her feet, fingers, wrists, and arms. Objective findings included inflammation on the joints, redness, and an inability to extend the joints. The pain was described as a sharp burning sensation. Blood pressure was 132/61 mmHg and heart rate of 73 beats per minute. The practitioner diagnosed this condition as qi and blood stagnation. ***Flex (GT)*** and ***Herbal ANG*** were prescribed. After taking the herbs and receiving acupuncture just a few times, the patient reported that her pain alleviated from a 9 to a 5 level. It was also noted that her range of motion had improved and was not as stiff as she was during the initial treatment. Submitted by J.C., Rosemead, California.
- A 42-year-old female nurse presented with chronic pain throughout her body, especially located in the neck and shoulder areas. The TCM diagnosis was Liver qi and blood stagnation along with Spleen and Heart deficiency. For treatment, ***Herbal ANG*** and ***Neck Shoulder (CR)*** were prescribed. After taking the herbs and receiving acupuncture treatment twice a week for a month, the patient found that her condition had improved more than it had by physiotherapy and anti-inflammatory drugs she had tried previously. Other findings in result of taking the herbs were increase of range of motion by 50% and softening of the muscles. Submitted by J.L., San Diego, California.
- L.S., a 27-year-old male electrician, complained of bad back spasms, which then lead to being unable to stand up straight for two days. This occurred after a recent job he had been bending over for while working and was in extreme pain. This condition was diagnosed as Liver yin deficiency. The patient was treated with ***Back Support (AC)*** and ***Herbal ANG*** four pills three times a day. It took one week for complete recovery, while the intensity of the pain decreased during the one week of treatment. Submitted by A.I., Hilo, Hawaii.
- N.T, a 41-year-old female patient, presented with neck pain, spasms, not being able to turn her head to the left, and waking up with pain in the morning. She was in severe pain and discomfort. This condition was diagnosed as Liver blood deficiency. Upon diagnosis, the patient was prescribed ***Neck Shoulder (AC)*** and ***Herbal ANG***. After taking the herbs for two days the neck pain decreased and the range of motion greatly improved. Submitted by A.I., Hilo, Hawaii.
- D.S., a 65-year-old female, presented with discomfort fluctuating between the areas of neck, shoulder, and lower back. It was noted that this condition had been affected by sitting at her desk job throughout the day. Objective findings included limited range of motion and a positive reaction when palpating her rotator muscles. The practitioner diagnosed this condition as damp-cold *bi zheng* (painful obstruction syndrome); her Western diagnosis was fibromyalgia. For treatment, ***Herbal ANG*** and ***Arm Support*** were prescribed. The patient continued to take the herbs as needed; however, she has reduced the amount of her anti-inflammatories and other prescription drugs by 70% after taking the herbs. An additional prescription was ***Back Support (CR)*** when her lower back pain was present. Overall, the patient reported her pain had decreased by 50% and she still wanted to continue taking the herbs for more relief. Submitted by J.L., San Diego, California.
- A 44-year-old female presented with chronic migraines, described as a tight sharp pain. It was mentioned that she had been having headaches for the past 30 years and she was also experiencing neck and arm pain. Objective findings included tight muscles upon palpation of the sternocleidomastoid, trapezius, biceps, and deltoid muscles. The TCM diagnosis was Liver qi stagnation along with qi and blood stagnation; Western diagnosis was repetitive muscle syndrome. ***Corydalin (CR)*** for headaches and ***Herbal ANG*** for muscle discomfort were prescribed and directed to take as needed. The patient had been treated on and off by these herbs for the past six months and had finally gotten off all her medications. She has sworn by them because they gave her better results than her anti-inflammatories. Submitted by J.L., San Diego, California.
- L.K., a 58-year-old female, presented with pain located on her left knee. Objective findings included limited range of motion, pain with movement, and limping. It was noted that her pain level was 7 out of 10 and the pain was only slightly alleviated with elevation or rest. The practitioner diagnosed this condition as qi and blood

Herbal ANG™

stagnation along with Liver and Kidney yin deficiencies. ***Knee & Ankle (CR)*** and ***Herbal ANG*** were prescribed upon diagnosis. After taking the herbs and receiving acupuncture, the patient's ROM was greater and her pain level had reduced. Submitted by J.C., Rosemead, California.

- J.B., an 83-year-old female, presented with upper right shoulder and low back pain. Her TCM diagnosis was qi and blood stagnation in the Urinary Bladder and Small Intestine channels. For treatment, ***Back Support (CR)*** and ***Herbal ANG*** were prescribed. The patient had reported a decrease in pain and an improvement in her quality of life. However, due to a removal of a shoulder muscle years back, she doesn't feel the pain may ever fully resolve. Submitted by B.S., Niceville, Florida.
- At a seminar in Providence, Rhode Island, a question was raised as whether *Yan Hu Suo* (Rhizoma Corydalis) would cause a person treated with this herb to test positive in a drug screen (as do a number of analgesic substances). A very small study was conducted in a laboratory at the Rhode Island Clinical Research Center: two people taking 6 capsules of ***Corydalin (AC)*** were screened for drugs three hours later. Both were completely negative in the seven drug panels. A solution of 5% *Yan Hu Suo* (Rhizoma Corydalis) powdered extract (freed from excessive carbohydrate) was also tested in the drug-screening test, again with negative results. It was concluded by the researchers that a person being treated for pain with the usual dosage of ***Corydalin (AC)*** would not risk testing positive for opiates, benzodiazepines, barbiturates, etc. [Note: *Yan Hu Suo* (Rhizoma Corydalis) is the main ingredient that is present in both ***Corydalin (AC)*** and ***Herbal ANG***.] Submitted by D.W., Hadley, Massachusetts.

PHARMACOLOGICAL AND CLINICAL RESEARCH

Herbal ANG is formulated specifically for relieving pain throughout the body. It contains ingredients that have shown exceptional analgesic and anti-inflammatory effects. Clinical applications include treatment of various aches and pains, swelling, inflammation, and external injuries.

Yan Hu Suo (Rhizoma Corydalis) is one of the strongest and most potent herbs for treatment of pain. Its effects are well documented in both historical references and modern research studies. According to classical texts, *Yan Hu Suo* (Rhizoma Corydalis) has been used to treat chest and hypochondriac pain, epigastric and abdominal pain, hernial pain, amenorrhea or menstrual pain, and pain of the extremities. According to laboratory studies, the extract of *Yan Hu Suo* (Rhizoma Corydalis) has been found to be effective in both acute and chronic phases of inflammation. The mechanism of its anti-inflammatory effect is attributed to its activity to inhibit the release of histamine and pro-inflammatory mediators.[5,6] Furthermore, it has a strong analgesic effect. With adjustment in dosage, the potency of *Yan Hu Suo* (Rhizoma Corydalis) has been compared to that of morphine. In fact, the analgesic effect of *Yan Hu Suo* (Rhizoma Corydalis) is so strong and reliable that it has been used with a satisfactory anesthetic effect in 98 out of 105 patients (93.4%) who underwent surgery.[7] The analgesic effect can be potentiated further with concurrent acupuncture therapy. In one research study, it is demonstrated that the analgesic effect is increased significantly with concurrent treatments using *Yan Hu Suo* (Rhizoma Corydalis) and electro-acupuncture, when compared to a control group, which received electro-acupuncture only.[8] Overall, it is well understood that *Yan Hu Suo* (Rhizoma Corydalis) has a marked effect to treat pain. Though the maximum analgesic effect of *Yan Hu Suo* (Rhizoma Corydalis) is not as strong as morphine, it has been determined that the herb is much safer, with significantly fewer side effects, less risk of tolerance, and no evidence of physical dependence even with long-term use.[9]

In addition to *Yan Hu Suo* (Rhizoma Corydalis), *Ru Xiang* (Gummi Olibanum) and *Mo Yao* (Myrrha) are added to enhance the effect to treat acute trauma and injuries. These two herbs have an analgesic effect to relieve pain and an anti-inflammatory effect to reduce swelling and inflammation.[10,11] They also showed an antiarthritic effect by reducing edema and decreasing arthritic scores in subjects with adjuvant-induced arthritis. The mechanism of action is attributed to the suppression of pro-inflammatory cytokines, such as tumor necrosis factor-alpha (TNF-α) and interleukin-1beta (IL-1β).[12] Furthermore, use of *Ru Xiang* (Gummi Olibanum) and *Mo Yao* (Myrrha) is also beneficial to facilitate wound healing by stimulating maturation and differentiation of white blood cells.[13] Clinically, they have been used effectively to treat various types of pain, such as trauma and external injuries,[14] chest pain, colicky or sharp pain,[15] and pain due to acute sprain of the lower back and legs.[16]

Dang Gui (Radix Angelicae Sinensis), another important herb in this formula, exerts both analgesic and anti-inflammatory effects through the inhibition of pro-inflammatory mediators, including nitric oxide and prostaglandin E2 in peritoneal macrophages.[17,18] In comparison with acetylsalicylic acid, the anti-inflammatory effect of *Dang Gui* (Radix Angelicae Sinensis) is approximately 1.1 times stronger, and its analgesic effect is approximately 1.7 times stronger.[19] According to clinical studies, *Dang Gui* (Radix Angelicae Sinensis) has been used successfully to treat menstrual pain in 112 patients,[20] migraine headache in 35 patients,[21] different types of headache in 36 patients,[22] and general complaint of pain in 105 patients.[23]

Lastly, *Sheng Ma* (Rhizoma Cimicifugae) has mild anti-inflammatory and analgesic effects.[24] *Sheng Ma* (Rhizoma Cimicifugae) also functions as a guiding herb, as it has the effects to reach the far ends of the body, such as the extremities. Its guiding function helps to enhance the overall effect of all the herbs in this formula.

In summary, ***Herbal ANG*** has marked analgesic and anti-inflammatory effects, and can be used individually or as an adjunct to another formula to treat pain of various onset, duration and characteristics.

Herbal ANG ™

COMPARATIVE ANALYSIS

Pain is a basic bodily sensation induced by a noxious stimulus that causes physical discomfort (as pricking, throbbing, or aching). Pain may be of acute or chronic state, and may be of nociceptive, neuropathic, or psychogenic origin. Two classes of drugs commonly used to treat pain include non-steroidal anti-inflammatory agents (NSAID) and opioid analgesics. NSAIDs [such as Motrin (ibuprofen) and Voltaren (diclofenac)] are generally used for mild to moderate pain, and are most effective to reduce inflammation and swelling. Though effective, they may cause such serious side effects as gastric ulcer, duodenal ulcer, gastrointestinal bleeding, tinnitus, blurred vision, dizziness and headache. Furthermore, the newer NSAIDs, also known as COX-2 inhibitors [such as Celebrex (celecoxib)], are associated with significantly higher risk of cardiovascular events, including heart attack and stroke. Opioid analgesics [such as Vicodin (APAP/hydrocodone) and morphine] are usually used for severe to excruciating pain. While they may be the most potent agents for pain, they also have the most serious risks and side effects, including but not limited to dizziness, lightheadedness, drowsiness, upset stomach, vomiting, constipation, stomach pain, rash, difficult urination, and respiratory depression resulting in difficult breathing. Furthermore, long-term use of these drugs leads to tolerance and addiction. In brief, it is important to remember that while drugs offer reliable and potent symptomatic pain relief, they should be used only if and when needed. Frequent use and abuse leads to unnecessary side effects and complications.

In TCM, treatment of pain is a sophisticated balance of art and science. Proper treatment of pain requires a careful evaluation of the type of disharmony (excess or deficiency, cold or heat, exterior or interior), characteristics (qi and/or blood stagnations), and locations (upper body, lower body, extremities, or internal organs). Furthermore, optimal treatment requires integrative use of herbs, acupuncture and *tui-na* therapies. All these therapies work together to tonify underlying deficiencies, strengthen the body, and facilitate recovery from chronic pain. TCM pain management targets both the symptoms and the causes of pain, and as such, often achieves immediate and long-term success. Furthermore, TCM pain management is often associated with few or no side effects.

For treatment of mild to severe pain due to various causes, TCM pain management offers similar treatment effects with significantly fewer side effects. However, as with any therapeutic modality, it is important to recognize the limitations of TCM pain management. In some cases, such as excruciating cancer pain in terminally ill patients, drugs are simply superior to herbs. Under these circumstances, immediate, potent and consistently reliable pain relief is the main objective, and this can be accomplished more effectively with drugs, such as intravenous injection of morphine. Herbs should be used to support the underlying constitution of the body, and to alleviate the side effects of the drugs.

References

1. Turk DC, Dworkin RH. What should be the core outcomes in chronic pain clinical trials?. Arthritis Res. Ther.. 2004;6(4):151–4.
2. Chan K, Lo AC, Yeung JH, Woo KS. Journal of Pharmacy and Pharmacology 1995 May;47(5):402-6.
3. Pharmacotherapy 1999 July;19(7):870-876.
4. European Journal of Drug Metabolism and Pharmacokinetics 1995; 20(1): 55-60.
5. *Biol Pharm Bull*, Feb 1994; 17(2):262-5.
6. Oh YC, Choi JG, Lee YS, Brice OO, Lee SC, Kwak HS, Byun YH, Kang OH, Rho JR, Shin DW, Kwon DY. Tetrahydropalmatine inhibits pro-inflammatory mediators in lipopolysaccharide-stimulated THP-1 cells. Department of Oriental Pharmacy, College of Pharmacy, Wonkwang University Wonkwang Oriental Medicines Research Institute, Iksan, Republic of Korea. J Med Food. 2010 Oct;13(5): 1125-32.
7. *He Bei Xin Yi Yao* (Hebei New Medicine and Herbology), 1973; 4:34.
8. *Chen Tzu Yen Chiu* (Acupuncture Research), 1994;19(1):55-8.
9. *Zhong Yao Yao Li Yu Ying Yong* (Pharmacology and Applications of Chinese Herbs), 1983; 447.
10. *Zhong Yao Xue* (Chinese Herbology), 1998; 539:540.
11. Yoshikawa M, Morikawa T, Oominami H, Matsuda H. Absolute stereostructures of olibanumols A, B, C, H, I, and J from olibanum, gum-resin of Boswellia carterii, and inhibitors of nitric oxide production in lipopolysaccharide-activated mouse peritoneal macrophages. Kyoto Pharmaceutical University, Japan. Chem Pharm Bull (Tokyo). 2009 Sep;57(9):957-64.
12. Fan AY, Lao L, Zhang RX, Zhou AN, Wang LB, Moudgil KD, Lee DY, Ma ZZ, Zhang WY, Berman BM. Effects of an acetone extract of Boswellia carterii Birdw. (Burseraceae) gum resin on adjuvant-induced arthritis in lewis rats. Center for Integrative Medicine, School of Medicine, University of Maryland, 3rd Floor, James Kernan Hospital Man, 2200 Kernan Drive, Baltimore, MD 21201, USA. J Ethnopharmacol. 2005 Oct 3;101(1-3):104-9.
13. Haffor A-S. 2010. Effect of myrrh (Commiphora molmol) on leukocyte levels before and during healing from gastric ulcer skin injury. J Immunotoxicol 7: 68-75.
14. *He Nan Zhong Yi Xue Yuan Xue Bao* (Journal of University of Henan School of Medicine), 1980; 3:38.
15. *Zhong Yao Xue* (Chinese Herbology), 1998; 540.
16. *He Nan Zhong Yi Xue Yuan Xue Bao* (Journal of University of Henan School of Medicine), 1980; 3:38.
17. *Xin Yi Yao Xue Za Zhi* (New Journal of Medicine and Herbology), 1975; (6):34.
18. Chao WW, Kuo YH, Li WC, Lin BF. The production of nitric oxide and prostaglandin E2 in peritoneal macrophages is inhibited by Andrographis paniculata, Angelica sinensis and Morus alba ethyl acetate fractions. Department of Biochemical Science and Technology, Institute of Microbiology and Biochemistry, National Taiwan University, Taipei 106, Taiwan, ROC. J Ethnopharmacol. 2009 Feb 25;122(1):68-75.
19. *Yao Xue Za Zhi* (Journal of Medicinals), 1971; (91):1098.
20. *Lan Zhou Yi Xue Yuan Xue Bao* (Journal of Lanzhou University of Medicine), 1988; 1:36.
21. *Bei Jing Yi Xue* (Beijing Medicine), 1988; 2:95.
22. *Hu Bei Zhong Yi Za Zhi* (Hubei Journal of Chinese Medicine), 1993; (2):9.
23. *Xin Yi Yao Xue Za Zhi* (New Journal of Medicine and Herbology), 1976; 12:26.
24. *Zhong Yao Xue* (Chinese Herbology), 1998; 106:108.

Herbal AVR™

CLINICAL APPLICATIONS

- **Viral infections** including the common cold, influenza (flu), oral herpes, genital herpes, herpes zoster (shingles), Epstein-Barr virus, viral hepatitis, infectious mononucleosis (mono), chickenpox, viral gastroenteritis, and viral pneumonia
- **Chronic, unresolved viral infections:** chronic unexplained fatigue, continued weight loss, low-grade fever, night sweats and chills, vague body aches and pain

WESTERN THERAPEUTIC ACTIONS

- Antiviral effect to inhibit viral replication
- Virucidal effect to kill viruses
- Immunostimulant to enhance the immune system

CHINESE THERAPEUTIC ACTIONS

- Releases wind-heat, clears deficiency heat
- Eliminates toxic heat
- Nourishes yin
- Tonifies qi and enhances the *wei* (defensive) *qi*

DOSAGE

Take 3 to 4 capsules three times daily on an empty stomach. The dosage may be increased up to 6 to 8 capsules every four to six hours as needed.

INGREDIENTS

Bai Shao (Radix Paeoniae Alba)
Ban Lan Gen (Radix Isatidis)
Bo He (Herba Menthae)
Chai Hu (Radix Bupleuri)
Chen Pi (Pericarpium Citri Reticulatae)
Fu Ling (Poria)
Gan Cao (Radix et Rhizoma Glycyrrhizae)
Huang Lian (Rhizoma Coptidis)
Huang Qi (Radix Astragali)
Huang Qin (Radix Scutellariae)
Jie Geng (Radix Platycodonis)
Jin Yin Hua (Flos Lonicerae Japonicae)
Lian Qiao (Fructus Forsythiae)
Ma Bo (Lasiosphaera seu Calvatia)
Mai Dong (Radix Ophiopogonis)
Niu Bang Zi (Fructus Arctii)
Nu Zhen Zi (Fructus Ligustri Lucidi)
Ren Shen (Radix et Rhizoma Ginseng)
Shan Yao (Rhizoma Dioscoreae)
Sheng Ma (Rhizoma Cimicifugae)
Xian He Cao (Herba Agrimoniae)
Xiang Chun Ye (Folium Toonae Sinensis)
Xuan Shen (Radix Scrophulariae)
Yu Xing Cao (Herba Houttuyniae)

BACKGROUND

Viruses are the smallest parasites composed of an RNA or DNA core and an outer cover of protein or lipid. There are several hundred different viruses, most of which infect humans via respiratory or enteric excretion, and some are transmitted via sexual contact or transfusion of blood. For infection to occur, the virus must attach and enter the host cell, replicate itself inside the host cell, and release new viruses to infect other host cells. Because viruses are made from RNA or DNA, covered by protein or lipid, and reside inside the host cell, they are very difficult to identify and kill. Treatment of viral infections with pharmaceutical drugs is mostly ineffective, or offers minimal benefits. In most cases, supportive care is given to alleviate signs, symptoms, and complications of viral infections. Vaccines are effective for prevention, but are available for only a few types of viruses. Protective measures, such as hand washing, proper food preparation, water treatment, and avoidance of contact with infected individuals, are important to prevent viral infections. All in all, the body's own immune system is the most effective way to prevent and treat viral infection.

FORMULA EXPLANATION

Viral infections become a problem when the host's protective immune mechanisms are compromised. Many of these patients experience persistent infections because the body is unable to clear the virus after the initial infection. Therefore, optimal treatment requires simultaneous efforts to treat the infection and strengthen the immunity. In traditional Chinese medicine (TCM), treating viral infections requires three strategies. First, use herbs to clear wind-heat and toxic heat. Second, tonify qi and enhance the body's immune system. Third, tonify yin to address symptoms of yin-deficient fire, such as low-grade fever in cases of chronic viral infections.

Herbal AVR contains herbs to clear wind-heat and eliminate toxins. Many of the following herbs show excellent antiviral effect. *Huang Qin* (Radix Scutellariae), *Huang Lian* (Rhizoma Coptidis), *Xuan Shen* (Radix Scrophulariae), *Ma Bo* (Lasiosphaera seu Calvatia), and *Ban Lan Gen* (Radix Isatidis) clear heat and eliminate toxins. *Niu Bang Zi* (Fructus Arctii) *Lian Qiao* (Fructus Forsythiae), and *Bo He* (Herba Menthae) disperse wind-heat accumulation. Also, they are excellent for fever, sore throat, and swollen glands. *Jie Geng* (Radix Platycodonis) and *Gan Cao* (Radix et Rhizoma Glycyrrhizae) act synergistically to relieve sore throat, thus helping the heat-clearing herbs. *Chen Pi* (Pericarpium Citri Reticulatae) regulates qi circulation to reduce swelling and inflammation. *Sheng Ma* (Rhizoma Cimicifugae) and *Chai Hu* (Radix Bupleuri), in addition to dispersing wind-heat, have an antipyretic effect to reduce body temperature. *Jin Yin Hua* (Flos Lonicerae Japonicae), *Xian He Cao* (Herba Agrimoniae), *Yu Xing Cao* (Herba Houttuyniae), and *Xiang Chun Ye* (Folium Toonae Sinensis) have an excellent antiviral effect and are included in this formula.

Herbal AVR™

The next two groups of herbs tonify qi and nourish yin of the body, which are often deficient from fighting a long-term viral infection. Chronic infection taxes the body and consumes yin. Patients often suffer from weight loss or emaciation and show symptoms of fatigue, tiredness, low-grade fever, loss of appetite, and weakness. The first group of herbs enhances the body's own *wei* (defensive) *qi* or immune system to fight against the infection. They include *Ren Shen* (Radix et Rhizoma Ginseng), *Shan Yao* (Rhizoma Dioscoreae), *Fu Ling* (Poria), and *Huang Qi* (Radix Astragali). Together, they strengthen the Spleen and boost the immune system while preventing the harsh properties of the heat-clearing herbs from injuring the digestive system. The second group of herbs, the yin tonics, addresses low-grade fever and other signs of deficiency heat. Herbs in this group include *Bai Shao* (Radix Paeoniae Alba), *Mai Dong* (Radix Ophiopogonis), and *Nu Zhen Zi* (Fructus Ligustri Lucidi). *Xuan Shen* (Radix Scrophulariae) is also effective to prevent the heat-clearing, damp-drying herbs from injuring the yin.

Together, ***Herbal AVR*** is a balanced formula to address acute and chronic viral infections by clearing heat and tonifying the body's own defense system.

CAUTIONS & CONTRAINDICATIONS

- This formula is contraindicated in cases of deficiency and coldness.
- For patients with a sensitive or weak digestive system, take the herbs 30 minutes after meals.
- This formula is contraindicated during pregnancy and nursing.

CLINICAL NOTES

- Though seasonal infections may be caused by either bacterial or viral infections, common cold and influenza (flu) are two of the most common forms of viral infections. It is important to keep in mind that antibacterial drugs should not be used for these viral infections because they are unnecessary and ineffective against viruses. The overuse of antibacterial drugs can weaken the patient, leaving the body more susceptible for future infections. Therefore, accurate diagnosis and proper prescriptions are absolutely essential for successful treatment of viral infections.
- ***Herbal AVR*** incorporates numerous antibiotic herbs for two important reasons. First, the use of multiple herbs within an herbal formula has been shown to increase the antibiotic effect more than tenfold. Second, isolated use of single ingredients is often ineffective and increases the risk of development of bacterial and viral resistance.[1] Given these two reasons, it is necessary to combine herbs with appropriate properties to ensure effectiveness in treating the infection and minimizing the potential risk of the micro-organisms developing resistance and/or mutation.
- Patients with encephalitis or meningitis should be sent to the emergency room for immediate medical treatment. Warning signs and symptoms of encephalitis or meningitis include fever, headache, stiff neck, sore throat, vomiting, and mental confusion. In addition to soreness, the stiffness is also characterized by severe pain with gentle taps to the neck, and extreme stiffness and immobility when the patient tries to lower the chin to the chest.

Pulse Diagnosis by Dr. Jimmy Chang:

- Viral infections predominantly show a weak pulse to reflect the body's weakened immune system.
- **Upper respiratory viral infection or influenza (flu):** deep and weak pulse on the right *cun*. (If the pulse on the right *cun* is superficial, forceful, and jumpy, then it is upper respiratory bacterial infection).
- **Weakened immune system:** tent pulse, a weak, convex-shaped pulse that collapses under pressure, on the right *cun*

SUPPLEMENTARY FORMULAS

- For respiratory infections, add ***Lonicera Complex***, ***Herbal ENT*** or ***Respitrol*** formulas.
- For oral herpes, add ***Lonicera Complex***.
- For genital herpes, add ***Gentiana Complex***.
- For herpes zoster, add ***Dermatrol (HZ)***.
- For viral infections of the gastrointestinal tract, add ***GI Care II***.
- For patients with weak immune system, add ***Immune +*** or ***Cordyceps 3***.
- For chronic fatigue syndrome, add ***Imperial Tonic***.
- To strengthen the immune system, add ***Immune +***.
- For chronic viral infection or post viral infection with yin deficiency, add ***Nourish*** or ***Balance (Heat)***.
- For hepatitis, add ***Liver DTX***.
- For genital human papillomavirus (HPV), add ***V-Support***. Use Yin Care externally as herbal wash is also beneficial.
- With more inflammation, add ***Astringent Complex***.
- With fever, add ***Gardenia Complex***.

ACUPUNCTURE POINTS

Traditional Points:

- Check under other formulas that treat the specific disease for the acupuncture protocol.

Balance Method by Dr. Richard Tan:

- Left side: *Houxi* (SI 3), *Xiaohai* (SI 8), *Taichong* (LR 3), *Ququan* (LR 8)
- Right side: *Shaohai* (HT 3), *Shenmen* (HT 7), *Yanglingquan* (GB 34), *Zulinqi* (GB 41)
- Left and right sides can be alternated from treatment to treatment.
- The above acupuncture prescription is for general inflammation. Please refer to other formulas for acupuncture points depending on each specific condition.

Ear Acupuncture:

- Check under other formulas that treat the specific disease for the ear acupuncture protocol.

Herbal AVR™

Auricular Medicine by Dr. Li-Chun Huang:

- **Enhance the immune functions:** Allergic Area, Endocrine, Adrenal Gland, Spleen, Liver, corresponding points (to the area affected). Bleed Ear Apex and Helix 1-6 (selective area).
- **Reduce body temperature:** Thalamus, Brain Stem, Lung, Sympathetic, Endocrine, corresponding points. Bleed Ear Apex, Tragic Apex and Adrenal Gland.
- Check under other formulas that treat the specific disease for the Auricular Medicine protocol.

NUTRITION

- Always eat breakfast! According to the TCM clock, the most optimal time for the digestive system is in the morning from 8:00 to 10:00 a.m.
- Drink plenty of water.
- Avoid sugar: any and all foods containing sugar such as cake, dessert, candy, chocolate, canned juice, soft drinks, stevia, sugar substitutes, agave, xylitol, and corn syrup.
- Avoid raw or cold food/beverages such as sashimi, sushi, salads, steak tartar, and seared meat. Eat all cooked vegetables and nothing straight from the refrigerator.
- Avoid carbohydrates like white rice or bread as they may damage the Spleen and in turn produce more dampness.
- No seafood, especially shellfish, like crabs, oyster, scallops, clams, lobster and shrimp (they enter the *yangming* Stomach channel). This is especially the case if suffering from skin disorder.
- Avoid fermented foods like cheese or fermented tofu.
- No dairy, including milk, cream, yogurt, cheese, and ice cream. Dairy products in general tend to create dampness and therefore should be consumed less. Milk, cheese and other dairy products should be avoided, especially if patients are lactose intolerant.
- Avoid deep-fried or greasy foods. No lamb, beef, goose or duck.
- Most melons (winter melon, watermelon, etc.), nightshades (eggplant, potato, bell and spicy peppers, tomato), bitter melon, seaweed, cucumber, grapefruit, papaya, and pineapple are too cold for the Spleen. Therefore, it's best to eat sparingly or not at all.
- Avoid the following fruits that are bad for the Spleen because they are cold in nature: plums, citrus, guava, pineapple, papaya, watermelon, honeydew.
- Avoid certain fruits like mango and durian that have heat producing effect, which aggravates the condition.
- Avoid spicy foods and stimulants like coffee, alcohol, and energy drinks.
- Avoid spicy/pungent/aromatic vegetables such as pepper, garlic, onions, basil, rosemary, cumin, funnel, anise, leeks, chives, scallions, thyme, saffron, wormwood, mustard, chili pepper, wasabi, and cardamom.
- Avoid foods and drinks with artificial coloring.
- Consume as few meat products as possible. Do not eat processed meats, such as lunch meats, hot dogs and sausages, as they contain nitrites that are associated with inflammation and chronic disease.

The Tao of Nutrition by Dr. Maoshing Ni and Cathy McNease:

- Increase consumption of dandelion greens, ginger, garlic, mung beans, daikons, carrots, mint, and lotus root.

LIFESTYLE INSTRUCTIONS

- Sleep by 10:00 p.m. In TCM, 11:00 p.m. to 1:00 a.m. is when the yin shifts to yang. It is crucial for the body to be at rest during this time for optimal health. There is no better way to restore or enhance the immune system other than resting and sleeping before 10:00 p.m.
- Afternoon naps for about 30 minutes are also recommended.

PHARMACOLOGICAL AND CLINICAL RESEARCH

Herbal AVR is an herbal antiviral formula that treats viral infections. Pharmacological effects of this formula include antiviral, virucidal, and immunostimulant effects.

Many herbs in ***Herbal AVR*** have shown excellent antiviral and virucidal effects. *Ban Lan Gen* (Radix Isatidis) has a wide range of antiviral effects. It exerts an antiviral effect against influenza A and B viruses through the inhibition of the hemagglutination to prevent infection.[2] It also has an antiviral effect against many different human or avian influenza viruses, as it has been shown to interfere with attachment of the virus to the host cell surface.[3] Indirubin, one of the biologically active compounds of *Ban Lan Gen* (Radix Isatidis), has shown significant cytotoxicity on swine pseudorabies virus,[4] as well as an inhibitory effect against influenza virus infection in the human bronchial epithelial cells.[5] Furthermore, isoformononetein from *Ban Lan Gen* (Radix Isatidis) shows antiviral activity *in vitro* against the influenza virus A/Hanfang/359/95 (H3N2), the herpes simplex virus 1 (HSV-1), and Coxsackie virus B3 (Cox-B3).[6] Lastly, clemastanin B, one of the major lignans from *Ban Lan Gen* (Radix Isatidis), has been shown to inhibit different subtypes of human (H1N1, including swine-origin H1N1; H3N2 and influenza B) and avian influenza viruses (H6N2, H7N3, H9N2). Furthermore, treatment with clemastanin B did not easily result in the emergence of viral resistance.[7]

Yu Xing Cao (Herba Houttuyniae) is another herb with significant antiviral activity in this formula. According to one study, injection of *Yu Xing Cao* (Herba Houttuyniae) has a remarkable preventive and treatment effect on H1N1 influenza virus.[8] According to another study, the water extract of *Yu Xing Cao* (Herba Houttuyniae) illustrates an antiviral effect to treat coronavirus in severe acute respiratory syndrome (SARS), a life-threatening form of pneumonia.[9] Furthermore, the hot water extract of *Yu Xing Cao* (Herba Houttuyniae) significantly inhibits the replication of herpes simplex virus (HSV), with a stronger antiviral effect against HSV-2 than HSV-1.[10] Norcepharadione B, a compound from *Yu Xing Cao* (Herba Houttuyniae), shows good inhibitory activity against the replication of herpes simplex virus type 1 (HSV-1).[11] In

FORMULAS

Herbal AVR™

addition, the injection of *Yu Xing Cao* (Herba Houttuyniae) demonstrates a direct inhibitory activity against pseudorabies herpesvirus *in vitro*.[12] Finally, the essential oils from *Yu Xing Cao* (Herba Houttuyniae) demonstrate inhibitory and virucidal activity against herpes simplex virus type 1 (HSV-1), influenza virus, and human immunodeficiency virus type 1 (HIV-1) by interfering with the function of the virus envelope.[13]

In addition, *Xiang Chun Ye* (Folium Toonae Sinensis) is an excellent herb with an antiviral effect against coronavirus (CoV) and SARS coronavirus (SARS-CoV), which cause severe acute respiratory syndrome (SARS), a life-threatening disease. According to a study that tested herbs from many references, including *Shang Han Lun* (Discussion of Cold-Induced Disorders) and *Wen Bing Tiao Bian* (Systematic Differentiation of Warm Disease), *Xiang Chun Ye* (Folium Toonae Sinensis) is the only herb found to have an evident effect against SARS-CoV. *Xiang Chun Ye* (Folium Toonae Sinensis) exerts its antiviral effect by inhibiting the replication of SARS coronavirus *in vitro*, and according to the researchers, is an important resource against SARS-CoV.[14]

Herbal AVR contains many other herbs with significant antiviral effects. *Xian He Cao* (Herba Agrimoniae) has highly-effective antiviral activity against all three subtypes of human influenza viruses, including H1N1 and H3N2 influenza A subtypes and influenza B virus. *Xian He Cao* (Herba Agrimoniae) also has a virucidal effect against influenza A and B viruses,[15] and an inhibitory effect against human immunodeficiency virus (HIV) type-1.[16] Extracts of *Huang Qin* (Radix Scutellariae) have displayed a wide spectrum of antiviral activity. Specifically, baicalein and wogonin, two compounds from the herb, boost innate antiviral immunity by stimulating the production of cytokines and increasing the resistance to viral infection in human leukocytes.[17] Lastly, shuangkangsu, a cyclic peroxide from *Jin Yin Hua* (Flos Lonicerae Japonicae), illustrates significant antiviral activities against influenza virus and respiratory syncytial virus.[18] Finally, other herbs with antiviral effects in this formula are *Chai Hu* (Radix Bupleuri),[19] *Huang Lian* (Rhizoma Coptidis),[20] and *Lian Qiao* (Fructus Forsythiae).[21]

Clinically, herbs in ***Herbal AVR*** have been used to treat various viral infections with great success. *Ban Lan Gen* (Radix Isatidis) has been used in herbal formulas to treat influenza, viral pneumonia, severe acute respiratory syndrome (SARS), acute tonsillitis, epidemic cerebrospinal meningitis, encephalitis B, herpes infection of the skin, and many others.[22,23,24,25] *Jin Yin Hua* (Flos Lonicerae Japonicae) and *Lian Qiao* (Fructus Forsythiae) have been used with excellent results to treat 1,150 patients with common colds or influenza.[26] The combination of *Huang Qin* (Radix Scutellariae), *Huang Qi* (Radix Astragali) and others has been shown in 21 patients with HIV/AIDS to significantly alleviate the symptoms, improve their immune function, inhibit HIV reproduction to a certain extent or keep it stable, and without obvious toxic or adverse reactions.[27]

In addition to direct antiviral and virucidal effects, many herbs in ***Herbal AVR*** stimulate the immune system to prevent and treat viral infections. Use of *Huang Qi* (Radix Astragali) increases white blood cells and multinuclear leukocytes,[28] enhances production of IgM,[29] and activates B cells and macrophages.[30] Furthermore, administration of *Huang Qi* (Radix Astragali) has been shown to prolong allograft survival associated with promotion of CD4+ and CD25+ regulatory T cells.[31] Administration of *Nu Zhen Zi* (Fructus Ligustri Lucidi) is associated with an increase in white blood cells. It is also effective in reversing neutropenia induced by chemotherapy treatment.[32] Lastly, *Ren Shen* (Radix et Rhizoma Ginseng) has immune-enhancing effects, as it increases the function of the reticuloendothelial system and increases the total count of IgM.[33] Clinically, use of *Huang Qi* (Radix Astragali) and others have been shown to prevent infections such as common colds and influenza,[34] pulmonary tract infection,[35] and upper respiratory tract infections.[36,37]

In summary, ***Herbal AVR*** is an excellent formula with marked antiviral, virucidal, and immunostimulant properties. It can be used individually for viral infections, or in combination with another formula to treat the infection and the related complications.

COMPARATIVE ANALYSIS

There are several hundred different viruses, with most infecting humans via respiratory or enteric excretion, and some transmitted via sexual contact or transfusion of blood. Viral infections are very difficult to treat because viruses are hard to identify (they are made from RNA or DNA and are covered by protein or lipid) and kill (many reside and replicate inside the host cell). Therefore, successful treatment of viral infections is a challenge to both Western and traditional Chinese medicines.

In Western medicine, there are many categories of antiviral drugs. Antiviral drugs are generally ineffective for respiratory viruses, such as influenza viruses, adenoviruses, respiratory syncytial virus, and rhinoviruses. In most cases, viral respiratory infection is treated only with supportive care or symptomatic treatment. Antiviral drugs are also mostly ineffective for gastrointestinal viruses, such as rotavirus, norovirus, adenovirus, and coronavirus. The main treatment for viral gastrointestinal infection is supportive care to prevent dehydration and symptomatic relief to alleviate nausea, vomiting, and diarrhea. Antiherpes drugs, such as Zovirax (acyclovir), are effective to inhibit the replication of herpes simplex virus, herpes zoster virus, and varicella. Interferons are sometimes prescribed to treat viral infections, such as hepatitis, hairy cell leukemia, and Kaposi's sarcoma, but they can cause serious adverse reactions such as depression, hepatitis, and bone marrow suppression. Overall, there are only few choices for antiviral drugs, and most have marginal effectiveness but significant toxic adverse effects.

In traditional Chinese medicine, through thousands of years of clinical trials and errors, many herbs and formulas have

Herbal AVR™

been tested and shown to effectively treat viral infections. Some herbs have antiviral effect to suppress the replication of viruses, some have virucidal effect to kill viruses, and others have immunostimulant effect to boost the immune system to clear the viral infection. Furthermore, many other herbs are available to offer supportive care and symptomatic treatment. Most importantly, most of these herbs are extremely safe, and do not have the same harsh side effects as drugs.

In conclusion, Western and traditional Chinese medicines are both effective to treat viral infections, they each have their own limitations. Therefore, despite amazing advances in Western medicine and thousands of years of human clinical experience in traditional Chinese medicine, human's own immune system is still the most effective and best treatment for viral infections.

References

1. *Zhong Yao Xue* (Chinese Herbology), 1988; 140:144.
2. Yang ZF, Wang YT, Qin S, Zhao SS, Zhao YS, Lin Q, Guan WD, Huang QD, Mo ZY, Li CY, Zhong NS. The effects of a hot water soluble extract (S-03) isolated from Isatis indigotica root on influenza A and B viruses in vitro. Bing Du Xue Bao. 2011 May;27(3):218-23.
3. Yang Z, Wang Y, Zhong S, Zhao S, Zeng X, Mo Z, Qin S, Guan W, Li C, Zhong N. In vitro inhibition of influenza virus infection by a crude extract from Isatis indigotica root resulting in the prevention of viral attachment. Mol Med Report. 2012 Mar;5(3):793-9.
4. Hsuan SL, Chang SC, Wang SY, Liao TL, Jong TT, Chien MS, Lee WC, Chen SS, Liao JW. The cytotoxicity to leukemia cells and antiviral effects of Isatis indigotica extracts on pseudorabies virus. J Ethnopharmacol. 2009 May 4;123(1):61-7.
5. Mak NK, Leung CY, Wei XY, Shen XL, Wong RN, Leung KN, Fung MC. Inhibition of RANTES expression by indirubin in influenza virus-infected human bronchial epithelial cells. Biochem Pharmacol. 2004 Jan 1;67(1):167-74.
6. Wang XL, et al. Chemical consitituents from root of Isatis indigotica. Zhongguo Zhong Yao Za Zhi. 2013 Apr;38(8):1172-82.
7. Yang Z, et al. Antiviral activity of Isatis indigotica root-derived clemastanin B against human and avian influenza A and B viruses in vitro. Int J Mol Med. 2013 Apr;31(4):867-73. doi: 10.3892/ijmm.2013.1274.
8. Liu FZ, et al. Pharmacodynamic experiment of the antivirus effect of houttuynia cordata injection on influenza virus in mice. Institute of Chinese Materia Medica, China Academy of Chinese Medical Sciences, Beijing 100700, China. Yao Xue Xue Bao. 2010 Mar;45(3):399-402.
9. Lau KM, et al. Immunomodulatory and anti-SARS activities of Houttuynia cordata. Institute of Chinese Medicine, The Chinese University of Hong Kong, Shatin, Hong Kong SAR, China. J Ethnopharmacol. 2008 Jun 19;118(1):79-85.
10. Chiang LC, Chang JS, Chen CC, Ng LT, Lin CC. Anti-Herpes simplex virus activity of Bidens pilosa and Houttuynia cordata. Department of Microbiology, College of Medicine, Kaohsiung Medical University, Kaohsiung 807, Taiwan. Am J Chin Med. 2003;31(3):355-62.
11. Chou SC, Su CR, Ku YC, Wu TS. The constituents and their bioactivities of Houttuynia cordata. Department of Chemistry, National Cheng Kung University, Tainan 701, Taiwan. Chem Pharm Bull (Tokyo). 2009 Nov;57(11):1227-30.
12. Ren X, Sui X, Yin J. The effect of Houttuynia cordata injection on pseudorabies herpesvirus (PrV) infection in vitro. Department of Preventive Medicine, College of Veterinary Medicine, Northeast Agricultural University, Harbin, China. Pharm Biol. 2011 Feb;49(2):161-6.
13. Hayashi K, Kamiya M, Hayashi T. Virucidal effects of the steam distillate from Houttuynia cordata and its components on HSV-1, influenza virus, and HIV. Department of Virology, Toyama Medical and Pharmaceutical University, Japan. Planta Med. 1995 Jun;61(3):237-41.
14. Chen CJ, Michaelis M, Hsu HK, Tsai CC, Yang KD, Wu YC, Cinatl J Jr, Doerr HW. Toona sinensis Roem tender leaf extract inhibits SARS coronavirus replication. J Ethnopharmacol. 2008 Oct 30;120(1):108-11.
15. Shin WJ, Lee KH, Park MH, Seong BL. Broad-spectrum antiviral effect of Agrimonia pilosa extract on influenza viruses. Department of Biotechnology, College of Life Science and Biotechnology, Yonsei University, Seoul 120-749, Korea. Microbiol Immunol. 2010;54(1):11-9.
16. Min B.S., Kim Y.H., Tomiyama M., Nakamura N., Miyashiro H., Otake T. & Hattori M. Inhibitory effects of Korean plants on HIV-1 activities. *Phytother Res.* 2001, 15(6): 481-486.
17. Błach-Olszewska Z, Jatczak B, Rak A, Lorenc M, Gulanowski B, Drobna A, Lamer-Zarawska E. Production of cytokines and stimulation of resistance to viral infection in human leukocytes by Scutellaria baicalensis flavones. Ludwik Hirszfeld Institute of Immunology and Experimental Therapy, Polish Academy of Sciences, Wrocław, Poland. J Interferon Cytokine Res. 2008 Sep;28(9): 571-81.
18. Yu DQ, Chen RY, Huang LJ, Xie FZ, Ming DS, Zhou K, Li HY, Tong KM. The structure and absolute configuration of Shuangkangsu: a novel natural cyclic peroxide from Lonicera japonica (Thunb.). The Key Laboratory of Bioactive Substances and Resources Utilization of Chinese Herbal Medicine, Ministry of Education, Peking Union Medical College, Beijing, China. J Asian Nat Prod Res. 2008 Sep-Oct;10(9-10):851-6.
19. *Zhong Yao Xue* (Chinese Herbology), 1998; 103:106.
20. Wang S., Fan M. & Bian Z. Experimental study of bacteriostatic activity of Chinese herbal medicines on primary cariogenic bacteria *in vitro* . *Zhonghua Kou Qiang Yi Xue Za Zhi.* 2001, 36(5): 385-387.
21. *Shan Xi Xin Yi Yao* (New Medicine and Herbology of Shanxi), 1980; 9(11):51.
22. *Zhong Yi Za Zhi* (Journal of Chinese Medicine), 1983; 24(11):19.
23. *Xian Dai Shi Yong Yao Xue* (Practical Applications of Modern Herbal Medicine), 221.
24. *Jiang Xi Yi Yao* (Jiangxi Medicine and Herbology), 1989; 24(5):315.
25. Tanaka T., Ikeda T., Kaku M., Zhu X.H., Okawa M., Yokomizo K., Uyeda M. & Nohara T. A new lignan glycoside and phenylethanoid glycosides from *Strobilanthes cusia* BREMEK. *Chem Pharm Bull.* (Tokyo). 2004, 52(10): 1242-1245.
26. *Guang Dong Zhong Yi* (Guangdong Chinese Medicine), 1962; 5:25.
27. Wei JA, Sun LM, Chen YX. Effects of Ailing Granule on immuno-reconstruction in HIV/AIDS patients. Zhongguo Zhong Xi Yi Jie He Za Zhi. 2006 Apr;26(4):319-21.
28. *Shan Xi Yi Yao Za Zhi* (Shanxi Journal of Medicine and Herbology), 1974; 5-6:57.
29. *Biol Pharm Bull*, 1977; 20(11)-1178-82.
30. Shao BM, Xu W, Dai H, Tu P, Li Z, Gao XM. A study on the immune receptors for polysaccharides from the roots of Astragalus membranaceus, a Chinese medicinal herb. Department of Immunology, School of Basic Medical Science, Peking University Health Science Center, Beijing, China. Biochem Biophys Res Commun. 2004 Aug 6;320(4):1103-11.
31. Qu LL, Su YL, Li CX, Hou GH. Astragalus membranaceus injection delayed allograft survival related with CD4+ CD25+ regulatory T cells. Department of Nuclear Medicine, Qilu Hospital of Shandong University, Jinan, Shandong, China. Transplant Proc. 2010 Nov;42(9):3793-7.
32. *Zhong Cheng Yao Yan Jiu* (Research of Chinese Patent Medicine), 1982; (1):42.
33. *Zhong Yao Xue* (Chinese Herbology), 1998; 729:736.
34. *Zhong Yi Za Zhi* (Journal of Chinese Medicine), 1980; 1:71.
35. *Hu Nan Zhong Yi Xue Yuan Xue Bao* (Journal of Hunan University of Traditional Chinese Medicine), 1987; 4:13.
36. *Shang Hai Zhong Yi Yao Za Zhi* (Shanghai Journal of Chinese Medicine and Herbology), 1983; 9:27.
37. *Jiang Su Zhong Yi* (Jiangsu Chinese Medicine), 1988; 9:32.

Herbal DRX™

CLINICAL APPLICATIONS

- **Edema and generalized water accumulation**
- **Swelling due to water accumulation**
- Feeling of heaviness or sluggishness in the body, preference to lay down or sleep all day
- *Tan yin* (phlegm retention) syndrome

WESTERN THERAPEUTIC ACTIONS

- Diuretic effect to eliminate water and treat edema

CHINESE THERAPEUTIC ACTIONS

- Strengthens the Spleen
- Resolves dampness
- Promotes urination and treats edema

DOSAGE

Take 3 to 4 capsules three times daily. For maximum effectiveness, take the herbs on an empty stomach.

INGREDIENTS

Bai Zhu (Rhizoma Atractylodis Macrocephalae)
Chen Pi (Pericarpium Citri Reticulatae)
Chi Fu Ling (Poria Rubra)
Chuan Mu Xiang (Radix Vladimiriae)
Fu Ling (Poria)
He Zi (Fructus Chebulae)
Hua Shi (Talcum)
Sheng Jiang Pi (Pericarpium Zingiberis Recens)
Wu Bei Zi (Galla Chinensis)
Yi Yi Ren (Semen Coicis)
Ze Xie (Rhizoma Alismatis)
Zhu Ling (Polyporus)

BACKGROUND

Edema is the swelling of soft tissues due to increased accumulation of water and fluids. Edema may be localized or generalized. Localized edema is usually caused by venous obstruction, lymphatic obstruction, or infection. Generalized edema is commonly due to heart failure, liver failure or kidney failure. In addition to water and fluid retention, other symptoms of edema may include feeling of tightness or fullness in the chest, feeling of heaviness or sluggishness in the body, and preference to lay down or sleep all day. Optimal treatment requires use of herbs to treat the cause and the symptoms.

FORMULA EXPLANATION

Herbal DRX is designed specifically to treat edema, water retention and swelling. It treats the cause of edema by strengthening the Spleen and resolving dampness. It treats the symptoms of edema by clearing damp-heat and draining water through urination.

In this formula, *Fu Ling* (Poria), *Bai Zhu* (Rhizoma Atractylodis Macrocephalae), and *Yi Yi Ren* (Semen Coicis) strengthen the Spleen to resolve dampness. *Fu Ling* (Poria), *Zhu Ling* (Polyporus), *Ze Xie* (Rhizoma Alismatis), and *Sheng Jiang Pi* (Pericarpium Zingiberis Recens) resolve dampness, regulate water circulation, and drain water accumulation. *Sheng Jiang Pi* (Pericarpium Zingiberis Recens) is especially good for water trapped in the superficial parts of the skin. *Hua Shi* (Talcum) and *Chi Fu Ling* (Poria Rubra) clear damp-heat to promote normal urination. *Chuan Mu Xiang* (Radix Vladimiriae) and *Chen Pi* (Pericarpium Citri Reticulatae) activate qi circulation, which is often stagnant in cases of water and damp accumulation. Lastly, *Wu Bei Zi* (Galla Chinensis) and *He Zi* (Fructus Chebulae) are astringent herbs that reduce swelling, and constrict and push the excess fluids out of the body.

In summary, ***Herbal DRX*** is an excellent formula to treat both the cause and symptoms of edema. This formula may be used individually, or in combination with others to treat the cause and/or complications of edema.

CAUTIONS & CONTRAINDICATIONS

- ***Herbal DRX*** is an excellent formula to eliminate accumulation of water and treat edema. However, in addition to elimination of excessive water, diuretic herbs may lead to excretion of some electrolytes. Therefore, if the formula is to be taken for more than two weeks, it is important to receive supplementation of additional electrolytes to prevent imbalance. Symptoms of electrolyte imbalance include muscle spasms and cramps. Common supplements include bananas, orange juice, multivitamins and minerals, and sports drinks.
- Concurrent use of diuretic herbs and diuretic drugs is not recommended as they have the same functions to eliminate water and electrolytes. Concurrent use may contribute to dehydration and electrolyte imbalance.
- This formula is contraindicated during pregnancy.

CLINICAL NOTES

- In comparison with pharmaceutical drugs, diuretic herbs have a moderate potency and a slower onset of action. Therefore, most patients will experience noticeable diuretic effect only after two to four weeks. This formula is designed as a long-term therapy for treatment and prevention of edema-related disorders. Acute conditions, such as acute nephritis with edema, should be treated with other methods and formulas.
- In addition to eliminating excessive water, some herbs in this formula have also shown a marked effect to reduce blood pressure, blood glucose levels, and cholesterol levels, and improve kidney functions.
- Severity of water retention can be easily checked by pressing the patient's shin bone [around the area of *Ligou* (LR 5)]. The deeper the indentation and the longer it stays without bouncing back, the more severe the condition is.

Herbal DRX ™

Pulse Diagnosis by Dr. Jimmy Wei-Yen Chang:
- Deep pulse on all three positions on both hands

SUPPLEMENTARY FORMULAS
- With excessive damp and phlegm, add ***Pinellia Complex***.
- For deficient types of hypertension with edema, combine with ***Gastrodia Complex***.
- For excess types of hypertension with edema, combine with ***Gentiana Complex***.
- For edema due to compromised kidney functions, combine with *Kidney DTX*.
- For obesity with edema, add ***Herbalite***.
- For Spleen deficiency with edema, add ***GI Tonic***.
- For high cholesterol with excessive dampness, add ***Cholisma*** or ***Cholisma (ES)***.
- For gallstones, add ***Dissolve (GS)***.
- For kidney stones, add ***Dissolve (KS)***.
- For cysts or fibroids in the uterus or ovaries, add ***Resolve (Lower)***.
- For fibroids in the breast with excessive dampness, combine with ***Resolve (Upper)***.
- For excessive dampness in conditions such as dysuria, vaginitis, yellow vaginal discharge, add ***V-Support***.
- For yang deficiency type of edema with coldness and possible low back pain, add *Zhen Wu Tang* (True Warrior Decoction).

ACUPUNCTURE TREATMENT
Traditional Points:
- *Lieque* (LU 7), *Hegu* (LI 4), *Piani* (LI 6), *Yinlingquan* (SP 9), *Weiyang* (BL 39), *Pishu* (BL 20), *Shenshu* (BL 23), *Shuifen* (CV 9), *Ciliao* (BL 32), *Guanyuan* (CV 4), *Shangqiu* (SP 5), *Fenglong* (ST 40)

Classic Master Tung's Points:
- **Edema (general):** *Dihuang* (T 77.19), *Tongshen* (T 88.09), *Tongwei* (T 88.10), *Shuiqu* (T 66.09), *Tongbei* (T 88.11)
- **Edema (face):** *Dihuang* (T 77.19), *Tianhuangfu [Shenguan]* (T 77.18), *Tongshen* (T 88.09), *Tongwei* (T 88.10), *Tongbei* (T 88.11), *Huoying* (T 66.03), *Shuijin* (T 1010.20) towards *Shuitong* (T 1010.19), *Xinling* (T 33.17)*
- **Edema (lower body):** *Fuchang* (T 77.12), *Shuiqu* (T 66.09)
- **Edema (pulmonary):** *Chongzi* (T 22.01), *Chongxian* (T 22.02), *Simazhong* (T 88.17), *Neiguan* (PC 6). Bleed the LU and HT area below the knee. Bleed before needling for best result.

Master Tung's Points by Dr. Chuan-Min Wang:
- **Edema:** *Shuiqu* (T 66.09), *Tongshen* (T 88.09)

Balance Method by Dr. Richard Tan:
- Left side: *Hegu* (LI 4), *Shaoze* (SI 1), *Wangu* (SI 4), *Yinlingquan* (SP 9), *Yinbai* (SP 1), *Gongsun* (SP 4)
- Right side: *Chize* (LU 5), *Jingqu* (LU 8), *Shaoshang* (LU 11), *Fenglong* (ST 40), *Weizhong* (BL 40), *Kunlun* (BL 60)
- Alternate sides in between treatments.

Auricular Medicine by Dr. Li-Chun Huang:
- Kidney, Spleen, Heart, *Sanjiao*, Endocrine, Ascites Point

NUTRITION
- A low-sodium diet is recommended, as sodium may cause fluid retention.
- Consume an adequate amount of vitamin B complex, which helps to reduce water retention.
- Consume a sufficient amount of free-form amino acid complex, as edema is sometimes caused by inadequate protein assimilation.
- Increase the consumption of foods that have natural diuretic effects, such as *Lu Dou* (Semen Phaseoli Radiati) and *Yi Yi Ren* (Semen Coicis).
- Avoid drinking ice, cold beverages or eating cold or raw foods.
- Avoid citrus and other foods that are cold in nature such as watermelon, salads, tomatoes, and cucumbers.
- Avoid eating fried, greasy or food high in fat content.
- Reduce the intake of dairy and sugar.

The Tao of Nutrition by Dr. Maoshing Ni and Cathy McNease:
- **Edema and swelling**
  - Recommendations: red (azuki) beans, corn, ginger skin, winter melon, winter melon skin, squash, apples, mulberries, peaches, tangerines, coconuts, seaweeds, fish, celery, green onions, garlic, bamboo shoots, spinach, water chestnuts, millet, wheat, black beans, pearl barley, carrots, watermelon, oats, and beef.
  - Avoid rich foods, salty foods, lamb, stimulating foods, wine, pepper, shellfish, fatty foods, and greasy foods.

LIFESTYLE INSTRUCTIONS
- Individuals with swelling and edema of legs and feet should sit with their legs up as much as possible. Wearing support hose will also reduce swelling in the legs.
- Exercise daily to help push fluids away from the legs and lower body.
- Avoid exposure to the rain. Do not engage in water sport activities while under treatment.

CASE STUDY
- S.S., a 31-year-old male patient, presented with a desire to lose weight, preferably 20 pounds. Symptoms included generalized weight gain and considerable swelling on his face and limbs. Pitting edema was seen upon inspection of the lower legs and hands. The practitioner diagnosed his condition as Spleen qi deficiency with dampness and food accumulation. ***Herbal DRX*** was prescribed at 4 capsules three times daily for two weeks and ***Herbalite*** at 4 capsules three times daily following the completion of ***Herbal DRX***. After taking ***Herbal DRX*** for two weeks, the patient noticed significant reduction in edema of the hands and legs as well as reduction in weight of six pounds. Submitted by A.G., Solana Beach, California.

Herbal DRX™

PHARMACOLOGICAL AND CLINICAL RESEARCH

Herbal DRX is designed to treat edema. To treat the symptom of edema, herbs with diuretic functions are used to increase urine output and water elimination. To manage the cause of edema, many herbs with beneficial effect for the heart, liver, and kidney are used to enhance their functions.

To treat the symptom of edema, many herbs with diuretic effects are used in ***Herbal DRX*** to eliminate excess water. According to one study, use of *Fu Ling* (Poria) is associated with a marked diuretic effect and a significant increase in urine output.[1] According to another study, use of *Fu Ling* (Poria) in an herbal formula is associated with marked effectiveness in treating 23 of 30 patients with edema.[2] *Zhu Ling* (Polyporus) and *Ze Xie* (Rhizoma Alismatis) also have a marked diuretic effect, and they increase the excretion of water, sodium, chloride, and potassium.[3,4] In fact, it has been shown that use of *Zhu Ling* (Polyporus) and Lasix (furosemide) for eight days have similar effect on diuresis, natriuresis and chloriuresis.[5] *Bai Zhu* (Rhizoma Atractylodis Macrocephalae) is also used frequently for its diuretic effect to treat edema. The mechanism of action for *Bai Zhu* (Rhizoma Atractylodis Macrocephalae) has been attributed to the inhibition of sodium re-absorption leading to increased diuresis.[6] Lastly, the use of *Shi Gao* (Gypsum Fibrosum) in an herbal formula has been shown to promote normal urination among 10 patients with urinary tract infection and dysuria.[7]

To manage the cause of edema, many herbs are used in ***Herbal DRX*** to treat heart, liver, and kidney dysfunctions. For heart disorders, *Chen Pi* (Pericarpium Citri Reticulatae), *Chuan Mu Xiang* (Radix Vladimiriae) and *Sheng Jiang* (Rhizoma Zingiberis Recens) are three herbs with beneficial cardiovascular effects.[8,9,10,11] For liver disorders, *Bai Zhu* (Rhizoma Atractylodis Macrocephalae), *Chuan Mu Xiang* (Radix Vladimiriae), *Ze Xie* (Rhizoma Alismatis) and *Zhu Ling* (Polyporus) are herbs with hepatoprotective effects. Furthermore, *Bai Zhu* (Rhizoma Atractylodis Macrocephalae) has been shown to treat specific liver disorders, such as ascites due to liver cirrhosis, hepatitis B, and liver damage caused by Tylenol (acetaminophen).[12,13,14] For kidney disorders, *He Zi* (Fructus Chebulae) has shown both hepatoprotective and nephroprotective effects. According to one study, use of *He Zi* (Fructus Chebulae) is associated with significantly lowered serum levels of the hepatic enzyme markers (AST and ALT) and reduced the indicators of oxidative stress in the liver, such as the glutathione disulfide content and lipid peroxidation, in a dose-dependent manner. In addition, *He Zi* (Fructus Chebulae) is effective to reduce the incidence of liver lesions, including hepatocyte swelling and neutrophilic infiltration. *He Zi* (Fructus Chebulae) can also repair necrosis induced by tert-butyl hydroperoxide.[15] According to another study, administration of *He Zi* (Fructus Chebulae) (125 mg/kg) and/or silymarin (25 mg/kg) offers significant protection for the liver and the kidneys by lowering the serum triglycerides, total cholesterol, blood urea nitrogen, serum creatinine, and aspartate transaminase activity.[16]

In summary, ***Herbal DRX*** is an effective formula to treat and prevent edema and its complications. Most herbs have direct diuretic functions to eliminate the accumulation of water. Others have cardiovascular, hepatoprotective, and nephroprotective effects to manage the cause of edema.

COMPARATIVE ANALYSIS

Water accumulation, as in edema, is a symptom that occurs in various diseases, such as hypertension, congestive heart failure, and nephropathy. This condition is usually treated in part with diuretic drugs, such as Lasix (furosemide), Aldactone (spironolactone), and Dyazide (HCTZ/triamterene). While these drugs all have diuretic effect to eliminate water, their risks include dizziness, vertigo, orthostatic hypotension, electrolyte imbalance, and in severe cases, agranulocytosis, leukopenia and thrombopenia. Furthermore, long-term use of these drugs may increase plasma levels of glucose and cholesterol level, thereby complicating overall management of cardiovascular and circulatory disorders. In short, diuretic drugs must be used carefully, as there are many potential side effects and adverse reactions.

In TCM, water accumulation is treated with herbs that treat both the symptoms and the causes. Diuretic herbs, known as herbs that regulate water and resolve dampness, have an excellent effect to facilitate elimination of water through urination. Furthermore, herbs are also used to strengthen the body and increase its own ability to regulate water circulation in and out of the body. Thus, the use of herbs is effective and achieves both short- and long-term benefits.

Drugs and herbs are both effective to drain water and treat edema. Drugs are more potent, and in severe cases, have a stronger and immediate onset of effect (especially with intravenous injection). However, diuretic drugs must be used and monitored carefully to ensure safe and effective use. Herbs, on the other hand, are gentle and effective. Though they are not as potent, they exert consistent and moderate diuretic effect over the course of therapy. Furthermore, herbs have a much better safety profile in comparison with drugs. In conclusion, selection of optimal treatment depends on the severity of the condition and the patient's risk tolerance.

References

1. *Chang Yong Zhong Yao Cheng Fen Yu Yao Li Shou Ce* (A Handbook of the Composition and Pharmacology of Common Chinese Drugs), 1994; 1383:1391.
2. *Shang Hai Zhong Yi Yao Za Zhi* (Shanghai Journal of Chinese Medicine and Herbology), 1986; 8:25.
3. *Yao Xue Xue Bao* (Journal of Herbology), 1964; 11(12):815.
4. *Sheng Yao Xue Za Zhi* (Journal of Raw Herbology), 1982; 36(2):150.
5. Zhang G, Zeng X, Han L, Wei JA, Huang H. Diuretic activity and kidney medulla AQP1, AQP2, AQP3, V2R expression of the aqueous extract of sclerotia of Polyporus umbellatus FRIES in normal rats. J Ethnopharmacol. 2010 Mar 24;128(2):433-7.

6. *Zhong Hua Yi Xue Za Zhi* (Chinese Journal of Medicine), 1961; 47(1):7.
7. *Liao Ning Yi Yao* (Liaoning Medicine and Herbology), 1976; (2):69.
8. *Journal of Pharmacol Exp Ther*, 1940; 69:309.
9. *Jiang Su Zhong Yi Za Zhi* (Jiangsu Journal of Chinese Medicine), 1981; (3):61.
10. *Zhong Yao Yao Li Yu Ying Yong* (Pharmacology and Applications of Chinese Herbs), 1983: 169.
11. *Zhong Yao Xue* (Chinese Herbology), 1998; 69:72.
12. *An Hui Zhong Yi Xue Yuan Xue Bao* (Journal of Anhui University School of Medicine), 1984; 2:25.
13. *Gan Su Zhong Yi* (Gansu Chinese Medicine), 1995; (1):19.
14. Xiong LL. Therapeutic effect of combined therapy of Salvia miltiorrhizae and Polyporus umbellatus polysaccharide in the treatment of chronic hepatitis B. Zhongguo Zhong Xi Yi Jie He Za Zhi. 1993 Sep;13(9):533-5, 516-7.
15. Lee HS, Won NH, Kim KH, Lee H, Jun W, Lee KW. Antioxidant effects of aqueous extract of Terminalia chebula in vivo and in vitro. Department of Food Science, College of Life & Environmental Sciences, Korea University, Seoul, Korea. Biol Pharm Bull. 2005 Sep;28(9):1639-44.
16. Gopi KS, Reddy AG, Jyothi K, Kumar BA. Acetaminophen-induced Hepato- and Nephrotoxicity and Amelioration by Silymarin and Terminalia chebula in Rats. Department of Pharmacology and Toxicology, College of Veterinary Science, Hyderabad - 500030, Andhra Pradesh, India. Toxicol Int. 2010 Jul;17(2):64-6.

Herbal DTX™

CLINICAL APPLICATIONS

- **Chronic chemical poisoning** (i.e., insecticide, pesticide, herbicide, artificial hormones and preservatives, chemical compounds, chemical solvents, plastics, cleaning products, pollutants, detergents, paint thinner, nail polish remover, new carpet fibers and any other products that may contain toxic fumes or fragrance)
- **Heavy metal poisoning** (i.e., arsenic, cadmium, lead, mercury)
- **Chronic poisoning from air pollution** (i.e., gas exhaust, fumes, perfumes, air freshener, burned plastic, and other airborne toxins)
- **Chronic food poisoning** (i.e., tetrodotoxin, snake, and mushrooms)
- **Chronic poisoning from accumulation of drugs and their metabolites**
- Note: Do ***not*** use this formula to treat acute or serious poisoning conditions. Call 911 and send the patient to the nearest emergency room immediately.

WESTERN THERAPEUTIC ACTIONS

- General detoxification effect to treat chronic exposure to and accumulation of unwanted substances, such as toxic chemicals, herbicides and pesticides, allergens, heavy metals, drugs, and other industrial pollutants and contaminants
- Hepatoprotective effect to protect the liver
- Nephroprotective effect to protect the kidneys

CHINESE THERAPEUTIC ACTIONS

- Clears heat and eliminates toxins
- Expels toxins through urine and stool
- Nourishes yin
- Tonifies Kidney and Heart

DOSAGE

Take 3 to 4 capsules three times daily with a large glass of water for six to twelve months for optimal effect. This formula is ineffective if taken only for a short period of time. Do not use this formula to treat acute poisoning.

INGREDIENTS

Bai Mao Gen (Rhizoma Imperatae)
Da Huang (Radix et Rhizoma Rhei)
Dan Shen (Radix et Rhizoma Salviae Miltiorrhizae)
Fang Feng (Radix Saposhnikoviae)
Gan Cao (Radix et Rhizoma Glycyrrhizae)
Gou Qi Zi (Fructus Lycii)
Lian Qiao (Fructus Forsythiae)
Lu Dou (Semen Phaseoli Radiati)

BACKGROUND

Poisoning is contact with a substance that causes toxicity. Acute poisoning generally has a direct cause-and-effect relationship, and is easy to diagnose and treat. Chronic poisoning is usually associated with long-term exposure to and accumulation of toxic substances, such as chemicals, herbicides and pesticides, allergens, heavy metals, drugs, and other industrial pollutants and contaminants. Chronic poisoning is difficult to identify as these toxic substances are ubiquitous in developed countries. The cause-and-effect relationship is hard to establish as substances become toxic with long-term exposure and accumulation, and not with one time contact. Therefore, detailed investigation into the personal life and medical history of the patient is absolutely necessary to identify the toxic substance. Optimal treatment requires avoidance of the toxic substances, and use of herbs to remove the toxic substance and manage the symptoms.

FORMULA EXPLANATION

Herbal DTX is designed to treat various symptoms related to chronic exposure to and accumulation of different kinds of chemicals, allergens, heavy metals, drugs and other toxins. Patients may exhibit symptoms of heat sensation, low-grade fever or high fever, thirst, dry mouth, headache, nasal congestion, allergy, irritability, nausea, vomiting, turbid urination or disorientation.

The key to treatment of poisoning is to accelerate the elimination of toxins in the body and protect the organs at the same time. *Lu Dou* (Semen Phaseoli Radiati) is sweet and cold, and clears heat and eliminates toxins. *Gan Cao* (Radix et Rhizoma Glycyrrhizae) is sweet and neutral, and is the most essential harmonizing herb to detoxify various substances. *Dan Shen* (Radix et Rhizoma Salviae Miltiorrhizae) is bitter and slightly cold, and has a great effect to invigorate blood and cleanse the toxicity from the blood. It also clears heat, reduces irritability and tranquilizes the Heart. *Bai Mao Gen* (Rhizoma Imperatae) is cold in property and clears heat and eliminates toxins through urination. It also prevents potential bleeding and protects the Kidney. *Lian Qiao* (Fructus Forsythiae) clears heat, detoxifies and further helps *Bai Mao Gen* (Rhizoma Imperatae) to dispel toxins through the Kidney. *Gou Qi Zi* (Fructus Lycii) is sweet, and is mainly used for nourishing the Stomach yin and generating body fluids. It has a unique effect to create a protective layer in the stomach to prevent the absorption of toxins from the digestive tract. *Da Huang* (Radix et Rhizoma Rhei) is a purgative herb that detoxifies and purges heat simultaneously by invigorating blood circulation and purging downwards. *Fang Feng* (Radix Saposhnikoviae) dispels internal Liver wind and is used to relieve stiffness, discomfort, and pain in the muscles associated with poisoning.

Herbal DTX is an excellent formula for the prevention and treatment of overdose and accumulation of harmful chemicals and toxins. ***Herbal DTX*** eliminates toxins through urination and defecation, invigorates blood circulation to accelerate recovery, and strengthens the body to increase its natural defensive ability.

Herbal DTX™

CAUTIONS & CONTRAINDICATIONS

- This formula is ***not*** recommended for the following conditions:
  - Patients with an acute overdose or severe poisoning should be treated in an emergency room or urgent care center. Call 911 and send the patient to the nearest emergency room immediately.
  - Patients with hematuria (blood in the urine) should be treated with extreme caution because this symptom may indicate the possibility of significant damage to the kidney.
  - Patients who are disorientated or having a seizure/epilepsy/convulsion associated with poisoning should consult their medical doctor immediately.
- This herbal formula contains herbs that invigorate blood circulation, such as *Dan Shen* (Radix et Rhizoma Salviae Miltiorrhizae). Therefore, patients who are on anticoagulant or antiplatelet therapies, such as Coumadin (warfarin), should use this formula with caution, or not at all, as there may be a higher risk of bleeding and bruising.[1]
- Patients with a sensitive stomach should take this formula with food. If stomach upset still occurs, reduce the dosage and increase the frequency.
- The following warning statement is required by the State of California: "This product contains *Da Huang* (Radix et Rhizoma Rhei). Read and follow directions carefully. Do not use if you have or develop diarrhea, loose stools, or abdominal pain because *Da Huang* (Radix et Rhizoma Rhei) may worsen these conditions and be harmful to your health. Consult your physician if you have frequent diarrhea or if you are pregnant, nursing, taking medication, or have a medical condition."

CLINICAL NOTES

- ***Herbal DTX*** is a good formula for individuals who have hypersensitivity to certain toxins, chemicals, and environmental factors because of its effect to eliminate the accumulation of toxins and enhance the functions of the liver and kidney. ***Herbal DTX*** contains herbs that will enhance the body's natural ability to break down and eliminate the buildup of toxins in the body. ***Herbal DTX*** is a gentle formula that gradually and continuously removes toxins from the body. It should be taken persistently for six to twelve months for optimal effect.
- General actions for acute poisoning are as follows:
  - For inhaled poison, open the doors and windows and get the person fresh air as quickly as possible.
  - For poison on the skin, remove the contaminated clothing and flood the skin with water for at least 10 minutes.
  - For poison in the eye, flood the affected eye(s) with lukewarm water poured from a glass two to three inches from the eye(s) and repeat for 15 minutes.
  - For swallowed poison, give a glass of water (two to eight ounces) immediately unless the person is unconscious, having convulsions, or cannot swallow. For more information, please contact the National Poison Control System at (800) 222-1222.

Pulse Diagnosis by Dr. Jimmy Wei-Yen Chang:

- Big pulse, a thick, expanding, forceful pulse on the left *guan* and both *chi* positions.

SUPPLEMENTARY FORMULAS

- For liver damage or hepatitis due to poisoning, add ***Liver DTX***.
- For kidney damage or nephritis due to poisoning, combine with ***Kidney DTX***.
- To detox the colon, add ***GI DTX***.
- For general signs and symptoms of heat and excess conditions, add ***Gardenia Complex***.
- For headaches, add ***Corydalin (AC)*** or ***Corydalin (CR)***.
- For toxicity manifesting in skin allergies, rashes or unexplainable itching of the skin, choose from ***Silerex, Dermatrol (Damp)*** or ***Dermatrol (Dry)***.
- For mild nasal congestion and post-nasal drip, combine with ***Magnolia Clear Sinus***.
- For severe nasal obstruction with yellow and sticky discharge, add ***Pueraria Clear Sinus***.
- For difficulty breathing and feeling of chest tightness, add ***Respitrol (Heat)*** or ***Respitrol (Deficient)***.
- For excess perspiration or fatigue, add ***Immune +***.
- For diarrhea with weakness, add ***GI Tonic*** or ***GI Care II***.
- *Zhu Dan* (Fel Porcus) and *Tu Fu Ling* (Rhizoma Smilacis Glabrae) can be added to detoxify poison in difficult cases. Dosage of *Tu Fu Ling* (Rhizoma Smilacis Glabrae) can be used up to 6 grams a day in addition to ***Herbal DTX*** to achieve desired effect.
- For unknown causes or strange symptoms of blood stagnation, add ***Circulation (SJ)***.

ACUPUNCTURE TREATMENT

Traditional Points:

- **To improve liver functions to metabolize toxins:** *Xingjian* (LR 2), *Taichong* (LR 3), *Ganshu* (BL 18), *Danshu* (BL 19), *Zusanli* (ST 36), *Fenglong* (ST 40), *Sanyinjiao* (SP 6)
- **To improve kidney functions to eliminate toxins:** *Sanyinjiao* (SP 6), *Zhigou* (TH 6), *Shuifen* (CV 9), *Guanyuan* (CV 4), *Feishu* (BL 13), *Hegu* (LI 4), *Zhongji* (CV 3), *Yinlingquan* (SP 9), *Zusanli* (ST 36)

Classic Master Tung's Points:

- *Fenzhishang* (T DT.01), *Fenzhixia* (T DT.02), *Ganmen* (T 33.11), *Minghuang* (T 88.12), *Huoquan* (T 88.16), *Qihuang* (T 88.14). Needle every day.

Master Tung's Points by Dr. Chuan-Min Wang:

- **Drugs, chemicals, heavy metal, toxin in the blood:** Bleed *Fenzhishang* (T DT.01), *Fenzhixia* (T DT.02). Needle *Jie* (T 88.28).

Balance Method by Dr. Richard Tan:

- Left side: *Dadun* (LR 1), *Yinbai* (SP 1), *Yongquan* (KI 1), *Hegu* (LI 4), *Zhongzhu* (TH 3), *Houxi* (SI 3)

Herbal DTX ™

- Right side: *Daling* (PC 7), *Lieque* (LU 7), *Lingdao* (HT 4), *Zusanli* (ST 36), *Yanglingquan* (GB 34), *Xialiao* (BL 34)
- Left and right sides can be alternated from treatment to treatment.

Auricular Medicine by Dr. Li-Chun Huang:

- **Drug addiction:** Sympathetic, *Shenmen*, Kidney, Liver, Lower Lung, Anxious, Nervous Subcortex. Bleed Ear Apex.

NUTRITION

- Organic products are highly recommended for patients who are suffering from poisoning.
- Take *Lactobacillus acidophilus* supplement to restore normal balance of intestinal flora.
- Drink plenty of water throughout the day to help flush out toxins.
- Avoid preserved foods such as ham, canned food, and peanut butter.

The Tao of Nutrition by Dr. Maoshing Ni and Cathy McNease:

- **Lead and copper poisoning:** consume daily 1 pound of fresh water chestnuts with 1/4 pound of peach kernels.
- **Allergic reaction to sulfites:** drink daily 3 cups of broth made from boiling equal portions of lima and mung beans.

LIFESTYLE INSTRUCTIONS

- Exposure to the offending toxins should be avoided as much as possible. Do not drink tap water if it contains high levels of heavy metals. Avoid eating foods that contain preservatives, artificial hormones, herbicides, and pesticides. Minimize outdoor activities if the air quality is poor in order to avoid inhalation of air pollutants. Avoid all products that may contain artificial scents and flavor. Lastly, individuals with hypersensitivity should avoid the use and inhalation of certain chemicals, such as hair spray and perfumes.
- The work environment should also be considered when determining the cause of poisoning. Chronic poisoning is sometimes related to the work environment.
- Taking deep breaths for ten minutes each day can enhance the elimination process of toxins in the body.

CASE STUDIES

- C.F., a 30-year-old male, presented with shortness of breath and had been experiencing asthma attacks while drinking, smoking, and painting an outside fence. Objective findings included a red face, swollen red tongue with cracks, and dry red coating. The practitioner diagnosed this condition as toxic heat due to toxic chemicals; Western diagnosis was acute asthma attack. ***Herbal DTX*** was prescribed for treatment. After taking the herbs for two weeks the patient reported that his shortness of breath had improved. He had mentioned he was going to continue taking the herbs to help him more. Submitted by M.P., Muskego, Wisconsin.
- W.G., a 23-year-old male, presented with toxicity due to recreational drugs. The TCM diagnosis was toxic heat in the Liver as well as throughout the entire body. For treatment, ***Liver DTX*** and ***Herbal DTX*** were prescribed. The patient noticed a significant detoxification in response to taking both formulas. In comparison, he had noticed the ***Liver DTX*** working more through the urine and the ***Herbal DTX*** working throughout the entire body. He was very in-tune with his body and testified that these formulas were very helpful to his condition. Submitted by B.S., Niceville, Florida.
- This formula has been used with great success in China for treatment of drug overdose (sedatives and hypnotics), accidental ingestion of rat poison, and adverse reactions associated with *Shang Lu* (Radix Phytolaccae). This formula has been used with excellent results by itself, in combination with drug treatment, or following gastric lavage. Submitted by W.C., Shanxi, China.

PHARMACOLOGICAL AND CLINICAL RESEARCH

Herbal DTX is designed to treat various kinds of chronic poisoning reactions, including but not limited to such toxins as environmental toxins, chemical compounds, heavy metals, drugs, insecticides, pesticides, herbicides, preservatives, gas exhaust, artificial hormones, air and water pollution. Acute poisonings are easy to diagnose, and are usually treated by physicians in the emergency room or urgent care center. Chronic poisonings, however, are far more difficult to diagnose as the signs and symptoms are often vague and non-conclusive. Chronic poisoning usually occurs following long-term exposure to toxic agents and their gradual accumulation in the body. Eventually, the accumulation of toxins will begin to interfere with the normal functions of the body to create various illnesses and diseases. Furthermore, since the liver and the kidneys are the two organs that are primarily responsible for metabolizing and eliminating foreign substances, it is extremely important to ensure that these organs are functioning properly. Individuals with chronic poisoning often have damaged liver and kidney functions. Therefore, optimal treatment must address both detoxification of the offending agent and healing of these two organs.

Gan Cao (Radix et Rhizoma Glycyrrhizae) is one of the most commonly used herbs for treatment of overdose and poisoning reactions. It has been proposed that *Gan Cao* (Radix et Rhizoma Glycyrrhizae) should be used as the first agent in cases where the identity of the ingested poison or the specific antidote is unknown.[2] Research and clinical reports have all confirmed *Gan Cao* (Radix et Rhizoma Glycyrrhizae) to have a marked effect to reduce the toxicity of numerous agents, such as toxic foods and plants.[3,4] More recently, it was reported that the use of *Gan Cao* (Radix et Rhizoma Glycyrrhizae) showed satisfactory results in treating 454 patients with various types of food poisoning.[5] In another report, 20 out of 22 patients with mushroom poisoning had complete recovery after being treated with an

Herbal DTX ™

herbal decoction of *Gan Cao* (Radix et Rhizoma Glycyrrhizae).[6] Furthermore, glycyrrhizin, generally considered one of the main constituents of *Gan Cao* (Radix et Rhizoma Glycyrrhizae), has a marked detoxifying effect to treat various kinds of poisonings, including but not limited to drug poisoning (chloral hydrate, urethane, cocaine, picrotoxin, caffeine, pilocarpine, nicotine, barbiturates, mercury and lead), food poisoning (tetrodotoxin, snake, and mushrooms), and others (herbicides, pesticides, enterotoxin).[7,8] In addition to *Gan Cao* (Radix et Rhizoma Glycyrrhizae), *Lu Dou* (Semen Phaseoli Radiati) has been used to treat cases of pesticide poisoning with complete recovery after only three doses.[9]

Herbal DTX also contains herbs that are effective for treating heavy metal poisoning. In one report, 278 patients were treated for arsenic poisoning with an herbal decoction twice daily consisting of *Fang Feng* (Radix Saposhnikoviae), *Lu Dou* (Semen Phaseoli Radiati), *Gan Cao* (Radix et Rhizoma Glycyrrhizae) and sugar. At the end of the 28-day treatment, 155 patients (55.76%) reported a significant improvement in subjective signs and symptoms, with normal levels of arsenic found through urinalysis.[10]

Herbal DTX contains many herbs, such as *Gan Cao* (Radix et Rhizoma Glycyrrhizae), *Dan Shen* (Radix et Rhizoma Salviae Miltiorrhizae) and *Da Huang* (Radix et Rhizoma Rhei), with marked hepatoprotective effects and can be used to treat various disorders related to the liver. In one report, 330 patients with hepatitis B were treated with glycyrrhizin with 77% effectiveness. The study reported that glycyrrhizin reduced the damage and death of liver cells, reduced inflammatory reaction, promoted the regeneration of liver cells, and decreased the risk of liver cirrhosis and necrosis.[11] The mechanism of action of *Gan Cao* (Radix et Rhizoma Glycyrrhizae) is attributed to the increase of enzyme cytochrome P450 in the liver, which is responsible for the protective effect of the herb on the liver against chemical- or tetrachloride-induced liver damage and liver cancer.[12] In addition, *Dan Shen* (Radix et Rhizoma Salviae Miltiorrhizae) is another herb with marked benefit to protect the liver and treat hepatitis. Administration of *Dan Shen* (Radix et Rhizoma Salviae Miltiorrhizae) is associated with a marked hepatoprotective effect against carbon tetrachloride by lowering liver enzyme levels.[13] The hepatoprotective function of *Dan Shen* (Radix et Rhizoma Salviae Miltiorrhizae) is due in part to its effect to improve blood circulation and promote regeneration of new liver cells.[14] Clinically, the use of *Dan Shen* (Radix et Rhizoma Salviae Miltiorrhizae) has been found to be 81.7% effective in treating acute viral hepatitis.[15] It is also used with great success in treating patients with chronic hepatitis.[16] Lastly, *Da Huang* (Radix et Rhizoma Rhei) can also be used to treat hepatitis and acute icteric hepatitis. *Da Huang* (Radix et Rhizoma Rhei) has a hepatoprotective effect by reducing the extent of liver damage (necrosis of hepatocytes), especially by carbon tetrachloride.[17] According to one study, 80 cases of acute icteric hepatitis were treated with a large dosage of *Da Huang* (Radix et Rhizoma Rhei) with 95% effective rate based on symptomatic evaluation and improvement of liver function.[18] According to another study, 67 patients with acute hepatitis A treated with *Da Huang* (Radix et Rhizoma Rhei) and *Qing Pi* (Pericarpium Citri Reticulatae Viride) resulted in recovery in 41 cases, significant improvement in 16 cases, moderate improvement in 7 cases, and no effect in 3 cases.[19]

Herbal DTX also has many herbs with remarkable nephroprotective effects to protect the kidney and treat kidney related disorders, including but not limited to acute and chronic nephritis, acute and chronic glomerulonephritis, and toxic uremia. Pharmacologically, *Da Huang* (Radix et Rhizoma Rhei) shows nephroprotective activity as it effectively reduces blood urea nitrogen (BUN) and creatinine in both *in vitro* and *in vivo* studies.[20] Clinically, an herbal formula with *Da Huang* (Radix et Rhizoma Rhei) and others was effective in treating 20 patients with various degrees of renal impairment by reducing the blood urea nitrogen and creatinine levels significantly.[21] Furthermore, one formula with *Bai Mao Gen* (Rhizoma Imperatae) as the main ingredient showed a marked effect for treating acute nephritis in children. Of 84 patients, 30 had complete recovery, 32 had significant improvement, 18 had moderate improvement, and 4 had no effect.[22] Chronic nephritis in 20 patients was treated with good success (significant improvement in 13 cases, moderate improvement in 2 cases, and slight improvement in 5 cases) using an herbal formula with *Dan Shen* (Radix et Rhizoma Salviae Miltiorrhizae) and other herbs in decoction.[23] For acute and chronic glomerulonephritis, one study of 60 patients reported 91.7% rate of effectiveness using an herbal decoction that contained *Dan Shen* (Radix et Rhizoma Salviae Miltiorrhizae), *Huang Qi* (Radix Astragali) and other herbs.[24] Lastly, 46 patients with toxic uremia were treated with 87.5% rate of effectiveness using an herbal formula that contained *Da Huang* (Radix et Rhizoma Rhei), *Huang Qi* (Radix Astragali) and others.[25]

In summary, ***Herbal DTX*** contains many herbs that have been used successfully to treat overdose and poisoning by many substances, as stated in the paragraphs above. Furthermore, herbs in ***Herbal DTX*** prevent and treat disorders of the liver and kidney caused by the accumulation of foreign and toxic substances. By restoring the normal functions of the liver and kidney, ***Herbal DTX*** ensures the healing and recovery from toxic reactions.

COMPARATIVE ANALYSIS

One striking difference between Western and traditional Chinese medicine is that Western medicine focuses on and excels in crisis management, while traditional Chinese medicine emphasizes on and shines in holistic and preventative treatments. Therefore, in emergencies, such as gunshot wounds or surgery, Western medicine is generally the treatment of choice. However, for treatment of chronic idiopathic illness of unknown origins,

Herbal DTX ™

where all lab tests are normal and a clear diagnosis cannot be made, traditional Chinese medicine is distinctly superior.

In cases of chronic poisoning (from chemicals, heavy metals, and various environmental toxins), there are often many vague, non-specific, non-diagnostic signs and symptoms accompanied by normal laboratory tests. Under these circumstances, Western medicine struggles to determine the exact diagnosis and corresponding treatments. On the other hand, traditional Chinese medicine is beneficial as it excels in regulating imbalances and alleviating associated signs and symptoms. This formula is extremely beneficial because many herbs in this formula have been shown to have a marked effect to detoxify various types of toxins, and to protect and restore normal functions of internal organs (liver and kidneys). This, however, is a gradual process that requires long-term commitment. Herbs should be taken continuously for 6 to 12 months for optimal success. By treating both symptoms and cause, herbal therapy effectively prevents deterioration and restores optimal health.

References

1. Chan K, Lo AC, Yeung JH, Woo KS. Journal of Pharmacy and Pharmacology 1995 May;47(5):402-406.
2. *Jin Gui Yao Lue* (Essentials from the Golden Cabinet) by Zhang Zhong-Jing in Eastern Han.
3. *Shang Hai Zhong Yi Yao Za Zhi* (Shanghai Journal of Chinese Medicine and Herbology), 1964; 8:22.
4. *Fu Jian Zhong Yi Yao* (Fujian Chinese Medicine and Herbology), 1965; 4:44.
5. *Xin Zhong Yi* (New Chinese Medicine), 1985; 2:34.
6. *Xin Zhong Yi* (New Chinese Medicine), 1978; 1:36.
7. *Zhong Yao Tong Bao* (Journal of Chinese Herbology), 1986; 11(10):54.
8. *Zhong Yao Tong Bao* (Journal of Chinese Herbology), 1986; 11(10):55.
9. *Zhe Jiang Zhong Yi Za Zhi* (Zhejiang Journal of Chinese Medicine), 1965; 7:7.
10. *Xin Yi Xue* (New Medicine), 1973; 7:6.
11. *Zhong Yao Tong Bao* (Journal of Chinese Herbology), 1987; 9:60.
12. *Zhong Yao Tong Bao* (Journal of Chinese Herbology), 1986; 11(10):55.
13. *Zhong Yi Za Zhi* (Journal of Chinese Medicine), 1982; (1):67.
14. *Zhong Xi Yi Jie He Za Zhi* (Journal of Integrated Chinese and Western Medicine), 1983; 3(3):180.
15. *Shan Xi Zhong Yi* (Shanxi Chinese Medicine), 1980; 6:15.
16. *Zhong Xi Yi Jie He Za Zhi* (Journal of Integrated Chinese and Western Medicine), 1984; 2:86.
17. *Zhong Guo Zhong Yao Za Zhi* (People's Republic of China Journal of Chinese Herbology), 1989; 14(10):46.
18. *Zhong Xi Yi Jie He Za Zhi* (Journal of Integrated Chinese and Western Medicine), 1983; 1:19.
19. *Si Chuan Zhong Yi* (Sichuan Chinese Medicine), 1994; (3):21.
20. *Chang Yong Zhong Yao Xian Dai Yan Jiu Yu Lin Chuang* (Recent Study & Clinical Application of Common Traditional Chinese Medicine), 1995; 181:190.
21. *Zhong Yi Za Zhi* (Journal of Chinese Medicine), 1981; 9:21.
22. *Yun Nan Zhong Yi Za Zhi* (Yunan Journal of Chinese Medicine), 1986; (4):19.
23. *Zhong Yao Lin Chuan Xin Yong* (New Clinical Applications of Chinese Medicine), 2001; 139.
24. *Zhong Yao Lin Chuan Xin Yong* (New Clinical Applications of Chinese Medicine), 2001; 139.
25. *Zhong Yao Lin Chuan Xin Yong* (New Clinical Applications of Chinese Medicine), 2001; 31-32.

Herbal ENT™

CLINICAL APPLICATIONS

- **Infection and inflammation in ears, nose, and throat** (ENT)
  - **Ear infection:** suppurative otitis media
  - **Nose infection:** sinus infection, sinusitis, and rhinitis
  - **Throat infection:** infectious parotitis, tonsillitis, pharyngitis, strep throat, severe sore throat, bad breath, and mouth ulcers
- Other infections: infectious mononucleosis, erysipelas, and sores and ulcerations in the oral cavity

WESTERN THERAPEUTIC ACTIONS

- Antiviral properties to treat viral infections
- Antibacterial properties to treat bacterial infections
- Antipyretic effect to reduce fever
- Anti-inflammatory effect to reduce swelling, relieve inflammation and alleviate pain

CHINESE THERAPEUTIC ACTIONS

- Clears heat in the head and the upper *jiao*
- Eliminates toxins

DOSAGE

Take 3 to 4 capsules three times daily on an empty stomach, with warm water. Dosage may be increased to 6 to 8 capsules three times daily, if necessary. The herbs should be taken with meals for those with a sensitive stomach.

INGREDIENTS

Ban Lan Gen (Radix Isatidis)
Bo He (Herba Menthae)
Chai Hu (Radix Bupleuri)
Chen Pi (Pericarpium Citri Reticulatae)
Gan Cao (Radix et Rhizoma Glycyrrhizae)
Huang Lian (Rhizoma Coptidis)
Huang Qin (Radix Scutellariae)
Jie Geng (Radix Platycodonis)
Lian Qiao (Fructus Forsythiae)
Ma Bo (Lasiosphaera seu Calvatia)
Niu Bang Zi (Fructus Arctii)
Xuan Shen (Radix Scrophulariae)
Zhe Bei Mu (Bulbus Fritillariae Thunbergii)

BACKGROUND

A healthy person has numerous defense mechanisms that protects against invasion of micro-organisms. These host defense mechanisms include natural barriers (i.e., skin), non-specific immunity (i.e., phagocytic cells) and specific immunity (i.e., antibodies). However, if the host defenses are defective or becomes disrupted, the micro-organisms may enter and affect various parts of the body. While infection may occur at any parts of the body, infection of the head is relatively common as the openings in the head (i.e., ear, nose and throat) directly connect the body to the outside world, and therefore, are often the first places affected by micro-organisms. Thus, optimal treatment of infective disorders affecting the ear, nose and throat requires use of treatment agents to kill the micro-organisms and preventative agents that block the spread of the infection.

FORMULA EXPLANATION

Herbal ENT is designed to treat wind, heat, and toxin invasion to the head region, leading to symptoms such as severe sore throat, redness and swelling of the face and head, difficulties opening the eyes, swollen glands, ear infection, and thirst. It contains herbs with actions to clear heat and eliminate toxins.

Huang Qin (Radix Scutellariae) and *Huang Lian* (Rhizoma Coptidis), the chief herbs of this formula, are used to clear heat in the head and eliminate toxins. *Niu Bang Zi* (Fructus Arctii), *Lian Qiao* (Fructus Forsythiae), and *Bo He* (Herba Menthae) disperse the accumulation of the wind-heat factor in the head. They are all crucial herbs in the treatment of sore throat. *Xuan Shen* (Radix Scrophulariae), *Ma Bo* (Lasiosphaera seu Calvatia) and *Ban Lan Gen* (Radix Isatidis) clear heat and eliminate toxins. *Ma Bo* (Lasiosphaera seu Calvatia) is especially effective for severe sore throat with difficulty to swallow. *Jie Geng* (Radix Platycodonis), *Zhe Bei Mu* (Bulbus Fritillariae Thunbergii) and *Gan Cao* (Radix et Rhizoma Glycyrrhizae) have a synergistic effect to soothe sore throat, thus helping the heat-clearing herbs. *Xuan Shen* (Radix Scrophulariae), besides benefiting the throat, also prevents the heat-clearing and dampness-drying herbs from injuring the yin. *Jie Geng* (Radix Platycodonis) also has an expectorant effect to bring out the sputum and prevent the spread of the infection deeper into the body. *Chen Pi* (Pericarpium Citri Reticulatae) descends Lung qi, relieves cough and eliminates phlegm. Finally, besides dispersing the wind-heat factor, *Chai Hu* (Radix Bupleuri), acts as a guiding herb to bring the other herbs upward to the head region, where the condition is most critical.

CAUTIONS & CONTRAINDICATIONS

- This formula is contraindicated during pregnancy and nursing.
- This formula should be used with caution in those with loose stools or diarrhea caused by Spleen qi deficiency. Take this formula after meals in patients who have a weak digestive system.
- Use this formula with caution in cases of yang and qi deficiencies.

CLINICAL NOTES

- If the condition does not improve after seven days, modification of the treatment may be necessary.
- There is no evidence thus far that use of heat-clearing herbs may permit secondary infections to arise (as is the case with antibiotic drugs). However, those who have recurrent infections should take acidophilus prophylactically, especially if they have a history of repeated antibiotic drug usage.
- ***Herbal ENT*** is stronger than ***Lonicera Complex*** in the treatment of wind-heat invasion. It is used in cases where there is severe sore throat accompanied with other wind-heat symptoms.

Herbal ENT™

- *Herbal ENT* incorporates numerous antibiotic herbs for two important reasons. First, the use of multiple herbs within an herbal formula has been shown to increase the antibiotic effect more than tenfold. Second, isolated use of single ingredients is often ineffective and increases the risk of development of bacterial and viral resistance.[1] Given these two reasons, it is necessary to combine herbs with appropriate properties to ensure effectiveness in treating the infection and minimizing the potential risk of the micro-organisms developing resistance and/or mutation.
- Patients with encephalitis or meningitis should be sent to the emergency room for immediate medical treatment. Warning signs and symptoms of encephalitis or meningitis include fever, headache, stiff neck, sore throat, vomiting, and mental confusion. In addition to soreness, the stiffness is also characterized by severe pain with gentle taps to the neck, and extreme stiffness and immobility when the patient tries to lower the chin to the chest.

Pulse Diagnosis by Dr. Jimmy Wei-Yen Chang:

- **Upper respiratory viral infection:** deep and weak pulse on the right *cun*
- **Upper respiratory bacterial infection:** superficial and forceful pulse on the right *cun*
- **Lower respiratory infection:** *Yangwei* pulse, a pulse extending distally from the *cun* position towards the thumb on the right hand. It is one of the eight extra meridian pulses.

SUPPLEMENTARY FORMULAS

- For common cold or influenza with sore throat, combine with ***Lonicera Complex*** .
- For sinus infections, combine with ***Magnolia Clear Sinus*** or ***Pueraria Clear Sinus***.
- For respiratory tract infections, combine with ***Respitrol (Heat)*** or ***Respitrol (Cold)***.
- For yellow or greenish phlegm due to respiratory tract infections, use with ***Pinellia XPT***.
- With more damp and phlegm in the body, add ***Pinellia Complex***.
- To enhance the antibiotic effect, add ***Herbal ABX***.
- To enhance the antiviral effect, add ***Herbal AVR***.
- With more inflammation, add ***Astringent Complex***.
- For high fever and excess heat in the body, combine with ***Gardenia Complex***.
- For headache, add ***Corydalin (AC)***.
- With severe infectious mononucleosis with swollen lymph nodes, add ***Resolve (AI)***.
- With severe suppurative otitis media, add ***Gentiana Complex***.
- With constipation, add ***Gentle Lax (Excess)***.

ACUPUNCTURE TREATMENT

Traditional Points:

- **Middle ear infection:** *Fengchi* (GB 20), *Yifeng* (TH 17), *Tinggong* (SI 19), *Hegu* (LI 4), *Waiguan* (TH 5), *Zulinqi* (GB 41), *Shenshu* (BL 23), *Quchi* (LI 11)
- **Sinus infection:**
  - *Feishu* (BL 13), *Hegu* (LI 4), *Quchi* (LI 11), *Shangyang* (LI 1), *Lingtai* (GV 10)
  - *Shaoshang* (LU 11), *Quchi* (LI 11), *Yingxiang* (LI 20)
- **Sore throat:**
  - *Tinghui* (GB 2), *Yifeng* (TH 17), *Jiache* (ST 6), *Hegu* (LI 4), *Lieque* (LU 7), *Fenglong* (ST 40), *Jiexi* (ST 41), *Shaoshang* (LU 11), *Jiaosun* (TH 20)
  - *Shaoshang* (LU 11), *Hegu* (LI 4), *Neiting* (ST 44), *Tianrong* (SI 17)

Classic Master Tung's Points:

- **Throat infection:** *Houjian* (T 44.29)*, *Linggu* (T 22.05), *Chongzi* (T 22.01), *Chongxian* (T 22.02), *Yizhong* (T 77.05), *Erzhong* (T 77.06), *Sanzhong* (T 77.07), *Zusanli* (ST 36), *Hegu* (LI 4), *Tongshen* (T 88.09), *Tongwei* (T 88.10), *Tongbei* (T 88.11). Bleed *Shaoshang* (LU 11) and also dark veins nearby *Yinlingquan* (SP 9) to *Xuehai* (SP 10), *Quling* (T 33.16), *Cesanli* (T 77.22), *Cexiasanli* (T 77.23) and the throat. Bleed before needling for best result.
- **Tonsillitis:** *Sanjian* (LI 3), *Mu* (T 11.17), *Qihu* (T 77.26), *Waisanguan* (T 77.27), *Xinling* (T 33.17)*, *Yizhong* (T 77.05), *Erzhong* (T 77.06), *Sanzhong* (T 77.07), *Hegu* (LI 4), *Linggu* (T 22.05), *Dabai* (T 22.04), *Tushui* (T 22.11), *Shiyin* (T 88.32), *Cesanli* (T 77.22), *Zuqianjin* (T 77.24). Bleed *Shaoshang* (LU 11) and also dark veins nearby *Yinlingquan* (SP 9) to *Xuehai* (SP 10). Bleed before needling for best result.
- **Middle ear infection:** *Wanshunyi* (T 22.08), *Linggu* (T 22.05), *Fugesan* (T 44.30)*, *Yizhong* (T 77.05), *Erzhong* (T 77.06), *Sanzhong* (T 77.07), *Huoying* (T 66.03), *Tianhuangfu [Shenguan]* (T 77.18). Bleed dark veins nearby 2 *cuns* above the lateral malleolus. Bleed before needling for best result.
- **Mumps:** *Linggu* (T 22.05), *Yizhong* (T 77.05), *Erzhong* (T 77.06), *Sanzhong* (T 77.07), *Shangquan* (T 88.22), *Zhongquan* (T 88.21), *Xiaquan* (T 88.20), *Waisanguan* (T 77.27). Bleed *Shaoshang* (LU 11). Bleed before needling for best result.
- **Influenza or common cold:** *Fugesan* (T 44.30)*, *Linggu* (T 22.05), *Hegu* (LI 4), *Ganmaoyi* (T 88.07), *Ganmaoer* (T 88.08), *Fugesan* (T 44.30)*, *Huofuhai* (T 33.07), *Mu* (T 11.17)

Master Tung's Points by Dr. Chuan-Min Wang:

- **Ear, nose, throat infection:** Needle *Dabai* (T 22.04), *Sanchasan* (T 22.17)*. Bleed *Yuji* (LU 10), *Shaoshang* (LU 11).

Balance Method by Dr. Richard Tan:

- Left side: *Tianjing* (TH 10), *Quchi* (LI 11), *ah shi* points from *Yanggu* (SI 5) to *Yanglao* (SI 6), *Yingu* (KI 10), *Ququan* (LR 8), *Yinlingquan* (SP 9)
- Right side: *Quze* (PC 3), *Shaofu* (HT 8), *ah shi* points from *Taiyuan* (LU 9) to *Yuji* (LU 10), *Yanglingquan* (GB 34), *Zusanli* (ST 36), *Weizhong* (BL 40)

Herbal ENT™

Ear Acupuncture:

- Kidney, Inner Ear, Endocrine, Outer Ear. Bleed any distended veins on the back of the ear.

Auricular Medicine by Dr. Li-Chun Huang:

- **Otitis media:** Internal Ear, External Ear, Temple, *San Jiao*, Endocrine, Spleen, Adrenal Gland. Bleed Ear Apex. Bleed Helix 5.
- **Earache:** Lesser Occipital Nerve, Large Auricular Nerve, Auriculotemporal Nerve, corresponding points (to the area of pain). Bleed Ear Apex and Helix 5.
- **Sore throat:** Pharynx, Larynx, Glottis, Mouth, Lung, Endocrine, Trachea. Bleed Ear Apex.
- **Tonsillitis:** Tonsil, Trachea, Throat, Larynx and Teeth, Mouth. Bleed Ear Apex and Helix 6.
- **Acute laryngeal pharyngitis:** Pharynx, Larynx, Mouth, *Sanjiao*, Endocrine, Teeth, Trachea. Bleed Ear Apex.
- **Chronic laryngeal pharyngitis:** Larynx, Pharynx, Lung, Teeth, Trachea, Spleen, *San Jiao*, Endocrine. Bleed Ear Apex.
- **Erysipelas:** Lung, Allergic Area, Liver, Spleen, Adrenal Gland, Endocrine. Bleed Ear Apex.

NUTRITION

- Food or beverages that are cool or cold in nature should be consumed. Among these are watermelon, lotus nodes, melon, seaweed, cranberries, celery, cucumber, cactus and winter melon.
- Drink plenty of water and urinate often.
- Increase supplementation with vitamin C and B complex.
- Increase intake of nourishing, cooling foods/roots such as Mexican yam, yam, radishes, potatoes, carrots, melons, cucumbers, beets, turnips, malanga, celeriac, taro, and rutabaga.
- Avoid spicy/pungent/aromatic vegetables such as pepper, garlic, onions, basil, rosemary, cumin, funnel, anise, leeks, chives, scallions, thyme, saffron, wormwood, mustard, chili pepper, wasabi.
- Avoid spicy, fried or greasy foods.

The Tao of Nutrition by Dr. Maoshing Ni and Cathy McNease:

- **Chronic sinusitis or rhinitis**
  - Recommendations: ginger, green onions, magnolia flower, bananas, garlic, black mushrooms, chrysanthemum flowers, mulberry leaves, and apricot kernel.
  - Avoid coffee and stop smoking.
- **Sore throat**
  - Recommendations: carrots, olives, daikon, celery, seaweed, licorice, Chinese prunes, cilantro, and mint. Drink a lot of water and gargle with warm salt water.
  - Avoid alcohol, smoking, pollution, sleeping with the mouth open, stimulating or spicy foods, and fatty foods.

LIFESTYLE INSTRUCTIONS

- It is important to build up a strong immune system. When not suffering from an infection, exercise regularly, take a short cold shower following a hot shower, and ingest tonic herbs to enhance the immune system.
- Adequate rest is essential for recovery. Stay away from wind by putting on more clothing. Individuals with infection should rest and recover in a separate room, to prevent spreading germs to other people. Ventilate the patient's room frequently – but make sure the patient is kept warm.
- Stop smoking and drinking, which weaken the immune system.
- Steam inhalation heals the throat, nasal passages, and bronchial tubes. During the acute phase, inhale the steam vapor for 15 minutes three times daily. During the chronic phase, inhale the steam vapor for 15 minutes before going to bed.

CASE STUDIES

- H.K., a 26-year-old female, presented with multiple symptoms of sore throat, fever, and slight sweating. Additional symptoms included sinus and chest congestion as well as headache and thirst. The TCM diagnosis was wind-heat obstructing the upper *jiao* with qi stagnation. For treatment, ***Herbal ENT*** was prescribed. She was a very active individual in an inhospitable climate where her symptoms had shown injury to her protective qi and body fluids. After taking the ***Herbal ENT*** for a week, the symptoms vanished. Submitted by H.C., Sydney, New York.
- S.F., a 45-year-old female, presented with pain in her left ear which became worse with any manipulation. Other symptoms included pain during swallowing and runny nose. Objective findings included redness and inflammation on the ear canal, yellow thick mucous, and redness on the throat. The practitioner diagnosed this condition as damp-heat in the upper *jiao*; Western diagnosis was upper respiratory infection. For treatment, ***Herbal ENT*** was prescribed. The patient experienced relief of symptoms after one week. She was able to experience more rest without the pain and her breathing had improved. Submitted by S.R., Waterbury, Connecticut.
- A.G., a 36-year-old male, presented with a combination of symptoms, including fever, chills, sore throat, and malaise. He was also experiencing ear pain and sinus congestion. It was also noted that the patient was allergic to sulfur drugs and was weary of taking Western medication. Pulse was superficial and rapid; tongue was swollen with a red tip. The practitioner diagnosed this condition as toxic heat. His Western diagnosis was laryngitis. After taking two bottles ***Herbal ABX*** and ***Herbal ENT***, the patient's symptoms had resolved. He still continued to use ***Herbal ABX*** periodically as it had worked well for him. Submitted by V.G., Virginia Beach, Virginia.

PHARMACOLOGICAL AND CLINICAL RESEARCH

Herbal ENT contains many herbs with wide-spectrum antibiotic effects to treat a wide variety of infectious disorders, including bacterial, viral or fungal infections. Furthermore, it also contains several herbs that address the related symptoms of infection

Herbal ENT™

that affect the upper parts of the body, such as fever, swelling, inflammation, and pain.

Many herbs in this formula have excellent antibiotic effects, including but not limited to *Huang Qin* (Radix Scutellariae),[2] *Huang Lian* (Rhizoma Coptidis),[3] *Xuan Shen* (Radix Scrophulariae),[4] *Lian Qiao* (Fructus Forsythiae),[5] *Chai Hu* (Radix Bupleuri),[6] *Ban Lan Gen* (Radix Isatidis),[7] and *Niu Bang Zi* (Fructus Arctii).[8] Among these herbs, *Huang Qin* (Radix Scutellariae) and *Huang Lian* (Rhizoma Coptidis) are generally considered as the most potent herbal antibiotics, as they are effective against micro-organisms such as *Bacillus anthracis, Bacillus dysenteriae, Bacillus proteus*, beta-hemolytic streptococcus, *Bordetella pertussis, Corynebacterium diphtheriae, Diplococcus meningitidis, Diplococcus pneumoniae, E. coli, Mycobacterium tuberculosis, Pseudomonas aeruginosa, Salmonella typhi, Staphylococcus aureus, Vibrio cholerae*.[9] Furthermore, berberine, a compound found in *Huang Lian* (Rhizoma Coptidis), showed antimicrobial activity against numerous strains of beta-lactam-resistant *Staphylococcus aureus* and methicillin-resistant *Staphylococcus aureus* (MRSA).[10] Berberine markedly lowered the minimum inhibition concentrations of ampicillin and oxacillin against MRSA. Berberine and ampicillin exhibited an additive effect, and berberine and oxacillin showed a synergistic effect against MRSA. These results suggest that berberine may have antimicrobial activity and the potential to restore the effectiveness of beta-lactam antibiotics against MRSA.[11] Lastly, in addition to having an antibacterial effect, these herbs also illustrated antiviral, antifungal and antimicrobial activities against a variety of organisms including bacteria, cariogenic bacteria, viruses, fungi, protozoans, helminths, chlamydia, and dermatophytes.[12,13,14]

In addition to treating the infection, ***Herbal ENT*** also contains many herbs that treat the related symptoms of infection. *Huang Qin* (Radix Scutellariae), *Huang Lian* (Rhizoma Coptidis), *Chen Pi* (Pericarpium Citri Reticulatae), *Jie Geng* (Radix Platycodonis) and *Lian Qiao* (Fructus Forsythiae) all have anti-inflammatory effects to reduce swelling, relieve inflammation, and alleviate pain.[15,16,17,18,19] *Huang Qin* (Radix Scutellariae) and *Huang Lian* (Rhizoma Coptidis) also have antipyretic effects to reduce fever.[20,21]

In regards to clinical applications, herbs in this formula have been used effectively to treat disorders such as common cold,[22] tonsillitis,[23] infectious parotitis,[24] pharyngitis,[25] suppurative otitis media,[26] cough,[27] respiratory tract infection,[28] upper respiratory tract infection,[29] chronic bronchitis,[30] pulmonary abscess,[31] pulmonary tuberculosis,[32] and severe acute respiratory syndrome (i.e., SARS).[33]

Overall, ***Herbal ENT*** is an excellent herbal antibiotic formula that treats infection and inflammation in the upper parts of the body. Clinically, it may be used for bacterial, viral or fungal infections. Its indications include treatment of ear, nose, throat and lung infections.

COMPARATIVE ANALYSIS

Discovery of antibiotic drugs is one of the major breakthroughs in modern medicine. It enables doctors to effectively treat many different types of infections. Unfortunately, decades of misuse and abuse have led to growing problems of bacterial mutation and resistance. At this moment, many of these "super bugs" can only be treated with the newest and most potent antibiotic drugs, and unfortunately, many of them have potent side effects as well. Due to the number of antibiotic drugs, and the various species of micro-organisms, it is beyond the scope of this monograph to discuss the benefits and risks of each individual drug. As a category, antibiotic drugs are extremely effective against most types of bacterial infections. The key points are to select the correct antibiotic drug with least potential side effects, and make sure that the patient finishes the entire course of therapy.

Herbs are also extremely effective for treatment of various infections. In fact, many modern pharmaceutical drugs were originally derived from natural sources, including penicillin [the oldest antibiotic] and gentamicin [one of the most potent]. One of the main benefits of using herbs is their wide spectrum of antibiotic effect, with indications for bacterial, viral and fungal infections. Furthermore, most of these herbs are extremely safe, and do not have the same harsh side effects as drugs.

Both drugs and herbs are effective to treat mild to moderate cases of bacterial infections. However, drugs are more appropriate for life-threatening infections, such as meningitis or encephalitis, because drugs are more immediately potent and can be prescribed with more laboratory precision (via cultures and sensitivity tests). On the other hand, use of herbs is far more effective than drugs for treating certain viral infections, such as the common cold and influenza, as drugs are essentially ineffective for these conditions. Most importantly, herbs are much gentler to the body and safer than drugs. In other words, herbs treat infection without damaging the patient's underlying constitution. This allows the patient to recover faster, and become more resistant to re-current or secondary infections.

References

1. *Zhong Yao Xue* (Chinese Herbology), 1988; 140:144.
2. *Zhong Yao Xue* (Chinese Herbology), 1988; 137:140.
3. *Zhong Yao Xue* (Chinese Herbology), 1988; 140:144.
4. *Zhong Yao Yao Li Yu Ying Yong* (Pharmacology and Applications of Chinese Herbs), 1983; 370.
5. *Shan Xi Xin Yi Yao* (New Medicine and Herbology of Shanxi), 1980; 9(11):51.
6. *Zhong Yao Xue* (Chinese Herbology), 1998; 103:106.
7. *Zhong Cheng Yao Yan Jiu* (Research of Chinese Patent Medicine), 1987; 12:9.
8. *Zhong Yao Zhi* (Chinese Herbology Journal), 1984; 250.
9. *J Pharm Pharmacol* 2000 Mar; 52(3):361-6.
10. *J Pharm Pharmacol* 2000 Mar; 52(3):361-6.
11. Yu HH, Kim KJ, Cha JD, Kim HK, Lee YE, Choi NY, You YO. Antimicrobial activity of berberine alone and in combination with ampicillin or oxacillin against methicillin-resistant Staphylococcus aureus. Department of Food and Nutrition, Kunsan National University, Kunsan. J Med Food. 2005 Winter;8(4):454-61.

12. Yu H.H., Kim K.J., Cha J.D., Kim H.K., Lee Y.E., Choi N.Y. & You Y.O. Antimicrobial Activity of Berberine Alone and in Combination with Ampicillin or Oxacillin Against Methicillin-Resistant *Staphylococcus aureus* . *J Med Food.* 2005, 8(4): 454-461.
13. Wang S., Fan M. & Bian Z. Experimental study of bacteriostatic activity of Chinese herbal medicines on primary cariogenic bacteria *in vitro* . *Zhonghua Kou Qiang Yi Xue Za Zhi.* 2001, 36(5): 385-387.
14. *Zhong Hua Yi Xue Za Zhi* (Chinese Journal of Medicine), 1958; 44(9):888.
15. *Chem Pharm Bull*, 1984; 32(7):2724.
16. *Yao Xue Za Zhi* (Journal of Medicinals), 1981; 101(10):883.
17. *Zhong Yao Yao Li Yu Ying Yong* (Pharmacology and Applications of Chinese Herbs), 1983; 567.
18. *Zhong Yao Yao Li Yu Ying Yong* (Pharmacology and Applications of Chinese Herbs), 1983; 866.
19. *Ke Yan Tong Xun* (Journal of Science and Research), 1982; (3):35.
20. *Zhong Hua Yi Xue Za Zhi* (Chinese Journal of Medicine), 1956; 42(10):964.
21. *Zhong Guo Bing Li Sheng Li Za Zhi* (Chinese Journal of Pathology and Biology), 1991; 7(3):264.
22. *Zhong Yi Za Zhi* (Journal of Chinese Medicine), 1985; 12:13.
23. *Yun Nan Zhong Yi Xue Yuan Xue Bao* (Journal of Yunnan University School of Medicine), 1983; 1:20.
24. *Zhong Yi Za Zhi* (Journal of Chinese Medicine), 1958; 7:463.
25. *Zhong Xi Yi Jie He Za Zhi* (Journal of Integrated Chinese and Western Medicine), 1991; (3):171.
26. *Zhong Hua Er Ke Za Zhi* (Chinese Journal of Pediatrics), 1954; 4:272.
27. *Zhong Yao Xue* (Chinese Herbology), 1998; 105.
28. *Guang Xi Zhong Yi Yao* (Guangxi Chinese Medicine and Herbology), 1989; (1):5.
29. *Zhong Yi Za Zhi* (Journal of Chinese Medicine), 1983; 24(11):19.
30. *Zhe Jiang Zhong Yi Za Zhi* (Zhejiang Journal of Chinese Medicine), 1985; 1:18.
31. *Jiang Su Zhong Yi Za Zhi* (Jiangsu Journal of Chinese Medicine), 1981; 3:35.
32. *Zhe Jiang Zhong Yi Za Zhi* (Zhejiang Journal of Chinese Medicine), 1964; 10:51.
33. Tanaka T., Ikeda T., Kaku M., Zhu X.H., Okawa M., Yokomizo K., Uyeda M. & Nohara T. A new lignan glycoside and phenylethanoid glycosides from *Strobilanthes cusia* BREMEK. *Chem Pharm Bull.* (Tokyo). 2004, 52(10): 1242-1245.

FORMULAS

Herbalite ™

CLINICAL APPLICATIONS

- **Obesity** with excess appetite and constant craving for food
- **Obesity** with elevated glucose and cholesterol levels

WESTERN THERAPEUTIC ACTIONS

- Increases energy level and promotes a sense of well-being
- Speeds up body metabolism to burn off excess fat and body weight
- Suppresses appetite to decrease unnecessary food intake
- Mild diuretic effect to eliminate water accumulation

CHINESE THERAPEUTIC ACTIONS

- Clears Stomach heat
- Cleanses the bowels
- Detoxifies residual toxins

DOSAGE

Take 3 to 4 capsules on an empty stomach half an hour before meals with a large glass of water. Avoid eating any food or snacks after dinner and within the last three to four hours before bedtime.

INGREDIENTS

Bai Shao (Radix Paeoniae Alba)
Cha Ye (Folium Camelliae)
Chai Hu (Radix Bupleuri)
Ci Wu Jia (Radix et Rhizoma seu Caulis Acanthopanacis Senticosi)
Da Huang (Radix et Rhizoma Rhei)
Da Zao (Fructus Jujubae)
He Ye (Folium Nelumbinis)
Huang Qi (Radix Astragali)
Huang Qin (Radix Scutellariae)
Ji Xue Cao (Herba Centellae)
Sheng Jiang (Rhizoma Zingiberis Recens)
Zao Jiao (Fructus Gleditsiae)
Zhi Shi (Fructus Aurantii Immaturus)

BACKGROUND

Obesity is excess body fat and body weight. Prevalence of obesity is high in developed countries and is continuing to increase. The cause of obesity is generally a combination of genetic predisposition and a chronic imbalance of energy intake (diet) and expenditure (exercise). There are many complications of obesity, including cardiovascular disorders, diabetes mellitus, fatty liver and cirrhosis, osteoarthritis, psychological disorders, and premature death. Treatment options include dietary modifications, lifestyle changes (exercise), and, if necessary, use of herbs and/or drugs.

FORMULA EXPLANATION

Herbalite is an herbal formula specifically designed for gradual yet effective weight loss. ***Herbalite*** contains herbs that suppress appetite, increase body metabolism, and speed up the breakdown of fatty tissues.

Chai Hu (Radix Bupleuri), the principle herb of this formula, is used with *Huang Qin* (Radix Scutellariae) to harmonize the *shaoyang* and clear heat from the Gallbladder (*shaoyang*). *Da Huang* (Radix et Rhizoma Rhei) and *Zhi Shi* (Fructus Aurantii Immaturus) purge heat from the Stomach (*yangming*). *Da Huang* (Radix et Rhizoma Rhei) and *Zhi Shi* (Fructus Aurantii Immaturus) also activate the qi circulation to dispel hardened stools. *Bai Shao* (Radix Paeoniae Alba) combines with *Da Huang* (Radix et Rhizoma Rhei) to relieve abdominal pain due to constipation. *Bai Shao* (Radix Paeoniae Alba) harmonizes qi and blood to help relieve depression and fidgeting. *He Ye* (Folium Nelumbinis) dissolves and eliminates dampness. *Da Zao* (Fructus Jujubae) and *Sheng Jiang* (Rhizoma Zingiberis Recens) harmonize all of the herbs in this formula. *Zao Jiao* (Fructus Gleditsiae) dries dampness and helps to break down fat through its function to dissipate phlegm stagnation. *Ci Wu Jia* (Radix et Rhizoma seu Caulis Acanthopanacis Senticosi) and *Huang Qi* (Radix Astragali) are used for their adaptogenic effects and to enhance overall well-being. Finally, *Cha Ye* (Folium Camelliae) and *Ji Xue Cao* (Herba Centellae) are added to increase the basal body metabolism and to burn excess fat.

CAUTIONS & CONTRAINDICATIONS

- *Cha Ye* (Folium Camelliae), commonly known as green tea, contains a small amount of caffeine as its natural ingredient.
- This formula is contraindicated during pregnancy and nursing.
- Discontinue ***Herbalite*** once the desired effect is achieved.
- The following warning statement is required by the State of California: "This product contains *Da Huang* (Radix et Rhizoma Rhei). Read and follow directions carefully. Do not use if you have or develop diarrhea, loose stools, or abdominal pain because *Da Huang* (Radix et Rhizoma Rhei) may worsen these conditions and be harmful to your health. Consult your physician if you have frequent diarrhea or if you are pregnant, nursing, taking medication, or have a medical condition."

CLINICAL NOTES

- ***Herbalite*** is designed to help with weight loss safely and gradually. Individuals who take ***Herbalite*** lose an average of one pound per week.
- Do not lose weight drastically. Rapid weight loss may be hazardous and is more likely to lead to rebound weight gain.
- It is extremely important to change the dietary and exercise habits to lose weight and avoid rebound weight gain.
- This formula is used mainly to reduce appetite in patients with Stomach heat. Should the overweight issue be due to some other diagnoses such as hormonal imbalance or thyroid dysfunction, another formula should be used instead.

Herbalite™

SUPPLEMENTARY FORMULAS

- For high cholesterol levels, add ***Cholisma***.
- For high cholesterol levels and fatty liver, add ***Cholisma (ES)***.
- For edema and water accumulation, add ***Herbal DRX***.
- With constipation, combine with ***Gentle Lax (Excess)*** or ***Gentle Lax (Deficient)***.
- For hypertension, add ***Gastrodia Complex*** or ***Gentiana Complex***.
- With diabetes, combine with ***Equilibrium***.
- To boost energy and raise the level of awareness, add ***Vibrant*** or ***Imperial Tonic***.
- For excess fire in the body, add ***Gardenia Complex***.
- For excess damp and phlegm, add ***Pinellia Complex***.
- For periodic intestinal detox, add ***GI DTX***.

ACUPUNCTURE TREATMENT

Traditional Points:

- *Shenmen* (HT 7), *Liangqiu* (ST 34), *Gongsun* (SP 4), *Tianshu* (ST 25), *Daling* (PC 7), *Qihai* (CV 6), *Guanyuan* (CV 4)

Classic Master Tung's Points:

- **Obesity (general):** *Linggu* (T 22.05), *Huaguyi* (T 55.02), *Huagusi* (T 55.05), *Yizhong* (T 77.05), *Erzhong* (T 77.06), *Sanzhong* (T 77.07), *Zusanli* (ST 36), *Menjin* (T 66.05), *Liangqiu* (ST 34), *Renhuang* (T 77.21), *Tongguan* (T 88.01), *Tianhuangfu [Shenguan]* (T 77.18), *Mufu* (T 88.38)*, *Minghuang* (T 88.12). Bleed SP and ST areas on the back and for dark veins nearby *Weizhong* (BL 40), *Sihuashang* (T 77.08), *Sihuazhong* (T 77.09), *Sihuaxia* (T 77.11), *Yizhong* (T 77.05), *Erzhong* (T 77.06) and *Sanzhong* (T 77.07). Bleed before needling for best result.
- **Hyperlipidemia:** *Fuding* (T 44.04), *Houzhi* (T 44.05), *Luotong* (T 44.14), *Zhitong* (T 44.13), *Xinling* (T 33.17)*, *Linggu* (T 22.05), *Jianzhong* (T 44.06), *Dizong* (T 44.09).
- **Diabetes:** *Tianhuang* (T 77.17), *Dihuang* (T 77.19), *Renhuang* (T 77.21), *Tianhuang* (T 88.13), *Minghuang* (T 88.12), *Qihuang* (T 88.14), *Tongshen* (T 88.09), *Tongwei* (T 88.10), *Shuijin* (T 1010.20), *Shuitong* (T 1010.19), *Piyi* (T 88.35)*, *Pier* (T 88.36)*, *Pisan* (T 88.37)*, *Tianhuangfu [Shenguan]* (T 77.18). Moxa *Tianhuangfu [Shenguan]* (T 77.18), *Zhongwan* (CV 12), *Guanyuan* (CV 4), *Zusanli* (ST 36).

Master Tung's Points by Dr. Chuan-Min Wang:

- **Obesity, excessive hunger, cravings:** Needle *Dabai* (T 22.04), *Linggu* (T 22.05), *Tushui* (T 22.11). Ear points Mouth, Small Intestine.

Balance Method by Dr. Richard Tan:

- Left side: *Waiguan* (TH 5), *Hegu* (LI 4), *Yinlingquan* (SP 9)
- Right side: *Zusanli* (ST 36), *Neiguan* (PC 6)
- Left and right sides can be alternated from treatment to treatment.

Ear Acupuncture:

- Stomach, Small Intestine, Kidney, Hypothalamus
- Embed ear seeds and massage the points for two to three minutes, thirty minutes before meals, to decrease appetite. Replace ear seeds once a week, and continue for five weeks per course of treatment. Rest for one to two weeks in between courses of treatments.
- The most effective ear seeds for weight loss are *Jie Zi* (Semen Sinapis) and *Wang Bu Liu Xing* (Semen Vaccariae).

Auricular Medicine by Dr. Li-Chun Huang:

- **Treating obesity by regulating endocrine function:** Pituitary, Endocrine.
  - Increase excitation: Forehead, Exciting Point
  - Heighten satiety: Hunger Point, Thalamus
  - Promote excretion: *San Jiao*, Kidney, Large Intestine, Lung
- **Treating obesity by reducing fat deposit:** Abdomen, Buttock, corresponding points of fat deposits
- **Obesity:** Pituitary, Endocrine, Forehead, Exciting, Hunger, Thalamus, *San Jiao*, Kidney, Large Intestine, Lung, Abdomen, Buttock

NUTRITION

- Include in the diet more complex carbohydrates, such as tofu, potatoes, sesame seeds, beans, brown rice, and whole grains.
- Consume large quantities of fresh fruits and vegetables.
- Drink six to eight glasses of water on a daily basis.
- Drink tea (especially *pu-er*, green, *oolong*, and black tea) as it helps to flush the oils from the intestines.
- Decrease the consumption of red meat, fatty foods, processed or fried foods, and sugary foods including soda, pastries, pies, doughnuts, and candy.
- Eat small, frequent meals throughout the day instead of a few large ones. Eat slowly and chew thoroughly.

The Tao of Nutrition by Dr. Maoshing Ni and Cathy McNease:

- Substitute quinoa for all other grains except amaranth.
- Eat sweet rice cake (mochi); a small amount is very filling.
- Eat spelt and oat bran cereals and eliminate all refined starch from the diet.

LIFESTYLE INSTRUCTIONS

- The importance of a regular exercise routine cannot be overemphasized. Exercise will stimulate the glands, improve energy levels, normalize metabolic functions, reduce fat, and burn calories.
- The following exercise can also be done in the shower to help weight loss. While in the shower, use a luffa to massage the body in circular motion starting from the toes to the heart, then the fingers to the heart. It is preferable to follow the channels while massaging to achieve maximum effect. Spend extra time to massage those places with the most fat deposits. Metabolism at those places where fat accumulates is usually slower and the surrounding muscles are not used as much. Therefore,

Herbalite™

massaging will enhance circulation to the area to help break up the stagnation. After the shower, drink one glass of water and soak in a tub with water that is warmer than 42°C (108°F). A high temperature bath stimulates the sympathetic nervous system and increases metabolism in a short period of time to help invigorate the body. However, this temperature is not suitable for long periods of soaking. One should not soak until he or she is dizzy. Finally, rinse off with cold water for at least 20 to 30 seconds to help tighten up muscle tone. [Note: For individuals who have *wei* (defensive) *qi* deficiency or those who catch colds frequently, it is not recommended to start this cold water rinsing regimen, as extreme changes in water temperature from high to low may trigger them to catch a cold. It is better to gradually lower the temperature, starting from warm then to cold water so the body can become accustomed to the change. Once the pores are conditioned to open and close with this temperature change, the body will become less susceptible to catching a cold.]

CASE STUDIES

- J.U., a 48-year-old female patient, presented with weight gain, strong appetite and low energy. No thyroid or other imbalances had been found. The patient's Western diagnosis was obesity and the TCM diagnosis was dampness. ***Herbalite*** was prescribed upon diagnosis and had been taking it for over a year. She has lost a considerable amount of weight, her appetite has decreased, and her energy has improved. This has allowed the patient to become more active and now has the ability to exercise more. She plans on continuing taking the herbs. Submitted by A.I. Hilo, Hawaii.
- M.L., a 59-year-old female, presented with obesity, experiencing difficulty losing weight after she had just gone through menopause. It was noted that she had cravings for sweets and had trouble controlling her diet. Her initial weight was 219 lbs and her height was 5'0". Pulse was deep and thready and tongue was swollen and pale. The TCM diagnosis was Spleen qi deficiency with Kidney yin deficiency. ***Herbalite*** was prescribed at 4 capsules two times daily. Within the first week the patient had lost 5 lbs; however, she gained back two pounds the following week. In continuation, the patient had lost 8 lbs during the third week and kept improving her diet and exercise. Submitted by M.P., Muskego, Wisconsin.
- J.P., a 52-year-old female, presented with obesity with a desire to lose weight. Her initial weight was 210 lbs and her blood pressure was 136/80 mmHg. Pulse was slippery and deep; tongue was swollen, pale and had scalloped sides. The TCM diagnosis was dampness and phlegm. ***Herbalite*** was prescribed at 4 capsules two times a day. After taking the herbs for two weeks, the patient had lost 2 lbs and noticed a decrease in her appetite. Submitted by M.P., Muskego, Wisconsin.
- A 53-year-old female business owner presented with low energy, muscle pain and low back pain. The patient was 45 pounds overweight. Pain was felt in her lumbar area upon palpation. The pulse was slow and the tongue was pale and swollen with a thin white coat. The practitioner diagnosed the condition as Kidney yang deficiency, qi deficiency and Liver yang excess. The practitioner also suspected a possibility of hypothyroidism, which had yet to be confirmed by lab tests. The patient was treated with ***Herbalite***, acupuncture, and diet modification. She then lost 43 pounds in four months and her energy level increased dramatically. The pain in her low back has also disappeared. ***Herbalite*** appeared to suppress her food cravings, increase her energy and improve her psychological status. The patient became more energetic, radiant, and positive. Submitted by T.S., East Providence, Rhode Island.
- A 58-year-old female was concerned about her voracious appetite, stress and inability to lose weight. The practitioner felt that the patient's overeating was directly caused by the patient's stress and her tendency to worry too much. The patient had problems with over-consumption of caffeine and sweets, which lead to her poor digestion and sluggish metabolism. Her diagnosis was Liver qi stagnation, Spleen qi deficiency and Kidney yin deficiency. After taking ***Herbalite***, the patient reported losing 7 lbs in the first two weeks. She felt that her excessive appetite tapered down considerably, especially at night. With ***Herbalite***, she reported a reduction for sweet cravings and a break from her detrimental eating cycle that was driven by emotions and stress. Submitted by S.A., Santa Fe, New Mexico.
- A 30-year-old female who worked in a computer company wanted to lose 10 pounds within one month. She was 5' 1" and weighed 125 pounds. She was instructed to take ***Herbalite*** (4 capsules three times daily on an empty stomach), along with recommendations to control her diet and engage in moderate exercise. On follow-up visits, she lost 6 pounds after two weeks, and a total of 11 pounds after four weeks. The patient was able to keep the weight off in a subsequent visit three months later. Submitted by J.C., Diamond Bar, California.
- A long history of battling weight gain had plagued a 34-year-old female teacher consequently causing her to feel low in energy along with bouts of depression. Diagnosis according to traditional Chinese medicine was damp and phlegm stagnation. Tongue analysis showed a "puffy" tongue body with a thick coating. The pulse was described as "rolling." Although she had encountered difficulties in losing weight in the past, she was able to lose 10 pounds in three months by using ***Herbalite***. Submitted Anonymously.
- A 32-year-old female computer technician who had gained almost 20 pounds within a year was diagnosed with damp and phlegm stagnation. Objective findings included a pale tongue body with teeth marks, a "rolling" pulse, low energy, and slow metabolism. Weight loss from taking ***Herbalite*** gradually appeared after two weeks of the initial intake of the formula. Within six months of ***Herbalite*** treatment, she had lost another 40 pounds, had increased energy level, and felt better about herself. Submitted by T.G., Albuquerque, NM.

Herbalite ™

- A 49-year-old perimenopausal female presented with cold extremities, easily fatigued, and weight gain. The practitioner diagnosed her condition as yang deficiency. After a little more than a week of taking ***Herbalite***, the patient lost 5 pounds. Along with the weight loss, she also felt more energized, had reduced appetite and felt warm sensations in her extremities. Dietary modifications, fluid intake, and exercise such as yoga were also implemented into her treatment protocol. Submitted by W.E., San Diego, California.
- D.K, a 33-year-old female, came to the office for weight loss. She had two children, ages three years and one year, and had not managed to drop the weight she had gained during her pregnancies. She was getting married in two months and wanted to be thinner for her wedding. Her weight-loss goal was 15 to 20 pounds. She did not feel that she had very good eating habits - she ate large portions and craved sweets. The patient said she was frequently irritable and exhausted. She also complained of constipation. Her blood pressure was 110/90 mmHg and her heart rate was 66 to 68 beats per minute. Her diagnosis according to traditional Chinese medicine was dampness in the Spleen with Liver qi stagnation. ***Herbalite*** was prescribed at 4 capsules three times a day. The patient took six bottles altogether. The first four bottles were without *Da Huang* (Radix et Rhizoma Rhei) since the patient was still nursing. The patient reported losing five pounds. She stated that ***Herbalite*** regulated her appetite sufficiently that she was able to be satisfied with smaller portions at meals. She also reduced her sugar consumption and increased her fiber intake. The client said that she took the herbs faithfully but she admitted that unless she greatly modified her diet and instituted an exercise regime, it was unlikely that she would succeed in meeting her weight loss goal. D.K was happy to report that ***Herbalite*** also relieved her constipation. Submitted by H.H., San Francisco, California.
- P.Z., a 61-year-old male patient, presented with obesity. He was 288 pounds and stated that he overate his whole life. Besides obesity, he also suffered from hypertension and high cholesterol and triglycerides levels. His blood pressure was 140/88 mmHg and his heart rate was 84 beats per minute. The diagnosis according to traditional Chinese medicine was damp accumulation. ***Herbalite*** was prescribed at 4 capsules three times daily. He lost a total of 66 pounds in approximately ten months. Patient was also given acupuncture treatment. Submitted by W.F., Bloomfield, New Jersey.

PHARMACOLOGICAL AND CLINICAL RESEARCH

Herbalite is designed to help with weight loss safely and gradually. ***Herbalite*** contains herbs that reduce body weight, lower blood glucose and cholesterols, and increase energy and body metabolism.

Cha Ye (Folium Camelliae), commonly known as tea leaf, has a wide range of therapeutic functions and is commonly used for obesity, hyperglycemia and hyperlipidemia. According to laboratory, epidemiological, and human intervention studies, consumption of *Cha Ye* (Folium Camelliae) and its polyphenols is useful to prevent obesity, type II diabetes, cardiovascular disease, and other chronic diseases.[1] The mechanism of action to reduce body fat is attributed to the simultaneous inhibition of the enzymes catechol-O-methyltransferase, acetyl-CoA carboxylase, fatty acid synthase and impeding absorption of fat via the gut.[2] Furthermore, administration of a preparation of *Cha Ye* (Folium Camelliae) shows a significant effect to lower plasma fasting glucose, triglycerides, and insulin concentrations. The mechanisms of action are attributed to the beneficial insulin sensitivity and antioxidant effects.[3] Therapeutic benefits of *Cha Ye* (Folium Camelliae) are equally impressive in clinical research. According to a randomized, double-blind, placebo-controlled, parallel study on 111 healthy adult volunteers, daily consumption of decaffeinated *Cha Ye* (Folium Camelliae) was associated with significant benefits in lowering cardiovascular risk factors, such as decreased blood pressure, LDL cholesterol, serum amyloid-α (a marker of chronic inflammation), and serum malondialdehyde (a marker of oxidative stress). Adverse effects associated with *Cha Ye* (Folium Camelliae) are mild and few and not different from placebo.[4] For treatment of hypercholesterolemia and dyslipidemia, one study showed that the consumption of nine or more cups of *Cha Ye* (Folium Camelliae) per day was associated with a decrease in total cholesterol level but no decrease in triglycerides or HDL-cholesterol.[5] Another randomized, placebo-controlled study in 33 patients with dyslipidemia demonstrated that daily consumption of *Cha Ye* (Folium Camelliae) for eight weeks was associated with a significant reduction of total cholesterol and LDL-cholesterol levels, but not HDL-cholesterol or triglycerides, when compared to the placebo group.[6]

He Ye (Folium Nelumbinis), also known as lotus leaf, also has excellent benefits to treat obesity, hyperglycemia and hyperlipidemia. For treatment of obesity, administration of *He Ye* (Folium Nelumbinis) reduces the body weight, body lipid accumulation, and activities of fatty acid synthase (FAS), glutamic oxaloacetic transaminase, and glutamic pyruvic transaminase. Enriched with flavonoids, *He Ye* (Folium Nelumbinis) extract is believed to target lipid-regulated enzymes and to reduce body lipid accumulation and prevent obesity.[7] According to another study, *He Ye* (Folium Nelumbinis) shows numerous mechanisms to suppress obesity, such as impairing digestion, inhibiting absorption of lipids and carbohydrates, accelerating lipid metabolism and up-regulating energy expenditure.[8] For management of hyperglycemia, *He Ye* (Folium Nelumbinis) and its active constituent catechin significantly and dose-dependently enhance insulin secretion to control hyperglycemia in non-insulin-dependent diabetes mellitus, according to a study in high-fat-diet-induced diabetic mice.[9] Furthermore, the extract of *He Ye* (Folium Nelumbinis) exerts potent antioxidant effects to protect against oxidative stress-related diseases and diabetic complications.[10] For treatment of hyperlipidemia, administration

Herbalite™

of *He Ye* (Folium Nelumbinis) effectively ameliorates lipid metabolic disorders (hyperlipidemia, hypercholesterolemia, and fatty liver) caused by a high fat diet, with efficacy similar to that of silymarin and Zocor (simvastatin).[11]

Herbalite contains many other herbs with significant therapeutic actions to treat complications of obesity, such as hyperglycemia and hyperlipidemia. *Bai Shao* (Radix Paeoniae Alba) has an antihyperglycemic effect that appears to be insulin independent, as the plasma insulin was not changed in normoglycemic subjects treated with this compound.[12] In addition, *Bai Shao* (Radix Paeoniae Alba) also has a significant effect to lower total cholesterol, low-density lipoprotein and triglyceride levels.[13] *Huang Qi* (Radix Astragali) has a hypoglycemic effect that lowers plasma glucose levels and alleviates insulin resistance. Furthermore, *Huang Qi* (Radix Astragali) also has antiobesity and hypolipidemic effects.[14] *Ci Wu Jia* (Radix et Rhizoma seu Caulis Acanthopanacis Senticosi) has a dose-dependent effect to lower plasma glucose levels. The mechanism of this hypoglycemic is attributed to the stimulation of pancreatic cells and augmentation of insulin release.[15] Clinical benefits of *Ci Wu Jia* (Radix et Rhizoma seu Caulis Acanthopanacis Senticosi) include an increase in energy level, protection against toxins and free radicals, and treatment of atherosclerosis.[16] One study demonstrated that *Ci Wu Jia* (Radix et Rhizoma seu Caulis Acanthopanacis Senticosi) reduces plasma sugar level and may be beneficial in treating diabetes.[17,18]

Finally, *Huang Qi* (Radix Astragali) and *Ci Wu Jia* (Radix et Rhizoma seu Caulis Acanthopanacis Senticosi) both have positive effects on the metabolic rate. Decoction of *Huang Qi* (Radix Astragali) has been shown to increase the basal metabolic rate and cAMP in laboratory studies.[19] The use of *Ci Wu Jia* (Radix et Rhizoma seu Caulis Acanthopanacis Senticosi) has been shown to effectively increase human physical working capacity.[20]

In summary, ***Herbalite*** is an excellent formula that contains herbs to treat obesity and related complications, such as high blood glucose levels, high blood cholesterol levels, and low energy and metabolic rate.

COMPARATIVE ANALYSIS

Obesity is an increasingly common health problem that has few treatment options available. Due to diet and lifestyle changes, many people in developed countries now struggle continual weight gain. Furthermore, there are few or no drug treatments available. Many older drugs, such as "fen-phen" (fenfluramine and phentermine) and dexfenfluramine, are now rarely used or withdrawn from the market because of serious and potentially life-threatening side effects, such as cardiac valvular dysfunction. Currently, there are very few drugs approved by the Food and Drug Administration for long-term weight loss, and they have serious side effects. Xenical (orlistat) reduces body weight by blocking absorption of fat in the digestive tract. Because it interferes with the normal absorption process, this drug is known to cause many gastrointestinal side effects, such as fecal incontinence, fecal urgency, flatulence with discharge, increased defecation, oily evacuation, oily rectal leakage, steatorrhea, and projectile diarrhea. Meridia (sibutramine) is a stimulant agent that causes weight loss by increasing metabolism and suppressing appetite. Similar to many other stimulant weight-loss drugs, use of Meridia (sibutramine) may cause anorexia, anxiety, constipation, dizziness, headache, insomnia, irritability, nervousness, rhinitis, xerostomia, hypertension, congestive heart failure, arrhythmias, seizure and stroke.

In TCM, obesity may be treated with herbs that suppress appetite, increase energy and metabolism, and eliminate accumulation of dampness and water. Use of herbs has been shown to be effective to slowly and steadily lower body weight. Based on clinical experience and case studies, most individuals lose an average of one or two pounds per week while taking this herbal formula. Therefore, this formula is considered a gentle formula that needs to be taken on a long-term basis for optimal results. For those who are grossly overweight and have immediate health risks, use of this formula is inappropriate and not recommended, as it will not cause instantaneous weight loss. Lastly, it is extremely important to remember there is no magic bullet for weight loss. Without commitment to changing diet and lifestyles, use of either drugs or herbs will have limited effectiveness. The practitioners and patients must work together to achieve significant and sustainable clinical results.

References

1. Grove KA, Lambert JD. Laboratory, epidemiological, and human intervention studies show that tea (Camellia sinensis) may be useful in the prevention of obesity. Department of Food Science, The Pennsylvania State University, University Park, PA 16802, USA. J Nutr. 2010 Mar;140(3):446-53.
2. Navamayooran Thavanesana. The putative effects of green tea on body fat: an evaluation of the evidence and a review of the potential mechanisms. British Journal of Nutrition. 14 November 2011 106: pp 1297-1309.
3. Hininger-Favier I, Benaraba R, Coves S, Anderson RA, Roussel A-M. 2009. Green tea extract decreases oxidative stress and improves insulin sensitivity in an animal model of insulin resistance, the fructose-fed rat. J Am Coll Nutr 28:355-61.
4. Nantz MP, Rowe CA, Bukowski JF, Percival SS. Standardized capsule of Camellia sinensis lowers cardiovascular risk factors in a randomized, double-blind, placebo-controlled study. Food Science and Human Nutrition Department, University of Florida, Gainesville, FL, USA. Nutrition. 2009 Feb;25(2):147-54.
5. Kono, S. et al., Green tea consumption and serum lipid profiles: a cross-sectional study in northern Kyushu, Japan. *Prev Med*, 1992; 21(4):526.
6. Batista Gde A, Cunha CL, Scartezini M, von der Heyde R, Bitencourt MG, Melo SF. Prospective double-blind crossover study of Camellia sinensis (green tea) in dyslipidemias. Universidade Federal do Paraná, PR, Brasil. Arq Bras Cardiol. 2009 Aug;93(2):128-34.
7. Wu CH, Yang MY, Chan KC, Chung PJ, Ou TT, Wang CJ. Improvement in high-fat diet-induced obesity and body fat accumulation by a Nelumbo nucifera leaf flavonoid-rich extract in mice. Institute of Biochemistry and Biotechnology, Chung Shan Medical University, No 110, Section 1, Chien-kauo N Road, Taichung, Taiwan. J Agric Food Chem. 2010 Jun 9;58(11):7075-81.
8. Ono Y, Hattori E, Fukaya Y, Imai S, Ohizumi Y. Anti-obesity effect of Nelumbo nucifera leaves extract in mice and rats. Matsuura Yakugyo Co. Ltd., Enjo-cho,

Showa-ku, Nagoya 459-8001, Japan. J Ethnopharmacol. 2006 Jun 30;106(2): 238-44.

9. Huang CF, Chen YW, Yang CY, Lin HY, Way TD, Chiang W, Liu SH. Extract of Lotus Leaf (Nelumbo nucifera) and Its Active Constituent Catechin with Insulin Secretagogue Activity. Graduate Institute of Chinese Medical Science, School of Chinese Medicine, College of Chinese Medicine, China Medical University , Taichung 40402, Taiwan. J Agric Food Chem. 2011 Feb 23;59(4):1087-94.
10. Jung HA, Jung YJ, Yoon NY, Jeong da M, Bae HJ, Kim DW, Na DH, Choi JS. Inhibitory effects of Nelumbo nucifera leaves on rat lens aldose reductase, advanced glycation endproducts formation, and oxidative stress. Division of Food Science and Biotechnology, Pukyong National University, Busan 608-737, South Korea. Food Chem Toxicol. 2008 Dec;46(12):3818-26.
11. Lin MC, Kao SH, Chung PJ, Chan KC, Yang MY, Wang CJ. Improvement for high fat diet-induced hepatic injuries and oxidative stress by flavonoid-enriched extract from Nelumbo nucifera leaf. Department of Internal Medicine, Chung-Shan Medical University Hospital, Taichung, Taiwan. J Agric Food Chem. 2009 Jul 8;57(13):5925-32.
12. Hsu FL, Lai CW, Cheng JT. Antihyperglycemic effects of paeoniflorin and 8-debenzoylpaeoniflorin, glucosides from the root of Paeonia lactiflora. Planta Med. 1997 Aug;63(4):323-5.
13. Yang HO, Ko WK, Kim JY, Ro HS. Paeoniflorin: an antihyperlipidemic agent from Paeonia lactiflora. Fitoterapia. 2004 Jan;75(1):45-9.
14. Mao XQ, Yu F, Wang N, Wu Y, Zou F, Wu K, Liu M, Ouyang JP. Hypoglycemic effect of polysaccharide enriched extract of Astragalus membranaceus in diet induced insulin resistant C57BL/6J mice and its potential mechanism. Department of Pathophysiology, Medical College of Wuhan University, Hubei Provincial Key Laboratory of Allergy and Immune-Related Diseases, Wuhan, China. Phytomedicine. 2009.May;16(5):416-25.
15. Liu KY, Wu YC, Liu IM, Yu WC, Cheng JT. Release of acetylcholine by syringin, an active principle of Eleutherococcus senticosus, to raise insulin secretion in Wistar rats. Graduate Institute of Natural Products, Kaohsiung Medical University, Kaohsiung City, Taiwan, ROC. Neurosci Lett. 2008 Mar 28;434(2):195-9.
16. Sprecher, E. Eleutherococcus Senticosus on the Way to Being a Phytopharmacon. *Pharma Ztg*; 134:9. 1989.
17. Hinino, H. et al. Isolation and Hypoglycemic Activity of Eleutherans A, B, C, D, E, F, and G: Glycans of Eleutherococcus senticosus roots. *J Nat Prod*; 49(2):293. 1986.
18. Molokovskii, DS. et al. The Action of Adaptogenic Plant Preparations in Experimental Alloxan Diabetes. *Probl Endokrinol*; 35(5):82. 1989.
19. *Zhong Yao Yao Li Yu Lin Chuang* (Pharmacology and Clinical Applications of Chinese Herbs), 1985:193.
20. Asano, K. et al. Effect of Eleutherococcus Senticosus Extract on Human Physical Working Capacity. *Planta Med*; 48(3):175. 1986.

FORMULAS

Immune + ™

CLINICAL APPLICATIONS

- **Weak or compromised immune system**
- **Frequent bacterial or viral infections,** such as common colds and/or influenza
- **Prolonged recovery period** from bacterial or viral infections
- **Cancer patients with weakened immune systems** from radiation or chemotherapy treatment
- **Individuals with no significant complaints, but desire to enhance their immunity**

WESTERN THERAPEUTIC ACTIONS

- Immunostimulant effect to enhance specific and non-specific immunities
- Immunomodulatory effect to improve humoral and cellular immune activities
- Antibacterial and antiviral effects to prevent and treat infections

CHINESE THERAPEUTIC ACTIONS

- Consolidates the *wei* (defensive) *qi* and dispels lingering pathogenic factors
- Tonifies normal qi and strengthens the body
- Tonifies the Lung, Spleen, and Kidney

DOSAGE

Treatment dosage: take 4 capsules three times daily. Maintenance dosage: take 2 capsules twice daily to enhance the immune system and prevent viral or bacterial infections.

INGREDIENTS

Bai Zhu (Rhizoma Atractylodis Macrocephalae)
Dong Chong Xia Cao (Cordyceps)
Fang Feng (Radix Saposhnikoviae)
Huang Qi (Radix Astragali)
Ling Zhi (Ganoderma)
Wu Wei Zi (Fructus Schisandrae Chinensis)

BACKGROUND

The immune system is a very important host defense mechanism that protects an individual from invasion of micro-organisms. If the immune system is defective or becomes disrupted, the micro-organisms can enter and affect various parts of the body. Therefore, optimal health is directly associated with a strong immunity.

FORMULA EXPLANATION

According to traditional Chinese medicine, *wei* (defensive) *qi* is located at the exterior surface of the body and provides the initial protection against foreign or pathogenic factors. When *wei* (defensive) *qi* is strong, pathogenic factors cannot penetrate the body. When it is weak, a wide variety of infections occur. Therefore, prevention of infections relies on normal functioning of *wei* (defensive) *qi*.

Huang Qi (Radix Astragali) is the chief herb in this formula. It fortifies the Lung, strengthens the *wei* (defensive) *qi* and indirectly protects against external pathogenic factors. *Ling Zhi* (Ganoderma) increases white blood cells and inhibits the growth of various viruses and bacteria. *Ling Zhi* (Ganoderma) has also been traditionally used to tonify blood and vital energy, which are essential in rebuilding the underlying constitution. *Dong Chong Xia Cao* (Cordyceps) has been used traditionally for chronically debilitated patients. It is an excellent herb to tonify Kidney yin and yang and improve overall bodily constitution. *Bai Zhu* (Rhizoma Atractylodis Macrocephalae) strengthens the Spleen, and *Wu Wei Zi* (Fructus Schisandrae Chinensis) closes the skin pores to stop sweating and prevent exterior attack of wind. *Fang Feng* (Radix Saposhnikoviae) circulates in the peripheral channels of the body and expels lingering pathogenic factors.

CAUTIONS & CONTRAINDICATIONS

- The main focus of this herbal formula is to enhance the immune system, not to treat infection. Patients with an active infection must be treated with other formulas accordingly.
- Since this formula may stimulant the immune system, it should be used with extreme caution in patients who have autoimmune disease or take immune suppressant drugs after organ transplant.

CLINICAL NOTES

- ***Immune +*** should ***not*** be used alone to treat infections.
- ***Immune +*** can be taken on a long-term basis to enhance the immune system in a normal or immuno-deficient person.
- ***Immune +*** is safe to use between infections for children who experience recurrent respiratory infections.

Pulse Diagnosis by Dr. Jimmy Wei-Yen Chang:

- Tent pulse, a convex-shaped pulse that is weak and collapses under pressure, on the right *cun*.

SUPPLEMENTARY FORMULAS

Use of this formula during remission:

- To tonify constitutional qi, blood, yin and yang, combine with ***Imperial Tonic***.
- For a quick boost of energy and awareness, use ***Vibrant***.
- To improve memory, add ***Enhance Memory***.
- To minimize the side effects of chemotherapy and radiation treatment, combine with ***C/R Support***.
- For end-stage cancer or cancer patients who are too weak to receive chemotherapy or radiation, add ***CA Support***.
- ***Cordyceps 3*** can be added to enhance the anticancer effect of ***Immune +***.
- For weaker, older patients who have asthma attacks, wheezing or dyspnea, use ***Respitrol (Deficient)*** instead.
- For cough, add ***Respitrol (CF)***.

Immune + ™

- For inflammation with swelling, add ***Resolve (AI)***.
  - With dryness and thirst, add ***Nourish (Fluids)***.
  - With Kidney yin deficiency, add ***Kidney Tonic (Yin)***.
  - With Kidney yang deficiency, add ***Kidney Tonic (Yang)***.

Use of this formula during infection and inflammation:

- Note: During infection and inflammation, patients should take formulas listed below. After the symptoms subside, patients may resume taking ***Immune +***.
- For bacterial or viral infections, use ***Herbal ABX*** or ***Herbal AVR*** instead of ***Immune +***.
- During the initial stages of cold and flu with sore throat, fever and/or headache, use ***Lonicera Complex*** instead of ***Immune +***.
- During the secondary stage of pathogenic invasion with Lung heat, use ***Respitrol (Heat)*** instead of ***Immune +***.
- For cold and flu with sneezing, clear nasal discharge, and chills, use ***Respitrol (Cold)*** instead of ***Immune +***.
- For cold and flu with profuse, yellow phlegm, and cough, use ***Pinellia XPT*** instead of ***Immune +***.
- For allergic conditions, sinus infection, and yellow nasal discharge, use ***Pueraria Clear Sinus*** instead of ***Immune +***.
- For allergic conditions, sinus headache, nasal obstruction, with or without white or clear nasal discharge, use ***Magnolia Clear Sinus*** instead of ***Immune +***.

ACUPUNCTURE TREATMENT

Traditional Points:

- *Zusanli* (ST 36), *Sanyinjiao* (SP 6), *Fengchi* (GB 20), *Fengmen* (BL 12), *Hegu* (LI 4)
- *Qihai* (CV 6), *Pishu* (BL 20), *Zhongwan* (CV 12), *Zusanli* (ST 36), *Hegu* (LI 4), *Weishu* (BL 21)

Master Tung's Points by Dr. Chuan-Min Wang:

- **Immune deficiency:** *Tongtian* (T 88.03), *Minghuang* (T 88.12), *Tongshen* (T 88.09)

Balance Method by Dr. Richard Tan:

- Left side: *Hegu* (LI 4), *Xuehai* (SP 10)
- Right side: *Chize* (LU 5), *Lieque* (LU 7), *Zusanli* (ST 36)
- Left and right sides can be alternated from treatment to treatment.

Ear Acupuncture:

- Nose, Spleen, Bone Marrow

Auricular Medicine by Dr. Li-Chun Huang:

- **Preventing common cold:** Spleen, Lung, Endocrine, Allergic Area, Adrenal Gland. Bleed Ear Apex.
- **Promoting immunity:** Allergic Area, Endocrine, Adrenal Gland, Spleen, Liver, corresponding point for the organ to be strengthened. Bleed Ear Apex and Helix 1-6.

NUTRITION

- Vitamins A, C, E and zinc are essential in promoting a healthy immune system.
- Drink plenty of fluids to ensure that the lymphatic system drains freely and circulates smoothly.
- Foods that are helpful to strengthen the body and fight infection include garlic, citrus fruits and green vegetables.
- Limit the intake of sweet foods and refined white sugar: they impair the body's ability to kill bacteria.

The Tao of Nutrition by Dr. Maoshing Ni and Cathy McNease:

- AIDS
  - Recommendations: Make brown rice porridge with pearl barley, mung beans, yams, and lotus seeds.
  - Avoid dairy, alcohol, sugar, coffee, fatty or deep-fried foods, overly spicy foods, cold or raw foods, tomato, eggplant, bell peppers, and shellfish.
- Cancer
  - Recommendations: Blend shiitake or ganoderma mushrooms and white fungus, boil and drink the soup three times a day.
  - Recommendations: Boil together mung beans, pearl barley, azuki beans, and figs. This makes a delicious dessert that will aid appetite and sustain energy level.
  - Avoid meat, chicken, coffee, cinnamon, anise, pepper, dairy products, spicy foods (except garlic), high fat foods, cooked oils, chemical additives, moldy foods, smoking, constipation, stress, and all irritations.
- **Susceptibility to common cold or influenza:** Make artichoke soup with generous amounts of garlic and onions and eat daily during the flu season.
- **Strengthen resistance against frequent colds:** Add one tablespoonful of bee pollen, lemon juice from 1/2 of a lemon, and one tablespoonful of honey into daily quinoa cereal in the morning.

LIFESTYLE INSTRUCTIONS

- Avoid over-exertion both mentally and physically, either of which can suppress the immune system.
- Wear appropriate clothing on cold, damp or windy days, and avoid becoming chilled or over-heated.
- Rest is essential in the recovery of a weak immune system or as protection against catching a cold.
- The skin is the largest organ of the body, and the first defense against pathogenic factors. Exercises that stimulate the skin will strengthen the immune system. Engage in such exercises as cold-water stepping, dew walking, dry brushing, and swimming in cold water. However, transition into these activities slowly to avoid catching a cold from sudden exposure.
- Regular exercise and adequate sleep (at least eight hours) are essential to maintaining a strong immune system.

Immune + ™

CASE STUDIES

- F.G., a 51-year-old male, presented with recurring colds, including excess phlegm usually white in color. It was noted that the patient works in an environment of smoke and smokes himself. The practitioner diagnosed this condition as Lung qi deficiency with phlegm. For treatment, ***Immune +*** was prescribed at 5 to 8 capsules three to four times a day. After taking the herbs, the patient noticed fewer colds over the next six months. Submitted by S.L., Yuma, Arizona.
- M.M., a 31-year-old male patient, presented with chronic cough and allergies after the hurricanes last year. The patient also worked in a bar that had mold damage. He was placed on a leave of absence from work to recover and was then placed on antibiotics. Other findings included pale face, low voice, and dark circles under the eyes, blue nail beds, weakness and lack of motivation. Western diagnosis was compromised immune system with lingering pathogenic factors. The TCM diagnosis was Lung qi, Spleen qi and *wei* (defensive) *qi* deficiencies. ***Immune +*** was prescribed at 6 capsules twice daily. After taking the herbs, the patient reported he regained his strength and had gone back to work after two months of acupuncture and herbs. He caught another cold during the two-month treatment period but was able to recover quickly. Submitted by M.H., West Palm Beach, Florida.
- A 20-year-old female student presented with a history of recurrent viral or bacterial infection since starting college. Other objective findings included lack of sleep, high stress, strep throat, bladder infection, and susceptibility to the flu. She was diagnosed as having qi deficiency and a weakened immune system. Within six months of taking ***Immune +***, her signs and symptoms decreased by 50%. The patient has noticed a marked decrease in recurrence of infection and sickness. Submitted by T.G., Albuquerque, New Mexico.
- N.T., a 36-year-old female patient, presented with a painful rash located on the center of her abdomen. She had been experiencing emotional stress as well. Her Western doctor had already diagnosed her with shingles and prescribed her an antiviral drug, which didn't seem to help and created lung pain. The TCM diagnosis was damp-heat, which the practitioner treated with ***Herbal ABX***. After taking the herbs daily and receiving acupuncture twice a week the patient's rash and pain disappeared in seven days. To maintain these results, the patient took ***Immune +*** to boost her immune system. Submitted by S.R., Waterbury, Connecticut.
- M.C., a 60-year-old male, presented with chronic sinusitis, consisting of yellow green discharge. Additional symptoms included sensation of heat in the upper neck area, some tightness in the chest, and a tickling of the throat but no cough. The practitioner diagnosed this condition as Lung qi deficiency and Kidney yin deficiency. Patient was given ***Herbal ABX*** when the discharge was present and ***Immune +*** when the discharge wasn't present. After taking the herbs, the patient stopped having sinus infections and bronchitis. The patient still came in for a follow ups occasionally. Submitted by B.L., Fort Myers, Florida.
- A 66-year-old female reported repeated episodes of respiratory infection that turned into asthma and bronchitis. The patient reported that she had allergy shots from her medical doctor because she could not take different drugs as they would give her irregular heartbeat. She could not take *Ma Huang* (Herba Ephedrae) or any other stimulants. Her blood pressure was 110/78 mmHg and her heart rate was 66 beats per minute. The diagnosis according to traditional Chinese medicine was *wei* (defensive) qi deficiency. ***Immune +*** was prescribed and after three months of treatment, the patient reported significantly less attacks of asthma. She was also advised to eat more vegetables and decrease the intake of dairy and gluten products. Submitted by D.W., Los Angeles, California.
- A 36-year-old female presented with fatigue, anxiety, and low immune function. She said she catches cold easily and frequently. Her pulse was weak and thready, and her tongue was purple. She was pale, with dark circles under her eyes. The TCM diagnosis was Lung and Kidney qi deficiencies. The patient was instructed to take ***Immune +***. After two months of ***Immune +*** and acupuncture treatment (every other week), the patient has not fallen ill from contact with her family and friends. She said prior to the treatments, she "would always get sick from others." Submitted by M.B., Bend, Oregon.
- S.C., a 42-year-old female, was over-worked and under constant stress. She wanted to enhance her immune system, as her health was compromised by stress and exhaustion. She was prescribed ***Immune +*** at two capsules, three times daily. During seven months of taking the herbs, she had no illnesses or symptoms. Submitted by C.L., Chino Hills, California.
- S.W. suffered from tiredness, restless sleep, and occasional, recurrent nasal congestion during allergy season. She was diagnosed with Kidney yin, yang, and *wei* (defensive) *qi* deficiencies. ***Immune +*** along with ***Vibrant*** were prescribed. ***Immune +*** was prescribed to build the *wei* (defensive) *qi* while ***Vibrant*** was used to sustain and build her Kidney yin and yang over time. The patient greatly commented on the positive results from ***Vibrant*** to increase her daily energy level and positive outlook. Submitted by J.P., Naples, Florida.
- A 59-year-old male physician presented with extreme fever (over 104°F), extreme difficulty in breathing, pain in the chest, shortness of breath aggravated by exertion, unsteady walk, dizziness, and inability to speak more than one word per breath. His tongue was pale with red tip and body, and his pulse was rapid and superficial. The diagnosis was phlegm heat in the Lung. The patient was treated with ***Pinellia XPT*** (6 capsules four times daily) and ***Immune +*** (6 capsules four times daily), along with other homeopathics and drugs (Combivent (albuterol/ipratropium) and aspirin). The patient had a definite response to the herbs. The respiration became much easier, energy level and sense of vitality enhanced, and cough was no

Immune + ™

longer productive. The practitioner commented that "While all protocols employed resulted in benefit – it is without question that the herbal formulas generated imminent benefit and long term recuperation." Submitted by I.B.J., Miami, Florida.

- A 54-year-old property manager presented with chronic sinus congestion and headache. Food allergies included E-95 panel to dairy, egg white, kidney beans and lima beans. The practitioner's diagnosis was Lung qi deficiency with excess damp. The patient stated that symptoms of sinus congestion and headaches would subside upon taking ***Immune*** +. Subsequently, he continued to use ***Immune*** + during allergy seasons, more in the fall, but as needed throughout the year. Submitted Anonymously.

PHARMACOLOGICAL AND CLINICAL RESEARCH

Immune + is an excellent formula to enhance immunity to treat many disorders associated with compromised or weakened immune system. ***Immune*** + contains herbs with immunostimulant effect to enhance the immune system, and antibacterial, and antiviral effects to prevent and treat infections.

Huang Qi (Radix Astragali) is one of the most frequently used Chinese herbs for its ability to tonify the *wei* (defensive) *qi*. From allopathic medical perspectives, modern research has confirmed in multiple studies that *Huang Qi* (Radix Astragali) increases both specific and non-specific immunity.[1,2,3] According to one study, the polysaccharides from *Huang Qi* (Radix Astragali) activated B cells and macrophages.[4] According to another study, administration of *Huang Qi* (Radix Astragali) prolonged allograft survival associated with promotion of CD4+ CD25+ regulatory T cells.[5] Furthermore, *Huang Qi* (Radix Astragali) has been shown to increase the production and maturity of blood cells from the bone marrow.[6] The therapeutic benefits of *Huang Qi* (Radix Astragali) are also well documented in clinical trials. According to one clinical trial of 115 leucopenic patients, it was found that the use of *Huang Qi* (Radix Astragali) is associated with an "obvious rise of the white blood cell (WBC) count" in a dose-dependent relationship.[7] According to another randomized, double-blind, controlled clinical trial on 36 adults who complained of chronic fatigue, the administration of *Huang Qi* (Radix Astragali) and *Dan Shen* (Radix et Rhizoma Salviae Miltiorrhizae) decreased the fatigue severity score, when comparing the herb group against the control group.[8]

Ling Zhi (Ganoderma) has a wide range of therapeutic effects. It has a marked immunostimulant effect to boost both humoral and cellular immune activities. The specific effects of *Ling Zhi* (Ganoderma) include an increase in monocytes, macrophages and T lymphocytes.[9,10,11,12] In addition, it also increases the production of cytokine, interleukin, tumor necrosis factor, and interferon. Furthermore, *Ling Zhi* (Ganoderma) has significant antitumor effect to inhibit tumor growth. Lastly, *Ling Zhi* (Ganoderma) has a broad spectrum of antibacterial activities and inhibits the growth of numerous bacteria. [13]

Dong Chong Xia Cao (Cordyceps) is another herb that has immunomodulatory and antitumor functions. *Dong Chong Xia Cao* (Cordyceps) enhances overall immunity by increasing the number of lymphocytes and natural killer cells and the production of interleukin, interferon, and tumor necrosis factor.[14,15,16,17,18] This immunomodulatory effect is attributed to the polysaccharides of *Dong Chong Xia Cao* (Cordyceps), which specifically interact with and activate surface receptors involved in innate immunity.[19] In addition to its immunomodulatory activities, *Dong Chong Xia Cao* (Cordyceps) also has an antitumor effect, and was found to significantly inhibit the proliferation of cancer cells.[20] In some instances, the growth inhibition rate of the cancer cells reached 78 to 83%.[21]

Bai Zhu (Rhizoma Atractylodis Macrocephalae), *Fang Feng* (Radix Saposhnikoviae) and *Wu Wei Zi* (Fructus Schisandrae Chinensis) are important herbs in this formula. *Bai Zhu* (Rhizoma Atractylodis Macrocephalae) and *Wu Wei Zi* (Fructus Schisandrae Chinensis) have immunostimulant effects. *Bai Zhu* (Rhizoma Atractylodis Macrocephalae) stimulates the activity of the macrophages and reticuloendothelial system, and increases the number of white blood cells, lymphocytes, and IgG.[22,23] Administration of *Wu Wei Zi* (Fructus Schisandrae Chinensis) is associated with stimulation of non-specific immunity.[24] *Wu Wei Zi* (Fructus Schisandrae Chinensis) also has an antibacterial effect to inhibit the growth of many bacteria.[25] Lastly, *Fang Feng* (Radix Saposhnikoviae) has both antibacterial and antiviral effects, and prevents individuals with compromised immune systems from contracting bacterial and viral infections.[26]

Overall, ***Immune*** + is an excellent formula that boosts the immune functions to prevent bacterial and viral infections, fight against cancer, and improve energy levels.

COMPARATIVE ANALYSIS

One striking difference between Western and traditional Chinese medicine is that Western medicine focuses on and excels in crisis management, while traditional Chinese medicine emphasizes and shines in holistic and preventative treatments. Therefore, in emergencies, such as gunshot wounds or surgery, Western medicine is generally the treatment of choice. However, for treatment of chronic idiopathic illness of unknown origins, where all lab tests are normal and a clear diagnosis cannot be made, traditional Chinese medicine is distinctly superior.

In cases of chronic immunodeficiency, even when confirmed with distinct symptoms (frequent and prolonged infections) and laboratory diagnosis (decreased white blood cells count), Western medicine has no drug treatment available. Though there is one drug available for acute immunosuppression, it is only indicated for treatment of bone marrow suppression in cancer patients receiving chemotherapy and radiation. In other words, patients with compromised immune system have few or no options for drug treatments. On the other hand, traditional Chinese medicine is beneficial as it excels in maintenance and preventative therapies. Herbs can be used to regulate imbalances

Immune + ™

and alleviate associated signs and symptoms. In this case, many herbs have been shown via *in vitro* and *in vivo* studies to have remarkable effect to boost both specific and non-specific immune systems. Therefore, herbal therapy should definitely be employed to restore optimal health and prevent contraction of infections.

References

1. Chu, DT. et al. Immunotherapy with Chinese medicinal herbs. I. Immune restoration of local xenogenetic graft-versus-host reaction in cancer patients by fractionated astragalus membranaceus in vitro. *Journal of Clinical & Laboratory Immunology*. 25(3):119-23, Mar. 1988.
2. Sun, Y. et al. Immune restoration and/or augmentation of local graft versus host reaction by traditional Chinese medicinal herbs. *Cancer*. 52(1):70-3, July 1, 1983.
3. Sun, Y. et al. Preliminary observations on the effects of the Chinese medicinal herbs Astragalus membranaceus and Ganoderma lucidum on lymphocyte blastogenic responses. *Journal of Biological Response Mopdifiers*. 2(3):227-37, 1983.
4. Shao BM, Xu W, Dai H, Tu P, Li Z, Gao XM. A study on the immune receptors for polysaccharides from the roots of Astragalus membranaceus, a Chinese medicinal herb. Department of Immunology, School of Basic Medical Science, Peking University Health Science Center, Beijing, China. Biochem Biophys Res Commun. 2004 Aug 6;320(4):1103-11.
5. Qu LL, Su YL, Li CX, Hou GH. Astragalus membranaceus injection delayed allograft survival related with CD4+ CD25+ regulatory T cells. Department of Nuclear Medicine, Qilu Hospital of Shandong University, Jinan, Shandong, China. Transplant Proc. 2010 Nov;42(9):3793-7.
6. *Nan Jing Zhong Yi Xue Yuan Xue Bao* (Journal of Nanjing University of Traditional Chinese Medicine), 1989; 1:43.
7. Weng, XS. *Chung Juo Chung Hsia I Chieh Ho Tsa Chih*, August 1995.
8. Cho JH, Cho CK, Shin JW, Son JY, Kang W, Son CG. Myelophil, an extract mix of Astragali Radix and Salviae Radix, ameliorates chronic fatigue: a randomised, double-blind, controlled pilot study. Complement Ther Med. 2009 Jun;17(3):141-6.
9. Wang, SY. et al. The anti-tumor effect of ganoderma lucidum is mediated by cytokines released from activated macrophages and T-lymphocytes. *International Journal of Cancer*. 70(6):699-705, Mar 17, 1997.
10. Van der Hem, LG. et al. Ling Zhi-8: studies of a new immunomodulating agent. *Transplantation*. 60(5):438-43, Sep 15, 1995.
11. Haak-Frendscho, M. et al. Ling Zhi-8: a novel T-cell mitogen induces cytokine production and upregulation of ICAM-1 expression. *Cellular Immunology*. 150(1):101-13, Aug. 1993.
12. Tanaka, S. et al. Complete amino acid sequence of a novel immunomodulatory protein, ling zhi-9. An immuno-modulator from a fungus, ganoderma lucidum, having similar effect to immunoglobulin variable regions.
13. Zhang J, Tang Q, Zhou C, Jia W, Da Silva L, Nguyen LD, Reutter W, Fan H. GLIS, a bioactive proteoglycan fraction from Ganoderma lucidum, displays anti-tumour activity by increasing both humoral and cellular immune response. Institut für Biochemie und Molekularbiologie, CBF, Charité-Universitätsmedizin Berlin, Germany. Life Sci. 2010 Nov 20;87(19-22):628-37.
14. Kuo, YC. et al. Cordyceps sinensis as an immunomodulatory agent. *American Journal of Chinese Medicine*. 24(2):111-25, 1996.
15. Guan, YJ. et al. Effect of Cordyceps sinensis on T-lymphocyte subsets in chronic renal failure. *Chung-Kuo Chung His I Chieh Ho Tsa Chih*. 12(6): 338-9,323, Jun. 1992.
16. Liu, C. et al. Effects of Cordyceps sinensis (CS) on in vitro natural killer cells. *Chung-Kuo Chung His I Chieh Ho Tsa Chih*. 12(5):267-9,259, May, 1992.
17. Xu, RH. et al. Effects of cordyceps sinensis on natural killer activity and colony formation of B16 melanoma. *Chinese Medical Journal*. 105(2):97-101, Feb. 1992.
18. Liu, P. et al. Influence of Cordyceps sinensis (Berk.) Sacc. and rat serum containing same medicine on IL-1, IFN and TNF produced by rat Kupffer's cells *Chung Kuo Chung Yao Tsa Chih*; 21(6):367-9, 384, Jun 1996.
19. Hsu TL, Cheng SC, Yang WB, Chin SW, Chen BH, Huang MT, Hsieh SL, Wong CH. Profiling carbohydrate-receptor interaction with recombinant innate immunity receptor-Fc fusion proteins. J Biol Chem. 2009 Dec 11;284(50): 34479-89.
20. Kuo, YC. et al. Growth inhibitors against tumor cells in Cordyceps sinensis other than cordycepin and polysaccharides. *Cancer Investigation*. 12(6): 611-5,1994.
21. Chen, YJ. et al. Effect of Cordyceps sinensis on the proliferation and differentiation of human leukemic U937 cells. *Life Sciences*. 60(25):2349-59, 1997.
22. *Jun Shi Yi Xue Jian Xun* (Military Medicine Notes), 1977; 2:5.
23. *Xin Yi Yao Xue Za Zhi* (New Journal of Medicine and Herbology), 1979; 6:60.
24. *Zhong Yao Xue* (Chinese Herbology), 1998; 878:881.
25. *Zhong Yao Xue* (Chinese Herbology), 1998; 878:881.
26. *Zhong Yao Tong Bao* (Journal of Chinese Herbology), 1988; 13(6):364.

Imperial Tonic™

CLINICAL APPLICATIONS

- **General tonic:** increases both mental and physical functions, enhances academic and sports performance
- **Recovery enhancement:** speeds up recovery from any event that contributes to mental or physical exhaustion, such as surgery, severe illness, and childbirth
- **Chronic fatigue:** constant tiredness, low energy, and lack of interest
- **Anemia:** with dizziness, fatigue, lack of energy or poor appetite

WESTERN THERAPEUTIC ACTIONS

- Adaptogenic function to enhance both mental and physical functions
- Enhances basal metabolic rate and increases the overall energy level
- Boosts the immune system, increases the number of white blood cells
- Treats anemia by increasing the number and function of red blood cells
- Anti-aging effect to enhance longevity and promote general wellness

CHINESE THERAPEUTIC ACTIONS

- Tonifies qi, blood, yin and yang
- Strengthens the overall constitution of the body

DOSAGE

The dosage for long-term administration is 2 to 4 capsules three times daily. The dosage may be increased up to 5 to 6 capsules three times daily for short-term use, for its adaptogenic effect or recovery enhancement.

INGREDIENTS

Bai Shao (Radix Paeoniae Alba)
Bai Zhu (Rhizoma Atractylodis Macrocephalae)
Chuan Xiong (Rhizoma Chuanxiong)
Da Zao (Fructus Jujubae)
Dang Gui (Radix Angelicae Sinensis)
Fu Ling (Poria)
Gui Xin (Cortex Rasus Cinnamomi)
Huang Qi (Radix Astragali)
Shan Yao (Rhizoma Dioscoreae)
Sheng Jiang (Rhizoma Zingiberis Recens)
Shu Di Huang (Radix Rehmanniae Praeparata)
Wu Wei Zi (Fructus Schisandrae Chinensis)
Xi Yang Shen (Radix Panacis Quinquefolii)
Zhi Gan Cao (Radix et Rhizoma Glycyrrhizae Praeparata cum Melle)

BACKGROUND

Imperial Tonic is an herbal formula specifically designed to treat qi, blood, yin and yang deficiencies. From Western medicine perspectives, this often corresponds to chronic deterioration in physical and physiological functions. During this stage, patients can subjectively feel deterioration in health, but physicians cannot objectively diagnose any disease. All laboratory tests may be within the normal range, yet the patients do not feel well as they experience many vague signs and symptoms, such as chronic fatigue, low energy, lack of appetite, dizziness, compromised mental and physical functions, frequent recurrence of infection, and prolonged recovery. To correct this physical and physiological decline in health, the use of herbs is essential to restore health.

FORMULA EXPLANATION

Imperial Tonic is one of the most comprehensive and most effective herbal formulas. It treats both specific and general constitutional disorders. ***Imperial Tonic*** contains herbs that tonify yin, yang, qi and blood. Clinically, it can be used to treat chronic fatigue, anemia, post-surgical recovery, postpartum recovery, and many other conditions characterized by general weakness and deficiency.

Huang Qi (Radix Astragali) strengthens the immune system and *Xi Yang Shen* (Radix Panacis Quinquefolii) tonifies the *yuan* (source) *qi* of the body. *Bai Zhu* (Rhizoma Atractylodis Macrocephalae) and *Fu Ling* (Poria) strengthen the Spleen and promote the absorption of nutrients from food. They work together to strengthen qi and the immune system. *Shu Di Huang* (Radix Rehmanniae Praeparata) tonifies the Liver and Kidney yin. *Dang Gui* (Radix Angelicae Sinensis), *Bai Shao* (Radix Paeoniae Alba), and *Chuan Xiong* (Rhizoma Chuanxiong) nourish and invigorate the blood. *Shan Yao* (Rhizoma Dioscoreae) tonifies the Spleen, the Lung, and the Kidney. *Gui Xin* (Cortex Rasus Cinnamomi) tonifies Kidney yang. *Wu Wei Zi* (Fructus Schisandrae Chinensis) has astringent and binding effects to prevent leakage of *jing* (essence). *Zhi Gan Cao* (Radix et Rhizoma Glycyrrhizae Praeparata cum Melle), *Sheng Jiang* (Rhizoma Zingiberis Recens), and *Da Zao* (Fructus Jujubae) harmonize the gastrointestinal tract.

In conclusion, ***Imperial Tonic*** tonifies qi, blood, yin and yang, and is one of the best formulas to treat both specific and general constitutional disorders.

CAUTIONS & CONTRAINDICATIONS

- ***Imperial Tonic*** is safe for long-term use. However, because it is a warm formula, it should be reduced in dosage or discontinued if it causes side effects characterized by heat, such as dry mouth, thirst, and nosebleeds.
- Since this formula may stimulant the immune system, it should be used with extreme caution in patients who have autoimmune disease or take immune suppressant drugs after organ transplant.
- This formula is contraindicated in cases of infection, inflammation, and other excess conditions.
- This herbal formula contains herbs that invigorate blood circulation, such as *Dang Gui* (Radix Angelicae Sinensis).

Imperial Tonic™

Therefore, patients who are on anticoagulant or antiplatelet therapies, such as Coumadin (warfarin), should use this formula with caution, or not at all, as there may be a higher risk of bleeding and bruising.[1,2,3]

CLINICAL NOTES

- ***Imperial Tonic*** is an excellent postpartum tonic. Women lose a tremendous amount of *jing* (essence) and blood after labor. The concept of replenishing the Kidney *jing* (essence) is not prevalent in the West. As a result, many women age faster than they should and suffer from low back pain or symptoms of Kidney yin or *jing* (essence) deficiency later in their lives. This is a great formula to use for one month starting one or two weeks after delivery. It helps to replenish qi, blood, yin and yang that were lost due to labor.
- Important Note: Before using ***Imperial Tonic*** as a postpartum tonic, *Sheng Hua Tang* (Generation and Transformation Decoction) should be used for three to five days (three days for natural birth, five days for Cesarean) to clear out residual blood stagnation and to relieve pain. This will prevent future gynecological complications due to blood stagnation in the pelvis.

Pulse Diagnosis by Dr. Jimmy Wei-Yen Chang:

- Tent pulse, a convex-shaped pulse that is weak and collapses upon pressure, on all three positions on both hands.

SUPPLEMENTARY FORMULAS

- To boost energy and awareness, use ***Vibrant***.
- To increase immunity, use ***Immune +***.
- For brittle, dry hair or scalp, or hair loss, combine with ***Polygonum 14***.
- For decreased sexual activity, low sex drive, and other sexual dysfunction in men and women, use ***Vitality***.
- For insomnia and anemia, combine with ***Schisandra ZZZ***.
- For menopause with hot flashes, mood swings, and excessive perspiration, combine ***Balance (Heat)*** with ***Nourish***.
- For supportive cancer therapy and to decrease the side effects of chemotherapy including nausea, vomiting, poor appetite, and fatigue, use with ***C/R Support***.
- For supportive therapy in patients with cancer who are too weak to receive chemotherapy or radiation, add ***CA Support***.
- ***Cordyceps 3*** can be added to enhance the overall antiaging effect.
- To enhance memory, add ***Enhance Memory***.
- To prevent osteoporosis, add ***Osteo 8***.
- To increase the shape and size of breasts, or to increase libido, use with ***Venus***.
- To strengthen the Spleen and the Stomach, add ***GI Tonic***.
- For stress and anxiety, add ***Calm***.
- For severe stress and anxiety, add ***Calm (ES)***.
- For stress, anxiety and insomnia with underlying deficiency, add ***Calm ZZZ***.
- For Kidney yang deficiency, add ***Kidney Tonic (Yang)***.
- For Kidney yin deficiency, add ***Kidney Tonic (Yin)***.
- For male infertility, add ***Vital Essence***.
- For female infertility, add ***Blossom (Phase 1-4)***.

ACUPUNCTURE TREATMENT

Traditional Points:

- *Zusanli* (ST 36), *Guanyuan* (CV 4), *Qihai* (CV 6), *Mingmen* (GV 4), *Shenshu* (BL 23)
- *Qihai* (CV 6), *Zhongwan* (CV 12), *Neiguan* (PC 6), *Gongsun* (SP 4), *Zusanli* (ST 36), *Geshu* (BL 17)

Classic Master Tung's Points:

- **Fatigue:** *Tianhuang* (T 77.17), *Dihuang* (T 77.19), *Renhuang* (T 77.21), *Minghuang* (T 88.12), *Tianhuang* (T 88.13), *Qihuang* (T 88.14), *Beimian* (T 44.07), *Sanyan* (T 11.21), *Zhitong* (T 44.13)

Master Tung's Points by Dr. Chuan-Min Wang:

- **Tonify qi, blood, yin, yang:** *Tianhuangfu [shenguan]* (T 77.18)

Balance Method by Dr. Richard Tan:

- Left side: *Hegu* (LI 4), *Zusanli* (ST 36), *Taixi* (KI 3), *Yinlingquan* (SP 9)
- Right side: *Lieque* (LU 7), *Tongli* (HT 5), *Zusanli* (ST 36)
- Left and right side can be alternated from treatment to treatment.

Auricular Medicine by Dr. Li-Chun Huang:

- **Fatigue:** Sympathetic, Kidney, Liver, Spleen, Speed Recovered Fatigue, *San Jiao*, Anxious, Nervous Subcortex, Thyroid. Bleed Ear Apex.
- **Replenishing the blood:** Spleen, Stomach, Heart, Kidney, *San Jiao*, Adrenal Gland, Blood, Endocrine
- **Hypotension:** Raise Blood Pressure, Adrenal Gland, Pituitary, Heart, Liver, Endocrine
- **Hypoglycemia:** Pancreas, Diabetes, Pituitary, Endocrine, Thalamus, Sympathetic, Duodenum, Digestive Subcortex

NUTRITION

- Increase the consumption of fresh fruits, vegetables, grains, seeds and nuts.
- Eat more fish and fish oils, onions, garlic, olives, olive oil, herbs, spices, soy products, tofu, yogurt, and fiber.
- Sea vegetables, such as kelp and seaweeds, replenish the body with minerals like magnesium, potassium, calcium, iodine and iron.
- Ensure adequate intake of vitamin B complex to process and utilize energy.
- Decrease intake of red meat, alcohol, fats, caffeine, and highly processed foods.
- Avoid the use of stimulants, such as coffee, caffeine, and high-sugar products.
- Food allergies or chemical hypersensitivity can drain energy and cause fatigue. Tests should be done to confirm or rule out allergy and/or hypersensitivity.

Imperial Tonic™

The Tao of Nutrition by Dr. Maoshing Ni and Cathy McNease:

- **Chronic fatigue syndrome**
  - Recommendations: winter melon, pumpkin, pumpkin seed, yam, sweet potato, lima bean, black bean, soy bean, strawberry, watermelon, pineapple, chestnut, papaya, figs, garlic, onions, and pearl barley.
  - Avoid dairy products, alcohol, coffee, sugar, fatty or deep-fried foods, overly spicy foods, cold and raw foods, tomato, eggplant, bell pepper, and shellfish.
- **Anemia:** Mix together and eat dried blueberries and raisins.
- **Weakness or anemia:** Cook one chicken with 30 grams of *Dang Gui* (Radix Angelicae Sinensis), and 6 1/2 cups of water. Simmer together for one hour. The darker meat birds, such as the Chinese black chicken (Silkie chicken), are the most tonifying.
- **Weakness, emaciation:** Cook pork in rice porridge.

LIFESTYLE INSTRUCTIONS

- Regular exercise and adequate rest are essential to optimal health.
- Take a hot bath for about 20 minutes prior to bedtime to relax. Sea salt or Epsom salts can be added to the bath water.
- Engage in activities such as *tai chi chuan* [*tai ji chuan*], walking, or meditation that allow calmness of mind without creating stagnation or excessive fatigue.
- Avoid exposure to heavy metal, such as lead, cadmium, aluminum, copper and arsenic, which can all suppress the immune system and cause fatigue.

CASE STUDIES

- R.B., a 63-year-old female, presented with fatigue (especially in the morning), constant need for a nap during the day, and an early bedtime. The condition was affected with mild activity, leading to emotional let down, and lack of being able to get things done. Her medical history consisted of brain tumor removal in 2009, followed by chemotherapy and radiation during each stage of her four cancer survivals. Objective findings include lack of shine in her eyes, poor focus, and poor memory. The practitioner diagnosed this condition as Kidney qi deficiency and blood deficiency; her Western diagnosis was fibromyalgia. For treatment, ***Imperial Tonic*** was prescribed three capsules three times a day for four weeks, followed by two capsules a day afterwards. As a result, the patient's energy is better than it has been for years. She can accomplish more during the day without the need of rest or a nap. Sleep is sound at night and there is even less muscle pain. The patient is thrilled and plans on taking the herbs for awhile. Submitted by L.M., Gresham, Oregon.
- L.B., a 47-year-old female, presented with pain located in the left knee and occasional low back pain when tired. It was also noted that she had slight night sweats, fatigue, caught colds easily, and breast tenderness during PMS. The blood pressure was 107/65 mmHg. The practitioner diagnosed the condition as Kidney qi deficiency with Liver qi stagnation. ***Imperial Tonic*** and *Jia Wei Xiao Yao San* (Augmented Rambling Powder) were prescribed to the patient for treatment. After taking the formulas, her overall energy and stamina increased, she didn't catch colds as easily, and any night sweats or breast tenderness were no longer occurring. With this condition the patient had to take the herbs consistently long term in order to maintain the results. Submitted by B.L., Fort Myers, Florida.
- J.L., a 66-year-old female, presented with multiple symptoms including low back pain, shallow breathing, some wheezing, fatigue, and unclear state of the mind. Her pulse was thin and thready, and her tongue was red with no coat and purplish color. The practitioner diagnosed this condition as Kidney yin deficiency and Lung qi deficiency. Upon diagnosis the patient was given ***Imperial Tonic***. As a result of taking the herbs, the patient reported her stamina and energy had improved as well as being able to think clearer. The patient has a tendency to dislike taking the herbs; however, was willing to continue taking them on a maintenance dosage for her condition. Submitted by B.L., Fort Myers, Florida.
- S.F., a 33-year-old female, presented with premenstrual symptoms consisting of fatigue and depression, three days before her cycle. The practitioner diagnosed this condition as qi deficiency with *shen* (spirit) disturbance. ***Imperial Tonic***, ***Calm***, and ***Shine*** were prescribed at 2 to 3 capsules each three times a day. As a result of taking ***Imperial Tonic*** for three weeks, she reported increase in energy and a more positive attitude. She only took the ***Calm*** and ***Shine*** for three months, and thereafter only continued with the ***Imperial Tonic*** as she felt recovered from her depression. Submitted by S.L., Yuma, Arizona.
- N.N., a 60-year-old female patient, presented with symptoms in recovering from something she had eaten two weeks prior. The fever and digestive disturbances were gone; however, low energy and "not feeling better" were still lingering. Western diagnosis was food poisoning; the TCM diagnosis was qi and blood deficiencies. ***Imperial Tonic*** was prescribed at three pills three times a day. Her energy and appetite picked up immediately within one day of taking the herbs. Submitted by A.I., Hilo, Hawaii.
- A.S., a 29-year-old female, presented with PCOS, consisting of multiple sacs, no ripening of the eggs, irregular cycles, and fatigue. It was also mentioned that she had two unsuccessful IUI's due to two chemical pregnancies. Additional symptoms included cystic ovaries, acne, increase facial body hair, deficiency of both vitamin D and DHEA, and short temperatured luteal phase. The TCM diagnosis was blood deficiency, damp and phlegm accumulation, Spleen and Kidney deficiencies, and dysregulation of the *ren* (conception) and *chong* (thoroughfare) channels. Her Western diagnosis was cystic ovaries infertility, low follicular and luteal temperatured irregular menstruation, and elevated prolactin. ***Blossom (Phases 1-4)*** were prescribed to her all month, ***Imperial Tonic*** to replenish the *jing* (essence), and ***Nourish*** to tonify the blood and Kidney yang. The six month

Imperial Tonic™

protocol was used to clear the heat, build the qi/blood/*jing* (essence), and regulate the cycle. As a result, her temperatures had re-established to create normal cycles. Secondly, after three months of a balanced cycle, her cystic ovaries had reduced; she also had increase of her qi/blood/*jing* (essence) as well as her additional deficiencies, which became restored. As a result she had a successful IUI and is now two months pregnant. ***Blossom (Phases 1-4)*** and ***Nourish*** were very helpful. Submitted by N.T., Bethesda, Maryland.

- L.H., a 33-year-old female, presented with postpartum symptoms consisting of weakness, fatigue, and anemia. Blood pressure was 98/60 mmHg and heart rate was 65 beats per minute. Tongue was pale, swollen, and shaking; pulse was thready and deep. The practitioner diagnosed this condition as Liver blood deficiency as well as deficiency of the Spleen and Kidney. ***Imperial Tonic*** was prescribed at 4 grams three times per day. After taking the herbs for two weeks, the patient's energy had improved. Postnatal eating habits were adjusted as well. Submitted by V.G., Virginia Beach, Virginia.
- A 35-year-old female patient presented with multiple symptoms consisting of low energy, feeling cold and underdeveloped breasts. It was also noted that she had infertility and insomnia. Blood pressure was 112/60 mmHg, and heart rate of 76 beats per minute. The practitioner diagnosed this condition as Kidney yang and *jing* (essence) deficiencies; the Western diagnosis was chronic fatigue syndrome. ***Venus*** was prescribed at 2 grams three times per day with ***Imperial Tonic*** at 2 grams daily three times per day. After three weeks the patient had returned with much improvement to her sleep, energy, and sex drive. She had also mentioned that her breasts were fuller. Submitted by L.W., Arroyo Grande, California.
- A tired and exhausted patient presented with general aches and pain in the neck and low back. There was also a history of poor sleep and digestion with no constipation. The practitioner felt the patient had over-worked herself throughout the years and that the condition was due to "wear and tear." The diagnosis was qi and blood deficiencies with underlying yin and yang deficiencies. ***Imperial Tonic***, ***Schisandra ZZZ*** and *Bu Zhong Yi Qi Tang* (Tonify the Middle and Augment the Qi Decoction) were given along with acupuncture and massage therapy. The treatment was concluded to be quite effective. Submitted by S.C., La Crescenta, California.
- A 44-year-old female with hepatitis C, necrosis of the liver, and diabetes (insulin-dependent) was treated with interferon, Rebetron (ribavirin and interferon α 2B), Zantac (ranitidine), Prozac (fluoxetine) and insulin. Her clinical manifestations included pain in the liver region, fatigue, insomnia, blurred vision, constipation, melancholy, frontal headache, dizziness, tremors, abdominal bloating, and a pale complexion. Her tongue was maroon in color, and the pulse was slippery. The diagnosis for this patient was dampness in the Liver and Gallbladder, with Liver overacting on the Spleen and the Stomach, hence disrupting the transformation and transportation of the digestive system. The patient was treated with two herbal formulas (***Liver DTX*** and ***Imperial Tonic***) and two homeopathic formulas (sarcode liver formula and oral insulin). The treatment also included acupuncture involving meridian treatment and extraordinary vessel treatment. After three weeks, the patient had significant improvements in her vitality, complexion, appetite, sleep, attitude and energy level. A dramatic reduction of her abdominal pain was also noted. Her insulin use was reduced by approximately 25%. Submitted by I.B., Miami, Florida.
- A 35-year-old female complained of the following symptoms: bedwetting, fatigue, low back pain, abdominal pain, loss of appetite and depression. The doctor diagnosed her with Kidney *jing* (essence), yin and yang deficiencies. ***Imperial Tonic*** and ***Vibrant*** were prescribed. The patient reported that bedwetting, depression and pain went away and the energy level went from 2 to 10. As an added and unexpected joy for her, the patient stated she also lost 10 pounds even though she had been eating more. Submitted by S.C., Santa Monica, California.
- R.D., a 54-year-old male patient, presented with the complaints of always being sick for long periods of time, always cold, weak and tired. Western diagnosis was chronic fatigue syndrome and immune dysfunction. His blood pressure was 110/70 mmHg and his heart rate was 66 beats per minute. The diagnosis was yang and qi deficiencies. ***Imperial Tonic*** was prescribed at 2 grams three times a day. After taking the herbs, the patient reported that he first began to feel more energy and a better sense of well being. He also noticed that he wasn't as sick as often and it did not last as long as before. The patient also received acupuncture treatment. The result of both the herbs and the acupuncture was evident within a few weeks. Submitted by W.F., Bloomfield, New Jersey.
- A 44-year-old, 215-pound male patient presented with excessive night sweats to the point he had to change his clothes twice every night. His blood pressure was 115/78 mmHg and his heart rate was 70 beats per minute. The patient also complained of pain in the big toe. The diagnosis was *wei* (defensive) *qi* and Lung qi deficiencies. *Sheng Mai San* (Generate the Pulse Powder) and ***Imperial Tonic*** were prescribed and the sweating stopped after using half a bottle of each formula. Submitted by H.K.C., Studio City, California.
- M.M., a 41-year-old female, complained of fatigue, malaise, cognitive problems, headache, slightly blurred vision, irritable bowel syndrome, muscle pain and constipation. The Western diagnosis was chronic fatigue syndrome; the TCM diagnosis was qi, blood and yin deficiencies. ***Imperial Tonic*** was prescribed, two capsules, three times daily. She took the herbs for nine weeks, and noted continual improvement, a significant decrease of fatigue and malaise, and an overall good constitution. Submitted by C.L., Chino Hills, California.

Imperial Tonic™

PHARMACOLOGICAL AND CLINICAL RESEARCH

Imperial Tonic is an herbal formula that incorporates herbs with a wide range of therapeutic benefits to treat various aspects of declining physical and physiological health.

Imperial Tonic has many herbs to restore health. *Xi Yang Shen* (Radix Panacis Quinquefolii) and *Bai Zhu* (Rhizoma Atractylodis Macrocephalae) both have adaptogenic effect to quickly help patients adapt to various conditions of mental and physical stress.[4,5] As demonstrated by human and animal studies, *Xi Yang Shen* (Radix Panacis Quinquefolii) prevents stress-induced ulcers, stimulates the proliferation of liver cells, increases natural killer cell activities, and enhances the secretion of interferons.[6] In addition to this short-term effect, ***Imperial Tonic*** contains many herbs with excellent gastrointestinal activities, such as *Bai Zhu* (Rhizoma Atractylodis Macrocephalae), *Gan Cao* (Radix et Rhizoma Glycyrrhizae), and *Sheng Jiang* (Rhizoma Zingiberis Recens), to restore normal digestive functions to absorb essential nutrients in foods.[7,8,9]

Reversal of declining health conditions requires proper blood circulation. In this formula, *Dang Gui* (Radix Angelicae Sinensis), *Huang Qi* (Radix Astragali) and *Shu Di Huang* (Radix Rehmanniae Praeparata) have hematopoietic effects to stimulate the bone marrow and increase the production of blood.[10,11] Furthermore, *Chuan Xiong* (Rhizoma Chuanxiong) is used to enhance the circulation of blood and increase blood perfusion to all parts of the body.[12,13] With adequate amount and proper circulation of blood, the body can begin its own healing process.

Imperial Tonic has many herbs to relieve stress and anxiety and improve cognitive functions. *Bai Shao* (Radix Paeoniae Alba) and *Fu Ling* (Poria) both have a calming effect on the central nervous system to relieve stress and improve sleep.[14,15] *Xi Yang Shen* (Radix Panacis Quinquefolii) and *Rou Gui* (Cortex Cinnamomi) exert an anxiolytic effect by regulating the serotonergic and GABAergic system to alleviate anxiety.[16,17] To improve cognitive function, *Bai Shao* (Radix Paeoniae Alba) and *Da Zao* (Fructus Jujubae) are used in this formula. Paeoniflorin, a compound from *Bai Shao* (Radix Paeoniae Alba), has been shown to enhance aging-induced learning deficit.[18] Oleamide, a compound from *Da Zao* (Fructus Jujubae), has a high activating effect (34.1%) on choline acetyltransferase and protects the brain from drug-induced amnesia.[19]

Individuals with deteriorating physical and physiological health often have a compromised immune system. They frequently contract infections, and require a prolonged period of time for recovery. ***Imperial Tonic*** contains many herbs with significant immunostimulant effects to boost the immune system and strengthen the body. *Huang Qi* (Radix Astragali) has a marked effect to increase both specific and non-specific immunity.[20,21,22] Administration of *Huang Qi* (Radix Astragali) has been shown to increase white blood cells,[23] enhance the production of IgM,[24] and activate B cells and macrophages.[25] *Bai Zhu* (Rhizoma Atractylodis Macrocephalae) also has a significant immunostimulant effect to increase the activity of the macrophages and reticuloendothelial system,[26] and boost the number of white blood cells, lymphocytes, and IgG.[27] Lastly, *Gan Cao* (Radix et Rhizoma Glycyrrhizae) and *Dang Gui* (Radix Angelicae Sinensis) both stimulate the phagocytic activity of macrophages.[28,29]

In addition to the health benefits listed above, herbs in ***Imperial Tonic*** have many other therapeutic effects to promote health and prevent disease. *Wu Wei Zi* (Fructus Schisandrae Chinensis), *Da Zao* (Fructus Jujubae) and *Gan Cao* (Radix et Rhizoma Glycyrrhizae) have hepatoprotective effects to protect the liver from various types of drugs and/or chemical-induced toxicity.[30,31,32] *Huang Qi* (Radix Astragali) and *Dang Gui* (Radix Angelicae Sinensis) have nephroprotective effects to reduce proteinuria, decrease the loss of capillaries, and improve microstructure dysfunction.[33] The nephroprotective effect is attributed in part to the antifibrosis activity of these two herbs to improve ischemic microvasculature and attenuate interstitial fibrosis.[34] *Shan Yao* (Rhizoma Dioscoreae) has a significant neuroprotective effect against neurotoxicity induced by scopolamine, glutamate and hydrogen peroxide, according to *in vivo* and *in vitro* studies.[35] Lastly, *Dang Gui* (Radix Angelicae Sinensis), *Chuan Xiong* (Rhizoma Chuanxiong) and *Wu Wei Zi* (Fructus Schisandrae Chinensis) also have neuroprotective effects, and show great benefits and potential for prevention and treatment of Alzheimer's disease because of their neuroprotective effect against beta-amyloid (Aβ).[36,37]

In summary, ***Imperial Tonic*** is an herbal formula with herbs that prevent and treat a wide range of disorders characterized by general decline in physical and physiological health.

COMPARATIVE ANALYSIS

One striking difference between Western and traditional Chinese medicine is that Western medicine focuses and excels in crisis management, while traditional Chinese medicine emphasizes and shines in holistic and preventative treatments. Therefore, in emergencies, such as gunshot wounds or surgery, Western medicine is generally the treatment of choice. However, for treatment of chronic idiopathic illness of unknown origins, where all lab tests are normal and a clear diagnosis cannot be made, traditional Chinese medicine is distinctly superior.

In cases of chronic energetic disorders, where all tests are normal but there are still general and non-diagnostic signs and symptoms, Western medicine offers few treatment options since there is not a clear diagnosis. On the other hand, traditional Chinese medicine is beneficial as it excels in maintainance and preventative therapies. Herbs can be used to regulate imbalances and alleviate associated signs and symptoms. Therefore, herbal therapy should definitely be employed to prevent deterioration and to restore optimal health.

Imperial Tonic ™

References

1. Chan K, Lo AC, Yeung JH, Woo KS. Journal of Pharmacy and Pharmacology 1995 May;47(5):402-6.
2. Pharmacotherapy 1999 July;19(7):870-876.
3. European Journal of Drug Metabolism and Pharmacokinetics 1995; 20(1):55-60.
4. *Zhong Yao Xue* (Chinese Herbology), 1998; 737:738.
5. *Xin Yi Yao Xue Za Zhi* (New Journal of Medicine and Herbology), 1974; 8:13.
6. Singh, VK. et al. *Planta Medica* 50:462, 1984.
7. *Chang Yong Zhong Yao Cheng Fen Yu Yao Li Shou Ce* (A Handbook of the Composition and Pharmacology of Common Chinese Drugs), 1994; 739:742.
8. *Zhong Yao Zhi* (Chinese Herbology Journal), 1993; 358.
9. *Xian Dai Zhong Yao Yao Li Xue* (Contemporary Pharmacology of Chinese Herbs), 1997; 66.
10. *Nan Jing Zhong Yi Xue Yuan Xue Bao* (Journal of Nanjing University of Traditional Chinese Medicine), 1989; 1:43.
11. Yuan Y, Hou S, Lian T, Han Y. Studies of Rehmannia glutinosa Libosch. f. hueichingensis as a blood tonic. Henan College of the Traditional Chinese Medicine, Zhengzhuo. Zhongguo Zhong Yao Za Zhi. 1992 Jun;17(6):366-8, inside backcover.
12. *Zhong Yao Xue* (Chinese Herbology), 1989; 535:539.
13. Tian JW, Fu FH, Jiang WL, Wang CY, Sun F, Zhang TP. Protective effect of ligusticum chuanxiong phthalides on focai cerebral ischemia in rats and its related mechanism of action. Zhongguo Zhong Yao Za Zhi. 2005 Mar;30(6):466-8.
14. *Zhong Yao Tong Bao* (Journal of Chinese Herbology), 1985; 10(6):43.
15. *Zhong Yao Da Ci Dian* (Dictionary of Chinese Herbs), 1977:1596.
16. Wei XY, et al. Anxiolytic effect of saponins from Panax quinquefolium in mice. Department of Pharmacology, Shenyang Pharmaceutical University, Shenyang 110016, PR China. J Ethnopharmacol. 2007 May 22;111(3):613-8.
17. Yu HS, Lee SY, Jang CG. Involvement of 5-HT1A and GABAA receptors in the anxiolytic-like effects of Cinnamomum cassia in mice. Department of Pharmacology, College of Pharmacy, Sungkyunkwan University, Suwon, Republic of Korea. Pharmacol Biochem Behav. 2007 May;87(1):164-70.
18. Ohta H., Matsumoto K., Shimizu M. & Watanabe H.Paeoniflorin attenuates learning impairment of aged rats in operant brightness discrimination task. *Pharmacol Biochem Behav.* 1994, 49(1): 213-217.
19. Heo HJ, Park YJ, Suh YM, Choi SJ, Kim MJ, Cho HY, Chang YJ, Hong B, Kim HK, Kim E, Kim CJ, Kim BG, Shin DH. Effects of oleamide on choline acetyltransferase and cognitive activities. Biosci Biotechnol Biochem. 2003 Jun;67(6):1284-91.
20. Chu, DT. et al. Immunotherapy with Chinese medicinal herbs: immune restoration of local xenogenetic graft-versus-host reaction in cancer patients by fractionated astragalus membranaceus in vitro. *Journal of Clinical & Laboratory Immunology*. 25(3):119-23, Mar. 1988.
21. Sun, Y. et al. Immune restoration and/or augmentation of local graft versus host reaction by traditional Chinese medicinal herbs. *Cancer*. 52(1):70-3, July 1, 1983.
22. Sun, Y. et al. Preliminary observations on the effects of the Chinese medicinal herbs astragalus membranaceus and Ganoderma lucidum on lymphocyte blastogenic responses. *Journal of Biological Response Modifiers*. 2(3):227-37, 1983.
23. *Shan Xi Yi Yao Za Zhi* (Shanxi Journal of Medicine and Herbology), 1974; 5-6:57.
24. *Biol Pharm Bull*, 1977; 20(11)-1178-82.
25. Shao BM, Xu W, Dai H, Tu P, Li Z, Gao XM. A study on the immune receptors for polysaccharides from the roots of Astragalus membranaceus, a Chinese medicinal herb. Department of Immunology, School of Basic Medical Science, Peking University Health Science Center, Beijing, China. Biochem Biophys Res Commun. 2004 Aug 6;320(4):1103-11.
26. *Jun Shi Yi Xue Jian Xun* (Military Medicine Notes), 1977; 2:5.
27. *Xin Yi Yao Xue Za Zhi* (New Journal of Medicine and Herbology), 1979; 6:60.
28. *Zhong Yao Xue* (Chinese Herbology), 1998; 759:766.
29. *Zhong Hua Yi Xue Za Zhi* (Chinese Journal of Medicine), 1978; 17(8):87.
30. *Zhong Hua Yi Xue Za Zhi* (Chinese Journal of Medicine), 1974; (5):275.
31. *Guang Dong Zhong Yi* (Guangdong Chinese Medicine), 1962; 5:1.
32. *Zhong Yao Tong Bao* (Journal of Chinese Herbology), 1986; 11(10):55.
33. Song J, Meng L, Li S, Qu L, Li X. A combination of Chinese herbs, Astragalus membranaceus var. mongholicus and Angelica sinensis, improved renal microvascular insufficiency in 5/6 nephrectomized rats. Renal Division, Department of Medicine, Peking University First Hospital, Beijing 100034, PR China. Vascul Pharmacol. 2009 May-Jun;50(5-6):185-93.
34. Meng L, Qu L, Tang J, Cai SQ, Wang H, Li X. A combination of Chinese herbs, Astragalus membranaceus var. mongholicus and Angelica sinensis, enhanced nitric oxide production in obstructed rat kidney. Renal Division, Department of Medicine, Peking University First Hospital, Beijing 100034 PR. China. Vascul Pharmacol. 2007 Aug-Sep;47(2-3):174-83.
35. Yang MH, Yoon KD, Chin YW, Park JH, Kim SH, Kim YC, Kim J. Neuroprotective effects of Dioscorea opposita on scopolamine-induced memory impairment in in vivo behavioral tests and in vitro assays. College of Pharmacy and Research Institute of Pharmaceutical Science, Seoul National University, Seoul, Republic of Korea. J Ethnopharmacol. 2009 Jan 12;121(1):130-4.
36. Cheng CY, Ho TY, Lee EJ, Su SY, Tang NY, Hsieh CL. Ferulic acid reduces cerebral infarct through its antioxidative and anti-inflammatory effects following transient focal cerebral ischemia in rats. Am J Chin Med. 2008; 36(6):1105-19.
37. Song JX, Lin X, Wong RN, Sze SC, Tong Y, Shaw PC, Zhang YB. Protective effects of dibenzocyclooctadiene lignans from Schisandra chinensis against beta-amyloid and homocysteine neurotoxicity in PC12 cells. The School of Chinese Medicine, LKS Faculty of Medicine, The University of Hong Kong, Pokfulam, Hong Kong SAR, China. Phytother Res. 2011 Mar;25(3):435-43. doi: 10.1002/ptr.3269.

Kidney DTX™

CLINICAL APPLICATIONS

- **Chronic nephritic syndrome** (nephritis, glomerulonephritis)
- **Chronic nephrotic syndrome** (nephropathy)
- **Chronic kidney disease** with signs and symptoms such as proteinuria, edema, soreness of the lower back, fatigue, emaciation, flabby tongue, greasy tongue coating, deep, thready or wiry pulse
- Note: This formula is ***not*** recommended for acute kidney disorders.

WESTERN THERAPEUTIC ACTIONS

- Nephroprotective benefit to restore the normal filtration and excretion functions of the kidney
- Nephroprotective effect to reduce the presence of protein and blood in the urine
- Antifibrotic activity to improve ischemic microvasculature and attenuate interstitial fibrosis
- Diuretic effect to increase urine output and eliminate water accumulation

CHINESE THERAPEUTIC ACTIONS

- Dispels dampness
- Tonifies Kidney yin
- Tonifies qi

DOSAGE

Take 3 to 4 capsules three times daily with warm water. For maximum effectiveness, take the herbs on an empty stomach. This formula is safe for long-term use.

INGREDIENTS

Bai Mao Gen (Rhizoma Imperatae)
Du Zhong (Cortex Eucommiae)
Fu Ling (Poria)
Huang Bo (Cortex Phellodendri Chinensis)
Huang Qi (Radix Astragali)
Jin Ying Zi (Fructus Rosae Laevigatae)
Lu Xian Cao (Herba Pyrolae)
Mu Li (Concha Ostreae)
Shan Zhu Yu (Fructus Corni)
Shi Wei (Folium Pyrrosiae)

BACKGROUND

Chronic nephritic syndrome and chronic nephrotic syndromes are two common kidney disorders characterized by the presence of blood (hematuria) and protein (proteinuria), respectively. Though the exact pathophysiology differs, these two syndromes do have considerable clinical overlap, and may occur separately or concurrently. Causes of these kidney disorders include heredity, infection (bacterial, viral and others), immunologic (autoimmune disorder), and drug-induced (i.e., gentamicin, tobramycin, NSAIDs). Optimal treatment requires proper management of the signs and symptoms, and identification and eliminate of the cause if possible.

FORMULA EXPLANATION

Chronic nephritic syndrome and chronic nephrotic syndrome in traditional Chinese medicine are considered a complicated disease as it involves both excess and deficiency. The excess refers to the clinical manifestation of the illness, which is the accumulation of dampness and turbidity in the lower *jiao*. The deficiency refers to the underlying cause, which are Kidney qi and yin deficiencies. Most patients are extremely Kidney deficient. Since Kidney is the organ that stores *jing* (essence), deficiency of the Kidney leads to its inability to retain the *jing* (essence). As a result, the *jing* (essence) is leaked out from the body in the form of serum protein, albumin, immunoglobulins, red blood cells, blood and trace minerals.

To treat patients with chronic nephritic syndrome and chronic nephrotic syndrome, ***Kidney DTX*** uses herbs to tonify the deficiency and drain the excess. *Huang Qi* (Radix Astragali) tonifies qi and regulates water metabolism in the body to reduce edema. *Shan Zhu Yu* (Fructus Corni) is sour, which consolidates Kidney *jing* (essence). It also has an excellent effect to tonify Kidney yin and *jing* (essence). *Du Zhong* (Cortex Eucommiae) tonifies the Kidney yang and strengthens the back to relieve soreness. *Shi Wei* (Folium Pyrrosiae) dispels dampness and stops bleeding in the urine. *Lu Xian Cao* (Herba Pyrolae) further helps to stop bleeding. *Huang Bo* (Cortex Phellodendri Chinensis) clears deficiency heat from the Kidney and reduces chronic inflammation. *Fu Ling* (Poria) and *Bai Mao Gen* (Rhizoma Imperatae) dispel dampness and promote urination to relieve edema. *Bai Mao Gen* (Rhizoma Imperatae) is frequently used for *lin zheng* (dysuria syndrome) to relieve blood in the urine. *Fu Ling* (Poria) and *Bai Mao Gen* (Rhizoma Imperatae) also help *Huang Bo* (Cortex Phellodendri Chinensis) to clear damp-heat in the lower *jiao* to dispel creatinine and blood urea nitrogen in the blood. *Mu Li* (Concha Ostreae) and *Jin Ying Zi* (Fructus Rosae Laevigatae) are astringent herbs used to prevent loss of Kidney *jing* (essence) through the urine. They also help to keep protein in the body and prevent the loss of protein and red blood cells through urine.

Kidney DTX is an excellent formula to treat kidney disorder because it tonifies without causing stagnation and sedates without injuring the body's constitution. Furthermore, it contains herbs to treat the cause and the symptoms of the illness, thereby offering both immediate and long-term therapeutic benefits.

CAUTIONS & CONTRAINDICATIONS

- ***Kidney DTX*** is ***not*** suitable for acute kidney disorders. Such conditions should be referred to a medical doctor for immediate treatment.
- This formula is contraindicated during pregnancy and nursing.

Kidney DTX™

CLINICAL NOTES

- To effectively treat kidney disorder, it is extremely important to identify and eliminate the cause(s). Disease conditions that are known to increase the risk and acceleration of kidney disorders, such as diabetes and lupus, must be properly controlled. Furthermore, certain drugs, toxins and heavy metals are known to cause kidney damage, and must be avoided as well. Examples of drugs include certain antibiotics, analgesics, and antiepileptics. Examples of environmental toxins include chemical solvents, biological agents, herbicides and pesticides. Examples of heavy metals include lead and cadmium. Avoidance of such factors will significantly improve both short- and long-term prognosis.
- It is prudent to monitor progress objectively with urine analysis. Such laboratory tests will confirm the effectiveness of the treatment and assist in the long-term treatment strategy.

Pulse Diagnosis by Dr. Jimmy Wei-Yen Chang:

- **Nephrotic syndrome and proteinuria** characterized by Kidney yang deficiency: deep, stagnating, and weak pulse on the left *chi*.
- **Chronic nephritis** characterized by Kidney fire: the brachial pulse is deep, thick, big, forceful, and hard. The patient may also present with a superficial, forceful, hard, *gu* pulse on the right *cun* and a deep, *chong* pulse on the right *chi*. *Gu* refers to the jump of a pulse when both the upward and downward beat of the pulse can be felt. *Chong* pulse is a long, thick, straight pulse that extends proximally to the *chi* position; it is one of the eight extra meridian pulses.

SUPPLEMENTARY FORMULAS

- For accumulation of environmental pollutant, chemical compounds, and other toxins in the body, add ***Herbal DTX***.
- For edema and water accumulation, add ***Herbal DRX***.
- For unknown cause of symptoms with blood stagnation in patients with excess condition, add ***Circulation (SJ)***.
- For excess fire in the body, add ***Gardenia Complex***.
- For *wei* (defensive) *qi* deficiency and frequent infections, add ***Immune +***.
- For dry mouth, deficiency heat symptoms, tinnitus or dizziness, add ***Nourish*** or ***Nourish (Fluids)***.
- For Kidney yang deficiency with frequent urination especially at night, soreness, weakness and coldness of the lower back and knees, add ***Kidney Tonic (Yang)***.
- For Spleen qi deficiency with poor appetite, add ***GI Tonic***.
- For high blood pressure, add ***Gastrodia Complex***.
- With compromised liver function, add ***Liver DTX***.
- With bleeding, add ***Notoginseng 9***.
- To detox the colon, add ***GI DTX***.

ACUPUNCTURE TREATMENT

Traditional Points:

- *Sanyinjiao* (SP 6), *Zhigou* (TH 6), *Shuifen* (CV 9), *Guanyuan* (CV 4), *Feishu* (BL 13), *Hegu* (LI 4), *Zhongji* (CV 3), *Yinlingquan* (SP 9), *Zusanli* (ST 36)

Classic Master Tung's Points:

- **Nephritis (chronic):** *Tianhuangfu [Shenguan]* (T 77.18), *Dihuang* (T 77.19), *Renhuang* (T 77.21), *Huoying* (T 66.03), *Tongshen* (T 88.09), *Houzhui* (T 44.02), *Shouying* (T 44.03), *Shuixiang* (T 66.14), *Shuixian* (T 66.15), *Tongwei* (T 88.10), *Tongbei* (T 88.11)
- **Pyelonephritis:** *Shuijin* (T 1010.20), *Shuitong* (T 1010.19), *Wanshunyi* (T 22.08), *Wanshuner* (T 22.09), *Tongshen* (T 88.09), *Tongguan* (T 88.01), *Houzhui* (T 44.02), *Shouying* (T 44.03)
- **Proteinuria:** *Tongshen* (T 88.09), *Tongwei* (T 88.10), *Tianhuang* (T 77.17), *Dihuang* (T 77.19), *Renhuang* (T 77.21), *Shuijin* (T 1010.20), *Shuitong* (T 1010.19), *Shuixiang* (T 66.14), *Shuixian* (T 66.15), *Tongbei* (T 88.11)

Master Tung's Points by Dr. Chuan-Min Wang:

- **Chronic nephritis, proteinuria, elevated creatinine, toxin in the Kidney:** *Tianhuang* (T 77.17), *Dihuang* (T 77.19), *Renhuang* (T 77.21)

Balance Method by Dr. Richard Tan:

- Left side: *Shenmen* (HT 7), *Lingdao* (HT 4), *Chize* (LU 5), *Feiyang* (BL 58), *Weizhong* (BL 40)
- Right side: *Zhubin* (KI 9), *Yingu* (KI 10), *Taichong* (LR 3), *Sanyangluo* (TH 8), Kidney point on the ear, *Linggu* (T 22.05).
- Left and right sides can be alternated from treatment to treatment.

Ear Acupuncture:

- Kidney and surrounding tender points. Leave needles in for four to six hours. Needle once a day for seven days. Stop all diuretic medications while under ear acupuncture therapy.

Auricular Medicine by Dr. Li-Chun Huang:

- **Nephritis:** Kidney, Nephritis Point, Endocrine, Adrenal Gland, Sympathetic, Spleen, *San Jiao*, Allergic Area, Coronary Vascular Subcortex. Bleed Ear Apex.
- **Pyelonephritis:** Kidney, Bladder, Urethra, Spleen, *San Jiao*, Adrenal Gland, Endocrine, Allergic Area. Bleed Ear Apex.

NUTRITION

- Intake of salt should be restricted to 1 to 2 grams per day, as excessive presence of salt will increase the severity of edema.
- Diet with restricted protein is recommended to reduce proteinuria and lower the stress on the kidneys. A high protein diet is discouraged since it accelerates the deterioration of kidney disease by increasing the intraglomerular pressure and urinary protein excretion.
- Vitamin D supplementation is encouraged in patients with clinical or biochemical evidence of vitamin D deficiency.
- Lotus nodes are recommended to be included in the diet.
- Do not eat sour and spicy foods.

Kidney DTX ™

The Tao of Nutrition by Dr. Maoshing Ni and Cathy McNease:

- **Nephritis (acute)**
  - Recommendations: black beans, mung beans, azuki beans, pearl barley, garlic, carp, winter melon, watermelon, watermelon rind, corn-silk, sweet rice, lotus root, and water chestnuts.
  - Cook soup with azuki beans, winter melon rind, watermelon rind and corn silk. Drink at least 3 to 4 times daily.
  - Make tea from lotus root; drink four large glasses daily.
  - Cook rice porridge with pearl barley, black beans, and water chestnuts.
  - Make juice from carrots, celery, cucumbers, and squash.
  - Avoid stimulating (sour, spicy, salty) foods, alcohol, caffeine, smoking, overworking, and high protein foods.
- **Nephritis (chronic)**
  - Recommendations: ginger, Chinese black dates, sweet rice, soybeans, winter melon, carp, yams, mung beans, and black beans.
  - Make rice porridge and add ginger, cinnamon, and Chinese black dates. Eat for breakfast and dinner.
  - Cook rice porridge with yams and eat for breakfast and dinner.
  - Steam together crab, garlic, and white wine. Eat once daily for fifteen days.
  - Avoid stimulating (sour, spicy, salty) foods, alcohol, caffeine, smoking, overworking, and high protein foods.

LIFESTYLE INSTRUCTIONS

- Adequate rest is essential to recovery. Strenuous exercise increases the stress of the kidneys and accelerates their deterioration.
- To minimize stress on the kidneys, encourage elimination of toxins through the lungs, skin, and bowel. Practice breathing exercises, ensure regular bowel movements, and take hot baths.
- Avoid smoking and drinking.

CASE STUDIES

- C.P., a 63-year-old female, presented with multiple symptoms including low energy, pain located in the areas of the elbow, hip, back, and neck. Additional symptoms included the face and other parts of the body being puffy. Objective findings were BUN level of 53.0 mg/dL, creatinine level of 2.6 mg/dL, and calcium level of 12 mg/dL. The practitioner diagnosed this condition as Kidney yin deficiency with dampness, along with Kidney failure at stage three. She was prescribed ***Kidney DTX*** and was advised to change her diet to a low protein diet. After four months of taking the herbs, her BUN level became normal, the creatinine level dropped but were still slightly high, and the calcium level became normal. The Western doctors involved with treating this patient were amazed at the change in values of BUN and creatinine as a result of the herbs. They had commented that they had never seen this happen before. Submitted by T. S. Tehachapi, California.
- W.P., a 45-year-old female, presented with pain in the kidney and liver areas. It was also noted that the patient had a history of Kidney infection and pancreatitis. She was also experiencing anxiety and depression, in regards to relationship issues. Pulse was weak and slightly slippery, and tongue was pale with a long center fissure. The practitioner diagnosed this condition as Liver qi stagnation with heat disturbing the *shen* (spirit), and toxins in the Kidney. Upon diagnosis the patient was prescribed ***Shine*** and ***Kidney DTX***. Within four weeks of taking the herbs the patient had noticed her mood was stable and was no longer experiencing pain in the liver and kidney areas. The patient had also made lifestyle changes in her diet and received acupuncture one time a week. Submitted by T.W., Perrysburg, Ohio.
- L.T., a 64-year-old female, presented with the beginning of kidney declination due to taking both her anti-inflammatories and high blood pressure medications for 20 years. Blood pressure was 130/80 mmHg and her heart beat was 72 beats per minute. The TCM diagnosis was Kidney and Liver yin deficiencies; the Western diagnosis was kidney failure (beginning stage). ***Kidney DTX*** was prescribed and directed to take for nine months. After going and seeing a Western doctor and being offered minimal help with a negative outlook, the patient lived an additional three years, which had been more than the Western doctor had predicted. Submitted by J.L., San Diego, California.
- An 82-year-old male has been living with type 2 diabetes for the past 40 years, with hypertension developing in the last 10 years and kidney function degradation in the last six years. These conditions were managed by various Western Medicine medications. In January 2013, patient's kidney function degraded significantly to the point of near renal failure, with blood urea nitrogen (BUN) level rising to 88 mg/dL (normal range 7 to 21 mg/dL) and creatinine level rising to 2.1 mg/dL (normal range 0.6 to 1.30 mg/dL). The patient was consequently hospitalized for a week in late January and again in late February. After being discharged from the hospital in late February 2013, the patient started to be administered with two doses of ***Kidney DTX*** on a daily basis with each dose containing 5 capsules. By late March 2013, the BUN level has been steadily reduced to 36 mg/dL and creatinine level has also been reduced to 1.46 mg/dL. The patient also reported better stamina and overall energy level, and without additional changes to the Western medicine hypertension medications, average systolic blood pressure has also reduced from 180 mm Hg to 160 mm Hg. Submitted by T.C., Hacienda Heights, California.
- A 40-year-old female presented with slow mental functions. She answered questions slowly, and reported hot flashes, acid reflux after eating spicy foods, and a history of alcoholism and smoking. Objective findings revealed that her ankles were slightly swollen. The TCM diagnosis was toxic damp-heat accumulation with yin deficiency. ***Kidney DTX*** was prescribed for one month with *Wu Pi Yin* (Five-Peel Decoction) and *Jia Wei Xiao Yao San* (Augmented Rambling Powder). After one month, the swelling in her legs was down and the woman felt less brain fog. She wanted to drink more water and less alcohol. After six months of

Kidney DTX ™

herbal, acupuncture and homeopathic treatment, she felt better all around. Submitted by M.C., Sarasota, Florida.

- A 51-years-old male had chronic recurrent nephritis for six years. In the past six months, the patient reported frequent urination at night (four to five times), soreness and pain of the lower back, tinnitus in both ears, fatigue, pale red and flabby tongue with teethmarks, white greasy tongue coat, and deep thready pulse. Objective tests confirmed the presence of protein (++) in the urine. The patient was diagnosed as qi and yin deficiencies of the Kidney with accumulation of dampness. After 50 days of herbal treatment, the patient reported a reduction of urination at night from four to five times down to one to two times, improvement of low back pain, reduction of tinnitus in the ears, and increased energy levels. Furthermore, urine analysis was negative for protein in three consecutive tests. The treatment was concluded to be effective. Submitted by W.J., Zhejiang, China.

PHARMACOLOGICAL AND CLINICAL RESEARCH

Kidney DTX is a carefully crafted formula that treats chronic and generalized kidney disorders in which the filtering and excretion functions are compromised. Compromised kidney function is often evident with the presence of protein, blood cells, and fat in the urine. In addition, chronic nephritic syndrome and chronic nephrotic syndrome will also cause edema, especially in the lower parts of the body. The causes for such kidney disorders vary and may include conditions such as diabetes, lupus, use of certain drugs, exposure to certain toxins, and chronic heavy metal poisoning. Therefore, optimal treatment requires comprehensive herbal therapy with appropriate adjustments in both lifestyle and dietary habits. ***Kidney DTX*** is a comprehensive formula with many herbs that address all aspects of chronic and generalized kidney disorders. Herbs in ***Kidney DTX*** have been shown to restore normal functions of the kidneys, reduce protein in the urine, promote normal urination, and eliminate edema.

Huang Qi (Radix Astragali) is used as the main herb in this formula, as it has a remarkable effect to treat kidney-related disorders, such as proteinuria, nephritis, nephropathy and glomerulonephritis. Pharmacologically, *Huang Qi* (Radix Astragali) exerts the nephroprotective effect by reducing fasting blood glucose and albuminuria levels, in reversing the glomerular hyperfiltration state, and in ameliorating the pathological changes of early diabetic nephropathy.[1] Administration of *Huang Qi* (Radix Astragali) via injection is associated with numerous benefits in patients with diabetic nephropathy, such as nephroprotective effect (BUN, SCr, CCr and urine protein) and systemic state improvement (serum albumin level).[2] One study showed that the oral use of *Huang Qi* (Radix Astragali) is effective to decrease the amount of protein present in urine.[3] Clinically, studies have also shown that *Huang Qi* (Radix Astragali) is effective in treating nephritis and glomerulonephritis by increasing the volume of urine and the elimination of chloride and ammonia.[4,5] In one clinical trial, use of *Huang Qi* (Radix Astragali) twice daily for 15 to 90 days was effective in treating 16 out of 20 patients with nephritis. Most patients also reported symptomatic improvement as well as a decrease of protein in the urine.[6] Furthermore, in another clinical study with 56 patients with chronic glomerulonephritis, use of *Huang Qi* (Radix Astragali) by intramuscular injection for one month had a 61.7% effective rate in improving the function of the kidneys and reducing the amount of protein in the urine.[7] All these clinical results clearly indicate that the use of *Huang Qi* (Radix Astragali) is effective in treating kidney disorders.

Huang Qi (Radix Astragali) is frequently used with other herbs for synergistic effect to treat various kidney disorders. In one study, the decoction of *Huang Qi* (Radix Astragali) and *Dang Gui* (Radix Angelicae Sinensis) shows marked effect to treat progressive chronic kidney disease by reducing proteinuria, decreasing the loss of capillaries, and improving microstructure dysfunction.[8] The nephroprotective effect is attributed in part to the antifibrotic activity of these two herbs to improve ischemic microvasculature and attenuate interstitial fibrosis.[9] In another study, twenty-one patients with type II diabetes with micro-albuminuria were treated with the decoction of *Huang Qi* (Radix Astragali) and *Chuan Xiong* (Rhizoma Chuanxiong) by mouth at 150 mL daily. After six months, there was a significant decrease of urinary albumin excretion and an improvement of endothelial dysfunction. The mechanism of action may relate with the therapeutic effects of herbs on anti-inflammation, antioxidation, and alleviation of the hypo-fibrinolytic/pro-thrombotic state.[10] Lastly, one study found that the combination of *Huang Qi* (Radix Astragali) and *Lu Xian Cao* (Herba Pyrolae) was effective in preventing drug-induced kidney and ear damages.[11]

Kidney DTX also contains herbs with marked diuretic effects since edema is a common complication of kidney disorder. *Bai Mao Gen* (Rhizoma Imperatae) has been shown to have a marked diuretic effect, especially if taken continuously for five to ten days.[12] *Bai Mao Gen* (Rhizoma Imperatae) has also been used in numerous formulas to successfully treat acute nephritis in adults and children.[13,14] *Fu Ling* (Poria) also has a marked diuretic effect to increase urine output.[15] In one clinical study, 30 patients with edema were treated with a preparation of *Fu Ling* (Poria) three times daily for seven days, with marked effectiveness in 23 cases and moderate effects in 7 cases.[16] Lastly, the extract of *Shan Zhu Yu* (Fructus Corni) has been shown to induce diuresis, and that this herb may be beneficial for the prevention and treatment of diabetic nephropathy.[17,18]

In summary, ***Kidney DTX*** is formulated with many herbs that have marked effects to treat kidney disorders, such as proteinuria, nephritis, nephropathy and glomerulonephritis. These herbs have been shown to protect the kidney, regulate water circulation, eliminate edema, reduce the presence of protein in the urine, and restore the normal filtration and excretion function of the kidney.

Kidney DTX™

COMPARATIVE ANALYSIS

Kidney diseases, such as chronic nephritic syndrome, chronic nephrotic syndrome and kidney failure, are serious and extremely complicated diseases. There are many potential causes of kidney diseases, and therefore, treatments vary depending on the exact etiology and prognosis. If the conditions continue to deteriorate, kidney dialysis, and eventually kidney transplant may become necessary. Kidney dialysis and transplant are generally considered to be the last options, but they do prolong life and offer additional hope.

Treatment of kidney diseases is a very challenging and complicated matter. However, many herbs have been shown to have a marked effect to relieve stress for the kidney by promoting elimination of water and other unwanted substances. Furthermore, certain herbs have been shown to restore normal functions of the kidney, thereby offering hope of a life free from kidney dialysis and kidney transplant. However, herbs are generally only effective for early- to mid-stage of kidney diseases, and only for those with mild to moderate severity. Furthermore, herbs are more suitable for chronic kidney diseases, and are not recommended for acute kidney failure. Nonetheless, for patients on kidney dialysis who have no options other than kidney transplant, use of herbal therapy offers one additional hope and option.

Kidney diseases are very challenging for both Western and traditional Chinese medicine. Both drugs and herbs offer hope to reverse the illness, especially in early stages of kidney diseases with mild to moderate severity. If the patient is already on kidney dialysis, it may still be worthwhile to explore herbal therapy, as there is a small possibility of recovery. When all else fails, kidney transplant is the final option.

References

1. Zhang J, Xie X, Li C, Fu P. Systematic review of the renal protective effect of Astragalus membranaceus (root) on diabetic nephropathy in animal models. Department of Nephrology, West China Hospital of Sichuan University, Chengdu 610041, China. J Ethnopharmacol. 2009 Nov 12;126(2):189-96.
2. Li M, Wang W, Xue J, Gu Y, Lin S. Meta-analysis of the clinical value of Astragalus membranaceus in diabetic nephropathy. Division of Nephrology, Huashan Hospital, Fudan University, Shanghai, China. J Ethnopharmacol. 2010 Oct 13.
3. *Chinese Convention on Biophysiology, 2nd Annual Convention*, 1963; 63.
4. *Zhong Hua Nei Ke Xue Za Zhi* (Journal of Chinese Internal Medicine), 1986; 25(4):222.
5. *Jiang Su Yi Xue* (Jiangsu Medical Journal), 1989; 15(11):12.
6. *Hei Long Jiang Zhong Yi Yao* (Heilongjiang Chinese Medicine and Herbology), 1982; 1:39.
7. *Zhong Xi Yi Jie He Za Zhi* (Journal of Integrated Chinese and Western Medicine), 1987; 7:403.
8. Song J, Meng L, Li S, Qu L, Li X. A combination of Chinese herbs, Astragalus membranaceus var. mongholicus and Angelica sinensis, improved renal microvascular insufficiency in 5/6 nephrectomized rats. Renal Division, Department of Medicine, Peking University First Hospital, Beijing 100034, PR China. Vascul Pharmacol. 2009 May-Jun;50(5-6):185-93.
9. Meng L, Qu L, Tang J, Cai SQ, Wang H, Li X. A combination of Chinese herbs, Astragalus membranaceus var. mongholicus and Angelica sinensis, enhanced nitric oxide production in obstructed rat kidney. Renal Division, Department of Medicine, Peking University First Hospital, Beijing 100034 PR. China. Vascul Pharmacol. 2007 Aug-Sep;47(2-3):174-83.
10. Lu ZM, Yu YR, Tang H, Zhang XX. The protective effects of Radix Astragali and Rhizoma Ligustici chuanxiong on endothelial dysfunction in type 2 diabetic patients with microalbuminuria. Sichuan Da Xue Xue Bao Yi Xue Ban. 2005 Jul;36(4):529-32.
11. Xuan, W., Dong, M., and Dong, M. *Annals of Otology, Rhinology and Laryngology*, May 1995; vol. 104(5): 374-80).
12. *Ren Min Wei Sheng Chu Ban She* (Journal of People's Public Health), 1983; 327.
13. *Shan Xi Zhong Yi* (Shanxi Chinese Medicine), 1986; (3):347.
14. *Yun Nan Zhong Yi Za Zhi* (Yunan Journal of Chinese Medicine), 1986; (4):19.
15. *Chang Yong Zhong Yao Cheng Fen Yu Yao Li Shou Ce* (A Handbook of the Composition and Pharmacology of Common Chinese Drugs), 1994; 1383:1391.
16. *Shang Hai Zhong Yi Yao Za Zhi* (Shanghai Journal of Chinese Medicine and Herbology), 1986; 8:25.
17. *Chang Yong Zhong Yao Cheng Fen Yu Yao Li Shou Ce* (A Handbook of the Composition and Pharmacology of Common Chinese Drugs), 1994, 368:376.
18. Xu H.Q. & Hao H.P. () Effects of iridoid total glycoside from *Cornus officinalis* on prevention of glomerular overexpression of transforming growth factor beta 1 and matrixes in an experimental diabetes model. *Biol Pharm Bull.* 2004, 27(7): 1014-1018.

Kidney Tonic (Yang)™

CLINICAL APPLICATIONS

- **Kidney yang deficiency** with diminished *ming men* (life gate) fire
- Clinical signs and symptoms: low energy and lethargy, aversion to cold, cold extremities, intolerance to cold, urinary incontinence, loose stools, diarrhea, early morning diarrhea, weakness of the lower back and knees, edema of the legs
- Clinical applications: infertility, impotence, spermatorrhea, frequent urination, incontinence, nephrotic syndrome, chronic nephritis, diabetes mellitus, bronchial asthma, sciatica, lumbago, and hypertrophic myelitis

WESTERN THERAPEUTIC ACTIONS

- Antiaging functions to stop premature or accelerated aging
- Improves genitourinary functions
- Nephroprotective effect to treat kidney disorders
- Adaptogenic effect to alleviate mental stress and physical stress
- Analgesic effect to alleviate musculoskeletal aches and pains

CHINESE THERAPEUTIC ACTIONS

- Warms and tonifies Kidney yang
- Replenishes *jing* (essence) and tonifies blood

DOSAGE

Take 3 to 4 capsules three times daily. Dosage can be increased up to 6 to 8 capsules three times daily as needed to treat more severe symptoms.

INGREDIENTS

Dang Gui (Radix Angelicae Sinensis)
Du Zhong (Cortex Eucommiae)
Fu Zi (Radix Aconiti Lateralis Praeparata)
Jiu Cai Zi (Semen Allii Tuberosi)
Lu Jiao Shuang (Cornu Cervi Degelatinatum)
Rou Gui (Cortex Cinnamomi)
Shan Yao (Rhizoma Dioscoreae)
Shan Zhu Yu (Fructus Corni)
Shu Di Huang (Radix Rehmanniae Praeparata)
Suo Yang (Herba Cynomorii)
Tu Si Zi (Semen Cuscutae)
Zhi Gan Cao (Radix et Rhizoma Glycyrrhizae Praeparata cum Melle)

BACKGROUND

The function of Kidney in traditional Chinese medicine is closely related to the physiology of the genitourinary system in Western medicine. In Western medicine, genitourinary disorders include a wide variety of disorders, such as infertility, low libido, sexual dysfunction, increased urinary frequency, polyuria, urinary incontinence, nephrotic syndrome, and chronic nephritis. In traditional Chinese medicine, these disorders are usually diagnosed as Kidney yang deficiency, Kidney yin deficiency, or both.

FORMULA EXPLANATION

Kidney Tonic (Yang) is designed to treat Kidney yang deficiency. Chronic illness may consume the yang qi of the body, causing low energy and lethargy. Deficiency of the Kidney yang may lead to internal coldness, resulting in aversion to cold and cold extremities. In males, Kidney yang deficiency often leads to sexual and reproductive disorders, such as impotence, premature ejaculation, spermatorrhea, and low sperm count. Kidney yang deficiency can also cause deficiency of the urinary function of the body, leading to frequent urination and urinary incontinence. Kidney yang deficiency may impair its functions to regulate water metabolism, leading to edema of the lower legs and loose stools. Because the kidney is located in the low back, Kidney deficiency may cause weakness of the lower back and knees.

Kidney Tonic (Yang) has *Rou Gui* (Cortex Cinnamomi), *Fu Zi* (Radix Aconiti Lateralis Praeparata), *Suo Yang* (Herba Cynomorii), *Jiu Cai Zi* (Semen Allii Tuberosi), and *Lu Jiao Shuang* (Cornu Cervi Degelatinatum) to warm the Kidney yang and raise the *ming men* (life gate) fire. *Du Zhong* (Cortex Eucommiae) enhances the Kidney to treat low back pain and soreness associated with yang deficiency. According to the yin-yang theory of mutual dependence, in order to effectively tonify the Kidney yang, the Kidney yin also needs to be nourished. Therefore, this formula also has *Shu Di Huang* (Radix Rehmanniae Praeparata), *Shan Zhu Yu* (Fructus Corni), *Shan Yao* (Rhizoma Dioscoreae), and *Tu Si Zi* (Semen Cuscutae) to nourish the yin and replenish *jing* (essence). *Dang Gui* (Radix Angelicae Sinensis) tonifies blood and nourishes the Liver. *Zhi Gan Cao* (Radix et Rhizoma Glycyrrhizae Praeparata cum Melle) harmonizes the entire formula.

In conclusion, ***Kidney Tonic (Yang)*** tonifies Kidney yang and treat related biomedical disorders.

CAUTIONS & CONTRAINDICATIONS

- This formula is contraindicated in cases of Kidney deficiency with dampness accumulation.
- This herbal formula contains herbs that invigorate blood circulation, such as *Dang Gui* (Radix Angelicae Sinensis). Therefore, patients who are on anticoagulant or antiplatelet therapies, such as Coumadin (warfarin), should use this formula with caution, or not at all, as there may be a higher risk of bleeding and bruising.[1,2,3]
- Patients who wear a pacemaker, or individuals who take anti-arrhythmic drugs [i.e., Tambocor (flecainide) and Procanbid (procainamide)] or cardiac glycosides [i.e., Lanoxin (digoxin)], should not take this formula. *Fu Zi* (Radix Aconiti Lateralis Praeparata) may interact with these drugs by affecting the rhythm and potentiating the contractile strength of the heart.[4]

CLINICAL NOTES

- This formula is relatively warm. It should be taken as needed to treat Kidney yang deficient conditions. However, once the

Kidney Tonic (Yang)™

desired effect is achieved, the dose should be lowered or the formula may be discontinued.

Pulse Diagnosis by Dr. Jimmy Wei-Yen Chang:

- **Urinary dysfunction** due to Kidney yang deficiency: deep and weak pulse on the right *chi*.
- **Reproductive dysfunction** due to Kidney yang deficiency: weak pulse on the left *chi*.

SUPPLEMENTARY FORMULAS

- With Kidney yin deficiency, add ***Kidney Tonic (Yin)***.
- For diarrhea due to Spleen qi and Kidney yang deficiency, add ***GI Tonic***.
- For extreme low energy, add ***Imperial Tonic***.
- For impotence or spermatorrhea, add ***Vitality***.
- For male infertility, add ***Vital Essence***.
- For female infertility, add ***Blossom (Phase 1-4)***.
- For edema, add ***Herbal DRX***.
- For hypothyroidism, add ***Thyro-forte***.
- For back pain, add ***Back Support (CR)***.
- For leg pain, add ***Knee & Ankle (CR)***.
- For low adrenal functions, add ***Adrenal +***.
- For asthma, add ***Cordyceps 3*** or ***Respitrol (Deficient)***.
- For osteoporosis, add ***Osteo 8***.
- For forgetfulness, add ***Enhance Memory***.
- For vaginal dryness, add ***Balance Spring***.

ACUPUNCTURE TREATMENT

Traditional Points:

- *Shenshu* (BL 23), *Taixi* (KI 3), *Ganshu* (BL 18), *Pishu* (BL 20), *Geshu* (BL 17), *Guanyuan* (CV 4), *Qihai* (CV 6), *Mingmen* (GV 4).

Classic Master Tung's Points:

- **Diarrhea:** *Qimen* (T 33.01), *Qijiao* (T 33.02), *Qizheng* (T 33.03), *Sihuashang* (T 77.08), *Sihuazhong* (T 77.09), *Sihuaxia* (T 77.11), *Menjin* (T 66.05), *Tianhuang* (T 77.17), *Dihuang* (T 77.19), *Renhuang* (T 77.21)
- **Back soreness/weakness:** *Linggu* (T 22.05), *Chongzi* (T 22.01), *Chongxian* (T 22.02), *Wanshunyi* (T 22.08), *Wanshuner* (T 22.09), *Zhongbai* (T 22.06), *Zhengjin* (T 77.01), *Zhengzong* (T 77.02), *Zhongjiuli* (T 88.25), *Tongshen* (T 88.09), *Tongwei* (T 88.10), *Simashang* (T 88.18), *Simazhong* (T 88.17), *Simaxia* (T 88.19), *Shuijin* (T 1010.20), *Shuitong* (T 1010.19), *Chengshan* (BL 57), *Biyi* (T 1010.22), *Zhitong* (T 44.13)
- **Edema of the legs:** *Fuchang* (T 77.12), *Shuiqu* (T 66.09)
- **Infertility (female):** *Fuke* (T 11.24), *Huanchao* (T 11.06), *Tongshen* (T 88.09), *Tongbei* (T 88.11), *Tianhuang* (T 77.17), *Dihuang* (T 77.19), *Renhuang* (T 77.21), *Jiemeiyi* (T 88.04), *Jiemeier* (T 88.05), *Jiemeisan* (T 88.06), *Mufu* (T 88.38)*, *Tianhuang* (T 88.13), *Minghuang* (T 88.12), *Qihuang* (T 88.14). Moxa lower abdomen.
- **Infertility (male):** *Tianhuang* (T 77.17), *Dihuang* (T 77.19), *Renhuang* (T 77.21), *Tianhuang* (T 88.13), *Minghuang* (T 88.12), *Qihuang* (T 88.14), and Endocrine, Kidney and Testicle points on the ear. Moxa *du* (governing) channel on the back.
- **Urinary incontinence:** *Tianhuang* (T 77.17), *Dihuang* (T 77.19), *Renhuang* (T 77.21), *Tongshen* (T 88.09), *Tongwei* (T 88.10)
- **Impotence:** *Tianhuang* (T 77.17), *Dihuang* (T 77.19), *Renhuang* (T 77.21), *Tianhuang* (T 88.13), *Minghuang* (T 88.12), *Qihuang* (T 88.14), *Tongshen* (T 88.09), *Tongwei* (T 88.10), *Sanshen* (T 44.27)*. Bleed tender points on the Kidney area of the back from L1-L5 with cupping. Bleed before needling for best result. Moxa for 30 minutes the Kidney area on the back from L1-L5, Guanyuan (CV 4), and Zhongji (CV 3).
- **Spermatorrhea:** *Tianhuang* (T 77.17), *Dihuang* (T 77.19), *Renhuang* (T 77.21), *Tongshen* (T 88.09), *Tongwei* (T 88.10), *Shuijin* (T 1010.20), *Shuitong* (T 1010.19), *Tianhuangfu [Shenguan]* (T 77.18). Moxa *Guanyuan* (CV 4), *Zhongji* (CV 3), *Zhongshu* (GV 7).
- **Nephritis (chronic):** *Tianhuangfu [Shenguan]* (T 77.18), *Dihuang* (T 77.19), *Renhuang* (T 77.21), *Huoying* (T 66.03), *Tongshen* (T 88.09), *Houzhui* (T 44.02), *Shouying* (T 44.03), *Shuixiang* (T 66.14), *Shuixian* (T 66.15), *Tongwei* (T 88.10), *Tongbei* (T 88.11)

Master Tung's Points by Dr. Chuan-Min Wang:

- **Kidney yang deficiency:** *Tianhuangfu [shenguan]* (T 77.18), *Dihuang* (T 77.19), *Renhuang* (T 77.21)

Balance Method by Dr. Richard Tan:

- Bilateral: *Rangu* (KI 2), *Dazhong* (KI 4), *Fuliu* (KI 7)
- Left side: *Shenmen* (HT 7), *Shaohai* (HT 3), *Zulinqi* (GB 41), *Yanglingquan* (GB 34), *Weizhong* (BL 40), *Shugu* (BL 65)
- Right side: *Zhongzhu* (TH 3), Tianjing (TH 10), *Houxi* (SI 3), *Xiaohai* (SI 8), *Taixi* (KI 3), *Yingu* (KI 10)

Auricular Medicine by Dr. Li-Chun Huang:

- **Enuresis:** Bladder, Urethra, Ear Center, Pituitary
  - For nocturia, add Forehead and Exciting Point.
  - For enuresis due to trauma of spinal cord, add Lumbosacral Vertebral.
- **Urinary incontinence:** Urethra, Occiput, Lumbosacral, Liver Pituitary, Bladder, Nervous Subcortex
- **Kidney deficiency:** Kidney, Pituitary, Endocrine, Liver, Heart, Thalamus, Adrenal Gland
- **Raynaud's disease:** Sympathetic, Hot, Finger, Lesser Occipital Nerve, Large Auricular Nerve, Coronary Vascular Nerve

NUTRITION

- Increase intake of the following warm foods and fruits such as lamb, lychee, longan fruit and spices such as pepper, garlic, onions, basil, rosemary, cumin, fennel, cardamon, anise, leeks, chives, scallions, thyme, saffron, wormwood, mustard, chili pepper, and wasabi.

Kidney Tonic (Yang)™

- Avoid raw or cold food/beverages such as sashimi, sushi, salads, steak tartar, and seared meat. Eat all cooked vegetables and nothing straight from the refrigerator.
- Avoid the following cooling foods: tofu, tomato, celery, asparagus, bamboo, seaweed, kelp, bitter melon, cucumber, gourd, luffa, winter melon, oranges, grapefruit, pear, banana, papaya, watermelon, white radish, mustard leaf, potherb mustard, Chinese kale, napa, bamboo sprout. Long-term use of cold fruits and vegetables like the ones listed above may be damaging to the Spleen. To make the property more neutral, one can add about 20 pieces of *Gou Qi Zi* (Fructus Lycii) when cooking.

The Tao of Nutrition by Dr. Maoshing Ni and Cathy McNease:

- Recommendations: warming foods, chicken, lamb, scallions, sesame seeds, fish, baked tofu, soybeans, walnuts, eggs, lentils, black beans, lotus seeds, a little wine, ginger, and cinnamon bark tea.
- Avoid cold foods, cold fruits, and raw foods.

LIFESTYLE INSTRUCTIONS

- Avoid exposure to the cold, such as water sports or exposure to cold and windy weather.

CASE STUDIES

- E.F., a 34-year-old female, presented with infertility. Additional symptoms included urinating seven to eight times each day and her periods had light cramping and white discharge. It was noted that her cycle was 32 days. Objective findings included pale face with cold hands. The TCM diagnosis was Spleen and Kidney yang deficiencies. It was noted that she had two years of unsuccessful IUIs and was just beginning IVF. ***Kidney Tonic (Yang)*** was prescribed at 3 capsules three times per day while on her IVF protocol. In result of taking the herbs, the patient experienced a successful IVF procedure and was currently six weeks pregnant. In addition, her urinary output became normalized. She was taken off the formula once she had become pregnant. Submitted by M.P., Muskego, Wisconsin.
- The patient had stopped taking birth control in 2009, which she had been using for nine years total. Currently she was having no periods, which had been occurring for the past 3.5 years. It was noted that she had implantation failure, two miscarriages, and infertility. Her doctors had stated that she had low estrogen as well as progesterone with no exogenous support. ***Blossom (Phases 1-4)*** for infertility and ***Kidney Tonic (Yang)*** to replenish *jing* (essence) were prescribed. Within six weeks of taking herbs and receiving acupuncture, she had a full five-day period with no clots. Her endometrial lining became 10 mm, where 8 mm is required, and ovulation was present. She and her husband were ready to conceive naturally. Submitted by N.T., Bethesda, Maryland.
- J.L., a 70-year-old male, presented with multiple symptoms including low energy, back pain, cold sensation, and frequent urination. Objective findings included difficult walking with weakness in the knees as well as a decreased range of motion. Blood pressure was 140/72 mmHg and heart rate was 77 beats per minute. The practitioner diagnosed this condition as Kidney yang deficiency. For treatment, ***Kidney Tonic (Yang)*** was prescribed. After taking the herbs for three weeks, the patient reported an increase in energy and decrease sensation of cold; however, coldness of extremities was still present upon palpation. He mentioned he would continue taking the herbs and receiving acupuncture. Submitted by J.C., Rosemead, California.
- A.P., a 55-year-old female, presented with multiple symptoms of always feeling cold, absence of thirst, tiredness, and loose stools. Blood pressure was 131/82 mmHg. Objective findings included cold abdomen and back. The TCM diagnosis was Kidney and Spleen yang deficiencies and ***Kidney Tonic (Yang)*** was prescribed with *Bu Zhong Yi Qi Tang* (Tonify the Middle and Augment the Qi Decoction) to treat the condition. After one month of taking the herbs, the patient began to have more energy, her stools were well formed, and she felt warmer overall. Submitted by J.M., Breckenridge, Colorado.
- A 73-year-old male presented with pain in the right leg around the thigh area; aggravation was noted after exertion such as walking. Slight relief was experienced with the application of heat as well as rest. Sleep and urination issues were also present. The practitioner diagnosed this condition as Kidney yang deficiency. For treatment, ***Kidney Tonic (Yang)*** was prescribed at 3 grams per day. As a result of taking the herbs, the patient noticed an increase in mobility, was able to decrease the amount of pain medication she was taking, and his pain level went from a level 7 to a level 1 out of 10. He was no longer waking up as much during his sleep and his flow of urination was more consistent. It was mentioned that 4 grams per day was too much as it seemed to aggravate his prostate/urination condition; 3 grams was more suitable for him. Submitted by L.M., Las Vegas, Nevada.

PHARMACOLOGICAL AND CLINICAL RESEARCH

Kidney Tonic (Yang) is formulated specifically to tonify Kidney yang and raise *ming men* (life gate) fire. From the Western perspective, this formula improves genitourinary functions, treats kidney disorders, and alleviates musculoskeletal aches and pains. Furthermore, ***Kidney Tonic (Yang)*** contains many herbs with general adaptogenic and antiaging functions.

Kidney Tonic (Yang) contains many herbs that strongly improve and treat sexual and reproductive disorders. *Jiu Cai Zi* (Semen Allii Tuberosi) has an aphrodisiac effect. According to one study on sexual behavior in male subjects, administration of *Jiu Cai Zi* (Semen Allii Tuberosi) is associated with an increase in mounting frequency, intromission frequency, and ejaculation frequency, and a decrease in mount latency, intromission latency, and ejaculation latency.[5] *Shan Zhu Yu* (Fructus Corni) and *Suo*

Kidney Tonic (Yang)™

Yang (Herba Cynomorii) have positive reproductive benefits. Administration of *Shan Zhu Yu* (Fructus Corni) is associated with substantial stimulatory effects on sperm motility from 25.8 +/- 7.7% to 42.8 +/- 10.3%.[6] Administration of *Suo Yang* (Herba Cynomorii) is associated with significant increase in spermatogenesis. It significantly increases in epididymal sperm count, absolute testes weights, and the expression of GDNF (glial cell-derived neurotrophic factor) at both the mRNA and protein levels in testes of male subjects.[7]

Kidney Tonic (Yang) also contains many herbs to treat urinary functions and kidney disorders. Pharmacologically, the extract of *Shan Zhu Yu* (Fructus Corni) has been shown to induce diuresis and lower blood pressure.[8,9] Clinically, use of these herbs, and others, showed effectiveness in one study to treat frequent urination in elderly patients characterized by Kidney yang deficiency. Of 64 patients who received herbal therapy for three weeks, 17 had complete recovery, 21 showed significant improvement, 21 showed slight improvement, and 5 showed no change.[10] According to another study, use of these herbs showed beneficial results to treat six patients with nephrotic syndrome unresponsive to drug treatment (steroids). Improvements included resolution of symptoms and reduction of protein in the urine.[11] For prevention and treatment of diabetic nephropathy, use of *Shan Zhu Yu* (Fructus Corni) showed beneficial effect.[12] Lastly, 12 patients with stones were treated with satisfactory results, using an herbal formula containing 30 grams of *Lu Jiao Shuang* (Cornu Cervi Degelatinatum) as the main ingredient. [13]

Many herbs in this formula have functions to relieve pain and treat musculoskeletal disorders. One report stated that *Dang Gui* (Radix Angelicae Sinensis) has marked analgesic and anti-inflammatory effects to relieve pain and reduce inflammation.[14] Another study showed that use of *Dang Gui* (Radix Angelicae Sinensis) and others via injection was associated with a 97% rate of effectiveness to relieve low back and leg pain.[15] Furthermore, use of *Rou Gui* (Cortex Cinnamomi) was associated with a 98% rate of effectiveness to treat low back pain.[16] Additionally, according to one report, 27 patients with severe pain of the back and legs were treated by local injection of a *Gan Cao* (Radix et Rhizoma Glycyrrhizae) solution, with complete relief of pain in 20 patients and moderate relief in 7 patients. Patients with acute conditions received injections every other day for four to seven treatments; those with chronic conditions received injections every other day, for eight to fourteen treatments.[17]

In summary, ***Kidney Tonic (Yang)*** is a great formula that improves genitourinary functions, treats kidney disorders, and alleviates musculoskeletal aches and pains. It also has general adaptogenic and antiaging effects to alleviate mental stress, physical stress, and premature aging.[18,19]

COMPARATIVE ANALYSIS

One striking difference between Western and traditional Chinese medicine is that Western medicine focuses and excels in crisis management, while traditional Chinese medicine emphasizes and shines in holistic and preventative treatments. Therefore, in emergencies, such as gunshot wounds or surgery, Western medicine is generally the treatment of choice. However, for treatment of chronic idiopathic illness of unknown origins, where all lab tests are normal and a clear diagnosis cannot be made, traditional Chinese medicine is distinctly superior.

In traditional Chinese medicine, Kidney yang is responsible for the proper functioning of the body and its energy, including growth, maturation, and aging processes. Therefore, a decline in Kidney yang leads to symptoms such as low energy and lethargy, aversion to cold, cold extremities, intolerance to cold, urinary incontinence, loose stools, diarrhea, early morning diarrhea, weakness of the lower back and knees, and edema of the legs. Specific indications include infertility, impotence, spermatorrhea, frequent urination, incontinence, and many others. In short, Kidney yang regulates many systems in the body, including but not limited to urinary, sexual and reproductive systems. Proper use of Kidney yang tonics ensures optimal health and prevents deterioration of these conditions.

Western medicine, on the other hand, considers many of these symptoms to be non-specific and non-diagnostic. Furthermore, laboratory tests are generally normal, despite the patients still having various signs and symptoms. Under these circumstances, Western medicine struggles to identify a specific diagnosis and appropriate treatment. As a result, these conditions continue to deteriorate, becoming increasingly debilitating on a daily basis.

References

1. Chan K, Lo AC, Yeung JH, Woo KS. Journal of Pharmacy and Pharmacology 1995 May;47(5):402-6.
2. Pharmacotherapy 1999 July;19(7):870-876.
3. European Journal of Drug Metabolism and Pharmacokinetics 1995; 20(1): 55-60.
4. *Forensic Science International*, 1994 June 28; 55-8.
5. Guohua H, Yanhua L, Rengang M, Dongzhi W, Zhengzhi M, Hua Z. Aphrodisiac properties of Allium tuberosum seeds extract. College of Life and Environment Science, Shanghai Normal University, Shanghai, PR China. J Ethnopharmacol. 2009 Apr 21;122(3):579-82.
6. Jeng H, Wu CM, Su SJ, Chang WC. A substance isolated from Cornus officinalis enhances the motility of human sperm. Department of Anatomy, Taipei Medical College, Taiwan. Am J Chin Med. 1997;25(3-4):301-6.
7. Yang WM, Kim HY, Park SY, Kim HM, Chang MS, Park SK. Cynomorium songaricum induces spermatogenesis with glial cell-derived neurotrophic factor (GDNF) enhancement in rat testes. Department of Prescriptionology, College of Oriental Medicine, Kyung Hee University, 1 Hoegi-dong, Dongdaemun-gu, Seoul 130-701, Republic of Korea. J Ethnopharmacol. 2010 Apr 21;128(3):693-6.
8. *Chang Yong Zhong Yao Cheng Fen Yu Yao Li Shou Ce* (A Handbook of the Composition and Pharmacology of Common Chinese Drugs), 1994, 368:376.
9. Li C.P. Chinese herbal medicine. A publication of the John E. Fogarty International Center for Advanced Study in the Health Sciences (US Depart of Health, Education & Welfare). 1974, 120 pp.
10. *Xin Zhong Yi* (New Chinese Medicine), 1997; 1:48.
11. *Shen De Yan Jiu* (Research of Kidney), 1981; 93.
12. Xu H.Q. & Hao H.P. () Effects of iridoid total glycoside from *Cornus officinalis* on prevention of glomerular overexpression of transforming growth factor beta

FORMULAS

Kidney Tonic (Yang)™

1 and matrixes in an experimental diabetes model. *Biol Pharm Bull.* 2004, 27(7): 1014-1018.

13. *Shang Hai Zhong Yi Yao Za Zhi* (Shanghai Journal of Chinese Medicine and Herbology), 1982; 10:3.
14. *Yao Xue Za Zhi* (Journal of Medicinals), 1971; (91):1098.
15. *Xin Zhong Yi* (New Chinese Medicine), 1980; 2:34.
16. *Zhong Xi Yi Jie He Za Zhi* (Journal of Integrated Chinese and Western Medicine), 1984; 2:115.
17. *Zhe Jiang Zhong Yi Za Zhi* (Zhejiang Journal of Chinese Medicine), 1980; 2:60.
18. *Zhong Yao Yao Li Yu Lin Chuang* (Pharmacology and Clinical Applications of Chinese Herbs), 1990; 6(4):6.
19. *Tong Ji Yi Ke Da Xue Xue Bao* (Journal of Tongji University of Medicine), 1989; (3):198.

Kidney Tonic (Yin)™

CLINICAL APPLICATIONS

- **Kidney yin deficiency** with depletion of the marrow and *jing* (essence)
- Clinical signs and symptoms: dizziness, vertigo, weakness of knees, soreness of the lower back, night and/or spontaneous sweating, spermatorrhea and/or nocturnal emission, tinnitus, dribbling of urine, thirst with desire to drink, dry mouth and throat, mirror-like tongue surface with little coating
- Clinical applications: male sexual dysfunction (spermatorrhea and nocturnal emission), infertility due to premature ovarian failure, uterine bleeding, amenorrhea, multiple neuritis, and polyneuritis

WESTERN THERAPEUTIC ACTIONS

- Antiaging function to stop premature aging
- Treats sexual and reproductive disorders
- Improves sensory and nerve functions
- Adaptogenic effect to alleviate mental and physical stress

CHINESE THERAPEUTIC ACTIONS

- Nourishes yin
- Tonifies the Kidney

DOSAGE

Take 3 to 4 capsules three times daily. Dosage can be increased up to 6 to 8 capsules three times daily to treat more severe symptoms.

INGREDIENTS

Fu Ling (Poria)
Gan Cao (Radix et Rhizoma Glycyrrhizae)
Gou Qi Zi (Fructus Lycii)
Gui Ban Jiao (Gelatinum Plastrum Testudinis)
Huang Jing (Rhizoma Polygonati)
Lu Jiao Shuang (Cornu Cervi Degelatinatum)
Niu Xi (Radix Achyranthis Bidentatae)
Nu Zhen Zi (Fructus Ligustri Lucidi)
Shan Yao (Rhizoma Dioscoreae)
Shan Zhu Yu (Fructus Corni)
Shu Di Huang (Radix Rehmanniae Praeparata)
Tu Si Zi (Semen Cuscutae)

BACKGROUND

The function of Kidney in traditional Chinese medicine is closely related to the physiology of the genitourinary system in Western medicine. In Western medicine, genitourinary disorders include a wide variety of disorders, such as infertility, low libido, sexual dysfunction, increased urinary frequency, polyuria, urinary incontinence, nephrotic syndrome, chronic nephritis, and others. In traditional Chinese medicine, these disorders are usually diagnosed as Kidney yang deficiency, Kidney yin deficiency, or both.

FORMULA EXPLANATION

Kidney Tonic (Yin) is designed to tonify the Kidney yin and replenish the marrow and *jing* (essence). Since the brain is the sea of marrow, deficiency of the marrow may lead to dizziness and vertigo. Deficiency of the Kidney often causes deficiency of the lower body, leading to weak knees and sore back. Night sweating, dry mouth and throat, and thirst indicate general yin deficiency and lack of body fluids. Nocturnal emission and spermatorrhea are the result of deficiency fire causing the *jing* (essence) to leak out. A mirror-like tongue surface with little coating indicates severe yin deficiency.

Kidney Tonic (Yin) has *Shu Di Huang* (Radix Rehmanniae Praeparata) to tonify the Kidney and replenish the Kidney yin. *Gou Qi Zi* (Fructus Lycii) tonifies *jing* (essence) and improves vision to relieve dizziness. *Shan Zhu Yu* (Fructus Corni) has a sour taste, and astringes the yin and body fluids to prevent further depletion. *Gui Ban Jiao* (Gelatinum Plastrum Testudinis) and *Lu Jiao Shuang* (Cornu Cervi Degelatinatum) are two animal substances that have a very strong effect to nourish the Kidney and tonify the *jing* (essence). *Tu Si Zi* (Semen Cuscutae) combines with *Niu Xi* (Radix Achyranthis Bidentatae) to tonify the Kidney and strengthen the lower body to relieve sore back and weak knees. *Shan Yao* (Rhizoma Dioscoreae) tonifies the Kidney and strengthens the Spleen. *Nu Zhen Zi* (Fructus Ligustri Lucidi) and *Huang Jing* (Rhizoma Polygonati) further replenish Kidney yin while *Fu Ling* (Poria) strengthens the Spleen to help with absorption of the tonics. Finally, *Gan Cao* (Radix et Rhizoma Glycyrrhizae) harmonizes the entire formula.

In conclusion, ***Kidney Tonic (Yin)*** tonifies Kidney yin and treat related biomedical disorders.

CAUTIONS & CONTRAINDICATIONS

- This formula is contraindicated in cases of excess, stagnation or fire, inflammation and infection.
- Patients with weak digestion should take this formula with caution as the yin tonic herbs may cause stagnation in the middle *jiao* and create bloating sensation.
- This formula is not recommended for prolonged use (more than two or three months). Switching to milder yin tonic formulas such as ***Nourish*** or ***Nourish (Fluids)*** is recommended.

CLINICAL NOTE

- This formula is heavy and full of nutrients to nourish the yin aspect of the body. For that reason, it is to be used for treatment purposes and stopped once desired effect is achieved. To consolidate the effect, switch to a milder yin tonic formula such as ***Nourish*** for better results.

SUPPLEMENTARY FORMULAS

- With Kidney yang deficiency, add ***Kidney Tonic (Yang)***.
- For hot flashes, tidal fever, and steaming bone sensations, add ***Balance (Heat)***.

Kidney Tonic (Yin)™

- For vaginal dryness, add ***Balance Spring***.
- For thirst and dryness, add ***Nourish (Fluids)***.
- For qi deficiency, add ***Cordyceps 3***.
- For qi and blood deficiencies, add ***Imperial Tonic***.
- For dry cough with scanty sputum, add ***Respitrol (CF)***.
- For dry stool, add ***Gentle Lax (Deficient)***.
- For infertility, add ***Blossom (Phase 1-4)***.
- For dizziness, vertigo or high blood pressure, combine with ***Gastrodia Complex***.
- For osteoporosis, add ***Osteo 8***.
- For degeneration of soft tissue (muscles, tendons, ligaments and cartilage), add ***Flex (MLT)***.
- For weakness and soreness of the back, add ***Back Support (CR)***.
- For weakness and soreness of the knees, add ***Knee & Ankle (CR)***.
- For hair loss, add ***Polygonum 14***.
- For visual disturbances, blurriness, redness or pain, combine with ***Lycium Support***.

ACUPUNCTURE TREATMENT

Traditional Points:

- *Shenshu* (BL 23), *Taixi* (KI 3), *Guanyuan* (CV 4), *Sanyinjiao* (SP 6), *Qihai* (CV 6), *Zhishi* (BL 52)

Classic Master Tung's Points:

- **Infertility (female):** *Fuke* (T 11.24), *Huanchao* (T 11.06), *Tongshen* (T 88.09), *Tongbei* (T 88.11), *Tianhuang* (T 77.17), *Dihuang* (T 77.19), *Renhuang* (T 77.21), *Jiemeiyi* (T 88.04), *Jiemeier* (T 88.05), *Jiemeisan* (T 88.06), *Mufu* (T 88.38)*, *Tianhuang* (T 88.13), *Minghuang* (T 88.12), *Qihuang* (T 88.14). Moxa lower abdomen.
- **Infertility (male):** *Tianhuang* (T 77.17), *Dihuang* (T 77.19), *Renhuang* (T 77.21), *Tianhuang* (T 88.13), *Minghuang* (T 88.12), *Qihuang* (T 88.14), Endocrine, Kidney and testicle point on the ear. Moxa *du* (governing) channel on the back.
- **Spermatorrhea:** *Tianhuang* (T 77.17), *Dihuang* (T 77.19), *Renhuang* (T 77.21), *Tongshen* (T 88.09), *Tongwei* (T 88.10), *Shuijin* (T 1010.20), *Shuitong* (T 1010.19), *Tianhuangfu [Shenguan]* (T 77.18). Moxa *Guanyuan* (CV 4), *Zhongji* (CV 3), *Zhongshu* (GV 7).
- **Dizziness:** *Linggu* (T 22.05), *Dabai* (T 22.04), *Zhenghui* (T 1010.01), *Wanshunyi* (T 22.08), *Wanshuner* (T 22.09), *Luotong* (T 44.14), two points on the sides of the first metacarpal joint of the thumb, *Fuding* (T 44.04), *Tongshen* (T 88.09), *Tongwei* (T 88.10), *Tongbei* (T 88.11), *Zhitong* (T 44.13)
- **Back soreness:** *Linggu* (T 22.05), *Chongzi* (T 22.01), *Chongxian* (T 22.02), *Wanshunyi* (T 22.08), *Wanshuner* (T 22.09), *Zhongbai* (T 22.06), *Zhengjin* (T 77.01), *Zhengzong* (T 77.02), *Zhongjiuli* (T 88.25), *Tongshen* (T 88.09), *Tongwei* (T 88.10), *Simashang* (T 88.18), *Simazhong* (T 88.17), *Simaxia* (T 88.19), *Shuijin* (T 1010.20), *Shuitong* (T 1010.19), *Chengshan* (BL 57), *Biyi* (T 1010.22), *Zhitong* (T 44.13)
- **Tinnitus:** *Mu* (T 11.17), *Wanshunyi* (T 22.08), *Wanshuner* (T 22.09), *Xiabai* (T 22.07), *Zhongbai* (T 22.06), *Simashang* (T 88.18), *Simazhong* (T 88.17), *Simaxia* (T 88.19), *Tianhuangfu [Shenguan]* (T 77.18), *Tongshen* (T 88.09), *Yizhong* (T 77.05), *Erzhong* (T 77.06), *Sanzhong* (T 77.07), *Menjin* (T 66.05), *Shuiqu* (T 66.09). Bleed dark veins on the lateral aspect of the lower limb. Bleed before needling for best result.
- **Dry mouth:** *Sanshen* (T 44.27)*, *Tongshen* (T 88.09), *Tongwei* (T 88.10), *Sihuashang* (T 77.08)
- **Amenorrhea:** *Fuke* (T 11.24), *Jiemeiyi* (T 88.04), *Jiemeier* (T 88.05), *Jiemeisan* (T 88.06), *Tianhuang* (T 77.17), *Dihuang* (T 77.19), *Renhuang* (T 77.21), *Tianhuang* (T 88.13), *Minghuang* (T 88.12), *Qihuang* (T 88.14)

Master Tung's Points by Dr. Chuan-Min Wang:

- **Kidney yin deficiency:** *Tongshen* (T 88.09), *Tongwei* (T 88.10), *Tongbei* (T 88.11)

Balance Method by Dr. Richard Tan:

- Bilateral: *Rangu* (KI 2), *Dazhong* (KI 4), *Fuliu* (KI 7)
- Left side: *Shenmen* (HT 7), *Shaohai* (HT 3), *Zulinqi* (GB 41), *Yanglingquan* (GB 34), *Weizhong* (BL 40), *Shugu* (BL 65)
- Right side: *Zhongzhu* (TH 3), Tianjing (TH 10), *Houxi* (SI 3), *Xiaohai* (SI 8), *Taixi* (KI 3), *Yingu* (KI 10)

Auricular Medicine by Dr. Li-Chun Huang:

- **Frequent micturition:** Urethra, Prostate, Pituitary, Internal Urethra (for female patients), Occiput
  - For inflammation due to frequent micturition, bleed Ear Apex.
  - For frequent micturition due to nervousness, add Nervous Subcortex and *Shenmen*.
- **Tinnitus:** Internal Ear, Temple (Auditory Center), *San Jiao*
  - For tinnitus due to excess, add Gallbladder and Liver. Bleed Ear Apex.
  - For tinnitus due to deficiency, add Kidney.
- **Kidney deficiency:** Kidney, Pituitary, Endocrine, Liver, Heart, Thalamus, Adrenal Gland
- **Excessive sweating:** Sympathetic, Thalamus, Heart, Lung, Spleen, Nervous Subcortex, corresponding sweating areas

NUTRITION

- Increase intake of nourishing roots such as Mexican yam, yam, radishes, potatoes, carrots, melons, cucumbers, beets, turnips, malanga, celeriac, taro, and rutabaga.
- Warm and hot natured foods that damage qi and yin should be avoided, such as:
  - certain fruits like mango and durian that produce heat.
  - stimulants like coffee, alcohol, and energy drinks.
  - spicy/pungent/aromatic vegetables such as pepper, garlic, onions, basil, rosemary, cumin, funnel, anise, leeks, chives, scallions, thyme, saffron, wormwood, mustard, chili pepper, and wasabi.
- Avoid food and drinks with artificial coloring.

Kidney Tonic (Yin)™

- Consume as few meat products as possible. Do not eat processed meats, such as lunch meats, hot dogs and sausages, as they contain nitrites that are associated with inflammation and chronic disease.

The Tao of Nutrition by Dr. Maoshing Ni and Cathy McNease:

- Recommendations: cooling foods, mulberries, apples, peaches, pears, fresh vegetables, mung beans, most beans, soybeans, tofu, soy sprouts, and chrysanthemum flowers.
- Avoid hot foods, spicy foods, smoking, alcohol, stress, and strong emotions.

CASE STUDIES

- L.S., a 45-year-old female, presented with hyperthyroidism, which she had been previously diagnosed with but for which she was not interested in receiving Western treatment. Her symptoms consisted of rapid heart beat, weight loss, hair loss, and exhaustion. Blood tests had also confirmed the indication of her hyperthyroidism as well. The patient had noted she had a tendency to always feel stressed at work. After diagnosing this condition as Kidney yin deficiency with Liver qi stagnation, the patient was prescribed both ***Kidney Tonic (Yin)*** and ***Thyrodex***. With taking the herbs the patient reported that most of her symptoms had stabilized; however, the hair loss was still present. She continued to take the herbs for additional improvement. Submitted by B.L., Fort Myers, Florida.
- C.R., a 56-year old female, presented with hot flashes. Additional symptoms included difficulty sleeping, dry mouth, anxiety, and depression. It was noted that her palpitations and sweating were constant. The practitioner diagnosed this condition as Kidney yin deficiency with heat. ***Nourish (Fluids)***, ***Kidney Tonic (Yin)***, and ***Balance (Heat)*** were prescribed. In result of taking the ***Kidney Tonic (Yin)*** with ***Balance (Heat)***, she noticed less heat sensation as well as decrease in both anxiety and sleep difficulty but was still sweating slightly. Afterwards, taking ***Kidney Tonic (Yin)*** with ***Nourish (Fluids)***, the patient was no longer experiencing the dry mouth and thirst. Submitted by J.C., Rosemead, California.

PHARMACOLOGICAL AND CLINICAL RESEARCH

Kidney Tonic (Yin) is formulated specifically to tonify Kidney yin and replenish marrow and *jing* (essence). From the Western perspectives, this formula treats sexual and reproductive disorders, and improves sensory and nerve functions. Furthermore, this formula contains many herbs with general adaptogenic and antiaging functions.

Many herbs in this formula have been used with great success to treat various sexual dysfunctions. For example, *Shu Di Huang* (Radix Rehmanniae Praeparata), *Shan Yao* (Rhizoma Dioscoreae), *Shan Zhu Yu* (Fructus Corni), *Tu Si Zi* (Semen Cuscutae) and others were found to effectively treat seven men with sexual dysfunction and decreased levels of testosterone. The herbal therapy effectively reversed signs and symptoms of sexual dysfunction, and raised the plasma testosterone level to normal.[1]

Kidney Tonic (Yin) also addresses reproductive disorders, including male and female infertility. Pharmacologically, administration of *Shan Zhu Yu* (Fructus Corni) is associated with substantial stimulatory effects on sperm motility from 25.8 +/- 7.7% to 42.8 +/- 10.3%.[2] Clinically, the herbs have been shown to effectively increase sperm count and improve sperm motility among 33 of 42 men within approximately two months. In follow-up visits two years after the initial treatment, all 33 men were successful in having children.[3] For female infertility, the herbs were used successfully to treat infertility caused by premature ovarian failure and secondary amenorrhea.[4]

Furthermore, this formula also treats menstrual disorders, such as amenorrhea and uterine bleeding. According to one study, use of these herbs for two to three months was successful in treating 9 of 14 patients with amenorrhea due to Kidney yin deficiency.[5] For uterine bleeding, one study reported significant improvement in 17 of 22 patients using these herbs to treat uterine bleeding characterized by Kidney yin and/or yang deficiency.[6] According to another study, use of these Kidney yin tonic herbs was associated with complete recovery in 38 of 45 patients with uterine bleeding.[7]

In addition to tonifying Kidney yin, this formula also replenishes the marrow and *jing* (essence) to treat sensory and nerve disorders. For sensory disorder, use of *Huang Jing* (Rhizoma Polygonati) enhanced auditory function and improved hearing in 100 patients with deafness.[8] For nerve disorders, use of many herbs in this formula has been shown to treat multiple neuritis,[9] polyneuritis,[10] and retrogressive myelitis.[11]

Lastly, in addition to specific effects, ***Kidney Tonic (Yin)*** uses many herbs with general adaptogenic and antiaging effect to alleviate mental stress, physical stress, and premature aging.[12,13]

COMPARATIVE ANALYSIS

One striking difference between Western and traditional Chinese medicine is that Western medicine focuses and excels in crisis management, while traditional Chinese medicine emphasizes and shines in holistic and preventative treatments. Therefore, in emergencies, such as gunshot wounds or surgery, Western medicine is generally the treatment of choice. However, for treatment of chronic idiopathic illness of unknown origins, where all lab tests are normal and a clear diagnosis cannot be made, traditional Chinese medicine is distinctly superior.

In traditional Chinese medicine, Kidney yin provides the substance needed for normal growth and functioning of the body. Therefore, a decline in Kidney yin leads to symptoms such as dizziness, vertigo, weakness of knees, soreness of the lower back, night and/or spontaneous sweating, spermatorrhea and/or nocturnal emission, tinnitus, dribbling of urine, thirst with desire to drink, dry mouth and throat, and a mirror-like tongue

Kidney Tonic (Yin)™

surface with little coating. Clinical applications include male sexual dysfunction (spermatorrhea and nocturnal emission), infertility due to premature ovarian failure, uterine bleeding, and amenorrhea. In short, Kidney yin affects many systems in the body, including the sexual and reproductive systems. Proper use of Kidney yin tonics ensures optimal health and prevents deterioration of these conditions.

Western medicine, on the other hand, considers many of these symptoms to be non-specific and non-diagnostic. Furthermore, laboratory tests are generally normal, despite the patients still having various signs and symptoms. Under these circumstances, Western medicine struggles to identify a specific diagnosis and appropriate treatment. As a result, these conditions continue to deteriorate, becoming increasingly debilitating on daily basis.

References

1. *Nan Jing Yi Xue Yuan Xue Bao* (Journal of Nanjing University of Medicine), 1988, 4:331.
2. Jeng H, Wu CM, Su SJ, Chang WC. A substance isolated from Cornus officinalis enhances the motility of human sperm. Department of Anatomy, Taipei Medical College, Taiwan. Am J Chin Med. 1997;25(3-4):301-6.
3. *Xin Zhong Yi* (New Chinese Medicine), 1988; 2:20.
4. Chao SL. Huang LW. Yen HR. Pregnancy in premature ovarian failure after therapy using Chinese herbal medicine. Chang Gung Medical Journal. 26(6):449-52, 2003 Jun.
5. *Zhong Yi Za Zhi* (Journal of Chinese Medicine), 1984; 7:35.
6. *Zhong Xi Yi Jie He Za Zhi* (Journal of Integrated Chinese and Western Medicine), 1984; 8:496.
7. *Hu Nan Zhong Yi Za Zhi* (Hunan Journal of Chinese Medicine), 1997; 3:57.
8. *Zhong Xi Yi Jie He Za Zhi* (Journal of Integrated Chinese and Western Medicine), 1982; 1:19.
9. *Zhong Hua Ren Min Gong He Guo Yao Dian* (Chinese Herbal Pharmacopoeia by People's Republic of China), 1995; 348.
10. *Zhong Yi Yao Xue Bao* (Report of Chinese Medicine and Herbology), 1993; 6:34.
11. *Liao Ning Zhong Yi Za Zhi* (Liaoning Journal of Chinese Medicine), 1982; 3:40.
12. *Zhong Yao Yao Li Du Li Yu Lin Chuang* (Pharmacology, Toxicology and Clinical Applications of Chinese Herbs), 1990; 6(3):28.
13. *Chang Yong Zhong Yao Cheng Fen Yu Yao Li Shou Ce* (A Handbook of the Composition and Pharmacology of Common Chinese Drugs), 1994; 1563:1564.

Knee & Ankle (AC)™

CLINICAL APPLICATIONS

- **Acute knee and ankle injuries:** sprain and strain, pain with swelling and inflammation
- **Acute leg injuries:** damages to the soft tissues, including muscles, ligaments, tendons, cartilages and bones

WESTERN THERAPEUTIC ACTIONS

- Analgesic effect to relieve pain
- Anti-inflammatory effect to reduce swelling and inflammation
- Antiarthritic effect to suppress pro-inflammatory cytokines
- Antirheumatic effect to protect against joint destruction

CHINESE THERAPEUTIC ACTIONS

- Clears heat
- Activates blood circulation
- Eliminates blood stasis
- Drains fluids

DOSAGE

Take 3 to 4 capsules three times daily. Dosage may be increased up to 5 to 6 capsules every four to six hours as needed. For quick and maximum effectiveness, take the herbs on an empty stomach with warm water.

INGREDIENTS

Chi Shao (Radix Paeoniae Rubrae)
Chuan Mu Xiang (Radix Vladimiriae)
Chuan Niu Xi (Radix Cyathulae)
Chuan Xiong (Rhizoma Chuanxiong)
Da Huang (Radix et Rhizoma Rhei)
Dang Gui (Radix Angelicae Sinensis)
Di Huang (Radix Rehmanniae)
Du Huo (Radix Angelicae Pubescentis)
Gan Cao (Radix et Rhizoma Glycyrrhizae)
Hong Hua (Flos Carthami)
Mo Yao (Myrrha)
Mu Gua (Fructus Chaenomelis)
Ru Xiang (Gummi Olibanum)
San Qi (Radix et Rhizoma Notoginseng)
Su Mu (Lignum Sappan)
Tao Ren (Semen Persicae)
Wu Yao (Radix Linderae)
Xu Duan (Radix Dipsaci)
Ze Lan (Herba Lycopi)

BACKGROUND

Musculoskeletal and connective tissue injuries lead to over 10 million clinic visits per year in the United States.[1] Causes of these injuries may be external (sports injuries, car accidents, trauma), internal (chronic wear and tear of muscles, ligaments and tendons; bones weakened by osteoporosis), or both. Acute injuries are characterized by severe pain, swelling and inflammation, and in some cases, internal bleeding. Treatment of acute injuries should focus on relieving pain, reducing swelling and inflammation, and stopping bleeding. Chronic injuries are characterized by dull pain, stiffness and numbness, and decreased muscle mass and strength. Treatment of chronic injuries includes relief of pain and restoration of physical and physiological functions.

FORMULA EXPLANATION

Knee & Ankle (AC) is designed to treat disorders of the knee and ankle characterized by swelling, inflammation, and pain. It contains herbs that activate qi and blood circulation, eliminate qi and blood stasis, clear heat, and reduce swelling and inflammation.

In this formula, many herbs are used to activate qi and blood circulation. *Dang Gui* (Radix Angelicae Sinensis), *Di Huang* (Radix Rehmanniae) and *Chuan Xiong* (Rhizoma Chuanxiong) are used to tonify blood and activate blood circulation. *Gan Cao* (Radix et Rhizoma Glycyrrhizae), *Chuan Mu Xiang* (Radix Vladimiriae) and *Wu Yao* (Radix Linderae) tonify qi and activate qi circulation. Furthermore, *San Qi* (Radix et Rhizoma Notoginseng), *Ze Lan* (Herba Lycopi), *Tao Ren* (Semen Persicae), *Chi Shao* (Radix Paeoniae Rubrae) and *Hong Hua* (Flos Carthami) activate blood circulation and eliminate blood stasis to treat pain. *Ze Lan* (Herba Lycopi) also has the ability to drain swelling associated with the inflammatory stage in acute pain conditions. *Su Mu* (Lignum Sappan), *Xu Duan* (Radix Dipsaci) and *Du Huo* (Radix Angelicae Pubescentis) open peripheral channels and collaterals to relieve pain. *Mu Gua* (Fructus Chaenomelis) relaxes the muscles to treat cramps, spasms, and stiffness. It helps repair damaged tendons and ligaments. *Da Huang* (Radix et Rhizoma Rhei) drains swelling and inflammation that often occur with acute physical injuries. It is one of the most commonly used herbs for acute trauma. Together, *Ru Xiang* (Gummi Olibanum) and *Mo Yao* (Myrrha) are used as a pair to dramatically reduce pain associated with external and trauma injuries. *Chuan Niu Xi* (Radix Cyathulae) and *Du Huo* (Radix Angelicae Pubescentis) act as channel-guiding herbs to direct the effect of the formula to the lower extremities and increase blood circulation to the area of the knees. Lastly, *Gan Cao* (Radix et Rhizoma Glycyrrhizae) tonifies qi and harmonizes the formula.

In summary, ***Knee & Ankle (AC)*** is an excellent formula to treat acute injuries of the knees and ankles with accompanying swelling, inflammation, and pain.

CAUTIONS & CONTRAINDICATIONS

- This formula is contraindicated during pregnancy and nursing.
- This herbal formula contains herbs that invigorate blood circulation, such as *Dang Gui* (Radix Angelicae Sinensis). Therefore, patients who are on anticoagulant or antiplatelet therapies, such as Coumadin (warfarin), should use this formula with caution, or not at all, as there may be a higher risk of bleeding and bruising.[2,3,4]

FORMULAS

Knee & Ankle (AC)™

- The following warning statement is required by the State of California: "This product contains *Da Huang* (Radix et Rhizoma Rhei). Read and follow directions carefully. Do not use if you have or develop diarrhea, loose stools, or abdominal pain because *Da Huang* (Radix et Rhizoma Rhei) may worsen these conditions and be harmful to your health. Consult your physician if you have frequent diarrhea or if you are pregnant, nursing, taking medication, or have a medical condition."

CLINICAL NOTES

- ***Knee & Ankle (AC)*** is most effective for knee disorders due to acute external or trauma injuries with swelling, inflammation and pain. These types of acute physical injury often affect both the bones and the soft tissues. Clinical applications of this formula include disorders of the bones (bone fracture, dislocation, or meniscus injury of the knees) and surrounding soft tissue damage [anterior cruciate ligament (ACL), posterior cruciate ligament (PCL), medial collateral ligament (MCL), and lateral collateral ligament (LCL)]. Anterior drawer test and posterior drawer test can also be performed to determine whether the ACL or the PCL is damaged.
- Patients with chronic knee disorders, such as with repetitive wear and tear of the joint leading to atrophy and degeneration, should be treated with ***Knee & Ankle (CR)*** and ***Flex (MLT)***.
- According to Dr. Jun-Qing Luo, a *tui-na* master from China, 70 to 80% of MCL and LCL damages involve a posterior shift of those ligaments. Treatment involves resetting the soft tissue in an upward motion towards the patella. The MCL/LCL should never be stroked downwards toward the popliteal fossa. Treating ACL and PCL injuries does not require excessive force, twisting or pulling motion. He also does not recommend using *tui-na* treatment during the acute inflammation stage of knee disorders. However, if left untreated, tendons and ligaments may adhere and make treatment more difficult and painful. According to Dr. Luo, ligament and meniscus injuries are better treated with *tui-na* and herbs instead of surgery.

  Furthermore, Dr. Luo's said that patients will often seek your help after their medical doctor confirmed that there is nothing wrong. However, patients still feel knee pain or discomfort. In such cases, the cause is likely just a minor ligament injury. In some cases, knee pain may not reflect where the problem is. It may be caused by problems elsewhere, such as in the greater trochanter causing radiating pain to the knee, the tensor fasciae latae and the iliotibial band, with physical structural changes to compensate for these imbalances that leads to the knee pain. Accurate diagnosis is essential to prescribing the correct formula.
- This formula is not the most suitable formula for knee disorders due to osteoarthritis or rheumatoid arthritis. Osteoarthritis should be treated with ***Osteo 8*** and ***Knee & Ankle (CR)***. Rheumatoid arthritis of the knees is more effectively treated with ***Flex (Heat)***.
- Because the meniscus is a cartilage and receives very little blood supply, it is important to increase blood supply to the knees so that the surrounding soft tissues receive an adequate supply of fresh blood and oxygen to facilitate healing. If blood stagnation is not removed, recovery time will be prolonged and adhesion is more likely to develop. Following this principle, blood-invigorating herbs are used extensively in this formula.
- ***Knee & Ankle (AC)*** is an adjunct formula to acupuncture treatment. Optimal results will occur with acupuncture, electro-stimulation and herbs are all included in the treatment regime.

SUPPLEMENTARY FORMULAS

- For severe pain, combine with ***Herbal ANG***.
- For severe inflammation and swelling, add ***Astringent Complex***.
- For knee and ankle disorder with heat manifestations or *re bi* (heat painful obstruction), combine with ***Flex (Heat)***.
- For knee and ankle disorder with cold and damp manifestations or *zhuo bi* (fixed painful obstruction), combine with ***Flex (CD)***.
- For knee and ankle disorders caused by acute injury or trauma or fracture of bones, use ***Flex (TMX)***.
- For ligament injury of the knee and ankle, add ***Flex (MLT)***.
- For knee and ankle disorders characterized by atrophy and degeneration, use ***Osteo 8***.
- For bone spurs, add ***Flex (SPR)***.

ACUPUNCTURE TREATMENT

Traditional Points:

- *Xiyan*, *Liangqiu* (ST 34), *Xiyangguan* (GB 33), *Jiexi* (ST 41), *Kunlun* (BL 60), *Qiuxu* (GB 40), *ah shi* points.

Classic Master Tung's Points:

- Needle contralateral to the pain. If the pain is in the center, needle bilaterally or the side with the more *ah shi* points. If the pain is bilateral, needle bilaterally.
- **General knee pain:** *Xiyan*, *Jianzhong* (T 44.06), *Xinxi* (T 11.09). Bleed around *Gaohuangshu* (BL 43) with cupping. Bleed before needling for best result.
- **Lateral knee pain:** *Xinxi* (T 11.09), *Jianzhong* (T 44.06)
- **Knee (coldness):** *Tongguan* (T 88.01), *Tongtian* (T 88.03), *Xiyan*. Use plum-blossom needle to bleed on and around the knee. Bleed before needling for best result.
- **Knee (ligament pain):** *Shenjian* (T 44.19), *Jianfeng* (T 44.31)*, *Shangqu* (T 44.16), *Jianzhong* (T 44.06), *Yunbai* (T 44.11), *Renzong* (T 44.08), *Quchi* (LI 11), *Xinling* (T 33.17)*
- **Chondromalacia patella:** *Jianfeng* (T 44.31)*, *Jianzhong* (T 44.06), *Huofuhai* (T 33.07), *Tianhuang* (T 77.17), *Dihuang* (T 77.19), *Renhuang* (T 77.21)
- **Knee arthritis:** *Linggu* (T 22.05), *Jianzhong* (T 44.06), *Shangqu* (T 44.16), *Xiaqu* (T 44.15), *Libai* (T 44.12), *Yunbai* (T 44.11)
- **Medial ankle pain:** *Xiabai* (T 22.07), *Minghuang* (T 88.12), *Tianhuang* (T 88.13), *Qihuang* (T 88.14), *Wuhu* (T 11.27), *ah shi* points around the MCP joint of the thumb, *Xiaojie* (T 22.13)*. Bleed the sprained ankle. Bleed before needling for best result.

Knee & Ankle (AC)™

- **Lateral ankle pain:** *Linggu* (T 22.05), *Qimen* (T 33.01), *Qihu* (T 77.26), *ah shi* points around the MCP joint of the thumb, *Xiaojie* (T 22.13)*. Bleed the sprained ankle. Bleed before needling for best result.

Master Tung's Points by Dr. Chuan-Min Wang:

- **Knee pain:** Needle contralaterally *Jianzhong* (T 44.06). Bleed *Chize* (LU 5) or *Quchi* (LI 11) area if acute.
- **Ankle pain:** Needle contralaterally *Zhongbai* (T 22.06), *Xiabai* (T 22.07), *Wuhu* 4, 5 (T 11.27).

Balance Method by Dr. Richard Tan:

- *Ah shi* points around *Quchi* (LI 11), *Chize* (LU 5) and *Shaohai* (HT 3). Needle the side that is more tender upon palpation. If the pain is deep on the knee, needle the elbow for up to 1.5 to 2 *cun* if necessary.

Ear Acupuncture:

- Select the respective points on the ear for the pain in addition to Subcortex, *Shenmen*, and Adrenals.

Auricular Medicine by Dr. Li-Chun Huang:

- **Knee pain:** Knee Joint. Bleed Ear Apex.
  - For external knee joint pain, add External Knee.
  - For internal knee joint pain, add Internal Knee Joint.
- **Heel pain:** Heel (front and back). Bleed Ear Apex.

NUTRITION

- Sulfur helps the absorption of calcium. Adequate intake and absorption of calcium is essential for the repair and the rebuilding of bones, tendons, cartilage, and connective tissues. Consume foods high in sulfur such as asparagus, eggs, fresh garlic, and onions.
- Histidine, an amino acid, is responsible for removing the high levels of copper and iron found in arthritic patients. Consume foods high in histidine, such as rice, wheat and rye.
- Fresh pineapples are recommended as they contain bromelain, an enzyme that is excellent in reducing inflammation.
- Fish oil may help alleviate pain associated with rheumatoid arthritis. It can be taken in conjunction with the herbs.
- Avoid spicy food, caffeine, citrus fruits, sugar, milk, dairy products and red meat.
- Decrease the intake of sour foods, drinks or fruits (citrus), as their nature constricts and may contribute to further stagnation in the channels and collaterals.

LIFESTYLE INSTRUCTIONS

- For obese patients, weight loss is suggested as it lessens the pressure on the joints, which can then help in relieving pain.
- Patients who are active in sports should take time off to rest the knee in order to gain full recovery.
- Patients with meniscus and ligament injuries are encouraged to rest and move the knee as little as possible to prevent recurrent injuries. Full movement or sports should not be performed until the knee is completely healed. Jumping or sudden landing are contraindicated.
- The above principles also apply to the ankles as well.

CASE STUDIES

- A 35-year-old male patient presented with acute ankle sprains due to sliding into second base at his softball game. Objective findings included swelling and bruising around both ankles. It was noted that he had iced and taken NSAIDs the night before. The practitioner diagnosed this condition as qi and blood stagnation. ***Knee & Ankle (AC)*** was prescribed at 5 capsules three times per day, along with rest and ice. Patient responded well with a full recovery after taking the herbs and receiving acupuncture for three weeks. Recommendation of stretching and warming up before games was also suggested to him for future prevention. Submitted by L.W., Arroyo Grande, California.
- S.V., a 30-year-old female, presented with knee pain, which had produced loss of range of motion and build up of scar tissue. It was noted that she had recently had surgery two weeks before coming in. Her blood pressure was 108/64 mmHg and her heart rate was 64 beats per minute. The practitioner diagnosed this condition as qi and blood stagnation. For treatment, ***Knee & Ankle (AC)*** was prescribed at 4 capsules four times per day. After taking the herbs for one week, the patient had reported the pain was less severe beginning after two days. The dosage was decreased after one week to 4 capsules twice per day, which she had continued taking for an additional week. Submitted by M.P., Muskego, Wisconsin.
- A.S., a 45-year-old female, presented with a right lateral ankle sprain that had occurred three days prior. Objective findings included purplish color and swelling around the ankle. The practitioner diagnosed this condition as local blood stagnation. For treatment, ***Flex (TMX)*** and ***Knee & Ankle (AC)*** were prescribed. After taking the herbs for three days, the patient reported her ankle was feeling 50% better. She discontinued taking the ***Flex (TMX)*** after 8 days since her ankle was then 90% better. For an additional week she continued to take the ***Knee & Ankle (CR)*** and her ankle was 100% better. Submitted by S.L., Yuma, Arizona.
- E.F., a 60-year-old male, presented with knee pain located above the right patella, beginning two days prior. X-rays had confirmed there was a bone spur present. It was noted that it became aggravated by any weight bearing or change of position. Objective findings included slight swelling and warm temperature. There was no trauma preceding the condition. The practitioner diagnosed this condition as qi and blood stagnation. ***Knee & Ankle (AC)*** and ***Flex (SPR)*** were prescribed at 2 capsules each three times per day. After taking the herbs for six weeks the condition had resolved. Submitted by L.L., Greenwich, Connecticut.

Knee & Ankle (AC)™

PHARMACOLOGICAL AND CLINICAL RESEARCH

Knee & Ankle (AC) is most effective for knee and ankle disorders due to acute trauma or external injuries with swelling, inflammation, and pain. Pharmacological effects of this formula include analgesic effect to relieve pain, anti-inflammatory action to reduce swelling, antiarthritic activity to suppress pro-inflammatory cytokines, and antirheumatic function to protect against joint destruction.

Several herbs in ***Knee & Ankle (AC)*** have significant analgesic effect to alleviate pain. *Ru Xiang* (Gummi Olibanum) and *Mo Yao* (Myrrha) have an analgesic effect to relieve pain and anti-inflammatory to reduce swelling and inflammation.[5,6] These two herbs also show an antiarthritic effect by reducing edema and decreasing arthritic scores in subjects with adjuvant-induced arthritis. The mechanism of action is attributed to the suppression of pro-inflammatory cytokines, such as tumor necrosis factor-alpha (TNF-α) and interleukin-1beta (IL-1β).[7] Furthermore, use of *Ru Xiang* (Gummi Olibanum) and *Mo Yao* (Myrrha) is also beneficial to facilitate wound healing by stimulating maturation and differentiation of white blood cells.[8] Clinically, these two herbs have been used effectively to treat pain associated with various types of trauma and external injuries.[9]

Knee & Ankle (AC) contains many herbs with both analgesic and anti-inflammatory effects. *Dang Gui* (Radix Angelicae Sinensis) alleviates pain and reduces inflammation through the inhibition of pro-inflammatory mediators, including nitric oxide and prostaglandin E2 in peritoneal macrophages.[10,11] In comparison with acetylsalicylic acid, the anti-inflammatory effect of *Dang Gui* (Radix Angelicae Sinensis) is approximately 1.1 times stronger, and its analgesic effect is approximately 1.7 times stronger.[12] In addition, *Du Huo* (Radix Angelicae Pubescentis) has a mild sedative effect and marked analgesic and anti-inflammatory activities.[13] Lastly, *Da Huang* (Radix et Rhizoma Rhei) has both analgesic and anti-inflammatory effects.[14] Emodin and rhein, two compounds from *Da Huang* (Radix et Rhizoma Rhei), exert their anti-inflammatory effect via inhibition of inducible nitric oxide synthase.[15]

Many herbs in ***Knee & Ankle (AC)*** have strong effects to reduce swelling and inflammation. *Chuan Xiong* (Rhizoma Chuanxiong) exerts its anti-inflammatory effect via an inhibitory activity on TNF-α production and bioactivity, and shows promising effect to treat inflammation and related diseases.[16] *Chuan Mu Xiang* (Radix Vladimiriae) exhibits an anti-inflammatory effect through significant inhibitory effects on INF-γ-induced nitric oxide production.[17] *San Qi* (Radix et Rhizoma Notoginseng) suppresses inflammation by inhibiting lipopolysaccharide-induced production of proinflammatory mediators, such as TNF-α, COX-2, IL-1, and IL-6.[18] *Su Mu* (Lignum Sappan) has both anti-inflammatory and antiarthritic effects. It suppresses inflammation through the inhibition of nitric oxide activity,[19] and attenuates collagen-induced arthritis by decreasing the levels of IL-1β, IL-6, TNF-α and PGE2 in serum and the expression of COX-2 and transcription factor NF-κB.[20] *Wu Yao* (Radix Linderae) has both anti-inflammatory and antirheumatic effects. It reduces inflammation via its inhibitory effects on the production of inflammatory mediators from macrophages by blocking NF-kappaB and MAPKs signaling pathways.[21] It treats rheumatism by protecting against joint destruction in type II collagen-induced model of rheumatoid arthritis.[22]

Di Huang (Radix Rehmanniae) and *Gan Cao* (Radix et Rhizoma Glycyrrhizae) also have anti-inflammatory effects, with different mechanism of action. *Di Huang* (Radix Rehmanniae) reduces swelling and inflammation through its influence on the endocrine system.[23] It has been shown that the use of *Di Huang* (Radix Rehmanniae) increases the plasma levels of adrenocortical hormones, even in the presence of dexamethasone.[24] *Gan Cao* (Radix et Rhizoma Glycyrrhizae) demonstrates marked anti-inflammatory effects by enhancing the effect of glucocorticoid through increased production and secretion as well as decreased metabolism by the liver.[25] In terms of anti-inflammatory actions, the comparison of cortisone to glycyrrhizin and glycyrrhetinic acid, two compounds from *Gan Cao* (Radix et Rhizoma Glycyrrhizae), is approximately 10:1.[26] Clinically, *Di Huang* (Radix Rehmanniae) has been used in an herbal formula to successfully treat 12 patients with rheumatoid arthritis.[27] *Gan Cao* (Radix et Rhizoma Glycyrrhizae) has been used with success to treat pain, inflammation, edema, arthritis, spasms, cramps and other related symptoms.[28,29]

Finally, many herbs are used in ***Knee & Ankle (AC)*** to facilitate healing and recovery from acute knee and ankle injuries. *San Qi* (Radix et Rhizoma Notoginseng) has an excellent osteogenic effect to treat bone fractures. *San Qi* (Radix et Rhizoma Notoginseng) promotes osteogenesis of bone marrow stromal cells by targeting osteogenesis-associated genes, which could be mediated by their actions on gap junction intercellular communication.[30] By improving the osteogenic differentiation of bone marrow stromal cells, *San Qi* (Radix et Rhizoma Notoginseng) is able to enhance bone mineral density and bone strength.[31] *Xu Duan* (Radix Dipsaci) has significant osteogenic and antiosteoporotic effects that promote generation of new bones and prevent osteoporosis. According to a bone cells culture experiment, administration of *Xu Duan* (Radix Dipsaci) shows potential effect to increase the proliferation and differentiation of the osteoblasts without affecting osteoclast activity. The researchers conclude that *Xu Duan* (Radix Dipsaci) can effectively increase the rate of tissue regeneration of damaged bones.[32]

In summary, ***Knee & Ankle (AC)*** is an excellent formula to use during the first days and weeks of leg injury to relieve pain, reduce swelling and inflammation, and facilitate recovery.

COMPARATIVE ANALYSIS

Pain is a basic bodily sensation induced by a noxious stimulus that causes physical discomfort (such as pricking, throbbing, or aching). Pain may be of acute or chronic states. For acute

Knee & Ankle (AC)™

pain of the legs (including knees and ankles), two classes of drugs commonly used for treatment include non-steroidal anti-inflammatory agents (NSAID) and opioid analgesics. NSAIDs [such as Motrin (ibuprofen) and Voltaren (diclofenac)] are generally used for mild to moderate pain, and are most effective to reduce inflammation and swelling. Though effective, they may cause such serious side effects as gastric ulcer, duodenal ulcer, gastrointestinal bleeding, tinnitus, blurred vision, dizziness and headache. Furthermore, the newer NSAIDs, also known as COX-2 inhibitors [such as Celebrex (celecoxib)], are associated with significantly higher risk of cardiovascular events, including heart attack and stroke. Opioid analgesics [such as Vicodin (APAP/hydrocodone) and morphine] are usually used for severe to excruciating pain. While they may be the most potent agents for pain, they also have the most serious risks and side effects, including but not limited to dizziness, lightheadedness, drowsiness, upset stomach, vomiting, constipation, stomach pain, rash, difficult urination, and respiratory depression resulting in difficult breathing. Furthermore, long-term use of these drugs leads to tolerance and addiction. In brief, it is important to remember that while drugs offer reliable and potent symptomatic pain relief, they should be used only if and when needed. Frequent use and abuse leads to unnecessary side effects and complications.

In TCM, treatment of pain is a sophisticated balance of art and science. Proper treatment of pain requires a careful evaluation of the type of disharmony (excess or deficiency, cold or heat, exterior or interior), characteristics (qi and/or blood stagnations), and location (upper body, lower body, extremities, or internal organs). Furthermore, optimal treatment requires integrative use of herbs, acupuncture, and *tui-na* therapies. All these therapies work together to tonify the underlying deficiencies, strengthen the body, and facilitate recovery from chronic pain. TCM pain management targets both the symptoms and causes of pain, and as such, often achieves immediate and long-term success. Furthermore, TCM pain management is often associated with few or no side effects.

For treatment of mild to severe pain due to various causes, TCM pain management offers similar treatment effects with significantly fewer side effects.

References

1. Berkow R. et al. The Merck Manual of Medical Information. Merck Research Laboratories. 1999 February.
2. Chan K, Lo AC, Yeung JH, Woo KS. Journal of Pharmacy and Pharmacology 1995 May;47(5):402-6.
3. Pharmacotherapy 1999 July;19(7):870-876.
4. European Journal of Drug Metabolism and Pharmacokinetics 1995; 20(1):55-60.
5. *Zhong Yao Xue* (Chinese Herbology), 1998; 539:540.
6. Yoshikawa M, Morikawa T, Oominami H, Matsuda H. Absolute stereostructures of olibanumols A, B, C, H, I, and J from olibanum, gum-resin of Boswellia carterii, and inhibitors of nitric oxide production in lipopolysaccharide-activated mouse peritoneal macrophages. Kyoto Pharmaceutical University, Japan. Chem Pharm Bull (Tokyo). 2009 Sep;57(9):957-64.
7. Fan AY, Lao L, Zhang RX, Zhou AN, Wang LB, Moudgil KD, Lee DY, Ma ZZ, Zhang WY, Berman BM. Effects of an acetone extract of Boswellia carterii Birdw. (Burseraceae) gum resin on adjuvant-induced arthritis in lewis rats. Center for Integrative Medicine, School of Medicine, University of Maryland, 3rd Floor, James Kernan Hospital Man, 2200 Kernan Drive, Baltimore, MD 21201, USA. J Ethnopharmacol. 2005 Oct 3;101(1-3):104-9.
8. Haffor A-S. 2010. Effect of myrrh (Commiphora molmol) on leukocyte levels before and during healing from gastric ulcer skin injury. J Immunotoxicol 7: 68-75.
9. *He Nan Zhong Yi Xue Yuan Xue Bao* (Journal of University of Henan School of Medicine), 1980; 3:38.
10. *Xin Yi Yao Xue Za Zhi* (New Journal of Medicine and Herbology), 1975; (6):34.
11. Chao WW, Kuo YH, Li WC, Lin BF. The production of nitric oxide and prostaglandin E2 in peritoneal macrophages is inhibited by Andrographis paniculata, Angelica sinensis and Morus alba ethyl acetate fractions. Department of Biochemical Science and Technology, Institute of Microbiology and Biochemistry, National Taiwan University, Taipei 106, Taiwan, ROC. J Ethnopharmacol. 2009 Feb 25;122(1):68-75.
12. *Yao Xue Za Zhi* (Journal of Medicinals), 1971; (91):1098.
13. *Zhong Yao Yao Li Yu Ying Yong* (Pharmacology and Applications of Chinese Herbs), 1983; 796.
14. *Chang Yong Zhong Yao Cheng Fen Yu Yao Li Shou Ce* (A Handbook of the Composition and Pharmacology of Common Chinese Drugs), 1994; 226:323.
15. Wang CC, Huang YJ, Chen LG, Lee LT, Yang LL. Inducible nitric oxide synthase inhibitors of Chinese herbs III. Rheum palmatum. Planta Med. 2002 Oct;68(10):869-74.
16. Liu L, Ning ZQ, Shan S, Zhang K, Deng T, Lu XP, Cheng YY. Phthalide Lactones from Ligusticum chuanxiong inhibit lipopolysaccharide-induced TNF-alpha production and TNF-alpha-mediated NF-kappaB Activation. Planta Med. 2005 Sep;71(9):808-13.
17. Xu J, Jin D, Shi D, Ma Y, Yang B, Zhao P, Guo Y. Sesquiterpenes from Vladimiria souliei and their inhibitory effects on NO production. Fitoterapia. 2011 Apr;82(3):508-11.
18. Rhule A, Navarro S, Smith JR, Shepherd DM. Panax notoginseng attenuates LPS-induced pro-inflammatory mediators in RAW264.7 cells. Department of Biomedical and Pharmaceutical Sciences, University of Montana, Missoula, MT 59812-1552, USA. J Ethnopharmacol. 2006 Jun 15;106(1):121-8.
19. Hong C.H., Hur S.K., Oh O.J., Kim S.S., Nam K.A. & Lee S.K. Evaluation of natural products on inhibition of inducible cyclooxygenase (COX-2) and nitric oxide synthase (iNOS) in cultured mouse macrophage cells. *J Ethnopharmacol.* 2002, 83(1-2): 153-159.
20. Wang YZ, Sun SQ, Zhou YB. Extract of the dried heartwood of Caesalpinia sappan L. attenuates collagen-induced arthritis. Department of Pharmacy, Daqing Campus of Harbin Medical University, Daqing 163319, China. J Ethnopharmacol. 2011 Jun 14;136(1):271-8.
21. Luo Y, Liu M, Yao X, Xia Y, Dai Y, Chou G, Wang Z. Total alkaloids from Radix Linderae prevent the production of inflammatory mediators in lipopolysaccharide-stimulated RAW 264.7 cells by suppressing NF-kappaB and MAPKs activation. Department of Pharmacology of Chinese Materia Medica, China Pharmaceutical University, 1 Shennong Road, Nanjing 210038, China. Cytokine. 2009 Apr;46(1):104-10.
22. Wang C, Dai Y, Yang J, Chou G, Wang C, Wang Z. Treatment with total alkaloids from Radix Linderae reduces inflammation and joint destruction in type II collagen-induced model for rheumatoid arthritis. Department of Pharmacology of Chinese Materia Medica, China Pharmaceutical University, 1 Shennong Road, Nanjing 210038, China. J Ethnopharmacol. 2007 May 4;111(2):322-8.
23. *Zhong Yao Yao Li Yu Ying Yong* (Pharmacology and Applications of Chinese Herbs), 1983: 400.
24. *Zhong Yao Xue* (Chinese Herbology), 1998; 156:158.
25. *Zhong Yao Zhi* (Chinese Herbology Journal), 1993; 358.
26. *Zhong Cao Yao* (Chinese Herbal Medicine), 1991; 22(10):452.

Knee & Ankle (AC)™

27. *Zhong Yao Lin Chuan Xin Yong* (New Clinical Applications of Chinese Medicine), 2001; 242-243.
28. *Zhe Jiang Zhong Yi Za Zhi* (Zhejiang Journal of Chinese Medicine), 1980; 2:60.
29. *Zhong Hua Nei Ke Za Zhi* (Chinese Journal of Internal Medicine), 1960; 4:354.
30. Li XD, Chang B, Chen B, Liu ZY, Liu DX, Wang JS, Hou GQ, Huang DY, Du SX. Panax notoginseng saponins potentiate osteogenesis of bone marrow stromal cells by modulating gap junction intercellular communication activities. Department of Orthopaedics, the First Affiliated Hospital, Shantou University Medical College, Shantou, PR China. Cell Physiol Biochem. 2010;26(6): 1081-92.
31. Shen Y, Li YQ, Li SP, Ma L, Ding LJ, Ji H. Alleviation of ovariectomy-induced osteoporosis in rats by Panax notoginseng saponins. Department of Pharmacology, China Pharmaceutical University, 24 Tong Jia Xiang, Nanjing, 210009, People's Republic of China. J Nat Med. 2010 Jul;64(3):336-45.
32. Yao CH, Tsai HM, Chen YS, Liu BS. Fabrication and evaluation of a new composite composed of tricalcium phosphate, gelatin, and Chinese medicine as a bone substitute. Institute of Biomedical Engineering and Material Science, Chungtai Institute of Health Science and Technology, Taichung, Taiwan, Republic of China. J Biomed Mater Res B Appl Biomater. 2005 Nov;75(2): 277-88.

Knee & Ankle (CR)™

CLINICAL APPLICATIONS

- **Chronic knee and ankle disorders** with atrophy and degeneration of the soft tissues (muscles, tendons and ligaments)
- **Chronic leg disorders** with weakness, stiffness, decreased range of motion and mobility of the joints
- Sprain, partial rupture, stretch or tear of ankle ligaments leading to instability and frequent re-injuries.

WESTERN THERAPEUTIC ACTIONS

- Chondroprotective function to protect joints and cartilages
- Osteogenic function to promote generation of new bones
- Anti-inflammatory effect to reduce swelling and inflammation
- Analgesic effect to relieve pain
- Muscle-relaxant effect to relieve spasms and cramps

CHINESE THERAPEUTIC ACTIONS

- Tonifies qi, blood and yin
- Activates qi and blood circulation
- Opens channels and collaterals of the lower limb to relieve pain

DOSAGE

Take 3 to 4 capsules three times daily. Depending on the nature and severity of the illness, the dosage may be increased up to 8 capsules three times daily for three or four days to relieve pain. For maximum effectiveness, take the herbs on an empty stomach with warm water. This formula should not be taken during the acute phases of injuries, where there is still bleeding, inflammation, and bruising.

INGREDIENTS

Bai Shao (Radix Paeoniae Alba)
Bai Zhu (Rhizoma Atractylodis Macrocephalae)
Chuan Niu Xi (Radix Cyathulae)
Da Zao (Fructus Jujubae)
Dan Shen (Radix et Rhizoma Salviae Miltiorrhizae)
Dang Gui (Radix Angelicae Sinensis)
Dang Shen (Radix Codonopsis)
Di Huang (Radix Rehmanniae)
Du Zhong (Cortex Eucommiae)
Fu Ling (Poria)
Gan Cao (Radix et Rhizoma Glycyrrhizae)
Huang Bo (Cortex Phellodendri Chinensis)
Ji Xue Teng (Caulis Spatholobi)
Mu Dan Pi (Cortex Moutan)
Qian Nian Jian (Rhizoma Homalomenae)
Shan Yao (Rhizoma Dioscoreae)
Shen Jin Cao (Herba Lycopodii)
Sheng Jiang (Rhizoma Zingiberis Recens)
Shu Di Huang (Radix Rehmanniae Praeparata)
Wu Jia Pi (Cortex Acanthopanacis)
Ze Xie (Rhizoma Alismatis)
Zhi Mu (Rhizoma Anemarrhenae)

BACKGROUND

Musculoskeletal and connective tissue injuries lead to over 10 million clinic visits per year in the United States.[1] Causes of these injuries may be external (sports injuries, car accidents, trauma), internal (chronic wear and tear of muscles, ligaments and tendons; bones weakened by osteoporosis), or both. Acute injuries are characterized by severe pain, swelling and inflammation, and in some cases, internal bleeding. Treatment of acute injuries should focus on relieving pain, reducing swelling and inflammation, and stopping bleeding. Chronic injuries are characterized by dull pain, stiffness and numbness, and decreased muscle mass and strength. Treatment of chronic injuries includes relief of pain and restoration of physical and physiological functions.

FORMULA EXPLANATION

Knee & Ankle (CR) is designed to treat chronic degenerative knee disorders with swelling, inflammation, and pain. This formula incorporates tonic herbs to address the chronic and degenerative nature of illness. Furthermore, it contains herbs that activate qi and blood circulation, clear heat to reduce swelling and inflammation, and open the channels and collaterals to relieve pain.

Dang Gui (Radix Angelicae Sinensis), *Di Huang* (Radix Rehmanniae), *Shu Di Huang* (Radix Rehmanniae Praeparata), and *Dan Shen* (Radix et Rhizoma Salviae Miltiorrhizae) tonify blood, activate blood circulation, and disperse blood stagnation. *Dang Shen* (Radix Codonopsis), *Bai Zhu* (Rhizoma Atractylodis Macrocephalae), and *Gan Cao* (Radix et Rhizoma Glycyrrhizae) tonify qi. *Bai Shao* (Radix Paeoniae Alba) and *Shan Yao* (Rhizoma Dioscoreae) nourish yin to relieve chronic *bi zheng* (painful obstruction syndrome) with underlying Kidney deficiencies. *Mu Dan Pi* (Cortex Moutan), *Zhi Mu* (Rhizoma Anemarrhenae), and *Huang Bo* (Cortex Phellodendri Chinensis) clear deficiency heat to reduce chronic swelling and inflammation. *Ze Xie* (Rhizoma Alismatis) and *Fu Ling* (Poria) eliminate water accumulation and reduce swelling. *Chuan Niu Xi* (Radix Cyathulae) dispels stagnation and opens the channels and collaterals.

As many patients experience pain or worsening of their condition prior to rainy days, antirheumatic herbs should be used. *Wu Jia Pi* (Cortex Acanthopanacis), *Qian Nian Jian* (Rhizoma Homalomenae), *Du Zhong* (Cortex Eucommiae) and *Shen Jin Cao* (Herba Lycopodii) dispel wind-damp to treat *bi zheng* (painful obstruction syndrome). *Shen Jin Cao* (Herba Lycopodii) also has the effect to relieve stiffness. *Sheng Jiang* (Rhizoma Zingiberis Recens), *Da Zao* (Fructus Jujubae) and *Gan Cao* (Radix et Rhizoma Glycyrrhizae) harmonize all the herbs in the formula. *Ji Xue Teng* (Caulis Spatholobi) moves blood, opens channels and collaterals, and enhances flexibility. Lastly, *Chuan Niu Xi* (Radix Cyathulae) also acts as a channel-guiding herb to direct the therapeutic qualities of the formula to the affected area in the lower extremities.

Knee & Ankle (CR)™

Overall, ***Knee & Ankle (CR)*** is a well-balanced formula that addresses chronic and degenerative aspects of chronic knee disorders.

CAUTIONS & CONTRAINDICATIONS

- This formula should ***not*** be used alone in patients with acute physical injuries of the knees, such as external injuries or trauma with actual damage to the soft tissues (muscles, tendons, and ligaments). Patients with acute physical injuries of the knees or ankles, such as external injuries or trauma with actual damage to the soft tissues (muscles, tendons, and ligaments), should be treated with ***Flex (TMX)***, ***Knee & Ankle (AC)*** or ***Herbal ANG***.
- This formula should ***not*** be used alone in patients with inflammatory knee disorders, such as rheumatoid arthritis, bursitis, synovitis and tenosynovitis. Patients with such conditions should be treated with ***Flex (Heat)***, ***Flex (CD)*** or others depending on the TCM diagnosis.
- This herbal formula contains herbs that invigorate blood circulation, such as *Dan Shen* (Radix et Rhizoma Salviae Miltiorrhizae) and *Dang Gui* (Radix Angelicae Sinensis). Therefore, patients who are on anticoagulant or antiplatelet therapies, such as Coumadin (warfarin), should use this formula with caution, or not at all, as there may be a higher risk of bleeding and bruising.[2,3,4]

CLINICAL NOTES

- This formula is an excellent adjunct formula to acupuncture treatment. Optimal results will occur when acupuncture, electro-stimulation, and herbs are all included in the treatment regimen.
- Patients with arthritis should avoid vigorous exercise of the knee. Mild exercise, such as *tai chi chuan* [*tai ji chuan*] and walking, are recommended.
- This formula is most effective when taken during the recovery and rehabilitation phases of treatment. Strengthening exercises help to ensure recovery of the integrity of the knee and ankle ligaments.
- In cases where acute sprain and strain of the knees and ankles are not treated properly, the ligaments and joints will become unstable and re-injury may occur more frequently. ***Knee & Ankle (CR)*** can ensure the repair of minor tears of the ligaments and can facilitate complete recovery to prevent the future possibility of re-injury.

SUPPLEMENTARY FORMULAS

- For acute injuries with severe pain, combine with ***Knee & Ankle (AC)*** or ***Herbal ANG***.
- For ligament injuries or degeneration of soft tissue, combine with ***Flex (MLT)***.
- For knee disorders with manifestations of heat or *re bi* (heat painful obstruction), combine with ***Flex (Heat)***.
- For knee disorders with manifestations of cold and damp or *zhuo bi* (fixed painful obstruction), combine with ***Flex (CD)***.
- For bone spurs, add ***Flex (SPR)***.
- For osteoarthritis of the knee, add ***Osteo 8***.
- For acute pain in the lower back, add ***Back Support (AC)***.
- For chronic pain in the lower back, add ***Back Support (CR)***.
- For spasms and cramps in the legs, combine with ***Flex (SC)***.

ACUPUNCTURE TREATMENT

Traditional Points:

- *Xiyan*, *Liangqiu* (ST 34), *Xiyangguan* (GB 33), *Jiexi* (ST 41), *Kunlun* (BL 60), *Qiuxu* (GB 40), relevant *ah shi* points

Classic Master Tung's Points:

- Needle contralateral to the pain. If the pain is in the center, needle bilaterally or the side with the more *ah shi* points. If the pain is bilateral, needle bilaterally.
- **General knee pain:** *Xiyan*, *Jianzhong* (T 44.06), *Xinxi* (T 11.09). Bleed around *Gaohuangshu* (BL 43) with cupping. Bleed before needling for best result.
- **Lateral knee pain:** *Xinxi* (T 11.09), *Jianzhong* (T 44.06)
- **Knee (coldness):** *Tongguan* (T 88.01), *Tongtian* (T 88.03), *Xiyan*. Use plum-blossom needle to bleed on and around the knee. Bleed before needling for best result.
- **Knee (ligament pain):** *Shenjian* (T 44.19), *Jianfeng* (T 44.31)*, *Shangqu* (T 44.16), *Jianzhong* (T 44.06), *Yunbai* (T 44.11), *Renzong* (T 44.08), *Quchi* (LI 11), *Xinling* (T 33.17)*
- **Chondromalacia patella:** *Jianfeng* (T 44.31)*, *Jianzhong* (T 44.06), *Huofuhai* (T 33.07), *Tianhuang* (T 77.17), *Dihuang* (T 77.19), *Renhuang* (T 77.21)
- **Knee arthritis:** *Linggu* (T 22.05), *Jianzhong* (T 44.06), *Shangqu* (T 44.16), *Xiaqu* (T 44.15), *Libai* (T 44.12), *Yunbai* (T 44.11)
- **Medial ankle pain:** *Xiabai* (T 22.07), *Minghuang* (T 88.12), *Tianhuang* (T 88.13), *Qihuang* (T 88.14), *Wuhu* (T 11.27), *ah shi* points around the MCP joint of the thumb, *Xiaojie* (T 22.13)*. Bleed the sprained ankle. Bleed before needling for best result.
- **Lateral ankle pain:** *Linggu* (T 22.05), *Qimen* (T 33.01), *Qihu* (T 77.26), *ah shi* points around the MCP joint of the thumb, *Xiaojie* (T 22.13)*. Bleed the sprained ankle. Bleed before needling for best result.

Master Tung's Points by Dr. Chuan-Min Wang:

- **Knee pain:** Needle contralaterally *Jianzhong* (T 44.06). Bleed *Chize* (LU 5) or *Quchi* (LI 11) area if acute.
- **Ankle pain:** Needle contralaterally *Zhongbai* (T 22.06), *Xiabai* (T 22.07), *Wuhu* 4, 5 (T 11.27).

Balance Method by Dr. Richard Tan:

- *Ah shi* points around *Quchi* (LI 11), *Chize* (LU 5) and *Shaohai* (HT 3). Needle the side that is more tender upon palpation. If the pain is deep in the knee, needle the elbow for up to 1.5 to 2 *cun* if necessary.

Knee & Ankle (CR)™

Ear Acupuncture:

- Select the respective points on the ear for the pain in addition to Subcortex, *Shenmen*, and Adrenals.

Auricular Medicine by Dr. Li-Chun Huang:

- **Knee pain:** Knee Joint. Bleed Ear Apex.
  - For external knee joint pain, add External Knee.
  - For internal knee joint pain, add Internal Knee Joint.
- **Heel pain:** Heel (front and back). Bleed Ear Apex.

NUTRITION

- Glucosamine sulfate and chondroitin sulfate are well recognized for their nutritional support, as they are important for the formation of bones, tendons, ligaments, and cartilages.
- Sea cucumber is very beneficial, as it contains a rich source of compounds that are needed in all connective tissues, especially synovial joints and joint fluids.
- It is important to consume an adequate amount of various vitamins and minerals, as they are essential to prevent bone loss and promote bone growth.

LIFESTYLE INSTRUCTIONS

- It is important to engage in gentle exercises daily. This will not only facilitate recovery, but will also prevent muscle atrophy and muscle wasting.
- Avoid activities with high impact or high risk of injury.

CASE STUDIES

- K.L., a 42-year-old male, presented with right hip and leg pain and numbness. He was using crutches with decreased and impaired mobility for the previous three months. Symptoms of stiff neck, frozen ankle, and pain affecting his sleep were present. The patient had a tendency to get injuries due to his poor balance. The practitioner diagnosed the condition as *bi zheng* (painful obstruction syndrome) with blood deficiency and blood stasis with qi constraint. His Western diagnosis was muscle atrophy. The patient was given ***Flex (MLT)*** for eight weeks with the addition of ***Knee & Ankle (CR)*** for four weeks. With both formulas and receiving acupuncture treatment for eight weeks, the patient regained 100% of his leg use, moving from crutches to a cane. The patient resumed sleeping flat after three weeks and riding a bicycle after eight weeks. Pain reduced from 10 to 0 on a 1-10 scale. The patient was very pleased with the herbs, has started a yoga practice and has become more enthusiastic about life. Submitted by K.F., Honolulu, Hawaii.
- L.K., a 58-year-old female, presented with pain located on her left knee. Objective findings included limited range of motion, pain with movement, and limping. It was noted that her pain level was 7 out of 10, and the pain was only slightly alleviated with elevation or rest. The practitioner diagnosed this condition as qi and blood stagnation along with Liver and Kidney yin deficiencies. ***Knee & Ankle (CR)*** and ***Herbal ANG*** were prescribed upon diagnosis. After taking the herbs and receiving acupuncture, the patient's ROM was greater and her pain level had reduced. Submitted by J.C., Rosemead, California.
- A.S., a 45-year-old female, presented with a right lateral ankle sprain that had occurred three days prior. Objective findings included purplish color and swelling around the ankle. The practitioner diagnosed this condition as local blood stagnation. For treatment, ***Flex (TMX)*** and ***Knee & Ankle (AC)*** were prescribed. After taking the herbs for three days, the patient reported her ankle was feeling 50% better. She discontinued taking the ***Flex (TMX)*** after eight days since her ankle was then 90% better. For an additional week she continued to take the ***Knee & Ankle (CR)*** and her ankle was 100% better. Submitted by S.L., Yuma, Arizona.

PHARMACOLOGICAL AND CLINICAL RESEARCH

Knee & Ankle (CR) is an excellent formula for rehabilitation from chronic knee or ankle disorders, such as repetitive knee injuries or long-term wear and tear of the joint. As a result, the chronic nature of this condition may eventually contribute to atrophy and degeneration of the knee joints, accompanied by decreased mobility of the joints, and generalized weakness and pain. This formula is designed specifically to treat this condition, as it contains herbs with chondroprotective functions to protect joint destruction and cartilage erosion, osteogenic functions to promote generation of new bones, anti-inflammatory effects to reduce swelling and inflammation, analgesic effects to relieve pain, and muscle-relaxant effects to relieve spasms and cramps.

To facilitate healing and recovery from chronic leg injuries, many herbs are used to promote healing of cartilages, nerves, and bones. *Chuan Niu Xi* (Radix Cyathulae) is an excellent herb to protect the cartilage from repetitive and stress-induced injuries. According to one study, the extract of *Chuan Niu Xi* (Radix Cyathulae) has a potent effect to inhibit the induction of MMP-13, an important enzyme for the degradation of the cartilage collagen matrix, especially under arthritic conditions. By down-regulating the MMP-13 activity, *Chuan Niu Xi* (Radix Cyathulae) shows great chondroprotective benefit against cartilage degrading disorders.[5] *Dang Shen* (Radix Codonopsis) promotes neuron regeneration in a dose-dependent manner. Specifically, it activates IGF-I and FGF-2 pathways to induce proliferation and migration effects in RSC96 Schwann cells.[6] *Dang Gui* (Radix Angelicae Sinensis), *Du Zhong* (Cortex Eucommiae), *Shu Di Huang* (Radix Rehmanniae Praeparata) and *Zhi Mu* (Rhizoma Anemarrhenae) all have beneficial effects on the bones. *Dang Gui* (Radix Angelicae Sinensis) is an effective herb to promote the generation of bones. According to one study, the water extract of *Dang Gui* (Radix Angelicae Sinensis) has been found to contribute to the formation of bones and treatment of bone injuries. It directly stimulates the proliferation, alkaline phosphatase activity, protein secretion and particularly type I collagen synthesis of human osteoprecursor cells in a

Knee & Ankle (CR)™

dose-dependent manner.[7] *Du Zhong* (Cortex Eucommiae) has significant osteogenic and antiosteoporotic effects that promote generation of new bones and prevent osteoporosis. According to a bone cells culture experiment, administration of *Du Zhong* (Cortex Eucommiae) shows a potential effect to increase the proliferation and differentiation of the osteoblasts without affecting osteoclasts activities. The researchers conclude that these herbs can effectively increase the rate of tissue regeneration of damaged bones.[8] *Shu Di Huang* (Radix Rehmanniae Praeparata) has an antiosteoporotic effect to prevent osteoporotic bone loss. This herb stimulates the proliferation and activities of osteoblasts, while inhibiting the generation and resorptive activities of osteoclasts.[9] Lastly, *Zhi Mu* (Rhizoma Anemarrhenae) has an osteoprotective effect. It is effective to prevent bone loss through the promotion of bone formation but not the inhibition of bone resorption.[10]

Knee & Ankle (CR) also contains herbs with marked analgesic and anti-inflammatory effects to relieve pain, and reduce swelling and inflammation. For example, *Dang Gui* (Radix Angelicae Sinensis) has marked analgesic and anti-inflammatory effects, with potency similar or stronger than that of acetylsalicylic acid.[11,12] *Wu Jia Pi* (Cortex Acanthopanacis) also has excellent analgesic and anti-inflammatory effects with the duration of action lasting up to five hours.[13,14] *Bai Shao* (Radix Paeoniae Alba) and *Di Huang* (Radix Rehmanniae) have anti-inflammatory and antipyretic effects, and are helpful to reduce inflammation and swelling, as well as relieve burning sensations in affected areas.[15,16] *Mu Dan Pi* (Cortex Moutan) and *Du Zhong* (Cortex Eucommiae) have strong anti-inflammatory actions.[17] Pharmacologically, the mechanisms behind the anti-inflammatory effects of these herbs vary, but most have been attributed primarily to the inhibition of prostaglandin synthesis and decreased permeability of the blood vessels.[18] Alternatively, some anti-inflammatory mechanisms involve stimulation of the endocrine system and consequent secretion of steroids from the adrenal cortex.[19] Clinically, these herbs have been used with great success to treat a wide variety of musculoskeletal conditions, including but not limited to muscle wasting, muscle atrophy, chronic soft tissue injuries, and various types of pain.[20,21]

Bai Shao (Radix Paeoniae Alba) has excellent muscle-relaxant effect to relieve spasms, cramps, and muscle stiffness.[22] This efficacy has been demonstrated in both smooth and skeletal muscles. In addition, *Bai Shao* (Radix Paeoniae Alba) and *Gan Cao* (Radix et Rhizoma Glycyrrhizae) are effective in treating neuralgia.[23] Furthermore, *Bai Shao* (Radix Paeoniae Alba) and *Gan Cao* (Radix et Rhizoma Glycyrrhizae) have shown marked effectiveness to treat pain of the entire body, especially in the lower back and legs.[24]

Lastly, ***Knee & Ankle (CR)*** uses many herbs with adaptogenic effects to facilitate both mental and physical aspects of rehabilitation. *Dang Shen* (Radix Codonopsis) has a regulatory effect on the central nervous system to help with adaptation to various stressful environments.[25] *Wu Jia Pi* (Cortex Acanthopanacis) enhances physical adaptation by increasing endurance and performance.[26]

In summary, ***Knee & Ankle (CR)*** is an excellent formula for chronic knee and ankle disorders. Degeneration of soft tissues (muscles, tendons, and ligaments) is often seen in chronic knee and ankle disorders that lead to decreased range of motion and mobility of the joints. With late-stage musculoskeletal injuries, muscle wasting and atrophy are present due to lack of exercise and physical movement. ***Knee & Ankle (CR)*** is developed specifically to address all of these conditions by using herbs that compliment the rehabilitation process and complete the recovery from these injuries.

COMPARATIVE ANALYSIS

Pain is a basic bodily sensation induced by a noxious stimulus that causes physical discomfort (such as pricking, throbbing, or aching). Pain may be of acute or chronic state, and may be of nociceptive, neuropathic, or psychogenic origin. For acute pain, use of non-steroidal anti-inflammatory agents (NSAID) and opioid analgesics offer immediate and reliable effects to relieve pain. Though these drugs have serious side effects, short-term use can be justified because the benefits often outweigh the risks. For chronic pain, on the other hand, use of NSAIDs and opioid analgesics are usually not the desired treatment options, as they symptomatically relieve pain, but do not change the underlying course of illness. Unfortunately, the convenience of these drugs contributes to the vicious cycle of pain, followed by continuous and repetitive use of drugs to symptomatically relieve pain. When the effect of the drugs dissipates, patients are often left with nothing but more pain and more complications from side effects. Therefore, it is important to understand that while these drugs may be beneficial for acute pain, they do not adequately address most cases of chronic pain. Additional treatment modalities must be incorporated to ensure effective and complete recovery from chronic pain conditions. [Note: Common side effects of NSAIDs include gastric ulcer, duodenal ulcer, gastrointestinal bleeding, tinnitus, blurred vision, dizziness and headache. Serious side effects of newer NSAIDs, also known as COX-2 inhibitors [such as Celebrex (celecoxib)], include significantly higher risk of cardiovascular events, including heart attack and stroke. Side effects of opioid analgesics [such as Vicodin (APAP/hydrocodone) and morphine] include dizziness, lightheadedness, drowsiness, upset stomach, vomiting, constipation, stomach pain, rash, difficult urination, and respiratory depression resulting in difficult breathing. Furthermore, long-term use of these drugs leads to tolerance and addiction.]

Treatment of chronic pain is a sophisticated balance of art and science. Proper treatment of pain requires a careful evaluation of the type of disharmony (excess or deficiency, cold or heat, exterior or interior), characteristics (qi and/or blood stagnations), and location (upper body, lower body, extremities,

Knee & Ankle (CR)™

or internal organs). Furthermore, optimal treatment requires integrative use of herbs, acupuncture and *tui-na* therapies. All these therapies work together to tonify the underlying deficiencies, strengthen the body, and facilitate recovery from chronic pain. TCM pain management targets both the symptom and the cause of pain, and as such, often achieves immediate and long-term success. Furthermore, TCM pain management is often associated with few or no side effects.

For treatment of mild to severe pain due to various causes, TCM pain management offers similar treatment effects with significantly fewer side effects. Though TCM therapies may not be as potent as drugs for acute pain management, they are often superior [better effects with fewer side effects] for chronic pain management.

References

1. Berkow R. et al. The Merck Manual of Medical Information. Merck Research Laboratories. 1999 February.
2. Chan K, Lo AC, Yeung JH, Woo KS. Journal of Pharmacy and Pharmacology 1995 May;47(5):402-6.
3. Pharmacotherapy 1999 July;19(7):870-876.
4. European Journal of Drug Metabolism and Pharmacokinetics 1995; 20(1):55-60.
5. Park HY, Lim H, Kim HP, Kwon YS. Downregulation of Matrix Metalloproteinase-13 by the Root Extract of Cyathula officinalis Kuan and its Constituents in IL-1β-treated Chondrocytes. College of Pharmacy, Kangwon National University, Chunchon, Korea. Planta Med. 2011 Feb 23.
6. Chen HT, Tsai YL, Chen YS, Jong GP, Chen WK, Wang HL, Tsai FJ, Tsai CH, Lai TY, Tzang BS, Huang CY, Lu CY. Dangshen (Codonopsis pilosula) activates IGF-I and FGF-2 pathways to induce proliferation and migration effects in RSC96 Schwann cells. Am J Chin Med. 2010;38(2):359-72.
7. Yang Q, Populo SM, Zhang J, Yang G, Kodama H. Effect of Angelica sinensis on the proliferation of human bone cells. Clin Chim Acta. 2002 Oct;324(1-2): 89-97.
8. Yao CH, Tsai HM, Chen YS, Liu BS. Fabrication and evaluation of a new composite composed of tricalcium phosphate, gelatin, and Chinese medicine as a bone substitute. Institute of Biomedical Engineering and Material Science, Chungtai Institute of Health Science and Technology, Taichung, Taiwan, Republic of China. J Biomed Mater Res B Appl Biomater. 2005 Nov;75(2): 277-88.
9. Oh KO, Kim SW, Kim JY, Ko SY, Kim HM, Baek JH, Ryoo HM, Kim JK. Effect of Rehmannia glutinosa Libosch extracts on bone metabolism. OCT Inc., 2-17, Omok-ri, Seonggeo-eup, Choongnam 330-831, Chonan, South Korea. Clin Chim Acta. 2003 Aug;334(1-2):185-95.
10. Nian H, Qin LP, Chen WS, Zhang QY, Zheng HC, Wang Y. Protective effect of steroidal saponins from rhizome of Anemarrhena asphodeloides on ovariectomy-induced bone loss in rats. Department of Pharmacognosy, School of Pharmacy, Second Military Medical University, Shanghai 200433, China. Acta Pharmacol Sin. 2006 Jun;27(6):728-34.
11. *Xin Yi Yao Xue Za Zhi* (New Journal of Medicine and Herbology), 1975; (6):34.
12. *Yao Xue Za Zhi* (Journal of Medicinals), 1971; (91):1098.
13. *Zhong Guo Yao Li Xue Tong Bao* (Journal of Chinese Herbal Pharmacology), 1986; 2(2):21.
14. *Zhong Cheng Yao Yan Jiu* (Research of Chinese Patent Medicine), 1984; 10:22.
15. *Zhong Yao Yao Li Yu Ying Yong* (Pharmacology and Applications of Chinese Herbs), 1983: 400.
16. *Zhong Yao Zhi* (Chinese Herbology Journal), 1993; 183.
17. *Sheng Yao Xue Za Zhi* (Journal of Raw Herbology), 1979; 33(3):178.
18. *Zhong Guo Yao Ke Da Xue Xue Bao* (Journal of University of Chinese Herbology), 1990; 21(4):222.
19. *Zhong Cao Yao* (Chinese Herbal Medicine), 1983; 14(8):27.
20. *Xin Yi Yao Xue Za Zhi* (New Journal of Medicine and Herbology), 1976; 12:26.
21. *Shang Hai Zhong Yi Yao Za Zhi* (Shanghai Journal of Chinese Medicine and Herbology), 1983; 4:14.
22. *Zhong Yi Za Zhi* (Journal of Chinese Medicine), 1983; 11:9.
23. *Zhong Yi Za Zhi* (Journal of Chinese Medicine), 1983; 11:9.
24. *Yun Nan Zhong Yi* (Yunnan Journal of Traditional Chinese Medicine), 1990; 4:15.
25. *Zhong Yao Tong Bao* (Journal of Chinese Herbology), 1986; 11(8):53.
26. *Zhong Cao Yao* (Chinese Herbal Medicine), 1987; 18(3):28.

Liver DTX ™

CLINICAL APPLICATIONS

- **Liver detoxification:** enhances the normal metabolic and detoxification functions of the liver
- **Liver damage** with elevated liver enzymes
- **Hepatitis** with or without jaundice
- **Liver cirrhosis** caused by alcohol, drugs or other chemicals
- **Addiction treatment:** detoxifies liver from alcohol, drugs, and other chemicals

WESTERN THERAPEUTIC ACTIONS

- Enhances the liver function by increasing the regeneration of liver cells
- Protects the liver from damage caused by alcohol, drugs or other chemicals
- Treats liver cirrhosis by preventing and repairing liver damage
- Antioxidant effects to neutralize free radicals and prevent cell damage
- Lowers elevated levels of hepatic enzymes

CHINESE THERAPEUTIC ACTIONS

- Clears heat and eliminates toxins
- Spreads the Liver qi
- Drains dampness
- Tonifies deficiency

DOSAGE

Take 3 to 4 capsules three times daily on an empty stomach with warm water.

INGREDIENTS

Bai Shao (Radix Paeoniae Alba)
Chai Hu (Radix Bupleuri)
Da Huang (Radix et Rhizoma Rhei)
Fu Ling (Poria)
Ge Hua (Flos Puerariae)
Hu Zhang (Rhizoma et Radix Polygoni Cuspidati)
Huang Qin (Radix Scutellariae)
Ma Bian Cao (Herba Verbenae)
Pu Tao Zi (Semen Vitis Vinifera)
Qing Pi (Pericarpium Citri Reticulatae Viride)
Shui Fei Ji (Fructus Silybi)
Wu Wei Zi (Fructus Schisandrae Chinensis)
Yin Chen (Herba Artemisiae Scopariae)
Yu Jin (Radix Curcumae)
Zhi Zi (Fructus Gardeniae)

BACKGROUND

The liver is an organ responsible for many metabolic functions: formation and excretion of bile, carbohydrate homeostasis, lipid synthesis, cholesterol metabolism, and metabolism or detoxification of drugs and other foreign substances. Liver disorders are often caused by infections, drugs, toxins, ischemia and autoimmune diseases. Liver disorders are characterized by abnormal laboratory test results (i.e., elevated ALT and AST) and symptoms (i.e., jaundice, right upper quadrant pain). Treatment varies depending on the exact disease and its cause.

FORMULA EXPLANATION

According to traditional Chinese medicine, liver disorders are characterized by damp-heat or toxic heat in the Liver. ***Liver DTX*** is formulated to eliminate damp-heat, clear toxic heat, and regulate Liver qi. Clinical applications include hepatitis, liver cirrhosis, and cholecystitis. It can also be used to protect the liver and lower liver enzymes secondary to the use of drugs and alcohol, and subsequent to viral infections.

To detoxify the liver, the treatment protocol is to strengthen the liver function. Capillarisin, one of the active ingredients of *Yin Chen* (Herba Artemisiae Scopariae), increases the secretion of bile, bile salts and bilirubin. It increases the regeneration of liver cells and is an indispensable herb when treating jaundice or cholecystitis. *Chai Hu* (Radix Bupleuri) is a channel-guiding herb and is also extremely effective in protecting the liver cells from denaturalization and necrosis. It is often used to decrease liver enzymes in patients with fatty liver or chronic hepatitis. *Ge Hua* (Flos Puerariae) relieves alcohol poisoning. *Hu Zhang* (Rhizoma et Radix Polygoni Cuspidati), *Zhi Zi* (Fructus Gardeniae), *Huang Qin* (Radix Scutellariae) and *Da Huang* (Radix et Rhizoma Rhei) clear heat, eliminate toxins and improve the liver function. *Bai Shao* (Radix Paeoniae Alba) nourishes the Liver blood. *Ma Bian Cao* (Herba Verbenae) enters the Liver channel to clear heat and detoxify. *Fu Ling* (Poria) strengthens the Spleen and promotes the excretion of toxins through urination. *Yu Jin* (Radix Curcumae) benefits the Gallbladder and the Liver in treating viral hepatitis. It also invigorates blood circulation to promote generation of new liver cells. *Qing Pi* (Pericarpium Citri Reticulatae Viride) spreads the stagnant Liver qi and relieves constraint. *Wu Wei Zi* (Fructus Schisandrae Chinensis) improves the Liver function in patients with hepatitis. Both *Pu Tao Zi* (Semen Vitis Vinifera) and *Shui Fei Ji* (Fructus Silybi) have excellent hepatoprotective and antioxidant functions.

In summary, ***Liver DTX*** eliminates damp-heat and clears toxic heat to enhance liver function and treat liver disorders.

CAUTIONS & CONTRAINDICATIONS

- ***Liver DTX*** is contraindicated during pregnancy and nursing. It should be used with caution in cases of qi and yang deficiencies.
- Do ***not*** use this formula to treat acute liver failure – such conditions must be sent to the emergency room for immediate medical care.
- Decrease the dosage to two capsules twice a day if there is loose stool after taking the herbs.
- The following warning statement is required by the State of California: "This product contains *Da Huang* (Radix et Rhizoma Rhei). Read and follow directions carefully. Do not use if you have or develop diarrhea, loose stools, or abdominal pain because

Liver DTX ™

Da Huang (Radix et Rhizoma Rhei) may worsen these conditions and be harmful to your health. Consult your physician if you have frequent diarrhea or if you are pregnant, nursing, taking medication, or have a medical condition."

CLINICAL NOTES

- Laboratory tests are extremely useful in diagnosis, treatment, and prognosis assessment for patients with liver dysfunction. Understanding the implications of laboratory tests empowers healthcare practitioners to effectively treat hepatic and gallbladder disorders.
- Elevation of liver enzymes is common in hepatitis. Though Western medicine has treatments for lowering liver enzymes, the results are often unsatisfactory, especially in chronic hepatitis B. Therefore, herbs that clear heat, remove dampness, strengthen the Spleen and regulate the Liver are used to normalize liver enzyme levels. In addition, small dosages of blood-activating and stasis-removing herbs can be used together for their synergistic effect. Patients should continue to take herbs for a period of time after liver enzyme levels return to normal to prevent a rebound increase of liver enzymes.
- Liver cirrhosis is a common complication of chronic hepatitis infection. To reduce the risk of developing cirrhosis of the liver in chronic hepatitis, use large dosages of *Dan Shen* (Radix et Rhizoma Salviae Miltiorrhizae) with regular dosages of *Hong Hua* (Flos Carthami). Addition of *Bie Jia* (Carapax Trionycis) to the herbal formula will further reduce the risk of developing liver cirrhosis.
- The five main reasons hepatitis B patients remain chronic carriers of the hepatitis B virus:
  1. Enhanced or suppressed immunity. Patients with irregular immune systems are less likely to become negative on the HBV exam. Indications of irregular immune system include high or low levels of IgG, IgM and IgA.
  2. Frequent infection of the oral region indicates a suppressed immunity. This can be treated with *Ye Ju Hua* (Flos Chrysanthemi Indici) and *Gan Cao* (Radix et Rhizoma Glycyrrhizae).
  3. Seasonal factors. The treatment of hepatitis is less effective in spring and summer. In spring, there is a higher incidence of Liver qi damaging the yin. In summer, the damp-heat in the environment may increase dampness and heat inside the body. Thus, the ideal seasons to treat hepatitis B are autumn and winter. To enhance the overall effectiveness of the treatment, *Yi Guan Jian* (Linking Decoction) can be added in autumn and *Liu Yi San* (Six-to-One Powder) can be added in summer.
  4. Increase in liver enzymes such as AST and ALT.
  5. Dietary restrictions. Patients should reduce their intake of alcohol, hot and spicy food, and any other foods that worsen the condition.

Pulse Diagnosis by Dr. Jimmy Wei-Yen Chang:

- Wiry, forceful, and deep pulse on the left *guan*

SUPPLEMENTARY FORMULAS

- For cholecystitis or gallstones with elevated liver enzymes, combine with ***Dissolve (GS)***.
- ***Gentiana Complex*** may be combined with ***Liver DTX*** for a synergistic effect to treat hepatic disorders.
- For fatty liver, add ***Cholisma (ES)***.
- With jaundice, add *Yin Chen Hao Tang* (Artemisia Scoparia Decoction).
- In early stage liver cirrhosis, add ***Resolve (AI)*** and ***Circulation (SJ)***.
- For nervousness, irritability, and stress, combine with ***Calm*** or ***Calm (ES)***.
- For excess fire signs and symptoms throughout the body, add ***Gardenia Complex***.
- For dark complexion and blood stagnation, add ***Circulation (SJ)***.
- To enhance the antibacterial function, add ***Herbal ABX***.
- To enhance the antiviral function, add ***Herbal AVR***.
- To reduce inflammation, add ***Astringent Complex***.
- For stomach discomfort, heartburn, and/or acid reflux, combine with ***GI Care***.
- With IBS or bloating, add ***GI Harmony***.
- To detox the colon, add ***GI DTX***.
- For heavy metal, chemical or environmental poisoning, add ***Herbal DTX***.
- For compromised kidney function, use ***Kidney DTX***.
- To enhance the immune system, add ***Immune +***.
- For a quick burst of energy and awareness, combine with ***Vibrant***.
- To tonify the underlying deficiencies of qi, blood, yin and yang, use ***Imperial Tonic***.
- For toxicity manifesting in skin allergies, rashes or unexplainable itching of the skin, choose from ***Silerex***, ***Dermatrol (Damp)*** or ***Dermatrol (Dry)***.
- With visual disorder, combine with ***Lycium Support*** or ***Nourish***.

ACUPUNCTURE TREATMENT

Traditional Points:

- *Taichong* (LR 3), *Xingjian* (LR 2), *Ganshu* (BL 18), *Zusanli* (ST 36)
- *Xingjian* (LR 2), *Taichong* (LR 3), *Fenglong* (ST 40), *Sanyinjiao* (SP 6), *Ganshu* (BL 18), *Danshu* (BL 19)

Classic Master Tung's Points:

- **Hepatitis (acute):** *Ganmen* (T 33.11), *Changmen* (T 33.10), *Xinmen* (T 33.12), *Linggu* (T 22.05), *Muyan* (T 11.20), *Ganlingsan* (T 33.18)*, *Tianhuang* (T 88.13), *Qihuang* (T 88.14), *Minghuang* (T 88.12), *Shuitong* (T 1010.19), *Tongguan* (T 88.01), *Shuijin* (T 1010.20), *Menjin* (T 66.05), *Muhuang* (T 88.47)*, *Muling* (T 11.29)*. Needle every other day. Bleed *Huobao* (T 55.01) or nearby dark veins. Bleed before needling for best result.

FORMULAS

Liver DTX ™

- **Hepatitis (toxins/medication):** *Fenzhishang* (T DT.01), *Fenzhixia* (T DT.02), *Ganmen* (T 33.11), *Minghuang* (T 88.12), *Huoquan* (T 88.16), *Qihuang* (T 88.14). Needle every day.
- **Liver cirrhosis:** *Ganlingsan* (T 33.18)*, *Minghuang* (T 88.12), *Qihuang* (T 88.14), *Tianhuang* (T 88.13), *Muyan* (T 11.20), *Yizhong* (T 77.05), *Erzhong* (T 77.06), *Sanzhong* (T 77.07), *Ganmen* (T 33.11), *Huozhi* (T 88.15), *Renhuang* (T 77.21), *Tianhuangfu [Shenguan]* (T 77.18). Needle everyday until condition stabilizes. Bleed *Shangqu* (T 44.16) or nearby dark veins. Bleed before needling for best result.

Master Tung's Points by Dr. Chuan-Min Wang:

- **Hepatitis:** *Changmen* (T 33.10), *Ganmen* (T 33.11)
- **Jaundice:** *Qihuang* (T 88.14), *Huozhi* (T 88.15), *Huoquan* (T 88.16)
- **Cirrhosis:** Needle *Ganmen* (T 33.11), *Minghuang* (T 88.12), *Tianhuang* (T 88.13), *Qihuang* (T 88.14). Bleed *Quchi* (LI 11).
- **Elevated liver enzymes, addiction, toxin in the Liver:** *Minghuang* (T 88.12), *Tianhuang* (T 88.13), *Qihuang* (T 88.14), *Ganmen* (T 33.11), *Fenjin* (T 44.01)

Balance Method by Dr. Richard Tan:

- Left side: *Hegu* (LI 4), *Zhizheng* (SI 7), *Ligou* (LR 5), *Ququan* (LR 8). *Ganmen*, Liver and Pancreas on the ear.
- Right side: *Neiguan* (PC 6), *Ximen* (PC 4) or *ah shi* points nearby, *Yanglingquan* (GB 34), *Zusanli* (ST 36) or *ah shi* points nearby. Liver and Pancreas on the ear.
- Left and right sides can be alternated from treatment to treatment.

Ear Acupuncture:

- **To detoxify the liver:** use three needles on the Liver or embed needles on the Liver point.

Auricular Medicine by Dr. Li-Chun Huang:

- **Hepatitis:** Liver, Gall Bladder, Rib Rim, Spleen, *San Jiao*, Endocrine, Abdominal Distension Area, Digestive Subcortex, Ear Center, Hepatitis

NUTRITION

- Patients with liver cirrhosis should increase the intake of vitamin K found in such foods as green leafy vegetables, almonds, bananas, kelp, prunes, raisins, rice, wheat bran, and seeds. They should increase their intake of vegetables, especially artichokes, carrots, and beets. Water intake should be increased.
- Artichokes contain cynarin, a substance that stimulates the bile flow and regulates the liver.
- Patients with hepatitis should avoid alcohol, sugar, fat, raw fish, shellfish and highly-processed foods with chemicals or food additives. Fat, butter, margarine, cheese, fish, fowl, meat, salt, soft drinks, sugar, tea, cod liver oil, vitamin A, and spicy and fried fried foods should be eliminated from the diet. Also avoid over-eating, cigarette smoking, alcohol, coffee, and drugs.
- Patients with jaundice should ***not*** consume alcohol, raw or undercooked fish, meat or poultry.

The Tao of Nutrition by Dr. Maoshing Ni and Cathy McNease:

- **Liver cleansing**
  - Drink beet top tea, or combine with dandelion herb and make tea.
  - To help liver detoxify, juice collard greens with kale, mustard greens, carrots, celery, and cucumber. Drink 1 to 2 glasses daily.
- **Liver toxicity**
  - Make vegetable juice from chard, kale, spinach, beet and carrot greens, carrot, apple and one tablespoonful of spirulina or chlorella. Consume one to two glasses daily.
- **Hepatitis**
  - Recommendations: rice, barley, millet, azuki beans, pearl barley, squash, cucumber, grapefruit, dandelion greens, beet greens, pears, water chestnut, carrot, cabbage, spinach, celery, winter melon, rice vinegar, pineapple, and lotus root.
  - Cook lotus root and puree, then cook into rice or millet porridge.
  - Juice watermelon, celery and pears.
  - Make mung bean soup with pearl barley.
  - Soak grapefruit and peel in rice vinegar overnight, then take one teaspoon in one cup of warm liquid.
  - Take cucumber juice on empty stomach every morning.
  - Avoid dairy products, alcohol, coffee, sugar, fatty and fried foods, overly spicy foods, cold and raw foods, tomato, eggplant, bell peppers, and shellfish.

LIFESTYLE INSTRUCTIONS

- Avoid physical and mental stress and exhaustion whenever possible. Maintain a cheerful and positive outlook and avoid dramatic emotional swings.
- Avoid exposure to toxins whenever possible, including but not limited to chemicals, heavy metals, herbicides, pesticides, and environmental pollutants.
- Physical stimulation to the back by scratching or intense massage will stimulate the liver to increase activity.

CASE STUDIES

- D.T., a 56-year-old male patient, presented with elevated liver enzymes and high cholesterol. The practitioner diagnosed the condition as Liver blood and yin deficiencies with blood stasis and Spleen deficiency. He was treated with ***Liver DTX*** at 4 capsules three times daily for one month, followed by ***Cholisma*** at 4 capsules three times daily for two months, gradually reducing thereafter. As a result of the treatment, his blood work revealed normal liver enzymes after one month of taking ***Liver DTX*** along with cholesterol levels within normal range after two months of taking ***Cholisma***. After one year his cholesterol levels remained great and he continued to take a maintenance dose of ***Cholisma***. Submitted by A.G., Solana Beach, California.

Liver DTX ™

- D.D., a 45-year old business owner, who was a single mom and had less than four hours of sleep each night, presented with chronic eczema and itchy skin. Objective findings were red and heavy eyes and the location of her rash was mainly on her hands and feet. She had recently lost over 50 pounds and was still trying to lose more weight. The practitioner diagnosed this condition as damp-heat and Liver disharmony. ***Dermatrol (PS)*** was prescribed at three pills three times daily along with ***Liver DTX*** at the same dosage. The results were positive; she experienced less itching and her rashes were less. However, during times of stress and lack of sleep the rash and itching symptoms would return. The patient's compliance with her lifestyle was needed for prolonged results. Submitted by L.W., Arroyo Grande, California.
- J.K., a 35-year-old male, presented with alcoholism, with a constant urge to drink. However, he did not want to do AA. Other than this, the patient was otherwise considered to be healthy. The patient had also just previously quit smoking cold turkey. For treatment the patient was given ***Calm (ES)*** and ***Liver DTX*** in conjunction with receiving acupuncture. As a result, the patient reported that he no longer had the urge to drink and was also being less reactive. The practitioner had also counseled the patient that this was not a stand alone treatment for alcoholism and advised the patient to go seek more help. Submitted by B.L., Fort Myers, Florida.
- W.G., a 23-year-old male, presented with toxicity due to recreational drugs. The TCM diagnosis was toxic heat in the Liver as well as throughout the entire body. For treatment, ***Liver DTX*** and ***Herbal DTX*** were prescribed. The patient noticed a significant detoxification in response to taking both formulas. In comparison, he had noticed the ***Liver DTX*** working more through the urine and the ***Herbal DTX*** working throughout the entire body. He was very in-tune with his body and testified that these formulas were very helpful to his condition. Submitted by B.S., Niceville, Florida.
- A 57-year-old female presented with an enlarged liver. There was a history of hepatitis and she had a cholecystectomy. Symptoms included shortness of breath, edema in the upper body, and liver enzyme elevation. The TCM diagnosis was Spleen qi deficiency with phlegm engendering the organs. ***Liver DTX*** and ***Cholisma (ES)*** were both prescribed for five months. Her liver was normal in size without any discrete mass. As a result of taking the herbs, the patient's overall condition had improved. It was confirmed through additional testing of her liver that it was back to normal. She hasn't had any issues since. Submitted by H.C., Sydney, New York.
- A 41-year-old male complained of occasional bouts of irritability. He had elevated liver enzymes, elevated HCT and was positive for Hepatitis C. The practitioner diagnosed his condition as damp-heat in the Liver and Gallbladder. After taking ***Liver DTX***, the liver enzyme levels tested within normal limits. The patient's medical doctor, after recognizing all supporting evidence, encouraged the herbal treatment wholeheartedly. Submitted by P.C., Stanwood, Washington.
- M.C., a 49-year-old highly-stressed executive, presented elevated SGPT, LDL and cholesterol levels. He stated he frequently checked his blood pressure and it ranged from 135-148/85-91 mmHg. He was never diagnosed with hypertension but had an upcoming insurance physical and wanted to lower his blood pressure naturally [without using drugs]. He also complained of low-grade temporal headaches, pressured feeling in the head, and neck and shoulder tension. His blood pressure at the time of examination was 148/94 mmHg and his heart rate was 72 beats per minute. He worried excessively, in part because his son was diagnosed with brain tumor ten years ago. He also suffered from insomnia, and fist clenching that lasted throughout the day. He said that his stress caused numbness and tension on his left shoulder and rhomboid area. The TCM diagnoses were Liver qi stagnation and Spleen qi deficiency. ***Cholisma*** at 4 capsules three times daily and ***Liver DTX*** at 5 capsules at night were prescribed. He reported after taking the herbs, he passed his exam for insurance. Blood pressure has stayed down at 120/72 mmHg. His stress was manageable and there were no more headaches. Energy level was also excellent. His cholesterol levels had also dropped from 216 to 186 mg/dL. The practitioner reported that the patient is now a believer of herbs. Submitted by M.H., West Palm Beach, Florida.
- A 45-year-old female with insulin-dependent diabetes presented with malaise, fatigue, night sweats, hot flashes and low back pain. She also had abdominal bloating, red eyes, weak nails and a pale complexion. She was diagnosed with hepatitis C. The practitioner prescribed ***Liver DTX*** (3 capsules three times daily) and ***Equilibrium*** (3 capsules three times daily). Also given was a pancreatic homeopathic remedy (10 drops 6 times a day) and another homeopathic remedy, Hepan Comp (1 drop three times daily). Two and a half months later, the patient discontinued her insulin use. Her viral load was almost within the normal range and she decided to discontinue all pharmaceuticals. There was a total reversal of her clinical picture. Submitted by I.B., Miami, Florida.
- A 68-year-old retired male complained of diminishing vision. In turn, he became frustrated with the fact that he was no longer able to play tennis as well as before or competitively. Other visual dysfunctions included a reduction in visual field and the inability to track objects. The practitioner diagnosed the patient's condition as Liver qi stagnation and Liver fire with underlying Liver yin deficiency. The practitioner suspected blood leakage into the post-retinal layer, which would have been indicative of a detached retina. The patient was given ***Liver DTX***. Along with the herbal treatment, the practitioner also stressed the importance of diet, especially devoid of alcohol and sugar. Although the patient was not completely compliant with the treatment, his visual compromise stabilized and the deterioration stopped. The practitioner observed a reversal of the patient's

Liver DTX ™

symptoms and anticipated an encouraging prognosis. Submitted by T.W., Santa Monica, California.

- J.J., a 45-year-old male, presented with tiredness, aching joints, occasional jaundice, bleeding gums and nose, thirst, foul and sticky bowel movements, short-temper, irritability, disturbed sleep, dry eyes and floaters. His tongue was red, quivering and the tip was red. His pulse was wiry on both sides. Blood pressure was 125/80 mmHg and the heart rate was 72 beats per minute. Western medical diagnosis was Hepatitis C. The TCM diagnosis was damp-heat in the Liver, Liver blood deficiency and Liver overacting on the Spleen. ***Liver DTX*** combined with *Huang Bo* (Cortex Phellodendri Chinensis) was prescribed totaling 12 grams a day. Omega-3 fatty acids were also recommended at 1 tablespoon per day. Patient had a very recent liver profile done before the treatment. Within three weeks of acupuncture and herbal treatments, his total liver profile (by a new blood test) imbalances were reduced by over 66%. He felt amazingly better. No bloating or hypochondrial pain. Digestion was much improved, as well as energy and well-being. Proper dietary recommendations were also implemented. The practitioner reported that he consistently found the ***Liver DTX*** to be an amazing and very powerful formula, especially with hepatitis. Submitted by M.N., Knoxville, Tennessee.
- A 44-year-old female with hepatitis C, necrosis of the liver, and diabetes (insulin-dependent) was treated with interferon, Rebetron (ribavirin and interferon α 2B), Zantac (ranitidine), Prozac (fluoxetine) and insulin. Her clinical manifestations included pain in the liver region, fatigue, insomnia, blurred vision, constipation, melancholy, frontal headache, dizziness, tremors, abdominal bloating, and a pale complexion. Her tongue was maroon in color, and the pulse was slippery. The diagnosis for this patient was dampness in the Liver and Gallbladder, with Liver overacting on the Spleen and the Stomach, hence disrupting the transformation and transportation of the digestive system. The patient was treated with two herbal formulas (***Liver DTX*** and ***Imperial Tonic***) and two homeopathic formulas (sarcode liver formula and oral insulin). The treatment also included acupuncture involving meridian treatment and extraordinary vessel treatment. After three weeks, the patient had significant improvements in her vitality, complexion, appetite, sleep, attitude and energy level. A dramatic reduction of her abdominal pain was also noted. Her insulin use was reduced by approximately 25%. Submitted by I.B., Miami, Florida.
- A 22-year-old female presented with high triglycerides and high ALT. The patient appeared thin and pale. Her limbs were always cold and she was easily agitated. Her blood pressure was 115/70 mmHg and the heart rate was 72 beats per minute. The TCM diagnosis was yang deficiency with heat in the Liver. ***Liver DTX*** at 3 capsules three times a day was prescribed with ***Cholisma*** at 2 capsules twice a day. She also received acupuncture. After six weeks, her liver enzymes and triglycerides levels returned to normal. Submitted by W.F., Bloomfield, New Jersey.
- M.C., a 49-year-old male, presented with elevated SGPT levels (72, normal 0-40) but his medical doctor told him it was normal. At age 8, this patient suffered from a blood disorder called "Fatty Bone Marrow" with no hemoglobins. He was treated but the results were reported to be moderate in effectiveness. There was negative history for any liver disorders. His blood pressure was 120/72 mmHg and his heart rate was 62 beats per minute. The TCM diagnoses were Spleen qi deficiency and Liver qi stagnation. He was instructed to take 5 capsules of ***Liver DTX*** at bedtime for three months. After the herbs, the SGOT level reduced to 21 and the SGPT level to 32. The patient was thrilled. Submitted by M.H., West Palm Beach, Florida .
- A 36-year-old female patient presented with severe hangover from excessive alcohol consumption. Clinical signs and symptoms included nausea, vomiting, anorexia, frontal headache, diarrhea, and extreme weakness and fatigue. Her tongue was pale and flabby, with a moist, greasy tongue coating. Her face was pale and puffy, with dark, sunken eyes. The Western diagnosis was acute alcohol intoxication; the TCM diagnosis was damp-heat in the Liver and Gallbladder, with qi deficiency. ***Liver DTX*** was prescribed at four capsules every four to six hours for one day. Within two hours after taking the first dose, the patient reported that she felt 98% improvement, and said that she had regained her strength and appetite. She stated that her headache, nausea, vomiting and diarrhea had all diminished. She took the second dose, ate a large meal, and recovered from alcohol intoxication. Submitted by C.L., Chino Hills, California.
- M.F., a 57-year-old female, presented with pain in the leg and big toe with pressure, metallic taste, absence of thirst, heat sensations except in the hands and feet, and upper body sweating. She had been exposed to toxic chemicals and pesticides for six months. The TCM diagnosis was yin deficiency with heat, damp-heat and toxic heat accumulation, and *bi zheng* (painful obstruction syndrome) of the legs. After six weeks of taking ***Liver DTX***, ***Balance (Heat)*** and ***Flex (NP)***, she experienced less leg pain, decreased sweating, subsiding heat sensations, and warmer hands. The patient still had a metallic taste in the mouth. The patient also increased her intake of carrot juice and cucumbers. Submitted by M.C., Sarasota, Florida.

PHARMACOLOGICAL AND CLINICAL RESEARCH

Liver DTX is formulated with herbs that enhance the normal metabolic rate and detoxification functions of the liver.[1] Herbs in ***Liver DTX*** have demonstrated functions to increase the regeneration of liver cells,[2] protect the liver from damage by foreign chemicals and substances,[1] prevent and repair liver damage,[3] and lower elevated levels of liver enzymes.[4]

Shui Fei Ji (Fructus Silybi), also known as milk thistle, is one of the main ingredients in ***Liver DTX***. The use of *Shui Fei Ji* (Fructus Silybi) can be traced back over 2,000 years to a Greek reference when Pliny the Elder (A.D. 23-79) first noted it had an excellent effect to "carry off bile."[5] Today, *Shui Fei Ji* (Fructus

Liver DTX ™

Silybi) is well documented for having both hepatoprotective and nephroprotective effects against Tylenol (acetaminophen)-induced liver and kidney toxicities.[6] The mechanism of action is attributed to its antiapoptotic, antioxidant and anti-inflammatory activities.[7] Silymarin, one active compound from *Shui Fei Ji* (Fructus Silybi), has been found to have hepatoprotective and antioxidant effects. Silymarin protects the liver by changing the outer liver cell membrane and preventing the entrance of toxins into the liver cells.[5,8] Specific indications for silymarin include cirrhosis and hepatitis. Silymarin was found to be effective in treating alcoholic cirrhosis as concluded by a 41-month double-blind study of 170 patients.[4] Silymarin also improved liver function in 20 patients with chronic active hepatitis.[9]

Wu Wei Zi (Fructus Schisandrae Chinensis) has a marked hepatoprotective effect and is frequently used to treat various liver disorders. Studies have shown that administration of *Wu Wei Zi* (Fructus Schisandrae Chinensis) is associated with a marked hepatoprotective effect against various types of drugs and/or chemical-induced toxicities.[10] In one study, a preparation of *Wu Wei Zi* (Fructus Schisandrae Chinensis) significantly lowered liver enzymes in subjects with elevated SGPT levels caused by intraperitoneal injection of 0.1% carbon tetrachloride. The mechanisms of hepatoprotective function of *Wu Wei Zi* (Fructus Schisandrae Chinensis) are attributed to the alteration of liver cell membrane permeability to prevent the entry of toxic substances, and increased blood flow to the liver and increased regeneration of liver cells.[11,12] Clinically, *Wu Wei Zi* (Fructus Schisandrae Chinensis) is frequently used to treat hepatitis and lower liver enzymes. In one study, oral ingestion of *Wu Wei Zi* (Fructus Schisandrae Chinensis) (3 to 6 grams in powdered herb mixed with honey) three times daily for one month per course of treatment effectively lowered liver enzyme levels to normal. Another study reported an 85.3% rate of effectiveness using 3g of powdered *Wu Wei Zi* (Fructus Schisandrae Chinensis) three times daily to treat 102 cases of non-icteric infectious hepatitis. Furthermore, one study reported that oral ingestion of *Wu Wei Zi* (Fructus Schisandrae Chinensis) in honey pills effectively lowered liver enzymes in 67 of 80 patients with chronic hepatitis.[13] Lastly, an herbal formula with *Wu Wei Zi* (Fructus Schisandrae Chinensis) was used with a 97% rate of effectiveness (33 out of 34 patients) in the treatment of chronic hepatitis.[14]

Yin Chen (Herba Artemisiae Scopariae), *Da Huang* (Radix et Rhizoma Rhei) and *Zhi Zi* (Fructus Gardeniae), three herbs used in *Yin Chen Hao Tang* (Artemisia Scoparia Decoction), are important herbs with significant activities to treat liver and gallbladder disorders. Pharmacologically, these three herbs have been shown in many studies to effectively protect the liver from various drug- or chemical-induced hepatitis, including Tylenol (acetaminophen), carbon tetrachloride, α-naphthylisothiocyanate (ANIT), and concanavalin A.[15,16,17] The mechanism of this action is attributed to inhibited production of inflammatory cytokines and enhanced production of anti-inflammatory cytokines. According to the research, administration of these three herbs may be useful for treating severe acute hepatitis accompanying cholestasis in cases of autoimmune hepatitis.[18] Clinically, these three herbs have been used successfully to treat acute infectious icteric hepatitis,[19] acute icteric hepatitis,[20] acute viral hepatitis,[21] jaundice,[22] and biliary atresia.[23]

Liver DTX contains many other herbs to directly and indirectly protect the liver and treat liver disorders. *Chai Hu* (Radix Bupleuri) has hepatoprotective activity that protects the liver against carbon tetrachloride-induced liver damages and inhibits the growth of liver cancer cells.[24,25] *Bai Shao* (Radix Paeoniae Alba) illustrates marked antiviral activity against hepatitis B virus (HBV) to inhibit the HBV multiplication and decrease the level of extracellular HBV.[26] Daidzin and daidzein, two compounds from *Ge Gen* (Radix Puerariae Lobatae) and *Ge Hua* (Flos Puerariae), have marked antialcoholic effects and help to treat liver damage associated with consumption of large amounts of ethanol.[27] *Hu Zhang* (Rhizoma et Radix Polygoni Cuspidati) contains resveratrol, which has demonstrated a hepatoprotective effect by lowering the liver enzymes SGOT and SGPT.[28] Clinical studies have shown *Hu Zhang* (Rhizoma et Radix Polygoni Cuspidati) to effectively treat chronic hepatitis with positive HbsAg.[29] *Huang Qin* (Radix Scutellariae) has a remarkable effect to protect and prevent various types of liver injuries. *Huang Qin* (Radix Scutellariae) protects against mutagenesis of liver cells induced by the mycotoxin aflatoxin-B_1.[30] It also protects against fibrosis and lipid peroxidation in the liver induced by bile duct ligation and scission or by carbon tetrachloride.[31] In one clinical study, 268 patients with infectious or chronic hepatitis were treated with *Huang Qin* (Radix Scutellariae) through oral administration and intramuscular injection. The duration of treatment was one month for both oral therapy (0.5 grams of baicalin three times daily) and injection therapy (60 to 120 mg of baicalin via intramuscular or intravenous injection). The effective rate was 63.6% for patients with infectious hepatitis and 73.3% for chronic hepatitis.[32]

In summary, ***Liver DTX*** is an excellent formula with numerous mechanisms of hepatoprotective effect to prevent and treat various liver disorders.

COMPARATIVE ANALYSIS

Liver diseases, such as hepatitis and liver cirrhosis, are serious and very complicated diseases. In Western medicine, these conditions are usually treated with interferon. These drugs, however, have limited success, but are extremely expensive and create significant number of serious side effects, including dizziness, confusion, coma, arrhythmia, heart failure, leukopenia, thrombocytopenia, and many others. In severe and life threatening cases, such as liver cirrhosis and liver cancer, surgery may be performed.

In traditional Chinese medicine, treatment of liver disorders is also a very challenging and complicated matter. These conditions are usually treated with herbs that drain damp-heat from the

Liver DTX™

Liver. Pharmacologically, these herbs have hepatoprotective effects that remove toxins from the liver, prevent the entrance of toxins into the liver cells, and increase blood circulation to the liver to facilitate recovery. In most cases, herbs are most effective in the early stages of liver disorder characterized by increased liver enzymes. Immediate and aggressive treatment with herbs generally lowers liver enzyme levels and reverses the illness. Once the disease progresses into various stages of hepatitis and/or liver cirrhosis, customized herbal treatments should be considered for maximum effectiveness.

Liver diseases, such as hepatitis and liver cirrhosis, are serious and very complicated diseases that are challenging to both Western and traditional Chinese medicine. Herbal treatment is generally more effective for the early stages of liver disease, and ones with mild to moderate severity. Drug treatment, such as with interferon, are generally not utilized unless there is moderate to severe liver disease, because the risk of side effects are generally greater than the potential benefits. Unfortunately, severe cases of liver diseases are extremely difficult to manage for both Western medicine and traditional Chinese medicine. Under these circumstances, customized treatment with careful supervision is most effective.

References

1. Olin, B. et al. *The Lawrence Reviews of Natural Products by Facts and Comparisons*. Milk Thistle, January 1997.
2. Sonnenbichler, J. et al. Proceedings of the International Bioflavonoid Symposium (Munich, Frg); 477. 1981.
3. Muzes, G. et al. *Orv Hetil*; 131 (16): 863-6. 1990.
4. Lang, I. et al. *Acta Med Hung*; 45 (3-4): 287-95. 1988.
5. Foster, S. Milk Thistle-Silybum Marianum, Botanical Series No. 305, Am. Botanical Council, Austin TX 1991; 3-7.
6. Gopi KS, Reddy AG, Jyothi K, Kumar BA. Acetaminophen-induced Hepato- and Nephrotoxicity and Amelioration by Silymarin and Terminalia chebula in Rats. Department of Pharmacology and Toxicology, College of Veterinary Science, Hyderabad - 500030, Andhra Pradesh, India. Toxicol Int. 2010 Jul;17(2):64-6.
7. Aghazadeh S, Amini R, Yazdanparast R, Ghaffari SH. Anti-apoptotic and anti-inflammatory effects of Silybum marianum in treatment of experimental steatohepatitis. Institute of Biochemistry and Biophysics, University of Tehran, P.O. Box 13145-1384, Tehran, Iran. Exp Toxicol Pathol. 2010 May 13.
8. Floersheim, GL. *Medical Toxicology*; 2:1. 1987.
9. Rumyantseva, Z. *Vrach Delo*; (5): 15-19. 1991.
10. *Zhong Hua Yi Xue Za Zhi* (Chinese Journal of Medicine), 1974; (5):275.
11. Nagai, H. et al. *Planta Medica*. 55(1):13-17. 1989.
12. Takeda, S. et al. *Nippon Yakurigaku Zasshi*. 88(4):321-30. 1986.
13. *Zhong Yao Lin Chuan Xin Yong* (New Clinical Applications of Chinese Medicine), 2001; 103.
14. *Shan Xi Zhong Yi* (Shanxi Chinese Medicine), 1988; 3:106.
15. *Zhong Yao Yao Li Yu Lin Chuang* (Pharmacology and Clinical Applications of Chinese Herbs) 1992;8:40.
16. *Shan Xi Yi Yao Za Zhi* (Shanxi Journal of Medicine and Herbology) 1975;3:79.
17. *Zhong Xi Yi Jie He Za Zhi* (Journal of Integrated Chinese and Western Medicine) 1985;6:56.
18. Yamashiki M, Mase A, Arai I, Huang XX, Nobori T, Nishimura A, Sakaguchi S, Inoue K. Effects of the Japanese herbal medicine 'Inchinko-to' (TJ-135) on concanavalin A-induced hepatitis in mice. Clin Sci (Lond) 2000 Nov;99(5): 421-31.
19. *Zhong Yi Ming Fang Lin Chuang Xin Yong* (Contemporary Clinical Applications of Classic Chinese Formulas) 2001;507.
20. *Shan Xi Zhong Yi* (Shanxi Chinese Medicine) 1998;3:19.
21. *Shan Xi Zhong Yi* (Shanxi Chinese Medicine) 1993;4:17.
22. *Zhong Yi Ming Fang Lin Chuang Xin Yong* (Contemporary Clinical Applications of Classic Chinese Formulas) 2001;508.
23. Kobayashi H, Horikoshi K, Yamataka A, Lane GJ, Yamamoto M, Miyano T. Beneficial effect of a traditional herbal medicine (inchin-ko-to) in postoperative biliary atresia patients. Pediatric Surgery International 2001 Jul;17(5-6):386-9.
24. *Zhong Yao Yao Li Yu Ying Yong* (Pharmacology and Applications of Chinese Herbs), 1983; 888.
25. Motoo Y. & Sawabu N. Antitumor effects of saikosaponins, baicalin and baicalein on human hepatoma cell lines. *Cancer Lett*. 1994, 86: 91-95.
26. Lee SJ, Lee HK, Jung MK, Mar W. In vitro antiviral activity of 1,2,3,4,6-penta-O-galloyl-beta-D-glucose against hepatitis B virus. Biol Pharm Bull. 2006 Oct;29(10):2131-4.
27. *Phytochemistry*. 47(4):499-506, 1998 Feb.
28. *Chem Pharm Bull*, 1982; 30(5):1766.
29. *Shan Dong Zhong Yi Za Zhi* (Shandong Journal of Chinese Medicine), 1982; 2:84.
30. de Boer JG, Quiney B, Walter PB, Thomas C, Hodgson K, Murch SJ, Saxena PK. Protection against aflatoxin-B1-induced liver mutagenesis by Scutellaria baicalensis. Centre for Biomedical Research, University of Victoria, P.O. Box 3020 STN CSC, Victoria, BC, Canada. Mutat Res. 2005 Oct 15;578(1-2):15-22.
31. Nan JX, Park EJ, Kim YC, Ko G, Sohn DH. Scutellaria baicalensis inhibits liver fibrosis induced by bile duct ligation or carbon tetrachloride in rats. Department of Pharmacy, Wonkwang University, Iksan, Cheonbuk, South Korea. J Pharm Pharmacol. 2002 Apr;54(4):555-63.
32. *Zhong Hua Nei Ke Za Zhi* (Chinese Journal of Internal Medicine), 1978; 2:127.

Lonicera Complex™

CLINICAL APPLICATIONS

- **Viral infections (early stages):** common cold, influenza, measles, oral herpes, cold sores, and fever blisters
- **Bacterial infections (early stages):** bronchitis, pneumonia
- **Throat infections:** soreness, swelling, and inflammation of the throat

WESTERN THERAPEUTIC ACTIONS

- Antiviral properties to treat viral infections
- Antibacterial properties to treat bacterial infections
- Antipyretic effect to lower body temperature
- Expectorant effect to eliminate sputum and phlegm
- Antitussive effect to suppress cough

CHINESE THERAPEUTIC ACTIONS

- Clears wind-heat
- Eliminates fire and heat toxins from the upper *jiao*
- Benefits the throat

DOSAGE

For treatment of viral or bacterial infections, take 4 capsules three times daily on an empty stomach with warm water. Begin herbal treatment with the first sign of viral or bacterial infection and continue for one to two weeks or until symptoms resolve. To shorten the duration of infection, take 6 capsules four times daily until symptoms resolve.

INGREDIENTS

Ban Lan Gen (Radix Isatidis)
Bo He (Herba Menthae)
Da Qing Ye (Folium Isatidis)
Dan Dou Chi (Semen Sojae Praeparatum)
Dan Zhu Ye (Herba Lophatheri)
Gan Cao (Radix et Rhizoma Glycyrrhizae)
Jie Geng (Radix Platycodonis)
Jin Yin Hua (Flos Lonicerae Japonicae)
Jing Jie (Herba Schizonepetae)
Lian Qiao (Fructus Forsythiae)
Lu Gen (Rhizoma Phragmitis)
Lysine
Niu Bang Zi (Fructus Arctii)
Pu Gong Ying (Herba Taraxaci)
Ye Ju Hua (Flos Chrysanthemi Indici)
Zi Hua Di Ding (Herba Violae)
Zi Zhui Ju (Herba Echinaceae)

BACKGROUND

A healthy person has numerous defense mechanisms that protects against invasion of micro-organisms. These host defense mechanisms include natural barriers (i.e., skin), non-specific immunity (i.e., phagocytic cells) and specific immunity (i.e., antibodies). However, if the host defenses are defective or becomes disrupted, the micro-organisms may enter and affect various parts of the body. Therefore, optimal treatment of infective disorders requires use of treatment agents to kill the micro-organisms and preventative agents that restore the host defense mechanisms.

FORMULA EXPLANATION

Lonicera Complex is an herbal formula designed to treat the early stages infections characterized by wind-heat, such as common cold, influenza, oral herpes, pneumonia, bronchitis, chickenpox, measles, tonsillitis, and pharyngitis.

Jin Yin Hua (Flos Lonicerae Japonicae) and *Lian Qiao* (Fructus Forsythiae) are the principle herbs in this formula. They have a broad spectrum of antibacterial and antiviral functions. *Jing Jie* (Herba Schizonepetae), *Dan Dou Chi* (Semen Sojae Praeparatum) and *Bo He* (Herba Menthae) relieve exterior pathogenic wind. *Niu Bang Zi* (Fructus Arctii) and *Ban Lan Gen* (Radix Isatidis) clear heat and treat acute tonsillitis. *Dan Zhu Ye* (Herba Lophatheri) and *Lu Gen* (Rhizoma Phragmitis) clear heat, generate body fluids and relieve thirst. *Ye Ju Hua* (Flos Chrysanthemi Indici), *Da Qing Ye* (Folium Isatidis), *Pu Gong Ying* (Herba Taraxaci), *Zi Hua Di Ding* (Herba Violae), and echinacea are antibacterial and antiviral herbs which clear toxic heat and treat infections. *Jie Geng* (Radix Platycodonis) dispels phlegm. Lysine reduces the duration of oral herpes outbreaks. Lastly, *Gan Cao* (Radix et Rhizoma Glycyrrhizae) harmonizes the formula.

In summary, ***Lonicera Complex*** clears wind-heat, and is a great herbal formula to treat the early stages infections.

CAUTIONS & CONTRAINDICATIONS

- ***Lonicera Complex*** is designed for patients with wind-heat attacks. Should the patient experience wind-cold symptoms such as clear nasal discharge, headache, or chills, use ***Respitrol (Cold)*** instead.
- Patients with encephalitis or meningitis should be sent to the emergency room for immediate medical treatment. Warning signs and symptoms of encephalitis or meningitis include fever, headache, stiff neck, sore throat, vomiting, and mental confusion. In addition to soreness, the stiffness is also characterized by severe pain with gentle taps to the neck, and extreme stiffness and immobility when the patient tries to lower the chin to the chest.

CLINICAL NOTES

- To enhance immunity in patients who are susceptible to catching colds, take ***Immune +*** at a low dose (1 to 2 capsules a day) on an empty stomach with warm water prior to the flu season.
- ***Lonicera Complex*** is derived from classic formula *Yin Qiao San* (Honeysuckle and Forsythia Powder). However, the classic formula has two major limitations. First, it is more specific for viral infections. Second, because of its long-term use, many pathogens have developed resistance to the formula. Therefore, ***Lonicera Complex*** is formulated with additional herbs to treat

Lonicera Complex™

both viral and bacterial infections, and to boost the overall antibiotic effect of the formula. For patients with infections that do not respond to the classic formulas, ***Lonicera Complex*** will often provide good clinical results.

- ***Lonicera Complex*** incorporates numerous antibiotic herbs for two important reasons. First, the use of multiple herbs within an herbal formula has been shown to increase the antibiotic effect more than tenfold. Second, isolated use of single ingredients is often ineffective and increases the risk of development of bacterial and viral resistance.[1] Given these two reasons, it is necessary to combine herbs with appropriate properties to ensure effectiveness in treating the infection and minimizing the potential risk of the micro-organisms developing resistance and/or mutation.

Pulse Diagnosis by Dr. Jimmy Wei-Yen Chang:

- **Common cold:** superficial and forceful pulse on the right *cun*.
- **Influenza:** deep and weak on the right *cun*.

SUPPLEMENTARY FORMULAS

- To enhance the overall antiviral function, add ***Herbal AVR***.
- To enhance the overall antibacterial function, add ***Herbal ABX***.
- To treat infection of ear, nose and throat, add ***Herbal ENT***.
- To treat cough, add ***Respitrol (CF)***.
- For respiratory infection with sore throat, fever, dyspnea, chest discomfort, use ***Respitrol (Heat)***.
- To treat cold type respiratory disorders with chills, clear nasal discharge, sneezing, nasal congestion, use ***Respitrol (Cold)***.
- For respiratory infection in patients with deficiency, combine with ***Respitrol (Deficient)***.
- For upper respiratory infection with profuse, yellow, thick sputum, combine with ***Pinellia XPT***.
- For sinusitis or rhinitis with yellow nasal discharge, use ***Pueraria Clear Sinus***.
- For sinusitis or rhinitis with clear nasal discharge, use ***Magnolia Clear Sinus***.
- For tonsillitis with swelling, add ***Resolve (AI)***.
- For stomach flu with diarrhea, add ***GI Care II***.
- For headache, add ***Corydalin (AC)*** or ***Corydalin (CR)***.
- For high fever, add ***Gardenia Complex***.
- For chickenpox with severe itching, add ***Silerex***.
- For shingles, add ***Dermatrol (HZ)***.
- ***Immune +*** can be used on a regular basis to strengthen the immune system and prevent bacterial or viral infections. However, ***Immune +*** should only be used after symptoms of cold and flu have completely subsided.

ACUPUNCTURE TREATMENT

Traditional Points:

- *Quchi* (LI 11), *Fengchi* (GB 20), *Chize* (LU 5), *Hegu* (LI 4), *Dazhui* (GV 14)

Classic Master Tung's Points:

- **Throat infection:** *Houjian* (T 44.29)*, *Linggu* (T 22.05), *Chongzi* (T 22.01), *Chongxian* (T 22.02), *Yizhong* (T 77.05), *Erzhong* (T 77.06), *Sanzhong* (T 77.07), *Zusanli* (ST 36), *Hegu* (LI 4), *Tongshen* (T 88.09), *Tongwei* (T 88.10), *Tongbei* (T 88.11). Bleed *Shaoshang* (LU 11) and also dark veins nearby *Yinlingquan* (SP 9) to *Xuehai* (SP 10), *Quling* (T 33.16), *Shaoshang* (LU 11), *Cesanli* (T 77.22), *Cexiasanli* (T 77.23) and the throat. Bleed before needling for best result.
- **Tonsillitis:** *Sanjian* (LI 3), *Mu* (T 11.17), *Qihu* (T 77.26), *Waisanguan* (T 77.27), *Xinling* (T 33.17)*, *Yizhong* (T 77.05), *Erzhong* (T 77.06), *Sanzhong* (T 77.07), *Hegu* (LI 4), *Linggu* (T 22.05), *Dabai* (T 22.04), *Tushui* (T 22.11), *Shiyin* (T 88.32), *Cesanli* (T 77.22), *Zuqianjin* (T 77.24). Bleed *Shaoshang* (LU 11) and also dark veins nearby *Yinlingquan* (SP 9) to *Xuehai* (SP 10), *Shaoshang* (LU 11). Bleed before needling for best result.
- **Herpes (oral):** *Shangchun* (T 77.15), *Xiachun* (T 77.16)
- **Influenza or common cold:** *Fugesan* (T 44.30)*, *Linggu* (T 22.05), *Hegu* (LI 4), *Ganmaoyi* (T 88.07), *Ganmaoer* (T 88.08), *Fugesan* (T 44.30)*, *Huofuhai* (T 33.07), *Mu* (T 11.17)
- **Bronchitis:** *Linggu* (T 22.05), *Dabai* (T 22.04), *Fenjin* (T 44.01), *Renshi* (T 33.13), *Dishi* (T 33.14), *Tianshi* (T 33.15), *Shuijin* (T 1010.20), *Shuitong* (T 1010.19), *Simazhong* (T 88.17), *Feiqiyi* (T 44.25)*, *Feiqier* (T 44.26)*, *Zhongjian* (T 11.05). Bleed the HT and LU area in the back. Bleed before needling for best result.
- **Pneumonia:** *Linggu* (T 22.05), *Dabai* (T 22.04), *Chongzi* (T 22.01), *Chongxian* (T 22.02), *Quling* (T 33.16), *Simashang* (T 88.18), *Simazhong* (T 88.17), *Simaxia* (T 88.19), *Zhongjian* (T 11.05). Bleed dark veins nearby the ST channel on the lower limb. Bleed the HT and LU areas on the upper back with cupping. Bleed before needling for best result.

Master Tung's Points by Dr. Chuan-Min Wang:

- **Common cold, flu**
  - Cold type: Needle *Fenjin* (T 44.01), *Huofuhai* (T 33.07). Bleed *Ganmaosan* (T DT.12).
  - Heat type: Needle *Dabai* (T 22.04), *Linggu* (T 22.05), *Sanchasan* (T 22.17)*. Bleed *Wuling* (T DT.04).

Balance Method by Dr. Richard Tan:

- Left side: *Chize* (LU 5), *Taiyuan* (LU 9), *Zusanli* (ST 36), *Xiangu* (ST 43)
- Right side: *Sanjian* (LI 3), *Quchi* (LI 11), *Taibai* (SP 3), *Yinlingquan* (SP 9)
- Left and right sides can be alternated from treatment to treatment.

Ear Acupuncture:

- Nose, Pharynx, Bronchi, Adrenal Gland. Needle for thirty minutes or embed needles on the points and switch ears every three days. Patient should be advised to press on the points three times daily for one to two minutes each time.

Lonicera Complex™

- **Acute tonsillitis:** Bleed the protruding vein in the back of the ear, and apex of the tragus once a day. Needle and strongly stimulate the Throat, Pharynx and Tonsils.

Auricular Medicine by Dr. Li-Chun Huang:

- **Common cold:** Lung, Internal Nose, Throat (Larynx, Pharynx)
  - For fever, bleed Ear Apex and Helix 1-6.
  - For dizziness, add Dizziness Area.
  - For pain and soreness all over the body, add Liver and Spleen. Bleed Helix 4.
  - For cough, add Trachea, Bronchus, and Stop Asthma.
- **Recurrent ulcerative stomatitis:** corresponding points (to the area of pain), Lower Palate, Upper Palate, Tongue, *San Jiao*, Mouth, Spleen, Allergic Area. Bleed Ear Apex.
- **Relieving sore throat:** Pharynx, Larynx, Glottis, Mouth, Lung, Endocrine, Trachea. Bleed Ear Apex.
- **Tonsillitis:** Tonsil, Trachea, Throat, Teeth & Larynx, Mouth. Bleed Ear Apex and Helix 6.
- **Acute laryngopharyngitis:** Pharynx, Larynx, Mouth, *San Jiao*, Endocrine, Teeth & Larynx, Trachea. Bleed Ear Apex.
- **Chronic laryngopharyngitis:** Larynx, Pharynx, Lung, Teeth & Larynx, Trachea, Spleen, *San Jiao*, Endocrine. Bleed Ear Apex.
- **Hoarseness:** Glottis, Larynx, Mouth, Trachea, Spleen, Lung, *San Jiao*, Endocrine.

NUTRITION

- For treatment of common cold or influenza, always drink plenty of water, juice, soup, and tea as they can help flush out the body and prevent dehydration. At least 6 to 8 glasses of water per day is recommended.
- Vitamin C is well recognized for its effect to prevent and treat common colds and influenza. Foods high in vitamin C, such as oranges, are strongly recommended.
- Vitamin A, a vital nutrient for the mucous membranes throughout the respiratory system, should also be consumed in adequate quantity. Foods rich in vitamin A include raw fruits and vegetables, such as carrots.
- To avoid infection, a diet high in garlic and onions is recommended as these two foods contain natural antibiotics.
- Phlegm-producing foods such as sweets, dairy products, and heavy or greasy foods are not recommended.
- Warm and hot natured foods that damage qi and yin should be avoided, such as:
  - certain fruits like mango and durian that produce heat.
  - stimulants like coffee, alcohol, and energy drinks.
  - spicy/pungent/aromatic vegetables such as pepper, garlic, onions, basil, rosemary, cumin, funnel, anise, leeks, chives, scallions, thyme, saffron, wormwood, mustard, chili pepper, and wasabi.
- Avoid food and drinks with artificial coloring.
- Consume as few meat products as possible. Do not eat processed meats, such as lunch meats, hot dogs and sausages, as they contain nitrites that are associated with inflammation and chronic disease.

The Tao of Nutrition by Dr. Maoshing Ni and Cathy McNease:

- **Common cold (wind-heat)**
  - Recommendations: mint, cabbage, chrysanthemum flowers, burdock root, cilantro, dandelion, apples, and bitter melon. Drink plenty of fluids and get lots of rest.
  - Drink cabbage broth freely.
  - Drink cilantro and mint tea.
  - Drink mint, chrysanthemum, and dandelion tea.
  - Drink mint, dandelion, and licorice tea.
  - Avoid shellfish, meats, vinegar, and hot foods.
- **Oral herpes or mouth sores**
  - Recommendations: mung beans, daikon, carrots, lotus root, persimmon caps, mint, and honeysuckle flower.
  - Make juice from carrots and lotus root and rinse the mouth three to four times a day for at least four days.
  - Take 5 to 6 persimmon caps and boil tea. When cool, rinse mouth four to five times a day.
  - Apply honey locally to help heal faster.
  - Boil mung bean soup and eat on an empty stomach.
  - Grind mung beans into powder, mix with honey; apply to the affected area.
  - Rub sea salt on the sores three times a day for two days. Also rinse mouth with salt water.
  - Avoid spicy foods, stimulating foods, smoking, stress, alcohol, coffee, and chocolate.
- **Sore throat**
  - Recommendations: carrots, olives, daikon, celery, seaweed, licorice, Chinese prunes, cilantro, and mint. Drink a lot of water and gargle with warm salt water.
  - Make tea from carrots and olives; drink three times daily for at least one week.
  - Make tea from daikon radish and green apples; drink twice daily.
  - Make tea from cilantro, one tablespoonful of green tea, and a little salt. Steep for about five minutes.
  - Avoid alcohol, smoking, pollution, sleeping with the mouth open, stimulating or spicy foods, and fatty foods.

LIFESTYLE INSTRUCTIONS

- Adequate rest is essential for recovery. Avoid exposure to wind by putting on more clothing. Covering the head and neck area is especially important. Fluctuation of temperature increases the risk of bacterial and viral infection. Installation of an air purifier is recommended for patients who repeatedly catch infectious respiratory disorders.
- Patients should be advised to stop smoking and drinking.
- It is recommended to take a hot shower or bath after taking the herbs to promote the diaphoretic function. Warm temperature

Lonicera Complex™

burns up and destroys the viruses. Low body temperature decreases resistance to viruses and bacteria.

- Steam inhalation heals the throat, nasal passages, and bronchial tubes. During the acute phase, inhale the steam vapor for 15 minutes three times daily. During the chronic phase, inhale the steam vapor for 15 minutes before going to bed.
- It is important to build up a strong immune system prior to the cold and flu season. Regular exercise, short cold shower following a hot shower, and ingestion of tonic herbs are all beneficial to strengthen the body and its immune system.
- Individuals with an infection should rest and recover in a separate room to prevent spreading germs to other people. Ventilate the room frequently – but make sure the patient is kept warm.
- Patients with oral herpes should stay away from heat, UV rays, over-exertion, stress, spicy or greasy foods, seafood, or anything that may trigger an attack. Conversely, they are advised to eat plenty of vegetables or fruits that are cold in nature (cucumber, pear, watermelon, tomatoes) and yogurt. Replacement of toothbrush is also recommended as some herpes virus may linger on the bristles.

CASE STUDIES

- J.H., a 28-year-old male patient, presented with flu symptoms for the previous two weeks. He had a temperature of 102.4°F and some breathing difficulty. The practitioner diagnosed the condition as viral pneumonia. In conjunction with acupuncture treatment, ***Lonicera Complex*** worked quite effectively after taking four pills every four hours the first day and three pills every four hours the second day. After two days, the patient reported he was sleeping well, the cough was almost completely absent, and his breathing was normal. Submitted by E.S., Muscatine, Iowa.
- K.M., a 37-year-old female, presented with symptoms consisting of fever, sore throat, and yellow mucus that had been occurring for one day. Pulse was rapid and tongue was red. The practitioner diagnosed this condition as wind-heat; her Western diagnosis was common cold. ***Lonicera Complex*** was prescribed at four capsules three times a day. After two days of taking the herbs and receiving acupuncture, the patient had healed. Since the patient tends to get frequent colds, she was directed to take ***Immune +*** after she had felt better. Submitted by S.L., Yuma, Arizona.
- M.Z., a 15-year-old male, presented with numerous pimples over his face. Objective findings included blemishes and dark discoloration on the cheeks, forehead, and chin. It was mentioned that he had already tried Western topical creams and antibiotics. The practitioner diagnosed this condition as damp-heat. For treatment, ***Lonicera Complex*** and ***Dermatrol (PS)*** were both prescribed. It was reported after three weeks that his condition had improved. The blemishes and purple patches had vanished. He continued taking ***Dermatrol (PS)*** 2 capsules daily for maintenance. Submitted by G.G., East Lansing, Michigan.
- F.L. is a 53-year-old female with a history of oral herpes that often began with tingling sensations of the lips that progressed to burning sensations and eruption of fever blisters lasting two to three weeks. Occasionally, an outbreak was associated with eruption of additional lesions. The patient was given specific instructions to begin taking ***Lonicera Complex*** at the initial onset of symptoms, at three capsules, three times daily. During a follow-up visit, the patient reported that ***Lonicera Complex*** was extremely effective. It stopped the exacerbation of oral blisters, there was no return of lesions, and no spread of lesions to other areas. The affected area on the lips simply changed to a small painless scab that healed quickly. Submitted by C.L., Chino Hills, California.
- A 33-year-old female presented with localized burning pain on her upper lip. The patient had a history of cold sores due to herpes simplex I. At the time, the practitioner classified the condition as wind-heat invasion. Once any signs of a cold sore outbreak could be sensed, ***Lonicera Complex*** was taken immediately. In addition to the herbal formula, a topical application of *San Huang Xie Xin Tang* (Three-Yellow Decoction to Sedate the Epigastrium) was supplemented. Unlike the previous resolution time of 14 days or longer, the cold sore disappeared within a total of five days, which was a significant improvement in recovery time. On a follow-up visit several months later, the patient noticed warning signs of a cold sore, and began taking ***Lonicera Complex*** without delay. After the ***Lonicera Complex*** treatment, the cold sore never presented itself. The practitioner concluded that the herbal formula was quite effective for prevention of cold sores. Submitted by S.A., Santa Fe, New Mexico.
- A robustly healthy female presented with flu symptoms. She had a sore throat and yellow mucus. The practitioner diagnosed her condition as wind-heat. In conjunction with acupuncture treatment, the practitioner also had the patient utilize a vaporizer for steaming her face. ***Lonicera Complex*** and ***Pueraria Clear Sinus*** worked quite effectively after taking them for three to four days at larger dosages. The practitioner also noted that *Pu Ji Xiao Du Yin* (Universal Benefit Decoction to Eliminate Toxin) could be used if the condition was more severe and had presence of heat and toxins. Submitted by S.C., La Crescenta, California.
- A 53-year-old female presented with a common cold. She had the typical cold symptoms such as headaches, sore throat, fever and a stiff neck. The practitioner diagnosed the condition as an upper respiratory tract infection due to wind-heat attack. ***Lonicera Complex*** was instantly administered. The following morning, her symptoms reduced dramatically. Within four days, almost all symptoms had abated. The practitioner stated that ***Lonicera Complex*** was quite effective in the treatment of common cold conditions. Submitted by S.K., Beverly Hills, California.
- A 28-year-old female on a one-day course of antibiotic treatment was recovering from strep throat. She had chills, fever and a sore throat. She was diagnosed with wind-heat invasion, which was indicative of her feverish complexion, red throat and rapid pulse.

Lonicera Complex™

The practitioner recommended ***Lonicera Complex***. Within one day, the patient felt her sore throat and pain reduced. By the end of the fifth day, her symptoms were totally diminished. Submitted by S.A., Santa Fe, New Mexico.

- M.M., a 41-year-old female, presented with sinus infection and frontal pain, sore throat, post-nasal drip and fatigue. The TCM diagnosis was wind-heat invasion. Within one or two days of taking ***Lonicera Complex*** (3 capsules of three times daily), the patient reported most symptoms resolved. This patient now uses ***Lonicera Complex*** whenever she feels early signs of infection. She reports that this stops the progress of symptoms. Submitted by C.L., Chino Hills, California.

PHARMACOLOGICAL AND CLINICAL RESEARCH

Lonicera Complex is an herbal formula designed to treat the early stages of viral or bacterial infections. It contains herbs with antiviral and antibacterial functions to treat infections. It also utilizes many herbs to treat other associated symptoms and complications.

Lonicera Complex utilizes many herbs with antiviral effects. *Jin Yin Hua* (Flos Lonicerae Japonicae) and *Lian Qiao* (Fructus Forsythiae) have significant antiviral activities against influenza virus and respiratory syncytial virus.[2,3] These two herbs have also been used successfully in herbal formulas to treat common colds or influenza.[4] *Ban Lan Gen* (Radix Isatidis) and *Da Qing Ye* (Folium Isatidis) also have significant antiviral activities against many viruses, such as swine pseudorabies virus,[5] influenza virus,[6] and encephalitis B virus.[7] Together, *Ban Lan Gen* (Radix Isatidis) and *Da Qing Ye* (Folium Isatidis) have been used to effectively treat common colds, influenza, acute laryngitis, bronchitis, pneumonia, tonsillitis and severe acute respiratory syndrome (SARS).[8,9]

Lonicera Complex also incorporates many herbs with antibacterial effects. *Jin Yin Hua* (Flos Lonicerae Japonicae) has demonstrated a broad spectrum of inhibitory actions against *Staphylococcus aureus*, beta-hemolytic streptococcus, *E. coli*, *Bacillus dysenteriae*, *Vibrio cholerae*, *Salmonella typhi*, *Diplococcus pneumoniae*, *Diplococcus meningitidis*, *Pseudomonas aeruginosa*, and *Mycobacterium tuberculosis*. Chlorogenic acid and isochlorogenic acid, two compounds from *Jin Yin Hua* (Flos Lonicerae Japonicae), have the strongest antibiotic effects.[10,11] *Lian Qiao* (Fructus Forsythiae) has illustrated a broad spectrum of inhibitory effects against *Staphylococcus aureus*, *Diplococcus pneumoniae*, *Bacillus dysenteriae*, α-hemolytic streptococcus, beta-hemolytic streptococcus, *Neisseria catarrhalis*, *Salmonella typhi*, *E. coli*, *Mycobacterium tuberculosis*, *Bacillus proteus*, *Bordetella pertussis*, *Corynebacterium diphtheriae*, leptospira, and some dermatophytes.[12] *Ban Lan Gen* (Radix Isatidis) has demonstrated marked antibacterial effects *in vitro* against *Staphylococcus aureus*, *Diplococcus pneumoniae*, *E. coli*, *Salmonella typhi*, and leptospira.[13] *Da Qing Ye* (Folium Isatidis) has broad-spectrum antibacterial effects against *Staphylococcus aureus*, α-hemolytic streptococcus, *Diplococcus meningitidis*, *Salmonella typhi*, *E. coli*, *Corynebacterium diphtheriae*, and *Bacillus dysenteriae*.[14,15] Other herbs with antibiotic effects include *Jing Jie* (Herba Schizonepetae),[16] *Niu Bang Zi* (Fructus Arctii),[17] *Pu Gong Ying* (Herba Taraxaci),[18] *Ye Ju Hua* (Flos Chrysanthemi Indici),[19] and *Zi Hua Di Ding* (Herba Violae).[20] Overall, these herbs have potent and broad-spectrum antibiotic effects and have been used successfully to treat a wide range of infectious diseases.

In addition to treating the infection, ***Lonicera Complex*** uses many herbs to treat the associated conditions and complications. *Jin Yin Hua* (Flos Lonicerae Japonicae),[21] *Da Qing Ye* (Folium Isatidis),[22] *Bo He* (Herba Menthae),[23] and *Dan Zhu Ye* (Herba Lophatheri) [24] all have antipyretic effects to lower body temperature and treat fever associated with infection. *Jie Geng* (Radix Platycodonis) has expectorant and antitussive effects to eliminate phlegm and suppress cough.[25] *Da Qing Ye* (Folium Isatidis) demonstrates an antiallergic effect by blocking mast cell degranulation,[26] while *Jie Geng* (Radix Platycodonis) illustrates an antiallergic effect by inhibiting the inflammatory cytokines and the Syk-dependent signaling cascades.[27] Finally, *Pu Gong Ying* (Herba Taraxaci) can be used symptomatically to treat acute tonsillitis and parotitis,[28,29] and *Ban Lan Gen* (Radix Isatidis) is effective to relieve sore throat.[30] Lastly, *Ye Ju Hua* (Flos Chrysanthemi Indici) has immunomodulatory properties on humoral and cellular immunity for long-term management of infectious diseases.[31]

In summary, ***Lonicera Complex*** is an herbal formula with both antibacterial and antiviral actions to treat early stages of bacterial and viral infections. It may be used individually, or with other formulas to treat associated conditions and complications.

COMPARATIVE ANALYSIS

The discovery of antibiotic drugs is one of the major breakthroughs in modern medicine. It enables doctors to effectively treat many different types of infections. Unfortunately, decades of abuse and misuse have led to growing problems of bacterial mutation and resistance. One of the key problems is the use of these antibacterial drugs to treat viral infections. These drugs offer nothing but placebo effect, as they are completely useless in treating virus infection. Despite all the advances in Western medicine, there is still no cure for the common cold, and the best treatment is still rest and water.

Herbs are also extremely effective for treatment of various infections. In fact, many modern pharmaceutical drugs were originally derived from natural sources, including penicillin [the oldest antibiotic] and gentamicin [one of the most potent]. One of the main benefits of using herbs is their wide spectrum of antibiotic effect, with indications for bacterial, viral and fungal infections. Furthermore, most of these herbs are extremely safe, and do not have the same harsh side effects as drugs.

Lonicera Complex™

Those who have a viral infection, such as common cold or influenza, should not be treated with antibiotic drugs since they are ineffective. Other drugs may be used, but only for symptomatic control. On the other hand, use of herbs is very effective, as they suppress replication of the virus, and reduce the duration of the infections. Furthermore, additional herbs may be prescribed to address the symptoms, such as nasal congestion, sore throat, and cough. Most importantly, herbs are much gentler to the body and safer than the drugs. In other words, use of herbs treats infection without damaging the underlying constitution of the patient. This allows the patient to recover faster, and become more resistant to secondary or recurrent infections.

References

1. *Zhong Yao Xue* (Chinese Herbology), 1988; 140:144
2. Yu DQ, Chen RY, Huang LJ, Xie FZ, Ming DS, Zhou K, Li HY, Tong KM. The structure and absolute configuration of Shuangkangsu: a novel natural cyclic peroxide from Lonicera japonica (Thunb.). The Key Laboratory of Bioactive Substances and Resources Utilization of Chinese Herbal Medicine, Ministry of Education, Peking Union Medical College, Beijing, China. J Asian Nat Prod Res. 2008 Sep-Oct;10(9-10):851-6.
3. *Shan Xi Xin Yi Yao* (New Medicine and Herbology of Shanxi), 1980; 9(11):51
4. *Guang Dong Zhong Yi* (Guangdong Chinese Medicine), 1962; 5:25
5. Hsuan SL, Chang SC, Wang SY, Liao TL, Jong TT, Chien MS, Lee WC, Chen SS, Liao JW. The cytotoxicity to leukemia cells and antiviral effects of Isatis indigotica extracts on pseudorabies virus. J Ethnopharmacol. 2009 May 4;123(1):61-7.
6. Biochem Pharmacol. 2004 Jan 1;67(1):167-74.Inhibition of RANTES expression by indirubin in influenza virus-infected human bronchial epithelial cells.Mak NK, Leung CY, Wei XY, Shen XL, Wong RN, Leung KN, Fung MC.
7. *Zhi Wu Yao You Xiao Cheng Fen Shou Ce* (Manual of Plant Medicinals and Their Active Constituents), 1986: 608,1084
8. *Fu Jian Zhong Yi Yao* (Fujian Chinese Medicine and Herbology), 1965; 4:14
9. Tanaka T., Ikeda T., Kaku M., Zhu X.H., Okawa M., Yokomizo K., Uyeda M. & Nohara T. A new lignan glycoside and phenylethanoid glycosides from *Strobilanthes cusia* BREMEK. *Chem Pharm Bull.* (Tokyo). 2004, 52(10): 1242-1245.
10. *Xin Yi Xue* (New Medicine), 1975; 6(3):155
11. *Jiang Xi Xin Yi Yao* (Jiangxi New Medicine and Herbology); 1960;(1):34
12. *Shan Xi Xin Yi Yao* (New Medicine and Herbology of Shanxi), 1980; 9(11):51
13. *Zhong Cheng Yao Yan Jiu* (Research of Chinese Patent Medicine), 1987; 12:9
14. *Zhong Yao Xue* (Chinese Herbology), 1998; 174:175
15. *Zhi Wu Yao You Xiao Cheng Fen Shou Ce* (Manual of Plant Medicinals and Their Active Constituents), 1986: 608,1084
16. *Zhong Yao Yao Li Yu Ying Yong* (Pharmacology and Applications of Chinese Herbs), 1983; 744
17. *Zhong Yao Zhi* (Chinese Herbology Journal), 1984; 250
18. *Zhong Yi Yao Xue Bao* (Report of Chinese Medicine and Herbology), 1991; (1):41
19. *Zhong Hua Yi Xue Za Zhi* (Chinese Journal of Medicine), 1962; 48(3):188
20. Xie C., Kokubun T., Houghton P.J. & Simmonds M.S. Antibacterial activity of the Chinese traditional medicine, Zi Hua Di Ding. *Phytother Res.* 2004, 18(6): 497-500.
21. *Shan Xi Yi Kan* (Shanxi Journal of Medicine), 1960;(10):22
22. *Zhong Yao Xue* (Chinese Herbology), 1998; 174:175
23. *Zhong Yao Xue* (Chinese Herbology), 1998; 89:91
24. *Zhong Yao Yao Li Yu Ying Yong* (Pharmacology and Applications of Chinese Herbs), 1977:2253
25. *Zhong Yao Yao Li Yu Ying Yong* (Pharmacology and Applications of Chinese Herbs), 1983; 866
26. Kiefer S, Mertz AC, Koryakina A, Hamburger M, Küenzi P. (E,Z)-3-(3',5'-Dimethoxy-4'-hydroxy-benzylidene)-2-indolinone blocks mast cell degranulation. Eur J Pharm Sci. 2010 May 12;40(2):143-7.
27. Han EH, Park JH, Kim JY, Chung YC, Jeong HG. Inhibitory mechanism of saponins derived from roots of Platycodon grandiflorum on anaphylactic reaction and IgE-mediated allergic response in mast cells. BK21 Project Team, Department of Pharmacy, College of Pharmacy, Chosun University, Gwangju, South Korea. Food Chem Toxicol. 2009 Feb 4.
28. *Xin Yi Yao Xue Za Zhi* (New Journal of Medicine and Herbology), 1977; 8:8
29. *New Medicine*, 1972; 10:49
30. *Liao Ning Zhong Yi Za Zhi* (Liaoning Journal of Chinese Medicine), 1988; 9:27
31. Cheng W, Li J, You T, Hu C. Anti-inflammatory and immunomodulatory activities of the extracts from the inflorescence of Chrysanthemum indicum Linné. Department of Chemistry, University of Science and Technology of China, Hefei 230026, China. J Ethnopharmacol. 2005 Oct 3;101(1-3):334-7.

LPS Support™

CLINICAL APPLICATIONS

- **Systemic lupus erythematosus (SLE)**
  - Lupus with inflammation in joints, tendons, and other connective tissues and organs
  - Lupus with arthritis, mouth sores, skin rash, facial rash, hair loss, depression, fever, sunlight sensitivity, extreme fatigue, joint pain, muscle pain and weakness, anemia, malar flush, headache, general malaise, and in severe cases, destruction of vital organs.
- **Autoimmune diseases with manifestations of heat and fire**

WESTERN THERAPEUTIC ACTIONS

- Inhibits and suppresses the growth and multiplications of cells
- Anti-inflammatory effect to reduce swelling and inflammation

CHINESE THERAPEUTIC ACTIONS

- Clears heat
- Eliminates toxins
- Nourishes yin, tonifies blood, and generates body fluids

DOSAGE

Take 4 to 6 capsules three times daily. For acute recurrences, the dosage may be increased to 6 capsules four times daily.

INGREDIENTS

Bai Hua She She Cao (Herba Hedyotis)
Ban Zhi Lian (Herba Scutellariae Barbatae)
Chi Shao (Radix Paeoniae Rubrae)
Di Huang (Radix Rehmanniae)
Hong Hua (Flos Carthami)
Hu Zhang (Rhizoma et Radix Polygoni Cuspidati)
Ji Xiang Teng (Caulis Paederiae)
Jin Yin Hua (Flos Lonicerae Japonicae)
Lian Qiao (Fructus Forsythiae)
Mo Han Lian (Herba Ecliptae)
Mu Dan Pi (Cortex Moutan)
Tao Ren (Semen Persicae)
Xuan Shen (Radix Scrophulariae)
Ye Ju Hua (Flos Chrysanthemi Indici)
Zhi Mu (Rhizoma Anemarrhenae)

BACKGROUND

Systemic lupus erythematosus (SLE) is an autoimmune disorder in which the immune system attacks many parts of the body, such as the heart, joints, skin, lungs, blood vessels, liver, kidneys, and nervous system, resulting in inflammation and tissue damage. Clinical signs and symptoms of lupus include, but are not limited to, malar rash, discoid rash, photosensitivity, oral ulcers, arthritis, serositis, leukopenia, renal disorder, and neurological disorder. The exact cause of lupus is unknown in Western medicine. Therefore, treatment is mainly focused on relieving the symptoms and preventing the relapse.

FORMULA EXPLANATION

From a traditional Chinese medicine perspective, lupus is a condition characterized by both excess and deficiency. Excess represents the inflammatory conditions of the body, with such symptoms as arthritis, mouth sores, skin rash, facial rash, and sunlight sensitivity. Deficiency represents the fundamental and underlying weakness, such as anemia, and dysfunction of the kidney, nerves or brain.

Most young girls suffering from lupus will show signs of excess heat in the blood level. Middle-aged women with lupus exhibit symptoms of chronic low-grade fever with exacerbation of symptoms upon exertion and tidal fever, flushed cheeks, petechiae spots on the skin, leg and heel pain, weakness of the limbs, night sweats, hair loss and thready and rapid pulse. Therefore, optimal treatment of lupus requires use of herbs to treat both the excess and the deficiency.

Di Huang (Radix Rehmanniae), *Chi Shao* (Radix Paeoniae Rubrae), *Mu Dan Pi* (Cortex Moutan), *Zhi Mu* (Rhizoma Anemarrhenae) and *Xuan Shen* (Radix Scrophulariae) clear heat and cool the blood to treat the fever, mouth sores and skin lesions. *Jin Yin Hua* (Flos Lonicerae Japonicae), *Lian Qiao* (Fructus Forsythiae), *Hu Zhang* (Rhizoma et Radix Polygoni Cuspidati), *Ye Ju Hua* (Flos Chrysanthemi Indici), *Bai Hua She She Cao* (Herba Hedyotis) and *Ban Zhi Lian* (Herba Scutellariae Barbatae) are added to clear heat, eliminate toxins and relieve inflammation. *Tao Ren* (Semen Persicae) and *Hong Hua* (Flos Carthami) activate blood circulation and eliminate blood stasis to relieve pain, and deliver the formula to the affected parts of the body. To nourish yin, tonify blood and promote the generation of body fluids, herbs such as *Di Huang* (Radix Rehmanniae), *Mo Han Lian* (Herba Ecliptae), *Xuan Shen* (Radix Scrophulariae), and *Mu Dan Pi* (Cortex Moutan) are used. *Ji Xiang Teng* (Caulis Paederiae) is used to relieve pain. By nourishing the body, symptoms of extreme fatigue, joint pain, muscle aches, anemia, and general malaise can be alleviated.

Overall, ***LPS Support*** is a balanced formula to address both the excess and the deficiency aspects of lupus. However, lupus is a complicated disorder with a wide variety of symptoms and severities. Therefore, additional formulas are often needed to address related symptoms and complications, as stated below in the Supplementary Formulas section.

CAUTIONS & CONTRAINDICATIONS

- The main emphasis of this formula is to use herbs to clear heat, eliminate toxins, and control the autoimmune and inflammatory conditions of lupus. Therefore, it contains many bitter and cold herbs, which may consume qi and yin. If the patient shows more signs and symptoms of such deficiencies, additional herbs and formulas should be given to strengthen the underlying constitutions. *See* Supplementary Formula section for details.
- Systemic lupus erythematosus is an autoimmune disorder. In theory, qi tonic herbs that stimulate the immune system, such

LPS Support™

as *Huang Qi* (Radix Astragali) and *Ren Shen* (Radix et Rhizoma Ginseng), should be used with caution. However, in clinical practice, these herbs may still be indicated based on differential diagnosis.

CLINICAL NOTES

- Lupus may develop after taking certain prescription medications. Symptoms generally disappear after the drug is discontinued. According to New England Journal of Medicine, up to 10% of lupus cases are related to drug reactions. Therefore, drugs that are most likely to cause lupus should be avoided, such as Apresoline (hydralazine), Procan (procainamide), and isoniazid. Certain birth control pills may also cause lupus to flare-up.

Pulse Diagnosis by Dr. Jimmy Wei-Yen Chang:

- **Inflammation:** big pulse, a thick, forceful, expanding pulse on all levels, in all three pulse positions

SUPPLEMENTARY FORMULAS

- With facial or skin rash, add ***Silerex*** or ***Dermatrol (PS)***.
- With mouth sores, use ***Lonicera Complex*** as a mouthwash and gargle with it for 5 minutes three times daily.
- With arthritis, combine with ***Flex (Heat)*** or ***Flex (CD)***.
- With nerve dysfunction, combine with ***Flex (NP)***.
- With kidney dysfunction or scanty yellow urination, combine with ***Kidney DTX***.
- With low white or red blood cell count, add ***Imperial Tonic***.
- With exterior wind-heat condition, add ***Lonicera Complex***.
- With cough, add ***Respitrol (CF)***.
- With constipation, add ***Gentle Lax (Excess)*** or ***Gentle Lax (Deficient)***.
- With high fever, add ***Gardenia Complex***.
- With thirst, dry eyes and mouth, add ***Nourish (Fluids)***.
- With Kidney yin deficiency manifesting chronic low-grade fever, flushed cheeks, body pain, purpura, add ***Balance (Heat)*** and ***Nourish***.
- With intermittent pulse, palpitation, anemia, and pale complexion, add ***Schisandra ZZZ***.
- With Kidney yang deficiency, add ***Kidney Tonic (Yang)***.
- With Kidney yin deficiency, add ***Kidney Tonic (Yin)***.
- With back pain, add ***Back Support (AC)*** or ***Back Support (CR)***.
- With jaundice, combine with *Yin Chen Hao Tang* (Artemisia Scoparia Decoction).

ACUPUNCTURE TREATMENT

Traditional Points:

- *Fengchi* (GB 20), *Jianshi* (PC 5), *Zusanli* (ST 36), *Dazhui* (GV 14), *Hegu* (LI 4), *Fuliu* (KI 7)
  - For heat and toxins: *Dazhui* (GV 14), *Weizhong* (BL 40), *Xiangu* (ST 43), *Daling* (PC 7), *Yanglingquan* (GB 34)
  - For yin and blood deficiencies: *Quchi* (LI 11), *Hegu* (LI 4), *Yingxiang* (LI 20), *Fengchi* (GB 20), *Laogong* (PC 8), *Yongquan* (KI 1)
  - For yang qi deficiency: *Quchi* (LI 11), *Hegu* (LI 4), *Zusanli* (ST 36), *Shangqiu* (SP 5), *Mingmen* (GV 4)
  - For qi stagnation and blood stasis: *Shanzhong* (CV 17), *Qihai* (CV 6), *Hegu* (LI 4), *Taichong* (LR 3), *Zhangmen* (LR 13), *Neiguan* (PC 6), *Yintang*

Classic Master Tung's Points:

- *Minghuang* (T 88.12), *Qihuang* (T 88.14), *Simazhong* (T 88.17), *Simashang* (T 88.18)

Master Tung's Points by Dr. Chuan-Min Wang:

- **Lupus:** *Minghuang* (T 88.12), *Tianhuang* (T 88.13), *Qihuang* (T 88.14), *Simazhong* (T 88.17), *Simashang* (T 88.18), *Simaxia* (T 88.19), *Zhongjiuli* (T 88.25), *Qili* (T 88.51)*

Balance Method by Dr. Richard Tan:

- Treatment Plan One:
  - Right side: *Hegu* (LI 4), *Houxi* (SI 3), *Zhongzhu* (TH 3), *Sanyinjiao* (SP 6), *Zhongfeng* (LR 4), *Taixi* (KI 3)
  - Left side: *Shaoshang* (LU 11), *Zhongchong* (PC 9), *Shaochong* (HT 9), *Zusanli* (ST 36), *Yanglingquan* (GB 34), *Weizhong* (BL 40)
- Treatment Plan Two:
  - Right side: *Shaoshang* (LU 11), *Zhongchong* (PC 9), *Shaochong* (HT 9), *Zusanli* (ST 36), *Yanglingquan* (GB 34), *Weizhong* (BL 40)
  - Left side: *Hegu* (LI 4), *Houxi* (SI 3), *Zhongzhu* (TH 3), *Sanyinjiao* (SP 6), *Zhongfeng* (LR 4)

Auricular Medicine by Dr. Li-Chun Huang:

- **Lupus erythematosus:** corresponding point (to the affected area), Kidney, Liver, Spleen, Lung, Endocrine, Allergic Area, *San Jiao*, Adrenal Gland. Bleed Ear Apex.

NUTRITION

- Adequate intake of calcium and magnesium is important, as they are necessary for pH balance and protection against bone loss.
- L-cysteine, L-methionine and L-lysine are important in skin formation and cellular protection and preservation.
- Diet low in fat, salt, and animal protein is less stressful to the kidneys. It also keeps the immune system from becoming overly reactive.
- Foods that contain sulfur, such as eggs, garlic and onions are essential for the repair and rebuilding of bones, cartilages, and connective tissues.
- Avoid caffeine, citrus fruits, salt, tobacco and foods that contain sugar.
- Raw, cold, greasy and salty foods are contraindicated.
- Barley, mung bean, mushrooms, lotus nodes, honey, soybeans and soy products, and duck are recommended.

LIFESTYLE INSTRUCTIONS

- Get an adequate amount of rest and exercise regularly to promote muscle tone and fitness.
- Use hypoallergenic soaps, lotions, and cosmetics.

LPS Support™

PHARMACOLOGICAL AND CLINICAL RESEARCH

Systemic lupus erythematosus (SLE), simply referred to as lupus, is a complicated autoimmune disorder that results in episodes of inflammation in joints, tendons, and other connective tissues and organs. It is complicated because the symptoms and their severity can differ drastically from person to person, ranging from mild to disabling to fatal. ***LPS Support*** contains many herbs with various actions: some address the autoimmune aspect of lupus by suppressing the multiplication of cells; others alleviate the symptoms of inflammation, rash, and dysfunction of the organs.

LPS Support incorporates many herbs that inhibit and suppress the growth and multiplication of cells to address the autoimmune aspect of lupus. Herbs with this therapeutic effect include *Bai Hua She She Cao* (Herba Hedyotis) and *Ban Zhi Lian* (Herba Scutellariae Barbatae).[1,2] By controlling the autoimmune aspect of lupus, these herbs help to control the underlying cause of the illness.

LPS Support has many herbs specifically to control the inflammatory symptoms of lupus. Many herbs in this formula have marked anti-inflammatory effects with multiple mechanisms of actions. *Jin Yin Hua* (Flos Lonicerae Japonicae) and *Lian Qiao* (Fructus Forsythiae) both have significant anti-inflammatory effects.[3,4] The mechanisms of action include inhibition of cylcooxygenase-2, inducible nitric oxide synthase, and 5-lipoxyfenase activities.[5] In addition, *Ye Ju Hua* (Flos Chrysanthemi Indici) has a marked anti-inflammatory effect to treat a variety of acute and chronic immune-related cutaneous inflammations. The anti-inflammatory properties of *Ye Ju Hua* (Flos Chrysanthemi Indici) are attributed to the inhibition of inflammatory mediators, such as nitric oxide, prostaglandin E(2), TNF-α, and IL-1beta.[6] Another study showed that *Ye Ju Hua* (Flos Chrysanthemi Indici) has immunomodulatory properties on humoral and cellular immunity.[7] Furthermore, *Tao Ren* (Semen Persicae) and *Hong Hua* (Flos Carthami) both have anti-inflammatory functions. *Tao Ren* (Semen Persicae) exerts its anti-inflammatory and antiallergic effects via reduction of histamine release from mast cells. *Hong Hua* (Flos Carthami) exerts its anti-inflammatory action via induction of heme oxygenase-1 expression.[8] *Mu Dan Pi* (Cortex Moutan) demonstrates a significant anti-inflammatory effect by suppressing histamine release and prostaglandin D(2) synthesis from mast cells.[9] Lastly, *Di Huang* (Radix Rehmanniae) has both anti-inflammatory and antiallergic effects by suppressing the expression of cytokines, chemokines, and adhesion molecules.[10]

With regards to clinical applications, many herbs in this formula have shown excellent results to treat related signs and symptoms of lupus, including but not limited to arthritis, skin disorders, and dysfunction of the internal organs. Clinically, *Di Huang* (Radix Rehmanniae) has been used to successfully treat 23 patients with rheumatoid arthritis in one study, and 37 patients with skin disorders (rashes, urticaria, and contact dermatitis) in another study.[11,12] *Zhi Mu* (Rhizoma Anemarrhenae) was used in one herbal formula to treat 56 patients with acute-onset rheumatism with 71.4% effectiveness.[13] Lastly, use of *Lian Qiao* (Fructus Forsythiae) in herbal formulas has been shown to be effective to treat nephropathy.[14]

In summary, lupus is a complicated disorder, as it is an autoimmune disorder that affects multiple areas of the body, leading to different symptoms of various severities. ***LPS Support*** integrates principles of traditional Chinese medicine and Western medicine, to address both the cause and the main symptoms of lupus.

COMPARATIVE ANALYSIS

Systemic lupus erythematosus (SLE) is an illness that poses great challenge for both Western and traditional Chinese medicines. It is quite challenging to manage lupus because the cause of the disease has not yet been clearly identified, and the illness may be complicated by its effect on tissues and organs in the body.

Drug treatments for lupus focus mainly on relieving the symptoms. Mild to moderate lupus is managed by use of non-steroidal anti-inflammatory agents (NSAIDs) to relieve pain and reduce inflammation. However, these drugs may cause such serious side effects as gastric ulcer, duodenal ulcer, gastrointestinal bleeding, tinnitus, blurred vision, dizziness and headache. Severe lupus is treated with corticosteroids, such as prednisone and immunosuppressant drugs. However, both of these types of medication have very serious side effects and must be used with extreme caution.

Heat-clearing herbs manage both the symptoms and the cause of lupus. These herbs have been shown to have an analgesic effect to relieve pain and an anti-inflammatory effect to reduce swelling and inflammation. Furthermore, certain herbs are also effective to suppress the immune system and help to control the autoimmune aspect of lupus.

Lupus is a challenging illness that has no cure at the present time, but may be managed with drugs and/or herbs. Drugs effectively suppress symptoms, but do not change the progress of illness or the underlying condition of the patients. Herbs help to manage symptoms and control the underlying cause of the illness. Both options should be explored to identify the most effective treatment.

References

1. *Zhong Yao Xue* (Chinese Herbology), 1998; 204.
2. *Ren Min Wei Sheng Chu Ban She* (Journal of People's Public Health), 1988; 302.
3. Kang OH, Choi JG, Lee JH, Kwon DY. Luteolin isolated from the flowers of Lonicera japonica suppresses inflammatory mediator release by blocking NF-kappaB and MAPKs activation pathways in HMC-1 cells. Department of Oriental Pharmacy, College of Pharmacy, Wonkwang University, Wonkwang Oriental Medicines Research Institute, Jeonbuk 570-749, Korea. Molecules. 2010 Jan 18;15(1):385-98.
4. Ozaki Y, Rui J, Tang Y, Satake M. Antiinflammatory effect of Forsythia suspensa Vahl and its active fraction. Biol Pharm Bull. 1997 Aug;20(8):861-4.
5. Ryu KH, Rhee HI, Kim JH, Yoo H, Lee BY, Um KA, Kim K, Noh JY, Lim KM, Chung JH. Anti-inflammatory and analgesic activities of SKLJI, a highly

FORMULAS

LPS Support™

purified and injectable herbal extract of Lonicera japonica. Pharmacology Team, Life Science R&D Center, SK Chemical Suwon, Korea. Biosci Biotechnol Biochem. 2010 Oct 23;74(10):2022-8.

6. Cheon MS, et al. Chrysanthemum indicum Linné extract inhibits the inflammatory response by suppressing NF-kappaB and MAPKs activation in lipopolysaccharide-induced RAW 264.7 macrophages. Department of Herbal Resources Research, Korea Institute of Oriental Medicine, Yuseong-gu, Daejeon, Republic of Korea. J Ethnopharmacol. 2009 Apr 21;122(3):473-7.
7. Cheng W, Li J, You T, Hu C. Anti-inflammatory and immunomodulatory activities of the extracts from the inflorescence of Chrysanthemum indicum Linné. Department of Chemistry, University of Science and Technology of China, Hefei 230026, China. J Ethnopharmacol. 2005 Oct 3;101(1-3):334-7.
8. Jun MS, Ha YM, Kim HS, Jang HJ, Kim YM, Lee YS, Kim HJ, Seo HG, Lee JH, Lee SH, Chang KC. Anti-inflammatory action of methanol extract of Carthamus tinctorius involves in heme oxygenase-1 induction. Department of Pharmacology, School of Medicine, and Institute of Health Sciences, Gyeongsang National University, 92 Chilam-dong, Jinju 660-751, Republic of Korea. J Ethnopharmacol. 2010 Oct 20.
9. Chan BC, Hon KL, Leung PC, Sam SW, Fung KP, Lee MY, Lau HY. Traditional Chinese medicine for atopic eczema: PentaHerbs formula suppresses inflammatory mediators release from mast cells. J Ethnopharmacol. 2008 Oct 30;120(1):85-91.
10. Sung YY, Yoon T, Jang JY, Park SJ, Kim HK. Topical application of Rehmannia glutinosa extract inhibits mite allergen-induced atopic dermatitis in NC/Nga mice. Center of Herbal Resources Research, Korea Institute of Oriental Medicine, Daejeon 305-811, Republic of Korea. J Ethnopharmacol. 2011 Mar 8;134(1):37-44.
11. *Zhong Yao Lin Chuan Xin Yong* (New Clinical Applications of Chinese Medicine), 2001; 242-243.
12. *Tian Jing Yi Xue Za Zhi* (Journal of Tianjing Medicine and Herbology), 1966; 3:209.
13. *Ji Lin Zhong Yi Yao* (Jilin Chinese Medicine and Herbology), 1992; (1):16.
14. *Jiang Xi Yi Yao* (Jiangxi Medicine and Herbology), 1961; 7:18.

Lycium Support™

CLINICAL APPLICATIONS

- **Atrophic and degenerative eye disorders:** macular degeneration, glaucoma, optic atrophy, cataracts, photophobia, retinitis, retinopathy and vitreous opacity
- **Deterioration of eye functions:** reduced visual acuity, diminished or impaired vision, blurred vision, night blindness
- Other eye conditions: dry eyes, red eyes, swelling and pain, spots in front of the eyes, excessive tearing, floaters, Lasik recovery

WESTERN THERAPEUTIC ACTIONS

- Prevents and treats degenerative eye disorders, such as age-related macular degeneration
- Prevents and treats diabetic retinopathy
- Prevents dry eyes by inhibiting local inflammation in lacrimal glands
- Lowers ocular pressure

CHINESE THERAPEUTIC ACTIONS

- Tonifies Liver and Kidney yin
- Brightens the vision

DOSAGE

Take 3 to 4 capsules three times daily. Dosage can be increased up to 6 to 8 capsules three times daily in severe cases. Serve with a pinch of salt and warm water.

INGREDIENTS

Che Qian Zi (Semen Plantaginis)
Chong Wei Zi (Fructus Leonuri)
Fu Ling (Poria)
Fu Pen Zi (Fructus Rubi)
Gou Qi Zi (Fructus Lycii)
Gu Jing Cao (Flos Eriocauli)
Gui Ban (Plastrum Testudinis)
Ju Hua (Flos Chrysanthemi)
Jue Ming Zi (Semen Cassiae)
Mi Meng Hua (Flos Buddlejae)
Mu Dan Pi (Cortex Moutan)
Qing Xiang Zi (Semen Celosiae)
Sha Yuan Zi (Semen Astragali Complanati)
Shan Yao (Rhizoma Dioscoreae)
Shan Zhu Yu (Fructus Corni)
Shu Di Huang (Radix Rehmanniae Praeparata)
Tu Si Zi (Semen Cuscutae)
Wu Wei Zi (Fructus Schisandrae Chinensis)
Ze Xie (Rhizoma Alismatis)

BACKGROUND

Good eye care and eye health are essential for preserving vision and protecting the overall health. The eyes are not only the "gateway to the soul," they are also the crystal ball that reflects external disorders and reveals internal diseases. External disorders that affect the eyes include infection, injuries, swellings, and inflammation. Internal diseases that affect the eyes include diabetes, cardiovascular diseases, thyroid disorders, and cancer. Therefore, optimal treatment requires accurate diagnosis, as well as treatment of external disorders and internal diseases.

FORMULA EXPLANATION

The Liver and the Kidney are the most important organs for eye health. The Liver organ manifests into the eyes; when there is heat in the Liver, it may manifest as redness, swelling, dryness, and even pain of the eyes. According to the five elements theory, the Kidney is the mother of Liver, and when there is Kidney yin deficiency, the Liver yin will also become deficient, leading to blurry vision, loss of visual acuity, and dryness of the eyes.

Lycium Support, based on *Liu Wei Di Huang Wan* (Six-Ingredient Pill with Rehmannia), contains *Shu Di Huang* (Radix Rehmanniae Praeparata), *Shan Yao* (Rhizoma Dioscoreae), *Shan Zhu Yu* (Fructus Corni), *Fu Ling* (Poria), *Ze Xie* (Rhizoma Alismatis) and *Mu Dan Pi* (Cortex Moutan) as a foundation to nourish Liver and Kidney yin. Vinegar-processed *Gui Ban* (Plastrum Testudinis) is added to further tonify the Liver and Kidney yin.

Gou Qi Zi (Fructus Lycii), *Wu Wei Zi* (Fructus Schisandrae Chinensis), *Sha Yuan Zi* (Semen Astragali Complanati), *Tu Si Zi* (Semen Cuscutae), and *Fu Pen Zi* (Fructus Rubi) tonify the Kidney and consolidate the *jing* (essence). They also nourish the Liver, brighten the eyes, and improve vision to treat deficiency signs of dryness, blurriness, and dizziness.

Ju Hua (Flos Chrysanthemi), *Jue Ming Zi* (Semen Cassiae), *Che Qian Zi* (Semen Plantaginis), *Chong Wei Zi* (Fructus Leonuri), *Gu Jing Cao* (Flos Eriocauli), and *Qing Xiang Zi* (Semen Celosiae) clear Liver heat and benefit the eyes to treat Liver fire rising causing redness, swelling, dryness, photophobia, cataracts, and night blindness. *Mi Meng Hua* (Flos Buddlejae) shows good results in treatment of eye disorders caused by either excess or deficiency syndromes.

In summary, ***Lycium Support*** is an excellent formula that nourishes Liver and Kidney yin to treat chronic and degenerative types of eye disorders.

CAUTIONS & CONTRAINDICATIONS

- ***Lycium Support*** is designed to treat atrophic and degenerative eye disorders. This formula is not suitable for acute eye disorders due to infection, external injuries, hemorrhage, or other causes.
- This formula is designed for oral ingestion. Do not apply it topically into the eyes.

CLINICAL NOTES

- It is helpful to provide more blood circulation to the eyes either by applying a heat pad or a moist hot towel over the area. Alternatively, one can also put some chrysanthemum flowers in a cup of hot water and let the steam treat the eyes.

Lycium Support™

- The following drugs are known to adversely affect the eyes:
  - Antibiotics (penicillins, tetracycline, and sulfonamide) can cause red, itchy and dry eyes, blurred vision, increased light sensitivity, and possible allergic reaction with red conjunctiva, tearing, and itching.
  - Antidepressants (tricyclic antidepressants or selective serotonin reuptake inhibitors) are known to cause dilated pupils, blurred vision, double vision, inability to focus, and dry eyes.
  - Antihistamines sometimes cause too much dryness in the eyes.
  - Appetite suppressants, such as amphetamine derivatives and similar stimulants, cause pupil dilation and impaired ability of the eyes to focus.
  - Hormone replacement therapy can cause superficial punctate keratitis, in which the eyes feel dry, gritty, irritated and tired.
  - Prednisone and other steroids increase the risk of cataracts and glaucoma.

SUPPLEMENTARY FORMULAS

- For visual disturbance from bacterial infections, add ***Herbal ABX***.
- For visual disturbance from viral infections, add ***Herbal AVR***.
- For visual disturbance from inflammation of the eyes, add ***Astringent Complex***.
- For visual disturbance due to diabetes, add ***Equilibrium***.
- For visual disturbance from glaucoma characterized by heat, add ***Gardenia Complex*** or ***Gentiana Complex***.
- For visual disturbance due to environmental toxins or pollutants, add ***Herbal DTX*** and ***Liver DTX***.
- For visual disturbance due to hypertension, add ***Gastrodia Complex*** or ***Gentiana Complex***.
- For visual disturbance from eye injuries, add ***Flex (TMX)***.
- With more Kidney and Liver yin deficiencies, combine with ***Kidney Tonic (Yin)***.
- With Kidney yin-deficient heat, add ***Nourish*** or ***Balance (Heat)***.
- With excessive heat, add ***Gardenia Complex***.

ACUPUNCTURE TREATMENT

Traditional Points:

- *Fengchi* (GB 20), *Hegu* (LI 4), *Jingming* (BL 1), *Shaoze* (SI 1), *Guangming* (GB 37), *Taixi* (KI 3), *Taichong* (LR 3), *Tinghui* (GB 2), *Zanzhu* (BL 2), *Sanyinjiao* (SP 6)
- *Xinming* #1, *Xinming* #2, *Touwei* (ST 8), *Fengchi* (GB 20), *Hegu* (LI 4).
- Note: *Xinming* #1 (新明1) is located in the back of the auricle, at the mid point of the skinfold behind the ear lobe, or at the point 0.5 *cun* above the introcession, between temporal apophysis and the posterior border of mandibular angle. *Xinming* #2 (新明2) is located on the forehead, 1 *cun* above tip of brow, and 0.5 *cun* lateral.

Classic Master Tung's Points:

- **Blurry vision:** *Tongshen* (T 88.09), *Tianhuang* (T 77.17), *Dihuang* (T 77.19), *Renhuang* (T 77.21), *Shangbai* (T 22.03), *Libai* (T 44.12), *Sifuyi* (T 1010.11), *Sifuer* (T 1010.10)
- **Optic nerve atrophy:** *Sanchayi* (T 22.15)*, two points on the sides of the first metacarpal joint of the thumb, *Sizhukong* (TH 23), *Tianhuangfu [Shenguan]* (T 77.18), *Zhenjing* (T 1010.08), *Zanzhu* (BL 2). Bleed dark veins nearby the temporal area. Bleed before needling for best result.
- **Glaucoma:** *Guangming* (GB 37), *Tianhuang* (T 77.17), *Dihuang* (T 77.19), *Renhuang* (T 77.21), *Shangbai* (T 22.03), *Wanshunyi* (T 22.08), *Minghuang* (T 88.12), *Tianhuang* (T 88.13), *Qihuang* (T 88.14), two points on the sides of the first metacarpal joint of the thumb. Bleed the dark veins nearby the temporal area. Bleed before needling for best result.
- **Cataract:** *Shangbai* (T 22.03), two points on the sides of the first metacarpal joint of the thumb, *Sihuashang* (T 77.08), *Huoying* (T 66.03), *Shuixiang* (T 66.14), *Minghuang* (T 88.12), *Tianhuang* (T 88.13), *Qihuang* (T 88.14), *Tianhuang* (T 77.17), *Dihuang* (T 77.19), *Renhuang* (T 77.21)
- **Astigmatism:** *Shangbai* (T 22.03), *Zhongbai* (T 22.06), *Xiabai* (T 22.07), *Wanshunyi* (T 22.08), *Wanshuner* (T 22.09), *Tongguan* (T 88.01), *Tongshan* (T 88.02), *Minghuang* (T 88.12), *Huozhi* (T 88.15), *Renhuang* (T 77.21), *Huoying* (T 66.03), *Tianhuangfu [Shenguan]* (T 77.18), two points on the sides of the first metacarpal joint of the thumb, *Tianhuang* (T 77.17), *Dihuang* (T 77.19)
- **Eyes (red):** *Linggu* (T 22.05), *Shangbai* (T 22.03), *Libai* (T 44.12), *Dabai* (T 22.04), *Huoying* (T 66.03), *Minghuang* (T 88.12), *Tianhuang* (T 88.13), *Qihuang* (T 88.14), *Simashang* (T 88.18), *Simazhong* (T 88.17), *Simaxia* (T 88.19). Bleed dark veins nearby the temporal area or tender points on the LR area of the back with cupping. Bleed before needling for best result.
- **Eyes (dry):** *Minghuang* (T 88.12), *Qihuang* (T 88.14), *Tianhuang* (T 88.13), *Guangming* (GB 37), *Shangbai* (T 22.03), two points on the sides of the first metacarpal joint of the thumb, *Tianhuangfu [Shenguan]* (T 77.18), *Sanchayi* (T 22.15)*, *Mu* (T 11.17)
- **Eyes (pain):** *Shangbai* (T 22.03), *Shangjiuli* (T 88.26), *Zhongjiuli* (T 88.25), *Xiajiuli* (T 88.27), *Shangli* (T 1010.09)
- **Eyes (tear):** *Shangbai* (T 22.03), *Huaguyi* (T 55.02), *Mu* (T 11.17), *Tongshen* (T 88.09), *Yizhong* (T 77.05), *Erzhong* (T 77.06), *Sanzhong* (T 77.07), *Tianhuangfu [Shenguan]* (T 77.18), two points on the sides of the first metacarpal joint of the thumb, *Huoying* (T 66.03), *Tianhuang* (T 77.17), *Dihuang* (T 77.19), *Renhuang* (T 77.21), *Shangli* (T 1010.09)
- **Eyes (floaters):** *Shangbai* (T 22.03), two points on the sides of the first metacarpal joint of the thumb, *Minghuang* (T 88.12), *Tianhuang* (T 88.13), *Qihuang* (T 88.14), *Tianhuangfu [Shenguan]* (T 77.18), *Shuixiang* (T 66.14), *Shuixian* (T 66.15), *Shangli* (T 1010.09), *Sifuyi* (T 1010.11), *Sifuer* (T 1010.10)
- **Lazy eyes:** *Huoquan* (T 88.16), *Qihuang* (T 88.14), *Huozhi* (T 88.15), *Renhuang* (T 77.21), *Tongshen* (T 88.09), *Huoying* (T 66.03)
- **Nearsightedness:** *Minghuang* (T 88.12), *Huozhi* (T 88.15), *Huoquan* (T 88.16), *Tianhuang* (T 88.13), *Tianhuangfu [Shenguan]* (T 77.18)

Lycium Support™

Master Tung's Points by Dr. Chuan-Min Wang:

- **Blurry vision, cataract, glaucoma, degenerative eye disorder:** *Tianhuangfu [shenguan]* (T 77.18), *Guangming* (T 77.28), *Shuixiang* (T 66.14)

Balance Method by Dr. Richard Tan:

- Left side: *Quchi* (LI 11), *Tianjing* (TH 10), *Yingu* (KI 10), *Ququan* (LR 8)
- Right side: *Quze* (PC 3), *Shaohai* (HT 3), *Dubi* (ST 35), *Xiyangguan* (GB 33)
- Left and right sides can be alternated from treatment to treatment.

Ear Acupuncture:

- Liver, Kidney, Eye, Vision #1, Vision #2, Endocrine, Adrenal

Auricular Medicine by Dr. Li-Chun Huang:

- **Improving vision:** Kidney, Liver, Vision 2, Eye, Sympathetic, Optic Center (Occiput). Bleed Ear Apex.
- **Ametropia:** Kidney, Liver, Occiput, Eye, Forehead, Vision 2, Sympathetic. Bleed Ear Apex.
- **Myopia:** Kidney, Liver, Spleen, Vision 2, Eye, Optic Center (Occiput), Sympathetic. Bleed Ear Apex.
- **Cataract:** Kidney, Liver, Eye, Vision 2, Endocrine, Sympathetic. Bleed Ear Apex.
- **Optic atrophy:** Kidney, Liver, Occiput, Vision 2, Eye, Sympathetic, Endocrine, Coronary Vascular Subcortex. Bleed Ear Apex.
- **Glaucoma:** Eye, Decrease BP Point, Kidney, Liver, Occiput, Vision 1, Coronary Vascular Subcortex. Bleed Ear Apex.

NUTRITION

- Make sure to drink at least 8 glasses of water per day.
- Try to select foods high in beta-carotene, such as carrots, sweet potatoes, spinach, kale, and butternut squash.
- Fish oil or the consumption of deep sea fish like salmon, sardines, and tuna is very good for the maintenance of eye health.
- Increase intake of nourishing roots such as Mexican yam, yam, radishes, potatoes, carrots, melons, cucumbers, beets, turnips, malanga, celeriac, taro, and rutabaga.
- Daily intake of the following supplements is beneficial for patients with macular degeneration, extensive drusen, pigment changes, or geographic atrophy: zinc oxide 80 mg, copper 2 mg, vitamin C 500 mg, vitamin E 400 IU, beta-carotene 15 mg (or vitamin A 28,000 IU).
- Avoid spicy foods, pungent foods, alcohol, and smoking.

The Tao of Nutrition by Dr. Maoshing Ni and Cathy McNease:

- **Cataracts:** increase the intake of chrysanthemum, cilantro, spinach, cloves, water chestnuts, yams, goji berries, black beans, and sesame seeds.
- Avoid any type of spices, salt, and garlic.

LIFESTYLE INSTRUCTIONS

- Avoid excessive use of the eyes. Take frequent breaks to rest the eyes when reading, watching television, or using the computer.
- Avoid excessive or prolonged exposure to ultraviolet light (sunlight, sunlamps, or welding arcs) or x-rays.
- Avoid wearing contact lenses for an excessive period of time.
- Avoid rubbing the eyes. Find the cause of eye irritation and treat accordingly.
- Make sure to intake enough fluids. Dehydration often contributes to dryness and discomfort of the eyes.
- Perform the following eye exercises:
  - In a quiet, relaxed environment, clear the mind and slowly look around in a circle with the eyes only, reversing the direction each time. This allows a person to exercise the muscles of the eyes in a healthy way.
  - Look far away: go outside into a natural clean environment and look as far away as possible. Relax the eyes, focus on one direction for 25 seconds at a time, and then focus on something that is close by. Repeat 20 times, three times a day. This allows the muscles and lens of the eyes to maintain their elasticity, and prevents premature changes in vision.

PHARMACOLOGICAL AND CLINICAL RESEARCH

Lycium Support is an herbal formula based on *Qi Ju Di Huang Wan* (Lycium Fruit, Chrysanthemum, and Rehmannia Pill). The traditional formula and the individual herbs have all shown excellent effect to treat various eye disorders.

Qi Ju Di Huang Wan (Lycium Fruit, Chrysanthemum, and Rehmannia Pill) has been shown to treat eye disorders such as retinitis and vitreous opacity. According to one study, the use of this formula in 140 patients with retinitis was associated with complete recovery in 22 patients, significant improvement in 21 patients, moderate improvement in 70 patients, and no benefit in 27 patients. The treatment protocol was to administer the herbs in decoction daily, for three weeks per course of treatment. The duration of treatment ranged from 30 to 118 days, with an average of 57 days.[1] According to another study, use of modified *Qi Ju Di Huang Wan* (Lycium Fruit, Chrysanthemum, and Rehmannia Pill) was successful to treat vitreous opacity in 34 patients (21 males and 13 females, between 38 to 76 years of age). The herbal formula contained *Gou Qi Zi* (Fructus Lycii) 15g, *Ju Hua* (Flos Chrysanthemi) 15g, *Shan Yao* (Rhizoma Dioscoreae) 15g, *Shan Zhu Yu* (Fructus Corni) 15g, *Shu Di Huang* (Radix Rehmanniae Praeparata) 20g, *Fu Ling* (Poria) 10g, *Ze Xie* (Rhizoma Alismatis) 10g, *Mu Dan Pi* (Cortex Moutan) 10g, *Tu Si Zi* (Semen Cuscutae) 10g, *Nu Zhen Zi* (Fructus Ligustri Lucidi) 10g, and *Jue Ming Zi* (Semen Cassiae) 10g. The treatment protocol was to cook the herbs in water, and administer the decoction in two equally-divided doses, two times daily for 30 days. Of 34 patients, the study reported significant improvement in 18 patients, moderate

Lycium Support™

improvement in 11 patients, and no benefit in 5 patients. The overall rate of effectiveness was 85.29%.[2]

In addition to the traditional formula, the individual ingredients, such as *Gou Qi Zi* (Fructus Lycii) and *Ju Hua* (Flos Chrysanthemi), have also illustrated marked benefit for the eyes. According to one up-to-date human trial, oral supplementation of *Gou Qi Zi* (Fructus Lycii) may be effective in prevention of age-related macular degeneration, a common disorder that causes irreversible loss of central vision. This beneficial effect is attributed to zeaxanthin, a compound that is present in *Gou Qi Zi* (Fructus Lycii), bioavailable to humans, and essential to prevent degenerative eye disorder.[3] According to another study, *Gou Qi Zi* (Fructus Lycii) extract and taurine (its major component) have a cytoprotective effect against glucose exposure in a human retinal epithelial cell line and provides beneficial effect to delay diabetic retinopathy progression. The mechanism of this effect is attributed to the reversal of the caspase-dependent apoptotic cytotoxicity pathway.[4] Another report attributes the beneficial effect of *Gou Qi Zi* (Fructus Lycii) to treat diabetic retinopathy on its effect to dose-dependently enhance peroxisome proliferator activated receptor-γ (PPAR-γ) in human retinal pigment epithelial cells.[5] Lastly, the combination of *Gou Qi Zi* (Fructus Lycii) and *Ju Hua* (Flos Chrysanthemi) has illustrated protective effects to treat diabetic retinopathy in streptozotocin-induced diabetes.[6]

Finally, *Mi Meng Hua* (Flos Buddlejae) and *Qing Xiang Zi* (Semen Celosiae) are two herbs that effectively treat "excess" conditions of the eyes, such as inflammation and increased ocular pressure. According to one study, topical application of *Mi Meng Hua* (Flos Buddlejae) as eye drops showed good results to treat dry eyes by inhibiting cell apoptosis in lacrimal glands.[7] According to another study, *Mi Meng Hua* (Flos Buddlejae) has a significant effect to prevent dry eyes by inhibiting local inflammation in lacrimal glands and reducing apoptosis of lacrimal gland cells.[8] Lastly, decoction of *Qing Xiang Zi* (Semen Celosiae) given daily for six days lowered ocular pressure.[9]

In summary, ***Lycium Support*** is an excellent herbal formula to treat various disorders of the eyes, including but not limited to macular degeneration, retinopathy, retinitis, inflammation of the eyes, and increased ocular pressure.

COMPARATIVE ANALYSIS

Optimal health of the eyes requires a careful balance of structure and function. Structural damages of the eyes include external injuries, burns, infection, and inflammation. Functional disorders of the eyes include acute and chronic loss of visual acuity, which may occur through aging, stress, prolonged exposure to computer monitors, television or sunlight, and internal causes such as diabetes, hypertension, and circulatory disorders. The structural and functional disorders of the eyes often occur together, as one inevitably affects the other.

Western medicine is generally more effective to treat structural damages and acute functional disorders of the eyes. Structural damages may include external injuries, hemorrhage, invasion of a foreign object, burns, and fractures. Acute functional disorders may include infection, inflammation, and retinal detachment. In these cases where the cause of acute structural and functional eye disorders is clearly defined, Western medicine provides effective and reliable treatment results.

Traditional Chinese medicine is usually more effective for atrophic and degenerative disorders that affect the functions of the eyes, such as blurred vision, reduced visual acuity, dry eyes, optic atrophy, and macular degeneration. Under these circumstances, Chinese herbs slow the aging process, reverse the atrophy or deterioration, and correct the underlying constitution. These atrophic and degenerative eye disorders occur over a long period of time, and therefore, may also require a long period of time to heal and recover.

References

1. *An Hui Zhong Yi Xue Yuan Xue Bao* (Journal of Anhui University School of Medicine) 1989;4:18.
2. *Zhong Yi Yao Xue Bao* (Report of Chinese Medicine and Herbology) 1995;2:25.
3. Cheng C.Y., Chung W.Y., Szeto Y.T. & Benzie I.F. Fasting plasma zeaxanthin response to *Fructus barbarum* L. (wolfberry; Kei Tze) in a food-based human supplementation trial. *Br J Nutr.* 2005, 93(1): 123-130.
4. Song MK, Roufogalis BD, Huang TH. Reversal of the Caspase-Dependent Apoptotic Cytotoxicity Pathway by Taurine from Lycium barbarum (Goji Berry) in Human Retinal Pigment Epithelial Cells: Potential Benefit in Diabetic Retinopathy. Herbal Medicine Group, Faculty of Pharmacy, The University of Sydney, Sydney, NSW 2006, Australia. Evid Based Complement Alternat Med. 2012;2012:323784.
5. Song MK, Salam NK, Roufogalis BD, Huang TH. Lycium barbarum (Goji Berry) extracts and its taurine component inhibit PPAR-γ-dependent gene transcription in human retinal pigment epithelial cells: Possible implications for diabetic retinopathy treatment. Faculty of Pharmacy, The University of Sydney, NSW 2006, Australia. Biochem Pharmacol. 2011 Nov 1;82(9):1209-18.
6. Hu CK, Lee YJ, Colitz CM, Chang CJ, Lin CT. The protective effects of Lycium barbarum and Chrysanthemum morifolum on diabetic retinopathies in rats. Vet Ophthalmol. 2012 Apr 5. doi: 10.1111/j.1463-5224.2012.01018.x.
7. Peng QH, Yao XL, Wu QL, Tan HY, Zhang JR. Effects of eye drops of Buddleja officinalis Maxim. extract on lacrimal gland cell apoptosis in castrated rats with dry eye. Key Department of Chinese Traditional Ophthalmology, the First Affiliated Hospital, Hunan University of Traditional Chinese Medicine, Changsha 410007, Hunan Province, China. Zhong Xi Yi Jie He Xue Bao. 2010 Mar;8(3):244-9.
8. Peng QH, Yao XL, Wu QL, Chen M. Effects of extract of Buddleja officinalis on prevention of dry eye in castrated rabbits. The First Hospital affiliated to Hunan University of TCM, Changsha 410007, China. Zhonghua Yan Ke Za Zhi. 2008 Nov;44(11):1011-9.
9. *Yun Nan Zhong Yi Za Zhi* (Yunan Journal of Chinese Medicine), 1990; 11(1):30.

Magnolia Clear Sinus ™

CLINICAL APPLICATIONS

- **Rhinitis or sinusitis** with clear, white nasal discharge
- **Seasonal allergies,** especially in spring
- **General nasal problems,** such as stuffy nose, sneezing, loss of smell, and clear watery nasal discharge

WESTERN THERAPEUTIC ACTIONS

- Antiallergic and antihistamine effects to treat sinusitis and/or rhinitis
- Anti-inflammatory effect to constrict the vessels in the nasal mucosa to treat rhinitis and/or sinusitis
- Antibiotic and antiviral effects to treat bacterial and viral infections

CHINESE THERAPEUTIC ACTIONS

- Unblocks nasal congestion and disperses wind-cold
- Transforms congested fluids
- Warms the Lung

DOSAGE

For treatment of sinusitis or rhinitis, take 4 to 6 capsules with warm water three times daily between meals. For prevention, begin taking 3 capsules three times daily just prior to the start of allergy season.

INGREDIENTS

Bai Zhi (Radix Angelicae Dahuricae)
Cang Er Zi (Fructus Xanthii), dry fried
Cha Ye (Folium Camelliae)
Che Qian Cao (Herba Plantaginis)
Chuan Xiong (Rhizoma Chuanxiong)
Fang Feng (Radix Saposhnikoviae)
Gan Cao (Radix et Rhizoma Glycyrrhizae)
Gan Jiang (Rhizoma Zingiberis)
Gao Ben (Rhizoma et Radix Ligustici)
Jie Geng (Radix Platycodonis)
Jing Jie (Herba Schizonepetae)
Sheng Ma (Rhizoma Cimicifugae)
Wu Wei Zi (Fructus Schisandrae Chinensis)
Xin Yi Hua (Flos Magnoliae)
Zhi Shi (Fructus Aurantii Immaturus)

BACKGROUND

Rhinitis and sinusitis are common disorders of the nose. Rhinitis is inflammation of the nasal mucous membrane with symptoms such as nasal congestion, rhinorrhea, itching, and sneezing. Rhinitis is usually caused by allergy, irritation, and viral infection. Sinusitis is the inflammation of the paranasal sinuses with symptoms such as nasal obstruction and congestion, purulent rhinorrhea, pain, fatigue and fever. Sinusitis may be caused by viral, bacterial or fungal infection.

FORMULA EXPLANATION

Magnolia Clear Sinus is formulated to treat rhinitis, sinusitis and allergies due to wind-cold and fluid congestion. Clinically, patients will have a stuffy nose, clear watery discharge, sneezing, loss of smell, and headache.

Xin Yi Hua (Flos Magnoliae) unblocks nasal congestion and treats loss of smell with its acrid, dispersing and warming properties. *Cang Er Zi* (Fructus Xanthii) helps *Xin Yi Hua* (Flos Magnoliae) to relieve allergy symptoms of sneezing, white watery nasal discharge, and/or nasal obstruction. *Bai Zhi* (Radix Angelicae Dahuricae), *Gao Ben* (Rhizoma et Radix Ligustici), and *Chuan Xiong* (Rhizoma Chuanxiong) are used to alleviate sinus pain and headache. *Gan Jiang* (Rhizoma Zingiberis) warms the interior, transforms congested fluids and dispels nasal congestion. *Jing Jie* (Herba Schizonepetae) and *Fang Feng* (Radix Saposhnikoviae) expel lingering pathogenic factors and prevent allergies from turning into a cold or triggering an asthma attack. With its ascending property, *Sheng Ma* (Rhizoma Cimicifugae) is used as a guiding herb. *Che Qian Cao* (Herba Plantaginis) drains nasal obstruction and postnasal drip caused by dampness and water congestion through diuresis. *Zhi Shi* (Fructus Aurantii Immaturus) unblocks sinus congestion by regulating qi, while *Jie Geng* (Radix Platycodonis) dispels phlegm, expands the chest, and relieves constipation. To counterbalance the strong dispersing property of this formula, a small amount of *Wu Wei Zi* (Fructus Schisandrae Chinensis) is added to prevent the leakage of Lung qi. *Cha Ye* (Folium Camelliae) is used to relieve sinus headaches commonly associated with sinus congestion. Lastly, *Gan Cao* (Radix et Rhizoma Glycyrrhizae) harmonizes the formula.

CAUTIONS & CONTRAINDICATIONS

- This formula is contraindicated during pregnancy and nursing.
- *Cang Er Zi* (Fructus Xanthii) used in this formula have been carefully dry fried at a high temperature until they appear dark brown or slightly charred, as dictated by Chinese *Materia Medica*. Dry frying is necessary because this process simultaneously increases the effect [by enhancing the extraction of active compounds] and decreases the side effects [by destroying the undesired glycosides]. Nonetheless, because *Cang Er Zi* (Fructus Xanthii) is metabolized by the liver and eliminated by the kidney, individuals with pre-exiting liver or kidney diseases should not take this formula.[1]

CLINICAL NOTES

- Approximately 25% of all sinusitis are related to food allergies. Therefore, it is extremely important to identify and avoid the allergy. Common allergens include milk, wheat, eggs, citrus fruits, corn, and peanuts.
- ***Magnolia Clear Sinus*** is more effective for sinusitis and rhinitis due to seasonal allergies. ***Pueraria Clear Sinus*** is more effective for sinus infections.

FORMULAS

Magnolia Clear Sinus™

Pulse Diagnosis by Dr. Jimmy Wei-Yen Chang:

- Tent pulse, a convex-shaped pulse that collapses upon pressure, on the right *cun*.
- *Yangqiao* pulse, a pulse extending distally from the *cun* position towards the middle finger on the right hand. It is one of the eight extra meridian pulses.

SUPPLEMENTARY FORMULAS

- For sinusitis or rhinitis with yellow nasal discharge, use ***Pueraria Clear Sinus***.
- For infection of the ear, nose and throat, add ***Herbal ENT***.
- With cough, add ***Respitrol (CF)***.
- To treat cold-type respiratory disorders with chills, clear nasal discharge, sneezing, or congestion, combine with ***Respitrol (Cold)***.
- For respiratory infection due to heat with yellow post-nasal discharge, add ***Respitrol (Heat)***.
- To enhance the overall antibacterial function, add ***Herbal ABX***.
- To enhance the overall antiviral function, add ***Herbal AVR***.
- With post-nasal drip or damp and phlegm in the lung, add ***Pinellia XPT***.
- With more underlying damp and phlegm with Spleen qi deficiency, add ***Pinellia Complex***.
- For nasal symptoms associated with environmental or toxic poisoning, add ***Herbal DTX***.
- For sinus congestion with sinus headache, add ***Corydalin (AC)***.
- To strengthen the overall constitution, use ***Imperial Tonic***.
- To enhance immunity against allergies, take ***Immune +*** at a low dose (1 to 2 capsules a day) during non-allergy seasons.

ACUPUNCTURE TREATMENT

Traditional Points:

- *Yingxiang* (LI 20), *Yintang* (Extra 1), *Fengchi* (GB 20), *Zusanli* (ST 36)
- *Lieque* (LU 7), *Hegu* (LI 4), *Yingxiang* (LI 20), *Fengchi* (GB 20), *Zanzhu* (BL 2)

Classic Master Tung's Points:

- **Allergy:** *Mu* (T 11.17), *Linggu* (T 22.05), *Tianshi* (T 33.15), *Dishi* (T 33.14), *Renshi* (T 33.13), *Simashang* (T 88.18), *Simazhong* (T 88.17), *Simaxia* (T 88.19), *Yingxiang* (LI 20), *Tongtian* (T 88.03), *Tongguan* (T 88.01), *Zhenjing* (T 1010.08), *Shangli* (T 1010.09), *Shuitong* (T 1010.19), *Shuijin* (T 1010.20), *Fenjin* (T 44.01), *Zhengben* (T 1010.12). Bleed dark veins nearby *Sihuawai* (T 77.14). Bleed before needling for best result.
- **Nose (stuffy):** *Linggu* (T 22.05), *Jianzhong* (T 44.06), *Mu* (T 11.17), *Tianshi* (T 33.15), *Dishi* (T 33.14), *Renshi* (T 33.13), *Zhenjing* (T 1010.08), *Simashang* (T 88.18), *Simazhong* (T 88.17), *Simaxia* (T 88.19)
- **Absence of smell:** *Fukuai* (T 1010.15), *Liukuai* (T 1010.16), *Simashang* (T 88.18), *Simazhong* (T 88.17), *Simaxia* (T 88.19). Bleed dark veins nearby *Sihuashang* (T 77.08), *Sihuazhong* (T 77.09), *Sihuaxia* (T 77.11) and *Weizhong* (BL 40). Bleed before needling for best result.

Master Tung's Points by Dr. Chuan-Min Wang:

- **Allergy, sinusitis, rhinitis:** Needle *Lianquan* (CV 23) using the Remove Dust 7 needling technique (from *Ling Shu*). Needle bilaterally *Tianrong* (SI 17), *Fenjin* (T 44.01), *Sanyinjiao* (SP 6).

Balance Method by Dr. Richard Tan:

- Left side: *Chize* (LU 5), *Taiyuan* (LU 9), *Zusanli* (ST 36), *Xiangu* (ST 43)
- Right side: *Sanjian* (LI 3), *Quchi* (LI 11), *Taibai* (SP 3), *Yinlingquan* (SP 9)
- Left and right sides can be alternated from treatment to treatment.

Ear Acupuncture:

- Nose, Adrenal Gland, Prostate Gland. Tape ear seeds and switch ears every three days.

Auricular Medicine by Dr. Li-Chun Huang:

- **Stuffy nose:** Lung, Internal Nose, Adrenal Gland, External Ear, Nasopharynx. Bleed Ear Apex.
- **Allergies:** Allergic Area, Endocrine, Adrenal Gland, Spleen. Bleed Ear Apex.
- **Allergic rhinitis:** Internal Nose, External Nose, Adrenal Gland, Endocrine, Allergic Area, Spleen, Lung, Sympathetic. Bleed Ear Apex.
- **Chronic rhinitis:** Internal Nose, External Ear, Lower Lung, Allergic Area, Adrenal Gland
- **Sinusitis:** Upper Jaw, Upper Palate, Forehead, Internal Nose, External Ear, *San Jiao*, Lung, Endocrine, Adrenal Gland, corresponding points
- **Loss of smell:** Internal Nose, Lower Lung, Brain Stem, Sympathetic, Endocrine, *San Jiao*, Large Intestine, Auriculotempo Nerve, Coronary Vascular Subcortex, Olfactory Center
- **Nasopharyngitis, post-nasal drip:** Nasopharynx, Sympathetic, Allergic Area, Lung, Endocrine, Trachea. Bleed Ear Apex.

NUTRITION

- Reduce or eliminate intake of dairy foods (i.e., milk, cream, yogurt, cheese, ice cream), as they create dampness and increase mucus production.
- Drink plenty of distilled water throughout the day to promote drainage.
- Make sure the diet is adequate in supplies of vitamin A and C. Vitamin A is essential for healthy mucous lining of the respiratory tract. Vitamin C is well recognized for its effect to prevent and treat infection.
- Avoid raw or cold food and beverages such as sashimi, sushi, salads, steak tartar, and seared meat. Eat cooked vegetables and nothing straight from the refrigerator.
- Avoid fried or greasy foods as they create dampness and phlegm.

Magnolia Clear Sinus™

- Avoid the following cooling foods: tofu, tomato, celery, asparagus, bamboo, seaweed, kelp, bitter melon, cucumber, gourd, luffa, winter melon, oranges, grapefruit, pear, banana, papaya, watermelon, white radish, mustard leaf, potherb mustard, cactus, Chinese kale, napa, and bamboo sprout. Long-term use of cold fruits and vegetables like the ones listed above may be damaging to the Spleen. To make the property more neutral, one can add about 20 pieces of *Gou Qi Zi* (Fructus Lycii) when cooking.

The Tao of Nutrition by Dr. Maoshing Ni and Cathy McNease:

- **Allergy**
  - Recommendations: ginger, onions, garlic, bamboo shoots, cabbage beets, beet top tea, carrots, leafy greens, yams, ganoderma mushroom.
  - Drink ginger tea to induce sweating.
  - Drink beet top tea as a water source.
  - Avoid wheat, citrus fruits, chocolate, shellfish, dairy products, eggs, potatoes, polluted meats, and polluted air.
- **Chronic sinusitis**
  - Recommendations: ginger, green onions, magnolia flower, bananas, garlic, black mushrooms, chrysanthemum flowers, mulberry leaves, and apricot kernel.
  - Make tea from magnolia flower, basil, ginger, and green onion. Drink three times daily for at least one week.
  - Combine magnolia flowers and eggs, cook and eat.
  - Make tea from mulberry leaves and chrysanthemums, then cook rice porridge in the tea, adding apricot kernels.
  - Boil tea of mint, basil, and ginger. While boiling the tea, inhale the steam through the nose, three times daily for at least two months.
  - Avoid coffee and stop smoking.

LIFESTYLE INSTRUCTIONS

- Avoid allergens that may trigger sinusitis and rhinitis whenever possible.
- Application of a saline solution to the nose three to four times daily helps to reduce nasal congestion.
- Strengthen the immune system by exercising, reducing worry and stress, and developing a normal sleep habit.
- Steam inhalation is helpful to drain sinus infection. Nasal septum flushing with cold saline water is helpful to desensitize the nose to temperature and common allergens. Repeatedly perform nasal flush for one to two minutes every morning.

CASE STUDIES

- T.W., a 34-year-old female, presented with chronic nasal congestion, allergies, headaches, and migraines. Her headaches were worse around the time of menses and when sinus pressure occurred she used nasal sprays and post nasal drips. She had been treated with birth control pills for 16 years with limited success. In addition, the patient had been taking Lexapro (escitalopram) for anxiety and was experiencing loose stools three times daily. The practitioner diagnosed this condition as damp and phlegm stagnation; the Western diagnosis was sinus pain and migraines. ***Magnolia Clear Sinus*** was prescribed at three pills three times daily together with ***Corydalin (AC)*** at the same dosage. The results were very positive. She reported her breathing was clearer through her nose, and did not get any headaches until two weeks later when she began teaching again at school. Submitted by L.W., Oceano, California.
- M.N., a 62-year-old female, presented with allergies. Symptoms included itchy red eyes, sneezing, and sinus congestion that was thick and yellow. Sinus pressure along the Stomach channel was also present. The practitioner diagnosed the condition as wind-heat and dryness. ***Magnolia Clear Sinus*** was given at three capsules three times a day and was switched to one capsule three times a day. The patient found the first dose of the herbs very drying, causing the headache to worsen. However, after the patient switched to one capsule dose, she felt that the formula was very effective at decreasing her allergy symptoms. Submitted by L.M., Lafayette, Colorado.
- L.A., a 55-year-old female, presented with chronic nasal drip. The patient was especially sensitive to dust and mold. It was also noted the symptoms worsened after eating ice cream and working in air conditioned environment. Symptoms of clear runny nose, cold sensation, itchy eyes, and foggy thinking were also present and they affected her sleep as well. Pulse was slow and slippery and the tongue had thick greasy white coating. The practitioner diagnosed the condition as Lung qi and Kidney qi deficiencies with phlegm and wind-cold. Her Western diagnosis was sinusitis. The patient was given ***Magnolia Clear Sinus*** and she took them for two months. With the ***Magnolia Clear Sinus*** both breathing and sleeping improved, her eyes got worse before they got better, and her blood pressure dropped after four weeks. The patient had also made changes to her diet and changed the air filter in the air conditioning system. Submitted by K.F., Honolulu, Hawaii.
- J.E., a 37-year-old female, presented with a combination of stuffy and congested nose, watery eyes, mild cough, and clear phlegm in the nose. The patient had a tendency to get seasonal allergies every year and had been taking supplements but no improvement was noted. The practitioner diagnosed the condition as Lung and Spleen qi deficiency with phlegm; her Western diagnosis was allergic rhinitis. After being prescribed ***Magnolia Clear Sinus*** at four capsules three times a day, her allergies disappeared immediately and lasted for about four hours. She reported that the herbs allowed her relief, but only while consistently taking the herbs. Submitted by L.M., Gresham, Oregon.
- K.T., a 26-year-old female, presented with seasonal allergies consisting of congestion, sneezing, and dry eyes. Tongue was pale red, slightly swollen and shaky. The practitioner diagnosed this condition as wind invasion; Western diagnosis was seasonal allergic rhinitis. Upon diagnosis the practitioner prescribed

Magnolia Clear Sinus™

Magnolia Clear Sinus at 4 capsules three times a day. The formula was very effective towards her condition; the patient rarely experiences any more allergy symptoms. Submitted by S.L., Yuma, Arizona.

- D.G., a 57-year-old female, presented with constant headaches located behind her right eye due to allergies. The TCM diagnosis was qi stagnation located in the Stomach, Gallbladder, and Large Intestine channels; external wind invasion was present as well. For treatment, ***Magnolia Clear Sinus*** was prescribed. After only taking the herbs for one week, the patient had reported improvement of her headaches with only slight discomfort after a few more weeks. It was mentioned that the acupuncture alone did not help as much as combined with taking the herbs. Submitted by B.S., Niceville, Florida.
- A 41-year-old male actor presented with chronic sinus infection and nasal congestion. Surgical procedure to scrape and drain the sinus cavity was done with post-surgical care required. The practitioner suspected that the patient's work environment exposed him to smoke particles that irritated the sinus cavity. The practitioner diagnosed the patient's condition as Lung qi deficiency with compromised *wei* (defensive) *qi*. He was given ***Magnolia Clear Sinus*** to address the sinus cavity irritation and keep it clear of mucus. In conjunction with the herbs, acupuncture treatment was employed as well. The results were quite effective. The patient was free of breathing difficulty and mucus drainage discomfort. The practitioner noted that ***Magnolia Clear Sinus*** also benefited other patients with similar conditions. Submitted by T.W., Santa Monica, California.
- A 50-year-old female patient presented with itchy and watery eyes. She had clear phlegm, headaches and wheezing. The patient was treated with Ventolin (albuterol) for wheezing, and Claritin (loratadine) for allergy. The practitioner diagnosed this as seasonal, allergic rhinitis due to phlegm-cold. The treatment protocol included both acupuncture and herbs. During the allergy season, acupuncture treatment was given every two weeks. In addition, the patient took ***Magnolia Clear Sinus***, 4 caps three times daily for ten days. After taking ***Magnolia Clear Sinus***, the patient no longer complained of wheezing and sneezing, and the headaches were less severe. The practitioner noted that the patient responded quite well to ***Magnolia Clear Sinus***, especially during allergic attacks with asthma. Submitted by M.K., Sherman Oaks, California.
- B.F., a 55-year-old male, presented with cough, thick nasal discharge, headache and fatigue. The tongue was pale, flabby and slightly purple. The pulse was slow. He was diagnosed with common cold and wind-cold invasion. ***Magnolia Clear Sinus***, ***Respitrol (Cold)*** and ***Herbal ABX*** were prescribed. The patient reported that the sinus cleared in three days. Submitted by B.F., Newport Beach, California.
- A 54-year-old female property manager presented with chronic sinus congestion and headaches. She had food allergies to dairy, egg whites, kidney beans and lima beans. The practitioner diagnosed the case as Lung qi deficiency with excess dampness. After taking ***Magnolia Clear Sinus***, the patient commented that the herbs were effective in treating headache and nasal congestion. The patient continued to take ***Magnolia Clear Sinus*** intermittently throughout the year, but more so during the fall season. Submitted by T.W., Santa Monica, California.
- A 41-year-old female presented with sinus pressure and swelling around the right eye. A one-inch diameter growth on the neck and a cyst-like lump on the right side of the head were also noted. Other symptoms included extreme fatigue, overall body pain, and frequent coldness. The practitioner diagnosed her condition as cold damp nasal congestion and wind-cold attack. Within one month of taking ***Magnolia Clear Sinus***, the eye swelling abated and the sinus pressure was reduced by almost 90%. The lump on the neck decreased to 20% the original size while the cyst on the head desiccated. Overall, her body pain diminished, energy level increased, and cold sensations stopped. Her sleep pattern was also much improved. Prior to the herbal treatment with ***Magnolia Clear Sinus***, the patient spent almost four months going to different specialists only to come up with no results. In addition to taking ***Magnolia Clear Sinus***, the treatment protocol included acupuncture as well as a diet devoid of any cold, raw foods. Submitted by S.T., Morgan Hill, California.
- J.C., a 34-year-old female, presented chronic allergic rhinitis with itchy, stuffy, runny nose, itchy eyes and aversion to wind. These symptoms started in her childhood and worsened during the morning and allergy seasons. Her blood pressure was 125/85 mmHg and her heart rate was 78 beats per minute. Her tongue was pink with normal thin white coating. Her pulse was moderate and slightly slippery. The diagnosis was Lung qi deficiency with underlying Kidney and Spleen deficiencies. ***Magnolia Clear Sinus*** was prescribed. After taking the herbs, the patient reported 70% decrease in allergy symptoms. She said she was able to wake up with clear nasal passage. Santa Ana winds still triggered the symptoms, but ***Magnolia Clear Sinus*** keeps it under control. Submitted by J.C., Whittier, California.
- I.L., a 35-year-old male with a history of seasonal allergies, presented with sinus congestion and orbital pain that had lasted two months. The TCM diagnosis was wind-cold invasion. After taking three capsules of ***Magnolia Clear Sinus*** three times daily for five days, the patient reported mild relief of symptoms, and complete resolution of symptoms after one week. Furthermore, the condition did not return in the three months following completion of this herbal regimen. Submitted by C.L., Chino Hills, California.
- H.M., a 59-year-old female, presented with seasonal nasal allergies, rhinitis, stuffy sinuses and profuse, clear, nasal mucus. She was allergic to mold and mildew. ***Herbal ABX*** and ***Magnolia Clear Sinus*** were prescribed. They brought about relief after ten days, when the patient would usually be battling the symptoms for months and would have to take antibiotics. Submitted by H.C., Stephens City, Virginia.

Magnolia Clear Sinus™

PHARMACOLOGICAL AND CLINICAL RESEARCH

Magnolia Clear Sinus is formulated to treat rhinitis, sinusitis, and seasonal allergies. The ingredients in this formula have antiallergic, antihistamine, anti-inflammatory, and antibiotic (antibacterial and antiviral) effects. Together, they effectively treat both the causes and the symptoms of rhinitis and sinusitis.

Magnolia Clear Sinus contains many herbs with antiallergic and antihistamine effects to treat allergy-induced rhinitis and sinusitis. *Xin Yi Hua* (Flos Magnoliae) has been used successfully used for management of allergic conditions. This herb shows an antiallergic effect by inducing mitochondria and caspase-dependent mast cell apoptosis.[2] In addition, *Xin Yi Hua* (Flos Magnoliae) and *Bai Zhi* (Radix Angelicae Dahuricae) have an antihistamine effect to inhibit histamine release and inflammation.[3,4] *Jie Geng* (Radix Platycodonis) also has an antiallergic effect, as it acts by inhibiting the inflammatory cytokines and the signaling cascades, according to *in vivo* and *in vitro* studies.[5] Lastly, *Jing Jie* (Herba Schizonepetae) and *Sheng Ma* (Rhizoma Cimicifugae) are incorporated in this formula for their antipruritic effect to relieve itching and irritation induced by substance P.[6]

Since inflammation is a primary condition in both rhinitis (inflammation nasal mucous membrane) and sinusitis (inflammation of paranasal sinus), many herbs with anti-inflammatory effects are used in this formula. *Fang Feng* (Radix Saposhnikoviae) and *Xin Yi Hua* (Flos Magnoliae) exert their anti-inflammatory effects via inhibition of nitric oxide production.[7,8] *Jing Jie* (Herba Schizonepetae) and *Wu Wei Zi* (Fructus Schisandrae Chinensis) demonstrate their anti-inflammatory activities by decreasing the levels of cyclo-oxygenase-2.[9,10] Lastly, *Sheng Ma* (Rhizoma Cimicifugae) shows an anti-inflammatory effect by inhibiting interleukin-8 production,[11] and *Chuan Xiong* (Rhizoma Chuanxiong) shows an anti-inflammatory effect by suppressing TNF-α production and bioactivity.[12]

Since infection may cause rhinitis and sinusitis, ***Magnolia Clear Sinus*** uses many herbs with antiviral and antibacterial effects to treat the cause. *Che Qian Zi* (Semen Plantaginis) has a strong antiviral effect against a series of viruses, namely herpesviruses (HSV-1 and HSV-2) and adenoviruses (ADV-3, ADV-8 and ADV-11).[13] *Fang Feng* (Radix Saposhnikoviae) and *Gao Ben* (Rhizoma et Radix Ligustici) have shown antiviral action against influenza viruses.[14,15] *Jing Jie* (Herba Schizonepetae) has an antibacterial effect against *Staphylococcus aureus*, *Corynebacterium diphtheriae*, *Bacillus anthracis*, beta-streptococcus, *Salmonella typhi*, *Bacillus dysenteriae*, *Pseudomonas aeruginosa*, and *Bacillus tuberculi*.[16] *Wu Wei Zi* (Fructus Schisandrae Chinensis) has an inhibitory effect against *Staphylococcus aureus*, *Bacillus anthracis*, *Salmonella typhi*, *Bacillus dysenteriae*, *Diplococcus pneumoniae*, *Vibrio cholerae*, and *Pseudomonas aeruginosa*.[17] Lastly, *Xin Yi Hua* (Flos Magnoliae) has an inhibitory effect on dermatomycoses, and some species of streptococcus and staphylococcus.[18]

Clinically, many herbs in this formula have been used with great success to treat rhinitis and sinusitis. According to one study, 46 patients with chronic sinusitis were treated with an herbal formula with marked effectiveness in 35 cases, moderate improvement in 8 cases, and no response in 3 cases. The herbal formula was given in decoction, once daily, for seven days per course of treatment. The herbal formula contained *Xin Yi Hua* (Flos Magnoliae), *Cang Er Zi* (Fructus Xanthii), *Gao Ben* (Rhizoma et Radix Ligustici), *Fang Feng* (Radix Saposhnikoviae), *Sheng Ma* (Rhizoma Cimicifugae), *Chuan Xiong* (Rhizoma Chuanxiong), *Bai Zhi* (Radix Angelicae Dahuricae) and others.[19] According to another study, 120 patients were treated with 95% rate of effectiveness using an herbal formula with *Xin Yi Hua* (Flos Magnoliae) as the chief ingredient.[20] In addition to oral ingestion, topical application of herbs also showed a marked treatment effect. Topical application of essential oil of *Xin Yi Hua* (Flos Magnoliae) has been associated with reduction of mucous secretion, reduction of inflammation, and relief of nasal obstruction.[21] In fact, 1,576 patients with chronic sinusitis were treated with 86.9% effective rate using topical application of an herbal formula made from *Xin Yi Hua* (Flos Magnoliae) and *Cang Er Zi* (Fructus Xanthii).[22] Finally, since many patients suffering from rhinitis and sinusitis will also have pain and headache, *Bai Zhi* (Radix Angelicae Dahuricae), *Chuan Xiong* (Rhizoma Chuanxiong), and *Gao Ben* (Rhizoma et Radix Ligustici) are added for their effect to treat headache and relieve pain.[23,24,25]

In summary, ***Magnolia Clear Sinus*** is an excellent formula to treat both the causes and the symptoms of rhinitis and sinusitis.

COMPARATIVE ANALYSIS

Rhinitis and sinusitis are two common nasal disorders. In Western medicine, these two conditions are primarily treated with vasoconstrictive drugs that promote drainage, such as pseudoephedrine. Though effective, it is a strong stimulant and may cause many side effects, such as nervousness, restlessness, dizziness, difficulty sleeping, upset stomach, difficulty breathing, fast or irregular heartbeat, muscle weakness, palpitations, tremors, and hallucinations. In addition to vasoconstrictive drugs, antihistamines, such as Claritin (loratadine), may be used to address allergic sinusitis and rhinitis. The main advantage of these two types of medications is that they are relatively effective, and reasonably safe, so long as they are used correctly.

Rhinitis and sinusitis are effectively treated with herbs that drain the sinus cavity, reduce nasal mucous secretions, and desensitize allergenic reactions. These herbs may be given before, during, and after episodes of sinusitis and rhinitis. These herbs are very effective, and do not have the stimulating side effects that drugs have.

In addition to using drugs or herbs to treat rhinitis and sinusitis, it is also important to identify the cause, especially in individuals with allergic rhinitis and sinusitis. Whenever possible,

Magnolia Clear Sinus ™

avoid or minimize exposure to these allergens. It is important to remember that drugs and herbs do not cure allergy, they are only effective as preventative and symptomatic treatments.

References

1. *Xian Dai Zhong Yao Du Li Xue* (Modern Toxicology of Chinese Materia Medica) 2005;63-65.
2. Kim G.C., Lee S.G., Park B.S., Kim J.Y., Song Y.S., Kim J.M., Yoo K.S., Huh G.Y., Jeong M.H., Lim Y.J., Kim H.M. & Yoo Y.H. Magnoliae flos induces apoptosis of RBL-2H3 cells via mitochondria and caspase. Int Arch Allergy Immunol. 2003 Jun;131(2):101-10.
3. Shen Y, Pang EC, Xue CC, Zhao ZZ, Lin JG, Li CG. Inhibitions of mast cell-derived histamine release by different Flos Magnoliae species in rat peritoneal mast cells. RMIT Chinese Medicine Research Group, School of Health Sciences, RMIT University, Victoria, Australia. Phytomedicine. 2008 Oct;15(10):808-14.
4. Chen Y., Fan G., Chen B., Xie Y., Wu H., Wu Y., Yan C. & Wang J. Separation and quantitative analysis of coumarin compounds from *Angelica dahurica* (Fisch. ex Hoffm) Benth. et Hook. f by pressurized capillary electrochromatography. *J Pharm Biomed Anal.* 2006, 41(1): 105-116.
5. Han EH, Park JH, Kim JY, Chung YC, Jeong HG. Inhibitory mechanism of saponins derived from roots of Platycodon grandiflorum on anaphylactic reaction and IgE-mediated allergic response in mast cells. BK21 Project Team, Department of Pharmacy, College of Pharmacy, Chosun University, Gwangju, South Korea. Food Chem Toxicol. 2009 Feb 4.
6. Tohda C, Kakihara Y, Komatsu K, Kuraishi Y. Inhibitory effects of methanol extracts of herbal medicines on substance P-induced itch-scratch response. Research Center for Ethnomedicines, Institute of Natural Medicine, Toyama Medical and Pharmaceutical University, Sugitani, Japan. Biol Pharm Bull. 2000 May;23(5):599-601.
7. Wang CC, Chen LG, Yang LL. Inducible nitric oxide synthase inhibitor of the Chinese herb I. Saposhnikovia divaricata (Turcz.) Schischk. Cancer Lett. 1999 Oct 18;145(1-2):151-7.
8. Noshita T, Funayama S, Hirakawa T, Kidachi Y, Ryoyama K. Machilin G and four neolignans from young fruits of Magnolia denudata show various degrees of inhibitory activity on nitric oxide (NO) production. Department of Clinical Pharmacy, Aomori University, Aomori, Japan. Biosci Biotechnol Biochem. 2008 Oct;72(10):2775-8.
9. Kim SJ, et al. Anti-inflammatory activity of Schizonepeta tenuifolia through the inhibition of MAPK phosphorylation in mouse peritoneal macrophages. Am J Chin Med. 2008;36(6):1145-58.
10. Guo LY, Hung TM, Bae KH, Shin EM, Zhou HY, Hong YN, Kang SS, Kim HP, Kim YS. Anti-inflammatory effects of schisandrin isolated from the fruit of Schisandra chinensis Baill. Natural Products Research Institute, College of Pharmacy, Seoul National University, Seoul 151-747, South Korea. Eur J Pharmacol. 2008 Sep 4;591(1-3):293-9.
11. Hirabayashi T, Ochiai H, Sakai S, Nakajima K, Terasawa K. Inhibitory effect of ferulic acid and isoferulic acid on murine interleukin-8 production in response to influenza virus infections in vitro and in vivo. Department of Japanese Oriental Medicine, Faculty of Medicine, Toyama Medical and Pharmaceutical University, Japan. Planta Med. 1995 Jun;61(3):221-6.
12. Liu L, Ning ZQ, Shan S, Zhang K, Deng T, Lu XP, Cheng YY. Phthalide Lactones from Ligusticum chuanxiong inhibit lipopolysaccharide-induced TNF-alpha production and TNF-alpha-mediated NF-kappaB Activation. Planta Med. 2005 Sep;71(9):808-13.
13. Chiang LC, Chiang W, Chang MY, Lin CC. In vitro cytotoxic, antiviral and immunomodulatory effects of Plantago major and Plantago asiatica. Am J Chin Med. 2003;31(2):225-34.
14. *Zhong Yao Tong Bao* (Journal of Chinese Herbology), 1988; 13(6):364.
15. *Zhong Cao Yao Xue* (Study of Chinese Herbal Medicine), 1976:779.
16. *Zhong Yao Yao Li Yu Ying Yong* (Pharmacology and Applications of Chinese Herbs), 1983; 744.
17. *Zhong Yao Xue* (Chinese Herbology), 1998; 878:881.
18. *Zhong Yao Xue* (Chinese Herbology), 1998; 84:85.
19. *Shan Xi Zhong Yi* (Shanxi Chinese Medicine), 1991; 12(4):177.
20. *Zhong Yao Tong Bao* (Journal of Chinese Herbology), 1985; 5:45.
21. *Zhong Yao Cai* (Study of Chinese Herbal Material), 1990; 13(9):33.
22. *Zhong Xi Yi Jie He Za Zhi* (Journal of Integrated Chinese and Western Medicine), 1984; 4:211.
23. *Hu Bei Zhong Yi Za Zhi* (Hubei Journal of Chinese Medicine), 1989; (1):8.
24. *Zhong Xi Yi Jie He Za Zhi* (Journal of Integrated Chinese and Western Medicine), 1991; (1):52.
25. *Ji Lin Zhong Yi Yao* (Jilin Chinese Medicine and Herbology), 1991; (5):14.

Menatrol™

CLINICAL APPLICATIONS

- **Amenorrhea**
- **Polycystic ovarian syndrome (PCOS)**
- **Infertility**
- **Irregular, delayed or scanty menstruation**
- Period with dark blood or clots
- Conditions above should be accompanied by dark purple tongue and cold signs and symptoms

WESTERN THERAPEUTIC ACTIONS

- Restores normal menstruation by removing physical obstructions
- Restores normal menstruation by regulating the hormones
- Relieves pain

CHINESE THERAPEUTIC ACTIONS

- Warms the *ming men* (life gate) fire, tonifies Kidney yang
- Nourishes the womb and the *chong* (thoroughfare) and *ren* (conception) channels
- Invigorates blood circulation in the lower *jiao* and the womb
- Tonifies Liver blood
- Tonifies *yuan* (source) *qi*

DOSAGE

Take 3 to 4 capsules three times daily on an empty stomach with warm water. Dosage may be increased to 6 to 8 capsules three times daily, if necessary. The minimum period for treatment with this formula is one to three months. For treatment of infertility, advise the patients to stop taking the herbs immediately once pregnancy is confirmed.

INGREDIENTS

Bai Shao (Radix Paeoniae Alba)
Chai Hu (Radix Bupleuri)
Chi Shao (Radix Paeoniae Rubrae)
Chuan Niu Xi (Radix Cyathulae)
Chuan Xiong (Rhizoma Chuanxiong)
Dang Gui (Radix Angelicae Sinensis)
Di Huang (Radix Rehmanniae)
Fu Ling (Poria)
Fu Zi (Radix Aconiti Lateralis Praeparata)
Gan Cao (Radix et Rhizoma Glycyrrhizae)
Gan Jiang (Rhizoma Zingiberis)
Gui Zhi (Ramulus Cinnamomi)
Hong Hua (Flos Carthami)
Mai Dong (Radix Ophiopogonis)
Mo Yao (Myrrha)
Mu Dan Pi (Cortex Moutan)
Pu Huang (Pollen Typhae)
Ren Shen (Radix et Rhizoma Ginseng)
Rou Gui (Cortex Cinnamomi)
Shan Yao (Rhizoma Dioscoreae)
Shan Zhu Yu (Fructus Corni)
Sheng Jiang (Rhizoma Zingiberis Recens)
Shu Di Huang (Radix Rehmanniae Praeparata)
Tao Ren (Semen Persicae)
Wu Zhu Yu (Fructus Evodiae)
Xiao Hui Xiang (Fructus Foeniculi)
Yan Hu Suo (Rhizoma Corydalis)
Ze Xie (Rhizoma Alismatis)
Zhi Qiao (Fructus Aurantii)

BACKGROUND

Amenorrhea, polycystic ovarian syndrome (PCOS), infertility, and irregular or scanty menstruation are common menstrual abnormalities. Though the disease names and the exact etiologies differ in Western medicine, these disorders all share in common hormonal imbalances and menstrual dysfunction. From perspectives of traditional Chinese medicine, such conditions are often diagnosed as patterns of "Kidney yang deficiency and blood stagnation."

FORMULA EXPLANATION

Menatrol is designed to treat amenorrhea and other gynecological disorders with underlying Kidney yang deficiency and blood stagnation. In addition, ***Menatrol*** also addresses such conditions as irregular menstrual cycles, delayed menstruation, spotting or scanty menstruation, weakness and soreness of the low back and knees, coldness of the extremities, accompanied by a pale purplish tongue.

If the Kidney is deficient, reproductive function will be impaired. This results in symptoms such as amenorrhea, irregular menstruation, vaginal dryness, infertility, decreased libido, habitual miscarriage, hair loss and fatigue. The Kidney also controls the "sea of marrow," that is, the brain, where the hypothalamus and pituitary gland are located. Kidney deficiency can be correlated with the inability of the hypothalamus to signal the pituitary gland to release hormones that cause ovaries to release eggs. In other words, the normal menstrual cycle will be disturbed. Therefore, optimal treatment requires use of herbs that tonify Kidney yang, yin, and *jing* (essence).

Fu Zi (Radix Aconiti Lateralis Praeparata) and *Rou Gui* (Cortex Cinnamomi) restore depleted Kidney yang, augment *ming men* (life gate) fire, and warm and open the channels to treat obstruction due to coldness. *Gan Jiang* (Rhizoma Zingiberis) enhances the warming action and decreases the toxicity of *Fu Zi* (Radix Aconiti Lateralis Praeparata). *Xiao Hui Xiang* (Fructus Foeniculi) and *Wu Zhu Yu* (Fructus Evodiae) are used to warm the Liver channel where it circulates around the genital organs.

Chi Shao (Radix Paeoniae Rubrae), *Gui Zhi* (Ramulus Cinnamomi), *Mu Dan Pi* (Cortex Moutan), *Tao Ren* (Semen Persicae), *Hong Hua* (Flos Carthami), *Chuan Niu Xi* (Radix Cyathulae), *Pu Huang* (Pollen Typhae), *Mo Yao* (Myrrha), *Yan Hu Suo* (Rhizoma Corydalis) and *Chuan Xiong* (Rhizoma Chuanxiong) are indispensable herbs for treating any obstetric/

Menatrol™

gynecologic disorders involving blood stagnation. Together, they invigorate blood circulation, dispel blood stasis, clear blood clots and relieve pain that may be caused by blood stagnation. The use of these herbs follows the same principles as the famous formulas *Gui Zhi Fu Ling Wan* (Cinnamon Twig and Poria Pill) and *Shao Fu Zhu Yu Tang* (Drive Out Blood Stasis in the Lower Abdomen Decoction).

The *chong* (thoroughfare) channel is known as "the sea of all twelve channels," and as "the sea of blood." The *ren* (conception) channel is known as "the sea of all yin channels." Therefore, in order to regulate menstruation and treat infertility, the *chong* (thoroughfare) and *ren* (conception) channels must be nourished. *Dang Gui* (Radix Angelicae Sinensis), *Bai Shao* (Radix Paeoniae Alba) and *Shu Di Huang* (Radix Rehmanniae Praeparata), the chief ingredients in *Si Wu Tang* (Four-Substance Decoction), are used to tonify blood. In addition, *Shan Zhu Yu* (Fructus Corni), *Shan Yao* (Rhizoma Dioscoreae) and *Di Huang* (Radix Rehmanniae) tonify Liver blood, replenish Kidney *jing* (essence) and nourish the *chong* (thoroughfare) and *ren* (conception) channels. Other tonic herbs here include *Ren Shen* (Radix et Rhizoma Ginseng) to tonify the *yuan* (source) *qi*, *Mai Dong* (Radix Ophiopogonis) to nourish yin, and *Fu Ling* (Poria) to strengthen the Spleen.

Zhi Qiao (Fructus Aurantii) and *Chai Hu* (Radix Bupleuri) are used to regulate Liver qi to ensure smooth flow. They are used to enhance the effectiveness of the blood invigorating herbs and also to prevent stagnation that may be caused by the tonic herbs. *Sheng Jiang* (Rhizoma Zingiberis Recens) and *Gan Cao* (Radix et Rhizoma Glycyrrhizae) are used to harmonize the formula.

In conclusion, ***Menatrol*** tonifies Kidney yang and eliminates blood stasis to treat amenorrhea and other gynecological disorders.

CAUTIONS & CONTRAINDICATIONS

- This formula is contraindicated during pregnancy and nursing.
- This formula is contraindicated in cases of heat and deficiency heat, and in cases of infection or inflammation.
- This herbal formula contains herbs that invigorate blood circulation, such as *Dang Gui* (Radix Angelicae Sinensis). Therefore, patients who are on anticoagulant or antiplatelet therapies, such as Coumadin (warfarin), should use this formula with caution, or not at all, as there may be a higher risk of bleeding and bruising.[1,2,3]
- Patients who wear a pacemaker, or individuals who take anti-arrhythmic drugs or cardiac glycosides such as Lanoxin (digoxin), should not take this formula. *Fu Zi* (Radix Aconiti Lateralis Praeparata) may interact with these drugs by affecting the rhythm and potentiating the contractile strength of the heart.[4]

CLINICAL NOTES

- Patients can massage the lower abdomen to increase blood circulation and warm the womb. Instruct the patient to fold her hands together [overlapping *Laogong* (PC 8)] and place her palm on her lower abdomen [at *Guanyuan* (CV 4)] and massage in a circular motion, moving clockwise 36 times and counterclockwise 36 times. Practice twice daily, once when waking in the morning and once before going to bed at night. Ideally, a male practitioner (yang energy) should massage the patient's abdomen (influencing yin). During massage of the abdomen, the patient should feel the pressure, but not pain or discomfort.
- Moxa the lower abdomen for at least 30 minutes every night to warm the uterus and dispel stasis.
- Patients with a long history of back pain may need additional diagnostic workups to rule out structural damage to the vertebrae causing amenorrhea, infertility or irregular menstruation.
- Patients with infertility should check to see if chlamydia is the cause. Scarring and inflammation of the tubes may be a cause of blockage leading to infertility.
- Patients experiencing infertility should monitor basal body temperature to track ovulation. If there is no change in the temperature profile after the patient has been taking herbs for two months, the practitioner should re-evaluate and consider modifying or changing the formula to properly address the patient's condition. If the patient does become pregnant, herbs should be stopped immediately as there are blood-invigorating herbs that may be too strong for the patient. Please refer to ***Blossom (Phase 1-4)*** for additional information on female infertility.
- Patients with infertility should not go on strict diets or exercise excessively. They should also be advised not to use a douche.

Pulse Diagnosis by Dr. Jimmy Wei-Yen Chang:

- **Endometriosis, adhesions, ovarian cysts, fibroids:** *ren* pulse, a thin, long, straight, wiry pulse on and proximal to the left *chi* that is deep to the bone. It is one of the eight extra meridians.
- **Polycystic ovaries:** turtle pulse, a convex-shaped pulse, on the left *chi*.
- **Blood stasis:** dispersing pulse on the left *chi*.

SUPPLEMENTARY FORMULAS

- For female infertility, add ***Blossom (Phase 1-4)***.
- For polycystic ovaries, endometriosis or fibroids, combine with ***Resolve (Lower)***.
- For severe Kidney yang deficiency, add ***Kidney Tonic (Yang)***.
- For severe Kidney yin deficiency, add ***Kidney Tonic (Yin)***.
- For lower abdominal pain during the period, combine with ***Mense-Ease***.
- For menopause, use with ***Balance (Heat)***.
- For fatigue and overall weakness, use with ***Imperial Tonic***.
- For amenorrhea due to stress, tension or Liver qi stagnation, use with ***Calm***.
- For amenorrhea due to Liver fire, use with ***Gentiana Complex***.
- For hyperthyroidism, combine with ***Thyrodex***.
- For severe blood stagnation, add ***Circulation (SJ)***.

Menatrol™

ACUPUNCTURE TREATMENT

Traditional Points:

- Needle *Sanyinjiao* (SP 6), *Geshu* (BL 17) and *Xuehai* (SP 10). Apply moxa to *Zusanli* (ST 36).
- *Qihai* (CV 6), *Shenque* (CV 8), *Xiawan* (CV 10), *Zhongwan* (CV 12), *Neiguan* (PC 6), *Gongsun* (SP 4), *Mingmen* (GV 4), *Sanyinjiao* (SP 6), *Dahe* (KI 12), *Zhongji* (CV 3)

Classic Master Tung's Points:

- **Amenorrhea:** *Fuke* (T 11.24), *Jiemeiyi* (T 88.04), *Jiemeier* (T 88.05), *Jiemeisan* (T 88.06), *Tianhuang* (T 77.17), *Dihuang* (T 77.19), *Renhuang* (T 77.21), *Tianhuang* (T 88.13), *Minghuang* (T 88.12), *Qihuang* (T 88.14)
- **Polycystic ovarian syndrome (PCOS):** *Huanchao* (T 11.06), *Waisanguan* (T 77.27), *Yizhong* (T 77.05), *Erzhong* (T 77.06), *Sanzhong* (T 77.07), *Jiemeiyi* (T 88.04), *Jiemeier* (T 88.05), *Jiemeisan* (T 88.06)
- **Infertility (deficiency):** *Fuke* (T 11.24), *Huanchao* (T 11.06), *Tongshen* (T 88.09), *Tongbei* (T 88.11), *Tianhuang* (T 77.17), *Dihuang* (T 77.19), *Renhuang* (T 77.21), *Jiemeiyi* (T 88.04), *Jiemeier* (T 88.05), *Jiemeisan* (T 88.06), *Mufu* (T 88.38)*, *Tianhuang* (T 88.13), *Minghuang* (T 88.12), *Qihuang* (T 88.14). Moxa the lower abdomen.
- **Infertility (damp):** *Fuke* (T 11.24), *Huanchao* (T 11.06), *Jiemeiyi* (T 88.04), *Jiemeier* (T 88.05), *Jiemeisan* (T 88.06), *Mufu* (T 88.38)*, *Tianhuang* (T 77.17), *Dihuang* (T 77.19), *Renhuang* (T 77.21), *Tianhuang* (T 88.13), *Minghuang* (T 88.12), *Qihuang* (T 88.14). Bleed dark veins on the sacral area, BL and ST channels on the lower limbs. Bleed before needling for best result.
- **Menstruation (scanty):** *Fuke* (T 11.24), *Wanshunyi* (T 22.08), *Wanshuner* (T 22.09), *Jiemeiyi* (T 88.04), *Jiemeier* (T 88.05), *Jiemeisan* (T 88.06), *Tianhuang* (T 77.17), *Dihuang* (T 77.19), *Renhuang* (T 77.21), *Tianhuang* (T 88.13), *Minghuang* (T 88.12), *Qihuang* (T 88.14)
- **Menstruation (delayed):** *Linggu* (T 22.05), *Renhuang* (T 77.21), *Sihuashang* (T 77.08), *Menjin* (T 66.05). Moxa the sacral area.
- **Dysmenorrhea:** *Fuke* (T 11.24), *Linggu* (T 22.05), *Tianhuang* (T 77.17), *Dihuang* (T 77.19), *Renhuang* (T 77.21), *Tianhuang* (T 88.13), *Minghuang* (T 88.12), *Qihuang* (T 88.14), *Simazhong* (T 88.17), *Sihuashang* (T 77.08), *Menjin* (T 66.05), *Sihuashang* (T 77.08), *Tianshu* (ST 25), *Zhongji* (CV 3)

Master Tung's Points by Dr. Chuan-Min Wang:

- **Amenorrhea, PCOS, infertility:** *Huanchao* (T 11.06), *Fuke* (T 11.24)

Balance Method by Dr. Richard Tan:

- Left side: *Yinlingquan* (SP 9), *Diji* (SP 8), *Sanyinjiao* (SP 6), *Hegu* (LI 4), *Linggu* (T 22.05)
- Right side: *Zusanli* (ST 36) or *ah shi* points nearby, *Chize* (LU 5), *Kongzui* (LU 6) or *ah shi* points nearby, *Diwuhui* (GB 42)
- Left and right sides can be alternated from treatment to treatment.

Ear Acupuncture:

- Uterus, Ovaries, Pituitary Gland, Hypothalamus
- Embed steel balls or needles. Switch ears every five days.

Auricular Medicine by Dr. Li-Chun Huang:

- **Menstrual disorder (menoxenia):** Gonadotropin, Uterus, Kidney, Liver, Pituitary, Ovary, Endocrine
- **Amenorrhea and hypomenorrhea:** Uterus, Ovary, Gonadotropin, Exciting Point, Pituitary Point, Endocrine, Kidney, Liver, Sympathetic, Coronary Vascular Subcortex, Nervous Subcortex
- **Dysmenorrhea:** Uterus, Pelvic, Liver, Sympathetic, Kidney, Ovary, Endocrine, Pituitary, Lower *Jiao*

NUTRITION

- Eat cooked food and drink warm or room temperature beverages.
- Foods that are warm, such as lamb, beef, chives, cinnamon and pepper are recommended. Nuts and seafood such as oyster, lobster and shrimp should be included, as they tonify the Kidney. Alcohol can be consumed in small amounts (1 oz.) daily, as it invigorates the blood and warms the body.
- Ensure there is an adequate intake of vitamin B complex and vitamin E, which are important for production of sex hormones. Deficiency in zinc may also contribute to irregular menstruation.
- Avoid raw or cold foods such as sushi, salad, cucumber, tomatoes, ice cream, and refrigerated or iced drinks. Excessive intake of fruits also may cause coldness. Refrain from eating sour fruits, such as grapefruit and oranges.

The Tao of Nutrition by Dr. Maoshing Ni and Cathy McNease:

- **Irregular menstruation due to coldness:** Stew together lamb, baked tofu, and ginger.

LIFESTYLE INSTRUCTIONS

- Avoid sports that may expose the body to cold environment, such as skiing or cold-water sports.
- Stress can sometimes lead to irregular or absence of menstruation. Avoid stressful situations, or engage in stress-reducing activities, whenever possible.
- A regular and healthy lifestyle with adequate rest and relaxation is the basic requirement for a normal menstrual cycle.
- Hot compresses on the abdomen increase blood circulation, relax abdominal muscles, and relieve pain.

CASE STUDIES

- A 41-year-old female presented with infertility and depression. Her practitioner diagnosed her as having Kidney deficiency and Liver qi deficiency. Poor egg quality was a secondary explanation to her infertility. The patient's treatment consisted of acupuncture once a week and ***Menatrol*** (4 capsules three times daily). Shortly after the treatment started, the patient's cold symptoms abated and her menstrual cycle became regular (from 32 days to 28

Menatrol™

days). She became pregnant after only two months of treatment. Submitted by L.M., San Diego, California.

- A 15-year-old female student presented with irregular periods for almost two years. Her period interval was noted to be eight days every four months. Tongue body appeared enlarged and purple with the sides slightly more pale. She also had a thick, white tongue coating and a "rolling" pulse. Her condition was diagnosed as damp stagnation with underlying deficiency. After being treated with ***Menatrol*** for two months, the patient started having her menses. Her period interval has changed from eight days every four months to five to seven days every one to one and one-half months. Submitted by T.G., Albuquerque, New Mexico.
- M.C., a 33-year-old female, presented with irregular menstruation for the past five years (about two to three times a year each time lasting four to five days). She complained of cramping pain, fatigue, lower back pain, bloating, poor circulation, dry skin and lips, and brittle nails. Her blood pressure was 139/90 mmHg and her heart rate was 92 beats per minute. Her tongue was slightly dusky, pale to pink in color, moist with a thin white coat. Her pulse was slippery. Her diagnosis was amenorrhea with blood deficiency, blood stagnation, and Spleen qi deficiency with phlegm and damp accumulation. ***Menatrol*** was prescribed. The patient's last period was in early January. After starting ***Menatrol***, she menstruated again the second week of February, which was an exciting and positive sign because she usually menstruates once every five to six months. She will continue taking ***Menatrol*** until her cycle becomes regular. She also received weekly acupuncture treatments and began walking three to four times a week. Submitted by J.C., Whittier, California.
- J.W., a 44-year-old patient, presented with infertility and a history of miscarriage. She experienced high stress which she "bottles up" inside. Her hands and feet were cold. She also had back pain, low energy, severe menstrual cramps and premenstrual syndrome (PMS). Her tongue was pale and purplish, swollen with teeth marks. The tip was red. Pulses were wiry on both sides and slippery on the right. Her blood pressure was 125/86 mmHg and heart rate was 83 beats per minute. Lab report showed she had low FSH levels. The diagnosis was Spleen and Kidney yang deficiencies with Liver qi and blood stagnation. ***Menatrol*** was prescribed. After one month on ***Menatrol***, the patient reported her menstrual cramping "miraculously disappeared" and her estrogen levels increased dramatically. She was afraid the herbs would interfere with her *in vitro* fertilization (IVF) procedure so she stopped taking them for six weeks. After the IVF was not successful and her tongue color became very purple in the center, the practitioner suggested she take the formula ***Calm***. She was open to it. Within a week, her stress level decreased and her energy level increased. Her tongue color changed from purple to pink and slightly dusky. She is presently continuing to take ***Calm*** and is actively trying to conceive naturally. Submitted by J.C.O., Whittier, California.

PHARMACOLOGICAL AND CLINICAL RESEARCH

Amenorrhea is defined as the absence or abnormal stoppage of the menses.[5] Other than pre-puberty, pregnancy, early lactation, and after menopause, amenorrhea is considered a pathologic condition and must be addressed.[6] Etiologies of amenorrhea include anatomical obstruction (such as stagnant accumulation of menstrual blood) and physiological abnormality (such as hormonal imbalance).[7] Therefore, optimal treatment must address both of these causes.

The excessive accumulation of menstrual blood leading to obstruction and pain is one of the most common presentations of amenorrhea. To address this condition, herbs are prescribed to eliminate the accumulated blood, improve blood circulation, and relieve pain. To eliminate accumulation of blood and clots, herbs with antiplatelet, anticoagulant, and thrombolytic functions are prescribed. Herbs with such functions include *Chi Shao* (Radix Paeoniae Rubrae), *Tao Ren* (Semen Persicae) and *Hong Hua* (Flos Carthami).[8,9,10] In fact, in one study, researchers found that herbs that activate blood circulation and eliminate blood stasis proved effective in inhibiting the formation of clots in 73.4% of the test cases.[11] Lastly, to improve circulation, *Chuan Xiong* (Rhizoma Chuanxiong) is added. *Chuan Xiong* (Rhizoma Chuanxiong) is one of the most effective herbs to improve the circulation of blood to the body's periphery.[12]

Because the accumulation of blood often leads to severe abdominal pain, herbs are prescribed to alleviate pain and discomfort. There are many herbs with marked analgesic effects, including (but not limited to) *Fu Zi* (Radix Aconiti Lateralis Praeparata), *Chuan Niu Xi* (Radix Cyathulae), *Dang Gui* (Radix Angelicae Sinensis), *Bai Shao* (Radix Paeoniae Alba), *Gan Cao* (Radix et Rhizoma Glycyrrhizae), and *Yan Hu Suo* (Rhizoma Corydalis), which have shown excellent *in vitro* and *in vivo* effects.[13,14,15,16,17] Of all these herbs, *Yan Hu Suo* (Rhizoma Corydalis) is especially effective against visceral pain, and its analgesic effect has been compared with that of morphine. Though morphine is still more potent and has a faster onset of action, *Yan Hu Suo* (Rhizoma Corydalis) has far fewer side effects, slower development of tolerance, and has shown no evidence of creating dependence.[18] Furthermore, it has synergistic effects in combination with electro-acupuncture.[19] Overall, these herbs offer safe, effective, and reliable pain relief.

Hormonal imbalance is another common cause of amenorrhea. Chronic anovulation may be caused by polycystic ovarian disease where there is an acyclic production of estrogen, or it may be due to hypogonadism where there is a low or absent production of estrogen. In either case, proper balance and regulation of the endocrine system is necessary to restore normal menstruation. Herbs in this formula have a two-directional effect on the endocrine system. They balance and regulate the endocrine system to restore equilibrium. *Di Huang* (Radix Rehmanniae), *Ren Shen* (Radix et Rhizoma Ginseng) and *Gan Cao* (Radix et Rhizoma

Menatrol ™

Glycyrrhizae) have all shown marked regulatory influence on the endocrine system. *Di Huang* (Radix Rehmanniae) and *Gan Cao* (Radix et Rhizoma Glycyrrhizae) are more specific to the adrenal glands,[20,21] while *Ren Shen* (Radix et Rhizoma Ginseng) has a more general influence on the entire endocrine system.[22] Specifically, administration of these herbs has been shown to regulate and balance the endocrine system by directly affecting the hypothalamus and the pituitary glands.[23]

Overall, ***Menatrol*** is an excellent formula to regulate the hormones and remove physical obstructions to treat conditions such as amenorrhea, polycystic ovarian syndrome, and infertility.

COMPARATIVE ANALYSIS

Amenorrhea and dysmenorrhea are conditions that almost all women suffer on an occasional basis. As common as the conditions are, there are few drug treatments available. On one hand, hormone drugs, such as birth control pills and patches, are prescribed to regulate menstrual cycles. Though they are more effective, they often cause serious side effects, such as weight gain, hyperkalemia, clotting disorders, retinal thrombosis, cancer, liver damage, hypertriglyceridemia, hypertension, bleeding, and fertility impairment. On the other hand, those with dysmenorrhea may take non-steroidal anti-inflammatory agents (NSAIDs) to relieve pain and reduce inflammation and swelling. Though effective, they cause such serious side effects as gastric ulcer, duodenal ulcer, gastrointestinal bleeding, tinnitus, blurred vision, dizziness, and headache. In short, drug treatment options are very limited between those that treat only symptoms and do not work well, and those that work well but may have significant side effects.

Herbal therapy is extremely effective to regulate menstruation and treat amenorrhea and dysmenorrhea. These herbs have analgesic effects to relieve pain, anti-inflammatory effects to reduce swelling and inflammation, and antispasmodic effects to relieve cramping. Furthermore, many herbs have been shown to have a marked effect to regulate hormones to promote normal menstruation. However, this effect requires continuous use of herbs for at least one to two cycles. In short, herbal therapy is extremely beneficial for treatment of menstrual disorder as it treats both the symptoms and the cause of PMS and dysmenorrhea.

Drugs offer limited options for treatment of amenorrhea and dysmenorrhea. Birth controls are effective, but these drugs carry significant short- and long-term side effects. NSAIDs relieve pain, but should be used as needed for only a short period of time. Herbs, on the other hand, are extremely effective for both immediate and prolonged benefits. Furthermore, they are very safe and are associated with few or no side effects. Individuals with such menstrual disorders should definitely explore these non-drug treatment options.

References

1. Chan K, Lo AC, Yeung JH, Woo KS. Journal of Pharmacy and Pharmacology 1995 May;47(5):402-6.
2. Pharmacotherapy 1999 July;19(7):870-876.
3. European Journal of Drug Metabolism and Pharmacokinetics 1995; 20(1): 55-60.
4. Chen J. Recognition & prevention of herb-drug interactions. Medical Acupuncture 1998/1999 Fall/Winter;10(2):9-13.
5. *Dorland's Illustrated Medical Dictionary 28th Edition*. W.B. Saunders Company 1994.
6. Berkow, R. *The Merck Manual of Diagnosis and Therapy 16th Edition*. 1992.
7. Fauci, A. et al. *Harrison's Principles of Internal Medicine 14th Edition*. McGraw-Hill Health Professions Division. 1998.
8. *Zhong Xi Yi Jie He Za Zhi* (Journal of Integrated Chinese and Western Medicine), 1984; 4(12):745.
9. *Zhong Xi Yi Jie He Za Zhi* (Journal of Integrated Chinese and Western Medicine), 1983; 2:109.
10. *Hua Xi Yi Xue Za Zhi* (Huaxi Medical Journal), 1993; 8(3):170.
11. *Zhong Cao Yao* (Chinese Herbal Medicine), 1983; 14(7):27.
12. *Zhong Yao Xue* (Chinese Herbology), 1989; 535:539.
13. *Zhong Guo Zhong Yao Za Zhi* (People's Republic of China Journal of Chinese Herbology), 1992; 17(2):104.
14. *Zhong Yao Tong Bao* (Journal of Chinese Herbology), 1988; 13(7):43.
15. *Xin Yi Yao Xue Za Zhi* (New Journal of Medicine and Herbology), 1975; (6):34.
16. *Yao Xue Za Zhi* (Journal of Medicinals), 1971; (91):1093.
17. *Hu Nan Zhong Yi* (Hunan Journal of Traditional Chinese Medicine), 1989; 2:7.
18. *Zhong Yao Yao Li Yu Ying Yong* (Pharmacology and Applications of Chinese Herbs), 1983; 447.
19. *Chen Tzu Yen Chiu* (Acupuncture Research), 1994; 19([illegible]):55-8.
20. *Zhong Yao Xue* (Chinese Herbology), 1998; 156:158.
21. *Zhong Hua Yi Xue Za Zhi* (Chinese Journal of Medicine), 1975; 10:718.
22. *Bai Qiu En Yi Ke Da Xue Xue Bao* (Journal of Baiqiuen University of Medicine), 1980; 6(2):32.
23. *Zhong Cheng Yao* (Study of Chinese Patent Medicine), 1989; 11(9):30.

Mense-Ease ™

CLINICAL APPLICATIONS

- **Pain in various gynecological disorders**
- **Dysmenorrhea** with bloating, cramping, pain or blood clots
- **Menstrual cramping and pain** due to endometriosis
- **Lower abdominal discomfort and pain** due to premenstrual syndrome (PMS) and polycystic ovarian syndrome (PCOS)
- **Postpartum pain**

WESTERN THERAPEUTIC ACTIONS

- Analgesic function to relieve pain
- Anti-inflammatory action to reduce swelling and inflammation
- Antispasmodic effect to relieve cramping

CHINESE THERAPEUTIC ACTIONS

- Relieves cramping and pain
- Invigorates blood circulation
- Disperses blood stagnation
- Activates qi circulation

DOSAGE

Take 3 to 4 capsules on an empty stomach three times daily with warm water. Dosage may be increased to 5 to 6 capsules every four hours as needed to relieve pain. For best results, combine ***Calm*** with ***Mense-Ease*** and begin herbal treatment three days before the first day of menstruation.

INGREDIENTS

Ai Ye (Folium Artemisiae Argyi)
Chi Shao (Radix Paeoniae Rubrae)
Chuan Xiong (Rhizoma Chuanxiong)
Dang Gui (Radix Angelicae Sinensis)
Gui Zhi (Ramulus Cinnamomi)
Hong Hua (Flos Carthami)
Mu Dan Pi (Cortex Moutan)
Niu Xi (Radix Achyranthis Bidentatae)
Pu Huang (Pollen Typhae)
Tao Ren (Semen Persicae)
Wu Yao (Radix Linderae)
Xiang Fu (Rhizoma Cyperi)
Yan Hu Suo (Rhizoma Corydalis)

BACKGROUND

Dysmenorrhea is uterine pain associated with menses, starting one to three days before the menses, peaks 24 hours after the menses, and subsides after two to three days. Dysmenorrhea may be primary or secondary. Primary dysmenorrhea is more common, is not associated with structural disorder, and is characterized by pain resulting from uterine contractions and ischemia mediated by prostaglandins and other inflammatory mediators. Secondary dysmenorrhea is less common, and is usually caused by pelvic abnormalities, such as endometriosis, fibroids, and uterine adenomyosis.

FORMULA EXPLANATION

Mense-Ease is formulated specifically to treat women's disorders, such as pain in various gynecological disorders like dysmenorrhea, endometriosis, premenstrual syndrome (PMS) and polycystic ovarian syndrome (PCOS). These women's disorders are considered as qi and blood stagnation in the lower *jiao*. ***Mense-Ease*** contains herbs that activate qi and blood circulation, remove qi and blood stagnation, and relieve pain and cramps.

Pu Huang (Pollen Typhae) has an excitatory action on the uterus and works to invigorate blood circulation and relieve pain by eliminating blood stasis. *Ai Ye* (Folium Artemisiae Argyi) and *Chi Shao* (Radix Paeoniae Rubrae) have antispasmodic effects on the smooth muscles to relieve pain. *Yan Hu Suo* (Rhizoma Corydalis), *Chuan Xiong* (Rhizoma Chuanxiong), *Mu Dan Pi* (Cortex Moutan), *Gui Zhi* (Ramulus Cinnamomi), *Tao Ren* (Semen Persicae), *Dang Gui* (Radix Angelicae Sinensis), *Niu Xi* (Radix Achyranthis Bidentatae), and *Hong Hua* (Flos Carthami) activate blood circulation, remove blood stasis, and relieve pain. *Wu Yao* (Radix Linderae) and *Xiang Fu* (Rhizoma Cyperi) are qi regulators that help to relieve abdominal bloating and distension.

In short, ***Mense-Ease*** moves qi and blood in the lower *jiao* to treat various gynecological disorders such as dysmenorrhea, endometriosis, PMS and PCOS.

CAUTIONS & CONTRAINDICATIONS

- This formula is contraindicated during pregnancy and nursing.
- This herbal formula contains herbs that invigorate blood circulation, such as *Dang Gui* (Radix Angelicae Sinensis). Therefore, patients who are on anticoagulant or antiplatelet therapies, such as Coumadin (warfarin), should use this formula with caution, or not at all, as there may be a higher risk of bleeding and bruising.[1,2,3]

CLINICAL NOTES

- ***Resolve (Lower)*** and ***Calm*** can be used one week prior to each menstrual cycle at 2 to 4 capsules each twice daily to help move qi and blood in the uterus and prepare for smooth shedding of the uterine wall during menstruation. Unless the patient is extremely deficient in qi or blood, this principle can be applied to all patients, especially those with blood stagnation.
- For most patients, heat pads or moxa will always relieve pain. Moxa treatments should be 30 minutes or longer for maximum effect.
- ***Imperial Tonic*** is an excellent postpartum tonic. Women lose a tremendous amount of *jing* (essence) and blood after labor. The concept of replenishing the Kidney *jing* (essence) is not prevalent in the West. As a result, many women age faster and suffer from low back pain or symptoms of Kidney yin or *jing* (essence) deficiency later in their lives. This is a great formula to start one or two weeks after delivery. It helps replenish qi, blood, yin and yang that may have been lost during labor. Also, it is beneficial

Mense-Ease ™

to nursing mothers, as more nutrients will be passed down to the baby. However, before tonifying the patient with ***Imperial Tonic***, *Sheng Hua Tang* (Generation and Transformation Decoction) should be used for one week to clear out residual blood stagnation and to relieve pain. This will prevent future gynecological complications due to blood stagnation in the pelvis.

- For individuals who had a cesarean section, ***Flex (TMX)*** can be used to relieve pain and facilitate recovery.

Pulse Diagnosis by Dr. Jimmy Wei-Yen Chang:

- *Ren* pulse, a thin, long, straight, wiry pulse on and proximal to the left *chi* that is deep to the bone. It is one of the eight extra meridians.
- **Polycystic ovaries:** turtle pulse, a convex-shaped pulse, on the left *chi*.
- **Blood stasis:** dispersing pulse in the left *chi*.

SUPPLEMENTARY FORMULAS

- To enhance the effect to relieve pain, add ***Herbal ANG***.
- For premenstrual syndrome (PMS), irritability, stress, or emotional disorders, add ***Calm***.
- For irritability, stress, or emotional disorders with insomnia in patients with deficiency, add ***Calm ZZZ***.
- For cystitis, urinary tract or lower *jiao* infections, use ***V-Support*** with ***Herbal ABX***.
- For fever and fire signs, add ***Gardenia Complex***.
- For cysts in the uterus and ovaries, fibroids or endometriosis, use ***Resolve (Lower)***.
- For back pain, use ***Back Support (CR)***.
- For menses with blood clots, add ***Resolve (Lower)***.
- For severe blood stagnation, add ***Circulation (SJ)***.
- For infertility, use ***Blossom (Phase 1-4)***.
- To stop bleeding, add ***Notoginseng 9***.
- For headache with blood deficiency, add ***Corydalin (CR)***.
- For gynecological pain due to scar tissue causing excessive qi and blood stagnation, add ***Flex (TMX)*** .
- For acne, add ***Dermatrol (Clear)***.

ACUPUNCTURE TREATMENT

Traditional Points:

- *Sanyinjiao* (SP 6), *Guilai* (ST 29), *Zhongji* (CV 3), *Zusanli* (ST 36), *Xuehai* (SP 10), *Qihai* (CV 6), *Geshu* (BL 17), *Diji* (SP 8), *Taichong* (LR 3), *Xingjian* (LR 2)
- Needle *Yinlingquan* (SP 9), *Lougu* (SP 7) and *Sanyinjiao* (SP 6). Massage local tender points around *Sanyinjiao* (SP 6).

Classic Master Tung's Points:

- **Dysmenorrhea:** *Fuke* (T 11.24), *Linggu* (T 22.05), *Tianhuang* (T 77.17), *Dihuang* (T 77.19), *Renhuang* (T 77.21), *Tianhuang* (T 88.13), *Minghuang* (T 88.12), *Qihuang* (T 88.14), *Simazhong* (T 88.17), *Sihuashang* (T 77.08), *Menjin* (T 66.05), *Tianshu* (ST 25), *Zhongji* (CV 3)
- **Polycystic ovarian syndrome (PCOS):** *Huanchao* (T 11.06), *Waisanguan* (T 77.27), *Yizhong* (T 77.05), *Erzhong* (T 77.06), *Sanzhong* (T 77.07), *Jiemeiyi* (T 88.04), *Jiemeier* (T 88.05), *Jiemeisan* (T 88.06)
- **Back pain from endometriosis:** *Fuke* (T 11.24), *Yunbai* (T 44.11), *Tongshen* (T 88.09), *Tianhuangfu [Shenguan]* (T 77.18)

Master Tung's Points by Dr. Chuan-Min Wang:

- **Dysmenorrhea:** Needle or bleed *Menjin* (T 66.05).

Balance Method by Dr. Richard Tan:

- Left side: *Yinlingquan* (SP 9), *Diji* (SP 8), *Sanyinjiao* (SP 6), *Hegu* (LI 4), *Linggu* (T 22.05)
- Right side: *Zusanli* (ST 36) or *ah shi* points nearby, *Chize* (LU 5), *Kongzui* (LU 6), *Lieque* (LU 7) or *ah shi* points nearby, *Diwuhui* (GB 42), *Zulinqi* (GB 41)
- Left and right sides can be alternated from treatment to treatment.

Ear Acupuncture:

- Ear seeds are very effective for relieving menstrual pain. The primary points to select are: *Shenmen*, Sympathetic, Uterus, Endocrine, Brain Stem and Ovary. Adjunct points can be used on other affected areas such as the Back for back pain, Spleen for diarrhea and so on.
- Ear seeds can be placed one week before each menstrual cycle. The patient should massage the points for five minutes three times each day or as frequently as possible. To prevent the seeds from falling out, advise the patient not to wash that ear during showers and not to rub the ear too hard with a towel while the ear is still wet. Each course of treatment is four months. Alternate ear each month.

Auricular Medicine by Dr. Li-Chun Huang:

- **Menstrual disorder (menoxenia):** Gonadotropin, Uterus, Kidney, Liver, Pituitary, Ovary, Endocrine
- **Amenorrhea and hypomenorrhea:** Uterus, Ovary, Gonadotropin, Exciting Point, Pituitary Point, Endocrine, Kidney, Liver, Sympathetic
- **Dysmenorrhea:** Uterus, Pelvic, Liver, Sympathetic, Kidney, Ovary, Endocrine, Pituitary, Lower *Jiao*, Cervix. Bleed Ear Apex.
- **Endometritis:** Uterus, Cervix, Kidney, Liver, Ovary, Pituitary, Thalamus, Endocrine, Gonadotropin, *San Jiao*.

NUTRITION

- Foods and fruits that are cold or sour in nature should be avoided, especially one week prior to or during menstruation. Cold and sour foods create more stagnation, and may worsen the pain.
- Decrease the consumption of salt, red meats, processed foods, junk foods, and foods with high sodium content. Caffeine should be avoided as it acts as a stimulant to excite the central nervous system and as a diuretic to deplete many important nutrients.

Mense-Ease ™

- Increase the consumption of whole-grain foods, broiled chicken, turkey, and fish.
- Drink a large quantity of distilled water daily before, during, and after the menstruation.
- Menstrual cramps due to calcium deficiency should be treated with ingestion of foods rich in calcium, such as green vegetables, legumes, and seaweeds.
- Ensure there is an adequate intake of vitamin B complex and vitamin E, which are important for production of sex hormones. Deficiency of zinc may also contribute to irregular menstruation.
- A folk remedy for menstrual pain uses a stalk of ginger (sliced) with 3 pieces of green onion, 30 grams of brown sugar and 3 cups of water. Bring the mixture to a boil and cook for five minutes. Add a teaspoon of white pepper and serve.

The Tao of Nutrition by Dr. Maoshing Ni and Cathy McNease:

- **Premenstrual syndrome,** including lower abdominal pain and bloating prior to menstruation: Make tea from cinnamon and hawthorn berries.
- **Menstrual pain:** Drink wine that was prepared with the herb motherwort (*Leonorus cardiaca*) prior to the onset of menses; the menstrual period will probably be a little heavier than usual.

LIFESTYLE INSTRUCTIONS

- Avoid sports that may expose the body to cold environments, such as snow skiing or cold-water sports.
- Hot baths or hot showers aimed at the abdomen help to relieve menstrual pain and cramps.
- Hot compresses on the abdomen increase blood circulation, relax abdominal muscles, and relieve pain.
- Stress can sometimes lead to irregular or no menstruation. Avoid stressful situations, or engage in stress-reducing activities.
- A regular and healthy lifestyle with adequate rest and relaxation is the basic requirement for a normal menstrual cycle.
- Wear clothes that fully cover the body and do not expose the belly or the abdomen to the cold environment. Avoid wearing tight pants.

CASE STUDIES

- G.E., a 44-year-old woman, presented with painful menstruation, starts and stops, and excessive flow with clotting. Other findings included pain upon palpation of the abdomen and a pulse that was deep, strong, and wiry. The Western diagnosis was menorrhagia; The TCM diagnosis was blood stasis. The patient was prescribed ***Mense-Ease*** and ***Resolve (Lower)***. Since this tends to happen every few months, the patient keeps the herbs on hand. Each time it resolves the pain, it is very helpful to her. Submitted by A.I., Hilo, Hawaii.
- L.C., a 50-year-old female, presented with macular degeneration, experiencing pain one week before her menses and waking up at night. Tinnitus, low back and abdominal pain were also present. Her menses consisted of a bright red color, sometimes dark brown, and some clots. Pulse was thready and weak and her tongue had teeth marks and a red tip. The practitioner diagnosed this condition as Liver and Kidney yin deficiencies with qi and blood stagnation in the lower *jiao*. Upon diagnosis the patient was prescribed ***Nourish*** and ***Mense-Ease***. After taking the herbs for two months, the patient no longer has pain with her menses and felt better overall. Submitted by T.W., Perrysburg, Ohio.
- S.T., a 27-year-old female, presented with PMS symptoms consisting of severe cramping and moodiness. Pulse was choppy and the tongue was purple. The practitioner diagnosed this condition as Liver qi and blood stagnation. ***Mense-Ease*** was prescribed at 4-6 capsules three times a day, along with ***Calm*** to take as needed. After taking ***Mense-Ease*** for one cycle, the patient reported less menstrual pain and less cramping and moodiness. In addition, she reported that ***Calm*** had immediate effectiveness. Submitted by S.L., Yuma, Arizona.
- S.H., a 19-year old female, presented with multiple symptoms consisting of cramps, fibrocystic breasts, moodiness, and headaches. Pulse was thready and wiry; tongue was swollen with a yellow coating. The practitioner diagnosed this condition as Liver blood and Spleen qi deficiencies with dampness of the Spleen. For treatment, ***Mense-Ease*** was prescribed. In result of taking the herbs, the patient's cramps and breast pain had dissipated within 24 hours. Overall, the pain had decreased from and an 8/10 to a 4/10 level. After two days, the pain decreased to a 1/10 level. Submitted by V.G., Virginia Beach, Virginia.
- A 27-year-old female office worker presented with pain in her lower abdomen. The pain was more prominent before and during menses. She also had occasional bloody stools. The patient had a history of chronic yeast infections and endometriosis, which were resolved by surgeries. The practitioner diagnosed the condition as blood and qi stagnation with damp-heat in the lower *jiao*. After taking ***Mense-Ease*** and ***Resolve (Lower)***, menstrual pain reduced and rectal bleeding abated. Submitted by N.H., Boulder, Colorado.
- A 51-year-old female postal worker noticed an irregularity in her menstrual cycle. For the past three years, she had noticed an increase in her menstrual irregularity. The patient noted moderate pain and heavy bleeding eight days out of her whole cycle. Computerized Electrodermal Screening (EAV) detected higher than average readings, which was indicative of stress or irritation to her glands. The practitioner diagnosed this as peri-menopausal dysmenorrhea/menorrhagia due to qi and blood stagnation in lower *jiao*. After two months of taking ***Mense-Ease*** (2 capsules with each meal), the patient's menstrual discomfort improved 75% and her excessive bleeding was completely resolved. Submitted by D.H., Fort Myers, Florida.
- L.L., a 27-year-old female, presented with severe menstrual cramps, numerous dark blood clots, headache, acne breakouts with periods, extreme fatigue which forced her to lie in bed all day on the first day of the period. She stated that she must fast

Mense-Ease™

the first day otherwise she has nausea and vomiting. The blood pressure was 110/72 mmHg and the heart rate was 76 beats per minute. Her teeth-marked tongue appeared dark purple with red dots on the tip and sides. Tongue coating was thin and white. The pulse was slippery and thin. The diagnosis was Liver blood stagnation with Spleen qi deficiency and Liver qi stagnation. ***Mense-Ease*** was prescribed. After taking it for two weeks, the patient's next period was much less debilitating. She reported fewer blood clots, no more headaches, normal body temperature, and less intense cramping. After two months, the symptoms have decreased by 50%. She was able to function and eat on day one of her period, whereas before, she was bed-ridden. Submitted by J.C.O., Whittier, California.

- S.M. presented with dysmenorrhea, cramping with dark blood clots, and fatigue. The tongue was purplish pale and the pulse was slippery and slow. She also had a pale complexion. The doctor diagnosed her with qi and blood stagnation and ***Mense-Ease*** was prescribed. After taking the formula, the patient reported relief of lower abdominal pain and reduction in blood clots. Submitted by B.F., Newport Beach, California.
- A 28-year-old female dental hygienist presented with a palpable lump on her lower abdomen near acupuncture point *Zigongxue* (Uterus). She had severe premenstrual syndrome (PMS) affecting her emotionally, as well as large dark clots in her menstrual discharge. She had one week of constant dull pain on her left lower abdomen especially after her period. She described the pain as a grabbing, shooting type of pain as though someone was tightening a rope around her belly. She had a history of candida. She sought to get pregnant, and therefore discontinued taking her birth control pills. Laparoscopy was done in 1995 to remove her right ovary and in 1999 to remove endometriosis. Scar tissue was present in her left lower abdomen from a hernia operation when she was a youngster. Cysts were also present on her left ovary. Lastly, the patient also had a history of hypothyroidism and hay fever. Her tongue color was unremarkable and her tongue coating appeared moist. Her tongue root coating would alternate from white to yellow. Her sublingual region was also unremarkable. The patient's pulse was constantly deep, thready and soft. The practitioner diagnosed this clinical picture as damp-heat in the lower *jiao* and Spleen qi deficiency leading to the accumulation of dampness. The practitioner prescribed ***Mense-Ease*** to regulate her menstruation, and ***Resolve (Lower)*** to treat endometriosis. The patient was instructed to take 3 to 5 capsules of each formula three times daily, starting three days before her period and to continue the dose throughout her menstrual flow and for one week afterwards. After taking the herbs, she became less emotional. She noted fewer episodes of cramps the first month and no pain during the second month of her herbal therapy. Although her lower abdominal pain lingered, the intensity lessened, the frequency reduced, and the affected area dwindled. The patient also finally discontinued her caffeine intake, which she also attributed to her pain. After three months of herbal treatment, surgery was done to remove two inches of tissue. Ultrasound confirmed the complete absence of ovarian cysts after three months of herbal therapy. Doppler ultrasound showed a favorable pulsatility index for uterine blood flow. There were no blockages present in her reproductive system. The practitioner concluded that ***Mense-Ease*** was quite effective in treating other patients with similar conditions. The efficacy of ***Resolve (Lower)*** was also proven clinically with ultrasound results. Submitted by T.K., Denver, Colorado.

PHARMACOLOGICAL AND CLINICAL RESEARCH

Mense-Ease is formulated specifically to treat pain in various gynecological disorders, such as dysmenorrhea, endometriosis, fibroids and postpartum pain. ***Mense-Ease*** contains many herbs that exert strong analgesic, anti-inflammatory and antispasmodic effects.

Mense-Ease contains many herbs with analgesic action to directly relieve pain. *Yan Hu Suo* (Rhizoma Corydalis) is one of the strongest and most potent herbs for the treatment of pain, and is commonly used to treat amenorrhea or menstrual pain, hernial pain, chest and hypochondriac pain, epigastric and abdominal pain, and pain of the extremities. According to laboratory studies, the extract of *Yan Hu Suo* (Rhizoma Corydalis) is effective in both acute and chronic phases of pain and inflammation. With adjustment in dosage, the analgesic potency of *Yan Hu Suo* (Rhizoma Corydalis) has been compared to that of morphine. Though the maximum analgesic effect of *Yan Hu Suo* (Rhizoma Corydalis) is not as strong as morphine, it has been determined that the herb is much safer, with significantly less side effects, less risk of tolerance, and no evidence of physical dependence even with long-term use.[4] In addition to *Yan Hu Suo* (Rhizoma Corydalis), *Xiang Fu* (Rhizoma Cyperi), *Dang Gui* (Radix Angelicae Sinensis) and *Niu Xi* (Radix Achyranthis Bidentatae) are three other herbs with analgesic effect to relieve pain.[5,6,7]

Mense-Ease also has many herbs with anti-inflammatory actions to reduce inflammation. *Dang Gui* (Radix Angelicae Sinensis) has an anti-inflammatory effect similar to that of acetylsalicylic acid. It decreases vascular permeability to reduce inflammation.[8] Its anti-inflammatory effect is approximately 1.1 times stronger than acetylsalicylic acid, and its analgesic effect is approximately 1.7 times stronger than acetylsalicylic acid.[9] The anti-inflammatory property of *Dang Gui* (Radix Angelicae Sinensis) is attributed to the inhibition of pro-inflammatory mediators, including nitric oxide and prostaglandin E2 in peritoneal macrophages.[10] *Mu Dan Pi* (Cortex Moutan) is another herb with strong anti-inflammatory actions. According to laboratory studies, the mechanism of the anti-inflammatory effect is attributed to inhibition of prostaglandin synthesis and decreased permeability of the blood vessels.[11,12] *Pu Huang* (Pollen Typhae) also demonstrates marked anti-inflammatory action through improved circulation and decreased permeability of

Mense-Ease™

blood vessels.[13] Lastly, *Wu Yao* (Radix Linderae) and *Xiang Fu* (Rhizoma Cyperi) are two other herbs that exert significant anti-inflammatory effects through their inhibitory activities on the production of inflammatory mediators.[14,15]

Since dysmenorrhea is directly associated with uterine contraction, herbs are used to relax muscle contraction and relieve pain. *Xiang Fu* (Rhizoma Cyperi) is a uterine relaxant that has an inhibitory effect on the uterus.[16] *Chi Shao* (Radix Paeoniae Rubra) has an inhibitory effect on the smooth muscles of the intestines and uterus.[17] Lastly, *Dang Gui* (Radix Angelicae Sinensis) has a dual effect to regulate the smooth muscle of the uterus. Clinical studies have shown that when the uterus is in a state of relaxation, *Dang Gui* (Radix Angelicae Sinensis) can induce contraction. Conversely, if the uterus is in a contracted state, then *Dang Gui* (Radix Angelicae Sinensis) promotes relaxation. This dual action is credited for the therapeutic effect of relieving spasms and stopping pain.[18]

Lastly, ***Mense-Ease*** incorporates many other herbs to treat associated conditions of dysmenorrhea. *Chi Shao* (Radix Paeoniae Rubra), *Hong Hua* (Flos Carthami) and *Tao Ren* (Semen Persicae) have antiplatelet and anticoagulant effects, and are effective to treat endometrial clots. *Chi Shao* (Radix Paeoniae Rubra) and *Yan Hu Suo* (Rhizoma Corydalis) have sedative and tranquilizing effects, and are helpful to alleviate irritability, anxiety and emotional instability.[19,20] Lastly, to relieve ischemia associated with uterine contraction and pain, *Gui Zhi* (Ramulus Cinnamomi) and *Mu Dan Pi* (Cortex Moutan) are used to relax and dilate blood vessels and promote blood circulation.[21,22]

In summary, ***Mense-Ease*** is a great formula to treat menses-related abnormalities, such as dysmenorrhea, pain in various gynecological disorders, cramping and pain due to endometriosis, postpartum pain, and PMS.

COMPARATIVE ANALYSIS

Dysmenorrhea is a condition that almost all women suffer on an occasional basis. As common as these conditions are, there are few drug treatments available. On one hand, there are over-the-counter (OTC) drugs such as Midol and Motrin (ibuprofen) that reduce swelling and inflammation. These drugs treat the symptoms, and do not regulate menstruation or change the long-term prognosis of the condition. Those who have dysmenorrhea are likely to have the same conditions on a monthly basis when treated with only these OTC drugs. On the other hand, there are prescription drugs such as birth control pills or patches that regulate menstrual cycles. Though they are more effective, they often cause serious side effects, such as weight gain, hyperkalemia, clotting disorders, retinal thrombosis, cancer, liver damage, hypertriglyceridemia, hypertension, bleeding, and fertility impairment. In short, drug treatment options are very limited between those that treat only symptoms and do not work well, and those that work well but may have significant side effects.

Herbal therapy is extremely effective to regulate menstruation and relieve PMS and dysmenorrhea. These herbs have analgesic effects to relieve pain, anti-inflammatory effects to reduce swelling and inflammation, and antispasmodic effects to relieve cramping. Furthermore, many herbs have been shown to have a marked effect to regulate hormones to promote normal menstruation. However, this effect requires continuous use of herbs for at least one to two cycles. In short, herbal therapy is extremely beneficial for treatment of menstrual disorders, as it treats both the symptoms and the cause of PMS and dysmenorrhea.

In conclusion, drugs offer limited options for the treatment of dysmenorrhea. OTC drugs are ineffective and do not have lasting effects. Birth control pills are effective, but these drugs carry significant short- and long-term side effects. Herbs, on the other hand, are extremely effective for both immediate and prolonged benefits. Furthermore, they are very safe and are associated with few or no side effects. Individuals with such menstrual disorders should definitely explore these non-drug treatment options.

References

1. Chan K, Lo AC, Yeung JH, Woo KS. Journal of Pharmacy and Pharmacology 1995 May;47(5):402-6.
2. Pharmacotherapy 1999 July;19(7):870-876.
3. European Journal of Drug Metabolism and Pharmacokinetics 1995; 20(1): 55-60.
4. *Zhong Yao Yao Li Yu Ying Yong* (Pharmacology and Applications of Chinese Herbs), 1983; 447.
5. *Gui Yang Yi Xue Yuan Xue Bao* (Journal of Guiyang Medical University), 1959:113.
6. *Yao Xue Za Zhi* (Journal of Medicinals), 1971; (91):1098.
7. *Zhong Yao Tong Bao* (Journal of Chinese Herbology), 1988; 13(7):43.
8. *Xin Yi Yao Xue Za Zhi* (New Journal of Medicine and Herbology), 1975; (6):34.
9. *Yao Xue Za Zhi* (Journal of Medicinals), 1971; (91):1098.
10. Chao WW, Kuo YH, Li WC, Lin BF. The production of nitric oxide and prostaglandin E2 in peritoneal macrophages is inhibited by Andrographis paniculata, Angelica sinensis and Morus alba ethyl acetate fractions. Department of Biochemical Science and Technology, Institute of Microbiology and Biochemistry, National Taiwan University, Taipei 106, Taiwan, ROC. J Ethnopharmacol. 2009 Feb 25;122(1):68-75.
11. *Sheng Yao Xue Za Zhi* (Journal of Raw Herbology), 1979; 33(3):178.
12. *Zhong Guo Yao Ke Da Xue Xue Bao* (Journal of University of Chinese Herbology), 1990; 21(4):222.
13. *Zhong Yao Xue* (Chinese Herbology), 1998; 519:522.
14. Luo Y, Liu M, Yao X, Xia Y, Dai Y, Chou G, Wang Z. Total alkaloids from Radix Linderae prevent the production of inflammatory mediators in lipopolysaccharide-stimulated RAW 264.7 cells by suppressing NF-kappaB and MAPKs activation. Department of Pharmacology of Chinese Materia Medica, China Pharmaceutical University, 1 Shennong Road, Nanjing 210038, China. Cytokine. 2009 Apr;46(1):104-10.
15. Seo WG, et al. Inhibitory effects of methanol extract of Cyperus rotundus rhizomes on nitric oxide and superoxide productions by murine macrophage cell line, RAW 264.7 cells. Department of Microbiology, Wonkwang University School of Medicine, Iksan, 570-749, Chonbuk, South Korea. J Ethnopharmacol. 2001 Jun;76(1):59-64.
16. *Zhong Hua Yi Xue Za Zhi* (Chinese Journal of Medicine), 1935; 12:1351.
17. *Zhong Cheng Yao Yan Jiu* (Research of Chinese Patent Medicine), 1980; 1:32.

Mense-Ease ™

18. *Zhong Yao Xue* (Chinese Herbology), 1998; 815:823.
19. *Zhong Cao Yao Xue* (Study of Chinese Herbal Medicine), 1976; 340.
20. *Zhong Yao Xue* (Chinese Herbology), 1998; 162:164.
21. *Zhong Yao Xue* (Chinese Herbology), 1998; 65:67.
22. Kang DG, Moon MK, Choi DH, Lee JK, Kwon TO, Lee HS. Vasodilatory and anti-inflammatory effects of the 1,2,3,4,6-penta-O-galloyl-beta-D-glucose (PGG) via a nitric oxide-cGMP pathway. Eur J Pharmacol. 2005 Nov 7;524 (1-3):111-9.

Neck & Shoulder (AC)™

CLINICAL APPLICATIONS

- **Acute neck and shoulder pain** due to sports injuries, car accidents, prolonged body posture in a fixed position (such as working in front of a computer or sleeping in a poor position)
- Neck and shoulder pain, possibly with redness, swelling, and inflammation
- Limited movement of the neck and shoulders, due to pain and stiffness
- Whiplash, muscle tightness and spasms
- Acute flare-ups of chronic neck and shoulder problems
- Pain associated with a slipped or bulging disk of the neck
- Frozen shoulder or pain in the shoulder and scapula regions

WESTERN THERAPEUTIC ACTIONS

- Analgesic effect to relieve pain
- Anti-inflammatory function to reduce inflammation and swelling
- Muscle-relaxant action to alleviate muscle spasms and cramps
- Osteogenic effect to promote formation of bones
- Chondroprotective effect to ameliorate joint destruction and prevent cartilage erosion

CHINESE THERAPEUTIC ACTIONS

- Invigorates qi and blood circulation, eliminates qi and blood stagnation
- Opens channels and collaterals and relieves pain
- Reduces swelling and inflammation

DOSAGE

Take 4 capsules three times daily for moderate pain, or 7 to 8 capsules three times daily for severe pain. For maximum effectiveness, take the herbs with 6 to 8 ounces of warm water on an empty stomach.

INGREDIENTS

Bai Shao (Radix Paeoniae Alba)
Chuan Xiong (Rhizoma Chuanxiong)
Dang Gui Wei (Extremitas Radix Angelicae Sinensis)
Gan Cao (Radix et Rhizoma Glycyrrhizae)
Ge Gen (Radix Puerariae Lobatae)
Hong Hua (Flos Carthami)
Qiang Huo (Rhizoma et Radix Notopterygii)
Wei Ling Xian (Radix et Rhizoma Clematidis)
Yan Hu Suo (Rhizoma Corydalis)

BACKGROUND

Musculoskeletal and connective tissue injuries lead to over 10 million clinic visits per year in the United States.[1] Causes of these injuries may be external (sports injuries, car accidents, trauma), internal (chronic wear and tear of muscles, ligaments and tendons; bones weakened by osteoporosis), or both. Acute injuries are characterized by severe pain, swelling and inflammation, and in some cases, internal bleeding. Treatment of acute injuries should focus on relieving pain, reducing swelling and inflammation, and stopping bleeding. Chronic injuries are characterized by dull pain, stiffness and numbness, and decreased muscle mass and strength. Treatment of chronic injuries includes relief of pain and restoration of physical and physiological functions.

FORMULA EXPLANATION

Neck & Shoulder (AC) is designed to treat acute neck and shoulder pain. Acute neck and shoulder problems are often caused by accidents, such as car accidents, whiplash injuries, and prolonged body posture in a fixed position. In addition to pain, there is sometimes redness, swelling and inflammation.

Bai Shao (Radix Paeoniae Alba) and *Ge Gen* (Radix Puerariae Lobatae) have strong antispasmodic effects to alleviate muscle spasms, cramps and pain. *Yan Hu Suo* (Rhizoma Corydalis) is a strong analgesic and is used in this formula to invigorate blood, activate qi and alleviate pain. To invigorate blood circulation and alleviate pain, *Hong Hua* (Flos Carthami), *Dang Gui Wei* (Extremitas Radix Angelicae Sinensis) and *Chuan Xiong* (Rhizoma Chuanxiong) are added. *Wei Ling Xian* (Radix et Rhizoma Clematidis) is used to alleviate pain, promote qi stagnation and unblock stagnation in the channels due to external wind obstruction. With its warm and aromatic properties, *Qiang Huo* (Rhizoma et Radix Notopterygii) opens the channels and alleviates pain in the upper body. Finally, *Gan Cao* (Radix et Rhizoma Glycyrrhizae) harmonizes the formula.

Together, herbs in ***Neck & Shoulder (AC)*** invigorates qi and blood circulation to treat acute neck and shoulder pain.

CAUTIONS & CONTRAINDICATIONS

- Acute neck and shoulder pain, such as in whiplash, may be accompanied by spinal or anatomical injuries. The patient should be checked for structural and anatomical abnormalities if the overall condition does not improve after taking this herbal formula for one to two weeks.
- This formula is contraindicated during pregnancy and nursing, as it contains strong qi and blood activating herbs.
- This herbal formula contains herbs that invigorate blood circulation, such as *Dang Gui Wei* (Extremitas Radix Angelicae Sinensis). Therefore, patients who are on anticoagulant or antiplatelet therapies, such as Coumadin (warfarin), should use this formula with caution, or not at all, as there may be a higher risk of bleeding and bruising.[2,3,4]

CLINICAL NOTES

- Dr. Alex Chen, a master of traditional Chinese medicine with over 30 years of clinical experience, formulated ***Neck & Shoulder (AC)*** specifically to relieve pain, reduce inflammation and stop muscle cramps. Herbs in this formula are routinely used in the trauma department of hospitals in China.
- Common causes of neck and shoulder injuries include traumas, such as car accidents, sports injuries and/or repetitive stress

Neck & Shoulder (AC)™

syndrome of the neck and shoulder (i.e., from prolonged sitting in an upright position and/or staring at a computer monitor).
- To consolidate the treatment effect, use ***Flex (MLT)*** or ***Neck & Shoulder (CR)*** for one week before discharging the patient.

Pulse Diagnosis by Dr. Jimmy Wei-Yen Chang:
- Thick and forceful pulse proximal to the right *chi* indicates pain on the upper *jiao*. This pulse feels like a toothpick underneath the skin. The more forceful the pulse, the more severe the condition is.

SUPPLEMENTARY FORMULAS
- To enhance the effect to relieve pain, add ***Herbal ANG***.
- For recent trauma or bone fractures, combine with ***Flex (TMX)*** initially, followed by ***Osteo 8***.
- For old injury or stubborn pain due to chronic blood stagnation, use ***Neck & Shoulder (CR)*** or add ***Circulation (SJ)***.
- With bone spurs or calcification, add ***Flex (SPR)***.
- For shooting pain radiating down the arms, add ***Arm Support***.
- For lower back, sciatic, or nerve pain, combine with ***Back Support (AC)*** or ***Back Support (CR)***.
- For joint pain or arthritis that worsens during cold and rainy weather, combine with ***Flex (CD)***.
- For joint inflammation with redness, swelling, and burning pain, combine with ***Flex (Heat)***.
- For severe spasms, combine with ***Flex (SC)***.
- With hypertension, combine with ***Gastrodia Complex***.
- With acute headache, add ***Corydalin (AC)***.
- With chronic headache, add ***Corydalin (CR)***.
- For stress-related neck pain, add ***Calm*** or ***Calm (ES)***.
- For stress-related neck pain with insomnia, add ***Calm ZZZ***.
- For osteoporosis, add ***Osteo 8***.
- For herniated disk, add ***Back Support (HD)***.
- For degeneration of muscles, tendons, ligaments and cartilage, add ***Flex (MLT)***.
- With severe inflammation, combine with ***Astringent Complex***.

ACUPUNCTURE TREATMENT
Traditional Points:
- *Houxi* (SI 3), *Shugu* (BL 65). Leave needles in for 15 minutes.
- *Hegu* (LI 4), *Shousanli* (LI 10), *Jianliao* (TH 14), *Chize* (LU 5), *Waiguan* (TH 5), *Quchi* (LI 11), *Fengchi* (GB 20), *Dazhui* (GV 14)

Classic Master Tung's Points:
- Needle contralateral to the pain. If the pain is in the center, needle bilaterally or the side with the more *ah shi* points. If the pain is bilateral, needle bilaterally.
- **Neck pain (bone spur):** *Wanshunyi* (T 22.08), *Wanshuner* (T 22.09), *Huochuan* (T 33.04), *Tianhuang* (T 88.13), *Sizhi* (T 77.20), *Minghuang* (T 88.12), *Qihuang* (T 88.14), *Guciyi* (T 44.21)*, *Gucier* (T 44.22)*, *Gucisan* (T 44.23)*, *Huofu* (T 88.41)*, *Huoliang* (T 88.42)*, *Huochang* (T 88.43)*, *Sojingdian* (T 22.19)*
- **Neck stiffness:** *Zhengjin* (T 77.01), *Zhengzong* (T 77.02), *Renhuang* (T 77.21), *Sojingdian* (T 22.19)*
- **Fallen pillow syndrome:** *Waisanguan* (T 77.27), *Tianhuang* (T 88.13), *Qihu* (T 77.26), *Wanshunyi* (T 22.08), *Wanshuner* (T 22.09), *Yanglao* (SI 6), *Sojingdian* (T 22.19)*
- **Shoulder pain:** *Tianhuang* (T 88.13), *Waisanguan* (T 77.27), *Fanhoujue* (T 22.12)*, *Renzong* (T 44.08), *Dizong* (T 44.09), *Tianzong* (T 44.10)
- **Frozen shoulder:** *Linggu* (T 22.05), *Dabai* (T 22.04), *Fanhoujue* (T 22.12)*, *Tianhuangfu [Shenguan]* (T 77.18), *Minghuang* (T 88.12), *Tianhuang* (T 88.13), *Qihuang* (T 88.14), *Quchi* (LI 11), *Xiyan*, *Huantiao* (GB 30), *Renhuang* (T 77.21), *Sihuashang* (T 77.08), *Waisanguan* (T 77.27), *Sizhi* (T 77.20), *ah shi* points around the second metacarpal phalangeal joint, *Baguansan* (T 11.30)*, *Baguansi* (T 11.31)*. Bleed the affected area with cupping. Bleed before needling for best result.

Master Tung's Points by Dr. Chuan-Min Wang:
- **Acute neck, shoulder pain:** Bleed trigger points of levator scapula muscle or upper trapezius muscle. Needle bilaterally *Shangbai* (T 22.03).
- **Chronic neck, shoulder pain:** Needle bilaterally *Shangbai* (T 22.03).

Balance Method by Dr. Richard Tan:
- Needle the following points on the side opposite the pain: *Lingdao* (HT 4), *Tongli* (HT 5), *Shenmen* (HT 7), *Xuanzhong* (GB 39), *Shugu* (BL 65)
- Needle the following points on the same side as the pain: *Houxi* (SI 3), *Zhongzhu* (TH 3), *Sanyinjiao* (SP 6) or *ah shi* points nearby
- After the needles are inserted, the patient should move his or her neck to loosen up the joint and the muscles.

Ear Acupuncture:
- **Neck pain:** Cervical Vertebrae, Neck, Shoulder, Shoulder Blades, Kidney. Embed ear seeds and instruct the patient to massage the points three to four times daily for two minutes each time. Switch ears every five days. Five treatments equal one course.
- **Frozen shoulder:** Shoulder, Shoulder Joint, Adrenal Gland; or Shoulder, Clavicle, Adrenal Gland, Liver, Spleen, Subcortex.
- **Torticollis or fallen pillow syndrome:** Neck, Cervical Vertebrae and all the tender points around the area. Strong stimulation for 60 minutes. Needle once a day. Most patients will experience relief once the needles are inserted. If the pain is along the Liver and Gallbladder channels, needle Liver and Gallbladder as well. Similarly, if the pain is on the *taiyang* Urinary Bladder or Small Intestine channel, needle the corresponding points accordingly.

Auricular Medicine by Dr. Li-Chun Huang:
- **Neck pain, acute sprain, contusion, fallen pillow syndrome:** Occiput, Lesser Occiput Nerve, Large Auricular Nerve, *Shenmen*,

Neck & Shoulder (AC)™

Triangle Area of Cervical Vertebrae on the front and back of the ear. Bleed Ear Apex.

- **Periarthritis of shoulder:** Shoulder, Shoulder Joint, Clavicle, Large Auricular Nerve. Bleed Ear Apex.
  - For pain of the shoulder upon abduction, use Clavicle, Shoulder (front and back of ear), Arm Pit.
  - For anterior shoulder pain, use Shoulder Joint (front of ear), Coronary Vascular Subcortex, Large Auricular Nerve.
  - For posterior shoulder pain, use Shoulder Joint (back of ear), Clavicle, Large Auricular Nerve.

NUTRITION

- Eat plenty of whole grains, seafood, dark green vegetables, and nuts. These foods are rich in vitamin B complex and magnesium, which are essential for nerve health and relaxation of tense muscles.
- Adequate intake of minerals, such as calcium and potassium, are essential for pain management. Deficiency of these minerals will lead to spasms, cramps, and tense muscles.

LIFESTYLE INSTRUCTIONS

- Patients should avoid exposing affected areas to cold or drafts. Scarves, turtlenecks or similar clothing should be worn to protect the neck and avoid exposing the shoulders.
- Patients with frozen shoulders should be encouraged to exercise their shoulders as much as possible.
- Patients should also be advised to check their pillow to make sure it is not too high or too low. Mattresses should also be assessed for firmness.
- Hot baths with Epsom salts help to relax tense muscles and withdraw toxins from the tissues. Rest and relax in the bath for about 30 minutes.

CASE STUDIES

- N.T, a 41-year-old female, presented with neck pain and spasms, unable to turn her head to the left, waking up with pain in the morning. She was in severe pain and discomfort. This condition was diagnosed as Liver blood deficiency. Upon diagnosis, the patient was prescribed ***Neck Shoulder (AC)*** and ***Herbal ANG***. After taking the herbs for two days, the neck pain decreased and the range of motion greatly improved. Submitted by A.I. Hilo, Hawaii.
- R.B., a 25-year-old female, presented with severe head and neck pain. The patient had also been experiencing tension headaches in the frontal and occipital area. Objective findings included a pain level of 7/10, decreased mobility, and increased heart rate. Diagnostic tests had been received, which ruled out infection and meningitis. She had also joined a yoga group and was receiving psychotherapy and massage. The practitioner diagnosed the condition as chronic neck and back pain; her Western diagnosis was occipital neuralgia. For treatment, the patient was instructed to make certain dietary changes, received acupuncture twice a week, and was prescribed ***Herbal ANG*** and ***Neck Shoulder (AC)***. The patient reported that with taking the herbs she experienced a slow, steady improvement to a healthier lifestyle. She felt her tendons and ligaments were getting stronger due to enhanced blood flow. She was very happy with the results of taking the herbs. Submitted by E.S., Castro Valley, California.
- S.P., a 32-year-old male, presented with pain located on his neck and back due to an injury while working out. The practitioner diagnosed this condition as qi and blood stagnation. ***Flex (TMX)*** was prescribed at 4 capsules three times a day, while also taking ***Neck Shoulder (AC)*** at 6 capsules three times a day. After taking the herbs, there was an immediate decrease in pain. The patient discontinued taking the ***Flex (TMX)*** after two weeks and continued taking the ***Neck Shoulder (AC)*** for an additional four weeks until the pain was gone. Submitted by S.L., Yuma, Arizona.
- L.P., a 77-year-old female, presented with severe pain in the left wrist and right rib cage after a fall. She had numbness of the wrist and palm where she landed on the cement. The patient showed bruises on the right eye. The right wrist was painful to light movement and palpation. There were tender points on the right subclavicular area. There were no visible contusions on the right rib cage. The diagnoses were qi and blood stagnation with soft tissue damage. ***Flex (TMX)***, ***Neck & Shoulder (AC)*** and ***Flex (SC)*** were prescribed at 2 capsules of each formula three times daily. The patient reported daily lowering of pain levels. Numbness was reduced to a light tingling after two days. She reported continuous and steady improvement each day. She was instructed to reduce the dosage to 2 capsules of each formula twice a day when the pain subsided. After the swelling was reduced, the patient was referred to a chiropractor for cervical and occipital adjustments. Submitted by M.H., West Palm Beach, Florida.
- A male presented with pain and decreased range of motion in the right shoulder. There was pain upon palpation on the Large Intestine and Small Intestine channels. The practitioner diagnosed the condition as *bi zheng* (painful obstruction syndrome) due to stagnation of qi and blood. The patient was instructed to take ***Neck & Shoulder (AC)***. Acupuncture treatments using Dr. Tan's Balance Method and *tui-na* massage using Dr. Alex Chen's techniques were also applied. After six acupuncture and herbal treatments, he regained full shoulder range of motion without pain. After the pain was completely resolved, the practitioner switched the prescription to ***Neck & Shoulder (CR)*** at 3 capsules per day for maintenance care. Upon recurrence of pain, the patient was instructed to increase the dosage, which in turn resolved the pain sensations. Submitted by K.S., Encinitas, California.
- A 44-year-old female police officer presented with chronic headaches located in the occipital/temporal regions. She stated that stress aggravated the problem. There was acute tenderness at the *Fengchi* (GB 20) area as well as in the cervical spine. She also experienced pain on her zygoma. The practitioner diagnosed the

Neck & Shoulder (AC)™

condition as qi and blood stagnation in the Gallbladder, Urinary Bladder, and Small Intestine channels in addition to myofascial syndrome, which was stress-induced because of the nature of her job. She was treated with ***Corydalin (AC)***, ***Neck & Shoulder (AC)*** and ***Calm (ES)***, which were all quite effective that they subsequently replaced her medication, Imitrex (sumatriptan). The practitioner concluded that a critical aspect in the treatment was to assist patients in coping with their stress, which in turn made the herbal treatment more effective. Submitted by S.C., La Crescenta, California.

- A 43-year-old female teacher presented with severe neck and shoulder muscle pain of two months' duration. She attributed her musculoskeletal pain to stress from her job. She had a red-purple tongue and a deep rolling pulse. The practitioner diagnosed her condition as qi and blood stagnation. Within a week of taking ***Neck & Shoulder (AC)***, her pain reduced to about 50 to 60%. As an adjunct to the herbal treatment, acupuncture, massage and yoga were also added. After three weeks on the treatment plan, the patient's pain was almost completely resolved. Submitted by T.G., Albuquerque, New Mexico.
- A 45-year-old female was involved in a car accident in August 1997. She was rear-ended by another vehicle, resulting in a whiplash. She had severe pain and inflammation on the back of her head and very limited movement of her neck. She could only move her head bilaterally 10 to 15 degrees. X-ray showed no structural damages. She started receiving *tui-na* treatments and taking ***Neck & Shoulder (AC)*** at 7 capsules three times daily. After two days, pain and inflammation were reduced significantly. After ten days, there was no inflammation and no pain at rest. She could now move her neck up to 40 degrees to the left, and 45 degrees to the right. She was able to return to work and drive safely on her own. Submitted by J.C., Diamond Bar, California.
- A 55-year-old horse trainer presented with a torn rotator cuff following a horse training accident. The pain in her left shoulder was so severe she was unable to sleep. NSAIDs were taken without any relief. The patient took ***Neck & Shoulder (AC)***. At the close of four days of herbs, 60% of her pain was relieved. After 2½ weeks, she had no difficulty sleeping and the pain was no longer present. Submitted by J.H., Fort Myers, Florida.
- An 18-year-old male chef presented with neck and shoulder pain from a skateboard fall. X-rays revealed a diminished cervical curvature as well as a hypokyphotic curve at T2 to T3. The practitioner diagnosed the condition as a cervical sprain/strain. The patient was treated with ***Neck & Shoulder (AC)*** and ***Flex (TMX)***, which produced a reduction in pain. The patient found it necessary to take the herbs with food to avoid stomach discomfort. Submitted by M.H., Jupiter, Florida.
- J.M., a 36-year-old female massage therapist, presented with pain from a recent automobile accident (second accident in six months). She exhibited neck, back, arm, and leg pain. Airbags bent her right thumb. Her blood pressure was 120/70 mmHg and her heart rate was 72 beats per minute. X-rays showed herniation and soft tissue damage. She also complained of muscle spasms, hot sensation on trigger points, inability to move the right thumb, and the range of motion for the neck and trunk were both decreased. ***Flex (TMX)***, ***Neck & Shoulder (AC)*** and ***Back Support (AC)*** were all prescribed at 2 capsules each three times daily. She responded quickly to these formulas and acupuncture treatments. Pain levels were reduced by half in a short period of time. Submitted by M.H., West Palm Beach, Florida.
- An 85-year-old retired female presented with excruciating pain in the neck and shoulder that caused difficulty sleeping. Objective findings included limited range of motion of the neck. The tongue had a dirty yellow coat and a red tip. The Western diagnosis included psoriatic arthritis, arthritis, fibromyalgia, hiatal hernia, hypertension, depression, chronic constipation, leaky gut syndrome, sciatica and insomnia. The patient was instructed to take ***Neck & Shoulder (AC)*** and ***Corydalin (AC)***, 3 capsules of each three times daily in between meals. ***Calm (ES)*** was given at night to help sleep. The patient responded that the formulas were effective in reducing the acute pain in the neck and shoulder region. After the acute phase two weeks later, the patient was switched to *Gan Mai Da Zao Tang* (Licorice, Wheat, and Jujube Decoction) and *Shao Yao Gan Cao Tang* (Peony and Licorice Decoction), a combination recommended by Dr. Richard Tan that consistently helps patients with fibromyalgia. Submitted by J.B., Camarillo, California.
- A 47-year-old female office manager complained of neck pain and low back pain that were aggravated by prolonged sitting. She has a past history of two whiplash injuries that also attributed to her neck pain. Upon examination, the practitioner found extreme spasms of the erector muscles, bilateral weakness of her sternocleidomastoid muscles and a lack of muscle tone in her lower back. With these symptoms, the patient was diagnosed with right-sided sciatica, arthralgia of the spine and stress-induced muscle spasms. The TCM diagnosis was Liver qi stagnation. The treatment included acupuncture, moxa, and infrared heat. ***Back Support (AC)*** and ***Neck & Shoulder (AC)*** were prescribed for this patient. The results were as follows:

  3/29/01: stress: 8; pain: 9-10 (on a scale of 1 to 10; 10 rating = worse condition)
  5/05/01: 50% improvement
  5/19/01: 70% improvement
  8/16/01: No more pain. However, slight intermittent flaring of her condition was noted.

  The practitioner and the patient both concluded that the ***Back Support (AC)*** and ***Neck & Shoulder (AC)*** have really helped. Submitted by T.W., Santa Monica, California.

PHARMACOLOGICAL AND CLINICAL RESEARCH

Neck & Shoulder (AC) is formulated to treat neck and shoulder pain and stiffness caused by trauma, sports injuries, sprains and strains, or subluxation. The herbs in this formula have an

Neck & Shoulder (AC)™

analgesic influence to relieve pain, anti-inflammatory action to reduce pain and inflammation, and an antispasmodic effect to relax muscles and tendons.

Yan Hu Suo (Rhizoma Corydalis) is one of the strongest and most potent herbs for treatment of pain. Its effects are well documented in both historical references and modern research studies. According to classical texts, *Yan Hu Suo* (Rhizoma Corydalis) has been used to treat chest and hypochondriac pain, epigastric and abdominal pain, hernial pain, amenorrhea or menstrual pain, and pain of the extremities. According to laboratory studies, the extract of *Yan Hu Suo* (Rhizoma Corydalis) has been found to be effective in both acute and chronic phases of inflammation. The mechanism of its anti-inflammatory effect is attributed to its inhibitory activities on the release of histamine and pro-inflammatory mediators.[5,6] Furthermore, it has a strong analgesic effect. With adjustment in dosage, the potency of *Yan Hu Suo* (Rhizoma Corydalis) has been compared to that of morphine. In fact, the analgesic effect of *Yan Hu Suo* (Rhizoma Corydalis) is so strong and reliable that it has been used with satisfactory anesthetic effect in 98 out of 105 patients (93.4%) who underwent surgery.[7] The analgesic effect can be potentiated further with concurrent acupuncture therapy. In one research study, it is demonstrated that the analgesic effect is increased significantly with concurrent treatments using *Yan Hu Suo* (Rhizoma Corydalis) and electro-acupuncture, when compared to a control group, which received electro-acupuncture only.[8] Overall, it is well understood that *Yan Hu Suo* (Rhizoma Corydalis) has a marked effect to treat pain. Though the maximum analgesic effect of *Yan Hu Suo* (Rhizoma Corydalis) is not as strong as morphine, it has been determined that the herb is much safer, with significantly less side effects, less risk of tolerance, and no evidence of physical dependence even with long-term use.[9]

In addition to *Yan Hu Suo* (Rhizoma Corydalis), many herbs in ***Neck & Shoulder (AC)*** have significant analgesic effects to relieve pain. *Ge Gen* (Radix Puerariae Lobatae) contains many isoflavonoid compounds which have significant analgesic and muscle-relaxant activities.[10] *Qiang Huo* (Rhizoma et Radix Notopterygii) has an analgesic effect to relieve muscle aches and pain.[11] *Dang Gui* (Radix Angelicae Sinensis) exerts both analgesic and anti-inflammatory effects through the inhibition of pro-inflammatory mediators, including nitric oxide and prostaglandin E2 in peritoneal macrophages.[12,13] In comparison with acetylsalicylic acid, the anti-inflammatory effect of *Dang Gui* (Radix Angelicae Sinensis) is approximately 1.1 times stronger, and its analgesic effect is approximately 1.7 times stronger.[14] Lastly, the combination of *Bai Shao* (Radix Paeoniae Alba) and *Gan Cao* (Radix et Rhizoma Glycyrrhizae) has a marked analgesic effect to relieve pain. The effectiveness is increased significantly when combined with acupuncture.[15] Clinically, these two herbs have been used successfully to treat conditions such as pain,[16] neuralgia,[17] trigeminal neuralgia,[18,19] neck pain,[20] acute back pain,[21] heel pain,[22] pain in the lower back and legs,[23] sciatica,[24] gastric and abdominal pain,[25] and dysmenorrhea.[26]

Neck & Shoulder (AC) also utilizes many herbs with excellent anti-inflammatory effects to reduce swelling and inflammation. *Qiang Huo* (Rhizoma et Radix Notopterygii) exerts its anti-inflammatory effect to reduce swelling and inflammation through the inhibition of 5-lipoxygenase and cyclo-oxygenase.[27] *Chuan Xiong* (Rhizoma Chuanxiong) illustrates an anti-inflammatory effect via an inhibitory activity on TNF-α production and TNF-α bioactivity, and shows a promising effect to treat inflammation and related diseases.[28] *Wei Ling Xian* (Radix et Rhizoma Clematidis) exerts a significant anti-inflammatory effect by blocking the production of the pro-inflammatory mediators, nitric oxide and prostaglandin E(2).[29] *Bai Shao* (Radix Paeoniae Alba) has an excellent anti-inflammatory effect to treat arthritis by modulating the pro-inflammatory mediators production from macrophage-like synoviocytes.[30] Lastly, *Gan Cao* (Radix et Rhizoma Glycyrrhizae) has demonstrated marked anti-inflammatory effects by enhancing the effect of glucocorticoids through increased production and secretion as well as decreased metabolism of glucocorticoids by the liver.[31] In terms of anti-inflammatory actions, the comparison of cortisone to glycyrrhizin and glycyrrhetinic acid, two compounds from *Gan Cao* (Radix et Rhizoma Glycyrrhizae), is approximately 10:1.[32] Clinical applications of *Gan Cao* (Radix et Rhizoma Glycyrrhizae) include pain, inflammation, edema, arthritis, spasms, cramps and others.[33,34]

To alleviate spasms and cramps commonly associated with acute injuries, *Bai Shao* (Radix Paeoniae Alba) and *Gan Cao* (Radix et Rhizoma Glycyrrhizae) are used in ***Neck & Shoulder (AC)*** for their excellent muscle-relaxant effect to relax both smooth and skeletal muscles.[35,36] Clinically, these two herbs have been used successfully to treat conditions such as leg cramps in the calf,[37] muscle cramps in hemodialysis,[38] restless leg syndrome,[39] intestinal spasm,[40] facial spasms and twitching,[41] and menstrual cramps and pain.[42]

Finally, to facilitate recovery from acute injuries, ***Neck & Shoulder (AC)*** uses many herbs to promote healing and recovery. *Dang Gui* (Radix Angelicae Sinensis) is an effective herb to promote the generation of bones. According to one study, the water extract of *Dang Gui* (Radix Angelicae Sinensis) was found to contribute to the formation of bones and treatment of bone injuries. It directly stimulates the proliferation, alkaline phosphatase activity, protein secretion and particularly type I collagen synthesis of human osteoprecursor cells in a dose-dependent manner.[43] *Wei Ling Xian* (Radix et Rhizoma Clematidis) has an excellent chondroprotective effect. One study shows that the saponin fraction from *Wei Ling Xian* (Radix et Rhizoma Clematidis) is effective in ameliorating joint destruction and cartilage erosion in subjects with osteoarthritis, and the mechanisms of action for protecting articular cartilage are through

Neck & Shoulder (AC)™

preventing extracellular matrix degradation and chondrocyte injury.[44] Another study demonstrates that the acetone extract of *Wei Ling Xian* (Radix et Rhizoma Clematidis) has significant and dose-dependent inhibitory effects on the pro-inflammatory and degradative mediators associated with inflammatory arthritis. *Wei Ling Xian* (Radix et Rhizoma Clematidis) has been shown to inhibit prostaglandin E(2), metalloproteinase (MMP-3 and -13) and cyclo-oxygenase-2 (COX-2) production by primary human chondrocytes stimulated by lipopolysaccharides.[45] Lastly, *Wei Ling Xian* (Radix et Rhizoma Clematidis) also has a beneficial effect for the treatment of osteoarthritis by preventing apoptosis in primary cultured articular chondrocytes induced by adenoviral TNF-related apoptosis inducing ligand.[46]

In summary, ***Neck & Shoulder (AC)*** is an excellent formula to use during the first days and weeks of neck and shoulder injuries to relieve pain, reduce swelling and inflammation, and facilitate recovery.

COMPARATIVE ANALYSIS

Pain is a basic bodily sensation induced by a noxious stimulus that causes physical discomfort (such as pricking, throbbing, or aching). Pain may be of acute or chronic states. For acute neck and shoulder pain, two classes of drugs commonly used for treatment include non-steroidal anti-inflammatory agents (NSAID) and opioid analgesics. NSAIDs [such as Motrin (ibuprofen) and Voltaren (diclofenac)] are generally used for mild to moderate pain, and are most effective to reduce inflammation and swelling. Though effective, they may cause such serious side effects as gastric ulcer, duodenal ulcer, gastrointestinal bleeding, tinnitus, blurred vision, dizziness and headache. Furthermore, the newer NSAIDs, also known as COX-2 inhibitors [such as Celebrex (celecoxib)], are associated with significantly higher risk of cardiovascular events, including heart attack and stroke. Opioid analgesics [such as Vicodin (APAP/hydrocodone) and morphine] are usually used for severe to excruciating pain. While they may be the most potent agents for pain, they also have the most serious risks and side effects, including but not limited to dizziness, lightheadedness, drowsiness, upset stomach, vomiting, constipation, stomach pain, rash, difficult urination, and respiratory depression resulting in difficult breathing. Furthermore, long-term use of these drugs leads to tolerance and addiction. In brief, it is important to remember that while drugs offer reliable and potent symptomatic pain relief, they should only be used if and when needed. Frequent use and abuse leads to unnecessary side effects and complications.

Treatment of pain is a sophisticated balance of art and science. Proper treatment of pain requires a careful evaluation of the type of disharmony (excess or deficiency, cold or heat, exterior or interior), characteristics (qi and/or blood stagnations), and location (upper body, lower body, extremities, or internal organs). Furthermore, optimal treatment requires integrative use of herbs, acupuncture and *tui-na* therapies. All these therapies work together to tonify underlying deficiencies, strengthen the body, and facilitate recovery from chronic pain. TCM pain management targets both symptoms and the causes of pain, and as such, often achieves immediate and long-term success. Furthermore, TCM pain management is often associated with few or no side effects.

For treatment of mild to severe pain due to various causes, TCM pain management offers similar treatment effects with significantly fewer side effects.

References

1. Berkow R. et al. The Merck Manual of Medical Information. Merck Research Laboratories. 1999 February.
2. Chan K, Lo AC, Yeung JH, Woo KS. Journal of Pharmacy and Pharmacology 1995 May;47(5):402-6.
3. Pharmacotherapy 1999 July;19(7):870-876.
4. European Journal of Drug Metabolism and Pharmacokinetics 1995; 20(1): 55-60.
5. *Biol Pharm Bull*, Feb 1994; 17(2):262-5.
6. Oh YC, Choi JG, Lee YS, Brice OO, Lee SC, Kwak HS, Byun YH, Kang OH, Rho JR, Shin DW, Kwon DY. Tetrahydropalmatine inhibits pro-inflammatory mediators in lipopolysaccharide-stimulated THP-1 cells. Department of Oriental Pharmacy, College of Pharmacy, Wonkwang University Wonkwang Oriental Medicines Research Institute, Iksan, Republic of Korea. J Med Food. 2010 Oct;13(5):1125-32.
7. *He Bei Xin Yi Yao* (Hebei New Medicine and Herbology), 1973; 4:34.
8. *Chen Tzu Yen Chiu* (Acupuncture Research), 1994;19(1):55-8.
9. *Zhong Yao Yao Li Yu Ying Yong* (Pharmacology and Applications of Chinese Herbs), 1983; 447.
10. Yasuda T, Endo M, Kon-no T, Kato T, Mitsuzuka M, Ohsawa K. Antipyretic, analgesic and muscle relaxant activities of pueraria isoflavonoids and their metabolites from Pueraria lobata Ohwi-a traditional Chinese drug. Biol Pharm Bull. 2005 Jul;28(7):1224-8.
11. *Zhong Cao Yao* (Chinese Herbal Medicine), 1991; 22(1):28.
12. *Xin Yi Yao Xue Za Zhi* (New Journal of Medicine and Herbology), 1975; (6):34.
13. Chao WW, Kuo YH, Li WC, Lin BF. The production of nitric oxide and prostaglandin E2 in peritoneal macrophages is inhibited by Andrographis paniculata, Angelica sinensis and Morus alba ethyl acetate fractions. Department of Biochemical Science and Technology, Institute of Microbiology and Biochemistry, National Taiwan University, Taipei 106, Taiwan, ROC. J Ethnopharmacol. 2009 Feb 25;122(1):68-75.
14. *Yao Xue Za Zhi* (Journal of Medicinals), 1971; (91):1098
15. *Guo Wai Yi Xue* (Foreign Medicine) 1984;6(1):58.
16. *Shang Hai Zhong Yi Yao Za Zhi* (Shanghai Journal of Chinese Medicine and Herbology), 1983; 4:14.
17. *Zhong Yi Ming Fang Lin Chuang Xin Yong* (Contemporary Clinical Applications of Classic Chinese Formulas) 2001;313.
18. *Jiang Xi Yi Yao* (Jiangxi Medicine and Herbology) 1965;5(7):909.
19. *Zhong Yi Za Zhi* (Journal of Chinese Medicine), 1983; 11:9.
20. *Jiang Su Zhong Yi* (Jiangsu Chinese Medicine), 1990; (10):29.
21. *Zhe Jiang Zhong Yi Za Zhi* (Zhejiang Journal of Chinese Medicine) 1995; (11):524.
22. *Si Chuan Zhong Yi* (Sichuan Chinese Medicine) 1996;11:38.
23. *Yun Nan Zhong Yi* (Yunnan Journal of Traditional Chinese Medicine), 1990; 4:15.
24. *Fu Jian Zhong Yi Yao* (Fujian Chinese Medicine and Herbology), 1994; (1):7.
25. *Fu Jian Zhong Yi Yao* (Fujian Chinese Medicine and Herbology) 1961;9(4):44.
26. Tanaka T. A novel anti-dysmenorrhea therapy with cyclic administration of two Japanese herbal medicines. Clinical & Experimental Obstetrics & Gynecology 2003;30(2-3):95-8.

Neck & Shoulder (AC)™

27. Zschocke S, Lehner M, Bauer R. 5-Lipoxygenase and cyclooxygenase inhibitory active constituents from Qianghuo (Notopterygium incisum). Planta Med. 1997 Jun;63(3):203-6.
28. Liu L, Ning ZQ, Shan S, Zhang K, Deng T, Lu XP, Cheng YY. Phthalide Lactones from Ligusticum chuanxiong inhibit lipopolysaccharide-induced TNF-alpha production and TNF-alpha-mediated NF-kappaB Activation. Planta Med. 2005 Sep;71(9):808-13.
29. Park EK, Ryu MH, Kim YH, Lee YA, Lee SH, Woo DH, Hong SJ, Han JS, Yoo MC, Yang HI, Kim KS. Anti-inflammatory effects of an ethanolic extract from Clematis mandshurica Rupr. East-West Bone and Joint Research Center, College of Medicine, Kyung Hee University, Hoegi-1 dong, Dongdaemun-gu, Seoul 130-701, South Korea. J Ethnopharmacol. 2006 Nov 3;108(1):142-7.
30. Zheng YQ, Wei W. Total glucosides of paeony suppresses adjuvant arthritis in rats and intervenes cytokine-signaling between different types of synoviocytes. Int Immunopharmacol. 2005 Sep;5(10):1560-73.
31. *Zhong Yao Zhi* (Chinese Herbology Journal), 1993; 358.
32. *Zhong Cao Yao* (Chinese Herbal Medicine), 1991; 22(10):452.
33. *Zhe Jiang Zhong Yi Za Zhi* (Zhejiang Journal of Chinese Medicine), 1980; 2:60.
34. *Zhong Hua Nei Ke Za Zhi* (Chinese Journal of Internal Medicine), 1960; 4:354.
35. *Guo Wai Yi Xue* (Foreign Medicine) 1984;6(1):58.
36. *He Nan Zhong Yi* (Henan Chinese Medicine) 1986;(6):15.
37. *Zhong Yi Za Zhi* (Journal of Chinese Medicine) 1985;6:450.
38. Inoshita F, Ogura Y, Suzuki Y, Hara S, Yamada A, Tanaka N, Yamashita A, Marumo F. Effect of orally administered shao-yao-gan-cao-tang (Shakuyaku-kanzo-to) on muscle cramps in maintenance hemodialysis patients: a preliminary study. American Journal of Chinese Medicine 2003;31(3):445-53.
39. *He Bei Zhong Yi* (Hebei Chinese Medicine) 1984;3:29.
40. *Zhong Yi Za Zhi* (Journal of Chinese Medicine), 1985; 6:50.
41. *Zhong Xi Yi Jie He Za Zhi* (Journal of Integrated Chinese and Western Medicine), 1991; (1):43.
42. *Bei Jing Zhong Yi* (Beijing Chinese Medicine) 1983;(1):33.
43. Yang Q, Populo SM, Zhang J, Yang G, Kodama H. Effect of Angelica sinensis on the proliferation of human bone cells. Clin Chim Acta. 2002 Oct;324(1-2):89-97.
44. Wu W, Xu X, Dai Y, Xia L. Therapeutic effect of the saponin fraction from Clematis chinensis Osbeck roots on osteoarthritis induced by monosodium iodoacetate through protecting articular cartilage. Department of Pharmacology of Chinese Materia Medica, College of Traditional Chinese Medicine, China Pharmaceutical University, Nanjing. Phytother Res. 2010 Apr;24(4):538-46.
45. Hsieh MS, Wang KT, Tseng SH, Lee CJ, Chen CH, Wang CC. Using (18)F-FDG microPET imaging to measure the inhibitory effects of Clematis chinensis Osbeck on the pro-inflammatory and degradative mediators associated with inflammatory arthritis. School of Medicine, Taipei Medical University, Taipei, Taiwan; Orthopedics Research Center, Taipei Medical University Hospital, Taipei, Taiwan. J Ethnopharmacol. 2010 Jul 3.
46. Lee SW, Lee HJ, Moon JB, Choi SM, Kim DK, Kim IR, Choi WC, Park BS. Purified extract from Clematis mandshurica prevents adenoviral-TRAIL induced apoptosis on rat articular chondrocytes. Department of Rheumatology, Dong-A University College of Medicine and Institute of Medical Science, Busan, South Korea. Am J Chin Med. 2008;36(2):399-410.

Neck & Shoulder (CR)™

CLINICAL APPLICATIONS

- **Chronic neck and shoulder pain**, including numbness and discomfort
- Limited movement of the neck and shoulders due to pain and stiffness
- Long-term neck and shoulder injuries with a slow recovery or continuing deterioration
- Injuries of the neck and shoulder muscles commonly caused by over-exertion
- Repetitive stress syndrome of the neck and shoulders (i.e., prolonged upright sitting position, or working in front of a computer)
- Arthritis of the neck

WESTERN THERAPEUTIC ACTIONS

- Chondroprotective function to protect joint destruction and cartilage erosion
- Osteogenic function to promote generation of new bones
- Anti-inflammatory effect to reduce inflammation and swelling
- Analgesic action to alleviate muscle pain
- Muscle-relaxant effect to relieve muscle cramps and spasms

CHINESE THERAPEUTIC ACTIONS

- Disperses painful obstruction, strengthens sinews and tendons
- Disperses residual qi and blood stagnation in the channels and collaterals
- Relieves pain and muscle spasms due to chronic *bi zheng* (painful obstruction syndrome) of the neck and shoulders

DOSAGE

Take 3 to 4 capsules three times daily. Depending on the nature and severity of the illness, the dosage may be increased up to 8 capsules three times daily for three or four days to relieve pain. For maximum effectiveness, take the herbs on an empty stomach with warm water. This formula should not be taken during the acute phases of injuries, where there is still bleeding, inflammation, and bruising.

INGREDIENTS

Bai Shao (Radix Paeoniae Alba)
Chuan Niu Xi (Radix Cyathulae)
Chuan Xiong (Rhizoma Chuanxiong)
Dang Gui Wei (Extremitas Radix Angelicae Sinensis)
Di Gu Pi (Cortex Lycii)
Di Huang (Radix Rehmanniae)
Gan Cao (Radix et Rhizoma Glycyrrhizae)
Ge Gen (Radix Puerariae Lobatae)
Hong Hua (Flos Carthami)
Mo Yao (Myrrha)
Mu Gua (Fructus Chaenomelis)
Qiang Huo (Rhizoma et Radix Notopterygii)
Qin Jiao (Radix Gentianae Macrophyllae)
Ru Xiang (Gummi Olibanum)
Sang Ji Sheng (Herba Taxilli)
Tao Ren (Semen Persicae)
Wu Jia Pi (Cortex Acanthopanacis)
Xu Duan (Radix Dipsaci)
Yan Hu Suo (Rhizoma Corydalis)

BACKGROUND

Musculoskeletal and connective tissue injuries lead to over 10 million clinic visits per year in the United States.[1] Causes of these injuries may be external (sports injuries, car accidents, trauma), internal (chronic wear and tear of muscles, ligaments and tendons; bones weakened by osteoporosis), or both. Acute injuries are characterized by severe pain, swelling and inflammation, and in some cases, internal bleeding. Treatment of acute injuries should focus on relieving pain, reducing swelling and inflammation, and stopping bleeding. Chronic injuries are characterized by dull pain, stiffness and numbness, and decreased muscle mass and strength. Treatment of chronic injuries includes relief of pain and restoration of physical and physiological functions.

FORMULA EXPLANATION

Neck & Shoulder (CR) is designed to treat chronic neck and shoulder problems characterized by pain, numbness, stiffness, discomfort, limited mobility, slow recovery or continuing deterioration. Effective treatment must focus on activating qi and blood circulation, opening the channels and collaterals, and nourishing the muscles and tendons.

Qiang Huo (Rhizoma et Radix Notopterygii) treats soreness, pain and numbness in the neck, upper back, and shoulders due to wind-damp obstruction. *Sang Ji Sheng* (Herba Taxilli), *Chuan Niu Xi* (Radix Cyathulae), *Di Huang* (Radix Rehmanniae) and *Xu Duan* (Radix Dipsaci) tonify the Kidney and the Liver, strengthen the tendons, and alleviate pain, stiffness and soreness of the muscles. *Mu Gua* (Fructus Chaenomelis) and *Qin Jiao* (Radix Gentianae Macrophyllae) dispel painful obstruction and cramping, relax the sinews and unblock the channels. *Wu Jia Pi* (Cortex Acanthopanacis) treats painful obstruction due to Liver and Kidney yin deficiencies. *Yan Hu Suo* (Rhizoma Corydalis) invigorates blood, activates qi and alleviates pain. *Tao Ren* (Semen Persicae), *Hong Hua* (Flos Carthami), *Ru Xiang* (Gummi Olibanum), *Mo Yao* (Myrrha), *Chuan Xiong* (Rhizoma Chuanxiong), and *Dang Gui Wei* (Extremitas Radix Angelicae Sinensis) invigorate blood and remove residual stasis in the channels and collaterals. *Ge Gen* (Radix Puerariae Lobatae) and *Bai Shao* (Radix Paeoniae Alba) have strong antispasmodic effects to alleviate muscle spasm, cramps and pain. Aside from its anti-inflammatory effects, *Gan Cao* (Radix et Rhizoma Glycyrrhizae) harmonizes the formula and alleviates muscle pain and spasms. *Di Huang* (Radix Rehmanniae) and *Di Gu Pi* (Cortex Lycii) tonify yin, clear deficiency heat, and keep the temperature of this formula cool.

Neck & Shoulder (CR)™

Together, ***Neck & Shoulder (CR)*** strengthens sinews and tendons to treat chronic neck and shoulder pain.

CAUTIONS & CONTRAINDICATIONS

- Chronic neck and shoulder pain may be accompanied by spinal or anatomical injuries. The patient should be checked for structural and anatomical abnormalities, especially if the overall condition does not improve after two to three weeks of herbal treatment.
- This herbal formula contains herbs that invigorate blood circulation, such as *Dang Gui Wei* (Extremitas Radix Angelicae Sinensis). Therefore, patients who are on anticoagulant or antiplatelet therapies, such as Coumadin (warfarin), should use this formula with caution, or not at all, as there may be a higher risk of bleeding and bruising.[2,3,4]

CLINICAL NOTES

- Dr. Alex Chen, a master of traditional Chinese medicine with over 30 years of clinical experience, formulated ***Neck & Shoulder (CR)*** specifically to relieve pain, reduce inflammation and stop muscle cramps. Herbs in this formula are routinely used in the trauma department of hospitals in China.

Pulse Diagnosis by Dr. Jimmy Wei-Yen Chang:

- Thick and forceful pulse proximal to the right *chi* indicates pain on the upper *jiao*. This pulse feels like a toothpick underneath the skin. If there is soft tissue damage, the pulse on or proximal to the right *chi* will feel like a "turtle shell."

SUPPLEMENTARY FORMULAS

- With bone spurs or calcification, add ***Flex (SPR)***.
- For joint pain or arthritis that worsens during cold and rainy weather, combine with ***Flex (CD)***.
- For joint inflammation with redness, swelling, and burning pain, combine with ***Flex (Heat)***.
- With severe spasms, combine with ***Flex (SC)***.
- To strengthen the soft tissues (muscles, tendons, ligaments), add ***Flex (MLT)***.
- For bone fractures, whiplash, or acute injuries, combine with ***Flex (TMX)***.
- To improve blood circulation, add ***Flex (NP)***.
- For lower back, sciatic, or nerve pain, add ***Back Support (AC)*** or ***Back Support (CR)***.
- With acute headache, add ***Corydalin (AC)***.
- With chronic headache, add ***Corydalin (CR)***.
- For osteoporosis, add ***Osteo 8***.
- To enhance the effect to relieve pain, add ***Herbal ANG***.
- For herniated disk, add ***Back Support (HD)***.
- For old injury or stubborn pain due to chronic blood stagnation, add ***Circulation (SJ)***.
- For shooting pain radiating down the arms, add ***Arm Support***.
- For stress-related neck pain with insomnia, add ***Calm ZZZ***.

ACUPUNCTURE TREATMENT

Traditional Points:

- *Ah shi* points
- *Shousanli* (LI 10), *Geshu* (BL 17), *Hegu* (LI 4), *Xuehai* (SP 10), *Jianliao* (TH 14)

Classic Master Tung's Points:

- Needle contralateral to the pain. If the pain is in the center, needle bilaterally or the side with the more *ah shi* points. If the pain is bilateral, needle bilaterally.
- **Neck pain (bone spur):** *Wanshunyi* (T 22.08), *Wanshuner* (T 22.09), *Huochuan* (T 33.04), *Tianhuang* (T 88.13), *Sizhi* (T 77.20), *Minghuang* (T 88.12), *Qihuang* (T 88.14), *Guciyi* (T 44.21)*, *Gucier* (T 44.22)*, *Gucisan* (T 44.23)*, *Huofu* (T 88.41)*, *Huoliang* (T 88.42)*, *Huochang* (T 88.43)*, *Sojingdian* (T 22.19)*
- **Neck stiffness:** *Zhengjin* (T 77.01), *Zhengzong* (T 77.02), *Renhuang* (T 77.21), *Sojingdian* (T 22.19)*
- **Fallen pillow syndrome:** *Waisanguan* (T 77.27), *Tianhuang* (T 88.13), *Qihu* (T 77.26), *Wanshunyi* (T 22.08), *Wanshuner* (T 22.09), *Yanglao* (SI 6), *Sojingdian* (T 22.19)*
- **Shoulder pain:** *Tianhuang* (T 88.13), *Waisanguan* (T 77.27), *Fanhoujue* (T 22.12)*, *Renzong* (T 44.08), *Dizong* (T 44.09), *Tianzong* (T 44.10)
- **Frozen shoulder:** *Linggu* (T 22.05), *Dabai* (T 22.04), *Fanhoujue* (T 22.12)*, *Tianhuangfu [Shenguan]* (T 77.18), *Minghuang* (T 88.12), *Tianhuang* (T 88.13), *Qihuang* (T 88.14), *Quchi* (LI 11), *Xiyan*, *Huantiao* (GB 30), *Renhuang* (T 77.21), *Sihuashang* (T 77.08), *Waisanguan* (T 77.27), *Sizhi* (T 77.20), *ah shi* points around the second metacarpal phalangeal joint, *Baguansan* (T 11.30)*, *Baguansi* (T 11.31)*. Bleed the affected area with cupping. Bleed before needling for best result.

Master Tung's Points by Dr. Chuan-Min Wang:

- **Primary points:** *Chongzi* (T 22.01), *Chongxian* (T 22.02), *Shangbai* (T 22.03), *Zhengjin* (T 77.01), *Zhengzong* (T 77.02), *Zhengshi* (T 77.03), *Yizhong* (T 77.05), *Erzhong* (T 77.06), *Sanzhong* (T 77.07), *Qihu* (T 77.26), *Sojingdian* (T 22.19)*
- **Secondary points:** *Feixin* (T 11.11), *Zhishen* (T 11.15), *Fuyuan* (T 11.22), *Shangbai* (T 22.03), *Huochuan* (T 33.04), *Sanchayi* (T 22.15)*, *Sanchaer* (T 22.16)*, *Sanchasan* (T 22.17)*, *Zhongjiuli* (T 88.25)

Balance Method by Dr. Richard Tan:

- Needle the following points on the side opposite the pain: *Lingdao* (HT 4), *Tongli* (HT 5), *Shenmen* (HT 7), *Xuanzhong* (GB 39), *Shugu* (BL 65)
- Needle the following points on the same side as the pain: *Houxi* (SI 3), *Zhongzhu* (TH 3), *Sanyinjiao* (SP 6) or *ah shi* points nearby.
- After the needles are inserted, the patient should move his or her neck to loosen up the joint and the muscles.

Neck & Shoulder (CR)™

Ear Acupuncture:

- **Neck pain:** Cervical Vertebrae, Neck, Shoulder, Shoulder Blades, Kidney. Embed ear seeds and instruct the patient to massage the points three to four times daily for two minutes each time. Switch ears every five days. Five treatments equal one course.
- **Frozen shoulder:** Shoulder, Shoulder Joint, Adrenal Gland, Clavicle, Liver, Spleen, Subcortex

Auricular Medicine by Dr. Li-Chun Huang:

- **Torticollis (strained neck):** Triangle Area of Cervical Vertebrae, Occiput, Lesser Occiput Nerve, Large Auricular Nerve
- **Periarthritis of shoulder:** Shoulder, Shoulder Joint, Clavicle, Large Auricular Nerve. Bleed Ear Apex or Helix 3-4.
  - For pain of the shoulder upon abduction, use Clavicle, Shoulder (front and back of ear), Arm Pit.
  - For anterior shoulder pain, use Shoulder Joint (front of ear), Coronary Vascular Subcortex, Large Auricular Nerve.
  - For posterior shoulder pain, use Shoulder Joint (back of ear), Clavicle, Large Auricular Nerve.
- **Cervical vertebral degeneration:** Triangle Area of Cervical, corresponding points (to the area of injury). Bleed Helix 4.

NUTRITION

- Eat plenty of whole grains, dark green vegetables, and nuts. These foods are rich in vitamin B complex and magnesium, which are essential for nerve health and relaxation of tense muscles.
- Adequate intake of minerals, such as calcium and potassium, are essential for pain management. Deficiency of these minerals will lead to spasms, cramps, and tense muscles.

LIFESTYLE INSTRUCTIONS

- Patients should avoid exposing affected areas to cold temperatures or drafts. Adequate clothing such as turtlenecks should be worn to cover the neck and shoulder areas.
- Patients with frozen shoulder should be encouraged to exercise the shoulders as much as possible. Increase the range of motion for the shoulder will help to prevent adhesions of the tendons and ligaments.
- Patients should also be advised to check their pillow height to make sure it is not too high or too low. Mattresses should also be assessed for firmness.
- Hot baths with Epsom salts help to relax tense muscles and withdraw toxins from the tissues. Rest and relax in the bath for about 30 minutes.

CASE STUDIES

- A 46-year-old female presented with left sided pain which originated at the C2 to C7 cervical region followed by a tingling sensation on the lateral side of the left forearm and hand. The practitioner had treated the patient for several years for the same condition. Initially, the pain was only isolated around the neck region with slight radiation towards the middle and lower trapezius. The patient was subsequently diagnosed with hypothyroidism accompanied by intermittent pain, which appeared usually after a couple of days. Administration of the ***Neck & Shoulder (CR)*** formula had provided the patient with great relief as well as making the recurrence less severe and not as abrupt. Consequently, she was able to discontinue taking Motrin (ibuprofen). The practitioner concluded that ***Neck & Shoulder (CR)*** was an excellent formula for degenerative disc disease. Submitted by C.H., San Jose, California.
- A 44-year-old female, who works as an accountant's assistant, presented with tightness to her neck and shoulders. She also complained of stress, depression and had a history of multiple surgeries. Her Western diagnosis was spinal stenosis. Her TCM practitioner diagnosed her condition as *bi zheng* (painful obstruction syndrome) of the neck and shoulders. Prior to taking ***Neck & Shoulder (CR)***, the practitioner prescribed *Ge Gen* (Radix Puerariae Lobatae) with little result. ***Neck & Shoulder (CR)*** was the only herbal formula to which the patient responded to favorably. Submitted by D.M., Raton, New Mexico.
- A 42-year-old female nurse presented with chronic pain throughout her body, especially located in the neck and shoulder areas. The TCM diagnosis was Liver qi and blood stagnation along with Spleen and Heart deficiency. For treatment, ***Herbal ANG*** and ***Neck Shoulder (CR)*** were prescribed. After taking the herbs and receiving acupuncture treatment twice a week for a month, the patient found that her condition had improved more than it had by physiotherapy and anti-inflammatories she had tried previously. Other findings in result of taking the herbs were increase of range of motion by 50% and softening of the muscles. Submitted by J.L., San Diego, California.
- A 53-year-old female presented with neck and shoulder pain which had been occurring for the previous 12 years. Current x-rays had shown a bone spur located in the C6-7 area. No curvature of the spine was seen. The practitioner had diagnosed the condition as yin and qi deficiencies with local qi and blood stagnation. ***Neck & Shoulder (CR)*** and ***Flex (SPR)*** were both prescribed. After taking the herbs, the patient had reported that her pain had decreased from a 7-8/10 to a 3-4/10 pain level. Submitted by H.C., Sydney, New York.
- A 22-year-old female presented with pain, tightness and tension in her neck, shoulders and upper back regions. The patient had been living with the condition for about the last six years. Initially her problems were due to stress; however, a severe car accident about 2½ years ago made the pain worse and constant. Symptoms exacerbated if under stress or when sick (sinus and head congestion). The pain on the right side of her back and neck was worse than her left. In particular, a point in her upper back where energy had been blocked since the car accident appeared quite weak. She had sought treatments from various physicians, chiropractors, physical therapists and massage therapists, which included *shiatsu*. Some of the treatments provided temporary relief but none had long-lasting effects. The patient was also

Neck & Shoulder (CR)™

taking birth control pills, zinc, echinacea, vitamin C, and Claritin (loratadine). Additionally, she was given antibiotics for her sinus infection, Prevacid (lansoprazole) for acid reflux, and a nasal spray prescription for her allergies. Her history and clinical picture directed the practitioner to diagnose the condition as qi and blood stagnation with *bi zheng* (painful obstruction syndrome) due to damp-cold. She was treated with acupuncture and began taking ***Neck & Shoulder (CR)***. The patient's neck muscles gradually became unconstrained over a period of 3½ months. Submitted by J.M., Baltimore, Maryland.

- A 40-year-old female presented with neck tension and pain. There was decreased range of motion in her cervical spine but all reflexes and DTR's were within normal limits bilaterally. Upon taking ***Neck & Shoulder (CR)***, the patient immediately noticed a diminished stiffness in her trapezius region. Submitted by G.P., Lawndale, California.
- A 47-year-old female presented with localized pinpoint pain situated 3 *cun* lateral to *Shendao* (GV 11) within the region of *Shentang* (BL 44). The patient also complained of insomnia, poor night vision, dry, itchy and flaky skin patches, ridged nails and clumps of falling hair. Her menstruation was regular at 28-days with no clots. Her tongue had teeth marks, a crack in the middle *jiao* and a white tongue coat. Her pulse was thin, wiry and rapid but slippery in the Spleen position. The Western diagnosis of her condition was reflex sympathetic dystrophy syndrome. The TCM diagnosis was qi and blood stagnation, Liver blood deficiency, and Kidney/Liver yin deficiency. After taking ***Neck & Shoulder (CR)***, her qi and blood stagnation subsided and her pain intensity decreased, as evident upon deep palpation. Her tongue cracks in the Spleen area also dwindled in size. Additionally, the patient reported improvement in sleep patterns because of pain relief. Submitted by M.D.P., Estes Park, Colorado.
- A male presented with pain and decreased range of motion in the right shoulder. There was pain upon palpation of the Large Intestine and Small Intestine channels. The practitioner diagnosed the condition as *bi zheng* (painful obstruction syndrome) due to stagnation of qi and blood. The patient was instructed to take ***Neck & Shoulder (AC)***. Acupuncture treatments using Dr. Tan's Balance Method and *tui-na* massage using Dr. Alex Chen's techniques were also applied. After six acupuncture and herbal treatments, he regained full shoulder range of motion and had no pain. After the pain was completely resolved, the practitioner switched the prescription to ***Neck & Shoulder (CR)*** at 3 capsules per day intended for maintenance care. Upon recurrence of pain, the patient was instructed to increase the dosage, which in turn resolved the pain sensation. Submitted by K.S., Encinitas, California.
- A 50-year-old retired male presented with severe neck and shoulder pain and stiffness, which is worse at night and disturbs sleep. The Western diagnosis included degenerative disk disease at C5 to C7. The diagnosis was blood stagnation, *bi zheng* (painful obstruction syndrome), and deficiencies of Spleen yang and Kidney *jing* (essence). The patient was instructed to take ***Neck & Shoulder (CR)*** (6 capsules three times daily) and ***Osteo 8*** (2 capsules three times daily). Upon return, the patient commented that ***Neck & Shoulder (CR)*** was effective for relieving pain. In fact, it was the only treatment that clearly helped. The patient remained under the care of an acupuncturist and a chiropractor, and continued to take the herbs. Submitted by J.B., Camarillo, California.
- A 41-year-old female housewife presented with neck and shoulder pain and occipital headaches. Severe muscle spasms bilateral to C4 to C7 were found as well as neck and shoulder tightness. The patient also reported anxiety and insomnia due to pain and depression. Her pulse was wiry and her tongue was purple. Past histories include eight surgeries to correct her condition. The practitioner diagnosed the presentation as blood and qi stagnation. After taking ***Neck & Shoulder (CR)***, a reduction in the severity of her neck and shoulder pain was noted. The patient also came to the realization that she was now less affected by damp and cold weather conditions. The practitioner also observed an improvement in the patient's neck range of motion. Submitted Anonymously.

PHARMACOLOGICAL AND CLINICAL RESEARCH

Neck & Shoulder (CR) is an excellent formula for rehabilitation from chronic neck and shoulder injuries, such as repetitive injuries or long-term wear and tear of the muscles and joints. As a result, the chronic nature of this condition may eventually contribute to atrophy and degeneration of the soft tissues, accompanied by decreased mobility of the joints, and generalized weakness and pain of the muscles. ***Neck & Shoulder (CR)*** contains herbs with chondroprotective and osteoprotective effects to facilitate recovery, anti-inflammatory effects to reduce swelling and inflammation, analgesic effects to relieve pain, and muscle-relaxant effects to relieve spasms and cramps.

Chronic pain is often associated with injuries to the muscles, tendons, ligaments, and bones, ***Neck & Shoulder (CR)*** contains many herbs to strengthen and rebuild the underlying structural damages. *Chuan Niu Xi* (Radix Cyathulae) is an excellent herb to protect the cartilage from repetitive and stress-induced injuries. According to one study, the extract of *Chuan Niu Xi* (Radix Cyathulae) has a potent effect to inhibit the induction of MMP-13, an important enzyme for the degradation of the cartilage collagen matrix, especially under arthritic conditions. By down-regulating the MMP-13 activity, *Chuan Niu Xi* (Radix Cyathulae) exerts great chondroprotection against cartilage degrading disorders.[5] *Dang Gui* (Radix Angelicae Sinensis) is an effective herb to promote the generation of bones. According to one study, the water extract of *Dang Gui* (Radix Angelicae Sinensis) has been found to contribute to the formation of bones and treatment of bone injuries. It directly stimulates the proliferation, alkaline phosphatase activity, protein secretion and particularly type I collagen synthesis of human osteoprecursor

Neck & Shoulder (CR)™

cells in a dose-dependent manner.[6] Lastly, *Sang Ji Sheng* (Herba Taxilli) and *Xu Duan* (Radix Dipsaci) have significant osteogenic and antiosteoporotic effects that promote the generation of new bones and prevent osteoporosis. According to a bone cells culture experiment, administration of *Sang Ji Sheng* (Herba Taxilli) shows a potential effect to increase the proliferation and differentiation of the osteoblasts without affecting osteoclast activity. The researchers conclude that these herbs can effectively increase the rate of tissue regeneration of damaged bones.[7]

Neck & Shoulder (CR) contains herbs with marked anti-inflammatory effect to reduce swelling and inflammation. *Dang Gui* (Radix Angelicae Sinensis) exerts both analgesic and anti-inflammatory effects through the inhibition of pro-inflammatory mediators, including nitric oxide and prostaglandin E2 in peritoneal macrophages.[8,9] In comparison with acetylsalicylic acid, the anti-inflammatory effect of *Dang Gui* (Radix Angelicae Sinensis) is approximately 1.1 times stronger, and its analgesic effect is approximately 1.7 times stronger.[10] *Chuan Xiong* (Rhizoma Chuanxiong) exerts its anti-inflammatory effect via an inhibitory activity on tumor necrosis factor-alpha (TNF-α) production and bioactivity, and shows promising effect to treat inflammation and related diseases.[11] *Qiang Huo* (Rhizoma et Radix Notopterygii) also has an anti-inflammatory effect to reduce swelling and inflammation. The mechanism is attributed to the inhibition of 5-lipoxygenase and cyclo-oxygenase.[12] Lastly, *Di Huang* (Radix Rehmanniae) and *Gan Cao* (Radix et Rhizoma Glycyrrhizae) exert their anti-inflammatory effect via the endocrine system. *Di Huang* (Radix Rehmanniae) reduces swelling and inflammation by influencing the endocrine system to increase the plasma levels of adrenocortical hormones,[13] even in the presence of dexamethasone.[14] Clinically, *Di Huang* (Radix Rehmanniae) has been used in an herbal formula to successfully treat 12 patients with rheumatoid arthritis.[15] *Gan Cao* (Radix et Rhizoma Glycyrrhizae) demonstrates marked anti-inflammatory effects by enhancing the effect of glucocorticoids through increased production and secretion as well as decreased metabolism by the liver.[16] In terms of anti-inflammatory actions, the comparison of cortisone to glycyrrhizin and glycyrrhetinic acid, two compounds from *Gan Cao* (Radix et Rhizoma Glycyrrhizae), is approximately 10:1.[17] Clinical applications of *Gan Cao* (Radix et Rhizoma Glycyrrhizae) include pain, inflammation, edema, arthritis, spasms, cramps and others.[18,19]

Neck & Shoulder (CR) incorporates many herbs with analgesic effects to relieve pain. *Yan Hu Suo* (Rhizoma Corydalis) is one of the strongest and most potent herbs for treatment of pain. It has a strong analgesic effect that is comparable to morphine. In fact, the analgesic effect of *Yan Hu Suo* (Rhizoma Corydalis) is so strong and reliable that it has been used with satisfactory anesthetic effect in 98 out of 105 patients (93.4%) who underwent surgery.[20] The analgesic effect can be potentiated further with concurrent acupuncture therapy. Overall, it is well understood that *Yan Hu Suo* (Rhizoma Corydalis) has a marked effect to treat pain. In addition, *Ru Xiang* (Gummi Olibanum) and *Mo Yao* (Myrrha) have an analgesic effect to relieve pain and anti-inflammatory to reduce swelling and inflammation.[21,22] These two herbs also showed an antiarthritic effect by reducing edema and decreasing arthritic scores in subjects with adjuvant-induced arthritis. The mechanism of action is attributed to the suppression of pro-inflammatory cytokines, such as TNF-α and interleukin-1beta (IL-1β).[23] Clinically, they have been used effectively to treat pain associated with various types of trauma and external injuries.[24] Furthermore, the combination of *Bai Shao* (Radix Paeoniae Alba) and *Gan Cao* (Radix et Rhizoma Glycyrrhizae) has a marked analgesic effect to relieve pain. The effectiveness is increased significantly when combined with acupuncture.[25] Clinically, these two herbs have been used successfully to treat conditions such as pain,[26] neuralgia,[27] trigeminal neuralgia,[28,29] neck pain,[30] acute back pain,[31] heel pain,[32] pain in the lower back and legs,[33] sciatica,[34] gastric and abdominal pain,[35] and dysmenorrhea.[36] Lastly, *Ge Gen* (Radix Puerariae Lobatae) contains many isoflavonoid compounds which have significant analgesic and muscle-relaxant activities.[37] It is also a guiding herb that enhances the effect of all the herbs in the formula.

To relieve spasms and cramps, *Bai Shao* (Radix Paeoniae Alba) and *Gan Cao* (Radix et Rhizoma Glycyrrhizae) are used for their excellent muscle-relaxant effect to relax both smooth and skeletal muscles.[38,39] Clinically, these two herbs have been used successfully to treat conditions such as leg cramps in the calf,[40] muscle cramps in hemodialysis,[41] restless leg syndrome,[42] intestinal spasm,[43] facial spasms and twitching,[44] and menstrual cramps and pain.[45]

In summary, ***Neck & Shoulder (CR)*** is an excellent formula that contains herbs with chondroprotective and osteogenic functions to repair cartilage erosion, protect joints from destruction, and promote generation of new bones. Furthermore, it also utilizes herbs with analgesic and anti-inflammatory effects to relieve pain and inflammation associated with back pain.

COMPARATIVE ANALYSIS

Pain is a basic bodily sensation induced by a noxious stimulus that causes physical discomfort (such as pricking, throbbing, or aching). Pain may be of acute or chronic state, and may be of nociceptive, neuropathic, or psychogenic origin. For acute pain, use of non-steroidal anti-inflammatory drugs (NSAIDs) and opioid analgesics offer immediate and reliable effects to relieve pain. Though these drugs have serious side effects, short-term use can be justified because the benefits often outweigh the risks. For chronic pain, on the other hand, use of NSAIDs and opioid analgesics are usually not the desired treatment options, as they symptomatically relieve pain, but do not change the underlying course of illness. Unfortunately, the convenience of these drugs contributes to the vicious cycle of pain, followed by continuous and repetitive use of drugs to symptomatically relieve pain. When the effect of the drugs dissipates, patients are often left with

Neck & Shoulder (CR)™

nothing but more pain and more complications from side effects. Therefore, it is important to understand that while these drugs may be beneficial for acute pain, they do not adequately address most cases of chronic pain. Additional treatment modalities must be incorporated to ensure effective and complete recovery from chronic pain conditions. [Note: Common side effects of NSAIDs include gastric ulcer, duodenal ulcer, gastrointestinal bleeding, tinnitus, blurred vision, dizziness and headache. Serious side effects of newer NSAIDs, also known as COX-2 inhibitors [such as Celebrex (celecoxib)], include significantly higher risk of cardiovascular events, including heart attack and stroke. Side effects of opioid analgesics [such as Vicodin (APAP/hydrocodone) and morphine] include dizziness, lightheadedness, drowsiness, upset stomach, vomiting, constipation, stomach pain, rash, difficult urination, and respiratory depression resulting in difficult breathing. Furthermore, long-term use of these drugs leads to tolerance and addiction.]

Treatment of chronic pain is a sophisticated balance of art and science. Proper treatment of pain requires a careful evaluation of the type of disharmony (excess or deficiency, cold or heat, exterior or interior), characteristics (qi and/or blood stagnations), and location (upper body, lower body, extremities, or internal organs). Furthermore, optimal treatment requires integrative use of herbs, acupuncture and *tui-na* therapies. All these therapies work together to tonify underlying deficiencies, strengthen the body, and facilitate recovery from chronic pain. TCM pain management targets both the symptoms and causes of pain, and as such, often achieves immediate and long-term success. Furthermore, TCM pain management is often associated with few or no side effects.

For treatment of mild to severe pain due to various causes, TCM pain management offers similar treatment effects with significantly fewer side effects. Though TCM therapies may not be as potent as drugs for acute pain management, they are often superior [better effects with fewer side effects] for chronic pain management.

References

1. Berkow R. et al. The Merck Manual of Medical Information. Merck Research Laboratories. 1999 February.
2. Chan K, Lo AC, Yeung JH, Woo KS. Journal of Pharmacy and Pharmacology 1995 May;47(5):402-6.
3. Pharmacotherapy 1999 July;19(7):870-876.
4. European Journal of Drug Metabolism and Pharmacokinetics 1995; 20(1):55-60.
5. Park HY, Lim H, Kim HP, Kwon YS. Downregulation of Matrix Metalloproteinase-13 by the Root Extract of Cyathula officinalis Kuan and its Constituents in IL-1β-treated Chondrocytes. College of Pharmacy, Kangwon National University, Chunchon, Korea. Planta Med. 2011 Feb 23.
6. Yang Q, Populo SM, Zhang J, Yang G, Kodama H. Effect of Angelica sinensis on the proliferation of human bone cells. Clin Chim Acta. 2002 Oct;324(1-2):89-97.
7. Yao CH, Tsai HM, Chen YS, Liu BS. Fabrication and evaluation of a new composite composed of tricalcium phosphate, gelatin, and Chinese medicine as a bone substitute. Institute of Biomedical Engineering and Material Science, Chungtai Institute of Health Science and Technology, Taichung, Taiwan, Republic of China. J Biomed Mater Res B Appl Biomater. 2005 Nov;75(2):277-88.
8. *Xin Yi Yao Xue Za Zhi* (New Journal of Medicine and Herbology), 1975; (6):34.
9. Chao WW, Kuo YH, Li WC, Lin BF. The production of nitric oxide and prostaglandin E2 in peritoneal macrophages is inhibited by Andrographis paniculata, Angelica sinensis and Morus alba ethyl acetate fractions. Department of Biochemical Science and Technology, Institute of Microbiology and Biochemistry, National Taiwan University, Taipei 106, Taiwan, ROC. J Ethnopharmacol. 2009 Feb 25;122(1):68-75.
10. *Yao Xue Za Zhi* (Journal of Medicinals), 1971; (91):1098.
11. Liu L, Ning ZQ, Shan S, Zhang K, Deng T, Lu XP, Cheng YY. Phthalide Lactones from Ligusticum chuanxiong inhibit lipopolysaccharide-induced TNF-alpha production and TNF-alpha-mediated NF-kappaB Activation. Planta Med. 2005 Sep;71(9):808-13.
12. Zschocke S, Lehner M, Bauer R. 5-Lipoxygenase and cyclooxygenase inhibitory active constituents from Qianghuo (Notopterygium incisum). Planta Med. 1997 Jun;63(3):203-6.
13. *Zhong Yao Yao Li Yu Ying Yong* (Pharmacology and Applications of Chinese Herbs), 1983: 400.
14. *Zhong Yao Xue* (Chinese Herbology), 1998; 156:158.
15. *Zhong Yao Lin Chuan Xin Yong* (New Clinical Applications of Chinese Medicine), 2001; 242-243.
16. *Zhong Yao Zhi* (Chinese Herbology Journal), 1993; 358.
17. *Zhong Cao Yao* (Chinese Herbal Medicine), 1991; 22(10):452.
18. *Zhe Jiang Zhong Yi Za Zhi* (Zhejiang Journal of Chinese Medicine), 1980; 2:60.
19. *Zhong Hua Nei Ke Za Zhi* (Chinese Journal of Internal Medicine), 1960; 4:354.
20. *He Bei Xin Yi Yao* (Hebei New Medicine and Herbology), 1973; 4:34.
21. *Zhong Yao Xue* (Chinese Herbology), 1998; 539:540.
22. Yoshikawa M, Morikawa T, Oominami H, Matsuda H. Absolute stereostructures of olibanumols A, B, C, H, I, and J from olibanum, gum-resin of Boswellia carterii, and inhibitors of nitric oxide production in lipopolysaccharide-activated mouse peritoneal macrophages. Kyoto Pharmaceutical University, Japan. Chem Pharm Bull (Tokyo). 2009 Sep;57(9):957-64.
23. Fan AY, Lao L, Zhang RX, Zhou AN, Wang LB, Moudgil KD, Lee DY, Ma ZZ, Zhang WY, Berman BM. Effects of an acetone extract of Boswellia carterii Birdw. (Burseraceae) gum resin on adjuvant-induced arthritis in lewis rats. Center for Integrative Medicine, School of Medicine, University of Maryland, 3rd Floor, James Kernan Hospital Man, 2200 Kernan Drive, Baltimore, MD 21201, USA. J Ethnopharmacol. 2005 Oct 3;101(1-3):104-9.
24. *He Nan Zhong Yi Xue Yuan Xue Bao* (Journal of University of Henan School of Medicine), 1980; 3:38.
25. *Guo Wai Yi Xue* (Foreign Medicine) 1984;6(1):58.
26. *Shang Hai Zhong Yi Yao Za Zhi* (Shanghai Journal of Chinese Medicine and Herbology), 1983; 4:14.
27. *Zhong Yi Ming Fang Lin Chuang Xin Yong* (Contemporary Clinical Applications of Classic Chinese Formulas) 2001;313.
28. *Jiang Xi Yi Yao* (Jiangxi Medicine and Herbology) 1965;5(7):909.
29. *Zhong Yi Za Zhi* (Journal of Chinese Medicine), 1983; 11:9.
30. *Jiang Su Zhong Yi* (Jiangsu Chinese Medicine), 1990; (10):29.
31. *Zhe Jiang Zhong Yi Za Zhi* (Zhejiang Journal of Chinese Medicine) 1995;(11):524.
32. *Si Chuan Zhong Yi* (Sichuan Chinese Medicine) 1996;11:38.
33. *Yun Nan Zhong Yi* (Yunnan Journal of Traditional Chinese Medicine), 1990; 4:15.
34. *Fu Jian Zhong Yi Yao* (Fujian Chinese Medicine and Herbology), 1994; (1):7.
35. *Fu Jian Zhong Yi Yao* (Fujian Chinese Medicine and Herbology) 1961;9(4):44.
36. Tanaka T. A novel anti-dysmenorrhea therapy with cyclic administration of two Japanese herbal medicines. Clinical & Experimental Obstetrics & Gynecology 2003;30(2-3):95-8.
37. Yasuda T, Endo M, Kon-no T, Kato T, Mitsuzuka M, Ohsawa K. Antipyretic, analgesic and muscle relaxant activities of pueraria isoflavonoids and their metabolites from Pueraria lobata Ohwi-a traditional Chinese drug. Biol Pharm Bull. 2005 Jul;28(7):1224-8.

Neck & Shoulder (CR)™

38. *Guo Wai Yi Xue* (Foreign Medicine) 1984;6(1):58.
39. *He Nan Zhong Yi* (Henan Chinese Medicine) 1986;(6):15.
40. *Zhong Yi Za Zhi* (Journal of Chinese Medicine) 1985;6:450.
41. Inoshita F, Ogura Y, Suzuki Y, Hara S, Yamada A, Tanaka N, Yamashita A, Marumo F. Effect of orally administered shao-yao-gan-cao-tang (Shakuyaku-kanzo-to) on muscle cramps in maintenance hemodialysis patients: a preliminary study. American Journal of Chinese Medicine 2003; 31(3):445-53.
42. *He Bei Zhong Yi* (Hebei Chinese Medicine) 1984;3:29.
43. *Zhong Yi Za Zhi* (Journal of Chinese Medicine), 1985; 6:50.
44. *Zhong Xi Yi Jie He Za Zhi* (Journal of Integrated Chinese and Western Medicine), 1991; (1):43.
45. *Bei Jing Zhong Yi* (Beijing Chinese Medicine) 1983;(1):33.

FORMULAS

Neuro Plus™

CLINICAL APPLICATIONS

- **Alzheimer's disease or dementia** with decreased mental and cognitive functions
- **Sequelae of stroke** with poor speech, muscle paralysis, urinary and bowel incontinence, and constipation
- **Neurodegenerative disorders with compromised mental functions:** forgetfulness, poor memory, difficulty concentrating, reduced comprehension, and possibly increased anxiety
- **Neurodegenerative disorders with compromised physical functions:** slurred speech, muscle rigidity, poor balance, difficulty walking, involuntary salivation, frequent urination, constipation, difficulty swallowing, or visual problems
- **Parkinson's disease** with compromised mental and physical functions
- **Multiple sclerosis (MS)**

WESTERN THERAPEUTIC ACTIONS

- Neuroprotective benefit to improve mental and physical functions
- Cognitive effect to improve and restore brain functions
- Circulatory effect to promote microcirculation and increase blood perfusion

CHINESE THERAPEUTIC ACTIONS

- Tonifies the Kidney yin, yang and *jing* (essence)
- Regulates qi and blood circulation and removes blood stagnation
- Opens the sensory orifices to promote awareness and alertness

DOSAGE

Take 2 to 3 capsules three times daily on an empty stomach with warm water during the first week of herbal treatment. After the first week, increase the dosage to 4 capsules three times daily. ***Neuro Plus*** should be taken continuously for at least one to two months prior to making an evaluation and prognosis.

INGREDIENTS

Ba Ji Tian (Radix Morindae Officinalis)
Bai Zhi (Radix Angelicae Dahuricae)
Bai Zhu (Rhizoma Atractylodis Macrocephalae)
Dan Shen (Radix et Rhizoma Salviae Miltiorrhizae)
Di Huang (Radix Rehmanniae)
Dong Chong Xia Cao (Cordyceps)
Du Zhong (Cortex Eucommiae)
Fen Bi Xie (Rhizoma Dioscoreae Hypoglaucae)
Fu Ling (Poria)
Gou Qi Zi (Fructus Lycii)
Gui Ban (Plastrum Testudinis)
Hong Hua (Flos Carthami)
Huang Qi (Radix Astragali)
Lu Jiao Shuang (Cornu Cervi Degelatinatum)
Meng Chong (Tabanus)
Qian Ceng Ta (Herba Lycopodii Serrati)
Ren Shen (Radix et Rhizoma Ginseng)
San Qi (Radix et Rhizoma Notoginseng)
Shan Yao (Rhizoma Dioscoreae)
Shan Zha (Fructus Crataegi)
Shan Zhu Yu (Fructus Corni)
Shi Chang Pu (Rhizoma Acori Tatarinowii)
Shu Di Huang (Radix Rehmanniae Praeparata)
Shui Zhi (Hirudo)
Tian Ma (Rhizoma Gastrodiae)
Tu Si Zi (Semen Cuscutae)
Wu Gong (Scolopendra)
Xi Yang Shen (Radix Panacis Quinquefolii)
Yi Zhi (Fructus Alpiniae Oxyphyllae)
Yin Xing Ye (Folium Ginkgo)
Yuan Zhi (Radix Polygalae)
Zhi He Shou Wu (Radix Polygoni Multiflori Praeparata)

BACKGROUND

Neurodegenerative disorders, such as dementia, Alzheimer's disease or Parkinson's disease, are neurologic disorders characterized by compromised mental and physical functions. Signs and symptoms include loss of memory, cognitive deficits, and behavior disorder (slurred speech, muscle rigidity, poor balance, difficulty walking). Causes of neurodegenerative disorders include trauma (i.e., hematoma), metabolic disorder (i.e., hypothyroidism), toxins (i.e., lead), and drugs.

FORMULA EXPLANATION

Neurodegenerative disorders are complex and pernicious diseases whose onset is insidious and is followed by progressive deterioration. The clinical manifestations are determined by the location and the seriousness of the disorder. The pathogenesis of neurodegenerative disorders is a mixture of deficient and excess conditions, represented by Kidney *jing* (essence) deficiency (a deficient condition), or blockage of the brain channel by blood stasis (an excess condition), or both.

Though it is the brain that shows the symptoms of neurodegenerative disorders, the cause lies in the Kidney. From the point of view of traditional Chinese medicine's disease differentiation through viscera and their inter-relations, the root of the disease is due to the deficiency of the Kidney and the bone marrow, whereas blood stasis and phlegm accumulation are considered symptoms, not the cause. Therefore, the keys to treat neurodegenerative disorders are to tonify the Kidney, eliminate phlegm, remove blood stasis, restore cognition, and promote perception.

Dong Chong Xia Cao (Cordyceps), *Ba Ji Tian* (Radix Morindae Officinalis), *Shu Di Huang* (Radix Rehmanniae Praeparata), *Du Zhong* (Cortex Eucommiae), *Gou Qi Zi* (Fructus Lycii), *Zhi He Shou Wu* (Radix Polygoni Multiflori Praeparata), *Yi Zhi* (Fructus Alpiniae Oxyphyllae), *Tu Si Zi* (Semen Cuscutae), and *Shan Zhu Yu* (Fructus Corni) are used in this formula to nourish both Kidney yin and yang. Hence, the production of *jing* (essence) and the marrow are increased. *Ren Shen* (Radix et Rhizoma Ginseng),

Neuro Plus™

Shan Yao (Rhizoma Dioscoreae), *Huang Qi* (Radix Astragali), *Xi Yang Shen* (Radix Panacis Quinquefolii), *Bai Zhu* (Rhizoma Atractylodis Macrocephalae), and *Fu Ling* (Poria) are used to reinforce the *yuan* (source) *qi*, calm the *shen* (spirit), and increase mental functions. *San Qi* (Radix et Rhizoma Notoginseng), *Shan Zha* (Fructus Crataegi), *Shui Zhi* (Hirudo), *Dan Shen* (Radix et Rhizoma Salviae Miltiorrhizae), *Hong Hua* (Flos Carthami), *Meng Chong* (Tabanus), *Tian Ma* (Rhizoma Gastrodiae), *Di Huang* (Radix Rehmanniae) and *Wu Gong* (Scolopendra) open the channels and collaterals, invigorate blood circulation, and remove blood stasis. *Yuan Zhi* (Radix Polygalae), *Shi Chang Pu* (Rhizoma Acori Tatarinowii) and *Bai Zhi* (Radix Angelicae Dahuricae) are used to open up the sensory orifices, eliminate phlegm, and calm *shen* (spirit). *Gui Ban* (Plastrum Testudinis) and *Lu Jiao Shuang* (Cornu Cervi Degelatinatum) tonify the true yin and yang of the Kidney and generate qi and blood flow. *Yin Xing Ye* (Folium Ginkgo) and *Qian Ceng Ta* (Herba Lycopodii Serrati) are used to improve memory functions in patients with dementia or Alzheimer's disease.

In conclusion, ***Neuro Plus*** is a great formula to treat both mental and physical deteriorations associated with neurodegenerative disorders, such as dementia, Alzheimer's disease or Parkinson's disease, and post stroke sequelae.

CAUTIONS & CONTRAINDICATIONS

- This formula is contraindicated during pregnancy and nursing.
- Stroke due to hemorrhage should ***not*** be treated with this herbal formula until the condition stabilizes.
- A slight increase in blood pressure has been observed in approximately 3 to 5% of patients, due in part to the warm herbs in the formula. Should this happen, reduce the dosage of the herbs. Increase in blood pressure associated with the herbs is self-limiting.
- This herbal formula contains herbs that invigorate blood circulation, such as *Dan Shen* (Radix et Rhizoma Salviae Miltiorrhizae). Therefore, patients who are on anticoagulant or antiplatelet therapies, such as Coumadin (warfarin), should use this formula with caution, or not at all, as there may be a higher risk of bleeding and bruising.[1]
- According to most textbooks and contemporary references, the classic entry of "*He Shou Wu*" is now separated into two entries: the <u>unprepared</u> *Sheng Shou Wu* (Radix Polygoni Multiflori) and the <u>prepared</u> *Zhi He Shou Wu* (Radix Polygoni Multiflori Praeparata), as they have significantly different therapeutic effects and side effects. *Sheng Shou Wu* (Radix Polygoni Multiflori) is a stimulant laxative that treats constipation, but may cause nausea, vomiting, abdominal pain, diarrhea, and in rare cases, liver disorder (dose- and time-dependent, and reversible upon discontinuation).[2] On the other hand, *Zhi He Shou Wu* (Radix Polygoni Multiflori Praeparata) is a tonic herb that is safe and well-tolerated. The dramatic changes in the therapeutic effect and safety profile are attributed to the long and complicated processing of the root with *Hei Dou* (Semen Sojae) through repeated blending, cooking, and drying procedures. When properly processed, the chemical composition of the root changes significantly. Many new compounds are generated from the Maillard reaction (four furanones, two furans, two nitrogen compounds, one pyran, one alcohol and one sulfur compound). Furthermore, the preparation process causes changes in the composition of sugars and 16 kinds of amino acids; it also reduces the pH of the herb from 6.28 to 5.61.[3,4] In summary, these changes give rise to the tonic effects of the <u>prepared</u> roots, and eliminate the adverse reactions associated with the <u>unprepared</u> roots. **Note:** Due to medical risks and legal liabilities, it is prudent to exercise caution and ***not*** use this herb in either <u>prepared</u> or <u>unprepared</u> forms in patients with pre-existing or risk factors of liver diseases.

CLINICAL NOTES

- Since neurodegenerative disorders are characterized by the chronic and deteriorating nature of the illness, herbal treatment is considered effective if there is: 1) improvement in the signs and symptoms, or 2) lack of deterioration or stabilization of the overall condition.
- It has been noted by many practitioners that ***Neuro Plus*** is effective in treating patients with multiple sclerosis. The general consensus is approximately one out of four patients will have a marked improvement, while the others showed only minimal changes.
- To prevent deterioration of cognitive function, take 1 to 2 capsule of ***Neuro Plus*** twice daily.

SUPPLEMENTARY FORMULAS

- For post-stroke patients with deviation of the eyes and mouth, add ***Symmetry***.
- To relieve constipation, combine with ***Gentle Lax (Excess)*** or ***Gentle Lax (Deficient)***.
- To minimize the risk of stroke in patients with hypertension, combine with ***Gastrodia Complex*** or ***Gentiana Complex***.
- For cardiovascular disorders, combine with ***Circulation***.
- For severe blood stagnation, add ***Circulation (SJ)***.
- For high blood pressure and fast heart rate due to excess fire, add ***Gardenia Complex***.
- For heavy metal poisoning, add ***Herbal DTX***.
- For adrenal insufficiency, add ***Adrenal +***.
- To enhance the effect to strengthen the constitution of the body, add ***Cordyceps 3***.
- For compromised kidney functions, add ***Kidney DTX***.
- With osteoporosis, add ***Osteo 8***.
- With qi and blood deficiencies, add ***Imperial Tonic***.
- With Kidney yang deficiency, add ***Kidney Tonic (Yang)***.
- With Kidney yin deficiency, add ***Kidney Tonic (Yin)***.
- For general forgetfulness not associated with Alzheimer's disease, use ***Enhance Memory*** instead.

Neuro Plus™

ACUPUNCTURE TREATMENT

Traditional Points:

1. **Main Points**: *Neiguan* (PC 6), *Renzhong* (GV 26), *Sanyinjiao* (SP 6). *Neiguan* (PC 6) nourishes the heart, calms the *shen* (spirit), and promotes smooth circulation of qi and blood. *Renzhong* (GV 26) opens up sensory orifices, stimulates the brain and awakens the *shen* (spirit). The combination of *Neiguan* (PC 6) and *Renzhong* (GV 26) has been found to increase the contractile strength of the heart and the cardiac output of blood circulation to the brain. *Sanyinjiao* (SP 6) is the meeting point of the three *yin* channels of foot. *Sanyinjiao* (SP 6) nourishes the Kidney, tonifies the *jing* (essence) and the marrow to improve the function of the brain.
2. **Local Points**: *Jiquan* (HT 1), *Chize* (LU 5), *Weizhong* (BL 40), and *Hegu* (LI 4) are local points that open up the channels and collaterals and improve the circulation of qi and blood. *Jiquan* (HT 1), *Chize* (LU 5), and *Hegu* (LI 4) are used for paralysis and tremor of the arms and the hands; and *Weizhong* (BL 40) is used for paralysis of the legs. *Fengchi* (GB 20), *Yifeng* (TH 17), *Wangu* (GB 12) and *Tianzhu* (BL 10) are four excellent points that help patients who have speech impairment or frequent aspiration of food particles, leading to respiratory infections.

   Shanshangdien (upper thunder point) and *Xiashangdien* (lower thunder point) are two extraordinary points that were discovered through clinical trial and experience. These two acupuncture points are very potent and should be reserved for those patients who have partial to complete paralysis.

   Shanshangdien (upper thunder point) is located on the lateral side of the neck, on the same level with Adam's apple, and between the sternal head and clavicular head of m. sternocleidomastoideus. It is three *cun* posterior to the Adam's apple and one *cun* posterior-inferior. It is located slightly inferior to *Futu* (LI 18). Its indications include frozen shoulder, shoulder pain, paralysis of the arm, stiff and rigid muscle of the arm, and tremor of the hand.

   Xiashangdien (lower thunder point) is located in the buttock region. *Xiashangdien* (lower thunder point) is the posterior tip of an equilateral triangle with greater trochanter and the iliac crest as the anterior two points. It is located slightly superior to *Huantiao* (GB 30). Its indications include pain in the lower back and hip region, muscular atrophy, sciatica, pain, weakness and muscular atrophy of the lower extremities, and hemiplegia.
3. **Needling Technique**: Stroke is an excess condition and sedation is warranted. This is because stroke is characterized by the *shen* (spirit) trapped inside the head with complete or partial closure of the sensory orifices. Therefore, the overall treatment focus should be to open up the sensory orifices, release *shen* (spirit), and awaken the brain.

   To achieve the maximum benefit from acupuncture, the location for some of the acupuncture points and their corresponding needling techniques are slightly different. *Neiguan* (PC 6) should be needled bilaterally first. Insert the needle 1 to 1.5 *cun*, then stimulate the point for at least one minute by slightly turning the needle and moving it up and down. The healthy side should be tonified while the diseased side should be sedated.

   Next, needle *Renzhong* (GV 26). Aim slightly upwards toward the top of the head and stimulate strongly until the patient shows tears in his or her eyes. Stimulation should be done with quick rapid movements, a motion similar to a woodpecker drilling trees.

   The third point is *Sanyinjiao* (SP 6). The point of insertion for *Sanyinjiao* (SP 6) should be moved 0.5 *cun* toward the dorsal side of the body (or towards Kidney channel) for greater stimulation. Tonify *Sanyinjiao* (SP 6) by moving the needle up and down until the patient shows a "jerking motion" of the lower leg three times.

   Jiquan (HT 1) should be needled with the patient raising his or her arm upward in the air. The point of insertion is moved 0.5 *cun* toward the fingers and away from the body. *Jiquan* (HT 1) should be sedated by moving the needle up and down until the patient shows "jerking motion" of the arm three times.

   Weizhong (BL 40) may be needled with the patient lying on the back or on the stomach. Point of insertion should be moved 0.5 *cun* higher toward the buttocks along the Urinary Bladder channel. The needle should be inserted 1 to 1.5 *cun* deep, and the point should be sedated until the leg shows a "jerking motion" three times.

   Hegu (LI 4) should be needled obliquely with the tip of the needle pointing toward *Sanjian* (LI 3). This point should be sedated until the index finger jerks three times.

   Shanshangdien (upper thunder point) should be needled perpendicularly 1 *cun* deep, and stimulated until there is an "electric sensation" that runs through the entire length of the arm. The needle is then withdrawn at that time. *Shanshangdien* (upper thunder point) should never be needled downward toward the lung as it may puncture the lung and cause pneumothorax.

   Lastly, *Xiashangdien* (lower thunder point) should be needled perpendicularly 1.5 to 3.0 *cun* deep, and stimulated until there is an "electric sensation" that runs through the entire length of the leg. The needle is then withdrawn at that time.

   For maximum effect, acupuncture treatment should be conducted daily for seven days during the first course of treatment, every other day for 3 weeks for the second course of treatment, and two to three times per week for the next two months of treatment. Three days of resting period is given between each course of treatment. Evaluations are made one month and three months after the initiation of treatment.

Classic Master Tung's Points:

- **Decreased mental and cognitive functions, forgetfulness:** *Dizong* (T 44.09), *Tianhuangfu [Shenguan]* (T 77.18), *Zhenghui* (T 1010.01), *Piyi* (T 88.35)*, *Pier* (T 88.36)*
- **Stroke:** *Linggu* (T 22.05), *Dabai* (T 22.04), *Zhongbai* (T 22.06), *Dizong* (T 44.09), *Waisanguan* (T 77.27), *Yizhong* (T 77.05), *Erzhong* (T 77.06), *Sanzhong* (T 77.07), *Sansheng* (T 55.07)*,

Neuro Plus™

Simashang (T 88.18), *Simazhong* (T 88.17), *Simaxia* (T 88.19), *Zhenghui* (T 1010.01), *Qianhui* (T 1010.05), *Minghuang* (T 88.12), *Tianhuang* (T 88.13), *Qihuang* (T 88.14), *Renhuang* (T 77.21), *Muhuo* (T 11.10), *Neitongguan* (T 88.29), *Neitongshan* (T 88.30), *Neitongtian* (T 88.31), *Zhongquan* (T 88.21). Bleed *du* (governing) channel and the back of the knee. Bleed before needling for best result. In emergency cases, bleed *Shixuan*.

- **Sequelae of stroke (incontinence):** *Minghuang* (T 88.12), *Tianhuang* (T 88.13), *Qihuang* (T 88.14), *Zhenghui* (T 1010.01), *Tianhuang* (T 77.17), *Dihuang* (T 77.19), *Renhuang* (T 77.21), *Tongshen* (T 88.09), *Majinshui* (T 1010.13), *Makuaishui* (T 1010.14)
- **Sequelae of stroke (tremor):** *Minghuang* (T 88.12), *Tianhuang* (T 88.13), *Qihuang* (T 88.14), *Zhenghui* (T 1010.01), *Qianhui* (T 1010.05), *Houhui* (T 1010.06), *Houxi* (SI 3) to *Laogong* (PC 8), *Gongsun* (SP 4) to *Yongquan* (KI 1), *Sanchayi* (T 22.15)*, *Sanchaer* (T 22.16)*, *Sanchasan* (T 22.17)*, *Bafeng*, *Baxie*
- **Sequelae of stroke (speech difficulties):** *Minghuang* (T 88.12), *Tianhuang* (T 88.13), *Qihuang* (T 88.14), *Zhenghui* (T 1010.01), *Qianhui* (T 1010.05), *Houhui* (T 1010.06), *Linggu* (T 22.05), *Dizong* (T 44.09)

Master Tung's Points by Dr. Chuan-Min Wang:

- **Alzheimer's:** *Shuixiang* (T 66.14), *Huochuan* (T 33.04), *Huoling* (T 33.05), *Huoshan* (T 33.06), *Zhenghui* (T 1010.01), *Qianhui* (T 1010.05), *Zhengben* (T 1010.12)
- **Parkinson's:** *Huochuan* (T 33.04), *Zhenghui* (T 1010.01), *Minghuang* (T 88.12), *Tianhuang* (T 88.13), *Qihuang* (T 88.14), *Tianhuangfu [shenguan]* (T 77.18), *Renzhong* (GV 26)
- **Post stroke**
  - Liver stroke: *Minghuang* (T 88.12), *Tianhuang* (T 88.13), *Qihuang* (T 88.14)
  - Heart stroke: *Neitongguan* (T 88.29), *Neitongshan* (T 88.30), *Neitongtian* (T 88.31)
  - Spleen stroke: *Yizhong* (T 77.05), *Erzhong* (T 77.06), *Sanzhong* (T 77.07)
  - Lung stroke: *Linggu* (T 22.05), *Dabai* (T 22.04)
  - Kidney stroke: *Tianhuang* (T 77.17), *Dihuang* (T 77.19), *Renhuang* (T 77.21)
  - Tightness of the limbs: *Chongzi* (T 22.01), *Chongxian* (T 22.02)
  - Weakness of the limbs: *Dabai* (T 22.04), *Linggu* (T 22.05)
  - Facial muscle paralysis: *Zhongjiuli* (T 88.25), *Qili* (T 88.51)*
  - Upper limb paralysis: *Jianzhong* (T 44.06), *Huofuhai* (T 33.07), *Linggu* (T 22.05)
  - Lower limb paralysis: *Zhongjiuli* (T 88.25), *Cesanli* (T 77.22), *Sihuazhong* (T 77.09)

Balance Method by Dr. Richard Tan:

- **Alzheimer's disease and dementia:**
  - Left side: *Yongquan* (KI 1), *Dazhong* (KI 4), *Shangyang* (LI 1), *Hegu* (LI 4)
  - Right side: *Shaoshang* (LU 11), *Jingqu* (LU 8), *Zhiyin* (BL 67), *Jinggu* (BL 64)
  - Left and right sides can be alternated from treatment to treatment.

Auricular Medicine by Dr. Li-Chun Huang:

- **Invigorating the brain function:** Brain, Thalamus, Pituitary, Forehead, Heart, Kidney, Smart, Nervous Subcortex, Groove of Brain Posterior

NUTRITION

- Small frequent meals are recommended, instead of a few large meals. Avoid overeating, and stop when approximately 80% fullness is achieved.
- They should lose weight if obese. Cholesterol levels should be reduced if elevated.
- Encourage more "white meat" and less "red meat."
- Consume adequate amounts of vegetables for vitamins A, B_1, B_2, C and E.
- Avoid fried, smoked or barbecued foods.
- Stop smoking and avoid drinking alcohol.
- Avoid contact and exposure to aluminum, which may be found in antacids, cookware, aluminum foil, and certain foods. Drinking steam-distilled water has a chelating effect in the blood to remove unwanted aluminum from the body.
- Encourage a diet with a diverse source of all nutrients, including raw fruits, vegetables, whole grains, nuts, and seeds. B vitamins are important to maintain nerve health.

LIFESTYLE INSTRUCTIONS

- Exercise daily and maintain a positive, hopeful outlook toward the future.
- Regular workout and deep breathing exercises are excellent ways to oxygenate the blood and improve circulation to all parts of the body to facilitate recovery.
- When recuperating from a stroke, engage in regular and mild exercises, such as walking and swimming. However, make sure the activities are supervised as the risk of another accident (i.e., slip and fall) is high during the earlier period of recovery.

CASE STUDIES

- A.H., a 61-year-old male, presented with foggy, unclear mind, difficulty concentrating on more than one task, poor memory, forgetfulness, decline of comprehension ability. Patient had also suffered from hypothyroidism for 12 years. The TCM diagnosis was Kidney qi deficiency. ***Neuro Plus*** was prescribed at 3 capsules twice daily. In two days, the patient showed remarkable improvement. His memory was extremely clear. He was able to recall information without looking at hand-written notes. His energy level increased and he was very alert. Best of all, he was able to multi-task three things at once (something that was totally impossible before). The patient also noticed an increase in libido. The patient had so much energy that his dosage was reduced to 2 capsules twice daily. The medical doctor reported she was very

Neuro Plus™

impressed with the results of this amazing formula. Submitted by M.H., West Palm Beach, Florida.

- A 78-year-old female with a past history of stroke presented with memory loss, insomnia, nightmares, and was easily frightened. She frequently woke up in the middle of the night because of her dreams, which disturbed the entire nursing home. Her Western medical diagnosis was dementia. The TCM diagnosis included qi and blood stagnation, Liver and Kidney yin deficiency, and Heart fire. She was given ***Calm (ES)*** and ***Neuro Plus***. After taking the herbs for approximately one month, the patient was able to recall the practitioner's name for the very first time! In addition, her sleep, mood, complexion, and energy level improved greatly. The patient was much calmer and less irritable. Despite the fact that she still did not know the name of her town or the correct month, there were many improvements in all other areas. The practitioner concluded that the combination of ***Calm (ES)*** and ***Neuro Plus*** has enhanced the patient's quality of life. Submitted by P.R., Encinitas, California.
- J.D. is an 83-year-old female who had a stroke two years ago. On the first visit, the patient shuffled into the clinic, sat down, and promptly fell asleep. She was unresponsive to questions. Clinical observation showed an extremely deficient and deep pulse. The tongue was pink and slightly dusky with greasy yellow-green tongue coat that was much thicker on her left side. J.D. started taking ***Neuro Plus*** daily (4 capsules three times daily) and received acupuncture treatment twice weekly. The points used were *Neiguan* (PC 6), *Sanyinjiao* (SP 6), *Yinlingquan* (SP 9), *Hegu* (LI 4) and *Taichong* (LR 3). The patient showed marked improvement. She can lift her feet, smile, and respond somewhat and stay awake throughout the entire treatment. The patient improved rapidly at two treatments per week. Her progress slowed when she had to reduce the treatment to once per week due to financial reasons. However, she continued to improve. Her tongue coat became granular and brownish, changing over the course of treatment to a slightly-thick, more even white, or slightly yellow coat. After four months of treatments she has able to converse more normally. Her friends are happy because she can now talk with them on the phone. Treatment continues. Submitted by S.K., Toluca Lake, California.
- K.L. is a 64-year-old retired male. The date of his first visit was January 29, 1995. Clinical manifestations included the following signs and symptoms: poor attention span, hand tremor, stiff tongue and inability to hold a rice bowl or chop sticks, poor balance and required help when walking. He also had partial urinary and fecal incontinence with frequent urination. A CT scan taken on December 22, 1995 confirmed cerebral atrophy. The patient's condition dramatically improved after taking ***Neuro Plus*** for only five days. On the sixth day, the patient's hand tremors stopped. He was much more energetic. His frequency of urination decreased, and he did not require assistance to walk. He commented that ***Neuro Plus*** was like a "magic bullet" - and he said it without stuttering. Submitted Anonymously.
- J.B., a 76-year-old male, presented with post-stroke symptoms which occurred eleven years prior. The patient had been experiencing aphasia to the point of only being able to speak a minimal amount of words or phrases. In addition to his frustration, he had also been taking Lipitor (atorvastatin) for elevated cholesterol levels. The TCM diagnosis was unsubstantial phlegm obstructing the sensory orifices as well as Kidney qi and yin deficiencies. ***Neuro Plus*** was prescribed at 2 grams three times daily for six months before the dosage was cut in half to combine the dosage with ***Cholisma*** at 1 gram three times daily. After one month of taking ***Neuro Plus***, the patient experienced increase in mental acuity and was able to put together sentences with more ease. He had also been receiving annual stem cell injections. However, these changes were above what his results were with the stem cell injections by themselves. The patient is now completely off Lipitor (atorvastatin) and his cholesterol levels are within normal range. ***Cholisma*** was added in after the ***Neuro Plus***, acupuncture, and lifestyle changes had been in place for more than a year. In addition, his recent physical had also revealed his blood circulation was great with minimal to no obstructions. The patient now takes 2 grams three times daily of three formulas combined together (***Neuro Plus***, ***Cholisma*** and ***Circulation***). Submitted by A.G., Solana Beach, California.
- D.D., a 72-year-old male, presented with shortness of breath and cough with frothy, clear white sputum. It was noted that this patient was diabetic, post stroke, with a heart function of 77%, and creatinine level of 1.8 mg/dL. Objective findings included left leg hot to the touch, right leg cold to the touch, and difficulty with inhaling. He had recently taken two rounds of antibiotics. The practitioner diagnosed this condition as Kidney not grasping the qi, Lung and Spleen qi deficiencies with phlegm accumulation; his Western diagnosis was COPD. For treatment he was given a combination of ***Cordyceps 3***, ***Respitrol (Deficient)***, ***Circulation (SJ)*** and ***Neuro Plus***, just one bottle at a time. The patient gradually improved, getting stronger each week and continued taking the herbs for about three months. Submitted by T.W., Perrysburg, Ohio.
- M.H., a 75-year-old male, presented with fatigue, was overworked, and had recently experienced a mini stroke in which he could not walk for 24 hours. Tongue was slightly deviated to the left and pulse was deep and slippery. The TCM diagnosis was Spleen and Kidney yang deficiencies; Western diagnosis was a 6 mm lesion in the poris medulla. After taking ***Symmetry*** and ***Neuro Plus***, the patient felt less confused, more focused, and was able to walk again without struggle. He continued to take the herbs for five months to maintain his results. Submitted by V.G., Virginia Beach, Virginia.
- J.B., 64-year-old male, presented with chorea, jerky gait, and impaired psychomotor function. Symptoms of muscle atrophy, slurred speech and weight loss were also present. Both his father and grandfather had a similar condition that had resulted in death. His Western diagnosis was a possible hereditary

Neuro Plus ™

genetic disorder called Huntington's disease. The patient had refused receiving any Huntington's muscle genetics testing. The practitioner diagnosed this condition as Kidney yin and *jing* (essence) deficiencies as well as wind in the channels. The patient was given ***Neuro Plus*** three capsules three times a day and took it for three months. At first, he was unable to be needled on distal points due to uncontrolled movement of the limbs, tremors and additional shaking. With ***Neuro Plus***, the patient's walking and balance improved. The patient reported improvement in his skin health, feels stronger overall, and gained ten pounds in three months. He remains active, drives, and works as a pottery craftsman. Submitted by K.F., Honolulu, Hawaii.

- A 52-year-old male presented with mania and anxiety due to working long hours and worrying too much about his finances. He had difficulty unwinding and sleeping at the end of the day. The patient also displayed unexpected bouts of hostility along with impulsive and belligerent outbursts of conversations. He had a family history of Alzheimer's disease. After taking low doses of ***Neuro Plus***, the patient appeared to have returned to normal. He reverted back to his easy-going personality, both in relation to his work and his general lifestyle. Though the long-term success of ***Neuro Plus*** was still inconclusive, the improvement towards the well being of this patient was encouraging up to this moment. Submitted by L.C., Santa Monica, California.
- R.V. is a 91-year-old female who suffers from poor memory and Sundowner's syndrome. She has no short-term memory and is agitated and uncooperative at dusk. The only other symptom is loose stool. MRI shows no brain atrophy. The practitioner diagnosed her with Alzheimer's with Kidney yin and yang deficiencies. ***Neuro Plus*** was taken for three years at 1 capsule twice a day. The practitioner reported that ***Neuro Plus*** appears to have slowed down the progression of Alzheimer's. The patient experiences no more agitation at dusk and the periods of agitation that she does experience is dramatically reduced. Submitted by D.V., Newark, California.
- A 62-year-old female diagnosed with Alzheimer's disease presented with memory loss, disorientation and repetitive nonsensical speech patterns. The practitioner diagnosed the condition as qi and blood stagnation and Kidney qi deficiency. After taking ***Neuro Plus***, the patient's speech and thoughts were more coherent, as well as a reduction of memory loss. Submitted by V.G., Carlsbad, California.
- A 45-year-old female presented with right-sided dyskinesis, lethargy, headaches and contractures. She was diagnosed with Parkinson's disease. After taking ***Neuro Plus***, the patient displayed improvements in energy level, thinking and movement, which in turn enhanced her ability to function in activities of daily living. The patient was continually prescribed ***Neuro Plus*** at 8 grams per day. Submitted by G.P., Brea, California.
- C.B. was a 56-year-old female who suffered from weight gain, right-side sciatic pain, insomnia, hot flashes and night sweats. She exhibited rapid, thin and thready pulse with peeled and cracked tongue. The practitioner diagnosed her with Kidney yin and blood deficiency with deficiency heat and blood stagnation. ***Neuro Plus*** and ***Balance (Heat)*** were prescribed. The patient reported the sciatic pain went away completely. Night sweats and hot flashes were reduced, therefore insomnia was no longer an issue. Submitted by S.C., Santa Monica, California.
- R.L., a 79-year-old female, presented with post-stroke symptoms of paralysis on the right side (leg, arm and face). Her blood pressure was 140/80 mmHg and the heart rate was 90 beats per minute. She also had high cholesterol. She was diagnosed with wind-stroke with blood stagnation. ***Neuro Plus*** and ***Cholisma*** were prescribed at 4.5 grams and 1.5 grams each day, respectively. This patient also received acupuncture. After ten weeks of treatment, the patient regained movement of her leg and partial movement of her arm and almost full movement of her face and mouth. ***Neuro Plus*** also helped the patient regain strength. These were very quick results. In addition, the cholesterol level dropped from 250 to 180 mg/dL. Submitted by W.F., Bloomfield, New Jersey.

PHARMACOLOGICAL AND CLINICAL RESEARCH

Neuro Plus is designed to treat dementia, Alzheimer's disease, Parkinson's disease, sequelae of stroke, and other neurodegenerative disorders with compromised mental functions. ***Neuro Plus*** contains herbs that exert positive actions in the treatment of neurodegenerative disorders. They promote blood circulation to the brain to facilitate repair and healing of brain cells, protect the nerves against toxic substances, and improve mental and physical functions.

Yin Xing Ye (Folium Ginkgo), one of the main herbs in this formula, has been used in China and Europe for treatment of dementia. Pharmacologically, it has an antiplatelet effect to reduce blood viscosity and vasodilative effect to increase perfusion to peripheral parts of the body, such as the brain.[5,6] In addition, it has also shown cognitive effect to improve attention and memory in 52 young, healthy volunteers.[7] Clinically, numerous studies have shown *Yin Xing Ye* (Folium Ginkgo) to be safe and effective in treating various types of neurodegenerative disorders. According to a placebo-controlled, double-blind, randomized clinical trial with 309 patients over 52 weeks, *Yin Xing Ye* (Folium Ginkgo) was concluded to be "safe" and capable of "improving the cognitive performance and the social functioning of demented patients for six months to one year." The study was published by JAMA in October 1997.[8] According to another randomized, placebo-controlled, double-blind clinical trial, 400 patients aged 50 years or above with dementia with neuropsychiatric features were treated with *Yin Xing Ye* (Folium Ginkgo) extract or placebo for 22 weeks. The results showed that *Yin Xing Ye* (Folium Ginkgo) extract was significantly superior to placebo on all secondary outcome measures, including the Neuropsychiatric Inventory and an activities-of-daily-living scale. Furthermore, *Yin Xing Ye* (Folium Ginkgo) extract was well tolerated. Incidents of adverse effects were comparable to placebo.[9] Another study conducted at the University of Southern California Keck School of Medicine also showed that use of *Yin Xing Ye* (Folium Ginkgo) is significantly better than placebo to improve cognitive performance and global assessment scores in patients with dementia accompanied by neuropsychiatric symptoms.[10]

Another important herb in this formula is *Qian Ceng Ta* (Herba Lycopodii Serrati). This herb is historically used to invigorate blood circulation and disperse blood stasis in Chinese herbal medicine. It contains huperzine A, a unique alkaloid that has shown remarkable neuroprotective, antidementia, and cognitive effects. Huperzine A has the ability to protect nerve cells against hydrogen peroxide, beta-amyloid protein (or peptide), glutamate, ischaemia and staurosporine-induced cytotoxicity and apoptosis.[11] In addition, it has reversible, potent and selective acetylcholine esterase (AChE) inhibitors, according to *in vitro* and *in vivo* pharmacological studies.[12,13] Huperzine A exhibits memory-enhancing activities in a broad range of cognitive models in animals.[14] It also shows a significant effect to improve learning and retrieval processes,[15] and improves short and long-term memory in patients with cerebral arteriosclerosis and memory impairment.[16]

Clinically, there are many studies to justify the use *Qian Ceng Ta* (Herba Lycopodii Serrati) to treat Alzheimer's disease, dementia, and other neurodegenerative disorders. According to one multicenter, prospective, double-blind, parallel, placebo-controlled and randomized method, daily administration of 0.2 mg of huperzine A in 50 patients with Alzheimer's disease was associated with improvements in their memory, cognitive, and behavioral functions, when compared with 53 patients on placebo. Furthermore, no severe side effects were found with huperzine A use.[17] More recently, huperzine A shows significant improvements to both cognitive function and the quality of life in patients with Alzheimer's disease, according to a double-blind, placebo-controlled clinical trial.[18] According to another clinical study, huperzine A showed a significant curative effect when used to treat 56 patients with multi-infarct dementia or senile dementia and 104 patients with senile and presenile simple memory disorders. The main side effect noted was slight dizziness in only a few patients, and this did not affect the therapeutic benefits.[19] Lastly, according to Phase IV clinical trials in China, huperzine A significantly relieves many conditions associated with memory deficits, including benign senescent forgetfulness, Alzheimer's disease and vascular dementia. In addition, use of huperzine A is associated with minimal peripheral cholinergic side effects when compared to other acetylcholinesterase drugs.[20] Overall, *Qian Ceng Ta* (Herba Lycopodii Serrati) has been used to treat approximately 100,000 patients with dementia in China. In short, while the mechanism of action of huperzine A in *Qian Ceng Ta* (Herba Lycopodii Serrati) is similar to that of Cognex (tacrine), the first drug approved in the United States for Alzheimer's, the researchers conclude that the herb may be more effective and cause fewer side effects than the drug.[21]

One of the main etiologies of neurodegenerative disorders is the lack of blood perfusion to the brain, which deprives it of essential nutrients and leads to deterioration in mental and physical functions. Many herbs are used in ***Neuro Plus*** to remedy this condition. *Dan Shen* (Radix et Rhizoma Salviae Miltiorrhizae) improves microcirculation and is commonly used to increase blood perfusion to the brain.[22] *Dan Shen* (Radix et Rhizoma Salviae Miltiorrhizae) has been shown in two studies to have a protective effect against cerebral ischemia by increasing cerebral perfusion and reducing ultra-structural abnormalities.[23,24] Other studies demonstrate that with an increase in cerebral perfusion, *Dan Shen* (Radix et Rhizoma Salviae Miltiorrhizae) reduces neurological deficits and repairs cellular damage.[25,26] Furthermore, *Dan Shen* (Radix et Rhizoma Salviae Miltiorrhizae), *Shui Zhi* (Hirudo) and *Hong Hua* (Flos Carthami) inhibit coagulation, activate fibrinolysis, and are especially effective in treating and/or preventing stroke caused by blood clots blocking the blood vessels in the brain.[27]

Wu Gong (Scolopendra) has an excellent effect in stopping muscle spasms and cramps. It is commonly used clinically to treat seizures, convulsions, diphtheria and other conditions that exhibit muscle stiffness and spasm. Though mechanisms of actions differ, *Tian Ma* (Rhizoma Gastrodiae) also has anticonvulsive and muscle-relaxant effects. These two herbs are used together in this herbal formula to address muscle spasms, tremors, muscle rigidity and general musculoskeletal problems.[28]

In summary, ***Neuro Plus*** is an excellent formula to treat various neurodegenerative disorders, including but not limited to dementia, Alzheimer's disease, Parkinson's disease, and sequelae of stroke.

COMPARATIVE ANALYSIS

Neurological disorders are complicated illnesses that encompass many different diseases, including but not limited to Alzheimer's disease, Parkinson's disease, and sequelae of stroke. From Western medical perspectives, these diseases are well defined and accurately diagnosed, but not successfully treated. Alzheimer's disease may be managed with Cognex (tacrine) and Namenda (memantine), which temporarily improves thinking but does not cure the disease nor alter its prognosis. However, Cognex (tacrine) may cause clumsiness, unsteadiness, diarrhea, loss of appetite, nausea, vomiting, and liver damage, and Namenda (memantine) may lead to extreme tiredness, dizziness, confusion, headache, sleepiness, constipation, vomiting, pain anywhere in the body, shortness of breath, and hallucination. Parkinson's disease may be managed with drugs that control symptoms, such as Sinemet (levodopa and carbidopa). However, these drugs only control symptoms, and do not cure the disease nor alter its prognosis. Common side effects include agitation, anxiety, nervousness, difficulty concentrating, dizziness or lightheadedness, headache,

Neuro Plus™

irritability, loss of appetite, nausea, blotchy spots on the skin, insomnia, and nightmares. Sequelae of stroke are only treated symptomatically with supportive care. Though there are drugs for treatment and prevention of stroke, there are none for management of stroke sequelae, such as poor speech, muscle paralysis, urinary and bowel incontinence, and constipation. In brief, drug treatment for these neurological disorders focus on treating symptoms, as there are no drugs that cure or alter the progression of these diseases.

TCM offers many options for treatment of these neurological disorders. ***Neuro Plus*** has been used in major hospitals in Tianjing, China with great success for treatment of Alzheimer's disease, Parkinson's disease, and stroke sequelae. Alzheimer's and Parkinson's diseases are chronic illnesses that develop over a long period of time, and therefore, require long-term use of herbs to slowly stabilize and stop deterioration of the illness. Stroke, on the other hand, is an acute, sudden illness that causes immediate and dramatic changes. Similarly, use of TCM treatments (acupuncture and herbs) is likely to have immediate and significant results. In fact, near-complete recovery from stroke sequelae is sometimes possible, especially if treatments are initiated early, frequently, and aggressively.

Alzheimer's and Parkinson's diseases are two challenging conditions to both Western and traditional Chinese medicine. Drugs and herbs may manage symptoms, but they do not reverse the course of these illnesses. Sequelae of stroke is poorly managed by Western medicine but effectively treated with traditional Chinese medicine. Therefore, for post-stroke patients, both acupuncture and herbal treatments must be initiated early, frequently, and aggressively to achieve maximum benefit and near-complete recovery.

References

1. Chan K, Lo AC, Yeung JH, Woo KS. Journal of Pharmacy and Pharmacology 1995 May;47(5):402-406.
2. Lei X, et al. Liver Damage Associated with Polygonum multiflorum Thunb.: A Systematic Review of Case Reports and Case Series. Evid Based Complement Alternat Med. 2015;2015:459749. doi: 10.1155/2015/459749.
3. Liu Z, Chao Z, Liu Y, Song Z, Lu A. Maillard reaction involved in the steaming process of the root of Polygonum multiflorum. Institution of Basic Theory, China Academy of Chinese Medical Sciences, Beijing, PR China. Planta Med. 2009 Jan;75(1):84-8. Epub 2008 Nov 25.
4. Liu Z, et al. In vitro antioxidant activities of maillard reaction products produced in the steaming process of Polygonum multiflorum root. Nat Prod Commun. 2011 Jan;6(1):55-8.
5. Kudolo GB, Wang W, Barrientos J, Elrod R, Blodgett J. The ingestion of Ginkgo biloba extract (EGb 761) inhibits arachidonic acid-mediated platelet aggregation and thromboxane B2 production in healthy volunteers. Department of Clinical Laboratory Sciences, MSC 6246, University of Texas HSC at San Antonio, 7703 Floyd Curl Drive, San Antonio, TX 78229-3900, USA. J Herb Pharmacother. 2004;4(4):13-26.
6. *Guo Wai Yi Xue Zhong Yi Zhong Yao Fen Ce* (Monograph of Chinese Herbology from Foreign Medicine), 1979; 4:200.
7. Elsabagh S, Hartley DE, Ali O, Williamson EM, File SE. Differential cognitive effects of Ginkgo biloba after acute and chronic treatment in healthy young volunteers. Psychopharmacology Research Unit, Centre for Neuroscience, Hodgkin Building, King's College London, Guy's Campus, London, SE1 1UL, UK. Psychopharmacology (Berl). 2005 May;179(2):437-46.
8. Le Bars, P. et al. A placebo-controlled, double-blind randomized trial of an extract of ginkgo biloba for dementia. *JAMA* (Journal of American Medical Association);278:1327-1332. October 22, 1997.
9. Napryeyenko O, Borzenko I; GINDEM-NP Study Group. Ginkgo biloba special extract in dementia with neuropsychiatric features. A randomised, placebo-controlled, double-blind clinical trial. Psychiatry Department, National Medical University, Kyiv, Ukraine. Arzneimittelforschung. 2007;57(1):4-11.
10. Schneider LS, DeKosky ST, Farlow MR, Tariot PN, Hoerr R, Kieser M. A randomized, double-blind, placebo-controlled trial of two doses of Ginkgo biloba extract in dementia of the Alzheimer's type. Curr Alzheimer Res. 2005 Dec;2(5):541-51.
11. Wang R. & Tang X.C. Neuroprotective effects of huperzine A. A natural cholinesterase inhibitor for the treatment of Alzheimer's disease. *Neurosignals.* 2005, 14(1-2): 71-82.
12. Guo B, Xu L, Wei Y, Liu C. Research advances of Huperzia serrata (Thunb.) Trev. College of Life Science, Northwest University, Xi'an 710069, China. Zhongguo Zhong Yao Za Zhi. 2009 Aug;34(16):2018-23.
13. Tang XC. Huperzine A (shuangyiping): a promising drug for Alzheimer's disease. Department of Pharmacology, State Key Laboratory of Drug Research, Shanghai Institute of Materia Medica, Chinese Academy of Sciences, China. Zhongguo Yao Li Xue Bao. 1996 Nov;17(6):481-4.
14. Tang X.C. Huperzine A (shuangyiping): a promising drug for Alzheimer's disease . *Zhongguo Yao Li Xue Bao.* 1996, 17(6): 481-484.
15. Zangara, A. The psychopharmacology of huperzine A: an alkaloid with cognitive enhancing and neuroprotective properties of interest in the treatment of Alzheimer's disease. *Pharmacol Biochem Behav.* 2003, 75(3): 675-686.
16. Zhu X.Z. (1991) Development of natural products as drugs acting on central nervous system. *Mem Inst Oswaldo Cruz.* , 86(2): 173-175.
17. Xu SS, Gao ZX, Weng Z, Du ZM, Xu WA, Yang JS, Zhang ML, Tong ZH, Fang YS, Chai XS, et al. Efficacy of tablet huperzine-A on memory, cognition, and behavior in Alzheimer's disease. Zhejiang Supervision and Detection Station of Drug Abuse, Zhejiang Medical University, Hangzhou, China. Zhongguo Yao Li Xue Bao. 1995 Sep;16(5):391-5.
18. Zangara A. (2003) The psychopharmacology of huperzine A: an alkaloid with cognitive enhancing and neuroprotective properties of interest in the treatment of Alzheimer's disease. *Pharmacol Biochem Behav.* , 75(3): 675-686.
19. Zhang RW, Tang XC, Han YY, Sang GW, Zhang YD, Ma YX, Zhang CL, Yang RM. Drug evaluation of huperzine A in the treatment of senile memory disorders. Zhejiang Academy of Medical Sciences, Hangzhou, China. Zhongguo Yao Li Xue Bao. 1991 May;12(3):250-2.
20. Wang R., Yan H. & Tang X.C. Progress in studies of huperzine A, a natural cholinesterase inhibitor from Chinese herbal medicine. *Acta Pharmacol Sin.* 2006, 27(1): 1-26.
21. Skolnick, A. Old Chinese herbal medicine used for fever yields possible new Alzheimer's disease therapy. *JAMA* (Journal of American Medical Association); 227:776. March 12, 1997.
22. Nagai, M. et al. Vasodilator effects of des(alpha-carboxy-3'4-dihydroxyphenethyl)lithospermic acid (8-epiblechnic acid)' a derivative of lithospermic acids in salviae miltiorrhizae radix. *Biol Pharm Bull*, 19(2):228-32 Feb. 1996.
23. Wu, W. et al. The effect of radix saliva miltiorrhizae on the changes of ultrastructure in rat brain after cerebral ischemia. *J. Tradit Chin Med*, 12(3):183-6 Sept. 1992.
24. Kuang, PG. et al. The effect of radix saliva miltiorrhizae on vasoactive intestinal peptide in cerebral ischemia: an animal experiment *J Tradit Chin Med*, 9(3):203-6 Sept. 1989.
25. Kuang, P. et al. Effect of radix saliva miltiorrhizae on nitric oxide in cerebral ischemia-reperfusion injury. *J Tradit Chin Med*, 16(3):224-7 Sept. 1996.
26. Protective effect of radix saliva miltiorrhizae on nitric oxide in cerebral ischemia-reperfusion injury. *J Tradit Chin Med*, 15(2):135-40. Jun. 1995.

Neuro Plus™

27. Yeung, HC. *Handbook of Chinese Herbs*. Institute of Chinese Medicine. 1996.

28. Bensky, D. et al. *Chinese Herbal Medicine Materia Medica*. Eastland Press. 1993.

Notoginseng 9™

CLINICAL APPLICATIONS

- **Bleeding**
- **Internal bleeding** (upper gastrointestinal bleeding, stomach bleeding, duodenal bleeding, hemoptysis, hematuria, epistaxis, and excessive or irregular menstrual bleeding)
- **External bleeding** (from external and traumatic injuries)

WESTERN THERAPEUTIC ACTIONS

- Hemostatic effect to stop bleeding
- Facilitates and accelerates wound healing

CHINESE THERAPEUTIC ACTIONS

- Cools the blood
- Disperses blood stasis
- Stops bleeding

DOSAGE

Take 6 to 8 capsules to stop bleeding. If necessary, the herbs may be repeated three to four times daily until the bleeding stops.

INGREDIENTS

Ai Ye (Folium Artemisiae Argyi), charred
Ce Bai Ye (Cacumen Platycladi), charred
Di Yu (Radix Sanguisorbae), charred
He Zi (Fructus Chebulae)
Jing Jie (Herba Schizonepetae), charred
Qian Cao (Radix et Rhizoma Rubiae)
San Qi (Radix et Rhizoma Notoginseng)
Wu Bei Zi (Galla Chinensis)
Xian He Cao (Herba Agrimoniae)

BACKGROUND

Bleeding may be caused by external injuries or internal factors. Bleeding from external injuries are simple to diagnose and straight-forward to treat. Bleeding from internal factors, on the other hand, are much more complex and may involve disorders from various organs and systems. Though the body has its own mechanism to stop bleeding, mechanical or medicinal intervention may be required if the bleeding is profuse, prolonged or uncontrolled.

FORMULA EXPLANATION

Notoginseng 9 is designed specifically to symptomatically stop bleeding. It contains herbs to cool the blood, disperse blood stasis, and stop bleeding in the upper, middle and lower *jiaos*.

San Qi (Radix et Rhizoma Notoginseng) is one of the most important herbs to stop bleeding. It has the dual function to activate blood circulation and stop bleeding, therefore preventing the risk of blood stasis. Charred *Ce Bai Ye* (Cacumen Platycladi) cools the blood and stops respiratory bleeding. *Qian Cao* (Radix et Rhizoma Rubiae) moves blood and stops irregular and excessive menstrual bleeding. Charred *Di Yu* (Radix Sanguisorbae) clears heat and cools the blood to stop bleeding in the gastrointestinal tract. Charred *Ai Ye* (Folium Artemisiae Argyi) warms the channels and collaterals, relieves pain and treats a variety of bleeding disorders. *Xian He Cao* (Herba Agrimoniae) has a good restraining function and is commonly used to treat various bleeding disorders. Charred *Jing Jie* (Herba Schizonepetae) also has an excellent hemostatic effect. *Wu Bei Zi* (Galla Chinensis) and *He Zi* (Fructus Chebulae) are astringent herbs to help stabilize and consolidate the effect.

In summary, ***Notoginseng 9*** is an excellent formula to stop bleeding due to various causes in the upper, middle and lower *jiaos*.

CAUTIONS & CONTRAINDICATIONS

- Patients with profuse bleeding from serious injuries (such as acute trauma or accidents) should be sent to the emergency room immediately.
- This formula is used primarily to stop the "symptom," not the "cause," of bleeding. Once bleeding stops, proper measures should be taken to identify and treat the cause of bleeding. This formula should not to be taken long-term. *See* Supplementary Formulas section for appropriate formulas to use once the cause is determined.
- This formula should ***not*** be used in patients who are on anti-coagulant or antiplatelet drugs, such as Coumadin (warfarin) and Plavix (clopidogrel), as it may counter the effectiveness of these drugs.
- Some drugs cause bleeding and prolong bleeding, and should be avoided. These drugs include aspirin and non-steroidal anti-inflammatory drugs, such as Motrin (ibuprofen) and Naprosyn (naproxen).

SUPPLEMENTARY FORMULAS

- For gastric or duodenal ulcer bleeding, combine with ***GI Care***.
- For colitis or intestinal bleeding with burning diarrhea, combine with ***GI Care II***.
- For bleeding from Crohn's disease or irritable bowel syndrome (IBS), combine with ***GI Harmony***.
- For bleeding due to ulcerative colitis, add ***GI Care (UC)***.
- For external bleeding from injuries and trauma, stop the bleeding first and then use ***Flex (TMX)***.
- For cough with blood-streaked sputum, add ***Respitrol (CF)***.
- For hemorrhoids, add ***GI Care (HMR)***.
- For urinary tract infection, cystitis or abnormal uterine bleeding due to heat, add ***V-Support***.
- For menstrual pain, add ***Mense-Ease***.
- For uterine fibroids or cysts, add ***Resolve (Lower)***.
- For bleeding with high fever and excess heat, combine with ***Gardenia Complex***.
- For blood stagnation, add ***Circulation (SJ)***.
- For dryness and thirst, add ***Nourish (Fluids)***.

FORMULAS

Notoginseng 9™

ACUPUNCTURE TREATMENT

Traditional Points:

- **Blood in the urine:** *Zhongji* (CV 3), *Xingjian* (LR 2), *Pangguangshu* (BL 28), *Yinlingquan* (SP 9), *Sanyinjiao* (SP 6), *Xuehai* (SP 10), *Shenshu* (BL 23), *Daling* (PC 7), *Shenmen* (HT 7)
- **Cough with blood:** *Xingjian* (LR 2), *Yuji* (LU 10), *Laogong* (PC 8), *Feishu* (BL 13), *Quze* (PC 3), *Kongzui* (LU 6), *Rangu* (KI 2), *Taixi* (KI 3)
- **Nosebleed:** *Shangxing* (GV 23), *Hegu* (LI 4), *Shaoshang* (LU 11), *Fengfu* (GV 16), *Tianfu* (LU 3)
- **Vomiting of blood:** *Shangxing* (GV 23), *Erjian*, *Zhongwan* (CV 12), *Yinbai* (SP 1)
- **Blood in the stool:** *Dachangshu* (BL 25), *Changqiang* (GV 1), *Pishu* (BL 20), *Xiajuxu* (ST 39), *Chengshan* (BL 57)
- **Bleeding from Spleen deficiency:** Needle and moxa *Zhongwan* (CV 12), *Zusanli* (ST 36), *Shenshu* (BL 23), *Yinbai* (SP 1), *Guanyuan* (CV 4), and *Taibai* (SP 3).

Classic Master Tung's Points:

- **Bleeding (during ovulation):** *Yunbai* (T 44.11), *Fuke* (T 11.24). Needle everyday except the week of and the week before menstruation.
- **Bleeding from trauma:** *Liuwan* (T 66.08)

Master Tung's Points by Dr. Chuan-Min Wang:

- **Bleeding:** *Liuwan* (T 66.08), *Huagusi* (T 55.05)

Balance Method by Dr. Richard Tan:

- Left side: *Hegu* (LI 4), *Yinlingquan* (SP 9)
- Right side: *Shaofu* (HT 8), *Laogong* (PC 8), *Zusanli* (ST 36)
- Alternate sides between treatments.

Ear Acupuncture:

- Needle the area or organ area corresponding to bleeding, in addition to Adrenal and Subcortex.

Auricular Medicine by Dr. Li-Chun Huang:

- **Stop bleeding:** Pituitary, Diaphragm, Adrenal Gland, Spleen, corresponding point where there is bleeding
- **Epistaxis:** Internal Nose, Diaphragm, Spleen, Pituitary, Lung, Adrenal Gland

NUTRITION

- Consume an adequate amount of calcium and magnesium, which are important for blood clotting.
- Consume an adequate amount of multivitamin, especially vitamin K, as they are essential for blood clotting. Foods rich in vitamin K include alfalfa, broccoli, cauliflower, egg yolks, kale, spinach, and all green leafy vegetables.

The Tao of Nutrition by Dr. Maoshing Ni and Cathy McNease:

- **Nosebleed and hypertension:** Drink lotus root juice daily.
- **Vomiting or defecating blood:** Cook 1/2 cup of lotus root starch with 1/2 cup rice porridge until jelly-like consistency and consume while lukewarm.
- **Blood in the urine:** Make tea of lotus root and bamboo leaves.
- **Bloody stools:** Juice fresh water chestnuts and mix with equal amount of rice wine and drink three times a day on an empty stomach. Results should be seen within three days.
- **Excess uterine bleeding:** Charcoal the water chestnuts, powder them and take with rice wine.
- **Abnormal bleeding, anemia:** Boil tea from black fungus and Chinese dates.

LIFESTYLE INSTRUCTIONS

- Avoid drinking alcohol, as it irritates the stomach and may cause ulcer and bleeding.
- Patients should find out the cause of bleeding and avoid it accordingly.

CASE STUDIES

- K.J., a 33-year-old-female, presented with excess menstrual flow for two days, consisting of red and slightly purple in color. Pain was also present upon palpation of the abdomen. The TCM diagnosis was blood heat, slight blood stagnation, and uterine hemorrhaging. ***Notoginseng 9*** was prescribed at four pills three times a day. The very next day the bleeding had stopped. The patient was able to compete the following night in her sport activity after her recovery from the help of what she described as an amazing herbal formula. Submitted by A.I., Hilo, Hawaii.
- L.B., a 45-year-old female, presented with excessive blood flow from menstruation, not in quantity but duration. The symptoms had been present for six months, bleeding very lightly but constantly. Doctors did not know what to do. The Western diagnosis was metrorrhagia, and the TCM diagnosis was blood heat. After the patient took ***Notoginseng 9*** for 1.5 weeks, the excessive flow completely resolved. She is now a firm believer of Chinese medicine. Since then it has not happened again. Submitted by A.I., Hilo, Hawaii.
- P.I., a 46-year-old female, presented with spotting and uterine bleeding between menstrual cycles, which were irregular short cycles ranging from 15 to 27 days long. She had been experiencing heavy bleeding, no clots during her cycles, night sweats, and chronic anxiety, which was worse before her menses. Her Western diagnosis was perimenopausal syndrome with chronic anxiety; and the TCM diagnosis was Liver and Kidney yin deficiencies with deficiency heat, blood stagnation, Liver qi stagnation, and *shen* (spirit) disturbance. The practitioner prescribed ***Calm (ES)***, two grams three times a day and has been taking this formula for anxiety the past two years. In addition, she was also prescribed ***Nourish*** and ***Notoginseng 9***, same dosage

Notoginseng 9 ™

as the other formula, for six months to stop the uterine bleeding. ***Notoginseng 9*** successfully stopped the irregular bleeding and night sweats, which had been gradually reduced over the six month period. Her periods have returned to normal with light flow and her anxiety is also much better ever since adding ***Nourish***. The patient had excellent wellness and lifestyle habits, including her diet and exercise, and she was very compliant with taking her herbs. Submitted by E.Z., Portland, Oregon.

PHARMACOLOGICAL AND CLINICAL RESEARCH

Notoginseng 9 is one of the most effective formulas to stop bleeding, as it contains many herbs with a fast onset of hemostatic effect. This formula has been used to treat various types of bleeding disorders, including internal and external bleeding.

San Qi (Radix et Rhizoma Notoginseng) is one of the most useful and unique herbs to stop bleeding, as it has an excellent effect to stop bleeding with minimal effect of creating blood clots. Pharmacologically, it has shown a marked hemostatic effect to decrease prothrombin time and stop bleeding.[1] Furthermore, the saponins of *San Qi* (Radix et Rhizoma Notoginseng) have been shown to have mild antiplatelet and anticoagulant effects, thereby minimizing the risks of clotting disorder.[2,3] Clinically, *San Qi* (Radix et Rhizoma Notoginseng) has been used to treat various bleeding disorders, including but not limited to, upper gastrointestinal bleeding,[4] stomach bleeding,[5] hemoptysis due to bronchiectasis, pulmonary tuberculosis or pulmonary abscess,[6] and hematuria.[7] In fact, one study reported satisfactory results for treatment of acute perforated stomach ulcer and bleeding using 6 grams of powdered *San Qi* (Radix et Rhizoma Notoginseng) and 20 grams of powdered *Bai Ji* (Rhizoma Bletillae) with acupuncture on *Tianzhu* (BL 10), *Zhongwan* (CV 12), and *Zusanli* (ST 36).[8]

In addition to *San Qi* (Radix et Rhizoma Notoginseng), *Xian He Cao* (Herba Agrimoniae) has also demonstrated a remarkable hemostatic effect, with its mechanism of action attributed to an increase in platelets and a reduction in bleeding time.[9] Clinical research has confirmed its effect to treat hemoptysis (coughing of blood), upper gastrointestinal bleeding and menstrual bleeding.[10,11,12] *Di Yu* (Radix Sanguisorbae) also has a good hemostatic effect, and has been shown in animal studies to reduce bleeding time by 31.9 to 45.5%.[13] In humans, *Di Yu* (Radix Sanguisorbae) is most effective for hemoptysis (coughing of blood),[14] hematochezia (blood in the stools),[15] upper gastrointestinal bleeding, and profuse menstrual bleeding.[16,17] *Ce Bai Ye* (Cacumen Platycladi) has demonstrated marked influence to shorten bleeding time,[18] and has been used effectively to treat bleeding ulcers in 100 patients and bleeding hemorrhoids in 8 patients.[19,20] Administration of *Qian Cao* (Radix et Rhizoma Rubiae) shows marked effectiveness in reducing bleeding time.[21] According to one study, it effectively stops profuse bleeding after tooth extraction in 41 patients within one to two minutes.[22] Lastly, *Jing Jie* (Herba Schizonepetae) and *Ai Ye* (Folium Artemisiae Argyi), in either fresh or charred form, have demonstrated a marked hemostatic effect to stop bleeding.[23,24]

While the main priority to treat bleeding disorders is to stop bleeding, it is also important to facilitate wound healing and promote recovery. *He Zi* (Fructus Chebulae) is a unique herb that has been shown to accelerate dermal wound healing, as indicated by improved rates of contraction and a decreased period of epithelialization. From a biochemical perspective, use of *He Zi* (Fructus Chebulae) is associated with a significant increase in total protein, DNA, and collagen contents in the granulation tissues of treated wounds.[25]

In summary, ***Notoginseng 9*** is an excellent formula to treat bleeding disorders as it contains herbs with remarkable hemostatic effects to stop bleeding without creating blood stasis, as well as an herb to facilitate wound healing and promote recovery. It may be used to treat all types of bleeding, including but not limited to upper gastrointestinal bleeding, stomach bleeding, duodenal bleeding, hemoptysis, hematuria, menstrual bleeding, and bleeding due to various external and traumatic injuries.

COMPARATIVE ANALYSIS

Bleeding is a very common condition that may be caused by external or internal injuries. Because of the wide variety of etiologies, each condition is managed differently. For example, according to Western medicine, treatments are different for uterine bleeding, gastrointestinal bleeding, bleeding from trauma, and bleeding from overdose of Coumadin (warfarin).

TCM identifies the causes of bleeding and treat them differently. However, in addition to specific treatments (which requires time to diagnose and prepare treatment), general treatment is also available to immediately stop bleeding. ***Notoginseng 9*** is a formula that is designed to symptomatically stop bleeding. Once bleeding stops, it is then necessary to identify the cause and treat accordingly.

References

1. *Zhong Cao Yao* (Chinese Herbal Medicine), 1986; 17(6):34.
2. *Xian Dai Zhong Yao Yao Li Xue* (Contemporary Pharmacology of Chinese Herbs), 1997; 282-283, 1997; 807:824.
3. Lau AJ, Toh DF, Chua TK, Pang YK, Woo SO, Koh HL. Antiplatelet and anticoagulant effects of Panax notoginseng: comparison of raw and steamed Panax notoginseng with Panax ginseng and Panax quinquefolium. Department of Pharmacy, National University of Singapore, 18 Science Drive 4, Singapore 117543, Singapore. J Ethnopharmacol. 2009 Sep 25;125(3):380-6.
4. *Shang Hai Zhong Yi Yao Za Zhi* (Shanghai Journal of Chinese Medicine and Herbology), 1983; 9:15.
5. *Yun Nan Zhong Yi Za Zhi* (Yunan Journal of Chinese Medicine), 1985; 1:28.
6. *Zhong Yi Za Zhi* (Journal of Chinese Medicine), 1965; 11:29.
7. *Ha Yi Da Xue Bao* (Journal of Ha Medical University), 1974; 7(2):51.
8. *Zhong Yi Za Zhi* (Journal of Chinese Medicine), 1994; (3):135.
9. *Zhong Yao Yao Li Yu Ying Yong* (Pharmacology and Applications of Chinese Herbs), 1983:323.
10. *Si Chuan Zhong Yi* (Sichuan Chinese Medicine), 1995; (8):33.

FORMULAS

Notoginseng 9 ™

11. *Shang Hai Zhong Yi Yao Za Zhi* (Shanghai Journal of Chinese Medicine and Herbology), 1979; 4:28.
12. *Shan Xi Zhong Yi* (Shanxi Chinese Medicine), 1985; 6(7):323.
13. *Zhong Yao Yao Li Yu Ying Yong* (Pharmacology and Applications of Chinese Herbs), 1983; 406.
14. *Zhong Yao Lin Chuan Xin Yong* (New Clinical Applications of Chinese Medicine), 2001; 247.
15. *Zhong Yao Lin Chuan Xin Yong* (New Clinical Applications of Chinese Medicine), 2001; 247.
16. *Zhe Jiang Zhong Yi Xue Yuan Xue Bao* (Journal of Zhejiang University of Chinese Medicine), 1985; 9(4):26.
17. *Zhe Jiang Zhong Yi Za Zhi* (Zhejiang Journal of Chinese Medicine), 1965; 8(3):4.
18. 18 *Zhong Yi Yao Yan Jiu Zi Liao* (Research and Resource of Chinese Medicine and Herbology), 1965; (3):48.
19. *Zhong Hua Nei Ke Xue Za Zhi* (Journal of Chinese Internal Medicine), 1960; 8(3):249.
20. *Zhong Guo Gang Chang Bing Za Zhi* (Chinese Journal of Proctology), 1985; 4:5.
21. *Zhong Yi Yao Yan Jiu* (Research of Chinese Medicine and Herbology), 1991; (3):54.
22. *Yi Xue Wei Sheng Tong Xun* (Journal of Medicine and Sanitation), 1974; 1:54.
23. *Zhong Yao Cai* (Study of Chinese Herbal Material), 1989; 12(6):37.
24. *Zhong Yao Cai* (Study of Chinese Herbal Material), 1992; 15(2):22.
25. Suguna L, Singh S, Sivakumar P, Sampath P, Chandrakasan G. Influence of Terminalia chebula on dermal wound healing in rats. Department of Biochemistry, Central Leather Research Institute, Adyar, Chennai, India. Phytother Res. 2002 May;16(3):227-31.

Nourish ™

CLINICAL APPLICATIONS

- **Menopause:** hot flashes, night sweats, fluctuation of body temperature
- **Kidney yin deficiency with mild deficiency heat conditions:**
  - Eyes and ears: blurry vision, dizziness, general visual disturbance, fatigue of the eyes, optic nerve atrophy, mild cases of glaucoma, and macular degeneration
  - Kidneys: chronic nephritis, nephrotic syndrome, chronic renal failure
  - Bladder: frequent urination, urinary incontinence
  - Liver: chronic hepatitis
  - Pancreas: diabetes mellitus
  - Skin: dryness with lack of elasticity of the skin throughout the body

WESTERN THERAPEUTIC ACTIONS

- Regulates endocrine functions to balance the hormones
- Revives eyes and ear functions
- Restores normal functions of internal organs, such as liver, kidneys, bladder, and pancreas

CHINESE THERAPEUTIC ACTIONS

- Nourishes Liver and Kidney yin
- Controls flare-ups of yin-deficient heat

DOSAGE

Take 3 to 4 capsules three times daily on an empty stomach with warm water. For prevention of chronic and recurrent infections in the genito-urinary region, take 2 to 3 capsules three times daily.

INGREDIENTS

Fu Ling (Poria)
Gou Qi Zi (Fructus Lycii)
Huang Bo (Cortex Phellodendri Chinensis)
Ju Hua (Flos Chrysanthemi)
Mu Dan Pi (Cortex Moutan)
Shan Yao (Rhizoma Dioscoreae)
Shan Zhu Yu (Fructus Corni)
Shu Di Huang (Radix Rehmanniae Praeparata)
Ze Xie (Rhizoma Alismatis)
Zhi Mu (Rhizoma Anemarrhenae)

BACKGROUND

Chronic or consumptive disorders are often characterized by weakness, dryness, and atrophy of the glands or organs. These chronic or consumptive disorders affect various parts of the body, especially internal organs and endocrine glands. As a result, the internal organs and endocrine glands atrophy and gradually lose their normal functions. From traditional Chinese medicine perspective, these types of chronic or consumptive disorders are diagnosed as "yin deficiency."

FORMULA EXPLANATION

Nourish is formulated to treat Kidney yin deficiency with deficiency heat. Clinically, these patients will show such symptoms as hot flashes, fluctuation of body temperature, night sweats, tinnitus, blurred vision, dry eyes, and dizziness. Furthermore, chronic bacterial or viral infections, such as urinary tract infections or genital herpes, will also show as Kidney yin deficiency with deficiency heat. Finally, aging is also a sign of Kidney yin deficiency, manifesting in symptoms such as soreness and weakness of the lower back and knees, tinnitus, vertigo, blurry vision, diminished hearing, heat sensations, thirst, and dryness of mucous membranes.

Shu Di Huang (Radix Rehmanniae Praeparata), *Shan Zhu Yu* (Fructus Corni), *Shan Yao* (Rhizoma Dioscoreae), *Ze Xie* (Rhizoma Alismatis), *Mu Dan Pi* (Cortex Moutan), and *Fu Ling* (Poria) compose the classic Kidney yin tonic formula *Liu Wei Di Huang Wan* (Six-Ingredient Pill with Rehmannia), one of the most famous herbal tonics. *Shu Di Huang* (Radix Rehmanniae Praeparata) tonifies the Kidney yin and the Kidney *jing* (essence). *Shan Zhu Yu* (Fructus Corni) nourishes the Liver and prevents the leakage of Kidney *jing* (essence). *Shan Yao* (Rhizoma Dioscoreae) tonifies the Spleen and stabilizes the Kidney *jing* (essence). *Ze Xie* (Rhizoma Alismatis) clears deficiency fire from the Kidney. *Mu Dan Pi* (Cortex Moutan) sedates Liver fire. *Fu Ling* (Poria) dissolves dampness from the Spleen. These six herbs are formulated with careful checks and balances to maximize the therapeutic effects and minimized unwanted side effects.

In addition to nourishing Kidney and Liver yin, *Zhi Mu* (Rhizoma Anemarrhenae) and *Huang Bo* (Cortex Phellodendri Chinensis) are added to sedate deficiency fire. *Gou Qi Zi* (Fructus Lycii) and *Ju Hua* (Flos Chrysanthemi) benefit the eyes and treat dry and blurry vision by nourishing the Liver and Kidney yin.

In short, ***Nourish*** tonifies Liver and Kidney yin to treat various disorders characterized by aging and deterioration.

CAUTIONS & CONTRAINDICATIONS

- This formula should not be used for yang deficiency with such symptoms as intolerance of cold with cold hands and feet.

CLINICAL NOTES

- In contrast with hormone replacement therapy, use of yam, such as *Shan Yao* (Rhizoma Dioscoreae) in this formula, is not only effective to treat menopause symptoms, but also safe in regards to risks of cancer and cardiovascular diseases. In one study, the extract of yam has been shown to act as a weak phytoestrogen and protects against proliferation in human breast cancer (MCF-7) cells.[1] In another study, use of yam was found to reduce the risk of breast cancer and cardiovascular diseases in postmenopausal women.[2]
- Most patients with chronic or debilitating illness have an underlying Kidney yin deficiency. ***Nourish*** can be used to change

Nourish™

the fundamental constitution of these patients so they respond better to the overall treatment.

- This formula can also be used to treat cataracts by nourishing the Kidney yin and the eyes. If the cataract is secondary to other disorders such as diabetes, hypertension or arteriosclerosis, additional herbal formulas should also be prescribed (*see* Supplementary Formulas).

SUPPLEMENTARY FORMULAS

- For menopause with deficiency heat symptoms (hot flashes and irritability), use with ***Balance (Heat)***.
- For vaginal dryness, add ***Balance Spring***.
- For Kidney yin deficiency without deficiency fire, use ***Kidney Tonic (Yin)*** instead.
- For irritability, stress, or anxiety, combine with ***Calm***.
- For menopause with stress or anxiety with insomnia and underlying deficiency, add ***Calm ZZZ***.
- For osteoporosis, add ***Osteo 8***.
- For excess fire with severe hot flashes, add ***Gardenia Complex***.
- As a constitutional tonic, combine with ***Imperial Tonic***.
- For back pain, add ***Back Support (CR)***.
- For dry hair, premature gray hair or hair loss, combine with ***Polygonum 14***.
- For general deterioration in both mental and physical functions, use ***Neuro Plus***.
- For hypertension, combine with ***Gastrodia Complex***.
- For irregular menstrual bleeding, add ***Notoginseng 9***.
- To relieve side effects from chemotherapy and/or radiation treatments, use ***C/R Support***.
- For acute attacks of herpes or urinary tract infection, use ***Gentiana Complex***.
- For forgetfulness and to improve memory, add ***Enhance Memory***.
- For adrenal insufficiency, add ***Adrenal +***.
- For lack of sexual interest and other sexual dysfunction, add ***Vitality***.
- To tonify the individual to remedy the underlying constitutional deficiency, add ***Cordyceps 3***.
- For visual disturbances, blurriness, redness or pain, combine with ***Lycium Support***.

ACUPUNCTURE TREATMENT

Traditional Points:

- *Ququan* (LR 8), *Taixi* (KI 3), *Sanyinjiao* (SP 6)
- *Jingming* (BL 1), *Taichong* (LR 3), *Xingjian* (LR 2), *Taiyang* (Extra 2), *Hegu* (LI 4), *Xiaxi* (GB 43)

Classic Master Tung's Points:

- **Menopause (general):** *Tianhuang* (T 77.17), *Dihuang* (T 77.19), *Renhuang* (T 77.21), *Tianhuang* (T 88.13), *Minghuang* (T 88.12), *Qihuang* (T 88.14), *Shuijin* (T 1010.20), *Zhenjing* (T 1010.08), *Xinling* (T 33.17)*, *Simashang* (T 88.18), *Simazhong* (T 88.17), *Simaxia* (T 88.19)
- **Hot flashes:** *Tianhuang* (T 77.17), *Dihuang* (T 77.19), *Renhuang* (T 77.21), *Tianhuang* (T 88.13), *Minghuang* (T 88.12), *Qihuang* (T 88.14), *Shuijin* (T 1010.20), *Zhenjing* (T 1010.08), *Xinling* (T 33.17)*, *Simashang* (T 88.18), *Simazhong* (T 88.17), *Simaxia* (T 88.19)
- **Mood swings:** *Tianhuang* (T 77.17), *Dihuang* (T 77.19), *Renhuang* (T 77.21), *Tianhuang* (T 88.13), *Minghuang* (T 88.12), *Qihuang* (T 88.14), *Shuijin* (T 1010.20), *Zhenjing* (T 1010.08), *Xinling* (T 33.17)*, *Simashang* (T 88.18), *Simazhong* (T 88.17), *Simaxia* (T 88.19), *Fuke* (T 11.24), *Shuixiang* (T 66.14)
- **Irregular menstruation:** *Fuke* (T 11.24), *Tianhuang* (T 77.17), *Dihuang* (T 77.19), *Renhuang* (T 77.21), *Tianhuang* (T 88.13), *Minghuang* (T 88.12), *Qihuang* (T 88.14), *Shuijin* (T 1010.20), *Zhenjing* (T 1010.08), *Xinling* (T 33.17)*, *Simashang* (T 88.18), *Simazhong* (T 88.17), *Simaxia* (T 88.19), *Wanshunyi* (T 22.08), *Wanshuner* (T 22.09)
- **Osteoporosis:** *Tianhuang* (T 77.17), *Dihuang* (T 77.19), *Renhuang* (T 77.21), *Tianhuang* (T 88.13), *Minghuang* (T 88.12), *Qihuang* (T 88.14), *Fuke* (T 11.24), *Zhengji* (T 44.24)*
- **Blurry vision:** *Tongshen* (T 88.09), *Tianhuang* (T 77.17), *Dihuang* (T 77.19), *Renhuang* (T 77.21), *Shangbai* (T 22.03), *Libai* (T 44.12), *Sifuyi* (T 1010.11), *Sifuer* (T 1010.10)
- **Optic nerve atrophy:** *Sanchayi* (T 22.15)*, two points on the first metacarpal joint of the thumb, *Sizhukong* (TH 23), *Tianhuangfu [Shenguan]* (T 77.18), *Zhenjing* (T 1010.08), *Zanzhu* (BL 2). Bleed dark veins nearby the temporal area. Bleed before needling for best result.
- **Glaucoma:** *Guangming* (GB 37), *Tianhuang* (T 77.17), *Dihuang* (T 77.19), *Renhuang* (T 77.21), *Shangbai* (T 22.03), *Wanshunyi* (T 22.08), *Minghuang* (T 88.12), *Tianhuang* (T 88.13), *Qihuang* (T 88.14), two points on the sides of the first metacarpal joint on the thumb. Bleed the dark veins nearby the temporal area. Bleed before needling for best result.

Master Tung's Points by Dr. Chuan-Min Wang:

- **Kidney yin deficiency:** *Tongshen* (T 88.09), *Tongwei* (T 88.10), *Tongbei* (T 88.11)

Balance Method by Dr. Richard Tan:

- Left side: *Hegu* (LI 4), *Tongli* (HT 5)
- Right side: *Zusanli* (ST 36), *Taixi* (KI 3), *Guanyuan* (CV 4), *Shimen* (CV 5), *Qihai* (CV 6)
- Left and right sides can be alternated from treatment to treatment.

Ear Acupuncture:

- **Menopause:** Uterus, Ovary, Endocrine, *Shenmen*, Sympathetic, Subcortex
  - For emotional disturbance, add *Shenmen* and Heart.
  - For palpitation and irregular heart beat, add Heart and Small Intestine.
  - For hypertension, add Depression point on the back of the ear.

Nourish ™

- For flushed cheeks and excess perspiration, add Sympathetic, Cheeks and Lung.

- **High pitched tinnitus:** Inner Ear, Temporal Lobe, Pons, Adrenal Gland, Pituitary Gland
- **Low pitched tinnitus:** Middle Ear, Ear Drum, Eustachian Tube, Adrenal Gland, Pituitary Gland

Auricular Medicine by Dr. Li-Chun Huang:

- **Menopause:** Uterus, Endocrine, Ovary, Gonadotropin, Pituitary, Sympathetic, Anxious, Kidney, Liver, Heart
- **Tinnitus:** Gallbladder, Kidney, *Sanjiao*, Internal Ear, Auditory Centre (Temple). Bleed Ear Apex.
  - **due to deficiency:** add Coronary Vascular Subcortex, Sympathetic
- **Improving the visual acuity:** Kidney, Liver, Vision 2, Eye, Sympathetic, Optic Center (Occiput). Bleed Ear Apex.
- **Improving hearing acuity:** Speed Hearing, *San Jiao*, Internal Ear, External Ear, Sympathetic, Kidney, Gallbladder, Vision 1, Auditory Center.
- **Cataract:** Kidney, Liver, Eye, Vision 2, Endocrine, Sympathetic. Bleed Ear Apex.

NUTRITION

- Eat a variety of fresh, organic fruits and vegetables of all colors.
- Incorporate more high-fiber whole grains and nuts into diet.
- Drink warm or hot liquids with meals. Putting cold and ice on any part of the body will immediately constrict the flow of blood to that region. Similarly, drinking cold or iced drinks with meals will hinder the natural peristaltic movements of the digestive system.
- Foods with antioxidant effects, such as vitamin A, C and E are beneficial as they neutralize the free radicals and minimize damage to cells. Beneficial foods include citrus fruits, carrots, green leaf vegetables, and green tea.
- Increase intake of foods that nourish yin and moisten dryness, such as yam, radishes, potatoes, carrots, melons, cucumbers, beets, turnips, malanga, celeriac, taro, and rutabaga.
- Chew food completely and thoroughly. The digestive tract can process and absorb smaller pieces of food much better than food that is incompletely chewed. Larger pieces of food can lead to incomplete digestion and digestive discomfort.
- Always eat breakfast. According to the TCM clock, the most optimal time for the digestive system is in the morning from 8 to 10 a.m.
- Give the body two to three hours between the last meal of the day and bedtime. During sleep, the digestive system slows down as well. Make sure the body has adequate time to digest the food before going into sleep mode.
- If the patient is allergic to any food or feels uncomfortable after eating certain foods, then avoid eating them.
- Avoid fast food, processed foods, junk food, foods with artificial colors or sugars, and carbonated drinks. Stay away from meat, greasy food, alcohol, caffeinated and energy drinks, dairy products (except for unsweetened low-fat yogurt), tap water, iron supplements and vegetables and fruits sprayed with pesticides.
- Avoid spicy/pungent/aromatic vegetables such as pepper, garlic, onions, basil, rosemary, cumin, funnel, anise, leeks, chives, scallions, thyme, saffron, wormwood, mustard, chili pepper, wasabi, and cardamom. Also avoid certain fruits that may produce heat and aggravate the condition, such as mango and durian.
- Consume as few meat products as possible. Do not eat processed meats, such as lunch meats, hot dogs and sausages, as they contain nitrites that are associated with inflammation and chronic disease.

The Tao of Nutrition by Dr. Maoshing Ni and Cathy McNease:

- **Menopause**
  - Recommendations: black beans, sesame seeds, soybeans, walnuts, lycium berries, mulberries, yams, licorice, lotus seeds, and chrysanthemum flowers.
  - Avoid stress, tension, and all stimulants.
- **Tinnitus**
  - Recommendations: black sesame seeds, black beans, walnuts, grapes, celery, oyster shells, pearl barley, azuki beans, Chinese black dates, yams, lotus seeds, chestnuts, and chrysanthemum. Get plenty of sleep, massage the neck and head area, and try to live in a quiet and peaceful place if possible.
  - Avoid loud noise, stress, tension, stimulating foods, spicy foods, smoking, alcohol, and coffee.
- **Cataract**
  - Recommendations: chrysanthemum, cilantro, spinach, cloves, water chestnuts, yams, lycium berries, black beans. Exercise the eyes regularly and get plenty of oxygen into the bloodstream. Steam the eyes over boiling spinach.
  - Avoid any type of spices, salt, and garlic. Avoid foods that may cause constipation.

LIFESTYLE INSTRUCTIONS

- Avoid stress, tension, and anxiety as much as possible.
- Avoid cigarette smoking or exposure to second-hand smoke as it may dry up yin and body fluids.

CASE STUDIES

- J.M., a 54-year-old female, presented with hot flashes, which were especially bad at night, causing her to wake up constantly throughout the night. Pulse was deep and thin, and her tongue was dusky pink with a center crack. The practitioner diagnosed this condition as Kidney yin deficiency; her Western diagnosis was menopause. Upon diagnosis, the patient was prescribed ***Nourish*** and ***Balance (Heat)*** up to five capsules three times a day. After taking the herbs for four weeks, the duration of the hot flashes was shorter and she was sleeping through the night. Submitted by T.W., Perrysburg, Ohio.

Nourish ™

- P.I., a 46-year-old female, presented with spotting and uterine bleeding between menstrual cycles, which were irregular short cycles ranging from 15 to 27 days long. She had been experiencing heavy bleeding, no clots during her cycles, night sweats, and chronic anxiety, which was worse before her menses. Her Western diagnosis was perimenopausal syndrome with chronic anxiety; the TCM diagnosis was Liver and Kidney yin deficiencies with deficiency heat, blood stagnation, Liver qi stagnation, and *shen* (spirit) disturbance. The practitioner prescribed ***Calm (ES)***, two grams three times a day and has been taking this formula for anxiety the past two years. In addition, she was also prescribed ***Nourish*** and ***Notoginseng 9***, same dosage as the other formula, for six months to stop the uterine bleeding. ***Notoginseng 9*** successfully stopped the irregular bleeding. ***Nourish*** helped with her night sweats, which had been gradually reduced over the six month period. Her periods have returned to normal with light flow and her anxiety is also much better ever since adding ***Nourish***. The patient had excellent wellness and lifestyle habits, including her diet and exercise, and she was very compliant with taking her herbs. Submitted by E.Z., Portland, Oregon.
- J.C., a 57-year-old female, presented with nervousness, insomnia, and anxiety with a desire to stop smoking. Night sweats were also present. Her tongue was red with no coating present. The practitioner diagnosed the condition as Kidney yin deficiency with heat and Liver qi stagnation. Her Western diagnosis was menopause and hypothyroidism. The patient was given a combination of ***Nourish***, ***Shine***, and ***Calm***. ***Nourish*** was taken daily while ***Shine*** and ***Calm*** were taken as needed. After taking the herbs for six months, the patient reported improvement in sleep; she was calmer and more balanced overall with a positive attitude. Submitted by K.F., Honolulu, Hawaii.
- L.C., a 50-year-old female, presented with macular degeneration, experiencing pain one week before her menses and waking up at night. Tinnitus, low back and abdominal pain were also present. Her menses consisted of a bright red color, sometimes dark brown, and some clots. Pulse was thready and weak and her tongue had teeth marks and a red tip. The practitioner diagnosed this condition as Liver and Kidney yin deficiencies with qi and blood stagnation in the lower *jiao*. Upon diagnosis the patient was prescribed ***Nourish*** and ***Mense-Ease***. After taking the herbs for two months, the patient no longer has pain with her menses and felt better overall. Submitted by T.W., Perrysburg, Ohio.
- A.S., a 29-year-old female, presented with PCOS, consisting of multiple sacs, no ripening of the eggs, irregular cycles, and fatigue. It was also mentioned that she had two unsuccessful IUIs due to two chemical pregnancies. Additional symptoms included cystic ovaries, acne, increase facial and body hair, deficiencies of both vitamin D and DHEA, and short temperatured luteal phase. The TCM diagnosis was blood deficiency, phlegm and damp accumulation, Spleen and Kidney deficiencies, and *ren* (conception) and *chong* (thoroughfare) channels dysregulation. Her Western diagnosis was cystic ovaries infertility, low follicular and luteal temperatured irregular menstruation, and elevated prolactin. ***Blossom (Phases 1-4)*** was prescribed to her all month, with ***Imperial Tonic*** to replenish the *jing* (essence), and ***Nourish*** to tonify the blood and Kidney yin. The six month protocol was used to clear heat, tonify the qi/blood/*jing* (essence), and regulate the cycle. As a result her temperatures had re-established to create normal cycles again. Secondly, after three months of balanced cycles, her cystic ovaries had reduced; she also had nourished her qi/blood/*jing* (essence), and her other deficiencies which were also restored. As a result she had a successful IUI and was now two months pregnant. The ***Blossom (Phases 1-4)*** and ***Nourish*** were very helpful. Submitted by N.T., Bethesda, Maryland.
- A 27-year-old female health care provider presented with genital herpes. The affected area in the genital region was itchy, red and swollen with thick white discharge. The patient also felt menstrual pain. Her pulse was slippery, deep and strong. Her tongue body was pale purple with a red tip, and the sides were swollen with scalloped edges. The practitioner diagnosed the condition as damp-heat in the Liver and Liver qi stagnation. After taking ***Nourish*** and ***Gentiana Complex***, a decrease in symptoms was noted. Symptoms flared up when the patient stopped using the formulas. Submitted by B.H., Pearl City, Hawaii.
- A 50-year-old male presented with hearing loss, ringing in the ear and diminished hearing. The TCM diagnosis was Kidney yin deficiency. The patient was prescribed ***Nourish*** with good results. The practitioner commented that ***Nourish*** works the best for such conditions. Submitted by R.C., MD, Ph.D., New York, New York.
- D.S., a 45-year-old female, presented with insomnia, mood swings, cramps and fatigue. The tongue was slightly purplish pale with teeth marks. The coating was thin and white. The pulse was deep and wiry. She was diagnosed with Spleen qi deficiency and blood deficiency. ***Nourish***, ***Calm***, and ***Schisandra ZZZ*** were prescribed. The patient reported her sleep pattern improved, her moods balanced and her energy level increased. She was very happy with the herbs. Submitted by B.F., Newport Beach, California.
- A 53-year-old female patient presented with anxiety, depression and pale complexion. Her pulse was thin, weak and deep in all positions. She had cyclical bouts of rage, fatigue, sleeplessness, anxiety and severe depression. Periods were irregular. Her tongue was puffy and pale. The TCM diagnosis was blood and yin deficiencies with Liver qi stagnation, Kidney yin and yang deficiencies. ***Shine*** and ***Nourish***, along with an iron supplement were prescribed. The patient noticed a change within the first ten days and more so around her cycle. She felt as if a cloud had been lifted from above. She found herself smiling more. Restlessness was still bothering her but her sleep was much better. This patient has suffered from depression for a long time and is very deficient. Submitted by N.V., Muir Beach, California.

PHARMACOLOGICAL AND CLINICAL RESEARCH

Nourish is a contemporary formula that is similar to classical

Nourish ™

formulas such as *Liu Wei Di Huang Wan* (Six-Ingredient Pill with Rehmannia), *Zhi Bai Di Huang Wan* (Anemarrhena, Phellodendron, and Rehmannia Pill) and *Qi Ju Di Huang Wan* (Lycium Fruit, Chrysanthemum, and Rehmannia Pill). ***Nourish*** is designed to tonify Liver and Kidney yin, a condition in traditional Chinese medicine that resembles deteriorations of internal organs and endocrine glands associated with chronic or consumptive disorders. To restore optimal health, ***Nourish*** utilizes many herbs to revive normal functions of eyes, ears, liver, kidneys, bladder, pancreas and skin.

Nourish incorporates herbs to treat disorders associated with declining functions of the reproductive organs (ovaries and testes) and their corresponding hormones (estrogen, testosterone). For women, many herbs in the formula *Liu Wei Di Huang Wan* (Six-Ingredient Pill with Rehmannia), effectively treated 23 patients with menopause (marked improvement in 9 patients and moderate improvement in 14 patients). Clinical improvements included relief of hot flashes, tidal fever, perspiration, palpitations, anxiety, restlessness, insomnia, forgetfulness, and others.[3] According to another study, *Qi Ju Di Huang Wan* (Lycium Fruit, Chrysanthemum, and Rehmannia Pill) successfully treated 144 women with menopausal symptoms. Of 144 patients, the study reported complete recovery in 12 patients, significant improvement in 48 patients, moderate improvement in 32 patients, and no benefit in 52 patients.[4] For men, herbs in this formula are also effective for treating sexual and reproductive disorders. Use of *Gou Qi Zi* (Fructus Lycii) is associated with improvements in sperm count and sperm motility.[5] Administration of modified *Liu Wei Di Huang Wan* (Six-Ingredient Pill with Rehmannia) was beneficial to treat impotence among 18 men (complete recovery in 12 patients, improvement in 4 patients, and no benefit in 2 patients).[6] Furthermore, one study reported 83.3% effectiveness using modified *Liu Wei Di Huang Wan* (Six-Ingredient Pill with Rehmannia) to treat 30 male patients with infertility.[7] Another study stated *Zhi Bai Di Huang Wan* (Anemarrhena, Phellodendron, and Rehmannia Pill) to be 92.2% effective in treating 220 men with infertility.[8] Lastly, modified *Liu Wei Di Huang Wan* (Six-Ingredient Pill with Rehmannia) was shown to effectively treat infertility in both men and women (16 males and 26 females between the ages of 22 to 37).[9]

Nourish utilizes herbs to restore optimal function to the eyes and ears. *Gou Qi Zi* (Fructus Lycii) has a positive ocular effect to improve and restore eye functions. According to an up-to-date human trial, oral supplementation of *Gou Qi Zi* (Fructus Lycii) is effective in prevention of age-related macular degeneration, a common disorder that causes irreversible loss of central vision. This beneficial effect is attributed to zeaxanthin, a compound present in *Gou Qi Zi* (Fructus Lycii) that is essential to prevent degenerative eye disorder.[10] *Shan Zhu Yu* (Fructus Corni) has a positive auditory function to improve and restore ear functions. The ursolic acid from *Shan Zhu Yu* (Fructus Corni) shows a marked antioxidant effect to protect the auditory cells from hydrogen peroxide-induced cytotoxicity through inhibition of lipid peroxidation and induction of antioxidant enzymes, catalase and glutathione peroxidase.[11] Clinically, herbs in ***Nourish*** have been used successfully to treat 140 patients with retinitis (complete recovery in 22 patients, significant improvement in 21 patients, moderate improvement in 70 patients, and no benefit in 27 patients). The duration of treatment ranged from 30 to 118 days, with an average of 57 days.[12]

Nourish is an excellent formula to restore kidney functions and treat kidney disorders. *Liu Wei Di Huang Wan* (Six-Ingredient Pill with Rehmannia) has been shown to increase blood perfusion to the kidneys, improve kidney functions, and reduced protein and uric acid in the urine.[13] Clinically, it has been used effectively to treat 6 patients with edema and proteinuria due to nephrotic syndrome,[14] 12 patients with chronic renal failure,[15] and 30 patients with nephrotic syndrome.[16]

Nourish contains many herbs with hepatoprotective effects to treat liver disorders. *Gou Qi Zi* (Fructus Lycii) has marked hepatoprotective effects against carbon tetrachloride-induced hepatotoxicity through the antioxidative activity and expressional regulation of cytochrome P450 2E1 (CYP2E1).[17] Another study reiterates the hepatoprotective effect by showing that *Gou Qi Zi* (Fructus Lycii) protects liver cells against oxidative stress cell damage by hydrogen peroxide via scavenging reactive oxygen species and enhancing antioxidant enzyme activity.[18] *Ze Xie* (Rhizoma Alismatis) exerts a hepatoprotective effect in subjects with non-alcoholic fatty liver disease induced by high-fat diet. Therapeutic benefits of the herb included a decrease of serum and liver lipids, a reduction of fasting serum glucose, and an improvement of insulin resistance.[19] Berberine, a compound present in *Huang Bo* (Cortex Phellodendri Chinensis), has a marked effect to reduce inflammation by inhibiting the production of proinflammatory cytokines in HepG2 cells, including interleukin-1beta and tumor necrosis factor-alpha (TNF-α).[20] As a formula, *Liu Wei Di Huang Wan* (Six-Ingredient Pill with Rehmannia) illustrates a hepatoprotective effect to protect the liver against damage induced by substances such as carbon tetrachloride, thioacetamide, and prednisolone.[21] Clinically, *Liu Wei Di Huang Wan* (Six-Ingredient Pill with Rehmannia) has been used effectively to treat 65 patients with chronic hepatitis.[22]

Nourish incorporates several herbs with marked influence on the pancreas, production of insulin, and treatment of diabetes mellitus. *Fu Ling* (Poria) has an antihyperglycemic effect. Administration of *Fu Ling* (Poria) is effective to reduce postprandial blood glucose levels via enhanced insulin sensitivity in subjects with streptozocin-induced diabetes.[23] *Gou Qi Zi* (Fructus Lycii) illustrates an antidiabetic benefit in subjects with non-insulin dependent diabetes mellitus. It lowers fasting plasma insulin levels, ameliorates insulin resistance and significantly increases the insulin sensitive index.[24] *Shan Yao* (Rhizoma

Nourish™

Dioscoreae) also has an antidiabetic effect to lower blood glucose levels. It controls the normally sharp increase of blood glucose following intraperitoneal injection of glucose.[25] The extract of *Shan Zhu Yu* (Fructus Corni) has been shown to promote the proliferation of islets and increase postprandial secretion of insulin to accelerate glucose transport in subjects with non-insulin-dependent diabetes mellitus.[26] Lastly, *Zhi Mu* (Rhizoma Anemarrhenae) exerts antidiabetic and hypoglycemic effects to lower blood glucose levels through increased insulin secretion and decreased insulin resistance.[27,28] Clinically, herbs in this formula have been used successfully to treat adult-onset diabetes,[29,30] and non-insulin dependant diabetes,[31,32] and diabetes with complications.[33]

Finally, ***Nourish*** is also beneficial for many other chronic and consumptive disorders. *Gou Qi Zi* (Fructus Lycii) has demonstrated a protective effect on the skin. The glycoconjugates of *Gou Qi Zi* (Fructus Lycii) show interesting antiapoptotic and antioxidant properties to promote the survival of human dermal fibroblasts.[34] The herbs in this formula are beneficial in geriatric patients to treat various complaints of dryness, such as a dry mouth, dry nose, and constipation.[35] Spontaneous perspiration also responds well to the herbs in this formula.[36] Finally, this formula may be used to treat frequent urination associated with declining bladder functions.[37]

In summary, ***Nourish*** is an excellent formula to revive and restore the normal functions of eyes, ears, skin, liver, kidneys, bladder, pancreas, and other internal organs and endocrine glands.

COMPARATIVE ANALYSIS

As life expectancy continues to increase, women are expected to spend more and more of their life in post-menopausal years. Therefore, it is becoming increasingly important to ensure a smooth transition during the menopausal years. Western medicine used to consider hormone replacement therapy (HRT) as the standard treatment for menopause and its related conditions. However, there is no longer a consensus as to when or how to use these drugs. While these drugs may alleviate hot flashes, they significantly increase risk of breast cancer, ovarian cancer, uterine cancer, and have a number of significant side effects. For most physicians and patients, the risks are simply far greater than the potential benefits. The bottom line is – synthetic hormone can never replace endogenous hormone. Therefore, no matter when or how they are prescribed, the potential for adverse reactions is always present.

TCM offers a gentle yet effective way to address menopause and its related conditions. Chinese herbs have demonstrated via numerous *in vivo* and *in vitro* studies to have a marked effect to alleviate hot flashes, vasomotor instability, loss of bone mass, and other conditions associated with menopause. Most importantly, they are much gentler and safer on the body. In conclusion, menopause is simply a transition in the journey of life. It is not a disease, and therefore, should not be treated with synthetic drugs that pose significantly higher risks of cancer and other side effects. Herbs should be considered the primary option, and not the secondary alternative, as they are safe and natural, and more than sufficient to address almost all cases of menopause.

References

1. Park MK, Kwon HY, Ahn WS, Bae S, Rhyu MR, Lee Y. Estrogen activities and the cellular effects of natural progesterone from wild yam extract in mcf-7 human breast cancer cells. Am J Chin Med. 2009;37(1):159-67.
2. Wu WH, Liu LY, Chung CJ, Jou HJ, Wang TA. Estrogenic effect of yam ingestion in healthy postmenopausal women. J Am Coll Nutr. 2005 Aug;24(4):235-43.
3. *Zhong Xi Yi Jie He Za Zhi* (Journal of Integrated Chinese and Western Medicine) 1986;6:336.
4. *Shi Zhen Guo Yao Yan Jiu* (Research of Shizhen Herbs) 1998;1:11.
5. *Xin Zhong Yi* (New Chinese Medicine), 1988; 2:20.
6. *Si Chuan Zhong Yi* (Sichuan Chinese Medicine) 1995;5:30.
7. *Hu Bei Zhong Yi Za Zhi* (Hubei Journal of Chinese Medicine) 1996;2:24.
8. *Guang Xi Zhong Yi Yao* (Guangxi Chinese Medicine and Herbology) 1996;2:43.
9. *Cheng Du Zhong Yi Xue Yuan Xue Bao* (Journal of Chengdu University of Traditional Chinese Medicine) 1993;1:20.
10. Cheng C.Y., Chung W.Y., Szeto Y.T. & Benzie I.F. Fasting plasma zeaxanthin response to *Fructus barbarum* L. (wolfberry; Kei Tze) in a food-based human supplementation trial. *Br J Nutr.* 2005, 93(1): 123-130.
11. Yu HH, Hur JM, Seo SJ, Moon HD, Kim HJ, Park RK, You YO. Protective effect of ursolic acid from Cornus officinalis on the hydrogen peroxide-induced damage of HEI-OC1 auditory cells. Department of Food and Nutrition, Kunsan National University, Kunsan, South Korea. Am J Chin Med. 2009;37(4):735-46.
12. *An Hui Zhong Yi Xue Yuan Xue Bao* (Journal of Anhui University School of Medicine) 1989;4:18.
13. *Zhong Yi Fang Ji Xian Dai Yan Jiu* (Modern Study of Medical Formulae in Traditional Chinese Medicine) 1997;710.
14. *Zhe Jiang Zhong Yi Za Zhi* (Zhejiang Journal of Chinese Medicine) 1988;6:244.
15. *Shi Yong Zhong Yi Nei Ke Za Zhi* (Journal of Practical Chinese Internal Medicine) 1993;3:142.
16. *Shi Yong Zhong Yi Za Zhi* (Journal of Practical Chinese Medicine) 1995;6:10.
17. Ha KT, Yoon SJ, Choi DY, Kim DW, Kim JK, Kim CH. Protective effect of Lycium chinense fruit on carbon tetrachloride-induced hepatotoxicity. J Ethnopharmacol. 2005 Jan 15;96(3):529-35.
18. Zhang R, Kang KA, Piao MJ, Kim KC, Kim AD, Chae S, Park JS, Youn UJ, Hyun JW. Cytoprotective effect of the fruits of Lycium chinense Miller against oxidative stress-induced hepatotoxicity. J Ethnopharmacol. 2010 Jul 20;130(2):299-306.
19. Hong X, Tang H, Wu L, Li L. Protective effects of the Alisma orientalis extract on the experimental nonalcoholic fatty liver disease. Institute of Chinese Herb Medicine, College of Pharmaceutical Sciences, Zhejiang University, Hangzhou, Zhejiang, 310031, PRC. J Pharm Pharmacol. 2006 Oct;58(10):1391-8.
20. Hsiang CY, Wu SL, Cheng SE, Ho TY. Acetaldehyde-induced interleukin-1beta and tumor necrosis factor-alpha production is inhibited by berberine through nuclear factor-kappaB signaling pathway in HepG2 cells. Graduate Institute of Medical Science, China Medical University, Taichung 404, Taiwan. J Biomed Sci. 2005 Oct;12(5):791-801.
21. *Zhong Guo Yao Ke Da Xue Xue Bao* (Journal of University of Chinese Herbology) 1989;6:951.
22. *Nei Meng Gu Zhong Yi Yao* (Traditional Chinese Medicine and Medicinals of Inner Mongolia) 1998;1:4.
23. Li TH, Hou CC, Chang CL, Yang WC. Anti-Hyperglycemic Properties of Crude Extract and Triterpenes from Poria cocos. Evid Based Complement Alternat Med. 2011;2011. pii: 128402.

Nourish ™

24. Zhao R, Li Q, Xiao B. Effect of Lycium barbarum polysaccharide on the improvement of insulin resistance in NIDDM rats. Yakugaku Zasshi. 2005 Dec;125(12):981-8.
25. *Zhong Guo Yao Ke Da Xue Xue Bao* (Journal of University of Chinese Herbology), 1991; 22(3):158.
26. Qian DS, Zhu YF, Zhu Q. Effect of alcohol extract of Cornus officinalis Sieb. et Zucc on GLUT4 expression in skeletal muscle in type 2 (non-insulin-dependent) diabetic mellitus rats. Department of Pharmacology, Nantong Medical College, Nantong, 226001 Jiangsu, China. Zhongguo Zhong Yao Za Zhi. 2001 Dec;26(12):859-62.
27. Hoa NK, Phan DV, Thuan ND, Ostenson CG. Insulin secretion is stimulated by ethanol extract of Anemarrhena asphodeloides in isolated islet of healthy Wistar and diabetic Goto-Kakizaki Rats. Department of Pharmacology, Hanoi Medical University, Hanoi, Vietnam. Exp Clin Endocrinol Diabetes. 2004 Oct;112(9):520-5.
28. Miura T, Ichiki H, Iwamoto N, Kato M, Kubo M, Sasaki H, Okada M, Ishida T, Seino Y, Tanigawa K. Antidiabetic activity of the rhizoma of Anemarrhena asphodeloides and active components, mangiferin and its glucoside. Department of Clinical Nutrition, Suzuka University of Medical Science, Mie, Japan. Biol Pharm Bull. 2001 Sep;24(9):1009-11.
29. *Yun Nan Yi Yao* (Yunan Medicine and Herbology) 1983;3:181.
30. *Hu Nan Zhong Yi Za Zhi* (Hunan Journal of Chinese Medicine) 1997;6:7.
31. *He Bei Zhong Yi* (Hebei Chinese Medicine) 1999;11:35.
32. *Hu Bei Zhong Yi Za Zhi* (Hubei Journal of Chinese Medicine) 1992;2:20.
33. *Shang Hai Zhong Yi Yao Za Zhi* (Shanghai Journal of Chinese Medicine and Herbology) 1991;10:23.
34. Zhao H, Alexeev A, Chang E, Greenburg G, Bojanowski K. Lycium barbarum glycoconjugates: effect on human skin and cultured dermal fibroblasts. Phytomedicine. 2005 Jan;12(1-2):131-7.
35. *Ji Lin Zhong Yi Yao* (Jilin Chinese Medicine and Herbology) 1993;3:24.
36. *Xin Zhong Yi* (New Chinese Medicine) 1999;11:44.
37. *Shang Hai Zhong Yi Yao Za Zhi* (Shanghai Journal of Chinese Medicine and Herbology) 1998;6:31.

FORMULAS

Nourish (Fluids)™

CLINICAL APPLICATIONS

- **Thirst and dryness** due to Lung and Stomach yin deficiencies
- **Chronic consumptive disorders** with dryness and body fluids deficiency
- **Lung disorders** with chronic consumptive characteristics: post-infective cough, chronic bronchitis, laryngitis, bronchiectasis, tuberculosis, non-specific pneumonia, and smoking-related complications
- **Stomach disorders** with chronic consumptive characteristics: oral lesions, thirst, dryness of the mouth, nausea, vomiting, stomach and duodenal ulcers, gastritis, constipation and dry stools
- **Cancer:** dryness and thirst associated with chemotherapy and radiation
- **Antibiotic-related side effects,** such as dryness, thirst, and weakness
- **Sjögren's syndrome** with dry eyes and mouth

WESTERN THERAPEUTIC ACTIONS

- General tonic effect to improve overall health
- Antitussive and expectorant effect to benefit the respiratory tract
- Antiulcer effect to benefit the gastrointestinal tract
- General hepatoprotective and detoxification effects
- Regulatory effect on the endocrine system to balance hormones

CHINESE THERAPEUTIC ACTIONS

- Nourishes Lung and Stomach yin
- Replenishes body fluids
- Harmonizes the middle *jiao*

DOSAGE

Take 3 to 4 capsules three times daily. For maximum effect, take the herbs on an empty stomach with one tall glass of warm water and honey.

INGREDIENTS

Bai He (Bulbus Lilii)
Bei Sha Shen (Radix Glehniae)
Da Zao (Fructus Jujubae)
Geng Mi (Semen Oryzae)
Mai Dong (Radix Ophiopogonis)
Nan Sha Shen (Radix Adenophorae)
Tian Dong (Radix Asparagi)
Xi Yang Shen (Radix Panacis Quinquefolii)
Zhi Gan Cao (Radix et Rhizoma Glycyrrhizae Praeparata cum Melle)

BACKGROUND

Chronic or consumptive disorders are often characterized by weakness, dryness, and lack of elasticity of the tissues. These chronic or consumptive disorders affect various parts of the body, including muscles and internal organs. As a result, the tissues lose their elasticity and become weak and dry. From traditional Chinese medicine perspective, these types of chronic or consumptive disorders are diagnosed as "dryness" with "body fluids deficiency."

FORMULA EXPLANATION

Nourish (Fluids) is designed to treat various disorders due to dryness and body fluid deficiencies. Such deficiencies often occur as a result of over-work, over-exhaustion, chronic illness, dietary imbalances and chronic exposure to environmental toxins. The purpose of this formula is to strengthen the body, moisten dryness, replenish body fluids, and restore the body to its optimal health.

Mai Dong (Radix Ophiopogonis) and *Tian Dong* (Radix Asparagi) are the chief herbs that enter the Lung and the Stomach to quickly replenish yin, relieve thirst and moisten dryness. *Bei Sha Shen* (Radix Glehniae), *Nan Sha Shen* (Radix Adenophorae) and *Bai He* (Bulbus Lilii) assist the chief herbs to nourish the yin and replenish the body fluids to relieve dryness. *Xi Yang Shen* (Radix Panacis Quinquefolii) nourishes both yin and qi to relieve fatigue or weakness that may be associated with yin deficiency. It is also slightly cool in property to clear the deficiency heat symptoms associated with yin deficiency. *Geng Mi* (Semen Oryzae), *Da Zao* (Fructus Jujubae), and *Zhi Gan Cao* (Radix et Rhizoma Glycyrrhizae Praeparata cum Melle) harmonize the formula and tonify the middle *jiao.*

In summary, this is an excellent formula to moisten dryness and replenish body fluids. It is most beneficial in individuals who have chronic consumptive disorders, or ones with such deficiencies caused by overwork or exhaustion.

CAUTIONS & CONTRAINDICATIONS

- This formula is contraindicated in cases of excess heat or dampness.

CLINICAL NOTES

- In addition to the clinical applications listed above, this is also an excellent formula to use in diseases characterized by yin and/or body fluid deficiency, such as bronchitis, bronchial asthma, pneumonia, laryngopharyngitis, hoarse voice, whooping cough, tuberculosis, diabetes mellitus, hypertension, and arteriosclerosis.
- However, this formula should not be taken by itself when there is an active infection or inflammation. Another formula is needed to treat infection and/or inflammation.

Pulse Diagnosis by Dr. Jimmy Wei-Yen Chang:

- **Dryness:** floating pulse, a pulse which can only be detected at the superficial (top) level with minimal pressure.

SUPPLEMENTARY FORMULAS

- For chronic respiratory disorder, add ***Respitrol (Deficient).***
- For stomach or duodenal ulcer, add ***GI Care.***
- For chronic constipation or constipation due to dryness, add ***Gentle Lax (Deficient).***
- For diabetes, add ***Equilibrium.***

Nourish (Fluids)™

- For hepatitis, add ***Liver DTX***.
- For hair loss, add ***Polygonum 14***.
- For nausea, vomiting and fatigue after chemotherapy and radiation therapy, add ***C/R Support***.
- For terminal stage cancer, add ***CA Support***.
- For qi, blood, yin and yang deficiencies, add ***Imperial Tonic***.
- For cough, add ***Respitrol (CF)***.
- For excess fire or fever, add ***Gardenia Complex***.
- For Sjögren's syndrome with swollen glands, add ***Herbal ENT*** and ***Resolve (AI)***.
- For menopause with yin-deficient heat, add ***Balance (Heat)***.
- For Kidney yin deficiency, add ***Nourish*** or ***Kidney Tonic (Yin)***.
- For vaginal dryness, add ***Balance Spring***.

ACUPUNCTURE TREATMENT

Traditional Points:

- *Fuliu* (KI 7), *Taixi* (KI 3), *Chize* (LU 5)
- *Feishu* (BL 13), *Pishu* (BL 20), *Lianquan* (CV 23)

Classic Master Tung's Points:

- **Bronchiectasis:** *Dajian* (T 11.01), *Xiaojian* (T 11.02), *Linggu* (T 22.05), *Dabai* (T 22.04), *Sanzhong* (T 77.07), *Chongzi* (T 22.01), *Chongxian* (T 22.02), *Feiqiyi* (T 44.25)*, *Feiqier* (T 44.26)*
- **Laryngitis:** *Linggu* (T 22.05), *Dabai* (T 22.04), *Chongzi* (T 22.01), *Chongxian* (T 22.02), *Yizhong* (T 77.05), *Erzhong* (T 77.06), *Sanzhong* (T 77.07), *Shiyin* (T 88.32), *Fenjin* (T 44.01), *Waisanguan* (T 77.27), *Zuqianjin* (T 77.24), *Zuwujin* (T 77.25). Bleed dark veins nearby *Quling* (T 33.16), *Shaoshang* (LU 11), *Cesanli* (T 77.22), *Cexiasanli* (T 77.23) and the throat. Bleed before needling for best result.
- **Tuberculosis:** *Feiqier* (T 44.26)*, *Linggu* (T 22.05), *Shuijin* (T 1010.20), *Shuitong* (T 1010.19), *Simashang* (T 88.18), *Simazhong* (T 88.17), *Simaxia* (T 88.19), *Sihuashang* (T 77.08), *Sihuazhong* (T 77.09), *Sihuaxia* (T 77.11). Bleed the HT and LU area in the back. Bleed before needling for best result.
- **Nausea:** *Tushui* (T 22.11), *Xinling* (T 33.17)*, *Sihuashang* (T 77.08), *Menjin* (T 66.05), *Linggu* (T 22.05), *Xinmen* (T 33.12), *Tianhuangfu [Shenguan]* (T 77.18)
- **Vomiting:** *Tushui* (T 22.11), *Xinling* (T 33.17)*, *Sihuashang* (T 77.08), *Menjin* (T 66.05), *Linggu* (T 22.05), *Xinmen* (T 33.12). Bleed near *Yamen* (GV 15). Bleed before needling for best result.
- **Duodenal ulcer:** *Linggu* (T 22.05), *Dabai* (T 22.04), *Tushui* (T 22.11), *Tongwei* (T 88.10), *Tongshen* (T 88.09), *Sihuashang* (T 77.08), *Shuitong* (T 1010.19), *Shuijin* (T 1010.20), *Xinmen* (T 33.12), *Changmen* (T 33.10), *Ganmen* (T 33.11). Bleed dark veins nearby the ST channel on the lower limb. Bleed before needling for best result.

Master Tung's Points by Dr. Chuan-Min Wang:

- **Chronic consumptive disorders, Stomach and Lung yin deficiency:** *Tongshen* (T 88.09), *Tongwei* (T 88.10), *Tongbei* (T 88.11), *Tianhuangfu [shenguan]* (T 77.18)

Balance Method by Dr. Richard Tan:

- Left side: *Linggu* (T 22.05), *Hegu* (LI 4), *Rangu* (KI 2), *Dazhong* (KI 4), *Fuliu* (KI 7)
- Right side: *Neiguan* (PC 6), *Zusanli* (ST 36), *Feiyang* (BL 58)
- Alternate sides in between treatments.

Auricular Medicine by Dr. Li-Chun Huang:

- **Hoarseness:** Glottis, Larynx, Mouth, Trachea, Spleen, Lung, *San Jiao*, Endocrine

NUTRITION

- Increase intake of foods that nourish yin and moisten dryness, such as Mexican yam, yam, radishes, potatoes, carrots, melons, cucumbers, beets, turnips, malanga, celeriac, taro, rutabaga, and millet.
- Decrease intake of warm and hot natured foods that damage qi and yin, such as:
  - certain fruits like mango and durian that produce heat.
  - stimulants like coffee, alcohol, and energy drinks.
  - spicy/pungent/aromatic vegetables such as pepper, garlic, onions, basil, rosemary, cumin, funnel, anise, leeks, chives, scallions, thyme, saffron, wormwood, mustard, chili pepper, and wasabi.
- Avoid food and drinks with artificial coloring.
- Consume as few meat products as possible. Do not eat processed meats, such as lunch meats, hot dogs and sausages, as they contain nitrites that are associated with inflammation and chronic disease.

The Tao of Nutrition by Dr. Maoshing Ni and Cathy McNease:

- **Thirst:** Drink bok choy and cucumber juice.
- **Thirst, irritability, and sore throat:** Drink fresh, raw watercress juice.
- **Yin and blood deficiencies:** Eat steamed chicken eggs.
- **Clear heat:** Eat lightly steamed broccoli.

LIFESTYLE INSTRUCTIONS

- Patients with chronic consumptive diseases (such as cancer and chronic disorders of lung or stomach) should receive concurrent treatments to eliminate the cause and replenish the fluids.
- Engage in regular exercise.
- Avoid stress whenever possible.

CASE STUDIES

- M.M., a 65-year-old male, presented with chronic dry cough. Symptoms of thirst, dryness, constipation, and poor appetite were also present. The patient had a tendency to overwork himself as a massage therapist with long hours. The patient had been treated with various medications including Concerta (methylphenidate) for attention deficit disorder (ADD) and BuSpar (buspirone) for depression. The practitioner diagnosed the condition as Kidney

Nourish (Fluids)™

yin deficiency and Liver blood deficiency. His Western diagnosis was ADD and bronchitis. The patient was given ***Nourish (Fluids)*** to nourish the yin. With the ***Nourish (Fluids)*** the patient experienced great results, including improvement in digestion and breathing. Additional areas that improved were gum health, urinary stream, and mental focus. The patient was very happy with the results of the formula. Submitted by K.F., Honolulu, Hawaii.

- C.R., a 56-year-old female, presented with hot flashes. Additional symptoms included difficulty sleeping, dry mouth, anxiety and depression. It was noted that her palpitations and sweating were constant. The practitioner diagnosed this condition as Kidney yin-deficient heat. ***Nourish (Fluids)***, ***Kidney Tonic (Yin)***, and ***Balance (Heat)*** were prescribed. As a result of taking the ***Kidney Tonic (Yin)*** with ***Balance (Heat)***, she noticed less heat sensation, decrease in both anxiety and sleep difficulty, but still sweating slightly. Afterwards, taking ***Kidney Tonic (Yin)*** with ***Nourish (Fluids)***, the patient was no longer experiencing the dry mouth and thirst. Submitted by J.C., Rosemead, California.
- J.N., a 59-year-old female, presented with a chronic, dry hacking cough. Additional symptoms included shortness of breath, dry hair and nails. Blood pressure was 120/80 mmHg and heart rate was 78 beats per minute. The practitioner diagnosed this condition as Lung and Kidney qi and yin deficiencies. ***Respitrol (Deficient)*** and ***Nourish (Fluids)*** were prescribed. As a result of taking the herbs, the cough became looser and not as painful. She was also able to cough a little sputum up and improvement of her hair and nails was also seen. Submitted by J.M., Breckenridge, Colorado.

PHARMACOLOGICAL AND CLINICAL RESEARCH

Nourish (Fluids) is a unique formula as it is composed of herbs that have general protective and restorative effects on various systems in the body. Herbs in this formula are very beneficial in individuals who are recovering from chronic consumptive disorders, or diseases characterized by dryness and deficiency of body fluids. Clinically, this is an excellent formula to treat chronic and consumptive illnesses characterized by compromised functions of the respiratory, gastrointestinal, hepatic, and endocrine systems.

Nourish (Fluids) contains many herbs with marked influences on the respiratory system. For example, *Bai He* (Bulbus Lilii) and *Zhi Gan Cao* (Radix et Rhizoma Glycyrrhizae Praeparata cum Melle) both have marked antitussive and expectorant effects.[1] Clinically, these herbs have shown beneficial effects to treat chronic consumptive lung diseases, such as chronic bronchitis, bronchiectasis, tuberculosis, non-specific pneumonia, pulmonary tuberculosis, and complications of smoking.[2]

Nourish (Fluids) has many herbs that influence and improve the overall gastrointestinal functions. Individuals with chronic illnesses often have dysfunction of the gastrointestinal system, where nutrients from foods cannot be properly digested and absorbed. For example, *Zhi Gan Cao* (Radix et Rhizoma Glycyrrhizae Praeparata cum Melle) has a marked effect on the gastrointestinal tract to prevent and treat peptic ulcers, with mechanisms such as inhibition of gastric acid secretion, binding and deactivation of gastric acid, and promotion of recovery from ulceration.[3] Clinically, many herbs in this formula may be used to treat gastrointestinal disorders, such as *Bai He* (Bulbus Lilii) for treatment of atrophic gastritis,[4] and *Zhi Gan Cao* (Radix et Rhizoma Glycyrrhizae Praeparata cum Melle) for treatment of peptic ulcer and intestinal spasms.[5,6]

Individuals with chronic liver disorders often have underlying weakness and deficiency of the hepatic system. ***Nourish (Fluids)*** utilizes herbs with hepatoprotective effects specifically to address such disorders. For example, the use of *Zhi Gan Cao* (Radix et Rhizoma Glycyrrhizae Praeparata cum Melle) is associated with an increased amount of cytochrome p450 in the liver, which is responsible for the protective effect of the herb on the liver against chemicals or tetrachloride-induced liver damage and liver cancer.[7] In addition, use of glycyrrhizin, an active component in *Zhi Gan Cao* (Radix et Rhizoma Glycyrrhizae Praeparata cum Melle), is associated with a 77% rate of effectiveness in treating 30 patients with hepatitis B. The mechanism of this effect has been attributed to the action of the herb to reduce the damage to and death of liver cells, decrease inflammatory reaction, promote regeneration of liver cells, and lower the risk of liver cirrhosis and necrosis.[8]

Chronic and consumptive disorders are often related in part to the dysfunction of the endocrine system and the related glands. According to one study, 8 out of 9 patients with declining pituitary function were treated successfully by taking an herbal combination that contains *Zhi Gan Cao* (Radix et Rhizoma Glycyrrhizae Praeparata cum Melle) as the main ingredient for two to three months.[9] Specifically, *Zhi Gan Cao* (Radix et Rhizoma Glycyrrhizae Praeparata cum Melle) has been shown to have a potent effect to stimulate the production of the adrenocortical hormones, such as glucocorticoids and mineralocorticoids. Administration of glycyrrhizin and glycyrrhetinic, two ingredients of *Gan Cao* (Radix et Rhizoma Glycyrrhizae), clearly prolonged the therapeutic effect of cortisone as demonstrated by various laboratory studies. The same components also increase the mineralocorticoid effect to balance the water and electrolyte levels in the body.[10]

Nourish (Fluids) contains herbs with general effects that improve the overall health and facilitate recovery from chronic illnesses. For example, use of *Zhi Gan Cao* (Radix et Rhizoma Glycyrrhizae Praeparata cum Melle) is associated with effects to increase body weight, muscle strength, and physical endurance.[11] *Xi Yang Shen* (Radix Panacis Quinquefolii) and *Bai He* (Bulbus Lilii) have an adaptogenic effect that improves both mental and physical health and performance.[12,13] Lastly, use of *Mai Dong* (Radix Ophiopogonis) daily in 100 geriatric patients is associated with a significant improvement in their overall health.[14]

Nourish (Fluids)™

Nourish (Fluids) incorporates many herbs that are beneficial for patients with cancer. Cancer is often diagnosed in traditional Chinese medicine as an excess condition (heat, phlegm, and toxins) that consume yin and body fluids. Furthermore, cancer treatments, such as chemotherapy and radiation, further damage the body and cause more weakness and deficiency. To address these conditions, this formula uses herbs to support patients with cancer and alleviate general side effects associated with chemotherapy and radiation. For example, *Tian Dong* (Radix Asparagi) has been shown to be very effective in supporting/treating 42 patients with breast cancer and malignant lymphoma.[15,16] Furthermore, according to one clinical study, use of *Xi Yang Shen* (Radix Panacis Quinquefolii) is associated with a significant reduction of side effects related to chemotherapy and radiation, such as dry mouth, nausea, and vomiting.[17]

In summary, ***Nourish (Fluids)*** is an excellent adjunct formula for treatment of chronic and consumptive illnesses characterized by compromised functions of the respiratory, gastrointestinal, hepatic, and endocrine systems.

COMPARATIVE ANALYSIS

One striking difference between Western and traditional Chinese medicine is that Western medicine focuses and excels in crisis management, while traditional Chinese medicine emphasizes and shines in holistic and preventative treatments. Therefore, in emergencies, such as gunshot wounds or surgery, Western medicine is generally the treatment of choice. However, for treatment of chronic idiopathic illness of unknown origins, where all lab tests are normal and a clear diagnosis cannot be made, traditional Chinese medicine is distinctly superior.

The general condition of "dryness and body fluids deficiencies" may be present in many different scenarios, such as in cases of chronic consumptive disorders, chronic lung and stomach disorders, and individuals who received antibiotic, chemotherapy, and radiation treatments. All these conditions are characterized by symptoms such as thirst, dryness, and the general presence of lack of body fluids and insufficient hydration of body tissues. These are non-specific and non-diagnostic signs and symptoms. Therefore, Western medicine struggles to identify a diagnosis and treatment. On the other hand, these are obvious presentations of "dryness and body fluid deficiencies" in traditional Chinese medicine. The use of herbs that nourish yin and promote generation of body fluids is extremely beneficial to correct these imbalances and restore normal health and body functions. From a prognostic perspective, use of this formula facilitates and shortens the course of recovery from many chronic and consumptive diseases.

References

1. *Pharmacology and Applications of Chinese Herbs*, 1983; 264.
2. *Jiang Xi Yi Yao* (Jiangxi Medicine and Herbology), 1965; 1:562.
3. *Zhong Yao Zhi* (Chinese Herbology Journal), 1993; 358.
4. *Liao Ning Zhong Yi Za Zhi* (Liaoning Journal of Chinese Medicine), 1988; 4:18.
5. *Zhong Hua Nei Ke Xue Za Zhi* (Journal of Chinese Internal Medicine), 1960; 3:226.
6. *Zhong Hua Nei Ke Za Zhi* (Chinese Journal of Internal Medicine), 1960; 4:354.
7. *Zhong Yao Tong Bao* (Journal of Chinese Herbology), 1986; 11(10):55.
8. *Zhong Yao Tong Bao* (Journal of Chinese Herbology), 1987; 9:60.
9. *Zhong Hua Yi Xue Za Zhi* (Chinese Journal of Medicine), 1975; 10:718.
10. *Zhong Yao Zhi* (Chinese Herbology Journal), 1993; 358.
11. *Guo Wai Yi Xue Zhong Yi Zhong Yao Fen Ce* (Monograph of Chinese Herbology from Foreign Medicine), 1985; 7(4):48.
12. *Zhong Yao Xue* (Chinese Herbology), 1998; 737:738.
13. *Zhong Yao Cai* (Study of Chinese Herbal Material), 1990; 13(6):31.
14. *Zhong Guo Zhong Yao Za Zhi* (People's Republic of China Journal of Chinese Herbology), 1992; 17(1):21.
15. *Jiang Su Yi Yao* (Jiangsu Journal of Medicine and Herbology), 1976; 4:33.
16. *Xin Yi Xue* (New Medicine), 1975; 4:193.
17. *Shang Hai Zhong Yi Yao Za Zhi* (Shanghai Journal of Chinese Medicine and Herbology), 1979; 4:29.

Osteo 8 ™

CLINICAL APPLICATIONS

- **Osteoporosis** with decreased bone strength, mass, and density
- Individuals with risk factors of osteoporosis, such as menopause, old age, and use of tobacco, alcohol, and drugs
- Maintenance for healthy and strong bones
- Soreness, weakness and pain in the bones, lower back and knees
- Inability to stand for a prolonged period of time
- Pain or soreness that is aggravated by weight-bearing activities
- **Recovery from bone fracture and broken bones**

WESTERN THERAPEUTIC ACTIONS

- Osteogenic effect to stimulate osteoblast proliferation and differentiation
- Osteoprotective effect to prevent and treat osteoporosis
- Increases absorption and utilization of calcium
- Increases bone mass and density
- Angiogenic effect to stimulate blood vessel formation, invigorate blood circulation, facilitate wound healing, enhance tissue regeneration, and facilitate healing of bone fractures

CHINESE THERAPEUTIC ACTIONS

- Replenishes Kidney *jing* (essence)
- Tonifies Kidney yang and yin
- Tonifies qi and blood

DOSAGE

Take 3 to 4 capsules three times daily on an empty stomach with warm water. For prevention in patients with higher risk of osteoporosis, take 2 capsules daily.

INGREDIENTS

Dang Gui (Radix Angelicae Sinensis)
E Jiao (Colla Corii Asini)
Gou Qi Zi (Fructus Lycii)
Gu Sui Bu (Rhizoma Drynariae)
Gui Ban (Plastrum Testudinis)
Lu Jiao (Cornu Cervi)
Ren Shen (Radix et Rhizoma Ginseng)
Xu Duan (Radix Dipsaci)

BACKGROUND

Osteoporosis is a disorder characterized by a reduction of bone mass density, leading to fractures after minimal trauma.[1] Osteoporosis is becoming one of the more common disorders as the population continues to age and life expectancies continue to increase. Osteoporosis occurs mostly in individuals between 51 to 75 years of age, and is six times more common in women than men.[2] There are numerous risk factors, including but not limited to aging, dietary habits, lifestyles, and family history. Chronic use of drugs also increases the risk of osteoporosis, with such examples as thyroid supplements, corticosteroids, ethanol, tobacco, and heparin. Therefore, optimal prevention and treatment of osteoporosis require modification to diet and exercise, and use of herbal medicine.

FORMULA EXPLANATION

Osteo 8 is a well-balanced formula designed for women and men of all ages who want to maintain healthy bones. It contains herbs that tonify qi, blood, yin and yang. The main function of the formula is to replenish the vital *jing* (essence) of the Kidney to strengthen bones, increase bone density, and promote healing.

Most herbs in ***Osteo 8*** enter the Kidney to revitalize the body and replenish *jing* (essence). Osteoporosis or weakness of sinews and bones are the result of Kidney and Liver deficiencies. According to traditional Chinese medicine, the Kidney stores the *jing* (essence) that is vital for strong bones, and the Liver stores blood and controls the sinews and tendons. If the Liver and Kidney are deficient, bone, sinews and joints become weak. Therefore, treatment of bone disorders requires tonification of the Liver and Kidney.

Lu Jiao (Cornu Cervi), one of the most effective and precious herbs, is the principle herb in ***Osteo 8***. It tonifies Kidney yang, replenishes Kidney *jing* (essence), nourishes blood and strengthens sinews and bones. *Gu Sui Bu* (Rhizoma Drynariae) and *Xu Duan* (Radix Dipsaci) are two herbs that tonify Kidney yang. *Gu Sui Bu* (Rhizoma Drynariae) and *Xu Duan* (Radix Dipsaci) strengthen the bones and are often used together to promote mending of bones and relieve soreness, weakness and pain of the bones. They are the best pair used to heal fractured bones and other injuries such as contusions, sprains, and ligament injuries due to trauma.

Gui Ban (Plastrum Testudinis), *Gou Qi Zi* (Fructus Lycii) and *E Jiao* (Colla Corii Asini) are used to tonify the Kidney yin and *jing* (essence). *Gui Ban* (Plastrum Testudinis) nourishes Kidney yin and strengthens the bones by filling the marrow with *jing* (essence). *Gou Qi Zi* (Fructus Lycii) tonifies the Liver and the Kidney yin to treat secondary symptoms such as dizziness, dryness, blurred vision, tinnitus, thirst, and night sweats. Neutral in property, it has a unique function to effectively nourish the different parts of the body without creating any stagnation. *E Jiao* (Colla Corii Asini), one of the essential herbs used in most antiaging formulas, tonifies blood and nourishes yin. Together, these three herbs replenish Kidney yin and *jing* (essence) to maintain healthy bones and treat weakness and soreness of the back, hips and knees.

Finally, to enhance the overall wellness of the body, *Ren Shen* (Radix et Rhizoma Ginseng) and *Dang Gui* (Radix Angelicae Sinensis) are added to tonify qi and blood.

CAUTIONS & CONTRAINDICATIONS

- This formula should be used with caution in patients with an excess condition or heat accumulation.
- This formula should be used with caution in patients with damp-heat in the lower *jiao*.

Osteo 8™

- This herbal formula contains herbs that invigorate blood circulation, such as *Dang Gui* (Radix Angelicae Sinensis). Therefore, patients who are on anticoagulant or antiplatelet therapies, such as Coumadin (warfarin), should use this formula with caution, or not at all, as there may be a higher risk of bleeding and bruising.[3,4,5]
- The safety status of using *Dang Gui* (Radix Angelicae Sinensis) in individuals with hormone-dependent cancer is unclear.[6,7,8] According to one reference, use of *Dang Gui* (Radix Angelicae Sinensis) is not associated with thickening of the endometrium or vaginal cell maturation, both of which would indicate an estrogenic effect. Furthermore, there is no confirmation of the presence of a phytoestrogen component or affect on hormone-dependent cancer, when ferulic acid is evaluated as the main component of *Dang Gui* (Radix Angelicae Sinensis).[9] According to another reference, the water extract of *Dang Gui* (Radix Angelicae Sinensis) has a weak estrogen-agonistic activity to stimulate the growth of breast cancer cells (MCF-7).[10] In summary, due to conflicting and insufficient data, use of *Dang Gui* (Radix Angelicae Sinensis) in patients with hormone-dependent cancer warrants caution pending further study.

CLINICAL NOTES

- Osteoporosis is six times more common in women than in men because a tremendous amount of *jing* (essence) is lost during the process of pregnancy and delivery. Post-menopausal osteoporosis is most common and happens between 51 to 75 years of age. Women who have children may see signs and symptoms of osteoporosis earlier than those who have fewer or no children.
- Men may not experience osteoporosis in the same way as women. Men lose *jing* (essence) with excessive sexual activities, and may show symptoms and signs of Kidney deficiency, such as hair loss, loose teeth, weakness and soreness of the back and knees.
- There are three excellent formulas for post-surgical recovery. ***Flex (TMX)*** should be taken after the surgery for 5 to 10 days to facilitate the immediate healing of wounds. Continue herbal treatment with ***Flex (MLT)*** and ***Osteo 8*** for one month to facilitate healing and recovery of soft tissues and bones, respectively.

SUPPLEMENTARY FORMULAS

- For soreness and pain of the low back and knees, combine with ***Back Support (CR)***.
- For neck and shoulder pain, use with ***Neck & Shoulder (CR)***.
- For arm pain, add ***Arm Support***.
- For bone spurs, add ***Flex (SPR)***.
- For arthritis due to heat with redness, swelling and burning of joints, use with ***Flex (Heat)***.
- For arthritis due to coldness, with pain that worsens during cold and rainy weather, use with ***Flex (CD)***.
- For gout, add ***Flex (GT)***.
- For bone fractures, use with ***Flex (TMX)***.
- For recovery from bone fracture with soft tissue injuries, use with ***Flex (MLT)***.
- For fatigue and overall deficiency, use with ***Imperial Tonic***.
- For menopause with hot flashes and night sweats, use with ***Balance (Heat)***.
- For menopause with dryness or yin deficiency, use with ***Nourish***.
- For vaginal dryness, add ***Balance Spring***.
- For menopause with irritability and insomnia, use with ***Calm***, ***Calm ZZZ***, or ***Calm (ES)***.
- For hair loss or premature gray hair, use with ***Polygonum 14***.
- For blood deficiency, insomnia and excessive dreams, use with ***Schisandra ZZZ***.
- For Kidney yang deficiency, add ***Kidney Tonic (Yang)***.
- For Kidney yin deficiency, add ***Kidney Tonic (Yin)***.
- For visual disturbances, blurriness, redness or pain, combine with ***Lycium Support***.

ACUPUNCTURE TREATMENT

Traditional Points:

- *Mingmen* (GV 4), *Dashu* (BL 11), *Shenshu* (BL 23)
- *Sanyinjiao* (SP 6), *Shenshu* (BL 23), *Guanyuan* (CV 4), *Pishu* (BL 20)

Classic Master Tung's Points:

- *Tianhuang* (T 77.17), *Dihuang* (T 77.19), *Renhuang* (T 77.21), *Tianhuang* (T 88.13), *Minghuang* (T 88.12), *Qihuang* (T 88.14), *Fuke* (T 11.24), *Zhengji* (T 44.24)*

Master Tung's Points by Dr. Chuan-Min Wang:

- **Osteoporosis:** *Linggu* (T 22.05), *Tianhuang* (T 77.17), *Dihuang* (T 77.19), *Renhuang* (T 77.21)
- **Osteoarthritis**
  - Knee: Needle contralaterally *Jianzhong* (T 44.06). Needle ipsilaterally medial knee eye and lateral knee eye.
  - Hip: Needle contralaterally *Jianzhong* (T 44.06), *Naoshu* (SI 10). Needle ipsilaterally *Huantiao* (GB 30).

Balance Method by Dr. Richard Tan:

- Left side: *Shenmai* (BL 62), *Weizhong* (BL 40), *Tongli* (HT 5), *Shaohai* (HT 3)
- Right side: *Taixi* (KI 3), *Yingu* (KI 10), *Houxi* (SI 3), *Xiaohai* (SI 8)
- Left and right sides can be alternated from treatment to treatment.

Auricular Medicine by Dr. Li-Chun Huang:

- **Osteoporosis and cervical vertebral degeneration:** corresponding points (to the area of degeneration), Triangle Area of Cervical Vertebra (back of ear), C6, C7, C3, C4; Large Auricular Nerve.
  - For dizziness, add Dizziness Area.
  - For shoulder pain, add Shoulder Joint.
  - For finger numbness, add Finger, Coronary Subcortex, and Large Auricular Nerve.

FORMULAS

Osteo 8 ™

- For back headache, add Occiput and Lesser Auricular Nerve. Bleed Ear Apex.

NUTRITION

- Consume a sufficient amount of calcium, either from diet or supplements. Make sure the supplement is of good quality so it breaks down and absorbs in the body. Calcium supplementation is most effective if it is combined with vitamin D and other minerals.
- Consumption of foods rich in plant estrogen is also beneficial, such as soybeans and yam.
- Consumption of oxtail, ox neck or bone-based soup with tomato and ginger is highly recommended.

The Tao of Nutrition by Dr. Maoshing Ni and Cathy McNease:

- Make hummus with black beans and goat milk yogurt. Eat as a snack in between meals regularly.

LIFESTYLE INSTRUCTIONS

- Patients are advised stop drinking alcohol, smoking tobacco, and limit sexual activities to prevent loss of *jing* (essence).
- Patients with osteoporosis have higher risk of bone fractures. They should refrain from activities with high risk of injury, such as lifting heavy objects or overexertion from strenuous exercises.
- Walking, *tai chi chuan [tai ji chuan]*, *qi gong*, and other mild exercises are recommended in order to strengthen the bones and joints without increased risk of injury. Weight-bearing exercise is especially effective to improve bone strength.

CASE STUDIES

- A 49-year-old female practitioner of Oriental medicine has family history of osteoporosis in maternal grandmother and mother. While her grandmother did not have any incidence of physical injury leading to bone fracture, her mother had an ankle fracture on the right side, and lost three inches in height. The patient sought treatment for prevention and treatment of osteoporosis. Upon evaluation, the diagnosis was blood deficiency without visible signs of bone loss. The patient started on ***Osteo 8*** at a dosage of 3 to 6 capsules per day. In addition, she also took a supplement of calcium, magnesium, and potassium (2 to 4 capsules per day). She exercised aerobically with weights three times a week. She also lowered her intake of high-fat foods and avoided caffeine. No other changes were made with the lifestyle. Prior to treatment, her baseline bone mass density (BMD) was 0.448 (on 9/19/01). After four month of treatment, her bone mass density (BMD) increased to 0.7 (1/16/02). The patient improved from "low normal" to "low risk" for osteoporosis. The practitioner commented that the "increase in bone density was remarkable." Submitted by C.C., Middletown, Connecticut.
- B.D., a 68-year-old female, wanted a natural alternative to Evista (raloxifene) for osteoporosis prevention. She appeared thin and pale. She had a history of osteoporosis in her mother's side of the family. The TCM diagnosis was Kidney qi, *jing* (essence), yin and yang deficiencies. ***Osteo 8*** was prescribed at 2 capsules a day. She had a bone mass density test done two years ago and it was slightly low, and was therefore placed on Evista (raloxifene). After one year on ***Osteo 8***, the bone density tested normal. She repeated the test one year later and the density tested normal again. Her medical doctor was quite impressed. [Note: This patient had a sensitive stomach. She started with 4 capsules daily but had to be reduced to 2 caps because of gastrointestinal discomfort.] Submitted by M.H., West Palm Beach, Florida.
- C.M., a 48-year-old female, presented with joint pain (hands, feet, knees) that worsened in cold and rainy weather, reporting a family history of arthritis and osteoporosis. She also suffered from tendonitis of both forearms. She had decreased range of motion, with calcification of joints in her fingers. Her Western diagnosis was rheumatoid arthritis; the TCM diagnosis was cold and damp obstruction. ***Osteo 8*** and ***Flex (CD)*** were prescribed at four capsules each, twice daily. Within one day, the symptoms began improving. After one week, joints and tendons were not stiff, and almost pain-free. During the winter (the season in which her condition usually deteriorated), the symptoms even improved. The patient reported later that if she stopped taking the herbs, the symptoms returned. Submitted by C.D., Phoenix, Oregon.

PHARMACOLOGICAL AND CLINICAL RESEARCH

Osteo 8 is an herbal formula specifically for osteoporosis and other bone-related disorders. It contains herbs that increase the utilization of calcium, strengthen the bones, prevent fractures, and promote healing.

Calcium is the most abundant mineral in the bones and the body. Therefore, health of the bones is directly associated with proper intake and absorption of calcium. However, most forms of calcium (i.e., calcium carbonate) are hard to digest, and there are many other factors that impede the absorption, such as caffeine, fat, excess dietary fiber, alcohol, cocoa (chocolate), and excessive amounts of protein. Therefore, efforts must be made to enhance the bioavailability of calcium through proper intake and absorption. *Lu Jiao* (Cornu Cervi) and *Gui Ban* (Plastrum Testudinis) are both rich in numerous minerals, including calcium and magnesium, which are essential for bone health.[11] *Gu Sui Bu* (Rhizoma Drynariae), traditionally used to treat patients with bone fractures, has been shown to increase the absorption of calcium.[12] Furthermore, daily ingestion of *E Jiao* (Colla Corii Asini) is associated with increased absorption and utilization of calcium, as well as elevated levels of calcium in the blood.[13] Thus, ingestion of ***Osteo 8*** will increase the intake, absorption, and utilization of calcium.

Osteo 8 contains many herbs that promote the generation of new bones. *Dang Gui* (Radix Angelicae Sinensis) has a marked effect on osteoblast proliferation and differentiation systems, as

Osteo 8 ™

well as in a fibroblast-secreted hyaluronic acid assay. It enhances the deposition of hyaluronic acid and proliferation of osteoblasts *in vitro*, as well as bone regeneration.[14] Furthermore, *Dang Gui* (Radix Angelicae Sinensis) has been shown to contribute to the formation of bones and treatment of bone injuries. It directly stimulates the proliferation, alkaline phosphatase activity, protein secretion and particularly type I collagen synthesis of human osteoprecursor cells in a dose-dependent manner.[15] *Xu Duan* (Radix Dipsaci), another herb in this formula, shows a potential effect to increase the proliferation and differentiation of the osteoblasts, and it does not affect osteoclast activity. The researchers concluded that these herbs can effectively increase the rate of tissue regeneration of damaged bones.[16] *Gu Sui Bu* (Rhizoma Drynariae) has a marked osteoprotective effect, and has been shown to effectively prevent and treat osteoporosis. According to *in vivo* and *in vitro* studies, the extract of *Gu Sui Bu* (Rhizoma Drynariae) exerts significant activity on both the proliferation of osteoblastic cells and promotion of bone mineral density (BMD).[17,18] In addition, *in vitro* and *in vivo* studies have shown *Gu Sui Bu* (Rhizoma Drynariae) to significantly influence both osteoblast and osteoclast activity to safely and effectively accelerate bone regeneration and enhance bone healing. *Gu Sui Bu* (Rhizoma Drynariae) increased osteoblast numbers, intracellular alkaline phosphatase (ALP) levels and nodule numbers without influencing osteoclast activity.[19] *Gu Sui Bu* (Rhizoma Drynariae) promotes osteoblast maturation by regulating bone differentiation-related gene expression and defending against nitrosative stress-induced apoptotic insults.[20] Clinically, *Gu Sui Bu* (Rhizoma Drynariae) has marked physiological effect to treat many bone-related disorders, including but not limited to postmenopausal osteoporosis,[21] osteoarthritis,[22] and periodontal diseases.[23,24] Another study showed that herbs that strengthen both the bones and the tendons, such as *Gu Sui Bu* (Rhizoma Drynariae), *Gou Qi Zi* (Fructus Lycii) and *Xu Duan* (Radix Dipsaci), have a positive effect in treating osteoporosis, with results better than that of calcium alone. The researchers in this study concluded that the use of herbs that tonify the Kidney is an "optimal method for osteoporotic treatment."[25] Finally, oral administration of polypeptides from *Lu Rong* (Cornu Cervi Pantotrichum) has been shown to reverse osteoporosis and prevent bone loss. The mechanisms of actions are attributed to the promotion of mitosis and the inhibition of interleukin-1 (IL-1) and interleukin-6 (IL-6). The researchers state that *Lu Rong* (Cornu Cervi Pantotrichum) can be a therapeutic agent for the treatment of postmenopausal osteoporosis.[26]

Ren Shen (Radix et Rhizoma Ginseng) and *Dang Gui* (Radix Angelicae Sinensis) are two representative herbs that tonify qi and blood in Chinese herbal medicine. As they improve the "function" and the "substance" aspects of the body, they lead to an increase in overall health and well-being. From a biomedical perspective, these two herbs both have an angiogenic effect to promote blood vessel formation, invigorate blood circulation, facilitate wound healing and enhance tissue regeneration.[27,28,29]

Overall, ***Osteo 8*** contains herbs that are rich in calcium, increase adsorption of calcium into bones, and promote the growth and healing of bones. It is an ideal formula for both the prevention and the treatment of decreased bone density, bone fractures, or other bone-related disorders.

COMPARATIVE ANALYSIS

Osteoporosis is a bone disorder that primarily affects elderly individuals as they gradually lose bone mass density. As a result of osteoporosis, their bones become weak and fragile, and they have a much higher risk of bone fracture from minor injuries. Furthermore, individuals with osteoporosis often require an extended period of time for recovery, which is often complicated by infection.

The drugs of choice for treating osteoporosis are bisphosphonates, a category of drugs that include Fosamax (alendronate), Actonel (risedronate), Didronel (etidronate), Aredia (pamidronate), and Skelid (tiludronate). On average, these drugs may increase bone mass density by 3 to 5% after continuous use for three years. However, they cause numerous side effects, such as stomach irritation, and may increase the risk of cancer (thyroid adenoma and adrenal pheochromocytoma) and fertility impairment (inhibition of ovulation, and testicular and epididymal atrophy). Furthermore, there is evidence that use of these drugs do not decrease the incidence of bone fracture. Though these drugs increase bone mass density, the bones remain brittle and are susceptible to fracture. This is evident as the use of biphosphonates is linked with increased risks of osteonecrosis of the jaw (1 in 952 cases) and subtrochanteric or femoral shaft fractures (274% increased risk).[30,31] In women with menopause, hormone replacement therapy may be used to decrease the loss of bone mass density. These drugs, however, must be prescribed and monitored very carefully, as use of these hormone substances have been shown to significantly increase risk of cancer, such as breast cancer (by 20 to 30%), endometrial cancer (by six to eight fold), and ovarian cancer (by 10 to 20%). Other side effects and adverse reactions of hormone replacement therapy include gallbladder disease, thromboembolitic disease, and photosensitivity.[32] In brief, treatment of osteoporosis requires careful evaluation of risks versus benefits by both practitioners and patients.

Herbs have been used with great success to nourish underlying deficiencies, and prevent and treat osteoporosis. In fact, according to one clinical study, use of herbs that tonifies Kidney *jing* (essence) for one year was associated with an average increase of 3.4% in bone mass density among 28 women in menopause (average age of 48.8 years). Furthermore, few or no side effects were reported throughout the study.

Drugs and herbs are both effective for the prevention and treatment of osteoporosis. However, herbs are safe and natural, and should be considered the treatment of choice. Furthermore,

Osteo 8 ™

patients are encouraged to adopt the dietary and lifestyle recommendations described above to maximize the overall efficacy of their treatment program.

References

1. *Dorland's Illustrated Medical Dictionary 28th Edition*, 1994.
2. Berkow, R et al. *The Merck Manual of Diagnosis and Therapy 16th Edition*, 1992.
3. Chan K, Lo AC, Yeung JH, Woo KS. Journal of Pharmacy and Pharmacology 1995 May;47(5):402-6.
4. Pharmacotherapy 1999 July;19(7):870-876.
5. European Journal of Drug Metabolism and Pharmacokinetics 1995; 20(1): 55-60.
6. Natural Standard (www.naturalstandard.com).
7. National Institutes of Health.
8. U.S National Library of Medicine.
9. American Herbal Pharmacopoeia. *Dang Gui* (Radix Angelicae Sinensis) monograph.
10. Lau CB, Ho TC, Chan TW, Kim SC. Use of dong quai (Angelica sinensis) to treat peri- or postmenopausal symptoms in women with breast cancer: is it appropriate? Menopause 2005 Nov-Dec;12(6):734-40.
11. *Chang Yong Zhong Yao Cheng Fen Yu Yao Li Shou Ce* (A Handbook of the Composition and Pharmacology of Common Chinese Drugs), 1994.
12. *Zhong Yao Xue* (Chinese Herbology), 1998; 802:803.
13. *Chin J Physiol*, 1935; 9(4):383.
14. Zhao H, Alexeev A, Sharma V, Guzman LD, Bojanowski K. Effect of SBD.4A--a defined multicomponent preparation of Angelica sinensis--in periodontal regeneration models. Phytother Res. 2008 Jul;22(7):923-8.
15. Yang Q, Populo SM, Zhang J, Yang G, Kodama H. Effect of Angelica sinensis on the proliferation of human bone cells. Clin Chim Acta. 2002 Oct;324(1-2): 89-97.
16. Yao CH, Tsai HM, Chen YS, Liu BS. Fabrication and evaluation of a new composite composed of tricalcium phosphate, gelatin, and Chinese medicine as a bone substitute. Institute of Biomedical Engineering and Material Science, Chungtai Institute of Health Science and Technology, Taichung, Taiwan, Republic of China. J Biomed Mater Res B Appl Biomater. 2005 Nov;75(2):277-88.
17. Wang XL, Wang NL, Zhang Y, Gao H, Pang WY, Wong MS, Zhang G, Qin L, Yao XS. Effects of eleven flavonoids from the osteoprotective fraction of Drynaria fortunei (KUNZE) J. SM. on osteoblastic proliferation using an osteoblast-like cell line. Chem Pharm Bull (Tokyo). 2008 Jan;56(1):46-51.
18. Tang Q, Chen LL, Yan J. Effects of traditional chinese medicine Drynaria fortunei smith on promoting the proliferation, differentiation and calcification of mouse osteoblastic MC3T3-E1 cells. Zhongguo Zhong Yao Za Zhi. 2004 Feb;29(2):164-8.
19. Dong GC, Chen HM, Yao CH. A novel bone substitute composite composed of tricalcium phosphate, gelatin and drynaria fortunei herbal extract. J Biomed Mater Res A. 2008 Jan;84(1):167-77.
20. Hung TY, Chen TL, Liao MH, Ho WP, Liu DZ, Chuang WC, Chen RM. Drynaria fortunei J. Sm. promotes osteoblast maturation by inducing differentiation-related gene expression and protecting against oxidative stress-induced apoptotic insults. Ethnopharmacol. 2010 Aug 19;131(1):70-7.
21. Yin J, Tezuka Y, Kouda K, Tran QL, Miyahara T, Chen Y, Kadota S. Antiosteoporotic activity of the water extract of Dioscorea spongiosa. Biol Pharm Bull. 2004 Apr;27(4):583-6.
22. *Zhong Yao Tong Bao* (Journal of Chinese Herbology), 1987; 12(10):41.
23. Hu QY, Chen LL, Wang RF. Traditional Chinese medicine Drynaria fortunei J. Smith naringin promotes proliferation and differentiation of human periodontal ligament cells. Zhejiang Da Xue Xue Bao Yi Xue Ban. 2010 Jan;39(1):79-83.
24. Jiang JQ, Ding Y, Li XY, Cai W, Wang ZC. Effects of Drynaria fortunei naringin on proliferation, alkaline phosphatase activity of human periodontal ligament cells. Hua Xi Kou Qiang Yi Xue Za Zhi. 2009 Oct;27(5):538-41.
25. Liu HD, Li E, Tong XX. Effects of replenishing kidney herbs on estrogen and 1,25-dihydroxyvitamin D3 of dexamethasone-induced rats model with osteoporosis. *Chung Kuo Chung His Chieh Ho Tsa Chih* 1993 Sep; 13(9): 544-5,518.
26. Zhang LZ, et al. The anti-osteoporotic effect of velvet antler polypeptides from Cervus elaphus Linnaeus in ovariectomized rats. J Ethnopharmacol. 2013 Oct 28;150(1):181-6. doi: 10.1016/j.jep.2013.08.029.
27. Lam HW, Lin HC, Lao SC, Gao JL, Hong SJ, Leong CW, Yue PY, Kwan YW, Leung AY, Wang YT, Lee SM. The angiogenic effects of Angelica sinensis extract on HUVEC in vitro and zebrafish in vivo. J Cell Biochem. 2008 Jan 1;103(1):195-211.
28. Yu LC, Chen SC, Chang WC, Huang YC, Lin KM, Lai PH, Sung HW. Stability of angiogenic agents, ginsenoside Rg1 and Re, isolated from Panax ginseng: in vitro and in vivo studies. Department of Chemical Engineering, National Tsing Hua University, Hsinchu 30013, Taiwan, ROC. Int J Pharm. 2007 Jan 10;328(2):168-76.
29. Huang YC, Chen CT, Chen SC, Lai PH, Liang HC, Chang Y, Yu LC, Sung HW. A natural compound (ginsenoside Re) isolated from Panax ginseng as a novel angiogenic agent for tissue regeneration. Department of Chemical Engineering, National Tsing Hua University, Hsinchu, Taiwan, Republic of China. Pharm Res. 2005 Apr;22(4):636-46.
30. Journal of Oral and Maxillofacial Surgery. Volume 68, Issue 2 , Pages 243-253, February 2010.
31. JAMA. February 23, 2011.
32. Estrogen Supplements. *Drug Facts and Comparison*, 1999.

Pinellia Complex™

CLINICAL APPLICATIONS

- **Damp and phlegm accumulation with Spleen and Stomach qi deficiency**
  - **Damp and phlegm accumulation:** profuse, white sputum that can be easily expectorated, a feeling of distension and a stifling sensation in the chest and epigastrium, nausea, vomiting, lassitude, weak extremities, possible vertigo, palpitations, white, moist or greasy tongue coating, and a slippery pulse
  - **Spleen and Stomach qi deficiencies:** pale face, sallow complexion, low voice, lassitude, weakness of the extremities, poor appetite, loose stools, pale tongue with teeth marks, and a fine, moderate pulse
- Mostly used as an adjunct formula to treat a variety of disorders if the diagnosis includes dampness and phlegm

WESTERN THERAPEUTIC ACTIONS

- Gastrointestinal activities to treat various digestive disorders
- Metabolic activities to treat obesity and diabetes mellitus
- Antitussive and expectorant functions to treat respiratory disorders
- Circulatory and cardiovascular effects to treat hyperlipidemia and atherosclerosis

CHINESE THERAPEUTIC ACTIONS

- Dries dampness and dissolves phlegm
- Regulates qi and harmonizes the middle *jiao*
- Tonifies Spleen qi

DOSAGE

Take 3 to 4 capsules three times daily on an empty stomach. The dosage may be increased up to 6 to 8 capsules every four to six hours as needed.

INGREDIENTS

Bai Zhu (Rhizoma Atractylodis Macrocephalae)
Ban Xia (Rhizoma Pinelliae)
Cang Zhu (Rhizoma Atractylodis)
Fu Ling (Poria)
Ju Hong (Exocarpium Citri Rubrum)
Sha Ren (Fructus Amomi)
Sheng Jiang (Rhizoma Zingiberis Recens)
Wu Mei (Fructus Mume)
Xiang Fu (Rhizoma Cyperi)
Zhi Gan Cao (Radix et Rhizoma Glycyrrhizae Praeparata cum Melle)
Zhi Qiao (Fructus Aurantii)
Zhu Ru (Caulis Bambusae in Taenia)

BACKGROUND

Damp and phlegm disorders are closely related to the functions of the organs that control water: the Spleen, Lung, and Kidney. The Spleen transforms water, the Lung distributes water, and the Kidney eliminates water. Disorders in any of these three organs will lead to the accumulation of water and dampness, and eventually, the formation of phlegm. Once phlegm is formed, it may affect virtually any part of the body, including but not limited to the chest, diaphragm, stomach, intestines, all four extremities, and every channel and collateral. Presentations of phlegm disorders include signs and symptoms such as cough, wheezing, hurried respiration, dizziness, vertigo, nausea, vomiting, seizures, epilepsy, *dian kuang* (mania and withdrawal), formation of hardness and nodules, and many others. In short, phlegm is commonly described in traditional Chinese medicine as the "mother of hundreds of disorders," causing imbalance in the *zang fu* organs as well as obstructions of the channels and collaterals. This is why herbal formulas that treat dampness and phlegm often have multiple pharmacological effects and can be used to address a wide range of indications.

FORMULA EXPLANATION

Pinellia Complex is based on *Er Chen Tang* (Two-Cured Decoction), the foundational formula for treating dampness and phlegm. According to traditional Chinese medicine theories, the Spleen sends clear fluids up to the upper *jiao*. If this function is impaired, dampness may accumulate in the Spleen and create phlegm. If the Spleen is deficient and full of dampness, its functions of transportation and transformation will be impaired, which will lead to insufficient supply of nutrients to the body and the extremities. The result will be lassitude and weak extremities. The Lung, on the other hand, stores phlegm. Phlegm accumulation in the Lung manifests as coughing with profuse sputum. A feeling of distension and oppression in the chest and epigastrium arises as a result of dampness and phlegm obstructing the chest. Nausea and vomiting are due to damp-phlegm obstructing Stomach qi and causing it to rise abnormally. If dampness and phlegm affect the ascent of yang qi, then palpitations and vertigo can occur.

Ban Xia (Rhizoma Pinelliae) acts as the chief herb in this formula because it is the best herb to break up and dissolve phlegm stagnation. Its acrid and warm properties dissolve phlegm, dry dampness, and open pathways for the qi to flow. In addition, it corrects the reversed flow of Stomach qi to relieve nausea and vomiting. *Ju Hong* (Exocarpium Citri Reticulatae) activates and regulates qi to remove residual phlegm and dampness. *Fu Ling* (Poria), *Bai Zhu* (Rhizoma Atractylodis Macrocephalae), and *Cang Zhu* (Rhizoma Atractylodis) strengthen the Spleen and dispel dampness. *Xiang Fu* (Rhizoma Cyperi) and *Sha Ren* (Fructus Amomi) are used to resolve dampness and promote qi circulation. *Zhu Ru* (Caulis Bambusae in Taenia) and *Zhi Qiao* (Fructus Aurantii) are used to clear heat, regulate qi, and eliminate phlegm. *Sheng Jiang* (Rhizoma Zingiberis Recens) relieves nausea and vomiting by guiding Stomach qi downward, and helps to detoxify *Ban Xia* (Rhizoma Pinelliae). A small amount of *Wu Mei* (Fructus Mume) is used to astringe the Lung to prevent qi loss. The restraining effect of *Wu Mei* (Fructus Mume) also balances the dispersing nature of *Ban Xia* (Rhizoma

Pinellia Complex™

Pinelliae), thereby minimizing the potential side effects of each others. *Zhi Gan Cao* (Radix et Rhizoma Glycyrrhizae Praeparata cum Melle) regulates the Lung and Spleen and harmonizes all of the herbs.

In summary, ***Pinellia Complex*** is an excellent formula to strengthen the Spleen and Stomach, dry up dampness, and eliminate phlegm.

CAUTIONS & CONTRAINDICATIONS

- ***Pinellia Complex*** is contraindicated in cases of yin deficiency, yin-deficient heat, qi stagnation, excess heat, high fever, or thirst conditions.
- Discontinue this formula when the desired effect is achieved. Continued use may cause yin deficiency and symptoms of dry mouth, dry tongue, thirst, or irritability.

CLINICAL NOTES

- Because damp and phlegm cause a wide variety of disorders, treatment is most effective if ***Pinellia Complex*** is used to dispel damp and phlegm, while another formula is used to treat the subsequent disorder.

Pulse Diagnosis by Dr. Jimmy Wei-Yen Chang:

- Deep *taiyin* pulse on the right *cun*. If the pulse is strong and deep, then there is damp-heat.

SUPPLEMENTARY FORMULAS

- For respiratory disorders with clear or white sputum, combine with ***Respitrol (Cold)***.
- For respiratory disorders with yellow sputum, add ***Pinellia XPT*** and/or ***Respitrol (Heat)***.
- For asthma in children caused by heat, add ***Respitrol (Heat)***.
- For nasal allergies, add ***Magnolia Clear Sinus*** or ***Pueraria Clear Sinus***.
- For dry-phlegm characterized by sputum that is yellow, thick, and difficult to expectorate, add ***Nourish (Fluids)***.
- With nausea and vomiting due to cold in the Stomach and a deficient body constitution, add ***GI Tonic***.
- With irritable bowel syndrome (IBS), add ***GI Harmony***.
- If accompanied by depression, add ***Shine*** or ***Shine (DS)***.
- For nodules caused by phlegm obstructing the channels, add ***Resolve (AI)***.
- For severe Spleen and Stomach qi deficiencies, or with diarrhea, add ***GI Tonic***.
- With edema due to Spleen deficiency, add ***Herbal DRX***.
- With qi and blood deficiencies, combine with ***Imperial Tonic***.
- With damp-type of lesions, add ***Dermatrol (Damp)***.
- For damp-heat in the lower *jiao*, add ***V-Support***.
- For plum-pit syndrome, add *Ban Xia Hou Po Tang* (Pinellia and Magnolia Bark Decoction).

ACUPUNCTURE TREATMENT

Traditional Points:

- *Yinlingquan* (SP 9), *Taibai* (SP 3), *Zusanli* (ST 36), *Zhigou* (TH 6), *Taiyuan* (LU 9), *Lieque* (LU 7), *Zhongwan* (CV 12)

Balance Method by Dr. Richard Tan:

- Left side: *Yinbai* (SP 1), *Yangchi* (TH 4), *Sanjian* (LI 3), *Hegu* (LI 4), *Quchi* (LI 11)
- Right side: *Yuji* (LU 10) , *Jingqu* (LU 8), *Lieque* (LU 7), *Fenglong* (ST 40)
- Alternate sides with each treatment.

Ear Acupuncture:

- Stomach, Spleen, Lung, Endocrine, Adrenal, *Shenmen*

Auricular Medicine by Dr. Li-Chun Huang:

- Nasopharynx, Sympathetic, Allergic Area, Lung, Endocrine, Trachea. Bleed Ear Apex.

NUTRITION

- Avoid any and all foods containing sugar, such as cake, dessert, candy, chocolate, cake, canned juice, soft drinks, stevia, sugar substitutes, agave, xylitol, and corn syrup.
- Avoid raw or cold food and beverages, such as sashimi, sushi, salads, steak tartar, and seared meat. Eat cooked vegetables and nothing straight from the refrigerator.
- Avoid carbohydrates like white rice or bread as they may damage the Spleen and in turn produce more dampness.
- Do not eat seafood, especially shellfish like crab, oyster, scallop, clam, lobster and shrimp, as they enter the *yangming* Stomach channel. This is especially important for individuals suffering from skin disorders.
- Avoid fermented foods like cheese or fermented tofu.
- Avoid dairy products, such as milk, cream, yogurt, cheese, and ice cream. Dairy products in general tend to create dampness and therefore should not be consumed. Milk, cheese and other dairy products should be avoided, especially if patients are lactose intolerant.
- Do not eat lamb, beef, goose or duck. Avoid deep-fried or greasy foods.
- Avoid the following foods that are cold in nature and may damage the Spleen: most melons (winter melon, watermelon, honeydew melon, etc.), nightshades (eggplant, potato, bell and spicy peppers, tomato), bitter melon, seaweed, cucumber, grapefruit, and citrus.

The Tao of Nutrition by Dr. Maoshing Ni and Cathy McNease:

- Hawthorn berries, papayas, oranges, apples, daikons, and parsley.
- Dry and age orange peel for about one month. Soak it in hot water to make tea and drink it after meals.
- Blend daikon radish juice and take after meals.

Pinella Complex™

LIFESTYLE INSTRUCTIONS

- Always eat breakfast! According to the TCM clock, the most optimal time for the digestive system is in the morning from 8:00 to 10:00 a.m.
- Drink warm or hot liquids with your meal. Putting cold and ice on any part of the body will immediately constrict the flow of blood to that region. Similarly, drinking cold or iced drinks with meals will hinder the natural peristaltic movements of the digestive system.
- Sleep by 10:00 p.m. In traditional Chinese medicine (TCM), 11:00 p.m. to 1:00 a.m. is when the yin shifts to yang. It is crucial for the body to be at rest during this time for optimal health.
- Give the body two to three hours between the last meal of the day and bedtime. When a person sleeps, the digestive system slows down as well. Make sure the body has adequate time to digest the food before going into sleep mode.

PHARMACOLOGICAL AND CLINICAL RESEARCH

"Damp and phlegm" are concepts in traditional Chinese medicine that describe a myriad of dysfunctions affecting various organ systems in the body, including but not limited to gastrointestinal, metabolic, respiratory, cardiovascular, and neurological systems. Similarly, herbs that dry dampness and eliminate phlegm have a wide range of pharmacological effects as well as multiple clinical applications.

"Damp and phlegm" are derived from foods that are fatty, oily, greasy, and/or deep-fried. These foods are low in nutrients, difficult to digest, and adversely affect the digestive system to cause symptoms such as indigestion, nausea, vomiting, pain, constipation, diarrhea, anorexia, and many others. Therefore, as a general principle, herbs that dry dampness and eliminate phlegm have remarkable gastrointestinal effects to treat various digestive disorders. *Bai Zhu* (Rhizoma Atractylodis Macrocephalae) and *Cang Zhu* (Rhizoma Atractylodis) have excellent effects to regulate the gastrointestinal tract. *Bai Zhu* (Rhizoma Atractylodis Macrocephalae) has a dual effect on the gastrointestinal tract to treat either constipation or diarrhea.[1,2,3] *Cang Zhu* (Rhizoma Atractylodis) also has a balancing effect: it can relax the gastrointestinal tract to relieve spasms and cramps,[4] or it can stimulate the gastrointestinal tract to increase gastric emptying or intestinal motility.[5] Similarly, *Sha Ren* (Fructus Amomi) has a regulatory effect on the gastrointestinal system: it has a stimulating effect at low doses and an inhibiting effect at high doses.[6] *Sheng Jiang* (Rhizoma Zingiberis Recens) and *Ban Xia* (Rhizoma Pinelliae) have a significant antiemetic effect,[7,8] and are commonly used to treat nausea and vomiting due to various causes.[9,10] *Wu Mei* (Fructus Mume), *Gan Cao* (Radix et Rhizoma Glycyrrhizae) and *Zhi Qiao* (Fructus Aurantii) all have a gastroprotective effect. *Wu Mei* (Fructus Mume) reduces mucosal inflammation and protects against chronic atrophic gastritis.[11] *Gan Cao* (Radix et Rhizoma Glycyrrhizae) stimulates the growth of intestinal crypt cells to facilitate intestinal mucosa repair.[12] *Zhi Qiao* (Fructus Aurantii) protects the gastric mucosa against lesions induced by ethanol and non-steroidal anti-inflammatory drugs (NSAIDs) by increasing the gastric mucus production.[13] Lastly, many herbs in this formula have been used with great success to treat conditions such as gastric or duodenal ulcers,[14] atrophic gastritis,[15] epigastric pain,[16] and many others.

After foods with "damp and phlegm" characteristics are absorbed, they directly affect the metabolic system by increasing body weight and blood glucose levels. *Ban Xia* (Rhizoma Pinelliae) and *Bai Zhu* (Rhizoma Atractylodis Macrocephalae) are two herbs with antiobesity effects. *Ban Xia* (Rhizoma Pinelliae) has been shown to decrease body weight by increasing thermogenesis and fatty acid oxidation.[17] *Bai Zhu* (Rhizoma Atractylodis Macrocephalae) reduces body weight associated with high fat diet by inhibiting adipogenesis.[18] Furthermore, many herbs in this formula have great functions to treat diabetes. *Bai Zhu* (Rhizoma Atractylodis Macrocephalae) and *Cang Zhu* (Rhizoma Atractylodis) have antidiabetic effects to lower plasma glucose levels and treat diabetes.[19,20] *Fu Ling* (Poria) has an antihyperglycemic effect to reduce postprandial blood glucose levels via enhanced insulin sensitivity.[21] *Sheng Jiang* (Rhizoma Zingiberis Recens) has multiple antidiabetic activities, including a marked effect to increase blood insulin level and enhance insulin sensitivity.[22] Finally, herbs in this formula have been shown to effectively treat diabetes mellitus as well as its complications, such as diabetic retinopathy, diabetic nephropathy, and "diabetic foot."[23,24,25]

Increased intake of "damp and phlegm" foods also increases risks of circulatory and cardiovascular disorders, such as hyperlipidemia and atherosclerosis. *Gan Cao* (Radix et Rhizoma Glycyrrhizae) is used for its antihyperlipidemic effect to lower plasma cholesterol levels,[26] and *Zhi Qiao* (Fructus Aurantii) is used for its antiatherogenic and anti-inflammatory properties to treat atherosclerosis.[27] Furthermore, many herbs in this formula have marked cardiovascular effects: *Cang Zhu* (Rhizoma Atractylodis) may decrease blood pressure,[28] *Xiang Fu* (Rhizoma Cyperi) may strengthen the heart beat and lower the heart rate,[29] *Gan Cao* (Radix et Rhizoma Glycyrrhizae) may restore normal heart rhythm,[30] and together, herbs in this formula may treat both acute episodes and sequelae of stroke.[31]

Though "damp and phlegm" is a pathological concept in traditional Chinese medicine, the presence of "sputum and phlegm" in the lungs is literally a pathological condition in Western medicine. The presence of sputum and phlegm is indicative of respiratory disorders, and therefore, must be treated accordingly. *Ban Xia* (Rhizoma Pinelliae) and *Gan Cao* (Radix et Rhizoma Glycyrrhizae) have marked and prolonged antitussive and expectorant effects to facilitate the elimination of phlegm.[32] *Ban Xia* (Rhizoma Pinelliae) and *Chen Pi* (Pericarpium Citri Reticulatae) have antiasthmatic effects to facilitate breathing.[33] Synephrine from *Zhi Qiao* (Fructus Aurantii) has a moderate effect to relax and dilate the airways.[34] Clinically, herbs in

Pinellia Complex ™

this formula have been used to treat various respiratory tract disorders, such as asthma, bronchitis,[35] bronchiolitis,[36] tuberculosis,[37] and others.

In summary, it has been said in TCM that "phlegm is the mother of hundreds of diseases." Phlegm may literally indicate sputum expelled from the lungs, or it may figuratively refer to various disorders affecting the gastrointestinal, metabolic, respiratory, cardiovascular, and circulatory systems. ***Pinellia Complex*** is an excellent formula to dry "damp" and eliminate "phlegm," and in turn, treat imbalances affecting these systems.

References

1. *Chang Yong Zhong Yao Cheng Fen Yu Yao Li Shou Ce* (A Handbook of the Composition and Pharmacology of Common Chinese Drugs), 1994; 739:742.
2. *Shan Dong Zhong Yi Za Zhi* (Shandong Journal of Chinese Medicine), 1982; 2:107.
3. *Xin Yi Yao Xue Za Zhi* (New Journal of Medicine and Herbology), 1979; 6:27.
4. *Zhong Cheng Yao Yan Jiu* (Research of Chinese Patent Medicine), 1983; (7):25.
5. Kimura Y, Sumiyoshi M. Effects of an Atractylodes lancea rhizome extract and a volatile component β-eudesmol on gastrointestinal motility in mice. J Ethnopharmacol. 2012 May 7;141(1):530-6.
6. *Zhong Yao Xue* (Chinese Herbology), 1998; 326:327.
7. Haniadka R, Rajeev AG, Palatty PL, Arora R, Baliga MS. Zingiber officinale (Ginger) as an Anti-Emetic in Cancer Chemotherapy: A Review. J Altern Complement Med. 2012 May;18(5):440-4.
8. *Jiang Su Zhong Yi Za Zhi* (Jiangsu Journal of Chinese Medicine), 1987; 3:16.
9. *Xin Zhong Yi* (New Chinese Medicine), 1986; 12:24.
10. *Dissertation Abstr Interant*, 1987, 8:3297.
11. Enomoto S, Yanaoka K, Utsunomiya H, Niwa T, Inada K, Deguchi H, Ueda K, Mukoubayashi C, Inoue I, Maekita T, Nakazawa K, Iguchi M, Arii K, Tamai H, Yoshimura N, Fujishiro M, Oka M, Ichinose M. Inhibitory effects of Japanese apricot (Prunus mume Siebold et Zucc.; Ume) on Helicobacter pylori-related chronic gastritis. Second Department of Internal Medicine, Wakayama Medical University, Wakayama, Japan. Eur J Clin Nutr. 2010 Jul;64(7):714-9.
12. He Y, Zhang X, Zeng X, Huang Y, Wei JA, Han L, Li CX, Zhang GW. HuR-mediated posttranscriptional regulation of p21 is involved in the effect of Glycyrrhiza uralensis licorice aqueous extract on polyamine-depleted intestinal crypt cells proliferation. J Nutr Biochem. 2012 Jan 2.
13. Moraes TM, et al. Effects of limonene and essential oil from Citrus aurantium on gastric mucosa: role of prostaglandins and gastric mucus secretion. São Paulo State University, Department of Physiology, Rubião Junior, cp 510, CEP 18618-000, Botucatu, São Paulo, Brazil. Chem Biol Interact. 2009 Aug 14;180(3):499-505.
14. *Zhong Yao Lin Chuan Xin Yong* (New Clinical Applications of Chinese Medicine), 2001; 163.
15. *Bei Jing Zhong Yi* (Beijing Chinese Medicine) 1990;1:5.
16. *Nei Meng Gu Zhong Yi Yao* (Traditional Chinese Medicine and Medicinals of Inner Mongolia) 1998;3:19.
17. Kim YJ, Shin YO, Ha YW, Lee S, Oh JK, Kim YS. Anti-obesity effect of Pinellia ternata extract in Zucker rats. Biol Pharm Bull. 2006 Jun;29(6):1278-81.
18. Kim CK, Kim M, Oh SD, Lee SM, Sun B, Choi GS, Kim SK, Bae H, Kang C, Min BI. Effects of Atractylodes macrocephala Koidzumi rhizome on 3T3-L1 adipogenesis and an animal model of obesity. J Ethnopharmacol. 2011 Sep 1;137(1):396-402.
19. Shan J.J. & Tian G.Y. Studies on physico-chemical properties and hypoglycemic activity of complex polysaccharide AMP-B from *Atractylodes macrocephala* Koidz. *Yao Xue Xue Bao.* 2003, 38(6): 438-441.
20. *Zhong Hua Yi Xue Za Zhi* (Chinese Journal of Medicine), 19858; 44(2):150.
21. Li TH, Hou CC, Chang CL, Yang WC. Anti-Hyperglycemic Properties of Crude Extract and Triterpenes from Poria cocos. Evid Based Complement Alternat Med. 2011;2011. pii: 128402.
22. Iranloye BO, Arikawe AP, Rotimi G, Sogbade AO. Anti-diabetic and anti-oxidant effects of Zingiber Officinale on alloxan-induced and insulin-resistant diabetic male rats. Niger J Physiol Sci. 2011 Nov 23;26(1):89-96.
23. *Zhe Jiang Zhong Yi Za Zhi* (Zhejiang Journal of Chinese Medicine) 1994;1:9.
24. *Zhong Yao Lin Chuan Xin Yong* (New Clinical Applications of Chinese Medicine), 2001; 309.
25. Gao L. Qi-promoting and phlegm-resolving method for treatment of diabetic microvascular complications. Journal of Traditional Chinese Medicine 2000 Jun;20(2):104-9.
26. *Zhong Yao Xue* (Chinese Herbology), 1998, 759:765.
27. Liu L, et al. Naringenin and hesperetin, two flavonoids derived from Citrus aurantium up-regulate transcription of adiponectin. Pharmaceutical Informatics Institute, College of Pharmaceutical Sciences, Zijin'gang Campus, Zhejiang University, Hangzhou, 310058, China. Phytother Res. 2008 Oct;22(10):1400-3.
28. *Chang Yong Zhong Yao Cheng Fen Yu Yao Li Shou Ce* (A Handbook of the Composition and Pharmacology of Common Chinese Drugs), 1994; 979:985.
29. *Zhong Guo Yao Ke Da Xue Xue Bao* (Journal of University of Chinese Herbology), 1989; 20(1):48
30. Ojha S, Golechha M, Kumari S, Bhatia J, Arya DS. Glycyrrhiza glabra protects from myocardial ischemia-reperfusion injury by improving hemodynamic, biochemical, histopathological and ventricular function. Exp Toxicol Pathol. 2011 Oct 3.
31. *Shan Xi Zhong Yi* (Shanxi Chinese Medicine) 1995;16(9):393.
32. *Zhong Yao Xian Dai Yan Jiu Yu Ying Yong* (Modern Study of Traditional Chinese Medicine) 1993;165, 199, 388, 490.
33. Ok IS, Kim SH, Kim BK, Lee JC, Lee YC. Pinellia ternata, Citrus reticulata, and their combinational prescription inhibit eosinophil infiltration and airway hyperresponsiveness by suppressing CCR3+ and Th2 cytokines production in the ovalbumin-induced asthma model. Mediators Inflamm. 2009;2009:413270.
34. *Zhi Wu Yao You Xiao Cheng Fen Shou Ce* (Manual of Plant Medicinals and Their Active Constituents), 1986; 1012.
35. *Jiang Xi Zhong Yi Yao* (Jiangxi Chinese Medicine and Herbology) 1988;1:16.
36. *Zhong Ji Yi Kan* (Medium Medical Journal) 1994;12:45.
37. *Jiang Xi Yi Yao* (Jiangxi Medicine and Herbology), 1965; 1:562.

Pinellia XPT™

CLINICAL APPLICATIONS

- **Profuse yellow or green sputum** from infection and/or inflammation of the respiratory tract
- **Cough and dyspnea** from pneumonia or bronchitis
- **Chest congestion and fullness** from respiratory disorders
- **Post-nasal drip**

WESTERN THERAPEUTIC ACTIONS

- Expectorant effect to expel phlegm and sputum from the upper respiratory tract
- Antitussive function to relieve cough
- Antibiotic effect to treat bacterial and viral infections

CHINESE THERAPEUTIC ACTIONS

- Clears Lung heat
- Regulates Lung qi
- Lowers the adverse rising qi and relieves cough
- Transforms phlegm

DOSAGE

Take 4 to 6 capsules three times daily on an empty stomach with warm water.

INGREDIENTS

Ban Xia (Rhizoma Pinelliae)
Chen Pi (Pericarpium Citri Reticulatae)
Da Zao (Fructus Jujubae)
Dan Nan Xing (Arisaema cum Bile)
Dong Gua Zi (Semen Benincasae)
Fu Ling (Poria)
Huang Qin (Radix Scutellariae)
Jie Geng (Radix Platycodonis)
Ku Xing Ren (Semen Armeniacae Amarum)
Ting Li Zi (Semen Descurainiae)
Yi Yi Ren (Semen Coicis)
Zhi Shi (Fructus Aurantii Immaturus)
Zhu Ru (Caulis Bambusae in Taenia)

BACKGROUND

Phlegm and sputum are secretion and discharge of the respiratory tract associated with infection and inflammation. Phlegm contains mucus with bacteria, debris, and inflammatory cells. When phlegm is expectorated via cough, it is called sputum. Phlegm and sputum generally indicates infection and inflammation of the respiratory tract. The presence of phlegm and sputum interferes with normal functions of the lung, and therefore, should be expelled via coughing or use of herbs.

FORMULA EXPLANATION

Pinellia XPT addresses the secondary stage of lung infection in which the superficial symptoms are no longer present. Instead there is an internal stagnation of phlegm and fire, which interferes with the descending function of Lung qi. Therefore, cough and profuse yellow or green sputum are the predominant symptoms.

Dan Nan Xing (Arisaema cum Bile) has a strong effect to treat blockage due to fire and phlegm. *Huang Qin* (Radix Scutellariae), *Ting Li Zi* (Semen Descurainiae) and *Jie Geng* (Radix Platycodonis) work together to drain Lung fire while transforming phlegm. *Bai Jie Zi* (Semen Sinapis) and *Ku Xing Ren* (Semen Armeniacae Amarum) eliminate phlegm, reverse rebellious Lung qi, and relieve cough. *Chen Pi* (Pericarpium Citri Reticulatae) and *Zhi Shi* (Fructus Aurantii Immaturus) regulate Lung qi and relieve chest congestion and fullness. *Zhu Ru* (Caulis Bambusae in Taenia) clears phlegm-heat to expel sputum and relieve the stifling sensation in the chest. *Fu Ling* (Poria), *Yi Yi Ren* (Semen Coicis) and *Dong Gua Zi* (Semen Benincasae) strengthen the Spleen and dispel phlegm through urination. *Da Zao* (Fructus Jujubae) is used to harmonize the Stomach and moderate the strong properties of *Dan Nan Xing* (Arisaema cum Bile) and *Ting Li Zi* (Semen Descurainiae).

In short, ***Pinellia XPT*** clears Lung heat and transforms phlegm to treat various respiratory tract with infection and inflammation.

CAUTIONS & CONTRAINDICATIONS

- This formula is designed for respiratory infections characterized by chest congestion with profuse yellow phlegm. It is not suitable for the initial stage of wind-heat or wind-cold.
- Some patients may experience stomach discomfort as a result of taking this formula. Should this occur, reduce the dosage or take the herbs with food.
- This formula is contraindicated during pregnancy and nursing.
- This formula is not recommended for long-term use. It should be discontinued when the desired effects are achieved.

CLINICAL NOTES

Pulse Diagnosis by Dr. Jimmy Wei-Yen Chang:

- **Upper respiratory tract infection:** superficial and forceful pulse on the right *cun*.
- **Lower respiratory tract infection:** shapeless *yangwei* pulse, a pulse extending distally from the *cun* position towards the thumb, on the left hand. It is one of the eight extra meridian pulses.

SUPPLEMENTARY FORMULAS

- With more underlying damp and phlegm due to Spleen qi deficiency, add ***Pinellia Complex***.
- For infection with fever, chest congestion, and dyspnea characterized by Lung heat, add ***Respitrol (Heat)***.
- For cough, add ***Respitrol (CF)***.
- For high fever, add ***Gardenia Complex***.
- To enhance the overall antibiotic effect, add ***Herbal ABX***.
- To enhance the overall antiviral effect, add ***Herbal AVR***.
- To treat infection of ear, nose and throat, add ***Herbal ENT***.

Pinellia XPT™

- For sinus infection with yellow nasal discharge, combine with ***Pueraria Clear Sinus***.
- For tonsillitis with swollen throat, combine with ***Resolve (AI)*** and ***Herbal ENT***.
- For wind-heat, add ***Lonicera Complex***.
- ***Immune +*** can be taken on a daily basis to build-up the immune system and prevent bacterial or viral infections. Start taking ***Immune +*** after symptoms of cold and influenza have subsided.
- For plum-pit syndrome, add *Ban Xia Hou Po Tang* (Pinellia and Magnolia Bark Decoction).

ACUPUNCTURE TREATMENT

Traditional Points:

- *Feishu* (BL 13), *Shanzhong* (CV 17), *Dazhui* (GV 14), *Zusanli* (ST 36)
- *Shanzhong* (CV 17), *Feishu* (BL 13), *Yuji* (LU 10)

Classic Master Tung's Points:

- **Pneumonia:** *Linggu* (T 22.05), *Dabai* (T 22.04), *Chongzi* (T 22.01), *Chongxian* (T 22.02), *Quling* (T 33.16), *Simashang* (T 88.18), *Simazhong* (T 88.17), *Simaxia* (T 88.19), *Zhongjian* (T 11.05). Bleed dark veins nearby the ST channel on the lower limb. Bleed the HT and LU areas on the upper back with cupping. Bleed before needling for best result.
- **Bronchitis:** *Linggu* (T 22.05), *Dabai* (T 22.04), *Fenjin* (T 44.01), *Renshi* (T 33.13), *Dishi* (T 33.14), *Tianshi* (T 33.15), *Shuijin* (T 1010.20), *Shuitong* (T 1010.19), *Simazhong* (T 88.17), *Feiqiyi* (T 44.25)*, *Feiqier* (T 44.26)*, *Zhongjian* (T 11.05). Bleed the HT and LU area in the back. Bleed before needling for best result.

Master Tung's Points by Dr. Chuan-Min Wang:

- **Yellow phlegm, post-nasal drip:** Bleed *Sihuawai* (T 77.14). Needle *Xiaojian* (T 11.02), *Dabai* (T 22.04).

Balance Method by Dr. Richard Tan:

- Left side: *Ligou* (LR 5), *Taibai* (SP 3), *Yinlingquan* (SP 9), *Zhubin* (KI 9), *Sanyinjiao* (SP 6), *Sanjian* (LI 3), *Hegu* (LI 4), *Quchi* (LI 11)
- Right side: *Chize* (LU 5), *Yuji* (LU 10), *Taiyuan* (LU 9), *Fenglong* (ST 40), *Chengshan* (BL 57)
- Left and right sides can be alternated from treatment to treatment.

Auricular Medicine by Dr. Li-Chun Huang:

- **Bronchial asthma:** Bronchus, Trachea, Lung, Chest, Stop Asthma, Sympathetic, Adrenal Gland, Allergic Area, Endocrine. Bleed Ear Apex.
- **Bronchiectasis:** Bronchus, Lung, Chest, Stop Asthma, Allergic Area, Sympathetic, Adrenal Gland, Spleen
- **Snoring and apnea:** Trachea, *San Jiao*, Lower Lung, Pharynx, Larynx, Sympathetic, Nasopharynx, Chest, Mouth, Esophagus, Larynx and Tooth
- **Nasopharyngitis, post-nasal drip:** Nasopharynx, Sympathetic, Allergic Area, Lung, Endocrine, Trachea. Bleed Ear Apex.

NUTRITION

- Avoid foods that are greasy or spicy in nature as they create more dampness and heat.
- To avoid infection, a diet high in garlic, onions, and water is recommended.
- Adequate intake of vitamin C is important as it is greatly consumed by white blood cells when fighting infections.
- Avoid smoking and exposure to second-hand smoke, alcohol, seafood, and phlegm-producing foods such as sweets, dairy products, heavy or greasy foods.
- Eat plenty of foods that contain vitamin A and C, which strengthen the lung tissue and improve resistance to infection, respectively.
- Spleen is responsible for generating post-natal qi and good Spleen function also contributes to a healthy immune system. Foods that damage the Spleen should be avoided:
  - Avoid any and all foods that contain sugar, such as cake, dessert, candy, chocolate, canned juice, soft drinks, caffeinated drinks, stevia, sugar substitutes, agave, xylitol, and corn syrup.
  - Avoid raw or uncooked meats, such as sashimi, sushi, steak tartar, and seared meat. Minimize consumption of foods that are cooling in nature, including tofu, tomato, celery, asparagus, bamboo, seaweed, kelp, bitter melon, cucumber, gourd, luffa, eggplant, winter melon, watermelon, honeydew, citrus, oranges, guava, grapefruit, pineapple, plums, pear, banana, papaya, white radish, mustard leaf, potherb mustard, Chinese kale, napa, bamboo sprout. Do not eat foods straight from the refrigerator. Long-term intake of cold fruits and vegetables like the ones listed above may be damaging to the Spleen. The cooling property of foods can be neutralized by cooking or adding 20 pieces of *Gou Qi Zi* (Fructus Lycii).
  - Avoid carbohydrates like white rice or bread as they may produce dampness.
  - No seafood especially shellfish, like crabs, oyster, scallops, clams, lobster and shrimp (they enter the *yangming* Stomach channel).
  - Avoid fermented foods like cheese or fermented tofu.
  - Do not eat dairy products, such as milk, cream, yogurt, cheese, and ice cream.
  - Avoid fried or greasy foods.
- Warm and hot natured foods that damage qi and yin should be avoided, such as:
  - certain fruits like mango and durian that produce heat.
  - stimulants like coffee, alcohol, and energy drinks.
  - spicy/pungent/aromatic vegetables such as pepper, garlic, onions, basil, rosemary, cumin, funnel, anise, leeks, chives, scallions, thyme, saffron, wormwood, mustard, chili pepper, and wasabi.
- Avoid food and drinks with artificial coloring.
- Consume as few meat products as possible. Do not eat processed meats, such as lunch meats, hot dogs and sausages, as they contain nitrites that are associated with inflammation and chronic disease.

Pinellia XPT™

The Tao of Nutrition by Dr. Maoshing Ni and Cathy McNease:

- **Dry cough with yellow sputum:** Take warm daikon and water chestnut juice with one teaspoon honey.
- **Cough with yellow sputum:** Drink apple juice.
- **Cough, mucus, and upper respiratory infection:** Put slices of onion over the nose like a mask and inhale the aroma for 30 minutes. Or steam the sliced onion and apply warm as a poultice to the chest area; cover to keep warm and leave on for 20 to 30 minutes.

LIFESTYLE INSTRUCTIONS

- Patients are encouraged to expel sputum out so that the airway can be cleared to facilitate normal respiration and relieve chest congestion.
- Installation of an air purifier at home is recommended for recurrent respiratory disorders.
- A humidifier will increase moisture in the air, hydrate the mucous membranes of the nose and the lung, and hence increase resistance to infection.

CASE STUDIES

- A 59-year-old female presented with copious congestion, chest tightness and yellow-greenish phlegm. The patient's condition was diagnosed as heat in the Lung with phlegm congestion. The practitioner prescribed ***Pinellia XPT***. Subsequently, the patient's phlegm resolved as well as her chest tightness and pain. Submitted by V.G., Carlsbad, California.
- A 59-year-old male physician presented with extreme fever (over 104°F), extreme difficulty breathing, pain in the chest, shortness of breath aggravated by exertion, unsteady walk, dizziness, and inability to speak more than one word per breath. His tongue was pale with a red tip and body, and his pulse was rapid and superficial. The diagnosis was phlegm heat in the Lung. The patient was treated with ***Pinellia XPT*** (6 capsules four times daily) and ***Immune +*** (6 capsules four times daily), along with other homeopathics and drugs [Combivent (albuterol/ipratropium) and aspirin]. The patient had a definite response to the herbs. The respiration became much easier, energy level and sense of vitality enhanced, and cough was no longer productive. The practitioner commented: "While all protocols employed resulted in benefit – it is without question that the herbal formulas generated imminent benefit and long term recuperation." Submitted by I.B.J., Miami, Florida.
- D.C., a 50-year-old female, presented common cold symptoms of cough, chest congestion and difficult to expectorate phlegm. She had a slight fever. The tongue was red with yellow coating. The pulse was rapid and slippery. The doctor diagnosed her with Lung heat. The two formulas prescribed were ***Respitrol (Heat)*** and ***Pinellia XPT***. In three days, the heat was relieved and the phlegm was cleared. Submitted by B.F., Newport Beach, California.

PHARMACOLOGICAL AND CLINICAL RESEARCH

Pinellia XPT is an expectorant formula designed to stop the production and eliminate the storage of phlegm in the respiratory tract. This formula contains herbs with expectorant effects to eliminate phlegm, antitussive effects to relieve cough, anti-inflammatory effects to reduce swelling and inflammation, and antibiotic effects to treat infection.

Many herbs in ***Pinellia XPT*** have an expectorant effect to eliminate phlegm, and an antitussive effect to suppress cough. *Ban Xia* (Rhizoma Pinelliae) has strong and prolonged antitussive effects, with the duration of action of approximately five hours.[1] *Dan Nan Xing* (Arisaema cum Bile) has expectorant properties and increases secretion of mucus in the respiratory tract. *Jie Geng* (Radix Platycodonis) has marked antitussive and expectorant effects to suppress and relieve cough.[2] *Bai Jie Zi* (Semen Sinapis) also has an expectorant effect.[3] Most importantly, *Ku Xing Ren* (Semen Armeniacae Amarum) has a remarkable antitussive effect, with its mechanism attributed to inhibition of the respiratory reflex in the brain.[4] Since the presence of phlegm in the lungs affects breathing, ***Pinellia XPT*** has herbs with antiasthmatic effects to facilitate breathing. The combination of *Ban Xia* (Rhizoma Pinelliae) and *Chen Pi* (Pericarpium Citri Reticulatae) shows a marked effect to treat artificially-induced asthma in one study.[5] Clinically, use of *Ban Xia* (Rhizoma Pinelliae) and *Ku Xing Ren* (Semen Armeniacae Amarum) exhibited a good effect in treating coughing from an exterior condition in 119 patients (82 with marked effect, 28 with moderate effect, and 6 with no effect).[6] An herbal formula with *Ting Li Zi* (Semen Descurainiae seu Lepidii) also showed a good effect to treat 30 children with cough and dyspnea from bronchitis.[7] Finally, one study of 10 patients showed that pulmonary abscesses can be treated with satisfactory results using *Jie Geng* (Radix Platycodonis) and *Gan Cao* (Radix et Rhizoma Glycyrrhizae).[8]

Pinellia XPT incorporates many herbs with anti-inflammatory effects to reduce the swelling and inflammation in the lungs. *Chen Pi* (Pericarpium Citri Reticulatae) decreases the permeability of the blood vessels and reduces inflammation from allergy.[9] *Jie Geng* (Radix Platycodonis) illustrates its anti-inflammatory effect by decreasing capillary permeability and suppressing sensitivity from allergic reactions.[10] Finally, *Huang Qin* (Radix Scutellariae) demonstrates significant and potent anti-inflammatory properties via inhibition of nitric oxide (NO), inducible NOS (iNOS), cyclo-oxygenase-2 (COX-2), prostaglandin E2 (PGE2), and proinflammatory cytokines.[11]

Lastly, ***Pinellia XPT*** contains many herbs with marked antibiotic effects to treat respiratory tract infections. For example, *Huang Qin* (Radix Scutellariae) has broad antimicrobial effects against *Staphylococcus aureus*, beta-hemolytic streptococcus, *Diplococcus pneumoniae*, *Pseudomonas aeruginosa*, *Bacillus dysenteriae*, *E. coli*, *Bordetella pertussis*, *Vibrio cholerae*, *Diplococcus meningitidis*, leptospira and various species of

Pinellia XPT ™

dermatophytes and influenza viruses. *Huang Qin* (Radix Scutellariae) is most effective against *Staphylococcus aureus* and *Pseudomonas aeruginosa.* Furthermore, it was discovered that the effectiveness of standard antibiotics such as ampicillin, amoxicillin, methicillin and cefotaxime can be potentiated with addition of baicalin, a flavone isolated from this herb. With the addition of baicalin, the effectiveness of these beta-lactam antibiotics was restored against beta-lactam-resistant *Staphylococcus aureus* and methicillin-resistant *Staphylococcus aureus* (MRSA).[12,13] In addition, *Huang Qin* (Radix Scutellariae) has antiviral activities and suppresses the replication of influenza A and B viruses.[14] Specifically, baicalein and wogonin, two compounds from *Huang Qin* (Radix Scutellariae), boost innate antiviral immunity by stimulating the production of cytokines and increasing the resistance to viral infection in human leukocytes.[15] Furthermore, pinelloside, an antimicrobial cerebroside isolated from *Ban Xia* (Rhizoma Pinelliae), inhibited the growth of *Bacillus subtilis, Staphylococcus aureus, Aspergillus niger* and *Candida albicans.*[16] Lastly, *Zhu Ru* (Caulis Bambusae in Taenia) also has an inhibitory effect against many pathogens, such as *Staphylococcus albus, Bacillus subtilis, E. coli,* and *Salmonella typhi.*[17]

In summary, ***Pinellia XPT*** is an excellent formula to treat sputum, cough, dyspnea, chest congestion, and fullness from respiratory tract infections.

COMPARATIVE ANALYSIS

Respiratory tract disorders (such as cough, dyspnea, and lung infection) are often complicated with the presence of phlegm, and swelling and inflammation of the lungs. Because the presence of phlegm in the lungs creates discomfort and delays recovery, it is often necessary to expectorate the phlegm.

There is only one approved expectorant available for treatment of phlegm – guaifenesin. This drug is mixed with other drug combinations, such as Robitussin and Triaminic, to treat the overall cold and flu complex of cough, nasal obstruction, chest congestion, and runny nose. Guaifenesin is relatively safe and free from side effects, but its potency is also limited.

Many herbs are extremely effective to stop the production, loosen the viscosity, and facilitate the elimination of phlegm. Similar to Western medicine, these herbs are often combined with others to treat other accompanying symptoms of illness, such as cough, nasal obstruction, and chest congestion.

Expectorants are effective to assist the elimination of phlegm in the chest, and are most effective when used with other medicinal substances to enhance the overall effect to treat various symptoms of respiratory tract disorders. Guaifenesin is the only drug option available, and is rather mild in potency. On the other hand, there are many herbs available to stop the production of phlegm and facilitate its elimination.

References

1. *Zhong Yao Yao Li Yu Ying Yong* (Pharmacology and Applications of Chinese Herbs), 1983: 383.
2. *Zhong Yao Yao Li Yu Ying Yong* (Pharmacology and Applications of Chinese Herbs), 1983; 866.
3. *Zhong Yao Xue* (Chinese Herbology), 1998; 608:610.
4. *Life Sci*, 1980; 27(8):659.
5. Ok IS, Kim SH, Kim BK, Lee JC, Lee YC. Pinellia ternata, Citrus reticulata, and their combinational prescription inhibit eosinophil infiltration and airway hyperresponsiveness by suppressing CCR3+ and Th2 cytokines production in the ovalbumin-induced asthma model. Mediators Inflamm. 2009;2009:413270.
6. *An Hui Zhong Yi Xue Yuan Xue Bao* (Journal of Anhui University School of Medicine), 1992; 1:45.
7. *Zhong Yi Za Zhi* (Journal of Chinese Medicine), 1984; 10:43.
8. *Jiang Su Zhong Yi Za Zhi* (Jiangsu Journal of Chinese Medicine), 1981; 3:35.
9. *Zhong Yao Yao Li Yu Ying Yong* (Pharmacology and Applications of Chinese Herbs), 1983; 567.
10. *Zhong Yao Yao Li Yu Ying Yong* (Pharmacology and Applications of Chinese Herbs), 1983; 866.
11. Kim EH, Shim B, Kang S, Jeong G, Lee JS, Yu YB, Chun M. Anti-inflammatory effects of Scutellaria baicalensis extract via suppression of immune modulators and MAP kinase signaling molecules. Department of Biological Sciences, Seoul National University, Seoul 151-742, Republic of Korea. J Ethnopharmacol. 2009 Nov 12;126(2):320-31.
12. *Zhong Yao Xue* (Chinese Herbology), 1988; 137:140.
13. *J Pharm Pharmacol* 2000 Mar;52(3):361-6.
14. Nagai et al. antiviral activity of plant flavonoid, 5,7,4'-trihydroxy-8-methoxyflavone, from scutellaria baicalensis against influenza A (H3N2) and B viruses. *Biol Pharm Bull*; 18(2):295-9. Feb. 1995.
15. Błach-Olszewska Z, Jatczak B, Rak A, Lorenc M, Gulanowski B, Drobna A, Lamer-Zarawska E. Production of cytokines and stimulation of resistance to viral infection in human leukocytes by Scutellaria baicalensis flavones. Ludwik Hirszfeld Institute of Immunology and Experimental Therapy, Polish Academy of Sciences, Wrocław, Poland. J Interferon Cytokine Res. 2008 Sep;28(9): 571-81.
16. Chen J.H., Cui G.Y., Liu J.Y. Tan R.X. Pinelloside, an antimicrobial cerebroside from *Pinellia ternata. Phytochemistry*. 2003, 64(4): 903-906.
17. *Zhong Yao Xue* (Chinese Herbology), 1998; 623:625.

Polygonum 14™

CLINICAL APPLICATIONS

- **Hair disorders:** alopecia (hair loss, baldness), premature gray hair, and brittle, unhealthy hair with split ends
- **Scalp, skin and nails:** dryness with unhealthy complexion
- Other deficiency conditions: anemia and osteoporosis

WESTERN THERAPEUTIC ACTIONS

- Increases blood circulation to the scalp
- Provides essential nutrients for hair growth
- Osteogenic effect to promote generation of bones
- Hematopoietic effect to stimulate the production of blood

CHINESE THERAPEUTIC ACTIONS

- Replenishes the *jing* (essence) and promotes the growth and maintains the health of hair, skin, nails, and bones
- Nourishes blood and promotes circulation to the scalp

DOSAGE

Take 4 capsules three times daily on an empty stomach with warm water. ***Polygonum 14*** should be taken continuously for two months prior to making an evaluation. Most patients report changes in hair texture within two months, and changes in hair color in four to six months.

INGREDIENTS

Bai Shao (Radix Paeoniae Alba)
Chuan Xiong (Rhizoma Chuanxiong)
Da Zao (Fructus Jujubae)
Dang Gui (Radix Angelicae Sinensis)
Gan Cao (Radix et Rhizoma Glycyrrhizae)
Ge Gen (Radix Puerariae Lobatae)
Gui Zhi (Ramulus Cinnamomi)
Hei Zhi Ma (Semen Sesami Nigrum)
Huang Qi (Radix Astragali)
Mo Han Lian (Herba Ecliptae)
Nu Zhen Zi (Fructus Ligustri Lucidi)
Sang Shen (Fructus Mori)
Shu Di Huang (Radix Rehmanniae Praeparata)
Zhi He Shou Wu (Radix Polygoni Multiflori Praeparata)

BACKGROUND

Hair disorders, such as alopecia (hair loss, baldness), premature gray hair and unhealthy hair, are common disorders affecting both men and women. Common causes of hair disorders include heredity, infection, endocrine disorder (i.e., hypothyroidism, hyperthyroidism, menopause), postpartum weakness, nutritional deficiencies, stress, and drugs (i.e., chemotherapy, radiation, anticoagulants, oral contraceptives, ACE inhibitors, beta blockers, anticonvulsants, lithium and others).

FORMULA EXPLANATION

Polygonum 14 is designed primarily to treat hair loss, premature gray hair, and brittleness with split ends, which are all signs of Kidney yin with Liver blood deficiency. ***Polygonum 14*** is formulated to nourish Kidney yin and Kidney *jing* (essence), tonify Liver blood, and increase blood circulation to the scalp.

Zhi He Shou Wu (Radix Polygoni Multiflori Praeparata) is an indispensable herb for treating any hair disorder. It replenishes the vital essence of the Liver and Kidney and tonifies the blood. *Mo Han Lian* (Herba Ecliptae), *Sang Shen* (Fructus Mori), and *Nu Zhen Zi* (Fructus Ligustri Lucidi) tonify the Liver and the Kidney yin to benefit the hair. *Shu Di Huang* (Radix Rehmanniae Praeparata), *Hei Zhi Ma* (Semen Sesami Nigrum) and *Bai Shao* (Radix Paeoniae Alba) are selected to tonify Liver blood and nourish the hair. Proper blood circulation to the scalp is also an important factor for healthy hair. *Huang Qi* (Radix Astragali), *Ge Gen* (Radix Puerariae Lobatae) and *Gui Zhi* (Ramulus Cinnamomi) have ascending properties that carry the therapeutic functions of this formula to the scalp. *Chuan Xiong* (Rhizoma Chuanxiong) and *Dang Gui* (Radix Angelicae Sinensis) improve microcirculation and nourish the blood. *Da Zao* (Fructus Jujubae) and *Gan Cao* (Radix et Rhizoma Glycyrrhizae) are used to harmonize the formula.

In short, ***Polygonum 14*** nourishes Kidney yin and Kidney *jing* (essence) to treat various disorders associated with aging and deterioration.

CAUTIONS & CONTRAINDICATIONS

- Because ***Polygonum 14*** is a rich and cloying formula, some patients may experience loose stools after taking it. This can be alleviated by lowering the dosage, or taking it with food.
- ***Polygonum 14*** is contraindicated in individuals with exterior or excess conditions.
- This herbal formula contains herbs that invigorate blood circulation, such as *Dang Gui* (Radix Angelicae Sinensis). Therefore, patients who are on anticoagulant or antiplatelet therapies, such as Coumadin (warfarin), should use this formula with caution, or not at all, as there may be a higher risk of bleeding and bruising.[1,2,3]
- According to most textbooks and contemporary references, the classic entry of "*He Shou Wu*" is now separated into two entries: the unprepared *Sheng Shou Wu* (Radix Polygoni Multiflori) and the prepared *Zhi He Shou Wu* (Radix Polygoni Multiflori Praeparata), as they have significantly different therapeutic effects and side effects. *Sheng Shou Wu* (Radix Polygoni Multiflori) is a stimulant laxative that treats constipation, but may cause nausea, vomiting, abdominal pain, diarrhea, and in rare cases, liver disorder (dose- and time-dependent, and reversible upon discontinuation).[4] On the other hand, *Zhi He Shou Wu* (Radix Polygoni Multiflori Praeparata) is a tonic herb that is safe and well-tolerated. The dramatic changes in the therapeutic effect and safety profile are attributed to the long and complicated processing of the root with *Hei Dou* (Semen Sojae) through repeated blending, cooking, and drying procedures.

Polygonum 14™

When properly processed, the chemical composition of the root changes significantly. Many new compounds are generated from the Maillard reaction (four furanones, two furans, two nitrogen compounds, one pyran, one alcohol and one sulfur compound). Furthermore, the preparation process causes changes in the composition of sugars and 16 kinds of amino acids; it also reduces the pH of the herb from 6.28 to 5.61.[5,6] In summary, these changes give rise to the tonic effects of the prepared roots, and eliminate the adverse reactions associated with the unprepared roots. **Note:** Due to medical risks and legal liabilities, it is prudent to exercise caution and ***not*** use this herb in either prepared or unprepared forms in patients with pre-existing or risk factors of liver diseases.

CLINICAL NOTES

- *Zhi He Shou Wu* (Radix Polygoni Multiflori Praeparata) has been known as a popular antiaging herb since the Ming dynasty (14th Century) in China. It is often used by the sages and Taoist monks to enhance longevity.
- ***Polygonum 14*** is an herbal formula originally developed for Empress *Chi-Xi*, the last empress in the history of China. It was developed in the 19th century by a private doctor in the Forbidden City who used a relatively large amount of *Zhi He Shou Wu* (Radix Polygoni Multiflori Praeparata) to enhance hair color and texture. Empress *Chi-Xi* took this formula throughout her life and it became the secret to her shiny, black hair even when she was in her eighties.
- ***Polygonum 14*** is a constitutional tonic that changes the fundamental color and texture of hair. Change in hair texture requires approximately one to two months, and change in hair color requires four to six months of continuous herbal treatment. Therefore, individuals who take ***Polygonum 14*** must be patient, as changes will not occur immediately.

SUPPLEMENTARY FORMULAS

- For hair loss due to chemotherapy and radiation, combine with ***C/R Support*** to minimize side effects.
- For hair loss due to stress, add ***Calm***.
- For post-partum hair loss, combine with ***Schisandra ZZZ*** or ***Imperial Tonic***.
- For low libido, add ***Vitality***.
- For vaginal dryness, add ***Balance Spring***.
- For prevention of osteoporosis, add ***Osteo 8***.
- For forgetfulness, add ***Enhance Memory***.
- To control appetite for weight loss, add ***Herbalite***.
- To improve the shape and increase the size of the breasts, combine with ***Venus***.
- To clear acne, add ***Dermatrol (Clear)***.
- To tonify blood, combine with ***Schisandra ZZZ***.
- For depression, use ***Shine*** or ***Shine (DS)***.
- For constipation, use ***Gentle Lax (Deficient)***.
- For blurry vision or tinnitus, combine with ***Nourish***.
- To tonify Kidney yang, add ***Kidney Tonic (Yang)***.
- To tonify Kidney yin, add ***Kidney Tonic (Yin)***.
- With blood stagnation, add ***Circulation (SJ)***.

ACUPUNCTURE TREATMENT

Traditional Points:

- *Shangxing* (GV 23), *Baihui* (GV 20), *Yinlingquan* (SP 9), *Sanyinjiao* (SP 6), *Taixi* (KI 3)
- *Baihui* (GV 20). Apply moxa to *Zusanli* (ST 36) and *Sanyinjiao* (SP 6).

Classic Master Tung's Points:

- *Qianhui* (T 1010.05), *Zhenghui* (T 1010.01), *Houhui* (T 1010.06), *Tianhuangfu [Shenguan]* (T 77.18), *Minghuang* (T 88.12), *Tianhuang* (T 88.13), *Qihuang* (T 88.14), *Simashang* (T 88.18), *Simaxia* (T 88.19), *Simazhong* (T 88.17). Bleed the LU and HT areas on the back, dark veins nearby *Weizhong* (BL 40), lateral side of the lower limb. Bleed before needling for best result.
- **Dry skin/wrinkles:** Needle along the lines of the wrinkle, *Shuijin* (T 1010.20), *Shuitong* (T 1010.19), *Yuhuo* (T 1010.21), *Zhenjing* (T 1010.08), *Muzhi* (T 1010.18), *Sifuyi* (T 1010.11), *Sifuer* (T 1010.10), *Makuaishui* (T 1010.14), *Liukuai* (T 1010.16), *Qikuai* (T 1010.17), *Tianhuang* (T 88.13), *Minghuang* (T 88.12), *Qihuang* (T 88.14), *Simashang* (T 88.18), *Simaxia* (T 88.19), *Simazhong* (T 88.17). Bleed the LR area T5 – T9 and KI area T9 – T12 on the back with cupping. Bleed before needling for best result.

Master Tung's Points by Dr. Chuan-Min Wang:

- **Hair loss, premature gray, dry nails:** Bleed *Qixing* (T DT.03). Needle *Minghuang* (T 88.12), *Tianhuang* (T 88.13), *Qihuang* (T 88.14), *Shuixiang* (T 66.14), *Shuixian* (T 66.15).

Auricular Medicine by Dr. Li-Chun Huang:

- **Alopecia:** Sympathetic, Kidney, Liver, Gallbladder, Spleen, Lung, Endocrine, Pituitary, Coronary Vascular Subcortex, corresponding points

NUTRITION

- Biotin, found in green peas, oats, soybeans, sunflower seeds and walnuts, is essential for healthy hair and skin. Kelp and seaweed are also excellent choices to include in the daily diet.
- Protein is the essential make-up of hair. Therefore, the intake of food high in protein such as milk, fish, egg, and beans is recommended.
- Foods that are high in collagen will improve the elasticity and shine of hair, such as wild yam, taro, lotus root, and tendons.
- Intake of vitamins A and B are also recommended, as they can improve circulation to the scalp and promote hair growth.
- Increase intake of water, vegetables, fruits, seeds and nuts for patients with dry skin.
- Those with dandruff can increase the intake of vitamin B_6 and B_{12}.

Polygonum 14™

- Consume adequate amounts of vegetables for vitamins, as they improve circulation to the scalp and promote hair growth.

LIFESTYLE INSTRUCTIONS

- Avoid cigarette smoking and second-hand smoke, sugar, alcohol, caffeine, and junk food.
- Stay out of the sun as it can dry and damage skin and hair.
- Stress can impair the delivery of nutrients to the scalp as it causes stagnation. Patient should be advised to stay away from stressful situations.
- Natural bristle brushes are recommended. Brushes with sharp tips should not be used as they might scrape the scalp. To invigorate circulation to the scalp, brush hair 100 times from the back of the head towards the front with the head down at least twice a day.
- Untangle hair with a brush before shampooing. Mild shampoo should also be selected to avoid overstimulation to the scalp. Water temperature should not be too hot to avoid further hair loss. The scalp can be massaged while shampooing. Be sure to rinse completely, leaving no shampoo or conditioning residues to clog up the hair pores. Hair should be dried by gently padding on the towel instead of rubbing back and forth.
- Blow-drying and use of hair products such as gel, mousse, and hairspray are not recommended. Chemical treatments, perms, and color should also be avoided.
- Avoid swimming as much as possible as chlorine will do much damage to the hair. If one cannot avoid swimming, it is recommended that the patient wear a cap or rub some baby oil into the hair.
- Get regular exercise and establish a normal pattern of sleep.

CASE STUDIES

- D.K, a 65-year-old female, complained of both dry skin and thinning hair. She would wake up to a pillow covered with hair. The TCM diagnosis was Kidney yang and Liver blood deficiency. She was treated with ***Polygonum 14***, instructed to take 2 capsules three times daily for the first week, gradually increasing the dosage to 4 capsules as the patient had a very sensitive digestive system. The patient noted no digestive upset from taking the herbs in this manner. After two months of taking ***Polygonum 14***, the patient noted that her hair was no longer falling out all over her pillow nor was the 'root' attached to the hairs that came out. The patient noticed her hair was beginning to thicken and soften in addition to having more moist skin. Additional treatment received included acupuncture for the Kidney yang deficiency. Submitted by C.V., Concord, North Carolina.
- A.T., a 35-year-old male, complained of gray hair that had been present since the previous year. He had a forceful pulse, yet it was weak in the Kidney areas. This condition was diagnosed as Kidney yin deficiency. The patient was treated with ***Polygonum 14*** at four capsules three times a day. Since he had been taking the formula he noticed less gray hair coming in. Patient is continuing to take the formula and his hair has been less gray ever since. Submitted by A.I., Hilo, Hawaii.
- T.W., a 47-year-old female, who had a habit of frequently coloring her own hair, presented with thinning of hair which was breaking off easily. The practitioner prescribed ***Polygonum 14*** at four capsules three times daily. After taking the herbs for many months, the patient reported she was very pleased with the results. She had also noticed new growth that had grown in more red than her normal color. Submitted by L.W., Arroyo Grande, California.
- Two females, ages 54- and 55-years-old, presented with hair loss. The practitioner attributed their hair loss to blood deficiency with some underlying Liver yin and Spleen qi deficiencies. They were both treated with the ***Polygonum 14*** formula. The patients reported new hair growth as well as normalization of bowel movements. The practitioner concluded ***Polygonum 14*** to be quite effective in treating hair loss due to aging. Submitted by D.N., Pacific Palisades, California.
- C.W., a 40-year-old male, presented with tiredness, poor sleep, constipation, gray hair, over-work, and high cholesterol. His blood pressure was 130/80 mmHg and his heart rate was 80 beats per minute. There was no Western diagnosis and the TCM diagnosis was found to be Liver blood deficiency. ***Polygonum 14*** was prescribed at 2 grams three times daily. This patient also received acupuncture as the overall treatment regime. The patient reported the quality of sleep improved after taking the herbs. Energy level increased and the constipation was relieved. Additionally, his cholesterol level dropped from 223 to 190 mg/dL. Submitted by W.F., Bloomfield, New Jersey.
- A 22-year-old male college student presented with dry skin and hair loss on the scalp, as noted by a patch near the vertex. He admitted to drug use and smoking, along with depression. His pulse was rapid and full while his tongue was crimson. The patient appeared restless. The practitioner diagnosed the condition as yin deficiency and fluid consumption, possibly from an overuse of stimulants. After taking ***Polygonum 14*** for less than one month, the patient observed that his hair felt less brittle and that he had not seen any hair strands on his pillow unlike in the past. The patch of lost hair was less noticeable and he detected new hair growth after 1½ months. The patient also reported an increased energy level, as well as a more cheerful disposition. He also appeared less restless. Additionally, he had refrained from drugs and smoking, from which he fortunately did not develop any withdrawal signs or cravings. Interestingly, with the use of ***Polygonum 14***, the patient's hair not only felt healthier but also became darker, although his hair was naturally dark blonde. Submitted by F.V., Orlando, Florida.
- A 35-year-old female singer presented with hair loss, fatigue and low energy. She had a pale tongue, soft pulse and cold feet. The practitioner diagnosed her condition as Kidney yang deficiency. The patient was instructed to take ***Polygonum 14***. The patient reported excellent results. The practitioner concluded

Polygonum 14™

that *Polygonum 14* had been quite effective in treatment of a variety of conditions, including Kidney yin deficiency and Spleen qi deficiency, but especially with hair loss symptoms. Submitted by L.T., Chicago, Illinois.

PHARMACOLOGICAL AND CLINICAL RESEARCH

Polygonum 14 is designed mainly to treat hair disorders, including hair loss, premature gray, and brittleness with split ends. As the herbs nourish the body, other associated benefits include increased production of blood, skin, nails, and bones.

The main ingredient of ***Polygonum 14*** is *Zhi He Shou Wu* (Radix Polygoni Multiflori Praeparata), an herb commonly used to tonify the Liver and Kidney *jing* (essence), nourish the blood, and treat various hair disorders. Pharmacologically, use of *Zhi He Shou Wu* (Radix Polygoni Multiflori Praeparata) via oral ingestion or topical application has been shown to promote hair growth and stimulate an increase in the number and the size of hair follicles. The mechanism of this action is attributed to the induction of the anagen phase in resting hair follicles.[7] Clinically, use of *Zhi He Shou Wu* (Radix Polygoni Multiflori Praeparata) has been shown to effectively treat both hair loss (alopecia) and poor hair quality (premature gray). According to one clinical trial, 24 patients with alopecia were treated with oral and topical applications of herbs with good results. For oral ingestion, all patients received an herbal formula that uses *Zhi He Shou Wu* (Radix Polygoni Multiflori Praeparata) as the main ingredient, with other additions and modifications as needed. For topical application, the patients were instructed to wash their hair with an herbal solution made from *Sang Ye* (Folium Mori) 60g and *Ma Ye* (Folium Cannabis) 60g.[8] According to another study, 36 patients with gray hair were treated to evaluate the effectiveness of herbs. Out of 36 patients, 20 had partial white discoloration of hair and 16 had complete white discoloration of hair. The herbs selected include *Zhi He Shou Wu* (Radix Polygoni Multiflori Praeparata), *Dang Gui* (Radix Angelicae Sinensis) and *Shu Di Huang* (Radix Rehmanniae Praeparata). The patients were advised to take the herbs once to twice daily continuously until there were significant changes, which could vary from one year to ten years. After ten years of clinical trial, it was concluded that the use of these herbs were 88.89% effective, with 24 out of 36 patients showing significant improvement, and 8 patients showing moderate improvement.[9]

Polygonum 14 also contains many herbs to promote generation of bones and prevent osteoporosis. Pharmacologically, *Di Huang* (Radix Rehmanniae) has an antiosteoporotic effect to stimulate the proliferation and activities of osteoblasts, while inhibiting the generation and resorptive activities of osteoclasts. It also shows preventive effects on osteoporotic bone loss induced by ovariectomy. In addition, the water extract of *Dang Gui* (Radix Angelicae Sinensis) has been found to contribute to the formation of bones and treatment of bone injuries. It directly stimulates the proliferation, alkaline phosphatase activity, protein secretion and particularly type I collagen synthesis of human osteoprecursor cells in a dose-dependent manner.[10] In another study, *Dang Gui* (Radix Angelicae Sinensis) shows a marked effect on osteoblast proliferation and differentiation systems, as well as in a fibroblast-secreted hyaluronic acid assay. It enhances the deposition of hyaluronic acid and proliferation of osteoblasts *in vitro*, as well as bone regeneration.[11,12] Clinically, an herbal formula that contains *Zhi He Shou Wu* (Radix Polygoni Multiflori Praeparata) as the main ingredient showed 90.8% effectiveness to treat osteoporosis. Out of 76 cases, the study reported significant improvement in 12 cases, moderate improvement in 57 cases, and no benefit in 7 cases.[13]

In addition to its function of nourishing hair, many herbs in ***Polygonum 14*** have remarkable effects to stimulate the production of blood and improve blood circulation. *Dang Gui* (Radix Angelicae Sinensis), *Nu Zhen Zi* (Fructus Ligustri Lucidi) and *Shu Di Huang* (Radix Rehmanniae Praeparata) have hematopoietic effects to stimulate the production of blood through expediting the multiplication and differentiation of bone marrow hematopoietic cells (CFU-S and CFU-E).[14,15] *Chuan Xiong* (Rhizoma Chuanxiong) increases peripheral blood circulation by reducing the agglutination and the peripheral activities of platelets.[16]

Lastly, ***Polygonum 14*** contains many herbs with antioxidant effects to prevent damage or death to cells. The extract of *Zhi He Shou Wu* (Radix Polygoni Multiflori Praeparata) has an antioxidant effect to treat skin damage induced by ultraviolet B irradiation (UVB). *Zhi He Shou Wu* (Radix Polygoni Multiflori Praeparata) strongly inhibits the destruction of superoxide dismutase by UVB and probably contains agents to slow down photo-aging of the skin.[17] *Shu Di Huang* (Radix Rehmanniae Praeparata) has been shown to scavenge reactive oxygen species and suppresses many adverse effects of ultraviolet radiation, such as DNA fragmentation, damage to mitochondrial function, modulation of apoptotic marker proteins, and UV-induced apoptosis of cells.[18] *Hei Zhi Ma* (Semen Sesami Nigrum) has antioxidant activity with a potency comparable to that of a standard antioxidant (ascorbic acid), according to *in vitro* assays.[19] *Dang Gui* (Radix Angelicae Sinensis) and *Chuan Xiong* (Rhizoma Chuanxiong) protect against endothelial cells damage induced by hydrogen peroxide by enhancing the antioxidative ability, activating ERK and eNOS signaling pathways.[20]

Overall, ***Polygonum 14*** is a great tonic formula to improve the quality and quantity of hair, bone, and blood.

COMPARATIVE ANALYSIS

One striking difference between Western and traditional Chinese medicine is that Western medicine focuses and excels in crisis management, while traditional Chinese medicine emphasizes and shines in holistic and preventative treatments. Therefore, in emergencies, such as gunshot wounds or surgery, Western medicine is generally the treatment of choice. However, for treatment of chronic idiopathic illness of unknown origins,

Polygonum 14™

where all lab tests are normal and a clear diagnosis cannot be made, traditional Chinese medicine is distinctly superior.

In regards to premature aging of the hair characterized by hair loss, premature gray hair, and unhealthy hair, there is very few drug treatments available in Western medicine. Rogaine (minoxidil) and Propecia (finasteride) are two of very limited options available, and their effects are often disappointing and side effects staggering. Limited hair growth may occur only after continuous use for several months. Furthermore, hair loss occurs after drug use is discontinued. Lastly, sexual dysfunction is common with the use of these medications. In short, drug treatment is only marginally beneficial and is only effective for a short period of time.

On the other hand, traditional Chinese medicine is significantly superior to Western medicine to restore normal appearance and texture of hair. Furthermore, when used continuously for four to six months, it also helps to promote lasting hair growth. In addition to improving texture and volume of hair, this formula also has an antiaging effect to improve overall well-being. Lastly, it is very safe and can be used for a prolonged period of time.

References

1. Chan K, Lo AC, Yeung JH, Woo KS. Journal of Pharmacy and Pharmacology 1995 May;47(5):402-6.
2. Pharmacotherapy 1999 July;19(7):870-876.
3. European Journal of Drug Metabolism and Pharmacokinetics 1995; 20(1): 55-60.
4. Lei X, et al. Liver Damage Associated with Polygonum multiflorum Thunb.: A Systematic Review of Case Reports and Case Series. Evid Based Complement Alternat Med. 2015;2015:459749. doi: 10.1155/2015/459749.
5. Liu Z, Chao Z, Liu Y, Song Z, Lu A. Maillard reaction involved in the steaming process of the root of Polygonum multiflorum. Institution of Basic Theory, China Academy of Chinese Medical Sciences, Beijing, PR China. Planta Med. 2009 Jan;75(1):84-8. Epub 2008 Nov 25.
6. Liu Z, et al. In vitro antioxidant activities of maillard reaction products produced in the steaming process of Polygonum multiflorum root. Nat Prod Commun. 2011 Jan;6(1):55-8.
7. Park HJ, Zhang N, Park DK. Topical application of Polygonum multiflorum extract induces hair growth of resting hair follicles through upregulating Shh and β-catenin expression in C57BL/6 mice. Department of Bioscience and Biotechnology, Konkuk University, 1 Hwayang-dong, Kwangjin-gu, Seoul 143-701, Republic of Korea. J Ethnopharmacol. 2011 Mar 17.
8. *Fu Jian Zhong Yi Yao* (Fujian Chinese Medicine and Herbology) 1983;5:19.
9. Zhao, HB. Treatment of white hair with polygonum (he shou wu) tincture. *Shangdong Journal of Traditional Chinese Medicine*. 4:41. 1983.
10. Yang Q, Populo SM, Zhang J, Yang G, Kodama H. Effect of Angelica sinensis on the proliferation of human bone cells. Clin Chim Acta. 2002 Oct;324(1-2): 89-97.
11. Zhao H, Alexeev A, Sharma V, Guzman LD, Bojanowski K. Effect of SBD.4A--a defined multicomponent preparation of Angelica sinensis--in periodontal regeneration models. Phytother Res. 2008 Jul;22(7):923-8.
12. Oh KO, Kim SW, Kim JY, Ko SY, Kim HM, Baek JH, Ryoo HM, Kim JK. Effect of Rehmannia glutinosa Libosch extracts on bone metabolism. OCT Inc., 2-17, Omok-ri, Seonggeo-eup, Choongnam 330-831, Chonan, South Korea. Clin Chim Acta. 2003 Aug;334(1-2):185-95.
13. *Hu Nan Zhong Yi Za Zhi* (Hunan Journal of Chinese Medicine) 1999;2:26.
14. *Zhong Yao Tong Bao* (Journal of Chinese Herbology), 1983; 8(6):35.
15. Yuan Y, Hou S, Lian T, Han Y. Studies of Rehmannia glutinosa Libosch. f. hueichingensis as a blood tonic. Henan College of the Traditional Chinese Medicine, Zhengzhuo. Zhongguo Zhong Yao Za Zhi. 1992 Jun;17(6):366-8, inside backcover.
16. Yeung, HC. *Handbook of Chinese Herbs*. Institute of Chinese Medicine. 1996.
17. Hwang IK, Yoo KY, Kim DW, Jeong SJ, Won CK, Moon WK, Kim YS, Kwon DY, Won MH, Kim DW. An extract of Polygonum multiflorum protects against free radical damage induced by ultraviolet B irradiation of the skin. Central Research Center, Natural F & P Co., Ltd., Chunchon, South Korea. Braz J Med Biol Res. 2006 Sep;39(9):1181-8.
18. Shin SW, Park CI, Yang CH, Park JW. Protective effect of Rehmannia glutinosa on the UV-induced apoptosis in U937 cells. School of Life Sciences and Biotechnology, College of Natural Sciences, Kyungpook National University, Taegu 702-701, Korea. Am J Chin Med. 2008;36(6):1159-70.
19. Nahar L, Rokonuzzaman. Investigation of the analgesic and antioxidant activity from an ethanol extract of seeds of Sesamum indicum. Department of Pharmacy, Southeast University, Banani, Dhaka, Bangladesh. Pak J Biol Sci. 2009 Apr 1;12(7):595-8.
20. Hou YZ, Zhao GR, Yang J, Yuan YJ, Zhu GG, Hiltunen R. Protective effect of Ligusticum chuanxiong and Angelica sinensis on endothelial cell damage induced by hydrogen peroxide. Life Sci. 2004 Aug 20;75(14):1775-86.

P-Support™

CLINICAL APPLICATIONS

- **Benign prostatic hyperplasia (BPH):** prostate enlargement with urinary frequency, urgency and nocturia; feeling of incomplete emptying, terminal dribbling, and pain with urination
- **Varicocele** with enlarged vein, pain within scrotum, and feeling of heaviness in the testicle(s)
- **Prostatitis** with dysuria and pain or discomfort of the penis or testicle(s)
- ***Lin zheng* (dysuria syndrome)** with urinary urgency, painful urination, difficult urination with inflammation

WESTERN THERAPEUTIC ACTIONS

- Reduces the size of the prostate gland
- Analgesic and anti-inflammatory effects to relieve pain and reduce inflammation associated with prostatic hyperplasia
- Diuretic effect to promote normal urination

CHINESE THERAPEUTIC ACTIONS

- Clears damp-heat
- Promotes normal urination
- Tonifies qi, blood and *jing* (essence)

DOSAGE

Take 3 to 4 capsules three times daily, with warm water, on an empty stomach. Dosage may be increased up to 8 to 10 capsules three times daily in acute conditions until symptoms subside, but for no more than four days. After relief of symptoms, dosage can then be reduced to 3 to 4 capsules daily. For prevention or maintenance, take 2 capsules twice daily.

INGREDIENTS

Chi Shao (Radix Paeoniae Rubrae)
Fu Ling (Poria)
Hu Po (Succinum)
Hua Shi (Talcum)
Huang Bo (Cortex Phellodendri Chinensis)
Huang Qi (Radix Astragali)
Mo Yao (Myrrha)
Pu Gong Ying (Herba Taraxaci)
Ru Xiang (Gummi Olibanum)
Tao Ren (Semen Persicae)
Tong Cao (Medulla Tetrapanacis)
Wang Bu Liu Xing (Semen Vaccariae)
Yi Yi Ren (Semen Coicis)

BACKGROUND

Benign prostatic hyperplasia is the enlargement of the prostate gland causing varying degrees of bladder outlet obstruction.[1] The exact etiology is unknown, but it is presumed to be linked to hormonal changes associated with aging. Clinically, patients often present with symptoms such as progressive urinary frequency, urgency and nocturia. Furthermore, many will experience a feeling of incomplete emptying, terminal dribbling, and pain with urination. Decreased size and force of the urinary stream is also commonly reported. Therefore, proper therapy requires treatment of both the cause and the symptoms.

FORMULA EXPLANATION

In traditional Chinese medicine, benign prostatic hyperplasia in geriatric men is a condition due to both excess and deficiency. Excess refers to the enlargement of the gland leading to stagnation of qi and blood and accumulation of damp-heat. Deficiency refers to the gradual depletion of qi, blood, and Kidney *jing* (essence) accompanying aging. Therefore, optimal treatment must use herbs that tonify the underlying deficiency, clear damp-heat, and promote normal urination.

In this formula, many herbs are used to break up and resolve the enlargement and disperse stagnation. *Ru Xiang* (Gummi Olibanum) and *Mo Yao* (Myrrha) have excellent functions to activate blood circulation and disperse blood stagnation. This pair is commonly used to disperse masses throughout the entire body – not just the prostate. *Chi Shao* (Radix Paeoniae Rubrae) and *Tao Ren* (Semen Persicae) are used to enhance the effect of softening the hardness and promoting normal urination. *Hu Po* (Succinum) is used to break up blood stagnation and open the orifices. Furthermore, *Tong Cao* (Medulla Tetrapanacis) and *Wang Bu Liu Xing* (Semen Vaccariae) are added to disperse and reduce swelling and inflammation. They also have excellent penetrating qualities to help restore healthy, continuous urinary flow. This combination exerts an excellent effect to resolve enlargement and disperse stagnation. In addition, *Huang Qi* (Radix Astragali) and *Fu Ling* (Poria) are markedly effective at tonifying qi and regulating water circulation. *Fu Ling* (Poria), *Hua Shi* (Talcum), *Tong Cao* (Medulla Tetrapanacis) and *Yi Yi Ren* (Semen Coicis) are diuretic herbs used to promote normal urination and relieve various discomforts associated with dampness and swelling. Bitter and cold, *Huang Bo* (Cortex Phellodendri Chinensis) and *Pu Gong Ying* (Herba Taraxaci) clear damp-heat and toxic heat from the lower *jiao*.

In conclusion, ***P-Support*** addresses both the cause and the symptoms of benign prostatic hyperplasia. It treats the cause by resolving enlargement of the prostate gland. It treats the symptoms by clearing damp-heat and promoting normal urination, alleviating discomfort and resolving or preventing inflammation. By targeting both the cause and the symptoms simultaneously, it offers both immediate and long-term support for these patients.

CAUTIONS & CONTRAINDICATIONS

- ***P-Support*** is designed to treat mild to moderate prostate enlargement. While it may help to promote normal urination, it is ***not*** suitable for the treatment of prostate cancer. Additional workup is necessary to confirm or rule out the diagnosis of prostate cancer.

P-Support™

- This formula is not designed for long-term use. It should be discontinued when the desired effects are achieved.
- If use of this formula is necessary for extended maintenance, use only a reduced dosage.

CLINICAL NOTES

- Benign prostatic hyperplasia is a condition that becomes progressively more common and severe with aging. While the incidence of benign prostatic hyperplasia is 40 to 50% in men aged 51 to 60 years, the incidence is 80% in men older than 80 years of age. Therefore, BPH should be treated as early as possible to prevent the occurrence and deterioration of the condition.
- ***P-Support*** is an excellent formula for prevention and/or maintenance, at two capsules twice daily.
- ***P-Support*** can be used for geriatric men who are beginning to develop enlarged prostates associated with aging and hormonal changes. ***P-Support*** treats BPH by draining damp-heat and tonifying qi and *jing* (essence).

Pulse Diagnosis by Dr. Jimmy Wei-Yen Chang:

- Turtle pulse, a convex-shaped pulse, found on both *chi* positions.

SUPPLEMENTARY FORMULAS

- For varicocele, add ***Resolve (Lower)***. The dosages of ***P-Support*** and ***Resolve (Lower)*** should be at a 3:1 ratio, respectively.
- For damp-heat accumulation with turbid, painful urination, use ***Gentiana Complex***.
- For bacterial prostatitis or infection of the urinary tract, use with ***V-Support*** or ***Herbal ABX***.
- For kidney stones, add ***Dissolve (KS)***.
- For compromised renal functions, add ***Kidney DTX***.
- For Kidney yang deficiency with coldness or impotence, add ***Kidney Tonic (Yang)***.
- For Kidney yin deficiency, add ***Kidney Tonic (Yin)***.
- For edema and water accumulation, add ***Herbal DRX***.
- For blood stagnation, add ***Circulation (SJ)***.
- With severe inflammation, combine with ***Astringent Complex***.

ACUPUNCTURE TREATMENT

Traditional Points:

- *Hegu* (LI 4), *Sanyinjiao* (SP 6), *Guanyuan* (CV 4), *Zhongji* (CV 3), *Yanglingquan* (GB 34), *Qugu* (CV 2), *Huiyin* (CV 1)
- Needle *Ciliao* (BL 32). Apply moxa to *Guanyuan* (CV 4) and *Zusanli* (ST 36).

Classic Master Tung's Points:

- **Benign prostatic hyperplasia (BPH):** *Tianhuang* (T 77.17), *Dihuang* (T 77.19), *Renhuang* (T 77.21), *Tianhuang* (T 88.13), *Minghuang* (T 88.12), *Qihuang* (T 88.14), *Yizhong* (T 77.05), *Erzhong* (T 77.06), *Sanzhong* (T 77.07), *Shuitong* (T 1010.19), *Shuijin* (T 1010.20). Bleed tender points on the KI area in the back with cupping. Bleed before needling for best result.
- **Urinary frequency:** *Tianhuang* (T 77.17), *Dihuang* (T 77.19), *Renhuang* (T 77.21), *Shuiqu* (T 66.09), *Huozhu* (T 66.04), *Makuaishui* (T 1010.14), *Tongshen* (T 88.09), *Tongwei* (T 88.10)
- ***Lin zheng*** **(dysuria syndrome):** *Fenzhishang* (T DT.01), *Fenzhixia* (T DT.02), *Tianhuang* (T 77.17), *Dihuang* (T 77.19), *Renhuang* (T 77.21), *Tongshen* (T 88.09), *Tongwei* (T 88.10), *Tongbei* (T 88.11)

Master Tung's Points by Dr. Chuan-Min Wang:

- **Prostate, urinary disorders:** *Shuitong* (T 1010.19), *Shuijin* (T 1010.20).

Balance Method by Dr. Richard Tan:

- Left side: *Dazhong* (KI 4), *Zhaohai* (KI 6), *Zhongfeng* (LR 4), *Yangxi* (LI 5), *Yangchi* (TH 4), Prostate point on the ear
- Right side: *Jiexi* (ST 41), *Shenmai* (BL 62), *Lieque* (LU 7), *Daling* (PC 7)
- Left and right sides can be alternated from treatment to treatment.

Auricular Medicine by Dr. Li-Chun Huang:

- **Prostatitis:** Prostate, Urethra, Pelvic, Kidney, Lower *Jiao*, Liver, Spleen, *San Jiao*, Endocrine. Bleed Ear Apex.
- **Hyperplasia of prostate:** Prostate, Urethra, Pelvic, Kidney, Liver, Lower *Jiao*, Pituitary, Endocrine, *San Jiao*, Gonadotropin.
- **Orchitis and epididymitis:** Testis, Endocrine, Adrenal Gland, Kidney, Liver, Prostate, Pelvic, Internal Genital, External Genital.
- **Urosis:** Urethra, M. Prostate, F. Internal Urethra, Liver, Adrenal Gland, Lower *Jiao*, Endocrine. Bleed Ear Apex.

NUTRITION

- Encourage the patient to eat foods rich in zinc, such as raw pumpkin seeds or pumpkin seed oil, and sunflower seeds. Studies have shown zinc deficiency to be linked to prostate disorders.
- Foods with phytoestrogens, such as soy and yams, have a beneficial effect for prostate health.
- Increase the consumption of the following foods beneficial for general prostate health: organic, fresh, leafy vegetables, whole grains and raw wheat germ, carrots, citrus fruits, tomatoes, and natural enzymes. It is also recommended to eat cooked vegetables instead of raw ones.
- Avoid fruits such as watermelon and citrus that are cold or sour in nature.
- Avoid tobacco smoking, alcoholic beverages, junk food, and spicy food. Reduce salt intake.

The Tao of Nutrition by Dr. Maoshing Ni and Cathy McNease:

- Recommendations: pumpkin seeds, anise, tangerines, cherries, figs, litchis, sunflower seeds, mangos, and seaweeds.
- Roast pumpkin seeds or boil into tea and incorporate into the diet, one large handful twice daily.
- Make tea from rhubarb root, peach kernels, winter melon seeds, pearl barley, azuki beans, and corn silk; drink three times daily.

P-Support™

- Boil fig tea.
- Avoid dairy products, rich foods, fatty foods; all stimulants such as alcohol, caffeine, and smoking; stress, tension, sex, and eating meat late in the day.

LIFESTYLE INSTRUCTIONS

- Take steps to reduce blood cholesterol levels if necessary. Studies have shown high cholesterol to be linked to prostate disorders.[2]
- Relaxation exercises help to relieve tension and facilitate bladder emptying.
- Abstain from sexual intercourse as much as possible until the condition is resolved, and then observe moderation in sexual activity.

CASE STUDIES

- A 61-year-old male patient complained of frequent urination, with incomplete sensation afterwards. He described it as he did not feel like he was completely empty. No lab reports were present, but he was diagnosed with an enlarged prostate. This condition was given a TCM diagnosis of Kidney yin deficiency and damp-heat. The patient was treated with ***P-Support*** at four capsules three times a day. The symptoms improved and the patient had reported that the formula does the job for him; urination is a lot easier for him and he feels more complete after. Submitted by A.I., Hilo, Hawaii.
- R.A., 78-year-old male, presented with frequent urination up to three to four times each night with urgency and difficulty in flow at times. The Western diagnosis was BPH; the TCM diagnosis was Kidney yin deficiency and qi stagnation in the Bladder. This condition was treated with ***P-Support*** at 12 capsules a day. After taking the herbs, the patient only needed to get up once each night. The dosage was lowered to 9 pills a day to maintain the results. Since then, there had only been a few times where the patient needed to increase the dosage for a short time. The patient continued to keep them on hand. Submitted by L.M., Portland, Oregon.

PHARMACOLOGICAL AND CLINICAL RESEARCH

P-Support is formulated to treat prostate enlargement and prostatitis with symptoms such as urinary frequency, urgency, nocturia, feeling of incomplete emptying, terminal dribbling, and pain with urination. ***P-Support*** contains herbs that effectively reduce the size of the prostate, promote normal urination, relieve pain, and reduce inflammation.

Many herbs in ***P-Support*** have been used with marked success to treat benign prostatic hyperplasia and prostatitis, along with their associated symptoms. Pharmacologically, *Huang Bo* (Cortex Phellodendri Chinensis) is one of the most effective herbs to treat benign prostatic hyperplasia. It has been used successfully to treat prostatic urethral obstruction by promoting the relaxation and inhibiting the contraction of smooth muscle in the prostate.[3] Clinically, one study reported a 90% rate of effectiveness for treatment of chronic prostatitis among 108 patients. The herbal formula was given in decoction, and contained many herbs, such as *Huang Bo* (Cortex Phellodendri Chinensis), *Wang Bu Liu Xing* (Semen Vaccariae), *Chi Shao* (Radix Paeoniae Rubra), *Pu Gong Ying* (Herba Taraxaci), and others.[4] According to another study on chronic prostatitis, use of herbs was associated with a 93.7% rate of effectiveness among 32 patients (13 with recovery, 10 with significant improvement, 7 with moderate improvement, and 2 had no effect). Lastly, according to a study on prostatic hyperplasia, 52 patients were treated with very positive results using a decoction made from *Huang Qi* (Radix Astragali), *Hua Shi* (Talcum) and *Hu Po* (Succinum). That study reported that 38 of 52 patients reported complete remission of symptoms, 13 reported improvement in flow rate and reduction in prostate size, and 1 reported no improvement.[5]

Since benign prostatic hyperplasia is often accompanied by inflammation of the prostate gland and painful urination, herbs are added to alleviate these conditions. *Ru Xiang* (Gummi Olibanum) and *Mo Yao* (Myrrha) have excellent analgesic effects, and are commonly used to treat various types of pain.[6,7,8] *Tao Ren* (Semen Persicae), *Tong Cao* (Medulla Tetrapanacis) and *Hu Po* (Succinum) show marked anti-inflammatory properties, and are used to reduce swelling and enlargement of the prostate gland.[9,10,11]

Altered patterns and distinct characteristics of urination are some of the most common symptoms of benign prostatic hyperplasia that must be addressed. Herbs with diuretic effect are often quite successful in reducing frequency and urgency of urination, improving the force of the urinary stream, and relieving dribbling and incontinence. Herbs with diuretic action that promote normal urination and increase urinary output include *Fu Ling* (Poria), *Tong Cao* (Medulla Tetrapanacis), and *Pu Gong Ying* (Herba Taraxaci).[12,13,14]

In summary, ***P-Support*** is carefully crafted to address both the cause and the symptoms of benign prostatic hyperplasia and prostatitis. ***P-Support*** contains herbs that treat the cause by reducing the size of the prostate gland, and herbs that treat the symptoms by promoting normal urination, relieving pain, and reducing inflammation.

COMPARATIVE ANALYSIS

Benign prostate hyperplasia (BPH) is a disorder that affects most men as they age. In Western medicine, BPH may be treated with drugs that relax the bladder muscle to improve urination [such as Minipress (prazosin)], or drugs that shrink the prostate [such as Proscar (finasteride)]. However, Minipress (prazosin) is an α-adrenergic drug originally used to treat hypertension, and may cause side effects such as hypotension, dizziness, lightheadedness, orthostatism, syncope, and if/when the drug is discontinued, rebound hypertension. Proscar (finasteride) is effective, but requires three months or more to take effect, and may cause sexual dysfunction with side effects such as

P-Support™

impotence, decreased libido, and decreased volume of ejaculate. In severe cases of prostate hyperplasia, a catheter is inserted through the penis into the bladder to drain urine. Finally, Western medicine considers surgical removal of the prostate to be the best option.

Many herbs can be used to effectively treat BPH. The main therapeutic benefits of this formula include an analgesic effect to relieve pain, an anti-inflammatory effect to reduce swelling and inflammation, and a diuretic effect to promote normal urination. Though this formula does not cure BPH, it is quite effective to reduce the size of the prostate gland and relieve the symptoms.

Both Western and traditional Chinese medicines are effective to treat BPH. Drug therapy is usually unsatisfactory, as its effectiveness is limited, and is associated with significant side effects. Herbal therapy, on the other hand, is both safe and effective, and has short- and long-term benefits. However, in serious cases of prostate cancer, patients should be referred to Western medicine, as use of herbs as a sole treatment modality is not recommended.

References

1. Beers, M. and Berkow, R. *The Merck Manual of Diagnosis and Therapy 19th Edition*. 2011.
2. Balch, J. and Balch, P. *Prescriptions for Nutritional Healing*. Avery Publishing Group. 1997.
3. Xu Y, Ventura S. Extracts of bark from the traditional Chinese herb Phellodendron amurense inhibit contractility of the isolated rat prostate gland. Prostate Research Co-operative, Medicinal Chemistry and Drug Action, Monash Institute of Pharmaceutical Sciences, Monash University, 381 Royal Parade, Parkville, Victoria 3052, Australia. J Ethnopharmacol. 2010 Jan 8;127(1):196-9.
4. *Zhong Yao Lin Chuan Xin Yong* (New Clinical Applications of Chinese Medicine), 2001; 114.
5. *Xin Zhong Yi* (New Chinese Medicine), 1987; 10:54.
6. *Zhong Yao Xue* (Chinese Herbology), 1998; 539:540.
7. *Zhong Yao Xue* (Chinese Herbology), 1998; 541:542.
8. Su S, Wang T, Duan JA, Zhou W, Hua YQ, Tang YP, Yu L, Qian DW. Anti-inflammatory and analgesic activity of different extracts of Commiphora myrrha. Jiangsu Key Laboratory for TCM Formulae Research, Nanjing University of Chinese Medicine, Nanjing 210046, PR China. J Ethnopharmacol. 2011 Mar 24;134(2):251-8.
9. *Zhong Yao Tong Bao* (Journal of Chinese Herbology), 1986; 11(11):37.
10. *Chang Yong Zhong Yao Cheng Fen Yu Yao Li Shou Ce* (A Handbook of the Composition and Pharmacology of Common Chinese Drugs), 1994; 1459:1462.
11. *Shang Hai Zhong Yi Yao Za Zhi* (Shanghai Journal of Chinese Medicine and Herbology), 1958; 11:33.
12. *Chang Yong Zhong Yao Cheng Fen Yu Yao Li Shou Ce* (A Handbook of the Composition and Pharmacology of Common Chinese Drugs), 1994; 1383:1391.
13. *Zhong Yao Cai* (Study of Chinese Herbal Material), 1991; 14(9):40.
14. *Zhong Yao Xue* (Chinese Herbology), 1988; 171:172.

Pueraria Clear Sinus™

CLINICAL APPLICATIONS

- **Sinusitis** or **rhinitis** with purulent, yellow nasal discharge
- **Sinus infection** with headache, pain, and nasal obstruction
- **General nasal problems** including stuffy nose, sneezing, loss of smell, and yellow sticky nasal discharge

WESTERN THERAPEUTIC ACTIONS

- Antiallergic and antihistamine effects to treat allergy-induced sinusitis or rhinitis
- Antibiotic (antibacterial and antiviral) activities to treat bacterial and viral infections of the nose and the sinus cavity
- Anti-inflammatory effect to constricts the vessels in the nasal mucosa to open up sinus passages
- Analgesic effect to relieve sinus headache and pain

CHINESE THERAPEUTIC ACTIONS

- Dispels damp-heat accumulation
- Removes fluid congestion
- Unblocks nasal obstruction
- Clears heat and dispels purulent infection
- Alleviates sinus pain

DOSAGE

For treatment of sinusitis, rhinitis or sinus infection, take 4 to 6 capsules three times daily with warm water on an empty stomach one hour before or two hours after meals. For maintenance or prevention, take 3 capsules two times daily.

INGREDIENTS

Bai Shao (Radix Paeoniae Alba)
Bai Zhi (Radix Angelicae Dahuricae)
Cang Er Zi (Fructus Xanthii), dry fried
Chuan Xiong (Rhizoma Chuanxiong)
Da Huang (Radix et Rhizoma Rhei)
Da Zao (Fructus Jujubae)
Gan Cao (Radix et Rhizoma Glycyrrhizae)
Ge Gen (Radix Puerariae Lobatae)
Gui Zhi (Ramulus Cinnamomi)
Huang Qin (Radix Scutellariae)
Jie Geng (Radix Platycodonis)
Sheng Jiang (Rhizoma Zingiberis Recens)
Shi Gao (Gypsum Fibrosum)
Xin Yi Hua (Flos Magnoliae)

BACKGROUND

Sinusitis and rhinitis are common disorders of the nose. Sinusitis is the inflammation of the paranasal sinuses with symptoms such as nasal obstruction and congestion, purulent rhinorrhea, pain, fatigue and fever. Sinusitis may be caused by viral, bacterial or fungal infection. Rhinitis is inflammation of the nasal mucous membrane with symptoms such as nasal congestion, rhinorrhea, itching and sneezing. Rhinitis is usually caused by allergy, irritation, and viral infection.

FORMULA EXPLANATION

Pueraria Clear Sinus is formulated to treat sinusitis, rhinitis or sinus infection due to damp-heat and fluid congestion. Clinically, common signs and symptoms include stuffy nose, sticky yellow discharge, loss of ability to smell, and sinus headache.

Xin Yi Hua (Flos Magnoliae) and *Cang Er Zi* (Fructus Xanthii) are the chief herbs in this formula. They have acrid, dispersing, and decongestant properties to unblock the nasal passages. *Huang Qin* (Radix Scutellariae), *Shi Gao* (Gypsum Fibrosum) and *Da Huang* (Radix et Rhizoma Rhei) clear heat, reduce inflammation and neutralize the warming properties of the chief herbs. *Gui Zhi* (Ramulus Cinnamomi) and *Bai Shao* (Radix Paeoniae Alba) harmonize the *wei* (defense) and *ying* (nutritive) levels to dispel external pathogenic influences. *Ge Gen* (Radix Puerariae Lobatae) dispels wind-heat and alleviates pain. *Chuan Xiong* (Rhizoma Chuanxiong) relieves sinus headache. *Jie Geng* (Radix Platycodonis) and *Bai Zhi* (Radix Angelicae Dahuricae) eliminate pus and resolve nasal discharge and post-nasal drip associated with sinus infection. *Da Zao* (Fructus Jujubae), *Sheng Jiang* (Rhizoma Zingiberis Recens), and *Gan Cao* (Radix et Rhizoma Glycyrrhizae) harmonize the formula and protect the middle *jiao*.

In short, ***Pueraria Clear Sinus*** clears damp-heat from the nose to treat sinusitis, rhinitis or sinus infection.

CAUTIONS & CONTRAINDICATIONS

- This formula is contraindicated during pregnancy and nursing.
- This formula is designed for sinusitis or rhinitis due to damp-heat with yellow and sticky discharge. Sinusitis or rhinitis due to wind-cold with clear watery discharge should be treated with ***Magnolia Clear Sinus***.
- *Cang Er Zi* (Fructus Xanthii) used in this formula has been carefully dry fried at high temperature until they appear dark brown or slightly charred, as dictated by Chinese *Materia Medica*. Dry frying is necessary because this process simultaneously increase the effect [by enhancing the extraction of active compounds] and decreases the side effects [by destroying the undesired glycosides]. Nonetheless, because *Cang Er Zi* (Fructus Xanthii) is metabolized by the liver and eliminated by the kidney, individuals with pre-exiting liver or kidney diseases should not take this formula.[1]
- The following warning statement is required by the State of California: "This product contains *Da Huang* (Radix et Rhizoma Rhei). Read and follow directions carefully. Do not use if you have or develop diarrhea, loose stools, or abdominal pain because *Da Huang* (Radix et Rhizoma Rhei) may worsen these conditions and be harmful to your health. Consult your physician if you have frequent diarrhea or if you are pregnant, nursing, taking medication, or have a medical condition."

Pueraria Clear Sinus ™

CLINICAL NOTES

- Approximately 25% of all sinusitis are related to food allergies. Therefore, it is extremely important to identify and avoid the allergen. Common allergens include milk, wheat, eggs, citrus fruits, corn and peanuts.
- Some patients may experience mild stomach discomfort while taking this herbal formula. If such a reaction occurs, ask the patient to reduce the dosage and increase the frequency of administration (instead of taking 4 capsules three times daily, take 2 capsules six times a day). Taking the herbs with food may prevent stomach discomfort.
- ***Pueraria Clear Sinus*** is more effective for sinus infections. ***Magnolia Clear Sinus*** is more effective for sinusitis and rhinitis due to seasonal allergies.

Pulse Diagnosis by Dr. Jimmy Wei-Yen Chang:

- Superficial and forceful pulse on the right *cun*.

SUPPLEMENTARY FORMULAS

- For infection of the ear, nose, and throat, add ***Herbal ENT***.
- To enhance the overall antibacterial function, add ***Herbal ABX***.
- To enhance the overall antiviral function, add ***Herbal AVR***.
- For profuse yellow phlegm, post-nasal drip, dyspnea, or chest congestion, use ***Pinellia XPT***.
- With more underlying damp and phlegm with Spleen qi deficiency, add ***Pinellia Complex***.
- For wind-heat at the exterior, add ***Lonicera Complex***.
- For Lung heat with cough, dyspnea, and fever, combine with ***Respitrol (Heat)***.
- For acute headache, add ***Corydalin (AC)***.
- For chronic headache due to deficiency, add ***Corydalin (CR)***.
- For nasal symptoms associated with environmental or toxic poisoning, add ***Herbal DTX***.
- For excess heat, add ***Gardenia Complex***.
- To strengthen the constitution of the body, use ***Imperial Tonic***.
- To enhance immunity against allergies, take ***Immune +*** at a low dose (1 to 2 capsules a day) during non-allergy seasons.
- With severe inflammation, combine with ***Astringent Complex***.

ACUPUNCTURE TREATMENT

Traditional Points:

- *Feishu* (BL 13), *Hegu* (LI 4), *Quchi* (LI 11), *Shangyang* (LI 1), *Lingtai* (GV 10)
- *Shaoshang* (LU 11), *Quchi* (LI 11), *Yingxiang* (LI 20)

Classic Master Tung's Points:

- **Allergy:** *Mu* (T 11.17), *Linggu* (T 22.05), *Tianshi* (T 33.15), *Dishi* (T 33.14), *Renshi* (T 33.13), *Simashang* (T 88.18), *Simazhong* (T 88.17), *Simaxia* (T 88.19), *Yingxiang* (LI 20), *Tongtian* (T 88.03), *Tongguan* (T 88.01), *Zhenjing* (T 1010.08), *Shangli* (T 1010.09), *Shuitong* (T 1010.19), *Shuijin* (T 1010.20), *Fenjin* (T 44.01), *Zhengben* (T 1010.12). Bleed dark veins nearby *Sihuawai* (T 77.14). Bleed before needling for best result.
- **Nose (stuffy):** *Linggu* (T 22.05), *Jianzhong* (T 44.06), *Mu* (T 11.17), *Tianshi* (T 33.15), *Dishi* (T 33.14), *Renshi* (T 33.13), *Zhenjing* (T 1010.08), *Simashang* (T 88.18), *Simazhong* (T 88.17), *Simaxia* (T 88.19)
- **Absence of smell:** *Fukuai* (T 1010.15), *Liukuai* (T 1010.16), *Simashang* (T 88.18), *Simazhong* (T 88.17), *Simaxia* (T 88.19). Bleed dark veins nearby *Sihuashang* (T 77.08), *Sihuazhong* (T 77.09), *Sihuaxia* (T 77.11) and *Weizhong* (BL 40). Bleed before needling for best result.

Master Tung's Points by Dr. Chuan-Min Wang:

- **Allergy, sinusitis, rhinitis:** Needle *Lianquan* (CV 23) using the Remove Dust 7 needling technique (from *Ling Shu*). Needle bilaterally *Tianrong* (SI 17), *Fenjin* (T 44.01), *Sanyinjiao* (SP 6).

Balance Method by Dr. Richard Tan:

- Left side: *Chize* (LU 5), *Taiyuan* (LU 9), *Zusanli* (ST 36), *Xiangu* (ST 43)
- Right side: *Sanjian* (LI 3), *Quchi* (LI 11), *Taibai* (SP 3), *Yinlingquan* (SP 9)
- Left and right sides can be alternated from treatment to treatment.

Auricular Medicine by Dr. Li-Chun Huang:

- **Stuffy nose:** Lung, Internal Nose, Adrenal Gland, External Ear, Nasopharynx. Bleed Ear Apex.
- **Allergies:** Allergic Area, Endocrine, Adrenal Gland, Spleen. Bleed Ear Apex.
- **Chronic rhinitis:** Internal Nose, External Ear, Lower Lung, Allergic Area, Adrenal Gland
- **Allergic rhinitis:** Internal Nose, External Ear, Adrenal Gland, Endocrine, Allergic Area, Spleen, Lung, Sympathetic. Bleed Ear Apex.
- **Sinusitis:** Upper Jaw, Upper Palate, Forehead, Internal Nose, External Ear, *San Jiao*, Lung, Endocrine, Adrenal Gland, corresponding points
- **Nasopharyngitis, post nasal drip:** Nasopharynx, Sympathetic, Allergic Area, Lung, Endocrine, Trachea. Bleed Ear Apex.
- **Snoring, apnea:** Trachea, *San Jiao*, Lower Lung, Pharynx, Larynx, Sympathetic, Nasopharynx, Chest, Mouth, Esophagus, Tooth

NUTRITION

- Reduce or eliminate the intake of dairy products, as they increase mucus production.
- Drink plenty of distilled water throughout the day to help drainage.
- Make sure the diet contains an adequate amount of vitamin A and C. Vitamin A is essential for healthy mucous lining of the respiratory tract. Vitamin C is well recognized for its effect to prevent and treat infection.

Pueraria Clear Sinus™

- The Spleen is responsible for generating post-natal qi and good Spleen function also contributes to a healthy immune system. Foods that damage the Spleen should be avoided:
  - Avoid any and all foods that contain sugar, such as cake, dessert, candy, chocolate, canned juice, soft drinks, caffeinated drinks, stevia, sugar substitutes, agave, xylitol, and corn syrup.
  - Avoid raw or uncooked meats, such as sashimi, sushi, steak tartar, and seared meat. Minimize consumption of foods that are cooling in nature, including tofu, tomato, celery, asparagus, bamboo, seaweed, kelp, bitter melon, cucumber, gourd, luffa, eggplant, winter melon, watermelon, honeydew, citrus, oranges, guava, grapefruit, pineapple, plums, pear, banana, papaya, white radish, mustard leaf, potherb mustard, Chinese kale, napa, and bamboo sprout. Do not eat foods straight from the refrigerator. Long-term intake of cold fruits and vegetables like the ones listed above may be damaging to the Spleen. The cooling property of foods can be neutralized by cooking or adding 20 pieces of *Gou Qi Zi* (Fructus Lycii).
  - Avoid carbohydrates like white rice or bread as they may produce dampness.
  - No seafood especially shellfish, like crabs, oyster, scallops, clams, lobster and shrimp (they enter the *yangming* Stomach channel).
  - Avoid fermented foods like cheese or fermented tofu.
  - Do not eat dairy products, such as milk, cream, yogurt, cheese, and ice cream.
  - No lamb, beef, goose or duck.
  - Avoid fried or greasy foods.
- Warm and hot natured foods that damage qi and yin should be avoided, such as:
  - certain fruits like mango and durian that produce heat.
  - stimulants like coffee, alcohol, and energy drinks.
  - spicy/pungent/aromatic vegetables such as pepper, garlic, onions, basil, rosemary, cumin, funnel, anise, leeks, chives, scallions, thyme, saffron, wormwood, mustard, chili pepper, and wasabi.
- Avoid food and drinks with artificial coloring.
- Consume as few meat products as possible. Do not eat processed meats, such as lunch meats, hot dogs and sausages, as they contain nitrites that are associated with inflammation and chronic disease.

The Tao of Nutrition by Dr. Maoshing Ni and Cathy McNease:

- **Allergy**
  - Recommendations: ginger, onions, garlic, bamboo shoots, cabbage beets, beet top tea, carrots, leafy greens, yams, and ganoderma mushroom.
  - Drink ginger tea to induce sweating.
  - Drink beet top tea as a water source.
  - Avoid wheat, citrus fruits, chocolate, shellfish, dairy products, eggs, potatoes, polluted meats, and polluted air.
- **Chronic sinusitis**
  - Recommendations: ginger, green onions, magnolia flower, bananas, garlic, black mushrooms, chrysanthemum flowers, mulberry leaves, and apricot kernel.
  - Make tea from magnolia flower, basil, ginger, and green onion. Drink three times daily for at least one week.
  - Combine magnolia flowers and eggs, cook and eat.
  - Make tea from mulberry leaves and chrysanthemums, then cook rice porridge in the tea, adding apricot kernels.
  - Boil tea of mint, basil, and ginger. While boiling the tea, inhale the steam through the nose, three times daily for at least two months.
  - Avoid coffee and stop smoking.

LIFESTYLE INSTRUCTIONS

- Avoid allergens that may trigger sinusitis and rhinitis.
- Application of saline solution to the nose three to four times daily helps to reduce nasal congestion.
- Strengthen the immune system by increasing exercise, reducing worry and stress, and developing a normal sleep pattern.
- Steam inhalation is helpful to drain sinus infections. Rinsing the nostrils with cold saline water is helpful to desensitize the nose to temperature and common allergens. Repeatedly suck in and blow out the cold saline water for one to two minutes every morning.

CASE STUDIES

- M.B., a 37-year-old male, presented with pain located on the forehead that had been occurring for three days. Additional symptoms included thick yellow mucus and a fever of 102°F. Pain was also found upon palpation of his sinal cavities. His Western diagnosis was sinusitis and the TCM diagnosis was wind-heat. Upon the diagnosis, the patient was administered ***Pueraria Clear Sinus*** and ***Herbal ABX***, both at four capsules three times a day. In one day the fever had cleared, followed by decreased in pain in two days. The sinuses finally resolved within a week. Submitted by A.I., Hilo, Hawaii.
- L.T., a 28-year-old male, presented with allergies, sneezing, occipital stiffness, and sinus headache along the Stomach and Gallbladder channels. Clear copious phlegm was also present. Pulse was wiry and big on the left side and slippery and big on the right side. The practitioner diagnosed this condition as wind-cold allergies with phlegm dampness. The patient was given ***Pueraria Clear Sinus*** at four capsules three times a day. With ***Pueraria Clear Sinus*** the allergies resolved within 1 week of taking the formula. He continues to take it whenever he experiences an allergic reaction. Submitted by L.M., Lafayette, Colorado.
- M.C., a 60-year-old male, presented with cough and nasal congestion with yellow discharge. He had been previously diagnosed with sinusitis and bronchitis and was currently taking antibiotics. There had been a chronic case of allergies triggering repeated episodes of his sinus infections and bronchitis. The

Pueraria Clear Sinus ™

patient would get an episode every 2 to 3 months and had been on a lot of antihistamine and cortisone medications. The practitioner diagnosed this condition as exterior wind-heat with phlegm heat. Upon diagnosis, the patient was prescribed ***Pueraria Clear Sinus*** and ***Herbal ABX***. With taking the herbs, the patient reported her sinusitis and bronchitis had cleared, the discharge lessened in amount and the color became clear. Submitted by B.L., Fort Myers, Florida.

- A robustly healthy female presented with flu symptoms. She had a sore throat and yellow mucus. The practitioner diagnosed her condition as wind-heat. In conjunction with acupuncture treatment, the practitioner also had the patient utilize a vaporizer for steaming her face. ***Lonicera Complex*** and ***Pueraria Clear Sinus*** worked quite effectively after taking them for three to four days at larger dosages. The practitioner also noted that *Pu Ji Xiao Du Yin* (Universal Benefit Decoction to Eliminate Toxin) could be used if the condition was more severe and had presence of heat and toxins. Submitted by S.C., La Crescenta, California.
- A 28-year-old male presented with dizziness, sinus drainage, ringing in the ears, bitter taste in the mouth, and night sweating for about five weeks. His tongue was dry with a red tip and a greasy yellow coating. His pulse was at 80 beats per minute, fast and superficial with Kidney, Spleen/Stomach deficient. His medical doctor diagnosed his condition to be caused by fluid in the ears. The practitioner diagnosed the condition as nasal obstruction due to heat. A combination herbal treatment of ***Pueraria Clear Sinus*** and *Zhi Bai Di Huang Wan* (Anemarrhena, Phellodendron, and Rehmannia Pills) was administered. Dizziness was resolved within two days of the treatment. The patient noted that the herbal formulas worked much better for his condition than the antihistamines. Submitted by S.T., San Jose, California.
- A 42-year-old midwife presented with sinus infection (for ten days) with yellow green discharge, increased pressure and pain in the sinus cavity and the ears, and severe pain. Upon examination, it was found that there was also lymph node swelling and pain. The TCM diagnosis was phlegm heat in the Lung and toxic heat in the throat. The patient was instructed to take ***Pueraria Clear Sinus*** (4 capsules three times daily) and ***Herbal ABX*** (4 capsules three times daily). Within one day, the patient responded that there was a lot less pain and marked decrease in swelling. She continued to improve with each dose and stated that she felt "all better" by the third day. The practitioner commented the formulas were "very amazing and powerful." Submitted by M.N., Knoxville, Tennessee.
- A 33-year-old male presented with frontal headaches with yellow nasal discharge. No body aches or fever were reported. His pulse was rapid. The practitioner diagnosed the condition as phlegm heat and wind-heat. The patient took ***Pueraria Clear Sinus*** for ten days (6 capsules three times daily). Subsequently, his phlegm and headaches resolved. Submitted by M.K., Sherman Oaks, California.

PHARMACOLOGICAL AND CLINICAL RESEARCH

Pueraria Clear Sinus is formulated to treat sinusitis, rhinitis or sinus infection. The ingredients in this formula have antibiotic (antibacterial, antiviral and antifungal) effects to treat infection, antiallergic and antihistamine effects to treat allergy, and anti-inflammatory effects to reduce swelling and inflammation. Together, they effectively treat both the causes and the symptoms of rhinitis and sinusitis.

Pueraria Clear Sinus uses many herbs with antibacterial effects to treat the cause of the disease. *Huang Qin* (Radix Scutellariae) has a wide-spectrum inhibitory effect against *Staphylococcus aureus*, beta-hemolytic streptococcus, *Diplococcus pneumoniae*, *Pseudomonas aeruginosa*, *Bacillus dysenteriae*, *E. coli*, *Bordetella pertussis*, *Vibrio cholerae*, *Diplococcus meningitidis*, leptospira and various species of dermatophytes and influenza viruses. *Huang Qin* (Radix Scutellariae) is most effective against *Staphylococcus aureus* and *Pseudomonas aeruginosa*. Furthermore, it was discovered that the effectiveness of standard antibiotics such as ampicillin, amoxicillin, methicillin and cefotaxime can be potentiated with addition of baicalin, a flavone isolated from this herb. With the addition of baicalin, the effectiveness of these beta-lactam antibiotics was restored against beta-lactam-resistant *Staphylococcus aureus* and methicillin-resistant *Staphylococcus aureus* (MRSA).[2,3] *Da Huang* (Radix et Rhizoma Rhei) also has a broad-spectrum antibiotic effect. It is most effective against the streptococcus and staphylococcus species of bacteria. It also inhibits the activity of *Corynebacterium diphtheriae*, *Bacillus subtilis*, *Salmonella typhi*, and *Bacillus dysenteriae*. Constituents responsible for the antibiotic effect include emodin, rhein, and aloe-emodin.[4] In fact, aloe-emodin, an anthraquinone from *Da Huang* (Radix et Rhizoma Rhei), has potent antibacterial activity and is effective against methicillin-resistant *Staphylococcus aureus* (MRSA).[5]

Furthermore, ***Pueraria Clear Sinus*** utilizes many herbs with antiviral effects to treat the cause of the disease. *Ge Gen* (Radix Puerariae Lobatae) has an inhibitory effect on enterovirus 71 (EV71) when given before, simultaneously with, or after viral infection. *Gui Zhi* (Ramulus Cinnamomi) has an antiviral effect against influenza viruses.[6] *Huang Qin* (Radix Scutellariae) has a wide spectrum of antiviral activity. Specifically, baicalein and wogonin, two compounds from the herb, boost innate antiviral immunity by stimulating the production of cytokines and increasing the resistance to viral infection in human leukocytes.[7]

Pueraria Clear Sinus also incorporates many herbs with antifungal effects to treat the cause of the disease. *Xin Yi Hua* (Flos Magnoliae) has an inhibitory effect on dermatomycoses.[8] *Gui Zhi* (Ramulus Cinnamomi) and *Huang Qin* (Radix Scutellariae) also have antifungal effect. *Gui Zhi* (Ramulus Cinnamomi) has a strong activity against murine oral candidiasis. Cinnamaldehyde, a compound from the plant, was the principal component responsible that inhibited the growth of *Candida albicans*. The researchers concluded that oral intake of a cassia preparation is

Pueraria Clear Sinus ™

a clinical candidate for a prophylactic or therapeutic tool against oral candida infection.[9] *Huang Qin* (Radix Scutellariae) has an *in vivo* antifungal effect against *Candida albicans*.[10]

In addition, ***Pueraria Clear Sinus*** contains many herbs to treat allergy-induced rhinitis and sinusitis. *Xin Yi Hua* (Flos Magnoliae) has been used successfully for the management of allergic diseases. This herb shows an antiallergic effect by inducing mitochondria and caspase-dependent mast cell apoptosis.[11] In addition, *Xin Yi Hua* (Flos Magnoliae) and *Bai Zhi* (Radix Angelicae Dahuricae) have an antihistamine effect to inhibit histamine release and inflammation.[12,13] *Jie Geng* (Radix Platycodonis) also has an antiallergic effect, as it acts by inhibiting the inflammatory cytokines and the signaling cascades, according to *in vivo* and *in vitro* studies.[14] Lastly, *Huang Qin* (Radix Scutellariae) shows a remarkable effect as an antiallergic agent. It inhibits histamine and leukotriene release from mast cells activated, with greater potency than Intal (cromolyn), a drug that prevents the release of inflammatory chemicals such as histamine from mast cells.[15]

Since inflammation is a primary condition in both rhinitis (inflammation nasal mucous membrane) and sinusitis (inflammation of paranasal sinus), many herbs with anti-inflammatory effects are used in ***Pueraria Clear Sinus***. *Da Huang* (Radix et Rhizoma Rhei) and *Xin Yi Hua* (Flos Magnoliae) exert their anti-inflammatory effects via inhibition of nitric oxide production.[16,17] *Huang Qin* (Radix Scutellariae) has significant and potent anti-inflammatory properties via inhibition of nitric oxide, cyclo-oxygenase-2, prostaglandin E2, and proinflammatory cytokines.[18] *Chuan Xiong* (Rhizoma Chuanxiong) shows its anti-inflammatory effect by suppressing TNF-α production and bioactivity.[19] *Bai Shao* (Radix Paeoniae Alba) has a significant effect to decrease the secretion of monocyte chemotactic proteins (MCP-1 and MCP-3), two potent chemokines that mediate allergic nasal inflammation.[20] Lastly, *Sheng Jiang* (Rhizoma Zingiberis Recens) has several mechanisms for its anti-inflammatory effect. It has inhibitory effects on prostaglandin biosynthesis, similar to that of non-steroidal anti-inflammatory drugs. Furthermore, it suppresses prostaglandin synthesis through inhibition of cyclo-oxygenase-1 and cyclo-oxygenase-2. Lastly, ginger suppresses leukotriene biosynthesis by inhibiting 5-lipoxygenase.[21]

Clinically, many herbs in ***Pueraria Clear Sinus*** have been used with great success to treat rhinitis and sinusitis. According to one study, 46 patients with chronic sinusitis were treated with an herbal formula with marked effectiveness in 35 cases, moderate improvement in 8 cases, and no response in 3 cases. The herbal formula was given in decoction, once daily, for seven days per course of treatment. The herbal formula contained *Xin Yi Hua* (Flos Magnoliae), *Cang Er Zi* (Fructus Xanthii), *Chuan Xiong* (Rhizoma Chuanxiong), *Bai Zhi* (Radix Angelicae Dahuricae) and others.[22] According to another study, 120 patients were treated with a 95% rate of effectiveness using an herbal formula with *Xin Yi Hua* (Flos Magnoliae) as the chief ingredient.[23] In addition to oral ingestion, topical application of herb also showed marked treatment effect. Topical application of essential oil of *Xin Yi Hua* (Flos Magnoliae) has been associated with reduction of mucous secretion, reduction of inflammation, and relief of nasal obstruction.[24] In fact, 1,576 patients with chronic sinusitis were treated with an 86.9% effective rate using topical application of an herbal formula made from *Xin Yi Hua* (Flos Magnoliae) and *Cang Er Zi* (Fructus Xanthii).[25] Finally, since many patients suffering from rhinitis and sinusitis will also have pain and headache, *Bai Zhi* (Radix Angelicae Dahuricae), *Chuan Xiong* (Rhizoma Chuanxiong), and *Ge Gen* (Radix Puerariae Lobatae) are added for their effect to treat headache and relieve pain.[26,27,28]

In summary, ***Pueraria Clear Sinus*** is an excellent formula to treat the causes and the symptoms of rhinitis and sinusitis.

COMPARATIVE ANALYSIS

Sinusitis, rhinitis, and sinus infection are common nasal disorders. In Western medicine, these conditions are primarily treated with vasoconstrictive drugs that promote drainage, such as pseudoephedrine. Though effective, it is a strong stimulant and may cause many side effects, such as nervousness, restlessness, dizziness, difficulty sleeping, upset stomach, difficulty breathing, fast or irregular heartbeat, muscle weakness, palpitations, tremors, and hallucinations. In addition to vasoconstrictive drugs, antibiotic drugs may be used to address infectious sinusitis, rhinitis, and sinus infection. The main advantage of these two types of medications is that they are relatively effective, and reasonably safe, so long as they are prescribed correctly and monitored carefully.

Sinusitis, rhinitis, and sinus infection are effectively treated with herbs that drain the sinus cavity, reduce nasal mucous secretions, and treat infection. These herbs may be given to treat acute or chronic infectious sinusitis and rhinitis. These herbs are very effective, and do not have the stimulating side effects that drugs have. Furthermore, antibiotic herbs are much safer and gentler than antibiotic drugs, and are able to treat infection without causing significant side effects or secondary infections. However, it is important to keep in mind that this formula is primarily a formula that treats sinusitis and rhinitis. Though it does have an antibiotic effect, its potency is only moderate, and may not be suitable in cases of severe sinus or respiratory tract infections.

Both drugs and herbs are effective to treat sinusitis and rhinitis. In most cases, use of herbs is more than sufficient, as they effectively treat both conditions with little risk of side effects and adverse reactions. In cases of severe and stubborn sinus infection, additional therapies may be needed, such as antibiotic drugs or another antibiotic herbal formula.

References

1. *Xian Dai Zhong Yao Du Li Xue* (Modern Toxicology of Chinese Materia Medica) 2005;63-65.

Pueraria Clear Sinus ™

2. *Zhong Yao Xue* (Chinese Herbology), 1988; 137:140.
3. *J Pharm Pharmacol* 2000 Mar;52(3):361-6.
4. *Zhong Yao Xue* (Chinese Herbology), 1998; 251:256.
5. Hatano T, Kusuda M, Inada K, Ogawa TO, Shiota S, Tsuchiya T, Yoshida T. Effects of tannins and related polyphenols on methicillin-resistant Staphylococcus aureus. Phytochemistry. 2005 Sep;66(17):2047-55.
6. *Zhong Yao Xue* (Chinese Herbology), 1998; 65:67.
7. Błach-Olszewska Z, Jatczak B, Rak A, Lorenc M, Gulanowski B, Drobna A, Lamer-Zarawska E. Production of cytokines and stimulation of resistance to viral infection in human leukocytes by Scutellaria baicalensis flavones. Ludwik Hirszfeld Institute of Immunology and Experimental Therapy, Polish Academy of Sciences, Wrocław, Poland. J Interferon Cytokine Res. 2008 Sep;28(9): 571-81.
8. *Zhong Yao Xue* (Chinese Herbology), 1998; 84:85.
9. Taguchi Y, Takizawa T, Ishibashi H, Sagawa T, Arai R, Inoue S, Yamaguchi H, Abe S. Therapeutic effects on murine oral candidiasis by oral administration of cassia (Cinnamomum cassia) preparation. Research and Product Development Division, S & B Foods Inc., Tokyo, Japan. Nippon Ishinkin Gakkai Zasshi. 2010;51(1):13-21.
10. Wong KS, Tsang WK. In vitro antifungal activity of the aqueous extract of Scutellaria baicalensis Georgi root against Candida albicans. Int J Antimicrob Agents. 2009 Sep;34(3):284-5.
11. Kim G.C., Lee S.G., Park B.S., Kim J.Y., Song Y.S., Kim J.M., Yoo K.S., Huh G.Y., Jeong M.H., Lim Y.J., Kim H.M. & Yoo Y.H. Magnoliae flos induces apoptosis of RBL-2H3 cells via mitochondria and caspase. Int Arch Allergy Immunol. 2003 Jun;131(2):101-10.
12. Shen Y, Pang EC, Xue CC, Zhao ZZ, Lin JG, Li CG. Inhibitions of mast cell-derived histamine release by different Flos Magnoliae species in rat peritoneal mast cells. RMIT Chinese Medicine Research Group, School of Health Sciences, RMIT University, Victoria, Australia. Phytomedicine. 2008 Oct;15(10):808-14.
13. Chen Y., Fan G., Chen B., Xie Y., Wu H., Wu Y., Yan C. & Wang J. Separation and quantitative analysis of coumarin compounds from *Angelica dahurica* (Fisch. ex Hoffm) Benth. et Hook. f by pressurized capillary electrochromatography. *J Pharm Biomed Anal.* 2006, 41(1): 105-116.
14. Han EH, Park JH, Kim JY, Chung YC, Jeong HG. Inhibitory mechanism of saponins derived from roots of Platycodon grandiflorum on anaphylactic reaction and IgE-mediated allergic response in mast cells. BK21 Project Team, Department of Pharmacy, College of Pharmacy, Chosun University, Gwangju, South Korea. Food Chem Toxicol. 2009 Feb 4.
15. Kim DS, Son EJ, Kim M, Heo YM, Nam JB, Ro JY, Woo SS. Antiallergic herbal composition from Scutellaria baicalensis and Phyllostachys edulis. Unigen Inc., Cheonan, 330-863 Chungnam, Korea. Planta Med. 2010 May;76(7):678-82.
16. Wang CC, Huang YJ, Chen LG, Lee LT, Yang LL. Inducible nitric oxide synthase inhibitors of Chinese herbs III. Rheum palmatum. Planta Med. 2002 Oct;68(10):869-74.
17. Noshita T, Funayama S, Hirakawa T, Kidachi Y, Ryoyama K. Machilin G and four neolignans from young fruits of Magnolia denudata show various degrees of inhibitory activity on nitric oxide (NO) production. Department of Clinical Pharmacy, Aomori University, Aomori, Japan. Biosci Biotechnol Biochem. 2008 Oct;72(10):2775-8.
18. Yoon SB, Lee YJ, Park SK, Kim HC, Bae H, Kim HM, Ko SG, Choi HY, Oh MS, Park W. Anti-inflammatory effects of Scutellaria baicalensis water extract on LPS-activated RAW 264.7 macrophages. Dept. of Herbology, College of Oriental Medicine, Kyungwon University, Seongnam 461-701, Republic of Korea. J Ethnopharmacol. 2009 Sep 7;125(2):286-90.
19. Liu L, Ning ZQ, Shan S, Zhang K, Deng T, Lu XP, Cheng YY. Phthalide Lactones from Ligusticum chuanxiong inhibit lipopolysaccharide-induced TNF-alpha production and TNF-alpha-mediated NF-kappaB Activation. Planta Med. 2005 Sep;71(9):808-13.
20. Leem K, Kim H, Boo Y, Lee HS, Kim JS, Yoo YC, Ahn HJ, Park HJ, Seo JC, Kim HK, Jin SY, Park HK, Chung JH, Cho JJ. Effects of Paeonia lactiflora root extracts on the secretions of monocyte chemotactic protein-1 and -3 in human nasal fibroblasts. Phytother Res. 2004 Mar;18(3):241-3.
21. Grzanna R, Lindmark L, Frondoza CG. Ginger - an herbal medicinal product with broad anti-inflammatory actions. J Med Food. 2005 Summer;8(2):125-32.
22. *Shan Xi Zhong Yi* (Shanxi Chinese Medicine), 1991; 12(4):177.
23. *Zhong Yao Tong Bao* (Journal of Chinese Herbology), 1985; 5:45.
24. *Zhong Yao Cai* (Study of Chinese Herbal Material), 1990; 13(9):33.
25. *Zhong Xi Yi Jie He Za Zhi* (Journal of Integrated Chinese and Western Medicine), 1984; 4:211.
26. *Hu Bei Zhong Yi Za Zhi* (Hubei Journal of Chinese Medicine), 1989; (1):8.
27. *Zhong Xi Yi Jie He Za Zhi* (Journal of Integrated Chinese and Western Medicine), 1991; (1):52.
28. *Zhong Yao Xue* (Chinese Herbology), 1998; 101:103.

Resolve (AI)™

CLINICAL APPLICATIONS

- **Infection and inflammation with swelling:** goiter, lymphedema, hemorrhoids, intestinal polyps, tonsillitis, appendicitis, diverticulitis, infected lesions, dermatological swellings, mastitis, sinusitis, osteomyelitis, cellulitis, and thrombophlebitis
- **Hardness and nodules:** any type of swelling, mass, enlargement, hardness, nodule, scrofula, boil, carbuncle, goiter, sore, lump, furuncle, abscess, polyp, hordeolum or hard-seated lesion in the body that may or may not have accompanying pus, pain or heat sensations
- **Lymphatic blockage:** this formula drains the lymphatic system to clear stagnation and treat lymph edema

WESTERN THERAPEUTIC ACTIONS

- Anti-infective (antibacterial and antiviral) properties to treat infection
- Anti-inflammatory action to reduce swelling and inflammation
- Antitumor and antiproliferative effects to resolve hardness and nodules
- Antipyretic influence to reduce fever
- Analgesic effect to relieve pain

CHINESE THERAPEUTIC ACTIONS

- Clears heat and detoxifies
- Reduces swelling and promotes discharge of pus
- Invigorates blood circulation and relieves pain

DOSAGE

Take 3 to 4 capsules three times daily on an empty stomach. For maximum effectiveness, take up to 6 to 8 capsules three times daily with two tall glasses of warm water. Herbs may be taken with meals if they cause upset on an empty stomach.

INGREDIENTS

Bai Zhi (Radix Angelicae Dahuricae)
Chen Pi (Pericarpium Citri Reticulatae)
Chi Shao (Radix Paeoniae Rubrae)
Dang Gui Wei (Extremitas Radix Angelicae Sinensis)
Fang Feng (Radix Saposhnikoviae)
Gan Cao (Radix et Rhizoma Glycyrrhizae)
Jin Yin Hua (Flos Lonicerae Japonicae)
Kun Bu (Thallus Eckloniae)
Mo Yao (Myrrha)
Ru Xiang (Gummi Olibanum)
Tong Cao (Medulla Tetrapanacis)
Xia Ku Cao (Spica Prunellae)
Zao Jiao (Fructus Gleditsiae)
Zao Jiao Ci (Spina Gleditsiae)
Zhe Bei Mu (Bulbus Fritillariae Thunbergii)

BACKGROUND

Nodules and hardness are general terms that are used to describe many different types of infectious and inflammatory disorders, such as sores, abscesses, boils, carbuncles, goiter, lymphedema, mastitis, sinusitis, tonsillitis, infected lesions, dermatological swellings, and many others. Though these conditions may have different etiology, they are all characterized by swelling, inflammation, and possible infection.

FORMULA EXPLANATION

Resolve (AI) has excellent anti-infective and anti-inflammatory effects to resolve various nodules and hardnesses. From traditional Chinese medicine perspectives, it clears heat, eliminates toxins, reduces swelling, and invigorates blood circulation. Clinically, it can be used as a primary formula or as an adjunct formula to treat various conditions due to infection and inflammation characterized by the formation of hardness, nodules, and swelling.

Jin Yin Hua (Flos Lonicerae Japonicae) is an indispensable anti-inflammatory herb when it comes to treating toxic heat accumulation in the body. *Zhe Bei Mu* (Bulbus Fritillariae Thunbergii), *Xia Ku Cao* (Spica Prunellae), and *Kun Bu* (Thallus Eckloniae) are used in ***Resolve (AI)*** to penetrate the channels, soften hardness and expel phlegm accumulation. *Zao Jiao* (Fructus Gleditsiae), *Zao Jiao Ci* (Spina Gleditsiae), and *Bai Zhi* (Radix Angelicae Dahuricae) drain pus. Blood invigorating herbs such as *Ru Xiang* (Gummi Olibanum), *Mo Yao* (Myrrha), *Dang Gui Wei* (Extremitas Radix Angelicae Sinensis), and *Chi Shao* (Radix Paeoniae Rubrae) are used to disperse stagnation, relieve pain, and help with the regeneration or healing process. *Chen Pi* (Pericarpium Citri Reticulatae) regulates qi, dispels phlegm and has a synergistic effect with the blood invigorating herbs to soften hardness and relieve pain. *Fang Feng* (Radix Saposhnikoviae) dispels lingering wind that may reside in the channels and reduce superficial swelling. *Tong Cao* (Medulla Tetrapanacis) drains and expels dampness through urination. *Gan Cao* (Radix et Rhizoma Glycyrrhizae) further helps with detoxification and also harmonizes the formula.

In conclusion, ***Resolve (AI)*** clears heat and resolves phlegm to treat various disorders with formation of hardness and nodules.

CAUTIONS & CONTRAINDICATIONS

- This formula is contraindicated in cases of yin-type (deep-rooted) furuncles or carbuncles where the appearance is grayish dark and shows no signs of redness or pain.
- This formula is contraindicated during pregnancy and nursing.
- Use with caution in cases of Spleen qi deficiency or yang deficiency with coldness of the extremities.
- This formula is not designed for long-term use. It should be discontinued when the desired effects are achieved.
- Though this formula has herbs with marked anti-infective and anti-inflammatory effects, certain conditions, such as acute

Resolve (AI)™

appendicitis, are still better treated with surgery to avoid rupture of the appendix.

- This herbal formula contains herbs that invigorate blood circulation, such as *Dang Gui Wei* (Extremitas Radix Angelicae Sinensis). Therefore, patients who are on anticoagulant or antiplatelet therapies, such as Coumadin (warfarin), should use this formula with caution, or not at all, as there may be a higher risk of bleeding and bruising.[1,2,3]

CLINICAL NOTES

- The primary effect of ***Resolve (AI)*** is to reduce inflammation and swelling to soften hardness and nodules. Though it contains herbs with anti-infective effects, use of this formula alone may not be sufficient in treating acute infection with inflammation, such as in tonsillitis or sinusitis. Instead, another formula with heat-clearing, anti-infective actions should be added to potentiate its effect.
- Inflammation of the lymphatic system will often cause sub-cutaneous formation of hardness and nodules. Such conditions can be effectively treated with ***Resolve (AI)***.

Pulse Diagnosis by Dr. Jimmy Wei-Yen Chang:

- Big and convex pulse, a pulse that is expanding and forceful on all levels.

SUPPLEMENTARY FORMULAS

- To enhance the antiviral effect, add ***Herbal AVR***.
- To enhance the antibacterial effect, add ***Herbal ABX***.
- With more underlying damp and phlegm due to Spleen qi deficiency, add ***Pinellia Complex***.
- For tonsillitis, add ***Herbal ENT***.
- For high blood pressure and fast heart rate due to excess fire, add ***Gardenia Complex***.
- For nasal polyps or sinusitis, add ***Magnolia Clear Sinus*** or ***Pueraria Clear Sinus***.
- For mastitis, add ***Resolve (Upper)***.
- For goiter due to hyperthyroidism, add ***Thyrodex***.
- For goiter due to hypothyrodism, add ***Thyro-forte***.
- For constipation, add ***Gentle Lax (Excess)***.
- For endometriosis, add ***Resolve (Lower)***.
- For prostate enlargement, add ***P-Support***.
- For lymphatic drainage, add ***Circulation (SJ)***.
- For herpes or shingles, combine with ***Gentiana Complex*** or ***Dermatrol (HZ)***.
- For joint enlargement due to inflammation, add ***Flex (Heat)***.
- For gout, add ***Flex (GT)***.
- For water retention, add ***Herbal DRX***.
- For chronic stubborn swelling with blood stagnation, add ***Circulation (SJ)***.
- For weepy skin conditions, add ***Dermatrol (Damp)***.
- For dry skin conditions, add ***Dermatrol (Dry)***.
- For non-healing open sores due to qi deficiency, add ***Immune +***.

ACUPUNCTURE TREATMENT

Traditional Points:

- *Weizhong* (BL 40), *Quchi* (LI 11), *Xuehai* (SP 10), *Shenzhu* (GV 12), *Lingtai* (GV 10), *Hegu* (LI 4), *ah shi* points
- Bleed veins around *Weizhong* (BL 40). Needle *xi* (cleft) points of the channel in which there is swelling.

Classic Master Tung's Points:

- **Appendicitis:** *Wanshunyi* (T 22.08), *Wanshüner* (T 22.09), *Shanggao* (T 22.21)*, *Xiagao* (T 22.22)*, *Sihuashang* (T 77.08)
- **Boil and carbuncle:** *Jianzhong* (T 44.06), *Waisanguan* (T 77.27), *Zhiwu* (T 11.26)
- **Cellulitis:** *Linggu* (T 22.05), *Yizhong* (T 77.05), *Erzhong* (T 77.06), *Sanzhong* (T 77.07), *Simashang* (T 88.18), *Simazhong* (T 88.17), *Simaxia* (T 88.19), *Minghuang* (T 88.12), *Tianhuang* (T 88.13), *Qihuang* (T 88.14)
- **Goiter:** *Simashang* (T 88.18), *Simazhong* (T 88.17), *Simaxia* (T 88.19), *Sanzhong* (T 77.07), *Xinling* (T 33.17)*, *Sihuashang* (T 77.08), *Cesanli* (T 77.22), *Jianyu* (LI 15), *Yizhong* (T 77.05), *Erzhong* (T 77.06), *Cexiasanli* (T 77.23). Bleed the LU area on the lower limb. Bleed the back of the neck. Bleed before needling for best result.
- **Hemorrhoids:** *Qimen* (T 33.01), *Qijiao* (T 33.02), *Qizheng* (T 33.03), *Waisanguan* (T 77.27), *Yizhong* (T 77.05), *Erzhong* (T 77.06), *Sanzhong* (T 77.07), *Kongzui* (LU 6), *Huofu* (T 88.41)*, *Huoliang* (T 88.42)*, *Huochang* (T 88.43)*. Bleed dark veins on the back of the knees. Bleed dark veins on the KI channel of the lower limb. Bleed before needling for best result.
- **Lymph blockage/swelling:** *Linggu* (T 22.05), *Jianzhong* (T 44.06), *Yizhong* (T 77.05), *Erzhong* (T 77.06), *Sanzhong* (T 77.07), *Menjin* (T 66.05), *Sihuaxia* (T 77.11)
- **Lipoma:** *Minghuang* (T 88.12), *Qihuang* (T 88.14). Bleed the lipoma for yellow fluids. Bleed before needling for best result.
- **Mastitis:** *Jianfeng* (T 44.31)*, *Jianzhong* (T 44.06), *Fenzhishang* (T DT.01), *Shuanglongyi* (T 77.29)*, *Shuanglonger* (T 77.30)*, *Yizhong* (T 77.05), *Erzhong* (T 77.06), *Sanzhong* (T 77.07). Bleed the HT, LU, LR areas on the back from T4-T7 with cupping. Bleed before needling for best result.
- **Osteomyelitis:** *Tongshen* (T 88.09), *Tongwei* (T 88.10), *Tongguan* (T 88.01), *Simashang* (T 88.18), *Simazhong* (T 88.17). Needle everyday. Bleed the affected area.
- **Tonsillitis:** *Sanjian* (LI 3), *Mu* (T 11.17), *Qihu* (T 77.26), *Waisanguan* (T 77.27), *Xinling* (T 33.17)*, *Yizhong* (T 77.05), *Erzhong* (T 77.06), *Sanzhong* (T 77.07), *Hegu* (LI 4), *Linggu* (T 22.05), *Dabai* (T 22.04), *Tushui* (T 22.11), *Shiyin* (T 88.32), *Cesanli* (T 77.22), *Zuqianjin* (T 77.24). Bleed *Shaoshang* (LU 11) and also dark veins nearby *Yinlingquan* (SP 9) to *Xuehai* (SP 10), *Shaoshang* (LU 11). Bleed before needling for best result.

Master Tung's Points by Dr. Chuan-Min Wang:

- **Lumps, nodules, lymphatic system detoxification:** *Tongguan* (T 88.01), *Tongshan* (T 88.02), *Waisanguan* (T 77.27)

Resolve (AI)™

Balance Method by Dr. Richard Tan:

- Bleed *Shaoze* (SI 1) and *Dadun* (LR 1).
- Depending on the case, select additional 'balance' points.

Ear Acupuncture:

- **Acute tonsillitis:** Bleed the protruding vein in the back of the ear and apex of the tragus once a day. Needle and strongly stimulate the Throat, Pharynx, and Tonsils.

Auricular Medicine by Dr. Li-Chun Huang:

- **Simple goiter:** Thyroid, Endocrine, Pituitary, Thalamus, *San Jiao*, Kidney, Liver
- **Appendicitis:** Appendix, Abdomen, Sympathetic, Endocrine, *Shenmen*, Occiput
- **Lymphadenitis:** *San Jiao*, Allergic Area, Adrenal Gland, Liver, Spleen, Endocrine. Bleed Ear Apex or Helix 4

NUTRITION

- Refrain from eating spicy, greasy, fried foods, BBQ, canned foods, fermentated or dairy products, seafood, alcohol, duck or the internal organs of any creature during the course of treatment.
- Drink plenty of water throughout the day.
- For tonsillitis, gargle with salt water for one minute, twice daily.
- The Spleen is responsible for generating post-natal qi, and good Spleen function also contributes to a healthy immune system. Foods that damage the Spleen should be avoided:
  - Avoid any and all foods that contain sugar, such as cake, dessert, candy, chocolate, canned juice, soft drinks, caffeinated drinks, stevia, sugar substitutes, agave, xylitol, and corn syrup.
  - Avoid raw or uncooked meats, such as sashimi, sushi, steak tartar, and seared meat. Minimize consumption of foods that are cooling in nature, including tofu, tomato, celery, asparagus, bamboo, seaweed, kelp, bitter melon, cucumber, gourd, luffa, eggplant, winter melon, watermelon, honeydew, citrus, oranges, guava, grapefruit, pineapple, plums, pear, banana, papaya, white radish, mustard leaf, potherb mustard, Chinese kale, napa, and bamboo sprout. Do not eat foods straight from the refrigerator. Long-term intake of cold fruits and vegetables like those listed above may be damaging to the Spleen. The cooling property of foods can be neutralized by cooking or adding 20 pieces of *Gou Qi Zi* (Fructus Lycii).
  - Avoid carbohydrates like white rice or bread as they may produce dampness.
  - No seafood especially shellfish, like crabs, oyster, scallops, clams, lobster and shrimp (they enter the *yangming* Stomach channel).
  - Avoid fermented foods like cheese or fermented tofu.
  - Do not eat dairy products, such as milk, cream, yogurt, cheese, and ice cream.
  - No lamb, beef, goose or duck.
  - Avoid fried or greasy foods.
- Warm and hot natured foods that damage qi and yin should be avoided, such as:
  - certain fruits like mango and durian that produce heat.
  - stimulants like coffee, alcohol, and energy drinks.
  - spicy/pungent/aromatic vegetables such as pepper, garlic, onions, basil, rosemary, cumin, funnel, anise, leeks, chives, scallions, thyme, saffron, wormwood, mustard, chili pepper, and wasabi.
- Avoid food and drinks with artificial coloring.
- Consume as few meat products as possible. Do not eat processed meats, such as lunch meats, hot dogs and sausages, as they contain nitrites that are associated with inflammation and chronic disease.

The Tao of Nutrition by Dr. Maoshing Ni and Cathy McNease:

- **Lumps, nodules, and tumors:** Make tea from seaweed, peach kernel and green orange peels to take internally. Externally, make poultice of seaweed, ginger, and dandelion, and apply locally.
- **Swollen lymph glands, nodules, scrofula, goiter, and tuberculosis:** Dry taro root, grind to powder, then take equal parts of water chestnuts and jellyfish and boil into tea. Take the liquid and mix with the taro root powder; roll into pills the size of mung beans, take two tablespoons of pills three times daily with warm water.

LIFESTYLE INSTRUCTIONS

- Mild exercise is recommended as it will help with qi and blood circulation in the body. However, individuals with dermatological swellings should avoid heavy exercise that induces sweating, as it may delay healing of sores on the skin.
- Do not scratch the lesions to avoid contraction of infection and formation of scars. When boils or cysts break and are draining, keep the local area clean to prevent infection to the other parts of the body. After handling a boil, hands should be washed thoroughly to avoid transferring infection to other areas.

CASE STUDIES

- M.I., a 29-year-old female, presented with pus-filled sores located on her scalp. It had been occurring for a week along with symptoms of pain, slight itching, and fever. The cause was unknown. The sores were described as filled with white pus and 3-4 mm width. Her Western diagnosis was seborrheic dermatitis (capiti); and the TCM diagnosis was blood heat with wind dryness. The patient was prescribed the combination of ***Resolve (AI)*** and ***Herbal ABX*** both at three capsules three times a day. After three days the inflammation and sores had gone down and within one week the sores had completely resolved. Submitted by A.I., Hilo, Hawaii.
- J.V., a 56-year-old female, with diabetes and overweight presented with sores located in the genital region. The sores were affected by her blood sugar levels. The TCM diagnoses included wind and damp-heat. ***Resolve (AI)*** and ***Herbal ABX*** at four capsules three times a day were prescribed. This condition is ongoing

Resolve (AI)™

and occurs each time the patient doesn't control her diet or blood sugar level. ***Resolve (AI)*** and ***Herbal ABX*** greatly reduced the sores and alleviated the discomfort when needed. She kept this combination on hand and they have always work for her. Submitted by A.I., Hilo, Hawaii.

- F.T., a 44-year-old female marathon runner, presented with a Baker's cyst on her left knee, previously diagnosed by an MRI, measuring out to be 4 cm in diameter. Objective findings were pain and swelling, limiting her ability to walk and run. The practitioner diagnosed this condition as stagnation of qi and blood within the channels, as well as heat toxin and accumulation of phlegm. ***Resolve (AI)*** and ***Flex (NP)*** were prescribed at three grams three times a day at a 2:1 ratio. After one month of taking the herbs, the cyst was almost completely resolved. The formula had been modified to address the residual inflammation of stagnation in the channels. Thereafter, the client was able to begin long distance running again without further problems. Other than that condition, the patient was in excellent health. She had eliminated coffee from her diet and started eating anti-inflammatory foods while being treated for the cyst. Submitted by E.Z., Portland, Oregon.
- L.L., a 52-year-old female, presented with body aches all over the entire body along with swelling of the legs. Additional symptoms included low-grade fever, sore throat, and low energy. The patient had been previously diagnosed with Lyme's disease. Her pulse was thin and weak and her tongue was pale and dull with thin white coating. The practitioner diagnosed this condition as general qi and blood stagnation with Spleen qi deficiency. For treatment, the patient was instructed to take ***Resolve (AI)*** and ***Flex (NP)*** in conjunction with acupuncture. As a result, the patient's energy had increased, the pain had lessened, and the sore throat was no longer present. Additional treatment the patient had received was lymphatic massage which also had helped her improve. Submitted by B.L., Fort Myers, Florida.
- B.S., a 34-year-old male, presented with feeling of fullness in the head due to a middle ear condition. No objective findings were found when taking a look at his ears, nose, and throat. The TCM diagnosis was phlegm fluid retention in the upper jaw obstructing the orifices. For treatment, a combination of ***Magnolia Clear Sinus***, ***Resolve (AI)***, and ***Circulation (SJ)*** were prescribed. Relief of his headaches was experienced immediately after taking ***Resolve (AI)***. However, the pain had returned. It was believed to be a structural/mechanical blockage within the middle ear, which required greater attention than an herbal prescription. Submitted by B.S., Niceville, Florida.
- D.C., a 45-year-old woman, presented with right-sided elbow pain that began after she received a cortisone injection. She also suffered from depression after having recently moved to a new location. The right elbow appeared swollen and slightly warm to the touch. Her hands and feet were always cold. The TCM diagnosis was *bi zheng* (painful obstruction syndrome) with Liver qi stagnation. After taking ***Resolve (AI)*** and *Si Ni San* (Frigid Extremities Powder), her elbow pain was 75% better and no longer hurt steadily. It worsened with work but was bearable. The patient also received acupuncture and homeopathic therapy. Submitted by M.C., Sarasota, Florida.
- M.S., a 41-year-old female, presented with an allergic reaction: both eyes were itchy and weeping thick yellow fluids. This worsened with exposure to dust or chemicals. The TCM diagnosis was yin deficiency with damp-heat accumulation. After taking ***Resolve (AI)*** with *Ming Mu Di Huang Wan* (Improve Vision Pill with Rehmannia), the patient was 95% better. She continued to take the herbs and noticed that the symptoms would return when she stopped the herbs. This patient did not receive any acupuncture treatment. Submitted by M.C., Sarasota, Florida.

PHARMACOLOGICAL AND CLINICAL RESEARCH

Resolve (AI) is formulated specifically to treat formation of hardness and nodules due to a wide variety of causes, including infection, inflammation, lymphatic obstruction, lipoma, and many others. The herbs in ***Resolve (AI)*** have demonstrated anti-infective properties to treat infection, anti-inflammatory action to reduce swelling and inflammation, and antitumor and antiproliferative effects to resolve hardness and nodules. ***Resolve (AI)*** is most effective in the treatment of swelling and inflammation due to infection, with the formation of abscesses, hardness and nodules.

Resolve (AI) contains many herbs with marked anti-infective (antibacterial and antiviral) functions. *Jin Yin Hua* (Flos Lonicerae Japonicae) has demonstrated a broad spectrum of inhibitory actions against *Staphylococcus aureus*, *beta-hemolytic streptococcus*, *E. coli*, *Bacillus dysenteriae*, *Vibrio cholerae*, *Salmonella typhi*, *Diplococcus pneumoniae*, *Diplococcus meningitidis*, *Pseudomonas aeruginosa*, and *Mycobacterium tuberculosis*.[4,5] Decoction of *Bai Zhi* (Radix Angelicae Dahuricae) has an inhibitory effect against *E. coli*, *Bacillus dysenteriae*, *Bacillus proteus*, *Salmonella typhi*, *Pseudomonas aeruginosa*, *Vibrio cholerae*, *Mycobacterium tuberculosis hominis*, and species of *Shigella*.[6] *Fang Feng* (Radix Saposhnikoviae) has an antibacterial effect against *Shigella spp.*, *Pseudomonas aeruginosa*, and *Staphylococcus aureus*, and an antiviral effect against influenza viruses.[7] *Xia Ku Cao* (Spica Prunellae) has demonstrated an inhibitory action against *Shigella spp.*, *Salmonella typhi*, *E. coli*, *Pseudomonas aeruginosa*, *Mycobacterium tuberculosis*, *Streptococcus*, and *dermatophytes*.[8] All together, herbs in ***Resolve (AI)*** provide a potent and wide-spectrum anti-infective effect to ensure complete and effective treatment of infection.

Many herbs in ***Resolve (AI)*** have with marked anti-inflammatory, antipyretic, and analgesic effects. This well-rounded action is necessary, as infection and inflammation are often accompanied by fever and pain. In this formula, *Bai Zhi* (Radix Angelicae Dahuricae) has potent anti-inflammatory effects.[9,10] *Jin Yin Hua* (Flos Lonicerae Japonicae) has both anti-inflammatory and antipyretic properties.[11] *Chen Pi* (Pericarpium Citri Reticulatae) also

Resolve (AI)™

exhibits anti-inflammatory activity to decrease the permeability of blood vessels, a symptom associated with inflammation or allergy.[12] *Dang Gui* (Radix Angelicae Sinensis), on the other hand, has anti-inflammatory and analgesic influence, and is commonly used to treat both pain and inflammation.[13] It has been shown that *Dang Gui* (Radix Angelicae Sinensis) is approximately 1.1 times stronger than aspirin to reduce inflammation, and 1.7 times stronger to relieve pain.[14] Lastly, *Gan Cao* (Radix et Rhizoma Glycyrrhizae) is regarded by many as one of the most potent herbs to reduce inflammation. Unlike most herbs, *Gan Cao* (Radix et Rhizoma Glycyrrhizae) exerts an anti-inflammatory effect by stimulating the production of glucocorticoids and slows down the rate of breakdown of the same substances. *Gan Cao* (Radix et Rhizoma Glycyrrhizae) has been used successfully for treatment of inflammation, edema, granuloma formation, edematous arthritis, and other conditions. The anti-inflammatory influence of glycyrrhizin and glycyrrhetinic acid is approximately 1/10th that of cortisone.[15]

Resolve (AI) contains many herbs that treat hardness and nodules due to various disorders. *Xia Ku Cao* (Spica Prunellae) has marked effectiveness in treating lipoma in animals.[16] *Bai Zhi* (Radix Angelicae Dahuricae) has an antitumor effect, and showed significant inhibition in a dose-dependent manner on many cultured human tumor cells *in vitro*.[17] *Fang Feng* (Radix Saposhnikoviae) possesses strong antiproliferative properties against several human tumor cell lines.[18] *Mo Yao* (Myrrha) has antiproliferative and antineoplastic effects against eight cancer cell-lines.[19] *Zao Jiao* (Fructus Gleditsiae) has an anticancer effect against various types of solid and non-solid tumor cell lines including esophageal squamous cell carcinoma.[20] According to another study, *Zao Jiao* (Fructus Gleditsiae) shows anticancer potential on various solid tumor and leukemia cell lines *in vitro*. The mechanism of this anticancer effect is attributed to its apoptotic activity, telomerase inhibition, antiangiogenesis, and suppression of cyclo-oxygenase-2 expression.[21,22] *Zao Jiao Ci* (Spina Gleditsiae) also has a significant anticancer effect, without any negative side effects.[23]

In summary, ***Resolve (AI)*** is comprised of herbs that are well-documented for their anti-infective, anti-inflammatory, antitumor and antiproliferative effects. The clinical applications include hardness and nodules due to infection and inflammation, with such presentation as fever, abscess, nodules, hardness, discharge, and related symptoms.

COMPARATIVE ANALYSIS

Nodules and hardness represent a wide range of disorders, including infection, inflammation, and obstruction. When infection is involved, anti-infectives may be used orally or topically. When there is pain and inflammation, analgesic or anti-inflammation drugs may be used for symptomatic treatment. Lastly, surgery may be performed to directly remove the nodule or hardened tissues.

These nodules are considered to be the stagnation of qi, blood, and phlegm. From a pharmacological perspective, these herbs have anti-infective effects to treat infection, and anti-inflammatory effects to reduce swelling and inflammation. Furthermore, these herbs are also effective for hardness and nodules where there are no signs of infection and inflammation. For this application, however, herbs must be taken continuously for a few months to slowly dissolve and disperse these nodules and hardened tissues.

Nodules and hardened tissues encompass a wide variety of clinical conditions. When the cause is unknown, Western medicine struggles to identify a diagnosis and a treatment. Traditional Chinese medicine, however, is quite effective as it offers a wide range of therapeutic substances to treat infection, reduce swelling and inflammation, and dissolve and disperse nodules and hardened tissues.

References

1. Chan K, Lo AC, Yeung JH, Woo KS. Journal of Pharmacy and Pharmacology 1995 May;47(5):402-6.
2. Pharmacotherapy 1999 July;19(7):870-876.
3. European Journal of Drug Metabolism and Pharmacokinetics 1995; 20(1): 55-60.
4. *Xin Yi Xue* (New Medicine), 1975; 6(3):155.
5. *Jiang Xi Xin Yi Yao* (Jiangxi New Medicine and Herbology); 1960; (1):34.
6. *Zhong Yao Yao Li Yu Ying Yong* (Pharmacology and Applications of Chinese Herbs), 1983; 796.
7. *Zhong Yao Tong Bao* (Journal of Chinese Herbology), 1988; 13(6):364.
8. *Zhong Yi Xue* (Chinese Herbal Medicine), 1989; 20(6):22.
9. *Chang Yong Zhong Yao Cheng Fen Yu Yao Li Shou Ce* (A Handbook of the Composition and Pharmacology of Common Chinese Drugs), 1994; 1459:1462.
10. *Zhong Guo Zhong Yao Za Zhi* (People's Republic of China Journal of Chinese Herbology), 1991; 16(9):560.
11. *Shan Xi Yi Kan* (Shanxi Journal of Medicine), 1960; (10):22.
12. *Zhong Yao Yao Li Yu Ying Yong* (Pharmacology and Applications of Chinese Herbs), 1983; 567.
13. *Xin Yi Yao Xue Za Zhi* (New Journal of Medicine and Herbology), 1975; (6):34.
14. *Yao Xue Za Zhi* (Journal of Medicinals), 1971; (91):1098.
15. *Zhong Cao Yao* (Chinese Herbal Medicine), 1991; 22(10):452.
16. *Zhong Cao Yao* (Chinese Herbal Medicine), 1989; 20(6):22.
17. Kim YK, Kim YS, Ryu SY. Antiproliferative effect of furanocoumarins from the root of Angelica dahurica on cultured human tumor cell lines. Phytother Res. 2007 Mar;21(3):288-90.
18. Tai J, Cheung S. Anti-proliferative and antioxidant activities of Saposhnikovia divaricata. Oncol Rep. 2007 Jul;18(1):227-34.
19. Shoemaker M., Hamilton B., Dairkee S.H., Cohen I. & Campbell M.J. *In vitro* anticancer activity of twelve Chinese medicinal herbs. *Phytother Res.* 2005, 19(7): 649-651.
20. Pak KC, Lam KY, Law S, Tang JC. The inhibitory effect of Gleditsia sinensis on cyclooxygenase-2 expression in human esophageal squamous cell carcinoma. Lo Ka Chung Centre for Natural Anti-cancer Drug Development, The Hong Kong Polytechnic University, Hong Kong SAR, P.R. China. Int J Mol Med. 2009 Jan;23(1):121-9.
21. Cheung F, Chui CH, Chan AS, Lau FY, Cheng GY, Wong RS, Kok SH, Teo IT, Cheng CH, Tang JC. Inhibition of proteasome activity in Gleditsia sinensis fruit extract-mediated apoptosis on human carcinoma cells. State Key Laboratory of Chinese Medicine and Molecular Pharmacology, Shenzhen, PR China. Int J Mol Med. 2005 Nov;16(5):925-9.

Resolve (AI)™

22. Chow LM, Chui CH, Tang JC, Teo IT, Lau FY, Cheng GY, Wong RS, Leung TW, Lai KB, Yau MY, Gou D, Chan AS. Gleditsia sinensis fruit extract is a potential chemotherapeutic agent in chronic and acute myelogenous leukemia. Department of Applied Biology and Chemical Technology, The Hong Kong Polytechnic University, Hung Hom, Hong Kong, China. Oncol Rep. 2003 Sep-Oct;10(5):1601-7.

23. Lee SJ, Park K, Ha SD, Kim WJ, Moon SK. Gleditsia sinensis thorn extract inhibits human colon cancer cells: the role of ERK1/2, G2/M-phase cell cycle arrest and p53 expression. Department of Biotechnology, Chungju National University, Chungju, Chungbuk 380-702, South Korea; Department of Food Science and Technology, Chung-Ang University, Ansung 72-1, Korea. Phytother Res. 2010 Dec;24(12):1870-6. doi: 10.1002/ptr.3214.

FORMULAS

Resolve (Lower)™

CLINICAL APPLICATIONS

- **Fibrocystic disorders in the lower abdominal region,** such as cysts and fibroids in the uterus and ovaries
- **Masses, myomas, and benign tumors** of the female reproductive organs
- **Endometriosis**
- **Female infertility** due to obstruction in the lower abdominal region (i.e., tubal obstruction)
- **Pelvic pain** due to obstruction in the lower abdominal region
- **Scarring** or blood stasis in the pelvic cavity from surgery
- **Varicocele** in men causing infertility

WESTERN THERAPEUTIC ACTIONS

- Antiproliferative effect to inhibit abnormal growth of connective tissue and dissolve masses and nodules
- Resolves cysts and fibroids in the uterus and ovaries
- Treats female infertility due to obstructions in the uterus and ovaries
- Antitumor effect to treat benign tumors of the female reproductive organs
- Analgesic and anti-inflammatory actions to relieve pain and swelling

CHINESE THERAPEUTIC ACTIONS

- Dispels blood stasis and disperses nodules and masses
- Invigorates the blood circulation and alleviates pain

DOSAGE

Take 3 to 4 capsules three times daily on an empty stomach with warm water. In cases of large fibroids, the dosage may be increased up to 8 to 10 capsules twice or three times daily. ***Resolve (Lower)*** should be taken continuously for one to two months prior to making a progress evaluation.

INGREDIENTS

Bie Jia (Carapax Trionycis)
Chi Shao (Radix Paeoniae Rubrae)
Chuan Xiong (Rhizoma Chuanxiong)
Dang Gui (Radix Angelicae Sinensis)
E Zhu (Rhizoma Curcumae)
Fu Ling (Poria)
Gui Zhi (Ramulus Cinnamomi)
Hong Hua (Flos Carthami)
Mu Dan Pi (Cortex Moutan)
Mu Li (Concha Ostreae)
Pu Huang (Pollen Typhae)
San Leng (Rhizoma Sparganii)
San Qi (Radix et Rhizoma Notoginseng)
Tao Ren (Semen Persicae)
Yan Hu Suo (Rhizoma Corydalis)
Zhe Bei Mu (Bulbus Fritillariae Thunbergii)

BACKGROUND

Cysts, fibroids, masses, myomas, endometriosis are all common gynecological disorders. Cysts are the growth of mucus-filled sacs. Fibroids are benign uterine growth of smooth muscles. Masses are abnormal growth of cysts and tumors. Myomas are smooth, benign tumors. Endometriosis is the growth of endometrial tissues outside the uterine cavity. Though the names differ in Western medicine, they all refer to abnormal growth of tissues in different places. According to traditional Chinese medicine, these abnormal tissues are diagnosed as "blood stasis and phlegm stagnation."

FORMULA EXPLANATION

According to traditional Chinese medicine, a palpable mass in the lower abdominal region is often diagnosed as blood stasis and phlegm stagnation. Fibrocystic disorders, such as endometriosis, fibroids, and cysts in the uterus and ovaries, are examples of blood and phlegm stagnation in the lower *jiao*. ***Resolve (Lower)*** contains herbs that activate blood circulation, remove blood and phlegm stagnation, warm the abdomen, and relieve pain.

Gui Zhi (Ramulus Cinnamomi), *Tao Ren* (Semen Persicae), *Hong Hua* (Flos Carthami) and *Chi Shao* (Radix Paeoniae Rubrae) unblock the blood vessels and remove blood stasis by promoting circulation. *Chuan Xiong* (Rhizoma Chuanxiong), *Dang Gui* (Radix Angelicae Sinensis), and *Mu Dan Pi* (Cortex Moutan) activate circulation, remove blood stasis and relieve pain. *Pu Huang* (Pollen Typhae) has an excitatory action on the uterus and works to invigorate the blood and relieve pain by eliminating blood stasis. *Yan Hu Suo* (Rhizoma Corydalis) is a strong analgesic and produces effects similar to morphine and codeine to relieve pain. *San Leng* (Rhizoma Sparganii) and *E Zhu* (Rhizoma Curcumae) have strong blood invigorating functions to dispel masses and alleviate pain. *Zhe Bei Mu* (Bulbus Fritillariae Thunbergii), *Mu Li* (Concha Ostreae) and *Bie Jia* (Carapax Trionycis) eliminate phlegm, soften abdominal masses, and dissipate nodules. *Fu Ling* (Poria) further helps to dispel phlegm and prevent the formation of dampness by strengthening the Spleen. *San Qi* (Radix et Rhizoma Notoginseng) invigorates blood circulation and stops bleeding to prevent hypermenorrhea.

In summary, these herbs work together to resolve blood stasis, eliminate phlegm stagnation, and remove abnormal and unhealthy growth of tissues.

CAUTIONS & CONTRAINDICATIONS

- This formula contains herbs that have strong blood-invigorating functions and should be used with caution in patients with deficiencies. Patients with underlying deficiencies should be treated concurrently with tonic formulas, such as ***Kidney Tonic (Yin)***, ***Kidney Tonic (Yang)***, ***C/R Support***, ***Imperial Tonic***, ***Schisandra ZZZ***, or ***Immune +***.
- This formula contains herbs that have strong blood-invigorating and stasis-removing functions. It is contraindicated for patients

Resolve (Lower)™

during pregnancy and nursing. It should be used with caution during menstruation, as bleeding may be increased.

- This formula should not be the only course of therapy. Consider surgical intervention if multiple masses exist, if the cyst is large, or if the fibroids do not respond to herbal therapy.
- This herbal formula contains herbs that invigorate blood circulation, such as *Dang Gui* (Radix Angelicae Sinensis). Therefore, patients who are on anticoagulant or antiplatelet therapies, such as Coumadin (warfarin), should use this formula with caution, or not at all, as there may be a higher risk of bleeding and bruising.[1,2,3]

CLINICAL NOTES

- ***Resolve (Lower)*** should be taken every day of the month except during menstruation to avoid profuse bleeding. During menstruation, either reduce the dosage by half or temporarily discontinue the formula.
- If pain is present during the period, ***Mense-Ease*** should be administered starting the first day of menstruation. If pain is present before the onset of each cycle, both formulas can be taken together to invigorate blood and relieve pain.
- ***Resolve (Lower)*** should be taken for three months prior to making an evaluation on the progress of the treatment. If the cysts, fibroids or mass reduce in size, continue giving the formula until the conditions are completely resolved. On the other hand, if the size remains constant, increase the dosage by 30 to 50% and continue for another three months prior to making the final evaluation. If the conditions still remain the same, other treatment options should be considered.

Pulse Diagnosis by Dr. Jimmy Wei-Yen Chang:

- *Yinqiao* pulse, a thin, long, wiry, and forceful pulse on or proximal to the left *chi*.

SUPPLEMENTARY FORMULAS

- For benign breast disorders, use with ***Resolve (Upper)***.
- For premenstrual syndrome (PMS) or irritability, use with ***Calm***.
- For stress and insomnia in patients with deficiency, add ***Calm ZZZ***.
- For dysmenorrhea, use ***Mense-Ease***.
- To treat infertility, use ***Blossom (Phase 1-4)***.
- To clear hot flashes in menopausal patients, combine with ***Balance (Heat)***.
- For infection in the genital area, add ***V-Support***.
- For presence of hardness and nodules in the chest area, combine with ***Resolve (AI)***.
- To improve blood circulation throughout the body and in severe cases of varicocele or varicose veins, add ***Circulation (SJ)***.
- With edema, water retention or swelling of the legs, combine with ***Herbal DRX***.
- For patients with cancer who have extreme weakness and deficiency and cannot tolerate chemotherapy or radiation treatment, use ***CA Support***.
- To minimize the side effects of chemotherapy and radiation treatment in patients with cancer, combine with ***C/R Support***.

ACUPUNCTURE TREATMENT

Traditional Points:

- *Neiguan* (PC 6), *Zhaohai* (KI 6), *Qimen* (LR 14), *Ganshu* (BL 18), *Taichong* (LR 3), *Xingjian* (LR 2), *Xuehai* (SP 10), *Geshu* (BL 17)

Classic Master Tung's Points:

- **Fibroids, cysts, myomas:** *Fuke* (T 11.24), *Jiemeiyi* (T 88.04), *Jiemeier* (T 88.05), *Jiemeisan* (T 88.06), *Yizhong* (T 77.05), *Erzhong* (T 77.06), *Sanzhong* (T 77.07). Bleed in the sacral region with cupping. Bleed before needling for best result.
- **Tumors of the fallopian tubes:** *Fuke* (T 11.24), *Huanchao* (T 11.06), *Sanzhong* (T 77.07), *Jiemeiyi* (T 88.04), *Jiemeier* (T 88.05), *Jiemeisan* (T 88.06), *Shuangling* (T 11.28)*, *Zhiwu* (T 11.26). Bleed dark veins nearby *Daling* (PC 7) and *Yinxi* (HT 6). Bleed before needling for best result. The more the blood is let out, the better the effect.
- **Tumor of the ovaries, cervix, uterus:** *Fuke* (T 11.24), *Huanchao* (T 11.06), *Zhiwu* (T 11.26), *Shuangling* (T 11.28)*, *Qimen* (T 33.01), *Qijiao* (T 33.02), *Qizheng* (T 33.03), *Yunbai* (T 44.11), *Menjin* (T 66.05), *Waisanguan* (T 77.27), *Tianhuang* (T 77.17), *Dihuang* (T 77.19), *Renhuang* (T 77.21), *Jiemeiyi* (T 88.04), *Jiemeier* (T 88.05), *Jiemeisan* (T 88.06), *Mufu* (T 88.38)*, *Tongshen* (T 88.09), *Tongbei* (T 88.11). Bleed the dark veins near the web between the first and second; and second and third toes. Bleed sacral area with cupping. Bleed before needling for best result. The more the blood is let out, the better the effect.
- **Endometriosis:** *Fuke* (T 11.24), *Linggu* (T 22.05), *Menjin* (T 66.05), *Minghuang* (T 88.12), *Tianhuang* (T 88.13), *Qihuang* (T 88.14), *Jiemeiyi* (T 88.04), *Jiemeier* (T 88.05)

Master Tung's Points by Dr. Chuan-Min Wang:

- **Ovarian / uterine cysts or fibroids:** *Mufu* (T 66.02), *Huanchao* (T 11.06)

Balance Method by Dr. Richard Tan:

- Left side: *Taichong* (LR 3), *Gongsun* (SP 4), *Zhaohai* (KI 6), *Waiguan* (TH 5), *Linggu* (T 22.05)
- Right side: *Tongli* (HT 5), *Neiguan* (PC 6), *Xiajuxu* (ST 39), *Fenglong* (ST 40)
- Left and right sides can be alternated from treatment to treatment.

Auricular Medicine by Dr. Li-Chun Huang:

- **Endometritis:** Uterus, Cervix, Kidney, Liver, Ovary, Pituitary, Thalamus, Endocrine, Gonadotropin, *San Jiao*. Bleed Ear Apex.
- **Irregular menstruation:** Gonadotropin, Uterus, Kidney, Liver, Pituitary, Ovary, Endocrine
- **Hypomenorrhea and amenorrhea:** Uterus, Ovary, Exciting, Pituitary, Endocrine, Kidney, Liver, Sympathetic, Gonadotropin, Coronary Vascular Subcortex, Nervous Subcortex

Resolve (Lower)™

- **Excessive menstruation or bleeding in between periods:** Uterus, Spleen, Diaphgram, Endocrine, Pituitary, Liver, Kidney, Ovary, Adrenal Gland

NUTRITION

- Avoid red meat, tap water, processed foods, junk foods, alcohol, dairy products (except for unsweetened low-fat yogurt), and those fruits and vegetables sprayed with pesticides.
- Avoid eating meats that have been treated with hormones, which may stimulate the growth of fibroids.
- Eliminate coffee from the diet as it may contribute to the growth of fibroids.
- Avoid cold and raw foods, such as watermelon, citrus, and sushi. Also refrain from drinking cold beverages, such as ice water.

LIFESTYLE INSTRUCTIONS

- Avoid or reduce exposure to radiation whenever possible, such as from microwave, television and computer monitors.
- Relaxation, maintaining a positive outlook on life and regular exercise are important to the recovery of cancer and to the progress in resolving fibroids and cysts, and for preventing recurrences.

CASE STUDIES

- G.E., a 44-year-old female, presented with painful menstruation that starts and stops, and excessive flow with clotting. Other findings included pain upon palpation of the abdomen and a pulse that was deep, strong, and wiry. The Western diagnosis was menorrhagia; the TCM diagnosis was blood stasis. The patient was prescribed ***Mense-Ease*** and ***Resolve (Lower)***. Since this tends to happen every few months, the patient keeps the herbs on hand. The herbs resolve the pain each time; they are very helpful to her. Submitted by A.I., Hilo, Hawaii.
- N.K, a 48-year-old female, presented with pain in the lower quadrant as well as constipation. The patient showed a history of a right cyst present one year ago on her radiology exam. However, there is no current evidence. Her gynecologist had confirmed that bilateral ovarian cysts were present; the left one measuring out to be 8.65/5.6/5.5 inches. The TCM diagnosis was qi, blood, and phlegm accumulation in the lower abdomen. The patient was prescribed ***Resolve (Lower)*** at six capsules three times daily; however, the patient only took three capsules two to three times daily, which was lower than directed to take. After six months of taking the herbs, she reported that the constipation had improved, the right cyst was no longer visible, and the left one was varying in size from test to test. Submitted by N. H., Chatsworth, California.
- N.T., a 34-year-old female, who was told she wouldn't be able to have children, presented with a Western diagnosis of polycystic ovarian disease and fibroids. The patient had been taking levothyroxine after a thyroidectomy in 2004. Patient experienced constipation, poor sleep, heavy menses, cramps, fatigue, and weight gain. The practitioner diagnosed the condition as phlegm and blood stagnation. She was treated with ***Resolve (Lower)*** at four capsules three times daily and directed not to take them during her menses. After taking the herbs for three months, while also receiving acupuncture and cupping one to three times a week, she became unexpectedly pregnant. She and her husband were very happy and thankful. Submitted by L.W., Arroyo Grande, California.
- A 36-year-old female presented with extreme headaches and lower abdominal cramping one week before her period. She also had heavy bleeding. The practitioner diagnosed the condition as blood stagnation in the lower *jiao* and in the *chong* (thoroughfare) and *ren* (conception) channels. Her gynecologist confirmed the presence of fibroids and endometriosis. Laproscopy was done on fibroid tumors, which were found in both ovaries. After taking ***Resolve (Lower)***, 4 capsules three times daily, for four cycles along with acupuncture treatments one to two times a week for five months, the patient's headaches and abdominal cramping abated. Her periods were no longer painful. The practitioner concluded that regular prescriptions of ***Resolve (Lower)*** were quite effective for his patients with endometriosis and fibroids, especially those patients with underlying blood stagnation. Submitted by M.K., Sherman Oaks, California.
- A 42-year-old female medical doctor presented with uterine fibroids and painful menses. Upon further inquiry, the irritable patient also noted dark clots. Her pulse was wiry and her tongue was light purple. The practitioner diagnosed the condition as blood and phlegm stagnation. After taking ***Resolve (Lower)***, the patient's menstrual pain and excessive bleeding lessened. The clots were smaller and the patient felt that the fibroids were dwindling in size. She was recommended for an MRI for confirmation. Submitted by D.M., Raton, New Mexico.
- A 27-year-old female office worker presented with pain in her lower abdomen. The pain was more prominent before and during menses. She also had occasional bloody stools. The patient had a history of chronic yeast infections and endometriosis, which were resolved by surgeries. The practitioner diagnosed the condition as blood and qi stagnation with damp-heat in the lower *jiao*. After taking ***Mense-Ease*** and ***Resolve (Lower)***, menstrual pain reduced and rectal bleeding abated. Submitted by N.H., Boulder, Colorado.
- A 28-year-old female dental hygienist presented with a palpable lump on her lower abdomen near acupuncture point *Zigongxue* (Uterus). She had severe premenstrual syndrome (PMS) affecting her emotionally as well as large dark clots in her menstrual discharge. She had one week of constant dull pain on her left lower abdomen especially after her period. She described the pain as a grabbing, shooting type of pain as though someone was tightening a rope around her belly. She had a history of candida. She sought to get pregnant, and therefore discontinued taking her birth control pills. Laparoscopy was done in 1995 to remove her right ovary and in 1999 to remove endometriosis. Scar tissue was present in her left lower abdomen from a hernia operation

Resolve (Lower)™

when she was a youngster. Cysts were also present on her left ovary. Lastly, the patient also had a history of hypothyroidism and hay fever. Her tongue color was unremarkable and her tongue coating appeared moist. Her tongue root coating would alternate from white to yellow. Her sublingual region was also unremarkable. The patient's pulse was constantly deep, thready and soft. The practitioner diagnosed this clinical picture as damp-heat in the lower *jiao* and Spleen qi deficiency leading to the accumulation of dampness. The practitioner prescribed ***Mense-Ease*** to regulate her menstruation, and ***Resolve (Lower)*** to treat endometriosis. The patient was instructed to take 3 to 5 capsules of each formula three times daily, starting three days before her period and continue the dose throughout her menstrual flow and for one week afterwards. After taking the herbs, she became less emotional. She noted fewer episodes of cramps the first month and no pain during the second month of her herbal therapy. Although her lower abdominal pain lingered, the intensity lessened, the frequency reduced, and the affected area dwindled. The patient also finally discontinued her caffeine intake, which she also attributed to her pain. After three months of herbal treatment, surgery was done to remove two inches of tissue. Ultrasound confirmed the complete absence of ovarian cysts after three months of herbal therapy. Doppler ultrasound showed a favorable pulsatility index for uterine blood flow. There were no blockages present in her reproductive system. The practitioner concluded that ***Mense-Ease*** was quite effective in treating other patients with similar conditions. The efficacy of ***Resolve (Lower)*** was also proven clinically with ultrasound results. Submitted by T.K., Denver, Colorado.

PHARMACOLOGICAL AND CLINICAL RESEARCH

Resolve (Lower) is designed to treat abnormal growth of cells and tissues in the lower abdominal regions, such as cysts, fibroids, masses, myomas, endometriosis and benign tumors. ***Resolve (Lower)*** contains herbs with significant functions to suppress the growth of abnormal cells and tissues, relieve pain, and reduce inflammation.

Resolve (Lower) contains many herbs with a marked effect to inhibit the growth and proliferation of cells and tissues. *Bie Jia* (Carapax Trionycis) has an antiproliferative effect to inhibit proliferation of connective tissue, and dissolve masses and nodules.[4] *Dang Gui* (Radix Angelicae Sinensis) demonstrates an anticancer effect in a dose-dependent manner by inducing cell cycle arrest and apoptosis on various types of cancer cells.[5] The mechanism of this anticancer effect is attributed to its strong cytotoxic and antiproliferative activities.[6] *Fu Ling* (Poria) has an antineoplastic effect against a variety of cancer cells.[7] *Yan Hu Suo* (Rhizoma Corydalis) illustrates anticancer and antimetastatic activities.[8] *Tao Ren* (Semen Persicae) shows an antitumor effect in both *in vitro* and *in vivo* assays by delaying the two-stage carcinogenesis.[9] Lastly, *San Leng* (Rhizoma Sparganii) and *E Zhu* (Rhizoma Curcumae) have antineoplastic and antitumor effects.[10] *E Zhu* (Rhizoma Curcumae) exerts an antitumor effect by inducing apoptosis and inhibiting proliferation of human cervical cancer cells *in vitro* and *in vivo* in a dose-dependent manner.[11] Furanodiene, a sesquiterpene from *E Zhu* (Rhizoma Curcumae), showed strong growth inhibition on many human cancer cell lines, including cervical cancer, uterine cervical cancer, and others.[12] The mechanism of this action is attributed in part to its antiangiogenic effect, which blocks the formation of new blood vessels to suppress tumour growth, invasion, and metastasis.[13]

Resolve (Lower) utilizes many herbs with analgesic effects to relieve pain. *Yan Hu Suo* (Rhizoma Corydalis) is one of the strongest and most potent herbs for treatment of pain, and is commonly used to treat chest and hypochondriac pain, epigastric and abdominal pain, hernial pain, amenorrhea or menstrual pain, and pain of the extremities. According to laboratory studies, the extract of *Yan Hu Suo* (Rhizoma Corydalis) is effective in both acute and chronic phases of pain and inflammation. With adjustment in dosage, the analgesic potency of *Yan Hu Suo* (Rhizoma Corydalis) has been compared to that of morphine. Though the maximum analgesic effect of *Yan Hu Suo* (Rhizoma Corydalis) is not as strong as morphine, it has been determined that the herb is much safer, with significantly fewer side effects, less risk of tolerance, and no evidence of physical dependence even with long-term use.[14] In addition to *Yan Hu Suo* (Rhizoma Corydalis), other herbs with analgesic effects include *San Leng* (Rhizoma Sparganii) and *Dang Gui* (Radix Angelicae Sinensis).[15,16]

Resolve (Lower) also incorporates many herbs with anti-inflammatory effects to reduce swelling and inflammation. *Mu Dan Pi* (Cortex Moutan) exerts strong anti-inflammatory actions through the inhibition of prostaglandin synthesis and decreased permeability of the blood vessels.[17,18] *San Qi* (Radix et Rhizoma Notoginseng) illustrates anti-inflammatory effects via the inhibition of nitric oxide and prostaglandin E2 production.[19] *Tao Ren* (Semen Persicae) and *Hong Hua* (Flos Carthami) are commonly used together as they both exert anti-inflammatory functions.[20,21] Lastly, *Dang Gui* (Radix Angelicae Sinensis) and *Chuan Xiong* (Rhizoma Chuanxiong) both have analgesic and anti-inflammatory effects. In fact, the analgesic effect of *Dang Gui* (Radix Angelicae Sinensis) is approximately 1.7 times stronger than acetylsalicylic acid, and its anti-inflammatory effect is approximately 1.1 times stronger than acetylsalicylic acid.[22]

Clinically, one formula showed 81% rate of effectiveness for treatment of endometriosis in 58 patients. The herbal formula contained *San Leng* (Rhizoma Sparganii), *E Zhu* (Rhizoma Curcumae), *Chi Shao* (Radix Paeoniae Rubra), *Zhe Bei Mu* (Bulbus Fritillariae Thunbergii), *Dang Gui* (Radix Angelicae Sinensis), *Bie Jia* (Carapax Trionycis) and others. The treatment protocol was to administer the herbs in decoction starting on the second or third day after the period ends, and continue until the period begins in the following menstrual cycle.[23]

Resolve (Lower)™

In summary, ***Resolve (Lower)*** is an excellent formula that contains herbs to suppress the growth of abnormal cells and tissues, such as cysts, fibroids, masses, myomas, endometriosis and other similar gynecological disorders.

COMPARATIVE ANALYSIS

Fibrocystic disorders in the lower abdomen, such as fibroids, cysts and endometriosis, are very common among women. These disorders may cause irregular menstruation, severe pain, and infertility.

These conditions are usually treated with hormonal drugs that suppress growth of these tissues. Unfortunately, these drugs have limited benefits but serious side effects, including breast tenderness, swelling, bleeding, thrombosis, embolism, depression, weight gain, elevated cholesterol and triglycerides, and many others. In many cases, an invasive procedure such as surgery is recommended to remove fibroids, cysts, and endometrial tissues.

These fibrocystic conditions are diagnosed as qi, blood, and phlegm stagnation. Use of these herbs has been shown to be extremely effective to dissolve, disperse, and disintegrate these tissues. These herbs have a potent and consistent effect, and generally show a marked effect after three months of therapy. However, the length of treatment may be longer depending on the size of the masses and the severity of the condition.

The best treatment for these fibrocystic conditions is the integration of Western and traditional Chinese medicine. Since drug benefits are often less than satisfactory and have significant side effects, herbs should be used as the first line of therapy. In most cases, improvements are noted within three to six months. If so, herbal therapy should be continued until the condition is resolved. If herbs do not work, then surgery may be employed as the last alternative.

References

1. Chan K, Lo AC, Yeung JH, Woo KS. Journal of Pharmacy and Pharmacology 1995 May;47(5):402-6.
2. Pharmacotherapy 1999 July;19(7):870-876.
3. European Journal of Drug Metabolism and Pharmacokinetics 1995; 20(1): 55-60.
4. *Zhong Cao Yao Xue* (Study of Chinese Herbal Medicine), 1980:1445.
5. Cheng YL, Chang WL, Lee SC, Liu YG, Chen CJ, Lin SZ, Tsai NM, Yu DS, Yen CY, Harn HJ. Acetone extract of Angelica sinensis inhibits proliferation of human cancer cells via inducing cell cycle arrest and apoptosis. Life Sci. 2004 Aug 13;75(13):1579-94.
6. Kan WL, Cho CH, Rudd JA, Lin G. Study of the anti-proliferative effects and synergy of phthalides from Angelica sinensis on colon cancer cells. J Ethnopharmacol. 2008 Oct 30;120(1):36-43.
7. *Zhong Cao Yao Xue* (Study of Chinese Herbal Medicine), 1976:15.
8. Gao JL, Shi JM, He K, Zhang QW, Li SP, Lee SM, Wang YT. Yanhusuo extract inhibits metastasis of breast cancer cells by modulating mitogen-activated protein kinase signaling pathways. Institute of Chinese Medical Sciences, University of Macau, Macau, P.R. China. Oncol Rep. 2008 Oct;20(4):819-24.
9. Fukuda T, Ito H, Mukainaka T, Tokuda H, Nishino H, Yoshida T. Anti-tumor promoting effect of glycosides from Prunus persica seeds. Faculty of Pharmaceutical Sciences, Okayama University, Kyoto, Japan. Biol Pharm Bull. 2003 Feb;26(2):271-3.
10. *Zhong Yao Xue* (Chinese Herbology), 1988; 549:550.
11. Lim CB, Ky N, Ng HM, Hamza MS, Zhao Y. Curcuma wenyujin extract induces apoptosis and inhibits proliferation of human cervical cancer cells in vitro and in vivo. Integr Cancer Ther. 2010 Mar;9(1):36-49.
12. Sun XY, Zheng YP, Lin DH, Zhang H, Zhao F, Yuan CS. Potential anti-cancer activities of Furanodiene, a Sesquiterpene from Curcuma wenyujin. Am J Chin Med. 2009;37(3):589-96.
13. Varinska L, Mirossay L, Mojzisova G, Mojzis J. Antiangogenic effect of selected phytochemicals. Pharmazie. 2010 Jan;65(1):57-63.
14. *Zhong Yao Yao Li Yu Ying Yong* (Pharmacology and Applications of Chinese Herbs), 1983; 447.
15. Lu T, Mao C, Qiu L. The research of analgestic action of different processed products of Sparganium stoloniferum. Nanjing Univesity of Traditional Chinese Medicine, Nanjing 210029. Zhong Yao Cai. 1997 Mar;20(3):135-7.
16. *Yao Xue Za Zhi* (Journal of Medicinals), 1971; (91):1098.
17. *Sheng Yao Xue Za Zhi* (Journal of Raw Herbology), 1979; 33(3):178.
18. *Zhong Guo Yao Ke Da Xue Xue Bao* (Journal of University of Chinese Herbology), 1990; 21(4):222.
19. Jin UH, Park SG, Suh SJ, Kim JK, Kim DS, Moon SK, Lee YC, Park WH, Kim CH. Inhibitory effect of Panax notoginseng on nitric oxide synthase, cyclo-oxygenase-2 and neutrophil functions. Department of Biological Sciences, Sungkyunkwan University, Chunchun-Dong, Suwon City, Kyunggi-Do 440-746, Korea. Phytother Res. 2007 Feb;21(2):142-8.
20. *Zhong Yao Tong Bao* (Journal of Chinese Herbology), 1986; 11(11):37.
21. Jun MS, Ha YM, Kim HS, Jang HJ, Kim YM, Lee YS, Kim HJ, Seo HG, Lee JH, Lee SH, Chang KC. Anti-inflammatory action of methanol extract of Carthamus tinctorius involves in heme oxygenase-1 induction. Department of Pharmacology, School of Medicine, and Institute of Health Sciences, Gyeongsang National University, 92 Chilam-dong, Jinju 660-751, Republic of Korea. J Ethnopharmacol. 2010 Oct 20.
22. *Yao Xue Za Zhi* (Journal of Medicinals), 1971; (91):1098.
23. *Zhong Yi Za Zhi* (Journal of Chinese Medicine), 1995; (5):291.

Resolve (Upper)™

CLINICAL APPLICATIONS

- **Fibrocystic disorders:** breast pain, breast cysts, breast lumps, and palpable masses of the breast
- **Fibroadenomas:** small, slippery, painless lumps of the breast
- **Mastitis:** breast infection with redness, swelling, distension and pain
- **Mastalgia:** breast pain that can be localized or diffuse, affect one or both breasts
- **Lymphadenopathy** characterized by swollen and enlarged lymph nodes with nodules or fibroids

WESTERN THERAPEUTIC ACTIONS

- Antitumor activities which cause degeneration and necrosis of tumor cells
- Antibiotic and anti-inflammatory functions to treat infection and inflammation

CHINESE THERAPEUTIC ACTIONS

- Dispels blood, qi and phlegm stasis
- Disperses nodules and masses
- Unblocks the stagnant Liver qi
- Clears heat and detoxifies

DOSAGE

Take 3 to 4 capsules three times daily on an empty stomach with warm water. Take ***Resolve (Upper)*** continuously for one to two months prior to making an evaluation of progress.

INGREDIENTS

Bai Hua She She Cao (Herba Hedyotis)
Chai Hu (Radix Bupleuri)
Dang Gui Wei (Extremitas Radix Angelicae Sinensis)
Feng Fang (Nidus Vespae)
Hou Po (Cortex Magnoliae Officinalis)
Lou Lu (Radix Rhapontici)
Niu Bang Zi (Fructus Arctii)
Pu Gong Ying (Herba Taraxaci)
Qing Pi (Pericarpium Citri Reticulatae Viride)
Tu Fu Ling (Rhizoma Smilacis Glabrae)
Wang Bu Liu Xing (Semen Vaccariae)
Zao Jiao Ci (Spina Gleditsiae)
Zhe Bei Mu (Bulbus Fritillariae Thunbergii)
Zhi Zi (Fructus Gardeniae)

BACKGROUND

Fibrocystic changes, fibroadenomas, mastalgia and mastitis are all common breast disorders. Fibrocystic changes include the presence of breast pain, breast cysts, breast lumps, and palpable masses of the breast. Fibroadenomas are the small, slippery, painless lumps of the breast. Mastalgia is breast pain that can be localized or diffuse, and can be present on one or both sides. Mastitis is breast infection with redness, swelling, distension and pain. Though the names differ in Western medicine, they all refer to abnormal growth of tissues that may be accompanied by pain and inflammation. According to traditional Chinese medicine, these abnormal tissues are diagnosed as "blood stasis and phlegm stagnation."

FORMULA EXPLANATION

In TCM, a palpable mass is diagnosed as blood stasis and phlegm stagnation. Fibrocystic disorders in the upper half of the body, such as breast nodules, fibroids or inflammation of the mammary glands, are often characterized by prolonged Liver qi stagnation with blood and phlegm obstruction.

Chai Hu (Radix Bupleuri), *Qing Pi* (Pericarpium Citri Reticulatae Viride) and *Hou Po* (Cortex Magnoliae Officinalis) unblock stagnant Liver qi, relieve distension, and alleviate pain. All of the above herbs enter the Liver meridian, which passes through the breast. *Zao Jiao Ci* (Spina Gleditsiae) dissolves phlegm and invigorates qi circulation in the chest. *Bai Hua She She Cao* (Herba Hedyotis) has an excellent antitumor effect. It increases white blood cells and inhibits the mitosis of tumor cells, causing the degeneration and necrosis of tumor cells. *Feng Fang* (Nidus Vespae) eliminates toxicity and has been used for mastitis to relieve inflammation of the mammary glands. *Lou Lu* (Radix Rhapontici) and *Zhe Bei Mu* (Bulbus Fritillariae Thunbergii) soften nodules to facilitate dissipation. *Tu Fu Ling* (Rhizoma Smilacis Glabrae) and *Pu Gong Ying* (Herba Taraxaci) clear toxic heat in the nodules. *Wang Bu Liu Xing* (Semen Vaccariae) and *Dang Gui Wei* (Extremitas Radix Angelicae Sinensis) have strong blood invigorating effects to dissolve stagnation and alleviate pain. *Niu Bang Zi* (Fructus Arctii) and *Zhi Zi* (Fructus Gardeniae) relieve toxic heat accumulation.

Together, these herbs dispel qi, blood, and phlegm stagnation to resolve hardness and masses in the upper parts of the body.

CAUTIONS & CONTRAINDICATIONS

- ***Resolve (Upper)*** is formulated for patients in the initial or early stages of masses in the breasts or lymphadenopathy. Patients with breast lump or large cyst should seek medical treatment to rule out tumor or cancer.
- ***Resolve (Upper)*** is contraindicated during pregnancy and nursing.
- ***Resolve (Upper)*** should be used with caution during menstruation as it may cause excessive bleeding.
- This formula is not designed for long-term use. It should be discontinued once the desired effects are achieved.
- ***Resolve (Upper)*** should be taken with food in individuals with a sensitive stomach.
- This herbal formula contains herbs that invigorate blood circulation, such as *Dang Gui Wei* (Extremitas Radix Angelicae Sinensis). Therefore, patients who are on anticoagulant or antiplatelet therapies, such as Coumadin (warfarin), should use this formula with caution, or not at all, as there may be a higher risk of bleeding and bruising.[1,2,3]

Resolve (Upper)™

- The safety status of using *Dang Gui* (Radix Angelicae Sinensis) in individuals with hormone-dependent cancer is unclear.[4,5,6] According to one reference, use of *Dang Gui* (Radix Angelicae Sinensis) is not associated with thickening of the endometrium or vaginal cell maturation, both of which would indicate an estrogenic effect. Furthermore, there is no confirmation of the presence of a phytoestrogen component or affect on hormone-dependent cancer, when ferulic acid is evaluated as the main component of *Dang Gui* (Radix Angelicae Sinensis).[7] According to another reference, the water extract of *Dang Gui* (Radix Angelicae Sinensis) has a weak estrogen-agonistic activity to stimulate the growth of breast cancer cells (MCF-7).[8] In summary, due to conflicting and insufficient data, use of *Dang Gui* (Radix Angelicae Sinensis) in patients with hormone-dependent cancer warrants caution pending further study.

CLINICAL NOTES

- Upon resolution of the cysts or fibroids, ***Resolve (Upper)*** should be taken for another two weeks to consolidate the effects.
- Patients with deficiencies or weak constitutions should be treated concurrently with ***Imperial Tonic***, ***C/R Support*** or ***Immune +*** to ensure maximum effectiveness.
- ***Resolve (Upper)*** is a strong formula and is best used at the beginning stages of the disease.
- Patients who are under constant stress and anxiety are at higher risk of developing Liver qi stagnation. Prolonged Liver qi stagnation prevents recovery and contributes to continued deterioration in the overall condition. If at all possible, they need to manage stress from their lives to achieve maximum clinical effect.

SUPPLEMENTARY FORMULAS

- Side effects of chemotherapy or radiation can be reduced by using ***C/R Support***.
- For fatigue and immune enhancement, use ***Immune +*** or ***Cordyceps 3***.
- For premenstrual syndrome (PMS), irritability, or anxiety, combine with ***Calm***.
- For stress with insomnia in patients with deficiency, combine with ***Calm ZZZ***.
- For an excess condition with stress, irritability, anxiety, and restlessness, add ***Calm (ES)***.
- For fatigue, dizziness, insomnia, excessive worrying or anemia, combine with ***Schisandra ZZZ***.
- For dysmenorrhea, use ***Mense-Ease***.
- For amenorrhea, use ***Menatrol*** after fibrocystic condition has resolved.
- For presence of hardness and nodules else where in the chest area, or swelling of the lymphatic system, combine with ***Resolve (AI)***.
- To improve blood circulation throughout the body, add ***Circulation (SJ)***.
- For infection or mastitis, add ***Herbal ABX***.
- For signs and symptoms of excess heat, add ***Gardenia Complex***.
- For patients with cancer who have extreme weakness and deficiency and cannot tolerate chemotherapy or radiation treatment, use ***CA Support***.
- To minimize the side effects of chemotherapy and radiation treatment in patients with cancer, combine with ***C/R Support***.

ACUPUNCTURE TREATMENT

Traditional Points:

- *Jianjing* (GB 21), *Rugen* (ST 18), *Qimen* (LR 14), *Houxi* (SI 3), *Neiguan* (PC 6), *Ganshu* (BL 18), *Chize* (LU 5), *Zusanli* (ST 36)
- *Shanzhong* (CV 17), *Yingchuang* (ST 16)

Classic Master Tung's Points:

- **Fibrocystic breasts:** *Jianfeng* (T 44.31)*, *Shuanglongyi* (T 77.29)*, *Shuanglonger* (T 77.30)*, *Waisanguan* (T 77.27). Bleed dark veins near the ST channel on the lower limb. Bleed before needling for best result.
- **Mastitis:** *Jianfeng* (T 44.31)*, *Jianzhong* (T 44.06), *Fenzhishang* (T DT.01), *Shuanglongyi* (T 77.29)*, *Shuanglonger* (T 77.30)*, *Yizhong* (T 77.05), *Erzhong* (T 77.06), *Sanzhong* (T 77.07). Bleed in the HT, LU, LR areas on the back from T4-T7 with cupping. Bleed before needling for best result.
- **Lymphadenopathy:** *Linggu* (T 22.05), *Jianzhong* (T 44.06), *Yizhong* (T 77.05), *Erzhong* (T 77.06), *Sanzhong* (T 77.07)

Master Tung's Points by Dr. Chuan-Min Wang:

- **Breast lumps or cysts:** *Yizhong* (T 77.05), *Erzhong* (T 77.06), *Sanzhong* (T 77.07)

Balance Method by Dr. Richard Tan:

- On the same side of the fibroid: *Neiguan* (PC 6), *Jianshi* (PC 5), *Ximen* (PC 4), *Lieque* (LU 7), *Tongli* (HT 5), *Xiajuxu* (ST 39) and *Fenglong* (ST 40).
- On the opposite side of the fibroid: *Sanjian* (LI 3), *Sanyinjiao* (SP 6), *Lougu* (SP 7) and *Diji* (SP 8) or *ah shi* points nearby.

Ear Acupuncture:

- Mammary Gland, *Shenmen*, Endocrine
- Needle both ears and leave needles in for two to three hours. Ten treatments equal one course.

Auricular Medicine by Dr. Li-Chun Huang:

- **Lobular breast hyperplasia:** Breast, Chest, Pituitary, Ovary, Endocrine, *San Jiao*, Liver
- **Mastitis:** Breast, Chest, Liver, Occiput, Allergic Area, Endocrine, Adrenal Gland. Bleed Ear Apex.
- **Lymphadenitis:** corresponding point (to the area affected), *San Jiao*, Allergic Area, Adrenal Gland, Liver, Spleen, and Endocrine. Bleed Ear Apex.

Resolve (Upper)™

NUTRITION

- A diet based on organic fresh fruits and vegetables is highly recommended. The following foods are very beneficial to patients with breast cancer: all mushrooms (shiitake especially), whole grains, broccoli, brussel sprouts, cabbage, cauliflower, yellow/orange vegetables (carrots, pumpkins, squash, sweet potatoes), garlic, onions, fresh berries, apples, cherries, grapes, and plums.
- Advise the patient to avoid red meat, tap water, processed foods, junk foods, alcohol, caffeine, dairy products (except for unsweetened low-fat yogurt), iron supplements and those fruits and vegetables sprayed with pesticides.
- Avoid eating meats that have been treated with hormones, which stimulate the growth of fibroids.
- Eliminate coffee from the diet, as it may contribute to the growth of fibroids.

The Tao of Nutrition by Dr. Maoshing Ni and Cathy McNease:

- **Mastitis**
  - Recommendations: cooling foods, cabbage, cucumber, dandelion, lettuce, malt, reed root, lotus root, and honeysuckle.
  - Make tea from malt (sprouted oat), drink three times daily.
  - Externally, take egg whites mixed with green onions and apply to the area, changing two to three times daily.
  - Make tea from dandelion and honey, drink three times daily for at least five days.
  - Make tea from honeysuckle, mint, and licorice. Drink tea and apply the solids locally.
  - Combine cabbage, lettuce, and dandelions to make a poultice for external application.
  - Avoid spicy, stimulating foods, coffee, smoking, alcohol, dairy products, and breast feeding.

LIFESTYLE INSTRUCTIONS

- Avoid all exposure to radiation, such as from microwave, television and computer monitors.
- Relaxation, maintaining a positive outlook on life, and regular exercise are important to the recovery of cancer and to the progress in resolving fibroids and cysts, and preventing recurrences.

CASE STUDY

- J.S., a 34-year-female, presented with a non-cancerous fibrocystic breast lump on the right side. She had it for eight months and it felt achy and tender before her period. She also felt tired from overworking. The TCM diagnosis was Spleen yang deficiency with phlegm accumulation. ***Resolve (Upper)*** at one capsule three times daily, and ***Immune +*** at three capsules, three times daily were prescribed. Two weeks later, the patient reported the breast felt much better and her energy level was great. One month later, patient experienced only slight tenderness in the breast. She went back to her medical doctor for an examination and found that the lump had diminished in size. The patient was also advised to not wear underwire bras, to avoid further local qi stagnation. Submitted by M.C., Sarasota, Florida.

PHARMACOLOGICAL AND CLINICAL RESEARCH

Resolve (Upper) is designed to treat many breast disorders, such as fibrocystic changes, fibroadenomas and mastitis. It contains herbs that have demonstrated significant activities to suppress growth of abnormal cells and tissues, relieve pain, and reduce inflammation.

Bai Hua She She Cao (Herba Hedyotis) and *Ban Zhi Lian* (Herba Scutellariae Barbatae) are two herbs commonly used together to strongly suppress tumor growth and increase survival rate in subjects with carcinoma.[9] *Bai Hua She She Cao* (Herba Hedyotis) has a strong effect to inhibit the growth of eight cancer cell lines by inducing apoptosis.[10] Methylanthraquinone, compound from this herb, exhibited potent anticancer activity in many kinds of cancer cells, including human breast cancer cells.[11] *Tu Fu Ling* (Rhizoma Smilacis Glabrae) is another herb with significant antiproliferative and proapoptotic activities. It has been shown to suppress the proliferation and induce the apoptosis of breast cancer cells.[12] *Zao Jiao Ci* (Spina Gleditsiae), *Zhe Bei Mu* (Bulbus Fritillariae Thunbergii) and *Zhi Zi* (Fructus Gardeniae) are three herbs with anticancer and antitumor activities, as they treat various types of cancer and tumor.[13,14,15] *Chai Hu* (Radix Bupleuri) and *Qing Pi* (Pericarpium Citri Reticulatae Viride) have strong antiproliferative properties against several human tumor cell lines.[16,17,18] Lastly, *Hou Po* (Cortex Magnoliae Officinalis), *Wang Bu Liu Xing* (Semen Vaccariae) and *Zhi Zi* (Fructus Gardeniae) have antiangiogenic activities in a variety of cancers.[19,20,21]

Resolve (Lower) incorporates many herbs with analgesic effects to relieve pain and anti-inflammatory effects to reduce swelling and inflammation. *Dang Gui* (Radix Angelicae Sinensis) has both analgesic and anti-inflammatory effects.[22] Its analgesic effect is approximately 1.7 times stronger than acetylsalicylic acid, and its anti-inflammatory effect is approximately 1.1 times stronger than acetylsalicylic acid.[23] *Niu Bang Zi* (Fructus Arctii) and *Tu Fu Ling* (Rhizoma Smilacis Glabrae) exert potent anti-inflammatory effects through inhibition on nitric oxide, tumor necrosis factor and interleukin.[24,25] *Hou Po* (Cortex Magnoliae Officinalis) and *Zao Jiao Ci* (Spina Gleditsiae) demonstrate anti-inflammatory properties through the inactivation of NF-kappaB, an important factor in inflammatory reactions.[26,27]

Clinically, *Feng Fang* (Nidus Vespae) is one of the best herbs to treat breast disorders. According to one study, four patients with acute mastitis were treated with *Feng Fang* (Nidus Vespae) with surprisingly good results. *Feng Fang* (Nidus Vespae) was prepared by dry-frying it until it was a light yellow color. The patients were given 1 to 2 grams of the powder every six hours with 30 mL of grain-based liquor. In a follow-up study to confirm effectiveness, the same treatment protocol was applied to 26 women with acute mastitis. The study reported complete

Resolve (Upper)™

recovery in 23 patients, significant improvement in 1 patient, and no response in 2 patients. The overall rate of effectiveness was 92.3%.[28]

In summary, ***Resolve (Upper)*** is an excellent formula that contains herbs to suppress the growth of abnormal cells and tissues, such as in breast cysts, breast lumps, mastitis, mastalgia, and palpable masses of the breast.

COMPARATIVE ANALYSIS

Fibrocystic disorders in the chest region, such as palpable masses and mastitis, are very common among women. These disorders may cause pain and discomfort, and must be addressed immediately and carefully. In Western medicine, antibiotic drugs are usually used to treat mastitis. Palpable masses are generally removed surgically.

These fibrocystic conditions are diagnosed as qi, blood, and phlegm stagnation. Use of these herbs has been shown to be extremely effective to dissolve, disperse, and disintegrate these tissues. These herbs have a potent and consistent effect, and generally show marked effect after three months of therapy. However, the length of treatment may be longer depending on the size of the masses and severity of the condition.

The best treatment for these fibrocystic conditions is the integration of Western and traditional Chinese medicine. Herbs should be used as the first line of therapy, as they effectively address both infection and inflammation. For palpable masses, improvements will be noted within three to six months. If so, herbal therapy should be continued until the condition is resolved. If herbs do not work, then surgery may be employed as the last alternative.

References

1. Chan K, Lo AC, Yeung JH, Woo KS. Journal of Pharmacy and Pharmacology 1995 May;47(5):402-6.
2. Pharmacotherapy 1999 July;19(7):870-876.
3. European Journal of Drug Metabolism and Pharmacokinetics 1995; 20(1): 55-60.
4. Natural Standard (www.naturalstandard.com).
5. National Institutes of Health.
6. U.S National Library of Medicine.
7. American Herbal Pharmacopoeia. *Dang Gui* (Radix Angelicae Sinensis) monograph.
8. Lau CB, Ho TC, Chan TW, Kim SC. Use of dong quai (Angelica sinensis) to treat peri- or postmenopausal symptoms in women with breast cancer: is it appropriate? Menopause 2005 Nov-Dec;12(6):734-40.
9. Yu Hsueh-Chiu, Suzuki S., Okubo T., Kawashima I., Tsuda M., Borai N.E., Yamamura M. & Yu H.C. Anti-tumor effect of Chinese herbal medicines " *Scutellaria barbata* and *Oldenlandia diffusa* " on cancer cell lines and C3H-AVy mouse with spontaneous hepatocellular carcinoma. *J of Traditional Medicines*. 2000, 17: 165-169.
10. Gupta S, Zhang D, Yi J, Shao J. Anticancer activities of Oldenlandia diffusa. J Herb Pharmacother. 2004;4(1):21-33.
11. Liu Z, Liu M, Liu M, Li J. Methylanthraquinone from Hedyotis diffusa WILLD induces Ca(2+)-mediated apoptosis in human breast cancer cells. Toxicol In Vitro. 2010 Feb;24(1):142-7.
12. Ooi LS, Wong EY, Chiu LC, Sun SS, Ooi VE. Antiviral and anti-proliferative glycoproteins from the rhizome of Smilax glabra Roxb (Liliaceae). Department of Biology, The Chinese University of Hong Kong, Shatin, N.T., Hong Kong, China. Am J Chin Med. 2008;36(1):185-95.
13. Lee SJ, Park K, Ha SD, Kim WJ, Moon SK. Gleditsia sinensis thorn extract inhibits human colon cancer cells: the role of ERK1/2, G2/M-phase cell cycle arrest and p53 expression. Department of Biotechnology, Chungju National University, Chungju, Chungbuk 380-702, South Korea; Department of Food Science and Technology, Chung-Ang University, Ansung 72-1, Korea. Phytother Res. 2010 Dec;24(12):1870-6. doi: 10.1002/ptr.3214.
14. Zheng Z, Li DY, Chen XY. Study on the compound Fritilaria thunbergii Miq particles to the subcellular accumulation ability and inducing apoptoais of K562/A02 cells. Zhongguo Zhong Xi Yi Jie He Za Zhi. 2010 Feb;30(2):167-9.
15. Lim W, Kim O, Jung J, Ko Y, Ha J, Oh H, Lim H, Kwon H, Kim I, Kim J, Kim M, Kim S, Kim BK, Kim S, Kang BC, Choi H, Kim O. Dichloromethane fraction from Gardenia jasminoides: DNA topoisomerase 1 inhibition and oral cancer cell death induction. Second Stage of Brain Korea 21 for School of Dentistry, Dental Science Research Institute, Chonnam National University, Bug-Gu, Gwangju, Korea. Pharm Biol. 2010 Dec;48(12):1354-60.
16. Cheng Y.L., Lee S.C., Lin S.Z., Chang W.L., Chen Y.L., Tsai N.M., Liu Y.C., Tzao C., Yu D.S. & Harn H.J. Anti-proliferative activity of *Bupleurum scrozonerifolium* in A549 human lung cancer cells *in vitro* and *in vivo*. *Cancer Lett.* 2005, 222(2): 183-193.
17. Kim MJ, Park HJ, Hong MS, Park HJ, Kim MS, Leem KH, Kim JB, Kim YJ, Kim HK. Citrus Reticulata blanco induces apoptosis in human gastric cancer cells SNU-668. Department of Obesity Management, Graduate School of Obesity Science, Dongduk Women's University, Seoul, 136-714, South Korea. Nutr Cancer. 2005;51(1):78-82.
18. Mak NK, Wong-Leung YL, Chan SC, Wen J, Leung KN, Fung MC. Isolation of anti-leukemia compounds from Citrus reticulata. Department of Biology, Hong Kong Baptist University. Life Sci. 1996;58(15):1269-76.
19. Tse A.K., Wan C.K., Shen X.L., Yang M. & Fong W.F. Honokiol inhibits TNF-alpha-stimulated NF- kappaB activation and NF-kappaB-regulated gene expression through suppression of IKK activation. *Biochem Pharmacol.* 2005, 70(10):1443-1457.
20. Feng L, Hua H, Qiu LY, Zhang LF, Jin J. Study on antiangiogenesis effect of Vaccaria segetalis. Laboratory of Natural Medicine, Ministry of Education, Jiangnan University, Wuxi 214122, China. Zhong Yao Cai. 2009 Aug;32(8): 1256-9.
21. Koo HJ, Lee S, Shin KH, Kim BC, Lim CJ, Park EH. Geniposide, an anti-angiogenic compound from the fruits of Gardenia jasminoides. College of Pharmacy, Sookmyung Women's University, Seoul, Korea. Planta Med. 2004 May;70(5):467-9.
22. *Xin Yi Yao Xue Za Zhi* (New Journal of Medicine and Herbology), 1975; (6):34.
23. *Yao Xue Za Zhi* (Journal of Medicinals), 1971; (91):1098.
24. Zhao F, Wang L, Liu K. In vitro anti-inflammatory effects of arctigenin, a lignan from Arctium lappa L., through inhibition on iNOS pathway. School of Pharmacy, Yantai University, Yantai, Shandong, China. J Ethnopharmacol. 2009 Apr 21;122(3):457-62.
25. Jiang J, Xu Q. Immunomodulatory activity of the aqueous extract from rhizome of Smilax glabra in the later phase of adjuvant-induced arthritis in rats. Department of Pharmacology for Chinese Materia Medica, China Pharmaceutical University, 24 Tong Jia Xiang, Nanjing 210009, PR China. J Ethnopharmacol. 2003 Mar;85(1):53-9.
26. Oh JH, Kang LL, Ban JO, Kim YH, Kim KH, Han SB, Hong JT. Anti-inflammatory effect of 4-O-methylhonokiol, compound isolated from Magnolia officinalis through inhibition of NF-kappaB. College of Pharmacy, CBITRC, Chungbuk National University, 12, Gaesin-dong, Heungduk-gu, Cheongju, Chungbuk 361-763, Republic of Korea. Chem Biol Interact. 2010 Dec 5;188(3):677.
27. Ha HH, Park SY, Ko WS, Kim Y. Gleditsia sinensis thorns inhibit the production of NO through NF-kappaB suppression in LPS-stimulated macrophages.

Resolve (Upper)™

Department of Molecular Biology, College of Natural Sciences, Pusan National University, Jangjeon-dong, Keumjeong-gu, Pusan, Republic of Korea. J Ethnopharmacol. 2008 Aug 13;118(3):429-34.

28. *Zhong Yi Za Zhi* (Journal of Chinese Medicine), 1959; 5:40.

Respitrol (CF)™

CLINICAL APPLICATIONS

- **Cough**
  - with associated symptoms such as sputum, chest congestion, wheezing and dyspnea
  - from acute conditions, such as common cold, influenza and lung infection
  - chronic cough induced by various conditions, such as post-nasal drip, infection, drugs, and smoking
  - cough in tuberculosis or lung cancer

WESTERN THERAPEUTIC ACTIONS

- Antitussive effect to suppress cough
- Expectorant effect to eliminate phlegm and reduce congestion
- Bronchodilating effect to relieve wheezing and dyspnea
- Antibiotic effect to treat cough with infection
- Antiallergic and antihistamine effects to dry up nasal discharge and stop post-nasal drip

CHINESE THERAPEUTIC ACTIONS

- Releases wind from the exterior
- Eliminates phlegm
- Nourishes yin
- Descends Lung qi

DOSAGE

The standard dosage for adults is 4 to 6 capsules three times daily. This is a potent formula; therefore, the dosage must be carefully adjusted based on age, body weight and severity of the condition, especially for pediatric and geriatric patients.

INGREDIENTS

Gan Cao (Radix et Rhizoma Glycyrrhizae)
Jie Zi (Semen Sinapis)
Ku Xing Ren (Semen Armeniacae Amarum)
Mai Dong (Radix Ophiopogonis)
Sheng Jiang (Rhizoma Zingiberis Recens)
Tian Zhu Zi (Fructus Nandina)
Wu Mei (Fructus Mume)
Zi Su Ye (Folium Perillae)
Zi Su Zi (Fructus Perillae)

BACKGROUND

Cough is an explosive expiratory maneuver intended to clear the airways. Acute cough is often caused by upper respiratory infection, postnasal drip, pneumonia or COPD exacerbation. Chronic cough is frequently due to postnasal drip, chronic bronchitis, airway hyper-responsiveness after resolution of an infection, or gastroesophageal reflux disease. Proper treatment of cough requires accurate diagnosis and treatment of the cause and the management of the symptoms.

FORMULA EXPLANATION

Respitrol (CF) is an empirical formula designed to treat cough due to various causes, including but not limited to external (wind-cold or wind-heat), or internal causes (heat, phlegm, or yin deficiency). This formula contains herbs that release wind from the exterior, eliminate phlegm, nourish yin, and descend Lung qi.

In this formula, *Zi Su Ye* (Folium Perillae) and *Sheng Jiang* (Rhizoma Zingiberis Recens) release wind-cold from the exterior, eliminate phlegm, and stop coughing. *Jie Zi* (Semen Sinapis) eliminates phlegm and opens the airways. *Tian Zhu Zi* (Fructus Nandina) and *Ku Xing Ren* (Semen Armeniacae Amarum) have a marked effect to suppress cough, as they cause Lung qi to descend. *Mai Dong* (Radix Ophiopogonis) nourishes yin and relieves chronic cough due to Lung deficiency. *Zi Su Zi* (Fructus Perillae) eliminates phlegm and descends Lung qi to relieve cough. Lastly, *Wu Mei* (Fructus Mume) astringes Lung qi and relieves cough. The use of *Mai Dong* (Radix Ophiopogonis) and *Wu Mei* (Fructus Mume) also help to control the warm, dispersing and drying nature of the formula from consuming yin and fluids. *Gan Cao* (Radix et Rhizoma Glycyrrhizae) harmonizes the formula.

In short, ***Respitrol (CF)*** is an excellent empirical formula to symptomatically treat cough. However, if the cause can be identified, the overall treatment will be more effective if another formula is used to address the cause.

CAUTIONS & CONTRAINDICATIONS

- Cough is a symptom that has many causes, such as infection (bronchitis or pneumonia), pre-existing diseases (tuberculosis or emphysema), airway irritation (smoke, dust and fumes), and aspiration (upper airway secretion or gastric contents). It is very important to identify and treat the underlying cause, in addition to treating the symptom.
- In cases of lung infection, cough is a beneficial protective mechanism for clearing respiratory secretions and foreign materials. Optimal treatment in these situations requires use of medicines to treat the infection and the cough (if necessary) concurrently. Suppressing the symptom without treating the cause may delay the overall recovery. Though this formula contains herbs with antibiotic effect, it is necessary to combine with additional formulas to reinforce the overall effect to treat infection.
- Do ***not*** use an excessive amount of this formula, as gross overdose of any medicinal substances will inevitably contribute to unwanted reactions. In this case, *Ku Xing Ren* (Semen Armeniacae Amarum) and *Tian Zhu Zi* (Fructus Nandina) have excellent functions to stop coughing by suppressing respiratory reflex in the brain. Hence, gross overdose of these two herbs may suppress respiration and cause difficulty breathing.[1,2] Other potential side effects associated with gross overdose include dizziness, weakness, nausea, vomiting, abdominal pain, burning

Respitrol (CF)™

sensations in the upper abdominal region, increased blood pressure, and increased respiration.[3] Due to the potent effect of these herbs, this formula should be used with caution for pediatric or geriatric patients, and is contraindicated during pregnancy and nursing.

CLINICAL NOTES

- ***Respitrol (CF)*** is most effective when:
  - The cause of the cough is not known or a specific treatment is not possible.
  - The cough performs no useful function, or causes significant discomfort.
  - If the cause if known, then this formula may be used as a useful adjunct to suppress cough.
- Certain drugs, such as angiotensin-converting enzyme (ACE) inhibitors [Capoten (captopril), Zestril (lisinopril) and Vasotec (enalapril)], may cause non-productive cough in up to 20% of patients. This drug-induced cough may begin as soon as one week after starting that therapy, but may be delayed by as much as six months.[4] This type of cough may be treated with ***Respitrol (CF)*** and ***Nourish (Fluids)***.
- Gastroesophageal reflux is a common cause of cough that should be remembered but is often overlooked.

SUPPLEMENTARY FORMULAS

- For cough due to common cold or influenza, combine with ***Lonicera Complex***.
- For cough caused by post-nasal drip, add ***Magnolia Clear Sinus*** or ***Pueraria Clear Sinus***.
- For cough due to lung infection (such as in bronchitis or pneumonia), use with ***Herbal ABX***.
- To enhance the overall antiviral function, add ***Herbal AVR***.
- For cough with sore throat from a sinus infection, combine with ***Herbal ENT***.
- For cough due to gastroesophageal reflux, combine with ***GI Care***.
- For cough due to airway hyper-responsiveness after resolution of an infection characterized by dryness and yin deficiency, add ***Nourish (Fluids)***.
- For cough with chest congestion and profuse phlegm, use with ***Pinellia XPT***.
- With more underlying damp and phlegm with Spleen qi deficiency, add ***Pinellia Complex***.
- For cough with wheezing and dyspnea due to Lung heat, use with ***Respitrol (Heat)***.
- For cough with wheezing and dyspnea due to Lung cold, use with ***Respitrol (Cold)***.
- For chronic cough with wheezing and dyspnea due to Lung deficiency, use with ***Respitrol (Deficient)*** or ***Cordyceps 3***.
- For high fever, add ***Gardenia Complex***.
- For cough due to stress, add ***Calm***.
- For immune deficiency, add ***Cordyceps 3*** or ***Immune +***.

ACUPUNCTURE TREATMENT

Traditional Points:

- **Cough in general:** *Lieque* (LU 7), *Hegu* (LI 4), *Feishu* (BL 13), *Chize* (LU 5), *Taiyuan* (LU 9), *Taibai* (SP 3), *Fenglong* (ST 40), *Yuji* (LU 10), *Xingjian* (LR 2)
- **Cough due to external factors** (wind-cold or wind-heat): *Lieque* (LU 7), *Hegu* (LI 4), *Feishu* (BL 13). Use strong stimulation for wind-heat. Use regular stimulation plus moxa for wind-cold.
- **Cough due to internal causes** (heat, phlegm, or yin deficiency): *Feishu* (BL 13), *Taiyuan* (LU 9), *Zhangmen* (LR 13)

Classic Master Tung's Points:

- **Cough, asthma:** *Dingke* (T 44.28)*, *Chongzi* (T 22.01), *Fugesan* (T 44.30)*, *Dabai* (T 22.04), *Tianshi* (T 33.15), *Dishi* (T 33.14), *Renshi* (T 33.13), *Feiqiyi* (T 44.25)*, *Feiqier* (T 44.26)*, *Huofuhai* (T 33.07), *Quling* (T 33.16), *Zhongjian* (T 11.05)
- **Common cold**: *Fugesan* (T 44.30)*, *Linggu* (T 22.05), *Hegu* (LI 4), *Ganmaoyi* (T 88.07), *Ganmaoer* (T 88.08), *Huofuhai* (T 33.07), *Mu* (T 11.17)
- **Tuberculosis:** *Feiqier* (T 44.26)*, *Linggu* (T 22.05), *Shuijin* (T 1010.20), *Shuitong* (T 1010.19), *Simashang* (T 88.18), *Simazhong* (T 88.17), *Simaxia* (T 88.19), *Sihuashang* (T 77.08), *Sihuazhong* (T 77.09), *Sihuaxia* (T 77.11). Bleed the HT and LU area in the back. Bleed before needling for best result.
- **Chest stuffiness:** *Linggu* (T 22.05), *Dabai* (T 22.04), *Tianshi* (T 33.15), *Dishi* (T 33.14), *Renshi* (T 33.13), *Zhenjing* (T 1010.08), *Shangli* (T 1010.09)
- **Lung cancer/tumor:** *Simashang* (T 88.18), *Simazhong* (T 88.17), *Simaxia* (T 88.19), *Linggu* (T 22.05), *Dabai* (T 22.04), *Shuangling* (T 11.28)*, *Waisanguan* (T 77.27), *Xinchang* (T 11.19), *Zhiwu* (T 11.26). Bleed the LU area below the knee. Bleed before needling for best result. The more the blood is let out, the better the effect. Bleed the LU and HT areas on the back (from T3 to T5) with cupping. Bleed before needling for best result.

Master Tung's Points by Dr. Chuan-Min Wang:

- **Cough:** Needle *Fenjin* (T 44.01), *Quchi* (LI 11), *Sanchasan* (T 22.17)*, *Chongzi* (T 22.01), *Chongxian* (T 22.02). Bleed *Ganmaosan* (T DT.12).

Balance Method by Dr. Richard Tan:

- Left side: *Jingqu* (LU 8), *Taiyuan* (LU 9), *Neiguan* (PC 6), *Xiajuxu* (ST 39), *Fenglong* (ST 40), *Jiexi* (ST 41)
- Right side: *Hegu* (LI 4), *Yangxi* (LI 5), *Sanyinjiao* (SP 6), *Jiaoxin* (KI 8)
- Alternate sides with each treatment.

Ear Acupuncture:

- Lung, Trachea, *Shenmen*, Liver, Spleen, Kidney

Respitrol (CF)™

Auricular Medicine by Dr. Li-Chun Huang:

- **Cough:** Trachea, Bronchus, Lung, *Shenmen*, Occiput, Stop Asthma, corresponding points of pain. Bleed Ear Apex.
- **Cough from common cold:** Lung, Internal Nose, Throat (Larynx, Pharynx), Trachea, Bronchus, Stop Asthma
- **Cough from bronchiectasis:** Bronchus, Lung, Chest, Stop Asthma, Allergic Area, Sympathetic, Adrenal Gland, Spleen

NUTRITION

- Individuals with a poor swallowing reflex should consume food and beverages slowly. Aspiration of these contents into the lungs increases the risk of cough and lung infection.
- Pear, loquat, lemon with honey, pineapples, lotus nodes and white radish are excellent foods to help reduce frequency and severity of cough.
- White radish is an excellent food to relieve cough. Take 1 white radish, approximately the size of a fist and cut it into thin slices. Mix it with 1 tablespoon of maltose and 1 cup of water and cook for 20 minutes. Serve the radish and the juice when they cool to room temperature. Another easier method is to mix the slices of white radish with honey. Wait for 30 minutes and drink the fluids that are secreted from the radish.
- Tea made from fresh ginger and honey (1:4 ratio) is also helpful to relieve both acute and chronic cough.
- Avoid drinking cold beverages, as they may constrict the airways and induce cough.
- Avoid foods that are acrid, spicy, aromatic or drying in nature. Do not eat foods that are heavy, greasy, or deep-fried.

The Tao of Nutrition by Dr. Maoshing Ni and Cathy McNease:

- **Cough**
  - Boil tea from watercress and apricot kernels (remove the apex) or almonds. Drink one cup three times daily.
  - Cook banana with a bit of sugar.
  - Drink ginger tea.
  - Mix honey with water and/or almonds.
  - Dice carrots, mix with molasses and leave it overnight; take two teaspoons three times daily.
- **Chronic cough:** Make tea with about 20 grapefruit seeds, adding a bit of honey; drink three times daily.
- **Dry cough**
  - Cook four grapefruit slices with either pork or cabbage.
  - Grind pine nuts and walnuts, add honey and slowly cook over low flame until thick; take two teaspoons with warm water.
  - Mash strawberries with brown sugar; steam and eat three times daily.
- **Dry cough with yellow sputum:** Take warm daikon and water chestnut juice with one teaspoon honey.
- **Productive cough:** Juice raw turnip, and mix with honey and warm water. Drink 2 to 3 cups a day.
- **Cough with yellow sputum:** Drink apple juice.
- **Cough with yellow phlegm:** Core Asian pear and fill with 3 grams of *Chuan Bei Mu* (Bulbus Fritillariae Cirrhosae) and a little rock sugar or brown sugar; steam about 30 minutes and eat completely.

LIFESTYLE INSTRUCTION

- Airway irritation (smoke, dust and fumes) is a very common cause of cough. Try to avoid exposure to these environments as much as possible. If necessary, install an air filter to clean the air.

PHARMACOLOGICAL AND CLINICAL RESEARCH

Respitrol (CF) is an empirical therapy for the symptomatic relief of cough. It contains many herbs with antitussive effects to suppress cough, expectorant effects to eliminate phlegm and reduce congestion, bronchodilating effects to relieve wheezing and dyspnea, and antibiotic effects to treat cough from infection.

Many herbs in ***Respitrol (CF)*** have excellent antitussive effects to suppress cough, such as *Ku Xing Ren* (Semen Armeniacae Amarum), *Tian Zhu Zi* (Fructus Nandina) and *Gan Cao* (Radix et Rhizoma Glycyrrhizae). *Ku Xing Ren* (Semen Armeniacae Amarum) suppresses cough via an inhibitory effect on the respiratory center in the brain, thereby exerting its antitussive effect.[5] *Tian Zhu Zi* (Fructus Nandina) has been used to treat various types of cough, including but not limited to acute bronchitis, whooping cough, and cough in children.[6] *Gan Cao* (Radix et Rhizoma Glycyrrhizae) has marked antitussive and expectorant effects, and the mechanism of action has been attributed to its effect on the central nervous system.[7]

Respitrol (CF) also incorporates many herbs to treat symptoms commonly associated with coughing, such as phlegm, chest congestion, wheezing, and dyspnea. For example, *Jie Zi* (Semen Sinapis) and *Gan Cao* (Radix et Rhizoma Glycyrrhizae) have expectorant effects to eliminate phlegm and relieve congestion.[8] *Zi Su Ye* (Folium Perillae) promotes bronchodilation to relieve bronchospasm. It also reduces secretions from the bronchioli.[9] Furthermore, *Gan Cao* (Radix et Rhizoma Glycyrrhizae) has an anti-inflammatory effect to reduce swelling and relieve chest congestion.[10] The mechanism of this action is attributed in part to the effect of *Gan Cao* (Radix et Rhizoma Glycyrrhizae) to stimulate the production of glucocorticoids by the adrenal glands and to delay their metabolism by the liver.[11]

Furthermore, because cough is often a symptom of respiratory tract infection, many herbs with antibiotic effects are used in ***Respitrol (CF)***, including *Zi Su Ye* (Folium Perillae),[12,13] *Sheng Jiang* (Rhizoma Zingiberis Recens),[14] *Mai Dong* (Radix Ophiopogonis),[15] and *Wu Mei* (Fructus Mume).[16,17]

Postnasal drip is a common cause of both acute and chronic cough. Therefore, *Zi Su Ye* (Folium Perillae) is used for its anti-allergic effect to dry up nasal discharge and ameliorate allergic inflammatory reactions. The mechanisms of the antiallergic and anti-inflammatory effects include decreased mast cell and eosinophil infiltration, reduced histamine levels, and inhibited expressions of interleukin (IL)-1β, IL-6 and tumor necrosis factor-α.[18]

In summary, ***Respitrol (CF)*** is an empirical formula that treats cough and its associated conditions. It is formulated with herbs that suppress cough, eliminate phlegm, reduce chest congestion, relieve wheezing and dyspnea, and treat infection.

COMPARATIVE ANALYSIS

Cough is a symptom that has many causes, such as infection, pre-existing diseases, airway irritation, and aspiration. Because cough is a natural reaction to eliminate foreign or harmful substance from the lungs, mild to moderate coughing is generally not treated. However, in cases where severe or constant cough interferes with resting and recovery, drugs and herbs should be used together to treat the symptom (cough) and the cause (numerous).

Cough is usually treated with opioids, such as dextromethorphan and narcotic antitussives (such as codeine). These drugs have a respiratory depressant effect to suppress cough. Though these drugs are effective, they may cause side effects such as hypersensitivity, tachycardia or bradycardia, syncope, respiratory depression, circulatory depression, nausea, vomiting, constipation, urinary retention, and in severe cases, tolerance and dependence.

Cough is usually treated with herbs that eliminate sputum, relieve chest congestion, and regulate the flow of Lung qi. In other words, herbs do not just suppress cough, but rather, they open up the airways and unblock chest congestion to relieve cough. Nonetheless, some herbs that relieve cough may have side effects, such as described above under Cautions & Contraindications.

It is generally not necessary to treat cough, as it is a natural defensive and desirable reaction. However, if treatment is deemed necessary, both the symptom and the cause must be addressed at the same time. In this case, both drugs and herbs are effective to treat cough. Drugs tend to "suppress" cough by depressing the respiratory tract. Herbs tend to "relieve" cough by opening the airways and unblocking obstruction. Both medicines have side effects, and must be carefully evaluated in choosing the most suitable therapy for the patient.

References

1. *Zhong Yao Bu Liang Fan Ying Yu Zhi Liao* (Adverse Reactions and Treatment of Chinese Herbal Medicine), 1996; 218:220, 1996; 213 217.
2. Kariyone. T. *Atlas of Medicinal Plants.*
3. *Zhong Yao Bu Liang Fan Ying Yu Zhi Liao* (Adverse Reactions and Treatment of Chinese Herbal Medicine), 1996; 218:220, 1996; 213:217.
4. Fauci, Braunwald, Isselbacher, et al. Harrison's Principles of Internal Medicine 14th Edition. McGraw-Hill, 1998.
5. *Life Sci*, 1980; 27(8):659.
6. Kariyone. T. *Atlas of Medicinal Plants.*
7. *Zhong Yao Yao Li Yu Ying Yong* (Pharmacology and Applications of Chinese Herbs), 1983; 264.
8. *Zhong Yao Xue* (Chinese Herbology), 1998; 608:610.
9. *Zhong Yao Xue* (Chinese Herbology), 1998; 67:68.
10. *Zhong Cao Yao* (Chinese Herbal Medicine), 1991; 22(10):452.
11. *Zhong Yao Zhi* (Chinese Herbology Journal), 1993; 358.
12. *Zhong Guo Zhong Yao Za Zhi* (People's Republic of China Journal of Chinese Herbology), 1990; 25(2):31.
13. Choi UK, Lee OH, Lim SI, Kim YC. Optimization of Antibacterial Activity of Perilla frutescens var. acuta Leaf against Pseudomonas aeruginosa Using the Evolutionary Operation-Factorial Design Technique. Pohang Center for Evaluation of Biomaterials, Pohang 790-834, Korea. Int J Mol Sci. 2010 Oct 14;11(10):3922-32.
14. *Zhong Yao Xue* (Chinese Herbology), 1998; 69:72.
15. *Zhong Yao Xue* (Chinese Herbology), 1998; 845:843.
16. *Zhong Yi Za Zhi* (Journal of Chinese Medicine), 1984; 262.
17. Yingsakmongkon S, Miyamoto D, Sriwilaijaroen N, Fujita K, Matsumoto K, Jampangern W, Hiramatsu H, Guo CT, Sawada T, Takahashi T, Hidari K, Suzuki T, Ito M, Ito Y, Suzuki Y. In vitro inhibition of human influenza A virus infection by fruit-juice concentrate of Japanese plum (Prunus mume SIEB. et ZUCC). Department of Biomedical Sciences, College of Life and Health Sciences, Chubu University, 1200 Matsumoto, Kasugai, Aichi 487-8501, Japan. Biol Pharm Bull. 2008 Mar;31(3):511-5.
18. Oh HA, Park CS, Ahn HJ, Park YS, Kim HM. Effect of Perilla frutescens var. acuta Kudo and rosmarinic acid on allergic inflammatory reactions. Department of Pharmacology, Institute of Oriental Medicine, College of Oriental Medicine, School of Medicine, Kyung Hee University, 1 Hoegi-dong, Dongdaemun-gu, Seoul 130-701, Republic of Korea. Exp Biol Med (Maywood). 2011 Jan;236(1):99-106.

Respitrol (Cold)™

CLINICAL APPLICATIONS

- **Respiratory disorders with cold manifestations:** wheezing, dyspnea, shortness of breath, coughing
- **Wind-cold or Lung cold** with sinus congestion, sneezing, watery eyes, and watery or white nasal discharge, white sputum
- **Wheezing and/or dyspnea** with intolerance to cold (temperature, food or drinks), grayish and cyanotic complexion of the face and body, chills, and absence of perspiration
- Used as immediate relief for sneezing and clear nasal discharge in people who are exposed to cold weather (i.e., rain or snow) or cold water (i.e., swimmers or divers)

WESTERN THERAPEUTIC ACTIONS

- Bronchodilating and antiasthmatic effects to relax the bronchial smooth muscle and relieve wheezing and dyspnea
- Antitussive effect to suppress cough
- Expectorant effect to eliminate phlegm
- Antibiotic action to treat bacterial and viral infections in the respiratory tract

CHINESE THERAPEUTIC ACTIONS

- Dispels cold, warms the interior
- Eliminates phlegm
- Regulates qi circulation to relieve wheezing and dyspnea

DOSAGE

Take 4 to 6 capsules three times a day with warm water on an empty stomach. For maximum effectiveness, start taking ***Respitrol (Cold)*** with the first sign of respiratory discomfort.

INGREDIENTS

Bai Shao (Radix Paeoniae Alba)
Cang Er Zi (Fructus Xanthii), dry fried
Gan Jiang (Rhizoma Zingiberis)
Gui Zhi (Ramulus Cinnamomi)
Hou Po (Cortex Magnoliae Officinalis)
Jie Zi (Semen Sinapis)
Ku Xing Ren (Semen Armeniacae Amarum)
Pi Pa Ye (Folium Eriobotryae)
Wu Wei Zi (Fructus Schisandrae Chinensis)
Zhi Gan Cao (Radix et Rhizoma Glycyrrhizae Praeparata cum Melle)
Zi Su Zi (Fructus Perillae)
Zi Wan (Radix et Rhizoma Asteris)

BACKGROUND

Lung inflammation and infection are two conditions that often occur together. Lung inflammation refers to the swelling of airways causing symptoms such as wheezing, dyspnea, chest tightness, cough, and presence of phlegm. Lung infection refers to invasion of the respiratory tract by micro-organisms such as bacteria, viruses, and fungi. If these lung inflammation and infection disorders are not properly treated, then the lung's structures and functions will be adversely affected, causing conditions such as mucus hypersecretion, mucus plugging, mucosal edema, loss of elasticity in the airways, peribronchial fibrosis, enlarged alveolar space, and loss of airway support. Chronic lung inflammation and infection with compromised functions and structures is generally described as Lung cold in traditional Chinese medicine.

FORMULA EXPLANATION

Respitrol (Cold) is formulated to treat cold-type respiratory disorders, including but not limited to, chronic asthma, chronic obstructive pulmonary disease, bronchitis, pneumonia, and inflammation and infection of the respiratory tract. Diagnostic signs and symptoms of cold include chills, clear watery nasal discharge, sneezing, intolerance to cold, absence of fever, and grayish and cyanotic complexion of the face and body. ***Respitrol (Cold)*** contains herbs with functions to dispel cold, warm the interior, eliminate phlegm, and regulate qi circulation.

In this formula, *Ku Xing Ren* (Semen Armeniacae Amarum) and *Hou Po* (Cortex Magnoliae Officinalis) eliminate phlegm, transform congested fluids, and reduce wheezing. *Zi Wan* (Radix et Rhizoma Asteris) expels wind and relieves dyspnea, chest discomfort, and wheezing. *Gui Zhi* (Ramulus Cinnamomi) works synergistically with *Bai Shao* (Radix Paeoniae Alba) to tonify and harmonize the qi in the *wei* (defense) and *ying* (nutritive) levels. Due to cold, water metabolism of the Lung may be impaired leading to a sudden blockage of fluids in the upper *jiao*. *Gan Jiang* (Rhizoma Zingiberis), *Jie Zi* (Semen Sinapis), *Zi Su Zi* (Fructus Perillae) and *Cang Er Zi* (Fructus Xanthii) warm the Lung, dispel the cold factor, arrest wheezing, and move water by regulating the qi flow of the Lung. *Wu Wei Zi* (Fructus Schisandrae Chinensis) is used to protect the Lung by preventing the leakage of qi. *Zhi Gan Cao* (Radix et Rhizoma Glycyrrhizae Praeparata cum Melle) and *Bai Shao* (Radix Paeoniae Alba) relieve bronchial spasms, alleviate pain, and harmonize the formula.

CAUTIONS & CONTRAINDICATIONS

- This formula is contraindicated during pregnancy and nursing.
- Patients with severe or acute asthma attacks may need additional herbal or drug treatment.
- Patients with heat- or deficient-type respiratory disorders should use ***Respitrol (Heat)*** or ***Respitrol (Deficient)***, respectively. See Supplementary Formulas for maintenance treatment of respiratory disorders.
- This formula is contraindicated for long-term use. It should be discontinued when the desired effects are achieved. For long-term treatment, consider using ***Respitrol (Deficient)*** or ***Cordyceps 3***.
- The *Cang Er Zi* (Fructus Xanthii) used in this formula has been carefully dry fried at high temperature until they appear dark brown or slightly charred, as dictated by the Chinese *Materia Medica*. Dry frying is necessary because this process

Respitrol (Cold)™

simultaneously increases the effect [by enhancing the extraction of active compounds] and decreases the side effects [by destroying the undesired glycosides]. Nonetheless, because *Cang Er Zi* (Fructus Xanthii) is metabolized by the liver and eliminated by the kidneys, individuals with pre-exiting liver or kidney diseases should not take this formula.[1]

CLINICAL NOTES

- ***Respitrol (Heat)*** or ***Respitrol (Cold)*** should be taken for respiratory disorders with wheezing, dyspnea, and shortness of breath. When the condition stabilizes, use ***Respitrol (Deficient)*** and ***Cordyceps 3*** during the remission stage of chronic respiratory disorders to strengthen the underlying constitution of the patient. ***Respitrol (Deficient)*** should not be taken during the acute stage of any respiratory disorder. Furthermore, ***Cordyceps 3*** is also very beneficial to strengthen the Lung and the Kidney, the two organs that are responsible for controlling respiration. Therefore, it is extremely important to ensure that the patient is compliant with taking ***Respitrol (Deficient)*** and/or ***Cordyceps 3*** to reduce the frequency and severity of asthma attacks.
- ***Respitrol (Cold)*** is suitable for common cold or influenza due to wind-cold. However, if the wind-cold transforms into wind-heat or Lung heat, ***Lonicera Complex*** or ***Respitrol (Heat)*** should be used, respectively.
- In cases where the patient is having an acute attack and the medication or inhaler is not readily available, two cups of coffee, hot cocoa, and chocolate bars are good alternatives to help alleviate symptoms of wheezing or dyspnea. Caffeine has a similar effect as the popular asthma drug theophylline.

Pulse Diagnosis by Dr. Jimmy Wei-Yen Chang:

- Pulse within a pulse or a constricting pulse, a pulse in which it feels like there is a bundle of thin, straight tight wires within the artery, on the right *cun*.
- *Yangwei* pulse, a pulse extending distally from the right *cun* towards the thumb. It is one of the eight extra meridian pulses.

SUPPLEMENTARY FORMULAS

- For allergies, sinus headache, nasal obstruction, and white watery nasal discharge, combine with ***Magnolia Clear Sinus***.
- For allergies, sinus headache, nasal obstruction, and sticky yellow nasal discharge, combine with ***Pueraria Clear Sinus***.
- For coughing, add ***Respitrol (CF)***.
- For infection of ear, nose, and throat, add ***Herbal ENT***.
- To enhance the overall antibacterial function, add ***Herbal ABX***.
- To enhance the overall antiviral function, add ***Herbal AVR***.
- For profuse, thick, yellow phlegm with chest congestion, combine with ***Pinellia XPT***.
- With more underlying damp and phlegm accumulation with Spleen qi deficiency, add ***Pinellia Complex***.
- For thirst, dry mouth and throat, add ***Nourish (Fluids)***.
- ***Immune +*** can be used as a maintenance formula for patients with underlying Lung deficiency manifesting in a weak immune system, recurrent colds and flu triggering asthma attacks.
- To tonify the overall constitution of the body, take ***Imperial Tonic*** on a daily basis.
- For maintenance and prevention of asthma attack, use ***Cordyceps 3*** and ***Respitrol (Deficient)***.

ACUPUNCTURE TREATMENT

Traditional Points:

- *Fengfu* (GV 16), *Fengchi* (GB 20), *Hegu* (LI 4), *Geshu* (BL 17), *Lieque* (LU 7), *Qihu* (ST 13), *Zhongfu* (LU 1)
- Apply moxa to *Dingchuan* (Extra 6), *Gaohuang*, and *Feishu* (BL 13)

Classic Master Tung's Points:

- *Dingke* (T 44.28)*, *Dajian* (T 11.01), *Zhongjian* (T 11.05), *Linggu* (T 22.05), *Dabai* (T 22.04), *Renshi* (T 33.13), *Dishi* (T 33.14), *Tianshi* (T 33.15), *Shuitong* (T 1010.19), *Shuijin* (T 1010.20), *Zhenjing* (T 1010.08), *Libai* (T 44.12), *Yunbai* (T 44.11). Bleed *Sihuawai* (T 77.14) or nearby dark veins. Bleed before needling for best result.
- **Chest stuffiness:** *Linggu* (T 22.05), *Dabai* (T 22.04), *Tianshi* (T 33.15), *Dishi* (T 33.14), *Renshi* (T 33.13), *Zhenjing* (T 1010.08), *Shangli* (T 1010.09)

Master Tung's Points by Dr. Chuan-Min Wang:

- **Common cold, flu**
  - Cold type: Needle *Fenjin* (T 44.01), *Huofuhai* (T 33.07). Bleed *Ganmaosan* (T DT.12).
  - Heat type: Needle *Dabai* (T 22.04), *Linggu* (T 22.05), *Sanchasan* (T 22.17)*. Bleed *Wuling* (T DT.04).
- **Asthma**
  - Kidney type: *Shuitong* (T 1010.19), *Shuijin* (T 1010.20)
  - Heart type: *Renshi* (T 33.13), *Dishi* (T 33.14), *Tianshi* (T 33.15)
  - Lung type: *Simazhong* (T 88.17), *Simashang* (T 88.18), *Simaxia* (T 88.19)

Balance Method by Dr. Richard Tan:

- Left side: *Shugu* (BL 65), *Jiexi* (ST 41), *Zusanli* (ST 36), *Jingqu* (LU 8)
- Right side: *Gongsun* (SP 4), *Sanyinjiao* (SP 6), *Hegu* (LI 4)
- Left and right sides can be alternated from treatment to treatment.

Ear Acupuncture:

- Bronchi, Lung, Adrenal Gland, Prostate Gland. Apply ear seeds to these points on both ears.

Auricular Medicine by Dr. Li-Chun Huang:

- **Bronchial asthma:** Bronchus, Trachea, Lung, Chest, Stop Asthma, Sympathetic, Adrenal Gland, Allergic Area, Endocrine. Bleed Ear Apex.
- **Common cold:** Lung, Internal Nose, Throat (Larynx, Pharynx)
  - For fever, bleed Ear Apex and Helix 1 to 6.

Respitrol (Cold)™

- For dizziness, add Dizziness Area.
- For pain and soreness all over the body, add Liver and Spleen. Bleed Helix 4.
- For cough, add Trachea, Bronchus, and Stop Asthma.

- **Bronchitis:** Bronchus, Trachea, Lung, Spleen, Stop Asthma, Sympathetic. Bleed Ear Apex.
- **Bronchiectasis:** Bronchus, Lung, Chest, Stop Asthma, Allergic Area, Sympathetic, Adrenal Gland, Spleen
- **Emphysema:** Sympathetic, Allergic Area, Chest, Lung, Bronchus, Stop Asthma, Spleen, Kidney, Endocrine
- **Cough:** Trachea, Bronchus, Lung, *Shenmen*, Occiput, Stop Asthma, corresponding points of pain. Bleed Ear Apex.

NUTRITION

- Eliminate all cold and raw foods and beverages from the diet as they constrict the bronchial tubes causing spasms.
- Since asthma may be allergy related, eliminate foods from the diet that commonly cause allergy, such as milk, eggs, shellfish, fish, and nuts. Sulfites – used commonly in restaurants to preserve salads, french fries, and avocado dips – are also linked to asthma attacks.
- White radish is an excellent food to relieve cough. Take 1 white radish, approximately the size of a fist and cut it into thin slices. Mix it with 1 tablespoon of maltose and 1 cup of water and cook for 20 minutes. Serve the radish and the juice when they cool to room temperature. Another easier method is to mix the slices of white radish with honey. Wait for 30 minutes and drink the fluids that are secreted from the radish.
- Lemon juice with honey is also very effective to relieve cough.
- A diet low in spicy, raw, greasy, and sweet foods is also recommended.
- Avoid the following cooling foods: tofu, tomato, celery, asparagus, bamboo, seaweed, kelp, cucumber, gourd, luffa, oranges, pear, banana, mustard leaf, potherb mustard, cactus, Chinese kale, napa, bamboo sprout. Most melons (such as watermelon), nightshades (eggplant, potato, bell and spicy peppers, tomato), bitter melon, grapefruit, papaya and pineapple are too cold for the Spleen. Therefore, it's best to eat sparingly or not at all. Long-term use of cold fruits and vegetables like the ones listed above may be damaging to the Spleen. To make the property more neutral, one can add about 20 pieces of *Gou Qi Zi* (Fructus Lycii) when cooking them.

The Tao of Nutrition by Dr. Maoshing Ni and Cathy McNease:

- **Asthma**
  - Recommendations: apricot kernels, almonds, walnuts, basil, carrots, pumpkins, sunflower seeds, loofah, squash, figs, and daikon.
  - Cut the top out of a small winter melon, remove the seeds, fill with molasses. Close the top with cheesecloth, and steam. Eat daily for seven days.
  - Take an unpeeled orange, pierce with a chopstick and roast until the peel blackens. Remove the peel and eat the fruit; one orange daily for seven days.
  - Mix 1/2 cup fig juice with 1/2 cup lukewarm water and drink daily.
  - Avoid mucus-producing foods, cold foods, fruits, salads, all shellfish, dairy products, watermelon, bananas, mung beans, salty foods, cold weather, and especially ice cream.
- **Common cold (wind-cold)**
  - Recommendations: ginger, garlic, mustard greens and seeds, grapefruit peel, cilantro, parsnip, scallions, cinnamon, basil, soupy rice porridge, and eat as little as possible so as not to burden the system with a lot to digest.
  - Lightly boil the following for five minutes: garlic, ginger, green onion, basil, mustard, or cinnamon. Drink the tea, go to bed and prepare to sweat.
  - Drink cilantro and green tea.
  - Drink scallion and basil tea.
  - Make tea from dried grapefruit peel.
  - Avoid shellfish, heavy proteins and fats, meats, and all vinegars.

LIFESTYLE INSTRUCTIONS

- Avoid exposure to pollen, dust, and drastic changes in temperature. Regular exercise with herbal therapy is the key to complete recovery.
- For asthma patients, vacuum and central heating filters should be changed frequently to keep dust, mold, and dust mites to a minimum. Installation of an air purifier is recommended for patients who have family members with infectious respiratory disorders. It is recommended to replace carpets with hard surface floors to prevent dust, molds, and other allergens from being trapped in the carpet. Bleach such as Clorox can be used to clear mold and fungus. Animal dander is also a major factor in causing allergies in patients. All contact (direct and indirect) with allergens should be avoided if possible to prevent allergic reactions.
- Patients should be advised to stop smoking, and stay away from secondhand smoke.
- Patients should strengthen their immune system and body resistance in between asthma attacks. A balance of exercise and rest is important. Alternation of hot and cold water in the shower is also effective to desensitize the body to changes in temperature. Herbs that enhance the immune system, such as ***Cordyceps 3*** or ***Immune +***, should also be taken on a regular basis.
- Patients are strongly encouraged to use hypo-allergenic products, and avoid those that contain artificial or chemical additives.

CASE STUDIES

- C.C., a 28-year-old male, presented with chronic asthma. Symptoms included tightness of the chest, loud wheezing, cough, and yellowish phlegm. The TCM diagnosis was wind-heat, and the patient was prescribed ***Respitrol (Cold)*** at four capsules three times a day. This is an ongoing cure, in which each time the

Respitrol (Cold)™

cough during asthma attacks gets less, as well as the phlegm and wheezing. He also took the herb at the beginning of a cold and it worked well for that too. Submitted by A.I., Hilo, Hawaii.

- B.F., a 55-year-old male, presented with cough, thick nasal discharge, headache, and fatigue. The tongue was pale, flabby, and slightly purple. The pulse was slow. He was diagnosed with common cold and wind-cold invasion. ***Magnolia Clear Sinus***, ***Respitrol (Cold)*** and ***Herbal ABX*** were prescribed. The patient reported that the sinus cleared in three days. Submitted by B.F., Newport Beach, California.

PHARMACOLOGICAL AND CLINICAL RESEARCH

Respitrol (Cold) is formulated to treat chronic respiratory disorders with cold signs and symptoms, such as wheezing, dyspnea, shortness of breath, watery or white nasal discharge, white sputum, intolerance to cold, grayish and cyanotic complexion of the face and body, chills, and absence of perspiration. ***Respitrol (Cold)*** contains herbs with a wide range of therapeutic effects, including antiasthmatic, bronchodilating, anti-inflammatory, expectorant, antitussive, and antibiotic functions.

Respitrol (Cold) has a marked effect to treat asthma, wheezing and dyspnea because many herbs in this formula have marked antiasthmatic and bronchodilating effects. For example, *Ku Xing Ren* (Semen Armeniacae Amarum) has an inhibitory effect on the respiratory center in the brain, thereby exerting its antiasthmatic effects.[2] *Hou Po* (Cortex Magnoliae Officinalis) has a stimulating effect on the respiratory system to relieve wheezing and dyspnea.[3] Magnolol and honokiol, two compounds from *Hou Po* (Cortex Magnoliae Officinalis), exert their antiasthmatic effect by relieving muscle spasms and inhibiting smooth muscle contraction in the trachea.[4,5] *Wu Wei Zi* (Fructus Schisandrae Chinensis) has been shown to stimulate the lungs to increase the depth of respiration. It also reverses respiratory depression associated with morphine.[6] Most importantly, *Gan Cao* (Radix et Rhizoma Glycyrrhizae) has a remarkable anti-inflammatory effect to reduce swelling and inflammation in the lungs. The proposed mechanism of anti-inflammatory action includes decreased permeability of the blood vessels, antihistamine functions, and decreased sensitivity to stimuli. The anti-inflammatory influence of glycyrrhizin and glycyrrhetinic acid is approximately 1/10th that of cortisone.[7]

Respitrol (Cold) also contains herbs that treat associated symptoms of respiratory disorders. For example, *Jie Zi* (Semen Sinapis) has an expectorant effect to facilitate discharge of phlegm and sputum.[8] *Pi Pa Ye* (Folium Eriobotryae) and *Cang Er Zi* (Fructus Xanthii) have good antitussive effects to suppress coughing.[9,10] *Gan Cao* (Radix et Rhizoma Glycyrrhizae) has antitussive and expectorant effects to relieve coughing and chest congestion.[11] In addition, *Gui Zhi* (Ramulus Cinnamomi) illustrates an antiallergic effect to serum IgE, histamine, and tumor necrosis factor-α.[12] Lastly, *Pi Pa Ye* (Folium Eriobotryae) demonstrates antiallergic and anti-inflammatory effects through its inhibitory effect on the mast cells and the pro-inflammatory cytokines.[13] This herb can be used to treat chronic bronchitis by inhibiting the inflammatory cytokine and mediator induction from alveolar macrophages.[14] Ursolic acid, one active component from *Pi Pa Ye* (Folium Eriobotryae), is especially effective in the treatment of pulmonary inflammation as it inhibited lipopolysaccharide-induced cytokines and inducible enzyme production in lung epithelial cells.[15]

Respitrol (Cold) utilizes many herbs with antibiotic effects (antibacterial, antiviral and antifungal) to treat lung infections. Herbs with antibacterial effects include *Zi Wan* (Radix et Rhizoma Asteris), *Hou Po* (Cortex Magnoliae Officinalis), *Bai Shao* (Radix Paeoniae Alba), *Gan Cao* (Radix et Rhizoma Glycyrrhizae), and *Wu Wei Zi* (Fructus Schisandrae Chinensis). *Zi Wan* (Radix et Rhizoma Asteris) has an inhibitory influence against *E. coli*, *Bacillus dysenteriae*, *Bacillus proteus*, *Salmonella typhi*, *Bacillus paratyphosus*, *Pseudomonas aeruginosa*, and *Vibrio cholerae*.[16] *Hou Po* (Cortex Magnoliae Officinalis) has an inhibitory effect against *Streptococcus matuans*, *Staphylococcus aureus*, *Bacillus subtilis*, *Diplococcus pneumoniae*, and *Bacillus dysenteriae*.[17,18,19] Furthermore, piperitylmagnolol and honokiol, two compounds from *Hou Po* (Cortex Magnoliae Officinalis), exhibited antibacterial activities against vancomycin-resistant enterococci (VRE) and methicillin-resistant *Staphylococcus aureus* (MRSA) in a time- and concentration-dependent manner.[20] *Bai Shao* (Radix Paeoniae Alba) has been shown to have an inhibitory action against *Bacillus dysenteriae*, *E. coli*, *Salmonella typhi*, *Pseudomonas aeruginosa*, *Staphylococcus aureus*, beta-hemolytic streptococcus, and *Diplococcus pneumoniae*.[21] *Gan Cao* (Radix et Rhizoma Glycyrrhizae) inhibits the growth of *Staphylococcus aureus*, *Mycobacterium tuberculosis*, *E. coli*, amoebae and *Trichomonas vaginalis*.[22] Lastly, *Wu Wei Zi* (Fructus Schisandrae Chinensis) has an inhibitory effect *in vitro* against *Staphylococcus aureus*, *Bacillus anthracis*, *Salmonella typhi*, *Bacillus dysenteriae*, *Diplococcus pneumoniae*, *Vibrio cholerae*, and *Pseudomonas aeruginosa*.[23] Herbs with antiviral effects include *Gui Zhi* (Ramulus Cinnamomi) and *Zi Wan* (Radix et Rhizoma Asteris). These two herbs both have an inhibitory effect against influenza viruses.[24,25] Finally, herbs with antifungal activities include *Ku Xing Ren* (Semen Armeniacae Amarum), *Jie Zi* (Semen Sinapis) and *Gui Zhi* (Ramulus Cinnamomi).[26,27,28]

Clinically, the herbs in ***Respitrol (Cold)*** have been used with great success to treat various types of respiratory disorders. One study uses *Wu Wei Zi* (Fructus Schisandrae Chinensis) in a formula to effectively treat 50 patients with asthma.[29] Another study shows that use of *Ku Xing Ren* (Semen Armeniacae Amarum) in *Xing Su San* (Apricot Kernel and Perilla Leaf Powder) is effective to treat coughing due to wind-cold in 50 patients.[30] *Ku Xing Ren* (Semen Armeniacae Amarum) also illustrates a 96.8% rate of effectiveness for treatment of chronic tracheitis in 124 patients (23 reported complete recovery, 66 reported marked effectiveness, 31 experienced some improvement, and 4 had no

Respitrol (Cold)™

response). The rate of effectiveness is 96.8%.[31] Lastly, use of *Zi Su Zi* (Fructus Perillae), *Jie Zi* (Semen Sinapis) and *Lai Fu Zi* (Semen Raphani) shows a marked effect for treatment of chronic and stubborn coughs. Out of 40 patients, the study reported marked improvement in 62.5%, and moderate improvement in 37.5%.[32]

In summary, ***Respitrol (Cold)*** is an excellent formula to treat respiratory disorders with cold manifestations. Not only does it have good therapeutic effect to treat respiratory tract inflammation and infection, it also contains many herbs to relieve the associated symptoms.

COMPARATIVE ANALYSIS

Treatment of wheezing and dyspnea is generally divided into acute and chronic management. In Western medicine, acute wheezing and dyspnea are treated by bronchodilators that open the airways and reverse obstruction. Chronic wheezing and dyspnea are managed by use of several categories of drugs, including bronchodilators, corticosteroids, theophylline, and cromolyn. Western medicine is extremely effective in treating acute wheezing and dyspnea, as use of bronchodilators [such as Proventil or Ventolin (albuterol) inhalers] generally reverses airway obstruction within minutes. However, Western medicine is not as successful in long-term management and prevention of wheezing and dyspnea. These drugs do not change the underlying condition of the disease, nor do they improve the constitution of the patient. Therefore, the long-term prognosis is often characterized by successful suppression of acute wheezing and dyspnea, but no change in frequency or severity of recurrent wheezing and dyspnea.

In TCM, wheezing and dyspnea are treated based on the urgency of the disease presentation and the underlying condition of the patients. Urgency refers to the acute or chronic nature of the disease, while underlying condition refers to the fundamental constitution of the patients. By addressing both the disease and the fundamental constitution, the use of herbs achieves both immediate and prolonged effects.

Both drugs and herbs are effective for the treatment of wheezing and dyspnea. Generally speaking, drugs are more effective for acute conditions, as they are more potent, and can be delivered via inhalation or intravenous injection to achieve a faster onset of relief. However, long-term treatment of wheezing and dyspnea with drugs is often less than optimal, as these drugs tend to create tolerance and dependence. Furthermore, they do not change the course of illness, and do not reduce the frequency and severity of recurrent attacks. On the other hand, herbs are better for long-term prevention and management of wheezing and dyspnea. Herbs strengthen the body and enhance its own ability to treat wheezing and dyspnea. However, use of herbs may not be appropriate for acute asthma because they are less immediately potent than some pharmaceuticals, and have a slower onset of action. In conclusion, optimal treatment of wheezing and dyspnea does not require choosing between drugs or herbs, but may be gained by embracing the benefits of both, by using drugs for acute treatment and herbs for long-term healing and prevention.

References

1. *Xian Dai Zhong Yao Du Li Xue* (Modern Toxicology of Chinese Materia Medica) 2005;63-65.
2. *Life Sci*, 1980; 27(8):659.
3. *Zhong Yao Xue* (Chinese Herbology), 1998; 320:323.
4. Chan SS, Zhao M, Lao L, Fong HH, Che CT. Magnolol and honokiol account for the anti-spasmodic effect of Magnolia officinalis in isolated guinea pig ileum. School of Chinese Medicine, The Chinese University of Hong Kong, Hong Kong, P.R. China. Planta Med. 2008 Mar;74(4):381-4.
5. Ko CH, Chen HH, Lin YR, Chan MH. Inhibition of smooth muscle contraction by magnolol and honokiol in porcine trachea. Planta Med. 2003 Jun;69(6): 532-6.
6. *Zhong Yao Yao Li Yu Ying Yong* (Pharmacology and Applications of Chinese Herbs), 1983, 1983: 177.
7. *Zhong Cao Yao* (Chinese Herbal Medicine), 1991; 22(10):452.
8. *Zhong Yao Xue* (Chinese Herbology), 1998; 608:610.
9. *Zhong Yao Xue* (Chinese Herbology), 1998; 651:653.
10. *Zhong Yao Xue* (Chinese Herbology), 1998; 81:83.
11. *Zhong Yao Yao Li Yu Ying Yong* (Pharmacology and Applications of Chinese Herbs), 1983; 264.
12. Sung YY, Yoon T, Jang JY, Park SJ, Gi-Hoon J, Kim HK. Inhibitory effects of Cinnamomum cassia extract on atopic dermatitis-like skin lesions induced by mite antigen in NC/Nga mice. Center of Herbal Resources Research, Korea Institute of Oriental Medicine, Daejeon 305-811, Republic of Korea. J Ethnopharmacol. 2010 Oct 28.
13. Kim SH, Shin TY. Anti-inflammatory effect of leaves of Eriobotrya japonica correlating with attenuation of p38 MAPK, ERK, and NF-kappaB activation in mast cells. CMRI, IHBR, Department of Pharmacology, School of Medicine, Kyungpook National University, Daegu 700-422, Republic of Korea. Toxicol In Vitro. 2009 Oct;23(7):1215-9.
14. Huang Y, Li J, Wang R, Wu Q, Li YH, Yu SC, Cheng WM, Wang YY. Effect of triterpene acids of Eriobotrya japonica (Thunb.) Lindl. leaf on inflammatory cytokine and mediator induction from alveolar macrophages of chronic bronchitic rats. School of Pharmacy, Anhui Medical University, Tunxi West Road, Hefei 230032, Anhui Province, China. Inflamm Res. 2007 Feb;56(2): 76-82.
15. Lee CH, Wu SL, Chen JC, Li CC, Lo HY, Cheng WY, Lin JG, Chang YH, Hsiang CY, Ho TY. Eriobotrya japonica leaf and its triterpenes inhibited lipopolysaccharide-induced cytokines and inducible enzyme production via the nuclear factor-kappaB signaling pathway in lung epithelial cells. Graduate Institute of Chinese Medical Science, China Medical University, Taichung 40402, Taiwan. Am J Chin Med. 2008;36(6):1185-98.
16. *Chang Yong Zhong Yao Cheng Fen Yu Yao Li Shou Ce* (A Handbook of the Composition and Pharmacology of Common Chinese Drugs), 1994; 1678:1681.
17. *Planta med*, 1982; 44(2):100.
18. *Yao Jian Gong Zuo Tong Xun* (Journal of Herbal Preparations), 1980; 10(4):209.
19. *Xin Hua Ben Cao Gang Mu* (New Chinese Materia Medica), 1988; 58.
20. Syu WJ, Shen CC, Lu JJ, Lee GH, Sun CM. Antimicrobial and cytotoxic activities of neolignans from Magnolia officinalis. Institute of Microbiology and Immunology, National Yang-Ming University, Taipei, Taiwan 112, Republic of China. Chem Biodivers. 2004 Mar;1(3):530-7.
21. *Xin Zhong Yi* (New Chinese Medicine), 1989; 21(3):51.
22. *Zhong Yao Zhi* (Chinese Herbology Journal), 1993; 358.
23. *Zhong Yao Xue* (Chinese Herbology), 1998; 878:881.
24. *Zhong Yao Xue* (Chinese Herbology), 1998; 65:67.
25. *Chang Yong Zhong Yao Cheng Fen Yu Yao Li Shou Ce* (A Handbook of the Composition and Pharmacology of Common Chinese Drugs), 1994; 1678: 1681.

Respitrol (Cold)™

26. Yiğit D, Yiğit N, Mavi A. Antioxidant and antimicrobial activities of bitter and sweet apricot (Prunus armeniaca L.) kernels. Department of Science Education, Education Faculty, Erzincan University, Erzincan, Turkey. Braz J Med Biol Res. 2009 Apr;42(4):346-52.
27. *Chang Yong Zhong Yao Xian Dai Yan Jiu Yu Lin Chuan* (Recent Study & Clinical Application of Common Traditional Chinese Medicine), 1995; 439:441.
28. Taguchi Y, Takizawa T, Ishibashi H, Sagawa T, Arai R, Inoue S, Yamaguchi H, Abe S. Therapeutic effects on murine oral candidiasis by oral administration of cassia (Cinnamomum cassia) preparation. Research and Product Development Division, S & B Foods Inc., Tokyo, Japan. Nippon Ishinkin Gakkai Zasshi. 2010;51(1):13-21.
29. *Zhong Yi Za Zhi* (Journal of Chinese Medicine), 1988; 9:47.
30. *Shi Yong Zhong Yi Nei Ke Za Zhi* (Journal of Practical Chinese Internal Medicine), 1993; 7(4):48.
31. *Zhong Yi Yan Jiu Yuan* (Research Hospital of Chinese Medicine), 1971; 34.
32. *Zhong Yao Tong Bao* (Journal of Chinese Herbology), 1986; 8:56.

FORMULAS

Respitrol (Deficient)™

CLINICAL APPLICATIONS

- **Chronic and deficient respiratory diseases**, such as asthma, respiratory allergies, occupational lung diseases, and environmental lung diseases
- Chronic respiratory disorders characterized by compromised breathing functions and damaged lung structures
- General symptoms and signs of deficiency including shortness of breath characterized by difficult inhalation but normal exhalation, wheezing and shortness of breath that becomes worse with physical exertion, snoring sounds in the throat due to phlegm accumulation, low-pitched rhonchi, audible wheezes, frail cough with sputum, dry throat, aversion to wind, spontaneous sweating, red cheeks, red tongue with scanty coating, and a thready, rapid pulse.

WESTERN THERAPEUTIC ACTIONS

- Antiasthmatic and bronchodilating effects to treat wheezing, dyspnea and asthma
- Antitussive function to stop coughing
- Expectorant function to eliminate sputum and phlegm
- Anti-inflammatory effect to reduce the swelling and inflammation in the lung

CHINESE THERAPEUTIC ACTIONS

- Relieves wheezing, arrests cough
- Eliminates phlegm
- Tonifies the Lung and the Kidney
- Tonifies the Kidney to grasp the qi downward

DOSAGE

Take 3 to 4 capsules three times daily on an empty stomach with warm water. This formula may be taken continuously on a long-term basis for the maintenance and prevention of asthma.

INGREDIENTS

Chai Hu (Radix Bupleuri)
Chen Pi (Pericarpium Citri Reticulatae)
Dang Gui (Radix Angelicae Sinensis)
Dong Chong Xia Cao (Cordyceps)
Hou Po (Cortex Magnoliae Officinalis)
Jie Zi (Semen Sinapis)
Ku Xing Ren (Semen Armeniacae Amarum)
Lai Fu Zi (Semen Raphani)
Rou Gui (Cortex Cinnamomi)
Ting Li Zi (Semen Descurainiae)
Wu Wei Zi (Fructus Schisandrae Chinensis)
Zao Jiao Ci (Spina Gleditsiae)
Zhi Gan Cao (Radix et Rhizoma Glycyrrhizae Praeparata cum Melle)
Zi Su Ye (Folium Perillae)
Zi Su Zi (Fructus Perillae)
Zi Wan (Radix et Rhizoma Asteris)

BACKGROUND

Chronic respiratory diseases are chronic diseases of the airways and other structures of the lung. Common examples include asthma, respiratory allergies, occupational lung diseases and environmental lung diseases. Causes of chronic respiratory diseases include tobacco smoking, indoor air pollution, outdoor air pollution, allergens, and occupational risks and vulnerability. As a result of chronic respiratory illness, the breathing functions become compromised and the lung structures are damaged, leading to Lung deficiency, as described in traditional Chinese medicine.

FORMULA EXPLANATION

Respitrol (Deficient) is formulated to treat deficient-types of respiratory disorders, including but not limited to, asthma, respiratory allergies, occupational lung diseases, environmental lung diseases, and other chronic and debilitating respiratory disorders. Diagnostic signs and symptoms of deficiency include dyspnea, shortness of breath, wheezing, difficulty with inhalation, fatigue with dyspnea on mild physical exertion, and weak and chronic types of respiratory illnesses. ***Respitrol (Deficient)*** contains herbs with functions to tonify the Kidney, regulate qi circulation, and eliminate phlegm.

Ku Xing Ren (Semen Armeniacae Amarum), *Zi Su Zi* (Fructus Perillae), *Zi Wan* (Radix et Rhizoma Asteris), *Jie Zi* (Semen Sinapis) and *Ting Li Zi* (Semen Descurainiae) direct Lung qi downwards, eliminate phlegm, and relieve coughing and wheezing. *Wu Wei Zi* (Fructus Schisandrae Chinensis) is an astringent herb that prevents the leakage of Lung qi. *Lai Fu Zi* (Semen Raphani) tonifies the Spleen and reduces the production of phlegm. *Chen Pi* (Pericarpium Citri Reticulatae) and *Zao Jiao Ci* (Spina Gleditsiae) are expectorants to eliminate the storage of phlegm. To prolong inhalation, *Rou Gui* (Cortex Cinnamomi) and *Dong Chong Xia Cao* (Cordyceps) warm the Kidney yang and restore its ability to grasp qi downward. *Hou Po* (Cortex Magnoliae Officinalis) and *Chai Hu* (Radix Bupleuri) regulate qi and relieve chest congestion. *Dang Gui* (Radix Angelicae Sinensis) nourishes the blood. *Zi Su Ye* (Folium Perillae) disperses coldness and dilates the Lung. *Zhi Gan Cao* (Radix et Rhizoma Glycyrrhizae Praeparata cum Melle) harmonizes the formula.

CAUTIONS & CONTRAINDICATIONS

- This formula is contraindicated during pregnancy and nursing.
- Patients with heat- or cold-type respiratory disorders should use ***Respitrol (Heat)*** or ***Respitrol (Cold)***, respectively. Please refer to Supplementary Formulas for maintenance treatment of respiratory disorders.
- Patients with severe or acute asthma attacks may need additional herbal or drug treatment.
- This herbal formula contains herbs that invigorate blood circulation, such as *Dang Gui* (Radix Angelicae Sinensis).

Respitrol (Deficient) ™

Therefore, patients who are on anticoagulant or antiplatelet therapies, such as Coumadin (warfarin), should use this formula with caution, or not at all, as there may be a higher risk of bleeding and bruising.[1,2,3]

CLINICAL NOTES

- ***Respitrol (Heat)*** or ***Respitrol (Cold)*** should be taken for respiratory disorders with wheezing, dyspnea and shortness of breath. When the condition stabilizes, take ***Respitrol (Deficient)*** and/or ***Cordyceps 3*** during the remission stage of chronic respiratory disorders to strengthen the underlying constitution of the patient. ***Respitrol (Deficient)*** should not be taken during the acute stage of any respiratory disorder. Furthermore, ***Cordyceps 3*** is also very beneficial to strengthen the Lung and the Kidney, the two organs that are responsible for controlling respiration. Therefore, it is extremely important to ensure that the patient is compliant with taking ***Respitrol (Deficient)*** and/or ***Cordyceps 3*** to reduce the frequency and severity of asthma attacks.
- In cases where the patient is having an acute attack and the medication or inhaler is not readily available, two cups of coffee, hot cocoa, and chocolate bars are good alternatives to help alleviate symptoms of wheezing or dyspnea. Caffeine has a similar effect as the popular asthma drug theophylline.[6]

SUPPLEMENTARY FORMULAS

- For maintenance and prevention of asthma attack, use with ***Cordyceps 3***.
- For coughing, add ***Respitrol (CF)***.
- For infection of ear, nose and throat, add ***Herbal ENT***.
- For thirst, dry mouth and throat, add ***Nourish (Fluids)***.
- Take with ***Immune +*** to enhance immunity.
- For respiratory infection with sore throat, fever, headache, use ***Lonicera Complex*** or ***Respitrol (Heat)*** instead.
- To treat cold-type respiratory disorders with chills, clear nasal discharge, sneezing, nasal congestion, use ***Respitrol (Cold)***.
- To treat allergies, use ***Magnolia Clear Sinus*** or ***Pueraria Clear Sinus***.
- For deficiency of qi, blood, yin or yang, combine ***Imperial Tonic*** with ***Respitrol (Deficient)*** as a preventative treatment for asthma during remission periods.
- For Kidney yang deficiency, combine ***Kidney Tonic (Yang)*** with ***Respitrol (Deficient)*** as a preventative treatment for asthma during remission periods.
- With more underlying damp and phlegm due to Spleen qi deficiency, add ***Pinellia Complex***.
- With more inflammation in the Lung, add ***Astringent Complex***.

ACUPUNCTURE TREATMENT

Traditional Points:

- *Zusanli* (ST 36), *Fenglong* (ST 40), *Feishu* (BL 13), *Dashu* (BL 11), *Shanzhong* (CV 17), *Shenshu* (BL 23), *Chize* (LU 5), *Kongzui* (LU 6), *Taixi* (KI 3), *Qihai* (CV 6)
- Apply moxa to *Guanyuan* (CV 4), *Mingmen* (GV 4), and *Dingchuan* (Extra 6).

Classic Master Tung's Points:

- *Dingke* (T 44.28)*, *Chongzi* (T 22.01), *Fugesan* (T 44.30)*, *Dabai* (T 22.04), *Tianshi* (T 33.15), *Dishi* (T 33.14), *Renshi* (T 33.13), *Feiqiyi* (T 44.25)*, *Feiqier* (T 44.26)*, *Huofuhai* (T 33.07), *Quling* (T 33.16), *Zhongjian* (T 11.05), *Tianhuangfu [Shenguan]* (T 77.18), *Tianhuang* (T 77.17), *Dihuang* (T 77.19), *Renhuang* (T 77.21)
- **Chest stuffiness:** *Linggu* (T 22.05), *Dabai* (T 22.04), *Tianshi* (T 33.15), *Dishi* (T 33.14), *Renshi* (T 33.13), *Zhenjing* (T 1010.08), *Shangli* (T 1010.09)

Master Tung's Points by Dr. Chuan-Min Wang:

- **Asthma**
  - Kidney type: *Shuitong* (T 1010.19), *Shuijin* (T 1010.20)
  - Heart type: *Renshi* (T 33.13), *Dishi* (T 33.14), *Tianshi* (T 33.15)
  - Lung type: *Simazhong* (T 88.17), *Simashang* (T 88.18), *Simaxia* (T 88.19)

Balance Method by Dr. Richard Tan:

- Left side: *Neiguan* (PC 6), *Kongzui* (LU 6), *Lingdao* (HT 4), *Fenglong* (ST 40), *Zusanli* (ST 36)
- Right side: *Sanjian* (LI 3), *Piani* (LI 6), *Jiaoxin* (KI 8), *Sanyinjiao* (SP 6), *Zhongfeng* (LR 4)
- Left and right sides can be alternated from treatment to treatment.

Ear Acupuncture:

- Bronchi, Lung, Adrenal Gland, Prostate Gland. Apply ear seeds to these points on both ears.

Auricular Medicine by Dr. Li-Chun Huang:

- **Asthma:** Bronchus, Trachea, Lung, Chest, Stop Asthma, Sympathetic, Adrenal Gland, Allergic Area, Endocrine. Bleed Ear Apex.
- **Common cold:** Lung, Internal Nose, Throat (Larynx, Pharynx)
  - For fever, bleed Ear Apex and Helix 1 to 6.
  - For dizziness, add Dizziness Area.
  - For pain and soreness all over the body, add Liver and Spleen. Bleed Helix 4.
  - For cough, add Trachea, Bronchus, and Stop Asthma.
- **Bronchitis:** Bronchus, Trachea, Lung, Spleen, Stop Asthma, Sympathetic. Bleed Ear Apex.
- **Bronchiectasis:** Bronchus, Lung, Chest, Stop Asthma, Allergic Area, Sympathetic, Adrenal Gland, Spleen
- **Emphysema:** Sympathetic, Allergic Area, Chest, Lung, Bronchus, Stop Asthma, Spleen, Kidney, Endocrine.
- **Cough:** Trachea, Bronchus, Lung, *Shenmen*, Occiput, Stop Asthma, corresponding points of pain. Bleed Ear Apex.
- **Snoring, apnea:** Trachea, *San Jiao*, Lower Lung, Pharynx, Larynx, Sympathetic, Nasopharynx, Chest, Mouth, Esophagus, Teeth and Larynx

FORMULAS

Respitrol (Deficient)™

NUTRITION

- Eliminate all cold and raw foods and beverages from the diet as they constrict the bronchial tubes causing spasms.
- Since asthma may be allergy related, eliminate foods from the diet that commonly cause allergy, such as milk, eggs, shellfish, fish, and nuts. Sulfites – used commonly in restaurants to preserve salads, French fries, and avocado dips – are also linked to asthma attacks.
- White radish is an excellent food to relieve cough. Take 1 white radish, approximately the size of a fist and cut it into thin slices. Mix it with 1 tablespoon of maltose and 1 cup of water and cook for 20 minutes. Serve the radish and the juice when they cool to room temperature. Another easier method is to mix the slices of white radish with honey. Wait for 30 minutes and drink the fluids that are secreted from the radish.
- Lemon juice with honey is also very effective to relieve cough.
- Avoid mucus-producing foods such as sugar, fried or greasy foods, dairy products including cheese, food additives (MSG, metabisulfite), white flour products, and junk food. Increase onion and garlic intake in the diet. A diet low in spicy, raw, greasy, and sweet foods is also recommended.

The Tao of Nutrition by Dr. Maoshing Ni and Cathy McNease:

- **Asthma**
  - Recommendations: apricot kernels, almonds, walnuts, basil, carrots, pumpkins, winter melon, sunflower seeds, loofah, squash, figs, and daikon.
  - Mix 1/2 cup fig juice with 1/2 cup lukewarm water and drink daily.
  - Cut the top out of a small winter melon, remove the seeds, and fill with molasses. Close the top with cheesecloth, and steam. Eat daily for seven days.
  - Take an unpeeled orange, pierce with a chopstick and roast until the peel blackens. Remove the peel and eat the fruit; eat one orange daily for seven days.
  - Drink fresh fig juice three times daily.
  - Avoid mucus-producing foods, cold foods, fruits, salads, all shellfish, dairy products, watermelon, bananas, mung beans, salty foods, cold weather, and especially ice cream.
- **Common cold (wind-cold)**
  - Recommendations: ginger, garlic, mustard greens and seeds, grapefruit peel, cilantro, parsnip, scallions, cinnamon, basil, and soupy rice porridge. Eat as little as possible so as not to burden the system with a lot to digest.
  - Lightly boil the following for five minutes: garlic, ginger, green onion, basil, mustard, or cinnamon. Drink the tea, go to bed and prepare to sweat.
  - Drink cilantro and green tea.
  - Drink scallion and basil tea.
  - Make tea from dried grapefruit peel.
  - Avoid shellfish, heavy proteins and fats, meats, and all vinegars.

LIFESTYLE INSTRUCTIONS

- Patients with emphysema should avoid cigarettes and secondhand smoke. Avoid air pollution, dust, mold, fur, animal dander, chemicals, or artificial fragrances.
- It is helpful to maintain a stable temperature environment. Avoid sudden and extremes of temperature, including heat, cold, humidity, or dryness whenever possible.
- Patients should strengthen their immune system and body resistance in between asthma attacks. A balance of exercise and rest is important. Alternation of hot and cold water in the shower is also effective to desensitize the body to changes in temperature. Herbs that enhance the immune system, such as ***Immune +*** or ***Cordyceps 3***, should also be taken on a regular basis.
- Regular exercise with herbal therapy is the key to complete recovery.
- For asthma patients, vacuum and central heating filters should be changed frequently to keep dust, mold, and dust mites to a minimum. Installation of an air purifier is recommended for patients who have family members with infectious respiratory disorders. It is recommended to replace carpets with hard surface floors to prevent dust, molds and other allergens from being trapped in the carpet. Bleach such as Clorox can be used to clear mold and fungus. Animal dander is also a major factor in causing allergies in patients. All contact (direct and indirect) with allergens should be avoided if possible to prevent allergic reactions.

CASE STUDIES

- J.D., a 41-year-old female, presented with asthma, allergies, and phlegm in the lungs. Additional symptoms included stress, weight gain, and fatigue. Coughing was triggered by lying down on her back at night and she would wake up in the morning with opaque mucus and yellow phlegm. The Western diagnosis was asthma and chronic bronchitis. The TCM diagnosis was Lung, Spleen and Kidney qi deficiencies with phlegm occupying the lung and nasal passages. This condition was treated with ***Respitrol (Deficient)*** at four spoonfuls twice daily. Patient did not take the herbs consistently, but completed the amount in three months. After taking them, her allergies improved, lungs became clearer, only flaring up if she caught a cold, and her energy increased. The patient was very pleased with the herbs and their results. Submitted by M.M., Alameda, California.
- S.F., a 74-year-old female, presented with chronic breathing difficulty. It was especially worse with exertion such as walking up stairs. Dry wheezing sounds and hoarse throat were also present. No phlegm was expectorated as noted by the patient. Blood pressure was 128/88 mmHg and heart rate was 80 beats per minute. The practitioner diagnosed the condition as Lung and Kidney yin deficiencies as well as Spleen qi deficiency. ***Respitrol (Deficient)*** was prescribed at three capsules three times a day. With taking ***Respitrol (Deficient)*** for two weeks, the patient was

Respitrol (Deficient)™

able to stop using her oxygen tank during the day. She could take deeper, easier breaths; however, she still has difficulty walking up stairs. With the patient being a type 2 diabetic, it was also noted that her fasting blood sugar levels had improved since taking this formula. Submitted by L.M., Lafayette, Colorado.

- D.D., a 72-year-old male, presented with shortness of breath and cough with frothy, clear white sputum. It was noted that this patient was diabetic, post-stroke, with a heart function of 77%, and creatinine level of 1.8 mg/dL. Objective findings included left leg hot to the touch, right leg cold to the touch, and difficulty with inhaling. He had recently taken two rounds of antibiotics. The practitioner diagnosed this condition as Kidney not grasping the qi, Lung and Spleen qi deficiencies with phlegm accumulation; his Western diagnosis was COPD. For treatment he was given a combination of ***Cordyceps 3***, ***Respitrol (Deficient)***, ***Circulation (SJ)*** and ***Neuro Plus***, just one bottle at a time. The patient gradually improved, getting stronger each week and continued taking the herbs for about three months. Submitted by T.W., Perrysburg, Ohio.
- J.N., a 59-year-old female, presented with a chronic, dry hacking cough. Additional symptoms included shortness of breath, dry hair and nails. Blood pressure was 120/80 mmHg and heart rate was 78 beats per minute. The practitioner diagnosed this condition as Lung and Kidney qi and yin deficiencies. ***Respitrol (Deficient)*** and ***Nourish (Fluids)*** were prescribed. As a result of taking the herbs, the cough became looser and not as painful. She was also able to cough a little sputum up and improvement of her hair and nails was also seen. Submitted by J.M., Breckenridge, Colorado.
- A 17-year-old male student presented with wheezing, shortness of breath and a dry, non-productive cough. It was worse with exertion and exposure to cold. He was extremely thin and unable to gain weight. The practitioner diagnosed the patient's condition as rebellious Lung qi with deficient Kidney not grasping Lung qi. The Western diagnosis was chronic asthma. After taking ***Respitrol (Deficient)***, he was able to restrain his wheezing and keep it under control. Utilization of his inhaler was reduced from three to four times a day to once or twice a week. While on ***Respitrol (Deficient)***, the patient also received acupuncture treatments twice a week for two weeks followed by once a week for two weeks. Submitted Anonymously.

PHARMACOLOGICAL AND CLINICAL RESEARCH

Respitrol (Deficient) is designed to treat chronic respiratory diseases characterized by compromised breathing functions and damaged lung structures, such as asthma, respiratory allergies, occupational lung diseases, and environmental lung diseases. It is formulated using herbs with antiasthmatic effects to relieve wheezing and dyspnea, antitussive effects to stop coughing, and expectorant effects to eliminate phlegm and sputum.

Respitrol (Deficient) has a marked effect to treat asthma, wheezing and dyspnea because many herbs in this formula have marked antiasthmatic and bronchodilating effects. For example, *Chen Pi* (Pericarpium Citri Reticulatae) has an antiasthmatic effect to suppress airway hyper-responsiveness in asthma.[4] *Ku Xing Ren* (Semen Armeniacae Amarum) has an inhibitory effect on the respiratory center in the brain, thereby exerting its antiasthmatic effects.[5] *Hou Po* (Cortex Magnoliae Officinalis) has a stimulating effect on the respiratory system to relieve wheezing and dyspnea.[6] Magnolol and honokiol, two compounds from *Hou Po* (Cortex Magnoliae Officinalis), exert their antiasthmatic effect by relieving muscle spasms and inhibiting smooth muscle contraction in trachea.[7,8] *Dang Gui* (Radix Angelicae Sinensis) also alleviates bronchospasm to treat wheezing and dyspnea.[9] *Zi Su Ye* (Folium Perillae) reduces secretions from the bronchioli to promote bronchodilation and relieve bronchospasm.[10] *Wu Wei Zi* (Fructus Schisandrae Chinensis) has been shown to stimulate the lungs to increase the rate and depth of respiration. It also reverses respiratory depression associated with morphine.[11] Furthermore, *Gan Cao* (Radix et Rhizoma Glycyrrhizae) has a remarkable anti-inflammatory effect to reduce swelling and inflammation in the lungs. The proposed mechanism of its anti-inflammatory action includes decreased permeability of the blood vessels, antihistamine functions, and decreased sensitivity to stimuli. The anti-inflammatory influence of glycyrrhizin and glycyrrhetinic acid is approximately 1/10th that of cortisone.[12] Lastly, *Dong Chong Xia Cao* (Cordyceps) has significant influences on the respiratory tract to treat asthma by dilating and relaxing the bronchial muscles.[13] The mechanism of this action is attributed to the stimulation and increased production of adrenal gland hormones.[14]

In addition to treating the cause, ***Respitrol (Deficient)*** is also formulated with herbs that treat the associated symptoms. For example, *Jie Zi* (Semen Sinapis) has an expectorant effect to facilitate the discharge of phlegm and sputum.[15] *Gan Cao* (Radix et Rhizoma Glycyrrhizae) has antitussive and expectorant effects to relieve coughing and chest congestion.[16] *Pi Pa Ye* (Folium Eriobotryae) has good antitussive effect to suppress coughing.[17] *Zi Su Ye* (Folium Perillae) and *Pi Pa Ye* (Folium Eriobotryae) demonstrate antiallergic and anti-inflammatory effects. The mechanisms of action for *Zi Su Ye* (Folium Perillae) include decreased mast cell and eosinophil infiltration, reduced histamine levels, and inhibited expressions of interleukin (IL)-1β, IL-6 and tumor necrosis factor-α.[18] The mechanisms of action for *Pi Pa Ye* (Folium Eriobotryae) include inhibitory effect on the mast cells and the pro-inflammatory cytokines.[19] Furthermore, *Pi Pa Ye* (Folium Eriobotryae) can be used to treat chronic bronchitis by inhibiting the inflammatory cytokine and mediator induction from alveolar macrophages.[20] Ursolic acid, one active component from *Pi Pa Ye* (Folium Eriobotryae), is especially effective in the treatment of pulmonary inflammation as it inhibits lipopolysaccharide-induced cytokines and inducible enzyme production in lung epithelial cells.[21]

Respitrol (Deficient)™

Clinically, the herbs in ***Respitrol (Deficient)*** have been used with great success to treat various types of respiratory disorders. In one study, 656 patients with chronic tracheitis were treated with *Dong Chong Xia Cao* (Cordyceps) three times daily for 40 days with good results.[22] In another study, administration of 6 grams of *Dong Chong Xia Cao* (Cordyceps) three times daily for four weeks showed a 93% effective rate in treating 43 patients with allergic rhinitis.[23] In addition, one study used *Wu Wei Zi* (Fructus Schisandrae Chinensis) in a formula to effectively treat 50 patients with asthma.[24] Another study showed that use of *Ku Xing Ren* (Semen Armeniacae Amarum) in *Xing Su San* (Apricot Kernel and Perilla Leaf Powder) was effective to treat coughing due to wind-cold in 50 patients.[25] *Ku Xing Ren* (Semen Armeniacae Amarum) also illustrated a 96.8% rate of effectiveness for treatment of chronic tracheitis in 124 patients (23 reported complete recovery, 66 reported marked effectiveness, 31 experienced some improvement, and 4 had no response). The rate of effectiveness was 96.8%.[26] Lastly, *Zi Su Zi* (Fructus Perillae), *Jie Zi* (Semen Sinapis) and *Lai Fu Zi* (Semen Raphani) are three herbs commonly used together to treat various respiratory tract disorders, including but not limited to bronchitis, bronchial asthma, emphysema, pediatric asthma, and spasms of the diaphragm.[27] In one study, use of these three herbs showed marked effect for the treatment of chronic and stubborn coughs. Out of 40 patients, the study reported marked improvement in 62.5%, and moderate improvement in 37.5%.[28]

In summary, ***Respitrol (Deficient)*** is an excellent formula to treat chronic respiratory disorders, as it contains herbs to dilate the bronchi, reverse airway obstruction, and relieve related symptoms.

COMPARATIVE ANALYSIS

Treatment of respiratory diseases is generally divided into acute and chronic management. In Western medicine, acute respiratory diseases are treated by bronchodilators that open the airways and reverse obstruction. Chronic respiratory diseases are managed by several categories of drugs, including bronchodilators, corticosteroids, theophylline, and cromolyn. Western medicine is extremely effective in treating acute respiratory diseases, as use of bronchodilators [such as Proventil or Ventolin (albuterol) inhalers] generally reverses airway obstruction within minutes. However, Western medicine is not as successful in long-term management and prevention of respiratory diseases. These drugs do not change the underlying condition of the disease, nor do they improve the constitution of the patient. Therefore, the long-term prognosis is often characterized by successful suppression of acute respiratory symptoms, but no change in frequency or severity of recurrent respiratory diseases.

In TCM, respiratory diseases are treated based on the urgency of the disease presentation and the underlying condition of the patients. Urgency refers to the acute or chronic nature of the disease, while underlying condition refers to the fundamental constitution of the patients. By addressing both the disease and the fundamental constitution, the use of herbs achieves both immediate and prolonged effects.

Both drugs and herbs are effective for the treatment of respiratory diseases. Generally speaking, drugs are more effective for acute conditions, as they are more potent, and can be delivered via inhalation or intravenous injection to achieve a faster onset of relief. However, long-term treatment of respiratory diseases with drugs is often less than optimal, as these drugs tend to create tolerance and dependence. Furthermore, they do not change the course of illness, and do not reduce the frequency and severity of recurrent attacks. On the other hand, herbs are better for long-term prevention and management of respiratory diseases. Herbs strengthen the body and enhance its own ability to manage respiratory diseases. However, use of herbs may not be appropriate for acute asthma because they are less immediately potent than some pharmaceuticals, and have a slower onset of action. In conclusion, optimal treatment of respiratory diseases does not require choosing between drugs or herbs, but may be gained by embracing the benefits of both, by using drugs for acute treatment and herbs for long-term healing and prevention.

References

1. Chan K, Lo AC, Yeung JH, Woo KS. Journal of Pharmacy and Pharmacology 1995 May;47(5):402-6.
2. Pharmacotherapy 1999 July;19(7):870-876.
3. European Journal of Drug Metabolism and Pharmacokinetics 1995; 20(1): 55-60.
4. Ok IS, Kim SH, Kim BK, Lee JC, Lee YC. Pinellia ternata, Citrus reticulata, and their combinational prescription inhibit eosinophil infiltration and airway hyperresponsiveness by suppressing CCR3+ and Th2 cytokines production in the ovalbumin-induced asthma model. Mediators Inflamm. 2009;2009: 413270.
5. *Life Sci*, 1980; 27(8):659.
6. *Zhong Yao Xue* (Chinese Herbology), 1998; 320:323.
7. Chan SS, Zhao M, Lao L, Fong HH, Che CT. Magnolol and honokiol account for the anti-spasmodic effect of Magnolia officinalis in isolated guinea pig ileum. School of Chinese Medicine, The Chinese University of Hong Kong, Hong Kong, P.R. China. Planta Med. 2008 Mar;74(4):381-4.
8. Ko CH, Chen HH, Lin YR, Chan MH. Inhibition of smooth muscle contraction by magnolol and honokiol in porcine trachea. Planta Med. 2003 Jun;69(6): 532-6.
9. *Zhong Cao Yao* (Chinese Herbal Medicine), 1983; 14(8):45.
10. *Zhong Yao Xue* (Chinese Herbology), 1998; 67:68.
11. *Zhong Yao Yao Li Yu Ying Yong* (Pharmacology and Applications of Chinese Herbs), 1983, 1983: 177.
12. *Zhong Cao Yao* (Chinese Herbal Medicine), 1991; 22(10):452.
13. *Fu Jian Yi Yao Za Zhi* (Fujian Journal of Medicine and Herbology), 1983; 5:311.
14. *Zhong Xi Yi Jie He Za Zhi* (Journal of Integrated Chinese and Western Medicine), 1990; 10(9):570.
15. *Zhong Yao Xue* (Chinese Herbology), 1998; 608:610.
16. *Zhong Yao Yao Li Yu Ying Yong* (Pharmacology and Applications of Chinese Herbs), 1983; 264.
17. *Zhong Yao Xue* (Chinese Herbology), 1998; 651:653.
18. Oh HA, Park CS, Ahn HJ, Park YS, Kim HM. Effect of Perilla frutescens var. acuta Kudo and rosmarinic acid on allergic inflammatory reactions. Department of Pharmacology, Institute of Oriental Medicine, College of Oriental Medicine, School of Medicine, Kyung Hee University, 1 Hoegi-dong,

Respitrol (Deficient)™

Dongdaemun-gu, Seoul 130-701, Republic of Korea. Exp Biol Med (Maywood). 2011 Jan;236(1):99-106.

19. Kim SH, Shin TY. Anti-inflammatory effect of leaves of Eriobotrya japonica correlating with attenuation of p38 MAPK, ERK, and NF-kappaB activation in mast cells. CMRI, IHBR, Department of Pharmacology, School of Medicine, Kyungpook National University, Daegu 700-422, Republic of Korea. Toxicol In Vitro. 2009 Oct;23(7):1215-9.
20. Huang Y, Li J, Wang R, Wu Q, Li YH, Yu SC, Cheng WM, Wang YY. Effect of triterpene acids of Eriobotrya japonica (Thunb.) Lindl. leaf on inflammatory cytokine and mediator induction from alveolar macrophages of chronic bronchitic rats. School of Pharmacy, Anhui Medical University, Tunxi West Road, Hefei 230032, Anhui Province, China. Inflamm Res. 2007 Feb;56(2): 76-82.
21. Lee CH, Wu SL, Chen JC, Li CC, Lo HY, Cheng WY, Lin JG, Chang YH, Hsiang CY, Ho TY. Eriobotrya japonica leaf and its triterpenes inhibited lipopolysaccharide-induced cytokines and inducible enzyme production via the nuclear factor-kappaB signaling pathway in lung epithelial cells. Graduate Institute of Chinese Medical Science, China Medical University, Taichung 40402, Taiwan. Am J Chin Med. 2008;36(6):1185-98.
22. *Zhong Cao Yao* (Chinese Herbal Medicine), 1987; 10:8.
23. *Zhong Xi Yi Jie He Za Zhi* (Journal of Integrated Chinese and Western Medicine), 1987; 1:43.
24. *Zhong Yi Za Zhi* (Journal of Chinese Medicine), 1988; 9:47.
25. *Shi Yong Zhong Yi Nei Ke Za Zhi* (Journal of Practical Chinese Internal Medicine), 1993; 7(4):48.
26. *Zhong Yi Yan Jiu Yuan* (Research Hospital of Chinese Medicine), 1971; 34.
27. Bensky, D. et al. *Chinese Herbal Medicine Formulas and Strategies*. Eastland Press. 1990.
28. *Zhong Yao Tong Bao* (Journal of Chinese Herbology), 1986; 8:56.

Respitrol (Heat)™

CLINICAL APPLICATIONS

- **Respiratory disorders with heat manifestations:** infection and inflammation of the lungs with wheezing, dyspnea, shortness of breath, cough, chest distension
- **Respiratory disorders with fever, thick yellow discharge** from the nose or the lungs
- **Wheezing and dyspnea** with a choking sensation, coughing with chest distension, fever, irritability, flushed face, and yellow sputum

WESTERN THERAPEUTIC ACTIONS

- Bronchodilating and antiasthmatic effects that relaxes the bronchial muscles and relieves wheezing and dyspnea
- Antitussive and expectorant functions to stop cough and eliminate sputum and phlegm
- Antihistamine effect to treat allergy-induced respiratory disorders
- Antipyretic action to reduce fever and body temperature
- Antibiotic effect to treat lung infections

CHINESE THERAPEUTIC ACTIONS

- Clears Lung heat
- Dissolves phlegm
- Regulates qi circulation to relieve wheezing and dyspnea

DOSAGE

Take 4 to 6 capsules three times a day with warm water on an empty stomach. Patients should begin taking ***Respitrol (Heat)*** with the first sign of respiratory discomfort for maximum effectiveness.

INGREDIENTS

Da Zao (Fructus Jujubae)
Di Gu Pi (Cortex Lycii)
Gan Cao (Radix et Rhizoma Glycyrrhizae)
Hou Po (Cortex Magnoliae Officinalis)
Jie Geng (Radix Platycodonis)
Ku Xing Ren (Semen Armeniacae Amarum)
Lian Qiao (Fructus Forsythiae)
Pi Pa Ye (Folium Eriobotryae)
Sang Bai Pi (Cortex Mori)
She Gan (Rhizoma Belamcandae)
Shi Gao (Gypsum Fibrosum)
Ting Li Zi (Semen Descurainiae)
Wu Wei Zi (Fructus Schisandrae Chinensis)

BACKGROUND

Lung inflammation and infection are two conditions that often occur together. Lung inflammation refers to swelling of the airways causing symptoms such as wheezing, dyspnea, chest tightness, cough, and presence of phlegm. Lung infection refers to invasion of the respiratory tract by micro-organisms such as bacteria, viruses, and fungi. In Western medicine, specific disease names for lung inflammation and infection include asthma, pneumonia, bronchitis, and lung abscess. In traditional Chinese medicine, the general description for this pattern of disharmony is Lung heat. Though the terminologies differ, they are essentially describing the same disorder.

FORMULA EXPLANATION

Respitrol (Heat) is formulated to treat heat-type respiratory disorders, including but not limited to asthma, bronchitis, pneumonia, and other conditions characterized by inflammation and infection of the respiratory tract. Diagnostic signs and symptoms of heat include fever, cough, dyspnea, chest tightness, flushed face, perspiration, and yellow sputum. ***Respitrol (Heat)*** contains herbs with functions to clear Lung heat, dissolve phlegm, and regulate qi circulation.

Shi Gao (Gypsum Fibrosum) clears Lung heat, reduces fever, and relieves coughing. *Ku Xing Ren* (Semen Armeniacae Amarum) stops coughing and calms wheezing. *Sang Bai Pi* (Cortex Mori) and *Di Gu Pi* (Cortex Lycii) clear Lung heat and stop coughing and wheezing. *Jie Geng* (Radix Platycodonis) clears Lung heat, expands the chest, and dissolves phlegm. *Hou Po* (Cortex Magnoliae Officinalis) helps *Jie Geng* (Radix Platycodonis) expand the chest and relieve congestion. *She Gan* (Rhizoma Belamcandae) and *Pi Pa Ye* (Folium Eriobotryae) clear heat, relieve toxicity, and eliminate sputum and phlegm from the upper respiratory tract. *Ting Li Zi* (Semen Descurainiae) drains the Lung, eliminates phlegm and reduces wheezing. *Da Zao* (Fructus Jujubae) minimizes the harsh effect of *Ting Li Zi* (Semen Descurainiae) to prevent damage to the Lung. *Lian Qiao* (Fructus Forsythiae) clears Lung heat and detoxifies. A small amount of *Wu Wei Zi* (Fructus Schisandrae Chinensis) is used to inhibit the leakage of Lung qi to prevent qi loss. *Gan Cao* (Radix et Rhizoma Glycyrrhizae) relieves spasms, supplements qi, and harmonizes all the herbs in this formula.

In summary, ***Respitrol (Heat)*** clears lung heat to treat various respiratory disorders with infection and inflammation.

CAUTIONS & CONTRAINDICATIONS

- Patients with cold or deficient respiratory disorders should use ***Respitrol (Cold)*** or ***Respitrol (Deficient)***, respectively. *See* Supplementary Formulas for maintenance treatment of respiratory disorders.
- Patients with severe or acute asthma attacks may need additional herbal or drug treatment.
- This formula is contraindicated during pregnancy and nursing.
- This formula is contraindicated for long-term use. It should be discontinued when the desired effects are achieved. For long-term treatment, consider using ***Respitrol (Deficient)*** or ***Cordyceps 3***.

CLINICAL NOTES

- ***Respitrol (Heat)*** or ***Respitrol (Cold)*** should be taken for acute

Respitrol (Heat)™

respiratory disorders with wheezing, dyspnea, and shortness of breath. When the condition stabilizes, use ***Respitrol (Deficient)*** and ***Cordyceps 3*** during the remission stage of chronic respiratory disorders to strengthen the underlying constitution of the patient. ***Respitrol (Deficient)*** should not be taken during the acute stage of any respiratory disorder. Furthermore, ***Cordyceps 3*** is also very beneficial to strengthen the Lung and the Kidney, the two organs that are responsible to control respiration. Therefore, it is extremely important to ensure that the patient is compliant with taking ***Respitrol (Deficient)*** and/or ***Cordyceps 3*** to reduce the frequency and severity of asthma attacks.
- Most cough during the day is due to heat or dryness. Cough at night is mostly due to Kidney deficiency, Spleen deficiency, or dampness.
- In cases where the patient is having an acute attack and the medication or inhaler is not readily available, two cups of coffee, hot cocoa, and chocolate bars are good alternatives to help alleviate symptoms of wheezing or dyspnea. Caffeine has similar effect as the popular asthma drug theophylline.[5]
- ***Respitrol (Heat)*** incorporates numerous antibiotic herbs for two important reasons. First, the use of multiple herbs within an herbal formula has been shown to increase the antibiotic effect more than tenfold. Second, isolated use of single ingredients is often ineffective and increases the risk of development of bacterial and viral resistance.[1] Given these two reasons, it is necessary to combine herbs with appropriate properties to ensure effectiveness in treating the infection and minimizing the potential risk of the micro-organisms developing resistance and/or mutation.

Pulse Diagnosis by Dr. Jimmy Wei-Yen Chang:
- Superficial and forceful pulse on the right *cun*.
- *Yangwei* pulse, a pulse extending distally from the right *cun* towards the thumb. It is one of the eight extra meridian pulses.

SUPPLEMENTARY FORMULAS
- To enhance the overall antibacterial function, add ***Herbal ABX***.
- To enhance the overall antiviral function, add ***Herbal AVR***.
- For sinus infections with yellow nasal discharge, combine with ***Pueraria Clear Sinus***.
- For profuse, thick, yellow phlegm with chest congestion, combine with ***Pinellia XPT***.
- With more underlying damp and phlegm accumulation with Spleen qi deficiency, add ***Pinellia Complex***.
- For coughing, add ***Respitrol (CF)***.
- For infection of ear, nose and throat, add ***Herbal ENT***.
- For thirst, dry mouth and throat, add ***Nourish (Fluids)***.
- For excess heat or fire, add ***Gardenia Complex***.
- To boost the immune system, take ***Immune +*** after cold/flu symptoms subside.
- For maintenance and prevention of asthma attack, use ***Cordyceps 3*** and ***Respitrol (Deficient)*** during remission.
- For dyspnea or chest tightness due to environmental or toxic poisoning, add ***Herbal DTX***.
- With severe inflammation, combine with ***Astringent Complex***.

ACUPUNCTURE TREATMENT
Traditional Points:
- *Feishu* (BL 13), *Lieque* (LU 7), *Hegu* (LI 4), *Taiyuan* (LU 9), *Taibai* (SP 3), *Fenglong* (ST 40), *Chize* (LU 5)
- *Ciliao* (BL 32), *Dazhui* (GV 14), *Feishu* (BL 13), *Kongzui* (LU 6)

Classic Master Tung's Points:
- *Dingke* (T 44.28)*, *Dajian* (T 11.01), *Zhongjian* (T 11.05), *Linggu* (T 22.05), *Dabai* (T 22.04), *Renshi* (T 33.13), *Dishi* (T 33.14), *Tianshi* (T 33.15), *Shuitong* (T 1010.19), *Shuijin* (T 1010.20), *Zhenjing* (T 1010.08), *Libai* (T 44.12), *Yunbai* (T 44.11), *Hegu* (LI 4), *Kongzui* (LU 6), *Quchi* (LI 11), *Chize* (LU 5), *Shousanli* (LI 10). Bleed *Sihuawai* (T 77.14) or dark veins nearby. Bleed before needling for best result.
- **Chest stuffiness:** *Linggu* (T 22.05), *Dabai* (T 22.04), *Tianshi* (T 33.15), *Dishi* (T 33.14), *Renshi* (T 33.13), *Zhenjing* (T 1010.08), *Shangli* (T 1010.09)

Master Tung's Points by Dr. Chuan-Min Wang:
- **Common cold, flu**
  - Cold type: Needle *Fenjin* (T 44.01), *Huofuhai* (T 33.07). Bleed *Ganmaosan* (T DT.12).
  - Heat type: Needle *Dabai* (T 22.04), *Linggu* (T 22.05), *Sanchasan* (T 22.17)*. Bleed *Wuling* (T DT.04).
- **Asthma**
  - Kidney type: *Shuitong* (T 1010.19), *Shuijin* (T 1010.20)
  - Heart type: *Renshi* (T 33.13), *Dishi* (T 33.14), *Tianshi* (T 33.15)
  - Lung type: *Simazhong* (T 88.17), *Simashang* (T 88.18), *Simaxia* (T 88.19)

Balance Method by Dr. Richard Tan:
- Left side: *Chize* (LU 5), *Taiyuan* (LU 9), *Zusanli* (ST 36), *Xiangu* (ST 43)
- Right side: *Sanjian* (LI 3), *Quchi* (LI 11), *Taibai* (SP 3), *Yinlingquan* (SP 9)
- Left and right sides can be alternated from treatment to treatment.

Ear Acupuncture:
- Bronchi, Lung, Adrenal Gland, Prostate Gland. Apply ear seeds to these points on both ears.

Auricular Medicine by Dr. Li-Chun Huang:
- **Bronchial asthma**: Bronchus, Trachea, Lung, Chest, Stop Asthma, Sympathetic, Adrenal Gland, Allergic Area, Endocrine. Bleed Ear Apex.
- **Common cold:** Lung, Internal Nose, Throat (Larynx, Pharynx)
  - For fever, bleed Ear Apex and Helix 1 to 6.
  - For dizziness, add Dizziness Area.

Respitrol (Heat)™

- For pain and soreness all over the body, add Liver and Spleen. Bleed Helix 4.
- For cough, add Trachea, Bronchus, Stop Asthma.

- **Cough:** Trachea, Bronchus, Lung, *Shenmen*, Occiput, Stop Asthma, corresponding points of pain. Bleed Ear Apex.
- **Bronchitis:** Bronchus, Trachea, Lung, Spleen, Stop Asthma, Sympathetic. Bleed Ear Apex.
- **Bronchiectasis:** Bronchus, Lung, Chest, Stop Asthma, Allergic Area, Sympathetic, Adrenal Gland, Spleen
- **Emphysema:** Sympathetic, Allergic Area, Chest, Lung, Bronchus, Stop Asthma, Spleen, Kidney, Endocrine
- **Tracheitis:** Bronchus, Trachea, Lung (Lower), Spleen, Stop Asthma, Sympathetic. Bleed Ear Apex.

NUTRITION

- Eliminate all spicy, cold and raw foods and beverages from the diet as they constrict the bronchial tubes causing spasms.
- A diet low in spicy, raw, greasy and sweet foods is also recommended.
- To avoid infection, a diet high in garlic, onions, and water is recommended. Stay away from cigarette smoke, alcohol, seafood, food additives (MSG, metabisulfite), and phlegm-producing foods such as sweets, dairy products, and heavy or greasy foods.
- Supplying the body with vitamin C is important, as it is greatly consumed by white blood cells when fighting infections.
- Drink plenty of fluids throughout the day to facilitate the elimination of heat, phlegm, and sputum.
- Since asthma may be allergy-related, eliminate foods from diet that commonly cause allergies, such as milk, eggs, shellfish, fish, and nuts. Sulfites – used commonly in restaurants to preserve salads, french fries, and avocado dips – are also linked to asthma attacks.
- White radish is an excellent food to relieve cough. Take 1 white radish, approximately the size of a fist and cut it into thin slices. Mix it with 1 tablespoon of maltose and 1 cup of water and cook for 20 minutes. Serve the radish and the juice when they cool to room temperature. Another easier method is to mix the slices of white radish with honey. Wait for 30 minutes and drink the fluids that are secreted from the radish.
- Lemon juice with honey is also very effective to relieve cough.
- Warm and hot natured foods that damage qi and yin should be avoided, such as:
  - certain fruits like mango and durian that produce heat.
  - stimulants like coffee, alcohol, and energy drinks.
  - spicy/pungent/aromatic vegetables such as pepper, garlic, onions, basil, rosemary, cumin, funnel, anise, leeks, chives, scallions, thyme, saffron, wormwood, mustard, chili pepper, and wasabi.
- Avoid food and drinks with artificial coloring.
- Consume as few meat products as possible. Do not eat processed meats, such as lunch meats, hot dogs and sausages, as they contain nitrites that are associated with inflammation and chronic disease.

The Tao of Nutrition by Dr. Maoshing Ni and Cathy McNease:

- **Asthma**
  - Recommendations: apricot kernels, almonds, walnuts, basil, carrots, pumpkins, winter melon, sunflower seeds, loofah, squash, figs, and daikon.
  - Mix 1/2 cup fig juice with 1/2 cup lukewarm water and drink daily.
  - Cut the top out of a small winter melon, remove the seeds, fill with molasses. Close the top with cheesecloth, and steam. Consume daily for seven days.
  - Take an unpeeled orange, pierce with a chopstick and roast until the peel blackens. Remove the peel and eat the fruit; one orange daily for seven days.
  - Drink fresh fig juice three times daily.
  - Avoid mucus-producing foods, cold foods, fruits, salads, all shellfish, dairy products, watermelon, bananas, mung beans, salty foods, cold weather, and especially ice cream.
- **Common cold (wind-heat)**
  - Recommendations: mint, cabbage, chrysanthemum flowers, burdock root, cilantro, dandelion, apples, and bitter melon. Drink plenty of fluids and get lots of rest.
  - Drink cabbage broth freely.
  - Drink cilantro and mint tea.
  - Drink mint, chrysanthemum, and dandelion tea.
  - Drink mint, dandelion, and licorice tea.
  - Avoid shellfish, meats, vinegar, and hot natured foods.
- **Chronic bronchitis**
  - Recommendations: carrots, apricot kernels, persimmons, white fungus, pears, honey jellyfish, ginger, water chestnuts, yams, sweet potatoes, daikon radish, walnuts, papaya, peach kernels, lotus roots, seaweed, and winter melon seeds. Always try to stay warm.
  - Cook carrots and apricot kernels in rice porridge. Eat three times daily for one month.
  - Remove cores of 2 to 3 pears and fill with honey, eat before bed every day for one month.
  - Mash together ginger, apricot kernels, pine nuts and walnuts; add rock sugar, and steam. Eat 2 to 3 tablespoons twice daily for at least two weeks.
  - Make juice from pineapple and lemon; drink before meals for immediate relief.
  - Peel a papaya, add some honey, steam and eat.
  - Cut banana into small pieces and cook with rock sugar until sugar melts. Eat 1 to 2 pieces of banana every evening for one week.
  - Avoid overworking, being chilled, stimulating foods, spicy foods, smoking, alcohol, caffeine, and cold drinks.

LIFESTYLE INSTRUCTIONS

- Avoid exposure to pollen, dust, and drastic changes in temperature. Regular exercise with herbal therapy is the key to complete recovery.

Respitrol (Heat)™

- For patients with asthma, vacuum and central heating filters should be changed frequently to keep dust, mold, and dust mites to a minimum. Installation of an air purifier is recommended for patients who have family members with infectious respiratory disorders. It is recommended to replace carpets with hard surface floors to prevent dust, molds, and other allergens from being trapped in the carpet. Bleach such as Clorox can be used to clear mold and fungus. Animal dander is also a major factor in causing allergies in patients. All contact (direct and indirect) with allergens should be avoided if possible to prevent allergic reactions.
- Patients should be advised to stop smoking, and stay away from second-hand smoke.
- Patients should strengthen their immune system and body resistance in between asthma attacks. A balance of exercise and rest is important. Alternation of hot and cold water in the shower is also effective to desensitize the body to changes in temperature. Herbs that enhance the immune system, such as ***Immune +*** or ***Cordyceps 3***, should also be taken on a regular basis.

CASE STUDIES

- S.Z., a 59-year-old female, presented with asthma, shortness of breath (SOB), and other respiratory symptoms. Blood pressure was 110/22 mmHg and her heart rate was 67 beats per minute. An objective finding was red face and chest. The practitioner diagnosed this condition as Lung heat and prescribed ***Respitrol (Heat)*** at three capsules three times per day. After only two days of taking the herbs, the patient noticed a reduction in the thick yellow phlegm she had been experiencing. The patient had also reported that after three weeks of taking the herbs her SOB and wheezing had improved. Submitted by M.P., Muskego, Wisconsin.
- A 36-year-old female computer technician presented with chills and fever, dry mouth and throat, body aches, and thirst. The chills and fever only lasted for one day. Tongue body was red with a thin, white tongue coating. Her pulse was superficial. Although warm to the touch, the patient complained of cold sensations. The practitioner diagnosed her condition as wind-heat invasion. The practitioner prescribed a full dose of ***Respitrol (Heat)*** for the first three days until the patient's symptoms subsided. The dose was subsequently reduced until all indications of the patient's condition were resolved. Submitted by T.G., Albuquerque, New Mexico.
- D.C., a 50-year-old female, presented common cold symptoms of cough, chest congestion and difficult-to-expectorate phlegm. She had a slight fever. The tongue was red with yellow coating. The pulse was rapid and slippery. The doctor diagnosed her with Lung heat. The two formulas prescribed were ***Respitrol (Heat)*** and ***Pinellia XPT***. In three days, the heat was relieved and the phlegm was cleared. Submitted by B.F., Newport Beach, California.
- S.O., a 3-year-old female, presented with constant coughing for two weeks. After being taken to the ER, she was diagnosed with whooping cough; however, no medication was prescribed. Other assessments included veins seen on her chest. The TCM diagnosis was Lung heat and the parents were instructed to give her ***Respitrol (Heat)*** and ***Herbal AEX*** mixed with juice. Initially there was no change noted. However after two days the symptoms began to lessen and she was back to normal within a week. Submitted by A.I., Hilo, Hawaii.

PHARMACOLOGICAL AND CLINICAL RESEARCH

Respitrol (Heat) is formulated specifically to treat respiratory disorders with signs and symptoms of heat. From the traditional Chinese medicine perspective, Lung heat is closely associated with lung infection and inflammation, with signs and symptoms such as wheezing, dyspnea, cough, chest distension, and yellow sticky phlegm. Therefore, to address both the cause and the symptoms of this disorder, ***Respitrol (Heat)*** uses herbs with antibiotic effects to treat the infection, anti-inflammatory effects to reduce swelling and inflammation, bronchodilating effects to relieve wheezing and dyspnea, and antitussive and expectorant activities to relieve the associated symptoms.

Respitrol (Heat) contains many herbs with significant antibiotic effects, including antibacterial, antiviral, and antifungal. Herbs with antibacterial effects include *Lian Qiao* (Fructus Forsythiae), *Hou Po* (Cortex Magnoliae Officinalis), *Gan Cao* (Radix et Rhizoma Glycyrrhizae) and *Wu Wei Zi* (Fructus Schisandrae Chinensis). *Lian Qiao* (Fructus Forsythiae) has a broad spectrum of inhibitory effects against *Staphylococcus aureus*, *Diplococcus pneumoniae*, *Bacillus dysenteriae*, α-hemolytic streptococcus, beta-hemolytic streptococcus, *Neisseria catarrhalis*, *Salmonella typhi*, *E. coli*, *Mycobacterium tuberculosis*, *Bacillus proteus*, *Bordetella pertussis*, and *Corynebacterium diphtheriae*.[2] *Hou Po* (Cortex Magnoliae Officinalis) has an inhibitory effect against *Streptococcus matuans*, *Staphylococcus aureus*, *Bacillus subtilis*, *Diplococcus pneumoniae*, and *Bacillus dysenteriae*.[3,4,5] Furthermore, piperitylmagnolol and honokiol, two compounds from *Hou Po* (Cortex Magnoliae Officinalis), have antibacterial activities against vancomycin-resistant enterococci (VRE) and methicillin-resistant *Staphylococcus aureus* (MRSA) in a time- and concentration-dependent manner.[6] *Gan Cao* (Radix et Rhizoma Glycyrrhizae) inhibits the growth of *Staphylococcus aureus*, *Mycobacterium tuberculosis*, *E. coli*, and *Trichomonas vaginalis*.[7] Lastly, *Wu Wei Zi* (Fructus Schisandrae Chinensis) has an inhibitory effect *in vitro* against *Staphylococcus aureus*, *Bacillus anthracis*, *Salmonella typhi*, *Bacillus dysenteriae*, *Diplococcus pneumoniae*, *Vibrio cholerae*, and *Pseudomonas aeruginosa*.[8] Herbs with antiviral effects include *She Gan* (Rhizoma Belamcandae), *Lian Qiao* (Fructus Forsythiae) and *Sang Bai Pi* (Cortex Mori). *She Gan* (Rhizoma Belamcandae) and *Lian Qiao* (Fructus Forsythiae) are most effective against influenza

FORMULAS

Respitrol (Heat)™

viruses.[9,10] *Sang Bai Pi* (Cortex Mori) has potent antiviral activity against herpes simplex type 1 virus (HSV-1).[11] Finally, *She Gan* (Rhizoma Belamcandae) and *Ku Xing Ren* (Semen Armeniacae Amarum) have antifungal activities.[12,13]

Respitrol (Heat) has a marked effect to treat asthma, wheezing and dyspnea because many herbs in this formula have marked antiasthmatic and bronchodilating effects. For example, *Ku Xing Ren* (Semen Armeniacae Amarum) has an inhibitory effect on the respiratory center in the brain, thereby exerting its antiasthmatic effects.[14] *Hou Po* (Cortex Magnoliae Officinalis) has a stimulating effect on the respiratory system to dilate the lungs and relieve wheezing and dyspnea.[15] Magnolol and honokiol, two compounds from *Hou Po* (Cortex Magnoliae Officinalis), exert their antiasthmatic effects by relieving muscle spasms and inhibiting smooth muscle contraction in trachea.[16,17] *Wu Wei Zi* (Fructus Schisandrae Chinensis) has been shown to stimulate the lungs to increase the rate and depth of respiration. It also reverses respiratory depression associated with morphine.[18] Most importantly, *Gan Cao* (Radix et Rhizoma Glycyrrhizae) has a remarkable anti-inflammatory effect to reduce swelling and inflammation in the lungs. The proposed mechanism of anti-inflammatory action includes decreased permeability of the blood vessels. The anti-inflammatory influence of glycyrrhizin and glycyrrhetinic acid is approximately $1/10^{th}$ that of cortisone.[19]

Respitrol (Heat) is formulated with herbs that treat the associated symptoms of lung infection and inflammation. For example, *Pi Pa Ye* (Folium Eriobotryae), *Gan Cao* (Radix et Rhizoma Glycyrrhizae) and *Jie Geng* (Radix Platycodonis) all have antitussive and expectorant effects to relieve coughing and chest congestion.[20,21,22] In addition, *Pi Pa Ye* (Folium Eriobotryae) showed antiallergic and anti-inflammatory effects through its inhibitory effect on the mast cells and the pro-inflammatory cytokines.[23] *Jie Geng* (Radix Platycodonis) illustrates significant antiallergic effect by inhibiting the inflammatory cytokines, suppressing the sensitivity for allergic reaction, and decreasing capillary permeability.[24,25] *Shi Gao* (Gypsum Fibrosum) and *Di Gu Pi* (Cortex Lycii) have antipyretic effects to lower body temperature to treat fever.[26,27] Lastly, *Sang Bai Pi* (Cortex Mori) and *She Gan* (Rhizoma Belamcandae) have demonstrated strong *in vitro* and *in vivo* anti-inflammatory effects to reduce swelling and inflammation.[28,29]

Clinically, the herbs in ***Respitrol (Heat)*** have been used with great success to treat various types of respiratory disorders. One study uses *Wu Wei Zi* (Fructus Schisandrae Chinensis) in a formula to effectively treat 50 patients with asthma.[30] Another study showed that use of *Ku Xing Ren* (Semen Armeniacae Amarum) in *Xing Su San* (Apricot Kernel and Perilla Leaf Powder) was effective to treat coughing due to wind-cold in 50 patients.[31] *Ku Xing Ren* (Semen Armeniacae Amarum) also illustrated a 96.8% rate of effectiveness for the treatment of chronic tracheitis in 124 patients (23 reported complete recovery, 66 reported marked effectiveness, 31 experienced some improvement, and 4 had no response). The rate of effectiveness was 96.8%.[32] Lastly, thirty children with cough and dyspnea from bronchitis were treated with a preparation of *Ting Li Zi* (6 to 15 grams) with a 96.7% success rate.[33]

In summary, ***Respitrol (Heat)*** is an excellent formula to treat respiratory disorders with signs and symptoms of heat. Not only does it have good antibiotic effect to treat respiratory tract infection, it also contains many herbs to relieve the associated symptoms.

COMPARATIVE ANALYSIS

Treatment of wheezing and dyspnea is generally divided into acute and chronic management. In Western medicine, acute wheezing and dyspnea are treated by bronchodilators that open the airways and reverse obstruction. Chronic wheezing and dyspnea are managed by use of several categories of drugs, including bronchodilators, corticosteroids, theophylline, and cromolyn. Western medicine is extremely effective in treating acute wheezing and dyspnea, as use of bronchodilators [such as Proventil or Ventolin (albuterol) inhalers] generally reverses airway obstruction within minutes. However, Western medicine is not as successful in long-term management and prevention of wheezing and dyspnea. These drugs do not change the underlying condition of the disease, nor do they improve the constitution of the patient. Therefore, the long-term prognosis is often characterized by successful suppression of acute wheezing and dyspnea, but no change in frequency or severity of recurrent wheezing and dyspnea.

In TCM, wheezing and dyspnea are treated based on the urgency of the disease presentation and the underlying condition of the patients. Urgency refers to the acute or chronic nature of the disease, while underlying condition refers to the fundamental constitution of the patients. By addressing both the disease and the fundamental constitution, the use of herbs achieves both immediate and prolonged effects.

Both drugs and herbs are effective for the treatment of wheezing and dyspnea. Generally speaking, drugs are more effective for acute conditions, as they are more potent, and can be delivered via inhalation or intravenous injection to achieve a faster onset of relief. However, long-term treatment of wheezing and dyspnea with drugs is often less than optimal, as these drugs tend to create tolerance and dependence. Furthermore, they do not change the course of illness, and do not reduce the frequency and severity of recurrent attacks. On the other hand, herbs are better for long-term prevention and management of wheezing and dyspnea. Herbs strengthen the body and enhance its own ability to manage wheezing and dyspnea. However, use of herbs may not be appropriate for acute asthma because they are less immediately potent than some pharmaceuticals, and have a slower onset of action. In conclusion, optimal treatment of wheezing and dyspnea does not require choosing between drugs or herbs, but may be gained by embracing the benefits of both, by using drugs for acute treatment and herbs for long-term healing and prevention.

References

1. *Zhong Yao Xue* (Chinese Herbology), 1988; 140:144
2. *Shan Xi Xin Yi Yao* (New Medicine and Herbology of Shanxi), 1980; 9(11):51
3. *Planta med*, 1982; 44(2):100
4. *Yao Jian Gong Zuo Tong Xun* (Journal of Herbal Preparations), 1980; 10(4):209
5. *Xin Hua Ben Cao Gang Mu* (New Chinese Materia Medica), 1988; 58
6. Syu WJ, Shen CC, Lu JJ, Lee GH, Sun CM. Antimicrobial and cytotoxic activities of neolignans from Magnolia officinalis. Institute of Microbiology and Immunology, National Yang-Ming University, Taipei, Taiwan 112, Republic of China. Chem Biodivers. 2004 Mar;1(3):530-7.
7. *Zhong Yao Zhi* (Chinese Herbology Journal), 1993; 358
8. *Zhong Yao Xue* (Chinese Herbology), 1998; 878:881
9. *Zhong Yao Yao Li Yu Ying Yong* (Pharmacology and Applications of Chinese Herbs), 1990; 6(6):28
10. *Shan Xi Xin Yi Yao* (New Medicine and Herbology of Shanxi), 1980; 9(11):51
11. Du J, He ZD, Jiang RW, Ye WC, Xu HX, But PP. Antiviral flavonoids from the root bark of Morus alba L. Department of Biology and Chemistry and Institute of Chinese Medicine, The Chinese University of Hong Kong, Shatin, Hong Kong, PR China. Phytochemistry. 2003 Apr;62(8):1235-8.
12. Oh KB, Kang H, Matsuoka H. Detection of antifungal activity in Belamcanda chinensis by a single-cell bioassay method and isolation of its active compound, tectorigenin. Natural Products Research Institute, Seoul National University, Jongro, Korea. Biosci Biotechnol Biochem. 2001 Apr;65(4):939-42.
13. Yiğit D, Yiğit N, Mavi A. Antioxidant and antimicrobial activities of bitter and sweet apricot (Prunus armeniaca L.) kernels. Department of Science Education, Education Faculty, Erzincan University, Erzincan, Turkey. Braz J Med Biol Res. 2009 Apr;42(4):346-52.
14. *Life Sci*, 1980; 27(8):659
15. *Zhong Yao Xue* (Chinese Herbology), 1998; 320:323
16. Chan SS, Zhao M, Lao L, Fong HH, Che CT. Magnolol and honokiol account for the anti-spasmodic effect of Magnolia officinalis in isolated guinea pig ileum. School of Chinese Medicine, The Chinese University of Hong Kong, Hong Kong, P.R. China. Planta Med. 2008 Mar;74(4):381-4.
17. Ko CH, Chen HH, Lin YR, Chan MH. Inhibition of smooth muscle contraction by magnolol and honokiol in porcine trachea. Planta Med. 2003 Jun;69(6): 532-6.
18. *Zhong Yao Yao Li Yu Ying Yong* (Pharmacology and Applications of Chinese Herbs), 1983, 1983: 177
19. *Zhong Cao Yao* (Chinese Herbal Medicine), 1991; 22(10):452
20. *Zhong Yao Xue* (Chinese Herbology), 1998; 651:653
21. *Zhong Yao Yao Li Yu Ying Yong* (Pharmacology and Applications of Chinese Herbs), 1983; 264
22. *Zhong Yao Yao Li Yu Ying Yong* (Pharmacology and Applications of Chinese Herbs), 1983; 866
23. Kim SH, Shin TY. Anti-inflammatory effect of leaves of Eriobotrya japonica correlating with attenuation of p38 MAPK, ERK, and NF-kappaB activation in mast cells. CMRI, IHBR, Department of Pharmacology, School of Medicine, Kyungpook National University, Daegu 700-422, Republic of Korea. Toxicol In Vitro. 2009 Oct;23(7):1215-9.
24. Han EH, Park JH, Kim JY, Chung YC, Jeong HG. Inhibitory mechanism of saponins derived from roots of Platycodon grandiflorum on anaphylactic reaction and IgE-mediated allergic response in mast cells. BK21 Project Team, Department of Pharmacy, College of Pharmacy, Chosun University, Gwangju, South Korea. Food Chem Toxicol. 2009 Feb 4.
25. *Zhong Yao Yao Li Yu Ying Yong* (Pharmacology and Applications of Chinese Herbs), 1983; 866
26. Hsu, HY. et al. *Oriental Materia Medica, A Concise Guide*. Oriental Healing Arts Institute. 1986.
27. *Yi Xue Zhong Yang Za Zhi* (Central Journal of Medicine), 1967; 223:664
28. Chung KO, Kim BY, Lee MH, Kim YR, Chung HY, Park JH, Moon JO. In-vitro and in-vivo anti-inflammatory effect of oxyresveratrol from Morus alba L. College of Pharmacy, Pusan National University, Keumjeonggu, Pusan 609-735, Korea. J Pharm Pharmacol. 2003 Dec;55(12):1695-700.
29. Ahn KS, Noh EJ, Cha KH, Kim YS, Lim SS, Shin KH, Jung SH. Inhibitory effects of Irigenin from the rhizomes of Belamcanda chinensis on nitric oxide and prostaglandin E(2) production in murine macrophage RAW 264.7 cells. Department of Experimental Therapeutics, The University of Texas M. D. Anderson Cancer Center, 1515 Holcombe Boulevard, Houston, USA. Life Sci. 2006 Apr 11;78(20):2336-42.
30. *Zhong Yi Za Zhi* (Journal of Chinese Medicine), 1988; 9:47
31. *Shi Yong Zhong Yi Nei Ke Za Zhi* (Journal of Practical Chinese Internal Medicine), 1993; 7(4):48
32. *Zhong Yi Yan Jiu Yuan* (Research Hospital of Chinese Medicine), 1971; 34
33. *Zhong Yi Za Zhi* (Journal of Chinese Medicine), 1984; 10:43

Schisandra ZZZ™

CLINICAL APPLICATIONS

- **Insomnia** with difficulty falling and staying asleep
- **Disturbed sleep** with excessive dreams and restlessness
- **Poor memory** with dizziness, weakness, fatigue, and anemia
- **Fragile mental state** with worries, fear, constant fatigue and tiredness
- **Postpartum depression** with weakness and anemia

WESTERN THERAPEUTIC ACTIONS

- Sedative and hypnotic effects to facilitate falling and staying asleep
- Anxiolytic effect to alleviate stress and anxiety
- Antidepressant effect to lift depression
- Adaptogenic effect to facilitate coping with mental and physical stress

CHINESE THERAPEUTIC ACTIONS

- Nourishes the Spleen and the Heart
- Tonifies qi and blood
- Tranquilizes the *shen* (spirit)

DOSAGE

Take 4 capsules three times daily with warm water on an empty stomach. For treatment of insomnia and disturbed sleep, take 8 capsules 30 to 60 minutes before bedtime.

INGREDIENTS

Bai Zhu (Rhizoma Atractylodis Macrocephalae)
Chuan Mu Xiang (Radix Vladimiriae)
Da Zao (Fructus Jujubae)
Dang Gui (Radix Angelicae Sinensis)
Fu Shen (Poria Paradicis)
Huang Qi (Radix Astragali)
Long Yan Rou (Arillus Longan)
Ren Shen (Radix et Rhizoma Ginseng)
Sheng Jiang (Rhizoma Zingiberis Recens)
Suan Zao Ren (Semen Ziziphi Spinosae)
Wu Wei Zi (Fructus Schisandrae Chinensis)
Xie Cao (Radix et Rhizoma Valerianae)
Yuan Zhi (Radix Polygalae)
Zhi Gan Cao (Radix et Rhizoma Glycyrrhizae Praeparata cum Melle)

BACKGROUND

Insomnia is defined as difficulty falling or staying asleep. There are many potential causes of insomnia, including but not limited to poor sleep hygiene (coffee, exercise or excitement near bedtime), psychiatric disorders (stress, depression), physical disorders (chronic pain, arthritis), sleep apnea, narcolepsy, restless leg syndrome, use of drugs (alcohol, stimulants, steroids, thyroid hormones) and withdrawal of drugs (alcohol, certain antidepressants, opioids, barbiturates, sedatives and illicit drugs). Insomnia should be treated as prolonged lack of sleep will adversely affect health and well-being.

FORMULA EXPLANATION

Schisandra ZZZ is formulated with herbs to nourish the Spleen and the Heart, tranquilize the *shen* (spirit), and tonify qi and blood. Clinical applications of ***Schisandra ZZZ*** include insomnia, difficulty falling asleep and staying asleep, poor memory, dizziness, weakness, constant fatigue, and postpartum depression due to anemia.

Wu Wei Zi (Fructus Schisandrae Chinensis) replenishes the vital energy and has a regulatory effect on the central nervous system (CNS). *Ren Shen* (Radix et Rhizoma Ginseng), *Huang Qi* (Radix Astragali), *Bai Zhu* (Rhizoma Atractylodis Macrocephalae) and *Fu Shen* (Poria Paradicis) tonify the Spleen qi and enable it to generate blood to nourish the *shen* (spirit) of the Heart. *Dang Gui* (Radix Angelicae Sinensis) and *Long Yan Rou* (Arillus Longan) tonify blood and calm the *shen* (spirit). *Suan Zao Ren* (Semen Ziziphi Spinosae) and *Yuan Zhi* (Radix Polygalae) are tranquilizing herbs with sedative and hypnotic effects. *Xie Cao* (Radix et Rhizoma Valerianae) is an herb that has tranquilizing and calming effects. *Zhi Gan Cao* (Radix et Rhizoma Glycyrrhizae Praeparata cum Melle), *Sheng Jiang* (Rhizoma Zingiberis Recens) and *Da Zao* (Fructus Jujubae) improve the appetite, harmonize, and strengthen the gastrointestinal tract. *Chuan Mu Xiang* (Radix Vladimiriae) revives the Spleen and dispels stagnation.

In summary, ***Schisandra ZZZ*** nourishes the blood and calms the *shen* (spirit) to treat insomnia and sleeping disorders.

CAUTIONS & CONTRAINDICATIONS

- This herbal formula may cause drowsiness in individuals who are sensitive to herbs. Patients are advised not to drive or operate heavy machinery while taking this herbal formula. Similarly, alcohol is not recommended as it may intensify the effect.
- This herbal formula contains herbs that invigorate blood circulation, such as *Dang Gui* (Radix Angelicae Sinensis). Therefore, patients who are on anticoagulant or antiplatelet therapies, such as Coumadin (warfarin), should use this formula with caution, or not at all, as there may be a higher risk of bleeding and bruising.[1,2,3]

CLINICAL NOTE

- ***Schisandra ZZZ*** is excellent to take for a week after each menstrual cycle. It replenishes the blood and qi lost during each period.

Pulse Diagnosis by Dr. Jimmy Wei-Yen Chang:

- **Insomnia due to Spleen and Heart yang deficiencies:** floating and weak pulse on left *cun* and right *guan*
- **Insomnia due to blood deficiency:** weak pulse on the right *cun*

SUPPLEMENTARY FORMULAS

- For depression, combine with ***Shine*** or ***Shine (DS)***.

Schisandra ZZZ™

- For Spleen qi deficiency with loose stool and poor appetite, add ***GI Tonic***.
- For Liver qi stagnation manifesting in irritability, restlessness, or PMS, combine with ***Calm***.
- For severe insomnia with disturbed *shen* (spirit) in excess patients, use ***Calm (ES)***.
- For insomnia due to stress in patients with deficiency, combine with ***Calm ZZZ***.
- For menopausal symptoms, combine with ***Balance (Heat)***.
- For dysmenorrhea, combine with ***Mense-Ease***.
- For hair loss, dry or brittle hair, combine with ***Polygonum 14***.
- To tonify the overall bodily constitution, add ***Imperial Tonic***.
- For forgetfulness, add ***Enhance Memory***.
- For Kidney yang deficiency, add ***Kidney Tonic (Yang)***.
- For Kidney yin deficiency, add ***Kidney Tonic (Yin)***.

ACUPUNCTURE TREATMENT

Traditional Points:

- *Shenmen* (HT 7), *Sanyinjiao* (SP 6), *Xinshu* (BL 15), *Pishu* (BL 20), *Taixi* (KI 3), *Weishu* (BL 21), *Zusanli* (ST 36)
- *Anmian* (extra point), *Shenmen* (HT 7), *Baihui* (GV 20)

Classic Master Tung's Points:

- **Insomnia, dreams:** *Linggu* (T 22.05), *Xinling* (T 33.17)*, *Shenjian* (T 44.19), *Zhenjing* (T 1010.08), *Zhenghui* (T 1010.01), *Tianhuang* (T 77.17), *Dihuang* (T 77.19), *Renhuang* (T 77.21), *Huoying* (T 66.03), *Tianhuangfu [Shenguan]* (T 77.18), *Shenmen* on the ear. Bleed *du* (governing) channel and back of the knee area. Bleed before needling for best result.
- **Weakness and fatigue:** *Tianhuang* (T 77.17), *Dihuang* (T 77.19), *Renhuang* (T 77.21), *Minghuang* (T 88.12), *Tianhuang* (T 88.13), *Qihuang* (T 88.14), *Beimian* (T 44.07), *Sanyan* (T 11.21), *Zhitong* (T 44.13)
- **Poor memory:** *Dizong* (T 44.09), *Tianhuangfu [Shenguan]* (T 77.18), *Zhenghui* (T 1010.01), *Piyi* (T 88.35)*, *Pier* (T 88.36)*
- **Dizziness:** *Linggu* (T 22.05), *Dabai* (T 22.04), *Zhenghui* (T 1010.01), *Wanshunyi* (T 22.08), *Wanshuner* (T 22.09), *Luotong* (T 44.14), two points on the sides of the first metacarpal joint of the thumb, *Fuding* (T 44.04), *Tongshen* (T 88.09), *Tongwei* (T 88.10), *Tongbei* (T 88.11), *Zhitong* (T 44.13)
- **Anemia:** *Shuitong* (T 1010.19), *Shuijin* (T 1010.20), *Tongtian* (T 88.03), *Zusanli* (ST 36), *Tuling* (T 88.46)*. Moxa *Huofuhai* (T 33.07) and *Zusanli* (ST 36).
- **Depression:** *Tongguan* (T 88.01), *Tongshen* (T 88.09), *Neiguan* (PC 6), *Tianhuangfu [Shenguan]* (T 77.18), *Huoying* (T 66.03), *Huoxi* (T 11.16). Bleed the HT and LU areas of the back with cupping. Bleed before needling for best result.

Master Tung's Points by Dr. Chuan-Min Wang:

- **Insomnia, excessive worries, pensiveness:** *Tongtian* (T 88.03), *Tongshen* (T 88.09)

Balance Method by Dr. Richard Tan:

- Left side: *Yinlingquan* (SP 9), *Xuehai* (SP 10), *Sanyinjiao* (SP 6), *Rangu* (KI 2), *Dazhong* (KI 4), *Fuliu* (KI 7), *Hegu* (LI 4), *Zhongzhu* (TH 3), *Zhizheng* (SI 7), ear *Shenmen*
- Right side: *Zusanli* (ST 36), *Jiexi* (ST 41), *Shaofu* (HT 8), *Tongli* (HT 5), *Shaohai* (HT 3)
- Left and right sides can be alternated from treatment to treatment.

Ear Acupuncture:

- **Insomnia:** Heart, Kidney, Parietal Lobe. Place magnetic ear balls or embed ear needles on one or both ears every evening and remove them in the morning. Five days equal one course of treatment.
- **Frequent dreams:** Heart, Kidney, Frontal Lobe. Embed needles and switch ear every three days. Patient should be instructed to massage those points at least three to four times each day for one to two minutes.
- **Anemia:** Bone Marrow, Kidney, Spleen, Ovaries or Testis, Adrenal Gland
- **Excessive worry or neurasthenia:**
  - Main points: *Shenmen*, Heart, Subcortex, Brain Stem
  - Adjunct points: Kidney, Spleen, Liver, Endocrine, Stomach

Auricular Medicine by Dr. Li-Chun Huang:

- **Dream-disturbed sleep or to improve sleep:** Dream-Disturbed Sleep Area, *Shenmen*, Occiput, Heart, Neurasthenia Area, Neurasthenia Point, Nervous Subcortex. Bleed Ear Apex.
  - For dream-disturbed sleep due to disharmony between the Heart and Kidney: add Kidney.
  - For dream-disturbed sleep due to deficiency of both Heart and Spleen: add Spleen.
  - For dream-disturbed sleep due to Liver qi stagnation: add Liver.
  - For nightmares: add Gallbladder.
- **Replenishing the blood:** Spleen, Stomach, Heart, Kidney, *San Jiao*, Adrenal Gland, Blood, Endocrine
- **Neurasthenia:** *Shenmen*, Heart, Occiput, Nervous Subcortex, Neurasthenia Area (front and back), Neurasthenia Point (front and back). Bleed Ear Apex.
- **Hypoglycemia:** Pancreas, Diabetes, Pituitary, Endocrine, Thalamus, Sympathetic, Duodenum, Digestive Subcortex
- **Dizziness from anemia:** Dizziness Area, External Sympathetic, Liver, Occiput, Spleen, *San Jiao*. Bleed Ear Apex.

NUTRITION

- Increase consumption of foods that contain high levels of tryptophan such as turkey, bananas, figs, dates, yogurt, milk, tuna, and whole grain crackers as they help promote sleep.
- Avoid foods that contain tyramine near bedtime. Tyramine increases the release of the brain stimulant norepinephrine. Foods with high content of tyramine include bacon, cheese, chocolate, eggplant, ham, potatoes, sugar, sausage, spinach, and tomatoes.
- A glass of warm milk with honey is helpful for mild insomnia.

Schisandra ZZZ™

The Tao of Nutrition by Dr. Maoshing Ni and Cathy McNease:

- Drink celery and beet tops tea in the evening, two hours prior to bedtime.
- Boil mulberry tea and drink 1/2 cup.
- Toast 1/4 cup amaranth in oven until slightly brown, remove and steep in a cup of hot water for five minutes and sip before bedtime.
- Eat soup for dinner made from lima beans with other calming foods like turkey and sage.

LIFESTYLE INSTRUCTIONS

- Especially at night, patients with insomnia should avoid alcohol, caffeine, and tobacco.
- If insomnia is due to overwork, do not work in the bedroom and remove anything that may be a reminder of the office or work. A warm bath or light snack before bedtime may also be helpful.
- Patient should be counseled to not worry about things they cannot control or change.

CASE STUDIES

- E.E. is a 30-year-old postpartum female who presented difficulty falling and staying asleep, restlessness, overactive mind, difficulty concentrating, fearfulness and anxiousness. The pulse was thin, weak and rapid. The tongue was very red with peeled edges and quivering at the same time. The face, ear and neck were red and flushed. The practitioner diagnosed her with postpartum depression with Heart fire and Spleen and Heart qi and blood deficiencies. ***Schisandra ZZZ*** was prescribed at 3 capsules three times daily. Within the first week, the patient noticed reduced anxiety. She was able to fall asleep and the mind was calmer. Submitted by S.S., Topanga, California.
- An 18-year-old patient presented with life-long insomnia. She often needed one hour to fall asleep. Her sleep quality was quite poor, and she remained sluggish throughout the day. The practitioner diagnosed the case as qi and blood deficiency. The patient took 6 capsules of ***Schisandra ZZZ*** 30 minutes before bedtime. After three weeks of treatment, the patient was able to fall asleep within 15 minutes and awaken with more energy. Submitted by M.K., Sherman Oaks, California.
- I.G., a 48-year-old female, presented with stress and insomnia. It was noted that the patient's son was getting married and she was experiencing lots of worries and stress surrounding the wedding. This caused the patient to have difficulty falling asleep at night, waking often, and becoming easily fatigued. Headaches were also present quite often. The patient was given 8 capsules of ***Schisandra ZZZ*** 30-60 minutes prior to sleep. With taking the herbs, the patient's sleep immediately got better. She was able to fall asleep within minutes and often stayed asleep the entire night. If she did wake, falling asleep was quicker and easier. Her headaches also got better. Submitted by L.M., Gresham, Oregon.
- A.B., a 22-year-old female, presented with anxiety and fear of failure. Additional symptoms she had been experiencing were depression, insomnia, and poor eating habits. It was noted that her *shen* (spirit) was not settled and she had dysglycemia. The practitioner diagnosed this condition as Liver qi stagnation and Spleen qi deficiency; Western diagnosis was low self-esteem along with low caloric diet. ***Calm (ES)*** was prescribed to take during the day and then ***Calm ZZZ*** to take at night. After two weeks she was then instructed to take ***Schisandra ZZZ*** at night and ***Shine*** during the day. *Bu Zhong Yi Qi Tang* (Tonify the Middle and Augment the Qi Decoction) was taken as well until she began eating at regular intervals. After one month of taking the herbs, the insomnia had resolved and regular sleeping habits were occurring. In addition, her depression was lifted. She started experiencing major changes in attitude, life purpose and direction. Six weeks later she maintained her results by taking ***Calm***. The anxiety had also reduced, only being anxious during stressful situations, which she had been resolving. She had also established regular eating habits, her energy had improved and her menses became regular without pain. Overall, the patient was very pleased with the outcome of taking the herbs. Submitted by N.T., Bethesda, Maryland.
- S.M., a 43-year-old female, presented with infertility. It was noted that the patient had other health concerns of weight gain, irritability due to high stress, and undergoing IVF cycles. She had been experiencing high risk pregnancy, consisting of nine failed IUIs, and was currently taking DHEA hormonal drugs. The TCM diagnosis was Heart qi and blood deficiencies, blood stagnation, Liver and Kidney yin deficiencies, and Spleen deficiency. Her Western diagnosis was undefined infertility, possibly due to old age. For treatment, ***Blossom (Phases 1-4)*** was prescribed with the addition of ***Schisandra ZZZ***. After 6 weeks of taking the herbs, she had successful conception implantation. The patient reported she was able to sleep more, moods were more stabilized, less fatigued, and her weight became more stable. As a result, she gave birth to a healthy baby girl. Submitted by N.T., Bethesda, Maryland.
- A tired and exhausted patient presented with general aches and pain in the neck and low back. There was also a history of poor sleep and digestion with no constipation. The practitioner felt the patient had over-worked herself throughout the years and that the condition was due to "wear and tear." The diagnosis was qi and blood deficiencies with underlying yin and yang deficiencies. ***Imperial Tonic***, ***Schisandra ZZZ*** and *Bu Zhong Yi Qi Tang* (Tonify the Middle and Augment the Qi Decoction) were given along with acupuncture and massage therapy. The treatment was concluded to be quite effective. Submitted by S.C., La Crescenta, California.
- D.S., a 45-year-old female, presented with insomnia, mood swings, cramps and fatigue. The tongue was slightly purplish and pale with teeth marks. The coating was thin and white. The pulse

Schisandra ZZZ™

was deep and wiry. She was diagnosed with Spleen qi deficiency and blood deficiency. ***Nourish***, ***Calm***, and ***Schisandra ZZZ*** were prescribed. The patient reported her sleep pattern improved, her moods balanced and her energy level increased. She was very happy with the herbs. Submitted by B.F., Newport Beach, California.

- L.A., a 37-year-old female patient, presented with insomnia, with difficulty falling and staying asleep. Other symptoms included neck and shoulder stiffness, TMJ pain, heavy menstrual flow, and cramping with blood clots. She complained of marital problems and held the stress and sadness within. She was also seeing a psychotherapist. The blood pressure was 123/86 mmHg and her heart rate was 88 beats per minute. The tongue appeared to be salmon pink in color, moist with numerous fissures from the center to the tip. The tongue was swollen and the tip was red. The pulse was slippery and thin. The TCM diagnosis was Spleen qi and Heart blood deficiencies with Liver qi stagnation. ***Calm*** was prescribed. ***Calm*** alone eased her tension, but did not help much with her energy. Her sleep improved slightly. The TMJ resolved after eight acupuncture treatments. After two months, ***Schisandra ZZZ*** was added. The patient then slept through the night much more soundly. However, she still complained about the neck and shoulder pain. Submitted by J.C.O., Whittier, California.
- H.G., a 55-year-old female, presented with agitation, anxiety, depression, and insomnia, and stated that she was easily angered. Her tongue was purple, with a thin white coating; her pulse was soft and wiry. The Western diagnosis was depressive-anxiety disorder; the TCM diagnosis was Liver fire rising with Liver qi stagnation. ***Calm (ES)*** was prescribed at three capsules, three times daily. Upon follow-up one week later, the patient reported a decrease of anxiety and agitation, but continuing insomnia. ***Schisandra ZZZ*** was added to her herbal regimen. One week later, the patient reported the insomnia completely resolved; but said that she experienced somnolence in the morning. She was told to reduce ***Schisandra ZZZ*** from three times daily to twice daily, eliminating the morning dose. After the dosage adjustment, the patient reported calm, uninterrupted sleep, and waking feeling energized, without lethargy or grogginess. She continues to take ***Schisandra ZZZ*** on an as-needed basis. Submitted by C.L., Chino Hills, California.
- A 53-year-old male miner presented with insomnia, depression, stress, anxiety and fatigue. He had difficulty falling asleep, which was aggravated by relentless worrying. Other symptoms included palpitations and occasional dizziness. A choppy pulse and a pale tongue were present, along with a pale complexion. The practitioner diagnosed the condition as Heart and Spleen blood deficiency. After the initial treatment, his sleep improved from two to three hours per night to five to six hours per night. The patient was no longer fatigued and felt much calmer. Because of his occupation and the nature of his condition, he was unable to take the Western medication since drowsiness was a side effect. The combination of ***Schisandra ZZZ*** and ***Calm (ES)*** made it possible to manage his condition with no known side effects. The practitioner recommended continuous application of the herbal combination of ***Schisandra ZZZ*** and ***Calm (ES)*** for his medical condition. Submitted by D.M., Raton, New Mexico.
- M.P., a 74-year-old female, presented with insomnia. She was prescribed Ambien (zolpidem) by her medical doctor but could not take it because of an allergy to the medication where her tongue would swell and burn. She was then put on Zyprexa (olanzapine) and Paxil (paroxetine). The patient reported she also had an allergic reaction (tongue swelling) to Zyprexa (Olanzapine). The patient, described by the practitioner, was a very anxious, nervous type of person who would hyperventilate when stressed. Her husband also has multiple medical problems and she stated she was worried about him. Her blood pressure was 120/70 mmHg and her heart rate was 70 beats per minute. The TCM diagnosis was Spleen and Heart disharmony with qi and blood deficiencies. ***Schisandra ZZZ*** was prescribed at 4 to 6 capsules at night. The patient reported that taking 4 capsules allowed her to sleep for four hours and then she was awake. Dosage was then increased to 6 capsules at night and she reported she was able to sleep five to six hours. The patient is still currently under care and the practitioner is adjusting the dose slowly. Submitted by M.H., West Palm Beach, Florida.
- A 42-year-old female presented with insomnia due to family-related stress. She reported having difficulty falling asleep due to excessive thoughts, thus creating morning fatigue that "feels like a hangover." The TCM diagnosis was insomnia due to Spleen and Heart qi deficiencies with *shen* (spirit) disturbance. After she began taking three capsules of ***Schisandra ZZZ*** at bedtime, the patient reported much improved sleep without difficulty falling or staying asleep. Submitted by C.L., Chino Hills, California.
- E.P., a 32-year-old female, presented with a 2½-year history of vertigo, associated with insomnia, palpitations, anxiety and nausea. She also suffered from irritable bowel syndrome with alternating diarrhea and constipation. She had an unsteady gait and was unable to drive. For the Western diagnosis of anxiety disorder, the TCM diagnosis was Liver fire. Initially, ***Calm*** and ***Gentiana Complex*** were prescribed at two capsules each, three times daily, but then the dosage was increased to three capsules of each, three times daily. After three weeks, the signs and symptoms of irritable bowel syndrome were resolved, and ***Gentiana Complex*** was discontinued. On the sixth treatment, the patient reported all symptoms improved. However, work-related stress anxiety remained. On the 15th visit, ***Calm*** was changed to ***Schisandra ZZZ*** to help with her insomnia. After taking this formula for nine days, the patient reported much improvement in her sleeping patterns, from five to six hours of interrupted sleep to six to seven hours of uninterrupted sleep. The patient was treated with acupuncture five times throughout the course of herbal treatment. Submitted by C.L., Chino Hills, California.

Schisandra ZZZ ™

A 50-year-old female public information specialist who was emotionally labile presented with pain in the shoulder, neck, thoracic, lumbar and foot. Her lumbar discs at L4 and L5 were herniated. In addition to migraines and bouts of constipation, she also complained of anxiety, depression and insomnia, all of which may be attributed to some side effects of taking multiple pharmaceuticals. The practitioner diagnosed her condition as qi and blood stagnation as well as Liver depression. ***Corydalin (AC)*** and ***Schisandra ZZZ*** were given. ***Corydalin (AC)*** significantly reduced her pain. She was able to lessen the use of oxycontin and Duragesic (fentanyl) patches significantly. In fact, the dosages of oxycontin and Duragesic (fentanyl) patches were reduced by as much as 75%. Furthermore, the practitioner observed that ***Corydalin (AC)*** was also effective to maintain other patients who suffered from occasional pain. The majority of patients (about 90%) who took ***Corydalin (AC)*** responded favorably, especially since most were experiencing digestive side effects with ibuprofen. Submitted by F.G., Sykesville, Maryland.

PHARMACOLOGICAL AND CLINICAL RESEARCH

Schisandra ZZZ is designed to treat insomnia with difficulty falling and staying asleep. It utilizes herbs with sedative and hypnotic effects to directly treat insomnia. Furthermore, since insomnia is frequently associated with emotional and mood disorders, herbs in this formula also have anxiolytic, antidepressant, and adaptogenic functions to enhance the overall effectiveness of the formula.

Schisandra ZZZ contains many herbs with sedative and hypnotic effects to directly treat insomnia. *Suan Zao Ren* (Semen Ziziphi Spinosae), *Fu Shen* (Poria Paradicis), *Da Zao* (Fructus Jujubae), and *Huang Qi* (Radix Astragali) all have sedative effects.[4,5,6,7] *Da Zao* (Fructus Jujubae) shows additional benefit to reduce spontaneous motor activities.[8] *Da Zao* (Fructus Jujubae) has a hypnotic effect to significantly increase the total sleep and non-REM sleep, while it shows no significant effect on REM sleep and slow wave sleep.[9] *Xie Cao* (Radix et Rhizoma Valerianae) and *Suan Zao Ren* (Semen Ziziphi Spinosae) have been shown to prolong sleeping time, reverse excitation caused by caffeine, and inhibit hyperactivity induced by morphine.[10,11] Specifically, the clinical effects of *Xie Cao* (Radix et Rhizoma Valerianae) are thought to be similar to those of short-acting benzodiazepines.[12]

According to the Merck Manual, 80% of patients with major depression report insomnia, and 40% of patients who suffer chronic insomnia have a mood disorder.[13] Therefore, successful treatment of insomnia often requires use of herbs to address mood disorders. ***Schisandra ZZZ*** utilizes many herbs to treat stress, anxiety and depression. *Xie Cao* (Radix et Rhizoma Valerianae) and *Yuan Zhi* (Radix Polygalae) both have antidepressant activities. According to one study, administration of various preparations of *Xie Cao* (Radix et Rhizoma Valerianae) has been associated with pronounced anxiolytic and antidepressant activities.[14] *Xie Cao* (Radix et Rhizoma Valerianae) and its active valerenic acid exert anxiolytic effects and reduce anxious behavior by interacting with the GABA(A)-ergic system, a mechanism of action similar to the benzodiazepine drugs.[15] According to another study, use of *Yuan Zhi* (Radix Polygalae) is associated with a marked antidepressant effect to reverse the harmful effects of chronic stress on mood and behaviors. The mechanism of this antidepressant effect is attributed in part to the neuroendocrine and neuropropective activities, as well as involvement of the hypothalamo-pituitary-adrenal system.[16] Furthermore, *Yuan Zhi* (Radix Polygalae) and *Long Yan Rou* (Arillus Longan) also showed anxiolytic, sedative and hypnotic activities.[17,18] Lastly, oral administration of *Suan Zao Ren* (Semen Ziziphi Spinosae) is associated with anxiolytic effects at lower dose and sedative effects at higher dose.[19]

Schisandra ZZZ also contains many other herbs that offer additional support to treat insomnia and related complications. *Ren Shen* (Radix et Rhizoma Ginseng) and *Bai Zhu* (Rhizoma Atractylodis Macrocephalae) have adaptogenic effects to help the patient manage mental and physical stress.[20,21,22] *Da Zao* (Fructus Jujubae), *Gan Cao* (Radix et Rhizoma Glycyrrhizae) and *Wu Wei Zi* (Fructus Schisandrae Chinensis) have cognitive effects to significantly reduce memory impairment.[23,24,25] *Yuan Zhi* (Radix Polygalae), *Suan Zao Ren* (Semen Ziziphi Spinosae) and *Wu Wei Zi* (Fructus Schisandrae Chinensis) have neuroprotective effects to inhibit acetylcholinesterase (AChE) activity,[26] protect the neurons from Abeta-induced neuronal damages,[27,28] and prevents neurotoxicity induced by glutamate.[29,30] Lastly, since lack of rest directly leads to fatigue and speeds the aging process, *Long Yan Rou* (Arillus Longan) is added for its antifatigue effect,[31] and *Ren Shen* (Radix et Rhizoma Ginseng) is incorporated for its antiaging effect.[32]

Clinically, many herbs in ***Schisandra ZZZ*** have been used with great success to treat insomnia. In a randomized, placebo-controlled, multi-center study, 121 patients were divided into either an herb group or a placebo group. Both groups received pills one hour before bedtime for 28 consecutive days. The subjects in the herb group received 600 mg of 70% alcohol extract of *Xie Cao* (Radix et Rhizoma Valerianae) standardized to 0.4 to 0.6% valerenic acid. At the end of the trial, the study reported good or very good results in 66% of subjects in the herb group, compared to only 29% in the placebo group.[33] In another double-blind crossover study of 128 participants, it was found that those who took *Xie Cao* (Radix et Rhizoma Valerianae) had a significant improvement in sleep quality with fewer awakenings and less somnolence the next morning.[34] Lastly, daily intake of 10 grams of *Suan Zao Ren* (Semen Ziziphi Spinosae) powder at night effectively treated 34 of 39 patients with insomnia within three to ten days. These patients were allowed to drink 15 grams of green tea at 8:00 a.m., but could not take other stimulants throughout the day.[35]

Schisandra ZZZ™

Overall, ***Schisandra** ZZZ* is a great formula to treat insomnia using herbs with sedative, hypnotic, anxiolytic and antidepressant functions.

COMPARATIVE ANALYSIS

Though there are many causes of insomnia, there is one overwhelming treatment - sedatives and hypnotics for short term relief. The sleeping pills most frequently used include benzodiazepines such as Halcion (triazolam), Restoril (temazepam), and Dalmane (flurazepam). The main advantages of these drugs are they are extremely potent, and generally induce sedation within 30 to 60 minutes. However, their effect generally lasts for a long period of time, resulting in drowsiness the following morning. Furthermore, if used for a long period of time, they cause tolerance and dependence, making it increasingly difficult to restore normal sleeping patterns. Finally, these drugs are also likely to cause other side effects, such as blurred vision, changes in sex drive or ability, shuffling walk, persistent, fine tremor or inability to sit still, difficulty breathing or swallowing, severe skin rash, yellowing of the skin or eyes, irregular heartbeat, and addiction. Therefore, these drugs should only be used when necessary for short-term treatment of insomnia, and not be relied upon on a long-term basis.

From a Chinese medical perspective, insomnia [inability to fall or stay asleep] is the direct result of *shen* (spirit) disturbance. Therefore, the main focus of this formula is to use herbs that calm the *shen* (spirit) to treat insomnia. Furthermore, lack of sleep over a long period of time contributes to deficiency. Therefore, many tonic herbs are also used to supplement such weakness and deficiencies. It is important to remember that herbs do not "sedate" the patient to treat insomnia. Rather, they calm the *shen* (spirit) and nourish the deficiency to restore normal waking / sleeping cycles. Therefore, herbs should be taken continuously for at least one week to restore normal waking / sleeping cycles, as they do not work on an "as needed" basis like sleeping pills.

It is important to re-evaluate the patients periodically. Individuals who continue to have insomnia should be examined for secondary causes, such as pain, anxiety, stress, depression, and withdrawal from drug or alcohol. While drugs and herbs are both effective, insomnia can only be treated successfully on a long-term basis when these secondary causes are removed.

References

1. Chan K, Lo AC, Yeung JH, Woo KS. Journal of Pharmacy and Pharmacology 1995 May;47(5):402-6.
2. Pharmacotherapy 1999 July;19(7):870-876.
3. European Journal of Drug Metabolism and Pharmacokinetics 1995; 20(1): 55-60.
4. *Chang Yong Zhong Yao Xian Dai Yan Jiu Yu Lin Chuan* (Recent Study & Clinical Application of Common Traditional Chinese Medicine), 1995; 489:491.
5. *Zhong Yao Da Ci Dian* (Dictionary of Chinese Herbs), 1977:1596.
6. *Guo Wai Yi Xue Zhong Yi Zhong Yao Fen Ce* (Monograph of Chinese Herbology from Foreign Medicine), 1985; 7(4):48.
7. *Zhong Yao Tong Bao* (Journal of Chinese Herbology), 1986; 11(9):47.
8. *Guo Wai Yi Xue Zhong Yi Zhong Yao Fen Ce* (Monograph of Chinese Herbology from Foreign Medicine), 1985; 7(4):48.
9. Cao JX, Zhang QY, Cui SY, Cui XY, Zhang J, Zhang YH, Bai YJ, Zhao YY. Hypnotic effect of jujubosides from Semen Ziziphi Spinosae. Department of Pharmacology, Peking University, School of Basic Medical Science, 38 Xueyuan Lu, Beijing 100191, China. J Ethnopharmacol. 2010 Jul 6;130(1):163-6.
10. *Xian Dai Zhong Yao Yao Li Xue* (Contemporary Pharmacology of Chinese Herbs), 1997; 1092.
11. *Chang Yong Zhong Yao Xian Dai Yan Jiu Yu Lin Chuan* (Recent Study & Clinical Application of Common Traditional Chinese Medicine), 1995; 489:491.
12. Von Eickstedt, KW. *Arzneimittelforschung*; 19:995. 1969.
13. Porter R, Kaplan J. The Merck Manual of Diagnosis and Therapy 19th Edition. Merck Sharp & Dohme Corp. 2011.
14. Hattesohl M, Feistel B, Sievers H, Lehnfeld R, Hegger M, Winterhoff H. Extracts of Valeriana officinalis L. s.l. show anxiolytic and antidepressant effects but neither sedative nor myorelaxant properties. Department of Pharmacology and Toxicology, Universitätsklinikum Münster, Westfälische Wilhelms-Universität Münster, Domagkstr. 12, 48149 Münster, Germany. Phytomedicine. 2008 Jan; 15(1-2):2-15.
15. Murphy K, Kubin ZJ, Shepherd JN, Ettinger RH. Valeriana officinalis root extracts have potent anxiolytic effects in laboratory rats. Department of Psychology, Eastern Oregon University, LaGrande, OR 97850, USA. Phytomedicine. 2010 Jul;17(8-9):674-8.
16. Hu Y, Liu P, Guo DH, Rahman K, Wang DX, Xie TT. Antidepressant effects of the extract YZ-50 from Polygala tenuifolia in chronic mild stress treated rats and its possible mechanisms. Dept. of Clinical Pharmacology, Pharmacy Care Center, Chinese PLA General Hospital, Beijing 100853, China. Pharm Biol. 2010 Jul;48(7):794-800.
17. Yao Y, Jia M, Wu JG, Zhang H, Sun LN, Chen WS, Rahman K. Anxiolytic and sedative-hypnotic activities of polygalasaponins from Polygala tenuifolia in mice. Department of Pharmacognosy, School of Pharmacy, Second Military Medical University, Shanghai, China. Pharm Biol. 2010 Jul;48(7):801-7.
18. Okuyama E, Ebihara H, Takeuchi H, Yamazaki M. Adenosine, the anxiolytic-like principle of the Arillus of Euphoria longana. Planta Med. 1999 Mar;65(2): 115-9.
19. Peng WH, Hsieh MT, Lee YS, Lin YC, Liao J. Anxiolytic effect of seed of Ziziphus jujuba in mouse models of anxiety. Institute of Chinese Pharmaceutical Sciences, China Medical College, Taichung, Taiwan, PR China. J Ethnopharmacol. 2000 Oct;72(3):435-41.
20. *Zhong Yao Ci Hai* (Encyclopedia of Chinese Herbs), 1994.
21. Reay JL, Kennedy DO, Scholey AB. Effects of Panax ginseng, consumed with and without glucose, on blood glucose levels and cognitive performance during sustained 'mentally demanding' tasks. Human Cognitive Neuroscience Unit, Northumbria University, Newcastle upon Tyne, NE1 8ST, UK. J Psychopharmacol. 2006 Nov;20(6):771-81.
22. *Xin Yi Yao Xue Za Zhi* (New Journal of Medicine and Herbology), 1974; 8:13.
23. Heo HJ, Park YJ, Suh YM, Choi SJ, Kim MJ, Cho HY, Chang YJ, Hong B, Kim HK, Kim E, Kim CJ, Kim BG, Shin DH. Effects of oleamide on choline acetyltransferase and cognitive activities. Biosci Biotechnol Biochem. 2003 Jun;67(6):1284-91.
24. Zhu Z, Li C, Wang X, Yang Z, Chen J, Hu L, Jiang H, Shen X. 2,2',4'-trihydroxychalcone from Glycyrrhiza glabra as a new specific BACE1 inhibitor efficiently ameliorates memory impairment in mice. J Neurochem. 2010 Jul;114(2):374-85.
25. Kang S.Y., Lee K.Y., Koo K.A., Yoon J.S., Lim S.W., Kim Y.C. & Sung S.H. ESP-102, a standardized combined extract of *Angelica gigas* , *Saururus chinensis* and *Schizandra chinensis* , significantly improved scopolamine-induced memory impairment in mice. *Life Sci.* 2005, 76(15): 1691-1705.
26. Park CH, Choi SH, Koo JW, Seo JH, Kim HS, Jeong SJ, Suh YH. Novel cognitive improving and neuroprotective activities of Polygala tenuifolia Willdenow extract, BT-11. Department of Pharmacology, College of Medicine,

National Creative Research Initiative Center for Alzheimer's Dementia and Neuroscience Research Institute, MRC, Seoul National University, Seoul, South Korea. J Neurosci Res. 2002 Nov 1;70(3):484-92.

27. Naito R, Tohda C. Characterization of anti-neurodegenerative effects of Polygala tenuifolia in Abeta(25-35)-treated cortical neurons. Division of Biofunctional Evaluation, Research Center for Ethnomedicine, Institute of Natural Medicine, University of Toyama, Toyoma, Japan. Biol Pharm Bull. 2006 Sep;29(9):1892-6.
28. Song JX, Lin X, Wong RN, Sze SC, Tong Y, Shaw PC, Zhang YB. Protective effects of dibenzocyclooctadiene lignans from Schisandra chinensis against beta-amyloid and homocysteine neurotoxicity in PC12 cells. The School of Chinese Medicine, LKS Faculty of Medicine, The University of Hong Kong, Pokfulam, Hong Kong SAR, China. Phytother Res. 2011 Mar;25(3):435-43. doi: 10.1002/ptr.3269.
29. Li C, Yang J, Yu S, Chen N, Xue W, Hu J, Zhang D. Triterpenoid saponins with neuroprotective effects from the roots of Polygala tenuifolia. Planta Med. 2008 Feb;74(2):133-41.
30. Park JH, Lee HJ, Koh SB, Ban JY, Seong YH. Protection of NMDA-induced neuronal cell damage by methanol extract of zizyphi spinosi semen in cultured rat cerebellar granule cells. College of Veterinary Medicine and Research Institute of Veterinary Medicine, Chungbuk National University, Cheongju, Chungbuk 361-763, South Korea. J Ethnopharmacol. 2004 Nov;95(1):39-45.
31. Zheng SQ, Jiang F, Gao HY, Zheng JG. Preliminary observations on the antifatigue effects of longan (Dimocarpus longan Lour.) seed polysaccharides. Fujian Fruit Breeding Engineering Technology Research Center for Longan and Loquat, Fuzhou, Fujian 350013, China. Phytother Res. 2010 Apr;24(4):622-4.
32. Lee J, Jung E, Lee J, Huh S, Kim J, Park M, So J, Ham Y, Jung K, Hyun CG, Kim YS, Park D. Panax ginseng induces human Type I collagen synthesis through activation of Smad signaling. Biospectrum Life Science Institute, 101-701 SK VENTIUM, 522 Dangjung Dong, Gunpo City, 435-833 Gyunggi Do, Republic of Korea. J Ethnopharmacol. 2007 Jan 3;109(1):29-34.
33. *PDR for Herbal Medicine*, 2nd Edition, Medical Economics Company, 2000; 783-786.
34. Leathwood, PD. et al. Aqueous extract of valerian root (Valeriana officinalis l.) improves sleep quality in man. *Pharmacol Biochem Behav*; 17:65. 1982.
35. *Shang Hai Zhong Yi Yao Za Zhi* (Shanghai Journal of Chinese Medicine and Herbology), 1984; (10):30.

Shine ™

CLINICAL APPLICATIONS

- **Depression** with low energy, prolonged sadness or irritability, and lack of interest in daily activities

WESTERN THERAPEUTIC ACTIONS

- Antidepressant effect to elevate mood and energy
- Promotes the digestion and utilization of energy

CHINESE THERAPEUTIC ACTIONS

- Relieves food, qi, blood, and phlegm stagnation
- Promotes movement of qi
- Releases constraint

DOSAGE

Take 4 capsules three times daily with warm water on an empty stomach. Dosage may be increased up to 5 to 7 capsules if the condition is severe.

INGREDIENTS

Cha Ye (Folium Camelliae)
Chai Hu (Radix Bupleuri)
Chuan Xiong (Rhizoma Chuanxiong)
Da Zao (Fructus Jujubae)
Gan Cao (Radix et Rhizoma Glycyrrhizae)
Guan Ye Jin Si Tao (Herba Hyperici Perforati)
He Huan Pi (Cortex Albiziae)
Long Gu (Os Draconis)
Mu Li (Concha Ostreae)
Shen Qu (Massa Fermentata)
Shi Chang Pu (Rhizoma Acori Tatarinowii)
Xiang Fu (Rhizoma Cyperi)
Yu Jin (Radix Curcumae)
Yuan Zhi (Radix Polygalae)
Zhi Zi (Fructus Gardeniae)

BACKGROUND

Depression is a mood disorder characterized by severe or prolonged sadness that interferes with energy levels, daily functions and quality of life. Depression is characterized by symptoms such as fatigue, poor concentration, loss of interest and pleasure, and absence of sexual desires. While the exact cause of depression is unknown, common contributing factors include heredity, endocrine disorders, neurological disorders, mental disorders, and use of certain medications.

FORMULA EXPLANATION

Shine is formulated specifically to treat depression, which according to traditional Chinese medicine is a disease caused by prolonged stagnation of qi, blood, dampness, and/or food. The treatment protocol is to break up all stagnation and nourish the internal organs.

Xiang Fu (Rhizoma Cyperi) and *Chai Hu* (Radix Bupleuri) promote the flow of Liver qi and reduce hypochondriac distension. *Yu Jin* (Radix Curcumae) and *Chuan Xiong* (Rhizoma Chuanxiong) relieve stagnation by invigorating blood flow. *Shen Qu* (Massa Fermentata) helps digestion by removing food stagnation. *Gan Cao* (Radix et Rhizoma Glycyrrhizae) and *Da Zao* (Fructus Jujubae) nourish the Heart and moisten internal dryness. *Yuan Zhi* (Radix Polygalae) and *He Huan Pi* (Cortex Albiziae) calm the *shen* (spirit) and relieve depression. *Cha Ye* (Folium Camelliae) lifts the mood. *Zhi Zi* (Fructus Gardeniae) sedates heat in the Heart and relieves irritability. *Shi Chang Pu* (Rhizoma Acori Tatarinowii) opens the orifices, eliminates phlegm to increase alertness, and calms the *shen* (spirit). *Long Gu* (Os Draconis) and *Mu Li* (Concha Ostreae) have tranquilizing functions to alleviate insomnia and dream-disturbed sleep. Finally, *Guan Ye Jin Si Tao* (Herba Hyperici Perforati), also known as St. John's Wort, is clinically found to be effective against depression, and enhances the overall effectiveness of this formula.

In short, ***Shine*** resolves food, qi, blood, and phlegm stagnation to lift depression.

CAUTIONS & CONTRAINDICATIONS

- This formula is contraindicated during pregnancy and nursing.
- Use of *Guan Ye Jin Si Tao* (Herba Hyperici Perforati) is sometimes associated with increased photosensitivity. Patients should avoid excessive exposure to UV irradiation (e.g., sunlight, tanning) when using this herb.
- Do not use *Guan Ye Jin Si Tao* (Herba Hyperici Perforati) while taking prescription drug(s) without advice of your prescribing physician. The following are two herb-drug interactions:
  - The concurrent use of *Guan Ye Jin Si Tao* (Herba Hyperici Perforati) and antidepressant drugs should be avoided, as the combination may lead to serotonin syndrome. *Guan Ye Jin Si Tao* (Herba Hyperici Perforati) has been shown to inhibit the uptake of serotonin, norepinephrine, and dopamine *in vitro* at high concentrations. The antidepressant drugs include monoamine oxidase inhibitors (MAOI), tricyclic antidepressants (TCA), and selective serotonin reuptake inhibitors (SSRI).[1]
  - Use of *Guan Ye Jin Si Tao* (Herba Hyperici Perforati) may induce the cytochrome P450 system of the liver, leading to increased metabolism and decreased plasma concentration of certain drugs, such as Sandimmune/Neoral (cyclosporine), combined oral contraceptive (ethinylestradiol and desogestrel), Theo-Dur (theophylline), Lanoxin (digoxin), and Crixivan (indinavir).[2]
- Allergy warning: *Shen Qu* (Massa Fermentata) used in this product contains wheat. Persons with allergy to wheat should not take this product.

CLINICAL NOTES

- Depression may be treated effectively with ***Shine*** or ***Shine (DS)***.
  - ***Shine*** is more effective for depression characterized by

FORMULAS

Shine™

stagnation (food, qi, blood and phlegm). ***Shine*** should not be used concurrently with antidepressant drugs, as this formula contains *Guan Ye Jin Si Tao* (Herba Hyperici Perforati), commonly known as St John's Wort.

- ***Shine (DS)*** is more effective for depression with stress characterized by Liver qi stagnation and Heart fire. ***Shine (DS)*** may be used concurrently with antidepressant drugs, as there are no known interactions.

- Discontinuation of antidepressant drugs, particularly abruptly, may cause certain withdrawal symptoms such as "electric shock" sensations (also known as "brain shivers" or "brain zaps"), dizziness, acute depressions and irritability. Therefore, it is best to taper off the drugs slowly, and offer herbal treatment simultaneously. ***Shine (DS)*** may be used concurrently with antidepressant drugs or during the tapering process. ***Shine*** should not be used until the antidepressant drugs have been discontinued for two weeks.

Pulse Diagnosis by Dr. Jimmy Wei-Yen Chang:

- Deep and concave pulse on the left *guan*

SUPPLEMENTARY FORMULAS

- For vegetative depression with withdrawal, no desire to speak, poor appetite, and insomnia, combine with ***Schisandra ZZZ***.
- For depression with stress, anxiety, restlessness (manic-depressives), add ***Calm (ES)***.
- For chronic depressive patients who do not respond to any of the above treatment or show little result, add ***Circulation (SJ)***.
- For a quick boost of energy and vitality, combine with ***Vibrant***.
- Post-partum or for constant fatigue and lack of energy, combine with ***Imperial Tonic***.
- To strengthen the constitutional weakness and deficiency, use with ***Cordyceps 3***.
- For loss of sexual desire, combine with ***Vitality***.
- For over-weight or excessive weight gain, combine with ***Herbalite***.
- For patients who are "burned out" with adrenal insufficiency, use with ***Adrenal +***.
- For difficulty with concentration, poor memory or forgetfulness, use with ***Enhance Memory***.
- With insomnia in patients who worry excessively or have anemia, ***Schisandra ZZZ***.
- For insomnia with stress in patients with deficiency, combine with ***Calm ZZZ***.
- Pre-menopausal and menopausal depression, add ***Balance (Heat)***.
- With headache, add ***Corydalin (AC)***.
- For heat sensations, irritability or nightmares due to excess fire, add ***Gardenia Complex***.

ACUPUNCTURE TREATMENT

Traditional Points:

- *Qimen* (LR 14), *Taichong* (LR 3), *Xingjian* (LR 2), *Guanyuan* (CV 4), *Shanzhong* (CV 17), *Ganshu* (BL 18)
- *Taichong* (LR 3), *Shuaigu* (GB 8), *Neiguan* (PC 6)

Classic Master Tung's Points:

- **Depression:** *Tongguan* (T 88.01), *Tongshen* (T 88.09), *Neiguan* (PC 6), *Tianhuangfu [Shenguan]* (T 77.18), *Huoying* (T 66.03), *Huoxi* (T 11.16). Bleed the HT and LU areas of the back with cupping. Bleed before needling for best result.

Master Tung's Points by Dr. Chuan-Min Wang:

- **Depression:** *Zhenjing* (T 1010.08), *Huoying* (T 66.03)

Balance Method by Dr. Richard Tan:

- Left side: *Zulinqi* (GB 41), *Yanglingquan* (GB 34), *Shenmen* (HT 7), *Tongli* (HT 5), *Shaohai* (HT 3), *Quze* (PC 3), *Daling* (PC 7)
- Right side: *Taichong* (LR 3), *Ligou* (LR 5), *Ququan* (LR 8), *Zhongzhu* (TH 3), *Waiguan* (TH 5), *Tianjing* (TH 10)
- Bilateral ear *Shenmen*, *Anmian*
- Alternate sides with each treatment.

Auricular Medicine by Dr. Li-Chun Huang:

- *Shenmen*, Liver, Heart, Occiput, Nervous Subcortex, Anxious Point, Be Happy Point. Bleed Ear Apex.

NUTRITION

- Depression may be due in part to nutritional deficiency. Foods such as white bread, flour, saturated animal fats, hydrogenated vegetable oils, sweets, soft drinks, and canned goods deprive the body of B vitamins and increase the probability of depression.
- Avoid a diet too low in complex carbohydrates as it may cause serotonin depletion and depression.

General Guidelines for a Healthy Diet

- Eat a variety of fresh, organic fruits and vegetables of all colors.
- Incorporate more high-fiber whole grains and nuts into diet.
- Drink warm or hot liquids with meals. Putting cold and ice on any part of the body will immediately constrict the flow of blood to that region. Similarly, drinking cold or iced drinks with meals will hinder the natural peristaltic movements of the digestive system.
- Foods with antioxidant effects, such as vitamin A, C and E are beneficial as they neutralize the free radicals and minimize damage to cells. Beneficial foods include citrus fruits, carrots, green leaf vegetables, and green tea.
- Chew food completely and thoroughly. The digestive tract can process and absorb smaller pieces of food much better than food that is incompletely chewed. Larger pieces of food can lead to incomplete digestion and digestive discomfort.
- Always eat breakfast. According to the TCM clock, the most optimal time for the digestive system is in the morning from 8 to 10 a.m.
- Give the body two to three hours between the last meal of the day and bedtime. During sleep, the digestive system slows down as well. Make sure the body has adequate time to digest the food before going into sleep mode.

Shine™

- If the patient is allergic to any food or feel uncomfortable after eating certain foods, then avoid eating them.
- Avoid fast food, processed foods, junk food, artificial sugars, and carbonated drinks. Stay away from meat, greasy food, alcohol, caffeine, dairy products (except for unsweetened low-fat yogurt), tap water, iron supplements and vegetables and fruits with pesticides.
- The Spleen is responsible for generating post-natal qi and good Spleen function also contributes to a healthy immune system. Foods that damage the Spleen should be avoided:
  - Avoid any and all foods that contain sugar, such as cake, dessert, candy, chocolate, canned juice, soft drinks, caffeinated drinks, stevia, sugar substitutes, agave, xylitol, and corn syrup.
  - Avoid raw or uncooked meats, such as sashimi, sushi, steak tartar, and seared meat. Minimize consumption of foods that are cooling in nature, including tofu, tomato, celery, asparagus, bamboo, seaweed, kelp, bitter melon, cucumber, gourd, luffa, eggplant, winter melon, watermelon, honeydew, citrus, oranges, guava, grapefruit, pineapple, plums, pear, banana, papaya, white radish, mustard leaf, potherb mustard, Chinese kale, napa, and bamboo sprout. Do not eat foods straight from the refrigerator. Long-term use of cold fruits and vegetables like the ones listed above may be damaging to the Spleen. To make the property more neutral, one can add about 20 pieces of *Gou Qi Zi* (Fructus Lycii) when cooking them.
- Warm and hot natured foods that damage qi and yin should be avoided, such as:
  - certain fruits like mango and durian that produce heat.
  - stimulants like coffee, alcohol, and energy drinks.
  - spicy/pungent/aromatic vegetables such as pepper, garlic, onions, basil, rosemary, cumin, funnel, anise, leeks, chives, scallions, thyme, saffron, wormwood, mustard, chili pepper, and wasabi.
- Avoid food and drinks with artificial coloring.
- Consume as few meat products as possible. Do not eat processed meats, such as lunch meats, hot dogs and sausages, as they contain nitrites that are associated with inflammation and chronic disease.

LIFESTYLE INSTRUCTIONS

- Exercise outdoors and under the sun will help to lift depression. It has been found that exercise helps people who are depressed by making them more energetic and stress-tolerant.
- A balanced lifestyle of work, rest and exercise is extremely important to achieve better mental and physical health.
- Massaging the nerves along the spine will help to relieve tension associated with depression.

CASE STUDIES

- S.J., 31-year-old female, presented with depression. Symptoms included no social desire, lack of energy in the mornings, and easily fatigued. Objective findings included black circles under the eyes, no shine to the eyes, and overweight. The practitioner diagnosed the condition as qi stagnation and Kidney qi deficiency. After taking ***Shine*** at three capsules three times a day, the patient felt immediate results of more energy and elevated mood. The most significant change was how she felt in the morning, saying how she bounced out of bed ready to start the day. Submitted by L.M., Gresham, Oregon.
- J.M., a 36-year-old female, presented with depression. She was a single mother with two children and a pending divorce. Her psychologist wanted her on medication. She had poor appetite for food but increased cravings for candy and carbohydrates and alcohol. She was crying, unfocused and said she felt scattered emotionally and deflated energetically. Her blood pressure was 118/72 mmHg and her heart rate was 78 beats per minute. The diagnosis was qi and blood stagnation with Liver and Spleen disharmony. ***Shine*** was prescribed at 4 capsules three times daily. Results were apparent within 24 hours. Her depression began lifting the next day. She reported that she felt more solid, grounded and focused again. She was also more interested in moving physically and felt emotionally more stable. As the symptoms resolved, the dosage was reduced to 4 capsules twice daily and finally, once daily. The practitioner reported that the patient had previously been seeing another acupuncturist, and was on an herbal formula from another company. She reported that with the other formula, she felt stuck and was unable to move forward. With ***Shine***, she felt the difference dramatically. Submitted by M.H., West Palm Beach, Florida.
- W.P., a 45-year-old female, presented with pain in the kidney and liver areas. It was also noted that the patient had a history of Kidney infection and pancreatitis. She was also experiencing anxiety and depression as a result of relationship issues. Pulse was weak and slightly slippery, and tongue was pale with a long center fissure. The practitioner diagnosed this condition as Liver qi stagnation with heat disturbing the *shen* (spirit), and toxins in the kidney. Upon diagnosis the patient was prescribed ***Shine*** and ***Kidney DTX***. Within four weeks of taking the herbs the patient had noticed her mood was stable and she was no longer experiencing pain in the liver and kidney areas. The patient had also made lifestyle changes in her diet and received acupuncture one time a week. Submitted by T.W., Perrysburg, Ohio.
- S.F., a 33-year-old female, presented with premenstrual symptoms consisting of fatigue and depression, three days before her cycle. The practitioner diagnosed this condition as qi deficiency with *shen* (spirit) disturbance. ***Imperial Tonic***, ***Calm*** and ***Shine*** were prescribed at 2 to 3 capsules each, three times a day. As a result of taking ***Imperial Tonic*** for three weeks, she reported increase in energy and a more positive attitude. She only took the ***Calm*** and ***Shine*** for three months, and thereafter only continued with the ***Imperial Tonic*** as she felt recovered from her depression. Submitted by S.L., Yuma, Arizona.
- A.B., a 22-year-old female, presented with anxiety and fear of failure. Additional symptoms she had been experiencing were depression, insomnia, and poor eating habits. It was noted that

Shine ™

her *shen* (spirit) was not settled and she had dysglycemia. The practitioner diagnosed this condition as Liver qi stagnation and Spleen qi deficiency; Western diagnosis was low self-esteem along with low caloric diet. ***Calm (ES)*** was prescribed to take during the day and then ***Calm ZZZ*** to take at night. After two weeks she was then instructed to take ***Schisandra ZZZ*** at night and ***Shine*** during the day. *Bu Zhong Yi Qi Tang* (Tonify the Middle and Augment the Qi Decoction) was taken as well until she began eating at regular intervals. After 1 month of taking the herbs, the insomnia had resolved and regular sleeping habits were occurring. In addition, her depression was lifted. She started experiencing major changes in attitude, life purpose and direction. Six weeks later she maintained her results by taking ***Calm***. The anxiety had also reduced, only being anxious during stressful situations, which she had been resolving. She had also established regular eating habits, her energy had improved and her menses became regular without pain. Overall, the patient was very pleased with the outcome of taking the herbs. Submitted by N.T., Bethesda, Maryland.

- A 26-year-old female presented with chronic depression, which may have been due to not working for a few years. She was diagnosed with bipolar disorder. Signs of depression manifested as constant somnolence and a lack of interest in any activity. According to traditional Chinese medicine, she was diagnosed with phlegm stagnation, evidenced by a "puffy" tongue body with a thick white tongue coating and a "rolling" pulse. Within a month of taking ***Shine***, her somnolence subsided and she became more active during the day, which in turn made her less depressed. Submitted by T.G., Albuquerque, New Mexico.
- A woman presented with depression and irritability. Her anxiety was enhanced upon hearing that her Western doctor was to discontinue her Vicodin (APAP/hydrocodone) prescription, and the consequence of withdrawal. Hence, she was quite angry with her doctor. Her diagnosis included hepatitis C, fibromyalgia and Liver qi stagnation. The patient began taking ***Shine***. In a separate event, a serious altercation with her spouse exacerbated her condition to a point where she considered suicide. After immediate administration of ***Shine***, she began feeling much calmer. A half hour after ingesting the herbs, she said that thoughts of suicide were dismissed. The practitioner concluded that ***Shine*** was quite effective in treating patients with similar conditions. Submitted by M.H., Jupiter, Florida.
- A 58-year-old male teacher presented with palpitations, which began one year ago following the death of his significant other. Stress or jogging appeared to exacerbate his condition. His symptoms were indicative of mitral valve prolapse. The diagnosis was Liver oppressing the Heart and Liver yang rising. The tongue was pink with a red tip and the pulse was wiry and pounding. Along with acupuncture treatment, the patient was given 4 capsules of ***Shine*** three times daily for about six months. The patient displayed a 75% (subjective) improvement within two weeks. The palpitations became less frequent. Feelings of stress reduced significantly along with a milder pounding sensation in the chest. After six weeks, the pulse was still full but had lost some of its wiry quality. The diagnosis was changed to Heart qi and blood deficiency. Within ten weeks, the pulse became slow and leisurely. Palpitations were also rare after seven months of treatment. Herbs were eventually discontinued with acupuncture maintenance every three to four weeks. The practitioner concluded that ***Shine*** was quite effective in reducing the stress level as well as the palpitations of the patient in a prompt and efficient manner. Submitted by C.C., Cromwell, Connecticut.
- A 42-year-old female finance administrator presented with "plum-pit" syndrome, belching, constipation, and irritability especially when angered. Her tongue was pale and her pulse was wiry. The patient's demeanor was always uptight or tense and short-tempered. In addition, the patient reported constant burping. The practitioner diagnosed the condition as follows: (1) Liver qi stagnation with dampness in the middle *jiao* and lower *jiao*, in turn, attacking the Stomach leading to continuous belching; (2) stagnation causing phlegm to congeal and stick, resulting in a "plum-pit" syndrome; and (3) stagnation of the Large Intestines causing constipation. The patient was instructed to take ***Shine***. As a result of taking one bottle of ***Shine*** during the course of the treatment, significant improvements in the elimination of "plum-pit" qi and constipation were noted. Belching was also relieved by 90%. Upon taking the second bottle of ***Shine***, the patient felt queasy and edgy and decided to stop taking the herbs. The patient however noted a positive change in mood and a more uplifted spirit. The practitioner concluded that the side effects might have been due to the fact that the patient had a deficient constitution. Submitted by P.L., San Diego, California.
- H.E., a 20-year-old female, presented with depression, difficulty with concentration, difficulty falling asleep, very active mind and short-temper. She startled easily. Her tongue was dry with white coating. Pulse was wiry. The diagnosis was Liver qi stagnation and Gallbladder/Heart disharmony. *Wen Dan Tang* (Warm the Gallbladder Decoction) and ***Shine*** were prescribed at 2 capsules each three times daily. Patient reported much improvement in symptoms after using herbs. She also reported that symptoms came back after stopping the herbs. Submitted by S.F., Greenbrae, California.
- A 53-year-old female patient presented with anxiety, depression and pale complexion. Her pulse was thin, weak and deep in all positions. She had cyclical bouts of rage, fatigue, sleeplessness, anxiety and severe depression. Periods were irregular. Her tongue was puffy and pale. The TCM diagnosis was blood and yin deficiencies with Liver qi stagnation, Kidney yin and yang deficiencies. ***Shine*** and ***Nourish***, along with an iron supplement were prescribed. The patient noticed a change within the first ten days and more so around her cycle. She felt as if a cloud had been lifted from above. She found herself smiling more. Restlessness

Shine™

was still bothering her but her sleep was much better. This patient has suffered from depression for a long time and is very deficient. Submitted by N.V., Muir Beach, California.

- J.C., a 57-year-old female, presented with nervousness, insomnia, and anxiety with a desire to stop smoking. Night sweats were also present. Her tongue was red with no coating present. The practitioner diagnosed the condition as Kidney yin deficiency with heat and Liver qi stagnation. Her Western diagnosis was menopause and hypothyroidism. The patient was given a combination of ***Nourish***, ***Shine***, and ***Calm***. ***Nourish*** was taken daily while ***Shine*** and ***Calm*** were taken as needed. After taking the herbs for six months, the patient reported improvement in sleep; she was calmer and more balanced overall with a positive attitude. Submitted by K.F., Honolulu, Hawaii.
- L.W., a 22-year-old male, presented with septic facial acne. Very depressed, he did not want to be seen in public. The TCM diagnosis was damp-heat with Liver qi stagnation. After one week of taking ***Dermatrol (PS)*** and ***Shine***, the acne was 80% resolved and the depression improving. After washing his face with a mild soap, the patient applied a topical skin wash (Yin Care) diluted with tea tree oil. The acne was gone in 28 days. The patient now socializes happily with family and friends. Submitted by H.C., Stephens City, Virginia.

PHARMACOLOGICAL AND CLINICAL RESEARCH

Shine is designed to treat depression by using herbs with demonstrated effectiveness to elevate mood, alleviate stress, and increase energy.

Guan Ye Jin Si Tao (Herba Hyperici Perforati), commonly known as St. John's Wort, is an herb used in both China and European countries dating back to the Middle Ages. It was used historically in treatment of inflammation, gastritis and insomnia; more recently, however, its use centers almost exclusively on the treatment of depression. Pharmacologically, *Guan Ye Jin Si Tao* (Herba Hyperici Perforati) works primarily by increasing the level of serotonin and secondarily by inhibiting the enzyme monoamine oxidase (MAO).[3,4] Another study shows that hyperforin, one of the main active compounds in the herb, also has the effect of inhibiting the reuptake of serotonin and other neurotransmitters, such as norepinephrine and dopamine.[5] Clinically, the effectiveness of this herb in treating depression has been demonstrated in many studies. One study using the Hamilton Depression Scale found *Guan Ye Jin Si Tao* (Herba Hyperici Perforati) to be clinically effective in the treatment of depression with ratings close to a 70% treatment response.[6,7,8,9] In another study, the long-term intake of the herb for up to one year among 517 patients was deemed as a safe and effective way to treat mild to moderate depression, and is especially suitable for a relapse prevention.[10] In comparison with Western medicine, *Guan Ye Jin Si Tao* (Herba Hyperici Perforati) has shown comparable effectiveness to many antidepressant drugs. According to a randomized, double-blind, comparative trial involving 149 outpatients with mild or moderate depression, *Guan Ye Jin Si Tao* (Herba Hyperici Perforati) and Prozac (fluoxetine) demonstrated equivalent therapeutic effect for treatment of depression. The duration of treatment was 6 weeks. Patients in the herb group received 800 mg of the extract per day, and patients in the drug group received 20 mg of Prozac (fluoxetine).[11] In another study with 1,757 mild-to-moderate depressed patients, *Guan Ye Jin Si Tao* (Herba Hyperici Perforati) was found to be significantly superior to placebo and "similarly effective" to antidepressant drugs.[12] Lastly, one study reported *Guan Ye Jin Si Tao* (Herba Hyperici Perforati) and Prozac (fluoxetine) to be therapeutically equivalent in the treatment of mild to moderate depression.[13] Side effects of *Guan Ye Jin Si Tao* (Herba Hyperici Perforati) are rare, with rash and photosensitivity being the most common.[14]

Yuan Zhi (Radix Polygalae) and *He Huan Pi* (Cortex Albiziae) are two other herbs in ***Shine*** that have also shown marked effects to treat depression. Use of *Yuan Zhi* (Radix Polygalae) is associated with marked antidepressant effects to reverse the harmful effects of chronic mild stress on mood and behaviors. The mechanism of this action is attributed in part to its neuroendocrine and neuropropective activities, as well as involvement of the hypothalamo-pituitary-adrenal system.[15] *He Huan Pi* (Cortex Albiziae) exerts its antidepressant effect via the 5-HT1A receptor system. Its therapeutic effect is comparable to Tofranil (imipramine), a tricyclic antidepressant drug.[16] Clinically, one study reported 81.8% rate of effectiveness in treating depression in 33 patient (12 with recovery, 15 with improvement, and 6 with no effect) using an herbal formula that contained *He Huan Pi* (Cortex Albiziae), *Shi Chang Pu* (Rhizoma Acori Tatarinowii), and others.[17]

Beyond using herbs to directly treat depression, ***Shine*** incorporates other herbs to support the patient and treat other aspects of depression. Since stress is a main contributor of depression, many herbs are used in this formula to calm the patient and alleviate depression, such as *Chai Hu* (Radix Bupleuri),[18] *Chuan Xiong* (Rhizoma Chuanxiong),[19] *Da Zao* (Fructus Jujubae),[20] and *Xiang Fu* (Rhizoma Cyperi).[21] To improve sleep pattern and treat insomnia, *Yuan Zhi* (Radix Polygalae) is added for its sedative effect.[22] To improve and increase energy, *Shen Qu* (Massa Fermentata) is used to improve digestion and absorption of nutrients, and *Cha Ye* (Folium Camelliae) is added to gently stimulant the central nervous system and increase body metabolism.[23,24,25]

In summary, ***Shine*** is a great formula to treat depression and its associated symptoms.

COMPARATIVE ANALYSIS

Depression is an emotional disorder that affects millions of people worldwide. In Western medicine, the biomedical understanding of depression is relatively new, as antidepressant drugs were mostly developed only in the last two decades. Though there are several categories of drugs for depression, the most commonly

Shine ™

used are the serotonin specific reuptake inhibitors (SSRI), such as Prozac (fluoxetine), Zoloft (sertraline), and Paxil (paroxetine). As the name implies, these drugs have the specific effect of increasing serotonin activities in the brain to lift depression. However, despite their specific mechanism, they often require six to eight weeks before they exert their effect to lift depression. Furthermore, they are associated with a great number of side effects, including but not limited to nausea, vomiting, weight loss, sexual dysfunction, and increased risk of suicide. Therefore, these drugs must be prescribed and monitored carefully to avoid such adverse reactions.

In TCM, depression is characterized by stagnation of qi, blood, food, and phlegm. Therefore, optimal treatment requires use of herbs to relieve such stagnation. These same herbs have also been found to have an excellent effect to increase energy levels and lift depression. Generally speaking, most patients begin to benefit within approximately two weeks. Most importantly, these herbs are safe and natural, and are associated with few or no side effects.

Depression is an emotional disorder that should be addressed cautiously. Though use of drugs is effective, one must carefully evaluate the potential benefits versus risks. Once decision is made to start drug therapy, the patient must be monitored carefully to ensure that the drugs do not cause serious side effects. In comparison, herbs are also effective, and definitely much safer. It provides an additional option that definitely should be explored. Furthermore, in addition to drug or herbal therapies, counseling and behavior therapy should be initiated as they are extremely helpful toward long-term improvement. Lastly, exercise is also helpful as this increases one's inherent ability to deal with stress and depression.

References

1. Muller WE, Schafer C er al., In-vitro-Studie uber Hypericum-Extrakt, Hyericin und Kampferol. *DAZ* 136(13):1015-1022.1996.
2. *PDR for Nutritional Supplements 1st Edition*, Medical Economics, 2001.
3. Bombardelli, E. et al. *Fitoterapia*; 66(1):43-68. 1995.
4. Suzuki, O. et al. *Planta Med*; 2:272. 1984.
5. Muller, WE et al., Hyperforin represents the neurotransmitter reuptake inhibiting constituent of Hypericum extract. *Pharmacopsychiatry* 1998 Jun;31 Suppl 1:16-21.
6. Ernst, E. *Fortschr Med*; 113(25): 354-55. 1995.
7. Mueller, W. et al. *Deutsche Apotheker Zeitung*; 136:17-22,24. Mar 28, 1996.
8. DeSmet, P. et al. *Br. Med J*; 313:241-42. Aug 3, 1996.
9. Harrer, G. et al. *Phytomedicine*; 1:3-8. 1994.
10. Brattström A. Long-term effects of St. John's wort (Hypericum perforatum) treatment: a 1-year safety study in mild to moderate depression. Max Zeller Söhne Zeller AG, Seeblickstr. 4, CH-8590 Romanshorn, Switzerland. Phytomedicine. 2009 Apr;16(4):277-83.
11. Harrer, G et al., Comparison of equivalence between the St. John's Wort extract LoHyp-57 and fluoxetine. *Arzneimittelforschung* 1999 Apr;(4):289-96.
12. Linde, K. et al. *Br Med J*; 313(7052):253-58. 1996.
13. Behnke K, Jensen GS, Graubaum HJ, Gruenwald J. Hypericum perforatum versus fluoxetine in the treatment of mild to moderate depression. PhytoPharm Consulting, Institute for Phytopharmaceuticals, Berlin, Germany. Adv Ther. 2002 Jan-Feb;19(1):43-52.
14. Muldner, VH. and Zoller, M. *Arzneimittelforschung*; 34:918. 1984.
15. Hu Y, Liu P, Guo DH, Rahman K, Wang DX, Xie TT. Antidepressant effects of the extract YZ-50 from Polygala tenuifolia in chronic mild stress treated rats and its possible mechanisms. Dept. of Clinical Pharmacology, Pharmacy Care Center, Chinese PLA General Hospital, Beijing 100853, China. Pharm Biol. 2010 Jul;48(7):794-800.
16. Kim JH, Kim SY, Lee SY, Jang CG. Antidepressant-like effects of Albizzia julibrissin in mice: involvement of the 5-HT1A receptor system. Department of Pharmacology, College of Pharmacy, Sungkyunkwan University, Suwon 440-746, Republic of Korea. Pharmacol Biochem Behav. 2007 May;87(1):41-7.
17. *Zhong Yao Lin Chuan Xin Yong* (New Clinical Applications of Chinese Medicine), 2001; 282.
18. *Zhong Yao Yao Li Yu Ying Yong* (Pharmacology and Applications of Chinese Herbs), 1983; 888.
19. *Zhong Yao Yao Li Yu Ying Yong* (Pharmacology and Applications of Chinese Herbs), 1983:123.
20. *Guo Wai Yi Xue Zhong Yi Zhong Yao Fen Ce* (Monograph of Chinese Herbology from Foreign Medicine), 1985; 7(4):48.
21. *Zhong Guo Yao Ke Da Xue Xue Bao* (Journal of University of Chinese Herbology), 1989; 20(1):48.
22. *Zhong Yao Yao Li Yu Ying Yong* (Pharmacology and Applications of Chinese Herbs), 1983; 477.
23. *Zhong Yao Xue* (Chinese Herbology), 1998; 436:437.
24. Tyler, V. *The New Honest Herbal. Philadelphia*, PA: G.F. Stickley Co., 1987.
25. Olin, R. et al. *The Lawrence Review of Natural Products by Facts and Comparison.* Green Tea. May 1993.

Shine (DS)™

CLINICAL APPLICATIONS

- **Depression/Stress**
- Anxiety, stress, irritability
- Sadness, lack of interest
- Possible chest distension, abdominal bloating, generalized weakness and/or discomfort
- **Note: This formula has no known interactions with anti-depressant drugs.**

WESTERN THERAPEUTIC ACTIONS

- Antidepressant effect to elevate mood and lift depression
- Anxiolytic effect to alleviate stress and anxiety
- Gastrointestinal effect to regulate and restore normal digestive system and improve energy

CHINESE THERAPEUTIC ACTIONS

- Spreads Liver qi
- Clears Heart fire

DOSAGE

Take 3 to 4 capsules three times daily on an empty stomach. The dosage may be increased up to 6 to 8 capsules every four to six hours as needed.

INGREDIENTS

Bai Shao (Radix Paeoniae Alba)
Bai Zhu (Rhizoma Atractylodis Macrocephalae)
Cang Zhu (Rhizoma Atractylodis)
Chai Hu (Radix Bupleuri)
Chuan Xiong (Rhizoma Chuanxiong)
Dang Gui (Radix Angelicae Sinensis)
Fu Ling (Poria)
He Huan Pi (Cortex Albiziae)
Mu Dan Pi (Cortex Moutan)
Shen Qu (Massa Fermentata)
Xiang Fu (Rhizoma Cyperi)
Yuan Zhi (Radix Polygalae)
Zhi Gan Cao (Radix et Rhizoma Glycyrrhizae Praeparata cum Melle)
Zhi Mu (Rhizoma Anemarrhenae)
Zhi Zi (Fructus Gardeniae)

BACKGROUND

Depression is a mood disorder that encompasses more than just sadness. Stress and anxiety are among the most common symptoms that also affect patients with depression, and more often than not, the symptoms from stress, anxiety, and depression are difficult to separate out.

Controlling depression with pharmaceuticals is difficult, and may require months of trial and error with different medications. Often a combination of two or more drugs is needed to keep depression under control. The disadvantages of using pharmaceuticals for the treatment of mood disorders include long-term dependency, and of course, the myriad side effects that may come with the medication, or the combination of medications. Traditional Chinese medicine (TCM) has a long history of dealing with mood disorders in an all-natural way. At the root of the issue is an imbalance of the internal organs; by correcting the relative imbalances of these organs, the individual's mood disorder should naturally improve. However, with TCM alone, it is often more difficult and time-consuming to treat serious mood disorders. Sometimes it is most effective to utilize a combination of Western and Chinese herbal medicine to gradually bring the patient back into health.

FORMULA EXPLANATION

Shine (DS) treats depression characterized by Liver qi stagnation accompanied by interior heat and underlying blood and Spleen deficiencies. Often, this constraint leads to other complications, such as stagnation of blood, phlegm, heat, dampness, and food. If the qi is stagnant in the chest and abdomen, qi is not able to ascend or descend freely; chest distension and oppression as well as abdominal fullness and pain may occur.

Chai Hu (Radix Bupleuri) and *Xiang Fu* (Rhizoma Cyperi) enter the Liver channel to activate qi circulation and relieve qi stagnation. *Mu Dan Pi* (Cortex Moutan), *Zhi Mu* (Rhizoma Anemarrhenae) and *Zhi Zi* (Fructus Gardeniae) sedate interior heat arising from Spleen and blood deficiencies, and from Liver qi stagnation. *Chuan Xiong* (Rhizoma Chuanxiong) activates blood circulation to dispel blood stagnation. *Bai Shao* (Radix Paeoniae Alba) and *Dang Gui* (Radix Angelicae Sinensis) tonify the yin and the blood to contain the fire in the body.

Bai Zhu (Rhizoma Atractylodis Macrocephalae), *Cang Zhu* (Rhizoma Atractylodis), and *Fu Ling* (Poria) strengthen the Spleen and dry dampness to clear damp and phlegm stagnation. When the Spleen is strong, the patient is less likely to worry and overthink. *He Huan Pi* (Cortex Albiziae) and *Yuan Zhi* (Radix Polygalae) calm the *shen* (spirit). *Shen Qu* (Massa Fermentata) promotes digestion, clears food stagnation and relieves the digestive symptoms arising from Liver overacting on the Spleen. Finally, *Zhi Gan Cao* (Radix et Rhizoma Glycyrrhizae Praeparata cum Melle) harmonizes the entire formula.

In conclusion, ***Shine (DS)*** treats depression and stress by regulating Liver qi and clearing interior heat.

CAUTIONS & CONTRAINDICATIONS

- This formula is contraindicated during pregnancy and nursing.
- Allergy warning: *Shen Qu* (Massa Fermentata) used in this product contains wheat. Persons with allergy to wheat should not take this product.
- This herbal formula contains herbs that invigorate blood circulation, such as *Dang Gui* (Radix Angelicae Sinensis). Therefore, patients who are on anticoagulant or antiplatelet therapies, such as Coumadin (warfarin), should use this formula

Shine (DS)™

with caution, or not at all, as there may be a higher risk of bleeding and bruising.[1,2,3]

CLINICAL NOTES

- Depression may be treated effectively with ***Shine*** or ***Shine (DS)***.
  - ***Shine*** is more effective for depression characterized by stagnation (food, qi, blood and phlegm). ***Shine*** should not be used concurrently with antidepressant drugs, as this formula contains *Guan Ye Jin Si Tao* (Herba Hyperici Perforati), commonly known as St John's Wort.
  - ***Shine (DS)*** is more effective for depression and stress characterized by Liver qi stagnation and Heart fire. ***Shine (DS)*** may be used concurrently with antidepressant drugs, as there are no known interactions.
- Discontinuation of antidepressant drugs, particularly abruptly, may cause certain withdrawal symptoms such as "electric shock" sensations (also known as "brain shivers" or "brain zaps"), dizziness, acute depression and irritability. Therefore, it is best to taper off the drugs slowly, and offer herbal treatment simultaneously. ***Shine (DS)*** may be used concurrently with antidepressant drugs or during the tapering process. ***Shine*** should not be used until the antidepressant drugs have been discontinued for two weeks.

Pulse Diagnosis by Dr. Jimmy Wei-Yen Chang:

- **Inward-directed mood disorders:** concave and deep pulse on the left *guan*
- **Outward-directed mood disorders:** convex and forceful on the left *guan*

SUPPLEMENTARY FORMULAS

- With stress, anxiety, restlessness, and bipolar disorders (manic-depressives), add ***Calm (ES)***.
- For purplish tongue, blood stasis or chronic depression, add ***Circulation (SJ)*** in the first month of treatment.
- With Liver blood deficiency and insomnia, add ***Calm ZZZ***.
- With overthinking or over worrying due to Spleen qi deficiency, add ***Schisandra ZZZ***.
- With indigestion and bloating, add ***GI Harmony***.
- For more phlegm, add ***Pinellia Complex***.
- For constipation, combine with ***Gentle Lax (Excess)*** or ***Gentle Lax (Deficient)***.
- For a quick boost of energy and vitality, combine with ***Vibrant***.
- For constant fatigue and lack of energy due to deficiency, combine with ***Imperial Tonic***.
- For loss of sexual desire, combine with ***Vitality***.
- For over-weight or obesity, combine with ***Herbalite***.
- For heat sensations, irritability or nightmares due to excess fire, add ***Gardenia Complex***.
- For chronic depressive patients who do not respond to any of the above treatment or show little result, add ***Circulation (SJ)*** for two months and re-evaluate.

ACUPUNCTURE POINTS

Traditional Points:

- *Taichong* (LR 3), *Yanglingquan* (GB 34), *Hegu* (LI 4), *Yintang*, *Taixi* (KI 3), *Qimen* (LR 14), *Zusanli* (ST 36), *Shenmen* (HT 7), *Neiguan* (PC 6)

Classic Master Tung's Points:

- **Depression:** *Tongguan* (T 88.01), *Tongshen* (T 88.09), *Neiguan* (PC 6), *Tianhuangfu [Shenguan]* (T 77.18), *Huoying* (T 66.03), *Huoxi* (T 11.16). Bleed the HT and LU areas of the back with cupping. Bleed before needling for best result.
- **Stress:** *Zhenjing* (T 1010.08), *Tianhuangfu [Shenguan]* (T 77.18), *Huoying* (T 66.03), *Dizong* (T 44.09), *Dan* (T 11.13)

Master Tung's Points by Dr. Chuan-Min Wang:

- **Depression:** *Zhenjing* (T 1010.08), *Huoying* (T 66.03)

Balance Method by Dr. Richard Tan:

- Left side: *Zulinqi* (GB 41), *Yanglingquan* (GB 34), *Shenmen* (HT 7), *Tongli* (HT 5), *Shaohai* (HT 3), *Quze* (PC 3), *Daling* (PC 7)
- Right side: *Taichong* (LR 3), *Ligou* (LR 5), *Ququan* (LR 8), *Zhongzhu* (TH 3), *Waiguan* (TH 5), *Tianjing* (TH 10)
- Bilateral ear *Shenmen*, *Anmian*
- Alternate sides with each treatment.

Ear Acupuncture:

- *Shenmen*, Endocrine, Subcortex, Sympathetic, Heart, Spleen, Kidney

Auricular Medicine by Dr. Li-Chun Huang:

- *Shenmen*, Liver, Heart, Occiput, Nervous Subcortex, Anxious Point, Be Happy Point. Bleed Ear Apex.

NUTRITION

- Depression may be due in part to nutritional deficiency. Foods such as white bread, flour, saturated animal fats, hydrogenated vegetable oils, sweets, soft drinks, and canned goods deprive the body of B vitamins and increase the probability of depression.
- Avoid a diet too low in complex carbohydrates as it may cause serotonin depletion and depression.

General Guidelines for a Healthy Diet

- Eat a variety of fresh, organic fruits and vegetables of all colors.
- Incorporate more high-fiber whole grains and nuts into diet.
- Drink warm or hot liquids with meals. Putting cold and ice on any part of the body will immediately constrict the flow of blood to that region. Similarly, drinking cold or iced drinks with meals will hinder the natural peristaltic movements of the digestive system.
- Foods with antioxidant effects, such as vitamin A, C and E are beneficial as they neutralize the free radicals and minimize

Shine (DS)™

damage to cells. Beneficial foods include citrus fruits, carrots, green leaf vegetables, and green tea.

- Chew food completely and thoroughly. The digestive tract can process and absorb smaller pieces of food much better than food that is incompletely chewed. Larger pieces of food can lead to incomplete digestion and digestive discomfort.
- Always eat breakfast. According to the TCM clock, the most optimal time for the digestive system is in the morning from 8 to 10 a.m.
- Give the body two to three hours between the last meal of the day and bedtime. During sleep, the digestive system slows down as well. Make sure the body has adequate time to digest the food before going into sleep mode.
- If the patient is allergic to any food or feel uncomfortable after eating certain foods, then avoid eating it.
- Avoid fast food, processed foods, junk food, artificial sugars, and carbonated drinks. Stay away from meat, greasy food, alcohol, caffeine, dairy products (except for unsweetened low-fat yogurt), tap water, iron supplements and vegetables and fruits with pesticides.
- Spleen is responsible for generating post-natal qi and good Spleen function also contributes to a healthy immune system. Foods that damage the Spleen should be avoided:
  - Avoid any and all foods that contain sugar, such as cake, dessert, candy, chocolate, canned juice, soft drinks, caffeinated drinks, stevia, sugar substitutes, agave, xylitol, and corn syrup.
  - Avoid raw or uncooked meats, such as sashimi, sushi, steak tartar, seared meat. Minimize consumption of foods that are cooling in nature, including tofu, tomato, celery, asparagus, bamboo, seaweed, kelp, bitter melon, cucumber, gourd, luffa, eggplant, winter melon, watermelon, honeydew, citrus, oranges, guava, grapefruit, pineapple, plums, pear, banana, papaya, white radish, mustard leaf, potherb mustard, Chinese kale, napa, bamboo sprout. Do not eat foods straight from the refrigerator. Long-term use of cold fruits and vegetables like the ones listed above may be damaging to the Spleen. To make the property more neutral, one can add about 20 pieces of *Gou Qi Zi* (Fructus Lycii) when cooking them.
- Warm and hot natured foods that damage qi and yin should be avoided, such as:
  - certain fruits like mango and durian that produce heat.
  - stimulants like coffee, alcohol, and energy drinks.
  - spicy/pungent/aromatic vegetables such as pepper, garlic, onions, basil, rosemary, cumin, funnel, anise, leeks, chives, scallions, thyme, saffron, wormwood, mustard, chili pepper, and wasabi.
- Avoid food and drinks with artificial coloring.
- Consume as few meat products as possible. Do not eat processed meats, such as lunch meats, hot dogs and sausages, as they contain nitrites that are associated with inflammation and chronic disease.

LIFESTYLE INSTRUCTIONS

- Regular use of steam rooms or saunas can help to eliminate toxins through sweating.
- Take a 30-minute walk after meals to help stimulate the circulatory and digestive systems.
- Incorporate some form of cardiovascular exercise.
- Do not postpone bowel movements, respond to the urge immediately.
- Sleep by 10:00 p.m. In traditional Chinese medicine (TCM), 11:00 p.m. to 1:00 a.m. is when the yin shifts to yang. It is crucial for the body to be at rest during this time for optimal health.
- Eliminate things that are unhealthy (e.g., alcohol, coffee, cigarettes, refined sugars, or saturated fats) or potentially toxic (e.g. chemical-based household cleaners and personal hygiene products).

MODERN RESEARCH

Shine (DS) is designed to treat depression by using herbs with demonstrated effectiveness to elevate mood, alleviate stress, and reduce anxiety.

Zhi Mu (Rhizoma Anemarrhenae), *Yuan Zhi* (Radix Polygalae), and *He Huan Pi* (Cortex Albiziae) are three herbs in this formula that have also shown marked effects to treat depression. *Zhi Mu* (Rhizoma Anemarrhenae) contains sarsasapogenin which have shown significant antidepressant activity on two experimental models of depression.[4] *Zhi Mu* (Rhizoma Anemarrhenae) exerts its antidepressant influences in both the hypothalamus and the hippocampus.[5] Furthermore, use of *Yuan Zhi* (Radix Polygalae) is associated with a marked antidepressant effect to reverse the harmful effects of chronic mild stress on mood and behavior. The mechanism of this action is attributed in part to its neuroendocrine and neuroprotective activities, as well as involvement of the hypothalamo-pituitary-adrenal system.[6] Lastly, *He Huan Pi* (Cortex Albiziae) exhibits comparable antidepressant effect to Tofranil (imipramine), a tricyclic antidepressant drug.[7] Clinically, one study reported an 81.8% rate of effectiveness in treating depression in 33 patient (12 with recovery, 15 with improvement, and 6 with no effect) using an herbal formula that contained *He Huan Pi* (Cortex Albiziae), *Shi Chang Pu* (Rhizoma Acori Tatarinowii), and others.[8]

Beyond using herbs to directly treat depression, ***Shine (DS)*** incorporates other herbs to support the patient and treat other aspects of depression. Since stress is a main contributor of depression, many herbs are used in this formula to calm the patient and alleviate depression, such as *Chai Hu* (Radix Bupleuri),[9] *Chuan Xiong* (Rhizoma Chuanxiong),[10] and *Xiang Fu* (Rhizoma Cyperi).[11] To improve sleep pattern and treat insomnia, *Yuan Zhi* (Radix Polygalae) is added for its sedative effect.[12] To improve and increase energy, *Shen Qu* (Massa Fermentata) is used to improve digestion and absorption of nutrients,[13] *Bai Zhu* (Rhizoma Atractylodis Macrocephalae) and *Cang Zhu* (Rhizoma Atractylodis) are incorporated to regulate and restore

Shine (DS)™

the digestive system,[14,15] and *Zhi Gan Cao* (Radix et Rhizoma Glycyrrhizae Praeparata cum Melle) is utilized to protect and repair the intestines.[16] Lastly, *Bai Zhu* (Rhizoma Atractylodis Macrocephalae) has an adaptogenic effect to facilitate adjustment to various mental and physical stress.[17]

In summary, ***Shine (DS)*** is a great formula to treat depression and its associated symptoms.

COMPARATIVE ANALYSIS

Depression is an emotional disorder that affects millions of people worldwide. In Western medicine, the biomedical understanding of depression is relatively new, as antidepressant drugs were mostly developed only in the last two decades. Though there are several categories of drugs for depression, the most commonly used are the serotonin specific reuptake inhibitors (SSRI), such as Prozac (fluoxetine), Zoloft (sertraline), and Paxil (paroxetine). As the name implies, these drugs have specific effects to increase serotonin activities in the brain to lift depression. However, despite their specific mechanism, they often require six to eight weeks before they exert their effect to lift depression. Furthermore, they are associated with a great number of side effects, including but not limited to nausea, vomiting, weight loss, sexual dysfunction, and increased risk of suicide. Therefore, these drugs must be prescribed and monitored carefully to avoid such adverse reactions.

In TCM, depression is characterized by stagnation of qi, blood, food, and phlegm. If untreated or poorly treated, these stagnations can create heat, causing Heart fire and *shen* (spirit) disturbance. Therefore, optimal treatment requires use of herbs to relieve stagnation and clear Heart fire. These same herbs have also been found to have an excellent effect to increase energy levels and lift depression. Generally speaking, most patients begin to benefit within approximately two weeks. Most importantly, these herbs are safe and natural, and are associated with few or no side effects.

Depression is an emotional disorder that should be addressed cautiously. Though use of drugs is effective, one must carefully evaluate the potential benefits against the potential risks. Once the decision is made to start drug therapy, the patient must be monitored carefully to ensure that the drugs do not cause serious side effects. In comparison, herbs are also effective, and definitely much safer. It provides an additional option that should be explored. Furthermore, in addition to drug or herbal therapies, counseling and behavior therapy should be initiated as they are extremely helpful toward long-term improvement. Lastly, exercise is also helpful as it increases one's inherent ability to deal with stress and depression.

References

1. Chan K, Lo AC, Yeung JH, Woo KS. Journal of Pharmacy and Pharmacology 1995 May;47(5):402-6.
2. Pharmacotherapy 1999 July;19(7):870-876.
3. European Journal of Drug Metabolism and Pharmacokinetics 1995; 20(1): 55-60.
4. Ren LX, Luo YF, Li X, Wu YL. Antidepressant activity of sarsasapogenin from Anemarrhena asphodeloides Bunge (Liliaceae). School of Pharmacy, Shenyang Pharmaceutical University, Shenyang, China. Pharmazie. 2007 Jan;62(1):78-9.
5. Ren LX, Luo YF, Li X, Zuo DY, Wu YL. Antidepressant-like effects of sarsasapogenin from Anemarrhena asphodeloides BUNGE (Liliaceae). School of Pharmacy, Shenyang Pharmaceutical University, China. Biol Pharm Bull. 2006 Nov;29(11):2304-6.
6. Hu Y, Liu P, Guo DH, Rahman K, Wang DX, Xie TT. Antidepressant effects of the extract YZ-50 from Polygala tenuifolia in chronic mild stress treated rats and its possible mechanisms. Dept. of Clinical Pharmacology, Pharmacy Care Center, Chinese PLA General Hospital, Beijing 100853, China. Pharm Biol. 2010 Jul;48(7):794-800.
7. Kim JH, Kim SY, Lee SY, Jang CG. Antidepressant-like effects of Albizzia julibrissin in mice: involvement of the 5-HT1A receptor system. Department of Pharmacology, College of Pharmacy, Sungkyunkwan University, Suwon 440-746, Republic of Korea. Pharmacol Biochem Behav. 2007 May;87(1):41-7.
8. *Zhong Yao Lin Chuan Xin Yong* (New Clinical Applications of Chinese Medicine), 2001; 282.
9. *Zhong Yao Yao Li Yu Ying Yong* (Pharmacology and Applications of Chinese Herbs), 1983; 888.
10. *Zhong Yao Yao Li Yu Ying Yong* (Pharmacology and Applications of Chinese Herbs), 1983:123.
11. *Zhong Guo Yao Ke Da Xue Xue Bao* (Journal of University of Chinese Herbology), 1989; 20(1):48.
12. *Zhong Yao Yao Li Yu Ying Yong* (Pharmacology and Applications of Chinese Herbs), 1983; 477.
13. *Zhong Yao Xue* (Chinese Herbology), 1998; 436:437.
14. *Chang Yong Zhong Yao Cheng Fen Yu Yao Li Shou Ce* (A Handbook of the Composition and Pharmacology of Common Chinese Drugs), 1994; 739:742.
15. Kimura Y, Sumiyoshi M. Effects of an Atractylodes lancea rhizome extract and a volatile component β-eudesmol on gastrointestinal motility in mice. J Ethnopharmacol. 2012 May 7;141(1):530-6.
16. He Y, Zhang X, Zeng X, Huang Y, Wei JA, Han L, Li CX, Zhang GW. HuR-mediated posttranscriptional regulation of p21 is involved in the effect of Glycyrrhiza uralensis licorice aqueous extract on polyamine-depleted intestinal crypt cells proliferation. J Nutr Biochem. 2012 Jan 2.
17. *Xin Yi Yao Xue Za Zhi* (New Journal of Medicine and Herbology), 1974; 8:13.

Silerex™

CLINICAL APPLICATIONS

- **Skin disorders:** itching, rash, urticaria, dermatitis, and eczema
- **Skin allergies** induced by drugs, chemicals or foods

WESTERN THERAPEUTIC ACTIONS

- Antihistamine and antipruritic effects to relieve itching and neutralize allergic reactions
- Anti-inflammatory effect to relieve swelling and inflammation
- Antibiotic properties to treat skin infections

CHINESE THERAPEUTIC ACTIONS

- Disperses the wind to relieve itching
- Clears heat, cools the blood
- Drains dampness

DOSAGE

Take 5 to 6 capsules with warm water on an empty stomach every six hours as needed. Using ***Silerex*** prior to exposure to the allergen may prevent or reduce the risk of developing an allergy.

INGREDIENTS

Bai Xian Pi (Cortex Dictamni)
Che Qian Zi (Semen Plantaginis)
Dang Gui (Radix Angelicae Sinensis)
Di Fu Zi (Fructus Kochiae)
Di Huang (Radix Rehmanniae)
Fang Feng (Radix Saposhnikoviae)
Ji Li (Fructus Tribuli)
Jing Jie (Herba Schizonepetae)
Ku Shen (Radix Sophorae Flavescentis)
Lian Qiao (Fructus Forsythiae)
Mu Dan Pi (Cortex Moutan)
Niu Bang Zi (Fructus Arctii)
Zhi Zi (Fructus Gardeniae)

BACKGROUND

Itching is a symptom that may be caused by external or internal disorders. External disorders that cause itching include atopic dermatitis, contact dermatitis, dry skin, infection, and urticaria. Internal disorders that cause itching include allergic reactions (i.e., to foods, drugs, chemicals), cholestasis, chronic renal failure, and others. While the symptom of itching can be treated effectively with herbs, efforts must be made to identify and eliminate the cause.

FORMULA EXPLANATION

Silerex is formulated to treat various dermatological disorders, including rash, itching, urticaria, eczema, dermatitis, and skin allergies to drugs, chemicals or foods. ***Silerex*** is comprised of herbs that disperse wind, clear heat, cool blood, and drain damp.

Commonly known as siler, *Fang Feng* (Radix Saposhnikoviae) is one of the best herbs to extinguishes wind and treat skin disorders such as itching, rash, urticaria, and eczema. *Jing Jie* (Herba Schizonepetae) and *Ji Li* (Fructus Tribuli) also release external wind to relieve itching. *Zhi Zi* (Fructus Gardeniae) clears heat to reduce redness and inflammation of the affected areas. *Mu Dan Pi* (Cortex Moutan), *Niu Bang Zi* (Fructus Arctii) and *Lian Qiao* (Fructus Forsythiae) cool and detoxify the blood to relieve itching. *Ku Shen* (Radix Sophorae Flavescentis), *Che Qian Zi* (Semen Plantaginis), and *Di Fu Zi* (Fructus Kochiae) drain dampness through urination and treat weepy lesions. *Bai Xian Pi* (Cortex Dictamni) has antifungal effects to relieve fire toxicity. Finally, *Dang Gui* (Radix Angelicae Sinensis) and *Di Huang* (Radix Rehmanniae) tonify and move the blood to extinguish wind to relieve rashes and itching.

In conclusion, ***Silerex*** dispels wind-heat from the exterior to treat rash, itching, urticaria, eczema, dermatitis, and other skin disorders.

CAUTIONS & CONTRAINDICATIONS

- The optimal treatment of allergies is to avoid the allergens. ***Silerex*** relieves the symptoms, but does not cure the allergy. Therefore, it is ***not*** recommended to take this formula for a long time simply to suppress the symptoms. Every effort should be made to identify and avoid the allergen.
- If the condition does not improve after using ***Silerex*** for two to three weeks, consider modifying the herbal formula.
- This herbal formula contains herbs that invigorate blood circulation, such as *Dang Gui* (Radix Angelicae Sinensis). Therefore, patients who are on anticoagulant or antiplatelet therapies, such as Coumadin (warfarin), should use this formula with caution, or not at all, as there may be a higher risk of bleeding and bruising.[1,2,3]

CLINICAL NOTES

- For itching of the genital region, use ***Gentiana Complex*** both internally and externally. For external treatment, wash the affected area with mild soap first. Then mix 5 grams each of *Ku Shen* (Radix Sophorae Flavescentis), *She Chuang Zi* (Fructus Cnidii Monnieri), and ***Gentiana Complex***, with 2 cups of warm water. Soak the affected area in the herbal solution for five minutes before rinsing off with water. Repeat the process once daily until itching is relieved.
- The optimal approach to address allergy is prevention, not treatment. Empirical wisdom suggests isolating the allergen and minimizing the patient's exposure to said allergen as much as possible.

Pulse Diagnosis by Dr. Jimmy Wei-Yen Chang:

- **Allergy lesions** due to fire and dryness in the Lung, Large Intestine and Liver: floating, forceful, and jumpy on the right *cun* and left *guan*.
- **Toxic lesions** due to Liver fire: thick, long, wiry, forceful, and jumpy on both *chi*; and floating, forceful, and jumpy on the left *guan*.

FORMULAS

Silerex™

- **Skin problems** due to stress: forceful on the left *guan*.
- **Wet skin lesions** due to damp-heat accumulation: deep and forceful pulse on all three pulse positions (*cun, guan, chi*).
- **Dry skin lesions** due to dryness and heat accumulation in the Lung and Large Intestine: floating and forceful pulse on the right *cun*.

SUPPLEMENTARY FORMULAS

- For signs and symptoms of excess fire, add ***Gardenia Complex***.
- For psoriasis, add ***Dermatrol (PS)***.
- For weepy skin conditions, add ***Dermatrol (Damp)***.
- For dry skin conditions, add ***Dermatrol (Dry)***.
- For heavy metal poisoning, chemical allergy or any other unknown allergy, combine with ***Herbal DTX***.
- For chronic cases of allergy due to accumulation of allergen in the body, use it with ***Liver DTX***.
- To enhance the overall antiviral function, add ***Herbal AVR***.
- To enhance the overall antibacterial function, use ***Herbal ABX***.
- For pus or swelling on the lesions, add ***Resolve (AI)***.
- For respiratory discomfort associated with allergies, add ***Respitrol (Heat)*** or ***Respitrol (Cold)***.
- For headache, add ***Corydalin (AC)*** or ***Corydalin (CR)***.
- If the allergy is due to ingestion of food, cleanse the colon with ***GI DTX***.
- For itching that worsens with stress, add ***Calm*** or ***Calm (ES)***.
- With yin deficiency and heat, add ***Nourish***.

ACUPUNCTURE TREATMENT

Traditional Points:

- *Xuehai* (SP 10), *Geshu* (BL 17), *Fengchi* (GB 20), *Chize* (LU 5)
- *Quchi* (LI 11), *Xuehai* (SP 10)

Classic Master Tung's Points:

- **Eczema:** *Simashang* (T 88.18), *Simazhong* (T 88.17), *Simaxia* (T 88.19), *Linggu* (T 22.05), *Minghuang* (T 88.12), *Tianhuang* (T 88.13), *Qihuang* (T 88.14), *Tianhuang* (T 77.17), *Dihuang* (T 77.19), *Renhuang* (T 77.21), *Jinqianshang* (T 88.24), *Jinqianxia* (T 88.23)
- **Atopic dermatitis:** *Simashang* (T 88.18), *Simazhong* (T 88.17), *Simaxia* (T 88.19), *Linggu* (T 22.05), *Zhisima* (T 11.07)
- **Herpes zoster:** *Linggu* (T 22.05), *Tianhuang* (T 88.13), *Minghuang* (T 88.12), *Qihuang* (T 88.14), *Simashang* (T 88.18), *Simazhong* (T 88.17), *Simaxia* (T 88.19), *Shuitong* (T 1010.19), *Shuijin* (T 1010.20)
- **Tinea versicolor:** *Tianhuang* (T 88.13), *Minghuang* (T 88.12), *Qihuang* (T 88.14), *Simashang* (T 88.18), *Simaxia* (T 88.19), *Simazhong* (T 88.17), *Shuijin* (T 1010.20), *Shuitong* (T 1010.19). Bleed the LR area T5 – T9 and KI area T9 – T12 on the back with cupping. Bleed before needling for best result.
- **Hives:** *Simashang* (T 88.18), *Simaxia* (T 88.19), *Simazhong* (T 88.17), *Tianhuang* (T 77.17), *Dihuang* (T 77.19), *Renhuang* (T 77.21), *Tianhuang* (T 88.13), *Minghuang* (T 88.12), *Qihuang* (T 88.14), *Zhisima* (T 11.07)
- **Poisoning from drugs or chemicals:** *Fenzhishang* (T DT.01), *Fenzhixia* (T DT.02), *Qihuang* (T 88.14), *Simazhong* (T 88.17), *Zhongjiuli* (T 88.25), *Zhisima* (T 11.07)

Master Tung's Points by Dr. Chuan-Min Wang:

- **Eczema, rash, urticaria:** Bleed Ear Apex. Needle *Simazhong* (T 88.17), *Simashang* (T 88.18), *Simaxia* (T 88.19).

Balance Method by Dr. Richard Tan:

- Left side: *Sanjian* (LI 3), *Quchi* (LI 11), *Gongsun* (SP 4), *Yinlingquan* (SP 9), *Taichong* (LR 3)
- Right side: *Fenglong* (ST 40), *Jiexi* (ST 41), *Diwuhui* (GB 42), *Taiyuan* (LU 9), *Chize* (LU 5)
- Left and right sides can be alternated from treatment to treatment.

Ear Acupuncture:

- Lung, Large Intestine, Adrenal Gland, corresponding point of the affected area(s)
- **Pruritus:** *Shenmen*, Lung, Subcortex, Adrenal Gland, Urticaria Point. Adjunct points: Liver, Spleen, Heart, Endocrine, Pancreas, Gallbladder, Ovary, Testicles. Select three to five points and needle both ears every other day. Five to ten days is one treatment course. Rest for one week in between treatment courses.
- **Urticaria:** Lung, Urticaria, Adrenal Gland, *Pingchuan*, Liver. Needle one to two points each time every other day. Ten treatments equal one course.

Auricular Medicine by Dr. Li-Chun Huang:

- **Rash and itching:** Allergy Area, *Shenmen*, Sympathetic, Occiput, Nervous Subcortex, Lung, Diaphragm, Spleen, Liver. Bleed Ear Apex.
- **Contact dermatitis:** Allergic Area, Sympathetic, Adrenal Gland, Liver, Spleen, Lung, Endocrine, corresponding points (to the area affected). Bleed Ear Apex.
  - For dermatitis with severe pain, add *Shenmen* and Occiput.
- **Eczema:** Allergic Area, Lung, Sympathetic, Spleen, *Shenmen*, Endocrine, Occiput, Diaphragm, corresponding points (to the area affected). Bleed Ear Apex.
- **Cutaneous pruritis:** *Shenmen*, Occiput, Liver, Spleen, Lung, Endocrine, Diaphragm, Allergic Area. Bleed Ear Apex.
- **Urticaria:** Liver, Lung, Spleen, Diaphragm, *Shenmen*, Occiput, Allergic Area, Sympathetic, Endocrine, Adrenal Gland. Bleed Ear Apex.
- **Severe itching:** Prick five times on the ear apex, five times each on the helix near the Great Auricular Nerve and Lesser Occipital Nerve.

NUTRITION

- Avoid seafood, sushi, duck, goose, onions, garlic, sugar, alcohol, and foods that are raw, spicy, fried, and greasy. Many meats and

Silerex™

dairy products increase skin irritation by increasing the acidity of body tissue.

- Increase the consumption of flax seed oil, which helps to reduce inflammation in the body.

The Tao of Nutrition by Dr. Maoshing Ni and Cathy McNease:

- Eczema
  - Recommendations: potatoes, broccoli, dandelion, mung bean, seaweed, pearl barley, cornsilk, water chestnut, winter melon, and watermelon.
  - Make fresh potato and apply locally, changing every four hours, for three days.
  - Apply honey to area.
  - Apply mashed daikon radish to area.
  - Make tea from mung beans and pearl barley and drink.
  - Boil soup from seaweed and winter melon, drinking at least once a day for ten days.
- Hives
  - Recommendations: winter melon rind, chrysanthemum, vinegar, papaya, ginger, dried prunes, black sesame, black beans, and pearl barley.
  - Take a sea salt bath, rubbing salt on the hives.
  - Cook together papaya, ginger, and rice vinegar until vinegar dries up. Eat the ginger and papaya twice daily for at least ten days.
  - Mix honey with rice wine and steam. Drink two tablespoons on an empty stomach every morning.
  - Cook together black sesame seeds, black beans, and Chinese black dates and eat at least once daily.
  - Eat two to three dried prunes daily.
  - Avoid shellfish and allergic foods.
- Allergy
  - Recommendations: ginger, onions, garlic, bamboo shoots, cabbage, beets, beet top tea, carrots, leafy greens, yams, ganoderma mushroom.
  - Drink ginger tea to induce sweating.
  - Drink beet top tea as a water source.
  - Avoid wheat, citrus fruits, chocolate, shellfish, dairy products, eggs, potatoes, polluted meats, and polluted air.

LIFESTYLE INSTRUCTIONS

- The best long-term treatment is to identify and avoid the allergen. In addition, balancing and strengthening one's health and immunity will also reduce the frequency of allergic reactions while strengthening the patient's immunological balance.
- Cotton or silk clothing is recommended over synthetic fibers for better ventilation.

CASE STUDIES

- K.B., a 62-year-old patient, presented with a chronic bilateral rash located on her arms. The rash occurred daily with a description of purple and dark in color. Daily lifestyle habits consisted of light alcohol drinking, cigarette smoking, and eating spicy foods. Other symptoms included pain with itching and peeling of the skin towards the end of the day. The TCM diagnosis was Lung and Liver fire. The practitioner administered ***Gardenia Complex*** and ***Silerex***, both at four capsules three times a day. Within two weeks, the patient reported that her skin had completely cleared up. The patient continued with the same herbal combination for an additional two months. Submitted by A I., Hilo, Hawaii.
- S.T., a 39-year-old female, presented with hives, which included symptoms of redness, itchiness, and blotchiness. Tongue was red and quivering, with a thin coat. The practitioner diagnosed this condition as wind-heat with dampness. ***Silerex*** was prescribed at 4 capsules three times a day. After two months of taking the herbs, she reported that the hives had lessened; however, if she stopped taking them the hives would come back strongly. The patient never found out the source of what caused the allergy but still continued taking the herbs. Submitted by S.L., Yuma, Arizona.

PHARMACOLOGICAL AND CLINICAL RESEARCH

Itching is a symptom associated with many external and internal disorders, including but not limited to dermatitis, contact dermatitis, infection, urticaria, and allergic reactions to foods, drugs, chemicals and other allergens. Proper treatment requires use of herbs with antipruritic effects to relieve itching, antiallergic and antihistamine activities to alleviate hypersensitivity reactions, and anti-inflammatory function to reduce swelling and inflammation.

Silerex contains many herbs with excellent antipruritic, antiallergic and antihistamine effects to directly stop itching associated with internal or external disorders. *Ku Shen* (Radix Sophorae Flavescentis) has an antipruritic effect to inhibit scratching in a dose-dependent manner.[4] The antipruritic effect of *Ku Shen* (Radix Sophorae Flavescentis) is attributed in part to its effect to reduce several eicosanoid-related skin inflammation disorders, such as atopic dermatitis.[5] *Jing Jie* (Herba Schizonepetae) exerts its antipruritic effect to inhibit itch-scratch response induced by substance P.[6] *Di Huang* (Radix Rehmanniae) has marked antiallergic activities to treat atopic dermatitis by suppressing the expression of cytokines, chemokines, and adhesion molecules.[7] *Niu Bang Zi* (Fructus Arctii) shows a marked antiallergic effect to inhibit the scratching behavior associated with atopic dermatitis and other allergy-related diseases. *Niu Bang Zi* (Fructus Arctii) also shows a marked effect to treat allergic diseases, including atopic dermatitis, by inhibiting the expression of IL-4 and IL-5.[8] Lastly, *Mu Dan Pi* (Cortex Moutan) has both antiallergic and antihistamine effects to treat allergy as it significantly suppresses histamine release and prostaglandin D(2) synthesis from mast cells.[9]

Silerex also contains many herbs with anti-inflammatory effects to reduce the swelling and inflammation of the skin. *Fang Feng* (Radix Saposhnikoviae) and *Che Qian Zi* (Semen

Silerex ™

Plantaginis) both exert their anti-inflammatory effects via their inhibitory effects on nitric oxide production.[10,11] *Mu Dan Pi* (Cortex Moutan), *Dang Gui* (Radix Angelicae Sinensis) and *Bai Xian Pi* (Cortex Dictamni) demonstrate anti-inflammatory effects by inhibiting prostaglandin synthesis and decreasing permeability of the blood vessels.[12,13,14] Lastly, *Di Fu Zi* (Fructus Kochiae) and *Zhi Zi* (Fructus Gardeniae) have strong anti-inflammatory activity as they suppress vascular inflammation via inhibition of tumor necrosis factor-alpha (TNF-α).[15,16]

Clinically, herbs in ***Silerex*** have been used to treat many skin disorders successfully. According to one study of 148 patients, dermatological disorders, such as rashes, itching and eczema, were treated with *Ku Shen* (Radix Sophorae Flavescentis) through oral decoction or intramuscular injection with a 79% effective rate.[17] According to another study, using *Di Huang* (Radix Rehmanniae) as the main ingredient in decoction, 37 patients with rashes, urticaria and contact dermatitis were treated, making a complete recovery in 28 cases, significant improvement in 3 cases, slight improvement in 5 cases, and no effect in one case.[18] In addition, 353 patients with various dermatological disorders were treated with a 90.7% effective rate, using injection of *Dang Gui* (Radix Angelicae Sinensis) on ear points every other day for 10 to 20 days per course of treatment.[19] Furthermore, application of *Jing Jie* (Herba Schizonepetae) powder topically showed a marked effect to treat various dermatological disorders, such as measles, pruritic rash and itching.[20] Finally, topical application of *Bai Xian Pi* (Cortex Dictamni) in fine powder form was 100% effective in treating 33 cases of suppurative dermatological disorders.[21]

In summary, ***Silerex*** contains herbs with antipruritic, anti-allergic and antihistamine activities, and can be used successfully to treat various dermatological conditions.

COMPARATIVE ANALYSIS

Skin disorders such as rash, itching, dermatitis, and eczema commonly occur as a result of oral ingestion of or direct physical contact with an incompatible substance. As a result, allergic and hypersensitive reactions occur either in localized areas or throughout the entire body. In Western medicine, these skin disorders are treated with drugs that symptomatically relieve itching and irritation. Commonly used drugs include antihistamines [such as Benadryl (diphenhydramine)] and corticosteroids [such as hydrocortisone]. In most cases, these drugs are used topically for a short period of time, and are therefore associated with limited side effects. However, oral use of these drugs is likely to cause more side effects. Furthermore, it is important to remember that the best way to avoid allergic skin reactions is to avoid the allergens whenever possible.

In TCM, skin disorders such as rash and eczema are characterized by wind-heat. Certain herbs that treat wind-heat have been shown to have marked antihistamine effects, and are excellent to alleviate skin itching and discomfort. Furthermore, many herbs also have anti-inflammatory effects to reduce swelling and inflammation. In short, oral ingestion of herbs is very effective to alleviate signs and symptoms of general skin disorders such as rash, eczema and dermatitis.

Drugs and herbs are both effective for treating skin disorders such as rash, dermatitis, and eczema. Though neither therapy "cures" allergy, they both effectively alleviate symptoms. Topical use of drugs alleviates symptoms safely and effectively, but oral use of the drugs tends to cause more side effects. On the other hand, herbs can be used safely and effectively via both oral and topical administrations.

References

1. Chan K, Lo AC, Yeung JH, Woo KS. Journal of Pharmacy and Pharmacology 1995 May;47(5):402-6.
2. Pharmacotherapy 1999 July;19(7):870-876.
3. European Journal of Drug Metabolism and Pharmacokinetics 1995; 20(1): 55-60.
4. Yamaguchi-Miyamoto T, Kawasuji T, Kuraishi Y, Suzuki H. Antipruritic effects of Sophora flavescens on acute and chronic itch-related responses in mice. Japan Society for the Promotion of Science, Domestic Research Fellow, Hon-machi, Kawaguchi, Saitama, Japan. Biol Pharm Bull. 2003 May;26(5):722-4.
5. Kim DW, Chi YS, Son KH, Chang HW, Kim JS, Kang SS, Kim HP. Effects of sophoraflavanone G, a prenylated flavonoid from Sophora flavescens, on cyclooxygenase-2 and in vivo inflammatory response. College of Pharmacy, Kangwon National University, Chunchon, Korea. Arch Pharm Res. 2002 Jun;25(3):329-35.
6. Tohda C, Kakihara Y, Komatsu K, Kuraishi Y. Inhibitory effects of methanol extracts of herbal medicines on substance P-induced itch-scratch response. Research Center for Ethnomedicines, Institute of Natural Medicine, Toyama Medical and Pharmaceutical University, Sugitani, Japan. Biol Pharm Bull. 2000 May;23(5):599-601.
7. Sung YY, Yoon T, Jang JY, Park SJ, Kim HK. Topical application of Rehmannia glutinosa extract inhibits mite allergen-induced atopic dermatitis in NC/Nga mice. Center of Herbal Resources Research, Korea Institute of Oriental Medicine, Daejeon 305-811, Republic of Korea. J Ethnopharmacol. 2011 Mar 8;134(1):37-44.
8. Sohn EH, Jang SA, Joo H, Park S, Kang SC, Lee CH, Kim SY. Anti-allergic and anti-inflammatory effects of butanol extract from Arctium Lappa L. Department of Pediatrics, College of Medicine, Hanyang University, Seoul, 133-792, Korea. Clin Mol Allergy. 2011 Feb 8;9(1):4.
9. Chan BC, Hon KL, Leung PC, Sam SW, Fung KP, Lee MY, Lau HY. Traditional Chinese medicine for atopic eczema: PentaHerbs formula suppresses inflammatory mediators release from mast cells. J Ethnopharmacol. 2008 Oct 30;120(1):85-91.
10. Wang CC, Chen LG, Yang LL. Inducible nitric oxide synthase inhibitor of the Chinese herb I. Saposhnikovia divaricata (Turcz.) Schischk. Cancer Lett. 1999 Oct 18;145(1-2):151-7.
11. Tezuka Y., Irikawa S., Kaneko T., Banskota A.H., Nagaoka T., Xiong Q., Hase K., Kadota S. Screening of Chinese herbal drug extracts for inhibitory activity on nitric oxide production and identification of an active compound of *Zanthoxylum bungeanum*. *J Ethnopharmacol.* 2001, 77(2-3): 209-217.
12. *Sheng Yao Xue Za Zhi* (Journal of Raw Herbology), 1979; 33(3):178.
13. Chao WW, Kuo YH, Li WC, Lin BF. The production of nitric oxide and prostaglandin E2 in peritoneal macrophages is inhibited by Andrographis paniculata, Angelica sinensis and Morus alba ethyl acetate fractions. Department of Biochemical Science and Technology, Institute of Microbiology and Biochemistry, National Taiwan University, Taipei 106, Taiwan, ROC. J Ethnopharmacol. 2009 Feb 25;122(1):68-75.
14. Kim JH, Park YM, Shin JS, Park SJ, Choi JH, Jung HJ, Park HJ, Lee KT. Fraxinellone inhibits lipopolysaccharide-induced inducible nitric oxide

synthase and cyclooxygenase-2 expression by negatively regulating nuclear factor-kappa B in RAW 264.7 macrophages cells. Biol Pharm Bull. 2009 Jun;32(6):1062-8.

15. Shin KM, Kim YH, Park WS, Kang I, Ha J, Choi JW, Park HJ, Lee KT. Inhibition of methanol extract from the fruits of Kochia scoparia on lipopolysaccharide-induced nitric oxide, prostaglandin [correction of prostagladin] E2, and tumor necrosis factor-alpha production from murine macrophage RAW 264.7 cells. Biol Pharm Bull. 2004 Apr;27(4):538-43.
16. Hwang SM, Lee YJ, Yoon JJ, Lee SM, Kang DG, Lee HS. Gardenia jasminoides inhibits tumor necrosis factor-alpha-induced vascular inflammation in endothelial cells. Professional Graduate School of Oriental Medicine, Wonkwang University, Chonbuk, Republic of Korea. Phytother Res. 2010 Jun;24 Suppl 2:S214-9.
17. *Zhong Cao Yao Tong Xun* (Journal of Chinese Herbal Medicine), 1976; 1:35.
18. *Tian Jing Yi Xue Za Zhi* (Journal of Tianjing Medicine and Herbology), 1966; 3:209.
19. *Shan Xi Yi Yao Za Zhi* (Shanxi Journal of Medicine and Herbology), 1975; 5:69.
20. *Zhong Yi Za Zhi* (Journal of Chinese Medicine), 12:18.
21. *Chi Jiao Yi Sheng Za Zhi* (Journal of Barefoot Doctors), 1975; 6:21.

Symmetry™

CLINICAL APPLICATIONS

- **Bell's palsy**
- **Facial paralysis**
- **TMJ (temporomandibular joint) pain**
- **Trigeminal neuralgia**
- **Migraine headache** due to wind, phlegm, and blood stagnation
- **Post-stroke sequelae,** such as twitching of muscles

WESTERN THERAPEUTIC ACTIONS

- Neurological benefits to treat facial paralysis, trigeminal neuralgia and migraine headache
- Analgesic effect to relieve pain
- Anti-inflammatory effect to reduce swelling and inflammation
- Antiseizure and antiepileptic effects to treat post-stroke sequelae and relieve nerve-related pain

CHINESE THERAPEUTIC ACTIONS

- Releases exterior wind
- Opens the channels and collaterals
- Activates qi and blood circulation

DOSAGE

Take 4 to 6 capsules three times daily. Herbal therapy should begin immediately on notice of the first warning signs. If necessary, the dosage may be increased to 8 capsules three times daily on day one of herbal therapy to achieve faster onset of action. If the herbs are irritating to the stomach where the patient reports nausea or epigastric discomfort, take the herbs after meals.

INGREDIENTS

Bai Fu Zi (Rhizoma Typhonii)
Bai Zhi (Radix Angelicae Dahuricae)
Chuan Xiong (Rhizoma Chuanxiong)
Dang Gui (Radix Angelicae Sinensis)
Fang Feng (Radix Saposhnikoviae)
Jiang Can (Bombyx Batryticatus)
Jing Jie (Herba Schizonepetae)
Quan Xie (Scorpio)
Si Gua Luo (Retinervus Luffae Fructus)
Wu Gong (Scolopendra)
Yan Hu Suo (Rhizoma Corydalis)

BACKGROUND

Bell's palsy, facial paralysis, trigeminal neuralgia, and TMJ (temporomandibular joint) disorder are complicated neurological disorders that affect the head region. These disorders affect different nerves in the face and the head, leading to numbness, pain, and loss of sensory or musculoskeletal functions. The causes are not always known, but are generally attributed to damage to the cranial nerves.

FORMULA EXPLANATION

According to traditional Chinese medicine, trigeminal neuralgia and facial paralysis are two conditions characterized by wind attacking the channels and collaterals in the facial regions, leading to blocked circulation of qi and blood. As a result, there is often severe pain, numbness, loss of muscle tone, and paralysis of the muscles. Optimal treatment of this condition requires use of herbs to release exterior wind, open the channels and collaterals, and activate qi and blood circulation.

Symmetry is formulated based on *Qian Zheng San* (Lead to Symmetry Powder), a classic formula that treats deviation of the eyes and mouth by restoring symmetry of the face. Following this general principle, ***Symmetry*** uses *Fang Feng* (Radix Saposhnikoviae), *Bai Zhi* (Radix Angelicae Dahuricae) and *Jing Jie* (Herba Schizonepetae) to release exterior wind, and *Quan Xie* (Scorpio) and *Wu Gong* (Scolopendra) to dispel interior Liver wind. In addition, *Bai Fu Zi* (Rhizoma Typhonii) and *Jiang Can* (Bombyx Batryticatus) dispel wind and eliminate phlegm obstruction. *Dang Gui* (Radix Angelicae Sinensis) tonifies blood in the channels and collaterals, and treats the underlying deficiency. *Yan Hu Suo* (Rhizoma Corydalis) and *Chuan Xiong* (Rhizoma Chuanxiong) activate qi and blood circulation and relieve pain. *Si Gua Luo* (Retinervus Luffae Fructus) opens the peripheral channels and collaterals.

Overall, ***Symmetry*** is a strong formula to treat various disorders of the face, including but not limited to trigeminal neuralgia, facial paralysis, TMJ disorder, and migraine headache.

CAUTIONS & CONTRAINDICATIONS

- This formula is strong and potent, and contains herbs that are considered slightly toxic in traditional Chinese medicine. Therefore, the dosage should be prescribed carefully according to the age, body weight and severity of the condition. For additional details, *see* Strategic Dosing Guidelines for age-to-dose and weight-to-dose charts on page 14.
- This formula is contraindicated during pregnancy and nursing. It should be used with extreme caution in pediatric and geriatric patients, and only when the benefits outweigh the risks.
- This herbal formula contains herbs that invigorate blood circulation, such as *Dang Gui* (Radix Angelicae Sinensis). Therefore, patients who are on anticoagulant or antiplatelet therapies, such as Coumadin (warfarin), should use this formula with caution, or not at all, as there may be a higher risk of bleeding and bruising.[1,2,3]

CLINICAL NOTES

- Early and frequent treatment of Bell's palsy will ensure proper recovery. Acupuncture and moxa are extremely effective to treat this condition. In acute cases, patients are recommended to receive acupuncture treatment three times a week. Moxa on the local area for at least 20 minutes each day will also enhance recovery.

Symmetry™

- Stress or Liver qi stagnation may be triggering factors for many women who suffer from Bell's palsy. In such cases, maintenance and preventative formulas such as ***Calm*** or ***Calm (ES)*** should be taken regularly to prevent repeated attacks in the future.
- Bell's palsy is the prodromal sign of a future stroke in some patients. After successfully treating the symptoms, patients should be put on another formula to nourish yin or lower Liver wind to prevent future attacks. *See* Supplementary Formulas.
- This formula is an adjunct formula to acupuncture treatment. Optimal results will occur when acupuncture, electro-stimulation and herbs are all included in the treatment regime.
- For deviation of the eyes and mouth, topical application of herbs is also beneficial. The topical preparation may be prepared by mixing extract powder of *Bai Jie Zi* (Semen Sinapis) with concentrated green tea. This herbal paste is to be applied topically to the affected area for four to eight hours (the affected side in Bell's palsy can be determined by the side of the eye that cannot close). This process may be repeated daily, or every other day.
- For trigeminal neuralgia, the topical use of herbs is also very beneficial. One topical preparation that has been used with great success contains *Ma Qian Zi* (Semen Strychni) 30g, *Zhi Chuan Wu* (Radix Aconiti Praeparata) 15g, *Zhi Cao Wu* (Radix Aconiti Kusnezoffii Praeparata) 15g, *Ru Xiang* (Gummi Olibanum) 15g, and *Mo Yao* (Myrrha) 15g. This topical preparation is made by grinding all the ingredients into a fine powder and then mixing it with oil to form an herbal paste. A small amount of herbal paste is to be applied topically to acupuncture points around the affected area, such as *Taiyang*, *Xiaguan* (ST 7), and *Jiache* (ST 6). [Note: These five herbs must be used only topically, and ***not*** internally, as internal ingestion of some of these herbs may be toxic.]

SUPPLEMENTARY FORMULAS

- For post-stroke patients with mental and physical deterioration, combine with ***Neuro Plus***.
- For severe nerve pain, combine with ***Flex (NP)***.
- For severe and acute migraine headache, add ***Corydalin (AC)***.
- For chronic and moderate migraine headache due to blood deficiency, combine with ***Corydalin (CR)***.
- With neck and shoulder pain, add ***Neck & Shoulder (AC)***.
- With excessive stress, add ***Calm*** or ***Calm (ES)***.
- For postpartum Bell's palsy with qi and blood deficiency, add ***Imperial Tonic***.
- With high blood pressure or prevention of stroke, combine with ***Gastrodia Complex*** or ***Gentiana Complex***.

ACUPUNCTURE TREATMENT

Traditional Points:

- **Bell's palsy or facial paralysis:**
  - Needle the affected side (the side with the eye and/or mouth that cannot close): *Jiache* (ST 6), *Dicang* (ST 4), *Xiaguan* (ST 7), *Sibai* (ST 2), *Yangbai* (GB 14), *Taiyang*, *Yingxiang* (LI 20), *Chengjiang* (CV 24), *Yifeng* (TH 17), *Fengchi* (GB 20), *Hegu* (LI 4), *Zanzhu* (BL 2)
  - In severe cases, more aggressive treatment is necessary. Thread the needle underneath the skin from *Dicang* (ST 4) towards *Jiache* (ST 6), *Yangbai* (GB 14) towards *Yuyao*, *Zanzhu* (BL 2) towards *Jingming* (BL 1), *Yingxiang* (LI 20) towards *Sibai* (ST 2), and *Renzhong* (GV 26) towards *Dicang* (ST 4). These points are needled subcutaneously at least 1 *cun* parallel to the skin. Once the needle is inserted, be careful to not have the tip of the needle penetrate out of the skin.
- **Trigeminal neuralgia**:
  - Strongly stimulate the following points: *Zanzhu* (BL 2), *Xiaguan* (ST 7), *Daying* (ST 5), *Yuyao*, *Sibai* (ST 2), *Chengjiang* (CV 24), *Yintang*, *Tinggong* (SI 19)
  - Alternate points in Group 1 and 2 from treatment to treatment. Needle and bleed these points.
  - Group 1: *Shangxing* (GV 23), *Wuchu* (BL 5), *Chengguang* (BL 6), *Tongtian* (BL 7), *Luoque* (BL 8)
  - Group 2: *Qianding* (GV 21), *Baihui* (GV 20), *Toulinqi* (GB 15), *Muchuang* (GB 16), *Zhengying* (GB 17), *Chengling* (GB 18)
  - Select a few points and alternate between them: *Hegu* (LI 4), *Taiyang*, *Yangbai* (GB 14), *Zanzhu* (BL 2), *Tongziliao* (GB 1), *Xiaguan* (ST 7), *Juliao* (GB 29), *Jiache* (ST 6), *Daying* (ST 5), and *Tinghui* (GB 2).

Classic Master Tung's Points:

- **Facial paralysis:** *Sanchasan* (T 22.17)*, *Wanshunyi* (T 22.08), *Wanshuner* (T 22.09), *Dizong* (T 44.09), *Cesanli* (T 77.22), *Cexiasanli* (T 77.23), *Yizhong* (T 77.05), *Erzhong* (T 77.06), *Sanzhong* (T 77.07), *Shangquan* (T 88.22). *Zhongquan* (T 88.21), *Xiaquan* (T 88.20) , *Zhenghui* (T 1010.01), *Dicang* (ST 4), *Jiache* (ST 6), *Zhisanzhong* (T 11.14). Bleed dark veins nearby the temporal area. Bleed before needling for best result.
- **TMJ (temporomandibular joint) pain:** *Tianhuang* (T 88.13), *Minghuang* (T 88.12), *Qihuang* (T 88.14), *Tongshen* (T 88.09), *Shangquan* (T 88.22), *Xiaquan* (T 88.20) *Wanshunyi* (T 22.08), *Wanshuner* (T 22.09), *Sanzhong* (T 77.07), *Huoying* (T 66.03)
- **Trigeminal neuralgia:** *Yizhong* (T 77.05), *Erzhong* (T 77.06), *Sanzhong* (T 77.07), *Shangquan* (T 88.22), *Zhongquan* (T 88.21), *Xiaquan* (T 88.20), *Cesanli* (T 77.22), *Zhongjiuli* (T 88.25). Bleed the ear lobe and the *ah shi* points. Bleed before needling for best result.
- **Migraine:** *Linggu* (T 22.05), *Dabai* (T 22.04), *Cesanli* (T 77.22), *Yizhong* (T 77.05), *Erzhong* (T 77.06). *Sanzhong* (T 77.07), *Liuwan* (T 66.08), *Zhongjiuli* (T 88.25)
- **Post-stroke sequelae (twitching of muscles):** *Minghuang* (T 88.12), *Tianhuang* (T 88.13), *Qihuang* (T 88.14), *Zhenghui* (T 1010.01), *Qianhui* (T 1010.05), *Houhui* (T 1010.06), *Houxi* (SI 3) to *Laogong* (PC 8), *Gongsun* (SP 4) to *Yongquan* (KI 1), *Sanchayi* (T 22.15)*, *Sanchaer* (T 22.16)*, *Sanchasan* (T 22.17)*, *Bafeng*, *Baxie*

Symmetry™

Balance Method by Dr. Richard Tan:

- Left side: *Sanjian* (LI 3), *Zhongzhu* (TH 3), *Ququan* (LR 8)
- Right side: *ah shi* points around *Chize* (LU 5) to *Kongzui* (LU 6), *Quze* (PC 3) to *Ximen* (PC 4), *Shaohai* (HT 3) to *Lingdao* (HT 4), *Zulinqi* (GB 41), *Xiangu* (ST 43)
- Alternate sides from treatment to treatment. Patient should receive acupuncture treatment at least twice a week for optimal result.

Auricular Medicine by Dr. Li-Chun Huang:

- **Trigeminal neuralgia:** Auricular Temporal Nerve, Brain Stem, *San Jiao*. Bleed Ear Apex.
  - For neuralgia of the first branch of the trigeminal nerve, add Forehead and Eye.
  - For neuralgia of the maxilla nerve, add Upper Jaw and Upper Palate.
  - For neuralgia of the mandibular nerve, add Lower Jaw and Lower Palate.
- **Facial paralysis:** Cheek Area, Brain Stem, *Sanjiao*, Endocrine, Adrenal Gland, Mouth, Sympathetic, Liver, Spleen, Coronary Vascular Subcortex. Bleed Ear Apex and Helix 5.
- **Epilepsy:** Epilepsy Point, Brain, Brain Stem, Nervous Subcortex, Occiput, *Shenmen*, Kidney, Liver. Bleed Ear Apex.
- **Temporomandibular joint (TMJ) pain:** TMJ (front and back), *San Jiao*, Teeth and Larynx, Mouth. Bleed Helix 4 or Helix 5.

NUTRITION

- Consume adequate amounts of vegetables for vitamins A, B_1, B_2, C and E.
- Encourage a diet with a diverse source of all nutrients, including raw fruits, vegetables, whole grains, nuts, and seeds. B vitamins are important to maintain nerve health.
- Avoid cold, icy food and beverages, fried, smoked or barbecued foods. Stop smoking and avoid drinking alcohol.
- Advise patients to avoid all aluminum products, which may be found in antacids, cookware, aluminum foil, and certain foods. Drinking steam-distilled water has a chelating effect in the blood to remove unwanted aluminum from the body.

LIFESTYLE INSTRUCTIONS

- Advise patients to exercise daily and maintain a positive, hopeful outlook toward the future.
- Regular workout and deep breathing exercises are excellent ways to oxygenate the blood and improve circulation to all parts of the body to facilitate recovery.
- When recovering from a stroke or Bell's palsy, engage in regular and mild exercises, such as walking and *tai chi chuan [tai ji chuan]*. However, it is important to advise the patient to avoid exposure to wind and cold. In addition, biking, and direct exposure to either fans or air conditioning is strictly prohibited.

CASE STUDIES

- B.T., a 33-year-old male, presented with Bell's palsy located on the left facial area without wrinkles on his forehead. The patient was able to close his left eye with effort and needed to wear an eye patch at night. The action he was unable to perform was lifting the left angle of his mouth or smile. Attempted treatments by ER doctors included short courses of prednisone and Zovirax (acyclovir). Previously, before it occurred, the patient had recently installed an air conditioner in his room in addition to experiencing increased stress. The client was not experiencing pain at this time. With the TCM diagnosis of invasion of wind and Liver qi stagnation, ***Symmetry*** was prescribed. After three treatments and five days of taking ***Symmetry***, the client was able to close his eye comfortably without needing the eye patch at night. He was also able to raise the left angle of his mouth and wrinkle his forehead by 30% of normal. Submitted by C.S., Hood River, Oregon.
- A 44-year-old male presented with Bell's palsy affecting the right side of his face, which had begun one week prior. Additional symptoms included left side frontal headache, fatigue, and stress. His medical reports ruled out possible ischemic and hemorrhagic strokes. Objective findings during his neurological exam were the patient being unable to pucker his lips, smile, or close and blink his right eye. The practitioner diagnosed this condition as wind phlegm and damp obstructing the channels of the face. ***Symmetry*** was prescribed at six capsules three times a day. He continued taking it for three bottles. Treatment of acupuncture was given four times a week with smokeless moxa as well on the right side of his face. After the first acupuncture treatment, his mouth was getting better and he was able to smile. Furthermore, after eleven days of contracting Bell's palsy, the patient had reported a 70% improvement. The patient's pucker and facial dimples returned and he no longer need to tape his eye closed at night after receiving three treatments of acupuncture and taking ***Symmetry***. Submitted by G.T., San Diego, California.
- S.H., a 54-year-old female, presented with acute symptoms of numbness of the tongue, pain and inability to close the mouth. Objective findings were drooping eyes and lips, affected smile, and tenderness on the left nostril. Her mother had died around the same age due to a stroke. She has a tendency to ride her bike to work, enjoying the wind, and works a stressful job. Pulse was wiry and tongue was deviated with thick greasy tongue coating. The practitioner diagnosed the condition as exterior wind attack blocking the channels. Her Western diagnosis was Bell's palsy with one-sided facial paralysis. The patient was given ***Symmetry*** for a period of two weeks. With ***Symmetry*** the patient returned to pre-stroke condition after just two weeks. Submitted by K.F., Honolulu, Hawaii.
- M.H., a 75-year-old male, presented with fatigue, overworked, and had recently experienced a mini-stroke in which he could not walk for 24 hours. Tongue was slightly deviated to the left and pulse was deep and slippery. The TCM diagnosis was Spleen

Symmetry™

and Kidney yang deficiencies; the Western diagnosis was a 6 mm lesion in the poris medulla. After taking ***Symmetry*** and ***Neuro Plus***, the patient felt less confused, more focused, and was able to walk again without struggle. He continued to take the herbs for five months to maintain his results. Submitted by V.G., Virginia Beach, Virginia.

☯ A 50-year-old female suffered from deviation of her eye and mouth on the right side of the face. The patient had yellow tongue coating, and a wiry, fine, slippery, and rapid pulse. Upon more inquiry, the condition was diagnosed as wind attacking the channels and collaterals, with underlying deficiencies. The patient was treated with both electro-acupuncture and modified ***Symmetry***. In addition, the patient was instructed to apply herbs topically to the affected area at night, removing them in the morning (the topical preparation was made by mixing *Bai Jie Zi* (Semen Sinapis) with concentrated green tea). After three courses of treatment, the overall condition was greatly improved. The deviation was not noticeable at rest, and only slightly noticeable when laughing. The patient continued to be treated on a regular basis, and eventually reported complete recovery. Submitted Anonymously.

PHARMACOLOGICAL AND CLINICAL RESEARCH

Symmetry is designed specifically to treat disorders affecting the facial regions, such as facial paralysis or hemiplegia in stroke sequelae, Bell's palsy, TMJ (temporomandibular joint) pain and trigeminal neuralgia. ***Symmetry*** contains herbs with neurological benefits to treat facial paralysis, analgesic effects to relieve pain, anti-inflammatory effects to reduce swelling and inflammation, and antiseizure and antiepileptic effects to treat post-stroke sequelae.

Bai Fu Zi (Rhizoma Typhonii), *Jiang Can* (Bombyx Batryticatus) and *Quan Xie* (Scorpio) are the three principle herbs in this formula. Together, these three herbs have shown remarkable effect via numerous clinical studies to treat facial paralysis, trigeminal neuralgia and migraine headache. According to one study, concurrent use of acupuncture and herbs [*Bai Fu Zi* (Rhizoma Typhonii), *Jiang Can* (Bombyx Batryticatus), *Quan Xie* (Scorpio) and others] were successful in treating 52 of 60 patients with facial paralysis.[4] According to another study, concurrent use of acupuncture and herbs [*Bai Fu Zi* (Rhizoma Typhonii), *Jiang Can* (Bombyx Batryticatus), *Quan Xie* (Scorpio) and others] for two days to one year was associated with 95% effective rate in 88 patients with facial paralysis.[5] In addition, use of these three herbs in an herbal formula successfully treated 50 patients with facial paralysis with a 98% rate of effectiveness (complete recovery in 44 cases, significant improvement in 3 cases, moderate improvement in 2 cases, and no effect in 1 case).[6] For trigeminal neuralgia, one study reported 94.2% rate of effectiveness among 52 patients when treated with *Bai Fu Zi* (Rhizoma Typhonii), *Jiang Can* (Bombyx Batryticatus), *Quan Xie* (Scorpio) and others.[7] Finally, these three herbs also showed good results to treat 25 patients with stubborn migraine headache. The overall rate of effectiveness was 92%.[8]

Symmetry also contains many herbs with analgesic effects to relieve pain and anti-inflammatory effects to reduce swelling and inflammation. *Yan Hu Suo* (Rhizoma Corydalis), *Bai Zhi* (Radix Angelicae Dahuricae) and *Dang Gui* (Radix Angelicae Sinensis) all have excellent analgesic and anti-inflammatory effects. *Yan Hu Suo* (Rhizoma Corydalis) may be used to treat pain of various origins.[9,10] *Bai Zhi* (Radix Angelicae Dahuricae) is most effective for treating headache.[11,12] *Dang Gui* (Radix Angelicae Sinensis) is excellent for migraine headache, with a potency comparable to that of acetylsalicylic acid.[13,14] *Chuan Xiong* (Rhizoma Chuanxiong) has been used in various formulas to treat headache (95.1% success rate),[15] vascular headache (96.3% rate of effectiveness),[16] trigeminal nerve pain (90.6% rate of effectiveness),[17] and trigeminal neuralgia.[18] Lastly, *Bai Fu Zi* (Rhizoma Typhonii) in formulas has been shown to have good success to treat numbness and pain of the facial nerves.[19]

Many herbs in ***Symmetry*** also have marked antiseizure and antiepileptic effects to prevent seizure and epilepsy, and to treat post-stroke sequelae. Herbs with such actions include *Jiang Can* (Bombyx Batryticatus),[20] *Quan Xie* (Scorpio),[21] and *Wu Gong* (Scolopendra).[22] In addition, use of these herbs is associated with very little toxicity in mice studies.[23]

In summary, ***Symmetry*** is an excellent formula to treat disorders affecting the face. It restores symmetry to the face for disorders such as facial paralysis and Bell's palsy. It also relieves pain to treat TMJ (temporomandibular joint) pain, trigeminal neuralgia, and migraine headache.

COMPARATIVE ANALYSIS

Neurological disorders are complicated illnesses that encompass many different diseases, including but not limited to Bell's palsy, facial paralysis, TMJ (temporomandibular joint) pain, and trigeminal neuralgia. From Western medicine perspectives, these diseases are well-defined and accurately diagnosed, but not successfully treated. Though there are some drugs available for symptomatic treatment, such as use of antiseizure or tricyclic antidepressants for nerve pain, none are very effective and all have serious side effects. Furthermore, there are simply no effective pharmaceutical treatments for either the symptoms or the cause of conditions such as Bell's palsy and facial paralysis. As a result, these conditions continue to deteriorate, creating more debilitation and suffering.

TCM has long excelled in the treatment of such neurological disorders with both acupuncture and herbs. There are numerous options available to stimulate the central and peripheral nervous systems to help relieve symptoms and restore normal functions. Generally speaking, the prognosis is excellent if treatment begins within three months from the onset of illness, positive within one year, and hopeful if within three years. TCM treatments using both acupuncture and herbs should be explored and aggressively implemented as early and as much as possible to achieve maximum results. Time delay before treatment only decreases the overall success rate.

TCM treatments offer safe and effective options for treatment of these neurological disorders, and are significantly superior to Western medicine.

References

1. Chan K, Lo AC, Yeung JH, Woo KS. Journal of Pharmacy and Pharmacology 1995 May;47(5):402-6.
2. Pharmacotherapy 1999 July;19(7):870-876.
3. European Journal of Drug Metabolism and Pharmacokinetics 1995; 20(1): 55-60.
4. *Nei Meng Gu Zhong Yi Yao* (Traditional Chinese Medicine and Medicinals of Inner Magnolia), 1990; 9(4):18.
5. *Shi Zhen Guo Yao Yan Jiu* (Research of Shizhen Herbs), 1996; 7(1):13.
6. *He Bei Zhong Yi* (Hebei Chinese Medicine) 1985;4:30.
7. *Si Chuan Zhong Yi* (Sichuan Chinese Medicine), 1998; 2:25.
8. *Shi Yong Zhong Yi Yao Za Zhi* (Journal of Practical Chinese Medicine and Medicinals) 1997;2:5.
9. *Zhong Yao Yao Li Yu Ying Yong* (Pharmacology and Applications of Chinese Herbs), 1983; 447.
10. *Biol Pharm Bull*, 1994:Feb; 17(2):262-5.
11. *Xin Yi Xue* (New Medicine), 1976; 1:8.
12. *Xin Yi Yao Xue Za Zhi* (New Journal of Medicine and Herbology), 1976; 8:35.
13. *Xin Yi Yao Xue Za Zhi* (New Journal of Medicine and Herbology), 1975; (6):34.
14. *Bei Jing Yi Xue* (Beijing Medicine), 1988; 2:95.
15. *Shan Xi Zhong Yi Za Zhi* (Shanxi Journal Chinese Medicine), 1985; 10:447.
16. *Si Chuan Zhong Yi* (Sichuan Chinese Medicine), 1996; (11):27.
17. *He Bei Zhong Yi Za Zhi* (Hebei Journal of Chinese Medicine), 1982; 4:34.
18. *Zhong Yao Lin Chuan Xin Yong* (New Clinical Applications of Chinese Medicine), 2001; 65.
19. *Hu Bei Zhong Yi Za Zhi* (Hubei Journal of Chinese Medicine), 1982; 1:33.
20. *Jiang Su Yi Yao* (Jiangsu Journal of Medicine and Herbology), 1976; 2:33.
21. *Si Chuan Zhong Yi* (Sichuan Chinese Medicine), 1991; 9(11):12.
22. *Zhong Yao Xue* (Chinese Herbology), 1998; 704:706.
23. Wang CG, et al. Molecular characterization of an anti-epilepsy peptide from the scorpion Buthus martensi Karsch. State Key Laboratory of Molecular Biology, Shanghai Institute of Biochemistry, China. Eur J Biochem. 2001 Apr;268(8):2480-5.

Thyrodex ™

CLINICAL APPLICATIONS

- **Hyperthyroidism**
  - with low-grade fever, tachycardia (90 to 120 heartbeats per minute), tremors of the tongue and fingers, enlarged thyroid gland, unilateral or bilateral swollen and bulging eyes
  - with palpitations or tachycardia, fatigue, weight loss, fidgeting, irritability, bad temper, aversion to heat, perspiration, hunger and increased appetite, and increased blood pressure

WESTERN THERAPEUTIC ACTIONS

- Lowers the level of thyroid hormone in the blood
- Reduces enlargement of the thyroid gland
- Treats the unwanted "sympathetic excess" signs and symptoms of hyperthyroidism

CHINESE THERAPEUTIC ACTIONS

- Softens hardness, resolves nodules, and eliminates phlegm
- Clears toxic heat and drains Liver fire
- Tranquilizes the *shen* (spirit)
- Tonifies qi and yin

DOSAGE

Take 3 to 4 capsules three times daily. However, the dosage may need to be adjusted based on age, body weight, severity of condition, and response to the treatment. Patients with hyperthyroidism (other than thyrotoxicosis) should notice dramatic improvement within one to one-and-a-half months of herbal treatment.

INGREDIENTS

Bie Jia (Carapax Trionycis)
Chuan Niu Xi (Radix Cyathulae)
Fang Feng (Radix Saposhnikoviae)
Gan Cao (Radix et Rhizoma Glycyrrhizae)
Huang Qi (Radix Astragali)
Mu Li (Concha Ostreae)
Xia Ku Cao (Spica Prunellae)
Xuan Shen (Radix Scrophulariae)
Yuan Zhi (Radix Polygalae)
Zhe Bei Mu (Bulbus Fritillariae Thunbergii)
Zhi Huang Qi (Radix Astragali Praeparata cum Melle)
Zhi Mu (Rhizoma Anemarrhenae)
Zhi Zi (Fructus Gardeniae)

BACKGROUND

Hyperthyroidism is thyroid hormone excess with clinical manifestations such tachycardia, fatigue, weight loss, nervousness, tremor, heat intolerance, increased appetite and hunger, and in some cases, unilateral or bilateral swollen and bulging eyes. Hyperthyroidism may be caused by autoimmune disorder (Grave's disease), iodine excess, and hyperfunctioning (toxic adenoma, toxic multinodular goiter) or inflammation (thyroiditis) of the thyroid glands. Optimal management requires treatment of the cause and balancing of the thyroid hormones.

FORMULA EXPLANATION

According to traditional Chinese medicine, hyperthyroidism is a combination of qi and yin deficiencies, Liver fire rising, and phlegm stagnation. The fundamental causes are qi and yin deficiencies while the symptoms and signs show Liver fire and phlegm stagnation. Treatment, therefore, must address both the cause and the symptoms simultaneously.

Bie Jia (Carapax Trionycis) nourishes yin and resolves hard lumps. *Xuan Shen* (Radix Scrophulariae) and *Zhi Mu* (Rhizoma Anemarrhenae) have three important functions: replenishing the *jing* (essence), clearing heat and resolving hard lumps in the body. *Zhi Zi* (Fructus Gardeniae) and *Xia Ku Cao* (Spica Prunellae) clear heat and purge Liver fire. They reduce the "sympathetic excess" signs and symptoms commonly associated with hyperthyroidism, such as increased heart rate, increased blood pressure, and tremor. *Zhe Bei Mu* (Bulbus Fritillariae Thunbergii) resolves phlegm and further assists *Xia Ku Cao* (Spica Prunellae) to disperse lumps and hardenings. Clinically, *Zhe Bei Mu* (Bulbus Fritillariae Thunbergii) and *Mu Li* (Concha Ostreae) are commonly used to treat goiter. *Chuan Niu Xi* (Radix Cyathulae) stimulates blood circulation and enhances the overall effectiveness of the formula. *Yuan Zhi* (Radix Polygalae) calms the *shen* (spirit) and relieves nervousness and anxiety. *Gan Cao* (Radix et Rhizoma Glycyrrhizae) harmonizes all the herbs of the formula. *Fang Feng* (Radix Saposhnikoviae) and *Huang Qi* (Radix Astragali), two principle herbs in the formula *Yu Ping Feng San* (Jade Windscreen Powder), have excellent effects to strengthen *wei* (defensive) *qi* and stop perspiration.

Together, herbs in ***Thyrodex*** effectively treat hyperthyroidism by clearing heat and fire, eliminate phlegm accumulation, and nourish qi and yin.

CAUTIONS & CONTRAINDICATIONS

- This formula is contraindicated during pregnancy and nursing.
- Patients with thyrotoxicosis or thyroid storm require emergency medical treatment. Warning signs and symptoms of thyroid storm or thyrotoxicosis include high fever, tachycardia, fidgeting, irritability, nausea, vomiting, obvious weight loss, profuse perspiration, delirium, and possible loss of unconsciousness.
- The etiology of Grave's disease is the excessive stimulation by the immune system of the thyroid gland to produce thyroid hormone. Therefore, during the acute inflammatory phase of the disease when the immune system is activated by the presence of pathogens, qi tonics that boost the immune system, such as *Huang Qi* (Radix Astragali) in this formula, should not be used since this herb may further stimulate the immune system. During this acute inflammatory phase, ***Gardenia Complex***

Thyrodex ™

is a more suitable formula as it has herbs that clear heat and fire to suppress the immune system and reduce inflammation throughout the entire body.

CLINICAL NOTES

- Patients with hyperthyroidism (other than thyrotoxicosis) should notice dramatic improvement within one to one-and-a-half months of herbal treatment. Most symptoms should completely subside within three to six months of treatment. Protrusion of the eye(s) may persist despite herbal treatment.
- Patients with hyperthyroidism can be treated with drugs, herbs, or both. However, if both drugs and herbs are used, it is important to monitor the patient's condition frequently to ensure proper control of the signs and symptoms. Over-dosage with drugs and/or herbs may cause "hypothyroid-like" signs and symptoms, and under-dosage may contribute to "hyperthyroid-like" signs and symptoms.
- Practitioners should suspect hyperthyroidism when the following manifestations are present:
  - Young adults (especially female) who have a bad temper, hunger with excessive appetite, palpitations, and profuse perspiration.
  - Young adults (especially female) who are fidgety and irritable, have early menses with a light flow, amenorrhea, and significant weight loss.
  - Young adults with sudden onset of difficulty with physical movement, numbness of legs, or possible collapse of leg muscles while walking.
- *Thyrodex* is an herbal formula developed by Professor Xiao-Ping Zhang of Anhui Hospital of Traditional Chinese Medicine. It is an empirical formula designed to treat patients with hyperthyroidism. It has been used for over 30 years in China and has helped several thousand patients with hyperthyroidism.

Pulse Diagnosis by Dr. Jimmy Wei-Yen Chang:

- **Hyperthyroidism caused by pituitary gland problem:** floating, rapid, weak pulse on the *cun* positions.
- **Hyperthyroidism related to stress:** floating, rapid, weak pulse on the left *guan*.

SUPPLEMENTARY FORMULAS

- For high blood pressure and fast heart rate due to excess fire, add ***Gardenia Complex***.
- For anxiety and nervousness, add ***Calm (ES)***.
- For insomnia, add ***Schisandra ZZZ*** or ***Calm ZZZ***.
- For hypertension, use ***Gastrodia Complex*** or ***Gentiana Complex***.
- For enlarged thyroid, use with ***Resolve (AI)***.
- For thirst with dry mouth and throat, add ***Nourish (Fluids)***.
- With Kidney yin deficiency, add ***Nourish*** or ***Kidney Tonic (Yin)***.
- With blood stagnation, add ***Circulation (SJ)***.
- For dysmenorrhea, use ***Mense-Ease***.

ACUPUNCTURE TREATMENT

Traditional Points:

- *Huatoujiaji* points (Extra 15), *Jianshi* (PC 5), *Sanyinjiao* (SP 6), *Yinxi* (HT 6), *Fuliu* (KI 7), *Taixi* (KI 3), *Neiguan* (PC 6)
- *Xingjian* (LR 2), *Quchi* (LI 11)

Classic Master Tung's Points:

- **Hyperthyroidism:** *Sanzhong* (T 77.07), *Tongguan* (T 88.01), *Simashang* (T 88.18), *Simazhong* (T 88.17), *Simaxia* (T 88.19), *Xinling* (T 33.17)*, *Sihuashang* (T 77.08), *Yizhong* (T 77.05), *Erzhong* (T 77.06). Bleed the Helix on the earlobe. Bleed before needling for best result.
- **With bulging eyes:** *Sanzhong* (T 77.07), *Tongguan* (T 88.01), *Simashang* (T 88.18), *Simazhong* (T 88.17), *Simaxia* (T 88.19), *Xinling* (T 33.17)*, *Sihuashang* (T 77.08), *Yizhong* (T 77.05), *Erzhong* (T 77.06). Bleed the Helix on the earlobe. Bleed before needling for best result.

Master Tung's Points by Dr. Chuan-Min Wang:

- **Hyperthyroid:** *Yizhong* (T 77.05), *Erzhong* (T 77.06), *Sanzhong* (T 77.07)

Balance Method by Dr. Richard Tan:

- Left side: *Guanchong* (TH 1), *Yangchi* (TH 4), *Taichong* (LR 3), *Ququan* (LR 8)
- Right side: *Neiguan* (PC 6), *Zhongchong* (PC 9), *Chongyang* (ST 42), *Lidui* (ST 45), *Yanglingquan* (GB 34), *Zulinqi* (GB 41)
- *Yintang*, bilateral ear *Shenmen* and *Anmian*
- Left and right sides can be alternated from treatment to treatment.

Auricular Medicine by Dr. Li-Chun Huang:

- **Hyperthyroidism:** Thyroid, Pituitary, Endocrine, Thalamus, Nervous Subcortex, Kidney, Liver, Heart, Occiput, *Shenmen*. Bleed Ear Apex.
- **Simple goiter:** Thyroid, Endocrine, Pituitary, Thalamus, *San Jiao*, Kidney, Liver

NUTRITION

- Consume plenty of the following foods: broccoli, brussel sprouts, cabbage, cauliflower, kale, mustard greens, peaches, pears, soybeans, spinach, and turnips. These foods may help to suppress thyroid hormone production.[1]
- Short-term consumption of foods rich in iodine will provide temporary relief of hyperthyroidism due to a negative feedback mechanism. Long-term consumption, however, is not recommended because foods rich in iodine will facilitate the production of thyroid hormone. Foods rich in iodine include sea salt, iodized salt, kelp, and sargassum.
- Eat a variety of fresh, organic fruits and vegetables of all colors.
- Incorporate more high-fiber whole grains and nuts into the diet.
- Drink warm or hot liquids with meals. Putting cold and ice on any part of the body will immediately constrict the flow of blood to

Thyrodex™

that region. Similarly, drinking cold or iced drinks with meals will hinder the natural peristaltic movements of the digestive system.

- Foods with antioxidant effects, such as vitamin A, C and E are beneficial as they neutralize the free radicals and minimize damage to cells. Beneficial foods include citrus fruits, carrots, green leaf vegetables, and green tea.
- Chew food completely and thoroughly. The digestive tract can process and absorb smaller pieces of food much better than food that is incompletely chewed. Larger pieces of food can lead to incomplete digestion and digestive discomfort.
- Always eat breakfast. According to the TCM clock, the most optimal time for the digestive system is in the morning from 8 to 10 a.m.
- Give the body two to three hours between the last meal of the day and bedtime. During sleep, the digestive system slows down as well. Make sure the body has adequate time to digest the food before going into sleep mode.
- If the patient is allergic to any food or feels uncomfortable after eating certain foods, then they should avoid eating these foods.
- Avoid fast food, processed foods, junk food, artificial sugars, and carbonated drinks. Stay away from meat, greasy food, alcohol, caffeine, tap water, iron supplements, and vegetables and fruits with pesticides.
- The Spleen is responsible for generating post-natal qi and good Spleen function also contributes to a healthy immune system. Foods that damage the Spleen should be avoided:
  - Avoid any and all foods that contain sugar, such as cake, dessert, candy, chocolate, canned juice, soft drinks, caffeinated drinks, stevia, sugar substitutes, agave, xylitol, and corn syrup.
  - Avoid raw or uncooked meats, such as sashimi, sushi, steak tartar, and seared meat. Minimize consumption of foods that are cooling in nature, including tofu, tomato, celery, asparagus, bamboo, seaweed, kelp, bitter melon, cucumber, gourd, luffa, eggplant, winter melon, watermelon, honeydew, citrus, oranges, guava, grapefruit, pineapple, plums, pear, banana, papaya, white radish, mustard leaf, potherb mustard, Chinese kale, napa, and bamboo sprout. Do not eat foods straight from the refrigerator. Long-term intake of cold fruits and vegetables like the ones listed above may be damaging to the Spleen. The cooling property of foods can be neutralized by cooking or adding 20 pieces of *Gou Qi Zi* (Fructus Lycii).
  - Avoid carbohydrates like white rice or bread as they may produce dampness.
  - No seafood especially shellfish, like crabs, oyster, scallops, clams, lobster and shrimp (they enter the *yangming* Stomach channel).
  - Avoid fermented foods like cheese or fermented tofu.
  - Do not eat dairy products, such as milk, cream, yogurt (except for unsweetened low-fat yogurt), cheese, and ice cream.
  - No lamb, beef, goose or duck.
  - Avoid deep-fried or greasy foods.
- Warm and hot natured foods that damage qi and yin should be avoided, such as:
  - certain fruits like mango and durian that produce heat.
  - stimulants like coffee, alcohol, and energy drinks.
  - spicy/pungent/aromatic vegetables such as pepper, garlic, onions, basil, rosemary, cumin, funnel, anise, leeks, chives, scallions, thyme, saffron, wormwood, mustard, chili pepper, and wasabi.
- Avoid food and drinks with artificial coloring.
- Consume as few meat products as possible. Do not eat processed meats, such as lunch meats, hot dogs and sausages, as they contain nitrites that are associated with inflammation and chronic disease.

The Tao of Nutrition by Dr. Maoshing Ni and Cathy McNease:

- **Goiter**
  - Make soup from dried (preferably green) orange peel, carrots, and seaweed.
  - Soak cherry pits in vinegar until they disintegrate, then apply locally.

LIFESTYLE INSTRUCTIONS

- Eliminate all stimulants, such as cigarette smoking, secondhand smoke, and caffeine from tea, coffee or soft drinks.
- Avoid vigorous exercise, hot tubs, and saunas.
- Advise the patients to engage in relaxing exercises, such as walking, *qi gong* or *tai chi chuan [tai ji chuan]*.
- Sleep by 10 p.m. In TCM, 11 p.m. to 1 a.m. is when the yin shifts to yang. It is crucial for the body to be at rest during this time for optimal health.

CASE STUDIES

- M.D., a 52-year-old female, presented with a nodule on the left thyroid, palpitation, agitation, shortness of breath with chest pressure, nausea, frequent urination, restless sleep and soft bowel movements. Her blood pressure was 110/70 mmHg and her heart rate was from 90 to 120 beats per minute. The Western diagnosis was hyperthyroidism. Her TCM diagnosis was Liver fire with Liver and Kidney yin deficiencies with phlegm stagnation. ***Thyrodex*** was prescribed. Within one week of acupuncture and herbs, the patients started to feel better Listed below is her lab report showing great improvement over a four-month period. All her symptoms continued to steadily and gradually improve. This is a great formula. Her medical doctor does not understand how her condition improved but had canceled her scheduled radiation treatment. She was very happy. Submitted by M.N., Knoxville, Tennessee.

Date	T4	T3	TSH
January	1.73	4.59	0.02
April	1.03	2.82	0.04

FORMULAS

Thyrodex™

- A 39-year-old female with hyperthyroidism had been diagnosed with Grave's disease. Subjective and objective signs and symptoms included goiter, exophthalmus, and insomnia. Objective laboratory analysis indicated elevation of thyroid hormone (T4) and decreased TSH. Conventional pharmaceutical and alternative medical treatments failed to improve her condition. When she sought Chinese medicine as a last measure prior to possible surgical intervention, she was instructed to take ***Thyrodex*** (4 capsules three times daily). After a short period of taking ***Thyrodex***, she noticed significant improvements in sleep habits and energy levels. The patient felt less irritable and anxious. Her eye discomfort also resolved. Furthermore, there were no side effects from the herbs whatsoever. The practitioner concluded an overall positive outcome and diminishing signs and symptoms of Grave's disease using ***Thyrodex***. Upon follow-ups visits, the lab results for thyroid hormones were within normal limits. Submitted by D. S., San Diego, California.
- A 46-year-old female with hyperthyroidism presented with the following symptoms: feelings of warmth and thirst, perspiration, fast metabolism, difficulty sleeping, chronic sore throat (worse at night), migraines, poor appetite in the morning, and frequent diarrhea. The pulse was thin and deep on the left side, and full on the right side. The tongue was pale and scalloped with a slightly thick white coat. The diagnosis was Kidney yin deficiency with Liver yang rising, accompanied by Spleen qi deficiency with dampness. The patient was instructed to take ***Thyrodex*** (4 capsules three times daily). After six months of treatment using ***Thyrodex***, the lab results showed normal levels of T4 and TSH (T3 was not tested). The patient's attitude and overall demeanor was quite upbeat. She continued to take ***Thyrodex*** (2 capsules three times daily). Both the medical doctor and the acupuncturist closely monitored her condition. Submitted by R.H., Ft. Collins, Colorado.
- M.C., a 55-year-old female, presented with trouble sleeping. Lab results showed hyperthyroidism, goiter and hypertension. Her blood pressure was 166/98 mmHg and her heart rate was 90 beats per minute. The diagnosis was Liver fire rising. ***Thyrodex*** was prescribed at 4 capsules three times a day. Thyroid hormones dropped from 10.34 to 4.88 in two months. Swelling in the neck was also better. Submitted by W.F., Bloomfield, New Jersey.
- D.E., a 49-year-old woman with a history of hyperthyroidism, presented with heart palpitations, sweating easily (especially at night), hunger, weight loss, and becoming easily agitated. Her blood pressure was 120/88 mmHg, with heart rate of 98 beats per minute. The Western diagnosis was hyperthyroidism; the TCM diagnosis was Stomach fire, Heart yin deficiency, and *wei* (defensive) *qi* deficiency. The patient was taking Tapazole at 2.5 to 5 mg per day. The practitioner prescribed ***Thyrodex*** at 3 to 4 capsules, three times daily, and acupuncture treatments. After commencing herbal treatment, the patient gradually reduced her Tapazole from 5.0 mg to 2.5 mg per day. In the course of two months of herbal treatment, the patient showed significant improvement with no more palpitations, sweating, or excessive hunger. Even with drug therapy reduced by 50%, TSH levels remained approximately the same while under herbal treatment. The patient continues to receive both herbal and acupuncture treatments. Submitted by D.L., Doylestown, Pennsylvania.
- L.S., a 45-year-old female, presented with hyperthyroidism, which she had been previously diagnosed with but was not interested in receiving Western treatment. Her symptoms consisted of rapid heart beat, weight loss, hair loss, and exhaustion. Blood tests had also confirmed the indication of her hyperthyroidism as well. The patient had noted she had a tendency to always feel stressed at work. After diagnosing this condition as Kidney yin deficiency with Liver qi stagnation, the patient was prescribed both ***Kidney Tonic (Yin)*** and ***Thyrodex***. With taking the herbs the patient reported that most of her symptoms had stabilized; however, the hair loss was still present. She continued to take the herbs for additional improvement. Submitted by B.L., Fort Myers, Florida.
- A 39-year-old female presented with elevated blood pressure, palpitations, hot flashes, anxiety, and swelling in her neck, with a heart rate of 92 beats per minute. The Western diagnosis was hyperthyroidism; the TCM diagnosis was Liver and Kidney yin deficiencies. After she began taking ***Thyrodex***, the patient experienced diminished hot flashes and anxiety. Her blood pressure remained unchanged but the goiter diminished in size. After ***Gastrodia Complex*** was added to the herbal treatment, the patient noticed improvement in her blood pressure after just one bottle. Submitted by P.W., Paulet, Vermont.

PHARMACOLOGICAL AND CLINICAL RESEARCH

Thyrodex is formulated to treat hyperthyroidism with increased thyroid hormone in the blood leading to many signs and symptoms similar to "sympathetic excess," such as increased blood pressure, tachycardia, and weight loss. Treatment should focus on reducing the amount of thyroid hormone, decreasing the enlargement of the thyroid gland, and relieving the signs and symptoms of hyperthyroidism.

Hyperthyroidism is characterized in part by the inflammation of the thyroid gland, such as thyroiditis. Therefore, herbs with anti-inflammatory effects are used in this formula to reduce the inflammation. *Fang Feng* (Radix Saposhnikoviae) has a marked effect to suppress inflammation via the inhibition of nitrite production by inducible nitric oxide synthase.[2] *Xia Ku Cao* (Spica Prunellae) shows anti-inflammatory activity by inhibiting lipopolysaccharide-induced prostaglandin E2 and nitric oxide in mouse macrophages.[3] *Zhi Zi* (Fructus Gardeniae) illustrates a dose-dependent effect to suppress vascular inflammation via inhibition of tumor necrosis factor-alpha (TNF-α).[4] *Zhi Mu* (Rhizoma Anemarrhenae) exhibits significant anti-inflammatory action by inhibiting cyclo-oxygenase-2, inducible nitric oxide synthase and 5-lipoxygenase.[5] Lastly, glycyrrhizin and glycyrrhetinic acid from *Gan Cao* (Radix et Rhizoma Glycyrrhizae) have demonstrated marked anti-inflammatory effects.

Thyrodex™

The proposed mechanism of anti-inflammatory action includes decreased permeability of the blood vessels, antihistamine functions, and decreased sensitivity to stimuli. The anti-inflammatory influence of glycyrrhizin and glycyrrhetinic acid is approximately 1/10th that of cortisone.[6]

Though the causes vary, the clinical signs and symptoms of hyperthyroidism are essentially the same: low-grade fever, heat intolerance, increased blood pressure, palpitations or tachycardia (90 to 120 heartbeats per minute), fidgeting, irritability, bad temper, fatigue, and enlarged thyroid gland. ***Thyrodex*** utilizes many herbs to specifically manage these symptoms of "sympathetic excess." *Fang Feng* (Radix Saposhnikoviae) and *Zhi Mu* (Rhizoma Anemarrhenae) have antipyretic effects to reduce fever.[7,8] *Xia Ku Cao* (Spica Prunellae) and *Xuan Shen* (Radix Scrophulariae) both have antihypertensive effects to reduce blood pressure. The mechanism of this antihypertensive effect is generally attributed to vasodilation.[9,10,11] *Zhi Zi* (Fructus Gardeniae) has a hypotensive effect. It stimulates the parasympathetic nervous system and decreases cardiac contractility and cardiac output.[12] *Yuan Zhi* (Radix Polygalae) and *Zhi Zi* (Fructus Gardeniae) have a suppressant effect on the central nervous system to treat anxiety, restlessness, insomnia, and other symptoms of hyperactivity.[13,14,15] *Huang Qi* (Radix Astragali) and *Gan Cao* (Radix et Rhizoma Glycyrrhizae) restore the digestive functions to improve energy and relieve fatigue.[16] Lastly, *Zhe Bei Mu* (Bulbus Fritillariae Thunbergii), *Mu Li* (Concha Ostreae), *Xuan Shen* (Radix Scrophulariae) and *Zhi Mu* (Rhizoma Anemarrhenae) are Chinese herbs historically prescribed to dissolve lumps and hardenings. Clinically, they have been used with great results for treating goiter and hyperthyroidism.[17,18]

In summary, ***Thyrodex*** is a great formula to treat hyperthyroidism with signs and symptoms of "sympathetic excess," such as increased blood pressure, tachycardia, heat intolerance, weight loss, and restlessness.

COMPARATIVE ANALYSIS

Hyperthyroidism is a common disorder that is well understood, but it only has limited treatment options: drugs or surgery. In most cases, patients prefer non-invasion drug therapy first. Unfortunately, these drugs [such as tapazole and propylthiouracil] are ineffective and cannot consistently control thyroid hormones within an optimal range. Fluctuation of thyroid hormone levels contributes to the presentation of hyperthyroidism or hypothyroidism, depending on whether the drug is under- or over-dosed, respectively. Eventually, most patients receive either surgery or radioactive iodine treatments. These treatments are invasive and irreversible, as they literally remove or destroy the thyroid gland to reduce its production of thyroid hormones. After these invasive treatments, many patients develop hypothyroidism, and must take synthetic thyroid hormone for the rest of their life.

Hyperthyroidism is a disorder characterized by Liver fire rising with underlying qi and yin deficiencies. Hyperthyroidism has been treated in China for thousands of years successfully by using herbs that suppress the sympathetic excess to control the symptoms, and herbs that nourish underlying deficiencies to regulate the endocrine system. By targeting both the symptoms and the cause, herbs exert immediate and long-term effectiveness for the management of hyperthyroidism. However, herbal therapy in this case has certain limitations. Patients in thyroid storm crisis must be referred to Western medicine for urgent treatment. Furthermore, use of herbs will not reverse protrusion of the eyes, no matter the dose or duration.

Hyperthyroidism can be treated with both Western medicine and traditional Chinese medicine. Ideally, all options should be explored (including drugs, herbs, and others), as many cases of mild to moderate hyperthyroidism respond well to such treatment. If these treatments are effective, they spare the patients emotional grief, financial burden, and unnecessary exposure to risks associated with surgery and radioactive iodine treatments. If all other options fail, then surgery or radioactive iodine treatments can be considered as last alternatives, as these treatments are invasive and irreversible. It is important that practitioners and patients are informed and educated to understand all available options so that they may decide together on the most appropriate therapy.

References

1. Balch, JF and Balch, PA. *Prescriptions for Nutritional Healing*. Avery Publishing Group. 1997.
2. Wang CN, Shiao YJ, Kuo YH, Chen CC, Lin YL. Inducible nitric oxide synthase inhibitors from Saposhnikovia divaricata and Panax quinquefolium. Planta Med. 2000 Oct;66(7):644-7.
3. Huang N, Hauck C, Yum MY, Rizshsky L, Widrlechner MP, McCoy JA, Murphy PA, Dixon PM, Nikolau BJ, Birt DF. Rosmarinic acid in Prunella vulgaris ethanol extract inhibits lipopolysaccharide-induced prostaglandin E2 and nitric oxide in RAW 264.7 mouse macrophages. The Center for Research on Botanical Dietary Supplements, Interdepartmental Graduate Program in Nutritional Sciences, Iowa State University, Ames, IA 50011, USA. J Agric Food Chem. 2009 Nov 25;57(22):10579-89.
4. Hwang SM, Lee YJ, Yoon JJ, Lee SM, Kang DG, Lee HS. Gardenia jasminoides inhibits tumor necrosis factor-alpha-induced vascular inflammation in endothelial cells. Professional Graduate School of Oriental Medicine, Wonkwang University, Chonbuk, Republic of Korea. Phytother Res. 2010 Jun;24 Suppl 2:S214-9.
5. Lim H, Nam JW, Seo EK, Kim YS, Kim HP. (-)-Nyasol (cis-hinokiresinol), a norneolignan from the rhizomes of Anemarrhena asphodeloides, is a broad spectrum inhibitor of eicosanoid and nitric oxide production. College of Pharmacy, Kangwon National University, Chunchon 200-701, Korea. Arch Pharm Res. 2009 Nov;32(11):1509-14.
6. *Zhong Cao Yao* (Chinese Herbal Medicine), 1991; 22(10):452.
7. *Zhong Yi Yao Xin Xi* (Information on Chinese Medicine and Herbology), 1990; (4):39.
8. *Zhong Yao Xue* (Chinese Herbology), 1998; 115:119.
9. *Zhong Yao Yao Li Yu Ying Yong* (Pharmacology and Applications of Chinese Herbs), 1983:883.
10. *Zhong Yao Xue* (Chinese Herbology), 1998; 128:130.
11. *Zhong Yao Yao Li Yu Ying Yong* (Pharmacology and Applications of Chinese Herbs), 1983: 370.

FORMULAS

Thyrodex™

12. *Zhong Yao Yao Li Yu Ying Yong* (Pharmacology and Applications of Chinese Herbs), 1983; 934.
13. Yao Y, Jia M, Wu JG, Zhang H, Sun LN, Chen WS, Rahman K. Anxiolytic and sedative-hypnotic activities of polygalasaponins from Polygala tenuifolia in mice. Department of Pharmacognosy, School of Pharmacy, Second Military Medical University, Shanghai, China. Pharm Biol. 2010 Jul;48(7):801-7.
14. *Jiang Su Zhong Yi* (Jiangsu Chinese Medicine), 1989, (1):29.
15. *Jiang Su Yi Yao* (Jiangsu Journal of Medicine and Herbology), 1976; (1):28.
16. Chen J, Chen T. Chinese Medical Herbology and Pharmacology. Art of Medicine Press. 2004.
17. Yeung, HC. *Handbook of Chinese Herbs*. Institute of Chinese Medicine. 1993.
18. Zhang, XP. Treatment of Endocrine Disorders with Herbs. Presentation given by Professor Zhang at the Seminar hosted by California Association of Acupuncture and Oriental Medicine. July 1998.

Thyro-forte ™

CLINICAL APPLICATIONS

- **Hypothyroidism:** fatigue, lack of energy, dull facial expression, hoarse voice, drooping eyelids, puffy and swollen eyes and face, weight gain, constipation, aversion to cold, dry hair and skin, low body temperature, decreased heart rate and blood pressure, muscle weakness or sluggishness, and other related symptoms
- **Chronic thyroiditis** or **Hashimoto's thyroiditis**

WESTERN THERAPEUTIC ACTIONS

- Regulates and restores the endocrine system
- Stimulates the production of thyroid hormones
- Increases basal metabolism and enhances energy levels
- Improves physiological functions

CHINESE THERAPEUTIC ACTIONS

- Tonify Kidney, Heart, and Spleen yang
- Nourish Liver and Kidney yin
- Tonify qi

DOSAGE

Take 4 capsules three times daily on an empty stomach. However, the dosage may need to be adjusted based on age, body weight, severity of condition, and response to the treatment.

INGREDIENTS

Fu Ling (Poria)
Fu Zi (Radix Aconiti Lateralis Praeparata)
Gou Qi Zi (Fructus Lycii)
Gui Ban (Plastrum Testudinis)
Hai Zao (Sargassum)
Kun Bu (Thallus Eckloniae)
Lu Jiao (Cornu Cervi)
Mu Dan Pi (Cortex Moutan)
Ren Shen (Radix et Rhizoma Ginseng)
Rou Gui (Cortex Cinnamomi)
Shan Yao (Rhizoma Dioscoreae)
Shan Zhu Yu (Fructus Corni)
Shu Di Huang (Radix Rehmanniae Praeparata)
Ze Xie (Rhizoma Alismatis)

BACKGROUND

Hypothyroidism is thyroid hormone deficiency with clinical manifestations such as fatigue, lack of energy, dull facial expression, forgetfulness, hoarse voice, drooping eyelids, puffy and swollen eyes and face, weight gain, constipation, cold intolerance, dry hair and skin, low body temperature, decreased heart rate and blood pressure, and muscle weakness or sluggishness. Hypothyroidism may occur at any age but is most common among the elderly. Hypothyroidism may be caused by autoimmune disorder (Hashimoto's thyroiditis), iodine deficiency, drugs (i.e., lithium, amiodarone, interferon-α), radiation, or hormone imbalance [i.e., insufficient production of thyrotropin-releasing hormone (TRH) or thyroid-stimulating hormone (TSH)]. Optimal management requires treatment of the cause and the symptoms.

FORMULA EXPLANATION

According to traditional Chinese medicine, hypothyroidism is a condition characterized by yang deficiency. While the fundamental etiology is Kidney yang deficiency, complications may involve yin deficiency of the Kidney and yang deficiencies of the Spleen and Heart. Treatment, therefore, must address both yang and yin deficiencies of the organs involved.

Rou Gui (Cortex Cinnamomi) and *Fu Zi* (Radix Aconiti Lateralis Praeparata) are two of the strongest and most commonly used herbs to fortify the yang of Kidney, Heart, and Spleen, the three organs implicated in patients with hypothyroidism. In addition, *Rou Gui* (Cortex Cinnamomi) treats insufficient *ming men* (life gate) fire, a condition characterized by accelerated aging. *Fu Zi* (Radix Aconiti Lateralis Praeparata) tonifies and restores depleted yang, a condition characterized by lower basal metabolism and compromised physiological functions. The combination of these two herbs has an excellent synergistic function to tonify yang and treat the underlying cause of hypothyroidism. *Lu Jiao* (Cornu Cervi) and *Gui Ban* (Plastrum Testudinis) are excellent herbs to tonify Kidney yang, Kidney yin, and Kidney *jing* (essence), and they are safe and effective when used at a large dose or for a long period of time.

Hai Zao (Sargassum) and *Kun Bu* (Thallus Eckloniae) dispel phlegm and soften nodules. In other words, they have great effect to reduce the hypertrophy and enlargement of the thyroid glands. In addition, these two herbs are rich in iodine and will stimulate the production of thyroid hormone, especially in cases of hypothyroidism due to lack of iodine in the diet.

Shu Di Huang (Radix Rehmanniae Praeparata), *Shan Zhu Yu* (Fructus Corni), *Shan Yao* (Rhizoma Dioscoreae), *Ze Xie* (Rhizoma Alismatis), *Mu Dan Pi* (Cortex Moutan), and *Fu Ling* (Poria) compose the classic Kidney yin tonic formula *Liu Wei Di Huang Wan* (Six-Ingredient Pill with Rehmannia), one of the most famous herbal tonics. *Shu Di Huang* (Radix Rehmanniae Praeparata) tonifies the Kidney yin and the Kidney *jing* (essence); *Shan Zhu Yu* (Fructus Corni) nourishes the Liver and prevents the leakage of Kidney *jing* (essence); and *Shan Yao* (Rhizoma Dioscoreae) tonifies the Spleen and stabilizes the Kidney *jing* (essence). *Ze Xie* (Rhizoma Alismatis) clears deficiency fire from the Kidney; *Mu Dan Pi* (Cortex Moutan) sedates Liver fire; and *Fu Ling* (Poria) dissolves dampness from the Spleen. These six herbs are formulated with careful checks and balances to maximize the therapeutic effects and minimize unwanted side effects. Furthermore, *Gou Qi Zi* (Fructus Lycii) is used to tonify Liver and Kidney yin. In addition to treating the underlying cause of the illness, *Ren Shen* (Radix et Rhizoma Ginseng) tonifies qi and immediately raises the energy level of hypothyroid patients.

Thyro-forte™

In conclusion, ***Thyro-forte*** is an excellent formula that tonifies Kidney, Heart, and Spleen yang and treats hypothyroidism.

CAUTIONS & CONTRAINDICATIONS

- This formula is contraindicated during pregnancy and nursing.
- Patients who wear a pacemaker, or individuals who take antiarrhythmic drugs [i.e., Tambocor (flecainide) and Procanbid (procainamide)] or cardiac glycosides [i.e., Lanoxin (digoxin)], should not take this formula. *Fu Zi* (Radix Aconiti Lateralis Praeparata) may interact with these drugs by affecting the rhythm and potentiating the contractile strength of the heart.[1]
- The etiology of Hashimoto's thyroiditis is excessive autoimmunity causing destruction of the thyroid gland and reducing production of thyroid hormone. Therefore, during the acute inflammatory phase of the disease when the immune system is activated by the presence of pathogens, qi tonics that boost the immune system, such as *Ren Shen* (Radix et Rhizoma Ginseng), should be used with caution as this herb may further stimulate the immune system. During this acute inflammatory phase, ***Nourish*** may be a more suitable formula as it contains herbs that nourish yin to support the thyroid gland, and herbs that clear deficiency heat to reduce inflammation.

CLINICAL NOTES

- Patients with hypothyroidism usually notice improvement within one month, starting with increased energy and elevated body temperature. Stabilization and maximum effect may not be observed until the individual has been ingesting the herbs for two months or longer.
- Patients with hypothyroidism can be treated with drugs, herbs, or both. However, if both drugs and herbs are used, it is important to monitor the patient's condition frequently to ensure proper control of the signs and symptoms. Over-dosage with drugs and/or herbs may cause hyperthyroid-like signs and symptoms, and under-dosage may contribute to hypothyroid-like signs and symptoms.
- Progress of hypothyroid treatment can be monitored by checking the body temperature, heart rate, and blood pressure. It is best to check these parameters first thing in the morning to avoid fluctuations.
- It is important to be aware that long-term use of thyroid supplements (such as levothyroxine) has been associated with loss of as much as 13% of bone mass. Therefore, patients who have been or are currently using thyroid supplements should take calcium supplements to replenish the loss of bone mass.

Pulse Diagnosis by Dr. Jimmy Wei-Yen Chang:

- Deep, stagnating, sluggish pulse with low amplitude, but forceful upon pressure.

SUPPLEMENTARY FORMULAS

- For an immediate energy boost, add ***Vibrant***.
- For edema and water accumulation, add ***Herbal DRX***.
- To tonify Kidney yang, add ***Kidney Tonic (Yang)***.
- To tonify Kidney yin, add ***Kidney Tonic (Yin)***.
- For long-term increase in energy, add ***Imperial Tonic***.
- For constipation, add ***Gentle Lax (Deficient)***.
- For dry hair and skin, add ***Polygonum 14***.
- For lack of libido in men or women, add ***Vitality***.
- For adrenal insufficiency, use with ***Adrenal +***.
- To strengthen constitutional weakness and deficiency, add ***Cordyceps 3***.
- For poor appetite or loose stool, add ***GI Tonic***.

ACUPUNCTURE TREATMENT

Traditional Points:

- *Pishu* (BL 20), *Shenshu* (BL 23), *Zusanli* (ST 36), *Guanyuan* (CV 4), *Qihai* (CV 6)
- Apply moxa to *Shenshu* (BL 23), *Guanyuan* (CV 4) and *Zusanli* (ST 36).

Classic Master Tung's Points:

- *Sanzhong* (T 77.07), *Tongguan* (T 88.01), *Simashang* (T 88.18), *Simazhong* (T 88.17), *Simaxia* (T 88.19), *Tongshan* (T 88.02)

Master Tung's Points by Dr. Chuan-Min Wang:

- **Hypothyroid:** *Tianhuang* (T 77.17), *Dihuang* (T 77.19), *Renhuang* (T 77.21)

Balance Method by Dr. Richard Tan:

- Left side: *Shaohai* (HT 3), *Shenmen* (HT 7), *Taixi* (KI 3), *Yingu* (KI 10)
- Right side: *Zhongzhu* (TH 3), Tianjing (TH 10), *Yanglingquan* (GB 34), *Zulinqi* (GB 41)
- Left and right sides can be alternated from treatment to treatment.

Auricular Medicine by Dr. Li-Chun Huang:

- **Hypothyroidism:** Thyroid, Pituitary, Exciting Point, Thalamus, Endocrine, Gonadotropin, *Sanjiao*, Kidney, Liver, Sympathetic
- **Simple goiter:** Thyroid, Endocrine, Pituitary, Thalamus, *San Jiao*, Kidney, Liver

NUTRITION

- Avoid fluoride and chlorine (which are found in many toothpastes and in tap water). These elements may block the iodine receptors in the thyroid glands, leading to reduced hormone production and eventually hypothyroidism. Drink steam-distilled water only.
- Minimize intake of foods that suppress the production of thyroid hormone, such as brussel sprouts, peaches, pears, spinach, turnips, cabbage, broccoli, kale and mustard greens.
- Encourage the consumption of foods (or supplements) rich in vitamin B complex to promote the proper generation and utilization of energy.

Thyro-forte ™

- Increase the intake of foods rich in iodine, such as seaweed. Iodine is the building block of thyroid hormone, and is essential for normal thyroid health.
- According to traditional Chinese medicine, vegetables are generally cold in nature and meats are usually warm. Since individuals with hypothyroidism often have yang deficiency and cold presentations, increased consumption of meats (especially lamb) will help warm up the body and dispel cold. Other foods that are warm include lycii, longan fruit and spices such as pepper, garlic, onions, basil, rosemary, cumin, funnel, anise, leeks, chives, scallions, thyme, saffron, wormwood, mustard, chili pepper, and wasabi.
- Avoid the following cooling foods: tofu, tomato, celery, asparagus, bamboo, seaweed, kelp, bitter melon, cucumber, gourd, luffa, winter melon, oranges, grapefruit, pear, banana, papaya, watermelon, white radish, mustard leaf, potherb mustard, cactus, Chinese kale, napa, and bamboo sprout. Long-term use of cold fruits and vegetables like the ones listed above may be damaging to the Spleen. To make the property more neutral, one can add about 20 pieces of *Gou Qi Zi* (Fructus Lycii) when cooking.

The Tao of Nutrition by Dr. Maoshing Ni and Cathy McNease:

- **Goiter**
  - Make soup from dried (preferably green) orange peel, carrots, and seaweed.
  - Soak cherry pits in vinegar until they disintegrate, then apply locally.

LIFESTYLE INSTRUCTIONS

- Regular exercise helps to stimulate thyroid hormone secretion and increases the tissue sensitivity to the hormone. Exercise is also beneficial by raising the basal body metabolism.
- Induce perspiration by taking hot water baths, saunas, or steam baths.

CASE STUDIES

- L.L., a 55-year-old female, presented with a fluctuating emotional state, frontal headache, elbow pain, and cramping in the neck area. She was also experiencing eczema on the scalp, heat in the face and neck, and irritability. The Western diagnosis was leaky gut syndrome and Hashimoto's thyroiditis; the TCM diagnosis was heat in the *San Jiao*. After taking ***Thyro-forte***, the lab test counts were normalized and the symptoms were alleviated. She is no longer taking the auto-immune supplement she had been taking previously. Submitted by T.B., Tucson, Arizona.
- C.T., a 44-year-old female, presented with constipation and bloating. Symptoms of stress, depression, cold body feeling, and fatigue were also present. She was having difficulty losing weight as well despite regular exercise. Testing of TSH levels showed 0.45 mU/L before the herbal treatment and 1.5 mU/L after three months of taking the herbs. The practitioner diagnosed the condition as Kidney yin deficiency, Spleen and Kidney yang deficiencies, and Liver qi stagnation. Her Western diagnosis was hypothyroid depression. The patient was given ***Thyro-forte*** three capsules three times a day for three months. As shown on her TSH tests, with the ***Thyro-forte***, the patient's TSH levels remained in a normal range. She felt a greater sense of energy and was able to increase her exercise. Stress remains an ongoing issue, however, due to her high stress work life. Constipation is still in progress of resolving but the thyroid TSH still remains normal. Submitted by L.M., Lafayette, Colorado.
- L.H, a 75-year-old female, presented with dry eyes, sweaty feet, tinnitus, and frequent urination with thirst. Additional symptoms included lower legs and knees being cold, and difficulty falling asleep. The Western diagnosis was hypothyroidism; the TCM diagnosis was Kidney yang deficiency and Liver blood deficiency. This condition was treated with ***Thyro-forte***. After three weeks of taking the herbs the symptoms alleviated. Submitted by T.B., Tucson, Arizona.
- G.A., a 35-year-old female, presented with multiple symptoms including fatigue, weight gain, anxiety, and cold sensation all the time. Recently the patient's blood tests showed signs of hypothyroidism, for which she was then started on medication for treatment. However the patient was warned that she could become dependant on it so she had stopped taking them and was looking into taking herbs instead. Blood pressure was 113/76 mmHg and pulse rate was 64 beats per minute. The practitioner diagnosed this condition as Heart yin deficiency and Spleen qi deficiency. Upon diagnosis, the patient was directed to take ***Thyro-forte***. The patient had informed her NP about stopping the medication and beginning to take the ***Thyro-forte***, in which the doctor had supported. After three months of taking the herbs, the patient felt she was no longer experiencing hypothyroidism symptoms. Her thyroid panel afterwards also showed her TSH levels were now normal. Submitted by R.C., Anchorage, Alaska.
- M.S., a 60-year-old female, presented with night sweats, insomnia, pimples, TMJ disorder, high blood pressure, chest pain, cough with phlegm, heartburn, neck pain, indigestion, urinary dribbling, and goiter. The Western diagnosis was hypothyroidism with improper treatment; the TCM diagnosis was Heart yin deficiency, phlegm accumulation, and stomach yin deficiency. This condition was treated with ***Thyro-forte***. After taking the herbs, the sweating, insomnia, indigestion, dribbling urine, and goiter were all either relieved or reduced. Submitted by T.B., Tucson, Arizona.
- T.T., a 50-year-old female, presented with multiple symptoms including fatigue, lack of motivation, bloating, and cold sensation. Blood pressure was 90/60 mmHg and heart beat was 54 beats per minute. The practitioner diagnosed this condition as qi and blood deficiency of the Spleen, Kidney, and Heart; her Western diagnosis was Hashimoto's disease. Upon diagnosis the patient was prescribed ***Thyro-forte***, and given both dietary and exercise plans to follow. After three months of taking the herbs and

Thyro-forte™

following her lifestyle changes, the patient had reported her thyroid levels were within normal range. Submitted by L.H., Chicago, Illinois.

- C.F., a 27-year-old female, presented with hypothyroidism, which included symptoms of low energy, weight gain, and cold sensation. Lab results showed decrease in thyroid activity. The practitioner diagnosed this condition as yang deficiency. ***Thyro-forte*** was prescribed at 4 capsules three times a day. After two and half months, she felt increase in energy, and less cold sensation. However, there was no effect towards her weight gain. Submitted by S.L., Yuma, Arizona
- S.H., a 60-year-old patient, presented with a variety of symptoms, including urinary incontinence, frequent urination, loss of hair, abdominal bloating, hip soreness, lumbar pain, sciatica, and a red pastel eczema on the lower legs. The Western diagnosis was hypothyroidism and bladder sphincter paralysis; the TCM diagnosis was Kidney qi sinking, Spleen qi deficiency, and Liver qi constraint. This condition was treated with ***Thyro-forte***. After taking the herbs, she experienced 70% improvement in urinary incontinence, and 100% relief in abdominal bloating, lumbar pain and frequent urination. The patient still takes the herbs once a week to maintain the results. Submitted by T.B., Tucson, Arizona.
- D.W., 34-year-old female, presented with fatigue and cold sensation. Her TSH level was 6.34 mU/L (normal: 0.4-4.2 mU/L). Blood pressure was 104/90 mmHg and her heart rate was 60 beats per minute. The practitioner diagnosed this condition as qi deficiency of the Spleen, Kidney, and Heart as well as Liver blood deficiency. For treatment, the patient was prescribed ***Thyro-forte***. After taking the herbs, the patient subjectively described an increase in energy, focus, and less cold sensation. Submitted by L.H., Chicago, Illinois.
- A 47-year-old female presented with low energy and excess uterine bleeding. She had been diagnosed with hypothyroid and uterine fibroids. The patient stated she wanted to get off Synthroid (levothyroxine). Her RBC, TSH and T4 levels were low. Her pulse was thready and her tongue was pale. The practitioner diagnosed the case as Kidney deficiency with Liver blood deficiency due to excess bleeding. A raw herbal formula was used to shrink the fibroids and control the uterine bleeding for six months. Once the bleeding and fibroids were under control, the patient was instructed to take ***Thyro-forte***. Immediately, the patient experienced an increase in energy and overall health. The combination of 4 capsules three times daily of ***Thyro-forte*** accompanied with Synthroid (levothyroxine) was too potent, so the dose was reduced to 3 capsules three times daily with positive results. Without the ***Thyro-forte*** treatment, the patient noticed a drop in energy level. Submitted by F.V., Orlando, Florida.
- A 30-year-old female diagnosed with hypothyroidism displayed signs and symptoms of low energy, diarrhea, depression, coldness, and a low body temperature of 96.9° F. She was given ***Thyro-forte***. Shortly after administering ***Thyro-forte***, she reported an enhanced energy level along with an increase of overall body warmth by over 50% (basal temperature was increased to 97.8° F). The patient's bouts with diarrhea and depression appeared to have resolved. She felt stronger, happier, and more energetic. Submitted by S.T., San Jose, California.
- L.D., a 31-year-old female, presented with fatigue, dizziness, low body temperature, coldness, and muscle weakness. Her blood pressure was 100/60 mmHg and her heart rate was 65 beats per minute. Her Western diagnoses were hypotension and hypoglycemia. Laboratory results showed she had decreased thyroid activity and adrenal medullary insufficiency. The diagnosis was yang deficiency. She was prescribed ***Thyro-forte*** and ***Adrenal +*** at 2.5 and 1.5 grams per day, respectively. She did not receive any acupuncture. After two months, she felt much more energized and the dizziness was gone. She no longer felt cold. Submitted by W.F., Bloomfield, New Jersey.
- T.M., a 53-year-old female, presented with constant fatigue, muscle aches and pain, dry skin and trouble with communication, with sensations of tightness in her throat. The Western diagnoses were fibromyalgia and a low T4 level; the TCM diagnosis was Spleen qi and blood deficiencies. ***Thyro-forte*** was prescribed along with *Si Ni San* (Frigid Extremities Powder), *Gui Pi Tang* (Restore the Spleen Decoction) and *An Mian Pian* pills. After nine months of treatment with acupuncture and herbs, the patient was able to completely cease use of thyroid drugs. Submitted by M.C., Sarasota, Florida.
- E.B., a 75-year-old female, presented with hypothyroidism. It started a number of years ago and she took Thyroxin until recently when a new medical doctor switched her, against her will, to Levoxyl that contains no T3. Thyroxin contains T3. The client attributed this to the severe reduction in her energy and recent weight gain despite a program of aerobic exercise five days a week, weight lifting, and careful attention to her diet. After 12 noon everyday she lost any desire to do anything. The patient described herself as lethargic and discouraged. The patient weighed 151 pounds. Her blood pressure was 148/80 mmHg with a heart rate of 56 beats per minute. A year ago, before switching to the new thyroid drug, she weighed 133 pounds. No lab reports were available. She presented with excellent spirits but was clearly distressed about her loss of energy and her weight gain. Her tongue was pale with a purplish cast. The Spleen pulse was large and empty. The TCM diagnosis was Spleen qi and yang deficiency with dampness. ***Thyro-forte*** was prescribed at 2 capsules three times daily. The patient reported increased energy levels to 8 out of 10 from the 2 out of 10 she rated herself before the herbal treatment. Her weight, however, did not change. About a year and a half after the herbal treatment, the patient persuaded her M.D. to put her back on Thyroxin and she then tapered off the ***Thyro-forte*** thereafter. Submitted by H.H., San Francisco, California.

Thyro-forte™

PHARMACOLOGICAL AND CLINICAL RESEARCH

Hypothyroidism is an endocrine disorder. The cause of hypothyroidism is often associated with insufficient production of thyrotropin-releasing hormone (TRH) from the hypothalamus or thyroid-stimulating hormone (TSH) from the pituitary. The effect of insufficient thyroid hormones is slowed metabolism throughout the body. Therefore, optimal treatment requires managing both the cause (i.e., balance the endocrine system) and the effect (increase the metabolism).

Thyro-forte is a contemporary herbal formula based on a classic herbal formula - *Jin Gui Shen Qi Wan* (Kidney Qi Pill from the Golden Cabinet) from *Jin Gui Yao Lue* (Essentials from the Golden Cabinet) by Zhang Zhong-Jing (150-219 CE). The classic formula has six herbs to balance the endocrine system (nourish Liver and Kidney yin) and two herbs to elevate the metabolism (tonify Kidney yang). Clinical applications of this formula include various endocrine disorders, such as thyroid disorder,[2] reproductive disorder,[3] diabetes mellitus,[4,5] and many others. The mechanism of action includes stimulating of the endocrine system to increase the production of hormones from the pituitary gland, hypothalamus, and other glands.[6]

Synthesis of thyroid hormone requires adequate quantities of iodine.[7] Without iodine as the raw material, the thyroid gland continually attempts to produce thyroid hormone without success. This eventually leads to hypertrophy and enlargement of the thyroid glands. Rich in iodine, *Hai Zao* (Sargassum) and *Kun Bu* (Thallus Eckloniae) will stimulate the production of thyroid hormone, and effectively reduce the hypertrophy and enlargement of the thyroid gland (in cases of hypothyroidism due to lack of iodine in diet).[8]

For optimal treatment of hypothyroidism, it is imperative to ensure that the basal metabolism is increased and the physiological functions are improved. Basal metabolism may be increased with yang tonic herbs. Studies have shown that *Rou Gui* (Cortex Cinnamomi) and *Fu Zi* (Radix Aconiti Lateralis Praeparata) have stimulating effects on the body, leading to excitation of the cardiovascular,[9] gastrointestinal,[10] and immune systems.[11] Furthermore, physiological insufficiencies can be replenished with yin tonic herbs. Numerous herbs in this formula have shown marked stimulating effects on the endocrine system to increase the production of various endogenous hormones, such as *Shu Di Huang* (Radix Rehmanniae Praeparata),[12] *Shan Zhu Yu* (Fructus Corni),[13] and *Shan Yao* (Rhizoma Dioscoreae).[14] *Ze Xie* (Rhizoma Alismatis), *Mu Dan Pi* (Cortex Moutan) and *Fu Ling* (Poria) are added to balance the tonic herbs and minimize any unwanted side effects.

Lastly, *Ren Shen* (Radix et Rhizoma Ginseng) is added to ***Thyro-forte*** as it has numerous physiologic effects. In addition to increasing energy, *Ren Shen* (Radix et Rhizoma Ginseng) improves learning and memory,[15] stimulates the pituitary gland to increase the release of various endogenous hormones,[16,17] balances the cardiovascular system by restoring homeostasis,[18] and enhances the immune system.[19]

Thyro-forte is an herbal formula developed specifically for patients with hypothyroidism. Herbs in this formula have been shown to regulate the endocrine system, stimulate the production of thyroid hormone, increase basal metabolism, and improve the overall physiological functions.

COMPARATIVE ANALYSIS

Hypothyroidism is one of the most common disorders in developed countries. The disease is well understood, and treatment is simple and straightforward. In Western medicine, hypothyroidism is the lack of thyroid hormone, and therefore, treatment is to use synthetic thyroid hormone to supplement the insufficiency. Synthroid (levothyroxine) is generally considered to be the drug of choice, and when used carefully, it is generally safe and effective. Because Synthroid (levothyroxine) is very potent, it must be monitored carefully, as inappropriate dosing contributes to hyper- or hypothyroid signs and symptoms. It has also been noted that Synthroid (levothyroxine) may contribute to hypersensitivity problems, presumably because it is synthetic and may have compatibility issues. Lastly, it has been observed that long-term use of synthetic thyroid hormones is associated with increased loss of bone mass density and higher risks of osteoporosis. In short, synthetic thyroid hormone is the only drug treatment available for hypothyroidism patients. Furthermore, once synthetic thyroid hormone therapy begins, endogenous production slowly decreases and the body becomes more and more dependant on the exogenous source. Eventually, the patient will become dependent on thyroid drugs for life. In conclusion, though synthetic thyroid hormone is effective, it must be prescribed correctly, monitored carefully, and potential complications must be address with preventative measures (such as taking calcium supplements daily to avoid developing osteoporosis).

Many herbs effectively treat hypothyroidism. Because this condition is diagnosed as Kidney yang deficiency, it is treated with warm herbs that tonify Kidney yang. These herbs have been shown to have a marked effect to increase body temperature, elevate body metabolism, and improve mood to alleviate many symptoms associated with hypothyroidism. Furthermore, these herbs also have marked effects to regulate endocrine system and stimulate thyroid glands to increase production of thyroid hormones. Because herbs are effective to treat both the symptoms and the cause, they often exert both immediate and long-lasting effects. However, there is one major limitation to herbal therapy. Because these herbs work primarily by stimulating the thyroid gland to produce thyroid hormone, those who cannot produce thyroid hormone (such as those who have had a complete thyroidectomy) will not benefit from herbs. They must be treated with synthetic thyroid hormone to ensure proper regulation of growth and metabolism.

Thyro-forte™

Both drugs and herbs treat hypothyroidism effectively. The main benefit of drug therapy is potency and consistency, and the main disadvantages are the potential adverse reactions and long-term dependence on the drugs. The main advantage of herbal therapy is its effectiveness to manage both symptoms and cause of hypothyroidism, and the main drawback is the absence of means to treat patients who can no longer produce thyroid hormone internally. Optimal treatment depends on complete understanding by an informed and educated practitioner *and* an equally informed patient who both know of the pros and cons of both modalities of medicines, deciding together on the most appropriate therapy.

References

1. *Forensic Science International*, 1994 June 28; 55-8.
2. *Shan Xi Zhong Yi* (Shanxi Chinese Medicine) 1995;16(11):485.
3. *Zhong Yi Fang Ji Xian Dai Yan Jiu* (Modern Study of Medical Formulae in Traditional Chinese Medicine) 1997;709.
4. *Hu Bei Zhong Yi Za Zhi* (Hubei Journal of Chinese Medicine) 1992;2:20.
5. *Zhong Cheng Yao Yan Jiu* (Research of Chinese Patent Medicine) 1984;11:25.
6. *Zhong Yi Fang Ji Xian Dai Yan Jiu* (Modern Study of Medical Formulae in Traditional Chinese Medicine) 1997;673.
7. Fauci, et al., *Harrison's Principles of Internal Medicine 14th Edition*, 1998; 2012:2019.
8. Yen, ZH, et al., *Chinese Herbology*, 1998; 629:631.
9. Zhou, YD, *Journal of Herbology*, 1983; 18(5):394.
10. Chen, Y, *Journal of Chinese Herbology*, 1981; 6(5):32.
11. Wang, YS, *Pharmacology and Applications of Chinese Herbs*, 1983; 443.
12. Yen, ZH, et al., *Chinese Herbology*, 1998; 156:158.
13. Jiang, Y, *Pharmacology and Clinical Applications of Chinese Herbs*, 1989; 5(1):36.
14. He, ZQ, *Journal of University of Chinese Herbology*, 1991; 22(3):158.
15. *Encyclopedia of Chinese Herbs*, 1994.
16. Song, R, *Journal of Baiqioen University of Medicine*, 1980; 6(2):32.
17. Shu, SK, *Study of Chinese Patent Medicine*, 1989; 11(9):30.
18. *CA*, 1992; 116:34223d.
19. Yen, ZH, et al., *Chinese Herbology*, 1998; 729:736.

Venus ™

CLINICAL APPLICATIONS

- **Breast augmentation:** enhances small or underdeveloped breasts, maintains healthy breast shape and size
- **Nursing:** promotes lactation in nursing women

WESTERN THERAPEUTIC ACTIONS

- Regulates the endocrine system to increase the production of sex hormones
- Stimulates the growth and development of breasts
- Improves blood circulation
- Increases the generation of new tissue

CHINESE THERAPEUTIC ACTIONS

- Tonifies Kidney yang and *jing* (essence)
- Opens channels in the breasts
- Invigorates blood circulation

DOSAGE

- **Breast augmentation:** Take 2 to 4 capsules on an empty stomach three times daily to enhance healthy breasts. To achieve maximum effectiveness, the exercises listed under Clinical Notes should be done twice daily.
- **Nursing:** Take 2 capsules daily. Discontinue the formula if the baby has diarrhea.

INGREDIENTS

Bai Zhi (Radix Angelicae Dahuricae)
Dang Gui (Radix Angelicae Sinensis)
Huang Qi (Radix Astragali)
Lu Rong (Cornu Cervi Pantotrichum)
Mu Tong (Caulis Akebiae)
Tong Cao (Medulla Tetrapanacis)
Wang Bu Liu Xing (Semen Vaccariae)
Yin Yang Huo (Herba Epimedii)

BACKGROUND

Female breasts develop over several stages. During adolescence, the first outward signs of breast development begin to appear. As the ovaries begin to secrete estrogen, fat in the connective tissue begins to accumulate causing the breasts to enlarge and the duct system to grow. When ovulation and menstruation begin, the breasts continue to grow with the formation of secretory glands at the end of the milk ducts. With pregnancy and lactation, the breasts mature and are capable of producing milk. Finally, as a woman reaches menopause, the level of estrogen decreases dramatically, leading to a reduction in the size and shape of the breasts.

FORMULA EXPLANATION

Venus is designed for women with small and/or underdeveloped breasts due to various reasons, such as degeneration, aging, over-developed pectoris muscles, malnutrition and sudden weight loss. Small breasts in women are usually due to heredity, interruption of growth during adolescence, and nutritional deficiencies.

Venus contains potent Kidney yang and *jing* (essence) tonics that will stimulate the growth of reproductive organs and increase libido. *Lu Rong* (Cornu Cervi Pantotrichum), the chief ingredient in ***Venus***, is often medically used for developmental delays in children. It tonifies the *ming men* (life gate) fire, replenishes *jing* (essence) and blood. In Western medical terminology, it stimulates the pituitary gland to release growth hormones that will promote the growth of reproductive organs, including the breasts. When Kidney yang is restored, sex drive also increases. *Yin Yang Huo* (Herba Epimedii) is also a well-known herb to tonify Kidney yang and enhance libido. The Spleen is the organ responsible for generating muscle and tissue, and *Huang Qi* (Radix Astragali) is used to tonify the Spleen and help with toning and firming the muscles around the breasts. *Dang Gui* (Radix Angelicae Sinensis) is well known as an herb that treats all types of obstetric and gynecologic disorders. It tonifies blood, promotes blood circulation, and regulates menstruation. Its phyto-estrogenic effect stimulates the estrogenic receptors of the breasts and helps them grow to their fullest potential. *Mu Tong* (Caulis Akebiae), *Tong Cao* (Medulla Tetrapanacis) and *Wang Bu Liu Xing* (Semen Vaccariae) invigorate blood circulation and promote lactation. Historically, they have been used on postpartum women to support mammary glands and promote lactation. In women who are not nursing, however, these herbs will simply enlarge the breast tissue. *Bai Zhi* (Radix Angelicae Dahuricae), an herb that enters the Stomach channel and passes through the breasts, is used as a channel-guiding herb to draw nutrients from the other tonic herbs to the breast area.

In conclusion, ***Venus*** contains many herbs that have remarkable influences on the hormones and development of the sex organs. In the past, these herbs were used mainly to promote lactation in nursing mothers. More recently, with the understanding of modern science, these herbs are known to have a great effect to enhance breast development to its fullest potential.

CAUTIONS & CONTRAINDICATIONS

- This formula is contraindicated during pregnancy.
- Menopausal patients should take this formula with caution, as it may be too warming.
- This formula should not be taken for more than six months as it has warming properties.
- This herbal formula contains herbs that invigorate blood circulation, such as *Dang Gui* (Radix Angelicae Sinensis). Therefore, patients who are on anticoagulant or antiplatelet therapies, such as Coumadin (warfarin), should use this formula with caution, or not at all, as there may be a higher risk of bleeding and bruising.[1,2,3]

Venus™

- This formula is contraindicated in patients with acute infection or heat accumulation, fibrocystic disorders of the breast, hormone-dependent cancer, or have a personal or family history of breast cancer or cancer of any gynecological organs.
- The safety status of using *Dang Gui* (Radix Angelicae Sinensis) in individuals with hormone-dependent cancer is unclear.[4,5,6] According to one reference, use of *Dang Gui* (Radix Angelicae Sinensis) is not associated with thickening of the endometrium or vaginal cell maturation, both of which would indicate an estrogenic effect. Furthermore, there is no confirmation of the presence of a phytoestrogen component or affect on hormone-dependent cancer, when ferulic acid is evaluated as the main component of *Dang Gui* (Radix Angelicae Sinensis).[7] According to another reference, the water extract of *Dang Gui* (Radix Angelicae Sinensis) has a weak estrogen-agonistic activity to stimulate the growth of breast cancer cells (MCF-7).[8] In summary, due to conflicting and insufficient data, use of *Dang Gui* (Radix Angelicae Sinensis) in patients with hormone-dependent cancer warrants caution pending further study.

CLINICAL NOTES

- **Exercises for the breasts**: Several exercises can be done to help promote healthier breast size and firmness. They help strengthen the connective tissues around the breasts and promote the growth of new cells. These exercises should be done twice daily in addition to taking the herbs for maximum shaping, toning, and lifting effects.
- ***Breast Massage***: The purpose of this massage is to maintain and achieve a healthy breast shape and firmness. There are two steps for this breast massage exercise.
  - Step 1: This exercise prevents ligament laxity that causes drooping of the breast. Massage the breasts in a circular motion going outwards. Gradually increase the size of the circular motion to cover the neck and shoulder. Repeat for three to five minutes (Picture 1).
  - Step 2: Stroke the bottom of one breast upward using right and left hands in alternating motion. Repeat 50 times for each breast and make sure to cover the entire bottom curve (Picture 2).
- ***Praying Style Exercise***: The purpose of this exercise is to strengthen the pectoral muscles to help bring circulation to the chest. First, stand up straight with palms together in a prayer position in front of chest. Make sure both elbows form a straight horizontal line across the chest (Picture 3). Next, push palms together to feel the muscles under the breasts contracting. While pushing the palms together, raise the arms up to forehead with the elbows still in a straight line and hold for two to three seconds (Picture 4). After two to three seconds, release contraction and bring back to the original position in middle of chest. Repeat this exercise ten times.
- ***Expand the Chest Exercise***: The purpose of this exercise is to strengthen the upper chest muscles to enhance breast firmness to prevent drooping. This exercise helps open the *Ren* (conception) channel, as per Shizuto Masunaga's meridian exercises. First, clasp hands behind your back with palms facing down (Picture 5). Next, take a deep breath in, thrust chest outward and lift clasped hands behind your back. Tighten your lower back muscles and arch your whole body including your neck (Picture 6). Return to a relaxed position with hands clasped behind the back. Repeat this procedure ten times.

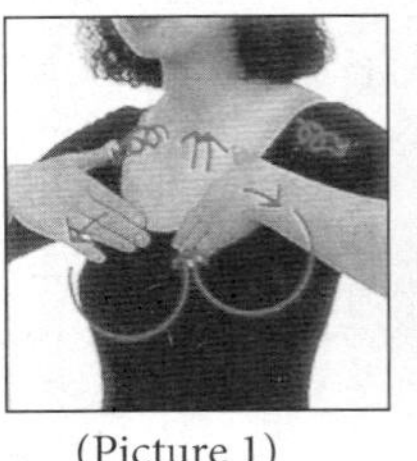
(Picture 1)

(Picture 2)

(Picture 3)

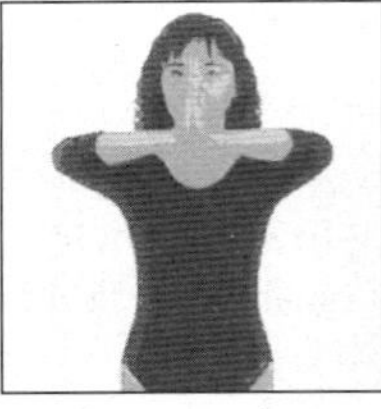
(Picture 4)

(Picture 5)

(Picture 6)

Some patients may notice breast tenderness after taking these herbs. That is an indication of growth and the patient should not be worried. Along with the exercises, patients should notice a difference in tone after 4 to 6 weeks, while actual growth may begin after 3 to 6 months. Full growth potential and desired results depend on body constitution, genetics, consistent intake of herbs, diet, and exercise. As is the case in not achieving desired weight loss, the main reason for lack of response to the herbs is from lapses in taking the herbs or doing exercise. Finally, patients should be advised that this formula and exercise could only enhance breasts to their maximum genetic potential and not beyond. A small-breasted woman from a family of small-breasted women may see improvement in the tone and shape of her breasts, but should not expect to greatly exceed her genetic inheritance.

SUPPLEMENTARY FORMULAS

- For healthy, shiny hair, add ***Polygonum 14***.
- For vaginal dryness, add ***Balance Spring***.
- For weight loss and to control the appetite, add ***Herbalite***.
- For fatigue and weakness or decrease in libido due to qi and blood deficiencies, add ***Imperial Tonic***.
- For postpartum recovery, add ***Imperial Tonic***.
- For anemia, dizziness or blood deficiency, add ***Schisandra ZZZ***.
- For low libido, add ***Vitality***.
- For decrease in libido due to stress, add ***Calm***.
- For menopause, add ***Balance (Heat)*** or ***Nourish***.
- For adrenal burnout, add ***Adrenal +***.

Venus ™

- For osteoporosis, add ***Osteo 8***.
- For Kidney yang deficiency, add ***Kidney Tonic (Yang)***.
- For Kidney yin deficiency, add ***Kidney Tonic (Yin)***.
- For infertility, add ***Blossom (Phase 1-4)***.

ACUPUNCTURE TREATMENT

Traditional Points:

- Needle *Shanzhong* (CV 17).
- Apply moxa to *Zusanli* (ST 36).
- Massage *Qihai* (CV 6), *Geshu* (BL 17), *Shanzhong* (CV 17), *Sanyinjiao* (SP 6), *Qimen* (LR 14), *Rugen* (ST 18), and *Shaoze* (SI 1).

Classic Master Tung's Points:

- **Breast augmentation:** *Yizhong* (T 77.05), *Erzhong* (T 77.06), *Sanzhong* (T 77.07), *Waisanguan* (T 77.27), *Shuanglongyi* (T 77.29)*, *Shuanglonger* (T 77.30)*. Moxa the LU, HT, SP and ST areas in the back. Massage the breasts.
- **Insufficient lactation:** *Linggu* (T 22.05), *Fuke* (T 11.24), *Shaoze* (SI 1), *Tongwei* (T 88.10), *Tongshen* (T 88.09).
  - Excess type: Bleed the LR area in the back. Bleed before needling for best result.
  - Deficiency type: Moxa *Shanzhong* (CV 17)

Master Tung's Points by Dr. Chuan-Min Wang:

- **Breast enhancement:** Bleed *Fenzhixia* (T DT.02). Needle *Jianzhong* (T 44.06), *Yizhong* (T 77.05), *Erzhong* (T 77.06), *Sanzhong* (T 77.07).
- **Insufficient lactation:** *Jiemeiyi* (T 88.04), *Jiemeier* (T 88.05), *Jiemeisan* (T 88.06)

Balance Method by Dr. Richard Tan:

- Left side: *Yinlingquan* (SP 9), *Lougu* (SP 7), *Sanyinjiao* (SP 6), *Sanjian* (LI 3), *Waiguan* (TH 5), the Breast point on the ear
- Right side: *Lieque* (LU 7), *Zusanli* (ST 36), *Xiajuxu* (ST 39)
- Left and right sides can be alternated from treatment to treatment.

Ear Acupuncture:

- Tender point on the Chest and Endocrine.
- Embed ear seeds.

Auricular Medicine by Dr. Li-Chun Huang:

- **Promoting secretion of milk:** Breast, Liver, Stomach, Pituitary, Endocrine, Thalamus, *San Jiao*

NUTRITION

- Patients are advised to eat a nutritious diet and increase the consumption of lamb because it is an excellent Kidney tonic. Intake of protein (such as beans and eggs) and foods high in collagen such as tendons, chicken wings, and animal skin can be increased. Other recommendations include lotus seeds, sunflower seeds, peanuts, strawberries, dates, yam, papaya, taro, onions, celery, chives, spinach, oranges, carrots, milk, and cheese.
- Fried, fatty food, sugar, dairy and caffeine should be avoided as much as possible.
- For low libido, intake of vitamin E can be increased. Foods high in vitamin E include wheat germ oil, almonds, sunflower seeds or oil, peanuts, soybeans, whole-wheat products and asparagus.
- Foods that are galactagogues that promote and increase production of breast milk include:
  - Grains, such as oats, barley, millet and brown rice.
  - Vegetables, including all the green, leafy vegetables.
  - Root vegetables such as carrot, beet and yam.
  - Garlic and ginger, to be used from the second week onwards and in moderation.
  - Green papaya, which is rich in oxytocin.
  - Salmon, a great source of essential fatty acids and omega-3 fatty acids.
  - Fenugreek and fennel, both of which have galactagogue effects.
  - Raw nuts, such as peanuts, almonds, macadamia and cashews.
  - Healthy fats from sources such as sesame oil or extra virgin olive oil.
  - Legumes and beans, including red beans (adzuki beans), black beans, kidney beans and tofu (made from soy beans).

LIFESTYLE INSTRUCTIONS

- Tight bras are not recommended since the constriction impairs proper circulation to the breasts.
- It is helpful to use cold water to shower the breasts to achieve a firming and massaging effect. Avoid using water that is too hot on the breasts as that may loosen surrounding tissue.
- Proper posture is important to prevent breasts from sagging. Swimming is recommended. Exercises that involve excessive vertical (up and down) movement of the breasts are not recommended as they might cause stretching or lengthening of the surrounding tendons and ligaments that support the breasts.

PHARMACOLOGICAL AND CLINICAL RESEARCH

Similar to the rest of the body, optimal development of the breasts is dependent on proper diet and nutrition. Just as bones require calcium and muscles need protein to grow, breasts need adequate nutrition and the proper environment to develop to their full potential. Most women never achieve their full potential because of interruptions during the developmental process, such as poor diet, hormonal imbalances, stress during adolescence, exposure to pollutants, pesticides and chemicals, and lack of certain vitamins and minerals during puberty. In reality, such interruptions are common events in daily life that affect many, many women.

To achieve the desired shape and size of the breast, ***Venus*** uses herbs that act to achieve the breasts' natural potential and stimulate additional growth. Herbs in ***Venus*** have been shown to have remarkable effects to regulate the endocrine system, increase the production of sex hormones and enhance the growth of the breasts.

Venus ™

To fulfill the natural growth potential of the breasts, *Lu Rong* (Cornu Cervi Pantotrichum) is used to stimulate the endocrine system and increase hormone production. Historically, it was used with great success to treat children with slow growth and development. More recently, it has been documented through *in vitro* and *in vivo* studies that it increases the production of hormones responsible for developing secondary sex characteristics.[9] In addition, *Wang Bu Liu Xing* (Semen Vaccariae) and *Mu Tong* (Caulis Akebiae) are commonly used together to stimulate the growth of the sex organs.[10] In fact, it has been found that *Wang Bu Liu Xing* (Semen Vaccariae) given on a daily basis was effective in promoting the growth and metabolism of breast tissue.[11,12] Furthermore, *Dang Gui* (Radix Angelicae Sinensis) is used in ***Venus*** to awaken the estrogen receptors in the breast to stimulate additional growth. One study found that *Dang Gui* (Radix Angelicae Sinensis) has an estrogen-like action and its use was associated with an increase in the sex organs.[13] In short, the use of these herbs restores natural growth potential and stimulates additional growth of the breasts.

In addition, many herbs are added to improve blood circulation and promote the generation of tissues. *Lu Rong* (Cornu Cervi Pantotrichum) and *Dang Gui* (Radix Angelicae Sinensis) are used to improve blood circulation throughout the body.[14] *Huang Qi* (Radix Astragali) is used to stimulate the growth of new tissues.[15] These herbs provide the essential nutrients and the optimal environment for proper and optimal development of the breasts.

In summary, the size and shape of the breasts are not predetermined solely by genetics. Various factors affect the growth and development of the breasts, and numerous methods can be employed to achieve the natural potential and to stimulate additional growth. ***Venus*** contains herbs that have been documented through research studies to regulate the endocrine system, increase the production of sex hormones, and enhance the growth of breasts.

COMPARATIVE ANALYSIS

In Western medicine, there is no drug treatment for insufficient lactation and breast enhancement.

This herbal formula has been used historically to address insufficient lactation, and is currently used for breast enhancement. This formula nourishes the body and promotes blood circulation to breast tissues. Historically, it has been used with great success to relieve pain and resolve insufficient lactation. Today, it is most useful to nourish breast tissues and increase their size. For insufficient lactation, improvement will be noted within days when ***Venus*** is combined with dietary recommendations listed above. For breast enhancement, improvement will be visible after three to six months of taking ***Venus*** combined with daily breast exercise.

References

1. Chan K, Lo AC, Yeung JH, Woo KS. Journal of Pharmacy and Pharmacology 1995 May;47(5):402-6.
2. Pharmacotherapy 1999 July;19(7):870-876.
3. European Journal of Drug Metabolism and Pharmacokinetics 1995; 20(1): 55-60.
4. Natural Standard (www.naturalstandard.com).
5. National Institutes of Health.
6. U.S National Library of Medicine.
7. American Herbal Pharmacopoeia. *Dang Gui* (Radix Angelicae Sinensis) monograph.
8. Lau CB, Ho TC, Chan TW, Kim SC. Use of dong quai (Angelica sinensis) to treat peri- or postmenopausal symptoms in women with breast cancer: is it appropriate? Menopause 2005 Nov-Dec;12(6):734-40.
9. *Chem Pharm Bull*, 1988; 36:2587:2593
10. *Zhong Yao Xue* (Chinese Herbology), 1998; 582:584
11. *Zhong Guo Zhong Yao Za Zhi* (People's Republic of China Journal of Chinese Herbology), 1990; 15(7): 52
12. *Chi Jiao Yi Sheng Za Zhi* (Journal of Barefoot Doctors), 1975; (8): 26
13. Liu, J. and Gong, H. Screening Some of the Estrogen-Like Herbs. The 5th Symposium on Research in Chinese
14. *Report of Medicine*, 1991; 26(9): 714
15. Xue, JX. et al. Effects of the combination of astragalus membranaceus (Fisch.) Bge. (AM), angelica sinensis (Oliv.) Diels (TAS), cyperus rotundus L. (CR), ligusticum chuanxiong Hort (LC) and paeonia veitchii lynch (PV) on the hemorrheological changes in "blood stagnating" rats. *Chung Kuo Chung Yao Tsa Chih*; 19(2): 108-10, 128. Feb 1994

Vibrant ™

CLINICAL APPLICATIONS

- **Tiredness, fatigue, lack of energy**
- **Chronic fatigue syndrome**
- **Sports formula:** to increase mental and physical performance

WESTERN THERAPEUTIC ACTIONS

- Increases basal metabolism to increase energy levels and sense of well-being
- Adaptogenic function help the patient adapt to stress, and improve mental and physical functions

CHINESE THERAPEUTIC ACTIONS

- Tonifies the *yuan* (source) *qi*
- Awakens the *shen* (spirit)

DOSAGE

Take 3 to 4 capsules up to three times daily on an empty stomach with warm water.

INGREDIENTS

Cha Ye (Folium Camelliae)
Ci Wu Jia (Radix et Rhizoma seu Caulis Acanthopanacis Senticosi)
Huang Qi (Radix Astragali)
Ji Xue Cao (Herba Centellae)

BACKGROUND

The modern lifestyle in developed country is one characterized by nonstop stress. When confronted with stress, the body responds with a burst of hormones to empower the organism to cope and survive. To facilitate this process, ***Vibrant*** contains herbs with excellent adaptogenic functions to improve both mental and physical performance.

FORMULA EXPLANATION

Vibrant is formulated to help people with demanding lifestyles cope with fatigue and lack of energy. In terms of traditional Chinese medicine, these herbs tonify the *yuan* (source) *qi*, strengthen the Spleen, and awaken the *shen* (spirit).

Ci Wu Jia (Radix et Rhizoma seu Caulis Acanthopanacis Senticosi) is one of the most commonly used herbs in Asia, Europe, and America. It is approved by the German Commission E as a tonic that has invigorating and fortifying effects to treat fatigue and debility. It also enhances the capacity for work and improves concentration. Its indications include convalescence, prevention of colds and flu, and chronic fatigue syndrome.

When used together, *Ci Wu Jia* (Radix et Rhizoma seu Caulis Acanthopanacis Senticosi) and *Huang Qi* (Radix Astragali) tonify the *yuan* (source) *qi* and have an excitatory effect on the central nervous system. They are both excellent herbs to promote well-being and health. *Huang Qi* (Radix Astragali) tonifies qi and ascends yang. It is especially helpful for patients who have shortness of breath, fatigue, and malaise.

Cha Ye (Folium Camelliae) is a beverage consumed in large quantities by people in Asian countries. It has excellent antibacterial, antiviral, immune-enhancing, and stimulating effects. Consumption of *Cha Ye* (Folium Camelliae) provides an immediate boost of energy to enhance both mental and physical performance.

Ji Xue Cao (Herba Centellae), also known as gotu kola, has adaptogenic effects, and is commonly used to address both mental and physical conditions. Numerous studies have demonstrated its effectiveness to improve memory and to overcome stress, fatigue, mental confusion, and deterioration in mental function.

CAUTIONS & CONTRAINDICATIONS

- Avoid drinking coffee or other beverages containing caffeine while taking ***Vibrant*** to prevent over-stimulation of the central nervous system.
- Possible side effects of ***Vibrant*** include dry mouth and a slight increase in blood pressure or heart rate.

CLINICAL NOTE

- ***Vibrant*** has a rapid onset of action and can be used on an as-needed basis in the early morning, late afternoon, before meetings, exams, or whenever there is fatigue or lack of energy.

SUPPLEMENTARY FORMULAS

- As a long-term, overall constitutional tonic, use with ***Imperial Tonic***.
- To enhance immunity, take with ***Immune +*** or ***Cordyceps 3***.
- For stress and anxiety, combine with ***Calm***.
- For anger and severe emotional disturbances, combine with ***Calm (ES)***.
- For stress and insomnia, take ***Calm ZZZ***.
- For difficulties falling asleep or staying asleep, take at bedtime ***Schisandra ZZZ***.
- To enhance memory and concentration, add ***Enhance Memory***.
- For Spleen qi deficiency, add ***GI Tonic***.
- For adrenal deficiency, add ***Adrenal +***.
- For Kidney yang deficiency, add ***Kidney Tonic (Yang)***.
- For Kidney yin deficiency, add ***Kidney Tonic (Yin)***.
- For sluggishness due to blood stagnation, add ***Circulation (SJ)***.

ACUPUNCTURE TREATMENT

Traditional Points:

- *Guanyuan* (CV 4), *Zhongwan* (CV 12), *Zhongji* (CV 3), *Pishu* (BL 20)
- Apply moxa to *Guanyuan* (CV 4), *Shenshu* (BL 23), *Mingmen* (GV 4) and *Zhongji* (CV 3).

Classic Master Tung's Points:

- **Fatigue:** *Tianhuang* (T 77.17), *Dihuang* (T 77.19), *Renhuang* (T 77.21), *Minghuang* (T 88.12), *Tianhuang* (T 88.13), *Qihuang* (T 88.14), *Beimian* (T 44.07), *Sanyan* (T 11.21), *Zhitong* (T 44.13)

Vibrant™

Master Tung's Points by Dr. Chuan-Min Wang:

- **Quick energy boost:** *Tianhuangfu [shenguan]* (T 77.18), *Huofuhai* (T 33.07)

Balance Method by Dr. Richard Tan:

- Left side: *Hegu* (LI 4), *Yinlingquan* (SP 9), *Waiguan* (TH 5), *Fuliu* (KI 7)
- Right side: *Lingdao* (HT 4), *Zusanli* (ST 36), *Lieque* (LU 7)
- Left and right sides can be alternated from treatment to treatment.

Auricular Medicine by Dr. Li-Chun Huang:

- **Fatigue:** Sympathetic, Kidney, Liver, Spleen, *San Jiao*, Anxious, Nervous Subcortex, Speed Recovered Fatigue. Bleed Ear Apex.

NUTRITION

- Advise the patient to eat a well-balanced diet with an adequate amount of raw foods, fruits and vegetables.
- Encourage the patients to drink at least 8 glasses of water daily.
- Eat more fish and fish oils, onions, garlic, olives, olive oil, herbs, spices, yogurt, fiber, tofu and other soy products.
- Sea vegetables, such as kelp and dulse, replenish the body with minerals like magnesium, potassium, calcium, iodine and iron.
- Decrease intake of red meat, alcohol, fats, caffeine, and highly processed foods. Avoid shellfish, fried foods, junk foods, and processed foods.
- Ensure adequate intake of vitamin B complex to process and utilize energy.
- Avoid the use of stimulants, such as coffee, caffeine, and high-sugar products.
- Food allergy or chemical hypersensitivity can drain energy and cause fatigue. Additional tests should be done to confirm or rule out allergy and/or hypersensitivity.

The Tao of Nutrition by Dr. Maoshing Ni and Cathy McNease:

- **Chronic fatigue syndrome**
  - Recommendations: winter melon, pumpkin, pumpkin seed, yam, sweet potato, lima bean, black bean, soy bean, strawberry, watermelon, pineapple, chestnut, papaya, figs, garlic, onions, and pearl barley.
  - Eat frequent, small meals, and drink more liquids.
  - Juice and drink daily: fresh water chestnut, lotus root, pear, watermelon, and carrots.
  - Make soup from lotus seed, white fungus and figs.
  - Chop garlic finely and stir-fry with egg white, parsley and diced yams.
  - Make chicken soup with garlic, onions, scallions, ginger and daikon radish. Drink soup or cook rice porridge with the broth.
  - Avoid dairy products, alcohol, coffee, sugar, fatty or fried foods, overly spicy foods, cold and raw foods, tomato, eggplant, bell pepper, and shellfish.

LIFESTYLE INSTRUCTIONS

- Daily exercise is advised to increase basal metabolic rate.
- Make sure the patient gets plenty of rest and goes to bed at a sensible hour.
- Get regular exercise and adequate rest.
- Take a bath for about 20 minutes prior to bedtime. Sea salt or Epsom salts can be added to the bath water.
- Engage in activities such as *tai chi chuan [tai ji chuan]*, walking or meditation that allow calmness of mind without creating stagnation or excessive fatigue.
- Avoid exposure to heavy metals, such as lead, cadmium, aluminum, copper and arsenic, all of which can suppress the immune system and cause fatigue.

CASE STUDIES

- D.H., a 24-year-old male, presented with occasional low energy. Pulse was deep and weak especially in the Lung position. The practitioner diagnosed this condition as qi deficiency and Lung qi deficiency. For treatment, ***Vibrant*** was prescribed at 4 capsules three times per day. After only one dose of ***Vibrant*** the patient reported an increase in energy. As a result of taking the herbs for two weeks, the patient reported he was feeling 70% better. The patient now only takes the herbs as needed and finds it works immediately for his fatigue. Submitted by S.L., Yuma, Arizona.
- A 35-year-old medical doctor complained of excessive stress and fatigue. He commented that he began to feel extremely tired around 11:00 a.m., and again at 3 p.m. (lunch hour was from 12 to 1 p.m.). Because the fatigue caused lack of concentration, it made working quite difficult. He began to take ***Vibrant***, 4 capsules in the morning and 4 capsules in the afternoon. He experienced an immediate increase in energy and concentration, which enabled him to work without any difficulty. Submitted by J.C., Diamond Bar, California.
- A 35-year-old female complained of bedwetting, fatigue, low back pain, abdominal pain, loss of appetite and depression. The doctor diagnosed her with Kidney *jing* (essence), yin and yang deficiencies. ***Imperial Tonic*** and ***Vibrant*** were prescribed. The patient reported that bedwetting, depression and pain went away and the energy level went from 2 to 10, on a scale of 1 to 10. As an added and unexpected joy for her, the patient stated she also lost ten pounds even though she had been eating more. Submitted by S.C., Santa Monica, California.
- S.W. suffered from tiredness, restless sleep, and occasional, recurrent nasal congestion during allergy season. She was diagnosed with Kidney yin and yang deficiency, and *wei* (defensive) *qi* deficiency. The practitioner prescribed ***Immune +*** to build the *wei* (defensive) *qi*, and ***Vibrant*** to sustain and build her Kidney yin and yang over time. The patient greatly commented on the positive results of ***Vibrant*** to increase her daily energy level and positive outlook. Submitted by J.P., Naples, Florida.

Vibrant™

PHARMACOLOGICAL AND CLINICAL RESEARCH

Vibrant is formulated to help individuals with demanding lifestyles cope with stress and fatigue. ***Vibrant*** has herbs which help the patient adapt to and overcome mental and physical stress, increase basal metabolism to boost energy, and stimulate the immune system to prevent infections.

Ci Wu Jia (Radix et Rhizoma seu Caulis Acanthopanacis Senticosi) has been used for centuries in both China and Russia for its "adaptogenic" effect to help people adapt to various types of mental and physical stress. Pharmacologically, this herb has a stimulant effect to increase energy and elevate the metabolic rate.[1] It also has a regulatory effect on the endocrine system, specifically the adrenal glands, thyroid, and pancreas. It has been used to treat subjects with adrenocortical insufficiency, enlarged thyroid, and hyperglycemia, with good results.[2,3] The mechanism of action is attributed to the sympatho-adrenal-system mediated stimulating effects, but without the side effects commonly associated with traditional stimulants.[4] Furthermore, this herb has a significant effect to enhance the immune system. Administration of *Ci Wu Jia* (Radix et Rhizoma seu Caulis Acanthopanacis Senticosi) is associated with an improvement of the immune system in both healthy and immune-suppressed subjects by increasing the production of white blood cells, interferon, and interleukin-6.[5,6,7,8] *Ci Wu Jia* (Radix et Rhizoma seu Caulis Acanthopanacis Senticosi) also has a mild sedative effect to calm the central nervous system and improve the quality and quantity of sleep.[9] Lastly, according to one study of more than 2,100 healthy human subjects, administration of *Ci Wu Jia* (Radix et Rhizoma seu Caulis Acanthopanacis Senticosi) is associated with marked adaptogenic effects to increase mental performance and physical working capacity in various stressful environments.[10] Eleutheroside E, a compound from *Ci Wu Jia* (Radix et Rhizoma seu Caulis Acanthopanacis Senticosi), is considered as the main compound that contributes to its adaptogenic and antifatigue actions.[11] According to another study, a randomized clinical trial of *Ci Wu Jia* (Radix et Rhizoma seu Caulis Acanthopanacis Senticosi) found that it safely improved some aspects of mental health and social functioning in elderly hypertensive human volunteers.[12]

Huang Qi (Radix Astragali) is one of the most frequently used Chinese herbs and is historically used for its function to tonify the *wei* (defensive) *qi*. From Western medicine perspectives, *Huang Qi* (Radix Astragali) has been shown to elevate the basal metabolic rate to increase energy levels.[13] Furthermore, it has an immunostimulant effect to increase the production of white blood cells,[14,15] and a hematopoietic effect to increase the production of red blood cells.[16] According to a clinical study of 115 leucopenic patients, it was found that the use of *Huang Qi* (Radix Astragali) is associated with an "obvious rise of the white blood cell count" in a dose-dependent relationship.[17]

Cha Ye (Folium Camelliae) has a wide range of functions and is commonly used in different clinical applications. It is an effective stimulant for the central nervous system as it increases body metabolism and boosts energy levels.[18] It has an immunostimulant effect to boost the immune system and its functions.[19,20] It also has an antiobesity effect to reduce body weight to prevent obesity, type II diabetes, cardiovascular disease, and other chronic diseases.[21] According to a randomized, double-blind, placebo-controlled, parallel study on 111 healthy adult volunteers, daily consumption of decaffeinated green tea is associated with significant benefits in lowering cardiovascular risk factors, such as decreased blood pressure, LDL cholesterol, serum amyloid-α (a marker of chronic inflammation), and serum malondialdehyde (a marker of oxidative stress). Furthermore, adverse effects associated with green tea were mild and few, and not different from placebo.[22] Overall, use of *Cha Ye* (Folium Camelliae) prolongs life span, contributes to longevity, and protects against life-threatening diseases.[23,24]

Ji Xue Cao (Herba Centellae) has adaptogenic effects, and is commonly used to address both mental and physical conditions. Numerous studies have demonstrated its effectiveness to improve memory and to overcome stress, fatigue, mental confusion,[25] and deterioration in mental function.[26,27] *Ji Xue Cao* (Herba Centellae) has also demonstrated a marked cognitive effect to ameliorate cognitive impairment in Alzheimer's disease.[28] The mechanism of action is attributed in part to its effect to improve blood circulation to peripheral parts of the organs and limbs.[29,30]

In summary, ***Vibrant*** is an excellent formula to help individuals with busy and demanding lifestyles cope with mental stress and physical fatigue. It contains herbs to calm the mind to relieve mental stress, along with herbs to stimulate the basal metabolic rate to increase energy levels. Indeed, it is an excellent formula to help individuals adapt to both mental and physical stress.

COMPARATIVE ANALYSIS

One striking difference between Western and traditional Chinese medicine is that Western medicine focuses and excels in crisis management, while traditional Chinese medicine emphasizes and shines in holistic and preventative treatments. Therefore, in emergencies, such as gunshot wounds or surgery, Western medicine is generally the treatment of choice. However, for treatment of chronic idiopathic illness of unknown origins, where all lab tests are normal and a clear diagnosis cannot be made, traditional Chinese medicine is distinctly superior.

In cases of chronic fatigue and tiredness where all tests are normal but there are still general and non-diagnostic signs and symptoms, Western medicine offers few treatment options since there is no clear diagnosis. On the other hand, traditional Chinese medicine is beneficial as it excels in maintenance and preventative therapies. Herbs can be used to regulate imbalances and alleviate associated signs and symptoms. Therefore, herbal therapy should definitely be employed to prevent deterioration and to restore optimal health.

Vibrant™

References

1. *CA*, 1967; 66:51311.
2. *CA*, 1964; 60:163896.
3. *CA*, 1967; 68:19237.
4. Panossian A. & Wagner H. Stimulating effect of adaptogens: an overview with particular reference to their efficacy following single dose administration. *Phytother Res.* 2005, 19(10): 819-838.
5. *Hei Long Jiang Zhong Yi Yao* (Heilongjiang Chinese Medicine and Herbology), 1981; (4):37.
6. *Zhong Cao Yao* (Chinese Herbal Medicine), 1990j; 21(1):27.
7. *CA*, 1972; 76:54331.
8. Steinmann GG, Esperester A, Joller P. Immunopharmacological in vitro effects of Eleutherococcus senticosus extracts. Arzneimittelforschung. 2001 Jan;51(1):76-83.
9. *Zhong Yi Yao Xue Bao* (Report of Chinese Medicine and Herbology), 1985; (2):29.
10. Werbach M. & Murray M. Botanical influences on illness - a sourcebook of clinical research. 2nd edition, Pub.- Third Line Press Inc. Tarzana California. 2000, 624 pp.
11. Kimura Y, Sumiyoshi M. Effects of various Eleutherococcus senticosus cortex on swimming time, natural killer activity and corticosterone level in forced swimming stressed mice. Second Department of Medical Biochemistry, School of Medicine, Ehime University. Shigenobu-cho, Onsen-gun, Ehime 719-0295, Japan. J Ethnopharmacol. 2004 Dec;95(2-3):447-53.
12. Cicero A.F., Derosa G., Brillante R., Bernardi R., Nascetti S. & Gaddi A. Effects of Siberian ginseng (*Eleutherococcus senticosus* maxim.) on elderly quality of life: a randomized clinical trial . *Arch Gerontol Geriatr Suppl.* 2004, 9: 69-73.
13. *Zhong Yao Yao Li Yu Lin Chuang* (Pharmacology and Clinical Applications of Chinese Herbs), 1985:193.
14. *Shan Xi Yi Yao Za Zhi* (Shanxi Journal of Medicine and Herbology), 1974; 5-6:57.
15. *Biol Pharm Bull*, 1977; 20(11)-1178-82.
16. *Nan Jing Zhong Yi Xue Yuan Xue Bao* (Journal of Nanjing University of Traditional Chinese Medicine), 1989; 1:43.
17. Weng, XS. *Chung Juo Chung Hsia I Chieh Ho Tsa Chih.* August 1995.
18. Olin, R. et al. *The Lawrence Review of Natural Products by Facts and Comparison.* Green Tea. May 1993.
19. Monobe M, Ema K, Tokuda Y, Maeda-Yamamoto M. Enhancement of the phagocytic activity of macrophage-like cells with a crude polysaccharide derived from green tea (Camellia sinensis) extract. National Institute of Vegetable and Tea Science, NARO, Shimada, Shizuoka, Japan. Biosci Biotechnol Biochem. 2010;74(6):1306-8.
20. Monobe M, Ema K, Kato F, Maeda-Yamamoto M. Immunostimulating activity of a crude polysaccharide derived from green tea (Camellia sinensis) extract. National Institute of Vegetable and Tea Science, NARO, Shizuoka, Japan. J Agric Food Chem. 2008 Feb 27;56(4):1423-7.
21. Grove KA, Lambert JD. Laboratory, epidemiological, and human intervention studies show that tea (Camellia sinensis) may be useful in the prevention of obesity. Department of Food Science, The Pennsylvania State University, University Park, PA 16802, USA. J Nutr. 2010 Mar;140(3):446-53.
22. Nantz MP, Rowe CA, Bukowski JF, Percival SS. Standardized capsule of Camellia sinensis lowers cardiovascular risk factors in a randomized, double-blind, placebo-controlled study. Food Science and Human Nutrition Department, University of Florida, Gainesville, FL, USA. Nutrition. 2009 Feb;25(2):147-54.
23. Uchida, S. et al. Radioprotective effects of (-)-epigallocatechin 3-0-gallate (green tea tannin) in mice. *Life Sci*;50(2):147. 1992.
24. Sadakata, S. et al. Mortality among female practitioners of Chanoyu (Japanese "tea-ceremony"). *Tohoku J Exp Med*; 166(4):475. 1992.
25. Bartram, T. *Encyclopedia of Herbal Medicine 1st edition.* Dorest, England: Grace Publishers. 1995.
26. Kapoor, LD. *CRC Handbook of Ayruvedic Medicinal Plants.* Boca Raton, FL: CRC Press. 1990 .
27. Murray, M. Centella asiatica (Gotu Kola) Monograph. *American Journal of Natural Medicine.* Volume 3, No. 6 Jul/Aug:22-26. 1996
28. Xu Y, Cao Z, Khan I, Luo Y. Gotu Kola (Centella Asiatica) extract enhances phosphorylation of cyclic AMP response element binding protein in neuroblastoma cells expressing amyloid beta peptide. J Alzheimers Dis. 2008 Apr;13(3):341-9.
29. Cesarone MR, Belcaro G, Rulo A, Griffin M, Ricci A, Ippolito E, De Sanctis MT, Incandela L, Bavera P, Cacchio M, Bucci M. Microcirculatory effects of total triterpenic fraction of Centella asiatica in chronic venous hypertension: measurement by laser Doppler, TcPO2-CO2, and leg volumetry. Irvine Vascular Laboratory, St Mary's Hospital and Imperial College, London, UK. Angiology. 2001 Oct;52 Suppl 2:S45-8.
30. Marastoni F., Baldo A., Redaelli G. & Ghiringhelli L. *Centella asiatica* extract in venous pathology of the lower limbs and its evaluation as compared with tribenoside. *Minerva Cardioangiol.* 1982, 30(4): 201-207.

Vital Essence ™

CLINICAL APPLICATIONS

- **Male infertility**
- **Male sexual and reproductive disorders,** such as infertility, low sperm count, poor sperm motility, mobility and morphology, premature ejaculation, and spermatorrhea

WESTERN THERAPEUTIC ACTIONS

- Regulates the sex organs and hormone production
- Balances hormone productions to treat sexual and reproductive disorders
- Antiaging and adaptogenic effects to improve general health

CHINESE THERAPEUTIC ACTIONS

- Tonifies Kidney yin and Liver blood
- Replenishes Kidney *jing* (essence)
- Revitalizes Kidney yang and *ming men* (life-gate) fire

DOSAGE

Take 3 to 4 capsules three times daily. Dosage can be increased up to 6 to 8 capsules three times daily. For optimal results, this formula should be taken continuously for two to three months, or until successful pregnancy of partner.

INGREDIENTS

Che Qian Zi (Semen Plantaginis)
Chuan Xiong (Rhizoma Chuanxiong)
Dang Gui (Radix Angelicae Sinensis)
Fu Ling (Poria)
Fu Pen Zi (Fructus Rubi)
Gou Qi Zi (Fructus Lycii)
Huang Qi (Radix Astragali)
Jiu Cai Zi (Semen Allii Tuberosi)
Shu Di Huang (Radix Rehmanniae Praeparata)
Tu Si Zi (Semen Cuscutae)
Wu Wei Zi (Fructus Schisandrae Chinensis)
Xian Mao (Rhizoma Curculiginis)
Yin Yang Huo (Herba Epimedii)
Zhi He Shou Wu (Radix Polygoni Multiflori Praeparata)

BACKGROUND

Infertility is the inability to conceive after one year of unprotected intercourse. Infertility may be due to sperm disorder (35%), decreased ovarian reserve or ovulatory dysfunction (20%), tubal dysfunction and pelvic lesions (30%), abnormal cervical mucus (5%), and unidentified causes (10%). Specifically, sperm disorder refers to defects in quality or quantity of sperm, which may be caused by endocrine disorders, genetic disorders, and drugs and toxins (anabolic steroids, corticosteroids, androgens, estrogens, aspirin, opioids, alcohol, nicotine, marijuana, and many others).[1]

FORMULA EXPLANATION

Vital Essence is mainly composed of herbs that tonify Kidney yin, yang and *jing* (essence). Tonifying Kidney yin will boost sperm count. Warming the Kidney yang will increase sperm mobility and motility. Replenishing Kidney *jing* (essence) will improve sperm morphology.

Gou Qi Zi (Fructus Lycii), *Shu Di Huang* (Radix Rehmanniae Praeparata) and *Dang Gui* (Radix Angelicae Sinensis) tonify Kidney yin and Liver blood. They replenish the foundation of the Kidney. *Jiu Cai Zi* (Semen Allii Tuberosi), *Tu Si Zi* (Semen Cuscutae), *Xian Mao* (Rhizoma Curculiginis) and *Yin Yang Huo* (Herba Epimedii) vitalize the Kidney yang, increase libido, and improve sperm mobility and motility. *Fu Pen Zi* (Fructus Rubi) and *Zhi He Shou Wu* (Radix Polygoni Multiflori Praeparata) are essential Kidney *jing* (essence) tonics for the treatment of male infertility. *Chuan Xiong* (Rhizoma Chuanxiong) moves blood and prevents the tonic herbs from creating stagnation in the body. *Huang Qi* (Radix Astragali) tonifies the *zhong* (central) *qi* to enhance energy. *Fu Ling* (Poria) and *Che Qian Zi* (Semen Plantaginis) are dampness-eliminating herbs that offset the cloying properties of the yin and *jing* (essence) tonics. *Fu Ling* (Poria) also strengthens the Spleen to ensure maximum absorption of the Kidney tonics. *Che Qian Zi* (Semen Plantaginis) ensures the absence of blockage in the lower *jiao*. Finally, *Wu Wei Zi* (Fructus Schisandrae Chinensis), an astringent, is added to prevent further leakage of *jing* (essence).

Together, the herbs in ***Vital Essence*** tonify Kidney yin, yang and *jing* (essence) to successfully treat male reproductive disorders.

CAUTIONS & CONTRAINDICATIONS

- It is important to remember that this formula is designed to treat infertility. They do ***not*** offer any protection against sexually transmitted diseases.
- Many drugs are known to damage and impair healthy sperm, including but not limited to anabolic steroids, corticosteroids, androgens, estrogens, aspirin, opioid analgesics, cimetidine, methotrexate, spirolactone, and sulfasalazine. Patients who take these medications should consult their physician to see if these drugs can be substituted or discontinued.
- This herbal formula contains herbs that invigorate blood circulation, such as *Dang Gui* (Radix Angelicae Sinensis). Therefore, patients who are on anticoagulant or antiplatelet therapies, such as Coumadin (warfarin), should use this formula with caution, or not at all, as there may be a higher risk of bleeding and bruising.[2,3,4]
- According to most textbooks and contemporary references, the classic entry of "*He Shou Wu*" is now separated into two entries: the unprepared *Sheng Shou Wu* (Radix Polygoni Multiflori) and the prepared *Zhi He Shou Wu* (Radix Polygoni Multiflori Praeparata), as they have significantly different therapeutic

Vital Essence™

effects and side effects. *Sheng Shou Wu* (Radix Polygoni Multiflori) is a stimulant laxative that treats constipation, but may cause nausea, vomiting, abdominal pain, diarrhea, and in rare cases, liver disorder (dose- and time-dependent, and reversible upon discontinuation).[5] On the other hand, *Zhi He Shou Wu* (Radix Polygoni Multiflori Praeparata) is a tonic herb that is safe and well-tolerated. The dramatic changes in the therapeutic effect and safety profile are attributed to the long and complicated processing of the root with *Hei Dou* (Semen Sojae) through repeated blending, cooking, and drying procedures. When properly processed, the chemical composition of the root changes significantly. Many new compounds are generated from the Maillard reaction (four furanones, two furans, two nitrogen compounds, one pyran, one alcohol and one sulfur compound). Furthermore, the preparation process causes changes in the composition of sugars and 16 kinds of amino acids; it also reduces the pH of the herb from 6.28 to 5.61.[6,7] In summary, these changes give rise to the tonic effects of the prepared roots, and eliminate the adverse reactions associated with the unprepared roots. **Note:** Due to medical risks and legal liabilities, it is prudent to exercise caution and ***not*** use this herb in either prepared or unprepared forms in patients with pre-existing or risk factors of liver diseases.

CLINICAL NOTES

- ***Vitality*** and ***Vital Essence*** are two formulas that are frequently combined together. ***Vitality*** tonifies Kidney yang to treat sexual dysfunction. ***Vital Essence*** replenishes Kidney yin and *jing* (essence) to treat reproductive disorders. Together, they complement and enhance the clinical success of each others.
- Semen analysis is extremely important, as sperm factors account for approximately 35% of all cases of infertility. Parameters evaluated include ejaculate volume, viscosity, appearance, pH balance, sperm count, motility, and sperm morphology. Semen composition of fructose less than 120 mg/dL is indicative of ejaculatory duct obstruction or agenesis of seminal vesicles. Most patients may already have an analysis. They should be instructed to re-test and compare the results after taking herbs for two to three months.
- Hormonal analysis is also important. Testosterone level studies are indicated for patients displaying loss of libido and possible hypogonadotropic abnormality. Normal FSH at baseline analysis correlates with improvement in semen parameters.
- Testicular volume estimation for impaired spermatogenic function or oligospermia should be performed.

Pulse Diagnosis by Dr. Jimmy Wei-Yen Chang:

- Deep and small pulse on the left *chi*.

SUPPLEMENTARY FORMULAS

- With impotence, erectile dysfunction or low libido, add ***Vitality***.
- For decreased sperm motility or mobility, combine with ***Kidney Tonic (Yang)***.
- For low sperm count, add ***Kidney Tonic (Yin)***.
- With premature ejaculation or spermatorrhea, add ***Vitality*** and *Jin Suo Gu Jing Wan* (Metal Lock Pill to Stabilize the Essence).
- For stress and anxiety, add ***Calm*** or ***Calm (ES)***.
- To improve the quality of sperm for *in vitro* fertilization (IVF), add ***Polygonum 14***.
- With difficulty in ejaculation, add *Wei Ling Xian* (Radix et Rhizoma Clematidis) and *Shi Chang Pu* (Rhizoma Acori Tatarinowii) with ***Resolve (Lower)***.
- With thick or condensed semen due to deficiency fire of the Kidney, add ***Nourish***.
- With prostatitis, add ***P-Support***.
- For varicocele, add ***Resolve (Lower)*** and ***P-Support***.

ACUPUNCTURE TREATMENT

Traditional Points:

- Needle and moxa: *Dahe* (KI 12), *Qugu* (CV 2), *Sanyinjiao* (SP 6), *Guanyuan* (CV 4), *Zhongji* (CV 3)
- Needle and moxa: *Qugu* (CV 2), *Yinlian* (LR 11), *Dadu* (SP 2), *Ciliao* (BL 32)
- Needle and moxa: *Shenshu* (BL 23), *Guanyuan* (CV 4), *Rangu* (KI 2), *Fuliu* (KI 7), *Zusanli* (ST 36), *Sanyinjiao* (SP 6)

Classic Master Tung's Points:

- **Infertility (male):** *Tianhuang* (T 77.17), *Dihuang* (T 77.19), *Renhuang* (T 77.21), *Tianhuang* (T 88.13), *Minghuang* (T 88.12), *Qihuang* (T 88.14); Endocrine, Kidney and Testicle points on the ear. Moxa *du* (governing) channel on the back
- **Spermatorrhea:** *Tianhuang* (T 77.17), *Dihuang* (T 77.19), *Renhuang* (T 77.21), *Tongshen* (T 88.09), *Tongwei* (T 88.10), *Shuijin* (T 1010.20), *Shuitong* (T 1010.19), *Tianhuangfu [Shenguan]* (T 77.18). Moxa *Guanyuan* (CV 4), *Zhongji* (CV 3), *Zhongshu* (GV 7)

Master Tung's Points by Dr. Chuan-Min Wang:

- **Low sperm count, poor motility, mobility, morphology:** *Tianhuangfu [shenguan]* (T 77.18), *Dihuang* (T 77.19), *Renhuang* (T 77.21)

Balance Method by Dr. Richard Tan:

- Left side: *Linggu* (T 22.05), *Lieque* (LU 7), *Shuiquan* (KI 5), *Sanyinjiao* (SP 6)
- Right side: *Yangxi* (LI 5), *Zusanli* (ST 36)
- Alternate sides from treatment to treatment

Auricular Medicine by Dr. Li-Chun Huang:

- **Emission:** *Shenmen*, Liver, Neurasthenia Point (front and back), Neurasthenia Area (front and back), Nervous Subcortex, Dream Disturbed Sleep Area, Heart, Kidney. Bleed Ear Apex.

Vital Essence™

NUTRITION

- Patients should be advised to eat more clams, oysters, sea cucumbers, and lamb.
- Excessive use of certain herbs such as echinacea, ginkgo biloba, and St. John's Wort have been associated with infertility and should be avoided.
- Consume an adequate amount of selenium (200 to 400 mcg daily), as deficiency has been associated with reduced sperm count and sterility in men.
- Consume an adequate amount of vitamin C and bioflavonoids (2,000 to 6,000 daily), as they are important in sperm production.
- Consume an adequate amount of vitamin E (200 to 400 IU daily), which helps to balance hormone production.
- Adequate intake of zinc (80 mg daily) is important for normal functioning of the reproductive organs.
- Avoid alcohol, coffee, and cigarette smoking.

The Tao of Nutrition by Dr. Maoshing Ni and Cathy McNease:

- **Infertility or inadequate sperm:** Eat three quail eggs before bedtime daily for one month.

LIFESTYLE INSTRUCTIONS

- Avoid excessive sexual intercourse or ejaculation. While taking herbs, sexual activity should be reduced to once a week until the sperm lab report is normal.
- Certain artificial lubricants may prevent the sperm from reaching the cervix. Saliva may also have a negative effect on spermatozoa.
- Avoid drinking alcohol, which reduces sperm count.
- Avoid smoking (and exposure to secondhand smoke of) cigarettes and marijuana, as they impair sperm production.
- Avoid stress as much as possible.

PHARMACOLOGICAL AND CLINICAL RESEARCH

Male sperm disorders account for approximately 35% of failed pregnancies. Disorders of sperm production can evolve from an assortment of conditions that include, but are not limited to, spermatogenesis, azoospermia, varicocele, retrograde ejaculation, in addition to endocrine, genetic, social, pharmaceutical and psychological factors. As men age, the sperm density and testosterone levels appear to decrease while estradiol and estrone levels increase.[8] Therefore, herbs must be used to regulate the endocrine system, balance the hormones, and promote blood circulation. ***Vital Essence*** is designed with such general and specific effects to treat male infertility.

Vital Essence has many herbs to increase the quantity and improve the quality of sperm. Pharmacologically, *Fu Pen Zi* (Fructus Rubi) and *Yin Yang Huo* (Herba Epimedii) have been shown to increase the production and release of testosterone.[9,10] *Xian Mao* (Rhizoma Curculiginis) stimulates the reproductive system to increase the weight of the testicles.[11] *Jiu Cai Zi* (Semen Allii Tuberosi) and *Xian Mao* (Rhizoma Curculiginis) have positive aphrodisiac properties that affect sexual behavior in male subjects, such as an increase in penile erection, mating performance, mount frequency, mount latency, and ejaculation frequency.[12,13] In addition, administration of *Yin Yang Huo* (Herba Epimedii) not only stimulates the sensory nerves and increases sexual desire and activity, it also increases sperm production.[14] Clinically, many herbs in ***Vital Essence*** have been used with great success to treat male infertility. According to one study, use of fresh *Gou Qi Zi* (Fructus Lycii) in a formula effectively increased sperm count and improved sperm motility. Of 42 patients, 33 successfully conceived children.[15] According to another study, one formula was reported to have a 95.3% rate of effectiveness in treating 129 males with poor sperm count using an herbal formula in decoction daily that contained 12 grams each of *Zhi He Shou Wu* (Radix Polygoni Multiflori Praeparata), *Huang Jing* (Rhizoma Polygonati), *Huang Qi* (Radix Astragali), *Yin Yang Huo* (Herba Epimedii), *Gou Qi Zi* (Fructus Lycii), *Tu Si Zi* (Semen Cuscutae), and *Zi He Che* (Placenta Hominis).[16]

Obstructed blood circulation may adversely affect sperm emission and spermatogenesis. Therefore, ***Vital Essence*** contains herbs to invigorate and improve blood circulation to peripheral parts of the body, such as *Dang Gui* (Radix Angelicae Sinensis) and *Chuan Xiong* (Rhizoma Chuanxiong). Use of *Dang Gui* (Radix Angelicae Sinensis) is associated with significant effects on angiogenesis, the physiological process that promotes blood vessel formation in various parts of the body.[17] It also improves overall blood circulation by decreasing the whole blood specific viscosity, or improving the hemorrheological changes associated with blood stagnation.[18] Administration of *Chuan Xiong* (Rhizoma Chuanxiong) is associated with increased blood perfusion.[19] The mechanism of this action is attributed mainly to its effect to inhibit thrombus formation and platelet aggregation.[20]

In this formula, *Zhi He Shou Wu* (Radix Polygoni Multiflori Praeparata) is well known for its antiaging effect as it demonstrated a marked effect to improve general health and increase life expectancy.[21] *Tu Si Zi* (Semen Cuscutae) has an adaptogenic effect to improve both mental and physical health.[22] Though these two herbs do not treat male infertility directly, they address the underlying deficiencies associated with many cases of infertility.

In summary, ***Vital Essence*** is one of the best formulas to treat male infertility. Not only does it treat the underlying sexual and reproductive disorders, it also restores the overall health and well-being of patients.

COMPARATIVE ANALYSIS

One striking difference between Western and traditional Chinese medicine is that Western medicine focuses and excels in crisis management, while traditional Chinese medicine emphasizes and shines in holistic and preventative treatments. Therefore, in emergencies, such as gunshot wounds or surgery, Western medicine is generally the treatment of choice. However, for treatment of chronic idiopathic illness of unknown origins, where

Vital Essence™

all lab tests are normal and a clear diagnosis cannot be made, traditional Chinese medicine is distinctly superior.

There is no drug treatment for male infertility. Those with sperm disorders (low sperm count, poor sperm motility, mobility and morphology) are usually treated with physical medicine, such as artificial insemination. However, there are no drug options available to increase sperm quantity and quality.

One main function of Kidney yang is regulation of sexual and reproductive functions. ***Vital Essence*** is a Kidney yang tonic formula that emphasizes more on maintaining reproductive functions and treating reproductive disorders, such as low sperm count, poor sperm motility, mobility, and morphology. Though this formula is definitely effective, it does not have an instantaneous effect, but rather requires continuous use for two to three months for maximum effect.

Reproductive disorder is perhaps best treated with integration of Western and traditional Chinese medicine. Herbal therapy has been found to be exceptionally effective for male infertility to increase sperm quantity and quality. In most cases, the use of herbal therapy is sufficient for mild to moderate cases of male infertility. In severe cases where herbs improve the condition but the patient still cannot achieve fertilization, artificial insemination can also be employed to enhance the success rate.

References

1. Beers, M. and Berkow, R. *The Merck Manual of Diagnosis and Therapy 19th Edition*. 2011.
2. Chan K, Lo AC, Yeung JH, Woo KS. Journal of Pharmacy and Pharmacology 1995 May;47(5):402-6.
3. Pharmacotherapy 1999 July;19(7):870-876.
4. European Journal of Drug Metabolism and Pharmacokinetics 1995; 20(1): 55-60.
5. Lei X, et al. Liver Damage Associated with Polygonum multiflorum Thunb.: A Systematic Review of Case Reports and Case Series. Evid Based Complement Alternat Med. 2015;2015:459749. doi: 10.1155/2015/459749.
6. Liu Z, Chao Z, Liu Y, Song Z, Lu A. Maillard reaction involved in the steaming process of the root of Polygonum multiflorum. Institution of Basic Theory, China Academy of Chinese Medical Sciences, Beijing, PR China. Planta Med. 2009 Jan;75(1):84-8. Epub 2008 Nov 25.
7. Liu Z, et al. In vitro antioxidant activities of maillard reaction products produced in the steaming process of Polygonum multiflorum root. Nat Prod Commun. 2011 Jan;6(1):55-8.
8. Beers, M. and Berkow, R. *The Merck Manual of Diagnosis and Therapy 19th Edition*. 2011.
9. Chen K, Fang J, Kuang X, Mo Q. Effects of the fruit of Rubus chingii Hu on hypothalamus-pituitary-sex gland axis in rats. Zhongguo Zhong Yao Za Zhi. 1996 Sep;21(9):560-2 inside back cover.
10. *Zhong Xi Yi Jie He Za Zhi* (Journal of Integrated Chinese and Western Medicine), 1989; 9(12):737-8,710.
11. *Zhong Guo Zhong Yao Za Zhi* (People's Republic of China Journal of Chinese Herbology), 1989; 14(10):42.
12. Guohua H, Yanhua L, Rengang M, Dongzhi W, Zhengzhi M, Hua Z. Aphrodisiac properties of Allium tuberosum seeds extract. College of Life and Environment Science, Shanghai Normal University, Shanghai, PR China. J Ethnopharmacol. 2009 Apr 21;122(3):579-82.
13. Chauhan NS, Rao ChV, Dixit VK. Effect of Curculigo orchioides rhizomes on sexual behaviour of male rats. Department of Pharmaceutical Sciences, Dr. H.S. Gour University Sagar (M.P.), India. Fitoterapia. 2007 Dec;78(7-8):530-4.
14. *Zhong Yao Da Ci Dian* (Dictionary of Chinese Herbs), 1977:2251.
15. *Xin Zhong Yi* (New Chinese Medicine), 1988; 2:20.
16. *Zhong Guo Zhong Xi Yi Jie He Za Zhi* (Chinese Journal of Integrative Chinese and Western Medicine), 1995; (1):43.
17. Lam HW, Lin HC, Lao SC, Gao JL, Hong SJ, Leong CW, Yue PY, Kwan YW, Leung AY, Wang YT, Lee SM. The angiogenic effects of Angelica sinensis extract on HUVEC in vitro and zebrafish in vivo. J Cell Biochem. 2008 Jan 1;103(1):195-211.
18. Xue, JX. et al. Effects of the combination of astragalus membranaceus (Fisch.) Bge. (AM), angelica sinensis (Oliv.) Diels (TAS), cyperus rotundus L. (CR), ligusticum chuanxiong Hort (LC) and paeonia veitchii lynch (PV) on the hemorrheological changes in "blood stagnating" rats. *Chung Kuo Chung Yao Tsa Chih*; 19(2):108-10, 128. Feb 1994.
19. *Zhong Yao Xue* (Chinese Herbology), 1989; 535:539.
20. Tian JW, Fu FH, Jiang WL, Wang CY, Sun F, Zhang TP. Protective effect of ligusticum chuanxiong phthalides on focai cerebral ischemia in rats and its related mechanism of action. Zhongguo Zhong Yao Za Zhi. 2005 Mar;30(6):466-8.
21. *Zhong Yao Yao Li Yu Lin Chuang* (Pharmacology and Clinical Applications of Chinese Herbs), 1989; 5(3):19.
22. *Chang Yong Zhong Yao Cheng Fen Yu Yao Li Shou Ce* (A Handbook of the Composition and Pharmacology of Common Chinese Drugs), 1994; 1563:1564.

Vitality™

CLINICAL APPLICATIONS

- **Sexual function and performance**
- **Sexual desire and arousal** in women and men
- **Sexual disorders:** low libido, impotence, erectile dysfunction, premature ejaculation, and spermatorrhea

WESTERN THERAPEUTIC ACTIONS

- Increases the secretion of endogenous hormones
- Increases the secretion of testosterone, corticosterone, and cortisol

CHINESE THERAPEUTIC ACTIONS

- Warms Kidney yang
- Replenishes Kidney *jing* (essence)
- Increases sexual desire

DOSAGE

Take 3 to 4 capsules three times daily on an empty stomach with warm water. The last dosage after dinner or before bedtime can be served with grain-based liquor such as vodka to enhance the overall effect, as this formula was traditionally prepared as an herbal tincture.

INGREDIENTS

Ba Ji Tian (Radix Morindae Officinalis)
Dang Gui (Radix Angelicae Sinensis)
Du Zhong (Cortex Eucommiae)
Fu Zi (Radix Aconiti Lateralis Praeparata)
Gou Qi Zi (Fructus Lycii)
Jiu Cai Zi (Semen Allii Tuberosi)
Ren Shen (Radix et Rhizoma Ginseng)
Rou Gui (Cortex Cinnamomi)
Shan Yao (Rhizoma Dioscoreae)
Shan Zhu Yu (Fructus Corni)
She Chuang Zi (Fructus Cnidii)
Shu Di Huang (Radix Rehmanniae Praeparata)
Suo Yang (Herba Cynomorii)
Tu Si Zi (Semen Cuscutae)
Yin Yang Huo (Herba Epimedii)

BACKGROUND

Sexual dysfunction is characterized by interference with interest or inability to engage in sexual intercourse. Common components of sexual dysfunction in men include decreased libido, lowered erectile dysfunction, inability to ejaculate and experience orgasm; and in women, female sexual dysfunction include lowered sexual desire, decreased sexual arousal, and absent or diminished orgasm. Possible causes of sexual dysfunction include stress, anxiety, depression, diabetes, endocrine disorders, circulatory disorders, and drugs (beta-blockers, diuretics, alcohol, antidepressants, hormones, and many others).

FORMULA EXPLANATION

Vitality is a formula with primary emphasis to treat sexual dysfunction in men and women. It is an excellent formula to tonify Kidney yang and Kidney *jing* (essence). Clinically, deficiencies of Kidney yang and Kidney *jing* (essence) are characterized by impotence, erectile dysfunction, premature ejaculation, low sperm count, low libido, and general sexual disorders. In Western terminology, these herbs increase the production of sex hormones; and in TCM terminology, these herbs tonify Kidney yang and Kidney *jing* (essence). This formula works to enhance libido in women as it boosts the testosterone levels and Kidney yang.

The direct translation of the chief herb *Yin Yang Huo* (Herba Epimedii) is "horny goat herb." It was originally discovered by a herder who noticed the increase in proliferation in one of his herds of goats that were grazing on this herb. *Yin Yang Huo* (Herba Epimedii) increases sexual activity, increases sperm production, stimulates the sensory nerves and therefore increases sexual desire. Weakness of Kidney yang and depletion of Kidney *jing* (essence) contribute to symptoms of impotence, decreased libido, spermatorrhea, premature ejaculation and other sexual dysfunctions. The treatment protocol is to increase the Kidney yang and tonify the Kidney *jing* (essence). *Fu Zi* (Radix Aconiti Lateralis Praeparata), *Rou Gui* (Cortex Cinnamomi), *Jiu Cai Zi* (Semen Allii Tuberosi), *Du Zhong* (Cortex Eucommiae), *Tu Si Zi* (Semen Cuscutae), *Ba Ji Tian* (Radix Morindae Officinalis), *Suo Yang* (Herba Cynomorii), and *She Chuang Zi* (Fructus Cnidii) warm and tonify the Kidney yang. *Shan Zhu Yu* (Fructus Corni), *Shu Di Huang* (Radix Rehmanniae Praeparata), *Gou Qi Zi* (Fructus Lycii), and *Shan Yao* (Rhizoma Dioscoreae) tonify Kidney *jing* (essence). *Dang Gui* (Radix Angelicae Sinensis) tonifies and moves blood, and directs the effect to the lower abdomen. *Ren Shen* (Radix et Rhizoma Ginseng) is used to replenish the vital energy and prolong stamina.

Together, the herbs in ***Vitality*** tonify Kidney yang and Kidney *jing* (essence) to effectively treat male and female sexual disorders.

CAUTIONS & CONTRAINDICATIONS

- This formula is contraindicated in individuals with exterior or excess conditions, such as infections or inflammations.
- Because this formula is warm to hot in property, prolonged use may be associated with reactions such as thirst, dry mouth, warm sensations, constipation, flushed face, and nosebleeds. To avoid these reactions, decrease the dosage or temporarily discontinue the formula.
- ***Vitality*** should be used with caution in patients with pre-existing hypertension, since many herbs in this formula are warm or hot in nature and may raise the blood pressure.

Vitality™

- Patients who wear a pacemaker, or individuals who take antiarrhythmic drugs or cardiac glycosides such as Lanoxin (digoxin), should not take this formula. *Fu Zi* (Radix Aconiti Lateralis Praeparata) may interact with these drugs by affecting the rhythm and potentiating the contractile strength of the heart.[1]
- This herbal formula contains herbs that invigorate blood circulation, such as *Dang Gui* (Radix Angelicae Sinensis). Therefore, patients who are on anticoagulant or antiplatelet therapies, such as Coumadin (warfarin), should use this formula with caution, or not at all, as there may be a higher risk of bleeding and bruising.[2,3]

CLINICAL NOTES

- ***Vitality*** and ***Vital Essence*** are two formulas that are frequently combined together. ***Vitality*** tonifies Kidney yang to treat sexual dysfunction. ***Vital Essence*** replenishes Kidney yin and *jing* (essence) to treat reproductive disorders. Together, they complement and enhance the clinical success of each others.
- ***Vitality*** is an excellent male and female tonic to increase sexual prowess and strengthen sexual energy. It is important to keep in mind that ***Vitality*** nourishes the body from within to change the underlying constitution of the person. It does not provide an immediate boost of sexual power.
- The practitioner may be able to find in chiropractic or medical supply catalogs a small piece of furniture that fits around the toilet to provide a safe, stable platform to support the feet several inches off the floor, promoting a more natural 'squatting' posture for the individual seated on the toilet. This may assist in promoting the complete evacuation of the bladder and bowels, enhancing the effort to strengthen the normal function and position of the reproductive organs.

Pulse Diagnosis by Dr. Jimmy Wei-Yen Chang:

- Deep and small pulse on the left *chi*.

SUPPLEMENTARY FORMULAS

- To treat male infertility, use with ***Vital Essence***.
- To treat female infertility, use ***Blossom (Phase 1-4)***.
- To tonify Kidney yin, add ***Kidney Tonic (Yin)***.
- To tonify Kidney yang, add ***Kidney Tonic (Yang)***.
- To boost energy and vitality, use with ***Vibrant*** or ***Imperial Tonic***.
- To strengthen constitutional weakness and deficiency, use with ***Cordyceps 3***.
- For adrenal deficiency, add ***Adrenal +***.
- For poor memory and forgetfulness, add ***Enhance Memory***.
- For vaginal dryness, add ***Balance Spring***.

ACUPUNCTURE TREATMENT

Traditional Points:

- *Shenshu* (BL 23), *Mingmen* (GV 4), *Guanyuan* (CV 4), *Rangu* (KI 2), *Sanyinjiao* (SP 6)

Classic Master Tung's Points:

- **Infertility (male):** *Tianhuang* (T 77.17), *Dihuang* (T 77.19), *Renhuang* (T 77.21), *Tianhuang* (T 88.13), *Minghuang* (T 88.12), *Qihuang* (T 88.14),); Endocrine, Kidney and Testicle points on the ear. Moxa *du* (governing) channel on the back.
- **Impotence:** *Tianhuang* (T 77.17), *Dihuang* (T 77.19), *Renhuang* (T 77.21), *Tianhuang* (T 88.13), *Minghuang* (T 88.12), *Qihuang* (T 88.14), *Tongshen* (T 88.09), *Tongwei* (T 88.10), *Sanshen* (T 44.27)*. Bleed tender points on the Kidney area of the back from L1-L5 with cupping. Bleed before needling for best result. Administer moxa for at least 30 minutes to the Kidney area on the back from L1-L5, *Guanyuan* (CV 4), *Zhongji* (CV 3).
- **Spermatorrhea:** *Tianhuang* (T 77.17), *Dihuang* (T 77.19), *Renhuang* (T 77.21), *Tongshen* (T 88.09), *Tongwei* (T 88.10), *Shuijin* (T 1010.20), *Shuitong* (T 1010.19), *Tianhuangfu [Shenguan]* (T 77.18). Moxa *Guanyuan* (CV 4), *Zhongji* (CV 3), *Zhongshu* (GV 7).

Balance Method by Dr. Richard Tan:

- Left side: *Xuehai* (SP 10), *Taixi* (KI 3), *Zhongfeng* (LR 4), *Yangxi* (LI 5), *Linggu* (T 22.05)
- Right side: *Lieque* (LU 7), *Daling* (PC 7), *Zusanli* (ST 36), *Shenmai* (BL 62), *Yanglingquan* (GB 34)
- Left and right sides can be alternated from treatment to treatment.

Auricular Medicine by Dr. Li-Chun Huang:

- **Impotence:** Internal Genital, External Genital, Gonadotropin Point, Kidney, Liver, Libido, Exciting Point, Endocrine, Pituitary
- **Emission:** *Shenmen*, Kidney, Liver, Heart, Neurasthenia Point (front and back), Neurasthenia Area (front and back), Nervous, Subcortex, Dream-Disturbed Sleep Area

NUTRITION

- Eliminate alcohol from the diet as it decreases the body's ability to produce testosterone.
- Intake of vitamin E should be increased. Foods high in vitamin E include wheat germ oil, almonds, sunflower seeds or oil, peanuts, soybeans, whole wheat products, and asparagus. Kiwis and fresh oysters can also be taken together as an aphrodisiac.
- Shellfish, oysters, shrimp, cashews, beef, and mushrooms are all foods that either contain high protein or zinc that may increase libido. However, these foods often are high in cholesterol and should not be over-consumed as they will otherwise cause blockage and lead to the opposite effect.
- Impotence is sometimes caused by circulatory problems. In such cases, increase the consumption of foods rich in niacin (eggs, peanut butter, avocado, and fish) and vitamin E (raw wheat germ and vegetable oil).
- Zinc is also beneficial in preventing impotence and reduced sperm count. Zinc is found in such foods as pumpkin seeds, sunflower seeds, oysters, soy, and eggs. Avoid eating foods that deplete the body of zinc, such as alcohol and coffee.

Vitality™

The Tao of Nutrition by Dr. Maoshing Ni and Cathy McNease:

- **Impotence**
  - Recommendations: scallions, scallion seeds, lamb, sea cucumber, shrimp, rooster, bitter melon seeds, ginseng, black beans, kidney beans, yams, and lycium fruit. Maintaining a calm composure.
  - Make lamb stew with daikon radish and Chinese black dates. Drink the broth and eat the lamb.
  - Steam rooster with ginger.
  - Make tea from walnuts, lotus seeds, pearl barley, Chinese black dates and goji berries. Drink three times daily.
  - Cook together scallions, shrimp, and egg. Eat with a shot of white liquor.
  - Avoid pornography, masturbation, overwork, and excessive sexual activities.
  - Reduce the intake of dairy products and sweets.

LIFESTYLE INSTRUCTIONS

- Avoid cigarette smoking or exposure to secondhand smoke.
- Vigorous exercise, hot tubs, saunas, and tight underwear lead to increased temperature in the testicles and reduced sperm count.
- Refrain from sexual activity when exhausted or under stress. Do not overindulge in sexual activity when any weakness in function or performance is present.
- Exercises for men with impotence and premature ejaculation: Tip-toe and clench one's teeth while urinating. This simple posture will tighten and strengthen the muscles surrounding the groin to help condition the Kidney qi. This is also a good exercise to help with terminal dripping in elderly patients. Women can practice this exercise by squatting and tip-toeing over the toilet while urinating. This exercise for women will strengthen and tighten the muscles and ligaments surrounding the reproductive organs to help treat prolapse of the bladder and uterus or frequent urinary urges due to Kidney yang deficiency. It also tightens the muscles surrounding the vagina and can be recommended to the partners of those taking ***Vitality*** or those who have low libido to enhance pleasure. Results can be expected in a few months if practiced daily and consistently.
- Exercises for women with low libido: Walk on the balls of the feet with the navel pulled towards the spine and the heels off the ground, taking care to breathe deeply. Engage in the Kegel exercise (attempting to use vaginal muscles to stop and start the flow of urine rapidly and frequently at each time of urinating) while also clenching the teeth and breathing through the nose. These exercises will be helpful if they are practiced regularly.
- There are five conditions when sexual activity should be avoided: when one is hungry, full, drunk, emotionally unstable (angry, sad, fearful, hateful or worried) or recovering from chronic illness.

CASE STUDIES

- A 65-year-old male presented with generalized male sexual dysfunction, possibly due to old age and/or use of high blood pressure medications. The diagnosis was Kidney yang and qi deficiencies. The patient was instructed to take ***Vitality*** with good results noted within one week. Submitted by R.C., M.D., Ph.D., New York, New York.
- R.R., a 61-year-old female, presented with multiple symptoms including low libido, low back pain, low energy, and brittle hair beginning to fall out. The practitioner diagnosed this condition as Kidney yang deficiency with *jing* (essence) deficiency. For treatment, ***Vitality*** was prescribed at three capsules three times a day. After taking the herbs for two months, she reported an increase in her sex drive. Her low back pain and energy improved as well. She had been receiving acupuncture treatments two to three times a week as well. No change was reported in the health of her hair. Submitted by S.L., Yuma, Arizona.
- T.S. is a female who presented with pain (especially of the joints of the limbs), coldness of the fingers and difficulty falling asleep. Objective findings revealed that her fingers were icy and cyanotic. Her leg muscles appeared to be abnormally tight. Her blood pressure was 110/80 mmHg and her heart rate was 78 beats per minute. She also received monthly rheumatoid arthritis shots. Western diagnosis for this patient was fibromyalgia. The TCM diagnosis was yang deficiency. ***Vitality*** was prescribed and the patient reported she felt the formula worked well in improving her condition and relieving the pain. Submitted by M.W., San Diego, California.

PHARMACOLOGICAL AND CLINICAL RESEARCH

Sexual dysfunction is characterized by interference with interest or inability to engage in sexual intercourse. Possible causes of sexual dysfunction include stress, anxiety, depression, diabetes, endocrine disorders, circulatory disorders, and drugs (beta-blockers, diuretics, alcohol, antidepressants, hormones, and many others). Optimal treatment requires use of herbs to balance the hormones, regulate the endocrine system, and promote blood circulation.

Vitality contains many herbs to treat both sexual and reproductive disorders. Pharmacologically, *Yin Yang Huo* (Herba Epimedii) has been shown to stimulate the sensory nerves, increase sexual desire and activity, and boost sperm production.[4] The mechanism of these actions is associated with the increased production and release of testosterone.[5] Furthermore, the extract of *Yin Yang Huo* (Herba Epimedii) shows a marked effect for the treatment of erectile dysfunction. The mechanism of this function is attributed to the relaxation of the corpus cavernosum smooth muscle through multi-targets in nitric oxide/cyclic guanosine monophosphate signaling pathway.[6] *Jiu Cai Zi* (Semen Allii Tuberosi) has positive aphrodisiac properties that affect sexual behavior in male subjects, such as an increase in penile erection, mating performance, mount frequency, mount latency, and ejaculation frequency.[7] *Shan Zhu Yu* (Fructus Corni) and *Suo Yang* (Herba Cynomorii) both have significant effects on

FORMULAS

Vitality™

the quality and quantity of sperm. *Shan Zhu Yu* (Fructus Corni) has a substantial stimulatory effect on sperm motility from 25.8 +/- 7.7% to 42.8 +/- 10.3%.[8] Administration of *Suo Yang* (Herba Cynomorii) is associated with a significant increase in spermatogenesis. It significantly increases the epididymal sperm count, absolute testes weights, and the expression of GDNF (glial cell-derived neurotrophic factor) at both the mRNA and protein levels in rat testes.[9]

Clinically, many herbs in this formula have been used to successfully treat sexual and reproductive disorders. According to one double-blind, placebo-controlled study, 143 male patients experiencing erectile dysfunction who were treated with *Ren Shen* (Radix et Rhizoma Ginseng) for eight weeks showed significantly higher erectile function and overall satisfaction scores in comparison with the placebo group.[10] According to another study, use of *Ren Shen* (Radix et Rhizoma Ginseng) effectively treated 24 of 27 patients with impotence.[11] Furthermore, use of fresh *Gou Qi Zi* (Fructus Lycii) in a formula effectively increased sperm count and improved sperm motility. Of 42 patients, 33 successfully conceived children.[12] Lastly, 78 men with impotence were treated with a 98% rate of effectiveness using an herbal formula that contained *Rou Gui* (Cortex Cinnamomi), *Jiu Cai Zi* (Semen Allii Tuberosi), *Yin Yang Huo* (Herba Epimedii), and others.[13]

Circulatory impairment is a major cause of erectile dysfunction and other sexual and reproductive disorders. Therefore, many herbs are used in ***Vitality*** to promote blood circulation. *Dang Gui* (Radix Angelicae Sinensis) has a direct and significant effect to stimulate angiogenesis, a physiological process that promotes blood vessel formation in various parts of the body.[14] It also improves overall blood circulation by decreasing the whole blood specific viscosity, or improving the hemorrheological changes associated with blood stagnation.[15] *Du Zhong* (Cortex Eucommiae) and *She Chuang Zi* (Fructus Cnidii) have vasorelaxant effects as they decrease resistance to blood flow.[16] Specifically, the ethanolic extract of *She Chuang Zi* (Fructus Cnidii) exhibits a vasorelaxant effect on the corpus cavernosum to improve blood circulation to the penis.[17]

Lastly, ***Vitality*** contains many herbs that treat sexual dysfunction due to the mind and the body. *Ba Ji Tian* (Radix Morindae Officinalis) is an excellent herb to treat chronic stress causing decreased plasma testosterone and increased plasma corticosterone.[18] It also contains constituents with marked antidepressant activities to treat depression.[19,20] In addition, *Ba Ji Tian* (Radix Morindae Officinalis) is shown in one study to have antifatigue activity as the polysaccharides (galacturonic acid, arabinose and galactose) of the herb improved the endurance of weight-loaded swimming subjects.[21]

In summary, ***Vitality*** is an excellent formula to treat various sexual and reproductive disorders, including, but not are limited to, decreased sexual desire and arousal, impotence, erectile dysfunction, and absence of or diminished orgasm.

COMPARATIVE ANALYSIS

One striking difference between Western and traditional Chinese medicine is that Western medicine focuses and excels in crisis management, while traditional Chinese medicine emphasizes and shines in holistic and preventative treatments. Therefore, in emergencies, such as gunshot wounds or surgery, Western medicine is generally the treatment of choice. However, for treatment of chronic idiopathic illness of unknown origins, where all lab tests are normal and a clear diagnosis cannot be made, traditional Chinese medicine is distinctly superior.

Sexual disorders, such as erectile disorders, are treated with drugs such as Viagra (sildenafil) and Cialis (tadalafil). These drugs generally have a quick onset of effect, and they work primarily by increasing blood flow to the penis. However, these drugs may cause side effects such as headache, upset stomach, diarrhea, dizziness or lightheadedness, flushing, nasal congestion, blindness, breast enlargement, rash, painful erection, prolonged erection, fainting, chest pain, and itching or burning during urination. Furthermore, these drugs are only effective for men, and not for women.

One main function of Kidney yang is the regulation of sexual and reproductive functions. ***Vitality*** is a Kidney yang tonic formula that emphasizes the maintenance of sexual functions and the treatment of sexual disorders, such as decreased libido in men and women, impotence, premature ejaculation, and spermatorrhea. Though this formula is very effective, it does not have an instantaneous effect, but rather requires continuous use for two to three months for maximum effect.

Both drugs and herbs are effective for treating sexual disorders. Drugs have a quick onset of action, but they only have one specific indication, are effective only for men, and have numerous significant side effects. Herbs have a gradual onset of action, but may be used in both men and women to treat a wide variety of sexual disorders. Furthermore, herbs are safe and natural, and have few or no side effects. Finally, it is important to remember that neither drugs nor herbs prevent pregnancy, nor do they protect either partner from sexually transmitted diseases and HIV.

References

1. *Forensic Science International*, 1994 June 28; 55-8.
2. Chan K, Lo AC, Yeung JH, Woo KS. Journal of Pharmacy and Pharmacology 1995 May;47(5):402-6.
3. Pharmacotherapy 1999 July;19(7):870-876; European Journal of Drug Metabolism and Pharmacokinetics 1995; 20(1):55-60.
4. *Zhong Yao Da Ci Dian* (Dictionary of Chinese Herbs), 1977:2251.
5. *Zhong Xi Yi Jie He Za Zhi* (Journal of Integrated Chinese and Western Medicine), 1989; 9(12):737-8,710.
6. Chiu JH, Chen KK, Chien TM, Chiou WF, Chen CC, Wang JY, Lui WY, Wu CW. Epimedium brevicornum Maxim extract relaxes rabbit corpus cavernosum through multitargets on nitric oxide/cyclic guanosine monophosphate signaling pathway. Institute of Traditional Medicine, School of Medicine, National Yang-Ming University, Peitou, Taipei, Taiwan, ROC. Int J Impot Res. 2006 Jul-Aug;18(4):335-42.

7. Guohua H, Yanhua L, Rengang M, Dongzhi W, Zhengzhi M, Hua Z. Aphrodisiac properties of Allium tuberosum seeds extract. College of Life and Environment Science, Shanghai Normal University, Shanghai, PR China. J Ethnopharmacol. 2009 Apr 21;122(3):579-82.
8. Jeng H, Wu CM, Su SJ, Chang WC. A substance isolated from Cornus officinalis enhances the motility of human sperm. Department of Anatomy, Taipei Medical College, Taiwan. Am J Chin Med. 1997;25(3-4):301-6.
9. Yang WM, Kim HY, Park SY, Kim HM, Chang MS, Park SK. Cynomorium songaricum induces spermatogenesis with glial cell-derived neurotrophic factor (GDNF) enhancement in rat testes. Department of Prescriptionology, College of Oriental Medicine, Kyung Hee University, 1 Hoegi-dong, Dongdaemun-gu, Seoul 130-701, Republic of Korea. J Ethnopharmacol. 2010 Apr 21;128(3):693-6.
10. Kim TH, Jeon SH, Hahn EJ, Paek KY, Park JK, Youn NY, Lee HL. Effects of tissue-cultured mountain ginseng (Panax ginseng CA Meyer) extract on male patients with erectile dysfunction. Department of Urology, School of Medicine, Kyung Hee University, Seoul 134-727, Korea. Asian J Androl. 2009 May;11(3):356-61.
11. *Ji Lin Yi Xue* (Jilin Medicine), 1983; 5:54.
12. *Xin Zhong Yi* (New Chinese Medicine), 1988; 2:20.
13. *Zhong Yi Yao Yan Jiu* (Research of Chinese Medicine and Herbology), 1997; (5):37.
14. Lam HW, Lin HC, Lao SC, Gao JL, Hong SJ, Leong CW, Yue PY, Kwan YW, Leung AY, Wang YT, Lee SM. The angiogenic effects of Angelica sinensis extract on HUVEC in vitro and zebrafish in vivo. J Cell Biochem. 2008 Jan 1;103(1):195-211.
15. Xue, JX. et al. Effects of the combination of astragalus membranaceus (Fisch.) Bge. (AM), angelica sinensis (Oliv.) Diels (TAS), cyperus rotundus L. (CR), ligusticum chuanxiong Hort (LC) and paeonia veitchii lynch (PV) on the hemorrheological changes in "blood stagnating" rats. *Chung Kuo Chung Yao Tsa Chih*; 19(2):108-10, 128. Feb 1994.
16. Kwan C.Y., Chen C.X., Deyama T. & Nishibe S. Endothelium-dependent vasorelaxant effects of the aqueous extracts of the *Eucommia ulmoides* Oliv. leaf and bark: implications on their antihypertensive action. *Vascul Pharmacol.* 2003, 40(5): 229-235.
17. Chiou WF, Huang YL, Chen CF, Chen CC. Vasorelaxing effect of coumarins from Cnidium monnieri on rabbit corpus cavernosum. Planta Med. 2001 Apr;67(3):282-4.
18. Li YF, Yuan L, Xu YK, Yang M, Zhao YM, Luo ZP. Antistress effect of oligosaccharides extracted from Morinda officinalis in mice and rats. Acta Pharmacol Sin. 2001 Dec;22(12):1084-8.
19. Cui C, Yang M, Yao Z, Cao B, Luo Z, Xu Y, Chen Y. Antidepressant active constituents in the roots of *Morinda officinalis* How. Zhongguo Zhong Yao Za Zhi. 1995 Jan;20(1):36-9, 62-3.
20. Zhang Z.Q., Yuan L., Yang M., Luo Z.P. & Zhao Y.M. The effect of *Morinda officinalis* How, a Chinese traditional medicinal plant, on the DRL 72-s schedule in rats and the forced swimming test in mice. *Pharmacol Biochem Behav.* 2002, 72(1-2): 39-43.
21. Zhang HL, Li J, Li G, Wang DM, Zhu LP, Yang DP. Structural characterization and anti-fatigue activity of polysaccharides from the roots of Morinda officinalis. Int J Biol Macromol. 2009 Apr 1;44(3):257-61.

FORMULAS

V-Support™

CLINICAL APPLICATIONS

- **Vaginitis**
- **Pelvic inflammatory disease (PID)**
- **Urinary tract infections (UTI)** in women and men
- **Genital eczema and itching, soreness and pain** in men or women
- **Yellow or green vaginal discharge** with offensive odor and cottage cheese consistency
- **Orchitis, epididymitis,** and infection and inflammation of the scrotum and male genital region
- **Pyelonephritis or cystitis** with dysuria, turbid, yellow urine
- **Candida yeast infection**
- **Infertility** due to inflammation and infection of the pelvis (ovaries, uterus, fallopian tubes)

WESTERN THERAPEUTIC ACTIONS

- Antibiotic effects to treat infection
- Anti-inflammatory effects to reduce inflammation and swelling
- Analgesic action to relieve pain
- Diuretic action to promote normal urination

CHINESE THERAPEUTIC ACTIONS

- Clears damp-heat in the lower *jiao*
- Clears damp-heat in the Liver, Gallbladder, and Urinary Bladder channels
- Promotes diuresis
- Invigorates blood circulation in the lower *jiao*

DOSAGE

Take 3 to 4 capsules three times daily with warm water on an empty stomach. Dosage may be increased to 6 to 8 capsules three times daily, if necessary. This formula should be taken consistently for at least one to two weeks to ensure complete eradication of the pathogen(s) and to avoid stimulating possible bacterial and viral resistance. It is important to advise the patient not to discontinue the use of herbs prior to completion of the whole course of herbal treatment.

INGREDIENTS

Bian Xu (Herba Polygoni Avicularis)
Chai Hu (Radix Bupleuri)
Che Qian Zi (Semen Plantaginis)
Da Huang (Radix et Rhizoma Rhei)
Dang Gui (Radix Angelicae Sinensis)
Deng Xin Cao (Medulla Junci)
Di Fu Zi (Fructus Kochiae)
Di Huang (Radix Rehmanniae)
Feng Wei Cao (Herba Pteris)
Gan Cao (Radix et Rhizoma Glycyrrhizae)
Hong Hua (Flos Carthami)
Hua Shi (Talcum)
Huang Qin (Radix Scutellariae)
Long Dan (Radix et Rhizoma Gentianae)
Niu Xi (Radix Achyranthis Bidentatae)
Pao Zai Cao (Herba Physalis Angulatae)
Qu Mai (Herba Dianthi)
Shui Ding Xiang (Herba Ludwigiae Prostratae)
Tao Ren (Semen Persicae)
Xian Feng Cao (Herba Bidentis)
Ya She Huang (Herba Lippiae)
Ze Xie (Rhizoma Alismatis)
Zhi Zi (Fructus Gardeniae)

BACKGROUND

V-Support is designed to treat infection and inflammation of the lower abdominal region, including conditions such as vaginitis, pelvic inflammatory disease, urinary tract infection, cystitis, dysuria and pyelonephritis. These disorders are characterized by the presence of infection and inflammation, and therefore, require the use of herbs with anti-infective and anti-inflammatory effects.

FORMULA EXPLANATION

V-Support treats damp-heat in the lower *jiao* manifesting in vaginitis, cystitis, urinary tract infection, pelvic inflammatory disease, vaginal discharge, genital itching, male genital infection, and pyelonephritis.

Long Dan (Radix et Rhizoma Gentianae) clears damp-heat from the Liver channel, which travels through the genital region. *Zhi Zi* (Fructus Gardeniae), *Da Huang* (Radix et Rhizoma Rhei) and *Huang Qin* (Radix Scutellariae) all clear damp-heat and treat infection. They work synergistically to relieve symptoms such as foul yellow vaginal discharge, dysuria, genital itching and male genital infection. *Feng Wei Cao* (Herba Pteris), *Ya She Huang* (Herba Lippiae), and *Pao Zai Cao* (Herba Physalis Angulatae), indigenous herbs from Taiwan, are used to detoxify and reduce inflammation and infection of the genital organs. *Di Fu Zi* (Fructus Kochiae) clears heat and relieves genital itching.

Shui Ding Xiang (Herba Ludwigiae Prostratae) and *Xian Feng Cao* (Herba Bidentis) are very strong herbs used in Taiwan to treat infections of the urinary system such as cystitis, urinary tract infection, nephritis, pyelonephritis, dysuria, and turbid yellow urine. These herbs reduce inflammation, clear heat, and promote diuresis.

Bian Xu (Herba Polygoni Avicularis), *Hua Shi* (Talcum), *Deng Xin Cao* (Medulla Junci), *Ze Xie* (Rhizoma Alismatis), *Che Qian Zi* (Semen Plantaginis), and *Qu Mai* (Herba Dianthi) dispel dampness in the lower *jiao* and promote urination. Together, they dispel water and treat *lin zheng* (dysuria syndrome). To prevent the diuretic herbs from draining too much fluid from the body, *Di Huang* (Radix Rehmanniae) and *Dang Gui* (Radix Angelicae Sinensis) are added to nourish yin and blood.

Chai Hu (Radix Bupleuri) is a guiding herb to the Liver channel, which passes through the genital region. *Niu Xi* (Radix Achyranthis Bidentatae), descending in nature, directs the overall

V-Support™

effect of the formula downward to the lower *jiao*, and thus, to the genital region.

To enhance the overall efficacy of the formula, *Tao Ren* (Semen Persicae) and *Hong Hua* (Flos Carthami) are added to increase blood circulation to the lower *jiao*. Proper blood circulation increases delivery of herbs to the affected area and in exchange helps to flush out toxins in the blood. Finally, *Gan Cao* (Radix et Rhizoma Glycyrrhizae) is used to harmonize the formula.

In conclusion, ***V-Support*** clears damp-heat in the lower *jiao* to treat infection and inflammation disorders affecting the genitourinary region.

CAUTIONS & CONTRAINDICATIONS

- This formula is contraindicated during pregnancy and nursing.
- This formula should be used with caution by patients with deficiency and cold of the Spleen and Stomach.
- This formula is contraindicated for long-term use. It should be discontinued when the desired effects are achieved.
- This herbal formula contains herbs that invigorate blood circulation, such as *Dang Gui* (Radix Angelicae Sinensis). Therefore, patients who are on anticoagulant or antiplatelet therapies, such as Coumadin (warfarin), should use this formula with caution, or not at all, as there may be a higher risk of bleeding and bruising.[1,2,3]
- The following warning statement is required by the State of California: "This product contains *Da Huang* (Radix et Rhizoma Rhei). Read and follow directions carefully. Do not use if you have or develop diarrhea, loose stools, or abdominal pain because *Da Huang* (Radix et Rhizoma Rhei) may worsen these conditions and be harmful to your health. Consult your physician if you have frequent diarrhea or if you are pregnant, nursing, taking medication, or have a medical condition."

CLINICAL NOTES

- The powder of *She Chuang Zi* (Fructus Cnidii) and *Ku Shen* (Radix Sophorae Flavescentis) can be applied topically to relieve itching. Wash the affected area thoroughly using a mild soap and apply 5 grams of each herb onto the external genitalia, leave for 3 to 5 minutes and rinse off. Repeat this procedure twice daily. Do not use internally.
- Vaginitis tends to recur in women who have diabetes or have frequently taken antibiotics.
- When a woman has frequent recurrences of lower *jiao* infections, the male partner should also be checked for urethral discharge, penile lesions, other infections, past venereal disease or parasitic infection. It is best to simultaneously treat both partners to prevent recurrences of vaginitis, urinary tract infection or cystitis.
- Patients who do not respond or improve after taking antibiotics or this formula consistently for two weeks usually have chronic vaginitis. They need to take ***Kidney Tonic (Yang)*** with ***V-Support*** at a 1:2 or 1:3 ratio, respectively.
- Vaginitis is common in women during the menopausal phase, as hormonal changes may disturb the pH balance of the vagina, leading to infections.
- Women with vaginitis should be careful before, during, and after menstruation, as this is when they are most susceptible to infection. Patients should pay extra attention to personal hygiene.
- Inflammation and infection of the reproductive organs may cause local swelling and obstruction, leading to infertility. This condition is similar to damp-heat in the lower *jiao* in traditional Chinese medicine.
- After a bowel movement, advise the patient to wipe from front to back to avoid infection.
- Patients should be advised to urinate after sexual intercourse to prevent bacteria from infecting the urethra and from causing urinary tract infection. ***V-Support*** incorporates numerous antibiotic herbs for two important reasons. First, the use of multiple herbs within an herbal formula has been shown to increase the antibiotic effect more than tenfold. Second, isolated use of single herbs is often ineffective and increases the risk of development of bacterial and viral resistance.[4] Given these two reasons, it is necessary to combine herbs with appropriate properties to ensure effectiveness in treating the infection and minimizing the potential risk of micro-organisms developing resistance and/or mutation.
- ***V-Support*** and ***Gentiana Complex*** both have strong effect to treat damp-heat affecting the lower *jiao*:
  - ***V-Support*** has a localized effect to treat damp-heat in the genital area.
  - ***Gentiana Complex*** has a broader effect to treat damp-heat along the Liver and Gallbladder channels from the head to the genital area.
- Vaginitis may be caused by different micro-organisms:
  - Bacterial vaginitis is more effectively treated with ***V-Support***.
  - Viral vaginitis is best treated with ***Gentiana Complex***.

Pulse Diagnosis by Dr. Jimmy Wei-Yen Chang:

- *Du* pulse, a forceful, thick, straight, and long pulse on and proximal to the left *chi*. It is one of the eight extra meridian pulses.

SUPPLEMENTARY FORMULAS

- To enhance the antibiotic effect to treat infection, use with ***Herbal ABX***.
- For yeast infection, add *Liu Jun Zi Tang* (Six-Gentlemen Decoction).
- For diabetes, use with ***Equilibrium***.
- For chronic recurrent vaginitis, use with ***Kidney Tonic (Yang)***.
- For menopausal patients, use with ***Balance (Heat)*** or ***Nourish***.
- For prostate disorders with burning urination, use with ***P-Support***.
- For patients who experience slight loose stools after taking ***V-Support***, combine with ***GI Tonic***.

V-Support™

- To activate blood circulation throughout the entire body, add ***Circulation (SJ)***.
- For signs and symptoms of excess fire, add ***Gardenia Complex***.
- For bleeding, add ***Notoginseng 9***.
- With more underlying damp and phlegm with Spleen qi deficiency, add ***Pinellia Complex***.

ACUPUNCTURE TREATMENT

Traditional Points:

- *Sanyinjiao* (SP 6), *Yinlingquan* (SP 9), *Qihaishu* (BL 24), *Shangliao* (BL 31), *Ciliao* (BL 32), *Zhongliao* (BL 33), *Xialiao* (BL 34), *Guanyuan* (CV 4), *Sanjiaoshu* (BL 22)
- *Zhongji* (CV 3), *Qugu* (CV 2), *Sanyinjiao* (SP 6)

Classic Master Tung's Points:

- **Urinary tract infection (UTI):** *Libai* (T 44.12), *Yunbai* (T 44.11), *Tianhuang* (T 77.17), *Dihuang* (T 77.19), *Renhuang* (T 77.21), *Simashang* (T 88.18), *Simazhong* (T 88.17), *Simaxia* (T 88.19), *Tongbei* (T 88.11), *Tongwei* (T 88.10), *Tongshen* (T 88.09), *Liukuai* (T 1010.16), *Qikuai* (T 1010.17), *Tianhuangfu [Shenguan]* (T 77.18). Bleed dark veins nearby the KI channel on the lower limb. Bleed before needling for best result.
- **Yeast infection:** *Fuke* (T 11.24), *Linggu* (T 22.05), *Yunbai* (T 44.11), *Libai* (T 44.12), *Simashang* (T 88.18), *Simazhong* (T 88.17), *Simaxia* (T 88.19), *Minghuang* (T 88.12), *Tianhuang* (T 88.13), *Qihuang* (T 88.14)
- **Genital itching:** *Fuke* (T 11.24), *Shoujie* (T 22.10), *Linggu* (T 22.05), *Tianzong* (T 44.10), *Yunbai* (T 44.11), *Libai* (T 44.12), *Tianhuang* (T 77.17), *Dihuang* (T 77.19), *Renhuang* (T 77.21), *Minghuang* (T 88.12), *Tianhuang* (T 88.13), *Qihuang* (T 88.14), *Simashang* (T 88.18), *Simazhong* (T 88.17), *Simaxia* (T 88.19), *Majinshui* (T 1010.13), *Makuaishui* (T 1010.14), *Zhenghui* (T 1010.01), *Renzong* (T 44.08), *Dizong* (T 44.09)
- **Genital swelling and infection:** *Huanchao* (T 11.06), *Fuke* (T 11.24), *Yunbai* (T 44.11), *Jiemeiyi* (T 88.04), *Jiemeier* (T 88.05), *Jiemeisan* (T 88.06), *Haibao* (T 66.01). Bleed sacral area with cupping. Bleed before needling for best result.
- **Vaginitis:** *Fuke* (T 11.24), *Huanchao* (T 11.06), *Jiemeiyi* (T 88.04), *Jiemeier* (T 88.05), *Jiemeisan* (T 88.06), *Libai* (T 44.12), *Yunbai* (T 44.11), *Jianzhong* (T 44.06), *Haibao* (T 66.01), *Renzong* (T 44.08), *Dizong* (T 44.09), *Tianzong* (T 44.10). Bleed tender points on the sacral region with cupping. Bleed before needling for best result.
- **Pelvic inflammatory disease (PID):** *Fuke* (T 11.24), *Huanchao* (T 11.06), *Qimen* (T 33.01), *Qijiao* (T 33.02), *Qizheng* (T 33.03), *Libai* (T 44.12), *Yunbai* (T 44.11), *Haibao* (T 66.01), *Huoying* (T 66.03), *Huozhu* (T 66.04), *Menjin* (T 66.05), *Jiemeiyi* (T 88.04), *Jiemeier* (T 88.05), *Jiemeisan* (T 88.06), *Mufu* (T 88.38)*, *Tongtian* (T 88.03), *Renhuang* (T 77.21), *Shuijing* (T 66.13)
- **Leukorrhea:** *Fuke* (T 11.24), *Yunbai* (T 44.11), *Libai* (T 44.12), *Tianhuang* (T 77.17), *Dihuang* (T 77.19), *Renhuang* (T 77.21), *Tianhuang* (T 88.13), *Minghuang* (T 88.12), *Qihuang* (T 88.14), *Jiemeiyi* (T 88.04), *Jiemeier* (T 88.05), *Jiemeisan* (T 88.06), *Qimen* (T 33.01), *Qijiao* (T 33.02), *Qizheng* (T 33.03), *Haibao* (T 66.01), *Tianhuangfu [Shenguan]* (T 77.18), *Mufu* (T 66.02), *Renzong* (T 44.08), *Dizong* (T 44.09), *Tianzong* (T 44.10). Bleed tender points on the low back and sacral regions with cupping. Bleed before needling for best result.
- **Pyelonephritis:** *Shuijin* (T 1010.20), *Shuitong* (T 1010.19), *Wanshunyi* (T 22.08), *Wanshuner* (T 22.09), *Tongshen* (T 88.09), *Tongguan* (T 88.01), *Houzhui* (T 44.02), *Shouying* (T 44.03)
- **Dysuria:** *Tianhuang* (T 77.17), *Dihuang* (T 77.19), *Renhuang* (T 77.21), *Yunbai* (T 44.11), *Libai* (T 44.12), *Majinshui* (T 1010.13), *Makuaishui* (T 1010.14), *Fenzhishang* (T DT.01), *Fenzhixia* (T DT.02)

Master Tung's Points by Dr. Chuan-Min Wang:

- **Yeast infection, damp-heat in the lower *jiao*:** *Shuixiang* (T 66.14), *Huoying* (T 66.03)

Balance Method by Dr. Richard Tan:

- Left side: *Dadu* (SP 2), *Taibai* (SP 3), *Taixi* (KI 3), *Dazhong* (KI 4), *Taichong* (LR 3), *Hegu* (LI 4), *Yangxi* (LI 5)
- Right side: *Zhiyin* (BL 67), *Zuqiaoyin* (GB 44), *Daling* (PC 7), *Lieque* (LU 7)

Auricular Medicine by Dr. Li-Chun Huang:

- **Vaginitis:** Allergic area, *Shenmen*, Occiput, Nervous Subcortex, Lung, Diaphragm, Spleen, Liver. Bleed Ear Apex.
- **Excessive vaginal discharge:** Uterus, Cervix, Kidney, Liver, Spleen, *San Jiao*, Endocrine, Lower *Jiao*, Adrenal Gland, Pelvic. Bleed Ear Apex.
- **Salpingitis (fallopian tube):** Fallopian Tube, Lower *Jiao*, Liver, *San Jiao*, Endocrine. Bleed Ear Apex.
- **Adnexitis:** Adnexa, Lower *Jiao*, Kidney, Liver, *San Jiao*, Endocrine. Bleed Ear Apex.
- **Cystitis:** Bladder, Urethra, Lower *Jiao*, Endocrine. Bleed Ear Apex.
- **Pelvic inflammation:** Pelvic, Kidney, Liver, *San Jiao*, Endocrine, Lower *Jiao*. Bleed Ear Apex.
- **Cervicitis:** Cervix, Kidney, Liver, Spleen, *San Jiao*, Endocrine, Lower *Jiao*. Bleed Ear Apex.
- **UTI:** Urethra, Male-Prostate, Female-Internal Urethra, Liver, Adrenal Gland, Lower *Jiao*, Endocrine. Bleed Ear Apex
- **Pyelonephritis:** Kidney, Bladder, Urethra, Spleen, *San Jiao*, Adrenal Gland, Endocrine, Allergic Area. Bleed Ear Apex.

NUTRITION

- Natural, plain yogurt with live cultures helps to minimize yeast infection by establishing a normal environment in the genital tract.
- Eat plenty of fruits and vegetables, which provide the nutrients needed to resist infection and facilitate healing.
- Regular consumption of unsweetened cranberry juice will help to prevent and treat urinary tract infection.

V-Support ™

- Warm and hot natured foods that damage qi and yin should be avoided, such as:
  - certain fruits like mango and durian that produce heat.
  - stimulants like coffee, alcohol, and energy drinks.
  - spicy/pungent/aromatic vegetables such as pepper, garlic, onions, basil, rosemary, cumin, funnel, anise, leeks, chives, scallions, thyme, saffron, wormwood, mustard, chili pepper, and wasabi.
- Avoid food and drinks with artificial coloring.
- Consume as few meat products as possible. Do not eat processed meats, such as lunch meats, hot dogs and sausages, as they contain nitrites that are associated with inflammation and chronic disease.

The Tao of Nutrition by Dr. Maoshing Ni and Cathy McNease:

- **Candida yeast infection**
  - Recommendations: dandelions, beet tops, carrot tops, barley, garlic, rice vinegar, mung beans, and citrus fruits.
  - Avoid sugar, excessive fruits, yeast-containing foods, processed foods, cheese, fermented foods, soy sauce, smoking, alcohol, and caffeine.
- **Chronic bladder infections**
  - Recommendations: watermelon, pears, carrots, celery, corn, mung beans, corn-silk, squash, wheat, water chestnuts, barley, red beans, millet, oranges, cantaloupe, grapes, strawberries, lotus roots, loquats, and plenty of water.
  - Drink watermelon and pear juice three times daily.
  - Drink carrot and celery juice three times daily.
  - Eat squash soup for at least seven days.
  - Drink blended mung bean juice.
  - Drink fresh strawberry or unsweetened cranberry juice.
  - Drink tea made from wheat and pearl barley.
  - Avoid heavy proteins, meat, dairy products, onions, scallions, ginger, black pepper, and alcohol.

LIFESTYLE INSTRUCTIONS

- During the treatment period, avoid sexual intercourse to prevent further irritation or infection, and to prevent spreading the infection to one's partner.
- Substances that irritate the genital area should be avoided, such as spermicides, lubricants, condoms, diaphragms, cervical caps, and contraceptive sponges. Select toilet tissue or feminine hygiene products that are not dyed, chlorine-bleached, or scented.
- Use hypo-allergenic or fragrance-free substances whenever possible, such as fabric softener, soap, laundry detergents, deodorant sprays, bathwater additives, shower gels, and related products.
- Candida cannot be killed with the normal washing and drying methods. Patients suffering from yeast infection can try to soak their underwear in bleach for 24 hours before washing them. Ironing may also be an alternative as candida is killed at high temperatures.
- Refrain from douching or the insertion of foreign objects in the vagina. In the case of severe itching, refrain from scratching or from *excessive* washing of the affected area.
- Wear loose clothing and refrain from wearing tight slacks, vinyl, or tight denim. Wear silk or cotton underwear for better ventilation. Avoid polyester, snug, nonporous or nonabsorbent underpants.
- Patients with urinary tract infections and cystitis should drink more water (more frequently) and urinate more often to prevent pathogens from lingering in the urinary tract and bladder.

CASE STUDIES

- M.D., a 42-year-old female, presented with an acute urinary tract infection (UTI) with symptoms of burning pain upon urination. The patient has had a history of Hodgkin's lymphoma, underwent chemotherapy, and continues getting UTIs. Usually cranberry juice prevents them; however, this time it was unsuccessful so the patient was thinking of getting antibiotics. The TCM diagnosis was damp-heat in the Urinary Bladder. This condition was treated with ***V-Support*** at four spoonfuls twice a day until her symptoms resolved. As symptoms of UTI resolved, the patient did not need to go get antibiotics. The patient was very happy. Submitted by M.M., Alameda, California.
- L.R., a 53-year-old female patient, who was a smoker and a fast-paced business woman, presented with frequent urinary tract infections (UTI) and herpes breakouts. Her eating habits consisted of spicy food, coffee, and wine. The patient had been experiencing burning and pressure, and had been taking antibiotics. The practitioner diagnosed the condition as damp-heat in the lower *jiao*. She was treated with ***Herbal ABX*** three pills four times daily along with ***V-Support*** at the same dosage. For topical treatment to the affected area, Yin Care was applied three times daily at 50% the recommended amount. After the infection had cleared, the patient was then directed to take ***Nourish*** at three pills three times daily. The patient healed quickly, complete relief of pain was present, and she had committed to eliminate smoking, coffee, and spicy food from her lifestyle. Submitted by L.W., Arroyo Grande, California.
- J.C., a 49-year-old female, presented with vaginal infection with symptoms of severe itching and burning within the area. Her blood pressure was 102/64 mmHg and heart rate was 57 beats per minute. Pulse was rapid and tongue was red with swollen sides and yellow coating. The TCM diagnosis was damp-heat in the lower *jiao*. ***V-Support*** was prescribed at 3 capsules two times per day. After taking the herbs for two weeks the infection had resolved. Submitted by M.P., Muskego, Wisconsin.
- A 27-year-old female clerk presented with bloating and inability to urinate. Pain and a burning sensation also followed upon urination. The color of her urine was yellow. She had a red

V-Support™

tongue color with a dry tongue coating, which appeared yellow towards the base. Pulse analysis was rapid and rolling. A Western diagnosis assessment of urinary tract infection (UTI) was concluded, with a TCM diagnosis of damp-heat in the lower *jiao*. The patient started urinating immediately after the treatment with ***V-Support***. Urinary tract infection was resolved within 10 days of continuous administration of ***V-Support***. Submitted by T.G., Albuquerque, New Mexico.

- J.H., an 83-year-old diabetic female, presented with a recent history of episodes of burning, painful, dribbling and frequent urination. The urgency and pressure woke her at night and she would have to get up to urinate several times between bedtime and morning. The patient reported that she has had bladder infections throughout her life but these were occurring more often than in the past. Her doctor was treating the infection with Cipro (ciprofloxacin) and the client was tired of taking drugs and afraid of its side effects. Actual lab work was not available but the patient reported the urine analysis showed very high bacteria count in which the practitioner suspected *E coli*. Her blood pressure was 153/82 mmHg and heart rate was 80 beats per minute. The diagnosis was damp-heat in the lower *jiao*, specifically the Urinary Bladder. ***V-Support*** was prescribed at 1 to 2 capsules twice daily. The patient began taking the herbs as soon as she finished the current prescription for Cipro (ciprofloxacin). She was pleased to report that she had been symptom-free and infection-free for nearly two years of taking the prophylactic dose of the herbs. She stated that she certainly did not miss either the pain or the infection or the repeated rounds of antibiotics. The practitioner concluded that this is an excellent example of the successful use of an herbal formula as a preventative measure. Submitted by H.H., San Francisco, California.
- A 31-year-old female presented with a family history of chronic psoriasis, and outbreaks mainly on her elbows, knees and sacrum. She also suffered from vaginal itching and burning sensations. The TCM diagnosis was toxic damp-heat in the Liver. ***V-Support*** and ***Dermatrol (PS)*** were prescribed. A topical wash, Yin Care, was prescribed for external application for the psoriasis and vaginally for local itching. The patient received acupuncture and herbal treatments for two years. She was advised to stop smoking, eat less spicy food, and refrain from alcohol intake, but was unable to change her lifestyle. Nonetheless, her condition continued to improve, and she noticed that if she did not take the herbs, the symptoms would return. Submitted by M.C., Sarasota, Florida.

PHARMACOLOGICAL AND CLINICAL RESEARCH

V-Support is designed to treat infection and inflammation of the lower abdominal region, such as vaginitis, pelvic inflammatory disease, urinary tract infection, cystitis, dysuria and pyelonephritis. It contains herbs with marked antibiotic effects to treat infection, anti-inflammatory activity to reduce inflammation, and diuretic effects to promote normal urination.

Many herbs in ***V-Support*** have marked antibiotic properties. *Huang Qin* (Radix Scutellariae) has a wide-spectrum of inhibitory effects against many bacteria and viruses. As an antibacterial agent, it is most effective against *Staphylococcus aureus* and *Pseudomonas aeruginosa.* It has also been shown that in cases where standard antibiotics drugs are ineffective due to pathogenic resistance, the addition of *Huang Qin* (Radix Scutellariae) will restore the bacteriocidal and bacteriostatic activities of the antibiotic drugs.[5] Furthermore, it was discovered that the effectiveness of standard antibiotics, such as ampicillin, amoxicillin, methicillin and cefotaxime, can be potentiated with the addition of baicalin, a flavone isolated from this herb. With the addition of baicalin, the effectiveness of these beta-lactam antibiotics was restored against beta-lactam-resistant *Staphylococcus aureus* and methicillin-resistant *Staphylococcus aureus* (MRSA).[6,7] *Huang Qin* (Radix Scutellariae) also has a wide spectrum of antiviral activities. Specifically, baicalein and wogonin, two compounds from the herb, boost innate antiviral immunity by stimulating the production of cytokines and increasing the resistance to viral infection in human leukocytes.[8] In addition to *Huang Qin* (Radix Scutellariae), other herbs with antibiotic properties include *Long Dan* (Radix et Rhizoma Gentianae),[9] *Zhi Zi* (Fructus Gardeniae),[10] *Da Huang* (Radix et Rhizoma Rhei),[11] *Bian Xu* (Herba Polygoni Avicularis),[12] *Chai Hu* (Radix Bupleuri),[13] and *Dang Gui* (Radix Angelicae Sinensis).[14] In fact, some of these herbs have potent, wide-spectrum inhibitory effects against micro-organisms that are most often found to cause genitourinary infections.[15]

In addition to having antibiotic properties, many herbs have potent effects to reduce inflammation and relieve pain. The combination of these herbs significantly suppresses capillary permeability, reduces inflammation and swelling, and alleviates pain. Herbs with marked anti-inflammatory effects include *Huang Qin* (Radix Scutellariae),[16] *Chai Hu* (Radix Bupleuri),[17] *Niu Xi* (Radix Achyranthis Bidentatae),[18] *Tao Ren* (Semen Persicae),[19] *Di Huang* (Radix Rehmanniae),[20] *Dang Gui* (Radix Angelicae Sinensis),[21] and *Gan Cao* (Radix et Rhizoma Glycyrrhizae).[22] Among the herbs having clearly-identified analgesic effects are *Dang Gui* (Radix Angelicae Sinensis), *Da Huang* (Radix et Rhizoma Rhei), *Zhi Zi* (Fructus Gardeniae), and *Gan Cao* (Radix et Rhizoma Glycyrrhizae).[23,24,25] Many herbs in ***V-Support*** promote normal urination to alleviate burning sensations and pain associated with infection and inflammation of the genito-urinary tract. Herbs with diuretic influence include *Long Dan* (Radix et Rhizoma Gentianae), *Bian Xu* (Herba Polygoni Avicularis), *Ze Xie* (Rhizoma Alismatis) and *Qu Mai* (Herba Dianthi).[26,27,28,29,30]

In addition to their general pharmacological effects, some herbs have specific influence against certain disorders. For example, the combination of *Hua Shi* (Talcum) and *Gan Cao* (Radix et Rhizoma Glycyrrhizae) was effective in treating 10

V-Support™

patients with urinary tract infection, within three to four days.[31] In another study, 58 patients with dysuria were successfully treated with an herbal formula that contained *Long Dan* (Radix et Rhizoma Gentianae), *Dang Gui* (Radix Angelicae Sinensis), *Chai Hu* (Radix Bupleuri), *Ze Xie* (Rhizoma Alismatis), *Zhi Zi* (Fructus Gardeniae), *Di Huang* (Radix Rehmanniae), and *Gan Cao* (Radix et Rhizoma Glycyrrhizae).[32] For chronic nephritis, the daily administration of 60 grams of *Deng Xin Cao* (Medulla Junci) was associated with complete recovery within thirty days in 25 out of 30 patients.[33] Lastly, 33 patients with acute nephritis were treated by injection of a 20% *Dang Gui* (Radix Angelicae Sinensis) solution to key acupuncture points once daily, with good results.[34]

In summary, ***V-Support*** is an excellent formula to treat infection and inflammation of the genitourinary tract, such as vaginitis, pelvic inflammatory disease, urinary tract infection, cystitis, dysuria, pyelonephritis, and infertility in women due to inflammation and infection.

COMPARATIVE ANALYSIS

There are many disorders characterized by infection and inflammation of genital regions, including vaginitis, cystitis, pelvic inflammatory disease, and urinary tract infection. In Western medicine, these conditions are generally treated with antibiotic drugs, including antibacterial, antiviral, and antifungal agents. As a category, these drugs are very effective to treat such infections and inflammations. However, these drugs are very potent, and may cause many side effects, such as secondary infection.

Herbal therapy is also very effective for treating these infections and inflammations. Many herbs have been shown to have marked antibacterial, antiviral, and antifungal properties. Furthermore, some have analgesic effects to relieve pain, and others have diuretic effects to relieve dysuria. Lastly, though these herbs are generally safe, they should be discontinued once the desired effects are achieved, as extended use may consume and weaken the body.

Drugs and herbs are both effective for treating infections and inflammations of the genitourinary system. In general, drugs are more effective for bacterial and fungal infections, but their safety profiles vary depending on the exact antibiotic prescribed. Herbs are equally effective for bacterial, viral, and fungal infections. For severe infections and inflammations, herbs are slightly less potent than drugs, but are much safer and have significantly fewer side effects. Lastly, in both therapies, the chosen substance(s) should always be taken until the course of therapy is completed. Those who have weakness and deficiency from the infection and/or its treatment should take tonic herbs to strengthen the body and facilitate recovery.

References

1. Chan K, Lo AC, Yeung JH, Woo KS. Journal of Pharmacy and Pharmacology 1995 May;47(5):402-6.
2. Pharmacotherapy 1999 July;19(7):870-876.
3. European Journal of Drug Metabolism and Pharmacokinetics 1995; 20(1): 55-60.
4. *Zhong Yao Xue* (Chinese Herbology), 1988; 140:144.
5. *J Pharm Pharmacol* 2000 Mar; 52(3):361-6.
6. *Zhong Yao Xue* (Chinese Herbology), 1988; 137:140.
7. *J Pharm Pharmacol* 2000 Mar;52(3):361-6.
8. Błach-Olszewska Z, Jatczak B, Rak A, Lorenc M, Gulanowski B, Drobna A, Lamer-Zarawska E. Production of cytokines and stimulation of resistance to viral infection in human leukocytes by Scutellaria baicalensis flavones. Ludwik Hirszfeld Institute of Immunology and Experimental Therapy, Polish Academy of Sciences, Wrocław, Poland. J Interferon Cytokine Res. 2008 Sep;28(9): 571-81.
9. *Zhong Yao Yao Li Yu Ying Yong* (Pharmacology and Applications of Chinese Herbs), 1983; 295.
10. *Zhong Yao Zhi* (Chinese Herbology Journal), 1984; 578.
11. *Zhong Yao Xue* (Chinese Herbology), 1988; 137:140.
12. *Yi Xue Xue Bao* (Report of Medicine), 1983; 18(9):700.
13. *Zhong Yao Xue* (Chinese Herbology), 1998; 103:106.
14. *Huo Xue Hua Yu Yan Jiu* (Research on Blood-Activating and Stasis-Eliminating Herbs), 1981; 335.
15. *Zhong Yao Xue* (Chinese Herbology),1998; 251:256.
16. *Chem Pharm Bull*, 1984; 32(7):2724.
17. *Zhong Yao Yao Li Yu Ying Yong* (Pharmacology and Applications of Chinese Herbs), 1983; 888.
18. *Zhong Yao Tong Bao* (Journal of Chinese Herbology), 1988; 13(7):43.
19. *Zhong Yao Tong Bao* (Journal of Chinese Herbology), 1986; 11(11):37.
20. *Zhong Yao Yao Li Yu Ying Yong* (Pharmacology and Applications of Chinese Herbs), 1983; 400.
21. *Xin Yi Yao Xue Za Zhi* (New Journal of Medicine and Herbology), 1975; (6):34.
22. *Zhong Cao Yao* (Chinese Herbal Medicine), 1991; 22(10):452.
23. *Si Chuan Zhong Yi* (Sichuan Chinese Medicine), 1988; 9:11.
24. *Shen Yang Yi Xue Yuan Xue Bao* (Journal of Shenyang University of Medicine), 1984; 1(3):214.
25. *Zhong Yao Xue* (Chinese Herbology),1998; 759:765.
26. *Zhong Yao Yao Li Yu Ying Yong* (Pharmacology and Applications of Chinese Herbs), 1983; 295.
27. *Chang Yong Zhong Yao Cheng Fen Yu Yao Li Shou Ce* (A Handbook of the Composition and Pharmacology of Common Chinese Drugs), 1994; 1665:1667.
28. *Sheng Yao Xue Za Zhi* (Journal of Raw Herbology), 1982; 36(2):150.
29. *Chang Yong Zhong Yao Xian Dai Yan Jiu Yu Lin Chuang* (Recent Study & Clinical Application of Common Traditional Chinese Medicine), 1995; 267:269.
30. *Zhong Yao Xue* (Chinese Herbology),1998; 353:354.
31. *Liao Ning Yi Yao* (Liaoning Medicine and Herbology), 1976; (2):69.
32. *Ji Lin Zhong Yi Yao* (Jilin Chinese Medicine and Herbology), 1991; (2):12.
33. *Fu Zhou Yi Yao* (Fuzhou Medicine and Medicinals), 1983; (3):30.
34. *Xin Yi Xue* (New Medicine), 1976; 6:294.

Section 6

Other Information

另外信息

Books by Lotus Speakers

Many Lotus speakers are authors of books related to **Acupuncture** and **Traditional Chinese Medicine (TCM)**. Below is a list of books written or recommended by our speakers. Please visit www.elotus.org to purchase these books.

Chinese Medical Herbology and Pharmacology by John Chen and Tina Chen

$89.95

As the most comprehensive and authoritative text of Chinese Herbal Medicine, this invaluable text contains 670 in-depth herb monographs and 1150 illustrations. It includes detailed descriptions of Chinese medicine (traditional uses, dosages), western science (pharmacological effects, research), and safety data (herb-drug interactions, toxicology).

1267 Pages

Chinese Herbal Formulas & Applications (Pharmacological Effects & Clinical Research) by John Chen and Tina Chen

$129.95

With over 664 formulas, this book takes the next step in presenting not only the traditional usage of Chinese herbal formulas, but also a combined perspective of the pharmacological effects of formulas themselves with clinically relevant research evidence.

1706 Pages

Chinese Herbal Formulas for Veterinarians by Signe Beebe, Michael Salewski, John Chen, and Tina Chen

$129.95

This book is the first of its kind in Western veterinary literature. The pharmacology and evidence-based research presented in this book offers a pragmatic rationale for the working of the formulas that practitioners use every day. This book is a "must-have" for those who practice or are interested in veterinary applications of Chinese Medicine.

1304 Pages

Say it Right CD - Chinese Medical Herbology and Pharmacology by Glenn Grossman and Hui Hong Xu

$10.00

Pinyin and Latin pronunciation guide for the herbs in the *Chinese Medical Herbology and Pharmacology*

Say it Right CD - Chinese Herbal Formulas and Applications by Glenn Grossman and Hui Hong Xu

$13.00

Pinyin and Latin pronunciation guide for the formulas in the *Chinese Herbal Formulas and Applications*

Pulsynergy by Wei-Yen (Jimmy) Chang and Marcus Brinkman

$27.00

This is an in-depth pulse diagnosis manual perfect for anyone with a genuine intent to make a clinical breakthrough in the modern clinic. In this book, Dr. Jimmy Wei-Yen Chang shares his highly efficient pulse-diagnosis system which allows practitioners to diagnose TCM syndromes and western biomedical conditions solely by pulse within seconds. This literature brings to light the missing links that have rendered pulse diagnosis a dying art.

166 Pages

Books by Lotus Speakers

Pulsynergy (written in Chinese) by Wei-Yen (Jimmy) Chang

$27.00

This is an in-depth pulse diagnosis manual perfect for anyone with a genuine intent to make a clinical breakthrough in the modern clinic. In this book, Dr. Jimmy Wei-Yen Chang shares his highly efficient pulse-diagnosis system which allows practitioners to diagnose TCM syndromes and western biomedical conditions solely by pulse within seconds. This literature brings to light the missing links that have rendered pulse diagnosis a dying art.

183 Pages

Dao of Chinese Medicine by Donald Kendall

$55.00

Dao of Chinese Medicine is the first Western text to reveal that Chinese medical theories are based on important physiological findings. This book offers a neurologic, scientific and evidence-based explanation of how and why acupuncture works. A must read for those interested in the western explanation of acupuncture.

356 Pages

Acupuncture 1,2,3 by Richard Tan

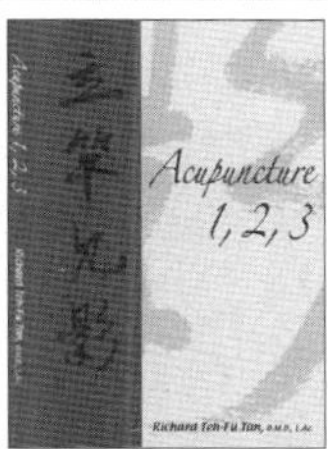

$37.00

Dr. Richard Teh-Fu Tan compiles years of experience into this simple and effective treatment manual in which he summarizes his popular Five Systems and provides an A-to-Z reference guide for common clinical complaints.

157 Pages

Dr. Tan's Strategy of Twelve Magical Points by Richard Tan

$32.00

This book will teach you how to treat complicated cases with exceptional clinical efficacy. It describes the mechanisms behind The Strategy of Twelve Magical Points and presents clinical cases to demonstrate its practical applications.

112 Pages

Twelve and Twelve in Acupuncture by Richard Tan and Stephen Rush

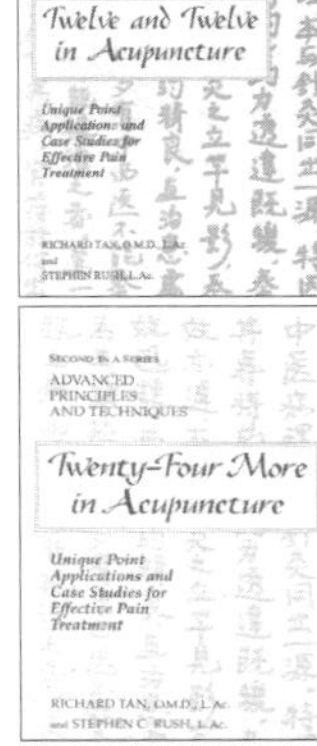

$30.00

This book shows you how Dr. Tan's Balance Method will dramatically improve your effectiveness in the treatment of many common pain conditions.

127 Pages

Twenty-Four More in Acupuncture by Richard Tan and Stephen Rush

$30.00

This book presents clinical cases with brilliant and innovative acupuncture strategies. It is also very well indexed, making for easy access to specific information.

128 Pages

Shower of Jewels by Richard Tan and Cheryl Warnke

$30.00

This practical guide to the ancient principles of art of placement is both fun and informative. Learn to improve your environment and your life through geo-energy manipulation, and possibly obtain great luck beyond your wildest dreams!!!

227 Pages

Books by Lotus Speakers

Introduction to Tung's Acupuncture by Chuan-Min Wang

$50.00

In this monumental work, a direct lineage disciple of Master Tung Ching-Chang, Dr. Chuan-Min Wang, reveals previously unpublished information regarding Master Tung's five *zang* channel system and illustrates how he used this method by providing several of Master Tung's medical cases. This book also illustrates the use of facial and palmar diagnosis as well as a general method for choosing Master Tung's points based on pulse diagnosis.

323 Pages

Illustrated Tung's Acupuncture Points by Wei-Chieh Young

$60.00

Learn the precise locations of Master Tung's acupuncture points from one of his best disciples, Dr. Wei-Chieh Young. In this book, Dr. Young helps you correctly locate Master Tung's points through anatomical location, as well as in relation to other Tung's points. In addition, he included more than 200 color photos showing these point locations.

82 Pages plus 54 pages of pictures

Lectures on Tung's Acupuncture: Points Study by Wei-Chieh Young

$70.00

In this book, Dr. Young explains the location, application, and mechanism of Master Tung's extraordinary points. He provides in great detail the locations of these points so they can be easily and correctly located. In addition, illustrations of each point are included to further assist you in locating the points. Dr. Young also elaborates on the indications of each point, with an emphasis on the mechanism of the indications. This explanation on the mechanism provides you with a better understanding for the reasons behind those indications, which helps you to obtain an even more remarkable effect.

283 Pages

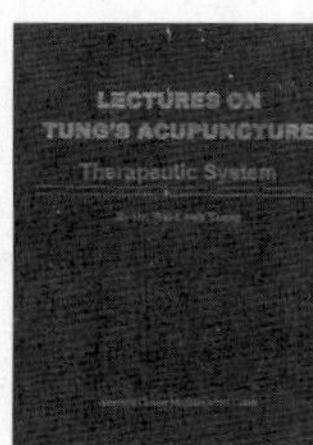

Lectures on Tung's Acupuncture: Therapeutic System by Wei-Chieh Young

$70.00

The therapeutic system of Master Tung's Acupuncture is the focus of this book. For each of the disorders discussed, Dr. Young includes point selections of Master Tung's acupuncture points and an analysis of why these points are used, as well as the theoretical principles. In addition, point selections from the 14 regular meridians and their explanation in accordance with classical acupuncture are explained. Dr. Young also provides a comparison of the therapeutic effect between the applications of the 14 regular meridians and Tung's Acupuncture, and explains which method (14 regular meridians, Tung's Acupuncture, or the combination of both) is best used for a specific disorder.

265 Pages

Advanced Tung Style Acupuncture: The Dao Ma Needling Technique of Master Tung Ching-Chang by James H. Maher

$98.00

This book presents a technique frequently employed by Dr. Tung - the *Dao Ma* needling technique. This book includes point description, palmar diagnosis, point groupings, needling sequence and needling depths, therapeutic enhancing techniques, such as 'Guiding the Movement of Qi', 'Massaging to Lead the Qi', and 'Blood Letting'.

339 Pages

Books by Lotus Speakers

Advanced Tung Style Acupuncture Vol. 2: Obstetrics & Gynecology by James H. Maher

$118.00

Volume 2 is concerned with the application of Master Tung's Acupuncture in obstetrics & gynecology. This volume contains over 400 diverse prescriptions and includes author-specific point locations, needling instructions, contraindications, and when available, clinical comments, herbal suggestions, lifestyle modifications, etc., all derived from the author's own personal clinical experiences with Master Tung's Acupuncture.

531 Pages

Advanced Tung Style Acupuncture Vol. 3: Nephrology Urology & Andrology by James H. Maher

$98.00

This volume is concerned with the application of Master Tung's Acupuncture to specific disorders of the upper and lower urinary tract in BOTH sexes. It includes disorders involving not only the actual anatomical substrates, but also the broader TCM organ/channel functions of the Kidney and Urinary Bladder. Disorders in this section include: nephrolithiasis, albuminuria, urethritis, cystitis, polyuria, edema, glomerulonephritis, nephritis, hematuria, nephrosis, frequent micturition, overactive bladder, diabetes insipidus, strangury, anuria, etc.

Section 2 of this volume – 'Andrology' – is directed toward disorders unique to the male such as: hernia, balanitis, phallalgia, cryptorchidism, orchitis, impotence, premature ejaculation, erectile dysfunction, spermatorrhea, etc.

365 Pages

Advanced Tung Style Acupuncture Vol. 4: Neurology by James H. Maher

$118.00

This volume is concerned with the application of Master Tung's Acupuncture in the treatment of neurological and neuropsychiatric disorders. This volume contains over 485 diverse prescriptions and includes author-specific point locations, needling instructions, contraindications, and when available, clinical comments, herbal suggestions, and lifestyle modifications, all derived from the author's own personal clinical experiences with Master Tung's Acupuncture.

496 Pages

Advanced Tung Style Acupuncture Vol. 5: Anesthesiology/Pain Management by James H. Maher

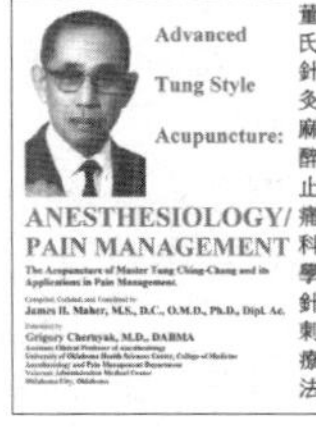

$88.00

This volume is concerned with the application of Master Tung's Acupuncture in the treatment of pain. This volume presents over 250 prescriptions and includes treatment suggestions directed towards usage in a pain management setting, much like that employed by an anesthesiologist in a pain management clinic.

261 Pages

Advanced Tung Style Acupuncture Vol. 6A: Internal Medicine by James H. Maher

$118.00

This volume of a 2-volume set is concerned with the application of Master Tung's Acupuncture in the treatment of internal medical disorders. Volume 6A of the set contains 5 chapters, 480+ pages of text, and addresses disorders of: the Cardiovascular System, the Respiratory System, the Liver, the Gallbladder, and the Blood.

542 Pages

Books by Lotus Speakers

Advanced Tung Style Acupuncture Vol. 6B: Internal Medicine by James H. Maher

$118.00

This volume of a 2-volume set is concerned with the application of Master Tung's Acupuncture in the treatment of internal medical disorders. Volume 6B of the set also contains 5 chapters, with 480+ pages of text, and addresses disorders of: the Gastrointestinal Tract, the Spleen, the Pancreas, the Endocrine System, and Miscellaneous Internal Medicine Disorders not found in the aforementioned chapters.

490 Pages

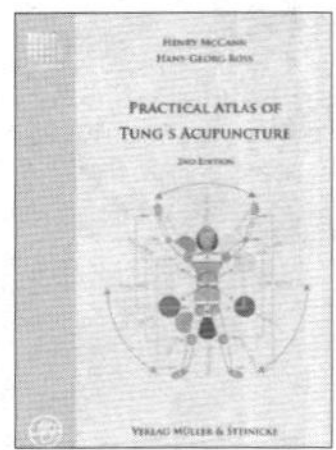

Practical Atlas of Tung's Acupuncture by Henry McCann and Hans-Georg Ross

$68.00

Throughout the history of Chinese medicine there have been several currents of medical practice. The Tung family lineage of acupuncture was a tradition of medical trade secrets that survived and even flourishes today. One special feature of Tung's system is that it uses hundreds of extra points not found in conventional acupuncture. Moreover, these points represent numerous microsystems over the entire body. This book on Tung's ancient system gives the reader a method of understanding how and when to use these unique points in the modern clinic. The book also explores the links between Tung's points, conventional acupuncture points and channels, and their connections to the classics of Chinese medicine. It is a must-have for both the beginning and advanced acupuncturist!

221 Pages

Pricking the Vessels: Bloodletting Therapy in Chinese Medicine by Henry McCann

$39.95

The first text on bloodletting therapy for Western practitioners of Chinese medicine, this authoritative text explores the theory and function of bloodletting, and provides detailed instruction on its clinical use. This book provides a concise overview of its theory, historical and contemporary relevance, and clinical guidance. The book also includes a chapter on the classical acupuncture techniques of Tung Ching-Chang whose work is attracting increasing attention in the West.

168 Pages

Mastering Tung Acupuncture: Distal Imaging for Fast Pain Relief by Brad Whisnant and Deborah Bleecker

$49.95

This book focuses on imaging and mirroring relationships, the concept, and the BEST image to use in your clinic. Honest, open, factual and clinically-effective based acupuncture tips for the 21st century. This book is the first of its kind written not by a scholar, but a practitioner who treats 110 patients per week. Learn what ideas work best in a Western patient based clinic so that you can see RESULTS.

180 Pages

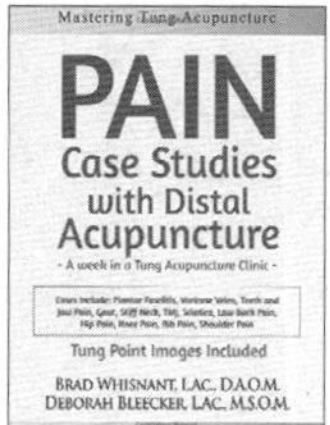

Pain Case Studies with Distal Acupuncture: A Week in a Tung Acupuncture Clinic by Brad Whisnant and Deborah Bleecker

$49.95

This book teaches you how to treat pain syndromes using Tung acupuncture with real cases from a clinic that treats 110 patients a week. Learn which points are the best choice and why. In Volume One, cases covered include: low back pain, sciatica, plantar fasciitis, hip pain, knee pain, rib pain, shoulder pain, neck pain, TMJ, gout, varicose veins, and teeth and jaw pain.

180 Pages

Books by Lotus Speakers

Pain Case Studies with Distal Acupuncture: Volume 2 by Brad Whisnant and Deborah Bleecker

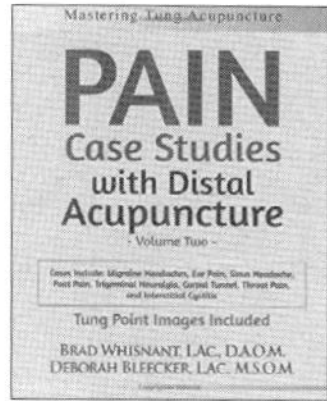

$49.95

This book teaches you how to treat pain syndromes using Tung acupuncture with real cases from a clinic that treats 110 patients a week. Learn which points are the best choice and why. In Volume Two, cases covered include: migraines, sinus headache, ear pain, trigeminal neuralgia, throat pain, interstitial cystitis, foot pain, carpal tunnel, and throat pain.

157 Pages

Auricular Medicine by Li-Chun Huang

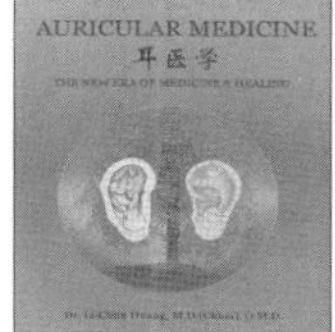

$115.00

This is by far the most complete textbook on Auricular Medicine. Dr. Li-Chun Huang revised the textbook from its first edition and added many new research results and clinical experiences. It covers all aspects of Auricular Medicine, including auricular diagnosis and auricular treatment.

627 Pages

Auricular Diagnosis with Color Photos by Li-Chun Huang

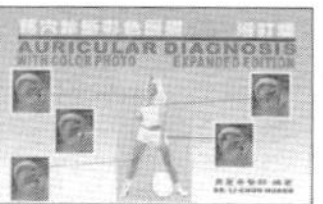

$100.00

This book shows reaction zones, depressions, protrusions, and trace marks that manifest in the ears in correlation with various conditions. With over 700 color photos referencing numerous disorders, this book makes auricular diagnosis much simpler.

400 Pages

Handbook of Auricular Treatment Prescriptions & Formulae by Li-Chun Huang

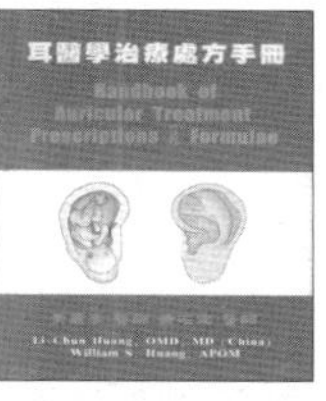

$45.00

This manual is a summary of the author's life-long auricular research and practice. Based on the author's clinical experience and research, this manual summarized 46 prescriptions which have been proved to be effective in treating common symptoms. Another 200 prescriptions are provided in the manual to help treat individual diseases. The prescriptions are illustrated with color ear pictures to help practitioners easily locate the auricular points. This manual is a great reference for TCM students, TCM practitioners, acupuncturists, and Auricular Medicine practitioners.

310 Pages

Color Atlas of Zhu's Scalp Acupuncture by Ming Qing Zhu and Moyee Siu

$59.00

This color atlas clearly presents the concepts and treatment locations of Zhu's Scalp Acupuncture in a unqiue layered format. It is an excellent reference and visual aid that will speed up your learning process of Zhu's scalp acupuncture.

64 Pages

Acupuncture Desk Reference Vol. 1 by David Kuoch

$34.95

This book provides information on more than 315 Chinese formulas, 370 single herbs, *zang fu* diagnosis, acupuncture points, clinical indications, methods, practice, and food as medicine for the most common ailments. One third of this book is devoted to Western Medicine, which contains information on drugs, herbal interactions, vitamins, nutrients and supplements, and labs. A resource section provides information for your everyday clinical practice, including insurance providers, suppliers, and general health forms for your practice.

416 Pages

Books by Lotus Speakers

Acupuncture Desk Reference Vol. 2 by David Kuoch

$34.95

ADR2, like the original, keeps concepts brief and easy to reference. This book includes symptoms, formulas, and points for conditions related to the 3 most common categories found in TCM. It also shows exercises to support wellness, and much, much more.

302 Pages

The Tao of Nutrition by Maoshing Ni and Cathy McNease

$19.95

Each meal is an opportunity to heal. *The Tao of Nutrition* provides information on making every meal therapeutic, teaching you how to make appropriate food choices for your ailments, your constitution, and the seasons of the year. Whether you are trying to become healthy or stay healthy, the authors guide you to a balanced way of eating. Included are delicious recipes and meal plans that have greatly benefited patients and families. This ancient knowledge from China provides guidance for the seasoned practitioner as well as the new student of healthy living.

255 Pages

Acupuncture and Chinese Herbal Medicine for Women's Health by Kathleen Albertson

$24.95

This book broadens your basic knowledge of women's reproductive health, acupuncture, and patterns of disease. An exceptional coverage of menstrual irregularities, fertility, pregnancy related issues, and menopause! Nutrition, lifestyle suggestions, discussion of tongue and pulse analysis, and research summaries will help you better educate your patients.

320 Pages

Oriental Medicine and You by Curry Chaudoir

$59.95

This book is not a complex text laden with medical terminology for use by medical and/or scientific academics who scour materials in search of what doesn't work; rather it is a work based upon: 1. the truths of Oriental Medicine as outlined in many texts used to train Acupuncture professionals, and 2. experience with thousands of patients and their reality. This book is intended as a reference for use by Acupuncturists who would like to offer their patients an understandable explanation of their particular symptom(s) prior to beginning care; it is also useful for patients who are curious about Acupuncture and Oriental Medicine.

218 Pages

Marijuana Syndromes: How to Balance and Optimize the Effects of Cannabis with Traditional Chinese Medicine by John Mini

$72.31

This book is a reference standard for healthcare professionals who work with people using marijuana. Perfect for acupuncturists, herbalists, physicians, psychotherapists, body workers and care givers who are familiar with the concepts of Traditional Chinese Medicine, *Marijuana Syndromes* will give you vital tools to work with the qualities and complications of marijuana use in a clinical setting. *Marijuana Syndromes* will help you spot marijuana syndromes in your clinical practice. It will give you a whole new set of easy-to-use tools in your diagnostics, radically improve your patients' healing, and boost your confidence, effectiveness and reputation as a practitioner.

824 Pages

Books by Lotus Speakers

Essential Chinese Formulas by Jake Paul Fratkin

$65.00

This book provides concise 2-page summations of 133 classical formulas, 83 modern formulas, and 9 single herbs. Within are formulas with ingredient percentages, clinical applications, historical origins, contraindications, and commentary. This book focuses on the 225 most important formulas in clinical practice, and references the various manufacturers for each formula. Its usefulness in the clinic will make this book a must-have for all practitioners and students of Traditional Chinese Herbal Medicine.

639 Pages

Huang Di Nei Jing Su Wen by Paul U. Unschuld

$84.00

The *Huang Di Nei Jing Su Wen*, known familiarly as the *Su Wen*, is a seminal text of ancient Chinese medicine, yet until now there has been no comprehensive, detailed analysis of its development and contents. At last Paul U. Unschuld offers entry into this still-vital artifact of China's cultural and intellectual past. Unschuld traces the history of the *Su Wen* to its origins in the final centuries B.C.E., when numerous authors wrote short medical essays to explain the foundations of human health and illness on the basis of the newly developed vessel theory. He examines the meaning of the title and the way the work has been received throughout Chinese medical history, both before and after the eleventh century when the text as it is known today emerged.

520 Pages

Eight Extraordinary Channels – Qi Jing Ba Mai: A Handbook for Clinical Practice and Nei Dan Inner Meditation by David Twicken

$39.95

The Eight Extraordinary channels are amongst the most fascinating, ambiguous, and clinically important aspects of Chinese medicine and *qi gong*. This book introduces the theory behind the channels, explains their clinical applications, and explores their psycho-emotional and spiritual qualities. The author also describes how to cultivate the channels through *nei gong*.

237 Pages

The Divergent Channels – Jing Bie: A Handbook for Clinical Practice and Five Shen Nei Dan Inner Meditation by David Twicken

$39.95

Rooted in the *Su Wen* and *Ling Shu*, Dr. Twicken integrates Chinese and Taoist medical philosophy, theories, and principles to clearly demonstrate that the Divergent Channels are an essential aspect of the clinical practice of acupuncture. He takes a step-by-step approach to assist practitioners in 'working out' the channels, and shows how this versatile channel system can be used in any acupuncture treatment. Twicken also includes instruction on Five *Shen Nei Dan* inner meditation to help practitioners gain a more profound emotional and spiritual understanding.

224 Pages

Auricular Chart

EAR CHARTS BY DR. LI CHUN HUANG

Laminated color ear charts are available. Please visit www.elotus.org to purchase these charts.

Note: Dr. Huang does not use acupuncture needles on the ear points. Instead, she uses vacarria seeds. She places two seeds per point to enhance the stimulation effect for better treatment outcome.

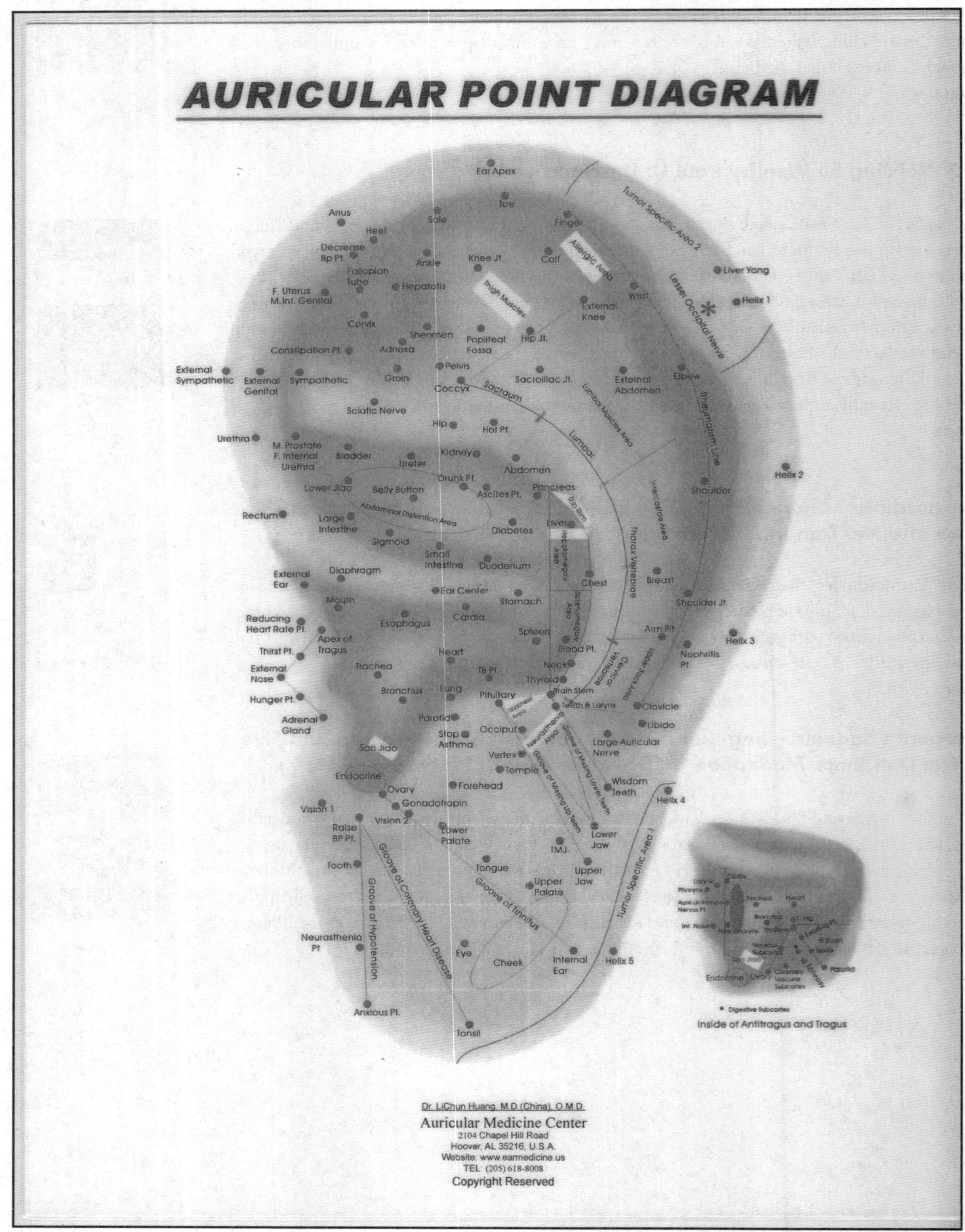

Auricular Chart

EAR CHARTS BY DR. LI CHUN HUANG

Laminated color ear charts are available. Please visit www.elotus.org to purchase these charts.

Note: Dr. Huang does not use acupuncture needles on the ear points. Instead, she uses vacarria seeds. She places two seeds per point to enhance the stimulation effect for better treatment outcome.

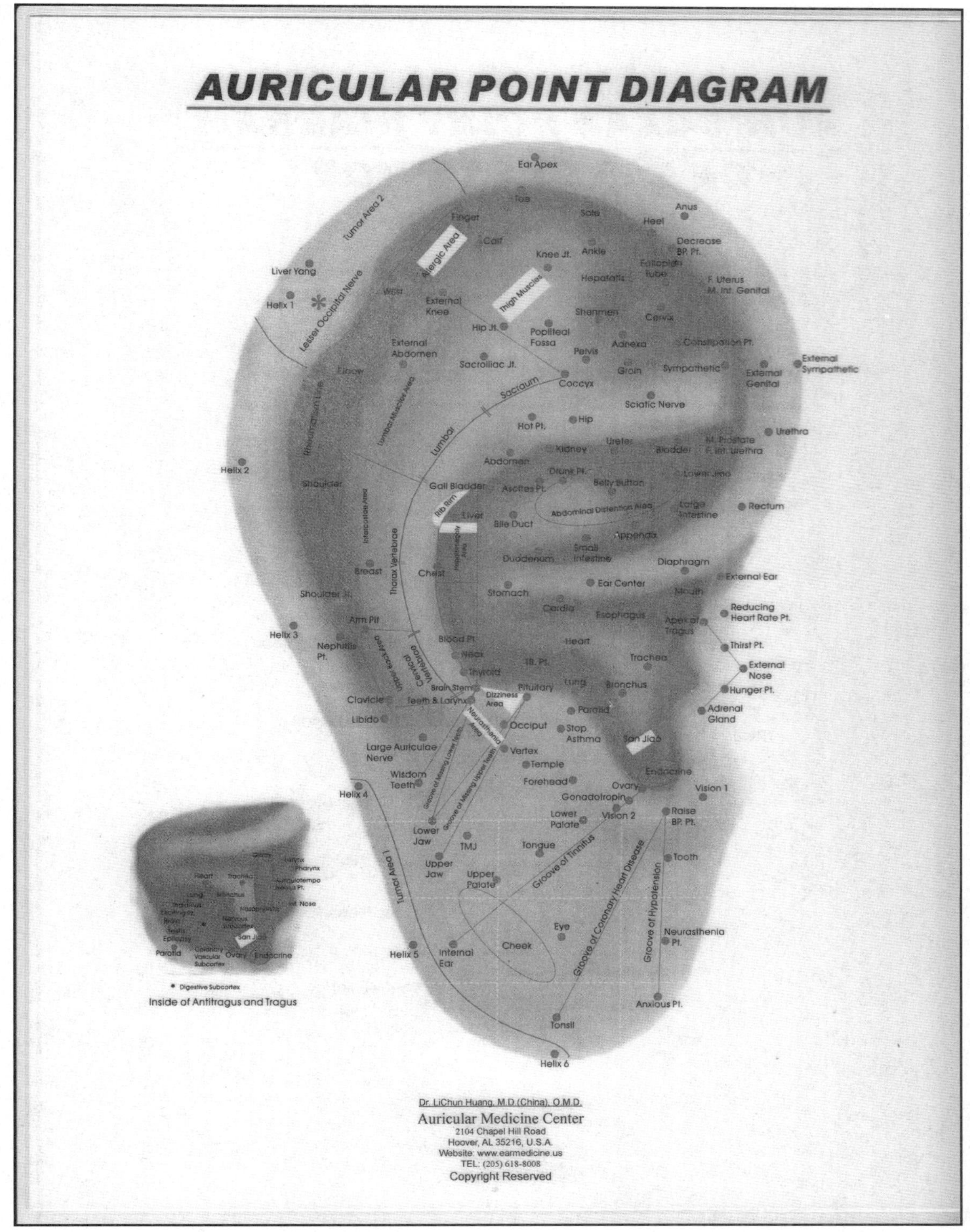

Auricular Chart

EAR CHARTS BY DR. LI CHUN HUANG

Laminated color ear charts are available. Please visit www.elotus.org to purchase these charts.

Note: Dr. Huang does not use acupuncture needles on the ear points. Instead, she uses vacarria seeds. She places two seeds per point to enhance the stimulation effect for better treatment outcome.

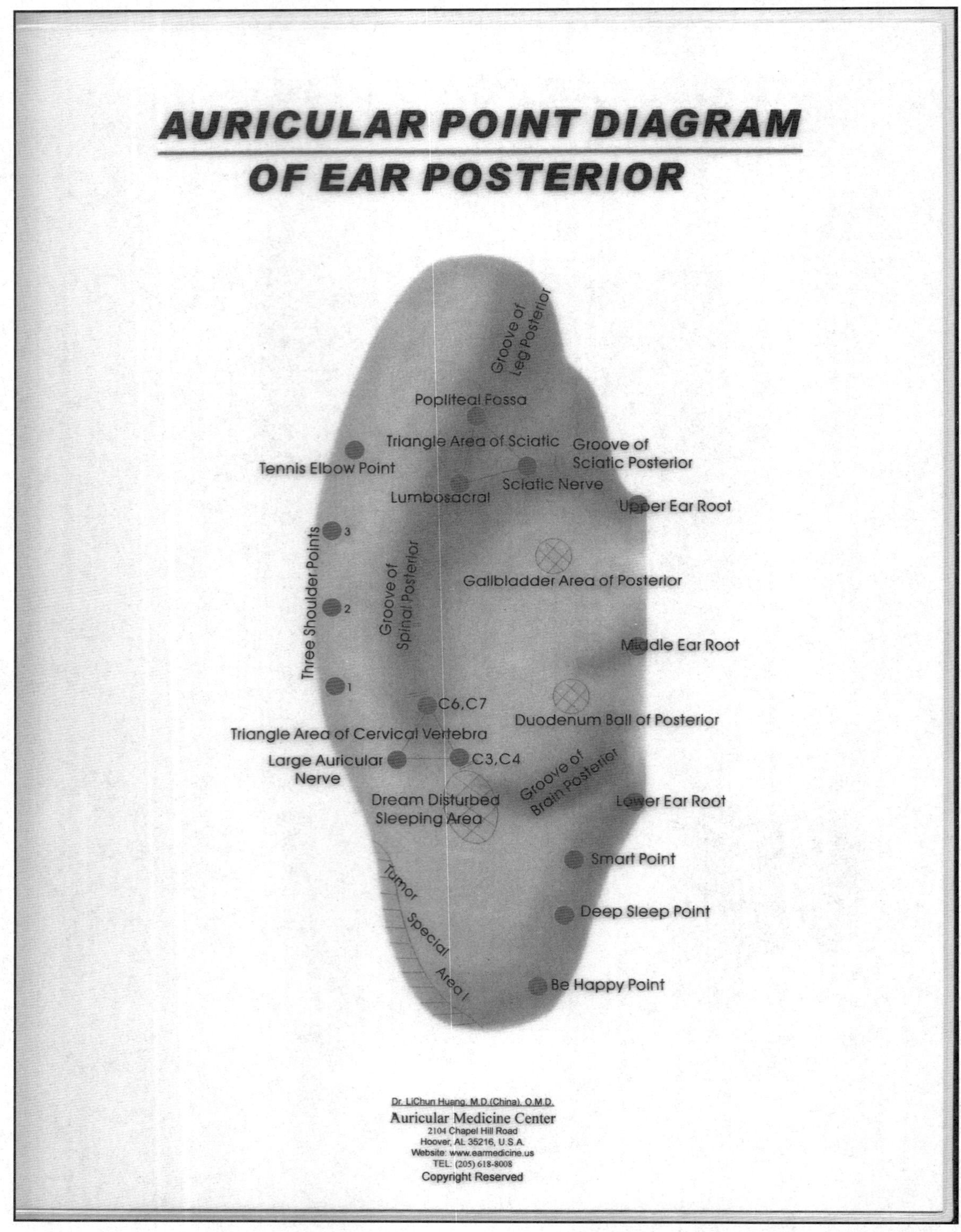

Auricular Chart

EAR CHARTS BY DR. LI CHUN HUANG

Laminated color ear charts are available. Please visit www.elotus.org to purchase these charts.

Note: Dr. Huang does not use acupuncture needles on the ear points. Instead, she uses vacarria seeds. She places two seeds per point to enhance the stimulation effect for better treatment outcome.

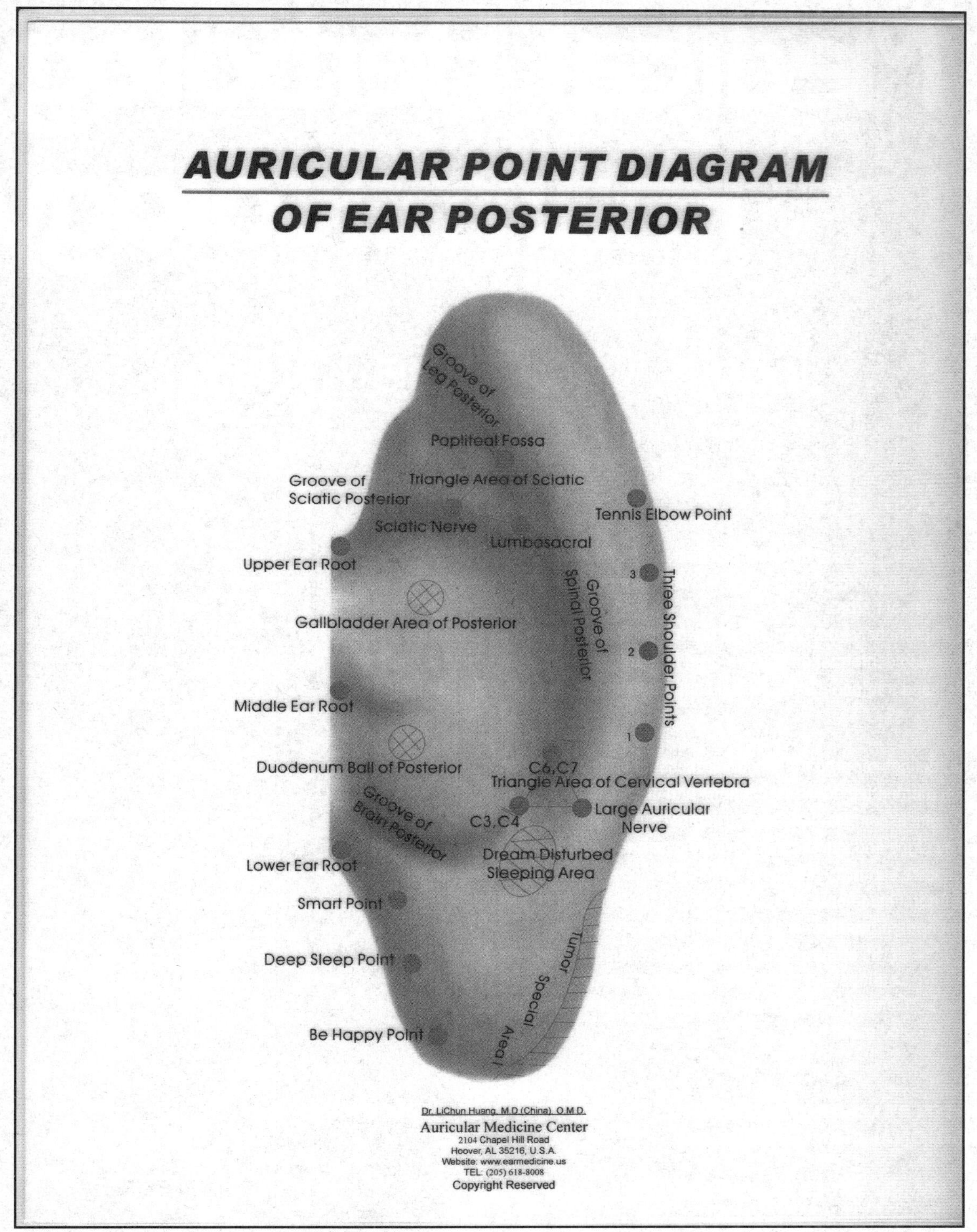

$89.95
ORDER NOW
www.evherbs.com

Chinese Medical Herbology and Pharmacology

John K. Chen • Tina T. Chen

OUTSTANDING FEATURES

- Over 1300 pages of detailed information on 670 herbs
- Over 1100 photos (colored & b/w), with color photographs for identifying and procuring correct species of herbs
- Comprehensive descriptions of pharmacological effects, clinical studies and research
- Invaluable information on herb-drug interactions, safety index, and toxicology
- Detailed traditional uses, herbal combinations and syndrome differentiation

PLUS:

- Guidelines for preparation and processing of Chinese herbs
- Recommended dosages, cautions and contraindications
- Chemical compositions and structure diagrams
- Key signs and symptoms of overdosage and treatments in such cases
- Concise summary tables for rapid clinical, classroom, or research differentiation
- Authors' comments on specific uses of herbs based on their clinical experiences
- In-depth information in ten wide-ranging appendices:
    - Herbs offering beneficial effects to support pregnancy
    - Cautions and contraindications for use of herbs during pregnancy
    - General dosing guidelines according to weight and age
    - and much more....

WRITTEN BY LEADING AUTHORITIES IN WESTERN PHARMACOLOGY AND TRADITIONAL CHINESE MEDICINE

VIEW SAMPLE PAGES AT WWW.AOMPRESS.COM
TO ORDER, VISIT WWW.EVHERBS.COM

$129.95
ORDER NOW
www.evherbs.com

Chinese Herbal Formulas and Applications

Pharmacological Effects & Clinical Research

John K. Chen • Tina T. Chen

OUTSTANDING FEATURES
(EXCLUSIVE TO CHINESE HERBAL FORMULAS AND APPLICATIONS)

- Over 1600 pages and 650 classical formulas.
- Comprehensive explanation of Pharmacological effects.
- Evidence resources from clinical studies and research.
- Historical backgrounds of famous influential doctors where the herbal formulas and philosophies developed are referenced to traditional patterns and diseases of today.
- Contributions from over 110 academic, clinical, research and regulatory professionals reviews complement the work of the authors.

PLUS:

- Thorough explanation of composition
- Concurrent uses of herbal medicinal formulas and pharmaceuticals
- Concise summary table for quick reference
- Detailed traditional and modern uses, preparation, administration, dosages, combinations, cautions and contraindications, toxicology
- Comparison and contrast of similar formulas and their clinical uses
- Authors' comments from clinical experiences
- Modifications to address changing conditions and enhance clinical efficacy
- In depth information in eleven practical useful appendices, including
    - Formulas used based on TCM patterns and western diagnosis
    - Cross references of the nomenclatures of both single herbs and formulas
    - Herbs and formulas affecting pregnancy (benefits/cautions)

THIS BOOK IS A "MUST HAVE" FOR THOSE WHO PRACTICE OR ARE INTERESTED IN CHINESE HERBAL MEDICINE.

Chinese Herbal Formulas and Applications
Pharmacological Effects & Clinical Research
John K. Chen • Tina T. Chen

Art of Medicine Press

TO VIEW SAMPLE PAGES, VISIT WWW.AOMPRESS.COM
TO ORDER, VISIT WWW.EVHERBS.COM

Introducing the Very First Comprehensive Veterinary Herbal Formulas Book!

$129.95

Chinese Herbal Formulas for Veterinarians

John K. Chen • Tina T. Chen

Signe Beebe • Michael Salewski

The first ever comprehensive veterinary herbal textbook is here! The ***Chinese Herbal Formulas for Veterinarians*** integrates foundations of Chinese herbal medicine with contemporary research, pharmacological interactions, and clinical applications. This book provides clear understanding for veterinarians who want to incorporate Chinese herbal medicine into their daily clinical practice.

OUTSTANDING FEATURES (EXCLUSIVE TO *CHINESE HERBAL FORMULAS FOR VETERINARIANS*)

- Over 1400 pages and 300 classical formulas
- Comprehensive explanation of pharmacological effects
- Veterinary clinical applications of Chinese herbal formulas
- Veterinary modifications
- Evidence resources from clinical studies and research
- Suggested acupuncture points for each formula

PLUS:

- Thorough explanation of composition
- Concurrent uses of herbal medicinal formulas and pharmaceuticals
- Concise summary table for quick reference
- Detailed traditional and modern uses, preparation, administration, dosages, combinations, cautions and contraindications
- Comparison and contrast of similar formulas and their clinical uses
- Authors' comments from clinical experiences
- Modifications to address changing conditions and enhance clinical efficacy
- In-depth information in eleven practical and useful appendices, including
  - Formulas used based on western diagnosis and TCM patterns
  - Cross references to the nomenclatures of both single herbs and formulas
  - Herbs & formulas affecting pregnancy (benefits/cautions)

THIS BOOK IS A "MUST HAVE" FOR THOSE WHO PRACTICE OR ARE INTERESTED IN VETERINARY APPLICATIONS OF CHINESE HERBAL MEDICINE.

The Best Value!

Get Unlimited CEUs for A Year

SAVE MONEY & TAKE ALL THE COURSES YOU WANT WITH THE HUA TUOS OF TODAY.

"This is the second year that I have had the Annual Pass and it has totally transformed my practice and my life. I have gained a new level of clinical effectiveness that I did not think possible."

– Alistair

WHAT YOU GET

- **VIP access to all webinars**, **videos**, **audios** and **articles** from **100+ experts**
- 1800+ hrs of online courses (more added monthly) (NCCAOM, CA, FL, IL, TX, IVAS, ABORM, AFPA, AHPRA, BAcC, CAAA, CTCMA, NZASA, NZRA, CA Chiro)
- Live chat and phone support, plus easy sign up and payment
- CEU/PDA Certificates issued immediately upon course completion
- Peer to peer support on our forums and live chat
- Risk-free 7-day trial*

order/learn more @ www.eLotus.org/Gold
toll-free (866) 905-6887 or scan with smart phone →

*The Gold Pass is an yearly contract non-refundable after the 7-day trial. Please read the product disclaimer in its entirety online prior to purchasing.

Lotus Institute Of Integrative Medicine
LEARN THE SCIENCE. PRACTICE THE ART. HEAL.

Website: www.eLotus.org
Toll-Free Tel: (866) 905-6887

Section 7

Index

Index

Index

Index

Index

Index

Index

Index

Index

Index

Index

Index

Index

Index

Index

Index

Index

Index

Index

Index

Index

Index

Index

Index

Index

Index

Index

Index

Index

Index

Index

Index